VOLUME ONE · THIRD EDITION

SCOTT, FORESMAN AND COMPANY   Chicago Atlanta Dallas Palo Alto Fair Lawn, N.J.

WALTER BLAIR
The University of Chicago

THEODORE HORNBERGER
University of Pennsylvania

RANDALL STEWART

JAMES E. MILLER, JR.
The University of Chicago

An anthology and history
From the Colonial Period through the American Renaissance

The Literature of the United States

ACKNOWLEDGMENTS

The editors are grateful to the publishers and editors who have given permission to reproduce the following materials:

American Antiquarian Society, Worcester, Massachusetts: "Of Being" by Jonathan Edwards, from *Proceedings of the American Antiquarian Society,* New Series, Vol. X, October 1895. William L. Clements Library, University of Michigan, Ann Arbor, Michigan: "Of the Nature and Manners of the People" and "Conclusion" from *A Briefe and True Report of the New Found Land of Virginia* by Thomas Hariot, ed. R. G. Adams, 1931. Colonial Society of Massachusetts: excerpt from Michael Wigglesworth's *Diary,* from *Publications of the Colonial Society of Massachusetts,* Vol. XXXV, 1951, ed. Edmund S. Morgan. Hendricks House, Inc., New York: "The Portent," "The House-Top," "The March to the Sea," "The Martyr," "The Tuft of Kelp," "After the Pleasure Party," "In a Garret," "Monody," "Lone Founts," "Art," and "Buddha" from *Collected Poems of Herman Melville,* ed. Howard Vincent O'Brien, 1947. The Huntington Library, San Marino, California: material from the manuscript of the *Autobiography of Benjamin Franklin.* Harold Jantz: excerpt from an elegy by John Fiske in *First Century of New England Verse,* ed. Harold Jantz, American Antiquarian Society, 1943; reprinted Russell & Russell Inc., 1962. The Macmillan Company, New York: Chapters I and III from the "Journal" and Chapters I and II from "A Plea for the Poor" from *The Journal and Essays of John Woolman,* ed. Amelia Gummere, 1925. *The New England Quarterly,* Brunswick, Maine: "The Agatha Letter," from *The New England Quarterly,* Vol. II, April 1929. The North Carolina Department of Archives and History, Raleigh, North Carolina: material from William Byrd's "Secret Journal," *William Byrd's Histories of the Dividing Line,* ed. W. K. Boyd, 1929. Princeton University Press, Princeton, New Jersey: material from *The Poetical Works of Edward Taylor,* ed. T. H. Johnson, 1939. G. P. Putnam's Sons, New York: material from *The Works of Alexander Hamilton,* ed. H. C. Lodge, 1904. The University of Chicago Press, Chicago, Illinois: *Billy Budd, Sailor* by Herman Melville, as edited by Harrison Hayford and Merton M. Sealts, Sr., 1962. Yale University Press, New Haven, Connecticut: "The American Belisarius," from *Sketches of Eighteenth Century America* by Michel Guillaume St. Jean de Crèvecoeur, eds. H. L. Bourdin, R. H. Gabriel, and S. T. Williams, 1925.

PREFACE

Throughout the world, interest in American literature has grown rapidly since World War II, and it appears likely to grow even more during the remaining decades of the twentieth century. Some idea of the high respect for American literature internationally may be gained by noticing the list of American Nobel prize winners in literature, seven in number during the last thirty years. And certainly it is true that the increasing interest penetrates beyond the modern period. The many books and articles that continue to appear on Hawthorne, Melville, James, Thoreau, Whitman, Twain, and Dickinson, and other nineteenth century writers offer indisputable evidence that our literature has come of age and has assumed a vitality in our culture with impact far beyond our national boundaries.

We Americans have reason to be proud of the concern with our culture and its literary interpreters, both contemporary and classic, in England and in France, in Germany and in Scandinavia, in India and in Japan — a concern the seriousness of which twenty years ago would have been inconceivable. We have also the duty to understand our own roots and diversity, our strengths and our weaknesses. The editors believe that the study of our literature, in breadth and in depth, is one of the best routes to such understanding. We hope that the users of this revised text will find it so.

The Literature of the United States has from the first been committed to the inclusion of enough variety so that the individual teacher can construct his favorite type of course. It provides the substance for a careful historical survey; it offers extensive selections from all major authors; it represents the major literary types; and it generously represents the development of characteristic American ideas and attitudes. It gives more space to minor authors, moreover, than is common in current anthologies, and it presents such genres as humor, folklore and the ballad, autobiography, the diary, and the sermon, of which the artistic values are often underestimated.

The new edition does not radically alter the original plan. In recent decades, however, a revolution in publishing — the rise of the paperback — has made unnecessary the inclusion of excerpts from novels. Political material, which loomed large in the wartime atmosphere wherein this anthology was first assembled, has been appreciably reduced. Other changes have been made in the light of current literary judgments and to meet contemporary classroom needs.

The result is the inclusion of a considerable amount of new material. Michael Wigglesworth has been added in the colonial period, with a generous selection from his recently published *Diary* and from *The Day of Doom*. Room has been found for two short novels: *Billy Budd* in Volume I and *The Red Badge of Courage* in Volume II, the former in the recent authentic edition prepared by Harrison

Hayford and Merton M. Sealts, Jr. Substantial additions have been made not only to selections from Melville and Crane but also to those from Poe, Thoreau, Hawthorne, Whitman, Dickinson, Twain, James, Frost, and Stevens. Ezra Pound, William Carlos Williams, E. E. Cummings, and Marianne Moore have been added to the substantial list of important poets of the early twentieth century poetic renaissance already included. It is still possible for the teacher who wants to stay within the covers of one book for his readings to find ample material, whatever his pedagogical purposes may be.

The most striking addition is, of course, the final chapter. Daily it is becoming clearer that World War II was a time of important conclusions and new beginnings, culturally as well as politically and scientifically. New elements — the Bomb in particular — have helped to shape, or reshape, the attitudes and feelings of American writers. The character and tempo of our life and literature have changed as the United States has assumed a new role, the leadership of the free world. Part of this leadership is reflected in the high level of contemporary writing and in the great respect for it abroad. There is ample justification, therefore, for the inclusion of the poetry of Theodore Roethke, Karl Shapiro, Robert Lowell, Richard Wilbur, and W. D. Snodgrass; of the fiction of Saul Bellow, Bernard Malamud, and John Updike; and of the drama of Edward Albee. No one can be sure, of course, which among these writers and their contemporaries will have the greatest reputations fifty years from now. But we already know that the writers of today are likely to make their time one of the most interesting and vigorous periods in our literary history.

The preface to this third edition of the two-volume version of our text must end on a note of grief. Randall Stewart, to whom *The Literature of the United States* owes much of its plan and quality, died on June 17, 1964. A graduate of Vanderbilt with advanced degrees from Harvard and Yale, Stewart was one of the most widely known teachers of his time. His chief posts were at Brown and Vanderbilt, but he was a popular summer lecturer, and is remembered affectionately by students at Texas, North Carolina, Harvard, Bread Loaf, Northwestern, Minnesota, Wyoming, Washington of Seattle, and Iowa. Hawthorne was his specialty; his biography of that author and his brilliant editing of the American and English *Notebooks* will not soon be forgotten. In the Modern Language Association of America, of whose American Literature Group he was chairman in 1951, he had innumerable friends, for he was always the most delightful of companions. A superb storyteller, he was also an attentive listener; and to be with him was invariably a heartwarming and memorable experience.

He was closely associated with two of the co-editors in this history and anthology for more than twenty years. He was always well informed in the trends of both historical scholarship and criticism. He was ingenious in helping to solve problems, efficient in making suggestions and in meeting deadlines. The breadth of his learning and the catholicity of his taste are reflected through the greater part of this book. Randall was the kind of man who could love both Sut Lovingood and Henry James.

Before Randall Stewart's death, James E. Miller, Jr., had consented to undertake editorial responsibilities for this new edition. All four editors therefore had a hand in planning the changes which are here embodied.

Walter Blair

Theodore Hornberger

Jas. E. Miller, Jr.

To indicate individual responsibility, the interchapters have been initialed, and the division of labor in the preparation of biographies, texts, headnotes and footnotes is shown in the following list:

W. B. (Walter Blair): John Smith, Sarah Kemble Knight, William Byrd, Samuel Peters, Singers of the Revolution, Hannah Foster, Richard Henry Wilde, Samuel Woodworth, Robert Bailey Thomas, Edgar Allan Poe, Henry Wadsworth Longfellow, Oliver Wendell Holmes, James Russell Lowell, Seba Smith, Morgan Neville, David Crockett, William Tappan Thompson, George Washington Harris, Singers of the West, Abraham Lincoln, Civil War Singers.

T.H. (Theodore Hornberger): Thomas Hariot, Thomas Morton, John Winthrop, Thomas Shepard, Roger Williams, Cotton Mather, John Wise, Jonathan Edwards, Charles Chauncy, Michael Wigglesworth, Benjamin Franklin, Michel Guillaume St. Jean de Crèvecoeur, John Woolman, William Bartram, Thomas Paine, Thomas Jefferson, Alexander Hamilton, H. H. Brackenridge, Joel Barlow, William Ellery Channing, Peter Cartwright, Philip Freneau, Timothy Dwight, Washington Irving, William Cullen Bryant.

R.S. (Randall Stewart): William Bradford, Samuel Sewall, Anne Bradstreet, Edward Taylor, Ralph Waldo Emerson, Henry David Thoreau, Nathaniel Hawthorne, Henry Timrod.

J. E. M. (James E. Miller, Jr.): James Fenimore Cooper, Herman Melville.

TABLE OF CONTENTS

Three details in editorial procedure require explanation: (1) The text of each selection is, in the judgment of the editors, the best available. The text has been specified, however, only when there has been some problem about the version to be adopted. (2) The first date where two dates appear after a selection, is that of composition; the second date is that of publication. Where one date appears, it is that of publication. (3) The titles of a few selections have been supplied by the editors.

Chapter 1 The English Colonies 1588–1765

The Promise of the New World
"Who can desire more content, that hath small
meanes; or but only his merit to advance his
fortunes, then to tread and plant that ground
he hath purchased by the hazard of his life? . . .
What so truely su[i]tes with honour and honestie,
as the discovering things unknowne? erecting
Townes, peopling Countries, informing the ignorant,
reforming things unjust, teaching virtue . . . ?"
                                        — *John Smith*

I. Intellectual Currents

The Pattern of Colonial Culture

Most Americans know the story of the colonial period of the United States. It extends from Columbus's first voyage in 1492 to the Stamp Act of 1765, which united in opposition to British policy thirteen decidedly dissimilar colonies, whose peoples had barely begun to be aware of common interests and growing strength.

Columbus, seeking a new route to the fabled gold and silks and spices of China and India, found instead what was quickly and appropriately called the New World. Upon the Americas were soon unleashed the ambitions of the nations arising from the ruin of medieval unity. Spain, Portugal, France, Holland, Sweden — every one of them looked westward across the Atlantic for more lands and strength. England entered rather belatedly into this contest for colonies. The voyages of John and Sebastian Cabot in the fifteenth century had given her some claim to the northern continent of the newly discovered hemisphere, but it was nearly a century before men like Walter Raleigh sought to make that claim good by actual occupation. As soon as it was clear that the eastern parts of North America offered no such easily portable loot as the gold and silver of Peru and Mexico, most Englishmen had little enthusiasm for colonization, and many were openly scornful of such costly failures as that at Roanoke Island in 1585. Ultimately, however, their patriotism (a curious blend of nationalism and Protestantism), their needs as a seafaring people, and their longings for land and wealth accounted for the establishment of permanent settlements at Jamestown in Virginia in 1607 and at Plymouth in Massachusetts in 1620.

The Pilgrims at Plymouth barely survived their first winter, and Jamestown came close to extinction in an Indian massacre in 1622. The future, however, remained doubtful for only a short time. Between 1628 and 1640, in what is known as the Great, or the Puritan, Migration, perhaps as many as twenty-five thousand persons settled in New England, giving to Massachusetts both a long-lasting economic and cultural leadership and the power to press effectively against the French in Canada and the Dutch in New Amsterdam. Virginian stability and growth were assured by a steadily growing taste for tobacco among Europeans, and by the end of the seventeenth century the plantation way of life was well established there. More color and variety in the growing colonial society came with the absorption of the Dutch along the Hudson and the Swedes on the Delaware, and from the determination of the Roman Catholic Lord Baltimore and the Quaker William Penn, who made Maryland and Pennsylvania havens from state-imposed religious conformity. Georgia, to cite one final example, was founded by James Edward Oglethorpe in part as a refuge for the poor and in part as a bastion against the Spaniards in Florida.

In short, villages and farms and plantations proliferated up and down the Atlantic coastline, and everywhere men sought to build that kind of life which seemed to them desirable, compromising always with the hard facts of their environment and the often conflicting ambitions of their neighbors. By 1700 the colonists numbered more than a quarter of a million; by 1765, approximately a million and three quarters. They had been fortunate in having been left largely to their own devices, or interfered with only sporadically and unsystematically. The difficulties of administering colonies from a distance of three thousand miles had been recognized by everyone, and all the colonies had their representative assemblies (the first of them in Virginia) comparable to the lower house of the English Parliament. For all their differences — and the colonies had many — they agreed upon one thing: they wanted to control their own affairs. We know now, as Americans in 1765 could not know, that the steps from such a conviction to Lexington and Bunker Hill and Independence Hall were inevitable, that the essential truth of the colonists' situation lay in Thomas Jefferson's epochal words: "When, in the course of human events, it becomes necessary for *one people*. . . ."

One people! Such the colonists in British America eventually became. Why and how they did so are still puzzling questions, despite the many words which have been written to explain the Revolution. The disintegrative forces of the colonial period were seemingly as powerful as those which operated for cohesion and unity. Intercolonial travel by land was difficult and uncommon. Personal and commercial connections between one colony and England were often closer than those between colony and colony. Marked religious differences prevailed, from Congregational New England to the Anglican establishments in Maryland, Virginia, and the Carolinas. Outside of New England there was little homogeneity of background, for by 1765 one out of every three Pennsylvanians was German, every other North Carolinian was of Scotch-Irish ancestry, Negro slaves made up almost half the population of Virginia, and in South Carolina and Georgia the whites were actually outnumbered. Nevertheless, in all regions there were characteristic political and social institutions and a literature of their own, which tells much of what they thought and argued and dreamed about.

Language, folklore, learning, the arts, literary tastes and types, legal, political, and educational institutions — everything except the land itself and a few skills acquired from the Indians — had been brought across the Atlantic Ocean. The process of transplantation had been sporadic, almost accidental; it had never been smoothly regular, almost never simple. Always involved in the process had been change, adaptation, modification to meet the peculiar circumstances of the new environment. The old ways never worked quite perfectly under the new conditions. Men came who knew how to build houses, but they had to work with the building materials they found — lime for plaster, for example, was hard to come by — and they had to meet the idiosyncrasies of climates unlike those to which they had been accustomed. Physicians arrived, their minds stored with botanical medicine, only to discover that America had a flora of its own, whose medicinal use had to be discovered by experiment or learned from the natives. Traditions lingered, but necessity forced the quicker-witted to improvisation and dependence on first-hand knowledge, and the problems in the lands from Maine to Georgia were so varied as to call forth all the ingenuity that experience could develop. Decade after decade the processes of transplantation and adaptation were repeated, with infinite variations. New men and women came from Europe, bringing new tools and talents and opinions and adapting them as best they could to what they found. Frontier succeeded frontier as immigrants pushed up the streams toward the mountains to find new farms and found new villages. Stability was short-lived, change incessant.

Nor was Europe static. In almost every realm of human thought the period was tumultuous, full of conflict and revolutionary change. In economics, the feudal system was giving way to modern capitalism. In politics, the theory of the divine right of kings was being superseded by constitutional and contractual concepts. In religion, the schisms and sectarian rivalries which were the aftermath of the Protestant Reformation were hardly yet softened by the principle of toleration, which was eventually to bring some degree of amity. In science, revolution was continuous as Copernicus, Galileo, Bacon, Descartes, Boyle, Ray, Newton, and their associates and disciples changed both the world-view of western man and his method of advancing his knowledge of the world in which he lived. In literature and the arts, the creative outpouring of the Renaissance was succeeded by the more orderly but far from barren reign of Neoclassicism.

The colonial era of the United States coincided, in other words, with the germinal period of what we call the modern world. Europe, of necessity the chief constant factor to the people who settled in America, was itself becoming a new world. The more intelligent colonists, busy though they were with their own concerns, never forgot that they were participants in affairs of mighty moment, in the rebuilding of an old society as well as in the creation of a new one.

Colonial literature was therefore written as often for European readers as for American. The men and women who wrote it had some immediate pressing purpose — economic, religious, or political — which could be furthered by writing.

The Economic Promise

The first and the greatest promise which the New World held out to Europeans was freedom from want. To landless men whose ancestors had for centuries been bound to someone else's soil, America offered freeholds. Here was room for a man to raise, on his own land, his own food and the fibers for his own clothing, a new chance to attain the security of overflowing granaries and well-stocked barnyards.

As Captain John Smith put it, "Who can desire more content, that hath small meanes; or but only his merit to advance his fortunes, then to tread and plant that ground he hath purchased by the hazard of his life?"

Colonial literature is understandably rich in accounts of the economic resources of the New World. The prospective immigrant wanted to know, in as much detail as possible, about his chances of earning a living. He did not always find accurate information, because the books about the colonies were often written by promoters whose evaluations were rosily optimistic rather than cautious. From the explorers, travelers, and settlers, however, as well as from the promoters, there came in time an enormous body of information on the climate, topography, soils, plants, animals, and minerals of the various regions of British America. These writings told what would and would not grow. They paid particular attention to timber, because England needed shipbuilding supplies and her great forests were playing out. They reported in detail on game and fur-bearing animals, on fisheries, on the prospects of mines.

The first selection in the present chapter is from the earliest English survey of a region now a part of the United States — Hariot's *Virginia* (1588). Thomas Hariot was Raleigh's protégé and a member of the Roanoke expedition of 1585; his book is not merely the first but also one of the fullest and most accurate prognostications of the various ways in which a living might be earned in the New World. Many of John Smith's writings were of the same nature as Hariot's, and both his *Map of Virginia* (1612) and his *Description of New England* (1616) were read carefully by men who were considering emigration. No colony was launched without a similar "Map" or "True Report" of economic possibilities, followed by a local literature of promotion which was in turn succeeded by reports of progress. Of the many other books which might be named, the most important are Francis Higginson's *New England's Plantation* (1630), William Wood's *New England's Prospect* (1634), Thomas Morton's *New English Canaan* (1637), John Hammond's *Leah and Rachel; or, The Two Fruitful Sisters, Virginia and Mary-Land* (1656), George Alsop's *Character of the Province of Mary-Land* (1666), Daniel Denton's *Brief Description of New-York* (1670), William Penn's *Brief Account of the Province of Pensilvania* (1681), Thomas Ashe's *Carolina* (1688), and Gabriel Thomas' *Historical and Geographical Account of the Province and Country of Pensilvania* (1698). These books all insist that the fundamental needs of food, clothing, and shelter could be satisfied rather more easily in America than in Europe, and they suggest over and over again that industry and ingenuity could produce an abundance of good things far beyond the experience of the common man in Europe.

That the New World was a land of marvels, of limitless economic opportunity, was taken almost for granted. The European mind had been prepared for this conviction over many centuries. The ancients had harbored traditions of wonderful western lands — the Elysian Fields where happy souls went after death and the Islands of the Hesperides where golden apples grew. In the west, too, lay Atlantis, the great island continent swallowed up by earthquakes and the sea long before the time of Plato, who probably invented it. In medieval times, men had written of inconceivably wealthy islands — Antillia and O'Brazil — somewhere in the western ocean, and the news had slowly circulated that the Norsemen had found a new, rich, western continent called Vinland. These stories, combined with the ineradicable faith that America was close to the legendary treasures of the Orient, had prepared Europeans for wonders, and they were duly delighted with the strange new plants and animals of which the explorers wrote.

Only a few were skeptical. Samuel Purchas, for one, expressed the belief in *Purchas His Pilgrimes* (1619) that America was not so wonderful as some people seemed to think. "For what haue they," he asked, "to oppose to our Elephants, Rhinocerotes, Camels, Horses, Kine, &c. Neither are the naturall fruits of America comparable to those of our World. Whence are their Spices, and best Fruits, but from hence, by transportation or transplantation? As for Arts, States, Literature, Diuine and Humane, multitudes of Cities, Lawes, and other Excellencies, our World enjoyeth still the priuiledge of the First-borne. America is a younger brother, and hath in these things almost no inheritance at all, till it bought somewhat hereof of the Spaniards, with the price of her Freedome." In the eighteenth century there were other skeptics, such as the Comte de Buffon and the Abbé Raynal, who were convinced that the American climate was so enervating that men and beasts degenerated in the New World. Thomas Jefferson sought to refute Buffon by compiling tables of the comparative weights of European and American animals and by assembling the skeleton of an American mastodon in his Paris apartments.

Most Europeans, however, were eager to look at America with unbounded optimism, especially when, as often happened, they grew impatient with the state of things in their own civilization. The prevailing temper was that of the English philosopher, George Berkeley, who pictured a Muse disgusted with Europe, waiting a better time

> In happy climes, where from the genial sun
> And virgin earth such scenes ensue,
> The force of art by nature seems outdone,
> And fancied beauties by the true.

Man was to be better treated by Nature in the western hemisphere than in Europe. He was, indeed, to rise to new heights, far more impressive than mere economic abundance could attain.

> Westward the course of empire takes its way,
> The four first Acts already past,
> The fifth shall close the Drama with the day;
> Time's noblest offspring is the last.

Only the presence of a savage people stood in the way of New World greatness. The Indians, it is true, were not very numerous and, with a few exceptions, not very dangerous. Some observers saw God's providence in a plague which had decimated the New England tribes just prior to the English settlement in that region; others argued that a few heathens should not be allowed to stand in the way of living room for good, civilized Christians. The prospective settler wanted, of course, to know about the Indians. They were an economic fact to be reckoned with — a possible source of wealth through trade or conquest, and a probable source of danger if they resented, as they easily might, the invasion of their hunting grounds by land-hungry Europeans. The Indians, therefore, have a conspicuous place in almost every book which surveyed New World resources. Hariot devoted one fourth of his tract to a description of them. Smith was at all times anxious to estimate their military strength. The English did not always deal justly with the aborigines; Roger Williams and William Penn were exceptional in their concern about obtaining land by purchase and treaty. Most of the settlers proceeded upon the expedient conviction that the Indians who stood in their path were treacherous and inferior animals, to be eliminated with as little compunction as the rattlesnakes, the wolves, and the bears. The story of the gradual dispossession of the Indians is one of the blackest in colonial annals.

Considerations other than economic appear in the literature about the Indians. Their novelty, the unsettled problem of their origin (were they, for instance, descendants of the Lost Ten Tribes of Israel?), their uncanny skill in woodcraft, their strange social and political organization, their stoic endurance of pain and their sadistic pleasure in torture, their heathen religious faith — all created interest amounting to fascination. The Pocahontas legend, whether or not Smith invented it out of whole cloth (see p. 49), epitomizes the tendency to create a "noble savage." Out of this grew the attitude known as primitivism, which glorified the unspoiled simplicity of the "uncivilized." Primitivism was basically an objection to the complexities and maladjustments of life in Europe, and appears more frequently in books written by Europeans than in those by persons who had actually been in contact with the savages, although Morton's *New English Canaan* (p. 69) is a noteworthy exception. Later, in the eighteenth century, primitivism appeared in the poems of Freneau (p. 509), the essays of Crèvecoeur (p. 328), and the *Travels* of William Bartram (p. 360). It continued well into the nineteenth century and is an essential element in the philosophical background of Cooper's Leather-Stocking tales and Longfellow's *Hiawatha*.

Colonial literature also records the economic processes by which simple home industries were gradually supplanted by a more specialized industrial system. The references to mining and ironworks in the writings of John Winthrop and William Byrd (see p. 105) give us a glimpse of the beginnings of industrialization, which was not to become general until many years after the achievement of political independence.

Most observers agree that the New World fulfilled its economic promise. Like the man in the folk tale whose three wishes were granted, but never quite as he expected them to be, the first Americans did not attain freedom from want as effortlessly as some of them had expected. They had to learn patience and thrift and the most efficient use of their vast new environment, and they had to adjust themselves to other than merely local circumstances. But in the end the colonists succeeded amazingly well, and their literature reveals both the nature and the realization of their economic dreams.

The Religious Life

Next to getting a living, the chief concern of great numbers of the colonists was religion. Some of them, indeed, regarded the saving of souls — their own and those of other people — as the most meaningful activity of life. To understand the men and women who established the pattern of American society, we need to know with some exactness their religious and theological background and its reflection in literature.

First it must be understood that most of the colonists, whatever their church, were keenly aware of the Reformation. The Bible in their own language had been in the hands of Englishmen only since 1535, and to most of them it was a fresh and inexhaustible revelation of the will of God. The persecutions of the reign of Queen Mary, the fear of a Spanish invasion (which it was believed would have been swiftly followed by an Inquisition in England), the memory of the Gunpowder Plot of Guy Fawkes, the vexing problem of the royal succession, and the endless debates about church government and ritual — all were closer to the English in the early seventeenth century than the hatreds of the Civil War are to present-day Americans.

The earliest attempts to colonize reflect the rivalry beween Catholics and Protestants. Both Hariot and Smith emphasized the heathenism of the Indians, implying that it was the sacred duty of the English to convert them to the true faith, that is, to Anglicanism, before they could be led astray by the Catholic Spaniards or French. Although the settlers who came to America with any such altruistic intentions were few and far between, a good deal of missionary work among the Indians was attempted. Harvard, William and Mary, and Dartmouth were all founded with an eye to the education of Indian youth, although in all of these colleges other purposes soon loomed much larger.

Six important settlements — Plymouth, Massachusetts Bay, Maryland, Rhode Island, New Haven, and Pennsylvania — were the work of religious groups or leaders to whom economic considerations were distinctly secondary. Some wanted the opportunity to organize and run a church-state, perhaps to improve upon John Calvin's experiment at Geneva; others wished only the toleration of non-conforming sects. All relate in one way or another to the peculiar circumstances of the Reformation in England.

Between Henry VIII's break with the Pope and the end of the reign of Elizabeth I, the Church of England had arrived at a *status quo* accurately described as moderate Protestantism. The break with Rome was complete. The ruler was the acknowledged head of the English church; monastic orders had been abolished, and most of the lands accumulated over the centuries by the Church had been seized and distributed by the Crown; church services were held in English rather than in Latin;

and the people had been provided with the English Bible and the English *Book of Common Prayer.* On the other hand, much that seemed "papist" to the more extreme Protestants remained — the hierarchy of parish priests, bishops, and archbishops, intimately connected with the structure of the civil state; richly ornamented churches and vestments; and set forms of prayer and worship.

English dissent or nonconformity (the terms are used interchangeably, although the latter connotes a somewhat more active position) consisted of innumerable groups and individuals who believed that the Reformation had not gone far enough. Some wanted to remove all vestiges of Catholic practices and rituals, placing more emphasis upon the sermon and the Bible as the chief means of bringing souls to Christ — these were the first English Puritans. Others desired to substitute a measure of lay control for the system of benefices, bishops, and archbishops, for which they found no Biblical precedent — these were the Presbyterians. Still others wished each congregation to decide for itself what form of worship it should follow — these were the Separatists, Independents, or Congregationalists, also sometimes called Brownists, after their first spokesman, Robert Browne (1550?-1633). In addition, there were many shades of opinion regarding the proper forms of worship and the most desirable form of church government. With the passage of time, differences of opinion about these matters multiplied rather than diminished, and the term "Puritan" began to be applied rather indiscriminately to all nonconformists.

The Anglican leaders sought continuously to enforce conformity to the *status quo.* Almost everyone regarded the church as an essential element to the stability of the state and could not envision a society tolerating diverse religious opinions. James I, therefore, in 1604, speaking of the Puritans, could announce, "I shall make them conform themselves or I will harry them out of the land, or else do worse." With the accession of Charles I in 1625, the more militant bishops had the support of a king with absolutist leanings, and the pressure on the Puritans increased enormously. Under William Laud, Bishop of London from 1628 until 1633, and thereafter Archbishop of Canterbury until his execution in 1645, clergymen who failed to follow the prescribed forms of worship were brought into church courts, tried, and if found guilty punished, most often (as in the case of Thomas Shepard) by being forbidden to exercise any clerical functions. Among these suspended clergy were many of the men who became the leaders of the New England colonies.

The Pilgrims who came to Plymouth were Separatists. Some of them had first emigrated to Holland, found the atmosphere there too foreign for their taste, and determined to settle in America. They were poor people and would not have been able to make the voyage in the *Mayflower* had not the necessary capital been provided by a group of "merchant adventurers" of London. William Bradford (see p. 54) was the mainstay of the settlement and church which they founded in Massachusetts. In 1692 Plymouth became a part of the Province of Massachusetts Bay.

The Puritans of the Massachusetts Bay Company came to New England when it became clear that further reform within the English Church, headed by Laud, was impossible. They took care to bring their charter with them, and they intended to establish a commonwealth in which the kind of church they wanted might thrive.

In contrast to the Pilgrims, they were wealthy and well educated, many of them being substantial property owners or professional men, university-trained as was their first governor, John Winthrop (see p. 72). Furthermore, they were numerous. Not all of them were as earnest in their religion as Winthrop and the ministers, but the Bay Colony leadership was far-sighted and effective. Social, political, and educational institutions were so securely established that no study of the genesis of American life can ignore the Puritan tradition. Before the Puritans had been long in New England, they agreed upon a form of church government which was more Congregational than Presbyterian. Whether the *Cambridge Platform* of 1649 was shaped by the example of the Separatist Pilgrims, or by Congregational tendencies among the Bay Colony leaders themselves, is a debatable question. By the time the *Cambridge Platform* was adopted, the Westminster Assembly had effected changes not wholly dissimilar within the Church of England, although they were largely annulled by the Restoration in 1660.

Puritanism, however, was more than an attitude toward forms of worship and church government. The term was used then, as it is now, to describe a strait-laced way of life, a concern with moral conduct so great as to lead some individuals to attempt what we now think of as unwarranted control of the personal lives of their neighbors, a rigid repression of acts and fashions that today are no longer considered evil. Such was Puritanism at its worst. At its best it provided men and women with a sense of social responsibility, an earnestness about life which had in it both intellectual conviction and intense, sometimes even mystic, piety.

Underlying Puritan earnestness was Calvinism, a stern and legalistic theology constructed by the Genevan reformer, John Calvin (1509-1564). Calvinism portrayed God as a sovereign whom man, in the person of Adam, had disobeyed, thereby breaking an inexpressibly sacred and solemn covenant. Upon Adam and all his race, retribution had justly fallen. Through Christ, however, man had been given a second chance, although that chance was extended only to those men whom God had "elected" to be saved. Most men were predestined to damnation, as they deserved. Although one could never be wholly sure of being among the fortunate few for whom salvation was foreordained, life was to be lived in a search for the divine will, as it might be expressed in one's own struggle for serenity, through one's spiritual growth, or as it might be interpreted from unusual events (or "special providences") in the external world. To walk uprightly in the sight of God and to seek to follow His will — these were the aims of the Calvinist and the origin, as has often been remarked, of the "New England conscience."

The "Five Points" upon which the Calvinists insisted were predestination, limited atonement, total depravity, irresistibility of grace, and perseverance of the saints. Although the vistas of human life which these terms represent are still observable, most of us discuss them in other terms, such as those of the existentialists. The American Puritans never tired of debating about them, nor of the two covenants which lay at the heart of their special version of Calvinism, often called "federal" or "covenant" theology. The covenant of works, which Adam broke, and the covenant of grace, which God offered through His son Jesus Christ, were enormously important in New England. One can see the idea of a covenant in the Mayflower Compact (see p. 62), and the intense concern with grace in the writings of Michael Wigglesworth (see p. 212), Edward Taylor (see p. 236), and Jonathan Edwards (see p. 165).

From the first, Calvinism had its opposition. Of the many challenging opponents four are so important to the student of literature that their description is a necessity. These four — Antinomianism, Arminianism, Quakerism, and Deism — had one thing in common: they granted human nature a more dignified role than the Calvinists were willing to grant it. Otherwise, they were most dissimilar. Antinomianism and Arminianism were merely theological positions, not necessarily concerned with a particular church any more than was Calvinism itself. Quakerism was and is the doctrine of a religious society, the Friends. Deism was neither a theology nor a church, but a philosophical position.

Antinomianism has approximately the place in religion that anarchy has in politics; that is to say, it is the denial of any authority over the individual. The Antinomian controversy which shook the Bay Colony to its foundations in 1636 and 1637 ended with the banishment of Anne Hutchinson for spreading, among other heresies, the doctrine that God revealed himself directly to individuals, so that a person could know whether or not he was of the "elect." Such thinking challenged both the Calvinistic conception of the Bible as God's final revelation and the social control which was basic in the thought of such leaders as Winthrop. Hawthorne's *The Scarlet Letter* is one of the works of literary art which owes something to Anne Hutchinson and Antinomianism.

Arminianism takes its name from a Dutch theologian, Jacobus Arminius (1560-1609), who held that one could achieve salvation in part through "good works," that is to say, through living a moral and upright life. It was regarded by the Calvinists as derogatory to the sovereignty of God and was one of the "errors" which Edwards was most anxious to refute in his *Freedom of Will* (p. 202). Although Arminianism was condemned by the Synod of Dort (1618-19), the body which established the "Five Points" of Calvinism, "good works" continued to appeal to the masses of men more widely than did the doctrines of abstruse theology, and when in the eighteenth century evangelical preachers took religion to the people, Arminianism flourished. The Methodist movement in particular had Arminian aspects.

Quakerism is the only one of the many radical Protestant opinions of the seventeenth century which has remained influential in its original form. The people who first called themselves "Children of Light," and later the Society of Friends, organized under the leadership of George Fox (1624-1691) in the late 1640's. Their popular name was given them in jest, after Fox had asserted in a courtroom that even magistrates would come to "tremble before the word of the Lord." The Friends believed that the duty of man is to follow the Bible and what was variously called "pure wisdom" or "the Inner Light," an "opening" from God. With a quietistic listening for God's guidance they combined the social control of "speaking out" in meeting, by which the promptings of the Inner Light were communicated to and passed upon by other Friends — a procedure which preserved them from the Antinomian lawlessness. They believed that all men are brethren, that all violence (and especially war) is evil, that worldly distinctions of class and dress are unfriendly, that the taking of oaths is blasphemous. They had no professional clergy, and they tended to distrust higher learning. Bitterly persecuted in New England as late as 1677, they established themselves in New Jersey and Pennsylvania, where they became a powerful force for the abolition of slavery and for many varieties of social reform. Although they wrote many narratives of their religious experience, they produced relatively few great writers (for the best of them, John Woolman, see p. 346), but their equalitarianism and humanitarianism have always been powerful factors in American life. Whittier was their chief spokesman in nineteenth-century American literature, but the Quaker tradition is strong in the work of Walt Whitman and many lesser authors.

Deism is ordinarily dated from the *De Veritate* (1624) of Lord Herbert of Cherbury, an English philosopher. Herbert approached religion from a purely rational angle, similar to what we would now call the comparative method. He found that in all times, whether pagan or Christian, men had agreed upon five axioms: (1) that there is a God; (2) that He ought to be worshipped; (3) that piety and virtue are the essentials of worship; (4) that man ought to repent his sins; and (5) that there are rewards and punishments in a future life. Veneration of the Bible as the revelation of God is wholly lacking in this view of religion; the distinguishing mark of Deistic thought is the rejection of revelation. In the latter part of the seventeenth century, rationalism spread rapidly, in part as a result of the advance of science, and there was widespread acceptance of the Deistic position that religious truth could be obtained by the use of reason. Although the Deistic controversy was primarily an English affair, Increase and Cotton Mather were attacking the Deists before 1700, and Edwards' *Divine and Supernatural Light* (p. 182) would not have been written had not the refutation of the Deistic emphasis upon the place of reason in religion seemed important. The best-known Deistic work by a colonial American is Benjamin Franklin's *Dissertation on Liberty and Necessity, Pleasure and Pain* (1725), which its author later accounted an "erratum" (see p. 273). No reader of Franklin is long in doubt about his basic agreement with Lord Herbert of Cherbury. The Deistic principles of many of the leaders of the Revolution, including Washington, Jefferson, Hamilton, and Ethan Allen, have led to the argument that there was an American "cult of reason" in the late eighteenth century, but that view, together with the mare's nest stirred up by Thomas Paine's *Age of Reason* (1794-1796), must await discussion in a later chapter.

Toleration and revivalism, probably the most distinctive features of American religion, also had their beginnings in the colonial period. Both remain, after all these years, the frequent concern of every thoughtful American.

Roger Williams, banished from Massachusetts Bay, founded Rhode Island in 1636 as a tiny refuge for those who might be persecuted by the civil state for their religious opinions. His only predecessor in the advocacy of liberty of conscience and the separation of church from state seems to have been an English Congregationalist, Leonard Busher, whose *Religious Peace* had been published in 1614. Rhode Island was far ahead of its time. Not until the chartering of Pennsylvania in 1681 was a second colony willing to receive all victims of religious persecution. Maryland, to be sure, passed a Toleration Act in 1649 as a protection for the Catholics, but Jews and Unitarians were not welcome. The other colonies, some of them reluctantly, bowed to the provisions of the Toleration Act passed by Parliament in 1689, and thereafter the principle of religious freedom received at least lip service. Nonconformists to the dominant pattern of religious life are by no means safe, however, even today, although in later years intolerance toward one group or another has been an aspect of economic competition as often, perhaps, as of religious conviction.

Revivalism, while not wholly native, has long been the most conspicuous emotional outlet of American Protestantism. Its origins may be found in the religious situation of colonies founded by earnest and pious folk who saw their children slipping away from religion as life became easier and more secular. This situation developed in New England shortly after 1650 and is signalized by the adoption of the Half-Way Covenant of 1662, which admitted the children of church members to church membership (although not to communion) without the previously required confession of "religious experience." For most of the sixty years thereafter, New England clergymen seized upon every possible opportunity to expound the decadence of religion, the necessity of a return to the ways of the founders (a renewal of covenant), the dangers of apostasy, and the innumerable signs of divine disfavor in comets, witchcraft, earthquakes, fires, and storms. Mrs. Knight's *Journal* (p. 93) is evidence of the trends which were viewed with alarm in Samuel Sewall's *Diary* (see p. 83) and in many tracts and sermons by the Mathers. Cotton Mather's *Magnalia Christi Americana* (p. 143) is the best-known and most sustained complaint of the decline of religion and the diminishing influence of the ministers.

After 1720, religion was reinvigorated by what is known as the "Great Awakening," a series of revivals which reached the young people and the lower classes in all the colonies. Through the Awakening, religion found new leaders and a somewhat broader base, becoming perceptibly less intellectual and more emotional. The excitement began in some Dutch Reformed churches of New Jersey in the 1720's. Similar revivals occurred in the Scotch-Irish Presbyterian churches of Pennsylvania, and by the 1730's appeared in New England, where Edwards was soon absorbed in their strange phenomena. Six times between 1729 and 1770 the colonies were visited by George Whitefield (1714-1770), an English evangelist who had been associated with the Wesleys in the early days of Methodism. Whitefield, who had the advantage of Calvinistic convictions, preached to vast crowds, often out-of-doors, and invariably aroused great enthusiasm. The Baptists and the Methodists found many converts through highly successful revivals, particularly in the South, in the decades just before the Revolution. Later the camp meeting and the brush-arbor church were to take revivalism westward.

The literature of revivalism is enormous; it is estimated that more than thirty-five thousand pieces relate to the Awakening. Best known, probably, are Edwards' *Some Thoughts Concerning the Present Revival of Religion in New England* (1742) and Charles Chauncy's *Seasonable Thoughts on the State of Religion in New-England* (p. 206).

The effect of revivalism was to make religion more the immediate concern of the common man than it had been before. That the development of revivalism coincided with the spread of a new sense of responsibility for the poor and the unfortunate is no accident. Revivalism was a democratizing phenomenon. It has remained typical of American Protestantism, despite the frowns of settled clergymen and of the higher economic levels of society. Although it may have tended to divide churches and to lend itself to the self-seeking of some unscrupulous evangelists, such as the one Sinclair Lewis portrayed in *Elmer Gantry,* revivalism has retained its appeal because of its recognition of the importance of emotional involvement as a part of religious experience.

Commonwealth-Building

A third great concern of the colonists, and a major theme in colonial literature, was the political hope which the New World offered. Americans were thinking, from the first, of the possibility of a new kind of state.

John Smith was not alone in observing a parallel between Europe in his time and the declining years of the Roman Empire (see p. 45). Although England had become a great and strong nation under Elizabeth I, there seemed to be more distressing poverty, more selfish wealth, more injustice and social unrest than there had ever been before. We now see, with the perspective of distance, that feudalism was still not wholly disintegrated, that hereditary and class privileges had survived longer than serfdom, and that capitalism had not yet generated sufficient social responsibility among men of wealth. Smith could say with conviction and a tinge of threat that "rich men for the most part are growne to that dotage, through their pride in their wealth, as though there were no accident could end it, or their life." In America, a land of greater plenty, merit and industry might find their fair rewards; and all men, Smith thought, might work together for the common weal.

Smith's frequent use of the word "commonwealth" is significant, for to his generation a commonwealth was a state in which all citizens — not merely a few — had an interest in the government. This is not to say that Smith was a democrat; he was not. He vaguely expressed the general dissatisfaction of his time with the political *status quo.* Men were dreaming of an ideal commonwealth, as they had not been dreaming since Plato in the fourth century B.C.

Thomas More's *Utopia* (1515-1516) and Francis Bacon's *New Atlantis* (c. 1617) suggest the political climate of opinion in the age of expansion to the New World. Such dreams of a new society were supported by the nostalgia of the primitivists, who looked back to a Golden Age in which men lived in amity, untroubled by such bickerings as those produced by the Reformation and the new national rivalries. Reformers in Switzerland, the Low Countries, and England were beginning to talk of church-states organized according to the Word of God and promising a speedy and complete reformation not merely of the church but of almost everything. In short, dreams of a "brave new world" were everywhere. So many were thinking of an ideal political organization that Shakespeare, in *The Tempest* (*c.* 1610), created an "honest old counsellor," Gonzalo, whose satirical remarks are worth recalling:

> I' th' commonwealth I would by contraries
> Execute all things; for nò kind of traffic
> Would I admit; no name of magistrate;
> Letters should not be known; riches, poverty,
> And use of service, none; . . .
> All things in common nature should produce
> Without sweat or endeavour; treason, felony,
> Sword, pike, knife, gun, or need of any engine,
> Would I not have, all foison, all abundance,
> To feed my innocent people. . . .
> I would with such perfection govern, sir,
> T' excel the golden age.

Eight American colonies — Plymouth, Massachusetts Bay, Maryland, Rhode Island, New Haven, Carolina, Pennsylvania, and Georgia — give evidence that their founders were thinking in terms of an ideal commonwealth. In most of the colonies economic and religious reasons were also involved, but at that time these could scarcely be separated from political intentions. The communistic beginnings of the Pilgrims, the theocracy of Massachusetts Bay and New Haven, the toleration principles of Rhode Island, John Locke's "ideal" constitution for Carolina, and Oglethorpe's notion of Georgia as a refuge for debtors — all had political implications. The most discussed experiment is that of Massachusetts Bay.

The full story of the transformation of the dream of an ideal commonwealth into the workaday institutions of British America, not ideal but on the whole far less aristocratic than those of Europe, is highly involved. We should remember, however, that colonial literature records at least three processes or developments: (1) the familiar pattern of transplantation and adaptation, in this case of English political and legal institutions; (2) the relative freedom from interference which was the result of unsettled problems of political authority in the mother country as well as of distance; and (3) the growth of democracy and local control, usually attributed to the influence of Separatism, which trained the humble to share in church government.

All are well illustrated in the picture which Winthrop gives us of the conflict between aristocracy and democracy in the Bay Colony. The aim of Winthrop and his associates was to found a theocracy, a state of which the head should be God, the fundamental law His word, the Bible. They wanted a Bible commonwealth in which civil authority should contribute in every way possible to the welfare of the Puritan churches. As John Eliot said in *The Christian Commonwealth* (1659), "there is undoubtedly a form of Civil Government, instituted by God himself in the holy Scriptures." This conviction, rather than any statutory provision, accounts for the leadership of the clergy in the seventeenth century. The magistrates consulted the "elders," that is, the ministers, about every important question of policy. Yet Winthrop had too much of a lawyer's respect for statute and for precedent to throw overboard the common law and the example of England, and it was not long before Massachusetts had a bicameral legislature and a legal code drawn from experience rather than from the Bible (as some ministers thought it should be). Because the Bay Company founders had the foresight to bring their charter with them, their government survived the chaotic changes of the Civil War in England. The independent attitude of the town of Hingham, finally, shows the early strength of the feeling for local autonomy in an era which had adopted a modified Congregational form of church government.

Bradford and Williams reveal in their writings much the same background. From Plymouth, the original Separatist community, we have the Mayflower Compact (see p. 62), earliest of American written constitutions and, like Winthrop's speech on liberty, a reflection of the covenant theology. In it the Pilgrims agreed to "solemnly & mutualy in yᵉ presence of God, and one of another, covenant & combine our selves togeather into a civill body politick, . . . and by vertue hearofto enacte . . . such just & equall lawes . . . as shall be thought most meete & convenient for yᵉ general good of yᵉ Colonie, unto which we promise all due submission and obedience." The Compact has a well-deserved distinction. It was Separatism, too, which led Williams to assert his doctrine that the power of the civil state must not serve the purposes of a single church (p. 128). The belief that government should rest upon the consent of the governed found practical application very early in American experience.

The conflict between the ideal of government by the few and the ideal of government by the many is reflected throughout American literature. In the colonial period it is best seen in the vast body of writings relating to the theocracy in Massachusetts. The belief of the ruling classes that things were not going well may be felt in Sewall's *Diary* and Mrs. Knight's *Journal* — both writers found the common people rowdy and obstreperous. William Byrd felt much the same way about the backcountry North Carolinians (see p. 101). Occasionally the common man found a defender, the most notable of whom was John Wise (p. 156), a vigorous champion of Congregationalism and democracy.

The colonies did not achieve the ideal commonwealth, but they present a consistent pattern of the effort to serve the common interest of all citizens, according to the lights of the leaders. "Their Cheif Red Letter day," Mrs. Knight wrote of the inhabitants of Connecticut, "is St. Election, which is annually Observed according to Charter, to choose their Governor; a blessing they can never be thankfull enough for, as they will find, if ever it be their hard fortune to loose it."

Superstition and Science

Anyone reading colonial literature notices that the texts are often punctuated with "It pleased God" or "a special providence of God appeared." These recognitions of the immediate concern of the Deity for His universe and people, always conspicuous in the historical works and diaries of the Puritans, may be found almost as readily in the reports of such hard-bitten gentlemen of fortune as Captain John Smith.

In the writings of Bradford, Winthrop, Sewall, and Mather, however, such references are often felt to be superstitious by latter-day readers, who live in a world which takes for granted an uninterrupted order of nature. We need to reflect briefly, therefore, upon the place of science in the thought of colonial Americans, especially when we encounter Sewall's comment on Cotton Mather's pulpit exposition of the Copernican hypothesis: "I think it inconvenient to assert such Problems."

The age unquestionably accepted the providential order of nature, a world in which the Lord intervened not merely to mark the sparrow's fall but to reward and punish in accordance with His inscrutable ends. We must not conclude too easily, however, that the seventeenth and eighteenth centuries were antiscientific. After all, they produced Bacon, Boyle, Descartes, Newton, Laplace, and many other first-rate scientists, whose search for truth was emulated, although not of course with such brilliant success, on this side of the Atlantic. Benjamin Franklin was not the first American to study natural phenomena, although he remains the most famous early experimenter and scientific theorist.

Colonial literature shows both a persistent scientific curiosity and a strong economic motive for the investigation of nature. Hariot impressed the Indians with mathematical instruments, the lodestone, and spring clocks (see p. 37), and Smith claimed to have fascinated Opechankanough with a sign-language exposition of astronomy and geography (see p. 50). Both men, moreover, classified and described natural phenomena in accordance with the best methods at their command, as did a great many of their successors among the travel writers and promoters. Bradford, as likely as anyone to perceive the hand of God in all events, found room to "leave it to naturallists to judge" the value of his hypothesis of the cause of earthquakes, and did not find his acceptance of providence inconsistent with speculation on the natural causes of the immoralities at Plymouth in 1642 (see p. 67). William Byrd's accounts of his travels in Virginia and North Carolina abound in botanical, zoological, and medicinal observations; Byrd, like Cotton Mather, was a Fellow of the Royal Society of London and a contributor to its *Philosophical Transactions,* the foremost British scientific journal.

The study of nature was not outlawed nor even greatly hampered by the prevalent sense of the nearness of God and the mysterious operations of His providence. Sewall's "inconvenient" was probably intended as an expression of the feeling that science and religion ought not to be mixed rather than as forthright opposition to scientific speculation. Actual mistrust of science is rarely encountered.

The Fine Arts

Architecture, painting, sculpture, and music, now often closely related to literature, were of relatively little interest to colonial writers. These arts are, however, a fascinating aspect of colonial culture as a whole, for they reveal its cosmopolitan origins, its inevitable pattern of transplantation and adaptation, and the centrality of religion in colonial society.

The most interesting of the arts is architecture, in which all three of the above elements are readily observable. The colonists learned little or nothing about house-building from the Indians and sometimes were far more uncomfortable in their first winters than they might have been had they looked about them. They had, of course, no architects and often no surplus of skilled artisans; so they built, in a sense, from memory. The more pretentious of the early New England houses imitated the half-timbered gables and overhangs of the late medieval English towns. New Amsterdam favored the small slanting dormer windows of the Dutch cottage. Along the Delaware the Swedes built log cabins — a type of structure which was to become the traditional makeshift shelter of the frontier. In the South the larger plantation houses reproduced the multiple-flued chimneys of the Jacobean period, and still further south Spanish St. Augustine introduced stuccoed walls and archways to North America. Many of these styles and a number of others, such as the Cape Cod cottage, are still being copied by conservative builders; American domestic architecture is a vast monument to our cosmopolitan origins.

Almost always, however, the transplanting of European styles had its difficulties. Chief among them was climate; England and indeed western Europe did not ordinarily have the extremes of heat and cold which characterize the eastern seaboard of North America. Materials varied, too; stone and brick were expensive and demanded a considerable degree of manual skill, but wood was plentiful, cheap, and fairly easily managed by amateur carpenters. Adaptation was therefore a necessity; to take a single example, the half-timbered and plaster house of England was almost immediately clapboarded in Massachusetts.

Finally, the dominance of religion in colonial culture is evident from the fact that the most conspicuous survivals of public architecture are the churches. In New England, especially, but to a degree in all the colonies, the church was the center of town and village life, its steeple the visible symbol of faith and aspiration.

Cosmopolitanism, adaptation, and the influence of religion are less obvious in the other arts, but there are traces of them everywhere. Painting was devoted almost exclusively to the portraiture of well-to-do families or much-loved clergymen. The really wealthy tended to have their portraits painted in England, but there were colonial "limners" from the middle of the seventeenth century who could turn out a portrait in an old-fashioned style or, if necessary, paint an inn sign or a coat of arms. One of the best known portraits is that of Samuel Sewall, by a native amateur. The first portrait engraving known to have been made in the British colonies was a wood-cut of Richard Mather dating from 1670; the first line engraving on copper, a portrait of Increase Mather made about 1701; the first mezzotint for framing, a portrait of Cotton Mather made in 1727.

Sculpture was confined, prior to the nineteenth century, to the carving of angel and of death's-heads, hourglasses, scythes, and other symbols of mortality upon tombstones, and to carving in wood. The stroller in colonial graveyards often comes away with a vivid sense of the fearlessness of death which accompanied profound faith, and the visitors to museums containing ships' figureheads and other wood-carvings can gain a first-hand impression of a seafaring, hand-skilled folk.

The first music consisted of the singing of psalms, in which the Puritans were deeply involved. The first book published in what is now the United States was the *Bay Psalm Book* (1640). With the Great Awakening came a renewed interest in church music, with a concern for hymns and choral singing. Even earlier, in Pennsylvania, the German pietistic sects had introduced instrumental music into their services. Secular music was rare before the Revolution, even in the South, and next to nothing is known about the music of the Negroes, beyond the fact that they brought both love of that art and ancient melodic patterns from their native Africa.

The Circumstances of Literary Production

Because the state of printing and the book trade are closely related to the health of literature, it is useful to recall something of the circumstances of the author in the years before 1765. Of particular importance were his close connection with Europe, his increasing opportunities as printing presses multiplied and a periodical press was established, and the changing nature of the reading public to which he addressed himself.

In the seventeenth century, as one would expect, most important books written by or relating to the colonists were printed in Europe. The colonial author wrote not so much for his immediate neighbors as for the larger world of which he felt himself a part.

For a time, indeed, colonial printing presses were both few in number and ill-equipped for book production. Printing was established in Massachusetts in 1639, but there were no presses in Maryland and Pennsylvania until 1685, none in New York until 1693. By 1763, however, printing had begun in all the thirteen original colonies. It was based upon the necessity for copies of the laws and other public papers. Almanacs, school textbooks, legal and business manuals, newspapers, and other useful but scarcely literary productions accounted for the bulk of the printed matter. Lengthy books were expensive, and very few of them were printed. Sermons, pamphlets, and small volumes of poems were fairly common. One common practice for those who admired a particular sermon was to subsidize its printing and then distribute copies to appreciative friends, as Samuel Sewall liked to do. Such distribution of a funeral sermon was apparently regarded as a suitable memorial to the departed. Much material was reprinted from English sources, sometimes, as in the case of textbooks, over and over again. The quantity of theological literature was greatest in New England, that of belles-lettres and political literature greatest in the middle colonies, and that of legal literature greatest in the South. In general, the production of the colonial printers was heavily utilitarian. Of the books represented in the present chapter only nine — Cotton Mather's *Wonders of the Invisible World* and *Manuductio,* Wise's *Vindication,* Edwards' two sermons and *Freedom of Will,* Chauncy's *Seasonable Thoughts,* Wigglesworth's *Day of Doom,* and the second edition of

Anne Bradstreet's poems — were printed in America in the years before 1765. Evidently it was not easy for colonial authors to rush into print. The book-buying public was relatively small; the average edition of books and pamphlets in the early part of the eighteenth century was probably between three and five hundred copies. As a matter of fact, much of what we now read as colonial literature, including the works here printed from the pens of Bradford, Winthrop, Sewall, Mrs. Knight, Byrd, and Edward Taylor, was not even in print prior to the Revolution.

Newspapers, although almost nonexistent in the seventeenth century, constituted the staple work of colonial printers by 1750. *Publick Occurrences,* which appeared at Boston in 1690, was suppressed after a single issue, so that the *Boston News-Letter,* established in 1704, is usually regarded as the first American newspaper and the *Boston Gazette* (1719) as the second. Other important early newspapers include the *American Weekly Mercury* of Philadelphia (founded 1719), the *New-England Courant* of Boston (1721), the *New-York Gazette* (1727), the *Maryland Gazette* of Baltimore (1727), the *Pennsylvania Gazette* (1730) — Franklin's journal and the best of colonial newspapers — the *South Carolina Gazette* of Charleston (1732), and the *Virginia Gazette* of Williamsburg (1736). Most of these papers were of modest size at first, and it was many years before there was much space for literary material. Sometimes, as in the case of James Franklin's *New-England Courant,* a printing shop became the center of an informal club of literary-minded gentlemen, and Benjamin Franklin used the *Pennsylvania Gazette* to promote the cooperative and political ends he had in mind. Gradually newspapers began to find room for letters to the editor, political articles, discussions of science and technology, even familiar essays and poetry. None of the selections in the present chapter, however, had a newspaper origin. Magazines were even less significant than newspapers, although in 1741 both Benjamin Franklin and his chief rival, Andrew Bradford, issued short-lived magazines in imitation of London periodicals.

The colonial printer was often bookseller and postmaster as well. Many books were imported, and as time went on their distribution was accomplished by peddlers and auctions as well as by bookshop sales. A few of the more expensive books were sold by subscriptions obtained before they were actually printed. All in all, it seems certain that most readers, like most serious authors, looked abroad for their fulfillment of literary life.

American traditions about censorship and the control of the press had their beginnings in this time. There were incidents in which governors or councils brought action against printers, but probably the colonial press was as free or even freer than that of England. As early as 1696 a Massachusetts jury refused to convict a printer for publishing a work which had offended the officials and the clergy, and in 1735 the famous trial of Peter Zenger in New York enhanced the precedent that libel laws were not to be readily used to suppress freedom of speech and freedom of the press. By the beginning of the Revolutionary period the colonial press was in a position to play what from some points of view may be regarded as a decisive part in the drama of political action that would lead ultimately to the independence of the United States.

II. Literary Trends

Moses Coit Tyler, in his *History of American Literature, 1607-1765* (1878), divided colonial books into two groups: those written for English readers and those composed for the Americans themselves. In the former group Tyler found six types of material: (1) books whose purpose was to send home tidings of "welfare or ill fare"; (2) books written to appeal legal or financial matters to superior tribunals in England; (3) apologetics, designed to defend the colonies against injurious aspersions by their enemies; (4) writings particularly devoted to the Indians; (5) "descriptions of nature in America"; and (6) accounts of gradual innovations in politics, laws, creeds, and religious and domestic usages. Among the writings composed for the colonists themselves Tyler found four types of material: (1) sermons and religious treatises; (2) histories; (3) poems; and (4) prose with miscellaneous purposes.

Tyler's classification is still useful, but its fundamental division violates the conclusion of later scholars that the colonists seldom wrote merely for themselves. As we turn now to problems of literary forms and excellence, we can describe the bulk of colonial writings under seven heads. The principle of division is still content, but we shall consider particularly the structural problems which faced colonial writers, and their solutions in: (1) accounts of voyages; (2) promotion tracts; (3) sermons; (4) polemical tracts and treatises; (5) histories and biographies; (6) diaries and autobiographies; and (7) poems. A brief explanation of the absence of plays and novels in colonial America will conclude this introduction.

Accounts of Voyages

Of the literary types common in the colonies, the simplest in structure was the account of a voyage, from which developed the later literature of travel. At first such accounts were plain narratives written by plain and barely literate men. The organization was chronological, presenting a sequence of events as recorded in the writer's memory, journal, or whatever notes he had thought worth making. He could expand whenever his interests or those of his prospective readers seemed to make expansion desirable. The letter in which Columbus reported upon his first voyage is a good example of the type; another is John Brereton's *Briefe and True Relation of the Discouerie of the North Part of Virginia* (1602), the earliest English account of the New England coast. The type dominates the great collections of voyages which were edited by Richard Hakluyt, Samuel Purchas, and John Harris (*Collection of Voyages and Travels*, 1705). Although written to provide information, the account of a voyage was seldom impersonal, and it sometimes achieved a sharpness of effect and a charm as great as if written by a literary artist.

Both Mrs. Knight's *Journal* and Byrd's "Progress to the Mines" adapt the type to a land journey with highly readable results. Byrd's versions of the *History of the Dividing Line* show how readily information and humor could be inserted into the elastic structure of the travel narrative.

Travel books constitute one of the largest classes of American literature. Although such books are closely related to the economic motives for colonization and westward migration, they are also valuable for the light they throw upon social life and customs. Often, moreover, they reveal interesting and lively personalities, some of them with a sense of humor and a talent for entertainment.

Promotion Tracts

The writer of a promotion tract almost invariably had to struggle with a topical arrangement. To generalize attractively about the resources of the region he was describing required persuasive division of material with which he was not always intimately acquainted. Furthermore, he could make only limited use of narrative, and he needed to appear judicious and relatively objective. Promotion tracts therefore vary considerably in structure, according to the individual solutions of these problems.

Hariot wisely followed his main interest — economic resources — in his account of Virginia. First he described commodities already found or raised in Virginia in quantities sufficient to be marketable: useful plants, minerals, and furs. He then listed commodities known to be plentiful enough to sustain life: grains, vegetables, fruits, game animals, fowl, and fish. A third section listed miscellaneous commodities. His account of the Indians (p. 35) followed, and the whole was concluded by a few pages of persuasion (p. 40).

Smith's *Description of New England* (p. 44) and *Map of Virginia* employed a far commoner structure. They both began with the general geographical features and then described the climate, winds, soils, rivers, settled places, plants, animals, birds, fish, minerals, and Indians. The *Map* was the more carefully organized; in his *Description* Smith himself realized that his enthusiasm had carried him away, and at one point he asks his readers to return a little with him, adding that he is not "sufficiently yet acquainted in those parts, to write fully the estate of the Sea, the Ayre, the Land, the Fruites, the Rocks, the People, the Gouernment, Religion, Territories and Limitations, Friends and Foes: but as I gathered from the niggardly relations in a broken language to my understanding, during the time I ranged those Countries." Smith, one may note, had a list of topics arranged in an order proceeding from the general to the particular. This systematic approach he probably derived from the geographical literature of his day, which in turn reflects the almost invariable approach of the medieval schoolmen to the study of the external world.

When the works of Aristotle were the highest authority in science, they were studied according to a settled system. A student began with the *Organon* and the *Physica,* which deal with logic and the general properties of natural bodies; next he examined the *De Caelo,* a description of the heavens; after that he took up the *De Generatione et Corruptione,* which treats the four elements — earth, water, air, and fire — and their various combinations and interactions; he then looked at the *Meteorologica,* which describes the various processes of change in the elements, and at various discussions of "perfectly mixed" and "imperfectly mixed" bodies of the inanimate kind (stones, metals, and minerals); and finally he came to the *De Anima* and the *Historia Animalium,* descriptions of animate bodies (plants and animals). Thus equipped, he could undertake the study of man.

Many promotion tracts besides Smith's were based upon this tradition, for it was the topical arrangement most familiar to educated men. Francis Higginson's *New England's Plantation* begins with the following statement: "And because the life and wel-fare of euerie Creature here below, and the commodiousnesse of the Countrey whereas such Creatures liue, doth by the most wise ordering of Gods prouidence, depend next vnto himselfe, vpon the temperature and disposition of the foure Elements, Earth, Water, Aire, and Fire. . . . Therefore I will indeauour to shew you what *New England* is by the consideration of these apart, and truly endeauour by Gods helpe to report nothing but the naked truth." Wood's *New England's Prospect* is similarly Aristotelian, in that it proceeds from the general to the particular. Morton's *New English Canaan* is less systematic.

Although the thoughtful reader will discover many minor variations, together with some amusing decisions about order and treatment, the promotion tracts are remarkably consistent in general outline. They are very numerous and are closely related to the "progress reports" sent back to those at home by actual settlers. Reports of progress contain a somewhat larger proportion of narrative, but do not differ greatly otherwise.

Sermons

The sermon was the most highly developed literary type in colonial literature, and a list of the sermons available in print and in manuscript would run literally into the thousands. Men and women listened to sermons every Sunday; often they went to lecture sermons during the week; they heard sermons on many public occasions — elections, thanksgiving and fast days, military trainings, funerals. The more serious kept diaries or notebooks, recording the texts and even the heads of the discourses to which they listened. Men and women who lived in an age when the pulpit was the center of intellectual life knew a good sermon when they heard one.

Two complete sermons are reprinted in this chapter in order to represent this important type more adequately than is possible with excerpts. That by Thomas Shepard is from the early seventeenth century; that by Jonathan Edwards was delivered in 1733. Both are systematically organized with doctrines drawn from the Scripture text, reasons given for those doctrines, and the uses or applications of the doctrines suggested. This structure is the most common by far in the sermons of the American Puritans. It could be varied, as Shepard's sermon shows, by inserting objections and answers or by subdivision, such as the nine easy ways to hell under Use 5. A present-day reader is likely to find the "firstlys," "secondlys," etc., wooden and pedantic, but earnest churchgoers in Shepard's time wanted to know where they were, so that they could go home and debate the soundness of his third or fourth or fifth use. The logical structure is also lightened by numerous homely illustrations and bursts of eloquence, and by the frequent citation of parallel texts from the Bible. All this is typical; the preachers made valiant efforts to relate their sermons to the experience of their hearers.

Some Puritan sermons reflect the system of logic developed by a sixteenth-century French humanist, Petrus Ramus, or Pierre de la Ramée. Ramus saw the world in terms of pairs or opposites, and he may well be responsible for the fondness for similitudes and antitheses which is evident in the sermons, even in that by Edwards.

The sermons raise questions, moreover, about prose style. The Puritans tended to favor the "plain" style, but some of them were fond of embellishing their discourses with tags of Latin, Greek, or even Hebrew, or with allusions to secular literature. Among the Americans, Cotton Mather was probably the most given to ornament. He seems to have had the idea that part of the preacher's job was to educate his unlettered congregation. A comparison of Shepard and Edwards reveals a sharp contrast between an almost brusque vigor and a polished smooth-flowing eloquence (cf. the paragraph beginning "The way of *Formality,*" p. 125, with that beginning "IF CHRIST should now appear," p. 192). One man is clearly of the Renaissance, the other a child of the Enlightenment.

Their purpose, however, was the same: to persuade men to consider honestly the state of their souls. The minister was to preach the gospel of Jesus Christ, to awaken his hearers to the supreme importance of faith and regeneration, to the urgent necessity of assuming an active part in the eternal warfare within man's soul between good and evil, the spirit and the flesh, God and the Devil. The sermon was the essence of Protestantism, more important than any theological dogma, form of worship, perhaps even more important than the sacraments (although the Lord's Supper was of enormous significance to such a man as Edward Taylor). Among the Calvinists, the sermon was the chief means of preserving believers from fatalistic acceptance of their destiny. That most men were foreordained to sin and damnation and that there was nothing the individual could do about it: these were doctrines which might easily have led to despair or indifference. The sermons, however, were based upon the even more powerful doctrines that divine grace did come to some men, and that to those who received it grace was a constant growth, an increasing understanding of perfection, an endless enlarging of one's capacity to deal with doubt and sin and temptation. Hence the soul searching of the Puritans, the esteem and affection for "soul-ravishing" preachers like Shepard, the vast respect for the sublime certainty with which Edwards testified to the "spiritual Light" which is "the dawning of the Light of Glory in the Heart." Puritans found sermons thrilling because sermons guided the analyzing and strengthening of their inner life.

The sermon was both an appeal to man's imperfect reason and a stirring of his emotion, both an intellectual experience and a glimpse of magnificent poetic vistas, opened by God's promise to the regenerate soul. Whenever and wherever religion was a vital and absorbing concern it called forth some of the best available literary talent. The sermon remains, moreover, the key to the religious life of the colonial era.

Beginning of Controversial Writing

Theological and political discussion also produced an extensive literature of controversy. Decisions had to be made about church government, institutional organization, governmental policy, and theological positions, and there were often wide divergences of opinion. Men with convictions expressed them in numerous tracts and treatises, represented in the following pages by Williams' *Bloudy Tenent,* Cotton Mather's *Manuductio ad Ministerium,* Wise's *Vindication,* Edwards' *Freedom of Will,* and Chauncy's *Seasonable Thoughts.* These, and other works like them, vary widely in their structure, which ordinarily grew directly out of the controversial issues with which they dealt.

Williams' use of the dialogue is not uncommon, and has the virtue of lending some drama to the issues, but topical organization is probably more usual. Polemical tracts were frequently a point-by-point refutation of a preceding pamphlet or treatise. Sometimes they were constructed as a series of queries, to which the author gave his well-considered answers. The fiction of a "letter" to a friend was used many times. To generalize about the literary form of the literature of controversy is, therefore, extremely difficult. Its most striking difference from similar material of today is perhaps that little of it appeared in magazines. The development of periodicals as a forum for discussion came in a later period.

The volume and variety of tracts and treatises can best be suggested by listing a few of the better-known titles, in addition to those by Williams, Eliot, Cotton Mather, Wise, Edwards, and Franklin which have already been mentioned. Among the books which still find readers are the following: Richard Mather's *Church Government and Church Covenant* (1643); John Cotton's *Way of the Churches of Christ in New-England* (1645); Nathaniel Ward's *Simple Cobler of Aggawam in America* (1647); Thomas Hooker's *Survey of the Summe of Church Discipline* (1648); Increase Mather's *Cases of Conscience concerning Evil Spirits Personating Men* (1693); Samuel Sewall's

Selling of Joseph (1700); Cotton Mather's *Essays to Do Good* (as *Bonifacius,* 1710) and *Christian Philosopher* (1721); Franklin's *Modest Inquiry into the Nature and Necessity of a Paper Currency* (1729) and *Proposals Relating to the Education of Youth in Pensilvania* (1749); Jared Eliot's *Essay on Field Husbandry in New England* (Part I, 1748); John Woolman's *Some Considerations on the Keeping of Negroes* (Part I, 1753); James Otis' *Vindication of the Conduct of the House of Representatives of Massachusetts* (1762) and *Rights of British Colonies Asserted and Proved* (1764). Religion, women's fashions, social reform, science, education, agriculture, politics — all are represented, and the list could easily be extended. This type of literature had its models in Europe, but its content is almost always peculiarly American. It is the basis of the tradition of free discussion and a free press and is perhaps, to the intellectual historian, the most significant part of colonial writing.

Histories and Biographies

History and biography are conspicuous in colonial literature because the settlers wanted, for several reasons, to preserve a record of what happened in the New World. In its simplest form such writing was annalistic, a simple statement of historical and biographical fact. The journals of Bradford and Winthrop and Nathaniel Morton's *New-England's Memoriall* (1669) follow the natural chronological order and set down the main facts of each year. This bare narration seldom satisfied the colonial writer of history, however; he conceived it his duty to interpret events, usually in terms of speculation about God's intentions.

Mixed motives appear in most colonial histories and biographies. Smith's account of Virginia (p. 49) was both a justification of his own actions and a defense of the somewhat unpopular movement for colonization. Smith also had a remarkably modern grasp of the connection between history and geography. Bradford's history of Plymouth (p. 55) was written for the children and grandchildren of the Pilgrims, that they might understand and perpetuate the piety of the little group of founders whose struggles had merited, so Bradford thought, the special favor of God. Winthrop's journal-history of the Bay Colony (p. 73), strongly flavored with the same providential view of events as Bradford's book, had in it also both the element of self-justification and a lawyer's respect for exact knowledge of precedents and experiments in institutional organization. Cotton Mather's biography of Burr (p. 144) amplified Bradford's admiration for the founders and concern for succeeding generations into a defense of the good old "New England Way." Byrd's histories of the Dividing Line (p. 98) and Peters' account of Connecticut (p. 110) had axes to grind as well as information to convey.

Much colonial historical writing was tinged with the belief in a providential order of nature, and hence took on a distinctly theological quality. If events were to be interpreted as the working out of the divine plan, which man could never know in its entirety, a monstrous birth might be quite as instructive as a victory in battle or a momentous political or religious compromise. To the modern reader, Winthrop seems to jump easily from affairs of great moment to the most trivial events, and to be scarcely aware of the operation of economic, political, and social forces upon a changing society. He was more interested in looking for moral meanings in events. The same attitude characterizes most seventeenth-century histories, appearing most vividly in Edward Johnson's *The Wonder-Working Providence of Sion's Saviour in New England* (1654) and reaching its culmination in Cotton Mather's *Magnalia Christi Americana* (1702). For the providential theory the colonists had the example of the Book of Kings, the Roman historian Livy, and many ecclesiastical annalists from the time of St. Augustine.

More rationalistic tendencies may also be observed in colonial historiography. We have already noted Bradford's analysis of the possible causes for an outbreak of immorality in 1642. Judicious and objective methods were foreshadowed in Thomas Prince's *Chronological History of New England in the Form of Annals* (2 vols., 1736, 1755), in William Stith's *History of the First Discovery of Virginia* (1747), and most notably in Thomas Hutchinson's *History of the Province of Massachusetts Bay* (3 vols., 1764, 1767, 1828). These works likewise had European models, although Hutchinson's was the only one to show traces of the regard for institutional development which made Voltaire's *Age of Louis XIV* (1751) a landmark.

Diaries and Autobiographies

An amazing number of colonists kept diaries or wrote autobiographies. Their purpose was sometimes practical — the desire to have a record of the weather, the planting and harvesting of crops, business transactions, and personal affairs. More often, perhaps, and almost always in the case of the autobiographies, the aim was fundamentally religious. Earnest churchgoers wished to study the state of their souls, and one of the best possible methods was to preserve a day-by-day or systematic account of temptations, struggles, and meditations.

The best example of a Puritan diary is that kept between February 1653, and May, 1657, by Michael Wigglesworth (p. 212), not printed until 1951. Its agonizing concern for the shortcomings of its author (and of his neighbors!) is pathological but probably typical. Cotton Mather's diary, better known and much longer, gives the impression of being dressed up for possible publication; he seems to have kept a regular day-by-day journal but edited it at the end of a year, keeping only the more "spiritual" passages. In the realm of autobiography, Jonathan Edwards' "Personal Narrative" is probably outstanding for its portrayal of a man absorbed in the problem of his relation to God. The autobiography and "Meditations and Spiritual Experience" of Thomas Shepard are earlier efforts in this genre. There are innumerable "testimonies" or spiritual autobiographies, especially among the Quakers, most of which concentrate on the experience of conversion. Two of the greatest of early American books — John Woolman's *Journal* (p. 348) and Benjamin Franklin's *Autobiography* (p. 273) — are in the direct line of descent from the simpler self-analyses.

Those diaries which are most treasured by later generations are the ones in which soul-searching is leavened by an interest in temporal affairs. Winthrop's journal and the travel journal of Mrs. Knight (p. 93) have this interest, but the two chief diaries are those by Samuel Sewall (p. 83) and William Byrd. Both preserve for us the customs, manners, and personalities of relatively worldly people. We learn from them of the food, the drink, the social life, the household appointments, the gardens, the crimes, the births, marriages, and deaths — the external life, in short, of seventeenth- and eighteenth-century Americans.

Sewall's diary is the better of the two, even though it does not compare with the great English diaries of John Evelyn and Samuel Pepys, written at about the same time. Sewall's world was more circumscribed than theirs. Like all good diarists, however, Sewall has the virtue of revealing himself as a human being, beset by frailties and inadequacies and little vanities.

Byrd (p. 98) kept his diary in shorthand; and except for those portions of it which he chose to expand into travel accounts or histories of the running of the Dividing Line, it has been only recently available. Its three volumes cover the years 1709-1712 (published 1941), 1717-1721 (1958), and 1739-1741 (1942). Although the entries are sometimes repetitious and trivial, they provide the most intimate acquaintance we now have with a leading number of the Virginia oligarchy, which was closely allied in its ambitions with the landed gentry of England. For Byrd London was a second home. Sewall went to London as a tourist.

Poems

American poetry prior to 1765 is, when compared to that of England in the same period, small in quantity and, with few exceptions, inferior in quality. No colonial poet, with the possible exception of Edward Taylor, reached the level of George Herbert, Robert Herrick, Abraham Cowley, Samuel Butler, Matthew Prior, Edward Young, or James Thomson, and none remotely approached the artistic achievement of Donne, Milton, Dryden, or Pope.

Nevertheless, the attitude toward early American verse has become much less apologetic in the last thirty years, thanks to the discovery of Taylor by Thomas H. Johnson (ed., *The Poetical Works of Edward Taylor*, 1939), and the investigation of Taylor's predecessors and contemporaries by Harold S. Jantz (*The First Century of New England Verse*, 1943). Poetry which nineteenth-century critics found either quaint or pedantic is now taken seriously and its tight-packed imagery admired. The style which Moses Coit Tyler spoke of as "fantastic perversion" (he preferred to call the school of Donne "fantastics" rather than "metaphysicals") is now labeled "Baroque" and studied with respect.

Seventeenth-century American verse can be divided roughly into two categories: that written to be memorized, and that written to dignify or embellish important occasions. The former is the best known and more naïve.

Puritan children apparently memorized maxims and stories in verse from the earliest days of the settlement. Among the pieces available for this purpose were rhymed accounts of English Protestant history by the Rev. John Wilson (see *Handkerchiefs from Paul,* ed. K. B. Murdock, 1927) and *The Day of Doom* (1662), the Rev. Michael Wigglesworth's famous summary of Calvinistic theology. Even the compilers of the *Bay Psalm Book* (1640), although their main purpose was to translate the Hebrew with the greatest possible exactness, chose to put the psalms to be sung in the New England churches in English meter, that is to say in the ballad stanza of folk poetry:

> The Lord to mee a shepheard is,
> want therefore shall not I.
> Hee in the folds of tender-grasse,
> doth cause mee downe to lie.
> To waters calme me gently leads
> Restore my soule doth hee:
> he doth in paths of righteousnes:
> for his names sake leade mee.

The use of the ballad stanza reveals the strength of the popular tradition in the face of novel conditions — in this instance the Puritan respect for the Hebrew text of the Psalms. Poetry as art suffered, but the meter of "Barbara Allan" was the one most easily remembered. Vaguely related to the mnemonic purpose, although essentially didactic in the same way as colonial historical writing, are the numerous historical poems of the period. Bradford himself tried his hand at this type of writing, but the best known examples are Benjamin Tompson's narratives of King Philip's War: *New Englands Crisis* (1676) and *New-Englands Tears for Her Present Miseries* (1676). Both display the providential theory of history in an elaborate form.

Many important events were commemorated in poetry (see *American Broadside Verse,* ed. Ola Elizabeth Winslow, 1930), but the one thing that most commonly called for the dignifying presence of verse was the death of a clergyman or other public figure. The anagrams and elegies thus evoked have been the butt of considerable humor, including Benjamin Franklin's recipe for the would-be elegist:

For the subject of your Elegy, Take one of your Neighbors who has lately departed this Life; it is no great matter of what Age the Party dy'd, but it will be best if he went away suddenly, being *Kill'd, Drown'd,* or *Frose to Death.*

Having chose the Person, take all his Virtues, Excellencies, &c. and if he have not enough, you may borrow some to make up a sufficient Quantity. To these add his last Words, dying Expressions, &c. if they are to be had; mix all these together, and be sure you strain them well. Then season all with a Handful or two of Melancholly Expressions, such as, *Dreadful, Deadly, cruel cold Death, unhappy Fate, weeping Eyes,* &c. . . . let them Ferment for the Space of a Fortnight, and by that Time they will be incorporated into a Body, which take out, and having prepared a sufficient Quantity of double Rhimes, such as *Power, Flower;*

Quiver, Shiver; Grieve us, Leave us; tell you, excel you; Expeditions, Physicians; Fatigue him, Intrigue him; &c. you must spread all upon Paper, and if you can procure a Scrap of Latin to put at the End, it will garnish it mightily; then having affixed your Name at the Bottom, with a *Moestus Composuit,* you will have an Excellent Elegy.

The quality of the Puritan funeral elegy no doubt deteriorated. In the early seventeenth century, however, it was, as Jantz has demonstrated, a sophisticated form. A number of the elegists began with an anagram of their subject's name (John Fiske, for example, took John Cotton [Iohn Kotton] and got "O, Honie knott"), then used this anagram as a basic image around which the elegy developed. The result was the kind of tight-packed imagery which is so much admired in the poems of Edward Taylor. Fiske's poem includes such passages as this:

> Hee who the knotts of Truth, of Mysteries
> sacred, most cleerely did ope' fore our eyes
> even hee who such a one, is ceas'd to bee
> 'twixt whose life, death, the most sweete harmony
> Knotts we doe meet with many a cue daily
> which crabbed anggry tough unpleasing bee
> but we as in a honi-comb a knott
> of Hony sweete, here had such sweetenes Gott
> the knotts and knobbs that on the Trees doe grow
> the bitterest excrescences we know.

The mnemonic verses and the elegies loom large in the seventeenth century, but they are not, of course, the whole story. Two poets, both represented in the present chapter, range fairly widely for their subject matter and, although they imitated French and English religious poets — the English Spenserians, Du Bartas, Donne, Herbert, Quarles, and Richard Crashaw — succeeded in conveying the intensity of their individual experience. Anne Bradstreet and Edward Taylor tell us much of the inner life of American Puritanism.

In the eighteenth century, American verse took on a more classical orientation, as the number of colleges increased and educated gentlemen followed the fashions set by Dryden and Pope. Latin verses continued to be composed, and translations constituted a common exercise. The "highbrow" versemaking reached its height in *Pietas et Gratulatio* (1761). Harvard College's tribute to the new king, George III, it contained three poems in Greek, sixteen in Latin, and twelve in English. Individuals trained in the classics were also interested in the work of the English Neoclassical school, and there were many colonial poems in the manner of the satires of Dryden and Pope, the mock-heroics of Butler, and the philosophical pieces of Thomson, Young, and Pomfret. These are often of interest for their content, although it is disconcerting to find colonial poets expressing boredom with court and city life, when, as someone said, five minutes' walking would have taken any one of them into a cow pasture. We may safely leave the works of Mather Byles, John Adams (the clergyman, not the statesman), George Webb, William Livingston, the younger Thomas Godfrey, Nathaniel Evans, Joseph Green, and other "wits" to the specialist, remembering, however, that they were the literati of their day and that they cherished the tradition of belles-lettres in a world frequently too busy for art.

Plays and Novels

Fiction and drama, which bulk large in later American literature, were almost nonexistent in the colonial period. Both were distrusted by serious-minded persons, in England as well as in America, although it is not just to ascribe their absence entirely to Puritan influence. A theater requires considerable capital and a public in the habit of playgoing, neither of which is often to be found except in the largest centers of population. As a class, moreover, actors were long mistrusted by civic authorities, as the history of the London theater shows. These factors alone would be enough to account for the antagonism to stage plays which appears in colonial laws forbidding their public performance. Virginia was one of the few colonies without such legislation, but the earliest mention of a play acted in the colonies suggests some prejudice even there. In 1665 three citizens of Accomac County were called upon to appear in costume and tell what they said in *Ye Bare and Ye Cubb.* They were discharged and their accuser forced to pay the court charges.

The Puritans, however, unquestionably delayed the development of an American drama. Their influence had closed the theaters in England for eighteen years, and many colonists shared the resentment of English Puritans for the ridicule of Puritanism in Elizabethan drama. Remembered also was the association of the theater with the immoralities of king and court and the vigorous attack on the theater by the church fathers of the latter days of the Roman empire. To the famous English attacks on the theater by Stubbs (1583), Prynne (1632), and Collier (1698) there was at least one American parallel: Increase Mather's *Testimony against Several Prophane and Superstitious Customs, Now Practised by Some in New England* (1687).

There was no effort to keep printed plays out of the college libraries, and as time went on there seems to have been sporadic interest in them in academic halls. There is some evidence that students at Harvard were thinking of histrionic things in the 1690's — a doubtful tradition that Benjamin Colman, later a prominent liberal clergyman, wrote a Latin play entitled *Gustavus Vasa* in 1690, and an allusion to examining "several of the Scholars about the Comedy" in Increase Mather's diary for 1698. The students at William and Mary offered a "pastoral colloquy" before the governor in 1702, and later in the eighteenth century undergraduates at Philadelphia, Princeton, New Haven, and Cambridge were frequently experimenting with dialogues and dramatic exercises. *The Prince of Parthia,* by the younger Thomas Godfrey, one of the literary group centering in the College of Philadelphia, was written in 1759, published in 1765, and actually produced on a professional stage in 1767. Imitative of the English heroic drama, it was a natural outgrowth of the discovery of belles-lettres by undergraduates and their friends.

New tastes and attitudes were accepted by the general public only gradually, despite the efforts of entranced amateurs, the visits of professional actors, and the changing tone of English drama. The first play to be printed was *Antroboros* (1714), a political satire published anonymously by Robert Hunter, governor of New York. Williamsburg built a theater in 1716, but there is no evidence that it was used until twenty years later. New York probably was entertained by a group of professional actors in 1732, and Charleston had a brief "season" in 1735. A company which performed Addison's *Cato* in Philadelphia in 1742 was arrested and forbidden to appear again. Going to New York, it performed *Richard III, The Beggar's Opera,* and other plays in 1750. An amateur performance scandalized conservative Boston in that same year, although George Lillo's bourgeois tragedy, *George Barnwell* (1731), had been reprinted in *The New-England Weekly Journal* within a year after its appearance in London. American theatrical history is usually said to have begun in 1752, with the arrival of Lewis Hallam's "American Company," which had continuous history in repertoire until 1774, when the Continental Congress forbade theatrical performances "for the duration." The American Company played at Williamsburg, New York, Philadelphia, Annapolis, Newport, Providence, Charleston, and several towns in Virginia, and succeeded (sometimes by such stratagems as offering *Othello* as a series of "Moral Dialogues") in familiarizing the more venturesome colonists with the plays of Shakespeare, Marlowe, Dryden, Congreve, Farquhar, Addison, Steele, Cibber, Ambrose Philips, and others. But there was no native drama.

Nor did colonial Americans produce either novels or novel-like narratives comparable to those of Bunyan, Defoe, and Swift. This is less surprising than that there should have been no drama, for the novel as a form had by no means reached its full maturity. The seriousness of the reading public left little time for long romances, although a good many of them appear on colonial book lists, and the pleasure in swift-moving narrative was partly provided for by the accounts of voyages and travels, the somewhat lurid accounts of captivity among the Indians, and the other factual material such as reports of the experiences and final hours of pirates and murderers and the descriptions of remarkable providences and witchcrafts. Many works of fiction which supposedly portrayed life must have seemed dull in comparison to more direct reporting. The prevalent attitude toward fiction is probably that of Cotton Mather in *Manuductio ad Ministerium,* where he advises divinity students to enjoy the recreation of poetry but not to be so set upon it

> as to be always poring on the *Passionate* and *Measured* Pages. Let not what should be *Sauce* rather than Food for you, Engross all your Application. . . . Indeed, not merely for the *Impurities* which they convey, but also on some other Accounts, the *Powers of Darkness* have a *Library* among us, whereof the *Poets* have been the most *Numerous* as well as the most *Venemous* Authors. Most of the modern *Plays,* as well as the *Romances* and *Novels,* and *Fictions,* which are a sort of *Poems,* do belong to the Catalogue of this cursed Library.   T.H.

1560—1621 Thomas Hariot

I n 1585 Thomas Hariot, a twenty-five-year-old Englishman already known in Oxford as a talented mathematician, landed on Roanoke Island, off the coast of what is now North Carolina, with the hundred-odd men involved in Sir Walter Raleigh's most ambitious attempt to establish a colony in North America. He stayed in Virginia (as all the territory claimed by the British had been named) for a little over a year, surveying its resources with scientific care. On his return to England he found it necessary to defend Raleigh's projects against slander from those members of the company who had been miserable in America because "there were not to bee found any English cities, nor such faire houses, nor at their owne wish any of their olde accustomed daintie food, nor any soft beds of downe or fethers." Hariot's defense of Raleigh and Virginia took the form of a forty-six-page pamphlet, *A Briefe and True Report of the New Found Land of Virginia* (London, 1588). Soon after it was published, he was pensioned by the Earl of Northumberland so that he could devote himself to mathematics and astronomy, and in his later years he was famous for his work in algebra.

Hariot knew that a living was to be had in America, and easily, but he knew also that men would have to learn to use the commodities which the country provided. His book, therefore, was one of the first "promotion tracts," designed to inform prospective emigrants of the opportunities the New World could offer to ambitious men. Like the real estate brochure of the present day, the promotion tract almost invariably emphasized the possibilities of vast profits and minimized the probable losses and hardships. Even Hariot, to whom the New World was less an earthly paradise than it was to some of his successors, assured his readers that in Virginia one man "may prepare and husband so much ground (having once borne corne before) with lesse than foure and twenty hours labour, as shall yeeld him victual in a large proportion for a twelvemoneth." Probably no one ever came to America actually believing that twenty-four hours of work would provide nearly enough food for a year, but the tenor of the promotion tracts was almost that optimistic. They pictured a land of limitless resources, unbounded fertility, and ideal climate, and contributed appreciably to the notion of America as a place where mankind's centuries-old dream of freedom from want might at last be realized.

Hariot was also among the earliest of English visitors to describe the American aborigines. Prospective settlers naturally wanted to know how numerous the Indians were and how friendly; but they had also a great curiosity about the new races and cultures to which the discovery of the New World had introduced Europeans. Among Hariot's companions on Roanoke Island was an artist, John White. In 1590, when Hariot's *Virginia* was reprinted at Frankfort, engravings from White's drawings were appended. Twenty-two of these engravings depicted the Indians, adding to Hariot's emphasis on their curious religious customs and suggesting what Hariot did not, that the savages were physically sturdy and handsome. Reading Hariot, one can grasp many of the motives for English colonization; looking at White's drawings, one can understand the long-lived literary tradition of the noble savage, whose simple, uncovetous life was to seem infinitely superior to that of supposedly civilized Europeans in the eyes of many seventeenth- and eighteenth-century writers.

Bernard Jaffe, **American Men of Science**, New York, 1944 · **The American Drawings of John White, 1577-1590**, 2 vols., Chapel Hill, 1964

from A Briefe and True Report of the New Found Land of Virginia

Hariot's Virginia *was divided into six sections, as follows: (1) an introduction, in which he explained his purpose in writing the book; (2) a section on "marchantable" commodities, that is to say, products such as ship supplies and furs for which a European market existed; (3) a section on commodities "for victuall and sustenance of mans life," in which he listed edible vegetables, animals, fish, and fowl, stating that many more had been observed and pictures made of them by White; (4) a brief section on materials for building and other uses; (5) an account of "the nature and manners of the people"; and (6) a conclusion in which the benefits of colonization are outlined. The fifth and sixth sections are here reprinted. Hariot's purpose in this tract was partly informative and partly persuasive. He wrote hurriedly, in all likelihood, but with the ease and freedom which characterize the best prose of Elizabethan England.*

In its original edition of 1588, Hariot's Virginia *is one of the rarest books relating to America. In 1600 Richard Hakluyt included Hariot's account in the third volume of his* Principall Nauigations, *and it was thereafter readily available to European and American readers.*

The apparent waywardness in spelling, punctuation, and abbreviation may be laid at the printer's door as much as at Hariot's; such things had not been standardized in the sixteenth century.

Of the Nature and Manners of the People

It resteth I speake a word or two of the naturall inhabitants, their natures and maners, leauing large discourse thereof vntill time more conuenient hereafter: nowe onely so farre foorth, as that you may know, how that they in respect of troubling our inhabiting and planting, are not to be feared; but that they shall haue cause both to feare and loue vs, that shall inhabite with them.

They are a people clothed with loose mantles made of Deere skins, & aprons of the same rounde about their middles; all els naked; of such a difference of statures only as wee in England; hauing no edge tooles or weapons of yron or steele to offend vs withall, neither know they how to make any: those weapons ỹ they haue, are onlie
10 bowes made of Witch hazle, & arrowes of reeds; flat edged truncheons also of wood about a yard long, neither haue they any thing to defēd thēselues but targets made of barks; and some armours made of stickes wickered together with thread.

Their townes are but small, & neere the sea coast but few, some containing but 10. or 12. houses: some 20. the greatest that we haue seene haue bene but of 30. houses: if they be walled it is only done with barks of trees made fast to stakes, or els with poles onely fixed vpright and close one by another.

Their houses are made of small poles made fast at the tops in rounde forme after the maner as is vsed in many arbories in our gardens of England, in most townes couered with barkes, and in some with artificiall mattes made of long rushes; from
20 the tops of the houses downe to the ground. The length of them is commonly double to the breadth, in some places they are but 12. and 16. yardes long, and in other some wee haue seene of foure and twentie.

In some places of the countrey one onely towne belongeth to the gouernment of a *Wiróans* or chiefe Lorde; in other some two or three, in some sixe, eight, & more; the greatest *Wiróans* that yet we had dealing with had but eighteene townes in his gouernment, and able to make not aboue seuen or eight hundred fighting men at the most: The language of euery gouernment is different from any other, and the farther they are distant the greater is the difference.

Their maner of warres amongst themselues is either by sudden surprising one an
30 other most comonly about the dawning of the day, or moone light; or els by ambushes, or some suttle deuises: Set battels are very rare, except it fall out where there are many trees, where eyther part may haue some hope of defence, after the deliuerie of euery arrow, in leaping behind some or other.

Text: from a facsimile of the 1588 edition prepared by R. G. Adams, Ann Arbor, 1931   9 ỹ, that. Elizabethan printers used the tilde or a superior horizontal line for omitted letters, usually consonants, and made frequent use of abbreviations; here the *y* is the Old English thorn, representing *th*, which came into use because the thorn resembled and was thus confused with the Roman *y*   24 **Wiróans**. Like other early travelers, Hariot tried to indicate the pronunciation of Indian words by phonetic spellings and accents. Most Indian tribes encountered from Maine to Virginia belonged to the Algonquian group, and some linguistic similarities are observable.

If there fall out any warres between vs & them, what their fight is likely to bee, we hauing aduantages against them so many maner of waies, as by our discipline, our strange weapons and deuises els; especially by ordinance great and small, it may be easily imagined; by the experience we haue had in some places, the turning vp of their heeles against vs in running away was their best defence.

In respect of vs they are a people poore, and for want of skill and iudgement in the knowledge and vse of our things, doe esteeme our trifles before thinges of greater value: Notwithstanding in their proper manner considering the want of such meanes as we haue, they seeme very ingenious; For although they haue no such tooles, nor any such craftes, sciences and artes as wee; yet in those thinges they doe, 10 they shewe excellencie of wit. And by howe much they vpon due consideration shall finde our manner of knowledges and craftes to exceede theirs in perfection, and speed for doing or execution, by so much the more is it probable that they shoulde desire our friendships & loue, and haue the greater respect for pleasing and obeying vs. Whereby may bee hoped if meanes of good gouernment bee vsed, that they may in short time be brought to ciuilitie, and the imbracing of true religion.

Some religion they haue alreadie, which although it be farre from the truth, yet beyng as it is, there is hope it may bee the easier and sooner reformed.

They beleeue that there are many Gods which they call *Mantóac,* but of different sortes and degrees; one onely chiefe and great God, which hath bene from all 20 eternitie. Who as they affirme when hee purposed to make the worlde, made first other goddes of a principall order to bee as meanes and instruments to bee vsed in the creation and gouernment to follow; and after the Sunne, Moone, and Starres, as pettie goddes and the instruments of the other order more principall. First they say were made waters, out of which by the gods was made all diuersitie of creatures that are visible or inuisible.

For mankind they say a woman was made first, which by the woorking of one of the goddes, conceiued and brought foorth children: And in such sort they say they had their beginning.

But how manie yeeres or ages haue passed since, they say they can make no 30 relatiõ, hauing no letters nor other such meanes as we to keepe recordes of the particularities of times past, but onelie tradition from father to sonne.

They thinke that all the gods are of humane shape, & therfore they represent them by images in the formes of men, which they call *Kewasówok* one alone is called *Kewás;* Them they place in houses appropriate or temples which they call *Machicómuck;* Where they woorship, praie, sing, and make manie times offerings vnto them. In some *Machicómuck* we haue seene but on *Kewás,* in some two, and in other some three; The common sort thinke them to be also gods.

They beleeue also the immortalitie of the soule, that after this life as soone as the soule is departed from the bodie according to the workes it hath done, it is eyther 40 carried to heauen the habitacle of gods, there to enjoy perpetuall blisse and happi-

---

7 **esteeme our trifles,** a reference to the pleasant Indian habit, observed from the time of Columbus, of exchanging gold and copper ornaments for bits of broken bottles and other gaudy objects   16 **true religion,** i.e. Anglicanism, as opposed to Roman Catholicism

nesse, or els to a great pitte or hole, which they thinke to be in the furthest partes
of their part of the worlde towarde the sunne set, there to burne continually: the
place they call *Popogusso.*

For the confirmation of this opinion, they tolde mee two stories of two men that
had been lately dead and reuiued againe, the one happened but few yeres before our
comming into the countrey of a wicked man which hauing beene dead and buried,
the next day the earth of the graue beeing seene to moue, was taken vp againe; Who
made declaration where his soule had beene, that is to saie very neere entring into
Popogusso, had not one of the gods saued him & gaue him leaue to returne againe,
10 and teach his friends what they should doe to auoid that terrible place of torment.

The other happened in the same yeere wee were there, but in a towne that was
threescore miles from vs, and it was tolde mee for straunge newes that one beeing
dead, buried and taken vp againe as the first, shewed that although his bodie had
lien dead in the graue, yet his soule was aliue, and had trauailed farre in a long broade
waie, on both sides whereof grewe most delicate and pleasaunt trees, bearing more rare
and excellent fruites then euer hee had seene before or was able to expresse, and at
length came to most braue and faire houses, neere which hee met his father, that
had beene dead before, who gaue him great charge to goe backe againe and shew
his friendes what good they were to doe to enjoy the pleasures of that place, which
20 when he had done he should after come againe.

What subtilty soeuer be in the *Wiróances* and Priestes, this opinion worketh so
much in manie of the common and simple sort of people that it maketh them haue
great respect to their Gouernours, and also great care what they do, to auoid torment after death, and to enioy blisse; although notwithstanding there is punishment
ordained for malefactours, as stealers, whoremoongers, and other sortes of wicked
doers; some punished with death, some with forfeitures, some with beating, according to the greatnes of the factes.

And this is the summe of their religiõ, which I learned by hauing special familiarity with some of their priestes. Wherein they were not so sure grounded, nor gaue
30 such credite to their traditions and stories but through conuersing with vs they were
brought into great doubts of their owne, and no small admiration of ours, with
earnest desire in many, to learne more than we had meanes for want of perfect vtterance in their language to expresse.

Most thinges they sawe with vs, as Mathematicall instruments, sea compasses, the
vertue of the loadstone in drawing yron, a perspective glasse whereby was shewed
manie strange sightes, burning glasses, wildefire woorkes, gunnes, bookes, writing
and reading, spring clocks that seeme to goe of themselves, and manie other thinges
that wee had, were so straunge vnto them, and so farre exceeded their capacities to
comprehend the reason and meanes how they should be made and done, that they
40 thought they were rather the works of gods then of men, or at the leastwise they

---

2 **towarde . . . set.** In the folklore of primitive peoples, the west is more often the abode of the blest than
of the damned. "Gone west," still a common euphemism for death, is a survival   34 **Mathematicall instruments,** the astrolabe and astrolabe quadrant, used to determine latitude by measurement of the angle
between a celestial body and the horizon   36 **wildefire,** Greek fire, combustible materials used to fire enemy
ships and for other warlike purposes

had bin giuen and taught vs of the gods. Which made manie of them to haue such opinion of vs, as that if they knew not the trueth of god and religion already, it was rather to be had from vs, whom God so specially loued then from a people that were so simple, as they found themselues to be in comparison of vs. Whereupon greater credite was giuen vnto that we spake of concerning such matters.

Manie times and in euery towne where I came, according as I was able, I made declaration of the contentes of the Bible; that therein was set foorth the true and onelie GOD, and his mightie woorkes, that therein was contayned the true doctrine of saluation through Christ, with manie particularities of Miracles and chiefe poyntes of religion, as I was able then to vtter, and thought fitte for the time. And although 10 I told them the booke materially & of it self was not of anie such vertue, as I thought they did conceiue, but onely the doctrine therein contained; yet would many be glad to touch it, to embrace it, to kisse it, to hold it to their brests and heades, and stroke ouer all their bodie with it; to shewe their hungrie desire of that knowledge which was spoken of.

The *Wiróans* with whom we dwelt called *Wingina,* and many of his people would be glad many times to be with vs at our praiers, and many times call vpon vs both in his owne towne, as also in others whither he sometimes accompanied vs, to pray and sing Psalmes; hoping thereby to bee partaker of the same effectes which wee by that meanes also expected.   20

Twise this *Wiróans* was so grieuously sicke that he was like to die, and as hee laie languishing, doubting of anie helpe by his owne priestes, and thinking he was in such daunger for offending vs and thereby our god, sent for some of vs to praie and bee a meanes to our God that it would please him either that he might liue or after death dwell with him in blisse, so likewise were the requestes of manie others in the like case.

On a time also when their corne began to wither by reason of a drouth which hap-pened extraordinarily, fearing that it had come to passe by reason that in some thing they had displeased vs, many woulde come to vs & desire vs to praie to our God of England, that he would preserue their corne, promising that when it was ripe we 30 also should be partakers of the fruite.

There could at no time happen any strange sicknesse, losses, hurtes, or any other crosse vnto them, but that they would impute to vs the cause or meanes thereof for offending or not pleasing vs.

One other rare and strange accident, leauing others, will I mention before I ende, which mooued the whole countrey that either knew or hearde of vs, to haue vs in wonderfull admiration.

There was no towne where we had any subtile deuise practised against vs, we leauing it vnpunished or not reuenged (because wee sought by all meanes pos-sible to win them by gentlenesse) but that within a few dayes after our departure 40 from euerie such towne, the people began to die very fast, and many in short space; in some townes about twentie, in some fourtie, in some sixtie, & in one six score, which in trueth was very manie in respect of their numbers. This happened in no place that wee coulde learne but where wee had bene, where they vsed some practise against vs, and after such time; The disease also so strange, that they neither knew what it was, nor how to cure it; the like by report of the oldest men in the countrey neuer happened before, time out of minde. A thing specially obserued by vs as also by the naturall inhabitants themselues.

Insomuch that when some of the inhabitantes which were our friends & especially the *Wiróans Wingina* had obserued such effects in foure or fiue towns to follow their wicked practises, they were perswaded that it was the worke of our God through our meanes, and that wee by him might kil and slaie whom wee would without weapons and not come neere them.

10   And thereupon when it had happened that they had vnderstanding that any of their enemies had abused vs in our iourneyes, hearing that wee had wrought no reuenge with our weapons, & fearing vpon some cause the matter should so rest: did come and intreate vs that we would bee a meanes to our God that they as others that had dealt ill with vs might in like sort die; alleaging howe much it would be for our credite and profite, as also theirs; and hoping furthermore that we would do so much at their requests in respect of the friendship we professe them.

Whose entreaties although wee shewed that they were vngodlie, affirming that our God would not subiect him selfe to anie such praiers and requestes of men: that in deede all thinges haue beene and were to be done according to his good pleas-
20 ure as he had ordained: and that we to shew our selues his true seruants ought rather to make petition for the contrarie, that they with them might liue together with vs, bee made partakers of his truth & serue him in righteousnes; but notwithstanding in such sort, that wee referre that as all other thinges, to bee done according to his diuine will & pleasure, and as by his wisedome he had ordained to be best.

Yet because the effect fell out so sodainly and shortly after according to their de-sires, they thought neuerthelesse it came to passe by our meanes, and that we in vsing such speeches vnto them did but dissemble the matter, and therefore camê vnto vs to giue vs thankes in their manner that although wee satisfied them not in promise, yet in deedes and effect we had fulfilled their desires.

30   This maruelous accident in all the countrie wrought so strange opinions of vs, that some people could not tel whether to think vs gods or men, and the rather because that all the space of their sicknesse, there was no man of ours knowne to die, or that was specially sicke: they noted also that we had no women amongst vs, neither that we did care for any of theirs.

Some therefore were of opinion that wee were not borne of women, and therefore not mortall, but that wee were men of an old generation many yeeres past then risen againe to immortalitie.

Some woulde likewise seeme to prophesie that there were more of our generation yet to come, to kill theirs and take their places, as some thought the purpose was
40 by that which was already done.

Those that were immediatly to come after vs they imagined to be in the aire, yet inuisible & without bodies, & that they by our intreaty & for the loue of vs did make the people to die in that sort as they did by shooting inuisible bullets into them.

To confirme this opinion their phisitions to excuse their ignorance in curing the disease, would not be ashamed to say, but earnestly make the simple people beleue, that the strings of blood that they sucked out of the sicke bodies, were the strings wherewithall the inuisible bullets were tied and cast.

Some also thought that we shot them our selues out of our pieces from the place where we dwelt, and killed the people in any such towne that had offended vs as we listed, how farre distant from vs soeuer it were.

And other some saide that it was the speciall woorke of God for our sakes, as wee our selues haue cause in some sorte to thinke no lesse, whatsoeuer some doe or maie imagine to the contrarie, specially some Astrologers knowing of the Eclipse of the Sunne which wee saw the same yeere before in our voyage thytherward, which vnto 10 them appeared very terrible. And also of a Comet which beganne to appeare but a few daies before the beginning of the said sicknesse. But to conclude them from being the speciall causes of so speciall an accident, there are farther reasons then I thinke fit at this present to bee alleadged.

These their opinions I haue set downe the more at large that it may appeare vnto you that there is good hope they may be brought through discreet dealing and gouernement to the imbracing of the trueth, and consequently to honour, obey, feare and loue vs.

And although some of our companie towardes the ende of the yeare, shewed them-selues too fierce, in slaying some of the people, in some towns, vpon causes that on 20 our part, might easily enough haue been borne withall: yet notwithstanding because it was on their part iustly deserued, the alteration of their opinions generally & for the most part concerning vs is the lesse to bee doubted. And whatsoeuer els they may be, by carefulnesse of our selues neede nothing at all to be feared.

The best neuerthelesse in this as in all actions besides is to be endeuoured and hoped, & of the worst that may happen notice to be taken with consideration, and as much as may be eschewed.

The Conclusion

Now I haue as I hope made relation not of so fewe and final things but that the countrey of men that are indifferent & wel disposed maie be sufficiently liked: If there were no more knowen then I haue mentioned, which doubtlesse and in great 30 reason is nothing to that which remaineth to bee discouered, neither the soile, nor commodities. As we haue reason so to gather by the differēce we found in our trauails; for although all which I haue before spokē of, haue bin discouered & ex-perimented not far frō the sea coast where was our abode & most of our trauailing: yet somtimes as we made our iourneies farther into the maine and countrey; we found the soyle to bee fatter; the trees greater and to growe thinner; the grounde more firme and deeper mould; more and larger champions; finer grasse and as good as euer we saw any in England; in some places rockie and farre more high and hillie ground; more plentie of their fruites; more abundance of beastes; the more inhab-

---

37 **champions,** champaigns; flat. open plains

ited with people, and of greater pollicie & larger dominions, with greater townes and houses.

Why may wee not then looke for in good hope from the inner parts of more and greater plentie, as well of other things, as of those which wee haue alreadie discouered? Vnto the Spaniardes happened the like in discouering the maine of the West Indies. The maine also of this countrey of *Virginia,* extending some wayes so many hundreds of leagues, as otherwise then by the relation of the inhabitants wee haue most certaine knowledge of, where yet no Christian Prince hath any possession or dealing, cannot but yeeld many kinds of excellent commodities, which we in our
10 discouerie haue not yet seene.

What hope there is els to be gathered of the nature of the climate, being answerable to the Iland of *Iapan,* the land of *China, Persia, Iury,* the Ilandes of *Cyprus* and *Candy,* the South parts of *Greece, Italy,* and *Spaine,* and of many other notable and famous countreis, because I meane not to be tedious, I leaue to your owne consideration.

Whereby also the excellent temperature of the ayre there at all seasons, much warmer then in England, and neuer so violently hot, as sometimes is vnder & between the Tropikes, or nere them; cannot bee vnknowne vnto you without farther relation.

20 For the holsomnesse thereof I neede to say but thus much: that for all the want of prouision, as first of English victuall; excepting for twentie daies, wee liued only by drinking water and by the victuall of the countrey, of which some sorts were very straunge vnto vs, and might haue bene thought to haue altered our temperatures in such sort as to haue brought vs into some greeuous and dangerous diseases: secõdly the want of English meanes, for the taking of beastes, fishe, and foule, which by the helpe only of the inhabitants and their meanes, coulde not bee so suddenly and easily prouided for vs, nor in so great numbers & quantities, nor of that choise as otherwise might haue bene to our better satisfaction and contentment. Some want also wee had of clothes. Furthermore, in all our trauailes which were most speciall and
30 often in the time of winter, our lodging was in the open aire vpon the grounde. And yet I say for all this, there were but foure of our whole company (being one hunddred and eight) that died all the yeere and that but at the latter ende thereof and vpon none of the aforesaide causes. For all foure especially three were feeble, weake, and sickly persons before euer they came thither, and those that knewe them much marueyled that they liued so long beeing in that case, or had aduentured to trauaile.

Seeing therefore the ayre there is so temperate and holsome, the soyle so fertile and yeelding such commodities as I haue before mentioned, the voyage also thither to and fro beeing sufficiently experimented, to bee perfourmed thrise a yeere with
40 ease and at any season thereof: And the dealing of *Sir Water Raleigh* so liberall in

5 **maine,** mainland as in "Spanish Main," the north coast of South America. Hariot had in mind the riches of Peru and Mexico   11 **answerable to,** in the same latitude as   12 **Iury** may possibly be "Jewry"   13 **Candy,** Candia or Crete   40 **Sir Water** [Walter] **Raleigh** (1552?-1618). Later colonists, Captain John Smith among them, were inclined to regard Raleigh as a grandiose dreamer who held out false hopes of easily won riches

large giuing and graunting lande there, as is alreadie knowne, with many helpes and furtherances els: (The least that hee hath graunted hath beene fiue hundred acres to a man onely for the aduenture of his person): I hope there remaine no cause wherby the action should be misliked.

If that those which shall thither trauaile to inhabite and plant bee but reasonably prouided for the first yere as those are which were transported the last, and beeing there doe vse but that diligence and care as is requisite, and as they may with ease: There is no doubt but for the time following they may haue victuals that is excellent good and plentie enough; some more Englishe sortes of cattaile also hereafter, as some haue bene before, and are there yet remaining, may and shall bee God will- 10 ing thither transported: So likewise our kinde of fruites, rootes, and hearbes may bee there planted and sowed, as some haue bene alreadie, and proue wel: And in short time also they may raise of those sortes of commodities which I haue spoken of as shall both enrich them selues, as also others that shall deale with them.

And this is all the fruites of our labours, that I haue thought necessary to aduertise you of at this present: what els concerneth the nature and manners of the inhabitants of *Virginia:* The number with the particularities of the voyages thither made; and of the actions of such that haue bene by *Sir Water Raleigh* therein and there imployed, many worthy to bee remembred; as of the first discouerers of the Countrey: of our Generall for the time *Sir Richard Greinuile;* and after his departure, 20 of our Gouernour there Master *Rafe Lane:* with diuers others directed and imployed vnder theyr gouernement: Of the Captaynes and Masters of the voyages made since for transportations; of the Gouernour and assistants of those alredie transported, as of many persons, accidents, and thinges els, I haue ready in a discourse by it self in maner of a Chronicle according to the course of times, and when time shall bee thought conuenient shall be also published.

Thus referring my relation to your fauourable constructions, expecting good successe of the action, from him which is to be acknowledged the authour and gouernour not only of this but of all things els, I take my leaue of you, this moneth of *February.* 1588.   30

                                                                                          1588

---

20 **Sir Richard Greinuile** [Grenville] (1542-1591) commanded the fleet of seven ships in which Hariot and his companions came to America. Tennyson's "The Revenge" is based on Grenville's heroic death a few years later   21 **Master Rafe** (Ralph) **Lane** (1530?-1603) was in command on Roanoke Island. His account of the settlement was printed in Hakluyt's *Principall Nauigations,* just before Hariot's book   24 **I . . . discourse.** Apparently the time for its publication did not arrive

1579–1631 *John Smith*

The band of Englishmen with whom John Smith sailed from London down the Thames and out to sea in 1606 was poorly fitted for battling the American wilderness. Only a few were workmen; the rest were all "poor gentlemen, tradesmen, serving-men, libertines, and such like." They, like Smith, had seen a chance to fatten their purses by setting up a new colony. Holding, perhaps, with the common contemporary notion that the new land was so rich that even dripping pans and handcuffs there were made of pure gold, they probably expected few hardships when in May 1607 they sailed into Hampton Roads, Virginia.

Apparently the colonizers were lucky to have Captain Smith's leadership on what turned out to be a heartbreaking although, in the long run, a successful venture — the establishment of the first permanent British colony on this continent. One must say "apparently," because what we know about Smith's ability and background he chiefly has told us, and the blustering soldier of fortune was not a man to underestimate his valor or to let literal truth spoil a good story. His account told how he had been born at Willoughby and educated in the free schools there, how he had broken family ties in his teens, had gone into military service in his twenties, and thereafter — rushing into the midst of any fighting in Europe or beyond its frontiers — had slain Turks, Tartars, or Indians with equal aplomb.

During his stay in Virginia from May 1607 to October 1609, Smith, according to his account, efficiently led the colonists, set up relationships with the Indians, and explored the country. In addition, somehow, he found time to write his first book and to send it overseas for publication. In the fall of 1609 Smith went back to England and remained there until 1614. That year, some six years before the settlement of Plymouth, he returned to America to explore New England minutely from the Penobscot River to Cape Cod. Believing that a territory of such extent deserved a name of its own, he christened it New England. At home he made an excellent map of the coast and dotted it with English names such as Cape Ann, Charles River, and Plymouth. In 1615 he sailed again for New England with a body of colonizers who traveled on two ships. This expedition, however, was cut short when French pirates stopped the vessels. Smith was captured and taken to Rochelle, but he shortly escaped and returned to his native country. His exploring days over, he remained there until his death in London, June 21, 1631.

Historians have pictured the mustachioed captain writing his first book in a sleazy wilderness tent by the light of a blazing pine-knot. However it was composed, *A True Relation* (1607) was a book wrought on the scene between clashes with redmen. It and books which followed it, notably *A Description of New England* (1616) and *The Generall Historie of Virginia, New England, and the Summer Isles* (1624), written to encourage and direct colonizing or to glorify Smith, reveal his gusto and his imaginativeness, combined with what seems to be vivid circumstantial detail. Thus the poetry and hardships of the colonizing adventure fuse in these accounts.

Smith's works are interesting for their characterization of the author, their picturing of happenings, and their style. The style is that of an educated — but not too educated — man, writing imaginatively about first-hand experiences. It has the varied rhythms, the homeliness fused with strangeness and stateliness, of prose in the age of the King James Bible. Callous-fisted soldier though he was, Smith produced several fine bits of prose like those which follow.

Captain John Smith, **Works,** 1608-1631, ed. Edward Arber, Birmingham, 1884 (re-edited by A. G. Bradley, 1910)   **Complete Works of John Smith,** ed. Kermit Goell, New York, 1963   M. C. Tyler, **History of American Literature, 1607-1765,** New York, 1878, I, 18-38   Philip L. Barbour, **The Three Worlds of Captain John Smith,** New York, 1964

from A Description of New England

[*Motives for Colonizing*]

The following selection from A Description of New England *(1616) shows Smith as the advocate of the colonizing adventure. Eight years later the passage was reprinted in* The Generall Historie. *Like much of the writing of the period and like many other passages by Smith, this has as its purpose the attraction of settlers to the new colonies. As he addresses several arguments to his countrymen, Smith puts into poetic words the attitudes of the adventurous explorers and settlers of his day.*

Who can desire more content, that hath small meanes; or but only his merit to advance his fortunes, then to tread and plant that ground he hath purchased by the hazard of his life? If he have but the taste of virtue and magnanimity, what to such a minde can bee more pleasant, then planting and building a foundation for his Posteritie, gotte from the rude earth, by Gods blessing and his owne industry without prejudice to any? If hee have any graine of faith or zeale in Religion, what can hee doe lesse hurtfull to any: or more agreeable to God, then to seeke to convert those poore Salvages to know Christ, and humanitie, whose labours with discretion will triple requite thy charge and paines? What so truely su[i]tes with honour and honestie, as the discovering things unknowne? erecting Townes, peopling Countries, 10 informing the ignorant, reforming things unjust, teaching virtue; and gaine to our

---

Text (for this and the following selection): **Captain John Smith, Works,** 1608-1613, ed. Edward Arber, The English Scholar's Library, No. 16, Birmingham, 1884

Native mother-countrie; a kingdom to attend her: finde imployment for those that
are idle, because they know not what to doe: so farre from wronging any, as
to cause posterity to remember thee; and remembering thee, ever honour that
remembrance with praise?

Consider: what were the beginnings and endings of the Monarkies of the *Chaldeans,*
the *Syrians,* the *Grecians,* and *Romanes,* but this one rule; What was it they would
not do for the good of their common weale, or their Mother-citie? For example:
Rome, What made her such a Monarchesse, but onely the adventures of her youth,
not in riots at home; but in dangers abroad? and the justice and judgement out of
10 their experiences, when they grewe aged. What was their ruine and hurt but this;
The excesse of idlenesse, the fondnesse of Parents, the want of experience in Magistrates, the admiration of their undeserved honours, the contempt of true merit,
their unjust jealo[u]sies, their politike incredulities, their hypocriticall seeming
goodnesse, and their deeds of secret lewdnesse? finally, in fine, growing onely formall temporists, all that their predecessors got in many yeeres they lost in a few
daies. Those by their pain and vertues became Lords of the world; they by their
ease and vices became slaves to their servants. This is the difference betwixt the use
of Armes in the field, and on the monuments of stones; the golden age and the
leaden age, prosperity and miserie, justice and corruption, substance and shadowes,
20 words and deeds, experience and imagination, making Commonwealths, and marring
Commonwealths, the fruits of virtue, and the conclusions of vice.

Then, who would live at home idly (or thinke in himselfe any worth to live)
onely to eate, drink and sleepe, and so die? Or by consuming that carelesly,
his friends got worthily? Or by using that miserably, that maintained vertue honestly? Or for being descended nobly, pine with the vaine vaunt of great kindred in
penurie? Or (to maintaine a silly shew of bravery) toyle out thy heart, soule, and
time, basely; by shifts, tricks, cards and dice? Or by relating newes of others actions,
sharke here and there for a dinner, or supper; deceive thy friends, by faire promises
and dissimulation, in borrowing where thou never intendest to pay; offend the
30 lawes, surfeit with excesse, burden thy Country, abuse thy selfe, despaire in want,
and then couzen thy kindred, yea even thy owne brother, and wish thy parents
death (I will not say damnation) to have their estates? though thou seest what
honours, and rewards, the world yet hath for them [who] will seeke them and
worthily deserve them.

I would bee sor[r]y to offend, or that any should mistake my honest meaning: for I
wish good to all, hurt to none. But rich men for the most part are growne to that
dotage, through their pride in their wealth, as though there were no accident could
end it, or their life.

And what hellish care do such take to make it their owne miserie and their
40 Countries spoile, especially when there is most neede of their imployment? drawing
by all manner of inventions, from the Prince and his honest subjects, even the vitall
spirits of their powers and estates: as if their Bagges, or Bragges were so powerfull
a defence, the malicious could not assault them; when they are the onely baite, to

31 **couzen,** cozen, cheat   42 **Bagges,** money bags

cause us not to bee onely assaulted; but betrayed and murdered in our owne security, ere wee well perceive it.

May not the miserable ruine of *Constantinople,* their impregnable walles, riches, and pleasures [at] last taken by the *Turke* (which were then but a bit, in comparison of their mightines) now remember us of the effects of private covetousnesse? at which time the good *Emperour* held himselfe rich enough, to have such rich subjects, so formall in all excesse of vanity, all kinde of delicacie and prodigalitie. His povertie when the *Turke* besieged, the citizens (whose merchandizing thoughts were onely to get wealth, little conceiving the desperate resolution of a valiant expert enemy) left the Emp[erour] so long to his conclusions, having spent all he had to   10 pay his young, raw, discontented Souldiers; that sodainly he, they, and their citie were all a prey to the devouring *Turke.* And what they would not spare for the maintenance of them who adventured their lives to defend them, did serve onely their enemies to torment them, their friends and countrey, and all Christendome to this present day. Let this lamentable example remember you that are rich (seeing there are such great theeves in the world to robbe you) not [to] grudge to lend some proportion, to breed them that have little, yet [are] willing to learne how to defend you: for, it is too late when the deed is a-doing.

The *Romanes* estate hath beene worse then this: for, the meere covetousnesse and extortion of a few of them, so moved the rest, that not having any imployment but   20 contemplation; their great judgements grew to so great malice, as themselves were sufficient to destroy themselves by faction: Let this move you to imbrace imployment for those whose educations, spirits, and judgements want but your purses; not onely to prevent such accustomed dangers, but also to gaine more thereby then you have.

And you fathers, that are either so foolishly fond, or so miserably coveteous, or so wilfully ignorant, or so negligently careless, as that you will rather maintaine your children in idle wantonness, till they grow your masters; or become so basely unkinde, as they wish nothing but your deaths; so that both sorts grow dissolute: and although you would wish them any where to escape the gallowes, and ease your   30 cares; though they spend you here one, two or three hundred pound[s] a yeer, you would grudge to give halfe so much in adventure with them to obtaine an estate, which in a small time, but with a little assistance of your providence, might bee better then your owne. But if an Angell should tell you, [that] any place yet unknowne can afford such fortunes; you would not beleeve it, no more then *Columbus* was beleeved there was any such Land as is now the well knowne abounding *America;* much lesse such large Regions as are yet unknowne, as well in *America,* as in *Affrica* and *Asia,* and *Terra incognita;* where were courses for gentlemen (and them that would be so reputed) more suiting their qualities, then begging from

---

3 **the miserable . . . Constantinople.** The fall of Constantinople, in 1453, followed a fierce forty-day siege. Historians agree with Smith that Constantine's inability to pay his troops contributed to their poor morale, but they disagree with Smith's claim that the defending force was larger than the attacking force   19 **The Romanes estate. . . .** This paragraph contains Smith's version of the causes for the fall of the Roman Empire

their Princes generous disposition, the labours of his subjects, and the very marrow of his maintenance.

I have not beene so ill bred, but I have tasted of *Plenty* and *Pleasure,* as well as *Want* and *Miserie:* nor doth necessitie yet, or occasion of discontent, force me to these endeavors: nor am I ignorant what small thanke[s] I shall have for my paines; or that many would have the Worlde imagine them to bee of great judgement, that can but blemish these my designes, by their witty objections and detractions: yet (I hope) my reasons with my deeds, will so prevaile with some, that I shall not want imployment in these affaires, to make the most blinde see his owne senselesnesse and
10 incredulity; Hoping that gaine will make them affect that which Religion, Charity and the Common good cannot. It were but a poore device in me, To deceive my selfe; much more the King, State, my Friends and Countrey, with these inducements, which seeing his Majestie hath given permission, I wish all sorts of worthie, honest, industrious spirits, would understand: and if they desire any further satisfaction, I will doe my best to give it: Not to perswade them to goe onely; but goe with them: Not leave them there; but live with them there.

I will not say, but by ill providing and undue managing, such courses may bee taken [that] may make us miserable enough: But if I may have the execution of what I have projected; if they want to eate, let them eat or never digest Mee. If I
20 performe what I say, I desire but that reward out of the gaines [which] may su[i]te my paines, quality, and condition. And if I abuse you with my tongue, take my head for satisfaction. If any dislike at the yeeres end, defraying their charge, by my consent they should freely returne. I feare not want of companie sufficient, were it but knowne what I know of these Countries; and by the proofe of that wealth I hope yeerely to returne, if God please to blesse me from such accidents, as are beyond my power in reason to prevent: For, I am not so simple to thinke, that ever any other motive then wealth, will ever erect there a Commonweale; or draw companie from their ease and humours at home, to stay in *New England* to effect my purposes.

30 And lest any should think the toile might be insupportable, though these things may bee had by labour, and diligence: I assure my selfe there are who delight extreamly in vaine pleasure, that take much more paines in *England* to enjoy it, then I should doe here [*New England*] to gaine wealth sufficient; and yet I thinke they should not have halfe such sweet content: for our pleasure here is still gaines, in *England* charges and losse. Heer nature and liberty affords us that freely, which in *England* we want, or it costeth us deerely. What pleasure can bee more, then (being tired with any occasion a-shore, in planting Vines, Fruits, or Hearbs, in contriving their owne grounds to the pleasure of their owne minds, their Fields, Gardens, Orchards, Buildings, Ships, and other workes, &c.) to recreate themselves before
40 their owne doores in their owne boates upon the Sea; where man, woman and childe, with a small hooke and line, by angling, may take divers sorts of excellent fish, at their pleasures? And is it not pretty sport, to pull up two pence, six pence, and twelve pence, as fast as you can ha[u]le and veare a line? He is a

---

19 **digest Mee,** endure me   43 **haule and veare,** pull in and let out

very bad Fisher [that] cannot kill in one day with his hooke and line, one, two,
or three hundred Cods: which dressed and dried, if they bee sold there for ten shillings a hundred, though in England they will give more than twentie, may not both
the servant, the master and marchant, be well content with this gaine? If a man
worke but three daies in seaven, he may get more than hee can spend unlesse he will
be excessive. Now that Carpenter, Mason, Gardiner, Taylor, Smith, Sailer, Forgers,
or what other, may they not make this a pretty recreation though they fish but an
houre in a day, to take more then they can eat in a weeke? or if they will not eat it,
because there is so much better choice; yet sell it, or change it, with the fishermen or
marchants for any thing they want. And what sport doth yeeld a more pleasing con-   10
tent, and lesse hurt and charge then angling with a hooke; and crossing the sweet
ayre from Ile to Ile, over the silent streames of a calme Sea? Wherein the most curious may finde pleasure, profit, and content.

    Thus, though all men be not fishers; yet all men, whatsoever, may in other mat-
ters doe as well. For necessity doth in these cases so rule a Commonwealth, and
each in their severall functions, as their labours in their qualities may be as profitable, because there is a necessary mutuall use of all.

    For Gentlemen, what exercise should more delight them, then ranging dayly these
unknowne parts, using fowling and fishing, for hunting and hawking? and yet you
shall see the wilde-haukes give you some pleasure, in seeing them stoope (six or seven   20
times after one another) an houre or two together, at the skuls of fish in the faire
harbours, as those a-shore at a foule, and never trouble nor torment yourselves, with
watching, mewing, feeding, and attending them: nor kill horse and man with running and crying, *See you not a hawk?* For hunting also: the woods, lakes and rivers
affoord not onely chase sufficient, for any that delights in that kinde of toile
or pleasure; but such beasts to hunt, that besides the delicacy of their bodies for
food, their skins are so rich, as they will recompence thy daily labour with a Captains pay.

    For labourers, if those that sowe hempe, rape, turnups, parsnips, carrats, cabidge,
and such like; give 20, 30, 40, 50 shillings yearely for an acre of ground, and meat[,]   30
drinke[,] and wages to use it, and yet grow rich; when better, or at least as good
ground may be had and cost nothing but labour; it seems strange to me, any such
should there grow poore.

    My purpose is not to perswade children from their parents; men from their wives;
nor servants from their masters: onely such as with free consent may be spared: But
that each parish, or village, in Citie, or Countrey, that will but apparell their father-
lesse children of thirteene or foureteene years of age, or young maried people that
have small wealth to live on, heere by their labour may live exceeding well: provided
alwaies, that first there bee a sufficient power to command them, houses to receive
them, meanes to defend them, and meet provisions necessarie for them; for any place   40
may bee over-lain: and it is most necessarie to have a fortresse (ere this grow to
practice) and sufficient masters, (as, Carpenters, Masons, Fishers, Fowlers, Gardiners,
Husbandmen, Sawyers, Smiths, Spinsters, Taylors, Weavers, and such like) to take

6 **excessive,** extravagant   20 **stoope,** dive   23 **mewing,** caging up   41 **over-lain,** overwhelmed

ten, twelve, or twentie, or as there is occasion, for Apprentises. The Masters by this may quicklie growe rich; these may learne their trades themselves, to doe the like; to a generall and an incredible benefit, for King, and Countrey, Master, and Servant.

1616

from The Generall Historie of Virginia [*Pocahontas*]

The passage recounting Smith's captivity and his rescue by Pocahontas, from The Generall Historie *(1624), gains in interest if it is placed alongside the account of the same events which had appeared in 1608 in his* A True Relation of Such Occurences and Accidents of Note as Hath Happened in Virginia. *Henry Adams notes that, according to the earlier version, Smith had shortly found that his captors were using him with kindness, but that in the later he constantly feared violence; that "eight guards, which had been sufficient in 1608, were multiplied to thirty or forty tall fellows in 1624," and so on. Such changes heightened the drama, making both the captain and his captors more formidable. The most notable changes added to the ferocity of Powhatan and showed Pocahontas in the act of rescuing the heroic captain. The modifications suggest that Smith was perhaps better qualified as a writer of historical fiction than as a sternly accurate historian. The passage, nevertheless, vividly re-creates the life of the colonists and reveals the character of its picturesque author. The zestful yet workaday style is typical.*

The next voyage hee proceeded so farre that with much labour by cutting of trees insunder he made his passage; but when his Barge could passe no farther, he left her in a broad bay out of danger of shot, commanding none should goe a shore till his returne: himselfe with two English and two Salvages went up higher in a Canowe, but hee was not long absent, but his men went a shore, whose want of government, gave both occasion and opportunity to the Salvages to surprise one *George Cassen,* whom they slew, and much failed not to have cut of[f] the boat and all the rest.

    Smith little dreaming of that accident, being got to the marshes at the rivers head,
10 twentie myles in the desert, had his two men slaine (as is supposed) sleeping by the Canowe, whilst himselfe by fowling sought them victuall, who finding he was beset with 200. Salvages, two of them hee slew, still defending himselfe, with the ayd of a Salvage his guid[e], whom he bound to his arme with his garters, and used him as a buckler, yet he was shot in his thigh a little, and had many arrowes that stucke in his cloathes but no great hurt, till at last they took him prisoner.

    When this newes came to *James* towne, much was their sorrow for his losse, fewe expecting what ensued.

    Sixe or seven weekes those Barbarians kept him prisoner, many strange triumphes and conjurations they made of him, yet hee so demeaned himselfe amongst them,
20 as he not onely diverted them from surprising the Fort, but procured his owne

---

1 **hee,** John Smith. The account is written in the third person   7 **much failed not . . . boat,** came near cutting off the boat   10 **two men slaine,** "Jehu Robinson and Thomas Emry slaine" (Smith's note)   18 **Sixe . . . weekes.** "More accurately about three weeks — Dec. 16, 1607-Jan. 8, 1608." (Arber's note)

libertie, and got himselfe and his company such estimation amongst them, that those Salvages admired him more then their owne *Quiyouckosucks.*

The manner how they used and delivered him, is as followeth.

The Salvages having drawne from *George Cassen* whether Captaine *Smith* was gone, prosecuting that opportunity they followed him with 300. bowmen, conducted by the King of *Pamaunkee,* who in divisions searching the turnings of the river, found Robinson and Emry by the fire side, those they shot full of arrowes and slew. Then finding the Captaine, as is said, that used the Salvage that was his guide as his shield (three of them being slaine and divers other so gauld) all the rest would not come neere him. Thinking thus to have returned to his boat, regarding them, as he 10 marched, more then his way, [Smith] slipped up to the middle in an oasie creeke & his Salvage with him, yet durst they not come to him till being neere dead with cold, he threw away his armes. Then according to their composition they drew him forth and led him to the fire, where his men were slaine. Diligently they chafed his benummed limbs.

He demanding for their Captaine, they shewed him *Opechankanough,* King of Pamaunkee, to whom he gave a round Ivory double compass Dyall. Much they marvailed at the playing of the Fly and Needle, which they could see so plainely, and yet not touch it, because of the glasse that covered them. But when he demonstrated by that Globe-like Jewell, the roundness of the earth, and skies, the spheare of the 20 Sunne, Moone, and Starres, and how the Sunne did chase the night round about the world continually; the greatnesse of the Land and Sea, the diversitie of Nations, varietie of complexions, and how we were to them Antipodes, and many other such like matters, they all stood as amazed with admiration.

Notwithstanding, within an houre after they tyed him to a tree, and as many as could stand about him prepared to shoot him, but the King holding up the Compass in his hand, they all laid downe their Bowes and Arrowes, and in a triumphant manner led him to Orapaks, where he was after their manner kindly feasted, and well used.

Their order in conducting him was thus; Drawing themselves all in fyle, the King 30 in the middest had all their Peeces and Swords borne before him. Captaine *Smith* was led after him by three great Salvages, holding him fast by each arme: and on each side six went in fyle with their Arrowes nocked. But arriving at the Towne (which was but onely thirtie or fortie hunting houses made of Mats, which they remove as they please, as we our tents) all the women and children staring to behold him, the souldiers first all in fyle performed the forme of a Bissom so well as could be, and on each flanke, officers as Serjeants to see them keepe their orders. A good time they continued this exercise, and then cast themselves in a ring, dauncing in such severall Postures, and singing and yelling out such hellish notes and screeches; being strangely painted, every one his quiver of Arrowes, and at his backe a club; on 40

---

2 **Quiyouckosucks.** Henry Spelman, in his *Relation of Virginea* (1613), wrote, "In yᵉ Patomecks country they have an other god whom they call Quioquascacke, and untᵘ ther Images they offer Beades and Copper if at any time they want Rayne or have to much. . . ."   4 **whether,** whither   9 **gauld,** galled   11 **oasie,** oozy   13 **composition,** agreement   36 **Bissom,** a military formation

his arme a Fox or an Otters skinne, or some such matter for his vambrace; their
heads and shoulders painted red, with Oyle and *Pocones* mingled together, which
Scarlet-like colour made an exceeding handsome shew; his Bow in his hand, and
the skinne of a Bird with her wings abroad dryed, tyed on his head, a peece of copper, a white shell, a long feather, with a small rattle growing at the tayles of their
snaks tyed to it, or some such like toy. All this while *Smith* and the King stood in
the middest guarded, as before is said; and after three dances they all departed. *Smith*
they conducted to a long house, where thirtie or fortie tall fellowes did guard him;
and ere long more bread and venison was brought him then would have served
10 twentie men, I thinke his stomacke at that time was not very good; what he left
they put in baskets and tyed over his head. About midnight they set the meate againe
before him, all this time not one of them would eate a bit with him, till the next
morning they brought him as much more, and then did they eate all the old, &
reserved the new as they had done the other, which made him thinke they would
fat him to eat him. Yet in this desperate estate to defend him from the cold, one
Maocassater brought him his gowne, in requitall of some beads and toyes Smith had
given him at his first arrivall in Virginia.

Two dayes after, a man would have slaine him (but that the guard prevented it)
for the death of his sonne, to whom they conducted him to recover the poore man
20 then breathing his last. *Smith* told them that at *James* towne he had a water would
doe it, if they would let him fetch it, but they would not permit that; but made all
the preparations they could to assault *James* towne, craving his advice, and for recompence he should have life, libertie, land, and women. In part of a table booke he
writ his minde to them at the Fort, what was intended, how they should follow that
direction to affright the messengers, and without fayle send him such things as he
writ for, and an inventory with them. The difficultie and danger he told the Salvages, of the Mines, great gunnes, and other Engins, exceedingly affrighted them;
yet according to his request they went to James towne, in as bitter weather as could
be of frost and snow, and within three dayes returned with an answer.

30 But when they came to *Jame*[*s*] towne, seeing men sally out as he had told them
they would, they fled; yet in the night they came againe to the same place where
he had told them they should receive an answer, and such things as he had promised them; which they found accordingly, and with which they returned with no
small expedition, to the wonder of them all that heard it, that he could either divine, or the paper could speake.

Then they led him to the *Youthtanunds* the *Mattapanients,* the *Payankatanks,* the
Nantaughtacunds, and *Onawmanients* upon the rivers of *Rapahanock,* and *Patawomek,*
over all those rivers, and backe againe by divers other severall Nations, to the Kings
habitation at Pamaunkee, where they entertained him with most strange and feare-
40 full Conjurations;

> As if neare led to hell,
> Amongst the Devils to dwell.

---

1 **vambrace,** a leather guard worn on the forearm   2 **Pocones,** bloodroot

Not long after, early in a morning a great fire was made in a long house, and a mat spread on the one side, as on the other; on the one they caused him to sit, and all the guard went out of the house, and presently came skipping in a great grim fellow, all painted over with coale, mingled with oyle; and many Snakes and Wesels skins stuffed with mosse, and all their tayles tyed together, so as they met on the crowne of his head in a tassell; and round about the tassell was as a Coronet of feathers, the skins hanging round about his head, backe, and shoulders, and in a manner covered his face; with a hellish voyce, and a rattle in his hand. With most strange gestures and passions he began his invocation, and environed the fire with a circle of meale; which done, three more such like devils   10 came rushing in with the like antique tricks, painted halfe blacke, halfe red: but all their eyes were painted white, and some red stroakes like Mutchato's along their cheekes. Round about him those fiends daunced a pretty while, and then came in three more as ugly as the rest, with red eyes, and white stroakes over their blacke faces. At last they all sat downe right against him, three of them on the one hand of the chiefe Priest, and three on the other. Then all with their rattles began a song, which ended, the chiefe Priest layd downe five wheat cornes; then strayning his armes and hands with such violence that he sweat, and his veynes swelled, he began a short Oration; at the conclusion they all gave a short groane, and they layd down three graines more. After that, began their song againe, and then another Oration, ever   20 laying downe so many cornes as before, till they had twice incirculed the fire; that done, they tooke a bunch of little stickes prepared for that purpose, continuing still their devotion, and at the end of every song and Oration, they layd downe a sticke betwixt the divisions of Corne. Till night, neither he nor they did either eate or drinke; and then they feasted merrily, with the best provisions they could make. Three dayes they used this Ceremony; the meaning whereof, they told him, was to know if he intended them well or no. The circle of meale signified their Country, the circles of corne the bounds of the Sea, and the stickes his Country. They imagined the world to be flat and round, like a trencher, and they in the middest.

After this they brought him a bagge of gunpowder, which they carefully preserved   30 till the next spring, to plant as they did their corne; because they would be acquainted with the nature of that seede.

Opitchapam the Kings brother, invited him to his house, where, with as many platters of bread, foule, and wild beasts as did environ him, he bid him wellcome; but not any of them would eate a bit with him, but put up all the remainder in Baskets.

At his return to Opechancanoughs, all the Kings women, and their children, flocked about him for their parts; as a due by Custome, to be merry with such fragments.

But his waking mind in hydeous dreames did oft see wondrous shapes,
Of bodies strange, and huge in growth, and of stupendious makes.   40

At last they brought him to *Meronocomoco,* where was *Powhatan,* their Emperor. Here more than two hundred of those grim Courtiers stood wondering at him, as

12 **Mutchato's,** mustachios

he had beene a monster; till *Powhatan* and his trayne had put themselves in their greatest braveries. Before a fire upon a seat like a bedsted, he sat covered with a great robe, made of *Rarowcun* skinnes, and all the tayles hanging by. On either hand did sit a young wench of 16 or 18 yeares, and along on each side the house, two rowes of men, and behind them as many women, with all their heads and shoulders painted red; many of their heads bedecked with the white downe of Birds; but every one with something, and a great chayne of white beads about their necks.

At his entrance before the King, all the people gave a great shout. The Queene of *Appamatuck* was appointed to bring him water to wash his hands, and another
10 brought him a bunch of feathers, in stead of a Towell, to dry them: having feasted him after their best barbarous manner they could, a long consultation was held; but the conclusion was, two great stones were brought before Powhatan: then as many as could layd hands on him, dragged him to them, and thereon laid his head, and being ready with their clubs, to beate out his braines, *Pocahontas,* the Kings dearest daughter, when no intreaty could prevaile, got his head in her armes, and laid her owne upon his to save him from death: whereat the Emperour was contented he should live to make him hatchets, and her bells, beads, and copper; for they thought him as well of all occupations as themselves. For the King himselfe will make his owne robes, shooes, bowes, arrowes, pots; plant, hunt, or doe any thing so well as
20 the rest.

> They say he bore a pleasant shew,
> But sure his heart was sad.
> For who can pleasant be, and rest,
> That lives in feare and dread:
> And having life suspected, doth
> It still suspected lead.

Two days after, *Powhatan*, having disguised himselfe in the most fearefullest manner he could, caused Captain *Smith* to be brought forth to a great house in the woods, and there upon a mat by the fire to be left alone. Not long after, from behinde a
30 mat that divided the house, was made the most dolefullest noyse he ever heard; then *Powhatan,* more like a devill then a man, with some two hundred more as blacke as himselfe, came unto him and told him now they were friends, and presently he should goe to *James* towne, to send him two great gunnes, and a gryndstone, for which he would give him the Country of *Capahowosick,* and for ever esteeme him as his sonne *Nantaquoud.*

So to *James* towne with 12 guides *Powhatan* sent him. That night they quarterd in the woods, he still expecting (as he had done all this long time of his imprisonment) every houre to be put to one death or other: for all their feasting. But almightie God (by his divine providence) had mollified the hearts of those sterne Bar-
40 barians with compassion. The next morning betimes they came to the Fort; where *Smith,* having used the Salvages with what kindnesse he could, he shewed *Rawhunt,*

---

3 **Rarowcun,** raccoon   18 **as well of,** as efficient at

Powhatans trusty servant, two demi-Culverings & a millstone to carry *Powhatan:* they found them somewhat too heavie; but when they did see him discharge them, being loaded with stones, among the boughs of a great tree loaded with Isickles, the yce and branches came so tumbling downe, that the poore Salvages ran away halfe dead with feare. But at last we regained some conference with them, and gave them such toyes; and sent to *Powhatan,* his women, and children such presents, as he gave them in generall full content.

Now in *James* Towne they were all in combustion, the strongest preparing once more to run away with the pinnace; which with the hazzard of his life, with Sakre falcon and musket shot, *Smith* forced now the third time to stay or sinke.   10

Some, no better then they should be, had plotted with the President, the next day to have put him to death by the Leviticall law, for the lives of *Robinson* and *Emry;* pretending the fault was his that had led them to their ends: but he quickly tooke such order with such Lawyers, that he layd them by the heeles till he sent some of them prisoners for *England.*

1623-1624

---

1 **demi-Culverings,** nine-pound cannons   9 **Sakre falcon,** a type of cannon   12 **Leviticall law,** as set forth in Leviticus 24: 17: "And he that killeth any man shall surely be put to death"

1590—1657 William Bradford

Villiam Bradford came of a family of prosperous farmers in Yorkshire, England. While still a boy, he joined the Separatist group which met in the house of William Brewster at Scrooby, and in 1609 he accompanied the Separatists to Holland, where they remained eleven years. He sailed on the *Mayflower* in 1620. Following the landing at Plymouth in December of that year, Bradford, as his *History* records, took a leading part in the affairs of the colony. He was chosen governor in the annual elections no less than thirty times, serving continuously from 1621 to 1656 except for five years, when he was relieved at his own urgent request. The record shows him to have been worthy of such confidence.

The manuscript of Bradford's work was probably not intended for publication. At any rate, although it was freely drawn upon by numerous New England historians in the seventeenth and eighteenth centuries (among them, Thomas Hutchinson), it was not published until 1856, shortly after it had been discovered in the library of the Bishop of London. It may have been taken to London by Hutchinson, a Loyalist, or by a British soldier. The manuscript was returned to Massachusetts in 1897 and has since reposed in the Massachusetts State Library.

Bradford's book tells the story of Plymouth Plantation through 1646. "There is no other document upon New England history," says Moses Coit Tyler, "that can take precedence of this either in time or in authority." It is a vivid record of the colonists' triumph over difficulties of many kinds. One cannot help being impressed by Bradford's sincerity, his exalted aims, and his lifelong dedication to religious truth as he conceived it. Although he was said by Cotton Mather to have mastered Latin and Greek and to have studied Hebrew ("because he would see with his own eyes the ancient oracles of God in their native beauty"), his study must have been predominantly in the English Bible, which he read in the Geneva version of 1560, for his style, like John Bunyan's, shows a strong Biblical influence. Whether his art was conscious or not, Bradford's prose is worthy of a distinguished place in the English tradition of his century.

Bradford's History of Plymouth Plantation, ed. Samuel E. Morison, New York, 1952   E. F. Bradford, "Conscious Art in Bradford's History of Plymouth Plantation," New England Quarterly, I (April 1928), 133-157

from The History of Plymouth Plantation

THE 9. CHAP.: *Of their vioage, & how they passed ye sea, and of their safe arrival at Cape Codd*

Septr. 6. [1620] These troubles being blowne over, and now all being compacte togeather in one shipe, they put to sea againe with a prosperus winde, which continued diverce days togeather, which was some incouragmente unto them; yet according to ye usuall maner many were afflicted with sea-sicknes. And I may not omite hear a spetiall worke of Gods providence. Ther was a proud & very profane yonge man, one of ye sea-men, of a lustie, able body, which made him the more hauty; he would allway be contemning ye poore people in their sicknes, & cursing them dayly with greeous execrations, and did not let to tell them, that he hoped to help to cast halfe of them over board before they came to their jurneys end, and to make mery 10 with what they had; and if he were by any gently reproved, he would curse and swear most bitterly. But it plased God before they came halfe seas over, to smite this yong man with a greevous disease, of which he dyed in a desperate maner, and so was him selfe ye first y^t was throwne overbord. Thus his curses light on his owne head; and it was an astonishmente to all his fellows, for they noted it to be ye just hand of God upon him.

After they had injoyed faire winds and weather for a season, they were incountred

---

2 **shipe,** the *Mayflower*   8 **let,** forbear

many times with crosse winds, and mette with many feirce stormes, with which yᵉ
shipe was shroudly shaken, and her upper works made very leakie; and one of the
maine beames in yᵉ midd ships was bowed & craked, which put them in some fear
that yᵉ shipe could not be able to performe yᵉ vioage. So some of yᵉ cheefe of yᵉ
company, perceiveing yᵉ mariners to feare yᵉ suffisiencie of yᵉ shipe, as appeared by
their mutterings, they entred into serious consulltation with yᵉ mʳ & other officers
of yᵉ ship, to consider in time of yᵉ danger; and rather to returne then to cast them
selves into a desperate & inevitable perill. And truly ther was great distraction &
differance of opinion amongst yᵉ mariners them selves; faine would they doe what
could be done for their wages sake, (being now halfe the seas over,) and on yᵉ other 10
hand they were loath to hazard their lives too desperatly. But in examening of all
opinions, the mʳ & others affirmed they knew yᵉ ship to be stronge & firme under
water; and for the buckling of yᵉ maine beame, ther was a great iron scrue yᵉ passengers brought out of Holland, which would raise yᵉ beame into his place; yᵉ which
being done, the carpenter & mʳ affirmed that with a post put under it, set firme in
yᵉ lower deck, & otherways bounde, he would make it sufficiente. And as for yᵉ decks
& uper workes they would calke them as well as they could, and though with yᵉ
workeing of yᵉ ship they would not longe keepe stanch, yet ther would otherwise
be no great danger, if they did not overpress her with sails. So they comited them
selves to yᵉ will of God, & resolved to proseede.   20

In sundrie of these stormes the winds were so feirce, & yᵉ seas so high, as they
could not beare a knote of saile, but were forced to hull, for diverce days togither.
And in one of them, as they thus lay at hull, in a mighty storme, a lustie yonge
man (called John Howland) coming upon some occasion above yᵉ grattings, was,
with a seele of yᵉ shipe throwne into [the] sea; but it pleased God yᵗ he caught
hould of yᵉ top-saile halliards, which hunge over board, & rane out at length; yet
he held his hould (though he was sundrie fadomes under water) till he was hald up
by yᵉ same rope to yᵉ brime of yᵉ water, and then with a boat hooke & other means
got into yᵉ shipe againe, & his life saved; and though he was something ill with it,
yet he lived many years after, and became a profitable member both in church & 30
comone wealthe. In all this viage ther died but one of yᵉ passengers, which was
William Butten, a youth, servant to Samuell Fuller, when they drew near yᵉ coast.
But to omite other things, (that I may be breefe,) after longe beating at sea they
fell with that land which is called Cape Cod; the which being made & certainly
knowne to be it, they were not a litle joyfull. After some deliberation had amongst
them selves & with yᵉ mʳ of yᵉ ship, they tacked aboute and resolved to stande for
yᵉ southward (yᵉ wind & weather being faire) to finde some place aboute Hudsons
river for their habitation. But after they had sailed yᵗ course aboute halfe yᵉ day,
they fell amongst deangerous shoulds and roring breakers, and they were so farr in-
tangled ther with as they conceived them selves in great danger; & yᵉ wind shrink- 40
ing upon them withall, they resolved to bear up againe for the Cape, and thought
them selves hapy to gett out of those dangers before night overtooke them, as by

---

2 **shroudly,** severely   6 **mʳ,** master or captain   22 **knote of sail,** enough sail to move the ship at a
speed of one knot   28 **brime,** brim   39 **shoulds,** shoals

Gods providence they did. And yᵉ next day they gott into yᵉ Cape-harbor wher they ridd in saftie. A word or too by yᵉ way of this cape; it was thus first named by Capten Gosnole & his company, Anᵒ: 1602, and after by Capten Smith was caled Cape James; but it retains yᵉ former name amongst sea-men. Also yᵗ pointe which first shewed those dangerous shoulds unto them, they called Pointe Care, & Tuckers Terrour; but yᵉ French & Dutch to this day call it Malabarr, by reason of those perilous shoulds, and the losses they have suffered their.

Being thus arived in a good harbor and brought safe to land, they fell upon their knees & blessed yᵉ God of heaven, who had brought them over yᵉ vast & furious
10 ocean, and delivered them from all yᵉ periles & miseries thereof, againe to set their feete on yᵉ firme and stable earth, their proper elemente. And no marvell if they were thus joyefull, seeing wise Seneca was so affected with sailing a few miles on yᵉ coast of his owne Italy; as he affirmed, that he had rather remaine twentie years on his way by land, then pass by sea to any place in a short time; so tedious & dreadfull was yᵉ same unto him.

But hear I cannot but stay and make a pause, and stand half amased at this poore peoples presente condition; and so I thinke will the reader too, when he well considers yᵉ same. Being thus passed yᵉ vast ocean, and a sea of troubles before in their preparation (as may be remembred by yᵗ which wente before), they had now no
20 freinds to wellcome them, nor inns to entertaine or refresh their weather-beaten bodys, no houses or much less townes to repaire too, to seeke for succoure. It is recorded in scripture as a mercie to yᵉ apostle & his shipwraked company, yᵗ the barbarians shewed them no smale kindness in refreshing them, but these savage barbarians, when they mette with them (as after will appeare) were readier to fill their sids full of arrows then otherwise. And for yᵉ season it was winter, and they that know yᵉ winters of yᵗ cuntrie know them to be sharp & violent, & subjecte to cruell & feirce stormes, deangerous to travill to known places, much more to serch an unknown coast. Besids, what could they see but a hidious & desolate wilderness, full of wild beasts & willd men? and what multituds ther might be of them they knew
30 not. Nether could they, as it were, goe up to yᵉ tope of Pisgah, to vew from this willdernes a more goodly cuntrie to feed their hops; for which way soever they turned their eys (save upward to yᵉ heavens) they could have litle solace or content in respecte of any outward objects. For sumer being done, all things stand upon them with a wetherbeaten face; and yᵉ whole countrie, full of woods & thickets, represented a wild & savage heiw. If they looked behind them, ther was yᵉ mighty ocean which they had passed, and was now as a maine barr & goulfe to seperate them from all yᵉ civill parts of yᵉ world. If it be said they had a ship to sucour them, it is trew; but what heard they daly from the mʳ & company? but yᵗ with speede they should looke out a place with their shallop, wher they would be at some near distance; for
40 yᵉ season was shuch as he would not stirr from thence till a safe harbor was discovered by them wher they would be, and he might goe without danger; and that victells consumed apace, but he must & would keepe sufficient for them selves &

---

2 **Capten Gosnole,** Bartholomew Gosnold (fl. 1572-1607) established the northern route to North America   22 **scripture.** See Acts 28:1-2

their returne. Yea, it was muttered by some, that if they gott not a place in time,
they would turne them & their goods ashore & leave them. Let it also be considred
what weake hopes of supply & succoure they left behinde them, y^t might bear up
their minds in this sade condition and trialls they were under; and they could not
but be very smale. It is true, indeed, ye affections & love of their brethren at Leyden
was cordiall & entire towards them, but they had litle power to help them, or them
selves; and how ye case stode betweene them & ye marchants at their coming away,
hath allready been declared. What could now sustaine them but ye spirite of God &
his grace? May not & ought not the children of these fathers rightly say: *Our faithers*
were Englishmen which came over this great ocean, and were ready to perish in this will-   10
dernes; but they cried unto ye Lord, and he heard their voyce, and looked on their adversitie,
&c. Let them therfore praise ye Lord, because he is good, & his mercies endure for ever. Yea,
let them which have been redeemed of ye Lord, shew how he hath delivered them from y^e
hand of the oppressour. When they wandered in ye deserte willdernes out of ye way, and
found no citie to dwell in, both hungrie, & thirstie, their sowle was overwhelmed in them.
Let them confess before ye Lord his loving kindness, and his wonderfull works before ye sons
of men.

Being thus arrived at Cap-Cod ye 11. of November, and necessitie calling them to
looke out a place for habitation, (as well as the maisters & mariners importunitie,)
they having brought a large shalop with them out of England, stowed in quarters   20
in ye ship, they now gott her out & sett their carpenters to worke to trime her up;
but being much brused & shatered in ye shipe wth foule weather, they saw she would
be longe in mending. Wherupon a few of them tendered them selves to goe by land
and discovere those nearest places, whilst ye shallop was in mending; and ye rather
because as they wente into y^t harbor ther seemed to be an opening some 2. or 3.
leagues of, which ye maister judged to be a river. It was conceived ther might be
some danger in ye attempte, yet seeing them resolute, they were permitted to goe,
being 16. of them well armed, under ye conduct of Captain Standish, having shuch
instructions given them as was thought meete. They sett forth ye 15. of Nove^{br}:
and when they had marched aboute ye space of a mile by ye sea side, they espied 5.   30
or 6. persons with a dogg coming towards them, who were salvages; but they fled
from them, & rane up into ye woods, and ye English followed them, partly to see if
they could speake with them, and partly to discover if ther might not be more of
them lying in ambush. But ye Indeans seeing them selves thus followed, they againe
forsooke the woods, & rane away on ye sands as hard as they could, so as they could
not come near them, but followed them by ye tracte of their feet sundrie miles, and
saw that they had come the same way. So, night coming on, they made their ran-
devous & set out ther sentinels, and rested in quiete y^t *night,* and the next morning
followed their tracte till they had headed a great creake, & so left the sands, & turned
an other way into ye woods. But they still followed them by geuss, hopeing to find   40

---

5 **Leyden,** in Holland, whence the most devout members of the group had come   9 **Our . . . &c.** The
sentence paraphrases Deuteronomy 26:7   12 **Let . . . men.** The passage paraphrases Psalms 107:1-8   28
Standish. Myles Standish (1584?-1656) was the colony's only professional soldier, and had been employed
by the Pilgrims in the Netherlands

their dwellings; but they soone lost both them & them selves, falling into shuch thickets as were ready to tear their cloaths & armore in peeces, but were most distresed for wante of drinke. But at length they found water & refreshed them selves, being ye first New-England water they drunke of, and was now in thir great thirste as pleasante unto them as wine or bear had been in for-times. Afterwards they directed their course to come to ye other shore, for they knew it was a necke of land they were to crosse over, and so at length gott to ye sea-side, and marched to this supposed river, & by ye way found a pond of clear fresh water, and shortly after a good quantitie of clear ground wher ye Indeans had formerly set corne, and some of their
10 graves. And proceeding furder they saw new-stuble wher corne had been set ye same year, also they found wher latly a house had been, wher some planks and a great ketle was remaining, and heaps of sand newly padled with their hands, which they, digging up, found in them diverce faire Indean baskets filled with corne, and some in eares, faire and good, of diverce collours, which seemed to them a very goodly sight, (haveing never seen any shuch before). This was near ye place of that supposed river they came to seeck; unto which they wente and found it to open it selfe into 2. armes with a high cliffe of sand in the enterance, but more like to be crikes of salte water then any fresh, for ought they saw; and that ther was good harborige for their shalope; leaving it further to be discovered by their shalop when she was
20 ready. So their time limeted them being expired, they returned to ye ship, least they should be in fear of their saftie; and tooke with them parte of ye corne, and buried up ye rest, and so like ye men from Eshcoll carried with them of ye fruits of ye land, & showed their breethren; of which, & their returne, they were marvelusly glad, and their harts incouraged.

    After this, ye shalop being got ready, they set out againe for ye better discovery of this place, & ye m^r. of ye ship desired to goe him selfe, so ther went some 30. men, but found it to be no harbor for ships but only for boats; ther was allso found 2. of their houses covered with matts, & sundrie of their implements in them, but ye people were rune away & could not be seen; also ther was found more of their corne,
30 & of their beans of various collours. The corne & beans they brought away, purposing to give them full satisfaction when they should meete with any of them (as about some 6. months afterward they did, to their good content). And here is to be noted a spetiall providence of God, and a great mercie to this poore people, that hear they gott seed to plant them corne ye next year, or els they might have starved, for they had none, nor any liklyhood to get any till ye season had beene past (as ye sequell did manyfest). Neither is it lickly they had had this, if ye first viage had not been made, for the ground was now all covered with snow, & hard frozen. But the Lord is never wanting unto his in their greatest needs; let his holy name have all ye praise.

    The month of November being spente in these affairs, & much foule weather fall-
40 ing in, the 6. of Desem^r: they sente out their shallop againe with 10. of their principall men, & some sea men, upon further discovery, intending to circulate that deepe bay of Cap-codd. The weather was very could, & it frose so hard as ye sprea of ye sea lighting on their coats, they were as if they had been glased; yet *that night* be-

---

22 **Eshcoll**, or Eshcol. See Numbers 13: 23-25

times they gott downe into ye botome of ye bay, and as they drue nere ye shore they saw some 10. or 12. Indeans very busie about some thing. They landed aboute a league or 2. from them, and had much a doe to put a shore any wher, it lay so full of flats. Being landed, it grew late, and they made them selves a barricade with loggs & bowes as well as they could in ye time, & set out their sentenill & betooke them to rest, and saw ye smoake of ye fire ye savages made y^t night. When *morning* was come they devided their company, some to coaste along ye shore in ye boate, and the rest marched throw ye woods to see ye land, if any fit place might be for their dwelling. They came allso to ye place wher they saw the Indans ye night be- fore, & found they had been cuting up a great fish like a grampus, being some 2. 10 inches thike of fate like a hogg, some peeces wher of they had left by ye way; and ye shallop found 2. more of these fishes dead on ye sands, a thing usuall after storms in y^t place, by reason of ye great flats of sand that lye of. So they ranged up and doune all y^t day, but found no people, nor any place they liked. When ye sune grue low, they hasted out of ye woods to meete with their shallop, to whom they had made signes to come to them into a *creeke* hardby, the which they did at highwater; of which they were very glad, for they had not seen each other all y^t day, since ye morning. So they made them a barricado (as usually they did every night) with loggs, staks, & thike pine bowes, ye height of a man, leaving it open to leeward, partly to shelter them from ye could & wind (making their fire in ye midle, & lying round 20 about it), and partly to defend them from any sudden assaults of ye savags, if they should surround them. So being very weary, they betooke them to rest. But aboute *midnight,* they heard a hideous & great crie, and their sentinell caled, "Arme, arme"; so they bestired them & stood to their armes, & shote of a cupple of moskets, and then the noys seased. They concluded it was a companie of wolves, or such like willd beasts; for one of ye sea men tould them he had often heard shuch a noyse in New-found land. So they rested till about 5. of ye clock in the *morning;* for ye tide, & ther purpos to goe from thence, made them be stiring betimes. So after praier they prepared for breakfast, and it being day dawning, it was thought best to be carring things downe to ye boate. But some said it was not best to carrie ye armes 30 downe, others said they would be the readier, for they had laped them up in their coats from ye dew. But some 3. or 4. would not cary theirs till they wente them selves, yet as it fell out, ye water being not high enough, they layed them downe on ye banke side, & came up to breakfast. But presently, all on ye sudain, they heard a great & strange crie, which they knew to be the same voyces they heard in ye night, though they varied their notes, & one of their company being abroad came runing in, & cried, "Men, Indeans, Indeans"; and w^{th}all, their arowes came flying amongst them. Their men rane with all speed to recover their armes, as by ye good provi- dence of God they did. In ye mean time, of those that were ther ready, tow muskets were discharged at them, & 2. more stood ready in ye enterance of ther randevoue, 40 but were comanded not to shoote till they could take full aime at them; & ye other 2. charged againe with all speed, for ther were only 4. had armes ther, & defended the baricado which was first assalted. The crie of ye Indeans was dreadful, espetially when they saw ther men rune out of ye randevoue towourds ye shallop, to recover

their armes, the Indeans wheeling aboute upon them. But some ruñing out with
coats of malle on, & cutlasses in their hands, they soone got their armes, & let flye
amongs them, and quickly stopped their violence. Yet ther was a lustie man, and
no less valiante, stood behind a tree within halfe a musket shot, and let his arrows
flie at them. He was seen shoot 3. arrowes, which were all avoyded. He stood 3.
shot of a musket, till one taking full aime at him, and made ye barke or splinters
of ye tree fly about his ears, after which he gave an extraordinary shrike, and away
they wente all of them. They left some to keep ye shalop, and followed them aboute
a quarter of a mille, and shouted once or twise, and shot of 2. or 3. peces, & so re-
10 turned. This they did, that they might conceive they were not affrade of them or any
way discouraged. Thus it pleased God to vanquish their enimies, and give them
deliverance; and by his spetiall providence so to dispose that not any one of them
were either hurte, or hitt, though their arrows came close by them, and on every
side them, and sundry of their coats, which hunge up in ye barocado, were shot throw
& throw. Aterwards they gave God sollamne thanks & praise for their deliverance,
& gathered up a bundle of their arrows, & sente them into England afterward by y^e
m^r. of ye ship, and called that place ye first encounter. From hence they departed, &
costed all along, but discerned no place likly for harbor; & therfore hasted to a place
that their pillote, (one M^r. Coppin who had bine in ye cuntrie before) did assure
20 them was a good harbor, which he had been in, and they might fetch it before night;
of which they were glad, for it begane to be foule weather. After some houres sailing, it begane to snow & raine, & about ye midle of ye afternoone, ye wind increased,
& ye sea became very rough, and they broake their rudder, & it was as much as 2.
men could doe to steere her with a cupple of oares. But their pillott bad them be
of good cheere, for he saw ye harbor; but ye storme increasing, & night drawing
on, they bore what saile they could to gett in, while they could see. But herwith
they broake their mast in 3. peeces, & their saill fell over bord, in a very grown
sea, so as they had like to have been cast away; yet by God's mercie they recovered
them selves, & having ye floud with them, struck into ye harbore. But when it came
30 too, ye pillott was deceived in the place, and said, ye Lord be mercifull unto them,
for his eys never saw y^t place before; & he & the m^r. mate would have rune her
ashore, in a cove full of breakers, before ye winde. But a lusty seaman which steered,
bad those which rowed, if they were men, about with her, or ells they were all cast
away; the which they did with speed. So he bid them be of good cheere & row lustly,
for ther was a faire sound before them, & he doubted not but they should find one
place or other wher they might ride in saftie. And though it was *very darke,* and
rained sore, yet in ye end they gott under ye lee of a smalle iland, and remained ther
all y^t night in saftie. But they knew not this to be an iland till morning, but were
devided in their minds; some would keepe ye boate for fear they might be amongst
40 ye Indians; others were so weake and could, they could not endure, but got a shore,
& with much adoe got fire, (all things being so wett,) and ye rest were glad to come
to them; for after midnight ye wind shifted to the north-west, & it frose hard. But

---

19 **Coppin.** Robert Coppin was second mate on the *Mayflower.* He may have had Captain John Smith's
map of 1616   27 **grown sea,** a sea running high

though this had been a day & night of much trouble & danger unto them, yet God gave them a *morning* of comforte & refreshing (as usually he doth to his children), for yᵉ next day was a fair sunshinīg day, and they found them sellvs to be on an iland secure from yᵉ Indeans, wher they might drie their stufe, fixe their peeces, & rest them selves, and gave God thanks for his mercies, in their manifould deliverances. And this being the *last day of yᵉ weeke,* they prepared ther to keepe yᵉ Sabath. On Munday they sounded yᵉ harbor, and founde it fitt for shipping; and marched into yᵉ land, & found diverse cornfeilds, & litle running brooks, a place (as they supposed) fitt for situation; at least it was yᵉ best they could find, and yᵉ season, & their present necessitie, made them glad to accepte of it. So they returned to their 10 shipp againe with this news to yᵉ rest of their people, which did much comforte their harts.

On yᵉ 15. of Desemʳ: they wayed anchor to goe to yᵉ place they had discovered, & came within 2. leagues of it, but were faine to bear up againe; but yᵉ 16. *day* yᵉ winde came faire, and they arrived safe in this harbor. And after wards tooke better view of yᵉ place, and resolved wher to pitch their dwelling; and yᵉ 25. *day* begane to erecte yᵉ first house for com̃one use to receive them and their goods.

THE 2. BOOKE

The rest of this History (if God give me life, & opportunitie) I shall, for brevitis sake, handle by ways of *annalls,* noteing only the heads of principall things, and 20 passages as they fell in order of time, and may seeme to be profitable to know, or to make use of. And this may be as yᵉ 2. Booke.

The remainder of Anº: 1620

I shall a litle returne backe and begine with a combination made by them before they came ashore, being yᵉ first foundation of their govermente in this place; occasioned partly by yᵉ discontented & mutinous speeches that some of the strangers amongst them had let fall from them in yᵉ ship — That when they came a shore they would use their owne libertie; for none had power to com̃and them, the patente they had being for Virginia, and not for New-england, which belonged to an other Goverment, with which yᵉ Virginia Company had nothing to doe. And partly that 30 shuch an acte by them done (this their condition considered) might be as firme as any patent, and in some respects more sure.

The forme was as followeth.

In yᵉ name of God, Amen. We whose names are underwriten, the loyall subjects of our dread soveraigne Lord, King James, by yᵉ grace of God, of Great Britaine, Franc, & Ireland king, defender of yᵉ faith, &c., haveing undertaken, for yᵉ glorie

---

7 **Munday.** Thus the Pilgrims came to the site of Plymouth   34 **In** . . . . **1620.** This document, known as the "Mayflower Compact," was an agreement signed by the Pilgrim Fathers to serve as a form of government because the Pilgrims had no charter

of God, and advancemente of ye Christian faith, and honour of our king & countrie, a voyage to plant ye first colonie in ye Northerne parts of Virginia, doe by these presents solemnly & mutualy in ye presence of God, and one of another, covenant & combine our selves togeather into a civill body politick, for our better ordering & preservation & furtherance of ye ends aforesaid; and by vertue hearof to enacte, constitute, and frame such just & equall lawes, ordinances, acts, constitutions, & offices, from time to time, as shall be thought most meete & convenient for ye generall good of ye Colonie, unto which we promise all due submission and obedience. In witnes wherof we have hereunder subscribed our names at Cap-Codd ye 11. of
10 November, in ye year of ye raigne of our soveraigne lord, King James, of England, France, & Ireland ye eighteenth, and of Scotland ye fiftie fourth.

An^o: Dom. 1620.

After this they chose, or rather confirmed, Mr. John Carver (a man godly & well approved amongst them) their Governour for that year. And after they had provided a place for their goods, or comone store, (which were long in unlading for want of boats, foulnes of winter weather, and sicknes of diverce,) and begune some small cottages for their habitation, as time would admitte, they mette and consulted of lawes & orders, both for their civill & military Govermente, as ye necessitie of their condition did require, still adding thereunto as urgent occasion in severall
20 times, and as cases did require.

In these hard & difficulte beginings they found some discontents & murmurings arise amongst some, and mutinous speeches & carriags in other; but they were soone quelled & overcome by ye wisdome, patience, and just & equall carrage of things by ye Govr and better part, wch clave faithfully togeather in ye maine. But that which was most sadd & lamentable was, that in 2. or 3. moneths time halfe of their company dyed, espetialy in Jan: & February, being ye depth of winter, and wanting houses & other comforts; being infected with ye scurvie & other diseases, which this long vioage & their inacomodate condition had brought upon them; so as ther dyed some times 2. or 3. of a day, in ye foresaid time; that of 100. & odd
30 persons, scarce 50. remained. And of these in ye time of most distres, ther was but 6. or 7. sound persons, who, to their great comendations be it spoken, spared no pains, night nor day, but with abundance of toyle and hazard of their owne health, fetched them woode, made them fires, drest them meat, made their beads, washed their lothsome cloaths, cloathed & uncloathed them; in a word, did all the homly & necessarie offices for them wch dainty & quesie stomacks cannot endure to hear named; and all this willingly & cherfully, without any grudging in ye least, shewing herein their true love unto their freinds & bretheren. A rare example & worthy to be remembred. Tow of these 7. were M^r. William Brewster, ther reverend Elder, & Myles Standish, ther Captein & military comander, unto whom my selfe, & many
40 others, were much beholden in our low & sicke condition. And yet the Lord so upheld these persons, as in this generally calamity they were not at all infected either with sicknes, or lamnes. And what I have said of these, I may say of many others

who dyed in this generall vissitation, & others yet living, that whilst they had
health, yea, or any strength continuing, they were not wanting to any that had need
of them. And I doute not but their recompence is with ye Lord. . . .

[1623] All this whille no supply was heard of, neither knew they when they might
expecte any. So they begane to thinke how they might raise as much corne as they
could, and obtaine a beter crope then they had done, that they might not still thus
languish in miserie. At length, after much debate of things, the Govr (with ye advise of ye cheefest amongest them) gave way that they should set corne every man
for his owne perticuler, and in that regard trust to them selves; in all other things
to goe on in ye generall way as before. And so assigned to every family a parcell of 10
land, according to the proportion of their number for that end, only for present use
(but made no devission for inheritance), and ranged all boys & youth under some
familie. This had very good success; for it made all hands very industrious, so as
much more corne was planted then other waise would have bene by any means y^e
Govr or any other could use, and saved him a great deall of trouble, and gave farr
better contente. The women now wente willingly into ye feild, and tooke their
litle-ons with them to set corne, which before would aledg weaknes, and inabilitie;
whom to have compelled would have bene thought great tiranie and oppression.

The experience that was had in this comone course and condition, tried sundrie
years, and that amongst godly and sober men, may well evince the vanitie of that 20
conceite of Platos & other ancients, applauded by some of later times; — that y^e
taking away of propertie, and bringing in comunitie into a comone wealth, would
make them happy and florishing; as if they were wiser then God. For this comunitie
(so farr as it was) was found to breed much confusion & discontent, and retard much
imploymēt that would have been to their benefite and comforte. For ye yongmen
that were most able and fitte for labour & service did repine that they should spend
their time & streingth to worke for other mens wives and children, with out any
recompence. The strong, or man of parts, had no more in devission of victails &
cloaths, then he that was weake and not able to doe a quarter ye other could; this
was thought injuestice. The aged and graver men to be ranked and equalised in 30
labours, and victails, cloaths, &c., with ye meaner and yonger sorte, thought it some
indignite and disrespect unto them. And for mens wives to be commanded to doe
servise for other men, as dresing their meate, washing their cloaths, &c., they deemd
it a kind of slaverie, neither could many husbands well brooke it. Upon ye poynte
all being to have alike, and all to doe alike, they thought them selves in ye like
condition, and one as good as another; and so, if it did not cut of those relations
that God hath set amongst men, yet it did at least much diminish and take of y^e
mutuall respects that should be preserved amongst them. And would have bene
worse if they had been men of another condition. Let none objecte this is men's
corruption, and nothing to ye course it selfe. I answer, seeing all men have this cor- 40
ruption in them, God in his wisdom saw another course fiter for them. . . .

[1628] Aboute some 3. or 4. years before this time, ther came over one Captaine
Wolastone, (a man of pretie parts) and with him 3. or 4. more of some eminencie,

19 **comōne course**, ownership in common   36 **of**, off

who brought with them a great many servants, with provissions & other implments
for to begine a plantation; and pitched them selves in a place within the Massachusets, which they called, after their Captains name, Mount-Wollaston. Amongst
whom was one M^r. Morton, who, it should seeme, had some small adventure (of
his owne or other mens) amongst them; but had litle respecte amongst them, and
was sleghted by ye meanest servants. Haveing continued ther some time, and not
finding things to answer their expectations, nor profite to arise as they looked for,
Captaine Wollaston takes a great part of ye sarvants, and transports them to Virginia, wher he puts them of at good rates, selling their time to other men; and
10 writs back to one M^r. Rassdall, one of his cheefe partners, and accounted their
marchant, to bring another parte of them to Verginia likewise, intending to put
them of ther as he had done ye rest. And he, wth ye consente of ye said Rasdall,
appoynted one Fitcher to be his Livetenante, and governe ye remaines of ye plantation, till he or Rasdall returned to take further order theraboute. But this Morton
abovesaid, haveing more craft than honestie, (who had been a kind of petiefogger,
of Furnefells Inne,) in ye absence, watches an oppertunitie, (commons being but
hard amongst them,) and gott some strong drinck and other junkats, & made them
a feast; and after they were merie, he begane to tell them, he would give them
good counsell. You see (saith he) that many of your fellows are carried to Virginia;
20 and if you stay till this Rasdall returne, you will also be carried away and sould for
slaves with ye rest. Therfore I would advise you to thruste out this Levetenant Fitcher;
and I, having a parte in the plantation, will receive you as my partners and con-
sociats; so may you be free from service, and we will converse, trad, plante, & live
togeather as equalls & supporte & protecte one another, or to like effecte. This
counsell was easily received; so they tooke oppertunitie, and thrust Levetenante
Fitcher out a dores, and would suffer him to come no more amongst them, but forct
him to seeke bread to eate, and other releefe from his neigbours, till he could gett
passage for England. After this they fell to great licenciousnes, and led a dissolute
life, powering out them selves into al profanenes. And Morton became lord of mis-
30 rule, and maintained (as it were) a schoole of Athisme. And after they had gott
some good into their hands, and gott much by trading with ye Indeans, they spent
it as vainly, in quaffing & drinking both wine & strong waters in great exsess, and,
as some reported, 10^{li s} worth in a morning. They allso set up a May-pole, drinking
and dancing aboute it many days togeather, inviting the Indean women, for their
consorts, dancing and frisking togither, (like so many fairies, or furies rather,) and
worse practises. As if they had anew revived and celebrated the feasts of ye Roman
Goddes Flora, or ye beasly practieses of ye madd Bacchinalians. Morton likewise (to

---

4 **M^r. Morton**, Thomas Morton, whose amusing and very different account in the *New English Canaan* (see
p. 69) should be compared with Bradford's   4 **small adventure**, pecuniary risk   15 **petiefogger**, pettifogger, and inferior lawyer   16 **Furnefells Inne**, Furnival's Inn, one of the Inns of Court in London occupied by "students and practicers" of the law   16 **commons**, food   29 **powering**, pouring   29
lord of misrule. The anti-Anglican protestants were particularly opposed to the secular Christmas revels,
over which this officer presided   33 **10^{li s}**, ten pounds   33 **May-pole**. This central object of the popular May Day celebration, about which the celebrants danced, was also objectionable to the anti-Anglican
protestants   37 **Bacchinalians**, followers of the Greek wine god Dionysius

shew his poetrie) composed sundry rimes & verses, some tending to lasciviousnes, and others to ye detraction and scandall of some persons, which he affixed to this idle or idoll May-polle. They chainged allso the name of their place, and in stead of calling it Mounte Wollaston, they called it Merie-mounte, as if this joylity would have lasted ever. But this continued not long, for after Morton was sent for England, (as follows to be declared,) shortly after came over that worthy gentlman, M^r. John Indecott, who brought over a patent under ye broad seall, for ye govermente of ye Massachusets, who visiting those parts caused y^t May-polle to be cutt downe, and rebuked them for their profannes, and admonished them to looke ther should be better walking; so they now, or others, changed ye name of their place again, 10 and called it Mounte-Dagon. . . .

[1633] M^r. Roger Williams (a man godly & zealous, having many precious parts, but very unsettled in judgmente) came over first to ye Massachusetts, but upon some discontente left y^t place, and came hither, (wher he was friñdly entertained, according to their poore abilitie,) and exercised his gifts amongst them, & after some time was admitted a member of ye church; and his teaching well approved, for ye benefite wherof I still blese God, and am thankfull to him, even for his sharpest admonitions & reproufs, so farr as they agreed with truth. He this year begane to fall into some strang oppīons, and from opinion to practise; which caused some controversie betweene ye church & him, and in ye end some discontente on 20 his parte, by occasion whereof he left them some thing abruptly. Yet after wards sued for his dismission to ye church of Salem, which was granted, with some caution to them concerning him, and what care they ought to have of him. But he soone fell into more things ther, both to their and ye governments troble & disturbance. I shall not need to name perticulers, they are too well knowen now to all, though for a time ye church here wente under some hard censure by his occasion, from some that afterwards smarted them selves. But he is to be pitied, and prayed for, and so I shall leave ye matter, and desire ye Lord to shew him his errors, and reduse him into ye way of truth, and give him a setled judgment and constancie in ye same; for I hope he belongs to ye Lord, and y^t he will shew him mercie. . . . 30

[1638] This year, aboute ye 1. or 2. of June, was a great & fearfull earthquake; it was in this place heard before it was felte. It came with a rumbling noyse, or low murmure, like unto remoate thunder; it came from ye norward, & pased southward. As ye noyse aproched nerer, they earth begane to shake, and came at length with that violence as caused platters, dishes, & such like things as stoode upon shelves, to clatter & fall downe; yea, persons were afraid of ye houses them selves. It so fell oute y^t at ye same time diverse of ye cheefe of this towne were mett together at one house, conferring with some of their freinds that were upon their removall from ye place, (as if ye Lord would herby shew ye signes of his displeasure, in their shaking a peeces & removalls one from an other.) How ever it was very terrible for ye time, 40 and as ye men were set talking in ye house, some women & others were without y^e

7 **Indecott**, John Endicott   11 **Mounte-Dagon**, Dagon was a god of the Philistines; see Judges 16:23   29 **Y^e . . . truth.** Banished from the Massachusetts Bay Colony in 1635, Roger Williams (see p. 126) migrated to the Narragansett country, where he founded Providence, Rhode Island

dores, and yᵉ earth shooke with yᵗ violence as they could not stand without catching hould of yᵉ posts & pails yᵗ stood next them; but yᵉ violence lasted not long. And about halfe an hower, or less, came an other noyse & shaking, but nether so loud nor strong as yᵉ former, but quickly passed over; and so it ceased. It was not only on yᵉ sea coast, but yᵉ Indeans felt it within land; and some ships that were upon yᵉ coast were shaken by it. So powerfull is yᵉ mighty hand of yᵉ Lord, as to make both the earth & sea to shake, and the mountaines to tremble before him, when he pleases; and who can stay his hand? It was observed that yᵉ somers, for divers years togeather after this earthquake, were not so hotte & seasonable for the
10 ripning of corne & other fruits as formerly; but more could & moyst, & subjecte to erly & untimly frosts, by which, many times, much Indean corne came not to maturitie; but whether this was any cause, I leave it to naturallists to judge. . . .

Anno Dom: 1642

Marvilous it may be to see and consider how some kind of wickednes did grow & breake forth here, in a land wher the same was so much witnesed against, and so narrowly looked unto, & severly punished when it was knowne; as in no place more, or so much, that I have known or heard of; insomuch as they have been somewhat censured, even by moderate and good men, for their severitie in punishments. And yet all this could not suppress yᵉ breaking out of sundrie notorious sins,
20 (as this year, besids other, gives us too many sad presidents and instances) espetially drunkennes and unclainnes; not only incontinencie betweene persons unmaried, for which many both men & women have been punished sharply enough, but some maried persons allso. But that which is worse, even sodomie and bugerie, (things fearfull to name,) have broak forth in this land, oftener then once. I say it may justly be marveled at, and cause us to fear & tremble at the consideration of our corrupte natures, which are so hardly bridled, subdued, & mortified; nay, cannot by any other means but yᵉ powerfull worke & grace of Gods spirite. But (besids this) one reason may be, that yᵉ Divell may carrie a greater spite against the churces of Christ and yᵉ gospell hear, by how much yᵉ more they indeaour to preserve holynes and
30 puritie amongst them, and strictly punisheth the contrary when it ariseth either in church or comone wealth; that he might cast a blemishe & staine upon them in the eyes of [yᵉ] world, who use to be rash in judgmente. I would rather thinke thus, then that Satane hath more power in these heathen lands, as som have thought, then in more Christian nations, espetially over Gods servants in them.

2. An other reason may be, that it may be in this case as it is with waters when their streames are stopped or damed up, when they gett passage they flow with more violence, and make more noys and disturbance, then when they are suffered to rune quietly in their owne chanels. So wikednes being here more stopped by strict laws, and yᵉ same more nerly looked unto, so as it cannot rune in a comone road of lib-
40 erty as it would, and is inclined, it searches ever wher, and at last breaks out wher it getts vente.

---

20 **presidents,** precedents

3. A third reason may be, hear (as I am verily perswaded) is not more evills in this kind, nor nothing nere so many by proportion, as in other places; but they are here more discovered and seen, and made publick by due serch, inquisition, and due punishment; for ye churches looke narrowly to their members, and ye magistrats over all, more strictly then in other places. Besids, here the people are but few in comparison of other places, which are full and populous, and lye hid, as it were, in a wood or thickett, and many horrible evills by y^t means are never seen nor knowne; whereas hear, they are, as it were, brought into ye light, and set in ye plaine feeld, or rather on a hill, made conspicuous to ye view of all. . . .

                                                                          1630-1657-1856

1580?—1646 Thomas Morton

The founding fathers of New England were serious rather than gay, austere rather than warmly humane. It is not hard, although perhaps not wholly fair, to picture them as humorless spoilsports. Even in colonial times, such a picture was drawn by Thomas Morton.

What manner of man Morton was is still debatable after three centuries. William Bradford's low opinion of him (see pp. 65-66) was not completely shared by Hawthorne, whose short story "The Maypole of Merry Mount" is the best-known literary use of Morton's story, nor by the historian John Lothrop Motley, who wrote a novel on the episode of Merry Mount, nor by Howard Hanson and Richard Stokes, who used it for the libretto of their opera *Merry Mount* (1933).

Little is known of Morton's life before 1625, when he became a part of a trading company at Mount Wollaston, near Plymouth, later renamed "Ma-re," or Merry, Mount. He had probably been a London lawyer, and made an earlier visit to New England. In 1627 he was arrested and deported, whether for the reasons given by Bradford or for those suggested by Morton himself the reader must decide. He returned, and in 1630 was again deported.

Morton's single book, the *New English Canaan, or New Canaan*, was first printed at Amsterdam in 1637. It consists of three parts. The first concerns the Indians, their origin and customs; the second is essentially a promotion tract, with an account of the country and its commodities; the third is an account of the English settlement, as seen from Morton's anti-Puritan position. Morton appears to have fancied himself as a writer, and his book is unusual among works of its type for its allusive literary, and sometimes overornamental style.

Morton was in America again in 1643, and was once more arrested. After many months in the Boston jail, he was released. He left Massachusetts, this time without being forced to, and found a retreat in Maine, where he died in 1646.

New English Canaan, or New Canaan, ed. C. F. Adams, Jr., Publications of the Prince Society, Boston, 1883

from New English Canaan

The following selection is the fifteenth chapter of Book III. It should be compared with Bradford's account of the same incident (pp. 65-66). Morton's none too happy efforts to give his writing an air of learning begin with the chapter title: "Of a Great Monster Supposed to Be at Ma-re-mount; and the Preparation Made to Destroy It." The style, indeed, is frequently a loud echo of that of the chivalric romances and their satirist, Cervantes. "Captaine Shrimp" is the famous but short military leader of Plymouth Colony, Captain Miles Standish.

The Seperatists, envying the prosperity and hope of the Plantation at Ma-re Mount, (which they perceaved beganne to come forward, and to be in a good way for gaine in the Beaver trade,) conspired together against mine Host especially, (who was the owner of that Plantation,) and made up a party against him; and mustred up what aide they could, accounting of him as of a great Monster.

Many threatening speeches were given out both against his person and his Habitation, which they divulged should be consumed with fire: And taking advantage of the time when his company, (which seemed little to regard theire threats,) were gone up into the Inlands to trade with the Salvages for Beaver, they set upon my
10 honest host at a place called Wessaguscus, where, by accident, they found him. The inhabitants there were in good hope of the subvertion of the plantation at Mare Mount, (which they principally aymed at;) and the rather because mine host was a man that indeavoured to advaunce the dignity of the Church of England; which they, (on the contrary part,) would laboure to vilifie with uncivile termes: enveying against the sacred booke of common prayer, and mine host that used it in a laudable manner amongst his family, as a practise of piety.

There hee would be a meanes to bring sacks to their mill, (such is the thirst after Beaver,) and helped the conspiratores to surprise mine host, (who was there all alone;) and they chargded him, (because they would seeme to have some reasonable
20 cause against him to sett a glosse upon their mallice,) with criminall things; which indeede had beene done by such a person, but was of their conspiracy; mine host demaunded of the conspirators who it was that was author of that information, that seemed to be their ground for what they now intended. And because they answered they would not tell him, hee as peremptorily replyed, that hee would not say whether he had, or he had not done as they had bin informed.

1 **Seperatists,** the Congregationalists of Plymouth (see p. 9)   10 **Wessaguscus,** present-day Weymouth; like Monoticut or Monatoquit (p. 70), present-day Braintree, a settlement a few miles south of what is now Boston, only a short distance from Wollaston or Merrymount

The answere made no matter, (as it seemed,) whether it had bin negatively or affirmatively made; for they had resolved that hee should suffer, because, (as they boasted,) they were now become the greater number: they had shaked of their shackles of servitude, and were become Masters, and masterles people.

It appears they were like beares whelpes in former time, when mine hosts plantation was of as much strength as theirs, but now, (theirs being stronger,) they, (like over-growne beares,) seemed monsterous. In breife, mine host must indure to be their prisoner untill they could contrive it so that they might send him for England, (as they said,) there to suffer according to the merrit of the fact which they intended to father upon him; supposing, (belike,) it would proove a hainous crime.   10

Much rejoycing was made that they had gotten their capitall enemy, (as they concluded him;) whome they purposed to hamper in such sort that hee should not be able to uphold his plantation at Ma-re Mount.

The Conspirators sported themselves at my honest host, that meant them no hurt, and were so joccund that they feasted their bodies, and fell to tippeling as if they had obtained a great prize; like the Trojans when they had the custody of Hippeus pinetree horse.

Mine host fained greefe, and could not be perswaded either to eate or drinke; be-cause hee knew emptines would be a meanes to make him as watchfull as the Geese kept in the Roman Cappitall: whereon, the contrary part, the conspirators would   20 be so drowsy that hee might have an opportunity to give them a slip, insteade of a tester. Six persons of the conspiracy were set to watch him at Wessaguscus: But hee kept waking; and in the dead of night, (one lying on the bed for further suerty,) up gets mine Host and got to the second dore that hee was to passe, which, notwith-standing the lock, hee got open, and shut it after him with such violence that it affrighted some of the conspirators.

The word, which was given with an alarme, was, ô he's gon, he's gon, what shall wee doe, he's gon! The rest, (halfe a sleepe,) start up in a maze, and, like rames, ran theire heads one at another full butt in the darke.

Theire grande leader, Captaine Shrimp, tooke on most furiously and tore his 30 clothes for anger, to see the empty nest, and their bird gone.

The rest were eager to have torne theire haire from theire heads; but it was so short that it would give them no hold. Now Captaine Shrimp thought in the losse of this prize, (which hee accoumpted his Master peece,) all his honor would be lost for ever.

In the meane time mine Host was got home to Ma-re Mount through the woods, eight miles round about the head of the river Monatoquit that parted the two Plan-tations, finding his way by the helpe of the lightening, (for it thundred as hee went terribly;) and there hee prepared powther, three pounds dried, for his present im-ployement, and foure good gunnes for him and the two assistants left at his howse, 40

---

16 **Trojans . . . pinetree horse,** an allusion to the trick by which Troy was finally taken after a ten-year siege. Morton is intentionally mock heroic; in the *Aeneid* (Bk. IV) Virgil says that the wooden horse was of fir   19 **Geese kept in the Roman Cappitall,** by the priests in charge of the auguries; in 390 B.C. their hissing is supposed to have aroused Marius Manlius, who was thus able to halt the attack of the Gauls on the Capitoline Hill

with bullets of severall sizes, three houndred or thereabouts, to be used if the conspirators should pursue him thether: and these two persons promised theire aides in
the quarrell, and confirmed that promise with health in good rosa solis.

Now Captaine Shrimp, the first Captaine in the Land, (as hee supposed,) must
doe some new act to repaire this losse, and, to vindicate his reputation, who had
sustained blemish by this oversight, begins now to study, how to repaire or survive
his honor: in this manner, callinge of Councell, they conclude.

Hee takes eight persons more to him, and, (like the nine Worthies of New
Canaan,) they imbarque with preparation against Ma-re Mount, where this Monster
10 of a man, as theire phrase was, had his denne; the whole number, had the rest not
bin from home, being but seaven, would have given Captaine Shrimpe, (a quondam
Drummer,) such a wellcome as would have made him wish for a Drume as bigg as
Diogenes tubb, that hee might have crept into it out of sight.

Now the nine Worthies are approached, and mine Host prepared: having intelligence by a Salvage, that hastened in love from Wessaguscus to give him notice of
their intent.

One of mine Hosts men prooved a craven: the other had prooved his wits to purchase a little valoure, before mine Host had observed his posture.

The nine worthies comming before the Denne of this supposed Monster, (this
20 seaven headed hydra, as they termed him,) and began, like Don Quixote against
the Windmill, to beate a parly, and to offer quarter, if mine Host would yeald; for
they resolved to send him for England; and bad him lay by his armes.

But hee, (who was the Sonne of a Souldier,) having taken up armes in his just
defence, replyed that hee would not lay by those armes, because they were so neede-
full at Sea, if hee should be sent over. Yet, to save the effusion of so much worty
bloud, as would have issued out of the vaynes of these 9. worthies of New Canaan,
if mine Host should have played upon them out at his port holes, (for they came
within danger like a flocke of wild geese, as if they had bin tayled one to another,
as coults to be sold at a faier,) mine Host was content to yeelde upon quarter; and
30 did capitulate with them in what manner it should be for more certainety, because
hee knew what Captaine Shrimpe was.

Hee expressed that no violence should be offered to his person, none to his goods,
nor any of his Howsehold: but that hee should have his armes, and what els was
requisit for the voyage: which theire Herald retornes, it was agreed upon, and
should be performed.

But mine Host no sooner had set open the dore, and issued out, but instantly
Captaine Shrimpe and the rest of the worthies stepped to him, layd hold of his armes,
and had him downe: and so eagerly was every man bent against him, (not regarding
any agreement made with such a carnall man,) that they fell upon him as if they

8 **nine** Worthies, medieval heroes: Hector, Alexander the Great, Julius Caesar, Joshua, David, Judas Mac-
cabeus, King Arthur, Charlemagne, Geoffrey of Boulogne. Again Morton is mock heroic   13 **Diogenes
tubb.** Diogenes the Cynic (412?-323 B.C.) believed that virtue was the avoidance of all physical comfort,
and so lived in a tub for a purpose not unlike Thoreau's at Walden Pond. But Morton is poking fun at
Captain Standish's small stature   20 **Don Quixote against the Windmill,** an allusion to the best known
episode in *Don Quixote* (1605-1615), picaresque romance by the Spanish author, Miguel de Cervantes Saa-
vedra (1547-1616)

would have eaten him: some of them were so violent that they would have a slice with scabbert, and all for haste; untill an old Souldier, (of the Queenes, as the Proverbe is,) that was there by accident, clapt his gunne under the weapons, and sharply rebuked these worthies for their unworthy practises. So the matter was taken into more deliberate consideration.

Captaine Shrimp, and the rest of the nine worthies, made themselves, (by this outragious riot,) Masters of mine Host of Ma-re Mount, and disposed of what hee had at his plantation.

This they knew, (in the eye of the Salvages,) would add to their glory, and diminish the reputation of mine honest Host; whome they practised to be ridd of 10 upon any termes, as willingly as if hee had bin the very Hidra of the time.

1637

1588—1649 *John Winthrop*

John Winthrop was past forty in 1629 when the Massachusetts Bay Company decided to take its charter to New England and chose him as its governor. A Suffolk County squire who had practiced law and quietly administered the very considerable estate left him by his father, Winthrop was a devout Puritan with an ambition, as he himself admitted, for public service. This ambition he satisfied unselfishly in Massachusetts, where for nineteen years he held high office, nine times chosen governor. He labored diligently for the good of the commonwealth, spent much of his private fortune in hospitality and charity, and frankly based his actions upon the social and religious obligations of an aristocratic ruling class. Besides providing the economic basis for what was long the most influential of the colonies, the group which Winthrop represented is memorable for its early development of educational and political institutions which have survived to the present day.

Of the many remarkable aspects of the Bay Colony, two are especially connected with Winthrop's career: the annual election provided for in the charter, which periodically brought to review the stewardship of public servants; and the development of governmental institutions roughly equivalent to those of England, notably a legislature of two houses and a system of courts, statutes, and common law. Both the annual election and the transference of English constitutional practice to the New World are contributions of a Puritan oligarchy which, although in some ways unenlightened according to twentieth-century standards, was remarkably astute in practice.

Winthrop's writings are somewhat varied in nature. A series of letters addressed to his third wife, Margaret, is perhaps the finest picture of a happy Puritan marriage in our literature. "A Modell of Christian Charity," a discourse composed for delivery on board the *Arbella,* flagship of the Puritan migration, is a careful exposition of his political philosophy: that "God Almightie in his most holy and wise providence hath soe disposed of the Condicion of mankinde, as in all times some must be rich some poore, some highe and eminent in power and dignitie; others meane and in subieccion." Winthrop is chiefly read, however, in his *Journal* or *History of New England,* which is a chronicle of events from 1630 until two months before his death in 1649.

The History of New England from 1630 to 1649, ed. James Savage, New Edition, 2 vols., Boston, 1853   Winthrop's Journal in the Original Narratives of Early American History series, ed. J. K. Hosmer, 2 vols., New York, 1908   Edmund S. Morgan, **The Puritan Dilemma: The Story of John Winthrop,** Boston, 1958   Richard S. Dunn, **Puritans and Yankees: The Winthrop Dynasty of New England,** Princeton, 1962

from The History of New England

William Hubbard, Cotton Mather, and Thomas Prince, among the earlier New England historians, knew of Winthrop's manuscript journal bound up in three volumes. The first two volumes, covering the period from 1630 to 1644, were published in 1790. The third, rediscovered in 1816, was turned over for editing, along with the previously published volumes, to James Savage. Before his edition appeared in 1825-1826, Volume II was destroyed by fire. There has never been an edition giving the exact reading of the manuscript, for Savage modernized Winthrop's spelling and wrote out the abbreviations in full — a fact which accounts for the relatively conventional text of the extracts which follow.

The selection which follows covers a period of extraordinary interest to students of Puritanism: the first months of the Long Parliament, whose moves toward "reformation" brought on the Civil War and the execution of Charles I. It seemed for a time that the ideal commonwealth which Winthrop and his companions hoped to establish in Massachusetts might be achieved in Old England. Immigration to the Bay Colony dropped off sharply, causing considerable economic distress. The New England way of life, however, had already established itself by 1640, and Winthrop, with his curiosity about "special providences" and his chronicling of events, great and small, tells us much about its developing patterns.

[December] 15, [1640] A pinnace called the Coach, being in her voyage to New Haven (late Quinipiack) between Salem and Cape Cod, sprang a leak, so as in the morning they found her hold half filled with water; whereupon the seamen and passengers betook themselves to their skiff, being a very small one, and the wind then growing very high at S. W. Only one Jackson, a godly man and an experienced seaman, would not leave the vessel before he had tried the utmost, so getting them in again, and laying the bark upon the contrary side, they fell to getting out the water, which, it pleased God, they overcame, and having a fine fresh gale, they got safe back to Salem.

Mr. Pelham's house in Cambridge took fire in the dead of the night by the chimney. A neighbor's wife hearing some noise among her hens, persuaded her husband to arise, which, being very cold, he was loth to do, yet through her great importunity he did, and so espied the fire, and came running in his shirt, and had much to do to awake any body, but he got them up at last, and so saved all. The fire being ready to lay hold upon the stairs, they had all been burnt in their chambers, if God had not by his special providence sent help at that very instant.

About this time a pinnace called the Make Shift, (so called because she was built of the wreck of a greater vessel at the Isle of Sable, and by that means the men saved,) being on a voyage to the southward, was cast away upon a ledge of rocks 10 near Long Island, the goods were all lost, but the men were saved. No winter but some vessels have been cast away in that voyage.

About this time there fell out a thing worthy of observation. Mr. Winthrop the younger, one of the magistrates, having many books in a chamber where there was corn of divers sorts, had among them one wherein the Greek testament, the psalms and the common prayer were bound together. He found the common prayer eaten with mice, every leaf of it, and not any of the two other touched, nor any other of his books, though there were above a thousand.

Quere, of the child at Cambridge killed by a cat.

Mo. 8 [October]. We received a letter at the general court from the magistrates 20 of Connecticut and New Haven and of Aquiday, wherein they declared their dislike of such as would have the Indians rooted out, as being of the cursed race of Ham, and their desire of our mutual accord in seeking to gain them by justice and kindness, and withal to watch over them to prevent any danger by them, &c. We returned answer of our consent with them in all things propounded, only we refused to include those of Aquiday in our answer, or to have any treaty with them.

Mo. 10 [December]. About the end of this month a fishing ship arrived at Isle of Shoals, and another soon after, and there came no more this season for fishing. They brought us news of the Scots entering into England, and the calling of a parliament, and the hope of a thorough reformation, &c. whereupon some among 30 us began to think of returning back to England. Others despairing of any more supply from thence, and yet not knowing how to live there, if they should return, bent their minds wholly to removal to the south parts, supposing they should find better means of subsistence there, and for this end put off their estates here at very low rates. These things, together with the scarcity of money, caused a sudden and

13 **the younger.** John Winthrop, Jr. (1606-1676) followed his father to Massachusetts in 1631. He interested himself in ironworks and other early industries, dabbled in chemistry and medicine, and was made a Fellow of the Royal Society. Settling in Connecticut in 1644, he was governor of that colony in 1657 and from 1659 until his death. He owned one of the largest libraries in seventeenth-century New England. Many commentators have been amused that the New England mice should share the Puritan prejudice against the Anglican Book of Common Prayer   20 **Mo. 8 [October],** before 1752, according to the Gregorian calendar, the year began in March not January, thus making October the eighth month   21 **Aquiday,** Aquidneck, the largest island in Narragansett Bay, Rhode Island. A number of exiles from the Massachusetts theocracy found refuge there, establishing the colony which first practiced religious toleration   27 **Isle of Shoals,** off the mouth of the Piscataqua River, in New Hampshire, then claimed by Massachusetts

very great abatement of the prices of all our own commodities. Corn (Indian) was sold ordinarily at three shillings the bushel, a good cow at seven or eight pounds, and some at £5, — and other things answerable . . . whereby it came to pass that men could not pay their debts, for no money nor beaver were to be had, and he who last year, or but three months before was worth £1000 could not now, if he should sell his whole estate, raise £200, whereby God taught us the vanity of all outward things, &c.

One Taylor of Linne, having a milch cow in the ship as he came over, sold the milk to the passengers for 2d the quart, and being after at a sermon wherein oppres-
10 sion was complained of, &c. he fell distracted. Quere, of the price, for 2d the quart was not dear at sea.

This evil was very notorious among all sorts of people, it being the common rule that most men walked by in all their commerce, to buy as cheap as they could, and to sell as dear.

A great ship called the Charles of above 300 tons brought passengers hither this year. The master was a plain quiet man, but his company were very wicked, and did wrong the passengers much, and being at Pascataquack to take in clapboards with another ship wherein Mr. Peter by occasion preached one Lord's day, the company of the Charles did use all the means they could do disturb the exercise, by hooting
20 and hallooing, but in their return they were set upon by the Turks and divers of them killed.

A wicked fellow, given up to bestiality, fearing to be taken by the hand of justice, fled to Long Island, and there was drowned. He had confessed to some, that he was so given up to that abomination, that he never saw any beast go before him but he lusted after it.

Mr. Nathaniel Eaton, of whom mention is made before, being come to Virginia, took upon him to be a minister, but was given up of God to extreme pride and sensuality, being usually drunken, as the custom is there. He sent for his wife and children. Her friends here persuaded her to stay a while, but she went notwithstand-
30 ing, and the vessel was never heard of after.

Mo. 12. 2. [February 2, 1641]. The church of Dorchester being furnished with a very godly and able pastor, one Mr. Mather, and having invited to them one Mr. Burr, who had been a minister in England, and of very good report there for piety and learning, with intent to call him also to office, after he was received a member in their church, and had given good proofs of his gifts and godliness to the satisfaction of the church, they gave him a call to office, which he deferring to accept,

---

17 **Pascataquack**, now Dover, New Hampshire. Four early settlements in New Hampshire were virtually independent colonies at the time Winthrop wrote   18 **Peter**. Hugh Peter or Peters (1598-1660), one of the most conspicuous figures in the Puritan movement, he succeeded Roger Williams as minister at Salem in 1636, took an active part in Massachusetts affairs before going to England on behalf of the colony in 1641, and played a leading role in the Cromwell era   26 **Eaton**. Nathaniel Eaton (1609?-1674), the black sheep of a family prominent in the founding of New Haven, Connecticut. He was the first teacher at Harvard College, but was quickly discharged for trying to make money at the expense of his students, whom he fed at fixed charges. Violence and drunkenness appeared in a number of unsavory episodes, and he left Boston owing some £ 1000. Winthrop displays some prejudice against Virginian parsons   32 **Mather . . . Burr.** See p. 148 for Cotton Mather's version of this incident

in the mean time he delivered some points savoring of familism, wherein the church desiring satisfaction, and he not so free to give it as was meet, it was agreed that Mr. Mather and he should confer together, and so the church should be informed wherein the difference lay. Accordingly Mr. Burr wrote his judgment in the points in difference, in such manner and terms as from some of his propositions there could no other be gathered but that he was erroneous; but this was again so qualified in other parts as might admit of a charitable construction. Mr. Mather reports to the church the errors which might be collected, without mentioning the qualification, or acquainting Mr. Burr with it before. When this was published, Mr. Burr disclaimed the errours, and Mr. Mather maintained them from his writings; 10 whereupon the church was divided, some joining with the one, and some with the other, so as it grew to some heat and alienation, and many days were spent for reconciliation, but all in vain. In the end they agreed to call in help from other churches, so this day there was a meeting at Dorchester of the governour and another of the magistrates, and about ten of the elders of the neighboring churches, wherein four days were spent in opening the cause, and such offences as had fallen out in the prosecution; and in conclusion the magistrates and elders declared their judgment and advice in the case to this effect; that both sides had cause to be humbled for their failings, more particularly Mr. Burr for his doubtful and unsafe expressions, and backwardness to give clear satisfaction, &c. and Mr. Mather 20 for his inconsideration both in not acquainting Mr. Burr with his collections before he had published them to the church, and in not certifying the qualifications of those errours which were in his writings: for which they were advised to set a day apart for reconciliation. Upon this Mr. Mather and Mr. Burr took the blame of their failings upon themselves, and freely submitted to the judgment and advice given, to which the rest of the church yielded a silent assent, and God was much glorified in the close thereof; and Mr. Burr did again fully renounce those erroneous opinions of which he had been suspected, confessing that he was in the dark about these points, till God, by occasion of this agitation, had cleared them to him, which he did with much meekness and many tears.   30

The church of Boston were necessitated to build a new meeting house, and a great difference arose about the place of situation, which had much troubled other churches on the like occasion, but after some debate it was referred to a committee and was quietly determined. It cost about £1000, which was raised out of the weekly voluntary contribution without any noise or complaint, when in some other churches which did it by way of rates, there was much difficulty and compulsion by levies to raise a far less sum.

The general fear of want of foreign commodities, now our money was gone, and that things were like to go well in England, set us on work to provide shipping of our own, for which end Mr. Peter, being a man of a very public spirit and singular 40 activity for all occasions, procured some to join for building a ship at Salem of 300 tons, and the inhabitants of Boston, stirred up by his example, set upon the building another at Boston of 150 tons. The work was hard to accomplish for want of money, &c. but our shipwrights were content to take such pay as the country could make. The shipwright at Salem, through want of care of his tackle, &c. occasioned the death of one Baker, who was desired with five or six more to help hale up a piece of timber, which, the rope breaking, fell down upon them. The rest by special providence were saved. This Baker, going forth in the morning very well, after he had prayed, told his wife he should see her no more, though he could not foresee any danger towards him.

The court having found by experience that it would not avail by any law to redress the excessive rates of labourers' and workmen's wages, &c. (for being restrained, they would either remove to other places where they might have more,
10 or else being able to live by planting and other employments of their own, they would not be hired at all,) it was therefore referred to the several towns to set down rates among themselves. This took better effect, so that in a voluntary way, by the counsel and persuasion of the elders, and example of some who led the way, they were brought to more moderation than they could be by compulsion. But it held not long.

Upon the great liberty which the king had left the parliament to in England, some of our friends there wrote to us advice to send over some to solicit for us in the parliament, giving us hope that we might obtain much, &c. But consulting about it, we declined the motion for this consideration, that if we should put our-
20 selves under the protection of the parliament, we must then be subject to all such laws as they should make, or at least such as they might impose upon us; in which course though they should intend our good, yet it might prove very prejudicial to us. But upon this occasion the court of assistants being assembled, and advising with some of the elders about some course to serve the providence of God in making use of present opportunity of a ship of our own being ready bound for England, it was thought fit to send some chosen men in her with commission to negotiate for us, as occasion should be offered, both in furthering the work of reformation of the churches there which was now like to be attempted, and to satisfy our countrymen of the true cause why our engagements there have not been
30 satisfied this year, as they were wont to be in all former time since we were here planted; and also to seek out some way, by procuring cotton from the West Indies, or other means that might be lawful, and not dishonorable to the gospel, for our present supply of clothing, &c. for the country was like to afford enough for food, &c. The persons designed hereto were Mr. Peter, pastor of the church of Salem, Mr. Welde, the pastor of the church of Roxbury, and Mr. Hibbins of Boston. For this end the governour and near all the rest of the magistrates and some of the elders wrote a letter to the church of Salem acquainting them with our intentions, and desiring them to spare their pastor for that service. The governour also moved the church of Roxbury for Mr. Welde, whom, after some time of consideration, they
40 freely yielded. But when it was propounded to the church of Salem, Mr. Endecott,

---

35 **Welde.** Thomas Weld (1595-1660/61) landed at Boston in 1632 and a month later became minister at Roxbury. Like Hugh Peter he was sent to England as a commissioner for the colony and never returned 35 **Hibbins.** William Hibbins, a well-to-do merchant of Boston, held a number of public posts, but is best known as the husband of Ann Hibbins, executed as a witch in 1656. She is a character in Hawthorne's *The Scarlet Letter* 40 **Endecott,** John Endecott (1589?-1665), a founder of Salem in 1628 and a long-time

being a member thereof, and having formerly opposed it, did now again the like in the church. Some reasons were there alleged, as that officers should not be taken from their churches for civil occasions, that the voyage would be long and dangerous, that it would be reported that we were in such want as we had sent to England to beg relief, which would be very dishonourable to religion, and that we ought to trust God who had never failed us hitherto, &c. But the main reason, indeed, which was privately intimated, was their fear lest he should be kept there, or diverted to the West Indies, for Mr. Humfrey intended to go with him, who was already engaged that way by the lord Say, &c. and therefore it was feared he should fall under strong temptations that way, being once in England; and Mr. Humfrey 10 discovered his intentions the more by falling foul upon Mr. Endecott in the open assembly at Salem for opposing this motion, and with that bitterness as gave great offence, and was like to have grown to a professed breach between them, but being both godly, and hearkening to seasonable counsel, they were soon reconciled, upon a free and public acknowledgment of such failings as had passed. But the church, not willing to let their pastor go, nor yet to give a plain denial to the magistrates' request, wrote an answer by way of excuse, tendering some reasons of their unsatisfiedness about his going, &c. The agitation of this business was soon about the country, whereby we perceived there would be sinister interpretations made of it, and the ship being suddenly to depart, we gave it over for that season.   20

Mo. 2. [April]. 13. A negro maid, servant to Mr. Stoughton of Dorchester, being well approved by divers years' experience, for sound knowledge and true godliness, was received into the church and baptized.

Some agitation fell out between us and Plimouth about Seacunk. Some of our people finding it fit for plantations, and thinking it out of our patent, which Plimouth men understanding, forbad them, and sent to us to signify that it was within their grant, and that we would therefore forbid ours to proceed. But the planters having acquainted us with their title, and offering to yield it to our jurisdiction, and assuring us that it could not be in the Plimouth patent, we made answer to Plimouth accordingly, and encouraged our neighbors to go on, so 30 as divers letters passing between us, and they sending some to take possession for them, at length we sent some to Plimouth to see their patent, who bringing us a copy of so much as concerned the thing in question, though we were not fully satisfied thereby, yet not being willing to strive for land, we sat still.

There fell out much trouble about this time at Pascataquack. Mr. Knolles had gathered a church of such as he could get, men very raw for the most part, &c.

---

governor of Massachusetts (1644, 1649, 1651-1653, 1655-1664). His bluff and courageous Puritanism is celebrated in Hawthorne's "Endicott and the Red Cross"   8 **Humfrey . . . lord Say.** William Fiennes, first Viscount Saye and Sele (1582-1662), was deeply involved in a number of large land patents, including one in New Hampshire. His proposal that Massachusetts adopt the British system of hereditary nobility was rejected by the colony   21 **Stoughton.** Israel Stoughton, a founder of Dorchester and one of the largest landholders in the colony. A son, William Stoughton, was later lieutenant governor and a benefactor of Harvard College   24 **Seacunk,** or Seaconk, a region in Rhode Island near present-day Providence   35 **Knolles.** Hanserd Knollys (1599?-1691), a particular (i.e., Calvinistic) Baptist, in New Hampshire only very briefly. He was later prominent in the Cromwell regime

Afterwards there came amongst them one Mr. Larkham, who had been a minister at Northam near Barnstable in England, a man not savoring the right way of church discipline, but being a man of good parts and wealthy, the people were soon taken with him, and the greater part were forward to cast off Mr. Knolles their pastor and to choose him, for they were not willing nor able to maintain two officers, so Mr. Knolles gave place to him, and he being thus chosen, did soon discover himself. He received into the church all that offered themselves, though men notoriously scandalous and ignorant, so they would promise amendment, and fell into contention with the people, and would take upon him to rule all, even the
10 magistrates (such as they were;) so as there soon grew sharp contention between him and Mr. Knolles, to whom the more religious still adhered, whereupon they were divided into two churches. Mr. Knolles and his company excommunicated Mr. Larkham, and he again laid violent hands upon Mr. Knolles. In this heat it began to grow to a tumult, some of their magistrates joined with Mr. Larkham and assembled a company to fetch Capt. Underhill (another of their magistrates and their captain) to their court, and he also gathered some of his neighbors to defend himself, and to see the peace kept; so they marched forth towards Mr. Larkham's, one carrying a Bible upon a staff for an ensign, and Mr. Knolles with them armed with a pistol. When Mr. Larkham and his company saw them thus provided, they
20 proceeded no further, but sent to Mr. Williams, who was governor of those in the lower part of the river, who came up with a company of armed men and beset Mr. Knolles' house, where Capt. Underhill then was, and they kept a guard upon them night and day, and in the mean time they called a court, and Mr. Williams sitting as judge, they found Capt. Underhill and his company guilty of a riot, and set great fines upon them, and ordered him and some others to depart the plantation. The cause of this eager prosecution of Capt. Underhill was, because he had procured a good part of the inhabitants there to offer themselves again to the government of the Massachusetts, who being thus prosecuted, they sent a petition to us for aid.

The governour and council considered of their petition, and gave commission to
30 Mr. Bradstreet, one of our magistrates, Mr. Peter and Mr. Dalton two of our elders, to go thither and to endeavor to reconcile them, and if they could not effect that, then to inquire how things stood, and to certify us, &c. They went accordingly, and finding both sides to be in fault, at length they brought matters to a peaceable end. Mr. Larkham was released of his excommunication and Capt. Underhill and the rest from their centures, and by occasion of these agitations Mr. Knolles was discovered to be an unclean person, and to have solicited the chastity of two maids, his servants, and to have used filthy dalliance with them, which he acknowledged

---

15 **Underhill.** John Underhill (1597?-1672), a military adventurer who led a stormy life in several of the colonies. He was the author of a history of the Pequot War of 1637, in which he served Connecticut. His military prowess and his work as trainer of the Massachusetts militia did not outweigh his unorthodox opinions. Banished for his connection with the Antinomian affair, he settled at Dover and was for a time governor of that tiny settlement   20 **Williams.** Francis Williams was governor of the rival settlement in New Hampshire, Strawberry Bank (later Portsmouth)   30 **Bradstreet.** Simon Bradstreet (1603-1697), husband of Anne (see p. 228), came to Massachusetts with Winthrop in 1630 and was never out of public employment until his death

before the church there, and so was dismissed, and removed from Pascataquack. This sin of his was the more notorious, because the fact, which was first discovered, was the same night after he had been exhorting the people by reasons and from scripture, to proceed against Capt. Underhill for his adultery. And it is very observable how God gave up these two, and some others who had held with Mrs. Hutchinson, in crying down all evidence from sanctification, &c. to fall into these unclean courses, whereby themselves and their erroneous opinions were laid open to the world.

Mr. Peter and Mr. Dalton, with one of Acomenticus, went from Pascataquack, with Mr. John Ward, who was to be entertained there for their minister; and 10 though it be but six miles, yet they lost their way, and wandered two days and one night without food or fire, in the snow and wet. But God heard their prayers, wherein they earnestly pressed him for the honour of his great name, and when they were even quite spent, he brought them to the seaside near the place they were to go to, blessed forever be his name.

Not long before a godly maid of the church of Linne, going in a deep snow from Meadford homeward, was lost and some of her clothes found after among the rocks.

One John Baker, a member of the church of Boston, removing from thence to Newbury for enlargement of his outward accommodation, being grown wealthy from nothing, grew there very disordered, fell into drunkenness and such violent 20 contention with another brother, maintaining the same by lying, and other evil courses, that the magistrates sent to have him apprehended. But he rescued himself out of the officer's hands and removed to Acomenticus, where he continued near two years, and now at this time he came to Boston, and humbled himself before the church confessing all his wickedness, with many tears, and showing how he had been followed with satan, and how he had labored to pacify his conscience by secret confessions to God, &c. but could have no peace, yet could not bring his heart to return and make public acknowledgment, until the hand of God fell upon one Swain his neighbor, who fell into despair, and would often utter dreadful speeches against himself, and cry out that he was all on fire under the wrath of God, but 30 would never discover any other heinous sin, but that having gotten about £40 by his labour, he went into England and there spent it in wicked company, and so continued, and after a small time hanged himself. This Baker coming in, and seeing him thus dead, was so struck with it as he could have no rest, till he came and made his peace with the church and court. Upon his confession the church was doubtful whether they ought not to cast him out, his offences being so scandalous, notwithstanding they were well persuaded of the truth of his repentance: but the judgment of the church was, that seeing he had excommunicated himself by deserting the church, and Christ had ratified it by giving him up to satan, whereby the ordinance had had its proper effect, therefore he ought now to be received and pardoned, 40 whereto the church agreed. Yet this man fell into gross distempers soon after.

---

6 **Hutchinson.** Anne Hutchinson (1591-1643), most famous of the Antinomians, was banished for holding that an individual could have direct revelation from God. She settled in Rhode Island   9 **Acomenticus,** or Agamenticus, now York, Maine, was settled in 1631

Mr. Cotton out of that in Revelations 15. none could enter into the temple until, &c. delivered, that neither Jews nor any more of the Gentiles should be called until Antichrist were destroyed, viz. to a church estate, though here and there a proselyte.

Upon the Lord's day at Concord two children were left at home alone, one lying in a cradle, the other having burned a cloth and fearing its mother should see it, thrust it into a hay stack by the door (the fire not being quite out) whereby the hay and house were burned and the child in the cradle before they came from the meeting. About the same time two houses were burned at Sudbury.

By occasion of these fires I may add another of a different kind, but of much
10 observation. A godly woman of the church of Boston, dwelling sometimes in London, brought with her a parcel of very fine linen of great value, which she set her heart too much upon, and had been at charge to have it all newly washed and curiously folded and pressed, and so left it in press in her parlour over night. She had a negro maid went into the room very late and let fall some snuff of the candle upon the linen, so as by the morning all the linen was burned to tinder, and the boards underneath, and some stools and a part of the wainscot burned, and never perceived by any in the house, though some lodged in the chamber over head, and no ceiling between. But it pleased God that the loss of this linen did her much good, both in taking off her heart from worldly comforts, and in preparing her for
20 a far greater affliction by the untimely death of her husband, who was slain not long after at Isle of Providence.

Mo. 4. [June]. 2. The court of elections, Richard Bellingaham, Esq. chosen governor. . . .

This year the two ships were finished, one at Salem of 300 tons and another at Boston of 160 tons.

The parliament of England setting upon a general reformation both of church and state, the earl of Strafford being beheaded, and the archbishop (our great enemy) and many others of the great officers and judges, bishops and others, imprisoned and called to account, this caused all men to stay in England in expectation of a
30 new world, so as few coming to us, all foreign commodities grew scarce, and our own of no price. Corn would buy nothing: a cow which cost last year £20 might now be bought for 4 or £5, &c. and many gone out of the country, so as no man could pay his debts, nor the merchants make return into England for their commodities, which occasioned many there to speak evil of us. These straits set our people on work to provide fish, clapboards, plank, &c. and to sow hemp and flax (which prospered very well) and to look out to the W. Indies for a trade for cotton. The general court also made orders about payment of debts, setting corn at the wonted price, and payable for all debts which should arise after a time prefixed.

1 **Cotton.** John Cotton (1584-1652), teacher of the Boston church from his arrival in 1633, was evidently preaching on Revelation 15:8 at the time Winthrop was writing. Cotton's *An Exposition upon the Thirteenth Chapter of the Revelation* was printed posthumously in 1655   22 **Bellingaham.** Richard Bellingham (1592?-1672) arrived in Massachusetts in 1634, serving in many posts in the colony, being governor in 1641, 1654, and 1665-1672. He, too, appears in *The Scarlet Letter*   27 **Strafford.** Sir Thomas Wentworth, first Earl of Strafford (1593-1641), was impeached by the House of Commons in 1640 and executed on Tower Hill on May 11, 1641. He had been one of the staunchest supporters of Charles I

They thought fit also to send some chosen men into England to congratulate the happy success there, and to satisfy our creditors of the true cause why we could not make so current payment now as in former years we had done, and to be ready to make use of any opportunity God should offer for the good of the country here, as also to give any advice, as it should be required, for the settling the right form of church discipline there, but with this caution, that they should not seek supply of our wants in any dishonourable way, as by begging or the like, for we were resolved to wait upon the Lord in the use of all means which were lawful and honourable.

1640-1641

1652 — 1730 Samuel Sewall

Samuel Sewall was born at Bishopstoke, England, but migrated to Boston when he was nine years old and spent the rest of his life there. For nearly sixty years following his graduation from Harvard in 1671 he was active in business and politics. For a period (1681-1684) he managed the colony's printing press; he spent a year in England (1688-1689), engaged in private business and assisted Increase Mather in his unsuccessful efforts to bring about the restoration of the colony's charter; he was captain, in 1701, of the Ancient and Honorable Artillery Company; and from 1718 to 1728 he was Chief Justice of the Superior Court of Massachusetts.

Sewall had fourteen children by his first wife (Hannah, daughter of John Hull, Master of the Mint), whom he married in 1676 and who died in 1717. A second wife, married in 1719, died May 26, 1720. During October and November 1720 he courted Madam Winthrop without success (see pp. 86-92). A third marriage — his last — occurred in 1722.

James Truslow Adams (in the *Dictionary of American Biography*) calls Sewall a "competent jurist of more than average liberality." His most famous, or infamous, juridical rôle was played at Salem in 1692 as one of three commissioners (William Stoughton and John Hathorne were the other two) appointed by the Royal Governor, Sir William Phips, to try the cases of witchcraft. Nineteen persons were sentenced to death. Sewall was the only one of the three judges ever to admit publicly that the court had been guilty of a tragic error. On January 14, 1697, the day appointed by the legislature as a day of penance for whatever had been done amiss at Salem, he stood up in the Old South Church while the Reverend Samuel Willard read Sewall's prepared statement of confession (see p. 84).

Sewall has been called unattractive names by more than one recent writer on colonial New England. Adams says that he was "mercenary"; Parrington speaks of his "tradesman's conception of religion"; socially minded historians have pointed to Sewall as an example of the unholy alliance between Puritanism and capitalism. It is true that Sewall was not the man to underestimate the value of a dollar honestly earned. At the same time, it is hardly possible for the careful reader of the *Diary* to question the sincerity of Sewall's religious convictions. His use of legal terminology in religious contexts was quite natural to a lawyer; moreover, the same usage occurs in the sermons of the least worldly ministers of the period, and Sewall was a great hearer and reader of sermons. A tradesman, yes; but the record of "a private day of Prayer with Fasting" (see entry of February 9, 1708, p. 84f.) shows him to have been a sincerely religious man — and an extraordinary tradesman. The passage is, to say the least, extraordinary.

Sewall was the author of several lesser works (among them, *The Selling of Joseph,* perhaps the earliest protest in this country against Negro slavery); but his fame rests upon the *Diary,* which remained unpublished until 1878. Begun in 1673 and continued through 1729, the *Diary* affords a rich and vivid picture of life in and around Boston for a period of about fifty-seven years. It is remarkably concise and suggestive. Indeed, its distinctive literary virtue lies in the writer's ability to suggest an unforgettable picture in a few words: the picture, for example, of a New England meeting house in winter, "This day so cold that the Sacramental Bread is frozen pretty hard, and rattles sadly as broken into the Plates." After these two hundred years and more, Sewall's *Diary,* in Parrington's words, "is still quick with life."

Samuel Sewall, **Diary**, Massachusetts Historical Society Collections, Series 5, Vols. V-VII, 1878-1882 **Samuel Sewall's Diary** (abridged), ed. Mark Van Doren, New York, 1927 Ola Elizabeth Winslow, **Samuel Sewall of Boston**, New York, 1964

from the Diary

July 8, 1677. New Meeting House *Mane:* In Sermon time there came in a female Quaker, in a Canvas Frock, her hair disshevelled and loose like a Periwigg, her face as black as ink, led by two other Quakers, and two other followed. It occasioned the greatest and most amazing uproar that I ever saw. . . .

[Nov. 12, 1685] . . . the Ministers of this Town Come to the Court and complain against a Dancing Master who seeks to set up here and hath mixt Dances, and his time of Meeting is Lecture-Day; and 'tis reported he should say that by one Play he

---

1 **Mane,** in the morning   1 a **female Quaker.** Interesting evidence is here afforded of a historical basis for Hawthorne's depiction of a fanatical Quakeress in "The Gentle Boy" (see p. 1237)   2 **Periwigg.** Sewall had a particular aversion to periwigs   7 **Lecture-Day,** every Thursday, when a sermon, or "lecture", was delivered   7 **one Play.** The theater, of course, was not permitted in colonial Boston

could teach more Divinity than Mr. Willard or the Old Testament. Mr. Moodey said 'twas not a time for N[ew] E[ngland] to dance. Mr. Mather struck at the Root, speaking against mixt Dances. . . .

Sabbath, Jany 24 [1686]. Friday night and Satterday were extream cold, so that the Harbour frozen up, and to the Castle. This day so cold that the Sacramental Bread is frozen pretty hard, and rattles sadly as broken into the Plates. . . .

Tuesday, Decr 21 [1686]. There is a meeting at Mr. Allen's, of the Ministers and four of each Congregation, to consider what answer to give the Governour; and 'twas agreed that could not with a good conscience consent that our Meeting-Houses should be made use of for the Common-Prayer Worship. . . .   10

[January 14, 1697]. Copy of the Bill I put up on the Fast day; giving it to Mr. Willard as he pass'd by, and standing up at the reading of it, and bowing when finished; in the Afternoon.

Samuel Sewall, sensible of the reiterated strokes of God upon himself and family; and being sensible, that as to the Guilt contracted upon the opening of the late Comission of Oyer and Terminer at Salem (to which the order for this Day relates) he is, upon many accounts, more concerned than any that he knows of, Desires to take the Blame and shame of it, Asking pardon of men, And especially desiring prayers that God, who has an Unlimited Authority, would pardon that sin and all other his sins; personal and Relative: And according to his infinite Benignity, 20 and Sovereignty, Not visit the sin of him, or of any other, upon himself or any of his, nor upon the Land: But that He would powerfully defend him against all Temptations to Sin, for the future; and vouchsafe him the efficacious, saving Conduct of his Word and Spirit. . . .

Lord's Day, June 10, 1705. The Learned and pious Mr. Michael Wigglesworth dies at Malden about 9 m. Had been sick about 10 days of a Fever; 73 years and 8 moneths old. He was the Author of the Poem entituled The Day of Doom, which has been so often printed: and was very useful as a Physician. . . .

Feby 9. 1708. The Apointment of a Judge for the Super. Court being to be made upon next Fifth day, Febr. 12, I pray'd God to Accept me in keeping a private day 30 of Prayer with Fasting for That and other Important Matters: I kept it upon the Third day Febr. 10. 1708 in the uper Chamber at the North-East end of the House, fastening the Shutters next the Street. — Perfect what is lacking in my Faith, and in the faith of my dear Yokefellow. Convert my children; especially Samuel and Hanah; Provide Rest and Settlement for Hanah: Recover Mary, Save Judith, Elisabeth and Joseph: Requite the Labour of Love of my Kinswoman Jane Tappin, Give her health, find out Rest for her. Make David a man after thy own heart, Let Susan

---

2 **Mr. Mather,** the Rev. Increase Mather, father of Cotton Mather   10 **Common-Prayer Worship,** the form of worship used by the Established Church of England. "I would not set up," Sewall wrote in his *Diary,* "that which the people of New England came over to avoid." Thus rebuffed, Sir Edmund Andros, the Royal Governor, and his Anglican associates founded King's Chapel, although the building was not completed until after Andros' expulsion from the colony in 1689   11 **the Bill.** The document is Sewall's public confession of error as one of the judges of the witchcraft cases in Salem in 1692   16 **Oyer and Terminer,** literally, to hear and determine; used of a writ or commission giving authority to judges   27 **The Day of Doom,** first published in 1662, was the most popular poem written in colonial New England (see p. 221)

live and be baptised with the Holy Ghost, and with fire. Relations. Steer the Government in this difficult time, when the Governour and many others are at so much Variance: Direct, incline, overrule on the Council-day fifth-day, Febr. 12. as to the special Work of it in filling the Super. Court with Justices; or any other thing of like nature. . . . Bless the Company for propagation of the Gospel, especiall Govr Ashurst &c. Revive the Business of Religion at Natick, and accept and bless John Neesnumin who went thither last week for that end. Mr. Rawson at Nantucket. Bless the South Church in preserving and spiriting our Pastor; in directing unto suitable Supply, and making the Church unanimous: Save the Town, College; Prov-
10 ince from Invasion of Enemies, open, Secret, and from false Brethren: Defend the Purity of Worship. Save Connecticut, bless their New Governour: Save the Reformation under N. York Governm^t. Reform all the European Plantations in America; Spanish, Portuguese, English, French, Dutch; Save this New World, that where Sin hath abounded, Grace may Superabound; that CHRIST who is stronger, would bind the strong man and spoil his house; and order the Word to be given, Babylon is fallen.———— Save our Queen, lengthen out her Life and Reign. Save France, make the Proud helper stoop, Save all Europe; Save Asia, Africa, Europe and America. These were gen^l heads of my Meditation and prayer; and through the bounteous Grace of GOD, I had a very Comfortable day of it. . . .
20   Augt 25 [1709]. Mr. Cotton Mather, Mr. Pemberton and wife, and others dine with us after Lecture. In the even I invited the Govr and Council to drink a Glass of Wine with me; About 20 came; viz. Govr Winthrop, Hathorne. . . . Gave them variety of good Drink, and at going away a large piece of Cake Wrap'd in Paper. They very heartily wish'd me Joy of my daughter's Marriage. . . .
   April 3 [1711]. I dine with the Court at Pullin's. Mr. Attorney treats us at his house with excellent Pipins, Anchovas, Olives, Nuts. I said I should be able to make no Judgment on the Pipins without a Review, which made the Company Laugh. Spake much of Negroes; I mention'd the problem, whether should be white after the Resurrection: Mr. Bolt took it up as absurd, because the body should be
30 void of all Colour, spake as if it should be a Spirit. I objected what Christ said to his Disciples after the Resurrection. He said twas not so after his Ascension. . . .
   Seventh Day [Saturday] Feby 6 [1714] [Queen Anne's birthday]. . . . My neighbour Colson knocks at our door about 9 or past to tell of the Disorders at the Tavern at the South-end in Mr. Addington's house, kept by John Wallis. He desired me that I would accompany Mr. Bromfield and Constable Howel thither. It was 35 Minutes past Nine at Night before Mr. Bromfield came; then we went. I took Aeneas Salter with me. Found much Company. They refus'd to go away. Said were there to drink the Queen's Health, and they had many other Healths to drink.

---

6 **Religion at Natick,** John Eliot had founded Natick as a "Praying Town" for Indians, but by this date there had been much falling away from the initial success   9 **College,** Harvard College   13 **where . . . Superabound.** Cf. Romans 5:20: "But where sin abounded, grace did much more abound." Sewall's language is often Biblical   14 **bind . . . house,** a paraphrase of Matthew 12:29   16 **Queen,** Anne, Queen of England, 1702-1714   17 **Proud . . . stoop,** a paraphrase of Job 9:13   22 **Hathorne,** John Hathorne, one of the "witch judges" and an ancestor of Nathaniel Hawthorne

Call'd for more Drink: drank to me, I took notice of the Affront to them. Said must and would stay upon that Solemn occasion. Mr. John Netmaker drank the Queen's health to me. I told him I drank none; upon that he ceas'd. Mr. Brinley put on his Hat to affront me. I made him take it off. I threaten'd to send some of them to prison; that did not move them. They said they could but pay their Fine, and doing that they might stay. I told them if they had not a care, they would be guilty of a Riot. Mr. Bromfield spake of raising a number of Men to Quell them, and was in some heat, ready to run into Street. But I did not like that. Not having Pen and Ink, I went to take their Names with my Pensil, and not knowing how to Spell their Names, they themselves of their own accord writ them. Mr. Netmaker, 10 reproaching the Province, said they had not made one good Law.

At last I address'd myself to Mr. Banister. I told him he had been longest an Inhabitant and Freeholder, I expected he should set a good Example in departing thence. Upon this he invited them to his own House, and away they went; and we, after them, went away. The Clock in the room struck a pretty while before they departed. I went directly home, and found it 25 Minutes past Ten at Night when I entred my own House. . . .

Decr 23 [1714]. Dr. C. Mather preaches excellently from Ps. 37. Trust in the Lord &c. only spake of the Sun being in the centre of our System. I think it inconvenient to assert such Problems. . . . 20

Octob^r 3. [1720]. Waited on Madam Winthrop again; 'twas a little while before she came in. Her daughter Noyes being there alone with me, I said, I hoped my Waiting on her Mother would not be disagreeable to her. She answer'd she should not be against that that might be for her Comfort. I Saluted her, and told her I perceiv'd I must shortly wish her a good Time; (her mother had told me, she was with Child, and within a Moneth or two of her time). By and by in came Mr. Airs, Chaplain of the Castle, and hang'd up his Hat, which I was a little startled at, it seeming as if he was to lodge there. At last Madam Winthrop came in too. After a considerable time, I went up to her and said, if it might not be inconvenient I desired to speak with her. She assented, and spake of going into another Room; but 30 Mr. Airs and Mrs. Noyes presently rose up, and went out, leaving us there alone. Then I usher'd in Discourse from the names in the Fore-seat; at last I pray'd that Katharine might be the person assign'd for me. She instantly took it up in the way of Denyal, as if she had catch'd at an Opportunity to do it, saying she could not do it before she was asked. Said that was her mind unless she should Change it, which she believed she should not; could not leave her Children. I express'd my Sorrow that she should do it so Speedily, pray'd her Consideration, and ask'd her when I should wait on her agen. She setting no time, I mention'd that day Sennight. Gave

---

5 **Fine.** A law of the colony "for the better observation and keeping of the Lord's Day" imposed a fine of five shillings on every person remaining in a public house, "drinking, or idly spending his time on Saturday night, after the sun is set, or on the Lord's Day, or the evening following" 21 **Waited . . . again.** Sewall's second wife had died May 26, 1720. At this time Sewall was 68; Madam Winthrop, 56. Twice a widow, she did not marry again 27 **Castle,** Castle Island, which was fortified, and where soldiers were stationed 32 **names . . . Fore-seat,** eligible widows, mentioned in a previous entry 33 **Katharine,** Madam Winthrop 38 **Sennight,** a week

her Mr. Willard's Fountain open'd with the little print and verses; saying, I hop'd if we did well read that book, we should meet together hereafter, if we did not now. She took the Book, and put it in her Pocket. Took Leave.

8ʳ 5. Midweek, I din'd with the Court; from thence went and visited Cousin Jonathon's wife, Lying in with her little Betty. Gave the Nurse 2ˢ. Although I had apointed to wait upon her, Mᵐ Winthrop, next Monday, yet I went from my Cousin Sewall's thither about 3. p.m. The Nurse told me Madam dined abroad at her daughter Noyes's, they were to go out together. I ask'd for the Maid, who was not within. Gave Katee a peny and a Kiss and came away. Accompanyed my Son and
10 dâter Cooper in their Remove to their New House. . . .

8ʳ 6ᵗʰ. . . . A little after 6. p. m. I went to Madam Winthrop's. She was not within. I gave Sarah Chickering the Maid 2ˢ, Juno, who brought in wood, 1ˢ. Afterward the Nurse came in, I gave her 18ᵈ, having no other small Bill. After awhile Dr. Noyes came in with his Mother; and quickly after his wife came in: They sat talking, I think, till eight a-clock. I said I fear'd I might be some Interruption to their Business: Dr. Noyes reply'd pleasantly: He fear'd they might be an Interruption to me, and went away. Madam seem'd to harp upon the same string. Must take care of her Children; could not leave that House and Neighbourhood where she had dwelt so long. I told her she might doe her children as much or more good by
20 bestowing what she laid out in Hous-keeping, upon them. Said her Son would be of age the 7ᵗʰ of August. I said it might be inconvenient for her to dwell with her Daughter-in-Law, who must be Mistress of the House. I gave her a piece of Mr. Belcher's Cake and Ginger-Bread wrapped up in a clean sheet of Paper; told her of her Father's kindness to me when Treasurer, and I Constable. My Daughter Judith was gon from me and I was more lonesom — might help to forward one another in our Journey to Canaan. — Mr. Eyre came within the door; I saluted him, ask'd how Mr. Clark did, and he went away. I took leave about 9 aclock. I told [her] I came now to refresh her Memory as to Monday-night; said she had not forgot it. In discourse with her, I ask'd leave to speak with her Sister; I meant to gain Madᵐ
30 Mico's favour to persuade her Sister. She seem'd surpris'd and displeas'd, and said she was in the same condition! . . .

8ʳ 10ᵗʰ. . . . In the Evening I visited Madam Winthrop, who treated me with a great deal of Curtesy; Wine, Marmalade. I gave her a News-Letter about the Thanksgiving Proposals, for sake of the verses for David Jeffries. She tells me Dr. Increase Mather visited her this day, in Mr. Hutchinson's Coach. . . .

8ʳ 11ᵗʰ I writ a few Lines to Madam Winthrop to this purpose: "Madam, These wait on you with Mr. Mayhew's Sermon, and Account of the state of the Indians on Martha's Vinyard. I thank you for your Unmerited Favours of yesterday; and hope to have the Hapiness of Waiting on you tomorrow before Eight a-clock after Noon.

---

1 **Fountain open'd.** Samuel Willard, *The Fountain Opened, or the Great Gospel Privilege of having Christ exhibited to Sinful Men* . . . , Boston, 1700   13 18ᵈ, the abbreviation for pence is derived from *denarius,* the name of Roman coin   33 **News-Letter.** The Boston *News-Letter,* founded in 1704, was the first newspaper in the colonies. The issue of October 3-10, 1720 contained "A Proclamation for a General Thanksgiving" issued by Governor Samuel Shute, calling for the observance of Thursday, October 27, and "forbidding all Servile Labour and Recreation" on that day   34 **Proposals,** an unidentified broadside, presumably

I pray GOD to keep you, and give you a joyful entrance upon the Two Hundred
and twenty ninth year of Christopher Columbus his Discovery; and take Leave, who
am, Madam, your humble Servt.

                                                                                    S. S.

Sent this by Deacon Green, who deliver'd it to Sarah Chickering, her Mistress
not being at home.

8^r 12. . . . Mrs. Anne Cotton came to door (twas before 8.) said Madam Winthrop
was within, directed me into the little Room, where she was full of work behind a
Stand; Mrs. Cotton came in and stood. Madam Winthrop pointed to her to set me
a Chair. Madam Winthrop's Countenance was much changed from what 'twas on 10
Monday, look'd dark and lowering. At last, the work, (black stuff or Silk) was taken
away, I got my Chair in place, had some Converse, but very Cold and indifferent to
what 'twas before. Ask'd her to acquit me of Rudeness if I drew off her Glove. Enquiring the reason, I told her twas great odds between handling a dead Goat, and a
living Lady. Got it off. I told her I had one Petition to ask of her, that was, that
she would take off the Negative she laid on me the third of October; She readily
answer'd she could not, and enlarg'd upon it; She told me of it so soon as she could;
could not leave her house, children, neighbours, business. I told her she might do
som Good to help and suport me. Mentioning Mrs. Gookin, Nath, the widow
Weld was spoken of; said I had visited Mrs. Denison. I told her Yes! Afterward I 20
said, If after a first and second Vagary she would Accept of me returning, Her Victorious Kindness and Good Will would be very Obliging. She thank'd me for my
Book, (Mr. Mayhew's Sermon), But said not a word of the Letter. When she insisted on the Negative, I pray'd there might be no more Thunder and Lightening,
I should not sleep all night. I gave her Dr. Preston, The Church's Marriage and
the Church's Carriage, which cost me 6^s at the Sale. The door standing open, Mr.
Airs came in, hung up his Hat, and sat down. After awhile, Madam Winthrop
moving, he went out. Jno Eyre look'd in, I said How do ye, or, your servant Mr.
Eyre: but heard no word from him. Sarah fill'd a Glass of Wine, she drank to me, I
to her, She sent Juno home with me with a good Lantern, I gave her 6^d and bid 30
her thank her Mistress. In some of our Discourse, I told her I had rather go to the
Stone-House adjoining to her, than to come to her against her mind. Told her the
reason why I came every other night was lest I should drink too deep draughts of
Pleasure. She had talk'd of Canary, her Kisses were to me better than the best
Canary. Explain'd the expression Concerning Columbus. . . .

8^r 17. . . . In the Evening I visited Madam Winthrop, who Treated me Courteously,
but not in Clean Linen as sometimes. She said, she did not know whether I would
come again, or no. I ask'd her how she could so impute inconstancy to me. (I had
not visited her since Wednesday night being unable to get over the Indisposition
received by the Treatment received that night, and I *must* in it seem'd to sound like 40
a made piece of Formality.) Gave her this day's Gazett. . . .

---

25 **Dr. Preston,** John Preston (1587-1628), English Puritan divine, much read by the early Puritans   30
Juno, an Indian servant   32 **Stone-House,** the prison near by   41 **Gazett,** The Boston *Gazette,* founded
in 1719

8^r 18. Visited Madam Mico, who came to me in a splendid Dress. I said, It may be you have heard of my Visiting Madam Winthrop, her Sister. She answered, Her Sister had told her of it. I ask'd her good Will in the Affair. She answer'd, If her Sister were for it, she should not hinder it. I gave her Mr. Homes's Sermon. She gave me a Glass of Canary, entertain'd me with good Discourse, and a Respectfull Remembrance of my first Wife. I took Leave.

8^r 19. Midweek, Visited Madam Winthrop; Sarah told me she was at Mr. Walley's, would not come home till late. I gave her Hanah 3 oranges with her Duty, not knowing whether I should find her or no. Was ready to go home: but said if I
10 knew she was there, I would go thither. Sarah seem'd to speak with pretty good Courage, She would be there. I went and found her there, with Mr. Walley and his wife in the little Room below. At 7 a-clock I mentioned going home; at 8. I put on my Coat, and quickly waited on her home. She found occasion to speak loud to the servant, as if she had a mind to be known. Was Courteous to me; but took occasion to speak pretty earnestly about my keeping a Coach: I said 'twould cost £100. per anum: she said twould cost but £40. Spake much against John Winthrop, his false-heartedness. Mr. Eyre came in and sat awhile; I offer'd him Dr. Incr. Mather's Sermons, whereof Mr. Apleton's Ordination Sermon was one; said he had them already. I said I would give him another. Exit. Came away somewhat late.
20 8^r 20. . . . Madam Winthrop not being at Lecture, I went thither first; found her very Serene with her dâter Noyes, Mrs. Dering, and the widow Shipreev sitting at a little Table, she in her arm'd Chair. She drank to me, and I to Mrs. Noyes. After awhile pray'd the favour to speak with her. She took one of the Candles, and went into the best Room, clos'd the shutters, sat down upon the Couch. She told me Madam Usher had been there, and said the Coach must be set on Wheels, and not by Rusting. She spake somthing of my needing a Wigg. Ask'd me what her Sister said to me. I told her, She said, If her Sister were for it, She would not hinder it. But I told her, she did say she would be glad to have me for her Brother. Said, I shall keep you in the Cold, and asked her if she would be within to morrow night,
30 for we had had but a running Feat. She said she could not tell whether she should or no. I took Leave. As were drinking at the Governour's, he said: In England the Ladies minded little more than that they might have Money, and Coaches to ride in. I said, And New-England brooks its Name. At which Mr. Dudley smiled. Govr said they were not quite so bad here.

8^r 21. Friday, My Son, the Minister, came to me p. m. by apointment and we pray one for another in the Old Chamber; more especially respecting my Courtship. About 6. a-clock I go to Madam Winthrop's; Sarah told me her Mistress was gon out, but did not tell me whither she went. She presently order'd me a Fire; so I went in, having Dr. Sibb's Bowels with me to read. I read the two first Sermons,
40 still no body came in: at last about 9. a-clock Mr. Jno Eyre came in; I took the oportunity to say to him as I had done to Mrs. Noyes before, that I hoped my Visiting his Mother would not be disagreeable to him; He answered me with much Respect.

---

39 **Dr. Sibb's Bowels,** Richard Sibbes, *Bowels Opened; or Discovery of the neere and deere Love between Christ and the Church,* 1639. An English Puritan, Sibbes was much read by the New England Puritans

When twas after 9. a-clock He of himself said he would go and call her, she was
but at one of his Brothers: A while after I heard Madam Winthrop's voice, enquiring something about John. After a good while and Claping the Garden door twice
or thrice, she came in. I mention'd somthing of the lateness; she banter'd me, and
said I was later. She receiv'd me Courteously. I ask'd when our proceedings should
be made publick: She said They were like to be no more publick than they were
already. Offer'd me no Wine that I remember. I rose up at 11 a-clock to come away,
saying I would put on my Coat. She offer'd not to help me. I pray'd her that Juno
might light me home, she open'd the Shutter, and said twas pretty light abroad;
Juno was weary and gon to bed. So I came hom by Star-light as well as I could. At   10
my first coming in, I gave Sarah five Shillings. I writ Mr. Eyre his Name in his
book with the date Octob^r 21. 1720. It cost me 8^s. Jehovah jireh! Madam told me
she had visited M. Mico, Wendell, and Wm Clark of the South [Church].
    Octob^r 22. Dâter Cooper visited me before my going out of Town, staid till
about Sun set. I brought her going near as far as the Orange Tree. Coming back,
near Leg's Corner, Little David Jeffries saw me, and looking upon me very lovingly,
ask'd me if I was going to see his Grandmother? I said, Not to-night. Gave him a
peny, and bid him present my Service to his Grandmother.
    Octob^r 24. I went in the Hackny Coach through the Comon, stop'd at Madam
Winthrop's (had told her I would take my departure from thence). Sarah came to   20
the door with Katee in her Arms: but I did not think to take notice of the Child.
Call'd her Mistress. I told her, being encourag'd by David Jeffries loving eyes, and
sweet Words, I was come to enquire whether she could find in her heart to leave
that House and Neighbourhood, and go and dwell with me at the South-end;
I think she said softly, Not yet. I told her It did not ly in my Lands to keep
a Coach. If I should, I should be in danger to be brought to keep company with
her Neighbour Brooker, (he was a little before sent to prison for Debt). Told her
I had an Antipathy against those who would pretend to give themselves; but nothing of their Estate. I would a proportion of my Estate with my self. And I supos'd
she would do so. As to a Perriwig, My best and greatest Friend, I could not possibly   30
have a greater, began to find me with Hair before I was born, and had continued to
do so ever since; and I could not find in my heart to go to another. She comended
the book I gave her, Dr. Preston, the Church Marriage; quoted him saying 'twas
inconvenient keeping out of a Fashion comonly used. I said the Time and Tide did
circumscribe my Visit. She gave me a Dram of Black-Cherry Brandy, and gave me a
lump of the Sugar that was in it. She wish'd me a good Journy. I pray'd God to
keep her, and came away. Had a very pleasant Journy to Salem. . . .
    31. . . . At night I visited Madam Winthrop about 6. p.m. They told me she was
gon to Madam Mico's. I went thither and found she was gon; so return'd to her
house, read the Epistles to the Galatians, Ephesians in Mr. Eyre's Latin Bible. After   40
the Clock struck 8. I began to read the 103. Psalm. Mr. Wendell came in from his
Warehouse. Ask'd me if I were alone? Spake very kindly to me, offer'd me to call

---

12 **Jehovah jireh,** the name which Abraham gave to the place where he found the ram and offered it up in
Isaac's stead (see Genesis 22:14). The meaning is "God will provide"

Madam Winthrop. I told him, She would be angry, had been at Mrs. Mico's; he help'd me on with my Coat and I came home: left the Gazett in the Bible, which told Sarah of, bid her present my Service to Mrs. Winthrop, and tell her I had been to wait on her if she had been at home.

Novr 1. I was so taken up that I could not go if I would.

Novr 2. Midweek, went again, and found Mrs. Alden there, who quickly went out. Gave her about ½ pound of Sugar Almonds, cost 3^s per £. Carried them on Monday. She seem'd pleas'd with them, ask'd what they cost. Spake of giving her a Hundred pounds per añum if I dy'd before her. Ask'd what sum she would give me, if she should dy first? Said I would give her time to Consider of it. She said she heard as if I had given all to my Children by Deeds of Gift. I told her 'twas a mistake, Point-Judith was mine &c. That in England, I own'd, my Father's desire was that it should go to my eldest Son; 'twas 20£ per añum; she thought 'twas forty. I think when I seem'd to excuse pressing this, she seem'd to think twas best to speak of it; a long winter was coming on. Gave me a Glass or two of Canary.

Novr 4th. Friday, Went again about 7. a-clock; found there Mr. John Walley and his wife: sat discoursing pleasantly. I shew'd them Isaac Moses's Writing. Madam W. serv'd Comfeits to us. After a-while a Table was spread, and Super was set. I urg'd Mr. Walley to Crave a Blessing; but he put it upon me. About 9. they went away. I ask'd Madam what fashioned Neck-lace I should present her with, She said, None at all. I ask'd her Whereabout we left off last time; mention'd what I had offer'd to give her; Ask'd her what she would give me; She said she could not Change her Condition: She had said so from the beginning; could not be so far from her Children, the Lecture. Quoted the Apostle Paul affirming that a single Life was better than a Married. I answer'd That was for the present Distress. Said she had not pleasure in things of that nature as formerly: I said, you are the fitter to make me a Wife. If she held in that mind, I must go home and bewail my Rashness in making more haste than good Speed. However, considering the Super, I desired her to be within next Monday night, if we liv'd so long. Assented. She charg'd me with saying, that she must put away Juno, if she came to me: I utterly deny'd it, it never came into my heart; yet she insisted upon it; saying it came in upon Discourse about the Indian woman that obtained her Freedom this Court. About 10. I said I would not disturb the good orders of her House, and came away. She not seeming pleas'd with my Coming away. Spake to her about David Jeffries, had not seen him.

Monday, Novr 7th. My Son pray'd in the Old Chamber. Our time had been taken up by Son and Daughter Cooper's Visit; so that I only read the 130th and 143. Psalm. Twas on the Account of my Courtship. I went to Mad. Winthrop; found her rocking her little Katee in the Cradle. I excus'd my Coming so late (near Eight). She set me an arm'd Chair and Cusheon; and so the Cradle was between her arm'd Chair and mine. Gave her the remnant of my Almonds; She did not eat of them as before; but laid them away; I said I came to enquire whether she had

---

5 **taken up,** busily occupied   25 **the present Distress,** 1 Corinthians 7:26 "I suppose therefore that this [the virgin estate] is good for the present distress"

alter'd her mind since Friday, or remained of the same mind still. She said, There-abouts. I told her I loved her, and was so fond as to think that she loved me: She said had a great respect for me. I told her, I had made her an offer, without asking any advice; she had so many to advise with, that twas a hindrance. The Fire was come to one short Brand beside the Block, which Brand was set up in end; at last it fell to pieces, and no Recruit was made: She gave me a Glass of Wine. I think I repeated again that I would go home and bewail my Rashness in making more haste than good Speed. I would endeavor to contain myself, and not go on to sollicit her to do that which she could not Consent to. Took leave of her. As came down the steps she bid me have a Care. Treated me Courteously. Told her she had enter'd 10 the 4th year of her Widowhood. I had given her the News-Letter before: I did not bid her draw off her glove as sometime I had done. Her dress was not so clean as sometime it had been. Jehovah jireh!

1677-1720, 1878-1882

1666—1727 Sarah Kemble Knight

The life of Sarah Kemble Knight shows that even in early colonial days a woman of enterprise and intelligence could make a career for herself. The daughter of a Boston merchant, Madam Knight, after her husband's death, efficiently attended to the business of the estate. In addition, she kept a dame's school which Benjamin Franklin is said to have attended, did a good deal of legal work and managed a rather large household. She lived in Boston until 1713, then moved to New London, Connecticut, and lived there until her death in 1727.

Mrs. Knight's *Journal* (October 1704-March 1705) — a record of a trip through Rhode Island and Connecticut to New York and thence back to Boston — differs greatly in its materials from the gloomy religious introspections characteristic of the diaries of her contemporaries. This "dame of Boston—buxom, blithe, and debonair—" writes amusingly of her journeying and of her stops along the way. Much of the humor is made possible by Mrs. Knight's sprightly fun with some of the religious concepts which weigh down other journals of the day. Pondering the crossing of a rough stream by boat, for instance, she pictured herself being doused "like a holy Sister Just come out of a Spiritual Bath in dripping Garments"; or learning that an innkeeper nearby was named Mr. Devil, she wondered whether she should "go to the Devil to be helpt out of affliction."

Madam Knight's sense of comedy plus her flair for observation gave her little book added importance as an early humorous depiction of the characters and manners of rural New England and New York. Her sketch of the Yankee bumpkin and his mate, in the selection which follows (the title has been supplied by the editors), vividly brings to life physical aspects, postures, and speech — a rare achievement for the period.

The Journal was first published in 1825.   The Journal of Madam Knight, ed. G. P. Winship, Boston, 1925   Sidney Gunn, "Sarah Kemble Knight," Dictionary of American Biography, X, 468-469, New York, 1933

from the Journal *[Life in Connecticut]*

Saturday, Oct 7ᵗʰ [1704]

. . . About two o'clock afternoon we arrived in New Haven, where I was received with all Posible Respects and civility. Here I discharged Mr. Wheeler with a reward to his satisfaction, and took some time to rest after so long and toilsome a Journey; And Inform'd myselfe of the manners and customs of the place, and at the same time employed myselfe in the afair I went there upon.

They are Govern'd by the same Laws as wee in Boston, (or little differing,) thr'out this whole Colony of Connecticot, And much the same way of Church Government, and many of them good, Sociable people, and I hope Religious too: but a
10 little too much Independent in their principalls, and, as I have been told, were formerly in their Zeal very Riggid in their Administrations towards such as their Lawes made Offenders, even to a harmless Kiss or Innocent merriment among Young people. Whipping being a frequent and counted an easy Punishment, about wᶜʰ as other Crimes, the Judges were absolute in their Sentences. They told mee a pleasant story about a pair of Justices in those parts, wᶜʰ I may not omit the relation of.

A Negro Slave belonging to a man in yᵉ Town, stole a hogs head from his master, and gave it or sold it to an Indian, native of the place. The Indian sold it in the neighbourhood, and so the theft was found out. Thereupon the Heathen was Seized,
20 and carried to the Justices House to be Examined. But his worship (it seems) was gone into the field, with a Brother in office, to gather in his Pompions. Whither the malefactor is hurried, And Complaint made, and satisfaction in the name of Justice demanded. Their Worships cann't proceed in form without a Bench: whereupon they Order one to be Imediately erected, which, for want of fitter materials, they made with pompions — which being finished, down setts their Worships, and the Malefactor call'd, and by the Senior Justice Interrogated after the following manner. You Indian why did You steal from this man? You sho'dn't do so — it's a Grandy wicked wicked thing to steal. Hol't Hol't cryes Justice Junʳ. Brother, You speak Negro to him. I'le ask him. You sirrah, why did You steal this man's Hoggs-

21 **Pompions**, pumpkins

head? Hoggshead? (replys the Indian,) me no stomany. No? says his Worship; and
pulling off his hatt, Patted his own head with his hand, sais, Tatapa — You, Tatapa
— you: all one this. Hah! says Netop, now me stomany that. Whereupon the
Company fell into a great fitt of Laughter, even to Roreing. Silence is comanded,
but to no effect: for they continued perfectly Shouting. Nay, said his worship, in an
angry tone, if it be so, *take mee off the Bench.*

Their Diversions in this part of the Country are on Lecture days and Training
days mostly: on the former there is Riding from town to town.

And on training dayes The Youth divert themselves by Shooting at the Target,
as they call it, (but it very much resembles a pillory,) where hee that hitts neerest 10
the white has some yards of Red Ribbin presented him wch being tied to his hatt-
band, the two ends streeming down his back, he is Led away in Triumph, wth great
applause, as the winners of the Olympiack Games. They generally marry very
young: the males oftener as I am told under twentie than above; they generally
make public weddings, and have a way something singular (as they say) in some of
them, *viz.* Just before Joynning hands the Bridegroom quitts the place, who is soon
followed by the Bridesmen, and as it were, [is] dragged back to duty — being the
reverse to ye former practice among us, to steal his Bride.

There are great plenty of Oysters all along by the sea side, as farr as I Rode in
the Collony, and those very good. And they Generally lived very well and comfort- 20
ably in their famelies. But too Indulgent (especially ye farmers) to their slaves: suffering too great familiarity from them, permitting them to sit at Table and eat with
them, (as they say to save time,) and into the dish goes the black hoof as freely as
the white hand. They told me there was a farmer lived nere the Town where
I lodgd who had some differences wth his slave, concerning something the master
had promised him and did not punctualy perform; wch caused some hard words
between them; But at length they put the matter of Arbitration and Bound themselves to stand to the award of such as they named — wch done, the Arbitra-
tors Having heard the Allegations of both parties, Order the master to pay 40^s to
black face, and acknowledge his fault. And so the matter ended: the poor master 30
very honestly standing to the award.

There are every where in the Towns as I passed, a Number of Indians the Natives of
the Country, and are the most salvage of all the salvages of that kind that I had
ever Seen: little or no care taken (as I heard upon enquiry) to make them otherwise. They have in some places Landes of their owne, and Govern'd by Law's of
their own making; — they marry many wives and at pleasure put them away, and
on the least dislike or fickle humour, on either side, saying *stand away* to one another is a sufficient Divorce. And indeed those uncomely *Stand aways* are too much
in Vougue among the English in this (Indulgent Colony) as their Records plentifully prove, and that on very trivial matters, of which some have been told me, but 40
are not proper to be Related by a Female pen, tho some of that foolish sex have
had too large a share in the story.

If the natives committ any crime on their own precincts among themselves, y^e

1 **stomany,** understand (?)   7 **Training days,** days on which the militia drilled

English takes no Cognezens of. But if on the English ground, they are punishable by our Laws. They mourn for their Dead by blackening their faces, and cutting their hair, after an Awkerd and frightfull manner; But can't bear You should mention the names of their dead Relations to them: they trade most for Rum, for wch theyd hazard their very lives; and the English fit them Generally as well, by seasoning it plentifully with water.

They give the title of merchant to every trader; who Rate their Goods according to the time and spetia they pay in: *viz.* Pay, mony, Pay as mony, and trusting. *Pay* is Grain, Pork, Beef, &c. at the prices sett by the General Court that Year; *mony* is
10 pieces of Eight, Ryalls, or Boston or Bay shillings (as they call them,) or Good hard money, as sometimes silver coin is termed by them; also Wampom, *vizt.* Indian beads wch serves for change. *Pay as mony* is provisions, as aforesd one Third cheaper then as the Assembly or Gen^{el} Court sets; and *Trust* as they and the merch^t agree for time.

Now, when the buyer comes to ask for a comodity, sometimes before the merchant answers that he has it, he sais, *is Your pay redy?* Perhaps the Chap Reply's Yes: what do You pay in? say's the merchant. The buyer having answered, then the price is set; as suppose he wants a sixpenny knife, in pay it is 12d — in pay as money eight pence, and hard money its own price, *viz.* 6d. It seems a very Intricate way of
20 trade and what *Lex Mercatoria* had not thought of.

Being at a merchants house, in comes a tall country fellow, wth his alfogeos full of Tobacco; for they seldom Loose their Cudd, but keep Chewing and Spitting as long as they'r eyes are open, — he advanc't to the midle of the Room, makes an Awkward Nodd, and spitting a Large deal of Aromatick Tincture, he gave a scrape with his shovel like shoo, leaving a small shovel full of dirt on the floor, made a full stop, Hugging his own pretty Body with his hands under his arms, Stood staring rown'd him, like a Catt let out of a Baskett. At last, like the creature Balaam Rode on, he opened his mouth and said: have You any Ribeinen for Hatbands to sell I pray? The Questions and Answers about the pay being past, the Ribin is bro't
30 and opened. Bumpkin Simpers, cryes its confounded Gay I vow; and beckning to the door, in comes Jone Tawdry, dropping about 50 curtsees, and stands by him: hee shows her the Ribin. *Law You,* sais shee, *its right Gent,* do You, take it, *tis dreadfull pretty.* Then she enquires, *have you any hood silk I pray?* wch being brought and bought, Have you any *thred silk to sew it wth* says shee, wch being accomodated wth they Departed. They Generaly stand after they come in a great while speachless and sometimes dont say a word till they are askt what they want, which I Impute to the Awe they stand in of the merchants, who they are constantly almost Indebted too; and must take what they bring without Liberty to choose for themselves; but they serve them as well, making the merchants stand long enough for their pay.
40 We may Observe here the great necessity and bennefitt both of Education and

---

5 **fit them,** punish them   8 **spetia,** species of money   10 **Ryalls,** Spanish reals   20 **Lex Mercatoria,** the usage and customs of merchants   21 **alfogeos,** Spanish alforjas, saddlebags — here meaning, of course, cheeks   27 **the creature Balaam Rode on,** the ass in the Biblical story of Balaam (see Numbers 22:28)   28 **Ribeinen,** ribbons   32 **Gent,** genteel

Conversation; for these people have as Large a portion of mother witt, and sometimes a Larger, than those who have bin brought up in Citties; But for want of improvements, Render themselves almost Ridiculos, as above. I should be glad if they
would leave such follies, and am sure all that Love Clean Houses (at least) would
be glad on't too.

They are generaly very plain in their dress, throuout all ye Colony, as I saw, and
follow one another in their modes; that You may know where they belong, especially
the women, meet them where you will.

Their Cheif Red Letter day is St. Election, wch is annually Observed according to
Charter, to choose their Govern^r; a blessing they can never be thankfull enough for, 10
as they will find, if ever it be their hard fortune to loose it. The present Governor
is the Honble John Winthrop Esq. A Gentleman of an Ancient and Honourable
Family, whose Father was Governor here sometime before, and his Grandfather had
bin Govr of the Massachusetts. This gentleman is a very curteous and afable person, much Given to Hospitality, and has by his Good services Gain'd the affection
of the people as much as any who had bin before him in that post.

1704-1705, 1825

_____

10 **a blessing** . . . Madam Knight is referring to the fact that Massachusetts, unlike Connecticut, at the time
was governed by appointees of the king

1674–1744 **William Byrd**

G entleman, scholar, and wit, William Byrd II, Esquire, of Westover Plantation, Virginia, vividly exemplifies colonial Southern aristocracy. Although
Byrd's birthplace was a tidewater plantation, he was educated in England and on the Continent. His training in business and the law prepared him to engage in what he called "projects for improving our infant colony"
and to administer his properties. His training in the social graces and in classical
and Neoclassical literature prepared him to live as an aristocrat and to write amusing literature.

Shortly after his return from England to America in 1692, Byrd assumed his place
as a member of the ruling circle of Virginia. He served several times as a representative in the House of Burgesses; on various occasions he represented the colony in
England; he was appointed a member of the Supreme Council and held that dignified position for the remainder of his life. With other large Virginia planters, he

engaged in the fight with Governor Spotswood over limiting the Council's power.

In addition to these political duties, Byrd had the task of running a vast plantation tended by numerous slaves and of supervising extensive scattered properties.
(He had title to 179,440 acres of land at the time of his death.) "Like one of the
patriarchs," he wrote a noble British friend, "I have my flocks and my herds, my
bondmen and my bondwomen, and every sort of trade amongst my own servants,
so that I live in a kind of independence of everyone but Providence. However, this
sort of life . . . is attended with a great deal of trouble. I must take care to keep all
my people to their duty, to set all the springs in motion, and to make everyone
draw his equal share to carry the marching forward." Some of Byrd's secret journals
which recently have been decoded and published make clear that, although he lived
in a princely style, he had more than his share of work and worry, including the
burden of debts incurred chiefly in the building of his Georgian mansion, "Westover."

Byrd's numerous tasks, however, did not keep him from living as he felt a gentleman should. His handsome brick mansion, with its fine gardens and its wide lawn
sloping to the river, was a show place. The manor house was furnished with the
costliest of furniture, cut glass, and silver imported from England, and on the walls
were hung not only family portraits but also paintings of the lords and ladies he
had met abroad. Having seen more of genteel society in London than any contemporaneous Virginian, Byrd thought of himself as a social leader — one who should
set the pace for the *beau monde*. "My doors," he wrote proudly, "are open to everybody"; and his hospitality was lavish.

But Byrd's idea of aristocratic living included pleasures in addition to those afforded by dancing, dining, and fox hunting. He is reported to have read Hebrew,
Greek, Latin, Italian, and French, and his library of over thirty-six hundred volumes
was one of the finest in colonial America. Thinking well of scholarship, for years he
corresponded with the Royal Society, of which he was a member; and almost daily
he took from the shelves of his admirable library some Latin, Greek, or Hebrew
classic to read and enjoy. And in his correspondence through the years with
his British friends he tried to give his phrases the sparkle, the wit, and the grace of
some of the urbane classical authors whom the most cursory reading of his work
shows that he greatly admired.

For many years, apparently, Byrd kept a diary in shorthand. Three good-sized sections of it have been deciphered and printed in the last twenty-five years; they cover
most of 1709-12, 1717-21, and 1739-41. That for 1717-21 is the most revealing,
juxtaposing (as do some of James Boswell's journals) the sophisticated and the
brutish aspects of eighteenth-century London. At times, moreover, Byrd seems to
have expanded his shorthand diaries into more elaborate works, which may have
circulated in manuscript among his friends. These include *The Secret History of the
Line* and *The History of the Dividing Line,* sharply varying accounts of a survey of
the Virginia-North Carolina boundary in 1728, and *A Progress to the Mines* and *A
Journey to the Land of Eden,* reports on trips in 1732 and 1733 to inspect his frontier
properties. Some of the material used to expand the diary notes was derived from
Byrd's reading, particularly that in natural history.

These writings show the ability to record in well-turned phrases the witty perceptions of an author who knew and admired such sophisticated British writers of the period as Wycherley, Swift, and Pope. They also demonstrate the personality of their author — a businessman, keenly observant of industry, commerce, and commercial possibilities; a Virginia aristocrat, given to taking sly digs at people of other social strata or other parts of the country, a charming and urbane man of the world.

History of the Dividing Line and Other Tracts, ed. T. H. Wynne, Richmond, 1866   The Writings of Colonel William Byrd of Westover in Virginia, Esq., ed. J. S. Basset, New York, 1901   William Byrd's Histories of the Dividing Line (including The Secret History), ed. W. K. Boyd, New York, 1929   R. C. Beatty, William Byrd of Westover, Boston, 1932   Louis Wright, "The Byrds' Progress from Trade to Genteel Elegance," The First Gentleman of Virginia, San Marino, 1940   The Secret Diary of William Byrd of Westover, 1709-1712, ed. L. B. Wright and Marion Tinling, Richmond, 1941   Another Secret Diary of William Byrd of Westover, 1739-1741, with Letters and Literary Exercises, 1696-1726, ed. M. H. Woodfin, tr. and collated by Marion Tinling, Richmond, 1942   The London Diary, 1717-1721, ed. L. B. Wright and Marion Tinling, London, 1958.

from The Secret History of the Line

The following entries in Byrd's secret journal tell of a part of the survey in 1728 to determine the line between Virginia and North Carolina. At the time the passage begins, the surveyors were going through the Dismal Swamp, and the commissioners, who had gone around the swamp, were awaiting their return. The passage, with its handling of a rather racy situation in the manner of an author of Restoration comedy, is typical of a good deal of Byrd's writing. It is noteworthy that Byrd gives his companions names generally used in the comedy of the period.

March] 25, [1728] The Air was chill'd with a N. Wester which favour'd our Dismalites who enter'd the Desert very early. It was not so kind to Meanwell who unreasonably kick't off the Bed Clothes & catch't An Ague. We killed the Time, by that great help to disagreeable Society, a Pack of Cards. Our Landlord had not the Good Fortune to please Firebrand with our Dinner, but surely when People do their best, a reasonable Man wou'd be satisfy'd. But he endeavour'd to mend his Entertainment by making hot Love to Ruth, who wou'd by no means be charm'd either with his Perswasion, or his Person. While the Master was employ'd in making Love to one Sister, the man made his Passion known to the other, Only he was more boisterous, & employ'd force, when he cou'd not succeed by fair means. Tho' one of the men 10 rescu'd the poor Girl from this violent Lover; but was so much his Friend as to

1 **Dismalites**, the surveyors in the Dismal Swamp   2 **Meanwell**, identified by Professor Boyd as William Dandridge, a Virginia commissioner   5 **Firebrand**, Richard Fitz-William, another Virginia commissioner

keep the shamefull Secret from those, whose Duty it wou'd have been to punish such Violations of Hospitality. Nor was this the only one this disorderly fellow was guilty of, for he broke upon a House where our Landlord kept the Fodder for his own use, upon the belief that it was better than what he allow'd us. This was in compliment to his Master's Horses I hope, & not in blind obedience to any order he receiv'd from him.

[March] 26. I persuaded Meanwell to take a Vomit of Ipocoacana which workt very kindly; I took all the care of him I cou'd, tho' Firebrand was so unfriendly as not to step once up Stairs to visit him. I also gave a Vomit to a poor Shoemaker
10 that belong'd to my Landlord, by which he reap't great benefit. Puzzlecause made a Journey to Edenton, & took our Chaplain with him to preach the Gospel to the Infidels of that Town, & to baptize some of their Children. I began to entertain with my Chocolate, which every body commended, but only he that commends nothing that don't belong to himself. In the Evening I took a Solitary walk, that I might have Leizure to think on my absent Friends, which I now grew impatient to see. Orion stuck as close to his Patron Firebrand, as the Itch does to the Fingers of many of his Country Folks.

[March] 27. Tho' it threaten'd Rain both Yesterday & today, yet Heaven was so kind to our Friends in the Dismal as to keep it from Falling. I perswaded Meanwell
20 to take the Bark, which He did with good Effect, tho' he continued very faint & low-Spirited. He took Firebrand's Neglect in great Dudgeon, and amidst all his good Nature cou'd not forbear a great deal of Resentment; but I won his Heart entirely by the tender Care I took of him in his illness. I also gain'd the Men's Affection by dressing their wounds, & giving them little Remedys for their complaints. Nor was I less in my Landlords Books, for acting the Doctor in his Family. Tho' I observ'd some Distempers in it, that were past my Skill to cure. For his Wife & Heir Apparent were so enclin'd to a cheerfull Cup, that our Liquor was very unsafe in their keeping. I had a long time observed that they made themselves happy every day, before the Sun had run one third of his course, which no doubt gave some un-
30 easiness to the Old Gentleman: but Custome that reconciles most Evils, made him bear it with Christian Patience.

As to the Young Gentleman, he seem'd to be as worthless as any homebred Squire I had ever met with, & much the worse for having a good Opinion of himself. His good Father intended him for the Mathematicks, but he never cou'd rise higher in that Study than to gage a Rum Cask. His Sisters were very sensible Industrious Damsels, who tho' they see Gentlemen but Seldom, have the Grace to resist their Importunitys, & tho' they are innocently free, will indulge them in no dangerous Libertys. However their cautious Father having some Notion of Female Frailty, from what he observed in their Mother, never suffers them to lie out of his
40 own Chamber.

1728, 1929

---

3 **Ipocoacana,** technical name for ipecac, the root of which is emetic   6 **Puzzlecause,** fictious name for Edward Moseley, a North Carolina commissioner   12 **Orion,** another Virginia commissioner   16 **the Bark,** quinine

from The History of the Dividing Line
[*An Aristocrat Describes Lubberland*]

Byrd's account, in The History of the Dividing Line, *of three of the days covered in the previous selection offers an interesting comparison with the less polite* Secret History. *Although in each passage the author has his eye on amusing literary effects, the second version, intended for publication, is less libelous and more polished. The second version, too, shows more of Byrd's prejudices — against infidels and New Englanders, for instance. The satirical description of the poor whites in the entry for March 27, the best-known passage in the diary, is an interesting early example of a kind of humor which later was to be widespread in America — humor which made sport of the people of this class.*

March 24, 1728.] This being Sunday, we had a Numerous congregation, which flocked to our Quarters from all the adjacent Country. The News that our Surveyors were come out of the Dismal, increas'd the Number very much, because it wou'd give them an Opportunity of guessing, at least, whereabouts the Line wou'd cut, whereby they might form Some Judgment whether they belong'd to Virginia or Carolina. Those who had taken up Land within the Disputed Bounds were in great pain lest it should be found to ly in Virginia; because this being done contrary to an Express Order of that government, the Patentees had great reason to fear they should in that case have lost their land. But their Apprehensions were now at an end, when they understood that all the Territory which had been controverted was   10 like to be left in Carolina. In the afternoon, those who were to re-enter the Dismal were furnished with the Necessary provisions, and Order'd to repair the Over-Night to their Landlord, Peter Brinkley's, that they might be ready to begin their Business early on Monday Morning. Mr. Irvin was excused from the fatigue, in compliment to his Lungs; but Mr. Mayo and Mr. Swan were Robust enough to return upon that painful Service, and, to do them Justice, they went with great Alacrity. The Truth was, they now knew the worst of it; and cou'd guess pretty near at the time when they might hope to return to Land again.

[March] 25th. The Air was chill'd this Morning with a Smart North-west Wind, which favour'd the Dismalites in their Dirty March. They return'd by the Path they   20 had made in coming out, and with great Industry arriv'd in the Evening at the Spot where the Line had been discontinued. After so long and laborious a Journey, they were glad to repose themselves on their couches of Cypress-bark, where their sleep was as sweet as it wou'd have been on a Bed of Finland Down. In the mean time, we who stay'd behind had nothing to do, but to make the best observations we cou'd upon that Part of the Country. The Soil of our Landlord's Plantation, though none of the best, seemed more fertile than any thereabouts, where the Ground is

1 **Numerous congregation,** ironic reference to the people of the district, gathered not for Sunday worship but to find where the line was to fall   8 **Patentees,** holders of land grants   26 **Landlord's Plantation,** the Speight plantation

near as Sandy as the Desarts of Affrica, and consequently barren. The Road leading from thence to Edenton, being in distance about 27 Miles, lies upon a ridge call'd Sandy-Ridge, which is so wretchedly Poor that it will not bring Potatoes.

The Pines in this part of the country are of a different Species from those that grow in Virginia: their bearded Leaves are much longer and their Cones much larger. Each Cell contains a Seed of the Size and Figure of a black-ey'd Pea, which, Shedding in November, is a very Good Mast for Hogs, and fattens them in a Short time. The smallest of these Pines are full of Cones, which are 8 or 9 Inches long, and each affords commonly 60 or 70 Seeds. This Kind of Mast has the Advantage
10 of all other, by being more constant, and less liable to be nippt by the Frost, or eaten by the Caterpillars. The Trees also abound more with Turpentine, and consequently yield more Tarr, than either the Yellow or the White Pine; and for the same reason make more durable Timber for building. The Inhabitants hereabouts pick up Knots of Lightwood in abundance, which they burn into tar, and then carry it to Norfolk or Nansemond for a Market. The Tar made in this method is the less Valuable, because it is said to burn the Cordage, tho' it is full as good for all other uses, as that made in Sweden and Muscovy.

Surely there is no place in the World where the Inhabitants live with less Labour than in N Carolina. It approaches nearer to the Description of Lubberland than any
20 other, by the great felicity of the Climate, the easiness of raising Provisions, and the Slothfulness of the People.

Indian corn is of so great increase, that a little Pains will Subsist a very large Family with Bread, and then they may have meat without any pains at all, by the Help of the Low Grounds, and the great Variety of Mast that grows on the High-land. The Men, for their Parts, just like the Indians, impose all the Work upon the poor Women. They make their Wives rise out of their Beds early in the Morning, at the same time that they lye and Snore, till the Sun has risen one-third of his course, and disperst all the unwholesome Damps. Then, after Stretching and Yawning for half an Hour, they light their Pipes, and, under the protection of a cloud of Smoak,
30 venture out into the open Air; tho', if it happens to be never so little cold, they quickly return Shivering into the Chimney corner. When the Weather is mild, they stand leaning with both their arms upon the cornfield fence, and gravely consider whether they had best go and take a Small Heat at the Hough but generally find reasons to put it off till another time.

Thus they loiter away their Lives, like Solomon's Sluggard, with their Arms across, and at the Winding up of the Year Scarcely have Bread to Eat. To speak the Truth, tis a thorough Aversion to Labor that makes People file off to N Carolina, where Plenty and a Warm Sun confirm them in their disposition to Laziness for their whole Lives.
40 [March] 26. Since we were like to be confin'd to this place, till the People return'd out of the Dismal, twas agreed that our Chaplain might Safely take a turn to Edenton, to preach the Gospel to the Infidels there, and Christen their Children. He was accom-

---

14 **Lightwood,** resinous pine   19 **Lubberland,** imaginary country where people live in idleness   33 **Hough,** hoe   35 **Solomon's Sluggard.** See Proverbs 6:9: "How long wilt thou sleep, O sluggard?"

pany'd thither by Mr. Little, One of the Carolina Commissioners, who, to shew his regard for the Church, offered to treat Him on the Road with a Fricassee of Rum. They fry'd half a Dozen Rashers of very fat Bacon in a Pint of Rum, both which being disht up together, serv'd the company at once both for meat and Drink. Most of the Rum they get in this country comes from New England, and is so bad and unwholesome, that it is not improperly called "Kill-Devil." It is distilled there from forreign molosses, which, if Skilfully manag'd, yields near Gallon for Gallon. Their molosses comes from the same country, and has the name of "Long Sugar" in Carolina, I suppose from the Ropiness of it, and Serves all the purposes of Sugar, both in their Eating and Drinking.   10

When they entertain their Friends bountifully, they fail not to set before them a Capacious Bowl of Bombo, so call'd from the Admiral of that name. This is a Compound of Rum and Water in Equal Parts, made palatable with the said long Sugar. As good humour begins to flow, and the Bowl to Ebb, they take Care to replenish it with Shear rum, of which there always is a Reserve under the Table. But such Generous doings happen only when that Balsam of life is plenty; for they have often such Melancholy times, that neither Land-graves nor Cassicks can procure one drop for their Wives, when they ly in, or are troubled with the Colick or Vapours. Very few in this Country have the Industry to plant Orchards, which, in a Dearth of Rum, might supply them with much better Liquor. The Truth is, there is one   20 Inconvenience that easily discourages lazy People from making This improvement: very often, in Autumn, when the Apples begin to ripen, they are visited with Numerous Flights of paraqueets, that bite all the Fruit to Pieces in a moment, for the sake of the Kernels. The Havock they make is sometimes so great, that whole orchards are laid waste in Spite of all the Noises that can be made, or Mawkins that can be dresst up, to fright 'em away. These Ravenous Birds visit North Carolina only during the warm Season, and so soon as the Cold begins to come on, retire back towards the Sun. They rarely Venture so far North as Virginia, except in a very hot Summer, when they visit the most Southern Parts of it. They are very Beautiful; but like some other pretty Creatures, are apt to be loud and mischievous.   30

[March] 27. Betwixt this and Edenton there are many thuckleberry Slashes, which afford a convenient Harbour for Wolves and Foxes. The first of these wild Beasts is not so large and fierce as they are in other countries more Northerly. He will not attack a Man in the Keenest of his Hunger, but run away from him as from an Animal more mischievous than himself. The Foxes are much bolder, and will Sometimes not only make a Stand, but likewise assault any one that would balk them of their Prey. The Inhabitants hereabouts take the trouble to dig abundance of Wolf-Pits, so deep and perpendicular, that when a Wolf is once tempted into them, he can no more Scramble out again, than a Husband who has taken the leap can Scramble out of Matrimony. Most of the Houses in this part of the country are Log-houses, cov- 40

---

17 **Land-graves nor Cassicks,** high officials provided for in John Locke's *The Fundamental Constitutions of Carolina* (1669). Byrd is here gibing at some of the stuffy titles suggested by Locke   25 **Mawkins,** scarecrows   31 **thuckleberry Slashes,** huckleberry swamps which, as Byrd goes on to say, drain into the Dismal Swamp

ered with Pine or Cypress shingles, 3 feet long, and one broad. They are hung upon
Laths with Peggs, and their doors too turn upon Wooden Hinges, and have wooden
Locks to Secure them, so that the Building is finisht without Nails or other Iron-
Work. They also set up their Pales without Nails at all, and indeed more Securely
than those that are nailed. There are 3 Rails mortis'd into the Posts, the lowest of
which serves as a Sill with a Groove in the Middle, big enough to receive the End
of the Pales: the middle Part of the pale rests against the Inside of the Next Rail,
and the Top of it is brought forward to the outside of the uppermost. Such Wreath-
ing of the Pales in and out makes them stand firm, and much harder to unfix than
10 when nail'd in the Ordinary way.

Within 3 or 4 miles of Edenton, the Soil appears to be a little more fertile, tho'
it is much cut with Slashes, which seem all to have a tendency towards the Dismal.
This Towne is Situate on the North side of Albemarle Sound, which is thereabout
5 miles over. A Dirty Slash runs all along the Back of it, which in the Summer is a
foul annoyance, and furnishes abundance of that Carolina plague, musquetas. There
may be 40 or 50 Houses, most of them Small, and built without Expense. A Citizen
here is counted Extravagant, if he has Ambition enough to aspire to a Brick-chimney.
Justice herself is but indifferently Lodged, the Court-House having much of the Air
of a common Tobacco-House. I believe this is the only Metropolis in the Christian
20 or Mahometan World, where there is neither Church, Chappel, Mosque, Synagogue,
or any other Place of Publick Worship of any Sect or Religion whatsoever. What
little Devotion there may happen to be is much more private than their vices. The
People seem easy without a Minister, as long as they are exempted from paying
Him. Sometimes the Society for propagating the Gospel has had the Charity to
send over Missionaries to this Country; but unfortunately the Priest has been too
Lewd for the people, or, which oftener happens, they too lewd for the Priest. For
these Reasons these Reverend Gentlemen have always left their Flocks as arrant
Heathen as they found them. Thus much however may be said for the Inhabitants
of Edenton, that not a Soul has the least taint of Hypocrisy, or Superstition, acting
30 very Frankly and aboveboard in all their Excesses.

Provisions here are extremely cheap, and extremely good, so that People may live
plentifully at a triffleing expense. Nothing is dear but Law, Physick, and Strong
Drink, which are all bad in their Kind, and the last they get with so much Difficulty, that they are never guilty of the Sin of Suffering it to Sour upon their Hands.
Their Vanity generally lies not so much in having a handsome Dining-Room, as a
Handsome House of Office: in this Kind of Structure they are really extravagant.
They are rarely guilty of Flattering or making Court to their governors, but treat
them with all the Excesses of Freedom and Familiarity. They are of Opinion their
rulers wou'd be apt to grow insolent, if they grew Rich, and for that reason take
40 care to keep them poorer, and more dependent, if possible, than the Saints in New
England used to do their Governors. They have very little corn, so they are forced
to carry on their Home-Traffick with Paper-Money. This is the only Cash that will

---

4 **Pales,** fence pales   26 **Lewd,** ignorant   40 **Saints in New England,** a gibe at New England
Puritanism

tarry in the Country, and for that reason the Discount goes on increasing between that and real Money, and will do so to the End of the Chapter.

[March] 28. Our Time passt heavily in our Quarters, where we were quite cloy'd with the Carolina Felicity of having nothing to do. It was really more insupportable than the greatest Fatigue, and made us even envy the Drudgery of our Friends in the Dismal. Besides, tho' the Men we had with us were kept in Exact Discipline, and behav'd without Reproach, yet our Landlord began to be tired of them, fearing they would breed a Famine in his Family. Indeed, so many keen Stomachs made great Havock amongst the Beef and Bacon which he had laid in for his Summer Provision, nor cou'd he easily purchase More at that time of the Year, with the Money 10 we paid him, because the People having no certain Market seldom provide any more of these Commodities than will barely supply their own Occasions. Besides the Weather was now grown too warm to lay in a fresh Stock so late in the Spring. These Considerations abated somewhat of that chearfulness with which he bidd us Welcome in the Beginning, and made him think the time quite as long as we did until the Surveyors return'd. While we were thus all Hands uneasy, we were comforted with the News that this Afternoon the Line was finisht through the Dismal. The Messenger told us it had been the hard work of three days to measure the Length of only 5 miles, and mark the Trees as they passt along, and by the most exact Survey they found the Breadth of the Dismal in this Place to be com- 20 pletely 15 miles. How wide it may be in other Parts, we can give no Account, but believe it grows narrower towards the North; possibly towards Albemarle Sound it may be something broader, where so many Rivers issue out of it. All we know for certain is, that from the Place where the line enter'd the Dismal, to where it came out, we found the Road round that Portion of it belongs to Virginia to be about 65 Miles. How great the Distance may be from Each of those Points, round that Part that falls within the Bounds of Carolina, we had no certain Information: Tho' tis conjectur'd it cannot be so little as 30 Miles. At which rate the whole Circuit must be about an Hundred. What a Mass of Mud and Dirt is treasur'd up within this filthy circumference, and what a Quantity of Water must perpetually drain into it 30 from the riseing ground that Surrounds it on every Side? Without taking the Exact level of the Dismal, we may be sure that it declines towards the Places where the Several Rivers take their Rise, in order to carry off the constant Supplies of Water. Were it not for such Discharges, the whole Swamp would long Since have been converted into a Lake. On the other Side this Declension must be very gentle, else it would be laid perfectly dry by so many continual drains; Whereas, on the contrary, the Ground seems everywhere to be thoroughly drenched even in the dryest Season of the Year. The Surveyors concluded this day's Work with running 25 chains up into the Firm Land, where they waited further Orders from the Commissioners.   40

1728, 1841

---

7 behav'd without Reproach. Compare *The Secret History*   39 chains, surveyor's chains, sixty feet long,
for measuring

from A Progress to the Mines

In September and October 1732 Byrd took a trip to inspect some of his mining properties and to collect what data he could on the cost of manufacturing iron. Along the way he stopped to inspect properties of his or to visit with various prosperous planters. This excerpt tells of the first two stops. He halted first at his father's old place near the falls of the James River, where he supervised some drilling and talked with the miller, the weaver, the overseer's wife, and the overseer. His second stop was at Colonel Randolph's home at Tuckahoe. There with Mrs. Fleming, another friend of the Randolphs, he was delayed for a time by rainy weather.

1732, Sept. 18. For the pleasure of the good company of Mrs. Byrd, and her little Governuor, my Son, I went about half way to the Falls in the Chariot. There we halted, not far from a purling Stream, and upon the Stump of a propagate Oak picket the Bones of a Piece of Roast Beef. By the Spirit which that gave me, I was the better able to part with the dear Companions of my Travels, and to perform the rest of my Journey on Horseback by myself. I reached Shaccoa's before 2 o'clock, and crost the River to the Mills. I had the Grief to find them both stand as still, for the want of Water, as a dead Woman's Tongue, for want of Breath. It had rain'd so little for many Weeks above the Falls, that the Naides had hardly Water enough
10 left to wash their Faces. However, as we ought to turn all our Misfortunes to the best Advantage, I directed Mr. Booker, my first Minister there, to make use of the lowness of the water for blowing up the Rocks at the Mouth of the Canal. For that purpose I order'd Iron Drills to be made about 2 foot long, pointed with Steel, Chizzel fashion, in order to make holes, into which we put our Cartridges of Powder, containing each about 3 Ounces. There wanted Skill among my Engineers to chuse the best parts of the Stone for boring, that we might blow to the most advantage. They made all their Holes quite perpendicular, whereas they should have humour'd the Grain of the Stone for the more effectual Execution. I order'd the points of the Drills to be made Chizzel way, rather than the Diamond, that they might need to be Sel-
20 domer repair'd, tho' in Stone the Diamond points would make the most despatch. The Water now flow'd out of the River so slowly, that the Miller was oblig'd to pond it up in the Canal, by setting open the Floodgates at the Mouth, and shutting those close at the Mill. By this contrivance, he was able at any time to grind two or three Bushels, either for his choice Customers, or for the use of my Plantations. Then I walkt to the place where they broke the Flax, which is wrought with much greater ease than the Hemp, and is much better for Spinning. From thence I paid a Visit to the Weaver, who needed a little of Minerva's Inspiration to make the most of a piece of fine Cloth. Then I lookt in upon my Caledonian Spinster, who was mended more in her looks than in her Humour. However, she promised much, tho'
30 at the same time intended to perform little. She is too high-Spirited for Mr. Booker,

9 Naides, naiads   27 **Minerva,** the goddess of spinning and weaving   28 **Caledonian Spinster,** the wife of the overseer

who hates to have his sweet Temper ruffled, and will rather suffer matters to go a little wrong sometimes, than give his righteous Spirit any uneasiness. He is very honest, and would make an admirable Overseer where Servants will do as they are bid. But Eye-Servants, who want abundance of overlooking, are not so proper to be committed to his Care. I found myself out of order, and for that reason retir'd Early; yet with all this precaution had a gentle feaver in the Night, but towards morning Nature set open all her Gates, and drove it out in a plentiful perspiration.

[Sept.] 19. The worst of this fever was, that it put me to the Necessity of taking another Ounce of Bark. I moisten'd every dose with a little Brandy, and fill'd the Glass up with Water, which is the least Nauseous way of taking this Popish Medi-   10
cine, and besides hinders it from Purging. After I had swallow'd a few Poacht Eggs, we rode down to the Mouth of the Canal, and from thence crost over to the broad Rock Island in a Canoe. Our errand was to view some Iron Ore, which we dug up in two places. That on the surface seemed very spongy and poor, which gave us no great Encouragement to search deeper, nor did the Quantity appear to be very great. However, for my greater Satisfaction, I order'd a hand to dig there for some time this Winter. We walkt from one End of the Island to the other, being about half a Mile in length, and found the Soil very good, and too high for any Flood, less than that of Deucalion, to do the least damage. There is a very wild prospect both upward and downward, the River being full of Rocks, over which the Stream tum-   20
bled with a Murmur, loud enough to drown the Notes of a Scolding Wife. This Island would make an agreeable Hermitage for any good Christian, who had a mind to retire from the World. Mr. Booker told me how Dr. Ireton had cured him once of a Looseness, which had been upon him two whole years. He order'd him a Dose of Rhubarb, with directions to take 25 Drops of Laudanum so Soon as he had had 2 Physical Stools. Then he rested one day, and the next order'd him another Dose of the same Quantity of Laudanum to be taken, also after the 2d Stool. When this was done, he finisht the Cure by giving him 20 drops of Laudanum every night for five Nights running. The Doctor insisted upon the necessity of Stopping the Operation of the Rhubarb before it workt quite off, that what remained behind might   30
strengthen the Bowels. I was punctual in Swallowing my Bark, and that I might use exercise upon it, rode to Prince's Folly, and my Lord's Islands, where I saw very fine Corn. In the meantime Vulcan came in Order to make the drills for boring the Rocks, And gave me his Parole he wou'd, by the grace of God, attend the works till they were finisht, which he perform'd as lamely as if he had been to labour for a dead Horse, and not for ready Money. I made a North Carolina dinner upon Fresh Pork, though we had a plate of Green Peas after it, by way of Desert, for the Safety of our Noses. Then my first minister and I had some serious Conversation about my affairs, and I find nothing disturb'd his peaceable Spirit so much as the misbehavior of the Spinster above-mention'd. I told him I cou'd not pity a Man, who   40
had it always in his Power to do himself and her Justice, and wou'd not. If she were

---

19 **Deucalion,** son of Prometheus. When Jupiter punished the race of men with a vast flood, Deucalion and his wife Pyrrha alone survived by finding refuge on towering Parnassus   33 **Vulcan,** god of fire, hence of the glow of the forge. Here, of course, the name is humorously applied to a very un-Vulcanlike worker

a Drunkard, a Scold, a Thief, or a Slanderer, we had wholesome Laws, that would make her Back Smart for the diversion of her other Members, and it was his Fault he had not put those wholesome Severities in Execution. I retired in decent time to my own Apartment, and Slept very comfortably upon my Bark, forgetting all the little crosses arising from Overseers and Negroes.

[Sept.] 20. I continued the Bark, and then tost down my Poacht Eggs, with as much ease as some good Breeders Slip Children into the World. About Nine I left the Prudentest Orders I could think of with my Visier, and then crost the River to Shacc's. I made a running Visit to 3 of my Quarters, where, besides finding all the
10 People well, I had the Pleasure to see better Crops than usual both of Corn and Tobacco. I parted there with my Intendant, and pursued my Journey to Mr. Randolph's, at Tuckahoe, without meeting with any Adventure by the way. Here I found Mrs. Fleming, who was packing up her Baggage with design to follow her Husband the next day, who was gone to a new Settlement in Goochland. Both he and She have been about Seaven Years persuading themselves to remove to that retired part of the Country, tho' they had the two strong Arguments of Health and Interest for doing so. The Widow smiled graciously upon me, and entertain'd me very handsomely. Here I learnt all the tragical Story of her Daughter's humble Marriage with her Uncle's Overseer. Besides the meanness of this mortal's Aspect, the Man has
20 not one visible Qualification, except Impudence, to recommend him to a Female's Inclinations. But there is sometimes such a Charm in that Hibernian Endowment, that frail Woman cannot withstand it, tho' it stand alone without any other Recommendation. Had she run away with a Gentleman or a pretty Fellow, there might have been some Excuse for her, tho' he were of inferior Fortune: but to stoop to a dirty Plebeian, without any kind of merit, is the lowest Prostitution. I found the Family justly enraged at it; and tho' I had more good Nature than to join in her Condemnation, yet I cou'd devise no Excuse for so senceless a Prank as this young Gentlewoman had play'd. Here good Drink was more Scarce than good Victuals, the Family being reduc'd to the last Bottle of Wine, which was therefore husbanded
30 very carefully. But the Water was excellent. The Heir of the Family did not come home till late in the Evening. He is a pretty Young Man, but had the misfortune to become his own master too soon. This puts young Fellows upon wrong pursuits, before they have Sence to Judge rightly for themselves. Tho' at the same time they have a strange conceit of their own Sufficiency, when they grow near 20 Years old, especially if they happen to have a small Smattering of Learning. Tis then they fancy themselves wiser than all their Tutors and Governors, which makes them headstrong to all advice, and above all Reproof and Admonition.

[Sept.] 21. I was sorry in the morning to find myself stopt in my Career by bad Weather brought upon us by a North-East Wind. This drives a World of Raw un-
40 kindly Vapours upon us from Newfoundland, laden with Blite, Coughs, and Pleurisys. However, I complain'd not, lest I might be suspected to be tir'd of the good Company. Tho' Mrs. Fleming was not so much upon her Guard, but mutiny'd strongly at the Rain, that hinder'd her from pursuing her dear Husband. I said what I cou'd

---

8 **Visier**, vizier

to comfort a Gentlewoman under so sad a Disappointment. I told her a husband, that staid so much at Home as her's did, cou'd be no such violent Rarity, as for a Woman to venture her precious Health, to go daggling thro' the Rain after him, or to be miserable if she happen'd to be prevented. That it was prudent for marry'd people to fast Sometimes from one another, that they might come together again with the better Stomach. That the best things in this World, if constantly us'd, are apt to be cloying, which a little absence and Abstinence wou'd prevent. This was Strange Doctrine to a fond Female, who fancys People shou'd love with as little Reason after Marriage as before. In the afternoon Monsieur Marij, the Minister of the Parish, came to make me a Visit. He had been a Romish Priest, but found Rea- 10 sons, either Spiritual or temporal, to quit that gay Religion. The fault of this new Convert is, that he looks for as much Respect from his Protestant Flock, as is paid to the Popish Clergy, which our ill-bred Hugonots dont understand. Madam Marij, had so much Curiosity as to want to come too; but another Horse was wanting, and she believ'd it would have too Vulgar an Air to ride behind her Husband. This Woman was of the true Exchange Breed, full of Discourse, but void of Discretion, and marry'd a Parson, with the Idle hopes he might some time or other come to be his Grace of Canterbury. The Gray Mare is the better Horse in that Family, and the poor man Submits to her wild Vagarys for Peace' Sake. She has just enough of the fine Lady, to run in debt, and be of no signification in her Household. And the only 20 thing that can prevent her from undoing her loving Husband will be, that nobody will trust them beyond the 16000, which is soon run out in a Goochland store. The way of Dealing there is, for some small Merchant or Pedler to buy a Scots Penny-worth of Goods, and clap 150 per cent upon that. At this Rate the Parson cant be paid much more for his preaching than tis worth. No sooner was our Visitor retired, but the facetious Widow was so kind as to let me into all this Secret History, but was at the same time exceedingly Sorry that the Woman should be so indiscreet, and the man so tame as to be govern'd by an unprofitable and fantastical Wife.

[Sept.] 22. We had another wet day, to try both Mrs. Fleming's Patience and my good Breeding. The N E Wind commonly sticks by us 3 or 4 days, filling the At- 30 mosphere with damps, injurious both to man and Beast. The worst of it was, we had no good Liquor to warm our Blood, and fortify our Spirits against so strong a Malignity. However, I was cheerful under all these Misfortunes, and expresst no Concern but a decent Fear lest my long visit might be troublesome. Since I was like to have thus much Leizure, I endeavour'd to find out what Subject a dull marry'd man cou'd introduce that might best bring the Widow to the Use of her Tongue. At length, I discover'd she was a notable Quack, and therefore paid that regard to her Knowledge, as to put some Questions to her about the bad distemper that raged then in the Country. I mean the Bloody Flux, that was brought us in the Negro-ship consigned to Colo. Braxton. She told me she made use of very Simple 40 remedys in that Case, with very good Success. She did the Business either with Hartshorn Drink, that had Plantain Leaves boil'd in it, or else with a Strong decoc-tion of St. Andrew's Cross, in New milk instead of Water. I agreed with her that

---

22 **16000.** Sixteen thousand pounds of tobacco was the legal salary of a minister

those remedys might be very good, but would be more effectual after a dose or two
of Indian Physick. But for fear this Conversation might be too grave for a Widow,
I turn'd the discourse, and began to talk of Plays, & finding her Taste lay most towards Comedy, I offer'd my Service to read one to Her, which she kindly accepted.
She produced the 2d part of the Beggar's Opera, which had diverted the Town for
40 nights successively, and gain'd four thousand pounds to the Author. This was
not owing altogether to the Wit or Humour that Sparkled in it, but to some Political Reflections, that seem'd to hit the Ministry. But the great Advantage of the
Author was, that his Interest was solicited by the Dutchess of Queensbury, which
10 no man could refuse who had but half an Eye in his head, or half a Guinea in his
Pocket. Her Grace, like Death, spared nobody, but even took my Lord Selkirk in
for 2 Guineas, to repair which Extravagance he liv'd upon Scots Herrings 2 Months
afterwards. But the best Story was, she made a very Smart Officer in his Majesty's
Guards give her a Guinea, who Swearing at the same time twas all he had in the
world, she sent him 50 for it the next day, to reward his Obedience. After having
acquainted my Company with the History of the Play, I read 3 Acts of it, and left
Mrs. Fleming and Mr. Randolph to finish it, who read as well as most Actors do at
a Rehearsal. Thus we kill'd the time, and triumpht over the bad Weather.

1732, 1866

---

5 **The Beggar's Opera** (1727), a play by John Gay (1688-1732) produced very successfully, as Byrd indicates, in London. Actually it ran for sixty-three successive nights   9 **the Dutchess of Queensbury,**
Catharine Douglas, the wife of the third Duke of Queensbury, Charles Douglas — a leading figure in London society and one of Gay's staunchest friends

1735—1826 Samuel *Peters*

Samuel Peters, an early writer of American "whoppers," was born in Hebron,
Connecticut, in 1735, the descendant of an old colonial Puritan family. He
graduated from Yale in 1757, went abroad, and was converted to Anglicanism. Following his ordination in 1760, he was appointed Rector of Hebron
and Hertford.

In the dispute between the colonies and England, Peters was persecuted because
of his Toryism. On one occasion, for instance, a mob, coming to his home, "fired
balls into the house, and with stones, bricks and clubs broke the doors, windows,
and furniture, wounding his mother, the nurse of his infant son, and his two

brothers, and seizing him, tore off his hat, wig, gown, and cassock, made him naked (except his breeches, stocking, and shoes), struck him with their staves and spat in his face," and threatened to tar and feather him. Imperiled by additional violence, he escaped to England in 1774 and did not return until 1805. He died in 1826.

In England, in 1781, Peters published his *General History of Connecticut,* which purposed, he said, "to bring to light truths long concealed," and which included "a description of the country, and many curious and interesting anecdotes." The scientific accuracy of the history and description in the book was somewhat militated against by Peters' prejudices. Furthermore the Rev. Peters had a sense of humor which caused him to enjoy working into a solemn description of a river the statement that it flowed so fast a crowbar would float on it.

The result was a book foreshadowing *Knickerbocker's History of New York* and the tall tales later to be published by Western writers. As Irving was to do, Peters maliciously satirized life in New England, emphasizing the harsh Blue Laws, the practice of bundling, and the foolishness of some of the inhabitants. He also threw in some "stretchers," included, apparently, for the pure joy of drawing a long bow. Such passages as the following have in them the fantasy and solemn-faced mendacity typical of much later American humor.

General History of Connecticut, ed. S. J. McCormick, New York, 1877   E. A. Duyckinck and G. L. Duyckinck, "Samuel Peters," Cyclopedia of American Literature, New York, 1856

from General History of Connecticut

Birds and Tree-frogs

The partridges in New England are near as large as a Dorking fowl; the quails, as an English partridge; and the robins twice as big as those in England. The dew-mink, so named from its articulating those syllables, is black and white, and of the size of an English robin. Its flesh is delicious. The humility is so called because it speaks the word *humility,* and seldom mounts high in the air. Its legs are long enough to enable it to outrun a dog for a little way; its wings long and narrow, body meager, and of the size of a blackbird's; plumage variegated with white, black, blue, and red. It lives on tadpoles, spawn, and worms; has an eye more piercing than the falcon, and the swiftness of an eagle. Hence it can never be shot: for it sees the sparks of fire even before they enkindle the powder, and by the extreme rapidity of 10 its flight, gets out of reach in an instant. It is never known to light upon a tree, but is always seen upon the ground or wing. These birds appear in New England in summer only; what becomes of them afterwards is not discovered. They are caught in snares, but can never be tamed.

4 robin . . . humility. The American robin, twice as large as the European robin and with only superficial resemblance save in the color of the breast, borrowed its name; dewmink (probably the towhee or chewink) and humility (an obsolete New England term for snipe) are American names for American birds

The whippoorwill has so named itself by its nocturnal songs. It is also called the pope, by reason of its darting with great swiftness from the clouds to the ground, and bawling out *Pope!* which alarms young people and the fanatics very much, especially as they know it to be an ominous bird. However, it has hitherto proved friendly, always giving travellers and others notice of an approaching storm, by saluting them every minute with *Pope! Pope!* It flies only a little before sunset, unless for this purpose of giving notice of a storm. It never deceives the people with false news. If the tempest is to continue long, the augurs appear in flocks, and nothing can be heard but the word *Pope! Pope!* The whippoorwill is about the size of a 10 cuckoo, has a short beak, long and narrow wings, a large head and mouth enormous, yet it is not a bird of prey. Under its throat is a pocket, which it fills with air at pleasure, whereby it sounds forth the fatal words *Pope* in the day, and *Whip-her-I-will* in the night. The superstitious inhabitants would have exorcised this harmless bird long ago, as an emissary from Rome and an enemy to the American vine, had they not found out that it frequents New England only in the summer, and prefers the wilderness to a palace. Nevertheless, many cannot but believe it a spy from some foreign court, an agent of Antichrist, a lover of persecution, and an enemy of Protestants, because it sings of *whipping,* and of the *Pope,* which they think portends misery and a change of religion.

20 The tree-frog cannot be called an insect, a reptile, or one of the winged host. He has four legs, the two foremost short, with claws as sharp as those of a squirrel: the hind legs five inches long, and folding by three joints. His body is about as big as the first joint of a man's thumb. Under his throat is a wind-bag, which assists him in singing the word *I-sa-ac,* all the night. When it rains and is very dark, he sings the loudest. His voice is not so pleasing as that of a nightingale; but this would be a venial imperfection if he would but keep silence on Saturday nights, and not forever prefer *I-sa-ac* to *Abraham* and *Jacob.* He has more elasticity in his long legs than any other creature yet known. By this means he will leap five yards up a tree, fastening himself to it by his fore feet; and in a moment will hop or spring as far as 30 from one tree to another. It is from the singing of the tree-frog that the Americans have acquired the name of *Little Isaac.* Indeed, like a certain part of them, the creature appears very devout, noisy, arbitrary, and phlegmatic, and associates with none but what agree with him in his ways.

The Frogs of Windham

Windham, the second county in the ancient kingdom of Sassacus, or colony of Saybrook, is hilly; but the soil being rich, has excellent butter, cheese, hemp, wheat, Indian corn, and horses. Its towns are twelve.

Windham resembles Rumford, and stands on Winnomantic river. Its meeting-house is elegant, and has a steeple, bell, and clock. Its court-house is scarcely to be

---

1 **whippoorwill.** In his remarks about this bird, Peters makes fun of the Puritan fear of popery 31 **like** . . . **them.** Here Peters makes fun of what he considers the fanaticism and dogmatism of the Puritans 38 **Winnomantic river,** the Willimantic

looked upon as an ornament. The township forms four parishes, and is ten miles square.

Strangers are very much terrified at the hideous noise made on summer evenings by the vast number of frogs in the brooks and ponds. There are about thirty different voices among them, some of which resemble the bellowing of a bull. The owls and whippoor-wills complete the rough concert, which may be heard several miles. Persons accustomed to such serenades are not disturbed by them at their proper stations; but one night, in July, 1758, the frogs of an artificial pond, three miles square, and about five from Windham, finding the water dried up, left the place in a body, and marched, or rather hopped, towards Winnomantic river. They were 10 under the necessity of taking the road and going through the town, which they entered about midnight. The bull frogs were the leaders, and the pipers followed without number. They filled a road 40 yards wide for four miles in length, and were for several hours, in passing through the town, unusually clamorous. The inhabitants were equally perplexed and frightened: some expected to find an army of French and Indians; others feared an earthquake, and dissolution of nature. The consternation was universal. Old and young, male and female, fled naked from their beds with worse shriekings than those of the frogs. The event was fatal to several women. The men, after a flight of half a mile, in which they met with many broken shins, finding no enemies in pursuit of them, made a halt and summoned resolution enough 20 to venture back to their wives and children; when they distinctly heard from the enemy's camp these words, *"Wight, Hilderken, Dier, Tete."* This last they thought meant *treaty;* and plucking up courage, they sent a triumvirate to capitulate with the supposed French and Indians. These three men approached in their shirts, and begged to speak with the General; but it being dark, and no answer given, they were sorely agitated for some time betwixt hope and fear; at length, however, they discovered that the dreaded inimical army was an army of thirsty frogs, going to the river for a little water.

Such an incursion was never known before nor since; and yet the people of Windham have been ridiculed for their timidity on this occasion. I verily believe an 30 army under the Duke of Marlborough would, under like circumstances, have acted no better than they did.

In 1768, the inhabitants on Connecticut river were as much alarmed at an army of caterpillars, as those of Windham were at the frogs; and no one found reason to jest at their fears. Those worms came in one night, and covered the earth on both sides of that river to an extent of three miles in front and two in depth. They marched with great speed and eat up everything green for the space of one hundred miles, in spite of rivers, ditches, fires, and the united efforts of 1,000 men. They were, in general, two inches long, had white bodies covered with thorns, and red throats. When they had finished their work, they went down to the river Con- 40 necticut, where they died, poisoning the waters until they were washed into the sea. This calamity was imputed by some to the vast number of trees and logs lying in the creeks, and to the cinders, smoke, and fires made to consume the waste wood for three or four hundred miles up the Connecticut; while others thought it augured

future evils similar to those in Egypt. The inhabitants of the Verdmonts would unavoidably have perished by famine in consequence of the devastation of these
worms, had not a remarkable providence filled the wilderness with wild pigeons,
which were killed by sticks as they sat on the branches of trees in such multitudes,
that 30,000 people lived on them for three weeks. If a natural cause may be assigned
for the coming of the frogs and caterpillars, yet the visit of the pigeons to a wilderness in August has been necessarily ascribed to an interposition of infinite power
and goodness. Happy will it be for America, if the smiling providence of Heaven
produces gratitude, repentance, and obedience amongst her children!

10 *Hebron*

Hebron is the center of the province; and it is remarkable that there are thirty-six
towns larger, and thirty-six less. It is situated between two ponds, about two miles in
length and one in breadth, and is intersected by two small rivers, one of which falls
into the Connecticut, the other into the Thames. A large meeting[-house] stands on a
square, where four roads meet. The town resembles Finchley. The township eight
miles square; five parishes, one is Episcopal. The number of houses is 400; of the inhabitants, 3,200. It pays one part out of seventy-three of all governmental taxes, and is
a bed of farmers on their own estates. Frequent suits about the Indian titles have
rendered them famous for their knowledge in law and self-preservation. In 1740,
20 Mr. George Whitefield gave them this laconic character: "Hebron," says he, "is the
stronghold of Satan; for its people mightily oppose the work of the Lord, being
more fond of earth than of heaven."

This town is honored by the residence of the Rev. Dr. Benjamin Pomeroy, an
excellent scholar, an exemplary gentleman, and a most˙thundering preacher of the
New Light order. His great abilities procured him the favor and honor of being the
instructor of Abimeleck, the present King of Mohegin. He is of a very persevering,
sovereign disposition; but just, polite, generous, charitable, and without dissimulation. — *Avis alba.*

Here also reside some of the descendants of William Peters, Esq., already spoken
30 of; among whom is the Rev. Samuel Peters, an Episcopal clergyman, who, by his
generosity and zeal for the Church of England and loyalty to the House of Hanover, has rendered himself famous both in New and Old England, and in some degree made an atonement for the fanaticism and treasons of his uncle Hugh, and of
his ancestor on his mother's side, Major-general Thomas Harrison, both hanged at
Charing-Cross in the last century. . . .

1781

---

1 **the Verdmonts,** Vermont   25 **New Light,** a particular sect of the Congregationalists   28 **Avis alba,**
a white bird. The modern equivalent would be "a rare bird"   30 **Samuel Peters.** The author speaks of
himself anonymously

RELIGIOUS THINKERS:
Shepard
Williams
Mather
Wise
Edwards
Chauncy

1604—1649 Thomas Shepard

Among the leaders of the New England colonies were many forceful clergymen, notably John Cotton of Boston, Richard Mather of Dorchester,
Thomas Hooker of Hartford, John Davenport of New Haven, and
Roger Williams of Providence. In piety, however, and in subsequent
influence, few exceeded that "gracious, sweet, heavenly minded and soul ravishing
minister," Thomas Shepard of Cambridge. A "poore, weake, pale-complectioned
man," he typified in many ways the religious life of first generation New England.

Shepard's career followed a familiar pattern. At twenty-three he left Emmanuel
College, Cambridge, sometimes called the cradle of the Puritan party, with both his
B.A. and his M.A. degrees. Because, like other Puritans, he disregarded prescribed
ritual in favor of evangelical sermonizing, Shepard was three years later brought
before William Laud, then Bishop of London, and forbidden to "preach, read,
marry, bury, or exercise any ministerial function" in that diocese. In 1635, after narrow escapes from Laud's agents and from storms at sea, he landed in Massachusetts,
with enough of a personal following to occupy Newton, or Cambridge, where he
remained for the rest of his life, preaching, writing, and overseeing the infant college named after another Emmanuel alumnus, John Harvard.

The core of Shepard's faith, and the great strength of Puritanism, was a spirituality which permeated every phase of living; a burning pietism which made the
things of this world insignificant when compared with the exhilarating problem of
the individual's relation to his God. "How many be there," Shepard asked in *The
Sound Believer* (London, 1645), "that believe in Christ, that they may live as they
list? If to drink, and whore, and scoff, and blaspheme; if to shake a lock, and follow
every fond fashion; if to cross and cringe before a piece of wood; . . . if to set our
hearts upon farms and merchandise, and so to be covetous; . . . if to have a name
to live, and yet be dead at the heart, — if this be to live the life of Love, we have
many that live this life; the Lord Jesus wants no love if this be to love. But O,
woe unto you, if you thus requite the Lord, foolish people and unwise."

Like his colleagues, Shepard was primarily interested in conversion, and at times played upon the emotions of his congregation with descriptions of the perils of the damned. His reputation rested, however, upon systematic accounts of Calvinistic doctrine, which were exceedingly popular in both England and America.

The Works of Thomas Shepard, 3 vols., Boston, 1853   S. E. Morison, Builders of the Bay Colony, Boston, 1930

from *The Sincere Convert*

The following complete sermon forms the fifth chapter of Shepard's first book, of which the full title is an excellent brief statement of the characteristic tenets of Calvinism, only that of foreordination being without explicit mention: The Sincere Convert: Discovering the Small Number of True Believers, and the Great Difficulty of Saving Conversion; Wherein Is Excellently and Plainly Opened These Choice and Divine Principles: 1. That There Is a God, and This God Is Most Glorious. 2. That God Made Man in a Blessed State. 3. Man's Misery by His Fall. 4. Christ the Only Redeemer by Price. 5. That Few Are Saved, and That with Difficulty.

The primacy of God, the depravity of man through Adam's sin, the mediation of Christ, the election of the few, and the just reprobation of the many — this was the theology which dominated the seventeenth and a large part of the eighteenth century. Thomas Shepard displays it in perhaps its most attractive form, wherein the rigors of the doctrine are softened by the spiritual security which he quite evidently found.

The systematic method of the following sermon is typical not only of Shepard but also of a fair majority of Puritan preachers. Note that he (1) takes a text from the Bible, (2) draws from it appropriate doctrines, (3) supports his doctrines by reasons and extensive Scriptural authority, and (4) concludes with an exhortation on the uses or practical application of the doctrine.

The fifth Principle. *That those that are saved are very few; and that those that are saved, are saved with very much difficulty. Strait is the gate, and narrow is the way that leadeth unto life, and few there be that finde it,* Mat. 7. 14.

Here are two parts.

1. The paucity of them that shall be saved: *few finde the way thither.*

2. The difficulty of being saved: *Strait and narrow is the way and gate unto life.*

Hence arise two Doctrines.

Doct. 1. 1. That the number of them that shall be saved is very small, *Luke* 13. 24. the Devill hath his drove, and swarmes to goe to hell, as fast as Bees to their Hive; Christ hath his *Flock,* and that is but *a little flock;* hence Gods children are called *Jewels, Mal. 3.* 17. which commonly are kept secret, in respect of the other lumber in the house; hence they are called *Strangers* and *Pilgrims,* which are very

10

---

1 **The fifth Principle.** In the text used, the London edition of 1655, "Corrected and much amended by the Author," there are two kinds of marginal matter: (1) organizational headings, as here, and (2) citations of sources: The first are here printed in the text in boldface; the second are printed, sometimes expanded, in the notes   10 **a little flock.** In margin: Luke 12.32

few in respect of the inhabitants of the countrey through which they passe: hence they are called *sonnes of God,* 1 *John* 3. 2. *Of the bloud Royall,* which are few in respect of common subjects.

But see the truth of this point in these two things.

Few saved in all ages. First, look to all ages and times of the world. Secondly, to all places and persons in the world, and we shall see few men were saved.

1. Look to all ages, and we shall find but a handfull saved. As soon as ever the Lord began to keep house, and there were but two families in it, there was a bloudy *Cain* living, and a good *Abel* slain. And as the world increased in number, so in wickednesse, *Gen.* 6. 12. it is said, *All flesh had corrupted their wayes,* and amongst so 10 many thousand men, not one righteous but *Noah,* and his family; and yet in the Ark there crept in a cursed *Cham.*

Afterwards as *Abrahams* posterity increased, so we see their sin abounded. When his posterity was in *Egypt,* where one would think, if ever men were good, now it would appear, being so heavily afflicted by *Pharaoh,* being by so many miracles miraculously delivered by the hand of *Moses,* yet most of these *God was wroth with, Heb.* 3. 12. and onely two of them, *Caleb* and *Joshua* went into *Canaan,* a type of heaven. Look into *Solomons* time, what glorious times! what great profession was there then! Yet after his death, *ten Tribes* fell to the odious sin of Idolatry, following the command of *Jeroboam* their King. Look further into *Isaiah's* time, where there were 20 multitudes of Sacrifices and prayers, *Isa.* 1. 11. yet then there was but a *remnant,* nay a very *little* remnant that should be saved. And look to the time of Christs coming in the flesh, (for I pick out the best time of all) when one would think by such Sermons he preached, such miracles he wrought, such a life as he led, all the *Jewes* would have entertained him, yet it is said, *He came unto his own, and they received him not.* So few, that Christ himself admires at one good *Nathaniel, behold an Israelite in whom there is no guile.* In the Apostles time, many indeed were converted, but few comparatively, and amongst the best Churches many bad: as that at *Philippi,* Phil. 3. 18. Many had a name to live, but were dead, and *few* only kept their garments unspotted. And presently after the Apostles time, *many grievous wolves came and* 30 *devoured the sheep;* and so in succeeding ages, *Rev.* 12. 9. *All the earth wondred at the whore in skarlet.*

Luther. And in *Luthers time,* when the light began to arise again, he saw so many carnal Gospellers, that he breaks out in one Sermon, into these speeches, *God grant I may never live to see those bloudy dayes that are coming upon an ungodly world. Latimer* heard so much prophanenesse in his time, that he thought verily dooms days was just at hand. And have not our ears heard censuring those in the *Palatinate,* where

---

9 **as the world . . . wickednesse.** Repeated in margin   12 **cursed Cham.** Ham, or Cham, a son of Noah, was accursed by his father because the son looked on Noah naked as he lay drunk. See Genesis 9: 18 ff.   21 **Isa. 1. 11.** In margin: Isai. 1. 9. The text citation is to the multitude of sacrifices; the marginal, to the remnant   25 **received.** In margin: Job 1. 2   27 **converted.** In margin: Rev. 3. 4   30 **grievous.** In margin: Acts 20. 28, 29, 30   33 **Luthers time.** The Pope excommunicated Martin Luther (1484-1546) in 1520, largely because of his vehement protests against abuses in the church   35 **Latimer,** Hugh Latimer (1480?-1535), English religious reformer   37 **Palatinate,** a district in southwest Germany where the struggle between Catholics and Protestants prolonged the Thirty Years' War (1618-1648)

(as 'tis reported) many have fallen from the glorious Gospell to Popery, as fast as leaves fall in *Autumn?* Who would have thought there had lurked such hearts under such a shew of detesting Popery, as was among them before? And at Christs comming, *shall he find faith on the earth?*

II. **Few shall be saved in all places.** 2. Let us look into all places and persons, and see how few shall be saved. The world is now split into four parts, *Europe, Asia, Africa,* and *America;* and the three biggest parts are drowned in a deluge of prophanenesse and superstition; they doe not so much as professe Christ; you may see the sentence of death written on these mens foreheads. *Jer.* 10. *ult.* But let us look upon
10 the best part of the world, and that is *Europe,* how few shall be saved there? First, the *Grecian* Church, howsoever now in these daies, their good patriarch of *Constantinople* is about a general Reformation among them, and hath done much good; yet are they for the present, and have been for the most part of them, without the saving means of knowledge. They content themselves with their old superstitions, having little or no preaching at all. And for the other parts, as *Italy, Spain, France, Germany,* for the most part they are Popish; and see the end of these men, 2 *Thes.* 2. 9, 10, 11, 12. And now amongst them that carry the badge of honesty, I will not speak what mine ears have heard, and my heart beleeves concerning other Churches: I will come into our own Church of *England,* which is the most flourishing Church
20 in the world: never had Church such Preachers, such means; yet have we not some Chappels and Churches stand as darke lanthorns without light, where people are led with blind, or idle, or licentious Ministers, and so both fall into the ditch?

Nay, even amongst them that have the means of grace, but few shall be saved. It may be sometimes amongst ninety nine in a parish, Christ sends a minister to call some *one* lost sheep among them, *Mat.* 13. Three grounds were bad where the seed was sown, and only one ground good. It's a strange speech of *Chrysostom* in his fourth Sermon to the people of *Antioch,* where he was much beloved and did much good: *How many do you think* (saith he) *shall be saved in this city? It will be an hard speech to you, but I will speak it; though here be so many thousands of you, yet there cannot*
30 *be found an hundred that shall be saved, and I doubt of them too; for what villany is there among youth? what sloth in old men?* and so he goes on. So say I, never tell me we are baptized, and are Christians, and trust to Christ; let us but separate the Goats from the sheep, and exclude none but such as the Scripture doth, and sets a crosse upon their doors, with, *Lord have mercy upon them,* and we shall see only few in the City shall be saved.

---

9 **Jer. 10. ult.** Jeremiah 10:25. In margin: Powre out thy fury upon the heathen that know thee not, and upon the families that call not upon thy name, &c.   11 **patriarch of Constantinople,** Cyril Lucar (1572-1638), holder of this office in the Greek Orthodox Church, 1620-1638. As a result of his friendship with a Swiss Calvinist, he published a strongly protestant confession of faith in 1631, and in 1638 assisted in translating the Bible into modern Greek. Repeatedly banished and reinstated, he was finally strangled by order of the sultan   20 **some Chappels.** In margin: Few shall be saved in England. I Cor. 1. 29   26 **Chrysostom** (345?-407), a famous preacher of Antioch in Asia Minor, 386-398, and patriarch of Constantinople, 398-404. In margin: Chrysostom thought in Antioch, an hundred could not be saved   32 **to Christ.** In margin: Those which the Scripture excludes from salvation   32 **separate . . . sheep.** A remarkably similar account of those men who will not be saved may be seen in Michael Wigglesworth's *Day of Doom* (1662), stanza 38 ff.

1. The profane. 1. Cast out all the *profane people* among us, as drunkards, swearers, whores, liers, which the Scripture brands for black sheep, and condemns them in an hundred places.

2. The civill men. 2. Set by all *Civill men,* that are but Wolves chained up, tame Devils, swine in a fair medow, that pay all they owe, and do no body any harm, yet do none any great good, that plead for themselvs and say, Who can say black is mine eye? These are righteous men, whom Christ never came to call; *For he came not to call the righteous, but sinners to repentance.*

3. The hypocrites. 3. Cast by all *Hypocrites,* that like stage-players, in the sight of others, act the parts of Kings, and honest men; when look upon them in their tyr-   10
ing hous, they are but base varlets.

4. The formall professors. 4. *Formall Professors,* and *Carnall Gospellers,* that have a thing like *faith* and like *sorrow,* and like *true repentance,* and like *good desires,* but yet they be but pictures, they deceive others and themselves too, 2 *Tim.* 3. 5.

Set by these four sorts, how few then are to be saved, even among them that are hatcht in the bosome of the Church?

Use 1. Of encouragement. First, here then is an Use of *encouragement.* Be not discouraged by the name of singularity. What? do you think your self wiser than others? and shall none be saved but such as are so precise as Ministers prate? Are you wiser than others that you think none shall go to heaven but your self? I tell   20
you if you would be saved, you must be singular men, not out of *faction,* but out of *conscience, Acts* 24. 16.

Use 2. Of terror. Secondly, here is matter of *terrour* to all those that be of opinion, that few shall be saved; and therefore when they are convinced of the danger of sin by the Word, they flie to this shelter, If I be damned, it will be woe to many more beside me then; as though most should not be damned. Oh yes, the most of them that live in the Church shall perish; and this made an *Hermit* which *Theodoret* mentions, to live 15 years in a cell in a desolate wildernesse, with nothing but bread and water, and yet doubted after all his sorrow, whether he should be saved or no. Oh! Gods wrath is heavy, which thou shalt one day bear.   30

Use 3. Of exhortation to all confident people. Thirdly, this ministreth *exhortation* to all *confident people,* that think they beleeve and say, they doubt not but to be saved, and hence doe not much fear death. Oh! learn hence to suspect and fear your estates, and fear it so much, that thou canst not be quiet untill thou hast got some assurance thou shalt be saved. When Christ told his Disciples that one of them should betray him, they all said, *Master, Is it I?* but if he had said, eleven of them should betray him, all except one, would they not all conclude, *Surely it is I?* If the Lord had said, only *Few* shall be damned, every man might fear, It may be it is I; but now he saies *most* shall, every man may cry out and say, Surely it is I. No humble heart, but is driven to and fro with many stinging fears this way; yet there is a   40

---

22 **Acts** 24. 16. In margin: Tit. 2. 14: "Who gave himself for us, that he might redeem us from all iniquity, and purify unto himself a peculiar people, zealous of good works"   27 **Theodoret** (393-457?), bishop of Cyrrhus, near Antioch, 423-449   40 **yet there.** In margin: Presumptuous men think of themselves as the Jews did of the Pharisees

generation of presumptuous, brazen-fac'd, bold people, that confidently think of themselves, as the *Jewes* of the *Pharisees* (being so holy and strict) that if God save but two in the world, they shall make one.

The childe of God indeed *is bold as a Lion;* but he hath Gods Spirit and promise, assuring him of his eternall welfare. But I speak of divers that have no sound ground to prove this point (which they pertinaciously defend) that they shall be saved. This confident humour rageth most of all in our old professors at large, who think, that's a jest indeed, that having been of a good belief so long, that they now should be so fare behind-hand, as to begin the work, and lay the foundation anew.
10 And not only among these, but amongst divers sorts of people whom the Devill never troubles, because he is sure of them already, and therefore cries peace in their ears, whose *consciences* never trouble them, because *that* hath shut its eyes; and hence they sleep, and sleeping dreame, that God is mercifull unto them, and will be so; yet never see they are deceived, untill they awake with the flames of hell about their ears; and the *world* troubles them not, they have their hearts desire here, because they are friends to it, and so enemies to God. And *Ministers* never trouble them, for they have none such as are fit for that work neer them; or if they have, they can sit and sleep in the Church, and chuse whether they will beleeve him. And their friends never trouble them, because they are afraid to displease them. And God himself
20 never troubles them, because that time is to come hereafter. This one truth well pondered and thought on, may damp thine heart and make thy conscience flie in thy face, and say, *Thou art the man;* it may be there are better in hell than thy self that art so confident; and therefore tell me what hast thou to say for thy self, that thou shalt be saved? In what thing hast thou gone beyond them that *think they are rich and want nothing, who yet are poor, blinde, miserable, and naked?*

Obj[ection] 1. Thou wilt say happily, first, I have left my sinnes I once lived in, and am now no drunkard, no swearer, no lier, &c.

Answ. I answer, thou mayest be washt from thy mire (the pollution of the world) and yet be a swine in Gods account, 2 *Pet.* 2. 20. thou mayest live a blamelesse, in-
30 nocent, honest, smooth life, and yet be a miserable creature still, *Phil.* 3. 6.

Obj. 2. But I pray, and that often.

Answ. This thou mayest doe, and yet never be saved, *Isai.* 1. 11. *To what purpose is your multitude of sacrifices?* Nay, thou mayest pray with much affection, with a good heart, as thou thinkest, yet a thousand miles off from being saved, *Prov.* 1. 28.

Obj. 3. But I fast sometimes, as well as pray.

Answ. So did the Scribes and Pharisees, even twice a week, which could not be publick, but private fasts. And yet this righteousnesse could never save them.

Obj. 4. But I hear the word of God, and like the best Preachers.

Answ. This thou mayst doe too, and yet never be saved. Nay, thou mayst so hear,
40 as to receive much *joy* and comfort in hearing, nay, to beleeve and catch hold on

---

8 that they. In margin: Confidence rages most in professors at large   11 cries peace. In margin: The devil never troubles some men, because he is sure of them already   18 And their friends. In margin: Friends never reprove some men, because of displeasing them   39 Nay, thou. In margin: Ezek. 33. 31, 32

Christ, and so say and think *he is thine,* and yet not be saved: as the stony ground did, *Matth.* 13. who heard the word with *joy,* and for a *season beleeved.*

Obj. 5. I read the Scriptures often.

Answ. This you may doe too, and yet never be saved; as the Pharisees, who were so perfect in reading the Bible, that Christ needed but only say, *It hath been said of old time,* for they knew the text and place well enough without intimation.

Obj. 6. But I am grieved and am sorrowfull, and repent for my sins past.

Answ. *Judas* did thus, *Mat.* 27. 3. he repents himself with a legall repentance for fear of hell, and with a naturall sorrow for dealing so unkindly with Christ, in betraying not only bloud, but innocent bloud. True humiliation is ever accompanyed with hearty reformation.

Obj. 7. Oh! but I love good men, and their company.

Answ. So did the *five foolish Virgins* love the company, and (at the time of *extremity)* the very *oyle* and grace of the *wise,* yet they were locked out of the gates of mercy.

Obj. 8. But God hath given me more *knowledge* than others, or than I my self had once.

Answ. This thou mayst have, and be able to teach others, and think so of thy self too, and yet never be saved.

Obj. 9. But I keep the Lords day strictly.

Answ. So did the Jewes, whom yet Christ condemned, and were never saved.

Obj. 10. I have very many *good desires* and *endeavours* to get heaven.

Answ. These thou and thousands may have, and yet misse of heaven.

Many shall seek to enter in at that narrow gate, and not be able.

Obj. 11. True, thou wilt say, many men doe many duties, but without any *life* or *zeal;* I am zealous.

Answ. So thou mayest be, and yet never be saved, as *Jehu; Paul* was zealous when he was a Pharisee, and if he was so for a false Religion, and a bad cause, why much more mayest thou be for a good cause; so zealous as not only to cry out against profanenesse in the wicked, but civill honesty of others, and hypocrisie of others, yea, even of the coldnesse of the best of Gods people: thou mayst be the fore-horse in the Team, and the Ring-leader of good exercises amongst the best men, (as *Joash* a wicked King was the first that complained of the negligence of his best Officers in not repairing the Temple) and so stirre them up unto it; nay, thou mayest be so forward, as to be persecuted, and not yeeld an inch, nor shrink in the wetting, but mayest manfully and courageously stand it out in time of persecution, as the *thorny ground* did: so zealous thou mayest be, as to like best of, and to flock most unto the most zealous Preachers, that search mens consciences best, as the whole countrey of *Judea* came flocking to *John's* Ministry, and delighted to hear him for a season; nay, thou mayest be zealous as to take sweet delight in doing of all these things, *Isa.* 58. 2, 3. *They delight in approaching near unto God,* yet come short of heaven.

Obj. 12. But thou wilt say, True, many a man rides post, that breaks his neck at

---

18 **This thou.** In margin: Rom. 2. 18   23 **these thou.** In margin: Luke 13.   27 **Paul.** In margin: Phil[ippians]. 3. 6. 11   33 **complained.** In margin: 2 Chron. 44. 4, 5, 6

last: many a man is zealous, but his fire is soon quench'd, and his zeal is soon spent; they hold not out; whereas I am constant, and persevere in godly courses.

Answ. So did that young man, yet he was a gracelesse man, *Mat.* 19. 20. *All these things have I done from my youth:* what lack I yet?

Obj. 13. It is true, hypocrites may persevere, but they know themselves *to be naught* all the while, and so deceive others: but I am perswaded that I am in *Gods* favour, and in a safe and happy estate, since I do all with a good heart for God.

Answ. This thou mayest verily think of thy self, and yet be deceived, and damned, and goe to the Devill at last. *There is a way* (saith *Solomon*) *that seemeth right to a man, but the end thereof is the way of death.* For he is an hypocrite not only that makes a seeming outward shew of what he hath not, but also that hath a true shew of what indeed there is not. The first sort of hypocrites deceive others onely; the later having some inward, yet common work, deceive themselves too, *Jam.* 1. 26. *If any man seem to be religious* (so many are, and so deceive the world,) but it is added, *deceiving his own soule.* Nay, thou mayst go so fairly, and live so honestly, that all the best Christians about thee may think well of thee, and never suspect thee, and so mayst passe through the world, and die with a deluded comfort, that thou shalt goe to heaven, and be canonized for a Saint in thy Funerall Sermon, and never know thou art counterfeit, till the Lord brings thee to thy strict and last examination, and so thou receivest that dreadfull sentence, *Go ye cursed.* So it was with the *five foolish Virgins* that were never discovered by the *wise,* nor by themselves, untill the gate of grace was shut upon them. If thou hast therefore no better evidences to shew for thy selfe, that thine estate is good, than these, Ile not give a pins point for all thy flattering false hopes of being saved: but it may be thou hast never yet come so farre as to this pitch; and if not, Lord, what will become of thee? Suspect thy self much, and when in this shipwrack of souls thou seest so many thousands sink, cry out, and conclude, It's a wonder of wonders, and a thousand and a thousand to one, if ever thou comest safe to shore.

Use 4. Strive to be saved. Oh! strive then to be one of them that shall be saved, though it cost thee thy bloud, and the losse of all that thou hast, labour to goe beyond all those that go so far, and yet perish at the last. Do not say, that seeing so few shall be saved, therefore this discourageth me from seeking, because all my labour may be in vain. Consider that Christ here makes another and a better use of it, *Luk.* 3. 24. *Seeing that many shall seek and not enter, therefore* (saith he) *strive to enter in at the strait gate;* venture at least, and try what the Lord will doe for thee.

Quest. Wherein doth the child of God, (and so how may I) go beyond these hypocrites that go so far?

Answ. In three things principally.

Wherein a childe of God goeth beyond an hypocrite. 1. No unregenerate man but lives in some known sin. First, no unregenerate man, though he go never so farre, let him do never so much, but he lives in some one sinne or other,

---

9 **way.** In margin: Prov. 14. 12   13 **work.** In margin: Some hypocrites deceive themselves, some deceive others   21 **Virgins.** In margin: Matt. 25. The five foolish virgins

secret or open, little or great. *Judas* went farre, but he was covetous. *Herod* went farre, but he loved his *Herodias*. Every dog hath his kennel, every swine hath his swill, and every wicked man his lust; for no unregenerate man hath fruition of God to content him, and there is no mans heart but it must have some good to content it, which good is to be found only in the fountain of all good, and that is God; or in the cistern, and that is in the creatures: hence a man having lost full content in God, he seeks for, and feeds upon contentment in the creature which he makes a God to him, and here lies his lust or sinne, which he must needs live in. Hence, aske those men that goe very far, and take their penny for good silver, and commend themselves for their good desires: I say, ask them, if they have no sin; Yes, say they, who can live without 10 sinne? and so they give way to sin, and therefore live in sin; Nay, commonly, all the duties, prayers, care, and zeal of the best hypocrites are to hide a lust; as the whore in the *Proverbs,* that wipes her mouth, and goes to the Temple, and paies her vowes; or to feed a lust, as *Jehu* his zeal against *Baal,* was to get a Kingdome. There remains a root of bitterness in the best hypocrites, which howsoever it be lopt off sometimes by sicknesse or horror of conscience, and a man hath purposes never to commit again, yet there it secretly lurks; and though it seemeth to be bound and conquered by the *Word,* or by *Prayer,* or by outward *Crosses,* or while the hand of God is upon a man, yet the inward strength and power of it remains still; and there-fore when temptations, like strong *Philistines,* are upon this man again, he breaks 20 all vowes, promises, bonds of God, and will save the life of his sin.

    2. **Unregenerate men are not poor in spirit.** Secondly, no unregenerate man or woman ever came to be poor in spirit, and so to be carried out of all duties unto Christ: if it were possible for them to forsake and break loose for ever from all sinne, yet here they stick as the Scribes and Pharisees, and so like zealous *Paul* before his conver-sion, they fasted and prayed, and kept the Sabbath, but they rested in their legall righteousnesse, and in the performance of these and the like duties. Take the best Hypocrit that hath the most strong perswasions of Gods love to him, and ask him, why he hopes to be saved. He will answer, *I pray, read, hear,* love *good men,* cry out *of the sinnes of the time.* And tell him again, that an Hypocrite may climb these stairs 30 and goe as farre; He will reply, true indeed, but they do not what they do with a sound heart, but to be seen of men. Mark now, how these men feel a good heart in themselves, and in all things they doe, and therefore feel not a want of all good, which is poverty of spirit, and therefore here they fall short. *Isai.* 66. 2. there were divers Hypocrites forward for the worship of God in the Temple, but God loathes these, because not poor in spirit, to them only it is said the Lord will look. I have seen many professors very forward for all good duties, but as ignorant of Christ when they are sifted, as blocks. And if a man (as few doe) know not Christ, he must rest in his duties, because he knowes not Christ, to whom he must goe and be carried if ever he be saved. I have heard of a man that being condemned to die, thought 40 to escape the gallowes, and to save himselfe from hanging by a certain gift he said

1 **Herod,** Herod Antipas,̓ who beheaded John the Baptist, hated by Herodias, Herod's wife (Mark 6: 14-29)   12 **lust.** In margin: Hypocrites like the whore in the Proverbs, or like Jehu, zealous against Baal, but for their own ends   35 **Hypocrites.** In margin: God looks on the poor in spirit

he had of whistling; so men seek to save themselves by their gifts of *knowledge*, gifts
of *memory*, gifts of *prayer*, and when they see they must die for their sinnes, this is
the ruine of many a soule, that though he forsake Egypt and his sins, and fleshpots
there, and will never be so as he hath been, yet he never cometh into *Canaan*, but
loseth himself and his soul in a wildernesse of many *duties*, and there perisheth.

3. **Unregenerate men never take their rest in Christ onely.** Thirdly, if any unregenerate man come unto *Christ*, he never gets into *Christ*, that is, never takes his *eternall
rest* and *lodging in Jesus Christ only, Heb.* 4. 4. *Judas followed Christ for the Bagge,* he would
have the *Bag* and *Christ* too. The young man came unto Christ to be his Disciple,
10 but he would have *Christ* and the *world* too; they will not content themselves with
Christ alone, nor with the world alone, but make their markets out of both, like
whorish wives, that wil please their hu[s]bands and others too. Men in distresse of
conscience, if they have comfort from Christ, they are contented; if they have salvation from hell by Christ, they are contented: but Christ himself contents them not.
Thus far an hypocrite goes not. So much for the first Doctrine observed out of the
Text. I come now to the second.

Doct. 2. Salvation difficult. Doct. 2. *That those that are saved, are saved with much
difficulty: or it is a wonderfull hard thing to be saved.*

The gate is strait, and therefore a man must sweat and strive to enter; both the
20 entrance is difficult, and the progresse of salvation too. *Jesus Christ* is not got with
a wet finger. It is not wishing and desiring to be saved, will bring men to heaven;
hells mouth is full of *good wishes*. It is not shedding a tear at a Sermon, or blubber-
ing now and then in a corner, and saying over thy prayers, and crying God mercy
for thy sins, will save thee. It is not *Lord have mercy upon us,* will doe thee good. It
is not coming constantly to Church; these are easie matters. But it is a tough work,
a wonderfull hard matter to be saved, 1 *Pet.* 4. 18. Hence the way to heaven is compared to a *Race*, where a man must put forth all his strength, and stretch every limb,
and all to get forward. Hence a Christians life is compared to *wrestling, Eph.* 6. 12.
All the policy and power of hell buckle together against a Christian, therefore he
30 must look to himself, or else he falls. Hence it is compared to *fighting*, 2 *Tim.* 4. 7.
a man must fight against the *Devill,* the *World, Himself;* who shoot poysoned bullets
in the soul, where a man must kill or be killed. God hath not lined the way to Christ
with velvet, nor strewed it with rushes. He will never feed a slothfull humour in
man, who will be saved if Christ and Heaven would drop into their mouthes, and
if any would bear their charges thither: If *Christ* might be bought for a few cold
wishes, and lazie desires, he would be of small reckoning amongst men, who would
say, *lightly come lightly goe.* Indeed *Christs yoke is easie* in it self, and when a man is got
into Christ, nothing is so sweet; but for a carnall dull heart, it is hard to draw in it; for,

There are 4 strait gates wch every one must pass through before he can enter
40 into heavẽ.

---

20 got . . . finger. The sense is either that salvation is not obtained by seeing which way the wind is blowing and accommodating oneself accordingly, or that thumbing through one's Bible, wetting one's finger to
turn the pages, is insufficient   30 fighting. In margin: Salvation compared to fighting   40 heavẽ. In
margin: Four strait gates to be past through before we can enter into heaven

1. **The strait gate of humiliation.** 1. There is the straight gate of *Humiliation:* God saveth none, but first he humbleth them; now it is hard to pass through the gates and flames of hell; for a heart as stiffe [as] a stake, to bow; as hard as a stone, to bleed for the least prick, not to mourne for one sin, but all sins; and not for a fit, but all a mans life time; Oh it is hard for a man to suffer himself to be loaden with sinne, and prest to death for sin, so as never to love sinne more, but to spit in the face of that which he once loved as dearly as his life. It is easie to drop a tear or two, and be Sermon-sick; but to have a heart rent *for* sinne, and *from* sinne, this is true humiliation, and this is hard.

2. **Of the strait gate of faith.** 2. The straight gate of *Faith, Eph.* 1. 19. It's an easie   10
matter to presume, but hard to beleeve in Christ. It is easie for a man that was never humbled, to beleeve and say, *'Tis but beleeving:* but it is an hard matter for a man humbled, when he sees all his sins in order before him, the *Devill* and *Conscience* roaring upon him, and crying out against him, and God frowning upon him, now to call God *Father,* is an hard work. *Judas* had rather be hang'd than believe. It is hard to see a Christ as a rock to stand upon, when we are overwhelmed with sorrow of heart for sinne. It is hard to prize Christ above ten thousand words of pearl: 'tis hard to desire Christ, and nothing but Christ; hard to follow Christ all the day long, and never to be quiet till he is got in thine armes, and then with *Simeon* to say, *Lord now lettest thou thy servant depart in peace.*   20

3. **Of the strait gate of repentance.** 3. The strait gate of *Repentance.* It is an easie matter for a man to confesse himselfe to be a sinner, and to cry God forgivenesse untill next time: but to have a bitter sorrow and to turn from all sin, and to return to God, and all the waies of God; which is true repentance indeed; this is hard.

4. **Strait opposition.** 4. The strait gate of *opposition of Devils,* the *World,* and a mans own *Self,* who knock a man down when he begins to look toward Christ and heaven.

Use 5. Of instruction. Hence learn, that every easie way to heaven is a false way, although ministers should preach it out of their Pulpits, and Angels should publish it out of heaven.

Now there are nine easie wayes to heaven, (as men think) all which lead to hell.   30

Nine false waies to salvation discovered. 1. The broad way. 1. The common broad way, wherein a whole parish may all goe a breadth in it; tell these people they shal be damned; their answer is, then woe to many more besides me.

2. **The way of civill education.** 2. The way of *Civill education,* whereby many wilde natures are by little and little tamed, and like wolves are chained up easily when they are young.

3. **The way of good wishes.** 3. *Balams* way of *good wishes,* whereby many people will confesse their ignorance, forgetfulnesse, and that they cannot make such shewes as others doe, but they thank God their hearts are as good, and God for his part accepts (say they) the will for the deed. And, *My son give me thine heart;* the heart is all in   40
all, and so long they hope to doe well enough. Poor deluded creatures thus think to break through armies of *sinnes, Devils, temptations,* and to break open the very gates of Heaven with a few good wishes; they think to come to their journeys end without legs, because their hearts are good to God.

4. The way of formality. 4. The way of *Formality,* whereby men rest in the *perform-ance* of most or of all *externall duties* without inward life, *Mark.* 1. 14. Every man must have some *Religion,* some fig-leaves to hide their nakednesse. Now this Reli-gion must be either true Religion, or the false one; if the true, he must either take up the power of it, but that he will not, because it is burdensome; or the *forme* of it, and this being easie men embrace it as their God, and will rather lose their lives than their Religion thus taken up. This form of Religion is the easiest Religion in the world; partly, because it easeth men of trouble of conscience, quieting that: Thou has sinned, saith conscience, and God is offended, take a book and pray, keep thy
10 conscience better, and bring thy Bible with thee. Now conscience is silent, being charmed down with the form of Religion, as the Devill is driven away (as they say) with holy water; partly also because the form of religion credits a man, partly be-cause it is easie in it self; it's of a light carriage, being but the shadow and picture of the substance of religion; as now, what an easie matter it is to come to Church? They hear (at least outwardly) very attentively an hour and more, and then to turn to a proof, and to turn down a leaf, here's the form. But now to spend Saturday night, and all the whole Sabbath day morning, in trimming the Lamp, and in getting oyle in the heart to meet the Bridegroom the next day, and so meet him in the Word, and there to tremble at the voice of God, and suck the brest while it is open,
20 and when the word is done, to goe aside privately, and there to chew upon the word, there to lament with tears all the vain thoughts in duties, deadnesse in *hearing,* this is hard, because this is the power of godlinesse, and this men will not take up: so for private *prayer,* what an easie matter is it for a man to say over a few prayers out of some *devout book,* or to repeat some old prayer got by heart since a childe, or to have two or three short winded wishes for Gods mercy in the morning and at night; this form is easie: but now to prepare the heart by serious meditation of God and mans self before he praies, then to come to God with a bleeding hunger-starved heart, not only with a desire, but with a warrant, I must have such or such a mercy, and there to wrestle with God, although it be an hour or two together for a bless-
30 ing, this is too hard; men think none doe thus, and therefore they will not.

5. The way of presumption. Fifthly, the way of *presumption,* whereby men having seen their sins, catch hold easily upon Gods mercy, and snatch comforts, before they are reached out unto them. There is no word of comfort in the book of God in-tended for such as *regard iniquity in their hearts,* though they doe not act it in their lives. Their only comfort is, that the sentence of damnation is not yet executed upon them.

6. The way of sloth. Sixthly, the way of *sloth,* whereby men lie still, and say God must doe all; If the Lord would set up a Pulpit at the Alehouse door, it may be they would hear oftner. If God will alwaies thunder, they will alwaye pray; if strike
40 them now and then with sicknesse, God shall be paid with good words and promises enow, that they will be better if they live; but as long as peace lasts, they will run to Hell as fast as they can; and if God will not catch them, they care not, they will not return.

---

10 **Bible.** In margin: The consciences of unregenerate men are often silenced with a form of religion

7. **The way of carelesnesse.** Seventhly, the way of *carelesnesse,* when men feeling many difficulties, pass through some of them, but not all, and what they cannot get *now,* they feed themselves with a false hope they shall *hereafter:* they are content to be called Precisions, and fools, and crazie brains, but they want brokennesse of heart, and they will pray (it may be) for it, and passe by that difficulty; but to keep the wound alwaies open, this they will not doe, to be alwaies sighing for help, and never to give themselves rest till their hearts are humbled; that they will not; *these have a name to live, yet are dead.*

8. **The way of moderation.** Eighthly, the way of *moderation* or honest discretion, *Rev.* 3. 16. which indeed is nothing but lukewarmnesse of the soul, and that is, when a   10
man contrives and cuts out such a way to Heaven, as he may be hated of none, but   please all, and so do any thing for a quiet life, and so sleep in a whole skin. The Lord saith, *He that will live godly, must suffer persecution:* No, not so, Lord. Surely (think they) if men were discreet and wise, it would prevent a great deal of trouble and oposition in good courses; this man will commend those that are most zealous, if they were but wise; if he meet with a black-mouth'd forswearer, he will not reprove him, lest he be displeased with him; if he meet with an honest man, hee'l yeeld to all he saith, that so he may commend him; and when he meets them both together, they shall be both alike welcome, (what ever hee thinks) to his house and table, because he would fain be at peace with all men.   20

9. **The way of self-love.** Ninthly, and lastly, the way of Self-love, whereby a man fearing terribly he shall be damned, useth diligently all means whereby he shall be saved. Here is the strongest difficulty of all, to row against the stream, and to hate a mans self, and then to follow Christ fully.

1641

1603?—1683 Roger Williams

R oger Williams has an honored place in American history as the first vigorous proponent of the principles which stand first in the Bill of Rights: "Congress shall make no law respecting the establishment of religion, or prohibiting the free exercise thereof." The separation of church from state and the complete toleration of religious opinions, whatever they may be, are so basic to American democracy that it is easy to forget how rare they once were, and how bitter and long-continued a battle was necessary to achieve their general acceptance.

As several events in the twentieth century have revealed, the struggle is not merely a historical episode. Religious freedom is not even yet secure the world over. Roger Williams, whose central conviction was that the power of the civil state must not be used to enforce a specious uniformity of religious belief, speaks of a matter still crucial in the tangled affairs of humanity.

The exact date of Williams' birth is unknown because of the destruction of records in the Great Fire of London in 1666. He was born between 1603 and 1606 in London, the son of a moderately prosperous merchant. Sometime in his teens he learned shorthand and became the protégé of one of England's greatest lawyers, Sir Edward Coke (1552-1634). Through Coke's influence he entered Charterhouse School in 1621 and there did so well that he won a scholarship. With it and other rewards for his distinction as a student, he was able to take his B.A. degree in 1627 as a member of Pembroke Hall, Cambridge, subscribing, as was required, to the authority of the King, the *Book of Common Prayer,* and the Thirty-Nine Articles (the accepted body of doctrine) in the Church of England.

It is probable that Williams went to the university with the intention of preparing for the law. After taking his degree, however, he continued at Cambridge as a student of divinity. Already Puritan in his sympathies, he was unable to accept the prospect presented by the ecclesiastical measures and appointments of Charles I, who obviously planned to suppress all nonconformity. In the winter of 1628-1629, therefore, Williams left the university to become the household chaplain of an Essex country gentleman who had connections with a number of the leading promoters of the Massachusetts Bay Colony. By May of 1629 he was considering migration to New England, and in December of 1630 he sailed for Massachusetts. Meanwhile he had suffered the humiliation of having his proposal of marriage to a young lady rejected by her aunt on the ground of his low social rank, and had married a lady's maid — on the rebound but, as it turned out, very happily. By 1630 he had arrived at Separatist convictions; he believed, that is to say, that the individual congregation should be the ultimate authority in church government and that the civil state should not be permitted to enforce uniformity.

Williams' religious and political convictions did not become apparent, however, until he arrived in New England. There, chosen teacher of the church in Boston, he refused the post because that congregation still wished to regard themselves as Anglicans. Chosen teacher at Salem, where the church was Separatist, he was unable to take the post after John Winthrop and other officials remonstrated with the Salem people. He then spent some two years at Plymouth, working as a laborer and acquainting himself with the language and customs of the Indians — a missionary work for which all New England had cause to be thankful later. In the latter part of 1633 he returned to Salem; here followed the series of events which brought Williams into conflict with the ruling oligarchy of the Bay Colony and eventually resulted in his banishment. Much has been written about these events, which are intricately bound up with the political development of Massachusetts; it is sufficient here to note that the main points at issue were two: the validity of the royal charter upon which were based all titles to land in the colony, and the power of the civil magistrates to enforce religious conformity. Williams, through his acquaintance with the customs of the Indians, had come to believe that their land had been unjustly taken from them, and he had strenuously denied the right of the General Court to make laws regulating the churches. His congregation at Salem supported him until the civil authorities and the more conservative clergy secured his banishment in 1635. He found refuge with friendly Indians in what is now Rhode Island.

The remainder of Williams' life is a complicated story of religious and political events in a frontier colony. He left Separatism to join the first Baptist church to be organized in America; but a few months later he decided that he could belong to no church and became a Seeker, acknowledging no authority but the Bible and the works of God and waiting for the light of revelation. At the same time, he devoted himself to organizing a new colony where all churches should be free from civil control. Circumstances favored him. To lands purchased from the Indians there came settlers, many of them exiles like himself from the more authoritarian colonies. In 1644 Williams visited England, where he found the temper of the Puritans in power more akin to his own than to that of the Bay Colony; he was able to obtain a charter granting full self-government to the Providence Plantations.

Roger Williams the man is much better remembered than Roger Williams the writer. *A Key into the Language of America* (London, 1643) is, however, one of the most readable of the seventeenth-century books about the Indians. He was also the author of a lengthy tract against the doctrines of the founder of the Society of Friends, *George Fox Digg'd out of His Burrowes* (Boston, 1676). His chief activity as a writer was connected with two periods of residence in London, on behalf of his fellow settlers in Rhode Island. He was there in 1643-1644 and again in 1652-1654. His associates in London included many famous men, among them John Milton. While there, he wrote a series of pamphlets in which he debated the subject of persecution for cause of conscience — or, freedom of thought — with John Cotton, one of those responsible for his banishment from Massachusetts.

The Works of Roger Williams, ed. Perry Miller, seven vols., New York, 1963 (a revision with additions of the six-volume Narragansett Publications edition, Providence, 1866-1874)   James Ernst, **The Political Thought of Roger Williams,** University of Washington Publications in Language and Literature, Vol. VII, No. 1, Seattle, 1929   Perry Miller, **Roger Williams, His Contribution to the American Tradition,** Indianapolis, 1953   Ola E. Winslow, **Master Roger Williams, A Biography,** New York, 1957

from The Bloudy Tenent *Of Persecution, for Cause of Conscience,*
Discussed, in a Conference Between Truth and Peace

The debate between John Cotton and Roger Williams on religious liberty began with the appearance of A Letter of Mr. John Cotton to Mr. Williams, *published in London in the fall of 1643, at a time when the Westminster Assembly was debating the reorganization of the Church of England. In it Cotton defended the Bay Colony for banishing Williams and incidentally argued in favor of enforced uniformity of religion. Williams countered in*

January with Mr. Cottons Letter Lately Printed, Examined and Answered, *following it the next month with* Queries of Highest Consideration, *in which he advocated separation of church and state. In July, moreover, he published* The Bloudy Tenent of Persecution for Cause of Conscience. *He was then in London and so sympathetic with the Levellers, one of the most democratic of the extreme Puritan parties, that he asserted in* The Bloudy Tenent *that the foundation of the civil power lies in the people and "that such Governments as are by them erected and established, have no more power, nor for no longer time, than the civill power or people consenting and agreeing shall betrust them with." Parliament decided that such remarks were dangerous enough to justify an order that the book be burned by the public hangman. It was perhaps fortunate for Williams that he published it anonymously.*

Cotton remained in Boston but the debate went on. His Keyes of the Kingdom of Heaven and Power Thereof, *an argument for a Congregational establishment, was published in 1644, and another work,* The Controversies Concerning Liberty of Conscience in Matters of Religion Truly Stated, *appeared in 1646. He answered Williams specifically in 1647 with* The Bloudy Tenent Washed, and Made White in the Bloud of the Lambe *and* A Reply to Mr. Williams His Examination, and Answer of the Letter Sent to Him by John Cotton. *The discussion was concluded five years later, in 1652, with Williams'* The Bloudy Tenent Yet More Bloody: By Mr. Cottons Endevour to Wash It White in the Blood of the Lambe.

Since all these books are interdependent, each being organized in terms of its predecessor, they are difficult to represent adequately in short space. The selection which follows consists of the introduction and the first two chapters of The Bloudy Tenent of Persecution for Cause of Conscience. *Only a part of Williams' argument is included, but the humanity of his position, the dialogue method which he used, and the occasional eloquence of his style are sufficiently evident.*

To every Courteous Reader.

While I plead the Cause of *Truth* and *Innocencie* against the bloody *Doctrine* of *Persecution* for cause of *conscience,* I judge it not unfit to give *alarme* to my selfe, and all men to prepare to be *persecuted* or hunted for cause of *conscience.*

Whether thou standest charged with 10 or but 2 *Talents,* if thou huntest any for cause of *conscience,* how canst thou say thou followest the *Lambe* of *God* who so abhorr'd that practice?

If *Paul,* if *Jesus Christ* were present here at *London,* and the *question* were proposed what *Religion* would they approve of: The *Papists, Prelatists, Presbyterians, Independents,*
10 &c. would each say, Of mine, of mine.

But put the second question, if one of the several sorts should by *major vote* attaine the *Sword* of steel: what weapons doth Christ Jesus authorize them to fight with in His cause? Doe not all men hate the *persecutor,* and every *conscience* true or false complaine of cruelty, tyranny? &c.

Two *mountaines* of crying *guilt* lye heavie upon the backes of All that name the name of *Christ* in the eyes of *Jewes, Turkes,* and *Pagans.*

Text: Narragansett Club Publications, ed. Samuel Caldwell, III, 1867   5 **Talents,** see Matthew 25: 14-30   9 **Papists . . . Independents,** forms of church governments, differing on whether the supreme authority should lie with the Pope, the King and his bishops, the presbyter, or individual congregations

First, The blasphemies of their *Idolatrous inventions, superstitions,* and most *unchristian conversations.*

Secondly, The bloody irreligious and inhumane *oppressions* and *destructions* under the maske or vaile of the Name of *Christ,* &c.

O how like is the *jealous Jehovah,* the consuming fire to end these present *slaughters* in a greater slaughter of the holy Witnesses? *Rev.* 11.

Six yeares preaching of so much Truth of *Christ* (as that time afforded in K. *Edwards* dayes) kindles the flames of Q. Marie's bloody *persecutions.*

Who can now but expect that after so many scores of yeares *preaching* and *professing* of more *Truth,* and amongst so many great *contentions* amongst the very best   10 of *Protestants,* a fierie furnace should be heat, and who sees not now the *fires* kindling?

I confesse I have little hopes till those flames are over, that this Discourse against the *doctrine* of *persecution* for cause of *conscience* should passe currant (I say not amongst the *Wolves* and *Lions,* but even amongst the *Sheep* of *Christ* themselves) yet *liberavi animam meam,* I have not hid within my *breast* my *souls* belief: And although sleeping on the bed either of the pleasures or profits of sinne thou thinkest thy conscience bound to smite at him that dares to waken thee? Yet in the middest of all these *civill* and *spirituall Wars* (I hope we shall agree in these particulars.)

First, how ever the proud (upon the advantage of an higher earth or ground) or'elooke the poore and cry out *Schismatickes, Hereticks,* &c. shall *blasphemers* and   20 *seducers* scape unpunished? &c. Yet there is a sorer punishment in the *Gospel* for despising of *Christ* then *Moses,* even when the despiser of *Moses* was put to death without mercie, *Heb.* 10. 28, 29. He that beleeveth not shall bee damned, *Marke* 16. 16.

Secondly, what ever Worship, Ministry, Ministration, the best and purest are practised without *faith* and true perswasion that they are the true institutions of God, they are sin, sinfull worships, Ministries, &c. And however in Civill things we may be servants unto men, yet in Divine and Spirituall things the poorest *pesant* must disdaine the service of the highest *Prince:* Be ye not the servants of men, I Cor. 14.

Thirdly, without search and triall no man attaines this faith and right perswasion,   30 I *Thes.* 5. Try all things.

In vaine have *English Parliaments* permitted *English Bibles* in the poorest *English* houses, and the simplest man or woman to search the Scriptures, if yet against their soules perswasion from the Scripture, they should be forced (as if they lived in *Spaine* or *Rome* it selfe without the sight of a *Bible*) to beleeve as the Church beleeves.

Fourthly, having tried, we must hold fast, I *Thessal.* 5. upon the losse of a Crowne, *Revel.* 13. we must not let goe for all the flea bitings of the present afflictions, &c. having bought Truth deare, we must not sell it cheape, not the least graine of it for the whole World, no not for the saving of Soules, though our owne most precious; least of all for the bitter sweetning of a little vanishing pleasure.   40

---

8 **K. Edwards dayes . . . persecutions.** The reign of Edward VI, 1547-1553, brought the *Book of Common Prayer* and the Forty-Two Articles; the reign of Mary, 1553-1558, in which an attempt was made to restore Roman Catholicism, saw about two hundred dissentients burned at the stake   14 **liberavi animam meam,** I have liberated my soul

For a little puffe of credit and reputation from the changeable breath of uncertaine sons of men.

For the broken bagges of Riches on Eagles wings: For a dreame of these, any or all of these which on our death-bed vanish and leave tormenting stings behinde them: Oh how much better is it from the love of Truth, from the love of the Father of lights, from whence it comes, from the love of the Sonne of God, who is the way and the Truth, to say as he, *John* 18. 37. For this end was I borne, and for this end came I into the World that I might beare witnesse to the Truth.

The Answer of Mr. Iohn Cotton of Boston in New-England, to the Aforesaid Arguments Against Persecution For Cause of Conscience Professedly Maintaining Persecution For Cause of Conscience

The *Question* which you put, is, Whether *Persecution* for cause of *Conscience,* be not against the *Doctrine* of *Jesus Christ* the *King of Kings.*

Now by *Persecution* for Cause of *Conscience,* I conceive you meane, either for professing some point of *Doctrine* which you believe in Conscience to be the Truth, or for practising some *Worke* which in *Conscience* you believe to be a *Religious Duty.*

Now in Points of *Doctrine* some are *fundamentall,* without right beliefe whereof a Man cannot be *saved:* Others are *circumstantiall* or lesse principall, wherein Men may differ in judgement, without prejudice of *salvation* on either part.

In like sort, in Points of *Practice,* some concerne the weightier Duties of the *Law,* as, What *God* we worship, and with what kinde of *Worship;* whether such, as if it be *Right,* fellowship with *God* is held; if *Corrupt,* fellowship with Him is lost.

Againe, in Points of *Doctrine* and *Worship* lesse Principall: either they are held forth in a meeke and *peaceable* way, though the Things be *Erroneous* or unlawfull: Or they are held forth with such *Arrogance* and *Impetuousnesse,* as tendeth and reacheth (even of it selfe) to the disturbance of *Civill Peace.*

Finally, let me adde this one distinction more: When we are persecuted for *Conscience* sake, It is either for *Conscience* rightly informed, or for erronious and blind *Conscience.* These things premised, I would lay down mine Answer to the Question in certaine *Conclusions.*

First, it is not lawfull to persecute any for *Conscience* sake *Rightly informed;* for in *persecuting* such, *Christ* himselfe is persecuted in them. *Acts* 9. 4.

Secondly, for an *Erronious* and *blind Conscience,* (even in fundamentall and weighty Points) It is not lawfull to persecute any, till after *Admonition* once or twice: and so the Apostle directeth, *Tit.* 3. 10. and giveth the Reason, that in *fundamentall* and principall points of Doctrine or Worship, the Word of *God* in such things is so cleare, that hee cannot but bee convinced in *Conscience* of the dangerous Errour of his way, after once or twice *Admonition,* wisely and faithfully dispensed. And then if any one persist, it is not out of *Conscience,* but against *his Conscience,* as the Apostle saieth, *vers.* 11. He is subverted and sinneth, being condemned of Himselfe, that is, of his owne *Conscience.* So that if such a Man after such Admonition shall still *per*sist in the *Errour* of his way, and be therefore punished; He is not *persecuted* for Cause of *Conscience*, but for sinning *against* his Owne *Conscience*.

A Reply to the Aforesaid Answer of Mr. Cotton in a Conference Betweene Truth and Peace

Chapter I

Truth. In what *darke corner* of the World *(sweet Peace)* are *we two* met? How hath this present evill *World* banished *Me* from all the Coasts & Quarters of it? and how hath the Righteous *God* in judgement taken *Thee* from the *Earth*, Rev. 6. 4.

Peace. 'Tis lamentably true *(blessed Truth)* the *foundations* of the *World* have long been out of course: the *Gates* of *Earth* and *Hell* have conspired together to intercept our joyfull *meeting* and our holy *kisses:* With what a wearied, *tyred Wing* have I flowne over *Nations, Kingdomes, Cities, Townes*, to finde out precious *Truth?*

Truth. The like enquiries in my flights and travells have I made for *Peace,* and still 10 am told, she hath left the *Earth*, and fled to *Heaven.*

Peace. Deare *Truth,* What is the *Earth* but a *dungeon of darknesse,* where *Truth* is not?

Truth. And what's the *Peace* thereof but a fleeting *dreame,* thine *Ape* and *Counterfeit?*

Peace. O where's the Promise of the *God* of *Heaven,* that *Righteousnes* and *Peace* shall *kisse* each other?

Truth. Patience (sweet *Peace*) these *Heavens* and *Earth* are growing *Old,* and shall be changed like a *Garment,* Psal. 102. They shall melt away, and be burnt up with all the *Works* that are therein; and the most high *Eternall Creatour,* shall gloriously 20 create *New Heavens* and *New Earth,* wherein dwells *Righteousnesse,* 2 Pet. 3. Our *kisses* then shall have their *endlesse* date of pure and sweetest ioyes? till then both *Thou* and *I* must hope, and wait, and beare the furie of the *Dragons* wrath, whose *monstrous Lies* and *Furies* shall with himselfe be cast into the *lake* of *Fire,* the *second death,* Revel. 20.

Peace. Most precious Truth, thou knowest we are both pursued and laid for: Mine *heart* is full of sighes, mine *eyes* with teares: Where can I better vent my full oppressed *bosome,* then into *thine,* whose faithfull *lips* may for these few houres revive my drooping wandring *spirits,* and here begin to *wipe Teares* from mine eyes, and the eyes of my dearest *Children?*   30

Truth. Sweet daughter of the *God* of *Peace,* begin; powre out thy *sorrowes,* vent thy *complaints:* how joyfull am I to improve these precious Minutes to revive our *Hearts,* both thine and mine, and the hearts of all that *love* the *Truth* and *Peace,* Zach. 8.

Answer, a paper written by Cotton (1585-1652) in answer to questions sent him, apparently, by a Baptist. It was not directly aimed at Williams' position. In logic and cocksureness it is typical of Cotton   7 **The Gates.** In margin: Truth and Peace rarely and seldom meete   23 **Dragons wrath,** Satan's wrath. Revelation 20:2: "And he laid hold on the dragon, that old serpent, which is the Devil, and Satan. . . ." There are many echoes of the Book of Revelation in this chapter

Peace. Deare Truth, I know thy *birth,* thy *nature,* thy *delight.* They that know thee, will *prize* thee farre above themselves and lives, and *sell themselves to buy thee.* Well spake that famous *Elizabeth* to her famous *attorney* Sir *Edward Coke:* Mr. *Attourney,* goe on as thou hast begun, and still plead, not *pro Domina Regina,* but *pro Domina Veritate.*

Truth. 'Tis true, my *Crowne* is high, my *Scepter's* strong to breake down *strongest holds,* to throw down highest *Crownes* of all that plead (though but in thought) against me. Some few there are, but oh how few are valiant for the *Truth,* and dare to *plead* my *Cause,* as my *Witnesses* in sack-cloth, Revel. 11. While all men's *Tongues*
10 are bent like *Bowes* to shoot out lying words against Me!

Peace. O how could I spend *eternall dayes* and *endlesse dates* at thy holy feet, in listning to the precious Oracles of thy mouth! All the Words of thy mouth are *Truth,* and there is no *iniquity* in them; Thy *lips* drop as the hony-combe. But oh! since we must part anon, let us (as thou saidst) improve our *Minutes,* and (according as thou promisedst) revive me with thy words, which are sweeter then the honey and the honey-combe.

Chapter II

Deare *Truth,* I have two sad *Complaints:*

First, the most sober of thy *Witnesses,* that dare to *plead* thy *Cause,* how are they charged to be *mine Enemies, contentious, turbulent, seditious?*
20 Secondly, Thine *Enemies,* though they speake and raile against thee, though they outragiously *pursue, imprison, banish, kill* thy faithfull *Witnesses,* yet how is all vermillion'd o're for *Justice* 'gainst the *Hereticks?* Yea, if they kindle coales, and blow the flames of *devouring Warres,* that leave neither *Spirituall* nor *Civill State,* but burns up *Branch* and *Root,* yet how doe all pretend an *holy War?* He that *kills,* and hee that's *killed,* they both cry out, It is for *God,* and for their *conscience.*

Tis true, nor one nor other seldome dare to plead the mighty Prince *Christ Jesus* for their *Authour,* yet both (both *Protestant* and *Papist*) pretend they have spoke with *Moses* and the *Prophets,* who all, say they (before *Christ* came) allowed such *holy persecutions, holy Warres* against the enemies of holy *Church.*
30 *Truth. Deare Peace* (to ease thy first *complaint*) tis true, thy dearest *Sons,* most like their mother, *Peace-keeping, Peace-making* Sons of God, have borne and still must beare the *blurs* of *troublers* of *Israel,* and turners of the *World* upside downe. And tis true againe, what *Salomon* once spake: The *beginning* of *strife* is as when one letteth out *Water,* therefore (saith he) leave off *contention* before it be medled with. This *Caveat* should keepe the *bankes* and *sluces* firme and strong, that *strife,* like a *breach of waters,* breake not in upon the sons of men.

Yet *strife* must be distinguished: It is *necessary* or *unnecessary, godly* or *ungodly, Christian* or *unchristian,* &c.

---

4 **pro . . . Veritate,** not for Mistress Queen, but for Mistress Truth   17 **Complaints.** In margin: Great complaints of Peace   26 **true.** In margin: Persecutors seldom plead Christ, but Moses for their Author   33 **Salomon.** See Proverbs 17:14   34 **Caveat,** warning   37 **strife.** In margin: Strife distinguished

1. **Ungodly strife.** It is *unnecessary, unlawfull, dishonourable, ungodly, unchristian,* in most cases in the world, for there is a *possibility* of keeping *sweet Peace* in most cases, and if it be *possible,* it is the expresse command of *God* that *Peace* be kept, *Rom.* 13.

2. **Godly strife.** Againe, it is *necessary, honourable, godly,* &c. with *civill* and earthly *weapons* to *defend* the *innocent,* and to *rescue* the oppressed from the violent *pawes* and *jaws* of oppressing persecuting *Nimrods,* Psal. 73. Job 29.

It is as *necessary,* yea more *honourable, godly,* and *Christian,* to *fight* the *fight* of *faith,* with *religious* and *spirituall Artillery,* and to *contend earnestly* for the *faith* of *Jesus, once* delivered to the *Saints* against all *opposers,* and the *gates* of *earth* and *hell, men* or *devils,* yea against *Paul* himselfe, or an *Angell* from *heaven,* if he bring any other *faith* or 10 *doctrine, Jude* vers. 4. *Gal.* 1. 8.

Peace. With the *clashing* of such *Armes* am I never *wakened.* Speake once againe (deare Truth) to my second *complaint* of bloody *persecution,* and devouring *wars,* marching under the colours of upright *Justice,* and holy *Zeale,* &c.

A threefold dolefull cry. *Truth.* Mine eares have long beene filled with a threefold dolefull *Outcry.*

First, of one hundred forty Foure thousand *Virgins* (*Rev.* 14.) forc'd and ravisht by *Emperours, Kings* and *Governours* to their beds of *worship* and *Religion,* set up (like *Absaloms*) on high in their severall *States* and *Countries.*

Secondly, the cry of those precious *soules* under the *Altar* (*Rev.* 6.) the *soules* of 20 such as have beene persecuted and slaine for the testimony and *witnesse* of *Jesus,* whose *bloud* hath beene spilt like *water* upon the *earth,* and that because they have held fast the *truth* and *witnesse* of *Jesus,* against the *worship* of the *States* and *Times,* compelling to an *uniformity* of *State Religion.*

These *cries* of *murthered Virgins* who can sit still and *heare?* Who can but run with zeale inflamed to prevent the *deflowring* of *chaste soules,* and spilling of the *bloud* of the *innocent?* *Humanity* stirs up and prompts the *Sonnes* of men to draw *materiall swords* for a *Virgins chastity* and *life,* against a *ravishing murtherer?* And *Piety* and *Christianity* must needs awaken the *Sons* of *God* to draw the *spirituall sword* (the Word of God) to preserve the *chastity* and *life* of *spirituall Virgins,* who abhorre the 30 spirituall *defilements* of *false worship, Rev.* 14.

Thirdly, the *cry* of the *whole earth,* made *drunke* with the *bloud* of its *inhabitants,* slaughtering each other in their *blinded zeale,* for *Conscience,* for *Religion,* against the *Catholickes,* against the *Lutherans,* &c.

What fearfull *cries* within these twenty years of hundred *thousands* men, women, children, fathers, mothers, husbands, wives, brethren, sisters, old and young, high and low, *plundred, ravished, slaughtered, murthered, famished?* And hence these cries, that men fling away the *spirituall sword* and *spirituall artillery* (in *spirituall* and *religious* causes) and rather trust for the suppressing of each others *God, Conscience,* and *Religion* (as they suppose) to an *arme* of *flesh,* and *sword* of *steele?*   40

Truth. Sweet Peace, what hast thou there?

Peace. *Arguments* against *persecution* for cause of *Conscience.*

Truth. And what there?

Peace. An *Answer* to such *Arguments,* contrarily maintaining such *persecution* for cause of *Conscience.*

Truth. These *Arguments* against such persecution, and the *Answer* pleading for it, written (as *Love* hopes) from godly *intentions, hearts,* and *hands,* yet in a marvellous different *stile* and *manner.* The *Arguments* against *persecution* in *milke,* the *Answer* for it (as I may say) in *bloud.*

The *Authour* of these *Arguments* (against *persecution*) (as I have beene informed)
10 being committed by *some* then in power, *close prisoner* to *Newgate,* for the witnesse of some *truths* of *Jesus,* and having not the use of *Pen* and *Inke,* wrote these *Arguments* in *Milke,* in sheets of Paper, brought to him by the *Woman* his *Keeper,* from a friend in *London,* as the *stopples* of his *Milk bottle.*

In such Paper written with *Milk* nothing will appear, but the way of reading it by *fire* being knowne to this *friend* who received the Papers, he transcribed and kept together the Papers, although the *Author* himselfe could not correct, nor view what himselfe had written.

It was in *milke,* tending to soule *nourishment,* even for *Babes* and Sucklings in *Christ.*

20 It was in *milke,* spiritually *white,* pure and innocent, like those *white horses* of the *Word* of *truth* and *meeknesse,* and the *white Linnen* or *Armour* of *righteousnesse,* in the *Army* of *Jesus. Rev.* 6. & 19.

It was in *milke,* soft, meeke, peaceable and gentle, tending both to the *peace* of *soules,* and the *peace* of *States* and Kingdomes.

Peace. The *Answer* (though I hope out of milkie pure intentions) is returned in *bloud: bloudy* & slaughterous *conclusions; bloudy* to the *souls* of all men, forc'd to the *Religion* and *Worship* which every civil State or Common-weale agrees on, and compells all subjects to in a dissembled *uniformitie.*

Bloudy to the *bodies,* first of the holy *witnesses* of *Christ Jesus,* who testifie against
30 such invented worships.

Secondly, of the *Nations* and Peoples slaughtering each other for their severall respective Religions and Consciences.

1644?, 1644

---

5 **These Arguments.** In margin: The wonderfull providéce of God in the writing of the Arguments against persecution in Milke   14 **way . . . fire,** that is, by heating the paper so that the writing appears   25 **The Answer.** In margin: The Answer writ in Bloud

1663–1728 Cotton Mather

Pedant, neurotic, megalomaniac, reactionary, benighted witch hunter — so has Cotton Mather come to be known to later generations, who have accepted him as the best example of New England Puritanism gone to seed. There is truth in the judgment, or enough so that no one is likely to grow fond of either the man or the writer; and yet to understand Cotton Mather is possibly a sure way to explore intellectual America between 1680 and 1728.

Mather's outward life was uneventful. He was born in Boston in 1663, the son of the Rev. Increase Mather and the grandson of the Rev. John Cotton. Of his boyhood, if it can be called that, we know very little except that he was incredibly pious and industrious and that he suffered from an impediment in his speech. Writing of his early life, for the benefit of his son, he lamented "early Ebullitions of *Original Sin*," but confessed that at the age of seven or eight he was composing forms of prayer for his schoolmates and rebuking them for "their wicked *words* and *ways.*" "And sometimes," he added, "I suffered from them, the persecution of not only *Scoffs* but Blows also for my Rebukes." At eleven, according to the same account, he wrote and spoke Latin with great facility, had gone through most of the New Testament in Greek, and had begun his Hebrew grammar. When he received his B.A. degree from Harvard College in 1678, he was fourteen, the youngest graduate then on record. His stammering relieved (convincing evidence to him of God's special favor), he put aside his plan of becoming a physician to follow his family's calling, the ministry. After taking his M.A. in 1681, also at Harvard, he continued to assist his father at the Second, or Old North, Church, where he was installed as co-minister in 1685. There he remained all his life, marrying three times, burying most of his fifteen children, preaching literally thousands of sermons, and writing untiringly. He published 444 separate items, and much is still in manuscript.

Outside of his personal idiosyncrasies, which were many and, at this distance, unpleasant, Mather was handicapped chiefly by nostalgia. He suffered from a lifelong yearning for the good old days when a New England clergyman wielded virtually sovereign power and regarded himself, quite rightly, as playing a leading rôle in a world-wide drama. Doubtless the good old days were never quite what Cotton Mather thought they were, and the Puritan Revolution not as all-important as it seemed. So intent was Mather upon preserving the "old New England way" that he was in many ways backward-looking, committed to a delaying action against new forces. Although he was never such a popular leader as his father, he was so prolific a writer that he has come to represent to many people the whole story of American Puritanism, a result which he himself would have regarded as unfortunate.

His most famous books, and indeed the bulk of his works, are best interpreted as efforts to strengthen the position of the church in a society which was growing steadily more worldly. *The Wonders of the Invisible World* (1693), the classic account of the tragedy of Salem witchcraft, is a monument to credulity; but it is also the result of a conviction, which Cotton Mather shared with pious and intelligent men on both sides of the Atlantic, that to give up a belief in spirits was to sell out to materialism. The vast *Magnalia Christi Americana* (1702) was designed to bind New Englanders to the religion of their forefathers by arousing pride in their spiritual inheritance. *The Christian Philosopher* (1721) sought to demonstrate that science was "no *Enemy,* but a mighty and wondrous *Incentive to Religion.*" And the *Manuductio ad Ministerium* (1726) was his mature advice to candidates for the ministry.

For all his efforts, Mather did not reinvigorate religion, as Jonathan Edwards was soon to do. He wrote too much and thought too little for that. His inveterate habit of paraphrasing freely from the books of others, on the theory that he could thereby edify his provincial audience, kept him almost always upon the surface of the world of ideas. There, however, he ranged widely, and often modified or shifted his intellectual position. *The Christian Philosopher, Manuductio ad Ministerium,* and *Bonifacius* (1710), better known as *Essays to Do Good,* show an amazing adjustment to scientific, humanitarian, and philanthropic movements which were, in the end, to build a new kind of society. Mather did not always understand their implications, but he was so anxious to be informative that his books mirror their age.

Sermons, biographies, theological treatises, essays, handbooks for his parishioners, letters, poems, and various other types of writing flowed steadily from his pen. He also kept one of the fullest and most self-revealing of Puritan diaries. He cultivated and defended an elaborate, allusion-studded style which modern readers are likely to find pedantic and antiquated. Both his literary forms and his style, however, sought to preserve provincial Boston's place in the sun.

Selections from Cotton Mather, ed. K. B. Murdock, New York, 1926   T. J. Holmes, Cotton Mather, A Bibliography of His Works, 3 vols., Cambridge, 1940   Barrett Wendell, Cotton Mather, the Puritan Priest, New York, 1891

from # The Wonders of the Invisible World

The Salem "witchcraft episode" began at Salem Village, now Danvers, Massachusetts, during the winter of 1691-1692, with the nine-year-old daughter, the eleven-year-old niece, and the West Indian servant, half Indian, half Negro, of the Rev. Samuel Parris. The children became "afflicted"; that is, they flew into fits and complained of being pricked, bitten, pinched, or choked by invisible hands, of being tormented by apparitions. When a gathering of ministers examined them and decided they were bewitched, they named, after much urging, three tormentors: an obvious neurotic, a miserable old woman, and Tituba, the West Indian servant. In March, publicly examined by Salem magistrates, Tituba confessed to the practice of witchcraft, naming the other two women as her accomplices. By May about one hundred persons were confined, awaiting trial.

To meet this situation the new governor, Sir William Phips, appointed a special court of oyer and terminer, to investigate and to try the witchcraft cases. On evidence such as appears in this selection, the seven magistrates sent Bridget Bishop to the gallows in June. In July five others were hanged; in August, six; in September, fourteen. One eighty-year-old man was pressed to death beneath heavy stones because, fearing that his conviction would forfeit the property he hoped to leave his family, he refused to plead either guilty or not guilty. Forty-five individuals confessed themselves witches and thus escaped death; all those who were executed maintained their innocence to the end. Altogether, more than two hundred persons were accused or suspected. At length the accusations became so numerous and so absurd that the prosecutions were abandoned and the confessed witches freed.

Scholars have disagreed violently about the extent to which Increase and Cotton Mather should be held responsible for this amazing episode. Their apologists point out (1) that the vast majority of educated men of the day, whatever their religious affiliations, believed in witchcraft; (2) that Increase Mather, who returned from England in the midst of the mania, urged the utmost caution in weighing the evidence; and (3) that Cotton Mather wrote his account of the trials out of friendship for the magistrates involved. Against these facts one must weigh the intangible effects of Increase Mather's Essay for the Recording of Illustrious Providences *(1684) and Cotton Mather's* Memorable Providences, Relating to Witchcrafts and Possessions *(1689). Both books collected accounts of Satan's activities against New England, with the intention of combating materialism and religious indifference. Although the Mathers were following in the footsteps of such English writers as Joseph Glanvill, Henry More, and Richard Baxter, possibly their books contributed to the state of mind which lay behind the explosion at Salem Village.*

The Wonders of the Invisible World, *for which many generations have condemned Cotton Mather as benighted and superstitious, was written in September and October 1692. Two Boston imprints appeared in 1693, and there were three London editions in the same year. More recently it has been several times reprinted, together with Robert Calef's* More Wonders of the Invisible World *(London, 1700), a rationalist attack on the outbreak.*

The Trial of Bridget Bishop, Alias, Oliver at the Court of Oyer and Terminer Held at Salem, June 2, 1692

I

She was Indicted for Bewitching of several persons in the Neighbourhood, the Indictment being drawn up, according to the *Form* in such Cases usual. And pleading, *Not Guilty,* there were brought in several persons, who had long undergone many kinds of Miseries, which were preternaturally Inflicted, and generally ascribed unto an horrible *Witchcraft.* There was little Occasion to prove the *Witchcraft;* it

---

Text: the first Boston edition, 1693   **Bridget Bishop,** previously married to a man named Oliver, had long had a bad reputation in Salem Village and had once before been accused of witchcraft. She was the first to be tried and hanged.   2 **the Form . . . usual,** based upon procedures of the English common law, developed during frequent prosecutions for witchcraft under statutes adopted in 1563 and 1604.

being Evident and Notorious to all Beholders. Now to fix the *Witchcraft* on the Prisoner at the Bar, the first thing used, was, the Testimony of the *Bewitched;* whereof, several Testify'd That the *Shape* of the Prisoner did oftentimes very grievously Pinch them, choak them, Bite them, & Afflict them; urging them to write their Names in a *Book,* which the said Spectre called, *Ours.* One of them did further Testify, that it was the *Shape* of this Prisoner, with another, which one Day took her from her Wheel, and carrying her to the River side, threatned there to Drown her, if she did not Sign to the Book mentioned: which yet she refused. Others of them did also Testify, that the said *Shape* did in her Threats brag to them that she
10 had been the Death of sundry persons, then by her Named; that she had *Ridden* a man, then likewise Named. Another Testify'd, the Apparition of *Ghosts* unto the Spectre of *Bishop,* crying out, *You Murdered us!* About the Truth whereof, there was in the matter of Fact, but too much Suspicion.

II. It was Testify'd, That at the Examination of the Prisoner, before the Magistrates, the Bewitched were extreamly Tortured. If she did but cast her Eyes on them, they were presently struck down; and this in such a manner as there could be no Collusion in the Business. But upon the Touch of her Hand upon them, when they lay in their Swoons, they would immediately Revive; and not upon the Touch of any ones else. Moreover, upon some Special Actions of her Body, as the shaking
20 of her Head, or the Turning of her Eyes, they presently and painfully fell into the like postures. And many of the like Accidents now fell out, while she was at the Bar. One at the same time testifying, That she said, *She could not be Troubled to see the Afflicted thus Tormented.*

III. There was Testimony likewise brought in, that a man striking once at the place, where a Bewitched person said, the *Shape* of this *Bishop* stood, the bewitched cryed out, that he had Tore her Coat, in the place then particularly specify'd; and the Womans Coat, was found to be Torn in that very place.

IV. One *Deliverance Hobbs,* who had Confessed her being a Witch, was now Tormented by the Spectres, for her Confession. And she now Testify'd, That this
30 *Bishop,* tempted her to Sign the *Book* again, and to Deny what she had Confess'd. She affirmed, that it was the Shape of this Prisoner, which whipped her with Iron Rods, to compel her thereunto. And she affirmed, that this *Bishop* was at a General Meeting of the Witches, in a Field at *Salem*-Village and there partook of a Diabolical Sacrament, in Bread and Wine then Administred!

---

3 **Shape . . . Prisoner.** The crucial point in the prosecutions was "spectral evidence." The magistrates acted on the assumption that evil spirits could not assume the shapes of innocent persons. Consequently if an accuser testified under oath to seeing the apparition of his tormentor, and identified it, his very accusation was accepted as proof of guilt.   5 **Book,** the large black book in which a witch inscribed his name to seal his contract with Satan. The signature was ordinarily made with the blood of the signer, as in the Faust legend.   7 **Wheel,** spinning wheel   10 **Ridden a man,** an allusion to the folk belief in incubi, from which the term "nightmare" is derived   15 **cast her Eyes,** an instance of the "evil eye," upon which the Salem judges pondered at some length   32 **General . . . Witches,** the Sabbat, the sacrilegious and obscene parody of the mass and other sacraments which constituted a central feature of the folklore of witchcraft. Goethe used it skillfully in *Faust,* and Hawthorne in "Goodman Brown" (see p. 1286); it survives in the Halloween figures of witches on broomsticks, on which they were supposed to ride to such meetings

V. To render it further Unquestionable, that the prisoner at the Bar, was the Person truly charged in THIS *Witchcraft,* there were produced many Evidences of OTHER *Witchcrafts,* by her perpetrated. For Instance, *John Cook* testify'd, that about five or six years ago, One morning, about Sun-Rise, he was in his Chamber assaulted by the *Shape* of this prisoner: which Look'd on him, grin'd at him, and very much hurt him, with a Blow on the side of the Head: and that on the same day, about Noon, the same *Shape* walked in the Room where he was, and an Apple strangely flew out of his Hand, into the Lap of his mother, six or eight foot from him.

VI. *Samuel Gray,* testify'd, That about fourteen years ago, he wak'd on a Night, & saw the Room where he lay, full of Light; & that he then saw plainly a Woman 10 between the Cradle, and the Bed-side, which look'd upon him. He Rose, and it vanished; tho' he found the Doors all fast. Looking out at the Entry-Door he saw the same Woman, in the same Garb again; and said, *In Gods Name, what do you come for?* He went to Bed, and had the same Woman again assaulting him. The Child in the Cradle gave a great schreech, and the Woman Disappeared. It was long before the Child could be quieted; and tho' it were a very likely thriving Child, yet from this time it pined away, and after divers months dy'd in a sad Condition. He knew not *Bishop,* nor her Name; but when he saw her after this, he knew by her Countenance, and Apparrel, and all Circumstances, that it was the Apparition of this *Bishop,* which had thus troubled him.   20

VII. *John Bly* and his wife, testify'd, that he bought a sow of *Edward Bishop,* the Husband of the prisoner; and was to pay the price agreed, unto another person. This Prisoner being Angry that she was thus hindred from fingring the money, Quarrell'd with *Bly.* Soon after which the Sow, was taken with strange Fits; Jumping, Leaping, and Knocking her head against the Fence; she seem'd Blind and Deaf, and would neither eat nor be suck'd. Whereupon a neighbour said, she believed the Creature was *Over-Looked;* & sundry other circumstances concurred, which made the Deponents Belive that *Bishop* had Bewitched it.

VIII. *Richard Coman* testify'd, that eight years ago, as he lay Awake in his Bed, with a Light Burning in the Room, he was annoy'd with the Apparition of this 30 *Bishop,* and of two more that were strangers to him; who came and oppressed him so that he could neither stir himself, nor wake any one else; and that he was the night after, molested again in the like manner; the said *Bishop* taking him by the Throat, and pulling him almost out of the Bed. His Kinsman offered for this cause to lodge with him; and that Night, as they were Awake, Discoursing together: this *Coman* was once more visited, by the Guests which had formerly been so troublesome; his kinsman being at the same time strook speechless and unable to move Hand or Foot. He had laid his sword by him; which these unhappy spectres, did strive much to wrest from him; only he held too fast for them. He then grew able to call the People of his house; but altho' they heard him, yet they had not power 40 to speak or stirr, until at last, one of the people crying out, *what's the matter!* the spectres all vanished.

---

9 **Samuel Gray,** who, according to Calef, repented his "wholly groundless" accusation on his deathbed

IX. *Samuel Shattock* testify'd, That in the Year 1680, this *Bridget Bishop,* often came to his house upon such frivolous and foolish errands, that they suspected she came indeed with a purpose of mischief. Presently whereupon his eldest child, which was of as promising Health & Sense, as any child of its Age, began to droop exceedingly; & the oftener that *Bishop* came to the House, the worse grew the Child. As the Child would be standing at the Door, he would be thrown and bruised against the Stones, by an Invisible Hand, and in like sort knock his Face against the sides of the House, and bruise it after a miserable manner. Afterwards this *Bishop* would bring him things to Dy, whereof he could not Imagine any use; and
10 when she paid him a piece of Money, the Purse and Money were unaccountably conveyed out of a Lock'd box, and never seen more. The Child was immediately hereupon taken with terrible fits, whereof his Friends thought he would have dyed: indeed he did almost nothing but cry and Sleep for several Months together: and at length his understanding was utterly taken away. Among other Symptoms of an Inchantment upon him, one was, that there was a Board in the Garden, whereon he would walk; and all the invitations in the world could never fetch him off. About Seventeen or Eighteen years after, there came a Stranger to Shattocks House, who seeing the Child, said, *This poor Child is Bewitched; and you have a Neighbour living not far off, who is a Witch.* He added, *Your Neighbour has had a falling out with your*
20 *Wife; and she said in her Heart, your Wife is a proud Woman, and she would bring down her Pride in this Child:* He then Remembred, that *Bishop* had parted from his Wife in muttering and menacing Terms, a little before the Child was taken Ill. The abovesaid Stranger would needs carry the Bewitched Boy with him, to *Bishops* House, on pretence of buying a pot of Cyder. The Woman Entertained him in furious manner; and flew also upon the Boy, scratching his Face till the Blood came, and saying, *Thou Rogue, what? dost thou bring this Fellow here to plague me?* Now it seems the man had said before he went, that he would fetch Blood of *her.* Even after the Boy was follow'd with grievous Fits, which the Doctors themselves generally ascribed unto *Witchcraft;* and wherein he would be thrown still into the *Fire*
30 or the *Water,* if he were not constantly look'd after; and it was verily believed that *Bishop* was the cause of it.

X. *John Louder* testify'd, that upon some little controversy with *Bishop* about her fowles, going well to Bed, he did awake in the Night by moonlight, and did see clearly the likeness of this woman grievously oppressing him; in which miserable condition she held him unable to help him self, till near Day. He told *Bishop* of this; but she deny'd it, and threatned him, very much. Quickly after this, being at home on a Lords Day, with the doors shutt about him, he saw a Black Pig approach him; at which he going to kick, it vanished away. Immediately after, sitting down, he saw a Black Thing Jump in at the Window, & come & stand before him. The
40 Body, was like that of a Monkey, the Feet like a Cocks, but the Face much like a mans. He being so extreemly affrighted, that he could not speak; this Monster spoke

---

32 **some little controversy,** suggestion that neighborhood quarrels and malice formed part of the explanation of the witchcraft episode   37 **Black Pig,** evidently the animal "familiar" of the witch, supposedly nourished by blood or by supernatural teat mentioned in Section XIII   39 **Black Thing,** the Devil

to him, and said, *I am a Messenger sent unto you, for I understand that you are in some Trouble of Mind, and if you will be ruled by me, you shall want for nothing in this world.* Whereupon he endeavoured to clap his hands upon it; but he could feel no substance, and it jumped out of the window again; but immediately came in by the Porch, though the Doors were shut, and said, *You had better take my Counsel!* He then struck at it with a stick, but struck only the Ground-sel, and broke the Stick. The Arm with which he struck was presently Disenabled, and it vanished away. He presently went out at the Back-Door, and spyed, this *Bishop,* in her Orchard, going toward her House; but he had not power to set one foot forward unto her. Whereupon returning into the House, he was immediately accosted by the Monster he 10 had seen before; which Goblin was now going to Fly at him: whereat he cry'd out, *The whole Armour of God, be between me and you!* So it sprang back, and flew over the Apple Tree; shaking many Apples off the Tree, in its flying over. At its Leap, it flung Dirt with its Feet, against the Stomack of the man; whereon he was then struck Dumb, and so continued for three Days together. Upon the producing of this Testimony, *Bishop* deny'd that she knew this Deponent: yet their two Orchards joined, and they had often had their Little Quarrels for some years together.

XI. *William Stacy, Testifyed,* That receiving Money of this *Bishop* for work done by him, he was gone but a matter of Three Rods from her, and looking for his money, found it unaccountably gone from him. Some time after, *Bishop* asked him 20 whether his Father would grind her grist for her? He demanded why? She Reply'd, *Because Folks count me a witch.* He answered, *No Question, but he will grind it for you.* Being then gone about six Rods from her, with a small Load in his Cart, suddenly the Off-wheel slump't and sunk down into an Hole, upon plain ground, so that the Deponent, was forced to get help for the Recovering of the wheel. But stepping Back to look for the Hole which might give him this disaster, there was none at all to be found. Some time after, he was waked in the Night; but it seem'd as Light as Day, and he perfectly saw the shape of this *Bishop,* in the Room, Troubling of him; but upon her going out, all was Dark again. He charg'd *Bishop* afterwards with it: and she deny'd it not; but was very angry. Quickly after, this Deponent having 30 been threatned by *Bishop,* as he was in a dark Night going to the Barn, he was very suddenly taken or lifted from the ground, and thrown against a stone wall; After that, he was again hoisted up and thrown down a Bank, at the end of his House. After this again, passing by this *Bishop,* his Horse with a small load, striving to Draw, all his Gears flew to pieces, and the Cart fell down; and this deponent going then to lift a Bag of corn, of about two Bushels; could not budge it, with all his might.

Many other pranks of this *Bishops,* this deponent was Ready to testify. He also testify'd, that he verily Believed, the said *Bishop,* was the Instrument of his Daughter, *Priscilla's* Death; of which suspicion, pregnant Reasons were assigned.   40

XII. To Crown all, *John Bly,* and *William Bly,* Testify'd, That being Employ'd by *Bridget Bishop,* to help take down the Cellar-wall of the old House, wherein she for-

---

6 **Ground-sel,** threshold   12 **The whole . . . God,** an allusion to the traditional protection from witchcraft: the name of God, the Bible, a crucifix or some other sacred object

merly Lived, they did in Holes of the said old Wall, find several *Poppets,* made up of Rags, and Hogs Brussels, with Headless Pins in them, the points being outward. Whereof she could now give no Account unto the Court, that was Reasonable or Tolerable.

XIII. One thing that made against the Prisoner was, her being evidently convicted of *Gross Lying* in the Court, several Times, while she was making her Plea. But besides this, a Jury of Women, found a preternatural Teat upon her Body; but upon a second search, within three or four Hours, there was no such thing to be seen. There was also an account of other people whom this woman had afflicted. 10 And there might have been many more, if they had been, enquired for. But there was no need of them.

XIV. There was one very strange thing more, with which the Court was newly Entertained. As this Woman was under a Guard, passing by the Great and Spacious Meeting-House of *Salem,* she gave a Look towards the House. And immediately a *Daemon* Invisibly Entring the Meeting-house, Tore down a part of it; so that tho' there were no person to be seen there, yet the people at the Noise running in, found a Board, which was strongly fastned with several Nails, transported unto another quarter of the House.

1692, 1693

------

1 **Poppets,** images. The practice described is commonplace in primitive magic and survives in voodooism

from Magnalia Christi Americana

Cotton Mather's best-known book is the Magnalia Christi Americana: or, The Ecclesiastical History of New-England, from Its First Planting in the Year 1620, unto the Year of Our Lord 1698. *It was begun in 1693 to bring together "Discoveries of the Divine Providence, in the Government of the World." Mather evidently hoped to continue the work begun by his father in the* Essay for the Recording of Illustrious Providences. *Soon, however, he was calling the project his "Church History of New England" and was working somewhat along the lines of Thomas Fuller's* Church-History of Britain *(1655) and John Vicars'* Magnalia Dei Anglicana *(1646). Largely completed by the end of 1696, the work was first published at London in 1702. Later editions appeared at Hartford in 1820 and in 1853-1855.*

The "great American deeds of Christ" are described in seven books: (1) a general account of the settlement of New England; (2) the lives of the governors; (3) the lives of the ministers; (4) an account of Harvard College and its leaders; (5) acts and monuments of the New England churches; (6) "Illustrious Discoveries and Demonstrations of the Divine Providence" (the remnant of the original plan); and (7) a description of the various church controversies and the troubles with the Indians. A vast storehouse of information on New England history, the Magnalia *shows its author at his best and worst. Vivid biographies and narratives are interspersed with pedantic quotations and allusions, accurate history with doubtful speculations. Yet it remains one of the great books of colonial America, and it will always be read appreciatively by those who wish to catch the flavor of the seventeenth century.*

The section which follows forms Chapter III of Book III, Part II. The Rev. Jonathan

Burr (1604-1641) was associated with Richard Mather, the author's grandfather, at Dorchester, for less than two years. His life is described as carefully, however, as that of the most conspicuous leaders of the Puritan Migration. Cotton Mather seldom expressed his attitude toward the laborers in the vineyard more clearly and happily.

Natus Ad Exemplar The Life of Mr. Jonathan Burr Exemplo Monstrante Viam

I

When the Interests of *David* were carried into a *Wilderness,* the Respects and Regards by his *Jonathan,* had thereunto were such, that he at last uttered this Exclamation thereupon, *Thy Love to me was wonderful!* The Interests of our *Jesus,* the true *David,* being lodged very much in an *American* Wilderness, there was a *Jonathan,* whose *Love* thereunto was indeed so *wonderful,* that it carried him through the *many Waters* of the *Atlantic* Ocean, to be serviceable thereunto; and this was Mr. *Jonathan Burr.*

2. He was born at *Redgrave,* in *Suffolk,* about the Year 1604; descended of Godly Parents, who gratified the Inclinations of this their Son, with a Learned Education. But altho' *Literature* did much adorn his Childhood, *Religion* did so much more; for he had *from a Child known the Holy Scriptures, which made him wise unto Salvation.* It is noted, that the *Rod* of *Aaron* was made of an *Almond-Tree;* of which 'twill be no *Plinyism* to observe (tho' *Pliny* observe it), that it flowers the first of all *Trees,* even in *January,* in the more Southern Countries, and bears in *March;* which has been sometimes employ'd as an Intimation, how *quickly* those that are designed for the Ministry, should *Blossom* towards Heaven, and be young *Jeremiahs,* and *Johns,* and *Timothies.* Thus did our *Jonathan.* Even in his very Childhood, so *studious* he was, as to leave his *Food* for his *Book,* but withal so *pious,* that he could neither Morning nor Evening dare to go without *Prayers* to God for his Blessing. And as it was his endeavour, whilst a Schoolboy, to be *every* Day in the *Fear of the Lord,* so he would on the *Lord's Day* discover a singular Measure of that *Fear;* not only by abstaining from the *Liberties* which others of his Age then use to take, to *pass the time away,* but also by *devoting the time* to the Exercises of *Devotion.* His Father, observing this Disposition of the *Child,* hoped, as well he might, that whatever was expended in fitting him for *Service,* would be well repaid, in the Service which might be done by him for the Church of God; and therefore after due Preparations for it, he sent him unto the University.

10

20

Text: the London edition of 1702   **Natus Ad Exemplar,** born to be an example (This and subsequent translations are those made by Lucius Robinson for the 1853-1855 edition.)   **Exemplo Monstrante Viam,** example shows the way   1 **Interests of David . . . wonderful!** See II Samuel 1:26   4 **true David.** Jesus was descended from David, who was at first regarded with messianic hope; see Matthew 1:1-17   12 **Rod of Aaron.** See Numbers 17   13 **Plinyism,** a statement of doubtful truth, such as might appear in the *Historia Naturalis* of Gaius Plinius Secundus (23-79). Mather's use of the word is the only one recorded in the *Oxford English Dictionary.* Pliny's statement about the almond tree appears in Bk. XVI, Chap. 42   27 **the University,** Cambridge, where Burr matriculated at Corpus Christi College in 1620. According to the records, he took his B.A. in 1623-1624; his M.A. in 1627

3. After he had spent three or four Years in *Academical* Studies, the Death of his *Father* fetch'd him sooner than he would have gone, into the country; where, thou' he kept a *School,* yet he pursued the Design of accomplishing himself with every part of Learning, that when those of his Years were to take their Degrees of *Mastership,* he was one of the *Moderators,* which place he discharged with great Acceptation. But he afterwards would say, That the awful and humbling Providence of God, in the Death of his *Father,* which hindred him from those Employments and Preferments in the *University,* for which he had a particular Fondness, had an effect upon him, for which he had Reason to admire the Wisdom of Heaven; inasmuch as it
10 reduced him to that modest, gracious, careful Frame, which made him the fitter for the Work of *turning many to Righteousness.*

4. Having for a while attended that Work at *Horninger,* near *Bury* in *Suffolk,* he afterwards undertook the Charge of *Reckingshal,* in the same County, wherein he did most exemplarily express the Spirit of a *Minister of the New Testament.* He would therein be sometimes ready to envy the more easie Condition of the *Husbandmen;* but in Submission and Obedience unto the Call of God, he now set his Hand unto the *Plough* of the Lord Jesus Christ: And therefore in the Form of a Solemn *Covenant,* he obliged himself unto the most Conscientious Discharge of his Ministerial Duties; in which Discharge he would always beg of God, that whatever *Exhortation*
20 he gave unto others, might first be shaped in his own *Experience:* And yet sometimes he would complain unto his Friends: *Alas, I preach not what I am, but what I ought to be.*

5. This *gracious* Man, was indeed a very *humble* Man, and his *Humility* carried him even into a *Dejection* of Spirit; especially when by Importunities he had been prevailed upon to *preach abroad.* Once particularly, there was a Person of Quality, for whose Conversion many Prayers had been put up to God, by those who hoped that God might have much *Honour* from a *Man of Honour* brought unto himself. Mr. *Burr* preaching at a place, far from his own Congregation, had a most happy Success in the Conversion of this Gentleman, who not only acknowledged this Change,
30 with much Thankfulness, both to God, and the Instrument; but also approved himself a *changed Man,* in the whole Frame of his After-Conversation. And yet coming home, from the Preaching of that Sermon, Mr. *Burr* had a particular Measure of his lowly and modest Reflections thereupon; adding, *I shall conclude, it is of God, if any Good be done by any thing preached by such an Unworthy Instrument.*

6. Hence on the *Lord's Day,* after he came home from his publick Work, it was his manner presently to *Retire,* and spend some time in *praying* to God, for the *pardon* of the Sins, which accompanied him in his Work, and in *praising* of God, for enabling him to go, in any measure, through it; with Petitions for the good Success of his Labours.
40 He then would come down to his *Family-Worship,* wherein he spent some Hours *instructing* of the *Family,* and performing of other Duties: And when his Wife desired him to abate of his excessive Pains, his Answer would be, *'Tis better to be worn out with Work, than to be eaten out with Rust.* It was indeed his *Joy,* to be spending his *Life* unto the uttermost for God, and for his People; yea, he would say, tho' he

should have no *Temporal Rewards.* Accordingly, when any that had been benefited
by his Ministry, sent him any *Tokens* of their Gratitude, he would (like *Luther*) beg
of God, *That he might not have his Portion in such things:* And he desired of his grateful Friends, *That if they had gotten any good of him, they would give unto God alone the
Glory of it.* Moreover, if he had understood, that any had gained in the Concern of
their Souls, by his Labours, he would mention it, in some of his privater Devotions,
with this Expression, *Lord, of thine own have I given, take then the Glory unto thy self:
As for me, let my Portion be in thy self, and not in the Things of this World.* But when
he was debarred of his Liberty to preach, he was even *like a Fish out of the Water;*
and his very *Body* languished through a Sympathy, with the Resentments of his 10
Mind; saying, *That his Preaching was his Life; and if he were laid aside from that, he
should quickly be dead.*

7. It was not on the *Lord's Day* only but *every Day,* that this good Man was usually,
In the Fear of the Lord all the Day long. He might say with the *Psalmist, When I awake,
I am still with God:* For at his first *awaking,* he would bless God for the Mercies of the
Night, and then pray, *That he might so number his Days, as to apply his Heart to Wisdom:* And if he awaked in the Night, it would commonly be with some *Thanksgivings* unto Heaven. Rising in the Morning, he would repair to his beloved *Study,*
where he began the Day with *Secret Prayer* before the Lord: After this he would read
a Chapter in the *Old Testament,* spending some time in Serious and Solemn, and 20
Heart-searching *Meditations* thereupon: He would then come down into his *Family;*
where, with his *Prayers,* he would then Read and Expound, and apply the same
Chapter unto his own Folks, and such of the Neighbours as would come in, to enjoy
his *Meditations,* at the usual Season of them. Retiring then to his *Study* again, he
would continue there, till called unto his *Dinner;* and if none came to speak with
him after Dinner, he would, after some Diversion for a while with his *Children,*
return to his Study, where he would then have a time to pray with his *Wife:* But
if at any time he were invited unto a Dinner abroad, he would have a time for *that*
Service in the Forenoon, before his going out.

As the Evening drew on, after the like manner, he would read a Chapter in the 30
New Testament, making his *Family* Partakers of his *Reflections,* with his Prayer upon
it. And before his going to Bed, he usually walked up and down the Room, for half
an Hour, or more, pondering upon *something,* which his Wife desiring to know,
What it was? He replied, *Seeing thou art so near me, if it may do thee good, I'll tell thee:
First,* He said, he called himself unto an Account, *How he had spent the day?* And
what sinful *Commissions,* or *Omissions,* he had been overtaken with; for which, he then,
begg'd Pardon of God. *Secondly,* He reckon'd up the particular *Mercies* he had received *in the Day,* rendring of Praises to Heaven for those Mercies. *Lastly,* He made
his *Petitions* to God, that he might be prepared for *sudden Death:* Unto which *Third
Article* in his Thoughts, that which gave more special Occasion was, the *sudden* 40
Death of his *Brother,* an eminent and excellent *Christian, whom,* he said, he *could
never forget.*

---

2 **Luther,** who, especially in the early days of the Reformation, refused the gifts of his admirers lest he be
criticized by his enemies

8. When he travelled abroad, he thought long to be *at home* again, through his Dissatisfaction at his not having elsewhere, so convenient Seasons for his *Communion* with God. And when he took any Journeys with his Friends, it was his manner to enquire, *What good had been done, or gained therein?* and *what good Examples had been seen?* and *what good Instructions had been heard?* and that there might be no loss of *time* in the Journeys, he would be full of *profitable Discourse,* especially by way of *Occasional Reflection,* upon things that then occurr'd unto Observation. What he was in a *Journey,* the same he was at the Table: even like the Fire, (what was once writ of *Athendorus*) Ἐξάπτων πάντα τὰ παρακείμενα. So that they who would bear
10 no part in a gracious *Communication,* would be *dumb,* where-ever he came; and some of the roughest and rudest Hearers, who have *Tears* fetched from their Eyes, at the Soul melting Expressions that passed from his Mouth. Moreover, at a *Feast* he would eat more sparingly than at another time, giving us his Reason for his Temperance, the Advice of the Wise Man: *Put a Knife to thy Throat:* And he would say, *Where there are many Varieties, there are many Temptations.*

9. It was his wont, before the *Lord's Supper,* to keep a Day of solemn *Fasting* and *Prayer* alone, with his *Wife,* as well to prepare themselves for that Sacred *Ordinance;* as to obtain the manifold Blessings of Heaven upon his Family and Neighbour-hood. Such was his *Piety.* And as for his *Charity,* he seldom visited the *Poor,* but
20 with *Spirituals,* he communicated also *Temporals* unto them: For which, when some of his Friends intimated, that he might err, in reserving no more for himself, he would answer, *I often think of those Words, he that soweth sparingly, shall reap sparingly.* It was also remarkable, to see how much his own Personal *Joys,* and *Griefs,* were swallowed up in the *Simpathy* which he had, with the Condition of the whole Church abroad: When he heard it was *well* with the Church, he would say, *Blessed be God, that it goes well with them, whatever becomes of me!* But if *ill,* none of his own private Prosperity kept him from feeling it, as a true Member of that *Mystical Body.* Finally, All the Graces which thus rendred him amiable to those that were about him, were attended with such *Mosaic Meekness,* as made him yet further amiable:
30 He would be *zealous,* when he saw Dishonour cast on the Name of God, but *patient* under Injury offer'd unto himself. If he were informed, that any thought meanly of him, he would not be moved at it, but say, *I think as meanly of my self, and therefore may well be content, that others think meanly of me:* And when *Evil* hath been charged on him, he has replied, *If Men see so much, what does God see?* Disgraceful and un-worthy Speeches bestowed upon him, he would call, *his Gains;* but it was his Trou-ble to find himself applauded. His Friends might indeed have said of him, as *Luther* of *Melancthon, Mihi plane videtur saltem in hoc errare, quod Christum ipse fingat longius abesse à Corde suo, quàm sit reverà, certè nimis Nullus in hoc est noster* Jonathan.

---

9 Ἐξάπτων . . . παρακείμενα, which troubles everything near it. The reference is probably to Athenodorus of Tarsus (74 B.C.-8 A.D.), teacher of Augustus and Tiberius, and friend of Cicero   14 **Put . . . Throat.** Proverbs 23:2: "And put a knife to thy throat, if thou be a man given to appetite"   36 **Luther of Melancthon,** Melancthon (Philip Schwarzerd, 1497-1560) was one of Luther's great allies in the German reformation. The sense of the quotation is: It is evident to me that he errs in pretending that Christ is far-ther from his heart than is really true. Surely in this my Jonathan seems to deprecate himself to an unrea-sonable extent

10. This bright *Star* must move *Westward.* He, with many Fellow-Sufferers for the *Testimony of Jesus,* being silenced in *England;* and foreseeing a dismal *Storm* a coming upon the Nation, till the overpassing whereof he saw many *Praying Saints* directed unto *America,* for *Chambers of Safety;* and willing to forego all Worldly Advantages, for the Enjoyment of Gospel Ordinances, administred without the mixtures of *Humane Inventions;* he removed into *New England,* having his three Children with him, and his Wife big with a Fourth, in his Remove; where arriving, it refreshed him not a little, to see the escaped People of God, with *Harps in their Hands,* there singing the *Song of Moses.* He came into *New-England,* at a time, when there was not so much want of *Lights,* as of *Golden Candlesticks,* wherein to place the *Lights;*   10 but he was not long there, before he was invited by the Church of *Dorchester,* to be an Assistant unto the well-known Mr. *Richard Mather.*

11. The *Evil One,* disturbed at the Happiness of Dorchester, very strongly endeavoured a *Misunderstanding* between Mr. *Mather* and Mr. *Burr;* and the *Misunderstanding* did proceed so far, as to produce a *Paroxism.*

It was judged by some of the Brethren in the Church, that Mr. *Burr* had expressed himself erroneously in certain Points, then much agitated throughout the Country; and Mr. *Mather,* upon their Desire, examining the Propositions which this Good Man had written, thought he could not altogether clear them from Exceptions. Hereupon grew such Alienations, that they could not be well Re-united, without   20 calling in the Help of Neighbour-Churches in a *Council;* which *Council* directing both Mr. *Mather* and Mr. *Burr,* to acknowledge what *Misunderstandings* were then discovered in this Business, those two Good Men set apart a Day for the *Reconciliation;* and with such Exemplary Expressions of *Humility* and *Affection,* Rectified all that had been out of Joint, that God was exceedingly Glorified, and the Peace of the *Church* effectually restored and maintained.

12. This true *Barnabas,* was not only to give the Churches of *New Engand* a Consolatory *Visit,* in his Passage unto Glory, that he might leave them an Example of that *Love, Patience, Holiness,* and *Fruitfulness,* which would make them an Happy People. Tho' he had not *Persecution* to try him in this Wilderness, yet he was not   30 without his Trials: For, as 'tis well observed in the Discourse, *De Duplici Martyrio,* which goes under the Name of *Cyprian; Si deest Tyrannus, si Tortor, si Spoliator, non deerit concupiscentia, Martyrii, Materiam quotidianam nobis exhibens.* The next Year after he came to *New-England,* he was taken Sick of the *Small-Pox;* out of which he nevertheless recovered, and came forth as *Gold that had been tryed in the Fire.* He then renewed and applied the *Covenant of Grace,* by the suitable Recognitions of the following *Instrument.*

---

9 Song of Moses. See Exodus 15:1   12 **Mr. Richard Mather** (1596-1669), Cotton Mather's grandfather   14 **a Misunderstanding.** Burr had been suspected of entertaining a belief in divine revelation directly to the individual. The Synod of 1657 had condemned eighty-two heresies of this nature   27 **Barnabas,** a contemporary of St. Paul, famous as a missionary (see I Corinthians 9:6)   31 **De Duplici Martyrio,** *Twofold Martyrdom,* a treatise attributed to Cyprian (200?-258), Church Father, martyr, and saint. It was probably composed by Erasmus   32 **Si deest Tyrannus,** etc. If there be no tyrant, no torturer, no robber, there will still be evil passions, furnishing daily occasions for martyrdom

'I *Jonathan Burr,* being brought in the Arms of Almighty God over the Vast
'*Ocean,* with my Family and Friends, and Graciously provided for in a Wilderness;
'and being sensible of my own *Unprofitableness* and *Self-seeking;* yet of Infinite
'Mercy, being called unto the Tremendous Work of *Feeding Souls,* and being of
'late with my Family deliver'd out of a Great Affliction of the *Small-Pox;* and hav-
'ing found the Fruit of that Affliction; God Tempering, Ordering, Mitigating the
'*Evil* thereof, so as I have been graciously and speedily deliver'd; I do promise
'and *vow* to him, that hath done all things for me; *First,* That I will aim only at
'his *Glory,* and the *Good* of *Souls,* and not *my self* and *Vain Glory:* And that, *Sec-*
10 '*ondly,* I will walk *Humbly,* with *lower Thoughts of my self,* considering what a poor
'Creature I am; a Puff of Breath, sustained only by the *Power* of his *Grace;* And
'therefore, *Thirdly,* I will be more *watchful* over my Heart, to *keep* it in a due
'Frame of *Holiness* and *Obedience,* without running out so far to the Creature; for I
'have seen, That he is mine only Help in time of need; *Fourthly,* That I will put
'more weight upon that *firm Promise,* and *sure Truth,* That God is a *God hearing*
'*Prayer: Fifthly,* That I will set up *God,* more in my *Family,* more in *my self, Wife,*
'*Children* and *Servants;* conversing with them in a more serious and constant man-
'ner; for *This,* God aimed at, in sending his Hand into my Family at this time.
Memento Mori.
20   '*In Meipso Nihil; in Christo Omne.'*

Nor was his *Heavenly Conversation* afterwards disagreeable to these Grateful Resolutions of his Devout Soul. By the same Token, that the famous Mr. *Thomas Hooker,*
being one of his Auditors, when he preached in a great Audience at *Charlestown,*
had this Expression about him. *Surely, this Man wont be long out of Heaven, for he*
preaches as if he were there already. And the most experienced Christians in the Country, found still in his *Ministry,* as well as in his whole *Behaviour,* the Breathing of
such a *Spirit,* as was very greatly to their Satisfaction. They could not but call him,
as *Dionysius* was once called, πετεινὸν τοὺς οὐρανοῖς, *The Bird of Heaven.* Had it
not been *Old Adam's World,* so Innocent, so Excellent, so Heavenly a Person, could
30 not have met with such *Exercises* as he and others like him, then sometimes did,
even from their *Truest Brethren.*

13. Having just been preaching about the *Redemption of Time,* he fell into a Sickness of *Ten Days* Continuance; during which Time, he expressed a wonderful
Patience, and Submission, upon all Occasions. His Wife perceiving his *Willingness*
to Die, asked him, *Whether he were desirous to leave her and his Children?* Whereto his
Anwer was, *Do not mistake me, I am not desirous of that; but I bless God, that now my*
Will is the Lord's Will: If he will have me to live yet with my dear Wife and Children, I
am willing. I will say to you my dear Wife and Children, as the Apostle says, It is better
for you, that I abide with you; but it is better for me to be dissolved and to be with Christ.
40 And perceiving his Wife's Disconsolation, he asked her, *If she could not be willing to*

---

19 **Memento Mori.** Keep death in mind, a common inscription on tombstones   20 **In** . . . **Omne.** In
myself, I am nothing; in Christ, I am all things   22 **Mr. Thomas Hooker** (1586-1647), the founder and
first minister of Hartford, Connecticut   28 **Dionysius,** probably Dionysius the Areopagite, mentioned in
Acts 17:34

part with him; whereupon, when she intimated how hard it was, he exhorted her to acquiesce in that God, who would be *Better than Ten Husbands:* Adding, *Our Parting is but for a Time, I am sure we shall one Day meet again.* Being discouraged by finding himself unable to put on his Clothes, one of his Friends told him, *his Work was now to lie still:* At which he complained, *I lie slugging a Bed, when others are at work!* But being minded of *God's Will,* That it should be so, *that* quieted him. Observing how diligently his Wife tended him, he said unto her, *Don't spend so much Time with me, but go thy way and spend some time in Prayer; thou knowest not what thou mayst obtain from God; I fear lest thou look too much upon this Affliction.* A Day or two before his Death, he blessed his Children; and the Night before he died, he was   10 overheard sometimes to say, *I will wait until my Change come;* and *Why art thou so loath to die?* A few Hours before his Death, it was observed, that he had a sore Conflict with the *Angel of Death,* who was now shooting his last *Arrows* at him; and when one of the Standers-by said, *The Sting of Death is taken away; the Lord Jesus Christ has overcome Death for you; this is one of Satan's last Assaults; his Work is now almost at an end; though he be a subtil Enemy, and would if it were possible, deceive the very Elect;* he presently laid hold on that last Expression, *If it were possible;* said he, *Blessed be God there is no Possibility!* After this, he requested the Company might withdraw, that so he might have an Opportunity to pray for a while by himself; but seeing the Company loth to leave the Room, he pray'd in Latin as long as he had   20 Strength to do it. When he was to Appearance just expiring, he called for his *Wife;* and stedfastly fixing his Eyes upon her, he said, *Cast thy Care upon God, for he careth for thee.* About half an Hour after this, when Death had been for some while drawing the Curtains about him, his last Words were those unto his Wife. *Hold Fast, Hold Fast!* So he finished his Pilgrimage, on *Aug.* 9. 1641.

14. Unto that Vertuous Gentlewoman his Wife, he expressed himself with great Confidence, *That God would certainly provide well for her;* and that Gentlewoman, shortly after being Honourably and Comfortably married unto another Gentleman of Good Estate, namely, *Richard Dummer,* Esq; once a Magistrate of the Colony, lived with him near Forty Years; and was more than Forty Years after alive to tes-   30 tify her Experience of the Accomplishment, which God had given unto that Faith of her *Dying Husband:* Who at his Death commended his Family to God, in Strains not unlike those of the Dying *Widerus;*

> CHRISTE, tibi soli mea pignora Viva relinquo,
> Quorum post Mortem Tu Pater esto meam.
> Qui cunctis Vitæ miserum me jugiter Annis
> Pavisti, Largam dans Mihi semper opem;
> Tu quoq; Pasce meos defende, tuere, doceq;
> Et tandem ad Coeli gaudia transfer.
>
>   Amen.

---

29 **Richard Dummer.** Their son, Jeremiah Dummer, became a famous colonial silversmith   33 **Widerus,** probably Count Herman van Weiden (1472-1552), archbishop of Cologne who was excommunicated by the Pope in 1546.

[Translation:
To thee, O Christ, this tender flock I leave;
  Be Thou their father when I am no more,
Thou from the morn of life until its eve
  Hast fed me with the riches of thy store.
These little ones so feed, protect, and love,
  And then translate them to thy rest above.]

Epitaphium
Mortuus hic Jacet, qui in Omnium Cordibus Vivit.
10   *Omnes Virtutes, quæ Vivunt post Funera,*
    In Unius BURRI *Funere invenerunt Sepulchrum.*

To make up his *Epitaph,* I will borrow a Line or two from the Tombstone of *Volkmarus.*

Hìc Jacet Exutis nimium citò BURRIUS *Annis,*
  Adjuga Suggestus, Magne MATHERE, *Tui*
Si magis Annosam licuisset condere Vitam,
  Ac Scriptis Animum notificare Libris,
Tot Verbis non esset opus hoc Scalpere Saxum,
  Sufficerent Quatuor, BURRIUS *hic situs est.*

1693-1698?, 1702

[Translation:
  Epitaphium
  Here he lies dead, but he lives in the hearts of all.
  All those great virtues, which the tomb defy,
  Now sleep within it, where our Burr doth lie.
  Here lieth Burr, whose span too soon was sped:
  Burr, whom in life our own great Mather led.
  Alas! had he but reached a riper age,
  And stamped his genius on some deathless page,
  No sculpture need upon this stone appear,
  Save one brief, meaning sentence: "Burr Lies Here."]

13 **Volkmarus,** an allusion the editor has been unable to identify. Mather was evidently paraphrasing from some book of epitaphs

from *Curiosa Americana*

Cotton Mather's curiosity about science won him election as Fellow of the Royal Society of London in 1713. Between 1712 and 1724 he sent to that organization over eighty letters on more or less scientific subjects. Some of his comments were summarized in the Philosophical Transactions. *The letter which follows was written to John Woodward (1655-1728), an*

English geologist who had undertaken a world-wide correspondence about fossil remains before publishing his Essay Toward a Natural History of the Earth *(1695). Professor Murdock has shown that Mather's facts were drawn from an account sent him by John Winthrop (1681-1747), a descendant of the famous governor of that name, on September 12, 1717.*

10 d. X m. 1717

Sr

Tho' we are gott so far onward at the Beginning of another Winter, yett we have not forgott the Last: which at the Latter End whereof, we were Entertained & overwhelmed with a *Snow,* which was attended with some Things that were uncommon enough, to afford matter for a letter from us. The *Winter* was not so bad as that wherein *Tacitus* tells us that *Corbulo* made his Expedition against the *Parthians.* Nor like that which proved so fatal to the Beasts & Birds, in the Days of the Emperour *Justinian* [nor?] that wherein the very Fishes were killed under the Freezing Sea, when *Phocas* did as much to the men whom Tyrants treat like the Fishes of the Sea. 10 But the Conclusion of our *Winter* was hard enough, & was too formidable to be easily forgotten: and of a peece with what you had in *Europe,* a year before. The *Snow* was the Chief Thing that made it so. For tho' rarely does a *Winter* pass us, wherein we may not say with *Pliny, Ingens Hyeme Nivis apud nos copia;* yett the Last *Winter* brought with it a *Snow* that Excelled them all. A *Snow* tis true, not equal to that which once fell and Lay Twenty Cubits high, about the Beginning of *October,* in the parts about the *Euxine Sea.* Nor to that, which the French Annals tell us, kept falling for twenty Nine weeks together. Nor to several mentioned by *Boethius,* wherein vast Numbers of people, and of Cattel, perished; Nor to those that *Strabo* finds upon *Caucasus* and *Rhodiginus* in *Armenia.* But yett such an one, and attended 20 with such Circumstances, as may deserve to be Remembred.

On the Twentieth of the Last *February,* there came on a *Snow,* which being added unto what had covered the ground a few Days before, made a Thicker Mantle for our Mother than what was usual: And the Storm with it, was for the following Day so violent, as to make all communication between the Neighbours every where to cease. People for some Hours could not pass from one side of a Street unto another, and the poor Women, who happened at this critical time to fall into Travail, were putt into Hardships which anon produced many odd Stories for us. But on the Twenty-fourth Day of the Month comes *Pelion* upon *Ossa.* Another *Snow* came on,

---

Text: from **Selections from Cotton Mather,** ed. K. B. Murdock   1 **10 d. X m. 1717,** December 10; see li. 20, p. 74   7 **Tacitus** (55?-117?), Roman historian. Corbulo, a famous general under Claudius and Nero, was executed at the latter's orders in 67 A.D. In all probability, Mather's allusions in his first paragraph were derived from some dictionary or classical encyclopedia which listed the great snows of antiquity   9 **Justinian** (483-565), Emperor of the eastern Roman Empire   10 **Phocas,** usurper of the empire of Constantinople, 602-610, and a notoriously cruel tyrant   14 **Ingens . . . copia.** We have had uncommonly heavy snows this winter   16 **Twenty Cubits,** thirty or more feet. The ancient cubit varied from eighteen to twenty-two inches   17 **Euxine Sea,** Black Sea   18 **Boethius** (475?-525?), Roman philosopher, author of a work on natural theology, *De Consolatione philosophia*   19 **Strabo** (60 B.C.?-24 A.D.?), Greek geographer   20 **Rhodiginus** (1450?-1525), Italian philologist, author of *Antiquae Lectiones* (1516)   29 **Pelion upon Ossa.** Both are mountains in Thessaly. In Greek mythology, the giants warring with the gods tried to pile one mountain upon the other. The expression, of course, means one great thing on top of another.

which almost buried the Memory of the former: With a Storm so furious, that Heaven laid an Interdict on the Religious Assemblies throughout the countrey on this Lords-day, the like whereunto had never been seen before. The Indians near an hundred years old, affirm, that their Fathers never told them of any thing that equall'd it. Vast Numbers of Cattel were destroy'd in this Calamity; Whereof some that were of the Stronger Sort, were found standing Dead on their Legs, as if they had been alive, many weeks after, when the Snow melted away. And others had their Eyes glazed over with Ice at such a rate, that being not far from the Sea, they went out of their way, and drowned them there.

10   One Gentleman, on whose Farms, there were now Lost above eleven hundred *Sheep,* which with other cattel were Interred (Shall I Say, or Inniv'd) in the Snow; writes me That there were Two *Sheep* very singularly circumstanced. For no Less than Eight & Twenty Days after the Storm, the people pulling out the Ruines of above an hundred Sheep, out of a Snow-bank, which Lay sixteen foot high drifted over them, there were Two found alive, which had been there all this time, & kept themselves alive by Eating the Wool of their Dead Companions. When they were taken out, they shed their own Fleeces, but soon gott into good Case again.

   Sheep were not the only creatures that Lived unaccountably for whole weeks without their usual Sustenance, entirely buried in the *Snow-drifts.* The *Swine* had a share 20 with the *Sheep* in Strange Survivals. A man had a couple of Young *Hogs,* which he gave over for Dead; But on the twenty-seventh day after their Burial, they made their way out of a *Snow-bank,* at the bottom of which they had found a Little Tansy to feed upon.

   The *Poultry* as unaccountably survived as these. *Hens* were found alive, after *Seven Days; Turkeys* were found alive, after *five & Twenty Days;* Buried in the *Snow,* and at a Distance from the Ground; and altogether destitute of any thing to feed them.

   The Number of Creatures, that kept a *Rigid Fast,* shutt up in *Snow,* for several weeks together, & were found alive after all, have yielded surprizing stories to us.

   The Wild Creaturss of the Woods, (the *Outgoings of the Evening)* made their 30 Descent as well as they could in this Time of Scarcity for them, towards the Sea-side. A vast multitude of Deer for the Same Cause taking the Same Course, & the Deep Snow Spoiling them of their only Defence: which is, *To Run,* they became such a prey to those Devourers, that it is thought, not one in Twenty Escaped.

   But here again occurr'd a Curiosity.

   These carniverous Sharpers, and especially the *Foxes,* would make their *Nocturnal Visits,* to the Pens, where the people had their Sheep defended from them. The poor Ewes big with young were so terrified with the frequent Approaches of the *Foxes,* & the Terror had such Impression on them, that most of the *Lambs* brought forth in the Spring following, were of Monsieur *Reinard's* complexion, when the 40 Dams were all either White or Black.

   It was remarkable, that immediately after the Fall of the Snow, an infinite multitude of Sparrows, made their Appearance; but then after a short continuance all disappeared.

---

11 **Inniv'd.** Mather is playing with the Latin words *terra* and *nix, nivis* (snow)

It is incredible, how much Damage was done to the *Orchards;* For the Snow freezing to a Crust, as high as the Boughs of the Trees, anon Splitt them to peeces. The Cattle also, walking on the Crusted Snow, a dozen foot from the Ground, so fed upon the Trees as very much to damnify them.

The Ocean was in a prodigious Ferment, and after it was over, Vast Heaps of Little Shells were driven ashore, where they were never seen before. Mighty Shoals of Porpoises, also kept a Playday in the Disturbed waves of our Harbours.

The odd Accidents befalling many poor people, whose Cottages were totally covered with the Snow, & the very tops of their Chimneys to be seen, would afford a Story; But there not being any Relacion to philosophy in them, I forbear them. 10 And now, *I am* Satis Terris Nivis. — And here is enough of my Winter-tale. If it serve to no other purpose, yett it will give me an opportunity to tell you, That Nine months ago, I did a thousand times wish myself with you in *Gresham-Colledge,* which is never so horribly Snow'd upon. But instead of so great a satisfaction, all I can attain to, is the pleasure of talking with you in this Epistolary way, and subscribing myself,

Syr, Yours with an Affection that knows no Winter

[Cotton Mather]

Dr Woodward

1717, 1926 20

---

11 **Satis Terris Nivis,** weary of the snow-covered ground   13 **Gresham-Colledge,** an institution founded with funds left by Sir Thomas Gresham (1519-1579). It was the early meeting place of the Royal Society of London

from Manuductio ad Ministerium

The Manuductio ad Ministerium, *or Directions for a Candidate of the Ministry (Boston, 1726), has been reprinted three times — in 1781, 1789, and by the Facsimile Text Society in 1938. It describes the proper studies for the prospective clergyman, evaluating all the arts and sciences. Professor Perry Miller has recently pointed out that it represents both a "mature tradition of Puritan scholarship in America" and certain striking departures from the seventeenth-century positions. Particularly forward-looking are Mather's emphasis on practical conduct, his minimizing of logic, his enthusiasm for science, and his failure to insist upon the traditional "doctrine-reasons-uses" pattern of the sermon. His comments on style, however, are a defense of the method and conviction of his own work, akin neither to the "plain style" of his predecessors nor to the fashions of the age of Addison and Steele. The passage is a digression in the course of Mather's comments on literature.*

There has been a deal of a do about a STYLE; So much, that I must offer you my Sentiments upon it. There is a *Way of Writing,* wherein the Author endeavours, that the Reader may have *something to the Purpose* in every Paragraph. There is not only a *Vigour* sensible in every *Sentence,* but the Paragraph is embellished with *Profitable*

Text: the Boston edition of 1726   1 **a deal . . . do,** particularly by the enthusiasts for the New Science of Francis Bacon, Robert Boyle, and the Royal Society

References, even to something beyond what is *directly spoken.* Formal and Painful *Quotations* are not studied; yet all that could be learnt from them is insinuated. The Writer pretends not unto *Reading,* yet he could not have writ as he does if he had not *Read* very much in his Time; and his Composures are not only a *Cloth of Gold,* but also stuck with as many *Jewels,* as the Gown of a Russian Embassador. This *Way of Writing* has been decried by many, and is at this Day more than ever so, for the same Reason, that in the old Story, the *Grapes* were decried, *That they were not Ripe.* A Lazy, Ignorant, Conceited Sett of Authors, would perswade the whole Tribe, to lay aside that *Way of Writing,* for the same Reason that one would have

10 perswaded his Brethren to part with the Encumbrance of their *Bushy Tails.* But however *Fashion* and *Humour* may prevail, they must not think that the Club at their *Coffee-House* is, *All the World;* but there will always be those, who will in this Case be governed by *Indisputable Reason;* And who will think, that the real Excellency of a Book will never ly in *saying of little;* That the less one has for his Money in a Book, 'tis really the more Valuable for it; and that the less one is instructed in a Book, and the more of Superfluous *Margin,* and Superficial *Harangue,* and the less of *Substantial Matter* one has in it, the more tis to be accounted of. And if a more Massy *Way of Writing* be never so much disgusted at This Day, a *Better Gust* will come on, as will some other Thing, *quæ jam Cecidere.* In the mean time, Nothing

20 appears to me more Impertinent and Ridiculous than the *Modern Way,* [I cannot say, *Rule;* For they have *None!*] of *Criticising.* The Blades that set up for *Criticks,* I know not who constituted or commission'd 'em! — they appear to me, for the most part as *Contemptible,* as they are a *Supercilious* Generation. For indeed no Two of them have the same *Style;* and they are as intollerably Cross-grain'd and severe in their Censures upon one another, as they are upon the rest of Mankind. But while each of them, conceitedly enough, sets up for the *Standard of Perfection,* we are entirely at a Loss which *Fire* to follow. Nor can you easily find any one thing wherein they agree for their *Style,* except perhaps a perpetual Care to give us Jejune and Empty Pages, without such *Touches of Erudition* (to speak in the *Style* of an In-

30 genious Traveller) as may make the Discourses less *Tedious,* and more *Enriching,* to the Mind of him that peruses them. There is much Talk of a *Florid Style,* obtaining among the Pens, that are most in Vogue; but how often would it puzzle one, even with the best Glasses to find the *Flowres!* And if they were to be Chastized for it, it would be with as much of Justice, as *Jerom* was, for being a *Ciceronian.* After all, Every Man will have his own *Style,* which will distinguish him as much as his *Gate:* And if you can attain to that which I have newly described, but always writing so as to give an *Easy Conveyance* unto your *Idea's,* I would not have you by any *Scourging* be driven out of your *Gate,* but if you must confess a *Fault* in it, make a Confession like that of the Lad, unto his Father while he was beating him for his

40 *Versifying.*

---

7 **the old Story,** of the fox and the grapes, in Aesop's *Fables,* a book which apparently was one of Mather's favorites. In 1692 he wrote and circulated in manuscript a number of "Political Fables."   18 **Gust,** taste   19 **quae jam Cecidere,** which now to cut short, i.e. so much for that   34 **Jerom,** St. Jerome (331?-420), famous as a stylist. The remark is attributed to Erasmus

However, since every Man will have his own Style, I would pray, that we may learn to treat one another with mutual *Civilities,* and *Condescensions,* and handsomely *indulge* one another in this, as *Gentlemen* do in other Matters.

I wonder what ails People, that they can't let *Cicero* write in the *Style* of *Cicero,* and *Seneca* write in the (much other!) *Style* of *Seneca;* and own that Both may please in their *several Ways.* — But I will freely tell you; what has made me consider the *Humourists* that set up for *Criticks upon Style,* as the most *Unregardable Set of Mortals* in the World, is This! Far more Illustrious *Criticks* than any of those to whom I am now bidding Defiance, and no less Men than your *Erasmus's,* and your *Grotius's,* have taxed the *Greek Style* of the *New Testament,* with I know not what *Solæcisms* 10 and *Barbarisms;* And, how many *learned Folks* have Obsequiously run away with the Notion! Whereas 'tis an Ignorant and an Insolent *Whimsey;* which they have been guilty of. It may be (and particularly by an Ingenious *Blackwal,* it has been) Demonstrated, That the Gentlemen are mistaken in every one of their pretended Instances, All the Unquestionable *Classicks,* may be brought in, to convince them of their Mistakes. Those Glorious Oracles are as *pure Greek* as ever was written in the World; and so Correct; so Noble, so Sublime is their *Style,* that never any thing under the Cope of Heaven, but the Old Testament, has equall'd it.

                                                                                 1726

---

5 **Seneca,** Lucius Annaeus Seneca (4 B.C.?-65 A.D.), noted for his short, epigrammatic sentences and rhetorical ornament, in marked contrast to the long sentences of Cicero   9 **Erasmus's . . . Grotius's,** Desiderius Erasmus (1467?-1536) and Hugo de Groot (1583-1645). Erasmus edited the New Testament in Greek, with a Latin translation; Grotius was the author of a commentary or "annotations" on the Bible   13 **Blackwal,** Anthony Blackwall (1674-1730), author of *The Sacred Classicks Defended* (1725)

1652–1725 John Wise

John Wise has been described by Moses Coit Tyler as "the most powerful and brilliant prose-writer produced in this country during the colonial time," and by Vernon Louis Parrington as "the keenest mind and the most trenchant pen of his generation of New Englanders." Without question, he was one of the first Americans to sense what was happening and to build a political philosophy outside the well-worn traditions of Plato, Aristotle, the Bible, and Covenant Theology.

Wise was graduated in 1673 from Harvard College, where he studied divinity. He settled later at Chebacco, in Ipswich, Massachusetts. An enormous man, he was renowned throughout New England as a wrestler, and served twice as a military chaplain. It is said that once a boat's crew from his parish was captured by pirates. Wise prayed for them earnestly on Sunday morning, finally saying, none too mildly: "Great God, if there is no other way, may they arise and butcher their enemies." Which is exactly what they did, at about the time Wise was praying — a coincidence not overlooked by the New England eye for God's providences.

Wise became involved in politics in 1687, when Governor Edmund Andros ordered the Massachusetts towns to appoint commissioners to collect taxes levied by the governor and council. Chebacco, with Wise as one of the leaders, refused. Wise was charged with sedition, jailed in Boston, fined, suspended from the ministry, and forced to post a bond for good behavior. In 1688, however, Edmund Andros was chased out of New England.

Wise became the champion of democratic, local control in church and, by implication, in state. We know of his convictions through two books: *The Churches Quarrel Espoused* (1710), and *A Vindication of the Government of New-England Churches* (1717). He was probably the author of several anonymously published pamphlets, but his reputation rests upon these two books.

The first denounced a proposal to establish associations of clergymen to gain power over the choice of new ministers and the setting up of new churches. The laity, Wise felt, should retain control of these things, and resist any step toward clerical domination.

The *Vindication* was planned to justify Congregationalism and is a landmark in the literature of that denomination. What makes it remarkable is that Wise argued not only in the patterns of a century-old debate on church government, but also in those of political philosophers. This is the first colonial book to portray men arriving at government through mutual consent, to discuss "natural rights," and to assume that man's reason is adequate to help in the construction of a good form of political organization. It is no wonder that Wise's two books were reprinted in 1772, in the midst of the Revolutionary crisis.

J. L. Sibley, **Biographical Sketches of the Graduates of Harvard University**, II, Cambridge, 1873   George Allan Cook, **John Wise, Early American Democrat**, New York, 1952

from A Vindication of the Government of New-England Churches

In the Preface, Wise outlined his book as follows: "The constitution of New-England Churches as settled by their Platform, may be fairly justified, from Antiquity; the Light of Nature; Holy Scripture; and from the Noble and Excellent Nature of the Constitution itself. And lastly from the Providence of GOD dignifying of it." The justification from the light of nature is the most remarkable portion because the theological frame of reference, which might be expected, is almost wholly absent. The seventeenth-century Puritans would have regarded Wise's dependence upon "right reason" as both foolish and dangerous, his easy dismissal of what has happened to man since his creation (that is to say, of Adam's fall) as heresy. Wise, in short, is very much a man of the new century.

I shall disclose several Principles of Natural Knowledge; plainly discovering the Law of Nature; or the true sentiments of Natural Reason, with Respect to Mans Being and Government. And in this Essay I shall peculiarly confine the discourse to two heads, *viz.*

1. Of the Natural [in distinction to the Civil] and then,

2. Of the Civil Being of Man. And I shall Principally take Baron *Puffendorff* for my Chief Guide and Spokesman. . . .

But to proceed under the head of a State of Natural Being, I shall more distinctly Explain the State of Humane Nature in its Original Capacity, as Man is placed on Earth by his Maker, and Cloathed with many investitures, and Immunities which 10 properly belong to Man separately considered. As,

1. The Prime Immunity in Mans State, is that he is most properly the Subject of the Law of Nature. He is the Favourite Animal on Earth; in that this Part of God's Image, *viz.* Reason is Congenate with his Nature, wherein by a Law Immutable, Instampt upon his Frame, God has provided a Rule for Men in all their Actions, obliging each one to the performance of that which is Right, not only as to Justice, but likewise as to all other Moral Vertues, the which is nothing but the Dictate of Right Reason founded in the Soul of Man. *Molloy, De Mao, Præf.* That which is to be drawn from Man's Reason, flowing from the true Current of that Faculty, when unperverted, may be said to be the Law of Nature; on which account, the Holy 20 Scriptures declare it written on Mens hearts. For being indowed with a Soul, you may know from your self, how, and what you ought to act, Rom. 2. 14. *These having not a Law, are a Law to themselves.* So that the meaning is, when we acknowledge the Law of Nature to be the dictate of Right Reason, we must mean that the Understanding of Man is Endowed with such a power, as to be able, from the Contemplation of humane Condition to discover a necessity of Living agreeably with this Law: And likewise to find out some Principle, by which the Precepts of it, may be clearly and solidly Demonstrated. The way to discover the Law of Nature in our own state, is by a narrow Watch, and accurate Contemplation of our Natural Condition, and propensions. Others say this is the way to find out the Law of Nature. 30 *scil.* If a Man any ways doubts, whether what he is going to do to another Man be agreeable to the Law of Nature, then let him suppose himself to be in that other Mans Room; And by this Rule effectually Executed. A Man must be a very dull Scholar to Nature not to make Proficiency in the Knowledge of her Laws. But more Particularly in pursuing our Condition for the discovery of the Law of Nature, this is very obvious to view, *viz.*

1. A Principle of Self-Love, & Self-Preservation, is very predominant in every Mans Being.

2. A Sociable Disposition.

3. An Affection or Love to Mankind in General. . . .   40

---

6 **Baron Puffendorff,** Samuel Pufendorf (1632-1694), German jurist-author of *De jure naturae et gentium* (1672), a work on natural and international law much read by colonial Americans   18 **Molloy, *De Mao,* Præf.,** a reference to the preface of *De jure maritimo* (1676), a legal work by Charles Molloy (1646-1690)   31 **scil.,** *scilicet.* namely

2. The Second Great Immunity of Man is an Original Liberty Instampt upon his Rational Nature. He that intrudes upon this Liberty, Violates the Law of Nature. In this Discourse I shall wave the Consideration of Mans Moral Turpitude, but shall view him Physically as a Creature which God has made and furnished essentially with many Enobling Immunities, which render him the most August Animal in the World, and still, whatever has happened since his Creation, he remains at the upper-end of Nature, and as such is a Creature of a very Noble Character. For as to his Dominion, the whole frame of the Lower Part of the Universe is devoted to his use, and at his Command; and his Liberty under the Conduct of Right Reason, is
10 equal with his trust. Which Liberty may be briefly Considered, Internally as to his Mind, and externally as to his Person.

1. The Internal Native Liberty of Mans Nature in general implies, a faculty of Doing or Omitting things according to the Direction of his Judgment. But in a more special meaning, this Liberty does not consist in a loose and ungovernable Freedom, or in an unbounded Licence of Acting. Such Licence is disagreeing with the condition and dignity of Man, and would make Man of a lower and meaner Constitution then Bruit Creatures; who in all their Liberties are kept under a better and more Rational Government, by their Instincts. Therefore as *Plutarch* says, *Those Persons only who live in Obedience to Reason, are worthy to be accounted free: They alone*
20 *live as they Will, who have Learnt what they ought to Will.* So that the true Natural Liberty of Man, such as really and truely agrees to him, must be understood, as he is Guided and Restrained by the Tyes of Reason, and Laws of Nature; all the rest is Brutal, if not worse.

2. Mans External Personal, Natural Liberty, Antecedent to all Humane parts, or Alliances must also be considered. And so every Man must be conceived to be perfectly in his own Power and disposal, and not to be controuled by the Authority of any other. And thus every Man, must be acknowledged equal to every Man, since all Subjection and all Command are equally banished on both sides; and considering all Men thus at Liberty, every Man has a Prerogative to Judge for himself, *viz.*
30 What shall be most for his Behoof, Happiness and Well-being.

3. The Third Capital Immunity belonging to Mans Nature, is an equality amongst Men; Which is not to be denied by the Law of Nature, till Man has Resigned himself with all his Rights for the sake of a Civil State; and then his Personal Liberty and Equality is to be cherished, and preserved to the highest degree, as will consist with all just distinctions amongst Men of Honour, and shall be agreeable with the publick Good. For Man has a high valuation of himself, and the passion seems to lay its first foundation [not in Pride, but] really in the high and admirable Frame and Constitution of Humane Nature. The Word Man, says my Author, is thought to carry somewhat of Dignity in its sound; and we commonly make use of this as
40 the most proper and prevailing Argument against a rude Insulter, *viz. I am not a*

---

3 **Consideration of Mans Moral Turpitude,** of original sin or the Fall. Note Wise's rather offhand dismissal of a basic Puritan belief — the innate evil of human nature   18 **Plutarch** (46?-120 A.D.), Greek biographer, author of *Parallel Lives of the Greeks and Romans,* one of the most famous books of its period   38 **my author,** Pufendorf

Beast or a Dog, but am a Man as well as your self. Since then Humane Nature agrees
equally with all persons; and since no one can live a Sociable Life with another that
does not own or Respect him as a Man; It follows as a Command of the Law of
Nature, that every Man Esteem and treat another as one who is naturally his Equal,
or who is a Man as well as he. There be many popular, or plausible Reasons that
greatly Illustrate this Equality, *viz.* that we all Derive our Being from one stock,
the same Common Father of humane Race. On this Consideration *Bœthius* checks
the pride of the Insulting Nobility.

> *Quid Genus et Proavos Strepitis?*
> *Si Primordia Vestra,*   10
> *Auteremque Deum Spectas,*
> *Nullus Degener Extat*
> *Nisi vitiis Perjura fovens,*
> *Proprium Deserat Ortum.*

> *Fondly our first Descent we Boast;*
> *If whence at first our Breath we Drew*
> *The common springs of Life we view,*
> *The Airy Notion soon is Lost.*

> *The Almighty made us equal all;*
> *But he that slavishly complyes*   20
> *To do the Drudgery of Vice,*
> *Denyes his high Original.*

And also that our Bodies are Composed of matter, frail, brittle, and lyable to be
destroyed by thousand Accidents; we all owe our Existence to the same Method of
propagation. The Noblest Mortal in his Entrance on to the Stage of Life, is not
distinguished by any pomp or of passage from the lowest of Mankind; and our Life
hastens to the same General Mark: Death observes no Ceremony, but Knocks as
loud at the Barriers of the Court, as at the Door of the Cottage. This Equality being admitted, bears a very great force in maintaining Peace and Friendship amongst
Men. For that he who would use the Assistance of others, in promoting his own 30
Advantage, ought as freely to be at their service, when they want his help on the
like Occasions. *One Good turn Requires another,* is the Common Proverb; for otherwise he must need esteem others unequal to himself, who constantly demands their
Aid, and as constantly denies his own. And whoever is of this Insolent Temper,
cannot but highly displease those about him, and soon give Occasion of the Breach
of the Common Peace. It was a Manly Reproof which *Charactacus* gave the *Romans,*
Num Si vos Omnibus &c. What! because you desire to be Masters of all Men, does it
follow therefore that all Men should desire to be your Slaves, for that it is a Command of Natures Law, that no Man that has not obtained a particular and special

---

7 **Boethius,** here quoted inaccurately   36 **Charactacus,** Caractacus, British chieftain who fought against
the Roman invaders until defeated in Wales, A.D. 50

Right, shall arrogate to himself a Larger share then his fellows, but shall admit others to equal Priviledges with himself. So that the Principle of Equality in a Natural State, is peculiarly transgressed by Pride, which is when a Man without sufficient reason prefers himself to others. And though as *Hensius,* Paraphrases upon *Aristotle's* Politicks to this Purpose. *viz. Nothing is more suitable to Nature, then that those who Excel in Understanding and Prudence, should Rule and Controul those who are less happy in those Advantages,* &c. Yet we must note, that there is room for an Answer, *scil.* That it would be the Greatest absurdity to believe, that Nature actually Invests the Wise with a Sovereignity over the weak; or with a Right of forcing
10 them against their Wills; for that no Sovereignty can be established, unless some Humane Deed, or Covenant Precede: Nor does Natural fitness for Government make a Man presently Governour over another; for that as *Ulpian* says, *by a Natural Right all Men are born free;* and Nature having set all Men upon a Level and made them Equals, no Servitude or Subjection can be conceived without Inequality; and this cannot be made without Usurpation or Force in others, or Voluntary Compliance in those who Resign their freedom, and give away their degree of Natural Being. And thus we come,

2. To consider Man in a Civil State of Being; wherein we shall observe the great difference between a Natural, and Political State; for in the Latter State many Great
20 disproportions appear, or at least many obvious distinctions are soon made amongst Men; which Doctrine is to be laid open under a few heads.

1. Every Man considered in a Natural State, must be allowed to be Free, and at his own dispose; yet to suit Mans Inclinations to Society; And in a peculiar manner to gratify the necessity he is in of publick Rule and Order, he is Impelled to enter into a Civil Community; and Divests himself of his Natural Freedom, and puts himself under Government; which amongst other things Comprehends the Power of Life and Death over Him; together with Authority to Injoyn him some things to which he has an utter Aversation, and to prohibit him other things, for which he may have as strong an Inclination; so that he may be often under this Authority,
30 obliged to Sacrifice his Private, for the Publick Good. So that though Man is inclined to Society, yet he is driven to a Combination by great necessity. For that the true and leading Cause of forming Governments, and yielding up Natural Liberty, and throwing Mans Equality into a Common Pile to be new Cast by the Rules of fellowship; was really and truly to guard themselves against the Injuries Men were lyable to Interchangeably; for none so Good to Man, as Man, and yet none a greater Enemy. So that,

2. The first Humane Subject and Original of Civil Power is the People. For as they have a Power every Man over himself in a Natural State, so upon a Combination they can and do bequeath this Power unto others; and settle it according as
40 their united decretion shall Determine. For that this is very plain, that when the Subject of Sovereign Power is quite Extinct, that Power returns to the People again. And when they are free, they may set up what species of Government they please;

---

4 **Hensius,** Daniel Hensius (1580-1655), a Dutch scholar   12 **Ulpian,** Domitius Ulpianus (d. 228 A.D.), Roman jurist, author of commentaries on the civil and criminal law

or if they rather incline to it, they may subside into a State of Natural Being, if it be plainly for the best. In the *Eastern* Country of the *Mogul,* we have some resemblance of the Case; for upon the Death of an absolute Monarch, they live so many days without a Civil Head; but in that *Interregnum,* those who survive the Vacancy, are glad to get into a Civil State again; and usually they are in a very Bloody Condition when they return under the Covert of a new Monarch; this project is to indear the People to a Tyranny, from the Experience they have so lately had of an Anarchy.

3. The formal Reason of Government is the Will of a Community, yielded up and surrendered to some other Subject, either of one particular Person, or more, Conveyed in the following manner.   10

Let us conceive in our Mind a multitude of Men, all Naturally Free & Equal; going about voluntarily, to Erect themselves into a new Common-Wealth. Now their Condition being such, to bring themselves into a Politick Body, they must needs Enter into divers Covenants.

1. They must Interchangeably each Man Covenant to joyn in one lasting Society, that they may be capable to concert the measures of their safety, by a Publick Vote.

2. A Vote or Decree must then nextly pass to set up some Particular species of Government over them. And if they are joyned in their first Compact upon absolute Terms to stand to the Decision of the first Vote concerning the Species of Government: Then all are bound by the Majority to acquiesce in that particular Form   20 thereby settled, though their own private Opinion, incline them to some other Model.

3. After a Decree has specified the Particular form of Government, then there will be need of a New Covenant, whereby those on whom Sovereignty is conferred, engage to take care of the Common Peace, and Welfare. And the Subjects on the other hand, to yield them faithful Obedience. In which Covenant is Included that Submission and Union of Wills, by which a State may be conceived to be but one Person. So that the most proper Definition of a Civil State, is this, *viz.* A Civil State is a Compound Moral Person, whose Will [United by those Covenants before passed] is the Will of all; to the end it may Use, and Apply the strength and riches of Private Persons towards maintaining the Common Peace, Security, and Well-   30 being of all. Which may be conceived as tho' the whole State was now become but one Man; in which the aforesaid Covenants may be supposed under Gods Providence, to be the Divine *Fiat,* Pronounced by God, let us make Man. And by way of resemblance the aforesaid Being may be thus Anatomized.

1. The Sovereign Power is the Soul infused, giving Life and Motion to the whole Body.

2. Subordinate Officers are the Joynts by which the Body moves.

3. Wealth and Riches are the Strength.

4. Equity and Laws are the Reason.

5. Councellors the Memory.   40

6. *Salus Populi,* or the Happiness of the People, is the End of its Being; or main Business to be attended and done.

---

2 **Mogul,** Mongol, ruler of the Moslem empire in India, with its capital at Delhi   14 **divers Covenants.** For a discussion of this subject, see p. 15

7. Concord amongst the Members, and all Estates, is the Health.

8. Sedition is Sickness, and Civil War Death.

4. The Parts of Sovereignty may be considered: So,

1. As it Prescribes the Rule of Action: It is rightly termed *Legislative Power.*

2. As it determines the Controversies of Subjects by the Standard of those Rules. So is it justly Termed Judiciary Power.

3. As it Arms the Subjects against Foreigners, or forbids Hostility, so its called the Power of Peace and War.

4. As it takes in Ministers for the discharge of Business, so it is called the Right of Appointing Magistrates. So that all great officers and Publick Servants, must needs owe their Original to the Creating Power of Sovereignty. So that those whose Right it is to Create, may Dissolve the being of those who are Created, unless they cast them into an Immortal Frame. And yet must needs be dissoluble if they justly forfeit their being to their Creators.

5. The Chief End of Civil Communities, is, that Men thus conjoyned, may be secured against the Injuries, they are lyable to from their own Kind. For if every Man could secure himself singly; It would be great folly for him, to Renounce his Natural Liberty, in which every Man is his own King and Protector.

6. The Sovereign Authority besides that it inheres in every State as in a Common and General Subject. So farther according as it resides in some One Person, or in a Council [consisting of some Select Persons, or of all the Members of a Community] as in a proper and particular Subject, so it produceth different Forms of Common-wealths, *viz.* Such as are either simple and regular, or mixt.

1. The Forms of a Regular State are three only, which Forms arise from the proper and particular Subject, in which the Supream Power Resides. As,

1. A Democracy, which is when the Sovereign Power is Lodged in a Council con-sisting of all the Members, and where every Member has the Priviledge of a Vote. This Form of Government, appears in the greatest part of the World to have been the most Ancient. For that Reason seems to shew it to be most probable, that when Men [being Originally in a condition of Natural Freedom and Equality] had thoughts of joyning in a Civil Body, would without question be inclined to Administer their common Affairs, by their common Judgment, and so must necessarily to gratifie that Inclination establish a Democracy; neither can it be rationally imagined, that Fathers of Families being yet Free and Independent, should in a moment, or little time take off their long delight in governing their own Affairs, & Devolve all upon some single Sovereign Commander; for that it seems to have been thought more Equitable, that what belonged to all, should be managed by all, when all had entered by Compact into one Community. The Original of our Government, says *Plato,* [speaking of the *Athenian* Common-wealth] *was taken from the Equality of our Race. Other States there are composed of different Blood, and of unequal Lines, the Conse-quence of which are disproportionable Soveraignty, Tyrannical or Oligarchycal Sway; under which men live in such a manner, as to Esteem themselves partly Lords, and partly Slaves to each other. But we and our Country men, being all Born Brethren of the same Mother,*

---

39 **Plato** (428?-348? B.C.), author of the *Republic,* here alluded to

*do not look upon our selves, to stand under so hard a Relation, as that of Lords, and Slaves;
but the Parity of our Descent incline us to keep up the like Parity by our Laws, and so
yield the precedency to nothing but to Superiour Vertue and Wisdome.* And moreover it
seems very manifest that most Civil Communities arose at first from the Union of
Families, that were nearly allyed in Race and Blood. And though Ancient Story
make frequent mention of Kings, yet it appears that most of them were such that
had an Influence rather in perswading, then in any Power of Commanding. So
Justin discribes that Kind of Government, as the most Primitive, which *Aristotle*
stiles an Heroical Kingdom. *viz.* Such as is no ways Inconsistent with a Democratical
State. *De Princip. Reru.* 1. *L.* 1. *C.*   10

A democracy is then Erected, when a Number of Free Persons, do Assemble together, in Order to enter into a Covenant for Uniting themselves in a Body: And
such a Preparative Assembly hath some appearance already of a Democracy; it is a
Democracy in *Embrio* properly in this Respect, that every Man hath the Priviledge
freely to deliver his Opinion concerning the Common Affairs. Yet he who dissents
from the Vote of the Majority, is not in the least obliged by what they determine,
till by a second Covenant, a Popular Form be actually Established; for not before
then can we call it a Democratical Government, *viz.* Till the Right of Determining
all matters relating to the publick Safety, is actually placed in a General Assembly
of the whole People; or by their own Compact and Mutual Agreement, Determine 20
themselves the proper Subject for the Exercise of Sovereign Power. And to compleat
this State, and render it capable to Exert its Power to answer the End of a Civil
State: These Conditions are necessary.

1. That a certain Time and Place be Assigned for Assembling.

2. That when the Assembly be Orderly met, as to Time and Place, that then the
Vote of the Majority must pass for the Vote of the whole Body.

3. That Magistrates be appointed to Exercise the Authority of the whole for the
better dispatch of Business, of every days Occurrence; who also may with more
Mature diligence, search into more Important Affairs; and if in case any thing happens of greater Consequence, may report it to the Assembly; and be peculiarly Serv- 30
iceable in putting all Publick Decrees into Execution. Because a large Body of
People is almost useless in Respect of the last Service, and of many others, as to the
more Particular Application and Exercise of Power. Therefore it is most agreeable
with the Law of Nature, that they Institute their Officers to act in their Name, and
Stead.

2. The Second Species of Regular Government, is an Aristocracy; and this is said
then to be Constituted when the People, or Assembly United by a first Covenant,
and having thereby cast themselves into the first Rudiments of a State; do then by
Common Decree, Devolve the Sovereign Power, on a Council consisting of some
Select Members; and these having accepted of the Designation, are then properly 40
invested with Sovereign Command; and then an Aristocracy is formed.

3. The Third Species of a Regular Government, is a Monarchy which is settled

---

8 **Justin**, Flavius Anicius Justinianus, Justinian I (483-565), emperor of the Eastern Roman Empire from
527 until his death, codifier of the Roman Law

when the Sovereign Power is confered on some one worthy Person. It differs from the former, because a Monarch who is but one Person in Natural, as well as in Moral account, & so is furnished with an Immediate Power of Exercising Sovereign Command in all Instances of Government; but the fore named must needs have Particular Time and Place assigned; but the Power and Authority is Equal in each.

2. Mixt Governments, which are various and of divers kinds [not now to be Enumerated] yet possibly the fairest in the World is that which has a Regular Monarchy; [in Distinction to what is Dispotick] settled upon a Noble Democracy as its Basis. And each part of the Government is so adjusted by Pacts and Laws
10 that renders the whole Constitution an *Elisium*. It is said of the *British* Empire, *That it is such a Monarchy, as that by the necessary subordinate Concurrence of the Lords and Commons, in the Making and Repealing all Statutes or Acts of Parliament; it hath the main advantages of an Aristocracy, and of a Democracy, and yet free from the Disadvantages and Evils of either. It is such a Monarchy, as by most Admirable Temperament affords very much to the Industry, Liberty, and Happiness of the Subject, and reserves enough for the Majesty and Prerogative of any King, who will own his People as Subjects, not as Slaves. It is a Kingdom, that of all the Kingdoms of the World, is most like to the Kingdom of Jesus Christ, whose Yoke is easie, and Burden light.* Present State of *England* 1st Part 64 *p* . . .

1717

1703–1758 *Jonathan Edwards*

To most Americans Jonathan Edwards is either the founder of the family often compared so favorably with the ill-fated Jukeses that it provides the stock argument for the importance of heredity and education or, and perhaps more commonly, the most sulphurous hellfire preacher of the colonial period. To the specialists, however, Edwards is the greatest theologian that America has yet produced, unquestionably one of the most original minds in our country's history. By uniting a passionate love for God and His authority with a genius for logic and system, he made himself the foremost reinterpreter of Calvinism in America; and he has remained, down to the present day, a great bulwark of religion through his powerful affirmation of faith in the reality and the primacy of spiritual experience. He has been compared with such church fathers as Tertullian, St. Augustine, and Calvin; with the philosophers Spinoza, Leibnitz, Berkeley, and

Kant; and, for his synthesis of the attitudes of an age, with such men as Dante and Emerson.

Edwards was born in 1703 at East Windsor, Connecticut, where his father was minister. Surrounded by sisters (he was the fifth child and the only son in a family of eleven), he received his early education at home. He was graduated from Yale College before he was seventeen. He spent two additional years at Yale in the study of theology and, after eight months during which he preached in a Presbyterian church in New York City, three more years as a tutor. Early in 1727 he joined his grandfather, the Rev. Solomon Stoddard, in the church at Northampton, Massachusetts, married, and became full minister at Stoddard's death in 1729.

As a clergyman Edwards developed an absorbing interest in what we would now call the psychology of religion. He welcomed the "awakenings" which came periodically in his church, and eventually announced that he could not conscientiously admit to communion those persons who had made no public relation of religious experience. His congregation were unwilling to accept this return to the stricter ways of the first generation in New England, and in 1750 Edwards was dismissed. From 1751 until 1757 he was pastor at Stockbridge, Massachusetts, at that time an Indian mission village on the frontier. He then accepted a call to the presidency of the College of New Jersey (now Princeton University), where he died of smallpox three months after his installation.

The rise of Edwards to leadership as a preacher and theologian is to be traced chiefly in his writings. His precocity as a thinker is demonstrated by a considerable body of philosophical papers written during his residence at Yale and published piecemeal after his death. "Of Insects," "Of Being," "Colours," and "Notes on the Mind" have often been cited as evidence of his genius for logical analysis. They show that he developed, independently of George Berkeley, the English philosopher, that philosophical position known as "subjective idealism," which holds that matter has reality only in terms of the perceiving mind. Although this position was fundamental to Edwards' entire intellectual life, he did not publish his conclusions and therefore had no genuine influence upon the philosophical thought of his age.

Soon after his settlement at Northampton, however, he began to publish sermons and case histories which show his absorption in the phenomena of conversion. *A Divine and Supernatural Light* (1734) carefully expounds his belief that a mystical faith is likewise the most logical. *A Faithful Narrative* (1737) describes the first great revival in his church. *Some Thoughts Concerning the Present Revival of Religion in New England* (1742) supports the activities of George Whitefield, an English Methodist who had preached with great effect throughout the colonies, in the face of ridicule by the leading ministers of Boston (see pp. 205-211). These works merit comparison with a famous book of the twentieth century: William James' *The Varieties of Religious Experience* (1902). Edwards must not be dismissed as a ranting revivalist, playing upon unstable individuals and reveling in the physical contortions of repenting sinners. He could be as skeptical of mass emotion as anyone, but he did believe thoroughly in the possibility and the supreme importance of true conversion. He had experienced it himself; he thought he could distinguish between the genuinely "awakened" and the momentarily excited. He lent his support, therefore, to those who sought to arouse men to the insufficiency of a comfortable Sunday pew unaccompanied by a deep-rooted, burning love of God. His justification of trust in religious experience and intuitive knowledge was enormously influential and helped to make evangelicalism and revivalism the prevailing pattern of American religion.

Finally, Edwards built for himself and his followers an impressively logical system of theology, powerfully reaffirming the principal heads of Calvinism but modifying their bases in accordance with the philosophy and psychology of his day. This system, which was largely responsible for his great posthumous reputation, was set forth in four treatises: *A Treatise Concerning Religious Affections* (1746); *A Careful and Strict Inquiry into the Modern Prevailing Notions of That Freedom of Will, Which Is Supposed To Be Essential to Moral Agency, Virtue and Vice, Reward and Punishment, Praise and Blame* (1754); *The Great Christian Doctrine of Original Sin Defended* (1758); and *Two Dissertations, I. Concerning the End for Which God Created the World. II. The Nature of True Virtue* (1765).

In the *Treatise Concerning Religious Affections* Edwards argued that the rational soul, or human mind, has two faculties: the Understanding, by which it discerns, views, or judges; and the Will or Inclination, by which it is turned toward or against the things perceived by the Understanding. Will, in other words, he regarded as closely akin to feeling or emotion; it is that aspect of mind which is described by the common phrase, to have a "heart" for this action or that one. The passions or affections of Will — love and hatred and their derivatives — were to Edwards the basis of religion; reason or judgment was not. Finally, he asserted that the religious affections, of which love was the most important, flowed from a "supernatural sense," communicated directly by God to the regenerate man. In this analysis, based partly upon traditional distinctions and partly upon his own experience, Edwards placed himself in opposition to those thinkers who laid most emphasis upon the element of reason in religion (the Deists and the Unitarians, for example), but he stopped short of the opinion of the Arminians (the followers of Jacobus Arminius, 1560-1609, a Dutch theologian) that the power of accepting or rejecting Divine grace rested in some measure in the Will itself.

The Arminians had long argued that unless the choice between good and evil is conceived of as lying with the individual there can be no real incentive to religion and virtue; they represented a growing opposition to the Calvinistic insistence upon predestination and the election of the few. Edwards' *Freedom of Will* is a lengthy consideration of this crucial point, in which he proved to his own satisfaction that the Will was passive. Although a man may be able to do what he pleases and so is to some degree free, each volitional act has a cause or motive which is outside his control. Edwards sought to maintain the glory of the Puritan God and, at the same time, to place some responsibility for conduct upon the individual. How successful he was depends upon his reader's willingness to accept his definition of terms.

Original Sin Defended answered *The Scripture-Doctrine of Original Sin Proposed to a Free and Candid Examination* (1738) by an English clergyman, John Taylor, who had drawn Isaac Watts, John Wesley, and other well-known divines into a controversy. Edwards once more reinforced the Calvinist positions by logical analysis and careful demolition of his opponent's arguments. His chief contributions were an ingenious explanation of general responsibility for Adam's sin, on the ground that all men are to Adam as buds and shoots are to the root or stock of a tree, and a description of the Fall as the withdrawal from man of the inclination toward virtue. At no point in his system was Edwards to be sooner challenged, for his portrayal of man's depravity and complete selfishness was in sharp contrast with the humanitarian trend of his times.

The glory of God was urged once more in the *Two Dissertations.* God created the world because of a "disposition to communicate His own fulness." "The beams of glory come from God, are something of God, and are refunded back again to their original." Virtue is "disinterested benevolence," a kind of beauty, exceedingly rare in man and attainable only by the grace of God. The discussion, as Professor Faust has shown, is closely related to the thought of the period, especially to Francis Hutcheson's *Inquiry into the Original of Our Ideas of Beauty and Virtue* (1725).

Doctrinally, in short, Edwards was at one with Thomas Shepard, and the title of *The Sincere Convert* (see p. 115) can stand for Edwards' theology as readily as for Shepard's. There were modifications, to be sure, but the Edwards theology is primarily a powerful reaffirmation, and comes at the middle point in the drift from Puritanism to Transcendentalism.

The Works of President Edwards, ed. Samuel Austin, 8 vols., Worcester, 1808   A new edition of Edwards' works, begun in 1957, is now being published by the Yale University Press   Jonathan Edwards: Representative Selections, ed. C. H. Faust and T. H. Johnson, Cincinnati, 1935   T. H. Johnson, The Printed Writings of Jonathan Edwards, 1703-1758, A Bibliography, Princeton, 1940   A. V. G. Allen, Jonathan Edwards, Boston, 1889   Ola E. Winslow, Jonathan Edwards, New York, 1940   Perry Miller, Jonathan Edwards, New York, 1949

Personal Narrative

Edwards' account of his "new sense of things" was written sometime after 1739, and was first printed in Samuel Hopkins' Life and Character of the Late Reverend Mr. Jonathan Edwards *(Boston, 1765). The manuscript has been lost. The "Personal Narrative" is much admired as one of the most glowing yet lucid descriptions of mystic experience in American literature. The invariable steps of conversion — a conviction of sin, a recognition of the justice and absolute sovereignty of God, and a surrender to Him — are followed by a description of results which most of us, whatever our faith, can find enviable. The exhilaration of the spirit which Edwards describes is what he lived for; his is one of the most vivid testimonies to the integrating power of religious ecstasy.*

I had a variety of concerns and exercises about my soul from my childhood; but had two more remarkable seasons of awakening, before I met with that change by which I was brought to those new dispositions, and that new sense of things, that I have since had. The first time was when I was a boy, some years before I went to

Text: the Austin edition of the *Works*, 1808   4 I . . . college. Edwards entered Yale in 1716

college, at a time of remarkable awakening in my father's congregation. I was then very much affected for many months, and concerned about the things of religion, and my soul's salvation; and was abundant in duties. I used to pray five times a day in secret, and to spend much time in religious talk with other boys; and used to meet with them to pray together. I experienced I know not what kind of delight in religion. My mind was much engaged in it, and had much selfrighteous pleasure; and it was my delight to abound in religious duties. I with some of my schoolmates joined together, and built a booth in a swamp, in a very retired spot, for a place of prayer. And besides, I had particular secret places of my own in the woods, where I used
10 to retire by myself; and was from time to time much affected. My affections seemed to be lively and easily moved, and I seemed to be in my element when engaged in religious duties. And I am ready to think, many are deceived with such affections, and such a kind of delight as I then had in religion, and mistake it for grace.

But in process of time, my convictions and affections wore off; and I entirely lost all those affections and delights and left off secret prayer, at least as to any constant performance of it; and returned like a dog to his vomit, and went on in the ways of sin. Indeed I was at times very uneasy, especially towards the latter part of my time at college; when it pleased God, to seize me with a pleurisy; in which he brought me nigh to the grave, and shook me over the pit of hell. And yet, it was not long
20 after my recovery, before I fell again into my old ways of sin. But God would not suffer me to go on with any quietness; I had great and violent inward struggles, till, after many conflicts with wicked inclinations, repeated resolutions, and bonds that I laid myself under by a kind of vows to God, I was brought wholly to break off all former wicked ways, and all ways of known outward sin; and to apply myself to seek salvation, and practise many religious duties; but without that kind of affection and delight which I had formerly experienced. My concern now wrought more by inward struggles and conflicts, and selfreflections. I made seeking my salvation the main business of my life. But yet, it seems to me, I sought after a miserable manner; which has made me sometimes since to question, whether ever it issued in that
30 which was saving; being ready to doubt, whether such miserable seeking ever succeeded. I was indeed brought to seek salvation in a manner that I never was before; I felt a spirit to part with all things in the world, for an interest in Christ. My concern continued and prevailed, with many exercising thoughts and inward struggles; but yet it never seemed to be proper to express that concern by the name of terror.

From my childhood up, my mind had been full of objections against the doctrine of God's sovereignty, in choosing whom he would to eternal life, and rejecting whom he pleased; leaving them eternally to perish, and be everlastingly tormented in hell. It used to appear like a horrible doctrine to me. But I remember the time very well, when I seemed to be convinced, and fully satisfied, as to this sovereignty
40 of God, and his justice in thus eternally disposing of men, according to his sovereign pleasure. But never could give an account, how, or by what means, I was thus convinced, not in the least imagining at the time, nor a long time after, that there was any extraordinary influence of God's Spirit in it; but only that now I saw further, and my reason apprehended the justice and reasonableness of it. However, my mind

rested in it; and it put an end to all those cavils and objections. And there has been ·
a wonderful alteration in my mind, with respect to the doctrine of God's sovereignty,
from that day to this; so that I scarce ever have found so much as the rising of an
objection against it, in the most absolute sense, in God's shewing mercy to whom
he will shew mercy, and hardening whom he will. God's absolute sovereignty and
justice, with respect to salvation and damnation, is what my mind seems to rest
assured of, as much as of any thing that I see with my eyes; at least it is so at times.
But I have often, since that first conviction, had quite another kind of sense
of God's sovereignty than I had then. I have often since had not only a conviction,
but a delightful conviction. The doctrine has very often appeared exceeding pleasant, 10
bright, and sweet. Absolute sovereignty is what I love to ascribe to God. But my
first conviction was not so.

The first instance that I remember of that sort of inward, sweet delight in God
and divine things that I have lived much in since, was on reading those words, 1
Tim. i.17. *Now unto the King eternal, immortal, invisible, the only wise God, be honor
and glory forever and ever, Amen.* As I read the words, there came into my soul, and
was as it were diffused through it, a sense of the glory of the Divine Being; a new
sense, quite different from any thing I ever experienced before. Never any words of
scripture seemed to me as these words did. I thought with myself, how excellent a
Being that was, and how happy I should be, if I might enjoy that God, and be rapt 20
up to him in heaven, and be as it were swallowed up in him for ever! I kept saying, and as it were singing over these words of scripture to myself; and went to
pray to God that I might enjoy him, and prayed in a manner quite different from
what I used to do; with a new sort of affection. But it never came into my thought,
that there was any thing spiritual, or of a saving nature in this.

From about that time, I began to have a new kind of apprehensions and ideas of
Christ, and the work of redemption, and the glorious way of salvation by him. An
inward, sweet sense of these things, at times, came into my heart; and my soul was
led away in pleasant views and contemplations of them. And my mind was greatly
engaged to spend my time in reading and meditating on Christ, on the beauty and 30
excellency of his person, and the lovely way of salvation by free grace in him.
I found no books so delightful to me, as those that treated of these subjects. Those
words Cant. ii.l, used to be abundantly with me, *I am the Rose of Sharon, and the
Lilly of the valleys.* The words seemed to me, sweetly to represent the loveliness and
beauty of Jesus Christ. The whole book of Canticles used to be pleasant to me, and
I used to be much in reading it, about that time; and found, from time to time, an
inward sweetness, that would carry me away, in my contemplations. This I know
not how to express otherwise, than by a calm, sweet abstraction of soul from all
the concerns of this world; and sometimes a kind of vision, or fixed ideas and
imaginations, of being alone in the mountains, or some solitary wilderness, far from 40
all mankind, sweetly conversing with Christ, and wrapt and swallowed up in God.
The sense I had of divine things, would often of a sudden kindle up, as it were, a
sweet burning in my heart; an ardor of soul, that I know not how to express.

---

33 **Cant. ii 1,** Canticles, Song of Solomon 2:1

Not long after I first began to experience these things, I gave an account to my father of some things that had passed in my mind. I was pretty much affected by the discourse we had together; and when the discourse was ended, I walked abroad alone, in a solitary place in my father's pasture, for contemplation. And as I was walking there, and looking up on the sky and clouds, there came into my mind so sweet a sense of the glorious *majesty* and *grace* of God, that I know not how to express. I seemed to see them both in a sweet conjunction; majesty and meekness joined together; it was a sweet, and gentle, and holy majesty; and also a majestic meekness; an awful sweetness; a high, and great, and holy gentleness.

10   After this my sense of divine things gradually increased, and became more and more lively, and had more of that inward sweetness. The appearance of every thing was altered; there seemed to be, as it were, a calm, sweet cast, or appearance of divine glory, in almost every thing. God's excellency, his wisdom, his purity and love, seemed to appear in every thing; in the sun, moon, and stars; in the clouds, and blue sky; in the grass, flowers, trees; in the water, and all nature; which used greatly to fix my mind. I often used to sit and view the moon for continuance; and in the day, spent much time in viewing the clouds and sky, to behold the sweet glory of God in these things; in the mean time, singing forth, with a low voice, my contemplations of the Creator and Redeemer. And scarce any thing, among all the
20   works of nature, was so sweet to me as thunder and lightning; formerly, nothing had been so terrible to me. Before, I used to be uncommonly terrified with thunder, and to be struck with terror when I saw a thunder storm rising; but now, on the contrary, it rejoiced me. I felt God, so to speak, at the first appearance of a thunder storm; and used to take the opportunity, at such times, to fix myself in order to view the clouds, and see the lightnings play, and hear the majestic and awful voice of God's thunder, which oftentimes was exceedingly entertaining, leading me to sweet contemplations of my great and glorious God. While thus engaged, it always seemed natural to me to sing, or chant for my meditations; or, to speak my thoughts in soliloquies with a singing voice.

30   I felt then great satisfaction, as to my good state; but that did not content me. I had vehement longings of soul after God and Christ, and after more holiness, wherewith my heart seemed to be full, and ready to break; which often brought to my mind the words of the Psalmist, Psal, cxix. 28. *My soul breaketh for the longing it hath.* I often felt a mourning and lamenting in my heart, that I had not turned to God sooner, that I might have had more time to grow in grace. My mind was greatly fixed on divine things; almost perpetually in the contemplation of them. I spent most of my time in thinking of divine things, year after year; often walking alone in the woods, and solitary places, for meditation, soliloquy, and prayer, and converse with God; and it was always my manner, at such times, to sing forth my
40   contemplations. I was almost constantly in ejaculatory prayer, wherever I was. Prayer seemed to be natural to me, as the breath by which the inward burnings of my heart had vent. The delights which I now felt in the things of religion, were of an exceeding different kind from those before mentioned, that I had when a boy; and what I then had no more notion of, than one born blind has of pleasant and

beautiful colors. They were of a more inward, pure, soul-animating and refreshing nature. Those former delights never reached the heart; and did not arise from any sight of the divine excellency of the things of God; or any taste of the soulsatisfying and life-giving good there is in them.

My sense of divine things seemed gradually to increase, until I went to preach at Newyork, which was about a year and a half after they began; and while I was there, I felt them, very sensibly, in a much higher degree than I had done before. My longings after God and holiness, were much increased. Pure and humble, holy and heavenly Christianity, appeared exceeding amiable to me. I felt a burning desire to be in every thing a complete Christian; and conform to the blessed image of Christ; 10 and that I might live, in all things, according to the pure, sweet and blessed rules of the gospel. I had an eager thirsting after progress in these things; which put me upon pursuing and pressing after them. It was my continual strife day and night, and constant inquiry, how I should *be* more holy, and *live* more holily, and more becoming a child of God, and a disciple of Christ. I now sought an increase of grace and holiness, and a holy life, with much more earnestness, than ever I sought grace before I had it. I used to be continually examining myself, and studying and contriving for likely ways and means, how I should live holily, with far greater diligence and earnestness, than ever I pursued any thing in my life; but yet with too great a dependance on my own strength; which afterwards proved a 20 great damage to me. My experience had not then taught me, as it has done since, my extreme feebleness and impotence, every manner of way; and the bottomless depths of secret corruption and deceit there was in my heart. However, I went on with my eager pursuit after more holiness, and conformity to Christ.

The heaven I desired was a heaven of holiness; to be with God, and to spend my eternity in divine love, and holy communion with Christ. My mind was very much taken up with contemplations' on heaven, and the enjoyments there; and living there in perfect holiness, humility and love: And it used at that time to appear a great part of the happiness of heaven, that there the saints could express their love to Christ. It appeared to me a great clog and burden, that what I felt within, I could 30 not express as I desired. The inward ardor of my soul, seemed to be hindered and pent up, and could not freely flame out as it would. I used often to think, how in heaven this principle should freely and fully vent and express itself. Heaven appeared exceedingly delightful, as a world of love; and that all happiness consisted in living in pure, humble, heavenly, divine love.

I remember the thoughts I used then to have of holiness; and said sometimes to myself, "I do certainly know that I love holiness, such as the gospel prescribes." It appeared to me, that there was nothing in it but what was ravishingly lovely; the highest beauty and amiableness — a *divine* beauty; far purer than any thing here upon earth; and that every thing else was like mire and defilement, in comparison 40 of it.

Holiness, as I then wrote down some of my contemplations on it, appeared to me

6 I . . . **Newyork.** He was in New York from August 1722 until April 1723. Little is known of his ministry there beyond what he says in this account

to be of a sweet, pleasant, charming, serene, calm nature; which brought an inexpressible purity, brightness, peacefulness and ravishment to the soul. In other words, that it made the soul like a field or garden of God, with all manner of pleasant flowers; all pleasant, delightful, and undisturbed; enjoying a sweet calm, and the gently vivifying beams of the sun. The soul of a true Christian, as I then wrote my meditations, appeared like such a little white flower as we see in the spring of the year; low and humble on the ground, opening its bosom to receive the pleasant beams of the sun's glory; rejoicing as it were in a calm rapture; diffusing around a sweet fragrancy; standing peacefully and lovingly, in the midst of other flowers
10 round about; all in like manner opening their bosoms, to drink in the light of the sun. There was no part of creature holiness, that I had so great a sense of its loveliness, as humility, brokenness of heart and poverty of spirit; and there was nothing that I so earnestly longed for. My heart panted after this, to lie low before God, as in the dust; that I might be nothing, and that God might be ALL, that I might become as a little child.

While at Newyork, I was sometimes much affected with reflections on my past life, considering how late it was before I began to be truly religious; and how wickedly I had lived till then; and once so as to weep abundantly, and for a considerable time together.
20 On *January* 12, 1723. I made a solemn dedication of myself to God, and wrote it down; giving up myself, and all that I had to God, to be for the future in no respect my own; to act as one that had no right to himself, in any respect. And solemnly vowed to take God for my whole portion and felicity; looking on nothing else as any part of my happiness, nor acting as if it were; and his law for the constant rule of my obedience; engaging to fight with all my might, against the world, the flesh and the devil, to the end of my life. But I have reason to be infinitely humbled, when I consider how much I have failed of answering my obligation.

I had then abundance of sweet religious conversation in the family where I lived, with Mr. John Smith and his pious mother. My heart was knit in affection to those
30 in whom were appearances of true piety; and I could bear the thoughts of no other companions, but such as were holy, and the disciples of the blessed Jesus. I had great longings for the advancement of Christ's kingdom in the world; and my secret prayer used to be, in great part, taken up in praying for it. If I heard the least hint of any thing that happened, in any part of the world, that appeared, in some respect or other, to have a favorable aspect on the interest of Christ's kingdom, my soul eagerly catched at it; and it would much animate and refresh me. I used to be eager to read public news letters, mainly for that end; to see if I could not find some news favorable to the interest of religion in the world.

I very frequently used to retire into a solitary place, on the banks of Hudson's
40 river, at some distance from the city, for contemplation on divine things, and secret converse with God; and had many sweet hours there. Sometimes Mr. Smith and I walked there together, to converse on the things of God; and our conversation used to turn much on the advancement of Christ's kingdom in the world, and the glorious things that God would accomplish for his church in the latter days. I had

then, and at other times the greatest delight in the holy scriptures, of any book whatsoever. Oftentimes in reading it, every word seemed to touch my heart. I felt a harmony between something in my heart, and those sweet and powerful words. I seemed often to see so much light exhibited by every sentence, and such a refreshing food communicated, that I could not get along in reading; often dwelling long on one sentence, to see the wonders contained in it; and yet almost every sentence seemed to be full of wonders.

I came away from Newyork in the month of April, 1723, and had a most bitter parting with Madam Smith and her son. My heart seemed to sink within me at leaving the family and city, where I had enjoyed so many sweet and pleasant days. 10 I went from Newyork to Weathersfield, by water, and as I sailed away, I kept sight of the city as long as I could. However, that night, after this sorrowful parting, I was greatly comforted in God at Westchester, where we went ashore to lodge; and had a pleasant time of it all the voyage to Saybrook. It was sweet to me to think of meeting dear Christians in heaven, where we should never part more. At Saybrook we went ashore to lodge, on Saturday, and there kept the Sabbath; where I had a sweet and refreshing season, walking alone in the fields.

After I came home to Windsor, I remained much in a like frame of mind, as when at Newyork; only sometimes I felt my heart ready to sink with the thoughts of my friends at Newyork. My support was in contemplations on the 20 heavenly state; as I find in my Diary of May 1, 1723. It was a comfort to think of that state, where there is fulness of joy; where reigns heavenly, calm, and delightful love, without alloy; where there are continually the dearest expressions of this love; where is the enjoyment of the persons loved, without ever parting; where those persons who appear so lovely in this world, will really be inexpressibly more lovely and full of love to us. And how sweetly will the mutual lovers join together to sing the praises of God and the Lamb! How will it fill us with joy to think, that this enjoyment, these sweet exercises will never cease, but will last to all eternity! — I continued much in the same frame, in the general, as when at Newyork, till I went to Newhaven as tutor to the college; particularly once at Bolton, on a journey from 30 Boston, while walking out alone in the fields. After I went to Newhaven I sunk in religion; my mind being diverted from my eager pursuits after holiness, by some affairs that greatly perplexed and distracted my thoughts.

In September, 1725, I was taken ill at Newhaven, and while endeavoring to go home to Windsor, was so ill at the North Village, that I could go no further; where I lay sick for about a quarter of a year. In this sickness God was pleased to visit me again with the sweet influences of his Spirit. My mind was greatly engaged there in divine, pleasant contemplations, and longings of soul. I observed that those who watched with me, would often be looking out wishfully for the morning; which brought to my mind those words of the psalmist, and which my soul with 40 delight made its own language, *My soul waiteth for the Lord, more than they that watch for the morning, I say, more than they that watch for the morning;* and when the light of day came in at the windows, it refreshed my soul from one morning to another. It seemed to be some image of the light of God's glory.

I remember, about that time, I used greatly to long for the conversion of some that I was concerned with; I could gladly honor them, and with delight be a servant to them, and lie at their feet, if they were but truly holy. But, some time after this, I was again greatly diverted in my mind with some temporal concerns that exceedingly took up my thoughts, greatly to the wounding of my soul; and went on through various exercises, that it would be tedious to relate, which gave me much more experience of my own heart, than ever I had before.

Since I came to this town, I have often had sweet complacency in God, in views of his glorious perfections and the excellency of Jesus Christ. God has appeared to me a glorious and lovely Being, chiefly on the account of his holiness. The holiness of God has always appeared to me the most lovely of all his attributes. The doctrines of God's absolute sovereignty, and free grace, in shewing mercy to whom he would shew mercy; and man's absolute dependance on the operations of God's Holy Spirit, have very often appeared to me as sweet and glorious doctrines. These doctrines have been much my delight. God's sovereignty has ever appeared to me, great part of his glory. It has often been my delight to approach God, and adore him as a sovereign God, and ask sovereign mercy of him.

I have loved the doctrines of the gospel; they have been to my soul like green pastures. The gospel has seemed to me the richest treasure; the treasure that I have most desired, and longed that it might dwell richly in me. The way of salvation by Christ has appeared, in a general way, glorious and excellent, most pleasant and most beautiful. It has often seemed to me, that it would in a great measure spoil heaven, to receive it in any other way. That text has often been affecting and delightful to me, Isa. xxxii. 2. *A man shall be an hiding place from the wind, and a covert from the tempest,* &c.

It has often appeared to me delightful, to be united to Christ; to have him for my head, and to be a member of his body; also to have Christ for my teacher and prophet. I very often think with sweetness, and longings, and pantings of soul, of being a little child, taking hold of Christ, to be led by him through the wilderness of this world. That text, Matth. xviii. 3, has often been sweet to me, *except ye be converted and become as little children,* &c. I love to think of coming to Christ, to receive salvation of him, poor in spirit, and quite empty of self, humbly exalting him alone; cut off entirely from my own root, in order to grow into, and out of Christ; to have God in Christ to be all in all; and to live by faith on the son of God, a life of humble, unfeigned confidence in him. That scripture has often been sweet to me, Psal. cxv. 1. *Not unto us, O Lord, not unto us, but unto thy name give glory, for thy mercy, and for thy truth's sake.* And those words of Christ, Luke x. 21. *In that hour Jesus rejoiced in spirit, and said, I thank thee, O Father, Lord of heaven and earth, that thou hast hid these things from the wise and prudent, and hast revealed them unto babes: Even so, Father, for so it seemed good in thy sight.* That sovereignty of God which Christ rejoiced in, seemed to me worthy of such joy; and that rejoicing seemed to shew the excellency of Christ, and of what spirit he was.

Sometimes, only mentioning a single word caused my heart to burn within me;

---

8 **this town,** Northampton

or only seeing the name of Christ, or the name of some attribute of God. And God has appeared glorious to me, on account of the Trinity. It has made me have exalting thoughts of God, that he subsists in three persons; Father, Son and Holy Ghost. The sweetest joys and delights I have experienced, have not been those that have arisen from a hope of my own good estate; but in a direct view of the glorious things of the gospel. When I enjoy this sweetness, it seems to carry me above the thoughts of my own estate; it seems at such times a loss that I cannot bear, to take off my eye from the glorious, pleasant object I behold without me, to turn my eye in upon myself, and my own good estate.

My heart has been much on the advancement of Christ's kingdom in the world. 10 The histories of the past advancement of Christ's kingdom have been sweet to me. When I have read histories of past ages, the pleasantest thing in all my reading has been, to read of the kingdom of Christ being promoted. And when I have expected, in my reading, to come to any such thing, I have rejoiced in the prospect, all the way as I read. And my mind has been much entertained and delighted with the scripture promises and prophecies, which relate to the future glorious advancement of Christ's kingdom upon earth.

I have sometimes had a sense of the excellent fulness of Christ, and his meetness and suitableness as a Saviour; whereby he has appeared to me, far above all, the chief of ten thousands. His blood and atonement have appeared sweet, and his 20 righteousness sweet; which was always accompanied with ardency of spirit; and inward strugglings and breathings, and groanings that cannot be uttered, to be emptied of myself, and swallowed up in Christ.

Once, as I rode out into the woods for my health, in 1737, having alighted from my horse in a retired place, as my manner commonly has been, to walk for divine contemplation and prayer, I had a view that for me was extraordinary, of the glory of the Son of God, as Mediator between God and man, and his wonderful, great, full, pure and sweet grace and love, and meek and gentle condescension. This grace that appeared so calm and sweet, appeared also great above the heavens. The person of Christ appeared ineffably excellent with an excellency great enough to swallow 30 up all thought and conception — which continued as near as I can judge, about an hour; which kept me the greater part of the time in a flood of tears, and weeping aloud. I felt an ardency of soul to be, what I know not otherwise how to express, emptied and annihilated; to lie in the dust, and to be full of Christ alone; to love him with a holy and pure love; to trust in him; to live upon him; to serve and follow him; and to be perfectly sanctified and made pure, with a divine and heavenly purity. I have, several other times, had views very much of the same nature, and which have had the same effects.

I have many times had a sense of the glory of the third person in the Trinity, in his office of Sanctifier; in his holy operations, communicating divine light and life 40 to the soul. God, in the communications of his Holy Spirit, has appeared as an infinite fountain of divine glory and sweetness; being full, and sufficient to fill and satisfy the soul; pouring forth itself in sweet communications; like the sun in its glory, sweetly and pleasantly diffusing light and life. And I have sometimes had an

affecting sense of the excellency of the word of God, as a word of life; as the light
of life; a sweet, excellent, life-giving word; accompanied with a thirsting after that
word, that it might dwell richly in my heart.

Often, since I lived in this town, I have had very affecting views of my own sinfulness and vileness; very frequently to such a degree as to hold me in a kind of
loud weeping, sometimes for a considerable time together; so that I have often been
forced to shut myself up. I have had a vastly greater sense of my own wickedness,
and the badness of my heart, than ever I had before my conversion. It has often appeared to me, that if God should mark iniquity against me, I should appear the
10 very worst of all mankind; of all that have been, since the beginning of the world
to this time; and that I should have by far the lowest place in hell. When others,
that have come to talk with me about their soul concerns, have expressed the sense
they have had of their own wickedness, by saying that it seemed to them, that they
were as bad as the devil himself; I thought their expression seemed exceeding faint
and feeble, to represent my wickedness.

My wickedness, as I am in myself, has long appeared to me perfectly ineffable,
and swallowing up all thought and imagination; like an infinite deluge, or mountains over my head. I know not how to express better what my sins appear to me
to be, than by heaping infinite upon infinite, and multiplying infinite by infinite.
20 Very often, for these many years, these expressions are in my mind, and in my
mouth, "Infinite upon infinite — Infinite upon infinite!" When I look into my
heart, and take a view of my wickedness, it looks like an abyss infinitely deeper than
hell. And it appears to me, that were it not for free grace, exalted and raised up to
the infinite height of all the fulness and glory of the great Jehovah, and the arm of
his power and grace stretched forth in all the majesty of his power, and in all the
glory of his sovereignty, I should appear sunk down in my sins below hell itself;
far beyond the sight of every thing, but the eye of sovereign grace, that can pierce
even down to such a depth. And yet it seems to me, that my conviction of sin is
exceeding small, and faint; it is enough to amaze me, that I have no more sense of
30 my sin. I know certainly, that I have very little sense of my sinfulness. When
I have had turns of weeping and crying for my sins I thought I knew at the time,
that my repentance was nothing to my sin.

I have greatly longed of late, for a broken heart, and to lie low before God; and,
when I ask for humility, I cannot bear the thoughts of being no more humble than
other Christians. It seems to me, that though their degrees of humility may be suitable for them, yet it would be a vile selfexaltation in me, not to be the lowest in
humility of all mankind. Others speak of their longing to be "humbled to the
dust;" that may be a proper expression for them, but I always think of myself, that
I ought, and it is an expression that has long been natural for me to use in prayer,
40 "to lie infinitely low before God." And it is affecting to think, how ignorant I was,
when a young Christian, of the bottomless, infinite depths of wickedness, pride,
hypocrisy and deceit, left in my heart.

I have a much greater sense of my universal, exceeding dependence on God's
grace and strength, and mere good pleasure, of late, than I used formerly to have;

and have experienced more of an abhorrence of my own righteousness. The very thought of any joy arising in me, on any consideration of my own amiableness, performances, or experiences, or any goodness of heart or life, is nauseous and detestable to me. And yet I am greatly afflicted with a proud and selfrighteous spirit, much more sensibly than I used to be formerly. I see that serpent rising and putting forth its head continually, every where, all around me.

Though it seems to me, that, in some respects, I was a far better Christian, for two or three years after my first conversion, than I am now; and lived in a more constant delight and pleasure; yet, of late years, I have had a more full and constant sense of the absolute sovereignty of God, and a delight in that sovereignty; and 10 have had more of a sense of the glory of Christ, as a Mediator revealed in the gospel. On one Saturday night, in particular, I had such a discovery of the excellency of the gospel above all other doctrines, that I could not but say to myself, "This is my chosen light, my chosen doctrine;" and of Christ, "This is my chosen Prophet." It appeared sweet, beyond all expression, to follow Christ, and to be taught, and enlightened, and instructed by him; to learn of him, and live to him. Another Saturday night, (*January*, 1739) I had such a sense, how sweet and blessed a thing it was to walk in the way of duty; to do that which was right and meet to be done, and agreeable to the holy mind of God; that it caused me to break forth into a kind of loud weeping, which held me some time, so that I was forced to shut myself up, 20 and fasten the doors. I could not but, as it were, cry out, "How happy are they which do that which is right in the sight of God! They are blessed indeed, they are the happy ones!" I had, at the same time, a very affecting sense, how meet and suitable it was that God should govern the world, and order all things according to his own pleasure; and I rejoiced in it, that God reigned, and that his will was done.

1739?, 1808

---

17 **January**, 1739, the only clue to the date of composition

Of Being

"Of Being" was written sometime between 1717 and 1720, shortly after Edwards had read for the first time John Locke's Essay Concerning Human Understanding. *Locke (Book II, Chapter 8) had said that "the ideas of primary qualities of bodies [i.e., solidity, extension, figure, motion or rest, and number] are resemblances of them, and their patterns do really exist in the bodies themselves; but the ideas produced in us by . . . secondary qualities [i.e., colors, sounds, tastes, etc.] have no resemblance of them at all. There is nothing like our ideas existing in the bodies themselves." Primary qualities, he continued (Chapter 23), are the chief basis of our ideas of corporeal substance, which can be no more and no less clear than our ideas of immaterial substance. Edwards, taking up the discussion at this point, concludes that what Locke called primary qualities depend, no less than those he called secondary, upon the perceiving mind. In other words, like George Berkeley, Edwards makes consciousness the only reality, transfers all "being" to the mind, and arrives at the basic principle of the philosophical system known as subjective idealism.*

That there should absolutely be nothing at all is utterly impossible, the Mind Can never Let it stretch its Conceptions ever so much bring it self to Conceive of a state of Perfect nothing, it put's the mind into mere Convulsion and Confusion to endeavour to think of such a state, and it Contradicts the very nature of the soul to think that it should be, and it is the Greatest Contradiction and the Aggregate of all Contradictions to say that there should not be, tis true we Cant so Distinctly show the Contradiction by words because we Cannot talk about it without Speaking horrid Nonsense and Contradicting our selve at every word, and because noth- ing is that whereby we Distinctly show other particular Contradictions, but here we
10 are Run up to Our first principle and have no other to explain the Nothingness or not being of nothing by, indeed we Can mean nothing else by nothing but a state of Absolute Contradiction; and If any man thinks that he Can think well Enough how there should be nothing I'll Engage that what he means by nothing is as much something as any thing that ever He thought of in his Life, and I believe that if he knew what nothing was it would be intuitively Evident to him that it Could not be. So that we see it is necessary some being should Eternally be and tis a more palpable Contradiction still to say that there must be being somewhere and not other- where for the words absolute nothing, and where, Contradict each other; and besides it Gives as great a shock to the mind to thin[k] of pure nothing being in
20 any one place, as it Does to think of it in all and it is self evident that there Can be nothing in one place as well as in another and so if there Can be in one there Can be in all. So that we see this necessary eternall being must be infinite and Omni- present. This Infinite And omnipresent being Cannot be solid. Let us see how Con- tradictory it is to say that an infinite being is solid, for Solidity surely is nothing but Resistance to other solidities.
Space is this Necessary eternal infinite and Omnipresent being, we find that we can with ease Conceive how all other beings should not be, we Can remove them out of our Minds and Place some Other in the Room of them, but Space is the very thing that we Can never Remove, and Conceive of its not being, If a man would imagine
30 space any where to be Divided So as there should be Nothing between the Divided parts, there Remains Space between notwithstanding and so the man Contradicts him- self, and it is self evident I believe to every man that space is necessary, eternal, infinite, & Omnipresent, but I had as Good speak Plain, I have already said as much as that Space is God, and it is indeed Clear to me, that all the Space there is not proper to body, all the space there is without ye Bounds of the Creation, all the space there was before the Creation, is God himself, and no body would in the Least stick at it if it were not because of the Gross Conceptions that we have of space.
A state of Absolute nothing is a state of Absolute Contradiction absolute nothing is the Aggregate of all the Absurd [?] contradictions in the World, a state wherein
40 there is neither body nor spirit, nor space neither empty space nor full space neither

Text: follows the transcription of the manuscript by Professor E. C. Smyth, printed in *Proceedings of the Anti- quarian Society*, New Series, X (1895)   22 **Omnipresent.** Interpolations and marginal notes in the manu- script suggest that Edwards regarded what he had said to this point as a preliminary proposition to be dem- onstrated more fully

little nor Great, narrow nor broad neither infinitely Great space, nor finite space, nor a mathematical point neither Up nor Down neither north nor south (I dont mean as it is with Respect to the body of the earth or some other Great body but no Contrary Point, nor Positions or Directions [)] no such thing as either here Or there this way or that way or only one way; When we Go About to form an idea of Perfect nothing we must shut Out all these things we must shut out of our minds both space that has something in it and space that has nothing in it we must not allow our selves to think of the least part of space never so small, nor must we Suffer our thoughts to take sanctuary in a mathematical point, when we Go to Expell body out of Our thoughts we must Cease not to leave empty space in the Room of 10 it and when we Go to Expell emptiness from Our thoughts we must not think to squeese it out by any thing Close hard and solid but we must think of the same that the sleeping Rocks Dream of and not till then shall we Get a Compleat idea of nothing

a state of nothing is a state wherein every Proposition in Euclid is not true, nor any of those self evident maxims by which they are Demonstrated & all other Eternal truths are neither true nor false

when we Go to Enquire whether or no there Can be absolutely nothing we speak nonsense in Enquiring the stating of the Question is Nonsense because we make a disjunction where there is none either being or absolute nothing is no Disjunction 20 no more than whether a t[r]iangle is a tiangle or not a tiangle there is no other way but Only for there to be existence there is no such thing as absolute nothing. There is such a thing as nothing with Respect to this Ink & paper there is such a thing as nothing with Respect to you & me there is such a thing as nothing with Respect to this Globe of Earth & with Respect to this Created universe there is another way besides these things having existence but there is no such thing as nothing with Respect to Entity or being absolutely Considered we don't know what we say if we say we think it Possible in it self that there should not be Entity and how Doth it Grate upon the mind to thin[k] that something should be from all Eternity, and nothing all the while be Conscious of it let us suppose to illustrate 30 it that the world had a being from all Eternity, and had many Great Changes and Wonderfull Revolutions, and all the while nothing knew, there was no knowledge in the Universe of any such thing, how is it possible to bring the mind to imagine, yea it is Really impossible it should be that Any thing should be and nothing know it then you'll say if it be so it is because nothing has Any existence any where else but in Consciousness no certainly no where else but either in Created or uncreated Consciousness Supposing there were Another Universe only of bodies Created at a Great Distance from this Created in excellent Order and harmonious motions, and a beautifull variety, and there was no Created intelligence in it nothing but senseless bodies, nothing but God knew anything of it I Demand in what Respect this 40 world has a being but only in the Divine Consciousness Certainly in no Respect there would be figures and magnitudes, and motions and Proportions but where where Else but in the almightie's knowledge how is it possible there should, then you'll say for the same Reason in a Room Close Shut Up that no body sees nor

hears nothing in it there is nothing any otherway than in Gods knowledge I answer Created beings are Conscious of the Effects of what is in the Room, for Perhaps there is not one leaf of a tree nor Spire of Grass but what has effects All over
the universe and will have to the End of Eternity but any otherwise there is nothing in a Room shut up but only in Gods Consciousness how Can Any thing be
there Any other way this will appear to be truly so to Any one that thinks of it
with the whole united strength of his mind. Let us suppose for illustration this impossibility that all the Spirits in the Universe to be for a time to be Deprived of
their Consciousness, and Gods Consciousness at the same time to be intermitted. I
10 say the Universe for that time would cease to be of it self and not only as we speak
because the almighty Could not attend to Uphold the world but because God knew
nothing of it tis our foolish imagination that will not suffer us to see we fancy there
may be figures and magnitudes Relations and properties without any ones knowing
of it, but it is our imagination hurts us we Dont know what figures and Properties
Are.

Our imagination makes us fancy we see Shapes an Colours and magnitudes tho no
body is there to behold it but to help our imagination Let us thus State the Case,
Let us suppose the world Deprived of Every Ray of light so that there should not
be the least Glimering of light in the Universe Now all will own that in such Case
20 the Universe would be immediately Really Deprived of all its Colours, one part of
the Universe is no More Red or blue, or Green or Yellow or black or white or light or
dark or transparent or opake there would be no visible Distinction between
the world and the Rest of the incomprehensible Void yea there would be no Difference in these Respect between the world and the infinite void, that is any Part
of that void would really be as light and as Dark, as white and as black as Red and
Green as blue and as brown as transparent and as opake as Any Part of the universe,
or as there would be in such Case no Difference between the world and nothing in
these Respects so there would be no Difference between one part of the world and
another all in these Respects is alike confounded with and undistinguishable from
30 infinite emptiness

At the same time also Let us suppose the Universe to be altogether Deprived of
motion, and all parts of it to be at perfec Rest (the same supposition is indeed included in this but we Distinguish them for better Clearness) then the Universe
would not Differ from the void in this Respect, there will be no more motion in
one than the other then also solidity would cease, all that we mean or Can
be meant by solidity is Resistance Resistance to touch, the Resistance of some parts
of Space, this is all the knowledge we Get of solidity by our senses and I am sure
all that we Can Get any other way, but solidity shall be shown to be nothing Else
more fully hereafter. but there Can be no Resistance if there is no motion, one body
40 Can [not] Resist another when there is perfect Rest Amongst them, but you'll say
tho there is not actuall Resistance yet there is potential existence, that is such and
such Parts of space would Resist upon occasion, but this Is all I would have that
there is no solidity now not but that God would Cause there to be on occasion
and if there is no solidity there is no extension for extension is the extenddness of

the solidity, then all figure, and magnitude and proportion immediately Ceases. put both these suppositions together that is Deprive the world of light and motion and the Case would stand thus with the world, there would [be] neither white nor black neither blew nor brown, bright nor shaded pellucid nor opake, no noise or sound neither heat nor Cold, neither fluid nor Wet nor Drie hard nor soft nor solidity nor Extension, nor figure, nor magnitude nor Proportion nor body nor spirit, what then [is] to become of the Universe Certainly it exists no where but in the Divine mind this will be Abundantly Clearer to one after having Read what I have further to say of solidity &c.

So that we see that a world without motion Can Exist no where Else but in the 10 mind either infinite or finite Corollary, it follows from hence that those beings which have knowledge and Consciousness are the Only Proper and Real And substantial beings, inasmuch as the being of other things is Only by these. from hence we may see the Gross mistake of those who think material things the most substantial beings and spirits more like a shadow, whereas spirits Only Are Properly Substance.

1720?, 1895

A Divine and Supernatural Light

Immediately Imparted to the Soul by the Spirit of God, Shown to Be Both a Scriptural, and Rational Doctrine; in a Sermon Preached at Northampton

This sermon was preached in August 1733 and published in Boston the following year. In form it follows the well-established "doctrine-reasons-uses" pattern, but it is remarkable for its ease and clarity and for its exposition of what was the central feature of Edwards' thought: the reality of supernatural principles communicated by God to the redeemed soul. The confidence in intuitive knowledge looks forward to that of Emerson and the other Transcendentalists two generations later (see pp. 696-700) and lends weight to the argument that much of the philosophy of the nineteenth century had its roots in Puritanism.

MATTHEW xvi. 17. *And* JESUS *answered and said unto him, blessed art thou Simon Barjona; for Flesh and Blood hath not revealed it unto thee, but my Father which is in Heaven.*

Christ says these Words to *Peter,* upon Occasion of his professing his Faith in him as the Son of GOD. Our Lord was enquiring of his Disciples, who Men said he was; not that he needed to be informed, but only to introduce and give Occasion to what follows. They answer, that some said he was *John* the *Baptist,* and some *Elias,* and others *Jeremias* or one of the Prophets. When they had thus given an Account who others said he was, CHRIST asks them, who they said he was. *Simon Peter,* whom

---

Text: the first edition, Boston, 1734   6 **John the Baptist . . . Elias . . . Jeremias.** Herod had said that Jesus was John the Baptist risen from the dead (Matthew 14:2; Luke 9:7); some also supposed that Elijah, Jeremiah, or some other Old Testament prophet was risen (Luke 9:8)

we find always zealous and forward, was the first to answer; he readily replied to the Question, *Thou art* CHRIST *the Son of the living* GOD.

UPON this Occasion CHRIST says as he does *to* him and *of* him in the Text: In which we may observe,

1. THAT *Peter* is pronounced blessed on this Account. *Blessed art thou* — "Thou "art an happy man, that thou art not ignorant of this, that I am CHRIST *the son of* "*the living God.* Thou art distinguishingly happy. Others are blinded, and have dark "and deluded Apprehensions, as you have now given an Account, some thinking "that I am *Elias,* and some that I am *Jeremias,* and some one thing, and some an-
10 "other; but none of them thinking right, all of them misled. Happy art thou, that "art so distinguished as to know the Truth in this Matter.

2. THE Evidence of this his Happiness declared; *viz.* That GOD and he *only* had *revealed it* to him. This is an Evidence of his being *blessed.*

First, As it shows how peculiarly favoured he was of GOD, above others. *q.d.* "How highly favored art thou, that others that are wise and great Men, the Scribes, "Pharisees, and Rulers, and the Nation in general, are left in Darkness, to follow "their own misguided Apprehensions, and that thou should'st be singled out, as it "were by Name, that my heavenly Father should thus set his Love on *thee Simon* "*Bar-jona.* This argues thee *blessed,* that thou should'st thus be the Object of GOD'S
20 "distinguishing Love.

Secondly, IT evidences his Blessedness also, as it intimates that this Knowlege is above any that *Flesh and Blood* can *reveal.* "This is such Knowlege as my *Father* "*which is in heaven* only can give: It is too high and excellent to be communicated "by such Means as other Knowlege is. Thou art *blessed,* that thou knowest that "which GOD alone can teach thee.

THE Original of this Knowlege is here declared; both negatively and positively. *Positively,* as GOD is here declared the Author of it. *Negatively,* as 'tis declared that *Flesh and Blood* had *not revealed it.* GOD is the Author of all Knowlege and Under-standing whatsoever: He is the Author of the Knowlege, that is obtained by hu-
30 man Learning: He is the Author of all moral Prudence, and of the Knowlege and Skill that Men have in their secular Business. Thus it is said of all in *Israel* that were *wisehearted,* and skill'd in Embroidering, that GOD had *fill'd* them *with the spirit of Wisdom.* Exod. 28.3

GOD is the Author of such Knowlege; but yet not so but that *Flesh and Blood reveals it.* Mortal Men are capable of imparting the Knowlege of human Arts and Sciences, and Skill in temporal Affairs. GOD is the Author of such Knowlege by those Means: *Flesh and Blood* is made use of by GOD as the *mediate* or *second* Cause of it; He conveys it by the Power and Influence of natural Means. But this spiritual Knowlege, spoken of in the Text, is what *God* is the Author of, and none else: He
40 *reveals it* and *Flesh and Blood reveals it not.* He imparts this Knowlege immediately, not making use of any intermediate natural Causes, as he does in other Knowlege.

What had passed in the preceding Discourse naturally occasioned CHRIST to ob-

---

14 **q.d.,** *quasi dicat,* as if he should say

serve this; because the Disciples had been telling, how others did not know him, but were generally mistaken about him, and divided and confounded in their Opinions of him; but *Peter* had declared his assured Faith that he was the *Son of GOD.* Now it was natural to observe, how it was not *Flesh and Blood* that had *revealed it to* him, but GOD; for if this knowlege were dependent on natural Causes or Means, how came it to pass that they, a Company of poor Fishermen, illiterate Men, and Persons of low Education, attain'd to the knowlege of the Truth; while the Scribes and Pharisees, Men of vastly higher advantages, and greater knowlege and sagacity in other matters, remain'd in Ignorance? This could be owing only to the gracious distinguishing Influence and Revelation of the SPIRIT of GOD. Hence, what I would 10 make the Subject of my present Discourse from these Words, is this

Doctrine, viz.

That there is such a thing, as A SPIRITUAL *and* DIVINE LIGHT, *immediately imparted to the Soul by* GOD, *of a different Nature from any that is obtain'd by natural Means.*
    IN what I say on this Subject at this Time, I would
    I. SHOW what this *divine Light* is.
    II. HOW it is given *Immediately by* GOD, and not *obtain'd by natural Means.*
    III. SHOW the Truth of the Doctrine.
    AND then conclude with a brief Improvement.   20
    I. I would show *what this* spiritual and divine Light *is.* And in order to it would show,
    First, IN a few things *what it is not.* And here,
    1. THOSE *Convictions that natural Men may have of their Sin and Misery* is not *this* spiritual and divine Light. Men in a natural Condition may have Convictions of the Guilt that lies upon them, and of the anger of GOD, and their Danger of divine Vengeance. Such Convictions are from *Light* or Sensibleness of Truth: That some Sinners have a greater Conviction of their Guilt and Misery than others, is because some have more *Light,* or more of an Apprehension of Truth than others. And this *Light* and Conviction may be from the Spirit of GOD; *the* SPIRIT *convinces* Men *of* 30 *Sin:* but yet nature is much more concern'd in it than in the Communication of that *spiritual and divine Light* that is spoken of in the *Doctrine;* 'tis from the Spirit of GOD only as assisting *natural Principles,* and not as infusing any new *Principles. Common Grace* differs from *special,* in that it influences only by assisting of *Nature;* and not by imparting *Grace,* or bestowing any thing *above* Nature. The *Light* that is obtain'd, is wholly *natural,* or of no superiour *Kind* to what meer *Nature* attains to; tho' more of *that kind* be obtained, than would be obtained if Men were left wholly to themselves. Or *in other Words, Common Grace* only assists the Faculties of the Soul to do that more fully, which they do by *Nature; as natural* Conscience, or Reason, will by meer *Nature* make a Man sensible of Guilt, and will accuse and 40 condemn him when he has done amiss. Conscience is a *Principle natural* to Men; and the Work that it doth *naturally,* or of itself, is to give an Apprehension of *right and wrong;* and to suggest to the Mind the Relation that there is between right and

wrong, and a Retribution. The Spirit of GOD, in those Convictions which unregenerate Men sometimes have, assists Conscience to do this Work in a further Degree,
than it would do if they were left to themselves: He helps it against those Things
that tend to stupify it, and obstruct its Exercise. But in the *renewing* and *sanctifying*
work of the HOLY GHOST, those things are wrought in the Soul that are *above*
Nature; and of which there is nothing of the like kind in the Soul *by* Nature; and
they are caused to exist in the Soul habitually, & according to such a stated Constitution or Law, that lays such a Foundation for Exercises in a continued Course,
as is called a *Principle* of nature. Not only are remaining *Principles* assisted to do
10 their work more freely and fully, but those *Principles* are restored that were utterly
destroyed by the Fall; and the mind thence-forward habitually exerts those acts that
the Dominion of Sin had made it as wholly destitute of, as a dead Body is of vital
Acts.

   THE Spirit of GOD acts in a very different manner in the one Case, from what he
doth in the other. He may indeed act *upon* the Mind of a natural Man; but he acts
in the Mind of a Saint as an *indwelling vital Principle*. He acts upon the Mind of an
unregenerate Person as an *extrinsick occasional Agent;* for in acting upon them he
doth not unite himself to them; for notwithstanding all his Influences that they
may be the Subjects of, they are still *sensual having not the Spirit. Jude* 19. But he
20 unites himself with the Mind of a Saint, takes him for his Temple, actuates and
influences him as a new, *supernatural Principle* of Life and Action. There is this Difference; that the Spirit of GOD in acting in the Soul of a Godly Man, exerts and
communicates himself there in his own proper Nature. Holiness is the proper Nature of the Spirit of GOD. The HOLY SPIRIT operates in the Minds of the Godly,
by uniting himself to them, and living in them, and exerting his own Nature in the
Exercise of their Faculties. The Spirit of GOD may act upon a Creature, and yet not,
in acting communicate himself. The Spirit of GOD may act upon inanimate Creatures; as the *Spirit moved upon the Face of the Waters,* in the Beginning of the
Creation: So the Spirit of GOD may act upon the minds of Men, many ways,
30 and communicate himself no more than when he acts upon an inanimate Creature.
For Instance. He may excite Thoughts in them, may assist their natural Reason and
Understanding, or may assist other natural Principles, and this without any Union
with the Soul, but may act, as it were, as upon an external Object. But as he acts
in his holy Influences, and spiritual Operations, he acts in a way of peculiar Communication of himself; so that the Subject is thence denominated *Spiritual.*

   2. THIS spiritual and divine Light *don't consist in any Impression made upon the
Imagination.* 'Tis no *Impression* upon the Mind, as tho' one saw any thing with the
bodily Eyes: 'Tis no *Imagination* or *Idea* of an outward *Light* or Glory, or any
Beauty of Form or Countenance, or a visible Lustre or Brightness of any Object.
40 The *Imagination* may be strongly impress'd with such things; but this is not *spiritual
Light.* Indeed when the Mind has a lively Discovery of spiritual things, and is greatly
affected by the Power of divine Light, it may, and probably very commonly doth,
much affect the *Imagination:* So that *Impressions* of an outward Beauty or Brightness,
may accompany those spiritual Discoveries. But *spiritual Light* is not that *Impression*

upon the Imagination, but an exceeding different thing from it. Natural Men may have lively *Impressions* on their *Imaginations;* and we cant determine but that the Devil, *who transforms himself into an Angel of Light,* may cause *Imaginations* of an outward Beauty, or visible Glory, and of Sounds and Speeches, and other such Things; but these are Things of a vastly inferiour Nature to *Spiritual Light.*

3. THIS spiritual Light *is not the suggesting of any new Truths, or Propositions not contain'd in the Word of* GOD. This suggesting of new Truths or Doctrines to the Mind, independent of any antecedent Revelation of those Propositions, either in Word or Writing, is Inspiration; such as the Prophets and Apostles had, and such as some Enthusiasts pretend to. But this *spiritual Light* that I am speaking of, is 10 quite a different thing from Inspiration: It reveals no new Doctrine, it suggests no new Proposition to the Mind, it teaches no new thing of GOD, or CHRIST, or another World, not taught in the Bible; but only gives a due Apprehension of those things that are taught in the word of GOD.

4. *'Tis not every affecting View that Men have of the Things of Religion, that is this* spiritual and divine Light. Men by meer Principles of Nature are capable of being *affected* with Things that have a special Relation to Religion, as well as other Things. A Person by meer Nature, for Instance, may be liable to be *affected* with the Story of JESUS CHRIST, and the sufferings he underwent, as well as by any other tragical Story: He may be the more *affected* with it from the Interest he conceives Mankind 20 to have in it: Yea he may be *affected* with it without believing it; as well as a Man may be *affected* with what he reads in a Romance, or see's acted in a Stage Play. He may be *affected* with a lively and eloquent description of many pleasant things that attend the state of the Blessed in Heaven; as well as his Imagination be entertain'd by a romantick description of the pleasantness of Fairy Land, or the like. And that common belief of the truth of *the things of Religion,* that Persons may have from Education, or otherwise, may help forward their *affection.* We read in Scripture of many that were greatly *affected* with things of a religious nature, who yet are there presented as wholly graceless, and many of them very ill Men. A Person therefore may have *affecting views of the things of Religion,* and yet be 30 very destitute of *spiritual Light. Flesh* and *Blood* may be the Author of this: One Man may give another an *affecting view* of divine things with but common assistance; but GOD alone can give a *spiritual* Discovery of them.

BUT I proceed to show,

Secondly, Positively, WHAT *this* spiritual and divine Light *is.*

AND it may be thus described, *A true sense of the divine Excellency of the things revealed in the Word of* GOD, *and a conviction of the truth and reality of them, thence arising.*

THIS *spiritual Light* primarily consists in the former of these, *viz.* a real sense and apprehension of the divine Excellency of things revealed in the Word of GOD. A spiritual and saving Conviction of the truth and reality of these things, arises from 40 such a sight of their divine Excellency and Glory; so that this Conviction of their truth is an effect and natural consequence of this sight of their divine Glory. There is therefore in this *spiritual Light,*

1. *A true sense of the divine and superlative excellency of the things of Religion;* a real

sense of the excellency of GOD and JESUS CHRIST, and of the work of Redemption, and the ways and works of GOD revealed in the Gospel. There is a *divine* and *superlative* Glory in these things; an Excellency that is of a vastly higher Kind, and more sublime Nature, than in other things; a Glory greatly distinguishing them from all that is earthly and temporal. He that is spiritually *enlightened* truly apprehends and sees it, or has a sense of it. He don't meerly rationally believe that GOD is Glorious, but he has a sense of the Gloriousness of GOD in his Heart. There is not only a rational belief that GOD is holy, and that Holiness is a good thing; but there is a sense of the Loveliness of GOD's Holiness. There is not only a speculatively judg-
10 ing that GOD is gracious, but a sense how amiable GOD is upon that Account; or a sense of the Beauty of this divine Attribute.

THERE is a twofold Understanding or Knowledge of Good that GOD has made the Mind of Man capable of. The *First*, that which is meerly *speculative* and *notional:* As when a Person only speculatively judges, that any thing is, which by the Agreement of Mankind, is called Good or Excellent, *viz.* that which is most to general Advantage, and between which and a Reward there is a suitableness; and the like. And the *other* is that which consists in the sense of the Heart: As when there is a sense of the Beauty, Amiableness, or Sweetness of a thing; so that the Heart is sensible of Pleasure and Delight in the presence of the *Idea* of it. In the *former* is exercised
20 meerly the speculative Faculty, or the Understanding strictly so called, or as spoken of in Distinction from the Will or Disposition of the Soul. In the *latter* the Will, or Inclination, or Heart, are mainly concern'd.

THUS there is a Difference between *having an Opinion* that GOD is holy and gracious, and *having a sense* of the Loveliness and Beauty of that Holiness and Grace. There is a Difference between *having a rational Judgment* that Honey is sweet, and *having a sense* of its sweetness. A Man may have the *Former,* that knows not how honey tasts; but a Man can't have the Latter unless he has an *Idea* of the tast of Honey in his Mind. So there is a difference between *believing* that a Person is Beautiful, and *having a* sense of his Beauty. The *Former* may be obtain'd by hear-say, but
30 the *Latter* only by seeing the Countenance. There is a wide difference between meer *speculative, rational Judging* any thing to be excellent, and *having* a sense of its Sweetness, and Beauty. The *Former* rests only in the Head, Speculation only is concern'd in it; but the Heart is concern'd in the *Latter.* When the Heart is sensible of the Beauty and Amiableness of a Thing, it necessarily feels Pleasure in the Apprehension. It is implied in a Persons being heartily sensible of the Loveliness of a thing, that the *Idea* of it is sweet and pleasant to his Soul; which is a far different thing from having a rational Opinion that it is excellent.

2. THERE *arises from this* sense of divine Excellency of Things contain'd in the Word of GOD, *a Conviction of the Truth and Reality of them: and that either* directly,
40 *or* indirectly.

First, *Indirectly,* and that two ways.

1. As *the Prejudices that are in the Heart, against* the truth of divine things, *are hereby removed; so that the Mind becomes susceptive of the due Force of rational Arguments for their Truth.* The Mind of Man is naturally full of *Prejudices against*

the Truth *of divine Things:* It is full of Enmity against the Doctrines of the Gospel; which is a disadvantage to those *Arguments* that prove their *Truth,* and causes them to lose their Force upon the Mind. But when a Person has discovered to him the divine excellency of Christian Doctrines, this destroys the Enmity, removes those *Prejudices,* and sanctifys the Reason, and causes it to lie open to the *Force of Arguments for their Truth.*

HENCE was the different Effect that CHRIST'S Miracles had to convince the Disciples, from what they had to convince the Scribes and Pharisees. Not that they had a stronger Reason, or had their Reason more improved; but their Reason was sanctified, and those blinding *Prejudices,* that the Scribes and Pharisees were under, were 10 removed by the sense they had of the Excellency of CHRIST, and his Doctrine.

2. IT *not only removes the Hinderances of Reason, but positively helps Reason.* It makes even the speculative Notions the more lively. It engages the attention of the Mind, with the more Fixedness and Intenseness to that Kind of Objects; which causes it to have a clearer View of them, and enables it more clearly to see their mutual Relations, and occasions it to take more Notice of them. The *Ideas* themselves that otherwise are dim, and obscure, are by this Means impress'd with the greater Strength, and have a Light cast upon them; so that the Mind can better judge of them. As he that beholds the Objects on the Face of the Earth, when the Light of the Sun is cast upon them, is under greater Advantage to discern them in their true 20 Forms, and mutual Relations, than he that sees them in a dim Star-light or Twilight.

The Mind having a sensibleness of the Excellency of divine Objects, dwells upon them with Delight; and the Powers of the Soul are more awaken'd and enliven'd to employ themselves in the Contemplation of them, and exert themselves more fully and much more to the Purpose. The Beauty and Sweetness of the Objects draws on the Faculties, and draws forth their Exercises: So that Reason it self is under far greater Advantages for its proper and free Exercises, and to attain its proper End, free of Darkness and Delusion. But,

SECONDLY, A true sense of the divine Excellency of the Things of GOD's Word doth more *directly* and *immediately* convince of the Truth of them; And that because 30 the Excellency of these things is so superlative. There is a Beauty in them that is so divine and Godlike, that is greatly and evidently distinguishing of them from things meerly human, or that Men are the Inventors and Authors of; a Glory that is so high and great, that when clearly seen, commands Assent to their Divinity and Reality. When there is an actual and lively Discovery of this Beauty and Excellency, it won't allow of any such Thought as that it is an Human work, or the Fruit of Mens Invention. This Evidence that they, that are spiritually *enlightned,* have of the Truth of the things of Religion, is a Kind of *intuitive* and *immediate* Evidence. They believe the Doctrines of GOD's Word to be divine, because they see Divinity in them, i.e. They see a divine, and transcendent, and most evidently distinguishing 40 Glory in them; such a Glory as, if clearly seen, don't leave Room to doubt of their being of GOD, and not of Men.

SUCH a Conviction of the Truth of Religion as this, arising, these Ways, from a sense of the divine Excellency of them, is that true spiritual Conviction, that there is in saving Faith. And this Original of it, is that by which it is most essentially distinguished from that common assent, which unregenerate Men are capable of.

II. I Proceed now to the second Thing proposed, *viz.* To show *how this Light is Immediately given by* GOD, *and not obtain'd by natural Means.* And here,

1. *'Tis not intended that the natural Faculties are not made Use of in it.* The *natural Faculties* are the Subject of this Light: And they are the Subject in such a Manner, that they are not meerly pasive, but active in it; the Acts and Exercises of Man's Understanding are concern'd and made use of in it. GOD in letting in this *Light* into the Soul, deals with Man according to his Nature, or as a rational Creature; and makes Use of his human *Faculties.* But yet this *Light* is not the less *immediately* from GOD for that; tho' the *Faculties are made Use of,* 'tis as the Subject and not as the Cause; and that acting of the *Faculties* in it, is not the Cause, but is either implied in the Thing it self, (in the *Light* that is imparted) or is the Consequence of it. As the Use that we make of our Eyes in beholding various Objects, when the Sun arises, is not the Cause of the Light that discovers those Objects to us.

2. *'Tis not intended that outward Means have no Concern in this Affair.* As I have observed already, 'tis not in this Affair, as it is in Inspiration, where new Truths are suggested: for here is by this *Light* only given a due Apprehension of the same Truths that are revealed in the Word of GOD; and therefore it is not given without the Word. The Gospel is made Use of in this Affair: This *Light* is the *Light of the Glorious Gospel of* CHRIST 2. *Cor.* iv. 4. The Gospel is as a Glass, by which this *Light* is conveyed to us. 1 *Cor.* xiii. 12. *Now we see through a Glass* — But,

3. WHEN it is said that this *Light* is given immediately by GOD, and not obtained by natural Means, *hereby is intended, that 'tis given by* GOD *without making Use of any Means that operate by their own Power, or a natural Force.* GOD makes Use of Means; but 'tis not as mediate Causes to produce this Effect. There are not truly any second Causes of it; but it is produced by GOD *immediately.* The Word of GOD is no proper Cause of this Effect: It don't operate by any *natural Force* in it. The Word of GOD is only made Use of to convey to the Mind the Subject matter of this saving Instruction: And this indeed it doth convey to us by *natural Force* or Influence. It conveys to our Minds these and those Doctrines; it is the Cause of the Notion of them in our Heads, but not of the sense of the divine Excellency of them in our Hearts. Indeed a Person can't have *spiritual Light* without the Word. But that don't argue, that the Word properly causes that *Light.* The Mind can't see the Excellency of any Doctrine, unless that Doctrine be first in the Mind; but the seeing the Excellency of the Doctrine may be immediately from the Spirit of GOD; tho' the conveying of the Doctrine or Proposition it self may be by the Word. So that the Notions that are the Subject matter of this *Light,* are conveyed to the Mind by the Word of GOD; but that due sense of the Heart, wherein this *Light* formally consists, is immediately by the Spirit of GOD. *As for Instance,* that Notion that there is a CHRIST and that CHRIST is holy and gracious, is conveyed to the Mind by the Word of GOD: But the sense of the Excellency of CHRIST by reason of that Holiness and Grace, is nevertheless immediately the Work of the HOLY SPIRIT. I come now,

III. To show *the Truth of the Doctrine;* that is to show *that there is such a Thing as that spiritual Light that has been described, thus immediately let into the Mind by* GOD. And here I would shew briefly, that this Doctrine is both *scriptural,* and *rational.*

First, 'TIS SCRIPTURAL. My Text is not only full to the Purpose, but 'tis a Doctrine that the Scripture abounds in. We are there abundantly taught, that the Saints differ from the Ungodly in this, that they have the Knowlege of GOD, and a sight of GOD, and of JESUS CHRIST. I shall mention but few Texts of many; 1 John 3. 6. *Whosoever sinneth hath not seen him, nor known him.* 3 John 11. *He that doth Good, is of God; but he that·doth Evil, hath not seen* GOD. John 14. 19. *The world seeth me no more; but ye see me.* John 17.   10

3. *And this is Eternal Life, that they might know thee, the only true* GOD, *and* JESUS CHRIST *whom thou hast sent.* This Knowlege, or sight of GOD and CHRIST, can't be a meer speculative Knowlege; because it is spoken of as a seeing and knowing, wherein they differ from the Ungodly. And by these Scriptures it must not only be a different Knowlege in Degree and Circumstances, and different in its Effects; but it must be entirely different in Nature and Kind.

AND this Light and Knowlege is always spoken of as immediately given of GOD Mat. 11. 25, 26, 27. *At that time* JESUS *answered and said, I thank thee O Father Lord of Heaven and Earth, because thou hast hid these things from the wise and prudent, and   20 hast revealed them unto Babes; even so Father, for so it seemed good in thy sight. All things are delivered unto me of my Father; and no Man knoweth the Son but the Father; neither knoweth any Man the Father, save the Son, and he to whomsoever the Son will reveal him.* Here this Effect is ascribed alone to the arbitrary Operation, and Gift of GOD, bestowing this Knowlege on whom he will, and distinguishing those with it, that have the least natural Advantage or Means for Knowlege, even *Babes,* when it is denied to the *Wise* and *Prudent.* And the imparting of the Knowlege of GOD is here appropriated to the Son of GOD, as his sole Prerogative. And again, 2 Cor. 4. 6. *For* GOD *who commanded the Light to shine out of Darkness, hath shined in our Hearts, to give the Light of the Knowlege of the Glory of* GOD *in the Face of* JESUS CHRIST. This   30 plainly shows, that there is such a thing as a discovery of the divine superlative Glory and Excellency of GOD and CHRIST; and that peculiar to the Saints: and also that 'tis as immediately from GOD, as Light from the Sun: and that 'tis the immediate Effect of his Power and Will; for 'tis compared to GOD'S creating the Light by his powerful Word in the beginning of the Creation; and is said to be by the Spirit of the LORD, in the 18th verse of the preceding Chapter. GOD is spoken of as giving the Knowlege of CHRIST in Conversion, as of what before was hidden and unseen in that Gal. 1. 15, 16. *But when it pleased* GOD, *who separated me from my Mothers Womb, and called me by his Grace, to reveal his Son in me —.* This Scripture also speaks plainly of such a Knowlege of the Word of GOD, as has been described,   40 as the immediate gift of GOD. Psal. 119. 18. *Open thou mine Eyes, that I may behold wondrous things out of thy Law.* What could the Psalmist mean, when he begged of GOD to *open* his *Eyes?* Was he ever blind? Might he not have Resort to the Law and see every Word and Sentence in it when he pleased? And what could he mean

by those *wondrous Things?* Was it the wonderful Stories of the Creation, and Deluge, and Israel's passing thro' the red Sea, and the like? were not his Eyes open to read these strange things when he would? Doubtless by *wondrous Things in* GOD's *Law,* he had Respect to those distinguishing and wonderful Excellencies, and marvellous Manifestations of the divine Perfections, and Glory, that there was in the Commands and Doctrines of the Word, and those Works and Counsels of GOD that were there revealed. So the Scripture speaks of a Knowlege of GOD's Dispensation, and Covenant of Mercy, and Way of Grace towards his People, as peculiar to the Saints, and given only by GOD, Psal. 25. 14. *The Secret of the* LORD *is with them that fear him;*
10 *and he will shew them his Covenant.*

AND that a true and saving Belief of the Truth of Religion is that which arises from such a Discovery, is also what the Scripture teaches. As John 6, 40. *And this is the will of him that sent me, that every one which* SEETH *the Son, and* BELIEVETH *on him, may have everlasting Life.* Where it is plain that a true Faith is what arises from a spiritual sight of CHRIST. And John 17. 6, 7, 8. *I have manifested thy Name unto the Men which thou gavest me out of the World* — —. *Now they have known that all things whatsoever thou hast given me, are of thee; for I have given unto them the words which thou gavest me, and they have received them, and have known surely that I came out from thee, and they have believed that thou didst send me.* Where CHRIST's *manifesting* GOD's
20 *Name* to the Disciples, or giving them the Knowlege of God, was that whereby they knew that CHRIST's Doctrine was *of* GOD, and that CHRIST himself was *of* him, proceeded *from* him, and was *sent* by him. Again John 12. 44, 45, 46. JESUS *cried and said, He that* believeth *on me,* believeth *not on me, but on him that sent me; And he that* seeth *me* seeth *him that sent me. I am come a* Light *into the World, that whosoever* Believeth *on me should not abide in* Darkness. Their Believing in CHRIST, and spiritually Seeing him, are spoken of as running parallel.

CHRIST condemns the Jews, that they did not know that he was the MESSIAH, and that his Doctrine was true, from an inward distinguishing Tast and Relish of what was divine, in *Luke* 12. 56, 57. He having there blamed the Jews, that though they
30 could *discern the Face of the Sky and of the Earth,* and Signs of the Weather, that yet they could not *discern* those *Times;* or as tis expressed in *Matthew, the Signs of* those *Times;* He adds, *yea and why even of your own selves, judge ye not what is right?* i. e. without extrinsick *Signs.* "Why have ye not that sense of true Excellency, whereby "ye may distinguish that which is holy and divine? Why have ye not that savour of "the things of GOD, by which you may see the distinguishing Glory, and evident "Divinity of me and my Doctrine?

THE Apostle *Peter* mentions it as what gave them (the Apostles) good and well grounded Assurance of the Truth of the Gospel, that they had seen the divine Glory of CHRIST. 2. *Pet.* 1. 16. *For we have not followed cunningly devised Fables, when we made*
40 *known unto you, the Power and Coming of our Lord* JESUS CHRIST, *but were Eye-witnesses of his Majesty.* The Apostle has Respect to that visible Glory of CHRIST which they saw in his Transfiguration: That Glory was so divine having such an ineffable Appearance and semblance of divine Holiness, Majesty, and Grace, that it evidently denoted him to be a divine Person. But if a sight of CHRIST's outward Glory might

give a rational Assurance of his Divinity, why may not an Apprehension of his spiritual Glory do so too. Doubtless CHRIST'S spiritual Glory is in itself as distinguishing, and as plainly shewing his Divinity, as his outward Glory; and a great deal more: for his spiritual Glory is that wherein his Divinity consists; and the outward Glory of his Transfiguration shew'd him to be divine, only as it was a Remarkable Image or Representation of that spiritual Glory. Doubtless therefore he that has had a clear sight of the spiritual Glory of CHRIST, may say, *I have not followed cunningly devised Fables, but* have been an *Eye-witness of his Majesty,* upon as good Grounds as the Apostle, when he had Respect to the outward Glory of Christ, that he had seen.   10

But this brings me to what was proposed next *viz.* to show that,

Secondly, THIS Doctrine is RATIONAL.

1. 'TIS rational *to suppose that there is really such an Excellency in divine things, that is so transcendent and exceedingly different from what is in other things, that if it were seen would most evidently distinguish them.* We can't *rationally* doubt but that Things that are *divine,* that appertain to the supreme Being, are vastly different from Things that are *human;* that there is that God-like, high, and glorious Excellency in them, that does most remarkably difference them from the things that are of Men; insomuch that if the difference were but seen, it would have a convincing, satisfying influence upon any one, that they are what they are, viz. *divine.* What Reason can be offered 20 against it? Unless we would argue that GOD is not remarkably distinguished in Glory from Men.

IF CHRIST should now appear to any One as he did on the Mount at his Transfiguration; or if he should appear to the World in the Glory that he now appears in Heaven, as he will do at the Day of Judgment; without doubt, the Glory and Majesty that he would appear in, would be such as would satisfy every One, that he was a divine Person, and that Religion was true: And it would be a most reasonable, and well grounded Conviction too. And why may there not be that Stamp of Divinity, or divine Glory on the word of GOD, on the Scheme and Doctrine of the Gospel, that may be in like manner distinguishing and as *rationally* convincing, pro- 30 vided it be but seen? 'Tis rational to suppose, that when GOD speaks to the World, there should be something in his Word or Speech vastly different from MEN'S Word. Supposing that GOD never had spoken to the World, but we had Noticed that He was about to do it; that he was about to Reveal himself from Heaven, and speak to us immediately himself, in divine Speeches or Discourses, as it were from his own Mouth; or that he should give us a Book of his own inditing; after what manner should we expect that he would speak? Would it not be *rational* to suppose, that his Speech would be exceeding different from Men's Speech, that he should speak like a GOD; that is, that there should be such an Excellency and sublimity in his Speech or Word, such a Stamp of Wisdom, Holiness, Majesty, and 40 other divine Perfections, that the word of Men, yea of the wisest of Men, should appear mean and base in Comparison of it? Doubtless it would be thought *rational* to expect this, and *unreasonable* to think otherwise. When a wise Man speaks in the Exercise of his Wisdom, there is something in every thing he says, that is very distinguishable from the Talk of a little Child. So, without doubt, and much more, is the Speech of GOD, (if there be any such Thing as the Speech of GOD,) to be distinguished from that of the wisest of Men; agreably to *Jer.* 23. 28, 29. GOD having there been reproving the false Prophets that prophesied in his Name, and pretended that what they spake was his Word, when indeed it was their own Word, says, *The Prophet that hath a Dream, let him tell a Dream; and he that hath my Word, let him speak my Word faithfully:* WHAT IS THE CHAFF TO THE WHEAT? *Saith the* LORD. *Is not my Word like as a Fire, saith the* LORD, *and like a Hammer that breaketh the Rock in Pieces?*

10   2. IF *there be such a distinguishing Excellency in divine things; 'tis* rational *to suppose that there may be such a thing as seeing it.* What should hinder but that it may be seen? 'Tis no Argument that there is no such Thing as such a distinguishing Excellency, or that, if there be, that it can't be seen, that some don't see it, tho' they may be discerning Men in temporal Matters. It is not *rational* to suppose, if there be any such Excellency in divine Things, that wicked Men should see it. 'Tis not *rational* to suppose, that those whose Minds are full of spiritual Pollution, and under the Power of filthy Lusts, should have any Relish or Sense of divine Beauty, or Excellency; or that their Minds should be susceptive of that *Light* that is in its own Nature so pure and heavenly. It need not seem at all strange, that Sin should 20 so blind the Mind, seeing that Mens particular natural Tempers and Dispositions will so much blind them in secular Matters; as when Mens natural Temper is melancholly, jealous, fearful, proud, or the like.

  3. 'TIS rational *to suppose that this Knowledge should be given immediately by* GOD, *and not be obtain'd by natural means.* Upon what account should it seem *unreasonable,* that there should be any immediate Communication between GOD and the Creature? 'Tis strange that Men should make any matter of difficulty of it. Why should not He that made all things, still have something *immediately* to do with the Things that he has made? Where lies the great difficulty, if we own the Being of a GOD, and that he created all things out of Nothing, of allowing some immediate Influ-30 ence of GOD on the Creation still. And if it be *reasonable* to suppose it with Respect to any Part of the Creation, 'tis Especially so with Respect to reasonable intelligent Creatures; who are next to GOD in the Gradation of the different Orders of Beings, and whose Business is most *immediately* with GOD; who were made on Purpose for those Exercises that do respect God, and wherein they have *nextly* to do with God: for *Reason* teaches that Man was made to serve and glorify his Creator. And if it be *rational* to suppose that GOD immediately communicates himself to Man in any Affair, it is in this. 'Tis *rational* to suppose that GOD would reserve that Knowledge and Wisdom, that is of such a divine and excellent Nature, to be bestowed *immediately* by himself, and that it should not be left in the Power of second Causes. 40 Spiritual Wisdom and Grace is the highest and most *excellent* Gift that ever GOD bestows on any Creature: In this the highest Excellency and Perfection of a rational Creature consists. 'Tis also immensely the most *important* of all divine Gifts: 'Tis that wherein Mans Happiness consists, and on which his everlasting Welfare depends. How *rational* is it to suppose that GOD, however he has left meaner Goods

and lower Gifts to second Causes, and in some sort in their Power, yet should reserve this most excellent, divine, and important of all divine Communications, in his own Hands, to be bestowed *immediately* by himself, as a thing too great for second Causes to be concern'd in? 'Tis *rational* to suppose that this Blessing should be *immediately* from GOD; for there is no Gift or Benefit that is in it self so nearly related to the divine Nature, there is nothing the Creature receives that is so much *of* GOD, *of* his Nature, so much a Participation of the Deity: 'Tis a Kind of Emanation of GOD's Beauty, and is related to GOD as the Light is to the Sun. 'Tis therefore congruous and fit, that when it is given of GOD, it should be nextly from himself, and by himself, according to his own Sovereign Will.   10

'TIS *rational* to suppose, that it should be beyond a Man's Power to obtain this Knowledge, and *Light,* by the meer Strength of natural Reason; for 'tis not a Thing that belongs to Reason, to see the Beauty and Loveliness of spiritual things; it is not a speculative thing, but depends on the Sense of the Heart. Reason indeed is necessary in order to it, as 'tis by Reason only that we are become the Subjects of the means of it; which means I have already shown to be necessary in order to it, though they have no proper causal Influence in the Affair. 'Tis by Reason that we become possessed of a notion of those Doctrines that are the Subject Matter of this *divine Light;* and Reason may many ways be indirectly, and remotely an Advantage to it. And Reason has also to do in the Acts that are immediately consequent on   20 this Discovery: A seeing the Truth of Religion from hence, is by Reason; though it be but by one step, and the Inference be immediate. So Reason has to do in that accepting of, and trusting in CHRIST, that is consequent on it. But if we take Reason strictly, not for the Faculty of mental Perception in general, but for Ratiocination, or a Power of Inferring by Arguments; I say if we take Reason thus, the perceiving of spiritual Beauty and Excellency no more belongs to Reason, than it belongs to the Sense of feeling to perceive Colors, or to the Power of seeing to perceive the Sweetness of Food. It is out of Reason's province to perceive the Beauty or Loveliness of any thing: Such a Perception don't belong to that Faculty. Reason's Work is to perceive Truth and not Excellency. 'Tis not Ratiocination that gives   30 Men the Perception of the Beauty and Amiableness of a Countenance; tho' it may be many ways indirectly an advantage to it; yet 'tis no more Reason that immediately perceives it, than it is Reason that perceives the Sweetness of Honey: It depends on the Sense of the Heart. Reason may determine that a Countenance is Beautiful to others, it may determine that Honey is sweet to others; but it will never give me a Perception of its Sweetness.

I will conclude with a very brief *Improvement* of what has been said.

FIRST. THIS Doctrine may lead us *to reflect* on the Goodness of GOD, that has so ordered it, that a saving Evidence of the Truth of the Gospel is such, as is attainable by Persons of mean Capacities, and Advantages, as well as those that are of   40 the greatest Parts and Learning. If the Evidence of the Gospel depended only on History, and such Reasonings as learned Men only are capable of, it would be above the Reach of far the greatest part of Mankind. But Persons, with but an ordinary Degree of Knowlege, are capable without a long and subtil Train of Reasoning, to see the divine Excellency of the things of Religion: They are capable of being taught by the Spirit of GOD, as well as learned Men. The Evidence that is this Way obtained, is vastly better and more satisfying, than all that can be obtain'd by the Arguings of those that are most Learned, and greatest Masters of Reason. And Babes are as capable of knowing these things, as [are] the wise and prudent; and they are often hid from these, when they are revealed to those. 1 Cor. 1. 26, 27. *For ye see your Calling Brethren, how that not many wise Men, after the Flesh, not many mighty, not many noble are called. But* GOD *hath chosen the foolish things of the World —.*

Secondly. THIS Doctrine may well put us upon *examining* ourselves, whether we
10 have ever had his *divine Light,* that has been described, let into our Souls. If there be such a thing indeed, and it ben't only a Notion or Whimsy of Persons of weak and distempered Brains, then doubtless 'tis a thing of great Importance, whether we have thus been taught by the Spirit of GOD; whether *the Light of the Glorious Gospel of* CHRIST, *who is the Image of* GOD *hath shined into us, giving us the Light of the Knowlege of the Glory of* GOD *in the Face of* JESUS CHRIST, whether we have *seen the Son, and believed on him,* or have that Faith of Gospel Doctrines that arises from a spiritual Sight of CHRIST.

Thirdly. ALL may hence be *exhorted,* earnestly *to seek* this *spiritual Light.* To influence and move to it, the following things may be consider'd.
20 1. THIS is the most *excellent and divine* Wisdom, that any Creature is capable of. 'Tis more excellent than any human Learning; 'Tis far more excellent than all the Knowlege of the greatest Philosophers or Statesmen. Yea the least Glimpse of *the Glory of* GOD *in the Face of* CHRIST doth more exalt and enoble the Soul, than all the Knowlege of those that have the greatest speculative Understanding in Divinity, without grace. This Knowlege has the most noble Object that is, or can be, *viz.* the divine Glory and Excellency of GOD, and CHRIST. The Knowlege of these Objects is that wherein consists the most excellent Knowlege of the Angels, yea, of GOD himself,

2. THIS Knowlege is that which is above all others *Sweet and Joyful.* Men have a
30 great deal of Pleasure in human Knowlege, in Studies of natural things; but this is nothing to that Joy which arises from this *divine Light* shining into the Soul. This *Light* gives a View of those things that are immensely the most exquisitely Beautiful, and capable of delighting the Eye of the Understanding. This *spiritual Light* is the dawning of the Light of Glory in the Heart. There is nothing so powerful as this to support Persons in Affliction, and to give the Mind Peace and Brightness, in this stormy and dark World.

3. THIS Light is such as *effectually influences the Inclination, and Changes the Nature of the Soul.* It assimilates the Nature to the divine Nature, and changes the Soul into an Image of the same Glory that is beheld. 2 Cor. 3. 18. *But we all with open*
40 *Face beholding as in a Glass the Glory of the Lord, are changed into the same Image, from Glory to Glory, even as by the Spirit of the Lord.* This Knowlege will wean from the World, and raise the Inclination to heavenly things. It will turn the Heart to GOD as the Fountain of Good, and to choose him for the only Portion. This *Light,* and this only, will bring the Soul to a saving Close with CHRIST. It conforms the Heart

to the Gospel, mortifies its Enmity and Opposition against the Scheme of Salvation therein revealed: It causes the Heart to embrace the joyful Tidings, and entirely to adhere to, and acquiesce in the Revelation of CHRIST as our Saviour: It causes the whole Soul to accord and Symphonize with it, admitting it with entire Credit and Respect, cleaving to it with full Inclination and Affection. And it effectually disposes the Soul to give up it self entirely to CHRIST.

4. THIS Light and this only *has its Fruit in a universal Holiness of Life.* No meerly notional or speculative Understanding of the Doctrines of Religion, will ever bring to this. But this *Light* as it reaches the bottom of the Heart, and changes the Nature, so it will effectually dispose to an universal Obedience. It shews GOD's worth- 10 iness to be obeyed and served. It draws forth the Heart in a sincere Love to GOD, which is the only Principle of a true, gracious and universal Obedience. And it convinces of the Reality of those glorious Rewards that GOD has promised to them that obey him.

1733, 1734

from Sinners in the Hands of an Angry God

Edwards' most notorious sermon, which gave him the reputation of a "hell-fire preacher," was delivered at Enfield, Connecticut, on July 8, 1741, in the early stages of the Great Awakening. The text, Deuteronomy 32:35 ("Their foot shall slide in due time") was a favorite of his; three previous treatments of it are extant in manuscript form. Although he was not a ranting preacher — his manner, in fact, was quiet and unemotional — his Enfield audience was moved to moans and shrieks so persistent that he was at times forced to halt his discourse. The doctrine he derived from his text was that there is "nothing that keeps wicked men at any one moment out of hell, but the mere pleasure of God." He supported his doctrine with ten "considerations" or reasons:

1. "There is no Want of *Power* in God to cast wicked Men into Hell at any Moment. . . ."
2. "They *deserve* to be cast into Hell; . . ."
3. "They are *already* under a Sentence of Condemnation to Hell. . . ."
4. "They are now the Objects of that very *same* Anger & Wrath of God that is expressed in the Torments of Hell: . . ."
5. "The *Devil* stands ready to fall upon them and seize them as his own, at what Moment God shall permit him. . . ."
6. "There are in the Souls of wicked Men those hellish *Principles* reigning, that would presently kindle and flame out into Hell Fire, if it were not for God's Restraints. . . ."
7. "It is no Security to wicked Men for one Moment, that there are no *visible Means of Death* at hand. . . ."
8. "Natural Men's *Prudence* and *Care* to preserve their own *Lives,* or the Care of others to preserve them, don't secure 'em a Moment. . . ."

Text: the 1741 edition

9. "All wicked Men's *Pains* and *Contrivance* they use to escape *Hell,* while they continue to reject Christ, and so remain wicked Men, don't secure 'em from Hell one Moment. . . ."

10. "God has laid himself under *no Obligation,* by any Promise to keep any natural Man out of Hell one Moment. God certainly has made no Promises either of eternal Life, or of any Deliverance or Preservation from eternal Death, but what are contained in the Covenant of Grace, the Promises that are given in Christ, in whom all the promises are Yea and Amen. . . ."

The selection which follows is the application of his doctrine, comprising somewhat more than half of the entire sermon. The rhetorical polish and the vivid imagery of this passage have fascinated, if not horrified, many generations of readers.

The USE may be of *Awakening* to unconverted Persons in this Congregation. This that you have heard is the Case of every one of you that are out of Christ. That World of Misery, that Lake of burning Brimstone is extended abroad under you. *There* is the dreadful Pit of the glowing Flames of the Wrath of God; there is Hell's wide gaping Mouth open; and you have nothing to stand upon, nor any Thing to take hold of: there is nothing between you and hell but the Air; 'tis only the Power and meer Pleasure of God that holds you up.

You probably are not sensible of this; you find you are kept out of Hell, but don't see the Hand of God in it, but look at other Things, as the good State of your bod-
10 ily Constitution, your Care of your own Life, and the Means you use for your own Preservation. But indeed these Things are nothing; if God should withdraw his Hand, they would avail no more to keep you from falling, than the thin Air to hold up a Person that is suspended in it.

Your Wickedness makes you as it were heavy as Lead, and to tend downwards with great Weight and Pressure towards Hell; and if God should let you go, you would immediately sink and swiftly descend & plunge into the bottomless Gulf, and your healthy Constitution, and your own Care and Prudence, and best Contrivance, and all your Righteousness, would have no more Influence to uphold you and keep you out of Hell, than a Spider's Web would have to stop a falling Rock. Were
20 it not that so is the sovereign Pleasure of God, the Earth would not bear you one Moment; for you are a Burden to it; the Creation groans with you; the Creature is made Subject to the Bondage of your Corruption, not willingly; the Sun don't willingly shine upon you to give you Light to serve Sin and Satan; the earth don't willingly yield her Increase to satisfy your Lusts; nor is it willingly a Stage for your Wickedness to be acted upon; the Air don't willingly serve you for Breath to maintain the Flame of Life in your Vitals, while you spend your Life in the Service of God's Enemies. God's Creatures are Good, and were made for Men to serve God with, and don't willingly subserve to any other Purpose, and groan when they are abused to Purposes so directly contrary to their Nature and End. And the World
30 would spue you out, were it not for the sovereign Hand of him who hath subjected it in Hope. There are the black Clouds of God's Wrath now hanging directly over your Heads, full of the dreadful Storm, and big with Thunder; and were it not for

the restraining Hand of God it would immediately burst forth upon you. The sovereign Pleasure of God for the present stays his rough Wind; otherwise it would come with Fury, and your Destruction would come like a Whirlwind, and you would be like the Chaff of the Summer threshing Floor.

The Wrath of God is like great Waters that are dammed for the present; they increase more and more, & rise higher and higher, till an outlet is given, and the longer the Stream is stop'd, the more rapid and mighty is it's Course, when once it is let loose. 'Tis true, that Judgment against your evil Works has not been executed hitherto; the Floods of God's Vengeance have been with-held; but your Guilt in the mean Time is constantly increasing, and you are every Day treasuring 10 up more Wrath; the Waters are continually rising and waxing more and more mighty; and there is nothing but the meer Pleasure of God that holds the Waters back that are unwilling to be stopped, and press hard to go forward; if God should only withdraw his Hand from the Flood-gate, it would immediately fly open, and the fiery Floods of the Fierceness and Wrath of God would rush forth with inconceivable Fury, and would come upon you with omnipotent Power; and if your Strength were ten thousand Times greater than it is, yea ten thousand Times greater than the Strength of the stoutest, sturdiest Devil in hell, it would be nothing to withstand or endure it.

The Bow of God's Wrath is bent, and the Arrow made ready on the String, and 20 Justice bends the Arrow at your Heart, and strains the Bow, and it is nothing but the meer Pleasure of God, and that of an angry God, without any Promise or Obligation at all, that keeps the Arrow one Moment from being made drunk with your Blood.

Thus are all you that never passed under a great Change of Heart, by the mighty Power of the SPIRIT of GOD upon your Souls; all that were never born again, and made new Creatures, and raised from being dead in Sin, to a State of new, and before altogether unexperienced Light and Life, (however you may have reformed your Life in many Things, and may have had religious Affections, and may keep up a Form of Religion in your Families and Closets, and in the House of God, and may 30 be strict in it,) you are thus in the Hands of an angry God; 'tis nothing but his meer Pleasure that keeps you from being this Moment swallowed up in everlasting Destruction.

However unconvinced you may now be of the Truth of what you hear, by & by you will be fully convinced of it. Those that are gone from being in the like Circumstances with you, see that it was so with them; for Destruction came suddenly upon most of them, when they expected nothing of it, and while they were saying, *Peace and Safety:* Now they see, that those Things that they depended on for Peace and Safety, were nothing but thin Air and empty Shadows.

The God that holds you over the Pit of Hell, much as one holds a Spider, or 40 some loathsome Insect, over the Fire, abhors you, and is dreadfully provoked; his Wrath towards you burns like Fire; he looks upon you as worthy of nothing else, but to be cast into the Fire; he is of purer Eyes than to bear to have you in his Sight; you are ten thousand Times so abominable in his Eyes as the most hateful

venemous Serpent is in ours. You have offended him infinitely more than a stubborn Rebel did his Prince: and yet 'tis nothing but his Hand that holds you from falling into the Fire every Moment: 'tis to be ascribed to nothing else, that you did not go to Hell the last Night; that you was suffer'd to awake again in this World, after you closed your Eyes to sleep: and there is no other Reason to be given why you have not dropped into Hell since you arose in the Morning, but that God's Hand has held you up: There is no other Reason to be given why you han't gone to Hell since you have sat here in the House of God, provoking his pure Eyes by your sinful wicked Manner of attending his solemn Worship: Yea, there is nothing
10 else that is to be given as a Reason why you don't this very Moment drop down into hell.

O Sinner! Consider the fearful Danger you are in: 'Tis a great Furnace of Wrath, a wide and bottomless Pit, full of the Fire of Wrath, that you are held over in the Hand of that God, whose Wrath is provoked and incensed as much against you as against many of the Damned in Hell: You hang by a slender Thread, with the Flames of divine Wrath flashing about it, and ready every moment to singe it, and burn it asunder; and you have no Interest in any Mediator, and nothing to lay hold of to save yourself, nothing to keep off the Flames of Wrath, nothing of your own, nothing that you have ever done, nothing that you can do, to induce God to spare
20 you one Moment.

And consider here more particularly several Things concerning that Wrath that you are in such Danger of.

1. *Whose* Wrath it is! It is the Wrath of the infinite GOD. If it were only the Wrath of Man, tho' it were of the most potent Prince, it would be comparatively little to be regarded. The Wrath of Kings is very much dreaded, especially of absolute Monarchs, that have the Possessions and Lives of their Subjects wholly in their Power, to be disposed of at their meer Will. Prov. 20. 2, *The Fear of a King is as the Roaring of a lion; whoso provoketh him to Anger, sinneth against his own Soul.* The Subject that very much enrages an arbitrary Prince, is liable to suffer the most extream
30 Torments, that human Art can invent or human Power can inflict. But the greatest earthly Potentates, in their greatest Majesty and Strength, and when cloathed in their greatest Terrors, are but feeble, despicable Worms of the Dust, in Comparison of the great and almighty Creator and King of Heaven and Earth: It is but little that they can do, when most enraged, and when they have exerted the utmost of their Fury. All the Kings of the Earth before GOD are as Grasshoppers, they are nothing and less than nothing: Both their Love and their Hatred is to be despised. The Wrath of the great King of Kings is as much more terrible than their's, as his Majesty is greater. Luke 12. 4, 5. *And I say unto you my Friends, be not afraid of them that kill the Body, and after that have no more that they can do: But I will forewarn you*
40 *whom ye shall fear; fear him, which after he hath killed, hath Power to cast into hell; yea, I say unto you, fear him.*

2. 'Tis the *Fierceness* of his Wrath that you are exposed to. We often read of the *Fury* of God; as in Isai. 59. 18. *According to their Deeds, accordingly will he repay Fury to his Adversaries.* So Isai. 66. 15. *For behold, the Lord will come with Fire, and with*

Chariots like a Whirlwind, to render his Anger with Fury, and his Rebukes with Flames of Fire. And so in many other Places. So we read of God's *Fierceness.* Rev. 19. 15. There we read of the *Winepress of the Fierceness and Wrath of Almighty God.* The Words are exceeding terrible: if it had only been said, *the Wrath of God,* the Words would have implied that which is infinitely dreadful: But 'tis not only said so, but *the fierceness and wrath of God:* the Fury of God! the Fierceness of Jehovah! Oh how dreadful that must be! Who can utter or conceive what such Expressions carry in them! But it is not only said so, but *the Fierceness and Wrath of ALMIGHTY GOD.* As tho' there would be a very great Manifestation of his almighty Power, in what the fierceness of his Wrath should inflict, as tho' Omnipotence should be as it 10 were enraged, and exerted, as Men are wont to exert their Strength in the fierceness of their Wrath. Oh! then, what will be the Consequence! What will become of the poor Worm that shall suffer it! Whose Hands can be strong? And whose Heart endure? To what a dreadful, inexpressible, inconceivable Depth of Misery must the poor creature be sunk, who shall be the Subject of this!

Consider this, you that are here present, that yet remain in an unregenerate State. That God will execute the fierceness of his Anger, implies that he will inflict Wrath without any Pity: when God beholds the ineffable Extremity of your Case, and sees your Torment so vastly disproportion'd to your Strength, and sees how your poor Soul is crushed and sinks down, as it were, into an infinite Gloom, he will have no 20 Compassion upon you, he will not forbear the Executions of his Wrath, or in the least lighten his Hand; there shall be no Moderation or Mercy, nor will God then at all stay his rough Wind; he will have no Regard to your Welfare, nor be at all careful lest you should suffer too much, in any other Sense than only that you shall not suffer beyond what strict Justice requires: nothing shall be with-held, because it's so hard for you to bear. Ezek. 8. 18, *Therefore will I also deal in* Fury; *mine Eye shall not spare, neither will I have Pity; and tho' they cry in mine Ears with a loud Voice, yet I will not hear them.* Now God stands ready to pity you; this is a Day of Mercy; you may cry now with some Encouragement of obtaining Mercy: but when once the Day of Mercy is past, your most lamentable and dolorous Cries and Shrieks will 30 be in vain; you will be wholly lost and thrown away of God, as to any Regard to your Welfare; God will have no other Use to put you to but only to suffer Misery; you shall be continued in Being to no other End; for you will be a Vessel of Wrath fitted to Destruction; and there will be no other Use of this Vessel but only to be filled full of Wrath: God will be so far from pitying you when you cry to him, that 'tis said he will only *Laugh and Mock,* Prov. 1. 25, 26, &c.

How awful are those Words, Isai. 63. 3. which are the Words of the great God: *I will tread them in mine Anger, and will trample them in my Fury, and their Blood shall be sprinkled upon my Garments, and I will stain all my Raiment.* 'Tis perhaps impossible to conceive of Words that carry in them greater Manifestations of these three 40 Things, *viz.* Contempt and Hatred, and fierceness of Indignation. If you cry to God to pity you, he will be so far from pitying you in your doleful Case, or shewing you the least Regard or Favour, that instead of that he'll only tread you under Foot: and tho' he will know that you can't bear the Weight of Omnipotence treading upon you, yet he won't regard that, but he will crush you under his Feet without Mercy; he will crush out your Blood, and make it fly, and it shall be sprinkled on his Garments, so as to stain all his Raiment. He will not only hate you, but he will have you in the utmost Contempt; no Place shall be thought fit for you, but under his Feet, to be trodden down as the Mire of the Streets.

    3. The Misery you are exposed to is that which God will inflict to that End, that he might *shew* what the *Wrath* of JEHOVAH is. God hath had it on his Heart to show to Angels and Men, both how excellent his Love is, and also how terrible his Wrath is. Sometimes earthly Kings have a Mind to shew how terrible *their* Wrath
10 is, by the extream Punishments they would execute on those that provoke 'em. *Nebuchadnezzar,* that mighty and haughty Monarch of the *Chaldean* Empire, was willing to shew *his* Wrath, when enraged with *Shadrach, Meschech,* and *Abednego;* and accordingly gave Order that the burning fiery Furnace should be het seven Times hotter than it was before; doubtless it was raised to the utmost Degree of Fierceness that humane art could raise it; But the great GOD is also willing to show *his Wrath,* and magnify his awful Majesty and mighty Power in the extream Sufferings of his Enemies. Rom. 9. 22, *What if God willing to shew* HIS *Wrath, and to make his Power known, endured with much Long-suffering the Vessels of Wrath fitted to Destruction?* And seeing this is his Design, and what he has determined, to shew
20 how terrible the unmixed, unrestrained Wrath, the Fury and Fierceness of JEHOVAH is, he will do it to Effect. There will be something accomplished and brought to pass, that will be dreadful with a Witness. When the great and angry God hath risen up and executed his awful Vengeance on the poor Sinner; and the Wretch is actually suffering the infinite Weight and Power of his Indignation, then will God call upon the whole Universe to behold that awful Majesty, and mighty Power that is to be seen in it. Isai. 33. 12, 13, 14. *And the People shall be as the burnings of Lime, as Thorns cut up shall they be burnt in the Fire. Hear ye that are far off what I have done; and ye that are near acknowledge my Might. The Sinners in Zion are afraid, fearfulness hath surprized the Hypocrites &c.*
30   Thus it will be with you that are in an unconverted State, if you continue in it; the infinite Might, and Majesty and Terribleness of the OMNIPOTENT GOD shall be magnified upon you, in the ineffable Strength of your Torments: You shall be tormented in the Presence of the holy Angels, and in the Presence of the Lamb; and when you shall be in this State of Suffering, the glorious Inhabitants of Heaven shall go forth and look on the awful Spectacle, that they may see what the Wrath and Fierceness of the Almighty is, and when they have seen it, they will fall down and adore that great Power and Majesty. Isai. 66. 23, 24, *And it shall come to pass, that from one new Moon to another, and from one Sabbath to another, shall all Flesh come to Worship before me, saith the Lord; and they shall go forth and look upon the Carcasses*
40 *of the Men that have transgressed against me; for their Worm shall not die, neither shall their Fire be quenched, and they shall be an abhorring unto all Flesh.*

    4. It is *everlasting* Wrath. It would be dreadful to suffer this Fierceness and Wrath of Almighty God one Moment; but you must suffer it to all Eternity: there will be

11 **Nebuchadnezzar.** See Daniel 3: 19-30 for the story of the fiery furnace

no End to this exquisite horrible Misery: When you look forward, you shall see a long Forever, a boundless Duration before you, which will swallow up your Thoughts, and amaze your Soul; and you will absolutely despair of ever having any Deliverance, any End, any Mitigation, any Rest at all; you will know certainly that you must wear out long Ages, Millions of Millions of Ages, in wrestling and conflicting with this almighty merciless Vengeance; and then when you have so done, when so many Ages have actually been spent by you in this Manner, you will know that all is but a Point to what remains. So that your Punishment will indeed be infinite. Oh who can express what the State of a Soul in such circumstances is! All that we can possibly say about it, gives but a very feeble faint Representation of it; 10 'tis inexpressible and inconceivable: for *who knows the Power of God's Anger?*

How dreadful is the State of those that are daily and hourly in Danger of this great Wrath, and infinite Misery! But this is the dismal Case of every Soul in this Congregation, that has not been born again, however moral and strict, sober and religious they may otherwise be. Oh that you would consider it, whether you be Young or Old. There is Reason to think, that there are many in this Congregation now hearing this Discourse, that will actually be the Subjects of this very Misery to all Eternity. We know not who they are, or in what Seats they sit, or what Thoughts they now have: it may be they are now at Ease, and hear all these Things without much Disturbance, and are now flattering themselves that they are not the Persons; 20 promising themselves that they shall escape. If we knew that there was one Person, and but one, in the whole Congregation that was to be the Subject of this Misery, what an awful Thing would it be to think of! If we knew who it was, what an awful Sight would it be to see such a Person! How might all the rest of the Congregation lift up a lamentable and bitter Cry over him! But alass! instead of one, how many is it likely will remember this Discourse in Hell! And it would be a Wonder if some that are now present, should not be in Hell in a very short Time, before this Year is out. And it would be no Wonder if some person that now sits here in some Seat of this Meeting-House in Health, and quiet & secure, should be there before to morrow Morning.   30

                                                                                               1741

from *Freedom of Will*

The following selection (Part I, Section 5) from the Freedom of Will *displays Edwards' skill in definition and logical distinctions. For his general position, see page 167.*

Concerning the Notion of Liberty, and of Moral Agency

The plain and obvious Meaning of the Words *Freedom* and *Liberty*, in common Speech, is *Power, Opportunity or Advantage, that any one has, to do as he pleases.* Or in other Words, his being free from Hindrance or Impediment in the Way of doing,

Text: the first edition, Boston, 1754

or conducting in any Respect, as he wills. And the contrary to Liberty, whatever Name we call that by, is a Person's being hinder'd or unable to conduct as he will, or being necessitated to do otherwise.

If this which I have mentioned be the Meaning of the Word Liberty, in the ordinary Use of language; as I trust that none that has ever learn'd to talk, and is unprejudiced, will deny; then it will follow, that in Propriety of Speech, neither Liberty, nor it's contrary, can properly be ascribed to any Being or Thing, but that which has such a Faculty, Power or Property, as is called will. For that which is possessed of no such Thing as *Will,* can't have any *Power* or *Opportunity* of doing
10 *according to it's Will,* nor be necessitated to act *contrary to its Will,* nor be restrained from acting agreeably to it. And therefore to talk of Liberty, or the contrary, as belonging to the *very Will it self,* is not to speak good Sense; if we judge of Sense, and Nonsense, by the original & proper Signification of Words. For the *Will it self* is not an Agent that *has a Will:* The Power of choosing, it self, has not a Power of chusing. That which has the Power of Volition or Choice is the Man or the Soul, and not the Power of Volition it self. And he that has the Liberty of doing according to his Will, is the Agent or Doer who is possessed of the Will; and not the Will which he is possessed of. We say with Propriety, that a Bird let loose has Power & Liberty to fly; but not that the Bird's Power of flying has a Power & Lib-
20 erty of flying. To be free is the Property of an Agent, who is possessed of Powers & Faculties, as much as to be cunning, valiant, bountiful, or zealous. But these Qualities are the Properties of Men or Persons; and not the Properties of Properties.

There are two Things that are contrary to this which is called Liberty in common Speech. One is *Constraint;* the same is otherwise called *Force, Compulsion,* & *Coaction;* which is a Person's being necessitated to do a Thing *contrary* to his Will. The other is *Restraint;* which is his being hindred, and not having Power to do *according* to his Will. But that which has no Will, can't be the Subject of these Things. — I need say the less on this Head, Mr. *Locke* having set the same Thing forth, with so great clearness, in his *Essay on the human Understanding.*
30 But one Thing more I would observe concerning what is vulgarly called *Liberty;* namely, that Power & Opportunity for one to do and conduct as he will, or according to his Choice, is all that is meant by it; without taking into the Meaning of the Word, any Thing of the Cause or Original of that Choice; or at all considering how the Person came to have such a Volition; whether it was caused by some external Motive or internal habitual Bias; whether it was determin'd by some internal antecedent Volition, or whether it happen'd without a Cause; whether it was necessarily connected with something foregoing, or not connected. Let the Person come by his Volition or Choice how he will, yet, if he is able, and there is Nothing in the Way to hinder his pursuing and executing his Will, the man is fully & per-
40 fectly free, according to the primary and common Notion of Freedom.

What has been said may be sufficient to show what is meant by *Liberty,* accord-

1 **wills.** "I say not only *doing,* but *conducting;* because a voluntary forbearing to do, sitting still, keeping Silence, &c. are Instances of Persons' *Conduct,* about which Liberty is exercised; tho' they are not so properly called *doing.*" — Edwards   28 **Mr. Locke,** in Bk. II, Chap. 21

ing to the common Notions of Mankind, and in the usual & primary Acceptation of the Word: but the Word, as used by *Arminians, Pelagians* & others, who oppose the *Calvinists,* has an entirely different Signification. These several Things belong to their Notion of Liberty. 1. That it consists in a *Self-determining Power* in the Will, or a certain Sovereignty the Will has over it self, and it's own Acts, whereby it determines it's own Volitions; so as not to be dependent in it's Determinations, on any Cause without it self, nor determined by any Thing prior to it's own Acts. 2. *Indifference* belongs to Liberty in their Notion of it, or that the Mind, previous to the Act of Volition be, *in iquilibrio.* 3. *Contingence* is another Thing that belongs and is essential to it; not in the common Acceptation of the Word, as that has been 10 already explain'd, but as opposed to all *Necessity,* or any fixed & certain Connection with some previous Ground or Reason of it's existence. They suppose the Essence of Liberty so much to consist in these Things, that unless the Will of Man be free in this Sense, he has no real Freedom, how much soever he may be at Liberty to act according to his will.

A *moral Agent* is a Being that is capable of those Actions that have a moral Quality, and which can properly be denominated good or evil in a moral Sense, vertuous or vicious, commendable or faulty. To moral Agency belongs a *moral Faculty,* or Sense of moral Good and Evil, or of such a Thing as Desert or Worthiness, of Praise or Blame, Reward or Punishment; and a Capacity which an Agent has of 20 being influenced in his Actions by moral Inducements or Motives, exhibited to the View of Understanding & Reason, to engage to a Conduct agreeable to the moral Faculty.

The Sun is very excellent & beneficial in it's Action and Influence on the Earth, in warming it, and causing it to bring forth it's Fruits; but it is not a moral Agent: It's Action, tho' good, is not vertuous or meritorious. Fire that breaks out in a City, and consumes great Part of it, is very mischievous in its Operation; but is not a moral Agent: what it does is not faulty or sinful, or deserving of any Punishment. The brute Creatures are not moral Agents: the actions of some of 'em are very profitable & pleasant; others are very hurtful: yet, seeing they have no moral Faculty, 30 or Sense of Desert, and don't act from Choice guided by Understanding, or with a Capacity of reasoning and reflecting, but only from Instinct, and are not capable of being influenced by moral Inducements, their Actions are not properly sinful or vertuous; nor are they properly the Subjects of any such moral Treatment for what they do, as moral Agents are for their Faults or good Deeds.

Here it may be noted, that there is a circumstantial Difference between the moral Agency of a *Ruler* and a *Subject.* I call it *circumstantial,* because it lies only in the Difference of moral Inducements they are capable of being influenced by, arising from the Difference of *Circumstances.* A Ruler, acting, in that Capacity only, is not capable of being influenced by a moral Law, and it's Sanctions of Threatnings and 40 Promises, Rewards and Punishments, as the *Subject* is; tho' both may be influenced by a Knowledge of moral Good and Evil. And therefore the moral Agency of the

---

2 **Pelagians,** followers of Pelagius (c. 360-c. 420), British theologian, who opposed free will to the Augustinian emphasis on total depravity

Supreme Being, who acts only in the Capacity of a *Ruler* towards his Creatures, and never as a *Subject,* differs in that Respect from the moral Agency of created intelligent Beings. God's Actions, and particularly those which he exerts as a moral Governour, have moral Qualifications, are morally good in the highest Degree. They are most perfectly holy & righteous; and we must conceive of Him as influenced in the highest Degree, by that which, above all others, is properly a moral Inducement, *viz.* the moral Good which He sees in such and such Things: And therefore He is, in the most proper Sense, a moral Agent, the Source of all moral Ability & Agency, the Fountain and Rule of all Vertue and moral Good; tho' by Reason of
10 his being Supreme over all, 'tis not possible He should be under the Influence of Law or Command, Promises or Threatnings, Rewards or Punishments, Counsels or Warnings. The essential Qualities of a moral Agent are in God, in the greatest possible Perfection; such as Understanding, to perceive the Difference between moral Good & Evil; a Capacity of discerning that moral Worthiness and Demerit, by which some Things are Praise-worthy, others deserving of Blame and Punishment; and also a Capacity of Choice, and Choice guided by Understanding, and a Power of acting according to his Choice or Pleasure, and being capable of doing those Things which are in the highest Sense Praise-worthy. And herein does very much consist that Image of God wherein he made Man, (which we read of *Gen.* I.
20 26, 27, & Chap. IX. 6.) by which God distinguished Man from the Beasts, *viz.* in those Faculties & Principles of Nature, whereby He is capable of moral Agency. Herein very much consists the *natural* Image of God; as his *spiritual* and *moral* Image, wherein Man was made at first, consisted in that moral Excellency, that he was endowed with.

1751-1754?, 1754

1705–1787 Charles Chauncy

A more shocking idea can scarce be given of the Deity than that which represents him as arbitrarily dooming the greater part of the race of men to eternal misery," wrote Charles Chauncy. To Thomas Shepard, to Cotton Mather, to Jonathan Edwards that statement would have seemed almost the ultimate in heresy, and it is not surprising that for most of his life Chauncy kept some of his theological opinions to himself or published them anonymously.

Yet everything in Chauncy's life and times tended to minimize the sterner Calvinistic doctrines of depravity and election — everything except the powerful reaffirmations of his great rival, Edwards.

For sixty years Chauncy was one of the ministers of the First Church in Boston. A poor preacher, if "exhorting" is the measure of pulpit success, he proved in his fifty-odd published books that no one in New England was his superior in knowledge of the church fathers, in staunch defense of Congregational church government, or in the exercise of a clear and functional style. He made worship dignified and intellectual; he expressed the social and political convictions of the dominantly Whig society in which he lived; he was outstanding among the controversialists of his day for unimpassioned detachment. Rational and somewhat cold, he is an excellent illustration of why Boston and eastern Massachusetts turned away from some of the most conspicuous aspects of Calvinism to the more comfortable but less emotional ways of Unitarianism and Universalism.

Although Chauncy is worth study both for his doctrine and for his part in the fight against the establishment of an Anglican episcopate (a fearful prospect to most of the New England clergy, and the issue which aligned them almost solidly with the Revolutionary party), he is perhaps at his best when he writes about religious experience. Without denying the part which emotion plays in regeneration and without deserting the authority of the Bible, he distrusted unbridled religious excitement and was convinced that the effects of semihysterical revival periods were seldom permanent. Lacking the passionate piety of Edwards, he had little use for "enthusiasm," and he stated his case against it in many places. Revivalism became, despite Chauncy, a characteristic feature of the religious life of America, but there have always been men like him, sure that the good life has most to do with rational conviction and the moral tone of daily living.

Williston Walker, **Ten New England Leaders,** New York and Chicago, 1901

from Seasonable Thoughts on the State of Religion in New-England

Between 1740 and 1745 over 150 New England towns felt the excitement of the "Great Awakening," a religious revival usually attributed to the influence of Jonathan Edwards and George Whitefield. Chauncy represents the urbane reaction to its remarkable physical manifestations and obvious dangers. His Seasonable Thoughts *(Boston, 1743), a treatise in five parts, presented (1) the "Things of a bad and dangerous Tendency" in the revival, i.e., such results as hysteria; (2) the obligations of pastors to help "suppress prevailing Disorders"; (3) instances of ill treatment of "Discouragers of Irregularities," i.e., persons who raised objections to uninhibited behavior; (4) what "ought to be corrected, or avoided," in testifying against the disorders; and (5) "what may be judged the best Expedients, to promote pure and undefiled Religion." The selection which follows is from the latter portion of Part I.*

I doubt not, but the *divine SPIRIT* often accompanies the *preached Word,* so as that, by *his Influence,* Sinners are awakened to a Sense *of Sin,* and filled with *deep Distress* of Soul: But the *blessed SPIRIT* must not, at Random, be made the Author of all those *Surprises,* operating in *strange Effects* upon the *Body,* which may be seen among People. They may be produced other Ways; yea, I trust, that has been already said, which makes it evident, they have actually been produced, even by the *wild and extravagant Conduct* of some *over-heated* Preachers.

It will, doubtless, be here said, these *Out-cries* have sometimes arisen, when no other than the great Truths of the Gospel have been urg'd upon the Consciences of Sinners; and this, in a *becoming Manner,* and by Preachers who have not been noted, either for the *Loudness of their Voice,* or the *Boisterousness of their Action.*

In Reply whereto, I deny not but this may have been the Case: But, at the same Time, think it worthy of Notice, that these bodily *Effects* were, at FIRST, produced, so far as I can learn, ONLY by *such Preachers* as were *remarkable* for their *terrible speaking,* both as to *Matter,* and *Manner:* Nor do I remember an Instance, in the Country, of *Out-cries,* by *any other Sort of Preachers,* 'till the Noise of such *extraordinary* Effects, as *Arguments* of an *immediate divine Power,* in one Place and another, had alarmed the People, and made many of them think, it was necessary they also should be in like Circumstances.

Besides, when these *Out-cries* have been effected by your more *moderate Preachers,* (which, by the Way, comparatively speaking, has been a rare Thing) have they not begun with one or two only, and from them been propagated to others? Nay, have not *these,* from whom they took Rise, *usually,* been such as were *before accustomed* to the Way of *screaming out?* And were they not, *at first,* brought to it, under a more terrible Kind of Preaching? I believe, upon Examination, this will be found to be *nearly* the Truth of the Case.

I shall only add further, that however distinguished the Minister who has preached has been, for his *exemplary Piety,* and *shining Gifts;* however agreeable to the Mind of CHRIST he has delivered the Truths of the Gospel; and however warmly he may have addrest himself to the *People's Passions,* if he wan't before known to have been a *Favourer* of these *Outcries,* he has not produced them: Nor do I believe, an Instance can be given in the Country, of their being brought forward by any Minister, of whom the People had a Suspicion, that he did not like them: Which to me, is not the best Argument of their being so wholly owing to the *divine Power,* as some may be too ready to imagine. But to proceed,

Another Thing that very much lessens my Opinion of these *religious Fears,* with the *strange Effects* of them is, that they are produced by the *Exhorters;* and this, in all Parts of the Land; and it may be, in more numerous Instances, than by the *Ministers* themselves. And if these *bodily Agitations* arise from the Influence of the SPIRIT, when produc'd by the *Ministers,* they are so when produced by the *Exhorters.* The Appearance is the same in both Cases; the like *inward Distress* is effected, and discovers it self in like *Cryings* and *Swoonings:* Nor is there any Reason to think well,

Text: the first edition, 1743

in the general, of the one, and not of the other. And yet, some of the best Friends
of *this Work,* both among the *Clergy* and *Laity,* think ill of these Things, as brought
forward by the *Exhorters:* Nay, one of the greatest Friends to the *good Work,* among
the Ministers in Town, freely declar'd concerning one of these *Exhorters,* who came
into this Place, and began the *Outcries* we were before Strangers to, that he feared
the Hand of Satan was in his coming here to throw Disgrace on the Work of GOD;
suggesting, that the Wonders wrought by the *Magicians* in *Egypt* were, to all
Appearance, like the *Miracles* wrought by MOSES. I see no Reason for such a Remark. The visible Effects of this young Man's exhorting here, and in the neighbouring Town of *Dorchester,* were just the same that are wrought by the most famous 10
Preachers in the *new Way:* And where there is no discernable Difference, there is no
Ground, in *Reason* or *Scripture,* to speak well of the one, and ill of the other. Such
are certainly inconsistent with themselves, who attribute these *Extraordinaries,* as
bro't forward by the *Exhorters,* to a *Spirit of Delusion,* or *Enthusiasm,* or any other
inferior Cause; while they can't bear to hear a Word said against them, when they are
the Produce of those who are called *Ministers.* For my self, I put them both on the
same Foot, as supposing they both arise from the same Cause: Only, the Appearance of these Things, in the same Kind and Degree, when the *Exhorters* are the Carriers on, administers just Ground of Fear, whether they are, in *general,* so much owing
to the *extraordinary Influence* of the *divine SPIRIT,* as some may be too ready 20
to im'agine. If they are not owing to the *wonderful Operation* of the HOLY GHOST,
when the *Exhorters* are the Occasion of them, they may easily be accounted for,
when produced by others: And it can't well be supposed, there should be the extraordinary Concurrence of the blessed SPIRIT with these *Exhorters.* For who are they
but such, concerning whom the *inspir'd Apostle* has said, *Not a Novice lest he be lifted
up with Pride, and fall into the Condemnation of the Devil?* Who are they but such, of
whom the same *Apostle* says, *they walk disorderly, working not at all, but are Busie-
Bodies?* With Respect to whom, he gives *Commandment by the LORD JESUS CHRIST,
that with Quietness they work and eat their own Bread.* Who are they but such, as set
themselves up in Opposition to their *Pastors,* though *sound in the Faith* and of a 30
good Conversation, contrary to the *Order of the Gospel,* and to the *Disturbance* of the
Churches? And can it be thought, that GOD would countenance the Conduct of
this Kind of Persons, by *extraordinary* Testimonies of his *Presence* from Heaven; and
this, while they are in a Method of acting that directly contradicts his own Appointments? Besides, may it not be said of these *Exhorters,* in the *general,* that they are
very *Babes in Understanding,* needing themselves to be *taught which be the first Principles of the Oracles of GOD?* That they are over-forward and conceited; taking that
upon them, they have neither a *Call* to, nor *Qualifications* for? Yea, is it not too true
of some of them, that they have acted under the Influence of an *over-heated Imagination:* or what is worse, from *low* and *base Views?* This is now so evident, that there 40

4 one . . . **Exhorters,** probably James Davenport (1716-1757), who visited Boston in 1742. Interviewed by
the ministers, and then excluded from the churches, he preached in the streets with such violence that he
was arrested and judged insane   25 **inspir'd Apostle.** Timothy; see I Timothy 3:6 and 5:13

is no Room for Debate upon the Matter. And of all Men, these, I should think, are the most unlikely to be distinguish'd with the *extraordinary Presence* of the HOLY GHOST.

There is yet another Thing that makes it look as though these *Terrors might* arise from a *lower Cause,* than that which is *Divine;* and that is, their happening in the *Night.* I don't mean, that there han't been *Outcries* in the *Day Time;* but the *Night* is more commonly the *Season,* when these Things are to be seen, and in their greatest Perfection. They are more *frequent,* and more *general,* and rais'd to a higher *Degree,* at the *Night Meetings,* when there are but *two* or *three* Candles in the Place of Worship, or they are wholly in the dark. I have often, in Conversation, heard this Remark made by those, who have been in the Way of these Things; and the same Observations I find in the *Letters* that have been sent me. Says one, speaking of these *Extraordinaries,* "They are more in the *Night* than in the Day;" Another, "They operate most strongly in their *Night Meetings;*" Another still, "They never happen'd (this must be understood of the particular Place, he is giving an Account of) to any considerable Degree, 'till the *Darkness* of the Night came on." And why should these *strange Effects* be more *frequent,* and *general,* in the *Gloominess* of the *Night,* if they were produc'd by the Agency of the *Divine SPIRIT?* Does he need the Advantage of the *dark* to fill Men's Hearts with Terror? This is certainly a shrew'd Sign, that there is more of the *Humane* in these Things, than some are willing to own. We know every Thing appears more dismal in the Night: Persons are more apt to be struck with Surprise and Consternation: And as this is a good Reason, it may be the true one, why a *doleful Voice,* and frightful *Managements* may take Effect more in the *Night* than at other Times.

The *Subjects* also of these *Terrors* may lead us to make the like Judgment about them; and these are *Children, Women,* and *youngerly* Persons. Not that others han't been wrought upon. Instances there have been of *Men;* and these, both *middle-aged,* and *advanced in Years,* who have both *cried out,* and *fallen down.* But 'tis among *Children, young People* and *Women,* whose Passions are soft and tender, and more easily thrown into a Commotion, that these Things *chiefly* prevail. I know, 'tis thus in those Places, where I have had Opportunity to make Inquiry. And from the Accounts transmitted to me from Friends, in other Places, it appears to have been so among them also. The Account I have from one Part of the Country is, "The Operation is principally among *Women* and *Girls;*" From another, "The Persons wrought upon were generally *Women* and *Children;*" From another, "These Effects have been most frequent in *Women* and *young* Persons." And are not these the very Persons, whose Passions according to *Nature,* it might be expected, would be alarmed? If *young* People are, in a moral Sense, more likely to be wrought upon by *Divine Grace,* than *old,* I see not that this is the Case with respect to *Women* in Distinction from *Men.* Men may as easily be overcome by the *Power* of the HOLY GHOST, as *Women;* and are as likely, in a *moral* View of the Matter, to be so: And what should then be the Reason that they should be, as it were, overlook'd, and *Women* generally the Persons thrown into these *Agitations* and *Terrors?* It certainly looks, as tho' the Weakness of their Nerves, and from hence their greater Liable-ness to be surpris'd, and overcome with Fear, was the true Account to be given of this Matter.

Moreover, the *Way* in which these *Terrors* spread themselves is a Circumstance, that does not much favour their *divine Origin.* They seem to be suddenly propagated, from one to another, as in a great Fright or Consternation. They often begin with a single Person, a *Child,* or *Woman,* or *Lad,* whose *Shrieks* set others a *Shrieking;* and so the Shrieks catch from one to another, 'till the whole Congregation is alarmed, and such an awful Scene, many Times, open'd, as no Imagination can paint to the Life. To this Purpose is that in the BOSTON-*Post-Boy* [Numb. 391.], when after an Account of the *terrible Language* made Use of by the Itinerants, 'tis added, "This 10 frequently frights the *little Children,* and sets them a Screaming; and that frights their *tender Mothers,* and sets them to Screaming, and by Degrees spreads over a great Part of the Congregation: And 40, 50, or an 100, of them screaming all together, makes such an awful and hideous Noise as will make a Man's Hair stand on End. Some will faint away, fall down upon the Floor, wallow and foam. Some Women will rend off their Caps, Handkerchiefs, and other Clothes, tear their Hair down about their Ears, and seem perfectly bereft of their Reason."

Appearances in this Kind, I have often had an Account of from those who have been present at them; and as begun by one or two Persons at first: And where this has been the Case, there is no great Difficulty in finding out the Cause: 'Tis far 20 more reasonable to look for it in *Nature,* than in *Grace.*

It may not be amiss to observe still further, that these *Terrors,* with their *Effects,* are *uniform all over the Country;* operating upon all in whom they take Place, much in the *same Way* and *Manner,* be their *moral* Character what it will. Whether the Subjects of them be *great* or *small* Sinners, whether the Sins they have committed be *more* or *less,* whether they have continued in Sin a *longer* or *shorter* Time, there is no Difference as to their *Fears,* and the *Operation* of them; but they are all indiscriminately thrown into the like *horrible* Circumstances; which it is not reasonable to think would be the Case, if they were put into this Condition by a *divine Influence:* Whereas, its the very Thing that might be expected, where *Nature* is suddenly sur- 30 pris'd, and over-come, as in a Fright.

In fine, it's a Circumstance no Ways favouring the *divine Rise* of these *Out-cries,* that many People now commonly make them, not as urg'd hereto from an *over-pouring* Sense of their *own* Sins, but the Sins of *others.* Having been *converted* themselves, their *Distress,* under the *Preaching of the Word,* is now raised to such a Height for the *unconverted Sinners in the Congregation,* that they can't help *screaming out;* and so *many of them,* sometimes at once, as that the *Worship* is *interrupted,* or greatly *disturb'd.* A *Concern* for others, whom we have Reason to fear, are in a State of Sin, is, no Doubt, reasonable; and there will be more or less of it, in the Heart of every sincere Christian. But are *Shriekings* a suitable Expression of this Concern; especially, 40

---

10 **Itinerants,** ministers not settled in a particular church; revivalists; clergymen of the Wesleyan, or Methodist, persuasion   17 **bereft . . . Reason.** "I should not have inserted this Account, it looks so *extravagant,* but that I have now by me two *Letters,* from Gentlemen of known *Worth* and *Integrity,* in the *Ministry,* who particularly refer to it, and say, 'tis a just one." — Chauncy

in the House of GOD? And can it be suppos'd, the *GOD of Order,* would, by the Exertment of his Power, raise this Concern to such a Height, as that his *own Worship* should be broke up upon the Account of it? 'Tis impossible. I never heard one *sober, solid* Person speak a Word, in Favour of *these Out-cries;* and am heartily sorry, any Thing has been *printed,* encouraging so gross an Extravagance. I hope none, from the *meer Sound* of some Texts, will justify *this same Distress for others,* as it begins now to discover it self, among some Persons, in *another* Form, in *Travail-Pains and Throws.* Of this, I have now an Account by me, in a *Letter* from a Friend, upon the Evidence of his *own Eyes and Ears;* which yet, I should not have mentioned, but
10 that I have since *personally* conversed with a *Minister* in the Country, who informed me of one, who had been in *Travail* two or three Times successively for him. i. e. Under all the *Signs of Distress,* that appear in *Women* upon such Occasions.

These are the Reasons, why I can't entertain so high an Opinion as some others do, of the *Terrors* appearing in strange *bodily* Effects, which have been so common of late in this Land.

1743?, 1743

1631—1705 Michael Wigglesworth

The author of *The Day of Doom, or a Poetical Description of the Great and Last Judgment,* the most widely read poem written in seventeenth-century New England, was born in Yorkshire but was brought to Connecticut by his parents before he was seven. Precocious but frail, he was sent to the Latin school at New Haven but was taken out when he was needed to help work his father's farm. Unfit by physique and temperament for farm labor, he was sent back to school after three years and in 1651 was graduated from Harvard College. He was uncertain of his calling. He seems to have thought first of studying medicine, but either the Cambridge environment or a religious experience turned him to theology and the ministry. He stayed on at Harvard as a fellow and tutor, began to preach occasionally, and from around 1654 had some assurance of the church at Malden, a town about four miles north of Boston. He married, after much soul searching, in 1655, and is believed to have been ordained at Malden two years later.

Afflicted apparently both by "preacher's sore throat" and hypochondria, and disturbed by strong sexual drives which he had difficulty in controlling, he was hardly a successful minister. From 1657 until 1686, in fact, he seems never to have performed regularly all the duties expected of a pastor, although he preached occasionally and practiced medicine among his neighbors. His first wife died in 1659, leaving him one daughter. In 1679 he remarried, complicating his standing among the townspeople and his fellow clergymen by choosing a woman who was neither a church member nor his social equal. She was, in fact, his housemaid, twenty-eight years his junior and six years younger than his daughter. She bore him six children before she died in 1690. A year later he married for a third time, now picking a widow. Their single child became the first Hollis professor of divinity at Harvard. For the last twenty years of his life, Wigglesworth recovered a large measure of his health and served his church effectively and faithfully, although he was remembered as "a little feeble shadow of a man."

Out of the travail of his long illness came three poems: *The Day of Doom* (usually dated 1662 although no copy is known from that year); *Meat Out of the Eater* (printed 1669); and "God's Controversy with New England" (not printed until 1873). There are more than a dozen lesser pieces.

Very possibly, however, Wigglesworth's future reputation will rest in large part upon his diary, although we have only a fragment of it. Partly written in shorthand, it was not printed until 1951, but no other Puritan document is as revealing of the profound depths of religious and personal insecurity.

The Day of Doom, ed. with an introduction by K. B. Murdock, New York, 1929   The Diary of Michael Wigglesworth, ed. with an introduction by Edmund S. Morgan, **Publications of the Colonial Society of Massachusetts**, XXXV, 310-444, Boston, 1951   Richard Crowder, **No Featherbed in Heaven: A Biography of Michael Wigglesworth, 1631-1705**, East Lansing, Mich., 1962   Harold S. Jantz, **The First Century of New England Verse**, New York, 1962

from Diary

September 16-November 19, 1653

That the Puritans were constantly under the impression that God walked with them every moment of their lives has been noted many times. Few illustrations of this rather egocentric view bring home its meaning more clearly than Wigglesworth's diary. His sense of guilt for his failures as a preacher and as a social being, for daydreaming while listening to sermons, and for his mixed feelings about his father's death now seems abnormal if not pathological. No other diary, however, so well conveys the bleak moods of Puritan introspection. Samuel Sewall (see p. 82) and Jonathan Edwards (see p. 165) seem, each in his own way, rays of sunshine by comparison.

Wigglesworth's diary from February 1653 to May 1657 exists in manuscript in the library of the Massachusetts Historical Society. The selection here is from the transcript made by Edmund S. Morgan. Those passages here italicized are in shorthand in the original. At the time of writing, Wigglesworth was a tutor in Harvard College.

[16 September ? 1653]

friday I find my usuall distempers pride and inordinate affection to the creature, weariness of gods worship, vain distractions in dutys, and manifold iniquitys breaking in like a flood. Lord in thy multitude of mercys pardon, heal, and take not thy holy spirit though grieved from me.

This hath bin a day of great temptation; though the Lord hath not let me be very much distracted; yet so awakened as solemly to fly to the throne of grace and cry with all my might for preservation out of temptation or at least that I might not be forsaken so as to sin against god wittingly by any vain words unsutable to the day. The reason of this temptation was the being here of a stranger what we could not but intertain both in the Hall and our chamber. The Lord hear'd my poor broken disordered chatterings, and in som measure kept my self, and hept me to administer to others occasion of religious discours. Yet I find so much of that plague of pride which my soul hateth: of a heart that cannot desire gret lettings out of christs love to me such as some times I haue felt which I dreadfully fear, such aptness to be weary of seeking god in his ordinances, to lose sence of my misery, of unbeleif: that I haue caus to sit downe astonied that such means produce so small effects in so long time. That which is wanting cannot be numbred; yet god is with me in his ordinances touching my heart in some measure with these things; oh that I could feel my owne emptiness so as not to know what to do without pardon and supply: as it was in the exigency above mentioned. Lord I bow the knees of my poor pining soul unto thy self my father, who art rich in mercy, compassionating oppressed sinners, that thou would seal to me pardon, and thy love and giue healing for thy faithfulness for thy glory, for thy son, for thy everlasting love sake.

I felt fears and misgiuings about my good estate. yet much pride got head in me; and presently the Lord let loos upon me some scruples of conscience which put me in fear least I went cross to gods will, and this to abase me.

25 I found besides much prevalency of pride, a heart apt to run after mirth and recreation. God assisted me much in my study. And now shall I again take his name in vain in this approaching sabbath, which I find I haue too too [*sic*] much accustomed to, and look't at it as a light matter, not watch't against it as I should haue done; especially grieving god by vain thoughts. Lord forgiue this trespass, and giue repentance for and deliverance from this with all other abominations.

26 I haue found much of gods presence in his ordinances this day: much stirring my heart in the forenoon by such sutable trueths. Concerning the good ground and the effects of the word therein: yet at noon my filthy vile heart could find room for pride: and vain thought after noon in the beginning of the sermon exceedingly prevail'd whereupon when Mr. Mitchel came to uses of strong consolation from gods constancy in his loue I begin to question gods love to me; and that one crevis of

---

16 **ordinances**, religious ceremonies, of which the sermon was the most important to the Puritan 38 **Mitchel**. Jonathan Mitchel (1624-1668), a graduate of Harvard College in 1747, succeeded Thomas Shepard as minister of the church at Cambridge in 1650. Mitchel was Wigglesworth's tutor, pastor, and close friend, later contributing prefatory verses to *The Day of Doom*

hope that hath chered my soul so long when other evidences fail'd, god plucks that from mee too, at least suffereth unbeleef to darken it vizt my renewed acts of closing with christ at his supper. and other times. when I look upon my vile ungrateful impenitent whorish heart I am ashamed to think that god should love or owne me. I abhor my self o Lord for these renewed incurable distempers. I could even take vengeance of my cursed heart that is so deceitful and desparately wicked in impenitent departure from god. Nevertheless through the riches of thy grace I am imboldned to ask peace with god and pardon and communion with God (which my heart breaths after, for that is my life) and a new heart after thy owne wil. Hide not (my father) thy face from me, lest I be like one of those that go down to the pit, lest I sink in discouragement and say 'tis a vain thing to seek the Lord.

27 There was an Artillery sermon here a munday. I found my heart secretly weary of the ordinance, and hankering after my studys or other occasions: a frame which I was exceedingly affraid of, and desire greatly to loath my self for. But Lord it puts me to a stand to think what mean's this that my heart is worst in appearance when I most earnestly strive but the day before for deliverance from these evils. How long oh Lord wilt thou be angry with my prayers? and withhold mercy from me. I feel a heart that hath no power to cleav to thee ready to fall utterly from thee. I fly, I cry I cast my soul o Lord into thy armes. Lusts and creatures shall not haue my heart through thy grace, noe I set them all at a defyance. thee I desire to chuse, o leav me not! let iniquity never never, never haue dominion over me. forgiue I beseech thee my trespasses and cause thy face to shine upon me, and so shall I be saved.

28 4th day. works of iniquity prevail against me; I am unworthy to lift up mine eys to heaven, becaus proud and vain and forgetful of god. yet verily thou art my father, as thou givest me ground of incouragement; because I find a daly restlesness under sin committed without renew'd repentance; my soul is breathing after god with my spirit within me I desire him; Emptiness are all things else; god cleareth up to me his calling of me, and causing me sundry times to come to his son and close with him upon gospel termes especially thrice at the Lords supper; and if called then justify'd, and then I shall be sanctify'd. Lord realize this grace of thine unto me, for my unbeleiving heart can scarce reach to make these things real to me.

October 2

On the sabbath I found both bodily spirits and spiritual desires much dead and down the wind, yet the Lord kept me desiring of him. he is the onely soul satisfying good.

3 Munday [*sic*] I found an unsavoury abominable spirit amidst godly persons and godly discours; and abundance of pride of the favour and acceptance I find with man. Outgoing of heart I fear too much after discours and dispute, and time mis-

---

12 **Artillery sermon.** The Ancient and Honorable Artillery Company of Boston was established in 1737. At its annual election of officers a sermon was a conspicuous feature of the ceremonies. It is not known who preached any of the sermons before 1659. Wigglesworth himself delivered that of 1686

pent therein. for these things I desire to abase and abhor my self; ah Lord hide not thy face, harden not my heart from thy fear.

4 Again some prevailings of pride, and imprudence in not redeeming opportunitys of profitable discours for my owne furtherance. I find a heart so hard that cannot be affected or humbled for such things a slight spirit in performance of holy dutys that hanker's after my studys through unbeleef, which finding my self so unable to make work off, and that indeed I can do nothing, I am loath to rely upon and therefore to seek earnestly gods assistance. o Lord I beseech thee forgiue and saue me from all these abominations, be thou my strength.

10   5 Mr Sims preaching at watertown upon this point a people that are near to god, may be not sought out but forsaken et contra; I haue not found more of the presence of god awakening and affecting me (even unto tears) for my sins, particularly of slighting and weariness of gods precious ordinances, unprofitableness under them, &c. my own iniquitys were so touch't; together with gods gradual departure from my self, and from this whole country, that took deep impression upon me. I was partly unwilling to goe to this lecture but company drew me on and I bless god that he forsakes not me though I be forsaking him. the desire of my soul is that the fruit of such meetings with god might continue. but woe is me I find the same weariness of spiritual dutys the same carnal, formal, heart at a private meeting the 20 same night, together with pride.

On friday I besought the Lord on purpose. for help in my studys finding some very difficult knot, and through mercy he help't me to se through it in some measure. the desire of my soul is after the Lord, but I find vain distractions so pestering me that I cannot seek him to purpose; pride prevail's also, and some mispence of time I fear. Lord forgiue and heal for thy mercy sake

Sabbath. Inumerable evils compass me about vain thoughts on gods day in his ordinances break in upon me like a flood. I am less than the least good thought. yet the evening before and this morning in prayer at the private meeting and in the hall god assisted me extraordinarily with his spirit in prayer; especially at our pri- 30 vate meeting melting my heart before him.

I was sadly assaulted after noon when I heard of gods trueth with doubting whether ever word of the scripture were infallible because of possibility of mistakes in the writings and because of the points in the Hebrew, and the various readings in the text and margent. for these things (o Lord) I crave pardon, and bring my blind eys and vile heart to thee for healing. thou art he whom my soul desires to enjoy, whose wil I desire to know and do o teach me thy wayes thou art my god

I went through much business, and found god above my strength carrying me through intricacys two hard for me, at my earnest intreaty. But an unthankful heart I haue; pride and a frothy light unsavoury spirit, and so much spiritual cooling of 40 affection toward god and his ordinances, little desire off opportunity to meditate off

---

10 **Sims.** Zachariah Symmes (1599-1671), a graduate of Cambridge University, became teacher of the church at Charlestown in 1634, succeeding Thomas James as its pastor in the year following. John Harvard was for a time Symmes' assistant   33 **Hebrew.** In the ancient Semitic languages only the consonants were writ- ten, the vowels being indicated by various dots or strokes. This practice admits considerable variation in reading and interpreting various scriptures

or hear god speak to me, all which are a burthen to me; and I am most affraid of a spirit so drown'd in my studys that savours not gods presence or ordinances. deliver me deliver me, O my father, from such iniquitys, pardon me for thy mercy sake, and faithfulness, heal my backslidings by converting grace, and love me freely, for thy love is better than wine. caus me really to se at once thy love and my own vileness.

12 Wednesday. Afore lecture the Lord much assisted my studys. At meeting I found as my natural spirits faint so my spiritual affections low, and heart little stird. yet after I came home I set my self seriously to cry to heaven for pardon and deliverance especially from a heart that cares not for, that is weary of gods or- 10 dinances and left to set light by them. It is a death to think of being left off gods spirit in his ordinances and left to set light by them. But Jehovah thou art my trust be thou my life.

14 friday morning. I had some fears in my spirit about the immutability of gods love in case I should fall away from him; but the Lord did in some measure clear the absolute stability thereof from the scripture. In the forenoon I met with great difficultys in my studys and my strength failed me, I besought the Lord for his help, and though in the forenoon I could make nothing off it, yet afternoon I was exceedingly helped and my work made marvelous easy. But ah! ungrateful heart, I take gods name in vain in my nearest approaches to him, and prophane his ordinances 20 for this I am not able to stand before him. God brought to my mind in special (being at a private meeting) my want of love and dutifulness to my parents, which I beg'd pardon of

15 And the very next morning news is brought me of my fathers death. whereupon I set my self to confess before the Lord my sins against him in want of naturall affections to, and sympathy with my afflicted parents, in my not prizing them and their life which god hath graciously continued so long. My great request is for pardon of all former sins, and present deliverance from a stupid frame of spirit unsensible of gods visitation and my owne loss in losing such friend. my humble supplication is to the Lord to sanctify his hand to me and all of us whom it concerns 30 and to become a father of the fatherless and husband to the widdow. my Father dyed the first of october.

16 On the sabbath I was earnest with the Lord not to giue me over unto a spirit senseless of his afflicting providence, and to forgiue all my sin in that kind; in not being so instant with god as I ought to haue bin for my fathers like &c. ut supra. I was much exercised with scruples of conscience in some old cases *(as Mister Mildmay's sword and Major Sedwick's son)* but I desired to lay down my soul at christs foot, and to know his wil that I might obey it. Lord lead and guid thou me in a right path. God discover'd that unto me. that makes me fear I haue faln far short

---

24 **fathers death** . . . Wigglesworth's relation to his father, who had been crippled since 1641, was never wholly comfortable   37 **Mildmay's sword** . . . **Sedwick's son.** William Mildmay, Harvard College, 1647, great-grandson of the founder of Emmanuel College, Cambridge, from which he transferred to Harvard, was none too bright. Major Robert Sedgwick of Charlestown gave Harvard its first Boston real estate in 1646; his son does not appear to have been admitted to the College

of my duty in making use of christs merit to plead for sanctifying grace. withhold
it not from me for that caus, o my god!

18 Tuesday morning. *I found the same cause of crying earnestly to the Lord and of
grace for a right spirit under God's afflicting hand that I might not be secretly glad that
my father was gone. I have given God much business this day and done much for others
but I have no confidence nor satisfaction in mine own doings but my soul longs for the Lord
When wilt thou come unto me Pardon I beseech thee my pride my stirring affections my
taking of thy name in vain in giving of thanks and seize at my soul with thy goodness.
The last night some filthiness in a vile dream escaped me for which I loathe myself and desire*
10 *to abase myself before my God O Lord deliver me from the power of that evil one.*

19-20 Wednesday. I was at Watertown lecture where the Lord awakned me with
the sence of that monstrous vileness of my heart that cannot desire heaven and communion with christ; and stird me up that night and the next morning and night to
cry and strive earnestly with god for redemption, giving me some weak measure of
faith to beleev that my seeking should not always be in vain.

24 The latter part of the week I spent in preparing to preach at Chalstown. In
my private studys the Lord much assisted me; But I spent near three days in the
same, whereas one day at Martins Vineyard sufficed me, Like those that gathered
manna, he that gathered much had nothing over, and he that gathered little had no
20 lack. When I came in publick the Lord much assisted me, and emboldned me, and
when I came to close application much inlarged me; As I return'd home that night
through some feared neglects of my duty, I had some ecclyps of my comfort in god
(who is my onely portion, whom I am not worthy to name) but god remov'd in some
measure those feares and how sweet was his returns to my soul? my heart blesseth
him that he takes any cours to make himself precious to me at any time; woe is
me! that it is so often otherwise through a spirit of whoardoms, ah Lord remember
not iniquitys against me for thy tender mercy sake, remove pride and apostacy of
heart far from me.

On the 2d day at night in my sleep I dream'd of the approach of the great and
30 dreadful day of judgment; and was thereby exceedingly awakned in spirit (as I
thought) to follow god with teares and crys until he gaue me some hopes of his
gracious good wil toward me.

25 The next day I found my self unable to make any work of it at my studys.
pride prevailing.

26 Wednesday. My iniquitys are extream pride which I am weary of as a body of
death and ashamed off before god; and a mind ful of distractions in holy dutys; neglect of improvement of opportunity of discours for advantage in my studys: negligence in not redeeming the opportunity to send a letter to Harford according to
promiss. I know not what to do but my eys are to thy son Jesus christ. hide not
40 thy face from me; my soul cleaveth after thee o Jehovah; I deserv to be confounded
by the; but let mercy pleas thee, thou art my god; thou wilt be my redeemer.

---

30 **day of judgment.** From this dream *The Day of Doom* presumably resulted   38 **Harford,** i.e., Hartford, Connecticut. The letter probably had something to do with one of Wigglesworth's several considerations of marriage

29 On the last day I went to Concord where I preach't out of Isaiah 57. 1. I had but extream short time. some few thoughts I had had of it before, but not resolved to take it till sunset the Last day night; gods assistance was here the more remarkable. Tuesday I drive the time of my return so long till it was so late they would not suffer me. wednesday. It began to snow exceedingly so that I saw god locking me up there to wait his pleasure; it continued snowing til it was knee deep, so that I knew not when I was likely to return: then I recall'd how in all the journeys of that nature I haue taken these many years god has cros't me remarkably, the Lord shew me his mind in it. I set my self seriously to seek the Lord, and he heard me and caused it to rain on thursday and that night so as abated the snow to the ankles 10 thereby giuing me a season of returning on friday. what shal I render to the Lord for all his benefits.

In this my journey I haue met with sundry trials and temptations. As 1st feares concerning my owne estate when I feel such a wicked heart as cannot love and de- sire communion with god, as can be weary of gods service, and be eager to be at other studys: this is an amazing consideration to me, and I know not what to do; but the Lord he awakens me to find some need of him by other providences that set me a seeking him with fear least any iniquity should separate me from him. *As in point of their not reading any part of God's word in public duties at Mister Bulkeley's I questioned exceeding whether I were not bound in conscience to speak something to him of* 20 *it   The scruple still remains Lord* assail *it*. be thou the strength of my heart and my portion for ever: for I find an end of all other perfection. Vanity of vanities all is vanity and vexation of spirit.

Saturday at night I was importuned to go preach at Roxbury because the Elders were both ill. I did so, and preacht out of the same text I had done at concord. the Lord assisting me more than formerly when I preach't the same.

Munday and tuesday the Lord mightily facilitated my studys and prosper'd me therein: yet takes off my affections from them, so that my soul longs for Jehovah. Behold I see an end of all perfection; vexation in studys when most succesful; in pupils, o Lord be thou my portion.   30

9 wednesday. I feel such distractions in holy dutys, such deadness of heart at lec- ture, such pride in divine assistance and in my own notions, even then when I haue bin taught to haue no confidence in the flesh, a pang of worldly desires amidst hear- ing the word, that I am ashamed to lift up my face to heaven: father forgiue or else I perish, Oh hide not thy face which is my life from me.

I think I haue found of late more ful purposing to follow the lord universally, and more longings after the return of his spirit to my soul after communion with him than formerly, especially since the discovery of my want of love to and desires after

1 Isaiah 57.1. "The righteous perisheth, and no man layeth it to heart: and merciful men are taken away from the evil to come."   9 to seek the Lord . . . This is perhaps the most remarkable of the numerous instances of Wigglesworth's belief in "special providences" — God's direct interference with the order of nature — here as an answer to prayer   19 Bulkeley's. Peter Bulkeley (1582-1659), graduate of St. John's College, Cambridge, was teacher of the church at Concord from its establishment in 1636. He was an an- cestor of Ralph Waldo Emerson   24 the Elders. The church at Roxbury was served at this date by John Eliot (1604-1690) and Samuel Danforth (1626-1674)

God at Concord. yet abundance of pride prevails and some whoarish affections, which
I am ashamed of before god. On the last day the Lord awakned me to seek him
earnestly both for pardon and grace against the evils of my owne heart, and
for mercy to this society.

But above all my vileness breakes forth again whilest I am hearing the word. An
Atheistic irreverent frame seizeth upon me; and whilest God is bidding me see his
glory I cannot see it; vile and unworthy conceptions concerning god come into my
mind. I cannot desire heaven because 'tis a place where I shall see and wonder at
and acknowledge the glory of god for ever; But I rather desire a heaven where I
10 might be doing for god than onely thinking and gazing on his excellency. Blind
mind! Carnal heart! I am affraid, ashamed, heavy laden under such cursed frames of
heart, as ever and anon beset me. My soul groans my body faints o Lord whilest I
pray and cry to the for pardon and redemption. Is there no baulm in Gilead? no
physician there? Look down and see my plague sores which I spread before thee my
saviour; wounds and old putrifyd sores which provoke the Lord, stink in his nos-
thrils, and poison the peace and comfort of my own soul. Behold I am vile, when
thou showest me any face I abhor my self. who can bring a clean thing out of filthiness, I was conceived bred brought up in sin. O redeem from these devouring Lyons
the hopeless shiftless soul that thou hast purchased! I deserv to be the stepping-
20 stone of thy wrath why behold I lay my self at the foot of mercy as low as thou
wouldst have me, confessing my self the cheeif of sinners. Lord what wouldst thou
haue me to doe? shew me thy wil, and bow my heart to obey it, and I haue what I
do desire. O lift up the light of thy countenance upon me and hear my prayer; shut
it not out for ever.

Munday. when I come in company affections dead toward god, and too much
savouring the creature. also pride; and aptness to be ensnared by my tongue hereupon fears and misgivings but the Lord in mercy scattered them.

15 Tuesday morning. I found special assistance in prayer. the Lord causing my
heart to love him. I fear least I should griev him in not obeying all his known wil, but
30 for this I wil trust him, who alone wil work all my works in me and for me.

16 Wednesday morning. I had bin much perplexed with the ill carriage of one of
my pupils, and had some thoughts of admonishing him openly, I besought the Lord
before hand and he guided me to act in a fairer way; and ishued my trouble to my
good satisfaction. But o pride pride, and outwandrings of heart from my resting
place. Lord lay them not to my charge; for thou art the desire of my soul hide not
thy face from me.

Thursday 17 yesterday I was in a doubt whether I should goe to watertown lecture or not because of multiplicity of business; I went nevertheless. And this day
through Gods assistance I haue done as much as I used to doe in two dayes
40 Friday morning the Lord let in some comfort in that, though I be sinful and impotent unto any thing that is good yet he hath made christ righteousness and strength
to me and accepts me through him. which was evidenced to me by my longings
and reachings of heart after the Lord not finding satisfaction any where else: And in
my desiring the promoting of Gods glory, that he may be advanced by my self and

many others. How can I loue the Lord or his glory except he haue lov'd me; and if
he haue so done he wil ever do the same.

Dies ult. The Lord's Supper being nigh: I am affraid at the thoughts of it; And
wel I may having a heart so vastly unsutable to be at any time near god, More fit
to ly lowest in Hel that I might be farthest from him. For upon search I find, (yea
I haue dayly found, though not sufficiently felt) 1: A blind mind, often questeoning
the most Palpable truth's and unable to clear them to my self though I would never
so fain. As whether God be: whither the scriptures be his word, and that alone without corruption, at least through errour crept into the text. How it appear's that the
Lords supper is a seal as wel as a sign; which doubt I was sorely assaulted 10
and buffeted with the last Lord's supper. Whither christ's purchase were of all the
good I need, or onely of pardon of sin and deliverance from wrath; other things being
freely giv'n of god without any purchase, though disposed by christ; this doubt I
am scarce able to extricate my self from by the word of god as yet, though I exceedingly desire it and do grope after the light. And so for light in my daly actions.
Fearful shakings frequently assail me, and I would stand fast upon the word of god
but I can find no foot-hold. My knowledge and faith is thus assaulted by the powers
of darkness when I should be nearest God to receiv much good from him; thus pit-
tifully am I made to stagger instead of coming to him. 2: Carnal security and hardness of heart all sence of want and misery gone, when I approach to the fountain 20
of mercy, especially in hearing the word. 3. whoarish affections apt to rest in the
bosom of creatures. 4. Want of dear love to the Lord Jesus and his appearing, a
Brutish swinish heart that cannot savour Heavenly things and spiritual ordinances.
5. Pride. 6. Slouth. 7. Vain distractions in holy dutys. 8. want of sence and sorrow
for my Fathers death, o Lord forgiue! 9. want of heart to seek Gods glory. 10. Un-
fruitfulness under so many means of grace, and daly visitations of gods spirit; who
having the like would not bring forth more fruit? I hope the Lord hath of late giv'n
me a little ground against inordinate affection to the creatures, and made my soul
to breath somewhat more after himself; which I sought him for in such opportunitys as these heretofore.   30

    I came to the Lord supper under the guilt of all these iniquitys, and with the
plague of a hard heart little affected or sensible of all this sin and misery considering it was so great. But I saw the more need of a saviour to deliver me from the
guilt of so fearful abominations and to save me from the power. I saw need of a
priest to reconcile me to god. and yet no less need of a prophet to teach, and of a
King to rule me, to bring all my lusts into subjection, such a christ I desired and
still desire to close with, and no other christ I would haue. God helpt me in some
measure against my blindness of mind, and doubts concerning the doctrin of god
which I besought him for and was affraid of; and sent me out of his presence. I hope
somewhat incouraged in the grace which he had made mine by his gift and my re- 40
ceiving yet afternoon I was assayled with feares in reference to my unsensibleness
under gods visitation in my fathers death and I feared least there should be some
root of bitterness that I were not willing to part with, unsearched out. But I know

3 **Dies ult.**, last day, i.e., Saturday

none, Lord search and try me, and make me upright before thee. yea blessed be thy name for Jesus christ in whom thou wilt redeem my soul from distruction, and crown me with loving kindness and tender mercys, Lord I beleiv help my unbeleif.

(1653, 1951)

from The Day of Doom
or, A Poetical Description of the Great and Last Judgment

Frank Luther Mott defined a "best seller" as a book with a total sale equal to one per cent of the population, but he allowed ten years of sales to be counted. Before 1690 his formula requires the sale of 1000 copies. Wigglesworth's The Day of Doom *is believed to have been printed in 1662 to the number of 1800 copies, all of them sold within a year. Later editions followed, and it has been said that for more than a century it was, except for the Bible, the most popular book in New England.*

The poem, written in ballad meter so that it could be readily memorized, is in three parts: (1) a description of what happens when Gabriel blows his horn and all the folk who have ever lived are called before God for His final judgment; (2) the separation of the sheep from the goats and the trial of the latter, group by group; and (3) the consignment of the damned to hell and the ascension of the elect to heaven. The first part is in some ways the most vivid; the second part is, from the point of view of Calvinistic theology, the most important; but the third part, here reprinted, is the best place to see the fears and hopes of the seventeenth-century Puritans. Hell is undeniably a little more real than heaven.

[201]

Ye sinfull wights, and cursed sprights,
    that work Iniquity,
Depart together from me for ever,
    to endless Misery;
Your portion take in yonder Lake,
    where Fire and Brimstone flameth:
Suffer the smart, which your desert
    as it's due wages claimeth.

[202]

Oh piercing words more sharp then swords:
    what, to depart from Thee,   10
Whose face before for evermore
    the best of Pleasures be!
What? to depart (unto our smart)

Text: the 1666 edition   1 **Ye sinfull wights.** . . . In the margin: The Judge prounceth the Sentence of condemnation. Mat. 25. 41. Luk. 13.27   11 **Whose face.** . . . In margin: The terrour of it.

from thee *Eternally:*
To be for ay banish'd away,
  with *Devils* company!

[*203*]

What? to be sent to *Punishment,*
  and flames of *Burning Fire,*
To be surrounded, & eke confounded
  with Gods *Revengful ire.*   20
What? to abide, not for a tide
  these Torments, but for *Ever:*
To be released, or to be eased,
  not after years, but *Never.*

[*204*]

Oh, *fearful Doom!* Now there's no room
  for hope, or help at all:
Sentence is past which aye shall last,
  Christ will not it recall.
There might you hear them rent and tear
  the Air with their out-cries: 30
The hideous noise of their sad voice
  ascendeth to the Skies.

[*205*]

They wring their hands, their caitiff-hands,
  and gnash their teeth for terrour:
They cry, they roar for anguish sore,
  and gnaw their tongues for horrour.
But get a way without delay,
  Christ pitties not your cry:
Depart to Hell, their may you yell,
  and roar Eternally.   40

[*206*]

That word, *Depart,* maugre their heart,
  drives every wicked one,
With mighty pow'r, the self-same hour,

---

33 **They wring.** . . . In margin: Luk. 13.28   39 **Depart.** . . . In margin: Prov. 1.26   41 **That word,** . . .
In margin: It is put in execution   41 **maugre,** in spite of

far from the Judge's Throne.
Away they're chaste by the strong blast
  of his Death-threatning mouth:
They flee full fast, as if in haste,
  although they be full loath.

[*207*]

As chaff that's dry, and dust doth fly
  before the Northern wind: 50
Right so are they chased away,
  and can no Refuge find.
They hasten to the Pit of Wo,
  guarded by Angels stout;
Who to fulfill Christ's holy will,
  attend this wicked Rout.

[*208*]

Whom having brought, as they are taught,
  unto the brink of Hell
(That dismal place far from Christ's face,
  where Death and Darkness dwell: 60
Where Gods fierce Ire kindleth the fire,
  and Vengeance feeds the flame
With piles of Wood, and Brimstone Flood,
  that none can quench the same,)

[*209*]

With Iron bands they bind their hands,
  and cursed feet together,
And cast them all, both great and small,
  into that Lake for ever.
Where day and night, without respite,
  they wail, and cry, and howl   70
For tort'ring pain, which they sustain
  in Body and in Soul.

[*210*]

For day and night, in their despight,
  their torments smoak ascendeth:

---

45 **Away they're chaste.** . . . In margin: Mat. 25.46   53 **They hasten.** . . . In margin: Matt. 13.41, 42   57
Whom having. . . . In margin: HELL. Mat. 25.30. Mark 9. 43. Isa. 30. 33. Rev. 21.8   65 **With Iron
bands.** . . . In margin: Wicked Men and Devils cast into it forever. Mat. 22. 13. & 25. 46   73 **For day.** . . .
In margin: Rev. 14. 10,11

Their pain and grief have no relief,
  their anguish never endeth.
There must they ly, and never dy,
  though dying every day:
There must they dying ever ly,
  and not consume away.   80

[*211*]

Dy fain they would, if dy they could,
  but Death will not be had;
God's direful wrath their bodies hath
  for ev'r Immortal made.
They live to ly in misery,
  and bear eternal wo;
And live they must whilst God is just,
  that he may plague them so.

[*212*]

But who can tell the plagues of Hell,
  and torments exquisite?   90
Who can relate their dismal state,
  and terrours infinite?
Who fare the best, and feel the least,
  yet feel that punishment
Whereby to nought they should be brought,
  if God did not prevent.

[*213*]

The least degree of miserie
  there felt's incomparable,
The lightest pain they there sustain
  more than intolerable: 100
But God's great pow'r from hour to hour
  upholds them in the fire,
That they shall not consume a jot,
  nor by it's force expire.

[*214*]

But ah, the wo they undergo
  (they more then all beside)

---

89 **But who.** . . . In margin: The unsufferable torments of the damned. Luk. 16. 24. Jude 7   99 **The lightest.** . . . In margin: Isa. 33. 14. Mark 9. 43, 44

Who had the light, and knew the right,
  yet would not it abide.
The sev'n-fold smart, which to their part,
  and portion doth fall,   110
Who Christ his Grace would not imbrace,
  nor harken to his call.

[215]

The *Amorites* and *Sodomites*
  although their plagues be sore,
Yet find some ease, compar'd to these,
  who feel a great deal more.
Almighty God, whose Iron Rod,
  to smart them never lins,
Doth most declare his Justice rare
  in plaguing these mens sins.   120

[216]

The pain of loss their Souls doth toss,
  and wond'rously distress,
To think what they have cast away,
  by wilful wickedness:
We might have bin redeem'd from sin
  think they, and liv'd above,
Being possest of heav'nly rest,
  and joying in God's love.

[217]

But wo, wo, wo our Souls unto!
  we would not happy be;   130
And therefore bear Gods Vengeance here
  to all Eternitee.
Experience and woful Sense
  must be our painfull teachers
Who n'ould believe, nor credit give,
  unto our faithful Preachers.

[218]

Thus shall they ly, and wail, and cry,

---

107 **Who had.** . . . In margin: Luk. 12. 47   113 **The Amorites.** . . . In margin: Mat. 11. 24   118
lins, stops   121 **The pain** . . . In margin: Luke. 16. 23, 25. Luk. 13. 28   129 **But wo.** . . . In margin: Luk. 13. 14   135 **n'ould,** wouldn't   137 **Thus shall** . . . In margin: Mark 9. 44. Rom. 2. 15

tormented, and tormenting
Their galled hearts with pois'ned darts
   but now too late repenting.   140
There let them dwell i'th' Flames of Hell;
   there leave we them to burn,
And back agen unto the men
   whom Christ acquits, return.

[*219*]

The Saints behold with courage bold,
   and thankful wonderment,
To see all those that were their foes
   thus sent to punishment:
Then do they sing unto their King
   a Song of endless Praise: 150
They praise his Name, and do proclaim
   that just are all his ways.

[*220*]

Thus with great joy and melody
   to Heav'n they all ascend,
Him there to praise with sweetest layes,
   and Hymns that never end,
Where with long Rest they shall be blest,
   and nought shall them annoy:
Where they shall see as seen they be,
   and whom they love enjoy.   160

[*221*]

O glorious Place! where face to face
   Jehovah may be seen,
By such as were sinners whilere
   and no dark vail between.
Where the Sun shine, & light Divine,
   of Gods bright Countenance,
Doth rest upon them every one,
   with sweetness influence.

---

145 **The Saints.** . . . In margin: The Saints rejoyce to see Judgment executed upon the wicked World. Ps.
58. 10. Rev. 19. 1, 2, 3   153 **Thus with.** . . . In margin: They ascend with Christ into Heaven triumphing. Mat. 25. 46. I Joh. 3. 2. I Cor. 13. 12   161 **O glorious.** . . . In margin: Their Eternal happiness and
incomparable Glory there   168 **sweetness.** Other editions read: sweetest

[222]

O blessed state of the Renate!
  O wondrous Happiness,   170
To which they're brought, beyond what thought
  can reach, or words express!
Griefs water-course, and sorrows sourse,
  are turn'd to joyful streams.
Their old distress and heaviness
  are vanished like dreams.

[223]

For God above in arms of love
  doth dearly them embrace,
And fills their sprights with such delights,
  and pleasures in his grace;   180
As shall not fail, nor yet grow stale
  through frequency of use:
Nor do they fear Gods favour there,
  to forfeit by abuse.

[224]

For there the Saints are perfect Saints,
  and holy ones indeed,
From all the sin that dwelt within
  their mortal bodies, freed:
Made Kings & Princes to *God* through Christs
  dear loves transcendency,   190
There to remain, and there to raign
  with him Eternally.

                   1666

---

169 **the Renate,** those reborn   173 **Griefs water-course.** . . . In margin: Rev. 21. 4   179 **And fills.** . . . In margin: Psal. 16. 11   185 **For there.** . . . In margin: Heb. 12. 23   189 **Made Kings.** . . . In margin: Rev. 1. 6. & 22. 5.   189 **Princes.** Other editions read "Priests," which the rhyme scheme supports

1612—1672 Anne Bradstreet

Anne Bradstreet was born at Northampton, England. Since her father, Thomas Dudley, was steward of the estate of the Earl of Lincoln, it is reasonable to suppose that Anne, as a young girl, enjoyed special advantages, including perhaps the use of books from the Earl's library. At the age of sixteen she was married to Simon Bradstreet, a graduate of Emmanuel College, Cambridge, and steward of the Countess of Warwick. Two years later the Dudleys and the Bradstreets came to Massachusetts with John Winthrop and other prominent first settlers of the Massachusetts Bay Colony on the good ship *Arbella.* In Anne's own words, "I changed my condition and was marryed, and came into this Country, where I found a new world and new manners, at which my heart rose. But after I was convinced it was the way of God, I submitted to it." Like Ruth, she was sick for home amid the alien corn.

After brief residences at Cambridge and Ipswich, the Bradstreets resided permanently at Andover. Both Thomas Dudley and Simon Bradstreet were prominent leaders in the affairs of the Massachusetts Bay Colony. Anne Bradstreet had eight children; hers was the busy, heroic life of a wife and mother in a pioneer community. She found time, nevertheless, for the writing of verse, a considerable quantity of which was published in London in 1650 with the title *The Tenth Muse Lately Sprung up in America.* In the Preface of this book the author is described as "a Woman, honoured, and esteemed where she lives, for her gracious demeanour, her eminent parts, her pious conversation, her courteous disposition, her exact diligence in her place, and discreet managing of her Family occasions."

The Tenth Muse consisted largely of long encyclopedic poems on "The Four Elements," "The Four Humours in Man's Constitution," "The Four Ages of Man," "The Four Seasons of the Year," and "The Four Monarchies." In these compositions the author seems to have been misled by her favorite poet, Guillaume du Bartas, whose works she read in Joshua Sylvester's translation (*Du Bartas, His Divine Weeks and Works,* London, 1605). Happily, she outgrew this influence in her later work. "Contemplations," her most finished poem, shows the influence of two Elizabethan poets, Sidney and Spenser.

Mrs. Bradstreet's most original poems, and some may think her best, are her private domestic pieces, unpublished until after her death, in which she reveals her religious difficulties and her wifely and maternal devotion. She was disturbed by religious doubt. "Many times," she confessed, "hath Satan troubled me concerning the verity of the scriptures, many times by Atheisme how I could know whether there was a God." She feared that her love of the pleasant things of this life was unchristian. The conflict is incisively presented in "The Flesh and the Spirit." The Spirit was victor; but the Flesh, even though vanquished, reasserted again and again its claims. Her poems to her husband — "On the Restoration of her Husband from an Ague," "On her Husband's going to England," "In her solitary hours in her Husband's absence," "In thankful remembrance of her Husband's safe arrival home," "A letter to her Husband, absent upon Publick employment," "To my Dear and loving Husband" — attest to her warm devotion; they contain surprisingly frank avowals of passionate love, and refute the notion, sometimes met with, that the New England Puritans were cold. Anne Bradstreet loved Simon Bradstreet and her children and God with a troubled realization that she fell short of God's "Thou shalt love the Lord thy God with *all* thy heart."

The **Works of Anne Bradstreet**, ed. J. H. Ellis, Charlestown, 1867 (reprinted, 1932)   Se. E. Morison, "Mistress Anne Bradstreet," **Builders of the Bay Colony**, Boston, 1930   John Berryman, **Homage to Mistress Bradstreet**, New York, 1956

In reference to her Children, June 23, 1656

I had eight birds hatcht in one nest,
Four Cocks there were, and Hens the rest,
I nurst them up with pain and care,
Nor cost, nor labour did I spare,
Till at the last they felt their wing.
Mounted the Trees, and learn'd to sing;
Chief of the Brood then took his flight,
To Regions far, and left me quite:
My mournful chirps I after send,
Till he return, or I do end,   10
Leave not thy nest, thy Dam and Sire,
Fly back and sing amidst this Quire.
My second bird did take her flight,
And with her mate flew out of sight;
Southward they both their course did bend,

---

7 **Chief . . . Brood,** Samuel, who spent four years in England   13 **second bird.** Dorothy married the Rev. Seaborn Cotton, who preached for awhile in Connecticut

And Seasons twain they there did spend:
Till after blown by Southern gales,
They Northward steer'd with filled sayles.
A prettier bird was no where seen,
Along the Beach among the treen.   20
I have a third of colour white,
On whom I plac'd no small delight;
Coupled with mate loving and true,
Hath also bid her Dam adieu:
And where Aurora first appears,
She now hath percht, to spend her years;
One to the Academy flew
To chat among that learned crew:
Ambition moves still in his breast
That he might chant above the rest,   30
Striving for more than to do well,
That nightingales he might excell.
My fifth, whose down is yet scarce gone
Is 'mongst the shrubs and bushes flown,
And as his wings increase in strength,
On higher boughs he'l pearch at length.
My other three, still with me nest,
Untill they'r grown, then as the rest,
Or here or there, they'l take their flight,
As is ordain'd, so shall they light.   40
If birds could weep, then would my tears
Let others know what are my fears
Lest this my brood some harm should catch,
And be surpriz'd for want of watch,
Whilst pecking corn, and void of care
They fall un'wares in Fowlers snare:
Or whilst on trees they sit and sing,
Some untoward boy at them do fling:
Or whilst allur'd with bell and glass,
The net be spread, and caught, alas.   50
Or least by Lime-twigs they be foyl'd,
Or by some greedy hawks be spoyl'd.
O would my young, ye saw my breast,
And knew what thoughts there sadly rest,
Great was my pain when I you bred,
Great was my care, when I you fed,
Long did I keep you soft and warm,
And with my wings kept off all harm,

21 **third.** Sarah married Richard Hubbard of Ipswich, Massachusetts   27 **One.** Simon was admitted to
Harvard College

My cares are more, and fears than ever,
My throbs such now, as 'fore were never: 60
Alas my birds, you wisdome want,
Of perils you are ignorant,
Oft times in grass, on trees, in flight,
Sore accidents on you may light.
O to your safety have an eye,
So happy may you live and die:
Mean while my dayes in tunes Ile spend,
Till my weak layes with me shall end.
In shady woods I'le sit and sing,
And things that past, to mind I'le bring   70
Once young and pleasant, as are you,
But former toyes (no joyes) adieu.
My age I will not once lament,
But sing, my time so near is spent.
And from the top bough take my flight,
Into a country beyond sight,
Where old ones, instantly grow young,
And there with Seraphims set song:
No seasons cold, nor storms they see;
But spring lasts to eternity,   80
When each of you shall in your nest
Among your young ones take your rest,
In chirping language, oft them tell,
You had a Dam that lov'd you well,
That did what could be done for young,
And nurst you up till you were strong,
And 'fore she once would let you fly,
She shew'd you joy and misery;
Taught what was good, and what was ill,
What would save life, and what would kill. 90
Thus gone, amongst you I may live,
And dead, yet speak, and counsel give:
Farewell my birds, farewell adieu,
I happy am, if well with you.
                                   1678

To my Dear and loving Husband

If ever two were one, then surely we.
If ever man were lov'd by wife, then thee;
If ever wife was happy in a man,
Compare with me ye women if you can.

I prize thy love more than whole Mines of gold,
Or all the riches that the East doth hold.
My love is such that Rivers cannot quench,
Nor ought but love from thee, give recompence.
Thy love is such I can no way repay,
The heavens reward thee manifold I pray.   10
Then while we live, in love lets so persever,
That when we live no more, we may live ever.

                                        1678

Verses upon the burning of her house, July 10, 1666

In silent night when rest I took,
For sorrow neer I did not look,
I waken'd was with thundring nois
And Piteous shrieks of dreadfull voice.
That fearfull sound of fire and fire,
Let no man know is my Desire.

I, starting up, the light did spye,
And to my God my heart did cry
To strengthen me in my Distresse
And not to leave me succourlesse.   10
Then coming out beheld a space,
The flame consume my dwelling place.

And, when I could no longer look,
I blest his Name that gave and took,
That layd my goods now in the dust:
Yea so it was, and so 'twas just.
It was his own: it was not mine;
Far be it that I should repine.

He might of All justly bereft,
But yet sufficient for us left.   20
When by the Ruines oft I past,
My sorrowing eyes aside did cast,
And here and there the places spye
Where oft I sate, and long did lye.

Here stood that Trunk, and there that chest;

---

14 **I . . . took.** Job 1:21: "The Lord gave, and the Lord hath taken away, blessed be the name of the Lord"

There lay that store I counted best:
My pleasant things in ashes lye,
And them behold no more shall I.
Under thy roof no guest shall sitt,
Nor at thy Table eat a bitt.   30

No pleasant tale shall 'ere be told,
Nor things recounted done of old.
No Candle 'ere shall shine in Thee,
Nor bridegroom's voice ere heard shall bee.
In silence ever shalt thou lye;
Adieu, Adieu; All's vanity.

Then streight I gin my heart to chide,
And did thy wealth on earth abide?
Didst fix thy hope on mouldring dust,
The arm of flesh didst make thy trust?   40
Raise up thy thoughts above the skye
That dunghill mists away may flie.

Thou hast an house on high erect,
Fram'd by that mighty Architect,
With glory richly furnished,
Stands permanent tho' this bee fled.
Its purchased, and paid for too
By him who hath enough to doe.

A Prise so vast as is unknown,
Yet, by his Gift, is made thine own.   50
Ther's wealth enough, I need no more;
Farewell my Pelf, farewell my Store.
The world no longer let me Love,
My hope and Treasure lyes Above.
                              1678

The Flesh and the Spirit

Samuel Eliot Morison, in what is perhaps the best essay on Mrs. Bradstreet ("Mistress Anne Bradstreet," Builders of the Bay Colony), said about the following poem: "Her mature poem on 'The Flesh and the Spirit' is one of the best expressions in English literature of the conflict described by Saint Paul in the eighth chapter of his Epistle to the Romans. It has a dramatic quality which can only have come of personal experience."

In secret place where once I stood
Close by the Banks of Lacrim flood
I heard two sisters reason on
Things that are past, and things to come;
One flesh was call'd, who had her eye
On worldly wealth and vanity;
The other Spirit, who did rear
Her thoughts unto a higher sphere:
Sister, quoth Flesh, what liv'st thou on
Nothing but Meditation?   10
Doth Contemplation feed thee so
Regardlessly to let earth goe?
Can Speculation satisfy
Notion without Reality?
Dost dream of things beyond the Moon
And dost thou hope to dwell there soon?
Hast treasures there laid up in store
That all in th' world thou count'st but poor?
Art fancy sick, or turn'd a Sot
To catch at shadowes which are not?   20
Come, come, Ile shew unto thy sence,
Industry hath its recompence.
What canst desire, but thou maist see
True substance in variety?
Dost honour like? acquire the same,
As some to their immortal fame:
And trophyes to thy name erect
Which wearing time shall ne're deject.
For riches dost thou long full sore?
Behold enough of precious store.   30
Earth hath more silver, pearls and gold,
Than eyes can see, or hands can hold.
Affect's thou pleasure? take thy fill,
Earth hath enough of what you will.
Then let not goe, what thou maist find,
For things unknown, only in mind.
Spir. Be still thou unregenerate part,
Disturb no more my setled heart,
For I have vow'd, (and so will doe)
Thee as a foe, still to pursue.   40
And combate with thee will and must,
Untill I see thee laid in th' dust.
Sisters we are, ye[a] twins we be,

---

2 **Lacrim,** from the Latin word *lacrimae,* tears

Yet deadly feud 'twixt thee and me;
For from one father are we not,
Thou by old Adam wast begot,
But my arise is from above,
Whence my dear father I do love.
Thou speakst me fair, but hatst me sore,
Thy flatt'ring shews Ile trust no more.   50
How oft thy slave, hast thou me made,
When I believ'd, what thou hast said,
And never had more cause of woe
Then when I did what thou bad'st doe.
Ile stop mine ears at these thy charms,
And count them for my deadly harms.
Thy sinfull pleasures I doe hate,
Thy riches are to me no bait,
Thine honours doe, nor will I love;
For my ambition lyes above.   60
My greatest honour it shall be
When I am victor over thee,
And triumph shall, with laurel head,
When thou my Captive shalt be led,
How I do live, thou need'st not scoff,
For I have meat thou know'st not off;
The hidden Manna I doe eat,
The word of life it is my meat.
My thoughts do yield me more content
Then can thy hours in pleasure spent.   70
Nor are they shadows which I catch,
Nor fancies vain at which I snatch,
But reach at things that are so high,
Beyond thy dull Capacity;
Eternal substance I do see,
With which inriched I would be:
Mine Eye doth pierce the heavens, and see
What is Invisible to thee.
My garments are not silk nor gold,
Nor such like trash which Earth doth hold, 80
But Royal Robes I shall have on,
More glorious than the glistring Sun;
My Crown not Diamonds, Pearls, and gold,
But such as Angels heads infold.
The City where I hope to dwell,

---

85 **The City.** The remainder of the poem is based on Revelation 21:2: "And I John saw the holy city, new Jerusalem, coming down from God out of heaven, prepared as a bride adorned for her husband"

There's none on Earth can parallel;
The stately Walls both high and strong,
Are made of pretious Jasper stone;
The Gates of Pearl, both rich and clear,
And Angels are for Porters there;   90
The Streets thereof transparent gold,
Such as no Eye did e're behold,
A Chrystal River there doth run,
Which doth proceed from the Lambs Throne:
Of Life, there are the waters sure,
Which shall remain for ever pure,
Nor Sun, nor Moon, they have no need,
For glory doth from God proceed:
No Candle there, nor yet Torch light,
For there shall be no darksome night.   100
From sickness and infirmity,
For evermore they shall be free,
Nor withering age shall e're come there,
But beauty shall be bright and clear;
This City pure is not for thee,
For things unclean there shall not be:
If I of Heaven may have my fill,
Take thou the world, and all that will.

                            1678

c. 1645—1729 Edward Taylor

Very few biographical facts concerning Edward Taylor are known. He was born in Coventry, England. In 1668, at the age of twenty-two or twenty-three, he left England, presumably for liberty of conscience, and came to Boston, where he was cordially received by Increase Mather. He was admitted to Harvard College and was graduated in the Class of 1671. A life-long friendship with Samuel Sewall, of the same class, dates from his college years. "He and I," Sewall wrote, "were Chamber fellows and Bed fellows in Harvard-College Two years: He being admitted into the College, drew me thither [i.e., to himself]." Following his graduation, Taylor became pastor of the church at Westfield, Massachusetts. He lived quietly at Westfield during the remaining fifty-eight years of his life, serving the community for that long period both as minister and as physician. Twice married, he had seven children by his first wife and six by his second. Ezra Stiles, his grandson (President of Yale, 1778-1795), described him as "a man of small stature but firm: of quick Passions — yet serious and grave."

Taylor did not write his poems for publication. They must have been read by very few during the poet's lifetime, and for more than two centuries after his death their existence was almost completely forgotten. The publication of a small portion of Taylor's manuscripts in 1939 greatly enriched our poetical heritage from colonial times. Indeed, Taylor's poetry takes rank not only as the best poetry written in America before the nineteenth century but as one of the classics of New England literature.

Taylor wrote in the "metaphysical" tradition, the tradition of Donne, Crashaw, and Herbert, and he must have been influenced by their poetry, particularly by Herbert's. His structure follows the "metaphysical" pattern; that is, to borrow T. S. Eliot's description, "the elaboration of a figure of speech to the farthest stage to which ingenuity can carry it" and "a development by rapid association of thought." His poetry, nevertheless, is in no real sense imitative, for the stuff of Taylor's poetry is indisputably his own. The thought and emotion are elaborated in homely metaphors drawn straight from the poet's own experience. The weaving of cloth affords the metaphorical vehicle in one poem; the making of bread, in another; the cultivation of flowers, in a third. Music and musical instruments are a rich source of figurative language — the many musical references help to refute the popular notion that the early Puritans were hostile to music.

Taylor's poems help to refute also the notion that Puritans were, without exception, grim and strenuously unhappy. Taylor celebrates the joys of the Christian life; to him the Christian experience was something quite delightful. His saints, unlike Bunyan's plodding pilgrim, are "encoached for Heaven," and they sing as they ride. The Christian life is a rich banquet with music. The water of life is "beer"; the bread of life, "Heaven's Sugar Cake." He experiences a mystical union with the divine. He describes in brilliant, ardent verses Christ's ascent into Heaven and longs for wings to follow after.

The Poems of Edward Taylor, ed. Donald E. Stanford, New Haven, 1960   **Edward Taylor's Christographia,** ed. Norman S. Grabo, New Haven, 1962   Norman S. Grabo, **Edward Taylor,** New York, 1961

from God's Determinations The Glory of and Grace in the Church Set Out

Come now behold
Within this Knot What Flowers do grow:
    Spanglde like gold:
Whence Wreaths of all Perfumes do flow.

Most Curious Colours of all Sorts you shall
With all Sweet Spirits scent. Yet that's not all.

    Oh! Look, and finde
These Choicest Flowers most richly Sweet
    Are Disciplinde
With Artificiall Angells meet.   10
An heap of Pearls is precious: but they Shall
When Set by Art Excell. Yet that's not all.

    Christ's Spirit showers
Down in his Word, and Sacraments
    Upon these Flowers
The Clouds of Grace Divine Contents.
Such things of Wealthy Blessings on them fall
As make them sweetly thrive. Yet that's not all.

    Yet Still behold!
All flourish not at once. We see   20
    While Some Unfold
Their blushing Leaves, some buds there bee.
Here's Faith, Hope, Charity in flower, which call
On yonders in the Bud. Yet that's not all.

    But as they stand
Like Beauties reeching in perfume
    A Divine Hand
Doth hand them up to Glories room:
Where Each in sweet'ned Songs all Praises shall
Sing all ore Heaven for aye. And that's but all.   30
                                1939

---

26 **reeching,** reeking. Obviously, the word does not have the unpleasant connotations of modern usage

The Joy of Church Fellowship Rightly Attended

In Heaven soaring up, I dropt an Eare
    On Earth: and oh! sweet Melody:
And listening found it was the Saints who were
    Encoacht for Heaven that sang for Joy.
    For in Christs Coach they sweetly sing,
    As they to Glory ride therein.

Oh! joyous hearts! Enfir'de with holy Flame!
    Is Speech thus tassled with praise?
Will not your inward fire of Joy contain;
    That it in open flames doth blaze?   10
    For in Christs Coach Saints sweetly sing,
    As they to Glory ride therein.

And if a string do slip, by Chance, they soon
    Do screw it up again: whereby
They set it in a more melodious Tune
    And a Diviner Harmony.
    For in Christs Coach they sweetly sing
    As they to Glory ride therein.

In all their Acts, publick and private, nay,
    And secret too, they praise impart.   20
But in their Acts Divine and Worship, they
    With Hymns do offer up their Heart.
    Thus in Christs Coach they sweetly sing
    As they to Glory ride therein.

Some few not in; and some whose Time and Place
    Block up this Coaches way do goe
As Travellers afoot: and so do trace
    The Road that gives them right thereto;
    While in this Coach these sweetly sing
    As they to Glory ride therein.   30

————————   1939

8 **tassled,** tasseled, adorned

Huswifery

The poem is a good example of Taylor's ingenious elaboration of a single metaphor.

Make me, O Lord, thy Spinning Wheele compleat.
    Thy Holy Worde my Distaff make for mee.
Make mine Affections thy Swift Flyers neate
    And make my Soule thy holy Spoole to bee.
    My Conversation make to be thy Reele
    And reele the yarn thereon Spun of thy Wheele.

Make me thy Loome then, knit therein this Twine:
    And make thy Holy Spirit, Lord, winde quills:

————————

Huswifery, housewifery   3 **Flyers,** the pair of arms in a spinning wheel which revolve around the
bobbin to twist the yarn   8 **quills,** spindles or spools

Then weave the Web thyselfe. The yarn is fine.
Thine Ordinances make my Fulling Mills.   10
Then dy the Same in Heavenly Colours Choice,
All pinkt with Varnisht Flowers of Paradise.

Then cloath therewith mine Understanding, Will,
Affections, Judgment, Conscience, Memory;
My Words, and Actions, that their shine may fill
My wayes with glory and thee glorify.
Then mine apparell shall display before yee
That I am Cloathd in Holy robes for glory.

                                                                        1939

---

10 **Fulling Mills,** mills for cleaning, shrinking, and thickening cloth. This is an especially happy analogy, since the ordinances of the church may be supposed to have a similarly purifying and fortifying effect

from Sacramental Meditations The Experience

The poem seems to express an authentic mystical experience, the union of the soul with God, and should be compared with an even more notable account of such an experience in Jonathan Edwards' "Personal Narrative."

Oh! that I always breath'd in such an aire,
    As I suckt in, feeding on sweet Content!
Disht up unto my Soul ev'n in that pray're
    Pour'de out to God over last Sacrament.
    What Beam of Light wrapt up my Sight to finde
    Me neerer God than ere Came in my minde?

Most Strange it was! But yet more Strange that shine
    Which filld my Soul then to the brim to spy
My nature with thy Nature all Divine
    Together joynd in Him thats Thou, and I.   10
    Flesh of my Flesh, Bone of my Bone: there's run
    Thy Godhead, and my Manhood in thy Son.

Oh! that that Flame which thou didst on me Cast
    Might me enflame, and Lighten everywhere.
Then Heaven to me would be less at last,
    So much of heaven I should have while here.
    Oh! Sweet though Short! I'le not forget the same.
    My neerness, Lord, to thee did me Enflame.

I'le Claim my Right: Give place, ye Angells Bright.
  Ye further from the Godhead stande than I.   20
My Nature is your Lord; and doth Unite
  Better than Yours unto the Deity.
  Gods Throne is first and mine is next; to you
  Onely the place of Waiting-men is due.

Oh! that my Heart thy Golden Harp might bee
  Well tun'd by Glorious Grace, that ev'ry string
Screw'd to the highest pitch, might unto thee
  All Praises wrapt in sweetest Musick bring.
  I praise thee, Lord, and better praise thee would
  If what I had, my heart might ever hold.   30
  ───────────   1939

27 **highest pitch.** The tightening of the strings of musical instruments is a favorite figure with Taylor   30
ever, always, constantly, thus repeating the thought of the first line

Meditation Eight

I kening through Astronomy Divine
  The Worlds bright Battlement, wherein I spy
A Golden Path my Pensill cannot line
  From that bright Throne unto my Threshold ly.
  And while my puzzled thoughts about it pore
  I finde the Bread of Life in't at my doore.

When that this Bird of Paradise put in
  This Wicker Cage (my Corps) to tweedle praise
Had peckt the Fruite forbid: and so did fling
  Away its Food: and lost its golden dayes,   10
  It fell into Celestiall Famine sore:
  And never could attain a morsell more.

Alas! alas! Poore Bird, what wilt thou doe?
  This Creatures field no food for Souls e're gave.
And if thou knock at Angells dores they show
  An Empty Barrell: they no Soul bread have.
  Alas! Poore Bird, the Worlds White Loafe is done.
  And cannot yield thee here the smallest Crumb.

In this sad state, Gods Tender Bowells run
  Out Streams of Grace: And he to end all strife   20

6 **Bread of Life.** John 6:35: "And Jesus said unto them, I am the bread of life. . . ."   7 **Bird of Para-**
dise, the soul   8 **tweedle,** sing   11 **Celestiall Famine,** a lack of spiritual food   14 **Creatures field,**
the world   19 **Bowells,** the seat of pity; hence, compassion

The Purest Wheate in Heaven, his deare-dear Son
  Grinds, and kneads up into this Bread of Life.
  Which Bread of Life from Heaven down came and stands
  Disht on thy Table up by Angells Hands.

Did God mould up this Bread in Heaven, and bake,
  Which from his Table came, and to thine goeth?
Doth he bespeake thee thus, This Soule Bread take;
  Come, Eate thy fill of this, thy Gods White Loafe?
  Its Food too fine for Angells, yet come, take
  And Eate thy fill. Its Heavens Sugar Cake.   30

What Grace is this knead in this Loafe? This thing
  Souls are but petty things it to admire.
Yee Angells, help: This fill would to the brim
  Heav'ns whelm'd-down Chrystall meele Bowle, yea and higher.
  This Bread of Life dropt in thy mouth doth Cry:
  Eate, Eate me, Soul, and thou shalt never dy.

                                                                   1939

_____
34 **whelm'd-down,** filled to overflowing

Meditation Twenty

The poem describes Christ's ascension to Heaven.

View, all ye eyes above, this sight which flings
  Seraphick Phancies in Chill Raptures high:
A Turffe of Clay, and yet bright Glories King:
  From dust to Glory Angell-like to fly.
  A Mortall Clod immortaliz'de, behold,
  Flyes through the skies swifter than Angells could.

Upon the Wings he of the Winde rode in
  His Bright Sedan, through all the Silver Skies,
And made the Azure Cloud, his Charriot, bring
  Him to the Mountain of Celestiall joyes.   10
  The Prince o'th'Aire durst not an Arrow spend,
  While through his Realm his Charriot did ascend.

He did not in a Fiery Charriot's shine,
  And Whirlewinde, like Elias upward goe.

_____
11 **Prince . . . Aire,** Satan, who is described in Ephesians 2:2 as "the prince of the power of the air"   14
Elias, Elijah, whose ascent to heaven is described in II Kings 2:11

But th' golden Ladders Jasper rounds did climbe
  Unto the Heavens high from Earth below.
  Each step had on a Golden Stepping Stone
  Of Deity unto his very Throne.

Methinks I see Heavens sparkling Courtiers fly,
  In flakes of Glory down him to attend;   20
And heare Heart Cramping notes of Melody
  Surround his Charriot as it did ascend:
  Mixing their Musick, making e'ry string
  More to inravish, as they this tune sing.

God is Gone up with a triumphant shout:
  The Lord with sounding Trumpets melodies:
Sing Praise, sing Praise, sing Praise, sing Praises out,
  Unto our King sing praise seraphick-wise!
  Lift up your Heads, ye lasting Doors, they sing.
  And let the King of Glory Enter in.   30

Art thou ascended up on high, my Lord,
  And must I be without thee here below?
Art thou the sweetest joy the Heavens afford?
  Oh! that I with thee was! what shall I do?
  Should I pluck Feathers from an Angells Wing,
  They could not waft me up to thee my King.

Lend me thy Wings, my Lord, I'st fly apace,
  My Soules Arms stud with thy strong Quills, true Faith;
My Quills then Feather with thy Saving Grace,
  My Wings will take the Winde thy Word displai'th.   40
  Then I shall fly up to thy glorious Throne
  With my strong Wings whose Feathers are thine own.

                                                                  1939
_____

29 **Lift . . . in,** based upon Psalms 24:7   37 **I'st,** I wouldst

Meditation Sixty, Second Series

This poem, whose theme is the "water of life," may be regarded as a companion piece to "Meditation Eight," whose theme is the "bread of life."

Ye Angells bright, pluck from your Wings a Quill;
  Make me a pen thereof that best will write:
Lende me your fancy and Angellick skill

To treate this Theme, more rich than Rubies bright.
My muddy Inke and Cloudy fancy dark
Will dull its glory, lacking highest Art.

An Eye at Centre righter may describe
The Worlds Circumferentiall glory vast,
As in its nutshell bed it snugs fast ti'de,
    Than any angells pen can glory Cast   10
Upon this Drink drawn from the Rock, tapt by
The Rod of God, in Horeb, typickly.

Sea water strain'd through Minerall, Rocks, and Sands,
    Well Clarifi'de by Sunbeams, Dulcifi'de,
Insipid,,Sordid, Swill, Dishwater stands.
    But here's a Rock of Aqua-Vitae tri'de!
When once God broacht it, out a River came
To bath and bibble in, for Israels train.

Some rocks have sweat. Some Pillars bled out tears,
    But here's a River in a Rock up tunn'd,   20
Not of Sea Water nor of Swill. It's beere!
    No Nectar like it! Yet it once unbungd,
A River down out runs through ages all,
A Fountain opte, to wash off Sin and Fall.

Christ is this Horebs Rock, the streames that slide
    A River is of Aqua Vitae Deare,
Yet costs us nothing, gushing from his side:
    Celestiall Wine our sinsunk souls to cleare.
This Rock and Water, Sacramentall Cup
Are made, Lords Supper Wine for us to sup.   30

This Rock's the Grape that Zions Vineyard bore,
    Which Moses Rod did smiting pound, and press,
Untill its blood, the brooke of Life, run ore:
    All Glorious Grace, and Gracious Righteousness.
We in this brook must bath: and with faiths quill
Suck Grace and Life out of this Rock our fill.

---

11 **Rock . . . Horeb,** an allusion to the smiting of the rock by Moses, recorded in Numbers 20:11   12
typickly. The rock from which the water flowed typified, or prefigured, Christ. Cf. I Corinthians 10:4: "And
did all drink the same spiritual drink: for they drank of that spiritual Rock that followed them: and that
Rock was Christ"   16 **Aqua-Vitae,** brandy   21 **beere.** Good Puritans had no aversion to alcoholic
beverages if moderately used. (Cf. Sewall's *Diary,* August 25, 1709.) One is nevertheless astonished at the
audacity of the poet in using beer as an emblem of the "spiritual drink"   24 **opte,** opened

Lord, oynt me with this Petro oyle: I'm sick.
  Make me drink Water of the Rock: I'm dry.
Me in this fountain wash: my filth is thick.
  I'm faint: give Aqua Vitae or I dy.   40
  If in this stream thou cleanse and Chearish mee,
  My Heart thy Hallelujahs Pipe shall bee.

                                          1939

---

37 **Petro,** of the rock

Meditation One Hundred and Ten, Second Series

The Angells sung a Carole at thy Birth,
  My Lord, and thou thyselfe didst sweetly sing
An Epinicioum at thy Death on Earth.
  And order'st thine, in memory of this thing,
  Thy Holy Supper, closing it at last
  Up with an Hymn, and Choakst the foe thou hast.

This Feast thou madst in memory of thy death:
  Which is disht up most graciously: and towers
Of reeching vapours from thy Grave (Sweet breath)
  Aromatize the Skies: That sweetest Showers,   10
  Richly perfumed by the Holy Ghost,
  Are rained thence upon the Churches Coast.

Thy Grave beares flowers to dress thy Church withall,
  In which thou dost thy Table dress for thine.
With Gospell Carpet, Chargers, Festivall
  And Spirituall Venison, White Bread and Wine:
  Being the Fruits thy Grave brings forth and hands
  Upon thy Table where thou waiting standst.

Dainties most rich, all spiced o're with Grace,
  That grow out of thy Grave do deck thy Table.   20
To entertain thy Guests, thou callst, and place
  Allowst, with welcome: (and this is no Fable),
  And with these Guests I am invited to't,
  And this rich banquet makes me thus a Poet.

Thy Cross planted within thy Coffin beares
  Sweet Blossoms and rich Fruits, whose steams do rise

---

3 **Epinicioum,** epinicion, a song of triumph   9 **reeching,** the "reeking" atmosphere, a cloud of incense

Out of thy Sepulcher and purge the aire
    Of all Sins damps and fogs that Choake the Skies.
    This Fume perfumes Saints hearts as it out peeps,
    Ascending up to bury thee in th'reechs.   30

Joy stands on tiptoes all the while thy Guests
    Sit at thy Table, ready forth to sing
Its Hallilujahs in sweet musicks dress,
    Waiting for Organs to imploy herein.
    Here matter is allowd to all, rich, high,
    My Lord, to tune thee Hymns melodiously.

Oh! make my heart thy Pipe: the Holy Ghost
    The Breath that fills the same and Spiritually.
Then play on mee, thy pipe, that is almost
    Worn out with piping tunes of Vanity.   40
    Winde musick is the best, if thou delight
    To play the same thyselfe, upon my pipe.

Hence make me, Lord, thy Golden Trumpet Choice,
    And trumpet thou thyselfe upon the same
Thy heart enravishing Hymns with Sweetest Voice.
    When thou thy Trumpet soundst, thy tunes will flame.
    My heart shall then sing forth thy praises sweet,
    When sounded thus with thy Sepulcher reech.

Make too my Soul thy Cittern, and its wyers
    Make my affections: and rub off their rust   50
With thy bright Grace: and screw my Strings up higher,
    And tune the same to tunes thy praise most Just.
    Ile close thy Supper then with Hymns most sweet,
    Burr'ing thy Grave in thy Sepulcher's reech.
                                                                       1939

31 **Joy . . . tiptoes.** Taylor's first editor, Thomas H. Johnson, suggests that the phrase owes something to George Herbert's "The Church Militant": "Religion stands on tip-toe in our land/Readie to pass to the American strand"   48 **thy Sepulcher reech,** the breath of thy Sepulcher   49 **Cittern,** cithern, a lute-like instrument played with a plectrum, or pick   54 **Burr'ing,** burying

Chapter 2 The New Republic 1765–1829

To Secure the Blessings of Liberty
"We, the people of the United States, in order to
form a more perfect union, establish justice, insure
domestic tranquillity, provide for the common welfare,
and secure the blessings of liberty to ourselves and
our posterity, do ordain and establish this constitution for the United States of America."
— *Constitution of the United States*

I. Intellectual Currents

A New and a Proud Nation

The most distinctive aspects of the second great stage of American development were the stabilization of independent political institutions and a fervent desire to outshine the older nations of Europe in every conceivable way. Just as republican government was to be better than monarchical, so republican society, republican art, and republican literature were expected to excel anything that the Old World had yet produced. In what has often been called the early national period (extending from the Stamp Act Congress in 1765 to the inauguration of Andrew Jackson as seventh President in 1829), the future destiny of America was almost incessantly discussed and in some ways determined. These years constituted the first great era of American nationalism, cultural as well as political. Behind it lay the age of colonialism, before it the period of a sectionalism which culminated in civil war.

Events between 1765 and 1829 crowded one upon another. The Stamp Act was the first of a series of political crises which showed Americans the power they had when they united. Then came the Revolutionary War itself, followed by Shays' Rebellion, the framing and ratification of the Constitution, the Whiskey Insurrection, the birth of the two-party system, the Louisiana Purchase, the War of 1812, the Monroe Doctrine, and the Missouri Compromise. Union and expansion went hand in hand, and few foresaw the grave danger in the unexpected and rapid spread of Negro slavery. In Europe, meanwhile, the industrial revolution transformed Great Britain, and the continent seethed with the destruction of the French monarchy and the rise and fall of Napoleon.

Like all periods of rapid change, this one was exceedingly complex. Many aristocratic institutions and philosophies were under attack, and in the arts neoclassicism was giving way to the almost indefinable but impressively power-charged mood which came to be called romanticism.

Politically, then as now, and in Europe as well as in America, the "haves" were ranged against the "have nots," the proponents of centralized control against those who wished more local autonomy, absolutists and authoritarians of all varieties against all colors of individualists and democrats. Time-worn but perennial conflicts are discernible in all the familiar oppositions — Mercantilism or Protectionism *vs.* Free Trade, Imperialism *vs.* Home Rule, Tory *vs.* Whig, and Federalist *vs.* Republican. Basic differences in political philosophies, such as those between the right and the left, are never decisively resolved. There are always compromises, and those made in the early national period were of crucial importance to Americans, because they so largely determined later lines of thought. However short of perfection they may have fallen, they embodied ideals that were considerably more democratic than was then common in other lands.

Consider first the assertions of the Declaration of Independence: that all men are created equal, and that government rests on the consent of the governed. Both notions seemed ridiculous and extremely dangerous to many Americans, and it is hard to know how fully they were believed in. Even Thomas Jefferson, next to Thomas Paine the most radical of the political thinkers of the period, owned Negro slaves. In 1776, however, equality and a greater respect for the ordinary man were ideals to conjure with, and they have remained central in American thought.

Consider, on the other hand, the preamble to the Constitution, where the emphasis is upon the government and its functions — justice, the preservation of order, and the promotion of the general welfare. The "liberty" whose blessings the preamble proposed to secure was so abstract, so far perhaps from the ideals of the Declaration, that by 1791 ten amendments (the Bill of Rights) had been adopted. The framers of the Constitution were convinced that the unity, stability, and continuity of the nation — indeed its very survival — depended upon more effective control of divisive elements, including misguided majorities. The founding fathers so arranged things, therefore, that "the governed" could not possibly make a hasty or ill-considered change. This kind of conservatism has also remained a powerful American ideal, and the Constitution has been amended only fourteen times since 1791.

American nationalism, then, encompassed from the first widely divergent views of human nature and the role of government. The "American way" was democratic up to a point — but it did not extend the ideal of equality to Negro slaves nor to women. It sought to keep government close to the people by maintaining a fine balance between the federal government on the one hand and the state governments on the other — but tipped the scales toward "big" government by specifying federal control of foreign affairs, coinage, foreign commerce, and military and naval forces. Two of the most persistent issues in American life — civil rights and states' rights — go back, in short, to the beginnings of the national experience.

It must be admitted, moreover, that emotion played a large role in the growth of nationalism. The Revolution was to a degree a social upheaval, in which distrust of British control was mingled with antipathy to the wealthy. Crèvecoeur's "The American Belisarius" (p. 334) vividly suggests the feelings which sometimes got out of control. The common man could take the ideal of equality seriously, and in his more aggressive moments take the law into his own hands. The idea of inferiority, and particularly of inferiority to Britain, was unendurable, and even the most thoughtful Americans were extraordinarily sensitive to criticism.

The train of events, moreover, was propitious for the growth of nationalism.

Such diverse factors as the Revolution itself, the conservative reaction to the events in France, the Napoleonic wars, and Westward expansion contributed to unity. Many democratic tendencies were accentuated or set in motion by the Revolution. Large estates were confiscated and divided; small business and manufacturing were stimulated; church establishments were attacked; slavery, imprisonment for debt, and humiliating punishments were looked at with growing disfavor; the idea of universal education at state expense was seriously proposed. Americans were not of one mind about these matters, but they recognized that such tendencies differentiated the United States from the older nations of Europe. Americans agreed, moreover, in insisting that they were now ready to manage their own affairs, and in being sublimely confident that they could manage them better than the British had. The Americans were a "new" people, as Crèvecoeur put it. They were ready to teach the rest of the world; they were weary of being taught.

The assertion of the rights of man by the revolutionists in France seemed at first a gratifying compliment to the example set in America. The blood bath of the Reign of Terror, however, evoked a strong reaction among the more conservative Americans, not yet sure that the Constitution had really solved the problem of internal tranquillity. The Federalists, who under the leadership of George Washington, John Adams, and Alexander Hamilton controlled the government from the adoption of the Constitution until 1801, were committed to a strong federal union, able to keep order at home and repel enemies from abroad. Events proved them right.

The Napoleonic wars, which disrupted commercial and diplomatic accord with Europe, made American isolation more complete than it had been since the Revolution and led to a second armed confrontation with Great Britain. Because the War of 1812 cut off the United States from the rest of the world, the nation achieved the economic self-sufficiency which had long been talked about. Textile and iron industries grew up quickly, and Americans faced westward expansion with assurance.

The West, despite its individualism, was even more nationalistic than the seaboard states. It looked to the federal government for its lands and the means of access to them, and its local ties were new and weak. The West tended to be least respectful of Europe, most certain that the United States could "lick" the entire Old World if necessary. "War hawks" favoring the War of 1812 were from the West.

From the perspective of the twentieth century it is clear that the ties with Europe were not cut sharply, despite the powerful influence of nationalism. The old pattern of transplantation and adaptation continued as such immigrants as Albert Gallatin, Eleuthère Irénée Du Pont, and Samuel Slater brought their talents to the new nation. In finance and in manufacturing Americans had still much to learn.

In literature, however, nationalism led Americans to attempt the impossible — the creation, overnight, of a tradition of belles-lettres. To the cultural nationalist the possession of a first-rate literature of politics and a highly reputable literature of religion was not enough; if poetry, fiction, and the drama were the marks of a great civilization, America must have them. If, as Aristotle had asserted, epic poetry is the height of literary art, the United States must have epic poems comparable in grandeur to the continent and the superior political institutions of the Republic.

This quixotic attempt is reflected in the work of many of the writers of the period — Philip Freneau, the Connecticut Wits, William Cullen Bryant, Washington Irving, and James Fenimore Cooper most particularly. In orations delivered at college commencements or on the Fourth of July, and in short-lived magazines with "United States" or "Columbian" or the name of a state or city in their titles, Americans hammered at the theme of intellectual independence, the creation of a literary culture better than that of monarchical Europe. They did not succeed in their effort, but it was not for want of trying.

National pride led to many pleas for more generous support of American writers and to many defenses of America against the supercilious remarks of British editors and travelers. This outpouring of protest, most voluminous after the War of 1812, has been labeled the "Paper War" and was not of lasting interest, although both Cooper and Irving contributed to it. The "War" had, however, one very important effect: it focused the attention of American writers more sharply on the native scene. What, they asked themselves, was unique in American life? In their effort to answer that question they became concerned with native types, dialects, manners, scenery, and institutions. Despite their frequent failure to solve the problem of fresh or appropriate forms in which to clothe their new literary material, they left a body of writing notable both for its variety and for its interpretation of American life.

Political Thought

The literature of politics, generously represented in the present chapter, may be conveniently summarized as it appeared in four stages of American history: (1) the debate about self-government which extended from the Stamp Act to the Declaration of Independence; (2) the Revolution itself; (3) the struggle for stability and an acceptable balance of the opposing political philosophies of Hamilton and Jefferson; and (4) the continuing battle of the common man for a share in the responsibilities and rewards of political office.

(1) The differences of opinion and of feeling which lay behind the Revolution may be seen in Franklin's "Edict by the King of Prussia" (p. 316) and "Rules by Which a Great Empire May Be Reduced to a Small One" (p. 310), as well as in Thomas Paine's *Common Sense* (p. 383) and the Declaration of Independence itself (p. 425). Franklin provides a description of the economic and political irritations, enumerated also in the Declaration; Paine offers insight into the emotions of the period.

These writings are only a small part of the literary debate of 1765-1776. Pamphlets, speeches, sermons, and state papers appeared in profusion. Outstanding among the Whig writers were Samuel Adams, John Adams, James Otis, Daniel Dulany, and John Dickinson, along with the then youthful Jefferson and Hamilton. The Tory position was maintained by such writers as Martin Howard, Daniel Leonard, Samuel Seabury, and Joseph Galloway. Patrick Henry's "Give me liberty or give me death" speech of March 1775 is a part of the full picture, as is Francis Hopkinson's *A Pretty*

Story (1774). In a little more than a decade a large body of polemical prose appeared, offering arguments based both upon specific legal or constitutional positions and upon abstract philosophies of government. The Declaration includes both types.

The legal position of the Patriots — denial of the authority of Parliament to levy "internal taxes" on the colonies, assertion of the doctrine of "no taxation without representation," and demands that the colonial legislatures be recognized as the only just means of obtaining "consent of the governed" — proved in the end less defensible than direct appeal to the right of revolution. For that and other "natural rights" specifically named in the Declaration, the Patriots had the precedents of the revolutions which had driven Charles I and James II from the English throne. The Americans knew their history and their political philosophy; their writings show close study of the theories of Thomas Hobbes, Sir Robert Filmer, John Locke, and many other English and European thinkers. Americans had behind them, moreover, a solid tradition of theological disputation. It is impossible to read their presentations of their case without respecting their mental caliber and clarity of exposition.

(2) The "clash of resounding arms" at Lexington ended the constitutional debate and brought forward more emotional and persuasive writers — propagandists they would now be called. Their task was to unite and hold in line a Revolutionary party which was probably never more than a two-thirds majority of the population. Their method was to appeal to the interests and the prejudices of as many different groups as they could. Master of them all was Paine, whose *Crisis* series (p. 412) ranks with the most successful propaganda ever written. Newspapers and magazines printed much similar material, including numerous poems, such as Freneau's "Memorable Victory" (p. 518), Hopkinson's "Battle of the Kegs" (p. 377), and Dwight's "Columbia, Columbia, to Glory Arise" (p. 535). Popular songs, ballads, and hymns all had their place in the literary war (see p. 372). There were also lengthy verse satires, of which the most famous was John Trumbull's *M'Fingal* (Part I, 1775), an imitation of a popular English attack on the Puritans, Samuel Butler's *Hudibras* (1663-1678). The Loyalists also had their propagandists, the best known being Joseph Stansbury, Jonathan Odell, and Jacob Bailey. They show clearly the social cleavage of the Revolution, for they almost invariably assumed a snobbish tone toward the "rabble." The Loyalists, however, had few printing presses available, and their opinions must be sought in letters, diaries, parodies of Patriot songs, and such accounts of affairs as were published in England after the war. Of these last, the most notable is Jonathan Boucher's *A View of the Causes and Consequences of the American Revolution* (1797). Neither party was averse to name-calling or scurrility.

(3) In the literature of the years between the end of the war and the stabilization of the new government, a rational and deliberate tone is again uppermost, although undertones of emotion are often heard. The great monument of these times, outside of the Constitution itself, is *The Federalist,* in the main the work of Hamilton (p. 435). Washington's *Farewell Address,* in which Hamilton had a hand, the inaugural addresses of Jefferson (p. 431), and Freneau's "Stanzas to an Alien" (p. 529) reflect a few of the issues of the day. A fuller picture would include *The Anarchiad* (1786-1787) and numerous other works by the Connecticut Wits, most of whom were

strongly Federalist in their convictions. Joel Barlow, author of *Advice to the Privileged Orders* (1791) and *The Conspiracy of Kings* (1792), was the great exception.

Especially interesting here is the repetition, with variations, of the age-old conflicts. Centralized control and local autonomy, government by the few and government by the many — these were again among the alternatives. Woodrow Wilson and others have suggested that the Constitution was based upon a political philosophy derived in part from Newtonian physics. Its framers, according to this view, sought to balance opposing political forces one against another, and conceived of the state as a matter of retaining equilibrium despite incessant change and movement. John Adams was the chief American spokesman for this philosophy; he distrusted unlimited democracy and believed that stable government required elaborate checks and balances among executive, aristocratic, and democratic forces. The French philosopher Montesquieu, a student of British constitutional development, had had much the same idea, and he is known to have been so widely read in America that he, rather than Newton, is often credited with the checks and balances theory.

(4) The Federalists, however right they may have been, were not always astute politicians. Some of them failed to disguise their belief that the masses counted for little, the *aristoi* for much, and they sometimes ignored local loyalties and conditions which they would have done well to study. The common people were not to be denied the respect which the ideal of equality promised them, and toward the end of the period they were receiving from most successful politicians the flattery which has ever since been theirs. The people wanted their leaders folksy and didn't care if words were not meticulously pronounced nor diplomatic protocol rigorously observed. In 1828, they elected Jackson, and "the age of the common man" began.

A number of important writers have described this last phase of the early national period. Most of them did not much like what they saw, for they were usually, by tradition and by education, on the side of urbanity and sophistication. That ignorant and illiterate backwoodsmen with vulgar manners should be elected to high office seemed to them to court disaster. In *Modern Chivalry,* written over the years between 1792 and 1815, H. H. Brackenridge (p. 498) worried considerably about the nature of the American electorate. James Fenimore Cooper, however, was probably the most critical observer of the Jacksonian revolution. His attitude was precisely that of the orderly man who surveys the litter in a public park after the Labor Day weekend. He doubted that the general public had a sufficient sense of responsibility to take care of its political heritage. In his novels (particularly *The Pioneers,* 1823, *Home as Found,* 1838, and *The Crater,* 1847) and in a little book on politics *(The American Democrat,* 1838; see p. 679) he showed clearly that he distrusted man in the mass.

Jackson himself learned that a working democracy is not easily achieved. In the peroration of his *Farewell Address* (1837) he expressed pride in the national accomplishment and assurance that there was no longer danger from abroad. Then he said, "It is from within, among yourselves, from cupidity, from corruption, from disappointed ambition, and inordinate thirst for power, that factions will be formed and liberty endangered. It is against such designs, whatever disguise the actors may assume, that you have especially to guard yourselves."

Economic Development

The problem of earning a living was not so frequently or so fully the concern of literature after 1765 as it had been before. Nevertheless, the later writing can be better understood with some knowledge of the economic thought and conflicts which distinguished American life in the early national period. Fundamental, of course, was the desire of individuals to "get on" in the world. Simple living, thrift, and industry, the ideals preached by Poor Richard (see p. 301), were the ideals of most men. They were praised by writers as diverse as Crèvecoeur, Washington, Jefferson, Dwight, and Barlow. "My Neighbor Freeport" (p. 560) and Rip Van Winkle (p. 591) were decidedly not heroes of the era. Americans were on their way to acceptance of the gospel proclaimed by Longfellow in "A Psalm of Life" (p. 855):

> Let us, then, be up and doing
> With a heart for any fate;
> Still achieving, still pursuing,
> Learn to labor and to wait.

Most Americans probably felt that money was the chief thing to be up and doing about, and they did not question the validity of that goal for the worker. John Woolman (p. 346) was an exception. Like Thoreau in a later generation Woolman wished to know the result of the pursuit of wealth. Far more averse to luxuries and pomp than many who cried out against them from higher places in the world, he reached a thought-provoking conclusion: "Wealth desired for its own sake Obstructs the increase of Virtue, and large possessions in the hands of selfish men have a bad tendency, for by their means too small a number of people are employed in things usefull, and therefore some of them are necessitated to labour too hard." A few other observers — Crèvecoeur and Dwight, for example — expressed a similar concern lest money-getting end in too wide a discrepancy between the very rich and the very poor. Poor Richard's disciples, however, could scarcely admit the possibility that men could work too hard.

What were the main features of the American economy? In 1765 the Americans were primarily an agricultural people, and they were still so in 1829, but in the interval the economy of the nation underwent great changes which had their due effect upon literature. Three such changes may be mentioned: (1) the shift from a colonial to a national economy, although with continuing conflicts between those who wanted a centralized control of commerce, manufactures, finance, and transportation and those who wanted a large measure of local control; (2) the far-reaching development of industry and the factory system; and (3) the creation, through expansion to the West, of an enormous domestic market.

The colonies in 1765 were dependencies of a nation which, insofar as it had a colonial policy, had accepted the Mercantilist doctrine that overseas possessions should supply the home country with raw materials and serve as a market for manufactured products. The trade regulations based upon this theory caused much hard feeling, as may readily be seen in Franklin's "Edict" and "Rules"; such policies were, of course, one of the principal causes of the Revolution. Mercantilism was also partly responsible for the British desire to limit expansion to the West, where the control of markets would be more difficult. That attitude aroused as much antagonism, probably, as either the trade regulations or the taxation which was sought to help pay for the French and Indian War. The Virginians were particularly unwilling to give up the West to the Indians. As Paine's *Common Sense* shows, the Americans had come to think in "continental" terms, and they were determined to control not merely their internal affairs but their economic life as well.

The success of the Revolution permitted the development of home manufactures and the opening of the West. The federal government gradually acquired title to the Western lands, and, with the Constitution, internal tariff barriers were removed. Washington's *Farewell Address* provides a good view of the hope that the natural economic rivalries of the various sections might be minimized, a hope echoed later by Jefferson and Jackson. Americans did not agree, however, on the extent to which the central government should aid the states in internal improvements or "protect" infant industries or control the financial structure of the nation. They never have agreed on these matters, but their disagreements were especially sharp in the age of Hamilton's *Report on Manufactures,* of the clamor of the West for roads and canals, and of Jackson's classic struggle against the Second Bank of the United States.

Industrialization was forced upon the United States by the war between France and Great Britain, waged almost continuously from 1795 to 1815. The unprecedented growth of American foreign trade involved the nation in its first attempt to make good its right to trade as a neutral with belligerent nations, in the face of Napoleon's Berlin and Milan Decrees and the British Orders in Council. The Embargo Act of 1807 and the War of 1812 are usually credited with effecting a large measure of self-sufficiency in manufactures, although the full effect of the factory system was not felt until several decades later.

The settling of the West began almost immediately after the Revolution, but it was enormously accelerated by the introduction of new means of transportation. The steamboat reached the Ohio River in 1811, only four years after Robert Fulton's first successful demonstration on the Hudson. Roads and canals followed swiftly; the Cumberland, or National, Road had reached Zanesville, Ohio, by 1825, the year in which the Erie Canal was completed. The railroad era was soon to come; construction of the Baltimore & Ohio began in 1828. The West soon had its own literature, reflecting the turbulence of the period, and from the time of the *Western Review* (1819-1821), published in Lexington, Kentucky, it had its own periodicals and a local literature. The early Western writers, such as Morgan Neville (p. 562) and Peter Cartwright (p. 478), are only half the story. The West was the scene of two of Cooper's novels (*The Prairie,* 1827, and *The Oak Openings,* 1848), and it fascinated other Eastern authors, notably William Cullen Bryant (see "The Prairies," p. 645).

Religion

Religion remained vastly important to Americans, although it did not occupy quite so central a position as it had in the colonial period. The disruption and damage of the Revolution perceptibly weakened the position of many churches; Congress was forbidden by the Constitution to make any laws leading toward the establishment of a state church; and the Bill of Rights asserted the principle of complete religious toleration. Disestablishment followed in those states which had supported particular churches, and the period as a whole displays that wide variety of religious thought to which Americans are now accustomed. Nationalistic tendencies may be discerned in various denominations and in the continued dominance of Protestantism, but they are of minor significance.

This is not to say that religious fervor lessened, or that sectarianism disappeared. The masses wanted churches, denominational rivalries were no less intense, and the literature of religion was still enormous. Calvinism remained a powerful force through the influence of such followers of Edwards as Dwight, and it may be seen in a watered-down form in certain lines of Bryant's "Inscription for the Entrance to a Wood" (p. 634) and "To a Waterfowl" (p. 636). Revivalism flourished at intervals throughout the period, especially in the West, as Cartwright's autobiography (p. 479) shows Quakerism found its best American exponent in Woolman.

From the standpoint of literary history, however, the distinctive feature of the age is the emergence of the rationalistic and humanitarian doctrines of Deism and Unitarianism. Neither was new; neither was widely popular. The virulence with which they were both attacked gives us some hint of their effect upon the age, and from this distance it is clear that their confidence in the powers of the mind and their tendency to present a man-centered universe expressed something basic.

Deism (see p. 12), which denied the revelation of God in the Bible, chose to seek religious truth through human reason. The chief religious duty, according to the Deists, was to serve one's fellow man. Franklin arrived at Deistic beliefs early in life and he seems never to have deserted them. After his *Dissertation on Liberty and Necessity* (1725), however, he never expounded them openly, having reached the conclusion, apparently, that the orthodox Christian churches operated as a desirable social control, doing more good than harm. Somewhat similar attitudes are to be seen in Crèvecoeur, Freneau, Jefferson, and even Washington. At the time of the French Revolution, Deism became momentarily a proselyting faith, spread by Deistic newspapers, magazines, and societies, as well as by more or less formal treatises. Three of the last are worth mention: Ethan Allen's *Reason the Only Oracle of God* (1784), for which the Revolutionary hero of Vermont was largely indebted to a Dr. Thomas Young; Paine's *The Age of Reason* (p. 448), and Elihu Palmer's *Principles of Nature* (1802). These works were the object of almost unbelievably violent attacks by such orthodox Christians as Dwight, who regarded Deism not only as the worst form of infidelity but also as the handmaiden of political radicalism. Deism was effectually destroyed, for the masses were unwilling to give up the authority of the Bible.

Unitarianism, the denial of the doctrine of the Trinity and the divinity of Jesus Christ, is fully explained in William Ellery Channing's sermon (p. 461). It had been common among the upper and more rationalistic classes in Boston and other large New England towns since the 1780's and became a matter for heated debate only after 1805, when a Unitarian was appointed to the professorship of divinity in Harvard College. Differing from Deism in its acceptance of revelation, it is chiefly significant for its similar emphasis upon human nature and reason and for its humanitarianism. The genesis of the succeeding age of reform, insofar as that reform was triggered by Transcendentalism (see p. 698), has often been found in Unitarianism. Closely related to it is Universalism, organized as a formal sect in 1794 with the central doctrine that God could never have intended other than that all men shall be saved — a position anticipated some years earlier by Chauncy (p. 205). These doctrines, though not widely popular challenged the dominance of Calvinism.

Science and Education

Americans were of two minds about science and education in the early national period. They usually spoke of them with respect, and some substantial steps were made in their development. Neither, however, was very generously supported, and one does not have to look far for evidence of anti-intellectualism.

This ambivalent attitude may be explained in part by the bitter party strife between the Federalists and the Republicans. Jefferson, a lifelong lover of gadgets and of science, helped to frame the Northwest Ordinance, which set the pattern for federal aid to schools, encouraged the Lewis and Clark Expedition, one of the earliest of many government-sponsored surveys of resources, and suggested the bureau which became the United States Coast and Geodetic Survey, the earliest national scientific agency. Yet Jefferson was ridiculed as a "philosopher," unfit to run a government. "Go, wretch," wrote William Cullen Bryant in *The Embargo* (1808),

> resign thy presidential chair,
> Disclose thy secret measures, foul or fair,
> Go, search with curious eyes for horned frogs,
> 'Mid the Wild wastes of Louisiana bogs;
> Or where the Ohio rolls his turbid stream
> Dig for huge bones, thy glory and thy theme.

The thirteen-year-old Bryant was echoing an opinion widely held in Federalist circles, as was Washington Irving when he lampooned Jefferson as Wilhelmus Kieft in the Knickerbocker *History of New York*. "I have known many universal geniuses in my time," Diedrich Knickerbocker says, "though to speak my mind freely I never

knew one, who, for the ordinary purposes of life, was worth his weight in straw —
but, for the purposes of government, a little sound judgment and plain common
sense, is worth all the sparkling genius that ever wrote poetry or invented theories."

Science, moreover, was becoming more specialized and more technical, and the gulf
between the educated and the unlearned was widening. The scientist, therefore, is
sometimes portrayed as a comic figure. In Cooper's *The Prairie,* for example, considerable space is given to Obed Bat, M.D., "fellow of several cis-Atlantic learned
societies." The new species of animal which he discovers, *Vespertilio Horribilis Ameri-
canus,* turns out to be a jackass.

Nevertheless, American science was growing and, despite its allegiance to a world-
wide community of learning, displaying distinctly nationalistic tendencies. To the
single lasting scientific society of the colonial period, the American Philosophical
Society, was added, in 1780, the American Academy of Arts and Sciences, as well as
innumerable local and state organizations. Those devoted to the study of natural
history were especially active. Scientific periodicals were established. One such journal, the *American Journal of Science and Arts,* was founded by Benjamin Silliman in
1818 with the express purpose of raising science to "the elevation of our national
character."

Neither the common schools nor the universities were given much genuine state
support before 1829; the democritization of education was to come somewhat later.
The principle that the state should educate its citizens and exert itself for the diffusion of knowledge was, however, vigorously enunciated by Washington, Jefferson,
John Adams, James Madison, and many others. At the Constitutional Convention,
Charles Pinckney proposed to give Congress the control of education and to establish
a national university. Many other schemes for nationalizing education were put forward; all of them failed to win popular support, probably because of the determination of the states to retain as many of their prerogatives as possible.

The Fine Arts

The fine arts, relatively unimportant in the colonial period, were especially susceptible to the later impulses toward nationalism. Their connection with literature,
moreover, was much more intimate than it had been before. While it cannot be
said that they attained great distinction before 1829, their development was extraordinary and well worth remarking.

The piety which had supported portraiture in the earlier age now became patriotic,
and the founders of the Republic were given generously such immortality as paint
could provide. The many portraits of Washington by Gilbert Stuart (1755-1828) are
the best known illustration of the demand which supported a dozen or more painters
at this time. Most of them were trained abroad, some under Benjamin West (1738-
1820) in London. West, an expatriate from Pennsylvania, was President of the Royal
Academy from 1792 until his death. Large historical paintings of events connected

with the Revolution were also popular, although the best known (and in some eyes the worst), Emanuel Leutze's "Washington Crossing the Delaware," was painted somewhat later. The largest national commission, for four twelve-by-eighteen-foot paintings for the rotunda in the ·Capitol, at $8000 each, was given to John Trumbull (1756-1843). His subjects were the surrender of Burgoyne at Saratoga, the surrender of Cornwallis at Yorktown, the Declaration of Independence, and the resignation of Washington.

More interesting to students of literature, because it paralleled the literary search for new material, is the development of landscape painting by the Hudson River School and its successors. The interconnections of literature and landscape painting at this point are numerous and fascinating. Bryant addressed a characteristic patriotic sonnet (p. 645) to Thomas Cole (1801-1848), with whom he shared a delight in un-spoiled nature and a propensity toward didacticism and allegory. "The Flood of Years" (p. 653) is a poem whose pictorial effect derives from a series of images markedly like those in Cole's ambitious series — the five paintings called "The Course of Empire" and the four entitled "The Voyage of Life." Cooper, too, had affinities with the landscape painters, most particularly a fondness for grand panoramic vistas; a good deal of the power of his wilderness scenes comes from his seeing them as a painter might.

As was the case with science, the period brought noteworthy cooperative enter-prises by artists — short-lived academies and associations, art schools, such museums as that established about 1780 by Charles Willson Peale (1741-1827). Not until 1826, however, was the still surviving National Academy of the Arts of Design established. Prominent among its founders was Samuel F. B. Morse (1791-1872), better known for his perfection of the electromagnetic telegraph. It was an age of versatility.

Sculpture had only begun to develop, although by 1829 a considerable number of Americans, among them Horatio Greenough (1805-1852), were studying that art in Rome. Many of them returned to help fill the halls of the Capitol at Washington with nationalistic statuary. Greenough's own colossal statue of Washington, with one naked shoulder and the flowing lines of a Roman toga, was commissioned in 1833 and completed ten years later. It now seems less interesting than some of the ship figureheads of the period, the work of unpretentious artisans.

Music became somewhat more popular in the early national period, although it was still closely bound to religion. The "singing schools" proliferated after the Revolution, spreading out from New England as New Englanders moved westward. They produced one memorable composer, William Billings (1746-1800), author of a number of original hymns in what was called the "fuguing" manner. Revivalism and the camp meetings were also the source of many popular hymns; some persons believe that the Negro spirituals owe a good deal to this activity. In the towns music grew more sophisticated as time went on. Choral societies were organized, as far west as Cincinnati; opera was introduced in the 1820's; music had a conspicuous place in the world of the theater. In all these developments, immigrants played a conspicuous part, and the music was, for the most part, imported. Nationalism in music was largely confined to patriotic songs, which were, of course, numerous. It is instructive to recall that both "Hail Columbia" and "The Star-Spangled Banner" (as well as "America") were probably imports, so far as their melodies go. The lyrics were written by Joseph Hopkinson (1770-1842) and Francis Scott Key (1779-1843).

In no area is cultural nationalism more obvious than in the architecture of public buildings from about 1790 down through the following century. Classical models were for the most part triumphant, partly because the founding fathers thought them most proper for a Republic and partly because they wanted impressive façades. Much of the enthusiasm stemmed from Jefferson, who fell in love with the Roman remains at Nîmes in southern France, and with the Maison Carré in particular. His taste is evident in the Virginia state capitol at Richmond, in his own home, Monticello, and in the old ranges of the University at Charlottesville. The extension of the classical forms to domestic architecture was much less happy, especially in northern climates. Greek revival houses were sometimes mere boxes with impressive columned fronts, which kept light from the interior and collected snow and ice on the roof. Colonial and Georgian styles survived, however, especially in the seaboard towns, and the great architect of the period is now acknowledged to have been Charles Bulfinch (1763-1844), designer of the State House at Boston.

II. Literary Trends

The Circumstances of Literary Publication

The literate American between 1765 and 1829 had great advantages over his colonial ancestors. He was the heir of an enormous expansion of printing, of the establishment of a periodical press scarcely rivaled elsewhere in the world, and of the acceptance to a degree previously unknown of the protection of literary property by copyright. None of these developments had reached its height by 1829, but their collective importance to literature can scarcely be overemphasized.

Almost all of the writing represented in the present chapter was printed in America for American readers. The exceptions — certain pieces by Franklin, Crèvecoeur's *Letters,* and Paine's *Age of Reason* — are those whose circumstances of publication were peculiar. Irving and Cooper, chief among the few writers who had audiences on both sides of the Atlantic, developed the profitable system of nearly simultaneous editions in London and New York.

The spread of printing can be suggested by statistics. In 1810 the census found 202 paper mills in the United States. Charles Evans, who sought in his *American Bibliography* to list all American imprints before 1820 (and did not complete the task), discovered 35,854 items before 1800, of which 25,634 were printed between 1766 and 1799 inclusive, as against 10,220 items between 1639 and 1765. He listed 329 imprints for 1765 and 784 for 1799. Nor was this steady increase concentrated in one locality; it was, indeed, less so than is the case today. The chief center of printing prior to the Revolution was Boston; Philadelphia then held the lead until the 1820's, when it went to New York. But there were presses in all the larger towns, including those in the West, and many of them were used to print books as well as newspapers and political material. All printing was still by hand, on flat-bed presses, but improvements and industrialization were in the offing. The Columbian Iron Press, developed about 1807, substituted the principle of the fulcrum for that of the screw. Steam and revolving cylinder presses were soon to be available; and one American, William Church (1778-1853), had patented in London in 1827 a typesetting and composing machine.

The stimulation to printing was primarily political, for this was the age of party journalism. Much of the political writing by Franklin, Adams, Paine, Jefferson, Hamilton, and Freneau first appeared in newspapers, which, despite paper shortages and military occupations, played an important role in the Revolution. The war over, newspapers multiplied; it is said that about 200 were published simultaneously by 1801. Dailies appeared in Philadelphia and New York in 1783 and 1785, when those cities had about 25,000 inhabitants. In the Hamilton-Jefferson period, party journalism swiftly came to maturity with the help of Freneau (see p. 509). Newspapers survived the Alien and Sedition Acts (see Freneau's "Stanzas to an Alien," p. 529); their place in political controversy is clarified by Jefferson's attention to them in his *Second Inaugural.* Bryant made his fortune as editor and part owner of the New York *Evening Post,* founded by Hamilton in 1801. Throughout the period, in short, newspapers increased rapidly in number (by 1829 there were probably more than a thousand of them), in size, and in influence.

Magazines developed more slowly. F. L. Mott has estimated that about seventy-five were begun between 1783 and 1801, several hundred more during the first third of the nineteenth century. Most of them were short-lived, but they played a large part in the rise of belles-lettres. Among those in which material reprinted in the following pages first appeared were the *United States Magazine* (Philadelphia, 1779, edited by H. H. Brackenridge), the *New-York Magazine* (1790-1797), and the *North American Review* (Boston, 1815-1939). Other important literary outlets included the *Farmer's Weekly Museum* (Walpole, N.H., 1793-1810, edited chiefly by Joseph Dennie), the *Columbian Magazine* (Philadelphia, 1786-1792), the *American Museum* (Philadelphia, 1787-1792), the *Massachusetts Magazine* (Boston, 1789-1796), and the *Port Folio* (Philadelphia, 1801-1827, edited by Dennie). These periodicals, and others like them all over the nation, provided a market for poems, essays, fiction, and literary criticism on a scale previously unknown. They were the background for the magazine world which supported Edgar Allan Poe in the next decade (see p. 746).

The American author, moreover, was favored after 1790 by a national copyright law protecting him from the unauthorized use of his work within the United States (but not, it will be noted, abroad) for a period of fourteen years, with the possibility of an extension for another fourteen. This law, based upon the similar statute passed in Great Britain in 1710 and upon legislation in Connecticut in 1783, was a great boon, although it did not protect American writers from the competition of pirated British books. International copyright was not achieved until 1891.

The book trade developed rapidly after the Revolution, and before the end of the period publishing, as now understood, was replacing the older methods of bridging the gap between author and reader. Bookstores and printing establishments transformed themselves into publishers, and some of the familiar names of present-day publishing appeared. The firm of Wiley was founded by Charles Wiley, a bookseller, in 1807; that of Harper by J. and J. Harper, printers, in 1817; that of Appleton by Daniel Appleton, who began business by keeping a general store, in 1825. Americans, nevertheless, were still largely dependent upon Great Britain for their reading; it has been estimated that American presses supplied only twenty per cent of current books in 1820, only thirty per cent in 1830.

Romanticism

The content of American literature between 1765 and 1829 was largely determined by the peculiar circumstances of American life and, as we have seen, reflects clearly the dominant nationalistic thought of the period. When we turn, however, to problems of literary intention and method, we are at once impressed by a quite dissimilar if not conflicting factor — the continuing influence of European and particularly British literary fashions. Our early national literature was written at approximately the same time as the so-called romantic revival, and its connections with that widespread movement are so numerous that many scholars have preferred to describe it as American romanticism in the early stages.

Most readers feel that Freneau, Bryant, Irving, and Cooper, when compared to the Connecticut Wits, represent something new, just as Cowper, Burns, Wordsworth, Coleridge, Scott, Byron, Shelley, and Keats represent something new when one compares them to Pope and Johnson. This "newness" is exceedingly difficult to describe, because it is a compound of many separate elements, no single one of which is an adequate means of differentiation. Yet there is a perceptible difference, both in degree and in the prevailing conception of a man's relation to the universe in which he lives. This difference, whether it be described in terms of mood or in terms of literary method, is what is called romanticism.

Like other large generalizations, the term *romanticism* has been used so loosely that some critics have wished to discard it altogether. A majority, however, has found it indispensable, and a great deal of effort has been expended in the attempt to find an acceptable definition. René Wellek has recently surveyed these labors and concluded that the "peculiarity" of romanticism lies in "that attempt, apparently doomed to failure and abandoned in our time, to identify subject and object, to reconcile man and nature, consciousness and unconsciousness by poetry which is 'the first and last of all knowledge.' "*

Wellek's definition works beautifully with the major writers of the 1829-1860 period: Emerson, Thoreau, and Whitman; Poe, Hawthorne, and Melville. Their writings are shaped by poetic symbolism (one of the chief means of identifying subject and object), by a faith in intuition, and by an exhilarating determination to place man in a satisfying relationship to nature and to God.

One can make a case for Cooper as another fairly complete romanticist by Wellek's definition, although the task is not as easy as with the writers just listed. Freneau, Bryant, and Irving, however, fit the definition only imperfectly. They use many of the themes which preoccupied their successors — nature and the picturesque, the common man, the legendary past — but they lack the underlying philosophy, the urge to identify and reconcile which Wellek isolates. This is why they are commonly called pre-romantics, corresponding to such British writers of the eighteenth century as Thomson, Crabbe, and Cowper.

Some American literary historians have lamented a tendency toward calling Bryant the "American Wordsworth" and Cooper the "American Scott." There can be no doubt, however, but that American writers were deeply influenced by the literary fashions of Great Britain. The imitation, however, was far less slavish than it was in the case of many works by the Connecticut Wits (cf. Dwight's *Greenfield Hill*, p. 536). Freneau, Bryant, Irving, and Cooper all had a fondness for native materials and occasional flashes of original insight. Americans contributed to romanticism as much, perhaps, as they derived from it. The interplay of forms, ideas, and mood was simply the continuation of a cultural bond with Europe which no degree of national pride could wholly sever. Always the American writer was drawn in two directions: to his own land, which usually furnished him with the unique materials of his writing; and to that cosmopolitan tradition which ordinarily furnished him with the forms and methods within which he worked.

Types of Diminishing Importance

A distinctive feature of the period is the rise to greater importance than ever before of poetry, the essay, drama, and fiction — those forms in which the ideas of the writer are shaped within a fairly well defined aesthetic pattern. It cannot be said that Americans uniformly displayed, within these forms, that cultural independence which they thought so desirable. The rise of belles-lettres nevertheless reflects the

---

* "Romanticism Re-examined," in *Romanticism Reconsidered: Selected Papers from the English Institute,* edited with a Foreword by Northrop Frye (New York and London: Columbia University Press, 1963), p. 133. The phrase quoted by Wellek is from the Preface to the second edition of Wordsworth and Coleridge's *Lyrical Ballads.* Professor Wellek's excellent survey of the vast literature on romanticism is also available in his *Concepts of Criticism* (New Haven, Yale University Press, 1963)

appearance of a class of men who thought of themselves as literary artists, and of a reading public ready for literature other than the merely informational or utilitarian. With the advent of more polished and more self-consciously "literary" writers, the distinctive ideas of the age were much more likely to find expression in belles-lettres than had previously been common. Accounts of voyages on land and sea, promotion tracts, sermons, histories, and biographies continued to be written, but their characteristics changed somewhat and they no longer held a separate place.

The only pieces closely related to the accounts of voyages and the promotion tracts reprinted in the following pages are Crèvecoeur's *Letters* and Bartram's *Travels*. The former is really a series of essays, and Bartram's book too has an essay-like flavor if one skips judiciously. Other examples of this type are such works as Jonathan Carver's *Travels* (1778), Jefferson's *Notes on the State of Virginia* (written about 1782), Timothy Flint's *Geography and History of the Mississippi Valley* (1827), and the travel books of Bryant, Cooper, and Irving.

Sermons similarly became freer and more polished, under the influence of ideals of composition like those expressed by Channing (see p. 461). They were still innumerable. Dwight's sermons are probably more typical of the time than Channing's, but the sermons of both and the hundreds of others published during the period are now seldom read. The methods of oral discourse developed in the pulpit had their influence upon political oratory, which, as we shall see, now came into great favor.

As one might expect, the nationalistic temper of the period had an immediate effect upon history and biography. The events of the Revolution were recorded, its heroes immortalized in such works as John Marshall's *Life of Washington* (1804-1807), and there was a flood of local histories, headed by Jeremy Belknap's *History of New Hampshire* (1784-1792). Little of this work was objective, and Irving's burlesque of antiquarianism and parochial pedantry in the Knickerbocker *History of New York* was doubtless needed. Not for several decades was history of literary merit and sound scholarship to be popularized by Prescott, Motley, and Parkman. Cooper's history of the United States Navy and Irving's many biographies should not be forgotten, however. These writings were thoroughly characteristic of the period in which these men matured.

Polemical Tracts and Treatises

The literature of persuasion was, of course, outstanding in an age of continuous political discussion. It had a conspicuous place from the first, as we have seen; now it reached a very high level indeed in such examples as Franklin's "Edict" and "Rules," John Adams' *Novanglus* (1775), Paine's *Common Sense, American Crisis,* and *Age of Reason,* Barlow's *Advice to the Privileged Orders,* and *The Federalist*. Many other works from the period might be named, for the great bulk of political writing belongs to this class, as do many theological treatises. Closely related to the tract and treatise on the one hand, and to the sermon on the other, are the innumerable political addresses and orations, such as Washington's *Farewell Address* and Jefferson's inaugurals (p. 431).

The structure of this material varies so greatly that few generalizations are possible. Certain new tendencies are evident, however. The development of newspapers and magazines made place for short pieces like Franklin's, and for lengthy series of essays and letters such as those by John Adams, Paine (in the *Crisis,* for example), and Hamilton. Such series were quite obviously imitative of the numerous British periodical essays.

Topical arrangement continued to dominate, with the nature of the controversy determining the pattern. Of especial interest is the meticulous planning of *The Federalist,* described in the first number of that series, and the variety which was achieved by Paine, both in *Common Sense* and in the *Crisis* series. The addresses and orations will be found to have remarkably similar structure, except that to the topical arrangement are added the speaker's invariable exordium (introduction) and peroration (conclusion). The modest beginning and the highly dignified conclusion, often embodying an appeal to divine guidance, which characterize all of the political speeches, are still a part of the pattern of discourse expected of our national leaders.

The rhetorical height of the period was unquestionably the Declaration of Independence, which combines the topical structure of the tract with the tones and methods of oratory. The revisions of Jefferson's first draft (p. 426) provide an opportunity to study the standards of the Revolutionary period. The careful balance of emotion and reason makes the Declaration a model of its kind, and it is not surprising that its phrases have never lost their vividness. Paine's writings have a similar oratorical ring, as do, though less frequently, Hamilton's. Unfortunately we have no authentic texts of the speeches with which James Otis and Patrick Henry electrified their audiences, but they too were doubtless masters of persuasion.

Diaries and Autobiographies

Franklin's *Autobiography* (p. 273) and Woolman's *Journal* (p. 347) will be found in any list of the great books of the period, and the enduring attraction of diaries and autobiographies is also evident from the inclusion in this chapter of works by Jefferson and Peter Cartwright. All these men had a didactic purpose, ethical, religious, or political, but Cartwright shows some wish to be entertaining. The structure of such writings is ordinarily chronological, with success depending almost wholly upon the attractiveness of the personality self-revealed. Woolman is of course the outstanding spiritual autobiographer; he should be compared with Jonathan Edwards (p. 165) as a witness to the reality of religious experience. Franklin, by contrast, reveals the secularization of American life; as a matter of fact, he did his reputation a disservice by telling so unblushingly the ways he devised to get ahead in the world. More than one reader has been repelled by the flavor of self-centeredness in Franklin's story, even though he was probably more civic-minded and socially useful than the vast majority of men in his time.

Poems

Poetry had been written in America from the first, but it now began to bulk much larger. The present chapter contains the work of two poets — Freneau and Bryant — who would be included in most lists of major American writers. Represented also are the poets of the Revolution, two of the Connecticut Wits (Dwight and Barlow), and two sentimentalists (Wilde and Woodworth).

The singers of the Revolution were more concerned with propaganda than with artistic finish, but the relatively greater sophistication of their work, when one compares it to the *Bay Psalm Book* or *The Day of Doom,* is immediately evident. Popular ballad meters were retained, together with such ballad devices as repetition and refrain, but both "Yankee Doodle" and "The Battle of the Kegs" consistently use feminine rhymes and "Nathan Hale," probably the finest of the anonymous ballads, has a subjectivity unusual in the type.

The Revolutionary songs are, in fact, somewhat more free and fresh in their forms than most of the poems by the Connecticut Wits, who regarded themselves as the "highbrows" of their time. The Wits had studied English literature and accepted the classical "rules," including that respect for established types which is sometimes described as the "tyranny of the genres." Dwight thought so highly of Denham, Pope, Thomson, and Goldsmith that he incorporated whole lines of theirs in *Greenfield Hill* and deliberately imitated their forms and diction, even though he was dealing with American themes and problems. Barlow, least conservative of the Wits, felt most at home in the mock-heroic and the iambic pentameter couplet perfected by Pope and his predecessors and contemporaries. Nor are the examples here the most flagrant instances of the way in which a reverence for the classical forms vitiated the sometimes original ideas of the Connecticut Wits. Their efforts in the epic — Dwight's *Conquest of Canaan* (1785) and Barlow's *Columbiad* (1807) — are the best known evidence of misguided nationalistic endeavor.

We may leave sentimentalism for definition in connection with fiction, remembering, however, that such pieces as "The Lament of the Captive" and "The Old Oaken Bucket" merely foreshadow the reign of tears and self-pity in the holiday gift-books of the 1830's and 1840's. These poems, because of their emotionalism, reflect the romanticism of the time, but they are unpretentious and designed for a public only casually concerned with literary art.

Freneau and Bryant, taken together, look forward to the triumph of romanticism. Both were precursors of the new mood, rather than consistently a part of it. Freneau began as an admirer of the classics, Milton, and Ossian (see "The Power of Fancy," p. 511), and was never really very venturesome in his verse forms. His political and religious views, on the other hand, were liberal for his time, and a number of his poems (see "The Indian Burying-Ground, p. 524) have the dream-like, "soft focus" quality which is one of the characteristics of romanticism. Bryant similarly had deep roots in the English poetic theory of the eighteenth century; his concept of the imagination and his emphasis upon the moral quality of beauty sometimes conflicted with his more romantic glorification of emotion. Bryant was forward-looking, also, in his experiments with anapestic substitutions in iambic meter.

Examination of the minor poetry written between 1765 and 1829 will strengthen any reader's impression of the transitional nature of the period. Such examination may be easily made in anthologies: Elihu Hubbard Smith's *American Poems, Selected and Original* (1793), *The Columbian Muse* (1794), and Samuel Kettell's *Specimens of American Poetry* (1829). The transition was far from over by 1829.

Essays

Newspapers and magazines played their part in the increase of poetic production, but they were most fundamental, perhaps, to the American development of the literary essay. The essay form had firmly established itself in England with *The Spectator* (begun 1717) of Addison and Steele, and its prestige was much enhanced by Samuel Johnson, Oliver Goldsmith, and other later authors. Its brevity and variety, together with the ease to which it could be adapted to didactic purposes, made it very attractive to Americans, who had had nothing quite like it before except the squibs in the almanacs (see Franklin's "Way to Wealth," p. 301, and the excerpts from Thomas' almanacs, p. 558). As early as 1722 Franklin was imitating *The Spectator* in his brother's newspaper, over the signature of "Silence Dogood." For many years thereafter the newspaper or magazine which lacked its "Theodore, the Hermit" (William Smith), "Tomo Cheeki" (Freneau), "Jonathan Oldstyle" (Irving), or "Oliver Oldschool" (Joseph Dennie) was a rarity. The attempt to maintain a dignified anonymity gave a sameness to these productions in a type which depends for its success upon the personality, even the idiosyncrasy, of the author. In Irving's *Sketch Book,* however, the essay achieved genuine distinction. Crèvecoeur, also, has some claim to regard as an essayist; he was among the first to write what might be called the nature essay.

Newspaper and magazine requirements were likewise responsible for the beginnings of American literary criticism, in reviews and leading articles. Bryant's lectures on poetry (p. 657), although prepared for oral delivery, might easily have taken the review form, as much of his other criticism did. The earliest American reviewers learned their trade from the British quarterlies, much as they deplored the strictures of those journals on American politics and culture.

Plays

Imitation and adaptation of European models, combined with the all-pervading nationalism, appeared also in the drama. Royall Tyler's *The Contrast* (1787) is an admirable illustration of the process. Tyler is supposed to have written his comedy within three weeks of seeing a play for the first time. What he saw was Richard

Brinsley Sheridan's *The School for Scandal;* the play that he wrote had as one of its characters Jonathan, a rural New Englander and the first of many "stage Yankees." The hero of *The Contrast,* Colonel Manly, is a patriotic former officer of the Revolutionary army.

Important changes in the theatrical situation should be noted. The repertoire company system which had grown up during the colonial period survived the closing of the principal theaters in the decade after 1774, but before 1829 it was giving way to the "star" system, which throughout the nineteenth century brought famous English actors to tour the chief American cities. Prejudice against the theater lessened, as is evident from the opening of an undisguised playhouse in Boston in 1794 and the repeal in 1789 of a long-ignored Pennsylvania law against stage plays. Neither public support nor copyright laws, however, yet favored a native drama. All that can be said is that the theater became firmly established, with an ever increasing number of native-born actors, managers, and playwrights.

Some native plays, now lost, may have been produced in the years just before the Revolution. During the conflict itself some political use was made of dramatic dialogues and satires, but few of them were actually acted. H. H. Brackenridge's *Battle of Bunkers Hill* (1776) is typical of such closet drama. Beginning with Tyler, however, American playwrights began to see their work on the professional stage. Many of them were amateurs like Tyler and James Nelson Barker (1784-1858) of Philadelphia. Two — William Dunlap (1766-1839) and John Howard Payne (1791-1852) — made the theater their profession, so that a brief description of their work will provide an impression of theatrical affairs and of the difficulties which lay in the way of native drama. Their plays were traditional in structure.

Dunlap, born in New Jersey, was a boy in New York City during the Revolution. Between 1784 and 1787 he was in London, studying painting under Benjamin West and seeing as many plays as he could. He began writing soon after his return to New York and had his first play produced in 1789. Before his death he wrote at least twenty-nine original plays, adapted and translated twenty-one more from the German and the French, and published, in 1832, the first history of the American theater. As manager of the Park Theater, New York, in 1796-1805, he turned largely to foreign themes and fashions, although his most famous tragedy, *André* (acted in 1798), was based upon the well-known spy story of the Revolution and exemplifies the tendency to use nationalistic material.

Payne's chief distinction rests upon his being the first successful actor to be trained in the American theaters. Like Washington Irving, he did most of his writing for the English audience and was inclined to be critical of the failure of his countrymen to support native authors. He went to England in 1813 and did not return for nineteen years. More than sixty plays have been attributed to Payne, the best known of which are the tragedy *Brutus* (1818), which became one of the widely popular plays of the nineteenth century; *Clari or the Maid of Milan* (1823), an adaptation from the French into which was inserted Payne's most famous composition, "Home, Sweet Home"; and *Charles the Second* (1826), a farce in which Irving was Payne's collaborator. As the titles indicate, Payne looked abroad for his themes and models.

At home, however, Tyler had numerous successors in the attempt to glorify the Revolutionary struggle and native American character types. Not many native playwrights had sufficient theatrical sense to succeed, and it may be added in their defense that the drama everywhere in western Europe was in the doldrums.

Novels and Short Stories

The prejudice against fiction which had marked the colonial period did not disappear in America until well after 1800. Jefferson, Dwight, and Noah Webster are only a few of the many who expressed belief that stories gave wholly false notions of life to impressionable youth. Nevertheless, fiction grew steadily more popular. In the late eighteenth century circulating libraries specializing in fiction prospered with the support of young ladies who demanded romance; and the new magazines, although expressing a pious editorial concern about the possible moral effect of fiction, could not afford to bar it from their pages. By the 1780's American authors were ready to help supply the market with native productions, often meeting the anticipated criticism by protestations that their tales were drawn from "real life," or pointing out that they invariably portrayed the awful consequences of sin and the fair rewards of virtue. That sin was made attractive was purely coincidental.

The prevailing nationalism was evident in the quest for American settings and characters, but the American novel in its first stages was nevertheless heavily indebted to British models. Three distinct trends may be discerned, in an order which is roughly chronological. (1) The earliest American novels were adaptations of the fiction of sentiment and sensibility which had made the reputations of Samuel Richardson and Laurence Sterne; Mrs. Hannah Webster Foster's *The Coquette* (p. 488) is generally regarded as the best example of the type. (2) Americans next imitated the sensationalism of the so-called Gothic romance, as practiced in its latter stages by Mrs. Ann Radcliffe, and the mystery-laden propaganda novel of which William Godwin's *Caleb Williams* (1794) is typical; this trend is illustrated by the work of Charles Brockden Brown (1771-1810) and, so far as propaganda is concerned, by H. H. Brackenridge's *Modern Chivalry* (p. 499). (3) Finally the society or domestic novel, for which Fanny Burney and Jane Austen were famous, and the historical romance as developed by Sir Walter Scott became naturalized; in these forms James Fenimore Cooper achieved the first really striking success.

Sentiment and sensibility — alike in their release of the "tender" emotions but differing in that sentimentalism was didactic and moral, sensibility deliberately throat-filling and tear-jerking — can scarcely be separated in *The Power of Sympathy; or, The Triumph of Nature* (1789), written "to expose the dangerous Consequences of Seduction and to set forth the advantages of female Education." Usually regarded as the first American novel, it was long attributed to Mrs. Sarah Wentworth Morton, but is now believed to have been the work of William Hill Brown. Mrs. Susanna Haswell Rowson's *Charlotte Temple, a Tale of Truth* (1791) was more popular. Many other sentimental novels might be named, and seduction and suicide and floods of tears filled many pages of fiction far into the nineteenth century. For most readers, however, *The Coquette* will be a sufficient introduction to the type. Its form — a series of letters — was derived from Richardson's *Pamela* and *Clarissa Harlowe* and, while not universal, was characteristic.

Charles Brockden Brown made use of the epistolary form in *Jane Talbot* (1801) and *Clara Howard* (1801), but he is better known for his "thrillers": *Wieland* (1798), *Ormond* (1799), *Arthur Mervyn* (1799-1800), and *Edgar Huntley* (1799). These are remarkable for their use of such mysteries as ventriloquism and sleepwalking, as well as for wonder-working heroes and deep-dyed villains. Brown's imitation of the Gothic romance and of Godwin is unmistakable but far from slavish. He learned how to tell a good story, and some of his methods and materials were borrowed later by Edgar Allan Poe. Brown's work also shows traces of social purpose, although that theme was best used by Brackenridge, whose models were *Don Quixote* and Henry Fielding. *Modern Chivalry* (p. 499) is a rambling book, partly a satirical tract on the times and partly a picaresque romance, with Teague O'Regan as its rogue hero.

The work of Cooper, although in some respects feeble, was a clear improvement over earlier attempts in the novel. His first effort, *Precaution* (1820), was an imitation of the Jane Austen type of domestic fiction, and foreshadowed his lifelong concern with social distinctions. *The Spy* (1821) was doubtless suggested by the success of the then unidentified author of *Waverley* (1814) and *Ivanhoe* (1820) in combining history with fiction. Nationalism helped to make Cooper's work popular, but he should have credit for his skill in obtaining suspense in those parts of his novels in which physical action dominates, and with advances in characterization and the use of setting. He excelled in the escape-pursuit pattern of adventure, which dominates the Leather-Stocking series; unfortunately he often tried to mix with it over-elaborate mysteries, as in *The Pioneers* and *The Prairie*. But he made the American novel respectable, and his work was paralleled by Lydia Maria Child (1802-1880), Catherine Maria Sedgwick (1769-1867), and James Kirke Paulding (1778-1860).

Unlike the novel, the short story was largely dependent upon the magazines, and therefore had a relatively even start in international competition. Its beginnings are closely connected with those of the essay and with "characters" (delineations of unusual or typical personalities). Franklin came close to the short story in "The Way to Wealth" and "The Ephemera," while Crevecoeur's "The American Belisarius" is half-essay, half-story. The British magazines, although full of Oriental and moral tales, widely imitated in America, had not perfected the short story by 1819, nor had the German and French storytellers. Irving's *The Sketch-Book*, therefore, is something of a landmark in world literature as well as in American. The story-sketches retained many of the characteristics of the essay: a sense of the author's presence and manipulation, leisurely movement, a fullness of detail that is sometimes almost digression, and the achievement of atmosphere rather than suspense and sharp climax. Although few of his contemporaries rivaled him, one can argue convincingly that with the short story American literature first came of age. "Rip Van Winkle" and "The Legend of Sleepy Hollow" are our first fictional masterpieces.

T. H.

1706–1790 Benjamin Franklin

Benjamin Franklin was one of the great men of the eighteenth century, famous far beyond the limits of the colonies which he helped unite into a nation. John Adams once remarked that Franklin was more renowned than Sir Isaac Newton, Frederick the Great, or Voltaire, and "more beloved and esteemed than any or all of them." There was a warmth in Franklin; his mind, inquiring rather than dogmatic, endeared him to an age which regarded itself as peculiarly "enlightened," the more so since his reasonableness and simplicity were combined with a generous flair for showmanship. His contemporaries, and to some extent their posterity, saw Franklin in a series of sharply dramatic pictures — flying his kite in a thunderstorm to demonstrate the identity of lightning with electricity, standing modest but unawed before the House of Commons to assert the justice of American complaints, beaming philosophically yet with obvious delight in the adulation of the ladies of the court of Louis XVI, suggesting to the Constitutional Convention that it break a deadlock in debate by an appeal for the guidance of the Supreme Being.

Unfortunately for his later reputation Franklin wrote an autobiography in which he reviewed his early life. It is a classic of its type — the first "rags-to-riches" success story in American literature — but it so glorified thrift, industry, conformity, and shrewd calculation of the material results of tact in personal relations that many sensitive readers have damned Franklin, on his own testimony, as selfishly opportunistic. Only those who accept unthinkingly the bourgeois standard that "getting ahead" is the be-all and end-all of life can whole-heartedly admire his self-portrait.

The truth of the matter is that Franklin was neither a great-souled philanthropist nor an unprincipled careerist. A somewhat enigmatic mixture of idealist and realist, he comes close to being the first example of the typical American. He could not well have emerged from the mass of people in any corner of the world other than colonial America, and his vanity in having worked his way up is both pardonable and widespread in a land where class lines have never been rigid. Not very many self-made men, however, have turned as Franklin did from the making of a fortune to the broadening of a mind. Blessed with an insatiable curiosity and an admirable gusto for living, he became so widely traveled and so universally acquainted that there was scarcely a nook of the age in which he lived where he was not at home. The details of his early life are familiar through his autobiography. There he tells of his ancestry and birth (in Boston in 1706), of his early apprenticeship to his printer brother, of the circumstances which led to his running off to Philadelphia when he was seventeen, of his disillusion there and in London concerning easy roads to wealth. In 1728 he founded his own printing firm, determined to make his fortune by hard work and thrift. Only men with financial security could afford to indulge themselves in the public service which he had in the back of his mind.

It took just twenty years for him to make enough money so that he could retire. Other men of forty-two would have gone on to pile up the pounds, shillings, and pence; Franklin, for all his preaching of the gospel of moneymaking, was not ambitious for mere financial power. He turned first to science, long one of his enthusiasms, and within a few years was internationally famous for his *Experiments & Observations on Electricity,* first published in London in 1751. Already, however, he was busy with public projects and political affairs, notable among them the founding of the Library Company of Philadelphia (1731), the organization of the American Philosophical Society (1743), the proposal for the Academy of Philadelphia, later the University of Pennsylvania (1749), and his service as clerk of the colonial legislature (1736-1751).

To recite, much less to evaluate, Franklin's activities during the remainder of his life would require many pages and the recapitulation of American history from the Albany Congress of 1754 to the ratification of the Constitution of the United States in 1789. There was scarcely a stage in the process of binding disparate colonies into a great nation wherein the calm counsel of Benjamin Franklin had no part. He was probably the first American to assert the principle of "no taxation without representation"; between 1757 and 1775 he was the chief representative of the colonial point of view in England; in 1775-1776 he was a key member of the Second Continental Congress, where he was one of the drafting committee for the Declaration of Independence; between 1777 and 1785 he was in France, where he was largely responsible for the alliance without which the Revolution could hardly have been successful and where he helped to negotiate the treaty of peace; and in 1787, back in Philadelphia, he ended his good works by acting as a balance wheel in the stormy Constitutional Convention.

Franklin would not have obtained the influence which he had if he had not been a writer. At sixteen he was contributing essays to his brother's newspaper, over the signature of "Silence Dogood." Thereafter he wrote steadily, with growing ease and polish. Most of his early work appeared in the newspapers and almanacs which helped him make his fortune; later he became a skillful writer of political pamphlets, many of them published anonymously; throughout his life he was an accomplished letter writer. In an age which tended to like ornate Latinate prose he cultivated simplicity in style and structure. He did not think of himself as an author in the belletristic sense, although all his life he had a critical eye for style both in prose and in poetry. His literary purposes, like those in politics, were utilitarian; "that is best wrote," he once said, "which is best adapted for obtaining the end of the writer." Never a writer of books, he succeeded in leaving papers which are only in our day being completely collected.

His literary ends were many and various. *A Dissertation on Liberty and Necessity, Pleasure and Pain* (1725) expressed his youthful convictions on the fundamentals of morality — Deistic convictions which he later decided were not "useful," however sound they may have been. *Plain Truth* (1747) marked his entrance into political pamphleteering, with a plea for measures to defend Pennsylvania from the French and Indians. *Experiments & Observations on Electricity* (1751; 2d ed., 1754; 4th ed., 1769) was composed of letters describing his scientific work and that of his friends. *The Interest of Great Britain Considered with Regard to Her Colonies* (1760) was representative of his long effort to persuade the British of the necessity for a home-rule policy. Most of his other pieces were composed for newspaper or periodical publication or for the entertainment and edification of his friends. The *Autobiography*, by far his most extended work, not published until long after his death, was written for his family as well as for his friends.

Franklin and his writings have meant many things to many men, and they will doubtless continue to attract commentators and special students. The problems which they present are universal problems in religion, education, economics, politics, and the social and physical sciences. To the general reader, moreover, Franklin, as much as any colonial American, has the fascinating power of a great and versatile personality. To understand the drives which found expression in his life and work is not only a means of understanding the eighteenth century but also a way of clarifying certain personal values. What should a man or woman seek to find in the vocation which he chooses to gain his livelihood? To what extent is self-aggrandizement compatible with self-respect? What, after all, is success? Franklin did not give an ultimate answer to these questions, but few persons will read his life or writings without reflecting upon them with new insight.

The Papers of Benjamin Franklin, ed. L. W. Labaree and others, I-VIII, New Haven, 1959-1965, thirty-two additional volumes expected   The Writings of Benjamin Franklin, ed. A. H. Smyth, 10 vols., New York, 1905-1907   Benjamin Franklin's Memoirs: A Parallel Text Edition, ed. Max Farrand, Berkeley, 1949   Autobiography, ed. L. W. Labaree and others, New Haven, 1964   P. L. Ford, Franklin Bibliography, Brooklyn, 1889   Carl Van Doren, Benjamin Franklin, New York, 1938

from the Autobiography

Franklin began writing his autobiography when he was sixty-five. Vacationing with his friend Jonathan Shipley, Bishop of St. Asaph's, in Hampshire, he determined to use his unwonted leisure to give an account of his ancestry and early life to his son William, then governor of New Jersey. After setting down a list of events and topics to be discussed, he composed eighty-six pages of manuscript, carrying the story of his life down to 1730. He may have sent this manuscript to his son, although there is no real proof that he did so. At any rate, busy with political affairs, he forgot about his memoirs for eleven years. In 1782, living at Passy, a suburb of Paris, he received a letter from an American friend in which was enclosed a copy of the first portion of the autobiography (how obtained no one knows), with the urgent sugges- tion that it be continued. After consultation with his French friends, who agreed that the project should be completed, Franklin wrote fourteen more pages in 1784. In this portion he described his effort to learn virtue by a chart system; he was over seventy-eight when he com- posed it. Four years later, back in Philadelphia, he added a third section of 117 pages, and in 1790, a few weeks before his death, he wrote still a fourth part of seven and one-half pages. Although his memoirs were eagerly awaited, it was, through circumstances too com- plicated to describe here, many years before there was an edition based upon the original manuscript. John Bigelow's transcription, first published in 1868, is now known to be far from accurate, so far as Franklin's capitalization, punctuation, and sentence structure are concerned. A definitive edition, based upon the original manuscript at the Henry E. Hunt- ington Library and prepared by the late Max Farrand, embodies careful study of the innu- merable interlinear changes.

The following selections include about one third of the portion of the Autobiography *written at Twyford in 1771, the larger part of the portion written at Passy in 1784, and a small part (that describing Franklin's success with the investigation of electricity) of the portion written at Philadelphia in 1788. The "preachy" tone of the Twyford and Passy sections may be explained in part by his desire to edify his son, for whom he had high ambi- tions, and by his penchant for moralizing, evident throughout his work. It should be remem- bered, however, that the* Autobiography, *with its strong suggestion that anyone who is willing to pay the price of caution and industry can succeed, is not, for all its frankness, a full revelation of Franklin.*

Twyford, at the Bishop of St. Asaph's, 1771

Dear Son, I have ever had a Pleasure in obtaining any little Anecdotes of my Ances- tors. You may remember the Enquiries I made among the Remains of my Relations when you were with me in England; and the journey I undertook for that purpose. Now imagining it may be equally agreable to you to know the Circumstances of *my* Life, many of which you are yet unacquainted with; and expecting a Weeks unin- terrupted Leisure in my present Country Retirement, I sit down to write them for you. To which I have besides some other Inducements. Having emerg'd from the Poverty and Obscurity in which I was born and bred, to a State of Affluence and some Degree of Reputation in the World, and having gone so far thro' Life with a 1C considerable Share of Felicity, the conducing Means I made use of, which, with the Blessing of God, so well succeeded, my Posterity may like to know, as they may find some of them suitable to their own Situations, and therefore fit to be imitated. That Felicity, when I reflected on it, has induc'd me sometimes to say, that were it offer'd to my Choice, I should have no Objection to a Repetition of the same Life from its Beginning, only asking the Advantages Authors have in a second Edition to correct some Faults of the first. So would I if I might, besides corr[ecting] the

Text: That of the first section is based upon the original manuscript as examined by F. L.Mott and C. E. Jorgenson, that of the second and third sections is from the Bigelow edition, Vol. I (1887)   1 **Twyford,** a village near Winchester, about fifty miles southwest of London   4 **with me.** William Franklin and his father made a genealogical tour into central England in 1758

Faults, change some sinister Accidents and Events of it for others more favourable, but tho' this were deny'd, I should still accept the Offer. However, since such a Repetition is not to be expected, the next Thing most like living one's Life over again, seems to be a *Recollection* of that Life; and to make that Recollection as durable as possible, the putting it down in Writing. Hereby, too, I shall indulge the Inclination so natural in old Men, to be talking of themselves and their own past Actions, and I shall indulge it, without being troublesome to others who thro' respect to Age might think themselves oblig'd to give me a Hearing, since this may be read or not as any one pleases. And lastly (I may as well confess it, since my Denial of it
10 will be believ'd by no Body) perhaps I shall a good deal gratify my own *Vanity*. Indeed I scarce ever heard or saw the introductory Words, *Without vanity I may say,* &c but some vain thing immediately follow'd. Most People dislike Vanity in others whatever share they have of it themselves, but I give it fair Quarter wherever I meet with it, being persuaded that it is often productive of Good to the Possessor and to others that are within his Sphere of Action: And therefore in many Cases it would not be quite absurd if a Man were to thank God for his Vanity among the other Comforts of Life. —

And now I speak of thanking God, I desire with all Humility to acknowledge, that I owe the mention'd Happiness of my past Life to his kind Providence, which
20 led me to the Means I us'd and gave them Success. My Belief of this, induces me to *hope,* tho' I must not *presume,* that the same Goodness will still be exercis'd towards me in continuing that Happiness, or in enabling me to bear a fatal Reverse, which I may experience as others have done, the Complexion of my future Fortune being known to him only: in whose Power it is to bless to us even our Afflictions.

The Notes one of my Uncles (who had the same kind of Curiosity in collecting Family Anecdotes) once put into my Hands, furnish'd me with several Particulars relating to our Ancestors. From these Notes I learnt that the Family had liv'd in the same Village, Ecton in Northamptonshire, for 300 Years, and how much longer he knew not (perhaps from the Time when the Name *Franklin* that before was the
30 name of an Order of People, was assum'd by them for a Surname, when others took surnames all over the kingdom)[,] on a Freehold of about 30 Acres, aided by the Smith's Business, which had continued in the Family till his Time, the eldest son being always bred to that Business[.] A Custom which he and my Father both followed as to their eldest Sons. — When I search'd the Register at Ecton, I found an Account of their Births, Marriages and Burials, from the Year 1555 only, there being no Register kept in that Parish at any time preceding. — By that Register I perceiv'd that I was the youngest Son of the youngest Son for 5 Generations back. My Grandfather Thomas, who was born in 1598, lived at Ecton till he grew too old to follow Business longer, when he went to live with his Son John, a Dyer at Banbury
40 in Oxfordshire, with whom my Father serv'd an Apprenticeship. There my Grandfather died and lies buried. We saw his Gravestone in 1758. His eldest Son Thomas

---

25 **one . . . Uncles,** Benjamin Franklin, who died in Boston in 1728   28 **Ecton,** about fifty miles north-northeast of London   30 **Order of People.** Franklins were small landowners in the English feudal society of the fourteenth and fifteenth centuries

liv'd in the House at Ecton, and left it with the Land to his only Child, a Daughter, who, with her Husband, one Fisher of Wellingborough sold it to Mr. Isted, now Lord of the Manor there. My Grandfather had 4 Sons that grew up, viz Thomas, John, Benjamin and Josiah. I will give you what Account I can of them at this distance from my Papers, and if these are not lost in my Absence, you will among them find many more Particulars. Thomas was bred a Smith under his Father, but being ingenious, and encourag'd in Learning (as all his Brothers likewise were) by an Esquire Palmer then the principal Gentleman in that Parish, he qualify'd himself for the Business of Scrivener, became a considerable Man in the County Affairs, was a chief Mover of all publick Spirited Undertakings for the County or Town 10 of Northampton and his own village, of which many instances were told us; and he was at Ecton much taken Notice of and patroniz'd by the then Lord Halifax. He died in 1702, Jan. 6, old Stile, just 4 Years to a Day before I was born. The Account we receiv'd of his Life and Character from some old People at Ecton, I remember struck you as something extraordinary, from its Similarity to what you knew of mine. Had he died on the same Day, you said one might have suppos'd a Transmigration. — John was bred a Dyer, I believe of Woollens. Benjamin, was bred a Silk Dyer, serving an Apprenticeship at London. He was an ingenious Man, I remember him well, for when I was a Boy he came over to my Father in Boston, and lived in the House with us some Years. He lived to a great Age. His Grandson Samuel 20 Franklin now lives in Boston. He left behind him two Quarto Volumes, M. S. of his own Poetry, consisting of little occasional Pieces address'd to his Friends and Relations, of which the following sent to me, is a Specimen. He had form'd a Shorthand of his own, which he taught me, but, never practising it I have now forgot it. I was nam'd after this Uncle, there being a particular Affection between him and my Father. He was very pious, a great Attender of Sermons of the best Preachers, which he took down in his Shorthand and had with him many Volumes of them. He was also much of a Politician, too much perhaps for his Station. There fell lately into my Hands in London a Collection he had made of all the principal Pamphlets relating to Publick Affairs from 1641 to 1717. Many of the Volumes are wanting, as 30 appears by the Numbering, but there still remains 8 Vols. Folio, and 24 in 4. ^{to} and 8. ^{vo}. — A Dealer in old Books met with them, and knowing me by my sometimes buying of him, he brought them to me. It seems my Uncle must have left them here when he went to America, which was about 50 years since. There are many of his Notes in the Margins. —

This obscure Family of ours was early in the Reformation, and continu'd Protestants thro' the Reign of Queen Mary, when they were sometimes in Danger of Trouble on Account of their Zeal against Popery. They had got an English Bible, and to conceal and secure it, it was fastened open with Tapes under and within the Frame of a Joint Stool. When my Great Great Grandfather read [it] to his Family, 40

12 **Lord Halifax,** Charles Montague, first Earl of Halifax (1661-1715), a noted financier   13 **old Stile,** the Julian calendar, superseded by the present Gregorian calendar in 1752. By modern reckoning, Franklin was born on January 17, 1706   23 **a Specimen,** which Franklin failed to insert, as a marginal note shows was intended. Examples of Uncle Benjamin's verses are printed in the Bigelow edition   37 **Reign . . . Mary,** 1553-1558   40 **Joint Stool,** a wooden footstool held together by pegged joints

he turn'd up the joint Stool upon his Knees, turning over the Leaves then under the Tapes. One of the Children stood at the Door to give Notice if he saw the Apparitor coming, who was an Officer of the Spiritual Court. In that Case the Stool was turn'd down again upon its feet, when the Bible remain'd conceal'd under it as before. This Anecdote I had from my Uncle Benjamin. — The Family continu'd all of the Church of England till about the End of Charles the 2^{ds} Reign, when some of the Ministers that had been outed for Nonconformity, holding Conventicles in Northamptonshire, Benjamin and Josiah adher'd to them, and so continu'd all their Lives. The rest of the Family remain'd with the Episcopal Church.

10   Josiah, my father, married young, and carried his Wife with three Children into New England, about 1682. The Conventicles having been forbidden by Law, and frequently disturbed, induced some considerable Men of his Acquaintance to remove to that Country, and he was prevail'd with to accompany them thither, where they expected to enjoy their Mode of Religion with Freedom. — By the same Wife he had 4 Children more born there, and by a second wife ten more, in all 17, of which I remember 13 sitting at one time at his Table, who all grew up to be Men and Women, and married. I was the youngest Son, and the youngest Child but two, and was born in Boston, N. England. My mother, the 2^d wife was Abiah Folger, a daughter of Peter Folger, one of the first Settlers of New England, of whom hon-
20 ourable mention is made by Cotton Mather, in his Church History of that Country, (entitled Magnalia Christi Americana) as *a godly learned Englishman,* if I remember the Words rightly. I have heard that he wrote sundry small occasional Pieces, but only one of them was printed which I saw now many years since. It was written in 1675, in the home-spun Verse of that Time and People, and address'd to those then concern'd in the Government there. It was in favour of Liberty of Conscience, and in behalf of the Baptists, Quakers, and other Sectaries, that had been under Persecu-tion; ascribing the Indian Wars and other Distresses, that had befallen the Country to that Persecution, as so many Judgments of God, to punish so heinous an Offense; and exhorting a Repeal of those uncharitable Laws. The whole appear'd to me as
30 written with a good deal of Decent Plainness and manly Freedom. The six last con-cluding Lines I remember, tho' I have forgotten the two first of the Stanza, but the Purport of them was that his Censures proceeded from Good will, and therefore he would be known as the Author,

> "Because to be a Libeller, (says he)
>   I hate it with my Heart.
> From Sherburne Town where now I dwell,
>   My Name I do put here,
> Without Offense, your real Friend,
>   It is Peter Folgier."

---

6 **Charles . . . Reign,** 1660-1685   7 **for Nonconformity,** that is, for refusing to read the prayer book as required by the Act of Uniformity of 1662   7 **Conventicles,** secret religious meetings, outlawed by the Conventicle Act of 1664   21 **a godly . . . Englishman,** actually "an Able Godly Englishman," mentioned very briefly in Bk. VI, Chap. VI, of the *Magnalia* (see p. 143)   23 **one . . . printed,** an allusion to *A Looking Glass for the Times: or, the Former Spirit of New England Revived in This Generation,* a pamphlet pub-lished at Boston in 1676   36 **Sherburne Town,** "In the Island of Nantucket." — Franklin

My elder Brothers were all put Apprentices to different Trades. I was put to the Grammar School at Eight Years of Age, my Father intending to devote me as the Tithe of his Sons to the Service of the Church. My early Readiness in learning to read (which must have been very early, as I do not remember when I could not read) and the Opinion of all his Friends that I should certainly make a good Scholar, encourag'd him in this Purpose of his. My Uncle Benjamin too approv'd of it, and propos'd to give me all his Shorthand Volumes of Sermons I suppose as a Stock to set up with, if I would learn his Character. I continu'd however at the Grammar School not quite one Year, tho' in that time I had risen gradually from the Middle of the Class of that Year to be the Head of it, and farther was remov'd into the next Class above it, in order to go with that into the third at the End of the Year. But my Father in the mean time, from a View of the Expence of a College Education which, having so large a Family, he could not well afford, and the mean Living many so educated were afterwards able to obtain, Reasons that he gave to his Friends in my Hearing, altered his first Intention, took me from the Grammar School, and sent me to a School for Writing and Arithmetic kept by a then famous Man, Mr. Geo. Brownell, very successful in his Profession generally, and that by mild encouraging Methods. Under him I acquired fair Writing pretty soon, but I fail'd in the Arithmetic, and made no Progress in it. — At Ten Years old, I was taken home to assist my Father in his Business, which was that of a Tallow Chandler and Sope Boiler. A Business he was not bred to, but had assumed on his Arrival in New England and on finding his Dying Trade would not maintain his Family, being in little Request. Accordingly I was employed in cutting Wick for the Candles, filling the Dipping Mold, and the Molds for cast Candles, attending the Shop, going of Errands, etc. — I dislik'd the Trade and had a strong Inclination for the Sea; but my Father declar'd against it; however, living near the Water, I was much in and about it, learnt early to swim well, and to manage Boats, and when in a Boat or Canoe with other Boys I was commonly allow'd to govern, especially in any case of Difficulty; and upon other Occasions I was generally a Leader among the Boys, and sometimes led them into Scrapes, of wch I will mention one Instance, as it shows an early projecting public Spirit, tho' not then justly conducted. There was a salt Marsh that bounded part of the Mill Pond, on the Edge of which at Highwater, we us'd to stand to fish for Min[n]ows. By much Trampling, we had made it a mere Quagmire. My Proposal was to build a Wharff there fit for us to stand upon, and I show'd my Comrades a large Heap of Stones which were intended for a new House near the Marsh, and which would very well suit our Purpose. Accordingly in the Evening when the Workmen were gone, I assembled a Number of my Playfellows; and working with them diligently like so many Emmets, sometimes two or three to a Stone, we brought them all away and built our little Wharff. — The next Morning the Workmen were surpriz'd at Missing the Stones; which were

2 **the Grammar School.** There were two grammar schools in Boston in 1714. Franklin is thought to have attended the older one, now known as the Boston Latin School   3 **Tithe.** Benjamin was Josiah Franklin's tenth son   17 **Mr. Geo. Brownell,** who taught private pupils in Boston between 1712 and 1734   31 **projecting,** promoting

found in our Wharff; Enquiry was made after the Removers; we were discovered and complain'd of; several of us were corrected by our Fathers; and tho' I pleaded the Usefulness of the Work, mine convinc'd me that nothing was useful which was not honest.

I think you may like to know something of his Person and Character. He had an excellent Constitution of Body, was of middle Stature, but well set and very strong. He was ingenious, could draw prettily, was skill'd a little in Music and had a clear pleasing Voice, so that when he play'd Psalm Tunes on his Violin and sung withal as he sometimes did in an Evening after the Business of the Day was over, it was
10 extreamly agreable to hear. He had a mechanical Genius too, and on occasion was very handy in the Use of other Tradesmen's Tools. But his great Excellence lay in a sound Understanding, and solid Judgment in prudential Matters, both in private and publick Affairs. In the latter indeed he was never employed, the numerous Family he had to educate and the straitness of his Circumstances, keeping him close to his Trade, but I remember well his being frequently visited by leading People, who consulted him for his Opinion in Affairs of the Town or of the Church he belong'd to and show'd a good deal of Respect for his Judgment and advice. He was also much consulted by private Persons about their affairs when any Difficulty occurr'd, and frequently chosen an Arbitrator between contending Parties. — At his Table he lik'd
20 to have as often as he could, some sensible Friend or Neighbour to converse with, and always took care to start some ingenious or useful Topic for Discourse, which might tend to improve the Minds of his Children. By this means he turn'd our Attention to what was good, just, and prudent in the Conduct of Life; and little or no Notice was ever taken of what related to the Victuals on the Table, whether it was well or ill drest, in or out of season, of good or bad flavour, preferable or inferior to this or that other thing of the kind; so that I was bro't up in such a perfect Inattention to those Matters as to be quite Indifferent what kind of Food was set before me, and so unobservant of it, that to this Day, if I am ask'd I can scarce tell a few Hours after Dinner, what I din'd upon. This has been a Convenience to me in travel-
30 ling, where my Companions have been sometimes very unhappy for want of a suitable Gratification of their more delicate[,] because better instructed[,] tastes and appetites.

My Mother had likewise an excellent Constitution. She suckled all her 10 Children. I never knew either my Father or Mother to have any Sickness but that of which they dy'd he at 89 and she at 85 years of age. They lie buried together at Boston, where I some years since placed a Marble Stone over their Grave with this Inscription:

JOSIAH FRANKLIN
And ABIAH his Wife
40 Lie here interred.
They lived lovingly together in Wedlock
Fifty-five Years.
Without an Estate or any gainful Employment,

By constant labour and Industry,
With God's blessing,
They maintained a large Family
Comfortably;
And brought up thirteen Children,
And seven Grandchildren
Reputably.
From this Instance, Reader,
Be encouraged to Diligence in thy Calling,
And Distrust not Providence.   10
He was a pious and prudent Man,
She a discreet and virtuous Woman.
Their youngest Son,
In filial Regard to their Memory,
Places this Stone.
J. F. born 1655 — Died 1744 —Ætat 89.
A. F. born 1667 — Died 1752 — 85.

By my rambling Digressions I perceive myself to be grown old. I us'd to write
more methodically. — But one does not dress for private Company as for a publick
Ball. 'Tis perhaps only Negligence. —   20
    To return. I continu'd thus employ'd in my Father's Business for two Years, that
is till I was 12 Years old; and my Brother John, who was bred to that Business having left my Father, married and set up for himself at Rhodeisland, there was all
Appearance that I was destin'd to supply his Place and be a Tallow Chandler. But
my Dislike to the Trade continuing, my Father was under Apprehensions that if he
did not find one for me more agreable, I should break away and get to Sea, as his
Son Josiah had done to his great Vexation. He therefore sometimes took me to walk
with him, and see Joiners, Bricklayers, Turners, Braziers, etc. at their Work, that he
might observe my Inclination, and endeavour to fix it on some Trade or other on
Land. It has ever since been a Pleasure to me to see good Workmen handle their 30
Tools; and it has been useful to me, having learnt so much by it, as to be able to
do little Jobs myself in my House, when a Workman could not readily be got; and
to construct little Machines for my Experiments while the Intention of making the
Experiment was fresh and warm in my Mind. My Father at last fix'd upon the Cut-
ler's Trade, and my Uncle Benjamin's Son Samuel was bred to that Business
in London[,] being about that time establish'd in Boston, I was sent to be with
him some time on liking. But his Expectations of a Fee with me displeasing my
Father, I was taken home again. —
    From a Child I was fond of Reading, and all the little Money that came into my
Hands was ever laid out in Books. Pleas'd with the Pilgrim's Progress, my first Col- 40
lection was of John Bunyan's Works, in separate little Volumes. I afterwards sold

40 **Pilgrim's Progress,** allegorical novel (1678) by John Bunyan (1628-1688), English nonconformist.
Bunyan's writings were not collected at this date; Franklin's purchases were probably early editions of
separate works

them to enable me to buy R. Burton's Historical Collections; they were small Chapmen's Books and cheap, 40 or 50 in all. — My Father's little Library consisted chiefly of Books in polemic Divinity, most of which I read, and have since often regretted, that at a time when I had such a Thirst for Knowledge, more proper Books had not fallen in my Way, since it was now resolv'd I should not be a Clergyman. Plutarch's Lives there was, in which I read abundantly, and I still think that time spent to great Advantage. There was also a Book of Defoe's, called an Essay on Projects, and another of Dr. Mather's, called Essays to do Good which perhaps gave me a Turn of thinking that had an influence on some of the principal future Events
10 of my Life.

This Bookish inclination at length determin'd my Father to make me a Printer, tho' he had already one Son (James) of that Profession. In 1717 my Brother James return'd from England with a Press and Letters to set up his Business in Boston. I lik'd it much better than that of my Father, but still had a Hankering for the Sea. — To prevent the apprehended Effect of such an Inclination, my Father was impatient to have me bound to my Brother. I stood out some time, but at last was persuaded and signed the Indentures, when I was yet but 12 Years old. — I was to serve as an Apprentice till I was 21 Years of Age, only I was to be allow'd Journeyman's Wages during the last Year. In a little time I made great Proficiency in the Business, and
20 became a useful Hand to my Brother. I now had Access to better Books. An Acquaintance with the Apprentices of Booksellers, enabled me sometimes to borrow a small one, which I was careful to return soon and clean. Often I sat up in my Room reading the greatest Part of the Night, when the Book was borrow'd in the Evening and to be return'd early in the Morning[,] lest it should be miss'd or wanted. And after some time an ingenious Tradesman Mr. Matthew Adams who had a pretty Collection of Books, and who frequented our Printing House, took Notice of me, invited me to his Library, and very kindly lent me such Books as I chose to read. I now took a Fancy to Poetry, and made some little Pieces. My Brother, thinking it might turn to account encourag'd me, and put me on composing two
30 occasional Ballads. One was called The *Lighthouse Tragedy,* and contained an Acc^t of the drowning of Capt. Worthilake with his Two Daughters; the other was a Sailor Song on the Taking of *Teach* or Blackbeard the Pirate. They were wretched Stuff, in the Grub-street Ballad Stile, and when they were printed he sent me about the town to sell them. The first sold wonderfully, the Event being recent, having made a great Noise. This flatter'd my Vanity. But my Father discourag'd me, by ridiculing my Performances, and telling me Verse-makers were generally Beggars; so I escap'd

1 **R. Burton's** . . . **Collections,** a series of compilations by an English publisher and hack writer, Nathaniel Crouch (1632?-1725). Sold at a shilling each by chapmen (peddlers) and bookdealers, they were widely popular in colonial America   6 **Plutarch's Lives,** the most famous collection of biographies of the Greeks and Romans, by a Greek who lived at Rome in the first century A.D.   7 **Essay on Projects** (1697) by Daniel Defoe (1661?-1731), English journalist and novelist. The book dealt with such matters as education and insurance   8 **Essays** . . . **Good,** contained the ideas of Cotton Mather (see p. 137) on cooperative societies for religious and humanitarian improvement   12 **James,** James Franklin (1696/7-1735)   31 **Capt. Worthilake** or Worthylake, first keeper of the Boston lighthouse. He and his wife and one daughter were drowned (Franklin's memory was at fault here) in November 1718   32 **Teach,** Edward Teach or Thatch, better known as Blackbeard, killed by a British naval officer in North Carolina in 1718

being a Poet, most probably a very bad one. But as Prose Writing has been of great Use to me in the Course of my Life, and was a principal Means of my Advancement, I shall tell you how in such a Situation I acquir'd what little Ability I have in that Way.

There was another Bookish Lad in the Town, John Collins by Name, with whom I was intimately acquainted. We sometimes disputed, and very fond we were of Argument, and very desirous of confuting one another. Which disputacious Turn, by the way, is apt to become a very bad Habit, making People often extreamly disagreeable in Company, by the Contradiction that is necessary to bring it into Practice, and thence, besides souring and spoiling the Conversation, is productive of 10 Disgusts and perhaps Enmities where you may have occasion for Friendship. I had caught it by reading my Father's Books of Dispute about Religion. Persons of good Sense, I have since observ'd, seldom fall into it, except Lawyers, University Men, and Men of all Sorts that have been bred at Edinborough. A Question was once some how or other started between Collins and me, of the Propriety of educating the Female Sex in Learning, and their Abilities for Study. He was of Opinion that it was improper, and that they were naturally unequal to it. I took the contrary Side, perhaps a little for Dispute['s] sake. He was naturally more eloquent, had a ready Plenty of Words, and sometimes as I thought bore me down more by his Fluency than by the Strength of his Reasons. As we parted without settling the Point, and 20 were not to see one another again for some time, I sat down to put my Arguments in Writing, which I copied fair and sent to him. He answer'd and I reply'd. Three of [or] four Letters of a Side had pass'd, when my Father happen'd to find my Papers, and read them. Without ent'ring into the Discussion, he took occasion to talk to me about the Manner of my Writing, observ'd that tho' I had the Advantage of my Antagonist in correct Spelling and pointing (which I ow'd to the Printing House) I fell far short in elegance of Expression, in Method and in Perspicuity, of which he convinc'd me by several Instances. I saw the Justice of his Remarks, and thence grew more attentive to the *Manner* in writing, and determin'd to endeavour at Improvement. —   30

About this time I met with an odd Volume of the Spectator. It was the Third. I had never before seen any of them. I bought it, read it over and over, and was much delighted with it. I thought the Writing excellent, and wish'd if possible to imitate it. With that View, I took some of the Papers, and making short Hints of the Sentiment in each Sentence, laid them by a few Days, and then without looking at the Book, try'd to compleat the Papers again, by expressing each hinted Sentiment at length, and as fully as it had been express'd before, in any suitable Words, that should come to hand.

Then I compar'd my Spectator with the Original, discover'd some of my Faults and corrected them. But I found I wanted a Stock of Words or a Readiness in recol- 40 lecting and using them, which I thought I should have acquir'd before that time, if I had gone on making Verses, since the continual Occasion for Words of the same

---

26 **pointing,** punctuating   31 **Spectator** (1711-1712; second series, 1714), English literary periodical conducted by Joseph Addison (1672-1719) and Sir Richard Steele (1672-1729)

Import but of different Length, to suit the Measure, or of different Sound for the Rhyme, would have laid me under a constant Necessity of searching for Variety, and also have tended to fix that Variety in my Mind, and make me Master of it. Therefore I took some of the Tales and turn'd them into Verse: And after a time, when I had pretty well forgotten the Prose, turn'd them back again. I also sometimes jumbled my Collections of Hints into Confusion, and after some Weeks, endeavour'd to reduce them into the best Order, before I began to form the full Sentences, and compleat the Paper. This was to teach me Method in the Arrangement of Thoughts. By comparing my work afterwards with the original, I discover'd
10 many faults and amended them; but I sometimes had the Pleasure of Fancying that in certain Particulars of small Import, I had been lucky enough to improve the Method or the Language and this encourag'd me to think I might possibly in time come to be a tolerable English Writer, of which I was extreamly ambitious.

My time for these Exercises and for Reading, was at Night, after Work or before it began in the Morning; or on Sundays, when I contrived to be in the Printing House alone, evading as much as I could the common Attendance on publick Worship, which my Father used to exact of me when I was under his Care: And which indeed I still thought a Duty; tho' I could not, as it seemed to me, afford the Time to practise it.

20 When about 16 Years of Age, I happen'd to meet with a Book, written by one Tryon, recommending a Vegetable Diet. I determined to go into it. My Brother being yet unmarried, did not keep House, but boarded himself and his Apprentices in another Family. My refusing to eat Flesh occasioned an Inconveniency, and I was frequently chid for my singularity. I made myself acquainted with Tryon's Manner of preparing some of his Dishes, such as Boiling Potatoes or Rice, making Hasty Pudding, and a few others, and then propos'd to my Brother, that if he would give me Weekly half the Money he paid for my Board I would board myself. He instantly agreed to it, and I presently found that I could save half what he paid me. This was an additional Fund for buying Books. But I had another Advantage in it. My Brother
30 and the rest going from the Printing House to their Meals, I remain'd there alone, and dispatching presently my light Repast, (which often was no more than a Bisket or a Slice of Bread, a Handful of Raisins or a Tart from the Pastry Cook's, and a Glass of Water) had the rest of the Time till their Return, for Study, in which I made the greater Progress from the greater Clearness of Head and quicker Apprehension which usually attend Temperance in Eating and Drinking. And now it was that being on some Occasion made asham'd of my Ignorance in Figures, which I had twice failed in Learning when at School, I took Cocker's Book of Arithmetick, and went thro' the whole by myself with great Ease. I also read Seller's and Sturmy's Books of Navigation, and became acquainted with the little Geometry they contain,

---

21 **Tryon**, Thomas Tryon (1634-1703), English mystic. Franklin probably read *Health's Grand Preservative* (1682)   37 **Cocker's.** Edward Cocker (1631-1675), English textbook writer, was the author of several different arithmetics, the most popular of which was first published in 1678, after Cocker's death   38 **Seller's.** John Seller (fl. 1700) was the author of *The English Pilot* (1671) and *Practical Navigation* (1718). The latter is the book which Franklin probably read   38 **Sturmy's**, presumably Samuel Sturmy's *The Mariner's Magazine* (1669)

but never proceeded far in that Science. — And I read about this Time Locke on Human Understanding, and the Art of Thinking by Mess[rs] du Port Royal.

While I was intent on improving my Language, I met with an English Grammar (I think it was Greenwood's) at the End of which there were two little Sketches of the Arts of Rhetoric and Logic, the latter finishing with a Specimen of a Dispute in the Socratic Method. And soon after I procur'd Xenophon's Memorable Things of Socrates, wherein there are many Instances of the same Method. I was charm'd with it, adopted it, dropt my abrupt Contradiction, and positive Argumentation, and put on the humble Enquirer and Doubter. And being then, from reading Shafts-bury and Collins, become a real Doubter in many Points of our religious Doctrine, 10 I found this Method safest for myself and very embarrassing to those against whom I us'd it, therefore I took a Delight in it, practis'd it continually and grew very art-ful and expert in drawing People even of superior Knowledge into Concessions the Consequences of which they did not forsee, entangling them in Difficulties out of which they could not extricate themselves, and so obtaining Victories that neither myself nor my Cause always deserved. — I continu'd this Method some few years, but gradually left it, retaining only the Habit of expressing myself in Terms of modest Diffidence, never using when I advance any thing that may possibly be disputed, the Words, *Certainly, undoubtedly;* or any others that give the Air of Positiveness to an Opinion; but rather say, I conceive, or I apprehend a Thing to be so or so, It appears 20 to me, or I should think it so or so for such and such Reasons, or I imagine it to be so, or it is so if I am not mistaken. This Habit I believe has been of great Ad-vantage to me, when I have had occasion to inculcate my Opinions and persuade Men into Measures that I have been from time to time engag'd in promoting. — And as the chief Ends of Conversation are to *inform,* or to be *informed,* to *please* or to *persuade,* I wish wellmeaning sensible Men would not lessen their Power of doing Good by a Positive assuming Manner that seldom fails to disgust, tends to create Opposition, and to defeat every one of those Purposes for which Speech was given us, to wit, giving or receiving Information, or Pleasure: For if you would *inform,* a positive dogmatical Manner in advancing your Sentiments, may provoke Contradic- 30 tion and prevent a candid Attention. If you wish Information and Improvement from the Knowledge of others and yet at the same time express yourself as firmly fix'd in your present Opinions, modest sensible Men, who do not love Disputation, will probably leave you undisturbed in the Possession of your Error; and by such a

---

1 **Locke . . . Understanding,** the best-known work of the English philosopher John Locke (1632-1704), *An Essay Concerning Human Understanding* (1690)   2 **Messrs . . . Royal.** Port-Royal, originally a nun-nery near Chevreuse in France, became in the seventeenth century the center of Jansenism, a movement within the Catholic Church with which were associated Bishop Cornelius Jansen (1585-1638) and philosopher Blaise Pascal (1623-1662). The book referred to by Franklin is *L'art de penser,* a logic first published in 1662   4 **Greenwood's,** *An Essay towards a Practical English Grammar* (1711) by James Greenwood (d. 1737), English grammarian   6 **Xenophon's . . . Socrates,** probably the translation by that title published in 1712 by Edward Bysshe, an English hack writer. Xenophon (444-354? B.C.) wrote his *Memorabilia* (in dialogue form) to defend Socrates against the charge that he had corrupted the youth of Athens   9 **Shaftesbury and Collins,** presumably a reference to *Characteristicks of Men, Manners, Opinions, and Times* (1711) by Anthony Ashley Cooper, third Earl of Shaftesbury (1671-1713), a moralist whose remarks on the Bible show Deistic tendencies, and the *Discourse of Freethinking* (1713) by Anthony Collins (1676-1729), in which he advanced the thesis that all belief should be based on reason

Manner you can seldom hope to recommend yourself in *pleasing* your Hearers, or to persuade those whose Concurrence you desire. — Pope says, judiciously,

> *Men should be taught as if you taught them not,*
> *And things unknown propos'd as things forgot,* —

farther recommending it to us,

> *To speak tho' sure, with seeming Diffidence.*

And he might have coupled with this Line that which he has coupled with another, I think less properly,

> *For want of Modesty is want of Sense.*

10 If you ask why *less properly*, I must repeat the lines;

> "Immodest Words admit of *no* Defence;
> *For* Want of Modesty is Want of Sense."

Now is not *Want of Sense* (where a Man is so unfortunate as to want it) some Apology for his *Want of Modesty?* and would not the Lines stand more justly thus?

> Immodest Words admit *but this* Defence,
> That Want of Modesty is Want of Sense.

This however I should submit to better Judgments. —

My Brother had in 1720 or 21, begun to print a Newspaper. It was the second that appear'd in America, and was called *The New England Courant.* The only one
20 before it, was *the Boston News Letter.* I remember his being dissuaded by some of his Friends from the Undertaking, as not likely to succeed, one Newspaper being in their Judgment enough for America. — At this time 1771 there are not less than five and twenty. — He went on however with the Undertaking, and after having work'd in composing the Types and printing off the Sheets, I was employ'd to carry the Papers thro' the Streets to the Customers. — He had some ingenious Men among his Friends who amus'd themselves by writing little Pieces for this Paper, which gain'd it Credit, and made it more in Demand; and these Gentlemen often visited us. — Hearing their Conversations, and their Accounts of the Approbation their Papers were receiv'd with, I was excited to try my Hand among them.

---

2 **Pope says,** in the *Essay on Criticism* (1711), Part II, 11. 574-575. Franklin substitutes "should" for "must" in the first line, evidently quoting from memory. The additional line is from the same poem, 1. 567   7 **another,** not actually by Pope. The couplet Franklin had in mind, concluding "For want of decency is want of sense," is from the *Essay on Translated Verse* (1684) by Wentworth Dillon, fourth Earl of Roscommon (1633?-1685)   18 **the second.** The *New-England Courant* had been preceded by three other newspapers (see p. 20)

But being still a Boy, and suspecting that my Brother would object to printing any Thing of mine in his Paper if he knew it to be mine, I contriv'd to disguise my Hand, and writing an anonymous Paper I put it in at Night under the Door of the Printing House. It was found in the Morning and communicated to his Writing Friends when they call'd in as usual. They read it, commented on it in my Hearing, and I had the exquisite Pleasure, of finding it met with their Approbation, and that in their different Guesses at the Author none were named but Men of some Character among us for Learning and Ingenuity. — I suppose now that I was rather lucky in my Judges: And that perhaps they were not really so very good ones as I then esteem'd them. Encourag'd however by this, I wrote and convey'd in the same 10 Way to the Press several more Papers, which were equally approv'd, and I kept my Secret till my small Fund of Sense for such Performances was pretty well exhausted, and then I discovered it; when I began to be considered a little more by my Brother's Acquaintance, and in a manner that did not quite please him, as he thought, probably with reason, that it tended to make me too vain. And perhaps this might be one Occasion of the Differences that we began to have about this Time. Tho' a Brother, he considered himself as my Master, and me as his Apprentice; and accordingly expected the same Services from me as he would from another; while I thought he demean'd me too much in some he requir'd of me, who from a Brother expected more Indulgence. Our Disputes were often brought before our 20 Father, and I fancy I was either generally in the right, or else a better Pleader, because the Judgment was generally in my favour. But my Brother was passionate and had often beaten me, which I took extreamly amiss; and thinking my Apprenticeship very tedious, I was continually wishing for some Opportunity of shortening it, which at length offered in a manner unexpected.

One of the Pieces in our Newspaper, on some political Point which I have now forgotten, gave Offence to the Assembly. He was taken up, censur'd and imprison'd for a Month by the Speaker's Warrant, I suppose because he would not discover his Author. I too was taken up and examin'd before the Council; but tho' I did not give them any Satisfaction, they contented themselves with admonishing me, 30 and dismiss'd me; considering me perhaps as an Apprentice who was bound to keep his Master's Secrets. During my Brother's Confinement, which I resented a good deal, notwithstanding our private Differences, I had the Management of the Paper, and I made bold to give our Rulers some Rubs in it, which my Brother took very kindly, while others began to consider me in an unfavourable Light, as a young Genius that had a Turn for Libelling and Satyr. My Brother's Discharge was accompany'd with an Order of the House, (a very odd one) *that James Franklin should*

---

25 **unexpected.** "I fancy his harsh and tyrannical treatment of me, might be a means of impressing me with that aversion to arbitrary power that has stuck to me thro' my whole life." — Franklin   26 **some political Point.** James Franklin's offense, hardly heinous from a present-day point of view, was to print a fictitious letter from Newport saying that pirates had been seen off the coast and that it was reported that the Massachusetts government was fitting out a ship to go after them, "wind and weather permitting." Franklin was arrested for contempt and released only after apology. The Order of the House came six months later, after James Franklin had printed (in January 1723) an article attacking "hypocritical pretenders to religion." Benjamin Franklin's name appeared as publisher from February 11, 1723, until fall, when he ran away to New York

no longer print the Paper called the New England Courant. There was a Consultation held in our Printing House among his Friends what he should do in this Case. Some propos'd to evade the Order by changing the Name of the Paper; but my Brother seeing Inconveniences in that, it was finally concluded on as a better Way, to let it be printed for the future under the Name of *Benjamin Franklin.* And to avoid the Censure of the Assembly that might fall on him, as still printing it by his Apprentice, the Contrivance was, that my old Indenture should be return'd to me with a full Discharge on the Back of it, to be shown on Occasion; but to secure to him the Benefit of my Service I was to sign new Indentures for the Remainder of
10 the Term, wch. were to be kept private. A very flimsy Scheme it was, but however it was immediately executed, and the Paper went on accordingly under my Name for several Months. At length a fresh Difference arising between my Brother and me, I took upon me to assert my Freedom, presuming that he would not venture to produce the new Indentures. It was not fair in me to take this Advantage, and this I therefore reckon one of the first Errata of my life: But the Unfairness of it weighed little with me, when under the Impressions of Resentment, for the Blows his Passion too often urg'd him to bestow upon me. Tho' he was otherwise not an ill-natur'd Man: Perhaps I was too saucy and provoking.
    When he found I would leave him, he took care to prevent my getting Employ-
20 ment in any other Printing-House of the Town, by going round and speaking to every Master, who accordingly refus'd to give me Work. I then thought of going to New York as the nearest Place where there was a Printer: and I was the rather inclin'd to leave Boston, when I reflected that I had already made myself a little obnoxious to the governing Party; and from the arbitrary Proceedings of the Assembly in my Brother's Case it was likely I might if I stay'd soon bring myself into Scrapes; and farther that my indiscrete Disputations about Religion began to make me pointed at with Horror by good People, as an Infidel or Atheist. I determin'd on the Point: but my Father now siding with my Brother, I was sensible that if I attempted to go openly, Means would be used to prevent me. My Friend Collins
30 therefore undertook to manage a little for me. He agreed with the Captain of a New York Sloop for my Passage, under the Notion of my being a young Acquaintance of his that had got a naughty Girl with Child, whose Friends would compel me to marry her, and therefore I could not appear or come away publickly. So I sold some of my Books to raise a little Money, Was taken on board privately, and as we had a fair Wind[,] in three Days I found myself in New York near 300 Miles from home, a Boy of but 17, without the least Recommendation to or Knowledge of any Person in the Place, and with very little Money in my Pocket.
    My Inclinations for the Sea, were by this time worne out, or I might now have gratify'd them. But having a Trade, and supposing myself a pretty good Workman,
40 I offer'd my Service to the Printer in the Place, old Mr. Wm Bradford, who had

---

40 old . . . Keith. William Bradford (1663-1752) was the pioneer printer of the middle colonies, having first visited Pennsylvania in 1682. In 1692 Bradford was arrested and tried for printing the "Christian Quaker" writings of George Keith (1639?-1716), regarded as seditious by the ruling faction. The jury failed to agree and he was discharged, but he moved to New York in 1693

been the first Printer in Pensilvania, but remov'd from thence upon the Quarrel of
Geo. Keith. — He could give me no Employment, having little to do, and Help
enough already: But, says he, my Son at Philadelphia has lately lost his principal
Hand, Aquila Rose, by Death. If you go thither I believe he may employ you. —
Philadelphia was 100 Miles farther. I set out, however, in a Boat for Amboy, leaving my Chest and Things to follow me round by Sea. In crossing the Bay we met
with a Squall that tore our rotten sails to pieces, prevented our getting into the
Kill, and drove us upon Long Island. In our Way a drunken Dutchman, who was
a Passenger too, fell overboard; when he was sinking I reach'd thro' the Water to
his shock Pate and drew him up so that we got him in again. His ducking sober'd 10
him a little, and he went to sleep, taking first out of his Pocket a Book which he
desir'd I would dry for him. It prov'd to be my old favourite Author Bunyan's Pilgrim's Progress in Dutch, finely printed on good Paper with copper Cuts, a Dress
better than I had ever seen it wear in its own Language. I have since found that it
has been translated into most of the Languages of Europe, and suppose it has been
more generally read than any other Book except perhaps the Bible. Honest John
was the first that I know of who mix'd Narration and Dialogue, a Method of
Writing very engaging to the Reader, who in the most interesting Parts finds himself, as it were brought into the Company, and present at the Discourse. De foe in
his Cruso, his Moll Flanders, Religious Courtship, Family Instructor, and other 20
Pieces, has imitated it with Success. And Richardson has done the same in his
Pamela, etc. —
     When we drew near the Island we found it was at a Place where there could be
no Landing, there being a great Surff on the stony Beach. So we dropt Anchor and
swung round towards the Shore. Some People came down to the Water Edge and
hallow'd to us, as we did to them. But the Wind was so high and the Surff so loud,
that we could not hear so as to understand each other. There were Canoes on the
Shore, and we made Signs and hallow'd that they should fetch us, but they either
did not understand us, or thought it impracticable. So they went away, and Night
coming on, we had no Remedy but to wait till the Wind should abate, and in the 30
mean time the Boatman and I concluded to sleep if we could, and so crouded into
the Scuttle with the Dutchman who was still wet, and the Spray beating over the
Head of our Boat, leak'd thro' to us, so that we were soon almost as wet as he. In
this Manner we lay all Night with very little Rest. But the Wind abating the next
Day, we made a Shift to reach Amboy before Night, having been 30 Hours on the
Water without Victuals, or any Drink but a Bottle of filthy Rum: The Water we
sail'd on being salt. —
     In the Evening I found myself very feverish, and went in to Bed. But having read

---

3 **my Son,** Andrew Bradford (1686-1742), for many years Franklin's chief rival in Philadelphia   4 **Aquila
Rose** (1695-1723), a minor poet, author of the posthumous *Poems on Several Occasions* (1740)   5 **Amboy,**
Perth Amboy, on the southern shore of Raritan Bay in New Jersey   19 **De foe . . . Pieces.** The references are to *Robinson Crusoe* (1719), *Moll Flanders* (1722), *Religious Courtship* (1722), and *The Family Instructor* (1715-1718) or *A New Family Instructor* (1727). Franklin's acquaintance with the works of Defoe has
interesting implications for the student of his style   21 **Richardson,** Samuel Richardson (1689-1761),
English novelist, whose *Pamela, or Virtue Rewarded* was first printed in 1740

somewhere that cold Water drank plentifully was good for a Fever, I follow'd the Prescription, sweat plentifully most of the Night, my Fever left me, and in the Morning crossing the Ferry, I proceeded on my Journey, on foot, having 50 Miles to Burlington, where I was told I should find Boats that would carry me the rest of the Way to Philadelphia.

It rain'd very hard all the Day, I was thoroughly soak'd, and by Noon a good deal tir'd, so I stopt at a poor Inn, where I staid all night, beginning now to wish I had never left home. I cut so miserable a Figure too, that I found by the Questions ask'd me I was suspected to be some runaway Servant, and in danger of being taken
10 up on that Suspicion. However I proceeded the next Day, and got in the Evening to an Inn within 8 or 10 Miles of Burlington, kept by one Dr. Brown. —

He ent[e]red into Conversation with me while I took some Refreshment, and finding I had read a little, became very sociable and friendly. Our Acquaintance continu'd as long as he liv'd. He had been, I imagine, an itinerant Doctor, for there was no Town in England, or Country in Europe, of which he could not give a very particular Account. He had some Letters, and was ingenious, but much of an Unbeliever, and wickedly undertook, some Years after to travesty the Bible in doggrel Verse as Cotton had done Virgil. By this means he set many of the Facts in a very ridiculous Light, and might have hurt weak minds if his Work had been publish'd:
20 — but it never was. — At his House I lay that Night, and the next Morning reach'd Burlington. — But had the Mortification to find that the regular Boats were gone, a little before my coming, and no other expected to go till Tuesday, this being Saturday. Wherefore I returned to an old Woman in the Town of whom I had bought Gingerbread to eat on the Water, and ask'd her Advice; she invited me to lodge at her House till a Passage by Water should offer: and being tired with my foot Travelling, I accepted the Invitation. She understanding I was a Printer, would have had me stay at that Town and follow my Business, being ignorant of the Stock necessary to begin with. She was very hospitable, gave me a Dinner of Ox Cheek with great Goodwill, accepting only of a Pot of Ale in return. And I thought my-
30 self fix'd till Tuesday should come. However walking in the Evening by the Side of the River, a Boat came by, which I found was going towards Philadelphia, with several People in her. They took me in, and as there was no wind, we row'd all the Way; and about Midnight not having yet seen the City, some of the Company were confident we must have pass'd it, and would row no farther, the others knew not where we were, so we put towards the Shore, got into a Creek, landed near an old Fence[,] with the Rails of which we made a Fire, the Night being cold, in October, and there we remain'd till Daylight. Then one of the Company knew the Place to be Cooper's Creek a little above Philadelphia, which we saw as soon as we got out of the Creek, and arriv'd there about 8 or 9 o'Clock, on the Sunday morning, and
40 landed at the Market Street Wharff. —

4 **Burlington,** on the Delaware River, northeast of Philadelphia   11 **Dr. Brown,** apparently an obscure physician, Dr. John Browne, who died in 1737   18 **as Cotton . . . Virgil,** an allusion to a burlesque poem, *Scarronides, or the First Book of Virgil Travestie* (1664), by Charles Cotton (1630-1687), English translater   38 **Cooper's Creek,** a small stream which empties into the Delaware at Camden, just above downtown Philadelphia

I have been the more particular in this Description of my Journey, and shall be so of my first Entry into that City, that you may in your Mind compare such unlikely Beginnings with the Figure I have since made there. I was in my Working Dress, my best Cloaths being to come round by Sea. I was dirty from my Journey; my Pockets were stuff'd out with Shirts and Stockings; I knew no Soul, nor where to look for Lodging. I was fatigued with Travelling, Rowing and Want of Rest. I was very hungry, and my whole Stock of Cash consisted of a Dutch Dollar and about a Shilling in Copper. The latter I gave the People of the Boat for my Passage, who at first refus'd it on Acc^t of my Rowing; but I insisted on their taking it, a Man being sometimes more generous when he has but a little Money than when 10 he has plenty, perhaps thro' Fear of being thought to have but little. Then I walk'd up the Street, gazing about, till near the Market House I met a Boy with Bread. I had made many a Meal on Bread, and inquiring where he got it, I went immediately to the Baker's he directed me to in Second Street; and ask'd for Bisket, intending such as we had in Boston, but they it seems were not made in Philadelphia, then I ask'd for a threepenny Loaf, and was told they had none such: so not considering or knowing the Difference of Money and the greater Cheapness nor the Names of his Bread, I bad[e] him give me threepenny worth of any sort. He gave me accordingly three great Puffy Rolls. I was surpriz'd at the Quantity, but took it, and having no room in my Pockets, walk'd off, with a Roll under each Arm, and 20 eating the other. Thus I went up Market Street as far as fourth Street, passing by the Door of Mr. Read, my future Wife's Father, when she standing at the Door saw me, and thought I made as I certainly did a most awkward ridiculous Appearance. Then I turn'd and went down Chestnut Street and part of Walnut Street, eating my Roll all the Way, and coming round found myself again at Market Street Wharff, near the Boat I came in, to which I went for a Draught of the River Water, and being fill'd with one of my Rolls, gave the other two to a Woman and her Child that came down the River in the Boat with us and were waiting to go farther. Thus refresh'd I walk'd again up the Street, which by this time had many clean dress'd People in it who were all walking the same Way; I join'd them, and thereby 30 was led into the great Meeting House of the Quakers near the Market. I sat down among them, and after looking round awhile and hearing nothing said; being very drowsy thro' Labour and want of Rest the preceding Night, I fell fast asleep, and continu'd so till the Meeting broke up, when one was kind enough to rouse me. This was therefore the first House I was in or slept in, in Philadelphia. —

. . . I had been religiously educated as a Presbyterian; and tho' some of the dogmas of that persuasion, such as *the eternal decrees of God, election, reprobation, etc.*, appeared to me unintelligible, others doubtful, and I early absented myself from the public assemblies of the sect, Sunday being my studying day, I never was without some religious principles. I never doubted, for instance, the existence of the Deity; 40 that he made the world, and govern'd it by his Providence; that the most acceptable

---

15 **Philadelphia.** The selection from the portion of the *Autobiography* written at Twyford ends here; Franklin went on to describe his first connections in Philadelphia, his voyage to England and his work there in 1724-1726, and his business life in Philadelphia down to 1730

service of God was the doing good to man; that our souls are immortal; and that all crime will be punished, and virtue rewarded, either here or hereafter. These I esteem'd the essentials of every religion; and, being to be found in all the religions we had in our country, I respected them all, tho' with different degrees of respect, as I found them more or less mix'd with other articles, which, without any tendency to inspire, promote, or confirm morality, serv'd principally to divide us, and make us unfriendly to one another. This respect to all, with an opinion that the worst had some good effects, induc'd me to avoid all discourse that might tend to lessen the good opinion another might have of his own religion; and as our province in-
10 creas'd in people, and new places of worship were continually wanted, and generally erected by voluntary contribution, my mite for such purpose, whatever might be the sect, was never refused.

Tho' I seldom attended any public worship, I had still an opinion of its propriety, and of its utility when rightly conducted, and I regularly paid my annual subscription for the support of the only Presbyterian minister or meeting we had in Philadelphia. He us'd to visit me sometimes as a friend, and admonish me to attend his administrations, and I was now and then prevail'd on to do so, once for five Sundays successively. Had he been in my opinion a good preacher, perhaps I might have continued, notwithstanding the occasion I had for the Sunday's leisure in my
20 course of study; but his discourses were chiefly either polemic arguments, or explications of the peculiar doctrines of our sect, and were all to me very dry, uninteresting, and unedifying, since not a single moral principle was inculcated or enforc'd, their aim seeming to be rather to make us Presbyterians than good citizens.

At length he took for his text that verse of the fourth chapter of Philippians: *"Finally, brethren, whatsoever things are true, honest, just, pure, lovely, or of good report, if there be any virtue, or any praise, think on these things."* And I imagin'd, in a sermon on such a text, we could not miss of having some morality. But he confin'd himself to five points only, as meant by the apostle, viz.: 1. Keeping holy the Sabbath day. 2. Being diligent in reading the holy Scriptures. 3. Attending duly the publick wor-
30 ship. 4. Partaking of the Sacrament. 5. Paying a due respect to God's ministers. These might be all good things; but, as they were not the kind of good things that I expected from that text, I despaired of ever meeting with them from any other, was disgusted, and attended his preaching no more. I had some years before compos'd a little Liturgy, or form of prayer, for my own private use (viz., in 1728), entitled, *Articles of Belief and Acts of Religion*. I return'd to the use of this, and went no more to the public assemblies. My conduct might be blameable, but I leave it, without attempting further to excuse it; my present purpose being to relate facts, and not to make apologies for them.

It was about this time I conceiv'd the bold and arduous project of arriving
40 at moral perfection. I wish'd to live without committing any fault at any time; I

---

3 the essentials . . . religion, derived, that is to say, from comparing the fundamentals of all faiths — a typical Deistic method. Note also that Franklin omits mention of the Bible as the revealed word of God, an omission which is the surest distinguishing mark of Deism   35 Articles . . . Religion, to be found in *Papers*, I, 101-109

would conquer all that either natural inclination, custom, or company might lead me into. As I knew, or thought I knew, what was right and wrong, I did not see why I might not always do the one and avoid the other. But I soon found I had undertaken a task of more difficulty than I had imagined. While my care was employ'd in guarding against one fault, I was often surprised by another; habit took the advantage of attention; inclination was sometimes too strong for reason. I concluded, at length, that the mere speculative conviction that it was our interest to be completely virtuous, was not sufficient to prevent our slipping; and that the contrary habits must be broken, and good ones acquired and established, before we can have any dependence on a steady, uniform rectitude of conduct. For this purpose I 10 therefore contrived the following method.

In the various enumerations of the moral virtues I had met with in my reading, I found the catalogue more or less numerous, as different writers included more or fewer ideas under the same name. Temperance, for example, was by some confined to eating and drinking, while by others it was extended to mean the moderating every other pleasure, appetite, inclination, or passion, bodily or mental, even to our avarice and ambition. I propos'd to myself, for the sake of clearness, to use rather more names, with fewer ideas annex'd to each, than a few names with more ideas; and I included under thirteen names of virtues all that at that time occurr'd to me as necessary or desirable, and annexed to each a short precept, which fully express'd 20 the extent I gave to its meaning.

These names of virtues, with their precepts, were:

1. *Temperance.*
Eat not to dullness; drink not to elevation.

2. *Silence.*
Speak not but what may benefit others or yourself; avoid trifling conversation.

3. *Order.*
Let all your things have their places; let each part of your business have its time.

4. *Resolution.*
Resolve to perform what you ought; perform without fail what you resolve.   30

5. *Frugality.*
Make no expense but to do good to others or yourself; *i.e.,* waste nothing.

6. *Industry.*
Lose no time; be always employ'd in something useful; cut off all unnecessary actions.

7. *Sincerity.*
Use no hurtful deceit; think innocently and justly, and, if you speak, speak accordingly.

8. Justice.
Wrong none by doing injuries, or omitting the benefits that are your duty.

9. Moderation.
Avoid extreams; forbear resenting injuries so much as you think they deserve.

10. Cleanliness.
Tolerate no uncleanliness in body, cloaths, or habitation.

11. Tranquillity.
Be not disturbed at trifles, or at accidents common or unavoidable.

12. Chastity.
10   Rarely use venery but for health or offspring, never to dulness, weakness, or the injury of your own or another's peace or reputation.

13. Humility.
Imitate Jesus and Socrates.

My intention being to acquire the *habitude* of all these virtues, I judg'd it would be well not to distract my attention by attempting the whole at once, but to fix it on one of them at a time; and, when I should be master of that, then to proceed to another, and so on, till I should have gone thro' the thirteen; and, as the previous acquisition of some might facilitate the acquisition of certain others, I arrang'd them with that view, as they stand above. Temperance first, as it tends to procure that
20   coolness and clearness of head, which is so necessary where constant vigilance was to be kept up, and guard maintained against the unremitting attraction of ancient habits, and the force of perpetual temptations. This being acquir'd and establish'd, Silence would be more easy; and my desire being to gain knowledge at the same time that I improv'd in virtue, and considering that in conversation it was obtain'd rather by the use of the ears than of the tongue, and therefore wishing to break a habit I was getting into of prattling, punning, and joking, which only made me acceptable to trifling company, I gave *Silence* the second place. This and the next, *Order,* I expected would allow me more time for attending to my project and my studies. *Resolution,* once become habitual, would keep me firm in my endeavors to
30   obtain all the subsequent virtues; *Frugality* and Industry freeing me from my remaining debt, and producing affluence and independence, would make more easy the practice of Sincerity and Justice, etc., etc. Conceiving then, that, agreeably to the advice of Pythagoras in his Golden Verses, daily examination would be necessary, I contrived the following method for conducting that examination.

---

33 **Pythagoras . . . Verses.** The Greek philosopher Pythagoras (fl. 54-512 B.C.) favored an ascetic discipline as a means of attaining spiritual perfection. A translation of the verses referred to by Franklin, showing remarkable similarity to the program here outlined, is given in Bigelow's *Complete Works,* I, 177-179. It seems probable that Franklin derived his Pythagorean ideas from Thomas Tryon, whose vegetarianism has been mentioned earlier

I made a little book, in which I allotted a page for each of the virtues. I rul'd each page with red ink, so as to have seven columns, one for each day of the week, marking each column with a letter for the day. I cross'd these columns with thirteen red lines, marking the beginning of each line with the first letter of one of the virtues, on which line, and in its proper column, I might mark, by a little black spot, every fault I found upon examination to have been committed respecting that virtue upon that day.

Form of the Pages

Temperance.							
Eat Not to Dulness; Drink Not to Elevation.							
	S.	M.	T.	W.	T.	F.	S.
T.							
S.	*	*		*		*	
O.	**	*	*		*	*	*
R.			*			*	
F.		*			*		
I.			*				
S.							
J.							
M.							
C.							
T.							
C.							
H.							

I determined to give a week's strict attention to each of the virtues successively. Thus, in the first week, my great guard was to avoid every the least offence against *Temperance,* leaving the other virtues to their ordinary chance, only marking every evening the faults of the day. Thus, if in the first week I could keep my first line, marked T, clear of spots, I suppos'd the habit of that virtue so much strengthen'd, and its opposite weaken'd, that I might venture extending my attention to include the next, and for the following week keep both lines clear of spots. Proceeding thus to the last, I could go thro' a course compleat in thirteen weeks, and four courses in a year. And like him who, having a garden to weed, does not attempt to eradicate all the bad herbs at once, which would exceed his reach and his strength, but works on one of the beds at a time, and, having accomplish'd the first, proceeds to a second, so I should have, I hoped, the encouraging pleasure of seeing on my pages the progress I made in virtue, by clearing successively my lines of their spots, till

1 **a little book,** which bears, according to William Temple Franklin, the date July 1, 1733

in the end, by a number of courses, I should be happy in viewing a clean book, after a thirteen weeks' daily examination.

This my little book had for its motto these lines from Addison's *Cato:*

> Here will I hold. If there's a power above us
> (And that there is, all nature cries aloud
> Thro' all her works), He must delight in virtue;
> And that which He delights in must be happy.

Another from Cicero,

O vitæ Philosophia dux! O virtutum indagatrix expultrixque vitiorum! Unus
10 dies, bene et ex præceptis tuis actus, peccanti immortalitati est anteponendus.

Another from the Proverbs of Solomon, speaking of wisdom or virtue:

Length of days is in her right hand, and in her left hand riches and honour. Her ways are ways of pleasantness, and all her paths are peace. — iii. 16, 17.

And conceiving God to be the fountain of wisdom, I thought it right and necessary to solicit his assistance for obtaining it; to this end I formed the following little prayer, which was prefix'd to my tables of examination, for daily use.

O powerful Goodness! bountiful Father! merciful Guide! Increase in me that wisdom which discovers my truest interest. Strengthen my resolutions to perform what that wisdom dictates. Accept my kind offices to thy other children as the only return in my power for thy contin-
20 *ual favours to me.*

I used also sometimes a little prayer which I took from Thomson's Poems, viz:

> Father of light and life, thou Good Supreme!
> O teach me what is good; teach me Thyself!
> Save me from folly, vanity, and vice,
> From every low pursuit; and fill my soul
> With knowledge, conscious peace, and virtue pure;
> Sacred, substantial, never-fading bliss!

---

3 **Addison's Cato,** a tragedy produced and published in 1713. The lines quoted (except for the "us" at the end of the first line) appear in a soliloquy by Cato on Plato's views of the immortality of the soul, at the beginning of Act V   8 **Cicero,** Marcus Tullius Cicero (106-43 B.C.), Roman orator and philosopher. The sentences, with a few lines intervening, are in Bk. V, Chap. II of the *Tusculan Disputations,* and may be translated as follows: "O philosophy, thou guide of life, O thou explorer of virtue and expeller of vice. One day well spent and in accordance with thy lessons is to be preferred to an eternity of errors"   21 **Thomson's Poems.** The lines are from *Winter* (1726), ll. 217-222, by the English poet James Thomson (1700-1748)

The precept of *Order* requiring that *every part of my business should have its allotted time,* one page in my little book contain'd the following scheme of employment for the twenty-four hours of a natural day.

THE MORNING. *Question.* What good shall I do this day?	5 6 7	Rise, wash and address *Powerful Goodness!* Contrive day's business, and take the resolution of the day; prosecute the present study, and breakfast.
	8 9 10 11	Work.
NOON.	12 1	Read, or overlook my accounts, and dine.
	2 3 4 5	Work.
EVENING. *Question.* What good have I done to-day?	6 7 8 9	Put things in their places. Supper. Music or diversion, or conversation. Examination of the day.
NIGHT.	10 11 12 1 2 3 4	Sleep.

I enter'd upon the execution of this plan for self-examination, and continu'd it with occasional intermissions for some time. I was surpris'd to find myself so much fuller of faults than I had imagined; but I had the satisfaction of seeing them diminish. To avoid the trouble of renewing now and then my little book, which, by scraping out the marks on the paper of old faults to make room for new ones in a new course, became full of holes, I transferr'd my tables and precepts to the ivory leaves of a memorandum book, on which the lines were drawn with red ink, that made a durable stain, and on those lines I mark'd my faults with a black-lead pencil, which marks I could easily wipe out with a wet sponge. After a while I went thro' one course only in a year, and afterward only one in several years, till at length I omitted them entirely, being employ'd in voyages and business abroad, with a multiplicity of affairs that interfered; but I always carried my little book with me.

My scheme of ORDER gave me the most trouble; and I found that, tho' it might be practicable where a man's business was such as to leave him the disposition of his time, that of a journeyman printer, for instance, it was not possible to be exactly observed by a master who must mix with the world and often receive people of business at their own hours. *Order,* too, with regard to places for things, papers, etc., I found extreamly difficult to acquire. I had not been early accustomed to it, and, having an exceeding good memory, I was not so sensible of the inconvenience 10 attending want of method. This article, therefore, cost me so much painful attention, and my faults in it vexed me so much, and I made so little progress in amendment, and had such frequent relapses, that I was almost ready to give up the attempt, and content myself with a faulty character in that respect, like the man who, in buying an ax of a smith, my neighbour, desired to have the whole of its surface as bright as the edge. The smith consented to grind it bright for him if he would turn the wheel; he turn'd, while the smith press'd the broad face of the ax hard and heavily on the stone, which made the turning of it very fatiguing. The man came every now and then from the wheel to see how the work went on, and at length would take his ax as it was, without farther grinding. "No," said the smith, 20 "turn on, turn on; we shall have it bright by-and-by; as yet, it is only speckled." "Yes," says the man, *"but I think I like a speckled ax best."* And I believe this may have been the case with many who, having, for want of some such means as I employ'd, found the difficulty of obtaining good and breaking bad habits in other points of vice and virtue, have given up the struggle, and concluded that *"a speckled ax was best";* for something, that pretended to be reason, was every now and then suggesting to me that such extream nicety as I exacted of myself might be a kind of foppery in morals, which, if it were known, would make me ridiculous; that a perfect character might be attended with the inconvenience of being envied and hated; and that a benevolent man should allow a few faults in himself, to keep his 30 friends in countenance.

In truth, I found myself incorrigible with respect to Order; and now I am grown old, and my memory bad, I feel very sensibly the want of it. But, on the whole, tho' I never arrived at the perfection I had been so ambitious of obtaining, but fell far short of it, yet I was, by the endeavour, a better and a happier man than I otherwise should have been if I had not attempted it; as those who aim at perfect writing by imitating the engraved copies, tho' they never reach the wish'd-for excellence of those copies, their hand is mended by the endeavour, and is tolerable while it continues fair and legible.

It may be well my posterity should be informed that to this little artifice, with 40 the blessing of God, their ancestor ow'd the constant felicity of his life, down to his 79th year, in which this is written. What reverses may attend the remainder is in the hand of Providence; but, if they arrive, the reflection on past happiness enjoy'd ought to help his bearing them with more resignation. To Temperance he ascribes his long-continued health, and what is still left to him of a good constitution; to

Industry and Frugality, the early easiness of his circumstances and acquisition of his fortune, with all that knowledge that enabled him to be a useful citizen, and obtained for him some degree of reputation among the learned; to Sincerity and Justice, the confidence of his country, and the honorable employs it conferred upon him; and to the joint influence of the whole mass of the virtues, even in the imperfect state he was able to acquire them, all that evenness of temper, and that cheerfulness in conversation, which makes his company still sought for, and agreeable even to his younger acquaintances. I hope, therefore, that some of my descendants may follow the example and reap the benefit. . . .

In 1746, being at Boston I met there with a Dr. Spence who was lately arrived 10 from Scotland, and show'd me some electric experiments. They were imperfectly perform'd as he was not very expert but, being on a subject quite new to me, they equally surpris'd and pleased me. Soon after my return to Philadelphia, our library company receiv'd from Mr. P. Collinson, Fellow of the Royal Society of London, a present of a glass tube with some account of the use of it in making such experiments. I eagerly seized the opportunity of repeating what I had seen at Boston; and, by much practice, acquir'd great readiness in performing those, also, which we had an account of from England, adding a number of new ones. I say much practice, for my house was continually full, for some time, with people who came to see these new wonders. 20

To divide a little this incumbrance among my friends, I caused a number of similar tubes to be blown at our glass-house, with which they furnished themselves, so that we had at length several performers. Among these, the principal was Mr. Kinnersley, an ingenious neighbor, who, being out of business, I encouraged to undertake showing the experiments for money, and drew up for him two lectures, in which the experiments were rang'd in such order, and accompanied with such explanations in such method, as that the foregoing should assist in comprehending the following. He procur'd an elegant apparatus for the purpose, in which all the little machines that I had roughly made for myself were nicely form'd by instrument-makers. His lectures were well attended, and gave great satisfaction, and after some 30 time he went thro' the colonies exhibiting them in every capital town and pick'd up some money. In the West India Islands, indeed, it was with difficulty the experiments could be made, from the general moisture of the air.

9 benefit. Here ends the selection from the portion of the *Autobiography* written at Passy in 1784. A few paragraphs, relating chiefly to a proposed book on the art of virtue, which Franklin never got around to writing, have been omitted   10 Dr. Spence has been identified by J. A. Leo Lerney (*Maryland Historical Magazine*, LIX, 1964) as the Rev. Archibald Spencer, who gave courses in experimental philosophy in Boston in 1743 and in Philadelphia in 1744. Franklin erred both in the date of his first acquaintance with electrical experiments and in the name of the man who first displayed them   14 Mr. P. Collinson, Peter Collinson (1694-1768), a Quaker merchant of London whose large trade with America enabled him to gratify a fondness for gardening and natural history. He formed intimate connections not only with Franklin but also with John Bartram, the father of William Bartram (see p. 359), and throughout his life imported exotic plants for his garden at Mill Hill, near London   23 Mr. Kinnersley, Ebenezer Kinnersley (1711-1778), one of Franklin's closest associates and himself a considerable contributor to electrical science. After 1751 he lectured, on a plan drawn up by Franklin, throughout the colonies and even in the West Indies

Oblig'd as we were to Mr. Collinson for his present of the tube, etc., I thought it right he should be inform'd of our success in using it, and wrote him several letters containing accounts of our experiments. He got them read in the Royal Society where they were not at first thought worth so much notice as to be printed in their Transactions. One paper, which I wrote for Mr. Kinnersley, on the sameness of lightning with electricity, I sent to Dr. Mitchel, an acquaintance of mine and one of the members also of that society, who wrote me word that it had been read, but was laughed at by the connoisseurs. The papers, however, being shown to Dr. Fothergill, he thought they were of too much value to be stifled, and advis'd
10 the printing of them. Mr. Collinson then gave them to Cave for publication in his *Gentleman's Magazine;* but he chose to print them separately in a pamphlet and Dr. Fothergill wrote the preface. Cave, it seems, judged rightly for his profit, for by the additions that arrived afterward, they swell'd to a quarto volume which has had five editions, and cost him nothing for copy-money.

It was, however, some time before those papers were much taken notice of in England. A copy of them happening to fall into the hands of the Count de Buffon, a philosopher deservedly of great reputation in France, and, indeed, all over Europe, he prevailed with M. Dalibard to translate them into French, and they were printed at Paris. The publication offended the Abbé Nollet, preceptor in Natural Philosophy
20 to the royal family, and an able experimenter, who had form'd and publish'd a theory of electricity, which then had the general vogue. He could not at first believe that such a work came from America, and said it must have been fabricated by his enemies at Paris, to decry his system. Afterwards, having been assur'd that there really existed such a person as Franklin at Philadelphia, which he had doubted, he wrote and published a volume of "Letters," chiefly address'd to me, defending his theory, and denying the verity of my experiments, and of the positions deduc'd from them.

I once purpos'd answering the abbé, and actually began the answer; but, on consideration that my writings contain'd a description of experiments which any one
30 might repeat and verify, and if not to be verifi'd, could not be defended; or of observations offer'd as conjectures, and not delivered dogmatically, therefore not laying me under any obligation to defend them; and reflecting that a dispute between two persons, writing in different languages, might be lengthened greatly by mistranslations and thence misconceptions of one another's meaning, much of one of

---

6 **Dr. Mitchel,** John Mitchell (d. 1768), an English physician and scientist who lived from about 1721 to 1747 or 1748 at Urbanna, Virginia. He is most famous for his map of North America, printed in 1755 9 **Dr. Fothergill,** John Fothergill (1712-1780), English Quaker physician. He had many close connections with the American colonies and subsidized William Bartram's expedition into the Floridas and Georgia in 1773-1777 (see pp. 360-371) 10 **Cave,** Edward Cave (1691-1754), English printer and founder of the *Gentleman's Magazine* (1731), probably the most widely circulated periodical of the eighteenth century 16 **Count de Buffon,** George Louis Leclerc, Comte de Buffon (1707-1785), one of the great natural philosophers of the age 18 **M. Dalibard,** Jean François Dalibard (1703-1799). His translation was printed in 1752; on May 10 of the same year he successfully carried out the experiment suggested by Franklin of drawing lightning from the clouds 19 **Abbé Nollet,** Jean Antoine Nollet (1700-1770), the chief French opponent to Franklin's theories. He appears to have been offended because Franklin ignored his earlier work in electricity

the abbé's letters being founded on an error in the translation, I concluded to let my papers shift for themselves, believing it was better to spend what time I could spare from public business in making new experiments, than in disputing about those already made. I therefore never answered M. Nollet, and the event gave me no cause to repent my silence; for my friend M. le Roy, of the Royal Academy of Sciences, took up my cause and refuted him; my book was translated into the Italian, German, and Latin languages; and the doctrine it contain'd was by degrees universally adopted by the philosophers of Europe in preference to that of the abbé; so that he lived to see himself the last of his sect, except Monsieur B————, of Paris, his *élève* and immediate disciple.   10

What gave my book the more sudden and general celebrity, was the success of one of its proposed experiments, made by Messrs. Dalibard and Delor at Marly, for drawing lightning from the clouds. This engag'd the public attention every where. M. Delor, who had an apparatus for experimental philosophy, and lectur'd in that branch of science, undertook to repeat what he called the *Philadelphia Experiments;* and, after they were performed before the king and court, all the curious of Paris flocked to see them. I will not swell this narrative with an account of that capital experiment, nor of the infinite pleasure I receiv'd in the success of a similar one I made soon after with a kite at Philadelphia, as both are to be found in the histories of electricity.   20

Dr. Wright, an English physician, when at Paris, wrote to a friend, who was of the Royal Society, an account of the high esteem my experiments were in among the learned abroad, and of their wonder that my writings had been so little noticed in England. The Society, on this, resum'd the consideration of the letters that had been read to them, and the celebrated Dr. Watson drew up a summary account of them and of all I had afterwards sent to England on the subject, which he accompanied with some praise of the writer. This summary was then printed in their Transactions; and some members of the Society in London, particularly the very ingenious Mr. Canton, having verified the experiment of procuring lightning from the clouds by a pointed rod, and acquainting them with the success, they soon made 30 me more than amends for the slight with which they had before treated me. Without my having made any application for that honor, they chose me a member, and voted that I should be excus'd the customary payments, which would have amounted to twenty-five guineas; and ever since have given me their Transactions gratis. They

---

5 **M. le Roy,** Jean Baptiste Le Roy (1719-1800), a French physician much interested in electricity   12
Delor. Of Delor, "master of experimental philosophy," little is known beyond the fact that he performed Franklin's experiments before the King and his courtiers and on May 18, 1752, repeated the experiment of drawing lightning from the clouds by using a ninety-foot iron rod   21 **Dr. Wright.** At this point Franklin's memory seems to have been badly in error. His writings were actually discussed before the Royal Society in June 1751 by Watson (see note below), some time before Franklin's book had reached France. The Dr. Wright referred to is possibly William Wright (1735-1819), later closely associated with Franklin's friends, Fothergill and Sir John Pringle (see p. 308)   25 **Dr. Watson,** Sir William Watson (1715-1787), who had begun to contribute papers on electricity to the Royal Society as early as 1745. His theories were very similar to Franklin's, although more vaguely expressed   29 **Mr. Canton,** John Canton (1718-1772), English schoolteacher and electrician, elected a Fellow of the Royal Society in 1749

also presented me with the gold medal of Sir Godfrey Copley for the year 1753, the delivery of which was accompanied by a very handsome speech of the president, Lord Macclesfield, wherein I was highly honoured.

1771-1788, 1868

1 **Sir Godfrey Copley** (d. 1709), left the Royal Society the sum of one hundred pounds, the income of which was expended after 1736 for the annual award of a gold medal to persons making notable contributions to natural knowledge   3 **Lord Macclesfield,** George Parker, second Earl of Macclesfield (1697-1764), astronomer and a president of the Royal Society. He was chiefly responsible for the English acceptance of the change of the calendar in 1752

The Way to Wealth

In 1757, on board ship en route to England, Franklin brought together into a single piece many of the aphorisms relating to industry, frugality, and prudence which had previously appeared in the pages of Poor Richard's Almanac. *Whether or not he had a file of the almanacs with him is uncertain; very possibly he had at hand a copy of* Gnomologia: Adagies and Proverbs; Wise Sentences and Witty Sayings, Ancient and Modern, Foreign and British *(London, 1732) by Thomas Fuller (1654-1734), a book which contains a great many of the sentences used by Franklin. In any case the compilation eventually proved to be one of Franklin's best-known works. As published in* Poor Richard Improved *for 1758 it had no title; it was reprinted in 1760 as* Father Abraham's Speech, *and in 1774 as* The Way to Wealth, *by which name it is now usually known. Thereafter it was published over and over again and translated into almost all of the modern languages; altogether nearly five hundred different editions are known. The explanation of such popularity lies partly in the age-old love for proverbs and partly in the dominance of the bourgeois philosophy of life during the nineteenth and twentieth centuries.*

The almanacs did not always contain such trustful worldly wisdom as appears here; Franklin had a streak of cynicism, and such adages as "Let thy maid-servant be faithful, strong, and homely," "Fish and visitors smell in three days," "An egg today is better than a hen tomorrow," and "He does not possess wealth, it possesses him" are not in quite the same spirit as those included here. It should be noted that Franklin did not claim to be original in his maxims (only one, "Three Removes is as bad as a Fire," is thought to have been completely his creation); he displayed admirable literary skill, however, in creating a character and background to make his piece more than a mere listing of wise sayings, and in polishing and humanizing the material he garnered from his predecessors. "The cat in gloves catches no mice" is, for example, a redaction of "A gloved cat was never a good mouser" (Scottish proverb) and "A muffled cat is no good mouser" (English).

Courteous Reader,

I have heard that nothing gives an Author so great Pleasure, as to find his Works respèctfully quoted by other learned Authors. This Pleasure I have seldom enjoyed; for tho' I have been, if I may say it without Vanity, an *eminent Author* of Almanacks annually now a full Quarter of a Century, my Brother Authors in the same Way,

Text: *Poor Richard Improved* for 1758   5 **Quarter . . . Century.** The first *Poor Richard* was compiled in 1732, for the year 1733

for what Reason I know not, have ever been very sparing in their Applauses; and no other Author has taken the least Notice of me, so that did not my Writings produce me some solid *Pudding,* the great Deficiency of *Praise* would have quite discouraged me.

I concluded at length, that the People were the best Judges of my Merit; for they buy my Works; and besides, in my Rambles, where I am not personally known, I have frequently heard one or other of my Adages repeated, with, *as Poor Richard says,* at the End on't; this gave me some Satisfaction, as it showed not only that my Instructions were regarded, but discovered likewise some Respect for my Authority; and I own, that to encourage the Practice of remembering and repeating those wise 10 Sentences, I have sometimes *quoted myself* with great Gravity.

Judge then how much I must have been gratified by an Incident I am going to relate to you. I stopt my Horse lately where a great Number of People were collected at a Vendue of Merchant Goods. The Hour of Sale not being come, they were conversing on the Badness of the Times, and one of the Company call'd to a plain clean old Man, with white Locks, *Pray, Father Abraham, what think you of the Times? Won't these heavy Taxes quite ruin the Country? How shall we ever be able to pay them? What would you advise us to?* — Father *Abraham* stood up, and reply'd, If you'd have my Advice, I'll give it you in short, for a *Word to the Wise is enough,* and *many Words won't fill a Bushel,* as *Poor Richard says.* They join'd in desiring him to speak his 20 Mind, and gathering round him, he proceeded as follows;

"Friends, says he, and Neighbours, the Taxes are indeed very heavy, and if those laid on by the Government were the only Ones we had to pay, we might more easily discharge them; but we have many others, and much more grievous to some of us. We are taxed twice as much by our *Idleness,* three times as much by our *Pride,* and four times as much by our *Folly,* and from these Taxes the Commissioners cannot ease or deliver us by allowing an Abatement. However let us hearken to good Advice, and something may be done for us; *God helps them that help themselves,* as *Poor Richard* says, in his Almanack of 1733.

It would be thought a hard Government that should tax its People one tenth Part 30 of their *Time,* to be employed in its Service. But *Idleness* taxes many of us much more, if we reckon all that is spent in absolute *Sloth,* or doing of nothing, with that which is spent in idle Employments or Amusements, that amount to nothing. *Sloth,* by bringing on Diseases, absolutely shortens Life. *Sloth, like Rust, consumes faster than Labour wears, while the used Key is always bright,* as *Poor Richard* says. But *dost thou love Life, then do not squander Time, for that's the Stuff Life is made of,* as *Poor Richard* says. — How much more than is necessary do we spend in Sleep! forgetting that *The sleeping Fox catches no Poultry,* and that *there will be sleeping enough in the Grave,* as *Poor Richard* says. If Time be of all Things the most precious, *wasting Time* must be, as *Poor Richard* says, *the greatest Prodigality,* since, as he elsewhere tells us, *Lost* 40 *Time is never found again;* and what we call *Time-enough, always proves little enough:*

---

3 **solid Pudding.** How much money Franklin made from *Poor Richard* is not known, but from the beginning his almanac was an enormous success, averaging perhaps ten thousand copies annually. It must have been one of his most reliable sources of income

Let us then up and be doing, and doing to the Purpose; so by Diligence shall we do more with less Perplexity. *Sloth makes all Things difficult, but Industry all easy,* as *Poor Richard* says; and *He that riseth late, must trot all Day, and shall scarce overtake his Business at Night.* While *Laziness travels so slowly, that Poverty soon overtakes him,* as we read in *Poor Richard,* who adds, *Drive thy Business, let not that drive thee;* and *Early to Bed, and early to rise, makes a Man healthy, wealthy and wise.*

So what signifies *wishing* and *hoping* for better Times. We may make these Times better if we bestir ourselves. *Industry need not wish,* as *Poor Richard* says, and *He that lives upon Hope will die fasting. There are no Gains, without Pains;* then *Help Hands,*
10 *for I have no Lands,* or if I have, they are smartly taxed. And, as *Poor Richard* likewise observes, *He that hath a Trade hath an Estate,* and *He that hath a Calling, hath an Office of Profit and Honour;* but then the *Trade* must be worked at, and the *Calling* well followed, or neither the *Estate,* nor the *Office,* will enable us to pay our Taxes. — If we are industrious we shall never starve; for, as *Poor Richard* says, *At the working Man's House* Hunger *looks in, but dares not enter.* Nor will the Bailiff or the Constable enter, for *Industry pays Debts, while Despair encreaseth them,* says *Poor Richard.* — What though you have found no Treasure, nor has any rich Relation left you a Legacy, *Diligence is the Mother of Good luck,* as *Poor Richard* says, *and God gives all Things to Industry.* Then *plough deep, while Sluggards sleep, and you shall have*
20 *Corn to sell and to keep,* says *Poor Dick.* Work while it is called To-day, for you know not how much you may be hindered To-morrow, which makes *Poor Richard* say, *One To-day is worth two To-morrows;* and farther, *Have you somewhat to do To-morrow, do it To-day.* If you were a Servant, would you not be ashamed that a good Master should catch you idle? Are you then your own Master, *be ashamed to catch yourself idle,* as *Poor Dick* says. When there is so much to be done for yourself, your Family, your Country, and your gracious King, be up by Peep of Day; *Let not the Sun look down and say, Inglorious here he lies.* Handle your Tools without Mittens; remember that *the Cat in Gloves catches no Mice,* as *Poor Richard* says. 'Tis true there is much to be done, and perhaps you are weak handed, but stick to it steadily, and you will see
30 great Effects, for *constant Dropping wears away Stones,* and by *Diligence and Patience the Mouse ate in two the Cable;* and *little Strokes fell great Oaks,* as *Poor Richard* says in his Almanack, the Year I cannot just now remember.

Methinks I hear some of you say, *Must a Man afford himself no Leisure?* — I will tell thee, my Friend, what *Poor Richard* says, *Employ thy Time well if thou meanest to gain Leisure;* and *since thou art not sure of a Minute, throw not away an Hour.* Leisure, is Time for doing something useful; this Leisure the diligent Man will obtain, but the lazy Man never; so that, as *Poor Richard* says, a *Life of Leisure and a Life of Laziness are two Things.* Do you imagine that Sloth will afford you more Comfort than Labour? No, for as *Poor Richard* says, *Trouble springs from Idleness, and grievous Toil*
40 *from needless Ease. Many without Labour, would live by their* WITS *only, but they break for want of Stock.* Whereas Industry gives Comfort, and Plenty, and Respect: *Fly Pleasures, and they'll follow you. The diligent Spinner has a large Shift;* and *now I have a Sheep and a Cow, every Body bids me Good morrow;* all which is well said by *Poor Richard.*

But with our Industry, we must likewise be *steady, settled* and *careful,* and oversee
our own Affairs *with our own Eyes,* and not trust too much to others; for, as *Poor
Richard* says,

> *I never saw an oft removed Tree,*
> *Nor yet an oft removed Family,*
> *That throve so well as those that settled be.*

And again, *Three Removes is as bad as a Fire;* and again, *Keep thy Shop, and thy Shop
will keep thee;* and again, *If you would have your Business done, go; If not, send.* And again,

> *He that by the Plough would thrive,*
> *Himself must either hold or drive.*   10

And again, *The Eye of a Master will do more Work than both his Hands;* and again,
Want of Care does us more Damage than Want of Knowledge; and again, *Not to oversee
Workmen, is to leave them your Purse open.* Trusting too much to others Care is the
Ruin of many; for, as the *Almanack* says, *In the Affairs of this World, Men are saved,
not by Faith, but by the Want of it;* but a Man's own Care is profitable; for, saith
Poor Dick, Learning is to the Studious, and *Riches to the Careful,* as well as *Power to the
Bold,* and *Heaven to the Virtuous.* And farther, *If you would have a faithful Servant,
and one that you like, serve yourself.* And again, he adviseth to Circumspection and
Care, even in the smallest Matters, because sometimes *a little Neglect may breed great
Mischief;* adding, *For want of a Nail the Shoe was lost; for want of a Shoe the Horse* 20
was lost; and for want of a Horse the Rider was lost, being overtaken and slain by the
Enemy, all for want of Care about a Horse shoe Nail.

So much for Industry, my Friends, and Attention to one's own Business; but to
these we must add *Frugality,* if we would make our *Industry* more certainly successful. A Man may, if he knows not how to save as he gets, *keep his Nose all his Life
to the Grindstone,* and die not worth a *Groat* at last. *A fat Kitchen makes a lean Will,*
as *Poor Richard* says; and,

> *Many Estates are spent in the Getting,*
> *Since Women for Tea forsook Spinning and Knitting,*
> *And Men for Punch forsook Hewing and Splitting.*   30

If you would be wealthy, says he, in another Almanack, *think of Saving as well as of
Getting: The* Indies *have not made* Spain *rich, because her* Outgoes *are greater than her*
Incomes. Away then with your expensive Follies, and you will not have so much
Cause to complain of hard Times, heavy Taxes, and chargeable Families; for, as *Poor
Dick* says,

> *Women and Wine, Game and Deceit,*
> *Make the Wealth small, and the Wants great.*

And farther, *What maintains one Vice, would bring up two Children.* You may think perhaps, That a *little* Tea, or a *little* Punch now and then, Diet a *little* more costly, Clothes a *little* finer, and a *little* Entertainment now and then, can be no *great* Matter; but remember what *Poor Richard* says, *Many* a Little *makes a Mickle;* and farther, *Beware* of little *Expences; a small Leak will sink a great Ship;* and again, *Who Dainties love, shall Beggars prove;* and moreover, *Fools make Feasts, and wise Men eat them.*

Here you are all got together at this Vendue of *Fineries* and *Knicknacks.* You call them *Goods,* but if you do not take Care, they will prove *Evils* to some of you. You expect they will be sold *cheap,* and perhaps they may for less than they cost; but if
10 you have no Occasion for them, they must be *dear* to you. Remember what *Poor Richard* says, *Buy what thou hast no Need of, and ere long thou shalt sell thy Necessaries.* And again, *At a great Pennyworth pause a while:* He means, that perhaps the Cheapness is *apparent* only, and not *real;* or the Bargain, by straitning thee in thy Business, may do thee more Harm than Good. For in another Place he says, *Many have been ruined by buying good Pennyworths.* Again, *Poor Richard* says, *'Tis foolish to lay out Money in a Purchase of Repentance;* and yet this Folly is practised every Day at Vendues, for want of minding the Almanack. *Wise Men,* as *Poor Dick* says, *learn by others Harms, Fools scarcely by their own;* but *Felix quem faciunt aliena Pericula cautum.* Many a one, for the Sake of Finery on the Back, have gone with a hungry Belly, and half starved their
20 Families; *Silks and Sattins, Scarlet and Velvets,* as *Poor Richard* says, *put out the Kitchen Fire.* These are not the *Necessaries* of Life; they can scarcely be called the *Conveniences,* and yet only because they look pretty, how many *want* to *have* them. The *artificial* Wants of Mankind thus become more numerous than the *natural;* and, as *Poor Dick* says, *For one* poor *Person, there are an hundred* indigent. By these, and other Extravagancies, the Genteel are reduced to Poverty, and forced to borrow of those whom they formerly despised, but who through *Industry* and *Frugality* have maintained their Standing; in which Case it appears plainly, that a *Ploughman on his Legs is higher than a Gentleman on his Knees,* as *Poor Richard* says. Perhaps they have had a small Estate left them which they knew not the Getting of; they think *'tis Day, and will*
30 *never be Night;* that a little to be spent out of *so much,* is not worth minding; *(a Child and a Fool, as Poor Richard says, imagine* Twenty Shillings *and Twenty Years can never be spent)* but, *always taking out of, the Meal-tub, and never putting in, soon comes to the Bottom;* then, as *Poor Dick* says, *When the Well's dry, they know the Worth of Water.* But this they might have known before, if they had taken his Advice; *If you would know the Value of Money, go and try to borrow some;* for, *he that goes a borrowing goes a sorrowing;* and indeed so does he that lends to such People, when he goes *to get it in again.* — *Poor Dick* farther advises, and says,

> *Fond* Pride of Dress *is sure a very Curse;*
> *E'er* Fancy *you consult, consult your Purse.*

40 And again, *Pride is as loud a Beggar as Want, and a great deal more saucy.* When you have bought one fine Thing you must buy ten more, that your Appearance may be

---

18 **Felix . . . cautum.** Fortunate is he whom the mistakes of others make wary

all of a Piece; but *Poor Dick* says, *'Tis easier to* suppress *the first Desire, than to* satisfy *all that follow it.* And 'tis as truly Folly for the Poor to ape the Rich, as for the Frog to swell, in order to equal the Ox.

> *Great Estates may venture more,*
> *But little Boats should keep near Shore.*

'Tis however a Folly soon punished; for *Pride that dines on Vanity sups on Contempt,* as *Poor Richard* says. And in another Place, *Pride breakfasted with Plenty, dined with Poverty, and supped with Infamy.* And after all, of what Use is this *Pride of Appearance,* for which so much is risked, so much is suffered? It cannot promote Health, or ease Pain; it makes no Increase of Merit in the Person, it creates Envy, it has- 10
tens Misfortune.

> *What is a Butterfly? At best*
> *He's but a Caterpillar drest.*
> *The gaudy Fop's his Picture just,*

as *Poor Richard* says.

But what Madness must it be to *run in Debt* for these Superfluities! We are offered, by the Terms of this Vendue, *Six Months Credit;* and that perhaps has induced some of us to attend it, because we cannot spare the ready Money, and hope now to be fine without it. But, ah, think what you do when you run in Debt; *You give to another, Power over your Liberty.* If you cannot pay at the Time, you will be ashamed 20
to see your Creditor; you will be in Fear when you speak to him; you will make poor pitiful sneaking Excuses, and by Degrees come to lose your Veracity, and sink into base downright lying; for, as *Poor Richard* says, *The second Vice is Lying, the first is running in Debt.* And again, to the same Purpose, *Lying rides upon Debt's Back.* Whereas a freeborn *Englishman* ought not to be ashamed or afraid to see or speak to any Man living. But Poverty often deprives a Man of all Spirit and Virtue: *'Tis hard for an empty Bag to stand upright,* as *Poor Richard* truly says. What would you think of that Prince, or that Government, who should issue an Edict forbidding you to dress like a Gentleman or a Gentlewoman, on Pain of Imprisonment or Servitude? Would you not say, that you are free, have a Right to dress as you please, 30
and that such an Edict would be a Breach of your Privileges, and such a Government tyrannical? And yet you are about to put yourself under that Tyranny when you run in Debt for such Dress! Your Creditor has Authority at his Pleasure to deprive you of your Liberty, by confining you in Gaol for Life, or to sell you for a Servant, if you should not be able to pay him! When you have got your Bargain, you may, perhaps, think little of Payment; but *Creditors, Poor Richard* tells us, *have better Memories than Debtors;* and in another Place says, *Creditors are a superstitious Sect, great Observers of set Days and Times.* The Day comes round before you are aware, and the Demand is made before you are prepared to satisfy it. Or if you bear your Debt in Mind, the Term which at first seemed so long, will, as it lessens, appear 40

extreamly short. *Time* will seem to have added Wings to his Heels as well as Shoulders. *Those have a short Lent,* saith *Poor Richard, who owe Money to be paid at Easter.* Then since, as he says, *The Borrower is a Slave to the Lender, and the Debtor to the Creditor,* disdain the Chain, preserve your Freedom; and maintain your Independency: Be *industrious* and *free;* be *frugal* and *free.* At present, perhaps, you may think yourself in thriving Circumstances, and that you can bear a little Extravagance without Injury; but,

> *For Age and Want, save while you may;*
> *No Morning Sun lasts a whole Day,*

¹⁰ as *Poor Richard* says — Gain may be temporary and uncertain, but ever while you live, Expence is constant and certain; and *'tis easier to build two Chimnies than to keep one in Fuel,* as *Poor Richard* says. So *rather go to Bed supperless than rise in Debt.*

> *Get what you can, and what you get hold;*
> *'Tis the Stone that will turn all your Lead into Gold,*

as *Poor Richard* says. And when you have got the Philosopher's Stone, sure you will no longer complain of bad Times, or the Difficulty of paying Taxes.

This Doctrine, my Friends, is *Reason* and *Wisdom;* but after all, do not depend too much upon your own *Industry,* and *Frugality,* and *Prudence,* though excellent Things, for they may all be blasted without the Blessing of Heaven; and therefore ²⁰ ask that Blessing humbly, and be not uncharitable to those that at present seem to want it, but comfort and help them. Remember *Job* suffered, and was afterwards prosperous.

And now to conclude, *Experience keeps a dear School, but Fools will learn in no other, and scarce in that;* for it is true, *we may give Advice, but we cannot give Conduct,* as *Poor Richard* says: However, remember this, *They that won't be counselled, can't be helped,* as *Poor Richard* says: And farther, That *if you will not hear Reason, she'll surely rap your Knuckles.*

Thus the old Gentleman ended his Harangue. The People heard it, and approved the Doctrine and immediately practised the contrary, just as if it had been a com-³⁰ mon Sermon; for the Vendue opened, and they began to buy extravagantly, notwithstanding all his Cautions, and their own Fear of Taxes. — I found the good Man had thoroughly studied my Almanacks, and digested all I had dropt on those Topicks during the Course of Five-and-twenty Years. The frequent Mention he made of me must have tired any one else, but my Vanity was wonderfully delighted with it, though I was conscious that not a tenth Part of the Wisdom was my own which he ascribed to me, but rather the *Gleanings* I had made of the Sense of all Ages and Nations. However, I resolved to be the better for the Echo of it; and though I had

---

36 **The Gleanings . . . Nations.** Not all of Franklin's adages can be traced to particular sources, but examination of earlier collections of proverbs will disclose most of them in some form similar to that he used

at first determined to buy Stuff for a new Coat, I went away resolved to wear my
old One a little longer. *Reader,* if thou wilt do the same, thy Profit will be as great
as mine.

> *I am, as ever,*
> *Thine to serve thee,*
>
> RICHARD SAUNDERS.

July 7, 1757

                                                                            1757, 1758

---

6 **Richard Saunders,** the fictitious compiler of *Poor Richard*

Letter to Sir John Pringle

*It is difficult to represent Franklin's scientific writing, particularly that which deals with
electricity, in small space. The following letter, however, illustrates both the clarity of his
explanatory style — a factor which had a great deal to do with the wide acceptance of his
theories and suggestions — and his talent for devising simple apparatus for the experimental
investigation of his hypotheses. His thinking in the field of hydrodynamics has been amply
justified by later expenditures to provide experimental tanks for the study of naval architecture and, although he did not foresee them, wind tunnels for the investigation of aerodynamics.
Sir John Pringle (1707-1782) was a Scottish physician and professor who served as president of the Royal Society of London from 1772 until 1778. He and Franklin traveled together on the continent in the summer of 1766. This letter was first printed in the 1769
edition of* Experiments & Observations on Electricity.

                                                       Craven Street, 10 May, 1768
    Sir: — You may remember that when we were travelling together in Holland,
you remarked that the *trackschuit* in one of the stages went slower than usual, and
inquired of the boatman what might be the reason; who answered that it had been
a dry season and the water in the canal was low. On being again asked if it was so
low that the boat touched the muddy bottom, he said no, not so low as that, but
so low as to make it harder for the horse to draw the boat. We neither of us at first
could conceive that if there was enough water for the boat to swim clear of the bottom, its being deeper would make any difference. But, as the man affirmed it seriously as a thing well known among them, and as the punctuality required in their 10
stages was likely to make such difference, if any there were, more readily observed
by them than by other watermen who did not pass so regularly and constantly backwards and forwards in the same track, I began to apprehend there might be something in it, and attempted to account for it from this consideration, that the boat,
in proceeding along the canal, must, in every boat's length of her course, move out
of her way a body of water equal in bulk to the room her bottom took up in the

---

Text: Bigelow, *Complete Works,* IV, 159-162   3 **trackshuit,** *trek-schuit,* the Dutch word for towboat water; that the water so moved must pass on each side of her and under her bottom to get behind her; that if the passage under her bottom was straitened by the shallows, more of that water must pass by her sides, and with a swifter motion, which would retard her, as moving the contrary way; or that the water becoming lower behind the boat than before, she was pressed back by the weight of its difference in height, and her motion retarded by having that weight constantly to overcome. But as it is often lost time to attempt accounting for uncerain facts, I determined to make an experiment of this when I should have convenient time and opportunity.

10   After our return to England, as often as I happened to be on the Thames, I enquired of our watermen whether they were sensible of any difference in rowing over shallow or deep water. I found them all agreeing in the fact that there was a very great difference, but they differed widely in expressing the quantity of the difference; some supposing it was equal to a mile in six, others to a mile in three, &c. As I did not recollect to have met with any mention of this matter in our philosophical books, and conceiving that if the difference should really be great it might be an object of consideration in the many projects now on foot for digging new navigable canals in this island, I lately put my design of making the experiment in execution, in the following manner.

20   I provided a trough of planed boards fourteen feet long, six inches wide, and six inches deep, in the clear, filled with water within half an inch of the edge, to represent a canal. I had a loose board of nearly the same length and breadth, that, being put into the water, might be sunk to any depth, and fixed by little wedges where I would choose to have it stay, in order to make different depths of water, leaving the surface at the same height with regard to the sides of the trough. I had a little boat in form of a lighter or boat of burthen, six inches long, two inches and a quarter wide, and one inch and a quarter deep. When swimming it drew one inch water. To give motion to the boat I fixed one end of a long silk thread to its bow, just even with the water's edge, the other end passed over a well-made brass pulley of

30   about an inch diameter, turning freely on a small axis; and a shilling was the weight. Then placing the boat at one end of the trough, the weight would draw it through the water to the other.

Not having a watch that shows seconds, in order to measure the time taken up by the boat in passing from end to end, I counted as fast as I could count to ten repeatedly, keeping an account of the number of tens on my fingers. And, as much as possible to correct any little inequalities in my counting, I repeated the experiment a number of times at each depth of water, that I might take the medium. And the following are the results: [see following page]

I made many other experiments, but the above are those in which I was most

40   exact; and they serve sufficiently to show that the difference is considerable. Between the deepest and shallowest it appears to be somewhat more than one fifth. So that, supposing large canals and boats and depths of water to bear the same proportions, and that four men or horses would draw a boat in deep water four leagues in four

---

17 **many . . . foot.** Most of the canals of Great Britain were constructed between 1760 and 1840

	Water 1½ inches deep.	2 inches.	4½ inches.
1st exp.	- - - - 100	- - - - - 94	- - - - - 79
2	- - - - - 104	- - - - - 93	- - - - - 78
3	- - - - - 104	- - - - - 91	- - - - - 77
4	- - - - - 106	- - - - - 87	- - - - - 79
5	- - - - - 100	- - - - - 88	- - - - - 79
6	- - ' - - - 99	- - - - - 86	- - - - - 80
7	- - - - - 100	- - - - - 90	- - - - - 79
8	- - - - - 100	- - - - - 88	- - - - - 81
	813	717	632
	Medium 101	Medium 89	Medium 79

hours, it would require five to draw the same boat in the same time as far in shallow water; or four would require five hours.

Whether this difference is of consequence enough to justify a greater expense in deepening canals, is a matter of calculation, which our ingenious engineers in that way will readily determine. I am, &c.,

B. FRANKLIN
1768, 1769

Rules by Which a Great Empire May be Reduced to a Small One

A large part of Franklin's time in the decade after the repeal of the Stamp Act (1766) was devoted to pleading the cause of the American colonies before the British public and the Tory government. Had his policy of mediation been successful, some scheme of home rule, foreshadowing the later colonial policy of Great Britain, might have been worked out. Franklin was ordinarily good-natured about the situation, but sometimes he grew impatient with the measures of men who did not know or wish to know the true state of affairs in America. The latter mood lay behind the "Rules by Which a Great Empire May be Reduced to a Small One," perhaps the most vitriolic of his satires, first published in a London newspaper, the Public Advertiser, *in 1773. Using his favorite method of irony, he displayed the worst features of the British colonial administration, which was based on favoritism and selfishness rather than on any desire for efficiency and competence. On the surface it was pointed most directly, perhaps, at William Legge, second Earl of Dartmouth (1731-1801), who had become, in August 1772, secretary of state for the colonies and president of board of trade and foreign plantations. Actually, however, the acts and policies listed form a scathing review of the record of Dartmouth's predecessor in those posts, Wills Hill, first Earl of Hillsborough (1718-1793), who served as the cabinet member chiefly responsible for American affairs from 1768 until 1772. Some printings, in fact, bear the half-title "Presented to a late Minister, when he entered upon his Administration."*

An ancient Sage boasted, that, tho' he could not fiddle, he knew how to make a *great city* of a *little one*. The science that I, a modern simpleton, am about to communicate, is the very reverse.

I address myself to all ministers who have the management of extensive dominions, which from their very greatness are become troublesome to govern, because the multiplicity of their affairs leaves no time for *fiddling*.

I. In the first place, gentlemen, you are to consider, that a great empire, like a great cake, is most easily diminished at the edges. Turn your attention, therefore, first to your remotest provinces; that, as you get rid of them, the next may follow in order.

10 II. That the possibility of this separation may always exist, take special care the provinces are never incorporated with the mother country; that they do not enjoy the same common rights, the same privileges in commerce; and that they are governed by *severer* laws, all of *your enacting,* without allowing them any share in the choice of the legislators. By carefully making and preserving such distinctions, you will (to keep to my simile of the cake) act like a wise gingerbread baker, who, to facilitate a division, cuts his dough half through in those places, where, when baked, he would have it *broken to pieces.*

III. These remote provinces have perhaps been acquired, purchased, or conquered, at the *sole expence* of the settlers or their ancestors, without the aid of the mother 20 country. If this should happen to increase her *strength* by their growing numbers ready to join in her wars; her *commerce,* by their growing demand for her manufactures, or her *naval power* by greater employment for her ships and seamen, they may probably suppose some merit in this, and that it entitles them to some favour; you are therefore to *forget it all,* or resent it as if they had done you injury. If they happen to be zealous Whigs, friends of liberty, nurtured in revolution principles, *remember all that* to their prejudice, and resolve to punish it; for such principles, after a revolution is thoroughly established, are of *no more use;* they are even *odious* and *abominable.*

IV. However peaceably your colonies have submitted to your government, shewn 30 their affection to your interests, and patiently borne their grievances; you are to *suppose* them always inclined to revolt, and treat them accordingly. Quarter troops among them, who by their insolence may *provoke* the rising of mobs, and by their bullets and bayonets *suppress* them. By this means, like the husband who uses his wife ill *from suspicion,* you may in time convert your *suspicions* into *realities.*

V. Remote provinces must have *Governors,* and *Judges,* to represent the Royal Person, and execute every where the delegated parts of his office and authority. You ministers know, that much of the strength of government depends on the *opinion* of the people; and much of that opinion on the choice of rulers placed immediately over them. If you send them wise and good men for governors, who study the interest 40 of the colonists, and advance their prosperity, they will think their King wise and

Text: from the *Gentleman's Magazine,* September 1773   25 **revolution principles,** an allusion to the Whig leadership in the "Glorious Revolution" of 1688, an event which was the chief precedent for those who believed in the supremacy of the people over the crown   31 **Quarter troops,** as in Boston, where their presence, on the recommendation of Governor Bernard, led eventually to the Boston Massacre of 1770

good, and that he wishes the welfare of his subjects. If you send them learned and
upright men for Judges, they will think him a lover of justice. This may attach
your provinces more to his government. You are, therefore, to be careful who you
recommend for those offices. — If you can find prodigals who have ruined their fortunes, broken gamesters or stock jobbers, these may do well as *governors;* for they
will probably be rapacious, and provoke the people by their extortions. Wrangling
proctors and pettifogging lawyers, too, are not amiss; for they will be for ever disputing and quarrelling with their little parliaments. If withal they should be ignorant,
wrong headed, and insolent, so much the better. Attornies clerks and Newgate solicitors will do for *Chief-Justices,* especially if they hold their places *during your pleasure.* 10
And all will contribute to impress those ideas of your government that are proper
for a people *you would wish to renounce it.*

VI. To confirm these impressions, and strike them deeper, whenever the injured
come to the capital with complaints of mal-administration, oppression, or injustice,
punish such suitors with long delay, enormous expence, and a final judgment in
favour of the oppressor. This will have an admirable effect every way. The trouble
of future complaints will be prevented, and Governors and Judges will be encouraged to farther acts of oppression and injustice; and thence the people may become
more disaffected, *and at length desperate.*

VII. When such Governors have crammed their coffers, and made themselves so 20
odious to the people that they can no longer remain among them in safety to their
persons, recal and *reward* them with pensions. You may make them *Baronets,* too, if
that respectable order should not think fit to resent it. All will contribute to encourage new governors in the same practices, and make the supreme government
detestable.

VIII. If, when you are engaged in war, your colonies should vie in liberal aids of
men and money against the common enemy, upon your simple requisition, and give
far beyond their abilities, reflect, that a penny taken from them by your power is
more honourable to you than a pound presented by their benevolence. Despise
therefore their voluntary grants, and resolve to harrass them with novel taxes. They 30
will probably complain to your parliaments, that they are taxed by a body in which
they have no representative, and that this is contrary to common right. They will
petition for redress. Let the Parliaments flout their claims, reject their petitions, refuse
even to suffer the reading of them, and treat the petitioners with the utmost contempt. Nothing can have a better effect in producing the alienation proposed; for
though many can forgive injuries, *none ever forgave contempt.*

IX. In laying these taxes, never regard the heavy burthens those remote people
already undergo, in defending their own frontiers, supporting their own provincial
governments, making new roads, building bridges, churches, and other public
edifices, which in old countries have been done to your hands by your ancestors, 40
but which occasion constant calls and demands on the purses of a new people. Forget the *restraints* you lay on their trade for *your own* benefit, and the advantage a

---

22 **Baronets.** Governor Francis Bernard (1714-1779) was created baronet after his recall from Massachusetts   30 **novel taxes,** such as the Stamp Tax of 1765

monopoly of this trade gives your exacting merchants. Think nothing of the wealth those merchants and your manufacturers acquire by the colony commerce; their encreased ability thereby to pay taxes at home; their accumulating, in the price of their commodities, most of those taxes, and so levying them from their consuming customers; all this, and the employment and support of thousands of your poor by the colonists, you are *intirely to forget*. But remember to make your arbitrary tax more grievous to your provinces, by public declarations importing that your power of taxing them has *no limits;* so that when you take from them without their consent one shilling in the pound, you have a clear right to the other nineteen. This will
10 probably weaken every idea of *security in their property* and convince them, that, under such a government, *they have nothing they can call their own;* which can scarce fail of producing *the happiest consequences!*

X. Possibly, indeed, some of them might still comfort themselves, and say, 'Though we have no property, we have yet *something* left that is valuable; we have 'constitutional *liberty* both of person and of conscience. This King, these Lords, and 'these Commons, who, it seems, are too remote from us to know us, and feel for 'us, cannot take from us our *Habeas-Corpus* right, or our right of trial *by a Jury of 'our neighbours;* they cannot deprive us of the exercise of our religion, alter our eccle- 'siastical constitution, and compel us to be Papists, if they please, or Mahometans.'
20 To annihilate this comfort, begin by laws to perplex their commerce with infinite regulations impossible to be remembered and observed; ordain seizures of their property for every failure; take away the trial of such property by Jury, and give it to arbitrary Judges of your own appointing, and of the lowest characters in the country, whose salaries and emoluments are to arise out of the duties or condemnations, and whose appointments are *during pleasure*. Then let there be a formal declaration of both houses, that opposition to your edicts is *treason;* and that any person suspected of treason in the provinces may, according to some obsolete law, be seized and sent to the metropolis of the empire for trial; and pass an act that those there charged with certain other offences shall be sent away in chains from their friends
30 and country to be tried in the same manner for felony. Then erect a new Court of Inquisition among them, accompanied by an armed force, with instructions to transport all such suspected persons, to be ruined by the expence if they bring over evidences to prove their innocence, or be found guilty and hanged if they cannot afford it. And, lest the people should think you cannot possibly go any farther, pass another solemn declaratory act, that 'King, Lords, and Commons had, hath, and of right 'ought to have, full power and authority to make statutes of sufficient force and 'validity to bind the unrepresented provinces IN ALL CASES WHATSOEVER.' This will include *spiritual* with temporal; and, taken together, must operate wonderfully to your purpose, by convincing them, that they are at present under a power some-
40 thing like that spoken of in the scriptures, which cannot only *kill their bodies,* but *damn their souls* to all eternity, by compelling them, if it pleases, *to worship the Devil.*

---

35 **declaratory act,** the Declaratory Act of 1766, passed immediately before the repeal of the Stamp Act. It was the answer of Parliament to the colonists' argument that they were not, under their royal charters, subject to control by a body in which they had no representation

XI. To make your taxes more odious, and more likely to procure resistance, send from the capital a board of officers to superintend the collection, composed of the most *indiscreet, ill-bred,* and *insolent,* you can find. Let these have large salaries out of the extorted revenue, and live in open grating luxury upon the sweat and blood of the industrious, whom they are to worry continually with groundless and expensive prosecutions before the above-mentioned arbitrary revenue Judges, all *at the cost of the party prosecuted,* tho' acquitted, because *the King is to pay no costs.* — Let these men, *by your order,* be exempted from all the common taxes and burthens of the province, though they and their property are protected by its laws. If any revenue officers are ·suspected of the least tenderness for the people, discard them. If others are justly com- 10 plained of, protect and reward them. If any of the under officers behave so as to provoke the people to drub them, promote those to better offices: this will encourage others to procure for themselves such profitable drubbings, by multiplying and enlarging such provocations, and *all will work towards the end you aim at.*

XII. Another way to make your tax odious, is to misapply the produce of it. If it was originally appropriated for the *defence* of the provinces, the better support of government, and the administration of justice where it may be *necessary,* then apply none of it to that *defence,* but bestow it where it is *not necessary,* in augmented salaries or pensions to every governor who has distinguished himself by his enmity to the people, and by calumniating them to their sovereign. This will make them pay it 20 more unwillingly, and be more apt to quarrel with those that collect it, and those that imposed it, who will quarrel again with them, and all shall contribute to your *main purpose,* of making them *weary of your government.*

XIII. If the people of any province have been accustomed to support their own Governors and Judges to satisfaction, you are to apprehend that such Governors and Judges may be thereby influenced to treat the people kindly, and to do them justice. This is another reason for applying part of that revenue in larger salaries to such Governors and Judges, given, as their commissions are, *during your pleasure* only, forbidding them to take any salaries from their provinces; that thus the people may no longer hope any kindness from their Governors, or (in Crown cases) 30 any justice from their Judges. And as the money thus misapplied in one province is extorted from all, probably *all will resent the misapplication.*

XIV. If the parliaments of your provinces should dare to claim rights, or complain of your administration, order them to be harrassed with repeated *dissolutions.* If the same men are continually returned by new elections, adjourn their meetings to some country village where they cannot be accommodated, and there keep them *during pleasure;* for this, you know, is your PREROGATIVE; and an excellent one it is, as you may manage it, to promote discontents among the people, diminish their respect, and *increase their disaffection.*

XV. Convert the brave, honest officers of your navy into pimping tide-waiters 40 and colony officers of the customs. Let those who, in time of war, fought gallantly

---

34 **dissolutions,** such as those in Massachusetts. Franklin seems to have had in mind the refusal of the House of Representatives in 1768 to rescind the circular letter sent to other colonial assemblies, although Hillsborough ordered them to do so or face dissolution

in defence of the commerce of their countrymen, in peace be taught to prey upon it. Let them learn to be corrupted by great and real smugglers; but (to shew their diligence) scour with armed boats every bay, harbour, river, creek, cove, or nook, throughout the coast of your colonies; stop and detain every coaster, every wood-boat, every fisherman, tumble their cargoes, and even their ballast, inside out, and upside down; and, if a penn'orth of pins is found un-entered, let the whole be seized and confiscated. Thus shall the trade of your colonists suffer more from their friends in time of peace, than it did from their enemies in war. Then let these boats crews land upon every farm in their way, rob the orchards, steal the pigs and the poultry, and
10 insult the inhabitants. If the injured and exasperated farmers, unable to procure other justice, should attack the agressors, drub them and burn their boats; you are to call this *high treason* and *rebellion,* order fleets and armies into their country, and threaten to carry all the offenders three thousand miles to be hanged, drawn, and quartered. *O! this will work admirably!*

XVI. If you are told of discontents in your colonies, never believe that they are general, or that you have given occasion for them; therefore, do not think of apply-ing any remedy, or of changing any offensive measure. Redress no grievance, lest they should be encouraged to demand the redress of some other grievance. Grant no request that is just and reasonable, lest they should make another that is unrea-
20 sonable. Take all your informations of the state of the colonies from your Governors and officers in enmity with them. Encourage and reward these *leasing makers;* secrete their lying accusations, lest they should be confuted; but act upon them as the clearest evidence, and believe nothing you hear from the friends of the people: suppose all *their* complaints to be invented and promoted by a few factious demagogues, whom if you could catch and hang, all would be quiet. Catch and hang a few of them ac-cordingly; and the *blood of the Martyrs* shall *work miracles* in favour of your purpose.

XVII. If you see *rival nations* rejoicing at the prospect of your disunion with your provinces, and endeavouring to promote it; if they translate, publish and applaud all the complaints of your discontented colonists, at the same time privately stimu-
30 lating you to severer measures, let not that *alarm* or offend you. Why should it? since you all mean *the same thing.*

XVIII. If any colony should, at their own charge, erect a fortress to secure their port against the fleets of a foreign enemy, get your Governor to betray that fortress into your hands. Never think of paying what it cost the country, for that would *look,* at least, like some regard for justice; but turn it into a citadel to awe the in-habitants, and curb their commerce. If they should have lodged in such fortress the very arms they bought and used to aid you in your conquests, seize them all; it will provoke like *ingratitude* added to *robbery.* One admirable effect of these operations will be, to discourage every other colony from erecting such defences, and so your

---

11 **burn their boats,** an allusion to the burning of the schooner *Gaspée,* June 10, 1772, an act of violence which called forth the threats mentioned   21 **leasing makers,** in Scottish law, a liar, specifically one who lies and slanders to alienate a king from his subjects   32 **a fortress,** Castle William in Boston Harbor, delivered to the British by Governor Thomas Hutchinson (1711-1780) in September 1770

enemies may more easily invade them, to the great disgrace of your government, and, of course, *the furtherance of your project.*

XIX. Send armies into their country under pretence of protecting the inhabitants; but, instead of garrisoning the forts on their frontiers with those troops, to prevent incursions, demolish those forts, and order the troops into the heart of the country, that the savages may be encouraged to attack the frontiers, and that the troops may be protected by the inhabitants: this will seem to proceed from your ill-will or your ignorance, and contribute farther to produce and strengthen an opinion among them, *that you are no longer fit to govern them.*

XX. Lastly, invest the General of your army in the provinces with great and uncon- 10
stitutional powers, and free him from the controul of even your own Civil Governors. Let him have troops enow under his command, with all the fortresses in his possession; and who knows but (like some provincial Generals in the Roman empire, and encouraged by the universal discontent you have produced) he may take it into his head to set up for himself. If he should, and you have carefully practised these few *excellent rules* of mine, take my word for it, all the provinces will immediately join him, and you will that day (if you have not done it sooner) get rid of the trouble of governing them, and all the *plagues* attending their *commerce* and connection, from thenceforth and for ever.

                                                          Q. E. D.   20
                                                          1773, 1773

────────────

20 Q.E.D., abbreviation of *quod erat demonstrandum,* that which was to be demonstrated

An Edict by the King of Prussia

A second satire of 1773, also published in the Public Advertiser, *is usually known as "An Edict by the King of Prussia." By skillfully paraphrasing actual laws by which Parliament had regulated trade in Ireland and America, Franklin dramatized the illogicality of the ministry's position in a way remarkable for its brevity and its effectiveness. Of the reception of the piece he left an account in one of his letters: "What made it the more noticed here was, that people in reading it were, as the phrase is, taken in, till they had got half through it, and imagined it a real edict, to which mistake I suppose the King of Prussia's character must have contributed. I was down at Lord Le Despencer's, when the post brought that day's papers. Mr. Whitehead was there, too [Paul Whitehead, the author of "Manners"], who runs early through all the papers, and tells the company what he finds remarkable. He had them in another room, and we were chatting in the breakfast parlour, when he came running in to us, out of breath, with the paper in his hand. 'Here!' says he, 'here's news for ye! Here's the King of Prussia claiming a right to this kingdom!' All stared, and I as much as anybody; and he went on to read it. When he had read two or three paragraphs, a gentleman present said, 'Damn his impudence. I dare say we shall hear by next post, that he is upon his march with one hundred thousand men to back this.' Whitehead, who is very shrewd, soon after began to smoke it, and looking in my face, said, 'I'll be hanged if this is not some of your American jokes upon us.' The reading went on, and ended with abundance of laughing, and a general verdict that it was a fair hit."*

Dantzick, Sept. 5

We have long wondered here at the supineness of the English nation, under the Prussian impositions upon its trade entering our port. We did not, till lately, know the claims, ancient and modern, that hang over that nation, and therefore could not suspect that it might submit to those impositions from a sense of duty, or from principles of equity. The following Edict, just made publick, may, if serious, throw some light upon this matter:

"FREDERICK, by the grace of God, King of Prussia, &c. &c. &c. to all present and to come, Health. The peace now enjoyed throughout our dominions, having
10 afforded us leisure to apply ourselves to the regulation of commerce, the improvement of our finances, and at the same time the easing our domestic subjects in their taxes: For these causes and other good considerations us thereunto moving, we hereby make known, that, after having deliberated these affairs in our council, present our dear brothers, and other great officers of the state, members of the same, we, of our certain knowledge, full power, and authority royal, have made and issued this present Edict, viz.

"Whereas it is well known to all the world, that the first German settlements made in the island of Britain were by colonies of people, subjects to our renowned ducal ancestors, and drawn from their dominions, under the conduct of Hengist,
20 Horsa, Hella, Uffa, Cerdicus, Ida, and others; and that the said colonies have flourished under the protection of our august house, for ages past; have never been emancipated therefrom; and yet have hitherto yielded little profit to the same: And whereas we ourself have in the last war fought for and defended the said colonies, against the power of France, and thereby enabled them to make conquests from the said power in America; for which we have not yet received adequate compensation: And whereas it is just and expedient that a revenue should be raised from the said colonies in Britain, towards our indemnification; and that those who are descendants of our ancient subjects, and thence still owe us due obedience, should contribute to the replenishing of our royal coffers, as they must have done, had their ancestors
30 remained in the territories now to us appertaining: We do therefore hereby ordain and command, that, from and after the date of these presents, there shall be levied, and paid to our officers of the customs, on all goods, wares, and merchandizes, and on all grain and other produce of the earth, exported from the said island of Britain, and on all goods of whatever kind imported into the same, a duty of four and a half per cent. ad valorem, for the use of us and our successors. And that the said duty may more effectually be collected, we do hereby ordain, that all ships or vessels bound from Great-Britain to any other part of the world, or from any other part of the world to Great-Britain, shall in their respective voyages touch at our

---

Text: *Gentleman's Magazine* for October 1773   8 to all . . . come. "A tous presens et a venir ORIGI-
NAL." — Franklin   19 Hengist . . . Ida, all leaders of the Germanic invasion of Britain, traditionally
dated as beginning in 449 A.D. Franklin seems to have read the *History of England* (1754-1762) by his friend
David Hume (1711-1776), wherein these names are mentioned in almost the same order. Hella should be
Ælla, or Ella

port of Koningsberg, there to be unladen, searched, and charged with the said duties.

"And whereas there hath been from time to time discovered in the said island of Great-Britain, by our colonists there, many mines or beds of iron stone; and sundry subjects of our ancient dominion, skilful in converting the said stone into metal, have in times past transported themselves thither, carrying with them and communicating that art; and the inhabitants of the said island, presuming that they had a natural right to make the best use they could of the natural productions of their country, for their own benefit, have not only built furnaces for smelting the said stone into iron, but have erected plating forges, slitting mills, and steel furnaces, for the more convenient manufacturing of the same, thereby endangering a diminu- 10 tion of the said manufacture in our ancient dominion; we do therefore hereby farther ordain, that, from and after the date hereof, no mill or other engine for slitting or rolling of iron, or any plating forge to work with a tilt-hammer, or any furnace for making steel, shall be erected or continued in the said island of Great-Britain: And the Lord-Lieutenant of every county in the said island is hereby commanded, on information of any such erection within his county, to order and by force to cause the same to be abated and destroyed, as he shall answer the neglect thereof to us at his peril. But we are nevertheless graciously pleased to permit the inhabitants of the said island to transport their iron into Prussia, there to be manufactured, and to them returned, they paying our Prussian subjects for the workman- 20 ship, with all the costs of commission, freight, and risk, coming and returning, any thing herein contained to the contrary notwithstanding.

"We do not, however, think fit to extend this our indulgence to the article of wool; but meaning to encourage not only the manufacturing of woolen cloth, but also the raising of wool, in our ancient dominions; and to prevent both, as much as may be, in our said island, we do hereby absolutely forbid the transportation of wool from thence even to the mother-country, Prussia; And that those islanders may be farther and more effectually restrained in making any advantage of their own wool, in the way of manufacture, we command that none shall be carried out of one county into another, nor shall any worsted, bay, or woollen-yarn, cloth, says, bays, kerseys, 30 serges, frizes, druggets, cloth-serges, shalloons, or any other drapery stuffs, or woollen manufactures whatsoever, made up or mixed with wool in any of the said counties, be carried into any other county, or be water-borne even across the smallest river or creek, on penalty of forfeiture of the same, together with the boats, carriages, horses, &c. that shall be employed in removing them. Nevertheless, our loving subjects there are hereby permitted (if they think proper) to use all their wool as manure, for the improvement of their lands.

"And whereas the art and mystery of making hats hath arrived at great perfection

---

1 **Koningsberg,** Königsberg, in East Prussia, peculiarly suitable to Franklin's purpose because of its remoteness. The hit is at the laws requiring American ships trading abroad to touch at an English port   3 **iron stone.** A parliamentary act of 23 George III, c. 29 (1749-1750) prohibited ironworks in the American colonies   9 **slitting mills,** mills for making nails or rods from iron bars   24 **wool.** An act of 10 and 11 William III, c. 10 (1698-1699) prevented the exportation of wool from Ireland and the colonies   38 **making hats.** The act of 5 George II, c. 22 (1731-1732) prohibited the conveyance of hats and felt from the colonies

in Prussia; and the making of hats by our remoter subjects ought to be as much as possible restrained: And forasmuch as the islanders before mentioned, being in possession of wool, beaver and other furs, have presumptuously conceived they had a right to make some advantage thereof, by manufacturing the same into hats, to the prejudice of our domestic manufacture: We do therefore hereby strictly command and ordain, that no hats or felts whatsoever, dyed or undyed, finished or unfinished, shall be loaden or put into or upon any vessel, cart, carriage, or horse, to be transported or conveyed out of one county in the said island into another county, or to any other place whatsoever, by any person or persons whatsoever, on pain of forfeit-
10 ing the same, with a penalty of five hundred pounds sterling for every offence. Nor shall any hat-maker, in any of the said counties, employ more than two apprentices, on penalty of five pounds sterling per month: we intending hereby that such hat-makers, being so restrained, both in the production and sale of their commodity, may find no advantage in continuing their business. But, lest the said islanders should suffer inconveniency by the want of hats, we are farther graciously pleased to permit them to send their beaver furs to Prussia; and we also permit hats made thereof to be exported from Prussia to Britain; the people thus favoured to pay all costs and charges of manufacturing, interest, commission to our merchants, insurance and freight going and returning, as in the case of iron.
20   "And lastly, being willing farther to favour our said colonies in Britain, we do hereby also ordain and command, that all the thieves, highway and street robbers, house-breakers, forgerers, murderers, s—d—tes, and villains of every denomination, who have forfeited their lives to the law in Prussia, but whom we, in our great clemency, do not think fit here to hang, shall be emptied out of our gaols into the said island of Great-Britain, for the better peopling of that country.

"We flatter ourselves, that these our royal regulations and commands will be thought just and reasonable by our much favoured colonists in England; the said regulations being copied from their own statutes, of 10 and 11 Will. III. c. 10.—5 Geo. II. c. 22—23 Geo. II c. 29—4 Geo. I. c. 11. and from other equitable laws
30 made by their parliaments, or from instructions given by their Princes, or from resolutions of both Houses, entered into for the good government of their own colonies in Ireland and America.

"And all persons in the said island are hereby cautioned not to oppose in any wise the execution of this our Edict, or any part thereof, such opposition being high-treason; of which all who are suspected shall be transported in fetters from Britain to Prussia, there to be tried and executed according to the Prussian law.

"Such is our pleasure.

"Given at Potsdam, this twenty-fifth day of the month of August, One thousand seven hundred and seventy-three, and in the thirty-third year of our reign.

40   "By the King, in his Council.
      "RECHTMAESSIG, Sec."

---

21 **thieves,** etc. See the act of 4 George II, c. 11 (1717-1718) relating to piracy   22 **s—d—tes,** sodomites

Some take this Edict to be merely one of the King's Jeux d'Esprit: others suppose it serious, and that he means a quarrel with England; but all here think the
assertion it concludes with, "that these regulations are copied from acts of the English parliament respecting their colonies," a very injurious one; it being impossible
to believe, that a people distinguished for their love of liberty, a nation so wise, so
liberal in its sentiments, so just and equitable towards its neighbours, should, from
mean and injudicious views of petty immediate profit, treat its own children in a
manner so arbitrary and tyrannical!

1773, 1773

The Ephemera *An Emblem of Human Life*

The Ephemera *was originally written in French for Madame Brillon de Jouy, one of
Franklin's neighbors during his residence at Passy, and is thought to have been first printed
on his private press there, about September 1778. Madame Brillon, perhaps forty years
Franklin's junior, was the wife of a government official, none too happy in her family responsibilities but possessed of an abundant share of that vivacity which is so common among
educated Frenchwomen. She and Franklin shared a fondness for music and for chess, and they
exchanged half-flirtatious, half-serious letters not unlike the more polished bagatelle which
follows. The familiar piece entitled* The Whistle *was also written for Madame Brillon.
    As appears from the introductory paragraph,* The Ephemera *was suggested by a visit to
the Moulin Joli, a small island in the Seine which was a part of the country estate
of Claude-Henri Watelet. Franklin later acknowledged that he owed something to his memory
of a newspaper essay on "Human Vanity," printed in the* Pennsylvania Gazette *for December 4, 1735. What makes* The Ephemera *an unusually pointed comment on the well-
worn theme of the transience of life is the reader's identification of the experienced Franklin
with the insect philosopher. Pathos has seldom been more delicately sustained.*

You may remember, my dear friend, that when we lately spent that happy day in
the delightful garden and sweet society of the Moulin Joly, I stopt a little in one
of our walks, and stayed some time behind the company. We had been shown numberless skeletons of a kind of little fly, called an ephemera, whose successive generations, we were told, were bred and expired within the day. I happened to see a living
company of them on a leaf, who appeared to be engaged in conversation. You know
I understand all the inferior animal tongues. My too great application to the study
of them is the best excuse I can give for the little progress I have made in your
charming language. I listened through curiosity to the discourse of these little creatures; but as they, in their national vivacity, spoke three or four together, I could   10
make but little of their conversation. I found, however, by some broken expressions
that I heard now and then, they were disputing warmly on the merit of two foreign

Text: Bigelow's *Complete Works*, VI, 237-239

musicians, one a *cousin,* the other a *moscheto;* in which dispute they spent their time, seemingly as regardless of the shortness of life as if they had been sure of living a month. Happy people! thought I; you are certainly under a wise, just, and mild government, since you have no public grievances to complain of, nor any subject of contention but the perfections and imperfections of foreign music. I turned my head from them to an old gray-headed one, who was single on another leaf, and talking to himself. Being amused with his soliloquy, I put it down in writing, in hopes it will likewise amuse her to whom I am so much indebted for the most pleasing of all amusements, her delicious company and heavenly harmony.

10   "It was," said he, "the opinion of learned philosophers of our race, who lived and flourished long before my time, that this vast world, the Moulin Joly, could not itself subsist more than eighteen hours; and I think there was some foundation for that opinion, since, by the apparent motion of the great luminary that gives life to all nature, and which in my time has evidently declined considerably towards the ocean at the end of our earth, it must then finish its course, be extinguished in the waters that surround us, and leave the world in cold and darkness, necessarily producing universal death and destruction. I have lived seven of those hours, a great age, being no less than four hundred and twenty minutes of time. How very few of us continue so long! I have seen generations born, flourish, and expire. My present
20 friends are the children and grandchildren of the friends of my youth, who are now, alas, no more! And I must soon follow them; for, by the course of nature, though still in health, I cannot expect to live above seven or eight minutes longer. What now avails all my toil and labor in amassing honey-dew on this leaf, which I cannot live to enjoy! What the political struggles I have been engaged in for the good of my compatriot inhabitants of this bush, or my philosophical studies for the benefit of our race in general! for in politics what can laws do without morals? Our present race of ephemeræ will in a course of minutes become corrupt, like those of other and older bushes, and consequently as wretched. And in philosophy how small our progress! Alas! art is long, and life is short! My friends would comfort me with the
30 idea of a name they say I shall leave behind me; and they tell me I have lived long enough to nature and to glory. But what will fame be to an ephemera who no longer exists? And what will become of all history in the eighteenth hour, when the world itself, even the whole Moulin Joly, shall come to an end, and be buried in universal ruin?"

To me, after all my eager pursuits, no solid pleasures now remain, but the reflection of a long life spent in meaning well, the sensible conversation of a few good lady ephemeræ, and now and then a kind smile and a tune from the ever amiable *Brillante.*

B. FRANKLIN
1778, 1778?

---

1 **one . . . moscheto,** one a gnat, the other a mosquito. In a letter to William Carmichael written June 17, 1780, Franklin said that at the time he wrote "The Ephemera" "all conversations at Paris were filled with disputes about the music of Gluck and Piccini, a German and an Italian musician, who divided the town into violent parties." The *Iphigénie en aulide* of C. W. Ritter von Gluck (1714-1787) was produced at Paris in 1774; Niccolò Piccini (1728-1800) was invited to Paris in 1776

Dialogue Between Franklin and the Gout

Like The Ephemera, *Franklin's dialogue with the gout was first written in French and may have been printed on the Passy press sometime in 1780. Although it is one of the simplest of the bagatelles, it is nevertheless a characteristic summary of Franklin's ideas on health, recreation, pleasure, and pain. The young man who sought to learn virtue by keeping a chart of his daily failings had come to accept the discomfort of paying for his pleasures. The numerous local allusions emphasize Franklin's real purpose, the amusement of his circle of friends, but he was a moralizer even in his lightest moments.*

Midnight, 22 October, 1780

FRANKLIN. Eh! oh! eh! What have I done to merit these cruel sufferings?

GOUT. Many things; you have ate and drank too freely, and too much indulged those legs of yours in their indolence.

FRANKLIN. Who is it that accuses me?

GOUT. It is I, even I, the Gout.

FRANKLIN. What! my enemy in person?

GOUT. No, not your enemy.

FRANKLIN. I repeat it; my enemy; for you would not only torment my body to death, but ruin my good name; you reproach me as a glutton and a tippler; now all 10 the world, that knows me, will allow that I am neither the one nor the other.

GOUT. The world may think as it pleases; it is always very complaisant to itself, and sometimes to its friends; but I very well know that the quantity of meat and drink proper for a man, who takes a reasonable degree of exercise, would be too much for another, who never takes any.

FRANKLIN. I take — eh! oh! — as much exercise — eh! — as I can, Madam Gout. You know my sedentary state, and on that account, it would seem, Madam Gout, as if you might spare me a little, seeing it is not altogether my own fault.

GOUT. Not a jot; your rhetoric and your politeness are thrown away; your apology avails nothing. If your situation in life is a sedentary one, your amusements, your 20 recreations, at least, should be active. You ought to walk or ride; or, if the weather prevents that, play at billiards. But let us examine your course of life. While the mornings are long, and you have leisure to go abroad, what do you do? Why, instead of gaining an appetite for breakfast, by salutary exercise, you amuse yourself with books, pamphlets, or newspapers, which commonly are not worth the reading. Yet you eat an inordinate breakfast, four dishes of tea, with cream, and one or two buttered toasts, with slices of hung beef, which I fancy are not things the most easily digested. Immediately afterwards you sit down to write at your desk, or converse with persons who apply to you on business. Thus the time passes till one, without any kind of bodily exercise. But all this I could pardon, in regard, as you say, to 30 your sedentary condition. But what is your practice after dinner? Walking in the beautiful gardens of those friends with whom you have dined would be the choice

of men of sense; yours is to be fixed down to chess, where you are found engaged for two or three hours! This is your perpetual recreation, which is the least eligible of any for a sedentary man, because, instead of accelerating the motion of the fluids, the rigid attention it requires helps to retard the circulation and obstruct internal secretions. Wrapt in the speculations of this wretched game, you destroy your constitution. What can be expected from such a course of living, but a body replete with stagnant humors, ready to fall a prey to all kinds of dangerous maladies, if I, the Gout, did not occasionally bring you relief by agitating those humors, and so purifying or dissipating them? If it was in some nook or alley in Paris, deprived of
10 walks, that you played awhile at chess after dinner, this might be excusable; but the same taste prevails with you in Passy, Auteuil, Montmartre, or Sanoy, places where there are the finest gardens and walks, a pure air, beautiful women, and most agreeable and instructive conversation; all which you might enjoy by frequenting the walks. But these are rejected for this abominable game of chess. Fie, then Mr. Franklin! But amidst my instructions, I had almost forgot to administer my wholesome corrections; so take that twinge, — and that.

FRANKLIN. Oh! eh! oh! ohhh! As much instruction as you please, Madam Gout, and as many reproaches; but pray, Madam, a truce with your corrections!

GOUT. No, Sir, no, — I will not abate a particle of what is so much for your good,
20 — therefore —

FRANKLIN. Oh! ehhh! — It is not fair to say I take no exercise, when I do very often, going out to dine and returning in my carriage.

GOUT. That, of all imaginable exercises, is the most slight and insignificant, if you allude to the motion of a carriage suspended on springs. By observing the degree of heat obtained by different kinds of motion, we may form an estimate of the quantity of exercise given by each. Thus, for example, if you turn out to walk in winter with cold feet, in an hour's time you will be in a glow all over; ride on horseback, the same effect will scarcely be perceived by four hours' round trotting; but if you loll in a carriage, such as you have mentioned, you may travel all day and gladly
30 enter the last inn to warm your feet by a fire. Flatter yourself then no longer, that half an hour's airing in your carriage deserves the name of exercise. Providence has appointed few to roll in carriages, while he has given to all a pair of legs, which are machines infinitely more commodious and serviceable. Be grateful, then, and make a proper use of yours. Would you know how they forward the circulation of your fluids, in the very action of transporting you from place to place; observe when you walk, that all your weight is alternately thrown from one leg to the other; this occasions a great pressure on the vessels of the foot, and repels their contents; when relieved, by the weight being thrown on the other foot, the vessels of the first are allowed to replenish, and, by a return of this weight, this repulsion again succeeds;

---

1 **chess**, of which Franklin, in his seventies, was so fond that he is said to have once played from six in the evening until sunrise. His *Morals of Chess*, written about the same time as this dialogue, is one of the classics of the game   11 **Auteuil, Montmartre, or Sanoy.** At the time Franklin wrote, all were suburban villages like Passy. Auteuil is a short distance down the Seine; Montmartre, a district in the northern part of the city; Sannois, still some miles north of the city limits

thus accelerating the circulation of the blood. The heat produced in any given time depends on the degree of this acceleration; the fluids are shaken, the humors attenuated, the secretions facilitated, and all goes well; the cheeks are ruddy, and health is established. Behold your fair friend at Auteuil; a lady who received from bounteous nature more really useful science than half a dozen such pretenders to philosophy as you have been able to extract from all your books. When she honors you with a visit, it is on foot. She walks all hours of the day, and leaves indolence, and its concomitant maladies, to be endured by her horses. In this, see at once the preservative of her health and personal charms. But when you go to Auteuil, you must have your carriage, though it is no further from Passy to Auteuil than from Auteuil to 10 Passy.

FRANKLIN. Your reasonings grow very tiresome.

GOUT. I stand corrected. I will be silent and continue my office; take that, and that.

FRANKLIN. Oh! Ohh! Talk on, I pray you!

GOUT. No, no; I have a good number of twinges for you to-night, and you may be sure of some more to-morrow.

FRANKLIN. What, with such a fever! I shall go distracted! Oh! eh! Can no one bear it for me?

GOUT. Ask that of your horses; they have served you faithfully.

FRANKLIN. How can you so cruelly sport with my torments?   20

GOUT. Sport! I am very serious. I have here a list of offences against your own health distinctly written, and can justify every stroke inflicted on you.

FRANKLIN. Read it then.

GOUT. It is too long a detail; but I will briefly mention some particulars.

FRANKLIN. Proceed. I am all attention.

GOUT. Do you remember how often you have promised yourself, the following morning, a walk in the grove of Boulogne, in the garden de la Muette, or in your own garden, and have violated your promise, alleging, at one time, it was too cold, at another too warm, too windy, too moist, or what else you pleased; when in truth it was too nothing, but your insuperable love of ease?   30

FRANKLIN. That I confess may have happened occasionally, probably ten times in a year.

GOUT. Your confession is very far short of the truth; the gross amount is one hundred and ninety-nine times.

FRANKLIN. Is it possible?

GOUT. So possible, that it is fact; you may rely on the accuracy of my statement. You know M. Brillon's gardens, and what fine walks they contain; you know the handsome flight of an hundred steps, which lead from the terrace above to the lawn below. You have been in the practice of visiting this amiable family twice a week, after dinner, and

---

4 **your fair friend**, Madame Helvétius, widow of a French philosopher, with whom Franklin was so intimate that he once addressed to her a half-serious proposal of marriage   27 **grove . . . Muette**, the Bois de Boulogne, just west of Passy, now perhaps the chief public park of Paris, and the garden of a royal chateau, La Muette, now largely built over. The first balloon ascension was made in the park of La Muette on November 21, 1783, Franklin being one of the spectators   37 **M. Brillon's gardens**, in Passy. See *The Ephemera*

it is a maxim of your own, that "a man may take as much exercise in walking a mile, up and down stairs, as in ten on level ground." What an opportunity was here for you to have had exercise in both these ways! Did you embrace it, and how often?

FRANKLIN. I cannot immediately answer that question.

GOUT. I will do it for you; not once.

FRANKLIN. Not once?

GOUT. Even so. During the summer you went there at six o'clock. You found the charming lady, with her lovely children and friends, eager to walk with you, and entertain you with their agreeable conversation; and what has been your choice? Why, to
10 sit on the terrace, satisfying yourself with the fine prospect, and passing your eye over the beauties of the garden below, without taking one step to descend and walk about in them. On the contrary, you call for tea and the chess-board; and lo! you are occupied in your seat till nine o'clock, and that besides two hours' play after dinner; and then, instead of walking home, which would have bestirred you a little, you step into your carriage. How absurd to suppose that all this carelessness can be reconcilable with health, without my interposition!

FRANKLIN. I am convinced now of the justness of poor Richard's remark, that "Our debts and our sins are always greater than we think for."

GOUT. So it is. You philosophers are sages in your maxims, and fools in your
20 conduct.

FRANKLIN. But do you charge among my crimes, that I return in a carriage from Mr. Brillon's?

GOUT. Certainly; for, having been seated all the while, you cannot object the fatigue of the day, and cannot want therefore the relief of a carriage.

FRANKLIN. What then would you have me do with my carriage?

GOUT. Burn it if you choose; you would at least get heat out of it once in this way; or, if you dislike that proposal, here's another for you; observe the poor peasants, who work in the vineyards and grounds about the villages of Passy, Auteuil, Chaillot, etc.; you may find every day among these deserving creatures, four
30 or five old men and women, bent and perhaps crippled by weight of years, and too long and too great labor. After a most fatiguing day, these people have to trudge a mile or two to their smoky huts. Order your coachman to set them down. This is an act that will be good for your soul; and, at the same time, after your visit to the Brillons, if you return on foot, that will be good for your body.

FRANKLIN. Ah! how tiresome you are!

GOUT. Well, then, to my office; it should not be forgotten that I am your physician. There.

FRANKLIN. Ohhh! what a devil of a physician!

GOUT. How ungrateful you are to say so! Is it not I who, in the character of your
40 physician, have saved you from the palsy, dropsy, and apoplexy? one or other of which would have done for you long ago, but for me.

FRANKLIN. I submit, and thank you for the past, but entreat the discontinuance of your visits for the future; for, in my mind, one had better die than be cured so

---

29 **Chaillot,** a village a short distance up the Seine from Passy

dolefully. Permit me just to hint, that I have also not been unfriendly to *you*. I never feed physician or quack of any kind, to enter the list against you; if then you do not leave me to my repose, it may be said you are ungrateful too.

GOUT. I can scarcely acknowledge that as any objection. As to quacks, I despise them; they may kill you indeed, but cannot injure me. And, as to regular physicians, they are at last convinced that the gout, in such a subject as you are, is no disease, but a remedy; and wherefore cure a remedy? — but to our business, — there.

FRANKLIN. Oh! oh! — for Heaven's sake leave me! and I promise faithfully never more to play at chess, but to take exercise daily, and live temperately.

GOUT. I know you too well. You promise fair; but, after a few months of good 10 health, you will return to your old habits; your fine promises will be forgotten like the forms of last year's clouds. Let us then finish the account, and I will go. But I leave you with an assurance of visiting you again at a proper time and place; for my object is your good, and you are sensible now that I am your *real friend*.

1780, 1780?

EARLY COMMENTATORS ON AMERICAN LIFE:
Crèvecoeur
Woolman
Bartram

1735–1813 Michel Guillaume St. Jean de Crèvecoeur

Michel Guillaume St. Jean de Crèvecoeur was born in France, near Caen. Educated first in a Jesuit school and then in England, he took ship for Canada before he was twenty and there enlisted in the army. He rose to the rank of lieutenant, making himself particularly useful as a mapmaker in the region of the lower Great Lakes. About 1759 Crèvecoeur drifted down through the English colonies, probably working as a surveyor, and in 1764 applied for naturalization in New York. He settled on an Orange County farm, married, and for approximately fifteen years lived as a gentleman farmer in a well-established and prosperous rural community. Soon after his marriage in 1769, he appears to have begun setting down his impressions of the country; and by 1780, when he was forced to leave America because his moderate opinions had made both Whigs and Tories suspicious of him, he had a small trunk full of manuscripts. He found a publisher for some of them in London, but the publisher was a Whig and probably selected for *Letters from an American Farmer* (1782) those pieces least critical of the Revolutionary party in America. A few others were published in a French translation in 1784, but a number of more obviously Tory papers remained in manuscript until 1925, when they were included in *Sketches of Eighteenth Century America.*

Crèvecoeur's *Letters* were popular in English, French, and German, and for a time he was a literary lion, the protégé in the Paris salons of Madame d'Houdetot, whom Rousseau had loved. Partly through her influence, the "sauvage" from America was sent back to New York as consul-general, and from 1783 until 1790 Crèvecoeur did his best to keep alive American gratitude to and friendship with France. The last twenty-three years of his life were spent in Europe.

Crèvecoeur expresses many of the revolutionary ideals which operated powerfully in the eighteenth century, first in America and then in France. He was a perfectionist, although he never recognized the paradox in his admiration for social progress and his equally high regard for the primitive and simple. He was more than a believer in religious freedom; he was anticlerical, with a distrust of organized religion almost as strong as Thomas Paine's. Like Benjamin Franklin and the Frenchmen who were weary of the old order, he was a physiocrat, believing that agriculture should be left largely free of taxation because it was the basis of wealth and a healthy economic life. Like Jefferson, he envisaged an agrarian society, free of governmental restrictions; free of the dangers of cities and of great wealth concentrated in the hands of the few; free, by and large, of the influence of clergymen and of lawyers; free of sickness, intemperance, and extravagance. In his most expansive moments, Crèvecoeur was capable of seeing America as "one diffusive scene of happiness reaching from the sea-shores to the last settlements on the borders of the wilderness."

Sometimes, particularly in the pieces which remained so long in manuscript, there is brief recognition of man's inhumanity to man, as exemplified by slavery and civil disturbances and war. Nature, usually beneficent, occasionally displays its crueler aspects, when the snakes fight to the death, the hummingbirds grow irascible, and storms and insects plague the determinedly happy farmer. Crèvecoeur, however, was fundamentally an optimist, and the pastoral tone prevails in his writing. His mind was keen and sensitive; an excellent observer, he had the power to communicate his emotional experience. If he overdramatized, he did so, one is convinced, without intent to deceive. The modern reader can understand the conviction of the friend who described Crèvecoeur as "a philanthropist; a man of serene temper and pure benevolence. The milk of human kindness circulated in every vein."

Crèvecoeur wrote well, although unevenly. The fashion of his day compelled him to shape his best-known book into a series of letters, but within these he displayed considerable command of three different forms: the prose essay, the short story, and the dramatic dialogue. His ideas are not unlike those of the promotion tracts and progress reports, but he had a sense of the form appropriate to his "sentiment and susceptibility." He therefore has his place both as a social philosopher and as one of the earliest American writers to experiment with the nature essay and with fiction as a medium for expression. Whether or not he was an "emotional liar," idealizing the simple life without regard to truth, may be a question for debate; there is almost no dissent, however, from the praise of his literary grace.

Letters from an American Farmer, ed. W. P. Trent and Ludwig Lewisohn, New York, 1904   Sketches of Eighteenth Century America, ed. H. L. Bourdin, R. H. Gabriel, and S. T. Williams, New Haven, 1925   Eighteenth Century Travels in Pennsylvania and New York, trans. and ed., Percy G. Adams, Lexington, Ky., 1961   Journey into Northern Pennsylvania and the State of New York, trans. and ed., Clarissa S. Bostelman, Ann Arbor, 1964

from Letters *from* an American Farmer

Letters from an American Farmer *(London, 1782) was reprinted, in the English version, five times before 1793, and there were three editions of the French expansion and two of the German translation.*

The twelve essays, or "letters," vary greatly in length, and it seems probable that the letter form was an after-thought of Crèvecoeur or his printer. The first three essays are a general and highly favorable view of American life, emphasizing the construction of a new and su-

perior society in sharp contrast with Europe, which he regarded as decadent, stratified, and priest-dominated. The next six essays are more particular; four of them deal with Nantucket, which Crèvecoeur regarded as "inhabited merely to prove what mankind can do when happily governed," one with Martha's Vineyard and the whale fishery, and one with Charleston and the deplorable institution of slavery. A nature essay, a description of the visit of a Russian gentleman to John Bartram, and "Distresses of a Frontier Man" complete the book. The final essay is the only one which contains hints of the "desolating consequences" of the Revolution, mentioned in the Preface and described so vividly in "The American Belisarius" (see p. 334).

The organization of the Letters *is loose; Crèvecoeur's strength lay in his paragraphs and stretches of dialogue. The selection which follows is approximately the first third of Letter III, "What Is an American?"*

I wish I could be acquainted with the feelings and thoughts which must agitate the heart and present themselves to the mind of an enlightened Englishman, when he first lands on this continent. He must greatly rejoice that he lived at a time to see this fair country discovered and settled; he must necessarily feel a share of national pride, when he views the chain of settlements which embellishes these extended shores. When he says to himself, this is the work of my countrymen, who, when convulsed by factions, afflicted by a variety of miseries and wants, restless and impatient, took refuge here. They brought along with them their national genius, to which they principally owe what liberty they enjoy, and what substance they possess. Here he sees the industry of his native country displayed in a new manner, and traces in their works the embrios of all the arts, sciences, and ingenuity which flourish in Europe. Here he beholds fair cities, substantial villages, extensive fields, an immense country filled with decent houses, good roads, orchards, meadows, and bridges, where an hundred years ago all was wild, woody and uncultivated! What a train of pleasing ideas this fair spectacle must suggest; it is a prospect which must inspire a good citizen with the most heartfelt pleasure. The difficulty consists in the manner of viewing so extensive a scene. He is arrived on a new continent; a modern society offers itself to his contemplations, different from what he had hitherto seen. It is not composed, as in Europe, of great lords who possess everything, and of a herd of people who have nothing. Here are no aristocratical families, no courts, no kings, no bishops, no ecclesiastical dominion, no invisible power giving to a few a very visible one; no great manufacturers employing thousands, no great refinements of luxury. The rich and the poor are not so far removed from each other as they are in Europe. Some few towns excepted, we are all tillers of the earth, from Nova Scotia to West Florida. We are a people of cultivators, scattered over an immense territory, communicating with each other by means of good roads and navigable rivers, united by the silken bands of mild government, all respecting the laws, without dreading their power, because they are equitable. We are all animated with the spirit of an industry which is unfettered and unrestrained, because each person works for himself. If he travels through our rural districts he views not the hostile castle, and the haughty mansion, contrasted with the clay-built hut and miserable cabbin, where cattle and men help to keep each other warm, and dwell in meanness, smoke, and indigence. A pleasing uniformity of decent competence appears throughout our habitations. The meanest of our log-houses is a dry and comfortable habitation. Lawyer or merchant are the fairest titles our towns afford; that of a farmer is the only appellation of the rural inhabitants of our country. It must take some time ere he can reconcile himself to our dictionary, which is but short in words of dignity, and names of honor. There, on a Sunday, he sees a congregation of respectable farmers and their wives, all clad in neat homespun, well mounted, or riding in their own humble waggons. There is not among them an esquire, saving the unlettered magistrate. There he sees a parson as simple as his flock, a farmer who does not riot on the labour of others. We have no princes, for whom we toil, starve, and bleed: we are the most perfect society now 1(existing in the world. Here man is free as he ought to be; nor is this pleasing equality so transitory as many others are. Many ages will not see the shores of our great lakes replenished with inland nations, nor the unknown bounds of North America entirely peopled. Who can tell how far it extends? Who can tell the millions of men whom it will feed and contain? for no European foot has as yet travelled half the extent of this mighty continent!

The next wish of the traveller will be to know whence came all these people? they are a mixture of English, Scotch, Irish, French, Dutch, Germans, and Swedes. From this promiscuous breed, that race now called Americans have arisen. The eastern provinces must indeed be excepted, as being the unmixed descendants of 2(Englishmen. I have heard many wish that they had been more intermixed also: for my part, I am no wisher, and think it much better as it has happened. They exhibit a most conspicuous figure in this great and variegated picture; they too enter for a great share in the pleasing perspective displayed in these thirteen provinces. I know it is fashionable to reflect on them, but I respect them for what they have done; for the accuracy and wisdom with which they have settled their territory; for the decency of their manners; for their early love of letters; their ancient college, the first in this hemisphere; for their industry; which to me who am but a farmer, is the criterion of everything. There never was a people, situated as they are, who with so ungrateful a soil have done more in so short a time. Do you think that the monar- 3(chical ingredients which are more prevalent in other governments, have purged them from all foul stains? Their histories assert the contrary.

In this great American asylum, the poor of Europe have by some means met together, and in consequence of various causes; to what purpose should they ask one another what countrymen they are? Alas, two thirds of them had no country. Can a wretch who wanders about, who works and starves, whose life is a continual scene of sore affliction or pinching penury; can that man call England or any other kingdom his country? A country that had no bread for him, whose fields procured him no harvest, who met with nothing but the frowns of the rich, the severity of the laws, with jails and punishments; who owned not a single foot of the extensive sur- 4(face of this planet? No! urged by a variety of motives, here they came. Every thing has tended to regenerate them; new laws, a new mode of living, a new social system;

Text: first London edition   20 **eastern provinces,** New England   27 **ancient college,** Harvard, founded in 1636

here they are become men: in Europe they were as so many useless plants, wanting vegitative mould, and refreshing showers; they withered, and were mowed down by want, hunger, and war; but now by the power of transplantation, like all other plants they have taken root and flourished! Formerly they were not numbered in any civil lists of their country, except in those of the poor; here they rank as citizens. By what invisible power has this surprising metamorphosis been performed? By that of the laws and that of their industry. The laws, the indulgent laws, protect them as they arrive, stamping on them the symbol of adoption; they receive ample rewards for their labours; these accumulated rewards procure them lands; those lands confer on
10 them the title of freemen, and to that title every benefit is affixed which men can possibly require. This is the great operation daily performed by our laws. From whence proceed these laws? From our government. Whence that government? It is derived from the original genius and strong desire of the people ratified and confirmed by the crown. This is the great chain which links us all, this is the picture which every province exhibits, Nova Scotia excepted. There the crown has done all; either there were no people who had genius, or it was not much attended to: the consequence is, that the province is very thinly inhabited indeed; the power of the crown in conjunction with the musketos has prevented men from settling there. Yet some parts of it flourished once; and it contained a mild harmless set of people. But for the
20 fault of a few leaders, the whole were banished. The greatest political error the crown ever committed in America, was to cut off men from a country which wanted nothing but men!

What attachment can a poor European emigrant have for a country where he had nothing? The knowledge of the language, the love of a few kindred as poor as himself, were the only cords that tied him: his country is now that which gives him land, bread, protection, and consequence: *Ubi panis ibi patria,* is the motto of all emigrants. What then is the American, this new man? He is either an European, or the descendant of an European, hence that strange mixture of blood, which you will find in no other country. I could point out to you a family whose grandfather was
30 an Englishman, whose wife was Dutch, whose son married a French woman, and whose present four sons have now four wives of different nations. *He* is an American, who leaving behind him all his ancient prejudices and manners, receives new ones from the new mode of life he has embraced, the new government he obeys, and the new rank he holds. He becomes an American by being received in the broad lap of our great *Alma Mater*. Here individuals of all nations are melted into a new race of men, whose labours and posterity will one day cause great changes in the world. Americans are the western pilgrims, who are carrying along with them that great mass of arts, sciences, vigour, and industry which began long since in the east; they will finish the great circle. The Americans were once scattered all over Europe; here
40 they are incorporated into one of the finest systems of population which has ever

15 **the crown . . . all.** Nova Scotia, the chief part of French Acadia, was conquered by the English in 1710. The authorities found it difficult to find English settlers, and the Acadians refused to take an oath of allegiance. In 1755, about ten thousand Acadians were removed and their lands given to English families. Both Crèvecoeur and Longfellow (in *Evangeline*) appear to have underestimated the difficulty of assimilation   26 **Ubi . . . patria.** One's fatherland is where there is bread

appeared, and which will hereafter become distinct by the power of the different
climates they inhabit. The American ought therefore to love this country much better
than that wherein either he or his forefathers were born. Here the rewards of his industry follow with equal steps the progress of his labour; his labour is founded on
the basis of nature, *self-interest;* can it want a stronger allurement? Wives and children, who before in vain demanded of him a morsel of bread, now, fat and frolick-
some, gladly help their father to clear those fields whence exuberant crops are to
arise to feed and to clothe them all; without any part being claimed, either by a
despotic prince, a rich abbott, or a mighty lord. Here religion demands but little of
him; a small voluntary salary to the minister, and gratitude to God; can he refuse 10
these? The American is a new man, who acts upon new principles; he must therefore
entertain new ideas, and form new opinions. From involuntary idleness, servile
dependence, penury, and useless labour, he has passed to toils of a very different
nature, rewarded by ample subsistence. — This is an American.

British America is divided into many provinces, forming a large association,
scattered along a coast 1500 miles extent and about 200 wide. This society I would
fain examine, at least such as it appears in the middle provinces; if it does not afford
that variety of tinges and gradations which may be observed in Europe, we have
colours peculiar to ourselves. For instance, it is natural to conceive that those who
live near the sea, must be very different from those who live in the woods; the inter- 20
mediate space will afford a separate and distinct class.

Men are like plants; the goodness and flavour of the fruit proceeds from the peculiar
soil and exposition in which they grow. We are nothing but what we derive from
the air we breathe, the climate we inhabit, the government we obey, the system of
religion we profess, and the nature of our employment. Here you will find but few
crimes; these have acquired as yet no root among us. I wish I were able to trace all
my ideas; if my ignorance prevents me from describing them properly, I hope I shall
be able to delineate a few of the outlines, which are all I propose.

Those who live near the sea, feed more on fish than on flesh, and often encounter
that boisterous element. This renders them more bold and enterprising; this leads 30
them to neglect the confined occupations of the land. They see and converse with a
variety of people; their intercourse with mankind becomes extensive. The sea inspires
them with a love of traffic, a desire of transporting produce from one place to another;
and leads them to a variety of resources which supply the place of labour. Those
who inhabit the middle settlements, by far the most numerous, must be very different; the simple cultivation of the earth purifies them, but the indulgences of the
government, the soft remonstrances of religion, the rank of independent freeholders,
must necessarily inspire them with sentiments, very little known in Europe among
people of the same class. What do I say? Europe has no such class of men; the early
knowledge they acquire, the early bargains they make, give them a great degree of 40
sagacity. As freemen they will be litigious; pride and obstinacy are often the cause

---

22 **Men . . . plants.** Crèvecoeur's frequent use of this analogy suggests some knowledge, at first or second
hand, of Montesquieu's *L'Esprit des lois* (1748), landmark in the literature of social and political science

of law suits; the nature of our laws and governments may be another. As citizens it is easy to imagine, that they will carefully read the newspapers, enter into every political disquisition, freely blame or censure governors and others. As farmers they will be careful and anxious to get as much as they can, because what they get is their own. As northern men they will love the chearful cup. As Christians, religion curbs them not in their opinions; the general indulgence leaves every one to think for themselves in spiritual matters; the laws inspect our actions, our thoughts are left to God. Industry, good living, selfishness, litigiousness, country politics, the pride of freemen, religious indifference, are their characteristics. If you recede still
10 farther from the sea, you will come into more modern settlements; they exhibit the same strong lineaments, in a ruder appearance. Religion seems to have still less influence, and their manners are less improved.

Now we arrive near the great woods, near the last inhabited districts; there men seem to be placed still farther beyond the reach of government, which in some measure leaves them to themselves. How can it pervade every corner; as they were driven there by misfortunes, necessity of beginnings, desire of acquiring large tracks of land, idleness, frequent want of economy, ancient debts; the re-union of such people does not afford a very pleasing spectacle. When discord, want of unity and friendship; when either drunkenness or idleness prevail in such remote districts;
20 contention, inactivity, and wretchedness must ensue. There are not the same remedies to these evils as in a long established community. The few magistrates they have, are in general little better than the rest; they are often in a perfect state of war; that of man against man, sometimes decided by blows, sometimes by means of the law; that of man against every inhabitant of these venerable woods, of which they are come to dispossess them. There men appear to be no better than carnivorous animals of a superior rank, living on the flesh of wild animals when they can catch them, and when they are not able, they subsist on grain. He who would wish to see America in its proper light, and have a true idea of its feeble beginnings and barbarous rudiments, must visit our extended line of frontiers where the last settlers
30 dwell, and where he may see the first labours of settlement, the mode of clearing the earth, in all their different appearances; where men are wholly left dependent on their native tempers, and on the spur of uncertain industry, which often fails when not sanctified by the efficacy of a few moral rules. There, remote from the power of example, and check of shame, many families exhibit the most hideous parts of our society. They are a kind of forlorn hope, preceding by ten or twelve years the most respectable army of veterans which come after them. In that space, prosperity will polish some, vice and the law will drive off the rest, who uniting again with others like themselves will recede still farther; making room for more industrious people, who will finish their improvements, convert the loghouse into a convenient habita-
40 tion, and rejoicing that the first heavy labours are finished, will change in a few years that hitherto barbarous country into a fine fertile, well regulated district. Such is our progress, such is the march of the Europeans toward the interior parts of this continent. In all societies there are off-casts; this impure part serves as our precursors

---

13 **the last . . . districts,** the frontier, noticeably unglorified in this description

or pioneers; my father himself was one of that class, but he came upon honest principles, and was therefore one of the few who held fast; by good conduct and
temperance, he transmitted to me his fair inheritance, when not above one in fourteen of his contemporaries had the same good fortune.

Forty years ago this smiling country was thus inhabited; it is now purged, a general
decency of manners prevails throughout, and such has been the fate of our best
countries.

Exclusive of those general characteristics, each province has its own, founded on the
government, climate, mode of husbandry, customs, and peculiarity of circumstances.
Europeans submit insensibly to these great powers, and become, in the course of a few   10
generations, not only Americans in general, but either Pennsylvanians, Virginians,
or provincials under some other name. Whoever traverses the continent must easily
observe those strong differences, which will grow more evident in time. The inhabitants of Canada, Massachusetts, the middle provinces, the southern ones will be as
different as their climates; their only points of unity will be those of religion and
language. . . .

                                                                          1780?, 1782
_____

1 **my father,** a fictional touch, as there is no evidence that Crèvecoeur's father was ever in America

from Sketches of Eighteenth Century America The American Belisarius

*Belisarius (505?-565) was the chief military genius in the reign of the Emperor Justinian.
After a long series of brilliant victories, he was accused of conspiracy and deprived of his
property; writers of a later period asserted that, his eyes put out by order of the Emperor,
Belisarius became a beggar in the streets. In truth, apparently, Justinian was not thus ungrateful, but believed in his general's innocence and restored his dignities. Crèvecoeur's implication in the title of the following story is that Americans did not always appreciate their
true leaders.*

*"The American Belisarius" is both an experiment in fiction, with so many allusions to
tears that it takes its place in the tradition of sentimentalism, and an excellent expression of
Crèvecoeur's Tory sympathies, which the reader of the* Letters *would scarcely expect. Probably
written before the end of the Revolution, it remained in manuscript until 1925. Sketches
of Eighteenth Century America, published more than a century after its author's death,
rehabilitated Crèvecoeur's reputation, so that he now ranks as one of the major figures of
eighteenth-century American literature.*

Journals, memoirs, elaborate essays shall not fail hereafter to commemorate the
heroes who have made their appearance on this new American stage, to the end that
Europe may either lavishly praise or severely censure their virtues and their faults.
It requires the inquisitive eye of an unnoticed individual mixing in crowds to find
out and select for private amusement more obscure, though not less pathetic scenes.
_____

Text: that established by H. L. Bourdin, R. H. Gabriel, and S. T. Williams, following Bourdin's discovery
of the Crèvecoeur papers in 1923

Scenes of sorrow and affliction are equally moving to the bowels of humanity. Find them where you will, there is a strange but peculiar sort of pleasure in contemplating them; it is a mournful feast for some particular souls.

A pile of ruins is always striking, but when the object of contemplation is too extensive, our divided and wearied faculties receive impressions proportionably feeble; we possess but a certain quantity of tears and compassion. But when the scale is diminished, when we descend from the destruction of an extensive government or nation to that of several individuals, to that of a once opulent, happy, virtuous family, there we pause, for it is more analogous to our own situation. We can better com-
10 prehend the woes, the distresses of a father, mother, and children immersed in the deepest calamities imagination can conceive, than if we had observed the overthrow of kings and great rulers.

After a violent storm of northwest wind I never see even a single oak overset, once majestic and lofty, without feeling some regret at the accident. I observe the knotty roots wrenched from the ground, the broken limbs, the scattered leaves. I revolve in my mind the amazing elemental force which must have occasioned so great an overthrow. I observe the humble bushes which grew under its shade. They felt the impression of the same storm, but in a proportion so much the less, as was that of their bulk when compared to that of the oak. I acknowledge that, were I to observe
20 a whole mountain thus divested of its trees by the impulse of the same gale, I should feel a superior degree of astonishment, but, at the same time, my observations could not be so minute nor so particular. It is not, therefore, those great and general calamities to the description of which my pencil is equal; it is the individual object as it lies lowly prostrate which I wish to describe. I can encompass it; I can view it in all situations; and the limited impressions admit within my mind a possibility of retracing them. Reserve this, therefore, for the hours, for the moments of your greatest philanthropy. The enormity may shock you. Here we are more used to it, and, having so many objects to feel for, one is able to feel so much the less for each.

The horror, the shocking details of the following tragedy, 'tis true, show mankind
30 in the worst light possible. But what can you expect when law, government, morality are become silent and inefficacious? When men are artfully brought into a chaos, in order, as they are taught to believe, that they may be raised from their former confined line to a much preferable state of existence? To make use of a modern simile: the action of ploughing seems to be laborious and dirty; numberless worms, insects, and wise republics of ants are destroyed by the operation. Yet these scenes of unknown disasters, of unnoticed murders and ruins happily tend to produce a rich harvest in the succeeding season.

In the township of _____ lived S. K., the son of a Dutch father and of an English mother. These mixtures are very frequent in this country. From his youth
40 he loved and delighted in hunting, and the skill he acquired confirmed his taste for that manly diversion. In one of the long excursions which he took in the mountains

---

4 **a pile of ruins.** This typically eighteenth-century reflection, best known, perhaps, through Shelley's "Ozymandias," found fullest expression in Comte de Volney's *Les Ruines, ou méditations sur les révolutions des empires* (1791)

of _____ (which he had never before explored), mixing the amusements of the chase with those of more useful contemplation, and viewing the grounds as an expert husbandman, he found among the wilds several beautiful vales formed by Nature in her most indulgent hours; when, weary with the creation of the surrounding cliffs and precipices, she condescended to exhibit something on which Man might live and flourish, — a singular contrast which you never fail to meet with in the mountains of America: the more rocky, barren, and asperous are the surrounding ridges, the richer and more fertile are the intervales and valleys which divide them. Struck with the singular beauty and luxuriance of one of these spots, he returned home, and soon after patented it. I think it contained about one thousand acres.   10

With cheerfulness he quitted the paternal estate he enjoyed, and prepared to begin the world anew in the bosom of this huge wilderness, where there was not even a path to guide him. He had a road to make, some temporary bridges to make, overset trees to remove, a house to raise, swamps to convert into meadows and to fit for the scythe, upland fields to clear for the plough, — such were the labours he had to undertake, such were the difficulties he had to overcome. He surmounted every obstacle; he was young, healthy, vigorous, and strong-handed. In a few years this part of the wilderness assumed a new face and wore a smiling aspect. The most abundant crops of grass, of fruit, and grain soon succeeded to the moss, to the acorn, to the wild berry, and to all the different fruits, natives of that soil. Soon after these first 20 successful essays the fame of his happy beginning drew abundance of inferior people to that neighbourhood. It was made a county, and in a short time grew populous, principally with poor people, whom some part of this barren soil could not render much richer. But the love of independence, that strong attachment to wives and children which is so powerful and natural, will people the tops of cliffs; and make them even prefer such settlements to the servitude of attendance, to the confinement of manufactories, or to the occupation of more menial labours.

There were in the neighbourhood two valuable pieces of land, less considerable indeed, but in point of fertility as good as his own. S. K. purchased them both and invited his two brothers-in-law to remove there; generously making them an offer 30 of the land, of his teams, and every other necessary assistance; requiring only to be paid the advanced capital whenever they should be enabled; giving up all pretensions to interest or any other compensation. This handsome overture did not pass unaccepted. They removed to the new patrimony which they had thus easily purchased and in this sequestered situation became to S. K. two valuable neighbours and friends. Their prosperity, which was his work, raised no jealousy in him. They all grew rich very fast. The virgin earth abundantly repaid them for their labours and advances; and they soon were enabled to return the borrowed capital which they had so industriously improved. This part of the scene is truly pleasing, pastoral, and edifying: three brothers, the founders of three opulent families, the creators of 40 three valuable plantations, the promoters of the succeeding settlements that took place around them. The most plentiful crops, the fattest cattle, the greatest number of hogs and horses, raised loose in his wilderness, yearly accumulated their wealth;

7 **asperous**, rugged

swelled their opulence and rendered them the most conspicuous families in this corner of the world. A perfect union prevailed not only from the ties of blood, but cemented by those of the strongest gratitude.

Among the great number of families which had taken up their residence in that vicinage it was not to be expected that they could all equally thrive. Prosperity is not the lot of every man; so many casualties occur that often prevent it. Some of them were placed, besides, on the most ungrateful soil, from which they could barely draw a subsistence. The industry of Man, the resources of a family are never tried in this cold country, never put to the proof, until they have undergone the severity of
10 a long winter. The rigours of this season generally require among this class of people every exertion of industry, as well as every fortunate circumstance that can possibly happen. A cow, perhaps, a few sheep, a couple of poor horses must be housed, must be fed through the inclement season; and you know that it is from the labour of the summer, from collected grasses and fodder, this must proceed. If the least accident through droughts, sickness, carelessness or want of activity happens, a general calamity ensues. The death of any one of these precious animals oversets the well-being of the family. Milk is wanting for the children; wood must be hauled; the fleeces of sheep cannot be dispensed with. What providence can replace these great deficiencies?
20   Happily S. K. lived in the neighbourhood. His extreme munificence and generosity had hitherto, like a gem, been buried, for he had never before lived in a country where the needy and the calamitous were so numerous. In their extreme indigence, in all their unexpected disasters, they repair to this princely farmer. He opens to them his granary; he lends them hay; he assists them in whatever they want; he cheers them with good counsel; he becomes a father to the poor of this wilderness. They promise him payment; he never demands it. The fame of his goodness reaches far and near. Every winter his house becomes an Egyptian granary, where each finds a supply proportioned to his wants. Figure to yourself a rich and opulent planter situated in an admirable vale, surrounded by a variety of distressed inhabitants, giving
30 and lending, in the midst of a severe winter, cloaks, wool, shoes, etc., to a great number of unfortunate families; relieving a mother who has not perhaps wherewithal to clothe her newborn infant; sending timely succour, medicines, victuals to a valetudinarian exhausted with fatigues and labours; giving a milch cow to a desolate father who has just lost his in a quagmire, as she went to graze the wild herbage for want of hay at home; giving employment; directing the labours and essays of these grateful but ignorant people towards a more prosperous industry. Such is the faithful picture of this man's conduct, for a series of years, to those around him. At home he was hospitable and kind, an indulgent father, a tender husband, a good master. This, one would have imagined, was an object on which the good genius
40 of America would have constantly smiled.

Upon an extraordinary demand of wheat from abroad, the dealers in this commodity would often come to his house and solicit from him the purchase of his abundant crops. "I have no wheat," said he, "for the rich; my harvest is for the poor.

---

5 **vicinage**, neighborhood   27 **an Egyptian granary.** See the story of Joseph, Genesis 47:12

What would the inhabitants of these mountains do, were I to divest myself of what superfluous grain I have?" "Consider, sir, you will receive your money in a lump, and God knows when you are to expect it from these needy people, whose indolence you rather encourage by your extreme bounty." "Some do pay me very punctually. The rest wish and try to do it, but they find it impossible; and pray, must they starve because they raise less grain than I do?" Would to God I were acquainted with the sequel of this humane conversation! I would recapitulate every phrase; I would dwell on every syllable. If Mercy herself could by the direction of the Supreme Being assume a visible appearance, such are the words which this celestial Being would probably utter for the example, for the edification of mankind. 'Tis really a necessary relief 10 and a great comfort to find in human society some such beings, lest in the crowd, which through experience we find so different, we should wholly lose sight of that beautiful original and of those heavenly dispositions, with which the heart of Man was once adorned.

One day as he was riding through his fields, he saw a poor man carrying a bushel of wheat on his back. "Where now, neighbour?"

"To mill, sir."

"Pray, how long since you are become a beast of burthen?"

"Since I had the misfortune of losing my jade."

"Have you neither spirit nor activity enough to catch one of my wild horses?"   20

"I dare not without your leave."

"Hark ye, friend, the first time I see you in that servile employment whilst I have so many useless ones about my farm, you shall receive from me a severe reprimand." The honest countryman took the hint, borrowed a little salt and a halter, and soon after appeared mounted on a spirited mare, which carried him where he wanted to go, and performed for him his necessary services at home.

In the fall of the year it was his usual custom to invite his neighbours in, helping him to hunt and to gather together the numerous heads of swine which were bred in his woods, that he might fat them with corn which he raised in the summer. He made it a rule to treat them handsomely, and to send them home each with a good 30 hog, as a reward for their trouble and attendance. In harvest and haying he neither hired nor sent for any man, but, trusting to the gratitude of the neighbourhood, always found his company of reapers and hay-makers more numerous than he wanted. It was truly a patriarchal harvest gathered for the benefit of his little world. Yet, notwithstanding his generosity, this man grew richer every crop; every agricultural scheme succeeded. What he gave did not appear to diminish his stores; it seemed but a mite, and immediately to be replaced by the hand of Providence. I have known Quakers in Pennsylvania who gave annually the tenth part of their income, and that was very great; but this man never counted, calculated, nor compared. The wants of the year, the calamities of his neighbourhood were the measure by which he pro- 40 portioned his bounty. The luxuriance of his meadows surpassed all belief; I have heard many people say, since his misfortunes, that they have often cut and cured three tons and half per acre. The produce of his grain was in proportion; the blessings of heaven prospered his labours and showered fertility over all his lands. Equally vigilant and industrious, he spared neither activity nor perseverance to accomplish his schemes of agriculture. Thus he lived for a great number of years, the father of the poor and the example of this part of the world. He aimed at no popular promotion, for he was a stranger to pride and arrogance. A simple commission as a militia-captain was all that distinguished him from his equals.

Unfortunate times came at last. What opinion he embraced in the beginning remains unknown. His brothers-in-law had long envied his great popularity, of which, however, he had never made the least abuse. They began to ridicule his generosity, and, from a contempt of his manner of living, they secretly passed to extreme hatred;
10 but hitherto they had taken care to conceal their rancour and resentment. At the dawn of this new revolution, they blazed forth. Fanned by the general impunity of the times, they, in an underhanded manner, endeavoured to represent him as inimical. They prevailed upon the leaders to deprive him of his commission (though fifty-six years of age), and even made him submit to the duties of a simple militiaman. They harassed his son by all the means which false zeal and uncontrollable power — [all] too unhappily — suggested to them. In short, they made themselves so obnoxious as to expose them to every contumely devised by the rage of party and the madness of the times.

As he was a great lover of peace and repose, he obeyed their commands and went
20 forth, as well as his son, whenever ordered. This unexpected compliance became a severe mortification and an insupportable disappointment to his enemies. They became, therefore, more openly outrageous. They began by causing his son to be deprived of a favourite rifle, a rifle that had constantly and successfully contributed to his father's youthful amusements. This outrage the old gentleman could not patiently endure. He seized on the house of the officer who had committed this act of violence. A great dispute ensued, in consequence of which he was cast (into prison) and severely fined. Innumerable other insults were offered to the youth, who, young, bold, and courageous, preferred at last a voluntary exile to so much insult and vexation. He joined the King's troops. This was what had been forseen, and [was] a
30 part of that plan which had been previously concerted by his brothers-in-law and his other enemies. Thus these people, from the wild fury of the times, contrived the means of S. K.'s destruction, which was to ensure them the possession of his fine estate. This elopement with the doubtful confirmed the preceding suspicions; realized the conjectures of his enemies. Among the more irascible the torch now blazed with redoubled heat. His life was immediately demanded by the fanatical, and his estate secured by the detestable devisers of his ruin.

What a situation for an honest, generous man! Despised, shunned, hated, calumniated, and reviled in the midst of a county of which he was the founder, in the midst of a people the poorest of which he had so often assisted and relieved; pur-
40 sued and overtaken by his brothers-in-law, whom he had raised from indigence! Gracious God, why permit so many virtues to be blasted in their greatest refulgency? Why permit the radiance of so many heavenly attributes to be eclipsed by men who impiously affix to their new, fictitious zeal the sacred name of liberty on purpose to blind the unwary, whilst, ignorant of Thee, they worship no deity but self-interest,

and to that idol sacrilegiously sacrifice so many virtues? If it is to reward him with never-fading happiness, condescend to manifest some faint ray of Thy design proportioned to the weakness of the comprehension of us, frail mortals and fellow-sufferers, that we may not despair, nor impious men may arraign Thy eternal justice. Yes, it is virtue Thou meanest to reward and to crown. The struggle, the contest, the ignominy to which it is now exposed, the greater disasters which will soon terminate this scene have some distant affinity with the suffering of Thy Son, the Moral Legislator, the Pattern of Mankind.

S. K. bore his misfortunes with a manly constancy. However, the absence of his son impaired his industry, and almost put an entire stop to his designs of improve- 10 ment. He saw but neglected his farm, his fields, his pastures, and his meadows; the ruinous and deplorable state in which the country was involved. His house, once the mansion of hospitality and kindness, was entered now but by secret emissaries, enemies, committeemen, etc. The few friends he had left dared not visit him, for they, too, were struggling with their difficulties; they dared not expose themselves to a declaration of their sentiments by soothing his oppressed mind, and comforting him in his adversity. He was taken ill. Nevertheless, militia-duty was demanded and required of him. He was fined forty pounds for every fortnight he had been absent. He recovered and resolved either to cease to be, or else to exist with more ease. He went towards New York, but the guards and other obstacles he met with prevented 20 him from accomplishing his design. He returned, but ere he reached his house, he heard the melancholy tidings that it had been plundered, and that there was a general order for the militia to hunt him through the woods. For a great number of days he had to escape their pursuit from hill to hill, from rocks to rocks, often wanting bread, and uncertain where to hide himself. By means of the mediation of some friends he was at last permitted to return home and remain there on bail. A dejected, melancholy wife, a desolated house, a half-ruined farm, a scarcity of everything struck him to the heart at his first coming, but his sorrow and affliction were all passive. These impressions, however, soon wore away; he insensibly grew more reconciled to his situation. His advanced age, his late sickness, his fatigues had wearied him down; 30 and his mind, partaking of the debility of his body, did no longer view these disagreeable images in the same keenness of light.

This happened in the fall. The following winter some poor people repaired to his house for relief and supplies as usual. "Alas, my friends, committees and rulers have made such a havoc here that I have no longer the means to relieve you. A little hay, perhaps, I may spare, for they have stolen all my horses. Pray, were not you one of those who hunted me whilst I was wild?"

"Yes, sir, I was unfortunately one of them, but I was compelled. I was driven to do it. You know as well as I the severity with which we poor militiamen are treated; exorbitant and arbitrary fines, corporal punishments. Every kind of terror is held out 40 to us. What could I do?"

"I know it, and am far from blaming you, though I greatly lament and pity your situation. Pray, have you been paid for your services against me?"

"No, sir."

"How many days have you been out?"

"Two."

"What! Two days in the woods and you have received no wages? Have neither committees nor captains ever settled that matter yet?"

"No, sir, our services are gratis, and we must, besides, find our victuals, our blankets, and the very ammunition we expend, — we must pay for it."

"I hate, and always did, to see poor men employed for nothing. Take two loads of hay for your two days' work. Will that satisfy you?"

"You were always a good man. God loves you yet though some men are dread-
10 fully set against you."

"Do tell me, would you really have killed me as you were ordered, if you had met me in the woods?" Here the poor man, hiding his face with his hat, shed tears and made no other answer.

The patience, the resignation with which he seemed now to bear his fate, greatly alarmed his enemies. They reproached themselves with the facility with which they suffered him to return and to procure bail; new devices, therefore, were made use of to push him to a final extremity. His determination of thus remaining at home, quiet and inoffensive, might abate that popular rage and malice which were the foundations of their hopes. The keen edge of popular clamour might become
20 blunted; there was a possibility of their being frustrated in their most favourite expectations. They, therefore, secretly propagated a report that he had harboured Indians on their way to New York. No sooner said than believed. Imprisonment, hanging were denounced against him by the voice of the public. This new clamour was principally encouraged by his brothers-in-law, the one now become a magistrate, and the other a captain of the militia.

Finding himself surrounded with new perils, without one friend either to advise or to comfort him; threatened with his final doom; accused of that which, though they could not prove, he could only deny; knowing of no power he could appeal to, either for justice or relief; seeing none but prejudiced enemies in his accusers,
30 judges, and neighbours; he at last determined to join the Indians who were nearest to him, not so much with the design of inciting them to blood and slaughter, as [of finding] a place of refuge and repose. This was what his enemies expected. His house, his farm, — all were seized, even the scanty remains of what had escaped their former avidity and plunder. All was sold, and the house and farm were rented to a variety of tenants until laws should be made to sell the lands.

> Such a house broke!
> So noble a master fallen! All gone! and not
> One friend to take his fortune by the arm,
40 > And go along with him.

It has been said since that this famed farm has ceased this year to bear as plentifully as usual; that the meadows have brought but little hay; that the grain has been scanty and poor. This is at least the tradition of the neighbourhood. It may be that these inconsiderate tenants neither plough nor cultivate it as it was formerly; that the meadows, late-fed and ill-fenced, have no time to bear a crop; and that in the short space of their lease they refuse the necessary manures and usual care, without which the best land produces nothing.

His wife, alas! has been hitherto overlooked and unnoticed, though you may be sure she has not been passive through these affecting scenes. In all these various calamities which have befallen her family she has borne the part of a tender mother, an affectionate wife. Judge of her situation at this particular and critical moment! The repeated shocks which she has sustained within these three years have impaired the tone of her nerves, — you know the delicacy of the female frame. Though her 10 cheerfulness was gone, the gleamings of home, the presence of her husband still supported her. This sudden and unexpected blow completed the horrid catastrophe. Soon after his elopement, when the armed men came to seize him, she fainted, and though she has since recovered the use of her limbs, her reason has never returned but in a few lucid intervals. She is now confined to a small room, her servants sold and gone; she is reduced to penury; she is become a poor tenant of that very house which in the better days of her husband's prosperous industry had glowed with the cheerful beams of benevolence. She is now an object of pity without exciting any. When her reason returns, it is only to hear herself and family reviled. "You your-selves have driven my son, my husband away," is all she can say. Could tears, could 20 wishes, could prayers relieve her, I'd shed a flood, I'd form a thousand, I'd proffer the most ardent ones to heaven. But who can stem the tide of Fate? It is the arbiter of kings and subjects; in spite of every impediment it will rise to its preordained height. She lives, happily unknown to herself, an example of the last degree of desola-tion which can overtake a once prosperous family, the object of raillery to those who are witnesses of her delirium. It would have been a miracle indeed, had her senses remained unimpaired amidst the jars, the shocks of so many perturbations. A Stoic himself would have required the spirit of Zeno to have withstood, placid and composed, the convulsions of so great a ruin.

One stroke of fortune is still wanting. S. K. in his flight met with a party of Indians 30 coming towards _____, which they intended to destroy. He accompanied them, never ceasing to beg of them that they would shed no blood and spare the lives of poor innocent farmers. The deaths of three or four, to which he was witness, shocked his humane soul. He quitted them and returned once more towards home, choosing rather to meet his final doom in his own country than be any longer a witness to the further mischiefs meditated by these incensed people. On his return he was soon informed of the deplorable state to which his wife was reduced and of the destruc-tion of his property. He balanced what to do, as if amidst so much evil there was still a possibility of choice. Sad, however, was the alternative: whether to venture and deliver himself up at all hazards, and thus end the suspense; or whether to live 40 a vagrant, a fugitive in these woods and mountains, with the paths and intricate ways of which he was so well-acquainted. But whence was he to procure subsistence? It

28 **Zeno** (fl. 300 B.C.), founder of the Stoic school of philosophy, held that the wise man should always be indifferent to external circumstances

could not be by the chase. Was he then to turn plunderer? Weary of life, he at last
found means to inform the rulers of his return and repentance; but he received no
other answer than what was soon afterwards delivered by the mouths of the dogs
and by the noise of the militia which was ordered out to search the woods for him.
He luckily escaped their pursuit, but hunger, his greatest enemy, at last overtook
him. He ventured towards a cabin, the tenants of which he had often relieved in
their adversity. They gave him some bread and advised him to fly. Soon afterwards,
by means of the indiscretion of a child, this mystery of generosity and gratitude was
revealed. The aged couple were severely whipped, being too poor to be fined. For a
10 long time he skulked from tree to tree, from rock to rock; now hid on the tops of
cliffs, seeing his pursuers below him; now creeping through the impervious ways
of marshes and swamps, the receptacle of bears less cruel than his enemies.

Ye angels of peace, ye genii of placid benevolence, ye invisible beings who are
appointed to preside over the good, the unjustly persecuted, is there no invisible ægis
in the high armouries of heaven? Gently cause one to descend, in order to shield
this mortal man, your image, from the muskets of his ancient friends and dependants,
— all aimed towards him. Whichsoever way he steers, he has to dread the smell of
dogs, now become his enemies. Where can he go to escape and live? But if
he lives, what life will it be? The goaded mind incessantly represents to itself and
20 compares the ancient days of ease, felicity, tranquillity, and wealth, with the present
hours of hunger, persecution, and general hatred; once the master and proprietor of
a good house, now reduced to the shelter of the woods and rocks; once surrounded
with servants and friends, now isolated and alone, afraid of the very animal which
used to be his companion in the chase. Such, however, was the fate of this man for
a long time, until, abandoning himself to despair, overpowered by the excess of
fatigue, debility, and hunger, he suffered himself to be taken. He was conducted to
gaol, where he expected he should not long languish. Mercy was now become useless to him. What good could it procure him, now that his wife was delirious, his
son gone, and all his property destroyed? His only remaining felicity was the remem-
30 brance of his ancient humane deeds which like a sweet ethereal dew must cast a
mist over the horrors of his confinement, and imperceptibly prepare him to appear
in that world which blesses the good, the merciful without measure, and has no
bitterness for such tenants.

The day of trial soon came, and to his great surprise, as well as to the astonishment of all, he was released on bail and permitted to go to work for his bread. Like
Belisarius of old, he is returned to live in that small part of his own house which
is allotted him for his habitation; there to behold once more the extensive havoc
which surrounds him; and to contemplate in gloomy despair the overthrow of his
wife's reason and the reunion of all the physical evil that could possibly befall him,
40 without resources and without hope.

Yet he lives; yet he bears it without murmuring. Life seems still to be precious
to him; 'tis a gift he has no thought of parting with. Strange! What is it good for
when thus embittered, when thus accompanied with so much acrimony, such irre-

---

14 **ægis,** the storm cloud or shield of Zeus; hence any powerful protection

trievable accidents? 'Tis a perpetual state of agony. Better part with it in a heavy, final groan and trust to Nature for the consequence than to drag so ponderous a chain. How much happier the felon, the murderer who at one fortunate blow ends the remembrance of his life and his crimes, and is delivered from chains, putrid holes, and all the other wants of Nature!

Compare now the fate of this man with that of his more fortunate persecutors. I appeal to the enlightened tribunals of Europe, to the casuistical doctors of the colleges of science, to the Divan, to the synods, to the presbyteries, and to all bodies and conventions of men reunited to judge of the various cases which the combined malice of men exhibit on the stage of the world, as well as of the various preven- 10 tives and punishments designed to check malice and evil deeds. I appeal to the American tribunals on that day when the mist of these times shall be dissipated. I ask them all on what principles can this man be punished? What has he done that can deserve so much severity? The graft, by the virulence of these times, is made to poison the parent stock; the vine is made to corrode the tutelar elm which has so long supported its entwined limbs and branches. 'Tis the jealousy, the avarice, the secret thirst of plunder, sanctified under new and deceiving names, which have found means to vilify this generous citizen, and have set the aspic tongues reviling this innocent man. Can it be? Can this be the reflected work of three years? Yes, it is. But for their demoniacal fury he might have remained at home passive and inoffen- 20 sive. The produce of his fertile farm might have served to support the cause. But this was not sufficient to satisfy the rage, the malice of an ignorant, prejudiced public.

Are ye not afraid, ye modern rulers, to attract the wrath of heaven, the vindictive fires of its eternal justice in thus trampling under, in thus disregarding the most essential laws of humanity, in thus neglecting the most indispensable ones contained in that code which ought to reign supreme, exclusive of all parties, factions, and revolutions? is not the deplorable state into which this man and all his family are reduced more than sufficient to atone for the popular offences he is supposed to have been guilty of? Must poverty, langour, and disease terminate in want, penury, and ignominy a life hitherto pursued on the most generous principles, a life which, con- 30 trary to the tenor of yours, has been so useful, so edifying?

But I am not pleading his cause; I am no biographer. I give way to an exuberance of thoughts which involuntarily crowd on my mind, unknown to all the world but its Ruler and yourself. I don't presume that this man was matchless, devoid of vices and faults. Like all other men, his cup was no doubt mixed with those ingredients which enter into the beverage of mortals. It is not the minutiæ of his life into which I want to descend. This unfortunate epoch is *that* alone which I want to select and to describe as a proof of his hard destiny, and as one of the characteristics of the times in which we live. Yet I am persuaded that there are several members in Congress and in every province who, moved into compassion at this relation, would 40 shed tears over the ashes of this ruin; but these men at a great distance direct the revolution of the new orb. It is the inferior satellites who crush, who dispel, and make such a havoc in the paths which it is to follow.

---

8 **the Divan,** the highest council of state among the Turks

Yet his enemies exult, triumph, and rule. They bear sway, are applauded, gather every harvest, and receive every incense which the world can give, whilst he bemoans his fate, and is obliged to support himself and his wife. His enemies, now become his masters, were before these times, mostly poor, obscure, and unnoticed; great psalm-singers, zealous religionists who would not have cracked a nut on the Sabbath, — no, not for any worldly consideration. They were meek, lowly Christians, always referring every accident to God's divine providence and peculiar appointment; humble in their deportment, composed in their carriage, prudent in their outward actions, careful of uttering offensive words; men of plausible countenances, sleek-

10 haired, but possessed at the same time of great duplicity of heart; shy in their common social intercourse, callous, — pushing, with an affected charitable language, from their doors the poor, the orphan, the widow.

I have known some of these country saints to tenaciously detain in gaol some debtors for twelve pounds, which S. K., unknown to everybody, would privately cause to be paid. These are the people who before these times were ostentatiously devout, laboriously exact in their morning prayers, reading, expoundings, etc. These are the men who now in the obscure parts of this country have assumed the iron sceptre and from religious hypocrites are become political tyrants. That affected meekness, that delusive softness of manners are now gone; they are discarded as useless.

20 They were formerly the high road to popularity, applause, and public respect, but this new zeal for their new cause must not, like the ancient one, moulder under the ashes and be afraid of sunshine and of air. It must burn, it must conflagrate; the more violent the flames, the thicker the smoke, the more meritorious. Whilst the unaffected good man, the sincere Christian, who proved his principles by his actions more than by his vain words and his disputations, is reprobated, shunned, despised, and punished, the secret liar, the hidden fornicator, the nocturnal drunkard, the stranger to charity and benevolence are uplifted on modern wings, and obtain the applause of the world which should be the reward of merit, of benefits conferred, of useful actions done.

30 Surely this points out the absolute necessity of future rewards and punishments. Were not I convinced of it, I would not suffer the rebukes, the taunts, the daily infamy, to which I have conscientiously exposed myself. I'd turn Manichean like so many others. I'd worship the demon of the times, trample on every law, break every duty, neglect every bond, overlook every obligation to which no punishment was annexed. I'd set myself calumniating my rich neighbours. I'd call all passive, inoffensive men by the name of inimical. I'd plunder or detain the entrusted deposits. I'd trade on public moneys, though contrary to my oath. Oath! Chaff for good Whigs, and only fit to bind a few conscientious Royalists! I'd build my new fortune on the depreciation of the money. I'd inform against every man who would make any dif-

40 ference betwixt it and silver, whilst I, secure from any discovery or suspicion by my

---

3 **His enemies.** The passage which follows suggests something of the class conflict which underlay the Revolution 32 **Manichean.** Manichaeism was a religion originating in Babylonia in the third century, with Mani or Manes. Long regarded as dangerous by the Christian church, it was often misrepresented. To Crèvecoeur, Manichaeism apparently meant the same thing as materialism, an equation which it did not deserve

good name, would privately exchange ten for one. I'd pocket the fines of poor militiamen extracted from their heart's blood. I'd become obdurate, merciless, and unjust. I'd grow rich, *"fas vel nefas."* I'd send others a-fighting, whilst I stayed at home to trade and to rule. I'd become a clamorous American, a modern Whig, and offer every night incense to the god Arimanes.

1780?, 1925

──────────

3 *"fas vel nefas,"* right or wrong   5 the god Arimanes, Ahriman, the Persian name for the Devil, or principle of evil

1720–1772 John Woolman

T he *Journal* of John Woolman has found enthusiastic readers ever since its first publication in 1774. Among those who have been charmed by its revelation of a man who for honesty, simplicity, and sweetness of temper merits comparison with St. Francis of Assisi and Jesus Christ must be counted Charles Lamb, the English essayist, Lamb's friend Crabb Robinson, diarist-historian of the Romantic era, William Ellery Channing (p. 459), and John Greenleaf Whittier. To many, Woolman has come to represent American Quakerism at its splendid best, a mystic faith whose outward starkness and lack of pomp accentuate great inward richness. More recently Woolman has been much admired for his unique grasp of the social and economic implications of the concept of the Society of Friends that the human race is one great family.

The brotherhood of man was to Woolman not an ideal but a reality, and as he grew older he sought to divorce himself, quietly but firmly, from all actions and institutions which even indirectly involved injustice to his fellow creatures. Although he made much of his living by drawing up legal documents, he refused to make out bills of sale for slaves. When he learned that plantation workers in the West Indies endured indescribable hardships, he did without sugar. Before he died he was examining every aspect, every purchase, of his daily life in the light of its social effect. He hit upon the methods of passive resistance, non-coöperation, and the economic boycott and, like Thoreau two generations later, learned to scale down his wants to fit his principles. Woolman did not reform society, but he tried to deal honestly with the exceedingly complicated problem of an individual's just relation to his fellow men. On occasion his methods have proved to be tremendously effective.

Woolman was born on a farm on Rancocas Creek, midway between Burlington and Mount Holly, New Jersey. There he lived until he was twenty, learning to love the Quaker way of life in his family, the village school, and the weekly Meeting. He then went into a shop in Mount Holly, five miles away, and in his spare time learned the tailor's trade. Diligent and thrifty, he might easily have grown wealthy, but his social conscience was obviously far greater than that of most of his associates. Soon he felt the call to visit other Meetings, as was the custom of those Friends who wished to become ministers and elders in a sect which had no professional clergy. During the last half of his life, except when he was ill, he made at least one journey a year, sometimes being away from home for as long as four months. Usually accompanied by another Friend, he visited and testified at Quaker meetings and in Quaker homes from New England to the Carolinas and westward into the Indian country, telling what was in his mind and heart and remonstrating with Quaker slaveholders and businessmen whose lives, in his judgment, fell short of what he called "pure wisdom." His tact, his literary skill, and, most of all, his unimpeachable sincerity made him successful in Quaker politics and action, and he was chiefly responsible for consolidating Quaker sentiment for the emancipation of Negro slaves. His inclination to help arouse the English Quakers to the importance of this cause sent him to England in 1772. He arrived in London in June, visited Friends there and in the neighborhood, and then, wishing to go to the North, chose characteristically to walk rather than have any part in the oppression of postboys and horses. He got as far as York, where he died of smallpox in September.

In the course of his life Woolman wrote more than a dozen essays on matters which he thought ought to be more fully considered by the Quakers. Some of them were published during his lifetime, usually by the Overseers of the Press of the Philadelphia Meeting, so that they were distributed among Quakers with some degree of authority. The *Essay on Some Considerations on the Keeping of Negroes* (Part I, 1754; Part II, 1762) and *Considerations on Pure Wisdom and Human Policy* (1758) are the most important. A few of the more radical essays and the *Journal* did not appear until after Woolman's death.

Woolman's writing is far from being as artless as it may seem at first glance. He gained precisely the effect of unpretentious directness that he wanted, and he revised some of his manuscripts with considerable care. His Quaker readers were suspicious of learning, of dependence upon close-knit logic or rhetorical devices. The sweet reasonableness of Woolman's tone and the apparent carelessness in organization clothe a keen and penetrating intellect, stored with the rich wisdom of the Bible and of personal experience and directed by convictions which are often revolutionary.

The Journal and Essays of John Woolman, ed. Amelia M. Gummere, New York, 1922   Janet Whitney, John Woolman, American Quaker, Boston, 1942

from The Journal and Essays of John Woolman

Woolman tells us that he began his journal when he was thirty-six. Presumably he kept some kind of day-by-day diary, but so far as is known none is extant. The Journal *has come down to us in two manuscripts, one of which includes a number of Woolman's essays and is the manuscript which he himself prepared for the publication committee of the Philadelphia Meeting. The Journal consists of eleven chapters: all of Chapter I and a part of Chapter III follow. Mrs. Whitney has shown in her biography, by reference to manuscript account books, that Woolman's dating of events, probably from memory, is not always to be relied upon. His account of his gradual progress toward spiritual enlightenment, "until I felt that rise which prepares the creature to Stand like a Trumpet, through which the Lord Speaks to his flock," is possibly the clearest exposition of the Quaker faith in our literature.*

Chapter I

I have often felt a motion of Love to leave some hints of my experience of the Goodness of God: and pursuant thereto, in the 36 year of my age, I begin this work.

I was Born in Northampton, in Burlington county, in West Jersey, in the year of our Lord 1720 & before I was seven years old, I began to be acquainted with the operations of Divine Love. Through the care of my Parents, I was taught to Read as soon as I was capable of it, and as I went from School one seventh-day, I remember, while my companions went to play by the way, I went forward out of sight, and seting down, I read the twenty second chapter of the Revelations: "He showed me a pure River of Water of Life, clear as Crystal, proceeding out of the Throne of God and of the Lamb," &c. and in the reading of it, my mind was drawn to seek 10 after that Pure Habitation, which I then believed God had prepared for his servants. The place where I sat, and the sweetness that attended my soul, remain fresh in my memory.

This, and the like Gracious Visitations, had that effect upon me, that when boys used ill language, it troubled me, & through the continued Mercies of God, I was preserved from it. The pious instructions of my Parents were often fresh in my mind when I happened to be among wicked children, and were of use to me.

My Parents haveing a large family of children, used frequently on first-days after meeting, to put us to read in the Holy Scriptures, or some religious books, one after another, the rest sitting by without much conversation, which I have since 20 often thought was a good practice. From what I had read, I believed there had been in past ages, people who Walked in Uprightness before God in a degree exceeding any that I knew, or heard of, now living: & the Apprehension of their being less Steadiness and firmness amongst people in this age than in past ages, often Troubled me while I was still young.

I had a Dream about the ninth year of my age as follows: I saw the Moon rise near the West, & run a regular course Eastward, so swift that in about a quarter of an hour, she reached our Meridian, when there descended from her a small Cloud on the Direct line to the Earth, which lighted on a pleasant Green about twenty yards from the Door of my Father's House (in which I thought I stood) and was 30 immediately turned into a Beautiful green Tree. The Moon appeared to run on with Equal swiftness, and soon set in the East, at which time the Sun arose at the place

18 **large family.** John Woolman was the fourth child and eldest son in a family of six girls and seven boys   26 **a Dream.** The symbolism of Woolman's dream is obscure, but presumably has something to do with his knowledge of good and evil

where it commonly doth in the Sumer, and Shineing with full Radiance in a Serene air, it appeared as plesant a morning as ever I saw.

All this time I stood still in the door, in an Awfull frame of mind, and I observed that as heat increased by the Riseing Sun, it wrought so powerfully on the little green Tree, that the leaves gradually withered, and before Noon it appear'd dry & dead. There then appeared a Being, Small of Size, moving Swift from the North Southward, called a *"Sun Worm."*

Tho' I was A Child, this dream was instructive to me.

Another thing remarkable in my childhood was, that once as I went to a neigh-
10 bour's house, I saw, on the way, a Robbin sitting on her nest, and as I came near she went off, but having young ones, flew about, and with many cries expressed her Concern for them. I stood and threw stones at her, till one striking her, she fell down dead. At first I was pleas'd with the Exploit, but after a few minutes was seized with Horror, as haveing in a sportive way kild an Innocent Creature while she was carefull for her young. I beheld her lying dead, & thought those young ones for which she was so carefull must now perish for want of their dam to nourish them; and after some painfull considerations on the subject, I climbed up the Tree, took all the young birds, and killed them supposing that better than to leave them to pine away and die miserably; and believ'd in this case, that scripture proverb was
20 fulfilled, "The tender mercies of the wicked are Cruel." I then went on my errand, but, for some hours, could think of little else but the Cruelties I had committed, and was much troubled.

Thus He whose tender Mercies are over all his works, hath placed that in the Human mind which incites to exercise goodness towards every liveing creature and This being singly attended to, people become tender-hearted and sympathizing; but being frequently & totally rejected, the mind shuts itself up in a Contrary disposition.

About the twelfth year of my age, my Father being abroad, my Mother reproved me for some misconduct, to which I made an Undutifull reply & the next first-day, as I was with my Father returning from Meeting, He told me he understood I had
30 behaved amis to my Mother, and Advised me to be more carefull in future. I knew myself blameable, and in shame and confusion remained silent. Being thus awakened to a sense of my Wickedness, I felt remorse in my mind, and geting home, I retired and prayed to the Lord to forgive me; and I do not remember that I ever after that, spoke unhandsomely to either of my Parents, however foolish in some other things.

Having attained the age of Sixteen, I began to love wanton company: and though I was preserved from profane language or Scandalous conduct, Still I perceived a plant in me which produced much wild grapes. Yet my Merciful Father forsook me not utterly, but at times through his grace I was brought seriously to consider my
40 ways, and the sight of my backsliding affected me with sorrow: but for want of rightly attending to the reproofs of Instruction, Vanity was added to Vanity, and Repentance. Upon the whole my mind was more and more Alienated from the Truth, and I has-

---

19 **scripture proverb,** Proverbs 10:12

tened towards Destruction. While I meditate on the Gulf towards which I traveled, and reflect on my youthful Disobedience, my heart is affected with Sorrow.

Advancing in age, the number of my Acquaintance increased, and thereby my way grew more difficult. Though I had heretofore found comfort in reading the Holy Scriptures, and thinking on heavenly things, I was now Estranged therefrom. I knew I was going from the flock of Christ, and had no resolution to return, hence serious reflections were uneasie to me, and Youthfull Vanities and Diversions my greatest pleasure. Runing in this Road I found many like myself, and we associated in that which is reverse to true Friendship: but in this swift race it pleased God to visit me with Sickness, so that I doubted of recovering: and then did Darkness, Horror and 10 Amazement, with full force seize me, even when my pain and distress of body was verry great: I thought it would have been better for me never to have had a being, than to see the day which I now saw. I was filled with Confusion, & in great affliction both of mind & body, I lay and bewailed myself. I had not confidence to lift up my cries to God, whom I had thus offended; but in a deep sense of my great folly I was humbled before Him, & at length that Word which is as a Fire and a Hamer, broke and dissolved my rebellious heart, and then my Cries were put up in contrition, and in the multitude of His mercies I found inward relief, and felt a close Engagement, that if he was pleased to Restore my health, I might walk Humbly before Him.   20

After my Recovery, this Exercise remained with me a considerable time, but, by degrees, giving way to youthfull vanities, they gained strength, and geting with wanton young people I lost ground. The Lord had been verry Gracious, and Spoke peace to me in the time of my distress, and I now most ungratefully turned again to folly, on which account, at times, I felt sharp reproof, but did not get low enough to Cry for help. I was not so hardy as to commit things scandalous, but to Exceed in Vanity, and promote myrth, was my chief study. Still I retained a love and esteem for pious people, and their company brought an Awe upon me. My Dear Parents several times Admonished me in the fear of the Lord, and their admonition entered into my heart, & had a good effect for a season, but not geting deep enough 30 to pray rightly, the tempter when he came found entrance. I remember once having spent a part of a day in wantonness, as I went to bed at night, there lay in a window near my bed a Bible, which I opened, and first cast my eye on the Text, "we lie down in our shame, and our confusion covers us." This I knew to be my case, and meeting with so unexpected a reproof, I was somewhat Affected with it, and went to bed under remorse of conscience, which I soon cast off again.

Thus time passed on, my heart was replenished with myrth and wantonness, while pleasing scenes of Vanity were presented to my Imagination, till I attain'd the age of Eighteen years, near which time I felt the Judgments of God in my soul like a consuming fire, and looking over my past life, the prospect was moveing. I was 40 often sad, and longed to be deliver'd from those vanities; then again my heart was Strongly Inclined to them, and there was in me a sore conflict. At times I turned to

---

33 **the Text,** Jeremiah 3:25

folly, and then again sorrow and confusion took hold of me. In a while I resolved totally to leave off some of my vanities, but there was a secret reserve in my heart, of the more refined part of them, and I was not low enough to find true peace. Thus for some months, I had great troubles and disquiet, there remaining in me an unsubjected will, which rendered my labours fruitless, till at length, through the Mercifull continuance of Heavenly Visitations, I was made to bow down in Spirit before the Most High. I remember one evening I had spent some time in reading a pious author, and walking out a lone, I humbly prayed to the Lord for his help, that I might be delivered from those vanities which so ensnared me. Thus being brought
10 low he helped me, and as I learned to bear the Cross, I felt refreshment to come from his Presence: but not keeping in that Strength which gave victory I lost ground again, The sense of which greatly afflicted me and I sought Desarts and lonely places, and there with tears did confess my Sins to God, and humbly craved help of HIM, and I may say with Reverence he was near to me in my troubles, and in those times of Humiliation opened my ear to Discipline.

I was now led to look seriously at the means by which I was drawn from the pure Truth, and I learned this. That if I would live in the life which the Faithful servants of God lived in, I must not go into company as heretofore in my own will, but all the cravings of Sense must be governed by a Divine principle. In times of
20 sorrow and abasement these Instructions were sealed upon me, and I felt the power of Christ prevail over all selfish desires, so that I was preserved in a good degree of steadiness, and being young and believing at that time that a single life was best for me, I was strengthened to keep from such company as had often been a snare to me.

I kept steady to meetings, spent first-days in the afternoon chiefly in reading the scriptures and other good Books, and was early convinced in my mind that true Religion consisted in an inward life, wherein the Heart doth Love and Reverence God the Creator, and learn to Exercise true Justice and Goodness, not only toward all men, but allso toward the Brute Creatures. That as the mind was moved by an
30 inward Principle to Love God as an invisible, Incomprehensible Being, by the same principle it was moved to love him in all his manifestations in the Visible world. That as by his breath the flame of life was kindled in all Animal and Sensible creatures, to say we Love God as unseen, and at the same time Exercise cruelty toward the least creature moving by his life, or by life derived from Him, was a Contradiction in itself.

I found no narrowness respecting Sects and Opinions, but believe that sincere upright-hearted people, in Every society who truly love God were accepted of HIM.

As I lived under the Cross, and simply followed the openings of Truth, my mind from day to day was more Enlightened, my former acquaintance were left to judge
40 of me as they would, for I found it safest for me to live in private and keep these things sealed up in my own breast. While I silently ponder on that change which was wrought in me, I find no language equal to it, nor any means to convey a clear idea of it. I looked upon the works of God in this Visible Creation, and an awfullness covered me: my heart was tender and often contrite, and a universal Love to

my fellow Creatures increased in me. This will be understood by such who have troden in the same path.

Some glances of Real beauty is percieveble in their faces, who dwell in true meekness. Some tincture of true Harmony in the sound of that voice to which Divine Love gives utterance, & Some appearance of right order in their temper and Conduct, whose passions are fully regulated, yet all these do not fully show forth that inward life to such who have not felt it; but this white stone and new name is known rightly to such only who have it.

Now tho' I had been thus Strengthened to bear the Cross, I still found myself in great danger, having many weaknesses Attending me, and strong Temptations to 10 wrestle with, in the feeling whereof I frequently withdrew into private places, and often with tears besought the Lord to help me, whose gracious ear was open to my cry.

All this time I lived with my Parents, and wrought on the plantation, and having had schooling pretty well for a planter, I used to improve winter evenings, and other leisure times, and being now in the Twenty first year of my age, a man in much business at Shopkeeping and Baking, asked me if I would hire with him to tend Shop and keep books. I acquainted my Father with the proposal, and, after some deliberation it was agreed for me to go. I had for a considerable time found my mind less given to Husbandry than heretofore, having often in view some other 20 way of living.

At home I had lived retired, and now having a prospect of being much in the way of company, I felt frequent and fervent Cries in my heart to God the Father of Mercies, that he would preserve me from all Taint & Corruption. That in this more public Employ, I might serve Him my Gracious Redeemer, in that Humility and self Denial with which I had been in a small degree exercised in a verry private life.

The man who employed me furnished a Shop in Mountholly, about five miles from my Father's house & Six from his own and there I lived alone, & tended his Shop. Shortly after my settlement here, I was visited by several young people, my former acquaintances, who knew not but vanities would be as agreeable to me now 30 as ever, and at these times I cryed unto the Lord in Secret for wisdom and Strength, for I felt myself Encompassed with difficulties, and had fresh Ocasion to bewail the follies of time past, in contracting a familiarity with Libertine people. And as I had now left my Fathers house outwardly, I found my Heavenly Father to be mercifull to me beyond what I can express.

By day I was much among people, and had many tryals to go through, but in evenings I was mostly alone, and may with thankfulness acknowledge, that in those times the Spirit of Supplication was often poured upon me, under which I was frequently exercised, and felt my Strength renewed.

In a few months after I came here, my Master bought several Scotch men-servants, 40 from on board a Vessel, and brought them to Mountholly to sell & having sold several the rest were left with me, one of which was taken sick, & died. The latter

---

7 **white stone ... name,** Revelations 2:17: "... To him that overcometh I will give ... him a white stone, and in the stone a new name, which no man knoweth saving he that receiveth it"

part of his sickness, he, being delirious, used to curse and Swear most sorrowfully, and after he was buried, I was left to sleep alone the next night in the same chamber where he died. I perceived in me a Timorousness: I knew however I had not injured the man, but had assisted in taking care of him according to my capacity, and I was not free to ask any one, on that occasion, to sleep with me: nature was feble, but every tryal was a fresh incitement to give myself up wholly to the service of God, for I found no helper like Him in times of Trouble.

After a while my former Acquaintance gave over Expecting me as one of their company, and I began to be known to some whose conversation was helpful to me.
10 And now, as I had Experienced the Love of God, through Jesus Christ, to Redeem me from many polutions, and to be a constant succour to me through a Sea of conflicts, with which no person was fully acquainted, and as my heart was often enlarged in this Heavenly Principle, so I felt a tender compassion for the youth who remain'd entangled in the same snares which had entangled me. From one month to another, this Love & tenderness increased, and my mind was more strongly engaged for the good of my fellow-creatures. I went to meetings in an awfull frame of mind, and endeavoured to be inwardly acquainted with the language of the True Shephered, and one day being under a strong Exercise of Spirit, I stood up, and said some words in a meeting, but not keeping close to the Divine opening, I said more than was
20 required of me & being soon sencible of my error, I was afflicted in mind some weeks, without any light or comfort, even to that degree that I could take satisfaction in nothing. I remembered God, and was troubled and in the depth of my distress he had pitty upon me, and sent the Comforter. I then felt forgiveness for my offence, and my mind became calm and quiet, being truly thankfull to my Gracious Redeemer for his mercies. And after this, feeling the spring of Divine Love opened, and a Concern to Speak, I said a few words in meeting in which I found peace; this I believe was about six weeks from the first time, and as I was thus humbled and disciplined under the Cross, my understanding became more strengthened to distinguish the language of the pure Spirit which inwardly moves upon the heart, and taught me
30 to wait in Silence sometimes many weeks together, until I felt that rise which prepares the creature to Stand like a Trumpet, through which the Lord Speaks to his flock.

From an inward purifying, and stedfast abiding under it, springs a lively operative · desire for the good of others. All faithful people are not called to the publick ministry but whoever are called to it, are called to minister of that which they have taisted and handled spiritually. The outward modes of worship are various, but wheresoever [men] are true Ministers of Jesus Christ, it is from the operation of his Spirit upon their hearts, first purifying them, and thus giving them a [feeling] sense of the conditions of others. This truth was early fixed in my mind, and I was taught to watch the pure opening, and to take heed least while I was standing to speak, my own
40 will should get upermost, and cause me to utter words from worldly wisdom, and depart from the Chanel of the true Gospel Ministry.

In the management of my outward affairs I may say with thankfulness I found Truth to be my Support, and I was respected in my Masters Family who came to live in Mountholly within two years after my going there [1742.]

About the twenty third year of my age I had many fresh and heavenly openings, in respect to the care and providence of the Almighty over his creatures in general, and over man as the most noble amongst those which are visible, and Being clearly convinced in my Judgmt that to place my whole trust in God was best for me, I felt renewed engagements that in all things I might act on an inward principle of Virtue, and pursue worldly business no further than as Truth open'd my way therein.

About the time called Christmas I observed many people from the Country, and dwellers in Town, who resorting to publick houses, spent their time in drinking and vain sports, tending to, corrupt one another, on which account I was much 10 troubled. At one house in particular there was much disorder, and I believed it was a duty laid on me to go and speak to the master of that house. I considered I was young, and that several Elderly friends in Town had opportunity to See these things, and though I would gladly have been excused, yet I could not feel my mind clear. The Exercise was heavy, and as I was Reading what the Almighty Said to Ezekiel, respecting his duty as a watchman, the matter was set home more clearly, and then with prayer and tears, I besought the Lord for his Assistance, who in loving kindness gave me a Resigned heart. Then at a sutable Opportunity, I went to the publick house, and Seeing the man amongst a company, I went to him and told him I wanted to speak with him, so we went aside, and there in the Fear and dread of the Almighty 20 I Exprest to him what rested on my mind, which he took kindly, and afterward showed more regard to me than before. In a few years after he died, midle-aged, and I often thought that had I neglected my duty in that case, it would have given me great trouble and I was humbly thankfull to my Gracious Father, who had supported me therein.

My Employer having a Negro woman sold her, and directed me to write a bill of Sale, The man being waiting who had bought her. The thing was Sudden, and though the thoughts of writing an Instrument of Slavery for one of my fellow creatures felt uneasie, yet I remembered I was hired by the year; that it was my master who directed me to do it, and that it was an Elderly man, a member of our society who bought 30 her, so through weakness I gave way, and wrote it, but at the Executing it I was so Afflicted in my mind, that I said before my Master and the friend, that I believed Slavekeeping to be a practice inconsistent with the Christian Religion: this in some degree abated my uneasiness, yet as often as I reflected seriously upon it I thought I should have been clearer, if I had desired to be Excused from it, as a thing against my conscience, for such it was. [And] some time after this a young man of our Society, spake to me to write [an instrument of Slavery], he having taken a Negro into his house. I told him I was not easie to write it, for though many [people] kept slaves in our society as in others, I still believed the practice was not right, and desired to be excused from doing the writing. I spoke to him in good will, and 40 he told me, that keeping slaves was not altogether agreable to his mind, but that the slave being a gift made to his wife, he had accepted of her.

---

15 **Ezekiel.** See Ezekiel 3:17-19

Chapter III

. . . Until the year 1756, I continued to retail goods, besides following my trade as a Taylor; about which time I grew uneasy on account of my business growing too cumbersome. I began with selling trimings for garments, and from thence proceeded to Sell cloaths and linens, and at length having got a considerable shop of goods, my trade increased every year, and the road to large business appeared open: but I felt a Stop in my mind.

Through the Mercies of the Almighty I had in a good degree learned to be content with a plain way of living. I had but a small family my outward Affairs had been prosperous and, on serious reflection I believed Truth did not require me to
10 engage in much cumbering affairs. It had generally been my practice to buy and sell things realy usefull. Things that served chiefly to please the vain mind in people, I was not easie to trade in; seldom did it, and whenever I did, I found it weaken me as a Christian.

The increase of business became my burthen, for though my natural inclination was towards merchandize, yet I believed Truth required me to live more free from outward cumbers. There was now a strife in my mind betwixt the two, and in this exercise my prayers were put up to the Lord, who Graciously heard me, and gave me a heart resigned to his Holy will; I then lessened my outward business; and as I had opportunity told my customers of my intention that they might consider what
20 shop to turn to: and so in a while, wholly laid down merchandize, following my trade as a Taylor, myself only, having no prentice. I also had a nursery of Apple trees, in which I spent a good deal of time, howing, grafting, triming & Inoculating.

In merchandize it is the custom, where I lived, to sell chiefly on credit; and poor people often get in debt, & when payment is expected haveing not wherewith to pay, & so their creditors often sue for it at Law: having often observed occurrences of this kind, I found it good for me to advise poor people to take such as were most useful & not costly.

In the time of trading I had an oportunity of seeing that a too liberal use of Spirituous liquors, and the Custom of wearing too costly apparrel, led some people into great
30 inconveniences: and these two things appear to be often connected one with the other; for by not attending to that use of things which is consistent with Universal Righteousness, there is a [necessary] increase of Labour which extends beyond what our Heavenly Father intends for us: and by great labour, and often by much sweting in the heat there is, even among such who are not drunkards, a craving of some liquor to revive the spirits: That partly by the wanton, Luxurious drinking of some, and partly by the drinking of others, led to it through immoderate labour, verry great quantities of Rum are annually expended in our Colonies, of which we should have no need, did we steadily Attend to pure Wisdom.

Where men take pleasure in feeling their minds elevated with strong drink, and
40 so indulge this appetite as to disorder their understanding, neglect their duty as mem-

---

22 **howing,** hoeing

bers in a family or civil society, and cast off all pretence to Religion, their case is much to be pittied; And where such whose lives are for the most part regular, and whose Examples have a strong influence on the minds of others, Adhere to some customs which powerfully draw toward the use of More strong liquor than pure wisdom [directeth the Use of,] this allso, as it hinders the spreading of the Spirit of meekness, and Strengthens the hands of the more Excessive drinkers, is a case to be lamented.

As [the least] degree of luxury hath some connection with evil, for those who profess to be disciples of Christ, and are looked upon as leaders of the people, to have that mind in them which was also in Him, & so stand separate from every 10 wrong way, is a means of help to the weaker. As I have sometimes been much spent in the heat, and taken spirits to revive me. I have found by Experience that the mind is not so calm in such circumstances, nor so fitly disposed for Divine meditation, as when all such extreams are avoided; and I have felt an increasing Care to attend to that Holy Spirit which sets right bounds to our desires, and leads those who faithfully follow it to apply all the gifts of Divine Providence to the purposes for which they were intended. Did such who have the care of great Estates, attend with singleness of heart to this Heavenly Instructor, which so opens and enlarges the mind that Men love their neighbours as themselves, They would have wisdom given them to manage, without ever finding occasion to employ some people in the Luxuries 20 of life, or to make it necessary for others to labour too hard: But for want of regarding steadily this Principle of Divine love, a selfish Spirit takes place in the minds of people, which is attended with darkness & manifold confusions in the world.

In the Course of my Tradeing, being somewhat affected at the Various Law Suits about collecting Money which I saw going forward; On aplying to a Constable, he gave me a List of his proceedings for one year as follows; to wit.

Served 267 Warrants, 103 Summonses, and 17 Executions! As to Writs Served by the Sheriff, I got no account of them.

I once had a Warrant for an Idle Man, who I believed was about to run away, which was the only time I applied to the Law to recover Money.   30

Through trading in things Usefull is an honest employ, yet through the great number of Superfluities which are commonly bought and sold, and through the corruptions of the times, they who apply to merchandize for a living, have great need to be well experienced in that precept which the prophet Jeremiah laid down for Baruc, his scribe: "Seekest thou great things for thyself? seek them not." . . .

                                                                                          1772?, 1774

_____

31 **Through.** Sense would seem to require "Though"   34 **precept.** See Jeremiah 45:5

from *A Plea for the Poor*

A Word of Remembrance and Caution to the Rich *(Dublin, 1793) first appeared under Woolman's simpler title in 1837. It was probably written during the winter of 1763-1764. None of Woolman's essays has attracted more attention recently; none shows more clearly the*

*amazing breadth of his humanitarianism. Abridged and published as Fabian Tract No. 79
(January 1898), it eventually had wide circulation in England, the editor remarking that it
contains "the most connected account" of Woolman's views on social questions. The same editor
described Woolman as "the voice in the wilderness, the John the Baptist of the Gospel of Socialism." In its entirety, the essay consists of sixteen chapters. The first two, reprinted here, give
Woolman's general position; in the others he discusses the responsibilities of the wealthy, the
dangers of overwork and avarice, the economic origin of war, the injustice of primogeniture, the
proper education of children, and the duties of masters to their servants and slaves.*

Chapter I

Wealth desired for its own sake Obstructs the increase of Virtue, and large possessions in the hands of selfish men have a bad tendency, for by their means too small a
number of people are employed in things usefull, and therefore some of them are
necessitated to labour too hard, while others would want business to earn their Bread,
were not employments invented, which having no real use, serve only to please the
vain mind.

Rents set on lands are often so high, that persons who have but small substance
are straitened in hiring a plantation and while Tenants are healthy, and prosperous
in business, they often find Occasion to labour harder than was intended by our
10 Gracious Creator.

Oxen & Horses are often seen at work, when through Heat & too much labour,
their eyes, and the emotion of their Bodies manifest that they are oppressed. Their
loads in Wagons are frequently so heavy, than when weary with halling it far, their
drivers find occasion in going up Hills, or through mire, to raise their spirits by
whiping to get forward. Many poor people are so thronged in their business, that it
is difficult for them to provide Shelter sutable for their animals, in great storms.
These things are common when in health; but through Sickness and inability to
labour through loss of Creatures, and miscarriage in business, many are straitened;
& much of their increase goes to pay rent or Interest, that they have not wherewith
20 to hire so much as their case requires. Hence one poor woman in attending on her
Children, providing for her family, & helping the sick, does as much business as
would for the time be Sutable Employment for two or three, and honest persons
are often straitened to give their children sutable learning.

The mony which the wealthy receive from the poor, who do more than a proper
share of business in raising it, is frequently paid to other poor people for doing business which is foreign to the true use of things.

Men who have large possessions, & live in the spirit of Charity, who carefully
inspect the circumstance of those who occupy their Estates, and, regardless of the
Customs of the times, regulate their demands agreeably to Universal Love: these by
30 being Righteous on a principle, do good to the poor without placing it as an act
of bounty. Their Example in avoiding superfluities tends to incite others to modera-

---

Text: Mrs. Gummere's edition   5 **having . . . use.** The objection to luxury, frequent in Woolman's writings and a characteristic eighteenth century notion, should be compared with that by Timothy Dwight,
p. 541

tion; their goodness, in not exacting what the Laws or Customs would support them in, tends to open the Channel to moderate Labour in useful Affairs, and to discourage those branches of business which have not their foundation in true wisdom.

To be busied in that which is but vanity, & serves only to please the unstable mind, tends to an alliance with those who promote that vanity, and is a snare in which many poor tradesmen are entangled.

To be employed in things connected with Virtue, is most agreeable with the Character and Inclination of an honest man.

While industrious frugal people are borne down with poverty, and opressed with too much labour in useful things, the way to apply mony, without promoting pride 10 and Vanity, remains open to such who truly Sympathize with them in their various Difficulties.

Chapter II

The Creator of the earth is the owner of it. He gave us being thereon, and our nature requires nourishment, which is the produce of it. As he is kind and merciful we, as his creatures, while we live answerable to the design of our creation, are so far Entitled to a convenient Subsistence, that no man may justly deprive us of it.

By the agreements and Contracts of Our Fathers and predecessors, and by doings and proceedings of our own, some claim a much greater share of this world than others: and while those possessions are Faithfully Improved to the good of the whole, it consists with Equity. But he who with a view to self-exaltation, causeth some 20 with their domestick Animals to labour immoderately, and, with the monys arising to him therefrom, employs others in the Luxuries of Life, Acts, contrary to the Gracious designs of Him who is the true owner of the Earth, nor can any possessions, either acquired or derived from Ancestors, justify such conduct.

Goodness Remains to be goodness, and the direction of pure wisdom is obligatory on all Reasonable Creatures: that Laws and Customs are no further a Standard for our proceedings than as their Foundation is on Universal Righteousness.

Though the poor Occupy our Estates by a bargain, to which they in their poor Circumstances agreed, and we ask even less than a punctual fulfilling of their agreement; yet if our views are to lay up riches, or to live in conformity to customs which 30 have not their Foundation in the Truth, and our demands are such as requires greater Toyl, or application to business in them, than is Consistent with pure Love, we invade their rights as Inhabitants of that World, of which a good and gracious God is proprietor, under whom we are Tennants.

Were all superfluities, and the desire of outward greatness laid aside, and the right use of things universally attended to, Such a number of people might be employed in things usefull, as that moderate labour, with the Blessing of Heaven, would answer all good purposes relating to people and their Animals, and a Sufficient number have time to attend to proper Affairs of Civil Society.

1763-1764?, 1793

1739—1823 William Bartram

Wilham Bartram could draw and color pictures of Pennsylvania turtles well enough to have them published in the *Gentleman's Magazine* in London, but he was not anxious to be apprenticed to an engraver. He failed to make his living either as a trader or as a farmer. Wandering with his father into the back country, collecting seeds and plants to send to wealthy gardening enthusiasts in England, he had learned a great many things, none of them especially profitable.

In another environment, perhaps, Bartram's meticulous observations might have made him a great botanist, ornithologist, geologist, or anthropologist, but he would not have been happy. In his time the study of nature was relatively unspecialized, and it was still possible to see a plant, a bird, a landscape, or an Indian as an individual rather than as a specimen. Nature to Bartram was animistic, sublime, unspoiled, and beautiful; his Seminoles and Cherokees were, except when corrupted by the white man, unblemished in their nobility, as became nature's children. The great adventure of his life was as much poetic as scientific — a series of excursions into the deep South between 1773 and 1777, when he walked and sailed and paddled through enchanting country, taking notes for a book wherein poetry is modestly hidden behind a prosaic title: *Travels Through North & South Carolina, Georgia, East & West Florida, the Cherokee Country, the Extensive Territories of the Muscogules, or Creek Confederacy, and the Country of the Chactaws; Containing an Account of the Soil and Natural Productions of Those Regions, Together with Observations on the Manners of the Indians* (Philadelphia, 1791).

The *Travels* was reprinted in London editions in 1792 and 1794, in a Dublin edition in 1793, and translations were soon available in German (1793), Dutch (1794-1797), and French (1799-1801). It has been frequently reprinted in recent years.

Because Bartram was able to communicate his delight in the world with disarming and attractive freshness, one can readily understand why he was a favorite among many leading writers of the Romantic period.

Ernest Earnest, **John and William Bartram, Botanists and Explorers,** Philadelphia, 1940   **The Travels of William Bartram,** ed. Mark Van Doren, with introduction by John L. Lowes, New York, 1940; Naturalist's Edition, ed. Francis Harper, New Haven, 1958   N. B. Fagin, **William Bartram, Interpreter of the American Landscape,** Baltimore, 1933.

from Travels

Part I of the Travels *describes a sea trip from Philadelphia to Savannah, with a stop at Charleston, and several excursions into what is now the interior of Georgia. Part II, the longest and most popular section, covers travels in northern Florida. Part III is an account of a trip from Charleston across South Carolina and northern Georgia into Alabama and Louisiana. Part IV is "An Account of the Persons, Manners, Customs and Government of the Muscogules or Creeks, &c. Aborigines of the Continent of North America."*

The first selection printed here is the first quarter of Chapter 5, Part II; it is an example both of Bartram's attitude toward nature and of his narrative skill. The second selection, from Chapter 3, Part III, illustrates Bartram's acquaintance with traditions of pastoral literature.

Being desirous of continuing my travels and observations, higher up the river, and having an invitation from a gentleman who was agent for, and resident at a large plantation, the property of an English gentleman, about sixty miles higher up, I resolved to pursue my researches to that place; and having engaged in my service a young Indian, nephew to the White Captain, he agreed to assist me in working my vessel up as high as a certain bluff, where I was, by agreement, to land him, on the West or Indian shore, whence he designed to go in quest of the camp of the White Trader, his relation.

Provisions and all necessaries being procured, and the morning pleasant, we went on board and stood up the river. We passed for several miles on the left, by islands 10 of high swamp land, exceedingly fertile, their banks for a good distance from the water, much higher than the interior part, and sufficiently so to build upon, and be out of the reach of inundations. They consist of a loose black mould, with a mixture of sand, shells and dissolved vegetables. The opposite Indian coast is a perpendicular bluff, ten or twelve feet high, consisting of a black sandy earth, mixed with a large proportion of shells, chiefly various species of fresh water Cochlea and Mytuli. Near the river, on this high shore, grew Corypha palma, Magnolia grandiflora, Live Oak, Callicarpa, Myrica cerifera, Hybiscus spinifex, and the beautiful evergreen shrub called Wild lime or Tallow nut. This last shrub grows six or eight feet high, many erect stems rising from a root; the leaves are lanciolate and intire, two or three inches 20 in length and one in breadth, of a deep green colour, and polished; at the foot of each leaf grows a stiff, sharp thorn; the flowers are small and in clusters, of a greenish yellow colour, and sweet scented; they are succeeded by a large oval fruit, of the shape and size of an ordinary plumb, of a fine yellow colour when ripe, a soft sweet pulp covers a nut which has a thin shell, enclosing a white kernel somewhat of the

---

1 **the river,** the St. John's River in northeastern Florida   5 **the White Captain,** a Seminole chief, mentioned in the preceding chapter   16 **Cochlea . . . Tallow nut.** Here, as elsewhere, Bartram's scientific terms are a curious mixture of the technical, the popular, the obsolete, and the current. His generic names usually follow the classification of Linnaeus (Carl von Linné, 1707-1778), Swedish dictator of eighteenth-century natural history   20 **lanciolate,** lanceolate, spearlike

consistence and taste of the sweet Almond, but more oily and very much like hard tallow, which induced my father when he first observed it, to call it the Tallow nut.

At the upper end of this bluff is a fine Orange grove. Here my Indian companion requested me to set him on shore, being already tired of rowing under a fervid sun, and having for some time intimated a dislike to his situation, I readily complied with his desire, knowing the impossibility of compelling an Indian against his own inclinations, or even prevailing upon him by reasonable arguments, when labour is in the question; before my vessel reached the shore, he sprang out of her and landed, when uttering a shrill and terrible whoop, he bounded off like a roebuck, and I lost

10 sight of him. I at first apprehended that as he took his gun with him, he intended to hunt for some game and return to me in the evening. The day being excessively hot and sultry, I concluded to take up my quarters here until next morning.

The Indian not returning this morning, I sat sail alone. The coasts on each side had much the same appearance as already described. The Palm trees here seem to be of a different species from the Cabbage tree; their strait trunks are sixty, eighty or ninety feet high, with a beautiful taper of a bright ash colour, until within six or seven feet of the top, where it is a fine green colour, crowned with an orb of rich green plumed leaves: I have measured the stem of these plumes fifteen feet in length, besides the plume, which is nearly of the same length.

20 The little lake, which is an expansion of the river, now appeared in view; on the East side are extensive marshes, and on the other high forests and Orange groves, and then a bay, lined with vast Cypress swamps, both coasts gradually approaching each other, to the opening of the river again, which is in this place about three hundred yards wide; evening now drawing on, I was anxious to reach some high bank of the river, where I intended to lodge, and agreeably to my wishes, I soon after discovered on the West shore, a little promontory, at the turning of the river, contracting it here to about one hundred and fifty yards in width. This promontory is a peninsula, containing about three acres of high ground, and is one entire Orange grove, with a few Live Oaks, Magnolias and Palms. Upon doubling the point, I arrived at the

30 landing, which is a circular harbour, at the foot of the bluff, the top of which is about twelve feet high; and back of it is a large Cypress swamp, that spreads each way, the right wing forming the West coast of the little lake, and the left stretching up the river many miles, and encompassing a vast space of low grassy marshes. From this promontory, looking Eastward across the river, we behold a landscape of low country, u[n]paralleled as I think; on the left is the East coast of the little lake, which I had just passed, and from the Orange bluff at the lower end, the high forests begin, and increase in breadth from the shore of the lake, making a circular sweep to the right, and contain many hundred thousand acres of meadow, and this grand sweep of high forests encircles, as I apprehend, at least twenty miles of these green

40 fields, interspersed with hommocks or islets of evergreen trees, where the sovereign Magnolia and lordly Palm stand conspicuous. The islets are high shelly knolls, on

---

2 **my father.** Bartram was retracing a route he had followed with his father in 1765. John Bartram's journal of that expedition, which has been called "a kind of first draft of the *Travels*," was printed in the third edition (1769) of William Stork's *Description of East Florida*

the sides of creeks or branches of the river, which wind about and drain off the super-abundant waters that cover these meadows, during the winter season.

The evening was temperately cool and calm. The crocodiles began to roar and appear in uncommon numbers along the shores and in the river. I fixed my camp in an open plain, near the utmost projection of the promontory, under the shelter of a large Live Oak, which stood on the highest part of the ground and but a few yards from my boat. From this open, high situation, I had a free prospect of the river, which was a matter of no trivial consideration to me, having good reason to dread the subtle attacks of the alligators, who were crouding about my harbour. Having collected a good quantity of wood for the purpose of keeping up a light 10 and smoke during the night, I began to think of preparing my supper, when, upon examining my stores, I found but a scanty provision, I thereupon determined, as the most expeditious way of supplying my necessities, to take my bob and try for some trout. About one hundred yards above my harbour, began a cove or bay of the river, out of which opened a large lagoon. The mouth or entrance from the river to it was narrow, but the waters soon after spread and formed a little lake, extending into the marches, its entrance and shores within I observed to be verged with floating lawns of the Pistia and Nymphea and other aquatic plants; these I knew were ex-cellent haunts for trout.

The verges and islets of the lagoon were elegantly embellished with flowering 20 plants and shrubs; the laughing coots with wings half spread were tripping over the little coves and hiding themselves in the tufts of grass; young broods of the painted summer teal, skimming the still surface of the waters, and following the watchful parent unconscious of danger, were frequently surprised by the voracious trout, and he in turn, as often by the subtle, greedy alligator. Behold him rushing forth from the flags and reeds. His enormous body swells. His plaited tail brandished high, floats upon the lake. The waters like a cataract descend from his opening jaws. Clouds of smoke issue from his dilated nostrils. The earth trembles with his thunder. When immediately from the opposite coast of the lagoon, emerges from the deep his rival champion. They suddenly dart upon each other. The boiling surface of the 30 lake marks their rapid course, and a terrific conflict commences. They now sink to the bottom folded together in horrid wreaths. The water becomes thick and dis-coloured. Again they rise, their jaws clap together, re-echoing through the deep sur-rounding forests. Again they sink, when the contest ends at the muddy bottom of the lake, and the vanquished makes a hazardous escape, hiding himself in the muddy turbulent waters and sedge on a distant shore. The proud victor exulting returns to the place of action. The shores and forests resound his dreadful roar, together with the triumphing shouts of the plaited tribes around, witnesses of the horrid combat.

My apprehensions were highly alarmed after being a spectator of so dreadful a battle; it was obvious that every delay would but tend to encrease my dangers and 40 difficulties, as the sun was near setting, and the alligators gathered around my har-bour from all quarters; from these considerations I concluded to be expeditious in my trip to the lagoon, in order to take some fish. Not thinking it prudent to take

13 **bob,** hooks covered with fur, feathers, and cloth

my fusee with me, lest I might lose it overboard in case of a battle, which I had
every reason to dread before my return, I therefore furnished myself with a club for
my defence, went on board, and penetrating the first line of those which surrounded
my harbour, they gave way; but being pursued by several very large ones, I kept
strictly on the watch, and paddled with all my might towards the entrance of the
lagoon, hoping to be sheltered there from the multitude of my assailants; but ere I
had half-way reached the place, I was attacked on all sides, several endeavouring to
overset the canoe. My situation now became precarious to the last degree: two very
large ones attacked me closely, at the same instant, rushing up with their heads and
10 part of their bodies above the water, roaring terribly and belching floods of water
over me. They struck their jaws together so close to my ears, as almost to stun me,
and I expected every moment to be dragged out of the boat and instantly devoured,
but I applied my weapons so effectually about me, though at random, that I was so
successful as to beat them off a little; when, finding that they designed to renew the
battle, I made for the shore, as the only means left me for my preservation, for, by
keeping close to it, I should have my enemies on one side of me only, whereas I
was before surrounded by them, and there was a probability, if pushed to the last
extremity, of saving myself, by jumping out of the canoe on shore, as it is easy to
outwalk them on land, although comparatively as swift as lightning in the water. I
20 found this last expedient alone could fully answer my expectations, for as soon as I
gained the shore they drew off and kept aloof. This was a happy relief, as my confidence was, in some degree, recovered by it. On recollecting myself, I discovered
that I had almost reached the entrance of the lagoon, and determined to venture in,
if possible to take a few fish and then return to my harbour, while day-light continued; for I could now, with caution and resolution, make my way with safety along
shore, and indeed there was no other way to regain my camp, without leaving my
boat and making my retreat through the marshes and reeds, which, if I could even
effect, would have been in a manner throwing myself away, for then there would
have been no hopes of ever recovering my bark, and returning in safety to any set-
30 tlements of men. I accordingly proceeded and made good my entrance into the lagoon,
though not without opposition from the alligators, who formed a line across the
entrance, but did not pursue me into it, nor was I molested by any there, though
there were some very large ones in a cove at the upper end. I soon caught more
trout than I had present occasion for, and the air was too hot and sultry to admit
of their being kept for many hours, even though salted or barbecued. I now prepared
for my return to camp, which I succeeded in with but little trouble, by keeping close
to the shore, yet I was opposed upon re-entering the river out of the lagoon, and
pursued near to my landing (though not closely attacked) particularly by an old
daring one, about twelve feet in length, who kept close after me, and when I stepped
40 on shore and turned about, in order to draw up my canoe, he rushed up near my
feet and lay there for some time, looking me in the face, his head and shoulders out
of water; I resolved he should pay for his temerity, and having a heavy load in my
fusee, I ran to my camp, and returning with my piece, found him with his foot on

1 fusee, a light musket or firelock

the gunwale of the boat, in search of fish, on my coming up he withdrew sullenly and slowly into the water, but soon returned and placed himself in his former position, looking at me and seeming neither fearful or any way disturbed. I soon dispatched him by lodging the contents of my gun in his head, and then proceeded to cleanse and prepare my fish for supper, and accordingly took them out of the boat, laid them down on the sand close to the water, and began to scale them, when, raising my head, I saw before me, through the clear water, the head and shoulders of a very large alligator, moving slowly towards me; I instantly stepped back, when, with a sweep of his tail, he brushed off several of my fish. It was certainly most providential that I looked up at that instant, as the monster would probably, in less than a minute,   10 have seized and dragged me into the river. This incredible boldness of the animal disturbed me greatly, supposing there could now be no reasonable safety for me during the night, but by keeping continually on the watch; I therefore, as soon as I had prepared the fish, proceeded to secure myself and effects in the best manner I could: in the first place, I hauled my bark upon the shore, almost clear out of the water, to prevent their oversetting or sinking her, after this every moveable was taken out and carried to my camp, which was but a few yards off; then ranging some dry wood in such order as was the most convenient, cleared the ground round about it, that there might be no impediment in my way, in case of an attack in the night, either from the water or the land; for I discovered by this time, that this small isthmus,   20 from its remote situation and fruitfulness, was resorted to by bears and wolves. Having prepared myself in the best manner I could, I charged my gun and proceeded to reconnoitre my camp and the adjacent grounds; when I discovered that the peninsula and grove, at the distance of about two hundred yards from my encampment, on the land side, were invested by a Cypress swamp, covered with water, which below was joined to the shore of the little lake, and above to the marshes surrounding the lagoon, so that I was confined to an islet exceedingly circumscribed, and I found there was no other retreat for me, in case of an attack, but by either ascending one of the large Oaks, or pushing off with my boat.

It was by this time dusk, and the alligators had nearly ceased their roar, when I   30 was again alarmed by a tumultuous noise that seemed to be in my harbour, and therefore engaged my immediate attention. Returning to my camp I found it undisturbed, and then continued on to the extreme point of the promontory, where I saw a scene, new and surprising, which at first threw my senses into such a tumult, that it was some time before I could comprehend what was the matter; however, I soon accounted for the prodigious assemblage of crocodiles at this place, which exceeded every thing of the kind I had ever heard of.

How shall I express myself so as to convey an adequate idea of it to the reader, and at the same time avoid raising suspicions of my want of veracity. Should I say, that the river (in this place) from shore to shore, and perhaps near half a mile above   40 and below me, appeared to be one solid bank of fish, of various kinds, pushing through this narrow pass of St. Juans into the little lake, on their return down the river, and that the alligators were in such incredible numbers, and so close together from shore to shore, that it would have been easy to have walked across on their

heads, had the animals been harmless. What expressions can sufficiently declare the shocking scene that for some minutes continued, whilst this mighty army of fish were forcing the pass? During this attempt, thousands, I may say hundreds of thousands of them were caught and swallowed by the devouring alligators. I have seen an alligator take up out of the water several great fish at a time, and just squeeze them betwixt his jaws, while the tails of the great trout flapped about his eyes and lips, ere he had swallowed them. The horrid noise of their closing jaws, their plunging amidst the broken banks of fish, and rising with their prey some feet upright above the water, the floods of water and blood rushing out of their mouths, and the clouds
10 of vapour issuing from their wide nostrils, were truly frightful. This scene continued at intervals during the night, as the fish came to the pass. After this sight, shocking and tremendous as it was, I found myself somewhat easier and more reconciled to my situation, being convinced that their extraordinary assemblage here, was owing to this annual feast of fish, and that they were so well employed in their own element, that I had little occasion to fear their paying me a visit.

It being now almost night, I returned to my camp, where I had left my fish broiling, and my kettle of rice stewing, and having with me, oil, pepper and salt, and excellent oranges hanging in abundance over my head (a valuable substitute for vinegar) I sat down and regaled myself chearfully; having finished my repast, I re-kindled
20 my fire for light, and whilst I was revising the notes of my past day's journey, I was suddenly roused with a noise behind me toward the main land; I sprang up on my feet, and listning, I distinctly heard some creature wading in the water of the isthmus; I seized my gun and went cautiously from my camp, directing my steps towards the noise; when I had advanced about thirty yards, I halted behind a coppice of Orange trees, and soon perceived two very large bears, which had made their way through the water, and had landed in the grove, about one hundred yards distance from me, and were advancing towards me. I waited until they were within thirty yards of me, they there began to snuff and look towards my camp, I snapped my piece, but it flashed, on which they both turned about and galloped off, plung-
30 ing through the water and swamp, never halting as I suppose, until they reached fast land, as I could hear them leaping and plunging a long time; they did not presume to return again, nor was I molested by any other creature, except being occasionally awakened by the whooping of owls, screaming of bitterns, or the wood-rats running amongst the leaves.

The wood-rat is a very curious animal, they are not half the size of the domestic rat; of a dark brown or black colour; their tail slender and shorter in proportion, and covered thinly with short hair; they are singular with respect to their ingenuity and great labour in the construction of their habitations, which are conical pyramids about three or four feet high, constructed with dry branches, which they collect with
40 great labour and perseverance, and pile up without any apparent order, yet they are so interwoven with one another, that it would take a bear or wild-cat some time to pull one of these castles to pieces, and allow the animals sufficient time to secure a retreat with their young.

The noise of the crocodiles kept me awake the greater part of the night, but when I arose in the morning, contrary to my expectations, there was perfect peace; very few of them to be seen, and those were asleep on the shore, yet I was not able to suppress my fears and apprehensions of being attacked by them in future; and indeed yesterday's combat with them, nothwithstanding I came off in a manner victorious, or at least made a safe retreat, had left sufficient impression on my mind to damp my courage, and it seemed too much for one of my strength, being alone in a very small boat to encounter such collected danger. To pursue my voyage up the river, and be obliged every evening to pass such dangerous defiles, appeared to me as perilous as running the gauntlet betwixt two rows of Indians armed with knives and fire brands; I however resolved to continue my voyage one day longer, if I pos- 10 sibly could with safety, and then return down the river, should I find the like difficulties to oppose. Accordingly I got every thing on board, charged my gun, and set sail cautiously along shore; as I passed by Battle lagoon, I began to tremble and keep a good look out, when suddenly a huge alligator rushed out of the reeds, and with a tremendous roar, came up, and darted as swift as an arrow under my boat, emerging upright on my lea quarter, with open jaws, and belching water and smoke that fell upon me like rain in a hurricane; I laid soundly about his head with my club and beat him off, and after plunging and darting about my boat, he went off on a strait line through the water, seemingly with the rapidity of lightning, and entered the cape of the lagoon; I now employed my time to the very best advantage 20 in paddling close along shore, but could not forbear looking now and then behind me, and presently perceived one of them coming up again; the water of the river hereabouts, was shoal and very clear, the monster came up with the usual roar and menaces, and passed close by the side of my boat, when I could distinctly see a young brood of alligators to the number of one hundred or more, following after her in a long train, they kept close together in a column without straggling off to the one side or the other, the young appeared to be of an equal size, about fifteen inches in length, almost black, with pale yellow transverse waved clouds or blotches, much like rattle snakes in colour. I now lost sight of my enemy again.

Still keeping close along shore; on turning a point or projection of the river bank, at 30 once I beheld a great number of hillocks or small pyramids, resembling hay cocks, ranged like an encampment along the banks, they stood fifteen or twenty yards distant from the water, on a high marsh, about four feet perpendicular above the water; I knew them to be the nests of the crocodile, having had a description of them before, and now expected a furious and general attack, as I saw several large crocodiles swimming abreast of these buildings. These nests being so great a curiosity to me, I was determined at all events immediately to land and examine them. Accordingly I ran my bark on shore at one of their landing places, which was a sort of nick or little dock, from which ascended a sloping path or road up to the edge of the meadow, where their nests were, most of them were deserted, and the great thick whitish 40 egg-shells lay broken and scattered upon the ground round about them.

The nests or hillocks are of the form of an obtuse cone, four feet high and four or five feet in diameter at their bases; they are constructed with mud, grass and herbage: at first they lay a floor of this kind of tempered mortar upon the ground, upon

which they deposit a layer of eggs, and upon this a stratum of mortar seven or eight inches in thickness, and then another layer of eggs, and in this manner one stratum upon another, nearly to the top: I believe they commonly lay from one to two hundred eggs in a nest: these are hatched I suppose by the heat of the sun, and perhaps the vegetable substances mixed with the earth, being acted upon by the sun, may cause a small degree of fermentation, and so increase the heat in those hillocks. The ground for several acres about these nests shewed evident marks of a continual resort of alligators; the grass was every where beaten down, hardly a blade or straw was left standing; whereas, all about, at a distance, it was five or six feet
10 high, and as thick as it could grow together. The female, as I imagine, carefully watches her own nest of eggs until they are all hatched, or perhaps while she is attending her own brood, she takes under her care and protection, as many as she can get at one time, either from her own particular nest or others: but certain it is, that the young are not left to shift for themselves, having had frequent opportunities of seeing the female alligator, leading about the shores her train of young ones, just like a hen does her chickens, and she is equally assiduous and courageous in defending the young, which are under their care, and providing for their subsistence; and when she is basking upon the warm banks, with her brood around her, you may hear the young ones continually whining and barking, like young puppies. I
20 believe but few of the brood live to the years of full growth and magnitude, as the old feed on the young as long as they can make prey of them.

The alligator when full grown is a very large and terrible creature, and of prodigious strength, activity and swiftness in the water. I have seen them twenty feet in length, and some are supposed to be twenty-two or twenty-three feet; their body is as large as that of a horse; their shape exactly resembles that of a lizard, except their tail, which is flat or cuniform, being compressed on each side, and gradually diminishing from the abdomen to the extremity, which, with the whole body is covered with horny plates or squammae, impenetrable when on the body of the live animal, even to a rifle ball, except about their head and just behind their fore-legs or
30 arms, where it is said they are only vulnerable. The head of a full grown one is about three feet, and the mouth opens nearly the same length, the eys are small in proportion and seem sunk deep in the head, by means of the prominency of the brows; the nostrils are large, inflated and prominent on the top, so that the head in the water, resembles, at a distance, a great chunk of wood floating about. Only the upper jaw moves, which they raise almost perpendicular, so as to form a right angle with the lower one. In the fore part of the upper jaw, on each side, just under the nostrils, are two very large, thick, strong teeth or tusks, not very sharp, but rather the shape of a cone, these are as white as the finest polished ivory, and are not covered by any skin or lips, and always in sight, which gives the creature a frightful
40 appearance; in the lower jaw are hols opposite to these teeth, to receive them; when they clap their jaws together it causes a surprising noise, like that which is made by forcing a heavy plank with violence upon the ground, and may be heard at a great distance.

But what is yet more surprising to a stranger, is the incredible loud and terrifying roar, which they are capable of making, especially in the spring season, their breeding time; it most resembles very heavy distant thunder, not only shaking the air and waters, but causing the earth to tremble; and when hundreds and thousands are roaring at the same time, you can scarcely be persuaded, but that the whole globe is violently and dangerously agitated.

An old champion, who is perhaps absolute sovereign of a little lake or lagoon (when fifty less than himself are obliged to content themselves with swelling and roaring in little coves round about) darts forth from the reedy coverts all at once, on the surface of the waters, in a right line; at first seemingly as swift as lightning, but gradually more slowly until he arrives at the center of the lake, when he stops; 10 he now swells himself by drawing in wind and water through his mouth, which causes a loud sonorous rattling in the throat for near a minute, but it is immediately forced out again through his mouth and nostrils, with a loud noise, brandishing his tail in the air, and the vapour ascending from his nostrils like smoke. At other times, when swolen to an extent ready to burst, his head and tail lifted up, he spins or twirls round on the surface of the water. He acts his part like an Indian chief, when rehearsing his feats of war, and then retiring, the exhibition is continued by others who dare to step forth, and strive to excel each other, to gain the attention of the favorite female.

Having gratified my curiosity at this general breeding place and nursery of 20 crocodiles, I continued my voyage up the river without being greatly disturbed by them: in my way I observed islets or floating fields of the bright green Pistia, decorated with other amphibious plants, as Senecio Jacobea, Persicaria amphibia, Coreopsis bidens, Hydrocotile fluitans, and many others of less note. . . .

I arrived at Cowe about noon; this settlement is esteemed the capital town; it is situated on the bases of the hills on both sides of the river, near to its bank, and here terminates the great vale of Cowe, exhibiting one of the most charming natural mountainous landscapes perhaps any where to be seen; ridges of hills rising grand and sublimely one above and beyond another, some boldly and majestically advancing into the verdant plains, their feet bathed with the silver flood of 30 the Tanase, whilst others far distant, veiled in blue mists, sublimely mount aloft, with yet greater majesty lift up their pompous crests and overlook vast regions. . . .

Next day after my arrival I crossed the river in a canoe, on a visit to a trader who resided amongst the habitations on the other shore.

After dinner, on his mentioning some curious scenes amongst the hills, some miles distance from the river, we agreed to spend the afternoon in observations on the mountains.

After riding near two miles through Indian plantations of Corn, which was well cultivated, kept clean of weeds and was well advanced, being near eighteen inches in height, and the Beans planted at the Corn-hills were above ground; we leave the 40 fields on our right, turning towards the mountains and ascending through a delightful green vale or lawn, which conducted us in amongst the pyramidal hills

---

25 **Cowe**, a Cherokee town, in what is now Oconee County, South Carolina, bordering northern Georgia   31 **Tanase**, Tennessee

and crossing a brisk flowing creek, meandering through the meads which continued
near two miles, dividing and branching in amongst the hills; we then mounted their
steep ascents, rising gradually by ridges or steps one above another, frequently
crossing narrow, fertile dales as we ascended; the air feels cool and animating, being
charged with the fragrant breath of the mountain beauties, the blooming mountain
cluster Rose, blushing Rhododendron and fair Lilly of the valley: having now attained the summit of this very elevated ridge, we enjoyed a fine prospect indeed;
the enchanting Vale of Keowe, perhaps as celebrated for fertility, fruitfulness and
beautiful prospects as the Fields of Pharsalia or the Vale of Tempe: the town, the
10 elevated peaks of the Jore mountains, a very distant prospect of the Jore village in
a beautiful lawn, lifted up many thousand feet higher than our present situation,
besides a view of many other villages and settlements on the sides of the mountains,
at various distances and elevations; the silver rivulets gliding by them and snow
white cataracts glimmering on the sides of the lofty hills; the bold promontories of
the Jore mountain stepping into the Tanase river, whilst his foaming waters rushed
between them.

After viewing this very entertaining scene we began to descend the mountain on
the other side, which exhibited the same order of gradations of ridges and vales as
on our ascent, and at length rested on a very expansive, fertile plain, amidst the
20 towering hills, over which we rode a long time, through magnificent high forests,
extensive green fields, meadows and lawns. Here had formerly been a very flourishing settlement, but the Indians deserted it in search of fresh planting land, which
they soon found in a rich vale but a few miles distance over a ridge of hills. Soon
after entering on these charming, sequestered, prolific fields, we came to a fine little
river, which crossing, and riding over fruitful strawberry beds and green lawns, on
the sides of a circular ridge of hills in front of us, and going around the bases of
this promontory, came to a fine meadow on an arm of the vale, through which
meandered a brook, its humid vapours bedewing the fragrant strawberries which hung
in heavy red clusters over the grassy verge; we crossed the rivulet, then rising
30 a sloping, green, turfy ascent, alighted on the borders of a grand forest of stately
trees, which we penetrated on foot a little distance to a horse-stamp, where was a
large squadron of those useful creatures, belonging to my friend and companion,
the trader, on the sight of whom they assembled together from all quarters; some at
a distance saluted him with shrill neighings of gratitude, or came prancing up to
lick the salt out of his hand; whilst the younger and more timorous came galloping onward, but coyly wheeled off, and fetching a circuit stood aloof, but as soon
as their lord and master strewed the chrystaline salty bait on the hard beaten
ground, they all, old and young, docile and timorous, soon formed themselves in
ranks and fell to licking up the delicious morsel.

40 It was a fine sight; more beautiful creatures I never saw; there were of them of

---

8 **Vale of Keowe.** The Keowee River forms the present boundary between Oconee and Pickens Counties   9 **Pharsalia,** the central plain of Thessaly in Greece, where Pompey was defeated by Cæsar
(48 B.C.)   9 **Tempe,** a valley in the north of Thessaly, between Mounts Olympus and Ossa, renowned
for its beauty   10 **Jore mountains,** apparently the southern extremity of the Blue Ridge   31 **horse-
stamp,** an enclosure or habitual standing-place for horses

all colours, sizes and dispositions. Every year as they become of age he sends off a troop of them down to Charleston, where they are sold to the highest bidder.

Having paid our attention to this usefull part of the creation, who, if they are under our dominion, have consequently a right to our protection and favour. We returned to our trusty servants that were regaling themselves in the exuberant sweet pastures and strawberry fields in sight, and mounted again; proceeding on our return to town, continued through part of this high forest skirting on the meadows; began to ascend the hills of a ridge which we were under the necessity of crossing, and having gained its summit, enjoyed a most enchanting view, a vast expanse of green meadows and strawberry fields; a meandering river gliding through, saluting 10 in its various turnings the swelling, green, turfy knolls, embellished with parterres of flowers and fruitful strawberry beds; flocks of turkies strolling about them; herds of deer prancing in the meads or bounding over the hills; companies of young, innocent Cherokee virgins, some busily gathering the rich fragrant fruit, others having already filled their baskets, lay reclined under the shade of floriferous and fragrant native bowers of Magnolia, Azalea, Philadelphus, perfumed Calycanthus, sweet Yellow Jessamine and cerulian Glycine frutescens, disclosing their beauties to the fluttering breeze, and bathing their limbs in the cool fleeting streams; whilst other parties, more gay and libertine, were yet collecting strawberries or wantonly chasing their companions, tantalizing them, staining their lips and cheeks with the 20 rich fruit.

This sylvan scene of primitive innocence was enchanting, and perhaps too enticing for hearty young men long to continue as idle spectators.

In fine, nature prevailing over reason, we wished at least to have a more active part in their delicious sports. Thus precipitately resolving, we cautiously made our approaches, yet undiscovered, almost to the joyous scene of action. Now, although we meant no other than an innocent frolic with this gay assembly of hamadryades, we shall leave it to the person of feeling and sensibility to form an idea to what lengths our passions might have hurried us, thus warmed and excited, had it not been for the vigilance and care of some envious matrons who lay in ambush, and 30 espying us gave the alarm, time enough for the nymphs to rally and assemble together; we however pursued and gained ground on a group of them, who had incautiously strolled to a greater distance from their guardians, and finding their retreat now like to be cut off, took shelter under cover of a little grove, but on perceiving themselves to be discovered by us, kept their station, peeping through the bushes; when observing our approaches, they confidently discovered themselves and decently advanced to meet us, half unveiling their blooming faces, incarnated with

---

13 **companies . . . virgins.** One stanza from Wordsworth's "Ruth," composed in 1799, will illustrate the use which the English romantics made of Bartram's book. The youth who broke Ruth's heart was from Georgia, and

> He told of girls — a happy rout!
> Who quit their folds with dance and shout,
> Their pleasant Indian towns,
> To gather strawberries all day long;
> Returning with a choral song
> When daylight is gone down.

the modest maiden blush, and with native innocence and cheerfulness, presented their little baskets, merrily telling us their fruit was ripe and sound.

We accepted a basket, sat down and regaled ourselves on the delicious fruit, encircled by the whole assembly of the innocently jocose sylvan nymphs; by this time the several parties under the conduct of the elder matrons, had disposed themselves in companies on the green, turfy banks.

My young companion, the trader, by concessions and suitable apologies for the bold intrusion, having compromised the matter with them, engaged them to bring their collections to his house at a stipulated price, we parted friendly.

And now taking leave of these Elysian fields, we again mounted the hills, which we crossed, and traversing obliquely their flowery beds, arrived in town in the cool of the evening.

1774?-1776?, 1791

Singers of the Revolution

B oth Tories and Continentals used songs and poems to urge their forces to victory, voice their arguments, and celebrate their heroes. Beginning with the passage of the Stamp Act, the verses showed more and more clearly the growth of unrest, then defiance, and finally hatred.

There was a contrast in the sentiments expressed, but not much difference in the forms employed by the opposing songsters. The reason is suggested by Professor Boynton in *Literature and American Life* when he says, "The most popular songs were all set to melodies then current in old England, sometimes occurring in sequence: the first a parody of the English song, the next the parody of a parody, and so on." He cites the fortunes of the tune of David Garrick's "Hearts of Oak," first sung on the stage in 1759. Seven years later, in America, the tune was outfitted with words of a conciliatory sort urging both loyalty and liberty. Then came a series of versions whose first lines show the alternating use of the tune by the two parties:

July 1768: "Come, join hand in hand, brave Americans all."
January 1769: "Come, cheer up, my lads, like a true British band."
1775: "Come, rouse up, my lads, and join the great cause."

These represent only a fraction of the songs which, down to 1812, made use of the Garrick tune.

Despite such typical resemblances the songs of the Revolution have many elements of interest. They vividly tell the story of the war and the feelings of the people about it. Further, like balladry in general — although many of them have an eighteenth-century polish not typical of the older ballads — they forcefully display human emotions and human character in times of stress.

Songs and Ballads of the American Revolution, ed. Frank Moore, New York, 1856   Gilbert Chase, America's Music from the Pilgrims to the Present, New York, 1955

Yankee Doodle

Anonymous

"The Yankee's Return from Camp" *was the title first given to this song, later generally known by its present title. Since it is an authentic ballad, there is no way of determining just who wrote it, when it was written, and what the original words were. The tune was known in the colonies as early as 1767, but the words — which varied in different versions — were composed later, probably by British soldiers or Tory sympathizers who wanted to ridicule the crude Yankees. The contrary Yankees in time apparently used it as a battle song of their own. It is interesting not only for its wartime history and for its lasting appeal to Americans but also for the way it created an American bumpkin by letting him talk his own dialect, later to be a very important procedure in the humor and fiction of the United States.*

Father and I went down to camp,
    Along with Captain Gooding,
And there we see the men and boys,
    As thick as hasty pudding.

      Chorus
           Yankee Doodle, keep it up,
           Yankee Doodle, dandy,
           Mind the music and the step,
           And with the girls be handy.

And there we see a thousand men,
    As rich as 'Squire David;   10
And what they wasted every day,
    I wish it could be saved.

The 'lasses they eat every day,
    Would keep a house a winter;
They have so much that, I'll be bound,
    They eat it when they're a mind to.

And there we see a swamping gun,
    Large as a log of maple,
Upon a deuced little cart,
    A load for father's cattle.   20

And every time they shoot it off,
    It takes a horn of powder,

And makes a noise like father's gun,
  Only a nation louder.

I went as nigh to one myself,
  As Siah's underpinning;
And father went as nigh again,
  I thought the deuce was in him.

Cousin Simon grew so bold,
  I thought he would have cock'd it; 30
It scar'd me so, I shrink'd it off,
  And hung by father's pocket.

And Captain Davis had a gun,
  He kind of clapped his hand on't,
And stuck a crooked stabbing iron
  Upon the little end on't.

And there I see a pumpkin shell
  As big as mother's basin;
And every time they touch'd it off,
  They scamper'd like the nation.   40

I see a little barrel too,
  The heads were made of leather,
They knock'd upon't with little clubs,
  And call'd the folks together.

And there was Captain Washington,
  And gentlefolks about him,
They say he's grown so tarnal proud,
  He will not ride without 'em.

He got him on his meeting clothes,
  Upon a slapping stallion,   50
He set the world along in rows,
  In hundreds and in millions.

The flaming ribbons in his hat,
  They look'd so tearing fine ah,
I wanted pockily to get,
  To give to my Jemimah.

I see another snarl of men
  A digging graves, they told me,

So tarnal long, so tarnal deep,
   They 'tended they should hold me. 60

It scar'd me so, I hook'd it off,
   Nor stopp'd, as I remember,
Nor turned about, till I got home,
   Lock'd up in mother's chamber.

                1775

Nathan Hale

Anonymous

After the retreat from Long Island in 1776, Washington tried to find among his men a "discreet and enterprising person to penetrate the enemy's camp" as a spy. Young Captain Nathan Hale, three years out of Yale College, undertook the mission. He went through the British lines, secured the information he wanted, and started to return. He was captured, however, and executed as a spy. The excellent ballad which tells of the event does not, surprisingly, make use of his reputed last words ("I regret that I have but one life to give for my country") or the alleged statement of the provost marshal that Hale's letters were destroyed "that the rebels should not know that they had a man in their army who could die with so much firmness." But the author perhaps saw that such details did not harmonize well with the rather elegiac account of the execution. Repetition, a typical ballad device, is notably used in this song.

The breezes went steadily thro' the tall pines,
   A saying "Oh hu-ush!" a saying "Oh hu-ush!"
As stilly stole by a bold legion of horse,
   For Hale in the bush, for Hale in the bush.

"Keep still!" said the thrush as she nestled her young,
   In a nest by the road, in a nest by the road;
"For the tyrants are near, and with them appear
   What bodes us no good, what bodes us no good."

The brave captain heard it and thought of his home,
   In a cot by the brook, in a cot by the brook,   10
With mother and sister and memories dear,
   He so gaily forsook, he so gaily forsook.

Cooling shades of the night were coming apace,
   The tattoo had beat, the tattoo had beat:
The noble one sprang from his dark lurking-place
   To make his retreat, to make his retreat.

He warily trod on the dry rustling leaves,
  As he pass'd thro' the wood, as he pass'd thro' the wood,
And silently gain'd his rude launch on the shore,
  As she play'd with the flood, as she play'd with the flood. 20

The guards of the camp, on that dark, dreary night,
  Had a murderous will, had a murderous will:
They took him and bore him afar from the shore,
  To a hut on the hill, to a hut on the hill.

No mother was there, nor a friend who could cheer,
  In that little stone cell, in that little stone cell.
But he trusted in love from his Father above;
  In his heart all was well, in his heart all was well.

An ominous owl with his solemn bass voice
  Sat moaning hard by, sat moaning hard by: 30
"The tyrant's proud minions most gladly rejoice,
  For he must soon die, for he must soon die."

The brave fellow told them, no thing he restrain'd,
  The cruel gen'ral, the cruel gen'ral;
His errand from camp, of the ends to be gain'd;
  And said that was all, and said that was all.

They took him and bound him and bore him away,
  Down the hill's grassy side, down the hill's grassy side.
'Twas there the base hirelings, in royal array,
  His cause did deride, his cause did deride.   40

Five minutes were given, short moments, no more,
  For him to repent, for him to repent.
He pray'd for his mother, he ask'd not another;
  To Heaven he went, to Heaven he went.

The faith of a martyr the tragedy shew'd,
  As he trod the last stage, as he trod the last stage;
And Britons will shudder at gallant Hale's blood,
  As his words do presage, as his words do presage:

"Thou pale king of terrors, thou life's gloomy foe,
  Go frighten the slave, go frighten the slave;   50
Tell tyrants to you their allegiance they owe;
  No fears for the brave, no fears for the brave."   1776

The Battle of the Kegs

Francis Hopkinson 1737 – 1791

The first floating mines ever to be launched against an enemy fleet were tried out by the Americans in January 1778. These mines were kegs of powder which exploded upon coming into contact with other objects. A number of mines sent down the Delaware failed to do much damage to the British ships because the British had drawn them up to docks, out of the way of floating ice. One keg did explode, however, and the colonists claimed that the British became so disturbed that for a while they fearfully fired at every keg floating along the river, including a keg of butter.

Francis Hopkinson, a young Philadelphian and author of many pamphlets and poems in behalf of the Continentals, saw a chance to show the British in a ridiculous light by writing a poem about the incident. His ballad, published in the Pennsylvania Packet *for March 4, became one of the most popular songs of the Revolution. It was set to music, perhaps by the author himself, and was sung by the American soldiers. The achievements of Hopkinson, an extraordinarily versatile man, are fully recounted in G. E. Hastings,* The Life and Works of Francis Hopkinson, *published in 1926.*

Gallants attend, and hear a friend,
   Trill forth harmonious ditty,
Strange things I'll tell, which late befell,
   In Philadelphia city.

'Twas early day, as poets say,
   Just when the sun was rising,
A soldier stood, on a log of wood,
   And saw a thing surprising.

As in amaze he stood to gaze,
   The truth can't be denied, sir,   10
He spied a score of kegs or more,
   Come floating down the tide, sir.

A sailor, too, in jerkin blue,
   This strange appearance viewing,
First damn'd his eyes, in great surprise,
   Then said, "some mischief's brewing.

"These kegs, I'm told, the rebels hold,
   Packed up like pickled herring,
And they're come down, t' attack the town,
   In this new way of ferrying."   20

The soldier flew, the sailor too,
    And scared almost to death, sir,
Wore out their shoes to spread the news,
    And ran till out of breath, sir.

Now up and down, throughout the town,
    Most frantic scenes were acted;
And some ran here, and others there,
    Like men almost distracted.

Some fire cried, which some denied,
    But said the earth had quakèd;   30
And girls and boys, with hideous noise,
    Ran through the streets half naked.

Sir William, he, snug as a flea,
    Lay all this time a snoring;
Nor dreamed of harm, as he lay warm,
    In bed with Mrs. L. . . .g.

Now in a fright, he starts upright,
    Awak'd by such a clatter;
He rubs his eyes, and boldly cries,
    "For God's sake, what's the matter?"   40

At his bedside he then espied,
    Sir Erskine at command, sir,
Upon one foot he had one boot,
    And t'other in his hand, sir.

"Arise! arise, Sir Erskine cries,
    The rebels — more's the pity —
Without a boat, are all afloat,
    And rang'd before the city.

"The motley crew, in vessels new,
    With Satan for their guide, sir,   50
Packed up in bags, or wooden kegs,
    Come driving down the tide, sir.

"Therefore prepare for bloody war;

---

33 **Sir William**, Sir William Howe (1729-1814), the much hated commander of the British Army   36
Mrs. L....g, the wife of Joshua Loring, a Loyalist refugee from Boston   42 **Sir Erskine**, Sir William Erskine, a British general

The kegs must all be routed,
Or surely we despis'd shall be,
    And British courage doubted."

The royal band, now ready stand,
    All ranged in dread array, sir,
With stomachs stout, to see it out,
    And make a bloody day, sir.   60

The cannons roar from shore to shore,
    The small arms make a rattle;
Since wars began, I'm sure no man
    Ere saw so strange a battle.

The rebel dales, the rebel vales,
    With rebel trees surrounded,
The distant woods, the hills and floods,
    With rebel echoes sounded.

The fish below swam to and fro,
    Attack'd from every quarter;   70
Why sure, thought they, the devil's to pay,
    'Mongst folks above the water.

The kegs, 'tis said, though strongly made
    Of rebel staves and hoops, sir,
Could not oppose their powerful foes,
    The conquering British troops, sir.

From morn till night, these men of might
    Display'd amazing courage;
And when the sun was fairly down,
    Retir'd to sup their porridge.   80

An hundred men, with each a pen,
    Or more, upon my word, sir,
It is most true would be too few,
    Their valor to record, sir.

Such feats did they perform that day,
    Against those wicked kegs, sir,
That years to come, if they get home,
    They'll make their boasts and brags, sir.
                1778

The Epilogue

Anonymous

In October 1778, when the British had possession of Philadelphia and the Continental Congress was meeting in Yorktown, Virginia, "The Epilogue," a Tory song, was published in a ballad sheet and posted in the streets of New York and Philadelphia.

Said a foreword: "There was lately exhibited in the city of Philadelphia, an admirable farce called Independence. *Who the author was is not positively known, but some are of the opinion that it is the work of a certain quack doctor called Franklin. Others assert that it is the joint production of the strolling company by whom it was acted; it is, however, generally allowed, that one Adams gave the first hint, contrived the plot, and cast the parts. It appeared in the exhibition so tragi-comical, that the audience were at a loss whether to laugh or cry. They were, however, well pleased with the catastrophe, and joined heartily in the following chorus. As the renowned Voltaire somewhere relates, that a song was the cause of the French reformation, the excellent actor who performed the part of the President took upon himself the plain song."*

Our farce is now finish'd, your sport's at an end,
But ere you depart, let the voice of a friend
By way of a chorus, the evening crown
With a song to the tune of a hey derry down,
    Derry down, down, hey derry down.

Old Shakspeare, a poet, who should not be spit on,
Altho' he was born in the island called Britain,
Hath said that mankind are all players at best,
A truth we'll admit of, for sake of the jest.

On this puny stage we've strutted our hour,   10
And have acted our parts to the best of our power;
That the farce hath concluded not perfectly well,
Was surely the fault of the devil in hell.

This devil, you know, out of spleen to the church,
Will oftentimes leave his best friends in the lurch,
And turn them adrift in the midst of their joy;
'Tis a difficult matter to cheat the Old Boy.

Since this is the case, we must e'en make the best
Of a game that is lost; let us turn it to jest;
We'll smile, nay, we'll laugh, we'll carouse and we'll sing, 20
And cheerfully drink life and health to the king.

Let Washington now from his mountains descend,
Who knows but in George he may still find a friend;
A Briton, altho' he loves bottle and wench,
Is an honester fellow than parle vous French.

Our great Independence we give to the wind,
And pray that Great Britain may once more be kind.
In this jovial song all hostility ends,
And Britons and we will for ever be friends.

Boys fill me a bumper! now join in the chorus!   30
There is happiness still in the prospect before us,
In this sparkling glass, all hostility ends,
And Britons and we will for ever be friends.

Good night! my good people, retire to your houses,
Fair ladies, I beg you, convince your dear spouses
That Britons and we are united in bliss,
And ratify all with a conjugal kiss.

Once more, here's a health to the king and queen!
Confusion to him, who in rancor and spleen,
Refuses to drink with an English friend,   40
Immutable amity to the world's end.

1778

1737—1809 Thomas Paine

T he career and reputation of Thomas Paine are tragic evidence of human frailty. His private hells of physical and mental torture were paved with the most altruistic of intentions, and those who have judged him saint or devil have usually been passionately sincere. He emerged from failure and obscurity to become the most powerful single voice of revolutionary thought in British America; pursuing the line of his principles a little farther, he was driven out of England, jailed in France, and insulted and ostracized in the United States.

Down through the years his name has called forth more diverse and violent comment than any other in literary history, not excepting Poe and Shelley.

Paine was born at Thetford in Norfolk, England, in 1737. His father was a Quaker farmer and staymaker; his mother a Church of England woman, older than her husband, a shade higher in the social scale, and discontented. Their son's childhood was unhappy, his early manhood scarcely less so. Leaving school at thirteen, he searched fruitlessly for a quarter of a century before he found an agreeable occupation. As sailor, corsetmaker, collector of the excise, schoolteacher, tobacconist, he was never quite fitted to his task. At twenty-two he married, only to have his wife die in childbirth within a year. A second marriage, at thirty-four, ended three years later in a legal separation. All that Paine had found at thirty-seven were an interest in science and a sympathy for the underdog in society, the result of his private reading and his futile championship of the plea of his fellow-excisemen for more pay from Parliament.

Penniless and unknown, Paine encountered Benjamin Franklin, who apparently encouraged him to try America, giving him a letter of introduction as an "ingenious worthy young man" who might well be employed as "clerk, or assistant tutor in a school, or assistant surveyor." Late in 1774, seriously ill, Paine was carried off a ship in Pennsylvania.

Within a year he had readied himself for a new profession by a series of contributions to the *Pennsylvania Magazine.* As "Atlanticus," "Vox Populi," "Æsop," and "An Englishman," Paine learned to shape his humanitarian sympathies into persuasive essays on dueling, marriage, the rights of women, the need of copyright, kindness to animals, and the injustice of slavery. Meanwhile he had to make up his mind about the Battle of Lexington and the events which swiftly followed. That was not difficult, despite his Quaker predilections. What reason had he to love England? In the autumn of 1775 he was writing *Common Sense* to convince his adopted countrymen that "nothing can settle our affairs so expeditiously as an open and determined *Declaration for Independence.*" The pamphlet's appearance and success demonstrated that the colonies had welcomed no mere bankrupt staymaker, but a propagandist of genius, whose skill in moving men to action has seldom been rivaled.

Common Sense, however, was only a beginning. The *Declaration* achieved, Paine joined the army in time to share the disheartening retreat across New Jersey in the fall of 1776. In the face of disaster, he wrote the first of a series of letter-pamphlets now known as *The American Crisis.* Published just before Christmas, its ringing denunciation of the "summer soldier and the sunshine patriot" was read to the troops who crossed the Delaware to surprise the Hessians at Trenton and thereby preserved the morale of the Americans during the first crucial winter of the war. Fifteen times thereafter, in the space of the next seven years, the need arose for a *Crisis* paper to hold the nation together or to arouse the support required for decisive action. Each of the sixteen numbers circulated in the tens of thousands. Finally, in 1783, Paine could write, " 'The times that tried men's souls' are over — and the greatest and completest revolution the world ever knew, gloriously and happily accomplished."

Paine's contributions had included various kinds of work for the Continental

Congress, such as a quick but valuable trip to France in 1781. The end of the war, however, found him as poor as at the beginning, and not without his enemies. Washington, remembering the effect of his propaganda pieces, was able to suggest a few rewards: a confiscated estate from New York, a gift of money from Pennsylvania, and $3000 from the Congress itself. Paine's pamphlets had been his free-will offering to the cause; he had never wished to profit from their sale. No place appearing for him in the public service, he devoted what funds he had to promoting one of his inventions — a single-span iron bridge which, he argued, would be more practicable for American rivers than arches on piers, against which ice could jam in the spring. In April 1787 he sailed for France to display his model to the engineering experts and investors there. He was not, however, to succeed as a promoter of his own fortunes.

To follow in detail Paine's fifteen years in Europe would require many pages describing the intricate events of the French Revolution and the conservative reaction in England. Paine was not content to busy himself with bridges. *The Rights of Man* (Part I, 1791; Part II, 1792), his answer to Edmund Burke's *Reflections on the Revolution in France,* is the fullest expression of his political convictions: that the best form of government is a representative republic, with universal manhood suffrage; and that the "natural rights" of men should be protected by written constitutions and legislation to prevent the development of aristocratic and hereditary privileges. For these views and for his free prediction of coming revolution, he was found guilty of libel and exiled from an England he had already left. English mobs hanged and burned his effigy.

If, as has been said, Paine's views were too French for the English, they were soon to prove too English for the French. As honorary citizen and member of the National Convention, he opposed the execution of Louis XVI; and by December 1793, no longer a hero, he was imprisoned as a foreigner. Gouverneur Morris, the American ambassador, failed to help him (some biographers, in fact, believe that Morris was in part responsible for Paine's imprisonment, because of personal enmity), and Paine was not released until ten months later, after Morris had been succeeded by James Monroe. Broken in health, his faith in political rationalism seriously damaged, Paine had still to meet the bitterest antagonisms of his career.

The Age of Reason (Part I, 1794; Part II, 1795) was written as Paine's "last offering" to mankind, to provide a religion compatible with the new political and social order which he believed was at hand despite the excesses of the Reign of Terror. Mankind was not only unappreciative; it was so shocked by the apparent blasphemy of his application of reason to religion that a goodly part of it was willing to burn Paine at the stake. To the masses, swayed by newspapers and pulpit pronouncements, Paine's name became a synonym for atheism and infidelity. His English publisher was prosecuted for blasphemy; he himself, after his return to the United States in 1802, was shot at through his window, insulted in the streets, and humiliated on his deathbed by clergymen who forced their way into his room. Even the Quakers refused to permit burial in their cemetery. Ten years later his bones were exhumed and taken to England, where William Cobbett hoped to exhibit them as part of a scheme to reform society there. Forbidden this final gruesome means of swaying men's minds, Paine's bones were, it is said, nearly sold at auction to satisfy the creditors of Cobbett's son before they finally disappeared.

Men still find moderation virtually impossible when evaluating Thomas Paine. He wrote always for a purpose, and some of his purposes are still anathema to large groups of people. Of his merits as a writer, however, there can be little disagreement. No man of his time was better able to express, simply and clearly, the views which effected vast changes in the political, social, and religious constitution of Western civilization. The force, directness, and variety of his appeals to reason and emotion made him the foremost propagandist-agitator of his time. A master of persuasion rather than a profound or original thinker, he will be studied as long as there are men who seek to understand the social functions of language and literature.

Selections from the Works of Thomas Paine, ed. A. W. Peach, New York, 1928   Thomas Paine: Representative Selections, ed. H. H. Clark, Cincinnati, 1944   M. D. Conway, The Life of Thomas Paine, 2 vols., New York, 1892   Hesketh Pearson, Tom Paine, Friend of Mankind, New York, 1937   A. O. Aldridge, Man of Reason, The Life of Thomas Paine, Philadelphia, 1959

Common Sense

Addressed to the Inhabitants of America, on the following Interesting Subjects, viz.:
I. Of the Origin and Design of Government in General; with Concise Remarks on the English Constitution.
II. Of Monarchy and Hereditary Succession.
III. Thoughts on the Present State of American Affairs.
IV. Of the Present Ability of America; with some Miscellaneous Reflections.

A pamphlet of seventy-nine pages, Common Sense *was published at Philadelphia in January 1776. The first open appeal for a declaration of independence, it achieved a sale estimated at 125,000 copies within three months and by the end of the year had appeared in fifteen or more editions.*

George Washington, commanding the army besieging Boston, wrote on January 31 of the "sound doctrine and unanswerable reasoning" of Paine's pamphlet, and it was unquestionably the greatest single force in convincing Americans of the wisdom of separation from England. Its shrewd analyses and arguments are punctuated by bursts of emotion-laden rhetoric, all bound together by a constant reiteration of the theme of "continental" destiny. In one way or another Paine appealed to almost every interest, selfish or benevolent, which could help to draw the colonists together.

The "sound doctrine" which Washington admired will be found upon examination to be largely that of John Locke (1632-1704), the English philosopher whose Two Treatises on Government *(1689-1690) formed a classic justification of the Glorious Revolution of 1688. It is not profitable, however, to trace the origins of Paine's political thought. He did not claim that it was original, and he did not intend that* Common Sense *should be read for its abstract principles. It was designed to bring action, and in achieving that end it was supremely successful. Independence was declared, and Paine had every reason to feel, as he did, that the inscription on his tombstone should read simply "Thomas Paine, Author of Common Sense."*

INTRODUCTION

Perhaps the sentiments contained in the following pages, are not *yet* sufficiently fashionable to procure them general favor; a long habit of not thinking a Thing *wrong,* gives it a superficial appearance of being *right,* and raises at first a formidable outcry in defence of Custom. But the tumult soon subsides. Time makes more converts than Reason.

As a long and violent abuse of Power is generally the means of calling the right of it in question, (and in matters too which might never have been thought of, had not the Sufferers been aggravated into the inquiry,) and as the king of England hath undertaken in his *own right,* to support the Parliament in what he calls *theirs,* and
10 as the good People of this country are grievously oppressed by the combination, they have an undoubted privilege to inquire into the pretensions of both, and equally to reject the usurpation of *either.*

In the following Sheets, the Author has studiously avoided every thing which is personal among ourselves. Compliments as well as Censure to individuals make no part thereof. The wise and the worthy need not the triumph of a pamphlet; and those whose sentiments are injudicious or unfriendly will cease of themselves, unless too much pains is bestowed upon their conversions.

The cause of America is in a great measure the cause of all mankind. Many circumstances have, and will arise, which are not local, but universal, and through
20 which the principles of all lovers of mankind are affected, and in the event of which their affections are interested. The laying a country desolate with fire and sword, declaring war against the natural rights of all mankind, and extirpating the defenders thereof from the face of the earth, is the concern of every man to whom nature hath given the power of feeling; of which class, regardless of party censure, is

THE AUTHOR

On the Origin and Design of Government in General, with Concise Remarks on the English Constitution

Some Writers have so confounded Society with government, as to leave little or no distinction between them; whereas they are not only different, but have different
30 origins. Society is produced by our wants and government by our wickedness; the former promotes our happiness *positively* by uniting our affections, the latter *negatively* by restraining our vices. The one encourages intercourse, the other creates distinctions. The first is a patron, the last a punisher.

Society in every state is a blessing, but government, even in its best state, is but a

---

Text: Professor Peach's version of the first edition, which eliminated "such typographical errors as were clearly destructive of the sense" necessary evil, in its worst state an intolerable one; for when we suffer, or are exposed to the same miseries *by a government,* which we might expect in a country *without Government,* our calamity is heightened by reflecting that we furnish the means by which we suffer. Government, like dress, is the badge of lost innocence; the palaces of kings are built upon the ruins of the bowers of paradise. For were the impulses of conscience clear, uniform and irresistibly obeyed, man would need no other law-giver; but that not being the case, he finds it necessary to surrender up a part of his property to furnish means for the protection of the rest; and this he is induced to do by the same prudence which in every other case advises him, out of two evils to choose the least. *Wherefore,* security being the true design and end of 10 government, it unanswerably follows that whatever *form* thereof appears most likely to ensure it to us, with the least expense and greatest benefit, is preferable to all others.

   In order to gain a clear and just idea of the design and end of government, let us suppose a small number of persons settled in some sequestered part of the earth, unconnected with the rest; they will then represent the first peopling of any country, or of the world. In this state of natural liberty, society will be their first thought. A thousand motives will excite them thereto; the strength of one man is so unequal to his wants, and his mind so unfitted for perpetual solitude, that he is soon obliged to seek assistance and relief of another, who in his turn requires the same. Four or five united would be able to raise a tolerable dwelling in the midst of a wilderness, 20 but *one* man might labor out the common period of life without accomplishing any thing; when he had felled his timber he could not remove it, nor erect it after it was removed; hunger in the mean time would urge him to quit his work, and every different want would call him a different way. Disease, nay even misfortune, would be death; for though neither might be mortal, yet either would disable him from living, and reduce him to a state in which he might rather be said to perish than to die.

   Thus necessity, like a gravitating power, would soon form our newly arrived emigrants into society, the reciprocal blessings of which would supersede, and render the obligations of law and government unnecessary while they remained perfectly 30 just to each other; but as nothing but Heaven is impregnable to vice, it will unavoidable happen that in proportion as they surmount the first difficulties of emigration, which bound them together in a common cause, they will begin to relax in their duty and attachment to each other: and this remissness will point out the necessity of establishing some form of government to supply the defect of moral virtue.

   Some convenient tree will afford them a State-House, under the branches of which the whole Colony may assemble to deliberate on public matters. It is more than probable that their first laws will have the title only of *Regulations* and be enforced by no other penalty than public disesteem. In this first parliament every man by natural right will have a seat. 40

   But as the colony increases, the public concerns will increase likewise, and the distance at which the members may be separated, will render it too inconvenient

---

16 **natural liberty.** Paine's phrase, like his account of the origin of society, shows his general agreement with John Locke's idea of presocial society

for all of them to meet on every occasion as at first, when their number was small, their habitations near, and the public concerns few and trifling. This will point out the convenience of their consenting to leave the legislative part to be managed by a select number chosen from the whole body, who are supposed to have the same concerns at stake which those have who appointed them, and who will act in the same manner as the whole body would act were they present. If the colony continue encreasing, it will become necessary to augment the number of representatives, and that the interest of every part of the colony may be attended to, it will be found best to divide the whole into convenient parts, each part sending its proper number: and that the *elected* might never form to themselves an interest separate from the *electors,* prudence will point out the propriety of having elections often: because as the *elected* might by that means return and mix again with the general body of the *electors* in a few months, their fidelity to the public will be secured by the prudent reflection of not making a rod for themselves. And as this frequent interchange will establish a common interest with every part of the community, they will mutually and naturally support each other, and on this, (not on the unmeaning name of king,) depends the *strength of Government, and the happiness of the governed.*

Here then is the origin and rise of government; namely, a mode rendered necessary by the inability of moral virtue to govern the world; here too is the design and end of government, viz. freedom and security. And however our eyes may be dazzled with show, or our ears deceived by sound; however prejudice may warp our wills, or interest darken our understanding, the simple voice of nature and reason will say, 'tis right.

I draw my idea of the form of government from a principle in nature which no art can overturn, viz. that the more simple any thing is, the less liable it is to be disordered, and the easier repaired when disordered; and with this maxim in view I offer a few remarks on the so much boasted Constitution of England. That it was noble for the dark and slavish times in which it was erected, is granted. When the world was overrun with tyranny the least remove therefrom was a glorious rescue. But that it is imperfect, subject to convulsions, and incapable of producing what it seems to promise, is easily demonstrated.

Absolute governments, (tho' the disgrace of human nature) have this advantage with them, they are simple: if the people suffer, they know the head from which their suffering springs; know likewise the remedy; and are not bewildered by a variety of causes and cures. But the Constitution of England is so exceedingly complex, that the nation may suffer for years together without being able to discover in which part the fault lies; some will say in one and some in another, and every political physician will advise a different medicine.

I know it is difficult to get over local or long standing prejudices, yet if we will suffer ourselves to examine the component parts of the English Constitution, we shall find them to be the base remains of two ancient tyrannies, compounded with some new Republican materials.

First. — The remains of Monarchical tyranny in the person of the King.

Secondly. — The remains of Aristocratical tyranny in the persons of the Peers.

Thirdly. — The new Republican materials, in the persons of the Commons, on whose virtue depends the freedom of England.

The two first, by being hereditary, are independent of the People; wherefore in a *constitutional sense* they contribute nothing towards the freedom of the State.

To say that the Constitution of England is an *union* of three powers, reciprocally *checking* each other, is farcical; either the words have no meaning, or they are flat contradictions.

To say that the Commons is a check upon the king, presupposes two things.

First. — That the king is not to be trusted without being looked after; or in other words, that a thirst for absolute power is the natural disease of Monarchy.   1

Secondly. — That the Commons, by being appointed for that purpose, are either wiser or more worthy of confidence than the crown.

But as the same constitution which gives the Commons a power to check the King by withholding the supplies, gives afterwards the King a power to check the Commons, by empowering him to reject their other bills; it again supposes that the king is wiser than those whom it has already supposed to be wiser than him. A mere absurdity!

There is something exceedingly ridiculous in the composition of Monarchy; it first excludes a man from the means of information, yet empowers him to act in cases where the highest judgment is required. The state of a King shuts him from 2 the World, yet the business of a king requires him to know it thoroughly; wherefore the different parts, by unnaturally opposing and destroying each other, prove the whole character to be absurd and useless.

Some writers have explained the English Constitution thus: the king say they is one, the People another; the Peers are a house in behalf of the King, the Commons in behalf of the People; But this hath all the distinctions of a house divided against itself; and tho' the expressions be pleasantly arranged, yet when examined they appear idle and ambiguous; and it will always happen, that the nicest construction that words are capable of, when applied to the description of something which either cannot exist, or is too incomprehensible to be within the compass of description, 3 will be words of sound only, and tho' they may amuse the ear, they cannot inform the mind: for this explanation includes a previous question, viz. *how came the king by a power which the people are afraid to trust, and always obliged to check?* Such a power could not be the gift of a wise People, neither can any Power, *which needs checking,* be from God; yet the provision which the Constitution makes supposes such a power to exist.

But the provision is unequal to the task; the means either cannot or will not accomplish the end, and the whole affair is a *Felo de se:* for as the greater weight will always carry up the less, and as all the wheels of a machine are put in motion by one, it only remains to know which power in the constitution has the most weight, 4 for that will govern: and tho' the others, or a part of them, may clog, or check the rapidity of its motion, yet so long as they cannot stop it, their endeavors will be

5 **reciprocally checking.** Montesquieu had held such a view of the British Constitution   38 **Felo de se,** murderer of itself

ineffectual: The first moving power will at last have its way, and what it wants in speed is supplied by time.

That the crown is this overbearing part in the English constitution needs not be mentioned, and that it derives its whole consequence merely from being the giver of places and pensions is self-evident; wherefore, tho' we have been wise enough to shut and lock a door against absolute Monarchy, we at the same time have been foolish enough to put the Crown in possession of the key.

The prejudice of Englishmen, in favor of their own government, by Kings, Lords and Commons, arises as much or more from national pride than reason. Individuals are undoubtedly safer in England than in some other Countries: but the Will of the King is as much the Law of the land in Britain as in France, with this difference, that instead of proceeding directly from his mouth, it is handed to the People under the formidable shape of an act of Parliament. For the fate of Charles the First hath only made kings more subtle — not more just.

Wherefore, laying aside all national pride and prejudice in favor of modes and forms, the plain truth is that *it is wholly to the constitution of the People, and not to the constitution of the Government* that the Crown is not as oppressive in England as in Turkey.

An inquiry into the *constitutional errors* in the English form of government, is at this time highly necessary; for as we are never in a proper condition of doing justice to others, while we continue under the influence of some leading partiality, so neither are we capable of doing it to ourselves while we remain fettered by any obstinate prejudice. And as a man who is attached to a prostitute is unfitted to choose or judge of a wife, so any prepossession in favor of a rotten constitution of government will disable us from discerning a good one.

Of Monarchy and Hereditary Succession

Mankind being originally equals in the order of creation, the equality could only be destroyed by some subsequent circumstance: the distinctions of rich and poor may in a great measure be accounted for, and that without having recourse to the harsh ill-sounding names of oppression and avarice. Oppression is often the *consequence*, but seldom or never the *means* of riches; and tho' avarice will preserve a man from being necessitously poor, it generally makes him too timorous to be wealthy.

But there is another and greater distinction for which no truly natural or religious reason can be assigned, and that is the distinction of men into *Kings* and *Subjects*. Male and female are the distinctions of nature, good and bad the distinctions of Heaven; but how a race of Men came into the World so exalted above the rest, and distinguished like some new species, is worth inquiring into, and whether they are the means of happiness or of misery to mankind.

In the early ages of the World, according to the Scripture chronology there were no Kings; the consequence of which was, there were no wars; it is the pride of Kings which throws mankind into confusion. Holland without a King hath enjoyed more peace for this last century than any of the Monarchical governments in Europe. Antiquity favors the same remark; for the quiet and rural lines of the first Patriarchs have a happy something in them, which vanishes when we come to the history of Jewish royalty.

Government by Kings was first introduced into the World by the Heathens, from whom the children of Israel copied the custom. It was the most prosperous invention the Devil ever set on foot for the promotion of idolatry. The heathens paid divine honors to their deceased Kings, and the Christian World has improved on the plan by doing the same to their living ones. How impious is the title of sacred Majesty applied to a worm, who in the midst of his splendor is crumbling into dust!

As the exalting one man so greatly above the rest cannot be justified on the equal 1️⃣ rights of nature, so neither can it be justified on the authority of scripture; for the will of the Almighty as declared by Gideon, and the prophet Samuel, expressly disapproves of Government by kings. All anti-monarchical parts of scripture have been very smoothly glossed over in monarchical governments, but they undoubtedly merit the attention of Countries which have their governments yet to form. *"Render unto Cæsar the things which are Cæsar's,"* is the scripture doctrine of Courts, yet it is no support of monarchical government, for the Jews at that time were without a king, and in a state of vassalage to the Romans.

Near three thousand years passed away, from the Mosaic account of the creation, till the Jews under a national delusion requested a king. Till then, their form of 2️⃣ government (except in extraordinary cases where the Almighty interposed) was a kind of Republic, administered by a judge and the elders of the tribes. Kings they had none, and it was held sinful to acknowledge any Being under that title but the Lord of Hosts. And when a man seriously reflects on the idolatrous homage which is paid to the persons of kings, he need not wonder that the Almighty, ever jealous of his honor, should disapprove a form of government which so impiously invades the prerogative of Heaven.

Monarchy is ranked in scripture as one of the sins of the Jews, for which a course in reserve is denounced against them. The history of that transaction is worth attending to.

The children of Israel being oppressed by the Midianites, Gideon marched against 3️⃣ them with a small army, and victory thro' the Divine interposition decided in his favor. The Jews elate with success and attributing it to the generalship of Gideon, proposed making him a king, saying, *Rule thou over us, thou and thy son, and thy son's son.* Here was temptation in its fullest extent; not a kingdom only, but a hereditary one; but Gideon in the piety of his soul replied, *I will not rule over you, neither shall my son rule over you.* THE LORD SHALL RULE OVER YOU. Words need not be more explicit; Gideon doth not *decline* the honor, but denieth their right to give it; neither doth he compliment them with invented declarations of his thanks, but in the positive style of a prophet charges them with disaffection to their proper Sovereign, the King of Heaven.
4️⃣

About one hundred and thirty years after this, they fell again into the same error. The hankering which the Jews had for the idolatrous customs of the Heathens, is

---

12 **Gideon . . . Samuel.** See Judges 8:22-23 and I Samuel 8:5-22, most of which Paine quotes directly   33
Rule . . . OVER YOU. See Judges 8:22-23

something exceedingly unaccountable; but so it was, that laying hold of the misconduct of Samuel's two sons, who were intrusted with some secular concerns, they
came in an abrupt and clamorous manner to Samuel, saying, *Behold, thou art old,
and thy sons walk not in thy ways, now make us a king to judge us like all the other nations.* And here we cannot but observe that their motives were bad, viz. that they
might be *like* unto other nations, i. e. the Heathens, whereas their true glory lay in
being as much *unlike* them as possible. *But the thing displeased Samuel when they said,
give us a king to judge us; and Samuel prayed unto the Lord, and the Lord said unto
Samuel, hearken unto the voice of the people in all that they say unto thee, for they have
not rejected thee, but they have rejected me.* THAT I SHOULD NOT REIGN OVER THEM.
*According to all the works which they have done since the day that I brought them up out
of Egypt even unto this day, wherewith they have forsaken me, and served other Gods: so
do they also unto thee. Now therefore hearken unto their voice, howbeit, protest solemnly unto
them and show them the manner of the king that shall reign over them,* i. e. not of any
particular King, but the general manner of the Kings of the Earth whom Israel was
so eagerly copying after. And notwithstanding the great distance of time and difference of manners, the character is still in fashion. *And Samuel told all the words of
the Lord unto the People, that asked of him a King. And he said, This shall be the manner of the King that shall reign over you. He will take your sons and appoint them for
himself for his chariots and to be his horsemen, and some shall run before his chariots* (This
description agrees with the present mode of impressing men) *and he will appoint
him captains over thousands and captains over fifties, will set them to ear his ground and
to reap his harvests, and to make his instruments of war, and instruments of his chariots.
And he will take your daughters to be confectionaries, and to be cooks, and to be bakers* (This
describes the expense and luxury as well as the oppression of Kings) *and he will
take your fields and your vineyards, and your olive yards, even the best of them, and give
them to his servants. And he will take the tenth of your seed, and of your vineyards, and
give them to his officers and to his servants* (By which we see that bribery, corruption,
and favouritism, are the standing vices of Kings) *and he will take the tenth of your
men servants, and your maid servants, and your goodliest young men, and your asses, and
put them to his work: and he will take the tenth of your sheep, and ye shall be his servants,
and ye shall cry out in that day because of your king which ye shall have chosen,* AND THE
LORD WILL NOT HEAR YOU IN THAT DAY. This accounts for the continuation of
Monarchy; neither do the characters of the few good Kings which have lived since,
either sanctify the title, or blot out the sinfulness of the origin; the high encomium
given of David takes no notice of him *officially as a King,* but only as a *Man* after
God's own heart. *Nevertheless the People refused to obey the voice of Samuel, and they said,
Nay but we will have a King over us, that we may be like all the nations, and that our
King may judge us, and go out before us and fight our battles.* Samuel continued to reason with them but to no purpose; he set before them their ingratitude, but all would
not avail; and seeing them fully bent on their folly, he cried out, *I will call unto the*

---

3 Behold . . . REIGN OVER THEM. I Samuel 8:5, 6-9   17 And Samuel . . . IN THAT DAY.
Samuel 8:10-17   36 David. I Kings 2:4   37 Nevertheless. . . . our battles. I Samuel 8:19-20   41
I will call. . . . ASK A KING. I Samuel 12:17-19

Lord, and he shall send thunder and rain (which was then a punishment, being in the time of wheat harvest) *that ye may perceive and see that your wickedness is great which ye have done in the sight of the Lord,* IN ASKING YOU A KING. *So Samuel called unto the Lord, and the Lord sent thunder and rain that day, and all the people greatly feared the Lord and Samuel. And all the people said unto Samuel, Pray for thy servants unto the Lord thy God that we die not, for* WE HAVE ADDED UNTO OUR SINS THIS EVIL, TO ASK A KING. These portions of scripture are direct and positive. They admit of no equivocal construction. That the Almighty hath here entered his protest against monarchical government is true, or the scripture is false. And a man hath good reason to believe that there is as much of king-craft as priestcraft in withholding the scripture from the public in popish countries. For monarchy in every instance is the popery of government.

To the evil of monarchy we have added that of hereditary succession; and as the first is a degradation and lessening of ourselves, so the second, claimed as a matter of right, is an insult and imposition on posterity. For all men being originally equals, no *one* by *birth* could have a right to set up his own family in perpetual preference to all others for ever, and tho' himself might deserve *some* decent degree of honors of his contemporaries, might be far too unworthy to inherit them. One of the strongest natural proofs of the folly of hereditary right in kings, is that nature disapproves it, otherwise she would not so frequently turn it into ridicule, by giving mankind an *ass for a lion.*

Secondly, as no man at first could possess any other public honors than were bestowed upon him, so the givers of those honors could have no power to give away the right of posterity, and though they might say "we choose you for our head," they could not without manifest injustice to their children say "that your children and your children's children shall reign over our's forever." Because such an unwise, unjust, unnatural compact might (perhaps) in the next succession put them under the government of a rogue or a fool. Most wise men in their private sentiments have ever treated hereditary right with contempt; yet it is one of those evils which when once established is not easily removed: many submit from fear, others from superstition, and the more powerful part shares with the king the plunder of the rest.

This is supposing the present race of kings in the world to have had an honorable origin: Whereas it is more than probable, that, could we take off the dark covering of antiquity and trace them to their first rise, we should find the first of them nothing better than the principal ruffian of some restless gang; whose savage manners or pre-eminence in subtility obtained him the title of chief among plunderers: and who by increasing in power and extending his depredations, over-awed the quiet and defenceless to purchase their safety by frequent contributions. Yet his electors could have no idea of giving hereditary right to his descendants, because such a perpetual exclusion of themselves was incompatible with the free and unrestrained principles they profess to live by. Wherefore, hereditary succession in the early ages of monarchy could not take place as a matter of claim, but as something casual or complemental; but as few or no records were extant in those days, and traditionary history stuff'd with fables, it was very easy, after the lapse of a few generations, to trump up some superstitious tale conveniently timed, Mahomet-like, to cram hereditary right down the throats of the vulgar. Perhaps the disorders which threatened, or seemed to threaten, on the decease of a leader and the choice of a new one (for elections among ruffians could not be very orderly) induced many at first to favour hereditary pretensions; by which means it happened, as it hath happened since, that what at first was submitted to as a convenience was afterwards claimed as a right.

England since the conquest hath known some few good monarchs, but groaned beneath a much larger number of bad ones; yet no man in his senses can say that their claim under William the Conqueror is a very honorable one. A French Bastard landing with an armed Banditti and establishing himself king of England against the consent of the natives, is in plain terms a very paltry rascally original. — It certainly hath no divinity in it. However it is needless to spend much time in exposing the folly of hereditary right; if there are any so weak as to believe it, let them promiscuously worship the Ass and the Lion, and welcome. I shall neither copy their humility, nor disturb their devotion.

Yet I should be glad to ask how they suppose Kings came at first? The question admits but of three answers, viz. either by lot, by election, or by usurpation. If the first king was taken by lot, it establishes a precedent for the next, which excludes hereditary succession. Saul was by lot, yet the succession was not hereditary, neither does it appear from that transaction that there was any intention it ever should. If the first king of any country was by election that likewise establishes a precedent for the next; for to say that the right of all future generations is taken away by the act of the first electors in their choice not only of a king, but of a family of kings for ever, hath no parallel in or out of scripture but the doctrine of original sin, which supposes the free will of all men lost in Adam; and from such comparison, and it will admit of no other, hereditary succession can derive no glory. For as in Adam all sinned, and as in the first electors all men obeyed; as in the one all mankind were subjected to Satan, and in the other to sovereignty; as our innocence was lost in the first, and our authority in the last; and as both disabled us from reassuming some former state and privilege, it unanswerably follows that original sin and hereditary succession are parallels. Dishonorable rank! inglorious connection! yet the most subtle sophist cannot produce a juster simile.

As to usurpation, no man will be so hardy as to defend it; and that William the Conqueror was an usurper is a fact not to be contradicted. The plain truth is, that the antiquity of English monarchy will not bear looking into.

But it is not so much the absurdity as the evil of hereditary succession which concerns mankind. Did it insure a race of good and wise men it would have the seal of divine authority, but as it opens a door to the *foolish,* the *wicked,* and the *improper,* it hath in it the nature of oppression. Men who look upon themselves born to reign, and others to obey, soon grow insolent. — Selected from the rest of mankind, their minds are early poisoned by importance; and the world they act in differs so materially from the world at large, that they have but little opportunity of

---

1 **Mahomet-like,** an allusion to the belief that Mohammed, prophet of Islam, carefully timed for political purposes the revelations upon which the Koran is based   19 **Saul . . . lot.** See I Kings 10:17-24

knowing its true interest, and when they succeed to the government are frequently the most ignorant and unfit of any throughout the dominions.

Another evil which attends hereditary succession is, that the throne is subject to be possessed by a minor at any age; all which time the regency acting under the cover of a king have every opportunity and inducement to betray their trust. The same national misfortune happens when a king worn out with age and infirmity enters the last stage of human weakness. In both these cases the public becomes a prey to every miscreant who can tamper successfully with the follies either of age or infancy.

The most plausible plea which hath ever been offered in favor of hereditary succession is, that it preserves a Nation from civil wars; and were this true, it would be weighty; whereas it is the most barefaced falsity ever imposed upon mankind. The whole history of England disowns the fact. Thirty kings and two minors have reigned in that distracted kingdom since the conquest, in which time there has been (including the Revolution) no less than eight civil wars and nineteen Rebellions. Wherefore, instead of making for peace, it makes against it, and destroys the very foundation it seems to stand upon.

The contest for monarchy and succession, between the houses of York and Lancaster, laid England in a scene of blood for many years. Twelve pitched battles besides skirmishes and sieges were fought between Henry and Edward. Twice was Henry prisoner to Edward, who in his turn was prisoner to Henry. And so uncertain is the fate of war and the temper of a Nation, when nothing but personal matters are the ground of a quarrel, that Henry was taken in triumph from a prison to a palace, and Edward obliged to fly from a palace to a foreign land; yet, as sudden transitions of temper are seldom lasting, Henry in his turn was driven from the throne, and Edward recalled to succeed him. The parliament always following the strongest side.

This contest began in the reign of Henry the 6th, and was not entirely extinguished till Henry the 7th, in whom the families were united. Including a period of 67 years, viz. from 1422 to 1489.

In short, monarchy and succession have laid (not this or that kingdom only) but the world in blood and ashes. 'Tis a form of government which the word of God bears testimony against, and blood will attend it.

If we inquire into the business of a King, we shall find that in some countries they may have none; and after sauntering away their lives without pleasure to themselves or advantages to the nation, withdraw from the scene, and leave their successors to tread the same idle round. In absolute monarchies the whole weight of business civil and military lies on the King; the children of Israel in their request for a King urged this plea, "that he may judge us, and go out before us and fight our battles." But in countries where he is neither a judge nor a general, as in England, a man would be puzzled to know what *is* his business.

---

18 **York and Lancaster,** the two houses which contended for the English throne after the deposition of Richard II in 1399. The period described by Paine is that of the War of the Roses, so called because the Lancastrian emblem was a red rose and the Yorkist a white one

The nearer any government approaches to a Republic, the less business there is
for a King. It is somewhat difficult to find a proper name for the government of
England. Sir William Meredith calls it a Republic; but in its present state it is unworthy of the name, because the corrupt influence of the Crown, by having all the
places in its disposal, hath so effectually swallowed up the power, and eaten out the
virtue of the House of Commons (the Republican part in the constitution) that
the government of England is nearly as monarchical as that of France or Spain. Men
fall out with names without understanding them. For 'tis the republican and not
the monarchical part of the constitution of England which Englishmen glory in,
10 viz. the liberty of choosing an house of commons from out of their own body —
and it is easy to see that when republican virtues fail, slavery ensues. Why is the
Constitution of England sickly? but because monarchy hath poisoned the Republic;
the crown has engrossed the Commons.

In England a king hath little more to do than to make war and give away places;
which in plain terms is to empoverish the nation and set it together by the ears. A
pretty business indeed for a man to be allowed eight hundred thousand sterling a
year for, and worshipped into the bargain! Of more worth is one honest man to
society, and in the sight of God, than all the crowned ruffians that ever lived.

Thoughts on the Present State of American Affairs

20   In the following pages I offer nothing more than simple facts, plain arguments,
and common sense: and have no other preliminaries to settle with the reader, than
that he will divest himself of prejudice and prepossession, and suffer his reason and
his feeling to determine for themselves: that he will put on, or rather that he will
not put off, the true character of a man, and generously enlarge his views beyond
the present day.

Volumes have been written on the subject of the struggle between England and
America. Men of all ranks have embarked in the controversy, from different motives,
and with various designs; but all have been ineffectual, and the period of debate is
closed. Arms as the last resource decide the contest; the appeal was the choice of
30 the King, and the continent has accepted the challenge.

It hath been reported of the late Mr. Pelham (who tho' an able minister was not
without his faults) that on his being attacked in the House of Commons on the
score that his measures were only of a temporary kind, replied, *"they will last my
time."* Should a thought so fatal and unmanly possess the Colonies in the present
contest, the name of Ancestors will be remembered by future generations
with detestation.

The Sun never shined on a cause of greater worth. 'Tis not the affair of a City, a
County, a Province, or a Kingdom; but of a Continent — of at least one eighth part

---

3 **Sir William Meredith** (1725?-1790), an English political leader, at one time prominent in the Whig opposition to the Tory ministry   31 **Mr. Pelham**, Henry Pelham (1694-1754), prime minister of Great
Britain, 1744-1754

of the habitable globe. 'Tis not the concern of a day, a year, or an age; posterity are virtually involved in the contest, and will be more or less affected even to the end of time by the proceedings now. Now is the seedtime of continental union, faith and honor. The least fracture now, will be like a name engraved with the point of a pin on the tender rind of a young oak; the wound would enlarge with the tree, and posterity read it in full grown characters.

By referring the matter from argument to arms, a new æra for politics is struck — a new method of thinking has arisen. All plans, proposals, &c. prior to the nineteenth of April, i. e. to the commencement of hostilities, are like the almanacks of last year; which though proper then, are superceded and useless now. Whatever was 10 advanced by the advocates on either side of the question then, terminated in one and the same point, viz. a union with Great Britain; the only difference between the parties was the method of effecting it; the one proposing force, the other friendship; but it has so far happened that the first has failed, and the second has withdrawn her influence.

As much has been said of the advantages of reconciliation, which, like an agreeable dream, has passed away and left us as we were, it is but right that we should examine the contrary side of the argument, and enquire into some of the many ma-terial injuries which these Colonies sustain, and always will sustain, by being connected with and dependant on Great Britain. To examine that connection and 20 dependance, on the principles of nature and common sense, to see what we have to trust to, if separated, and what we are to expect, if dependant.

I have heard it asserted by some, that as America has flourished under her former connection with Great Britain, the same connection is necessary toward her future happiness, and will always have the same effect. — Nothing can be more fallacious than this kind of argument. — We may as well assert that because a child has thrived upon milk, that it is never to have meat, or that the first twenty years of our lives is to become a precedent for the next twenty. But even this is admitting more than is true; for I answer roundly, that America would have flourished as much, and probably much more, had no European power taken any notice of her. The commerce 30 by which she hath enriched herself are the necessaries of life, and will always have a market while eating is the custom of Europe.

But she has protected us, say some. That she hath engrossed us is true, and defended the Continent at our expence as well as her own, is admitted, and she would have defended Turkey from the same motive, *viz.* for the sake of trade and dominion.

Alas! we have been long led away by ancient prejudices and made large sacrifices to superstition. We have boasted the protection of Great Britain, without considering, that her motive was *interest* not *attachment;* and that she did not protect us from *our enemies* on *our account,* but from her enemies on her own account, from those who had no quarrel with us on any *other account,* and who will always be our enemies 40 on the *same account.* Let Britain waive her pretensions to the continent, or the continent throw off the dependance, and we should be at peace with France and Spain

---

8 **nineteenth of April**, the date of the engagement at Lexington

were they at war with Britain. The miseries of Hanover's last war ought to warn us against connections.

It hath lately been asserted in Parliament, that the colonies have no relation to each other but through the parent country, i. e. that Pennsylvania and the Jerseys, and so on for the rest, are sister colonies by the way of England; this is certainly a very roundabout way of proving relationship, but it is the nearest and only true way of proving enmity (or enemyship, if I may so call it). France and Spain never were, nor perhaps ever will be, our enemies as *Americans,* but as our being the *subjects of Great Britain.*

10   But Britain is the parent country, say some. Then the more shame upon her conduct. Even brutes do not devour their young, nor savages make war upon their families; wherefore, the assertion, if true, turns to her reproach; but it happens not to be true, or only partly so, and the phrase *parent* or *mother country* hath been jesuitically adopted by the King and his parasites, with a low papistical design of gaining an unfair bias on the credulous weakness of our minds. Europe, and not England, is the parent country of America. This new world hath been the asylum for the persecuted lovers of civil and religious liberty from *every part* of Europe. Hither have they fled, not from the tender embraces of the mother, but from the cruelty of the monster; and it is so far true of England, that the same tyranny which
20   drove the first emigrants from home, pursues their descendants still.

In this extensive quarter of the globe, we forget the narrow limits of three hundred and sixty miles (the extent of England) and carry our friendship on a larger scale; we claim brotherhood with every European Christian, and triumph in the generosity of the sentiment.

It is pleasant to observe by what regular gradations we surmount the force of local prejudices, as we enlarge our acquaintance with the world. A man born in any town in England divided into parishes, will naturally associate most with his fellow parishioners (because their interests in many cases will be common) and distinguish him by the name of *neighbor;* if he meet him but a few miles from home, he drops
30   the narrow idea of a street, and salutes him by the name of *townsman;* if he travel out of the county and meet him in any other, he forgets the minor divisions of street and town, and calls him *country-man, i.e. county-man;* but if in their foreign excursions they should associate in France, or any other part of *Europe,* their local remembrance would be enlarged into that of *Englishman.* And by a just parity of reasoning, all Europeans meeting in America, or any other quarter of the globe, are *countrymen;* for England, Holland, Germany, or Sweden, when compared with the whole, stand in the same places on the larger scale, which the divisions of street, town, and county do on the smaller ones; Distinctions too limited for Continental minds. Not one third of the inhabitants, even of this province are of English descent.
40 Wherefore, I reprobate the phrase of parent or mother country applied to England only, as being false, selfish, narrow and ungenerous.

But, admitting that we were all of English descent, what does it amount to? Noth-

---

1 **Hanover's last war,** the Seven Years' War (1756-1763), estimated to have cost 900,000 lives   39 **this province,** Pennsylvania

ing. Britain, being now an open enemy, extinguishes every other name and title: and to say that reconciliation is our duty, is truly farcical. The first king of England, of the present line (William the Conqueror) was a Frenchman, and half the Peers of England are descendants from the same country; wherefore, by the same method of reasoning, England ought to be governed by France.

Much hath been said of the united strength of Britain and the Colonies, that in conjunction they might bid defiance to the world: But this is mere presumption, the fate of war is uncertain, neither do the expressions mean any thing, for this Continent would never suffer itself to be drained of inhabitants, to support the British arms in either Asia, Africa or Europe.   10

Besides, what have we to do with setting the world at defiance? Our plan is commerce, and that, well attended to, will secure us the peace and friendship of all Europe; because it is the enterest of all Europe to have America a *free port*. Her trade will always be a protection, and her barrenness of gold and silver secure her from invaders.

I challenge the warmest advocate of reconciliation to show a single advantage that this Continent can reap, by being connected with Great Britain. I repeat the challenge, not a single advantage is derived. Our corn will fetch its price in any market in Europe, and our imported goods must be paid for buy them where we will.

But the injuries and disadvantages which we sustain by that connection, are with- 20 out number; and our duty to mankind at large, as well as to ourselves, instruct us to renounce the alliance: Because, any submission to, or dependance on, Great Britain, tends directly to involve this Continent in European wars and quarrels, and set us at variance with nations who would otherwise seek our friendship, and against whom we have neither anger nor complaint. As Europe is our market for trade, we ought to form no partial connection with any part of it. 'Tis the true interest of America to steer clear of European contentions, which she can never do, while by her dependance on Britain, she is made the make-weight in the scale of British politics.

Europe is too thickly planted with kingdoms to be long at peace, and whenever a war breaks out between England and any foreign power, the trade of America goes 30 to ruin, *because of her connection with Britain.* The next war may not turn out like the last, and should it not, the advocates for reconciliation now will be wishing for separation then, because neutrality in that case would be a safer convoy than a man of war. Everything that is right or reasonable pleads for separation. The blood of the slain, the weeping voice of nature cries, 'TIS TIME TO PART. Even the distance at which the Almighty hath placed England and America is a strong and natural proof that the authority of the one over the other, was never the design of heaven. The time likewise at which the Continent was discovered, adds weight to the argument, and the manner in which it was peopled, encreases the force of it. — The Reformation was preceded by the discovery of America: As if the Almighty graciously meant 40 to open a sanctuary to the persecuted in future years, when home should afford neither friendship nor safety.

The authority of Great Britain over this Continent, is a form of government, which sooner or later must have an end. And a serious mind can draw no true pleasure by looking forward, under the painful and positive conviction that what he calls "the present constitution" is merely temporary. As parents, we can have no joy, knowing that *this government* is not sufficiently lasting to insure any thing which we may bequeath to posterity: And by a plain method of argument, as we are running the next generation into debt, we ought to do the work of it, otherwise we use them meanly and pitifully. In order to discover the line of our duty rightly, we should take our children in our hand, and fix our station a few years farther into life; that eminence will present a prospect which a few present fears and prejudices conceal from our sight.

10   Though I would carefully avoid giving unnecessary offence, yet I am inclined to believe, that all those who espouse the doctrine of reconciliation, may be included within the following descriptions.

Interested men, who are not to be trusted, weak men who *cannot* see, prejudiced men who *will not* see, and a certain set of moderate men who think better of the European world than it deserves; and this last class, by an ill-judged deliberation, will be the cause of more calamities to this continent than all the other three.

It is the good fortune of many to live distant from the scene of present sorrow; the evil is not sufficiently brought to *their* doors to make *them* feel the precariousness with which all American property is possessed. But let our imaginations transport us a few moments to Boston; that seat of wretchedness will teach us wisdom, and instruct us for ever to renounce a power in whom we can have no trust. The inhabitants of that unfortunate city who but a few months ago were in ease and affluence, have now no other alternative than to stay and starve, or turn out to beg. Endangered by the fire of their friends if they continue within the city, and plundered by the soldiery if they leave it, in their present situation they are prisoners without the hope of redemption, and in a general attack for their relief they would be exposed to the fury of both armies.

Men of passive tempers look somewhat lightly over the offences of Great Britain, and, still hoping for the best, are apt to call out, *come, come, we shall be friends again* 30 *for all this*. But examine the passions and feelings of mankind: Bring the doctrine of reconciliation to the touchstone of nature, and then tell me whether you can hereafter love, honor, and faithfully serve the power that hath carried fire and sword into your land? If you cannot do all these, then are you only deceiving yourselves, and by your delay bringing ruin upon posterity. Your future connection with Britain, whom you can neither love nor honor, will be forced and unnatural, and being formed only on the plan of present convenience, will in a little time fall into a relapse more wretched than the first. But if you say, you can still pass the violations over, then I ask, Hath your house been burnt? Hath your property been destroyed before your face? Are your wife and children destitute of a bed to lie on, or 40 bread to live on? Have you lost a parent or child by their hands, and yourself the ruined and wretched survivor? If you have not, then are you not a judge of those who have. But if you have, and can still shake hands with the murderers, then are

---

20 **Boston,** besieged from July 1775 until March 1776

you unworthy the name of husband, father, friend, or lover, and whatever may be your rank or title in life, you have the heart of a coward, and the spirit of a sycophant. This is not inflaming or exaggerating matters, but trying them by those feelings and affections which nature justifies, and without which we should be incapable of discharging the social duties of life, or enjoying the felicities of it. I mean not to exhibit horror for the purpose of provoking revenge, but to awaken us from fatal and unmanly slumbers, that we may pursue determinately some fixed object. 'Tis not in the power of Britain or of Europe to conquer America, if she doth not conquer herself by *delay* and *timidity.* The present winter is worth an age if rightly employed, but if lost or neglected the whole continent will partake of the misfortune; 10 and there is no punishment which that man doth not deserve, be he who, or what, or where he will, that may be the means of sacrificing a season so precious and useful.

'Tis repugnant to reason, to the universal order of things; to all examples from former ages, to suppose, that this continent can long remain subject to any external power. The most sanguine in Britain doth not think so. The utmost stretch of human wisdom cannot, at this time, compass a plan, short of separation, which can promise the continent even a year's security. Reconciliation is *now* a fallacious dream. Nature has deserted the connection, and art cannot supply her place. For, as Milton wisely expresses, "never can true reconcilement grow where wounds of deadly hate have pierced so deep."   20

Every quiet method for peace hath been ineffectual. Our prayers have been rejected with disdain; and hath tended to convince us that nothing flatters vanity or confirms obstinacy in Kings more than repeated petitioning — and nothing hath contributed more than that very measure to make the Kings of Europe absolute. Witness Denmark and Sweden. Wherefore, since nothing but blows will do, for God's sake let us come to a final separation, and not leave the next generation to be cutting throats under the violated unmeaning names of parent and child.

To say they will never attempt it again is idle and visionary; we thought so at the repeal of the stamp act, yet a year or two undeceived us; as well may we suppose that nations which have been once defeated will never renew the quarrel.   30

As to government matters, 'tis not in the power of Britain to do this Continent justice: the business of it will soon be too weighty and intricate to be managed with any tolerable degree of convenience, by a power so distant from us, and so very ignorant of us; for if they cannot conquer us they cannot govern us. To be always running three or four thousand miles with a tale or a petition, waiting four or five months for an answer, which, when obtained, requires five or six more to explain it in, will in a few years be looked upon as folly and childishness. — There was a time when it was proper, and there is a proper time for it to cease.

Small islands not capable of protecting themselves, are the proper objects for government to take under their care; but there is something absurd in supposing 40 a Continent to be perpetually governed by an island. In no instance hath nature

---

19 **Milton.** See *Paradise Lost,* Bk. IV, ll. 98-99   24 **Denmark and Sweden,** where quarrels among the nobles had led to the establishment of absolute monarchy under Frederick III of Denmark in 1660 and Gustavus III of Sweden in 1772

made the satellite larger than its primary planet; and as England and America, with respect to each other, reverse the common order of nature, it is evident that they belong to different systems. England to Europe: America to itself.

I am not induced by motives of pride, party or resentment to espouse the doctrine of separation and independance; I am clearly, positively, and conscientiously persuaded that 'tis the true interest of this continent to be so; that everything short of *that* is mere patchwork, that it can afford no lasting felicity — that it is leaving the sword to our children, and shrinking back at a time when a little more, a little further, would have rendered this continent the glory of the earth.

10   As Britain hath not manifested the least inclination towards a compromise, we may be assured that no terms can be obtained worthy the acceptance of the continent, or any ways equal to the expence of blood and treasure we have been already put to.

The object contended for, ought always to bear some just proportion to the expence. The removal of North, or the whole detestable junto, is a matter unworthy the millions we have expended. A temporary stoppage of trade was an inconvenience, which would have sufficiently balanced the repeal of all the acts complained of, had such repeals been obtained; but if the whole Continent must take up arms, if every man must be a soldier, 'tis scarcely worth our while to fight against a con-
20 temptible ministry only. Dearly, dearly do we pay for the repeal of the acts, if that is all we fight for; for, in a just estimation 'tis as great a folly to pay a bunker-hill price for law as for land. As I have always considered the independancy of this Continent, as an event which sooner or later must arrive, so from the late rapid progress of the Continent to maturity, the event cannot be far off. Wherefore, on the breaking out of hostilities, it was not worth the while to have disputed a matter which time would have finally redressed, unless we meant to be in earnest: otherwise it is like wasting an estate on a suit at law, to regulate the trespasses of a tenant whose lease is just expiring. No man was a warmer wisher for a reconciliation than myself, before the fatal nineteenth of April, 1775, but the moment the event of that
30 day was made known, I rejected the hardened, sullen-tempered Pharaoh of England for ever; and disdain the wretch, that with the pretended title of FATHER OF HIS PEOPLE can unfeelingly hear of their slaughter, and composedly sleep with their blood upon his soul.

But admitting that matters were now made up, what would be the event? I answer, the ruin of the continent. And that for several reasons.

First. The powers of governing still remaining in the hands of the king, he will have a negative over the whole legislation of this Continent. And as he hath shown himself such an inveterate enemy to liberty, and discovered such a thirst for arbitrary power, is he, or is he not, a proper person to say to these Colonies, *You shall make*
40 *no laws but what I please!?* And is there any inhabitant of America so ignorant as not to know, that according to what is called the *present Constitution,* this Continent

---

15 **North,** Lord North (1733-1792), prime minister of Great Britain, 1770-1782   21 **bunker-hill price.**
Killed and wounded numbered nearly a third of the troops engaged on both sides

can make no laws but what the king gives leave to; and is there any man so unwise as not to see, that (considering what has happened) he will suffer no law to be made here but such as suits his purpose? We may be as effectually enslaved by the want of laws in America, as by submitting to laws made for us in England. After matters are made up, (as it is called) can there be any doubt, but the whole power of the crown will be exerted to keep this Continent as low and humble as possible? Instead of going forward we shall go backward, or be perpetually quarrelling, or ridiculously petitioning. — We are already greater than the King wishes us to be, and will he not hereafter endeavor to make us less? To bring the matter to one point, Is the power who is jealous of our prosperity, a proper power to govern us? 10 Whoever says No, to this question, is an Independent for independency means no more than this, whether we shall make our own laws, or, whether the King, the greatest enemy this Continent hath, or can have, shall tell us *"there shall be no laws but such as I like."*

But the King, you'll say, has a negative in England; the people there can make no laws without his consent. In point of right and good order, it is something very ridiculous that a youth of twenty-one (which hath often happened) shall say to several millions of people older and wiser than himself, "I forbid this or that act of yours to be law." But in this place I decline this sort of reply, tho' I will never cease to expose the absurdity of it, and only answer that England being the King's 20 residence, and America not so, makes quite another case. The King's negative here is ten times more dangerous and fatal than it can be in England; for *there* he will scarcely refuse his consent to a bill for putting England into as strong a state of defence as possible, and in America he would never suffer such a bill to be passed.

America is only a secondary object in the system of British politics, England consults the good of *this* country no further than it answers her *own* purpose. Wherefore, her own interest leads her to suppress the growth of *ours,* in every case which doth not promote *her* advantage, or in the least interfere with it. A pretty state we should soon be in under such a second-hand government, considering what has happened! Men do not change from enemies to friends by the alteration of a name: 30 And in order to show that reconciliation *now* is a dangerous doctrine, I affirm, *that it would be policy in the king at this time to repeal the acts, for the sake of reinstating himself in the government of the provinces;* In order that HE MAY ACCOMPLISH BY CRAFT AND SUBTLETY, IN THE LONG RUN, WHAT HE CANNOT DO BY FORCE AND VIOLENCE IN THE SHORT ONE. Reconciliation and ruin are nearly related.

Secondly. — That as even the best terms which we can expect to obtain can amount to no more than a temporary expedient, or a kind of government by guardianship, which can last no longer than till the Colonies come of age, so the general face and state of things in the interim will be unsettled and unpromising: Emigrants of property will not choose to come to a country whose form of government hangs 40 but by a thread, and who is every day tottering on the brink of commotion and disturbance: And numbers of the present inhabitants would lay hold of the interval to dispose of their effects, and quit the continent.

But the most powerful of all arguments is, that nothing but independence, i. e. a continental form of government, can keep the peace of the continent and preserve it inviolate from civil wars. I dread the event of a reconciliation with Britain *now,* as it is more than probable that it will be followed by a revolt some where or other, the consequences of which may be far more fatal than all malice of Britain.

Thousands are already ruined by British barbarity; (thousands more will probably suffer the same fate). Those men have other feelings than us who have nothing suffered. All they *now* possess is liberty; what they have before enjoyed is sacrificed to its service, and having nothing more to lose they disdain submission. Besides, the general temper of the colonies, towards a British government will be like that
10 of a youth who is nearly out of his time; they will care very little about her: And a government which cannot preserve the peace is no government at all, and in that case we pay our money for nothing; and pray what is it that Britain can do, whose power will be wholly on paper, should a civil tumult break out the very day after reconciliation? I have heard some men say, many of whom I believe spoke without thinking, that they dreaded an independence, fearing that it would produce civil wars: It is but seldom that our first thoughts are truly correct, and that is the case here; for there is ten times more to dread from a patched up connection than from independence. I make the sufferer's case my own, and I protest, that were I driven from house and home, my property destroyed, and my circumstances ruined, that
20 as a man, sensible of injuries, I could never relish the doctrine of reconciliation, or consider myself bound thereby.

The colonies have manifested such a spirit of good order and obedience to continental government, as is sufficient to make every reasonable person easy and happy on that head. No man can assign the least pretence for his fears, on any other grounds, than such as are truly childish and ridiculous, viz., that one colony will be striving for superiority over another.

Where there are no distinctions there can be no superiority; perfect equality affords no temptation. The Republics of Europe are all (and we may say always) in peace. Holland and Switzerland are without wars, foreign or domestic: Monarchical
30 governments, it is true, are never long at rest: the crown itself is a temptation to enterprising ruffians at *home;* and that degree of pride and insolence ever attendant on regal authority, swells into a rupture with foreign powers in instances where a republican government, by being formed on more natural principles, would negociate the mistake.

If there is any true cause of fear regarding independence, it is because no plan is yet laid down. Men do not see their way out. — Wherefore, as an opening into that business I offer the following hints; at the same time modestly affirming, that I have no other opinion of them myself, than that they may be the means of giving rise to something better. Could the straggling thoughts of individuals be col-
40 lected, they would frequently form materials for wise and able men to improve into useful matter.

---

29 **Holland and Switzerland.** The United Netherlands (northern Holland) was a republic until 1814; it and Switzerland were frequently cited by Americans as precedents in their anti-monarchical arguments

LET the assemblies be annual, with a president only. The representation more equal, their business wholly domestic, and subject to the authority of a Continental Congress.

Let each Colony be divided into six, eight, or ten, convenient districts, each district to send a proper number of Delegates to Congress, so that each Colony send at least thirty. The whole number in Congress will be at least 390. Each Congress to sit and to choose a President by the following method. When the Delegates are met, let a colony be taken from the whole thirteen Colonies by lot, after which let the Congress choose (by ballot) a president from out of the Delegates of that province. In the next Congress, let a Colony be taken by lot from twelve only, 10 omitting that Colony from which the president was taken in the former Congress, and so proceeding on till the whole thirteen shall have had their proper rotation. And in order that nothing may pass into a law but what is satisfactorily just, not less than three fifths of the Congress to be called a majority. — He that will promote discord, under a government so equally formed as this, would have joined Lucifer in his revolt.

But as there is a peculiar delicacy from whom, or in what manner, this business must first arise, and as it seems most agreeable and consistent that it should come from some intermediate body between the governed and the governors, that is, between the Congress and the People, Let a CONTINENTAL CONFERENCE be held in 20 the following manner, and for the following purpose.

A Committee of twenty six members of Congress, *viz.* Two for each colony. Two members from each house or Assembly, or Provincial convention; and five Representatives of the people at large, to be chosen in the capital city or town of each Province, for, and in behalf of the whole Province, by as many qualified voters as shall think proper to attend from all parts of the Province for that purpose; or, if more convenient, the Representatives may be chosen in two or three of the most populous parts thereof. In this CONFERENCE, thus assembled, will be united the two grand principles of business, *knowledge* and *power*. The members of Congress, Assemblies, or Conventions, by having had experience in national concerns, will be 30 able and useful counsellors, and the whole, being impowered by the people, will have a truly legal authority.

The conferring members being met, let their business be to frame a CONTINENTAL CHARTER, or Charter of the United Colonies; (answering to what is called the Magna Charta of England) fixing the number and manner of choosing members of Congress, Members of Assembly, with their date of sitting; and drawing the line of business and jurisdiction between them: Always remembering, that our strength is continental, not provincial. Securing freedom and property to all men, and above all things, the free exercise of religion, according to the dictates of conscience; with such other matter as it is necessary for a charter to contain. Immediately after which, 40

---

1 **a president only.** Paine's fear of monarchy was accompanied by such a strong distrust of executive power that he favored abolishing the office of governor of an individual state. It is also evident from his proposed scheme of government that he was opposed both to a bicameral legislature and to the principle of checks and balances

the said conference to dissolve, and the bodies which shall be chosen conformable to the said charter, to be the legislators and governors of this continent for the time being: Whose peace and happiness, may God preserve. AMEN.

Should any body of men be hereafter delegated for this or some similar purpose, I offer them the following extracts from that wise observer on governments, DRAGONETTI. "The science," says he, "of the politician consists in fixing the true point of happiness and freedom. Those men would deserve the gratitude of ages, who should discover a mode of government that contained the greatest sum of individual happiness, with the least national expense."

But where, say some, is the king of America? I'll tell you, Friend, he reigns above, and doth not make havoc of mankind like the Royal Brute of Great Britain. Yet that we may not appear to be defective even in earthly honors, let a day be solemnly set apart for proclaiming the Charter; let it be brought forth placed on the divine law, the Word of God; let a Crown be placed thereon, by which the world may know, that so far as we approve of monarchy, that in America THE LAW IS KING. For as in absolute governments the king is law, so in free countries the law *ought* to BE king, and there ought to be no other. But lest any ill use should afterwards arise, let the Crown at the conclusion of the ceremony be demolished, and scattered among the People whose right it is.

A government of our own is our natural right: and when a man seriously reflects on the precariousness of human affairs, he will become convinced, that it is infinitely wiser and safer, to form a Constitution of our own in a cool deliberate manner, while we have it in our power, than to trust such an interesting event to time and chance. If we omit it now, some Massanello may hereafter arise, who, laying hold of popular disquietudes, may collect together the desperate and the discontented, and by assuming to themselves the powers of government, finally sweep away the liberties of the Continent like a deluge. Should the government of America return again into the hands of Britain, the tottering situation of things will be a temptation for some desperate adventurer to try his fortune; and in such a case, what relief can Britain give? Ere she could hear the news, the fatal business might be done; and ourselves suffering like the wretched Britons under the oppression of the conqueror. Ye that oppose independance now, ye know not what ye do; ye are opening a door to eternal tyranny, by keeping vacant the seat of government. There are thousands and tens of thousands, who would think it glorious to expel from the Continent, that barbarous and hellish power, which hath stirred up the Indians and the Negroes to destroy us; the cruelty hath a double guilt, it is dealing brutally by us, and treacherously by them.

To talk of friendship with those in whom our reason forbids us to have faith, and our affections wounded thro' a thousand pores instruct us to detest, is madness and folly. Every day wears out the little remains of kindred between us and them;

---

6 **Dragonetti,** Giacinto, Marquis degl' Dragonetti (1738-1818), a Neapolitan jurist   9 **expense.** "Dragonetti on 'Virtues and Rewards.'" — Paine   24 **Massanello.** "Thomas Anello, otherwise Massanello, a fisherman of Naples, who after spiriting up his countrymen in the public market place, against the oppression of the Spaniards, to whom the place was then subject, prompted them to revolts, and in the space of a day became king." — Paine, in later editions.

and can there be any reason to hope, that as the relationship expires, the affection will increase, or that we shall agree better when we have ten times more and greater concerns to quarrel over than ever?

Ye that tell us of harmony and reconciliation, can ye restore to us the time that is past? Can ye give to prostitution its former innocence? neither can ye reconcile Britain and America. The last cord now is broken, the people of England are presenting addresses against us. There are injuries which nature cannot forgive; she would cease to be nature if she did. As well can the lover forgive the ravisher of his mistress, as the Continent forgive the murders of Britain. The Almighty hath implanted in us these inextinguishable feelings for good and wise purposes. They are the guardians of his image in our hearts. They distinguish us from the herd of common animals. The social compact would dissolve, and justice be extirpated from the earth, or have only a casual existence were we callous to the touches of affection. The robber and the murderer would often escape unpunished, did not the injuries which our tempers sustain, provoke us into justice.

O! ye that love mankind! Ye that dare oppose not only the tyranny but the tyrant, stand forth! Every spot of the old world is over-run with oppression. Freedom hath been hunted round the globe. Asia and Africa have long expelled her. — Europe regards her like a stranger, and England hath given her warning to depart. O receive the fugitive, and prepare in time an asylum for mankind.

Of the Present Ability of America with Some Miscellaneous Reflections

I have never met a man either in England or America, who hath not confessed his opinion, that a separation between the countries would take place, one time or other: And there is no instance, in which we have shown less judgment; than in endeavoring to describe, what we call, the ripeness or fitness of the Continent for independance.

As all men allow the measure, and vary only in their opinion of the time, let us, in order to remove mistakes, take a general survey of things, and endeavor if possible to find out the very time. But I need not go far, the inquiry ceases at once, for the *time hath found us.* The general concurrence, the glorious union of all things, proves the fact.

'Tis not in numbers but in unity that our great strength lies; yet our present numbers are sufficient to repel the force of all the world. The Continent has at this time the largest body of armed and disciplined men of any power under Heaven: and is just arrived at that pitch of strength, in which no single Colony is able to support itself, and the whole, when united, is able to do any thing. Our land force is more than sufficient, and as to naval affairs, we cannot be insensible that Britain would never suffer an American man of war to be built, while the Continent remained in her hands. Wherefore, we should be no forwarder a hundred years hence in that branch than we are now; but the truth is, we should be less so, because the timber of the country is every day diminishing.

Were the Continent crowded with inhabitants, her sufferings under the present circumstances would be intolerable. The more seaport-towns we had, the more should we have both to defend and to lose. Our present numbers are so happily proportioned to our wants, that no man need be idle. The diminution of trade affords an army, and the necessities of an army create a new trade.

Debts we have none; and whatever we may contract on this account will serve as a glorious memento of our virtue. Can we but leave posterity with a settled form of government, an independent constitution of its own, the purchase at any price will be cheap. But to expend millions for the sake of getting a few vile acts repealed, and routing the present ministry only, is unworthy the charge, and is using posterity with the utmost cruelty; because it is leaving them the great work to do, and a debt upon their backs from which they derive no advantage. Such a thought's unworthy a man of honor, and is the true characteristic of a narrow heart and a pidling politician.

The debt we may contract doth not deserve our regard if the work be but accomplished. No nation ought to be without a debt. A national debt is a national bond; and when it bears no interest, it is in no case a grievance. Britain is oppressed with a debt of upwards of one hundred and forty millions sterling, for which she pays upwards of four millions interest. And as a compensation for her debt, she has a large navy. America is without a debt, and without a navy; yet for a twentieth part of the English national debt, could have a navy as large again. The navy of England is not worth at this time more than three millions and a half sterling.

No country on the globe is so happily situated, or so internally capable of raising a fleet as America. Tar, timber, iron and cordage are her natural produce. We need go abroad for nothing. Whereas the Dutch, who make large profits by hiring out their ships of war to the Spaniards and Portuguese, are obliged to import most of the materials they use. We ought to view the building a fleet as an article of commerce, it being the natural manufactory of this country. 'Tis the best money we can lay out. A navy when finished is worth more than it cost: And is that nice point in national policy, in which commerce and protection are united. Let us build; if we want them not, we can sell; and by that means re-place our paper currency with ready gold and silver.

In point of manning a fleet, people in general run into great errors; it is not necessary that one fourth part should be sailors. The Terrible privateer, Captain Death, stood the hottest engagement of any ship last war, yet had not twenty sailors on board, though her complement of men was upwards of two hundred. A few able and social sailors will soon instruct a sufficient number of active landsmen in the common work of a ship. Wherefore we never can be more capable of beginning on maritime matters than now, while our timber is standing, our fisheries blocked up, and our sailors and shipwrights out of employ. Men of war, of seventy and eighty guns, were built forty years ago in New England, and why not the same now? Ship building is America's greatest pride, and in which she will, in time, excel the whole

---

33 **Captain Death,** a pseudonym for the commander of the *Terrible,* a British privateer captured by the French on December 28, 1756, after a murderous battle in which about four hundred were killed. His lieutenants bore the pseudonyms "Spirit" and "Ghost'"

world. The great empires of the east are mostly inland, and consequently excluded from the possibility of rivalling her. Africa is in a state of barbarism; and no power in Europe, hath either such an extent of coast, or such an internal supply of materials. Where nature hath given the one, she hath withheld the other; to America only hath she been liberal to both. The vast empire of Russia is almost shut out from the sea; wherefore her boundless forests, her tar, iron, and cordage are only articles of commerce.

In point of safety, ought we to be without a fleet? We are not the little people now, which we were sixty years ago; at that time we might have trusted our property in the streets, or fields rather, and slept securely without locks or bolts to our 1⁰ doors and windows. The case is now altered, and our methods of defence ought to improve with our encrease of property. A common pirate, twelve months ago, might have come up the Delaware, and laid the city of Philadelphia under contribution for what sum he pleased; and the same might have happened to other places. Nay, any daring fellow, in a brig of 14 or 16 guns, might have robbed the whole continent, and carried off half a million of money. These are circumstances which demand our attention, and point out the necessity of naval protection.

Some perhaps will say, that after we have made it up with Britain, she will protect us. Can they be so unwise as to mean, that she will keep a navy in our harbors for that purpose? Common sense will tell us, that the power which hath endeavored 2⁰ to subdue us, is of all others, the most improper to defend us. Conquest may be effected under the pretence of friendship; and ourselves, after a long and brave resistance, be at last cheated into slavery. And if her ships are not to be admitted into our harbors, I would ask, how is she to protect us? A navy three or four thousand miles off can be of little use, and on sudden emergencies, none at all. Wherefore if we must hereafter protect ourselves, why not do it for ourselves? Why do it for another?

The English list of ships of war, is long and formidable, but not a tenth part of them are at any one time fit for service, numbers of them are not in being; yet their names are pompously continued in the list, if only a plank be left of the ship; and 3⁰ not a fifth part of such as are fit for service, can be spared on any one station at one time. The East and West Indies, Mediterranean, Africa, and other parts, over which Britain extends her claim, make large demands upon her navy. From a mixture of prejudice and inattention, we have contracted a false notion respecting the navy of England, and have talked as if we should have the whole of it to encounter at once, and, for that reason, supposed that we must have one as large; which not being instantly practicable, has been made use of by a set of disguised Tories to discourage our beginning thereon. Nothing can be further from truth than this; for if America had only a twentieth part of the naval force of Britain, she would be by far an over-match for her; because, as we neither have, nor claim any foreign domin- 4⁰ ion, our whole force would be employed on our own coast, where we should, in the long run, have two to one the advantage of those who had three or four thousand miles to sail over, before they could attack us, and the same distance to return in order to refit and recruit. And although Britain, by her fleet, hath a check over our trade to Europe, we have as large a one over her trade to the West Indies, which, by laying in the neighborhood of the Continent lies entirely at its mercy.

Some method might be fallen on to keep up a naval force in time of peace, if we should not judge it necessary to support a constant navy. If premiums were to be given to merchants to build and employ in their service, ships mounted with 20, 30, 40, or 50 guns, (the premiums to be in proportion to the loss of bulk to the merchant,) fifty or sixty of those ships, with a few guardships on constant duty, would keep up a sufficient navy, and that without burdening ourselves with the evil so loudly complained of in England, of suffering their fleet in time of peace to lie rotting in the docks. To unite the sinews of commerce and defence is sound policy; for when our strength and our riches play into each other's hand, we need fear no external enemy.

In almost every article of defence we abound. Hemp flourishes even to rankness, so that we need not want cordage. Our iron is superior to that of other countries. Our small arms equal to any in the world. Cannon we can cast at pleasure. Saltpeter and gunpowder we are every day producing. Our knowledge is hourly improving. Resolution is our inherent character, and courage has never yet forsaken us. Wherefore, what is it that we want? Why is it that we hesitate? From Britain we can expect nothing but ruin. If she is once admitted to the government of America again, this continent will not be worth living in. Jealousies will be always arising; insurrections will be constantly happening; and who will go forth to quell them? Who will venture his life to reduce his own countrymen to a foreign obedience? The difference between Pennsylvania and Connecticut, respecting some unlocated lands, shows the insignificance of a British government, and fully proves that nothing but Continental authority can regulate Continental matters.

Another reason why the present time is preferable to all others, is, that the fewer our numbers are, the more land there is yet unoccupied, which, instead of being lavished by the king on his worthless dependants, may be hereafter supplied, not only to the discharge of the present debt, but to the constant support of government. No nation under Heaven hath such an advantage as this.

The infant state of the Colonies, as it is called, so far from being against is an argument in favor of independance. We are sufficiently numerous, and were we more so we might be less united. 'Tis a matter worthy of observation, that the more a country is peopled, the smaller their armies are. In military numbers, the ancients far exceeded the moderns: and the reason is evident, for trade being the consequence of population, men became too much absorbed thereby to attend to any thing else. Commerce diminishes the spirit both of Patriotism and military defence. And history sufficiently informs us, that the bravest achievements were always accomplished in the nonage of a nation. With the increase of commerce England hath lost its spirit. The city of London, notwithstanding its numbers, submits to continued insults with the patience of a coward. The more men have to lose, the less willing are they to venture. The rich are in general slaves to fear, and submit to courtly power with the trembling duplicity of a spaniel.

Youth is the seed-time of good habits as well in nations as in individuals. It might

be difficult, if not impossible, to form the Continent into one Government half a
century hence. The vast variety of interests, occasioned by an increase of trade and
population, would create confusion. Colony would be against Colony. Each being
able would scorn each other's assistance: and while the proud and foolish gloried
in their little distinctions, the wise would lament that the union had not been formed
before. Wherefore the present time is the true time for establishing it. The intimacy
which is contracted in infancy, and the friendship which is formed in misfortune,
are of all others the most lasting and unalterable. Our present union is marked with
both these characters: we are young, and we have been distressed; but our concord
hath withstood our troubles, and fixes a memorable Æra for posterity to glory in. 1(

The present time likewise, is that peculiar time which never happens to a nation
but once, viz. the time of forming itself into a government. Most nations have let
slip the opportunity, and by that means have been compelled to receive laws from
their conquerors, instead of making laws for themselves. First, they had a king, and
then a form of government; whereas the articles or charter of government should
be formed first, and men delegated to execute them afterwards: but from the errors
of other nations let us learn wisdom, and lay hold of the present opportunity — *To
begin Government at the right end.*

When William the Conqueror subdued England, he gave them law at the point
of the sword; and, until we consent that the seat of government in America 2(
be legally and authoritatively occupied, we shall be in danger of having it filled by
some fortunate ruffian, who may treat us in the same manner, and then, where will
be our freedom? where our property?

As to religion, I hold it to be the indispensible duty of government to protect all
conscientious professors thereof, and I know of no other business which government has to do therewith. Let a man throw aside that narrowness of soul, that selfishness of principle, which the niggards of all professions are so unwilling to part
with, and he will be at once delivered of his fears on that head. Suspicion is the
companion of mean souls, and the bane of all good society. For myself, I fully and
conscientiously believe, that it is the will of the Almighty that there should be a 3(
diversity of religious opinions among us. It affords a larger field for our christian
kindness: were we all of one way of thinking, our religious dispositions would want
matter for probation; and on this liberal principle I look on the various denominations among us, to be like children of the same family, differing only in what is
called their Christian names.

In pages 343 and 344 I threw out a few thoughts on the propriety of a continental
charter (for I only presume to offer hints, not plans) and in this place, I take the
liberty of re-mentioning the subject, by observing, that a charter is to be understood
as a bond of solemn obligation, which the whole enters into, to support the right
of every separate part, whether of religion, professional freedom, or property. A right 4(
reckoning makes long friends.

I have heretofore likewise mentioned the necessity of a large and equal representation; and there is no political matter which more deserves our attention. A small
number of electors, or a small number of representatives, are equally dangerous. But

if the number of representatives be not only small, but unequal, the danger is encreased. As an instance of this, I mention the following; when the petition of the associates was before the House of Assembly of Pennsylvania, twenty-eight members only were present; all the Bucks county members, being eight, voted against it, and had seven of the Chester members done the same, this whole province had been governed by two counties only; and this danger it is always exposed to. The unwarrantable stretch likewise, which the house made in their last sitting, to gain an undue authority over the Delegates of that Province, ought to warn the people at large, how they trust power out of their hands. A set of instructions for their
10 Delegates were put together, which in point of sense and business would have dishonoured a school-boy, and after being approved by a few, a very few, without doors, were carried into the house, and there passed in behalf of the whole Colony; whereas, did the whole Colony know with what ill-will that house had entered on some necessary public measures, they would not hesitate a moment to think them unworthy of such a trust.

Immediate necessity makes many things convenient, which if continued would grow into oppressions. Expedience and right are different things. When the calamities of America required a consultation, there was no method so ready, or at that time so proper, as to appoint persons from the several houses of Assembly for that pur-
20 pose; and the wisdom with which they have proceeded hath preserved this Continent from ruin. But as it is more than probable that we shall never be without a CONGRESS, every well wisher to good order must own that the mode for choosing members of that body, deserves consideration. And I put it as a question to those who make a study of mankind, whether representation and election is not too great a power for one and the same body of men to possess? When we are planning for posterity, we ought to remember that virtue is not hereditary.

It is from our enemies that we often gain excellent maxims, and are frequently surprised into reason by their mistakes. Mr. Cornwall (one of the Lords of the Treasury) treated the petition of the New-York Assembly with contempt, because
30 *that* house, he said, consisted but of twenty-six members, which trifling number, he argued, could not with decency be put for the whole. We thank him for his involuntary honesty.

TO CONCLUDE, however strange it may appear to some, or however unwilling they may be to think so, matters not, but many strong and striking reasons may be given to shew, that nothing can settle our affairs so expeditiously as an open and determined DECLARATION FOR INDEPENDANCE. Some of which are,

First. — It is the custom of Nations, when any two are at war, for some other powers, not engaged in the quarrel, to step in as mediators, and bring about the

---

2 **petition . . . associates,** an allusion, apparently, to the Association of 1774, a series of nonimportation, nonconsumption, and nonexportation resolutions adopted by the First Continental Congress   28 **Mr. Cornwall,** Charles Wolfram Cornwall (1735-1789), Lord of the Treasury in North's cabinet, 1774-1780, later speaker of the House of Commons, 1780-1789   32 **honesty.** "Those who would fully understand of what great consequence a large and equal representation is to a State, should read Burgh's Political Disquisitions." — Paine. The reference is to a work in three volumes published in 1774-1775 by James Burgh (1714-1775), a British reformer friendly to the American colonists

Preliminaries of a Peace: but while America calls herself the Subject of Great Britain, no power, however well disposed she may be, can offer her Mediation. Wherefore, in our present state we may quarrel on for ever.

Secondly. — It is unreasonable to suppose, that France or Spain will give us any kind of assistance, if we mean only to make use of that assistance for the purpose of repairing the breach, and strengthening the connection between Britain and America; because, those powers would be sufferers by the consequences.

Thirdly. — While we profess ourselves the Subjects of Britain, we must, in the eyes of foreign nations, be considered as Rebels. The precedent is somewhat dangerous to *their peace,* for men to be in arms under the name of Subjects: we, on the 10 spot, can solve the paradox; but to unite resistance and subjection, requires an idea much too refined for common understanding.

Fourthly. — Were a manifesto to be published, and despatched to foreign Courts, setting forth the miseries we have endured, and the peaceful methods which we have ineffectually used for redress; declaring at the same time, that not being able any longer to live happily or safely under the cruel disposition of the British court, we have been driven to the necessity of breaking off all connections with her; at the same time, assuring all such Courts of our peaceable disposition towards them, and of our desire of entering into trade with them; such a memorial would produce more good effects to this Continent, than if a ship were freighted with petitions 20 to Britain.

Under our present denomination of British Subjects, we can neither be received nor heard abroad: the custom of All courts is against us, and will be so, until by an independence we take rank with other Nations.

These proceedings may at first seem strange and difficult, but like all other steps which we have already passed over, will in a little time become familiar and agreeable: and until an Independance is declared, the Continent will feel itself like a man who continues putting off some unpleasant business from day to day, yet knows it must be done, hates to set about it, wishes it over, and is continually haunted with the thoughts of its necessity.   30

1775-1776

from *The American Crisis*

The first Crisis *appeared in the* Pennsylvania Journal *for December 19, 1776, and was almost immediately issued as a pamphlet. New Jersey was at the time well-nigh lost and Philadelphia panic-stricken. Washington had even written to his brother that "if every nerve is not strained to recruit the new army with all possible expedition, I think the game is pretty nearly up." No one would ever guess from Paine's stirring remarks that the situation was so serious. His courage, faith, and righteous wrath are here embodied in rhetoric which can yet stir Americans after all these many years. The use of alliteration, antithesis, balance, the rhetorical question, Biblical echoes, and other oratorical devices shows how well Paine had learned the first lesson of the propagandist — to aim straight at the apathetic, timid, individual reader. Never again, perhaps, did he attain such heights as a phrase-maker. The New York legislature made no mistake in giving Paine a farm because "his literary works, and those especially under the signature of Common Sense, and the Crisis, inspired the citizens of this state with unanimity, confirmed their confidence in the rectitude of their cause, and have ultimately contributed to the freedom, sovereignty, and independence of the United States."*

Number 1

These are the times that try men's souls: The summer soldier and the sunshine patriot will in this crisis, shrink from the service of his country; but he that stands it NOW, deserves the love and thanks of man and woman. Tyranny, like hell, is not easily conquered; yet we have this consolation with us, that the harder the conflict, the more glorious the triumph. What we obtain too cheap, we esteem too lightly: — 'Tis dearness only that gives everything its value. Heaven knows how to put a proper price upon its goods; and it would be strange indeed, if so celestial an article as FREEDOM should not be highly rated. Britain, with an army to enforce her tyranny, has declared that she has a right (*not only to*) TAX but "to BIND *us in* ALL CASES
10 WHATSOEVER," and if being *bound in that manner,* is not slavery, then is there not such a thing as slavery upon earth. Even the expression is impious, for so unlimited a power can belong only to GOD.

Whether the Independence of the Continent was declared too soon, or delayed too long, I will not now enter into as an argument; my own simple opinion is, that had it been eight months earlier, it would have been much better. We did not make a proper use of last winter, neither could we, while we were in a dependent state. However, the fault, if it were one, was all our own; we have none to blame but ourselves. But no great deal is lost yet; all that Howe has been doing for this month past, is rather a ravage than a conquest, which the spirit of the Jersies a year ago
20 would have quickly repulsed, and which time and a little resolution will soon recover.

I have as little superstition in me as any man living, but my secret opinion has ever been, and still is, that God Almighty will not give up a people to military destruction, or leave them unsupportedly to perish, who have so earnestly and so repeatedly sought to avoid the calamities of war, by every decent method which wisdom could invent. Neither have I so much of the infidel in me, as to suppose that he has relinquished the government of the world, and given us up to the care of devils; and as I do not, I cannot see on what grounds the king of Britain can look up to Heaven for help against us: a common murderer, a highwayman, or a house-breaker, has as good a pretence as he.
30 'Tis surprising to see how rapidly a panic will sometimes run through a country.

Text: an impression dated December 23, 1776, regarded by Professor Peach as the most authentic of its early pamphlet appearances   18 **Howe.** See note, p. 378   19 **The Jersies,** East Jersey, whose economic center was New York City, and West Jersey, which looked toward Philadelphia. East Jersey had most of the "spirit" for independence; West Jersey was predominantly Quaker

All nations and ages have been subject to them: Britain has trembled like an ague at the report of a French fleet of flat-bottomed boats; and in the fourteenth century the whole English army, after ravaging the kingdom of France, was driven back like men petrified with fear; and this brave exploit was performed by a few broken forces collected and headed by a woman, Joan of Arc. Would that heaven might inspire some Jersey maid to spirit up her countrymen, and save her fair fellow sufferers from ravage and ravishment! Yet panics, in some cases, have their uses; they produce as much good as hurt. Their duration is always short; the mind soon grows through them, and acquires a firmer habit than before. But their peculiar advantage is, that they are the touchstones of sincerity and hypocrisy, and bring things and men to 10 light, which might otherwise have lain forever undiscovered. In fact, they have the same effect on secret traitors which an imaginary apparition would have upon a private murderer. They sift out the hidden thoughts of man, and hold them up in public to the world. Many a disguised tory has lately shown his head, that shall penitentially solemnize with curses the day on which Howe arrived upon the Delaware.

As I was with the troops at Fort-Lee, and marched with them to the edge of Pennsylvania, I am well acquainted with many circumstances, which those who live at a distance, know but little or nothing of. Our situation there, was exceedingly cramped, the place being a narrow neck of land between the North-River and the Hackensack. Our force was inconsiderable, being not one-fourth so great as Howe could 20 bring against us. We had no army at hand to have relieved the garrison, had we shut ourselves up and stood on our defence. Our ammunition, light artillery, and the best part of our stores, had been removed, on the apprehension that Howe would endeavor to penetrate the Jerseys, in which case Fort Lee could be of no use to us; for it must occur to every thinking man, whether in the army or not, that these kind of field forts are only for temporary purposes, and last in use no longer than the enemy directs his force against the particular object, which such forts are raised to defend. Such was our situation and condition at Fort-Lee on the morning of the 20th of November, when an officer arrived with information that the enemy with 200 boats had landed about seven miles above: Major General Green, who com- 30 manded the garrison, immediately ordered them under arms, and sent express to General Washington at the town of Hackensack, distant by the way of the ferry, six miles. Our first object was to secure the bridge over the Hackensack, which laid up the river between the enemy and us, about six miles from us, three from them. General Washington arrived in about three-quarters of an hour, and marched at the head of the troops towards the bridge, which place I expected we should have a brush for; however, they did not choose to dispute it with us, and the greatest part of our troops went over the bridge, the rest over the ferry, except some which passed

2 **a French fleet,** assembled at Havre and other ports in 1759, during the Seven Years' War. The projected invasion was halted by British naval victories at Lagos and Quiberon Bay   2 **the fourteenth century.** Conway remarks that Paine "had no cyclopaedia in his knapsack" and hence placed Joan of Arc (1412-1431) in the wrong century   16 **Fort-Lee,** on the western shore of the Hudson, opposite Manhattan Island. It was hastily evacuated on November 20, the Americans even leaving their dinners cooking   30 **Major General Green,** Nathanael Greene (1742-1786). See Freneau's poem "To the Memory of the Brave Americans," p. 522

at a mill on a small creek, between the bridge and the ferry, and made their way through some marshy grounds up to the town of Hackensack, and there passed the river. We brought off as much baggage as the wagons could contain, the rest was lost. The simple object was to bring off the garrison, and march them on till they could be strengthened by the Jersey or Pennsylvania militia, so as to be enabled to make a stand. We staid four days at Newark, collected our out-posts with some of the Jersey militia, and marched out twice to meet the enemy, on being informed that they were advancing, though our numbers were greatly inferior to theirs. Howe, in my little opinion, committed a great error in generalship in not throwing a body
10 of forces off from Staten-Island through Amboy, by which means he might have seized all our stores at Brunswick, and intercepted our march into Pennsylvania; but if we believe the power of hell to be limited, we must likewise believe that their agents are under some providential control.

I shall not now attempt to give all the particulars of our retreat to the Delaware; suffice it for the present to say, that both officers and men, though greatly harassed and fatigued, frequently without rest, covering, or provision, the inevitable consequences of a long retreat, bore it with a manly and martial spirit. All their wishes centred in one, which was, that the country would turn out and help them to drive the enemy back. *Voltaire* has remarked that King William never appeared to full
20 advantage but in difficulties and in action; the same remark may be made on General Washington, for the character fits him. There is a natural firmness in some minds which cannot be unlocked by trifles, but which, when unlocked, discovers a cabinet of fortitude; and I reckon it among those kind of public blessings, which we do not immediately see, that GOD hath blessed him with uninterrupted health, and given him a mind that can even flourish upon care.

I shall conclude this paper with some miscellaneous remarks on the state of our affairs; and shall begin with asking the following question, Why is it that the enemy have left the New-England provinces, and made these middle ones the seat of war? The answer is easy: New England is not infested with tories, and we are. I have
30 been tender in raising the cry against these men, and used numberless arguments to show them their danger, but it will not do to sacrifice a world either to their folly or their baseness. The period is now arrived, in which either they or we must change our sentiments, or one or both must fall. And what is a tory? Good GOD! what is he? I should not be afraid to go with a hundred Whigs against a thousand tories, were they to attempt to get into arms. Every tory is a coward; for servile, slavish, self-interested fear is the foundation of Toryism; and a man under such influence, though he may be cruel, never can be brave.

But, before the line of irrecoverable separation be drawn between us, let us reason the matter together: Your conduct is an invitation to the enemy, yet not one in a
40 thousand of you has heart enough to join him. Howe is as much deceived by you as the American cause is injured by you. He expects you will all take up arms, and flock to his standard, with muskets on your shoulders. Your opinions are of no use

---

19 **Voltaire** (1694-1778) remarked that William III (1650-1702) was "jamais vif que dans un jour de combat," mettlesome only on a day of battle; see *Le Siècle de Louis XIV* (1751), Chap. 17

to him, unless you support him personally, for 'tis soldiers, and not tories, that he wants.

I once felt all that kind of anger, which a man ought to feel against the mean principles that are held by the tories: A noted one, who kept a tavern at Amboy, was standing at his door, with as pretty a child in his hand, about eight or nine years old, as I ever saw, and after speaking his mind as freely as he thought was prudent, finished with this unfatherly expression, *"Well! give me peace in my day."* Not a man lives on the continent but fully believes that a separation must some time or other finally take place, and a generous parent should have said, *"If there must be trouble, let it be in my day, that my child may have peace:"* and this single re- 10 flection, well applied, is sufficient to awaken every man to duty. Not a place upon earth might be so happy as America. Her situation is remote from all the wrangling world, and she has nothing to do but to trade with them. A man can distinguish himself between temper and principle, and I am as confident, as I am that GOD governs the world, that America will never be happy till she gets clear of foreign dominion. Wars, without ceasing, will break out till that period arrives, and the continent must in the end be conqueror; for though the flame of liberty may some- times cease to shine, the coal can never expire.

America did not, nor does not want force; but she wanted a proper application of that force. Wisdom is not the purchase of a day, and it is no wonder that we should 20 err at the first setting off. From an excess of tenderness, we were unwilling to raise an army, and trusted our cause to the temporary defence of a well-meaning militia. A summer's experience has now taught us better; yet with those troops, while they were collected, we were able to set bounds to the progress of the enemy, and, thank God! they are again assembling. I always considered militia as the best troops in the world for a sudden exertion, but they will not do for a long campaign. Howe, it is probable, will make an attempt on this city; should he fail on this side the Delaware, he is ruined. If he succeeds, our cause is not ruined. He stakes all on his side against a part on ours; admitting he succeeds, the consequences will be, that armies from both ends of the continent will march to assist their suffering friends 30 in the middle states; for he cannot go everywhere, it is impossible. I consider Howe as the greatest enemy the Tories have; he is bringing war into their country, which, had it not been for him and partly for themselves, they had been clear of. Should he now be expelled, I wish with all the devotion of a Christian, that the names of Whig and Tory may never more be mentioned; but should the Tories give him encouragement to come, or assistance if he come, I as sincerely wish that our next year's arms may expel them from the continent, and the Congress appropriate their possessions to the relief of those who have suffered in well-doing. A single success- ful battle next year will settle the whole. America could carry on a two years' war by the confiscation of the property of disaffected persons, and be made happy by 40 their expulsion. Say not that this is revenge, call it rather the soft resentment of a

---

27 **this city**, Philadelphia. Paine's prediction was borne out in September 1777, but Howe's capture of the city so weakened the British position in the north that the Americans were able to defeat Burgoyne

suffering people, who, having no object in view but the GOOD of ALL, have staked their OWN ALL upon a seemingly doubtful event. Yet it is folly to argue against determined hardness; eloquence may strike the ear, and the language of sorrow draw forth the tear of compassion, but nothing can reach the heart that is steeled with prejudice.

Quitting this class of men, I turn with the warm ardor of a friend to those who have nobly stood, and are yet determined to stand the matter out: I call not upon a few, but upon all: not in THIS state or THAT state, but on EVERY state: up and help us; lay your shoulders to the wheel; better have too much force than too little, when
10 so great an object is at stake. Let it be told to the future world, that in the depth of winter, when nothing but hope and virtue could survive, that the city and country, alarmed at one common danger, came forth to meet and to repulse it. Say not that thousands are gone, turn out your tens of thousands; throw not the burden of the day upon Providence, but *"shew your faith by your works,"* that God may bless you. It matters not where you live, or what rank of life you hold, the evil or the blessing will reach you all. The far and the near, the home counties and the back, the rich and the poor, will suffer or rejoice alike. The heart that feels not now is dead; the blood of his children will curse his cowardice, who shrinks back at a time when a little might have saved the whole, and made *them* happy. I love the man
20 that can smile in trouble, that can gather strength from distress, and grow brave by reflection. 'Tis the business of little minds to shrink; but he whose heart is firm, and whose conscience approves his conduct, will pursue his principles unto death. My own line of reasoning is to myself as straight and clear as a ray of light. Not all the treasures of the world, so far as I believe, could have induced me to support an offensive war, for I think it murder; but if a thief breaks into my house, burns and destroys my property, and kills or threatens to kill me, or those that are in it, and to *"bind me in all cases whatsoever"* to his absolute will, am I to suffer it? What signifies it to me, whether he who does it is a king or a common man; my countryman or not my countryman; whether it be done by an individual villain, or
30 an army of them? If we reason to the root of things we shall find no difference; neither can any just cause be assigned why we should punish in the one case and pardon in the other. Let them call me rebel and welcome, I feel no concern from it; but I should suffer the misery of devils, were I to make a whore of my soul by swearing allegiance to one whose character is that of a sottish, stupid, stubborn, worthless, brutish man. I conceive likewise a horrid idea in receiving mercy from a being, who at the last day shall be shrieking to the rocks and mountains to cover him, and fleeing with terror from the orphan, the widow, and the slain of America.

There are cases which cannot be overdone by language, and this is one. There are persons, too, who see not the full extent of the evil which threatens them; they
40 solace themselves with hopes that the enemy, if he succeed, will be merciful. It is the madness of folly, to expect mercy from those who have refused to do justice; and even mercy, where conquest is the object, is only a trick of war: The cunning

---

14 "shew . . . works." See James 2:18   16 the home . . . back, the seaboard and the frontier, already divergent in attitudes and economic interests

of the fox is as murderous as the violence of the wolf, and we ought to guard equally against both. Howe's first object is, partly by threats and partly by promises, to terrify or seduce the people to deliver up their arms and receive mercy. The ministry recommended the same plan to Gage, and this is what the tories call making their peace, *"a peace which passeth all understanding," indeed!* A peace which would be the immediate forerunner of a worse ruin than any we have yet thought of. Ye men of Pennsylvania, do reason upon these things! Were the back counties to give up their arms, they would fall an easy prey to the Indians, who are all armed: this perhaps is what some tories would not be sorry for. Were the home counties to deliver up their arms, they would be exposed to the resentment of the back counties, who would 10 then have it in their power to chastise their defection at pleasure. And were any one state to give up its arms, THAT state must be garrisoned by all Howe's army of Britons and Hessians to preserve it from the anger of the rest. Mutual fear is the principal link in the chain of mutual love, and woe be to that state that breaks the compact. Howe is mercifully inviting you to barbarous destruction, and men must be either rogues or fools that will not see it. I dwell not upon the vapors of imagination; I bring reason to your ears, and, in language as plain as A, B, C, hold up truth to your eyes.

I thank *God* that I fear not. I see no real cause for fear. I know our situation well, and can see the way out of it. While our army was collected, Howe dared not risk 20 a battle; and it is no credit to him that he decamped from the White Plains, and waited a mean opportunity to ravage the defenceless Jerseys; but it is great credit to us, that, with a handful of men, we sustained an orderly retreat for near an hundred miles, brought off our ammunition, all our field-pieces, the greatest part of our stores, and had four rivers to pass. None can say that our retreat was precipitate, for we were near three weeks in performing it, that the country might have time to come in. Twice we marched back to meet the enemy, and remained out till dark. The sign of fear was not seen in our camp, and had not some of the cowardly and disaffected inhabitants spread false alarms through the country, the Jersies had never been ravaged. Once more we are again collected and collecting, our new army at 30 both ends of the continent is recruiting fast, and we shall be able to open the next campaign with sixty thousand men, well armed and clothed. This is our situation, and who will may know it. By perseverance and fortitude we have the prospect of a glorious issue; by cowardice and submission, the sad choice of a variety of evils — a ravaged country — a depopulated city — habitations without safety, and slavery without hope — our homes turned into barracks and bawdy-houses for Hessians,

---

4 **Gage,** Thomas Gage (1721-1787), Howe's predecessor, had been commander in chief in North America from 1763 to 1775. He ordered the march on Concord and the attack on Bunker Hill   5 "a peace . . . **understanding."** See Philippians 4:7   13 **Hessians,** German mercenaries from six states (over half of them from Hesse-Cassel and Hesse-Hanau). About thirty thousand were brought to America by the British   21 **the White Plains,** in Westchester County, New York, where Howe had attacked American positions on October 28-29. On October 30, the Americans withdrew to Newcastle without opposition and were able to cross the Hudson to New Jersey, across which they slowly retreated, to take positions on the western bank of the Delaware   26 **the country,** the militia

and a future race to provide for, whose fathers we shall doubt of. Look on this picture and weep over it! and if there yet remains one thoughtless wretch who believes it not, let him suffer it unlamented.

COMMON SENSE

DECEMBER 23, 1776

1776

1743—1826 *Thomas Jefferson*

Thomas Jefferson, the third President of the United States, remains to this day the chief symbol for what has come to be called the "American way of life." Politicians quote him to lend authority to the most diverse points of view imaginable; to attack Jeffersonian principles would be well-nigh blasphemous. His words are the scriptures of our faith in democracy and the common man ("We hold these truths to be self-evident: that all men are created equal; that they are endowed by their creator with certain inalienable rights; that among these are life, liberty, and the pursuit of happiness"); of our abiding trust in popular education ("Religion, morality, and knowledge being necessary to good government and the happiness of mankind, schools and the means of education shall forever be encouraged"); of our deep-rooted individualism ("I have sworn upon the altar of God eternal hostility against every form of tyranny over the mind of man"). Nor is Jefferson's influence merely a matter of words; he has left his mark upon American political and educational institutions, even upon our public architecture, which reflects his enthusiasm for Greek and Roman models. Yet Jefferson is more than an oracle, more than a builder of the institutional foundations of American society. He himself would have deprecated the use of any man's words or actions to lend credit to any particular political or social program, for he had a sure grasp of the fact that every day is a new day, not merely to be endured but to be lived with as much intelligence and zest as an individual or nation can command. "The earth belongs always to the living generation. They may manage it then and what proceeds from it as they please during their usufruct. They are masters too of their own persons and consequently may govern them as they please."

It would take many pages to describe how Jefferson attained, through painful experience, such wisdom. The outline of his career tells only the outward story, not the inward, mental growth. He was born near Charlottesville, Virginia, in 1743, his father being a planter who had married into the famous Randolph family. At fourteen he inherited nearly three thousand acres of land and a considerable number of slaves. He studied hard at William and Mary during 1760-1762, but he was also a social leader, welcome at the dinner table of the colonial governor and other Williamsburg notables. He read law, was admitted to the bar in 1767, and succeeded in combining his profession with the management of large estates. On New Year's Day, 1772, he married Martha Wayles Skelton, an attractive widow with whom he was deeply in love. About a year later she inherited forty thousand acres of land and one hundred and thirty-five slaves. Not many revolutionists have come from such a background, and it would no doubt have been easy for Jefferson to spend his energies in plantation and family life, of which he was very fond, and to let the world go its own way. The record of his public service is, considering his tastes and his ability to satisfy them, one of the most remarkable in American history.

Member of the Virginia House of Burgesses, 1769-1774, member of the Virginia Conventions of 1774 and 1775, Virginia delegate to the Second Continental Congress, 1775-1776, member of the legislature of the new state of Virginia, 1776-1779, governor of Virginia, 1779-1781, member of Congress under the Articles of Confederation, 1783-1784, American minister to France, 1784-1789, secretary of state, 1790-1793, vice-president, 1797-1801, President of the United States, 1801-1809 — the list by itself is a thumbnail sketch of the birth and youth of a new nation. Jefferson was in the forefront of most of the great political developments of his age. His *Summary of the Rights of British America* (1774) was one of the notable assertions of the right of the colonists to self-government; he wrote, at thirty-three, the first draft of the *Declaration of Independence;* he led the attack on the state-supported church and the aristocracy-breeding institutions of primogeniture and entail in Virginia; he, more than any other single man, was responsible for the two-party system of government under the Constitution; as Chief Executive he engineered one of the great real-estate deals in history, the Louisiana Purchase; and throughout his life he was an earnest advocate of universal education for citizenship, of generous support of all the arts and sciences, of the emancipation of slaves, and of as large a measure of local self-government as was compatible with the common good of the whole nation.

One of the many paradoxes in his life is that he should be remembered for the studied sentences of his public papers, for he was inclined to distrust rhetoric and oratory. Behind the words of his great state papers, however, are both the maturing of a great people and a deep faith in the integrity of the common man. Jefferson's dream was of a world wherein reason and justice should prevail over brute force and selfishness. To know his writings is to fortify oneself against any shallow interpretation of the much-abused term "Americanism."

The Works of Thomas Jefferson, ed. P. L. Ford, Federal Edition, 12 vols., New York, 1892-1894   The Papers of Thomas Jefferson, ed. J. P. Boyd and others, I-XVI, Princeton, 1950-1961 (36 additional volumes are awaited)   Gilbert Chinard, Thomas Jefferson, the Apostle of Americanism, Boston, 1929   S. K. Padover, Jefferson, New York, 1942   Carl Becker, The Declaration of Independence, New York, 1922   M. D. Peterson, The Jefferson Image in the American Mind, New York, 1960   Dumas Malone, Jefferson and His Time, I-III, Boston, 1948-1962, a further volume expected

from *Autobiography*

Between January 6 and July 29, 1821, Jefferson spent some time composing the paper known as the "Autobiography," an account of his life up to 1790, when he arrived in New York to begin his work as secretary of state under President Washington. It was first printed in Memoirs, Correspondence, and Miscellanies *(1829), edited by his grandson, T. J. Randolph. The portion here reprinted was written many years before, however, perhaps as early as August 1776. It is the most authoritative account of the composition and adoption of the* Declaration of Independence, *which Jefferson rightly regarded as the contribution for which he was most likely to be remembered by later generations. Neither he nor his contemporaries regarded the* Declaration *as an original composition; it expressed the philosophy of natural rights which had been everywhere accepted in the colonies, and largely in Great Britain, since the Glorious Revolution of 1688. Jefferson denied, however, that he had turned to any book or pamphlet while writing it, and the similarities to John Locke's* Two Treatises on Government *(1689-1690) and James Otis'* The Rights of the British Colonies Asserted and Proved *(1764) were doubtless coincidental. The tone of its appeal to the high court of world opinion and the ingenious concentration of responsibility upon King George III — always a useful device in propaganda — make it an unexcelled model of skillful rhetoric.*

In Congress, Friday June 7. 1776. The delegates from Virginia moved in obedience to instructions from their constituents that the Congress should declare that these United colonies are & of right ought to be free & independent states, that they are absolved from all allegiance to the British crown, and that all political connection between them & the state of Great Britain is & ought to be, totally dissolved; that measures should be immediately taken for procuring the assistance of foreign powers, and a Confederation be formed to bind the colonies more closely together.

The house being obliged to attend at that time to some other business, the proposition was referred to the next day, when the members were ordered to attend punctually at ten o'clock.

Saturday June 8. They proceeded to take it into consideration and referred it to a committee of the whole, into which they immediately resolved themselves, and passed that day & Monday the 10th in debating on the subject.

It was argued by Wilson, Robert R. Livingston, E. Rutledge, Dickinson and others

---

Text: Ford's edition of the Works, Vol. I   1 **Congress,** the Second Continental Congress, which convened in Philadelphia, May 10, 1775, to direct the contest which had already become, with the Battle of Lexington, open war   1 **moved,** by Richard Henry Lee (1732-1794), later one of the first two United States senators from Virginia. The motion was seconded by John Adams of Massachusetts (1735-1826), later second President, commissioner to France during the War and vice president under Washington   14 **Wilson,** James Wilson (1742-1798) of Pennsylvania, later associate justice of the Supreme Court   14 **Robert R. Livingston** (1746-1813) of New York, minister to France (1801-1804) at the time of the Louisiana Purchase   14 **E. Rutledge,** Edward Rutledge (1749-1800) of South Carolina, later a U.S. senator   14 **Dickinson,** John Dickinson (1732-1808) of Pennsylvania, author of the popular *Letters from a Farmer in Pennsylvania* (1768)

That tho' they were friends to the measures themselves, and saw the impossibility that we should ever again be united with Gr. Britain, yet they were against adopting them at this time:

That the conduct we had formerly observed was wise & proper now, of deferring to take any capital step till the voice of the people drove us into it:

That they were our power, & without them our declarations could not be carried into effect;

That the people of the middle colonies (Maryland, Delaware, Pennsylva, the Jerseys & N. York) were not yet ripe for bidding adieu to British connection, but that they were fast ripening & in a short time would join in the general voice of America: 10

That the resolution entered into by this house on the 15th of May for suppressing the exercise of all powers derived from the crown, had shown, by the ferment into which it had thrown these middle colonies, that they had not yet accomodated their minds to a separation from the mother country:

That some of them had expressly forbidden their delegates to consent to such a declaration, and others had given no instructions, & consequently no powers to give such consent:

That if the delegates of any particular colony had no power to declare such colony independant, certain they were the others could not declare it for them; the colonies being as yet perfectly independant of each other: 20

That the assembly of Pennsylvania was now sitting above stairs, their convention would sit within a few days, the convention of New York was now sitting, & those of the Jerseys & Delaware counties would meet on the Monday following, & it was probable these bodies would take up the question of Independance & would declare to their delegates the voice of their state:

That if such a declaration should now be agreed to, these delegates must retire & possibly their colonies might secede from the Union:

That such a secession would weaken us more than could be compensated by any foreign alliance:

That in the event of such a division, foreign powers would either refuse to join 30 themselves to our fortunes, or, having us so much in their power as that desperate declaration would place us, they would insist on terms proportionably more hard and prejudicial:

That we had little reason to expect an alliance with those to whom alone as yet we had cast our eyes:

That France & Spain had reason to be jealous of that rising power which would one day certainly strip them of all their American possessions:

That it was more likely they should form a connection with the British court, who, if they should find themselves unable otherwise to extricate themselves from their difficulties, would agree to a partition of our territories, restoring Canada to 40 France, & the Floridas to Spain, to accomplish for themselves a recovery of these colonies:

That it would not be long before we should receive certain information of the

11 **resolution,** declaring "that every kind of authority under the said crown should be totally suppressed"

disposition of the French court, from the agent whom we had sent to Paris for that purpose:

That if this disposition should be favorable, by waiting the event of the present campaign, which we all hoped would be successful, we should have reason to expect an alliance on better terms:

That this would in fact work no delay of any effectual aid from such ally, as, from the advance of the season & distance of our situation, it was impossible we could receive any assistance during this campaign:

That it was prudent to fix among ourselves the terms on which we should form alliance, before we declared we would form one at all events:

And that if these were agreed on, & our Declaration of Independance ready by the time our Ambassador should be prepared to sail, it would be as well to go into that Declaration at this day.

On the other side it was urged by J. Adams, Lee, Wythe, and others

That no gentleman had argued against the policy or the right of separation from Britain, nor had supposed it possible we should ever renew our connection; that they had only opposed its being now declared:

That the question was not whether, by a declaration of independance, we should make ourselves what we are not; but whether we should declare a fact which already exists:

That as to the people or parliament of England, we had alwais been independent of them, their restraints on our trade deriving efficacy from our acquiescence only, & not from any rights they possessed of imposing them, & that so far our connection had been federal only & was now dissolved by the commencement of hostilities:

That as to the King, we had been bound to him by allegiance, but that this bond was now dissolved by his assent to the late act of parliament, by which he declares us out of his protection, and by his levying war on us, a fact which had long ago proved us out of his protection; it being a certain position in law that allegiance & protection are reciprocal, the one ceasing when the other is withdrawn:

That James the IId. never declared the people of England out of his protection yet his actions proved it & the parliament declared it:

No delegates then can be denied, or ever want, a power of declaring an existing truth:

That the delegates from the Delaware counties having declared their constituents ready to join, there are only two colonies Pennsylvania & Maryland whose delegates are absolutely tied up, and that these had by their instructions only reserved a right of confirming or rejecting the measure:

That the instructions from Pennsylvania might be accounted for from the times in which they were drawn, near a twelvemonth ago since which the face of affairs has totally changed:

---

1 **the agent,** Silas Deane (1737-1789), who went to Paris under instructions dated March 1776   3 **present campaign,** to defend New York and the Hudson River. At the time of these deliberations Washington was busy constructing fortifications commanding New York Harbor   14 **Wythe,** George Wythe (1726-1806) of Virginia, in whose office Jefferson had studied law; among his other famous pupils were Chief Justice John Marshall, President James Monroe, and Henry Clay

That within that time it had become apparent that Britain was determined to accept nothing less than a carte-blanche, and that the King's answer to the Lord Mayor Aldermen & common council of London, which had come to hand four days ago, must have satisfied every one of this point:

That the people wait for us to lead the way:

That *they* are in favour of the measure, tho' the instructions given by some of their *representatives* are not:

That the voice of the representatives is not always consonant with the voice of the people, and that this is remarkably the case in these middle colonies:

That the effect of the resolution of the 15th of May has proved this, which, rais- ▶ ing the murmurs of some in the colonies of Pennsylvania & Maryland, called forth the opposing voice of the freer part of the people, & proved them to be the majority, even in these colonies:

That the backwardness of these two colonies might be ascribed partly to the influence of proprietary power & connections, & partly to their having not yet been attacked by the enemy:

That these causes were not likely to be soon removed, as there seemed no probability that the enemy would make either of these the seat of this summer's war:

That it would be vain to wait either weeks or months for perfect unanimity, since it was impossible that all men should ever become of one sentiment on any question: 2

That the conduct of some colonies from the beginning of this contest, had given reason to suspect it was their settled policy to keep in the rear of the confederacy, that their particular prospect might be better, even in the worst event:

That therefore it was necessary for those colonies who had thrown themselves forward & hazarded all from the beginning, to come forward now also, and put all again to their own hazard:

That the history of the Dutch revolution, of whom three states only confederated at first proved that a secession of some colonies would not be so dangerous as some apprehended:

That a declaration of Independence alone could render it consistent with European 3 delicacy for European powers to treat with us, or even to receive an Ambassador from us:

That till this they would not receive our vessels into their ports, nor acknowledge the adjudications of our courts of admiralty to be legitimate, in cases of capture of British vessels:

That though France & Spain may be jealous of our rising power, they must think it will be much more formidable with the addition of Great Britain; and will therefore see it their interest to prevent a coalition; but should they refuse, we shall be but where we are; whereas without trying we shall never know whether they will aid us or not:

That the present campaign may be unsuccessful, & therefore we had better propose an alliance while our affairs wear a hopeful aspect:

2 **King's answer,** one of George III's rejections of petitions addressed to him on behalf of the colonies   27
Dutch revolution, of 1576. The United Netherlands Confederation was formed three years later

That to await the event of this campaign will certainly work delay, because during this summer France may assist us effectually by cutting off those supplies of provisions from England & Ireland on which the enemy's armies here are to depend; or by setting in motion the great power they have collected in the West Indies, & calling our enemy to the defence of the possessions they have there:

That it would be idle to lose time in settling the terms of alliance, till we had first determined we would enter into alliance:

That it is necessary to lose no time in opening a trade for our people, who will want clothes, and will want money too for the paiment of taxes:

And that the only misfortune is that we did not enter into alliance with France six months sooner, as besides opening their ports for the vent of our last year's produce, they might have marched an army into Germany and prevented the petty princes there from selling their unhappy subjects to subdue us.

It appearing in the course of these debates that the colonies of N. York, New Jersey, Pennsylvania, Delaware, Maryland, and South Carolina were not yet matured for falling from the parent stem, but that they were fast advancing to that state, it was thought most prudent to wait a while for them, and to postpone the final decision to July 1. but that this might occasion as little delay as possible a committee was appointed to prepare a declaration of independence. The commee were J. Adams, Dr. Franklin, Roger Sherman, Robert R. Livingston & myself. Committees were also appointed at the same time to prepare a plan of confederation for the colonies, and to state the terms proper to be proposed for foreign alliance. The committee for drawing the declaration of Independence desired me to do it. It was accordingly done, and being approved by them, I reported it to the house on Friday the 28th of June when it was read and ordered to lie on the table. On Monday, the 1st of July the House resolved itself into a commee of the whole & resumed the consideration of the original motion made by the delegates of Virginia, which being again debated through the day, was carried in the affirmative by the votes of N. Hampshire, Connecticut, Massachusetts, Rhode Island, N. Jersey, Maryland, Virginia, N. Carolina, & Georgia. S. Carolina and Pennsylvania voted against it. Delaware having but two members present, they were divided. The delegates for New York declared they were for it themselves & were assured their constituents were for it, but that their instructions having been drawn near a twelvemonth before, when reconciliation was still the general object, they were enjoined by them to do nothing which should impede that object. They therefore thought themselves not justifiable in voting on either side, and asked leave to withdraw from the question, which was given them. The commee rose & reported their resolution to the house. Mr. Edward Rutledge of S. Carolina then requested the determination might be put off to

---

11 **six months sooner.** The tone here suggests what is generally thought to be the fact: that the colonists had received some assurances of secret assistance from France as early as the autumn of 1775   12 **petty princes.** The British ministry sent agents to employ mercenary troops from the German princes late in 1775, with the obvious intention of settling the American revolt in 1776   20 **Roger Sherman** (1721-1793) of Connecticut, later U. S. senator   20 **myself.** Although he was only thirty-three, Jefferson received more votes for appointment on this committee than any other member, probably because of his reputation as a writer

the next day, as he believed his colleagues, tho' they disapproved of the resolution, would then join in it for the sake of unanimity. The ultimate question whether the house would agree to the resolution of the committee was accordingly postponed to the next day, when it was again moved and S. Carolina concurred in voting for it. In the meantime a third member had come post from the Delaware counties and turned the vote of that colony in favour of the resolution. Members of a different sentiment attending that morning from Pennsylvania also, her vote was changed, so that the whole 12 colonies who were authorized to vote at all, gave their voices for it; and within a few days, the convention of N. York approved of it and thus supplied the void occasioned by the withdrawing of her delegates from the vote.   1(

Congress proceeded the same day to consider the declaration of Independance which had been reported & lain on the table the Friday preceding, and on Monday referred to a commee of the whole. The pusillanimous idea that we had friends in England worth keeping terms with, still haunted the minds of many. For this reason those passages which conveyed censures on the people of England were struck out, lest they should give them offence. The clause too, reprobating the enslaving the inhabitants of Africa, was struck out in complaisance to South Carolina and Georgia, who had never attempted to restrain the importation of slaves, and who on the contrary still wished to continue it. Our northern brethren also I believe felt a little tender under those censures; for tho' their people had very few slaves them- 2(
selves yet they had been pretty considerable carriers of them to others. The debates having taken up the greater parts of the 2d 3d & 4th days of July were, on the evening of the last, closed the declaration was reported by the commee, agreed to by the house and signed by every member present except Mr. Dickinson. As the sentiments of men are known not only by what they receive, but what they reject also, I will state the form of the declaration as originally reported. The parts struck out by Congress shall be distinguished by a black line drawn under them; and those inserted by them shall be placed in the margin or in a concurrent column.

A Declaration by the Representatives of the United States
of America, in General Congress Assembled

When in the course of human events it becomes necessary for
one people to dissolve the political bands which have con- 3(
nected them with another, and to assume among the powers
of the earth the separate & equal station to which the laws of
nature and of nature's God entitle them, a decent respect to
the opinions of mankind requires that they should declare the
causes which impel them to the separation.

We hold these truths to be self-evident: that all men are

9 **few days,** July 9   11 **same day,** Tuesday, July 2   24 **signed . . . Dickinson.** Historians are agreed that Jefferson's memory was at fault on this point and that the Declaration was only "authenticated" by the signature of the president and the secretary on July 4. The formal signing took place on August 2   27 **a black line.** In the present text the excisions are italicized and enclosed within brackets

created equal; that they are endowed by their creator with
[*inherent and*] inalienable rights; that among these are life,   certain
liberty, & the pursuit of happiness: that to secure these rights,
governments are instituted among men, deriving their just
powers from the consent of the governed; that whenever any
form of government becomes destructive of these ends, it is
the right of the people to alter or to abolish it, & to institute
new government, laying it's foundation on such principles, &
organizing it's powers in such form, as to them shall seem
10 most likely to effect their safety & happiness. Prudence indeed
will dictate that governments long established should not be
changed for light & transient causes; and accordingly all experience hath shewn that mankind are more disposed to suffer
while evils are sufferable, than to right themselves by abolishing the forms to which they are accustomed. But when a long
train of abuses & usurpations [*begun at a distinguished period
and*] pursuing invariably the same object, evinces a design to
reduce them under absolute despotism, it is their right, it is
their duty to throw off such government, & to provide new
20 guards for their future security. Such has been the patient
sufferance of these colonies; & such is now the necessity which
constrains them to [*expunge*] their former systems of govern-   alter
ment. The history of the present king of Great Britain is a
history of [*unremitting*] injuries & usurpations, [*among which*   repeated/all having
appears no solitary fact to contradict the uniform tenor of the rest
but all have*] in direct object the establishment of an absolute
tyranny over these states. To prove this let facts be submitted
to a candid world [*for the truth of which we pledge a faith yet
unsullied by falsehood*].
30   He has refused his assent to laws the most wholesome &
necessary for the public good.
     He has forbidden his governors to pass laws of immediate
& pressing importance, unless suspended in their operation
till his assent should be obtained; & when so suspended, he
has utterly neglected to attend to them.
     He has refused to pass other laws for the accommodation
of large districts of people, unless those people would relinquish the right of representation in the legislature, a right inestimable to them, & formidable to tyrants only.
40   He has called together legislative bodies at places unusual,
uncomfortable, and distant from the depository of their public
records, for the sole purpose of fatiguing them into compliance with his measures.
     He has dissolved representative houses repeatedly [*& con-*

tinually] for opposing with manly firmness his invasions on the rights of the people.

He has refused for a long time after such dissolutions to cause others to be elected, whereby the legislative powers, incapable of annihilation, have returned to the people at large for their exercise, the state remaining in the meantime exposed to all the dangers of invasion from without & convulsions within.

He has endeavored to prevent the population of these states; for that purpose obstructing the laws for naturalization of 10 foreigners, refusing to pass others to encourage their migrations hither, & raising the conditions of new appropriations of lands.

obstructed   He has [*suffered*] the administration of justice [*totally to*
by   *cease in some of these states*] refusing his assent to laws for establishing judiciary powers.

He has made [*our*] judges dependant on his will alone, for the tenure of their offices, & the amount and paiment of their salaries.

He has erected a multitude of new offices [*by a self-assumed* 20 *power*] and sent hither swarms of new officers to harass our people and eat out their substance.

He has kept among us in times of peace standing armies [*and ships of war*] without the consent of our legislatures.

He has affected to render the military independant of, & superior to the civil power.

He has combined with others to subject us to a jurisdiction foreign to our constitutions & unacknowledged by our laws, giving his assent to their acts of pretended legislation for quartering large bodies of armed troops among us; for pro- 30 tecting them by a mock-trial from punishment for any murders which they should commit on the inhabitants of these states; for cutting off our trade with all parts of the world; for im-
in many cases   posing taxes on us without our consent; for depriving us [ ] of the benefits of trial by jury; for transporting us beyond seas to be tried for pretended offences; for abolishing the free system of English laws in a neighboring province, establishing therein an arbitrary government, and enlarging it's boundaries, so as to render it at once an example and fit instrument for
colonies   introducing the same absolute rule into these [*states*]; for tak- 40 ing away our charters, abolishing our most valuable laws, and altering fundamentally the forms of our governments; for suspending our own legislatures, & declaring themselves invested with power to legislate for us in all cases whatsoever.

He has abdicated government here [*withdrawing his governors, and declaring us out of his allegiance & protection*]. *by declaring us out of his protection, and waging war against us.*

He has plundered our seas, ravaged our coasts, burnt our towns, & destroyed the lives of our people.

He is at this time transporting large armies of foreign mercenaries to compleat the works of death, desolation & tyranny already begun with circumstances of cruelty and perfidy [ ] unworthy the head of a civilized nation. *scarcely paralleled in the most barbarous ages, & totally*

He has constrained our fellow citizens taken captive on the high seas to bear arms against their country, to become the executioners of their friends & brethren, or to fall themselves by their hands.

He has [ ] endeavored to bring on the inhabitants of our frontiers the merciless Indian savages, whose known rule of warfare is an undistinguished destruction of all ages, sexes, & condition [*of existence*]. *excited domestic insurrections among us, & has*

[*He has incited treasonable insurrections of our fellow-citizens, with the allurements of forfeiture & confiscation of our property.*

He has waged cruel war against human nature itself, violating it's most sacred rights of life and liberty in the persons of a distant people who never offended him, captivating & carrying them into slavery in another hemisphere, or to incur miserable death in their transportation thither. This piratical warfare, the opprobrium of INFIDEL *powers, is the warfare of the* CHRISTIAN *king of Great Britain. Determined to keep open a market where* MEN *should be bought & sold, he has prostituted his negative for suppressing every legislative attempt to prohibit or to restrain this execrable commerce. And that this assemblage of horrors might want no fact of distinguished die, he is now exciting those very people to rise in arms among us, and to purchase that liberty of which he has deprived them, by murdering the people on whom he also obtruded them: thus paying off former crimes committed against the* LIBERTIES *of one people, with crimes which he urges them to commit against the* LIVES *of another.*]

In every stage of these oppressions we have petitioned for redress in the most humble terms: our repeated petitions have been answered only by repeated injuries.

A prince whose character is thus marked by every act which may define a tyrant is unfit to be the ruler of a [ ] people *free* [*who mean to be free. Future ages will scarcely believe that the hardiness of one man adventured, within the short compass of twelve years only, to lay a foundation so broad & so undisguised for tyranny over a people fostered & fixed in principles of freedom*].

Nor have we been wanting in attentions to our British

brethren. We have warned them from time to time of at-
an unwarrantable tempts by their legislature to extend [*a*] jurisdiction over
us [*these our states*]. We have reminded them of the circumstances
of our emigration & settlement here, [*no one of which could
warrant so strange a pretension: that these were effected at the expense of our own blood & treasure, unassisted by the wealth or the
strength of Great Britain: that in constituting indeed our several
forms of government, we had adopted one common king, thereby laying a foundation for perpetual league & amity with them: but that
submission to their parliament was no part of our constitution, nor* 10
have *ever in idea, if history may be credited: and,*] we [   ] appealed
and we have to their native justice and magnanimity [*as well as to*] the ties
conjured them by of our common kindred to disavow these usurpations which
would inevitably [*were likely to*] interrupt our connection and correspondence.
They too have been deaf to the voice of justice & of consanguinity, [*and when occasions have been given them, by the regular
course of their laws, of removing from their councils the disturbers
of our harmony, they have, by their free election, re-established them
in power. At this very time too they are permitting their chief magistrate to send over not only soldiers of our common blood, but Scotch* 20
*& foreign mercenaries to invade & destroy us. These facts have
given the last stab to agonizing affection, and manly spirit bids us
to renounce forever these unfeeling brethren. We must endeavor to
forget our former love for them, and hold them as we hold the rest
of mankind, enemies in war, in peace friends. We might have been
a free and a great people together; but a communication of grandeur
& of freedom it seems is below their dignity. Be it so, since they will*
We must therefore *have it. The road to happiness & to glory is open to us too. We will
tread it apart from them, and*] acquiesce in the necessity which
and hold them as we denounces our [*eternal*] separation [   ]!   30
hold the rest of man-
kind, enemies in war,
in peace friends.

We therefore the representatives of   We therefore the representatives of the
the United States of America in General   United States of America in General
Congress assembled do in the name &   Congress assembled, appealing to the su-
by the authority of the good people of   preme judge of the world for the recti-
these [*states reject & renounce all allegiance*   tude of our intentions, do in the name, &
& subjection to the kings of Great Britain   by the authority of the good people of
& all others who may hereafter claim by,   these colonies, solemnly publish & de-
through or under them: we utterly dissolve   clare that these united colonies are & of
all political connection which may heretofore right ought to be free & independent
have subsisted between us & the people or   states; that they are absolved from all 40

31 **We therefore.** The version in the right-hand column is that adopted

parliament of Great Britain: & finally we do assert & declare these colonies to be free & independent states,] & that as free & independent states, they have full power to levy war, conclude peace, contract alliances, establish commerce, & to do all other acts & things which independent states may of right do.

And for the support of this declaration
10 we mutually pledge to each other our lives, our fortunes, & our sacred honour.

allegiance to the British crown, and that all political connection between them & the state of Great Britain is, & ought to be, totally dissolved; & that as free and independent states they have full power to levy war, conclude peace, contract alliances, establish commerce & to do all other acts & things which independant states may of right do.

And for the support of this declaration, with a firm reliance on the protection of divine providence we mutually pledge to each other our lives, our fortunes, & our sacred honor.

The Declaration thus signed on the 4th, on paper was engrossed on parchment, & signed again on the 2d. of August. . . .

1776?, 1829

13 **The Declaration.** This last sentence was added by Jefferson later, when he knew that his account of the signing had been called into question

First Inaugural Address

Jefferson's program as President was set forth simply and directly in his First Inaugural Address, *delivered in the Senate chamber on March 4, 1801. His eloquent plea for harmony and unity did not save him from the criticism of the Federalists, but even they could hardly question his list of the essential principles of democratic government. The brevity and pointedness of Jefferson's phrases make his* First Inaugural *one of the most memorable statements of the American concept of a free, self-governing people. It was immediately printed everywhere in the nation, both in the newspapers and separately.*

Friends & Fellow Citizens

Called upon to undertake the duties of the first Executive office of our country, I avail myself of the presence of that portion of my fellow citizens which is here assembled to express my grateful thanks for the favor with which they have been pleased to look towards me, to declare a sincere consciousness that the task is above my talents, & that I approach it with those anxious & awful presentiments, which the greatness of the charge, & the weakness of my powers so justly inspire.

A rising nation spread over a wide & fruitful land, traversing all the seas with the rich productions of their industry, engaged in commerce with nations who feel

Text: that established by P. L. Ford from the first draft, *Works,* Vol. IX. For the sake of ease in reading, however, most of the many abbreviations have here been spelled out and a few marks of punctuation added in brackets

power and forget right, advancing rapidly to destinies beyond the reach of mortal eye; when I contemplate these transcendent objects, & see the honor, the happiness, & the hopes of this beloved country committed to the issue & the auspices of this day, I shrink from the contemplation, & humble myself before the magnitude of the undertaking.

Utterly indeed should I despair, did not the presence of many whom I here see, remind me, that in the other high authorities provided by our constitution, I shall find resources of wisdom, of virtue & of zeal, on which to rely under all difficulties.

To you then, gentlemen who are charged with the sovereign functions of legisla- tion & to those associated with you, I look with encouragement for that guidance 10 & support which may enable us to steer with safety, the vessel in which we are all embarked amidst the conflicting elements of a troubled sea.

During the contest of opinion through which we have passed, the animation of discussions and of exertions, has sometimes worn an aspect which might impose on strangers unused to think freely, & to speak & to write what they think.

But this being now decided by the voice of the nation, enounced according to the rules of the constitution, all will of course arrange themselves under the will of the law, & unite in common efforts for the common good. All too will bear in mind this sacred principle that though the will of the Majority is in all cases to prevail, that will, to be rightful, must be reasonable: that the Minority possess their equal 20 rights, which equal laws must protect, & to violate would be oppression.

Let us then, fellow citizens, unite with one heart & one mind; let us restore to social intercourse that harmony & affection, without which Liberty, & even Life itself, are but dreary things.

And let us reflect that having banished from our land that religious intolerance under which mankind so long bled & suffered we have yet gained little, if we countenance a political intolerance, as despotic[,] as wicked [,] & capable of as bit- ter & bloody persecution.

During the throes and convulsions of the antient world, during the agonised spasms of infuriated man, seeking through blood & slaughter his long lost liberty, 30 it was not wonderful that the agitation of the billows should reach even this dis- tant & peaceful shore that this should be more felt & feared by some, & less by others, & should divide opinions as to measures of safety.

But every difference of opinion, is not a difference of principle. We have called, by different names, brethren of the same principle. We are all republicans: we are all federalists.

If there be any among us who wish to dissolve this union, or to change its re- publican form, let them stand undisturbed, as monuments of the safety with which error of opinion may be tolerated where reason is left free to combat it.

I know indeed that some honest men have feared that a republican government 40 cannot be strong; that this government is not strong enough. But would the honest patriot, in the full tide of successful experiment abandon a government which has

---

29 **throes and convulsions.** The Federalist editors, anxious to find fault, made much capital of the mixed metaphor in this sentence — the "agonised spasms" which change so abruptly to "billows"

so far kept us free & firm on the theoretic & visionary fear that this government, the world's best hope may, by possibility, want energy to preserve itself?

I trust not. I believe this, on the contrary, the strongest government on earth.

I believe it the only one where every man, at the call of the law, would fly to the standard of the law; would meet invasions of public order, as his own personal concern.

Some times it is said that Man cannot be trusted with the government of himself. — Can he then be trusted with the government of others? Or have we found angels in the form of kings to govern him? — Let History answer this question.

Let us then pursue with courage & confidence our own federal & republican
10 principles[,] our attachment to Union and Representative government.

Kindly separated by nature, & a wide ocean, from the exterminating havoc of one quarter of the globe,

Too high-minded to endure the degradations of the others;

Possessing a chosen country, with room enough for our descendants to the thousandth & thousandth generation;

Entertaining a due sense of our equal right, to the use of our own faculties, to the acquisitions of our own industry, to honor & confidence from our fellow citizens resulting not from birth, but from our actions & their sense of them, enlightened by a benign religion, professed indeed & practiced in various forms, yet all of
20 them inculcating honesty, truth, temperance[,] gratitude, & the love of man, acknowledging & adoring an overruling providence, which by all it's dispensations proves that it delights in the happiness of man here, & his greater happiness hereafter:

With all these blessings, what more is necessary to make us a happy and a prosperous people? Still one thing more, fellow citizens[,] a wise & frugal government, which shall restrain men from injuring one another, shall leave them otherwise free to regulate their own pursuits of industry & improvement, and shall not take from the mouth of labor the bread it has earned.

This is the sum of good government, & this is necessary to close the circle of our felicities.

30 About to enter[,] fellow citizens[,] on the exercise of duties, which comprehend everything dear & valuable to you, it is proper you should understand what I deem the essential principle of this government and consequently those which ought to shape it's administration.

I will compress them in the narrowest compass they will bear, stating the general principle, but not all it's limitations.

Equal & exact justice to all men, of whatever state or persuasion, religious or political:

Peace, commerce, & honest friendship with all nations, entangling alliances with none:

40 The support of the State governments in all their rights, as the most competent administrations for our domestic concerns, and the surest bulwarks against antirepublican tendencies:

The preservation of the General government, in it's whole constitutional vigor, as the sheet anchor of our peace at home, and safety abroad.

A jealous care of the right of election by the people, a mild & safe corrective of abuses, which are lopped by the sword of revolution, where peacable remedies are unprovided.

Absolute acquiescence in the decisions of the Majority[,] the vital principle of republics, from which is no appeal but to force, the vital principle & immediate parent of despotism.

A well disciplined militia, our best reliance in peace, & for the first moments of war, till regulars may relieve them: The Supremacy of the Civil over the Military authority:

Economy in public expense, that labor may be lightly burthened: 10

The honest paiment of our debts and sacred preservation of the public faith:

Encouragement of Agriculture, & of Commerce, as it's handmaid:

The diffusion of information, & arraignment of all abuses at the bar of the public reason:

Freedom of Religion, freedom of the press, & freedom of Person under the protection of the Habeas corpus: And trial by juries, impartially selected.

These Principles form the bright constellation which has gone before us, & guided our steps, thro' an age of Revolution and Reformation: The wisdom of our Sages, & blood of our Heroes, have been devoted to their attainment: they should be the Creed of our political faith, the Text of civic instruction, the Touchstone by   20 which to try the services of those we trust; and should we wander from them, in moments of error or alarm, let us hasten to retrace our steps and to regain the road which alone leads to Peace, Liberty & Safety.

I repair then, fellow citizens[,] to the post which you have assigned me.

With experience enough in subordinate stations to know the difficulties of this the greatest of all, I have learnt to expect that it will rarely fall to the lot of imperfect man to retire from this station with the reputation & the favor which bring him into it.

Without pretensions to that high confidence you reposed in our first & greatest revolutionary character whose preeminent services had entitled him to the first place 30 in his country's love, and had destined for him the fairest page in the volume of faithful history, I ask so much confidence only as may give firmness & effect to the legal administration of your affairs.

I shall often go wrong thro' defect of judgment: when right, I shall often be thought wrong by those whose positions will not command a view of the whole ground.

I ask your indulgence for my own errors, which will never be intentional: & your support against the errors of others who may condemn what they would not if seen in all it's parts.

The approbation implied by your suffrage, is a great consolation to me for the 40 past; and my future solicitude will be to retain the good opinion of those who have bestowed it in advance, to conciliate that of others, by doing them all the good in my power, and to be instrumental to the happiness & freedom of all.

---

29 **first** . . . **character,** Washington

Relying then on the patronage of your good will, I advance with obedience to the work, ready to retire from it whenever you become sensible how much better choice it is in your power to make.

And may that infinite power which rules the destinies of the universe lead our councils to what is best, and give them a favorable issue for your peace & prosperity.

1801

1757—1804 *Alexander Hamilton*

Much of the stability of the government of the United States, as we know it even today, must be attributed to the labors of Alexander Hamilton. Soldier, statesman, lawyer, and practical politician, he was only incidentally a writer. Yet, assisted by James Madison and John Jay, he planned and executed *The Federalist,* which Jefferson called, in a letter to Madison, "the best commentary on the principles of government that ever was written." The broader, more speculative papers in the series, notably No. X, were often Madison's, but Hamilton's shrewd realism helped to give the work the high place which it holds in the political literature of Western civilization.

Hamilton was born in the West Indies in 1757. At an early age he displayed an amazing talent for business, so that interested elders sent him to New York to finish his education. In 1774, when he was an undergraduate at King's College (now Columbia University), he joined the Whig opposition to the British and soon distinguished himself as a speaker and pamphleteer. The first indications of his mastery of constitutional history and the intricacies of political action appeared in *A Full Vindication of the Measures of the Congress from the Calumnies of Their Enemies* (1774) and *The Farmer Refuted* (1775), pamphlets written to refute the arguments of the American Tory writer Samuel Seabury and published anonymously. In March 1776 he joined the Continental Army with the rank of captain of an artillery company; in a year he was a lieutenant colonel and Washington's aide-de-camp. Despite a temporary break with his commander in chief (Hamilton is supposed to have been offended at what he regarded as an unjust reprimand from Washington), he served brilliantly to the end of the war and thereafter was a nationally known lawyer and public servant. His most important contributions to government were his draft of the call for the Constitutional Convention, his success in obtaining the ratification of the new form of government by New York, his term as first secretary of the treasury in 1789-1795 (usually regarded as having laid the foundations of the fiscal policy, and the chief party issues, of the United States), and his influence as Washington's most trusted adviser. Hamilton's opposition to Aaron Burr, first in the Presidential election of 1800, which was decided in favor of Jefferson in the House of Representatives, and later in the contest of 1804 for the governorship of New York, resulted in the famous duel in which Hamilton was killed.

The inevitable contrast between Hamilton and Jefferson has frequently obscured the former's greatness. The self-made man, relatively narrow in his interests and distrustful of the masses — "The people," he once remarked, "is a great beast!" — has suffered by the comparison with a versatile philosopher who, gracefully minimizing his own wealth and family connections, believed that all men are created equal. Men like Washington, however, quite evidently trusted Hamilton more than they did Jefferson; he had a solid quality, a realism which was wholly honest and direct. A comparison of No. I of *The Federalist* with Jefferson's *First Inaugural Address* brings the men closer together than might be expected, although it also reveals their mutual suspicions. Hamilton wanted a strong government, safe from attack from without and from disorder within; a political system which would place responsible and efficient men in public office, pay its own way, provide for the public good without partiality, and, above all, work smoothly. A shrewd judge of men's motives and a careful calculator of probabilities, he was more aware of the difficulties of obtaining such a system than was Jefferson, whose aim was, after all, not much different. To Hamilton, however, government was almost an end in itself; to Jefferson, as to most men, it was only a necessary means to other ends.

On political questions Hamilton was always well-informed, and he wrote clearly and effectively for the audience to which he addressed himself. There are few better practitioners of argument in American literature.

The Papers of Alexander Hamilton, 1786-1790, ed. Harold C. Syrett and Jacob E. Cooke, 7 vols., New York, 1961-1963   The Federalist, ed. Benjamin F. Wright, Cambridge, Mass., 1961; ed. Jacob E. Cooke, Middletown, Conn., 1961   Broadus Mitchell, **Alexander Hamilton: Youth to Maturity, 1755-1788,** New York, 1957, and **Alexander Hamilton: The National Adventure, 1788-1804,** New York, 1962   Bower Aly, **The Rhetoric of Alexander Hamilton,** New York, 1941

from The Federalist

The Federalist *consists of eighty-five essays, all but the last eight of which originally appeared in New York City newspapers between October 27, 1787, and April 4, 1788. They were at once collected and published in two volumes, presumably with Hamilton's supervision. There have since been many reprints, some of which incorporate verbal changes of doubtful authenticity. Although all of the essays were published under the pseudonym Publius, it was generally known that Hamilton, Madison, and Jay were the authors. Since the men had similar views and since Hamilton and Madison had remarkably similar styles, final determination of authorship of all the essays with any certainty is impossible. Both Hamilton and Madison left lists or otherwise ascribed various essays, but even the same man's lists do not always agree. Both, but especially Madison, had a real interest in preserving their anonymity because their political positions later shifted. Jay's contribution of five is least disputed; Hamilton's authorship of fifty-one of the papers is generally acknowledged, as is Madison's of at least fifteen. The remainder are ascribed to either Hamilton or Madison or to both with varying degrees of collaboration.*

The series was begun in answer to newspaper essays and pamphlets in opposition to the ratification of the Constitution (see Pamphlets on the Constitution of the United States, *1888, and* Essays on the Constitution of the United States, *1892, ed. P. L. Ford). In New York, Hamilton was the only delegate to the Constitutional Convention who supported the proposed new form of government; Robert Yates and John Lansing, joined by Governor George Clinton, vigorously opposed it.* The Federalist *is credited with having carried the issue in New York, and it may have had influence elsewhere. In the course of its creation, however, the series became something more than mere debate; it enabled Hamilton to bring to fruition his thorough study of constitutional problems. Of the three essays here reprinted, No. I shows his realistic philosophy of politics, No. XXIII his skill in logical argument, and No. LXIX his thorough knowledge of the early state constitutions, eleven of which had been adopted between 1776 and 1784.*

No. I

To the People of the State of New York:

   After an unequivocal experience of the inefficiency of the subsisting federal government, you are called upon to deliberate on a new Constitution for the United States of America. The subject speaks its own importance; comprehending in its consequences nothing less than the existence of the UNION, the safety and welfare of the parts of which it is composed, the fate of an empire in many respects the most interesting in the world. It has been frequently remarked that it seems to have been reserved to the people of this country, by their conduct and example, to decide
10 the important question, whether societies of men are really capable or not of establishing good government from reflection and choice, or whether they are forever destined to depend for their political constitutions on accident and force. If there be any truth in the remark, the crisis at which we are arrived may with propriety be regarded as the era in which that decision is to be made; and a wrong election of the part we shall act may, in this view, deserve to be considered as the general misfortune of mankind.

   This idea will add the inducements of philanthropy to those of patriotism, to heighten the solicitude which all considerate and good men must feel for the event. Happy will it be if our choice should be directed by a judicious estimate of our true interests, unperplexed and unbiassed by considerations not connected with the pub-
20 lic good. But this is a thing more ardently to be wished than seriously to be expected. The plan offered to our deliberations affects too many particular interests, innovates upon too many local institutions, not to involve in its discussion a variety of objects foreign to its merits, and of views, passions and prejudices little favorable to the discovery of truth.

Text: the Lodge edition of the *Works,* 1904, Vols. XI and XII   2 **the subsisting federal government,** under the Articles of Confederation   21 **The plan,** the Constitution

Among the most formidable of the obstacles which the new Constitution will have to encounter may readily be distinguished the obvious interest of a certain class of men in every State to resist all changes which may hazard a diminution of the power, emolument, and consequence of the offices they hold under the State establishments; and the perverted ambition of another class of men, who will either hope to aggrandise themselves by the confusions of their country, or will flatter themselves with fairer prospects of elevation from the subdivision of the empire into several partial confederacies than from its union under one government.

It is not, however, my design to dwell upon observations of this nature. I am well aware that it would be disingenuous to resolve indiscriminately the opposition of   10
any set of men (merely because their situations might subject them to suspicion) into interested or ambitious views. Candor will oblige us to admit that even such men may be actuated by upright intentions; and it cannot be doubted that much of the opposition which has made its appearance, or may hereafter make its appearance, will spring from sources, blameless at least, if not respectable — the honest errors of minds led astray by preconceived jealousies and fears. So numerous indeed and so powerful are the causes which serve to give a false bias to the judgment, that we, upon many occasions, see wise and good men on the wrong as well as on the right side of questions of the first magnitude to society. This circumstance, if duly attended to, would furnish a lesson of moderation to those who are ever so much   20
persuaded of their being in the right in any controversy. And a further reason for caution, in this respect, might be drawn from the reflection that we are not always sure that those who advocate the truth are influenced by purer principles than their antagonists. Ambition, avarice, personal animosity, party opposition, and many other motives not more laudable than these, are apt to operate as well upon those who support as those who oppose the right side of a question. Were there not even these inducements to moderation, nothing could be more ill-judged than that intolerant spirit which has, at all times, characterized political parties. For in politics, as in religion, it is equally absurd to aim at making proselytes by fire and sword. Heresies in either can rarely be cured by persecution.   30

And yet, however just these sentiments will be allowed to be, we have already sufficient indications that it will happen in this as in all former cases of great national discussion. A torrent of angry and malignant passions will be let loose. To judge from the conduct of the opposite parties, we shall be led to conclude that they will mutually hope to evince the justness of their opinions, and to increase the number of their converts by the loudness of their declamations and the bitterness of their invectives. An enlightened zeal for the energy and efficiency of government will be stigmatized as the offspring of a temper fond of despotic power and hostile to the principles of liberty. An over-scrupulous jealousy of danger to the rights of the people, which is more commonly the fault of the head than of the heart, will be repre-   40
sented as mere pretence and artifice, the stale bait for popularity at the expense of the public good. It will be forgotten, on the one hand, that jealousy is the usual concomitant of love, and that the noble enthusiasm of liberty is apt to be infected with a spirit of narrow and illiberal distrust. On the other hand, it will be equally

forgotten that the vigor of government is essential to the security of liberty; that, in the contemplation of a sound and well-informed judgment, their interest can never be separated; and that a dangerous ambition more often lurks behind the specious mask of zeal for the rights of the people than under the forbidding appearance of zeal for the firmness and efficiency of government. History will teach us that the former has been found a much more certain road to the introduction of despotism than the latter, and that of those men who have overturned the liberties of republics, the greatest number have begun their career by paying an obsequious court to the people; commencing demagogues, and ending tyrants.

10   In the course of the preceding observations, I have had an eye, my fellow-citizens, to putting you upon your guard against all attempts, from whatever quarter, to influence your decision in a matter of the utmost moment to your welfare, by any impressions other than those which may result from the evidence of truth. You will, no doubt, at the same time, have collected from the general scope of them, that they proceed from a source not unfriendly to the new Constitution. Yes, my countrymen, I own to you that, after having given it an attentive consideration, I am clearly of opinion it is your interest to adopt it. I am convinced that this is the safest course for your liberty, your dignity, and your happiness. I affect not reserves which I do not feel. I will not amuse you with an appearance of deliberation when I have
20   decided. I frankly acknowledge to you my convictions, and I will freely lay before you the reasons on which they are founded. The consciousness of good intentions disdains ambiguity. I shall not, however, multiply professions on this head. My motives must remain in the depository of my own breast. My arguments will be open to all, and may be judged of by all. They shall at least be offered in a spirit which will not disgrace the cause of truth.

I propose, in a series of papers, to discuss the following interesting particulars: — *The utility of the UNION to your political prosperity — The insufficiency of the present Confederation to preserve that Union — The necessity of a government at least equally energetic with the one proposed, to the attainment of this object — The conformity of the proposed*
30   *Constitution to the true principles of republican government — Its analogy to your own State constitution — and lastly, The additional security which its adoption will afford to the preservation of that species of government, to liberty, and to property.*

In the progress of this discussion I shall endeavor to give a satisfactory answer to all the objections which shall have made their appearance, that may seem to have any claim to your attention.

It may perhaps be thought superfluous to offer arguments to prove the utility of the UNION, a point, no doubt, deeply engraved on the hearts of the great body of the people in every State, and one, which it may be imagined, has no adversaries. But the fact is, that we already hear it whispered in the private circles of those who
40   oppose the new Constitution, that the thirteen States are of too great extent for any general system, and that we must of necessity resort to separate confederacies of

---

26 **particulars.** The outline covers only the first fifty-one essays; the scheme was later expanded to include analyses of the House of Representatives, the Senate, the Executive (see p. 443), and the Judiciary

distinct portions of the whole. This doctrine will, in all probability, be gradually propagated, till it has votaries enough to countenance an open avowal of it. For nothing can be more evident, to those who are able to take an enlarged view of the subject, than the alternative of an adoption of the new Constitution or a dismemberment of the Union. It will therefore be of use to begin by examining the advantages of that Union, the certain evils, and the probable dangers, to which every State will be exposed from its dissolution. This shall accordingly constitute the subject of my next address.

PUBLIUS

No. XXIII

To the People of the State of New York: 10
The necessity of a Constitution, at least equally energetic with the one proposed, to the preservation of the Union, is the point at the examination of which we are now arrived.

This inquiry will naturally divide itself into three branches — the objects to be provided for by the federal government, the quantity of power necessary to the accomplishment of those objects, the persons upon whom that power ought to operate. Its distribution and organization will more properly claim our attention under the succeeding head.

The principal purposes to be answered by union are these — the common defence of the members; the preservation of the public peace, as well against internal con- 20 vulsions as external attacks; the regulation of commerce with other nations and between the States; the superintendence of our intercourse, political and commercial, with foreign countries.

The authorities essential to the common defence are these: to raise armies; to build and equip fleets; to prescribe rules for the government of both; to direct their operations; to provide for their support. These powers ought to exist without limitation, *because it is impossible to foresee or define the extent and variety of national exigencies, or the correspondent extent and variety of the means which may be necessary to satisfy them.* The circumstances that endanger the safety of nations are infinite, and for this reason no constitutional shackles can wisely be imposed on the power to which the 30 care of it is committed. This power ought to be co-extensive with all the possible combinations of such circumstances; and ought to be under the direction of the same councils which are appointed to preside over the common defence.

This is one of those truths which, to a correct and unprejudiced mind, carries its own evidence along with it; and may be obscured, but cannot be made plainer by argument or reasoning. It rests upon axioms as simple as they are universal; the *means* ought to be proportioned to the *end;* the persons, from whose agency the

---

1 **the whole.** "The same idea, tracing the arguments to their consequences, is held out in several of the late publications against the new Constitution." — Publius. Madison had dealt with this "territorial" objection in No. XIV, and Hamilton returns to it briefly in No. XXIII. One conspicuous use of it by the opposition was in the popular **Letters from the Federal Farmer to the Republican** (1787) by Richard Henry Lee of Virginia

attainment of any *end* is expected, ought to possess the *means* by which it is to be attained.

Whether there ought to be a federal government intrusted with the care of the common defence, is a question in the first instance, open for discussion; but the moment it is decided in the affirmative, it will follow, that that government ought to be clothed with all the powers requisite to complete execution of its trust. And unless it can be shown that the circumstances which may affect the public safety are reducible within certain determinate limits; unless the contrary of this position can be fairly and rationally disputed, it must be admitted, as a necessary consequence, that there can be no limitation of that authority which is to provide for the defence and protection of the community, in any matter essential to its efficacy — that is, in any matter essential to the *formation, direction,* or *support* of the NATIONAL FORCES.

Defective as the present Confederation has been proved to be, this principle appears to have been fully recognised by the framers of it; though they have not made proper or adequate provision for its exercise. Congress have an unlimited discretion to make requisitions of men and money; to govern the army and navy; to direct their operations. As their requisitions are made constitutionally binding upon the States, who are in fact under the most solemn obligations to furnish the supplies required of them, the intention evidently was, that the United States should command whatever resources were by them judged requisite to the "common defence and general welfare." It was presumed that a sense of their true interests, and a regard to the dictates of good faith, would be found sufficient pledges for the punctual performance of the duty of the members to the federal head.

The experiment has, however, demonstrated that this expectation was ill-founded and illusory; and the observations, made under the last head, will, I imagine, have sufficed to convince the impartial and discerning, that there is an absolute necessity for an entire change in the first principles of the system; that if we are in earnest about giving the Union energy and duration, we must abandon the vain project of legislating upon the States in their collective capacities; we must extend the laws of the federal government to the individual citizens of America; we must discard the fallacious scheme of quotas and requisitions, as equally impracticable and unjust. The result from all this is that the Union ought to be invested with full power to levy troops; to build and equip fleets; and to raise the revenues which will be required for the formation and support of an army and navy, in the customary and ordinary modes practised in other governments.

If the circumstances of our country are such as to demand a compound instead of a simple, a confederate instead of a sole, government, the essential point which will remain to be adjusted will be to discriminate the OBJECTS, as far as it can be done, which shall appertain to the different provinces or departments of power; allowing to each the most ample authority for fulfilling the objects committed to its charge. Shall the Union be constituted the guardian of the common safety? Are fleets and armies and revenues necessary to this purpose? The government of the Union must be empowered to pass all laws, and to make all regulations which have relation to

---

25 **the last head.** Nos. XV-XXII deal with the insufficiency and defects of the Confederation

them. The same must be the case in respect to commerce, and to every other matter to which its jurisdiction is permitted to extend. Is the administration of justice between the citizens of the same State the proper department of the local governments? These must possess all the authorities which are connected with this object, and with every other that may be allotted to their particular cognizance and direction. Not to confer in each case a degree of power commensurate to the end, would be to violate the most obvious rules of prudence and propriety, and improvidently to trust the great interests of the nation to hands which are disabled from managing them with vigor and success.

Who so likely to make suitable provisions for the public defence, as that body to 10 which the guardianship of the public safety is confided; which, as the centre of information, will best understand the extent and urgency of the dangers that threaten; as the representative of the WHOLE, will feel itself most deeply interested in the preservation of every part; which, from the responsibility implied in the duty assigned to it, will be most sensibly impressed with the necessity of proper exertions; and which, by the extension of its authority throughout the States, can alone establish uniformity and concert in the plans and measures by which the common safety is to be secured? Is there not a manifest inconsistency in devolving upon the federal government the care of the general defence, and leaving in the State governments the *effective* powers by which it is to be provided for? Is not a want of co-operation 20 the infallible consequence of such a system? And will not weakness, disorder, an undue distribution of the burdens and calamities of war, an unnecessary and intolerable increase of expense, be its natural and inevitable concomitants? Have we not had unequivocal experience of its effects in the course of the revolution which we have just accomplished?

Every view we may take of the subject, as candid inquirers after truth, will serve to convince us, that it is both unwise and dangerous to deny the federal government an unconfined authority, as to all those objects which are intrusted to its management. It will indeed deserve the most vigilant and careful attention of the people, to see that it be modelled in such a manner as to admit of its being safely vested 30 with the requisite powers. If any plan which has been, or may be, offered to our consideration, should not, upon a dispassionate inspection, be found to answer this description, it ought to be rejected. A government, the constitution of which renders it unfit to be trusted with all the powers which a free people *ought to delegate to any government,* would be an unsafe and improper depositary of the NATIONAL INTERESTS. Wherever THESE can with propriety be confided, the coincident powers may safely accompany them. This is the true result of all just reasoning upon the subject. And the adversaries of the plan promulgated by the convention ought to have confined themselves to showing, that the internal structure of the proposed government was such as to render it unworthy of the confidence of the people. They 40 ought not to have wandered into inflammatory declamations and unmeaning cavils about the extent of the powers. The POWERS are not too extensive for the OBJECTS of federal administration, or, in other words, for the management of our NATIONAL INTERESTS; nor can any satisfactory argument be framed to show that they are

chargeable with such an excess. If it be true, as has been insinuated by some of the writers on the other side, that the difficulty arises from the nature of the thing, and that the extent of the country will not permit us to form a government in which such ample powers can safely be reposed, it would prove that we ought to contract our views, and resort to the expedient of separate confederacies, which will move within more practicable spheres. For the absurdity must continually stare us in the face of confiding to a government the direction of the most essential national interests, without daring to trust to it the authorities which are indispensable to their proper and efficient management. Let us not attempt to reconcile contradictions,
10 but firmly embrace a rational alternative.

I trust, however, that the impracticability of one general system cannot be shown. I am greatly mistaken, if anything of weight has yet been advanced of this tendency; and I flatter myself, that the observations which have been made in the course of these papers have served to place the reverse of that position in as clear a light as any matter still in the womb of time and experience can be susceptible of. This, at all events, must be evident, that the very difficulty itself, drawn from the extent of the country, is the strongest argument in favour of an energetic government; for any other can certainly never preserve the Union of so large an empire. If we embrace the tenets of those who oppose the adoption of the proposed Constitution, as
20 the standard of our political creed, we cannot fail to verify the gloomy doctrines which predict the impracticability of a national system pervading the entire limits of the present Confederacy.

PUBLIUS

No. LXIX

To the People of the State of New York:

I proceed now to trace the real characters of the proposed Executive, as they are marked out in the plan of the convention. This will serve to place in a strong light the unfairness of the representations which have been made in regard to it.

The first thing which strikes our attention is, that the executive authority, with few exceptions, is to be vested in a single magistrate. This will scarcely, however,
30 be considered as a point upon which any comparison can be grounded; for if, in this particular, there be a resemblance to the king of Great Britain, there is not less a resemblance to the Grand Seignior, to the khan of Tartary, to the Man of the Seven Mountains, or to the governor of New York.

That magistrate is to be elected for *four* years; and is to be reëligible as often as the people of the United States shall think him worthy of their confidence. In these circumstances there is a total dissimilitude between *him* and a king of Great Britain, who is an *hereditary* monarch, possessing the crown as a patrimony descendible to his heirs forever; but there is a close analogy between *him* and a governor of New York, who is elected for *three* years, and is reëligible without limitation or inter-

---

32 **the Grand Seignior . . . Seven Mountains,** in turn earlier rulers of Turkey, of the Tatars, and perhaps of the Assassins, the Old Man of the Mountains, Hasan ibn al-Sabbah, head of a sect of the Ismaili Islam

mission. If we consider how much less time would be requisite for establishing a dangerous influence in a single State, than for establishing a like influence throughout the United States we must conclude that a duration of *four* years for the Chief Magistrate of the Union is a degree of permanency far less to be dreaded in that office, than a duration of *three* years for a corresponding office in a single State.

The President of the United States would be liable to be impeached, tried, and, upon conviction of treason, bribery, or other high crimes or misdemeanors, removed from office; and would afterwards be liable to prosecution and punishment in the ordinary course of law. The person of the king of Great Britain is sacred and inviolable; there is no constitutional tribunal to which he is amenable; no punish- 10 ment to which he can be subjected without involving the crisis of a national revolution. In this delicate and important circumstance of personal responsibility, the President of Confederated America would stand upon no better ground than a governor of New York, and upon worse ground than the governors of Maryland and Delaware.

The President of the United States is to have power to return a bill, which shall have passed the two branches of the legislature, for reconsideration; and the bill so returned is to become a law, if, upon that reconsideration, it be approved by two thirds of both houses. The king of Great Britain, on his part, has an absolute negative upon the acts of the two houses of Parliament. The disuse of that power for a 20 considerable time past does not affect the reality of its existence; and is to be ascribed wholly to the crown's having found the means of substituting influence to authority, or the art of gaining a majority in one or the other of the two houses, to the necessity of exerting a prerogative which could seldom be exerted without hazarding some degree of national agitation. The qualified negative of the President differs widely from this absolute negative of the British sovereign; and tallies exactly with the revisionary authority of the council of revision of this State, of which the governor is a constituent part. In this respect the power of the President would exceed that of the governor of New York, because the former would possess, singly, what the latter shares with the chancellor and judges; but it would be precisely the same with 30 that of the governor of Massachusetts, whose constitution, as to this article, seems to have been the original from which the convention have copied.

The President is to be the "commander-in-chief of the army and navy of the United States, and of the militia of the several States, when called into the actual service of the United States. He is to have power to grant reprieves and pardons for offences against the United States, *except in cases of impeachment;* to recommend to the consideration of Congress such measures as he shall judge necessary and expedient; to convene, on extraordinary occasions, both houses of the legislature, or either of them, and, in case of disagreement between them *with respect to the time of adjournment,* to adjourn them to such time as he shall think proper; to take care that the laws be 40 faithfully executed; and to commission all officers of the United States." In most of these particulars, the power of the President will resemble equally that of the king

---

14 **Maryland and Delaware.** The constitutions of Maryland and Delaware had no specific provisions for impeachment; the governor of New York could be impeached

of Great Britain and of the governor of New York. The most material points of difference are these: — *First.* The President will have only the occasional command of such part of the militia of the nation as by legislative provision may be called into the actual service of the Union. The king of Great Britain and the governor of New York have at all times the entire command of all the militia within their several jurisdictions. In this article, therefore, the power of the President would be inferior to that of either the monarch or the governor. *Secondly.* The President is to be commander-in-chief of the army and navy of the United States. In this respect his authority would be nominally the same with that of the king of Great Britain,
10 but in substance much inferior to it. It would amount to nothing more than the supreme command and direction of the military and naval forces, as first General and admiral of the Confederacy; while that of the British king extends to the *declaring* of war and to the *raising* and *regulating* of fleets and armies, — all which, by the Constitution under consideration, would appertain to the legislature. The governor of New York, on the other hand, is by the constitution of the State vested only with the command of its militia and navy. But the constitutions of several of the States expressly declare their governors to be commanders-in-chief, as well of the army as navy; and it may well be a question, whether those of New Hampshire and Massachusetts, in particular, do not, in this instance, confer larger powers
20 upon their respective governors, than could be claimed by a President of the United States. *Thirdly.* The power of the President, in respect to pardons, would extend to all cases, *except those of impeachment.* The governor of New York may pardon in all cases, even in those of impeachment, except for treason and murder. Is not the power of the governor, in this article, on a calculation of political consequences, greater than that of the President? All conspiracies and plots against the government, which have not been matured into actual treason, may be screened from punishment of every kind, by the interposition of the prerogative of pardoning. If a governor of New York, therefore, should be at the head of any such conspiracy, until the design had been ripened into actual hostility he could insure his accomplices and adherents
30 an entire impunity. A President of the Union, on the other hand, though he may even pardon treason, when prosecuted in the ordinary course of law, could shelter no offender, in any degree, from the effects of impeachment and conviction. Would not the prospect of a total indemnity for all the preliminary steps be a greater temptation to undertake and persevere in an enterprise against the public liberty, than the mere prospect of an exemption from death and confiscation, if the final execution

---

14 **legislature.** "A writer in a Pennsylvania paper, under the signature of *Tamony,* has asserted that the king of Great Britain owes his prerogative as commander-in-chief to an annual mutiny bill. The truth is, on the contrary, that his prerogative, in this respect, is immemorial, and was only disputed 'contrary to all reason and precedent,' as Blackstone, vol. i, page 262, expresses it, by the Long Parliament of Charles I.; but by the statute the 13th of Charles II, chap. 6, it was declared to be in the king alone, for that the sole supreme government and command of the militia within his majesty's realms and dominions, and of all forces by sea and land, and of all forts and places of strength, EVER WAS AND IS the undoubted right of his majesty and his royal predecessors, kings and queens of England, and that both or either house of Parliament cannot nor ought to pretend to the same." — Publius. The reference is to *Commentaries on the Laws of England* (1765) by Sir William Blackstone (1723-1780), one of the chief sources of Hamilton's political philosophy

of the design, upon an actual appeal to arms, should miscarry? Would this last expectation have any influence at all, when the probability was computed, that the
person who was to afford that exemption might himself be involved in the consequences of the measure, and might be incapacitated by his agency in it from affording the desired impunity? The better to judge of this matter, it will be necessary to
recollect that, by the proposed Constitution, the offence of treason is limited "to
levying war upon the United States, and adhering to their enemies, giving them
aid and comfort"; and that by the laws of New York it is confined with similar
bounds. *Fourthly.* The President can only adjourn the national legislature in the
single case of disagreement about the time of adjournment. The British monarch   10
may prorogue or even dissolve the Parliament. The governor of New York may
also prorogue the legislature of this State for a limited time; a power which, in certain situations, may be employed to very important purposes.

   The President is to have power, with the advice and consent of the Senate, to
make treaties, provided two thirds of the senators present concur. The king of Great
Britain is the sole and absolute representative of the nation in all foreign transactions.
He can of his own accord make treaties of peace, commerce, alliance, and of every
other description. It has been insinuated, that his authority in this respect is not
conclusive, and that his conventions with foreign powers are subject to the revision, and stand in need of the ratification, of Parliament. But I believe this doctrine   20
was never heard of until it was broached upon the present occasion. Every jurist of
that kingdom, and every other man acquainted with its Constitution, knows, as an
established fact, that the prerogative of making treaties exists in the crown in its
utmost plenitude; and that the compacts entered into by the royal authority have
the most complete legal validity and perfection, independent of any other sanction.
The Parliament, it is true, is sometimes seen employing itself in altering the existing laws to conform them to the stipulations in a new treaty; and this may have
possibly given birth to the imagination, that its coöperation was necessary to the
obligatory efficacy of the treaty. But this parliamentary interposition proceeds from
a different cause: from the necessity of adjusting a most artificial and intricate sys-   30
tem of revenue and commercial laws, to the changes made in them by the operation of the treaty; and of adapting new provisions and precautions to the new state
of things, to keep the machine from running into disorder. In this respect, therefore, there is no comparison between the intended power of the President and the
actual power of the British sovereign. The one can perform alone what the other
can do only with the concurrence of a branch of the legislature. It must be admitted, that, in this instance, the power of the federal Executive would exceed that of
any State Executive. But this arises naturally from the sovereign power which
relates to treaties. If the Confederacy were to be dissolved, it would become a question, whether the Executives of the several States were not solely invested with that   40
delicate and important prerogative.

   The President is also to be authorized to receive ambassadors and other public
ministers. This, though it has been a rich theme of declamation, is more a matter

<hr />

21 **jurist.** *"Vide* Blackstone's *Commentaries,* vol. i, p. 257." — Publius

of dignity than of authority. It is a circumstance which will be without consequence in the administration of the government; and it was far more convenient that it should be arranged in this manner, than that there should be a necessity of convening the legislature, or one of its branches, upon every arrival of a foreign minister, though it were merely to take the place of a departed predecessor.

The President is to nominate and, *with the advice and consent of the Senate,* to appoint ambassadors and other public ministers, judges of the Supreme Court, and in general all officers of the United States established by law, and whose appointments are not otherwise provided for by the Constitution. The king of Great Britain is em-
10 phatically and truly styled the fountain of honor. He not only appoints to all offices, but can create offices. He can confer titles of nobility at pleasure; and has the disposal of an immense number of church preferments. There is evidently a great inferiority in the power of the President, in this particular, to that of the British king; nor is it equal to that of the governor of New York, if we are to interpret the meaning of the constitution of the State by the practice which has obtained under it. The power of appointment is with us lodged in a council, composed of the governor and four members of the Senate, chosen by the Assembly. The governor *claims,* and has frequently *exercised,* the right of nomination, and is *entitled* to a casting vote in the appointment. If he really has the right of nominating,
20 his authority is in this respect equal to that of the President, and exceeds it in the article of the casting vote. In the national government, if the Senate should be divided, no appointment could be made; in the government of New York, if the council should be divided, the governor can turn the scale, and confirm his own nomination. If we compare the publicity which must necessarily attend the mode of appointment by the President and an entire branch of the national legislature, with the privacy in the mode of appointment by the governor of New York, closeted in a secret apartment with at most four, and frequently with only two persons; and if we at the same time consider how much more easy it must be to influence the small number of which a council of appointment consists, than the considerable number of which the na-
30 tional Senate would consist, we cannot hesitate to pronounce that the power of the chief magistrate of this State, in the disposition of offices, must, in practice, be greatly superior to that of the Chief Magistrate of the Union.

Hence it appears that, except as to the concurrent authority of the President in the article of treaties, it would be difficult to determine whether that magistrate would, in the aggregate, possess more or less power than the Governor of New York. And it appears yet more unequivocally, that there is no pretence for the parallel which has been attempted between him and the king of Great Britain. But to render the contrast in this respect still more striking, it may be of use to throw the principal circumstances of dissimilitude into a closer group.
40 The President of the United States would be an officer elected by the people for *four* years; the king of Great Britain is a perpetual and *hereditary* prince. The one would be amenable to personal punishment and disgrace; the person of the other is sacred and inviolable. The one would have a *qualified* negative upon the acts of the legislative body; the other has an *absolute* negative. The one would have a right to

command the military and naval forces of the nation; the other, in addition to this right, possesses that of *declaring* war, and of *raising* and *regulating* fleets and armies by his own authority. The one would have a concurrent power with a branch of the legislature in the formation of treaties; the other is the *sole possessor* of the power of making treaties. The one would have a like concurrent authority in appointing to offices; the other is the sole author of all appointments. The one can confer no privileges whatever: the other can make denizens of aliens, noblemen of commoners; can erect corporations with all the rights incident to corporate bodies. The one can prescribe no rules concerning the commerce or currency of the nation; the other is in several respects the arbiter of commerce, and in this capacity can estab-   10 lish markets and fairs, can regulate weights and measures, can lay embargoes for a limited time, can coin money, can authorize or prohibit the circulation of foreign coin. The one has no particle of spiritual jurisdiction; the other is the supreme head and governor of the national church! What answer shall we give to those who would persuade us that things so unlike resemble each other? The same that ought to be given to those who tell us that a government, the whole power of which would be in the hands of the elective and periodical servants of the people, is an aristocracy, a monarchy, and a despotism.

Publius

1787-1788, 1788

1737—1809 Thomas Paine

from The Age of Reason

When Paine was arrested in Paris in December 1793, a part of The Age of Reason *was in the hands of his printer, and on his way to prison he was allowed to turn over the remainder of the manuscript of Part I to Joel Barlow. A few copies were printed in January 1794. Part II, begun under the shadow of the guillotine and finished in the home of James Monroe, was added, and the whole work was published in 1795.*

Paine's outspoken Deism (see p. 256 for a discussion of Deism) and anticlericalism were tempered by an earnest belief in a benevolent God and the perfectibility of man; he was neither an atheist nor a supporter of such mummery as the worship of an actress as representative of the Goddess of Reason — one of the actual incidents of the French Revolution. His book, indeed, was written partly to protest against the excesses of the Reign of Terror under Robespierre. It appeared, however, almost simultaneously with a new wave of evangelical fervor in America (see Peter Cartwright, pp. 478-486), and was used to embarrass the Jeffersonian Republicans, whose opponents linked infidelity with political radicalism for the purpose of getting votes. To the orthodox, Paine's attack on some of the most cherished doctrines of Christianity was sheer blasphemy.

The modern reader will wonder chiefly at Paine's persistently literal interpretation of the Bible and his unquestioning assumption that human beings wish to be rational in their beliefs. In both respects he was a child of his time, which ordinarily demanded order and consistency, and was thoroughly committed to the mathematical world-view of Sir Isaac Newton, who pictured the universe as a smooth-running, rationally conducted machine.

It has been my intention, for several years past, to publish my thoughts upon Religion. I am well aware of the difficulties that attend the subject; and, from that consideration, had reserved it to a more advanced period of life. I intended it to be the last offering I should make to my fellow-citizens of all nations; and that at a time when the purity of the motive that induced me to it could not admit of a question, even by those who might disapprove of the work.

Text: that established by Professor Peach on the basis of the 1795 edition

The circumstance that has now taken place in France, of the total abolition of the whole national order of priesthood and of everything appertaining to compulsive systems of religion, and compulsive articles of faith, has not only precipitated my intention, but rendered a work of this kind exceedingly necessary; lest, in the general wreck of superstition, of false systems of government, and false theology, we lose sight of morality, of humanity, and of the theology that is true.

As several of my colleagues, and others of my fellow-citizens of France, have given me the example of making their voluntary and individual profession of faith, I also will make mine; and I do this with all that sincerity and frankness with which the mind of man communicates with itself.   10

I believe in one God, and no more; and I hope for happiness beyond this life.

I believe in the equality of man, and I believe that religious duties consist in doing justice, loving mercy, and endeavoring to make our fellow-creatures happy.

But, lest it should be supposed that I believe many other things in addition to these, I shall, in the progress of this work, declare the things I do not believe, and my reasons for not believing them.

I do not believe in the creed professed by the Jewish church, by the Roman church, by the Greek church, by the Turkish church, by the Protestant church, nor by any church that I know of. My own mind is my own church.

All national institutions of churches — whether Jewish, Christian, or Turkish — 20 appear to me no other than human inventions set up to terrify and enslave mankind and monopolize power and profit.

I do not mean by this declaration to condemn those who believe otherwise. They have the same right to their belief as I have to mine. But it is necessary to the happiness of man, that he be mentally faithful to himself. Infidelity does not consist in believing, or in disbelieving; it consists in professing to believe what he does not believe.

It is impossible to calculate the moral mischief, if I may so express it, that mental lying has produced in society. When a man has so far corrupted and prostituted the chastity of his mind, as to subscribe his professional belief to things he does not 30 believe, he has prepared himself for the commission of every other crime. He takes up the trade of a priest for the sake of gain, and, in order to *qualify* himself for that trade, he begins with a perjury. Can we conceive anything more destructive to morality than this?

Soon after I had published the pamphlet, COMMON SENSE, in America, I saw the exceeding probability that a Revolution in the System of Government would be followed by a revolution in the system of religion. The adulterous connection of church and state, wherever it had taken place, whether Jewish, Christian, or Turkish, had so effectually prohibited, by pains and penalties, every discussion upon established creeds, and upon first principles of religion, that until the system of govern- 40 ment should be changed those subjects could not be brought fairly and openly before the world; but that whenever this should be done, a revolution in the sys-

---

1 **The circumstance,** a reference to the acts of the National Convention between 1792 and the time of writing

tem of religion would follow. Human inventions and priest-craft would be detected, and man would return to the pure, unmixed, and unadulterated belief of one God, and no more.

Every national church or religion has established itself by pretending some special mission from God, communicated to certain individuals. The Jews have their Moses; the Christians their Jesus Christ, their apostles and saints; and the Turks their Mahomet — as if the way to God was not open to every man alike.

Each of those churches show certain books which they call *revelation,* or the word of God. The Jews say that their word of God was given by God to Moses face to
10 face; the Christians say that their word of God came by divine inspiration; and the Turks say that their word of God (the Koran) was brought by an angel from heaven. Each of those churches accuse the other of unbelief; and, for my own part, I disbelieve them all.

As it is necessary to affix right ideas to words, I will, before I proceed further into the subject, offer some observations on the word *revelation.* Revelation, when applied to religion, means something communicated *immediately* from God to man.

No one will deny or dispute the power of the Almighty to make such a communication, if he pleases. But admitting, for the sake of a case, that something has been revealed to a certain person, and not revealed to any other person, it is revelation to
20 that person only. When he tells it to a second person, a second to a third, a third to a fourth, and so on, it ceases to be a revelation to all those persons. It is revelation to the first person only, and *hearsay* to every other; and, consequently, they are not obliged to believe it.

It is a contradiction in terms and ideas to call anything a revelation that comes to us at secondhand, either verbally or in writing. Revelation is necessarily limited to the first communication. After this, it is only an account of something which that person says was a revelation made to him; and though he may find himself obliged to believe it, it cannot be incumbent upon me to believe it in the same manner, for it was not a revelation to *me,* and I have only his word for it that it was made to *him.*
30 When Moses told the children of Israel that he received the two tables of the commandments from the hand of God, they were not obliged to believe him, because they had no other authority for it than his telling them so; and I have no other authority for it than some historian telling me so. The Commandments carry no internal evidence of divinity with them. They contain some good moral precepts, such as any man qualified to be a lawgiver, or legislator, could produce himself, without having recourse to supernatural intervention.

When I am told that the Koran was written in heaven, and brought to Mahomet by an angel, the account comes to near the same kind of hearsay evidence and second-hand authority as the former. I did not see the angel myself, and therefore I
40 have a right not to believe it.

When also I am told that a woman, called the Virgin Mary said, or gave out,

---

36 **supernatural intervention.** "It is, however, necessary to except the declaration which says that God visits the sins of the fathers upon the children. This is contrary to every principle of moral justice." — Paine

that she was with child without any cohabitation with a man, and that her betrothed husband, Joseph, said, that an angel told him so, I have a right to believe them or not; such a circumstance required a much stronger evidence than their bare word for it; but we have not even this; for neither Joseph nor Mary wrote any such matter themselves. It is only reported by others that *they said so.* It is hearsay upon hearsay, and I do not chuse to rest my belief upon such evidence.

It is, however, not difficult to account for the credit that was given to the story of Jesus Christ being the Son of God. He was born at a time when the heathen mythology had still some fashion and repute in the world, and that mythology had prepared the people for the belief of such a story. Almost all the extraordinary men 10 that ever lived under the heathen mythology were reputed to be the sons of some of their gods. It was not a new thing, at that time, to believe a man to have been celestially begotten; the intercourse of gods with women was then a matter of familiar opinion. Their Jupiter, according to their accounts, had cohabited with hundreds; the story therefore had nothing in it either new, wonderful, or obscene; it was conformable to the opinions that then prevailed among the people called Gentiles, or mythologists, and it was those people only that believed it. The Jews, who had kept strictly to the belief of one God and no more, and who had always rejected the heathen mythology, never credited the story.

It is curious to observe how the theory of what is called the Christian church 20 sprung out of the tail of the heathen mythology. A direct incorporation took place, in the first instance, by making the reputed founder to be celestially begotten. The trinity of gods that then followed was no other than a reduction of the former plurality, which was about twenty or thirty thousand. The statue of Mary succeeded the statue of Diana of Ephesus. The deification of heroes changed into the canonization of saints. The mythologists had gods for everything; the Christian mythologists had saints for everything. The church became as crouded with the one as the pantheon had been with the other; and Rome was the place of both. The Christian theory is little else than the idolatry of the ancient mythologists, accommodated to the purposes of power and revenue; and it yet remains to reason and philosophy to 30 abolish the amphibious fraud.

Nothing that is here said can apply, even with the most distant disrespect, to the real character of Jesus Christ. He was a virtuous and an amiable man. The morality that he preached and practiced was of the most benevolent kind; and though similar systems of morality had been preached by Confucius, and by some of the Greek philosophers, many years before; by the Quakers since, and by many good men in all ages, it has not been exceeded by any.

Jesus Christ wrote no account of himself, of his birth, parentage, or anything else. Not a line of what is called the New Testament is of his writing. The history of him is altogether the work of other people; and as to the account given of his resur- 40 rection and ascension, it was the necessary counterpart to the story of his birth. His historians, having brought him into the world in supernatural manner, were obliged

---

25 **Diana of Ephesus,** whose shrine was one of the seven wonders of the ancient world. See Acts 19   35
Confucius, the Chinese philosopher (551?-478 B.C.)

to take him out again in the same manner, or the first part of the story must have fallen to the ground.

The wretched contrivance with which this latter part is told exceeds everything that went before it. The first part, that of the miraculous conception, was not a thing that admitted of publicity; and therefore the tellers of this part of the story, had this advantage, that though they might not be credited they could not be detected. They could not be expected to prove it, because it was not one of those things that admitted of proof, and it was impossible that the person of whom it was told could prove it himself.

10   But the resurrection of a dead person from the grave, and his ascension through the air, is a thing very different, as to the evidence it admits of, to the invisible conception of a child in the womb. The resurrection and ascension, supposing them to have taken place, admitted of public and ocular demonstration, like that of the ascension of a balloon, or the sun at noonday, to all Jerusalem at least. A thing which everybody is required to believe, requires that the proof and evidence of it should be equal to all, and universal; and as the public visibility of this last related act was the only evidence that could give sanction to the former part, the whole of it falls to the ground because that evidence never was given. Instead of this, a small number of persons, not more than eight or nine, are introduced as proxies for the
20 whole world, to say they *saw it,* and all the rest of the world are called upon to believe it. But it appears that Thomas did not believe the resurrection; and, as they say, would not believe without having ocular and manual demonstration himself. *So neither will I;* and the reason is equally as good for me, and for every other person, as for Thomas.

It is in vain to palliate or disguise this matter. The story, so far as relates to the supernatural part, has every mark of fraud and imposition stamped upon the face of it. Who were the authors of it is as impossible for us now to know, as it is for us to be assured that the books in which the account is related were written by the persons whose names they bear. The best surviving evidence we now have respect-
30 ing this affair is the Jews. They are regularly descended from the people who lived in the times this resurrection and ascension is said to have happened, and they say, *it is not true.* It has long appeared to me a strange inconsistency to cite the Jews as a proof of the truth of the story. It is the same as if a man were to say, I will prove the truth of what I have told you by producing the people who say it is false.

That such a person as Jesus Christ existed, and that he was crucified, which was the mode of execution at that day, are historical relations strictly within the limits of probability. He preached most excellent morality, and the equality of man; but he preached also against the corruptions and avarice of the Jewish priests; and this brought upon him the hatred and vengeance of the whole order of priest-hood. The
40 accusation which those priests brought against him was that of sedition and conspiracy against the Roman government, to which the Jews were then subject and tributary; and it is not improbable that the Roman government might have some secret apprehension of the effects of his doctrine as well as the Jewish priests;

---

21 **Thomas.** See John 20:24-29; whence the epithet "doubting Thomas"

neither is it improbable that Jesus Christ had in contemplation the delivery of the Jewish nation from the bondage of the Romans. Between the two, however, this virtuous reformer and revolutionist lost his life.

It is upon this plain narrative of facts, together with another case I am going to mention, that the Christian mythologists, calling themselves the Christian church, have erected their fable, which for absurdity and extravagance is not exceeded by anything that is to be found in the mythology of the ancients.

The ancient mythologists tell that the race of Giants made war against Jupiter, and that one of them threw an hundred rocks against him at one throw; that Jupiter defeated him with thunder, and confined him afterwards under Mount Etna; and   10 that every time the Giant turns himself, Mount Etna belches fire. It is here easy to see that the circumstance of the mountain, that of its being a volcano, suggested the idea of the fable; and that the fable is made to fit and wind itself up with that circumstance.

The Christian mythologists tell that their Satan made war against the Almighty, who defeated him, and confined him afterwards, not under a mountain, but in a pit. It is here easy to see that the first fable suggested the idea of the second; for the fable of Jupiter and the Giants was told many hundred years before that of Satan.

Thus far the ancient and the Christian mythologists differ very little from each other. But the latter have contrived to carry the matter much farther. They have contrived to connect the fabulous part of the story of Jesus Christ, with the fable   20 originating from Mount Etna; and, in order to make all the parts of the story ty together, they have taken to their aid the tradition of the Jews; for the Christian mythology is made up partly from the ancient mythology and partly from the Jewish traditions.

The Christian mythologists, after having confined Satan in a pit, were obliged to let him out again, to bring on the sequel of the fable. He is then introduced into the garden of Eden in the shape of a snake, or a serpent, and in that shape he enters into familiar conversation with Eve, who is not in any way surprised to hear a snake talk, and the issue of this *tête-à-tête* is, that he persuades her to eat an apple, and the eating of that apple, damns all mankind.   30

After giving Satan this triumph over the whole creation, one would have supposed that the church mythologists would have been kind enough to send him back again to the pit; or, if they had not done this, that they would have put a mountain upon him (for they say their faith can remove a mountain) or have him put *under* a mountain, as the former mythologists had done, to prevent his getting again among the women and doing more mischief. But instead of this, they leave him at large without even obliging him to give his parole. The secret of which is, that they could not do without him; and after being at the trouble of making him, they bribed him to stay. They promised him ALL the Jews, ALL the Turks by anticipation, nine-tenths of the world beside, and Mahomet into the bargain. After   40 this, who can doubt the bountifulness of the Christian mythology?

Having thus made an insurrection and a battle in heaven, in which none of the

---

23 **Jewish traditions,** especially as found in the Cabala, or mystic books of the Jews, some of which are related to the Apocrypha. The idea of Satan is largely non-Biblical

combatants could be either killed or wounded — put Satan into the pit — let him out again — given him a triumph over the whole creation — damned all mankind by the eating of an apple, these Christian mythologists bring the two ends of their fable together. They represent this virtuous and amiable man, Jesus Christ, to be at once both God and man, and also the Son of God, celestially begotten on purpose to be sacrificed, because they say, that Eve in her longing had eaten an apple.

Putting aside everything that might excite laughter by its absurdity, or detestation by its prophaneness, and confining ourselves merely to an examination of the parts, it is impossible to conceive a story more derogatory to the Almighty, more
10 inconsistent with his wisdom, more contradictory to his power, than this story is.

In order to make for it a foundation to rise upon, the inventors were under the necessity of giving to the being whom they call Satan a power equally as great, if not greater, than they attribute to the Almighty. They have not only given him the power of liberating himself from the pit, after what they call his fall, but they have made that power increase afterwards to infinity. Before this fall, they represent him only as an angel of limited existence, as they represent the rest. After his fall, he becomes, by their account, omnipresent. He exists everywhere, and at the same time. He occupies the whole immensity of space.

Not content with this deification of Satan, they represent him as defeating, by
20 strategem, in the shape of an animal of the creation, all the power and wisdom of the Almighty. They represent him as having compelled the Almighty to the *direct necessity* either of surrendering the whole of the creation to the government and sovereignty of this Satan or of capitulating for its redemption by coming down upon earth and exhibiting himself upon a cross in the shape of a man.

Had the inventors of this story told it the contrary way — that is, had they represented the Almighty as compelling Satan to exhibit *himself* on a cross in the shape of a snake, as a punishment for his new transgression, the story would have been less absurd, less contradictory. But, instead of this, they make the transgressor triumph and the Almighty fall.
30 That many good men have believed this strange fable, and lived very good lives under that belief (for credulity is not a crime) is what I have no doubt of. In the first place, they were educated to believe it, and they would have believed anything else in the same manner. There are also many who have been so enthusiastically enraptured by what they conceived to be the infinite love of God to man in making a sacrifice of himself, that the vehemence of the idea has forbidden and deterred them from examining into the absurdity and prophaneness of the story. The more unnatural anything is, the more is it capable of becoming the object of dismal admiration.

But if objects for gratitude and admiration are our desire, do they not present themselves every hour to our eyes? Do we not see a fair creation prepared to receive us
40 the instant we were born — a world furnished to our hands that cost us nothing? Is it we that light up the sun, that pour down the rain, and fill the earth with abundance? Whether we sleep or wake the vast machinery of the universe still goes on. Are these things, and the blessings they indicate in future, nothing to us? Can our gross feelings be excited by no other subjects than tragedy and suicide? Or is the

gloomy pride of man become so intolerable that nothing can flatter it but the sacrifice of the Creator?

I know that this bold investigation will alarm many, but it would be paying too great a compliment to their credulity to forbear it upon that account. The times and the subject demand it to be done. The suspicion that the theory of what is called the Christian church is fabulous is becoming very extensive in all countries; and it will be a consolation to men staggering under that suspicion, and doubting what to believe and what to disbelieve, to see the subject freely investigated. I therefore pass on to an examination of the books called the Old and the New Testament. . . .

[Most of the remainder of Part I, and a large portion of Part II, here omitted, either display the "true theology" which Paine found in the works of creation, or attack the divine authority of the Bible by citation of conflicting texts and "absurd" stories. His chief argument is that mystery, miracle, and prophecy have been used in all ages to impose priesthood upon mankind. His positive Deism is summarized in the "Conclusion" to Part II, the latter part of which follows.]

Of all the systems of religion that ever were invented, there is none more derogatory 10
to the Almighty, more unedifying to man, more repugnant to reason, and more contradictory in itself, than this thing called Christianity. Too absurd for belief, too impossible to convince, and too inconsistent for practice, it renders the heart torpid or produces only atheists and fanatics. As an engine of power, it serves the purpose of despotism; and as a means of wealth, the avarice of priests; but so far as respects the good of man in general, it leads to nothing here or hereafter.

The only religion that has not been invented, and that has in it every evidence of divine originality, is pure and simple Deism. It must have been the first, and will probably be the last, that man believes. But pure and simple Deism does not answer the purpose of despotic governments. They cannot lay hold of religion as an 20
engine, but by mixing it with human inventions, and making their own authority a part; neither does it answer the avarice of priests but by incorporating themselves and their functions with it, and becoming, like the government, a party in the system. It is that that forms the otherwise mysterious connection of church and state; the church human, and the state tyrannic.

Were man impressed as fully and strongly as he ought to be with the belief of a God, his moral life would be regulated by the force of that belief; he would stand in awe of God and of himself, and would not do the thing that could not be concealed from either. To give this belief the full opportunity of force, it is necessary that it act alone. This is Deism.   30

But when, according to the Christian trinitarian scheme, one part of God is represented by a dying man, and another part, called the Holy Ghost, by a flying pigeon, it is impossible that belief can attach itself to such wild conceits.

---

33 **wild conceits.** "The book called the book of Matthew says (III, 16) that *the Holy Ghost descended in the shape of a dove.* It might as well have said a goose; the creatures are equally harmless, and the one is as much a nonsensical lie as the other. Acts II, 2, 3, says that it descended in a mighty *rushing wind,* in the shape of *cloven tongues;* perhaps it was cloven feet. Such absurd stuff is only fit for tales of witches and wizards." — Paine

It has been the scheme of the Christian church, and of all the other invented systems of religion, to hold man in ignorance of the Creator, as it is of government to hold him in ignorance of his rights. The systems of the one are as false as those of the other, and are calculated for mutual support. The study of theology, as it stands for Christian churches, is the study of nothing; it is founded on nothing; it rests on no principles; it proceeds by no authorities, it has no data; it can demonstrate nothing, and admits of no conclusion. Not any thing can be studied as a science without our being in possession of the principles upon which it is founded; and as this is not the case with Christian theology, it is therefore the study of nothing.

10   Instead, then, of studying theology, as is now done, out of the Bible and Testament, the meanings of which books are always controverted, and the authenticity of which is disproved, it is necessary that we refer to the Bible of the creation. The principles we discover there are eternal, and of divine origin; they are the foundation of all the science that exists in the world, and must be the foundation of theology.

We can know God only through his works. We cannot have a conception of any one attribute but by following some principle that leads to it. We have only a confused idea of his powers if we have not the means of comprehending something of its immensity. We can have no idea of his wisdom but by knowing the order and manner in which it acts. The principles of science lead to this knowledge; for the
20 Creator of man is the Creator of science; and it is through that medium that man can see God, as it were, face to face.

Could a man be placed in a situation, and endowed with the power of vision, to behold at one view, and to contemplate deliberately, the structure of the universe; to mark the movements of the several planets, the cause of their varying appearances, the unerring order in which they revolve, even to the remotest comet; their connection and dependence on each other, and to know the system of laws established by the Creator that governs and regulates the whole; he would then conceive, far beyond what any church theology can teach him, the power, the wisdom, the vastness, the munificence of the Creator. He would then see that all the knowledge
30 man has of science, and that all the mechanical arts by which he renders his situation comfortable here, are derived from that source; his mind, exalted by the scene and convinced by the fact, would increase in gratitude as it increased in knowledge; his religion or his worship would become united with his improvement as a man; any employment he followed that had connection with the principles of the crea-

---

5 **the study of nothing.** "The Bible-makers have undertaken to give us, in the first chapter of Genesis, an account of the creation; and in doing this they have demonstrated nothing but their ignorance. They make there to have been three days and three nights, evenings, and mornings, before there was any sun; when it is the presence or absence of the sun that is the cause of day and night — and what is called his rising and setting, that of morning and evening. Besides it is a puerile and pitiful idea to suppose the Almighty to say, 'Let there be light.' It is the imperative manner of speaking that a conjuror uses when he says to his cups and balls, 'Presto be gone' and most probably has been taken from it, as Moses and his rod are a conjuror and his wand. Longinus calls this expression the sublime; and by the same rule the conjuror is sublime too; for the manner of speaking is expressively and grammatically the same. When authors and critics talk of the sublime, they see not how nearly it borders on the ridiculous. The sublime of the critics, like some parts of Edmund Burke's sublime and beautiful, is like a windmill just visible in a fog, which imagination might distort into a flying mountain, or an archangel, or a flock of wild geese." — Paine

tion, as everything of agriculture, of science, and of the mechanical arts has, would teach him more of God and of the gratitude he owes to him than any theological Christian sermon he now hears. Great objects inspire great thoughts; great munificence excites great gratitude; but the groveling tales and doctrines of the Bible and the Testament are fit only to excite contempt.

Though man cannot arrive, at least in this life, at the actual scene I have described, he can demonstrate it because he has a knowledge of the principles upon which the creation is constructed. We know that the greatest works can be represented in model, and that the universe can be represented by the same means. The same principles by which we measure an inch or an acre of ground will measure to millions in extent. 10 A circle of an inch diameter has the same geometrical properties as a circle that would circumscribe the universe. The same properties of a triangle that will demonstrate upon paper the course of a ship, will do it on the ocean, and, when applied to what are called the heavenly bodies, will ascertain to a minute the time of an eclipse, though those bodies are millions of miles distant from us. This knowledge is of divine origin, and it is from the Bible of the creation that man has learned it, and not from the stupid Bible of the church that teacheth man nothing.

All the knowledge man has of science and of machinery, by the aid of which his existence is rendered comfortable upon earth, and without which he would be scarcely distinguishable in appearance and condition from a common animal, comes 20 from the great machine and structure of the universe. The constant and unwearied observations of our ancestors upon the movements and revolutions of the heavenly bodies, in what are supposed to have been the early ages of the world, have brought this knowledge upon earth. It is not Moses and the prophets nor Jesus Christ, nor his apostles that have done it. The Almighty is the great mechanic of the creation; the first philosopher and original teacher of all science. Let us then learn to reverence our master, and not forget the labor of our ancestors.

Had we, at this day, no knowledge of machinery, and were it possible that man could have a view, as I have before described, of the structure and machinery of the universe, he would soon conceive the idea of constructing some at least of the 30 mechanical works we now have; and the idea so conceived would progressively advance in practice. Or could a model of the universe, such as is called orrery, be presented before him and put in motion, his mind would arrive at the same idea. Such an object and such a subject would, whilst it improved him in knowledge useful to himself as a man and a member of society, as well as entertaining, afford far better matter for impressing him with a knowledge of and a belief in the Creator, and of the reverence and gratitude that a man owes to him, than the stupid texts of the Bible and the Testament, from which, be the talents of the preacher what they may, only stupid sermons can be preached. If man must preach, let him preach something that is edifying, and from the texts that are known to be true.   40

The Bible of the Creation is inexhaustible in texts. Every part of the science, whether connected with the geometry of the universe, with the systems of animal and vegetable life, or with the properties of inanimate matter, is a text as well for devotion as for philosophy — for gratitude as for human improvement. It will perhaps be said that if such a revolution in the system of religion takes place, every preacher ought to be a philosopher. *Most certainly;* and every house of devotion a school of science.

It has been by wandering from the immutable laws of science and the light of reason, and setting up an invented thing called revealed religion, that so many wild and blasphemous conceits have been formed of the Almighty. The Jews have made him the assassin of the human species, to make room for the religion of the Jews. The Christians have made him the murderer of himself, and the founder of a new religion, to supersede and expel the Jewish religion. And to find pretense and admis-
10 sion for these things, they must have supposed his power or his wisdom imperfect, or his will changeable; and the changeableness of the will is the imperfection of the judgment. The philosopher knows that the laws of the Creator have never changed with respect either to the principles of science or the properties of matter. Why, then, is it to be supposed they have changed with respect to man?

I here close the subject. I have shown in all the foregoing parts of this work that the bible and testament are impositions and forgeries; and I leave the evidence I have produced in proof of it to be refuted, if anyone can do it; and I leave the ideas that are suggested in the conclusion of the work to rest on the mind of the reader; certain, as I am, that when opinions are free, either in matters of government or
20 religion, truth will finally and powerfully prevail.

1793, 1794-1795

1780—1842 William Ellery Channing

William Ellery Channing entered Harvard College in 1794, just in time to encounter the unrest which was leading to the conservative reaction against the French Revolution. In later years he recalled that the "old foundations of social order, loyalty, tradition, habit, reverence for antiquity, were everywhere shaken, if not subverted. The authority of the past was gone. The old forms were outgrown, and new ones had not taken their place. The tone of books and conversation was presumptuous and daring. The tendency of all classes was to scepticism." That last decade of the eighteenth century was indeed a trying era. In 1796 the Harvard Corporation thought it wise to provide every student with a copy of Richard Watson's Apology for the Bible, *ablest of the replies to Paine's* The Age of Reason, *and at New Haven, Timothy Dwight (p. 533) discoursed to Yale seniors on* The Nature, and Danger, of Infidel Philosophy *(1798). Religion and politics were poised precariously between old ways and new.*

Channing gradually emerged as the spokesman for almost every liberal humanitarian doctrine of his age. More intellectual than Dwight, temperamentally averse to controversy, and for the most of his life an invalid, Channing had leadership thrust upon him, the kind of leadership that comes sometimes to studious, thoughtful men who are also unselfish and fearless. Slowly and coolly he spoke out his convictions: that human values and the moral law laid down by God are essentially the same; that personal liberty and absolute freedom of speech are the basis of political health; that slavery and war should be abolished; that the working classes should be protected and educated by the state. Fear of the future, in this world or the next, had no place in his thoughts.

To this position Channing came only gradually. He was born at Newport, Rhode Island, in 1780. After his graduation from Harvard in 1798 he spent a year and a half as a tutor in the home of Daniel Meade Randolph of Richmond, Virginia. There he was disturbed by his glimpses of the institution of slavery but impressed by the political preoccupations of John Marshall and other Virginians. Under their influence he read works he had not encountered at Harvard: modern history, the Deistic writers of the early eighteenth century, and the political radicals — Mary Wollstonecraft, Jean Jacques Rousseau, and William Godwin. When he returned to New England in July 1800, he was, in his quiet way, a perfectionist with a strong sense of social duty.

At Newport and at Cambridge he studied theology with unusual earnestness and independence. In 1803, he was ordained as minister of the Federal Street Church, Boston, where he was soon renowned for his concern with charity and his willingness to bring controversial topics into his pulpit. In 1810, for example, he denounced the military despotism of Napoleon, and in 1812 he spoke out against the declaration of war against England. Self-defense, however, he regarded as a righteous cause, and he stood for resistance when New England was threatened with invasion in 1814.

As early as 1806 Channing was thinking of himself as a "liberal" Christian, and he probably did not share the concern of the conservative, orthodox Congregationalists when Henry Ware, a Unitarian, was appointed to the Hollis professorship of divinity at Harvard in 1805. Particularly disturbed by a proposal to erect "ecclesiastical tribunals" for the purpose, presumably, of reading the liberals out of the Congregational Church, Channing, in The System of Exclusion and Denunciation in Religion Considered *(1815), defended the position of the "Liberal Christians," although he did not like that name. By 1819 he was ready to state his doctrine positively, and* Unitarian Christianity *marks the break with the conservative faction. Channing was thereafter the acknowledged leader of a new church. He helped organize the American Unitarian Association in 1825, preached many ordination sermons before Unitarian societies, and was one of the chief contributors to* The Christian Examiner, *which became one of the most influential religious reviews of the period. In its pages appeared such famous essays as "The Moral Argument Against Calvinism" (1820), "Remarks on the Character and Writings of John Milton" (1826), and "The Importance and Means of a National Literature" (1830).*

Channing's literary theories, and his anticipation of many of the fundamental positions of the Transcendentalists, are well expressed in a single paragraph from his private journal, composed at about the time of Unitarian Christianity. *"Good preaching never enraptures an audience by beauties of style, elocution, or gesture," he wrote. "An easy, unbalanced, unlabored style should be the common mode of expression. This will give relief and prominence to more important parts, and insure variety. Composition should resemble nature. Dazzling objects soon fatigue the eye. Simple truth, in plain, perspicuous words, should form the body of the discourse, and all appeals of peculiarly solemnizing, melting, invigorating character should be introduced in the way of transition. By simple truth, staleness and tameness are not meant, for there should always be richness of thought. A sermon should never be a barren sand-level of commonplaces, but a fresh, fertile field, verdant and well watered. In style, as in music, there should be a key, which should change with the topic. Let clearness, dignity, unstrained vigor, elevation without turgidness, purity without primness, pathos without whining, characterize my style. Let me study to be filled with the spirit of the truth I am to utter, and I shall speak as I ought. A slow, distinct, and rather low enunciation should form the ground of delivery. It is better to require exertion on the part of the hearer, than to stun him with clamor."*

The Works of William E. Channing, D.D., 6 vols., Boston, 1841-1843   W. H. Channing, The Life of William Ellery Channing, D.D., Centenary Memorial Edition, Boston, 1880   David P. Edgell, William Ellery Channing, an Intellectual Portrait, Boston, 1954   A. W. Brown, Always Young for Liberty: A Biography of William Ellery Channing, Syracuse, 1956   Madeleine H. Rice, Federal Street Pastor: The Life of William Ellery Channing, New York, 1961

Unitarian Christianity

Discourse at the Ordination of the Rev. Jared Sparks

The following sermon, delivered at Baltimore in 1819, began a theological controversy in which the chief works were attacks by Moses Stuart and Leonard Woods of the Andover Theological Seminary and defenses by Andrews Norton and Henry Ware of the liberal faction. Jared Sparks (1789-1866), at whose ordination the discourse was delivered, left the Baltimore pulpit in 1823, and later distinguished himself as an editor, historian, and president of Harvard (1849-1853). It will be observed that Channing does not preach directly upon his text, although he retains a systematic method reminiscent of earlier sermons. The simplicity and clarity are typical of all his best work.

1 THES. v. 21: "Prove all things; hold fast that which is good."

The peculiar circumstances of this occasion not only justify, but seem to demand a departure from the course generally followed by preachers at the introduction of a brother into the sacred office. It is usual to speak of the nature, design, duties, and advantages of the Christian ministry; and on these topics I should now be happy to insist, did I not remember that a minister is to be given this day to a religious society, whose peculiarities of opinion have drawn upon them much remark, and may I not add, much reproach. Many good minds, many sincere Christians, I am aware, are apprehensive that the solemnities of this day are to give a degree of influence to principles which they deem false and injurious. The fears and anxieties 10 of such men I respect; and, believing that they are grounded in part on mistake, I have thought it my duty to lay before you, as clearly as I can, some of the distin-

Text: *Works*, Vol. III, 8th ed., 1848   7 **much reproach.** Unitarianism, although not openly professed by many clergymen, had long been regarded as a dangerous heresy in New England and had been vigorously attacked in *The Panoplist* since 1815

guishing opinions of that class of Christians in our country, who are known to sympathize with this religious society. I must ask your patience, for such a subject is not to be despatched in a narrow compass. I must also ask you to remember, that it is impossible to exhibit, in a single discourse, our views of every doctrine of Revelation, much less the differences of opinion which are known to subsist among ourselves. I shall confine myself to topics, on which our sentiments have been misrepresented, or which distinguish us most widely from others. May I not hope to be heard with candor? God deliver us all from prejudice and unkindness, and fill us with the love of truth and virtue.

There are two natural divisions under which my thoughts will be arranged. I shall 10 endeavour to unfold, 1st, The principles which we adopt in interpreting the Scriptures. And 2dly, Some of the doctrines, which the Scriptures, so interpreted, seem to us clearly to express.

I. We regard the Scriptures as the records of God's successive revelations to mankind, and particularly of the last and most perfect revelation of his will by Jesus Christ. Whatever doctrines seem to us to be clearly taught in the Scriptures, we receive without reserve or exception. We do not, however, attach equal importance to all the books in this collection. Our religion, we believe, lies chiefly in the New Testament. The dispensation of Moses, compared with that of Jesus, we consider as adapted to the childhood of the human race, a preparation for a nobler system, and 20 chiefly useful now as serving to confirm and illustrate the Christian Scriptures. Jesus Christ is the only master of Christians, and whatever he taught, either during his personal ministry, or by his inspired Apostles, we regard as of divine authority, and profess to make the rule of our lives.

This authority, which we give to the Scriptures, is a reason, we conceive, for studying them with peculiar care, and for inquiring anxiously into the principles of interpretation, by which their true meaning may be ascertained. The principles adopted by the class of Christians in whose name I speak, need to be explained, because they are often misunderstood. We are particularly accused of making an unwarrantable use of reason in the interpretation of Scripture. We are said to exalt 30 reason above revelation, to prefer our own wisdom to God's. Loose and undefined charges of this kind are circulated so freely, that we think it due to ourselves, and to the cause of truth, to express our views with some particularity.

Our leading principle in interpreting Scripture is this, that the Bible is a book written for men, in the language of men, and that its meaning is to be sought in the same manner as that of other books. We believe that God, when he speaks to the human race, conforms, if we may so say, to the established rules of speaking and writing. How else would the Scriptures avail us more, than if communicated in an unknown tongue?

Now all books, and all conversation, require in the reader or hearer the constant 40 exercise of reason; or their true import is only to be obtained by continual comparison and inference. Human language, you well know, admits various interpretations; and every word and every sentence must be modified and explained according to the subject which is discussed, according to the purposes, feelings, circumstances, and principles of the writer, and according to the genius and idioms of the language which he uses. These are acknowledged principles in the interpretation of human writings; and a man, whose words we should explain without reference to these principles, would reproach us justly with a criminal want of candor, and an intention of obscuring or distorting his meaning.

Were the Bible written in a language and style of its own, did it consist of words, which admit but a single sense, and of sentences wholly detached from each other, there would be no place for the principles now laid down. We could not reason about it, as about other writings. But such a book would be of little worth; and

10 perhaps, of all books, the Scriptures correspond least to this description. The Word of God bears the stamp of the same hand, which we see in his works. It has infinite connexions and dependences. Every proposition is linked with others, and is to be compared with others; that its full and precise import may be understood. Nothing stands alone. The New Testament is built on the Old. The Christian dispensation is a continuation of the Jewish, the completion of a vast scheme of providence, requiring great extent of view in the reader. Still more, the Bible treats of subjects on which we receive ideas from other sources besides itself; such subjects as the nature, passions, relations, and duties of man; and it expects us to restrain and modify its language by the known truths, which observation and experience furnish

20 on these topics.

We profess not to know a book, which demands a more frequent exercise of reason than the Bible. In addition to the remarks now made on its infinite connexions, we may observe, that its style nowhere affects the precision of science, or the accuracy of definition. Its language is singularly glowing, bold, and figurative, demanding more frequent departures from the literal sense, than that of our own age and country, and consequently demanding more continual exercise of judgment. — We find, too, that the different portions of this book, instead of being confined to general truths, refer perpetually to the times when they were written, to states of society, to modes of thinking, to controversies in the church, to feelings and usages

30 which have passed away, and without the knowledge of which we are constantly in danger of extending to all times, and places, what was of temporary and local application. — We find, too, that some of these books are strongly marked by the genius and character of their respective writers, that the Holy Spirit did not so guide the Apostles as to suspend the peculiarities of their minds, and that a knowledge of their feelings, and of the influences under which they were placed, is one of the preparations for understanding their writings. With these views of the Bible, we feel it our bounden duty to exercise our reason upon it perpetually, to compare, to infer, to look beyond the letter to the spirit, to seek in the nature of the subject, and the aim of the writer, his true meaning; and, in general, to make use of what

40 is known, for explaining what is difficult, and for discovering new truths. . . .

II. Having thus stated the principles according to which we interpret Scripture, I now proceed to the second great head of this discourse, which is, to state some of

---

40 **truths.** . . . Seven paragraphs, in defense of human reason, are here omitted

the views we derive from that sacred book, particularly those which distinguish us from other Christians.

1. In the first place, we believe in the doctrine of God's UNITY, or that there is one God, and one only. To this truth we give infinite importance, and we feel ourselves bound to take heed, lest any man spoil us of it by vain philosophy. The proposition, that there is one God, seems to us exceedingly plain. We understand by it, that there is one being, one mind, one person, one intelligent agent, and one only, to whom underived and infinite perfection and dominion belong. We conceive, that these words could have conveyed no other meaning to the simple and uncultivated people, who were set apart to be the depositaries of this great truth, and who were 10 utterly incapable of understanding those hair-breadth distinctions between being and person, which the sagacity of later ages has discovered. We find no intimation, that this language was to be taken in an unusual sense, or that God's unity was a quite different thing from the oneness of other intelligent beings. . . .

2. Having thus given our views of the unity of God, I proceed in the second place to observe, that we believe in the unity of Jesus Christ. We believe that Jesus is one mind, one soul, one being, as truly one as we are, and equally distinct from the one God. We complain of the doctrine of the Trinity, that, not satisfied with making God three beings, it makes Jesus Christ two beings, and thus introduces infinite confusion into our conceptions of his character. This corruption of Chris- 20 tianity, alike repugnant to common sense and to the general strain of Scripture, is a remarkable proof of the power of a false philosophy in disfiguring the simple truth of Jesus.

According to this doctine, Jesus Christ, instead of being one mind, one conscious intelligent principle, whom we can understand, consists of two souls, two minds; the one divine, the other human; the one weak, the other almighty; the one ignorant, the other omniscient. Now we maintain, that this is to make Christ two beings. To denominate him one person, one being, and yet to suppose him made up of two minds, infinitely different from each other, is to abuse and confound language, and to throw darkness over all our conceptions of intelligent natures. According to 30 the common doctrine, each of these two minds in Christ has its own consciousness, its own will, its own perceptions. They have, in fact, no common properties. The divine mind feels none of the wants and sorrows of the human, and the human is infinitely removed from the perfection and happiness of the divine. Can you conceive of two beings in the universe more distinct? We have always thought that one person was constituted and distinguished by one consciousness. The doctrine, that one and the same person should have two consciousnesses, two wills, two souls, infinitely different from each other, this we think an enormous tax on human credulity.

We say, that if a doctrine, so strange, so difficult, so remote from all the previous conceptions of men, be indeed a part and an essential part of revelation, it must be 40 taught with great distinctness, and we ask our brethren to point to some plain, direct passage, where Christ is said to be composed of two minds infinitely different, yet

---

14 **intelligent beings.** . . . Six paragraphs, an argument that the Trinitarian doctrine subverts the unity of God, are omitted

constituting one person. We find none. Other Christians, indeed, tell us, that this doctrine is necessary to the harmony of the Scriptures, that some texts ascribe to Jesus Christ human, and others divine properties, and that to reconcile these, we must suppose two minds, to which these properties may be referred. In other words, for the purpose of reconciling certain difficult passages, which a just criticism can in a great degree, if not wholly, explain, we must invent an hypothesis vastly more difficult, and involving gross absurdity. We are to find our way out of a labyrinth, by a clue which conducts us into mazes infinitely more inextricable.

Surely, if Jesus Christ felt that he consisted of two minds, and that this was a
10 leading feature of his religion, his phraseology respecting himself would have been colored by this peculiarity. The universal language of men is framed upon the idea, that one person is one person, is one mind, and one soul; and when the multitude heard this language from the lips of Jesus, they must have taken it in its usual sense, and must have referred to a single soul all which he spoke, unless expressly instructed to interpret it differently. But where do we find this instruction? Where do you meet, in the New Testament, the phraseology which abounds in Trinitarian books, and which necessarily grows from the doctrine of two natures in Jesus? Where does this divine teacher say, "This I speak as God, and this as man; this is true only of human mind, this only of my divine"? Where do we find in the
20 Epistles a trace of this strange phraseology? Nowhere. It was not needed in that day. It was demanded by the errors of a later age.

We believe, then, that Christ is one mind, one being, and, I add, a being distinct from the one God. That Christ is not the one God, not the same being with the Father, is a necessary inference from our former head, in which we saw that the doctrine of three persons in God is a fiction. But on so important a subject, I would add a few remarks. We wish, that those from whom we differ, would weigh one striking fact. Jesus, in his preaching, continually spoke of God. The word was always in his mouth. We ask, does he, by this word, ever mean himself? We say, never. On the contrary, he most plainly distinguishes between God and him-
30 self, and so do his disciples. How this is to be reconciled with the idea, that the manifestation of Christ, as God, was a primary object of Christianity, our adversaries must determine.

If we examine the passages in which Jesus is distinguished from God, we shall see, that they not only speak of him as another being, but seem to labor to express his inferiority. He is continually spoken of as the Son of God, sent of God, receiving all his powers from God, working miracles because God was with him, judging justly because God taught him, having claims on our belief, because he was anointed and sealed by God, and as able of himself to do nothing. The New Testament is filled with this language. Now we ask, what impression this language was fitted
40 and intended to make? Could any, who heard it, have imagined that Jesus was the very God to whom he was so industriously declared to be inferior; the very Being by whom he was sent, and from whom he professed to have received his message and power? Let it here be remembered, that the human birth, and bodily form, and humble circumstances, and mortal sufferings of Jesus, must all have prepared men

to interpret, in the most unqualified manner, the language in which his inferiority to God was declared. Why, then, was this language used so continually, and without limitation, if Jesus were the Supreme Deity, and if this truth were an essential part of his religion? I repeat it, the human condition and sufferings of Christ tended strongly to exclude from men's minds the idea of his proper Godhead; and of course, we should expect to find in the New Testament perpetual care and effort to counteract this tendency, to hold him forth as the same being with his Father, if this doctrine were, as is pretended, the soul and centre of his religion. We should expect to find the phraseology of Scripture cast into the mould of this doctrine, to hear familiarly of God the Son, of our Lord God Jesus, and to be told, that to us 10 there is one God, even Jesus. But, instead of this, the inferiority of Christ pervades the New Testament. It is not only implied in the general phraseology, but repeatedly and decidedly expressed, and unaccompanied with any admonition to prevent its application to his whole nature. Could it, then, have been the great design of the sacred writers to exhibit Jesus as the Supreme God?

I am aware that these remarks will be met by two or three texts, in which Christ is called God, and by a class of passages, not very numerous, in which divine properties are said to be ascribed to him. To these we offer one plain answer. We say, that it is one of the most established and obvious principles of criticism, that language is to be explained according to the known properties of the subject to which 20 it is applied. Every man knows, that the same words convey very different ideas, when used in relation to different beings. Thus, Solomon *built* the temple in a different manner from the architect whom he employed; and God *repents* differently from man. Now we maintain, that the known properties and circumstances of Christ, his birth, sufferings, and death, his constant habit of speaking of God as a distinct being from himself, his praying to God, his ascribing to God all his power and offices, these acknowledged properties of Christ, we say, oblige us to interpret the comparatively few passages which are thought to make him the Supreme God, in a manner consistent with his distinct and inferior nature. It is our duty to explain such texts by the rule which we apply to other texts, in which human beings 30 are called gods, and are said to be partakers of the divine nature, to know and possess all things, and to be filled with all God's fulness. These latter passages we do not hesitate to modify, and restrain, and turn from the most obvious sense, because this sense is opposed to the known properties of the beings to whom they relate; and we maintain, that we adhere to the same principle, and use no greater latitude, in explaining, as we do, the passages which are thought to support the Godhead of Christ.

Trinitarians profess to derive some important advantages from their mode of viewing Christ. It furnishes them, they tell us, with an infinite atonement, for it shows them an infinite being suffering for their sins. The confidence with which 40

---

39 **infinite atonement.** The doctrine of the atonement had long been one of the central problems in New England theology and has always led to wide diversity of opinion. Did Christ suffer death on the cross to expiate the sins of the human race or to satisfy the honor of God? Interpretation of the atonement involves the Christian's whole conception of God and of the processes of salvation

this fallacy is repeated astonishes us. When pressed with the question, whether they really believe, that the infinite and unchangeable God suffered and died on the cross, they acknowledge that this is not true, but that Christ's human mind alone sustained the pains of death. How have we, then, an infinite sufferer? This language seems to us an imposition on common minds, and very derogatory to God's justice, as if this attribute could be satisfied by a sophism and a fiction.

We are also told, that Christ is a more interesting object, that his love and mercy are more felt, when he is viewed as the Supreme God, who left his glory to take humanity and to suffer for men. That Trinitarians are strongly moved by this representation, we do not mean to deny; but we think their emotions altogether founded on a misapprehension of their own doctrines. They talk of the second person of the Trinity's leaving his glory and his Father's bosom, to visit and save the world. But this second person, being the unchangeable and infinite God, was evidently incapable of parting with the least degree of his perfection and felicity. At the moment of his taking flesh, he was as intimately present with his Father as before, and equally with his Father filled heaven, and earth, and immensity. This Trinitarians acknowledge; and still they profess to be touched and overwhelmed by the amazing humiliation of this immutable being! But not only does their doctrine, when fully explained, reduce Christ's humiliation to a fiction, it almost wholly destroys the impressions with which his cross ought to be viewed. According to their doctrine, Christ was comparatively no sufferer at all. It is true, his human mind suffered; but this, they tell us, was an infinitely small part of Jesus, bearing no more proportion to his whole nature, than a single hair of our heads to the whole body, or than a drop to the ocean. The divine mind of Christ, that which was most properly himself, was infinitely happy, at the very moment of the suffering of his humanity. Whilst hanging on the cross, he was the happiest being in the universe, as happy as the infinite Father; so that his pains, compared with his felicity, were nothing. This Trinitarians do, and must, acknowledge. It follows necessarily from the immutableness of the divine nature, which they ascribe to Christ; so that their system, justly viewed, robs his death of interest, weakens our sympathy with his sufferings, and is, of all others, most unfavorable to a love of Christ, founded on a sense of his sacrifices for mankind. We esteem our own views to be vastly more affecting. It is our belief, that Christ's humiliation was real and entire, that the whole Saviour, and not a part of him, suffered, that his crucifixion was a scene of deep and unmixed agony. As we stand round his cross, our minds are not distracted, nor our sensibility weakened, by contemplating him as composed of incongruous and infinitely differing minds, and as having a balance of infinite felicity. We recognize in the dying Jesus but one mind. This, we think, renders his sufferings, and his patience and love in bearing them, incomparably more impressive and affecting than the system we oppose.

3. Having thus given our belief on two great points, namely, that there is one God, and that Jesus Christ is a being distinct from, and inferior to, God, I now proceed to another point, on which we lay still greater stress. We believe in the *moral perfection of God.* We consider no part of theology so important as that which

treats of God's moral character; and we value our views of Christianity chiefly as they assert his amiable and venerable attributes.

It may be said, that, in regard to this subject, all Christians agree, that all ascribe to the Supreme Being infinite justice, goodness, and holiness. We reply, that it is very possible to speak of God magnificently, and to think of him meanly; to apply to his person high-sounding epithets, and to his government, principles which make him odious. The Heathens called Jupiter the greatest and the best; but his history was black with cruelty and lust. We cannot judge of men's real ideas of God by their general language, for in all ages they have hoped to soothe the Deity by adulation. We must inquire into their particular views of his purposes, of the principles of his administration, and of his disposition towards his creatures.

We conceive that Christians have generally leaned towards a very injurious view of the Supreme Being. They have too often felt as if he were raised, by his greatness and sovereignty, above the principles of morality, above those eternal laws of equity and rectitude, to which all other beings are subjected. We believe that in no being is the sense of right so strong, so omnipotent, as in God. We believe that his almighty power is entirely submitted to his perceptions of rectitude; and this is the ground of our piety. It is not because he is our Creator merely, but because he created us for good and holy purposes; it is not because his will is irresistible, but because his will is the perfection of virtue, that we pay him allegiance. We cannot bow before a being, however great and powerful, who governs tyrannically. We respect nothing but excellence, whether on earth or in heaven. We venerate not the loftiness of God's throne, but the equity and goodness in which it is established.

We believe that God is infinitely good, kind, benevolent, in the proper sense of these words; good in disposition, as well as in act; good, not to a few, but to all; good to every individual, as well as to the general system.

We believe, too, that God is just; but we never forget, that his justice is the justice of a good being, dwelling in the same mind, and acting in harmony, with perfect benevolence. By this attribute, we understand God's infinite regard to virtue or moral worth, expressed in a moral government; that is, in giving excellent and equitable laws, and in conferring such rewards, and inflicting such punishments, as are best fitted to secure their observance. God's justice has for its end the highest virtue of the creation, and it punishes for this end alone, and thus it coincides with benevolence; for virtue and happiness, though not the same, are inseparably conjoined.

God's justice thus viewed, appears to us to be in perfect harmony with his mercy. According to the prevalent systems of theology, these attributes are so discordant and jarring, that to reconcile them is the hardest task, and the most wonderful achievement, of infinite wisdom. To us they seem to be intimate friends, always at peace, breathing the same spirit, and seeking the same end. By God's mercy, we understand not a blind instinctive compassion, which forgives without reflection, and without regard to the interests of virtue. This, we acknowledge, would be incompatible with justice, and also with enlightened benevolence. God's mercy, as we understand it, desires strongly the happiness of the guilty, but only through

---

12 **injurious . . . Being.** The point made here was expanded by Channing in "The Moral Argument against Calvinism"

their penitence. It has a regard to character as truly as his justice. It defers punishment, and suffers long, that the sinner may return to his duty, but leaves the impenitent and unyielding, to the fearful retribution threatened in God's Word.

To give our views of God in one word, we believe in his Parental character. We ascribe to him, not only the name, but the dispositions and principles of a father. We believe that he has a father's concern for his creatures, a father's desire for their improvement, a father's equity in proportioning his commands to their powers, a father's joy in their progress, a father's readiness to receive the penitent, and a father's justice for the incorrigible. We look upon this world as a place of education, in which he is training men by prosperity and adversity, by aids and obstructions, by conflicts of reason and passion, by motives to duty and temptations to sin, by a various discipline suited to free and moral beings, for union with himself, and for a sublime and ever-growing virtue in heaven.

Now, we object to the systems of religion, which prevail among us, that they are adverse, in a greater or less degree, to these purifying, comforting, and honorable views of God; that they take from us our Father in heaven, and substitute for him a being, whom we cannot love if we would, and whom we ought not to love if we could. We object, particularly on this ground, to that system, which arrogates to itself the name of Orthodoxy, and which is now industriously propagated through our country. This system indeed takes various shapes, but in all it casts dishonor on the Creator. According to its old and genuine form, it teaches, that God brings us into life wholly depraved, so that under the innocent features of our childhood is hidden a nature averse to all good and propense to all evil, a nature which exposes us to God's displeasure and wrath, even before we have acquired power to understand our duties, or to reflect upon our actions. According to a more modern exposition, it teaches, that we came from the hands of our Maker with such a constitution, and are placed under such influences and circumstances, as to render certain and infallible the total depravity of every human being, from the first moment of his moral agency; and it also teaches, that the offence of the child, who brings into life this ceaseless tendency to unmingled crime, exposes him to the sentence of everlasting damnation. Now, according to the plainest principles of morality, we maintain, that a natural constitution of the mind, unfailingly disposing it to evil and to evil alone, would absolve it from guilt; that to give existence under this condition would argue unspeakable cruelty; and that to punish the sin of this unhappily constituted child with endless ruin, would be a wrong unparalleled by the most merciless despotism.

This system also teaches, that God selects from this corrupt mass a number to be saved, and plucks them, by a special influence, from the common ruin; that the rest of mankind, though left without that special grace which their conversion requires, are commanded to repent, under penalty of aggravated woe; and that forgiveness is promised them, on terms which their very constitution infallibly disposes them to reject, and in rejecting which they awfully enhance the punishments of hell. These proffers of forgiveness and exhortations of amendment, to beings

---

18 **that system,** Calvinism

born under a blighting curse, fill our minds with a horror which we want words to express.

That this religious system does not produce all the effects on character, which might be anticipated, we most joyfully admit. It is often, very often, counteracted by nature, conscience, common sense, by the general strain of Scripture, by the mild example and precepts of Christ, and by the many positive declarations of God's universal kindness and perfect equity. But still we think that we see its unhappy influence. It tends to discourage the timid, to give excuses to the bad, to feed the vanity of the fanatical, and to offer shelter to the bad feelings of the malignant. By shocking, as it does, the fundamental principles of morality, and by exhibiting a severe and partial Deity, it tends strongly to pervert the moral faculty, to form a gloomy, forbidding, and servile religion, and to lead men to substitute censoriousness, bitterness, and persecution, for a tender and impartial charity. We think, too, that this system, which begins with degrading human nature, may be expected to end in pride; for pride grows out of a consciousness of high distinctions, however obtained, and no distinction is so great as that which is made between the elected and abandoned of God.

The false and dishonorable views of God, which have now been stated, we feel ourselves bound to resist unceasingly. Other errors we can pass over with comparative indifference. But we ask our opponents to leave to us a GOD, worthy of our love and trust, in whom our moral sentiments may delight, in whom our weaknesses and sorrows may find refuge. We cling to the Divine perfections. We meet them everywhere in creation, we read them in the Scriptures, we see a lovely image of them in Jesus Christ; and gratitude, love, and veneration call on us to assert them. Reproached, as we often are, by men, it is our consolation and happiness, that one of our chief offences is the zeal with which we vindicate the dishonored goodness and rectitude of God.

4. Having thus spoken of the unity of God; of the unity of Jesus, and his inferiority to God; and of the perfections of the Divine character; I now proceed to give our views of the mediation of Christ, and of the purposes of his mission. With regard to the great object which Jesus came to accomplish, there seems to be no possibility of mistake. We believe, that he was sent by the Father to effect a moral, or spiritual deliverance of mankind; that is, to rescue men from sin and its consequences, and to bring them to a state of everlasting purity and happiness. We believe, too, that he accomplishes this sublime purpose by a variety of methods; by his instructions respecting God's unity, parental character, and moral government, which are admirably fitted to reclaim the world from idolatry and impiety, to the knowledge, love, and obedience of the Creator; by his promises of pardon to the penitent, and of divine assistance to those who labor for progress in moral excellence; by the light which he has thrown on the path of duty; by his own spotless example, in which the loveliness and sublimity of virtue shine forth to warm and quicken, as well as guide us to perfection; by his threatenings against incorrigible guilt; by his glorious discoveries of immortality; by his sufferings and death; by that signal event, the resurrection, which powerfully bore witness to his divine mis-

sion, and brought down to men's senses a future life; by his continual intercession, which obtains for us spiritual aid and blessings; and by the power with which he is invested of raising the dead, judging the world, and conferring the everlasting rewards promised to the faithful.

We have no desire to conceal the fact, that a difference of opinion exists among us, in regard to an interesting part of Christ's mediation; I mean, in regard to the precise influence of his death on our forgiveness. Many suppose, that this event contributes to our pardon, as it was a principal means of confirming his religion, and of giving it a power over the mind; in other words, that it procures forgiveness by leading to that repentance and virtue, which is the great and only condition on which forgiveness is bestowed. Many of us are dissatisfied with this explanation, and think that the Scriptures ascribe the remission of sins to Christ's death, with an emphasis so peculiar, that we ought to consider this event as having a special influence in removing punishment, though the Scriptures may not reveal the way in which it contributes to this end.

Whilst, however, we differ in explaining the connexion between Christ's death and human forgiveness, a connexion which we all gratefully acknowledge, we agree in rejecting many sentiments which prevail in regard to his mediation. The idea, which is conveyed to common minds by the popular system, that Christ's death has an influence in making God placable, or merciful, in awakening his kindness towards men, we reject with strong disapprobation. We are happy to find, that this very dishonorable notion is disowned by intelligent Christians of that class from which we differ. We recollect, however, that, not long ago, it was common to hear of Christ, as having died to appease God's wrath, and to pay the debt of sinners to his inflexible justice; and we have a strong persuasion that the language of popular religious books, and the common mode of stating the doctrine of Christ's mediation, still communicate very degrading views of God's character. They give to multitudes the impression, that the death of Jesus produces a change in the mind of God towards man, and that in this its efficacy chiefly consists. No error seems to us more pernicious. We can endure no shade over the pure goodness of God. We earnestly maintain, that Jesus, instead of calling forth, in any way or degree, the mercy of the Father, was sent by that mercy, to be our Saviour; that he is nothing to the human race, but what he is by God's appointment; that he communicates nothing but what God empowers him to bestow; that our Father in heaven is originally, essentially, and eternally placable, and disposed to forgive; and that his unborrowed, underived, and unchangeable love is the only fountain of what flows to us through his Son. We conceive, that Jesus is dishonored, not glorified, by ascribing to him an influence, which clouds the splendor of Divine benevolence.

We farther agree in rejecting, as unscriptural and absurd, the explanation given by the popular system, of the manner in which Christ's death procures forgiveness for men. This system used to teach as its fundamental principle, that man, having sinned against an infinite Being, has contracted infinite guilt, and is consequently exposed to an infinite penalty. We believe, however, that this reasoning, if reason-

---

5 **a difference of opinion,** on the doctrine of the atonement

ing it may be called, which overlooks the obvious maxim, that the guilt of a being must be proportioned to his nature and powers, has fallen into disuse. Still the system teaches, that sin, of whatever degree, exposes to endless punishment, and that the whole human race, being infallibly involved by their nature in sin, owe this awful penalty to the justice of their Creator. It teaches, that this penalty cannot be remitted, in consistency with the honor of the divine law, unless a substitute be found to endure it or to suffer an equivalent. It also teaches, that, from the nature of the case, no substitute is adequate to this work, save the infinite God himself; and accordingly, God, in his second person, took on him human nature, that he might pay to his own justice the debt of punishment incurred by men, and might thus reconcile forgiveness with the claims and threatenings of his law. Such is the prevalent system. Now, to us, this doctrine seems to carry on its front strong marks of absurdity; and we maintain that Christianity ought not to be encumbered with it, unless it be laid down in the New Testament fully and expressly. We ask our adversaries, then, to point to some plain passages where it is taught. We ask for one text, in which we are told, that God took human nature that he might make an infinite satisfaction to his own justice; for one text, which tells us, that human guilt requires an infinite substitute; that Christ's sufferings owe their efficacy to their being borne by an infinite being; or that his divine nature gives infinite value to the sufferings of the human. Not *one word* of this description can we find in the Scriptures; not a text, which even hints at these strange doctrines. They are altogether, we believe, the fictions of theologians. Christianity is in no degree responsible for them. We are astonished at their prevalence. What can be plainer, than that God cannot, in any sense, be a sufferer, or bear a penalty in the room of his creatures? How dishonorable to him is the supposition, that his justice is now so severe, as to exact infinite punishment for the sins of frail and feeble men, and now so easy and yielding, as to accept the limited pains of Christ's human soul, as a full equivalent for the endless woes due from the world? How plain is it also, according to this doctrine, that God, instead of being plenteous in forgiveness, never forgives; for it seems absurd to speak of men as forgiven, when their whole punishment, or an equivalent to it, is borne by a substitute? A scheme more fitted to obscure the brightness of Christianity and the mercy of God, or less suited to give comfort to a guilty and troubled mind, could not, we think, be easily framed.

We believe, too, that this system is unfavorable to the character. It naturally leads men to think, that Christ came to change God's mind rather than their own; that the highest object of his mission was to avert punishment, rather than to communicate holiness; and that a large part of religion consists in disparaging good works and human virtue, for the purpose of magnifying the value of Christ's vicarious sufferings. In this way, a sense of the infinite importance and indispensable necessity of personal improvement is weakened, and high-sounding praises of Christ's cross seem often to be substituted for obedience to his precepts. For ourselves, we have not so learned Jesus. Whilst we gratefully acknowledge, that he came to rescue us from punishment, we believe, that he was sent on a still nobler errand, namely, to deliver us from sin itself, and to form us to a sublime and heavenly virtue. We regard him as a Saviour, chiefly as he is the light, physician, and guide of the dark, diseased, and wandering mind. No influence in the universe seems to us so glorious, as that over the character; and no redemption so worthy of thankfulness, as the restoration of the soul to purity. Without this, pardon, were it possible, would be of little value. Why pluck the sinner from hell, if a hell be left to burn in his own breast? Why raise him to heaven, if he remain a stranger to its sanctity and love? With these impressions, we are accustomed to value the Gospel chiefly as it abounds in effectual aids, motives, excitements to a generous and divine virtue. In this virtue, as in a common centre, we see all its doctrines, precepts, promises meet; and we believe, that faith in this religion is of no worth, and contributes nothing to salvation, any farther than as it uses these doctrines, precepts, promises, and the whole life, character, sufferings, and triumphs of Jesus, as the means of purifying the mind, of changing it into the likeness of his celestial excellence.

5. Having thus stated our views of the highest object of Christ's mission, that it is the recovery of men to virtue, or holiness, I shall now, in the last place, give our views of the nature of Christian virtue, or true holiness. We believe that all virtue has its foundation in the moral nature of man, that is, in conscience, or his sense of duty, and in the power of forming his temper and life according to conscience. We believe that these moral faculties are the grounds of responsibility, and the highest distinctions of human nature, and that no act is praiseworthy, any farther than it springs from their exertion. We believe, that no dispositions infused into us without our own moral activity, are of the nature of virtue, and therefore, we reject the doctrine of irresistible divine influence on the human mind, moulding it into goodness, as marble is hewn into a statue. Such goodness, if this word may be used, would not be the object of moral approbation, any more than the instinctive affections of inferior animals, or the constitutional amiableness of human beings.

By these remarks, we do not mean to deny the importance of God's aid or Spirit; but by his Spirit, we mean a moral, illuminating, and persuasive influence, not physical, not compulsory, not involving a necessity of virtue. We object, strongly, to the idea of many Christians respecting man's impotence and God's irresistible agency on the heart, believing that they subvert our responsibility and the laws of our moral nature, that they make men machines, that they cast on God the blame of all evil deeds, that they discourage good minds, and inflate the fanatical with wild conceits of immediate and sensible inspiration.

Among the virtues, we give the first place to the love of God. We believe, that this principle is the true end and happiness of our being, that we were made for union with our Creator, that his infinite perfection is the only sufficient object and true resting-place for the insatiable desires and unlimited capacities of the human mind, and that, without him, our noblest sentiments, admiration, veneration, hope, and love, would wither and decay. We believe, too, that the love of God is not only essential to happiness, but to the strength and perfection of all the virtues; that conscience, without the sanction of God's authority and retributive justice, would be a weak director; that benevolence, unless nourished by communion with his goodness, and encouraged by his smile, could not thrive amidst the selfishness and thank-

lessness of the world; and that self-government, without a sense of the divine inspection, would hardly extend beyond an outward and partial purity. God, as he is
essentially goodness, holiness, justice, and virtue, so he is the life, motive, and sus-
tainer of virtue in the human soul.

But, whilst we earnestly inculcate the love of God, we believe that great care is
necessary to distinguish it from counterfeits. We think that much which is called
piety is worthless. Many have fallen into the error, that there can be no excess in
feelings which have God for their object; and, distrusting as coldness that self-
possession, without which virtue and devotion lose all their dignity, they have abandoned themselves to extravagances, which have brought contempt on piety. Most   10
certainly, if the love of God be that which often bears its name, the less we have
of it the better. If religion be the shipwreck of understanding, we cannot keep too
far from it. On this subject, we always speak plainly. We cannot sacrifice our reason to the reputation of zeal. We owe it to truth and religion to maintain, that
fanaticism, partial insanity, sudden impressions, and ungovernable transports, are
any thing rather than piety.

We conceive, that the true love of God is a moral sentiment, founded on a clear
perception, and consisting in a high esteem and veneration, of his moral perfections.
Thus, it perfectly coincides, and is in fact the same thing, with the love of virtue,
rectitude, and goodness. You will easily judge, then, what we esteem the surest and   20
only decisive signs of piety. We lay no stress on strong excitements. We esteem
him, and him only a pious man, who practically conforms to God's moral perfections and government; who shows his delight in God's benevolence, by loving and
serving his neighbour; his delight in God's justice, by being resolutely upright; his
sense of God's purity, by regulating his thoughts, imagination, and desires; and
whose conversation, business, and domestic life are swayed by a regard to God's
presence and authority. In all things else men may deceive themselves. Disordered
nerves may give them strange sights, and sounds, and impressions. Texts of Scripture may come to them as from Heaven. Their whole souls may be moved, and
their confidence in God's favor be undoubting. But in all this there is no religion.   30
The question is, Do they love God's commands, in which his character is fully
expressed, and give up to these their habits and passions? Without this, ecstasy is
a mockery. One surrender of desire to God's will, is worth a thousand transports.
We do not judge of the bent of men's minds by their raptures, any more than we
judge of the natural direction of a tree during a storm. We rather suspect loud profession, for we have observed, that deep feeling is generally noiseless, and least
seeks display.

We would not, by these remarks, be understood as wishing to exclude from religion warmth, and even transport. We honor, and highly value, true religious sensibility. We believe, that Christianity is intended to act powerfully on our whole   40

---

21 **We . . . excitements.** Late in life, asked whether or not he had ever experienced conversion, Channing
replied, "I should say not, unless the whole of my life may be called, as it truly has been a *process* of conversion."
He merits comparison in this respect with Edwards, Chauncy, and Cartwright (see pp. 165, 205, 478)

nature, on the heart as well as the understanding and the conscience. We conceive of heaven as a state where the love of God will be exalted into an unbounded fervor and joy; and we desire, in our pilgrimage here, to drink into the spirit of that better world. But we think, that religious warmth is only to be valued, when it springs naturally from an improved character, when it comes unforced, when it is the recompence of obedience, when it is the warmth of a mind which understands God by being like him, and when, instead of disordering, it exalts the understanding, invigorates conscience, gives a pleasure to common duties, and is seen to exist in connexion with cheerfulness, judiciousness, and a reasonable frame of mind. When we
10 observe a fervor, called religious, in men whose general character expresses little refinement and elevation, and whose piety seems at war with reason, we pay it little respect. We honor religion too much to give its sacred name to a feverish, forced, fluctuating zeal, which has little power over the life.

Another important branch of virtue, we believe to be love to Christ. The greatness of the work of Jesus, the spirit with which he executed it, and the sufferings which he bore for our salvation, we feel to be strong claims on our gratitude and veneration. We see in nature no beauty to be compared with the loveliness of his character, nor do we find on earth a benefactor to whom we owe an equal debt. We read his history with delight, and learn from it the perfection of our nature. We are
20 particularly touched by his death, which was endured for our redemption, and by that strength of charity which triumphed over his pains. His resurrection is the foundation of our hope of immortality. His intercession gives us boldness to draw nigh to the throne of grace, and we look up to heaven with new desire, when we think, that, if we follow him here, we shall there see his benignant countenance, and enjoy his friendship for ever.

I need not express to you our views on the subject of the benevolent virtues. We attach such importance to these, that we are sometimes reproached with exalting them above piety. We regard the spirit of love, charity, meekness, forgiveness, liberality, and beneficence, as the badge and distinction of Christians, as the brightest
30 image we can bear of God, as the best proof of piety. On this subject, I need not, and cannot enlarge; but there is one branch of benevolence which I ought not to pass over in silence, because we think that we conceive of it more highly and justly than many of our brethren. I refer to the duty of candor, charitable judgment, especially towards those who differ in religious opinion. We think, that in nothing have Christians so widely departed from their religion, as in this particular. We read with astonishment and horror, the history of the church; and sometimes when we look back on the fires of persecution, and on the zeal of Christians, in building up walls of separation, and in giving up one another to perdition, we feel as if we were reading the records of an infernal, rather than a heavenly kingdom. An enemy to every
40 religion, if asked to describe a Christian, would, with some show of reason, depict him as an idolater of his own distinguishing opinions, covered with badges of party, shutting his eyes on the virtues, and his ears on the arguments, of his opponents, arrogating all excellence to his own sect and all saving power to his own creed, sheltering under the name of pious zeal the love of domination, the conceit of infal-

libility, and the spirit of intolerance, and trampling on men's rights under the pretence of saving their souls.

We can hardly conceive of a plainer obligation on beings of our frail and fallible nature, who are instructed in the duty of candid judgment, than to abstain from condemning men of apparent conscientiousness and sincerity, who are chargeable with no crime but that of differing from us in the interpretation of the Scriptures, and differing, too, on topics of great and acknowledged obscurity. We are astonished at the hardihood of those, who, with Christ's warnings sounding in their ears, take on them the responsibility of making creeds for his church, and cast out professors of virtuous lives for imagined errors, for the guilt of thinking for themselves. We 10 know that zeal for truth is the cover for this usurpation of Christ's prerogative; but we think that zeal for truth, as it is called, is very suspicious, except in men, whose capacities and advantages, whose patient deliberation, and whose improvements in humility, mildness, and candor, give them a right to hope that their views are more just than those of their neighbors. Much of what passes for a zeal for truth, we look upon with little respect, for it often appears to thrive most luxuriantly where other virtues shoot up thinly and feebly; and we have no gratitude for those reformers, who would force upon us a doctrine which has not sweetened their own tempers, or made them better men than their neighbours.

We are accustomed to think much of the difficulties attending religious inquiries; 20 difficulties springing from the slow development of our minds, from the power of early impressions, from the state of society, from human authority, from the general neglect of the reasoning powers, from the want of just principles of criticism and of important helps in interpreting Scripture, and from various other causes. We find, that on no subject have men, and even good men, ingrafted so many strange conceits, wild theories, and fictions of fancy, as on religion; and remembering, as we do, that we ourselves are sharers of the common frailty, we dare not assume infallibility in the treatment of our fellow-Christians, or encourage in common Christians, who have little time for investigation, the habit of denouncing and contemning other denominations, perhaps more enlightened and virtuous than their own. 30 Charity, forbearance, a delight in the virtues of different sects, a backwardness to censure and condemn, these are virtues, which, however poorly practised by us, we admire and recommend; and we would rather join ourselves to the church in which they abound, than to any other communion, however elated with the belief of its own orthodoxy, however strict in guarding its creed, however burning with zeal against imagined error.

I have thus given the distinguishing views of those Christians in whose names I have spoken. We have embraced this system, not hastily or lightly, but after much deliberation; and we hold it fast, not merely because we believe it to be true, but because we regard it as purifying truth, as a doctrine according to godliness, as able 40 to "work mightily" and to "bring forth fruit" in them who believe. That we wish to spread it, we have no desire to conceal; but we think, that we wish its diffusion, because we regard it as more friendly to practical piety and pure morals than the opposite doctrines, because it gives clearer and nobler views of duty, and stronger motives to its performance, because it recommends religion at once to the understanding and the heart, because it asserts the lovely and venerable attributes of God, because it tends to restore the benevolent spirit of Jesus to his divided and afflicted church, and because it cuts off every hope of God's favor, except that which springs from practical conformity to the life and precepts of Christ. We see nothing in our views to give offence, save their purity, and it is their purity which makes us seek and hope their extension through the world.

My friend and brother; — You are this day to take upon you important duties; to be clothed with an office, which the Son of God did not disdain; to devote yourself
10 to that religion, which the most hallowed lips have preached, and the most precious blood sealed. We trust that you will bring to this work a willing mind, a firm purpose, a martyr's spirit, a readiness to toil and suffer for the truth, a devotion of your best powers to the interests of piety and virtue. I have spoken of the doctrines which you will probably preach; but I do not mean, that you are to give yourself to controversy. You will remember, that good practice is the end of preaching, and will labor to make your people holy livers, rather than skilful disputants. Be careful, lest the desire of defending what you deem truth, and of repelling reproach and misrepresentation, turn you aside from your great business, which is to fix in men's minds a living conviction of the obligation, sublimity, and happiness of Christian
20 virtue. The best way to vindicate your sentiments, is to show, in your preaching and life, their intimate connexion with Christian morals, with a high and delicate sense of duty, with candor towards your opposers, with inflexible integrity, and with an habitual reverence for God. If any light can pierce and scatter the clouds of prejudice, it is that of a pure example. My brother, may your life preach more loudly than your lips. Be to this people a pattern of all good works, and may your instructions derive authority from a well-grounded belief in your hearers, that you speak from the heart, that you preach from experience, that the truth which you dispense has wrought powerfully in your own heart, that God, and Jesus, and heaven, are not merely words on your lips, but most affecting realities to your mind, and
30 springs of hope and consolation, and strength, in all your trials. Thus laboring, may you reap abundantly, and have a testimony of your faithfulness, not only in your own conscience, but in the esteem, love, virtues, and improvements of your people.

To all who hear me, I would say, with the Apostle, Prove all things, hold fast that which is good. Do not, brethren, shrink from the duty of searching God's Word for yourselves, through fear of human censure and denunciation. Do not think, that you may innocently follow the opinions which prevail around you, without investigation, on the ground, that Christianity is now so purified from errors, as to need no laborious research. There is much reason to believe, that Christianity is at this moment dishonored by gross and cherished corruptions. If you remember the dark-
40 ness which hung over the Gospel for ages; if you consider the impure union, which still subsists in almost every Christian country, between the church and state, and which enlists men's selfishness and ambition on the side of established error; if you recollect in what degree the spirit of intolerance has checked free inquiry, not only be-

fore, but since the Reformation; you will see that Christianity cannot have freed itself from all the human inventions, which disfigured it under the Papal tyranny. No. Much stubble is yet to be burned; more rubbish to be removed; many gaudy decorations, which a false taste has hung around Christianity, must be swept away; and the earth-born fogs, which have long shrouded it, must be scattered, before this divine fabric will rise before us in its native and awful majesty, in its harmonious proportions, in its mild and celestial splendors. This glorious reformation in the church, we hope, under God's blessing, from the progress of the human intellect, from the moral progress of society, from the consequent decline of prejudice and bigotry, and, though last not least, from the subversion of human authority in matters of reli- 10 gion, from the fall of those hierarchies, and other human institutions, by which the minds of individuals are oppressed under the weight of numbers, and a Papal dominion is perpetuated in the Protestant church. Our earnest prayer to God is, that he will overturn, and overturn, and overturn the strongholds of spiritual usurpation, until HE shall come, whose right it is to rule the minds of men; that the conspiracy of ages against the liberty of Christians may be brought to an end; that the servile assent, so long yielded to human creeds, may give place to honest and devout inquiry into the Scriptures; and that Christianity, thus purified from error, may put forth its almighty energy, and prove itself, by its ennobling influence on the mind, to be indeed "the power of God unto salvation."

1819

---

19 **the power** . . . **salvation.** See Romans 1:16

1785—1872 Peter Cartwright

A bout 1800, thanks to the camp meeting, an ingenious new method of bringing religion to the sparsely settled frontier, eastern Tennessee and Kentucky felt the first effects of a great religious revival. In the next few years it attained enormous proportions and probably had a greater effect upon the religious life of America than did the "Great Awakening" (see p. 13) sixty years previously. In tumultuous open-air gatherings, marked by "jerks," "shouting," and other obvious signs of emotional release, what was then the West adopted by acclamation an evangelical faith in which there was much excitement and little subtlety. It dramatized the good life as open battle with sin — drinking, fighting, vice, and unbelief; it promised the repentant sinner rewards appropriate to good behavior.

From the new demand that religion should be exciting and dramatic the Methodists profited most, because they perfected an organization which was the quintessence of drama — the circuit-rider system. Peter Cartwright, perhaps the most colorful of the circuit riders, was converted to Methodism in 1801. He was then a large-framed and spirited sixteen-year-old, uneducated except in the wiles of card-playing and dance steps. Born in Virginia, he had moved with his family to Kentucky when he was five and had grown up in Logan County, near the Tennessee border. Physically powerful, quick-witted, and, after his conversion, naïvely certain of what was good and what was evil, he was soon a preacher made for his time and place. "I do not wish," he wrote in later life, "to undervalue education, but really I have seen so many of these educated preachers who forcibly reminded me of lettuce growing under the shade of a peach-tree, or like a gosling that had got the straddles by wading in the dew, that I turn away sick and faint." Like many of his fellow workers and successors, Cartwright was a believer in direct methods when sweet persuasion failed; he could fight guile with guile, but he rather enjoyed using his fists. "In general," he once remarked, "I have made it a rule not to back down to the devil or his imps, whether he appears in male or female form."

From the time he was eighteen Cartwright traveled his appointed circuit, in Tennessee or Ohio or Kentucky. In 1824, distressed by slavery, he asked to be transferred to Illinois, where he was a leader in his church and in politics for nearly fifty years. Twice he was elected to the state legislature; in 1846 he was defeated in a campaign for election to the national House of Representatives by an "infidel" opponent, Abraham Lincoln. Methodism he defined as the preaching of the gospel by itinerant preachers, and he distrusted any move toward a settled ministry and any apparent desertion of the Bible. Doctrinally he was unimportant, although he occasionally attacked the theology of competing denominations, notably in a famous letter "To the Right Honorable, the Devil," whom he pictures as enjoying the predestinarian preaching of the Presbyterians. In practical religion or morality, however, he was a guiding light, famous for his shrewdness and his mother wit. His writing, although far from polished, is direct, vivid, and dramatic.

Autobiography of Peter Cartwright, the Backwoods Preacher, ed. W. P. Strickland, New York, 1856   Fifty Years as a Presiding Elder, ed. Rev. W. S. Hooper, Cincinnati, 1871

from the Autobiography

Cartwright's autobiography is a long, ill-organized, often ungrammatical book, in which anecdotes are inserted with little apparent art. In the Preface he expressed his regret that he had not kept a journal, as he had once started to do, and thus avoided many imperfections and inaccuracies. Nevertheless, his account of his experiences very probably retains the qualities which made his sermons famous, especially his flair for effective illustration and his use of dialogue, suspense, and climax.

At the close of this conference year, 1806, I met the Kentucky preachers at Lexington, and headed by William Burke, about twenty of us started for conference, which was held in East Tennessee, at Ebenezer Church, Nollichuckie, September 15th. Our membership had increased to twelve thousand six hundred and seventy; our net increase was about eight hundred.

This year another presiding-elder district was added to the Western Conference, called the Mississippi District. The number of our traveling preachers increased from thirty-eight to forty-nine. Bishop Asbury attended the Conference. There were thirteen of us elected and ordained deacons. According to the printed Minutes, this was placed in 1807, but it was in the fall of 1806. Two years before there were eighteen 10 of us admitted on trial; that number, in this short space of time, had fallen to thirteen; the other five were discontinued at their own request, or from sickness, or were reduced to suffering circumstances, and compelled to desist from traveling for want of the means of support.

I think I received about forty dollars this year, but many of our preachers did not receive half that amount. These were hard times in those Western wilds; *many,* very *many,* pious and useful preachers, were literally starved into a location. I do not mean that they were starved for want of food; for although it was rough, yet the preachers generally got enough to eat. But they did not generally receive in a whole year money enough to get them a suit of clothes; and if people, and preachers too, had not dressed 20 in home-spun clothing, and the good sisters had not made and presented their preachers with clothing, they generally must retire from itinerant life, and go to work and clothe themselves. Money was very scarce in the country at this early day, but some of the best men God ever made, breasted the storms, endured poverty, and triumphantly planted Methodism in this Western world.

When we were ordained deacons at this Conference, Bishop Asbury presented me with a parchment certifying my ordination in the following words, namely:

"Know all by these presents, That I, Francis Asbury, *Bishop of the Methodist Episcopal Church* in America, under the protection of Almighty God, and with a single eye to his glory, by the imposition of my hands and prayer, have this day set 30 apart Peter Cartwright for the office of a DEACON in the said Methodist Episcopal Church; a man whom I judge to be well qualified for that work; and do hereby recommend him to all whom it may concern, as a proper person to administer the ordinances of baptism, marriage, and the burial of the dead, in the absence of an elder, and to feed the flock of Christ, so long as his spirit and practice are such as become the Gospel of Christ, and he continueth to hold fast the form of sound words, according to the established doctrine of the Gospel.

"In testimony whereof, I have hereunto set my hand and seal this sixteenth day of September, in the year of our Lord one thousand eight hundred and six.

"FRANCIS ASBURY." 40

Text: the edition of 1856, edited by W. P. Strickland   2 **William Burke** (1770-1855), first secretary of the Western Conference of the Methodist Episcopal Church, 1800-1811   3 **Nollichuckie,** a river and settlement in the present Greene County, east of Knoxville   8 **Bishop Asbury,** Francis Asbury (1745-1816), the chief organizer of the Methodist Church in America

I had traveled from Zanesville, in Ohio, to East Tennessee to conference, a distance of over five hundred miles; and when our appointments were read out, I was sent to Marietta Circuit, almost right back, but still further east. Marietta was at the mouth of the Muskingum River, where it emptied into the Ohio. The circuit extended along the north bank of the Ohio, one hundred and fifty miles, crossed over the Ohio River, at the mouth of the Little Kanawha, and up that stream to Hughes River, then east to Middle Island. I suppose it was three hundred miles round. I had to cross the Ohio River four times every round.

It was a poor and hard circuit at that time. Marietta and the country round were
10 settled at an early day by a colony of Yankees. At the time of my appointment I had never seen a Yankee, and I had heard dismal stories about them. It was said they lived almost entirely on pumpkins, molasses, fat meat, and bohea tea; moreover, that they could not bear loud and zealous sermons, and they had brought on their learned preachers with them, and they read their sermons, and were always criticising us poor backwoods preachers. When my appointment was read out, it distressed me greatly. I went to Bishop Asbury and begged him to supply my place, and let me go home. The old father took me in his arms, and said,

"O no, my son; go in the name of the Lord. It will make a man of you."

Ah, thought I, if this is the way to make men, I do not want to be a man. I cried
20 over it bitterly, and prayed too. But on I started, cheered by my presiding elder, Brother J. Sale. If ever I saw hard times, surely it was this year; yet many of the people were kind, and treated me friendly. I had hard work to keep soul and body together. The first Methodist house I came to, I found the brother a Universalist. I crossed over the Muskingum River to Marietta. The first Methodist family I stopped with there, the lady was a member of the Methodist Episcopal Church, but a thorough Universalist. She was a thin-faced, Roman-nosed loquacious Yankee, glib on the tongue, and you may depend on it, I had a hard race to keep up with her, though I found it a good school, for it set me to reading my Bible. And here permit me to say, of all the isms that I ever heard of, they were here. These descendants of
30 the Puritans were generally educated, but their ancestors were rigid predestinarians; and as they were sometimes favored with a little light on their moral powers, and could just "see men as trees walking," they jumped into Deism, Universalism, Unitarianism, etc., etc. I verily believe it was the best school I ever entered. They waked me up on all sides; Methodism was feeble, and I had to battle or run, and I resolved on the former.

There was here in Marietta a preacher by the name of A. Sargent; he had been a Universalist preacher, but finding such a motley gang, as I have above mentioned, he thought (and thought correctly too) that they were proper subjects for his im-

---

12 **bohea tea,** black tea   23 **Universalist,** a believer in the doctrine that all men will eventually repent of their sins, and so all will be saved. Individuals of many denominations (Charles Chauncy, for example) leaned toward this doctrine in the late eighteenth century; after 1779, separate Universalist churches were established in America. In 1960 the Universalist Church and the American Unitarian Association consolidated into the Unitarian Universalist Association   32 **"see men . . . walking."** This is the first remark of the blind man whose sight Jesus restored (Mark 8:24) before his sight was fully regained

posture. Accordingly, he assumed the name of Halcyon Church, and proclaimed himself the millennial messenger. He professed to see visions, fall into trances, and to converse with angels. His followers were numerous in the town and country. The Presbyterian and Congregational ministers were afraid of him. He had men preachers and women preachers. The Methodists had no meeting-house in Marietta. We had to preach in the court-house when we could get a chance. We battled pretty severely. The Congregationalists opened their Academy for me to preach in. I pre-pared myself, and gave battle to the Halcyons. This made a mighty commotion. In the meantime we had a camp-meeting in the suburbs of Marietta. Brother Sale, our presiding elder, was there. Mr. Sargent came, and hung around and wanted to preach, but Brother Sale never noticed him. I have said before that he professed to go into trances and have visions. He would swoon away, fall, and lay a long time; and when he would come to, he would tell what mighty things he had seen and heard.

On Sunday night, at our camp-meeting, Sargent got some powder, and lit a cigar, and then walked down to the bank of the river, one hundred yards, where stood a large stump. He put his powder on the stump, and touched it with his cigar. The flash of the powder was seen by many at the camp; at least the light. When the powder flashed, down fell Sargent; there he lay a good while. In the meantime, the people found him lying there, and gathered around him. At length he came to, and said he had a message from God to us Methodists. He said God had come down to him in a flash of light, and he fell under the power of God, and thus received his vision.

Seeing so many gathered around him there, I took a light, and went down to see what was going on. As soon as I came near the stump, I smelled the sulphur of the powder; and stepping up to the stump, there was clearly the sign of powder, and hard by lay the cigar with which he had ignited it. He was now busy deliver-ing his message. I stepped up to him, and asked him if an angel had appeared to him in that flash of light.

He said, "Yes."

Said I, "Sargent, did not that angel smell of brimstone?"   30

"Why," said he, "do you ask me such a foolish question?"

"Because," said I, "if an angel has spoken to you at all, he was from the lake that burneth with fire and brimstone!" and raising my voice, I said, "I smell sulphur now!" I walked up to the stump, and called on the people to come and see for them-selves. The people rushed up, and soon saw through the trick, and began to abuse Sargent for a vile imposter. He soon left, and we were troubled no more with him or his brimstone angels.

I will beg leave to remark here, that while I was battling successfully against the Halcyons, I was treated with great respect by the Congregational minister and his people, and the Academy was always open for me to preach in; but as soon as I   40

---

2 **millenial,** pertaining to the thousand years of Satan's bondage mentioned in Revelation 20. The pertinent verse is the sixth: "Blessed and holy is he that hath part in the first resurrection: on such the second death hath no power, but they shall be priests of God and of Christ, and shall reign with him a thousand years."

triumphed over and vanquished them, one of the elders of the Congregational Church waited on me, and informed me that it was not convenient for me to preach any more in their Academy. I begged the privilege to make one more appointment in the Academy, till I could get some other place to preach in. This favor, as it was only one more time, was granted.

I then prepared myself; and when my appointed day rolled around, the house was crowded; and I leveled my whole Arminian artillery against their Calvinism; and challenged their minister, who was present, to public debate; but he thought prudence the better part of valor, and declined. This effort secured me many friends,
10 and some persecution; but my way was opened, and we raised a little class, and had a name among the living.

I will here mention a special case of wild fanaticism that took place with one of these Halcyon preachers while I was on this circuit. He worked himself up into the belief that he could live so holy in this life, that his animal nature would become immortal, and that he would never die; and he conceived that he had gained this immortality, and could live without eating. In despite of all arguments and persuasion of his friends, he refused to eat or drink. He stood it sixteen days and nights, and then died a suicidal death. His death put a stop to this foolish delusion, and threw a damper over the whole Halcyon fanaticism.
20 I will here state something like the circumstances I found myself in, at the close of my labors on this hard circuit. I had been from my father's house about three years; was five hundred miles from my home; my horse had gone blind; my saddle was worn out; my bridle reins had been eaten up and replaced, (after a sort) at least a dozen times; and my clothes had been patched till it was difficult to detect the original. I had concluded to try to make my way home, and get another outfit. I was in Marietta, and had just seventy-five cents in my pocket. How I would get home and pay my way I could not tell.

But it was of no use to parley about it; go I must, or do worse; so I concluded to go as far as I could, and then stop and work for more means, till I got home. I
30 had some few friends on the way, but not many; so I cast ahead.

My first day's travel was through my circuit. At about thirty-five miles' distance there lived a brother, with whom I intended to stay all night. I started, and late in the evening, within five miles of my stopping-place, fell in with a widow lady, not a member of the Church, who lived several miles off my road. She had attended my appointments in that settlement all the year. After the usual salutations, she asked me if I was leaving the circuit.

I told her I was, and had started for my father's.

"Well," said she, "how are you off for money? I expect you have received but little on this circuit."
40 I told her I had but seventy-five cents in the world. She invited me home with her, and told me she would give me a little to help me on. But I told her I had my places fixed to stop every night till I got to Maysville; and if I went home with her, it would derange all my stages, and throw me among strangers. She then handed

---

7 **Arminian.** See p. 11

me a dollar, saying it was all she had with her, but if I would go home with her she would give me more. I declined going with her, thanked her for the dollar, bade her farewell, moved on, and reached my lodging-place.

By the time I reached the Ohio River, opposite Maysville, my money was all gone. I was in trouble about how to get over the river, for I had nothing to pay my ferriage.

I was acquainted with Brother J. Armstrong, a merchant in Maysville, and concluded to tell the ferryman that I had no money, but if he would ferry me over, I could borrow twenty-five cents from Armstrong, and would pay him. Just as I got to the bank of the river he landed, on my side, with a man and a horse; and when 10 the man reached the bank, I saw it was Colonel M. Shelby, brother to Governor Shelby, of Kentucky. He was a lively exhorter in the Methodist Episcopal Church, and an old acquaintance and neighbor of my father's.

When he saw me he exclaimed:

"Peter! is that you?"

"Yes, Moses," said I, "what little is left of me."

"Well," said he, "from your appearance you must have seen hard times. Are you trying to get home?"

"Yes," I answered.

"How are you off for money, Peter?" said he.   20

"Well, Moses," said I, "I have not a cent in the world."

"Well," said he, "here are three dollars, and I will give you a bill of the road and a letter of introduction till you get down into the barrens, at the Pilot Knobb."

You may be sure my spirits greatly rejoiced. So I passed on very well for several days and nights on the colonel's money and credit, but when I came to the first tavern beyond the Pilot Knobb my money was out. What to do I did not know, but I rode up and asked for quarters. I told the landlord I had no money; had been three years from home, and was trying to get back to my father's. I also told him I had a little old watch, and a few good books in my saddle-bags, and I would compensate him in some way. He bade me alight and be easy.   30

On inquiry I found this family had lived here from an early day, totally destitute of the Gospel and all religious privileges. There were three rooms in this habitation, below — the dining-room, and a back bedroom, and the kitchen. The kitchen was separated from the other lower rooms by a thin, plank partition, set up on an end; and the planks had shrunk and left considerable cracks between them.

When we were about to retire to bed, I asked the landlord if he had any objection to our praying before we laid down. He said, "None at all;" and stepped into the kitchen, as I supposed, to bring in the family. He quickly returned with a candle in his hand, and said, "Follow me." I followed into the back bedroom. Whereupon he set down the candle, and bade me good night, saying, "There, you can 40 pray as much as you please."

I stood, and felt foolish. He had completely ousted me; but it immediately occurred to me that I would kneel down and pray with full and open voice; so down

11 **Governor Shelby,** Isaac Shelby (1750-1826), first governor of Kentucky, 1792-1796

I knelt, and commenced praying audibly. I soon found, from the commotion created in the kitchen, that they were taken by surprise as much as I had been. I distinctly heard the landlady say, "He is crazy, and will kill us all this night. Go, husband, and see what is the matter." But he was slow to approach; and when I ceased praying he came in, and asked me what was the cause of my acting in this strange way. I replied, "Sir, did you not give me the privilege to pray as much as I pleased?" "Yes," said he, "but I did not expect you would pray out." I told him I wanted the family to hear prayer, and as he had deprived me of that privilege, I knew of no better way to accomplish my object than to do as I had done, and I hoped he would
10 not be offended.

I found he thought me deranged, but we fell into a free conversation on the subject of religion, and, I think, I fully satisfied him that I was not beside myself, but spoke forth the words of truth with soberness.

Next morning I rose early, intending to go fifteen miles to an acquaintance for breakfast, but as I was getting my horse out of the stable the landlord came out, and insisted that I should not leave till after breakfast. I yielded, but he would not have anything for my fare, and urged me to call on him if ever I traveled that way again. I will just say here, that in less than six months I called on this landlord, and he and his lady were happily converted, dating their conviction from the ex-
20 traordinary circumstances of the memorable night I spent with them.

I found other friends on my journey till I reached Hopkinsville, Christian County, within thirty miles of my father's, and I had just six and a quarter cents left. This was a new and dreadfully wicked place. I put up at a tavern kept by an old Mr. M'. The landlord knew my father. I told him I had not money to pay my bill, but as soon as I got home I would send it to him. He said, "Very well," and made me welcome. His lady was a sister of the apostate Dr. Allen whom I have elsewhere mentioned.

Shortly after I laid down I fell asleep. Suddenly I was aroused by a piercing scream, or screams, of a female. I supposed that somebody was actually committing murder.
30 I sprung from my bed, and, after getting half dressed, ran into the room from whence issued the piercing screams, and called out, "What's the matter here?" The old gentleman replied, that his wife was subject to spasms, and often had them. I commenced a conversation with her about religion. I found she was under deep concern about her soul. I asked if I might pray for her. "O, yes," she replied, "for there is no one in this place that cares for my soul."

I knelt and prayed, and then commenced singing, and directed her to Christ as an all-sufficient Saviour, and prayed again. She suddenly sprung out of the bed and shouted, "Glory to God! he has blessed my soul." It was a happy time indeed. The old gentleman wept like a child. We sung and shouted, prayed and praised, nearly
40 all night. Next morning the old landlord told me my bill was paid tenfold, and that all he charged me was, every time I passed that way, to call and stay with them.

---

26 **the apostate Dr. Allen,** one of two Baptist ministers mentioned by Cartwright in Chap. 3. One embraced the "blasphemous doctrine" of Universalism; the other "took to open drunkenness, and with him his salvation by water expired." Which one was Allen is not clear

Next day I reached home with the six and a quarter cents unexpended. Thus I have given you a very imperfect little sketch of the early travel of a Methodist preacher in the Western Conference. My parents received me joyfully. I tarried with them several weeks. My father gave me a fresh horse, a bridle and saddle, some new clothes, and forty dollars in cash. Thus equipped, I was ready for another three years' absence.

1856

THE AMERICAN SCENE:
Foster
Brackenridge
Wilde
Woodworth
Freneau
Dwight
Barlow
Tyler
Thomas

1758—1840 Hannah Foster

M rs. Hannah Webster Foster was born in Salisbury, Massachusetts, in 1758, the daughter of a merchant. As numerous learned and literary allusions in her writings attest, she was "highly educated for the times." In 1785 she married a minister, John Foster, a cousin of the woman upon whose sad story her best-known novel, *The Coquette; or, the History of Eliza Wharton* (1797), was based. Her only other book, another epistolary work, was *The Boarding School* (1798).

The excerpts which follow typify a group of fictional works produced by the hundreds and read widely in this country between 1789 and 1860. These "sentimental novels" were important as a literary form which influenced in various ways such famous narrative writers as Henry Wadsworth Longfellow, Harriet Beecher Stowe, Edgar Allan Poe, and Nathaniel Hawthorne. *The Coquette* is one of the best of these narratives of sensibility.

The title page of *The Coquette,* like that of many a novel of the time, proclaimed that it was "founded on fact." To some extent this proclamation, like the moralizing which dotted its pages, helped overcome a widespread prejudice against fiction. In addition, its many tempestuous emotional scenes, centering around a seduction, were sure to touch the heart of sensibility. Mrs. Foster told her story in a way then much admired, using the letter method which had been made famous by the great Samuel Richardson.

The plot, typical of this kind of novel, tells how the Rev. J. Boyer, a good and sincere (but rather dull) man, tries to win the hand of Eliza Wharton. Eliza, too fond for her own good of "the scenes of festive mirth and the dissipating amusements of the gay world," is more taken with dashing Major Sanford, a rake whose dangerousness is enhanced by both his shrewdness and his charm. Eliza loses her chance to marry Boyer by showing too much interest in the Major. Even after San-

R. L. Shurter, "Mrs. Hannah Webster Foster and the Early American Novel," **American Literature,** IV (Nov. 1932)   H. R. Brown, "Introduction," **The Coquette,** Facsimile Text Society Edition, New York, 1939; **The Sentimental Novel in America, 1789-1860,** Durham, N.C., 1959

ford marries, she continues to see him, and eventually he seduces her. The following letters take up the story at this point, but the letters describing Eliza's pathetic death and the moralizing about it are not included.

from The Coquette

Letter LXV

To Mr. Charles Deighton

Hartford

Good news, Charles, good news! I have arrived to the utmost bounds of my wishes; the full possession of my adorable Eliza! I have heard a quotation from a certain book; but what book it was I have forgotten, if I ever knew. No matter for that; the quotation is, that "stolen waters are sweet, and bread eaten in secret is pleasant." If it has reference to the pleasures, which I have enjoyed with Eliza, I like it hugely, as Tristram Shandy's father said of Yorick's sermon; and I think it fully verified.

I had a long and tedious siege. Every method which love could suggest, or art 10 invent, was adopted. I was sometimes ready to despair, under an idea that her resolution was unconquerable, her virtue impregnable. Indeed, I should have given over the pursuit long ago, but for the hopes of success I entertained from her parlying with me, and in reliance upon her own strength, endeavoring to combat, and counteract my designs. Whenever this has been the case, Charles, I have never yet been defeated in my plan. If a lady will consent to enter the lists against the antagonist of her honor, she may be sure of loosing the prize. Besides, were her delicacy genuine, she would banish the man at once, who presumed to doubt, which he certainly does, who attempts to vanquish it!

But, far be it from me to criticise the pretensions of the sex. If I gain the rich 20 reward of my dissimulation and gallantry, that you know is all I want.

To return then to the point. An unlucky, but not a miraculous accident, has taken place, which must soon expose our amour. What can be done? At the first discovery, absolute distraction seized the soul of Eliza, which has since terminated in a fixed melancholy. Her health too is much impaired. She thinks herself rapidly declining; and I tremble when I see her emaciated form!

My wife has been reduced very low, of late. She brought me a boy a few weeks past, a dead one though.

These circumstances give me neither pain nor pleasure. I am too much ingrossed by my divinity to take an interest in any thing else. True, I have lately suffered 30 myself to be somewhat engaged here and there, by a few jovial lads, who assist me

---

6 "stolen . . . pleasant." See Proverbs 9:17   8 **Tristram Shandy,** a character in *The Life and Opinions of Tristram Shandy* (1760), an English sentimental novel, the fictional masterpiece of Laurence Sterne (1713-1768)

in dispelling the anxious thoughts, which my perplexed situation excites. I must, however, seek some means to relieve Eliza's distress. My finances are low; but the last fraction shall be expended in her service, if she need it.

Julia Granby is expected at Mr. Wharton's every hour. I fear that her inquisitorial eye will soon detect our intrigue, and obstruct its continuation. Now there's a girl, Charles, I should never attempt to seduce; yet she is a most alluring object, I assure you. But the dignity of her manners forbid all assaults upon her virtue. Why, the very expression of her eye, blasts in the bud, every thought, derogatory to her honor; and tells you plainly, that the first insinuation of the kind, would be punished with eternal banishment and displeasure! Of her there is no danger! But I can write no more, except that I am, &c.   PETER SANFORD

Letter LXVI

To Mrs. Lucy Sumner

Hartford

Oh, my friend! I have a tale to unfold; a tale which will rend every nerve of sympathizing pity, which will rack the breast of sensibility, and unspeakably distress your benevolent heart! Eliza — oh, the ruined, lost Eliza!

I want words to express the emotions of indignation, and grief which oppress me. But I will endeavor to compose myself; and relate the circumstances as they came to my knowledge.

After my last letter, Eliza remained much in the same gloomy situation as I found her. She refused to go, agreeably to her promise, to visit your mamma; and under one pretext or another, has constantly declined accompanying me any where else, since my arrival.

Till last Thursday night she slept in the same bed with me; when she excused herself, by saying she was restless, and should disturb my repose. I yielded to her humor of taking a different apartment, little suspecting the real cause! She frequently walked out, and though I sometimes followed, I very seldom found her. Two or three times, when I happened to be awake, I heard her go down stairs; and on inquiry in the morning, she told me that she was very thirsty, and went down for water. I observed a degree of hesitancy in her answers, for which I could not account. But last night, the dreadful mystery was developed! A little before day, I heard the front door opened with great caution. I sprang from my bed, and running to the window, saw by the light of the moon, a man going from the house. Soon after I perceived a footstep upon the stairs, which carefully approached and entered Eliza's chamber.

Judge of my astonishment, my surprise, my feelings, upon this occasion! I doubted not but Major Sanford was the person I had seen; and the discovery of Eliza's guilt, in this infamous intrigue, almost deprived me of thought and recollection! My blood thrilled with horror at this sacrifice of virtue! After a while I recovered myself, and put on my clothes. But what to do, I knew not; whether to go directly to her chamber and let her know that she was detected; or to wait another opportunity.

I resolved on the first. The day had now dawned. I tapped at her door; and she

bid me come in. She was sitting in an easy chair by the side of her bed. As I entered she withdrew her handkerchief from her face; and looking earnestly at me,
said, what procures me the favor of a visit, at this early hour, Miss Granby? I was
disturbed, said I, and wished not to return to my bed. But what breaks your rest;
and calls you up so unseasonably, Eliza? Remorse, and despair, answered she, weeping. After what I have witnessed, this morning, rejoined I, I cannot wonder at it!
Was it not Major Sanford whom I saw go from the house some time ago? She was
silent, but tears flowed abundantly. It is too late, continued I, to deny, or evade. Answer my question sincerely; for, believe me, Eliza, it is not malice, but concern for
you, which prompts it. I will answer you, Julia, said she. You have discovered a 10
secret, which harrows up my very soul! A secret, which I wished you to know, but
could not exert resolution to reveal! Yes! It was Major Sanford; the man who has
robbed me of my peace; who has triumphed in my destruction; and who will cause
my sun to sit at noon!

I shudder, said I, at your confession! Wretched, deluded girl! Is this a return for
your parent's love, and assiduous care; for your friends' solicitude, and premonitory
advice? You are ruined, you say! You have sacrificed your virtue to an abandoned,
despicable profligate! And you live to acknowledge and bear your infamy! I do, said
she; but not long shall I support this burden! See you not, Julia, my decaying frame,
my faded cheek, and tottering limbs? Soon shall I be insensible to censure and 20
reproach! Soon shall I be sequestered in that mansion, "where the wicked cease from
troubling, and where the weary are at rest!" Rest! said I, can you expect to find rest
either in this world, or another, with such a weight of guilt on your head? She exclaimed, with great emotion, add not to the upbraidings of a wounded spirit! Have
pity upon me, Oh! my friend, have pity upon me!

Could you know what I suffer, you would think me sufficiently punished! I wish
you no other punishment, said I, than what may effect your repentance and reformation. But your mother, Eliza! She cannot long be ignorant of your fall; and I
tremble to think of her distress! It will break her widowed heart! How has she loved;
how has she doated upon you! Dreadful is the requital which you have made! My 30
mother, rejoined she — Oh, name her not! The very sound is distraction to me!
Oh! my Julia, if your heart be not shut against mercy and compassion towards me,
aid me through this trying scene! Let my situation call forth your pity, and induce
you, undeserving as I am, to exert it in my behalf!

During this time, I had walked the chamber. My spirits had been raised above
their natural key, and were exhausted. I sat down, but thought I should have
fainted, till a copious flood of tears gave me relief. Eliza was extremely affected. The
appearance of calamity which she exhibited would have softened the most obdurate
anger. Indeed, I feared some immediate and fatal effect. I therefore seated myself
beside her; and assuming an air of kindness, compose yourself, Eliza, said I; I repeat 40
what I told you before, it is the purest friendship, which thus interests me in your
concerns. This, under the direction of charity, induces me again to offer you my
hand. Yet you have erred against knowledge and reason; against warning and coun-

---

22 "where . . . at rest." See Job 3:17

sel. You have forfeited the favor of your friends; and reluctant will be their forgiveness. I plead guilty, said she, to all your charges. From the general voice I expect no clemency. If I can make my peace with my mother, it is all I seek or wish on this side the grave.

In your benevolence I confide for this. In you I hope to find an intercessor. By the remembrance of our former affection and happiness, I conjure you, refuse me not. At present, I entreat you to conceal from her this distressing tale. A short reprieve is all I ask. Why said I, should you defer it? When the painful task is over, you may find relief in her lenient kindness. After she knows my condition, I cannot see
10 her, resumed she, till I am assured of her forgiveness. I have not strength to support the appearance of her anger and grief. I will write to her what I cannot speak. You must bear the melancholy message, and plead for me, that her displeasure may not follow me to the grave; whither I am rapidly hastening. Be assured, replied I, that I will keep your secret as long as prudence requires. But I must leave you now; your mamma will wonder at our being thus closetted together. When opportunity presents, we will converse further on the subject. In the mean time, keep yourself as composed as possible, if you would avoid suspicion. She raised her clasped hands, and with a piteous look, threw her handkerchief over her face, and reclined in her chair, without speaking a word. I returned to my chamber, and endeavored
20 to dissipate every idea which might tend to disorder my countenance, and break the silence I wished to observe, relative to what had happened.

When I went down, Mrs. Wharton desired me to step up, and inform Eliza that breakfast was ready. She told me she could not yet compose herself sufficiently to see her mamma; she begged me to excuse her absence as I thought proper. I accordingly returned for answer to Mrs. Wharton, that Eliza had rested but indifferently, and being somewhat indisposed, would not come down, but wished me to bring her a bowl of chocolate, when we had breakfasted. I was obliged studiously to suppress even my thoughts concerning her, lest the emotions they excited might be observed. Mrs. Wharton conversed much of her daughter, and expressed great concern
30 about her health and state of mind. Her return to this state of dejection, after having recovered her spirits and cheerfulness, in a great degree, was owing, she feared, to some cause unknown to her; and she entreated me to extract the secret, if possible. I assured her of my best endeavors, and doubted not, I told her, but I should be able in a few days to effect what she wished.

Eliza came down and walked in the garden before dinner; at which she commanded herself much better than I expected. She said that a little ride might, she imagined, be of service to her; and asked me if I would accompany her a few miles in the afternoon. Her mamma was much pleased with the proposition; and the chaise was accordingly ordered.

40 I observed to Eliza, as we rode, that with her natural and acquired abilities, with her advantages of education, with her opportunities of knowing the world, and of tracing the virtues and vices of mankind to their origin, I was surprised at her becoming the prey of an insidious libertine, with whose character she was well acquainted, and whose principles she was fully apprised would prompt him to deceive

and betray her. Your surprise is very natural, said she. The same will doubtless be felt and expressed by every one to whom my sad story is related. But the cause may be found in that unrestrained levity of disposition, that fondness for dissipation and coquetry which alienated the affections of Mr. Boyer from me. This event fatally depressed, and enfeebled my mind. I embraced with avidity the consoling power of friendship, ensnaringly offered by my seducer; vainly inferring from his marriage with a virtuous woman, that he had seen the error of his ways, and forsaken his licentious practices, as he affirmed, and I, fool that I was, believed it!

It is needless for me to rehearse the perfidious arts, by which he insinuated himself into my affections, and gained my confidence. Suffice it to say, he effected his 10 purpose! But not long did I continue in the delusive dream of sensual gratification. I soon awoke to a most poignant sense of his baseness, and of my own crime and misery. I would have fled from him; I would have renounced him forever; and by a life of sincere humility and repentance, endeavored to make my peace with heaven, and to obliterate, by the rectitude of my future conduct, the guilt I had incurred; but I found it too late! My circumstances called for attention; and I had no one to participate my cares, to witness my distress, and to alleviate my sorrows, but him. I could not therefore prevail on myself, wholly to renounce his society. At times I have admitted his visits; always meeting him in the garden, or grove adjoining; till of late, the weather, and my ill health induced me to comply with his solicitations, 20 and receive him into the parlor.

Not long, however, shall I be subject to these embarrassments. Grief has undermined my constitution. My health has fallen a sacrifice to a disordered mind. But I regret not its departure! I have not a single wish to live. Nothing which the world affords can restore my former serenity and happiness!

The little innocent I bear, will quickly disclose its mother's shame! God Almighty grant it may not live as a monument of my guilt, and a partaker of the infamy and sorrow, which is all I have to bequeath it! Should it be continued in life, it will never know the tenderness of a parent; and, perhaps, want and disgrace may be its wretched portion! The greatest consolation I can have, will be to carry it with me 30 to a state of eternal rest; which, vile as I am, I hope to obtain, through the infinite mercy of heaven, as revealed in the gospel of Christ.

I must see Major Sanford again. It is necessary to converse further with him, in order to carry my plan of operation into execution. What is this plan of operation, Eliza? said I. I am on the rack of anxiety for your safety. Be patient, continued she, and you shall soon be informed. Tomorrow I shall write my dreadful story to my mother. She will be acquainted with my future intentions; and you shall know, at the same time, the destination of your lost friend. I hope, said I, that you have formed no resolution against your own life. God forbid, rejoined she. My breath is in his hands, let him do what seemeth good in his sight! Keep my secret one day longer, 40 and I will never more impose so painful a silence upon you.

By this time we had reached home. She drank tea with composure, and soon retired to rest. Mrs. Wharton eagerly inquired whether I had found out the cause of Eliza's melancholy. I have urged her, said I, on the subject; but she alleges that she has particular reasons for present concealment. She has, notwithstanding, promised to let me know, the day after to-morrow. Oh, said she, I shall not rest till the period arrives. Dear, good woman, said I to myself, I fear you will never rest afterwards!

This is our present situation. Think what a scene rises to the view of your Julia! She must share the distresses of others, though her own feelings, on this unhappy occasion, are too keen to admit a moment's serenity! My greatest relief is in writing to you; which I shall do again by the next post. In the mean time, I must beg leave to subscribe myself, sincerely yours,   JULIA GRANBY

Letter LXVII

To the same
10   Hartford

All is now lost; lost, indeed! She is gone! Yes, my dear friend, our beloved Eliza, is gone! Never more shall we behold this once amiable companion, this once innocent and happy girl. She has forsaken, and, as she says, bid an everlasting adieu to her home, her afflicted parent and her friends! But I will take up my melancholy story where I left it in my last.

She went, as she told me she expected, into the garden, and met her detestable paramour. In about an hour she returned, and went directly to her chamber. At one o'clock I went up, and found her writing, and weeping. I begged her to compose herself, and go down to dinner. No, she said, she could not eat; and was not fit to
20 appear before any body. I remonstrated against her immoderate grief; represented the injury she must sustain by the indulgence of it, and conjured her to suppress the violence of its emotions.

She entreated me to excuse her to her mamma; said she was writing to her, and found it a task too painful to be performed with any degree of composure; that she was almost ready to sink under the weight of her affliction; but hoped and prayed for support, both in this, and another trying scene, which awaited her. In compliance with her desire, I now left her; and told her mamma that she was very busy in writing; wished not to be interrupted at present; but would take some refreshment, an hour or two hence. I visited her again about four o'clock; when she
30 appeared more calm and tranquil.

It is finished, said she, as I entered her apartment, it is finished. What said I, is finished? No matter, replied she; you will know all to-morrow, Julia. She complained of excessive fatigue, and expressed an inclination to lie down; in which I assisted her, and then retired. Some time after, her mamma went up, and found her still on the bed. She rose, however, and accompanied her down stairs. I met her at the door of the parlor, and taking her by the hand, inquired how she did? Oh, Julia, miserably indeed, said she. How severely does my mother's kindness reproach me! How insupportably it increases my self-condemnation! She wept; she wrung her hands, and walked the room in the greatest agony! Mrs. Wharton was exceedingly dis-
40 tressed by her appearance. Tell me, Eliza, said she, tell me the cause of your trouble! Oh, kill me not by your mysterious concealment! My dear child, let me, by sharing,

alleviate your affliction! Ask me not, madam, said she; O my mother, I conjure you not to insist on my divulging to night, the fatal secret which engrosses and distracts my mind! To morrow I will hide nothing from you. I will press you no further, rejoined her mamma. Chuse your own time, my dear; but remember, I must participate your grief, though I know not the cause.

Supper was brought in; and we endeavored to prevail on Eliza to eat, but in vain. She sat down, in compliance with our united importunities; but neither of us tasted food. It was removed untouched. For a while, Mrs. Wharton and I gazed in silent anguish upon the spectacle of woe, before us! At length, Eliza rose to retire. Julia, said she, will you call at my chamber as you pass to your own? I assented. She then 10 approached her mamma, fell upon her knees before her, and clasping her hand, said, in broken accents, Oh madam! can you forgive a wretch, who has forfeited your love, your kindness, and your compassion? Surely, Eliza, said she, you are not that being! No, it is impossible! But however great your transgression, be assured of my forgiveness, my compassion, and my continued love! Saying this, she threw her arms about her daughter's neck, and affectionately kissed her. Eliza struggled from her embrace, and looking at her with wild despair, exclaimed, this is too much! Oh, this unmerited goodness is more than I can bear! She then rushed precipitately out of the room, and left us overwhelmed in sympathy and astonishment!

When Mrs. Wharton had recovered herself a little, she observed, that Eliza's brain 20 was evidently disordered. Nothing else, continued she, could impel her to act in this extraordinary manner. At first she was resolved to follow her; but I dissuaded her from it, alledging, that as she had desired me to come into her chamber, I thought it better for me to go alone. She acquiesced; but said she should not think of going to bed; but would, however, retire to her chamber, and seek consolation there. I bade her good night; and went up to Eliza, who took me by the hand and led me to the toilet, upon which she laid the two inclosed letters, the one to her mamma, and the other to me. These, said she, contain what I had not resolution to express. Promise me, Julia, that they shall not be opened till to morrow morning. I will, said I. I have thought and wept, continued she, till I have almost exhausted my 30 strength, and my reason. I would now obtain a little respite, that I may prepare my mind for the account I am one day to give at a higher tribunal than that of earthly friends. For this purpose, what I have written, and what I shall yet say to you, must close the account between you and me. I have certainly no balance against you, said I. In my breast you are fully acquitted. Your penitential tears have obliterated your guilt, and blotted out your errors with your Julia. Henceforth, be they all forgotten. Live, and be happy. Talk not, said she, of life. It would be a vain hope, though I cherished it myself.

> "That I must die, it is my only comfort;
> Death is the privilege of human nature;   40
> And life without it were not worth our taking.
> Thither the poor, the prisoner and the mourner
> Fly for relief, and lay their burden down!"

You have forgiven me, Julia; my mother has assured me of her forgiveness, and what have I more to wish? my heart is much lightened by these kind assurances; they will be a great support to me in the dreadful hour which awaits me! What mean you, Eliza? said I. I fear some dreadful purpose labors in your mind. Oh, no, she replied; you may be assured your fear is groundless. I know not what I say: my brain is on fire; I am all confusion! Leave me, Julia; when I have had a little rest, I shall be composed. These letters have almost distracted me; but they are written, and I am comparatively easy. I will not leave you, Eliza, said I, unless you will go directly to bed, and endeavor to rest. I will, said she, and the sooner the better. I
10 tenderly embraced her, and retired, though not to bed. About an hour after, I returned to her chamber, and opening the door very softly, found her apparently asleep. I acquainted Mrs. Wharton with her situation, which was a great consolation to us both; and encouraged us to go to bed. Having suffered much in my mind, and being much fatigued, I soon fell asleep; but the rattling of a carriage, which appeared to stop a little distance from the house, awoke me. I listened a moment, and heard the door turn slowly on its hinges. I sprang from my bed, and reached the window just in time to see a female handed into a chaise by a man who hastily followed her, and drove furiously away! I at once concluded they could be no other than Eliza and Major Sanford. Under this impression I made no delay, but ran imme-
20 diately to her chamber. A candle was burning on the table; but Eliza was not there! I thought it best to acquaint her mamma with the melancholy discovery; and stepping to her apartment for the purpose, found her rising. She had heard me walk, and was anxious to know the cause. What is the matter, Julia, said she; what is the matter? Dear madam, said I, arm yourself with fortitude! What new occurrence demands it? rejoined she. Eliza has left us! Left us! what mean you? She is just gone! I saw her handed into a chaise, which instantly disappeared!

At this intelligence she gave a shriek, and fell back on her bed! I alarmed the family, and by their assistance soon recovered her. She desired me to inform her of every particular relative to her elopement, which I did; and then delivered her the letter
30 which Eliza had left for her. I suspect, said she, as she took it; I have long suspected, what I dared not believe! The anguish of my mind has been known only to myself, and my God! I could not answer her, and therefore withdrew. When I had read Eliza's letter to me, and wept over the sad fall; and, as I fear the total loss of this once amiable and accomplished girl, I returned to Mrs. Wharton. She was sitting in her easy chair; and still held the fatal letter in her hand. When I entered, she fixed her streaming eyes upon me, and exclaimed, O Julia, this is more than the bitterness of death! True, madam, said I, your affliction must be great; yet that all-gracious Being, who controls every event, is able, and I trust, disposed to support you! To Him, replied she, I desire humbly to resign myself; but I think I could
40 have borne almost any other calamity with greater resignation and composure than this. With how much comparative ease could I have followed her to the grave, at any period since her birth! Oh, my child, my child! dear, very dear hast thou been to my fond heart! Little did I think it possible for you to prepare so dreadful a cup of sorrow for your widowed mother! But where, continued she, where can the poor

fugitive have fled? Where can she find that protection and tenderness, which, not-withstanding her great apostacy, I should never have withheld? From whom can she receive those kind attentions, which her situation demands.

The agitation of her mind had exhausted her strength; and I prevailed on her to refresh, and endeavor to compose herself to rest; assuring her of my utmost exertions to find out Eliza's retreat, and restore her to a mother's arms.

I am obliged to suppress my own emotions; and to bend all my thoughts towards the alleviation of Mrs. Wharton's anxiety and grief.

Major Sanford is from home, as I expected; and I am determined, if he return, to see him myself, and extort from him the place of Eliza's concealment. Her flight, in 10 her present state of health, is inexpressibly distressing to her mother; and unless we find her soon, I dread the effects!

I shall not close this, till I have seen or heard from the vile miscreant who has involved a worthy family in wretchedness!

Friday morning. — Two days have elapsed without affording us much relief. Last evening, I was told that Major Sanford was at home. I immediately wrote him a billet, entreating and conjuring him to let me know where the hapless Eliza had fled. He returned me the following answer.

"Miss Granby need be under no apprehensions, respecting the situation of our be-loved Eliza. She is well provided for, conveniently accommodated, and has every 20 thing to make her happy, which love or affluence can give.

Major Sanford has solemnly sworn not to discover her retreat. She wishes to avoid the accusations of her friends, till she is better able to bear them.

Her mother may rest assured of immediate information, should any danger threaten her amiable daughter; and also of having seasonable notice of her safety."

Although little dependence can be placed upon this man; yet these assurances have, in a great degree, calmed our minds. We are, however, contriving means to explore the refuge of the wanderer; and hope, by tracing his steps, to accomplish our purpose. This we have engaged a friend to do.

I know, my dear Mrs. Sumner, the kind interest you will take in this disastrous 30 affair. I tremble to think what the event may be! To relieve your suspense, how-ever, I shall write you every circumstance, as it occurs. But at present, I shall only enclose Eliza's letters to her mamma, and me, and, subscribe myself your sincere and obliged friend,

JULIA GRANBY

Letter LXVIII

To Mrs. M. Wharton

Tuesday

My Honored and Dear Mamma,

In what words, in what language shall I address you? What shall I say on a sub-ject which deprives me of the power of expression? Would to God I had been totally 40 deprived of that power before so fatal a subject required its exertion? Repentance comes too late, when it cannot prevent the evil lamented. For your kindness, your more than maternal affection towards me, from my infancy to the present moment, a long life of filial duty and unerring rectitude could hardly compensate. How greatly deficient in gratitude must I appear then, while I confess, that precept and example, counsel and advice, instruction and admonition, have been all lost upon me!

Your kind endeavors to promote my happiness have been repaid by the inexcusable folly of sacrificing it. The various emotions of shame, and remorse, penitence and regret, which torture and distract my guilty breast, exceed description. Yes, madam, your Eliza has fallen; fallen, indeed! She has become the victim of her own
10 indiscretion, and of the intrigue and artifice of a designing libertine, who is the husband of another! She is polluted, and no more worthy of her parentage! She flies from you, not to conceal her guilt, that she humbly and penitently owns; but to avoid what she has never experienced, and feels herself unable to support, a mother's frown; to escape the heart-rending sight of a parent's grief, occasioned by the crimes of her guilty child!

I have become a reproach and disgrace to my friends. The consciousness of having forfeited their favor, and incurred their disapprobation and resentment, induces me to conceal from them the place of my retirement; but, lest your benevolence should render you anxious for my comfort in my present situation, I take the liberty to
20 assure you that I am amply provided for.

I have no claim even upon your pity; but from my long experience of your tenderness, I presume to hope it will be extended to me. Oh, my mother, if you knew what the state of my mind is, and has been, for months past, you would surely compassionate my case! Could tears efface the stain, which I have brought upon my family, it would long since have been washed away! But, alas, tears are vain; and vain is my bitter repentance! It cannot obliterate my crime, nor restore me to innocence and peace! In this life I have no ideas of happiness. These I have wholly resigned! The only hope which affords me any solace, is that of your forgiveness. If the deepest contrition can make an atonement; if the severest pains, both of body
30 and mind, can restore me to your charity, you will not be inexorable! Oh, let my sufferings be deemed a sufficient punishment; and add not the insupportable weight of a parent's wrath! At present, I cannot see you. The effect of my crime is too obvious to be longer concealed, to elude the invidious eye of curiosity. This night, therefore, I leave your hospitable mansion! This night I become a wretched wanderer from thy paternal roof! Oh, that the grave were this night to be my lodging! Then should I lie down and be at rest! Trusting in the mercy of God, through the mediation of his son; I think I could meet my heavenly father with more composure and confidence, than my earthly parent!

Let not the faults and misfortunes of your daughter oppress your mind. Rather
40 let the conviction of having faithfully discharged your duty to your lost child, support and console you in this trying scene.

Since I wrote the above, you have kindly granted me your forgiveness, though you knew not how great, how aggravated was my offence! You forgive me, you say: Oh, the harmonious, the transporting sound! It has revived my drooping spirits;

and will enable me to encounter, with resolution, the trials before me!

Farewell, my dear mamma! pity and pray for your ruined child; and be assured, that affection and gratitude will be the last sentiments, which expire in the breast of your repenting daughter,

Eliza Wharton

1797

1748—1816 Hugh Henry Brackenridge

As farm boy, schoolteacher, divinity student, army chaplain, lawyer, legislator, and judge, Hugh Henry Brackenridge, "our first back-country writer," rubbed shoulders with Americans of many persuasions. He did not find democracy an unmixed blessing, but he believed in it, possibly because it offered opportunity to him. He remains perhaps the best contemporary observer of the true "rising glory" of America in the last quarter of the eighteenth century: the freedom of the individual to choose his own occupation and to improve his condition without the handicap of rigid class distinction.

Brackenridge was born in Scotland in 1748 and came to York County, Pennsylvania, then a frontier region, when he was five. At fifteen he was teaching school in Maryland; at the age of twenty he entered the College of New Jersey (now Princeton), where he was a classmate of James Madison and Philip Freneau (p. 509). Before his graduation in 1771, he had dabbled in satirical verse and fiction. Although he returned to schoolteaching, he had literary ambitions, and within a few years published *The Rising Glory of America* (1772), a Commencement poem in which Freneau had had a hand, *A Poem on Divine Revelation* (1774), which he read when he took his M.A. degree, and *The Battle of Bunkers-Hill* (1776), a poetic drama supposedly recited by his pupils in a Maryland academy. Whig by conviction, he turned his theological studies to good use by becoming a chaplain in 1776-1778 and attacking the Tories in *Six Political Discourses Founded on the Scripture* (1778). Then, for a year, he tried magazine publishing in Philadelphia. When *The United States Magazine* folded up, he was reading law; and by 1785 he was settled in Pittsburgh, with the ambition of becoming a legislator and political leader. The move did not bring him tranquillity, but it deposited a thoughtful democrat with literary tastes in a turbulent center of frontier democracy. The result was *Modern Chivalry,* of which the first volume appeared in 1792, and the whole in finally revised form in 1815. There is no better record of the society which rebelled against Alexander Hamilton's internal revenue measures in the so-called Whiskey Insurrection of 1791-1794.

Brackenridge's political career as state assemblyman and justice of the state Supreme Court was never smooth, because, seeing justice on both sides, he pleased neither for very long. He could never go all the way with either Federalists or Republicans, with national or local interests; and more than once he found himself defeated at the polls, vilified in the local newspapers, and suspected by his party leaders. His recourse, fortunately, was to satire, both in verse and in prose.

His son remarked that Brackenridge "appeared to live more in the world of books than of men," and there is much evidence of his delight in the classics of all literatures. His particular enthusiasms were Cervantes, Rabelais, Samuel Butler, Swift, Fielding, Le Sage, Smollett, and Sterne — a list which reveals his liking for the earthy and vigorous in fiction and satire. Perhaps because of this taste, *Modern Chivalry* does not seem so weakly imitative as the productions of such men as Timothy Dwight (p. 533), even though it is a picaresque novel obviously modeled on *Don Quixote,* with chapters of author's commentary in the manner of Swift's *The Tale of a Tub* and Fielding's *Tom Jones.* The subject matter dominates the form, and *Modern Chivalry,* though sprawling and uneven, retains vitality.

Modern Chivalry, ed. C. M. Newlin, New York, 1937   C. M. Newlin, The Life and Writings of Hugh Henry Brackenridge, Princeton, 1932   R. J. Ferguson, Early Western Pennsylvania Politics, Pittsburgh, 1938

from Modern Chivalry

Modern Chivalry: Containing the Adventures of Captain John Farrago, and Teague O'Regan, His Servant *was originally published in four installments and six volumes. The first two volumes (Philadelphia, 1792) and the third (Pittsburgh, 1793) describe the frontier's exaltation of the common man, personified by Teague, the ignorant Irish immigrant, without regard to his merits. A fourth volume (Philadelphia, 1797) was based on the Whiskey Insurrection. The fifth and sixth volumes (Carlisle, 1804, 1805) satirize political journalism and the popular distrust of courts and lawyers. A new complete edition, with still further additions, was printed in four volumes in 1815. Brackenridge's satire is directed against both the absurdities of classification in biological science and the pettifogging aspects of the law. Teague O'Regan, with Captain Farrago's assistance, has become an excise officer, commissioned by the President to see that the whiskey-making inhabitants of western Pennsylvania paid the revenue tax levied on their product. Shouting "Liberty and no excise; down with all excise officers," the crowd had, in a preceding chapter, seized Teague, tarred and feathered him, and borne him off on a cart. What we have here is the aftermath. The text is from the Wilmington, 1815 edition.*

The evening the outrage had been committed on him, he had run several miles, naked as he was; if a man may be said to be naked, that is invested with a layer of viscous fluid, and the adhesion of birds feathers to cover him; through much danger from the country people, who were ill affected to his office: He had at length gained the recesses of a forest, where he thought himself safe for the night; until near morning, when the barking of wolves at no great distance, as he thought, led him to apprehend the being devoured by these animals, who might take him for an object of their prey. To escape this, he had thought it adviseable to climb a spreading beech tree, and there remained until after sun-rise, when two hunters coming along at that early hour, descried him among the branches; and not without much surprize and astonishment. At first they took him for a bear; but seeing the feathers, it was decided that he must be of the fowl kind. Nevertheless his face and form, 10 which appeared to be human, made him a monster in creation, or at least a new species of animal, never before known in these woods.

They at first hesitated whether to take him down by a shot, or to pass on and leave him unmolested. But at length it was determined to pass on for the present, as if they had not seen him, and to rouse the settlement, to take him with dogs, and the help of men. It would be a valuable acquisition to have such a creature to carry to the great towns for a show. It might be a fortune to a man. This being resolved on, one of the hunters was despatched to rouse the settlement, while his comrade in the mean time, had taken his station on an eminence at no great distance, to watch the motions of the wild creature, and give information of his change 20 of situation. The officer in much melancholy of mind had descended from the beech, and was sitting on the point of a rock, looking about him like a bald eagle, when a couple of stout fellows came suddenly behind him, with the folds of ropes, and entrapped his body, so that he could not move his arms, which they took to be wings, but was as tightly laced as a ship's yard arm, when the sails are furled to prepare for a tempest.

A cage having been made and put into the bed of a waggon, he was conveyed to the capital, when the proprietors, after having published an advertisement, began to exhibit him as a curiosity, for the sum of a quarter dollar to each grown person, and an eighth of a dollar to the children of families whose parents brought them 30 with them.

In a short time, this uncommon creature, as it was thought to be, became the subject of general conversation; and the Philosophical Society heard of it. Having called a special meeting, they despatched two members to ascertain and report the nature of the animal, in a memoir to be inserted in their transactions.

The two members accordingly requested of the proprietors an opportunity of a leisurely examination of the animal, and paid them a quarter dollar each extraordinary, for this indulgence. The proprietors were disposed, as was natural, to assist with some particulars of fiction, the singular qualities of the animal they had in charge. They related, that when they first saw it, in its flying from the mountain, 40 it was just alighting on the tree top; that having taken it, they had at first offered it boiled and roasted flesh, but this it refused; but that at length it had come to eat

28 **capital,** Philadelphia   33 **Philosophical Society,** The American Philosophical Society, founded by Benjamin Franklin in 1743, was chartered by the state in 1780

flesh both roasted and sodden, with considerable gout, and sometimes even with rapacity. This was false, by the bye, for they had tried the officer with raw flesh at first, which he had refused, and would eat only roasted or boiled.

The proprietors informed, that when first taken, its cries, or voice, was of a mixed sound, between that of a wild cat and heron; but that it had come to have some imitation of the human voice, and even articulation, and might from that circumstance be probably a species of the parrot.

The philosophers noted all this, and doubtless made a proper use of the particulars, in determining the genus of the animal. For the last thing that a virtuoso
10 ought to question, is the truth of facts. It is by taking facts as granted, that an hypothesis is most easily established.

The transactions of the Society have not yet been published. Nevertheless we have been favoured with the report of the members on this occasion, with leave to publish it, having so immediate a relation to this work. It is as follows:

"The animal of which an account is now to be given, was asleep when we made our visit; and the keepers were unwilling to disturb him, having been kept awake, they said, too much for some time past, by the frequency of people coming to see him. However, this circumstance gave us an opportunity which we would not otherwise have had, of observing him while asleep. He lay with his head upon his right
20 shoulder, and his hinder legs, drawn up to his belly, in the manner of the dog, or bear. He has hair upon his head, with a mixture of feathers; but upon his body there is nothing but feathers, not in the manner of other fowls, if fowl this may be called, smooth and clean, but growing through a viscous substance resembling tar, and intermixed with it; in this particular differing from the bird kind in general, who by means of a spinal gland secrete an oily substance, with which they besmear and dress their feathers; for here the oily or viscous substance is itself mixed with the feathers, and oozing from the skin. Nor are the feathers here, as in fowls in general, lying all one way, but in various directions, as if nature had given them to sprout out at random. But what is most extraordinary, the stems are frequently pro-
30 truded, and the downy part inserted in the skin.

Such were our observations while he lay asleep.

After half an hour the keepers having awakened him, he got up from his straw by turning on his back, stretching out his fore legs, or wings, if they may be so called, raising himself on his rump, and then by resting on one paw, rising with a slow and easy motion, to his feet. It may seem a catachresis in language to talk of the face of a beast; nevertheless we shall use this phrase, for though in great part covered with feathers, and the same viscous matter with the body, yet in shape it has the appearance of a human face, full as much or more, than the baboon, or others of the ape species. It cannot be said to laugh, but rather grin, though once or twice
40 in our presence, you would have thought that it exhibited a dilatation of the oscular muscles, as if attempting to laugh.

The eye is of a grey colour, and the look wild, but steady, like that of a person under an impression of amazement and wonder. The neck, and whole form of the body, and

---

1 **sodden**, boiled   1 **gout**, gusto

even the hinder legs, have a strong resemblance of the human. Were it not for the feathers, a person on a superficial view might mistake the wings for arms, being attached to the body by a shoulder blade, and the claws resembling the fingers of a Negro.

If this animal is to be referred to the quadruped, or beast kind, it would naturally be classed with the Ouran Outang, or Wild Man of Africa: If with the bird kind, we shall be totally at a loss to assign the genus. For though it has a head and face not unlike the ouzel, or the grey owl, yet in the body it has no resemblance. Nevertheless we should certainly give it a place amongst fowls, were it not that it has ribs instead of the lamina, or side plates, which are peculiar to the winged race alone: 10 as also, because we have some reason to think it has an epiglottis, from the articulation of its sounds, by which it has come to imitate our speech, with a pronunciation not unlike that kind of brogue, which we remark in some of the west country Irish. It appears to want the ingluvies or crow [craw]; but has a gizzard, and digests its food by the dissolving power of the gastric juices.

All things considered, we incline to think that it is an animal of a species wholly new, and of a middle nature between a bird and a beast; yet so widely differing from a bat, as not to be classed with it.

This discovery leads to new and important considerations. We do not undertake to decide for the Society; but shall venture to suggest some particulars.   20

This animal would seem to form the link between the brutal and the human species; being nearer to it in some particulars then the Ouran Outang itself; and especially in the evident articulation of certain sounds. Articulation was with the ancients, the distinguishing characteristic of the human kind. The poet Homer has the epithet frequently, *Meropon, Anthropon*: articulate, speaking men. Yet we find from this discovery, that articulation, at least to some extent, is not peculiar to man alone. This is an incidental characteristic, given by the poet; but the distinguishing marks has been given with more subtilty of observation, by the philosopher Plato; whose definition is that of *Animal bipes implumis.* A two legged, unfeathered animal: For though it might be contended with some plausibility, that this animal has 30 two legs; yet it is evidently feathered; not indeed with the long and strong plumage of the ostrich, but with the down of a goose, or duck. This animal, like man, has not a tail. Nevertheless it has the oc coccygis, or termination of the spinal bone, longer than in man; as was ascertained by one of us, who in the interval of his sleeping, felt his rump. Not that we would draw from this any conclusion in favour of the hypothesis of Monboddo, that men had once tails; but that in the scale of animals, there is a gradual nearing of distance, from having long tails, to the having no tail at all.

The most important enquiry comes now to be investigated, namely, whether this be an animal new to discovery, or actually new to the world, and just lately come 40 into existence in the natural kingdom. No account of it having been heretofore

---

14 **ingluvies,** crop   33 **oc [os] coccygis,** the coccyx   36 **Monboddo.** James Burnett, Lord Monboddo (1714-1799) was the source of much amusement in the eighteenth century for his speculations on the similarities between men and monkeys

given by any traveller in America, either from the information of the natives, or personal observation of their own, founds a strong presumption that it is a novel breed of creatures; but that it is prepared to preserve its species, with a female, may be inferred, from the circumstance of nature having furnished it with testicles.

The idea of original production, involves in it the late hypothesis of Macilhattan, in his treatise, *De Seminibus,* that nature has within herself an aboriginal productive power; so that as some animals disappear from the earth, the mammoth for instance, others spring up, that were never known before. Which hypothesis, by the bye, so far as respects the extinction of animals, receives considerable countenance from the
10 ancient relations of the gorgon, the hydra, &c. and the less remote allusions to winged gryphins, orchs, &c. If this should be found to be the fact, it may be suggested whether it would be going too far to say, that it might be in the compass of human research, to discover the subtil combination of causes and effects, necessary to the production of life, and the formation of a living creature; and that the time might not be far distant, when ingenious chymists might undertake and accomplish the analysis of matter, and synthesis of composition, so as to be able to make animals, to those who should bespeak them; as a workman would make articles of furniture for a hall or assembly room. This would save much expence, in feeding, and providing them for food, or for the purposes of labour, and burdens.
20 We have thought it sufficient to suggest this, and propose it to the industry and ingenuity of the learned in philosophic science."

So far the memoir.

The society expressed their approbation of it; and it was proposed to make a purchase of this animal, for the purpose of examining it more fully, in their own hall, and possibly of sending it to the societies abroad, for their examination also. This proposition was adopted, and the same members appointed to drive a bargain with the proprietors, for the subject of their shew.

When the deputation came forward, and began to traffic with the keepers, proposing a purchase of the curiosity in their possession, the revenue officer, in the
30 cage just by, raised what is called the Irish howl, in a most pitiable manner; recollecting what the Captain had told him, on a former occasion, with regard to the use to which they would apply him, when they should have him in their power.

Dear love your shouls, my dear masters, said he, dat have taken me in de wild woods. I care not fat you make o'd me, a wild baste, or a turky buzzard; or a fish o'd de vater, while I gat good mate to ate, and clane straw to ly down upon; but for de sake o'd de holy faders do not sell me to dese filosophers, dat will cut me up as you would a dead cat, and put my skin upon a pitchfork, just to plase der own fancies; rader let me stay where I am, and shew me to de good paple, dat gape and stare, but keep deir teeth in deir mouths, and luke foolish, but dont affer to bite.
40 The philosophers assured him, that his apprehensions were without foundation; having not the least intention of dissecting, at least until he died a natural death. Doubtless, it might be an object, to ascertain from the internal structure of his body, to what genus or class of animals he might belong: nevertheless, they were per-

---

5 **Macilhattan.** This gentleman and his treatise seem to be Brackenridge's invention

suaded, the society would content themselves, with the observations drawn from external structure, at least for some time. On this turning round to the proprietors, they resumed the conversation relative to a purchase; the supposed animal continuing to vociferate and roar horribly.

In the mean time, the affair of this wild man, beast, bird, fish, or whatever it was, began to make a noise in the town; the people who had come to see it, being divided in opinion; some believing it to be a monster, or new animal in the creation; others disposed to be of opinion, and others confidently asserting, that it was a real man.

Coming to the ear of the chief justice of the state, it occurred to him, that if a 10 man, the confining him in that manner was a restraint upon the liberty of the subject; and ought not to be permitted in a country where the laws govern. Accordingly, he had issued his writ of habeas corpus to the keepers, commanding them forthwith to bring before him, the animal in their possession, and to assign the cause of this detainer. The officer came forward at the moment the keepers were about to close the bargain with the philosophers, and shewed his writ. They were obliged to obey; and came forward with their charge before the chief justice and associate justices, in open court then sitting, alleging property in themselves by caption, and employing counsel to support this allegation.

The court having assigned counsel to support the Habeas Corpus, the argument 20 began: Counsellor Patch first.

May it please your honours,

I take this to be an animal in which there can be no property absolute or qualified, being *feræ naturæ,* or of an untamed nature, such as a panther, or a buffalo; of which it is laid down no larceny can be committed, as not being the subject of property. 4 Black. 235; referring for authorities to 1 Hal. P. C. 511. Fost. 366. 1 Hawk. P. C. 94. Here counsellor Patch read the authorities.

Counsellor Catch in reply: But by the same authorities, it is laid down, that animals *feræ naturæ,* or wild, when reclaimed, or confined, and may serve for food, may be the subject of property, as deer inclosed in a park, fish in a trunk, or pheas- 30 ants or partridges in a mew.

But is it conceded, that this animal can *serve for food?* rejoined counsellor Patch.

The question to be considered in the first place, interrupted the chief justice, is whether this creature is of the brutal or the human kind. Speak to that point.

Counsellor Scratch, as *amicus curiæ* observed, that this being a question of fact, was most properly determinable by a jury.

Counsellor Patch thought not, as the trial by inspection in the case of infancy, which was within the province of the court, was analogous to this. The court were of opinion with counsellor Scratch, and proposed to the counsel for the thing in custody, to bring a writ *de homine replegiando* or *replevin,* for the body of a man, as 40

---

19 **caption,** seizure   30 **trunk,** a submerged, perforated box   35 **amicus curiæ,** friend of the court   40
replevin, a process by which property taken from a person is returned to him upon his giving security that
his rightful ownership will be decided in a court and the property returned if the judgment is against him

the proper writ to bring the case before a jury; or that an issue might be made upon the return to the *habeas corpus,* by consent; and in that shape let it be tried. It was agreed; property pleaded, the issue made up, and the jury about to be empannelled.

Counsellor Patch under the principle of an alien having a right to a jury *de medieta-tæ linguæ,* demanded, that the jury should consist of one half beasts.

Curia advisari vult, and in the mean time desired the counsel to search for precedents. No instance was found of the jury *de medietatæ linguæ,* being carried so far as this, and the motion was overruled.

The jury being now sworn, the counsel for the keepers, offered the two members
10 of the philosophical society, who had examined him, to establish his brutality; this evidence was offered on the principle, that it was peculiarly within the province of their studies to ascertain a point of this nature, and were therefore the proper witnesses; as in a case within the custom of merchants, individuals of this occupation are usually called. According to the maxim of the civil law, *Unicuique, in arte sua, perito credendum est.*

Exception to this evidence, that they were interested, having had an eye to the purchase of this thing, and actually in negociation for it.

The objection was overruled, as going to the credibility, not the competency.

The witnesses were clear that this thing was not of the human race, though to
20 what class of brute animals it was to be referred, they were not yet prepared to decide.

To the weight of this evidence counsellor Catch opposed the evidence of nature herself; the thing had a human voice and speech, that of a west country Irishman; no instance of which was to be found in any natural historian that had ever written. He would call upon the gentleman to produce any authority to that effect.

Counsellor Patch, was not prepared with an authority to prove, that beasts had been found that could speak Irish; but that it was no uncommon thing in early ages, and in many countries, for beasts to speak some language; such as Latin, Greek; for which he might refer the gentleman to the Æsopi Fabulæ, or those of
30 Phedrus; nor was he without an authority at hand, to prove that even in more modern times, there were many beasts who could speak English; this authority was that well known book, The History of Reynard the Fox; which he now produced, and from which he read passages.

The court thought the authority in point, and the evidence not to be got over, and directed the jury to find accordingly; which they did, in favour of the keepers, and the Habeas Corpus, was dismissed, and the thing remanded to custody.

The members after this, struck a bargain the more easily with the keepers; as they had been a good deal alarmed at the risk they had run of having this property taken from them. The Society after having retained the curiosity a year or so, and ascer-
40 tained its structure and properties, proposed sending it to some of the foreign

---

4 **de medietatæ linguæ,** of divided language   6 **Curia advisari vult,** the court wished to be advised   14 **Unicuique. . . .** The expert, unique in his occupation, must be believed   30 **Phedrus,** or **Phædrus** (fl. 1st century A.D.), a Roman author who versified the fables of Aesop, adding much of his own   32 **The History of Reynard the Fox,** a medieval beast epic, best known to students through Chaucer's Nun's Priest's Tale

societies, who had expressed a wish to have an ocular examination of it also. The preference was given to the societies of France; and it was accordingly shipped in a brig of Blair M'Clenachen, that was bound to Nantz. At this place on coming ashore, by rolling and tumbling in it, having worn off the tar and feathers from his back-side, he was mistaken for a sans culotte; and the mob rising broke the inclosure, and let him out. I have not heard whether he joined the army of the patriots, or is on his way home again to this country.

1797, 1815

_____

5 **sans culotte**, without breeches, a term applied to the most violent of the revolutionists

1789—1847 **Richard Henry Wilde**

From the time it was first printed about 1815, without the author's consent, "The Lament of the Captive" (sometimes titled "Stanzas") was well liked by nineteenth-century Americans. It was frequently reprinted, not only in the United States but in Scotland and Ireland as well, and at least six composers wrote musical settings for it. It is a fine example of the self-pity which characterizes much sentimental writing.

Wilde was born in Dublin, Ireland, the son of an Irish merchant and of Mary Newitt Wilde, whose Tory family had left America at the beginning of the Revolution. The Wildes came to this country when Richard was a boy of eight, lived in Baltimore for five years, and then in Georgia. Wilde became a lawyer, then turned to politics and served several terms in the United States Congress. He spent a number of years in Italy, studying the lives of Tasso and Dante. Though he wrote a great deal, he is remembered chiefly for the poem which follows.

C. C. Jones, **The Life, Literary Labors, and Neglected Grave of Richard Henry Wilde**, 1887   T. W. Koch, **Dante in America**

The Lament of the Captive

My life is like the summer rose,
    That opens to the morning sky,
But, ere the shades of evening close,
    Is scattered on the ground — to die!
Yet on the rose's humble bed

The sweetest dews of night are shed,
As if she wept the waste to see —
But none shall weep a tear for me!

My life is like the autumn leaf
    That trembles in the moon's pale ray: 10
Its hold is frail — its date is brief,
    Restless — and soon to pass away!
Yet, ere that leaf shall fall and fade,
The parent tree will mourn its shade,
The winds bewail the leafless tree —
But none shall breathe a sigh for me!

My life is like the prints which feet
    Have left on Tampa's desert strand;
Soon as the rising tide shall beat,
    All trace will vanish from the sand;   20
Yet, as if grieving to efface
All vestige of the human race,
On that lone shore loud moans the sea —
But none, alas! shall mourn for me!
                    1814?, 1815?

---

18 **Tampa's desert strand.** The poem, written as a part of a larger work, was supposedly the song of a captive in Florida

1785—1842 Samuel Woodworth

S cituate, Massachusetts, was the birthplace of Samuel Woodworth and the scene of a childhood which, contrary to the claims of his most famous poem, was a rather unhappy one. After somewhat scanty formal schooling, Woodworth became a printer, then a literary man, well-known in his day as editor, playwright, fictionist, and poet.

His most famous song, originally called "The Bucket," published in the New York *Republican Chronicle,* June 3, 1818, was immediately reprinted widely and hailed as a masterpiece. The poem was written to be sung to the melody of "The

Flower of Dunblane," but another musical setting by George Kiallmark (1781-1835) became popularly associated with it and helped spread and maintain its fame.

William Leggett's criticism of this piece, written in 1828, indicated the contemporary appeal of the song: "Its merit consists in the graphic accuracy of the description, the simplicity and nature of its sentiments, and the melodious flow of the versification. It appeals to feelings cherished in every human bosom . . . and forms around us, with the delusive power of a dream, a chain of young and heart-hoarded circumstances. . . ."

S. J. Kunitz and Howard Haycraft, **American Authors 1600-1900**, New York, 1938   A. H. Quinn, **A History of the American Drama from the Beginning to the Civil War**, New York, 1943

The Old Oaken Bucket

How dear to this heart are the scenes of my childhood,
    When fond recollection presents them to view!
The orchard, the meadow, the deep-tangled wild-wood,
    And every loved spot which my infancy knew!
The wide-spreading pond, and the mill that stood by it,
    The bridge, and the rock where the cataract fell,
The cot of my father, the dairy-house nigh it,
    And e'en the rude bucket that hung in the well —
The old oaken bucket, the iron-bound bucket,
The moss-covered bucket which hung in the well.   10

That moss-covered vessel I hail'd as a treasure,
    For often at noon, when return'd from the field,
I found it the source of an exquisite pleasure,
    The purest and sweetest that nature can yield.
How ardent I seized it, with hands that were glowing,
    And quick to the white-pebbled bottom it fell;
Then soon, with the emblem of truth overflowing,
    And dripping with coolness, it rose from the well —
The old oaken bucket, the iron-bound bucket,
The moss-covered bucket, arose from the well.   20

How sweet from the green mossy brim to receive it,
    As poised on the curb it inclined to my lips!
Not a full blushing goblet could tempt me to leave it
    The brightest that beauty or revelry sips.
And now, far removed from the loved habitation,
    The tear of regret will intrusively swell,
As fancy reverts to my father's plantation,

And sighs for the bucket that hangs in the well —
The old oaken bucket, the iron-bound bucket,
The moss-covered bucket that hangs in the well!   30

1818

1752—1832 Philip Freneau

P
hilip Freneau's relatively high rank in American literary history is based upon three different aspects of his work, none of which would by itself justify his being regarded as almost a major writer. Taken together, however, his poems of romantic fancy, his ballads and satires in behalf of American independence, and his work as editor in the interest of Jeffersonian Republicanism reveal a fluent, versatile, and sometimes powerful man of letters. That he never attained the height of genius was perhaps as much an accident of his time as of his talent.

In his youth Freneau had the advantages of wealth, as they were understood at that time in New York and New Jersey. When he entered Princeton at sixteen, he was well grounded in Latin and hoped to prepare for the ministry. In college, as the close friend of James Madison, Hugh Henry Brackenridge (see p. 498), and William Bradford, Freneau acquired Whig principles and literary ambitions. He began to write, imitating the classics and the English poets. In collaboration with Brackenridge he wrote part of a novel, "Father Bombo's Pilgrimage to Mecca in Arabia," and a Commencement poem, *The Rising Glory of America.* He had every reason to think the future would hold great things for him.

The next decade, however, brought unusual problems as well as the commonplace one of making a living (for Freneau's family resources steadily dwindled after his father's death in 1767). Theology proved unsatisfying; two ventures at teaching even more so. There was no livelihood in literature, although both the Commencement poem and one other, *The American Village,* were printed in 1772. For the next two years or more Freneau's movements are obscure. He was evidently restless, for, although he turned up in New York in 1775, writing satires against General Gage and the British, he was off the next year to the West Indies. For about two years he lived on Santa Cruz, in the Virgin Islands, writing some of his most fanciful poems: "The Jamaica Funeral," "The Beauties of Santa Cruz," and "The House of Night." In 1778, after several voyages to Bermuda and at least one tour of the lower Gulf of Mexico, he started back for New Jersey. His ship was captured off the Carolinas by the British, but he was permitted to land near his home and promptly enlisted in the militia. Capture, apparently, had brought the war close home to him. The *United States Magazine,* edited by Brackenridge, soon printed some of Freneau's best West Indian poems, together with "King George the Third's Soliloquy," but his work as a propagandist did not become important until 1780. By that time he had left the army to become a blockade runner and had made two more trips to the West Indies. He was starting out on a fourth voyage, this time as third mate, when he was captured and confined for six weeks on prison and hospital ships in New York Harbor. That experience made Freneau a boiling, bitter, hate-marked patriot, and *The British Prison-Ship* (1781) was followed by a flood of propaganda, most of it published in the *Freeman's Journal,* a Philadelphia weekly. In satire and in ballads he expressed the hopes and the hates of his countrymen.

The war over, Freneau turned again to the sea to make his living, and between 1784 and 1790 was engaged chiefly in coastwise shipping, most of the time as ship's captain. In port, at Charleston, Philadelphia, or New York, he occasionally offered a new poem to a newspaper or magazine, and he presumably found some satisfaction in seeing in his cabin *The Poems of Philip Freneau* (Philadelphia, 1786) and *The Miscellaneous Works of Mr. Philip Freneau Containing His Essays and Additional Poems* (Philadelphia, 1788).

In April 1790 Freneau married and settled in New York, to try once more to make his living as a writer. While editing the *Daily Advertiser,* he made plans to establish a country paper of his own in New Jersey. Through the influence of James Madison, however, he was offered a part-time clerkship as translator in the Department of State, under Jefferson. In October 1791, encouraged by Madison and Jefferson, Freneau founded in Philadelphia the *National Gazette,* designed to rival the strongly Federalist *Gazette of the United States,* and to provide a focal point for the opposition to the policies of Alexander Hamilton. Freneau and his friends regarded the financial measures of Hamilton as favorable to the wealthy and dangerous to the common people; his frankness in saying so soon plunged him into the midst of the bitterest incidents attending the birth of party politics in the United States. He supported Jefferson with all the force of direct attack, satire, and abuse, and came to epitomize to Hamilton and his party the rabble-rousing journalist. "That rascal Freneau!" Washington is reported to have exclaimed. In the end Freneau's enthusiasm for the French Revolution and his support of Citizen Genêt, after that gentleman had alienated even Jefferson, lost him support, and the *National Gazette* expired in the fall of 1793. There can be no doubt, however, of Freneau's mighty contribution to the establishment of party government and party journalism.

During the last thirty-nine years of his life, Freneau was in almost constant financial difficulty. His chief editorial ventures were on the *Jersey Chronicle* of Mount Pleasant in 1795-1796, where he published his "Tomo Cheeki" essays and failed to collect from his subscribers, and a New York periodical, *The Time-Piece; and Literary Companion,* in 1797-1798. In 1803-1807 he was forced once more to return to the sea. Before his death in a blizzard in 1832, he published three more collections of his work.

Although Freneau was obviously imitative in his forms and themes — most of the famous English poets of the eighteenth century were among his literary mentors — he is remembered for his discovery of American plants and birds, for his primitivistic idealization of the Indian, for his feeling for the sea, on which he spent so much of his life. As a precursor of Bryant, Emerson, Poe, Whittier, and Longfellow, he has historic interest; but he is memorable also for his revelation of himself — a man who lived in stirring, restless, difficult times, fighting, not always judiciously, for the ways of life in which he believed.

The Poems of Philip Freneau, ed. F. L. Pattee, 3 vols., Princeton, 1902-1907   Poems of Freneau, ed. H. H. Clark, New York, 1929   The Prose of Philip Freneau, ed. Philip Marsh, New Brunswick, N.J., 1955   Lewis Leary, That Rascal Freneau: A Study in Literary Failure, New Brunswick, N.J., 1941   N. F. Adkins, Philip Freneau and the Cosmic Enigma, New York, 1950

The Power of Fancy

"The Power of Fancy" is perhaps the most interesting of the poems which Freneau wrote as an undergraduate at Princeton. The many literary allusions emphasize his reading of the classics, and the delight in distant places exemplifies his romantic tendency. His concept of poetic fancy, which is characteristic of eighteenth-century thought, was probably derived from the "Ode to Fancy" by Joseph Warton (1722-1800), one of the earliest of English "romantic" poets (see H. H. Clark, "Literary Influences on Philip Freneau," Studies in Philology, *January 1925). Freneau's enthusiasm for Milton, and especially for "Il Penseroso," is more self-evident (see T. P. Haviland, "A Measure for the Early Freneau's Debt to Milton,"* Publications of the Modern Language Association, *December 1940).*

WAKEFUL, vagrant, restless thing,
Ever wandering on the wing,
Who thy wondrous source can find,
FANCY, regent of the mind;
A spark from Jove's resplendent throne,
But thy nature all unknown.
THIS spark of bright, celestial flame,
From Jove's seraphic altar came,
And hence alone in man we trace,
Resemblance to the immortal race.   10
Ah! what is all this mighty WHOLE,
These suns and stars that round us roll!
What are they all, where'er they shine,
But *Fancies* of the Power Divine!
What is this *globe,* these *lands,* and *seas,*
And *heat,* and *cold,* and *flowers,* and *trees,*

Text: the 1786 edition. In the 1795 edition and thereafter Freneau printed 11.1-20 and 141-154 as "Ode to Fancy," using the remainder in a much revised form as a poem entitled "Fancy's Ramble"

And *life,* and *death,* and *beast,* and *man,*
And *time,* — that with the *sun* began —
But thoughts on reason's scale combin'd,
Ideas of the Almighty mind?   20
   On the surface of the brain
Night after night she walks unseen,
Noble fabrics doth she raise
In the woods or on the seas,
On some high, steep, pointed rock,
Where the billows loudly knock
And the dreary tempests sweep
Clouds along the uncivil deep.
   Lo! she walks upon the moon,
Listens to the chimy tune   30
Of the bright, harmonious spheres,
And the song of angels hears;
Sees this earth a distant star,
Pendant, floating in the air;
Leads me to some lonely dome,
Where Religion loves to come,
Where the bride of Jesus dwells,
And the deep ton'd organ swells
In notes with lofty anthems join'd,
Notes that half distract the mind.   40
   Now like lightning she descends
To the prison of the fiends,
Hears the rattling of their chains,
Feels their never ceasing pains —
But, O never may she tell
Half the frightfulness of hell.
   Now she views Arcadian rocks,
Where the shepherds guard their flocks,
And, while yet her wings she spreads,
Sees chrystal streams and coral beds,   50
Wanders to some desert deep,
Or some dark, enchanted steep,
By the full moon light doth shew
Forests of a dusky blue,

---

20 **Ideas . . . mind?** The notion here, essentially Platonic, was common in eighteenth-century philosophy. The emphasis on reason in line 19 and the implications of line 18 are evidence of Freneau's Deistic ideas (p. 256)   30 **chimy . . . spheres.** The Aristotelian and Ptolemaic systems conceived of the universe as a succession of concentric spheres, something like the layers of an onion, which, as they rubbed together, produced a mighty musical harmony   33 **star,** "Milton's Paradise Lost, B.II, v. 1052." — Freneau   47 **Arcadian,** pastoral, from a mountainous area in ancient Greece, praised by the poets for its idyllic simplicity

Where, upon some mossy bed,
Innocence reclines her head.
   SWIFT, she stretches o'er the seas
To the far off Hebrides,
Canvas on the lofty mast
Could not travel half so fast —   60
Swifter than the eagle's flight
Or instantaneous rays of light!
Lo! contemplative she stands
On Norwegia's rocky lands —
Fickle Goddess, set me down
Where the rugged winters frown
Upon Orca's howling steep,
Nodding o'er the northern deep,
Where the winds tumultuous roar,
Vext that *Ossian* sings no more.   70
Fancy, to that land repair,
Sweetest Ossian slumbers there;
Waft me far to southern isles
Where the soften'd winter smiles,
To Bermuda's orange shades,
Or Demarara's lovely glades;
Bear me o'er the sounding cape,
Painting death in every shape,
Where daring *Anson* spread the sail
Shatter'd by the stormy gale —   80
Lo! she leads me wide and far,
Sense can never follow her —
Shape thy course o'er land and sea,
Help me to keep pace with thee,
Lead me to yon chalky cliff,
Over rock and over reef,
Into Britain's fertile land,
Stretching far her proud command.

---

58 **Hebrides,** islands off the coast of Scotland   67 **Orca's,** perhaps a reference to the Orchades or Orkney Islands, to the north of Scotland. In the later version of the poem, "Fancy's Ramble," Freneau substituted *Hecla,* a mountain in Iceland. In either case Fancy's flight is somewhat erratic   70 **Ossian,** a legendary Gaelic poet who celebrated the deeds of his father, Finn, or Find, who lived, presumably, in the third century. The Ossianic poems exist in fifteenth-century manuscripts, but their fame rests upon the attempt of James MacPherson (1736-1796) to create a Gaelic epic. His *Fingal* (1762) is now known to have been based largely upon forged manuscripts, but in Freneau's time it was accepted as authentic   76 **Demerara's,** now the name of both a county and a river in British Guiana; it was also once the name for Georgetown, the capital of that South American country   79 **Anson,** George Anson (1697-1762), leader of a British naval expedition to the South Pacific, 1740-1744, which, after raiding Peru and a Spanish treasure ship off Acapulco in Mexico, continued westward around the world

Look back and view, thro' many a year,
Cæsar, Julius Cæsar, there.   90
   Now to Tempe's verdant wood,
Over the mid ocean flood
Lo! the islands of the sea
— Sappho, Lesbos mourns for thee:
Greece, arouse thy humbled head,
Where are all thy mighty dead,
Who states to endless ruin hurl'd
And carried vengeance through the world? —
Troy, thy vanish'd pomp resume,
Or, weeping at thy Hector's tomb,   100
Yet those faded scenes renew,
Whose memory is to *Homer* due.
Fancy, lead me wandering still
Up to Ida's cloud-topt hill;
Not a laurel there doth grow
But in vision thou shalt show, —
Every sprig on Virgil's tomb
Shall in livelier colours bloom,
And every triumph Rome has seen
Flourish on the years between.   110
   Now she bears me far away
In the east to meet the day,
Leads me over Ganges' streams,
Mother of the morning beams —
O'er the ocean hath she ran,
Places me on *Tinian;*
Farther, farther in the east,
Till it almost meets the west,
Let us wandering both be lost
On Taitis sea-beat coast,   120
Bear me from that distant strand,
Over ocean, over land,
To California's golden shore —
Fancy, stop, and rove no more.
   Now, tho' late, returning home,

---

90 **there,** i.e., in Britain, where Caesar landed in 55 B.C.   91 **Tempe's.** See note, p. 369   94 **Sappho, Lesbos.** Sappho (fl. 630-570 B.C.), most famous of the women poets of Lesbos or Mytilini, off the coast of Asia Minor   95 **humbled head.** From 1715 until 1821 Greece was occupied by the Turks. An insurrection in 1770 may have suggested Freneau's phrase   104 **Ida's.** The gods watched the battles around Troy, described in Homer's *Iliad,* from the summit of Mount Ida   116 **Tinian,** an island in the Marianas, well-known to Americans through its occupation in World War II. Anson was there for two months in 1742   120 **Taitis,** Tahiti, in the Society Islands, well-known to eighteenth-century readers through the expedition of Captain James Cook, who observed the Transit of Venus of 1769 at that spot

Lead me to *Belinda's* tomb;
Let me glide as well as you
Through the shroud and coffin too,
And behold, a moment, there,
All that once was good and fair —   130
Who doth here so soundly sleep?
Shall we break this prison deep? —
Thunders cannot wake the maid,
Lightnings cannot pierce the shade,
And tho' wintry tempests roar,
Tempests shall disturb no more.
   YET must those eyes in darkness stay,
That once were rivals to the day — ?
Like heaven's bright lamp beneath the main
They are but set to rise again.   140
   FANCY, thou the muses' pride,
In thy painted realms reside
Endless images of things,
Fluttering each on golden wings,
Ideal objects, such a store,
The universe could hold no more:
Fancy, to thy power I owe
Half my happiness below;
By thee Elysian groves were made,
Thine were the notes that Orpheus play'd;   150
By thee was Pluto charm'd so well
While rapture seiz'd the sons of hell —
Come, O come — perceiv'd by none,
You and I will walk alone.

           1770, 1786

---

126 **Belinda's,** a common name in Neoclassical poetry   149 **Elysian groves,** the abode of the blessed in classical mythology, a land of eternal spring and happiness   150 **Orpheus,** a mythical Greek poet who, by petitioning Pluto with song and lyre, won back his wife Eurydice from Hades, only to lose her again by disobeying the injunction not to look at her until they reached the upper air

George the Third's Soliloquy

As *"King George the Third's Soliloquy," this poem first appeared in the* United States Magazine *for May 1779, and was reprinted almost at once in the* Pennsylvania Packet *for June 5. Freneau revised it extensively for the 1786 edition of his* Poems, *changing the order of the lines, omitting some passages, and adding others. He then entitled it "George III. His Soliloquy for 1779." The present title and text first appeared in 1795. The 1809 edition shows minor variations in spelling, but no further changes. In its combination of bitterness, ridicule, and confidence in the ultimate triumph of the American cause, it probably typifies the attitude and methods of the Whig leaders.*

What mean these dreams, and hideous forms that rise
Night after night, tormenting to my eyes —
No real foes these horrid shapes can be,
But thrice as much they vex and torture me.
    How cursed is he — how doubly curs'd am I —
Who lives in pain, and yet who dares not die;
To him no joy this world of Nature brings,
In vain the wild rose blooms, the daisy springs.
Is this a prelude to some new disgrace,
Some baleful omen to my name and race —!   10
It may be so — ere mighty Cesar died
Presaging Nature felt his doom, and sigh'd;
A bellowing voice through midnight groves was heard,
And threatening ghosts at dusk of eve appear'd —
Ere Brutus fell, to adverse fates a prey,
His evil genius met him on the way,
And so may mine! — but who would yield so soon
A prize, some luckier hour may make my own? —
Shame seize my crown, ere such a deed be mine —
No — to the last my squadrons shall combine,   20
And slay my foes, while foes remain to slay,
Or *heaven* shall grant me one successful day.
    Is there a robber close in Newgate hemm'd,
Is there a cut-throat, fetter'd and condemn'd?
Haste, loyal slaves, to George's standard come,
Attend his lectures when you hear the drum;
Your chains I break — for better days prepare,
Come out, my friends, from prison and from care,
Far to the west I plan your desperate sway,
There 'tis no sin to ravage, burn, and slay.   30
There, without fear, your bloody aims pursue,
And show mankind what English thieves can do.
    That day, when first I mounted to the throne,
I swore to let all foreign foes alone.
Through love of peace to terms did I advance,

Text: the 1795 edition   12 **Presaging Nature.** Plutarch and Strabo, Roman historians, tell of many wonders seen before Caesar's death, these among them   16 **His evil . . . him.** According to Plutarch, Brutus was visited one night by an apparition, who identified himself as "thy evil genius. We shall meet again at Philippi." On the eve of the second battle of Philippi the apparition reappeared; next day, defeated, Brutus fell on his sword   23 **Newgate.** A famous London prison

And made, they say, a shameful league with France
But different scenes rise horrid to my view,
I charg'd my hosts to plunder and subdue —
At first, indeed, I thought short wars to wage
And sent some jail-birds to be led by Gage.   40
For 'twas but right, that those we mark'd for slaves
Should be reduc'd by cowards, fools, and knaves:
Awhile, directed by his feeble hand,
Those *troops* were kick'd and pelted through the land,
Or starv'd in Boston, curs'd the unlucky hour
They left their dungeons for that fatal shore.
    France aids them now, a desperate game I play,
And hostile Spain will do the same, they say;
My armies vanquish'd, and my heroes fled,
My people murmuring, and my commerce dead,   50
My shattered navy pelted, bruis'd, and clubb'd,
By Dutchmen bullied, and by Frenchmen drubb'd,
My name abhorr'd, my nation in disgrace,
How should I act in such a mournful case!
My hopes and joys are vanish'd with my coin,
My ruin'd army, and my lost Burgoyne!
What shall I do — confess my labours vain,
Or whet my tusks, and to the charge again!
But where's my force — my choicest troops are fled,
Some thousand crippled, and a myriad dead —   60
If I were own'd the boldest of mankind,
And hell with all her flames inspir'd my mind,
Could I at once with Spain and France contend,
And fight the *rebels,* on the world's green end? —
The pangs of *parting* I can ne'er endure,
Yet *part* we must, and part to meet no more!
Oh! blast this *Congress,* blast each upstart STATE,
On whose commands ten thousand captains wait;
From various climes that dire *Assembly* came,
True to their trust, as hostile to my fame,   70
'Tis these, ah these, have ruin'd half my sway,
Disgrac'd my arms, and led my slaves astray —
Curs'd be the day, when first I saw the sun,

---

36 **a shameful . . . France.** Shameful because in making peace with France, the Earl of Bute, King George's teacher and first prime minister, deserted Frederick the Great of Prussia, who had been fighting the three great absolutist monarchies: Austria, Russia, and France   40 **Gage,** Thomas Gage. See note, p. 418. In the 1786 edition, this line read: "And sent a scoundrel by the name of Gage"   56 **Burgoyne.** John Burgoyne arrived in Boston to reinforce Gage in September 1774   67 **Oh! . . .** In the 1779 version, this line began the poem. Freneau's chief addition in 1786 consisted of ll. 1-22, but there was considerable rearrangement

Curs'd be the hour, when I these wars begun:
The fiends of darkness then possess'd my mind,
And powers unfriendly to the human kind.
To wasting grief, and sullen rage a prey,
To *Scotland's* utmost verge I'll take my way,
There with eternal storms due concert keep
And while the billows rage, as fiercely weep —   80
Ye highland lads, my rugged fate bemoan,
Assist me with one sympathizing groan,
For late I find the nations are my foes,
I must submit, and that with bloody nose,
Or, like our James, fly basely from the state,
Or share, what still is worse — old *Charles's* fate.

                                                        1779, 1795

85 **James** II decamped to the Continent when his political downfall seemed imminent in 1688   86 **old
Charles's fate,** an allusion to the execution of Charles I in 1649

On the Memorable Victory

Obtained by the Gallant Captain John Paul Jones, of the Bon Homme Richard,
over the Seraphis, *under the command of Captain Pearson*

This poem was first published in the Freeman's Journal, *August 8, 1781. It relates the
action of September 23, 1779, within sight of the east coast of* England, *in which John Paul
Jones (1747-1792) won his greatest victory. The* Bon Homme Richard, *named for Benjamin Franklin, "Poor Richard," was a converted merchantman; only her officers were Americans. The raiding force of which it was the flagship encountered, off Scarborough, a large
convoy from the Baltic, guarded by the* Serapis, *under the command of Richard Pearson
(1731-1806). Jones, handicapped by inferior arms and equipment, was skillful in placing
his deck guns and directing his boarding party, but his triumph came largely from the fact
that he never thought of accepting defeat. Freneau, curiously enough, does not use exactly
Jones' classic reply to Pearson's demand that he strike his colors. "I have not," he said, "begun to fight."*

O'ER the rough main, with flowing sheet,
The guardian of a numerous fleet,
  Seraphis from the Baltic came;
A ship of less tremendous force
Sail'd by her side the self-same course,
  Countess of Scarb'ro' was her name.

And now their native coasts appear,

Text: the 1795 edition

Britannia's hills their summit rear
  Above the German main:
Fond to suppose their dangers o'er,   10
They southward coast along the shore,
  Thy waters, gentle Thames, to gain.

Full forty guns Seraphis bore,
And Scarb'ro's Countess twenty-four,
  Mann'd with Old England's boldest tars —
What flag that rides the Gallic seas
Shall dare attack such piles as these,
  Design'd for tumults and for wars!

Now from the top-mast's giddy height
A seaman cry'd — "Four sail in sight   20
  "Approach with favouring gales,"
Pearson, resolv'd to save the fleet,
Stood off to sea, these ships to meet,
  And closely brac'd his shivering sails.

With him advanc'd the Countess bold,
Like a black tar in wars grown old:
  And now these floating piles drew nigh;
But, muse, unfold, what chief of fame
In the other warlike squadron came,
  Whose standards at his mast head fly.   30

'Twas JONES, brave JONES, to battle led
As bold a crew as ever bled
  Upon the sky-surrounded main;
The standards of the western world
Were to the willing winds unfurl'd,
  Denying Britain's tyrant reign.

The *Good-Man-Richard* led the line;
The *Alliance* next: with these combine
  The Gallic ship they *Pallas* call,
The *Vengeance,* arm'd with sword and flame; 40
These to attack the Britons came —
  But *two* accomplish'd all.

---

42 **two accomplish'd all.** The *Bon Homme Richard* took the *Serapis;* the *Pallas,* the *Countess of Scarborough.*
The *Vengeance* had no part in the action, and the *Alliance,* commanded by Captain Landis (d. 1818), who
was later judged insane, not only failed to help but also fired occasionally, so Jones said, at the *Bon Homme
Richard*

Now Phoebus sought his pearly bed:
But who can tell the scenes of dread,
   The horrors of that fatal night!
Close up those floating castles came;
The Good-Man-Richard bursts in flame;
   Seraphis trembled at the sight.

She felt the fury of *her* ball:
Down, prostrate, down the Britons fall;   50
   The decks were strew'd with slain:
JONES to the foe his vessel lash'd;
And, while the black artillery flash'd,
   Loud thunders shook the main.

Alas! that mortals should employ
Such murdering engines, to destroy
   That frame by heaven so nicely join'd;
Alas! that e'er the god decreed
That brother should by brother bleed,
   And pour'd such madness in the mind.   60

But thou, brave JONES, no blame shalt bear;
The rights of men demand your care:
   For *these* you dare the greedy waves —
No tyrant, on destruction bent,
Has plann'd thy conquests — thou art sent
   To humble tyrants and their slaves.

See! — dread Seraphis flames again —
And art thou, JONES, among the slain,
   And sunk to Neptune's caves below —
He lives — though crowds around him fall,   70
Still he, unhurt, survives them all;
   Almost alone he fights the foe.

And can thy ship these strokes sustain?
Behold thy brave companions slain,
   All clasped in ocean's dark embrace.
STRIKE, OR BE SUNK — the Briton cries —
SINK IF YOU CAN — the chief replies,
   Fierce lightnings blazing in his face.

Then to the side three guns he drew,
(Almost deserted by his crew)   80

---

43 **Phoebus**, the sun. The battle raged for several hours after sunset

And charg'd them deep with woe:
By *Pearson's* flash he aimed hot balls;
His main-mast totters — down it falls —
   O'erwhelming half below.

Pearson had yet disdain'd to yield,
But scarce his secret fears conceal'd,
   And thus was heard to cry —
"With hell, not mortals, I contend;
"What art thou — human or a fiend,
   "That dost my force defy? 90

"Return, my lads, the fight renew!" —
So call'd bold Pearson to his crew;
   But call'd, alas, in vain;
Some on the decks lay maim'd and dead;
Some to their deep recesses fled,
   And more were shrouded in the main.

Distress'd, forsaken, and alone,
He haul'd his tatter'd standard down,
   And yielded to his gallant foe;
Bold *Pallas* soon the *Countess* took, — 100
Thus both their haughty colours struck,
   Confessing what the brave can do.

But, JONES, too dearly didst thou buy
These ships possest so gloriously,
   Too many deaths disgrac'd the fray:
Thy barque that bore the conquering flame,
That the proud Briton overcame,
   Even she forsook thee on thy way;

For when the morn began to shine,
Fatal to her, the ocean brine 110
   Pour'd through each spacious wound;
Quick in the deep she disappear'd,
But JONES to friendly Belgia steer'd,
   With conquest and with glory crown'd.

Go on, great man, to scourge the foe,
And bid the haughty Britons know
   They to our *Thirteen Stars* shall bend;

---

113 **Belgia,** here Holland. Jones took his prizes to Texel, largest of the West Frisian Islands

The *Stars* that, veil'd in dark attire,
Long glimmer'd with a feeble fire,
　　But radiant now ascend.   120

Bend to the Stars that flaming rise
On western worlds, more brilliant skies.
　　Fair Freedom's reign restor'd —
So when the Magi, come from far,
Beheld the God-attending Star,
　　They trembled and ador'd.

　　　　　　　　　　　　　　　　　　1781

────────

124 **the Magi,** the wise men from the East who found the child Jesus in Bethlehem

To the Memory

Of the Brave Americans, under General Greene, in South Carolina, *Who Fell in the Action of* September 8, 1781

Since its appearance in the Freeman's Journal *of November 21, 1781, and in the edition of 1786, this has been one of Freneau's best-known poems. It combines the patriotic theme with that gentle melancholy which is most familiar through Gray's "Elegy Written in a Country Churchyard." The battle on which the poem is based was an attack by General Nathanael Greene (1742-1786) and his force upon a British outpost, commanded by Georgia-born General John Stuart (1759-1815). Retreating to another position, the British re-formed their line and this time repulsed the overanxious Americans, killing and wounding an estimated five to seven hundred men. Greene's attack was one of many which contributed to the failure of the British to hold South Carolina.*

At EUTAW springs the valiant died:
Their limbs with dust are cover'd o'er —
Weep on, ye springs, your tearful tide;
How many heroes are no more!

If in this wreck of ruin, they
Can yet be thought to claim a tear,
O smite thy gentle breast, and say
The friends of freedom slumber here!

Thou, who shalt trace this bloody plain,
If goodness rules thy generous breast,   10
Sigh for the wasted rural reign;
Sigh for the shepherds, sunk to rest!

────────

Text: the 1795 edition   1 **Eutaw springs,** on the Santee River, midway between Charlestown and Columbia, South Carolina

Stranger, their humble graves adorn;
You too may fall, and ask a tear:
'Tis not the beauty of the morn
That proves the evening shall be clear —

They saw their injur'd country's woe;
The flaming town, the wasted field;
Then rush'd to meet the insulting foe;
They took the spear — but left the shield, 20

Led by thy conquering genius, GREENE,
The Britons they compell'd to fly:
None distant view'd the fatal plain,
None griev'd, in such a cause, to die —

But, like the Parthian, fam'd of old,
Who, flying, still their arrows threw;
These routed Britons, full as bold,
Retreated, and retreating slew.

Now rest in peace, our patriot band;
Though far from Nature's limits thrown, 30
We trust, they find a happier land,
A brighter sun-shine of their own.

                                        1781
_____

19 **Then rush'd.** Professor Pattee has noted that Sir Walter Scott borrowed this and the following line for the introduction to Canto III of *Marmion:* "When Prussia hurried to the field, And snatch'd the spear, but left the shield."   25 **the Parthian.** The horsemen of Parthia, a region in ancient Persia, used the stratagem of pretended retreat; when their enemies were scattered, they turned to the attack

The Wild Honey Suckle

"These stanzas," writes Professor Leary, "placed Freneau, beyond the reach of calumny or special pleading, chronologically at the head of America's procession of poets." They were first printed over the signature "K" in the Columbian Herald, *July 6, 1786. Other printings followed in the* Pennsylvania Packet, *the* Freeman's Journal, *and the* Massachusetts Centinel. *There is no better evidence of Freneau's independence of the classical tradition and of his fresh perception of nature.*

Fair flower, that dost so comely grow,
Hid in this silent, dull retreat,
Untouch'd thy honey'd blossoms blow,
Unseen thy little branches greet:
_____

Text: the 1795 edition, with changes of wording indicated on the basis of Professor Leary's text of the original printing (*That Rascal Freneau*, p. 144). Variations in punctuation have not all been described

No roving foot shall crush thee here,
No busy hand provoke a tear.

By Nature's self in white array'd,
She bade thee shun the vulgar eye,
And planted here the guardian shade,
And sent soft waters murmuring by;   10
    Thus quietly thy summer goes,
    Thy days declining to repose.

Smit with those charms, that must decay,
I grieve to see your future doom;
They died — nor were those flowers less gay,
The flowers that did in Eden bloom;
    Unpitying frosts, and Autumn's power
    Shall leave no vestige of this flower.

From morning suns and evening dews
At first thy little being came: 20
If nothing once, you nothing lose,
For when you die you are the same;
    The space between, is but an hour,
    The frail duration of a flower.

                                    1786

_____

5 **crush.** 1786, find   15 **They died.** In the 1786 version the following two lines are in parentheses   15
less. 1786, more   24 **frail duration.** 1786, empty image

The Indian Burying-Ground

"Lines occasioned by a visit to an old Indian burying ground" appeared in the American
Museum *for November 1787 and in Freneau's* Miscellaneous Works *(1788). This poem
is usually regarded as one of the earliest idealizations of the Indian.*

In spite of all the learn'd have said,
I still my old opinion keep;
The *posture,* that *we* give the dead,
Points out the soul's eternal sleep.

Not so the ancients of these lands —
The Indian, when from life releas'd,
Again is seated with his friends,
And shares again the joyous feast.

_____

Text: the 1795 edition

His imag'd birds, and painted bowl,
And ven'son, for a journey dress'd,   10
Bespeak the nature of the soul,
ACTIVITY, that knows no rest.

His bow, for action ready bent,
And arrows, with a head of stone,
Can only mean that life is spent,
And not the finer essence gone.

Thou, stranger, that shalt come this way,
No fraud upon the dead commit —
Observe the swelling turf, and say
They do not *lie,* but here they *sit.*   20

Here still a lofty rock remains,
On which the curious eye may trace
(Now wasted, half, by wearing rains)
The fancies of a ruder race.

Here still an aged elm aspires,
Beneath whose far-projecting shade
(And which the shepherd still admires)
The children of the forest play'd!

There oft a restless Indian queen
(Pale *Shebah,* with her braided hair)   30
And many a barbarous form is seen
To chide the man that lingers there.

By midnight moons, o'er moistening dews,
In habit for the chace array'd,
The hunter still the deer pursues,
The hunter and the deer, a shade!

And long shall timorous fancy see
The painted chief, and pointed spear,
And Reason's self shall bow the knee
To shadows and delusions here.   40

        1787

---

8 **joyous feast.** "The North American Indians bury their dead in a sitting posture; decorating the corpse with wampum, the images of birds, quadrupeds, &c: And (if that of a warrior) with bows, arrows, toma-hawks, and other military weapons." — Freneau   16 **finer essence.** 1809, old ideas   36 **the hunter . . . shade!** Professor Pattee points out that the English poet Thomas Campbell borrowed this line in the fourth stanza of "O'Connor's Child": "Now o'er the hills in chase he flits, The hunter and the deer a shade!"

Lines by H. Salem, On His Return from Calcutta

No representative selection from Freneau would be complete without some poem of the sea, where he spent so many years of his life. There is no evidence that Freneau ever visited Calcutta, but this poem leaves no doubt of how he felt about the mariner's life. It first appeared as "A Mistake Rectified" over the signature of "Sinbat the Sailor," in the National Gazette, *and was soon reprinted in the Philadelphia* Daily Advertiser *and the* Charleston City Gazette. *In the 1795 edition it was called "Epistle to a Desponding Sea-man." Hezekiah Salem appears as a character or spokesman in several other poems by Freneau.*

Your men of the land, from the king to Jack Ketch,
All join in supposing the sailor a wretch;
That his life is a round of vexation and woe,
With always too much or too little to do:
In the dead of the night, when other men sleep,
He, starboard and larboard, his watches must keep;
Imprisoned by Neptune, he lives like a dog;
And to know where he is, must depend on a LOG;
Must fret in a calm, and be sad in a storm;
In winter much trouble to keep himself warm: 10

Through the heat of the summer pursuing his trade,
No trees, but his topmasts, to yield him a shade:
Then, add to the list of the mariner's evils,
The water corrupted, the bread full of weevils;
Salt-junk to be eat, be it better or worse,
And, often bull beef of an Irishman's horse:
Whosoever is free, he must still be a slave,
(Despotic is always the rule on the wave;)
Not relished on water, your lords of the main
Abhor the republican doctrines of PAINE,   20
And each, like the despot of Prussia, may say
That his crew has no right, but the right to obey.
Such things say the lubbers, and sigh when they've said 'em,
But things are not so bad as their fancies persuade 'em:

Text: the 1809 edition   1 **Jack Ketch,** a barbarous executioner, 1663?-1686, whose name became the popular appellation for the hangman   15 **Salt-junk,** salt meat used on long voyages   16 **bull beef,** flesh of bulls, exceedingly tough   20 **Paine.** Freneau admired Thomas Paine, as appears from a poem "On Mr. Paine's Rights of Man" (1795). Paine had left Philadelphia before Freneau had many associations there   21 **the despot of Prussia,** probably Frederick the Great (1712-1786), famous for his reluctance to delegate his powers

There ne'er was a task but afforded some ease,
Nor a calling in life, but had something to please.
If the sea has its storms, it has also its calms,
A time to sing songs and a time to sing psalms. —
Yes — give me a vessel well timbered and sound,
Her bottom good plank, and in rigging well found,   30
If her spars are but staunch, and her oakham swelled tight,
From tempests and storms I'll extract some delight —
At sea I would rather have Neptune my jailor,
Than a lubber on shore, that despises a sailor.
Do they ask me what pleasure I find on the sea? —
Why, absence from land is a pleasure to me:
A hamper of porter, and plenty of grog,
A friend, when too sleepy, to give me a jog,
A coop that will always some poult[r]y afford,
Some bottles of gin, and no parson on board,   40
A crew that is brisk when it happens to blow,
One compass on deck and another below,
A girl, with more sense than the girl at the head,
To read me a novel, or make up my bed —
The man that has these, has a treasure in store
That millions possess not, who live upon shore:
But if it should happen that commerce grew dull,
Or Neptune, ill-humoured, should batter our hull,
Should damage my cargo, or heave me aground,
Or pay me with farthings instead of a pound: 50
Should I always be left in the rear of the race,
And this be forever — forever the case;
Why then, if the honest plain truth I may tell,
I would clew up my topsails, and bid him farewell.

1791

---

31 **oakham,** oakum, loose fiber from old rope, used to calk ships' seams   42 **another below.** Probably
the commonplace instrument for making a circle, used in plotting a course   43 **the girl . . . head,** the
figurehead at the bow of the ship   54 **clew up,** draw up for furling

On Passing by an Old Church-Yard

*This poem first appeared as "Melancholy reflections in passing by a burying place in the
neighbourhood of Philadelphia" in the* Time-Piece, *September 15, 1797. It is a good example of the republicanism which sustained Freneau's distrust of pomp and aristocracy throughout the period of the French Revolution.*

Pensive, on this green turf I cast my eye,
And almost feel inclined to muse and sigh:
Such tokens of mortality so nigh.

But hold, — who knows if these who soundly sleep,
Would not, alive, have made some orphan weep,
Or plunged some slumbering victim in the deep.

There may be here, who once were virtue's foes,
A curse through life, the cause of many woes,
Who wrong'd the widow, and disturb'd repose.

There may be here, who with malicious aim   10
Did all they could to wound another's fame,
Steal character, and filch away good name.

Perhaps yond' solitary turf invests
Some who, when living, were the social pests,
Patrons of ribands, titles, crowns and crests.

Can we on such a kindred tear bestow?
They, who, in life, were every just man's foe,
A plague to all about them! — oh, no, no.

What though sepultured with the funeral whine;
Why, sorrowing on such tombs should we recline,   20
Where truth, perhaps, has hardly penn'd a line.

— Yet, what if here some honest man is laid
Whom nature of her best materials made,
Who all respect to sacred honor paid.

Gentle, humane, benevolent and just,
(Though now forgot and mingled with the dust,
There may be such, and such there are we trust.)

Yes — for the sake of that one honest man
We would on knaves themselves bestow a tear,
Think nature form'd them on some crooked plan,   30
And say *peace rest on all that slumber here.*

                                                  1797

_____

Text: the 1815 edition

Stanzas to an Alien,

Who After a Series of Persecutions Emigrated to the South Western Country.
—— *1799.* ——

Freneau and his friends of Jefferson's party were thoroughly suspicious of the conservative reaction to the French Revolution, exemplified by the Alien and Sedition Acts of 1798. This poem, first published as "To an Alien" in the Time-Piece *for July 13, 1798, shows Freneau's party spirit as well as his sympathy with political exiles. The "alien" has been identified by Professor Leary as John Daly Burk (1775?-1808), an Irishman who arrived in the United States in 1796. He had some reputation as an editor and dramatist and, after some trouble in New York, settled in Petersburg, Virginia.*

Remote, beneath a sultry star
Where Mississippi flows afar
I see you rambling, God knows where.

Sometimes, beneath a cypress bough
When met in dreams, with spirits low,
I long to tell you what I know.

How matters go, in this our day,
When monarchy renews her sway,
And royalty begins her play.

I thought you wrong to come so far   10
Till you had seen our western star
Above the mists ascended clear.

I thought you right, to speed your sails
If you were fond of loathsome jails,
And justice with uneven scales.

And so you came and spoke too free
And soon they made you bend the knee,
And lodged you under lock and key.

Discharged at last, you made your peace
With all you had, and left the place   20
With empty purse and meagre face. —

You sped your way to other climes
And left me here to teaze with rhymes
The worst of men in worst of times.

Text: the 1815 edition

Where you are gone the soil is free
And freedom sings from every tree,
"Come quit the crowd and live with me!"

Where I must stay, no joys are found;
Excisemen haunt the hateful ground,
And chains are forged for all around.   30

The scheming men, with brazen throat,
Would set a murdering tribe afloat
To hang you for the lines you wrote.

If you are safe beyond their rage
Thank heaven, and not our *ruling sage,*
Who shuts us up in jail and cage.

Perdition seize that odious race
Who, aiming at distinguish'd place,
Would life and liberty efface;

With iron rod would rule the ball   40
And, at their shrine, debase us all,
Bid devils rise and angels fall

Oh wish them ill, and wish them long
To be as usual in the wrong
In scheming for a chain too strong.

So will the happy time arrive
When coming home, if then alive,
You'll see them to the devil drive.   1798

35 **our ruling sage,** John Adams, the President. One of the acts relating to aliens gave him for two years
the power to deport any aliens he deemed dangerous

To a Caty-Did

In a branch of a willow hid
Sings the evening Caty-did:
From the lofty locust bough

Text: the 1815 edition, apparently the first printing of this poem. In the table of contents it is entitled
"Stanzas to a Caty-Did, the precursor of winter"   2 **Caty-Did.** "A well-known insect, when full grown,
about two inches in length, and of the exact color of a green leaf. It is of the genus cicada, or grasshopper
kind, inhabiting the green foliage of trees and singing such a note as *Caty-Did* in the evening, towards autumn." — Freneau

Feeding on a drop of dew,
In her suit of green array'd
Hear her singing in the shade
    Caty-did, Caty-did, Caty-did!

    While upon a leaf you tread,
Or repose your little head,
On your sheet of shadows laid,   10
All the day you nothing said:
Half the night your cheery tongue
Revell'd out its little song,
    Nothing else but Caty-did.

    From your lodgings on the leaf
Did you utter joy or grief — ?
Did you only mean to say,
I have had my summer's day,
And am passing, soon, away
To the grave of Caty-did: —   20
    Poor, unhappy Caty-did!

    But you would have utter'd more
Had you known of nature's power —
From the world when you retreat,
And a leaf's your winding sheet,
Long before your spirit fled,
Who can tell but nature said,
Live again, my Caty-did!
    Live, and chatter Caty-did.

    Tell me, what did Caty do?   30
Did she mean to trouble you? —
Why was Caty not forbid
To trouble little Caty-did? —
Wrong, indeed at you to fling,
Hurting no one while you sing
    Caty-did! Caty-did! Caty-did!

    Why continue to complain?
Caty tells me, she again
Will not give you plague or pain: — 40

---

30 **Caty do.** Here is introduced another Caty than the Caty-did addressed from the second stanza on, perhaps Freneau's third daughter Catherine, born in 1783, who is the recipient of the subsidiary moral lesson here

Caty says you may be hid
Caty will not go to bed
While you sing us Caty-did.
    Caty-did! Caty-did! Caty-did!

    But, while singing, you forgot
To tell us what did Caty *not:*
Caty-did not think of cold,
Flocks retiring to the fold,
Winter, with his wrinkles old,
Winter, that yourself foretold   50
    When you gave us Caty-did.

    Stay securely in your nest;
Caty now, will do her best,
All she can, to make you blest;
But, you want no human aid —
Nature, when she form'd you, said,
"Independent you are made,
My dear little Caty-did:
Soon yourself must disappear
With the verdure of the year," —   60
And to go, we know not where,
    With your song of Caty-did.
                                    1815

On the Uniformity and Perfection of Nature

*Freneau's views of God, man, and nature are fairly well summarized in this poem. The
reference to the "great first cause" and the acceptance of an uninterrupted order of nature
are Deistic in tendency, and it is possible to regard Freneau as philosophically akin to Franklin,
Paine, and Jefferson. He had perhaps less faith in man than they; as Professor Leary says,
his philosophy is one of "optimistic resignation."*

On one fix'd point all nature moves,
Nor deviates from the track she loves;
Her system, drawn from reason's source,
She scorns to change her wonted course.

Could she descend from that great plan
To work unusual things for man,
To suit the insect of an hour —
This would betray a want of power,

Text: the 1815 edition

Unsettled in its first design
And erring, when it did combine   10
The parts that form the vast machine,
The figures sketch'd on nature's scene.

Perfections of the great first cause
Submit to no contracted laws,
But all-sufficient, all-supreme,
Include no trivial views in them.

Who looks through nature with an eye
That would the scheme of heaven descry,
Observes her constant, still the same,
In all her laws, through all her frame.   20

No imperfection can be found
In all that is, above, around, —
All, nature made, in reason's sight
Is order all, and *all is right.*   1815

---

24 **all is right.** See the last lines of the first Epistle of Pope's *Essay on Man* (1732):
 "All Nature is but Art, unknown to thee;
 All Chance, Direction, which thou canst not see;
 All Discord, Harmony not understood;
 All partial Evil, universal Good:
 And, spite of Pride, in erring Reason's spite,
 One truth is clear, *Whatever is, is right.*"

1752–1817 Timothy Dwight

The solid rock of orthodoxy in the generation of the Connecticut Wits was Timothy Dwight, president of Yale College from 1795 until his death in 1817. Self-assured, immensely industrious, and a forthright warrior against all forms of religious infidelity, Dwight was the ideal college leader of his day. In conversation and in the pulpit he seemed the very fount of wisdom; and despite having ruined his eyesight by his college studies he managed to publish more than twenty-five titles, including a ten-thousand-line epic poem, *The Conquest of Canaan* (1785). Later generations have wondered at the veneration in which he was held by his contemporaries, because, as V. L. Parrington put it, his "mind was closed as tight as his study windows in January." Yet there can be no doubt of Dwight's claim to attention as the chief spokesman of conservative opinion in his period.

Dwight was an extraordinarily precocious student. Entering Yale at thirteen, he was graduated in 1769 and returned as tutor two years later, after some teaching experience in a New Haven grammar school. An exceedingly popular tutor, he helped to turn undergraduate attention to public speaking and belles-lettres and was the students' choice for president when that post fell vacant in 1777. But he was only twenty-five and was not thought experienced enough by the governing board.

By that time Dwight had decided upon theology in preference to law, and late in 1777 he resigned his tutorship to become an army chaplain. He did well in that capacity, writing patriotic songs as well as sermons, among them "Columbia, Columbia, to Glory Arise." Family responsibilities forced him to leave the army early in 1779, and for the next fifteen years he worked feverishly, first as farm manager, preacher, teacher, and legislator at Northampton, Massachusetts, and after 1783 as pastor of the Congregational Church at Greenfield, Connecticut. His preaching did not keep him from conducting one of the most famous schools of the day, an academy which accepted both boys and girls and drew pupils from Charleston and Jamaica as well as from close at hand. Meanwhile he found time to complete his long-projected epic, *The Conquest of Canaan* (1785), to loose a verse satire against the Deists, *The Triumph of Infidelity* (1788), and to finish *Greenfield Hill: A Poem, in Seven Parts* (1794).

Dwight was appointed to the Yale presidency in 1795. There his influence proved strong enough to check Deistic tendencies. He preached twice each Sunday, as well as on special occasions, and reviewed for each student generation the Calvinistic system as it was then understood. Although he emphasized practical ethics, he was no great thinker; his power was evangelical. Thanks to him, Yale and Connecticut shared in the widespread revival of religion at the turn of the century, and Yale-trained ministers continued to hold conspicuous places in the religious life of the nation. *The Nature, and Danger, of Infidel Philosophy* (1798) and *Theology: Explained and Defended* (5 vols., 1818-1819) are the record of a contribution seldom equaled by either theologians or college executives. The practical bent of Dwight's mind is also evident in his posthumous *Travels; in New-England and New-York* (4 vols., 1821-1822), a vast mine of information for the historian of the early years of the century. But his prose is more diffuse than his poetry and is difficult to present in selections.

Not since Cotton Mather had there been such an indefatigable, universally curious New England clergyman. The two were much alike in their defense of the *status quo,* their flashes of foresight, and the derivative quality of their minds. Dwight never sensed that he might be fighting a losing battle. Those who cannot accept his theological, political, or literary principles must perforce marvel at the certainties by which he lived.

The Connecticut Wits, ed. V. L. Parrington, New York, 1926   Charles E. Cuningham, Timothy Dwight, 1752-1817, A Biography, New York, 1942   Leon Howard, The Connecticut Wits, Chicago, 1943

Columbia, Columbia, to Glory Arise

Although this song is believed to have been written in 1778, while Dwight was a chaplain in the army, it was first printed in 1793. The tune, probably composed by Dwight himself, was first printed in Andrew Wright's The American Musical Miscellany *(Northampton, 1798).*

Columbia, Columbia, to glory arise,
The queen of the world, and child of the skies!
Thy genius commands thee; with rapture behold,
While ages on ages thy splendors unfold.
Thy reign is the last, and the noblest of time,
Most fruitful thy soil, most inviting thy clime;
Let the crimes of the east ne'er encrimson thy name,
Be freedom, and science, and virtue, thy fame.

To conquest, and slaughter, let Europe aspire;
Whelm nations in blood, and wrap cities in fire;   10
Thy heroes the rights of mankind shall defend,
And triumph pursue them, and glory attend.
A world is thy realm: for a world be thy laws,
Enlarg'd as thine empire, and just as thy cause;
On Freedom's broad basis, that empire shall rise,
Extend with the main, and dissolve with the skies.

Fair Science her gates to thy sons shall unbar,
And the east see thy morn hide the beams of her star.
New bards, and new sages, unrival'd shall soar
To fame, unextinguish'd, when time is no more;   20
To thee, the last refuge of virtue design'd,
Shall fly from all nations the best of mankind;
Here, grateful to heaven, with transport shall bring
Their incense, more fragrant than odours of spring.

Nor less shall thy fair ones to glory ascend,
And Genius and Beauty in harmony blend;
The graces of form shall awake pure desire,
And the charms of the soul ever cherish the fire;

Text: the first printing, in *American Poems, Selected and Original,* Litchfield, Connecticut, 1793, an anthology prepared by Dr. Elihu Hubbard Smith (1771-1798), one of the minor members of the Connecticut group

Their sweetness unmingled, their manners refin'd
And virtue's bright image, instamp'd on the mind,   30
With peace, and soft rapture, shall teach life to glow,
And light up a smile in the aspect of woe.

Thy fleets to all regions thy pow'r shall display,
The nations admire, and the ocean obey;
Each shore to thy glory its tribute unfold,
And the east and the south yield their spices and gold,
As the day-spring unbounded, thy splendor shall flow,
And earth's little kingdoms before thee shall bow,
While the ensigns of union, in triumph unfurl'd,
Hush the tumult of war, and give peace to the world.   40

Thus, as down a lone valley, with cedars o'erspread,
From war's dread confusion I pensively stray'd —
The gloom from the face of fair heav'n retir'd;
The winds ceas'd to murmur; the thunders expir'd;
Perfumes, as of Eden, flow'd sweetly along,
And a voice, as of angels, enchantingly sung:
"Columbia, Columbia, to glory arise,
The queen of the world, and the child of the skies."

                                              1793

from *Greenfield Hill*

Greenfield Hill *was published at New York in 1794, with a dedication to John Adams, then vice-president. "The greater part of it," Dwight says in his introduction, "was written seven years ago." His original intention was to imitate one of the great English poets in each of the seven sections; but that scheme was abandoned, and Dwight characteristically sought to "contribute to the innocent amusement of his countrymen, and to their improvement in manners, and in economical, political, and moral sentiments." Those who read his book doubtless found more improvement than innocent amusement. Among Dwight's favorite poems were Sir John Denham's* Cooper's Hill *(1642), Alexander Pope's* Windsor Forest *(1713), James Thomson's* The Seasons *(1730), and Oliver Goldsmith's* The Deserted Village *(1779). The last of these is admittedly the model for "The Flourishing Village," Part II of* Greenfield Hill, *of which about one fourth is here reprinted. The amazing slavishness of Dwight's imitation is obvious from his own notes; his didactic aims are apparent both there and in the "Argument" which preceded this and each of the other sections. There is enough detail in his description to show his knowledge and genuine liking for New England rural life, comparable to Whittier's as displayed over seventy years later in* Snow-Bound. *Dwight's lengthy note to his first line indicates, however, that he had other things on his mind than an account of rural delights.*

Part II The Flourishing Village

Fair Verna! loveliest village of the west;
Of every joy, and every charm, possess'd;
How pleas'd amid thy varied walks I rove,
Sweet, cheerful walks of innocence, and love,
And o'er thy smiling prospects cast my eyes,
And see the seats of peace, and pleasure, rise,
And hear the voice of Industry resound,
And mark the smile of Competence, around!
Hail, happy village! O'er thy cheerful lawns,
With earliest beauty, spring delighted dawns;   10
The northward sun begins his vernal smile;
The spring-bird carols o'er the cressy rill:
The shower, that patters in the ruffled stream,
The ploughboy's voice, that chides the lingering team,
The bee, industrious, with his busy song,
The woodman's axe, the distant groves among,
The waggon, rattling down the rugged steep,
The light wind, lulling every care to sleep,
All these, with mingled music, from below,
Deceive intruding sorrow, as I go.   20

Text: the original edition (1794)   1 **Fair Verna.** "Sweet Auburn, loveliest village of the plain! *Gold-smith.*" — Dwight   1 **village . . . west.** "This part of the poem, although appropriated to the parish of Greenfield, may be considered as a general description of the towns and villages of New England; those only excepted, which are either commercial, new, or situated on a barren soil. Morose and gloomy persons, and perhaps some others, may think the description too highly coloured. Persons of moderation and candour may possibly think otherwise. In its full extent, the writer supposes it applicable to the best inhabitants only; but he believes the number of these to be great; to others he thinks it partially applicable. Poetical representations are usually esteemed flattering; possibly this is as little so, as most of them. The inhabitants of New England notwithstanding some modern instances of declension, are, at least in the writer's opinion, a singular example of virtue and happiness.

"It will be easily discovered by the reader, that this part of the poem is designed to illustrate the effects of a state of property, which is the counter part to that, so beautifully exhibited by Dr. Goldsmith, in the Deserted Village. That excellent writer, in a most interesting manner, displays the wretched condition of the many, where enormous wealth, splendour, and luxury, constitute the state of the few. In this imperfect attempt, the writer wished to exhibit the blessings, which flow from an equal division of property, and a general competence.

"Whenever an *equal division of property* is mentioned, in this Work, the Reader is requested to remember, that that state of things only is intended, in which every citizen is secured in the avails of his industry and prudence, and in which property descends, by law, in equal shares, to the proprietor's children." — Dwight. The Connecticut law that all children should share equally in the family estate was passed in 1699   12 **spring-bird.** "A small bird, called, in some parts of New England, by that name; which appeared, very early in the spring, on the banks of brooks and small rivers, and sings a very sweet and sprightly note." — Dwight. Possibly the horned lark.   12 **cressy,** abounding in watercress

How pleas'd, fond Recollection, with a smile,
Surveys the varied round of wintery toil!
How pleas'd, amid the flowers, that scent the plain,
Recalls the vanish'd frost, and sleeted rain;
The chilling damp, the ice-endangering street,
And treacherous earth that slump'd beneath the feet.

 Yet even stern winter's glooms could joy inspire:
Then social circles grac'd the nutwood fire;
The axe resounded, at the sunny door;
The swain, industrious, trimm'd his flaxen store;   30
Or thresh'd, with vigorous flail, the bounding wheat,
His poultry round him pilfering for their meat;
Or slid his firewood on the creaking snow;
Or bore his produce to the main below;
Or o'er his rich returns exulting laugh'd;
Or pledg'd the healthful orchard's sparkling draught:
While, on his board, for friends and neighbours spread,
The turkey smoak'd, his busy housewife fed;
And Hospitality look'd smiling round,
And Leisure told his tale, with gleeful sound.   40

 Then too, the rough road hid beneath the sleigh,
The distant friend despis'd a length of way,
And join'd the warm embrace, and mingling smile,
And told of all his bliss, and all his toil;
And, many a month elaps'd, was pleas'd to view
How well the houshold far'd, the children grew;
While tales of sympathy deceiv'd the hour,
And Sleep, amus'd, resign'd his wonted power.

 Yes! let the proud despise, the rich deride,
These humble joys, to Competence allied: 50
To me, they bloom, all fragrant to my heart,
Nor ask the pomp of wealth, nor gloss of art.
And as a bird, in prison long confin'd,
Springs from his open'd cage, and mounts the wind,
Thro' fields of flowers, and fragrance, gaily flies,
Or re-assumes his birth-right, in the skies:

---

26 **slump'd**. "This word, said, in England, to be of North Country original, is customarily used in New England, to denote the sudden sinking of the foot in earth, when partially thawn, as in the month of March. It is also used to denote the sudden sinking of the earth under the foot." — Dwight 28 **nutwood**, "hickory." — Dwight 45 **And . . . view**. "And, many a year elapsed, return'd to view. *Goldsmith.*" — Dwight 49 **Yes! . . . proud**. "Yes, let the rich deride, the proud disdain. *Goldsmith.*" — Dwight 52 **gloss of art**. "*Goldsmith.*" — Dwight

Unprison'd thus from artificial joys,
Where pomp fatigues, and fussful fashion cloys,
The soul, reviving, loves to wander free
Thro' native scenes of sweet simplicity;   60
Thro' Peace' low vale, where Pleasure lingers long,
And every songster tunes his sweetest song,
And Zephyr hastes, to breathe his first perfume,
And Autumn stays, to drop his latest bloom:
'Till grown mature, and gathering strength to roam,
She lifts her lengthen'd wings, and seeks her home.

But now the wintery glooms are vanish'd all;
The lingering drift behind the shady wall;
The dark-brown spots, that patch'd the snowy field;
The surly frost, that every bud conceal'd;   70
The russet veil, the way with slime o'erspread,
And all the saddening scenes of March are fled.

Sweet-smiling village! loveliest of the hills!
How green thy groves! How pure thy glassy rills!
With what new joy, I walk thy verdant streets!
How often pause, to breathe thy gale of sweets;
To mark thy well-built walls! thy budding fields!
And every charm, that rural nature yields;
And every joy, to Competence allied,
And every good, that Virtue gains from Pride!   80

No griping landlord here alarms the door,
To halve, for rent, the poor man's little store.
No haughty owner drives the humble swain
To some far refuge from his dread domain;
Nor wastes, upon his robe of useless pride,
The wealth, which shivering thousands want beside;
Nor in one palace sinks a hundred cots;
Nor in one manor drowns a thousand lots;
Nor, on one table, spread for death and pain,
Devours what would a village well sustain.   90

O Competence, thou bless'd by Heaven's decree,

_____

63 **Zephyr,** the west wind   68 **The lingering drift.** "And parting summer's lingering blooms delayed. *Goldsmith."* — Dwight   73 **Sweet-smiling village!** "Sweet-smiling village! loveliest of the lawn. *Goldsmith."* — Dwight   75 **streets.** "In several parts of this country, the roads through the villages are called streets." —   79 **And every joy.** . . . "And every want, to opulence allied, and every pang that folly pays to pride. *Goldsmith."* — Dwight   87 **cots,** cottages   91 **O Competence.** "O luxury! thou curst by heaven's decree *Goldsmith.* Men in middling circumstance appear greatly to excel the rich, in piety, charity, and public spirit; nor will a critical observer of human life, hesitate to believe, that they enjoy more happiness." — Dwight

How well exchang'd is empty pride for thee!
Oft to thy cot my feet delighted turn,
To meet thy chearful smile, at peep of morn;
To join thy toils, that bid the earth look gay;
To mark thy sports, that hail the eve of May;
To see thy ruddy children, at thy board,
And share thy temperate meal, and frugal hoard;
And every joy, by winning prattlers giv'n,
And every earnest of a future Heaven.   100

There the poor wanderer finds a table spread,
The fireside welcome, and the peaceful bed.
The needy neighbour, oft by wealth denied,
There finds the little aids of life supplied;
The horse, that bears to mill the hard-earn'd grain;
The day's work given, to reap the ripen'd plain;
The useful team, to house the precious food,
And all the offices of real good.

There too, divine Religion is a guest,
And all the Virtues join the daily feast.   110
Kind Hospitality attends the door,
To welcome in the stranger and the poor;
Sweet Chastity, still blushing as she goes;
And Patience smiling at her train of woes;
And meek-eyed Innocence, and Truth refin'd,
And Fortitude, of bold, but gentle mind.

Thou pay'st the tax, the rich man will not pay;
Thou feed'st the poor, the rich man drives away.
Thy sons, for freedom, hazard limbs, and life,
While pride applauds, but shuns the manly strife: 120
Thou prop'st religion's cause, the world around,
And shew'st thy faith in works, and not in sound.

Say, child of passion! while, with idiot stare,
Thou seest proud grandeur wheel her sunny car;
While kings, and nobles, roll bespangled by,
And the tall palace lessens in the sky;
Say, while with pomp thy giddy brain runs round,
What joys, like these, in splendour can be found?
Ah, yonder turn thy wealth-inchanted eyes,
Where that poor, friendless wretch expiring lies!   130
Hear his sad partner shriek, beside his bed,

And call down curses on her landlord's head,
Who drove, from yon small cot, her household sweet,
To pine with want, and perish in the street.
See the pale tradesman toil, the livelong day,
To deck imperious lords, who never pay!
Who waste, at dice, their boundless breadth of soil,
But grudge the scanty meed of honest toil.
See hounds and horses riot on the store,
By HEAVEN created for the hapless poor!   140
See half a realm one tyrant scarce sustain,
While meagre thousands round him glean the plain!
See, for his mistress' robe, a village sold,
Whose matrons shrink from nakedness and cold!
See too the Farmer prowl around the shed,
To rob the starving houshold of their bread;
And seize, with cruel fangs, the helpless swain,
While wives, and daughters, plead, and weep, in vain;
Or yield to infamy themselves, to save
Their sire from prison, famine, and the grave.   150

    There too foul luxury taints the putrid mind,
And slavery there imbrutes the reasoning kind:
There humble worth, in damps of deep despair,
Is bound by poverty's eternal bar:
No motives bright the etherial aim impart,
Nor one fair ray of hope allures the heart.

    But, O sweet Competence! how chang'd the scene,
Where thy soft footsteps lightly print the green!
Where Freedom walks erect, with manly port,
And all the blessings to his side resort,   160
In every hamlet, Learning builds her schools,
And beggars' children gain her arts, and rules;
And mild Simplicity o'er manners reigns,
And blameless morals Purity sustains.

    From thee the rich enjoyments round me spring,
Where every farmer reigns a little king;
Where all to comfort, none to danger, rise;
Where pride finds few, but nature all supplies;
Where peace and sweet civility are seen,

---

145 **the Farmer.** "Farmer of revenue: A superior kind of tax-gatherer, in some countries of Europe." —
Dwight   154 **poverty's eternal bar.** "By poverty's unconquerable bar. *Beattie."* — Dwight. The line appears in the first stanza of *The Minstrel* (1771) by James Beattie (1735-1803)

And meek good-neighbourhood endears the green.   170
Here every class (if classes those we call,
Where one extended class embraces all,
All mingling, as the rainbow's beauty blends,
Unknown where every hue begins or ends)
Each following, each, with uninvidious strife,
Wears every feature of improving life.
Each gains from other comeliness of dress,
And learns, with gentle mein to win and bless,
With welcome mild the stranger to receive,
And with plain, pleasing decency to live;   180
Refinement hence even humblest life improves;
Not the loose fair, that form and frippery loves;
But she, whose mansion is the gentle mind,
Is thought, and action, virtuously refin'd.
Hence, wives and husbands act a lovelier part,
More just the conduct, and more kind the heart;
Hence brother, sister, parent, child, and friend,
The harmony of life more sweetly blend;
Hence labour brightens every rural scene;
Hence cheerful plenty lives along the green;   190
Still Prudence eyes her hoard, with watchful care,
And robes of thrift and neatness, all things wear.

. . . .

    Thrice bless'd the life, in this glad region spent,
In peace, in competence, and still content;
Where bright, and brighter, all things daily smile,
And rare and scanty, flow the streams of ill;
Where undecaying youth sits blooming round,
And Spring looks lovely on the happy ground;   640
Improvement glows, along life's cheerful way,
And with soft lustre makes the passage gay
Thus oft, on yonder Sound, when evening gales
Breath'd o'er th' expanse, and gently fill'd the sails,
The world was still, the heavens were dress'd in smiles,
And the clear moon-beam tipp'd the distant isles,
On the blue plain a lucid image gave,
And capp'd, with silver light, each little wave;

192 **all things wear.** According to Dwight's "Argument" the next 445 lines, omitted here, contain the following matter: "Africa appears — State of Negro Slavery in Connecticut — Effects of Slavery on the African, from his childhood through life — Slavery generally characterized — West-Indian Slavery — True cause of the calamities of the West-Indies — Church — Effects of the Sabbath — Academic School — Schoolmaster — House of Sloth — Female Worthy — Inferior Schools — Female Visit — What is not, and what is, a social female visit." As may be imagined, the tone is highly moral and didactic

The silent splendour, floating at our side,
Mov'd as we mov'd, and wanton'd on the tide;   650
While shadowy points, and havens, met the eye,
And the faint-glimmering landmark told us home was nigh.

    Ah, dire reverse! in yonder eastern clime,
Where heavy drags the sluggish car of time;
The world unalter'd by the change of years,
Age after age, the same dull aspect wears;
On the bold mind the weight of system spread,
Resistless lies, a cumbrous load of lead;
One beaten course, the wheels politic keep,
And slaves of custom, lose their woes in sleep;   660
Stagnant is social life; no bright design,
Quickens the sloth, or checks the sad decline.
The friend of man casts round a wishful eye,
And hopes, in vain, improving scenes to spy;
Slow o'er his head, the dragging moments roll,
And damp each cheerful purpose of the soul.

    Thus the bewilder'd traveler, forc'd to roam
Through a lone forest, leaves his friends, and home;
Dun evening hangs the sky; the woods around
Join their sad umbrage o'er the russet ground;   670
At every step, new gloom inshrouds the skies;
His path grows doubtful, and his fears arise:
No woodland songstress soothes his mournful way;
No taper gilds the gloom with cheering ray;
On the cold earth he lays his head forlorn,
And watching, looks, and looks, to spy the lingering morn.
And when new regions prompt their feet to roam,
And fix, in untrod fields, another home,
No dreary realms our happy race explore,
Nor mourn their exile from their native shore.   680
For there no endless frosts the glebe deform,
Nor blows, with icy breath, perpetual storm:
No wrathful suns, with sickly splendour glare,
Nor moors, impoison'd, taint the balmy air,
But medial climates change the healthful year;
Pure streamlets wind, and gales of Eden cheer;
In misty pomp the sky-topp'd mountains stand,
And with green bosom humbler hills expand:
With flowery brilliance smiles the woodland glade;

Full teems the soil, and fragrant twines the shade.   690
There cheaper fields the numerous household charm,
And the glad sire gives every son a farm;
In falling forests, Labour's axe resounds;
Opes the new field; and winds the fence's bounds;
The green wheat sparkles; nods the towering corn;
And meads, and pastures, lessening wastes adorn.
Where howl'd the forest, herds unnumber'd low;
The fleecy wanderers fear no prowling foe;
The village springs; the humble school aspires;
And the church brightens in the morning fires!   700
Young Freedom wantons; Art exalts her head;
And infant Science prattles through the shade.
There changing neighbours learn their manners mild;
And toil and prudence dress th' improving wild:
The savage shrinks, nor dares the bliss annoy;
And the glad traveller wonders at the joy.

    All hail, thou western world! by heaven design'd
Th' example bright, to renovate mankind.
Soon shall thy sons across the mainland roam;
And claim, on far Pacific shores, their home;   710
Their rule, religion, manners, arts, convey,
And spread their freedom to the Asian sea.
Where erst six thousand suns have roll'd the year
O'er plains of slaughter, and o'er wilds of fear,
Towns, cities, fanes, shall lift their towery pride;
The village bloom, on every streamlets side;
Proud Commerce' mole the western surges lave;
The long, white spire lie imag'd on the wave;
O'er morn's pellucid main expand their sails,
And the starr'd ensign court Korean gales.   720
Then nobler thoughts shall savage trains inform;
Then barbarous passions cease the heart to storm:
No more the captive circling flames devour;
Through the war path the Indian creep no more;
No midnight scout the slumbering village fire;
Nor the scalp'd infant stain his gasping sire:
But peace, and truth, illume the twilight mind,
The gospel's sunshine, and the purpose kind.
Where marshes teem'd with death, shall meads unfold;
Untrodden cliffs resign their stores of gold;   730

---

712 **Asian sea,** "Pacific ocean." — Dwight   720 **Korean.** "Korea is a large peninsula on the eastern shore of Asia." — Dwight

The dance refin'd on Albion's margin move,
And her lone bowers rehearse the tale of love.
Where slept perennial night, shall science rise,
And new-born Oxfords cheer the evening skies;
Miltonic strains the Mexic hills prolong,
And Louis murmur to Sicilian song.

    Then to new climes the bliss shall trace its way,
And Tartar desarts hail the rising day;
From the long torpor startled China wake;
Her chains of misery rous'd Peruvia break;   740
Man link to man; with bosom bosom twine;
And one great bond the house of Adam join:
The sacred promise full completion know,
And peace, and piety, the world o'erflow. 1787?, 1794

---

731 **Albion's margin.** "New Albion, a very desirable country, on the western shore of America, discovered by Sir Francis Drake." — Dwight. The California coast bore this name on the maps of America well into the nineteenth century   735 **Mexic hills.** "A range of mountains, running from north to south, at the distance of several hundred miles, westward of the Mississippi." — Dwight   736 **Louis,** "The Mississippi." — Dwight   736 **Sicilian song,** "Pastoral poetry." — Dwight

1754—1812 Joel Barlow

hilanthropist, statesman, philosopher, poet — such is the order in which his biographer ranks the various capacities in which Barlow distinguished himself. There can be little objection to the judgment; but it records the failure of a great ambition. Barlow wanted to be an epic poet; he spent a large part of his life planning, composing, and revising a long philosophical poem on the importance of American history. Some of it was written in 1780; two years later he was taking subscriptions for its publication. It appeared as *The Vision of Columbus* in 1787, and the final version, *The Columbiad,* was published in 1807, nearly thirty years after Barlow had conceived it. Later generations have regretted that the time spent on *The Columbiad* did not go into such relatively unpretentious portrayals of life and manners as *The Hasty-Pudding.*

    Barlow was born at Redding, Connecticut, in 1754, and was graduated from Yale College with the Class of 1778. His college career was distinguished chiefly by at least one vacation spent in the army and a Commencement poem, *The Prospect of Peace.* Settling down in the atmosphere of revolution proved somewhat difficult. He studied law for a time, then served as an unordained chaplain from September 1780 until the end of the war. Choosing Hartford for his home, he then tried his hand at teaching and editing before being admitted to the bar in 1786. In the year following he helped organize the Scioto Company, which planned to buy lands in Ohio and sell them at a large profit to European immigrants. Going abroad as a promoter in 1788, Barlow found London apathetic, but in Paris with the aid of enticing circulars, he created a speculative flurry in Ohio real estate. Unfortunately the titles which he sold were not clear, and the Frenchmen who occupied Gallipolis in 1790 found that they had been swindled. The fault, however, lay more with others than with Barlow, if not, indeed, with the French themselves, who were gulled by dreams of a Utopia in the wilderness.

Barlow was caught in Paris by the French Revolution. Somewhat surprisingly for a son of Federalist Connecticut who had collaborated in *The Anarchiad* (1786), an attack on populist tendencies in government, Barlow emerged in 1792 as an ardent radical. He expected a general revolution in the political and social structure of Europe along the lines of the American system. His *Advice to the Privileged Orders* — a pamphlet attack on monarchy, an established church, inequalities in taxation and access to the courts, and standing armies — helped precipitate the conservative reaction in England, of which Edmund Burke was leader. A poem entitled *The Conspiracy of Kings* made him anathema to cautious Englishmen. Another pamphlet, *A Letter to the National Convention of France,* won him the honor of French citizenship. Barlow lived through the Terror without inconvenience and was able to befriend Thomas Paine in one serious crisis. From 1795 to 1797 he served as American consul in Algiers, engineering a treaty with the pirates there; he then returned to Paris and by judicious speculation in securities made a comfortable fortune. From 1805 until 1811 he lived in considerable splendor near Washington, D. C., polishing what he regarded as his great epic and entertaining his wide circle of friends. President Madison sent him once more to France in 1811, as ambassador, and in the following year Barlow died in Poland, where he had gone to confer with Napoleon on matters of state.

The Connecticut Wits, ed. V. L. Parrington, New York, 1926   C. B. Todd, Life and Letters of Joel Barlow, New York, 1886   T. A. Zunder, The Early Days of Joel Barlow, a Connecticut Wit, New Haven, 1934   V. C. Miller, Joel Barlow: Revolutionist, London, 1791-1792, Hamburg, 1932   Leon Howard, The Connecticut Wits, Chicago, 1943   James L. Woodress, Yankee Odyssey: The Life of Joel Barlow, New York, 1958

The Hasty-Pudding

A Poem, in Three Cantos, Written at Chambery in Savoy, January, 1793

In January 1793, the month of the execution of Louis XVI, Barlow was in Savoy, apparently hoping to become a deputy to the National Convention from a new department or election district being organized there. In a spell of homesickness, brought on by encountering unexpectedly the most familiar porridge of his New England boyhood, he composed The

Hasty-Pudding, *which imitates the mock-heroic and pastoral veins of the age of Pope. The burlesque of the traditional epic invocation to the Muse, the rhetorical passages on exceedingly homely subjects, the numerous allusions — all reveal Barlow's familiarity with literature. Yet the poem, typical of the productions of the Connecticut group in its backward-looking tendencies, has a verve and an abundant local reference which save it from dullness. One might argue, indeed, that Barlow's democratic sympathies are as well expressed in his praise of simplicity as in his radical pamphlets. At any rate, to remember the most popular of Barlow's work is not wholly, as V. L. Parrington's remarks tend to suggest, to "make a mush" of an "honest thinker."*

> Omne tulit punctum qui miscuit utile dulci.
> *He makes a good breakfast who mixes pudding*
> *with molasses.*

Preface

A simplicity in diet, whether it be considered with reference to the happiness of individuals or the prosperity of a nation, is of more consequence than we are apt to imagine. In recommending so important an object to the rational part of mankind, I wish it were in my power to do it in such a manner as would be likely to gain their attention. I am sensible that it is one of those subjects in which example has
10 infinitely more power than the most convincing arguments or the highest charms of poetry. Goldsmith's *Deserted Village,* though possessing these two advantages in a greater degree than any other work of the kind, has not prevented villages in England from being deserted. The apparent *interest* of the rich individuals, who form the taste as well as the laws in that country, has been against him; and with that interest it has been vain to contend.

The vicious habits which in this little piece I endeavor to combat, seem to me not so difficult to cure. No class of people has any interest in supporting them, unless it be the interest which certain families feel in vying with each other in sumptuous entertainments. There may indeed be some instances of depraved appetites, which
20 no arguments will conquer; but these must be rare. There are very few persons but what would always prefer a plain dish for themselves, and would prefer it likewise for their guests, if there were no risk of reputation in the case. This difficulty can only be removed by example; and the example should proceed from those whose

---

Text: that which appeared in the January 1796 issue of the *New-York Magazine.* The first separate publication was apparently at New Haven; it contains an "advertisement" dated in April. The New Haven edition reveals several changes: the Preface became a dedication to Martha Washington; greater particularity was obtained by making "our sires" "my sire" throughout; four lines (following 264) were added; a prose note was appended and numerous changes made in punctuation, spelling, and italics. Possibly Barlow sent back two manuscripts; it is also possible that the dedication to Mrs. Washington was someone else's idea   1 **Omne . . . dulci.** The motto is from Horace, *Ars Poetica,* 1. 343, and may be translated: He has gained all approval who has mingled the useful with the agreeable   13 **apparent interest.** A distinction between the "interests" of privileged groups and the interests of the masses is the basis of Barlow's argument in *Advice to the Privileged Orders* (1792). In it he sought to appeal to the enlightened self-interest of all readers

situation enables them to take the lead in forming the manners of a nation. Persons of this description in America, I should hope, are neither above nor below the influence of truth and reason, when conveyed in language suited to the subject.

Whether the manner I have chosen to address my arguments to them be such as to promise any success is what I cannot decide. But I certainly had hopes of doing some good, or I should not have taken the pains of putting so many rhymes together. — The example of domestic virtues has doubtless a great effect. I only wish to rank *simplicity of diet* among the virtues. In that case I should hope it will be cherished and more esteemed by others than it is at present.

THE AUTHOR

Canto I

Ye Alps audacious, thro' the heav'ns that rise,
To cramp the day and hide me from the skies;
Ye Gallic flags, that o'er their heights unfurl'd,
Bear death to kings, and freedom to the world,
I sing not you. A softer theme I chuse,
A virgin theme, unconscious of the Muse,
But fruitful, rich, well suited to inspire
The purest frenzy of poetic fire.
   Despise it not, ye Bards to terror steel'd,
Who hurl your thunders round the epic field;   10
Nor ye who strain your midnight throats to sing
Joys that the vineyard and the still-house bring;
Or on some distant fair your notes employ,
And speak of raptures that you ne'er enjoy.
I sing the sweets I know, the charms I feel,
My morning incense, and my evening meal,
The sweets of Hasty-Pudding. Come, dear bowl,
Glide o'er my palate, and inspire my soul.
The milk beside thee, smoking from the kine,
Its substance mingled, married in with thine,   20
Shall cool and temper thy superior heat,
And save the pains of blowing while I eat.
   Oh! could the smooth, the emblematic song
Flow like thy genial juices o'er my tongue,
Could those mild morsels in my numbers chime,
And, as they roll in substance, roll in rhyme,
No more thy aukward unpoetic name
Should shun the Muse, or prejudice thy fame;
But rising grateful to th' accustom'd ear,

---

3 **Gallic flags,** French standards. At the beginning of the French Revolution, Savoy was part of the Kingdom of Sardinia; it was invaded and taken by the French in 1792   12 **still-house,** distillery

All Bards should catch it, and all realms revere.   30
   Assist me first with pious toil to trace
Thro' wrecks of time thy lineage and thy race;
Declare what lovely squaw, in dayes of yore,
(Ere great Columbus sought thy native shore)
First gave thee to the world; her works of fame
Have liv'd indeed, but liv'd without a name.
Some tawny Ceres, goddess of her days
First learn'd with stones to crack the well dry'd maise,
Thro' the rough seive to shake the golden show'r,
In boiling water stir the yellow flour: 40
The yellow flour, bestrew'd and stir'd with haste,
Swells in the flood and thickens to a paste,
Then puffs and wallops, rises to the brim,
Drinks the dry knobs that on the surface swim;
The knobs at last the busy ladle breaks,
And the whole mass its true consistence takes.
   Could but her sacred name unknown so long,
Rise, like her labors, to the son of song,
To her, to them, I'd consecrate my lays,
And blow her pudding with the breath of praise.   50
If 'twas Oella, whom I sang before,
I here ascribe her one great virtue more.
Not thro' the rich Peruvian realms alone
The fame of Sol's sweet daughter should be known,
But o'er the world's wide clime should live secure,
Far as his rays extend, as long as they endure.
   Dear Hasty-Pudding, what unpromis'd joy
Expands my heart, to meet thee in Savoy!
Doom'd o'er the world thro' devious paths to roam,
Each clime my country, and each house my home,   60
My soul is sooth'd, my cares have found an end,
I greet my long-lost, unforgotten friend.
   For Thee thro' Paris, that corrupted town,
How long in vain I wandered up and down,
Where shameless Bacchus, with his drenching hoard,
Cold from his cave usurps the morning board.
London is lost in smoke and steep'd in tea;
No Yankey there can lisp the name of thee;

---

37 **Ceres,** goddess of grain   43 **wallops,** bubbles (dialect)   51 **Oella . . . before.** In Bks. II and III of
The Vision of Columbus and *The Columbiad,* Barlow made great use of the legend that the Incas of Peru originated with two children of the Sun, Manco Capac and his sister-wife, Mama Oella. This legend, derived
from the history of Peru by Garcilaso de la Vega (1540-1616), made Oella the originator of spinning and
other useful arts   65 **Bacchus,** god of wine

The uncouth word, a libel on the town,
Would call a proclamation from the crown.   70
For climes oblique, that fear the sun's full rays,
Chill'd in their fogs, exclude the generous maize;
A grain whose rich luxuriant growth requires
Short gentle showers, and bright etherial fires.
    But here, tho' distant from our native shore,
With mutual glee we meet and laugh once more.
The same! I know thee by that yellow face,
That strong complexion of true Indian race.
Which time can never change, nor soil impair,
Nor Alpine snows, nor Turkey's morbid air;   80
For endless years, thro' every mild domain,
Where grows the maize, there thou art sure to reign.
    But man, more fickle, the bold licence claims,
In different realms to give thee different names.
Thee the soft nations round the warm Levant
Polanta call, the French of course *Polante.*
Ev'n in thy native regions, how I blush
To hear the Pennsylvanians call thee *Mush!*
On Hudson's banks, while men of Belgic spawn
Insult and eat thee by the name *Suppawn.*   90
Thy name is *Hasty-Pudding!* thus our sires
Were wont to greet thee fuming from their fires,
And while they argu'd in thy just defence
With logic clear, they thus explain'd the sense: —
"In *haste* the boiling cauldron, o'er the blaze,
"Receives and cooks the ready-powder'd maize;
"In *haste* 'tis served, and then in equal *haste,*
"With cooling milk, we make the sweet repast.
"No carving to be done, no knife to grate
"The tender ear, and wound the stony plate;   100
"But the smooth spoon, just fitted to the lip,
"And taught with art the yielding mass to dip,
"By frequent journeys to the bowl well stor'd,
"Performs the hasty honors of the board."
Such is thy name, significant and clear,
A name, a sound to every Yankey dear,
But most to me, whose heart and palate chaste

---

70 **crown.** "A certain king, at the time when this was written, was publishing proclamations to prevent American principles from being propagated in his country." — Barlow. The allusion is probably to a royal proclamation against seditious publications issued in England in May 1792, which forced Barlow to publish Part II of *Advice to the Privileged Orders* (1793) in Paris   85 **Levant,** countries of the eastern Mediterranean   89 **Belgic spawn,** the Dutch   90 **Suppawn,** supawn, a word of American Indian origin

Preserve my pure hereditary taste.
    There are who strive to stamp with disrepute
The luscious food, because it feeds the brute;   110
In tropes of high-strain'd wit, while gaudy prigs
Compare thy nursling man to pamper'd pigs;
With sovereign scorn I treat the vulgar jest,
Nor fear to share thy bounties with the beast.
What though the generous cow gives me to quaff
The milk nutritious; am I then a calf?
Or can the genius of the noisy swine,
Though nurs'd on pudding, thence lay claim to mine?
Sure the sweet song, I fashion to thy praise,
Runs more melodious than the notes they raise.   120
    My song resounding in its grateful glee,
No merit claims; I praise myself in thee.
My father lov'd thee thro' his length of days;
For thee his fields were shaded o'er with maize;
From thee what health, what vigor he possesst,
Ten sturdy freemen from his loins attest;
Thy constellation rul'd my natal morn,
And all my bones were made of Indian corn.
Delicious grain! whatever form it take,
To roast or boil, to smother or to bake,   130
In every dish 'tis welcome still to me,
But most, my *Hasty-Pudding,* most in thee.
    Let the green Succatash with thee contend,
Let beans and corn their sweetest juices blend,
Let butter drench them in its yellow tide,
And a long slice of bacon grace their side;
Not all the plate, how fam'd soe'er it be,
Can please my palate like a bowl of thee.
    Some talk of Hoe-Cake, fair Virginia's pride,
Rich Johnny-Cake this mouth has often tri'd;   140
Both please me well, their virtues much the same;
Alike their fabric, as allied their fame,
Except in dear New-England, where the last
Receives a dash of pumpkin in the paste,
To give it sweetness and improve the taste.
But place them all before me, smoaking hot,
The big, round dumplin rolling from the pot;
The pudding of the bag, whose quivering breast,
With suet lin'd, leads on the Yankey feast;

126 **Ten sturdy freemen.** Only nine Barlow children are accounted for. "Still," says Professor Zunder, "Joel must have known the truth"

The Charlotte brown, within whose crusty sides   150
A belly soft the pulpy apple hides;
The yellow bread, whose face like amber glows,
And all of Indian that the bake-pan knows —
You tempt me not, my fav'rite greets my eyes,
To that lov'd bowl my spoon by instinct flies.

Canto II

  To mix the food by vicious rules of art,
To kill the stomach and to sink the heart,
To make mankind to social virtue sour,
Cram o'er each dish, and be what they devour;
For this the kitchen Muse first fram'd her book,   160
Commanding sweat to stream from every cook;
Children no more their antic gambols tri'd,
And friends to physic wonder'd why they died.
  Not so the Yankey — his abundant feast,
With simples furnish'd, and with plainness drest,
A numerous offspring gathers round the board,
And cheers alike the servant and the lord;
Whose well-bought hunger prompts the joyous taste,
And health attends them from the short repast.
  While the full pail rewards the milk-maid's toil,   170
The mother sees the morning cauldron boil;
To stir the pudding next demands their care,
To spread the table and the bowls prepare;
To feed the children, as their portions cool,
And comb their heads, and send them off to school.
  Yet may the simplest dish some rules impart,
For nature scorns not all the aids of art.
Ev'n Hasty-Pudding, purest of all food,
May still be bad, indifferent, or good,
As sage experience the short process guides,   180
Or want of skill, or want of care presides.
Whoe'er would form it on the surest plan,
To rear the child and long sustain the man;
To shield the morals while it mends the size,
And all the powers of every food supplies,
Attend the lessons that the Muse shall bring,
Suspend your spoons, and listen while I sing.
  But since, O man! thy life and health demand

---

150 **Charlotte,** a sweet enclosed in a cake, crust, or crumbs, such as charlotte russe. Barlow probably picked up the word in Europe, although he may have been describing a kind of apple pie

Not food alone, but labour from thy hand,
First in the field, beneath the sun's strong rays,　　　190
Ask of thy mother earth the needful maize;
She loves the race that courts her yielding soil,
And gives her bounties to the sons of toil.
　When now the ox, obedient to thy call,
Repays the loan that fill'd the winter stall,
Pursue his traces o'er the furrow'd plain,
And plant in measur'd hills the golden grain.
But when the tender germe begins to shoot,
And the green spire declares the sprouting root,
Then guard your nursling from each greedy foe,　　　200
Th' insidious worm, the all-devouring crow.
A little ashes, sprinkled round the spire,
Soon steep'd in rain, will bid the worm retire;
The feather'd robber with his hungry maw
Swift flies the field before your man of straw,
A frightful image, such as school-boys bring
When met to burn the Pope, or hang the King.
　Thrice in each season, through each variant row
Wield the strong plow-share and the faithful hoe;
The faithful hoe; a double task that takes,　　　210
To till the summer corn, and roast the winter cakes.
　Slow springs the blade, while check'd by chilling rains,
Ere yet the sun the seat of Cancer gains;
But when his fiercest fires emblaze the land,
Then start the juices, then the roots expand;
Then, like a column of Corinthian mould,
The stalk struts upward, and the leaves unfold;
The busy branches all the ridges fill,
Entwine their arms, and kiss from hill to hill.
Here cease to vex them, all your cares are done;　　　220
Leave the last labors to the parent sun;
Beneath his genial smiles, the well-drest field,
When autumn calls, a plenteous crop shall yield.
　Now the strong foliage bears the standards high,
And shoots the tall top-gallants to the sky;
The suckling ears their silky fringes bend,
And pregnant grown, their swelling coats distend;
The loaded stalk, while still the burthen grows,

---

207 **burn . . . King.** The allusion is probably to the traditional celebration of Guy Fawkes Day, November 5, the anniversary of the discovery of the Gunpowder Plot in 1605. English children still ask "a penny for the Guy"; American boys probably cared little for distinctions between Fawkes, Pope, and King　　213 **Cancer,** the zodiacal sign marking the summer solstice or longest day of the year, about June 21　　216 **Corinthian mould,** the most ornamental of the Greek capital orders

O'erhangs the space that runs between the rows;
High as a hop-field waves the silent grove,   230
A safe retreat for little thefts of love,
When the pledg'd roasting-ears invite the maid,
To meet her swain beneath the new-form'd shade;
His generous hand unloads the cumbrous hill,
And the green spoils her ready basket fill;
Small compensation for the two-fold bliss,
The promis'd wedding and the present kiss.
  Slight depredations these; but now the moon
Calls from his hollow tree the sly raccoon;
And while by night he bears his prize away,   240
The bolder squirrel labors thro' the day.
Both thieves alike, but provident of time,
A virtue rare, that almost hides their crime.
Then let them steal the little stores they can,
And fill their gran'ries from the toils of man;
We've one advantage where they take no part, —
With all their wiles they ne'er have found the art
To boil the Hasty-Pudding; here we shine
Superior far to tenants of the pine;
This envy'd boon to man shall still belong,   250
Unshar'd by them in substance or in song.
  At last the closing season browns the plain,
And ripe October gathers in the grain;
Deep loaded carts the spacious corn-house fill,
The sack distended marches to the mill;
The lab'ring mill beneath the burthen groans,
And show'rs the future pudding from the stones;
Till the glad house-wife greets the powder'd gold,
And the new crop exterminates the old.

Canto III

  The days grow short; but tho' the falling sun   260
To the glad swain proclaims his day's work done,
Night's pleasing shades his various tasks prolong,
And yield new subjects to my various song.

---

259 **the old.** The New Haven ed. inserts:
  Ah, who can sing what every wight must feel,
  The joy that enters with the bag of meal,
  A general jubilee pervades the house,
  Wakes every child and gladdens every mouse.

For now, the corn-house fill'd, the harvest home,
Th' invited neighbors to the *Husking* come;
A frolic scene, where work, and mirth, and play,
Unite their charms, to chace the hours away.
    Where the huge heap lies center'd in the hall,
The lamp suspended from the cheerful wall,
Brown corn-fed nymphs, and strong hard-handed beaux, 270
Alternate rang'd, extend in circling rows,
Assume their seats, the solid mass attack;
The dry husks rustle, and the corn-cobs crack;
The song, the laugh, alternate notes resound,
And the sweet cider trips in silence round.
    The laws of Husking every wight can tell;
And sure no laws he ever keeps so well:
For each red ear a general kiss he gains,
With each smut ear he smuts the luckless swains;
But when to some sweet maid a prize is cast,   280
Red as her lips, and taper as her waist,
She walks the round, and culls one favor'd beau,
Who leaps, the luscious tribute to bestow.
Various the sport, as are the wits and brains
Of well-pleas'd lasses and contending swains;
Till the vast mound of corn is swept away,
And he that gets the last ear, wins the day.
    Meanwhile the house-wife urges all her care,
The well-earn'd feast to hasten and prepare.
The sifted meal already waits her hand.   290
The milk is strain'd, the bowls in order stand,
The fire flames high; and, as a pool (that takes
The headlong stream that o'er the mill-dam breaks)
Foams, roars, and rages, with incessant toils,
So the vext cauldron rages, roars and boils.
    First with clean salt she seasons well the food,
Then strews the flour, and thickens all the flood.
Long o'er the simmering fire she lets it stand;
To stir it well demands a stronger hand;
The husband takes his turn and round and round   300
The ladle flies; at last the toil is crown'd;
When to the board the thronging huskers pour,
And take their seats as at the corn before.
    I leave them to their feast. There still belong
More copious matters to my faithful song.
For rules there are, tho' ne'er unfolded yet,
Nice rules and wise, how pudding should be ate.
    Some with molasses grace the luscious treat,

And mix, like Bards, the useful with the sweet.
A wholesome dish, and well deserving praise,   310
A great resource in those bleak wintry days,
When the chill'd earth lies buried deep in snow,
And raging Boreas dries the shivering cow.
   Blest cow! thy praise shall still my notes employ,
Great source of health, the only source of joy;
Mother of Egypt's God, — but sure, for me,
Were I to leave my God, I'd worship thee.
How oft thy teats these pious hands have prest!
How oft thy bounties proved my only feast!
How oft I've fed thee with my fav'rite grain!   320
And roar'd, like thee, to find thy children slain!
   Ye swains who know her various worth to prize,
Ah! house her well from Winter's angry skies.
Potatoes, pumpkins, should her sadness cheer,
Corn from your crib, and mashes from your beer;
When spring returns she'll well acquit the loan,
And nurse at once your infants and her own.
   Milk then with pudding I should always chuse;
To this in future I confine my Muse,
Till she in haste some farther hints unfold,   330
Well for the young, nor useless to the old.
First in your bowl the milk abundant take,
Then drop with care along the silver lake
Your flakes of pudding; these at first will hide
Their little bulk beneath the swelling tide;
But when their growing mass no more can sink,
When the soft island looms above the brink,
Then check your hand; you've got the portion's due,
So taught our sires, and what they taught is true.
   There is a choice in spoons. Tho' small appear   340
The nice distinction, yet to me 'tis clear.
The deep-bowl'd Gallic spoon, contriv'd to scoop
In ample draughts the thin diluted soup,
Performs not well in these substantial things,
Whose mass adhesive to the metal clings;
Where the strong labial muscles must embrace,
The gentle curve, and sweep the hollow space.
With ease to enter and discharge the freight,
A bowl less concave but still more dilate,
Becomes the pudding best. The shape, the size,   350
A secret rests unknown to vulgar eyes.

---

316 **Mother . . . God,** Nut, mother of Osiris, was often represented as a cow

Experienc'd feeders can alone impart
A rule so much above the lore of art.
These tuneful lips, that thousand spoons have tried,
With just precision could the point decide.
Tho' not in song; the muse but poorly shines
In cones, and cubes, and geometric lines,
Yet the true form, as near as she can tell,
Is that small section of a goose-egg shell,
Which in two equal portions shall divide   360
The distance from the centre to the side.
　　Fear not to slaver; 'tis no deadly sin.
Like the free Frenchman, from your joyous chin
Suspend the ready napkin; or, like me,
Poise with one hand your bowl upon your knee;
Just in the zenith your wise head project,
Your full spoon, rising in a line direct,
Bold as a bucket, heeds no drops that fall,
The wide-mouth'd bowl will surely catch them all!   1793, 1796

---

369 **catch them all.** New Haven ed. inserts a note: "There are various ways of preparing and eating it; with
molasses, butter, sugar, cream, and fried. Why so excellent a thing cannot be eaten alone? Nothing is perfect alone, even man who boasts of so much perfection is nothing without his fellow substance. In eating,
beware of the lurking heat that lies deep in the mass; dip your spoon gentle, take shallow dips and cool it
by degrees. It is sometimes necessary to blow. This is indicated by certain signs which every experienced
feeder knows. They should be taught to young beginners. I have known a child's tongue blistered for want
of this attention, and then the schooldame would insist that the poor thing had told a lie. A mistake: the
falsehood was in the faithless pudding. A prudent mother will cool it for her child with her own sweet ·
breath. The husband, seeing this, pretends his own wants blowing too from the same lips. A sly deceit of
love. She knows the cheat, but feigning ignorance, lends her pouting lips and gives a gentle blast, which
warms the husband's heart more than it cools his pudding."

1766—1846 Robert Bailey Thomas

The first number of *The Farmer's Almanack,* later called *The Old Farmer's
Almanack,* was the issue of 1793; the publication is still flourishing.
Founder of this long-lived publication and its chief genius during the
years when farmers bought 100,000 copies of it each winter was Robert
Bailey Thomas. Thomas was born in Massachusetts in 1766, the son of a New Eng-
lander who had a varied career as schoolmaster, tradesman, soldier, and farmer. Hav-

ing inherited some of his father's versatility, Thomas, after a moderate amount of schooling, became a schoolmaster, then a bookbinder, then a bookseller, then a Boston publisher and author.

As a publisher, he made the annual issuance of his almanac an important and highly profitable task. He compiled its astronomical predictions, its calendars, its various useful charts; he selected and edited contributions sent in by clever readers; and he wrote a large amount of copy himself. "A man," as a co-worker testified, "of strong practical good sense," Thomas early began to include in each issue a column for every month called "Farmer's Calendar." Here, using and displaying his sound horse sense, he handed out seasonable advice, sometimes in proverb form, sometimes in the form of sketches or fables. A selection from these direct and apparently artless little pieces will show that, incidentally and quite unpretentiously, Thomas achieved in them a surprisingly inclusive portrait of New England life and manners.

Clarence Brigham, An Account of American Almanacs and Their Value for Historical Study, American Antiquarian Society, Worcester, 1925   J. H. Fitts, "The Thomas Almanacs," Historical Collections of the Essex Institute, XII, 243-270, October 1874   G. L. Kittredge, The Old Farmer and His Almanack, Boston, 1904

from The Farmer's Almanack

[NEIGHBOR BRAGGADOCIA]

I have more pork in my cellar, said neighbor Braggadocia, *than all the Almanack makers in christendom. Fie on your larnin, and all that stuff; I want none of your nonsense. No man shall teach me, faith.* Now I forebore to dispute with this great man; for the proverb says, *you cannot make a silken purse out of a sow's ear.*   July 1807

[BREAD AND CHEESE]

Cut your early winter grain while the blades are yellow and the joints are green. Gather herbs. About five o'clock let the boy carry out some bread and cheese. It is the most agreeable time in the whole day to eat; and such a rural repast, which needs not take but a few moments, will do your workmen more good than a barrel 10 of flip. I would not however have you be sparing of your liquor.   July 1807

[FARMER-SOLDIERS]

Now if you have been a good husband, and kept your sheep well thro' the winter, you may wash and shear them about this time. Let spring calves go to grass and salt them well. "Every farmer," says my old friend Tom, "should be soldier enough to understand the word attention."   May 1809

[*THE HAPPY FARMER*]

The farmer now must be as busy as a woman with twins. See daddy Spriggins! he considers the importance of strict attention to business. He is up at the peep of the dawn — the boys are called, and Tabathy has long ago been at milking! What pleasure exceeds that of the farmer? Now he exultingly beholds the fair fruits of his labour. He picks his apples; he gathers his corn; he digs his potatoes, and dances around the cider mill with a delight that kings and emperors cannot enjoy with all their pompous parade and tinsel splendor.   October 1809

[*NOVEMBER CHORES*]

10 The maltsters are calling for your barley — so make haste to thresh it. Breed horses and fat cattle. It will do to thresh all your grain. You may set fruit trees. Secure cellars from frost. Rack off cyder — put it into clean casks. See that your loose boards are nailed. Take care of your bees by sheltering them. Do not let geese, turkeys, &c. suffer for want of food. Be not impatient to get away to the grog shop.
November 1809

[*MINDING THE MAIN CHANCE*]

"There, there! run, John, the hogs are in the cornfield," cried old lady Lookout, as she stood slipshod over the cheese-tub. "I told your father, John, that this would be the case; but he would rather go day after day up to 'Squire Plunket's to drink
20 grog and swap horses, than go to a little pains to stop the gap in the wall, by which he might prevent the destruction of our beautiful cornfield; and then, Jonny, you know if we have corn to sell we can afford to rig up a little and go and see your aunt Winnypucker's folks."

"Aye, aye, mother, let us mind the main chance, as our minister told us the other day. You look to your cheese-tubs, I'll see to the hogs, and with a little good luck, by jinks, mother, we may be able to hold up our heads yet."   July 1812

[*SLIPPERY TIMES*]

"Slippery times, slippery times," cried father Simpkins, when he saw his neighbor's mare fall and break her leg for want of shoeing.
30   A blacksmith is of great use to a neighborhood. Farmer Heedless acknowledges this, yet he seldom employs one. 'Tis but a few days since I visited him. When I entered the house the good woman was complaining to him of his negligence.

"There," said she, "it is going on five years since you broke the crane in heating water to scald the hogs, and all this time I have had to set my kettle on the coals! Look at these tongs — they have been broke ever since Caleb was born! And as for the andirons, you have soaked them so much in your flip-pitcher that they have been useless this long time. John, take the mare over to Captain Smite's and have her shod all over, for the poor creature ha'n't had but a piece of a shoe on since last June, when I rode her up to your uncle Clumpet's. Ask him when he can shoe the oxen. O, by jingo! I wish I was a man — I would make business fly, like a hornet's nest in a pair of breeches, as the saying is," &c, &c, &c, &c.

February 1813

[*MY NEIGHBOR FREEPORT*]

My neighbor Freeport had a knack at telling a story, cracking a joke and singing a song, and these talents made him a favourite of his townsmen. Every town meeting 10 and training was sure to gather round him a crowd of jovial fellows, and my neighbour pretty soon added to his other acquisitions that of handsomely swigging a glass of grog. The demands for stories, jokes and songs encreased with the reward he received for them; and Freeport had not a heart to refuse either, till the tavern became his common resort. But while Freeport was so musical at the tavern his affairs got out of tune at home. His wife took a high pitch, and often gave him an unwelcome solo. Her stories had much of pith, and her sarcasms were of the keenest sort. She insisted that their affairs were going to rack and ruin. Sometimes the neighbour's cattle had broken into the corn — the rye had been ruined by laying out in the storm — the hogs had broken in and rooted up the garden — the hay was half 20 lost for want of attention — the fences were broken down, &c. &c. And then the children —

Alas! the poor children were shoeless, coatless and heartless; for they had become the scoff and sport of their little companions by reason of their father's neglect to provide them with decent and comfortable apparel. They were unable to read, for they had no books. The sheep — here the poor woman sorely wept — were sold by the collector to pay taxes. So there was no chance for any wool to knit the children's stockings. No flax had been raised, and of course they could have no shirts. To hear all this and ten times more was not very welcome to the ears of Freeport, whose heart was naturally tender and humane, so to get rid of it, he used to return 30 to the tavern like a sow to her wallowing. His shop bills run up fast, while his character was running down. In this way he went on about two years, till old Scrapewell and Screwpenny got his farm; for all this time these usurers had been lending him money, and thus encouraging him to pursue this dreadful course.

Old Capt. Gripe also came in for a share of poor Freeport's estate; and there was Plunket, the cobler, he had lent him nine pence several times and now had cobbled it up to a court demand. Bob Raikins had swapped watches with him, and came in for the boot. The widow Nippet had lent him her mare twice to mill and once to a funeral, and had sold the boys an old tow jacket for a peck of whortleberries, and also given them a mess of turnips, and so she made out her account and got a writ. 40 Tom Teazer, well known at the grog shops for a dabster at shoemaker loo,

---

11 **training.** See note, p. 94

old Jeremiah Jenkins, the Jew, Stephen Staball, the butcher, and all the village
moon-cursers came in for their portion of the wreck. So poor Freeport gave up vessel
and cargo to these land pirates, sent his disconsolate wife again to her father with
one of their babes, the rest were provided for by the town; and as for himself, miserable wretch, he became an outcast, a vagabond, and died drunk in the
highway!   October-December 1813

[*TURBULENT MARCH*]

'Tis almost as much as any one can do to keep his hat upon his head, and his head
upon his shoulders, during this turbulent month! See old aunt Betty Beeswax half
10 leg deep in splash, combating a gust of wind that has laid seige to her petticoat!
Alas, poor Betty! These are searching, saucy and pitiless winds. Take heed from
this and have mercy on those poor wretches whose characters you have a thousand
times thus belabored and writhed and twisted and turned topsyturvy. Perhaps you
are now on some *backbitical* expedition.

Take no alarm, ladies. Every fair dairy maid is not as Betty Beeswax, but lest some
of you should wax warm and with a vengeance tear up my Calendar, I will change
to a sweeter theme and sing of Maple Sugar. *Come thou sweet, delicious juice, and from
the pregnant maple pour and fill my cauldrons. The sweat and tears of sorrowing slaves
shall ne'er impair thy charming flavour!*   March 1815

20 [*TOM TWILIGHT*]

Through drifting snow and cutting sleet
I've trudged and toiled my friends to greet;
And tug'd beneath my lumb'ring gear,
To wish you all a *happy year.*
Ye, gentle folks, shall I unpack,
The precious store upon my back,
My wallet, crowded to the brim,
And all the wealth of *Pedlar Tim!*
I've books of various sorts and sizes;
30   Come, buy just as your fancy prizes!

Walk up, gemmen! Now's your time to make a fortune! Come, who takes this?
Here is Thacher's Orchardist; a book that ought to be in the possession of every
farmer. The price one dollar, and Capt. Thrifty says he would give five dollars rather
than be without one. Here's another excellent work, a Treatise on Gardening, by
William Cobbett, the great Porcupine! Be not afraid of his quills. The tiger is sof-

---

18 **sorrowing slaves,** slave labor in the West Indies produced molasses   32 **Thacher's Orchardist,** by
James Thacher (1754-1844), physician and miscellaneous writer, published in 1822   35 **the great Porcupine,** Cobbett titled his autobiography *The Life and Adventures of Peter Porcupine* with his pamphleteering
pseudonym

tened to the lamb. He was once as fierce as a bull; but now he is as calm as a sheep. His arrows were as sharp as a pitchfork; but now they are as blunt as a beetle! Now, my friends, is the time to read books, crack nuts and tell stories — so here's another of my Almanacks, which contains as much as the former ones, and is, I hope, as entertaining.   January 1824

[*THE PREMIUMS*]

This is the month for cattle shows, and other agricultural exhibitions — Premiums are offered by various societies for the greatest crops; the best stock, and the best domestic manufactures, and thousands are pulling away for the prize, with all their might.   10
    The great Bull of farmer Lumpkins is a nonsuch!
    Peter Nibble has raised a monstrous field of white beans!
    Jo Lucky's acre of corn has seven stout ears to the stalk!
    Dolly Dilligence has outstript all in the bonnet line!
    Tabitha Twistem's hearth rug is up to all Market-street!
    The Linsey-Woolsey Manufacturing Company have made the finest piece of satinet that ever mortals set eyes on!
    There is the widow Clacket's heifer, she is to be driven!
    And, O, if you could only see, Squire Trulliber's great boar! They say it is as big as a full grown rhinoceros!   20
    Huzza, huzza for the premiums! Here's to the girl that can best darn a stocking, and to the lad that shall raise the biggest pumpkin!   October 1824

1783—1840 Morgan Neville

The first fictionist of note to hail from west of the Alleghenies, Morgan Neville was born in Pittsburgh in 1783. He was the descendant of a family which for many years had been important in western Pennsylvania and which had included two Revolutionary War heroes. After studying at the Pittsburgh Academy, he began a varied career typical of the West of the day. At various times he was a lawyer, a bank cashier, a sheriff, a business secretary, a journalist, and an editor.

Neville's writings included — in addition to newspaper editorials and lyric poems, happily forgotten — a number of sketches and tales. One of these, still remembered, is "Reminiscence of Pittsburgh" (1831), a story of a French *émigré* who wandered to Pittsburgh in the days of the French Revolution and became the proprietor of a confectionery shop there. His most famous story is "The Last of the Boatmen," published in a Cincinnati giftbook, *The Western Souvenir,* in 1828.

"The Last of the Boatmen" is a portrayal of the famed Mike Fink (1770?-1823). Mike had been one of the keelboatmen on the Ohio and Mississippi rivers and later one of the trappers operating in the country far to the west of St. Louis. He became a representative, in popular thought, of the frontier, and during his lifetime and after his death he was the hero of much lore retailed by word of mouth up and down the rivers. Young Abe Lincoln and young Sam Clemens were destined to hear traditional yarns about him, and Clemens was to consider putting a passage about him in *Huckleberry Finn.*

Mike's story, as Neville told it, was transitional in the way much fiction of the 1820's and 1830's was — a combination of the elegant and leisurely method of the essay with the salty materials of the campfire yarn. Despite its stiffness and its embroidered elegance, it pointed the way for later writers who were to portray more and more indigenous American characters in a style like that of the fireside storyteller. Neville's work, in other words, was preparatory for that of some of the best humorists of the prewar period. That readers of the day were interested in subject matter such as Neville developed here is clearly shown by very frequent reprintings of this sketch in periodicals and books.

Walter Blair and F. J. Meine, eds., Half Horse Half Alligator: The Growth of the Mike Fink Legend, Chicago, 1956   J. T. Flanagan, "Morgan Neville, Early Western Chronicler," **Western Pennsylvania Historical Magazine,** December 1938, XXI, 255-266

The Last of the Boatmen

I embarked a few years since, at Pittsburgh, for Cincinnati, on board of a steam boat — more with a view of realising the possibility of a speedy return against the current, than in obedience to the call of either business or pleasure. It was a voyage of speculation. I was born on the banks of the Ohio, and the only vessels associated with my early recollections were the canoes of the Indians, which brought to Fort Pitt their annual cargoes of skins and bear's oil. The Flat boat of Kentucky, destined only to float with the current, next appeared; and after many years of interval, the Keel boat of the Ohio, and the Barge of the Mississippi were introduced for the convenience of the infant commerce of the West.

6 **Flat boat,** a boat used by pioneers in moving down river. These were flat-bottomed, boxlike structures of green oak fastened with wooden pins to timber frames, averaging about forty feet long, twelve feet wide, and eight feet deep   8 **Keel boat,** a vessel used for transporting cargoes not only downstream but upstream as well. These boats, averaging about fifty feet in length and nine feet or less in width, were built on a keel covered with planks. They had a draught of only twenty or thirty inches, and could be poled, bushwhacked, rowed, sailed, or cordelled — by manpower — upstream   8 **Barge,** a long boat, similar to a keelboat, sixty feet long, propelled by fifty oars

At the period, at which I have dated my trip to Cincinnati, the steam boat had made but few voyages back to Pittsburgh. We were generally skeptics as to its practicability. The mind was not prepared for the change that was about to take place in the West. It is now consummated; and we yet look back with astonishment at the result.

The rudest inhabitants of our forests; — the man whose mind is least of all imbued with a relish for the picturesque — who would gaze with vacant stare at the finest painting — listen with apathy to the softest melody, and turn with indifference from a mere display of ingenious mechanism, is struck with the sublime power and self-moving majesty of a steam boat; — lingers on the shore where it passes — and fol- 10 lows its rapid, and almost magic course with silent admiration. The steam engine in five years has enabled us to anticipate a state of things, which, in the ordinary course of events, it would have required a century to have produced. The art of printing scarcely surpassed it in its beneficial consequences.

In the old world, the places of the greatest interest to the philosophic traveller are ruins, and monuments, that speak of faded splendour, and departed glory. The broken columns of Tadmor — the shapeless ruins of Babylon, are rich in matter for almost endless speculation. Far different is the case in the western regions of America. The stranger views here, with wonder, the rapidity with which cities spring up in forests; and with which barbarism retreats before the approach of art and civiliza- 20 tion. The reflection possessing the most intense interest is — not what has been the character of the country, but what shall be her future destiny.

As we coasted along this cheerful scene, one reflection crossed my mind to diminish the pleasure it excited. This was caused by the sight of the ruins of the once splendid mansion of Blennerhassett. I had spent some happy hours here, when it was the favourite residence of taste and hospitality. I had seen it when a lovely and accomplished woman presided — shedding a charm around, which made it as inviting, though not so dangerous, as the island of Calypso; — when its liberal and polished owner made it the resort of every stranger, who had any pretensions to literature or science. I had beheld it again under more inauspicious circumstances: — 30 when its proprietor, in a moment of visionary speculation, had abandoned this earthly paradise to follow an adventurer — himself the dupe of others. A military banditti held possession, acting "by authority." The embellishments of art and taste disappeared beneath the touch of a band of Vandals, and the beautiful domain which presented the imposing appearance of a palace, and which had cost a fortune in the erection, was changed in one night, into a scene of devastation! The chimneys of the house remained for some years — the insulated monument of the folly of their owner, and pointed out to the stranger the place where once stood the temple of

---

17 **Tadmor,** an ancient city, said to have been built by Solomon (see II Chronicles 8:64), famous for its ruins, now called Palmyra   25 **mansion of Blennerhassett.** On an island in the Ohio, about fourteen miles below Marietta, the rich Irish emigrant, Harman Blennerhassett, built his expensive and showy mansion. He joined Aaron Burr in his conspiracy and was arrested with him in 1806. After the arrest, the mansion, deserted and neglected, became a picturesque ruin   28 **island of Calypso.** Calypso was a sea nymph visited by Ulysses during his wanderings. She fell in love with the Greek hero and tried to make him stay with her forever

hospitality. Driftwood covered the pleasure grounds; and the massive, cut stone, that formed the columns of the gateway, were scattered more widely than the fragments of the Egyptian Memnon.

When we left Pittsburgh, the season was not far advanced in vegetation. But as we proceeded, the change was more rapid than the difference of latitude justified. I had frequently observed this in former voyages, but it never was so striking, as on the present occasion. The old mode of travelling, in the sluggish flat boat seemed to give time for the change of season; but now a few hours carried us into a different climate. We met spring with all her laughing train of flowers and verdure, rapidly advancing from the south. The buck-eye, cottonwood, and maple, had already assumed, in this region, the rich livery of summer. The thousand varieties of the floral kingdom spread a gay carpet over the luxuriant bottoms on each side of the river. The thick woods resounded with the notes of the feathered tribe — each striving to out-do his neighbor in noise, if not in melody. We had not yet reached the region of paroquets; but the clear toned whistle of the cardinal was heard in every bush; and the cat-bird was endeavouring, with its usual zeal, to rival the powers of the more gifted mocking-bird.

A few hours brought us to one of those stopping points, known by the name of "wooding places." It was situated immediately above Letart's Falls. The boat, obedient to the wheel of the pilot, made a graceful sweep towards the island above the chute, and rounding to, approached the wood pile. As the boat drew near the shore, the escape steam reverberated through the forest and hills, like the chafed bellowing of the caged tiger. The root of a tree, concealed beneath the water, prevented the boat from getting sufficiently near the bank, and it became necessary to use the paddles to take a different position.

"Back out! Mannee — and try it again!" exclaimed a voice from the shore. "Throw your pole wide — and brace off — or you'll run against a snag!"

This was a kind of language long familiar to us on the Ohio. It was a sample of the slang of the keelboatmen.

The speaker was immediately cheered by a dozen of voices from the deck; and I recognized in him the person of an old acquaintance, familiarly known to me from my boyhood. He was leaning carelessly against a large beech; and as his left arm negligently pressed a rifle to his side, presented a figure, that Salvator would have chosen from a million, as a model for his wild and gloomy pencil. His stature was upwards of six feet, his proportions perfectly symmetrical, and exhibiting the evidence of Herculean powers. To a stranger, he would have seemed a complete mulatto. Long exposure to the sun and weather on the lower Ohio and Mississippi had changed his skin; and, but for the fine European cast of his countenance, he might have passed for the principal warrior of some powerful tribe. Although at least fifty years of age,

---

3 **Egyptian Memnon,** a huge statue erected on the banks of the Nile to honor the king of the Ethiopians. See note, p. 842   26 **Mannee,** river-slang term for crew member   26 **"Throw your pole wide . . ."** refers to the manipulation of keelboats with long poles. None was used, of course, on steamboats   27 **snag,** an uprooted tree which, lying upon river shoals, menaced river traffic   33 **Salvator,** Salvator Rosa (1615-1673),·an Italian painter famed for his romantic landscapes

his hair was as black as the wing of the raven. Next to his skin he wore a red flan-
nel shirt, covered by a blue capot, ornamented with white fringe. On his feet were
moccasins, and a broad leathern belt, from which hung, suspended in a sheath, a
large knife, encircled his waist.

As soon as the steam boat became stationary, the cabin passengers jumped on
shore. On ascending the bank, the figure I have just described advanced to offer me
his hand.

"How are you, MIKE?" said I.

"How goes it?" replied the boatman — grasping my hand with a squeeze, that I
can compare to nothing, but that of a blacksmith's vice.   10

"I am glad to see you, Mannee!" — continued he in his abrupt manner. "I am
going to shoot at the tin cup for a quart — off hand — and you must be judge."

I understood Mike at once, and on any other occasion, should have remonstrated,
and prevented the daring trial of skill. But I was accompanied by a couple of English
tourists, who had scarcely ever been beyond the sound of Bow Bells; and who were
travelling post over the United States to make up a book of observations, on our
manners and customs. There were, also, among the passengers, a few bloods from
Philadelphia and Baltimore, who could conceive of nothing equal to Chestnut or
Howard streets; and who expressed great disappointment at not being able to find
terrapins and oysters at every village — marvelously lauding the comforts of Rubi- 20
cum's. My tramontane pride was aroused; and I resolved to give them an opportunity of seeing a Western Lion — for such Mike undoubtedly was — in all his glory.
The philanthropist may start, and accuse me of want of humanity. I deny the charge,
and refer for apology to one of the best understood principles of human nature.

Mike, followed by several of his crew, led the way to a beech grove, some little
distance from the landing. I invited my fellow passengers to witness the scene. On
arriving at the spot, a stout bull-headed boatman, dressed in a hunting shirt — but
bare-footed — in whom I recognised a younger brother of Mike, drew a line with
his toe; and stepping off thirty yards — turned round fronting his brother — took a
tin cup, which hung from his belt, and placed it on his head. Although I had seen 30
this feat performed before, I acknowledge, I felt uneasy, whilst this silent preparation was going on. But I had not much time for reflection; for this second Albert
exclaimed —

"Blaze away, Mike! and let's have the quart."

My "compagnons de voyage," as soon as they recovered from the first effect of
their astonishment, exhibited a disposition to interfere. But Mike, throwing back
his left leg, levelled the rifle at the head of his brother. In this horizontal position
the weapon remained for some seconds as immovable, as if the arm which held it,
was affected by no pulsation.

"Elevate your piece a little lower, Mike! or you will pay the corn," cried the im- 40
perturbable brother.

I know not if the advice was obeyed or not; but the sharp crack of the rifle imme-

---

1 **red . . . capot,** parts of the boatman's typical costume   15 **Bow Bells,** the bells of Bow Church (St.
Mary-in-Arcubus) in Cheapside, London

diately followed, and the cup flew off thirty or forty yards — rendered unfit for future service. There was a cry of admiration from the strangers, who pressed forward to see, if the fool-hardy boatman was really safe. He remained as immoveable, as if he had been a figure hewn out of stone. He had not even winked, when the ball struck within two inches of his skull.

"Mike has won!" I exclaimed; and my decision was the signal which, according to their rules, permitted him of the target to move from his position. No more sensation was exhibited among the boatmen, than if a common wager had been won. The bet being decided, they hurried back to their boat, giving me and my friends 10 an invitation to partake of "the treat." We declined, and took leave of the thoughtless creatures. In a few minutes afterwards, we observed their "Keel" wheeling into the current, — the gigantic form of Mike, bestriding the large steering oar, and the others arranging themselves in their places in front of the cabin, that extended nearly the whole length of the boat, covering merchandize of immense value. As they left the shore, they gave the Indian yell; and broke out into a sort of unconnected chorus — commencing with —

> "Hard upon the beech oar! —
> She moves too slow! —
> All the way to Shawneetown,
20 Long while ago."

In a few moments the boat "took the chute" of Letart's Falls, and disappeared behind the point, with the rapidity of an Arabian courser.

Our travellers returned to the boat, lost in speculation on the scene, and the beings they had just beheld; and, no doubt, the circumstance has been related a thousand times with all the necessary amplifications of finished tourists.

Mike Fink may be viewed, as the correct representative of a class of men now extinct; but who once possessed as marked a character, as that of the Gipsies of England, or the Lazaroni of Naples. The period of their existence was not more than the third of a century. The character was created by the introduction of trade on 30 the Western waters; and ceased with the successful establishment of the steam boat.

There is something inexplicable in the fact, that there could be men found, for ordinary wages, who would abandon the systematic, but not laborious pursuits of agriculture, to follow a life, of all others, except that of the soldier, distinguished by the greatest exposure and privation. The occupation of a boatman was more calculated to destroy the constitution, and to shorten life, than any other business. In ascending the river, it was a continued series of toil, rendered more irksome by the snail like rate, at which they moved. The boat was propelled by poles, against which the shoulder was placed; and the whole strength, and skill of the individual were applied in this manner. As the boatmen moved along the running board, with their 40 heads nearly touching the plank on which they walked, the effect produced on the mind of an observer was similar to that, on beholding the ox, rocking before an

---

28 **Lazaroni,** the lazzaroni are homeless beggars and transient beggars of Naples

overloaded cart. Their bodies, naked to their waist for the purpose of moving with greater ease, and of enjoying the breeze of the river, were exposed to the burning suns of summer, and to the rains of autumn. — After a hard day's push, they would take their "fillee," or ration of whiskey, and having swallowed a miserable supper of meat half burnt, and of bread half baked, stretch themselves, without covering, on the deck, and slumber till the steersman's call invited them to the morning "fillee." Notwithstanding this, the boatman's life had charms as irresistible, as those presented by the splendid illusion of the stage. Sons abandoned the comfortable farms of their fathers, and apprentices fled from the service of their masters. There was a captivation in the idea of "going down the river;" and the youthful boatman who 10 had "pushed a keel" from New Orleans, felt all the pride of a young merchant, after his first voyage to an English sea port. From an exclusive association together, they had formed a kind of slang peculiar to themselves; and from the constant exercise of wit, with "the squatters" on shore, and crews of other boats, they acquired a quickness, and smartness of vulgar retort, that was quite amusing. The frequent battles they were engaged in with the boatmen of different parts of the river, and with the less civilized inhabitants of the lower Ohio, and Mississippi, invested them with that ferocious reputation, which has made them spoken of throughout Europe.

On board of the boats thus navigated, our merchants entrusted valuable cargoes, without insurance, and with no other guarantee than the receipt of the steersman, 20 who possessed no property but his boat; and the confidence so reposed was seldom abused.

Among these men, Mike Fink stood an acknowledged leader for many years. Endowed by nature with those qualities of intellect, that give the possessor influence, he would have been a conspicuous member of any society, in which his lot might have been cast. An acute observer of human nature has said — "Opportunity alone makes the hero. Change but their situations, and Caesar would have been but the best wrestler on the green." With a figure cast in a mould that added much of the symmetry of an Apollo to the limbs of a Hercules, he possessed gigantic strength; and accustomed from an early period of life to brave the dangers of a frontier life, 30 his character was noted for the most daring intrepidity. At the court of Charlemagne, he might have been a Roland; with the Crusaders, he would have been the favourite of the Knight of the Lion-heart; and in our revolution, he would have ranked with the Morgans and the Putnams of the day. He was the hero of a hundred fights, and the leader in a thousand daring adventures. From Pittsburgh to St. Louis, and New Orleans, his fame was established. Every farmer on the shore kept on good terms with Mike; otherwise, there was no safety for his property. Wherever he was an enemy, like his great prototype, Rob Roy, he levied the contribution of Black Mail for the use of his boat. Often at night, when his tired companions slept, he would take an excursion of five or six miles, and return before morning, rich in spoil. On 40

14 "**the squatters**," settlers who occupied land without paying for it   32 **Roland**, a hero of the army of Charlemagne which invaded Spain in 778   33 **Knight of the Lion-heart**, Richard Coeur de Lion, King of England, 1189-1199   34 **Morgans and Putnams**, Daniel Morgan (1736?-1802) and Israel Putnam (1718-1790) were Revolutionary War heroes   38 **Rob Roy**, says Walter Scott, was "the Robin Hood of Scotland — the dread of the wealthy and the friend of the poor"

the Ohio, he was known among his companions by the appellation of the "Snapping Turtle;" and on the Mississippi, he was called "The Snag."

At the early age of seventeen, Mike's character was displayed, by enlisting himself in a corps of Scouts — a body of irregular rangers, which was employed on the Northwestern frontiers of Pennsylvania, to watch the Indians, and to give notice of any threatened inroad.

At that time, Pittsburgh was on the extreme verge of white population, and the spies, who were constantly employed, generally extended their explorations forty or fifty miles to the west of this post. They went out, singly, lived as did the Indian,
10 and in every respect, became perfectly assimilated in habits, taste, and feeling, with the red men of the desert. A kind of border warfare was kept up, and the scout thought it as praiseworthy to bring in the scalp of a Shawnee, as the skin of a panther. He would remain in the woods for weeks together, using parched corn for bread, and depending on his rifle for his meat — and slept at night in perfect comfort, rolled in his blanket.

In this corps, whilst yet a stripling, Mike acquired a reputation for boldness, and cunning, far beyond his companions. A thousand legends illustrate the fearlessness of his character. There was one, which he told, himself, with much pride, and which made an indelible impression on my boyish memory. He had been out on the hills
20 of Mahoning, when, to use his own words, "he saw signs of Indians being about." — He had discovered the recent print of the moccasin on the grass; and found drops of the fresh blood of a deer on the green bush. He became cautious, skulked for some time in the deepest thickets of hazel and briar, and, for several days, did not discharge his rifle. He subsisted patiently on parched corn and jerk, which he had dried on his first coming into the woods. He gave no alarm to the settlements, because he discovered with perfect certainty, that the enemy consisted of a small hunting party, who were receding from the Alleghany.

As he was creeping along one morning, with the stealthy tread of a cat, his eye fell upon a beautiful buck, browsing on the edge of a barren spot, three hundred
30 yards distant. The temptation was too strong for the woodsman, and he resolved to have a shot at every hazard. — Re-priming his gun, and picking his flint, he made his approaches in the usual noiseless manner. At the moment he reached the spot, from which he meant to take his aim, he observed a large savage, intent upon the same object, advancing from a direction a little different from his own. Mike shrunk behind a tree, with the quickness of thought, and keeping his eye fixed on the hunter, waited the result with patience. — In a few moments, the Indian halted within fifty paces, and levelled his piece at the deer. In the meanwhile, Mike presented his rifle at the body of the savage; and at the moment the smoke issued from the gun of the latter, the bullet of Fink passed through the red man's breast. He uttered a yell,
40 and fell dead at the same instant with the deer. Mike re-loaded his rifle, and remained in his covert for some minutes, to ascertain whether there were more enemies at hand. He then stepped up to the prostrate savage, and having satisfied himself, that life was extinguished, turned his attention to the buck, and took from the carcass those pieces, suited to the process of jerking.

In the meantime, the country was filling up with a white population; and in a few years the red men, with the exception of a few fractions of tribes, gradually receded to the Lakes and beyond the Mississippi. The corps of Scouts was abolished, after having acquired habits, which unfitted them for the pursuits of civilized society. Some incorporated themselves with the Indians; and others, from a strong attachment to their erratic mode of life, joined the boatmen, then just becoming a distinct class. Among these was our hero, Mike Fink, whose talents were soon developed; and for many years, he was as celebrated on the rivers of the West, as he had been in the woods.

I gave to my fellow travellers the substance of the foregoing narrative, as we sat 10 on deck by moonlight, and cut swiftly through the magnificent sheet of water between Letart and the Great Kanhawa. It was one of those beautiful nights, which permitted every thing to be seen with sufficient distinctness to avoid danger; — yet created a certain degree of illusion, that gave reins to the imagination. The outline of the river hills lost all its harshness; and the occasional bark of the house dog from the shore, and the distant scream of the solitary loon, gave increased effect to the scene. It was altogether so delightful, that the hours till morning flew swiftly by, whilst our travellers dwelt with rapture on the surrounding scenery, which shifted every moment like the capricious changes of the kaleidoscope — and listening to tales of border warfare, as they were brought to mind, by passing the places where 20 they happened. The celebrated Hunter's Leap, and the bloody battle of Kanhawa, were not forgotten.

The afternoon of the next day brought us to the beautiful city of Cincinnati, which, in the course of thirty years, has risen from a village of soldiers' huts to a town, — giving promise of future splendour, equal to any on the sea-board.

Some years after the period, at which I have dated my visit to Cincinnati, business called me to New Orleans. On board of the steam boat, on which I had embarked, at Louisville, I recognized, in the person of the pilot, one of those men, who had formerly been a patroon, or keel boat captain. I entered into conversation with him on the subject of his former associates.   30

"They are scattered in all directions," said he. "A few, who had capacity, have become pilots of steam boats. Many have joined the trading parties that cross the Rocky mountains; and a few have settled down as farmers."

"What has become," I asked, "of my old acquaintance, Mike Fink?"

"Mike was killed in a skrimmage," replied the pilot. "He had refused several good offers on steam boats. He said he could not bear the hissing of steam, and he wanted room to throw his pole. He went to the Missouri, and about a year since he was shooting the tin cup, when he had corned too heavy. He elevated too low, and shot his companion through the head. A friend of the deceased, who was present, suspecting foul play, shot Mike through the heart, before he had time to re- 40 load his rifle."

With Mike Fink expired the spirit of the Boatmen.

                                                                                1828

1783—1859 Washington Irving

Washington Irving was both the most polished and the most popular American prose writer of his generation. Not a profound thinker and heavily indebted for his tastes and skills to European models, he was nevertheless a gifted observer of surface details, and he developed a style which justly earned him lasting fame. Wherever the short story is read, men, women, and children continue to enjoy "Rip Van Winkle," "The Legend of Sleepy Hollow," and other story sketches by Irving. They are both historically important, being among the first mature examples of American fiction, and charmingly untouched by time, revealing their author as a man who understood the amenities of life in a world which is not always orderly and reasonable.

Irving's career is best understood when divided into three periods: (1) 1783-1815, a rather lengthy but youthful groping for a profession which would satisfy his somewhat dilettantish tastes; (2) 1815-1832, a seventeen-year residence in Europe, where he achieved international recognition as one of the romantic rediscoverers of the past; and (3) 1832-1859, in which, established as a fashionable author, he wrote chiefly as a biographer and historian.

He was born in New York City on April 3, 1783, the eleventh and last son of Scotch-English parents. The staunch Presbyterianism of his father, a well-to-do merchant, played little part in Washington Irving's unsystematic education. A delicate boy, he found his chief pleasures in light literature, the theater, art, travel, and, most particularly, in good company. At nineteen, while reading law, he contributed a series of essays dealing largely with the theater to his brother Peter's newspaper, the *Morning Chronicle,* signing them in the eighteenth-century manner as "Jonathan Oldstyle." Between 1804 and 1806 he traveled in Europe, curiously unconcerned about the political turmoil in Napoleon's empire, but much impressed with such new friends as Washington Allston, the painter.

Back in New York and admitted to the bar, he joined his brother and James Kirke Paulding in a series of satirical essays and poems, *Salmagundi,* which ran for twenty numbers in 1807-1808. A more extended burlesque, begun with Peter Irving, resulted in *A History of New York . . . By Diedrich Knickerbocker* (1809), a satire so elaborate that the law must have been much neglected during its composition. In his twenties, as a matter of fact, Irving was doubtless uncertain of himself and of his aims.

He enjoyed the convivial society of New York's younger set, shared some responsibility in the family hardware business, and dabbled occasionally in Federalist politics, meanwhile pursuing a gentlemanly interest in literature. A moot question in Irving's biography is the importance of his romantic attachment to Matilda Hoffman, who died of consumption in 1809. Had he married, Irving might conceivably have settled down to the law or to the editing of literary magazines. Matilda's death made roving possible. A bachelor all his life, he cherished as he grew older a sentimental memory which did not entirely outlaw mild flirtations with living ladies.

In 1815 he went to Liverpool on business and found that family affairs there were in great disorder because of a brother's illness. Three years later the Irving firm was bankrupt, and his great decision — to make his living by authorship — was more or less forced upon him. The results were impressive: *The Sketch Book,* published serially in 1819-1820; *Bracebridge Hall* (1822); *Tales of a Traveller* (1824); and, after a stay in Spain as a diplomatic attaché, *The Alhambra* (1832). These and other books, together with his many social connections, brought fame and considerable fortune. Irving was at home in London, Paris, Dresden, and Madrid; he met and was accepted by many of the leading literary folk of Europe; he became, in short, a great success, bringing to the United States what the new nation most ardently desired in a man of letters — the respect of the Old World. Like Sir Walter Scott, whom he much admired, Irving worked hard but insisted on preserving the pleasant fiction that authorship was something that a gentleman accomplished with his left hand.

In this attitude he had the assistance of various governmental appointments which were urged upon him in his later years. He wisely refused offers of nominations to a seat in Congress, to the post of mayor of New York, to the secretaryship of the Navy. In 1841, however, he accepted the appointment of minister to Spain, and was again in Madrid between 1842 and 1845, when he resigned. The last years of his life were devoted to several relatively minor books dealing with the American West ("A Tour on the Prairies" in *The Crayon Miscellany,* 1835; *Astoria,* written in collaboration with his nephew, Pierre, 1836; and *Adventures of Captain Bonneville,* 1837), as well as to the biographical works which display his literary and political nostalgias (*Life of Oliver Goldsmith,* 1840, and *Life of Washington,* 5 vols., 1855-1859). Much of his time after 1835 was spent in the rambling, stepped-gabled cottage at Sunnyside, near Tarrytown and Sleepy Hollow, where he died on November 28, 1859.

Irving's historical work exemplifies the antiquarian spirit which he shared with Scott and other romanticists, but he is most significant for bringing American fiction into the main stream of world literature. He wrote with full knowledge of his immediate predecessors and contemporaries, and his work held its own in direct comparison with theirs. Irving owed much to Fielding, Sterne, Goldsmith, and Scott; he owed much, also, to such German romanticists as Ludwig Tieck and E. T. A. Hoffman. When all his literary obligations are recognized, however, there is much in Irving that is his own: a feeling for place and local customs; good-humored acceptance of eccentricities in human beings and divergent ways of looking at the world; a persistent refusal to take either himself or society too seriously; and, not least of all, a delicate balance between conformity and independence which, if not originality in the strictest sense, is still creative and individual. These are virtues which Americans have always liked to think characteristic of their nation.

Irving's **Works**, Author's Revised Edition, 40 vols., New York, 1848   **Washington Irving: Representative Selections**, ed. H. A. Pochmann, Cincinnati, 1934   P. M. Irving, **The Life and Letters of Washington Irving**, 4 vols., New York, 1862-1864   S. T. Williams, **The Life of Washington Irving**, 2 vols., New York, 1935   Van Wyck Brooks, **The World of Washington Irving**, New York, 1944   Edward Wagenknecht, **Washington Irving: Moderation Displayed**, Oxford, 1962

from A History of New York *by* Diedrich Knickerbocker

Soon after the conclusion of the Salmagundi *series in January 1808, Irving and his brother Peter planned to parody Samuel Latham Mitchill's* The Picture of New York *(1807) with a historical sketch, "followed by notices of the customs, manners, and institutions of the city; written in a serio-comic vein, and treating local errors, follies, and abuses with good-humored satire" ("The Author's Apology," in the 1848 edition). But Peter went to Europe, and in the spring of 1809, Washington Irving took up the task alone. First discarding the plan of a parody in favor of a comic history, he eventually confined himself to an account of the period of Dutch domination, in seven books. As he wrote, Irving discovered that the history of New York as a Dutch colony had never been adequately written, and he spent many hours with dusty books and manuscripts in the New York Historical Society and other libraries. Despite his humorous and satirical purposes, his account embodied fact as well as fiction, and, as he said in later life, his work provoked research into the forgotten archives of the province.*

When, in October, he was ready to publish, he and his close friends devised a newspaper hoax to attract attention to the forthcoming book. An advertisement in the Evening Post *announced that "a small elderly gentleman, dressed in an old black coat and cocked hat, by the name of KNICKERBOCKER," was missing from his lodgings; ten days later a letter to the same paper conveyed news of a person of this description seen on the Albany stage; in another ten days came the announcement that Mr. Knickerbocker had left a curious manuscript in his room at the Independent Hotel, which might be printed to pay Seth Handaside, the proprietor, for board and lodging. Thus, the* History *was published on December 6, 1809, with a dedication to the New York Historical Society and an account of the author signed by the fictitious Seth Handaside.*

As Professor Williams has said, the History *is without question "the most allusive of all American literary compositions written before 1825." Almost every page reflects Irving's wide reading of classical and English literature. He parodies or imitates Homer, Cervantes, Malory, Fielding, Sterne, Swift, and many other favorites; the work is, in effect, a patchwork quilt of references, echoes, burlesques. Footnotes cite all kinds of material, some of it created out of Irving's imagination; part of Irving's purpose was to poke fun at pompous learning.*

No one can read Irving's History *without feeling its youthful, undisciplined, irreverent buoyancy; never again, perhaps, did he write so effortlessly and at the same time so artfully. The aping of various literary models is accomplished with such verve and evident pleasure that its occasional lack of restraint and proportion is easily forgiven. The book should be received as Irving wished it to be, "with good-humored indulgence," to "be thumbed and chuckled over by the family fireside." It is literary rather than native humor; it produces not belly laughs but appreciative smiles, and the more one reads the more smiles it offers.*

Book VI *Containing the Second Part of the Reign of Peter the Headstrong, and His Gallant Achievements on the Delaware*

Chapter VII *Showing the Great Advantage That the Author Has over His Reader in Time of Battle — Together with Divers Portentous Movements; Which Betoken That Something Terrible Is About To Happen*

Like as a mighty alderman, when at a corporation feast the first spoonful of turtle-soup salutes his palate, feels his appetite but tenfold quickened, and redoubles his vigorous attacks upon the tureen; while his projecting eyes roll greedily round, devouring everything at table — so did the mettlesome Peter Stuyvesant feel that hunger for martial glory, which raged within his bowels, inflamed by the capture of 10 Fort Casimir, and nothing could allay it but the conquest of all New Sweden. No sooner, therefore, had he secured his conquest, than he stumped resolutely on, flushed with success, to gather fresh laurels at Fort Christina.

This was the grand Swedish post, established on a small river (or, as it is improperly termed, creek) of the same name; and here that crafty governor Jan Risingh lay grimly drawn up, like a gray-bearded spider in the citadel of his web.

But before we hurry into the direful scenes which must attend the meeting of two such potent chieftains, it is advisable to pause for a moment, and hold a kind of warlike council. Battles should not be rushed into precipitately by the historian and his readers, any more than by the general and his soldiers. The great commanders 20 of antiquity never engaged the enemy without previously preparing the minds of their followers by animating harangues; spiriting them up to heroic deeds assuring them of the protection of the gods, and inspiring them with a confidence in the prowess of their leaders. So the historian should awaken the attention and enlist the passions of his readers; and having set them all on fire with the importance of his subject, he should put himself at their head, flourish his pen, and lead them on to the thickest of the fight.

An illustrious example of this rule may be seen in that mirror of historians, the immortal Thucydides. Having arrived at the breaking out of the Peloponnesian war, one of his commentators observes that "he sounds the charge in all the disposition 30 and spirit of Homer. He catalogues the allies on both sides. He awakens our expectations, and fast engages our attention. All mankind are concerned in the important point now going to be decided. Endeavors are made to disclose futurity. Heaven itself is interested in the dispute. The earth totters, and nature seems to labor with

---

Text: the 1848 edition   11 **Fort Casimir,** a small post established by the Dutch in 1651 on the Delaware River near the present site of New Castle. Surrendered to the Swedes in 1654, it was recaptured by Stuyvesant in 1655   13 **Fort Christina.** "At present a flourishing town, called Christiana, or Christeen, about thirty-seven miles from Philadelphia, on the postroad to Baltimore." — Irving. This fort, established in 1638, is usually said to have been at Wilmington   14 **improperly termed,** creek. See p. 684   15 **Jan Risingh,** Johann Classon Rising (1617-1672), director-general of New-Sweden, 1654-1655

the great event. This is his solemn, sublime manner of setting out. Thus he mag-
nifies a war between two, as Rapin styles them, petty states; and thus artfully he
supports a little subject by treating it in a great and noble method."

In like manner, having conducted my readers into the very teeth of peril — having followed the adventurous Peter and his band into foreign regions — surrounded
by foes, and stunned by the horrid din of arms — at this important moment, while
darkness and doubt hang o'er each coming chapter, I hold it meet to harangue them,
and prepare them for the events that are to follow.

And here I would premise one great advantage which, as historian, I possess over
10 my reader; and this it is, that though I cannot save the life of my favorite hero, nor
absolutely contradict the event of a battle (both which liberties, though often taken
by the French writers of the present reign, I hold to be utterly unworthy of a scrupulous historian), yet I can now and then make him bestow on his enemy a sturdy
back-stroke sufficient to fell a giant; though, in honest truth, he may never have
done anything of the kind — or I can drive his antagonist clear round and round
the field, as did Homer make that fine fellow Hector scamper like a poltroon round
the walls of Troy; for which, if ever they have encountered one another in the Elysian
fields, I'll warrant the prince of poets has had to make the most humble apology.

I am aware that many conscientious readers will be ready to cry out "foul play!"
20 whenever I render a little assistance to my hero — but I consider it one of those
privileges exercised by historians of all ages — and one which has never been disputed. An historian is, in fact, as it were, bound in honor to stand by his hero —
the fame of the latter is intrusted to his hands, and it is his duty to do the best by
it he can. Never was there a general, an admiral, or any other commander, who, in
giving account of any battle he had fought, did not sorely belabor the enemy; and
I have no doubt that, had my heroes written the history of their own achievements,
they would have dealt much harder blows than any that I shall recount. Standing
forth, therefore, as the guardian of their fame, it behooves me to do them the same
justice they would have done themselves; and if I happen to be a little hard upon
30 the Swedes, I give free leave to any of their descendants, who may write a story of
the State of Delaware, to take fair retaliation, and belabor Peter Stuyvesant as hard
as they please.

Therefore stand by for broken heads and bloody noses! — My pen hath long itched
for a battle — siege after siege have I carried on without blows or bloodshed; but
now I have at length got a chance, and I vow to Heaven and St. Nicholas, that, let
the chronicles of the times say what they please, neither Sallust, Livy, Tacitus, Polybius, nor any other historian, did ever record a fiercer fight than that in which my
valiant chieftains are now about to engage.

And you, oh most excellent readers, whom, for your faithful adherence, I could
40 cherish in the warmest corner of my heart — be not uneasy — trust the fate of our

---

2 **Rapin**, René Rapin (1621-1687), French humanist   35 **St. Nicholas.** The Dutch introduced this saint
to America after having transmuted him into the Nordic magician better known later as Santa Claus   36
Sallust . . . Polybius, ancient historians. Polybius was a Greek, the others Romans

favorite Stuyvesant with me — for by the rood, come what may, I'll stick by Hard-koppig Piet to the last. I'll make him drive about these losels vile, as did the re-nowned Launcelot of the Lake a herd of recreant Cornish knights — and if he does fall, let me never draw my pen to fight another battle in behalf of a brave man, if I don't make these lubberly Swedes pay for it!

No sooner had Peter Stuyvesant arrived at Fort Christina than he proceeded with-out delay to intrench himself, and immediately on running his first parallel, dis-patched Antony Van Corlear to summon the fortress to surrender. Van Corlear was received with all due formality, hoodwinked at the portal, and conducted through a pestiferous smell of salt fish and onions to the citadel, a substantial hut built of 10 pine logs. His eyes were here uncovered, and he found himself in the august pres-ence of Governor Risingh. This chieftain, as I have before noted, was a very giantly man; and was clad in a coarse blue coat, strapped round the waist with a leathern belt, which caused the enormous skirts and pockets to set off with a very warlike sweep. His ponderous legs were cased in a pair of foxy-colored jackboots, and he was straddling in the attitude of the Colossus of Rhodes before a bit of broken looking-glass, shaving himself with a villanously dull razor. This afflicting operation caused him to make a series of horrible grimaces, which heightened exceedingly the grisly terrors of his visage. On Antony Van Corlear's being announced, the grim commander paused for a moment, in the midst of one of his most hard-favored con- 20 tortions, and after eying him askance over the shoulder, with a kind of snarling grin on his countenance, resumed his labors at the glass.

This iron harvest being reaped, he turned once more to the trumpeter, and de-manded the purport of his errand. Antony Van Corlear delivered in a few words, being a kind of short-hand speaker, a long message from his excellency, recounting the whole history of the province, with a recapitulation of grievances, and enumera-tion of claims, and concluding with a peremptory demand of instant surrender; which done, he turned aside, took his nose between his thumb and fingers, and blew a tremendous blast, not unlike the flourish of a trumpet of defiance — which it had doubtless learned from a long and intimate neighborhood with the melodious 30 instrument.

Governor Risingh heard him through, trumpet and all, but with infinite impatience; leaning at times, as was his usual custom, on the pommel of his sword, and at times twirling a huge steel watch-chain, or snapping his fingers. Van Corlear having fin-ished, he bluntly replied, that Peter Stuyvesant and his summons might go to the

---

1 **Hardkoppig Piet,** Stuyvesant's Dutch nickname, Hardheaded Pete   2 **losels,** worthless fellows (archaic)   3 **Launcelot . . . Lake,** an echo of the *Morte d'arthur* by Thomas Malory (d. 1471). The "driving about" of Cornish knights occurs chiefly in Bk. IX   8 **Antony Van Corlear,** or Van Curler, a figure more renowned in folklore than in history. As governor's trumpeter, he is supposed by Irving to have given his name to Anthony's Nose, a mountain across the Hudson from West Point, and to have died in 1644 on a mission from Stuyvesant. Sent to arouse the Dutch colonists to their danger from the British, he discovered that the creek separating Manhattan from the Bronx was swollen with rain. Swearing to swim it "en spuyt den Duyvil," he started out, but was seized halfway across by the Devil. He freed himself once by a blast on his trumpet, but the Devil, recovering from surprise, dragged him down. Hence the name Spuyten Duyvil Creek   16 **Colossus of Rhodes,** a statue of Apollo over one hundred feet high which in ancient times stood astride the entrance to the harbor of that Aegean island

d......l, whither he hoped to send him and his crew of ragamuffins before supper-time. Then unsheathing his brass-hilted sword, and throwing away the scabbard — " 'Fore gad," quod he, "but I will not sheathe thee again until I make a scabbard of the smoke-dried leathern hide of this runagate Dutchman." Then having flung a fierce defiance in the teeth of his adversary by the lips of his messenger, the latter was reconducted to the portal, with all the ceremonious civility due to the trumpeter, squire, and ambassador of so great a commander; and being again unblinded, was courteously dismissed with a tweak of the nose, to assist him in recollecting his message.

10   No sooner did the gallant Peter receive this insolent reply than he let fly a tremendous volley of red-hot execrations, which would infallibly have battered down the fortifications, and blown up the powder magazine about the ears of the fiery Swede, had not the ramparts been remarkably strong, and the magazine bomb-proof. Perceiving that the works withstood this terrific blast, and that it was utterly impossible (as it really was in those unphilosophic days) to carry on a war with words, he ordered his merry men all to prepare for an immediate assault. But here a strange murmur broke out among his troops, beginning with the tribe of the Van Bummels, those valiant trenchermen of the Bronx, and spreading from man to man, accompanied with certain mutinous looks and discontented murmurs. For once in his life,
20   and only for once, did the great Peter turn pale, for he verily thought his warriors were going to falter in this hour of perilous trial, and thus to tarnish forever the fame of the province of New Netherlands.

But soon did he discover, to his great joy, that in his suspicion he deeply wronged his most undaunted army; for the cause of this agitation and uneasiness simply was, that the hour of dinner was at hand, and it would have almost broken the hearts of these regular Dutch warriors to have broken in upon the invariable routine of their habits. Besides, it was an established rule among our ancestors always to fight upon a full stomach; and to this may be doubtless attributed the circumstance that they came to be so renowned in arms.

30   And now are the hearty men of the Manhattoes, and their no less hearty comrades, all lustily engaged under the trees, buffeting stoutly with the contents of their wallets, and taking such affectionate embraces of their canteens and pottles, as though they verily believed they were to be the last. And as I foresee we shall have hot work in a page or two, I advise my readers to do the same, for which purpose I will bring this chapter to a close; giving them my word of honor, that no advantage shall be taken of this armistice to surprise, or in any wise molest, the honest Nederlanders, while at their vigorous repast.

Chapter VIII   Containing the Most Horrible Battle Ever Recorded in Poetry or Prose; With the Admirable Exploits of Peter the Headstrong

"Now had the Dutchmen snatched a huge repast," and finding themselves wonderfully encouraged and animated thereby, prepared to take the field. Expectation, says

---

30 **Manhattoes,** the inhabitants of Manhattan. The origin of the name, spelled variously as Monados, Manadoes, Natoes, and Manhates, is obscure; one theory is that it came from Spanish *monados,* drunken man

the writer of the Stuyvesant manuscript — Expectation now stood on stilts. The world forgot to turn round, or rather stood still, that it might witness the affray; like a round-bellied alderman, watching the combat of two chivalrous flies upon his jerkin. The eyes of all mankind, as usual in such cases, were turned upon Fort Christina. The sun, like a little man in a crowd at a puppet-show, scampered about the heavens, popping his head here and there, and endeavoring to get a peep between the unmannerly clouds that obtruded themselves in his way. The historians filled their inkhorns — the poets went without their dinners, either that they might buy paper and goose-quills, or because they could not get anything to eat. Antiquity scowled sulkily out of its grave, to see itself outdone — while even Posterity stood mute, gazing in 10 gaping ecstasy of retrospection on the eventful field.

The immortal deities, who whilom had seen service at the "affair" of Troy — now mounted their feather-bed clouds, and sailed over the plain, or mingled among the combatants in different disguises, all itching to have a finger in the pie. Jupiter sent off his thunderbolt to a noted coppersmith, to have it furbished up for the direful occasion. Venus vowed by her chastity to patronize the Swedes, and in semblance of a blear-eyed trull paraded the battlements of Fort Christina, accompanied by Diana, as a sergeant's widow, of cracked reputation. The noted bully, Mars, stuck two horse-pistols into his belt, shouldered a rusty firelock, and gallantly swaggered at their elbow, as a drunken corporal — while Apollo trudged in their rear, as a bandy-legged 20 fifer, playing most villanously out of tune.

On the other side, the ox-eyed Juno, who had gained a pair of black eyes over night, in one of her curtain lectures with old Jupiter, displayed her haughty beauties on a baggage-wagon — Minerva, as a brawny gin-suttler, tucked up her skirts, brandished her fists, and swore most heroically, in exceeding bad Dutch (having but lately studied the language,) by way of keeping up the spirits of the soldiers; while Vulcan halted as a club-footed blacksmith, lately promoted to be a captain of militia. All was silent awe, or bustling preparation: war reared his horrid front, gnashed loud his iron fangs, and shook his direful crest of bristling bayonets.

And now the mighty chieftains marshalled out their hosts. Here stood stout 30 Risingh, firm as a thousand rocks — incrusted with stockades, and intrenched to the chin in mud batteries. His valiant soldiery lined the breastwork in grim array, each having his mustachios fiercely greased, and his hair pomatumed back, and queued so stiffly, that he grinned above the ramparts like a grisly death's head.

There came on the intrepid Peter — his brows knit, his teeth set, his fists clenched, almost breathing forth volumes of smoke, so fierce was the fire that raged within his bosom. His faithful squire Van Corlear trudged valiantly at his heels, with his trumpet gorgeously bedecked with red and yellow ribbons, the remembrances of his fair mistresses at the Manhattoes. Then came waddling on the sturdy chivalry of the Hudson. There were the Van Wycks, and the Van Dycks, and the Ten Eycks — the Van 40

---

1 **Stuyvesant manuscript,** described in Irving's Preface as "an elaborate manuscript written in exceeding pure and classic low Dutch, excepting a few errors in orthography, which was found in the archives of the Stuyvesant family." It is apparently one of Irving's fictitious authorities   12 **the "affair" of Troy.** In this and the following paragraph Irving burlesques Bk. V of Homer's *Iliad*   24 **gin-suttler,** gin-selling camp-follower   40 **Van Wycks,** etc. See the catalogue of ships in Bk. I

Nesses, the Van Tassels, the Van Grolls; the Van Hoesens, the Van Giesons and the Van Blarcoms — the Van Warts, the Van Winkles, the Van Dams; the Van Pelts, the Van Rippers, and the Van Brunts. There were the Van Hornes, the Van Hooks, the Van Bunschotens; the Van Gelders, the Van Arsdales, and the Van Bummels; the Vander Belts, the Vander Hoofs, the Vander Voorts, the Vander Lyns, the Vander Pools, and the Vander Spiegles — then came the Hoffmans, the Hooghlands, the Hoppers, the Cloppers, the Ryckmans, the Dyckmans, the Hogebooms, the Rosebooms, the Oothouts, the Quackenbosses, the Roerbacks, the Garrebrantzes, the Bensons, the Brouwers, the Waldrons, the Onderdonks, the Varra Vangers, the
10 Schermerhorns, the Stoutenburghs, the Brinkerhoffs, the Bontecous, the Knickerbockers, the Hockstrassers, the Ten Breecheses and the Tough Breecheses, with a host more of worthies, whose names are too crabbed to be written, or if they could be written, it would be impossible for man to utter — all fortified with a mighty dinner, and, to use the words of a great Dutch poet,

"Brimful of wrath and cabbage."

For an instant the mighty Peter paused in the midst of his career, and mounting on a stump, addressed his troops in eloquent Low Dutch, exhorting them to fight like *duyvels,* and assuring them that if they conquered, they should get plenty of booty — if they fell, they should be allowed the satisfaction, while dying, of reflect-
20 ing that it was in the service of their country — and after they were dead, of seeing their names inscribed in the temple of renown, and handed down, in company with all the other great men of the year, for the admiration of posterity. — Finally, he swore to them, on the word of a governor (and they knew him too well to doubt it for a moment), that if he caught any mother's son of them looking pale, or playing craven, he would curry his hide till he made him run out of it like a snake in spring time. Then lugging out his trusty sabre, he brandished it three times over his head, ordered Van Corlear to sound a charge, and shouting the words "St. Nicholas and the Manhattoes!" courageously dashed forwards. His warlike followers, who had employed the interval in lighting their pipes, instantly stuck them into
30 their mouths, gave a furious puff, and charged gallantly under cover of the smoke.

The Swedish garrison, ordered by the cunning Risingh not to fire until they could distinguish the whites of their assailants' eyes, stood in horrid silence on the covertway, until the eager Dutchmen had ascended the glacis. Then did they pour into them such a tremendous volley, that the very hills quaked around, and were terrified even unto an incontinence of water, insomuch that certain springs burst forth from their sides, which continue to run unto the present day. Not a Dutchman but would have bitten the dust beneath that dreadful fire, had not the protecting Minerva kindly taken care that the Swedes should, one and all, observe their usual custom of shutting their eyes and turning away their heads at the moment of discharge.

---

32 **covert-way** . . . **glacis.** Irving's familiarity with the scientific terms of military fortification was probably derived from one of his favorite books, *Tristram Shandy.* (See note, p. 488.) The covert-way is a covered passage in the counterscarp, or outer wall of a trench; the glacis is the open slope in front of that wall

The Swedes followed up their fire by leaping the counterscarp, and falling tooth and nail upon the foe with furious outcries. And now might be seen prodigies of valor, unmatched in history or song. Here was the sturdy Stoffel Brinkerhoff brandishing his quarter-staff, like the giant Blanderon his oak tree (for he scorned to carry any other weapon), and drumming a horrific tune upon the hard heads of the Swedish soldiery. There were the Van Kortlandts, posted at a distance, like the Locrian archers of yore, and plying it most potently with the longbow, for which they were so justly renowned. On a rising knoll were gathered the valiant men of Sing-Sing, assisting marvellously in the fight, by chanting the great song of St. Nicholas; but as to the Gardeniers of Hudson, they were absent on a marauding 10 party, laying waste the neighboring watermelon patches.

In a different part of the field were the Van Grolls of Antony's Nose, struggling to get to the thickest of the fight, but horribly perplexed in a defile between two hills, by reason of the length of their noses. So also the Van Bunschotens of Nyack and Kakiat, so renowned for kicking with the left foot, were brought to a stand for want of wind, in consequence of the hearty dinner they had eaten, and would have been put to utter rout but for the arrival of a gallant corps of voltigeurs, composed of the Hoppers, who advanced nimbly to their assistance on one foot. Nor must I omit to mention the valiant achievements of Antony Van Corlear, who, for a good quarter of an hour, waged stubborn fight with a little pursy Swedish drum- 20 mer; whose hide he drummed most magnificently, and whom he would infallibly have annihilated on the spot, but that he had come into the battle with no other weapon but his trumpet.

But now the combat thickened. — On came the mighty Jacobus Varra Vanger and the fighting men of the Wallabout; after them thundered the Van Pelts of Esopus, together with the Van Rippers and the Van Brunts, bearing down all before them — then the Suy Dams, and the Van Dams, pressing forward with many a blustering oath, at the head of the warriors of Hell-gate, clad in their thunder and lightning gaberdines; and lastly, the standard-bearers and body-guard of Peter Stuyvesant, bearing the great beaver of the Manhattoes.   30

And now commenced the horrid din, the desperate struggle, the maddening ferocity, the frantic desperation, the confusion and self-abandonment of war. Dutchman and Swede commingled, tugged, panted, and blowed. The heavens were darkened with a tempest of missiles. Bang! went the guns — whack! went the broad-swords — thump! went the cudgels — crash! went the musket-stocks — blows — kicks — cuffs — scratches — black eyes and bloody noses swelling the horrors of the scene! Thick thwack, cut and hack, helter-skelter, higgledy-piggledy, hurly-burly, head over heels, rough and tumble! — Dunder and blixum! swore the Dutchmen — splitter

---

4 **the giant Blanderon,** a name apparently invented by Irving. Perhaps he had in mind the giants of Greek mythology who revolted against Jupiter, using tree trunks for weapons   7 **Locrian archers.** The Locrians were the most ancient of Greek peoples   17 **voltigeurs,** members of a special skirmishing company attached to a French infantry regiment (obsolete)   38 **Dunder and blixum!... splitter and splutter.** The first phrase is the anglicized form of Dutch *donder en bliksem,* thunder and lightning, a mild oath; the latter is evidently merely imitative of the sound of Dutch

and splutter! cried the Swedes — Storm the works! shouted Hardkoppig Peter —Fire the mine! roared stout Risingh — Tanta-rarra-ra! twanged the trumpet of Antony Van Corlear — until all voice and sound became unintelligible — grunts of pain, yells of fury, and shouts of triumph mingling in one hideous clamor. The earth shook as if struck with a paralytic stroke — trees shrunk aghast, and withered at the sight — rocks burrowed in the ground like rabbits — and even Christina creek turned from its course, and ran up a hill in breathless terror!

Long hung the contest doubtful, for though a heavy shower of rain, sent by the "cloud-compelling Jove," in some measure cooled their ardor, as doth a bucket of
10 water thrown on a group of fighting mastiffs, yet did they but pause for a moment, to return with tenfold fury to the charge. Just at this juncture a vast and dense column of smoke was seen slowly rolling toward the scene of battle. The combatants paused for a moment, gazing in mute astonishment, until the wind, dispelling the murky cloud, revealed the flaunting banner of Michael Paw, the Patroon of Communipaw. That valiant chieftain came fearlessly on at the head of a phalanx of oyster-fed Pavonians and a corps de reserve of the Van Arsdales and Van Bummels, who had remained behind to digest the enormous dinner they had eaten. These now trudged manfully forward, smoking their pipes with outrageous vigor, so as to raise the awful cloud that has been mentioned; but marching exceedingly slow, being
20 short of leg, and of great rotundity in the belt.

And now the deities who watched over the fortunes of the Nederlanders having unthinkingly left the field, and stepped into a neighboring tavern to refresh themselves with a pot of beer, a direful catastrophe had well-nigh ensued. Scarce had the myrmidons of Michael Paw attained the front of battle, when the Swedes, instructed by the cunning Risingh, levelled a shower of blows full at their tobacco-pipes. Astounded at this assault, and dismayed at the havoc of their pipes, these ponderous warriors gave way, and like a drove of frightened elephants broke through the ranks of their own army. The little Hoppers were borne down in the surge: the sacred banner emblazoned with the gigantic oyster of Communipaw was trampled in the
30 dirt: on blundered and thundered the heavy-sterned fugitives, the Swedes pressing on their rear and applying their feet *a parte poste* of the Van Arsdales and the Van Brummels with a vigor that prodigiously accelerated their movements — nor did the renowned Michael Paw himself fail to receive divers grievous and dishonorable visitations of shoe-leather.

But what, oh Muse! was the rage of Peter Stuyvesant, when from afar he saw his army giving way! In the transports of his wrath he sent forth a roar, enough to shake the very hills. The men of the Manhattoes plucked up new courage at the sound; or rather, they rallied at the voice of their leader, of whom they stood more in awe than of all the Swedes in Christendom. Without waiting for their aid, the daring
40 Peter dashed sword in hand into the thickest of the foe. Then might be seen achievements worthy of the days of the giants. Wherever he went, the enemy shrank be-

---

16 **corps de reserve,** reserve corps   31 **a parte poste,** from the part after, here meaning to the backsides

fore him; the Swedes fled to right and left, or were driven, like dogs, into their own ditch; but as he pushed forward singly with headlong courage, the foe closed behind and hung upon his rear. One aimed a blow full at his heart; but the protecting power which watches over the great and good turned aside the hostile blade and directed it to a side-pocket, where reposed an enormous iron tobacco-box, endowed, like the shield of Achilles, with supernatural powers, doubtless from bearing the portrait of the blessed St. Nicholas. Peter Stuyvesant turned like an angry bear upon the foe, and seizing him as he fled, by an immeasurable queue, "Ah, whoreson caterpillar," roared he, "here's what shall make worms' meat of thee!" So saying, he whirled his sword, and dealt a blow that would have decapitated the varlet,   10 but that the pitying steel struck short and shaved the queue forever from his crown. At this moment an arquebusier levelled his piece from a neighboring mound, with deadly aim; but the watchful Minerva, who had just stopped to tie up her garter, seeing the peril of her favorite hero, sent old Boreas with his bellows, who, as the match descended to the pan, gave a blast that blew the priming from the touch-hole.

Thus waged the fight, when the stout Risingh, surveying the field from the top of a little ravelin, perceived his troops banged, beaten, and kicked by the invincible Peter. Drawing his falchion and uttering a thousand anathemas, he strode down to the scene of combat with some such thundering strides as Jupiter is said by Hesiod to have taken, when he strode down the spheres to hurl his thunder-bolts at   20 the Titans.

When the rival heroes came face to face, each made a prodigious start in the style of a veteran stage-champion. Then did they regard each other for a moment with the bitter aspect of two furious ram-cats on the point of a clapper-clawing. Then did they throw themselves into one attitude, then into another, striking their swords on the ground, first on the right side, then on the left — at last at it they went, with incredible ferocity. Words cannot tell the prodigies of strength and valor displayed in this direful encounter — an encounter compared to which the far-famed battles of Ajax with Hector, of Æneas with Turnus, Orlando with Rodomont, Guy of Warwick with Colbrand the Dane, or of that renowned Welsh knight, Sir Owen of the   30 Mountains with the giant Guylon, were all gentle sports and holiday recreations. At length the valiant Peter, watching his opportunity, aimed a blow, enough to cleave his adversary to the very chine; but Risingh, nimbly raising his sword, warded it off so narrowly, that glancing on one side, it shaved away a huge canteen in which he carried his liquor; thence pursuing its trenchant course, it severed off a deep coat pocket, stored with bread and cheese — which provant rolling among the armies, occasioned a fearful scrambling between the Swedes and Dutchmen, and made the general battle to wax more furious than ever.

Enraged to see his military stores laid waste, the stout Risingh, collecting all his

---

19 **Hesiod** (fl. 900 B.C.), Greek poet   24 **ramcats . . . clapper-clawing,** tomcats about to fight (dialectal)   29 **Ajax . . . Guylon,** a list of famous combats in literature. Irving's ultimate sources were Bk. XIV of the *Orlando Inamorato* of Matteo Maria Boiardo (1434-1494); the metrical romance, *Guy of Warwick* (thirteenth century); and *The Mabinogion* (twelfth century)   36 **provant,** provender, an allowance of food

forces, aimed a mighty blow full at the hero's crest. In vain did his fierce little cocked hat oppose its course. The biting steel clove through the stubborn ram beaver, and would have cracked the crown of any one not endowed with supernatural hardness of head; but the brittle weapon shivered in pieces on the skull of Hardkoppig Piet, shedding a thousand sparks, like beams of glory, round his grizzly visage.

The good Peter reeled with the blow, and turning up his eyes beheld a thousand suns, besides moons and stars, dancing about the firmament — at length, missing his footing, by reason of his wooden leg, down he came on his seat of honor with a crash which shook the surrounding hills, and might have wrecked his frame, had 10 he not been received into a cushion softer than velvet, which Providence, or Minerva, or St. Nicholas, or some cow, had benevolently prepared for his reception.

The furious Risingh, in spite of the maxim, cherished by all true knights, that "fair play is a jewel," hastened to take advantage of the hero's fall; but, as he stooped to give a fatal blow, Peter Stuyvesant dealt him a thwack over the sconce with his wooden leg, which set a chime of bells ringing triple bob majors in his cerebellum. The bewildered Swede staggered with the blow, and the wary Peter seizing a pocket pistol, which lay hard by, discharged it full at the head of the reeling Risingh. Let not my reader mistake; it was not a murderous weapon loaded with powder and ball; but a little sturdy stone pottle charged to the muzzle with a double dram of 20 true Dutch courage, which the knowing Antony Van Corlear carried about him by way of replenishing his valor; and which had dropped from his wallet during his furious encounter with the drummer. The hideous weapon sang through the air, and true to its course as was the fragment of rock discharged at Hector by bully Ajax, encountered the head of the gigantic Swede with matchless violence.

This heaven-directed blow decided the battle. The ponderous pericranium of General Jan Risingh sank upon his breast; his knees tottered under him; a deathlike torpor seized upon his frame, and he tumbled to the earth with such violence, that old Pluto started with affright, lest he should have broken through the roof of his infernal palace.

30 His fall was the signal of defeat and victory — the Swedes gave way — the Dutch pressed forward; the former took to their heels, the latter hotly pursued. — Some entered with them, pell-mell, through the sally-port — others stormed the bastion, and others scrambled over the curtain. Thus in a little while the fortress of Fort Christina, which, like another Troy, had stood a siege of full ten hours, was carried by assault, without the loss of a single man on either side. Victory, in the likeness of a gigantic ox-fly, sat perched upon the cocked hat of the gallant Stuyvesant; and it was declared, by all the writers whom he hired to write the history of his expedition, that on this memorable day he gained a sufficient quantity of glory to immortalize a dozen of the greatest heroes in Christendom.

---

2 **ram beaver,** man's hat   12 **maxim,** usually attributed to Scott in *Redgauntlet* (1824). Since Irving's use is earlier, both authors probably drew on some source in chivalric literature   15 **triple bob majors,** a bell-ringing term. Bob-majors are rung upon eight bells, a treble bob being a method which produces a dodging or irregular effect   32 **sally-port . . . bastion . . . curtain.** The sally-port is a small concealed gate in a fortification; the bastion, a projection; the curtain, the wall between bastions

Chapter IX   In Which the Author and the Reader, While Reposing after the Battle, Fall into a Very Grave Discourse — after Which Is Recorded the Conduct of Peter Stuyvesant after His Victory.

Thanks to St. Nicholas, we have safely finished this tremendous battle: let us sit down, my worthy reader, and cool ourselves, for I am in a prodigious sweat and agitation — truly this fighting of battles is hot work! and if your great commanders did but know what trouble they give their historians, they would not have the con- science to achieve so many horrible victories. But methinks I hear my reader com- plain, that throughout this boasted battle there is not the least slaughter, nor a single individual maimed, if we except the unhappy Swede, who was shorn of his queue 10 by the trenchant blade of Peter Stuyvesant; all which, he observes, is a great out- rage on probability, and highly injurious to the interest of the narration.

This is certainly an objection of no little moment, but it arises entirely from the obscurity enveloping the remote periods of time about which I have undertaken to write. Thus, though doubtless, from the importance of the object, and the prowess of the parties concerned, there must have been terrible carnage, and prodigies of valor displayed before the walls of Christina, yet, notwithstanding that I have con- sulted every history, manuscript, and tradition, touching this memorable though long-forgotten battle, I cannot find mention made of a single man killed or wounded in the whole affair.   20

This is, without doubt, owing to the extreme modesty of our forefathers, who, unlike their descendants, were never prone to vaunt of their achievements; but it is a virtue which places their historian in a most embarrassing predicament; for, hav- ing promised my readers a hideous and unparalleled battle, and having worked them up into a warlike and bloodthirsty state of mind, to put them off without any havoc and slaughter would have been as bitter a disappointment as to summon a multi- tude of good people to attend an execution, and then cruelly balk them by a reprieve.

Had the fates only allowed me some half a score of dead men, I had been content; for I would have made them such heroes as abounded in the olden time, but whose race is now unfortunately extinct; any one of whom, if we may believe those 30 authentic writers, the poets, could drive great armies, like sheep, before him, and conquer and desolate whole cities by his single arm.

But seeing that I had not a single life at my disposal, all that was left me was to make the most I could of my battle, by means of kicks, and cuffs, and bruises, and such like ignoble wounds. And here I cannot but compare my dilemma, in some sort, to that of the divine Milton, who, having arrayed with sublime preparation his immortal hosts against each other, is sadly put to it how to manage them, and how he shall make the end of his battle answer to the beginning, inasmuch as, being mere spirits, he cannot deal a mortal blow, nor even give a flesh wound to any of his combatants. For my part, the greatest difficulty I found was, when I had once 40 put my warriors in a passion, and let them loose into the midst of the enemy, to

36 **Milton.** See Bk. VI of *Paradise Lost*

keep them from doing mischief. Many a time had I to restrain the sturdy Peter from cleaving a gigantic Swede to the very waistband, or spitting half a dozen little fellows on his sword, like so many sparrows. And when I had set some hundred of missives flying in the air, I did not dare to suffer one of them to reach the ground, lest it should have put an end to some unlucky Dutchman.

The reader cannot conceive how mortifying it is to a writer thus in a manner to have his hands tied, and how many tempting opportunities I had to wink at, where I might have made as fine a death-blow as any recorded in history or song.

From my own experience I begin to doubt most potently of the authenticity of
10 many of Homer's stories. I verily believe, that when he had once launched one of his favorite heroes among a crowd of the enemy, he cut down many an honest fellow, without any authority for so doing, excepting that he presented a fair mark — and that often a poor fellow was sent to grim Pluto's domains, merely because he had a name that would give a sounding turn to a period. But I disclaim all such unprincipled liberties — let me but have truth and the law on my side, and no man would fight harder than myself — but since the various records I consulted did not warrant it, I had too much conscience to kill a single soldier. By St. Nicholas, but it would have been a pretty piece of business! My enemies, the critics, who I foresee will be ready enough to lay any crime they can discover at my door, might have
20 charged me with murder outright — and I should have esteemed myself lucky to escape with no harsher verdict than manslaughter!

And now, gentle reader, that we are tranquilly sitting down here, smoking our pipes, permit me to indulge in a melancholy reflection which at this moment passes across my mind. How vain, how fleeting, how uncertain are all those gaudy bubbles after which we are panting and toiling in this world of fair delusions! The wealth which the miser has amassed with so many weary days, so many sleepless nights, a spendthrift here may squander away in joyless prodigality; the noblest monuments which pride has ever reared to perpetuate a name, the hand of time will shortly tumble into ruins — and even the brightest laurels, gained by feats of arms, may
30 wither, and be forever blighted by the chilling neglect of mankind. "How many illustrious heroes," says the good Boëtius, "who were once the pride and glory of the age, hath the silence of historians buried in eternal oblivion!" And this it was that induced the Spartans, when they went to battle, solemnly to sacrifice to the Muses, supplicating that their achievements might be worthily recorded. Had not Homer tuned his lofty lyre, observes the elegant Cicero, that valor of Achilles had remained unsung. And such, too, after all the toils and perils he had braved, after all the gallant actions he had achieved, such too had nearly been the fate of the chivalric Peter Stuyvesant, but that I fortunately stepped in and engraved his name on the indelible tablet of history, just as the caitiff Time was silently brushing it
40 away forever!

The more I reflect, the more I am astonished at the important character of the historian. He is the sovereign censor to decide upon the renown or infamy of his

13 **Pluto's domains,** Hades   31 **Boëtius.** The remark appears in Bk. II, Prose VII of *The Consolations of Philosophy,* written early in the sixth century   35 **Cicero.** See *Pro Archia Poeta,* Chap. X

fellow men. He is the patron of kings and conquerors, on whom it depends whether they shall live in after ages, or be forgotten as were their ancestors before them. The tyrant may oppress while the object of his tyranny exists; but the historian possesses superior might, for his power extends even beyond the grave. The shades of departed and long-forgotten heroes anxiously bend down from above, while he writes, watching each movement of his pen, whether it shall pass by their names with neglect, or inscribe them on the deathless pages of renown. Even the drop of ink which hangs trembling on his pen, which he may either dash upon the floor, or waste in idle scrawlings — that very drop, which to him is not worth the twentieth part of a farthing, may be of incalculable value to some departed worthy — may elevate 10 half a score, in one moment, to immortality, who would have given worlds, had they possessed them, to insure the glorious meed.

Let not my readers imagine, however, that I am indulging in vainglorious boastings, or am anxious to blazon forth the importance of my tribe. On the contrary, I shrink when I reflect on the awful responsibility we historians assume — I shudder to think what direful commotions and calamities we occasion in the world — I swear to thee, honest reader, as I am a man, I weep at the very idea! Why, let me ask, are so many illustrious men daily tearing themselves away from the embraces of their families — slighting the smiles of beauty — despising the allurements of fortune, and exposing themselves to the miseries of war? — Why are kings desolating 20 empires, and depopulating whole countries? In short, what induces all great men of all ages and countries to commit so many victories and misdeeds, and inflict so many miseries upon mankind and upon themselves, but the mere hope that some historian will kindly take them into notice, and admit them into a corner of his volume? For, in short, the mighty object of all their toils, their hardships, and privations, is nothing but *immortal fame.* And what is immortal fame? — why, half a page of dirty paper! — alas! alas! how humiliating the idea — that the renown of so great a man as Peter Stuyvesant would depend upon the pen of so little a man as Diedrich Knickerbocker!

And now, having refreshed ourselves after the fatigues and perils of the field, it 30 behooves us to return once more to the scene of conflict, and inquire what were the results of this renowned conquest. The fortress of Christina being the fair metropolis, and in a manner the key to New Sweden, its capture was speedily followed by the entire subjugation of the province. This was not a little promoted by the gallant and courteous deportment of the chivalric Peter. Though a man terrible in battle, yet in the hour of victory was he endued with a spirit generous, merciful, and humane. He vaunted not over his enemies, nor did he make defeat more galling by unmanly insults; for like that mirror of knightly virtue, the renowned Paladin Orlando, he was more anxious to do great actions than to talk of them after they were done. He put no man to death; ordered no houses to be burnt down; permit- 40 ted no ravages to be perpetrated on the property of the vanquished; and even gave one of his bravest officers a severe admonishment with his walking staff, for having been detected in the act of sacking a hen-roost.

---

38 **Paladin Orlando,** or Roland, hero of romance, celebrated in the *Chanson de Roland*

He moreover issued a proclamation, inviting the inhabitants to submit to the authority of their High Mightinesses; but declaring, with unexampled clemency, that whoever refused should be lodged at the public expense in a goodly castle provided for the purpose, and have an armed retinue to wait on them in the bargain. In consequence of these beneficent terms, about thirty Swedes stepped manfully forward and took the oath of allegiance; in reward for which they were graciously permitted to remain on the banks of the Delaware, where their descendants reside at this very day. I am told, however, by divers observant travellers, that they have never been able to get over the chap-fallen looks of their ancestors; but that they still do strangely
10 transmit from father to son manifest marks of the sound drubbing given them by the sturdy Amsterdammers.

The whole country of New Sweden, having thus yielded to the arms of the triumphant Peter, was reduced to a colony called South River, and placed under the superintendence of a lieutenant-governor, subject to the control of the supreme government of New Amsterdam. This great dignitary was called Mynheer William Beekman, or rather *Beck*-man, who derived his surname, as did Ovidious Naso of yore, from the lordly dimensions of his nose, which projected from the centre of his countenance, like the beak of a parrot. He was the great progenitor of the tribe of the Beekmans, one of the most ancient and honorable families of the province; the
20 members of which do gratefully commemorate the origin of their dignity; not as your noble families in England would do, by having a glowing proboscis emblazoned in their escutcheon, but by one and all wearing a right goodly nose, stuck in the very middle of their faces.

Thus was this perilous enterprise gloriously terminated, with the loss of only two men — Wolfert Van Horne, a tall spare man, who was knocked overboard by the boom of a sloop in a flaw of wind; and fat Brom Van Bummel, who was suddenly carried off by an indigestion; both, however, were immortalized, as having bravely fallen in the service of their country. True it is, Peter Stuyvesant had one of his limbs terribly fractured in the act of storming the fortress; but as it was fortunately his
30 wooden leg, the wound was promptly and effectually healed.

And now nothing remains to this branch of my history but to mention that this immaculate hero, and his victorious army, returned joyously to the Manhattoes; where they made a solemn and triumphant entry, bearing with them the conquered Risingh, and the remnant of his battered crew, who had refused allegiance; for it appears that the gigantic Swede had only fallen into a swoon, at the end of the battle, from which he was speedily restored by a wholesome tweak of the nose.

These captive heroes were lodged, according to the promise of the governor, at the public expense, in a fair and spacious castle; being the prison of state, of which Stoffel Brinkerhoff, the immortal conqueror of Oyster Bay, was appointed governor;
40 and which has ever since remained in the possession of his descendants.

It was a pleasant and goodly sight to witness the joy of the people of New Am-

---

9 **chap-fallen,** with drooping jaws   16 **Ovidious Naso,** better known as Ovid (43 B.C.-17 A.D.?), Roman poet   26 **flaw,** gust, squall   40 **descendants.** "This castle, though very much altered and modernized, is still in being, and stands at the corner of Pearl Street, facing Coentie's slip." — Irving

sterdam, at beholding their warriors once more return from this war in the wilderness. The old women thronged round Antony Van Corlear, who gave the whole history of the campaign with matchless accuracy; saving that he took the credit of fighting the whole battle himself, and especially of vanquishing the stout Risingh; which he considered himself as clearly entitled to, seeing that it was effected by his own stone pottle.

The schoolmasters throughout the town gave holiday to their little urchins, who followed in droves after the drums, with paper caps on their heads, and sticks in their breeches, thus taking the first lesson in the art of war. As to the sturdy rabble, they thronged at the heels of Peter Stuyvesant wherever he went, waving their greasy 10 hats in the air, and shouting "Hardkoppig Piet forever!"

It was indeed a day of roaring rout and jubilee. A huge dinner was prepared at the Stadthouse in honor of the conquerors, where were assembled in one glorious constellation the great and little luminaries of New Amsterdam. There were the lordly Schout and his obsequious deputy — the burgomasters with their officious schepens at their elbows — the subaltern officers at the elbows of the schepens, and so on down to the lowest hanger-on of police: every tag having his rag at his side, to finish his pipe, drink off his heel-taps, and laugh at his flights of immortal dullness. In short — for a city feast is a city feast all the world over, and has been a city feast ever since the creation — the dinner went off much the same as do our great corporation junketings and Fourth of July banquets. Loads of fish, flesh, and fowl 20 were devoured, oceans of liquor drank, thousands of pipes smoked, and many a dull joke honored with much obstreperous fat-sided laughter.

I must not omit to mention, that to this far-famed victory Peter Stuyvesant was indebted for another of his many titles — for so hugely delighted were the honest burghers with his achievements, that they unanimously honored him with the name of *Pieter de Groodt*, that is to say, Peter the Great, or, as it was translated into English by the people of New Amsterdam, for the benefit of their New England visitors, *Piet de pig* — an appellation which he maintained even unto the day of his death.   1809

15 **Schout** . . . **burgomasters** . . . **schepens,** Dutch administrative officers. A schout was a magistrate; a burgomaster (master of a borough) corresponded to a mayor; a schepen was an alderman

The Author's Account of Himself

The Sketchbook of Geoffrey Crayon, Gent. *was first published in seven numbers in New York, between June 23, 1819, and September 13, 1820. In his Preface to the revised edition of 1848, Irving said that most of the essays and stories therein were part of an intended series which, before his plan had matured, he was compelled by circumstances to send piecemeal to the United States.*

In addition to "The Author's Account of Himself" and "L'Envoy," collected editions usually contain thirty-two pieces; the original seven numbers offered only twenty-five. Among the additions were "Traits of Indian Character" and "Philip of Pokanoket," previously

printed in the Analectic Magazine *of Philadelphia. The greater part of* The Sketch Book *is composed of essays on English life and manners with a decidedly nostalgic flavor. Among the more famous are "Rural Life in England" (in No. II), "The Boar's Head Tavern, Eastcheap" (No. III), a series on Christmas customs at the country house of a Yorkshire squire, "Bracebridge Hall" (in No. V), "John Bull" (No. VI), and "Westminster Abbey" and "Stratford-on-Avon" (No. VII). Their emphasis upon the common literary and social heritage of Americans and Englishmen doubtless contributed to international good will in an era when misunderstanding seemed inevitable. That Irving was no sycophantic Anglophile was shown by his vigorous "English Writers on America" (No. II), a frank warning to England that "should those reverses overtake her, from which the proudest empires have not been exempt," she might regret having lost the friendship of the United States. The Sketch Book has remained a classic, however, largely because of two sketches or short stories, "Rip Van Winkle" (No. I) and "The Legend of Sleepy Hollow" (No. VI), which are unquestionably among the best-known tales in the English language.*

Both stories were written in England in 1818, while Irving was absorbed in what he called "the rich mine of German literature," whose discovery he probably owed to the enthusiasm of Scott. Scholarly investigation has shown that Irving followed German legends for both plots (see especially H. A. Pochmann's article in Studies in Philology *for July 1930); his many allusions and tags of quotation reveal, in fact, how conscious he was of literary tradition. Yet, bookish as they are, both tales are skillfully localized and depend for their effect upon much the same feeling for history and folk life which characterizes the* History of New York. *Both of them, it will be noted, continue the pleasant fiction of Diedrich Knickerbocker; both, although thin in plot and unremarkable for characterization, display a perfection of tone and the delight in details of living which are Irving's finest qualities.*

"I am of this mind with Homer, that as the snaile that crept out of her shel was turned eftsoons into a toad, and thereby was forced to make a stoole to sit on; so the traveller that stragleth from his owne country is in a short time transformed into so monstrous a shape, that he is faine to alter his mansion with his manners, and to live where he can, not where he would." — LYLY'S EUPHUES.

I was always fond of visiting new scenes, and observing strange characters and manners. Even when a mere child I began my travels, and made many tours of discovery into foreign parts and unknown regions of my native city, to the frequent alarm of my parents, and the emolument of the town-crier. As I grew into boyhood,
10 I extended the range of my observations. My holiday afternoons were spent in rambles about the surrounding country. I made myself familiar with all its places famous in history or fable. I knew every spot where a murder or robbery had been committed, or a ghost seen. I visited the neighboring villages, and added greatly to my stock of knowledge, by noting their habits and customs, and conversing with their sages and great men. I even journeyed one long summer's day to the summit of the most distant hill, whence I stretched my eye over many a mile of terra incognita, and was astonished to find how vast a globe I inhabited.

Text: the revised edition of 1848   5 **Lyly's Euphues.** The quotation is from near the beginning of *Euphues and His England* (1580) by John Lyly (1553?-1606), English author of prose romances and courtly comedies

This rambling propensity strengthened with my years. Books of voyages and travels became my passion, and in devouring their contents, I neglected the regular exercises of the school. How wistfully would I wander about the pier-heads in fine weather, and watch the parting ships bound to distant climes — with what longing eyes would I gaze after their lessening sails, and waft myself in imagination to the ends of the earth!

Further reading and thinking, though they brought this vague inclination into more reasonable bounds, only served to make it more decided. I visited various parts of my own country; and had I been merely a lover of fine scenery, I should have felt little desire to seek elsewhere its gratification, for on no country have the charms 10 of nature been more prodigally lavished. Her mighty lakes, like oceans of liquid silver; her mountains, with their bright aerial tints; her valleys, teeming with wild fertility; her tremendous cataracts, thundering in their solitudes; her boundless plains, waving with spontaneous verdure; her broad deep rivers, rolling in solemn silence to the ocean; her trackless forests, where vegetation puts forth all its magnificence; her skies, kindling with the magic of summer clouds and glorious sunshine; — no, never need an American look beyond his own country for the sublime and beautiful of natural scenery.

But Europe held forth the charms of storied and poetical association. There were to be seen the masterpieces of art, the refinements of highly-cultivated society, the 20 quaint peculiarities of ancient and local custom. My native country was full of youthful promise: Europe was rich in the accumulated treasures of age. Her very ruins told the history of times gone by, and every mouldering stone was a chronicle. I longed to wander over the scenes of renowned achievement — to tread, as it were, in the footsteps of antiquity — to loiter about the ruined castle — to meditate on the falling tower — to escape, in short, from the common-place realities of the present, and lose myself among the shadowy grandeurs of the past.

I had, beside all this, an earnest desire to see the great men of the earth. We have, it is true, our great men in America: not a city but has an ample share of them. I have mingled among them in my time, and been almost withered by the shade into 30 which they cast me; for there is nothing so baleful to a small man as the shade of a great one, particularly the great man of a city. But I was anxious to see the great men of Europe; for I had read in the works of various philosophers, that all animals degenerated in America, and man among the number. A great man of Europe, thought I, must therefore be as superior to a great man of America, as a peak of the Alps to a highland of the Hudson; and in this idea I was confirmed, by observing the comparative importance and swelling magnitude of many English travellers

---

33 **philosophers,** e.g., the Comte de Buffon (see note, p. 299), who theorized on the harmful effects of the American climate   37 **English travellers.** Irving was keenly aware of the "Paper War" in which his countrymen had been defending themselves against the attacks of Englishmen. Here he echoes the judgment of John Bristed (*The Resources of the United States*, New York, 1816), that among the "vilest and silliest" of those who had abused America were *"Parkinson,* an English farmer; *Ashe, a soi-disant* military officer; and one Jansen [Janson], a *non-descript."* For a full account see Jane L. Mesick, *The English Traveler in America, 1785-1835* (New York, 1922), and see "English Writers on America" in No. II of *The Sketch Book*

among us, who, I was assured, were very little people in their own country. I will visit this land of wonders, thought I, and see the gigantic race from which I am degenerated.

It has been either my good or evil lot to have my roving passion gratified. I have wandered through different countries, and witnessed many of the shifting scenes of life. I cannot say that I have studied them with the eye of a philosopher; but rather with the sauntering gaze with which humble lovers of the picturesque stroll from the window of one print-shop to another; caught sometimes by the delineations of beauty, sometimes by the distortions of caricature, and sometimes
10 by the loveliness of landscape. As it is the fashion for modern tourists to travel pencil in hand, and bring home their port-folios filled with sketches, I am disposed to get up a few for the entertainment of my friends. When, however, I look over the hints and memorandums I have taken down for the purpose, my heart almost fails me at finding how my idle humor has led me aside from the great objects studied by every regular traveller who would make a book. I fear I shall give equal disappointment with an unlucky landscape painter, who had travelled on the continent, but, following the bent of his vagrant inclination, had sketched in nooks, and corners, and by-places. His sketchbook was accordingly crowded with cottages, and landscapes, and obscure ruins; but he had neglected to paint St. Peter's, or the
20 Coliseum; the cascade of Terni, or the bay of Naples; and had not a single glacier or volcano in his whole collection. 1819

20 **cascade of Terni,** artificial waterfalls in the Apennines, about fifty miles north of Rome. They had been described by Byron in *Childe Harold's Pilgrimage,* Canto IV (1818), stanzas lxix-lxxii

Rip Van Winkle

A Posthumous Writing of Diedrich Knickerbocker

By Woden, God of Saxons,
From whence comes Wensday, that is Wodensday.
Truth is a thing that ever I will keep
Unto thylke day in which I creep into
My sepulchre. — CARTWRIGHT

[The following Tale was found among the papers of the late Diedrich Knickerbocker, an old gentleman of New York, who was very curious in the Dutch history of the province, and the manners of the descendants from its primitive settlers. His historical researches, however, did not lie so much among books as among men;
10 for the former are lamentably scanty on his favorite topics; whereas he found the old burghers, and still more their wives, rich in that legendary lore, so invaluable

1 **Woden,** Odin, Teutonic god of storms and battles   5 **Cartwright,** possibly William Cartwright (1610-1643), English poet   6 **The following Tale.** The present foreword did not appear in the original of 1819

to true history. Whenever, therefore, he happened upon a genuine Dutch family, snugly shut up in its low-roofed farmhouse, under a spreading sycamore, he looked upon it as a little clasped volume of black-letter, and studied it with the zeal of a book-worm.

The result of all these researches was a history of the province during the reign of the Dutch governors, which he published some years since. There have been various opinions as to the literary character of his work, and, to tell the truth, it is not a whit better than it should be. Its chief merit is its scrupulous accuracy, which indeed was a little questioned on its first appearance, but has since been completely established; and it is now admitted into all historical collections, as a book of un- 10 questionable authority.

The old gentleman died shortly after the publication of his work, and now that he is dead and gone, it cannot do much harm to his memory to say that his time might have been much better employed in weightier labors. He, however, was apt to ride his hobby his own way; and though it did now and then kick up the dust a little in the eyes of his neighbors, and grieve the spirit of some friends, for whom he felt the truest deference and affection; yet his errors and follies are remembered "more in sorrow than in anger," and it begins to be suspected, that he never intended to injure or offend. But however his memory may be appreciated by critics, it is still held dear by many folk, whose good opinion is well worth having; 20 particularly by certain biscuit-bakers, who have gone so far as to imprint his likeness on their new-year cakes; and have thus given him a chance for immortality, almost equal to the being stamped on a Waterloo Medal, or a Queen Anne's Farthing.]

Whoever has made a voyage up the Hudson must remember the Kaatskill mountains. They are a dismembered branch of the great Appalachian family, and are seen away to the west of the river, swelling up to a noble height, and lording it over the surrounding country. Every change of season, every change of weather, indeed, every hour of the day, produces some change in the magical hues and shapes of these mountains, and they are regarded by all the good wives, far and near, as 30 perfect barometers. When the weather is fair and settled, they are clothed in blue and purple, and print their bold outlines on the clear evening sky; but, sometimes, when the rest of the landscape is cloudless, they will gather a hood of gray vapors about their summits, which, in the last rays of the setting sun, will glow and light up like a crown of glory.

At the foot of these fairy mountains, the voyager may have descried the light smoke curling up from a village, whose shingle-roofs gleam among the trees, just where the blue tints of the upland melt away into the fresh green of the nearer landscape. It is a little village, of great antiquity, having been founded by some of the Dutch colonists, in the early times of the province, just about the beginning of the 40

3 **black-letter,** a heavy-faced type used by early printers, now called Gothic or Old English   18 **"more in sorrow than in anger,"** *Hamlet,* Act I, sc.ii, l. 232   23 **Waterloo Medal,** struck off to commemorate the defeat of Napoleon on June 18, 1815. It was given to all British soldiers engaged in that action and bore the likeness of the Prince Regent (later King George IV)   23 **Queen Anne's Farthing,** a copper coin minted in the latter part of the reign of Anne (1702-1714)

government of the good Peter Stuyvesant (may he rest in peace!) and there were some of the houses of the original settlers standing within a few years, built of small yellow bricks brought from Holland, having latticed windows and gabled fronts, surmounted with weather-cocks.

In that same village, and in one of these very houses (which, to tell the precise truth, was sadly time-worn and weather-beaten), there lived many years since, while the country was yet a province of Great Britain, a simple good-natured fellow, of the name of Rip Van Winkle. He was a descendant of the Van Winkles who figured so gallantly in the chivalrous days of Peter Stuyvesant, and accompanied
10 him to the siege of Fort Christina. He inherited, however, but little of the martial character of his ancestors. I have observed that he was a simple good-natured man; he was, moreover, a kind neighbor, and an obedient hen-pecked husband. Indeed, to the latter circumstance might be owing that meekness of spirit which gained him such universal popularity; for those men are most apt to be obsequious and conciliating abroad, who are under the discipline of shrews at home. Their tempers, doubtless, are rendered pliant and malleable in the fiery furnace of domestic tribulation; and a curtain lecture is worth all the sermons in the world for teaching the virtues of patience and long-suffering. A termagant wife may, therefore, in some respects, be considered a tolerable blessing; and if so, Rip Van Winkle was thrice
20 blessed.

Certain it is, that he was a great favorite among all the good wives of the village, who, as usual, with the amiable sex, took his part in all family squabbles; and never failed, whenever they talked those matters over in their evening gossipings, to lay all the blame on Dame Van Winkle. The children of the village, too, would shout with joy whenever he approached. He assisted at their sports, made their playthings, taught them to fly kites and shoot marbles, and told them long stories of ghosts, witches, and Indians. Whenever he went dodging about the village, he was surrounded by a troop of them, hanging on his skirts, clambering on his back, and playing a thousand tricks on him with impunity; and not a dog would bark at him
30 throughout the neighborhood.

The great error in Rip's composition was an insuperable aversion to all kinds of profitable labor. It could not be from the want of assiduity or perseverance; for he would sit on a wet rock, with a rod as long and heavy as a Tartar's lance, and fish all day without a murmur, even though he should not be encouraged by a single nibble. He would carry a fowling-piece on his shoulder for hours together, trudging through woods and swamps, and up hill and down dale, to shoot a few squirrels or wild pigeons. He would never refuse to assist a neighbor even in the roughest toil, and was a foremost man at all country frolics for husking Indian corn, or building stone-fences; the women of the village, too, used to employ him to run their er-
40 rands, and to do such little odd jobs as their less obliging husbands would not do for them. In a word Rip was ready to attend to anybody's business but his own; but as to doing family duty, and keeping his farm in order, he found it impossible.

In fact, he declared it was of no use to work on his farm; it was the most pestilent

10 **Fort Christina,** see note, p. 574

little piece of ground in the whole country; every thing about it went wrong, and would go wrong, in spite of him. His fences were continually falling to pieces; his cow would either go astray, or get among the cabbages; weeds were sure to grow quicker in his fields than anywhere else; the rain always made a point of setting in just as he had some out-door work to do; so that though his patrimonial estate had dwindled away under his management, acre by acre, until there was little more left than a mere patch of Indian corn and potatoes, yet it was the worst conditioned farm in the neighborhood.

His children, too, were as ragged and wild as if they belonged to nobody. His son Rip, an urchin begotten in his own likeness, promised to inherit the habits, 10 with the old clothes of his father. He was generally seen trooping like a colt at his mother's heels, equipped in a pair of his father's cast-off galligaskins, which he had much ado to hold up with one hand, as a fine lady does her train in bad weather.

Rip Van Winkle, however, was one of those happy mortals, of foolish, well-oiled dispositions, who take the world easy, eat white bread or brown, whichever can be got with least thought and trouble, and would rather starve on a penny than work for a pound. If left to himself, he would have whistled life away in perfect content-ment; but his wife kept continually dinning in his ears about his idleness, his care-lessness, and the ruin he was bringing on his family. Morning, noon, and night, her tongue was incessantly going, and every thing he said or did was sure to pro- 20 duce a torrent of household eloquence. Rip had but one way of replying to all lec-tures of the kind, and that, by frequent use, had grown into a habit. He shrugged his shoulders, shook his head, cast up his eyes, but said nothing. This, however, always provoked a fresh volley from his wife; so that he was fain to draw off his forces, and take to the outside of the house — the only side which, in truth, belongs to a hen-pecked husband.

Rip's sole domestic adherent was his dog Wolf, who was as much hen-pecked as his master; for Dame Van Winkle regarded them as companions in idleness, and even looked upon Wolf with an evil eye, as the cause of his master's going so often astray. True it is, in all points of spirit befitting an honorable dog, he was as courageous 30 an animal as ever scoured the woods — but what courage can withstand the ever-during and all-besetting terrors of a woman's tongue? The moment Wolf entered the house his crest fell, his tail drooped to the ground, or curled between his legs, he sneaked about with a gallows air, casting many a sidelong glance at Dame Van Winkle, and at the least flourish of a broomstick or ladle, he would fly to the door with yelping precipitation.

Times grew worse and worse with Rip Van Winkle as years of matrimony rolled on; a tart temper never mellows with age, and a sharp tongue is the only edged tool that grows keener with constant use. For a long time he used to console him-self, when driven from home, by frequenting a kind of perpetual club of the sages, 40 philosophers, and other idle personages of the village; which held its sessions on a bench before a small inn, designated by a rubicund portrait of His Majesty George

---

12 **galligaskins,** loose, wide trousers

the Third. Here they used to sit in the shade through a long lazy summer's day, talking listlessly over village gossip, or telling endless sleepy stories about nothing. But it would have been worth any statesman's money to have heard the profound discussions that sometimes took place, when by chance an old newspaper fell into their hands from some passing traveller. How solemnly they would listen to the contents, as drawled out by Derrick Van Bummel, the schoolmaster, a dapper learned little man, who was not to be daunted by the most gigantic word in the dictionary; and how sagely they would deliberate upon public events some months after they had taken place.

10   The opinions of this junto were completely controlled by Nicholas Vedder, a patriarch of the village, and landlord of the inn, at the door of which he took his seat from morning till night, just moving sufficiently to avoid the sun and keep in the shade of a large tree; so that the neighbors could tell the hour by his movements as accurately as by a sun-dial. It is true he was rarely heard to speak, but smoked his pipe incessantly. His adherents, however (for every great man has his adherents), perfectly understood him, and knew how to gather his opinions. When any thing that was read or related displeased him, he was observed to smoke his pipe vehemently, and to send forth short, frequent and angry puffs; but when pleased, he would inhale the smoke slowly and tranquilly, and emit it in light and 20 placid clouds; and sometimes, taking the pipe from his mouth, and letting the fragrant vapor curl about his nose, would gravely nod his head in token of perfect approbation.

From even this stronghold the unlucky Rip was at length routed by his termagant wife, who would suddenly break in upon the tranquillity of the assemblage and call the members all to naught; nor was that august personage, Nicholas Vedder himself, sacred from the daring tongue of this terrible virago, who charged him outright with encouraging her husband in habits of idleness.

Poor Rip was at last reduced almost to despair; and his only alternative, to escape from the labor of the farm and clamor of his wife, was to take gun in hand and 30 stroll away into the woods. Here he would sometimes seat himself at the foot of a tree, and share the contents of his wallet with Wolf, with whom he sympathized as a fellow-sufferer in persecution. "Poor Wolf," he would say, "thy mistress leads thee a dog's life of it; but never mind, my lad, whilst I live thou shalt never want a friend to stand by thee!" Wolf would wag his tail, look wistfully in his master's face, and if dogs can feel pity I verily believe he reciprocated the sentiment with all his heart.

In a long ramble of the kind on a fine autumnal day, Rip had unconsciously scrambled to one of the highest parts of the Kaatskill mountains. He was after his favorite sport of squirrel shooting, and the still solitudes had echoed and re-echoed 40 with the reports of his gun. Panting and fatigued, he threw himself, late in the afternoon, on a green knoll, covered with mountain herbage, that crowned the brow of a precipice. From an opening between the trees he could overlook all the lower country for many a mile of rich woodland. He saw at a distance the lordly Hudson, far, far below him, moving on its silent but majestic course, with the reflection of a purple cloud, or the sail of a lagging bark, here and there sleeping on its glassy bosom, and at last losing itself in the blue highlands.

On the other side he looked down into a deep mountain glen, wild, lonely, and shagged, the bottom filled with fragments from the impending cliffs, and scarcely lighted by the reflected rays of the setting sun. For some time Rip lay musing on this scene; evening was gradually advancing; the mountains began to throw their long blue shadows over the valleys; he saw that it would be dark long before he could reach the village, and he heaved a heavy sigh when he thought of encountering the terrors of Dame Van Winkle.

As he was about to descend, he heard a voice from a distance, hallooing, "Rip 10 Van Winkle! Rip Van Winkle!" He looked round, but could see nothing but a crow winging its solitary flight across the mountain. He thought his fancy must have deceived him, and turned again to descend, when he heard the same cry ring through the still evening air; "Rip Van Winkle! Rip Van Winkle!" — at the same time Wolf bristled up his back, and giving a low growl, skulked to his master's side, looking fearfully down into the glen. Rip now felt a vague apprehension stealing over him; he looked anxiously in the same direction, and perceived a strange figure slowly toiling up the rocks, and bending under the weight of something he carried on his back. He was surprised to see any human being in this lonely and unfrequented place, but supposing it to be some one of the neighborhood in need of his 20 assistance, he hastened down to yield it.

On nearer approach he was still more surprised at the singularity of the stranger's appearance. He was a short square-built old fellow, with thick bushy hair, and a grizzled beard. His dress was of the antique Dutch fashion — a cloth jerkin strapped round the waist — several pair of breeches, the outer one of ample volume, decorated with rows of buttons down the sides, and bunches at the knees. He bore on his shoulder a stout keg, that seemed full of liquor, and made signs for Rip to approach and assist him with the load. Though rather shy and distrustful of this new acquaintance, Rip complied with his usual alacrity; and mutually relieving one another, they clambered up a narrow gully, apparently the dry bed of a mountain tor- 30 rent. As they ascended, Rip every now and then heard long rolling peals, like distant thunder, that seemed to issue out of a deep ravine, or rather cleft, between lofty rocks toward which their rugged path conducted. He paused for an instant, but supposing it to be the muttering of one of those transient thunder-showers which often take place in mountain heights, he proceeded. Passing through the ravine, they came to a hollow, like a small amphitheatre, surrounded by perpendicular precipices, over the brinks of which impending trees shot their branches, so that you only caught glimpses of the azure sky and the bright evening-cloud. During the whole time Rip and his companion had labored on in silence; for though the former marvelled greatly what could be the object of carrying a keg of liquor up 40 this wild mountain, yet there was something strange and incomprehensible about the unknown, that inspired awe and checked familiarity.

On entering the amphitheatre, new objects of wonder presented themselves. On a level spot in the centre was a company of odd-looking personages playing at

nine-pins. They were dressed in a quaint outlandish fashion; some wore short doublets, others jerkins, with long knives in their belts, and most of them had enormous breeches, of similar style with that of the guide's. Their visages, too, were peculiar: one had a large beard, broad face, and small piggish eyes: the face of another seemed to consist entirely of nose, and was surmounted by a white sugar-loaf hat, set off with a little red cock's tail. They all had beards, of various shapes and colors. There was one who seemed to be the commander. He was a stout old gentleman, with a weather-beaten countenance; he wore a laced doublet, broad belt and hanger, high crowned hat and feather, red stockings, and high-heeled shoes,
10 with roses in them. The whole group reminded Rip of the figures in an old Flemish painting, in the parlor of Dominie Van Schaick, the village parson, and which had been brought over from Holland at the time of the settlement.

What seemed particularly odd to Rip was, that though these folks were evidently amusing themselves, yet they maintained the gravest faces, the most mysterious silence, and were, withal, the most melancholy party of pleasure he had ever witnessed. Nothing interrupted the stillness of the scene but the noise of the balls, which, whenever they were rolled, echoed along the mountains like rumbling peals of thunder.

As Rip and his companion approached them, they suddenly desisted from their
20 play, and stared at him with such fixed statue-like gaze, and such strange, uncouth, lack-lustre countenances, that his heart turned within him, and his knees smote together. His companion now emptied the contents of the keg into large flagons, and made signs to him to wait upon the company. He obeyed with fear and trembling; they quaffed the liquor in profound silence, and then returned to their game.

By degrees Rip's awe and apprehension subsided. He even ventured, when no eye was fixed upon him, to taste the beverage, which he found had much of the flavor of excellent Hollands. He was naturally a thirsty soul, and was soon tempted to repeat the draught. One taste provoked another; and he reiterated his visits to the flagon so often that at length his senses were overpowered, his eyes swam in
30 his head, his head gradually declined, and he fell into a deep sleep.

On waking, he found himself on the green knoll whence he had first seen the old man of the glen. He rubbed his eyes — it was a bright sunny morning. The birds were hopping and twittering among the bushes, and the eagle was wheeling aloft, and breasting the pure mountain breeze. "Surely," thought Rip, "I have not slept here all night." He recalled the occurrences before he fell asleep. The strange man with a keg of liquor — the mountain ravine — the wild retreat among the rocks — the wobegone party at nine-pins — the flagon — "Oh! that flagon! that wicked flagon!" thought Rip — "what excuse shall I make to Dame Van Winkle!"

He looked round for his gun, but in place of the clean well-oiled fowling-piece,
40 he found an old firelock lying by him, the barrel incrusted with rust, the lock falling off, and the stock worm-eaten. He now suspected that the grave roysters of the mountain had put a trick upon him, and, having dosed him with liquor had robbed

---

4 **beard,** 1819: head. The 1848 text is probably in error   10 **roses,** rosettes   27 **Hollands,** Dutch gin   41 **roysters,** revellers, roisterers

him of his gun. Wolf, too, had disappeared, but he might have strayed away after a squirrel or partridge. He whistled after him and shouted his name, but all in vain; the echoes repeated his whistle and shout, but no dog was to be seen.

He determined to revisit the scene of the last evening's gambol, and if he met with any of the party, to demand his dog and gun. As he rose to walk, he found himself stiff in the joints, and wanting in his usual activity. "These mountain beds do not agree with me," thought Rip, "and if this frolic should lay me up with a fit of the rheumatism, I shall have a blessed time with Dame Van Winkle." With some difficulty he got down into the glen: he found the gully up which he and his companion had ascended the preceding evening; but to his astonishment a moun- 10 tain stream was now foaming down it, leaping from rock to rock, and filling the glen with babbling murmurs. He, however, made shift to scramble up its sides, working his toilsome way through thickets of birch, sassafras, and witch-hazel, and sometimes tripped up or entangled by the wild grapevines that twisted their coils or tendrils from tree to tree, and spread a kind of network in his path.

At length he reached to where the ravine had opened through the cliffs to the amphitheatre; but no traces of such opening remained. The rocks presented a high impenetrable wall over which the torrent came tumbling in a sheet of feathery foam, and fell into a broad deep basin, black from the shadows of the surrounding forest. Here, then, poor Rip was brought to a stand. He again called and whistled 20 after his dog; he was only answered by the cawing of a flock of idle crows, sporting high in air about a dry tree that overhung a sunny precipice; and who, secure in their elevation, seemed to look down and scoff at the poor man's perplexities. What was to be done? the morning was passing away, and Rip felt famished for want of his breakfast. He grieved to give up his dog and gun; he dreaded to meet his wife; but it would not do to starve among the mountains. He shook his head, shouldered the rusty firelock, and, with a heart full of trouble and anxiety, turned his steps homeward.

As he approached the village he met a number of people, but none whom he knew, which somewhat surprised him, for he had thought himself acquainted with 30 every one in the country round. Their dress, too, was of a different fashion from that to which he was accustomed. They all stared at him with equal marks of surprise, and whenever they cast their eyes upon him, invariably stroked their chins. The constant recurrence of this gesture induced Rip, involuntarily, to do the same, when, to his astonishment, he found his beard had grown a foot long!

He had now entered the skirts of the village. A troop of strange children ran at his heels, hooting after him, and pointing at his gray beard. The dogs, too, not one of which he recognized for an old acquaintance, barked at him as he passed. The very village was altered; it was larger and more populous. There were rows of houses which he had never seen before, and those which had been his familiar 40 haunts had disappeared. Strange names were over the doors — strange faces at the windows — every thing was strange. His mind now misgave him; he began to doubt whether both he and the world around him were not bewitched. Surely this was his native village, which he had left but the day before. There stood the Kaatskill mountains — there ran the silvery Hudson at a distance — there was every hill and dale precisely as it had always been — Rip was sorely perplexed — "That flagon last night," thought he, "has addled my poor head sadly."

It was with some difficulty that he found the way to his own house, which he approached with silent awe, expecting every moment to hear the shrill voice of Dame Van Winkle. He found the house gone to decay — the roof fallen in, the windows shattered, and the doors off the hinges. A half-starved dog that looked like Wolf was skulking about it. Rip called him by name, but the cur snarled, showed his teeth, and passed on. This was an unkind cut indeed — "My very dog," sighed
10 poor Rip, "has forgotten me!"

He entered the house, which, to tell the truth, Dame Van Winkle had always kept in neat order. It was empty, forlorn, and apparently abandoned. This desolateness overcame all his connubial fears — he called loudly for his wife and children — the lonely chambers rang for a moment with his voice, and then all again was silence.

He now hurried forth, and hastened to his old resort, the village inn — but it too was gone. A large rickety wooden building stood in its place, with great gaping windows, some of them broken and mended with old hats and petticoats, and over the door was painted, "the Union Hotel, by Jonathan Doolittle." Instead of the great tree that used to shelter the quiet little Dutch inn of yore, there was now
20 reared a tall naked pole, with something on the top that looked like a red nightcap, and from it was fluttering a flag, on which was a singular assemblage of stars and stripes — all this was strange and incomprehensible. He recognized on the sign, however, the ruby face of King George, under which he had smoked so many a peaceful pipe; but even this was singularly metamorphosed. The red coat was changed for one of blue and buff, a sword was held in the hand instead of a sceptre, the head was decorated with a cocked hat, and underneath was painted in large characters, GENERAL WASHINGTON.

There was, as usual, a crowd of folk about the door, but none that Rip recollected. The very character of the people seemed changed. There was a busy, bus-
30 tling, disputatious tone about it, instead of the accustomed phlegm and drowsy tranquillity. He looked in vain for the sage Nicholas Vedder, with his broad face, double chin, and fair long pipe, uttering clouds of tobacco-smoke instead of idle speeches; or Van Bummel, the schoolmaster, doling forth the contents of an ancient newspaper. In place of these, a lean, bilious-looking fellow, with his pockets full of handbills, was haranguing vehemently about rights of citizens — elections — members of congress — liberty — Bunker's Hill — heroes of seventy-six — and other words, which were a perfect Babylonish jargon to the bewildered Van Winkle.

The appearance of Rip, with his long grizzled beard, his rusty fowling-piece, his uncouth dress, and an army of women and children at his heels, soon attracted the
40 attention of the tavern politicians. They crowded round him, eyeing him from head to foot with great curiosity. The orator bustled up to him, and, drawing him partly aside, inquired "on which side he voted?" Rip stared in vacant stupidity. Another

---

20 **red night-cap,** the "liberty cap," popular in the French Revolution   37 **Babylonish jargon,** unintelligible speech, apparently an allusion to the Tower of Babel, Genesis 11:1-9

short but busy little fellow pulled him by the arm, and, rising on tiptoe, inquired in his ear, "Whether he was Federal or Democrat?" Rip was equally at a loss to comprehend the question; when a knowing, self-important old gentleman, in a sharp cocked hat, made his way through the crowd, putting them to the right and left with his elbows as he passed, and planting himself before Van Winkle, with one arm akimbo, the other resting on his cane, his keen eyes and sharp hat penetrating, as it were, into his very soul, demanded in an austere tone, "what brought him to the election with a gun on his shoulder, and a mob at his heels, and whether he meant to breed a riot in the village?" — "Alas! gentlemen," cried Rip, somewhat dismayed, "I am a poor quiet man, a native of the place, and a loyal subject of the   10 king, God bless him!"

Here a general shout burst from the by-standers — "A tory! a tory! a spy! a refu- gee! hustle him! away with him!" It was with great difficulty that the self-impor- tant man in the cocked hat restored order; and, having assumed a tenfold austerity of brow, demanded again of the unknown culprit, what he came there for, and whom he was seeking? The poor man humbly assured him that he meant no harm, but merely came there in search of some of his neighbors, who used to keep about the tavern.

"Well — who are they? — name them."

Rip bethought himself a moment, and inquired, "Where's Nicholas Vedder?"

There was a silence for a little while, when an old man replied, in a thin piping   20 voice, "Nicholas Vedder! why, he is dead and gone these eighteen years! There was a wooden tombstone in the church-yard that used to tell all about him, but that's rotten and gone too."

"Where's Brom Dutcher?"

"Oh, he went off to the army in the beginning of the war; some say he was killed at the storming of Stony Point — others say he was drowned in a squall at the foot of Anthony's Nose. I don't know — he never came back again."

"Where's Van Bummel, the schoolmaster?"

"He went off to the wars too, was a great militia general, and is now in congress."

Rip's heart died away at hearing of these sad changes in his home and friends,   30 and finding himself thus alone in the world. Every answer puzzled him, too, by treating of such enormous lapses of time, and of matters which he could not under- stand: war — congress — Stony Point; — he had no courage to ask after any more friends, but cried out in despair, "Does nobody here know Rip Van Winkle?"

"Oh, Rip Van Winkle!" exclaimed two or three, "Oh, to be sure! that's Rip Van Winkle yonder, leaning against the tree."

Rip looked, and beheld a precise counterpart of himself, as he went up the moun- tain: apparently as lazy, and certainly as ragged. The poor fellow was now com- pletely confounded. He doubted his own identity, and whether he was himself or another man. In the midst of his bewilderment, the man in the cocked hat demanded   40 who he was, and what was his name?

---

2 **Federal or Democrat?** i.e., a Federalist or a supporter of Jefferson   26 **Stony Point,** a rocky headland on the west bank of the Hudson a few miles below West Point   27 **Anthony's Nose,** see note, p. 576

"God knows," exclaimed he, at his wit's end; "I'm not myself — I'm somebody else — that's me yonder — no — that's somebody else got into my shoes — I was myself last night, but I fell asleep on the mountain, and they've changed my gun, and every thing's changed, and I'm changed, and I can't tell what's my name, or who I am."

The by-standers began now to look at each other, nod, wink significantly, and tap their fingers against their foreheads. There was a whisper, also, about securing the gun, and keeping the old fellow from doing mischief, at the very suggestion of which the self-important man in the cocked hat retired with some precipitation. At this

10 critical moment a fresh comely woman pressed through the throng to get a peep at the gray-bearded man. She had a chubby child in her arms, which, frightened at his looks, began to cry. "Hush, Rip," cried she, "hush, you little fool; the old man won't hurt you." The name of the child, the air of the mother, the tone of her voice, all awakened a train of recollections in his mind. "What is your name, my good woman?" asked he.

"Judith Gardenier."

"And your father's name?"

"Ah, poor man, Rip Van Winkle was his name, but it's twenty years since he went away from home with his gun, and never has been heard of since — his dog

20 came home without him; but whether he shot himself, or was carried away by the Indians, nobody can tell. I was then but a little girl."

Rip had but one more question to ask; but he put it with a faltering voice:

"Where's your mother?"

"Oh, she too had died but a short time since; she broke a blood-vessel in a fit of passion at a New-England peddler."

There was a drop of comfort, at least, in this intelligence. The honest man could contain himself no longer. He caught his daughter and her child in his arms. "I am your father!" cried he — "Young Rip Van Winkle once — old Rip Van Winkle now! — Does nobody know poor Rip Van Winkle?"

30 All stood amazed, until an old woman, tottering out from among the crowd, put her hand to her brow, and peering under it in his face for a moment, exclaimed, "Sure enough! it is Rip Van Winkle — it is himself! — Welcome home again, old neighbor — Why, where have you been these twenty long years?"

Rip's story was soon told, for the whole twenty years had been to him but as one night. The neighbors stared when they heard it; some were seen to wink at each other, and put their tongues in their cheeks: and the self-important man in the cocked hat, who, when the alarm was over, had returned to the field, screwed down the corners of his mouth, and shook his head — upon which there was a general shaking of the head throughout the assemblage.

40 It was determined, however, to take the opinion of old Peter Vanderdonk, who was seen slowly advancing up the road. He was a descendant of the historian of that name, who wrote one of the earliest accounts of the province. Peter was the most ancient inhabitant of the village, and well versed in all the wonderful events and traditions of the neighborhood. He recollected Rip at once, and corroborated

his story in the most satisfactory manner. He assured the company that it was a fact, handed down from his ancestor the historian, that the Kaatskill mountains had always been haunted by strange beings. That it was affirmed that the great Hendrick Hudson, the first discoverer of the river and country, kept a kind of vigil there every twenty years, with his crew of the Half-moon; being permitted in this way to revisit the scenes of his enterprise, and keep a guardian eye upon the river, and the great city called by his name. That his father had once seen them in their old Dutch dresses playing at nine-pins in a hollow of the mountain; and that he himself had heard, one summer afternoon, the sound of their balls, like distant peals of thunder.   10

To make a long story short, the company broke up, and returned to the more important concerns of the election. Rip's daughter took him home to live with her; she had a snug, well-furnished house, and a stout cheery farmer for a husband, whom Rip recollected for one of the urchins that used to climb upon his back. As to Rip's son and heir, who was the ditto of himself, seen leaning against the tree, he was employed to work on the farm; but evinced an hereditary disposition to attend to any thing else but his business.

Rip now resumed his old walks and habits; he soon found many of his former cronies, though all rather the worse for the wear and tear of time; and preferred making friends among the rising generation, with whom he soon grew into great   20 favor.

Having nothing to do at home, and being arrived at that happy age when a man can be idle with impunity, he took his place once more on the bench at the inn door, and was reverenced as one of the patriarchs of the village, and a chronicle of the old times "before the war." It was some time before he could get into the regular track of gossip, or could be made to comprehend the strange events that had taken place during his torpor. How that there had been a revolutionary war — that the country had thrown off the yoke of old England — and that, instead of being a subject of his Majesty George the Third, he was now a free citizen of the United States. Rip, in fact, was no politician; the changes of states and empires made but little   30 impression on him; but there was one species of despotism under which he had long groaned, and that was — petticoat government. Happily that was at an end; he had got his neck out of the yoke of matrimony, and could go in and out whenever he pleased, without dreading the tyranny of Dame Van Winkle. Whenever her name was mentioned, however, he shook his head, shrugged his shoulders, and cast up his eyes; which might pass either for an expression of resignation to his fate, or joy at his deliverance.

He used to tell his story to every stranger that arrived at Mr. Doolittle's hotel. He was observed, at first, to vary on some points every time he told it, which was, doubtless, owing to his having so recently awaked. It at last settled down precisely   40 to the tale I have related, and not a man, woman, or child in the neighborhood,

---

2 **the historian**, Adriaen Van der Donck (1620-1655?), author of a description of New Netherland, in Dutch, published at Amsterdam in 1655   7 **great city**. Hudson, on the east bank of the river, was a thriving shipping center in Irving's day

but knew it by heart. Some always pretended to doubt the reality of it, and insisted that Rip had been out of his head, and that this was one point on which he always remained flighty. The old Dutch inhabitants, however, almost universally gave it full credit. Even to this day they never hear a thunderstorm of a summer afternoon about the Kaatskill, but they say Hendrick Hudson and his crew are at their game of nine-pins; and it is a common wish of all henpecked husbands in the neighborhood, when life hangs heavy on their hands, that they might have a quieting draught out of Rip Van Winkle's flagon.

Note

10 The foregoing Tale, one would suspect, had been suggested to Mr. Knickerbocker by a little German superstition about the Emperor Frederick *der Rothbart,* and the Kypphauser mountain: the subjoined note, however, which he had appended to the tale, shows that it is an absolute fact, narrated with his usual fidelity:
  "The story of Rip Van Winkle may seem incredible to many, but nevertheless I give it my full belief, for I know the vicinity of our old Dutch settlements to have been very subject to marvellous events and appearances. Indeed, I have heard many stranger stories than this, in the villages along the Hudson; all of which were too well authenticated to admit of a doubt. I have even talked with Rip Van Winkle myself, who, when last I saw him, was a very venerable old man, and so perfectly
20 rational and consistent on every other point, that I think no conscientious person could refuse to take this into the bargain; nay, I have seen a certificate on the subject taken before a country justice and signed with a cross, in the justice's own handwriting. The story, therefore, is beyond the possibility of doubt.
                                                                                    D.K."

Postscript

The following are travelling notes from a memorandum-book of Mr. Knickerbocker:
  The Kaatsberg, or Catskill Mountains, have always been a region full of fable. The Indians considered them the abode of spirits, who influenced the weather, spreading sunshine or clouds over the landscape, and sending good or bad hunting sea-
30 sons. They were ruled by an old squaw spirit, said to be their mother. She dwelt on the highest peak of the Catskills, and had charge of the doors of day and night to open and shut them at the proper hour. She hung up the new moons in the skies, and cut up the old ones into stars. In times of drought, if properly propitiated, she would spin light summer clouds out of cobwebs and morning dew, and send them off from the crest of the mountain, flake after flake, like flakes of carded cotton, to float in the air; until, dissolved by the heat of the sun, they would fall in gentle showers, causing the grass to spring, the fruits to ripen, and the corn to grow

---

11 **der Rothbart,** the Redbeard, Frederick I (better known as Frederick Barbarossa), emperor of the Holy Roman Empire, 1152-1190. He sleeps, according to peasant tradition, in a mountain in central Germany
Postscript, added after 1819

an inch an hour. If displeased, however, she would brew up clouds black as ink, sitting in the midst of them like a bottle-bellied spider in the midst of its web; and when these clouds broke, wo betide the valleys!

In old times, say the Indian traditions, there was a kind of Manitou or Spirit, who kept about the wildest recesses of the Catskill Mountains, and took a mischievous pleasure in wreaking all kinds of evils and vexations upon the red men. Sometimes he would assume the form of a bear, a panther, or a deer, lead the bewildered hunter a weary chase through tangled forests and among ragged rocks; and then spring off with a loud ho! ho! leaving him aghast on the brink of a beetling precipice or raging torrent. 10

The favorite abode of this Manitou is still shown. It is a great rock or cliff on the loneliest part of the mountains, and, from the flowering vines which clamber about it, and the wild flowers which abound in its neighborhood, is known by the name of the Garden Rock. Near the foot of it is a small lake, the haunt of the solitary bittern, with water-snakes basking in the sun on the leaves of the pond-lilies which lie on the surface. This place was held in great awe by the Indians, insomuch that the boldest hunter would not pursue his game within its precincts. Once upon a time, however, a hunter who had lost his way, penetrated to the garden rock, where he beheld a number of gourds placed in the crotches of trees. One of these he seized and made off with it, but in the hurry of his retreat he let it fall among the rocks, 20 when a great stream gushed forth, which washed him away and swept him down precipices, where he was dashed to pieces, and the stream made its way to the Hudson, and continues to flow to the present day; being the identical stream known by the name of the Kaaterskill. 1818, 1819

The Legend of Sleepy Hollow

Found Among the Papers of the Late Diedrich Knickerbocker

A pleasing land of drowsy head it was,
Of dreams that wave before the half-shut eye;
And of gay castles in the clouds that pass,
For ever flushing round a summer sky.

CASTLE OF INDOLENCE

In the bosom of one of those spacious coves which indent the eastern shore of the Hudson, at that broad expansion of the river denominated by the ancient Dutch navigators the Tappan Zee, and where they always prudently shortened sail, and implored the protection of St. Nicholas when they crossed, there lies a small market-town or rural port, which by some is called Greensburgh, but which is more 10 generally and properly known by the name of Tarry Town. This name was given,

5 **Castle of Indolence** (1748), an English poem in imitation of Spenser, by James Thomson (1700-1748), Canto I, ll. 46-49   11 **Tarry Town,** one of the first Dutch settlements on the Hudson. It was Irving's home after 1835, and he was buried in the cemetery at Sleepy Hollow

we are told, in former days, by the good housewives of the adjacent country, from
the inveterate propensity of their husbands to linger about the village tavern on
market days. Be that as it may, I do not vouch for the fact, but merely advert to it,
for the sake of being precise and authentic. Not far from this village, perhaps about
two miles, there is a little valley, or rather lap of land, among high hills, which is
one of the quietest places in the whole world. A small brook glides through it, with
just murmur enough to lull one to repose; and the occasional whistle of a quail, or
tapping of a woodpecker, is almost the only sound that ever breaks in upon the
uniform tranquillity.

10   I recollect that, when a stripling, my first exploit in squirrel-shooting was in a
grove of tall walnut-trees that shades one side of the valley. I had wandered into it
at noon time, when all nature is peculiarly quiet, and was startled by the roar of
my own gun, as it broke the Sabbath stillness around, and was prolonged and reverberated by the angry echoes. If ever I should wish for a retreat, whither I might
steal from the world and its distractions, and dream quietly away the remnant of a
troubled life, I know of none more promising than this little valley.

    From the listless repose of the place, and the peculiar character of its inhabitants,
who are descendants from the original Dutch settlers, this sequestered glen has long
been known by the name of SLEEPY HOLLOW, and its rustic lads are called the Sleepy
20 Hollow Boys throughout all the neighboring country. A drowsy, dreamy influence
seems to hang over the land, and to pervade the very atmosphere. Some say that
the place was bewitched by a high German doctor, during the early days of the settlement; others, that an old Indian chief, the prophet or wizard of his tribe, held
his powwows there before the country was discovered by Master Hendrick Hudson.
Certain it is, the place still continues under the sway of some witching power, that
holds a spell over the minds of the good people, causing them to walk in a continual reverie. They are given to all kinds of marvellous beliefs; are subject to trances
and visions; and frequently see strange sights, and hear music and voices in the air.
The whole neighborhood abounds with local tales, haunted spots, and twilight
30 superstitions; stars shoot and meteors glare oftener across the valley than in any
other part of the country, and the nightmare, with her whole nine fold, seems to
make it the favorite scene of her gambols.

    The dominant spirit, however, that haunts this enchanted region, and seems to be
commander-in-chief of all the powers of the air, is the apparition of a figure on
horseback without a head. It is said by some to be the ghost of a Hessian trooper,
whose head had been carried away by a cannon-ball, in some nameless battle during
the revolutionary war; and who is ever and anon seen by the country folk, hurrying
along in the gloom of night, as if on the wings of the wind. His haunts are not
confined to the valley, but extend at times to the adjacent roads, and especially to
40 the vicinity of a church at no great distance. Indeed, certain of the most authentic

---

5 **lap,** surface or bosom (archaic and poetic)   22 **high German,** southern or highland German   24
Hendrick Hudson (d. 1611?) entered the river bearing his name in 1609   31 **nine fold,** an allusion to
line 126 in *King Lear,* Act II, Scene iv. In folk belief the nightmare was a demon; nine fold refers to her
offspring (from foals) or familiars. See notes, p. 139 and 141

historians of those parts, who have been careful in collecting and collating the floating facts concerning this spectre, allege that the body of the trooper, having been buried in the church-yard, the ghost rides forth to the scene of battle in nightly quest of his head; and that the rushing speed with which he sometimes passes along the Hollow, like a midnight blast, is owing to his being belated, and in a hurry to get back to the church-yard before daybreak.

Such is the general purport of this legendary superstition, which has furnished materials for many a wild story in that region of shadows; and the spectre is known, at all the country firesides, by the name of the Headless Horseman of Sleepy Hollow.

It is remarkable that the visionary propensity I have mentioned is not confined to 10 the native inhabitants of the valley, but is unconsciously imbibed by every one who resides there for a time. However wide awake they may have been before they entered that sleepy region, they are sure, in a little time, to inhale the witching influence of the air, and begin to grow imaginative — to dream dreams, and see apparitions.

I mention this peaceful spot with all possible laud; for it is in such little retired Dutch valleys, found here and there embosomed in the great State of New-York, that population, manners, and customs, remain fixed; while the great torrent of migration and improvement, which is making such incessant changes in other parts of this restless country, sweeps by them unobserved. They are like those little nooks of still water which border a rapid stream; where we may see the straw and bubble 20 riding quietly at anchor, or slowly revolving in their mimic harbor, undisturbed by the rush of the passing current. Though many years have elapsed since I trod the drowsy shades of Sleepy Hollow, yet I question whether I should not still find the same trees and the same families vegetating in its sheltered bosom.

In this by-place of nature, there abode, in a remote period of American history, that is to say, some thirty years since, a worthy wight of the name of Ichabod Crane; who sojourned, or, as he expressed it, "tarried," in Sleepy Hollow, for the purpose of instructing the children of the vicinity. He was a native of Connecticut; a State which supplies the Union with pioneers for the mind as well as for the forest, and sends forth yearly its legions of frontier woodsmen and country schoolmasters. The 30 cognomen of Crane was not inapplicable to his person. He was tall, but exceedingly lank, with narrow shoulders, long arms and legs, hands that dangled a mile out of his sleeves, feet that might have served for shovels, and his whole frame most loosely hung together. His head was small, and flat at top, with huge ears, large green glassy eyes, and a long snipe nose, so that it looked like a weather-cock, perched upon his spindle neck, to tell which way the wind blew. To see him striding along the profile of a hill on a windy day, with his clothes bagging and fluttering about him, one might have mistaken him for the genius of famine descending upon the earth, or some scarecrow eloped from a cornfield.

His school-house was a low building of one large room, rudely constructed of 40 logs; the windows partly glazed, and partly patched with leaves of old copy-books. It was most ingeniously secured at vacant hours, by a withe twisted in the handle of the door, and stakes set against the window shutters; so that, though a thief might

6 **before daybreak.** See the actions of the ghost of Hamlet's father in *Hamlet,* Act I

get in with perfect ease, he would find some embarrassment in getting out; an idea most probably borrowed by the architect, Yost Van Houten, from the mystery of an eel-pot. The school-house stood in a rather lonely but pleasant situation, just at the foot of a woody hill, with a brook running close by, and a formidable birch tree growing at one end of it. From hence the low murmur of his pupils' voices, conning over their lessons, might be heard in a drowsy summer's day, like the hum of a bee-hive; interrupted now and then by the authoritative voice of the master, in the tone of menace or command; or, peradventure, by the appalling sound of the birch, as he urged some tardy loiterer along the flowery path of knowledge. Truth
10 to say, he was a conscientious man, and ever bore in mind the golden maxim, "Spare the rod and spoil the child." — Ichabod Crane's scholars certainly were not spoiled.

I would not have it imagined, however, that he was one of those cruel potentates of the school, who joy in the smart of their subjects; on the contrary, he administered justice with discrimination rather than severity; taking the burthen off the backs of the weak, and laying it on those of the strong. Your mere puny stripling, that winced at the least flourish of the rod, was passed by with indulgence; but the claims of justice were satisfied by inflicting a double portion on some little, tough, wrong-headed, broad-skirted Dutch urchin, who sulked and swelled and grew dogged and sullen beneath the birch. All this he called "doing his duty by their parents;"
20 and he never inflicted a chastisement without following it by the assurance, so consolatory to the smarting urchin, that "he would remember it, and thank him for it the longest day he had to live."

When school hours were over, he was even the companion and playmate of the larger boys; and on holiday afternoons would convoy some of the smaller ones home, who happened to have pretty sisters, or good housewives for mothers, noted for the comforts of the cupboard. Indeed it behooved him to keep on good terms with his pupils. The revenue arising from his school was small, and would have been scarcely sufficient to furnish him with daily bread, for he was a huge feeder, and though lank, had the dilating powers of an anaconda; but to help out his maintenance, he
30 was, according to country custom in those parts, boarded and lodged at the houses of the farmers, whose children he instructed. With these he lived successively a week at a time; thus going the rounds of the neighborhood, with all his worldly effects tied up in a cotton handkerchief.

That all this might not be too onerous on the purses of his rustic patrons, who are apt to consider the costs of schooling a grievous burden, and schoolmasters as mere drones, he had various ways of rendering himself both useful and agreeable. He assisted the farmers occasionally in the lighter labors of their farms; helped to make hay; mended the fences, took the horses to water; drove the cows from pasture; and cut wood for the winter fire. He laid aside, too, all the dominant dignity
40 and absolute sway with which he lorded it in his little empire, the school, and became wonderfully gentle and ingratiating. He found favor in the eyes of the mothers,

---

10 **Spare . . . child.**" See Proverbs 13:24: "He that spareth his rod hateth his son." In the form used here the maxim first appeared in Part II (1664) of *Hudibras* by Samuel Butler (1612-1680), an English satirical poet

by petting the children, particularly the youngest; and like the lion bold, which
whilom so magnanimously the lamb did hold, he would sit with a child on one
knee, and rock a cradle with his foot for whole hours together.

In addition to his other vocations, he was the singing-master of the neighborhood,
and picked up many bright shillings by instructing the young folks in psalmody. It
was a matter of no little vanity to him, on Sundays, to take his station in front of
the church gallery, with a band of chosen singers; where, in his own mind, he completely carried away the palm from the parson. Certain it is, his voice resounded
far above all the rest of the congregation; and there are peculiar quavers still to be
heard in that church, and which may even be heard half a mile off, quite to the 10
opposite side of the mill-pond, on a still Sunday morning, which are said to be
legitimately descended from the nose of Ichabod Crane. Thus, by divers little make-
shifts in that ingenious way which is commonly denominated "by hook and by
crook," the worthy pedagogue got on tolerably enough, and was thought, by all
who understood nothing of the labor of headwork, to have a wonderfully easy
life of it.

The schoolmaster is generally a man of some importance in the female circle of
a rural neighborhood; being considered a kind of idle gentlemanlike personage, of
vastly superior taste and accomplishments to the rough country swains, and, indeed,
inferior in learning only to the parson. His appearance, therefore, is apt to occasion 20
some little stir at the tea-table of a farmhouse, and the addition of a supernumerary
dish of cakes or sweetmeats, or, peradventure, the parade of a silver tea-pot. Our
man of letters, therefore, was peculiarly happy in the smiles of all the country damsels.
How he would figure among them in the church-yard, between services on Sundays! gathering grapes for them from the wild vines that overrun the surrounding
trees; reciting for their amusement all the epitaphs on the tombstones; or sauntering, with a whole bevy of them, along the banks of the adjacent mill-pond; while
the more bashful country bumpkins hung sheepishly back, envying his superior
elegance and address.

From his half itinerant life, also, he was a kind of travelling gazette, carrying the 30
whole budget of local gossip from house to house; so that his appearance was always greeted with satisfaction. He was, moreover, esteemed by the women as a man
of great erudition, for he had read several books quite through, and was a perfect
master of Cotton Mather's history of New-England Witchcraft, in which, by the
way, he most firmly and potently believed.

He was, in fact, an odd mixture of small shrewdness and simple credulity. His
appetite for the marvellous, and his powers of digesting it, were equally extraordinary; and both had been increased by his residence in this spellbound region. No
tale was too gross or monstrous for his capacious swallow. It was often his delight,
after his school was dismissed in the afternoon, to stretch himself on the rich bed 40

1 the lion bold . . ., from a couplet which appears in the 1747 edition of *The New England Primer*   13
"by . . . crook," a phrase from "Colyn Cloute" (1523), by the English poet John Skelton (1460?-
1529)   34 **Cotton Mather's history,** a reference either to the *Memorable Providences* (1689) or to *Wonders
of the Invisible World* (1693). See p. 138

of clover, bordering the little brook that whimpered by his school-house, and there con over old Mather's direful tales, until the gathering dusk of the evening made the printed page a mere mist before his eyes. Then, as he wended his way, by swamp and stream and awful woodland, to the farmhouse where he happened to be quartered, every sound of nature, at that witching hour, fluttered his excited imagination: the moan of the whip-poor-will from the hill-side; the boding cry of the tree-toad, that harbinger of storm; the dreary hooting of the screech-owl, or the sudden rustling in the thicket of birds frightened from their roost. The fire-flies, too, which sparkled most vividly in the darkest places, now and then startled him, as one of uncommon brightness would stream across his path; and if, by chance, a huge blockhead of a beetle came winging his blundering flight against him, the poor varlet was ready to give up the ghost, with the idea that he was struck with a witch's token. His only resource on such occasions, either to drown thought, or drive away evil spirits, was to sing psalm tunes; — and the good people of Sleepy Hollow, as they sat by their doors of an evening, were often filled with awe, at hearing his nasal melody, "in linked sweetness long drawn out," floating from the distant hill, or along the dusky road.

Another of his sources of fearful pleasure was, to pass long winter evenings with the old Dutch wives, as they sat spinning by the fire, with a row of apples roasting and spluttering along the hearth, and listen to their marvellous tales of ghosts and goblins, and haunted fields, and haunted brooks, and haunted bridges, and haunted houses, and particularly of the headless horseman, or galloping Hessian of the Hollow, as they sometimes called him. He would delight them equally by his anecdotes of witchcraft, and of the direful omens and portentous sights and sounds in the air, which prevailed in the earlier times of Connecticut; and would frighten them wofully with speculations upon comets and shooting stars; and with the alarming fact that the world did absolutely turn round, and that they were half the time topsy-turvy!

But if there was a pleasure in all this, while snugly cuddling in the chimney corner of a chamber that was all of a ruddy glow from the crackling wood fire, and where, of course, no spectre dared to show his face, it was dearly purchased by the terrors of his subsequent walk homewards. What fearful shapes and shadows beset his path amidst the dim and ghastly glare of a snowy night! — With what wistful look did he eye every trembling ray of light streaming across the waste fields from some distant window! — How often was he appalled by some shrub covered with snow, which, like a sheeted spectre, beset his very path! — How often did he shrink with curdling awe at the sound of his own steps on the frosty crust beneath his feet; and dread to look over his shoulder, lest he should behold some uncouth being tramping close behind him! — and how often was he thrown into complete dismay by some rushing blast, howling among the trees, in the idea that it was the Galloping Hessian on one of his nightly scourings!

All these, however, were mere terrors of the night, phantoms of the mind that

---

6 **whip-poor-will.** "The whip-poor-will is a bird which is only heard at night. It receives its name from its note, which is thought to resemble those words." (Irving's note, added after 1820)   16 "**in linked . . . out,**" from "L'Allegro," l. 140, by John Milton (1608-1674)

walk in darkness; and though he had seen many spectres in his time, and been more than once beset by Satan in divers shapes, in his lonely perambulations, yet daylight put an end to all these evils; and he would have passed a pleasant life of it, in despite of the devil and all his works, if his path had not been crossed by a being that causes more perplexity to mortal man than ghosts, goblins, and the whole race of witches put together, and that was — a woman.

Among the musical disciples who assembled, one evening in each week, to receive his instructions in psalmody, was Katrina Van Tassel, the daughter and only child of a substantial Dutch farmer. She was a blooming lass of fresh eighteen; plump as a partridge; ripe and melting and rosy cheeked as one of her father's peaches, and 10 universally famed, not merely for her beauty, but her vast expectations. She was withal a little of a coquette, as might be perceived even in her dress, which was a mixture of ancient and modern fashions, as most suited to set off her charms. She wore the ornaments of pure yellow gold, which her great-great-grandmother had brought over from Saardam; the tempting stomacher of the olden time; and withal a provokingly short petticoat, to display the prettiest foot and ankle in the country round.

Ichabod Crane had a soft and foolish heart towards the sex; and it is not to be wondered at, that so tempting a morsel soon found favor in his eyes; more especially after he had visited her in her paternal mansion. Old Baltus Van Tassel was 20 a perfect picture of a thriving, contented, liberal-hearted farmer. He seldom, it is true, sent either his eyes or his thoughts beyond the boundaries of his own farm; but within those every thing was snug, happy, and well-conditioned. He was satisfied with his wealth, but not proud of it; and piqued himself upon the hearty abundance, rather than the style in which he lived. His stronghold was situated on the banks of the Hudson, in one of those green, sheltered, fertile nooks, in which the Dutch farmers are so fond of nestling. A great elm-tree spread its broad branches over it; at the foot of which bubbled up a spring of the softest and sweetest water, in a little well, formed of a barrel; and then stole sparkling away through the grass, to a neighboring brook, that bubbled along among alders and dwarf willows. Hard by the farm- 30 house was a vast barn, that might have served for a church; every window and crevice of which seemed bursting forth with the treasures of the farm; the flail was busily resounding within it from morning to night; swallows and martins skimmed twittering about the eaves; and rows of pigeons, some with one eye turned up, as if watching the weather, some with their heads under their wings, or buried in their bosoms, and others swelling, and cooing, and bowing about their dames, were enjoying the sunshine on the roof. Sleek unwieldy porkers were grunting in the repose and abundance of their pens; whence sallied forth, now and then, troops of sucking pigs, as if to snuff the air. A stately squadron of snowy geese were riding in an adjoining pond, convoying whole fleets of ducks; regiments of turkeys were 40 gobbling through the farmyard, and guinea fowls fretting about it, like ill-tempered housewives, with their peevish discontented cry. Before the barn door strutted the gallant cock, that pattern of a husband, a warrior, and a fine gentleman, clapping

---

15 **Saardam,** modern Zaandam, a village in northern Holland a few miles north of Amsterdam

his burnished wings, and crowing in the pride and gladness of his heart — sometimes tearing up the earth with his feet, and then generously calling his ever-hungry family of wives and children to enjoy the rich morsel which he had discovered.

The pedagogue's mouth watered, as he looked upon this sumptuous promise of luxurious winter fare. In his devouring mind's eye, he pictured to himself every roasting-pig running about with a pudding in his belly, and an apple in his mouth; the pigeons were snugly put to bed in a comfortable pie, and tucked in with a coverlet of crust; the geese were swimming in their own gravy; and the ducks pairing cosily in dishes, like snug married couples, with a decent competency of onion
10 sauce. In the porkers he saw carved out the future sleek side of bacon, and juicy relishing ham; not a turkey but he beheld daintily trussed up, with its gizzard under its wing, and, peradventure, a necklace of savory sausages; and even bright chanticleer himself lay sprawling on his back, in a side-dish, with uplifted claws, as if craving that quarter which his chivalrous spirit disdained to ask while living.

As the enraptured Ichabod fancied all this and as he rolled his great green eyes over the fat meadow-lands, the rich fields of wheat, of rye, of buckwheat, and Indian corn, and the orchards burthened with ruddy fruit, which surrounded the warm tenement of Van Tassel, his heart yearned after the damsel who was to inherit these domains, and his imagination expanded with the idea, how they might be readily
20 turned into cash, and the money invested in immense tracts of wild land, and shingle palaces in the wilderness. Nay, his busy fancy already realized his hopes, and presented to him the blooming Katrina, with a whole family of children, mounted on the top of a wagon loaded with household trumpery, with pots and kettles dangling beneath; and he beheld himself bestriding a pacing mare, with a colt at her heels, setting out for Kentucky, Tennessee, or the Lord knows where.

When he entered the house the conquest of his heart was complete. It was one of those spacious farmhouses, with high-ridged, but lowly-sloping roofs, built in the style handed down from the first Dutch settlers; the low projecting eaves forming a piazza along the front, capable of being closed up in bad weather. Under this
30 were hung flails, harness, various utensils of husbandry, and nets for fishing in the neighboring river. Benches were built along the sides for summer use; and a great spinning-wheel at one end, and a churn at the other, showed the various uses to which this important porch might be devoted. From this piazza the wondering Ichabod entered the hall, which formed the centre of the mansion and the place of usual residence. Here, rows of resplendent pewter, ranged on a long dresser, dazzled his eyes. In one corner stood a huge bag of wool ready to be spun; in another a quantity of linsey-woolsey just from the loom; ears of Indian corn, and strings of dried apples and peaches, hung in gay festoons along the walls, mingled with the gaud of red peppers; and a door left ajar gave him a peep into the best parlor, where
40 the claw-footed chairs, and dark mahogany tables, shone like mirrors; and irons, with their accompanying shovel and tongs, glistened from their covert of asparagus tops; mock-oranges and conch-shells decorated the mantelpiece; strings of various

---

40 **and irons.** 1820: andirons. The 1848 text is probably in error.   41 **asparagus tops,** fern-like sprays   42 **mock-oranges,** probably syringas

colored birds' eggs were suspended above it: a great ostrich egg was hung from the centre of the room, and a corner cupboard, knowingly left open, displayed immense treasures of old silver and well-mended china.

From the moment Ichabod laid his eyes upon these regions of delight, the peace of his mind was at an end, and his only study was how to gain the affections of the peerless daughter of Van Tassel. In this enterprise, however, he had more real difficulties than generally fell to the lot of a knight-errant of yore, who seldom had any thing but giants, enchanters, fiery dragons, and such like easily-conquered adversaries, to contend with; and had to make his way merely through gates of iron and brass, and walls of adamant, to the castle keep, where the lady of his heart was 10 confined; all which he achieved as easily as a man would carve his way to the centre of a Christmas pie; and then the lady gave him her hand as a matter of course. Ichabod, on the contrary, had to win his way to the heart of a country coquette, beset with a labyrinth of whims and caprices, which were for ever presenting new difficulties and impediments; and he had to encounter a host of fearful adversaries of real flesh and blood, the numerous rustic admirers, who beset every portal to her heart; keeping a watchful and angry eye upon each other, but ready to fly out in the common cause against any new competitor.

Among these the most formidable was a burly, roaring, roystering blade, of the name of Abraham, or, according to the Dutch abbreviation, Brom Van Brunt, the 20 hero of the country round, which rang with his feats of strength and hardihood. He was broad-shouldered and double-jointed, with short curly black hair, and a bluff, but not unpleasant countenance, having a mingled air of fun and arrogance. From his Herculean frame and great powers of limb, he had received the nickname of BROM BONES, by which he was universally known. He was famed for great knowledge and skill in horsemanship, being as dexterous on horseback as a Tartar. He was foremost at all races and cock-fights; and, with the ascendency which bodily strength acquires in rustic life, was the umpire in all disputes, setting his hat on one side, and giving his decisions with an air and tone admitting of no gainsay or appeal. He was always ready for either a fight or a frolic; but had more mischief 30 than ill-will in his composition; and, with all his overbearing roughness, there was a strong dash of waggish good humor at bottom. He had three or four boon companions, who regarded him as their model, and at the head of whom he scoured the country, attending every scene of feud or merriment for miles round. In cold weather he was distinguished by a fur cap, surmounted with a flaunting fox's tail; and when the folks at a country gathering descried this well-known crest at a distance, whisking about among a squad of hard riders, they always stood by for a squall. Sometimes his crew would be heard dashing along past the farmhouses at midnight, with whoop and halloo, like a troop of Don Cossacks; and the old dames, startled out of their sleep, would listen for a moment till the hurry-scurry 40 had clattered by, and then exclaim, "Ay, there goes Brom Bones and his gang!" The

---

39 **Don Cossacks,** Cossacks of the Don River region of Russia. The Cossacks were originally tribes notable for their strong military (and especially their cavalry) organization; the name is variously interpreted as meaning "adventurers," "freebooters," and "plunderers"

neighbors looked upon him with a mixture of awe, admiration, and good-will; and when any madcap prank, or rustic brawl, occurred in the vicinity, always shook their heads, and warranted Brom Bones was at the bottom of it.

This rantipole hero had for some time singled out the blooming Katrina for the object of his uncouth gallantries, and though his amorous toyings were something like the gentle caresses and endearments of a bear, yet it was whispered that she did not altogether discourage his hopes. Certain it is, his advances were signals for rival candidates to retire, who felt no inclination to cross a lion in his amours; insomuch, that when his horse was seen tied to Van Tassel's paling, on a Sunday
10 night, a sure sign that his master was courting, or, as it is termed, "sparking," within all other suitors passed by in despair, and carried the war into other quarters.

Such was the formidable rival with whom Ichabod Crane had to contend, and, considering all things, a stouter man than he would have shrunk from the competition, and a wiser man would have despaired. He had, however, a happy mixture of pliability and perseverance in his nature; he was in form and spirit like a supplejack — yielding, but tough; though he bent, he never broke; and though he bowed beneath the slightest pressure, yet, the moment it was away — jerk! he was erect, and carried his head as high as ever.

To have taken the field openly against his rival would have been madness; for he
20 was not a man to be thwarted in his amours, any more than that stormy lover, Achilles. Ichabod, therefore, made his advances in a quiet and gently-insinuating manner. Under cover of his character of singing-master, he made frequent visits at the farmhouse; not that he had any thing to apprehend from the meddlesome interference of parents, which is so often a stumbling-block in the path of lovers. Balt Van Tassel was an easy indulgent soul; he loved his daughter better even than his pipe, and, like a reasonable man and an excellent father, let her have her way in every thing. His notable little wife, too, had enough to do to attend to her housekeeping and manage her poultry; for, as she sagely observed, ducks and geese are foolish things, and must be looked after, but girls can take care of themselves. Thus while
30 the busy dame bustled about the house, or plied her spinning-wheel at one end of the piazza, honest Balt would sit smoking his evening pipe at the other, watching the achievements of a little wooden warrior, who, armed with a sword in each hand, was most valiantly fighting the wind on the pinnacle of the barn. In the mean time, Ichabod would carry on his suit with the daughter by the side of the spring under the great elm, or sauntering along in the twilight, that hour so favorable to the lover's eloquence.

I profess not to know how women's hearts are wooed and won. To me they have always been matters of riddle and admiration. Some seem to have but one vulnerable point, or door of access; while others have a thousand avenues, and may be
40 captured in a thousand different ways. It is a great triumph of skill to gain

---

4 **rantipole,** reckless, wild (rare)   15 **supplejack,** a walking-stick, cut from a climbing vine   21 **Achilles,** an allusion to his passion for Polyxena, daughter of Priam, the Trojan. Slain while arranging for the marriage, which was expected to bring peace, Achilles or his shade returned after death to demand his promised bride; she was accordingly sacrificed by the Greeks

the former, but a still greater proof of generalship to maintain possession of the latter, for the man must battle for his fortress at every door and window. He who wins a thousand common hearts is therefore entitled to some renown; but he who keeps undisputed sway over the heart of a coquette, is indeed a hero. Certain it is, this was not the case with the redoubtable Brom Bones; and from the moment Ichabod Crane made his advances, the interests of the former evidently declined; his horse was no longer seen tied at the palings on Sunday nights, and a deadly feud gradually arose between him and the preceptor of Sleepy Hollow.

Brom, who had a degree of rough chivalry in his nature, would fain have carried matters to open warfare, and have settled their pretensions to the lady, according to 10 the mode of those most concise and simple reasoners, the knights-errant of yore — by single combat; but Ichabod was too conscious of the superior might of his adversary to enter the lists against him: he had overheard a boast of Bones, that he would "double the schoolmaster up, and lay him on a shelf of his own school-house;" and he was too wary to give him an opportunity. There was something extremely provoking in this obstinately pacific system; it left Brom no alternative but to draw upon the funds of rustic waggery in his disposition, and to play off boorish practical jokes upon his rival. Ichabod became the object of whimsical persecution to Bones, and his gang of rough riders. They harried his hitherto peaceful domains; smoked out his singing school, by stopping up the chimney; broke into the school- 20 house at night, in spite of its formidable fastenings of withe and window stakes, and turned every thing topsy-turvy: so that the poor schoolmaster began to think all the witches in the country held their meetings there. But what was still more annoying, Brom took all opportunities of turning him into ridicule in presence of his mistress, and had a scoundrel dog whom he taught to whine in the most ludicrous manner, and introduced as a rival of Ichabod's to instruct her in psalmody.

In this way matters went on for some time, without producing any material effect on the relative situation of the contending powers. On a fine autumnal afternoon, Ichabod, in pensive mood, sat enthroned on a lofty stool whence he usually watched all the concerns of his little literary realm. In his hand he swayed a ferule, that sceptre 30 of despotic power; the birch of justice reposed on three nails, behind the throne, a constant terror to evil doers; while on the desk before him might be seen sundry contraband articles and prohibited weapons, detected upon the persons of idle urchins; such as half-munched apples, popguns, whirligigs, fly-cages, and whole legions of rampant little paper game-cocks. Apparently there had been some appalling act of justice recently inflicted, for his scholars were all busily intent upon their books, or slyly whispering behind them with one eye kept upon the master; and a kind of buzzing stillness reigned throughout the school-room. It was suddenly interrupted by the appearance of a Negro, in tow-cloth jacket and trowsers, a round-crowned fragment of a hat, like the cap of Mercury, and mounted on the back of a 40 ragged, wild, half-broken colt, which he managed with a rope by way of halter. He came clattering up to the school door with an invitation to Ichabod to attend a merrymaking or "quilting frolic," to be held that evening at Mynheer Van Tassel's;

---

40 **cap of Mercury**, the Patasus, or winged hat, symbol of speed as messenger of the gods

and having delivered his message with that air of importance, and effort at fine language, which a Negro is apt to display on petty embassies of the kind, he dashed
over the brook, and was seen scampering away up the hollow, full of the importance
and hurry of his mission.

All was now bustle and hubbub in the late quiet school-room. The scholars were
hurried through their lessons, without stopping at trifles; those who were nimble
skipped over half with impunity, and those were tardy, had a smart application
now and then in the rear, to quicken their speed, or help them over a tall word.
Books were flung aside without being put away on the shelves, inkstands were
10 overturned, benches thrown down, and the whole school was turned loose an hour
before the usual time; bursting forth like a legion of young imps, yelping and
racketing about the green, in joy at their early emancipation.

The gallant Ichabod now spent at least an extra half hour at his toilet, brushing
and furbishing up his best, and indeed only suit of rusty black, and arranging his
looks by a bit of broken looking-glass, that hung up in the school-house. That he
might make his appearance before his mistress in the true style of a cavalier, he
borrowed a horse from the farmer with whom he was domiciliated, a choleric old
Dutchman, of the name of Hans Van Ripper, and, thus gallantly mounted, issued
forth, like a knight-errant in quest of adventures. But it is meet I should, in the
20 true spirit of romantic story, give some account of the looks and equipments of my
hero and his steed. The animal he bestrode was a broken-down plough-horse, that
had outlived almost every thing but his viciousness. He was gaunt and shagged,
with a ewe neck and a head like a hammer; his rusty mane and tail were tangled
and knotted with burrs; one eye had lost its pupil, and was glaring and spectral;
but the other had the gleam of a genuine devil in it. Still he must have had fire
and mettle in his day, if we may judge from the name he bore of Gunpowder. He
had, in fact, been a favorite steed of his master's, the choleric Van Ripper, who was
a furious rider, and had infused, very probably, some of his own spirit into the
animal; for, old and broken-down as he looked, there was more of the lurking devil
30 in him than in any young filly in the country.

Ichabod was a suitable figure for such a steed. He rode with short stirrups, which
brought his knees nearly up to the pommel of the saddle; his sharp elbows stuck
out like grasshoppers'; he carried his whip perpendicularly in his hand, like a
sceptre, and, as his horse jogged on, the motion of his arms was not unlike the
flapping of a pair of wings. A small wool hat rested on the top of his nose, for so
his scanty strip of forehead might be called; and the skirts of his black coat fluttered
out almost to the horse's tail. Such was the appearance of Ichabod and his steed, as
they shambled out of the gate of Hans Van Ripper, and it was altogether such an
apparition as is seldom to be met with in broad daylight.
40 It was, as I have said, a fine autumnal day, the sky was clear and serene, and nature wore that rich and golden livery which we always associate with the idea of
abundance. The forests had put on their sober brown and yellow, while some trees
of the tenderer kind had been nipped by the frosts into brilliant dyes of orange,
purple, and scarlet. Streaming files of wild ducks began to make their appearance

high in the air; the bark of the squirrel might be heard from the groves of beech
and hickory nuts, and the pensive whistle of the quail at intervals from the neighboring stubble-field.

The small birds were taking their farewell banquets. In the fulness of their revelry,
they fluttered, chirping and frolicking, from bush to bush, and tree to tree, capricious from the very profusion and variety around them. There was the honest cock-
robin, the favorite game of stripling sportsmen, with its loud querulous note; and
the twittering blackbirds flying in sable clouds; and the golden-winged woodpecker,
with his crimson crest, his broad black gorget, and splendid plumage; and the cedar
bird, with its red-tipt wings and yellow-tipt tail, and its little monteiro cap of 10
feathers; and the blue jay, that noisy coxcomb, in his gay light-blue coat and white
under-clothes; screaming and chattering, nodding and bobbing and bowing, and
pretending to be on good terms with every songster of the grove.

As Ichabod jogged slowly on his way, his eye, ever open to every symptom of
culinary abundance, ranged with delight over the treasures of jolly autumn. On all
sides he beheld vast store of apples; some hanging in oppressive opulence on the
trees; some gathered into baskets and barrels for the market; others heaped up in
rich piles for the cider-press. Farther on he beheld great fields of Indian corn, with
its golden ears peeping from their leafy coverts, and holding out the promise of
cakes and hasty pudding; and the yellow pumpkins lying beneath them, turning up 20
their fair round bellies to the sun, and giving ample prospects of the most luxurious
of pies; and anon he passed the fragrant buckwheat fields, breathing the odor of the
bee-hive, and as he beheld them, soft anticipation stole over his mind of dainty
slapjacks, well buttered, and garnished with honey or treacle, by the delicate little
dimpled hand of Katrina Van Tassel.

Thus feeding his mind with many sweet thoughts and "sugar suppositions," he
journeyed along the sides of a range of hills which look out upon some of
the goodliest scenes of the mighty Hudson. The sun gradually wheeled his broad
disk down into the west. The wide bosom of the Tappan Zee lay motionless and
glassy, excepting that here and there a gentle undulation waved and prolonged the 30
blue shadow of the distant mountain. A few amber clouds floated in the sky, without a breath of air to move them. The horizon was of a fine golden tint, changing
gradually into a pure apple green, and from that into the deep blue of the mid-
heaven. A slanting ray lingered on the woody crests of the precipices that overhung
some parts of the river, giving greater depth to the dark-gray and purple of their
rocky sides. A sloop was loitering in the distance, dropping slowly down with the
tide, her sail hanging uselessly against the mast; and as the reflection of the sky
gleamed along the still water, it seemed as if the vessel was suspended in the air.

It was toward evening that Ichabod arrived at the castle of the Heer Van Tassel,
which he found thronged with the pride and flower of the adjacent country. Old 40
farmers, a spare leathern-faced race, in homespun coats and breeches, blue stockings,
huge shoes, and magnificent pewter buckles. Their brisk withered little dames, in
close crimped caps, long-waisted short-gowns, homespun petticoats, with scissors

---

10 **monteiro cap,** a hunting-cap with a flap

and pincushions, and gay calico pockets hanging on the outside. Buxom lasses, almost as antiquated as their mothers, excepting where a straw hat, a fine ribbon or perhaps a white frock, gave symptoms of city innovation. The sons, in short square-skirted coats with rows of stupendous brass buttons, and their hair generally queued in the fashion of the times, especially if they could procure an eel-skin for the purpose, it being esteemed, throughout the country, as a potent nourisher and strengthener of the hair.

Brom Bones, however, was the hero of the scene, having come to the gathering on his favorite steed Daredevil, a creature, like himself, full of mettle and mischief,
10 and which no one but himself could manage. He was, in fact, noted for preferring vicious animals, given to all kinds of tricks, which kept the rider in constant risk of his neck, for he held a tractable well-broken horse as unworthy of a lad of spirit.

Fain would I pause to dwell upon the world of charms that burst upon the enraptured gaze of my hero, as he entered the state parlor of Van Tassel's mansion. Not those of the bevy of buxom lasses, with their luxurious display of red and white: but the ample charms of a genuine Dutch country tea-table, in the sumptuous time of autumn. Such heaped-up platters of cakes of various and almost indescribable kinds, known only to experienced Dutch housewives! There was the doughty doughnut, the tenderer oly koek, and the crisp and crumbling cruller; sweet cakes
20 and short cakes, ginger cakes and honey cakes, and the whole family of cakes. And then there were apple pies and peach pies and pumpkin pies; besides slices of ham and smoked beef; and moreover delectable dishes of preserved plums, and peaches, and pears, and quinces; not to mention broiled shad and roasted chickens; together with bowls of milk and cream, all mingled higgledy-piggledy, pretty much as I have enumerated them, with the motherly tea-pot sending up its clouds of vapor from the midst — Heaven bless the mark! I want breath and time to discuss this banquet as it deserves, and am too eager to get on with my story. Happily, Ichabod Crane was not in so great a hurry as his historian, but did ample justice to every dainty.

He was a kind and thankful creature, whose heart dilated in proportion as his
30 skin was filled with good cheer; and whose spirits rose with eating as some men's do with drink. He could not help, too, rolling his large eyes round him as he ate, and chuckling with the possibility that he might one day be lord of all this scene of almost unimaginable luxury and splendor. Then, he thought, how soon he'd turn his back upon the old school-house; snap his fingers in the face of Hans Van Ripper, and every other niggardly patron, and kick any itinerant pedagogue out of doors that should dare to call him comrade!

Old Baltus Van Tassel moved about among his guests with a face dilated with content and good humor, round and jolly as the harvest moon. His hospitable attentions were brief, but expressive, being confined to a shake of the hand, a slap
40 on the shoulder, a loud laugh, and a pressing invitation to "fall to, and help themselves."

And now the sound of the music from the common room or hall, summoned to

---

19 **doughnut . . . oly koek . . . cruller,** all of them fried in deep fat, but varying in composition. Oly koek, from the Dutch, is known chiefly in New York

the dance. The musician was an old grayheaded Negro, who had been the itinerant orchestra of the neighborhood for more than half a century. His instrument was as old and battered as himself. The greater part of the time he scraped on two or three strings, accompanying every movement of the bow with a motion of the head; bowing almost to the ground, and stamping with his foot whenever a fresh couple were to start.

Ichabod prided himself upon his dancing as much as upon his vocal powers. Not a limb, not a fibre about him was idle; and to have seen his loosely hung frame in full motion, and clattering about the room, you would have thought Saint Vitus himself, that blessed patron of the dance, was figuring before you in person. He 10 was the admiration of all the Negroes; who having gathered, of all ages and sizes, from the farm and the neighborhood, stood forming a pyramid of shining black faces at every door and window, gazing with delight at the scene, rolling their white eye-balls, and showing grinning rows of ivory from ear to ear. How could the flogger of urchins be otherwise than animated and joyous? the lady of his heart was his partner in the dance; and smiling graciously in reply to all his amorous oglings; while Brom Bones, sorely smitten with love and jealousy, sat brooding by himself in one corner.

When the dance was at an end, Ichabod was attracted to a knot of the sager folks, who, with old Van Tassel, sat smoking at one end of the piazza, gossiping over 20 former times, and drawing out long stories about the war.

This neighborhood, at the time of which I am speaking, was one of those highly-favored places which abound with chronicle and great men. The British and American line had run near it during the war; it had, therefore, been the scene of marauding, and infested with refugees, cow-boys, and all kinds of border chivalry. Just sufficient time had elapsed to enable each story-teller to dress up his tale with a little becoming fiction, and, in the indistinctness of his recollection, to make himself the hero of every exploit.

There was the story of Doffue Martling, a large blue bearded Dutchman, who had nearly taken a British frigate with an old iron nine-pounder from a mud breast- 30 work, only that his gun burst at the sixth discharge. And there was an old gentleman who shall be nameless, being too rich a mynheer to be lightly mentioned, who, in the battle of Whiteplains, being an excellent master of defence, parried a musket ball with a small sword, insomuch that he absolutely felt it whiz round the blade, and glance off at the hilt: in proof of which, he was ready at any time to show the sword, with the hilt a little bent. There were several more that had been equally great in the field, not one of whom but was persuaded that he had a considerable hand in bringing the war to a happy termination.

But all these were nothing to the tales of ghosts and apparitions that succeeded. The neighborhood is rich in legendary treasures of the kind. Local tales and super- 40 stitions thrive best in these sheltered long-settled retreats; but are trampled under

---

9 **Saint Vitus,** according to legend a Christian martyr of the third century, especially venerated in medieval Germany   25 **cow-boys,** bands of Tory guerrillas who operated near New York City during the Revolution

foot by the shifting throng that forms the population of most of our country places. Besides, there is no encouragement for ghosts in most of our villages, for they have scarcely had time to finish their first nap, and turn themselves in their graves, before their surviving friends have travelled away from the neighborhood; so that when they turn out at night to walk their rounds, they have no acquaintance left to call upon. This is perhaps the reason why we so seldom hear of ghosts except in our long-established Dutch communities.

The immediate cause, however, of the prevalence of supernatural stories in these parts, was doubtless owing to the vicinity of Sleepy Hollow. There was a contagion
10 in the very air that blew from that haunted region; it breathed forth an atmosphere of dreams and fancies infecting all the land. Several of the Sleepy Hollow people were present at Van Tassel's, and, as usual, were doling out their wild and wonderful legends. Many dismal tales were told about funeral trains, and mourning cries and wailings heard and seen about the great tree where the unfortunate Major André was taken, and which stood in the neighborhood. Some mention was made also of the woman in white, that haunted the dark glen at Raven Rock, and was often heard to shriek on winter nights before a storm, having perished there in the snow. The chief part of the stories, however, turned upon the favorite spectre of Sleepy Hollow, the headless horseman, who had been heard several times of late, patrolling
20 the country; and, it was said, tethered his horse nightly among the graves in the church-yard.

The sequestered situation of this church seems always to have made it a favorite haunt of troubled spirits. It stands on a knoll, surrounded by locust-trees and lofty elms, from among which its decent, whitewashed walls shine modestly forth, like Christian purity beaming through the shades of retirement. A gentle slope descends from it to a silver sheet of water, bordered by high trees, between which, peeps may be caught at the blue hills of the Hudson. To look upon its grass-grown yard, where the sunbeams seem to sleep so quietly, one would think that there at least the dead might rest in peace. On one side of the church extends a wide woody dell,
30 along which raves a large brook among broken rocks and trunks of fallen trees. Over a deep black part of the stream, not far from the church, was formerly thrown a wooden bridge; the road that led to it, and the bridge itself, were thickly shaded by overhanging trees, which cast a gloom about it, even in the daytime; but occasioned a fearful darkness at night. This was one of the favorite haunts of the headless horseman; and the place where he was most frequently encountered. The tale was told of old Brouwer, a most heretical disbeliever in ghosts, how he met the horseman returning from his foray into Sleepy Hollow, and was obliged to get up behind him; how they galloped over bush and brake, over hill and swamp, until they reached the bridge; when the horseman suddenly turned into a skeleton, threw old
40 Brouwer into the brook, and sprang away over the tree-tops with a clap of thunder.

This story was immediately matched by a thrice marvellous adventure of Brom

---

14 **Major André** (1751-1780), executed at Tappan, across the Hudson a few miles below Tarrytown, following his capture with the plans of West Point and evidence of the treason of Benedict Arnold. A monument now stands near the place of his capture at Tarrytown

Bones, who made light of the galloping Hessian as an arrant jockey. He affirmed that, on returning one night from the neighboring village of Sing Sing, he had been overtaken by this midnight trooper; that he had offered to race with him for a bowl of punch, and should have won it too, for Daredevil beat the goblin horse all hollow, but, just as they came to the church bridge, the Hessian bolted, and vanished in a flash of fire.

All these tales, told in that drowsy undertone with which men talk in the dark, the countenances of the listeners only now and then receiving a casual gleam from the glare of a pipe, sank deep in the mind of Ichabod. He repaid them in kind with large extracts from his invaluable author, Cotton Mather, and added many marvellous 10 events that had taken place in his native State of Connecticut, and fearful sights which he had seen in his nightly walks about Sleepy Hollow.

The revel now gradually broke up. The old farmers gathered together their families in their wagons, and were heard for some time rattling along the hollow roads, and over the distant hills. Some of the damsels mounted on pillions behind their favorite swains, and their light-hearted laughter, mingling with the clatter of hoofs, echoed along the silent woodlands, sounding fainter and fainter until they gradually died away — and the late scene of noise and frolic was all silent and deserted. Ichabod only lingered behind, according to the custom of country lovers, to have a tête-à-tête with the heiress; fully convinced that he was now on the high road to 20 success. What passed at this interview I will not pretend to say, for in fact I do not know. Something, however, I fear me, must have gone wrong, for he certainly sallied forth, after no very great interval, with an air quite desolate and chop-fallen. — Oh these women! these women! Could that girl have been playing off any of her coquettish tricks? — Was her encouragement of the poor pedagogue all a mere sham to secure her conquest of his rival? — Heaven only knows, not I! — Let it suffice to say, Ichabod stole forth with the air of one who had been sacking a henroost, rather than a fair lady's heart. Without looking to the right or left to notice the scene of rural wealth, on which he had so often gloated, he went straight to the stable, and with several hearty cuffs and kicks, roused his steed most uncour- 30 teously from the comfortable quarters in which he was soundly sleeping, dreaming of mountains of corn and oats, and whole valleys of timothy and clover.

It was the very witching time of night that Ichabod, heavy-hearted and crest-fallen, pursued his travel homewards, along the sides of the lofty hills which rise above Tarry Town, and which he had traversed so cheerily in the afternoon. The hour was as dismal as himself. Far below him, the Tappan Zee spread its dusky and indistinct waste of waters, with here and there the tall mast of a sloop, riding quietly at anchor under the land. In the dead hush of midnight, he could even hear the barking of the watch dog from the opposite shore of the Hudson; but it was so vague and faint as only to give an idea of his distance from this faithful companion 40 of man. Now and then, too, the long-drawn crowing of a cock, accidentally awakened, would sound far, far off, from some farmhouse away among the hills — but it was like a dreaming sound in his ear. No signs of life occurred near him, but occasionally the melancholy chirp of a cricket, or perhaps the guttural twang of a bull-frog, from a neighboring marsh, as if sleeping uncomfortably, and turning suddenly in his bed.

All the stories of ghosts and goblins that he had heard in the afternoon, now came crowding upon his recollection. The night grew darker and darker; the stars seemed to sink deeper in the sky, and driving clouds occasionally hid them from his sight. He had never felt so lonely and dismal. He was, moreover, approaching the very place where many of the scenes of the ghost stories had been laid. In the centre of the road stood an enormous tulip-tree, which towered like a giant above all the other trees of the neighborhood, and formed a kind of landmark. Its limbs were gnarled, and fantastic, large enough to form trunks for ordinary trees, twisting down almost to the earth, and rising again into the air. It was connected with the tragical story of the unfortunate André, who had been taken prisoner hard by; and was universally known by the name of Major André's tree. The common people regarded it with a mixture of respect and superstition, partly out of sympathy for the fate of its ill-starred namesake, and partly from the tales of strange sights and doleful lamentations told concerning it.

As Ichabod approached this fearful tree, he began to whistle; he thought his whistle was answered — it was but a blast sweeping sharply through the dry branches. As he approached a little nearer, he thought he saw something white, hanging in the midst of the tree — he paused and ceased whistling; but on looking more narrowly, perceived that it was a place where the tree had been scathed by lightning, and the white wood laid bare. Suddenly he heard a groan — his teeth chattered and his knees smote against the saddle: it was but the rubbing of one huge bough upon another, as they were swayed about by the breeze. He passed the tree in safety, but new perils lay before him.

About two hundred yards from the tree a small brook crossed the road, and ran into a marshy and thickly-wooded glen, known by the name of Wiley's swamp. A few rough logs, laid side by side, served for a bridge over this stream. On that side of the road where the brook entered the wood, a group of oaks and chestnuts, matted thick with wild grapevines, threw a cavernous gloom over it. To pass this bridge was the severest trial. It was at this identical spot that the unfortunate André was captured, and under the covert of those chestnuts and vines were the sturdy yeomen concealed who surprised him. This has ever since been considered a haunted stream, and fearful are the feelings of the schoolboy who has to pass it alone after dark.

As he approached the stream, his heart began to thump; he summoned up, however, all his resolution, gave his horse half a score of kicks in the ribs, and attempted to dash briskly across the bridge; but instead of starting forward, the perverse old animal made a lateral movement, and ran broadside against the fence. Ichabod, whose fears increased with the delay, jerked the reins on the other side, and kicked lustily with the contrary foot: it was all in vain; his steed started, it is true, but it was only to plunge to the opposite side of the road into a thicket of brambles and alder bushes. The schoolmaster now bestowed both whip and heel upon the starveling ribs of old Gunpowder, who dashed forward, snuffling and snorting, but came to a stand just by the bridge, with a suddenness that had nearly sent his rider sprawling over his head. Just at this moment a plashy tramp by the side of the bridge caught the sensitive ear of Ichabod. In the dark shadow of the grove, on the margin of the brook, he beheld something huge, misshapen, black and towering. It stirred not, but seemed gathered up in the gloom, like some gigantic monster ready to spring upon the traveller.

The hair of the affrighted pedagogue rose upon his head with terror. What was to be done? To turn and fly was now too late; and besides, what chance was there of escaping ghost or goblin, if such it was, which could ride upon the wings of the wind? Summoning up, therefore, a show of courage, he demanded in stammering accents — "Who are you?" He received no reply. He repeated his demand in a 10 still more agitated voice. Still there was no answer. Once more he cudgelled the sides of the inflexible Gunpowder, and, shutting his eyes, broke forth with involuntary fervor into a psalm tune. Just then the shadowy object of alarm put itself in motion, and, with a scramble and a bound, stood at once in the middle of the road. Though the night was dark and dismal, yet the form of the unknown might now in some degree be ascertained. He appeared to be a horseman of large dimensions, and mounted on a black horse of powerful frame. He made no offer of molestation or sociability, but kept aloof on one side of the road, jogging along on the blind side of old Gunpowder, who had now got over his fright and waywardness.

Ichabod, who had no relish for this strange midnight companion, and bethought 20 himself of the adventure of Brom Bones with the Galloping Hessian, now quickened his steed, in hopes of leaving him behind. The stranger, however, quickened his horse to an equal pace. Ichabod pulled up, and fell into a walk, thinking to lag behind — the other did the same. His heart began to sink within him; he endeavored to resume his psalm tune, but his parched tongue clove to the roof of his mouth, and he could not utter a stave. There was something in the moody and dogged silence of this pertinacious companion, that was mysterious and appalling. It was soon fearfully accounted for. On mounting a rising ground, which brought the figure of his fellow-traveller in relief against the sky, gigantic in height, and muffled in a cloak, Ichabod was horror-struck, on perceiving that he was headless! — but 30 his horror was still more increased, on observing that the head, which should have rested on his shoulders, was carried before him on the pommel of the saddle: his terror rose to desperation; he rained a shower of kicks and blows upon Gunpowder, hoping, by a sudden movement, to give his companion the slip — but the spectre started full jump with him. Away then they dashed, through thick and thin; stones flying, and sparks flashing at every bound. Ichabod's flimsy garments fluttered in the air, as he stretched his long lank body away over his horse's head, in the eagerness of his flight.

They had now reached the road which turns off to Sleepy Hollow; but Gunpowder, who seemed possessed with a demon, instead of keeping up it, made an opposite 40 turn, and plunged headlong down hill to the left. This road leads through a sandy hollow, shaded by trees for about a quarter of a mile, where it crosses the bridge famous in goblin story, and just beyond swells the green knoll on which stands the whitewashed church.

As yet the panic of the steed had given his unskilful rider an apparent advantage in the chase; but just as he had got half way through the hollow, the girths of the saddle gave way, and he felt it slipping from under him. He seized it by the pommel, and endeavored to hold it firm, but in vain; and had just time to save himself by clasping old Gunpowder round the neck, when the saddle fell to the earth, and he heard it trampled under foot by his pursuer. For a moment the terror of Hans Van Ripper's wrath passed across his mind — for it was his Sunday saddle; but this was no time for petty fears; the goblin was hard on his haunches; and (unskilful rider that he was!) he had much ado to maintain his seat; sometimes slipping on 10 one side, sometimes on another, and sometimes jolted on the high ridge of his horse's backbone, with a violence that he verily feared would cleave him asunder.

An opening in the trees now cheered him with the hopes that the church bridge was at hand. The wavering reflection of a silver star in the bosom of the brook told him that he was not mistaken. He saw the walls of the church dimly glaring under the trees beyond. He recollected the place where Brom Bones's ghostly competitor had disappeared. "If I can but reach that bridge," thought Ichabod, "I am safe." Just then he heard the black steed panting and blowing close behind him; he even fancied that he felt his hot breath. Another convulsive kick in the ribs, and old Gunpowder sprang upon the bridge; he thundered over the resounding planks; he 20 gained the opposite side; and now Ichabod cast a look behind to see if his pursuer should vanish, according to rule, in a flash of fire and brimstone. Just then he saw the goblin rising in his stirrups, and in the very act of hurling his head at him. Ichabod endeavored to dodge the horrible missile, but too late. It encountered his cranium with a tremendous crash — he was tumbled headlong into the dust, and Gunpowder, the black steed, and the goblin rider, passed by like a whirlwind.

The next morning the old horse was found without his saddle, and with the bridle under his feet, soberly cropping the grass at his master's gate. Ichabod did not make his appearance at breakfast — dinner-hour came, but no Ichabod. The boys assembled at the school-house, and strolled idly about the banks of the brook; but no 30 schoolmaster. Hans Van Ripper now began to feel some uneasiness about the fate of poor Ichabod, and his saddle. An inquiry was set on foot, and after diligent investigation they came upon his traces. In one part of the road leading to the church was found the saddle trampled in the dirt; the tracks of horses' hoofs deeply dented in the road, and evidently at furious speed, were traced to the bridge, beyond which, on the bank of a broad part of the brook, where the water ran deep and black, was found the hat of the unfortunate Ichabod, and close beside it a shattered pumpkin.

The brook was searched, but the body of the schoolmaster was not to be discovered. Hans Van Ripper, as executor of his estate, examined the bundle which contained all his worldly effects. They consisted of two shirts and a half; two stocks for the 40 neck; a pair or two of worsted stockings; an old pair of corduroy small-clothes; a rusty razor; a book of psalm tunes, full of dogs' ears; and a broken pitchpipe. As to the books and furniture of the school-house, they belonged to the community, excepting Cotton Mather's History of Witchcraft, a New England Almanac, and a book of dreams and fortunetelling; in which last was a sheet of foolscap much scribbled and blotted in several fruitless attempts to make a copy of verses in honor of the heiress of Van Tassel. These magic books and the poetic scrawl were forthwith consigned to the flames by Hans Van Ripper; who from that time forward determined to send his children no more to school; observing, that he never knew any good come of this same reading and writing. Whatever money the schoolmaster possessed, and he had received his quarter's pay but a day or two before, he must have had about his person at the time of his disappearance.

The mysterious event caused much speculation at the church on the following Sunday. Knots of gazers and gossips were collected in the churchyard, at the bridge, and at the spot where the hat and pumpkin had been found. The stories of Brouwer, 10 of Bones, and a whole budget of others, were called to mind; and when they had diligently considered them all, and compared them with the symptoms of the present case, they shook their heads, and came to the conclusion that Ichabod had been carried off by the galloping Hessian. As he was a bachelor, and in nobody's debt, nobody troubled his head any more about him. The school was removed to a different quarter of the hollow, and another pedagogue reigned in his stead.

It is true, an old farmer, who had been down to New-York on a visit several years after, and from whom this account of the ghostly adventure was received, brought home the intelligence that Ichabod Crane was still alive; that he had left the neighborhood, partly through fear of the goblin and Hans Van Ripper, and partly 20 in mortification at having been suddenly dismissed by the heiress; that he had changed his quarters to a distant part of the country; had kept school and studied law at the same time, had been admitted to the bar, turned politician, electioneered, written for the newspapers, and finally had been made a justice of the Ten Pound Court. Brom Bones too, who, shortly after his rival's disappearance, conducted the blooming Katrina in triumph to the altar, was observed to look exceedingly knowing whenever the story of Ichabod was related, and always burst into a hearty laugh at the mention of the pumpkin; which led some to suspect that he knew more about the matter than he chose to tell.

The old country wives, however, who are the best judges of these matters, main- 30 tain to this day that Ichabod was spirited away by supernatural means; and it is a favorite story often told about the neighborhood round the winter evening fire. The bridge became more than ever an object of superstitious awe, and that may be the reason why the road has been altered of late years, so as to approach the church by the border of the millpond. The school-house being deserted, soon fell to decay, and was reported to be haunted by the ghost of the unfortunate pedagogue; and the plough boy, loitering homeward of a still summer evening, has often fancied his voice at a distance, chanting a melancholy psalm tune among the tranquil solitudes of Sleepy Hollow.

Postscript, Found in the Handwriting of Mr. Knickerbocker   40

The preceding Tale is given, almost in the precise words in which I heard it related at a Corporation meeting of the ancient city of Manhattoes, at which were present

---

24 **Ten Pound Court,** in which cases involving not more than ten pounds were tried by a justice

many of its sagest and most illustrious burghers. The narrator was a pleasant, shabby, gentlemanly old fellow, in pepper-and-salt clothes, with a sadly humorous face; and one whom I strongly suspected of being poor, — he made such efforts to be entertaining. When his story was concluded, there was much laughter and approbation, particularly from two or three deputy aldermen, who had been asleep the greater part of the time. There was, however, one tall, dry-looking old gentleman, with beetling eyebrows, who maintained a grave and rather severe face throughout: now and then folding his arms, inclining his head, and looking down upon the floor, as if turning a doubt over in his mind. He was one of your wary men, who never laugh,
10 but upon good grounds — when they have reason and the law on their side. When the mirth of the rest of the company had subsided, and silence was restored, he leaned one arm on the elbow of his chair, and sticking the other akimbo, demanded, with a slight, but exceedingly sage motion of the head, and contraction of the brow, what was the moral of the story, and what it went to prove?

The story-teller, who was just putting a glass of wine to his lips, as a refreshment after his toils, paused for a moment, looked at his inquirer with an air of infinite deference, and, lowering the glass slowly to the table, observed, that the story was intended most logically to prove: —

"That there is no situation in life but has its advantages and pleasures — provided
20 we will but take a joke as we find it:

"That, therefore, he that runs races with goblin troopers is likely to have rough riding of it.

"Ergo, for a country schoolmaster to be refused the hand of a Dutch heiress, is a certain step to high preferment, in the state."

The cautious old gentleman knit his brows tenfold closer after this explanation, being sorely puzzled by the ratiocination of the syllogism; while, methought, the one in pepper-and-salt eyed him with something of a triumphant leer. At length he observed, that all this was very well, but still he thought the story a little on the extravagant — there were one or two points on which he had his doubts.
30 "Faith, sir," replied the story-teller, "as to that matter, I don't believe one-half of it myself."

D. K.   1818, 1820

Adventure of the German Student

During his long residence abroad Irving returned occasionally in his imagination to Dutch New York and Diedrich Knickerbocker, most notably in "Dolph Heyliger" in Bracebridge Hall *and in "The Devil and Tom Walker" in* Tales of a Traveller. *His taste for the picturesque and his mastery of the tale relying for success upon suspense and sensation are best exemplified, however, in those stories which have their setting in Europe. Although briefer than most, "Adventure of the German Student" is an excellent example of the work which followed* The Sketch Book.

On a stormy night, in the tempestuous times of the French revolution, a young German was returning to his lodgings, at a late hour, across the old part of Paris. The lightning gleamed, and the loud claps of thunder rattled through the lofty streets — but I should first tell you something about this young German.

Gottfried Wolfgang was a young man of good family. He had studied for some time at Göttingen, but being of a visionary and enthusiastic character, he had wandered into those wild and speculative doctrines which have so often bewildered German students. His secluded life, his intense application, and the singular nature of his studies, had an effect on both mind and body. His health was impaired; his imagination diseased. He had been indulging in fanciful speculations on spiritual 10 essences, until, like Swedenborg, he had an ideal world of his own around him. He took up a notion, I do not know from what cause, that there was an evil influence hanging over him; an evil genius or spirit seeking to ensnare him and ensure his perdition. Such an idea working on his melancholy temperament, produced the most gloomy effects. He became haggard and desponding. His friends discovered the mental malady preying upon him, and determined that the best cure was a change of scene; he was sent, therefore, to finish his studies amid the splendors and gayeties of Paris.

Wolfgang arrived at Paris at the breaking out of the revolution. The popular delirium at first caught his enthusiastic mind, and he was captivated by the political 20 and philosophical theories of the day: but the scenes of blood which followed shocked his sensitive nature, disgusted him with society and the world, and made him more than ever a recluse. He shut himself up in a solitary apartment in the *Pays Latin,* the quarter of the students. There, in a gloomy street not far from the monastic walls of the Sorbonne, he pursued his favorite speculations. Sometimes he spent hours together in the great libraries of Paris, those catacombs of departed authors, rummaging among their hoards of dusty and obsolete works in quest of food for his unhealthy appetite. He was, in a manner, a literary ghoul, feeding in the charnel-house of decayed literature.

Wolfgang, though solitary and recluse, was of an ardent temperament, but for a 30 time it operated merely upon his imagination. He was too shy and ignorant of the world to make any advances to the fair, but he was a passionate admirer of female beauty, and in his lonely chamber would often lose himself in reveries on forms and faces which he had seen, and his fancy would deck out images of loveliness far surpassing the reality.

While his mind was in this excited and sublimated state, a dream produced an extraordinary effect upon him. It was of a female face of transcendent beauty. So strong was the impression made, that he dreamt of it again and again. It haunted his thoughts by day, his slumbers by night; in fine, he became passionately enamoured of this shadow of a dream. This lasted so long that it became one of those 40

----

6 **Göttingen,** a town in Hanover, West Germany. Its university was founded in 1734   11 **Swedenborg,** Emanuel Swedenborg (1688-1772), Swedish mystic and theologian   24 **Pays Latin,** the Latin Quarter, on the south bank of the Seine, for centuries inhabited by students and artists

fixed ideas which haunt the minds of melancholy men, and are at times mistaken for madness.

Such was Gottfried Wolfgang, and such his situation at the time I mentioned. He was returning home late one stormy night, through some of the old and gloomy streets of the *Marais,* the ancient part of Paris. The loud claps of thunder rattled among the high houses of the narrow streets. He came to the Place de Grève, the square where public executions are performed. The lightning quivered about the pinnacles of the ancient Hotel de Ville, and shed flickering gleams over the open space in front. As Wolfgang was crossing the square, he shrank back with horror
10 at finding himself close by the guillotine. It was the height of the reign of terror, when this dreadful instrument of death stood ever ready, and its scaffold was continually running with the blood of the virtuous and the brave. It had that very day been actively employed in the work of carnage, and there it stood in grim array, amidst a silent and sleeping city, waiting for fresh victims.

Wolfgang's heart sickened within him, and he was turning shuddering from the horrible engine, when he beheld a shadowy form, cowering as it were at the foot of the steps which led up to the scaffold. A succession of vivid flashes of lightning revealed it more distinctly. It was a female figure, dressed in black. She was seated on one of the lower steps of the scaffold, leaning forward, her face hid in her lap;
20 and her long dishevelled tresses hanging to the ground, streaming with the rain which fell in torrents. Wolfgang paused. There was something awful in this solitary monument of woe. The female had the appearance of being above the common order. He knew the times to be full of vicissitude, and that many a fair head, which had once been pillowed on down, now wandered houseless. Perhaps this was some poor mourner whom the dreadful axe had rendered desolate, and who sat here heartbroken on the strand of existence, from which all that was dear to her had been launched into eternity.

He approached, and addressed her in the accents of sympathy. She raised her head and gazed wildly at him. What was his astonishment at beholding, by the bright
30 glare of the lightning, the very face which had haunted him in his dreams. It was pale and disconsolate, but ravishingly beautiful.

Trembling with violent and conflicting emotions, Wolfgang again accosted her. He spoke something of her being exposed at such an hour of the night, and to the fury of such a storm, and offered to conduct her to her friends. She pointed to the guillotine with a gesture of dreadful significance.

"I have no friend on earth!" said she.

"But you have a home," said Wolfgang.

"Yes — in the grave!"

The heart of the student melted at the words.
40 "If a stranger dare make an offer," said he, "without danger of being misunderstood, I would offer my humble dwelling as a shelter; myself as a devoted friend. I am friendless myself in Paris, and a stranger in the land; but if my life could be of service, it is at your disposal, and should be sacrificed before harm or indignity should come to you."

There was an honest earnestness in the young man's manner that had its effect. His foreign accent, too, was in his favor; it showed him not to be a hackneyed inhabitant of Paris. Indeed, there is an eloquence in true enthusiasm that is not to be doubted. The homeless stranger confided herself implicitly to the protection of the student.

He supported her faltering steps across the Pont Neuf, and by the place where the statue of Henry the Fourth had been overthrown by the populace. The storm had abated, and the thunder rumbled at a distance. All Paris was quiet; that great volcano of human passion slumbered for a while, to gather fresh strength for the next day's eruption. The student conducted his charge through the ancient streets 10 of the *Pays Latin,* and by the dusky walls of the Sorbonne, to the great dingy hotel which he inhabited. The old portress who admitted them stared with surprise at the unusual sight of the melancholy Wolfgang with a female companion.

On entering his apartment, the student, for the first time, blushed at the scantiness and indifference of his dwelling. He had but one chamber — an old-fashioned saloon — heavily carved, and fantastically furnished with the remains of former magnificence, for it was one of those hotels in the quarter of the Luxembourg palace, which had once belonged to nobility. It was lumbered with books and papers, and all the usual apparatus of a student, and his bed stood in a recess at one end.

When lights were brought, and Wolfgang had a better opportunity of contem- 20 plating the stranger, he was more than ever intoxicated by her beauty. Her face was pale, but of a dazzling fairness, set off by a profusion of raven hair that hung clustering about it. Her eyes were large and brilliant, with a singular expression approaching almost to wildness. As far as her black dress permitted her shape to be seen, it was of perfect symmetry. Her whole appearance was highly striking, though she was dressed in the simplest style. The only thing approaching to an ornament which she wore, was a broad black band round her neck, clasped by diamonds.

The perplexity now commenced with the student how to dispose of the helpless being thus thrown upon his protection. He thought of abandoning his chamber to her, and seeking shelter for himself elsewhere. Still, he was so fascinated by her 30 charms, there seemed to be such a spell upon his thoughts and senses, that he could not tear himself from her presence. Her manner, too, was singular and unaccountable. She spoke no more of the guillotine. Her grief had abated. The attentions of the student had first won her confidence, and then, apparently, her heart. She was evidently an enthusiast like himself, and enthusiasts soon understand each other.

In the infatuation of the moment, Wolfgang avowed his passion for her. He told her the story of his mysterious dream, and how she had possessed his heart before he had ever seen her. She was strangely affected by his recital, and acknowledged to have felt an impulse towards him equally unaccountable. It was the time for wild theory and wild actions. Old prejudices and superstitions were done away; every- 40 thing was under the sway of the "Goddess of Reason." Among other rubbish of the old times, the forms and ceremonies of marriage began to be considered superfluous bonds for honorable minds. Social compacts were the vogue. Wolfgang was too much of a theorist not to be tainted by the liberal doctrines of the day.

"Why should we separate?" said he: "our hearts are united; in the eye of reason and honor we are as one. What need is there of sordid forms to bind high souls together?"

The stranger listened with emotion; she had evidently received illumination at the same school.

"You have no home nor family," continued he: "let me be everything to you, or rather let us be everything to one another. If form is necessary, form shall be observed — there is my hand. I pledge myself to you forever."

"Forever?" said the stranger, solemnly.

"Forever!" replied Wolfgang.

The stranger clasped the hand extended to her: "Then I am yours," murmured she, and sank upon his bosom.

The next morning the student left his bride sleeping, and sallied forth at an early hour to seek more spacious apartments suitable to the change in his situation. When he returned, he found the stranger lying with her head hanging over the bed, and one arm thrown over it. He spoke to her, but received no reply. He advanced to awaken her from her uneasy posture. On taking her hand, it was cold — there was no pulsation — her face was pallid and ghastly. In a word, she was a corpse.

Horrified and frantic, he alarmed the house. A scene of confusion ensued. The police was summoned. As the officer of police entered the room, he started back on beholding the corpse.

"Great heaven!" cried he, "how did this woman come here?"

"Do you know anything about her?" said Wolfgang eagerly.

"Do I?" exclaimed the officer: "she was guillotined yesterday."

He stepped forward; undid the black collar round the neck of the corpse, and the head rolled on the floor!

The student burst into a frenzy. "The fiend! the fiend has gained possession of me!" shrieked he: "I am lost forever."

They tried to soothe him, but in vain. He was possessed with the frightful belief that an evil spirit had reanimated the dead body to ensnare him. He went distracted, and died in a mad-house.

Here the old gentleman with the haunted head finished his narrative.

"And is this really a fact?" said the inquisitive gentleman.

"A fact not to be doubted," replied the other. "I had it from the best authority. The student told it me himself. I saw him in a mad-house in Paris."

1824

1794–1878 William Cullen Bryant

When William Cullen Bryant was born, during Washington's second term as President, there were fifteen states in the Union, with Kentucky the only one west of the Alleghenies. When Bryant died, twenty-two of the thirty-eight states were "western," and the first transcontinental railroad had been in operation for nearly a decade. In this period of unparalleled expansion, Bryant, as a public-spirited citizen and the editor of an influential newspaper, had a conspicuous place and would be remembered even had he not written poetry. Sober, dignified, earnest in urging principles and policies in which he believed, he was recognized as a great liberal, and it is likely that he will command respect from each succeeding generation of Americans.

As a poet, Bryant has suffered from being called the American Wordsworth, or a belated representative of New England Puritanism, or a cold child of the eighteenth century, only slightly affected by the warming influences of the Romantic movement. That there is some justice in each of these judgments cannot be denied, but Bryant may be better understood against the background of American expansion. His love of nature was typical of an age which was discovering the wildness and variety of American scenery; his moral earnestness was shared by the vast majority of his countrymen, although few of them, perhaps, were as untouched by denominational bigotry; and his conservative tastes in the arts were in large part the result of the uncertain groping of his generation toward standards and traditions. In Bryant's poetry, moreover, we can observe the two magnetic poles of his time: the past, Europe, and the idea of continuity on the one hand; and on the other the future, the manifest destiny of America, and the hope of a more perfect world.

Bryant was born at Cummington, in western Massachusetts, November 3, 1794. Brought up in a Calvinistic and Federalist environment, he took himself and the world very seriously as soon as he knew anything about them. His first verses appeared in a newspaper when he was ten, and he saw his first book in print five years later, when his father arranged for the publication of The Embargo, an attack on Jefferson's methods of avoiding entanglement in the Napoleonic conflict. He had only one year of college, at Williams, and then, because there was no livelihood in poetry, he turned to the study of law. Admitted to the bar in 1814, he practiced in several Massachusetts towns with moderate success, occasionally using his leisure for composing poems. After 1817, when his father sent some of his poems to a Boston friend and "Thanatopsis" came out in the *North American Review,* he became known as poet and reviewer for that periodical and others. In 1821 he married Fanny Fairchild, the "fairest of the rural maids"; theirs was an unusually happy marriage. During a visit to Boston in that same year, to read "The Ages" before the Phi Beta Kappa society at Harvard, Bryant arranged for the first collection of his poems, a thin volume of only eight pieces. It remains a landmark in American literary history.

Then, in 1825, Bryant had the courage to give up the law for the uncertainties of a literary life and deserted Massachusetts for New York City. Within a few months he formed a connection with the *Evening Post,* a daily newspaper which had been founded by Alexander Hamilton; in 1829 he became its editor-in-chief. Thereafter until his death in 1878 he was first of all the editor of the *Evening Post;* as a part owner he grew wealthy and was able to afford much European travel for himself and his family, as well as to establish a comfortable home at Roslyn on Long Island. His liberalism was most marked in his lifelong devotion to free trade; it may also be followed in his treatment of both national and local politics. In editorials, travel letters, and public discourses he persistently and fearlessly spoke out for what he regarded the best interests of the American people, upholding the right of working-men to organize, the abolition of slavery, and the rejected plans of Lincoln and Johnson for reconstruction of the South. He performed many public services, having a part in the establishment of New York City's Central Park and Metropolitan Museum of Art, and close connections with the National Academy of Design.

Busy as he was, Bryant continued to write poetry throughout his life, although not in great quantity. After 1821, the chief editions of his poems were those of 1832, 1836, 1847, 1854, 1871, and 1876. Other volumes of importance included *The Fountain and Other Poems* (1842), *The White Footed Deer and Other Poems* (1844), and *Thirty Poems* (1864). He also translated the *Iliad* and the *Odyssey* and published three volumes of travel letters as well as numerous commemorative discourses.

Bryant's poetry, although apparently simple, presents some very complicated problems, inadequately suggested by the familiar terms "classical" and "romantic." Lowell's famous description in *A Fable for Critics* (". . . Bryant, as quiet, as cool, and as dignified, / As a smooth, silent iceberg, that never is ignified") hints at the "classic" qualities of Bryant: his concern for form and clarity, harmony and serenity. That Bryant owed much to such English poets as James Thomson and William Cowper is clear. Yet his poetic theories and, more particularly, his themes — the past, death, freedom, nature — have much in them that is ordinarily called "romantic." Thoughtful consideration of his work will show how largely a matter of degree is the distinction between the classical and the romantic, and, for most readers, will bring respect for the mind of a man who was much more than a transition figure.

The Life and Works of William Cullen Bryant, ed. Parke Godwin, 6 vols., New York, 1883-1884   William Cullen Bryant: Representative Selections, ed. Tremaine McDowell, Cincinnati, 1935   Prose Writings, New York, 1964   W. A. Bradley, William Cullen Bryant, English Men of Letters Series, New York, 1905   H. H. Peckham, Gotham Yankee, A Biography of William Cullen Bryant, New York, 1951   G. W. Arms, Fields Were Green, Stanford, 1953   C. S. Johnson, Politics and a Belly-full, New York, 1962

Thanatopsis

Bryant's best-known poem, "Thanatopsis" (meaning "view of death"), probably written about 1815, when he was about twenty. A year later, without his knowledge, his father sent it and other pieces to the North American Review. *The story goes that Richard Henry Dana, later one of Bryant's closest friends, remarked on seeing the manuscript that no one in America was capable of writing such verses. Thinking that another poem on death, consisting of four stanzas in iambic tetrameter rhyming* abab, *was a part of "Thanatopsis," the editors of the* North American *published both under one title in the issue for September 1817. When Bryant prepared the* Poems *of 1821, he added lines 1-17 (to "Yet a few days") as an introduction, and sixteen lines at the end (beginning with "As the long train").*

The poem should be read in the light of both literary tradition and Bryant's own religious background. From the English poets (notably Henry Kirke White, Robert Blair, Bishop Beilby Porteus, Robert Southey, and William Cowper) he learned of the possibilities of blank verse and the themes of the "graveyard school" of writers. Even had he not read these poets, however, he would have had, from his Puritan background, a predilection for the funereal. Note, however, that Bryant's concept of Man's long sleep is more Stoic than Christian, with no hint of the resurrection or immortality of the soul.

To him who in the love of Nature holds
Communion with her visible forms, she speaks
A various language; for his gayer hours
She has a voice of gladness, and a smile
And eloquence of beauty, and she glides
Into his darker musings, with a mild
And healing sympathy, that steals away
Their sharpness, ere he is aware. When thoughts
Of the last bitter hour come like a blight
Over thy spirit, and sad images   10
Of the stern agony, and shroud, and pall,
And breathless darkness, and the narrow house,
Make thee to shudder, and grow sick at heart; —
Go forth, under the open sky, and list
To Nature's teachings, while from all around —
Earth and her waters, and the depths of air —
Comes a still voice — Yet a few days, and thee
The all-beholding sun shall see no more
In all his course; nor yet in the cold ground,
Where thy pale form was laid, with many tears,   20
Nor in the embrace of ocean, shall exist
Thy image. Earth, that nourished thee, shall claim

Text: here, as in the poems which follow, the 1876 edition

Thy growth, to be resolved to earth again,
And, lost each human trace, surrendering up
Thine individual being, shalt thou go
To mix for ever with the elements,
To be a brother to the insensible rock
And to the sluggish clod, which the rude swain
Turns with his share, and treads upon. The oak
Shall send his roots abroad, and pierce thy mould.   30

   Yet not to thine eternal resting-place
Shalt thou retire alone, nor couldst thou wish
Couch more magnificent. Thou shalt lie down
With patriarchs of the infant world — with kings,
The powerful of the earth — the wise, the good,
Fair forms, and hoary seers of ages past,
All in one mighty sepulchre. The hills
Rock-ribbed and ancient as the sun, — the vales
Stretching in pensive quietness between;
The venerable woods — rivers that move   40
In majesty, and the complaining brooks
That make the meadows green; and, poured round all,
Old Ocean's gray and melancholy waste, —
Are but the solemn decorations all
Of the great tomb of man. The golden sun,
The planets, all the infinite host of heaven,
Are shining on the sad abodes of death,
Through the still lapse of ages. All that tread
The globe are but a handful to the tribes
That slumber in its bosom. — Take the wings   50
Of morning, pierce the Barcan wilderness,
Or lose thyself in the continuous woods
Where rolls the Oregon, and hears no sound,
Save his own dashings — yet the dead are there:
And millions in those solitudes, since first
The flight of years began, have laid them down
In their last sleep — the dead reign there alone.
So shalt thou rest, and what if thou withdraw
In silence from the living, and no friend

---

51 **pierce . . . wilderness.** *North American:* and the Borean desert pierce; 1821, 1832, 1847: and the Barcan desert pierce; 1854: traverse Barca's desert sands; present reading, 1871. Borean refers to the area just below the Arctic. Barca is the ancient name of that part of Libya east of Tripoli, its capital being Bengazi. Bryant seems to have had the idea common in his time, that there was a Sahara-like desert west of the Mississippi   53 **Where . . . and.** *NA:* That veil Oregon, where he; 1821: Where rolls the Oregon, and. The Oregon is Bryant's name for the Columbia River   58 **withdraw.** *NA,* 1821, 1832: shalt fall   59 **In silence from.** *NA,* 1821: Unnoticed by; 1832, 1847: unheeded by

Take note of thy departure? All that breathe   60
Will share thy destiny. The gay will laugh
When thou art gone, the solemn brood of care
Plod on, and each one as before will chase
His favorite phantom; yet all these shall leave
Their mirth and their employments, and shall come
And make their bed with thee. As the long train
Of ages glide away, the sons of men,
The youth in life's green spring, and he who goes
In the full strength of years, matron and maid,
The speechless babe, and the gray-headed man —   70
Shall one by one be gathered to thy side,
By those, who in their turn shall follow them.
   So live, that when thy summons comes to join
The innumerable caravan, which moves
To that mysterious realm, where each shall take
His chamber in the silent halls of death,
Thou go not, like the quarry-slave at night,
Scourged to his dungeon, but, sustained and soothed
By an unfaltering trust, approach thy grave,
Like one who wraps the drapery of his couch   80
About him, and lies down to pleasant dreams.
                                            1815?, 1817, 1821

60 **All that breathe.** *NA:* Thousands more   61 **The gay . . . care.** *NA:* the tittering world. Dance to
the grave. The busy brood of care.   63 **as . . . chase.** *NA:* chases as before   70 **The speechless . . .
man —.** 1821: the bow'd with age, the infant in the smiles; 1832, 1847, 1854: And the sweet babe, and the
gray-headed man   74 **which.** 1821, 1832, 1847: that   75 **that mysterious realm.** 1821: the pale realms
of shade

Inscription for the Entrance to a Wood

Nowhere, perhaps, does Bryant express more happily the romantic view of nature than in "A
Fragment," which first appeared in the North American Review *for September 1817 with*
"Thanatopsis." In the Poems *of 1821 it was entitled "Inscription for the Entrance into a*
Wood." Note that nature is a joy and a solace to man, not, as the post-Darwinians tell us,
an arena for the struggle to survive.

   Stranger, if thou hast learned a truth which needs
No school of long experience, that the world
Is full of guilt and misery, and hast seen
Enough of all its sorrows, crimes, and cares,
To tire thee of it, enter this wild wood

1 **learned.** Until 1847: learnt   2 **No . . . experience.** Until 1832: Experience more than reason   3
seen. Until 1832: known

And view the haunts of Nature. The calm shade
Shall bring a kindred calm, and the sweet breeze
That makes the green leaves dance, shall waft a balm
To thy sick heart. Thou wilt find nothing here
Of all that pained thee in the haunts of men,   10
And made thee loathe thy life. The primal curse
Fell, it is true, upon the unsinning earth,
But not in vengeance. God hath yoked to guilt
Her pale tormentor, misery. Hence, these shades
Are still the abodes of gladness; the thick roof
Of green and stirring branches is alive
And musical with birds, that sing and sport
In wantonness of spirit; while below
The squirrel, with raised paws and form erect,
Chirps merrily. Throngs of insects in the shade   20
Try their thin wings and dance in the warm beam
That waked them into life. Even the green trees
Partake the deep contentment; as they bend
To the soft winds, the sun from the blue sky
Looks in and sheds a blessing on the scene.
Scarce less the cleft-born wild-flower seems to enjoy
Existence, than the wingèd plunderer
That sucks its sweets. The mossy rocks themselves,
And the old and ponderous trunks of prostrate trees
That lead from knoll to knoll a causey rude   30
Or bridge the sunken brook, and their dark roots,
With all their earth upon them, twisting high,
Breathe fixed tranquillity. The rivulet
Sends forth glad sounds, and tripping o'er its bed
Of pebbly sands, or leaping down the rocks,
Seems, with continuous laughter, to rejoice

---

7 **kindred.** 1817: kinder   9 **Thou . . . here.** 1817: Here thou wilt nothing find   13 **God . . . life.**
1817:   Misery is wed
   To guilt. Hence in these shades we still behold
   The abodes of gladness, here from tree to tree
   And through the rustling branches flit the birds
   In wantonness of spirit; — theirs are strains
   Of no dissembled rapture — while below
   The squirrel with rais'd paws and form erect
   Chirps merrily. In the warm glade the throngs
   Of dancing insects sport in the mild beam
   That wak'd them into life.
1821:   Misery is wed
   To guilt. And hence the shades are still the abodes
   Of undissembled gladness; the thick roof . . .
which is followed by the present version except for the use of "glade" instead of "shade" in line 20. By
1832 Bryant had come to the present reading   25 **Looks.** 1817: peeps   28 **mossy.** Until 1854:
massy   30 **causey.** 1817: causeway   31 **brook.** 1817: stream

In its own being. Softly tread the marge,
Lest from her midway perch thou scare the wren
That dips her bill in water. The cool wind,
That stirs the stream in play, shall come to thee,   40
Like one that loves thee nor will let thee pass
Ungreeted, and shall give its light embrace.
_____   1817

39 **in water.** The 1817 version ends with these words

To a Waterfowl

This poem, which Matthew Arnold believed the finest of its length in the English language,
was composed by Bryant after a walk from Cummington to Plainfield, Massachusetts, in
December 1815. It was first published in the North American Review *for March 1818*
and collected in the Poems *of 1821. The clarity of the central image and the aptness and*
simplicity of the moral analogy have always been admired, even by those who dislike "preach-
ing" in poetry. The effect of the stanza form has been described as "gliding," appropriate to
the visual image of the second stanza.

    Whither, midst falling dew,
While glow the heavens with the last steps of day,
Far, through their rosy depths, dost thou pursue
    Thy solitary way?

    Vainly the fowler's eye
Might mark thy distant flight to do thee wrong,
As, darkly seen against the crimson sky,
    Thy figure floats along.

    Seek'st thou the plashy brink
Of weedy lake, or marge of river wide,   10
Or where the rocking billows rise and sink
    On the chafed ocean-side?

    There is a Power whose care
Teaches thy way along that pathless coast —
The desert and illimitable air —
    Lone wandering, but not lost.

    All day thy wings have fanned,
At that far height, the cold, thin atmosphere,
Yet stoop not, weary, to the welcome land,
    Though the dark night is near.   20

And soon that toil shall end;
Soon shalt thou find a summer home, and rest,
And scream among thy fellows; reeds shall bend,
    Soon, o'er thy sheltered nest.

Thou'rt gone, the abyss of heaven
Hath swallowed up thy form; yet, on my heart
Deeply hath sunk the lesson thou hast given,
    And shall not soon depart.

He who, from zone to zone,
Guides through the boundless sky thy certain flight, 30
In the long way that I must tread alone,
    Will lead my steps aright.

                    1815, 1818

Forest Hymn

"A Hymn" first appeared in the United States Literary Gazette *for April 1, 1825, over the signature of "B." It was reprinted as "Forest Hymn" in the* Poems *of 1832. Except for minor changes in capitalization, punctuation, and spelling, Bryant left the poem pretty well alone down through the years. Thought to have been composed at Great Barrington early in 1825, it has always been praised for the simplicity and sincerity of its quiet love of the revelation of God in external nature.*

The groves were God's first temples. Ere man learned
To hew the shaft, and lay the architrave,
And spread the roof above them — ere he framed
The lofty vault, to gather and roll back
The sound of anthems; in the darkling wood,
Amid the cool and silence, he knelt down,
And offered to the Mightiest solemn thanks
And supplication. For his simple heart
Might not resist the sacred influences
Which, from the stilly twilight of the place,   10
And from the gray old trunks that high in heaven
Mingled their mossy boughs, and from the sound
Of the invisible breath that swayed at once
All their green tops, stole over him, and bowed
His spirit with the thought of boundless power

---

2 **shaft,** column   2 **architrave,** in classical architecture that part of the entablature, or lintel, lying between the capital and the frieze. Bryant was thinking first of the Greek temple and then ("lofty vault", l. 4) of the Gothic cathedral

And inaccessible majesty. Ah, why
Should we, in the world's riper years, neglect
God's ancient sanctuaries, and adore
Only among the crowd, and under roofs
That our frail hands have raised? Let me, at least,   20
Here, in the shadow of this aged wood,
Offer one hymn — thrice happy, if it find
Acceptance in His ear.
                    Father, thy hand
Hath reared these venerable columns, thou
Didst weave this verdant roof. Thou didst look down
Upon the naked earth, and, forthwith, rose
All these fair ranks of trees. They, in thy sun,
Budded, and shook their green leaves in thy breeze,
And shot toward heaven. The century-living crow   30
Whose birth was in their tops, grew old and died
Among their branches, till, at last, they stood,
As now they stand, massy, and tall, and dark,
Fit shrine for humble worshipper to hold
Communion with his Maker. These dim vaults,
These winding aisles, of human pomp or pride
Report not. No fantastic carvings show
The boast of our vain race to change the form
Of thy fair works. But thou art here — thou fill'st
The solitude. Thou art in the soft winds   40
That run along the summit of these trees
In music; thou art in the cooler breath
That from the inmost darkness of the place
Comes, scarcely felt; the barky trunks, the ground,
The fresh moist ground, are all instinct with thee.
Here is continual worship; — Nature, here,
In the tranquillity that thou dost love,
Enjoys thy presence. Noiselessly, around,
From perch to perch, the solitary bird
Passes; and yon clear spring, that, midst its herbs,   50
Wells softly forth and wandering steeps the roots
Of half the mighty forest, tells no tale
Of all the good it does. Thou hast not left
Thyself without a witness, in these shades,
Of thy perfections. Grandeur, strength, and grace,
Are here to speak of thee. This mighty oak —

---

30 **century-living crow.** The long life of the crow is traditional; there are said to be instances of a captive crow living nearly a hundred years   37 **fantastic carvings.** At this period of his life, Bryant evidently cared little for Gothic architecture

By whose immovable stem I stand and seem
Almost annihilated — not a prince,
In all that proud old world beyond the deep,
E'er wore his crown as loftily as he   60
Wears the green coronal of leaves with which
Thy hand has graced him. Nestled at his root
Is beauty, such as blooms not in the glare
Of the broad sun. That delicate forest flower,
With scented breath and look so like a smile,
Seems, as it issues from the shapeless mould,
An emanation of the indwelling Life,
A visible token of the upholding Love,
That are the soul of this great universe.

    My heart is awed within me when I think   70
Of the great miracle that still goes on,
In silence, round me — the perpetual work
Of thy creation, finished, yet renewed
Forever. Written on thy works I read
The lesson of thy own eternity.
Lo! all grow old and die — but see again,
How on the faltering footsteps of decay
Youth presses — ever-gay and beautiful youth
In all its beautiful forms. These lofty trees
Wave not less proudly that their ancestors   80
Moulder beneath them. Oh, there is not lost
One of earth's charms: upon her bosom yet,
After the flight of untold centuries,
The freshness of her far beginning lies
And yet shall lie. Life mocks the idle hate
Of his arch-enemy Death — yea, seats himself
Upon the tyrant's throne — the sepulchre,
And of the triumphs of his ghastly foe
Makes his own nourishment. For he came forth
From thine own bosom, and shall have no end.   90

    There have been holy men who hid themselves
Deep in the woody wilderness, and gave
Their lives to thought and prayer, till they outlived
The generation born with them, nor seemed
Less aged than the hoary trees and rocks
Around them; — and there have been holy men
Who deemed it were not well to pass life thus.
But let me often to these solitudes

Retire, and in thy presence reassure
My feeble virtue. Here its enemies,   100
The passions, at thy plainer footsteps shrink
And tremble and are still. Oh, God! when thou
Dost scare the world with tempests, set on fire
The heavens with falling thunderbolts, or fill,
With all the waters of the firmament,
The swift dark whirlwind that uproots the woods
And drowns the villages; when, at thy call,
Uprises the great deep and throws himself
Upon the continent, and overwhelms
Its cities — who forgets not, at the sight   110
Of these tremendous tokens of thy power,
His pride, and lays his strifes and follies by?
Oh, from these sterner aspects of thy face
Spare me and mine, nor let us need the wrath
Of the mad, unchained elements to teach
Who rules them. Be it ours to meditate,
In these calm shades, thy milder majesty,
And to the beautiful order of thy works
Learn to conform the order of our lives.   1825

I Cannot Forget with What Fervid Devotion

Nine "Stanzas" by "X. X." appeared in the New-York Review and Atheneum Magazine *for February 1826. When Bryant prepared the 1832 edition of his poems, he condensed
this piece to seven stanzas. The poem is thought to have been written at Cummington in
1815, when Bryant was only twenty-one, but the nostalgia of a man of affairs for the dreams
of his early youth was apparently recurrent throughout his life.*

I cannot forget with what fervid devotion
  I worshipped the visions of verse and of fame;
Each gaze at the glories of earth, sky, and ocean,
  To my kindled emotions, was wind over flame.

And deep were my musings in life's early blossom,
  'Mid the twilight of mountain-groves wandering long;
How thrilled my young veins, and how throbbed my full bosom,
  When o'er me descended the spirit of song!

'Mong the deep-cloven fells that for ages had listened
  To the rush of the pebble-paved river between,   10

---
9 **fells,** mountains, rocky uplands

Where the kingfisher screamed and gray precipice glistened,
All breathless with awe have I gazed on the scene;

Till I felt the dark power o'er my reveries stealing,
From the gloom of the thickets that over me hung,
And the thoughts that awoke, in that rapture of feeling,
Were formed into verse as they rose to my tongue.

Bright visions! I mixed with the world, and ye faded,
No longer your pure rural worshipper now;
In the haunts your continual presence pervaded,
Ye shrink from the signet of care on my brow.   20

In the old mossy groves on the breast of the mountain,
In deep lonely glens where the waters complain,
By the shade of the rock, by the gush of the fountain,
I seek your loved footsteps, but seek them in vain.

Oh, leave not forlorn and forever forsaken,
Your pupil and victim to life and its tears!
But sometimes return, and in mercy awaken
The glories ye showed to his earlier years.   1815?, 1826

---

14 **1832:**   From his throne in the depth of that stern solitude,
          And he breathed through my lips, in that tempest of feeling,
          Strains warm with his spirit, though artless and rude.

A Meditation on Rhode Island Coal

Humor and awareness of the technological advances of the age are pleasantly combined in "A Meditation on Rhode Island Coal," first published in the New-York Review and Atheneum Magazine *for April 1826.*

"Decolor, obscurus, vilis, non ille repexam
  Cesariem regum, non candida virginis ornat
  Colla, nec insigni splendet per cingula morsu
  Sed nova si nigri videas miracula saxi,
  Tunc superat pulchros cultus et quicquid Eois
  Indus litoribus rubra scrutatur in alga." — CLAUDIAN

Claudian The epigraph is from a poem on the magnet by Claudianus (365?-408) in his *Carminum Minorum Corpusculum* (XXIX, 11. 10-15). The sense is: Black, dull, and common, it does not adorn the braided hair of kings nor the snowy necks of girls, nor shine in the jewelled buckles of warrior's belts. But consider the marvelous properties of this dull-looking stone and you will see that it is of more worth than lovely gems and any pearl sought of Indian amid the seaweed on the Red Sea's shore

I sat beside the glowing grate, fresh heaped
   With Newport coal, and as the flame grew bright
— The many-colored flame — and played and leaped,
   I thought of rainbows, and the northern light,
Moore's Lalla Rookh, the Treasury Report,
And other brilliant matters of the sort.

And last I thought of that fair isle which sent
   The mineral fuel; on a summer day
I saw it once, with heat and travel spent,
   And scratched by dwarf-oaks in the hollow way.   10
Now dragged through sand, now jolted over stone —
A rugged road 'through rugged Tiverton.

And hotter grew the air, and hollower grew
   The deep-worn path, and horror-struck, I thought,
Where will this dreary passage lead me to?
   This long dull road, so narrow, deep, and hot?
I looked to see it dive in earth outright;
I looked — but saw a far more welcome sight.

Like a soft mist upon the evening shore,
   At once a lovely isle before me lay,   20
Smooth, and with tender verdure covered o'er,
   As if just risen from its calm inland bay;
Sloped each way gently to the grassy edge,
And the small waves that dallied with the sedge.

The barley was just reaped; the heavy sheaves
   Lay on the stubble-field; the tall maize stood
Dark in its summer growth, and shook its leaves,
   And bright the sunlight played on the young wood —
For fifty years ago, the old men say,
The Briton hewed their ancient groves away.   30

I saw where fountains freshened the green land,
   And where the pleasant road, from door to door,

---

2 **Newport coal.** Rhode Island coal was actually mined near Portsmouth on the northern part of the island in Narragansett Bay called Aquidneck by the Indians, on which Newport is located   5 **Lalla Rookh.** Part III of this poem by Thomas Moore (1779-1852) deals with Oriental fire worshipers   5 **the Treasury Report.** Since 1800, the law has required the secretary of state to make an annual report of the state of finances   12 **Tiverton,** on the mainland north and east of Rhode Island proper   29 **fifty years ago,** during the British occupation of Newport, between 1776 and 1779, when much timber was cut for firewood   31 **fountains,** springs

With rows of cherry-trees on either hand,
  Went wandering all that fertile region o'er —
Rogue's Island once — but when the rogues were dead,
Rhode Island was the name it took instead.

Beautiful island! then it only seemed
  A lovely stranger; it has grown a friend.
I gazed on its smooth slopes, but never dreamed
  How soon that green and quiet isle would send   40
The treasures of its womb across the sea,
To warm a poet's room and boil his tea.

Dark anthracite! that reddenest on my hearth,
  Thou in those island mines didst slumber long;
But now thou art come forth to move the earth,
  And put to shame the men that mean thee wrong:
Thou shalt be coals of fire to those that hate thee,
And warm the shins of all that underrate thee.

Yea, they did wrong thee foully — they who mocked
  Thy honest face, and said thou wouldst not burn;   50
Of hewing thee to chimney-pieces talked,
  And grew profane, and swore, in bitter scorn,
That men might to thy inner caves retire,
And there, unsinged, abide the day of fire.

Yet is thy greatness nigh. I pause to state,
  That I too have seen greatness — even I —
Shook hands with Adams, stared at La Fayette,
  When, bareheaded, in the hot noon of July,
He would not let the umbrella be held o'er him,
For which three cheers burst from the mob before him. 60

And I have seen — not many months ago —
  An Eastern Governor in chapeau bras

35 **Rogue's Island.** Bryant's etymology is not admitted by Rhode Island natives, who attribute the name to Giovanni da Verrazano, a Florentine sailing under the French flag, who visited Narragansett Bay in 1524 and thought it looked like the extensive harbors of the island of Rhodes in the Mediterranean   43 **anthracite.** Rhode Island coal is so compressed that it is much more hard to ignite than other hard coal; it is no longer commercially mined   57 **Shook . . . La Fayette.** Bryant probably saw Lafayette when he took part in the Fourth of July celebration at New York in 1825, near the end of his triumphal tour of the United States; the other reference is probably to John Adams, still living in Quincy, Massachusetts, when the poem was written   62 **Eastern . . . chapeau bras,** that is, in a three-cornered hat of the late-eighteenth-century fashion. The governor was perhaps De Witt Clinton (1769-1828)

And military coat, a glorious show!
  Ride forth to visit the reviews, and ah!
How oft he smiled and bowed to Jonathan!
How many hands were shook and votes were won!

'Twas a great Governor; thou too shalt be
  Great in thy turn, and wide shall spread thy fame
And swiftly; farthest Maine shall hear of thee,
  And cold New Brunswick gladden at thy name;   70
And, faintly through its sleets, the weeping isle
That sends the Boston folks their cod shall smile.

For thou shalt forge vast railways, and shalt heat
  The hissing rivers into steam, and drive
Huge masses from thy mines, on iron feet,
  Walking their steady way, as if alive,
Northward, till everlasting ice besets thee,
And South as far as the grim Spaniard lets thee.

Thou shalt make mighty engines swim the sea,
  Like its own monsters — boats that for a guinea   80
Will take a man to Havre — and shalt be
  The moving soul of many a spinning-jenny,
And ply thy shuttles, till a bard can wear
As good a suit of broadcloth as the mayor.

Then we will laugh at winter when we hear
  The grim old churl about our dwellings rave:
Thou, from that "ruler of the inverted year,"
  Shalt pluck the knotty sceptre Cowper gave,
And pull him from his sledge, and drag him in,
And melt the icicles from off his chin.   90
                                             1826

---

65 **Jonathan.** Brother Jonathan was a national character, preceding Uncle Sam and more resembling today's
John Q. Public in meaning   71 **weeping isle,** Newfoundland, notorious for its fogs   87 **"ruler . . .
year,"** from Bk. IV, l. 120 of Cowper's *The Task* (1785)   90 **his chin.** In the *New-York Review* there was
an additional stanza, somewhat more convivial and topical than those Bryant retained; it refers to the fa-
mous punch of Newport and the "Lunch" — the Bread and Cheese Club in which James Fenimore Cooper
was the leading spirit:
  Heat will be cheap — a small consideration
    Will put one in a way to raise his punch,
  Set lemon-trees, and have a cane plantation —
    'Twill be a pretty saving to the *Lunch.*
  Then the West India Negroes may go play
  The banjo and keep endless holiday

To Cole, the Painter, Departing for Europe

Thomas Cole (1801-1848), lionized in New York City in the 1820's for his discovery of native subjects for landscape paintings, was one of Bryant's numerous friends in the world of art. The two men, companions on walking tours in the Catskills, were remarkably similar in their tastes and accomplishments. From the Hudson River scenes which gave him reputa-tion Cole turned to allegories and moralizing in such series of paintings as "The Course of Empire" and "The Voyage of Life," both remarkably like Bryant's "The Flood of Years." Cole, born in England, came to the United States at eighteen, and in later life is said to have remarked that he would give his left hand to have been a native American. The na-tionalistic tone of Bryant's tribute is therefore quite appropriate.

Thine eyes shall see the light of distant skies;
   Yet, COLE! thy heart shall bear to Europe's strand
   A living image of our own bright land,
Such as upon thy glorious canvas lies;
Lone lakes — savannas where the bison roves —
   Rocks rich with summer garlands — solemn streams —
   Skies, where the desert eagle wheels and screams —
Spring bloom and autumn blaze of boundless groves.
Fair scenes shall greet thee where thou goest — fair,
   But different — everywhere the trace of men,   10
Paths, homes, graves, ruins, from the lowest glen
To where life shrinks from the fierce Alpine air —
   Gaze on them, till the tears shall dim thy sight,
   But keep that earlier, wilder image bright.

                                       1829

------

3 **our own bright.** Bryant seems not to have known at this time that Cole was English-born. He knew better when he delivered a funeral oration on Cole before the National Academy of Design in 1848

The Prairies

About 1830, two of Bryant's younger brothers went west to take up land, eventually settling at Princeton, Illinois. Visiting them in the summer of 1832, the poet rode on horseback northward a hundred miles from Jacksonville. "The Prairies," in which he combined his impressions on this trip with his well-tried themes of the ruins of empire and the transience of human life, was first published in the Knickerbocker *for December 1833. The last lines suggest that he believed it was the "manifest destiny" of the United States to occupy the en-tire North American continent.*

   These are the garden of the Desert, these
The unshorn fields, boundless and beautiful,
For which the speech of England has no name —
The Prairies. I behold them for the first,
And my heart swells, while the dilated sight
Takes in the encircling vastness. Lo! they stretch
In airy undulations, far away,
As if the Ocean, in his gentlest swell,
Stood still, with all his rounded billows fixed,
And motionless for ever. Motionless? —   10
No — they are all unchained again. The clouds
Sweep over with their shadows, and, beneath,
The surface rolls and fluctuates to the eye;
Dark hollows seem to glide along and chase
The sunny ridges. Breezes of the South!
Who toss the golden and the flame-like flowers,
And pass the prairie-hawk that, poised on high,
Flaps his broad wings, yet moves not — ye have played
Among the palms of Mexico and vines
Of Texas, and have crisped the limpid brooks   20
That from the fountains of Sonora glide
Into the calm Pacific — have ye fanned
A nobler or a lovelier scene than this?
Man hath no part in all this glorious work:
The hand that built the firmament hath heaved
And smoothed these verdant swells, and sown their slopes
With herbage, planted them with island-groves,
And hedged them round with forests. Fitting floor
For this magnificent temple of the sky —
With flowers whose glory and whose multitude   30
Rival the constellations! The great heavens
Seem to stoop down upon the scene in love, —
A nearer vault, and of a tenderer blue,
Than that which bends above our Eastern hills.

   As o'er the verdant waste I guide my steed,
Among the high rank grass that sweeps his sides
The hollow beating of his footstep seems

---

3 **no name.** "Prairie," French in origin, seems to have come into general use in American English before
the Revolution   13 **The surface . . . eye.** "The prairies of the West, with an undulating surface, *rolling
prairies,* as they are called, present to the unaccustomed eye a singular spectacle when the shadows of the
clouds are passing rapidly over them. The face of the ground seems to fluctuate and toss like billows of the
sea." — Bryant   17 **the prairie-hawk . . . not.** "I have seen the prairie-hawk balancing himself in the
air for hours together, apparently over the same spot; probably watching his prey." — Bryant   21 **Sonora,**
a state in the northwestern part of Mexico

A sacrilegious sound. I think of those
Upon whose rest he tramples. Are they here —
The dead of other days? — and did the dust 40
Of these fair solitudes once stir with life
And burn with passion? Let the mighty mounds
That overlook the rivers, or that rise
In the dim forest crowded with old oaks,
Answer. A race, that long has passed away,
Built them; a disciplined and populous race
Heaped, with long toil, the earth, while yet the Greek
Was hewing the Pentelicus to forms
Of symmetry, and rearing on its rock
The glittering Parthenon. These ample fields 50
Nourished their harvests, here their herds were fed,
When haply by their stalls the bison lowed,
And bowed his manèd shoulder to the yoke.
All day this desert murmured with their toils,
Till twilight blushed, and lovers walked, and wooed
In a forgotten language, and old tunes,
From instruments of unremembered form,
Gave the soft winds a voice. The red-man came —
The roaming hunter-tribes, warlike and fierce,
And the mound-builders vanished from the earth. 60
The solitude of centuries untold
Has settled where they dwelt. The prairie-wolf
Hunts in their meadows, and his fresh-dug den
Yawns by my path. The gopher mines the ground
Where stood their swarming cities. All is gone;
All — save the piles of earth that hold their bones,
The platforms where they worshipped unknown gods,
The barriers which they builded from the soil
To keep the foe at bay — till o'er the walls
The wild beleaguerers broke, and, one by one, 70
The strongholds of the plain were forced, and heaped
With corpses. The brown vultures of the wood

---

42 **mighty mounds.** In the forty-two lines which follow, Bryant builds upon the theory, common in his time but now generally rejected, that the burial, ceremonial, and earthwork mounds of the Mississippi Valley were not constructed by the ancestors of the Indians, but by an extinct race, the Mound Builders. There are said to be ten thousand such mounds in Illinois alone; Bryant's letters reveal that he had examined some near St. Louis   48 **Pentelicus,** a mountain range some miles northeast of Athens, where an unusually white marble was quarried   50 **Parthenon,** a temple dedicated to Athena Parthenos on the Acropolis in Athens. Completed about 435 B.C., it is still one of the great monuments of the ancient world   50 **These . . . harvests.** "The size and extent of the mounds in the valley of the Mississippi indicate the existence, at a remote period, of a nation once populous and laborious, and therefore probably subsisting by agriculture." — Bryant   52 **bison.** There is little evidence that the bison, commonly called buffalo, was ever domesticated

Flocked to those vast uncovered sepulchres,
And sat, unscared and silent, at their feast.
Haply some solitary fugitive,
Lurking in marsh and forest, till the sense
Of desolation and of fear became
Bitterer than death, yielded himself to die.
Man's better nature triumphed then. Kind words
Welcomed and soothed him; the rude conquerors   80
Seated the captive with their chiefs; he chose
A bride among their maidens, and at length
Seemed to forget — yet ne'er forgot — the wife
Of his first love, and her sweet little ones,
Butchered, amid their shrieks, with all his race.

   Thus change the forms of being. Thus arise
Races of living things, glorious in strength,
And perish, as the quickening breath of God
Fills them, or is withdrawn. The red-man, too,
Has left the blooming wilds he ranged so long,   90
And, nearer to the Rocky Mountains, sought
A wilder hunting-ground. The beaver builds
No longer by these streams, but far away,
On waters whose blue surface ne'er gave back
The white man's face — among Missouri's springs,
And pools whose issues swell the Oregon,
He rears his little Venice. In these plains
The bison feeds no more. Twice twenty leagues
Beyond remotest smoke of hunter's camp,
Roams the majestic brute, in herds that shake   100
The earth with thundering steps — yet here I meet
His ancient footprints stamped beside the pool.

   Still this great solitude is quick with life.
Myriads of insects, gaudy as the flowers
They flutter over, gentle quadrupeds,
And birds, that scarce have learned the fear of man,
Are here, and sliding reptiles of the ground,
Startlingly beautiful. The graceful deer
Bounds to the wood at my approach. The bee,
A more adventurous colonist than man,   110
With whom he came across the eastern deep,

---

80 **the rude . . . chiefs.** "Instances are not wanting of generosity like this among the North American Indians toward a captive or survivor of a hostile tribe on which the greatest cruelties had been exercised." — Bryant

Fills the savannas with his murmurings,
And hides his sweets, as in the golden age,
Within the hollow oak. I listen long
To his domestic hum, and think I hear
The sound of that advancing multitude
Which soon shall fill these deserts. From the ground
Comes up the laugh of children, the soft voice
Of maidens, and the sweet and solemn hymn
Of Sabbath worshippers. The low of herds   120
Blends with the rustling of the heavy grain
Over the dark-brown furrows. All at once
A fresher wind sweeps by, and breaks my dream,
And I am in the wilderness alone.

                                         1832, 1833

Robert of Lincoln

Bryant's pleasure in the bobolink is characteristically combined with a quiet comment on the round of human life. "Robert of Lincoln" is about as close as the sober Bryant ever gets to the carpe diem *theme — the glorification, that is to say, of the enjoyment of the present moment.*

Merrily swinging on brier and weed,
    Near to the nest of his little dame,
Over the mountain-side or mead,
    Robert of Lincoln is telling his name:
        Bob-o'-link, bob-o'-link,
        Spink, spank, spink;
    Snug and safe is that nest of ours,
Hidden among the summer flowers.
                Chee, chee, chee.

Robert of Lincoln is gayly drest,   10
    Wearing a bright black wedding-coat;
White are his shoulders and white his crest,
    Hear him call in his merry note:
        Bob-o'-link, bob-o'-link,
        Spink, spank, spink.
Look, what a nice new coat is mine,
Sure there was never a bird so fine.
                Chee, chee, chee.

Robert of Lincoln's Quaker wife,
   Pretty and quiet, with plain brown wings, 20
Passing at home a patient life,
   Broods in grass while her husband sings:
     Bob-o'-link, bob-o'-link,
     Spink, spank, spink;
Brood, kind creature; you need not fear
Thieves and robbers while I am here.
          Chee, chee, chee.

Modest and shy as a nun is she;
   One weak chirp is her only note.
Braggart and prince of braggarts is he,   30
   Pouring boasts from his little throat:
     Bob-o'-link, bob-o'-link,
     Spink, spank, spink;
Never was I afraid of man;
Catch me, cowardly knaves, if you can!
          Chee, chee, chee.

Six white eggs on a bed of hay,
   Flecked with purple, a pretty sight!
There as the mother sits all day,
   Robert is singing with all his might: 40
     Bob-o'-link, bob-o'-link,
     Spink, spank, spink;
Nice good wife, that never goes out,
Keeping house while I frolic about.
          Chee, chee, chee.

Soon as the little ones chip the shell
   Six wide mouths are open for food;
Robert of Lincoln bestirs him well,
   Gathering seeds for the hungry brood.
     Bob-o'-link, bob-o'-link,   50
     Spink, spank, spink;
This new life is likely to be
Hard for a gay young fellow like me.
          Chee, chee, chee.

Robert of Lincoln at length is made
   Sober with work, and silent with care;

---

49 **Gathering seeds,** John Burroughs in an essay "Nature and the Poets," challenged Bryant's natural history. The bobolink, he said, "is an insectivorous bird in the North, or until its brood has flown"

Off is his holiday garment laid,
  Half forgotten that merry air:
    Bob-o'-link, bob-o'-link,
    Spink, spank, spink;   60
Nobody knows but my mate and I
Where our nest and our nestlings lie.
              Chee, chee, chee.

Summer wanes; the children are grown;
  Fun and frolic no more he knows;
Robert of Lincoln's a humdrum crone;
  Off he flies, and we sing as he goes:
    Bob-o'-link, bob-o'-link,
    Spink, spank, spink;
When you can pipe that merry old strain, 70
Robert of Lincoln, come back again.
              Chee, chee, chee.

                    1855

_____

66 **crone,** a withered old woman. Bryant refers to the annual loss by the male bobolink (the rice-bird of the South) of his glossy black, buff, and white plumage, together with his song, so that at summer's end he is almost indistinguishable from the female

The Poet

Godwin informs us that "The Poet," the expression of Bryant's conviction that poetry depends primarily upon emotion, was written in 1863. As early as 1826, in his lectures on poetry before the American Atheneum Society, Bryant had asserted that "the great spring of poetry is emotion," although he also acknowledged the importance of appealing to the imagination and the understanding. His theories are similar to but somewhat less mystical than those of Emerson (see p. 1112) and Whitman. The extent to which he followed his own advice about revision is debatable, for textual study reveals that he often changed his mind about his diction. Textual revisions are indicated in the footnotes for "Thanatopsis" and "Inscription for the Entrance to a Wood."

Thou, who wouldst wear the name
  Of poet mid thy brethren of mankind,
And clothe in words of flame
  Thoughts that shall live within the general mind!
Deem not the framing of a deathless lay
The pastime of a drowsy summer day.

But gather all thy powers,
  And wreak them on the verse that thou dost weave,

_____

8 **wreak them on,** release them completely

And in thy lonely hours,
  At silent morning or at wakeful eve,   10
While the warm current tingles through thy veins,
Set forth the burning words in fluent strains.

No smooth array of phrase,
  Artfully sought and ordered though it be,
Which the cold rhymer lays
  Upon his page with languid industry,
Can wake the listless pulse to livelier speed,
Or fill with sudden tears the eyes that read.

The secret wouldst thou know
  To touch the heart or fire the blood at will?   20
Let thine own eyes o'erflow;
  Let thy lips quiver with the passionate thrill;
Seize the great thought, ere yet its power be past,
And bind, in words, the fleet emotion fast.

Then, should thy verse appear
  Halting and harsh, and all unaptly wrought,
Touch the crude line with fear,
  Save in the moment of impassioned thought;
Then summon back the original glow, and mend
The strain with rapture that with fire was penned. 30

Yet let no empty gust
  Of passion find an utterance in thy lay,
A blast that whirls the dust
  Along the howling street and dies away;
But feelings of calm power and mighty sweep,
Like currents journeying through the windless deep.

Seek'st thou, in living lays,
  To limn the beauty of the earth and sky?
Before thine inner gaze
  Let all that beauty in clear vision lie;   40
Look on it with exceeding love, and write
The words inspired by wonder and delight.

Of tempests wouldst thou sing,
  Or tell of battles — make thyself a part
Of the great tumult; cling
  To the tossed wreck with terror in thy heart;

Scale, with the assaulting host, the rampart's height,
And strike and struggle in the thickest fight.

So shalt thou frame a lay
   That haply may endure from age to age,   50
And they who read shall say:
   "What witchery hangs upon this poet's page!
What art is his the written spells to find
That sway from mood to mood the willing mind!"
                             1863, 1864

The Flood of Years

Many of Bryant's poems express a humanistic sense of the stream of life. "The Flood of Years," written in his eighty-first year, is one of the few places where he indicated a belief in the doctrine of personal immortality. One can understand the motive of the reader who wrote to ask if the closing lines represented Bryant's real convictions. He was answered as follows: "Certainly I believe all that is said in the lines you have quoted: otherwise I could not have written them. I believe in the everlasting life of the soul, and it seems to me that immortality would be but an imperfect gift without the recognition in the life to come of those who are dear to us here."

The central figure is remarkably similar to Addison's in "The Vision of Mirza," The Spectator, No. 159.

A mighty Hand, from an exhaustless Urn,
Pours forth the never-ending Flood of Years,
Among the nations. How the rushing waves
Bear all before them! On their foremost edge,
And there alone, is Life. The Present there
Tosses and foams and fills the air with roar
Of mingled noises. There are they who toil,
And they who strive, and they who feast, and they
Who hurry to and fro. The sturdy swain —
Woodman and delver with the spade — is there,   10
And busy artisan beside his bench,
And pallid student with his written roll.
A moment on the mounting billow seen,
The flood sweeps over them and they are gone.
There groups of revellers whose brows are twined
With roses, ride the topmost swell awhile,
And as they raise their flowing cups and touch
The clinking brim to brim, are whirled beneath
The waves and disappear. I hear the jar

Of beaten drums, and thunders that break forth   20
From cannon, where the advancing billow sends
Up to the sight long files of armèd men,
That hurry to the charge through flame and smoke.
The torrent bears them under, whelmed and hid
Slayer and slain, in heaps of bloody foam.
Down go the steed and rider, the plumed chief
Sinks with his followers; the head that wears
The imperial diadem goes down beside
The felon's with cropped ear and branded cheek.
A funeral-train — the torrent sweeps away   30
Bearers and bier and mourners. By the bed
Of one who dies men gather sorrowing,
And women weep aloud; the flood rolls on;
The wail is stifled and the sobbing group
Borne under. Hark to that shrill, sudden shout,
The cry of an applauding multitude,
Swayed by some loud-voiced orator who wields
The living mass as if he were its soul!
The waters choke the shout and all is still.
Lo! next a kneeling crowd, and one who spreads   40
The hands in prayer, the engulfing wave o'ertakes
And swallows them and him. A sculptor wields
The chisel, and the stricken marble grows
To beauty; at his easel, eager-eyed,
A painter stands, and sunshine at his touch
Gathers upon his canvas, and life glows;
A poet, as he paces to and fro,
Murmurs his sounding lines. Awhile they ride
The advancing billow, till its tossing crest
Strikes them and flings them under, while their tasks 50
Are yet unfinished. See a mother smile
On her young babe that smiles to her again;
The torrent wrests it from her arms; she shrieks
And weeps, and midst her tears is carried down.
A beam like that of moonlight turns the spray
To glistening pearls; two lovers, hand in hand,
Rise on the billowy swell and fondly look
Into each other's eyes. The rushing flood
Flings them apart: the youth goes down; the maid
With hands outstretched in vain, and streaming eyes, 60

---

26 **plumed chief.** Bryant perhaps had in mind James G. Blaine, "the plumed knight," so named at his
nomination for the Presidency in 1876 by Col. Robert G. Ingersoll   29 **cropped . . . cheek.** These dis-
figurements were routine punishments for criminals in the eighteenth century

Waits for the next high wave to follow him.
An aged man succeeds; his bending form
Sinks slowly. Mingling with the sullen stream
Gleam the white locks, and then are seen no more.
    Lo! wider grows the stream — a sea-like flood
Saps earth's walled cities; massive palaces
Crumble before it; fortresses and towers
Dissolve in the swift waters; populous realms
Swept by the torrent see their ancient tribes
Engulfed and lost; their very languages   70
Stifled, and never to be uttered more.
    I pause and turn my eyes, and looking back
Where that tumultous flood has been, I see
The silent ocean of the Past, a waste
Of waters weltering over graves, its shores
Strewn with the wreck of fleets where mast and hull
Drop away piecemeal; battlemented walls
Frown idly, green with moss, and temples stand
Unroofed, forsaken by the worshipper.
There lie memorial stones, whence time has gnawed   80
The graven legends, thrones of kings o'erturned,
The broken altars of forgotten gods,
Foundations of old cities and long streets
Where never fall of human foot is heard,
On all the desolate pavement. I behold
Dim glimmerings of lost jewels, far within
The sleeping waters, diamond, sardonyx,
Ruby and topaz, pearl and chrysolite,
Once glittering at the banquet on fair brows
That long ago were dust, and all around   90
Strewn on the surface of that silent sea
Are withering bridal wreaths, and glossy locks
Shorn from dear brows, by loving hands, and scrolls
O'er written, haply with fond words of love
And vows of friendship, and fair pages flung
Fresh from the printer's engine. There they lie
A moment, and then sink away from sight.
    I look, and the quick tears are in my eyes,
For I behold in every one of these
A blighted hope, a separate history   100
Of human sorrows, telling of dear ties
Suddenly broken, dreams of happiness
Dissolved in air, and happy days too brief
That sorrowfully ended, and I think

How painfully must the poor heart have beat
In bosoms without number, as the blow
Was struck that slew their hope and broke their peace.
    Sadly I turn and look before, where yet
The Flood must pass, and I behold a mist
Where swarm dissolving forms, the brood of Hope,   110
Divinely fair, that rest on banks of flowers,
Or wander among rainbows, fading soon
And reappearing, haply giving place
To forms of grisly aspect such as Fear
Shapes from the idle air — where serpents lift
The head to strike, and skeletons stretch forth
The bony arm in menace. Further on
A belt of darkness seems to bar the way
Long, low, and distant, where the Life to come
Touches the Life that is. The Flood of Years   120
Rolls toward it near and nearer. It must pass
That dismal barrier. What is there beyond?
Hear what the wise and good have said. Beyond
That belt of darkness, still the Years roll on
More gently, but with not less mighty sweep.
They gather up again and softly bear
All the sweet lives that late were overwhelmed
And lost to sight, all that in them was good,
Noble, and truly great, and worthy of love —
The lives of infants and ingenuous youths,   130
Sages and saintly women who have made
Their households happy; all are raised and borne
By that great current in its onward sweep,
Wandering and rippling with caressing waves
Around green islands fragrant with the breath
Of flowers that never wither. So they pass,
From stage to stage along the shining course
Of that bright river, broadening like a sea.
As its smooth eddies curl along their way
They bring old friends together; hands are clasped   140
In joy unspeakable; the mother's arms
Again are folded round the child she loved
And lost. Old sorrows are forgotten now,
Or but remembered to make sweet the hour
That overpays them; wounded hearts that bled
Or broke are healed forever. In the room
Of this grief-shadowed present, there shall be
A Present in whose reign no grief shall gnaw

The heart, and never shall a tender tie
Be broken; in whose reign the eternal Change 150
That waits on growth and action shall proceed
With everlasting Concord hand in hand.

1876

On the Nature of Poetry

In April 1826, Bryant delivered a series of four lectures before the New York Atheneum. The lecture here reprinted was followed by one on the value and uses of poetry, one on poetry "in Relation to Our Age and Country" which is another reflection of Bryant's nationalism, and one on originality and imitation. The critical questions which crop out in this first lecture are ageless, and the ideas which Bryant expresses can best be described as a complex patchwork of Neoclassical and romantic theories. His remarks here should be compared with "The Poet" and, for further study, with his introduction to A Library of Poetry and Song *(1871). See also William Charvat,* Origins of American Critical Thought, 1810-1835 *(Philadelphia, 1935); and William Palmer Hudson, "Archibald Alison and William Cullen Bryant,"* American Literature, *XII (March 1940), 59-68.*

In treating of the subject which has been assigned me, it is obvious that it will be impossible for me to compress into four lectures anything like a complete view of it. I am to speak of one of the most ancient of all arts, of the very earliest and most venerable branch of literature — one which even now exists in many countries that have no other; one, which although it has not in every period been cultivated with the same degree of success, has yet in no age of the world ceased to attract a large degree of the attention of mankind. Not only have the writers of poetry been exceedingly numerous — more so, perhaps, than those of any other class — but poetry has shot forth another branch of literature, her handmaid and satellite, and
10 raised up a large body of authors, who speculate upon what the poets have written, who define the elements and investigate the principles of the art, and fix the degrees of estimation in which its several productions should be held. Not only has the poetry of one age been exceedingly different from that of another, but different styles of poetry have prevailed at the same time in different nations, different schools of poetry have arisen in the same nation, and different forms of poetical composition have been preferred by the several writers of the same school. So much poetry has been written, and that poetry has been the subject of so much criticism, so much matter for speculation has been collected, and so many reasonings and theories have been framed out of it, that the subject has grown to be one of the
20 most comprehensive in the whole province of literature.
If I were to treat of either of its great subdivisions — if, for example, I were to attempt its history from its earliest origin, through its various stages, to the present time; if I were to analyze the several forms of poetical composition, or to point out

the characteristics of the various kinds of poetry that have prevailed at different periods, or to compare the genius of the most illustrious poets — in either case, I could do little more than pass rapidly over the principal topics. The view would be so brief that it would seem like a dry table of the contents of a large work, and would become tedious from its very brevity. I shall, therefore, in the short course of lectures which I have undertaken, attempt no entire view of the subject assigned to me; but shall only endeavor to select a few of the topics which seem to me among the most interesting, and on which I may imagine that I shall weary you the least.

Of the nature of poetry different ideas have been entertained. The ancient critics seemed to suppose that they did something toward giving a tolerable notion of it 10 by calling it a mimetic or imitative art, and classing it with sculpture and painting. Of its affinity with these arts there can be no doubt; but that affinity seems to me to consist almost wholly in the principles by which they all produce their effect, and not in the manner in which those principles are reduced to practice. There is no propriety in applying to poetry the term *imitative* in a literal and philosophical sense, as there is in applying it to painting and sculpture. The latter speak to the senses; poetry speaks directly to the mind. They reproduce sensible objects, and, by means of these, suggest the feeling or sentiment connected with them; poetry, by the symbols of words, suggests both the sensible object and the association. I should be glad to learn how a poem descriptive of a scene or an event is any more 20 an imitation of that scene or that event than a prose description would be. A prose composition giving an account of the proportions and dimensions of a building, and the materials of which it is constructed, is certainly, so far as mere exactness is concerned, a better imitation of it than the finest poem that could be written about it. Yet who, after all, ever thought of giving such a composition the name of an imitation? The truth is, painting and sculpture are, literally, imitative arts, while poetry is only metaphorically so. The epithet as applied to poetry may be well enough, perhaps, as a figure of speech, but to make a metaphor the foundation of a philosophical classification is putting it to a service in which it is sure to confuse what it professes to make clear.   30

I would rather call poetry a suggestive art. Its power of affecting the mind by pure suggestion, and employing, instead of a visible or tangible imitation, arbitrary symbols, as unlike as possible to the things with which it deals, is what distinguishes this from its two sister arts. It is owing to its operation by means of suggestion that it affects different minds with such different degrees of force. In a picture or a statue the colors and forms employed by the artist impress the senses with the greatest distinctness. In painting, there is little — in sculpture, there is less — for the imagination to supply. It is true that different minds, according to their several degrees of cultivation, will receive different degrees of pleasure from the production of these arts, and that the moral associations they suggest will be variously felt, 40 and in some instances variously interpreted. Still, the impression made on the senses is in all cases the same; the same figures, the same lights and shades, are seen

9 **ancient critics,** notably Aristotle, whose ideas on imitation appear in the first part of the *Poetics*. See also Bk. X of Plato's *Republic*.

by all the beholders alike. But the creations of Poetry have in themselves nothing of this precision and fixedness of form, and depend greatly for their vividness and clearness of impression upon the mind to which they are presented. Language, the great machine with which her miracles are wrought, is contrived to have an application to all possible things; and wonderful as this contrivance is, and numerous and varied as are its combinations, it is still limited and imperfect, and, in point of comprehensiveness, distinctness, and variety, falls infinitely short of the mighty and diversified world of matter and mind of which it professes to be the representative. It is, however, to the very limitation of this power of language, as it seems to me, that Poetry owes her magic. The most detailed of her descriptions, which, by the way, are not always the most striking, are composed of a few touches; they are glimpses of things thrown into the mind; here and there a trace of the outline; here a gleam of light, and there a dash of shade. But these very touches act like a spell upon the imagination and awaken it to greater activity, and fill it, perhaps, with greater delight than the best defined objects could do. The imagination is the most active and the least susceptible of fatigue of all the faculties of the human mind; its more intense exercise is tremendous, and sometimes unsettles the reason; its repose is only a gentle sort of activity; nor am I certain that it is ever quite unemployed, for even in our sleep it is still awake and busy, and amuses itself with fabricating our dreams. To this restless faculty — which is unsatisfied when the whole of its work is done to its hands, and which is ever wandering from the combination of ideas directly presented to it to other combinations of its own — it is the office of poetry to furnish the exercise in which it delights. Poetry is that art which selects and arranges the symbols of thought in such a manner as to excite it the most powerfully and delightfully. The imagination of the reader is guided, it is true, by the poet, and it is his business to guide it skilfully and agreeably; but the imagination in the mean time is by no means passive. It pursues the path which the poet only points out, and shapes its visions from the scenes and allusions which he gives. It fills up his sketches of beauty with what suits its own highest conceptions of the beautiful, and completes his outline of grandeur with the noblest images its own stores can furnish. It is obvious that the degree of perfection with which this is done must depend greatly upon the strength and cultivation of that faculty. For example, in the following passage, in which Milton describes the general mother passing to her daily task among the flowers:

> "With goddess-like demeanor forth she went
> Not unattended, for on her as queen
> A pomp of winning graces waited still."

16 **The imagination.** Bryant's notion is deeply influenced by eighteenth-century thought, as developed by Addison in Nos. 411-414 of *The Spectator* and by the followers of the "association" psychology of David Hartley (1705-1757). Among the books which Bryant read and which elaborate on the nature and function of the imagination is Archibald Alison's *Essays on the Nature and Principles of Taste* (1790)   34 **general mother,** Eve   36 **"With goddess-like . . . still."** *Paradise Lost,* Bk. VIII, ll. 59-61

The coldest imagination on reading it, will figure to itself, in the person of Eve, the finest forms, attitudes, and movements of female loveliness and dignity, which, after all, are not described, but only hinted at by the poet. A warmer fancy, kindling at the delicate allusions in these lines, will not only bestow these attractions on the principal figure, but will fill the air around her with beauty, and people it with the airy forms of the graces; it will see the delicate proportions of their limbs, the lustre of their flowing hair, and the soft light of their eyes. Take, also, the following passage from the same poet, in which, speaking of Satan, he says:

> "His face
> Deep scars of thunder had entrenched, and care   10
> Sat on his faded cheek — but under brows
> Of dauntless courage and considerate pride
> Waiting revenge; cruel his eye but cast
> Signs of remorse and passion to behold
> The fellows of his crime, the followers rather,
> (Far other once beheld in bliss), condemned
> For evermore to have their lot in pain."

The imagination of the reader is stimulated by the hints in this powerful passage 20 to form to itself an idea of the features in which reside this strong expression of malignity and dejection — the brow, the cheek, the eye of the fallen angel, bespeaking courage, pride, the settled purpose of revenge, anxiety, sorrow for the fate of his followers, and fearfully marked with the wrath of the Almighty. There can be no doubt that the picture which this passage calls up in the minds of different individuals will vary accordingly as the imagination is more or less vivid, or more or less excited in the perusal. It will vary, also, accordingly as the individual is more or less experienced in the visible expression of strong passion, and as he is in the habit of associating the idea of certain emotions with certain configurations of the countenance.   30

There is no question that one principal office of poetry is to excite the imagination, but this is not its sole, nor perhaps its chief province; another of its ends is to touch the heart, and, as I expect to show in this lecture, it has something to do with the understanding. I know that some critics have made poetry to consist solely in the exercise of the imagination. They distinguish poetry from pathos. They talk of pure poetry, and by this phrase they mean passages of mere imagery, with the least possible infusion of human emotion. I do not know by what authority these gentlemen take the term poetry from the people, and thus limit its meaning.

In its ordinary acceptation, it has, in all ages and all countries, included something more. When we speak of a poem, we do not mean merely a tissue of striking 40 images. The most beautiful poetry is that which takes the strongest hold of the feelings, and, if it is really the most beautiful, then it is poetry in the highest sense. Poetry is constantly resorting to the language of the passions to heighten the effect

---

9 "His face . . . in pain." *Paradise Lost,* Bk. I, ll. 600-608

of her pictures; and, if this be not enough to entitle that language to the appellation of poetical, I am not aware of the meaning of the term. Is there no poetry in the wrath of Achilles? Is there no poetry in the passage where Lear, in the tent of Cordelia, just recovered from his frenzy, his senses yet infirm and unassured, addresses his daughter as she kneels to ask his blessing?

> "Pray do not mock me;
> I am a very foolish, fond old man,
> Fourscore and upward:
> Not an hour more or less, and to deal plainly
> I fear I am not in my perfect mind."

Is there no poetry in the remorse of Othello, in the terrible consciousness of guilt which haunts Macbeth, or the lamentations of Anthony over the body of his friend, the devoted love of Juliet, and the self-sacrificing affection of Cleopatra? In the immortal work of Milton, is there no poetry in the penitence of Adam, or in the sorrows of Eve at being excluded from Paradise? The truth is, that poetry which does not find its way to the heart is scarcely deserving of the name; it may be brilliant and ingenious, but it soon wearies the attention. The feelings and the imagination, when skilfully touched, act reciprocally on each other. For example, when the poet introduces Ophelia, young, beautiful, and unfortunate, the wildness of frenzy in her eye, dressed with fantastic garlands of wild flowers, and singing snatches of old tunes, there is a picture for the imagination, but it is one which affects the heart. But when, in the midst of her incoherent talk, she utters some simple allusion to her own sorrows, as when she says,

> "We know what we are, but know not what we may be,"

this touching sentence, addressed merely to our sympathy, strongly excites the imagination. It sets before us the days when she knew sorrow only by name, before her father was slain by the hand of her lover, and before her lover was estranged, and makes us feel the heaviness of that affliction which crushed a being so gentle and innocent and happy.

Those poems, however, as I have already hinted, which are apparently the most affluent of imagery, are not always those which most kindle the reader's imagination. It is because the ornaments with which they abound are not naturally suggested by the subject, not poured forth from a mind warmed and occupied by it; but a forced fruit of the fancy, produced by labor, without spontaneity or excitement.

The language of passion is naturally figurative, but its figures are only employed to heighten the intensity of the expression; they are never introduced for their own sake. Important, therefore, as may be the office of the imagination in poetry, the great spring of poetry is emotion. It is this power that holds the key of the storehouse where the mind has laid up its images, and that alone can open it without violence. All the forms of fancy stand ever in its sight, ready to execute its bidding.

---

6 "**Pray . . . mind.**" *Lear,* Act IV, Sc. vii, ll. 59-63   24 "**We know . . . be.**" *Hamlet,* Act IV, Sc. iv, ll. 42-43

Indeed, I doubt not that most of the offences against good taste in this kind of composition are to be traced to the absence of emotion. A desire to treat agreeably or impressively a subject by which the writer is himself little moved, leads him into great mistakes about the means of effecting his purpose. This is the origin of cold conceits, of prosing reflections, of the minute painting of uninteresting circumstances, and of the opposite extremes of tameness and extravagance. On the other hand, strong feeling is always a sure guide. It rarely offends against good taste, because it instinctively chooses the most effectual means of communicating itself to others. It gives a variety to the composition it inspires, with which the severest taste is delighted. It may sometimes transgress arbitrary rules, or offend against local associations, but it speaks a language which reaches the heart in all countries and all times. Everywhere are the sentiments of fortitude and magnanimity uttered in strains that brace our own nerves, and the dead mourned in accents that draw our tears.

But poetry not only addresses the passions and the imagination; it appeals to the understanding also. So far as this position relates to the principles of taste which lie at the foundation of all poetry, and by which its merits are tried, I believe its truth will not be doubted. These principles have their origin in the reason of things, and are investigated and applied by the judgment. True it is that they may be observed by one who has never speculated about them, but it is no less true that their observance always gratifies the understanding with the fitness, the symmetry, and the congruity it produces. To write fine poetry requires intellectual faculties of the highest order, and among these, not the least important, is the faculty of reason. Poetry is the worst mask in the world behind which folly and stupidity could attempt to hide their features. Fitter, safer, and more congenial to them is the solemn discussion of unprofitable questions. Any obtuseness of apprehension or incapacity for drawing conclusions, which shows a deficiency or want of cultivation of the reasoning power, is sure to expose the unfortunate poet to contempt and ridicule.

But there is another point of view in which poetry may be said to address the understanding — I mean in the direct lessons of wisdom that it delivers. Remember that it does not concern itself with abstract reasonings, nor with any course of investigation that fatigues the mind. Nor is it merely didactic; but this does not prevent it from teaching truths which the mind instinctively acknowledges. The elements of moral truth are few and simple, but their combinations with human actions are as innumerable and diversified as the combinations of language. Thousands of inductions resulting from the application of great principles to human life and conduct lie, as it were, latent in our minds, which we have never drawn for ourselves, but which we admit the moment they are hinted at, and which, though not abstruse, are yet new. Nor are these of less value because they require no laborious research to discover them. The best riches of the earth are produced on its surface, and we need no reasoning to teach us the folly of a people who should leave its harvest ungathered to dig for its ores. The truths of which I have spoken, when possessing any peculiar force or beauty, are properly within the province of the art of which I am treating, and, when recommended by harmony of numbers, become poetry of the highest kind. Accordingly, they abound in the works of the most celebrated poets. When Shakespeare says of mercy,

> "it is twice blessed —
> It blesses him that gives and him that takes,"

does he not utter beautiful poetry as well as unquestionable truth? There are passages also in Milton of the same kind, which sink into the heart like the words of an oracle. For instance:

> "Evil into the mind of God or man
> May come and go so unapproved, and leave
> No spot or blame behind."

10

Take, also, the following example from Cowper, in which he bears witness against the guilt and folly of princes:

> "War is a game which, were their subjects wise,
> Kings should not play at. Nations would do well
> To extort their truncheons from the puny hands
> Of heroes whose infirm and baby minds
> Are gratified with mischief, and who spoil,
> Because men suffer it, their toy — the world."

I call these passages poetry, because the mind instantly acknowledges their truth
20 and feels their force, and is moved and filled and elevated by them. Nor does poetry refuse to carry on a sort of process of reasoning by deducing one truth from another. Her demonstrations differ, however, from ordinary ones by requiring that each step should be in itself beautiful or striking, and that they all should carry the mind to the final conclusion without the consciousness of labor.

All the ways by which poetry affects the mind are open also to the prose-writer. All that kindles the imagination, all that excites emotion, all those moral truths that find an echo in our bosoms, are his property as well as that of the poet. It is true that in the ornaments of style the poet is allowed a greater license, but there are many excellent poems which are not distinguished by any liberal use of the fig-
30 ures of speech from prose writings composed with the same degree of excitement. What, then, is the ground of the distinction between prose and poetry? This is a question about which there has been much debate, but one which seems to me of easy solution to those who are not too ambitious of distinguishing themselves by profound researches into things already sufficiently clear. I suppose that poetry differs from prose, in the first place, by the employment of metrical harmony. It differs from it, in the next place, by excluding all that disgusts, all that tasks and fatigues

---

3 "it is . . . takes," *Merchant of Venice.* Act IV, Sc. i, ll. 86-87   8 "Evil . . . behind." *Paradise Lost,* Bk. V, ll. 117-119. Bryant has missed Milton's comma after "go"   11 from Cowper. The passage is from "The Winter Morning, Walk," Bk. V of *The Task*   32 much debate. Coleridge's *Biographia Literaria* (1817) had much about the difference between poetry and prose, building upon Wordsworth's remarks in his Preface to the second edition (1800) of the *Lyrical Ballads*

the understanding, and all matters which are too trivial and common to excite any emotion whatever. Some of these, verse cannot raise into dignity; to others, verse is an encumbrance: they are, therefore, all unfit for poetry; put them into verse, and they are prose still.

A distinction has been attempted to be made between poetry and eloquence, and I acknowledge that there is one; but it seems to me that it consists solely in metrical arrangement. Eloquence is the poetry of prose; poetry is the eloquence of verse. The maxim that the poet is born and the orator made is a pretty antithesis, but a moment's reflection will convince us that one can become neither without natural gifts improved by cultivation. By eloquence I do not mean mere persuasiveness: there are 10 many processes of argument that are not susceptible of eloquence, because they require close and painful attention. But by eloquence I understand those appeals to our moral perceptions that produce emotion as soon as they are uttered. It is in these that the orator is himself affected with the feelings he would communicate, that his eyes glisten, and his frame seems to dilate, and his voice acquires an unwonted melody, and his sentences arrange themselves into a sort of measure and harmony, and the listener is chained in involuntary and breathless attention. This is the very enthusiasm that is the parent of poetry. Let the same man go to his closet and clothe in numbers conceptions full of the same fire and spirit, and they will be poetry.   20

In conclusion, I will observe that the elements of poetry make a part of our natures, and that every individual is more or less a poet. In this "bank-note world," as it has been happily denominated, we sometimes meet with individuals who declare that they have no taste for poetry. But by their leave I will assert they are mistaken; they have it, although they may have never cultivated it. Is there any one among them who will confess himself insensible to the beauty of order or to the pleasure of variety — two principles, the happy mingling of which makes the perfection of poetic numbers? Is there any one whose eye is undelighted with beautiful forms and colors, whose ear is not charmed by sweet sounds, and who sees no loveliness in the returns of light and darkness, and the changes of the seasons? Is there any 30 one for whom the works of Nature have no associations but such as relate to his animal wants? Is there any one for whom her great courses and operations show no majesty, to whom they impart no knowledge, and from whom they hide no secrets? Is there any one who is attached by no ties to his fellow-beings, who has no hopes for the future, and no memory of the past? Have they all forgotten the days and the friends of their childhood, and do they all shut their eyes to the advances of age? Have they nothing to desire and nothing to lament, and are their minds never darkened with the shadows of fear? Is it, in short, for these men that life has no pleasures and no pains, the grave no solemnity, and the world to come no mysteries? All these things are the sources of poetry, and they are not only part of our- 40 selves, but of the universe, and will expire only with the last of the creatures of God.

                                                                                          1826, 1884

---

22 **"bank-note world,"** from Fitz-Greene Halleck's "Alnwick Castle," St. 7

1789–1851 James Fenimore Cooper

James Cooper (he became "James Fenimore-Cooper" by a legislative act in 1826 and later dropped the hyphen) was born at Burlington, New Jersey, in 1789. In the previous year his father had laid out the site of Cooperstown at the foot of Otsego Lake, in New York, and in 1790 he settled there with his family. The son was brought up in a community in which the Coopers were by far the most important personages; his future was from the first defined as that of a landowner and estate manager. To prepare for it he had the education of a gentleman, first under a private tutor in Albany, and then in Yale College, which expelled him for too much pleasure-seeking in 1806. His further education consisted of shipping to England as a common sailor in 1806-1807 and three years' service as a midshipman in the United States Navy, from which he resigned shortly after his marriage, in 1811, to Susan Augusta De Lancey, daughter of a wealthy family in Mamaroneck, Westchester County. Both he and his wife had money of their own, and there was more in prospect. They settled down to raising a family and supervising their interests, living for some time at Cooperstown, and later in Westchester. In 1819, when Cooper was thirty, he was a gentleman farmer and a small capitalist, with neither the ambition nor the necessity for authorship.

Seldom, perhaps, has a novelist developed more casually. The tradition is that, reading aloud to his wife a story of English country life, he remarked that he could do as well himself and set out to make good his boast. The result was *Precaution,* a novel picturing English society and abounding with moral sentiment on marriage. It was published in 1820, and, although, not especially successful, it led directly to *The Spy* (1821), which was enormously so. The course of Cooper's life was changed abruptly from that natural to a country gentleman to the uncertain peregrinations of a writer. Possessing both a fertile imagination and a ready pen, he began to produce a stream of books which, at the time of his death in 1851, consisted of thirty-three novels and numerous volumes of social comment, naval history, and travel.

The relation between his life and his writing is highly complicated. In general, however, three periods are clearly distinguishable. Between 1820 and 1826 he explored the possibilities of the novel of romantic action, in emulation of Sir Walter Scott; living in New York City after 1822, the center of the congenial "Lunch" or Bread and Cheese Club, he sent forth to the world, in rapid succession, *The Pioneers*

(1823), *The Pilot* (1824), *Lionel Lincoln* (1825), and *The Last of the Mohicans* (1826). Between 1826 and 1833 he lived in Europe, where, under the tutelage of Lafayette, he became deeply interested in political philosophy, particularly as it appeared in the contrast between American and European institutions. An ardent patriot, he wrote a trilogy in opposition to Scott's glorification of medievalism, but *The Bravo* (1831), *The Heidenmauer* (1832), and *The Headsman* (1833) disappointed the public, in America as well as in Europe, and inaugurated a disillusion in their author which grew steadily with the years. From 1834 until his death Cooper lived half of each year in Cooperstown, spending the other six months in New York City. He had left the United States in the administration of John Quincy Adams; when he returned, the Jacksonian revolution had materially changed the social and political complexion of the nation. Cooper, an aristocrat by birth, by education, and by temperament, did not find the change wholly admirable; indeed, the last seventeen years of his life were spent in an unhappy battle for aristocratic principles which his countrymen found objectionable. Occasionally, as in *The Pathfinder* (1840) and *The Deerslayer* (1841), Cooper returned to his earlier vein, but his more characteristic works were social satires, such as *Home as Found* (1838), and the problem novels, *Satanstoe* (1845), *The Chainbearer* (1845), and *The Redskins* (1846), based upon the opposition of New Yorkers to the continuance of the tenant farm system of the patroons. Sometimes, indeed, he deserted fiction to present directly his social and political beliefs, among them his conviction that individual liberty can only be achieved by a constitutional government which protects property as well as human rights. In *Notions of the Americans* (1828) he played the role of a traveler from abroad reporting on his findings on the new nation to friends in Europe; in *The American Democrat* (1838) he argued for an aristocracy of merit not unlike that envisaged by Hamilton.

Cooper was unpopular in his later years because of his criticism of democracy. The tale of his innumerable libel suits against those critics who unjustly defamed his character is lengthy and inappropriate here, but it should be said that he was usually in the right and won his cases. Professor Spiller's claim that Cooper was the "most thoroughly critical mind that early America produced" is just. Few men of his time realized as he did that democracy, misunderstood, can be tyrannical; that the glorification of mediocrity and numbers work against distinction and quality.

It is not as a social critic, however, that Cooper has won his fame, and another age than the present may well forget his problem novels. He lives, as his friend Bryant said, as the American Hesiod or Theocritus, a poet of the youth of a nation, a nation which was wresting a continent from nature and the Indians, not always intelligently, not always justly, but with full awareness of the imaginative "lift" of the great open spaces and the epic quality of man's struggle with the wilderness. His claim to fame as the first great American novelist can scarcely be challenged.

James Fenimore Cooper: Representative Selections, ed. R. E. Spiller, Cincinnati, 1936   The Letters and Journals of James Fenimore Cooper, ed. James Franklin Beard, 4 vols., Cambridge, 1960-1964   R. E. Spiller and P. C. Blackburn, A Descriptive Bibliography of the Writings of James Fenimore Cooper, New York, 1934   T. R. Lounsbury, James Fenimore Cooper, American Men of Letters Series, Boston, 1882   R. E. Spiller, Fenimore Cooper, Critic of His Times, New York, 1931   "James Fenimore Cooper: A Re-appraisal," New York History, XXXV, special issue, 1954 (11 articles)

from Notions of the Americans

During his European sojourn from 1826 to 1833, Cooper became disturbed by the large number of superficial accounts of America written by English travelers. He began in 1827 a work which would provide a more accurate, less prejudiced picture of his native country. He chose the same form used by those he would answer — the travel book — and he adopted the guise of a cultivated Englishman (a "travelling bachelor") writing letters to fellow European members of a bachelor's club. The book appeared in 1828, first in England, later in America, as Notions of the Americans.

Letter XXIII [Literature and the Arts] is devoted to a survey of the American intellectual scene, with emphasis on education, periodicals and the press, and literature. Of particular interest is Cooper's explanation of the "powerful obstacles" to literature in the United States — the preference of American publishers for British works available free of charge, and the "poverty of materials" at hand for the American writer. The latter complaint was to be echoed later by such a writer as Hawthorne. Cooper himself provides one of the best examples of a writer who overcame the handicap by discovering — in a sense, creating — new and genuinely native materials.

Literature and the Arts

Letter XXIII: To the Abbate Giromachi, &c. &c.

Washington, _____

You ask me to write freely on the subject of the literature and the arts of the United States. The subjects are so meagre as to render it a task that would require no small portion of the talents necessary to figure in either, in order to render them of interest. Still, as the request has come in so urgent a form, I shall endeavour to oblige you.

The Americans have been placed, as respects moral and intellectual advancement, different from all other infant nations. They have never been without the wants of civilization, nor have they ever been entirely without the means of a supply. Thus pictures, and books, and statuary, and every thing else which appertains to elegant life, have always been known to them in an abundance, and of a quality exactly proportioned to their cost. Books, being the cheapest, and the nation having great leisure and prodigious zest for information, are not only the most common, as you will readily suppose, but they are probably more common than among any other people. I scarcely remember ever to have entered an American dwelling, however humble, without finding fewer or more books. As they form the most essential division of the subject, not only on account of their greater frequency, but on account of their far greater importance, I shall give them the first notice in this letter.

Unlike the progress of the two professions in the countries of our hemisphere, in America the printer came into existence before the author. Reprints of English works gave the first employment to the press. Then came almanacs, psalm-books, religious tracts, sermons, journals, political essays, and even rude attempts at poetry. All these preceded the revolution. The first journal was established in Boston at the commencement of the last century. There are several original polemical works of great originality and power that belong to the same period. I do not know that more learning and talents existed at that early day in the States of New-England than in Virginia, Maryland and the Carolinas, but there was certainly a stronger desire to exhibit them.

The colleges or universities, as they were somewhat prematurely called, date very far back in the brief history of the country. There is no stronger evidence of the 10 intellectual character, or of the judicious ambition of these people, than what this simple fact furnishes. Harvard College, now the university of Cambridge — (it better deserves the title at this day) — was founded in 1638; within less than *twenty years* after the landing of the first settlers in New-England! Yale (in Connecticut) was founded in 1701. Columbia (in the city of New-York) was founded in 1754. Nassau Hall (in New-Jersey) in 1738; and William and Mary (in Virginia) as far back as 1691. These are the oldest literary institutions in the United States, and all but the last are in flourishing conditions to the present hour. The first has given degrees to about five thousand graduates, and rarely has less than three hundred and fifty or four hundred students. Yale is about as well attended. The others contain 20 from a hundred and fifty to two hundred under-graduates. But these are not a moiety of the present colleges, or universities, (as they all aspire to be called,) existing in the country. There is no State, except a few of the newest, without at least one, and several have two or three.

Less attention is paid to classical learning here than in Europe; and, as the term of residence rarely exceeds four years, profound scholars are by no means common. This country possesses neither the population nor the endowments to maintain a large class of learned idlers, in order that one man in a hundred may contribute a mite to the growing stock of general knowledge. There is a luxury in this expenditure of animal force, to which the Americans have not yet attained. The good is far 30 too problematical and remote, and the expense of man too certain, to be prematurely sought. I have heard, I will confess, an American legislator quote Horace and Cicero; but it is far from being the humour of the country. I thought the taste of the orator questionable. A learned quotation is rarely of any use in an argument, since few men are fools enough not to see that the application of any maxim to politics is liable to a thousand practical objections, and, nine times in ten, they are evidences of the want of a direct, natural, and vigorous train of thought. They are the affectations, but rarely the ebullitions of true talent. When a man feels strongly, or thinks strongly, or speaks strongly, he is just as apt to do it in his native tongue as he is to laugh when he is tickled, or to weep when in sorrow. The Americans 40 are strong speakers and acute thinkers, but no great quoters of the morals and axioms of a heathen age, because they happen to be recorded in Latin.

---

12 **Harvard College . . . William and Mary.** Professor Spiller points out the correct dates for establishment of Harvard, 1636; Princeton (founded as Nassau Hall), 1746; William and Mary, 1693

The higher branches of learning are certainly on the advance in this country. The gentlemen of the middle and southern States, before the revolution, were very generally educated in Europe, and they were consequently, in this particular, like our own people. Those who came into life during the struggle, and shortly after, fared worse. Even the next generation had little to boast of in the way of instruction. I find that boys entered the colleges so late as the commencement of the present century, who had read a part of the Greek Testament, and a few books of Cicero and Virgil, with perhaps a little of Horace. But great changes have been made, and are still making, in the degree of previous qualification.

10 Still, it would be premature to say that there is any one of the American universities where classical knowledge, or even science, is profoundly attained, even at the present day. Some of the professors push their studies, for a life, certainly; and you well know, after all, that little short of a life, and a long one too, will make any man a good general scholar. In 1820, near eight thousand graduates of the twelve oldest colleges of this country (according to their catalogues) were then living. Of this number, 1,406 were clergymen. As some of the catalogues consulted were several years old, this number was of necessity greatly within the truth. Between the years 1800 and 1810, it is found that of 2,792 graduates, four hundred and fifty-three became clergymen. Here is pretty good evidence that religion is not neglected in 20 America, and that its ministers are not, as a matter of course, absolutely ignorant.

But the effects of the literary institutions of the United States are somewhat peculiar. Few men devote their lives to scholarship. The knowledge that is actually acquired, is perhaps quite sufficient for the more practical and useful pursuits. Thousands of young men, who have read the more familiar classics, who have gone through enough of mathematics to obtain a sense of their own tastes, and of the value of precision, who have cultivated *belles lettres* to a reasonable extent, and who have been moderately instructed in the arts of composition, and in the rules of taste, are given forth to the country to mingle in its active employments. I am inclined to believe that a class of American graduates carries away with it quite as much general and 30 diversified knowledge, as a class from one of our own universities. The excellence in particular branches is commonly wanting; but the deficiency is more than supplied by variety of information. The youth who has passed four years within the walls of a college, goes into the office of a lawyer for a few more. The profession of the law is not subdivided in America. The same man is counsellor, attorney, and conveyancer. Here the student gets a general insight into the principles, and a familiarity with the practice of the law, rather than an acquaintance with the study as a science. With this instruction he enters the world as a practitioner. Instead of existing in a state of dreaming retrospection, lost in a maze of theories, he is at once turned loose into the jostlings of the world. If perchance he encounters an antagonist 40 a little more erudite than himself, he seizes the natural truth for his sheet-anchor, and leaves precedent and quaint follies to him who has made them his study and delight. No doubt he often blunders, and is frequently, of necessity, defeated. But

---

34 **subdivided.** In England, only barristers plead in the courtroom; solicitors act as legal advisers outside the courts

in the course of this irreverent treatment, usages and opinions, which are bottomed in no better foundation than antiquity, and which are as inapplicable to the present state of the world, as the present state of the world is, or ought to be, unfavourable to all feudal absurdities, come to receive their death-warrants. In the mean time, by dint of sheer experience, and by the collision of intellects, the practitioner gets a stock of learning, that is acquired in the best possible school; and, what is of far more importance, the laws themselves get a dress which brings them within the fashions of the day. This same man becomes a legislator perhaps, and, if particularly clever, he is made to take an active part in the framing of laws that are not to harmonize with the other parts of an elaborate theory, but which are intended to 10 make men comfortable and happy. Now, taken with more or less qualification, this is the history of thousands in this country, and it is also an important part of the history of the country itself.

In considering the course of instruction in the United States, you are always to commence at the foundation. The common schools, which so generally exist, have certainly elevated the population above that of any other country, and are still elevating it higher, as they improve and increase in numbers. Law is getting every day to be more of a science, but it is a science that is forming rules better adapted to the spirit of the age. Medicine is improving, and in the cities it is, perhaps now, in point of practice, quite on a level with that of Europe. Indeed, the well-educated Ameri- 20 can physician very commonly enjoys an advantage that is little known in Europe. After obtaining a degree in his own country, he passes a few years in London, Edinburgh, Paris, and frequently in Germany, and returns with his gleanings from their several schools. This is not the case with one individual, but with many, annually. Indeed, there is so much of a fashion in it, and the custom is attended by so many positive advantages, that its neglect would be a serious obstacle to any very eminent success. Good operators are by no means scarce, and as surgery and medicine are united in the same person, there is great judgment in their practice. Human life is something more valuable in America than in Europe, and I think a critical attention to patients more common here than with us, especially when the sufferer be- 30 longs to an inferior condition in life. The profession is highly respectable; and in all parts of the country the better sort of its practitioners mingle, on terms of perfect equality, with the highest classes of society. There are several physicians in Congress, and a great many in the different State legislatures.

Of the ministry it is unnecessary to speak. The clergy are of all denominations, and they are educated, or not, precisely as they belong to sects which consider the gift of human knowledge of any importance. You have already seen how large a proportion of the graduates of some of the colleges enter the desk.

As respects authorship, there is not much to be said. Compared to the books that are printed and read, those of native origin are few indeed. The principal reason of 40 this poverty of original writers, is owing to the circumstance that men are not yet driven to their wits for bread. The United States are the first nation that possessed institutions, and, of course, distinctive opinions of its own, that was ever dependent on a foreign people for its literature. Speaking the same language as the English,

and long in the habit of importing their books from the mother country, the revolution effected no immediate change in the nature of their studies, or mental amusements. The works were re-printed, it is true, for the purposes of economy, but they
still continued English. Had the latter nation used this powerful engine with tolerable address, I think they would have secured such an ally in this country as would
have rendered their own decline not only more secure, but as illustrious as had been
their rise. There are many theories entertained as to the effect produced in this country by the falsehoods and jealous calumnies which have been undeniably uttered in
the mother country, by means of the press, concerning her republican descendant.
10 It is my opinion that, like all other ridiculous absurdities, they have defeated themselves, and that they are now more laughed at and derided, even here, than resented.
By all that I can learn, twenty years ago, the Americans were, perhaps, far too much
disposed to receive the opinions and to adopt the prejudices of their relatives;
whereas, I think it is very apparent that they are now beginning to receive them
with singular distrust. It is not worth our while to enter further into this subject,
except as it has had, or is likely to have, an influence on the national literature.

It is quite obvious, that, so far as taste and forms alone are concerned, the literature of England and that of America must be fashioned after the same models. The
authors, previously to the revolution, are common property, and it is quite idle to
20 say that the American has not just as good a right to claim Milton, and Shakspeare,
and all the old masters of the language, for his countrymen, as an Englishman. The
Americans having continued to cultivate, and to cultivate extensively, an acquaintance with the writers of the mother country, since the separation, it is evident they
must have kept pace with the trifling changes of the day. The only peculiarity that
can, or ought to be expected in their literature, is that which is connected with the
promulgation of their distinctive political opinions. They have not been remiss in
this duty, as any one may see, who chooses to examine their books. But we will
devote a few minutes to a more minute account of the actual condition of American literature.

30 The first, and the most important, though certainly the most familiar branch of
this subject, is connected with the public journals. It is not easy to say how many
newspapers are printed in the United States. The estimated number varies from six
hundred to a thousand. In the State of New-York there are more than fifty counties.
Now, it is rare that a county, in a State as old as that of New-York, (especially in
the more northern parts of the country), does not possess one paper at least. The
cities have many. The smaller towns sometimes have three or four, and very many
of the counties four or five. There cannot be many less than one hundred and fifty
journals in the State of New-York alone. Pennsylvania is said to possess eighty. But
we will suppose that these two States publish two hundred journals. They contain
40 about 3,000,000 of inhabitants. As the former is an enlightened State, and the latter

---

29 **literature.** "The writer might give, in proof of his opinion, one fact. He is led to believe that, so lately
as within ten years, several English periodical works were re-printed, and much read in the United States,
and that now they patronize their own, while the former are far less sought, though the demand, by means
of the increased population, should have been nearly doubled. Some of the works are no longer even
re-printed." — Cooper

rather below the scale of the general intelligence of the nation, it may not be a very bad average of the whole population. This rate would give eight hundred journals for the United States, which is probably something within the truth. I confess, however, this manner of equalizing estimates in America, is very uncertain in general, since a great deal, in such a question, must depend on the progress of society in each particular section of the country.

As might be expected, there is nearly every degree of merit to be found in these journals. No one of them has the benefit of that collected talent which is so often enlisted in the support of the more important journals of Europe. There is not often more than one editor to the best; but he is usually some man who has seen, in his 10 own person, enough of men and things to enable him to speak with tolerable discretion on passing events. The usefulness of the American journals, however, does not consist in their giving the tone to the public mind, in politics and morals, but in imparting facts. It is certain that, could the journals agree, they might, by their united efforts, give a powerful inclination to the common will. But, in point of fact, they do not agree on any one subject, or set of subjects, except, perhaps, on those which directly affect their own interests. They, consequently, counteract, instead of aiding each other, on all points of disputed policy; and it is in the bold and sturdy discussions that follow, that men arrive at the truth. The occasional union in their own favour, is a thing too easily seen through to do either good or harm. So far, 20 then, from the journals succeeding in leading the public opinion astray, they are invariably obliged to submit to it. They serve to keep it alive, by furnishing the means for its expression, but they rarely do more. Of course, the influence of each particular press is in proportion to the constancy and the ability with which it is found to support what is thought to be sound principles; but those principles must be in accordance with the private opinions of men, or most of their labour is lost.

The public press in America is rather more decent than that of England, and less decorous than that of France. The tone of the nation, and the respect for private feelings, which are, perhaps, in some measure, the consequence of a less artificial state of society, produce the former; and the liberty, which is a necessary attendant 30 of fearless discussion, is, I think, the cause of the latter. The affairs of an individual are rarely touched upon in the journals of this country; never, unless it is thought they have a direct connexion with the public interests, or from a wish to do him good. Still there is a habit, getting into use in America, no less than in France, that is borrowed from the English, which proves that the more unworthy feelings of our nature are common to men under all systems, and only need opportunity to find encouragement. I allude to the practice of repeating the proceedings of the courts of justice, in order to cater to a vicious appetite for amusement in the public.

It is pretended that, as a court of justice is open to the world, there can be no harm in giving the utmost publicity to its proceedings. It is strange the courts should 40 act so rigidly on the principles, that it is better a dozen guilty men should go free, than that one innocent man should suffer, and yet permit the gross injustice that is daily done by means of this practice. One would think, that if a court of justice is so open to the world, that it should be the business of the people of the world to enter it, in order that they might be certain that the information they crave should be without colouring or exaggeration. It is idle to say that the reports are accurate, and that he who reads is enabled to do justice to the accused, by comparing the facts that are laid before him. A reporter may give the expression of the tongue; but can he convey that of the eye, of the countenance, or of the form? — without regarding all of which, no man is perfectly master of the degree of credibility that is due to any witness of whose character he is necessarily ignorant. But every man has an infallible means of assuring himself of the value of these reports. Who has ever read a dozen of them without meeting with one (or perhaps more,) in which

10 the decision of the court and jury is to him a matter of surprise? It is true he assumes, that those who were present knew best, and as he has no great interest in the matter, he is commonly satisfied. But how is it with the unfortunate man who is wrongfully brought out of his retirement to repel an unjust attack against his person, his property, or his character? If he be a man of virtue, he is a man of sensibility; and not only he, but, what is far worse, those tender beings, whose existence is wrapped up in his own, are to be wounded daily and hourly, for weeks at a time, in order that a depraved appetite should be glutted. It is enough for justice that her proceedings should be so public as to prevent the danger of corruption; but we pervert a blessing to a curse, in making that which was intended for our protection, the means

20 of so much individual misery. It is an unavoidable evil of the law that it necessarily works some wrong, in order to do much good; but it is cruel that even the acquittal of a man should be unnecessarily circulated, in a manner to make all men remember that he had been accused. We have proof of the consequences of this practice in England. Men daily shrink from resistance to base frauds, rather than expose themselves to the observations and comments of those who enliven their breakfasts by sporting with these exhibitions of their fellow-creatures. There are, undoubtedly, cases of that magnitude which require some sacrifice of private feelings, in order that the community should reap the advantage; but the regular books are sufficient for authorities — the decisions of the courts are sufficient for justice — and the

30 utmost possible oblivion should prove as nearly sufficient as may be to serve the ends of a prudent and righteous humanity.

Nothing can be more free than the press of this country, on all subjects connected with politics. Treason cannot be written, unless by communicating with an open enemy. There is no other protection to a public man than that which is given by an independent jury, which punishes, of course, in proportion to the dignity and importance of the injured party. But the utmost lenity is always used in construing the right of the press to canvass the public acts of public men. Mere commonplace charges defeat themselves, and get into discredit so soon as to be lost, while graver accusations are met by grave replies. There is no doubt that the complacency of

40 individuals is sometimes disturbed by these liberties; but they serve to keep the officers of the government to their work, while they rarely do any lasting, or even temporary injury. Serious and criminal accusations against a public man, if groundless, are, by the law of reason, a crime against the community, and, as such, they are punished. The general principle observed in these matters is very simple. If A.

accuse B. of an act that is an offence against law, he may be called on for his proof, and if he fail he must take the consequences. But an editor of a paper, or any one else, who should bring a criminal charge, no matter how grave, against the President, and who could prove it, is just as certain of doing it with impunity, as if he held the whole power in his own hands. He would be protected by the invincible shield of public opinion, which is not only in consonance with the law, but which, in this country, makes law.

Actions for injuries done by the press, considering the number of journals, are astonishingly rare in America. When one remembers the usual difficulty of obtaining legal proof, which is a constant temptation, even to the guilty, to appeal to the 10 courts; and, on the other hand, the great freedom of the press, which is a constant temptation to abuse the trust, this fact, in itself, furnishes irresistible evidence of the general tone of decency which predominates in this nation. The truth is, that public opinion, among its other laws, has imperiously prescribed that, amidst the utmost latitude of discussion, certain limits shall not be passed; and public opinion, which is so completely the offspring of a free press, must be obeyed in this, as well as in other matters.

Leaving the journals, we come to those publications which make their appearance periodically. Of these there are a good many, some few of which are well supported. There are several scientific works, that are printed monthly, or quarterly, of respect- 20 able merit, and four or five reviews. Magazines of a more general character are not much encouraged. England, which is teeming with educated men, who are glad to make their bread by writing for these works, still affords too strong a competition for the success of any American attempts, in this species of literature. Though few, perhaps no English magazine is actually republished in America, a vast number are imported and read in the towns, where the support for any similar original production must first be found.

The literature of the United States, has indeed, too [two] powerful obstacles to conquer before (to use a mercantile expression) it can ever enter the markets of its own country on terms of perfect equality with that of England. Solitary and indi- 30 vidual works of genius may, indeed, be occasionally brought to light, under the impulses of the high feeling which has conceived them; but, I fear, a good, wholesome, profitable and continued pecuniary support, is the applause that talent most craves. The fact, that an American publisher can get an English work without money, must, for a few years longer, (unless legislative protection shall be extended to their own authors,) have a tendency to repress a national literature. No man will pay a writer for an epic, a tragedy, a sonnet, a history, or a romance, when he can get a work of equal merit for nothing. I have conversed with those who are conversant on the subject, and, I confess, I have been astonished at the information they imparted.

A capital American publisher has assured me that there are not a dozen writers in 40 this country, whose works he should feel confidence in publishing at all, while he reprints hundreds of English books without the least hesitation. This preference is

---

34 **without money.** There was no international copyright protection until the Bern Convention went into effect in 1887

by no means so much owing to any difference in merit, as to the fact that, when the price of the original author is to be added to the uniform hazard which accompanies all literary speculations, the risk becomes too great. The general taste of the reading world in this country is better than that of England. The fact is both proved and explained by the circumstance that thousands of works that are printed and read in the mother country, are not printed and read here. The publisher on this side of the Atlantic has the advantage of seeing the reviews of every book he wishes to print, and, what is of far more importance, he knows, with the exception of books that he is sure of selling, by means of a name, the decision of the English critics
10 before he makes his choice. Nine times in ten, popularity, which is all he looks for, is a sufficient test of general merit. Thus, while you find every English work of character, or notoriety, on the shelves of an American book-store, you may ask in vain for most of the trash that is so greedily devoured in the circulating libraries of the mother country, and which would be just as eagerly devoured here, had not a better taste been created by a compelled abstinence. That taste must now be overcome before such works could be sold at all.

When I say that books are not rejected here, from any want of talent in the writers, perhaps I ought to explain. I wish to express something a little different. Talent is sure of too many avenues to wealth and honours, in America, to seek, unnecessarily,
20 an unknown and hazardous path. It is better paid in the ordinary pursuits of life, than it would be likely to be paid by an adventure in which an extraordinary and skilful, because practised, foreign competition is certain. Perhaps high talent does not often make the trial with the American bookseller; but it is precisely for the reason I have named.

The second obstacle against which American literature has to contend, is in the poverty of materials. There is scarcely an ore which contributes to the wealth of the author, that is found, here, in veins as rich as in Europe. There are no annals for the historian; no follies (beyond the most vulgar and commonplace) for the satirist; no manners for the dramatist; no obscure fictions for the writer of romance;
30 no gross and hardy offences against decorum for the moralist; nor any of the rich artificial auxiliaries of poetry. The weakest hand can extract a spark from the flint, but it would baffle the strength of a giant to attempt kindling a flame with a pudding-stone. I very well know there are theorists who assume that the society and institutions of this country are, or ought to be, particularly favourable to novelties and variety. But the experience of one month, in these States, is sufficient to show any observant man the falsity of their position. The effect of a promiscuous assemblage any where, is to create a standard of deportment; and great liberty permits every one to aim at its attainment. I have never seen a nation so much alike in my life, as the people of the United States, and what is more, they are not only like
40 each other, but they are remarkably like that which common sense tells them they ought to resemble. No doubt, traits of character that are a little peculiar, without,

---

4 **England.** "The writer does not mean that the best taste of America is better than that of England; perhaps it is not quite so good; but, as a whole, the American reading world requires better books than the whole of the English reading world." — Cooper

however, being either very poetical, or very rich, are to be found in remote districts; but they are rare, and not always happy exceptions. In short, it is not possible to conceive a state of society in which more of the attributes of plain good sense, or fewer of the artificial absurdities of life, are to be found, than here. There is no custume for the peasant, (there is scarcely a peasant at all,) no wig for the judge, no baton for the general, no diadem for the chief magistrate. The darkest ages of their history are illuminated by the light of truth; the utmost efforts of their chivalry are limited by the laws of God; and even the deeds of their sages and heroes are to be sung in a language that would differ but little from a version of the ten commandments. However useful and respectable all this may be in actual life, it indicates 10 but one direction to the man of genius.

It is very true there are a few young poets now living in this country, who have known how to extract sweets from even these wholesome, but scentless native plants. They have, however, been compelled to seek their inspiration in the universal laws of nature, and they have succeeded, precisely in proportion as they have been most general in their application. Among these gifted young men, there is one (Halleck) who is remarkable for an exquisite vein of ironical wit, mingled with a fine, poetical, and, frequently, a lofty expression. This gentleman commenced his career as a satirist in one of the journals of New-York. Heaven knows, his materials were none of the richest; and yet the melody of his verse, the quaintness and force of his compari- 20 sons, and the exceeding humour of his strong points, brought him instantly into notice. He then attempted a general satire, by giving the history of the early days of a *belle.* He was again successful, though every body, at least every body of any talent, felt that he wrote in leading-strings. But he happened, shortly after the appearance of the little volume just named, (Fanny,) to visit England. Here his spirit was properly excited, and, probably on a rainy day, he was induced to try his hand at a *jeu d'esprit,* in the mother country. The result was one of the finest semi-heroic ironical descriptions to be found in the English language. This simple fact, in itself, proves the truth of a great deal of what I have just been writing, since it shows the effect a superiority of material can produce on the efforts of a man of 30 true genius.

Notwithstanding the difficulties of the subject, talent has even done more than in the instance of Mr. Halleck. I could mention several other young poets of this country of rare merit. By mentioning Bryant, Percival, and Sprague, I shall direct your attention to the names of those whose works would be most likely to give you pleasure. Unfortunately they are not yet known in Italian, but I think even you would not turn in distaste from the task of translation which the best of their effusions will invite.

The next, though certainly an inferior branch of imaginative writing, is fictitious composition. From the facts just named, you cannot expect that the novelists, or 40

16 **Halleck.** Fitz-Greene Halleck (1790-1867) wrote *Fanny* (1819), a satire of New York society, and *Alnwick Castle, with Other Poems* (1827)   28 **language.** "This little morceau of pleasant irony is called Alnwick Castle." — Cooper   34 **Bryant . . . Sprague.** William Cullen Bryant (1794-1878) had attained early fame for his "Thanatopsis"; James Gates Percival (1795-1856) had published *Poems* (1821); Charles Sprague (1791-1875), a Boston poet, was an imitator of the English Graveyard school

romance writers of the United States, should be very successful. The same reason will be likely, for a long time to come, to repress the ardour of dramatic genius. Still, tales and plays are no novelties in the literature of this country. Of the former, there are many as old as soon after the revolution; and a vast number have been published within the last five years. One of their authors of romance, who curbed his talents by as few allusions as possible to actual society, is distinguished for power and comprehensiveness of thought. I remember to have read one of his books (Wieland) when a boy, and I take it to be a never-failing evidence of genius, that, amid a thousand similar pictures which have succeeded, the images it has left, still
10 stand distinct and prominent in my recollection. This author (Mr. Brockden Brown) enjoys a high reputation among his countrymen, whose opinions are sufficiently impartial, since he flattered no particular prejudice of the nation in any of his works.

The reputation of Irving is well known to you. He is an author distinguished for a quality (humour) that has been denied his countrymen; and his merit is the more rare, that it has been shown in a state of society so cold and so restrained. Besides these writers, there are many others of a similar character, who enjoy a greater or less degree of favour in their own country. The works of two or three have even been translated (into French) in Europe, and a great many are reprinted in England. Though every writer of fiction in America has to contend against the difficulties I
20 have named, there is a certain interest in the novelty of the subject, which is not without its charm. I think, however, it will be found that they have all been successful, or the reverse, just as they have drawn warily, or freely, on the distinctive habits of their own country. I now speak of their success purely as writers of romance. It certainly would be possible for an American to give a description of the manners of his own country, in a book that he might choose to call a romance, which should be read, because the world is curious on the subject, but which would certainly never be read for that nearly indefinable poetical interest which attaches itself to a description of manners less bald and uniform. All the attempts to blend history with romance in America, have been comparatively failures, (and perhaps
30 fortunately,) since the subjects are too familiar to be treated with the freedom that the imagination absolutely requires. Some of the descriptions of the progress of society on the borders, have had a rather better success, since there is a positive, though no very poetical, novelty in the subject; but, on the whole, the books which have been best received, are those in which the authors have trusted most to their own conceptions of character, and to qualities that are common to the rest of the world and to human nature. This fact, if its truth be admitted, will serve to prove that the American writer must seek his renown in the exhibition of qualities that are general, while he is confessedly compelled to limit his observations to a state of society that has a wonderful tendency not only to repress passion, but to equalize
40 humours.

The Americans have always been prolific writers on polemics and politics. Their

---

5 **One of their authors,** Charles Brockden Brown (1771-1810), author of such Gothic romances as *Wieland* (1798) and *Edgar Huntly* (1799)   32 **society on the borders.** Throughout this passage, Cooper is referring to his own romances

sermons and fourth of July orations are numberless. Their historians, without being very classical or very profound, are remarkable for truth and good sense. There is not, perhaps, in the language a closer reasoner in metaphysics than Edwards; and their theological writers find great favour among the sectarians of their respective schools.

The stage of the United States is decidedly English. Both plays and players, with few exceptions, are imported. Theatres are numerous, and they are to be found in places where a traveller would little expect to meet them. Of course they are of all sizes, and of every degree of decoration and architectural beauty known in Europe, below the very highest. The façade of the principal theatre in Philadelphia, is a chaste 10 specimen in marble, of the Ionic, if my memory is correct. In New-York, there are two theatres about as large as the Théâtre Français (in the interior), and not much inferior in embellishments. Besides these, there is a very pretty little theatre, where lighter pieces are performed, and another with a vast stage for melodramas. There are also one or two other places of dramatic representation in this city, in which horses and men contend for the bays.

The Americans pay well for dramatic talent. Cooke, the greatest English tragedian of our age, died on this side of the Atlantic; and there are few players of eminence in the mother country who are not tempted, at some time or other, to cross the ocean. Shakspeare is, of course, the great author of America, as he is of England, 20 and I think he is quite as well relished here as there. In point of taste, if all the rest of the world be any thing against England, that of America is the best, since it unquestionably approaches nearest to that of the continent of Europe. Nearly one-half of the theatrical taste of the English is condemned by their own judgments, since the stage is not much supported by those who have had an opportunity of seeing any other. You will be apt to ask me how it happens, then, that the American taste is better? Because the people, being less exaggerated in their habits, are less disposed to tolerate caricatures, and because the theatres are not yet sufficiently numerous (though that hour is near) to admit of a representation that shall not be subject to the control of a certain degree of intelligence. I have heard an English 30 player complain that he never saw such a dull audience as the one before which he had just been exhibiting; and I heard the same audience complain that they never listened to such dull jokes. Now, there was talent enough in both parties; but the one had formed his taste in a coarse school, and the others had formed theirs under the dominion of common sense. Independently of this peculiarity, there is a vast deal of acquired, travelled taste in this country. English tragedy, and high English comedy, both of which, you know, are excellent, never fail here, if well played; that is, they never fail under the usual limits of all amusement. One will cloy of sweets. But the fact of the taste and judgment of these people, in theatrical exhibitions, is proved by the number of their good theatres, compared to their population.   40

Of dramatic writers there are none, or next to none. The remarks I have made in respect to novels apply with double force to this species of composition. A witty and successful American comedy could only proceed from extraordinary talent. There

---

17 **Cooke,** George Frederick Cooke (1756-1811), noted for his Shakespearian roles

would be less difficulty, certainly, with a tragedy; but still, there is rather too much foreign competition, and too much domestic employment in other pursuits, to invite genius to so doubtful an enterprise. The very baldness of ordinary American life is in deadly hostility to scenic representation. The character must be supported solely by its intrinsic power. The judge, the footman, the clown, the lawyer, the belle, or the beau, can receive no great assistance from dress. Melo-dramas, except the scene should be laid in the woods, are out of the question. It would be necessary to seek the great clock, which is to strike the portentous twelve blows, in the nearest church; a vaulted passage would degenerate into a cellar; and, as for ghosts, the country was
10 discovered, since their visitations have ceased. The smallest departure from the incidents of ordinary life would do violence to every man's experience; and, as already mentioned, the passions which belong to human nature must be delineated, in America, subject to the influence of that despot — common sense.

Notwithstanding the overwhelming influence of British publications, and all the difficulties I have named, original books are getting to be numerous in the United States. The impulses of talent and intelligence are bearing down a thousand obstacles. I think the new works will increase rapidly, and that they are destined to produce a powerful influence on the world. We will pursue this subject another time. — Adieu.

1828

from The American Democrat

Cooper's most penetrating commentary on American society and American institutions appeared in The American Democrat, *published in 1838. In his long period of residence abroad, Cooper had the opportunity to closely observe European culture and its relation to the European political systems. In his* Gleanings *volumes of 1837 and 1838, he had reported his observations in France, England, and Italy. It is natural that he should turn next to his own country and a reëxamination of its institutions in the light of his European experience.*

Although Cooper's is a small book, it bears comparison with one of the great analyses of American culture, Alexis de Tocqueville's Democracy in America, *which was translated into English and published in America in 1835. Although de Tocqueville's work seems epic in scope and Cooper's book appears a kind of primer, both writers made valuable and sometimes similar appraisals of the effect of the democratic political system on America's institutions and culture. Like de Tocqueville's book, Cooper's has had currency in the twentieth century. It was reissued in 1931, with an introduction of high praise by H. L. Mencken, and again in 1956.*

Cooper's point of view throughout The American Democrat *may be described as that of the enlightened conservative. Again and again, he comes back to property rights as the foundation for his position, and he takes a realistic — almost pessimistic — rather than idealistic view of the nature and condition of man. There is, he says, "one true mode of viewing life": ". . . it is a state of probation in which the trials exceed the enjoyments, and . . . while it is lawful to endeavor to increase the latter, more especially if of an intellectual and elevated kind, both form but insignificant interests in the great march of time."*

In the five chapters of The American Democrat *reprinted here, Cooper displays that ingenious combination of political liberalism and social conservatism that could derive only from a deep commitment to American democracy balanced by strong dedication to culture and art. It is astonishing how little of what he says seems dated, how much seems applicable to our own time. Whether commenting on prejudice or deportment (that is, manners), Cooper seems frequently and strikingly relevant to the twentieth-century American. Even on language, where he sounds most old-fashioned and quaint, he makes some astute observations — as, for example, when he says, "society is always a loser in mistaking names for things," or, more bluntly, "The love of turgid expressions is gaining ground, and ought to be corrected."*

On Prejudice

Prejudice is the cause of most of the mistakes of bodies of men. It influences our conduct and warps our judgment, in politics, religion, habits, tastes and opinions. We confide in one statesman and oppose another, as often from unfounded antipathies, as from reason; religion is tainted with uncharitableness and hostilities, without examination; usages are contemned; tastes ridiculed, and we decide wrong, from the practice of submitting to a preconceived and an unfounded prejudice, the most active and the most pernicious of all the hostile agents of the human mind.

The migratory propensities of the American people, and the manner in which the country has been settled by immigrants from all parts of the christian world, have an effect in diminishing prejudices of a particular kind, though, in other respects, few nations are more bigotted or provincial in their notions. Innovations on the usages connected with the arts of life are made here with less difficulty than common, reason, interest and enterprise proving too strong for prejudice; but in morals, habits and tastes, few nations have less liberality to boast of, than this. 10

America owes most of its social prejudices to the exaggerated religious opinions of the different sects which were so instrumental in establishing the colonies. The quakers, or friends, proscribed the delightful and elevated accomplishment of music, as, indeed, did the puritans, with the exception of psalmody. The latter confined marriage ceremonies to the magistrates, lest religion should be brought into disrepute! Most of those innocent recreations which help the charities, and serve to meliorate manners, were also forbidden, until an unnatural and monastic austerity, with a caustic habit of censoriousness, got to be considered as the only outward signs of that religious hope, which is so peculiarly adapted to render us joyous and benevolent. 20

False and extravagant notions on the subject of manners, never fail to injure a sound morality, by mistaking the shadow for the substance. Positive vice is known by all, for happily, conscience and revelation have made us acquainted with the laws of virtue, but it is as indiscreet unnecessarily to enlarge the circle of sins, as it is to expose ourselves to temptations that experience has shown we are unable to resist.

The most obvious American prejudices, connected with morality, are the notions that prevail on the subject of mispending time. That time may be mispent is undeniable, and few are they who ought not to reproach themselves with this neglect, 30 but the human mind needs relaxation and amusement, as well as the human body. These are to be sought in the different expedients of classes, each finding the most satisfaction in those indulgences that conform the nearest to their respective tastes. It is the proper duty of the legislator to endeavor to elevate these tastes, and not to prevent their indulgence. Those nations in which the cord of moral discipline, according to the dogmas of fanatics, has been drawn the tightest, usually exhibit the gravest scenes of depravity, on the part of those who break loose from restraints so ill judged and unnatural. On the other hand, the lower classes of society, in nations where amusements are tolerated, are commonly remarkable for possessing some of the tastes that denote cultivation and refinement. Thus do we find in catholic countries, that the men who in protestant nations, would pass their leisure in the coarsest indulgences, frequent operas and theatrical representations, classes of amusements which, well conducted, may be made powerful auxiliaries of virtue, and which generally have a tendency to improve the tastes. It is to be remarked that these exhibitions themselves are usually less gross, and more intellectual in catholic, than in protestant countries, a result of this improvement in manners.

The condition of this country is peculiar, and requires greater exertions than common, in extricating the mind from prejudices. The intimate connexion between popular opinion and positive law is one reason, since under a union so close there is danger that the latter may be colored by motives that have no sufficient foundation in justice. It is vain to boast of liberty, if the ordinances of society are to receive the impression of sectarianism, or of a provincial and narrow morality.

Another motive peculiar to the country, for freeing the mind from prejudice, is the mixed character of the population. Natives of different sections of the United States, and of various parts of Europe are brought in close contact, and without a disposition to bear with each other's habits, association becomes unpleasant, and enmities are engendered. The main result is to liberalize the mind, beyond a question, yet we see neighborhoods, in which oppressive intolerance is manifested by the greater number, for the time being, to the habits of the less. This is a sore grievance, more especially, when, as is quite frequently the case, the minority happen to be in possession of usages that mark the highest stage of civilization. It ought never to be forgotten, therefore, that every citizen is entitled to indulge without comment, or persecution, in all his customs and practices that are lawful and moral. Neither is morality to be regulated by the prejudices of sects, or social classes, but it is to be left strictly to the control of the laws, divine and human. To assume the contrary is to make prejudice, and prejudice of a local origin too, more imperious than the institutions. The justice, not to say necessity of these liberal concessions, is rendered more apparent when we remember that the parties meet as emigrants on what may be termed neutral territory, for it would be the height of presumption for the native of New York, for instance, to insist on his own peculiar customs, customs that other portions of the country perhaps repudiate, within the territory of New England, in opposition not only to the wishes of many of their brother emigrants, but to those of the natives themselves.

1838

An Aristocrat and a Democrat

We live in an age, when the words aristocrat and democrat are much used, without regard to the real significations. An aristocrat is one of a few, who possess the political power of a country; a democrat, one of the many. The words are also properly applied to those who entertain notions favorable to aristocratical, or democratical forms of government. Such persons are not, necessarily, either aristocrats, or democrats in fact, but merely so in opinion. Thus a member of a democratical government may have an aristocratical bias, and *vice versa*.

To call a man who has the habits and opinions of a gentleman, an aristocrat, from that fact alone, is an abuse of terms, and betrays ignorance of the true principles of government, as well as of the world. It must be an equivocal freedom, under which 10 every one is not the master of his own innocent acts and associations, and he is a sneaking democrat, indeed, who will submit to be dictated to, in those habits over which neither law nor morality assumes a right of control.

Some men fancy that a democrat can only be one who seeks the level, social, mental and moral, of the majority, a rule that would at once exclude all men of refinement, education and taste from the class. These persons are enemies of democracy, as they at once render it impracticable. They are usually great sticklers for their own associations and habits, too, though unable to comprehend any of a nature that are superior. They are, in truth, aristocrats in principle, though assuming a contrary pretension; the ground work of all their feelings and arguments being self. Such 20 is not the intention of liberty, whose aim is to leave every man to be the master of his own acts; denying hereditary honors, it is true, as unjust and unnecessary, but not denying the inevitable consequences of civilization.

The law of God is the only rule of conduct, in this, as in other matters. Each man should do as he would be done by. Were the question put to the greatest advocate of indiscriminate association, whether he would submit to have his company and habits dictated to him, he would be one of the first to resist the tyranny; for they, who are the most rigid in maintaining their own claims, in such matters, are usually the loudest in decrying those whom they fancy to be better off than themselves. Indeed, it may be taken as a rule in social intercourse, that he who is the most 30 apt to question the pretensions of others, is the most conscious of the doubtful position he himself occupies; thus establishing the very claims he affects to deny, by letting his jealousy of it be seen. Manners, education and refinement, are positive things, and they bring with them innocent tastes which are productive of high enjoyments; and it is as unjust to deny their possessors their indulgence, as it would be to insist on the less fortunate's passing the time they would rather devote to athletic amusements, in listening to operas for which they have no relish, sung in a language they do not understand.

All that democracy means, is as equal a participation in rights as is practicable; and to pretend that social equality is a condition of popular institutions, is to assume 40

that the latter are destructive of civilization, for, as nothing is more self-evident than the impossibility of raising all men to the highest standard of tastes and refinement, the alternative would be to reduce the entire community to the lowest. The whole embarrassment on this point exists in the difficulty of making men comprehend qualities they do not themselves possess. We can all perceive the difference between ourselves and our inferiors, but when it comes to a question of the difference between us and our superiors, we fail to appreciate merits of which we have no proper conceptions. In face of this obvious difficulty, there is the safe and just governing rule, already mentioned, or that of permitting every one to be the undisturbed judge
10 of his own habits and associations, so long as they are innocent, and do not impair the rights of others to be equally judges for themselves. It follows, that social intercourse must regulate itself, independently of institutions, with the exception that the latter, while they withhold no natural, bestow no factitious advantages beyond those which are inseparable from the rights of property, and general civilization.

In a democracy, men are just as free to aim at the highest attainable places in society, as to obtain the largest fortunes; and it would be clearly unworthy of all noble sentiment to say, that the grovelling competition for money shall alone be free, while that which enlists all the liberal acquirements and elevated sentiments of
20 the race, is denied the democrat. Such an avowal would be at once, a declaration of the inferiority of the system, since nothing but ignorance and vulgarity could be its fruits.

The democratic gentleman must differ in many essential particulars, from the aristocratical gentleman, though in their ordinary habits and tastes they are virtually identical. Their principles vary; and, to a slight degree, their deportment accordingly. The democrat, recognizing the right of all to participate in power, will be more liberal in his general sentiments, a quality of superiority in itself; but, in conceding this much to his fellow man, he will proudly maintain his own independence of vulgar domination, as indispensable to his personal habits. The same principles
30 and manliness that would induce him to depose a royal despot, would induce him to resist a vulgar tyrant.

There is no more capital, though more common error, than to suppose him an aristocrat who maintains his independence of habits; for democracy asserts the control of the majority, only, in matters of law, and not in matters of custom. The very object of the institution is the utmost practicable personal liberty, and to affirm the contrary, would be sacrificing the end to the means.

An aristocrat, therefore, is merely one who fortifies his exclusive privileges by positive institutions, and a democrat, one who is willing to admit of a free competition, in all things. To say, however, that the last supposes this competition will
40 lead to nothing, is an assumption that means are employed without any reference to an end. He is the purest democrat who best maintains his rights, and no rights can be dearer to a man of cultivation, than exemptions from unseasonable invasions on his time, by the coarse-minded and ignorant.

1838

On Language

Language being the medium of thought, its use enters into our most familiar practices. A just, clear and simple expression of our ideas is a necessary accomplishment for all who aspire to be classed with gentlemen and ladies. It renders all more respectable, besides making intercourse more intelligible, safer and more agreeable.

The common faults of American language are an ambition of effect, a want of simplicity, and a turgid abuse of terms. To these may be added ambiguity of expression. Many perversions of significations also exist, and a formality of speech, which, while it renders conversation ungraceful, and destroys its playfulness, seriously weakens the power of the language, by applying to ordinary ideas, words that are suited only to themes of gravity and dignity.   10

While it is true that the great body of the American people use their language more correctly than the mass of any other considerable nation, it is equally true that a smaller proportion than common attain to elegance in this accomplishment, especially in speech. Contrary to the general law in such matters, the women of the country have a less agreeable utterance than the men, a defect that great care should be taken to remedy, as the nursery is the birth-place of so many of our habits.

The limits of this work will not permit an enumeration of the popular abuses of significations, but a few shall be mentioned, in order that the student may possess a general clue to the faults. "Creek," a word that signifies an *inlet* of the sea, or of a lake, is misapplied to running streams, and frequently to the *outlets* of lakes. A 20 "square," is called a "park;" "lakes," are often called "ponds;" and "arms of the sea," are sometimes termed "rivers."

In pronunciation, the faults are still more numerous, partaking decidedly of provincialisms. The letter *u*, sounded like double *o*, or *oo*, or like *i*, as in vir*too*, for*tin*, for*tinate;* and *ew*, pronounced also like *oo*, are common errors. This is an exceedingly vicious pronunciation, rendering the language mean and vulgar. "New," pronounced as *"noo,"* is an example, and "few," as *"foo;"* the true sounds are *"nu"* and *"fu,"* the *u* retaining its proper soft sound, and not that of *"oo."*

The attempt to reduce the pronunciation of the English language to a common rule, produces much confusion, and taking the usages of polite life as the standard, 30 many uncouth innovations. All know the pronunciation of p l o u g h; but it will scarcely do to take this sound as the only power of the same combination of final letters, for we should be compelled to call t h o u g h, thou; t h r o u g h, throu; and t o u g h, tou.

False accentuation is a common American fault. Ensign (insin,) is called en*syne,* an engine (injin,) en*gyne.* Indeed, it is a common fault of narrow associations, to suppose that words are to be pronounced as they are spelled.

Many words are in a state of mutation, the pronunciation being unsettled even in the best society, a result that must often arise where language is as variable and

---

19 creek . . . rivers. *Creek* and *pond* in these meanings are Americanisms, dating back to 1622. *Park* and *river* are not.

undetermined as the English. To this class belong "clerk," "cucumber" and "gold," which are often pronounced as spelt, though it were better and more in conformity with polite usage to say "clark," "*cow*cumber," (not cow*cum*ber,) and "goold." For *loote*nant (lieutenant) there is not sufficient authority, the true pronunciation being "*levte*nant." By making a familiar compound of this word, we see the uselessness of attempting to reduce the language to any other laws than those of the usages of polite life, for they who affect to say *loote*nant, do not say "*loote*nant-co-lo-nel," but "*loote*nant-kurnel."

The polite pronunciation of "either" and "neither," is "i-ther" and "ni-ther," and
10 not "eether" and "neether." This is a case in which the better usage of the language has respected derivations, for "*ei*," in German are pronounced as in "height" and "sleight," "*ie*" making the sound of "*ee*." We see the arbitrary usages of the English, however, by comparing these legitimate sounds with those of the words "lieu-tenant colonel," which are derived from the French, in which language the latter word is called "*co-lo-nel*."

Some changes of the language are to be regretted, as they lead to false inferences, and society is always a loser by mistaking names for things. Life is a fact, and it is seldom any good arises from a misapprehension of the real circumstances under which we exist. The word "gentleman" has a positive and limited signification. It
20 means one elevated above the mass of society by his birth, manners, attainments, characters and social condition. As no civilized society can exist without these social differences, nothing is gained by denying the use of the term. If blackguards were to be *called* "gentlemen," and "gentlemen," "blackguards," the difference between them would be as obvious as it is today.

The word "gentleman," is derived from the French gentilhomme, which originally signified one of noble birth. This was at a time when the characteristics of the condition were never found beyond a caste. As society advanced, ordinary men attained the qualifications of nobility, without that of birth, and the meaning of the word was extended. It is now possible to be a gentleman without birth, though, even in
30 America, where such distinctions are purely conditional, they who have birth, except in extraordinary instances, are classed with gentlemen. To call a laborer, one who has neither education, manners, accomplishments, tastes, associations, nor any one of the ordinary requisites, a gentleman, is just as absurd as to call one who is thus qualified, a fellow. The word must have some especial signification, or it would be synonymous with man. One may have gentlemanlike feelings, principles and appearance, without possessing the liberal attainments that distinguish the gentleman. Least of all does money alone make a gentleman, though, as it becomes a means of obtaining the other requisites, it is usual to give it a place in the claims of the class. Men may be, and often are, very rich, without having the smallest title to be deemed
40 gentlemen. A man may be a distinguished gentleman, and not possess as much money as his own footman.

This word, however, is sometimes used instead of the old terms, "sirs," "my masters," &c. &c., as in addressing bodies of men. Thus we say "gentlemen," in addressing a publick meeting, in complaisance, and as, by possibility, some gentlemen may be present. This is a license that may be tolerated, though he who should insist that all present were, as individuals, gentlemen, would hardly escape ridicule.

What has just been said of the word gentleman, is equally true with that of lady. The standard of these two classes, rises as society becomes more civilized and refined; the man who might pass for a gentleman in one nation, or community, not being able to maintain the same position in another.

The inefficiency of the effort to subvert things by names, is shown in the fact that, in all civilized communities, there is a class of men, who silently and quietly recognize each other, as gentlemen; who associate together freely and without reserve, and who admit each other's claims without scruple or distrust. This class 10 may be limited by prejudice and arbitrary enactments, as in Europe, or it may have no other rules than those of taste, sentiment and the silent laws of usage, as in America.

The same observations may be made in relation to the words master and servant. He who employs laborers, with the right to command, is a master, and he who lets himself to work, with an obligation to obey, a servant. Thus there are house, or domestic servants, farm servants, shop servants, and various other servants; the term master being in all these cases the correlative.

In consequence of the domestic servants of America having once been negro-slaves, a prejudice has arisen among the laboring classes of the whites, who not only dis- 20 like the term servant, but have also rejected that of master. So far has this prejudice gone, that in lieu of the latter, they have resorted to the use of the word *boss,* which has precisely the same meaning in Dutch! How far a subterfuge of this nature is worthy of a manly and common sense peoples, will admit of question.

A similar objection may be made to the use of the word "help," which is not only an innovation on a just and established term, but which does not properly convey the meaning intended. They who aid their masters in the toil may be deemed "helps," but they who perform all the labor do not assist, or help to do the thing, but they do it themselves. A man does not usually hire his cook to *help* him cook his dinner, but to cook it herself. Nothing is therefore gained, while something is 30 lost in simplicity and clearness by the substitution of new and imperfect terms, for the long established words of the language. In all cases in which the people of America have retained the *things* of their ancestors, they should not be ashamed to keep the *names.*

The love of turgid expressions is gaining ground, and ought to be corrected. One of the most certain evidences of a man of high breeding, is his simplicity of speech; a simplicity that is equally removed from vulgarity and exaggeration. He calls a spade, a "spade." His enunciation, while clear, deliberate and dignified, is totally without strut, showing his familiarity with the world, and, in some degree, reflect- ing the qualities of his mind, which is polished without being addicted to senti- 40 mentalism, or any other bloated feeling. He never calls his wife, "his lady," but "his wife," and he is not afraid of lessening the dignity of the human race, by styl- ing the most elevated and refined of his fellow creatures, "men and women." He does not say, in speaking of a dance, that "the attire of the ladies was exceedingly elegant and peculiarly becoming at the late assembly," but that "the women were well dressed at the last ball;" nor is he apt to remark, "that the Rev. Mr. G— gave us an elegant and searching discourse the past sabbath," but, that "the parson preached a good sermon last sunday."

The utterance of a gentleman ought to be deliberate and clear, without being measured. All idea of effort should be banished, though nothing lost for want of distinctness. His emphasis ought to be almost imperceptible; never halting, or abrupt; and least of all, so placed as to give an idea of his own sense of cleverness; but regulated by those slight intonations that give point to wit, and force to reason.
10 His language should rise with the subject, and, as he must be an educated and accomplished man, he cannot but know that the highest quality of eloquence, and all sublimity, is in the thought, rather than in the words, though there must be an adaptation of the one to the other.

This is still more true of women than of men, since the former are the natural agents in maintaining the refinement of a people.

All cannot reach the highest standard in such matters, for it depends on early habit, and particularly on early associations. The children of gentlemen are as readily distinguished from other children by these peculiarities, as by the greater delicacy of their minds, and higher tact in breeding. But we are not to abandon all improve-
20 ment, because perfection is reached but by few. Simplicity should be the first aim, after one is removed from vulgarity, and let the finer shades of accomplishment be acquired as they can be attained. In no case, however, can one who aims at turgid language, exaggerated sentiment, or pedantic utterance, lay claim to be either a man or a woman of the world.

1838

On Deportment

Much of the pleasure of social communication depends on the laws of deportment. Deportment may be divided into that, which, by marking refinement and polish, is termed breeding; and that, which, though less distinguished for finesse and finish, denoting a sense of civility and respect, is usually termed manners. The first can
30 only be expected in men and women of the world, or those who are properly styled gentlemen and ladies; while an absence of the last is a proof of vulgarity and coarseness, that every citizen of a free state should be desirous of avoiding. Breeding is always pleasant, though often arbitrary in its rules; but manners are indispensable to civilization. It is just as unreasonable to expect high breeding in any but those who are trained to it, from youth upward, as it would be to expect learning without education; but a tone of manners, that shall mark equally self-respect and a proper regard for others, is as easily acquired as reading and writing.

The gentleman should aim at a standard of deportment that is refined by sentiment and taste, without the sickliness of overstrained feelings; and those beneath
40 him in condition, at a manly humanity, that shall not pretend to distinctions the

party does not comprehend, while it carefully respects all the commoner observances of civilized intercourse.

A refined simplicity is the characteristic of all high bred deportment, in every country, and a considerate humanity should be the aim of all beneath it.

1838

On American Deportment

The American people are superior in deportment, in several particulars, to the people of Europe, and inferior in others. The gentlemen have less finesse, but more frankness of manner, while the other classes have less vulgarity and servility, relieved by an agreeable attention to each other's rights, and to the laws of humanity in general. On the whole, the national deportment is good, without being polished, 10 supplying the deficiency in this last essential, by great kindness and civility. In that part of deportment which affects the rights of all, such as the admission of general and common laws of civility, the absence of social selfishness, and a strict regard to the wants and feebleness of woman, all other nations might be benefitted by imitating this.

The defects in American deportment are, notwithstanding, numerous and palpable. Among the first, may be ranked insubordination in children, and a general want of respect for age. The former vice may be ascribed to the business habits of the country, which leave so little time for parental instruction, and perhaps, in some degree, to the arts of political agents, who, with their own advantage in view, among 20 the other expedients of their cunning, have resorted to the artifice of separating children from the natural advisers, by calling meetings of the young, to decide on the fortunes and policy of the country. Every advertisement calling assemblies of the young, to deliberate on national concerns, ought to be deemed an insult to the good sense, the modesty, and the filial piety of the class to which it is addressed.

The Americans are reproached, also, with the want of a proper deference for social station; the lower classes manifesting their indifference by an unnecessary insolence. As a rule, this charge is unmerited, civility being an inherent quality of the American character; still, there are some who mistake a vulgar audacity for independence. Men and women of this disposition, require to be told that, in thus betraying their 30 propensities, they are giving the strongest possible proofs that they are not what their idle vanity would give reason to suppose they fancy themselves, the equals of those whom they insult by their coarseness.

More of this class err from ignorance, want of reflection, or a loose habit of regulating their conduct in their intercourse with others, than from design. The following anecdote will give an instance of what is meant, and, as the circumstance related is true, the reader will perceive the ludicrous impression that is left, by these gross improprieties of behaviour. A gentleman, who shall be called Winfield, perceiving a girl of eight or ten years of age, endeavoring to find an entrance to his house, enquired her errand. "I have some hats for *Winfield's girls,*" was the answer. Although 40 shocked at this rudeness, Mr. Winfield told the child, that by going to a certain door, she would find a servant to receive her. "Oh!" replied the girl, "I have already seen the *Irish lady,* in the kitchen." This Irish *lady,* was the cook, a very good woman in her way, but one who had no pretensions to be so termed!

Such a confusion in the ideas of this child, is a certain proof of a want of training, for the young ladies who were treated so disrespectfully, were not the less ladies, nor did the cook become more than a cook, for the vulgarity. Facts are not to be changed by words, and all they obtain, who fancy their language and deportment can alter the relations of society, is an exposure of their own ignorance.

The entire complexion, and in many respects, the well being of society, depends
10 on the deportment of its different members, to each other. It behooves the master to be kind to the servant, the servant to be respectful and obedient to his master; the young and inexperienced to defer to the aged and experienced; the ignorant to attend to the admonitions of the wise, and the unpolished to respect the tastes and habits of the refined.

In other countries, where positive ordinances create social distinctions in furtherance of these ends, it is believed they cannot be obtained in any other manner; but it is to be hoped that America is destined to prove, that common sense and the convictions of propriety and fitness, are as powerful agents as force. The servility and arrogance of a highly artificial social scale are not to be desired, but, having
20 positive social facts, also, which cannot be dispensed with, it is vain to resist them. Civility and respect are the sure accompaniments of a high civilization, and the admission of obvious facts is an indispensable requisite of common sense, as their denial is evidence of infatuation and folly.

There is a moral obligation in every man to conduct himself with civility to all around him. Neither are his particular notions of what is proper, to be taken as an excuse for his rudeness and insults. Refinement and the finesse of breeding are not expected from the majority, but none are so ignorant, in this country, as not to distinguish between what is proper and what is improper in deportment.

Some men imagine they have a right to ridicule what are termed "airs," in others.
30 If it could be clearly established what are "airs," and what not, a corrective of this sort might not be misapplied. But the term is conventional, one man experiencing disgust at what enters into the daily habits of another. It is exceedingly hazardous, therefore, for any but those who are familiar with the best usages of the world, to pronounce any thing "airs," because it is new to them, since what has this appearance to such persons may be no more than a proof of cultivation and of a good tone of manners.

On the other hand, many who have been thrown accidentally and for short periods, into the society of the more refined classes, adopt their usages without feeling or understanding their reasons and advantages, caricaturing delicacy and sentiment, and
40 laying stress on habits, which, though possibly convenient in themselves, are not deemed at all essential by men and women of the world. These affectations of breeding are laughed at, as the "silver-forkisms" of pretenders. To the man of the world it is unnecessary to point out the want of taste in placing such undue stress on these immaterial things, but it may not be unnecessary to the novice in the usages

of the better circles, to warn him that his ignorance will be more easily seen by his
exaggerations, than by his deficiencies of manner. The Duc de Richlieu is said to
have detected an impostor by his *not* taking olives with his fingers.

But these are points of little interest with the mass, while civility and decency lie
at the root of civilization. There is no doubt that, in general, America has retro-
graded in manners within the last thirty years. Boys, and even men, wear their hats
in the houses of all classes, and before persons of all ages and conditions. This is
not independence, but vulgarity, for nothing sooner distinguishes a gentleman from
a blackguard, than the habitual attention of the former to the minor civilities established by custom. It has been truly said, that the man who is well dressed·respects   10
himself more, and behaves himself better, than the man that is ill dressed; but it is
still more true that the man who commences with a strict observance of the commoner civilities, will be the most apt to admit of the influence of refinement on his
whole character.   1838

---

2 **Richlieu,** Armand Jean du Plessis, duc de Richelieu (1585-1642), French statesman and cardinal

Preface to the Leather-Stocking Tales

Leather-Stocking — or Natty Bumppo — appears in and binds together five novels: The
Pioneers *(1823),* The Last of the Mohicans *(1826),* The Prairie *(1827),* The Pathfinder *(1840), and* The Deerslayer *(1841). Cooper did not plan these novels organically,
however, and they are held together only as parts of a biographical whole which has numerous discrepancies. In point of biographical time* The Deerslayer *should be read first; its
action takes place on Otsego Lake between 1740 and 1745. Next comes* The Last of the
Mohicans, *which occurs on Lake George in 1757; then* The Pathfinder, *whose scene is
Lake Ontario in 1760. After* The Pioneers, *portraying the New York frontier of Otsego
County in 1793, comes* The Prairie, *in which the nameless hero — his dog Hector, stuffed
by an Indian taxidermist, at his side — dies in 1804 amid the scenic splendor of the Paw-
nee country.*

*In 1850, a decade after finishing the last novel of the series, Cooper placed the books in
proper sequence to make an episodic biography of Bumppo, and published them with a general Preface, reprinted here. In the Preface, Cooper attempts to show, in brief summary, the
essence of Bumppo's character and meaning, and he makes a succinct defense of his idealized
portrayal of the Indian. As in his social observations, Cooper is concise and pointed in explaining his own aims as a novelist and in defending his technique as a romanticist.*

This series of Stories, which has obtained the name of "The Leather-Stocking
Tales," has been written in a very desultory and inartificial manner. The order in
which the several books appeared was essentially different from that in which they
would have been presented to the world, had the regular course of their incidents
been consulted. In the Pioneers, the first of the series written, the Leather-Stocking
is represented as already old, and driven from his early haunts in the forest, by the

sound of the axe, and the smoke of the settler. "The Last of the Mohicans," the next book in the order of publication, carried the readers back to a much earlier period in the history of our hero, representing him as middle-aged, and in the full-est vigor of manhood. In the Prairie, his career terminates, and he is laid in his grave. There, it was originally the intention to leave him, in the expectation that, as in the case of the human mass, he would soon be forgotten. But a latent regard for this character induced the author to resuscitate him in "The Pathfinder," a book that was not long after succeeded by "The Deerslayer," thus completing the series as it now exists.

10   While the five books that have been written were originally published in the order just mentioned, that of the incidents, insomuch as they are connected with the career of their principal character, is, as has been stated, very different. Taking the life of the Leather-Stocking as a guide, "The Deerslayer" should have been the opening book, for in that work he is seen just emerging into manhood; to be succeeded by "The Last of the Mohicans," "The Pathfinder," "The Pioneers," and "The Prairie." This arrangement embraces the order of events, though far from being that in which the books at first appeared. "The Pioneers" was published in 1822; "The Deerslayer" in 1841; making the interval between them nineteen years. Whether these progres-sive years have had a tendency to lessen the value of the last-named book by lessen-
20   ing the native fire of its author, or of adding somewhat in the way of improved taste and a more matured judgment, is for others to decide.

If anything from the pen of the writer of these romances is at all to outlive him-self, it is, unquestionably, the series of "The Leather-Stocking Tales." To say this, is not to predict a very lasting reputation for the series itself, but simply to express the belief it will outlast any, or all, of the works from the same hand.

It is undeniable that the desultory manner in which "The Leather-Stocking Tales" were written, has, in a measure, impaired their harmony, and otherwise lessened their interest. This is proved by the fate of the two books last published, though probably the two most worthy an enlightened and cultivated reader's notice. If the
30   facts could be ascertained, it is probable the result would show that of all those (in America, in particular) who have read the three first books of the series, not one in ten has a knowledge of the existence even of the two last. Several causes have tended to produce this result. The long interval of time between the appearance of "The Prairie" and that of "The Pathfinder," was itself a reason why the later books of the series should be overlooked. There was no longer novelty to attract attention, and the interest was materially impaired by the manner in which events were neces-sarily anticipated, in laying the last of the series first before the world. With the generation that is now coming on the stage this fault will be partially removed by the edition contained in the present work, in which the several tales will be
40   arranged solely in reference to their connexion with each other.

The author has often been asked if he had any original in his mind, for the char-acter of Leather-Stocking. In a physical sense, different individuals known to the writer in early life, certainly presented themselves as models, through his recollec-tions; but in a moral sense this man of the forest is purely a creation. The idea of

delineating a character that possessed little of civilization but its highest principles as they are exhibited in the uneducated, and all of savage life that is not incompatible with these great rules of conduct, is perhaps natural to the situation in which Natty was placed. He is too proud of his origin to sink into the condition of the wild Indian, and too much a man of the woods not to imbibe as much as was at all desirable, from his friends and companions. In a moral point of view it was the intention to illustrate the effect of seed scattered by the way side. To use his own language, his "gifts" were "white gifts," and he was not disposed to bring on them discredit. On the other hand, removed from nearly all the temptations of civilized life, placed in the best associations of that which is deemed savage, and favor-   10
ably disposed by nature to improve such advantages, it appeared to the writer that his hero was a fit subject to represent the better qualities of both conditions, without pushing either to extremes.

There was no violent stretch of the imagination, perhaps, in supposing one of civilized associations in childhood, retaining many of his earliest lessons amid the scenes of the forest. Had these early impressions, however, not been sustained by continued, though casual connexion with men of his own color, if not of his own caste, all our information goes to show he would soon have lost every trace of his origin. It is believed that sufficient attention was paid to the particular circumstances in which this individual was placed to justify the picture of his qualities that has   20
been drawn. The Delawares early attracted the attention of missionaries, and were a tribe unusually influenced by their precepts and example. In many instances they became Christians, and cases occurred in which their subsequent lives gave proof of the efficacy of the great moral changes that had taken place within them.

A leading character in a work of fiction has a fair right to the aid which can be obtained from a poetical view of the subject. It is in this view, rather than in one more strictly circumstantial, that Leather-Stocking has been drawn. The imagination has no great task in portraying to itself a being removed from the every-day inducements to err, which abound in civilized life, while he retains the best and simplest of his early impressions; who sees God in the forest; hears him in the winds; bows   30
to him in the firmament that o'ercanopies all; submits to his sway in a humble belief of his justice and mercy; in a word, a being who finds the impress of the Deity in all the works of nature, without any of the blots produced by the expedients, and passion, and mistakes of man. This is the most that has been attempted in the character of Leather-Stocking. Had this been done without any of the drawbacks of humanity, the picture would have been, in all probability, more pleasing than just. In order to preserve the *vrai-semblable,* therefore, traits derived from the prejudices, tastes, and even the weaknesses of his youth, have been mixed up with these higher qualities and longings, in a way, it is hoped, to represent a reasonable picture of human nature, without offering to the spectator a "monster of goodness."   40

It has been objected to these books that they give a more favorable picture of the red man than he deserves. The writer apprehends that much of this objection arises from the habits of those who have made it. One of his critics, on the appearance of the first work in which Indian character was portrayed, objected that its "characters

were Indians of the school of Heckewelder, rather than of the school of nature."
These words quite probably contain the substance of the true answer to the objection. Heckewelder was an ardent, benevolent missionary, bent on the good of the
red man, and seeing in him one who had the soul, reason, and characteristics of a
fellow-being. The critic is understood to have been a very distinguished agent of the
government, one very familiar with Indians, as they are seen at the councils to treat
for the sale of their lands, where little or none of their domestic qualities come in
play, and where, indeed, their evil passions are known to have the fullest scope. As
just would it be to draw conclusions of the general state of American society from
10 the scenes of the capital, as to suppose that the negotiating of one of these treaties
is a fair picture of Indian life.

It is the privilege of all writers of fiction, more particularly when their works
aspire to the elevation of romances, to present the *beau-idéal* of their characters to
the reader. This it is which constitutes poetry, and to suppose that the red man is
to be represented only in the squalid misery or in the degraded moral state that certainly more or less belongs to his condition, is, we apprehend, taking a very narrow
view of an author's privileges. Such criticism would have deprived the world of
even Homer.   1850

---

1 **Heckewelder,** John Gottlieb Heckewelder (1743-1823), a Moravian missionary to the Indians, published
Account of the History, Manners, and Customs of the Indian Nations Who Once Inhabited Pennsylvania (1819)

Chapter 3 The American Renaissance 1829–1860

We Will Speak Our Own Minds.

"We will walk on our own feet;
we will work with our own hands;
we will speak our own minds."
> — *Emerson*

I. Intellectual Currents

Between the triumph of the frontier in Jackson's election and the days of the Civil War, the United States emerged a flourishing nation — a nation for the common man, a nation with a culture, a nation of promises.

This was the period of renaissance, the period of awakening and development, when Americans at last began speaking their own minds. The writers of the era represented in this chapter belong mostly to New England; and indeed the New England writers loom large in any survey of American literature during the years from 1829 to 1865. Three great writers of the period were outside the New England orbit: Edgar Allan Poe, Herman Melville, and Abraham Lincoln. None of these was unmindful of New England, for Poe was sharply critical of Transcendentalists and abolitionists; Melville was profoundly affected by one of New England's chief writers, Nathaniel Hawthorne; and Lincoln was the spokesman for the cause which New England's writers eloquently supported.

New England in Its Golden Day

The period in New England has had applied to it a variety of happy designations: Barrett Wendell called it "The Renaissance of New England," Lewis Mumford, "The Golden Day." But by whatever name it is known, it was the greatest literary period in the history of New England. This was a rich period, and in their writings the men of Boston and Cambridge, Concord and Salem set forth their all-embracing ideas and attitudes on religion and the conception of human nature, democracy and the common man, industry and the expanding frontier, slavery and the Civil War, science and human progress.

Changing Concepts of God and Man

The most important development in the religious thought of New England in this period was the break with Calvinism. Boston clergymen had become increasingly liberal in the eighteenth century (as shown in the opposition between Chauncy and Edwards), but it was not until the beginning of the nineteenth century that Unitarianism was strongly established. The appointment in 1805 of an avowed Unitarian to the chair of Divinity at Harvard, hitherto occupied by staunch Calvinists, may be taken as marking the transition. And yet the change from Calvinism to Unitarianism was perhaps not so complete, even in eastern Massachusetts, as some have supposed. That William Ellery Channing, the most influential of the early Unitarians, should have delivered his famous "Moral Argument Against Calvinism" as late as 1820 would seem to suggest the tenacity of the old orthodox beliefs. Preaching from his Unitarian pulpit in 1831, Emerson designated the Calvinistic and Unitarian groups as the "rigid" and the "liberal" parties, respectively, and urged his hearers to "borrow something of eternal truth from both of these opinions."

The chief points of difference between Calvinism and Unitarianism as expounded by Channing and his successors can be summarized briefly: (1) The two beliefs differed in their conceptions of the Deity. Calvinism emphasized God's inexorable justice; Unitarianism stressed His benevolence. The Unitarians questioned the justice of the doctrine of election: a God who says (according to Wigglesworth) "I do save none but mine own elect" seemed arbitrary and capricious. (2) The two beliefs differed in their conceptions of Christ. According to Calvinism, Christ is literally the Son of God, the second member of the Holy Trinity. According to Unitarianism, Christ is divine only in the sense in which all men are divine or have an element, however small, of divinity in their nature. The difference between Christ and ordinary mortals becomes one of degree, not of kind. (3) The two beliefs differed in their conceptions of man. Calvinism asserted the innate depravity of man, his predestination, and the necessity of his salvation through the atoning death of Christ. Unitarianism insisted upon man's innate goodness and his spiritual freedom. The Atonement became unnecessary to Unitarians, who preferred to point to Christ's life as an example to be emulated by men already potentially good.

As a young man Channing lived for two years in Virginia, where he presumably absorbed French romantic philosophy. From Rousseau and writers of his school, Channing probably derived, and imported into the Boston of the early 1800's, the ideas of the excellence of human nature and its infinite perfectibility. The inscription on the base of Channing's statue in Boston aptly summarizes his contribution to the religious thought of New England: "He breathed into theology a humane spirit and proclaimed anew the divinity of man." In his *The Flowering of New England* Van Wyck Brooks justly declares, "By raising the general estimate of human nature, which the old religion had despised, Channing gave a prodigious impulse to the creative life."

By 1820 Channing could say, "Calvinism is giving place to better views. We think the decline of Calvinism one of the most encouraging facts in our passing history." Unitarianism became the religion particularly of the fashionable and the well-to-do in and around Boston. "Whoever clung to the older faith," remarks Barrett Wendell, "did so at his social peril." Unitarianism, however, did not conquer the whole of New England. There were scattered Unitarian outposts, such as the parish of Sylvester Judd in Augusta, Maine, but the older faith continued dominant in the regions west and north of Boston.

Apart from both Calvinists and Unitarians, the Quakers were a comparatively small but important group. In early New England, Quakers were apt to be obstreperously fanatical (witness the Quakeress in Hawthorne's "Gentle Boy," p. 1237); but by the time of John Woolman (1720-1772) their fanaticism had diminished, and in nineteenth-century New England they were, in the words of one historian, "inconspicuous and inoffensive."

Like the Calvinists, the Quakers believed in the divinity of Christ and in the Bible as the inspired word of God. Like the Calvinists, too, they insisted upon the essential sinfulness of man: "Too dark ye cannot paint the sin," said Whittier, their chief representative in literature, in "The Eternal Goodness," his best poetical statement of the Quaker belief. But Whittier in the poem objects to the "iron creeds" of the Calvinists and to their emphasis upon God's wrath; he prefers to think of "our Lord's beatitudes." The Quakers emphasized the "Inner Light," which God, they believed, gave to all human beings and which afforded an infallible guide to a righteous life. Quakerism was more benevolent and humanitarian than Calvinism, and more pietistic than Unitarianism. A mere layman might experience some difficulty in distinguishing between the doctrine of the Inner Light and the Emersonian doctrine of intuition.

Emerson, after less than three years in the Unitarian ministry, resigned his pulpit in 1832 because of a growing dissatisfaction with the official rôle of the clergyman and the formalities of the church. Unitarianism, he felt, was good as far as it went; but it did not go far enough toward the rehabilitation of the individual. The new doctrine of which Emerson became the chief interpreter is known as Transcendentalism. Emerson's *Nature* (p. 1040), published in 1836, was the bible of the early Transcendentalists, and the "Transcendental Club" was, from 1836 until about 1844, a center of activity. Another focus was a quarterly magazine, *The Dial* (edited 1840-1842 by Margaret Fuller, and 1842-1844 by Emerson), which published many contributions by Transcendentalists during its lifetime of four years. The group as a whole was greatly influenced by the idealistic philosophies of other lands and ages: by Plato and the Neo-platonists, by the Oriental Scriptures, by Kant and other German idealists — particularly as interpreted by Coleridge and Carlyle.

Transcendentalism has been defined philosophically as "the recognition in man of the capacity of knowing truth intuitively, or of attaining knowledge transcending the reach of the senses." It has been described historically as having been "produced by the importing of German idealism into American Unitarianism." The last definition indicates an important relation between Transcendentalism and Unitarianism and requires a consideration of the similarities and differences between the two.

Unitarianism prepared the way for Transcendentalism by insisting that man is essentially good and may trust his own perceptions of religious truth. Channing spoke of "the confidence which is due to our rational and moral faculties in religion" and said that "the ultimate reliance of a human being is and must be on his own mind." But it is important to observe two points of difference: (1) Channing, the Unitarian, expressed confidence in "our *rational* faculties." Emerson, the Transcendentalist, drew a sharp distinction between the "Understanding," by which he meant the rational faculty, and the "Reason," by which he meant the suprarational or intuitive faculty; and he regarded the "Reason" as much more authoritative in spiritual matters than the "Understanding." (2) The Transcendentalists carried this reliance upon the intuitive perceptions of the individual much further than conventional Unitarianism would warrant — carried it so far as to set aside even the authority of the Christian Bible. "Make your own Bible," said Emerson. "Select and collect all the words and sentences that in all your reading have been to you like the blast of a trumpet, out of Shakespeare, Seneca, Moses, John, and Paul." Emerson would renounce all authority, all standards and laws externally imposed: "Nothing is at last sacred but the integrity of your own mind." He proclaimed this glorification of intuition and the repudiation of all external religious authority to a Unitarian audience at Harvard in 1838: "Thank God for these good men [meaning the Saints and the Prophets] but say 'I also am a man.'" The result was a storm of protest. Emerson's Transcendentalism had gone far beyond the bounds even of liberal Unitarianism.

Transcendental thought in the abstract can be best studied in Emerson. His disciples, of whom there were many, were usually interested more in practice than in theory and attempted to apply Emerson's individualistic doctrines in various practical ways. George Ripley, for example, organized the famous utopian community at Brook Farm; Theodore Parker militantly espoused reforms in church and state; Margaret Fuller advocated the emancipation of women; Henry Thoreau made a famous experiment in living at Walden Pond.

Many passages in Thoreau seem echoes of Emerson, though Thoreau's expression of the thought is always more concrete than Emerson's. "The fact is," Thoreau wrote in his journal in 1853, "I am a mystic, a transcendentalist, and a natural philosopher to boot" — meaning by "natural philosopher" a scientific student of nature. The emphasis in the statement is significant. Mystical, transcendental passages abound in Thoreau, especially in his earlier writings, as they abound everywhere in Emerson. But as Thoreau grew older, his interest in the observation and description of the world of nature became more and more absorbing. He became — as his journals of the 1850's attest — more of the natural philosopher and somewhat less of the Transcendentalist.

Transcendental ideas scarcely touched the writers of Boston and Cambridge. Influenced by his medical studies, Dr. Holmes approached religious problems from the scientific point of view. He objected to the Calvinistic condemnation of sinners because he believed that wrongdoing is often the result of an unfortunate heredity; bad men, he thought, should be treated as if they were insane. On the positive side, he had no transcendental ardor, but rather a rationalistic belief in the ability of the soul, in favorable circumstances, to "build more stately mansions." Longfellow's religious thought — such as it was — was mildly Unitarian, pleasantly optimistic about life and death. And Lowell, although he could write appreciatively of the stimulating effect of Emerson (". . . he made us conscious of the supreme and everlasting originality of whatever bit of soul might be in any of us"), was not a disciple; nor was he in sympathy with Transcendental ideas. "The word 'transcendental,'" he declared in the unsympathetic essay on Thoreau, "was the maid of all work for those who could not think." The men of Boston and Cambridge found the Concord air too rarefied for their mundane needs.

The chief spokesman of the opposition to Transcendentalism, however, was Hawthorne, who returned, in part at least, to the Calvinist position. He satirized utopian reforms on the ground that superficial reform measures avail nothing so long as the human heart, which is innately sinful, remains unregenerated. "Purify that inward sphere," he advised in "Earth's Holocaust," "and the many shapes of evil that haunt the outward will vanish of their own accord." He satirized Unitarianism and Transcendentalism in "The Celestial Railroad" (p. 1305); Bunyan's arduous pilgrimage seemed to him still the best way of reaching the Celestial City. In stories and novels he showed that evil is an ever-present reality, not an illusion to be brushed aside, and that self-reliant individualism alone does not save man from disaster. Hawthorne is a striking example of the persistence of the Puritan point of view in an age of liberalism and progressivism.

But it would be a mistake to suppose that the Puritan inheritance affected Hawthorne alone. It was everywhere present, giving native roots and indigenous strength to New England's flowering. The religious emphasis was a Puritan trait, as was the emphasis on books and reading. The Transcendental pursuit of perfection was the old Puritan pursuit of perfection in a new guise and on different terms. The diaries of Emerson, Thoreau, and Hawthorne continued an old Puritan practice; and the soul searchings in Emerson and Thoreau recall passages in Cotton Mather and Jonathan Edwards. When Emerson said that the poet "must drink water out of a wooden bowl," he was quoting the austerest of English Puritans, John Milton. The austerity of Emerson and Thoreau, and of Hawthorne, too, was of the essence of Puritanism. If this Puritan essence was considerably diluted in the other writers of the period, it nevertheless made itself felt. It came out in the ethical earnestness of Longfellow and Lowell and in their native attachments. In sum, the great period of New England literature would have been impossible without the two centuries of Puritan inheritance. It is hardly an accident that the three New England writers of the period whose works seem most likely to endure — Emerson, Thoreau, and Hawthorne — are the writers whose roots were deepest in New England's Puritan past.

Democracy, Industrialism, Expansion

From 1829 to 1860 the two major political parties in the United States were the Whigs and the Democrats. Conservative men of property in New England were likely to be Whigs; liberals and men of little or no property were likely to be Democrats.

The election of Andrew Jackson of Tennessee by the Democrats in 1828 is one of the great landmarks in the evolution of American democracy. The common man, whether backwoodsman, farmer, or small merchant, regarded Jackson, the conqueror of the Creek Indians and the hero of New Orleans, as a popular champion. Jackson's Whig opponent, the "aristocratic" John Quincy Adams, carried only New England and the North Atlantic states; the South and West went solidly for "Old Hickory." During the Jacksonian period, government in America became more democratic. The movement toward democracy, which had begun with the War of Independence and which had been arrested somewhat in the 1790's owing to a certain apprehension caused by the excesses of the French Revolution, now resumed its onward course. State constitutions were liberalized. Religious tests and property qualifications for holding office were at last removed, and manhood suffrage was adopted generally.

New England Looks at the New Democracy

To many New Englanders Jackson and his supporters seemed the dregs of democracy. Emerson wrote to Carlyle, "A most unfit person in the Presidency has been doing the worst things; and the worse he grew, the more popular." But it would not be fair to Emerson to suppose that this snobbish statement represents his real attitude. Like most educated men, he doubted at times the wisdom of the uneducated masses. "The mass," he wrote in a skeptical moment, "are animal, in state of pupilage, and nearer the chimpanzee." But despite moments of skepticism, he held firmly to his faith in the ultimate wisdom of the people. The belief that "God is in every man" was to him "the highest revelation." And he said in another passage on the subject, "The great mass understand what's what." It should be remembered that Emerson took sharp issue with his friend Carlyle on the subject of democracy: when Carlyle advocated what we today should call a fascist doctrine, Emerson vigorously dissented. He could think of many benefits that might come from even the "rank rabble party, the Jacksonism of the country." For one thing, this new democracy of the West might cure America of its slavish dependence upon Old World literature and Old World traditions, might "root out the hollow dilettantism of our cultivation." And he came ultimately to an admiration of Jackson himself. Writing in 1862 of the truly memorable things which he associated with the national capital, he mentioned along with the eloquence of Webster and the "sublime behaviour" of John Quincy Adams, the "fine military energy of Jackson in his presidency."

Jackson's fine military energy appealed also to James Russell Lowell, who wrote in his "Latest Views of Mr. Biglow":

Ole Hick'ry wouldn't ha' stood see-saw
    'Bout doin' things till they wuz done with, —
H'd smashed the tables o' the Law
    In time o' need to load his gun with;
He couldn't see but jest one side, —
    Ef his, 'twuz God's, an' thet wuz plenty;
An' so his *'Forrards'* multiplied
    An army's fightin' weight by twenty.

It must have required a great adjustment for the New England mind to appreciate a man like Andrew Jackson. Emerson and Lowell were capable of making the necessary accommodation, and Nathaniel Hawthorne, alone among the major New England writers, was a loyal member of the Democratic party and a staunch supporter of Jackson. Late in life he recorded in his journal the considered judgment, "Surely Jackson was a great man." But despite the personal challenge of Jackson himself, Emerson spoke for the generality of educated New Englanders when he said that the Whig party had the "best men"; the Democratic party, he added, had the "best cause."

The "best cause" became more and more pervasive in the literature of the period. An earlier democratic impetus had been supplied by the English Romantic Movement. When Emerson, in *The American Scholar* (p. 1068), hailed as one of the "auspicious signs" the exploring and poetizing of "the near, the low, the common," he was thinking particularly of the English Romantic poets. And when Longfellow celebrated the village blacksmith, and Whittier, the barefoot boy, the inspiration was at least partly derived from Burns and Wordsworth. Thus initiated, the democratic movement in literature was broadened and deepened and made more American by the fresh impetus of Jacksonian Democracy. Lowell affords a good illustration, for with him the democratic attitude evolved from the romantic and literary to the realistic and American. His celebration of Lincoln in 1865 as "New birth of our new soil, the first American" is a landmark in the democratic evolution of the New England mind. His full development in this direction is seen in his famous address "Democracy" (p. 980), in which he said:

> I recollect hearing a sagacious old gentleman say in 1840 that the doing away with the property qualification for suffrage twenty years before had been the ruin of the State of Massachusetts. . . . I lived to see that Commonwealth twenty odd years later paying the interest on her bonds in gold. . . . To the door of every generation there comes a knocking, and unless the household, like the Thane of Cawdor and his wife, have been doing some deed without a name, they need not shudder. It turns out at worst to be a poor relation who wishes to come in out of the cold.

Thus Lowell, the Brahmin, spoke for democracy and the forgotten man.

Another Brahmin, Oliver Wendell Holmes, was not visibly touched by the evolution of democratic thought in America. In *The Autocrat of the Breakfast-Table* (p. 908), he clung tenaciously to his aristocratic bias: "Self-made men? — Well, yes. Of course everybody likes and respects self-made men. It is a great deal better to be made in that way than not to be made at all. . . . But *other things being equal,* in most relations of life I prefer a man of family." His favorite subjects in poetry were aristocratic types ("Dorothy Q," "The Last Leaf," p. 902) and aristocratic heirlooms ("On Lending a Punch-Bowl"). It is not without significance in this connection that many of the writings of Dr. Holmes seem less vital and less important today than those of his more democratic contemporaries.

The Machine vs. Self-Reliance

The Jacksonian revolution affected the entire country; the industrial revolution was confined largely to the Northern states, and its effects became especially important in New England. After the War of 1812, business capital and initiative in New England were diverted from commerce to manufacturing, and the abundance of water power and skilled labor guaranteed the success of the factory system. The most striking new feature of the New England landscape about 1820 was the factory village, built near some waterfall and consisting of mills and houses for the "operatives." Conditions were much more agreeable in the new factory villages of New England than in the older manufacturing centers of England. Workers in the New England factories were mostly farmers' daughters from the surrounding country. Hawthorne in one of his rambles about the countryside remarked on the bright, cheerful faces looking out through the factory windows. A notable instance was Lowell, Massachusetts (founded in 1822), where the factory girls dressed neatly, were properly chaperoned, and published a literary weekly. By 1840 there were some 1200 cotton factories in the United States, two thirds of which were in New England.

One result of the industrial revolution in New England was the accumulation of wealth, a good deal of which was used for cultural purposes. Many New Englanders studied in Europe. The colleges of New England grew in resources and prestige. Almost every town had its free public library and its Lyceum, where an instructive course of lectures was given during the winter. Emerson, and even Thoreau, lectured on many Lyceum platforms. In the cities, mechanics' institutes offered vocational training. The Lowell family might be cited as illustrating the happy marriage of wealth and culture: one uncle of James Russell Lowell founded the manufacturing city which bears his name; another uncle established the famous Lowell Institute in Boston, where lectures have been given for more than a century by distinguished scientists, scholars, and men of letters.

To most New England writers of the period the industrial revolution no doubt seemed more beneficent than otherwise. One major writer, however — Henry David Thoreau — spoke out loud and bold against the mechanization of American life. Thoreau's objection was based upon the fundamental principle, Emerson's principle, of self-reliance. A man ought to do for himself the things which more and more were being done by machines: he ought to walk instead of riding on the train; he ought to build his own house, make his own clothes, bake his own bread. The machine brought on the division of labor which reduced men from integers to fractions. "Where is this division of labor to end?" Thoreau cried in *Walden;* and he added a statement the force of which is only today becoming apparent: "No doubt another *may* also think for me; but it is not therefore desirable that he should do so to the exclusion of my thinking for myself."

Compared with Thoreau's, the comments of other writers on the advancing machine age seem less decisive. Emerson entered a mild demurrer in *Self-Reliance* (p. 1094), warning that "the harm of the improved machinery may compensate its good";

but, in the long run, he was willing to accept the machine as part of the "beneficent tendency." Hawthorne seems to have been apprehensive of evil results; to him, apparently, the machine was a malevolent monster. One finds in his journal the following note for a story: "A steam engine in a factory to be supposed to possess a malignant spirit; it catches one man's arm and pulls it off; seizes another by the coat-tails, and almost grapples him bodily; catches a girl by the hair, and scalps her; and finally draws a man and crushes him to death." Here was a conception out of which Hawthorne might easily have developed a tale of Gothic horror, and perhaps also of social prophecy.

A conspicuous and characteristic product of the industrial revolution in America was the man of big business, the captain of industry. The subject received scant attention in the literature of the period. One passage, however, is of particular interest — a passage in Emerson's *Journals* which expresses the writer's great admiration of John M. Forbes, a builder of railroads in the West in the 1860's:

> He is an American to be proud of. Never was such force, good meaning, good sense, good action, combined with such domestic lovely behaviour. . . . Wherever he moves, he is the benefactor. It is of course that he should shoot well, ride well, sail well, administer railroads well, carve well, keep house well, but he was the best talker also in the company. . . .

The type has suffered at the hands of later writers. Perhaps Emerson was naïve; or possibly the type deteriorated in the post-Civil War period; or, quite likely, the American businessman was given less than justice by the satirists and "debunkers" of the 1920's.

New England Looks West with Mixed Feelings

Thinking in New England along political, economic, and social lines was conditioned not only by Jacksonian Democracy and the industrial revolution; it was conditioned also by the Westward movement. Some of the details of the movement are reserved for a later chapter. Our concern for the moment is with its effect upon New England attitudes.

In the early years of the century New Englanders had settled in western New York and Ohio; by the 1840's they not only had occupied Indiana, Illinois, and southern Michigan, but had ventured as far as Wisconsin, Minnesota, and Iowa. A popular song summed up the invitation to the West:

> Come all ye Yankee farmers who wish
>   to change your lot,
> Who've spunk enough to travel beyond
>   your native spot. . . .

Despite the ties between New England and the West, conservative New Englanders were inclined to deprecate the Westward migration. There were economic reasons for this attitude: the draining off of energetic young people tended to keep high the price of factory labor, and the revenue from the sale of public lands in the West furnished an argument to Southerners for lowering the tariff. There were moral reasons also. The appeal to "spunk" to leave "your native spot" in the song quoted above was reversible since one might argue that more spunk was required to succeed in one's native place, particularly if that place was a New England farm. "The wise man stays at home," said Emerson. And possibly Whittier was thinking of those who were tempted by the West when he emphasized the noble austerity of life in New England:

> Then ask not why to these bleak hills
> I cling, as clings the tufted moss . . .
> Better with naked nerve to bear
> The needles of this goading air,
> Than, in the lap of sensual ease, forego
> The godlike power to do, the godlike aim to know.

Migration to the West was regarded by many high-minded New Englanders as a decline to a lower level. Some reformers, on the other hand, made the point that Westward migration might be checked if certain improvements were made at home. Sylvester Judd said of his fictional utopia, described in *Margaret: A Tale of the Real and Ideal* (1845), that "the mania for removing to the West, which prevails all over New England, has here subsided."

The Western theme does not bulk very large in the writings and memoirs of the authors of New England's Renaissance, but a few details may be of interest to suggest their views and attitudes. Hawthorne was interested in the West, although his knowledge of the subject was not great. In the 1830's he traveled by stagecoach and canal boat as far as Niagara Falls and recorded his observations in a few slight but revealing sketches. While American consul at Liverpool, he met more Westerners than he had ever seen in Salem or Concord, some of whom he viewed with disapproval. A Mr. Lilley from Ohio, for example, he described in his notebooks as "a very unfavorable specimen of American manners — an outrageous tobacco chewer and atrocious spitter on carpets." But some years later in Concord he met young William Dean Howells, an Ohioan, whose manners were irreproachable. Hawthorne was (as Howells recorded) "curious about the West, which he seemed to fancy much more purely American, and said he would like to see some part of the country on which the damned shadow of Europe had not fallen."

To Lowell, as to Hawthorne, the West seemed more purely American because it was freer from European influences. (The same point was to be made at the end of the century by the historian Frederick Jackson Turner.) When "Nature" made Lincoln, Lowell said in his "Commemoration Ode" (p. 969),

> For him her Old-World moulds aside she threw,
> And choosing sweet clay from the breast
> Of the unexhausted West,
> With stuff untainted shaped a hero new . . .
> Nothing of Europe here. . . .

The great Americans in the early history of the Republic — Franklin, Washington, Jefferson, and the rest — possessed a culture which was largely European; but the culture of Lincoln was "untainted" by the Old World. Lowell's appreciation of this fact is all the more remarkable because, as a lifelong student of the Romance languages and literatures, he himself was an embodiment of European culture. Such an insight into the significance of the West was beyond the reach of another devotee of European literature, Longfellow, whose conception of the subject, as revealed in *Hiawatha* and *Evangeline,* was literary and romantic.

Unlike Longfellow, Thoreau was a tough, realistic writer who was qualified by temperament and personal habits to appreciate the values of the Western frontier. From Thoreau's point of view, life in New England had become too sophisticated; he spoke repeatedly of "these degenerate days." "We need the tonic of wildness," he declared in *Walden* (p. 1192); and in "Walking," he said, "The West is but another name for the Wild." He praised the sturdy self-reliance of the pioneer. If the race is to retain its vigor, men must live "a primitive and frontier life." Such a life had been lived by the settlers of New England, and Thoreau liked to quote from the colonial historians, particularly from Edward Johnson, who told how the first inhabitants of Concord were forced to live in a cave and "cut their bread very thin." Such a Spartan existence was enjoyed also, he supposed, by the Western frontiersman. "Adam in Paradise," he declared, "was not so favorably situated on the whole as is the backwoodsman in America." The backwoodsman whom Thoreau envisaged, we may be sure, was not of the lawless or mercenary sort; rather he was the sober New Englander dedicated to plain living and high thinking on a farm in Michigan or Illinois. The gold rush to California was quite another matter. The greed and the gambling instinct therein displayed, he thought, were a "disgrace on mankind." The California spectacle of 1849, he said, made of God "a moneyed gentleman who scatters a handful of pennies in order to see mankind scramble for them."

If Thoreau praised the West for its primitive qualities, Emerson praised it for its astonishingly rapid acquisition of culture. He lectured many times throughout the Middle West in the 1850's, going as far as Beloit, Wisconsin, where on January 9, 1856, he found an interested audience despite a temperature of thirty degrees below zero. The spread of culture on the frontier was to him indeed remarkable. Having heard piano music on one of his Western travels, he wrote:

> Witness the mute all hail
> The joyful traveller gives, when on the verge
> Of craggy Indian wilderness he hears
> From a log cabin stream Beethoven's notes
> On the piano, played with master's hand.

The college in Evanston blew down one night (Emerson recorded in his journal in 1857), but so great were the energy and progressivism of the founders of Northwestern that "they raised it again the next day, or built another." To Emerson, the West seemed the country of the future. He warned his Eastern readers that some day the sturdy Westerner would "gather all their laurels in his strong hands." Emerson's treatment of the West (which one finds chiefly in his *Journals*) emphasizes his identification not only with New England but with all America as well.

Slavery and Civil War

Still another influence on New England thought about political, economic, and social problems was the growing controversy over Negro slavery in the South and the tragic climax of the Civil War. The details of the anti-slavery movement and the rôle of Whittier as New England's chief abolitionist in literature are reserved for a later chapter, where the two sides — Northern and Southern — may more conveniently be brought together. Here we are concerned with the movement as a stimulus to thought and with the reactions of the major New England writers, Whittier excepted, to that stimulus.

Longfellow, as we might expect, was only mildly responsive. His sentiments were broadly and sincerely humanitarian; he believed that slavery was a great evil. But he was not active in reform, for he disliked controversy and preferred to write his poems on other subjects. Longfellow did, however, compose a few poems on slavery, of which "The Slave's Dream" (p. 862) may be regarded as typical of his attitude and method of treatment. The slave in the poem falls asleep in a rice field and dreams of his former life in Africa, where he had been a king and had ridden a spirited horse bridled with golden reins. The description would be more applicable to a knight of medieval romance and it reflects Longfellow's preoccupation with European romantic literature. When the Union was threatened by the sectional dispute, he wrote the noble and justly famous poem "The Building of the Ship" (1850), which was a poetical plea — matching Webster's plea in prose — for the preservation of the Union:

> Thou too sail on, O Ship of State!
> Sail on, O Union, strong and great!

Lowell was much more vocal than his fellow Cantabrigian. He had well-defined political convictions, and he enjoyed being in the thick of the fray. In the first series of *The Biglow Papers* (p. 945), he vigorously opposed the Mexican War, which Northern abolitionists unanimously regarded as having been precipitated by Southern strategists with the aim of extending slave territory in the Southwest:

> They jest want this Californy
> So's to lug new slave states in. . . .

He declared himself opposed to all war, "Ez fer war, I call it murder . . ," and preferred the separation of the North and South to slavery:

> Ef I'd my way I hed ruther
> We should go to work an' part. . . .

In the second series of *The Biglow Papers* (p. 957), written in 1862 when the Army of the Potomac had met with ill success, he abandoned his early pacifism and argued for a more vigorous prosecution of the War by the North:

> Oh for three weeks o' Crommle an' the Lord!
> Up, Isr'el to your tents an' grind the sword!

After the Civil War, however, Lowell directed his best poetical efforts toward reunion. Writing in 1875 in commemoration of the one hundredth anniversary of Washington's taking command of the colonial army, he extended the hand of reconciliation from Massachusetts to Virginia:

> Virginia gave us this imperial man . . .
> She gave us this unblemished gentleman.
> What shall we give her back but love and praise
> As in the dear old unestranged days. . . .

Ever responsive to changing conditions, Lowell's attitudes show, it seems fair to say, his flexibility, adaptability, and capacity for growth in his thinking on political questions.

It so happened that Lowell was usually on the side of the majority; Thoreau had a predilection for the side of the minority, often a minority of one. He had the rare personal courage to carry his convictions to their logical conclusion, even if that conclusion meant the defiance of civil law. He refused to pay taxes to a government which allowed slavery, and as a consequence spent a night in the Concord jail. The record of this episode is given in "Civil Disobedience" (p. 1176). He records in his journal that, contrary to the Fugitive Slave Law, on at least one occasion he helped a slave escape into Canada. While John Brown was in prison awaiting execution, Thoreau made a speech in Brown's behalf at Concord, and again at Boston and at Worcester, to unsympathetic audiences. In his famous "Plea for Captain John Brown" he said, "It was his peculiar doctrine that a man has a perfect right to interfere by force with the slaveholder, in order to rescue the slave. I agree with him." Thoreau is the best example in American literature of the extremely individualistic position: that a man must do what he believes to be right with utter disregard for the conventions of society and the laws of the state.

Emerson was as individualistic in theory, though in practice a good deal more amenable to laws and conventions. Nor did he have the crusading spirit of Thoreau. He was nevertheless an active opponent of slavery after 1850, and, like Thoreau, he spoke publicly in defense of John Brown. The high point in his participation in public affairs came on January 1, 1863, when he read the "Boston Hymn" at a meeting to celebrate the Emancipation Proclamation and was interrupted by the cheering crowd at the famous lines:

> Who is the owner? The slave is owner,
> And ever was. Pay *him*.

Alone among the great New England writers, Hawthorne did not give his approval to the antislavery movement. Possibly, from the Calvinistic point of view, chattel slavery seemed not the greatest of evils: all mankind were victims of a worse bondage — the bondage of sin. He was distrustful of reforms and reformers: reformers were likely to be impractical fanatics; reforms were superficial and as often as not proposed remedies which were worse than the disease. After the manner of the old Puritans, he believed that an inscrutable Providence would bring about the needed reform "at some brighter period, when the world should have grown ripe for it." Furthermore, as a loyal member of the Democratic party of James K. Polk and Franklin Pierce, Hawthorne subscribed to the conventional party arguments that (1) slavery was entitled to recognition and protection under the Constitution; (2) the Union was threatened with disruption by the activities of the abolitionists; and (3) the welfare and happiness of the Negro himself would be jeopardized by his emancipation. During the Civil War he found his position as a Northern Democrat embarrassing; he was looked at askance by friends and neighbors. He did not, however, join those Northern Democrats, known as Copperheads, who opposed the prosecution of the War and advocated a return to the *status quo ante bellum*. "I always thought that the War should have been avoided," he wrote in 1863, "although since it has broken out, I have longed for military success as much as any man or woman of the North." Devoted as he was to the older Union established by the founding fathers, he felt in 1863 that the permanent separation of North and South was inevitable, and persuaded himself "to be content with half the soil that was once our broad inheritance." He did not live to see the end of the War.

Science and Human Progress

Natural science advanced with remarkable rapidity in the nineteenth century, and its effects became more and more pervasive. In England — to mention only two of many notable publications in the scientific field — Sir Charles Lyell's *Principles of Geology* (1830-1833, 3 vols.) established the antiquity of the earth and the gradual evolution of its surface, and Charles Darwin's *Origin of Species* (1859) presented the theory of the evolution of man through a process of natural selection. In New England, as well as elsewhere in America, scientific activity in all of the fields kept pace with developments in the Old World. Benjamin Silliman at Yale published his *Elements of Chemistry* in 1830; Asa Gray at Harvard brought out a notable *Manual of the Botany of the Northern United States* in 1848; Louis Agassiz of Switzerland began in 1846 a distinguished career at Harvard in the field of comparative zoölogy. The Harvard Astronomical Observatory in 1846 was equipped with the world's largest telescope; and in 1847 the American Association for the Advancement of Science was organized in Boston in order "to promote intercourse between American scientists, to give a strong and more systematic impulse to research, and to procure for the labors of scientific men increased facilities and wider usefulness." New England writers were aware of these scientific developments, and their writings reflect, in various ways and degrees, the influence of the new facts and the new theories of experimental science.

Emerson greeted the scientific movement with enthusiasm. "One of the distinctions of our century," he wrote, "has been the devotion of cultivated men to natural science; the benefits thence derived to the arts and to civilization are signal and immense." Late in life he declared, "If absolute leisure were offered me, I should run to the college or the scientific school which offered the best lectures on Geology, Chemistry, Minerals, and Botany." Although one cannot be sure that Emerson read all of the scientists to whom he refers in his writings, his scientific reading was remarkably wide and certainly included, among other things, the works of Newton, Linnæus, Buffon, Lamarck, Lyell, Gray, Agassiz, and Darwin. But Emerson was not himself a scientist, nor was he interested in science for its own sake. Science was of value to him for the moral and spiritual implications which scientific fact and theory suggested to his mind — a quite unscientific reason. He liked to draw illustrations of spiritual truth from physical phenomena ("The axioms of physics translate the law of ethics," he said), and his pages abound in analogies between natural and spiritual laws. He was delighted, furthermore, by the doctrine of evolution, particularly by the earlier evolutionary theory of Lamarck, which seemed to him to confirm his optimistic hope for mankind. Paraphrasing Lamarck, he wrote as a motto for *Nature:*

> And striving to be man, the worm
> Mounts through all the spires of form.

If the worm might become man, if the caterpillar might evolve into a philosopher, then the future of the constantly evolving human race became glorious to contemplate.

Thoreau's relation to science was much more intimate than Emerson's. Thoreau was interested in nature for its own sake quite as much as for its Transcendental meanings. A student of botany and zoölogy, he liked to use the Latin names of plants and animals when he wrote about them. He sent to Agassiz for identification specimens of fishes and turtles, some of which were unknown to the Harvard professor. Thoreau did not have, however, either the equipment or the temperament of the genuine scientist. He did not go beyond description of behavior and classification. He would not murder to dissect. A hawk could be best studied, he maintained, not as a "dead specimen," but free and soaring above the fields. In short, Thoreau was, to use the phrase of his friend Ellery Channing (a nephew of William Ellery Channing), "the *poet*-naturalist."

Among the Brahmins, Longfellow and Lowell gave little attention to science, though Longfellow shared the general faith in the contributions of science to human progress. Lowell, on one occasion, twitted the Darwinians upon their arrogant assumption that evolution had supplanted God in the modern world (see his "Credidimus Jovem Regnare"). A third Brahmin, however, achieved a real distinction in science. Oliver Wendell Holmes studied medicine in Paris and from 1847 to 1882 was professor of anatomy and physiology in the Harvard Medical School. His most famous contribution to medical science was his essay on "The Contagiousness of Puerperal Fever" (1842), which materially aided the efforts of the medical profession to reduce the mortality of women in childbirth. Holmes' medical training gave him a scientific approach to his literary subjects. He became particularly interested in the problem of the bearing of heredity upon moral responsibility, which is the subject of his novel *Elsie Venner* (1861) and of other writings. He stated the problem as follows in the Preface to the novel:

> Was Elsie Venner, poisoned by the venom of a crotalus [rattlesnake] before she was born, morally responsible for the 'volitional' aberrations, which translated into acts become what is known as sin, and, it may be, what is punished as crime? If, on presentation of the evidence, she becomes by the verdict of the human conscience a proper object of divine pity and not of divine wrath, as a subject of moral poisoning, wherein lies the difference between her position at the bar of judgment, human or divine, and that of the unfortunate victim who received a moral poison from a remote ancestor before he drew his first breath?

Holmes anticipated by at least a generation the approach of modern neurology. He was the author of many volumes of popular novels, essays, and verse, but he nevertheless considered his article on childbed fever his best title to fame.

Hawthorne, once again, is found perversely at odds with this self-confident, progressive, optimistic age. He discovered a danger in the new emphasis upon experimental science. In "Rappaccini's Daughter" (p. 1335), in "Ethan Brand," and elsewhere, he examined the scientist and discovered that the scientist had been dehumanized. Of Dr. Rappaccini, "as true a man of science as ever distilled his own heart in an alembic," Hawthorne wrote: "His patients are interesting to him only as subjects for some new experiment. He would sacrifice human life, his own among the rest, or whatever else was dearest to him, for the sake of adding so much as a grain of mustard seed to the great heap of his accumulated knowledge." Likewise, Ethan Brand, a scientist in the field of experimental psychology, became "a cold observer, looking on mankind as the subject of his experiment"; he "lost his hold of the magnetic chain of humanity"; he became "a fiend." Hawthorne seemed to think that the exclusive cultivation of the scientific faculty produces atrophy of soul, and creates and lets loose in the world an agent which is "fiendish" because utterly unmoral. The mid-nineteenth century did not take the warning seriously. Now, a hundred years later, Hawthorne's point becomes more plainly perceptible.

Herman Melville: Explorer of the World and Enigmas

After a boyhood in New York City and Albany, a voyage to Liverpool, three years in the South Seas, a brief second residence in New York City, and a journey to London and Paris, the much-traveled Herman Melville settled in 1850, at the age of thirty-one, at "Arrowhead" near Pittsfield, Massachusetts. Obviously he was not a product of Massachusetts nor a part of the literary movement of New England, but his Massachusetts residence — which lasted, with interruptions for other travels, for more than twenty years — brought him within the sphere of influence of the New England Renaissance. He met in the Berkshires many of the New England writers and struck up a stimulating and sympathetic friendship with Hawthorne, who in 1850-1851 resided at nearby Lenox. It is significant that Melville wrote his greatest book, *Moby Dick,* during the months of his close association with Hawthorne and that he dedicated the book to Hawthorne.

Like Hawthorne, Melville was concerned with the darker side of human fate. Both insisted upon the reality of evil in the world; both were skeptical of the optimism of Emerson and his benevolent theory of the Universe; both presented the tragedies of the mind and soul. Hawthorne agreed with Bunyan's *Pilgrim's Progress,* where man is represented as going through life weighed down by a burden of sin. Melville called Ecclesiastes "the truest of all books . . . the fine hammered steel of woe."

Melville dwelt much upon the evil in the world. He had seen at first hand the brutality of ship captains, the depravity of Old World cities, the vices brought to the South Sea islanders by "civilized" invaders. More than that, evil appeared triumphant (as in *Pierre*), even when man's motives were virtuous. Why, Melville asked, did a good God — if indeed He is good — permit evil in His world? Melville could not accept the Universe with as much resignation as his friend Hawthorne. He persisted in challenging the sphinx riddle, courageously, defiantly.

In *Moby Dick,* which is a compendium of Melville's metaphysical speculation, Captain Ahab relentlessly pursues the White Whale only to be destroyed in the end. The allegory is susceptible of many interpretations. To Ahab "all evil was visibly personified and made practically assailable in Moby Dick." Ahab, however, is not the embodiment of unmixed good: his conduct is irrational and foolhardy; it is contrary to the well-being of others; it is motivated by revenge. Elsewhere, Ahab (and perhaps Melville) saw in Moby Dick "outrageous strength with an inscrutable malice sinewing it," and he hated chiefly the *inscrutability* of the whale. The story perhaps represents man's hopeless but heroic attempt to search out the inscrutable, to know the unknowable; the tragedy of man becomes the tragedy of his limited comprehension. But whatever the interpretation — and each reader must make his own, for the allegory with its countless ramifications is too complex to admit of a simple, categorical definition — Melville's Ahab, like Ethan Brand and other characters of Hawthorne, becomes completely obsessed with this one pursuit and sacrifices everything else to it. If the tragedy of man is his inability to possess complete knowledge of himself and his destiny, Ahab's tragedy is his monomania, the narrow range of his interests.

Melville's chief concern was with the profound enigmas — the nature of God and man, the mystery of "Providence, Foreknowledge, Will and Fate" — and like Milton's philosophers he "found no end, in wandering mazes lost." He was not, however, indifferent to the more mundane problems of modern society, and scattered through his works one finds abundant evidence of his awareness of contemporary social questions.

His own observation of tyranny on shipboard and the exploitation of the native population on the Pacific islands had awakened in him a flaming passion for social justice in a truly democratic society. This passion expressed itself angrily in *White-Jacket,* where he condemned the naval practice of flogging, and philosophically and satirically in *Mardi,* where he surveyed the governments, beliefs, and manners of much of the nineteenth-century world.

The latter book is of special importance for the student of Melville's social ideas with reference to his own country. He was critical of America's faults. "Vivenza [the United States] was a braggadocio": boastfulness was getting to be a national habit; after all, God should be given some credit for our mountains and rivers. The existence of slavery nullified our noble *Declaration of Independence.* The war against Mexico was foisted upon the nation by the imperialistic action of the President. The California of the gold rush was a "golden Hell." And speaking more radically, Melville pointed out the incompleteness of our freedom: political freedom alone was not enough, for "freedom is more social than political." But despite these and many other imperfections, the young American democracy inspired in Melville an ardent faith. The West was a source of fresh hope — Westerners "were a fine young tribe; like strong new wine they worked violently in becoming clear." "In its better aspect," he declared, "Vivenza was a noble land": "Like a young tropic tree she stood, laden down with greenness, myriad blossoms, and the ripened fruit thick-hanging from one bough. She was promising as the morning. Or Vivenza might be likened to St. John, feeding on locusts and wild honey, and with prophetic voice, crying to the nations from the wilderness. Or, childlike, standing among the old robed kings and emperors of the Archipelago, Vivenza seemed a young Messiah, to whose discourse the bearded Rabbis bowed." Like Hawthorne, Melville was a philosophical pessimist and a political optimist. It was possible to believe in original sin and still be a democrat.

Edgar Allan Poe, Southerner

The greatest writer of the ante-bellum South, Edgar Allan Poe, has usually been thought of as completely aloof from the intellectual currents of his time. V. L. Parrington confirmed this view in his famous pronouncement, "The problem of Poe, fascinating as it is, lies quite outside the main current of American thought. . . ."

It is true that Poe was not a philosopher, like Emerson, or a political propagandist, like Lowell, or a critic of society, like Thoreau. But it does not follow that he was without ideas and attitudes which are relevant both to his own work and to the history of American thought.

The late Professor Margaret Alterton summed up Poe's social and political attitudes as follows:

> Poe rejected democracy, social reform, and the doctrine of progress. . . . He had no faith in democratic institutions and no belief in human perfectibility or natural goodness. He despised the mob. . . . He endorsed and defended the institution of slavery, and regarded the abolition movement with horror as an envious attack on the rights of property.

Poe, in short, went to the aristocratic extreme.

One reason for Poe's attitudes, no doubt, was his proud, fastidious temperament; another, his desire to identify himself with, and be accepted by, the aristocracy of his adopted region, the South. His repeated attacks on New Englanders seem to have been motivated, in part, by regional prejudice — the following attack on Lowell, for example: "Mr. Lowell is one of the most rabid of the abolition fanatics, and no Southerner who does not wish to be insulted . . . should ever touch a volume of this author."

If Poe's aristocratic sentiments seem a little artificial and stagey, they nevertheless colored his view of life and conditioned the kind of fiction he wrote. "The House of Usher" is a typical Poe symbol of an aristocracy decadent but beautiful. The decay of the Usher line contained no seeds of a democratic birth. The attitude is, at bottom, perhaps the Gothic-aristocratic admiration of a noble and picturesque ruin.

Poe was so completely the artist that any discussion of his ideas and attitudes is likely to impinge upon the discussion of his literary achievements, for his ideas and attitudes can hardly be treated apart from their embodiment in his poetry and fiction. Two aspects of his thought, however, may be mentioned. These aspects are separable, and yet in the ultimate reaches of Poe's thought they seem to unite in a mystic union.

One is a scientific rationalism, which is best illustrated in *Eureka*. In this quasi-philosophical work, Poe attempted an analysis of the universe based upon Newtonian principles. He was concerned with such philosophical pairs as repulsion-attraction, diffusion-gravitation, variety-unity. The universe, Poe believed, had a mathematical beauty and precision in which one might catch a glimpse of the divine. He said, characteristically: "The plots of God are perfect. The Universe is a plot of God." Poe may have thought that in his own plot structures he was embodying a divine principle.

Another aspect of Poe's thought might be called imaginative idealism. It would be interesting and instructive to compare the idealisms of Poe and Emerson. Though both owed something to Coleridge, Poe's idealism was essentially different from Emerson's. "Beauty," Emerson said with staid Puritan accent, "is the mark God sets upon virtue." Poe, on the other hand, spoke of "the human aspiration for Supernal Beauty," in the contemplation of which one experiences "an elevating excitement of the soul." Poetry could give, Poe thought, a vision of this supernal beauty: in the reading of poetry, he said, "we are often made to feel, with a shivering delight, that from an earthly harp are stricken notes which cannot have been unfamiliar to the angels." Although it may not be true that he was confusing an excitement of the nerves with a true vision of the Ideal, it seems fair enough to say that whereas Emerson's idealism was profoundly moral, Poe's was narrowly, possibly morbidly, aesthetic.

Poe, then, was not divorced from his age, but reflected important facets of the American mind. His social and political conservatism was buttressed by the scientific analogy of a perfect and stable universe. His aestheticism was, on its negative side, a protest against the Puritan overemphasis on the moralistic in literature. His concept of the Idea was a union of mathematics and music — a "supernal beauty" pure and unearthly. And Poe himself became our chief symbol of the American artist who is at odds with the crass world about him.

Religion and Politics among the Southern Gentry

Religious questions were not nearly so vital in Southern literature as in the literature of New England and in the writings of Melville. Southern writers, in general, did not concern themselves with spiritual laws, like Emerson; or with the remorse for sin, like Hawthorne; or with metaphysical speculation, like Melville. Indeed, in religious matters the cultivated Southerner was likely to be tolerant to the point of indifference. John Pendleton Kennedy's account of Frank Meriwether in *Swallow Barn* (1832) may be regarded as fairly typical of the gentry of the Old South:

> If my worthy cousin be somewhat over-argumentative as a politician, he restores the equilibrium of his character by a considerate coolness in religious matters. He piques himself upon being a high-churchman, but is not the most diligent frequenter of places of worship, and very seldom permits himself to get into a dispute upon points of faith. If Mr. Chub, the Presbyterian tutor in the family, ever succeeds in drawing him into this field, as he occasionally has the address to do, Meriwether is sure to fly the course; he gets puzzled with scripture names, and makes some odd mistakes between Peter and Paul, and then generally turns the parson over to his wife, who, he says, has an astonishing memory.

Good form, however, required a decent respect for the outward observances of religion. Among the aristocracy, the Episcopal Church was the best form; the Presbyterian, though less good, was socially acceptable. Meanwhile, it should be noted, the revivalistic evangelism of the Methodists and Baptists flourished on the frontiers west of Charleston and Richmond, and by the time of the Civil War had enlisted such a large following as to change materially the religious complexion of the South.

The conservative Southerner was likely to consider the Puritan a disagreeable fellow — crabbed in temperament, morbid in the pursuit of virtue. William Gilmore Simms preferred the Cavalier type. If religious ideas became articulate in the Charleston of Simms or the Baltimore of Kennedy, they were likely to take on a rationalistic, eighteenth-century flavor. A statement by Kennedy on his sixty-fifth birthday might have come from Franklin or Jefferson: "I endeavor to avoid the un-charitableness of sectarian opinion, and maintain an equal mind toward the various forms in which an earnest piety shapes the divisions of the world of believers — tolerating honest differences as the right of all sincere thinkers, and looking only to the kindly nature of Christian principle as it influences the personal lives and con-duct of men, as the substantial and true test of a sound religion."

Politics, however, were another matter. The Old South had a genius for politics, and nothing delighted the Charleston lawyer or the Virginia planter more than a political discussion. The hero of *Swallow Barn* was a Jeffersonian Democrat who supported the rights of the states and preferred the agrarianism of the South to the mercantilism and industrialism of the North. In early life Kennedy doubtless agreed with his hero; but he later opposed the new Jacksonian Democracy, satirizing it vigorously in *Quodlibet* (1840). As a result of his connections with the business in-terests of Baltimore, he became a Whig advocate of the protective tariff for manu-facturers and ended a staunch Unionist and Republican.

Simms' political course was the reverse of Kennedy's: he began as a Unionist and became an ardent champion of states' rights. New occasions teach new duties, Simms might have said. When he opposed nullification in South Carolina in 1832, he was supporting Old Hickory and the issue was the tariff. When he advocated nullification in South Carolina twenty years later, he was supporting Calhoun and the issue was slavery.

Although Simms was more democratic in his sympathies than Kennedy — pos-sibly because of youthful experiences on the Southwestern frontier — the two men agreed that the business of government belonged in the abler hands of the ruling class, ordinarily the planter aristocracy. As to the subject races — the Indian and the Negro — writers like Kennedy and Simms believed that their state of subjection argued their intrinsic inferiority and that the white superiors of the blacks should maintain them in humane tutelage until some distant time when emancipation might prove feasible. Kennedy painted a disarming picture of the master-slave rela-tionship at Swallow Barn, where he found "an air of contentment and good humor and kind family attachment." He looked forward to gradual emancipation and the possible success of colonizing experiments. Simms' early view was substantially the same. His later violent championship of slavery as "a wisely devised institu-tion of heaven" can be understood only in the light of the sectional controversy of the 1850's.

The Irrepressible Conflict

The issues in dispute before and during the Civil War, the bloodiest conflict which the world had seen up to that time, were complex and confused. On the Northern side, the primary objective of the abolitionists was the destruction of slavery as an institution, while the aim of the nationalists was the preservation of the Union. On the Southern side, many fought to defend slavery — an institution whose rights had been guaranteed by the Constitution — while others believed that the basic issue was the vindication of the sovereignty of the individual state. Beneath these immediate issues lay the conflict between two radically different forms of society: the democratic, industrial economy of the North and the aristocratic, agrarian economy of the South. Although the causes of conflict were deeply imbedded in the American past, a series of dramatic events in the 1850's precipitated the outbreak of war in 1861.

The Fugitive Slave Law of 1850, which compelled the return of runaway slaves to their owners, fanned the fires of abolitionism. Emerson declared that he would not obey it; Thoreau actually helped at least one fugitive slave to escape into Canada; and the gentle-souled Whitman implied in one of his poems that he would aid all such fugitives with his "firelock" if the occasion should arise. A decisive incident occurred in Boston in 1854, when an infuriated mob attempted to rescue Anthony Burns, a fugitive slave, from the police, and United States troops intervened to enforce the law.

The rival efforts of Northerners and Southerners to control Kansas, where the issue of slavery was to be decided by popular vote, resulted in bloody strife in that territory in 1855. In a speech called "The Crime Against Kansas," Senator Charles Sumner of Massachusetts spoke too harshly of Senator Butler of South Carolina; whereupon Butler's young kinsman, Preston Brooks, assaulted Sumner on the floor of the Senate and inflicted an injury from which Sumner never fully recovered. The controversy over Kansas hastened the organization, in 1856, of the Republican party, with a platform opposing the extension of slavery.

Sectional bitterness was increased still further in 1857 by the Dred Scott decision of Chief Justice Taney. Having been taken by his owner into a free state and then brought back into a slave state, Dred sued for his freedom. The Supreme Court denied his petition, declaring that since a Negro was not a citizen, he did not have access to the courts. The decision was attacked by Lincoln in his famous debates with Stephen A. Douglas. Still more dramatic and more far-reaching in its effects was the attempt of John Brown, a fanatical abolitionist, to foment an insurrection of slaves in Virginia. After having captured the federal arsenal at Harper's Ferry in October 1859, he was arrested by a company of marines under Colonel Robert E. Lee, and was later tried and executed. Emerson and Thoreau spoke out in Brown's defense, while Southerners were horrified by the threat of a black uprising. The "martyrdom" of Brown contributed enormously to the rise of sectional feeling. He became the subject of a stirring battle song (p. 1594) which Northern soldiers were to sing during the war: "John Brown's body lies a-moldering in the grave,/His soul is marching on!"

The election to the Presidency in 1860 of the Republican nominee, Abraham Lincoln, precipitated the secession movement in the South. The new party was exclusively the party of the North; political lines were more completely sectional than ever before. Since Lincoln had declared that "this government cannot endure permanently half slave and half free," and the Republican party vigorously opposed the extension of slavery, Southern extremists believed that they were forced to choose between abolition and secession. South Carolina seceded from the Union in December 1860, and by February 1861, Georgia, Alabama, Florida, Mississippi, Louisiana, and Texas had followed her example. Shortly thereafter, the Confederate States of America was organized in Montgomery, Alabama, with Jefferson Davis as president. On April 12, 1861, the Confederate batteries in Charleston harbor fired on the federal garrison in Fort Sumter, which surrendered the next day. Soon after this decisive event marking the opening of the war, Virginia, Arkansas, Tennessee, and North Carolina joined the Confederacy.

The choice between state and nation was a difficult one for many Southerners. The old constitutional argument that the states were older than the Union (true of course of only the original thirteen) and that the Union consequently derived its authority from the states was no doubt intellectually convincing to some. But loyalty is based in the emotions rather than in the intellect. The most distinguished officer of the Confederate army, Robert E. Lee, resigned his commission in the United States Army when Virginia seceded because, as he put it, "I have been unable to make up my mind to raise my hand against my native state, my relatives, my children, and my home." A New England writer, Hawthorne, expressed sympathy with Lee's view when he said, with a touch of irony: "If a man loves his own State and is content to be ruined with her, let us shoot him if we can, but allow him an honorable burial in the soil he fights for."

At the outset of the war, the South believed that cotton alone was a guarantee of victory; that if deprived of cotton, the textile industry — and therefore the entire economy — of the North and of England would collapse. The Southern expectation was not realized. England, though on the point of doing so in 1862, never recognized the Confederacy. The issue was to be decided by arms alone, and the overwhelming superiority of the North in population and resources permitted little doubt of the eventual outcome. It is hardly necessary here to recount the shifting tides of battle during the four years of war. The turning point came in July 1863, when Lee was defeated at Gettysburg and Grant captured Vicksburg after a long siege. The surrender of Lee to Grant at Appomattox on April 9, 1865, in effect terminated the war. The assassination of Lincoln five days later plunged the nation into the turmoil of reconstruction, which for the South proved to be more trying in many ways than the war itself.

Attackers and Defenders of Slavery

From the foregoing brief survey it is clear that slavery was the great issue before the American people, and it is not surprising that slavery was the subject of much of the literature, both Northern and Southern, during the decade which preceded the Civil War.

In the North, the two chief representatives of antislavery literature were John Greenleaf Whittier (p. 995) and Mrs. Harriet Beecher Stowe. Both writers were motivated by a sincere devotion to the cause of human freedom. Whittier's poems were characterized by a fiery intensity rarely equaled even in polemical verse. His "Ichabod" (p. 1000) was a scorching condemnation of Daniel Webster for his support of the Fugitive Slave Law:

> Let not the land once proud of him
> 	Insult him now,
> Nor brand with deeper shame his dim,
> 	Dishonored brow.

A better, though equally partisan, poem was his "Massachusetts to Virginia" (p. 997), with its swinging rhythm and its impressive roll call of the Massachusetts counties. If the author's zeal caused him to forget that New Englanders had once been actively engaged in the slave trade — as when he said to Virginia,

> But that one dark loathsome burden ye must stagger with alone,
> And reap the bitter harvest which ye yourselves have sown! —

the poem was none the less effective both as an indictment of the South and as a summons to action at home. Mrs. Stowe's *Uncle Tom's Cabin* (1852) reached a larger number of readers than did all of Whittier's poems combined; indeed, the novel immediately became, and remained for many years, a best seller. It was dramatized and was long successful on the stage. Mrs. Stowe's appeal was more sentimental than Whittier's; her book emphasized the pathos of the traffic in Christian souls.

In the South, John Pendleton Kennedy's *Swallow Barn,* published in 1832, as has been indicated, presented a reassuring picture of the friendly relations which existed between master and slaves on a Virginia plantation. It was revised and reissued in 1851. But the abolitionist attacks of the 1840's and 1850's called forth a more elaborate and more vigorous defense. Calhoun pointed out that slavery was a necessary part of the Southern economy and that its abolition would destroy the South:

> The Southern States are an aggregate, in fact, of communities, not of individuals.
> Every plantation is a little community, with the master at its head, who concen-

trates in himself the united interests of capital and labor, of which he is the common representative. These small communities aggregated make the State in all, whose action, labor, and capital is equally represented and perfectly harmonized. Hence the harmony, the union, the stability of that section.

With the rising tide of sectional feeling, Southern apologists carried the argument to still greater extremes. William Gilmore Simms doubtless spoke for a substantial body of Southern opinion when he declared in 1852 that "slavery is a wisely devised institution of heaven devised for the benefit, improvement, and safety, morally, socially, and physically, of a barbarous and inferior race, who would otherwise perish by famine or by filth, by the sword, by disease, by waste, and destinies forever gnawing, consuming, and finally destroying."

The final step in the Southern defense carried the war to the enemy. The condition of the slaves on Southern plantations, it was argued, was infinitely better than that of the workers, or wage-slaves, in Northern factories and mines. William J. Grayson's *The Hireling and the Slave* (1854) pointed the contrast in Pope-like couplets: in Northern industrial communities,

> Gaunt Famine prowls around his pauper prey,
> And daily sweeps his ghastly hosts away;
> Unburied corpses taint the summer air,
> And crime and outrage revel with despair . . .

while on the Southern plantation,

> Warm social joys surround the Negro's cot,
> The evening dance its merriment imparts,
> Love, with its rapture, fills their youthful hearts,
> And placid age, the task of labor done,
> Enjoys the summer shade, the winter sun.

A middle position between the extremes of Northern abolitionism and Southern eulogy was taken by Webster and Lincoln. Throughout the controversy the aim of both men was not to destroy slavery but to preserve the Union, and both incurred the ill will of the abolitionists. Although they believed that slavery was an evil and opposed its extension, they were willing to respect its constitutional rights in the slave states if thereby the Union might be saved. Webster's desire for his country was best expressed in the noble peroration, "Liberty and Union, one and inseparable, now and forever." Lincoln's attitude as late as August 1862 was expressed in the famous letter to Horace Greeley (p. 1606): "My paramount object in this struggle is to save the Union, and is not either to save or to destroy slavery. . . . What I do about slavery and the colored race, I do because I believe it helps to save the Union." The Emancipation Proclamation, announced on January 1, 1863, was a shrewd political weapon as well as a great humanitarian document. It united the cause of the

Negro with that of the Union and gave to the Civil War in the eyes of the world the dignity of a crusade for human liberty.

The Literature of the War Years

Much of our best literature dealing with the Civil War was not written until many years later — Stephen Crane's *The Red Badge of Courage* in the 1890's, for example, and Stephen Vincent Benét's *John Brown's Body* in the 1930's. During the war itself, the memorable literature on the subject of the war was small in amount: a few poems by Whittier and Henry Timrod, several popular songs, the speeches of Lincoln, and Whitman's collection of poems, *Drum-Taps*.

Since Whittier's work as propagandist had been largely accomplished before the outbreak of the war, he was content during its course to write an occasional poem. In "Laus Deo" he rejoiced at the passage of the constitutional amendment abolishing slavery. The amendment marked the final triumph of the cause for which he had labored, with energy and self-sacrifice, for thirty years.

While Whittier did his best work before and after the war, actual hostilities had the magical effect on Henry Timrod (p. 1573), the Southern poet, of calling forth poems far superior to anything else he ever wrote. "Ethnogenesis" (p. 1574) and "The Cotton Boll" (p. 1577) are compositions which entitle Timrod to a higher rank among our poets than he has yet been accorded. In these poems he reiterated many of the traditional Southern arguments: the Constitution recognized slavery, and the Bible did not prohibit it; the bond slave of the South was treated more humanely than the wage-slave of the North; Southern cotton was necessary to the prosperity and happiness of the world. In eloquent, moving verse he described his conception of the South's mission and of the Southern character. The exportation of cotton under a system of free trade, he thought, would bind the nations together in lasting peace. The Southern character and its influence on the rest of the world were typified for him in the Gulf Stream, which ". . . through the cold, untempered ocean pours its genial streams."

The war also called forth Lincoln's first utterances. In the *First Inaugural Address* (p. 1598) he faced the difficult situation already created by the secession of seven Southern states. Lincoln asserted that the Union was indissoluble, and promised that no force other than that necessary to hold federal property and collect federal duties would be used against the erring states. He concluded with an appeal "to the better angels of our nature." *The Gettysburg Address* (p. 1607), second only to the Declaration of Independence, is our most classic expression of the American democratic ideal; it was so phrased as to be always applicable. America was "conceived in liberty and dedicated to the proposition that all men are created equal." Americans should "highly resolve . . . that this nation, under God, shall have a new birth of freedom; and that government of the people, by the people, and for the people, shall not perish from the earth." Delivered a little more than a month before Lee's surrender and the author's death, the *Second Inaugural Address* (p. 1608) regarded the war as the righteous judgment of God on both North and South for the sin of slavery. The task before us, he said, was to proceed, "with malice toward none, with charity for all . . . to bind up the nation's wounds . . . to do all which may achieve and cherish a just and lasting peace among ourselves, and with all nations." Lincoln's humane and wise view of postwar policy made his death a tragic loss to the South.

II. Literary Trends

Foreign and Domestic Impulses

The period of 1829-1865 was rich not only in ideas but also in artistic expression. Although New England produced more than its share of great artists, other sections also nurtured authors of whom they might well be proud. The Southwest was represented notably by a great group of humorists. Both the South and the East were the background for Edgar Allan Poe. New York was represented by Herman Melville, whose best fiction ranks with the finest our country has produced, and also by a preëminent poet, Walt Whitman. The consideration of Whitman, whose notable career began near the end of this period, in 1855, and extended until 1892, we postpone until later.

In designating this period the American Renaissance, critics have had in mind, doubtless, certain similarities it had to the English Renaissance. The English period, which preceded the American by about two and a half centuries, had produced a host of great writers and literary masterpieces. In the literary productions, whether they were created by giants such as Marlowe, Spenser, and Shakespeare or by lesser men, two impulses had been operative, one foreign and the other native. The exciting discovery of foreign literary works, both old and new, had accounted in part for such works as Shakespeare's *Julius Caesar,* based upon the *Lives* by the Greek biographer-historian Plutarch (translated by North in 1579), and his *Othello,* derived from an Italian *novella* by Cinthio which had first appeared during Shakespeare's lifetime. The patriotic enthusiasm of the day, which had soared during the reign of Queen Elizabeth, found expression in Shakespeare's historical plays such as *Henry IV* and *Henry V* as well as in many of his dramas with foreign settings.

Similarly, during the American Renaissance both foreign and domestic influences, old and new, were notable. Respectful study of ancient and contemporary foreign works and travel abroad, which acquainted authors with European culture, left their marks upon not only the stuff but also the form of our literature. At the same time, proud of their unique democratic system and of the vast nation whose beauty and strength they were coming to know, many authors recounted the history of their land and attempted to depict accurately native scenes and characters.

The Essay—a Standard Form Takes on New Qualities

In this period, as in the preceding one, the essay was an important literary form; but a combination of old and new influences, as well as the personal predilections of each author, gave the type distinctive qualities.

Poe, Critic and Journalist

Poe's essays and articles show kinship in two ways with writings of authors across the seas. For one thing, he was in the tradition of European authors who alternated between the rôles of critics and creators. Such German predecessors as Goethe (1749-1832), Schlegel (1767-1845), Tieck (1773-1853), and Schelling (1775-1854) were critics and philosophers as well as poets. And so were several British authors known by Poe: Coleridge, who wrote his literary autobiography and several fine lyrics; Wordsworth, who theorized about his poems in critical prefaces; Shelley, who wrote a *Defence of Poesy* and lyrics of great excellence; Byron, who wrote *English Bards and Scotch Reviewers* and who also wrote lyrics which Poe admired greatly. Poe, similarly, philosophized about literature and criticized it, justifying poetry in general and his own poetry in particular — in works such as "Letter to B —" (p. 748) and "The Philosophy of Composition" (p. 759) and in numerous published reviews.

Poe worked frequently in the tradition of important Britons and Scots who were reviewers for influential periodicals such as *Blackwood's Magazine, The Quarterly Review,* and *The Edinburgh Review.* Such men as Francis Jeffrey (1773-1850), William Hazlitt (1778-1830), Leigh Hunt (1784-1859), John Wilson (1785-1854), Thomas De Quincey (1785-1859), and J. G. Lockhart (1794-1854) were journalists whose work for magazines enhanced their literary reputations. Poe's reviews of current books, such as *Twice-Told Tales* (p. 754), were journalistic contributions resembling overseas reviews in procedure and tone. At times they were as ferocious as any in the notoriously stern British reviews, but generally they were intelligent estimates which augmented Poe's fame as a critic.

Lowell: Critical, Reminiscent

Of the famous Massachusetts men, perhaps the nearest to traditional essayists was James Russell Lowell. Yet the patterns he followed were not those of relatively impersonal essays such as some British authors had written in the eighteenth century.

What he wrote was, as a rule, quite personal. A large share of his prose, which dealt with issues of the day — candidacies, governmental policies, political theories — might have appeared in newspapers and did appear in magazines which took stands on current affairs.

Such prose, though it served its purpose in its time, has interest now for political rather than literary historians. The prose by Lowell most important as literature is critical or reminiscent — "Shakespeare," "Keats" (p. 951), "Hawthorne's *The Marble Faun*" (p. 954), or "A Good Word for Winter," "Cambridge Thirty Years Ago," and the like. In both critical and reminiscent essays an important factor is the revelation of Lowell's personality — his wit, his learning, his enthusiasm, his sensitivity, his novel way of putting things. One of his volumes bore a title which might have been used for many — "Fireside Travels." He wrote as if he were putting on paper the sort of talk an informed professor, blessed with humor, might deliver to an intelligent student who had dropped in for an evening chat by the library fire in Elmwood. Lowell poured out enthusiasms, drove home points by quoting now and then from old books pulled down from towering tiers of shelves, frolicked with classical allusions or Latin quotations, rolled felicitous phrases over his tongue. In particular, Lowell was a master of the epigram — a condensation of his observation and judgment into witty or striking phrases and sentences. Despite some unevenness in his achievements, Lowell's work in the field of the personal essay was outstanding.

Holmes: Conversational, Neoclassical

Holmes, like Lowell, wrote much prose of a frankly utilitarian kind — in his case, prose which made use of the doctor's scientific interests and training. (See "Mechanism in Thought and Morals," p. 919.) Whatever such writing contributed to the thought of the period — many believe a great deal — the prose which showed Holmes at his inimitable best was more like the informal talk of a New England drawing room or boarding house than like a medical school lecture. Such work took the unique form employed in the *Breakfast-Table* series (p. 908).

The literature which Holmes knew as a boy did its part to shape his essays. He was fond of remarking how much it had meant to him to have been born and reared "among books and those who knew what was in books," to have had a chance, as a youngster, to page through first editions of eighteenth-century classics in the large library which his forbears had collected. "All men are afraid of books," he claimed, "who have not handled them from infancy." The form of his essays had its parallels with those of the period with which he felt a spiritual kinship — the eighteenth century. This had been the period of his boyhood idols, Addison and Steele, authors of *The Spectator*, which as *The New Yorker* of its day reviewed, laughed at, or philosophized about people and events of eighteenth-century London.

The Autocrat, the Professor, and the Poet of Holmes' series were Spectators commenting upon contemporary manners; and boarding-house society, like the club to which the Spectator had belonged, was "very luckily composed of such persons as were engaged in different ways of life, and deputed as it were out of the most conspicuous classes of mankind." Sketches introduced characters in such a way as to catch *Spectator*-like types — the landlady's daughter, for instance: "(Aet. 19 +. Tender-eyed blonde. Long ringlets. Cameo pin. Gold pencil-case on a chain. Locket. Bracelet. Album. Autograph book. Accordeon. Reads Byron, Tupper, and Sylvanus Cobb, Junior, while her mother makes the puddings. Says 'Yes?' when you tell her anything.)" Essays in the form of conversation — dialogues — had been used frequently in the eighteenth century: by Shaftesbury to comment upon ethics; by Berkeley, on philosophy; and by Franklin, on a variety of subjects. (See "Dialogue Between Franklin and the Gout," p. 332.) In a similar manner the *Autocrat* papers record conversations of the boarding-house members. James Boswell (1740-1795) had reported the sparkling talk and what Holmes called the "bow-wow manner" of Samuel Johnson; and Holmes acknowledged indebtedness in the subtitle of the *Autocrat — Every Man His Own Boswell.* In *Tristram Shandy* (1760) Sterne had recorded meandering talk interspersed with personal essays and punctuated in a manner foreshadowing Holmes' eccentric punctuation.

Nineteenth-century publications, too, probably suggested devices which gave the *Autocrat* papers novelty. Possibly the magazine or the annual (which achieved remarkable popularity in this period), with its alternation of story, essay, and poems, suggested a similar intermingling of types. The dramatic interplay between personalities common to fiction may have suggested the author's habit of giving his conversations a dramatic quality and of running a plot (like one in a magazine serial story) through his papers. Like Lowell, Holmes no doubt followed the example of nineteenth-century English essayists such as Lamb and Hazlitt in talking intimately of life, personal prejudices, feelings. The Autocrat is, in effect, Holmes airing his own views to fellow boarders. "He was a well-behaved gentleman at table," testified the Autocrat's landlady, "only talked a good deal, and pretty loud sometimes, and had a way of turnin' up his nose when he didn't like what folks said. . . . Many's the time I've seen that gentleman keepin' two or three of the boarders settin' round the breakfast table after the rest had swallered their meal, and things was cleared off . . . and there the little man would set . . . a-talkin' and a-talkin', — and sometimes he would laugh, and sometimes the tears would come into his eyes. . . . He was a master hand to talk when he got a-goin'."

Thoreau and Emerson: Philosophical, Transcendental

A kind of discourse distantly related to informal talk left its imprint upon Thoreau's prose works, whether short pieces or longer ones in which numerous essays were linked, such as *Walden* (p. 1192). Thoreau kept a detailed journal in which, from day to day, he set down experiences, observations, and thoughts, and from this he drew materials as needed. These diaries were written with artistic care, the passages in them were carefully integrated with other parts of essays in which they were used, and the sentences were scrupulously polished, so that in the end there was less improvisation than there appeared to be. In learning to shape sentences to his needs — by studying the metaphysical poets, by translating Greek dramas and from Greek poems, by aping English prose masters — Thoreau became indebted to earlier authors. "Every sentence," he wrote, with these models in mind, "is the result of long probation, and should be read as if its author, had he held a plough instead of a pen, could have drawn a furrow deep and straight to the end."

Since the conveying of rich personal experience and meaning by straight furrow expressions was, in Thoreau's opinion, the chief task of the writer, what shaped his prose style more than anything else was his philosophy. To see what Thoreau was trying to do, the reader must understand that, despite all his accumulations of scientific data, Thoreau's way of thinking led him to care little for strictly scientific writing. He attempted, instead, in his finished works, to write in the rôle of a philosopher. The scientist, according to Transcendental beliefs, recorded the workings of the mere intellect — the "Understanding." The great writer, the man of vision, by contrast, recorded the discoveries of a faculty above mind and more important — the "Imagination" or the "Reason," which intuitively perceived in natural objects the truth of which they were symbols. Said Thoreau:

> It is the subject of the vision, the truth alone, that concerns me. The philosopher for whom rainbows, etc., can be explained never saw them. With regard to such objects, I find that it is not they themselves (with which men of science deal) that concern me; the point of interest is somewhere *between* me and them (i.e., the objects). . . .

Seeing the inner meanings of natural phenomena, the great writer employed those phenomena, Thoreau believed, to communicate those meanings. "My thought," he explained, "is a part of the meaning of the world, and hence I use a part of the world to express my thought."

When he filled his pages with vivid details, he attempted to present them so as to make them illuminating in the Transcendental sense: he wanted to set down particular instances of the universal law so that readers might find his own sense of "reality" — the higher kind — in them. His stay at Walden was a search "for the essential facts of life," and his circumstantial record of the stay (or more precisely of an ideal stay based upon sixteen years of records in his journal) was an attempt to convey his insights in meaningful symbols. And elsewhere than in *Walden* his practice was to show the eternally true in terms of the particular. "There was an excellent wisdom in him, proper to a rare class of men, which showed him the material world as a means and a symbol," wrote Emerson. "To him there was no such thing as size. The pond was a small ocean; the Atlantic, a large Walden Pond." Certain that the small stood for the large, Thoreau expounded higher meanings sometimes in his writings by using paradoxes or philosophical generalizations, but mainly he trusted minute, concrete details on page after page to convey his meaning.

Emerson, though extraordinarily concrete for a philosopher, was more abstract than Thoreau. "In reading Thoreau," he said, "I find the same thought, the same spirit that is in me, but he takes a step beyond and illustrates by excellent images that which I should have conveyed in a sleepy generality." Trained in the composition of sermons and lectures, Emerson, in speeches such as "The Divinity School Address" (p. 1082) and in essays often largely derived from his lectures, had the interest that preachers and lecturers frequently have in generalizing, in following lines of reasoning. Perhaps it is not inaccurate to say that while Thoreau's emphasis was particularly on concrete things, Emerson's was on philosophical relationships.

Emerson set forth what he conceived to be the task of the philosopher in his study of his idol Plato: it was to follow the natural course of the mind as it related the One which was the Oversoul to the Many, or as it related the Many to the One.

> The mind [he wrote] is urged to ask for one cause of many effects; then for the cause of that; and again the cause . . . self-assured that it will arrive at an absolute and sufficient one, — a one that shall be all. . . . Urged by an opposite necessity, the mind returns from the one to that which is not one, but . . . many; from cause to effect; and affirms the necessary existence of variety, the self-existence of both, as each is involved in the other. These strictly-blended elements it is the problem of thought to separate and reconcile.

Such was the idea Emerson had of the method of his essays, and a reader who has patience and skill in dialectic can, indeed, see that the essays are constructed according to this pattern.* Most readers, however, will not care to follow the involvements of his peculiar Transcendental structure. They will find that, though some of Emerson's essays have organizations such as they have seen in other compositions, most appear to lack coherence and unity. These readers will agree with Carlyle's remarks to Emerson in a letter about the *Essays: First Series*:

> The sentences . . . did not . . . always entirely cohere for me. Pure genuine Saxon; strong and simple; of a clearness, of a beauty — But they did not, sometimes, rightly stick to their foregoers and their followers: the paragraph not as a beaten *ingot,* but as a beautiful square *bag of duckshot* held together by canvas!

For them, the virtue of the essays will be found chiefly in individual sentences — sentences excellent for their extraordinary proverbial quality, for their compact expression of profound thoughts. Even such small units as sentences, however, show that Emerson, like other essayists of his day, combined old materials and methods with newly discovered ones, thereby making his purposeful writing seem a new thing.

American Fiction Comes into Its Own

When authors of the period 1829-1865 wrote fiction, they were inclined to consider whether the setting of their narratives should be remote or near at hand in time and space. Both kinds of settings were popular in literature which was generally admired.

---

*For some analyses of Emerson's essays according to this principle see W. T. Harris, "Ralph Waldo Emerson," **Atlantic**, 1882, CL, 238-252, and Walter Blair and Clarence Faust, "Emerson's Literary Method," **Modern Philology**, 1944, XLII, 79-95

German and British Gothic romances — or tales of terror — utilizing exotic backgrounds were extremely popular; so were Sir Walter Scott's historical novels, the last of which appeared in 1832. Across the ocean, in addition, flourished fiction which portrayed the manners and talk of common folk. This fiction had a large audience in the United States: Sir Walter Scott, Maria Edgeworth (1767-1849), and Charles Dickens (1812-1870), who wrote about common folk, were the most popular authors in this country — native authors included — during this period. Our authors adapted both types of settings and characterizations to their own purposes.

Poe: Skilled Craftsman

Early in his career as a fictionist, Poe wrote a letter to T. W. White, owner of the *Southern Literary Messenger,* explaining how he had happened to write one of his weird stories. He had been reading successful magazines, foreign and American, and had found that a certain kind of story was in demand. He mentioned "The Spectre in the Log Hut" *(Dublin University Review),* "The Last Man" *(Blackwood's),* "The Suicide" and "The Dance of Death" *(Godey's),* and "The Spectre Fire Ship" *(Knickerbocker).* All these were in the tradition of the Gothic tale of terror, which had flourished since the mid-eighteenth century. The most popular tales, Poe said, represented "the ludicrous heightened into the grotesque; the fearful colored into the horrible; the witty exaggerated into the burlesque; and the singular heightened into the strange and mystical." Poe could turn out stories with any of these effects, but he was at his best in creating the second and fourth of them. Such spine-tingling tales as "The Fall of the House of Usher" (p. 768), "Ligeia" (p. 783), "The Man of the Crowd" (p. 795), "The Masque of the Red Death" (p. 826), and "The Cask of Amontillado" (p. 830) owe much to the Gothic romances.

They also owe much to Poe's self-conscious craftsmanship. Thinking in terms of the faculty psychology and of the "science" of phrenology, widely accepted during his day, Poe devised a theory about writing tales which, fortunately, retained some of its validity after these "sciences" had lost theirs. Poe conceived of two elements in a tale — incident and tone — as stimuli to a response by the reader. The skillful artist, therefore, was one who carefully formulated exactly the effect he wished to achieve, then invented and combined events and told of them in words chosen to establish the preconceived effect. A tale so wrought, he felt, could not fail to "leave in the mind of him who contemplated it with a kindred art, a sense of the fullest satisfaction." The process, some have thought, was a somewhat mechanical one; but Poe's skill in both invention and execution, when he followed his formula, made possible achievements which, in particular genres, have not been surpassed. Subordinating everything in the tale to the effect, Poe skillfully utilized characteristic backgrounds, characters, and incidents of Gothic romance.

Hawthorne: Romance and Allegory

In believing that the most soul-stirring effect could be achieved by blurred rather than precise details, Poe, of course, differed from Hawthorne, whom he greatly admired and at times rather badly misread — differed, as a matter of fact, from most

New Englanders. In this period, one who saw a Yankee village from a distance noticed first of all the tidy white-spired churches which were an important and recurrent motif in the quiet green landscape — a motif which stood for a great force in the life of the section. Founded by zealots, New England for decades had produced moralizing literature, and it continued to produce it even when its authors wrote fiction. For Hawthorne, preëminent among New England fictionists, the theme of the tale was tremendously important. Although the Gothic influence was almost as pronounced on Hawthorne as it was on Poe and though sentimental fiction and allegorical narrative were important in shaping his fiction, these devices were subordinated to Hawthorne's own New England purpose.

As has frequently been noticed, paraphernalia of the tale of terror — animated ancestral portraits, fiendlike villains, men who sold their souls to the devil, witches, unnatural portents — figured notably in this author's tales and novels. The influence of sentimental fiction, too, is clear — even in such a masterpiece as *The Scarlet Letter.* The penalty of seduction, a chief stock in trade of the sentimentalists (see p. 487), is the chief substance of this great romance. A typical character of the fiction of sensibility — a child bringing sunshine into the home and gently leading parents to virtue — is little Pearl, an important character in the work. The misled feminist and the ministering angel popular in fourth-rate novels are combined in the portrayal of Hester. Calvinistic villainy common in sentimental fiction was bestowed upon Chillingworth. The sensibility of the minister and his dying glimpses of heavenly glory are hackneyed motifs in the sentimental pattern. And in the tales, as in the longer works, one familiar with the fiction of feeling will see its stuff used by Hawthorne.

Hawthorne was further influenced by a type of fiction not of his own time so much as of the past — the allegorical narrative, which, from childhood, he had read with much pleasure. When in 1843 he listed the authors he considered most notable, along with such conventional choices as Homer, Cervantes, Shakespeare, and Milton he named masters of fable and allegory: Aesop, Ariosto, Spenser, and "Bunyan, moulded of homeliest clay, but instinct with celestial fire." Other influences in addition to his liking for these authors encouraged him to borrow from them. Like Emerson, he had ideas about the artist's duty to give meaning to natural objects when he depicts them. The artist, he felt, cannot exactly reproduce the grandeur of nature which itself suggested truth. His "only resource," he decided, was to substitute something "that may stand instead of and suggest the truth." His Preface to *The House of the Seven Gables* (p. 1374) suggested that a great advantage of a Romance was that it "has fairly a right to present . . . truth under circumstances, to a great extent, of the author's own choosing or creation." This truth, moreover, might be the unifying element. "In all my stories, I think," he remarked, "there is one idea running through them like an iron rod, and to which all other ideas are referred and subordinate. . . ." Lowell's comment noted the same ideational unity: "It is commonly true of Hawthorne's romances that the interest centres in one strongly defined protagonist, — perhaps we should rather say a ruling Idea, of which all the characters are fragmentary embodiments."

Subtly adapted devices of allegorical fiction — for the portrayal of background and character and the selection of incidents — made possible Hawthorne's amalgamation of Gothic and sentimental elements in impressive fiction. Reminiscent of Spenser's Forest of Error or Bower of Bliss, in which details of background are made to stand for the author's concepts, are Hawthorne's descriptions of the Pearson cottage in "The Gentle Boy" and of the garden in "Rappaccini's Daughter" (p. 1336). Characters, too, are embodiments of ideas according to allegorical formulas. Sometimes older allegorists associated significant articles or details of dress with a character: in *Pilgrim's Progress* Christian labors under his heavy burden; in *The Faerie Queene* the knight has his "bloudie crosse." In "The Minister's Black Veil" (p. 1295) Hooper wears his meaningful bit of crepe. Again, older allegorists at times showed physical deformities which betokened spiritual deformities, as in the cases of Bunyan's Giant Despair and Spenser's Malbecco. Similarly, Hawthorne made the boy who alone could not yield to the "gentle boy's" influence a twisted cripple. Hawthorne ingeniously conceived other symbolic attributes of characters to signify their import: the gleaming smile of Minister Hooper and the perfume of Beatrice, to cite only two examples.

"The Artist of the Beautiful" (p. 1317) embodies and expounds Hawthorne's critical theory. The story treats, as its author says, "the troubled life of those who strive to create the beautiful," and the opening paragraph establishes a contrast — between the artist, working in light, and the thwarters of the artist, standing in darkness — important throughout the tale. Warland, who is given the attributes of the eternal artist, is the creator of a butterfly the beauty of which "represented the intellect, the sensibility, the soul" of such a creator. Each other character is, in one way or another, a thwarter of the artist, and each is so presented as to signify one of the hostile forces which work against art. All the details, images, and happenings in the tale are richly fused with the meaning, in a manner which is typical of the unique art which Hawthorne discovered for himself.

Melville: Symbol and Actuality

In 1850 Hawthorne and Melville, living a few miles apart but not yet acquainted, read one another's writings and found them good. What each said about the other indicates likenesses and differences. Melville admired Hawthorne for confronting the darker aspects of life. (See "Hawthorne and His Mosses," p. 1380.) Hawthorne wrote:

> I have read Melville's works with progressive appreciation of the author. No writer ever put reality before the reader more unflinchingly than he does in *Redburn* and *White-Jacket*. *Mardi* is a rich book, with depths here and there that compel a man to swim for his life. It is so good that one scarcely pardons the writer for not having brooded long over it, so as to make it a good deal better.

Clearly there was a kinship between Melville and Hawthorne in artistry as well as in philosophy. Both thought that the theme of a fictional work was very important. Both thought that an author should manipulate imagery, characterization, and plot to convey his ideas. But Hawthorne indicated a difference when he complained that his neighbor had not "brooded" enough over his material. Melville's fiction, if we may employ Hawthorne's terms, did not subdue "the Actual." "He felt instinctively," as William Ellery Sedgewick asserts, "that the effective use of a fact as symbol, having both inward and outward reference, depended on the preservation of its outward reality." Melville's aim — comparable with the way of writing which Hawthorne contrasted with his own in the Preface to *The Scarlet Letter* — was "to diffuse thought and imagination through the opaque substance of today, and thus to make it a bright transparency . . . to seek, resolutely, the true and indestructible value that lay hidden in the petty and wearisome incidents, and ordinary characters. . . ." Though Hawthorne could not write thus, could not thus simultaneously convey meaning and a sense of actuality, he could admire others who were able to, since he recognized that such writing achieved a similar end in contrasting fashion.

Billy Budd (p. 1469), not too representative of Melville's typical procedure, is closer to the New Englander's conception of "the Romance" (p. 1374) than almost anything else that Melville wrote. Romance though it is, it has a factual basis and includes a few more earthy details than Hawthorne would have been apt to include.

And when one turns to other, more typical works by Melville — works in which he presents many particular and vivid details based on fact and experience and representing the everyday lives of seamen — the contrast becomes quite clear. His selection and presentation of such facts made them actual, near at hand rather than remote, and at the same time meaningful. "Benito Cereno" (p. 1398), not only one of Melville's most typical stories but also one of his best, is a good example. Based as it is upon a first-hand account of Captain Delano's real experience, it loses little of its factuality when it is transformed into fiction. At the same time the changes in the nature of the details and in the structure of the narrative make possible the development of a significant theme.

Native American Humor

It remained for the humorists of the day, though, to get the largest amount of common life into their picturings. Two sections were rich in their humor between 1829 and 1865, New England and the old Southwest — Tennessee, Georgia, Alabama, Louisiana, Mississippi, Arkansas, and Missouri. The humorists' techniques for showing scenes from ordinary life were, in important ways, the freshest of the period because humor, in a romantic era, naturally moved in the direction of realism.

Earlier writers of course affected the humorists. Eighteenth-century essayists who portrayed "characters" and eccentrics doubtless influenced comic writers in both sections, particularly those in the Southwest. Type characterizations in travel books and almanacs — of acute Yankee peddlers, slow-witted Dutchmen, rambunctious frontiersmen, haughty and hard-drinking aristocrats and naïve Negro slaves — helped humorists, particularly the earlier ones, individualize characters in different sections. Walter Scott and other British authors who represented "low" characters by the depiction of manners, dress, and speech had value as models. And English sporting journals which combined native characterizations with accounts of hunts and horse races were read and imitated by Southwestern lovers of sports.

But two influences did much to Americanize the humor. One was a basic, widespread, and lasting belief. The other was a popular American folk art — that of the oral tale.

The belief was defined similarly by three great observers of life in the United States — Tocqueville from France in the 1830's, Schurz from Germany in the 1850's, and Bryce from England in the 1870's and 1880's. Bryce defined it most succinctly: "Truth is identified with common sense, the quality which the average American is most proud of possessing." Common sense, also called horse sense, native wit, and gumption, was generally considered to be that precious quality which enabled a man or woman with a keen mind and with wide experience in the world of men, rather than book learning, to see to the heart of any problem, solve it, and convincingly announce its solution.

Franklin's Poor Richard had revealed the quality early in the eighteenth century; the farm, the mechanic's shop, and the frontier had nurtured it over the years, and in this period its triumph in Jacksonian politics gave it enlarged prestige. Now it shaped the representation of humorous characters.

Incorrigible moralizers, New Englanders used horse-sensible characters to preach. Seba Smith showed how this might be done when in 1830 he launched his creation, rustic Jack Downing, upon a career destined to last (with some interruptions) until the eve of the Civil War. In letters which he wrote to home folk or to newspapers Jack told of his adventures in politics — in the state capital, in Washington, or on the battlefront during the Mexican War; and now and then the home folk wrote to tell Jack how things were going in Downingville. Keen eyes perceived the foibles of politicos, and sharp minds provided commentaries upon current issues.

So wide a following did Jack gain that a number of other Down East humorists created and depicted similar humble commentators: Matthew F. Whittier, creator of Ethan Spike, B. P. Shillaber, whose creation was Mrs. Partington, and others. In the days of the war with Mexico, James Russell Lowell looked around for a way of effectively conveying his views to a wide public. He hit upon the idea of having an imaginary unlearned farmer, Hosea Biglow, whom he described as "common sense vivified and heated by conscience," speak for him. The resulting Biglow Papers were the most popular of all Lowell's writings. Although all the characters were invented to serve as mouthpieces, their creators tended increasingly to give them palpable and lifelike backgrounds, and to endow them with traits which made them droll, human, and persuasive. Their comments in dialect showed what kinds of minds they had, what their experiences had been, and what they had figured out on the basis of their experiences. So the matter as well as the manner of the fiction about them was native and novel, and moved towards realism.

On the frontier, a similar distrust of learning and respect for pawkiness flourished.

Davy Crockett of the Tennessee canebrakes had a meteoric rise in politics largely because his neighbors knew that he had not been unduly educated and believed that he was strong in native wit. In politics, he was exploited first by the Jacksonian Democrats and later, when he switched parties, by the Whigs, for both parties sought the support of the great masses of voters in the horse-sensible camp. William Tappan Thompson invented Major Joseph Jones and, like Seba Smith before him, used his canny letter-writer to convey his political views. Other Southwestern humorists, such as George Washington Harris and T. B. Thorpe, less convinced that mother wit was a key to truth, nevertheless, in painting mountaineers, settlers, and hunters, showed liking for its worshipers and amusement with their foibles.

In both the Northeast and the Southwest, the native humor was much influenced by a favorite frontier pastime, yarnspinning. In the homes, country stores, and taverns of New England an important diversion was the swapping of oral tales. Traveling across country, moving down or up the rivers, resting at night by campfires or household firesides, the people of the Southwest found that good stories pleasantly passed the time. Able yarnspinners were greatly admired, and masters of the art such as Davy Crockett and Abe Lincoln found that well-told anecdotes, some aptly illustrating points which they wished to make, were political assets.

The stories ranged from wild fantasy to fairly accurate accounts of everyday happenings. Playful lies comparable to their modern descendants, "fish stories" or animated cartoons, celebrated the fertility of the soil or encounters with huge beasts; an example was Doggett's monologue in "The Big Bear of Arkansas" (p. 1557). Or they dealt with gigantic comic demigods such as keelboatman Mike Fink (p. 563) or the mythical Crockett of the almanacs (p. 1538). Fantastic details were a product of the soaring frontier imagination. But an incongruity which did much to make the tales comic was the incongruity between the actual and the impossible. Thus, though whole sequences of events were completely impossible, happening was made to arise from happening in a completely logical fashion. An earthy dialect style rather than the majestic language of poetry matter-of-factly recounted astonishing feats. Details painstakingly rendered — highly authentic details — gave added verisimilitude. Sometimes, even touches which were quite vulgar heightened contrasts between the earthy and the unearthly. A few lines after Jim Doggett has poetically evoked a giant bear which "looms like a black mist," Jim is shamefacedly telling about losing his pants. And often, though the tale was impossible by any sane standards, the character of the teller and his motives for inventing his lie were plausibly rendered. The playfulness of tall tales was underlined, in short, by constant reminders of actuality.

Even more of actuality entered into stories of another sort told by Western firesides and eventually translated into print — comic tales about more commonplace frontier characters and happenings. Several reasons for authenticity in such narratives may be cited. There was a desire on the part of some sophisticated storytellers and writers to show that they, like eighteenth-century British humorists, could detachedly perceive and appreciate "originals." Again, there was a wish, on the part of many, to write history — as A. B. Longstreet put it, in his pioneer book, *Georgia Scenes,*

". . . to supply a chasm in history which has always been overlooked — the manners, customs, amusements, wit, dialect, as they appear in all grades of society to an eye and ear witness. . . ." Finally, of course, there was a desire to entertain one's fellows. Lawyers, for instance, riding the circuits, said Samuel A. Hammett, in 1853, "living as they do in the thinly inhabited portion of our land, and among a class of persons generally their inferiors in point of education . . . are apt to seek for amusement in listening to the droll stories and odd things always to be heard at the country store or bar-room."

Whatever their motivation, authors who wrote such tales managed among them to record in extraordinary detail many aspects of frontier life. Franklin J. Meine, in his excellent anthology, *Tall Tales of the Southwest,* lists a group of subjects that is strikingly inclusive — local customs, games, courtships, weddings, law circuits, political life, hunting, travel, medicine, gambling, religion, fights, and oddities in character. As Bernard De Voto claims in *Mark Twain's America,* "No aspect of the life in the simpler America is missing from this literature." The details about backgrounds, costumes, mores, and dialect are plentiful and vivid. Regardless of their crudities and exaggerations, such authors as Crockett, Thorpe, Thompson, and G. W. Harris represent an early American achievement of what later was called "realism."

The Oratory of Lincoln

Some humorous writings of the period 1829-1865 had affiliations with political speeches. An unsigned comic skit which went the rounds in newspapers during the 1840's purported to be a speech of one Candidate Earth, who wanted backwoods neighbors to elect him sheriff. Said he:

> Now gentlemen, don't you think they ought to make me sheriff? I say, if Bob Black has floated farther on a log, killed more Injuns, or stayed longer under water than I have, elect him; if not, I say what has he done to qualify him for the office of sheriff? Did any of you ever know him to call for a quart? I never did; I have known him to call for several half-pints in the course of a day, but I never did know him to step forward manfully and say, "Give us a quart of your best." Then I say again, what has Bob Black done to qualify him for sheriff?

In similar (though often less literate) language, Crockett and other backwoods or rural candidates regularly appealed for votes. And the very simplicity of the diction, its very freedom from adornment, recommended the speakers to constituents who preferred gumption to book learning.

A very different kind of oratory, nevertheless, was also much admired — that, say, of Daniel Webster, Wendell Phillips, Henry Clay, and of other orators not so well remembered. William Cullen Bryant, stating a general belief in 1826, noticed important likenesses between the orator and the poet: both were inspired, both deeply moved, and both were deeply moving as they appealed to "moral perceptions of listeners." The orator's voice, said Bryant, "acquires an unwonted melody, and his sentences arrange themselves in a sort of measure and harmony, and the listener is chained in involuntary and breathless attention." Some of the most admired passages in the oratory of the day, consequently, were remarkably florid, figurative, and rhythmic." Particularly admired, for instance, was the conclusion of Webster's most celebrated speech in the Senate, the "Reply to Hayne" of 1830:

> When my eyes shall be turned to behold for the last time the sun in heaven, may I not see him shining on the broken and dishonored fragments of a once glorious Union; on States dissevered, discordant, belligerent; on a land rent with civil feuds, or drenched, it may be, in fraternal blood! Let their last feeble and lingering glance rather behold the gorgeous ensign of the republic, now known and honored throughout the earth, still full high advanced, its arms and trophies streaming in their original lustre, not a stripe erased or polluted, nor a single star obscured, bearing for its motto, no such miserable interrogatory as "What is all this worth?" nor those other words of delusion and folly, "Liberty first and Union afterwards"; but everywhere, spread all over it in characters of living light, blazing on all its ample folds, as they float over the sea and the land, and in every wind under the whole heavens, that other sentiment, dear to every true American heart, — Liberty *and* Union, now and for ever, one and inseparable!

Many who commended the great oratory of the day cited this passage or similar ones. Our appreciation for such flights is tepid. The reason is that there has been a change in taste during the last century.

In the years before the Civil War, there were already some portents of the change in taste which eventually was to take place. In 1857, Edward G. Parker, in his book *The Golden Age of American Oratory,* indicated that the age which he had in mind was about to end. He saw two reasons for its conclusion. First, what he called "the age of chivalry" was closing and, said he, "A brazen age, anti-sentimental, succeeds. . . ." Secondly, "the growing taste of our people for reading" was bringing into prominence "accurate rhetorical composition, rather than the dashing vigor and vivacious sparkle of spontaneous oratory."

Whether for the reasons he suggested or not, Parker's prophecy was, in general, to come true. Even as he wrote, some had begun to lose their liking for what Parker characterized as "oratory . . . bursting from the lips of Prophets" and to perfer "the less contagious influences of logic, and figures and facts." Addresses of Calhoun and of Webster delivered in 1850 represent, in style, the transitional period.

By 1850, Webster had developed what students call his "mature style" — a style which, compared with his earliest efforts, had greatly gained in simplicity. Edwin P. Whipple, in 1879, wrote: "The mature style of Webster is perfect of its kind, being in words the express image of his mind and character, — plain, terse, clear, forcible;

and rising to the level of lucid statement and argument into passages of superlative eloquence only when his whole nature is stirred by some grand sentiment. . . ." Modern readers, of course, shy away from the passages of "superlative eloquence" which Whipple obviously admired. But they find that Webster does not indulge in such eloquence too often and that the bulk of his oratory is concerned with expressing thoughts clearly. They find that most of his famous speech of March 7, 1850, is devoted to Webster's version of history, to arguments justifying his attitude, set forth massively to be sure, but for the most part simply and moderately — at least for the time. John C. Calhoun, generally ranked below Webster at the time, may be preferred by readers today. The reason was suggested by a comment made upon his style by a critic of oratory in 1849. "Mr. Calhoun," E. L. Magoon wrote, "flaunts in no gaudy rhetorical robes of scarlet and gold, but comes into the forum clothed in the simplest garb, with firm hands grasping the reins of fancy, and intent only on giving a reason for the faith that is in him." Readers today will admire the relatively simple dress and the tight grip upon the reins, will find Calhoun's logic and his clarity admirable.

Although modern readers can endure the reading of Webster and Calhoun, they find more moving the one speaker of the Golden Age of Oratory who, by general consent, has become a classic author — Abraham Lincoln. At least four of Lincoln's speeches — *Farewell Address at Springfield, First Inaugural Address, Gettysburg Address,* and *Second Inaugural Address* (see pp. 1598-1610) — whether one agrees or disagrees with their interpretation of history, were great utterances.

A student of Lincoln's collected speeches will find that a surprising amount of his work is far below these masterpieces in excellence. His first speech, delivered in 1832 when, as a gangling, ill-dressed youth of twenty-three, he was running for the state legislature, went this way:

> I presume you-all know who I am. I am humble Abe Lincoln. I have been solicited by many friends to become a candidate for the legislature. My politics are short and sweet like the old woman's dance. I am in favor of a national bank. I am in favor of the internal improvements system, and a high protective tariff. These are my sentiments and political principles. If elected I shall be thankful. If not it will be all the same.

The speech, to be sure, is somewhat better than that of Candidate Earth, but clearly its eloquence is in a similar style. And many of Lincoln's later speeches, among them the historic debates with Douglas, now appear to have little more than a certain homespun straightforwardness, well adapted to public debate, to recommend them. At times, by contrast, especially during his early career, Lincoln indulged in spread-eagle melodramatic oratory as tawdry as any produced at the time. An instance is a campaign speech of 1840, in which he said:

> I know that the great volcano at Washington, aroused and directed by the spirit that reigns there, is belching forth the lava of political corruption in a current

broad and deep, which is sweeping with frightful velocity over the whole length and breadth of the land, bidding fair to leave unscathed no green spot or living thing; while on its bosom are riding, like demons on the wave of hell, the imps of the evil spirit, and fiendishly taunting all who dare to resist its destroying course with the hopelessness of their efforts; and knowing this, I cannot deny that all may be swept away. Broken by it, I, too, may be; bow to it, I never will.

Obviously the figurative language here used was meant to appeal to the current taste. But although many contemporaries did not sufficiently appreciate him, Lincoln did manage, at least in his later years, to achieve greatness as a composer of speeches.

Just why Lincoln managed to steer away from both the crude utterances of a small-town politician and the fustian elegance of the popular orator is something of a problem. The very fact that he, unlike many of the leaders of the day, was self-schooled probably was important. While others among his contemporaries had studied the classical rules and examples of oratory, Lincoln had learned his art chiefly in frontier political debates and in clashes in law courts. Because he relied upon the teachings of experience, he shared the democratic belief in common sense and its direct expression, and that fact, too, was significant. Literary influences upon Lincoln, nevertheless, were important, and fortunately some of the most notable were those of authors who achieved forceful expression by means of simplicity and restraint — Robert Burns, William Shakespeare, and the translators of the Bible into the King James version. Finally, Lincoln's own character and feeling, as they developed during the trying years of his Presidency, were strongly reflected in his thought and the form of its expression. As Edgar Dewitt Jones remarks, somewhat flossily, in his study of orators, *Lords of Speech,* "The graces of an orator's presence, the charm of his voice and manner, are ephemeral; while the grandeur of his thoughts, the magnanimity of his soul and the soundness of his reasoning live after him. It is the substance of his speeches, together with the chaste beauty of a style which matches the sheer beauty of his spirit, that lift Abraham Lincoln into the small and elect company of the world's supreme masters of public speech." Lincoln, despite the intemperance of the times in which he lived, was a temperate man, and he was an extremely sincere man. He was also something of a poet. His utterances, therefore, could outlast both the crude mouthings of the folksy politicians and the highly ornate orations of less temperate, less sincere, and less poetic speakers.

Poetry: A Combination of the Old and the New

Poets, like the orators of the period, employed two styles, both related to the past as well as to their time. The Singers of the West (pp. 1566-1572) followed the tradition of ancient balladry: their songs were composed by the people (or by an artist who felt, spoke, and thought as they did), for the people, and were kept alive by the people. Some popular songs of Civil War days show how both a vernacular style and a more ornate literary style might be adapted to a single tune — the two versions of "Dixie" (p. 1589) for instance, and "John Brown's Body" and "The Battle Hymn of the Republic" (p. 1594). At the time little attention was paid to poems which used the phrasings of daily speech, but later scholars would collect such songs and serious poets would learn much about art and life from such earthy and vigorous songs.

Two respected authors, though, showed kinship with the popular singers. James Russell Lowell's *Biglow Papers,* as has been indicated, used diction and characterizations related to those in popular humor. John Greenleaf Whittier (p. 995) tried at times to write formidably literary verse, and his conscious use of dialect in poetry was infrequent. Nevertheless, at his most effective he was a writer of songs which were remarkably simple — almost in the manner of folk songs — both in metrical form and in the kind of words used. The country poet's country rearing, his brief schooling, and his particular admiration for the seemingly artless songs of Robert Burns all led him to write unpretentious poems. Never, it appears, did he give much consideration to matters of technique. His aim, as he stated it, was

> To paint, forgetful of the tricks of art,
> With pencil dipped alone in colors of the heart.

As a rule, no sign appeared of his striving for novelty. All his life, his favorite measures were ballad measure, octosyllabics, and iambic pentameter — quite conventional forms of verse — and he used a vocabulary and figures of speech which were far from complex. Because of their almost rustic directness and simplicity, his poems appealed greatly to many untutored readers.

Most poets eminent in the period were less simple and immediate, more elegant and remote. The background of the cultured New England poets led them to think of poetry as the height of elegance. Among the books which Holmes listed as obligatory reading for a boy of a good Boston or Cambridge family was "Pope, original edition, 15 volumes, London, 1717." The superstition that eighteenth-century Alexander Pope was "the greatest poet that ever lived" was, Lowell confessed, inculcated in him by childhood teachers; and, similarly, the other famous New England authors from babyhood to manhood listened to encomiums of the older poets. Others who had learned to like literature as youngsters in ancestral libraries had a natural tendency to worship somewhat old-fashioned literary gods. Bowdoin and Harvard were likely to encourage this tendency with their classical curriculums and their courses in writing based upon Blair's old-fashioned, square-toed *Rhetoric.* When Emerson was in Latin school, his favorite declamation was from the "Pleasures of Hope," a typical eighteenth-century philosophizing poem written by Campbell in heroic couplets.

But the tradition of culture, though it fostered approval of old ideas and models, also fostered the discovery and development of new ones. The new forces it put to work made certain that the prominent authors would modify, in various fashions, the ways of looking at things and the ways of voicing attitudes. In the South,

Henry Timrod acknowledged the influence of seventeenth-century Milton, but he also saw that he was influenced by ninteenth-century Wordsworth and Tennyson. In some poems ("Charleston," p. 1584; "Ode," p. 1587) he used the simple ballad stanza much liked by Wordsworth or a slight adaptation of it; in others ("Ethnogenesis," p. 1574; "The Cotton Boll," p. 1577) he used the irregular ode form which had been used with marked success by Wordsworth and Tennyson. Poe, who lived in England briefly during his youth, avidly read books and magazines from overseas. Literary men of Massachusetts might be sketchily informed about the nation to the West and to the South, but they were likely to widen their horizons by traveling extensively in the Old World. As Parrington has noticed, the New England Renaissance "involved three major strands: the social Utopianism that came from revolutionary France; the idealistic metaphysics that emerged from revolutionary Germany; and the new culture that spread with the development of literary romanticism . . . these strands . . . are but different, new world phases of a comprehensive European movement. . . ." The widespread revolutionary spirit invaded not only the quiet Cambridge libraries but also the woods by Walden Pond.

From the old and new books discovered abroad and at home, American authors took hints about poetic techniques. They learned procedures in writing from modern writers such as Wordsworth, Coleridge, Byron, Shelley, and Keats and from those of other times, such as the Norse epic poets, the authors of ancient Oriental works, and Plato and the Neo-platonists. In much of the poetry of the section, as a result, there was a combination of the old and the new — and every author's individual conception of poetry determined the nature of the combinations which he produced.

Poe: Poet of Unearthly Beauty

Poe, as Professor Killis Campbell observed,

> began his career as a poet by imitating Byron and Moore; he came a little later under the spell of Shelley; and both in his theorizing as to poetry and in the application of those theories to his own art he proclaimed himself the ardent disciple of Coleridge. In . . . 'The Raven,' 'The Haunted Palace,' and 'Annabel Lee' he followed, even though afar off, in the footsteps of the balladists; . . . and there is an unmistakable Gothic strain both in his earlier and some of his later verses.

Thus Poe was indebted to his immediate predecessors, and he was indebted, also, to some of his contemporaries, notably Mrs. Browning and an American poet now pretty well forgotten, Thomas Holley Chivers.

Despite such relationships, Poe wrote poetry which was, in some ways, unique. This was partly because of his ability to imagine and portray scenes of unearthly beauty — dreamlands, fairylands, cities in the sea, ghoul-haunted woodlands, and the like. It was partly because he wrote in accordance with rather precise theories — theories about the "single effect" of poetry, about the handling of metre and sound, and about the indirect ways "meaning" or "truth" should be hinted, though not articulated, in poetry.

Holmes: "Florist in Verse"

Much of Holmes' poetry had such a periwig-and-velvet-breeches quality about it, like that of Goldsmith, Pope, Gray, Campbell, and Gay, that Holmes appeared, as one critic put it, "less a revival of the eighteenth century than its latest survival."

Holmes' kinship with the coffee-house gentry was in part the result of his paying them the tribute of imitation, in part the consequence of his seeing poetry, as they often had, as a graceful social accomplishment. "I'm a florist in verse," he sang, "and what would people say, if I came to a banquet without my bouquet?" So successful was he at writing "by request of friends" that around Boston, almost invariably, first-class celebrations, anniversaries, banquets, receptions, and professional meetings were likely to program an appearance of Dr. Holmes, poem in hand.

All this meant a good deal about his poems. For *vers de société* or *vers d'occasion,* he saw as well as had the Neoclassicists, had to have certain qualities of tone and form. In it deep emotion was as out of place as it would be in a social group; the tone had to be light — wit and pathos were better than deep feeling. Much depended upon exactly the right phrasing — polished but conversational, witty, condensed. With all this in mind, Holmes wrote some of the finest American familiar verse.

Yet Holmes himself in the end considered his most typical poems evidences of his talent rather than of his genius. Eventually he came to feel that his earliest conception of poetry, that of a young man "trained after the schools of classical English verse," had represented "simple and partial views," since it had dealt too exclusively with "the constructive side of the poet's function." "I should rather say," he continued, "if I were called upon now to define that which makes a poet, it is the power of transfiguring the experience and shows of life into an aspect which comes from his imagination and kindles that of others." His occasional poems, he told Lowell, were "for the most part to poetry as the beating of a drum or tinkling of a triangle is to the harmony of a band." True poetry, he believed, was inspired in thought and to some extent in form (see p. 898). Only once did he feel sure that he had written such poetry — in "The Chambered Nautilus" (p. 907).

This romantic concept of the inspired poet was shared by all the famous New England literary men, both those of Cambridge and those of Concord. These men differed only in their ideas about the extent to which a poem was inspired as compared with the extent to which it was consciously contrived. The Brahmins rather tended, with Holmes, to see careful artistry playing an important part. They also joined him in allowing the older conception of poet as teacher to shape their writings.

Longfellow: Master of Words and Accents

Longfellow in particular has been praised by recent scholars for his technique and scolded for his didacticism. His prosodic skill was developed most definitely, perhaps, by his achievement of the exacting task of changing over to English, without signs of painful effort, the *chansons* of French troubadours, the *lieder* of German lyricists, the *terza rima* and sonnets of Italians, the sagas of Finnish bards. However he acquired his skills, as Professor Shepard says, "Together with his thought, he had at the same moment a clear notion of the form in which it could be expressed most effectively . . . and it is for this reason that in his better work the thought seems to fill the form without crowding or inflation."

Longfellow's art concealed art largely because of its simple naturalness. Unlike most poets, he managed to get both rhyme and rhythm without using many unusual words and, as a rule, without changing the normal order of phrases and sentences. What Professor Allen, in his *American Prosody,* says about the hackneyed poem "The Village Blacksmith" hints at similar compliments which might be paid to more important achievements: "Its severe simplicity of diction and regularity of rhythm is likely to make us underestimate the technical achievements. . . . There are only two inversions in the whole piece: 'a mighty man is he' and 'onward through life he goes.' The natural speech and syntax . . . was practically unique in American versification in 1839." The representative poems by Longfellow in this volume show his simple diction and natural grammatical arrangement. Also, it happens, they show him using without ostentation or evident difficulty each of the ordinary meters (iambic, anapestic, dactylic, and trochaic), some of them in unusual ways, and combining them with several metrical devices which are quite extraordinary. (Note the refrain of "My Lost Youth," and the spacing of accented syllables in "The Skeleton in Armor," "Jugurtha," and "The Tide Rises.")

This master of words and accents could, at times, make each word, each line do its job. The plots of his best narratives he developed in excellent order. His best lyrics — whatever might be said against their preachments — at least have the unity which development of a single thought or sentiment gives them. The unity of thought in such poems as "The Rainy Day," "The Arrow and the Song," and "Jugurtha" cannot be surpassed; in each the first part offers some image, and the second part suggests, usually with the aid of incremental repetition, the spiritual connotation in a detailed parallel. Similarly, "The Bridge" starts with a description of a scene, then passes to the meaning of the scene to the poet, and ends by applying the meaning to all men. In such simple structures, there is integration of the sort important in sonnets, a form particularly well handled by Longfellow.

Despite such prosodic skill and such unity and coherence of thought, Longfellow often failed to please for three reasons. The thought which held together a lyric of his was too often platitudinous. Secondly, more even than Holmes or Lowell, he was a bookish, library poet. One sees why Whitman complained of Longfellow's poetry being "reminiscent, polish'd, elegant, with the air of finest conventional library, picture-gallery or parlor, with ladies and gentlemen in them. . . ." Finally, although his poems were logically constructed, they were likely to be badly put together emotionally — or connotatively. That similes and metaphors should be more than handsome ornaments — that they should be as organic to the poem as the thought — he apparently did not conceive. Hence in many of his poems he used imagery which modern readers find incongruous, and in only a few did he avoid jarring connotations.

Lowell: Pioneer in Freedom of Verse Form

Professor Howard Mumford Jones has noticed that "readers do not turn to Lowell as they do to Longfellow, for a body of verse; and though certain lyrics are individual favorites, they are such as two or three other poets might have written. 'To the Dandelion' is Keatsian; many readers confuse 'The First Snowfall' with Bryant's poem on the same theme, and 'The Present Crisis' inevitably suggests Whittier." This comparison can be carried further: *A Fable for Critics,* with its Pope-like critiques, suggests Holmes; and "Auspex" might well have been written by Longfellow. Lowell perhaps busied himself too much with other matters to develop a poetic style all his own.

Yet in some of Lowell's work there are merits not discoverable in Holmes or Longfellow. His *Biglow Papers* are the most effective political satire in verse yet written in America, and *A Fable for Critics* combines sharply phrased wit with shrewd literary judgments as no other poetry in this country has. In his famous "Commemoration Ode" he showed ability in shaping a long contemplative poem beyond the skill of his fellow Brahmins. He had exactly the perception of the emotional relationship that Longfellow lacked. "My notion of a true lyric," he said, "is that the meaning should float steadfast in the centre of every stanza, while the vapory emotions . . . float up to it and over it, and wreathe it with an opal halo which seems their own, but is truly its own work. The shades of emotion over, there floats the meaning, clear and sole and sharp-cut in its luminous integrity. . . ." Lowell wrote some poems in which the figurative language thus related the emotion it connoted to the meaning as a whole: "To the Dandelion," "The Courtin'," and "Auspex" are instances. Finally, Lowell did make the sort of technical contribution to American versification best suggested by his irregular "Ode Recited at the Harvard Commemoration." In Professor Allen's words, this poet's prosody "introduced into American poetry the freedom which we find in the first two or three decades of nineteenth-century English poetry. . . . This freedom includes a more varied placing of accents and the combination of different kinds of feet to produce a suggestiveness of tone and cadence. . . . Yet . . . Lowell's versification is more important for the lessons it teaches than for the poetic beauty it achieved."

Emerson and Thoreau: Rebels Against Nineteenth-Century Forms

Some free verse lines of the Transcendentalist Ralph Waldo Emerson serve to set off his aims in poetry from those of the Brahmins:

> I will not read a pretty tale
> To pretty people in a nice saloon
> Borrowed from their expectation,
> But I will sing aloud and free
> From the heart of the world.

Thoreau, another Transcendentalist, also stated a view of writing at variance with that of the genteel Cambridge men when he wrote: "Enough has been said in these days of the charm of fluent writing. . . . The surliness with which the woodchopper speaks of his woods, handling them as indifferently as his axe, is better than the mealy-mouthed enthusiasm of the lover of nature. Better that the primrose by the river's brim be a yellow primrose, and nothing more, than that it be something less." In some ways, so far as form and substance were concerned, the most radical of the ante-bellum New England versifiers were the Transcendentalists, Emerson in a few great poems and Thoreau in even fewer.

"The form [of Transcendental poetry]," Cooke notes, "is often rugged, the verse is halting and defective. The metres stumble, and . . . rhymes are not correct. The poems are . . . metaphysical, subtle, and complicated in their thought. . . ." Unlike Longfellow, who acquired his free and easy ways with verse by echoing foreign metrical schemes, or Lowell, who came late enough to learn lessons from Shelley, the Transcendentalists found their chief models in a seventeenth-century school of unorthodox versifiers. From the metaphysical poets — Marvell, Crashaw, Donne, and others — who had rebelled against the dulcet melodiousness of Elizabethan lyricists, these rebels against the nineteenth-century saccharinity learned something about the forcefulness which results from breaking up regular patterns. It may be true, as some critics claim, that the very infrequency of the Concord men's excursions into verse had something to do with the harshness of their songs. But the most important cause for their radicalism, probably, was that the nature of Transcendental poetry, like that of Transcendental prose, was influenced strongly by the philosophy of its creators.

According to this philosophy the matter and the expression of a poem, one and inseparable, were both spontaneously inspired. Theoretically, this would lead a Transcendentalist, trusting his "instinct," to set down his songs without change; actually, it did cause them to tinker with initial expressions less than other poets did. And the intuitive expression, in their opinion, would carry to others the message the poets themselves had been vouchsafed. It would do this because the poets would pass on to readers the same symbols which originally had suggested eternal verities to the poets. "Things," said Emerson, "admit of being used as symbols, because nature is a symbol, in the whole, and in every part." The whole theory of Emerson and his group has been admirably summarized by Jean Gorely:

Emerson . . . believed that poetry . . . comes into being as the result of inspiration. In that moment the poet sees the very essence of things. . . . The poet makes the unseen visible by means of language. But he is not the conscious creator. Vision, also, shows him the symbols and the thought takes its own form in language that is rhythmical. Because of this, there is a certain indwelling beauty of poetry . . . poetry is spiritual and forms a link between the visible and invisible worlds.

Thus the symbols were important, and the ideas or deep perceptions for which the symbols stood were even more important — so significant that, as in earlier metaphysical poetry, they controlled everything else in a poem. The sentiment often cultivated by the Brahmin poets was practically crowded out by the thought. Since only imagery which developed such a thought was relevant, merely ornamental imagery was avoided. And the concept being expressed determined the general structure of the poem. "It is no metres, but metre-making argument," said Emerson, "that makes a poem, — a thought so passionate and alive, that, like the spirit of a plant or an animal, it has an architecture of its own and adorns nature with a new thing." This theory suggested the four chief methods for ordering material used by Emerson and Thoreau: (1) as in "The Snow-Storm" (p. 1147) or "Though All the Fates" (p. 1234), the poet might give a description of an object or scene which embodied and implied meaning; (2) as in "Brahma" (p. 1161) or "The Summer Rain" (p. 1229), the poet might list a number of parallel phenomena; (3) as in "Each and All" (p. 1143) or "Inspiration" (p. 1231), the poet might record the process by which he arrived at a great truth; (4) as in "Rumors from an Æolian Harp" (p. 1229), the poet might record a state of inspiration.

Logically, the meter in such poems should be appropriate for the emphasis of both the symbols and the truths for which the symbols stand. "There is a soberness," wrote Thoreau, "in a rough aspect, as of unhewn granite, which addresses a depth in us, but a polished surface hits only the ball of the eye." And Emerson, in "Merlin" (p. 1149), pointed out that:

> The kingly bard
> Must strike the chords rudely and hard,
> As with hammer or with mace;
> That they may render back
> Artful thunder, which conveys
> Secrets of the solar track. . . .

In these ways, the Transcendental poetry of Emerson and Thoreau looked backward to seventeenth-century metaphysical poetry, forward to the type of poetry admired most in the middle decades of the present century.

Melville: Poet in Private

Although Melville's contemporaries did not read his poetry, and in fact were largely unaware that he wrote it, the twentieth century has brought it forth from manuscripts and from his various volumes, mostly privately printed, to discover its peculiarly modern qualities. Radically different from the smooth flowing verse of Longfellow or Lowell, closer in effect to the jarring dissonance of Emerson or Thoreau, Melville's poetry represents a unique personal vision — sometimes direct, sometimes angular. Though Melville's poetic voice seems occasionally to stammer, it is distinctively his own. Melville turned to the writing of poetry only after he had exhausted his fictional vein, and he chose as his first subject the Civil War, attempting to embody it in ballad and song. Disappointed in the public indifference to his poetry, he turned in his old age to his inner feelings and to the left-over scraps of his youthful experiences for poetic material. His collected poems make a surprisingly large volume, but the memorable poems are not as numerous as the exuberant poetic-prose of *Moby Dick* would lead one to expect. Robert Penn Warren has written, "Perhaps the violence, the distortions, the wrenchings in the versification of some of these poems are to be interpreted not so much as a result of mere ineptitude as the result of a conscious effort to develop a nervous, dramatic, masculine style." What struck the ear of Melville's contemporary as awkward strikes the modern ear as thematically harmonious. For example, in a poem like "Housetop," one of his Civil War poems, Melville seems more akin in meaning and metaphor to, say, T. S. Eliot than to Walt Whitman, one of his contemporaries who also wrote of the Civil War (*Drum-Taps*, 1865). As in his great novels, in his poetry Melville was in advance of his time. His poems, frequently oblique, often crabbed, had to await an audience with the temperament to enjoy and the patience to ferret out their cryptic ironies and paradoxes.

Thus in the essay, in fiction, in oratory, and in poetry, the authors of the period 1829-1865 combined old and new materials and techniques. As a result, these writers gave memorable expression to the ideas about which our countrymen were excited during the American Renaissance, one of the richest periods in our literary history.

W.B.

1809–1849 Edgar Allan Poe

Probably more than any other American author, Edgar Allan Poe — as a personality — has appealed to popular imagination. Generally, people think of him ás a figure who might have emerged from one of his stories or poems — mysterious, wild, abnormal. There are, to be sure, elements of strangeness in the life of this neurotic genius. But it is dangerous to guess that his tales were merely autobiographical exploitations of his weird way of living. For one thing, it is easy to see that he deliberately tried to make people look upon him as a Byronic, enigmatic poet. For another, his highly logical criticisms and the tales themselves show that he used his extraordinary mind to work out his literary effects with almost mathematical exactitude.

Poe's tragic life was a product of bad luck and instability. The son of a wandering theatrical family, he was orphaned at two and became the ward of the John Allan family of Richmond, Virginia. Never legally adopted, he could not live quite the normal life of a son in a well-to-do family. Although in his early years both Mr. and Mrs. Allan did what they could to spoil him, friction grew between him and his foster father until he was withdrawn from the University of Virginia after less than a year of attendance. There followed a period of service in the army (1827-1829), an unhappy brief career at West Point (1830-1831), and a final break with Allan (1832).

Before the break Poe had published three books of poetry — *Tamerlane and Other Poems* (1827), *Al Aaraaf, Tamerlane, and Minor Poems* (1829), and *Poems* (Second Edition, 1831, — none very successful financially. Now driven to try to make a living with his pen, he began writing tales. A sign that he had some success was that one of them, "The MS. Found in a Bottle," won a one-hundred dollar prize in 1833. Befriended by one of the contest judges, John Pendleton Kennedy, he began a career as editor, serving on the staff of the *Southern Literary Messenger* (1835-1837), *Burton's Gentleman's Magazine* (1839), *Graham's Magazine* (1841-1842), and other periodicals. Other tales won repute for him, and he was an alert and canny editor; but his poverty, his fiery temper, and his instability worked against his success.

Although Poe was not at all times the brooding, gloomy person tradition has painted, his life was on the whole an unhappy one. In 1831 he found a home with Mrs. Maria Clemm, mother of Poe's cousin, Virginia — a home in which, although members of the family were devoted to one another, poverty and sickness made life hard. In 1835 he married thirteen-year old Virginia, a fragile child who suffered from a devastating illness destined to end her life when she was twenty-six. To forget financial troubles or what seemed bad treatment by the world, Poe periodically went on drinking sprees which completely disorganized his high-strung nerves. He drank little, but was so constituted that small amounts of alcohol were ruinous in effect. Between such outbreaks there were periods of sorrowful remorse. Proud because of his aristocratic upbringing and because of the high opinion he had of his abilities, he was bitter about not doing better in the world. His pay as an editor was usually small, less than $16 a week, for instance, for his very successful work as editor of *Graham's*. Even in 1845, after he had won wide popularity, a collection of his verse, *The Raven and Other Poems,* and a volume of his stories, *Tales of the Grotesque and Arabesque,* did not have much financial success. He died, in mysterious circumstances, in Baltimore, October 7, 1849.

Poe was outstanding as a critic, as a fiction-writer, and as a poet. As a critic, he was perceptive, independent, and articulate. Though at times he was ferocious in his attacks upon poorer writers of the day, he made evaluations which have, in general, been justified, and offered acute arguments supporting them. His evaluations, based upon a detailed, logical system, made much use of the concepts of psychology current during Poe's day. "A first requisite of a critic," he held, was knowledge of "the machinery of his own thoughts and the thoughts of other men." Whether Poe was discussing the work of another author or creating a work of his own, he carefully considered the content and form of the literary work in relation to its impact upon readers.

When Poe was about to start his career as a writer of tales, he evidently studied successful magazine stories with great care to find a formula for marketable fiction. He saw that, because of a complicated international copyright situation, the most remunerative market was the one for short narratives. He also found that in all the magazines — even the delicate *Godey's Lady's Book* — the tale of terror was thriving. Using the keen mind which eventually was to make him the outstanding journalistic critic of his day, he figured out a highly successful way of contriving such tales. This formula was that of the single effect, set forth in his "Review of *Twice-Told Tales.*" The writer of a tale, Poe held, should subordinate everything in it to the effect he wanted the narrative to have upon the reader. This formula he employed so well that the tales he wrote have outlasted all the less skillful narratives which originally had been his models. Two elements in the tales chiefly accounted for their success: the climactic arrangement of happenings in them and a poetic style appropriate to their unfolding.

This poetic style and a similar "single effect" formula were also important in molding Poe's poems. Using words carefully chosen for their connotations and making the most of his mastery of rhythm and tone color, he wrote a number of memorable lyrics. Some of these are too showy in technique, too deliberately blurred in meaning to satisfy modern taste; but others, such as "Romance," "To Helen," "Israfel," and "To One in Paradise," still stand as masterpieces of their kind.

Complete Works of Edgar Allan Poe, 17 vols., ed. J. A. Harrison, New York, 1902   The Poems of Edgar Allan Poe, ed. Killis Campbell, Boston, 1917; New York, 1962   Killis Campbell, The Mind of Poe, Cambridge, 1933   A. H. Quinn, Edgar Allan Poe, New York, 1941   Joseph Chiari, Symbolisme from Poe to Mallarmé: The Growth of a Myth, New York, 1957   S. P. Moss, Poe's Literary Battles, Durham, N.C., 1963   Edward Wagenknecht, Edgar Allan Poe: The Man Behind the Legend, Fair Lawn, N.J., 1963

"Letter to B_____"

Since Poe's critical writings are of peculiar value in explaining the nature of his works, and are particularly useful for the study of his technical skill, they are presented before the selections from the creative writings themselves. The tales and then the poems follow, each group chronologically arranged.

With the title "Letter to Mr. _____ _____" and dated "West Point, _____, 1831," this letter introduced Poe's Poems *in 1831. It began "Dear B_____" and in an opening paragraph discussed the poems in the volume. In July 1836, the revised version here reproduced was published in the* Southern Literary Messenger *with this note: "These detached passages form part of the preface to a small volume printed some years ago for private circulation. They have vigor and much originality — but of course we shall not be called upon to endorse all the writer's opinions." "B" may have been Poe's publisher, Elam Bliss.*

This letter has interest as Poe's first published critical discussion — one which states some beliefs that he held throughout his career and others which he later modified. He would continue to believe that theory and practice were closely related, that there were hierarchies of writers and readers, that only the poetic could truly appreciate poetry, that the best poems are short, non-philosophical, and indefinite in meaning. An opinion which he would not endorse at a later time was that thought and reason should not be used in composing a poem. Thus early, despite his criticisms of Samuel Taylor Coleridge, it is evident that this critic and poet was to be important as a shaper of Poe's critical theories.

It has been said that a good critique on a poem may be written by one who is no poet himself. This, according to *your* idea and *mine* of poetry, I feel to be false — the less poetical the critic, the less just the critique, and the converse. On this account, and because there are but few B_____'s in the world, I would be as much ashamed of the world's good opinion as proud of your own. Another than yourself might here observe, "Shakspeare is in possession of the world's good opinion, and yet Shakspeare is the greatest of poets. It appears then that the world judge correctly, why should you be ashamed of their favorable judgment?" The difficulty lies in the interpretation of the word "judgment" or "opinion." The opinion is the world's, truly, but it may be called theirs as a man would call a book his, having bought it; 10 he did not write the book, but it is his; they did not originate the opinion, but it is theirs. A fool, for example, thinks Shakspeare a great poet — yet the fool has never

read Shakspeare. But the fool's neighbor, who is a step higher on the Andes of the mind, whose head (that is to say his more exalted thought) is too far above the fool to be seen or understood, but whose feet (by which I mean his every-day actions) are sufficiently near to be discerned, and by means of which that superiority is ascertained, which but for them would never have been discovered — this neighbor asserts that Shakspeare is a great poet — the fool believes him, and it is henceforward his *opinion.* This neighbor's own opinion has, in like manner, been adopted from one above *him,* and so, ascendingly, to a few gifted individuals, who kneel around the summit, beholding, face to face, the master spirit who stands upon
10 the pinnacle.   *   *   *   *   *

You are aware of the great barrier in the path of an American writer. He is read, if at all, in preference to the combined and established wit of the world. I say established; for it is with literature as with law or empire — an established name is an estate in tenure, or a throne in possession. Besides, one might suppose that books, like their authors, improve by travel — their having crossed the sea is, with us, so great a distinction. Our antiquaries abandon time for distance; our very fops glance from the binding to the bottom of the title-page, where the mystic characters which spell London, Paris, or Genoa, are precisely so many letters of recommendation.
                              *   *   *   *   *
I mentioned just now a vulgar error as regards criticism. I think the notion that
20 no poet can form a correct estimate of his own writings is another. I remarked before, that in proportion to the poetical talent, would be the justice of a critique upon poetry. Therefore, a bad poet would, I grant, make a false critique, and his self-love would infallibly bias his little judgment in his favor; but a poet, who is indeed a poet, could not, I think, fail of making a just critique. Whatever should be deducted on the score of self-love, might be replaced on account of his intimate acquaintance with the subject; in short, we have more instances of false criticism than of just, where one's own writings are the test, simply because we have more bad poets than good. There are of course many objections to what I say: Milton is a great example of the contrary; but his opinion with respect to the Paradise Re-
30 gained, is by no means fairly ascertained. By what trivial circumstances men are often led to assert what they do not really believe! Perhaps an inadvertent word has descended to posterity. But, in fact, the Paradise Regained is little, if at all, inferior to the Paradise Lost, and is only supposed so to be, because men do not like epics, whatever they may say to the contrary, and reading those of Milton in their natural order, are too much wearied with the first to derive any pleasure from the second. I dare say Milton preferred Comus to either — if so — justly.
                              *   *   *   *   *
As I am speaking of poetry, it will not be amiss to touch slightly upon the most singular heresy in its modern history — the heresy of what is called very foolishly,

---

28 **Milton . . . . justly.** As David Masson remarks in *The Life of John Milton* (1880), VI, 655, it was commonly stated that the poet preferred his epic *Paradise Regained* to *Paradise Lost;* but there is no historical evidence that he did. Poe's conjecture that Milton preferred the shorter poem *Comus* to either epic is also without evidence

the Lake School. Some years ago I might have been induced, by an occasion like the present, to attempt a formal refutation of their doctrine; at present it would be a work of supererogation. The wise must bow to the wisdom of such men as Coleridge and Southey, but being wise, have laughed at poetical theories so prosaically exemplified.

Aristotle, with singular assurance, has declared poetry the most philosophical of all writing — but it required a Wordsworth to pronounce it the most metaphysical. He seems to think that the end of poetry is, or should be, instruction — yet it is a truism that the end of our existence is happiness; if so, the end of every separate part of our existence — every thing connected with our existence should be still   10 happiness. Therefore the end of instruction should be happiness; and happiness is another name for pleasure; — therefore the end of instruction should be pleasure: yet we see the above mentioned opinion implies precisely the reverse.

To proceed: ceteris paribus, he who pleases, is of more importance to his fellow men than he who instructs, since utility is happiness, and pleasure is the end already obtained which instruction is merely the means of obtaining.

I see no reason, then, why our metaphysical poets should plume themselves so much on the utility of their works, unless indeed they refer to instruction with eternity in view; in which case, sincere respect for their piety would not allow me to express my contempt for their judgment; contempt which it would be difficult   20 to conceal, since their writings are professedly to be understood by the few, and it is the many who stand in need of salvation. In such case I should no doubt be tempted to think of the devil in Melmoth, who labors indefatigably through three octavo volumes, to accomplish the destruction of one or two souls, while any common devil would have demolished one or two thousand.

*   *   *   *   *

Against the subtleties which would make poetry a study — not a passion — it becomes the metaphysician to reason — but the poet to protest. Yet Wordsworth and Coleridge are men in years; the one imbued in contemplation from his childhood, the other a giant in intellect and learning. The diffidence, then, with which I venture to dispute their authority, would be overwhelming, did I not feel, from the   30 bottom of my heart, that learning has little to do with the imagination — intellect with the passions — or age with poetry.

*   *   *   *   *

"Trifles, like straws, upon the surface flow,
He who would search for pearls must dive below,"

---

1 **Lake School,** a group of Romantic poets who lived in the Lake District of England: Samuel Taylor Coleridge (1772-1834), William Wordsworth (1770-1850), and Robert Southey (1774-1843)   6 **Aristotle . . . writing.** Poe appended a note quoting the Greek phrase which he has translated from *Poetics,* ix, 3. Wordsworth in the Preface to *Lyrical Ballads* (1800) had referred to the same passage   14 **ceteris paribus,** other things being equal   23 **Melmoth,** *Melmoth the Wanderer* (1820), a Gothic novel by Charles Robert Maturin, in which a man who has sold his soul to the Devil engages in a long search to find someone to take his place   33 **Trifles . . . below,** from the Prologue to John Dryden's play *All for Love* (1677). Dryden's lines concern not "Trifles" but "Errors"

are lines which have done much mischief. As regards the greater truths, men oftener err by seeking them at the bottom than at the top; the depth lies in the huge abysses where wisdom is sought — not in the palpable palaces where she is found. The ancients were not always right in hiding the goddess in a well: witness the light which Bacon has thrown upon philosophy; witness the principles of our divine faith — that moral mechanism by which the simplicity of a child may overbalance the wisdom of a man.

We see an instance of Coleridge's liability to err, in his *Biographia Literaria* — professedly his literary life and opinions, but, in fact, a treatise *de omni scibili et qui-*
10 *busdam aliis.* He goes wrong by reason of his very profundity, and of his error we have a natural type in the contemplation of a star. He who regards it directly and intensely sees, it is true, the star, but it is the star without a ray — while he who surveys it less inquisitively is conscious of all for which the star is useful to us below — its brilliancy and its beauty.

*   *   *   *   *

As to Wordsworth, I have no faith in him. That he had, in youth, the feelings of a poet I believe — for there are glimpses of extreme delicacy in his writings — (and delicacy is the poet's own kingdom) — his *El Dorado* — but they have the appearance of a better day recollected; and glimpses, at best, are little evidence of present poetic fire — we know that a few straggling flowers spring up daily in the crevices
20 of the glacier.

He was to blame in wearing away his youth in contemplation with the end of poetizing in his manhood. With the increase of his judgment the light which should make it apparent has faded away. His judgment consequently is too correct. This may not be understood, — but the old Goths of Germany would have understood it, who used to debate matters of importance to their State twice, once when drunk, and once when sober — sober that they might not be deficient in formality — drunk lest they should be destitute of vigor.

The long wordy discussions by which he tries to reason us into admiration of his poetry, speak very little in his favor: they are full of such assertions as this — (I
30 have opened one of his volumes at random) "Of genius the only proof is the act of doing well what is worthy to be done, and what was never done before" — indeed! then it follows that in doing what is *un*worthy to be done, or what *has* been done before, no genius can be evinced: yet the picking of pockets is an unworthy act, pockets have been picked time immemorial, and Barrington, the pick-pocket, in point of genius, would have thought hard of a comparison with William Wordsworth, the poet.

---

4 **goddess.** Democritus (c. 460- c. 370 B.C.), a Greek philosopher, stated that truth lay at the bottom of a well   5 **Bacon,** Francis (1561-1626), English philosopher who played an important role in initiating scientific methods   9 **de . . . aliis,** regarding all that can be written about and certain other things as well   17 **El Dorado,** a place of fabulous wealth   30 **Of genius . . . before,** quoted from "Essay, Supplementary to the Preface," written in 1815   34 **Barrington,** pseudonym of George Waldron (1755-1840?), an Irish author who was also a notorious pickpocket

Again — in estimating the merit of certain poems, whether they be Ossian's or M'Pherson's, can surely be of little consequence, yet, in order to prove their worthlessness, Mr. W. has expended many pages in the controversy. *Tantæne animis?* Can great minds descend to such absurdity? But worse still: that he may bear down every argument in favor of these poems, he triumphantly drags forward a passage, in his abomination of which he expects the reader to sympathize. It is the beginning of the epic poem "*Temora.*" "The blue waves of Ullin roll in light; the green hills are covered with day; trees shake their dusky heads in the breeze." And this — this gorgeous, yet simple imagery — where all is alive and panting with immortality — this — William Wordsworth, the author of Peter Bell, has *selected* for his contempt. We   10
shall see what better he, in his own person, has to offer. Imprimis:

> "And now she's at the pony's head,
> And now she's at the pony's tail,
> On that side now, and now on this,
> And almost stifled her with bliss —
> A few sad tears does Betty shed,
> She pats the pony where or when
> She knows not: happy Betty Foy!
> O Johnny! never mind the Doctor!"

Secondly: 20

> "The dew was falling fast, the — stars began to blink,
> I heard a voice, it said — drink, pretty creature, drink;
> And looking o'er the hedge, be — fore me I espied
> A snow-white mountain lamb with a — maiden at its side,
> No other sheep were near, the lamb was all alone,
> And by a slender cord was — tether'd to a stone."

Now we have no doubt this is all true; we *will* believe it, indeed we will, Mr. W. Is it sympathy for the sheep you wish to excite? I love a sheep from the bottom of my heart.

*   *   *   *   *

But there *are* occasions, dear B———, there are occasions when even Wordsworth 30
is reasonable. Even Stamboul, it is said, shall have an end, and the most unlucky blunders must come to a conclusion. Here is an extract from his preface —
"Those who have been accustomed to the phraseology of modern writers, if they

---

1 **Ossian's or M'Pherson's** refers to purported translations by James Macpherson (1736-1796) of *Fingal* and *Temora,* allegedly written by a third-century bard named Ossian. Wordsworth took part in the controversy about their authenticity, and criticized the opening lines of *Temora,* lines which Poe admired   3 **Tantaene animis?** Why all the resentment?   12 **And now . . . Doctor!** is a passage from an early version of Wordsworth's "The Idiot Boy"   21 **"The dew . . . stone."** Wordsworth's "The Pet Lamb," with dashes added by Poe   33 **"Those who . . . title."** Poe quotes somewhat inaccurately from the 1800 Preface to *Lyrical Ballads*

persist in reading this book to a conclusion (*impossible!*) will, no doubt, have to struggle with feelings of awkwardness; (ha! ha! ha!) they will look round for poetry (ha! ha! ha! ha!) and will be induced to inquire by what species of courtesy these attempts have been permitted to assume that title." Ha! ha! ha! ha! ha!

Yet let not Mr. W. despair; he has given immortality to a wagon, and the bee Sophocles has transmitted to eternity a sore toe, and dignified a tragedy with a chorus of turkeys.

* * * * *

Of Coleridge I cannot speak but with reverence. His towering intellect! his gigantic power! He is one more evidence of the fact *"que la plupart des sectes ont*
10 *raison dans une bonne partie de ce qu'elles avancent, mais non pas en ce qu'elles nient."* He has imprisoned his own conceptions by the barrier he has erected against those of others. It is lamentable to think that such a mind should be buried in metaphysics, and, like the Nyctanthes, waste its perfume upon the night alone. In reading his poetry I tremble — like one who stands upon a volcano, conscious, from the very darkness bursting from the crater, of the fire and the light that are weltering below.

* * * * *

What is Poetry? — Poetry! that Proteus-like idea, with as many appellations as the nine-titled Corcyra! Give me, I demanded of a scholar some time ago, give me a definition of poetry? *"Tres-volontiers,"* — and he proceeded to his library, brought me a Dr. Johnson, and overwhelmed me with a definition. Shade of the immortal
20 Shakspeare! I imagined to myself the scowl of your spiritual eye upon the profanity of that scurrilous Ursa Major. Think of poetry, dear B—, think of poetry, and then think of — Dr. Samuel Johnson! Think of all that is airy and fairy-like, and then of all that is hideous and unwieldy; think of his huge bulk, the Elephant! and then — and then think of the *Tempest* — the *Midsummer Night's Dream* — Prospero — Oberon — and Titania!

* * * * *

A poem, in my opinion, is opposed to a work of science by having, for its *imme-diate* object, pleasure, not truth; to romance, by having for its object an *indefinite*

---

5 **wagon,** alludes to Wordsworth's "The Waggoner"   5 **the bee Sophocles,** referring to the designation of the Greek dramatist as "the Attic bee." The "sore toe" refers to the Oedipus plays   6 **chorus of turkeys,** refers to Sophocles' alleged introduction of guinea fowls to lament the death of a character   9 **que la plupart . . . nient,** for the most part sects are right in what they affirm but not in what they deny   13 **Nyctanthes,** night-blooming plant   16 **Proteus,** a Greek god who frequently changed his appearance   17 **Corcyra,** the Greek island Corfu, which went under different names at different times   18 **Tres-volontiers,** very willingly   19 **Dr. Johnson,** Samuel Johnson (1709-1784), English neoclassic critic and poet of whom Romanticists had a low opinion   21 **Ursa Major,** the constellation the Great Bear, here applied to Johnson because of his burly figure and his way of growling his opinions   24 **the Tempest . . . Titania,** refers to fanciful plays by Shakespeare and imaginative portrayals of characters in them, *The Tempest* (1611) in which the magician Prospero appears, and *Midsummer Night's Dream* (1596), which pictures Oberon and Titania, king and queen of the fairies   26 **A poem . . . conception.** Cf. Coleridge's definition in *Biographia Literaria,* chap. xiv: "A poem is that species of composition, which is opposed to works of science, by proposing for its immediate object pleasure, not truth; and from all other species (having this object in common with it) it is discriminated by proposing to itself such delight from the whole, as is compatible with a distinct gratification from each component part." Coleridge, like Poe, distinguishes between romance and poem

instead of a *definite* pleasure, being a poem only so far as this object is attained; romance presenting perceptible images with definite, poetry with *in*definite sensations, to which end music is an *essential,* since the comprehension of sweet sound is our most indefinite conception. Music, when combined with a pleasurable idea, is poetry; music without the idea is simply music; the idea without the music is prose from its very definitiveness.

What was meant by the invective against him who had no music in his soul?

*   *   *   *   *

To sum up this long rigmarole, I have, dear B____, what you no doubt perceive, for the metaphysical poets, *as* poets, the most sovereign contempt. That they have followers proves nothing —   10

> No Indian prince has to his palace
> More followers than a thief to the gallows.

1831-1835

----

7 **invective.** See *Merchant of Venice,* Act V, Sc. i, 11. 81-88   11 **No Indian . . . gallows.** From *Hudibras* (1663-1678), a satirical poem by Samuel Butler (1612-1680)

Review of "Twice-Told Tales"

The criticism of Hawthorne's book typifies Poe's overwhelming interest in "effect" — the impact which a work has upon the reader — an interest which leads him not only to rank Hawthorne as an essayist in exactly the way he does but also to give essays, poems, and tales their respective ranks in a literary hierarchy. Even the talk about originality is talk about effect, since Poe thought of originality — as he said elsewhere — as "the reader's sense of the new." And clearly, poems are given their preëminent place because they have the greatest effect upon the highest faculty of the reader.

The most famous passage in this essay is the paragraph beginning with the words, "A skilful literary artist has constructed a tale" — a passage almost inevitably quoted in any book on the short story. Here, very specifically, Poe asserts that everything in a tale — every incident, every combination of events, every word — must aid the author in achieving a preconceived emotional effect. In a revision of the passage five years later, Poe was to make the second sentence even more specific by revising it to read in part: "He then invents such incidents, he then combines such events, and discusses them in such tone as may best serve him in establishing this preconceived effect." (The roman type indicates the addition.) What Poe means by "tone" perhaps was indicated in an earlier article in which he noted that Hawthorne's "tone is singularly effective — wild, plaintive, thoughtful, and in full accordance with his themes."

This review was published in Graham's Magazine, *May 1842. Parts of it were revised and included in an article, "Tale-Writing," in* Godey's Lady's Book, *November 1847, which shows some interesting modifications of Poe's judgments of Hawthorne.*

We said a few hurried words about Mr. Hawthorne in our last number, with the design of speaking more fully in the present. We are still, however, pressed for room, and must necessarily discuss his volumes more briefly and more at random than their high merits deserve.

The book professes to be a collection of *tales,* yet is, in two respects, misnamed. These pieces are now in their third republication, and, of course, are thrice-told. Moreover, they are by no means *all* tales, either in the ordinary or in the legitimate understanding of the term. Many of them are pure essays; for example, "Sights from a Steeple," "Sunday at Home," "Little Annie's Ramble," "A Rill from the Town 10 Pump," "The Toll-Gatherer's Day," "The Haunted Mind," "The Sister Years," "Snow-Flakes," "Night Sketches," and "Foot-Prints on the Sea-Shore." We mention these matters chiefly on account of their discrepancy with that marked precision and finish by which the body of the work is distinguished.

Of the essays just named, we must be content to speak in brief. They are each and all beautiful, without being characterised by the polish and adaptation so visible in the tales proper. A painter would at once note their leading or predominant feature, and style it *repose.* There is no attempt at effect. All is quiet, thoughtful, subdued. Yet this repose may exist simultaneously with high originality of thought; and Mr. Hawthorne has demonstrated the fact. At every turn we meet with novel 20 combinations; yet these combinations never surpass the limits of the quiet. We are soothed as we read; and withal is a calm astonishment that ideas so apparently obvious have never occurred or been presented to us before. Herein our author differs materially from Lamb or Hunt or Hazlitt — who, with vivid originality of manner and expression, have less of the true novelty of thought than is generally supposed, and whose originality, at best, has an uneasy and meretricious quaintness, replete with startling effects unfounded in nature, and inducing trains of reflection which lead to no satisfactory result. The Essays of Hawthorne have much of the character of Irving, with more of originality, and less of finish; while, compared with the Spectator, they have a vast superiority at all points. The Spectator, Mr. 30 Irving, and Mr. Hawthorne have in common that tranquil and subdued manner which we have chosen to denominate *repose;* but, in the case of the two former, this repose is attained rather by the absence of novel combination, or of originality, than otherwise, and consists chiefly in the calm, quiet, unostentatious expression of common-place thoughts, in an unambitious, unadulterated Saxon. In them, by strong effort, we are made to conceive the absence of all. In the essays before us the absence of effort is too obvious to be mistaken, and a strong under current of *suggestion* runs continuously beneath the upper stream of the tranquil thesis. In short, these effusions of Mr. Hawthorne are the product of a truly imaginative intellect, restrained,

---

1 **a few . . . words,** in a notice published in the April issue of *Graham's Magazine,* available in *Works,* ed. Harrison (hereafter referred to as *Works*), XI, 102-104. The earlier review makes several of the same points made by the later one. It is notable, however, that in the first review Poe says that, despite its fame, "A Rill from the Town Pump" is "the *least* meritorious" of Hawthorne's compositions and that the best include, in addition to those cited in this second review, "David Swan"   23 **Lamb . . . Hazlitt.** Charles Lamb (1775-1834), Leigh Hunt (1784-1859), and William Hazlitt (1778-1830) were outstanding English essayists

and in some measure repressed, by fastidiousness of taste, by constitutional melancholy and by indolence.

But it is of his tales that we desire principally to speak. The tale proper, in our opinion, affords unquestionably the fairest field for the exercise of the loftiest talent, which can be afforded by the wide domains of mere prose. Were we bidden to say how the highest genius could be most advantageously employed for the best display of its own powers, we should answer, without hesitation — in the composition of a rhymed poem, not to exceed in length what might be perused in an hour. Within this limit alone can the highest order of true poetry exist. We need only here say, upon this topic, that, in almost all classes of composition, the unity of effect or im- 10 pression is a point of the greatest importance. It is clear, moreover, that this unity cannot be thoroughly preserved in productions whose perusal cannot be completed at one sitting. We may continue the reading of a prose composition, from the very nature of prose itself, much longer than we can persevere, to any good purpose, in the perusal of a poem. This latter, if truly fulfilling the demands of the poetic sentiment, induces an exaltation of the soul which cannot be long sustained. All high excitements are necessarily transient. Thus a long poem is a paradox. And, without unity of impression, the deepest effects cannot be brought about. Epics were the offspring of an imperfect sense of Art, and their reign is no more. A poem *too* brief may produce a vivid, but never an intense or enduring impression. Without a cer- 20 tain continuity of effort — without a certain duration or repetition of purpose — the soul is never deeply moved. There must be the dropping of the water upon the rock. De Beranger has wrought brilliant things — pungent and spirit-stirring — but, like all immassive bodies, they lack *momentum,* and thus fail to satisfy the Poetic Sentiment. They sparkle and excite, but, from want of continuity, fail deeply to impress. Extreme brevity will degenerate into epigrammatism; but the sin of extreme length is even more unpardonable. *In medio tutissimus ibis.*

Were we called upon, however, to designate that class of composition which, next to such a poem as we have suggested, should best fulfil the demands of high genius — should offer it the most advantageous field of exertion — we should unhesitatingly 30 speak of the prose tale, as Mr. Hawthorne has here exemplified it. We allude to the short prose narrative, requiring from a half-hour to one or two hours in its perusal. The ordinary novel is objectionable, from its length, for reasons already stated in substance. As it cannot be read at one sitting, it deprives itself, of course, of the immense force derivable from *totality.* Worldly interests intervening during the pauses of perusal, modify, annul, or counteract, in a greater or less degree, the impressions of the book. But simple cessation in reading, would, of itself, be sufficient to destroy the true unity. In the brief tale, however, the author is enabled to carry out the fullness of his intention, be it what it may. During the hour of perusal the soul of the reader is at the writer's control. There are no external or extrinsic influences — 40 resulting from weariness or interruption.

A skilful literary artist has constructed a tale. If wise, he has not fashioned his

---

23 **De Beranger,** Pierre Jean de Béranger (1780-1857), a French poet   27 **In medio . . . ibis.** You will go most safely in the middle path

thoughts to accommodate his incidents; but having conceived, with deliberate care, a certain unique or single *effect* to be wrought out, he then invents such incidents — he then combines such events as may best aid him in establishing this preconceived effect. If his very initial sentence tend not to the outbringing of this effect, then he has failed in his first step. In the whole composition there should be no word written, of which the tendency, direct or indirect, is not to the one preestablished design. And by such means, with such care and skill, a picture is at length painted which leaves in the mind of him who contemplates it with a kindred art, a sense of the fullest satisfaction. The idea of the tale has been presented unblemished, because undisturbed; and this is an end unattainable by the novel. Undue brevity is just as exceptionable here as in the poem, but undue length is yet more to be avoided.

We have said that the tale has a point of superiority even over the poem. In fact, while the *rhythm* of this latter is an essential aid in the development of the poet's highest idea — the idea of the Beautiful — the artificialities of this rhythm are an inseparable bar to the development of all points of thought or expression which have their basis in *Truth*. But Truth is often, and in very great degree, the aim of the tale. Some of the finest tales are tales of ratiocination. Thus the field of this species of composition, if not in so elevated a region on the mountain of Mind, is a table-land of far vaster extent than the domain of the mere poem. Its products are never so rich, but infinitely more numerous, and more appreciable by the mass of mankind. The writer of the prose tale, in short, may bring to his theme a vast variety of modes or inflections of thought and expression — (the ratiocinative, for example, the sarcastic, or the humorous) which are not only antagonistical to the nature of the poem, but absolutely forbidden by one of its most peculiar and indispensable adjuncts; we allude, of course, to rhythm. It may be added here, *par parenthèse,* that the author who aims at the purely beautiful in a prose tale is laboring at great disadvantage. For Beauty can be better treated in a poem. Not so with terror, or passion, or horror, or a multitude of such other points. And here it will be seen how full of prejudice are the usual animadversions against those *tales of effect,* many fine examples of which were found in the earlier numbers of Blackwood. The impressions produced were wrought in a legitimate sphere of action, and constituted a legitimate although sometimes an exaggerated interest. They were relished by every man of genius; although there were found many men of genius who condemned them without just ground. The true critic will but demand that the design intended be accomplished, to the fullest extent, by the means most advantageously applicable.

We have very few American tales of real merit — we may say, indeed, none, with the exception of "The Tales of a Traveller" of Washington Irving, and these "Twice-Told Tales" of Mr. Hawthorne. Some of the pieces of Mr. John Neal abound in vigor and originality; but in general, his compositions of this class are excessively diffuse, extravagant, and indicative of an imperfect sentiment of Art. Articles at

---

25 **par parenthèse,** by way of parenthesis   30 **Blackwood,** a magazine in which Poe found a great deal of Gothic fiction. A tale which he wrote "à la Blackwood" parodied the Gothic technique   39 **Mr. John Neal** (1793-1876), an American fiction writer

random are, now and then, met with in our periodicals which might be advantageously compared with the best effusions of the British Magazines; but, upon the
whole, we are far behind our progenitors in this department of literature.

Of Mr. Hawthorne's Tales we would say, emphatically, that they belong to the
highest region of Art — an Art subservient to genius of a very lofty order. We had
supposed, with good reason for so supposing, that he had been thrust into his present position by one of the impudent *cliques* which beset our literature, and whose
pretensions it is our full purpose to expose at the earliest opportunity; but we have
been most agreeably mistaken. We know of few compositions which the critic can
more honestly commend than these "Twice-Told Tales." As Americans, we feel 10
proud of the book.

Mr. Hawthorne's distinctive trait is invention, creation, imagination, originality —
a trait which, in the literature of fiction, is positively worth all the rest. But the
nature of originality, so far as regards its manifestation in letters, is but imperfectly
understood. The inventive or original mind as frequently displays itself in novelty
of *tone* as in novelty of matter. Mr. Hawthorne is original at *all* points.

It would be a matter of some difficulty to designate the best of these tales; we
repeat that, without exception, they are beautful. "Wakefield" is remarkable for the
skill with which an old idea — a well-known incident — is worked up or discussed.
A man of whims conceives the purpose of quitting his wife and residing *incognito,* 20
for twenty years, in her immediate neighborhood. Something of this kind actually
happened in London. The force of Mr. Hawthorne's tale lies in the analysis of the
motives which must or might have impelled the husband to such folly, in the first
instance, with the possible causes of his perseverance. Upon this thesis a sketch of
singular power has been constructed.

"The Wedding Knell" is full of the boldest imagination — an imagination fully
controlled by taste. The most captious critic could find no flaw in this production.

"The Minister's Black Veil" is a masterly composition of which the sole defect is
that to the rabble its exquisite skill will be *caviare.* The *obvious* meaning of this article
will be found to smother its insinuated one. The *moral* put into the mouth of the 30
dying minister will be supposed to convey the *true* import of the narrative; and that
a crime of dark dye (having reference to the "young lady"), has been committed, is
a point which only minds congenial with that of the author will perceive.

"Mr. Higginbotham's Catastrophe" is vividly original and managed most dex-
terously.

"Dr. Heidegger's Experiment" is exceedingly well imagined, and executed with
surpassing ability. The artist breathes in every line of it.

"The White Old Maid" is objectionable, even more than the "Minister's Black
Veil," on the score of its mysticism. Even with the thoughtful and analytic, there
will be much trouble in penetrating its entire import.   40

"The Hollow of the Three Hills" we would quote in full, had we space; — not as
evincing higher talent than any of the other pieces, but as affording an excellent
example of the author's peculiar ability. The subject is commonplace. A witch subjects the Distant and the Past to the view of a mourner. It has been the fashion to

describe, in such cases, a mirror in which the images of the absent appear; or a cloud of smoke is made to arise, and thence the figures are gradually unfolded. Mr. Hawthorne has wonderfully heightened his effect by making the ear, in place of the eye, the medium by which the fantasy is conveyed. The head of the mourner is enveloped in the cloak of the witch, and within its magic folds there arise sounds which have an all-sufficient intelligence. Throughout this article also, the artist is conspicuous — not more in positive than in negative merits. Not only is all done that should be done, but (what perhaps is an end with more difficulty attained) there is nothing done which should not be. Every word *tells,* and there is not a word that does
10 *not* tell. . . .

In the way of objection we have scarcely a word to say of these tales. There is, perhaps, a somewhat too general or prevalent *tone* — a tone of melancholy and mysticism. The subjects are insufficiently varied. There is not so much of *versatility* evinced as we might well be warranted in expecting from the high powers of Mr. Hawthorne. But beyond these trivial exceptions we have really none to make. The style is purity itself. Force abounds. High imagination gleams from every page. Mr. Hawthorne is a man of the truest genius. We only regret that the limits of our Magazine will not permit us to pay him that full tribute of commendation, which, under other circumstances, we should be so eager to pay.

1842

---

9 **Every word . . . tell.** . . . The omitted passage hints that Hawthorne plagiarized from Poe in "Howe's Masquerade." The accusation is unfounded

The Philosophy of Composition

What the "Review of Twice-Told Tales" *does for Poe's theory of the tale, this essay does for his theory of the poem. Here is his account of the way he composed his most famous poem, "The Raven." Critics have argued interminably about the accuracy of this account, and of course there is no way of settling the dispute. Three points perhaps are worthy of emphasis: (1) that in the essay Poe himself labels irrelevant the primary circumstance or the necessity of composing the poem, thus dismissing in a curt paragraph an aspect of the poetic process with which literary historians are frequently most concerned; (2) that the account is perfectly in harmony with Poe's theories about the nature of artistic creations; (3) that, as Hervey Allen points out in his biography of Poe,* Israfel: *"The long period over which the composition of 'The Raven' stretched, a period of four years at least, shows that into the arrangement and composition of it went a great deal of critical thinking, artistic analysis, a logical arrangement of effects, and a painstaking construction of the spinal narrative which no mere emotion could have provided."*

Whether the account is factual or not, it does suggest what its author was likely to have in mind as he composed or studied a poem: the relationship between happenings, details, rhythms, refrains — everything in the poem — and the effect. Moreover, this essay, which Poe called "my best specimen of analysis," offers an excellent example of his critical mind at work.

Charles Dickens, in a note now lying before me, alluding to an examination I once made of the mechanism of "Barnaby Rudge," says — "By the way, are you aware that Godwin wrote his 'Caleb Williams' backwards? He first involved his hero in a web of difficulties, forming the second volume, and then, for the first, cast about him for some mode of accounting for what had been done."

I cannot think this the *precise* mode of procedure on the part of Godwin — and indeed what he himself acknowledges is not altogether in accordance with Mr. Dickens's idea; but the author of "Caleb Williams" was too good an artist not to perceive the advantage derivable from at least a somewhat similar process. Nothing is more clear than that every plot, worth the name, must be elaborated to its 10 *dénouement* before anything be attempted with the pen. It is only with the *dénouement* constantly in view that we can give a plot its indispensable air of consequence, or causation, by making the incidents, and especially the tone at all points, tend to the development of the intention.

There is a radical error, I think, in the usual mode of constructing a story. Either history affords a thesis, or one is suggested by an incident of the day, or, at best, the author sets himself to work, in the combination of striking events to form merely the basis of his narrative, designing, generally, to fill in with description, dialogue, or autorial comment whatever crevices of fact or action may from page to page render themselves apparent.   20

I prefer commencing with the consideration of an *effect*. Keeping originality *always* in view — for he is false to himself who ventures to dispense with so obvious and so easily attainable a source of interest — I say to myself, in the first place, — "Of the innumerable effects, or impressions, of which the heart, the intellect, or (more generally) the soul is susceptible, what one shall I, on the present occasion, select?" Having chosen a novel, first, and secondly a vivid effect, I consider whether it can be best wrought by incident or tone — whether by ordinary incidents and peculiar tone, or the converse, or by peculiarity both of incident and tone — afterward looking about me (or rather within) for such combinations of event, or tone, as shall best aid me in the construction of the effect.   30

I have often thought how interesting a magazine paper might be written by any author who would — that is to say, who could — detail, step by step, the processes by which any one of his compositions attained its ultimate point of completion. Why such a paper has never been given to the world, I am much at a loss to say; but, perhaps, the authorial vanity has had more to do with the omission than any one other cause. Most writers — poets in especial — prefer having it understood that they compose by a species of fine frenzy — an ecstatic intuition; and would posi-

---

1 **an examination . . . made,** "a prospective review," published in 1841, of *Barnaby Rudge,* when the novel was still coming out serially. Poe guessed the identity of the murderer and thus proved that Dickens had not deceived the reader as the author of a ratiocinative tale should do   3 **Godwin.** William Godwin testifies in the Preface to *Caleb Williams* that he wrote the book thus: "I formed the conception of a book of fictitious adventure, that should in some way be distinguished by a very powerful interest. Pursuing this idea, I invented first the third volume of my tale, then the second, and last of all the first . . ."   11 **dé-nouement,** from the French *dénouer* — to untie; hence, the unraveling of a plot

tively shudder at letting the public take a peep behind the scenes at the elaborate and vacillating crudities of thought, at the true purposes seized only at the last moment, at the innumerable glimpses of idea that arrived not at the maturity of full view, at the fully matured fancies discarded in despair as unmanageable, at the cautious selections and rejections, at the painful erasures and interpolations — in a word, at the wheels and pinions, the tackle for scene-shifting, the step-ladders and demon-traps, the cock's feathers, the red paint and the black patches, which in ninety-nine cases out of the hundred constitute the properties of the literary *histrio*.

10   I am aware on the other hand, that the case is by no means common in which an author is at all in condition to retrace the steps by which his conclusions have been attained. In general, suggestions, having arisen pell-mell, are pursued and forgotten in a similar manner.

    For my own part, I have neither sympathy with the repugnance alluded to, nor at any time the least difficulty in recalling to mind the progressive steps of any of my compositions; and, since the interest of an analysis, or reconstruction, such as I have considered a *desideratum,* is quite independent of any real or fancied interest in the thing analyzed, it will not be regarded as a breach of decorum on my part to show the *modus operandi* by which some one of my own works was put together. 20 I select "The Raven" as most generally known. It is my design to render it manifest that no one point in its composition is referable either to accident or intuition; that the work proceeded, step by step, to its completion with the precision and rigid consequence of a mathematical problem.

    Let us dismiss, as irrelevant to the poem *per se,* the circumstance — or say, the necessity — which in the first place gave rise to the intention of composing *a* poem that should suit at once the popular and the critical taste.

    We commence, then, with this intention.

    The initial consideration was that of extent. If any literary work is too long to be read at one sitting, we must be content to dispense with the immensely important effect derivable from unity of impression; for, if two sittings be required, the affairs 30 of the world interfere, and everything like totality is at once destroyed. But since, *ceteris paribus,* no poet can afford to dispense with *anything* that may advance his design, it but remains to be seen whether there is, in extent, any advantage to counterbalance the loss of unity which attends it. Here I say no, at once. What we term a long poem is, in fact, merely a succession of brief ones — that is to say, of brief poetical effects. It is needless to demonstrate that a poem is such, only inasmuch as it intensely excites, by elevating, the soul; and all intense excitements are, through a psychal necessity, brief. For this reason, at least one half of the "Paradise Lost" is essentially prose — a succession of poetical excitements interspersed, *inevitably,* with corresponding depressions — the whole being deprived, through the extremeness of 40 its length, of the vastly important artistic element, totality, or unity, of effect.

---

8 **histrio,** actor   18 **modus operandi,** method of working   23 **per se,** by itself   31 **ceteris paribus.**
See note, p. 750   37 **psychal,** pertaining to the soul. The necessity for brevity in poetry, for the reason suggested in this sentence, is one of Poe's favorite ideas

It appears evident, then, that there is a distinct limit, as regards length, to all works of literary art — the limit of a single sitting; and that, although in certain classes of prose composition, such as "Robinson Crusoe" (demanding no unity), this limit may be advantageously overpassed, it can never properly be overpassed in a poem. Within this limit, the extent of a poem may be made to bear mathematical relation to its merit — in other words, to the excitement or elevation — again, in other words, to the degree of the true poetical effect which it is capable of inducing; for it is clear that the brevity must be in direct ratio of the intensity of the intended effect: — this, with one proviso — that a certain degree of duration is absolutely requisite for the production of any effect at all.   10

Holding in view these considerations, as well as that degree of excitement which I deemed not above the popular while not below the critical taste, I reached at once what I conceived the proper *length* for my intended poem — a length of about one hundred lines. It is, in fact, a hundred and eight.

My next thought concerned the choice of an impression, or effect, to be conveyed: and here I may as well observe that, throughout the construction, I kept steadily in view the design of rendering the work *universally* appreciable. I should be carried too far out of my immediate topic were I to demonstrate a point upon which I have repeatedly insisted, and which with the poetical stands not in the slightest need of demonstration — the point, I mean, that Beauty is the sole legitimate province of 20 the poem. A few words, however, in elucidation of my real meaning, which some of my friends have evinced a disposition to misrepresent. That pleasure which is at once the most intense, the most elevating, and the most pure, is, I believe, found in the contemplation of the beautiful. When, indeed, men speak of Beauty, they mean, precisely, not a quality, as is supposed, but an effect; they refer, in short, just to that intense and pure elevation of *soul* — *not* of intellect, or of heart — upon which I have commented, and which is experienced in consequence of contemplating "the beautiful." Now I designate Beauty as the province of the poem, merely because it is an obvious rule of Art that effects should be made to spring from direct causes — that objects should be attained through means best adapted for their attainment — 30 no one as yet having been weak enough to deny that the peculiar elevation alluded to is *most readily* attained in the poem. Now the object, Truth, or the satisfaction of the intellect, and the object, Passion, or the excitement of the heart, are, although attainable to a certain extent in poetry, far more readily attainable in prose. Truth, in fact, demands a precision, and Passion a *homeliness* (the truly passionate will comprehend me), which are absolutely antagonistic to that Beauty which, I maintain, is the excitement or pleasurable elevation, of the soul. It by no means follows from anything here said that passion, or even truth, may not be introduced, and even profitably introduced, into a poem — for they may serve in elucidation, or aid the general effect, as do discords in music, by contrast; but the true artist will always 40

---

20 **Beauty.** . . . Compare Poe's statement in "The Poetic Principle": "I would define, in brief, the Poetry of words as *The Rhythmical Creation of Beauty*. Its sole arbiter is Taste. With the Intellect or with the Conscience, it has only collateral relations. Unless incidentally, it has no concern whatever with Duty or with Truth"

contrive, first, to tone them into proper subservience to the predominant aim, and, secondly, to enveil them, as far as possible, in that Beauty which is the atmosphere and the essence of the poem.

Regarding, then, Beauty as my province, my next question referred to the *tone* of its highest manifestation; and all experience has shown that this tone is one of *sadness*. Beauty of whatever kind, in its supreme development, invariably excites the sensitive soul to tears. Melancholy is thus the most legitimate of all poetical tones.

The length, the province, and the tone, being thus determined, I betook myself to ordinary induction, with the view of obtaining some artistic piquancy which might
10 serve me as a key-note in the construction of the poem — some pivot upon which the whole structure might turn. In carefully thinking over all the usual artistic effects — I did not fail to perceive immediately that no one had been so universally employed as that of the *refrain*. The universality of its employment sufficed to assure me of its intrinsic value, and spared me the necessity of submitting it to analysis. I considered it, however, with regard to its susceptibility of improvement, and soon saw it to be in a primitive condition. As commonly used, the *refrain,* or burden, not only is limited to lyric verse, but depends for its impression upon the force of monotone — both in sound and thought. The pleasure is deduced solely from the sense of identity — of repetition. I resolved to diversify, and so heighten, the effect, by
20 adhering, in general, to the monotone of sound, while I continually varied that of thought: that is to say, I determined to produce continuously novel effects, by the variation of *the application* of the *refrain* — the refrain itself remaining, for the most part, unvaried.

These points being settled, I next bethought me of the *nature* of my *refrain*. Since its application was to be repeatedly varied, it was clear that the *refrain* itself must be brief, for there would have been an insurmountable difficulty in frequent variations of application in any sentence of length. In proportion to the brevity of the sentence, would, of course, be the facility of the variation. This led me at once to a single word as the best *refrain.*

30 The question now arose as to the *character* of the word. Having made up my mind to a *refrain,* the division of the poem into stanzas was, of course, a corollary: the *refrain* forming the close to each stanza. That such a close, to have force, must be sonorous and susceptible of protracted emphasis, admitted no doubt; and these considerations inevitably led me to the long *o* as the most sonorous vowel in connection with *r* as the most producible consonant.

The sound of the *refrain* being thus determined, it became necessary to select a word embodying this sound and at the same time in the fullest possible keeping with that melancholy which I had predetermined as the tone of the poem. In such a search it would have been absolutely impossible to overlook the word "Never-
40 more." In fact, it was the very first which presented itself.

The next desideratum was a pretext for the continuous use of the one word "Nevermore." In observing the difficulty which I at once found in inventing a sufficiently plausible reason for its continuous repetition, I did not fail to perceive that this difficulty arose solely from the pre-assumption that the word was to be so continuously or monotonously spoken by a *human* being; I did not fail to perceive, in short, that the difficulty lay in the reconciliation of this monotony with the exercise of reason on the part of the creature repeating the word. Here, then, immediately arose the idea of a *non*-reasoning creature capable of speech; and, very naturally, a parrot, in the first instance, suggested itself, but was superseded forthwith by a Raven as equally capable of speech, and infinitely more in keeping with the intended *tone.*

I had now gone so far as the conception of a Raven — the bird of ill-omen — monotonously repeating the one word, "Nevermore," at the conclusion of each stanza, in a poem of melancholy tone, and in length about one hundred lines. Now, 10 never losing sight of the object *supremeness,* or perfection, at all points, I asked my-self — "Of all melancholy topics, what, according to the *universal* understanding of mankind, is the *most* melancholy?" Death — was the obvious reply. "And when," I said, "is this most melancholy of topics most poetical?" From what I have already explained at some length, the answer here also is obvious — "When it most closely allies itself to *Beauty;* the death, then, of a beautiful woman, is unquestionably, the most poetical topic in the world — and equally is it beyond doubt that the lips best suited for such a topic are those of a bereaved lover."

I had now to combine the two ideas, of a lover lamenting his deceased mistress and a Raven continuously repeating the word "Nevermore." I had to combine these, 20 bearing in mind my design of varying at every turn the *application* of the word re-peated; but the only intelligible mode of such combination is that of imagining the Raven employing the word in answer to the queries of the lover. And here it was that I saw at once the opportunity afforded for the effect on which I had been de-pending — that is to say, the effect of the *variation of application.* I saw that I could make the first query propounded by the lover — the first query to which the Raven should reply "Nevermore" — that I could make this first query a commonplace one, the second less so, the third still less, and so on, until at length the lover, startled from his original nonchalance by the melancholy character of the word itself, by its frequent repetition and by a consideration of the ominous reputation of the fowl 30 that uttered it, is at length excited to superstition, and wildly propounds queries of a far different character — queries whose solution he has passionately at heart — propounds them half in superstition and half in that species of despair which delights in self-torture — propounds them, not altogether because he believes in the prophetic or demoniac character of the bird (which, reason assures him, is merely repeating a lesson learned by rote), but because he experiences a frenzied pleasure in so modelling his questions as to receive from the *expected* "Nevermore" the most delicious because the most intolerable of sorrow. Perceiving the oppor-tunity thus afforded me — or, more strictly, thus forced upon me in the progress of the construction — I first established in mind the climax, or concluding query — 40 that query to which "Nevermore" should be in the last place an answer — that query in reply to which this word "Nevermore" should involve the utmost con-ceivable amount of sorrow and despair.

Here then the poem may be said to have its beginning — at the end, where all works of art should begin — for it was here, at this point of my preconsiderations, that I first put pen to paper in the composition of the stanza:

> "Prophet," said I, "thing of evil! prophet still if bird or devil!
> By that heaven that bends above us — by that God we both adore,
> Tell this soul with sorrow laden, if within the distant Aidenn,
> It shall clasp a sainted maiden whom the angels name Lenore —
> Clasp a rare and radiant maiden whom the angels name Lenore."
> Quoth the Raven, "Nevermore."

I composed this stanza, at this point, first, that by establishing the climax, I
10 might the better vary and graduate, as regards seriousness and importance, the preceding queries of the lover; and secondly, that I might definitely settle the rhythm, the meter, and the length and general arrangement of the stanza, — as well as graduate the stanzas which were to precede, so that none of them might surpass this in rhythmical effect. Had I been able, in the subsequent composition, to construct more vigorous stanzas, I should, without scruple, have purposely enfeebled them, so as not to interfere with the climacteric effect.

And here I may as well say a few words of the versification. My first object (as usual) was originality. The extent to which this has been neglected, in versification, is one of the most unaccountable things in the world. Admitting that there is little
20 possibility of variety in mere *rhythm,* it is still clear that the possible varieties of meter and stanza are absolutely infinite — and yet, *for centuries, no man, in verse, has ever done, or ever seemed to think of doing, an original thing.* The fact is, that originality (unless in minds of very unusual force) is by no means a matter, as some suppose, of impulse or intuition. In general, to be found, it must be elaborately sought, and although a positive merit of the highest class, demands in its attainment less of invention than negation.

Of course, I pretend to no originality in either the rhythm or meter of *The Raven.* The former is trochaic — the latter is octameter acatelectic, alternating with heptameter catalectic repeated in the refrain of the fifth verse, and terminating with tetra-
30 meter catalectic. Less pedantically — the feet employed throughout (trochees) consist of a long syllable followed by a short: the first line of the stanza consists of eight of these feet — the second of seven and a half (in effect two-thirds) — the third of eight — the fourth of seven and a half — the fifth the same — the sixth three and a half. Now, each of these lines, taken individually, has been employed before; and what originality *The Raven* has, is in their *combination into stanza;* nothing even remotely approaching this combination has ever been attempted. The effect of this originality of combination is aided by other unusual, and some altogether novel effects, arising from an extension of the application of the principles of rhyme and alliteration.

40 The next point to be considered was the mode of bringing together the lover and the Raven — and the first branch of this consideration was the *locale.* For this the most natural suggestion might seem to be a forest, or the fields — but it has always

appeared to me that a close *circumscription of space* is absolutely necessary to the effect of insulated incident: — it has the force of a frame to a picture. It has an indisputable moral power in keeping concentrated the attention, and, of course, must not be confounded with mere unity of place.

I determined, then, to place the lover in his chamber — in a chamber rendered sacred to him by memories of her who had frequented it. The room is represented as richly furnished — this in mere pursuance of the ideas I have already explained on the subject of Beauty, as the sole true poetical thesis.

The *locale* being thus determined, I had now to introduce the bird — and the thought of introducing him through the window, was inevitable. The idea of mak- 10 ing the lover suppose, in the first instance, that the flapping of the wings of the bird against the shutter, is a "tapping" at the door, originated in a wish to increase, by prolonging, the reader's curiosity, and in a desire to admit the incidental effect arising from the lover's throwing open the door, finding all dark, and thence adopting the half-fancy that it was the spirit of his mistress that knocked.

I made the night tempestuous, first, to account for the Raven's seeking admission, and secondly, for the effect of contrast with the (physical) serenity within the chamber.

I made the bird alight on the bust of Pallas, also for the effect of contrast between the marble and the plumage — it being understood that the bust was absolutely 20 *suggested* by the bird — the bust of *Pallas* being chosen, first, as most in keeping with the scholarship of the lover, and secondly, for the sonorousness of the word, *Pallas,* itself.

About the middle of the poem, also, I have availed myself of the force of contrast, with a view of deepening the ultimate impression. For example, an air of the fantastic — approaching as nearly to the ludicrous as was admissible — is given to the Raven's entrance. He comes in "with many a flirt and flutter."

> Not the *least obeisance made he* — not a moment stopped or stayed he,
> But with *mien of lord or lady,* perched above my chamber door.

In the two stanzas which follow, the design is more obviously carried out: —   30

> Then this ebony bird beguiling my sad fancy into smiling
> By the *grave and stern decorum of the countenance it wore,*
> "Though thy *crest be shorn and shaven* thou," I said, "art sure no craven,
> Ghastly grim and ancient Raven wandering from the nightly shore —
> Tell me what thy lordly name is on the Night's Plutonian shore?"
>   Quoth the Raven, "Nevermore."

> Much I marvelled *this ungainly fowl* to hear discourse so plainly
> Though its answer little meaning — little relevancy bore;
> For we cannot help agreeing that no living human being

---

1 **circumscription of space,** i.e., a limitation of the scene

> Ever yet was blessed with seeing bird above his chamber door —
> Bird or beast upon the sculptured bust above his chamber door,
>   With such name as "Nevermore."

The effect of the *dénouement* being thus provided for, I immediately drop the fantastic for a tone of the most profound seriousness — this tone commencing in the stanza directly following the one last quoted, with the line,

> But the Raven, sitting lonely on that placid bust, spoke only, etc.

From this epoch the lover no longer jests — no longer sees any thing even of the fantastic in the Raven's demeanor. He speaks of him as a "grim, ungainly, ghastly,
10 gaunt, and ominous bird of yore," and feels the "fiery eyes" burning into his "bosom's core." This revolution of thought, or fancy, on the lover's part, is intended to induce a similar one on the part of the reader — to bring the mind into a proper frame for the *dénouement* — which is now brought about as rapidly and as *directly* as possible.

With the *dénouement* proper — with the Raven's reply, "Nevermore," to the lover's final demand if he shall meet his mistress in another world — the poem, in its obvious phase, that of a simple narrative, may be said to have its completion. So far, every thing is within the limits of the accountable — of the real. A raven, having learned by rote the single word "Nevermore," and having escaped from the
20 custody of its owner, is driven at midnight, through the violence of a storm, to seek admission at a window from which a light still gleams — the chamber-window of a student, occupied half in poring over a volume, half in dreaming of a beloved mistress deceased. The casement being thrown open at the fluttering of the bird's wings, the bird itself perches on the most convenient seat out of the immediate reach of the student, who, amused by the incident and the oddity of the visitor's demeanor, demands of it, in jest and without looking for a reply, its name. The raven addressed, answers with its customary word, "Nevermore" — a word which finds immediate echo in the melancholy heart of the student, who, giving utterance aloud to certain thoughts suggested by the occasion, is again startled by the fowl's
30 repetition of "Nevermore." The student now guesses the state of the case, but is impelled, as I have before explained, by the human thirst for self-torture, and in part by superstition, to propound such queries to the bird as will bring him, the lover, the most of the luxury of sorrow, through the anticipated answer "Nevermore." With the indulgence, to the extreme, of this self-torture, the narration, in what I have termed its first or obvious phase, has a natural termination, and so far there has been no overstepping of the limits of the real.

But in subjects so handled, however skillfully, or with however vivid an array of incident, there is always a certain hardness or nakedness, which repels the artistical eye. Two things are invariably required — first, some amount of complexity,
40 or more properly, adaptation; and, secondly, some amount of suggestiveness — some undercurrent, however indefinite, of meaning. It is this latter, in especial, which

imparts to a work of art so much of that *richness* (to borrow from colloquy a forcible term) which we are too fond of confounding with *the ideal.* It is the *excess* of the suggested meaning — it is the rendering this the upper instead of the under current of the theme — which turns into prose (and that of the very flattest kind) the so-called poetry of the so-called transcendentalists.

Holding these opinions, I added the two concluding stanzas of the poem — their suggestiveness being thus made to pervade all the narrative which has preceded them. The undercurrent of meaning is rendered first apparent in the lines —

> "Take thy beak from out *my heart,* and take thy form from off my door!"
> Quoth the Raven, "Nevermore!"   10

It will be observed that the words, "from out my heart," involve the first metaphorical expression in the poem. They, with the answer, "Nevermore," dispose the mind to seek a moral in all that has been previously narrated. The reader begins now to regard the Raven as emblematical — but it is not until the very last line of the very last stanza, that the intention of making him emblematical of *Mournful and Never-ending Remembrance* is permitted distinctly to be seen:

> And the Raven, never flitting, still is sitting, still is sitting,
> On the pallid bust of Pallas, just above my chamber door;
> And his eyes have all the seeming of a demon's that is dreaming,
> And the lamplight o'er him streaming throws his shadow on the floor;   20
> And my soul *from out that shadow* that lies floating on the floor
> > Shall be lifted — nevermore.
> > > 1846

The Fall of the House of Usher

Some of the things Poe said in "The Philosophy of Composition" imply something about his methods in this most famous of his tales."It is an obvious rule of art," he said, "that effects should be made to spring from direct causes — that objects should be attained through means best adapted for their attainment. . . ." It might be said, therefore, that, in modern psychological terms, he regarded the work of art as a stimulus setting up a response in the reader. How does this relationship come about? Another passage suggests that the reader reacts in certain ways in sympathy with a character in the story. ("This revolution of thought, or fancy, on the lover's part," said Poe, "is intended to induce a similar one on the part of the reader. . . .")

Thus a chain is set up: incidents in the narrative cause the character to have certain emotions, and the reader experiences similar emotions. When the character's reaction changes or develops, so does that of the reader. So that a story may be climactic, Poe may "vary and graduate, as regards seriousness and importance," the parts of his narrative. Thus a story may·have two interrelated narrative strands, each climactically arranged — a set of incidents

*or stimuli and a set of effects or responses to those stimuli by the character and consequently
by the sympathetic reader.*

*These details about Poe's method of constructing a story, applied to "The Fall of the House
of Usher," indicate that the reader may well notice its two interrelated strands of narrative —
the one dealing with the emotions of the "affected" character and the one dealing with the
incidents which have the effects. Studying the character (here undoubtedly the narrator), the
reader will find that though, at the beginning of the tale, the "I" of the story is disturbed
by "a sense of insufferable gloom," he can stand aside, as it were, and detachedly attempt to
discover why he feels as he does. But as the happenings unfold, his uneasiness changes to
fear, his fear grows, and his detachment decreases, until at the end he "flees aghast" and
his "brain reels" as the "walls of the house rush asunder." Poe's assumption probably is
that the record of this developing emotion arouses "in the mind of him who contemplates it
with a kindred art" a similarly developing emotion.*

*Now the incidents in the tale, of course, should be appropriate causes for such a develop-
ing emotion. As one examines the tale, one may see in the strange appearance of the house,
the actions of its mad inmate, Usher, the strange burial and return to life of Madeline,
and the dissolution of the house, incidents likely to stimulate mounting terror. But a more
subtle and unified thread of narrative, some of it connoted by the "tone" of the story, does
even more to suggest the reason for increasing terror. This is made up of a series of increasingly weird identifications. There is an identification, for instance, between the house and
its inmates, at first detachedly called by the narrator a "quaint" identification by the
"peasantry" but later discovered to be something much more weird than a mere "equivocal
appellation." There are the identifications between Usher and his sister, between works of art
and actual happenings, and finally between the madness of Usher and the (at least momentary) madness of the narrator. These, more than the explicitly detailed incidents, account for the crescendo of horror which ends the tale.*

> *Son coeur est un luth suspendu;*
> *Sitot qu'on le touche il resonne.* — BÉRANGER

During the whole of a dull, dark, and soundless day in the autumn of the year,
when the clouds hung oppressively low in the heavens, I had been passing alone,
on horseback, through a singularly dreary tract of country; and at length found myself, as the shades of the evening drew on, within view of the melancholy House of
Usher. I know not how it was, but, with the first glimpse of the building, a sense
of insufferable gloom pervaded my spirit. I say insufferable; for the feeling was un-
relieved by any of that half pleasurable, because poetic, sentiment with which the
10 mind usually receives even the sternest natural images of the desolate or terrible. I
looked upon the scene before me — upon the mere house, and the simple landscape
features of the domain, upon the bleak walls, upon the vacant eyelike windows,
upon a few rank sedges, and upon a few white trunks of decayed trees — with an
utter depression of soul which I can compare to no earthly sensation more properly
than to the afterdream of the reveler upon opium: the bitter lapse into everyday
life, the hideous dropping off of the veil. There was an iciness, a sinking, a sicken-

1 **Son coeur . . . resonné.** His heart is a suspended lute which resounds as soon as it is touched. The
quotation is from Béranger's poem "Le Refus"

ing of the heart, an unredeemed dreariness of thought, which no goading of the imagination could torture into aught of the sublime. What was it — I paused to think — what was it that so unnerved me in the contemplation of the House of Usher? It was a mystery all insoluble; nor could I grapple with the shadowy fancies that crowded upon me as I pondered. I was forced to fall back upon the unsatisfactory conclusion that while, beyond doubt, there *are* combinations of very simple natural objects which have the power of thus affecting us, still the analysis of this power lies among considerations beyond our depth. It was possible, I reflected, that a mere different arrangement of the particulars of the scene, of the details of the picture, would be sufficient to modify, or perhaps to annihilate, its 10 capacity for sorrowful impression, and, acting upon this idea, I reined my horse to the precipitous brink of a black and lurid tarn that lay in unruffled luster by the dwelling, and gazed down — but with a shudder even more thrilling than before — upon the remodeled and inverted images of the gray sedge, and the ghastly tree-stems, and the vacant and eyelike windows.

Nevertheless, in this mansion of gloom I now proposed to myself a sojourn of some weeks. Its proprietor, Roderick Usher, had been one of my boon companions in boyhood; but many years had elapsed since our last meeting. A letter, however, had lately reached me in a distant part of the country — a letter from him — which in its wildly importunate nature had admitted of no other than a personal reply. 20 The MS. gave evidence of nervous agitation. The writer spoke of acute bodily illness, of a mental disorder which oppressed him, and of an earnest desire to see me, as his best and indeed his only personal friend, with a view of attempting, by the cheerfulness of my society, some alleviation of his malady. It was the manner in which all this, and much more, was said — it was the apparent *heart* that went with his request — which allowed me no room for hestitation; and I accordingly obeyed forthwith what I still considered a very singular summons.

Although as boys we had been even intimate associates, yet I really knew little of my friend. His reserve had been always excessive and habitual. I was aware, however, that his very ancient family had been noted, time out of mind, for a peculiar 30 sensibility of temperament, displaying itself, through long ages, in many works of exalted art, and manifested of late in repeated deeds of munificent yet unobtrusive charity, as well as in a passionate devotion to the intricacies, perhaps even more than to the orthodox and easily recognizable beauties, of musical science. I had learned, too, the very remarkable fact that the stem of the Usher race, all time-honored as it was, had put forth at no period any enduring branch; in other words, that the entire family lay in the direct line of descent, and had always, with a very trifling and very temporary variation, so lain. It was this deficiency, I considered, while running over in thought the perfect keeping of the character of the premises with the accredited character of the people, and while speculating upon the possible 40 influence which the one, in the long lapse of centuries, might have exercised upon the other — it was this deficiency, perhaps, of collateral issue, and the consequent undeviating transmission from sire to son of the patrimony with the name, which had at length so identified the two as to merge the original title of the estate in the quaint and equivocal appellation of the "House of Usher" — an appellation which seemed to include, in the minds of the peasantry who used it, both the family and the family mansion.

I have said that the sole effect of my somewhat childish experiment, that of looking down within the tarn, had been to deepen the first singular impression. There can be no doubt that the consciousness of the rapid increase of my superstition — for why should I not so term it? — served mainly to accelerate the increase itself. Such, I have long known, is the paradoxical law of all sentiments having terror as a basis. And it might have been for this reason only, that, when I again uplifted my
10 eyes to the house itself from its image in the pool, there grew in my mind a strange fancy — a fancy so ridiculous, indeed, that I but mention it to show the vivid force of the sensations which oppressed me. I had so worked upon my imagination as really to believe that about the whole mansion and domain there hung an atmosphere peculiar to themselves and their immediate vicinity: an atmosphere which had no affinity with the air of heaven, but which had reeked up from the decayed trees, and the gray wall, and the silent tarn; a pestilent and mystic vapor, dull, sluggish, faintly discernible, and leaden-hued.

Shaking off from my spirit what *must* have been a dream, I scanned more narrowly the real aspect of the building. Its principal feature seemed to be that of an
20 excessive antiquity. The discoloration of ages had been great. Minute fungi overspread the whole exterior, hanging in a fine tangled webwork from the eaves. Yet all this was apart from any extraordinary dilapidation. No portion of the masonry had fallen; and there appeared to be a wild inconsistency between its still perfect adaptation of parts and the crumbling condition of the individual stones. In this there was much that reminded me of the specious totality of old woodwork which has rotted for long years in some neglected vault, with no disturbance from the breath of the external air. Beyond this indication of extensive decay, however, the fabric gave little token of instability. Perhaps the eye of a scrutinizing observer might have discovered a barely perceptible fissure, which, extending from the roof of the
30 building in front, made its way down the wall in a zigzag direction, until it became lost in the sullen waters of the tarn.

Noticing these things, I rode over a short causeway to the house. A servant in waiting took my horse, and I entered the Gothic archway of the hall. A valet, of stealthy step, thence conducted me in silence through many dark and intricate passages in my progress to the *studio* of his master. Much that I encountered on the way contributed, I know not how, to heighten the vague sentiments of which I have already spoken. While the objects around me — while the carvings of the ceiling, the somber tapestries of the walls, the ebon blackness of the floors, and the phantasmagoric armorial trophies which rattled as I strode, were but matters to
40 which, or to such as which, I had been accustomed from my infancy, — while I hesitated not to acknowledge how familiar was all this, I still wondered to find how unfamiliar were the fancies which ordinary images were stirring up. On one of the staircases I met the physician of the family. His countenance, I thought, wore a mingled expression of low cunning and perplexity. He accosted me with trepida-

tion and passed on. The valet now threw open a door and ushered me into the presence of his master.

The room in which I found myself was very large and lofty. The windows were long, narrow, and pointed, and at so vast a distance from the black oaken floor as to be altogether inaccessible from within. Feeble gleams of encrimsoned light made their way through the trellised panes, and served to render sufficiently distinct the more prominent objects around; the eye, however, struggled in vain to reach the remoter angles of the chamber, or the recesses of the vaulted and fretted ceiling. Dark draperies hung upon the walls. The general furniture was profuse, comfortless, antique, and tattered. Many books and musical instruments lay scattered about, but 10 failed to give any vitality to the scene. I felt that I breathed an atmosphere of sorrow. An air of stern, deep, and irredeemable gloom hung over and pervaded all.

Upon my entrance, Usher arose from a sofa on which he had been lying at full length, and greeted me with a vivacious warmth which had much in it, I at first thought, of an overdone cordiality — of the constrained effort of the *ennuyé* man of the world. A glance, however, at his countenance, convinced me of his perfect sincerity. We sat down; and for some moments, while he spoke not, I gazed upon him with a feeling half of pity, half of awe. Surely man had never before so terribly altered, in so brief a period, as had Roderick Usher! It was with difficulty that I could bring myself to admit the identity of the wan being before me with the com- 20 panion of my early boyhood. Yet the character of his face had been at all times remarkable. A cadaverousness of complexion; an eye large, liquid, and luminous beyond comparison; lips somewhat thin and very pallid, but of a surpassingly beautiful curve; a nose of a delicate Hebrew model, but with a breadth of nostril unusual in similar formations; a finely-molded chin, speaking, in its want of prominence, of a want of moral energy; hair of a more than weblike softness and tenuity, — these features, with an inordinate expansion above the regions of the temple, made up altogether a countenance not easily to be forgotten. And now in the mere exaggeration of the prevailing character of these features, and of the expression they were wont to convey, lay so much of change that I doubted to whom I spoke. The 30 now ghastly pallor of the skin, and the now miraculous luster of the eye, above all things startled and even awed me. The silken hair, too, had been suffered to grow all unheeded, and as, in its wild gossamer texture, it floated rather than fell about the face, I could not, even with effort, connect its arabesque expression with any idea of simple humanity.

In the manner of my friend I was at once struck with an incoherence, an inconsistency; and I soon found this to arise from a series of feeble and futile struggles to overcome an habitual trepidancy, an excessive nervous agitation. For something of this nature I had indeed been prepared, no less by his letter than by reminscences of certain boyish traits, and by conclusions deduced from his peculiar physical con- 40 formation and temperament. His action was alternately vivacious and sullen. His

---

21 **the character . . . face.** As critics have noted, the description of Usher is remarkably like one appropriate for Poe. The "inordinate expansion," according to phrenologists of the day, indicated "ideality"

voice varied rapidly from a tremulous indecision (when the animal spirits seemed utterly in abeyance) to that species of energetic concision — that abrupt, weighty, unhurried, and hollow-sounding enunciation, that leaden, self-balanced, and perfectly modulated guttural utterance — which may be observed in the lost drunkard, or the irreclaimable eater of opium, during the periods of his most intense excitement.

It was thus that he spoke of the object of my visit, of his earnest desire to see me, and of the solace he expected me to afford him. He entered at some length into what he conceived to be the nature of his malady. It was, he said, a constitutional and a family evil, and one for which he despaired to find a remedy — a mere nerv-
10 ous affection, he immediately added, which would undoubtedly soon pass off. It displayed itself in a host of unnatural sensations. Some of these, as he detailed them, interested and bewildered me; although, perhaps, the terms and the general manner of the narration had their weight. He suffered much from a morbid acuteness of the senses; the most insipid food was alone endurable; he could wear only garments of certain texture; the odors of all flowers were oppressive; his eyes were tortured by even faint light; and there were but peculiar sounds, and these from stringed instruments, which did not inspire him with horror.

To an anomalous species of terror I found him a bounden slave. "I shall perish," said he, "I *must* perish in this deplorable folly. Thus, thus, and not otherwise, shall
20 I be lost. I dread the events of the future, not in themselves, but in their results. I shudder at the thought of any, even the most trivial, incident, which may operate upon this intolerable agitation of soul. I have, indeed, no abhorrence of danger, except in its absolute effect, — in terror. In this unnerved, in this pitable condition, I feel that the period will sooner or later arrive when I must abandon life and reason together in some struggle with the grim phantasm, FEAR."

I learned moreover at intervals, and through broken and equivocal hints, another singular feature of his mental condition. He was enchained by certain superstitious impressions in regard to the dwelling which he tenanted, and whence for many years he had never ventured forth, in regard to an influence whose supposititious force
30 was conveyed in terms too shadowy here to be restated, — an influence which some peculiarities in the mere form and substance of his family mansion had, by dint of long sufferance, he said, obtained over his spirit; an effect which the *physique* of the gray walls and turrets, and of the dim tarn into which they all looked down, had at length brought about upon the *morale* of his existence.

He admitted, however, although with hestitation, that much of the peculiar gloom which thus afflicted him could be traced to a more natural and far more palpable origin, — to the severe and long-continued illness, indeed to the evidently approaching dissolution, of a tenderly beloved sister, his sole companion for long years, his last and only relative on earth. "Her decease," he said, with a bitterness which I
40 can never forget, "would leave him (him, the hopeless and the frail) the last of the ancient race of the Ushers." While he spoke, the lady Madeline (for so was she called) passed slowly through a remote portion of the apartment, and, without having noticed my presence, disappeared. I regarded her with an utter astonishment not unmingled with dread, and yet I found it impossible to account for such feel-

ings. A sensation of stupor oppressed me, as my eyes followed her retreating steps. When a door, at length, closed upon her, my glance sought instinctively and eagerly the countenance of the brother; but he had buried his face in his hands, and I could only perceive that a far more than ordinary wanness had overspread the emaciated fingers through which trickled many passionate tears.

The disease of the lady Madeline had long baffled the skill of her physicians. A settled apathy, a gradual wasting away of the person, and frequent although transient affections of a partially cataleptical character, were the unusual diagnosis. Hitherto she had steadily borne up against the pressure of her malady, and had not betaken herself finally to bed; but, on the closing-in of the evening of my arrival   10 at the house, she succumbed (as her brother told me at night with inexpressible agitation) to the prostrating power of the destroyer; and I learned that the glimpse I had obtained of her person would thus probably be the last I should obtain, — that the lady, at least while living, would be seen by me no more.

For several days ensuing, her name was unmentioned by either Usher or myself; and during this period I was busied in earnest endeavors to alleviate the melancholy of my friend. We painted and read together; or I listened, as if in a dream, to the wild improvisations of his speaking guitar. And thus, as a closer and still closer intimacy admitted me more unreservedly into the recesses of his spirit, the more bitterly did I perceive the futility of all attempt at cheering a mind from which   20 darkness, as if an inherent positive quality, poured forth upon all objects of the moral and physical universe, in one unceasing radiation of gloom.

I shall ever bear about me a memory of the many solemn hours I thus spent alone with the master of the House of Usher. Yet I should fail in my attempt to convey an idea of the exact character of the studies, or of the occupations, in which he involved me, or led me the way. An excited and highly distempered ideality threw a sulphureous luster over all. His long, improvised dirges will ring forever in my ears. Among other things, I hold painfully in mind a certain singular perversion and amplification of the wild air of the last waltz of Von Weber. From the painting over which his elaborate fancy brooded, and which grew, touch by touch, into   30 vaguenesses at which I shuddered the more thrillingly because I shuddered knowing not why, — from these paintings (vivid as their images now are before me) I would in vain endeavor to educe more than a small portion which should lie within the compass of merely written words. By the utter simplicity, by the nakedness of his designs, he arrested and over-awed attention. If ever mortal painted an idea, that mortal was Roderick Usher. For me at least, in the circumstances then surrounding me, there arose, out of the pure abstractions which the hypochondriac contrived to throw upon his canvas, an intensity of intolerable awe, no shadow of which felt I ever yet in the contemplation of the certainly glowing yet too concrete reveries of Fuseli.   40

One of the phantasmagoric conceptions of my friend, partaking not so rigidly of

---

29 **the last . . . Von Weber,** No. 5 of *Danses brillantes* by Karl Gottlieb Reissiger (1798-1859), based on Von Weber's last waltz   40 **Fuseli,** Heinrich Fuseli, a Swiss painter who was taught in the Royal Academy at London

the spirit of abstraction, may be shadowed forth, although feebly, in words. A small picture presented the interior of an immensely long and rectangular vault or tunnel, with low walls, smooth, white, and without interruption or device. Certain accessory points of the design served well to convey the idea that this excavation lay at an exceeding depth below the surface of the earth. No outlet was observed in any portion of its vast extent, and no torch, or other artificial source of light, was discernible; yet a flood of intense rays rolled throughout, and bathed the whole in a ghastly and inappropriate splendor.

I have just spoken of that morbid condition of the auditory nerve which rendered
10 all music intolerable to the sufferer, with the exception of certain effects of stringed instruments. It was, perhaps, the narrow limits to which he thus confined himself upon the guitar, which gave birth, in great measure, to the fantastic character of his performances. But the fervid *facility* of his *impromptus* could not be so accounted for. They must have been, and were, in the notes as well as in the words of his wild fantasias (for he not unfrequently accompanied himself with rimed verbal improvisations), the result of that intense mental collectedness and concentration to which I have previously alluded as observable only in particular moments of the highest artificial excitement. The words of one of these rhapsodies I have easily remembered. I was, perhaps, the more forcibly impressed with it as he gave it, because, in
20 the under or mystic current of its meaning, I fancied that I perceived, and for the first time, a full consciousness, on the part of Usher, of the tottering of his lofty reason upon her throne. The verses, which were entitled "The Haunted Palace," ran very nearly, if not accurately, thus: —

I

In the greenest of our valleys
 By good angels tenanted,
Once a fair and stately palace —
 Radiant palace — reared its head.
In the monarch Thought's dominion,
 It stood there;
30 Never seraph spread a pinion
 Over fabric half so fair.

II

Banners yellow, glorious, golden,
 On its roof did float and flow
(This — all this — was in the olden
 Time long ago),
And every gentle air that dallied,

---

1 **A small picture.** Compare the vault in which the body of Madeline is placed later in the story   22
"**The Haunted Palace.**" Poe said this poem was intended "to imply a mind haunted by phantoms." It
should be compared with the description of Usher in the eighth paragraph of the story

In that sweet day,
Along the ramparts plumed and pallid,
A winged odor went away.

III

Wanderers in that happy valley
  Through two luminous windows saw
Spirits moving musically
  To a lute's well-tuned law,
Round about a throne, where sitting,
  Porphyrogene,
In state his glory well befitting,   10
  The ruler of the realm was seen.

IV

And all with pearl and ruby glowing
  Was the fair palace door,
Through which came flowing, flowing, flowing,
  And sparkling evermore,
A troop of Echoes, whose sweet duty
  Was but to sing,
In voices of surpassing beauty,
  The wit and wisdom of their king.

V

But evil things, in robes of sorrow,   20
  Assailed the monarch's high estate;
(Ah, let us mourn, for never morrow
  Shall dawn upon him, desolate!)
And, round about his home, the glory
  That blushed and bloomed
Is but a dim-remembered story
  Of the old time entombed.

VI

And travelers now within that valley
  Through the red-litten windows see
Vast forms that move fantastically   30
  To a discordant melody;
While, like a ghastly rapid river,
  Through the pale door,
A hideous throng rush out forever,
  And laugh — but smile no more.

---

9 **Porphyrogene**, a name meaning "born to the purple"

I well remember that suggestions arising from this ballad led us into a train of thought, wherein there became manifest an opinion of Usher's which I mention, not so much on account of its novelty (for other men have thought thus) as on account of the pertinacity with which he maintained it. This opinion, in its general form, was that of the sentience of all vegetable things. But in his disordered fancy, the idea had assumed a more daring character, and trespassed, under certain conditions, upon the kingdom of inorganization. I lack words to express the full extent or the earnest *abandon* of his persuasion. The belief, however, was connected (as I have previously hinted) with the gray stones of the home of his forefathers. The

10 conditions of the sentience had been here, he imagined, fulfilled in the method of collocation of these stones, — in the order of their arrangement, as well as in that of the many fungi which overspread them, and of the decayed trees which stood around; above all, in the long undisturbed endurance of this arrangement, and in its reduplication in the still waters of the tarn. Its evidence — the evidence of the sentience — was to be seen, he said (and I here started as he spoke), in the gradual yet certain condensation of an atmosphere of their own about the waters and the walls. The result was discoverable, he added, in that silent yet importunate and terrible influence which for centuries had molded the destinies of his family, and which made *him* what I now saw him, — what he was. Such opinions need no comment, and

20 I will make none.

Our books — the books which for years had formed no small portion of the mental existence of the invalid — were, as might be supposed, in strict keeping with this character of phantasm. We pored together over such works as the Ververt and Chartreuse of Gresset; the Belphegor of Machiavelli; the Heaven and Hell of Swedenborg; the Subterranean Voyage of Nicholas Klimm by Holberg; the Chiromancy of Robert Flud, of Jean D'Indagine, and of De la Chambre; the Journey into the Blue Distance of Tieck; and the City of the Sun of Campanella. One favorite volume was a small octavo edition of the *Directorium Inquisitorum,* by the Dominician Eymeric de Gironne; and there were passages in Pomponius Mela, about the old

3 **other men,** "Watson, Dr. Percival, Spallanzani, and especially the Bishop of Llandaff." — Poe. See *Chemical Essays,* Vol. V   23 **Ververt and Chartreuse,** anticlerical and licentious poems by Jean Baptiste Gresset (1709-1777)   24 **Belphegor,** a novel by Machiavelli (1469-1527) which tells how the archdemon Balfagor visited the earth and then returned to hell   24 **Swedenborg,** Emmanuel Swedenborg (1688-1772), Swedish mystic   25 **Holberg,** Ludwig Holberg (1684-1754), who published the book mentioned in Latin in 1741. The title brings in another mention of a journey into supernatural realms   25 **Chiromancy,** palmistry   26 **Robert Flud** (1547-1637), English physician and writer on pseudoscience   26 **Jean D'Indagine,** author of *Chiromantia* (1522), a work on palmistry   26 **De la Chambre,** Maria Cireau de la Chambre (1594-1669), French writer on palmistry   27 **Tieck,** Ludwig Tieck (1773-1853), German writer. Poe here refers to the subtitle of a book called *Das Alte Buch; oder Reise ins Blaue hinein.* Better than the main title, this repeats the motif of the journey from one world to the other, thus foreshadowing Madeline's reward after death   27 **Campanella,** Tommaso Campanella (1568-1639), Italian philosopher. His *Civitas Solis,* actually a Utopian treatise, serves here, by title, to connote the world beyond   28 **Directorium Inquisitorum** (1503) was by Nicholas Eymeric de Girone, inquisitor-general for Castile in 1536. The book gives in detail an account of the tortures of the Inquisition, and the title not only augments the suggestion of the exoticism of Usher's reading but also foreshadows the torture Madeline is to undergo   29 **Pomponius Mela** (first century A.D.), author of a geography often concerned with strange beasts. Here a journey into distant lands, instead of a journey into the other world, is suggested

African Satyrs and Aegipans, over which Usher would sit dreaming for hours. His chief delight, however, was found in the perusal of an exceedingly rare and curious book in quarto Gothic, — the manual of a forgotten church, — the *Vigiliæ Mortuorum secundum Chorum Ecclesiæ Maguntinæ.*

I could not help thinking of the wild ritual of this work, and of its probable influence upon the hypochondriac, when one evening, having informed me abruptly that the lady Madeline was no more, he stated his intention of preserving her corpse for a fortnight, (previously to its final interment) in one of the numerous vaults within the main walls of the building. The worldly reason, however, assigned for this sin-gular proceeding was one which I did not feel at liberty to dispute. The brother 10 had been led to his resolution (so he told me) by consideration of the unusual char-acter of the malady of the deceased, of certain obtrusive and eager inquiries on the part of her medical men, and of the remote and exposed situation of the burial ground of the family. I will not deny that when I called to mind the sinister countenance of the person whom I met upon the staircase, on the day of my arrival at the house, I had no desire to oppose what I regarded as at best but a harmless, and by no means an unnatural, precaution.

At the request of Usher, I personally aided him in the arrangement for the tem-porary entombment. The body having been encoffined, we two alone bore it to its rest. The vault in which we placed it (and which had been so long unopened that 20 our torches, half smothered in its oppressive atmosphere, gave us little opportunity for investigation) was small, damp, and entirely without means of admission for light; lying, at great depth, immediately beneath that portion of the building in which was my own sleeping apartment. It had been used apparently, in remote feudal times, for the worst purposes of a donjon keep, and in later days as a place of de-posit for powder, or some other highly combustible substance, as a portion of its floor, and the whole interior of a long archway through which we reached it, were carefully sheathed with copper. The door, of massive iron, had been also similarly protected. Its immense weight caused an unusually sharp grating sound as it moved upon its hinges.   30

Having deposited our mournful burden upon tressels within this region of horror, we partially turned aside the yet unscrewed lid of the coffin, and looked upon the face of the tenant. A striking similitude between the brother and sister now first arrested my attention; and Usher, divining, perhaps, my thoughts, murmured out some few words from which I learned that the deceased and himself had been twins, and that sympathies existed between them. Our glances, however, rested not long

---

1 **Aegipans,** goat-god Pan   3 **Vigiliæ Mortuorum . . .,** "The Watches of the Dead according to the Choir of the Church of Mayence." As Poe points out, this title is definitely related to what happens in the next paragraph. It is also related to the nightly torments of Usher and his guest later in the tale   17 **pre-caution.** The medical man, briefly glimpsed at the start of the story, at this point serves his sole purpose in the narrative. Usher's fear of "body-snatching" causes the temporary entombment of Madeline within the House of Usher. The earlier characterization of the doctor is meager but sufficient: his "mingled expression of perplexity and cunning" motivates Usher's apprehension

upon the dead, for we could not regard her unawed. The disease which had thus entombed the lady in the maturity of youth, had left, as usual in all maladies of a strictly cataleptical character, the mockery of a faint blush upon the bosom and the face, and that suspiciously lingering smile upon the lip which is so terrible in death. We replaced and screwed down the lid, and having secured the door of iron, made our way, with toil, into the scarcely less gloomy apartments of the upper portion of the house.

And now, some days of bitter grief having elapsed, an observable change came over the features of the mental disorder of my friend. His ordinary manner had van-
10 ished. His ordinary occupations were neglected or forgotten. He roamed from chamber to chamber with hurried, unequal, and objectless step. The pallor of his countenance had assumed, if possible, a more ghastly hue, but the luminousness of his eye had utterly gone out. The once occasional huskiness of his tone was heard no more; and a tremulous quaver, as if of extreme terror, habitually characterized his utterance. There were times, indeed, when I thought his unceasingly agitated mind was laboring with some oppressive secret, to divulge which he struggled for the necessary courage. At times, again, I was obliged to resolve all into the mere inexplicable vagaries of madness, for I beheld him gazing upon vacancy for long hours, in an attitude of the profoundest attention, as if listening to some imaginary
20 sound. It was no wonder that his condition terrified — that it infected me. I felt creeping upon me, by slow yet certain degrees, the wild influences of his own fantastic yet impressive superstitions.

It was, especially, upon retiring to bed late in the night of the seventh or eighth day after the placing of the lady Madeline within the donjon, that I experienced the full power of such feelings. Sleep came not near my couch, while the hours waned and waned away. I struggled to reason off the nervousness which had dominion over me. I endeavored to believe that much if not all of what I felt was due to the bewildering influence of the gloomy furniture of the room, — of the dark and tattered draperies which, tortured into motion by the breath of a rising tempest, swayed fit-
30 fully to and fro upon the walls, and rustled uneasily about the decorations of the bed. But my efforts were fruitless. An irrepressible tremor gradually pervaded my frame; and at length there sat upon my very heart an incubus of utterly causeless alarm. Shaking this off with a gasp and a struggle, I uplifted myself upon the pillows, and, peering earnestly within the intense darkness of the chamber, hearkened — I know not why, except that an instinctive spirit prompted me — to certain low and indefinite sounds which came, through the pauses of the storm, at long intervals, I knew not whence. Overpowered by an intense sentiment of horror, unaccountable yet unendurable, I threw on my clothes with haste (for I felt that I should sleep no more during the night), and endeavored to arouse myself from the pitiable
40 condition to which I had fallen, by pacing rapidly to and fro through the apartment.

I had taken but few turns in this manner, when a light step on an adjoining staircase arrested my attention. I presently recognized it as that of Usher. In an instant afterward he rapped with a gentle touch at my door, and entered, bearing a lamp. His countenance was, as usual, cadaverously wan — but, moreover, there was a species of mad hilarity in his eyes, — an evidently restrained hysteria in his whole demeanor. His air appalled me — but anything was preferable to the solitude which I had so long endured, and I even welcomed his presence as a relief.

"And you have not seen it?" he said abruptly, after having stared about him for some moments in silence, — "you have not then seen it? — but, stay! you shall." Thus speaking, and having carefully shaded his lamp, he hurried to one of the casements, and threw it freely open to the storm.

The impetuous fury of the entering gust nearly lifted us from our feet. It was, indeed, a tempestuous yet sternly beautiful night, and one wildly singular in its terror and its beauty. A whirlwind had apparently collected its force in our vicinity, for there were frequent and violent alterations in the direction of the wind; and the exceeding density of the clouds (which hung so low as to press upon the turrets of the house) did not prevent our perceiving the lifelike velocity with which they flew careering from all points against each other, without passing away into the distance. I say that even their exceeding density did not prevent our perceiving this; yet we had no glimpse of the moon or stars, nor was there any flashing forth of the lightning. But the under surfaces of the huge masses of agitated vapor, as well as all terrestrial objects immediately around us, were glowing in the unnatural light of a faintly luminous and distinctly visible gaseous exhalation which hung about and enshrouded the mansion.

"You must not — you shall not behold this!" said I shudderingly, to Usher, as I led him with a gentle violence from the window to a seat. "These appearances, which bewilder you, are merely electrical phenomena not uncommon — or it may be that they have their ghastly origin in the rank miasma of the tarn. Let us close this casement; the air is chilling and dangerous to your frame. Here is one of your favorite romances. I will read, and you shall listen; — and so we will pass away this terrible night together."

The antique volume which I had taken up was the "Mad Trist" of Sir Launcelot Canning, but I had called it a favorite of Usher's more in sad jest than in earnest; for, in truth, there is little in its uncouth and unimaginative prolixity which could have had interest for the lofty and spiritual ideality of my friend. It was, however, the only book immediately at hand; and I indulged a vague hope that the excitement which now agitated the hypochondriac might find relief (for the history of mental disorder is full of similar anomalies) even in the extremeness of the folly which I should read. Could I have judged, indeed, by the wild, overstrained air of vivacity with which he hearkened, or apparently hearkened, to the words of the tale, I might well have congratulated myself upon the success of my design.

I had arrived at that well-known portion of the story where Ethelred, the hero of the Trist, having sought in vain for peaceable admission into the dwelling of the hermit, proceeds to make good an entrance by force. Here, it will be remembered, the words of the narrative run thus: —

"And Ethelred, who was by nature of a doughty heart, and who was now mighty withal on account of the powerfulness of the wine which he had drunken, waited no longer to hold parley with the hermit, who, in sooth, was of an obstinate and maliceful turn, but, feeling the rain upon his shoulders, and fearing the rising of the tempest, uplifted his mace outright, and with blows made quickly room in the plankings of the door for his gauntleted hand; and now, pulling therewith sturdily, he so cracked, and ripped, and tore all asunder, that the noise of the dry and hollow-sounding wood alarumed and reverberated through the forest."

At the termination of this sentence I started, and for a moment paused; for it appeared to me (although I at once concluded that my excited fancy had deceived me) — it appeared to me that from some very remote portion of the mansion there came, indistinctly, to my ears, what might have been in its exact similarity of char-
10 acter the echo (but a stifled and dull one certainly) of the very cracking and ripping sound which Sir Launcelot had so particularly described. It was, beyond doubt, the coincidence alone which had arrested my attention; for amid the rattling of the sashes of the casements, and the ordinary commingled noises of the still increasing storm, the sound, in itself, had nothing, surely, which should have interested or disturbed me. I continued the story: —

"But the good champion Ethelred, now entering within the door, was sore enraged and amazed to perceive no signal of the maliceful hermit; but, in the stead thereof, a dragon of a scaly and prodigious demeanor, and of a fiery tongue, which sate in guard before a palace of gold with a floor of silver, and upon the wall there
20 hung a shield of shining brass with this legend enwritten: —

> *Who entereth herein, a conqueror hath bin;*
> *Who slayeth the dragon, the shield he shall win.*

And Ethelred uplifted his mace, and struck upon the head of the dragon, which fell before him, and gave up his pesty breath, with a shriek so horrid and harsh, and withal so piercing, that Ethelred had fain to close his ears with his hands against the dreadful noise of it, the like whereof was never before heard."

Here again I paused abruptly, and now with a feeling of wild amazement, for there could be no doubt whatever that, in this instance, I did actually hear (although from what direction it proceeded I found it impossible to say) a low and apparently
30 distant, but harsh, protracted, and most unusual screaming or grating sound, — the exact counterpart of what my fancy had already conjured up for the dragon's unnatural shriek as described by the romancer.

Oppressed as I certainly was, upon the occurrence of this second and most extraordinary coincidence, by a thousand conflicting sensations, in which wonder and extreme terror were predominant, I still retained sufficient presence of mind to avoid exciting, by any observation, the sensitive nervousness of my companion. I was by no means certain that he had noticed the sounds in question; although, assuredly, a strange alteration had during the last few minutes taken place in his demeanor. From a position fronting my own, he had gradually brought round his chair, so as to sit
40 with his face to the door of the chamber; and thus I could but partially perceive his features, although I saw that his lips trembled as if he were murmuring inaudibly. His head had dropped upon his breast; yet I knew that he was not asleep,

from the wide rigid opening of the eyes as I caught a glance of it in profile. The motion of his body, too, was at variance with this idea, for he rocked from side to side with a gentle yet constant and uniform sway. Having rapidly taken notice of all this, I resumed the narrative of Sir Launcelot, which thus proceeded: —

"And now the champion, having escaped from the terrible fury of the dragon, bethinking himself of the brazen shield, and of the breaking up of the enchantment which was upon it, removed the carcass from out of the way before him, and approached valorously over the silver pavement of the castle to where the shield was upon the wall; which in sooth tarried not for his full coming, but fell down at his feet upon the silver floor, with a mighty great and terrible ringing sound." 10

No sooner had these syllables passed my lips than — as if a shield of brass had indeed, at the moment, fallen heavily upon a floor of silver — I became aware of a distinct, hollow, metallic, and clangorous yet apparently muffled reverberation. Completely unnerved, I leaped to my feet; but the measured rocking movement of Usher was undisturbed. I rushed to the chair in which he sat. His eyes were bent fixedly before him, and throughout his whole countenance there reigned a stony rigidity. But, as I placed my hand upon his shoulder, there came a strong shudder over his whole person; a sickly smile quivered about his lips; and I saw that he spoke in a low, hurried, and gibbering murmur, as if unconscious of my presence. Bending closely over him, I at length drank in the hideous import of his words. 20

"Not hear it? — yes, I hear it, and *have* heard it. Long — long — long — many minutes, many hours, many days, have I heard it, yet I dared not — oh, pity me, miserable wretch that I am! — I dared not — I *dared* not speak! *We have put her living in the tomb!* Said I not that my senses were acute? I *now* tell you that I have heard her first feeble movements in the hollow coffin. I heard them — many, many days ago — yet I dared not — I *dared not speak!* And now — tonight — Ethelred — ha! ha! — the breaking of the hermit's door, and the deathcry of the dragon, and the clangor of the shield! — say, rather, the rending of her coffin, and the grating of the iron hinges of her prison, and her struggles within the coppered archway of the vault! Oh, whither shall I fly? Will she not be here anon? Is she not hurrying 30 to upbraid me for my haste? Have I not heard her footstep on the stair? Do I not distinguish that heavy and horrible beating of her heart? Madman!" — here he sprang furiously to his feet, and shrieked out his syllables, as if in the effort he were giving up his soul — *"Madman! I tell you that she now stands without the door!"*

As if in the superhuman energy of his utterance there had been found the potency of a spell, the huge antique panels to which the speaker pointed threw slowly back, upon the instant, their ponderous and ebony jaws. It was the work of the rushing gust — but then without those doors there *did* stand the lofty and enshrouded figure of the lady Madeline of Usher! There was blood upon her white robes, and the evidence of some bitter struggle upon every portion of her emaciated frame. For a 40 moment she remained trembling and reeling to and fro upon the threshold — then, with a low moaning cry, fell heavily inward upon the person of her brother, and in her violent and now final death agonies, bore him to the floor a corpse, and a victim to the terrors he had anticipated.

From that chamber and from that mansion I fled aghast. The storm was still abroad in all its wrath as I found myself crossing the old causeway. Suddenly there shot along the path a wild light, and I turned to see whence a gleam so unusual could have issued; for the vast house and its shadows were alone behind me. The radiance was that of the full, setting, and blood-red moon, which now shone vividly through that once barely discernible fissure, of which I have before spoken as extending from the roof of the building, in a zigzag direction, to the base. While I gazed, this fissure rapidly widened — there came a fierce breath of the whirlwind — the entire orb of the satellite burst at once upon my sight — my brain reeled as I saw the mighty walls rushing asunder — there was a long, tumultuous shouting sound like the voice of a thousand waters — and the deep and dank tarn at my feet closed sullenly and silently over the fragments of the *"House of Usher."*   1839

Ligeia

Poe believed that this was his best story, and at least some readers who are at times distressed by Poe's lack of subtlety may share his preference. One problem he faced (one he had previously tried to cope with in a similar story, "Morella") was that of unifying a narrative which tended to break into two disunited parts — one telling of the life and death of his chief character; and another telling of her return, several years later, to the world of the living.

He did this by (1) creating, in the first part, the character Ligeia, whose characteristics were of exactly the sort to give fictional probability to her strange conquest of death in the second part; (2) emphasizing throughout the theme of metempsychosis — the belief in transmigration of souls; (3) "discussing" — as he might have put it — his incidents "in such tone as best served him in establishing the preconceived effect." In making subtle use of this last device, Poe caused a series of highly suggestive words and images, associated with Ligeia in the first portion of the narrative, to prepare for and slowly build up to her weird return in the second.

This story was published in the American Museum, *September 1838, and was included in* Tales of the Grotesque and Arabesque *(1840). Since some of the revisions in the last half of the tale interestingly suggest how Poe improved his narrative, a few are pointed out in the footnotes.*

And the will therein lieth, which dieth not. Who knoweth the mysteries of the will, with its vigor? For God is but a great will pervading all things by nature of its intentness. Man doth not yield himself to the angels, nor unto death utterly, save only through the weakness of his feeble will. — JOSEPH GLANVILL

I cannot, for my soul, remember how, when, or even precisely where, I first became acquainted with the lady Ligeia. Long years have since elapsed, and my memory

---

Text: the revised version printed in the *Broadway Journal,* September 27, 1845   4 **Joseph Glanvill,** English philosopher (1636-1680), associated with the Cambridge Platonists. The quotation has not been located

is feeble through much suffering. Or, perhaps, I cannot *now* bring these points to mind, because, in truth, the character of my beloved, her rare learning, her singular yet placid cast of beauty, and the thrilling and enthralling eloquence of her low musical language, made their way into my heart by paces so steadily and stealthily progressive that they have been unnoticed and unknown. Yet I believe that I met her first and most frequently in some large, old decaying city near the Rhine. Of her family — I have surely heard her speak. That it is of a remotely ancient date cannot be doubted. Ligeia! Ligeia! Buried in studies of a nature more than all else adapted to deaden impressions of the outward world, it is by that sweet word alone — by Ligeia — that I bring before mine eyes in fancy the image of her who is no more. 10 And now, while I write, a recollection flashes upon me that I have *never known* the paternal name of her who was my friend and my betrothed, and who became the partner of my studies, and finally the wife of my bosom. Was it a playful charge on the part of my Ligeia? or was it a test of my strength of affection, that I should institute no inquiries upon this point? or was it rather a caprice of my own — a wildly romantic offering on the shrine of the most passionate devotion? I but indistinctly recall the fact myself — what wonder that I have utterly forgotten the circumstances which originated or attended it? And, indeed, if ever that spirit which is entitled *Romance* — if ever she, the wan and the misty-winged *Ashtophet* of idolatrous Egypt, presided, as they tell, over marriages ill-omened, then most surely 20 she presided over mine.

There is one dear topic, however, on which my memory fails me not. It is the *person* of Ligeia. In stature she was tall, somewhat slender, and, in her latter days, even emaciated. I would in vain attempt to portray the majesty, the quiet ease, of her demeanor, or the incomprehensible lightness and elasticity of her footfall. She came and departed as a shadow. I was never made aware of her entrance into my closed study save by the dear music of her low sweet voice, as she placed her marble hand upon my shoulder. In beauty of her face no maiden ever equalled her. It was the radiance of an opium dream — an airy and spirit-lifting vision more wildly divine than the phantasies which hovered about the slumbering souls of the daugh- 30 ters of Delos. Yet her features were not of that regular mould which we have been falsely taught to worship in the classical labors of the heathen. "There is no exquisite beauty," says Bacon, Lord Verulam, speaking truly of all the forms and *genera* of beauty, "without some *strangeness* in the proportion." Yet, although I saw that the features of Ligeia were not of a classic regularity — although I perceived that her loveliness was indeed "exquisite," and felt that there was much of "strangeness" pervading it, yet I have tried in vain to detect the irregularity and to trace home my own perception of "the strange." I examined the contour of the lofty and pale forehead — it was faultless — how cold indeed that word when applied to a majesty so divine! — the skin rivalling the purest ivory, the commanding extent and repose, 40

---

19 **Ashtophet,** probably Ashtoreth, a Canaanitish deity who, after adoption in Egypt, had the significance Poe suggests   30 **daughters of Delos,** an obscure reference, perhaps to Greek maidens who made offerings in the temple on the isle of Delos   33 **Bacon,** a slight misquotation, since Bacon's word is not "exquisite" but "excellent"

the gentle prominence of the regions above the temples; and then the raven-black, the glossy, the luxuriant and naturally-curling tresses, setting forth the full force of the Homeric epithet, "hyacinthe"! I looked at the delicate outlines of the nose — and nowhere but in the graceful medallions of the Hebrews had I beheld a similar perfection. There were the same luxurious smoothness of surface, the same scarcely perceptible tendency to the aquiline, the same harmoniously curved nostrils speaking the free spirit. I regarded the sweet mouth. Here was indeed the triumph of all things heavenly — the magnificent turn of the short upper lip — the soft, voluptuous slumber of the under — the dimples which sported, and the color which spoke — the teeth glancing back, with a brilliancy almost startling, every ray of the holy light which fell upon them in her serene and placid, yet most exultingly radiant of all smiles. I scrutinized the formation of the chin — and here, too, I found the gentleness of breadth, the softness and the majesty, the fullness and the spirituality, of the Greek — the contour which the God Apollo revealed but in a dream, to Cleomenes, the son of the Athenian. And then I peered into the large eyes of Ligeia.

For eyes we have no models in the remotely antique. It might have been, too, that in these eyes of my beloved lay the secret to which Lord Verulam alludes. They were, I must believe, far larger than the ordinary eyes of our own race. They were even fuller than the fullest of the gazelle eyes of the tribe of the valley of Nourjahad. Yet it was only at intervals — in moments of intense excitement — that this peculiarity became more than slightly noticeable in Ligeia. And at such moments was her beauty — in my heated fancy thus it appeared perhaps — the beauty of being either above or apart from the earth — the beauty of the Fabulous Houri of the Turk. The hue of the orbs was the most brilliant of black, and, far over them, hung jetty lashes of great length. The brows, slightly irregular in outline, had the same tint. The "strangeness," however, which I found in the eyes, was of a nature distinct from the formation, or the color, or the brilliancy of the features, and must, after all, be referred to the *expression*. Ah, word of no meaning! behind whose vast latitude of mere sound we intrench our ignorance of so much of the spiritual. The expression of the eyes of Ligeia! How for long hours have I pondered upon it! How have I, through the whole of a midsummer night, struggled to fathom it! What was it — that something more profound than the well of Democritus — which lay far within the pupils of my beloved? What *was* it? I was possessed with a passion to discover. Those eyes! those large, those shining, those divine orbs! they became to me twin stars of Leda, and I to them devoutest of astrologers.

There is no point, among the many incomprehensible anomalies of the science of mind, more thrillingly exciting than the fact — never, I believe, noticed in the schools — that, in our endeavors to recall to memory something long forgotten, we often

1 **gentle . . . temples,** in Poe's day, according to phrenological lore, signified "love of life"   4 **medallions . . . Hebrews,** the Roman bas-reliefs of the Jews   15 **Cleomenes,** an Athenian sculptor whose most famous work is the Venus of Medici. There is no legend of a revelation by Apollo to Cleomenes   20 **Nourjahad** refers to an Oriental novel, *The History of Nourjahad* (1767) by Mrs. Frances Sheridan   24 **Fabulous Houri,** the beautiful women who inhabit the Moslem heaven   33 **Democritus,** a Greek philosopher who said that truth lies in a deep well

find ourselves *upon the very verge* of remembrance, without being able, in the end, to remember. And thus how frequently, in my intense scrutiny of Ligeia's eyes, have I felt approaching the full knowledge of their expression — felt it approaching — yet not quite be mine — and so at length entirely depart! And (strange, oh strangest mystery of all!) I found, in the commonest objects of the universe, a circle of analogies to that expression. I mean to say that, subsequently to the period when Ligeia's beauty passed into my spirit, there dwelling as in a shrine, I derived, from many existences in the material world, a sentiment such as I felt always aroused within me by her large and luminous orbs. Yet not the more could I define that sentiment, or analyze, or even steadily view it. I recognized it, let me repeat, some- 10 times in the survey of a rapidly-growing vine — in the contemplation of a moth, a butterfly, a chrysalis, a stream of running water. I have felt it in the ocean; in the falling of a meteor. I have felt it in the glances of unusually aged people. And there are one or two stars in heaven — (one especially, a star of the sixth magnitude, double and changeable, to be found near the large star in Lyra) in a telescopic scrutiny of which I have been made aware of the feeling. I have been filled with it by certain sounds from stringed instruments, and not unfrequently by passages from books. Among innumerable other instances, I well remember something in a volume of Joseph Glanvill, which (perhaps merely from its quaintness — who shall say?) never failed to inspire me with the sentiment; — "And the will therein lieth, which dieth 20 not. Who knoweth the mysteries of the will, with its vigor? For God is but a great will pervading all things by nature of its intentness. Man doth not yield him to the angels, nor unto death utterly, save only through the weakness of his feeble will."

Length of years, and subsequent reflection, have enabled me to trace, indeed, some remote connection between this passage in the English moralist and a portion of the character of Ligeia. An *intensity* in thought, action, or speech, was possibly, in her, a result, or at least an index of that gigantic volition which, during our long intercourse, failed to give other and more immediate evidence of its existence. Of all the women whom I have ever known, she, the outwardly calm, the ever-placid Ligeia, was the most violently a prey to the tumultuous vultures of stern passion. 30 And of such passion I could form no estimate, save by the miraculous expansion of those eyes which at once so delighted and appalled me — by the almost magical melody, modulation, distinctness, and placidity of her very low voice — and by the fierce energy (rendered doubly effective by contrast with her manner of utterance) of the wild words which she habitually uttered.

I have spoken of the learning of Ligeia: it was immense — such as I have never known in woman. In the classical tongues was she deeply proficient, and as far as my own acquaintance extended in regard to the modern dialects of Europe, I have never known her at fault. Indeed upon any theme of the most admired, because simply the most abstruse of the boasted erudition of the academy, have I *ever* found 40 Ligeia at fault? How singularly — how thrillingly, this one point in the nature of my wife forced itself, at this late period only, upon my attention! I said her knowledge was such as I have never known in woman — but where breathes the man who has

---

15 **Lyra,** a constellation containing a binary star known as Epsilon Lyra

traversed, and successfully, *all* the wide areas of moral, physical, and mathematical science? I saw not then what I now clearly perceive, that the acquisitions of Ligeia were gigantic, were astounding; yet I was sufficiently aware of her infinite suprem-acy to resign myself, with a child-like confidence, to her guidance through the chaotic world of metaphysical investigation at which I was most busily occupied during the earlier years of our marriage. With how vast a triumph — with how vivid a de-light — with how much of all that is ethereal in hope — did I *feel*, as she bent over me in studies but little sought — but less known — that delicious vista by slow degrees expanding before me, down whose long, gorgeous, and all untrodden path, I might at length pass onward to the goal of a wisdom too divinely precious not to be forbidden!

How poignant, then, must have been the grief with which, after some years, I be-held my well-grounded expectations take wings to themselves and fly away! With-out Ligeia I was but as a child groping benighted. Her presence, her readings alone, rendered vividly luminous the many mysteries of the transcendentalism in which we were immersed. Wanting the radiant lustre of her eyes, letters, lambent and golden, grew duller than Saturnian lead. And now those eyes shone less and less frequently upon the pages over which I pored. Ligeia grew ill. The wild eyes blazed with a too-too glorious effulgence; the pale fingers became of the transparent waxen hue of the grave, and the blue veins upon the lofty forehead swelled and sank impetuously with the tides of the most gentle emotion. I saw that she must die — and I strug-gled desperately in spirit with the grim Azrael. And the struggles of the passionate wife were, to my astonishment, even more energetic than my own. There had been much in her stern nature to impress me with the belief that, to her, death would have come without its terrors; — but not so. Words are impotent to convey any just idea of the fierceness of resistance with which she wrestled with the Shadow. I groaned in anguish at the pitiable spectacle. I would have soothed — I would have reasoned; but, in the intensity of her wild desire for life, — for life — *but* for life — solace and reason were alike the utmost of folly. Yet not until the last instance, amid the most convulsive writhings of her fierce spirit, was shaken the external placidity of her demeanor. Her voice grew more gentle — grew more low — yet I would not wish to dwell upon the wild meaning of the quietly uttered words. My brain reeled as I hearkened entranced, to a melody more than mortal — to assumptions and aspirations which mortality had never before known.

That she loved me I should not have doubted; and I might have been easily aware that, in a bosom such as hers, love would have reigned no ordinary passion. But in death only, was I fully impressed with the strength of her affection. For long hours, detaining my hand, would she pour out before me the overflowing of a heart whose more than passionate devotion amounted to idolatry. How had I deserved to be so blessed by such confessions? — how had I deserved to be so cursed with the removal of my beloved in the hour of her making them? But upon this subject I cannot

---

15 **transcendentalism** refers less to the specific beliefs of the Concord school than to the vague, the strange in philosophy   17 **Saturnian,** pertaining to Saturn, Roman god renowned in fable as a king during a golden age   22 **Azrael,** the angel of death, who separates the soul from the body

bear to dilate. Let me say only, that in Ligeia's more than womanly abandonment to a love, alas! all unmerited, all unworthily bestowed, I at length recognized the principle of her longing with so wildly earnest a desire for the life which was now fleeing so rapidly away. It is this wild longing — it is this eager vehemence of desire for life — *but* for life — that I have no power to portray — no utterance capable of expressing.

At high noon of the night in which she departed, beckoning me, peremptorily, to her side, she bade me repeat certain verses composed by herself not many days before. I obeyed her. — They were these:

> Lo! 'tis a gala night   10
>   Within the lonesome latter years!
> An angel throng, bewinged, bedight
>   In veils, and drowned in tears,
> Sit in a theatre, to see
>   A play of hopes and fears,
> While the orchestra breathes fitfully
>   The music of the spheres.
>
> Mimes, in the form of God on high,
>   Mutter and mumble low,
> And hither and thither fly —   20
>   Mere puppets they, who come and go
> At bidding of vast formless things
>   That shift the scenery to and fro,
> Flapping from out their Condor wings
>   Invisible Woe!
>
> That motley drama! — oh, be sure
>   It shall not be forgot!
> With its Phantom chased forevermore,
>   By a crowd that seized it not,
> Through a circle that ever returneth in   30
>   To the self-same spot,
> And much of madness and more of Sin
>   And Horror the soul of the plot.

---

7 **At high noon** marks the beginning of a passage, including the poem and the two paragraphs following it, which replaced the paragraph telling of Ligeia's death in the first version of the story. This version read: "Methinks I again behold the terrific struggles of her lofty, her nearly idealized nature, with the might and terror, and the majesty, of the great Shadow. But she perished. The giant *will* succumbed to a power more stern. And I thought, as I gazed upon the corpse, of the wild passage in Joseph Glanville: 'The will therein lieth, which dieth not. Who knoweth the mysteries of the will, with its vigor? For God is but a great will pervading all things by the nature of its intentness. Man doth not yield him to the angels, *nor unto death utterly,* save only through the weakness of his feeble will'"

> But see, amid the mimic rout,
>   A crawling shape intrude!
> A blood-red thing that writhes from out
>   The scenic solitude!
> It writhes! — it writhes! — with mortal pangs
>   The mimes become its food,
> And the seraphs sob at vermin fangs
>   In human gore imbued.
>
> Out — out are the lights — out all!
>   And over each quivering form,
> The curtain, a funeral pall,
>   Comes down with the rush of a storm,
> And the angels, all pallid and wan,
>   Uprising, unveiling, affirm
> That the play is the tragedy, "Man,"
>   And its hero the Conqueror Worm.

"O God!" half shrieked Ligeia, leaping to her feet and extending her arms aloft with a spasmodic movement, as I made an end of these lines — "O God! O Divine Father! — shall these things be undeviatingly so? — shall this Conqueror be not once conquered? Are we not part and parcel of Thee? Who — who knoweth the mysteries of the will with its vigor? Man doth not yield him to the angels, *nor unto death utterly* save only through the weakness of his feeble will."

And now, as if exhausted with emotion, she suffered her white arms to fall, and returned solemnly to her bed of death. And as she breathed her last sighs, there came mingled with them a low murmur from her lips. I bent to them my ear and distinguished, again, the concluding words of the passage in Glanvill — *"Man doth not yield him to the angels, nor unto death utterly, save only through the weakness of his feeble will."*

She died; — and I, crushed into the very dust with sorrow, could no longer endure the lonely desolation of my dwelling in the dim and decaying city by the Rhine. I had no lack of what the world calls wealth. Ligeia had brought me far more, very far more than ordinarily falls to the lot of mortals. After a few months, therefore, of weary and aimless wandering, I purchased, and put in some repair, an abbey, which I shall not name, in one of the wildest and least frequented portions of fair England. The gloomy and dreary grandeur of the building, the almost savage aspect of the domain, the many melancholy and time-honored memories connected with both, had much in unison with the feelings of utter abandonment which had driven me into that remote and unsocial region of the country. Yet although the external abbey, with its verdant decay hanging about it, suffered but little alteration, I gave way, with a childlike perversity, and perchance with a faint hope of alleviating my sorrows, to a display of more than regal magnificence within. — For such follies, even in childhood, I had imbibed a taste and now they came back to me as if in the dotage of grief. Alas, I feel how much even of incipient madness might have been discovered in the gorgeous and fantastic draperies, in the solemn carvings of Egypt, in the wild cornices and furniture, in the Bedlam patterns of the carpets of tufted gold! I had become a bounden slave in the trammels of opium, and my labors and my orders had taken a coloring from my dreams. But these absurdities I must not pause to detail. Let me speak only of that one chamber, ever accursed, whither in a moment of mental alienation, I led from the altar as my bride — as the successor of the unforgotten Ligeia — the fair-haired and blue-eyed Lady Rowena Trevanion, of Tremaine.

There is no individual portion of the architecture and decoration of that bridal 10 chamber which is not now visibly before me. Where were the souls of the haughty family of the bride, when, through thirst of gold, they permitted to pass the threshold of an apartment *so* bedecked, a maiden and a daughter so beloved? I have said that I minutely remember the details of the chamber — yet I am sadly forgetful on topics of deep moment — and here there was no system, no keeping, in the fantastic display, to take hold upon the memory. The room lay in a high turret of the castellated abbey, was pentagonal in shape, and of capacious size. Occupying the whole southern face of the pentagon was the sole window — an immense sheet of unbroken glass from Venice — a single pane, and tinted of a leaden hue, so that the rays of either the sun or moon, passing through it, fell with a ghastly lustre on the objects 20 within. Over the upper portion of this huge window, extended the trellis-work of an aged vine, which clambered up the massy walls of the turret. The ceiling, of gloomy-looking oak, was excessively lofty, vaulted, and elaborately fretted with the wildest and most grotesque specimens of a semi-Gothic, semi-Druidical device. From out the most central recess of this melancholy vaulting, depended, by a single chain of gold with long links, a huge censer of the same metal, Saracenic in pattern, and with many perforations so contrived that there writhed in and out of them, as if endued with a serpent vitality, a continual succession of parti-colored fires.

Some few ottomans and golden candelabra, of Eastern figure, were in various stations about — and there was the couch, too — the bridal couch — of an Indian model, 30 and low, and sculptured of solid ebony, with a pall-like canopy above. In each of the angles of the chamber stood on end a gigantic sarcophagus of black granite, from the tombs of the kings over against Luxor, with their aged lids full of immemorial sculpture. But in draping of the apartment lay, alas! the chief phantasy of all. The lofty walls, gigantic in height — even unproportionably so — were hung from summit to foot, in vast folds, with a heavy and massive-looking tapestry — tapestry of a material which was found alike as a carpet on the floor, as a covering for the ottomans and the ebony bed, as a canopy for the bed, and as the gorgeous volutes of the curtains which partially shaded the window. The material was the richest cloth of gold. It was spotted all over, at irregular intervals, with arabesque 40 figures, about a foot in diameter, and wrought upon the cloth in patterns of the

---

3 **Bedlam,** insane; derived from Bedlam, an asylum in London   31 **pall-like,** added to the earlier version, which spoke simply of "a canopy"   33 **Luxor,** a center of archaeological research near Thebes

most jetty black. But these figures partook of the true character of the arabesque only when regarded from a single point of view. By a contrivance now common, and indeed traceable to a very remote period of antiquity, they were made changeable in aspect. To one entering the room, they bore the appearance of simple monstrosities; but upon a farther advance, this appearance gradually departed; and step by step, as the visitor moved his station in the chamber, he saw himself surrounded by an endless succession of the ghastly forms which belong to the superstition of the Norman, or arise in the guilty slumbers of the monk. The phantasmagoric effect was vastly heightened by the artificial introduction of a strong continual current of
10 wind behind the draperies — giving a hideous and uneasy animation to the whole.

In halls such as these — in a bridal chamber such as this — I passed, with the lady of Tremaine, the unhallowed hours of the first month of our marriage — passed them with but little disquietude. That my wife dreaded the fierce moodiness of my temper — that she shunned me and loved me but little — I could not help perceiving; but it gave me rather pleasure than otherwise. I loathed her with a hatred belonging more to demon than to man. My memory flew back (oh, with what intensity of regret!) to Ligeia, the beloved, the august, the beautiful, the entombed. I revelled in recollections of her purity, of her wisdom, of her lofty, her ethereal nature, of her passionate, her idolatrous love. Now, then, did my spirit fully and freely burn
20 with more than all the fires of her own. In the excitement of my opium dreams (for I was habitually fettered in the shackles of the drug) I would call aloud upon her name, during the silence of the night, or among the sheltered recesses of the glens by day, as if, through the wild eagerness, the solemn passion, the consuming ardor of my longing for the departed, I could restore her to the pathway she had abandoned — ah, *could* it be forever? — upon the earth.

About the commencement of the second month of the marriage, the Lady Rowena was attacked with sudden illness, from which her recovery was slow. The fever which consumed her rendered her nights uneasy; and in her perturbed state of half-slumber, she spoke of sounds, and of motions in and about the chamber of the tur-
30 ret, which I concluded had no origin save in the distemper of her fancy, or perhaps in the phantasmagoric influences of the chamber itself. She became at length convalescent — finally well. Yet but a brief period elapsed, ere a second more violent disorder again threw her upon a bed of suffering; and from this attack her frame, at all times feeble, never altogether recovered. Her illnesses were, after this epoch, of alarming character, and of more alarming recurrence, defying alike the knowledge and the great exertions of her physicians. With the increase of the chronic disease which had thus, apparently, taken too sure hold upon her constitution to be eradicated by human means, I could not fail to observe a similar increase in the nervous irritation of her temperament, and in her excitability by trivial causes of fear. She
40 spoke again, and now more frequently and pertinaciously, of the sounds — of the

---

17 **the august,** added in the later version   39 **fear,** followed in the earlier version with the sentence, "Indeed reason seemed fast tottering from her throne." By cutting out the sentence, Poe casts less doubt upon the perceptions of Lady Rowena, thus more effectively preparing for the reincarnation of Ligeia

slight sounds — and of the unusual motions among the tapestries, to which she had formerly alluded.

One night, near the closing in of September, she pressed this distressing subject with more than usual emphasis upon my attention. She had just awakened from an unquiet slumber, and I had been watching, with feelings half of anxiety, half of vague terror, the workings of her emaciated countenance. I sat by the side of her ebony bed, upon one of the ottomans of India. She partly arose, and spoke, in an earnest low whisper, of sounds which she *then* heard, but which I could not hear — and of motions which she *then* saw, but which I could not perceive. The wind was rushing hurriedly behind the tapestries, and I wished to show her (what, let me confess it, I could not *all* believe) that those almost inarticulate breathings, and those very gentle variations of the figures upon the wall, were but the natural effects of that customary rushing of the wind. But a deadly pallor, overspreading her face, had proved to me that my exertions to reassure her would be fruitless. She appeared to be fainting, and no attendants were within call. I remembered where was deposited a decanter of light wine which had been ordered by her physicians, and hastened across the chamber to procure it. But, as I stepped beneath the light of the censer, two circumstances of a startling nature attracted my attention. I had felt that some palpable although invisible object had passed lightly by my person; and I saw that there lay upon the golden carpet, in the very middle of the rich lustre thrown from the censer, a shadow — a faint, indefinite shadow of angelic aspect — such as might be fancied for the shadow of a shade. But I was wild with the excitement of an immoderate dose of opium, and heeded these things but little, nor spoke of them to Rowena. Having found the wine, I recrossed the chamber and poured out a gobletful, which I held to the lips of the fainting lady. She had now partially recovered, however, and took the vessel herself, while I sank upon an ottoman near me, with my eyes fastened upon her person. It was then that I became distinctly aware of a gentle foot-fall upon the carpet, and near the couch; and in a second thereafter, as Rowena was in the act of raising the wine to her lips, I saw, or may have dreamed that I saw, fall within the goblet, as if from some invisible spring in the atmosphere of the room, three or four large drops of a brilliant and ruby colored fluid. If this I saw — not so Rowena. She swallowed the wine unhesitatingly, and I forbore to speak to her of a circumstance which must, after all, I considered, have been but the suggestion of a vivid imagination, rendered morbidly active by the terror of the lady, by the opium, and by the hour.

Yet I cannot conceal it from my own perception that, immediately subsequent to the fall of the ruby-drops, a rapid change for the worse took place in the disorder of my wife; so that, on the third subsequent night, the hands of her menials prepared her for the tomb, and on the fourth, I sat alone, with her shrouded body, in that fantastic chamber which had received her as my bride. Wild visions, opium-engendered, flitted, shadow-like, before me. I gazed with unquiet eye upon the sarcophagi in the angles of the room, upon the varying figures of the drapery, and upon the writhing of the parti-colored fires in the censer overhead. My eyes then fell, as I called to mind the circumstances of a former night, to the spot beneath the glare of the censer where I had seen the faint traces of the shadow. It was there, however, no longer; and breathing with greater freedom, I turned my glances to the pallid and rigid figure upon the bed. Then rushed upon me a thousand memories of Ligeia — and then came back upon my heart, with the turbulent violence of a flood, the whole of that unutterable woe with which I had regarded *her* thus enshrouded. The night waned; and still, with a bosom full of bitter thoughts of the one only and supremely beloved, I remained gazing upon the body of Rowena.

It might have been midnight, or perhaps earlier, or later, for I had taken no note of time, when a sob, low, gentle, but very distinct, startled me from my revery. — I
10 *felt* that it came from the bed of ebony — the bed of death. I listened in an agony of superstitious terror — but there was no repetition of the sound. I strained my vision to detect any motion in the corpse — but there was not the slightest perceptible. Yet I could not have been deceived. I *had* heard the noise, however faint, and my soul was awakened within me. I resolutely and perseveringly kept my attention riveted upon the body. Many minutes elapsed before any circumstance occurred tending to throw light upon the mystery. At length it became evident that a slight, a very feeble, and barely noticeable tinge of color had flushed up within the cheeks, and along the sunken small veins of the eyelids. Through a species of unutterable horror and awe, for which the language of mortality has no sufficiently energetic
20 expression, I felt my heart cease to beat, my limbs grow rigid where I sat. Yet a sense of duty finally operated to restore my self-possession. I could no longer doubt that we had been precipitate in our preparations — that Rowena still lived. It was necessary that some immediate exertion be made; yet the turret was altogether apart from the portion of the abbey tenanted by the servants — there were none within call — I had no means of summoning them to my aid without leaving the room for many minutes — and this I could not venture to do. I therefore struggled alone in my endeavors to call back the spirit still hovering. In a short period it was certain, however, that a relapse had taken place; the color disappeared from both eyelid and cheek, leaving a wanness even more than that of marble; the lips became doubly
30 shrivelled and pinched up in the ghastly expression of death; a repulsive clamminess and coldness overspread rapidly the surface of the body; and all the usual rigorous stiffness immediately supervened. I fell back with a shudder upon the couch from which I had been so startlingly aroused, and again gave myself up to passionate waking visions of Ligeia.

An hour thus elapsed when (could it be possible?) I was a second time aware of some vague sound issuing from the region of the bed. I listened — in extremity of horror. The sound came again — it was a sigh. Rushing to the corpse, I saw — distinctly saw — a tremor upon the lips. In a minute afterward they relaxed, disclosing a bright line of the pearly teeth. Amazement now struggled in my bosom with the
40 profound awe which had hitherto reigned there alone. I felt that my vision grew dim, that my reason wandered; and it was only by a violent effort that I at length succeeded in nerving myself to the task which duty thus once more had pointed out. There was now a partial glow upon the forehead and upon the cheek and throat; a perceptible warmth pervaded the whole frame; there was even a slight pulsation at

the heart. The lady *lived;* and with redoubled ardor I betook myself to the task of restoration. I chafed and bathed the temples and the hands, and used every exertion which experience, and no little medical reading, could suggest. But in vain. Suddenly, the color fled, the pulsation ceased, the lips resumed the expression of the dead, and in an instant afterward, the whole body took upon itself the icy chilliness, the livid hue, the intense rigidity, the sunken outline, and all the loathsome peculiarities of that which has been, for many days, a tenant of the tomb.

And again I sunk into visions of Ligeia — and again (what marvel that I shudder while I write?), *again* there reached my ears a low sob from the region of the ebony bed. But why shall I minutely detail the unspeakable horrors of that night? Why 10 shall I pause to relate how, time after time, until near the period of the gray dawn, this hideous drama of revivification was repeated; how each terrific relapse was only into a sterner and apparently more irredeemable death; how each agony wore the aspect of a struggle with some invisible foe; and how each struggle was succeeded by I know not what wild change in the personal appearance of the corpse? Let me hurry to a conclusion.

The greater part of the fearful night had worn away, and she who had been dead, once again stirred — and now more vigorously than hitherto, although arousing from a dissolution more appalling in its utter hopelessness than any. I had long ceased to struggle or to move, and remained sitting rigidly upon the ottoman, a 20 helpless prey to a whirl of violent emotions, of which extreme awe was perhaps the least terrible, the least consuming. The corpse, I repeat, stirred and now more vigorously than before. The hues of life flushed up with unwonted energy into the countenance — the limbs relaxed — and, save that the eyelids were yet pressed heavily together, and that the bandages and draperies of the grave still imparted their charnel character to the figure, I might have dreamed that Rowena had indeed shaken off, utterly, the fetters of Death. But if this idea was not, even then, altogether adopted, I could at least doubt no longer, when arising from the bed, tottering, with feeble steps, with closed eyes, and with the manner of one bewildered in a dream, the thing that was enshrouded advanced boldly and palpably into the mid- 30 dle of the apartment.

I trembled not — I stirred not — for a crowd of unutterable fancies connected with the air, the stature, the demeanor of the figure, rushing hurriedly through my brain, had paralyzed — had chilled me into stone. I stirred not — but gazed upon the apparition. There was a mad disorder in my thoughts — a tumult unappeasable. Could it, indeed, be the *living* Rowena who confronted me? Could it indeed be Rowena *at all* — the fair-haired, the blue-eyed Lady Rowena Trevanion of Tremaine? Why, *why* should I doubt it? The bandage lay heavily about the mouth

---

13 **how each agony,** and the remainder of this sentence, did not appear in the earlier version   17 **she . . . dead,** in the later version, replaced "the corpse of Rowena." By making this change and the one next noted, Poe prepared for the reappearance of Ligeia by using ambiguous words to refer to the corpse   30 **the thing . . . enshrouded,** in the later version, replaced "the Lady of Tremaine" in the earlier   33 **the stature,** added in the second version, perhaps to indicate more definitely that the change had taken place   36 **Could it indeed,** and the rest of this sentence, added in the revised version. This change emphasizes the contrast, which now becomes important

— but then might it not be the mouth of the breathing Lady of Tremaine? And the cheeks — there were the roses as in her noon of life — yes, these might indeed be the fair cheeks of the living Lady of Tremaine. And the chin, with its dimples, as in health, might it not be hers? — but *had she then grown taller since her malady?* What inexpressible madness seized me with that thought? One bound, and I had reached her feet! Shrinking from my touch, she let fall from her head, unloosened, the ghastly cerements which had confined it, and there streamed forth, into the rushing atmosphere of the chamber, huge masses of long and dishevelled hair; *it was blacker than the raven wings of the midnight!* And now slowly opened *the eyes* of
10 the figure which stood before me. "Here then, at least," I shrieked aloud, "never can I be mistaken — these are the full, and the black, and the wild eyes — of my lost love — of the lady — of the LADY LIGEIA!"

1838, 1845

The Man of the Crowd

This story was published in the December 1840 issue of Burton's Gentleman's Magazine *and was slightly revised for inclusion in* Tales of the Grotesque and Arabesque *in 1845. It has interesting resemblances to Hawthorne's "Wakefield" (1835) and Melville's "Bartleby the Scrivener" (1853) which also portray men enigmatically and irretrievably alienated by some deep psychic necessity from human fellowship. (Hawthorne calls Wakefield an "Outcast of the Universe.") Anticipating the many portrayals in recent fiction of nonentities inexplicably lost in the mass of humanity, it is a story which has of late been increasingly appreciated. Modern critics also find it interesting because of Poe's handling of the point of view in a way essential to the development of his theme. The narrator has perceptivity, ratiocinative powers, and sensitivity similar to those which Poe would assign to his great detective Dupin a year later. But when this narrator tries to comprehend the one man in the milling London throng whose nature he is unable to fathom immediately, although he follows him closely through nightmare streets from dusk to dawn, he is driven to conclude that the man is still an enigma. The enigma is one of hidden sin, guilt, loss of will, and alienation. And the narrator, too, commands attention because his feverish interest in his quarry, as well as other details in his narrative, imply that his journey through the darkness is motivated by a desire for self discovery.*

Ce grand malheur, de ne pouvoir être seul.

La Bruyère

It was well said of a certain German book that *"es lässt sich nicht lesen"* — it does not permit itself to be read. There are some secrets which do not permit themselves to be told. Men die nightly in their beds, wringing the hands of ghostly confessors, and looking them piteously in the eyes — die with despair of heart and convulsion

---

1 **Ce grand malheur.** . . . The great misfortune, to be unable to be alone. Jean de La Bruyere (1645-1696), the French moralist, is slightly misquoted but his sense is not distorted

of throat, on account of the hideousness of mysteries which will not *suffer themselves* to be revealed. Now and then, alas, the conscience of man takes up a burden so heavy in horror that it can be thrown down only into the grave. And thus the essence of all crime is undivulged.

Not long ago, about the closing in of an evening in autumn, I sat at the large bow window of the D——Coffee-House in London. For some months I had been ill in health, but was now convalescent, and, with returning strength, found myself in one of those happy moods which are so precisely the converse of *ennui* — moods of the keenest appetency, when the film from the mental vision departs — the ἀχλὺς ἣ πρὶν ἐπῆεν — and the intellect, electrified, surpasses as greatly its every- 10 day condition, as does the vivid yet candid reason of Leibnitz, the mad and flimsy rhetoric of Gorgias. Merely to breathe was enjoyment; and I derived positive pleasure even from many of the legitimate sources of pain. I felt a calm but inquisitive interest in every thing. With a cigar in my mouth and a newspaper in my lap, I had been amusing myself for the greater part of the afternoon, now in poring over advertisements, now in observing the promiscuous company in the room, and now in peering through the smoky panes into the street.

This latter is one of the principal thoroughfares of the city, and had been very much crowded during the whole day. But, as the darkness came on, the throng momently increased; and, by the time the lamps were well lighted, two dense and con- 20 tinuous tides of population were rushing past the door. At this particular period of the evening I had never before been in a similar situation, and the tumultuous sea of human heads filled me, therefore, with a delicious novelty of emotion. I gave up, at length, all care of things within the hotel, and became absorbed in contemplation of the scene without.

At first my observations took an abstract and generalizing turn. I looked at the passengers in masses, and thought of them in their aggregate relations. Soon, however, I descended to details, and regarded with minute interest the innumerable varieties of figure, dress, air, gait, visage, and expression of countenance.

By far the greater number of those who went by had a satisfied business-like de- 30 meanor, and seemed to be thinking only of making their way through the press. Their brows were knit, and their eyes rolled quickly; when pushed against by fellow-wayfarers they evinced no symptom of impatience, but adjusted their clothes and hurried on. Others, still a numerous class, were restless in their movements, had flushed faces, and talked and gesticulated to themselves, as if feeling in solitude on account of the very denseness of the company around. When impeded in their progress, these people suddenly ceased muttering, but redoubled their gesticulations, and awaited, with an absent and overdone smile upon the lips, the course of the persons impeding them. If jostled, they bowed profusely to the jostlers, and appeared overwhelmed with confusion. — There was nothing very distinctive about these two 40 large classes beyond what I have noted. Their habiliments belonged to that order

---

9 **the . . . 'επῆεν**, the mist that before was upon it, from the *Iliad,* Bk. V, 1. 127   11 **Leibnitz,** Baron Gottfried Wilhelm von Leibnitz (1646-1716), German philosopher and mathematician   12 **Gorgias** (c. 483-376 B.C.), Sicilian rhetorician

which is pointedly termed the decent. They were undoubtedly noblemen, merchants, attorneys, tradesmen, stock-jobbers — the Eupatrids and the commonplaces of society — men of leisure and men actively engaged in affairs of their own — conducting business upon their own responsibility. They did not greatly excite my attention.

The tribe of clerks was an obvious one; and here I discerned two remarkable divisions. There were the junior clerks of flash houses — young gentlemen with tight coats, bright boots, well-oiled hair, and supercilious lips. Setting aside a certain dapperness of carriage, which may be termed *deskism* for want of a better word,
10 the manner of these persons seemed to me an exact facsimile of what had been the perfection of *bon ton* about twelve or eighteen months before. They wore the cast-off graces of the gentry; — and this, I believe, involves the best definition of the class.

The division of the upper clerks of staunch firms, or of the "steady old fellows," it was not possible to mistake. These were known by their coats and pantaloons of black or brown, made to sit comfortably, with white cravats and waistcoats, broad solid-looking shoes, and thick hose or gaiters. — They had all slightly bald heads, from which the right ears, long used to pen-holding, had an odd habit of standing off on end. I observed that they always removed or settled their hats with both hands, and wore watches, with short gold chains of a substantial and ancient pat-
20 tern. Theirs was the affectation of respectability; — if indeed there be an affectation so honorable.

There were many individuals of dashing appearance, whom I easily understood as belonging to the race of swell pick-pockets, with which all great cities are infested. I watched these gentry with much inquisitiveness, and found it difficult to imagine how they should ever be mistaken for gentlemen by gentlemen themselves. Their voluminousness of wristband, with an air of excessive frankness, should betray them at once.

The gamblers, of whom I descried not a few, were still more easily recognisable. They wore every variety of dress, from that of the desperate thimble-rig bully, with
30 velvet waistcoat, fancy neckerchief, gilt chains, and filigreed buttons, to that of the scrupulously inornate clergyman than which nothing could be less liable to suspicion. Still all were distinguished by a certain sodden swarthiness of complexion, a filmy dimness of eye, and pallor and compression of lip. There were two other traits, moreover, by which I could always detect them; — a guarded lowness of tone in conversation, and a more than ordinary extension of the thumb in a direction at right angles with the fingers. — Very often, in company with these sharpers, I observed an order of men somewhat different in habits, but still birds of a kindred feather. They may be defined as the gentlemen who live by their wits. They seem to prey upon the public in two battalions — that of the dandies and that of the
40 military men. Of the first grade the leading features are long locks and smiles; of the second, frogged coats and frowns.

---

2 **Eupatrids,** sons of noble fathers, the ancient nobility of Attica in Greece   29 **thimble-rig,** a swindling game in which the cheat fools the spectator by deftly shifting a pea or small ball from under one of three cups and bets the dupe he cannot locate the pea

Descending in the scale of what is termed gentility, I found darker and deeper themes for speculation. I saw Jew pedlars, with hawk eyes flashing from countenances whose every other feature wore only an expression of abject humility; sturdy professional street beggars scowling upon mendicants of a better stamp, whom despair alone had driven forth into the night for charity; feeble and ghastly invalids, upon whom death had placed a sure hand, and who sidled and tottered through the mob, looking every one beseechingly in the face, as if in search of some chance consolation, some lost hope; modest young girls returning from long and late labor to a cheerless home, and shrinking more tearfully than indignantly from the glances of ruffians, whose direct contact, even, could not be avoided; women of the town of   10
all kinds and of all ages — the unequivocal beauty in the prime of her womanhood, putting one in mind of the statue in Lucian, with the surface of Parian marble, and the interior filled with filth — the loathsome and utterly lost leper in rags — the wrinkled, bejewelled and paint-begrimed beldame, making a last effort at youth — the mere child of immature form, yet, from long association, an adept in the dreadful coquetries of her trade, and burning with a rabid ambition to be ranked the equal of her elders in vice; drunkards innumerable and indescribable — some in shreds and patches, reeling, inarticulate, with bruised visage and lacklustre eyes — some in whole although filthy garments, with a slightly unsteady swagger, thick sensual lips, and hearty-looking rubicund faces — others clothed in materials which   20
had once been good, and which even now were scrupulously well brushed — men who walked with a more than naturally firm and springy step, but whose countenances were fearfully pale, whose eyes were hideously wild and red, and who clutched with quivering fingers, as they strode through the crowd, at every object which came within their reach; beside these, pie-men, porters, coal-heavers, sweeps; organ-grinders, monkey-exhibitors and ballad-mongers, those who vended with those who sang; ragged artizans and exhausted laborers of every description, and all full of a noisy and inordinate vivacity which jarred discordantly upon the ear, and gave an aching sensation to the eye.

As the night deepened, so deepened to me the interest of the scene; for not only   30
did the general character of the crowd materially alter (its gentler features retiring in the gradual withdrawal of the more orderly portion of the people, and its harsher ones coming out into bolder relief, as the late hour brought forth every species of infamy from its den,) but the rays of the gas-lamps, feeble at first in their struggle with the dying day, had now at length gained ascendancy, and threw over every thing a fitful and garish lustre. All was dark yet splendid — as that ebony to which has been likened the style of Tertullian.

The wild effects of the light enchained me to an examination of individual faces; and although the rapidity with which the world of light flitted before the window, prevented me from casting more than a glance upon each visage, still it seemed that,   40
in my then peculiar mental state, I could frequently read, even in that brief interval of a glance, the history of long years.

---

12 **Lucian** (2nd century A.D.), Greek satirist   37 **Tertullian** (160?-230? A.D.), a church father noted as a Latin stylist

With my brow to the glass, I was thus occupied in scrutinizing the mob, when suddenly there came into view a countenance (that of a decrepid old man, some sixty-five or seventy years of age,) — a countenance which at once arrested and absorbed my whole attention, on account of the absolute idiosyncrasy of its expression. Any thing even remotely resembling that expression I had never seen before. I well remember that my first thought, upon beholding it, was that Retszch, had he viewed it, would have greatly preferred it to his own pictural incarnations of the fiend. As I endeavored, during the brief minute of my original survey, to form some analysis of the meaning conveyed, there arose confusedly and paradoxically

10 within my mind, the ideas of vast mental power, of caution, of penuriousness, of avarice, of coolness, of malice, of blood-thirstiness, of triumph, of merriment, of excessive terror, of intense — of extreme despair. I felt singularly aroused, startled, fascinated. "How wild a history," I said to myself, "is written within that bosom!" Then came a craving desire to keep the man in view — to know more of him. Hurriedly putting on an overcoat, and seizing my hat and cane, I made my way into the street, and pushed through the crowd in the direction which I had seen him take; for he had already disappeared. With some little difficulty I at length came within sight of him, approached, and followed him closely, yet cautiously, so as not to attract his attention.

20 I had now a good opportunity of examining his person. He was short in stature, very thin, and apparently very feeble. His clothes, generally, were filthy and ragged; but as he came, now and then, within the strong glare of a lamp, I perceived that his linen, although dirty, was of beautiful texture; and my vision deceived me, or, through a rent in a closely-buttoned and evidently second-hand *roquelaire* which enveloped him, I caught a glimpse both of a diamond and of a dagger. These observations heightened my curiosity, and I resolved to follow the stranger whithersoever he should go.

It was now fully night-fall, and a thick humid fog hung over the city, soon ending in a settled and heavy rain. This change of weather had an odd effect upon the

30 crowd, the whole of which was at once put into new commotion, and overshadowed by a world of umbrellas. The waver, the jostle, and the hum increased in a tenfold degree. For my own part I did not much regard the rain — the lurking of an old fever in my system rendering the moisture somewhat too dangerously pleasant. Tying a handkerchief about my mouth, I kept on. For half an hour the old man held his way with difficulty along the great thoroughfare; and I here walked close at his elbow through fear of losing sight of him. Never once turning his head to look back, he did not observe me. By and bye he passed into a cross street, which, although densely filled with people, was not quite so much thronged as the main one he had quitted. Here a change in his demeanor became evident. He walked

40 more slowly and with less object than before — more hesitatingly. He crossed and re-crossed the way repeatedly without apparent aim; and the press was still so thick, that, at every such movement, I was obliged to follow him closely. The street was

---

6 **Retszch,** Moritz Retszch (1779-1857), German artist who illustrated Goethe's *Faust*   24 **roquelaire,** a knee-length cloak

a narrow and long one, and his course lay within it for nearly an hour, during which
the passengers had gradually diminished to about that number which is ordinarily
seen at noon on Broadway near the Park — so vast a difference is there between a
London populace and that of the most frequented American city. A second turn
brought us into a square, brilliantly lighted, and overflowing with life. The old
manner of the stranger reappeared. His chin fell upon his breast, while his eyes
rolled wildly from under his knit brows, in every direction, upon those who hemmed
him in. He urged his way steadily and perseveringly. I was surprised, however, to
find, upon his having made the circuit of the square, that he turned and retraced
his steps. Still more was I astonished to see him repeat the same walk several times   10
— once nearly detecting me as he came round with a sudden movement.

In this exercise he spent another hour, at the end of which we met with far less
interruption from passengers than at first. The rain fell fast; the air grew cool; and
the people were retiring to their homes. With a gesture of impatience, the wanderer
passed into a by-street comparatively deserted. Down this, some quarter of a mile
long, he rushed with an activity I could not have dreamed of seeing in one so aged,
and which put me to much trouble in pursuit. A few minutes brought us to a large
and busy bazaar, with the localities of which the stranger appeared well acquainted,
and where his original demeanor again became apparent, as he forced his way to
and fro, without aim, among the host of buyers and sellers.   20

During the hour and a half, or thereabouts, which we passed in this place, it required much caution on my part to keep him within reach without attracting his
observation. Luckily I wore a pair of caoutchouc over-shoes, and could move about
in perfect silence. At no moment did he see that I watched him. He entered shop
after shop, priced nothing, spoke no word, and looked at all objects with a wild
and vacant stare. I was now utterly amazed at his behaviour, and firmly resolved
that we should not part until I had satisfied myself in some measure respecting him.

A loud-toned clock struck eleven, and the company were fast deserting the bazaar.
A shop-keeper, in putting up a shutter, jostled the old man, and at the instant I saw a
strong shudder come over his frame. He hurried into the street, looked anxiously   30
around him for an instant, and then ran with incredible swiftness through many
crooked and people-less lanes, until we emerged once more upon the great thoroughfare whence we had started — the street of the D—— Hotel. It no longer wore,
however, the same aspect. It was still brilliant with gas; but the rain fell fiercely,
and there were few persons to be seen. The stranger grew pale. He walked moodily
some paces up the once populous avenue, then, with a heavy sigh, turned in the
direction of the river, and, plunging through a great variety of devious ways, came
out, at length, in view of one of the principal theatres. It was about being closed,
and the audience were thronging from the doors. I saw the old man gasp as if for
breath while he threw himself amid the crowd; but I thought that the intense   40
agony of his countenance had, in some measure, abated. His head again fell upon
his breast; he appeared as I had seen him at first. I observed that he now took the

---

23 **caoutchouc,** rubber

course in which had gone the greater number of the audience — but, upon the whole, I was at a loss to comprehend the waywardness of his actions.

As he proceeded, the company grew more scattered, and his old uneasiness and vacillation were resumed. For some time he followed closely a party of some ten or twelve roisterers; but from this number one by one dropped off, until three only remained together, in a narrow and gloomy lane little frequented. The stranger paused, and, for a moment, seemed lost in thought; then, with every mark of agitation, pursued rapidly a route which brought us to the verge of the city, amid regions very different from those we had hitherto traversed. It was the most noisome
10 quarter of London, where everything wore the worst impress of the most deplorable poverty, and of the most desperate crime. By the dim light of an accidental lamp, tall, antique, worm-eaten, wooden tenements were seen tottering to their fall, in directions so many and capricious that scarce the semblance of a passage was discernible between them. The paving-stones lay at random, displaced from their beds by the rankly growing grass. Horrible filth festered in the dammed-up gutters. The whole atmosphere teemed with desolation. Yet, as we proceeded, the sounds of human life revived by sure degrees, and at length large bands of the most abandoned of a London populace were seen reeling to and fro. The spirits of the old man again flickered up, as a lamp which is near its death-hour. Once more he strode onward
20 with elastic tread. Suddenly a corner was turned, a blaze of light burst upon our sight, and we stood before one of the huge suburban temples of Intemperance — one of the palaces of the fiend, Gin.

It was now nearly day-break; but a number of wretched inebriates still pressed in and out of the flaunting entrance. With a half shriek of joy the old man forced a passage within, resumed at once his original bearing, and stalked backward and forward, without apparent object, among the throng. He had not been thus long occupied, however, before a rush to the doors gave token that the host was closing them for the night. It was something even more intense than despair that I then observed upon the countenance of the singular being whom I had watched so
30 pertinaciously. Yet he did not hesitate in his career, but, with a mad energy, retraced his steps at once, to the heart of the mighty London. Long and swiftly he fled, while I followed him in the wildest amazement, resolute not to abandon a scrutiny in which I now felt an interest all-absorbing. The sun arose while we proceeded, and, when we had once again reached that most thronged mart of the populous town, the street of the D—— Hotel, it presented an appearance of human bustle and activity scarcely inferior to what I had seen on the evening before. And here, long, amid the momently increasing confusion, did I persist in my pursuit of the stranger. But, as usual, he walked to and fro, and during the day did not pass from out the turmoil of that street. And, as the shades of the second eve-
40 ning came on, I grew wearied unto death, and, stopping fully in front of the wanderer, gazed at him steadfastly in the face. He noticed me not, but resumed his solemn walk, while I, ceasing to follow, remained absorbed in contemplation. "This old man," I said at length, "is the type and the genius of deep crime. He refuses to be alone. *He is the man of the crowd.* It will be in vain to follow; for I shall learn

no more of him, nor of his deeds. The worst heart of the world is a grosser book than the 'Hortulus Animæ,' and perhaps it is but one of the great mercies of God that *'es lässt sich nicht lesen.'* "   1840, 1845

2 **"Hortulus Animæ,"** identified by Poe as *Hortulus Animæ cum Oratiumculus Aliquibus Superadditis* (Little Garden of the Soul), published by Johannes Grünninger, a Strasbourg printer in 1500   3 "es lässt. . . ." it doesn't allow itself to be read

The Murders in the Rue Morgue

Mr. Howard Haycraft, in his history of detective fiction, Murder for Pleasure, *calls this "the world's first detective story," and in 1941 many authors and lovers of this kind of narrative paid a centenary tribute to Poe as the inventor of the form. Besides originating the general form, in his experiment Poe originated practically all the important technical devices constantly used in narratives of crime and detection. Among such devices, Mr. Haycraft lists "the transcendent and eccentric detective; the admiring and slightly stupid foil; the well-intentioned blundering and unimaginativeness of the official guardians of the law; the locked room convention; the pointing finger of unjust suspicion; the solution by surprise; deduction by putting one's self in another's position (now called psychology); concealment by means of the ultra-obvious; the staged ruse to force the culprit's hand; even the expansive and condescending explanation when the chase is done."*

The technique of the story is clearly related to that of Poe's horror stories. Here, too, events have an effect upon a sympathetic character, the narrator, and supposedly a similar effect upon the reader. Here, however, the events — Dupin's acts and deductions — presumably have their chief effect not on the "soul" or "heart" but on the "mind." The rather slow start, with its emphasis upon the deductive process, is therefore appropriate.

What song the Syrens sang, or what name Achilles assumed when he hid himself among women, although puzzling questions, are not beyond *all* conjecture. — SIR THOMAS BROWNE

The mental features discoursed of as the analytical, are, in themselves, but little susceptible of analysis. We appreciate them only in their effects. We know of them, among other things, that they are always to their possessor, when inordinately possessed, a source of the liveliest enjoyment. As the strong man exults in his physical ability, delighting in such exercises as call his muscles into action, so glories the analyst in that moral activity which *disentangles.* He derives pleasure from even the most trivial occupations bringing his talent into play. He is fond of enigmas, of conundrums, of hieroglyphics; exhibiting in his solutions of each a degree of *acumen* which appears to the ordinary apprehension præternatural. His results, brought about by the very soul and essence of method, have, in truth, the whole air of intuition.

The faculty of re-solution is possibly much invigorated by mathematical study, and especially by that highest branch of it which, unjustly, and merely on account

What song . . . . The quotation is from Chap. 5 of *Hydrotaphia, or Urn-Burial* (1658)

of its retrograde operations, has been called, as if *par excellence,* analysis. Yet to calculate is not in itself to analyse. A chess-player, for example, does the one without
effort at the other. It follows that the game of chess, in its effects upon mental character, is greatly misunderstood. I am not writing a treatise, but simply prefacing a
somewhat peculiar narrative by observations very much at random; I will, therefore,
take occasion to assert that the higher powers of the reflective intellect are more decidedly and more usefully tasked by the unostentatious game of draughts than by
all the elaborate frivolity of chess. In this latter, where the pieces have different and
bizarre motions, with various and variable values, what is only complex is mistaken
10 (a not unusual error) for what is profound. The *attention* is here called powerfully
into play. If it flag for an instant, an oversight is committed, resulting in injury or
defeat. The possible moves being not only manifold but involute, the chances of
such oversights are multiplied; and in nine cases out of ten it is the more concentrative rather than the more acute player who conquers. In draughts, on the contrary,
where the movers are *unique* and have but little variation, the probabilities of inadvertence are diminished, and the mere attention being left comparatively unemployed,
what advantages are obtained by either party are obtained by superior *acumen.* To be
less abstract — Let us suppose a game of draughts where the pieces are reduced to
four kings, and where, of course, no oversight is to be expected. It is obvious that
20 here the victory can be decided (the players being at all equal) only by some
recherché movement, the result of some strong exertion of the intellect. Deprived of
ordinary resources, the analyst throws himself into the spirit of his opponent, identifies himself therewith, and not unfrequently sees thus, at a glance, the sole methods
(sometimes indeed absurdly simple ones) by which he may seduce into error or
hurry into miscalculation.

    Whist has long been noted for its influence upon what is termed the calculating
power; and men of the highest order of intellect have been known to take an apparently unaccountable delight in it, while eschewing chess as frivolous. Beyond
doubt there is nothing of a similar nature so greatly tasking the faculty of analysis.
30 The best chess-player in Christendom *may* be little more than the best player of
chess; but proficiency in whist implies capacity for success in all those more important undertakings where mind struggles with mind. When I say proficiency, I mean
that perfection in the game which includes a comprehension of *all* the sources
whence legitimate advantage may be derived. These are not only manifold but
multiform, and lie frequently among recesses of thought altogether inaccessible to
the ordinary understanding. To observe attentively is to remember distinctly; and,
so far, the concentrative chess-player will do very well at whist; while the rules of
Hoyle (themselves based upon the mere mechanism of the game) are sufficiently
and generally comprehensible. Thus to have a retentive memory, and to proceed by
40 "the book," are points commonly regarded as the sum total of good playing. But it
is in matters beyond the limits of mere rule that the skill of the analyst is evinced.
He makes, in silence, a host of observations and inferences. So, perhaps, do
his companions; and the difference in the extent of the information obtained, lies

---

1 **par excellence,** preëminently

not so much in the validity of the inference as in the quality of the observation. The necessary knowledge is that of *what* to observe. Our player confines himself not at all; nor, because the game is the object, does he reject deductions from things external to the game. He examines the countenance of his partner, comparing it carefully with that of each of his opponents. He considers the mode of assorting the cards in each hand; often counting trump by trump, and honor by honor, through the glances bestowed by their holders upon each. He notes every variation of face as the play progresses, gathering a fund of thought from the differences in the expression of certainty, of surprise, of triumph, or chagrin. From the manner of gathering up a trick he judges whether the person taking it can make another in the suit. He recognises what is played through feint, by the air with which it is thrown upon the table. A casual or inadvertent word; the accidental dropping or turning of a card, with the accompanying anxiety or carelessness in regard to its concealment; the counting of the tricks, with the order of their arrangement; embarrassment, hesitation, eagerness, or trepidation — all afford, to his apparently intuitive perception, indications of the true state of affairs. The first two or three rounds having been played, he is in full possession of the contents of each hand, and thenceforward puts down his cards with as absolute a precision of purpose as if the rest of the party had turned outward the faces of their own.

The analytical power should not be confounded with simple ingenuity; for while the analyst is necessarily ingenious, the ingenious man is often remarkably incapable of analysis. The constructive or combining power, by which ingenuity is usually manifested, and to which the phrenologists (I believe erroneously) have assigned a separate organ, supposing it a primitive faculty, has been so frequently seen in those whose intellect bordered otherwise upon idiocy, as to have attracted general observation among writers on morals. Between ingenuity and the analytic ability there exists a difference far greater indeed, than that between the fancy and the imagination, but of a character very strictly analogous. It will be found, in fact, that the ingenious are always fanciful, and the *truly* imaginative never otherwise than analytic.

The narrative which follows will appear to the reader somewhat in the light of a commentary upon the propositions just advanced.

Residing in Paris during the spring and part of the summer of 18—, I there became acquainted with a Monsieur C. Auguste Dupin. This young gentleman was of an excellent — indeed of an illustrious family, but, by a variety of untoward events, had been reduced to such poverty that the energy of his character succumbed beneath it, and he ceased to bestir himself in the world, or to care for the retrieval of his fortunes. By courtesy of his creditors, there still remained in his possession a small remnant of his patrimony; and, upon the income arising from this, he managed, by means of a rigorous economy, to procure the necessaries of life, without troubling himself about its superfluities. Books, indeed, were his sole luxuries, and in Paris these are easily obtained.

10

20

30

40

---

33 **Dupin.** In France at that time "an illustrious family" bore that name. André Marie Jean Jacques Dupin, president of the Chamber of Deputies in 1840 and a writer on French criminal procedure, may have suggested the name to Poe

Our first meeting was at an obscure library in the Rue Montmartre, where the accident of our both being in search of the same very rare and very remarkable volume, brought us into closer communion. We saw each other again and again. I was deeply interested in the little family history which he detailed to me with all that candor which a Frenchman indulges whenever mere self is his theme. I was astonished, too, at the vast extent of his reading; and, above all, I felt my soul enkindled within me by the wild fervor, and the vivid freshness of his imagination. Seeking in Paris the objects I then sought, I felt that the society of such a man would be a treasure beyond price; and this feeling I frankly confided to him. It was at length

10 arranged that we should live together during my stay in the city; and as my worldly circumstances were somewhat less embarrassed than his own, I was permitted to be at the expense of renting, and furnishing in a style which suited the rather fantastic gloom of our common temper, a time-eaten and grotesque mansion, long deserted through superstitions into which we did not inquire, and tottering to its fall in a retired and desolate portion of the Faubourg St. Germain.

Had the routine of our life at this place been known to the world, we should have been regarded as madmen — although, perhaps, as madmen of a harmless nature. Our seclusion was perfect. We admitted no visitors. Indeed the locality of our retirement had been carefully kept a secret from my own former associates; and it had

20 been many years since Dupin had ceased to know or be known in Paris. We existed within ourselves alone.

It was a freak of fancy in my friend (for what else shall I call it?) to be enamored of the Night for her own sake; and into this *bizarrerie,* as into all his others, I quietly fell, giving myself up to his wild whims with a perfect *abandon.* The sable divinity would not herself dwell with us always; but we could counterfeit her presence. At the first dawn of the morning we closed all the massy shutters of our old building; lighting a couple of tapers which, strongly perfumed, threw out only the ghastliest and feeblest of rays. By the aid of these we then busied our souls in dreams — reading, writing, or conversing, until warned by the clock of the advent of the true Dark-

30 ness. Then we sallied forth into the streets, arm in arm, continuing the topics of the day, or roaming far and wide until a late hour, seeking amid the wild lights and shadows of the populous city, that infinity of mental excitement which quiet observation can afford.

At such times I could not help remarking and admiring (although from his rich ideality I had been prepared to expect it) a peculiar analytic ability in Dupin. He seemed, too, to take an eager delight in its exercise — if not exactly in its display — and did not hesitate to confess the pleasure thus derived. He boasted to me, with a low chuckling laugh, that most men, in respect to himself, wore windows in their bosoms, and was wont to follow up such assertions by direct and very startling proofs

40 of his intimate knowledge of my own. His manner at these moments was frigid and abstract; his eyes were vacant in expression; while his voice, usually a rich tenor, rose into a treble which would have sounded petulantly but for the deliberateness and entire distinctness of the enunciation. Observing him in these moods, I often

---

15 **Faubourg St. Germain,** a fashionable district on the south bank of the Seine

dwelt meditatively upon the old philosophy of the Bi-Part Soul, and amused myself with the fancy of a double Dupin — the creative and the resolvent.

Let it not be supposed, from what I have just said, that I am detailing any mystery, or penning any romance. What I have described in the Frenchman, was merely the result of an excited, or perhaps of a diseased intelligence. But of the character of his remarks at the periods in question an example will best convey the idea.

We were strolling one night down a long dirty street, in the vicinity of the Palais Royal. Being both, apparently, occupied with thought, neither of us had spoken a syllable for fifteen minutes at least. All at once Dupin broke forth with these words:

"He is a very little fellow, that's true, and would do better for the *Théâtre des* 10 *Variétés.*"

"There can be no doubt of that," I replied unwittingly and not at first observing (so much had I been absorbed in reflection) the extraordinary manner in which the speaker had chimed in with my meditations. In an instant afterward I recollected myself, and my astonishment was profound.

"Dupin," said I, gravely, "this is beyond my comprehension. I do not hesitate to say that I am amazed, and can scarcely credit my senses. How was it possible you should know I was thinking of — ?" Here I paused, to ascertain beyond a doubt whether he really knew of whom I thought.

"— of Chantilly," said he, "why do you pause? You were remarking to yourself 20 that his diminutive figure unfitted him for tragedy."

This was precisely what had formed the subject of my reflections. Chantilly was a *quondam* cobbler of the Rue St. Denis, who, becoming stage-mad, had attempted the *role* of Xerxes, in Crébillon's tragedy so called, and been notoriously Pasquinaded for his pains.

"Tell me, for Heaven's sake," I exclaimed, "the method — if method there is — by which you have been enabled to fathom my soul in this matter." In fact I was even more startled than I would have been willing to express.

"It was the fruiterer," replied my friend, "who brought you to the conclusion that the mender of soles was not of sufficient height for Xerxes *et id genus omne.*" 30

"The fruiterer! — you astonish me — I know no fruiterer whomsoever."

"The man who ran up against you as we entered the street — it may have been fifteen minutes ago."

I now remembered that, in fact, a fruiterer, carrying upon his head a large basket of apples, had nearly thrown me down, by accident, as we passed from the Rue C— into the thoroughfare where we stood; but what this had to do with Chantilly I could not possibly understand.

There was not a particle of *charlatanerie* about Dupin. "I will explain," he said, "and that you may comprehend all clearly, we will first retrace the course of your meditations, from the moment in which I spoke to you until that of the *rencontre* 40

---

10 **Théâtre des Variétés,** French vaudeville theater   23 **Rue St. Denis,** a street in Paris   24 **Crébillon,** Prosper Jolyot de Crébillon (1674-1762), a French tragic dramatist. His *Xerxes* was written in 1714   30 **et . . . omne,** and all of that sort

with the fruiterer in question. The larger links of the chain run thus — Chantilly, Orion, Dr. Nichols, Epicurus, Stereotomy, the street stones, the fruiterer."

There are few persons who have not, at some period of their lives, amused themselves in retracing the steps by which particular conclusions of their own minds have been attained. The occupation is often full of interest; and he who attempts it for the first time is astonished by the apparently illimitable distance and incoherence between the starting-point and the goal. What, then, must have been my amazement when I heard the Frenchman speak what he had just spoken, and when I could not help acknowledging that he had spoken the truth. He continued:

10 "We had been talking of horses, if I remember aright, just before leaving the Rue C—. This was the last subject we discussed. As we crossed into the street, a fruiterer, with a large basket upon his head, brushing quickly past us, thrust you upon a pile of paving-stones collected at a point where the causeway is undergoing repair. You stepped upon one of the loose fragments, slipped slightly, strained your ankle, appeared vexed or sulky, muttered a few words, turned to look at the pile, and then proceeded in silence. I was not particularly attentive to what you did; but observation has become with me, of late, a species of necessity.

"You kept your eyes upon the ground — glancing, with a petulant expression, at the holes and ruts in the pavement (so that I saw you were still thinking of the 20 stones), until we reached the little alley called Lamartine, which has been paved, by way of experiment, with the overlapping and riveted blocks. Here your countenance brightened up, and, perceiving your lips move, I could not doubt that you murmured the word 'stereotomy' a term very affectedly applied to this species of pavement. I knew that you could not say to yourself 'stereotomy' without being brought to think of atomies, and thus of the theories of Epicurus; and since, when we discussed this subject not very long ago, I mentioned to you how singularly, yet with how little notice, the vague guesses of that noble Greek had met with confirmation in the late nebular cosmogony, I felt that you could not avoid casting your eyes upward to the great *nebula* in Orion, and I certainly expected that you would do so. You did 30 look up, and I was assured that I had correctly followed your steps. But in that bitter *tirade* upon Chantilly, which appeared in yesterday's *'Musee,'* the satirist, making some disgraceful allusions to the cobbler's change of name upon assuming the buskin, quoted a Latin line about which we have often conversed. I mean the line

Perdidit antiquum litera prima sonum.

I had told you that this was in reference to Orion, formerly written Urion; and from certain pungencies connected with this explanation, I was aware that you could not have forgotten it. It was clear, therefore, that you would not fail to combine the two ideas of Orion and Chantilly. That you did combine them I saw by the character of the smile which passed over your lips. You thought of the poor cobbler's 40 immolation. So far you had been stooping in your gait; but now I saw you draw

2 **Orion,** a constellation   2 **Epicurus,** Greek philosopher (342?-270 B.C.)   34 **Perdidit . . . sonum.** The first letter destroys the antique sound

yourself up to your full height. I was then sure that you reflected upon the diminutive figure of Chantilly. At this point I interrupted your meditations to remark that as, in fact, he *was* a very little fellow — that Chantilly — he would do better at the *Théâtre des Variétés."*

Not long after this, we were looking over an evening edition of the *Gazette des Tribunaux,* when the following paragraphs arrested our attention.

"EXTRAORDINARY MURDERS. — This morning, about three o'clock, the inhabitants of the Quartier St. Roch were aroused from sleep by a succession of terrific shrieks, issuing, apparently, from the fourth story of a house in the Rue Morgue, known to be in the sole occupancy of one Madame L'Espanaye, and her daughter, Mademoi- 10
selle Camille L'Espanaye. After some delay, occasioned by a fruitless attempt to procure admission in the usual manner, the gateway was broken in with a crowbar, and eight or ten of the neighbors entered, accompanied by two *gendarmes.* By this time the cries had ceased; but, as the party rushed up the first flight of stairs, two or more rough voices, in angry contention, were distinguished, and seemed to proceed from the upper part of the house. As the second landing was reached, these sounds, also, had ceased, and everything remained perfectly quiet. The party spread themselves, and hurried from room to room. Upon arriving at a large back chamber in the fourth story (the door of which, being found locked, with the key inside, was forced open,) a spectacle presented itself which struck every one present not less with hor- 20
ror than with astonishment.

"The apartment was in the wildest disorder — the furniture broken and thrown about in all directions. There was only one bedstead; and from this the bed had been removed, and thrown into the middle of the floor. On a chair lay a razor, besmeared with blood. On the hearth were two or three long and thick tresses of grey human hair, also dabbled in blood, and seeming to have been pulled out by the roots. On the floor were found four Napoleons, an ear-ring of topaz, three large silver spoons, three smaller of *metal d'Alger,* and two bags, containing nearly four thousand francs in gold. The drawers of a *bureau,* which stood in one corner, were open, and had been, apparently, rifled, although many articles still.remained in them. A 30
small iron safe was discovered under the *bed* (not under the bedstead). It was open, with the key still in the door. It had no contents beyond a few old letters, and other papers of little consequence.

"Of Madame L'Espanaye no traces were here seen; but an unusual quantity of soot being observed in the fire-place, a search was made in the chimney, and (horrible to relate!) the corpse of the daughter, head downward, was dragged therefrom; it having been thus forced up the narrow aperture for a considerable distance. The body was quite warm. Upon examining it, many excoriations were perceived, no doubt occasioned by the violence with which it had been thrust up and disengaged. Upon the face were many severe scratches, and, upon the throat, dark bruises, and 40
deep indentations of fingernails, as if the deceased had been throttled to death.

"After a thorough investigation of every portion of the house, without farther discovery, the party made its way into a small paved yard in the rear of the build-

28 **metal d'Alger,** an alloy used in imitation of silver

ing, where lay the corpse of the old lady, with her throat so entirely cut that, upon an attempt to raise her, the head fell off. The body, as well as the head, was fearfully mutilated — the former so much so as scarcely to retain any semblance of humanity.

"To this horrible mystery there is not as yet, we believe, the slightest clew."

The next day's paper had these additional particulars.

"The Tragedy in the Rue Morgue. Many individuals have been examined in relation to this most extraordinary and frightful affair" [the word *'affaire'* has not yet, in France, that levity of import which it conveys with us], "but nothing whatever has 10 transpired to throw light upon it. We give below all the material testimony elicited.

"Pauline Dubourg, laundress, deposes that she has known both the deceased for three years, having washed for them during that period. The old lady and her daughter seemed on good terms — very affectionate towards each other. They were excellent pay. Could not speak in regard to their mode or means of living. Believed that Madame L. told fortunes for means of living. Was reputed to have money put by. Never met any persons in the house when she called for the clothes or took them home. Was sure that they had no servant in employ. There appeared to be no furniture in any part of the building except in the fourth story.

"Pierre Moreau, tobacconist, deposes that he has been in the habit of selling small 20 quantities of tobacco and snuff to Madame L'Espanaye for nearly four years. Was born in the neighborhood, and has always resided there. The deceased and her daughter had occupied the house in which the corpses were found, for more than six years. It was formerly occupied by a jeweller, who under-let the upper rooms to various persons. The house was the property of Madame L. She became dissatisfied with the abuse of the premises by her tenant, and moved into them herself, refusing to let any portion. The old lady was childish. Witness had seen the daughter some five or six times during the six years. The two lived an exceedingly retired life — were reputed to have money. Had heard it said among the neighbors that Madame L. told fortunes — did not believe it. Had never seen any person enter the door 30 except the old lady and her daughter, a porter once or twice, and a physician some eight or ten times.

"Many other persons, neighbors, gave evidence to the same effect. No one was spoken of as frequenting the house. It was not known whether there were any living connexions of Madame L. and her daughter. The shutters of the front windows were seldom opened. Those in the rear were always closed, with the exception of the large back room, fourth story. The house was a good house — not very old.

"Isidore Muset, gendarme, deposes that he was called to the house about three o'clock in the morning, and found some twenty or thirty persons at the gateway, endeavoring to gain admittance. Forced it open, at length, with a bayonet — not with 40 a crowbar. Had but little difficulty in getting it open, on account of its being a double or folding gate, and bolted neither at bottom nor top. The shrieks were continued until the gate was forced — and then suddenly ceased. They seemed to be screams of some person (or persons) in great agony — were loud and drawn out, not short and quick. Witness led the way upstairs. Upon reaching the first landing,

heard two voices in loud and angry contention — the one a gruff voice, the other much shriller — a very strange voice. Could distinguish some words of the former, which was that of a Frenchman. Was positive that it was not a woman's voice. Could distinguish the words 'sacré' and 'diable.' The shrill voice was that of a foreigner. Could not be sure whether it was the voice of a man or of a woman. Could not make out what was said, but believed the language to be Spanish. The state of the room and of the bodies was described by this witness as we described them yesterday.

"*Henri Duval,* a neighbor, and by trade a silver-smith, deposes that he was one of the party who first entered the house. Corroborates the testimony of Muset in general. As soon as they forced an entrance, they reclosed the door, to keep out the crowd, which collected very fast, notwithstanding the lateness of the hour. The shrill voice, this witness thinks, was that of an Italian. Was certain it was not French. Could not be sure that it was a man's voice. It might have been a woman's. Was not acquainted with the Italian language. Could not distinguish the words, but was convinced by the intonation that the speaker was an Italian. Knew Madame L. and her daughter. Had conversed with both frequently. Was sure that the shrill voice was not that of either of the deceased.

"——*Odenheimer, restaurateur.* This witness volunteered his testimony. Not speaking French, was examined through an interpreter. Is a native of Amsterdam. Was passing the house at the time of the shrieks. They lasted for several minutes — probably ten. They were long and loud — very awful and distressing. Was one of those who entered the building. Corroborated the previous evidence in every respect but one. Was sure that the shrill voice was that of a man — of a Frenchman. Could not distinguish the words uttered. They were loud and quick — unequal — spoken apparently in fear as well as in anger. The voice was harsh — not so shrill as harsh. Could not call it a shrill voice. The gruff voice said repeatedly 'sacré,' 'diable,' and once 'mon Dieu.'

"*Jules Mignaud,* banker, of the firm of Mignaud et Fils, Rue Deloraine. Is the elder Mignaud. Madame L'Espanaye had some property. Had opened an account with his banking house in the spring of the year — (eight years previously). Made frequent deposits in small sums. Had checked for nothing until the third day before her death, when she took out in person the sum of 4000 francs. This sum was paid in gold, and a clerk sent home with the money.

"*Adolphe Le Bon,* clerk to Mignaud et Fils, deposes that on the day in question, about noon, he accompanied Madame L'Espanaye to her residence with the 4000 francs, put up in two bags. Upon the door being opened, Mademoiselle L. appeared and took from his hands one of the bags, while the old lady relieved him of the other. He then bowed and departed. Did not see any person in the street at the time. It is a byestreet — very lonely.

"*William Bird,* tailor, deposes that he was one of the party who entered the house. Is an Englishman. Has lived in Paris two years. Was one of the first to ascend the stairs. Heard the voices in contention. The gruff voice was that of a Frenchman. Could make out several words, but cannot now remember all. Heard distinctly '*sacré,*' and '*mon Dieu.*' There was a sound at the moment as if of several persons struggling — a scraping and scuffling sound. The shrill voice was very loud — louder than the gruff one. Is sure that it was not the voice of an Englishman. Appeared to be that of a German. Might have been a woman's voice. Does not understand German.

"Four of the above-named witnesses, being recalled, deposed that the door of the chamber in which was found the body of Mademoiselle L. was locked on the inside when the party reached it. Every thing was perfectly silent — no groans or noises of any kind. Upon forcing the door no person was seen. The windows, both of the back and the front room, were down and firmly fastened from within. A door between the two rooms was closed, but not locked. The door leading from the front
10 room into the passage was locked, with the key on the inside. A small room in the front of the house, on the fourth story, at the head of the passage, was open, the door being ajar. This room was crowded with old beds, boxes, and so forth. These were carefully removed and searched. There was not an inch of any portion of the house which was not carefully searched. Sweeps were sent up and down the chimneys. The house was a four story one, with garrets *(mansardes)*. A trapdoor on the roof was nailed down securely — did not appear to have been opened for years. The time elapsing between the hearing of the voices in contention and the breaking open of the room door, was variously stated by the witnesses. Some made it as short as three minutes — some as long as five. The door was opened with difficulty.

20 "*Alfonzo Garcio,* undertaker, deposes that he resides in the Rue Morgue. Is a native of Spain. Was one of the party who entered the house. Did not proceed up stairs. Is nervous, and was apprehensive of the consequences of agitation. Heard the voices in contention. The gruff voice was that of a Frenchman. Could not distinguish what was said. The shrill voice was that of an Englishman — is sure of this. Does not understand the English language, but judges by the intonation.

"*Alberto Montani,* confectioner, deposes that he was among the first to ascend the stairs. Heard the voices in question. The gruff voice was that of a Frenchman. Distinguished several words. The speaker appeared to be expostulating. Could not make out the words of the shrill voice. Spoke quick and unevenly. Thinks it the voice of
30 a Russian. Corroborates the general testimony. Is an Italian. Never conversed with a native of Russia.

"Several witnesses, recalled, here testified that the chimneys of all the rooms on the fourth story were too narrow to admit the passage of a human being. By 'sweeps' were meant cylindrical sweeping-brushes, such as are employed by those who clean chimneys. These brushes were passed up and down every flue in the house. There is no back passage by which any one could have descended while the party proceeded upstairs. The body of Mademoiselle L'Espanaye was so firmly wedged in the chimney that it could not be got down until four or five of the party united their strength.

40 "*Paul Dumas,* physician, deposes that he was called to view the bodies about daybreak. They were both then lying on the sacking of the bedstead in the chamber where Mademoiselle L. was found. The corpse of the young lady was much bruised and excoriated. The fact that it had been thrust up the chimney would sufficiently account for these appearances. The throat was greatly chafed. There were several

deep scratches just below the chin, together with a series of livid spots which were evidently the impressions of fingers. The face was fearfully discolored and the eyeballs protruded. The tongue had been partially bitten through. A large bruise was discovered upon the pit of the stomach, produced, apparently, by the pressure of a knee. In the opinion of M. Dumas, Mademoiselle L'Espanaye had been throttled to death by some person or persons unknown. The corpse of the mother was horribly mutilated. All the bones of the right leg and arm were more or less shattered. The left *tibia* much splintered, as well as all the ribs of the left side. Whole body dreadfully bruised and discolored. It was not possible to say how the injuries had been inflicted. A heavy club of wood, or a broad bar of iron — a chair — any large, 10 heavy, and obtuse weapon would have produced such results, if wielded by the hands of a very powerful man. No woman could have inflicted the blows with any weapon. The head of the deceased, when seen by witness, was entirely separated from the body, and was also greatly shattered. The throat had evidently been cut with some very sharp instrument, — probably with a razor.

   "Alexandre Etienne, surgeon, was called with M. Dumas to view the bodies. Corroborated the testimony and opinions of M. Dumas.

   "Nothing farther of importance was elicited, although several other persons were examined. A murder so mysterious, and so perplexing in all its particulars, was never before committed in Paris — if indeed a murder has been committed at all. The 20 police are entirely at fault — an unusual occurrence in affairs of this nature. There is not, however, the shadow of a clew apparent."

   The evening edition of the paper stated that the greatest excitement still continued in the Quartier St. Roch — that the premises in question had been carefully researched, and fresh examinations of witnesses instituted, but all to no purpose. A postscript, however, mentioned that Adolphe Le Bon had been arrested and imprisoned — although nothing appeared to criminate him, beyond the facts already detailed.

   Dupin seemed singularly interested in the progress of this affair — at least so I judged from his manner, for he made no comments. It was only after the announce- 30 ment that Le Bon had been imprisoned, that he asked me my opinion respecting the murders.

   I could merely agree with all Paris in considering them an insoluble mystery. I saw no means by which it would be possible to trace the murderer.

   "We must not judge of the means," said Dupin, "by this shell of an examination. The Parisian police, so much extolled for *acumen,* are cunning, but no more. There is no method in their proceedings, beyond the method of the moment. They make a vast parade of measures; but, not unfrequently, these are so ill adapted to the objects proposed, as to put us in mind of Monsieur Jourdain's calling for his *robe-de-chambre — pour mieux entendre la musique.* The results attained by them are 40 not unfrequently surprising, but, for the most part, are brought about by simple diligence and activity. When these qualities are unavailing, their schemes fail.

---

39 **Monsieur Jourdain,** a naïve character in Molière's play *Le bourgeois gentilhomme,* who, as the quotation indicates, calls for his dressing gown "in order that he may listen better to the music"

Vidocq, for example, was a good guesser and a persevering man. But, without educated thought, he erred continually by the very intensity of his investigations. He impaired his vision by holding the object too close. He might see, perhaps, one or two points with unusual clearness, but in so doing he, necessarily, lost sight of the matter as a whole. Thus there is such a thing as being too profound. Truth is not always in a well. In fact, as regards the more important knowledge, I do believe that she is invariably superficial. The depth lies in the valleys where we seek her, and not upon the mountain-tops where she is found. The modes and sources of this kind of error are well typified in the contemplation of the heavenly bodies. To look
10 at a star by glances — to view it in a side-long way, by turning toward it the exterior portions of the *retina* (more susceptible of feeble impressions of light than the interior), is to behold the star distinctly — is to have the best appreciation of its lustre — a lustre which grows dim just in proportion as we turn our vision *fully* upon it. A greater number of rays actually fall upon the eye in the latter case, but, in the former, there is the more refined capacity for comprehension. By undue profundity we perplex and enfeeble thought; and it is possible to make even Venus herself vanish from the firmament by a scrutiny too sustained, too concentrated, or too direct.

"As for these murders, let us enter into some examinations for ourselves, before
20 we make up an opinion respecting them. An inquiry will afford us amusement" [I thought this an odd term, so applied, but said nothing], "and, besides, Le Bon once rendered me a service for which I am not ungrateful. We will go and see the premises with our own eyes. I know G—, the Prefect of Police, and shall have no difficulty in obtaining the necessary permission."

The permission was obtained, and we proceeded at once to the Rue Morgue. This is one of those miserable thoroughfares which intervene between the Rue Richelieu and the Rue St. Roch. It was late in the afternoon when we reached it; as this quarter is at a great distance from that in which we resided. The house was readily found; for there were still many persons gazing up at the closed shutters, with an object-
30 less curiosity, from the opposite side of the way. It was an ordinary Parisian house, with a gateway, on one side of which was a glazed watchbox, with a sliding panel in the window, indicating a *loge de concierge*. Before going in we walked up the street, turned down an alley, and then, again turning, passed in the rear of the building — Dupin, meanwhile, examining the whole neighborhood, as well as the house, with a minuteness of attention for which I could see no possible object.

Retracing our steps, we came again to the front of the dwelling, rang, and, having shown our credentials, were admitted by the agents in charge. We went up stairs — into the chamber where the body of Mademoiselle L'Espanaye had been found, and where both the deceased still lay. I saw nothing beyond what had been
40 stated in the *Gazette des Tribunaux.* Dupin scrutinized everything — not excepting the bodies of the victims. We then went into the other rooms, and into the yard; a

---

1 **Vidocq,** Eugène François Vidocq (1775-1857), a French detective whose picturesque *Mémoires* (1829) were doubtless of great value to Poe in suggesting methods of writing about crime   32 **loge de concierge,** janitor's lodge

gendarme accompanying us throughout. The examination occupied us until dark, when we took our departure. On our way home my companion stepped in for a moment at the office of one of the daily papers. I have said that the whims of my friend were manifold, and *Je les ménageais;* — for this phrase there is no English equivalent. It was his humor, now, to decline all conversation on the subject of the murder, until about noon the next day. He then asked me, suddenly, if I had ob-served anything *peculiar* at the scene of the atrocity.

There was something in his manner of emphasizing the word "peculiar," which caused me to shudder, without knowing why.

"No, nothing *peculiar*," I said; "nothing more, at least, than we both saw stated   10
in the paper."

"The *Gazette*," he replied, "has not entered, I fear, into the unusual horror of the thing. But dismiss the idle opinions of this print. It appears to me that this mys-tery is considered insoluble, for the very reason which should cause it to be re-garded as easy of solution — I mean for the *outre* character of its features. The police are confounded by the seeming absence of motive — not for the murder itself — but for the atrocity of the murder. They are puzzled, too, by the seeming impossibility of reconciling the voices heard in contention, with the facts that no one was dis-covered upstairs but the assassinated Mademoiselle L'Espanaye, and that there was no means of egress without the notice of the party ascending. The wild disorder of   20
the room; the corpse thrust, with the head downward, up the chimney; the fright-ful mutilation of the body of the old lady; these considerations, with those just mentioned, and others which I need not mention, have sufficed to paralyze the powers, by putting completely at fault the boasted *acumen,* of the government agents. They have fallen into the gross but common error of confounding the unusual with the abstruse. But it is by these deviations from the plane of the ordinary, that reason feels its way, if at all, in its search for the true. In investigations such as we are now pursuing, it should not be so much asked 'what has occurred,' as 'what has occurred that has never occurred before.' In fact, the facility with which I shall arrive, or have arrived, at the solution of this mystery, is in the direct ratio of its apparent   30
insolubility in the eyes of the police."

I stared at the speaker in mute astonishment.

"I am now awaiting," continued he, looking toward the door of our apartment — "I am now awaiting a person who, although perhaps not the perpetrator of these butcheries, must have been in some measure implicated in their perpetration. Of the worst portion of the crimes committed, it is probable that he is innocent. I hope that I am right in this supposition; for upon it I build my expectation of read-ing the entire riddle. I look for the man here — in this room — every moment. It is true that he may not arrive, but the probability is that he will. Should he come, it will be necessary to detain him. Here are pistols; and we both know how to use   40
them when occasion demands their use."

I took the pistols, scarcely knowing what I did, or believing what I heard, while

---

4 **Je les ménageais,** I humored them cautiously

Dupin went on, very much as if in a soliloquy. I have already spoken of his abstract manner at such times. His discourse was addressed to myself; but his voice, although by no means loud, had that intonation which is commonly employed in speaking to some one at a great distance. His eyes, vacant in expression, regarded only the wall.

"That the voices heard in contention," he said, "by the party upon the stairs, were not the voices of the women themselves, was fully proved by the evidence. This relieves us of all doubt upon the question whether the old lady could have first destroyed the daughter, and afterward have committed suicide. I speak of this
10 point chiefly for the sake of method; for the strength of Madame L'Espanaye would have been utterly unequal to the task of thrusting her daughter's corpse up the chimney as it was found; and the nature of the wounds upon her own person entirely precludes the idea of self-destruction. Murder, then, has been committed by some third party; and the voices of this third party were those heard in contention. Let me now advert — not to the whole testimony respecting these voices — but to what was *peculiar* in that testimony. Did you observe any thing peculiar about it?"

I remarked that, while all the witnesses agreed in supposing the gruff voice to be that of a Frenchman, there was much disagreement in regard to the shrill, or, as one individual termed it, the harsh voice.

20 "That was evidence itself," said Dupin, "but it was not the peculiarity of the evidence. You have observed nothing distinctive. Yet there *was* something to be observed. The witnesses, as you remark, agreed about the gruff voice; they were here unanimous. But in regard to the shrill voice, the peculiarity is — not that they disagreed — but that, while an Italian, an Englishman, a Spaniard, a Hollander, and a Frenchman attempted to describe it, each one spoke of it as that *of a foreigner*. Each is sure that it was not the voice of one of his own countrymen. Each likens it — not to the voice of an individual of any nation with whose language he is conversant — but the converse. The Frenchman supposes it the voice of a Spaniard, and might have distinguished some words *'had he been acquainted with the Spanish.'* The
30 Dutchman maintains it to have been that of a Frenchman; but we find it stated that *'not understanding French this witness was examined through an interpreter.'* The Englishman thinks it is the voice of a German, and *'does not understand German.'* The Spaniard 'is sure' that it was that of an Englishman, but 'judges by the intonation' altogether, *'as he has no knowledge of the English.'* The Italian believes it the voice of a Russian, but *'has never conversed with a native of Russia.'* A second Frenchman differs, moreover with the first, and is positive that the voice was that of an Italian; but, *not being cognizant of that tongue,* is, like the Spaniard, 'convinced by the intonation.' Now, how strangely unusual must that voice have really been, about which such testimony as this *could* have been elicited! — in whose tones, even,
40 denizens of the five great divisions of Europe could recognize nothing familiar! You will say that it might have been the voice of an Asiatic — of an African. Neither Asiatics nor Africans abound in Paris; but, without denying the inference, I will merely call your attention to three points. The voice is termed by one witness 'harsh rather than shrill.' It is represented by two others to have been 'quick and *unequal.'*

No words — no sound resembling words — were by any witness mentioned as distinguishable.

"I know not," continued Dupin, "what impression I may have made so far, upon your own understanding; but I do not hesitate to say that legitimate deductions even from this portion of the testimony — the portion respecting the gruff and shrill voices — are in themselves sufficient to engender a suspicion which should give direction to all farther progress in the investigation of the mystery. I said 'legitimate deductions;' but my meaning is not thus fully expressed. I designed to imply that the deductions are the *sole* proper ones, and that the suspicion arises *inevitably* from them as the single result. What the suspicion is, however, I will not say just 10 yet. I merely wish you to bear in mind that, with myself, it was sufficiently forcible to give a definite form — a certain tendency — to my inquiries in the chamber.

"Let us now transport ourselves, in fancy, to this chamber. What shall we first seek here? The means of egress employed by the murderers. It is not too much to say that neither of us believe in præternatural events. Madame and Mademoiselle L'Espanaye were not destroyed by spirits. The doers of the deed were material, and escaped materially. Then how? Fortunately, there is but one mode of reasoning upon the point, and that mode *must* lead to a definite decision. — Let us examine, each by each, the possible means of egress. It is clear that the assassins were in the room where Mademoiselle L'Espanaye was found, or at least in the room adjoining, when 20 the party ascended the stairs. It is then only from these two apartments that we have to seek issues. The police have laid bare the floors, the ceilings, and the masonry of the walls, in every direction. No *secret* issues could have escaped their vigilance. But not trusting to *their* eyes, I examined with my own. There were, then, *no* secret issues. Both doors leading from the rooms into the passage were securely locked, with the keys inside. Let us turn to the chimneys. These, although of ordinary width for some eight or ten feet above the hearths, will not admit, throughout their extent, the body of a large cat. The impossibility of egress, by means already stated, being thus absolute, we are reduced to the windows. Through those of the front room no one could have escaped without the notice of the crowd in the street. 30 The murderers *must* have passed, then, through those of the back room. Now, brought to this conclusion in so unequivocal manner as we are, it is not our part as reasoners, to reject it on account of apparent impossibilities. It is only left for us to prove that these apparent 'impossibilities' are, in reality, not such.

"There are two windows in the chamber. One of them is unobstructed by furniture, and is wholly visible. The lower portion of the other is hidden from view by the head of the unwieldy bedstead which is thrust close up against it. The former was found securely fastened from within. It resisted the utmost force of those who endeavored to raise it. A large gimlet-hole had been pierced in its frame to the left, and a very stout nail was found fitted therein, nearly to the head. Upon examining 40 the other window, a similar nail was seen similarly fitted in it; and a vigourous attempt to raise this sash, failed also. The police were now entirely satisfied that egress had not been in these directions. And, *therefore,* it was thought a matter of supererogation to withdraw the nails and open the windows.

"My own examination was somewhat more particular, and was so for the reason I have just given — because here it was, I knew, that all apparent impossibilities *must* be proved to be not such in reality.

"I proceeded to think thus — *a posteriori*. The murderers *did* escape from one of these windows. This being so, they could not have re-fastened the sashes from the inside, as they were found fastened; — the consideration which put a stop, through its obviousness, to the scrutiny of the police in this quarter. Yet the sashes *were* fastened. They *must*, then, have the power of fastening themselves. There was no escape from this conclusion. I stepped to the unobstructed casement, withdrew the nail
10 with some difficulty, and attempted to raise the sash. It resisted all my efforts, as I had anticipated. A concealed spring must, I now knew, exist; and this corroboration of my idea convinced me that my premises, at least, were correct, however mysterious still appeared the circumstances attending the nails. A careful search soon brought to light the hidden spring. I pressed it, and satisfied with the discovery, forbore to upraise the sash.

"I now replaced the nail and regarded it attentively. A person passing out through this window might have reclosed it, and the spring would have caught — but the nail could not have been replaced. The conclusion was plain, and again narrowed in the field of my investigations. The assassins *must* have escaped through the other
20 window. Supposing, then, the springs upon each sash to be the same, as was probable, there *must* be found a difference between the nails, or at least between the modes of their fixture. Getting upon the sacking of the bedstead, I looked over the headboard minutely at the second casement. Passing my hand down behind the board, I readily discovered and pressed the spring, which was, as I had supposed, identical in character with its neighbor. I now looked at the nail. It was as stout as the other, and apparently fitted in the same manner — driven in nearly up to the head.

"You will say that I was puzzled; but, if you think so, you must have misunderstood the nature of the inductions. To use a sporting phrase, I had not been once 'at fault.' The scent had never for an instant been lost. There was no flaw in any
30 link of the chain. I had traced the secret to its ultimate result, — and that result was *the nail*. It had, I say, in every respect, the appearance of its fellow in the other window; but this fact was an absolute nullity (conclusive as it might seem to be) when compared with the consideration that here, at this point, terminated the clew. 'There *must* be something wrong,' I said, 'about the nail.' I touched it; and the head, with about a quarter of an inch of the shank, came off in my fingers. The rest of the shank was in the gimlet-hole where it had been broken off. The fracture was an old one (for its edges were incrusted with rust), and had apparently been accomplished by the blow of a hammer, which had partially imbedded, in the top of the bottom sash, the head portion of the nail. I now carefully replaced this head por-
40 tion in the indentation whence I had taken it, and the resemblance to a perfect nail was complete — the fissure was invisible. Pressing the spring, I gently raised the sash for a few inches; the head went up with it, remaining firm in its bed. I closed the window, and the semblance of the whole nail was again perfect.

"The riddle, so far, was now unriddled. The assassin had escaped through the window which looked upon the bed. Dropping of its own accord upon his exit (or perhaps purposely closed), it had become fastened by the spring; and it was the retention of this spring which had been mistaken by the police for that of the nail, — farther inquiry being thus considered unnecessary.

"The next question is that of the mode of descent. Upon this point I had been satisfied in my walk with you around the building. About five feet and a half from the casement in question there runs a lightning-rod. From this rod it would have been impossible for any one to reach the window itself, to say nothing of entering it. I observed, however, that the shutters of the fourth story were of the peculiar kind called by Parisian carpenters *ferrades* — a kind rarely employed at the present 10 day, but frequently seen upon very old mansions at Lyons and Bordeaux. They are in the form of an ordinary door (a single, not a folding door), except that the upper half is latticed or worked in open trellis — thus affording an excellent hold for the hands. In the present instance these shutters are fully three feet and a half broad. When we saw them from the rear of the house, they were both about half open — that is to say, they stood off at right angles from the wall. It is probable that the police, as well as myself, examined the back of the tenement; but, if so, in looking at these *ferrades* in the line of their breadth, (as they must have done), they did not perceive this great breadth itself, or, at all events, failed to take it into due consideration. In fact, having once satisfied themselves that no egress could have been 20 made in this quarter, they would naturally bestow here a very cursory examination. It was clear to me, however, that the shutter belonging to the window at the head of the bed, would, if swung fully back to the wall, reach to within two feet of the lightning-rod. It was also evident that, by exertion of a very unusual degree of activity and courage, an entrance into the window, from the rod, might have been thus effected. — By reaching to the distance of two feet and a half (we now suppose the shutter open to its whole extent) a robber might have taken a firm grasp upon the trellis-work. Letting go, then, his hold upon the rod, placing his feet securely against the wall, and springing boldly from it, he might have swung the shutter so as to close it, and, if we imagine the window open at the time, might even have 30 swung himself into the room.

"I wish you to bear especially in mind that I have spoken of a *very* unusual degree of activity as requisite to success in so hazardous and so difficult a feat. It is my design to show you, first, that the thing might possibly have been accomplished: — but, secondly and *chiefly,* I wish to impress upon your understanding the *very extraordinary* — the almost præternatural character of that agility which could have accomplished it.

"You will say, no doubt, using the language of the law, that 'to make out my case' I should rather under-value, than insist upon a full estimation of the activity required in this matter. This may be the practice in law, but it is not the usage of reason. My ultimate object is only the truth. My immediate purpose is to lead you 40 to place in juxtaposition that *very unusual* activity of which I have just spoken, with that *very peculiar* shrill (or harsh) and *unequal* voice, about whose nationality no two persons could be found to agree, and in whose utterance no syllabification could be detected."

At these words a vague and half-formed conception of the meaning of Dupin flitted over my mind. I seemed to be upon the verge of comprehension, without power to comprehend — as men, at times, find themselves upon the brink of remembrance, without being able, in the end, to remember. My friend went on with his discourse.

"You will see," he said, "that I have shifted the question from the mode of egress to that of ingress. It was my design to suggest that both were effected in the same manner, at the same point. Let us now revert to the interior of the room. Let us survey the appearances here. The drawer of the bureau, it is said, had been rifled, although many articles of apparel still remained in them. The conclusion here is absurd. It is a mere guess — a very silly one — and no more. How are we to know that the articles found in the drawers were not all these drawers had originally contained? Madame L'Espanaye and her daughter lived an exceedingly retired life — saw no company — seldom went out — had little use for numerous changes of habiliment. Those found were at least of as good quality as any likely to be possessed by these ladies. If a thief had taken any, why did he not take the best, why did he not take all? In a word, why did he abandon four thousand francs in gold to encumber himself with a bundle of linen? The gold *was* abandoned. Nearly the whole sum mentioned by Monsieur Mignaud, the banker, was discovered, in bags, upon the floor. I wish you, therefore, to discard from your thoughts the blundering idea of *motive,* engendered in the brains of the police by that portion of the evidence which speaks of money delivered at the door of the house. Coincidences ten times as remarkable as this (the delivery of the money, and the murder committed within three days upon the party receiving it), happen to all of us every hour of our lives, without attracting even momentary notice. Coincidences, in general, are great stumbling-blocks in the way of that class of thinkers who have been educated to know nothing of the theory of probabilities — that theory to which most of the most glorious objects of human research are indebted for the most glorious of illustration. In the present instance, had the gold been gone, the fact of its delivery three days before would have formed something more than a coincidence. It would have been corroborative of this idea of motive. But, under the real circumstances of the case, if we are to suppose gold the motive of this outrage, we must also imagine the perpetrator so vacillating an idiot as to have abandoned his gold and his motive together.

"Keeping now steadily in mind the points to which I have drawn your attention — that peculiar voice, that unusual agility, and that startling absence of motive in a murder so singularly atrocious as this — let us glance at the butchery itself. Here is a woman strangled to death by manual strength, and thrust up a chimney, head downward. Ordinary assassins employ no such modes of murder such as this. Least of all, do they thus dispose of the murdered. In the manner of thrusting the corpse up the chimney, you will admit that there was something *excessively outré* — something altogether irreconcilable with our common notions of human action, even when we suppose the actors the most depraved of men. Think, too, how great must have been that strength which could have thrust the body *up* such an aperture so forcibly that the united vigor of several persons was found barely sufficient to drag it *down!*

"Turn, now, to other indications of the employment of a vigor most marvellous. On the hearth were thick tresses — very thick tresses — of grey human hair. These had been torn out by the roots. You are aware of the great force necessary in tearing thus from the head even twenty or thirty hairs together. You saw the locks in question as well as myself. Their roots (a hideous sight!) were clotted with fragments of the flesh of the scalp — sure token of the prodigious power which had been exerted in uprooting perhaps half a million of hairs at a time. The throat of the old lady was not merely cut, but the head absolutely severed from the body; the instrument was a mere razor. I wish you also to look at the *brutal* ferocity of these deeds. Of the bruises upon the body of Madame L'Espanaye I do not speak. Monsieur 10 Dumas, and his worthy coadjutor Monsieur Etienne, have pronounced that they were inflicted by some obtuse instrument; and so far these gentlemen are very correct. The obtuse instrument was clearly the stone pavement in the yard, upon which the victim had fallen from the window which looked in upon the bed. This idea, however simple it may seem, escaped the police for the same reason that the breadth of the shutters escaped them — because, by the affair of the nails, their perceptions had been hermetically sealed against the possibility of the windows having ever been opened at all.

"If now, in addition to all these things, you have properly reflected upon the odd disorder of the chamber, we have gone so far as to combine the ideas of an agility 20 astounding, a strength super-human, a ferocity brutal, a butchery without a motive, a *grotesquerie* in horror absolutely alien from humanity, and a voice foreign in tone to the ears of men of many nations, and devoid of all distinct or intelligible syllabification. What result, then, has ensued? What impression have I made upon your fancy?"

I felt a creeping of the flesh as Dupin asked me the question. "A madman," I said, "has done this deed — some raving maniac, escaped from a neighboring *Maison de Santé.*"

"In some respects," he replied, "your idea is not irrelevant. But the voices of madmen, even in their wildest paroxysms, are never found to tally with that peculiar 30 voice heard upon the stairs. Madmen are of some nation, and their language, however incoherent in its words, has always the coherence of syllabification. Besides, the hair of a madman is not such as I now hold in my hand. I disentangled this little tuft from the rigidly clutched fingers of Madame L'Espanaye. Tell me what you can make of it."

"Dupin!" I said, completely unnerved; "this hair is most unusual — this is no *human* hair."

"I have not asserted that it is," said he; "but, before we decide this point, I wish you to glance at the little sketch I have here traced upon this paper. It is a *facsimile* drawing of what has been described in one portion of the testimony as 'dark bruises, 40 and deep indentations of finger nails,' upon the throat of Mademoiselle L'Espanaye, and in another (by Messrs. Dumas and Etienne), as a 'series of livid spots, evidently the impression of fingers.'

"You will perceive," continued my friend, spreading out the paper upon the table before us, "that this drawing gives the idea of a firm and fixed hold. There is no *slipping* apparent. Each finger has retained — possibly until the death of the victim — the fearful grasp by which it originally imbedded itself. Attempt, now, to place all your fingers, at the same time, in the respective impressions as you see them."

I made the attempt in vain.

"We are possibly not giving this matter a fair trial," he said. "The paper is spread out upon a plane surface; but the human throat is cylindrical. Here is a billet of wood, the circumference of which is about that of the throat. Wrap the drawing around it and try the experiment again."

10   I did so; but the difficulty was even more obvious than before.

"This," I said, "is the mark of no human hand."

"Read now," replied Dupin, "this passage from Cuvier."

It was a minute anatomical and generally descriptive account of the large fulvous Ourang-Outang of the East Indian Islands. The gigantic stature, the prodigious strength and activity, the wild ferocity, and the imitative propensities of these mammalia are sufficiently well known to all. I understood the full horrors of the murder at once.

"The description of the digits," said I, as I made an end of reading, "is in exact accordance with this drawing. I see that no animal but an Ourang-Outang, of the
20   species here mentioned, could have impressed the indentations as you have traced them. This tuft of tawny hair, too, is identical in character with that of the beast of Cuvier. But I cannot possibly comprehend the particulars of this frightful mystery. Besides, there were *two* voices heard in contention, and one of them was unquestionably the voice of a Frenchman."

"True; and you will remember an expression attributed almost unanimously, by the evidence, to this voice, — the expression, *'mon Dieu!'* This, under the circumstances, has been justly characterized by one of the witnesses (Montani, the confectioner), as an expression of remonstrance or expostulation. Upon these two words, therefore, I have mainly built my hopes of a full solution of the riddle. A French-
30   man was cognizant of the murder. It is possible — indeed it is far more than probable — that he was innocent of all participation in the bloody transactions which took place. The Ourang-Outang may have escaped from him. He may have traced it to the chamber; but, under the agitating circumstances which ensued, he could never have re-captured it. It is still at large. I will not pursue these guesses — for I have no right to call them more — since the shades of reflection upon which they are based are scarcely of sufficient depth to be appreciable by my own intellect, and since I could not pretend to make them intelligible to the understanding of another. If the Frenchman in question is indeed, as I suppose, innocent of this atrocity, this advertisement, which I left last night, upon our return home, at the office of *Le*
40   *Monde* (a paper devoted to the shipping interest, and much sought by sailors), will bring him to our residence."

---

12 **Cuvier**, Georges Léopold Chrétien Frédéric Dagobert Cuvier (1769-1832), French naturalist, the founder of comparative anatomy and paleontology, was famous for his reconstruction of the fleshy parts of extinct animals from fossil remains

He handed me a paper, and I read thus:

CAUGHT — *In the Bois de Boulogne, early this morning of the — inst.* (the morning of the murder), *a very large, tawny Ourang-Outang of the Bornese species. The owner (who is ascertained to be a sailor, belonging to a Maltese vessel), may have the animal again, upon identifying it satisfactorily and paying a few charges arising from its capture and keeping. Call at No. —, Rue —, Faubourg, St. Germain — au troisième.*

"How was it possible," I asked, "that you should know the man to be a sailor, and belonging to a Maltese vessel?"

"I do *not* know it," said Dupin. "I am not *sure* of it. Here, however, is a small piece of ribbon, which from its form, and from its greasy appearance, has evidently 10 been used in tying the hair in one of those long *queues* of which sailors are so fond. Moreover, this knot is one which few besides sailors can tie, and is peculiar to the Maltese. I picked the ribbon up at the foot of the lightning-rod. It could not have belonged to either of the deceased. Now if, after all, I am wrong in my induction from this ribbon, that the Frenchman was a sailor belonging to a Maltese vessel, still I can have done no harm in saying what I did in the advertisement. If I am in error, he will merely suppose that I have been misled by some circumstance into which he will not take the trouble to inquire. But if I am right, a great point is gained. Cognizant although innocent of the murder, the Frenchman will naturally hesitate about replying to the advertisement — about demanding the Ourang-Outang. 20 He will reason thus: — 'I am innocent; I am poor; my Ourang-Outang is of great value — to one in my circumstances a fortune of itself — why should I lose it through idle apprehensions of danger? Here it is, within my grasp. It was found in the Bois de Boulogne — at a vast distance from the scene of that butchery. How can it ever be suspected that a brute beast should have done the deed? The police are at fault — they have failed to procure the slightest clew. Should they even trace the animal, it would be impossible to prove me cognizant of the murder, or to implicate me in guilt on account of that cognizance. Above all, *I am known.* The advertiser designates me as the possessor of the beast. I am not sure to what limit his knowledge may extend. Should I avoid claiming a property of so great value, 30 which it is known that I possess, I will render the animal, at least, liable to suspicion. It is not my policy to attract attention either to myself or to the beast. I will answer the advertisement, get the Ourang-Outang, and keep it close until this matter has blown over.' "

At this moment we heard a step upon the stairs.

"Be ready," said Dupin, "with your pistols, but neither use them nor show them until at a signal from myself."

The front door of the house had been left open, and the visitor had entered, without ringing, and advanced several steps upon the staircase. Now, however, he seemed to hesitate. Presently we heard him descending. Dupin was moving quickly 40 to the door, when we again heard him coming up. He did not turn back a second time, but stepped up with decision, and rapped at the door of our chamber.

"Come in," said Dupin, in a cheerful and hearty tone.

A man entered. He was a sailor, evidently, — a tall, stout, and muscular-looking person, with a certain daredevil expression of countenance, not altogether unprepossessing. His face, greatly sunburnt, was more than half hidden by whisker and *mustachio*. He had with him a huge oaken cudgel, but appeared to be otherwise unarmed. He bowed awkwardly, and bade us "good evening," in French accents, which, although somewhat Neufchatelish, were still sufficiently indicative of a Parisian origin.

"Sit down, my friend," said Dupin. "I suppose you have called about the Ourang-
10 Outang. Upon my word, I almost envy you the possession of him; a remarkably fine, and no doubt a very valuable animal. How old do you suppose him to be?"

The sailor drew a long breath, with the air of a man relieved of some intolerable burden, and then replied, in an assured tone:

"I have no way of telling — but he can't be more than four or five years old. Have you got him here?"

"Oh no; we had no conveniences for keeping him here. He is at a livery stable in the Rue Dubourg, just by. You can get him in the morning. Of course you are prepared to identify the property?"

"To be sure I am, sir."

20 "I shall be sorry to part with him," said Dupin.

"I don't mean that you should be at all this trouble for nothing, sir," said the man. "Couldn't expect it. Am very willing to pay a reward for the finding of the animal — that is to say, anything in reason."

"Well," replied my friend, "that is all very fair, to be sure. Let me think! — what shall I have? Oh! I will tell you. My reward shall be this. You shall give me all the information in your power about these murders in the Rue Morgue."

Dupin said the last words in a very low tone, and very quietly. Just as quietly, too, he walked toward the door, locked it, and put the key in his pocket. He then drew a pistol from his bosom and placed it, without the least flurry, upon the table.
30 The sailor's face flushed up as if he were struggling with suffocation. He started to his feet and grasped his cudgel; but the next moment he fell back into his seat, trembling violently, and with the countenance of death itself. He spoke not a word. I pitied him from the bottom of my heart.

"My friend," said Dupin, in a kind tone, "you are alarming yourself unnecessarily — you are indeed. We mean you no harm whatever. I pledge you the honor of a gentleman and of a Frenchman, that we intend you no injury. I perfectly well know that you are innocent of the atrocities in the Rue Morgue. It will not do, however, to deny that you are in some measure implicated in them. From what I have already said, you must know that I have had means of information about this matter —
40 means of which you could never have dreamed. Now the thing stands thus. You have done nothing which you could have avoided — nothing, certainly, which renders you culpable. You were not even guilty of robbery, when you might have

---

7 **Neufchatelish,** characteristic of Neufchâtel, a city in northern France

robbed with impunity. You have nothing to conceal. You have no reason for concealment. On the other hand, you are bound by every principle of honor to confess all you know. An innocent man is now imprisoned, charged with that crime of which you can point out the perpetrator."

The sailor had recovered his presence of mind, in a great measure, while Dupin uttered these words; but his original boldness of bearing was all gone.

"So help me God," said he, after a brief pause, "I *will* tell you all I know about this affair; — but I do not expect you to believe one half I say — I would be a fool indeed if I did. Still, I *am* innocent, and I will make a clean breast if I die for it."

What he stated was, in substance, this. He had lately made a voyage to the Indian 10 Archipelago. A party, of which he formed one, landed at Borneo, and passed into the interior on an excursion of pleasure. Himself and a companion had captured the Ourang-Outang. This companion dying, the animal fell into his own exclusive possession. After great trouble, occasioned by the intractable ferocity of his captive during the home voyage, he at length succeeded in lodging it safely at his own residence in Paris, where, not to attract toward himself the unpleasant curiosity of his neighbors, he kept it carefully secluded, until such time as it should recover from a wound in the foot, received from a splinter on board ship. His ultimate design was to sell it.

Returning home from some sailors' frolic on the night, or rather in the morning 20 of the murder, he found the beast occupying his own bed-room, into which it had broken from a closet adjoining, where it had been, as was thought, securely confined. Razor in hand, and fully lathered, it was sitting before a looking-glass, attempting the operation of shaving, in which it had no doubt previously watched its master through the keyhole of the closet. Terrified at the sight of so dangerous a weapon in the possession of an animal so ferocious, and so well able to use it, the man, for some moments, was at a loss what to do. He had been accustomed however, to quiet the creature, even in its fiercest moods, by the use of a whip, and to this he now resorted. Upon sight of it, the Ourang-Outang sprang at once through the door of the chamber, down the stairs, and thence, through a window, unfortunately open, 30 into the street.

The Frenchman followed in despair; the ape, razor still in hand, occasionally stopping to look back and gesticulate at its pursuer, until the latter had nearly come up with it. It then again made off. In this manner the chase continued for a long time. The streets were profoundly quiet, as it was nearly three o'clock in the morning. In passing down an alley in the rear of the Rue Morgue, the fugitive's attention was arrested by a light gleaming from the open window of Madame L'Espanaye's chamber, in the fourth story of her house. Rushing to the building, it perceived the lightning-rod, clambered up with inconceivable agility, grasped the shutter, which was thrown fully back against the wall, and, by its means, swung itself 40 directly upon the headboard of the bed. The whole feat did not occupy a minute. The shutter was kicked open again by the Ourang-Outang as it entered the room.

The sailor, in the meantime, was both rejoiced and perplexed. He had strong hopes of now recapturing the brute, as it could scarcely escape from the trap into

which it had ventured, except by the rod, where it might be intercepted as it came down. On the other hand, there was much cause for anxiety as to what it might do in the house. This latter reflection urged the man still to follow the fugitive. A lightning-rod is ascended without difficulty, especially by a sailor; but, when he had arrived as high as the window, which lay far to his left, his career was stopped; the most that he could accomplish was to reach over so as to obtain a glimpse of the interior of the room. At this glimpse he nearly fell from his hold through excess of horror. Now it was that those hideous shrieks arose upon the night, which had startled from slumber the inmates of the Rue Morgue. Madame L'Espanaye and her
10 daughter, habited in their night clothes, had apparently been occupied in arranging some papers in the iron chest already mentioned, which had been wheeled into the middle of the room. It was open, and its contents lay beside it on the floor. The victims must have been sitting with their backs toward the window; and, from the time elapsing between the ingress of the beast and the screams, it seems probable that it was not immediately perceived. The flapping-to of the shutter would naturally have been attributed to the wind.

As the sailor looked in, the gigantic animal had seized Madame L'Espanaye by the hair (which was loose, as she had been combing it), and was flourishing the razor about her face, in imitation of the motions of a barber. The daughter
20 lay prostrate and motionless; she had swooned. The screams and struggles of the old lady (during which the hair was torn from her head) had the effect of changing the probably pacific purposes of the Ourang-Outang into those of wrath. With one determined sweep of its muscular arm it nearly severed her head from her body. The sight of blood inflamed its anger into phrenzy. Gnashing its teeth, and flashing fire from its eyes, it flew upon the body of the girl, and imbedded its fearful talons in her throat, retaining its grasp until she expired. Its wandering and wild glances fell at this moment upon the head of the bed, over which the face of its master, rigid with horror, was just discernible. The fury of the beast, who no doubt bore still in mind the dreaded whip, was instantly converted into fear. Conscious of
30 having deserved punishment, it seemed desirous of concealing its bloody deeds, and skipped about the chamber in an agony of nervous agitation; throwing down and breaking the furniture as it moved, and dragging the bed from the bedstead. In conclusion, it seized first the corpse of the daughter, and thrust it up the chimney, as it was found; then that of the old lady, which it immediately hurled through the window headlong.

As the ape approached the casement with its mutilated burden, the sailor shrank aghast to the rod, and, rather gliding than clambering down it, hurried at once home — dreading the consequences of the butchery, and gladly abandoning, in his terror, all solicitude about the fate of the Ourang-Outang. The words heard by the
40 party upon the staircase were the Frenchman's exclamations of horror and affright, commingled with the fiendish jabberings of the brute.

I have scarcely anything to add. The Ourang-Outang must have escaped from the chamber, by the rod, just before the breaking of the door. It must have closed the window as it passed through it. It was subsequently caught by the owner himself, who obtained for it a very large sum of the *Jardin des Plantes.* Le Bon was instantly released, upon our narration of the circumstances (with some comments from Dupin) at the *bureau* of the Prefect of Police. This functionary, however well disposed to my friend, could not altogether conceal his chagrin at the turn which affairs had taken, and was fain to indulge in a sarcasm or two, about the propriety of every person minding his own business.

"Let him talk," said Dupin, who had not thought it necessary to reply. "Let him discourse; it will ease his conscience. I am satisfied with having defeated him in his own castle. Nevertheless, that he failed in the solution of this mystery, is by no means that matter for wonder which he supposes it; for, in truth, our friend the   10
Prefect is somewhat too cunning to be profound. In his wisdom is no *stamen.* It is all head and no body, like the pictures of the Goddess Laverna, — or, at best, all head and shoulders, like a codfish. But he is a good creature after all. I like him especially for one master stroke of cant by which he has attained his reputation for ingenuity. I mean the way he has *'de nier ce qui est, et d'expliquer ce qui n'est pas.'* "

1841

---

1 **Jardin des Plantes,** French zoölogical gardens   15 **de nier** . . ., of denying what is said and explaining what is not. Poe, in a footnote, attributes the phrase to Rousseau's *Nouvelle Heloise*

The Masque of the Red Death

Once the exposition has been presented in the opening three paragraphs, this story of the masque so orders its happenings as to make them increasingly horrifying. The prince and his associates are given only enough characteristics to show increasingly contagious reactions of terror. The account of the ball falls into three climactically arranged parts, each terrifying in its own peculiar way — paragraphs four and five, then paragraphs six and seven, and then the remainder of the tale. The "tone" is handled to give different emotional significance to each of these sections. The tone, by repeating symbols of death and of fleeting time, also adds allegorical implications concerning the inevitable triumph of death over mankind.

The "Red Death" had long devastated the country. No pestilence had ever been so fatal, or so hideous. Blood was its avatar and its seal — the redness and the horror of blood. There were sharp pains, and sudden dizziness, and then profuse bleeding at the pores, with dissolution. The scarlet stains upon the body, and especially upon the face, of the victim were the pest ban which shut him out from the aid and from the sympathy of his fellow men. And the whole seizure, progress, and termination of the disease were the incidents of half an hour.

But the Prince Prospero was happy and dauntless and sagacious. When his dominions were half depopulated he summoned to his presence a thousand hale and lighthearted friends from among the knights and dames of his court, and with   10
these retired to the deep seclusion of one of his castellated abbeys. This was an ex-

---

Text: the *Broadway Journal,* July 19, 1845

tensive and magnificent structure, the creation of the prince's own eccentric yet august taste. A strong and lofty wall girdled it in. This wall had gates of iron. The courtiers, having entered, brought furnaces and massy hammers, and welded the bolts. They resolved to leave means neither of ingress or egress to the sudden impulses of despair or of phrenzy from within. The abbey was amply provisioned. With such precautions the courtiers might bid defiance to contagion. The external world could take care of itself. In the meantime it was folly to grieve, or to think. The prince had provided all the appliances of pleasure. There were buffoons, there were improvisatori, there were ballet-dancers, there were musicians, there was Beauty,
10 there was wine. All these and security were within. Without was the Red Death.

It was toward the close of the fifth or sixth month of his seclusion, and while the pestilence raged most furiously abroad, that the Prince Prospero entertained his thousand friends at a masked ball of the most unusual magnificence.

It was a voluptuous scene, that masquerade. But first let me tell of the rooms in which it was held. There were seven — an imperial suite. In many palaces, however, such suites form a long and straight vista, while the sliding doors slide back nearly to the walls on either hand, so that the view of the whole extent is scarcely impeded. Here the case was very different, as might have been expected from the prince's love of the bizarre. The apartments were so irregularly disposed that the vision embraced
20 but little more than one at a time. There was a sharp turn at every twenty or thirty yards, and at each turn a novel effect. To the right and left, in the middle of each wall, a tall and narrow Gothic window looked out upon a closed corridor which pursued the windings of the suite. These windows were of stained glass, whose color varied in accordance with the prevailing hue of the decorations of the chamber into which it opened. That at the eastern extremity was hung, for example, in blue — and vividly blue were its windows. The second chamber was purple in its ornaments and tapestries, and here the panes were purple. The third was green throughout, and so were the casements. The fourth was furnished and lighted with orange, the fifth with white, the sixth with violet. The seventh apartment was closely
30 shrouded in black velvet tapestries that hung all over the ceiling and down the walls, falling in heavy folds upon a carpet of the same material and hue. But, in this chamber only, the color of the windows failed to correspond with the decorations. The panes here were scarlet — a deep blood-color. Now in no one of the seven apartments was there any lamp or candelabrum, amid the profusion of golden ornaments that lay scattered to and fro or depended from the roof. There was no light of any kind emanating from lamp or candle within the suite of chambers. But in the corridors that followed the suite there stood, opposite to each window, a heavy tripod, bearing a brazier of fire, that projected its rays through the tinted glass and so glaringly illumined the room. And thus were produced a multitude of gaudy
40 and fantastic appearances. But in the western or black chamber the effect of the firelight that streamed upon the dark hanging through the blood-tinted panes was ghastly in the extreme, and produced so wild a look upon the countenances

---

9 **improvisatori,** composers and singers of extemporaneous songs   19 **irregularly disposed.** The arrangement of the rooms is of a sort to distress anyone with a tendency to claustrophobia

of those who entered that there were few of the company bold enough to set foot within its precincts at all.

It was in this apartment, also, that there stood against the western wall a gigantic clock of ebony. Its pendulum swung to and fro with a dull, heavy, monotonous clang; and when the minute hand made the circuit of the face, and the hour was to be stricken, there came from the brazen lungs of the clock a sound which was clear and loud and deep and exceedingly musical, but of so peculiar a note and emphasis that, at each lapse of an hour, the musicians of the orchestra were constrained to pause, momentarily, in their performance, to hearken to the sound; and thus the waltzers perforce ceased their evolutions; and there was a brief disconcert of the   10
whole gay company; and, while the chimes of the clock yet rang, it was observed that the giddiest grew pale, and the more aged and sedate passed their hands over their brows as if in confused revery or meditation. But when the echoes had fully ceased, a light laughter at once pervaded the assembly; the musicians looked at each other and smiled as if at their own nervousness and folly, and made whispering vows, each to the other, that the next chiming of the clock should produce in them no similar emotion and then, after the lapse of sixty minutes (which embrace three thousand and six hundred seconds of the Time that flies) there came yet another chiming of the clock, and then were the same disconcert and tremulousness and meditation as before.   20

But, in spite of these things, it was a gay and magnificent revel. The tastes of the prince were peculiar. He had a fine eye for colors and effects. He disregarded the *decora* of mere fashion. His plans were bold and fiery, and his conceptions glowed with barbaric luster. There are some who would have thought him mad. His followers felt that he was not. It was necessary to hear and see and touch him to be *sure* that he was not.

He had directed, in great part, the movable embellishments of the seven chambers, upon occasion of this great fete; and it was his own guiding taste which had given character to the masqueraders. Be sure they were grotesque. There were much glare and glitter and piquancy and phantasm — much of what has been since seen   30
in *Hernani*. There were arabesque figures with unsuited limbs and appointments. There were delirious fancies such as the madman fashions. There was much of the beautiful, much of the wanton, much of the bizarre, something of the terrible, and not a little of that which might have excited disgust. To and fro in the seven chambers there stalked, in fact, a multitude of dreams. And these — the dreams — writhed in and about, taking hue from the rooms, and causing the wild music of the orchestra to seem as the echo of their steps. And, anon, there strikes the ebony clock which stands in the hall of the velvet. And then, for a moment, all is still, and all is silent save the voice of the clock. The dreams are stiff frozen as they stand. But the echoes of the chime die away — they have endured but an instant — and a   40
light, half-subdued laughter floats after them as they depart. And now again the music swells, and the dreams live, and writhe to and fro more merrily than ever, taking hue from the many-tinted windows through which stream the rays from the

31 **Hernani** (1830), a lavishly costumed romantic play by Victor Hugo

tripods. But to the chamber which lies most westwardly of the seven, there are now none of the maskers who venture; for the night is waning away, and there flows a ruddier light through the blood-colored panes; and the blackness of the sable drapery appals; and to him whose foot falls upon the sable carpet, there comes from the near clock of ebony a muffled peal more solemnly emphatic than any which reaches their ears who indulge in the more remote gaieties of the other apartments.

But these other apartments were densely crowded, and in them beat feverishly the heart of life. And the revel went whirlingly on, until at length there commenced the sounding of midnight upon the clock. And then the music ceased, as I have 10 told; and the evolutions of the waltzers were quieted; and there was an uneasy cessation of all things as before. But now there were twelve strokes to be sounded by the bell of the clock; and thus it happened, perhaps, that before the last echoes of the last chime had utterly sunk into silence, there were many individuals in the crowd who had found leisure to become aware of the presence of a masked figure which had arrested the attention of no single individual before. And the rumor of this new presence having spread itself whisperingly around, there arose at length from the whole company a buzz, or murmur, expressive of disapprobation and surprise — then, finally, of terror, of horror, and of disgust.

In an assembly of phantasms such as I have painted, it may well be supposed 20 that no ordinary appearance could have excited such sensation. In truth the masquerade license of the night was nearly unlimited; but the figure in question had outHeroded Herod, and gone beyond the bound of even the prince's indefinite decorum. There are chords in the hearts of the most reckless which cannot be touched without emotion. Even with the utterly lost, to whom life and death are equally jests, there are matters of which no jest can be made. The whole company, indeed, seemed now deeply to feel that in the costume and bearing of the stranger neither wit nor propriety existed. The figure was tall and gaunt, and shrouded from head to foot in the habiliments of the grave. The mask which concealed the visage was made so nearly to resemble the countenance of a stiffened corpse that the closest 30 scrutiny must have had difficulty in detecting the cheat. And yet all this might have been endured, if not approved, by the mad revelers around. But the mummer had gone so far as to assume the type of the Red Death. His vesture was dabbled in *blood* — and his broad brow, with all the features of the face, was besprinkled with the scarlet horror.

When the eyes of Prince Prospero fell upon this spectral image (which with a slow and solemn movement, as if more fully to sustain its role, stalked to and fro among the waltzers) he was seen to be convulsed, in the first moment, with a strong shudder either of terror or distaste; but, in the next, his brow reddened with rage.

"Who dares?" he demanded hoarsely of the courtiers who stood near him — "who 40 dares insult us with this blasphemous mockery? Seize him and unmask him — that we may know whom we have to hang at sunrise, from the battlements!"

---

10 **the waltzers.** It is important to know that since in 1842 many considered the waltz an immoral dance, mention of waltzers adds to the depiction of revelry   21 **had outHeroded Herod,** a quotation from Hamlet's speech to the players, meaning, in this context, "had gone beyond the extremes of this orgy"

It was in the eastern or blue chamber in which stood the Prince Prospero as he uttered these words. They rang throughout the seven rooms loudly and clearly — for the prince was a bold and robust man, and the music had become hushed at the waving of his hand.

It was in the blue room where stood the prince, with a group of pale courtiers by his side. At first, as he spoke, there was a slight rushing movement of this group in the direction of the intruder, who at the moment was also near at hand, and now, with deliberate and stately step, made closer approach to the speaker. But from a certain nameless awe with which the mad assumptions of the mummer had inspired the whole party, there were found none who put forth hand to seize him; so that, unimpeded, he passed within a yard of the prince's person; and while the vast assembly as if with one impulse, shrank from the centers of the rooms to the walls, he made his way uninterruptedly, but with the same solemn and measured step which had distinguished him from the first, through the blue chamber to the purple — through the purple to the green — through the green to the orange — through this again to the white — and even thence to the violet, ere a decided movement had been made to arrest him. It was then, however, that the Prince Prospero, maddening with rage and the shame of his own momentary cowardice, rushed hurriedly through the six chambers, while none followed him on account of a deadly terror that had seized upon all. He bore aloft a drawn dagger, and had approached, in rapid impetuosity, to within three or four feet of the retreating figure, when the latter, having attained the extremity of the velvet apartment, turned suddenly and confronted his pursuer. There was a sharp cry — and the dagger dropped gleaming upon the sable carpet, upon which, instantly afterwards, fell prostrate in death the Prince Prospero. Then, summoning the wild courage of despair, a throng of the revelers at once threw themselves into the black apartment, and, seizing the mummer, whose tall figure stood erect and motionless within the shadow of the ebony clock, gasped in unutterable horror at finding the grave cerements and corpselike mask, which they handled with so violent a rudeness, untenanted by any tangible form.

And now was acknowledged the presence of the Red Death. He had come like a thief in the night. And one by one dropped the revelers in the blood-bedewed halls of their revel, and died each in the despairing posture of his fall. And the life of the ebony clock went out with that of the last of the gay. And the flames of the tripods expired. And Darkness and Decay and the Red Death held illimitable dominion over all.

1842

The Cask of Amontillado

The thousand injuries of Fortunato I had borne as I best could; but when he ventured upon insult, I vowed revenge. You, who so well know the nature of my soul, will not suppose, however, that I gave utterance to a threat. *At length* I would be avenged; this was a point definitively settled — but the very definitiveness with which it was resolved precluded the idea of risk. I must not only punish, but punish with impunity. A wrong is unredressed when retribution overtakes its redresser. It is equally unredressed when the avenger fails to make himself felt as such to him who has done the wrong.

It must be understood that neither by word nor deed had I given Fortunato cause to doubt my good will. I continued, as was my wont, to smile in his face, and he did not perceive that my smile *now* was at the thought of his immolation.

He had a weak point — this Fortunato — although in other regards he was a man to be respected and even feared. He prided himself on his connoisseurship in
10 wine. Few Italians have the true virtuoso spirit. For the most part their enthusiasm is adopted to suit the time and opportunity — to practice imposture upon the British and Austrian millionaires. In painting and gemmary, Fortunato, like his countrymen, was a quack — but in the matter of old wines he was sincere. In this respect I did not differ from him materially: I was skillful in the Italian vintages myself, and bought largely whenever I could.

It was about dusk, one evening during the supreme madness of the carnival season, that I encountered my friend. He accosted me with excessive warmth, for he had been drinking much. The man wore motley. He had on a tight-fitting parti-striped dress, and his head was surmounted by the conical cap and bells. I was so
20 pleased to see him that I thought I should never have done wringing his hand.

I said to him, "My dear Fortunato, you are luckily met. How remarkably well you are looking today! But I have received a pipe of what passes for Amontillado, and I have my doubts."

"How?" said he. "Amontillado? A pipe? Impossible! And in the middle of the carnival!"

"I have my doubts," I replied; "and I was silly enough to pay the full Amontillado price without consulting you in the matter. You were not to be found, and I was fearful of losing a bargain."

"Amontillado!"
30 "I have my doubts."

"Amontillado!"

"And I must satisfy them."

"Amontillado!"

"As you are engaged, I am on my way to Luchresi. If any one has a critical turn, it is he. He will tell me —"

"Luchresi cannot tell Amontillado from Sherry."

"And yet some fools will have it that his taste is a match for your own."

"Come, let us go."

"Whither?"
40 "To your vaults."

"My friend, no; I will not impose upon your good nature. I perceive you have an engagement. Luchresi —"

"I have no engagement; — come."

---

12 **gemmary,** knowledge of precious stones   22 **pipe,** large barrel   22 **Amontillado,** a Spanish sherry

"My friend, no. It is not the engagement, but the severe cold with which I perceive you are afflicted. The vaults are insufferably damp. They are incrusted with niter."

"Let us go, nevertheless. The cold is merely nothing. Amontillado! You have been imposed upon. And as for Luchresi, he cannot distinguish Sherry from Amontillado."

Thus speaking, Fortunato possessed himself of my arm. Putting on a mask of black silk, and drawing a *roquelaire* closely about my person, I suffered him to hurry me to my palazzo.

There were no attendants at home; they had absconded to make merry in honor of the time. I had told them that I should not return until the morning, and had 10 given them explicit orders not to stir from the house. These orders were sufficient, I well knew, to insure their immediate disappearance, one and all, as soon as my back was turned.

I took from their sconces two flambeaus, and giving one to Fortunato, bowed him through several suites of rooms to the archway that led into the vaults. I passed down a long and winding staircase, requesting him to be cautious as he followed. We came at length to the foot of the descent, and stood together on the damp ground of the catacombs of the Monstresors.

The gait of my friend was unsteady, and the bells upon his cap jingled as he strode.

"The pipe," said he.   20

"It is farther on," said I; "but observe the white webwork which gleams from these cavern walls."

He turned towards me, and looked into my eyes with two filmy orbs that distilled the rheum of intoxication.

"Niter?" he asked at length.

"Niter," I replied. "How long have you had that cough?"

"Ugh! ugh! ugh! — ugh! ugh! ugh! — ugh! ugh! ugh! — ugh! ugh! ugh! — ugh! ugh! ugh!"

My poor friend found it impossible to reply for many minutes.

"It is nothing," he said, at last.   30

"Come," I said, with decision, "we will go back; your health is precious. You are rich, respected, admired, beloved; you are happy, as once I was. You are a man to be missed. For me it is no matter. We will go back; you will be ill, and I cannot be responsible. Besides, there is Luchresi — "

"Enough," he said; "the cough is a mere nothing; it will not kill me. I shall not die of a cough."

"True — true," I replied; "and, indeed, I had no intention of alarming you unnecessarily — but you should use all proper caution. A draught of this Medoc will defend us from the damps."

Here I knocked off the neck of a bottle which I drew from a long row of its fel- 40 lows that lay upon the mold.

"Drink," I said, presenting him the wine.

---

7 **roquelaire**, see note to line 24, p. 799   38 **Medoc**, wine from a particular region in France

He raised it to his lips with a leer. He paused and nodded to me familiarly, while his bells jingled.

"I drink," he said, "to the buried that repose around us."

"And I to your long life."

He again took my arm, and we proceeded.

"These vaults," he said, "are extensive."

"The Montresors," I replied, "were a great and numerous family."

"I forget your arms."

"A huge human foot d'or, in a field azure; the foot crushes a serpent rampant
10 whose fangs are embedded in the heel."

"And the motto?"

"Nemo me impune lacessit."

"Good!" he said.

The wine sparkled in his eyes and the bells jingled. My own fancy grew warm with the Medoc. We had passed through long walls of piled skeletons, with casks and puncheons intermingling, into the inmost recesses of the catacombs. I paused again, and this time I made bold to seize Fortunato by an arm above the elbow.

"The niter!" I said; "see, it increases. It hangs like moss upon the vaults. We are below the river's bed. The drops of moisture trickle among the bones. Come, we
20 will go back ere it is too late. Your cough —"

"It is nothing," he said; "let us go on. But first, another draught of the Medoc."

I broke and reached him a flagon of De Grâve. He emptied it at a breath. His eyes flashed with a fierce light. He laughed and threw the bottle upwards with a gesticulation I did not understand.

I looked at him in surprise. He repeated the movement — a grotesque one.

"You do not comprehend?" he said.

"Not I," I replied.

"Then you are not of the brotherhood."

"How?"

30 "You are not of the masons."

"Yes, yes," I said, "yes, yes."

"You? Impossible! A mason?"

"A mason," I replied.

"A sign," he said, "a sign."

"It is this," I answered, producing from beneath the folds of my *roquelaire,* a trowel.

"You jest," he exclaimed, recoiling a few paces. "But let us proceed to the Amontillado."

"Be it so," I said, replacing the tool beneath the cloak, and again offering him
40 my arm. He leaned upon it heavily. We continued our route in search of the Amon-

---

8 **arms,** coat of arms. That described by the narrator — a golden foot on a blue field, crushing a serpent — is symbolic, from his point of view, of the action of his story   12 **Nemo . . . lacessit.** No one attacks me with impunity — a reiteration of the vengeful attitude of the narrator   22 **De Grâve,** more accurately, Graves, a Bordeaux wine

tillado. We passed through a range of low arches, descended, passed on, and, descending again, arrived at a deep crypt, in which the foulness of the air caused our flambeaus rather to glow than flame.

At the most remote end of the crypt there appeared another less spacious. Its walls had been lined with human remains, piled to the vault overhead, in the fashion of the great catacombs of Paris. Three sides of this interior crypt were still ornamented in this manner. From the fourth the bones had been thrown down, and lay promiscuously upon the earth, forming at one point a mound of some size. Within the wall thus exposed by the displacing of the bones, we perceived a still interior recess, in depth about four feet, in width three, in height six or seven. 10 It seemed to have been constructed for no especial use within itself, but formed merely the interval between two of the colossal supports of the roof of the catacombs, and was backed by one of their circumscribing walls of solid granite.

It was in vain that Fortunato, uplifting his dull torch, endeavored to pry into the depth of the recess. Its termination the feeble light did not enable us to see.

"Proceed," I said; "herein is the Amontillado. As for Luchresi —"

"He is an ignoramus," interrupted my friend, as he stepped unsteadily forward, while I followed immediately at his heels. In an instant he had reached the extremity of the niche, and finding his progress arrested by the rock stood stupidly bewildered. A moment more and I had fettered him to the granite. In its surface were two iron 20 staples, distant from each other about two feet, horizontally. From one of these depended a short chain, from the other a padlock. Throwing the links about his waist, it was but the work of a few seconds to secure it. He was too much astounded to resist. Withdrawing the key, I stepped back from the recess.

"Pass your hand," I said, "over the wall; you cannot help feeling the niter. Indeed it is *very* damp. Once more let me *implore* you to return. No? Then I must positively leave you. But I must first render you all the little attentions in my power."

"The Amontillado!" ejaculated my friend, not yet recovered from his astonishment.   30

"True," I replied; "the Amontillado."

As I said these words I busied myself among the pile of bones of which I have before spoken. Throwing them aside, I soon uncovered a quantity of building stone and mortar. With these materials and with the aid of my trowel, I began vigorously to wall up the entrance of the niche.

I had scarcely laid the first tier of the masonry when I discovered that the intoxication of Fortunato had in a great measure worn off. The earliest indication I had of this was a low moaning cry from the depth of the recess. It was *not* the cry of a drunken man. There was then a long and obstinate silence. I laid the second tier, and the third, and the fourth; and then I heard the furious vibrations of the chain. The 40 noise lasted for several minutes, during which, that I might hearken to it with the more satisfaction, I ceased my labors and sat down upon the bones. When at last the clanking subsided, I resumed the trowel, and finished without interruption the fifth, the sixth, and the seventh tier. The wall was now nearly upon a level with my breast. I again paused, and holding the flambeaus over the mason work, threw a few feeble rays upon the figure within.

A succession of loud and shrill screams, bursting suddenly from the throat of the chained form, seemed to thrust me violently back. For a brief moment I hesitated — I trembled. Unsheathing my rapier, I began to grope with it about the recess; but the thought of an instant reassured me. I placed my hand upon the solid fabric of the catacombs, and felt satisfied. I reapproached the wall. I replied to the yells of him who clamored. I re-echoed — I aided — I surpassed them in volume and in strength. I did this, and the clamorer grew still.

10   It was now midnight, and my task was drawing to a close. I had completed the eighth, the ninth, and the tenth tier. I had finished a portion of the last and the eleventh; there remained but a single stone to be fitted and plastered in. I struggled with its weight; I placed it partially in its destined position. But now there came from out the niche a low laugh that erected the hairs upon my head. It was succeeded by a sad voice, which I had difficulty in recognizing as that of the noble Fortunato. The voice said —

"Ha! ha! ha! — he! he! he! — a very good joke indeed — an excellent jest. We will have many a rich laugh about it at the palazzo — he! he! he! — over our wine — he! he! he!"

20   "The Amontillado!" I said.

"He! he! he! — he! he! he! — yes, the Amontillado. But is it not getting late? Will not they be awaiting us at the palazzo, — the Lady Fortunato and the rest? Let us be gone."

"Yes," I said, "let us be gone."

"For the love of God, Montresor!"

"Yes," I said, "for the love of God!"

But to these words I hearkened in vain for a reply. I grew impatient. I called aloud —

"Fortunato!"

30   No answer. I called again —

"Fortunato!"

No answer still. I thrust a torch through the remaining aperture and let it fall within. There came forth in return only a jingling of the bells. My heart grew sick — on account of the dampness of the catacombs. I hastened to make an end of my labor. I forced the last stone into its position; I plastered it up. Against the new masonry I re-erected the old rampart of bones. For the half of a century no mortal has disturbed them. *In pace requiescat.*

1846

---

37 **In pace requiescat.** In peace may he rest

Romance

First published in 1829, this poem, like many by Poe, underwent a great deal of revision. In 1831 it was extended to about three times its original length; then, in later versions (1843, 1845), it returned to approximately its first form. Professor Killis Campbell says that the passages added in 1831 "are largely personal in nature — a fact which probably explains their omission in subsequent editions." Equally important, perhaps, is the fact that they were unduly repetitious. In a letter to John Neal, Poe characterized this poem as the "best thing," in every respect save "sound," in the 1829 volume. He was "certain," he said, that the five opening lines of the second stanza had "never been surpassed." The theme is much like that of Byron's "To Romance": in each poem the author renounces romance and swears allegiance to truth.

Romance, who loves to nod and sing,
With drowsy head and folded wing,
Among the green leaves as they shake
Far down within some shadowy lake,
To me a painted paroquet
Hath been — a most familiar bird —
Taught me my alphabet to say,
To lisp my very earliest word,
While in the wild wood I did lie,
A child — with a most knowing eye.   10

Of late, eternal Condor years
So shake the very Heaven on high
With tumult as they thunder by,
I have no time for idle cares
Through gazing on the unquiet sky.
And when an hour with calmer wings
Its down upon my spirit flings —
That little time with lyre and rhyme
To while away — forbidden things!
My heart would feel to be a crime   20
Unless it trembled with the strings.

                                        1829

Sonnet — To Science

Probably composed in the spring or summer of 1829, "Sonnet — To Science" echoes ideas of John Keats and Samuel Taylor Coleridge. "Do not all charms fly," asked Keats, in "Lamia," "at the merest touch of cold philosophy?" The opening lines of "Lamia" show some interesting parallels to lines 9-14 of this poem. Similarly, in Chapter XIV of his Biographia Literaria, *Coleridge had discoursed on science versus poetry.*

Science! true daughter of Old Time thou art!
Who alterest all things with thy peering eyes,
Why preyest thou thus upon the poet's heart,
Vulture, whose wings are dull realities?
How should he love thee? or how deem thee wise,
Who wouldst not leave him in his wandering
To seek for treasure in the jewelled skies,
Albeit he soared with an undaunted wing?
Hast thou not dragged Diana from her car?
And driven the Hamadryad from the wood   10
To seek a shelter in some happier star?
Hast thou not torn the Naiad from her flood,
The Elfin from the green grass, and from me
The summer dream beneath the tamarind tree?

                  1829

To Helen

Although Poe tacitly sanctioned the claim that this poem was written when he was only fourteen, it seems more likely that it was produced between 1829 and the year when it was published, 1831. It is, nevertheless, a tribute to Poe's boyhood idol, Mrs. Jane Stith Stanard of Richmond, who died in 1824, and whom he called "the first pure ideal love of my soul." As the notes suggest, some lines were felicitously revised in the 1845 edition, here reproduced.

*   The unity of this poem derives from both its feeling and its metaphorical expression. The imagery not only makes its heroine a haven for a desperate wanderer in darkness; it also increasingly associates Helen's type of classical beauty with the immortal splendor of Greece and Rome. In the first stanza, Helen's beauty is like "barks of yore," which carried the wanderer to his homeland, and the words "Nicean," "perfumed," and "weary, wayworn wanderer" (Ulysses) vaguely connote classical associations. In stanza two the classical quality of Helen's beauty is more clearly suggested, and "home" becomes "the glory that was Greece and the grandeur that was Rome." These opening stanzas hark back to the past; the third stanza, in the present tense, likens Helen to a statue standing in a lighted window-niche, thus attributing to her not only physical beauty but also immortal beauty of soul.*

Helen, thy beauty is to me
  Like those Nicean barks of yore,
That gently, o'er a perfumed sea,
  The weary, wayworn wanderer bore
    To his own native shore.

On desperate seas long wont to roam,
  Thy hyacinth hair, thy classic face,

---

2 **Nicean**, a word about which there has been much scholarly argument. The suggestion of J. J. Jones that it is derived from the Latin poetry of Catullus seems likely   7 **hyacinth** harks back to "Hyacinthine," a Homeric epithet for hair, probably meaning "curly ringlets"

Thy Naiad airs, have brought me home
   To the Glory that was Greece
And the grandeur that was Rome.   10

Lo! in yon brilliant window-niche
   How statue-like I see thee stand,
   The agate lamp within thy hand!
Ah, Psyche, from the regions which
   Are Holy Land!

                1829?, 1831

---

9 **To the Glory . . . Rome,** read, in the 1831 version, "To the beauty of fair Greece, and the grandeur of old Rome"   11 **brilliant window-niche,** in the original version, was "that little window-niche." The change set off the heroine in light from the poet in darkness   13 **agate lamp,** in the original, was "golden scroll." The lamp gives more of an impression of permanence and adds to the light associated with the figure of the woman

The City in the Sea

Lo! Death has reared himself a throne
In a strange city lying alone
Far down within the dim West,
Where the good and the bad and the worst and the best
Have gone to their eternal rest.
There shrines and palaces and towers
(Time-eaten towers that tremble not)
Resemble nothing that is ours.
Around, by lifting winds forgot,
Resignedly beneath the sky   10
The melancholy waters lie.

No rays from the holy heaven come down
On the long night-time of that town;
But light from out the lurid sea
Streams up the turrets silently,
Gleams up the pinnacles far and free:
Up domes, up spires, up kingly halls;
Up fanes, up Babylon-like walls,
Up shadowy long-forgotten bowers
Of sculptured ivy and stone flowers,   20
Up many and many a marvelous shrine
Whose wreathed friezes intertwine
The viol, the violet, and the vine.

Resignedly beneath the sky
The melancholy waters lie.
So blend the turrets and shadows there
That all seem pendulous in air,
While from a proud tower in the town
Death looks gigantically down.

There open fanes and gaping graves   30
Yawn level with the luminous waves;
But not the riches there that lie
In each idol's diamond eye, —
Not the gayly-jewelled dead,
Tempt the waters from their bed;
For no ripples curl, alas,
Along that wilderness of glass;
No swellings tell that winds may be
Upon some far-off happier sea;
No heavings hint that winds have been   40
On seas less hideously serene!

But lo, a stir is in the air!
The wave — there is a movement there!
As if the towers had thrust aside,
In slightly sinking, the dull tide;
As if their tops had feebly given
A void within the filmy Heaven!
The waves have now a redder glow,
The hours are breathing faint and low;
And when, amid no earthly moans,   50
Down, down that town shall settle hence,
Hell, rising from a thousand thrones,
Shall do it reverence.

                    1831

Israfel

Poe, in the motto, took a few liberties with the description of Israfel in Sale's "Preliminary Discourse" on the Koran, thereby making the phrases of the motto more appropriate than the original phrases had been. The words added in this revision, "whose heart-strings are a lute," were probably suggested by a passage in a poem by Béranger, also used as a motto for "The Fall of the House of Usher."

The song embodies some of Poe's theories about poetry — that a true poet writes from his heart, that his song is melodious and inspiring. The final stanzas voice despair concerning a poet's hampering environment.

And the angel Israfel, whose heart-strings are a lute, and who has the sweetest voice of all God's creatures. — KORAN

In Heaven a spirit doth dwell
  "Whose heart-strings are a lute;"
None sing so wildly well
As the angel Israfel,
And the giddy stars (so legends tell)
Ceasing their hymns, attend the spell
  Of his voice, all mute.

Tottering above
  In her highest noon,
  The enamoured moon   10
Blushes with love,
  While, to listen, the red levin
  (With the rapid Pleiads, even,
  Which were seven,)
  Pauses in Heaven.

And they say (the starry choir
  And the other listening things)
That Israfeli's fire
Is owing to that lyre
  By which he sits and sings —   20
The trembling living wire
Of those unusual strings.

But the skies that angel trod,
  Where deep thoughts are a duty —
Where Love's a grown-up God —
  Where the Houri glances are
Imbued with all the beauty
  Which we worship in a star.

Therefore, thou art not wrong,
  Israfeli, who despisest   30
An unimpassioned song;
To thee the laurels belong,
  Best bard, because the wisest!
Merrily live, and long!

Text: the 1845 volume   12 **levin,** lightning   13 **Pleiades,** a group of stars which according to Greek legend are the transformed seven daughters of Atlas

The ecstasies above
  With thy burning measures suit —
Thy grief, thy joy, thy hate, thy love,
  With the fervour of thy lute —
  Well may the stars be mute!

Yes, Heaven is thine; but this   40
  Is a world of sweets and sours;
  Our flowers are merely — flowers,
And the shadow of thy perfect bliss
  Is the sunshine of ours.

If I could dwell
Where Israfel
  Hath dwelt, and he where I,
He might not sing so wildly well
  A mortal melody,
While a bolder note than this might swell 50
  From my lyre within the sky.

                          1831

The Coliseum

This poem, which was at one time a soliloquy of the hero of Poe's drama, Politian, *was first published in* The Visiter *in 1833. It is interesting in two ways: as evidence of Byron's influence on Poe and as the earliest known example of Poe's use of blank verse. The first two stanzas announce the spell to be worked by the ancient ruin; the second two show the "silence, desolation, and dim night" with a series of appropriate images; and the final stanza evokes the light and the melody which give the scene immortal power.*

Type of the antique Rome! Rich reliquary
Of lofty contemplation left to Time
By buried centuries of pomp and power!
At length — at length — after so many days
Of weary pilgrimage and burning thirst
(Thirst for the springs of lore that in thee lie),
I kneel, an altered and an humble man,
Amid thy shadows, and so drink within
My very soul thy grandeur, gloom, and glory!

Vastness! and Age! and Memories of Eld!   10
Silence! and Desolation! and dim Night!

---

1 **Type**, emblem

I feel ye now — I feel ye in your strength —
O spells more sure than e'er Judaen king
Taught in the gardens of Gethsemane!
O charms more potent than the rapt Chaldee
Ever drew down from out the quiet stars!

Here, where a hero fell, a column falls!
Here, where the mimic eagle glared in gold,
A midnight vigil holds the swarthy bat!
Here, where the dames of Rome their gilded hair   20
Waved to the wind, now wave the reed and thistle!
Here, where on golden throne the monarch lolled,
Glides, spectre-like, unto his marble home,
Lit by the wan light of the horned moon,
The swift and silent lizard of the stones!

But stay! these walls — these ivy-clad arcades —
These mouldering plinths — these sad and blackened shafts —
These vague entablatures — this crumbling frieze —
These shattered cornices — this wreck — this ruin —
These stones — alas! these gray stones — are they all —   30
All of the famed and the colossal left
By the corrosive Hours to Fate and me?

"Not all"— the Echoes answer me — "not all!
Prophetic sounds and loud, arise forever
From us, and from all Ruin, unto the wise,
As melody from Memnon to the Sun.
We rule the hearts of mightiest men — we rule
With a despotic sway all giant minds.
We are not impotent — we pallid stones.
Not all our power is gone — not all our fame —   40
Not all the magic of our high renown —
Not all the wonder that encircles us —
Not all the mysteries that in us lie —
Not all the memories that hang upon
And cling around about us as a garment,
Clothing us in a robe of more than glory."

                                                        1833

13 **Judaen king,** Christ   14 **Gethsemane,** the garden near Jerusalem which was the scene of the agony
and arrest of Christ, as recorded in Matthew 26:36   15 **Chaldee** refers to the fame of the Chaldeans as
astrologers and wizards   18 **mimic eagle,** the standard of the Roman legions   20 **gilded hair** refers
to the gilt wigs worn by fashionable Roman ladies, and continues the association of departed gold with the
vanished folk of the ancient world   36 **Memnon,** son of Aurora and Tithonus — the king of the Ethiopians. His statue was reputed to give forth a harplike sound at sunrise

To One in Paradise

This song first appeared, without title, in a story published in January 1834. After numerous revisions, it appeared in 1845 with the present text and title. The most fortunate revision discarded this final stanza which had reduced a melodious and moving poem to the level of sentimentality:

> *Alas! for that accursed time*
> *They bore thee o'er the billow,*
> *From Love to titled age and crime,*
> *And an unholy pillow —*
> *From me, and from our misty clime,*
> *Where weeps the silver willow!*

Thou wast all that to me, love,
  For which my soul did pine:
A green isle in the sea, love,
  A fountain and a shrine,
All wreathed with fairy fruits and flowers,
  And all the flowers were mine.

Ah, dream too bright to last!
  Ah, starry Hope, that didst arise
But to be overcast!
  A voice from out the Future cries,   10
"On! on!" — but o'er the Past
  (Dim gulf!) my spirit hovering lies
Mute, motionless, aghast!

For, alas! alas! with me
  The light of Life is o'er!
No more — no more — no more —
  (Such language holds the solemn sea
  To the sands upon the shore)
Shall bloom the thunder-blasted tree,
  Or the stricken eagle soar!   20

And all my days are trances,
  And all my nightly dreams
Are where thy gray eye glances,
  And where thy footstep gleams —
In what ethereal dances,
  By what eternal streams.

1833, 1834

Sonnet – Silence

About the phrase "the corporate Silence" in line 10 of this irregular sonnet, Professor Campbell wrote this illuminating note: "That is, I take it, the physical death, the death which we can perceive with the senses. His shadow (1. 13), incorporate Silence, is, then, to be construed as the tyrant that rules in the nether world, in which the spirits of the unrighteous remain till the Day of Judgment."

There are some qualities — some incorporate things,
   That have a double life, which thus is made
A type of that twin entity which springs
   From matter and light, evinced in solid and shade.
There is a two-fold *Silence* — sea and shore —
   Body and soul. One dwells in lonely places,
   Newly with grass o'ergrown; some solemn graces,
Some human memories and tearful lore,
Render him terrorless: his name's "No More."
He is the corporate Silence: dread him not!   10
   No power hath he of evil in himself;
But should some urgent fate (untimely lot!)
   Bring thee to meet his shadow (nameless elf,
That haunteth the lone regions where hath trod
No foot of man), commend thyself to God!

                                       1840

_____

Text: the 1845 volume

Dream-Land

In this poem, published in Graham's Magazine, *June 1, 1844, Poe hit upon what critics called his later manner — the repetitive and rhythmic style of such lyrical works as "The Raven" and "Ulalume." The romantic depiction of a land "out of space, out of time" is representative of many of Poe's poetic descriptions. The identification of the land as the kingdom of death adds a touch highly characteristic of the author.*

   By a route obscure and lonely,
   Haunted by ill angels only,
   Where an Eidolon, named NIGHT,
   On a black throne reigns upright,
     I have reached these lands but newly

_____

3 **Eidolon,** phantom   3 **NIGHT,** here personified, as in many poems by Poe and others, as Death

From an ultimate dim Thule —
From a wild weird clime that lieth, sublime,
　　　Out of SPACE — out of TIME.

Bottomless vales and boundless floods,
　　And chasms, and caves, and Titan woods,　10
With forms that no man can discover
For the tears that drip all over;
Mountains toppling evermore
Into seas without a shore;
Seas that restlessly aspire,
Surging, unto skies of fire;
Lakes that endlessly outspread
Their lone waters, lone and dead, —
Their still waters, still and chilly
With the snows of the lolling lily.　　20

By the lakes that thus outspread
Their lone waters, lone and dead, —
Their sad waters, sad and chilly
With the snows of the lolling lily, —
By the mountains — near the river
Murmuring lowly, murmuring ever, —
By the grey woods, — by the swamp
Where the toad and the newt encamp, —
By the dismal tarns and pools
　　　Where dwell the Ghouls, —　　30
By each spot the most unholy —
In each nook most melancholy, —
There the traveller meets, aghast,
Sheeted Memories of the Past —
Shrouded forms that start and sigh
As they pass the wanderer by —
White-robed forms of friends long given,
In agony, to the Earth — and Heaven.

For the heart whose woes are legion
'Tis a peaceful, soothing region —　　40
For the spirit that walks in shadow
'Tis — oh, 'tis an Eldorado!
But the traveller, travelling through it,
May not — dare not openly view it;

---

6 **ultimate dim Thule,** from Latin *ultima Thule,* the farthest land　　10 **Titan,** gigantic and ancient　　30
Ghouls, demons which rob graves and feed upon corpses　　42 **Eldorado.** See headnote p. 853

Never its mysteries are exposed
To the weak human eye unclosed;
So wills its King, who hath forbid
The uplifting of the fringed lid;
And thus the sad Soul that here passes
Beholds it but through darkened glasses.   50

By a route obscure and lonely,
Haunted by ill angels only,
Where an Eidolon, named NIGHT,
On a black throne reigns upright,
I have wandered home but newly
From this ultimate dim Thule.

                                          1844

The Raven

When, in 1841, Poe reviewed Dickens' Barnaby Rudge, *he said: "The raven [in this novel], too, intensely amusing as it is, might have been made, more than we now see it, a portion of the conception of the fantastic Barnaby. Its croakings might have been prophetically heard in the course of the drama. Its character might have performed, in regard to that of the idiot, much the same part as does, in music, the accompaniment in respect to the air." This passage has led to the suggestion that, as early as 1841, Poe had some inklings of the sort of story told in his most famous poem. The best deduction from contradictory data regarding the time he composed the poem, however, sets the date of beginning composition not earlier than 1842 and the date of completion not before the middle of 1844.*

"The Philosophy of Composition," regardless of its literal accuracy as an account of the writing of the poem, offers most illuminating suggestions about the structure and the thought.

Once upon a midnight dreary, while I pondered, weak and weary,
Over many a quaint and curious volume of forgotten lore —
While I nodded, nearly napping, suddenly there came a tapping,
As of some one gently rapping, rapping at my chamber door.
" 'Tis some visitor," I muttered, "tapping at my chamber door —
     Only this and nothing more."

Ah, distinctly I remember it was in the bleak December;
And each separate dying ember wrought its ghost upon the floor.
Eagerly I wished the morrow; — vainly I had sought to borrow
From my books surcease of sorrow — sorrow for the lost Lenore —   10
For the rare and radiant maiden whom the angels named Lenore —
     Nameless *here* for evermore.

Text: the 1845 version as corrected by the author in his personal copy

And the silken, sad, uncertain rustling of each purple curtain
Thrilled me — filled me with fantastic terrors never felt before;
So that now, to still the beating of my heart, I stood repeating
" 'Tis some visitor entreating entrance at my chamber door,
Some late visitor entreating entrance at my chamber door:
    This it is and nothing more."

Presently my soul grew stronger; hesitating then no longer,
"Sir," said I, "or Madam, truly your forgiveness I implore: 20
But the fact is I was napping, and so gently you came rapping,
And so faintly you came tapping, tapping at my chamber door,
That I scarce was sure I heard you" — here I opened wide the door; —
    Darkness there and nothing more.

Deep into that darkness peering, long I stood there wondering, fearing,
Doubting, dreaming dreams no mortals ever dared to dream before:
But the silence was unbroken, and the stillness gave no token,
And the only word there spoken was the whispered word, "Lenore?"
This I whispered, and an echo murmured back the word, "Lenore!"
    Merely this and nothing more.   30

Back into the chamber turning, all my soul within me burning,
Soon again I heard a tapping somewhat louder than before.
"Surely," said I, "surely that is something at my window lattice;
Let me see, then, what thereat is, and this mystery explore;
Let my heart be still a moment and this mystery explore:
    'Tis the wind and nothing more!"

Open here I flung the shutter, when, with many a flirt and flutter,
In there stepped a stately Raven of the saintly days of yore;
Not the least obeisance made he; not a minute stopped or stayed he;
But with mien of lord or lady, perched above my chamber door,   40
Perched upon a bust of Pallas just above my chamber door:
    Perched, and sat, and nothing more.

Then this ebon bird beguiling all my fancy into smiling
By the grave and stern decorum of the countenance it wore,
"Though thy crest be shorn and shaven, thou," I said, "art sure no craven,
Ghastly grim and ancient Raven wandering from the Nightly shore —
Tell me what thy lordly name is on the Night's Plutonian shore!"
    Quoth the Raven "Nevermore."

---

41 **Pallas,** Pallas Athene, the goddess of wisdom   43 **all my fancy,** substituted for the "all my mad soul"
of an earlier version

Much I marveled this ungainly fowl to hear discourse so plainly,
Though its answer little meaning — little relevancy bore;   50
For we cannot help agreeing that no living human being
Ever yet was blessed with seeing bird above his chamber door,
Bird or beast upon the sculptured bust above his chamber door,
    With such name as "Nevermore."

But the Raven, sitting lonely on the placid bust, spoke only
That one word, as if his soul in that one word he did outpour,
Nothing further then he uttered, not a feather then he fluttered,
Till I scarcely more than muttered, — "Other friends have flown before;
On the morrow *he* will leave me, as my Hopes have flown before."
    Then the bird said "Nevermore."   60

Startled at the stillness broken by reply so aptly spoken,
"Doubtless," said I, "what it utters is its only stock and store,
Caught from some unhappy master whom unmerciful Disaster
Followed fast and followed faster till his songs one burden bore —
Till the dirges of his Hope that melancholy burden bore
    Of 'Never— nevermore.' "

But the Raven still beguiling all my fancy into smiling,
Straight I wheeled a cushioned seat in front of bird and bust and door;
Then, upon the velvet sinking, I betook myself to linking
Fancy unto fancy, thinking what this ominous bird of yore,   70
What this grim, ungainly, ghastly, gaunt, and ominous bird of yore
    Meant in croaking "Nevermore."

This I sat engaged in guessing, but no syllable expressing
To the fowl whose fiery eyes now burned into my bosom's core;
This and more I sat divining, with my head at ease reclining
On the cushion's velvet lining that the lamp-light gloated o'er,
But whose velvet violet lining with the lamp-light gloating o'er
    She shall press, ah, nevermore!

Then, methought, the air grew denser, perfumed from an unseen censer
Swung by Seraphim whose foot-falls tinkled on the tufted floor.   80
"Wretch," I cried, "thy God hath lent thee — by these angels he hath sent thee
Respite — respite and nepenthe, from thy memories of Lenore,
Quaff, oh quaff this kind nepenthe and forget this lost Lenore!"
    Quoth the Raven "Nevermore."

76 **gloated.** "Gloat" has as one of its unusual meanings, "to refract light"   80 **Seraphim whose foot-falls,** a correction from "angels whose faint foot-falls"   80 **tinkled,** defended by Poe as a word description of foot-falls, "because I saw that it had . . . been suggested to my mind by the sense of the *supernatural* with which it was, at the moment, filled"   83 **nepenthe,** a drink which banishes sorrow

"Prophet!" said I, "thing of evil! prophet still, if bird or devil!
Whether Tempter sent, or whether tempest tossed thee here ashore,
Desolate yet all undaunted, on this desert land enchanted —
On this home by Horror haunted — tell me truly, I implore:
Is there — *is* there balm in Gilead? — tell me — tell me, I implore!"
   Quoth the Raven "Nevermore."   90

"Prophet," said I, "thing of evil — prophet still, if bird or devil!
By that Heaven that bends above us, by that God we both adore,
Tell this soul with sorrow laden if, within the distant Aidenn,
It shall clasp a sainted maiden whom the angels name Lenore —
Clasp a rare and radiant maiden whom the angels name Lenore!"
   Quoth the Raven "Nevermore."

"Be that word our sign of parting, bird or fiend!" I shrieked, up-starting:
"Get thee back into the tempest and the Night's Plutonian shore!
Leave no black plume as a token of that lie thy soul hath spoken!
Leave my loneliness unbroken! quit the bust above my door!   100
Take thy beak from out my heart, and take thy form from off my door!"
   Quoth the Raven "Nevermore."

And the Raven, never flitting, still is sitting, *still* is sitting
On the pallid bust of Pallas just above my chamber door;
And his eyes have all the seeming of a demon's that is dreaming,
And the lamplight o'er him streaming throws his shadow on the floor;
And my soul from out that shadow that lies floating on the floor
   Shall be lifted — nevermore!

                                1845

---

89 **balm in Gilead.** See Jeremiah 8:22   93 **Aidenn,** a place of pleasure — variant of Eden or Aden   98
Plutonian, characteristic of Pluto or the nether world   106 **shadow,** justified by Poe thus: "For
the purposes of poetry it is quite sufficient that a thing is possible, or at least that the improbability be not
offensively glaring. It is true that in several ways, . . . the lamp might have thrown the bird's shadow on
the floor. *My* conception was that of the bracket candelabrum affixed against the wall, high up above the
door and bust . . ."

Ulalume

*For a time after the first publication of "Ulalume" (American Whig Review, December
1847), Poe liked the poem best without the tenth stanza. In his final published version of
the poem, however, the last ten lines were included, and they therefore appear in this text.*
   *The first nine stanzas build up admirably the tale of a growing uneasiness, and a grow-
ing perception of the cause of that uneasiness, on the part of the narrator. Then comes a
stanza which, so far as a large number of readers are concerned, hovers so close to the ridiculous as to spoil the effect. Perhaps Poe added the final stanza, as he said he did the final*

stanzas of "The Raven," to avoid repelling "the artistical eye" with "a certain hardness and nakedness." Whatever his reason for writing the last stanza, many will feel that his impulse to drop it was sounder than his final impulse.

The skies they were ashen and sober;
  The leaves they were crisped and sere,
  The leaves they were withering and sere;
It was night in the lonesome October
  Of my most immemorial year;
It was hard by the dim lake of Auber,
  In the misty mid region of Weir:
It was down by the dank tarn of Auber,
  In the ghoul-haunted woodland of Weir.

Here once, through an alley Titanic   10
  Of cypress, I roamed with my Soul —
  Of cypress, with Psyche, my Soul.
These were days when my heart was volcanic
  As the scoriac rivers that roll,
  As the lavas that restlessly roll
Their sulphurous currents down Yaanek
  In the ultimate climes of the Pole,
That groan as they roll down Mount Yaanek
  In the realms of the Boreal Pole.

Our talk had been serious and sober,   20
  But our thoughts they were palsied and sere,
  Our memories were treacherous and sere,
For we knew not the month was October,
  And we marked not the night of the year,
  (Ah, night of all nights in the year!)
We noted not the dim lake of Auber
  (Though once we had journeyed down here),
Remembered not the dank tarn of Auber,
  Nor the ghoul-haunted woodland of Weir.

And now, as the night was senescent   30
  And star-dials pointed to morn,

---

6 **Auber,** a geographic name, like Weir and Yaanek in the lines which follow, evidently invented by Poe   11
cypress, a species of tree often planted about tombs. The occurrence of an alley of such trees anticipates
the narrator's grim discovery   14 **scoriac,** volcanic, a word harking back to "ashen," "crisped," and "sere"
in the first stanza, words suggestive of burning   19 **Boreal,** northern, combining the suggestion of the
blighting cold of October with the burning brightness of the aurora borealis

As the star-dials hinted of morn,
At the end of our path a liquescent
  And nebulous lustre was born,
Out of which a miraculous crescent
  Arose, with a duplicate horn,
Astarte's bediamonded crescent
  Distinct with its duplicate horn.

And I said — "She is warmer than Dian:
  She rolls through an ether of sighs,   40
  She revels in a region of sighs:
She has seen that the tears are not dry on
  These cheeks, where the worm never dies,
And has come past the stars of the Lion
  To point us the path to the skies,
  To the Lethean peace of the skies:
Come up, in despite of the Lion,
  To shine on us with her bright eyes:
Come up through the lair of the Lion,
  With love in her luminous eyes."   50

But Psyche, uplifting her finger,
  Said — "Sadly this star I mistrust,
  Her pallor I strangely mistrust:
Oh, hasten! — oh, let us not linger!
  Oh, fly! — let us fly! — for we must."
In terror she spoke, letting sink her
  Wings till they trailed in the dust;
In agony sobbed, letting sink her
  Plumes till they trailed in the dust,
  Till they sorrowfully trailed in the dust.   60

I replied — "This is nothing but dreaming:
  Let us on by this tremulous light!
  Let us bathe in this crystalline light!
Its sibyllic splendor is beaming

---

37 **Astarte,** or Ashtoreth, Phoenician goddess associated with earthly love, see note, p. 784   39 **Dian,** Diana, goddess of the moon; with the Romans, chaste huntress typifying pure love   43 **where . . . dies.** See Isaiah 66:24   44 **the Lion,** constellation of Leo, here used to signify danger   46 **Lethean,** referring to Lethe, a legendary river of forgetfulness   52 **I mistrust.** This phrase of Psyche forecasts the distressing discovery at the end of the poem   64 **sibyllic,** oracular. In this stanza the narrator is attempting to prove that this "crystalline light" promises good fortune. Yet his talk of "tremulous light" which "flickers" actually admits distrust. Here, perhaps, as in "The Raven," at about the middle of the poem, the author "availed himself of the force of contrast, with a view of deepening the ultimate impression"

With hope and in beauty tonight:
  See, it flickers up the sky through the night!
Ah, we safely may trust to its gleaming,
  And be sure it will lead us aright:
We safely may trust to a gleaming
  That cannot but guide us aright,   70
  Since it flickers up to Heaven through the night."

Thus I pacified Psyche and kissed her,
  And tempted her out of her gloom,
  And conquered her scruples and gloom;
And we passed to the end of the vista,
  But were stopped by the door of a tomb,
  By the door of a legended tomb;
And I said — "What is written, sweet sister,
  On the door of this legended tomb?"
  She replied — "Ulalume — Ulalume —   80
  'Tis the vault of thy lost Ulalume!"

Then my heart it grew ashen and sober
  As the leaves that were crisped and sere,
  As the leaves that were withering and sere,
And I cried — "It was surely October
  On this very night of last year
  That I journeyed — I journeyed down here! —
  That I brought a dread burden down here —
  On this night of all nights in the year,
  Ah, what demon has tempted me here?   90
Well I know, now, this dim lake of Auber,
  This misty mid region of Weir:
Well I know, now, this dank tarn of Auber,
  This ghoul-haunted woodland of Weir.

Said we, then — the two, then: "Ah can it
  Have been that the woodlandish ghouls —
  The pitiful, the merciful ghouls —
To bar up our way and to ban it
  From the secret that lies in these wolds —
  From the thing that lies hidden in these wolds —   100
Have drawn up the spectre of a planet
  From the limbo of lunary souls —
This sinfully scintillant planet
  From the Hell of the planetary souls?"

                         1847

Eldorado

Written in the late winter or early spring of 1849, this poem was first published in Flag of
Our Union, *April 21, 1849. Eldorado was a fabulously rich city which early explorers of
the Western world vainly sought. In 1849 the name was frequently applied to California
gold fields.*

Gayly bedight,
A gallant knight,
In sunshine and in shadow,
Had journeyed long,
Singing a song,
In search of Eldorado.

But he grew old,
This knight so bold,
And o'er his heart a shadow
Fell as he found
No spot of ground
That looked like Eldorado.

And, as his strength
Failed him at length,
He met a pilgrim shadow —
"Shadow," said he,
"Where can it be,
This land of Eldorado?"

"Over the Mountains
Of the Moon,
Down the Valley of the Shadow,
Ride, boldly ride,"
The shade replied,
"If you seek for Eldorado!"

1849

THE BRAHMINS:
Longfellow
Holmes
Lowell

1807—1882 Henry Wadsworth Longfellow

During his lifetime Henry Wadsworth Longfellow was the best-loved American poet, and even today his poetry is popular because it says what many people want to be told in ways generally considered "poetic." Critics who disapprove of a large share of Longfellow's verse do so because they feel that its thought is commonplace, its mood sentimental, and its form not well related to its substance. Such critics are likely to admit, however, that at his infrequent best he wrote poetry which deserves to be treasured by fastidious readers.

Longfellow was born in Portland, Maine, on February 27, 1807. He was educated at Bowdoin and abroad, and he taught modern languages at Bowdoin (1829-1835) and then, after a second trip abroad, at Harvard (1837-1854). Meanwhile, his fame, which had begun to flourish when *Voices of the Night* was published in 1839, was augmented by such books as *Ballads and Other Poems* (1841) and *Evangeline* (1847). Works published after his retirement from Harvard — *Hiawatha* (1855), *The Courtship of Miles Standish* (1858), *Tales of a Wayside Inn* (1863, 1872, 1873), and *Christus: A Mystery* (1872) — brought still greater appreciation. Carefully sheltered in childhood and early manhood, never worried by poverty, the poet lived most of his days in peaceful old Craigie House in Cambridge. Odell Shepard has pictured him there as "he sat by the fireside writing verse on his knee with his eyes closed, now and then striding to the window to look down the vista of bristling elms to where the River Charles was 'writing the last letter of his name.'" When Howells saw him at the height of fame, he thought he was perfectly characterized as "the white Mr. Longfellow."

These and other similar details have long caused scholars to think of Longfellow's life as always sheltered and placid. Recent study, however, has shown that Longfellow won such peacefulness only after a youth full of storm and struggle. His fight, against odds, to become an author, his desperate sorrow following the death of his first wife in 1835, and his torture of spirit during the seven-year courtship of his second wife, Frances Appleton, all left their imprint on his life and work.

Because Europe was the background for some of his deepest emotional experiences and because he discovered new possibilities in literature during his study there, Longfellow was impelled to acquaint his countrymen with the Old World as he saw it. Culture-starved, painfully aware of their crudeness as European travel-book writers showed it, Americans were delighted with Longfellow's translations of European poems and his romantic depictions of the picturesque Old World. When he turned to the depiction of the America of the past (as he frequently did), one of his services was, in a sense, to "Europeanize" it — to show that this country, too, had mellow legends which might be given something like Old World treatments.

Much of Longfellow's verse has a simple pattern: a story is told, an object or scene is described, and then a moral which figuratively makes use of the story, object, or scene concludes the poem. The morals, some derived from German authors, have popular appeal; typical ones are: "Fight on"; "Others sorrow, too"; and "Sorrow must end." Many times there are striking figures of speech not only in the closing lines but also in earlier lines, but too often these are not related to one another or — in a basic way, at least — to the poem as a whole. The poems are written in relatively simple (sometimes prosaic) words and in memorable rhythms. When Longfellow avoids obvious preachments, sentimental tone, flat words, and loosely related figures, he does his best work. Sometimes, as in *The Courtship of Miles Standish* and certain narrative poems included in *Tales from a Wayside Inn,* he tells a story masterfully and employs humor with excellent effect. At other times, as in some sonnets and in some lyrics — "Hymn to the Night" and "The Tide Rises," for instance — his economically managed imagery, his emotional restraint, his sure diction, and his masterfully handled rhythms create memorable verse.

Complete Poetical Works, ed. H. E. Scudder, Boston, 1893   Samuel Longfellow, **The Life of Henry Wadsworth Longfellow,** 3 vols., Boston, 1891   Edward Wagenknecht, **Longfellow, A Full-Length Portrait,** New York, 1955   Newton Arvin, **Longfellow: His Life and Work,** Boston, 1963

A Psalm of Life

When, in 1838, Longfellow gave a new course, "Literature and the Literary Life," at Harvard, his study of Goethe was particularly useful in helping him to formulate a workable philosophy. The period was a trying one in Longfellow's life. His first wife's death had been and still was the cause of much sorrow. His courtship of Frances Appleton seemed doomed to failure. In Goethe, Longfellow found a suggestion for living when "the time is out of joint" — "to bear one's self doughtily in Life's battle: and make the best of things." This was the message expressed in "A Psalm of Life." "I kept it some time in manuscript," he wrote, "unwilling to show it to any one, it being a voice from my inmost heart, and expressing my feelings at a time when I was rallying from the depression of disappointment." Many repetitions have robbed the poem of its early fire, but it is important to remember that at the time it appeared this attack on acquiescence fostered by either dreamy romanticism or Calvinistic fatalism said something important to many readers.

Tell me not, in mournful numbers,
　　Life is but an empty dream!
For the soul is dead that slumbers,
　　And things are not what they seem.

Life is real! Life is earnest!
　　And the grave is not its goal;
Dust thou art, to dust returnest,
　　Was not spoken of the soul.

Not enjoyment, and not sorrow,
　　Is our destined end or way;   10
But to act, that each to-morrow
　　Find us farther than today.

Art is long, and Time is fleeting,
　　And our hearts, though stout and brave,
Still, like muffled drums, are beating
　　Funeral marches to the grave.

In the world's broad field of battle,
　　In the bivouac of Life,
Be not like dumb, driven cattle!
　　Be a hero in the strife!   20

Trust no Future, howe'er pleasant!
　　Let the dead Past bury its dead!
Act, — act in the living Present!
　　Heart within, and God o'erhead!

Lives of great men all remind us
　　We can make our lives sublime,
And, departing, leave behind us
　　Footprints on the sands of time;

Footprints, that perhaps another,
　　Sailing o'er life's solemn main,   30
A forlorn and shipwrecked brother,
　　Seeing, shall take heart again.

Let us, then, be up and doing,
　　With a heart for any fate;
Still achieving, still pursuing,
　　Learn to labor and to wait.   1838

Hymn to the Night

'Ασπασίη, τρίλλιστος

Longfellow said he wrote this poem in the summer of 1839, "while sitting at my chamber window, on one of the balmiest nights of the year. I endeavored to reproduce the impression of the hour and scene." The poem offers a way of coping with sorrow contrasting with the one suggested in "Psalm of Life." Here nighttime reveries, rather than heroic action, bring surcease of sorrow.

I heard the trailing garments of the Night
    Sweep through her marble halls!
I saw her sable skirts all fringed with light
    From the celestial walls!

I felt her presence, by its spell of might,
    Stoop o'er me from above;
The calm, majestic presence of the Night,
    As of the one I love.

I heard the sounds of sorrow and delight,
    The manifold, soft chimes,   10
That fill the haunted chambers of the Night,
    Like some old poet's rhymes.

From the cool cisterns of the midnight air
    My spirit drank repose;
The fountain of perpetual peace flows there, —
    From those deep cisterns flows.

O holy Night! from thee I learn to bear
    What man has borne before!
Thou layest thy finger on the lips of Care,
    And they complain no more.   20

Peace! Peace! Orestes-like I breathe this prayer!
    Descend with broad-winged flight,
The welcome, the thrice-prayed for, the most fair,
    The best-beloved Night!

                      1839

'Ασπασίη, τρίλλιστος, Welcome, three times prayed for   21 **Orestes-like** refers to the character Orestes in the plays of Aeschylus. At the end of the tragedy *The Choephorae*, Orestes, having avenged his father by murdering his mother, is pursued by the Furies. In a sequel, *The Eumenides*, he finds peace

The Skeleton in Armor

In a letter to his father written in December 1840, Longfellow announced that he had prepared this ballad, "which has been lying by me for some time," for the press. "It is connected," he said, "with the old Round Tower at Newport. The skeleton in armor really exists. It was dug up near Fall River, where I saw it some two years ago. I suppose it to be the remains of one of the old Northern searovers. . . . Of course, I make the tradition myself; and I think I have succeeded in giving the whole a Northern air."

Reviewing Ballads and Other Poems *(1841), in which the ballad was published, Poe said: "In 'The Skeleton in Armor' we find a pure and perfect thesis artistically treated. . . . The metre is simple, sonorous, well-balanced, and fully adapted to the subject." Scholars have pointed out Longfellow's indebtedness in this ballad to Michael Drayton's poem on the battle of Agincourt and to Shelley's "The Fugitives."*

"Speak! speak! thou fearful guest!
Who, with thy hollow breast,
Still in rude armor drest,
    Comest to daunt me!
Wrapt not in Eastern balms,
But with thy fleshless palms
Stretched, as if asking alms,
    Why dost thou haunt me?"

Then from those cavernous eyes
Pale flashes seemed to rise,   10
As when the Northern skies
    Gleam in December;
And, like the water's flow
Under December's snow,
Came a dull voice of woe
    From the heart's chamber.

"I was a Viking old!
My deeds, though manifold,
No Skald in song has told,
    No Saga taught thee!   20
Take heed that in thy verse
Thou dost the tale rehearse,
Else dread a dead man's curse;
    For this I sought thee.

"Far in the Northern Land,
By the wild Baltic's strand,

I, with my childish hand,
   Tamed the gerfalcon;
And, with my skates fast-bound,
Skimmed the half-frozen Sound,   30
That the poor whimpering hound
   Trembled to walk on.

"Oft to his frozen lair
Tracked I the grisly bear,
While from my path the hare
   Fled like a shadow;
Oft through the forest dark
Followed the were-wolf's bark,
Until the soaring lark
   Sang from the meadow.   40

"But when I older grew,
Joining a corsair's crew,
O'er the dark sea I flew
   With the marauders.
Wild was the life we led;
Many the souls that sped,
Many the hearts that bled,
   By our stern orders.

"Many a wassail-bout
Wore the long winter out;   50
Often our midnight shout
   Set the cocks crowing,
As we the Berserk's tale
Measured in cups of ale,
Draining the oaken pail
   Filled to o'erflowing.

"Once as I told in glee
Tales of the stormy sea,
Soft eyes did gaze on me,
   Burning yet tender;   60
And as the white stars shine
On the dark Norway pine,
On that dark heart of mine
   Fell their soft splendor.

---

53 **Berserk's,** a legendary invincible warrior

"I wooed the blue-eyed maid,
Yielding, yet half afraid,
And in the forest's shade
   Our vows were plighted.
Under its loosened vest
Fluttered her little breast,   70
Like birds within their nest
   By the hawk frighted.

"Bright in her father's hall
Shields gleamed upon the wall,
Loud sang the minstrels all,
   Chanting his glory;
When of old Hildebrand
I asked his daughter's hand,
Mute did the minstrels stand
   To hear my story.   80

"While the brown ale he quaffed,
Loud then the champion laughed,
And as the wind-gusts waft
   The sea-foam brightly,
So the loud laugh of scorn
Out of those lips unshorn,
From the deep drinking-horn
   Blew the foam lightly.

"She was a Prince's child,
I but a Viking wild,   90
And though she blushed and smiled,
   I was discarded!
Should not the dove so white
Follow the sea-mew's flight?
Why did they leave that night
   Her nest unguarded?

"Scarce had I put to sea,
Bearing the maid with me,
Fairest of all was she
   Among the Norsemen!   100
When on the white sea-strand,
Waving his armèd hand,
Saw we old Hildebrand,
   With twenty horsemen.

"Then launched they to the blast,
Bent like a reed each mast,
Yet we were gaining fast,
   When the wind failed us;
And with a sudden flaw
Came round the gusty Skaw,   110
So that our foe we saw
   Laugh as he hailed us.

"And as to catch the gale
Round veered the flapping sail,
'Death!' was the helmsman's hail,
   'Death without quarter!'
Midships with iron keel
Struck we her ribs of steel;
Down her black hulk did reel
   Through the black water!   120

"As with his wings aslant,
Sails the fierce cormorant,
Seeking some rocky haunt,
   With his prey laden, —
So toward the open main,
Beating to sea again,
Through the wild hurricane,
   Bore I the maiden.

"Three weeks we westward bore,
And when the storm was o'er,   130
Cloud-like we saw the shore
   Stretching to leeward;
There for my lady's bower
Built I the lofty tower,
Which, to this very hour,
   Stands looking seaward,

"There lived we many years;
Time dried the maiden's tears;
She had forgot her fears,
   She was a mother;   140
Death closed her mild blue eyes;
Under that tower she lies;
Ne'er shall the sun arise
   On such another!

110 **Skaw**, Cape Skagen, the northern point of Jutland in Denmark

"Still grew my bosom then,
Still as a stagnant fen!
Hateful to me were men,
    The sunlight hateful;
In the vast forest here,
Clad in my warlike gear,   150
Fell I upon my spear,
    Oh, death was grateful!

"Thus, seamed with many scars,
Bursting these prison bars
Up to its native stars
    My soul ascended!
There from the flowing bowl
Deep drinks the warrior's soul,
Skoal! to the Northland! *skoal!"*
    Thus the tale ended.   160
                    1840, 1841

<hr>

159 **Skoal,** "the customary salutation for drinking a health in Scandinavia" — Longfellow

The Slave's Dream

Returning from a trip abroad in 1842, Longfellow had a stormy journey. "I was not out of my berth more than twelve hours for the first twelve days," he recorded. "I was in the forward part of the vessel, where all the great waves struck and broke with voices of thunder. There, 'cribbed, cabined, and confined,' I passed fifteen days. During this time I wrote seven poems on slavery; I meditated upon them in the stormy, sleepless nights, and wrote them down with a pencil in the morning."

Shortly after arriving in America, he published these poems and one other in a volume called Poems on Slavery *— his contribution to the antislavery crusade. In a period when most of the New Englanders of good family were saying as little as possible about this controversy, it was rather brave for him thus to speak out.*

Beside the ungathered rice he lay,
    His sickle in his hand;
His breast was bare, his matted hair
    Was buried in the sand.
Again, in the mist and shadow of sleep,
    He saw his Native Land.

Wide through the landscape of his dreams
    The lordly Niger flowed;
Beneath the palm-trees on the plain

Once more a king he strode;   10
And heard the tinkling caravans
    Descend the mountain road.

He saw once more his dark-eyed queen
    Among her children stand;
They clasped his neck, they kissed his cheeks,
    They held him by the hand! —
A tear burst from the sleeper's lids
    And fell into the sand.

And then at furious speed he rode
    Along the Niger's bank;   20
His bridle-reins were golden chains,
    And, with a martial clank,
At each leap he could feel his scabbard of steel
    Smiting his stallion's flank.

Before him, like a blood-red flag,
    The bright flamingoes flew;
From morn till night he followed their flight,
    O'er plains where the tamarind grew,
Till he saw the roofs of Caffre huts,
    And the ocean rose to view.   30

At night he heard the lion roar,
    And the hyena scream,
And the river-horse, as he crushed the reeds
    Beside some hidden stream;
And it passed, like a glorious roll of drums,
    Through the triumph of his dream.

The forests, with their myriad tongues,
    Shouted of liberty;
And the Blast of the Desert cried aloud,
    With a voice so wild and free,   40
That he started in his sleep and smiled
    At their tempestuous glee.

He did not feel the driver's whip,
    Nor the burning heat of day;
For Death had illumined the Land of Sleep,
    And his lifeless body lay

---

29 **Caffre**, Kaffir, South African Negro   33 **river-horse**, hippopotamus

A worn-out fetter, that the soul
  Had broken and thrown away!

                                        1842

The Rainy Day

The day is cold, and dark, and dreary;
It rains, and the wind is never weary;
The vine still clings to the mouldering wall,
But at every gust the dead leaves fall,
  And the day is dark and dreary.

My life is cold, and dark, and dreary;
It rains, and the wind is never weary;
My thoughts still cling to the mouldering Past,
But the hopes of youth fall thick in the blast,
  And the days are dark and dreary.   10

Be still, sad heart! and cease repining;
Behind the clouds is the sun still shining;
Thy fate is the common fate of all,
Into each life some rain must fall,
  Some days must be dark and dreary.

                                        1842

The Bridge

I stood on the bridge at midnight
  As the clocks were striking the hour,
And the moon rose o'er the city,
  Behind the dark church-tower.

I saw her bright reflection
  In the waters under me,
Like a golden goblet falling
  And sinking into the sea.

And far in the hazy distance
  Of that lovely night in June,   10

The blaze of the flaming furnace
　Gleamed redder than the moon.

Among the long, black rafters
　The wavering shadows lay,
And the current that came from the ocean
　Seemed to lift and bear them away;

As sweeping and eddying through them,
　Rose the belated tide,
And, streaming into the moonlight,
　The seaweed floated wide.　　　　　20

And like those waters rushing
　Among the wooden piers,
A flood of thoughts came o'er me
　That filled my eyes with tears.

How often, oh how often,
　In the days that had gone by,
I had stood on that bridge at midnight
　And gazed on that wave and sky!

How often, oh how often,
　I had wished that the ebbing tide　　30
Would bear me away on its bosom
　O'er the ocean wild and wide!

For my heart was hot and restless,
　And my life was full of care,
And the burden laid upon me
　Seemed greater than I could bear.

But now it has fallen from me,
　It is buried in the sea;
And only the sorrows of others
　Throws its shadow over me.　　　　40

Yet whenever I cross the river
　On its bridge with wooden piers,
Like the odor of brine from the ocean
　Comes the thought of other years.

And I think how many thousands
　Of care-encumbered men,

Each bearing his burden of sorrow
   Have crossed the bridge since then.

I see the long procession
   Still passing to and fro,   50
The young heart hot and restless,
   And the old subdued and slow!

And forever and forever,
   As long as the river flows,
As long as the heart has passions,
   As long as life has woes;

The moon and its broken reflection
   And its shadow shall appear,
As the symbol of love in heaven,
   And its wavering image here.   60
              1845

The Arrow and the Song

The following is Longfellow's account of the writing of this poem: "October 16, 1845. Before church, wrote 'The Arrow and the Song,' which came into my mind as I stood with my back to the fire, and glanced onto the paper with an arrow's speed. Literally an improvisation."

I shot an arrow into the air,
It fell to earth, I knew not where;
For, so swiftly it flew, the sight
Could not follow it in its flight.

I breathed a song into the air,
It fell to earth, I knew not where;
For who has sight so keen and strong,
That it can follow the flight of song?

Long, long afterward, in an oak
I found the arrow, still unbroke;   10
And the song, from beginning to end,
I found again in the heart of a friend.
              1845

The Jewish Cemetery at Newport

An entry in Longfellow's journal for June 9, 1852, tells of the visit to the cemetery which suggested this poem. "There are few graves," he wrote; "nearly all are low tombstones of marble, with Hebrew inscriptions, and a few words added in English or Portuguese. . . . It is a shady nook, at the corner of two dusty, frequented streets. . . ."

Professor Shepard comments: "The poem . . . is written in the difficult stanza of Gray's 'Elegy' and in the mood of that poem. Comparison will show that Longfellow is as much superior to Gray in thought-structure and 'sense of the whole' as he is inferior in vividness and intensity of phrase and image."

How strange it seems! These Hebrews in their graves,
    Close by the street of this fair seaport town,
Silent beside the never-silent waves,
    At rest in all this moving up and down!

The trees are white with dust, that o'er their sleep
    Wave their broad curtains in the south-wind's breath,
While underneath these leafy tents they keep
    The long, mysterious Exodus of Death.

And these sepulchral stones, so old and brown,
    That pave with level flags their burial-place,   10
Seem like the tablets of the Law, thrown down
    And broken by Moses at the mountain's base.

The very names recorded here are strange,
    Of foreign accent, and of different climes;
Alvares and Rivera interchange
    With Abraham and Jacob of old times.

"Blessed be God, for he created Death!"
    The mourners said, "and Death is rest and peace;"
Then added, in the certainty of faith,
    "And giveth Life that nevermore shall cease."   20

Closed are the portals of their Synagogue,
    No Psalms of David now the silence break,
No Rabbi reads the ancient Decalogue
    In the grand dialect the Prophets spake.

---

8 **Exodus** refers to the book of Exodus, which recounts the journey of the Israelites from Egypt under Moses

Gone are the living, but the dead remain,
    And not neglected; for a hand unseen,
Scattering its bounty, like a summer rain,
    Still keeps their graves and their remembrance green.

How came they here? What burst of Christian hate,
    What persecution, merciless and blind,   30
Drove o'er the sea — that desert desolate —
    These Ishmaels and Hagars of mankind?

They lived in narrow streets and lanes obscure,
    Ghetto and Judenstrass, in mirk and mire;
Taught in the school of patience to endure
    The life of anguish and the death of fire.

All their lives long, with the unleavened bread
    And bitter herbs of exile and its fears,
The wasting famine of the heart they fed,
    And slaked its thirst with marah of their tears.   40

Anathema maranatha! was the cry
    That rang from town to town, from street to street:
At every gate the accursed Mordecai
    Was mocked and jeered, and spurned by Christian feet.

Pride and humiliation hand in hand
    Walked with them through the world where'er they went;
Trampled and beaten were they as the sand,
    And yet unshaken as the continent.

For in the background figures vague and vast
    Of patriarchs and of prophets rose sublime,   50
And all the great traditions of the Past
    They saw reflected in the coming time.

And thus forever with reverted look
    The mystic volume of the world they read,
Spelling it backward, like a Hebrew book,
    Till life became a Legend of the Dead.

---

32 **Ishmaels and Hagars.** See Genesis 16, 21. Hagar, a concubine of Abraham, was driven into the desert with Ishmael, her son by him   34 **Ghetto and Judenstrass,** quarters in which Jews are segregated   40 **marah,** bitter water   41 **Anathema maranatha,** an expression found in I Corinthians, formerly thought to be a double curse   43 **Mordecai,** the cousin of Esther. See the Book of Esther   55 **Spelling it backward.** Hebrew is printed so as to be read from right to left in contrast with other languages reading from left to right

But ah! what once has been shall be no more!
   The groaning earth in travail and in pain
Brings forth its races, but does not restore,
   And the dead nations never rise again.

1852

My Lost Youth

During a visit to Portland in 1846 Longfellow took a long walk around Munjoy's hill and down to old Fort Lawrence. Then, he says, "I lay down in one of the embrasures and listened to the lashing, lulling sound of the sea just at my feet. It was a beautiful afternoon, and the harbor was full of white sails, coming and departing." He considered writing a poem at the time, but not until 1855 did these two entries in his journal record its composition:
   "March 29. A day of pain; cowering over the fire. At night, as I lie in bed, a poem comes into my mind, — a memory of Portland, — my native town, the city by the sea. . . .
   "March 30. Wrote the poem; and am rather pleased with it, and with the bringing in of the two lines of the old Lapland song. . . ."
   The song may be found in a book by John Scheffer, The History of Lapland *(1674). The important passage is:*
> *"A youth's desire is the desire of the wind,*
>   *All his essaies*
>   *Are long delaies,*
>   *No issue can they find."*

Often I think of the beautiful town
   That is seated by the sea;
Often in thought go up and down
The pleasant streets of that dear old town,
   And my youth comes back to me.
     And a verse of a Lapland song
     Is haunting my memory still:
     "A boy's will is the wind's will,
And the thoughts of youth are long, long thoughts."

I can see the shadowy lines of its trees,   10
   And catch, in sudden gleams,
The sheen of the far-surrounding seas,
And islands that were the Hesperides
   Of all my boyish dreams.
     And the burden of that old song,
     It murmurs and whispers still:
     "A boy's will is the wind's will,
And the thoughts of youth are long, long thoughts."

---

13 **Hesperides,** paradise-like gardens in Greek legend where golden apples, guarded by maidens, grew

I remember the black wharves and the slips,
 And the sea-tides tossing free;   20
And Spanish sailors with bearded lips,
And the beauty and mystery of the ships,
 And the magic of the sea.
  And the voice of that wayward song
  Is singing and saying still:
  "A boy's will is the wind's will,
And the thoughts of youth are long, long thoughts."

I remember the bulwarks by the shore,
 And the fort upon the hill;
The sunrise gun, with its hollow roar,   30
The drumbeat repeated o'er and o'er,
 And the bugle wild and shrill.
  And the music of that old song
  Throbs in my memory still:
  "A boy's will is the wind's will,
And the thoughts of youth are long, long thoughts."

I remember the sea-fight far away,
 How it thundered o'er the tide!
And the dead captains, as they lay
In their graves, o'erlooking the tranquil bay 40
 Where they in battle died.
  And the sound of that mournful song
  Goes through me with a thrill:
  "A boy's will is the wind's will,
And the thoughts of youth are long, long thoughts."

I can see the breezy dome of groves,
 The shadows of Deering's Woods;
And the friendships old and the early loves
Come back with a Sabbath sound, as of doves
 In quiet neighborhoods.   50
  And the verse of that sweet old song,
  It flutters and murmurs still:
  "A boy's will is the wind's will,
And the thoughts of youth are long, long thoughts."

I remember the gleams and glooms that dart
 Across the schoolboy's brain;
The song and the silence in the heart,
That in part are prophecies, and in part

· Are longings wild and vain.
    And the voice of that fitful song   60
    Sings on, and is never still:
    "A boy's will is the wind's will,
And the thoughts of youth are long, long thoughts."

There are things of which I may not speak;
    There are dreams that cannot die;
There are thoughts that make the strong heart weak,
And bring a pallor into the cheek,
    And a mist before the eye.
      And the words of that fatal song
      Come over me like a chill: 70
      "A boy's will is the wind's will,
And the thoughts of youth are long, long thoughts."

Strange to me now are the forms I meet,
    When I visit the dear old town;
But the native air is pure and sweet,
And the trees that o'ershadow each well-known street,
    As they balance up and down,
      Are singing the beautiful song,
      Are singing and whispering still:
      "A boy's will is the wind's will,   80
And the thoughts of youth are long, long thoughts."

And Deering's Woods are fresh and fair,
    And with joy that is almost pain
My heart goes back to wander there,
And among the dreams of the days that were,
    I find my lost youth again.
      And the strange and beautiful song,
      Sings on, and is never still:
      "A boy's will is the wind's will,
And the thoughts of youth are long, long thoughts."   90
                        1855

The Poet's Tale

The Birds of Killingworth

When in his mid-fifties, Longfellow formulated an ambitious plan — to make a book out of a number of tales told by a group of men gathered in the parlor of the Red Horse Inn, in Sudsbury, Mass., and to relate the tales to the setting and to the tellers by means of narra-

tive verse preceding and following the tales. His models would be Boccaccio's Decameron
(c. 1349-1350), from which he took one of the tales, and Chaucer's Canterbury Tales *(c.
1387-1400). The members of the party, three Europeans and four Americans, would be
characterized by the framework passages and by the tales which they chose to tell.*

Tales of a Wayside Inn *originally consisted of one evening's storytelling, but because
this first group of tales was much admired when it was published in 1863 and because the
poet found extending the work an enjoyable task, he added Parts II and III, which recorded
later storytelling sessions, in 1872 and 1873. The twenty-two tales in the final version were
drawn from a great variety of European and American sources. They ranged from the
comic to the tragic, and they showed Longfellow's versatility by employing many metrical
forms, each appropriate to the tale in which it was used. The tales also displayed his remarkable
skill, already indicated in his longer poems, as a narrative poet.*

"The Poet's Tale" was first published in the Atlantic Monthly, *December, 1863. Like
the other storytellers, the poet's character was based upon an actual person, Thomas William
Parsons (1819-1892), author of a much admired "Ode on a Bust of Dante" and a translator of Dante's* Inferno. *Unlike the other tales, this one had no analogue; it was based
upon a legend which held that for several years the men of Kenilworth, Conn., annually
slaughtered birds which attacked their corn crop, and it came to Longfellow by word of
mouth. Written in eight-line stanzas such as Ariosto, Tasso, Keats, and Byron had used,
it seems effortless and appropriately light-hearted. The satiric portraits as well as the kindlier
picture of the bemused Preceptor show Longfellow's talent for succinct characterization; and
the accounts of the town meeting, the massacre, the discovery of the townsmen's error, and
the Preceptor's romance are given with characteristic grace and playfulness.*

It was the season, when through all the land
    The merle and mavis build, and building sing
Those lovely lyrics, written by His hand,
    Whom Saxon Cædmon calls the Blitheheart King;
When on the boughs the purple buds expand,
    The banners of the vanguard of the Spring,
And rivulets, rejoicing, rush and leap,
And wave their fluttering signals from the steep.

The robin and the bluebird, piping loud,
    Filled all the blossoming orchards with their glee;   10
The sparrows chirped as if they still were proud
    Their race in Holy Writ should mentioned be;
And hungry crows, assembled in a crowd,
    Clamored their piteous prayer incessantly,
Knowing who hears the ravens cry, and said:
"Give us, O Lord, this day, our daily bread!"

---

2 **merle and mavis,** the European blackbird and song thrush   4 **Cædmon,** seventh-century Anglo-Saxon
paraphraser of parts of the Bible. The reference is to a passage in his *Genesis*   11 **sparrows.** See Matthew
10:29   15 **ravens.** See Psalms 147:9   16 **'Give . . . bread!'** See Matthew 6:11

Across the Sound the birds of passage sailed,
   Speaking some unknown language strange and sweet
Of tropic isle remote, and passing hailed
   The village with the cheers of all their fleet;   20
Or quarrelling together, laughed and railed
   Like foreign sailors, landed in the street
Of seaport town, and with outlandish noise
Of oaths and gibberish frightening girls and boys.

Thus came the jocund Spring in Killingworth,
   In fabulous days, some hundred years ago;
And thrifty farmers, as they tilled the earth,
   Heard with alarm the cawing of the crow,
That mingled with the universal mirth,
   Cassandra-like, prognosticating woe;   30
They shook their heads, and doomed with dreadful words
To swift destruction the whole race of birds.

And a town-meeting was convened straightway
   To set a price upon the guilty heads
Of these marauders, who, in lieu of pay,
   Levied black-mail upon the garden beds
And cornfields, and beheld without dismay
   The awful scarecrow, with his fluttering shreds;
The skeleton that waited at their feast,
Whereby their sinful pleasure was increased.   40

Then from his house, a temple painted white,
   With fluted columns, and a roof of red,
The Squire came forth, august and splendid sight!
   Slowly descending, with majestic tread,
Three flights of steps, nor looking left nor right,
   Down the long street he walked, as one who said,
"A town that boasts inhabitants like me
Can have no lack of good society!"

The Parson, too, appeared, a man austere,
   The instinct of whose nature was to kill;   50
The wrath of God he preached from year to year,

---

17 **Sound,** Long Island Sound   25 **Killingworth,** originally Kenilworth, but corrupted to this form in time to be uncannily appropriate for the happenings of the tale   30 **Cassandra-like,** Cassandra, daughter of King Priam of Troy, prophesied dire happenings   41 **temple,** referring to the resemblance of some colonial mansions to Greek temples, thereby underlining the delusion of the Squire that he was god-like   51 **wrath of God,** a topic much discussed in Calvinistic sermons

And read, with fervor, Edwards on the Will;
His favorite pastime was to slay the deer
  In Summer on some Adirondac hill;
E'en now, while walking down the rural lane,
He lopped the wayside lilies with his cane.

From the Academy, whose belfry crowned
  The hill of Science with its vane of brass,
Came the Preceptor, gazing idly round,
  Now at the clouds, and now at the green grass,   60
And all absorbed in reveries profound
  Of fair Almira in the upper class,
Who was, as in a sonnet he had said,
As pure as water, and as good as bread.

And next the Deacon issued from his door,
  In his voluminous neck-cloth, white as snow;
A suit of sable bombazine he wore;
  His form was ponderous, and his step was slow;
There never was so wise a man before;
  He seemed the incarnate "Well, I told you so!"   70
And to perpetuate his great renown
There was a street named after him in town.

These came together in the new town-hall,
  With sundry farmers from the region round.
The Squire presided, dignified and tall,
  His air impressive and his reasoning sound;
Ill fared it with the birds, both great and small;
  Hardly a friend in all that crowd they found,
But enemies enough, who every one
Charged them with all the crimes beneath the sun.   80

When they had ended, from his place apart
  Rose the Preceptor, to redress the wrong,
And, trembling like a steed before the start,
  Looked round bewildered on the expectant throng;
Then thought of fair Almira, and took heart
  To speak out what was in him, clear and strong,
Alike regardless of their smile or frown,
And quite determined not to be laughed down.

---

52 **Edwards on the Will.** See p. 202   54 **Adirondac,** a mountain range in northern New York   57
Academy, the secondary school of the village in colonial times   67 **bombazine,** a black silk fabric in
twill weave

"Plato, anticipating the Reviewers,
    From his Republic banished without pity   90
The Poets; in this little town of yours,
    You put to death, by means of a Committee,
The ballad-singers and the Troubadours,
The street-musicians of the heavenly city,
The birds, who make sweet music for us all
In our dark hours, as David did for Saul.

"The thrush that carols at the dawn of day
    From the green steeples of the piny wood;
The oriole in the elm; the noisy jay,
    Jargoning like a foreigner at his food;   100
The bluebird balanced on some topmost spray,
    Flooding with melody the neighborhood;
Linnet and meadow-lark, and all the throng
That dwell in nests, and have the gift of song.

"You slay them all! and wherefore? for the gain
    Of a scant handful more or less of wheat,
Or rye, or barley, or some other grain,
    Scratched up at random by industrious feet,
Searching for worm or weevil after rain!
    Or a few cherries, that are not so sweet   110
As are the songs these uninvited guests
Sing at their feast with comfortable breasts.

"Do you ne'er think what wondrous beings these?
    Do you ne'er think who made them, and who taught
The dialect they speak, where melodies
    Alone are the interpreters of thought?
Whose household words are songs in many keys,
    Sweeter than instrument of man e'er caught!
Whose habitations in the tree-tops even
Are half-way houses on the road to heaven!   120

"Think, every morning when the sun peeps through
    The dim, leaf-latticed windows of the grove,
How jubilant the happy birds renew
    Their old, melodious madrigals of love!

---

89 **Plato . . . Reviewers,** refers to Plato, Greek philosopher (427-347 B.C.), who by banishing poets from
his ideal republic anticipated the harsh British reviewers of poets in the nineteenth century   93 **Troubadours,** medieval poet-musicians who lived in southern France and northern Italy   96 **David . . . Saul.**
See I Samuel 16:14-23

And when you think of this, remember too
   'T is always morning somewhere, and above
The awakening continents, from shore to shore,
Somewhere the birds are singing evermore.

"Think of your woods and orchards without birds!
   Of empty nests that cling to boughs and beams   130
As in an idiot's brain remembered words
   Hang empty 'mid the cobwebs of his dreams!
Will bleat of flocks or bellowing of herds
   Make up for the lost music, when your teams
Drag home the stingy harvest, and no more
The feathered gleaners follow to your door?

"What! would you rather see the incessant stir
   Of insects in the windrows of the hay,
And hear the locust and the grasshopper
   Their melancholy hurdy-gurdies play?   140
Is this more pleasant to you than the whir
   Of meadow-lark, and her sweet roundelay,
Or twitter of little field-fares, as you take
Your nooning in the shade of bush and brake?

"You call them thieves and pillagers; but know,
   They are the wingèd wardens of your farms,
Who from the cornfields drive the insidious foe,
   And from your harvests keep a hundred harms;
Even the blackest of them all, the crow,
   Renders good service as your man-at-arms,   150
Crushing the beetle in his coat of mail,
And crying havoc on the slug and snail.

"How can I teach your children gentleness,
   And mercy to the weak, and reverence
For Life, which, in its weakness or excess,
   Is still a gleam of God's omnipotence,
Or Death, which, seeming darkness, is no less
   The selfsame light, although averted hence,
When by your laws, your actions, and your speech,
You contradict the very things I teach?"   160

With this he closed; and through the audience went
   A murmur, like the rustle of dead leaves;

---

143 **field-fares**, a European thrush   144 **nooning**, a time for rest and refreshment at noon-time

The farmers laughed and nodded, and some bent
   Their yellow heads together like their sheaves;
Men have no faith in fine-spun sentiment
   Who put their trust in bullocks and in beeves.
The birds were doomed; and, as the record shows,
A bounty offered for the heads of crows.

There was another audience out of reach,
   Who had no voice nor vote in making laws,   170
But in the papers read his little speech,
   And crowned his modest temples with applause;
They made him conscious, each one more than each,
   He still was victor, vanquished in their cause.
Sweetest of all the applause he won from thee,
O fair Almira at the Academy!

And so the dreadful massacre began;
   O'er fields and orchards, and o'er woodland crests,
The ceaseless fusillade of terror ran.
   Dead fell the birds, with blood-stains on their breasts, 180
Or wounded crept away from sight of man,
   While the young died of famine in their nests;
A slaughter to be told in groans, not words,
The very St. Bartholomew of Birds!

The Summer came, and all the birds were dead;
   The days were like hot coals; the very ground
Was burned to ashes; in the orchards fed
   Myriads of caterpillars, and around
The cultivated fields and garden beds
   Hosts of devouring insects crawled, and found   190
No foe to check their march, till they had made
The land a desert without leaf or shade.

Devoured by worms, like Herod, was the town,
   Because, like Herod, it had ruthlessly
Slaughtered the Innocents. From the trees spun down
   The canker-worms upon the passers-by,
Upon each woman's bonnet, shawl, and gown,
   Who shook them off with just a little cry;
They were the terror of each favorite walk,
The endless theme of all the village talk.   200

---

184 **St. Bartholomew**, a massacre of French Huguenots by Catholics occurred on St. Bartholomew's Eve,
1572   192 **land.** See Acts 12:23   193 **Herod,** Matthew 2:16

The farmers grew impatient, but a few
   Confessed their error, and would not complain,
For after all, the best thing one can do
   When it is raining, is to let it rain.
Then they repealed the law, although they knew
   It would not call the dead to life again;
As school-boys, finding their mistake too late,
Draw a wet sponge across the accusing slate.

That year in Killingworth the Autumn came
   Without the light of his majestic look,   210
The wonder of the falling tongues of flame,
   The illumined pages of his Doom's-Day book.
A few lost leaves blushed crimson with their shame,
   And drowned themselves despairing in the brook,
While the wild wind went moaning everywhere,
Lamenting the dead children of the air!

But the next Spring a stranger sight was seen,
   A sight that never yet by bard was sung,
As great a wonder as it would have been
   If some dumb animal had found a tongue!   220
A wagon, overarched with evergreen,
   Upon whose boughs were wicker cages hung,
All full of singing birds, came down the street,
Filling the air with music wild and sweet.

From all the country round these birds were brought,
   By order of the town, with anxious quest,
And, loosened from their wicker prisons, sought
   In woods and fields the places they loved best,
Singing loud canticles, which many thought
   Were satires to the authorities addressed,   230
While others, listening in green lanes, averred
Such lovely music never had been heard!

But blither still and louder carolled they
   Upon the morrow, for they seemed to know
It was the fair Almira's wedding-day,
   And everywhere, around, above, below,
When the Preceptor bore his bride away,

---

211 **tongues.** See Acts 2:3   212 **Doom's-Day book,** a digest of the census of England, compiled in 1086 by William I, so-called because it resembled in inclusiveness the records to be scanned on the day of the Last Judgment

Their songs burst forth in joyous overflow,
And a new heaven bent over a new earth
Amid the sunny farms of Killingworth.   240

                                        1863

The Landlord's Tale

The Rhyme of Sir Christopher

Sir Christopher Gardiner, the protagonist of the final narrative in Tales of a Wayside
Inn, *was a legendary figure of precisely the sort to appeal to Longfellow. As Charles Francis
Adams says, "Who the man was, and why or whither he subsequently went, are mysteries
. . . but he stands out in picturesque incongruity against the monotonous background of
colonial life." Several historians had provided a few details about him, among them Jeremy
Belknap, whose* American Biography *appeared in several editions between 1794 and 1855
— almost certainly one of the poet's sources. Gardiner had appeared, too, in several fictional
works including the novel* Merrymount *(1840) by Longfellow's friend, the historian
John L. Motley.*

*The prototype of the narrator was a bachelor, Lyman Howe, descendant of proprietors of
the Red Horse Inn since the seventeenth century and the proprietor in Longfellow's time. He
had told the first of the tales, the stirring "Paul Revere's Ride."*

*The vein of humor may surprise some modern readers, since the supposedly prissy Long-
fellow writes with patent amusement about Gardiner's mistress and his bigamy. But by
sending both the mistress and the knight back to England, he does end the story more neatly
and properly than history had. Actually, some time after her capture in 1631, the mistress
married one Thomas Purchase in Boston and accompanied him to his home in Maine; there
not only she but also Sir Christopher (for several months at least) lived with her husband.
When Sir Christopher returned to England, it was apparently on his own volition. Mrs.
Purchase, evidently without ever returning to England, died in Boston in 1656. Longfellow's
evocation of the colonial scene, of "the little lady with golden hair" in the knight's rustic
"castle," and his account of the Puritan governor's dealings with the interlopers all show
his skill as a narrator.*

It was Sir Christopher Gardiner,
Knight of the Holy Sepulchre,
From Merry England over the sea,
Who stepped upon this continent
As if his august presence lent
A glory to the colony.

You should have seen him in the street
Of the little Boston of Winthrop's time,

---

2 **Knight** of the Holy Sepulchre, a papal order of knighthood, one of several titles dubiously claimed by
Sir Christopher

His rapier dangling at his feet,
Doublet and hose and boots complete,   10
Prince Rupert hat with ostrich plume,
Gloves that exhaled a faint perfume,
Luxuriant curls and air sublime,
And superior manners now obsolete!

He had a way of saying things
That made one think of courts and kings,
And lords and ladies of high degree;
So that not having been at court
Seemed something very little short
Of treason or lese-majesty,   20
Such an accomplished knight was he.

His dwelling was just beyond the town,
At what he called his country-seat;
For, careless of Fortune's smile or frown,
And weary grown of the world and its ways,
He wished to pass the rest of his days
In a private life and a calm retreat.

But a double life was the life he led,
And, while professing to be in search
Of a godly course, and willing, he said,   30
Nay, anxious to join the Puritan church,
He made of all this but small account,
And passed his idle hours instead
With roystering Morton of Merry Mount,
That pettifogger from Furnival's Inn,
Lord of misrule and riot and sin,
Who looked on the wine when it was red.

This country-seat was little more
Than a cabin of logs; but in front of the door
A modest flower-bed thickly sown   40
With sweet alyssum and columbine
Made those who saw it at once divine
The touch of some other hand than his own.
And first it was whispered, and then it was known,
That he in secret was harboring there
A little lady with golden hair,

---

11 **Prince Rupert hat,** a hat made fashionable (somewhat after the time of the story) by Prince Rupert
(1619-1682), a nephew of Charles I of England   34 **Morton of Merry Mount.** See p. 68

Whom he called his cousin, but whom he had wed
In the Italian manner, as men said,
And great was the scandal everywhere.

But worse than this was the vague surmise,   50
Though none could vouch for it or aver,
That the Knight of the Holy Sepulchre
Was only a Papist in disguise;
And the more to imbitter their bitter lives,
And the more to trouble the public mind,
Came letters from England, from two other wives,
Whom he had carelessly left behind;
Both of them letters of such a kind
As made the governor hold his breath;
The one imploring him straight to send   60
The husband home, that he might amend;
The other asking his instant death,
As the only way to make an end.

The wary governor deemed it right,
When all this wickedness was revealed,
To send his warrant signed and sealed,
And take the body of the knight.
Armed with this mighty instrument,
The marshal, mounting his gallant steed,
Rode forth from town at the top of his speed,   70
And followed by all his bailiffs bold,
As if on high achievement bent,
To storm some castle or stronghold,
Challenge the warders on the wall,
And seize in his ancestral hall
A robber-baron grim and old.

But when through all the dust and heat
He came to Sir Christopher's country-seat,
No knight he found, nor warder there,
But the little lady with golden hair,   80
Who was gathering in the bright sunshine
The sweet alyssum and columbine;
While gallant Sir Christopher, all so gay,
Being forewarned, through the postern gate

---

47 **wed . . . manner,** a catch-phrase for simply living with a woman   53 **a Papist in disguise.** Sir Christopher, despite his denials, was a Catholic; he was in New England as an agent for John Gorges, who claimed that he had been defrauded of a large tract in Massachusetts

Of his castle wall had tripped away,
And was keeping a little holiday
In the forests, that bounded his estate.

Then as a trusty squire and true
The marshal searched the castle through,
Not crediting what the lady said;   90
Searched from cellar to garret in vain,
And, finding no knight, came out again
And arrested the golden damsel instead,
And bore her in triumph into the town,
While from her eyes the tears rolled down
On the sweet alyssum and columbine,
That she held in her fingers white and fine.

The governor's heart was moved to see
So fair a creature caught within
The snares of Satan and of sin,   100
And he read her a little homily
On the folly and wickedness of the lives
Of women half cousins and half wives;
But, seeing that naught his words availed,
He sent her away in a ship that sailed
For Merry England over the sea,
To the other two wives in the old countree,
To search her further, since he had failed
To come at the heart of the mystery.

Meanwhile Sir Christopher wandered away   110
Through pathless woods for a month and a day,
Shooting pigeons, and sleeping at night
With the noble savage, who took delight
In his feathered hat and his velvet vest,
His gun and his rapier and the rest.
But as soon as the noble savage heard
That a bounty was offered for this gay bird,
He wanted to slay him out of hand,
And bring in his beautiful scalp for a show,
Like the glossy head of a kite or crow,   120
Until he was made to understand
They wanted the bird alive, not dead;
Then he followed him withersoever he fled,
Through forest and field, and hunted him down,
And brought him prisoner into the town.

---

107 **old countree.** Longfellow playfully uses a spelling common in old ballads

Alas! it was a rueful sight,
To see this melancholy knight
In such a dismal and hapless case;
His hat deformed by stain and dent,
His plumage broken, his doublet rent,   130
His beard and flowing locks forlorn,
Matted, dishevelled, and unshorn,
His boots with dust and mire besprent;
But dignified in his disgrace,
And wearing an unblushing face.
And thus before the magistrate
He stood to hear the doom of fate.
In vain he strove with wonted ease
To modify and extenuate
His evil deeds in church and state,   140
For gone was now his power to please;
And his pompous words had no more weight
Than feathers flying in the breeze.

With suavity equal to his own
The governor lent a patient ear
To the speech evasive and high-flown,
In which he endeavored to make clear
That colonial laws were too severe
When applied to a gallant cavalier,
A gentleman born, and so well known,   150
And accustomed to move in a higher sphere.

All this the Puritan governor heard,
And deigned in answer never a word;
But in summary manner shipped away,
In a vessel that sailed from Salem Bay,
This splendid and famous cavalier,
With his Rupert hat and his popery,
To Merry England over the sea,
As being unmeet to inhabit here.

Thus endeth the Rhyme of Sir Christopher,   160
Knight of the Holy Sepulchre,
The first who furnished this barren land
With apples of Sodom and ropes of sand.

                    1873

---

163 **apples . . . sand.** Two Puritan symbols of the merely apparent nature of Catholic faith. Apples of Sodom were legendary fruit that turned to ashes in the mouth

Divina Commedia

The six sonnets under this title prefaced the three parts of Longfellow's translation of Dante's masterpiece — I and II, the "Inferno"; III and IV, the "Purgatorio"; and V and VI, the "Paradiso." They at once comment on Dante's poem and reveal what it meant to Longfellow when, in the years of his grief over the death of his second wife, the years, also, of the Civil War, he translated the poem. The pairs of sonnets have appropriateness to the respective sections which they preface — Inferno, Purgatory, and Paradise.

I

Oft have I seen at some cathedral door
  A laborer, pausing in the dust and heat,
  Lay down his burden, and with reverent feet
  Enter, and cross himself, and on the floor
Kneel to repeat his paternoster o'er;
  Far off the noises of the world retreat;
  The loud vociferations of the street
  Become an undistinguishable roar.
So, as I enter here from day to day,
  And leave my burden at this minster gate,   10
  Kneeling in prayer, and not ashamed to pray,
The tumult of the time disconsolate
  To inarticulate murmurs dies away,
  While the eternal ages watch and wait.

                       1865

II

How strange the sculptures that adorn these towers!
  This crowd of statues, in whose folded sleeves
  Birds build their nests; while canopied with leaves
  Parvis and portal bloom like trellised bowers,
And the vast minster seems a cross of flowers!
  But fiends and dragons on the gargoyled eaves   20
  Watch the dead Christ between the living thieves,
  And, underneath, the traitor Judas lowers!
Ah! from what agonies of heart and brain,
  What exultations trampling on despair,
  What tenderness, what tears, what hate of wrong,

---

5 **paternoster,** literally, "Our Father"   10 **minster gate,** cathedral door   12 **time disconsolate** refers to the Civil War   18 **Parvis,** the church porch   20 **fiends,** a richly allusive reference, literally to the gargoyles in the church, figuratively to man in a world of evil and to the sufferers in the "Inferno"

What passionate outcry of a soul in pain,
  Uprose this poem of the earth and air,
  This medieval miracle of song!

               1865

III

I enter, and I see thee in the gloom
  Of the long aisles, O poet saturnine!   30
  And strive to make my steps keep pace with thine.
  The air is filled with some unknown perfume;
The congregation of the dead make room
  For thee to pass; the votive tapers shine;
  Like rooks that haunt Ravenna's groves of pine
  The hovering echoes fly from tomb to tomb.
From the confessionals I hear arise
  Rehearsals of forgotten tragedies,
  And lamentations from the crypts below;
And then a voice celestial that begins   40
  With the pathetic words, "Although your sins
  As scarlet be," and end with "as the snow."

               1866

IV

With snow-white veil and garments as of flame,
  She stands before thee, who so long ago
  Filled thy young heart with passion and the woe
From which thy song and all its splendors came;
And while with stern rebuke she speaks thy name,
  The ice about thy heart melts as the snow
  On mountain heights, and in swift overflow
  Comes gushing from thy lips in sobs of shame.   50
Thou makest full confession; and a gleam,
  As of the dawn on some dark forest cast,
  Seems on thy lifted forehead to increase;
Lethe and Eunoë — the remembered dream
  And the forgotten sorrow — bring at last
  That perfect pardon which is perfect peace.

               1866

---

27 **this poem . . . air,** the *Divine Comedy*. Here the poet combines the images of the opening five lines of this sonnet with those describing the "fiends and dragons"   30 **poet saturnine,** Dante   35 **Ravenna,** a city in Italy frequently mentioned by Dante   41 **"Although . . . snow."** See Isaiah 1:18   44 **She,** Beatrice   54 **Lethe and Eunoë.** In classical mythology the Lethe is the river of forgetfulness and the Eunoë, the river of the memory of the good. At the summit of the mountain of Purgatory, Dante drinks from these rivers

V

I lift mine eyes, and all the windows blaze
    With forms of Saints and holy men who died,
    Here martyred and hereafter glorified;
    And the great Rose upon its leaves displays   60
Christ's Triumph, and the angelic roundelays,
    With splendor upon splendor multiplied;
    And Beatrice again at Dante's side
    No more rebukes, but smiles her words of praise.
And then the organ sounds, and unseen choirs
    Sing the old Latin hymns of peace and love
    And benedictions of the Holy Ghost;
And the melodious bells among the spires
    O'er all the housetops and through heaven above
    Proclaim the elevation of the Host!   70

                                                      1867

VI

O star of morning and of liberty!
    O bringer of the light, whose splendor shines
    Above the darkness of the Apennines,
    Forerunner of the day that is to be!
The voices of the city and the sea,
    The voices of the mountains and the pines,
    Repeat thy song, till the familiar lines
    Are footpaths for the thought of Italy!
Thy flame is blown abroad from all the heights,
    Through all the nations, and a sound is heard,   80
    As of a mighty wind, and men devout,
Strangers of Rome, and the new proselytes,
    In their own language hear the wondrous word,
    And many are amazed and many doubt.

                                                      1867

Morituri Salutamus

*When he was sixty-seven, Longfellow composed this poem for delivery at the fiftieth-anniversary
celebration of the Class of 1825, Bowdoin College. The title, which means "We who are
about to die salute you," was the legendary cry of gladiators to the emperor as they were
about to enter the arena. The poem is said to have been suggested by a painting of the French*

---

60 **Rose** refers not only to the windows of the cathedral but also to the end of Dante's journey in the "Paradiso," when he sees the Trinity and the Blessed in the form of a rose   70 **the . . . Host,** the climax of
the celebration of the Mass when the Host is lifted high   71 **star,** Dante

artist Léon Gérome (1824-1904). Longfellow prefixed the poem with a quotation from Ovid which, translated, reads "Time passes away, we grow old with the quiet years, and the days fly with no delaying check."

"O Caesar, we who are about to die
Salute you!" was the gladiators' cry
In the arena, standing face to face
With death and with the Roman populace.

O ye familiar scenes, — ye groves of pine,
That once were mine and are no longer mine, —
Thou river, widening through the meadows green
To the vast sea, so near and yet unseen, —
Ye halls, in whose seclusion and repose
Phantoms of fame, like exhalations, rose   10
And vanished, — we who are about to die,
Salute you; earth and air and sea and sky,
And the Imperial Sun that scatters down
His sovereign splendors upon grove and town.

Ye do not answer us! ye do not hear!
We are forgotten; and in your austere
And calm indifference, ye little care
Whether we come or go, or whence or where.
What passing generations fill these halls,
What passing voices echo from these walls,   20
Ye heed not; we are only as the blast,
A moment heard, and then forever past.

Not so the teachers who in earlier days
Led our bewildered feet through learning's maze;
They answer us — alas! what have I said?
What greetings come there from the voiceless dead?
What salutation, welcome, or reply?
What pressure from the hands that lifeless lie?
They are no longer here; they all are gone
Into the land of shadows, — all save one.   30
Honor and reverence, and the good repute
That follows faithful service as its fruit,
Be unto him, whom living we salute.

The great Italian poet, when he made
His dreadful journey to the realms of shade,

---

30 **one,** Professor A. S. Packard

Met there the old instructor of his youth,
And cried in tone of pity and of ruth:
"Oh, never from the memory of my heart
Your dear, paternal image shall depart,
Who while on earth, ere yet by death surprised,   40
Taught me how mortals are immortalized;
How grateful am I for that patient care
All my life long my language shall declare."

Today we make the poet's words our own,
And utter them in plaintive undertone;
Nor to the living only be they said,
But to the other living called the dead,
Whose dear, paternal images appear
Not wrapped in gloom, but roped in sunshine here;
Whose simple lives, complete and without flaw,   50
Were part and parcel of great Nature's law;
Who said not to their Lord, as if afraid,
"Here is thy talent in a napkin laid."
But labored in their sphere, as men who live
In the delight that work alone can give.
Peace be to them; eternal peace and rest,
And the fulfillment of the great behest:
"Ye have been faithful over a few things,
Over ten cities shall ye reign as kings."

And ye who fill the places we once filled,   60
And follow in the furrows that we tilled,
Young men, whose generous hearts are beating high,
We who are old, and are about to die,
Salute you; hail you; take your hands in ours,
And crown you with our welcome as with flowers!
How beautiful is youth! how bright it gleams
With its illusions, aspirations, dreams!
Book of Beginnings, Story without End,
Each maid a heroine, and each man a friend!

Aladdin's Lamp, and Fortunatus' Purse,   70
That holds the treasures of the universe!

---

36 **the old instructor,** Brunetto Latini. Lines 38-43 are a translation of a speech in the "Inferno"   53
"Here . . . laid." See Matthew 25:14-20   58 **"Ye . . . kings."** See Matthew 25:21   70 **Fortunatus'
Purse,** an inexhaustible purse which, according to an old tale, was given to Fortunatus by Fortune

All possibilities are in its hands,
No danger daunts it, and no foe withstands;
In its sublime audacity of faith,
"Be thou removed," it to the mountain saith,
And with ambitious feet, secure and proud,
Ascends the ladder leaning on the cloud!

As ancient Priam at the Scæan gate
Sat on the walls of Troy in regal state
With the old men, too old and weak to fight,   80
Chirping like grasshoppers in their delight
To see the embattled hosts, with spear and shield,
Of Trojans and Achaians in the field;
So from the snowy summits of our years
We see you in the plain, as each appears,
And question of you; asking, "Who is he
That towers above the others? Which may be
Atreides, Menelaus, Odysseus,
Ajax the great, or bold Idomeneus?"

Let him not boast who puts his armor on   90
As he who puts it off, the battle done.
Study yourselves; and most of all note well
Wherein kind Nature meant you to excel.
Not every blossom ripens into fruit;
Minerva, the inventress of the flute,
Flung it aside, when she her face surveyed
Distorted in a fountain as she played;
The unlucky Marsyas found it, and his fate
Was one to make the bravest hesitate.
Write on your doors the saying wise and old,   100
"Be bold! be bold!" and everywhere, "Be bold;
Be not too bold!" Yet better the excess
Than the defect; better the more than less;
Better like Hector in the field to die,
Than like a perfumed Paris turn and fly.

And now, my classmates; ye remaining few
That number not the half of those we knew,

---

75 **"Be thou. . . ."** See Matthew 17:20   78 **As ancient Priam. . . .** The incident treated in ll. 78-83 occurs in the *Iliad,* Bk. III   98 **Marsyas,** a presumptuous Greek poet who challenged Apollo to a musical contest, lost, and was flayed alive   104 **Hector,** a Grecian hero who bravely met his death at the hands of Achilles. For Hector's bravery, and Paris' less admirable activity, see the *Iliad,* Bks. III and XXII

Ye, against whose familiar names not yet
The fatal asterisk of death is set,
Ye I salute! The horologe of Time   110
Strikes the half-century with a solemn chime,
And summons us together once again,
The joy of meeting not unmixed with pain.
Where are the others? Voices from the deep
Caverns of darkness answer me: "They sleep!"
I name no names; instinctively I feel
Each at some well-remembered grave will kneel,
And from the inscription wipe the weeds and moss,
For every heart best knoweth its own loss.
I see their scattered gravestones gleaming white   120
Through the pale dusk of the impending night;
O'er all alike the impartial sunset throws
Its golden lilies mingled with the rose;
We give to each a tender thought, and pass
Out of the graveyards with their tangled grass,
Unto these scenes frequented by our feet
When we were young, and life was fresh and sweet.

What shall I say to you? What can I say
Better than silence is? When I survey
This throng of faces turned to meet my own,   130
Friendly and fair, and yet to me unknown,
Transformed the very landscape seems to be;
It is the same, yet not the same to me.
So many memories crowd upon my brain,
So many ghosts are in the wooded plain,
I fain would steal away, with noiseless tread,
As from a house where someone lieth dead.
I cannot go; — I pause; — I hesitate;
My feet reluctant linger at the gate;
As one who struggles in a troubled dream   140
To speak and cannot, to myself I seem.

Vanish the dream! Vanish the idle fears!
Vanish the rolling mists of fifty years!
Whatever time or space may intervene,
I will not be a stranger in this scene.
Here every doubt, all indecision, ends;
Hail, my companions, comrades, classmates, friends!

---

109 **fatal asterisk,** a reference to the custom of indicating which members of a college class have died by
marking their names with asterisks

Ah me! the fifty years since last we met
Seem to me fifty folios bound and set
By Time, the great transcriber, on his shelves,   150
Wherein are written the histories of ourselves.
What tragedies, what comedies, are there;
What joy and grief, what rapture and despair!
What chronicles of triumph and defeat,
Of struggle, and temptation, and retreat!
What records of regrets, and doubts, and fears!
What pages blotted, blistered by our tears!
What lovely landscapes on the margin shine,
What sweet, angelic faces, what divine
And holy images of love and trust,   160
Undimmed by age, unsoiled by damp or dust!
Whose hand shall dare to open and explore
These volumes, closed and clasped forevermore?
Not mine. With reverential feet I pass;
I hear a voice that cries, "Alas! alas!
Whatever hath been written shall remain,
Nor be erased nor written o'er again;
The unwritten only still belongs to thee:
Take heed, and ponder well what that shall be."

As children frightened by a thunder-cloud   170
Are reassured if some one reads aloud
A tale of wonder, with enchantment fraught,
Or wild adventure, that diverts their thought,
Let me endeavor with a tale to chase
The gathering shadows of the time and place,
And banish what we all too deeply feel
Wholly to say, or wholly to conceal.

In medieval Rome, I know not where,
There stood an image with its arm in air,
And on its lifted finger, shining clear,   180
A golden ring with the device, "Strike here!"
Greatly the people wondered, though none guessed
The meaning that these words but half expressed,
Until a learned clerk, who at noonday
With downcast eyes was passing on his way,
Paused, and observed the spot, and marked it well,
Whereon the shadow of the finger fell;

---

174 **tale,** in the famous medieval collection, *Gesta Romanorum,* Tale CVII

And, coming back at midnight, delved, and found
A secret stairway leading underground.
Down this he passed into a spacious hall,   190
Lit by a flaming jewel on the wall;
And opposite, in threatening attitude,
With bow and shaft a brazen statue stood.
Upon its forehead, like a coronet,
Were these mysterious words of menace set:
"That which I am, I am; my fatal aim
None can escape, not even yon luminous flame!"

Midway the hall was a fair table placed,
With cloth of gold, and golden cups enchased
With rubies, and the plates and knives were gold,   200
And gold the bread and viands manifold.
Around it, silent, motionless, and sad,
Were seated gallant knights in armor clad,
And ladies beautiful with plume and zone,
But they were stone, their hearts within were stone;
And the vast hall was filled in every part
With silent crowds, stony in face and heart.

Long at the scene, bewildered and amazed,
The trembling clerk in speechless wonder gazed;
Then from the table, by his greed made bold,   210
He seized a goblet and a knife of gold,
And suddenly from their seats the guests upsprang,
The vaulted ceiling with loud clamors rang,
The archer sped his arrow, at their call,
Shattering the lambent jewel on the wall,
And all was dark around and overhead; —
Stark on the floor the luckless clerk lay dead.

The writer of this legend then records
Its ghostly application in these words:
The image is the Adversary old,   220
Whose beckoning finger points to realms of gold;
Our lusts and passions are the downward stair
That leads the soul from a diviner air;
The archer, Death; the flaming jewel, Life;
Terrestrial goods, the goblet and the knife;
The knights and ladies, all whose flesh and bone
By avarice have been hardened into stone;
The clerk, the scholar whom the love of pelf
Tempts from his books and from his nobler self.

The scholar and the world! The endless strife, 230
The discord in the harmonies of life!
The love of learning, the sequestered nooks,
And all the sweet serenity of books;
The market-place, the eager love of gain,
Whose aim is vanity, and whose end is pain!

But why, you ask me, should this tale be told
To men grown old, or who are growing old?
It is too late! Ah, nothing is too late
Till the tired heart shall cease to palpitate.
Cato learned Greek at eighty; Sophocles 240
Wrote his grand Œdipus, and Simonides
Bore off the prize of verse from his compeers,
When each had numbered more than fourscore years,
And Theophrastus, at fourscore and ten,
Had but begun his "Characters of Men."
Chaucer, at Woodstock with the nightingales,
At sixty wrote the Canterbury Tales;
Goethe at Weimar, toiling to the last,
Completed Faust when eighty years were past.
These are indeed exceptions; but they show 250
How far the gulf-stream of our youth may flow
Into the arctic regions of our lives,
Where little else than life itself survives.

As the barometer foretells the storm
While still the skies are clear, the weather warm,
So something in us, as old age draws near,
Betrays the pressure of the atmosphere.
The nimble mercury, ere we are aware,
Descends the elastic ladder of the air;
The telltale blood in artery and vein 260
Sinks from its higher levels in the brain;
Whatever poet, orator, or sage
May say of it, old age is still old age.
It is the waning, not the crescent moon;
The dusk of evening, not the blaze of noon;
It is not strength, but weakness; not desire,

---

240 **Cato**, Cato the Censor (234-149 B.C.) 240 **Sophocles** (495-405 B.C.) is said to have written *Oedipus at Colonus* shortly before his death 241 **Simonides** (556-467 B.C.), great Greek lyric poet 244 **Theophrastus** (382-297 B.C.), author of *Moral Characters* 246 **Chaucer . . . sixty.** At the time Longfellow wrote, it was thought Chaucer had been born in 1320. Modern scholars believe that 1340 was nearer the date of his birth 248 **Goethe** began work on *Faust* in 1773, but the conclusion did not appear until 1833

But its surcease; not the fierce heat of fire,
The burning and consuming element,
But that of ashes and of embers spent,
In which some living sparks we still discern,   270
Enough to warm, but not enough to burn.

What then? Shall we sit idly down and say
The night hath come; it is no longer day?
The night hath not yet come; we are not quite
Cut off from labor by the failing light;
Something remains for us to do or dare;
Even the oldest tree some fruit may bear;
Not Œdipus Coloneus, or Greek Ode,
Or tales of pilgrims that one morning rode
Out of the gateway of the Tabard Inn,   280
But other something, would we but begin;
For age is opportunity no less
Than youth itself, though in another dress,
And as the evening twilight fades away
The sky is filled with stars, invisible by day.

                                             1874, 1875

Chaucer

An old man in a lodge within a park;
    The chamber walls depicted all around
    With portraitures of huntsman, hawk, and hound,
    And the hurt deer. He listeneth to the lark,
Whose song comes with the sunshine through the dark
    Of painted glass in leaden lattice bound;
He listeneth and he laugheth at the sound,
    Then writeth in a book like any clerk.
He is the poet of the dawn, who wrote
    The Canterbury Tales, and his old age   10
    Made beautiful with song; and as I read
I hear the crowing cock, I hear the note
    Of lark and linnet, and from every page
    Rise odors of ploughed field or flowery mead.

                                             1873, 1875

---

8 **clerk**, in Chaucer's day, a scholar. The "clerk of Oxenford" is affectionately portrayed in *The Canterbury
Tales* (c. 1387-1400)

Milton

I pace the sounding sea-beach and behold
  How the voluminous billows roll and run,
  Upheaving and subsiding, while the sun
  Shines through their sheeted emerald far unrolled,
And the ninth wave, slow gathering fold by fold
  All its loose-flowing garments into one,
  Plunges upon the shore, and floods the dun
  Pale reach of sands, and changes them to gold.
So in majestic cadence rise and fall
  The mighty undulations of thy song,   10
  O sightless bard, England's Mæonides!
And ever and anon, high over all
  Uplifted, a ninth wave superb and strong,
  Floods all the soul with its melodious seas.

                          1873, 1875

5 **ninth wave.** According to folklore, the ninth wave was the mightiest of a series. Longfellow perhaps refers to Milton's Petrarchan sonnets, in which the ninth line was the climactic one, and to the sonorous periodic sentences of his epics   11 **Mæonides,** Homer, so called because tradition made him the son of Mæon. Milton resembled him in being blind and in being the author of great epic poems

Sleep

Lull me to sleep, ye winds, whose fitful sound
  Seems from some faint Æolian harp-string caught;
  Seal up the hundred wakeful eyes of thought
  As Hermes with his lyre in sleep profound
The hundred wakeful eyes of Argus bound;
  For I am weary, and am overwrought
  With too much toil, with too much care distraught,
  And with the iron crown of anguish crowned.
Lay thy soft hand upon my brow and cheek,
  O peaceful Sleep! until from pain released   10
  I breathe again uninterrupted breath!
Ah, with what subtle meaning did the Greek
  Call thee the lesser mystery at the feast
Whereof the greater mystery is death!

                      1875

2 **Æolian harp,** an ancient harp played by air currents   4 **Hermes,** son of Jupiter and the inventor of the lyre   5 **Argus,** the hundred-eyed son of Zeus, who had a habit of sleeping with only two eyes at a time. Hermes, by playing wonderful music, put all his eyes to sleep at once and then slew him

Jugurtha

The incident treated here is based on Plutarch's life of Marius, the Roman general. In Plutarch's account Jugurtha, a Numidian king defeated by the Romans, addresses his words to Hercules. But the name Apollo, the god of manly youth and beauty, of poetry, music, and oracles, and of healing and sudden death, has more poetic associations for modern readers.

How cold are thy baths, Apollo!
  Cried the African monarch, the splendid,
As down to his death in the hollow
  Dark dungeons of Rome he descended,
  Uncrowned, unthroned, unattended;
How cold are thy baths, Apollo!

How cold are thy baths, Apollo!
  Cried the Poet, unknown, unbefriended,
As the vision that lured him to follow
  With the mist and the darkness blended,   10
  And the dream and his life was ended;
How cold are thy baths, Apollo!
                      1879, 1880

The Tide Rises, the Tide Falls

The tide rises, the tide falls,
The twilight darkens, the curlew calls;
Along the sea-sands damp and brown
The traveller hastens toward the town,
  And the tide rises, the tide falls.

Darkness settles on roofs and walls,
But the sea, the sea in the darkness calls;
The little waves, with their soft, white hands,
Efface the footprints in the sands,
  And the tide rises, the tide falls.   10

The morning breaks; the steeds in their stalls
Stamp and neigh, as the hostler calls;
The day returns, but nevermore
Returns the traveller to the shore,
  And the tide rises, the tide falls.
                1879, 1880

1809—1894 Oliver Wendell Holmes

I have always been good company for myself," said Oliver Wendell Holmes. Because he was also good company — almost always — for others, Holmes' chief contribution to our letters probably was the infusion into them of a social grace that, in those days, flourished most notably in Europe. For this reason historians have pointed out that, like the two other famed Cambridge authors, Longfellow and Lowell, in his own unique way Holmes helped adapt European culture to American needs.

It was Holmes who dubbed the social group to which he belonged "Brahmins." A Brahmin is defined in the dictionary as "a Hindu of the highest, or priestly, caste." That Holmes belonged to the highest caste in New England there can be no doubt. His birth and his rearing were in accord with the tradition of his class. He was born in an old house which had historical associations with important battles of the Revolution. He was what he called "a man of family" — one "who inherits family traditions and the cumulative humanities of at least five generations." He was educated at a leading private school, at Harvard, and abroad. In his profession, medicine, he won honors first as a scholar and later (1847-1882) as a noted professor at Harvard.

But there was nothing priestly about little Doctor Holmes. To be sure, in some of his poems, like "The Chambered Nautilus" and various hymns, he preached what he considered inspired truths in a fashion much like that of Longfellow. His scientific training, however, led him to hit out fiercely at older religious attitudes and to distinguish sharply between acts for which man was responsible and acts determined by heredity and environment. Unlike many religious folk of his day, he refused to blame men for the results of their inherited qualities and their upbringing. Perhaps his chief contribution to American thought was the exposition of the deterministic philosophy which stressed the way a man's nature and upbringing molded his life. Furthermore, he was enough of a conservative in his social attitude during this great period of reform to attack vigorously any notions of human regeneration. Finally, much of his most admired verse is worldly, polished, amusing, rather than profound or preachy; and such papers as *The Autocrat of the Breakfast-Table* (1858) and *Over the Teacups* (1891) thrive chiefly because they gracefully transfer Holmes' charming talk to the printed page.

Strung together on slender threads of fiction, these collections of papers from the *Atlantic Monthly* happily combine the informal essay with informal conversation. A group of boarding-house characters who now and then voice opinions or ask questions are, for the most part, useful foils for the Autocrat, the Professor, or the Poet as each carries on his interrupted monologues. Each of the monologuists, since he has various aspects of Holmes' character, can, like his creator, talk shrewdly and wittily about hosts of subjects. In books of this type, rather than in novels such as *Elsie Venner* (1861), Holmes excelled. The novels — "medicated" novels, he called them — deal more seriously but less successfully with scientific and ethical problems. Their chief interest, aside from the ideas they express, derives from their gropings toward the form of something like the psychological fiction Henry James was later to write.

Holmes' verse, like his prose, is at its best when it is most informal. With a taste for eighteenth-century authors formed by childhood reading in his father's library, Holmes for a long time scoffed at the idea of poetic inspiration. Although in time he came to believe that the best poetry was inspired, as a rule he himself was content to write after the models of the sociable Neoclassical authors who flourished in England between 1660 and 1720. His numerous occasional verses, his use of the mock-heroic form, his preference for ballad stanzas and heroic couplets show his kinship with the Queen Anne "gentlemen who writ with ease." "I hold it to be a gift of a certain value," he wrote Lowell, "to give that slight passing spasm of pleasure which a few ringing couplets often cause, read at the right moment. Though they are for the most part to poetry as the beating of a drum or the tinkling of a triangle is to the harmony of a band, yet it is not everybody who can get their limited significance out of these humble instruments."

Prose Works of Oliver Wendell Holmes, Riverside Edition, Boston, 1891   **Poetical Works of Oliver Wendell Holmes,** Cambridge Edition, Boston, 1895   J. T. Morse, **The Life and Letters of Oliver Wendell Holmes,** 2 vols., Boston, 1896   W. S. Knickerbocker, "His Own Boswell: A Note on the Poetry of Oliver Wendell Holmes," **Sewanee Review,** October-December 1933, XLI, 454-466   Eleanor M. Tilton, **Amiable Autocrat,** New York, 1947

Old Ironsides

When, in September 1830, Holmes read a newspaper report that the old and unseaworthy frigate Constitution, *the conqueror of the* Guerrière *in the War of 1812, had been ordered destroyed, he wrote this indignant protest. Published first in the September 16, 1830 issue of the Boston* Daily Advertiser, *the poem was reprinted in many newspapers and was circulated in handbill form in Washington, D. C. The stir started by the poem caused the order to be retracted.*

Ay, tear her tattered ensign down!
   Long has it waved on high,
And many an eye has danced to see
   That banner in the sky;
Beneath it rung the battle shout,
   And burst the cannon's roar; —
The meteor of the ocean air
   Shall sweep the clouds no more!

Her deck, once red with heroes' blood,
   Where knelt the vanquished foe,   10
When winds were hurrying o'er the flood,
   And waves were white below,
No more shall feel the victor's tread,
   Or know the conquered knee; —
The harpies of the shore shall pluck
   The eagle of the sea!

Oh, better that her shattered hulk
   Should sink beneath the wave;
Her thunder shook the mighty deep,
   And there should be her grave;   20
Nail to the mast her holy flag,
   Set every threadbare sail,
And give her to the god of storms,
   The lightning and the gale!

          1830

The Ballad of the Oysterman

This mock-heroic poem emphasizes Holmes' indebtedness to the eighteenth-century light verse writers, such as Prior and Gray, who frequently wrote amusing poetry of this sort. An excellent example of the pretentious treatment of a nonheroic subject, it uses epic and ballad conventions to emphasize the incongruous elements in some of the sentimental love poetry of the 1830's.

It was a tall young oysterman lived by the river-side,
His shop was just upon the bank, his boat was on the tide;
The daughter of a fisherman, that was so straight and slim,
Lived over on the other bank, right opposite to him.

It was the pensive oysterman that saw a lovely maid,
Upon a moonlight evening, a-sitting in the shade;

He saw her wave her handkerchief, as much as if to say,
"I'm wide awake, young oysterman, and all the folks away."

Then up arose the oysterman, and to himself said he,
"I guess I'll leave the skiff at home, for fear that folks should see;   10
I read it in the story-book, that, for to kiss his dear,
Leander swam the Hellespont, — and I will swim this here."

And he has leaped into the waves, and crossed the shining stream,
And he has clambered up the bank, all in the moonlight gleam;
Oh there were kisses sweet as dew, and words as soft as rain, —
But they have heard her father's step, and in he leaps again!

Out spoke the ancient fisherman, — "Oh, what was that, my daughter?"
" 'Twas nothing but a pebble, sir, I threw into the water."
"And what is that, pray tell me, love, that paddles off so fast?"
"It's nothing but a porpoise, sir, that's been a-swimming past."   20

Out spoke the ancient fisherman, — "Now bring me my harpoon!
I'll get into my fishing-boat, and fix the fellow soon."
Down fell that pretty innocent, as falls a snow-white lamb,
Her hair drooped round her pallid cheeks, like seaweed on a clam.

Alas for those two loving ones! she waked not from her swound.
And he was taken with the cramp, and in the waves was drowned;
But Fate has metamorphosed them, in pity of their woe,
And now they keep an oyster-shop for mermaids down below.

                                                                1830

---

12 **Leander,** according to Greek legend, nightly swam the Hellespont to visit Hero, a priestess of Aphrodite. When Leander was drowned, Hero threw herself into the sea. The comparison of the humble oysterman to this character is a typical incongruous touch

My Aunt

My aunt! my dear unmarried aunt!
    Long years have o'er her flown;
Yet still she strains the aching clasp
    That binds her virgin zone;
I know it hurts her, — though she looks
    As cheerful as she can;

---

4 **zone,** belt

Her waist is ampler than her life,
   For life is but a span.

My aunt! my poor deluded aunt!
   Her hair is almost gray;   10
Why will she train that winter curl
   In such a spring-like way?
How can she lay her glasses down,
   And say she reads as well,
When through a double convex lens
   She just makes out to spell?

Her father — grandpapa! forgive
   This erring lip its smiles —
Vowed she should make the finest girl
   Within a hundred miles;   20
He sent her to a stylish school;
   'Twas in her thirteenth June;
And with her, as the rules required,
   "Two towels and a spoon."

They braced my aunt against a board,
   To make her straight and tall;
They laced her up, they starved her down,
   To make her light and small;
They pinched her feet, they singed her hair,
   They screwed it up with pins; —   30
Oh, never mortal suffered more
   In penance for her sins.

So, when my precious aunt was done,
   My grandsire brought her back;
(By daylight, lest some rabid youth
   Might follow on the track;)
"Ah!" said my grandsire, as he shook
   Some powder in his pan,
"What could this lovely creature do
   Against a desperate man!"   40

Alas! nor chariot, nor barouche,
   Nor bandit cavalcade,

---

8 **span,** Holmes puns on the meaning of span as the distance from the end of the thumb to the tip of the little finger of an outstretched hand, or nine inches   38 **pan,** the hollow in the loading part of a musket where powder is placed

Tore from the trembling father's arms
   His all-accomplished maid.
For her how happy had it been!
   And Heaven had spared to me
To see one sad, ungathered rose
   On my ancestral tree.

1831

The Last Leaf

A note preceding this poem, first published in the Amateur *for March 23, 1831, remarks that it "was suggested by the appearance in one of our streets of a venerable relic of the Revolution, said to be one of the party that threw the tea overboard in Boston Harbor." Students of American literature have been interested to learn that the subject was old Major Thomas Melville, Herman Melville's grandfather.*

   This is one of the most famous examples of Holmes' admirable light verse. Actually, the material might have been used in a very sentimental poem, but the exaggerated and incongruous imagery and the tripping verse form save it from mawkishness. Of the metrical scheme, Holmes said: "I do not recall any earlier example of this form of verse, which was commended by the fastidious Edgar Allan Poe, who made a copy of the poem which I have in his own handwriting."

I saw him once before,
As he passed by the door,
   And again
The pavement stones resound,
As he totters o'er the ground
   With his cane.

They say that in his prime,
Ere the pruning-knife of Time
   Cut him down,
Not a better man was found   10
By the Crier on his round
   Through the town.

But now he walks the streets,
And he looks at all he meets
   Sad and wan,
And he shakes his feeble head,
That it seems as if he said,
   "They are gone."

The mossy marbles rest
On the lips that he has prest   20

In their bloom,
And the names he loved to hear
Have been carved for many a year
    On the tomb.

My grandmamma has said —
Poor old lady, she is dead
    Long ago —
That he had a Roman nose,
And his cheek was like a rose
    In the snow;   30

But now his nose is thin,
And it rests upon his chin
    Like a staff,
And a crook is in his back,
And a melancholy crack
    In his laugh.

I know it is a sin
For me to sit and grin
    At him here;
But the old three-cornered hat,   40
And the breeches, and all that,
    Are so queer!

And if I should live to be
The last leaf upon the tree
    In the spring,
Let them smile, as I do now,
At the old forsaken bough
    Where I cling.

                    1831

The Deacon's Masterpiece

or, The Wonderful "One-Hoss Shay" A Logical Story

A satire on the great logical system of theology worked out by Calvinists and on the downfall of Calvinism, this poem was published in the Atlantic Monthly *of September 1858 as part of one of the* Autocrat *papers. The date of the building of the deacon's masterpiece, 1755, was the year after the publication of Jonathan Edwards' greatest defense of Calvinism,* Freedom of the Will; *the year, too, of the Lisbon earthquake, which provoked many arguments favorable to the Calvinistic system.*

Have you heard of the wonderful one-hoss shay,
That was built in such a logical way
It ran a hundred years to a day,
And then, of a sudden, it — ah, but stay,
I'll tell you what happened without delay,
Scaring the parson into fits,
Frightening people out of their wits, —
Have you ever heard of that, I say?

Seventeen hundred and fifty-five.
Georgius Secundus was then alive, —   10
Snuffy old drone from the German hive.
That was the year when Lisbon-town
.Saw the earth open and gulp her down,
And Braddock's army was done so brown,
Left without a scalp to its crown.
It was on the terrible Earthquake-day
That the Deacon finished the one-hoss shay.

Now in building of chaises, I tell you what,
There is always *somewhere* a weakest spot, —
In hub, tire, felloe, in spring or thill,   20
In panel, or crossbar, or floor, or sill,
In screw, bolt, thoroughbrace, — lurking still,
Find it somewhere you must and will, —
Above or below, or within or without, —
And that's the reason, beyond a doubt,
That a chaise *breaks down,* but doesn't *wear out.*

But the Deacon swore (as Deacons do,
With an "I dew vum," or an "I tell *yeou*")
He would build one shay to beat the taown
'N' the keounty 'n' all the kentry raoun';   30
It should be so built that it *could n'* break daown;
"Fur," said the Deacon, "'t's mighty plain
Thut the weakes' place mus' stan' the strain;
'N' the way t' fix it, uz I maintain,
        Is only jest
T' make that place uz strong uz the rest."

So the Deacon inquired of the village folk
Where he could find the strongest oak,
That could n't be split nor bent nor broke, —

---

14 **Braddock's army.** In an ambush near Duquesne, the General and his army barely escaped annihilation

That was for spokes and floors and sills;   40
He sent for lancewood to make the thills;
The crossbars were ash, from the straightest trees,
The panels of white-wood, that cuts like cheese,
But lasts like iron for things like these;
The hubs of logs from the "Settler's ellum," —
Last of its timber, — they could n't sell 'em,

Never an axe had seen their chips,
And the wedges flew from between their lips,
Their blunt ends frizzled like celery-tips;
Step and prop-iron, bolt and screw,   50
Spring, tire, axle, and linchpin too,
Steel of the finest, bright and blue;
Thoroughbrace bison-skin, thick and wide;
Boot, top, dasher, from tough old hide
Found in the pit when the tanner died.
That was the way he "put her through."
"There!" said the Deacon, "naow she'll dew!"

Do! I tell you, I rather guess
She was a wonder, and nothing less!
Colts grew horses, beards turned gray,   60
Deacon and deaconess dropped away,
Children and grandchildren — where were they?
But there stood the stout old one-hoss shay
As fresh as on Lisbon-earthquake-day!

EIGHTEEN HUNDRED; — it came and found
The Deacon's masterpiece strong and sound.
Eighteen hundred increased by ten; —
"Hahnsum kerridge" they called it then.
Eighteen hundred and twenty came; —
Running as usual; much the same.   70
Thirty and forty at last arrive,
And then come fifty, and FIFTY-FIVE.

Little of all we value here
Wakes on the morn of its hundredth year
Without both feeling and looking queer.
In fact, there 's nothing that keeps its youth,
So far as I know, but a tree and truth.
(This is a moral that runs at large;
Take it. — You 're welcome. — No extra charge.)

45 "**Settler's ellum.**" See *settler's elm* in *Dictionary of Americanisms*, ed. Mitford M. Mathews

FIRST OF NOVEMBER, — the Earthquake-day, —   80
There are traces of age in the one-hoss shay,
A general flavor of mild decay,
But nothing local, as one may say.
There could n't be, — for the Deacon's art
Had made it so like in every part
That there wasn't a chance for one to start.
For the wheels were just as strong as the thills,
And the floor was just as strong as the sills,
And the panels just as strong as the floor,
And the whipple-tree neither less nor more,   90
And the back crossbar as strong as the fore,
And spring and axle and hub *encore.*
And yet, *as a whole,* it is past a doubt
In another hour it will be *worn out!*

First of November, 'Fifty-five!
This morning the parson takes a drive.
Now, small boys, get out of the way!
Here comes the wonderful one-hoss shay,
Drawn by a rat-tailed, ewe-necked bay.
"Huddup!" said the parson. — Off went they.   100
The parson was working his Sunday's text, —
Had got to *fifthly,* and stopped perplexed
At what the — Moses — was coming next.
All at once the horse stood still,
Close by the meet'n'-house on the hill.
First a shiver, and then a thrill,
Then something decidedly like a spill, —
And the parson was sitting upon a rock,
At half past nine by the meet'n'-house clock —
Just the hour of the Earthquake shock!   110
What do you think the parson found,
When he got up and stared around?
The poor old chaise in a heap or mound,
As if it had been to the mill and ground!
You see, of course, if you're not a dunce,
How it went to pieces all at once, —
All at once, and nothing first, —
Just as bubbles do when they burst.

End of the wonderful one-hoss shay.
Logic is logic. That 's all I say.   120

1858

The Chambered Nautilus

The paragraph preceding this poem when it appeared at the end of a section of The Autocrat *gave the necessary facts about the background of the poem: "If you will look into Roget's*
Bridgewater Treatise, *you will find a figure of one of these shells [the nautilus], and a
section of it. The last will show you the series of enlarging compartments successively dwelt
in by the animal that inhabits the shell, which is built in a widening spiral. Can you find
no lesson in this?"*

*Of "The Chambered Nautilus," Holmes wrote: "I am as willing to submit this to criti-
cism as any [poem] I have written, in form as well as substance, and I have not seen any
English verse of just the same pattern." It was one work of his which he avowed had been
inspired.*

*"The Chambered Nautilus" is unusually suggestive of Longfellow's poems. Like "Excel-
sior" or "The Builders," it preaches a sermon with the text "Onward and upward." The
form, too, resembles Longfellow's: an object is described in the three opening stanzas, and
then, in the two stanzas addressed to the nautilus at the end, the moral is drawn. Holmes
seems to have been bothered very little by the incongruity — distressing to careful readers —
of some of his images.*

This is the ship of pearl, which, poets feign,
    Sails the unshadowed main, —
    The venturous bark that flings
On the sweet summer wind its purpled wings
In gulfs enchanted, where the Siren sings,
    And coral reefs lie bare,
Where the cold sea-maids rise to sun their streaming hair.

Its webs of living gauze no more unfurl;
    Wrecked is the ship of pearl!
Where its dim dreaming life was wont to dwell,   10
As the frail tenant shaped his growing shell,
    And every chambered cell,
    Before thee lies revealed, —
Its irised ceiling rent, its sunless crypt unsealed!

Year after year beheld the silent toil
    That spread his lustrous coil;
    Still, as the spiral grew,
He left the past year's dwelling for the new,
Stole with soft step its shining archway through,
    Built up its idle door,   20
Stretched in his last-found home, and knew the old no more.

Thanks for the heavenly message brought by thee,
    Child of the wandering sea,
    Cast from her lap, forlorn!
From thy dead lips a clearer note is born
Than ever Triton blew from wreathed horn!
    While on mine ear it rings,
Through the deep caves of thought I hear a voice that sings: —

Build thee more stately mansions, O my soul,
    As the swift seasons roll!   30
    Leave thy low-vaulted past!
Let each new temple, nobler than the last,
Shut thee from heaven with a dome more vast,
    Till thou at length art free,
Leaving thine outgrown shell by life's unresting sea!

                                1858

from The Autocrat of the Breakfast-Table

When Holmes was nearly fifty, Lowell, urged to edit the new Atlantic Monthly, *"made it a condition precedent" to his acceptance that Holmes should be "the first contributor to be engaged." Since Holmes was hardly a towering figure in the literary world, though he did have a fine reputation in medicine, the request rather surprised him.* The Autocrat of the Breakfast-Table, *which he contributed in monthly installments, established his literary reputation and did much to establish that of the magazine.*

    The Autocrat *papers, like the other series which followed them, are unique in form. Each paper is a printed account of a conversation, informal because of its chatty tone and because of interruptions — the author's own asides and the remarks of other boarders who sit at the table. In a sense, furthermore, the papers have some of the appeals of fiction: they have the slightest of plots running through them, and they reveal characters and the interplay between diverse personalities.*

    Since the speakers differ greatly, there is a good deal of variety in the attitudes expressed. Variety is also provided by the wide range of subjects discussed. A glance at the Index to The Autocrat *reveals that Holmes, interested in all sorts of matters, treated, among hundreds of other subjects, Aristocracy, Boating, Calamities, Drunkenness, Ears (Voluntary Movement of), Family, Hysterics, Jailers, Keats, Logical Minds, Maine (Willows in), Nerve-tapping, Old Age, Punning, Quantity, Racing (Horse), Sporting Men, Travel, Unloved, Voices, Women, and Zimmerman's Treatise on Solitude. The talk is witty and learned, allusive to both the classics and contemporary events — an excellent key to the appeal of Holmes as a talker.*

    A lyric conception — my friend, the Poet, said — hits me like a bullet in the forehead. I have often had the blood drop from my cheeks when it struck, and felt that I turned as white as death. Then comes a creeping as of centipedes running down the spine, — then a gasp and a great jump of the heart, — then a sudden flush and a beating in the vessels of the head, — then a long sigh, — and the poem is written.

It is an impromptu, I suppose, then, if you write it so suddenly, — I replied.

No, said he, — far from it. I said written, but I did not say *copied*. Every such poem has a soul and a body, and it is the body of it, or the copy, that men read and publishers pay for. The soul of it is born in an instant in the poet's soul. It comes to him a thought, tangled in the meshes of a few sweet words, — words that
10 have loved each other from the cradle of the language, but have never been wedded until now. Whether it will ever fully embody itself in a bridal train of a dozen stanzas or not is uncertain; but it exists potentially from the instant that the poet turns pale with it. It is enough to stun and scare anybody, to have a hot thought come crashing into his brain, and ploughing up those parallel ruts where the wagon trains of common ideas were jogging along in their regular sequences of association. No wonder the ancients made the poetical impulse wholly external. Μῆνιν ἄειδε Θεά. Goddess, — Muse, — divine afflatus, — something outside always. *I* never wrote any verses worth reading. I can't. I am too stupid. If I ever copied any that were worth reading, I was only a medium.

20 [I was talking all this time to our boarders, you understand, — telling them what this poet told me. The company listened rather attentively, I thought, considering the literary character of the remarks.]

The old gentleman opposite all at once asked me if I ever read anything better than Pope's "Essay on Man"? Had I ever perused McFingal? He was fond of poetry when he was a boy, — his mother taught him to say many little pieces, — he remembered one beautiful hymn; — and the old gentleman began, in a clear, loud voice, for his years, —

"The spacious firmament on high,
With all the blue ethereal sky,
30 And spangled heavens," —

He stopped, as if startled by our silence, and a faint flush ran up beneath the thin white hairs that fell upon his cheek. As I looked round, I was reminded of a show I once saw at the Museum, — the Sleeping Beauty, I think they called it. The old man's sudden breaking out in this way turned every face towards him, and each kept his posture as if changed to stone. Our Celtic Bridget, or Biddy, is not a foolish fat scullion to burst out crying for a sentiment. She is of the serviceable, red-handed, broad-and-high-shouldered type; one of those imported female servants who are known in public by their amorphous style of person, their stoop forwards, and a headlong and as it were precipitous walk, — the waist plunging downwards into
40 the rocking pelvis at every heavy foot-fall. Bridget, constituted for action, not for emotion, was about to deposit a plate heaped with something upon the table, when I saw the coarse arm stretched by my shoulder arrested, — motionless as the arm of

---

16 Μῆνιν ἄειδε Θεά, the opening words of the *Iliad*, "Goddess, sing of the wrath [of Achilles]"   28
The spacious firmament . . . , opening lines of "Hymn" by Joseph Addison (1672-1719)

a terra-cotta caryatid; she couldn't set the plate down while the old gentleman was speaking!

He was quite silent after this, still wearing the slight flush on his cheek. Don't ever think the poetry is dead in an old man because his forehead is wrinkled, or that his manhood has left him when his hand trembles! If they ever *were* there, they *are* there still!

By and by we got talking again. — Does a poet love the verses written through him, do you think, Sir? — said the divinity-student.

So long as they are warm from his mind, — carry any of his animal heat about them, I *know* he loves them, — I answered. When they have had time to cool, he is 10 more indifferent.

A good deal as it is with buckwheat cakes, — said the young fellow whom they call John.

The last words, only, reached the ear of the economically organized female in black bombazine. — Buckwheat is skerce and high, — she remarked. [Must be a poor relation sponging on our landlady — pays nothing, — so she must stand by the guns and be ready to repel boarders.]

I liked the turn the conversation had taken, for I had some things I wanted to say, and so, after waiting a minute, I began again. — I don't think the poems I read you sometimes can be fairly appreciated, given to you as they are in the green state. 20

— You don't know what I mean by the *green state?* Well, then, I will tell you. Certain things are good for nothing until they have been kept a long while; and some are good for nothing until they have been long kept and *used.* Of the first, wine is the illustrious and immortal example. Of those which must be kept and used I will name three, — meerschaum pipes, violins, and poems. The meerschaum is but a poor affair until it has burned a thousand offerings to the cloud-compelling deities. It comes to us without complexion or flavor, — born of the sea-foam, like Aphrodite, but colorless as *pallida Mors* herself. The fire is lighted in its central shrine, and gradually the juices which the broad leaves of the Great Vegetable had sucked up from an acre and curdled into a drachm are diffused through its thirsting 30 pores. First a discoloration, then a stain, and at last a rich, glowing, umber tint spreading over the whole surface. Nature true to her old brown autumnal hue, you see, — as true in the fire of the meerschaum as in the sunshine of October! And then the cumulative wealth of its fragrant reminiscences! he who inhales its vapors takes a thousand whiffs in a single breath; and one cannot touch it without awakening the old joys that hang around it as the smell of flowers clings to the dresses of the daughters of the house of Farina!

[Don't think I use a meerschaum myself, for I *do not,* though I have owned a calumet since my childhood, which from a naked Pict (of the Mohawk species) my grandsire won, together with a tomahawk and beaded knife-sheath; paying for the 40 lot with a bullet-mark on his right cheek. On the maternal side I inherit the love-

---

28 **pallida Mors,** pale Death   37 **Farina.** George Meredith's *Farina, A Legend of Cologne* (1857) ends with the invention of *eau de cologne* by the hero, Farina   39 **calumet,** peacepipe   39 **Pict . . . species).** Holmes combines incongruously a North Britain and an American Indian primitive

liest silver-mounted tobacco-stopper you ever saw. It is a little box-wood Triton,
carved with charming liveliness and truth; I have often compared it to a figure in
Raphael's "Triumph of Galatea." It came to me in an ancient shagreen case, — how
old it is I do not know, — but it must have been made since Sir Walter Raleigh's
time. If you are curious, you shall see it any day. Neither will I pretend that I am
so unused to the more perishable smoking contrivance that a few whiffs would
make me feel as if I lay in a ground-swell on the Bay of Biscay. I am not
unacquainted with that fusiform, spiral-wound bundle of chopped stems and miscellaneous incombustibles, the *cigar,* so called, of the shops, — which to "draw"
10 asks the suction-power of a nursling infant Hercules, and to relish, the leathery palate of an old Silenus. I do not advise you, young man, even if my illustration strike
your fancy, to consecrate the flower of your life to painting the bowl of a pipe, for,
let me assure you, the stain of a reverie-breeding narcotic may strike deeper than
you thing for. I have seen the green leaf of early promise grow brown before its
time under such Nicotian regimen, and thought the umbered meerschaum was
dearly bought at the cost of a brain enfeebled and a will enslaved.]

Violins, too, — the sweet old Amati! — the divine Stradivarius! Played on by ancient *maestros* until the bow-hand lost its power and the flying fingers stiffened. Be-
queathed to the passionate young enthusiast, who made it whisper his hidden love,
20 and cry his inarticulate longings, and scream his untold agonies, and wail his
monotonous despair. Passed from his dying hand to the cold *virtuoso,* who let it
slumber in its case for a generation, till, when his hoard was broken up, it came
forth once more and rode the stormy symphonies of royal orchestras, beneath the
rushing bow of their lord and leader. Into lonely prisons with improvident artists;
into convents from which arose, day and night, the holy hymns with which its tones
were blended; and back again to orgies in which it learned to howl and laugh as if
a legion of devils were shut up in it; then again to the gentle *dilettante* who calmed
it down with easy melodies until it answered him softly as in the days of the old
maestros. And so given into our hands, its pores all full of music; stained, like the
30 meerschaum, through and through, with the concentrated hue and sweetness of all
the harmonies which have kindled and faded on its strings.

Now I tell you a poem must be kept *and used,* like a meerschaum, or a violin. A
poem is just as porous as the meerschaum; — the more porous it is, the better. I
mean to say that a genuine poem is capable of absorbing an indefinite amount of
the essence of our own humanity, — its tenderness, its heroism, its regrets, its aspirations, so as to be gradually stained through with a divine secondary color derived
from ourselves. So you see it must take time to bring the sentiment of a poem into
harmony with our nature, by staining ourselves through every thought and image
our being can penetrate.

---

3 **Triumph of Galatea,** a famous painting of the Naiad   7 **Bay of Biscay,** on the Cantabrian Sea, noted
for the fierce waves stirred upon it by strong winds   10 **Hercules,** legendary Greek hero famous for his
strength from birth; as a babe he strangled two serpents   11 **Silenus,** the foster-father of Bacchus, Roman
god of wine, and a proverbial drunkard   17 **Amati,** Nicoló Amati (1596-1684), a great violin maker, teacher
of Antonio Stradivarius   17 **Stradivarius** (1644-1737), the most famous of the family famous as violin
makers in Cremona

Then again as to the mere music of a new poem; why, who can expect anything more from that than from the music of a violin fresh from the maker's hands? Now you know very well that there are no less than fifty-eight different pieces in a violin. These pieces are strangers to each other, and it takes a century, more or less, to make them thoroughly acquainted. At last they learn to vibrate in harmony and the instrument becomes an organic whole, as if it were a great seed-capsule which had grown from a garden-bed in Cremona, or elsewhere. Besides, the wood ·is juicy and full of sap for fifty years or so, but at the end of fifty or a hundred more gets tolerably dry and comparatively resonant.

Don't you see that all this is just as true of a poem? Counting each word 10 as a piece, there are more pieces in an average copy of verses than in a violin. The poet has forced all these words together, and fastened them, and they don't understand it at first. But let the poem be repeated aloud and murmured over in the mind's muffled whisper often enough, and at length the parts become knit together in such absolute solidarity that you could not change a syllable without the whole world's crying out against you for meddling with the harmonious fabric. Observe, too, how the drying process takes place in the stuff of a poem just as in that of a violin. Here is a Tyrolese fiddle that is just coming to its hundredth birthday, — (Pedro Klauss, Tyroli, fecit, 1760), — the sap is pretty well out of it. And here is the song of an old poet whom Neæra cheated: —   20

> "Nox erat, et cœlo fulgebat Luna sereno
>   Inter minora sidera,
> Cum tu magnorum numen læsura deorum
>   In verba jurabas mea."

Don't you perceive the sonorousness of these old dead Latin phrases? Now I tell you that every word fresh from the dictionary brings with it a certain succulence; and though I cannot expect the sheets of the "Pactolian," in which, as I told you, I sometimes print my verses, to get so dry as the crisp papyrus that held those words of Horatius Flaccus, yet you may be sure, that, while the sheets are damp, and while the lines hold their sap, you can't fairly judge of my performances, and that, if made 30 of the true stuff, they will ring better after a while.

[There was silence for a brief space, after my somewhat elaborate exposition of these self-evident analogies. Presently *a person* turned towards me — I do not choose to designate the individual — and said that he rather expected my pieces had given pretty good "sahtisfahction" — I had, up to this moment, considered this complimentary phrase as sacred to the use of secretaries of lyceums, and, as it has been usually accompanied by a small pecuniary testimonial, have acquired a certain relish

---

19 **Pedro Klauss . . . fecit, 1760,** made by Pedro Klauss in 1760   21 **Nox erat . . . mea.** From Horace, *Epodes,* XV. The lines have been translated thus by G. E. Bennett: " 'Twas night, and in a cloudless sky the moon was shining amid the lesser lights, when thou, soon to outrage the majesty of the mighty gods, didst pledge thy loyalty. . . ."   27 **Pactolian,** from Pactolus, a small Lydian stream, celebrated in antiquity for golden sands, the source of the wealth of Croesus. Holmes refers to an imaginary magazine, giving it a name which helps develop his point

for this moderately tepid and unstimulating expression of enthusiasm. But as a reward for gratuitous services, I confess I thought it a little below that blood-heat standard which a man's breath ought to have, whether silent, or vocal and articulate. I waited for a favorable opportunity, however, before making the remarks which follow.]

— There are single expressions, as I have told you already, that fix a man's position for you before you have done shaking hands with him. Allow me to expand a little. There are several things, very slight in themselves, yet implying other things not so unimportant. Thus, your French servant has *dévalisé* your premises and got
10 caught. *Excusez,* says the *sergent-de-ville,* as he politely relieves him of his upper garments and displays his bust in the full day-light. Good shoulders enough, — a little marked, — traces of smallpox, perhaps, — but white. . . . *Crac!* from the *sergent-de-ville's* broad palm on the white shoulder! Now look! *Vogue la galère!* Out comes the big red V — mark of the hot iron; — he had blistered it out pretty nearly, — hadn't he? — the old rascal VOLEUR, branded in the galleys at Marseilles! [Don't! What if he has got something like this? — nobody supposes I *invented* such a story.]

My man John, who used to drive two of those six equine females which I told you I had owned, — for, look you, my friends, simple though I stand here, I am one that has been driven in his "kerridge," — not using that term, as liberal shep-
20 herds do, for any battered old shabby-genteel go-cart which has more than one wheel, but meaning thereby a four-wheeled vehicle *with a pole,* — my man John, I say, was a retired soldier. He retired unostentatiously, as many of Her Majesty's modest servants have done before and since. John told me, that when an officer thinks he recognizes one of these retiring heroes, and would know if he has really been in the service, that he may restore him, if possible, to a grateful country, he comes suddenly upon him, and says, sharply, "Strap!" If he has ever worn the shoulderstrap, he has learned the reprimand for its ill adjustment. The old word of command flashes through his muscles, and his hand goes up in an instant to the place where the strap used to be.
30 [I was all the time preparing for my grand *coup,* you understand; but I saw they were not quite ready for it, and so continued, — always in illustration of the general principle I had laid down.]

Yes, odd things come out in ways that nobody thinks of. There was a legend, that, when the Danish pirates made descents upon the English coast, they caught a few Tartars occasionally, in the shape of Saxons, who would not let them go, — on the contrary, insisted on their staying, and, to make sure of it, treated them as Apollo treated Marsyas, or as Bartholinus has treated a fellow-creature in his titlepage, and, having divested them of the one essential and perfectly fitting garment, indispensable in the mildest climates, nailed the same on the church-door as we do
40 the banns of marriage, *in terrorem.*

---

9 dévalisé, plundered   10 Excusez, beg pardon   10 sergent-de-ville, bailiff   13 Vogue la galère!
Come what will!   15 Voleur, thief   30 coup, stroke   37 Apollo . . . Marsyas. See note on p.
889   37 Bartholinus, Thomas Bartholinus (1619-1680), Danish physician, author of a number of works
on anatomy   40 in terrorem, in terror

[There was a laugh at this among some of the young folks; but as I looked at our landlady, I saw that "the water stood in her eyes," as it did in Christiana's when the interpreter asked her about the spider, and I fancied, but wasn't quite sure that the schoolmistress blushed, as Mercy did in the same conversation, as you remember.]

That sounds like a cock-and-bull-story, — said the young fellow whom they call John. I abstained from making Hamlet's remark to Horatio, and continued.

Not long since, the church-wardens were repairing and beautifying an old Saxon church in a certain English village, and among other things thought the doors should be attended to. One of them particularly, the front-door, looked very badly, crusted, as it were, and as if it would be all the better for scraping. There happened 10 to be a microscopist in the village who had heard the old pirate story, and he took it into his head to examine the crust on this door. There was no mistake about it; it was a genuine historical document, of the Ziska drum-head pattern, — a real *cutis humana,* stripped from some old Scandinavian filibuster, and the legend was true.

My friend, the Professor, settled an important historical and financial question once by the aid of an exceedingly minute fragment of a similar document. Behind the pane of plate-glass which bore his name and title burned a modest lamp, signifying to the passers-by that at all hours of the night the slightest favors (or fevers) were welcome. A youth who had freely partaken of the cup which cheers and like- 20 wise inebriates, following a moth-like impulse very natural under the circumstances, dashed his fist at the light and quenched the meek luminary, — breaking through the plate-glass, of course, to reach it. Now I don't want to go into *minutiæ* at table, you know, but a naked hand can no more go through a pane of thick glass without leaving some of its cuticle, to say the least, behind it, than a butterfly can go through a sausage-machine without looking the worse for it. The Professor gathered up the fragments of glass, and with them certain very minute but entirely satisfactory documents which would have identified and hanged any rogue in Christendom who had parted with them. — The historical question, *Who did it?* and the financial question, *Who paid for it?* were both settled before the new lamp was lighted the next evening.   30

You see, my friends, what immense conclusions, touching our lives, our fortunes, and our sacred honor, may be reached by means of very insignificant premises. This is eminently true of manners and forms of speech; a movement or a phrase often tells you all you want to know about a person. Thus, "How's your health?" (commonly pronounced *haälth*) instead of, How do you do? or, How are you? Or calling your little dark entry a "hall," and your old rickety one-horse wagon a "kerridge." Or telling a person who has been trying to please you that he has given you pretty good "sahtisfahction." Or saying that you "remember of " such a thing, or that you

---

2 **Christiana,** wife of Christian in *Pilgrim's Progress*   6 **Hamlet's remark.** Act I, Scene v, ll. 166-167:
There are more things in heaven and earth, Horatio,
Than are dreamt of in our philosophy.
13 **Ziska drum-head,** named after John Zizka (1360?-1424), Bohemian Hussite leader who was frequently
cruel in the punishment of his foes   13 **cutis humana,** human skin   18 **the slightest favors (or fevers),**
a pun of which Holmes himself had been guilty in the early days of his medical career   22 **minutiae,**
minor details   31 **touching . . . honor,** the conclusion of the *Declaration of Independence*

have been "stoppin'" at Deacon Somebody's,— and other such expressions. One of my friends had a little marble statuette of Cupid in the parlor of his country-house, — bow, arrows, wings, and all complete. A visitor, indigenous to the region, looking pensively at the figure, asked the lady of the house "if that was a statoo of her deceased infant?" What a delicious, though somewhat voluminous biography, social, educational, and aesthetic, in that brief question!

[Please observe with what Machiavellian astuteness I smuggled in the particular offence which it was my object to hold up to my fellow-boarders, without too personal an attack on the individual at whose door it lay.]

10   That was an exceedingly dull person who made the remark, *Ex pede Herculem.* He might as well have said, "from a peck of apples you may judge of the barrel." *Ex* PEDE, to be sure! Read, instead, *Ex ungue minimi digiti pedis, Herculem, ejusque patrem, matrem, avos et proavos, filios, nepotes et pronepotes!* Talk to me about your δὸς πού στῶ! Tell me about Cuvier's getting up a megatherium from a tooth, or Agassiz's drawing a portrait of an undiscovered fish from a single scale! As the "O" revealed Giotto, — as the one word "moi" betrayed the Stratford atte-Bowe-taught Anglais, — so all a man's antecedents and possibilities are summed up in a single utterance which gives at once the gauge of his education and his mental organization.

Possibilities, Sir? — said the divinity-student; can't a man who says *Haöw?* arrive
20 at distinction?

Sir, — I replied, — in a republic all things are possible. But the man *with a future* has almost of necessity sense enough to see that any odious trick of speech or manners must be got rid of. Doesn't Sydney Smith say that a public man in England never gets over a false quantity uttered in early life? *Our* public men are in little danger of this fatal misstep, as few of them are in the habit of introducing Latin into their speeches, — for good and sufficient reasons. But they are bound to speak decent English, — unless, indeed, they are rough old campaigners, like General Jackson or General Taylor; in which case, a few scars on Priscian's head are pardoned to old fellows who have quite as many on their own, and a constituency of thirty
30 empires is not at all particular, provided they do not swear in their Presidential Messages.

---

10 **Ex pede Herculem** — "By the foot alone of Hercules," you may know him   12 **Ex . . . pronepotes!** By the nail of the smallest toe [you may know] Hercules, his father, mother, grandfathers and great-grandfathers, sons, nephews and grand-nephews   13 δὸς πού στῶ! refers to the famous remark of Archimedes, "Give me a place where I can stand, and I will move the world"   14 **Cuvier.** See note, p. 821   14 **megatherium,** an extinct genus of giant slothlike animals   14 **Agassiz's,** Louis John Rudolph Agassiz (1807-1873), Swiss naturalist who taught at Harvard, had been a student of Cuvier   16 **Giotto** (1276?-1337?), Florentine painter and architect who reputedly could draw, free hand, a perfect circle   16 **Stratford . . . Anglais.** The reference is to the prioress in the *Canterbury Tales,* of whom Chaucer said:
    And Frenssh she spake ful faire and fetisly [neatly]
    After the scole [school] of Stratford atte Bowe. . . .
Stratford-atte-Bowe was a Benedictine nunnery at Stratford, London, E., which taught Anglo-French differing from Parisian French. Therefore, the way she pronounced *"moi"* would show her origin   23 **Sydney Smith** (1771-1845), English divine, writer, and wit   27 **General Jackson,** Andrew Jackson (1767-1845), seventh President (1829-1837) of the United States   28 **General Taylor,** Zachary Taylor (1784-1850), twelfth President (1849-1850)   28 **Priscian,** Latin grammarian of the sixth century

However, it is not for me to talk. I have made mistakes enough in conversation and print. I never find them out until they are stereotyped, and then I think they rarely escape me. I have no doubt I shall make half a dozen slips before this breakfast is over, and remember them all before another. How one does tremble with rage at his own intense momentary stupidity about things he knows perfectly well, and to think how he lays himself open to the impertinences of the *captatores verborum,* those useful but humble scavengers of the language, whose business it is to pick up what might offend or injure, and remove it, hugging and feeding on it as they go! I don't want to speak too slightingly of these verbal critics; — how can I, who am so fond of talking about errors and vulgarisms of speech? Only there is a 10 difference between those clerical blunders which almost every man commits, knowing better, and that habitual grossness or meanness of speech which is unendurable to educated persons, from anybody that wears silk or broadcloth.

[I write down the above remarks this morning, January 26th, making this record of the date that nobody may think it was written in wrath, on account of any particular grievance suffered from the invasion of any *individual scarabœus grammaticus.*]

— I wonder if anybody ever finds fault with anything I say at this table when it is repeated? I hope they do, I am sure. I should be very certain that I had said nothing of much significance, if they did not.

Did you never, in walking in the fields, come across a large flat stone, which had 20 lain, nobody knows how long, just where you found it, with the grass forming a little hedge, as it were, all round it, close to its edges, — and have you not, in obedience to a kind of feeling that told you it had been lying there long enough, insinuated your stick or your foot or your fingers under its edge and turned it over as a housewife turns a cake, when she says to herself, "It's done brown enough by this time"? What an odd revelation, and what an unforeseen and unpleasant surprise to a small community, the very existence of which you had not suspected, until the sudden dismay and scattering among its members produced by your turning the old stone over! Blades of grass flattened down, colorless, ironed; hideous crawling creatures, some of them coleopterous or horny-shelled, — turtle-bugs one wants to call 30 them, some of them softer, but cunningly spread out and compressed like Lepine watches; (Nature never loses a crack or a crevice, mind you, or a joint in a tavern bedstead, but she always has one of her flat-pattern live timekeepers to slide into it); black glossy crickets, with their long filaments sticking out like the whips of four-horse stage-coaches; motionless, slug-like creatures, young larvæ, perhaps more horrible in their pulpy stillness than even in the infernal wriggle of maturity. But no sooner is the stone turned and the wholesome light of day let upon this compressed and blinded community of creeping things, than all of them which enjoy the luxury of legs — and some of them have a good many — rush round wildly, butting each other and everything in their way, and end in a general stampede for 40

---

6 **captatores verborum,** word hunters   16 **scarabœus grammaticus,** grammar beetle, or book-worm   30 **coleopterous,** belonging to the beetle order of insects   31 **Lepine watches.** Jean Antoine Lepine (1720-1814), French watchmaker, in 1744 reduced the thickness of watches by half

underground retreats from the region poisoned by sunshine. *Next year* you will find the grass growing tall and green where the stone lay; the ground-bird builds her nest where the beetle had his hole; the dandelion and the buttercup are growing there, and the broad fans of insect-angels open and shut over their golden disks, as the rhythmic waves of blissful consciousness pulsate through their glorified being.

— The young fellow whom they call John saw fit to say, in his very familiar way, — at which I do not choose to take offence, but which I sometimes think it necessary to repress, that I was coming it rather strong on the butterflies.

No, I replied; there is meaning in each of those images, — the butterfly as well as the others. The stone is ancient error. The grass is human nature borne down and bleached of all its colour by it. The shapes which are found beneath are the crafty beings that thrive in darkness, and the weaker organisms kept helpless by it. He who turns the stone over is whosoever puts the staff of truth to the old lying incubus, no matter whether he do it with a serious face or a laughing one. The next year stands for the coming time. Then shall the nature which had lain blanched and broken rise in its full stature and native hues in the sunshine. Then shall God's minstrels build their nests in the hearts of a newborn humanity. Then shall beauty — Divinity taking outlines and color — light upon the souls of men as the butterfly, image of the beatified spirit rising from the dust, soars from the shell that held a poor grub, which would never have found wings, had not the stone been lifted.

You never need think you can turn over any old falsehood without a terrible squirming and scattering of the horrid little population that dwells under it.

— Every real thought on every subject knocks the wind out of somebody or other. As soon as his breath comes back, he very probably begins to expend it in hard words. These are the best evidence a man can have that he has said something it was time to say. Dr. Johnson was disappointed in the effect of one of his pamphlets. "I think I have not been attacked enough for it," he said; — "attack is the reaction; I never think I have hit hard unless it rebounds."

— If a fellow attacked my opinions in print, would I reply? Not I. Do you think I don't understand what my friend, the Professor, long ago called *the hydrostatic paradox of controversy?*

Don't know what that means? — Well, I will tell you. You know, that, if you had a bent tube, one arm of which was of the size of a pipe-stem, and the other big enough to hold the ocean, water would stand at the same height in one as in the other. Controversy equalizes fools and wise men in the same way — *and the fools know it.*

— No, but I often read what they say about other people. There are about a dozen phrases which all come tumbling along together, like the tongs, and the shovel, and the poker, and the brush, and the bellows, in one of those domestic avalanches that everybody knows. If you get one, you get the whole lot.

What are they? — Oh, that depends a good deal on latitude and longitude. Epithets follow the isothermal lines pretty accurately. Grouping them in two families, one finds himself a clever, genial, witty, wise, brilliant, sparkling, thoughtful, distinguished, celebrated, illustrious scholar and perfect gentleman, and first writer of the age; or a dull, foolish, wicked, pert, shallow, ignorant, insolent, traitorous, black-hearted outcast, and disgrace to civilization.

What do I think determines the set of phrases a man gets? — Well, I should say a set of influences something like these: — 1st. Relationships, political, religious, social, domestic. 2nd. Oysters, in the form of suppers given to gentlemen connected with criticism. I believe in the school, the college, and the clergy; but my sovereign logic, for regulating public opinion — which means commonly the opinion of half a dozen of the critical gentry — is the following. *Major proposition.* Oysters *au naturel.* *Minor proposition.* The same "scalloped." *Conclusion.* That — (here insert entertainer's name) is clever, witty, wise, brilliant, — and the rest.

— No, it isn't exactly bribery. One man has oysters, and another epithets. It is an exchange of hospitalities; one gives a "spread" on linen, and the other on paper, — that is all. Don't you think you and I should be apt to do just so, if we were in the critical line? I am sure I couldn't resist the softening influences of hospitality. I don't like to dine out, you know, — I dine so well at our own table, [our landlady looked radiant,] and the company is so pleasant [a rustling movement of satisfaction among the boarders]; but if I did partake of a man's salt, with such additions as that article of food requires to make it palatable, I could never abuse him, and if I had to speak of him, I suppose I should hang my set of jingling epithets round him like a string of sleigh-bells. Good feeling helps society to make liars of most of us, — not absolute liars, but such careless handlers of truth that its sharp corners get terribly rounded. I love truth as chiefest among the virtues; I trust it runs in my blood; but I would never be a critic, because I know I could not always tell it. I might write a criticism of a book that happened to please me; that is another matter.

— Listen, Benjamin Franklin! This is for you, and such others of tender age as you may tell it to.

When we are as yet small children, long before the time when those two grown ladies offer us the choice of Hercules, there comes up to us a youthful angel, holding in his right hand cubes like dice, and in his left spheres like marbles. The cubes are of stainless ivory, and on each is written in letters of gold — TRUTH. The spheres are veined and streaked and spotted beneath, with a dark crimson flush above, where the light falls on them, and in a certain aspect you can make out upon every one of them the three letters L, I, E. The child to whom they are offered very probably clutches at both. The spheres are the most convenient things in the world; they roll with the least possible impulse just where the child would have them. The cubes will not roll at all; they have a great talent for standing still, and always keep right side up. But very soon the young philosopher finds that things which roll so easily are very apt to roll into the wrong corner, and to get out of his way when he most wants them, while he always knows where to find the others, which stay where they are left. Thus he learns — thus we learn — to drop the streaked and speckled globes of falsehood and to hold fast the white angular blocks of truth. But then comes

---

8 **au naturel,** in a natural state   25 **Benjamin Franklin,** the landlady's youngest son   28 **choice of Hercules.** As a youth, according to legend, Hercules had to choose, at a meeting of the ways, between two women — Pleasure and Duty

Timidity, and after her Good-nature, and last of all Polite-behavior, all insisting that truth must *roll*, or nobody can do anything with it; and so the first with her coarse rasp, and the second with her broad file, and the third with her silken sleeve, do so round off and smooth and polish the snow-white cubes of truth, that, when they have got a little dingy by use, it becomes hard to tell them from the rolling spheres of falsehood.

The schoolmistress was polite enough to say that she was pleased with this, and that she would read it to her little flock the next day. But she should tell the children, she said, that there were better reasons for truth than could be found in mere experience of its convenience and the inconvenience of lying.

Yes,— I said, — but education always begins through the senses, and works up to the idea of absolute right and wrong. The first thing the child has to learn about this matter is, that lying is unprofitable, — afterwards, that it is against the peace and dignity of the universe.

1858

From *Mechanism in Thought and Morals*

"Mechanism in Thought and Morals," an address delivered June 29, 1870, before the Phi Beta Kappa Society of Harvard University, summarizes as well as any other single piece by Holmes his ideas, radical for the time, on moral responsibility. Conservative in his social attitudes, in his conception of what was worth-while in literature, Holmes was led by scientific study and speculation to attack fiercely the current attitudes toward sin and its punishment. The deterministic doctrines here advanced figure importantly in many of his writings — in some of his breakfast-table papers, in several essays, and in his "medicated" novels, the most notable of which is Elsie Venner. *It was perhaps in the advocacy of these views that Holmes had his most profound and widespread effect upon the thought of his time.*

Limitations of space have made it necessary to present this wandering essay in a somewhat abbreviated form. The opening two paragraphs and other passages, at the points indicated, have been omitted.

I ask your attention to some considerations on the true mechanical relations of the thinking principle, and to a few hints as to the false mechanical relations which have intruded themselves into the sphere of moral self-determination.

I call that part of mental and bodily life mechanical which is independent of our volition. The beating of our hearts and the secretions of our internal organs will go on, without and in spite of any voluntary effort of ours, as long as we live. Respiration is partially under our control: we can change the rate and special mode of breathing, and even hold our breath for a time; but the most determined suicide cannot strangle himself without the aid of a noose or other contrivance which shall effect what his mere will cannot do. The flow of thought is, like breathing, essentially mechanical and necessary, but incidentally capable of being modified to a greater or less extent by conscious effort. Our natural instincts and tastes have a

basis which can no more be reached by the will than the sense of light and darkness, or that of heat and cold. All these things we feel justified in referring to the
great First Cause: they belong to the "laws of Nature," as we call them, for which
we are not accountable.

Whatever may be our opinions as to the relations between "mind" and "matter,"
our observation only extends to thought and emotion as connected with the living
body, and, according to the general verdict of consciousness, more especially with
certain parts of the body; namely, the central organs of the nervous system. . . . The
brain is an instrument, necessary, so far as our direct observation extends, to thought.
The "materialist" believes it to be wound up by the ordinary cosmic forces, and to 1
give them out again as mental products: the "spiritualist" believes in a conscious
entity, not interchangeable with motive force, which plays upon this instrument.
But the instrument must be studied by the one as much as by the other: the piano
which the master touches must be as thoroughly understood as the musical box or
clock which goes of itself by a spring or weight. A slight congestion or softening
of the brain shows the least materialistic of philosophers that he must recognize
the strict dependence of mind upon its organ in the only condition of life with which
we are experimentally acquainted. And what all recognize as soon as disease forces it
upon their attention, all thinkers should recognize, without waiting for such an
irresistible demonstration. They should see that the study of the organ of thought, 2
microscopically, chemically, experimentally, on the lower animals, in individuals
and races, in health and in disease, in every aspect of external observation, as well
as by internal consciousness, is just as necessary as if mind were known to be nothing more than a function of the brain, in the same way as digestion is of the
stomach. . . .

The resemblance of the act of intelligence to that of vision is remarkably shown
in the terms we borrow from one to describe the other. We *see* a truth; we *throw
light* on a subject; we *elucidate* a proposition; we *darken* counsel; we are *blinded* by
prejudice; we take a *narrow view* of things; we look at our neighbor with a *jaundiced
eye.* These are familiar expressions; but we can go much farther. We have intellec- 3
tual myopes, nearsighted specialists, and philosophers who are purblind to all but
the distant abstract. We have judicial intellects as nearly achromatic as the organ of
vision, eyes that are color-blind, and minds that seem hardly to have the sense of
beauty. The old brain thinks the world grows worse, as the old retina thinks the
eyes of needles and the fractions in the printed sales of stocks grow smaller. Just
as the eye seeks to refresh itself by resting on neutral tints after looking at brilliant
colors, the mind turns from the glare of intellectual brilliancy to the solace of gentle dulness; the tranquillizing green of the sweet human qualities, which do not make
us shade our eyes like the spangles of conversational gymnasts and *figurantes.* . . .

The more we examine the mechanism of thought, the more we shall see that the 4
automatic, unconscious action of the mind enters largely into all its processes. Our
definite ideas are stepping-stones; how we get from one to the other, we do not
know: something carries us; we do not take the step. A creating and informing
spirit which is with us, and not of us, is recognized everywhere in real and in storied

life. It is the Zeus that kindled the rage of Achilles; it is the Muse of Homer; it is the Daimon of Socrates; it is the inspiration of the seer; it is the mocking devil that whispers to Margaret as she kneels at the altar; and the hobgoblin that cried, "Sell him, sell him!" in the ear of John Bunyan: it shaped the forms that filled the soul of Michael Angelo when he saw the figure of the great Lawgiver in the yet unhewn marble, and the dome of the world's yet unbuilt basilica against the blank horizon; it comes to the least of us, as a voice that will be heard; it tells us what we must believe; it frames our sentences; it lends a sudden gleam of sense or eloquence to the dullest of us all, so that, like Katterfelto with his hair on end, we
10 wonder at ourselves, or rather not at ourselves, but at this divine visitor, who chooses our brain as his dwelling-place, and invests our naked thought with the purple of the kings of speech or song.

After all, the mystery of unconscious mental action is exemplified, as I have said, in every act of mental association. What happens when one idea brings up another? Some internal movement, of which we are wholly unconscious, and which we only know by its effect. What is this action, which in Dame Quickly agglutinates contiguous circumstances by their surfaces; in men of wit and fancy, connects remote ideas by partial resemblances; in men of imagination, by the vital identity which underlies phenomenal diversity; in the man of science, groups the objects of thought
20 in sequences of maximum resemblance? Not one of them can answer. There is a Delphi and a Pythoness in every human breast.

The poet sits down to his desk with an odd conceit in his brain; and presently his eyes fill with tears, his thought slides into the minor key, and his heart is full of sad and plaintive melodies. Or he goes to his work, saying, "To-night I would have tears;" and, before he rises from his table he has written a burlesque, such as he might think fit to send to one of the comic papers, if these were not so commonly cemeteries of hilarity interspersed with cenotaphs of wit and humor. These strange hysterics of the intelligence, which make us pass from weeping to laughter, and from laughter back again to weeping, must be familiar to every impressible
30 nature; and all is as automatic, involuntary, as entirely self-evolved by a hidden organic process, as are the changing moods of the laughing and crying woman. The poet always recognizes a dictation *ab extra;* and we hardly think it a figure of speech when we talk of his inspiration.

The mental attitude of the poet while writing, if I may venture to define it, is that of the "nun breathless with adoration." Mental stillness is the first condition of

---

1 **Achilles**, Trojan hero in the battle of Troy, was inspired to wrath by Zeus   2 **Daimon**, an inspiring spirit   3 **Margaret**, the heroine of *Faust*   4 "**Sell him!**" Bunyan suffered for years a hallucination that a devil was after him to sell Christ   5 **great Lawgiver**, Moses, pictured in one of Michelangelo's most famous murals   9 **Katterfelto**, a London quack of the eighteenth century who advertised with the slogan "Wonders! Wonders!" Cowper described him with his hair on end in *The Task*, Bk. IV, 1. 86   16 **Dame Quickly**, scatterbrained hostess of a tavern in Eastcheap, a character in Shakespeare's *Henry IV* and *Merry Wives of Windsor*   21 **Delphi**, dwelling place of a Greek oracle   21 **Pythoness**, the Delphic oracle   27 **cenotaphs**, tombs or monuments of those buried elsewhere, i. e., the writer hesitates to contribute to the comic papers because they carry so much material picked up elsewhere   32 **ab extra**, from without   35 "**nun . . . adoration.**" From William Wordsworth's sonnet "It is a beauteous evening," 11. 2-3: "The holy time is quiet as a Nun/ Breathless with adoration. . . ."

the listening state; and I think my friends the poets will recognize that the sense of effort, which is often felt, accompanies the mental spasm by which the mind is maintained in a state at once passive to the influx from without, and active in seizing only that which will serve its purpose. It is not strange that remembered ideas should often take advantage of the crowd of thoughts, and smuggle themselves in as original. Honest thinkers are always stealing unconsciously from each other. Our minds are full of waifs and estrays which we think are our own. Innocent plagiarism turns up everywhere. Our best musical critic tells me that a few notes of the air of "Shoo Fly" are borrowed from a movement in one of the magnificent harmonies of Beethoven.   10

And so the orator, — I do not mean the poor slave of a manuscript, who takes his thought chilled and stiffened from its mould, but the impassioned speaker who pours it forth as it flows coruscating from the furnace, — the orator only becomes our master at the moment when he himself is surprised, captured, taken possession of, by a sudden rush of fresh inspiration. How well we know the flash of the eye, the thrill of the voice, which are the signature and symbol of nascent thought, — thought just emerging into consciousness, in which condition, as is the case with the chemist's elements, it has a combining force at other times wholly unknown!

But we are all more or less improvisators. We all have a double, who is wiser and better than we are, and who puts thoughts into our heads, and words into our   20 mouths. Do we not all commune with our own hearts upon our beds? Do we not all divide ourselves, and go to buffets on questions of right or wrong, of wisdom or folly? Who or what is it that resolves the stately parliament of the day, with all its forms and conventionalities and pretences, and the great Me presiding, into the committee of a whole, with Conscience in the chair, that holds its solemn session through the watches of the night? . . .

The mechanical co-efficient of mental action may be therefore considered a molecular movement in the nervous centres, attended with waste of material conveyed thither in the form of blood, — not a mere tremor like the quiver of a bell, but a process more like combustion; the blood carrying off the oxidated particles, and   30 bringing in fresh matter to take their place.

This part of the complex process must, of course, enter into the category of the correlated forces. The brain must be fed in order to work; and according to the amount of waste of material will be that of the food required to repair losses. So much logic, so much beef; so much poetry, so much pudding: and, as we all know that growing things are but sponges soaked full of old sunshine, Apollo becomes as important in the world of letters as ever.

But the intellectual product does not belong to the category of force at all, as defined by physicists. It does not answer their definition as "that which is expended in producing or resisting motion." It is not reconvertible into other forms of force.   40 One cannot lift a weight with a logical demonstration, or make a tea-kettle boil by

---

9 **Shoo Fly**, a popular song with a catchy air, the burden of its lyrics being that the fly is not to bother the singer   36 **Apollo**, the sun god as well as patron of music and poetry

writing an ode to it. A given amount of molecular action in two brains represents a certain equivalent of food, but by no means an equivalent of intellectual product. Bavius and Mævius were very probably as good feeders as Virgil and Horace, and wasted as much brain-tissue in producing their *carmina* as the two great masters wasted in producing theirs. It may be doubted whether the present Laureate of England consumed more oxidable material in the shape of nourishment for every page of "Maud" or of "In Memoriam" than his predecessor Nahum Tate, whose masterpiece gets no better eulogy than that it is "the least miserable of his productions," in eliminating an equal amount of verse.

10   As mental labor, in distinction from the passive flow of thought, implies an exercise of will, and as mental labor is shown to be attended by an increased waste, the presumption is that this waste is in some degree referable to the material requirements of the act of volition. We see why the latter should be attended by a sense of effort, and followed by a feeling of fatigue. . . .

The connection between thought and the structure and condition of the brain is evidently so close that all we have to do is to study it. It is not in this direction that materialism is to be feared: we do not find Hamlet and Faust, right or wrong, the valor of men and the purity of women, by testing for albumen, or examining fibres in microscopes.

20   It is in the moral world that materialism has worked the strangest confusion. In various forms, under imposing names and aspects, it has thrust itself into the moral relations, until one hardly knows where to look for any first principles without upsetting everything in searching for them.

The moral universe includes nothing but the exercise of choice: all else is machinery. What we can help and what we cannot help are on two sides of a line which separates the sphere of human responsibility from that of the Being who has arranged and controls the order of things.

The question of the freedom of the will has been an open one, from the days of Milton's demons in conclave to the recent most noteworthy essay of Mr. Hazard,
30   our Rhode Island neighbor. It still hangs suspended between the seemingly exhaustive strongest motive argument and certain residual convictions. The sense that we are, to a limited extent, self-determining; the sense of effort in willing; the sense of responsibility in view of the future, and the verdict of conscience in review of the past, — all of these are open to the accusation of fallacy; but they all leave a certain undischarged balance in most minds. We can invoke the strong arm of the *Deus ex machina,* as Mr. Hazard, and Kant and others, before him, have done. Our will may be a primary initiating cause or force, as unexplainable, as unreducible, as indecomposable, as impossible if you choose, but as real to our belief, as the *æternitas a parte ante.* The divine fore-knowledge is no more in the way of delegated choice than the

---

2 **Bavius and Mævius,** minor Latin poets   2 **Virgil and Horace,** major Latin poets   3 **carmina,** poems   4 **Laureate,** Tennyson   6 **Nahum Tate** (1652-1715), poet laureate (1692-1715), of whose verse Pope said: "It is not poetry, but prose run mad"   28 **Milton's . . . conclave,** *Paradise Lost,* Bk. II, ll. 1-505   28 **Mr. Hazard,** Rowland Gibson Hazard (1801-1888), a highly successful manufacturer who also wrote on philosophical subjects. William Ellery Channing suggested to him that he refute Edwards' *Freedom of Will*   34 **Deus ex machina,** a god out of a machine; the supernatural assistant of man in classical drama   37 **æternitas . . . ante,** before eternity

divine omnipotence is in the way of delegated power. The Infinite can surely slip the cable of the finite if it choose so to do.

It is one thing to prove a proposition like the doctrine of necessity in terms, and another thing to accept it as an article of faith. There are cases in which I would oppose to the *credo quia impossibile est* a paradox as bold and as serviceable, — *nego quia probatum est*. Even Mr. Huxley, who throws quite as much responsibility on protoplasm as it will bear, allows that "our volition counts for something as a condition of the course of events."

I reject, therefore, the mechanical doctrine which makes me the slave of outside influences, whether it work with the logic of Edwards, or the averages of Buckle; 10 whether it come in the shape of the Greek's destiny, or the Mahometan's fatalism; or in that other aspect, dear to the band of believers, whom Beesly of Everton, speaking in the character of John Wesley, characterized as

"The crocodile crew that believe in election."

But I claim the right to eliminate all mechanical ideas which have crowded into the sphere of intelligent choice between right and wrong. The pound of flesh I will grant to Nemesis; but, in the name of human nature, not one drop of blood, — not one drop.

Moral chaos began with the idea of transmissible responsibility. It seems the stalest of truisms to say that every moral act, depending as it does on choice, is in its nature 20 exclusively personal; that its penalty, if it have any, is payable, not to bearer, not to order, but only to the creditor himself. To treat a mal-volition, which is inseparably involved with an internal condition, as capable of external transfer from one person to another, is simply to materialize it. When we can take dimensions of virtue by triangulation; when we can literally weigh Justice in her own scales; when we can speak of specific gravity of truth, or the square root of honesty; when we can send a statesman his integrity in a package to Washington, if he happen to have left it behind, — then we may begin to speak of the moral character of inherited tendencies, which belong to the machinery for which the Sovereign Power alone is responsible. The misfortune of perverse instincts, which adhere to us as congenital inheritances, 30 should go to our side of the account, if the books of heaven are kept, as the great Church of Christendom maintains they are, by double entry. But the absurdity which has been held up to ridicule in the nursery has been enforced as the highest reason upon older children. Did our forefathers tolerate Æsop among them? "I cannot trouble the water where you are," says the lamb to the wolf: "don't you see that I am farther down the stream?" — "But a year ago you called me ill names." — "Oh sir! a year ago I was not born." — "Sirrah," replies the wolf, "if it was not you, it was your father, and that is all one;" and finishes with the usual practical application.

---

5 **credo** . . . **est.** I believe because it is impossible   5 **nego** . . . **est.** I disbelieve because it has been proved   6 **Huxley,** Thomas Henry Huxley (1825-1895), famous exponent of the Darwinian hypothesis   10 **Buckle,** Henry Thomas Buckle (1821-1862), English historian   13 **John Wesley** (1703-1791), English preacher and founder of Methodism   15 **The crocodile crew,** "Southey's *Life of Wesley,* Vol. II, note 28." — Holmes   17 **Nemesis,** the righteous anger of the gods   32 **the absurdity . . . nursery,** in the fable of Æsop cited at the end of the paragraph

If a created being has no rights which his Creator is bound to respect, there is an end to all moral relations between them. Good Father Abraham thought he had, and did not hesitate to give his opinion. "Far be it from Thee," he says, to do so and so. And Pascal, whose reverence amounted to theophobia, could treat of the duties of the Supreme to the dependent being. If we suffer for anything except our own wrong-doing, to call it punishment is like speaking of a yard of veracity or a square inch of magnanimity.

So to rate the gravity of a mal-volition by its consequences is the merest sensational materialism. A little child takes a prohibited friction-match: it kindles a con-
10 flagration with it, which burns down the house, and perishes itself in the flames. Mechanically, this child was an incendiary and a suicide; morally, neither. Shall we hesitate to speak as charitably of multitudes of weak and ignorant grown-up children, moving about on a planet whose air is a deadly poison, which kills all that breathe it four or five scores of years?

Closely allied to this is the pretence that the liabilities incurred by any act of mal-volition are to be measured on the scale of the Infinite, and not on that of the total moral capacity of the finite agent, — a mechanical application of the Oriental way of dealing with offences. The sheik or sultan chops a man's head off for a look he does not like: it is not the amount of wrong, but the importance of the personage
20 who has been outraged. We have none of those moral relations with power, as such, which the habitual Eastern modes of speech seem to imply.

The next movement in moral materialism is to establish a kind of scale of equivalents between perverse moral choice and physical suffering. Pain often cures *ignorance,* as we know, — as when a child learns not to handle fire by burning its fingers, — but it does not change the moral nature. Children may be whipped into obedience, but not into virtue; and it is not pretended that the penal colony of heaven has sent back a single reformed criminal. We hang men for our convenience or safety; sometimes shoot them for revenge. Thus we come to associate the infliction of injury with offences as their satisfactory settlement, — a kind of neutraliza-
30 tion of them, as of an acid with an alkali: so that we feel as if a jarring moral universe would be all right if only suffering enough were added to it. This scheme of chemical equivalents seems to me, I confess, a worse materialism than making protoplasm master of arts and doctor of divinity.

Another mechanical notion is that which treats moral evil as bodily disease has so long been treated, — as being a distinct entity, a demon to be expelled, a load to be got rid of, instead of a condition, or the result of a condition. But what is most singular in the case of moral disease is, that it has been forgotten that it is a living creature in which it occurs, and that all living creatures are the subjects of natural and spontaneous healing processes. A broken vase cannot mend itself; but a broken

---

3 **so and so.** Genesis 18:25. "That be far from thee to do after this manner, to slay the righteous with the wicked." Abraham was pleading for Sodom   4 **Pascal,** Blaise Pascal (1623-1662), French philosopher   4 **theophobia.** "I use this term to designate a state of mind thus described by Jeremy Taylor: 'There are some persons so miserable and scrupulous, such perpetual tormentors of themselves with unnecessary fears, that their meat and drink is a snare to their consciences. These persons do not believe noble things of God.'" — Holmes

bone can. Nature, that is, the Divinity, in his every-day working methods, will soon make it as strong as ever.

Suppose the beneficent self-healing process to have repaired the wound in the moral nature: is it never to become an honest scar, but always liable to be re-opened? Is there no outlawry of an obsolete self-determination? If the President of the Society for the Prevention of Cruelty to Animals impaled a fly on a pin when he was ten years old, is it to stand against him, crying for a stake through his body, *in sæcula sæculorum?* The most popular hymn of Protestantism, and the "Dies Iræ" of Romanism, are based on this assumption: *Nil inultum remanebit.* So it is that a condition of a conscious being has been materialized into a purely inorganic brute 10 fact, — not merely dehumanized, but deanimalized and devitalized.

Here it was that Swedenborg, whose whole secret I will not pretend to have fully opened, though I have tried with the key of a thinker whom I love and honor, — that Swedenborg, I say, seems to have come in, if not with a new revelation, at least infusing new life into the earlier ones. *What we are* will determine the company we are to keep, and not the avoirdupois weight of our moral exuviæ, strapped on our shoulders like a porter's burden.

Having once materialized the whole province of self-determination and its conse-quences, the next thing is, of course, to materialize the methods of avoiding these consequences. We are all, more or less, idolaters, and believers in quackery. We love 20 specifics better than regimen, and observances better than self-government. The mo-ment our belief divorces itself from character, the mechanical element begins to gain upon it, and tends to its logical conclusion in the Japanese prayermill.

Brothers of the Phi Beta Kappa Society, my slight task is finished. I have always regarded these occasions as giving an opportunity of furnishing hints for future study, rather than of exhibiting the detailed results of thought. I cannot but hope that I have thrown some ray of suggestion, or brought out some clink of question-able soundness, which will justify me for appearing with the lantern and the hammer.

The hardest and most painful task of the student of to-day is to occidentalize and modernize the Asiatic modes of thought which have come down to us closely wed- 30 ded to mediæval interpretations. We are called upon to assert the rights and dig-nity of our humanity, if it were only that our worship might be worthy the accept-ance of a wise and magnanimous Sovereign. Self-abasement is the proper sign of homage to superiors with the Oriental. The Occidental demands self-respect in his inferiors as a condition of accepting their tribute to him as of any value. The *kotou* in all its forms, the pitiful acts of *creeping, crawling, fawning, like a dog at his mas-ter's feet* (which acts are signified by the word we translate *worship,* according to the learned editor of "The Comprehensive Commentary"), are offensive, not gratifying to him. Does not the man of science who accepts with true manly reverence the facts of Nature, in the face of all his venerated traditions, offer a more acceptable 40

---

8 **in sæcula sæculorum,** for ages of ages   8 **Dies Iræ,** Day of Wrath   9 **Nil inultum remanebit.** Nothing will remain unavenged   12 **Swedenborg,** see note, p. 777   13 **a thinker,** Henry James, Sr., *The Secret of Swedenborg* (1869)   23 **Japanese prayermill,** a wheel each turn of which is supposed to sub-stitute for an uttered prayer   35 **kotou,** kowtow, the Chinese form of obeisance

service than he who repeats the formulæ, and copies the gestures, derived from the language and customs of despots, and their subjects? The attitude of modern Science is erect, her aspect serene, her determination inexorable, her onward movement unflinching; because she believes herself, in the order of Providence, the true successor of the men of old who brought down the light of heaven to men. She has reclaimed astronomy and cosmogony, and is already laying a firm hand on anthropology, over which another battle must be fought, with the usual result, to come sooner or later. Humility may be taken for granted as existing in every human being; but it may be that it most truly manifests itself to-day in the readiness with which we bow to new truths as they come from the scholars, the teachers, to whom the inspiration of the Almighty giveth understanding. If a man should try to show it in the way good men did of old, — by covering himself with tow-cloth, sitting on an ash-heap, and disfiguring his person, — we should send him straightway to Worcester or Somerville; and if he began to "rend his garments" it would suggest the need of a strait-jacket.

Our rocky New England and old rocky Judæa always seem to have a kind of yearning for each other: Jerusalem governs Massachusetts, and Massachusetts would like to colonize Jerusalem.

> "The pine-tree dreameth of the palm,
> The palm-tree of the pine."

But political freedom inevitably generates a new type of religious character, as the conclave that contemplates endowing a dotard with infallibility has found out, we trust, before this time. The American of to-day may challenge for himself the noble frankness in his highest relations which did honor to the courage of the Father of the Faithful. . . .

Our dwellings are built on the shell-heaps, the kitchen-middens of the age of stone. Inherited beliefs, as obscure in their origin as the parentage of the cave-dwellers, are stronger with many minds than the evidence of the senses and the simplest deductions of the intelligence. Persons outside of Bedlam can talk of the "dreadful depravity of lunatics," — the sufferers whom we have learned to treat with the tenderest care, as the most to be pitied of all God's children. Mr. Gosse can believe that a fossil skeleton, with the remains of food in its interiors, was never part of a living creature, but was made just as we find it, — a kind of stage-property, a clever cheat, got up by the great Manager of the original Globe Theatre. All we can say of such persons is, that their "illative sense," to use Dr. Newman's phrase, seems to most of us abnormal and unhealthy. We cannot help looking at them as affected with a kind of mental Daltonism.

---

12 **men . . . old.** Job is the classic example   13 **Worcester or Somerville,** sites of Massachusetts mental institutions   29 **Bedlam,** an English lunatic asylum   31 **Gosse,** Philip Henry Gosse, a nineteenth-century naturalist. Holmes cites as his source "Owen, in *Encyc. Brit.* 8th edition, art. 'Paleontology,' p. 124, note"   34 **Globe Theatre,** a punning reference to the Elizabethan theater in which Shakespeare's plays were produced and to the deity as a theatrical producer on the globe   35 **illative sense,** what John Henry Newman in *Grammar of Assent* described as the ratiocinative sense   37 **Daltonism,** congenital red-green blindness, discovered by John Dalton

"Believing ignorance," said an old Scotch divine, "is much better than rash and presumptuous knowledge." But which is most likely to be presumptuous, ignorance, or knowledge? True faith and true philosophy ought to be one; and those disputes, — *à double vérité*, — those statements, "true according to philosophy, and false according to faith," condemned by the last Council of Lateran, ought not to find a place in the records of an age like our own. Yet so enlightened a philosopher as Faraday could say in a letter to one of his correspondents, "I claim an absolute distinction between a religious and an ordinary belief. If I am reproached for weakness in refusing to apply those mental operations, which I think good in high things, to the very highest, I am content to bear the reproach."   10

We must bestir ourselves; for the new generation is upon us, — the marrow-bone-splitting descendants of the old cannibal troglodytes. Civilized as well as savage races live upon their parents and grandparents. Each generation strangles and devours its predecessor. The young Feejeean carries a cord in his girdle for his father's neck; the young American, a string of propositions or syllogisms in his brains to finish the same relative. The old man says, "Son, I have swallowed and digested the wisdom of the past." The young man says, "Sire, I proceed to swallow and digest thee with all thou knowest." There never was a sandglass, nor a clepsydra, nor a horologe, that counted the hours and days and years with such terrible significance as this academic chronograph which has just completed a revolution. The prologue 20 of life is finished here at twenty: then come five acts of a decade each, and the play is over, with now and then a pleasant or a tedious afterpiece, when half the lights are put out, and half the orchestra is gone. . . .

                                                                                    1870

---

4 **à double vérité**, twofaced truth   5 **Lateran**, the cathedral church of Rome. Holmes cites as a reference, "Leibnitz, *Consid. sur la Doctrine d'un Esprit Universel*"   7 **Faraday**, Michael Faraday (1791-1867), English chemist and physicist   12 **troglodytes**, primitive cave dwellers   18 **clepsydra**, a device which measures time by a flow of water   20 **academic chronograph**, the school year

1819—1891 James Russell Lowell

James Russell Lowell's background and training seemed fairly certain to make him exactly the conservative in politics and literature that his neighbor Holmes was. For several reasons, however, he diverged notably from the Brahmin pattern. Born ten years after Holmes, he belonged to a generation which was beginning to rebel against an established style of thinking and living. Moreover, his reading of foreign literature differed from that of Longfellow and Holmes and led him to form different notions about the most important tasks and methods of great writers. Finally, his acquaintanceships and friendships influenced him to depart from beaten paths in New England literature.

Lowell was born February 22, 1819, at Elmwood, a large pre-Revolutionary mansion in Cambridge, Massachusetts, on what was called "Tory Row." A member of one of the most honored Brahmin families, he had the usual sort of education at home (dame's school and Harvard) and abroad. When Longfellow retired, Lowell took the distinguished chair which Longfellow had held at Harvard and served there from 1856 until 1877. He was not only a teacher, a critic, and a poet but also an editor of the *Atlantic Monthly* (1857-1861) and of the *North American Review* (1864-1872), a minister to Spain (1877-1880), and a minister to England (1880-1885). After his return to America, Lowell continued to express himself in political essays, criticism, and poetry to the time of his death, at Elmwood, August 12, 1891. The wide range of activity represented in his life is paralleled by the wide range in the writings of this most versatile of the Cambridge authors.

In the years before his appointment at Harvard, Lowell, largely because of the influence of his first wife, Maria White, became a leading writer in behalf of abolition. His *Biglow Papers* (first series, 1848; second series, 1867) in Yankee dialect was his chief contribution to antislavery literature. These writings, in the crackerbox philosopher tradition of Jack Downing (see p. 1527) and others, effectively argued for Lowell's beliefs on the basis of common sense. Most notable of his other political writings are *On a Certain Condescension in Foreigners* (1869) and *Democracy* (1884), which have a mannered elegance very strikingly different from the Yankee diatribes.

In the field of belles-lettres, Lowell wrote both criticism and poetry. His earliest criticism was largely a report of enthusiasms for various literary works. It was frankly subjective and impressionistic, deriving whatever value it had from Lowell's sensitivity and his ability to state his reactions in striking phrases. In *A Fable for Critics* (1848) brilliantly rhymed and witty commentaries on his contemporaries marked the height of this kind of criticism. Beginning in the 1850's, however, his study of the classic critics, of Goethe, and of Coleridge led him to adopt less impressionistic methods when he dealt with authors. His later criticism, stressing the relationship between the period and the author, between the author and his work, and between the details and the whole composition, was best represented in such collections of critical essays as *Among My Books* (first series, 1870; second series, 1876) and *My Study Windows* (1871). The essays in these volumes deal with the great authors of various lands and periods from the Middle Ages to the nineteenth century — Dante, Chaucer, Shakespeare, Milton, Wordsworth, Swinburne, and others. They not only communicate Lowell's judgments in memorable terms but also employ rather systematic tests of literary excellence and many illuminating comparisons or contrasts.

Lowell's students declare that his literary essays and his classroom talk were quite similar. Professor Will D. Howe in his "Introduction" to *Selected Literary Essays from James Russell Lowell* (Boston, 1914) quotes Barrett Wendell's testimony: "Now and again, some word or some passage would suggest to him a line of thought —

sometimes very earnest, sometimes paradoxically comical — that it would never have suggested to any one else. And he would lean back in his chair and talk away across country till he felt like stopping; or he would thrust his hands into the pockets of his rather shabby sack-coat, and pace the end of the room in his heavy laced boots, and look at nothing in particular, and discourse of things in general." A learned man, he was at ease with his learning; a scholar, he did not let pedantry overwhelm either his sense of humor or his saltiness of phrase.

Much of the poetry which Lowell wrote might have been written by either Long-fellow or Holmes: it had similar material, a similar arrangement, and a similar form. In some of his other poems, though, he showed his kinship with the new genera-tion, which included such writers as Emily Dickinson and Walt Whitman, by de-parting more frequently than his famous fellow townsmen from the well-established verse patterns. His versification, for example, like that of both British and American poets of the day, often fell into lines of uneven length and of varied meters. As a poet Lowell was versatile enough to publish the rustic Biglow verses, the sparklingly witty *Fable for Critics,* and the moralizing metrical romance, *The Vision of Sir Launfal,* all in one year. Although his versatility somewhat diffused his energies, he did write some good poetry. Lowell was at his poetic best, perhaps, in some of his nature poems and in some of his odes.

The Writings of James Russell Lowell, 10 vols., Boston, 1890   F. H. Underwood, **The Poet and the Man,** Boston, 1893   H. E. Scudder, **James Russell Lowell,** Boston, 1906   **Letters of James Russell Lowell,** ed. C. E. Norton, 2 vols., New York, 1906   Leon Howard, **Victorian Knight-Errant: A Study of the Early Literary Career of James Russell Lowell,** Berkeley, 1952

To the Dandelion

America, in the early forties, developed a great passion for democracy — a passion shared by Lowell and his bride of 1844. In the early days of their marriage this couple had astonished some of their neighbors by insisting that old family servants sit at the table with them at mealtime. Lowell worked sentences praising democracy into his critical articles and into his editorials. Expressive of his current enthusiasm for democracy, this song uses the humble flower as a symbol of the glory of the common man. The choice of imagery, except perhaps in part of the fourth stanza, is highly appropriate to the development of the thought. In this poem, published in Graham's Magazine *in January 1845, Lowell showed that now and then he could write a lyric poem which had both richness and unity.*

    Dear common flower, that grow'st beside the way,
Fringing the dusty road with harmless gold,
      First pledge of blithesome May,
Which children pluck, and, full of pride, uphold,
      High-hearted buccaneers, o'erjoyed that they
An Eldorado in the grass have found,
      Which not the rich earth's ample round

May match in wealth, — thou art more dear to me
Than all the prouder summer-blooms may be.

Gold such as thine ne'er drew the Spanish prow   10
Through the primeval hush of Indian seas,
    Nor wrinkled the lean brow
Of age, to rob the lover's heart of ease,
  'Tis the spring's largess, which she scatters now
To rich and poor alike, with lavish hand,
    Though most hearts never understand
    To take it at God's value, but pass by
  The offered wealth with unrewarded eye.

Thou art my tropics and mine Italy;
To look at thee unlocks a warmer clime;   20
    The eyes thou givest me
Are in the heart, and heed not space or time:
  Not in mid June the golden cuirassed bee
Feels a more summer-like warm ravishment
    In the white lily's breezy tent,
    His fragrant Sybaris, than I, when first
  From the dark green thy yellow circles burst.

Then think I of deep shadows on the grass,
Of meadows where in sun the cattle graze,
    Where, as the breezes pass,   30
The gleaming rushes lean a thousand ways,
  Of leaves that slumber in a cloudy mass,
Or whiten in the wind, of waters blue
    That from the distance sparkle through
    Some woodland gap, and of a sky above,
  Where one white cloud like a stray lamb doth move.

My childhood's earliest thoughts are linked with thee;
The sight of thee calls back the robin's song,
    Who, from the dark old tree
Beside the door, sang clearly all day long,   40
    And I, secure in childish piety,
Listened as if I heard an angel sing
    With news from heaven, which he could bring
    Fresh every day to my untainted ears,
  When birds and flowers and I were happy peers.

---

26 **Sybaris**, an ancient Greek city famous for its luxury and for the voluptuousness which flourished in its mild climate

How like a prodigal doth nature seem,
When thou, for all thy gold, so common art!
   Thou teachest me to deem
More sacredly of every human heart,
   Since each reflects in joy its scanty gleam   50
Of heaven and, could some wondrous secret show
   Did we but pay the love we owe,
And with a child's undoubting wisdom look
On all these living pages of God's book.

                                                                        1845

from A Fable for Critics

Lowell wrote that "this jeu d'esprit was extemporized, I may say, so rapidly was it writ-
ten. . . . I sent daily installments to a friend in New York, the late Charles Briggs. He
urged me to let it be printed, and I at last consented to its anonymous publication."
   As Lowell said at the outset of the poem, its plot,

                  . . . like an icicle, 's slender and slippery,
                  Every moment more slender, and likely to slip awry. . . .

In the main, it presents a critic explaining to Apollo what American authors of the period
were like. The passages below (the titles were supplied by the editors) are the critic's remarks
about the leading figures dealt with in the poem, as well as those about two minor authors
famous at the time, Dana and Neal.
   A long line of ancestors might be cited for the poem, notably Byron's "English Bards and
Scotch Reviewers" and a poem which Lowell had enjoyed reading not long before 1847 —
Leigh Hunt's "Feast of the Poets." For discernment, liveliness, and wit, Lowell's poem com-
pares very favorably with these predecessors.

Emerson

"There comes Emerson first, whose rich words, every one,
Are like gold nails in temples to hang trophies on,
Whose prose is grand verse, while his verse, the Lord knows,
Is some of it pr— No, 't is not even prose;
I'm speaking of metres; some poems have welled
From those rare depths of soul that have ne'er been excelled;
They're not epics, but that doesn't matter a pin,
In creating, the only hard thing's to begin;
A grass-blade's no easier to make than an oak;
If you've once found the way, you've achieved the grand stroke; 10

---

2 **gold nails.** See Ecclesiastes 12:11: "The words of the wise are as . . . nails fastened by the masters of assemblies . . ."   5 **metres,** a reference to Emerson's rather bumpy versification

In the worst of his poems are mines of rich matter,
But thrown in a heap with a crash and a clatter;
Now it is not one thing nor another alone
Makes a poem, but rather the general tone,
The something pervading, uniting the whole,
The before unconceived, unconceivable soul,
So that just in removing this trifle or that, you
Take away, as it were, a chief limb of the statue;
Roots, wood, bark, and leaves singly perfect may be,
But, clapt hodge-podge together, they don't make a tree.   20

"But, to come back to Emerson (whom, by the way,
I believe we left waiting), — his is, we may say,
A Greek head on right Yankee shoulders, whose range
Has Olympus for one pole, for t'other the Exchange;
He seems, to my thinking (although I'm afraid
The comparison must, long ere this, have been made),
A Plotinus-Montaigne, where the Egyptian's gold mist
And the Gascon's shrewd wit cheek-by-jowl coexist;
All admire, and yet scarcely six converts he's got
To I don't (nor they either) exactly know what;   30
For though he builds glorious temples, 'tis odd
He leaves never a doorway to get in a god.
'T is refreshing to old-fashioned people like me
To meet such a primitive Pagan as he,
In whose mind all creation is duly respected
As parts of himself — just a little projected;
And who's willing to worship the stars and the sun,
A convert to — nothing but Emerson.
So perfect a balance there is in his head,
That he talks of things sometimes as if they were dead;   40
Life, nature, love, God, and affairs of that sort,
He looks at as merely ideas; in short,
As if they were fossils stuck round in a cabinet,
Of such vast extent that our earth's a mere dab in it;
Composed just as he is inclined to conjecture her,
Namely, one part pure earth, ninety-nine parts pure lecturer;
You are filled with delight at his clear demonstration,
Each figure, word, gesture, just fits the occasion,

---

24 **Olympus**, dwelling place of the Grecian gods. Here Lowell is referring to Emerson's Platonic idealism   24 **Exchange**, symbol of Emerson's practicality. When a typical Brahmin praised a Transcendentalist, he was likely to laud him for not being too impractical   27 **Plotinus-Montaigne** repeats the claim
that Emerson was a happy mixture of idealism and practicality. Plotinus (205?-270?) was the most famous
of the neo-Platonic philosophers. Michel Eyquem de Montaigne (1533-1592) was a French skeptic, essayist,
and moralist

With the quiet precision of science he'll sort 'em,
But you can't help suspecting the whole a *post mortem*.   50

  "There are persons, mole-blind to the soul's make and style,
Who insist on a likeness 'twixt him and Carlyle;
To compare him with Plato would be vastly fairer,
Carlyle's the more burly, but E. is the rarer;
He sees fewer objects, but clearlier, truelier,
If C.'s as original, E.'s more peculiar;
That he's more of a man you might say of the one,
Of the other he's more of an Emerson;
C.'s the Titan, as shaggy of mind as of limb, —
E. the clear-eyed Olympian, rapid and slim;   60
The one's two thirds Norseman, the other half Greek,
Where the one's most abounding, the other's to seek;
C.'s generals require to be seen in the mass, —
E.'s specialties gain if enlarged by the glass;
C. gives nature and God his own fits of the blues,
And rims common-sense things with mystical hues, —
E. sits in a mystery calm and intense,
And looks coolly around him with sharp common-sense;
C. shows you how every-day matters unite
With the dim transdiurnal recesses of night, —   70
While E., in a plain, preternatural way,
Makes mysteries matters of mere every day;
C. draws all his characters quite *a la* Fuseli, —
Not sketching their bundles of muscles and thews illy,
He paints with a brush so untamed and profuse,
They seem nothing but bundles of muscles and thews;
E. is rather like Flaxman, lines strait and severe,
And a colorless outline, but full, round, and clear; —
To the men he thinks worthy he frankly accords
The design of a white marble statue in words.   80
C. labors to get at the centre, and then
Take a reckoning from there of his actions and men;
E. calmly assumes the said centre as granted,
And, given himself, has whatever is wanted.

  "He has imitators in scores, who omit
No part of the man but his wisdom and wit, —

---

52 **Carlyle,** Thomas Carlyle (1795-1881), English essayist. After they met in 1832 he and Emerson shared many interests   59 **Titan,** earth-born giant, contrasted here with the heaven-born Olympian   63 **generals,** generalizations   73 **Fuseli,** Heinrich Fuseli (1742?-1825), a German-Swiss painter, was noted for his distortions of form and the extravagance of his colors   77 **Flaxman,** John Flaxman (1755-1826), an English sculptor who followed classic models

Who go carefully o'er the sky-blue of his brain,
And when he has skimmed it once, skim it again;
If at all they resemble him, you may be sure it is
Because their shoals mirror his mists and obscurities,   90
As a mud-puddle seems deep as heaven for a minute,
While a cloud that floats o'er is reflected within it.

Bryant

"There is Bryant, as quiet, as cool, and as dignified,
As a smooth, silent iceberg, that never is ignified,
Save when by reflection 'tis kindled o' nights
With a semblance of flame by the chill Northern Lights.
He may rank (Griswold says so) first bard of your nation
(There's no doubt that he stands in supreme ice-olation),
Your topmost Parnassus he may set his heel on,
But no warm applauses come, peal following peal on, —   100
He's too smooth and too polished to hang any zeal on:
Unqualified merits, I'll grant, if you choose, he has 'em,
But he lacks the one merit of kindling enthusiasm;
If he stir you at all, it is just, on my soul,
Like being stirred up with the very North Pole.

"He is very nice reading in summer, but *inter*
Nos, we don't want *extra* freezing in winter,
Take him up in the depth of July, my advice is,
When you feel an Egyptian devotion to ices.
But, deduct all you can, there's enough that's right good in him, 110
He has a true soul for field, river, and wood in him;
And his heart, in the midst of brick walls, or where'er it is,
Glows, softens, and thrills with the tenderest charities —
To you mortals that delve in this trade-ridden planet?
No, to old Berkshire's hills, with their limestone and granite.
If you're one who *in loco* (add *foco* here) *desipis,*
You will get of his outermost heart (as I guess) a piece;
But you'd get deeper down if you came as a precipice,
And would break the last seal of its inwardest fountain,
If you only could palm yourself off for a mountain.   120
Mr. Quivis, or somebody quite as discerning,
Some scholar who's hourly expecting his learning,

---

94 **ignified,** set on fire   97 **Griswold,** Rufus Griswold (1815-1857), a leading nineteenth-century anthologist   106 **inter Nos,** between ourselves   116 **in . . . desipis.** You can be foolish in a particular place. The "add *foco* here" adds a rather complicated pun, referring not only to "one's own fireside" but also to the then-famous Loco-foco political party   121 **Mr. Quivis,** Mr. Anybody

Calls B. the American Wordsworth; but Wordsworth
May be rated at more than your whole tuneful herd's worth.
No, don't be absurd, he's an excellent Bryant;
But, my friends, you'll endanger the life of your client,
By attempting to stretch him up into a giant:
If you choose to compare him, I think there are two per-
    sons fit for a parallel — Thompson and Cowper;
I don't mean exactly — there's something of each,   130
There's T.'s love of nature, C.'s penchant to preach;
Just mix up their minds so that C.'s spice of craziness
Shall balance and neutralize T.'s turn for laziness,
And it gives you a brain cool, quite frictionless, quiet,
Whose internal police nips the buds of all riot, —
A brain like a permanent straight-jacket put on
The heart that strives vainly to burst off a button, —
A brain which, without being slow or mechanic,
Does more than a larger less drilled, more volcanic;
He's a Cowper condensed, with no craziness bitten,   140
And the advantage that Wordsworth before him had written.

    "But, my dear little bardlings, don't prick up your ears
Nor suppose I would rank you and Bryant as peers;
If I call him an iceberg, I don't mean to say
There is nothing in that which is grand in its way;
He is almost the one of your poets that knows
How much grace, strength, and dignity lie in Repose;
If he sometimes fall short, he is too wise to mar
His thought's modest fulness by going too far;
'T would be well if your authors should all make a trial   150
Of what virtue there is in severe self-denial,
And measure their writings by Hesiod's staff,
Which teaches that all has less value than half.

Whittier

    "There is Whittier, whose swelling and vehement heart
Strains the strait-breasted drab of the Quaker apart,
And reveals the live Man, still supreme and erect,
Underneath the bemummying wrappers of sect;

---

129 **Thompson,** properly spelled Thomson, James (1700-1748), author of *The Seasons*   129 **Cowper,**
William Cowper (1731-1800), author of *The Task.* Lowell wrote this rhymed footnote:
    To demonstrate quickly and easily how per-
    versely absurd 'tis to sound his *Cowper*
    As people in general call him named *super* [above]
    I remark that he rhymes it himself with horse-trooper.
152 **Hesiod** (fl. 766 B.C.), a Greek poet, author of *Works and Days*

There was ne'er a man born who had more of the swing
Of the true lyric bard and all that kind of thing;
And his failures arise (though he seem not to know it)   160
From the very same cause that has made him a poet, —
A fervor of mind which knows no separation
'Twixt simple excitement and pure inspiration,
As my Pythoness erst sometimes erred from not knowing
If 'twere I or mere wind through her tripod was blowing;
Let his mind once get head in its favorite direction
And the torrent of verse bursts the dams of reflection,
While, borne with the rush of the metre along,
The poet may chance to go right or go wrong,
Content with the whirl and delirium of song;   170
Then his grammar's not always correct, nor his rhymes,
And he's prone to repeat his own lyrics sometimes,
Not his best, though, for those are struck off at whiteheats
When the heart in his breast like a trip-hammer beats,
And can ne'er be repeated again any more
Than they could have been carefully plotted before:
Like old what's-his-name there at the battle of Hastings
(Who, however, gave more than mere rhythmical bastings),
Our Quaker leads off metaphorical fights
For reform and whatever they call human rights,   180
Both singing and striking in front of the war,
And hitting his foes with the mallet of Thor;
Anne haec, one exclaims, on beholding his knocks,
Vestis filii tui, O leather-clad Fox?
Can that be thy son, in the battle's mid din,
Preaching brotherly love and then driving it in
To the brain of the tough old Goliath of sin,
With the smoothest of pebbles from Castaly's spring
Impressed on his hard moral sense with a sling?

"All honor and praise to the right-hearted bard   190
Who was true to The Voice when such service was hard,
Who himself was so free he dared sing for the slave
When to look but a protest in silence was brave;
All honor and praise to the women and men
Who spoke out for the dumb and the down-trodden then!
It needs not to name them, already for each

---

164 **Pythoness.** See note p. 921   177 **old what's-his-name,** Taillefer, a minstrel who rode into the battle
of Hastings (1066) singing of Roland   182 **Thor,** Norse god of war and thunder   183 **Anne haec ...
tui.** Is this indeed the robe of thy son?   184 **Fox,** George Fox (1624-1691), English founder of the Society of Friends, or Quakers   187 **Goliath . . . pebbles.** See I Samuel 17:39-40   188 **Castaly's spring,**
a spring on Mount Parnassus   191 **The Voice** of God

I see History preparing the statue and niche;
They were harsh, but shall *you* be so shocked at hard words
Who have beaten your pruning-hooks up into swords,
Whose rewards and hurrahs men are surer to gain   200
By the reaping of men and of women than grain?
Why should *you* stand aghast at their fierce wordy war, if
You scalp one another for Bank or for Tariff?
Your calling them cut-throats and knaves all day long
Doesn't prove that the use of hard language is wrong;
While the World's heart beats quicker to think of such men
As signed Tyranny's doom with a bloody steel-pen,
While on Fourth-of-Julys beardless orators fright one
With hints at Harmodius and Aristogeiton,
You need not look shy at your sisters and brothers   210
Who stab with sharp words for the freedom of others; —
No, a wreath, twine a wreath for the loyal and true
Who, for sake of the many, dared stand with the few,
Not of blood-spattered laurel for enemies braved,
But of broad, peaceful oak-leaves for citizens saved!

Dana

   "Here comes Dana, abstractedly loitering along,
Involved in a paulo-post-future of song,
Who'll be going to write what'll never be written
Till the Muse, ere he think of it, gives him the mitten, —
Who is so well aware of how things should be done,   220
That his own works displease him before they're begun, —
Who so well all that makes up good poetry knows,
That the best of his poems is written in prose;
All saddled and bridled stood Pegasus waiting,
He was booted and spurred, but he loitered debating;
In a very grave question his soul was immersed, —
Which foot in the stirrup he ought to put first;
And, while this point and that he judicially dwelt on,
He, somehow or other, had written Paul Felton,
Whose beauties or faults, whichsoever you see there,   230
You'll allow only genius could hit upon either.
That he once was the Idle Man none will deplore,

---

203 **Bank or for Tariff.** Two of the hottest political issues of the period were the United States Bank and
the protective tariff   209 **Harmodius and Aristogeiton,** sixth-century Greeks who slew Hipparchus, tyrant of Athens   216 **Dana.** The fame of Richard Henry Dana, Sr. (1787-1879) has been eclipsed by his
son, Richard Henry, Jr., author of *Two Years Before the Mast.* Poet and essayist, the elder Dana, somewhat
too academic to win widespread fame, was important for his work on the influential *North American Review*   229 **Paul Felton,** a tale by Dana   232 **Idle Man,** a periodical edited by Dana in 1824. Lowell
mentions the pseudonym in relation to Dana's literary retirement (1840)

But I fear he will never be anything more;
The ocean of song heaves and glitters before him,
The depth and the vastness and longing sweep o'er him,
He knows every breaker and shoal on the chart,
He has the Coast Pilot and so on by heart,
Yet he spends his whole life, like the man in the fable,
In learning to swim on his library-table.

Neal

"There swaggers John Neal, who has wasted in Maine   240
The sinews and cords of his pugilist brain,
Who might have been poet, but that, in its stead, he
Preferred to believe that he was so already;
Too hasty to wait till Art's ripe fruit should drop,
He must pelt down an unripe and colicky crop;
Who took to the law, and had this sterling plea for it,
It required him to quarrel, and paid him a fee for it;
A man who's made less than he might have, because
He always has thought himself more than he was, —
Who, with very good natural gifts as a bard,   250
Broke the strings of his lyre out by striking too hard,
And cracked half the notes of a truly fine voice,
Because song drew less instant attention than noise.
Ah, men do not know how much strength is in poise,
That he goes the farthest who goes far enough,
And that all beyond that is just bother and stuff.
No vain man matures, he makes too much new wood;
His blooms are too thick for the fruit to be good;
'Tis the modest man ripens, 'tis he that achieves,
Just what's needed of sunshine and shade he receives;   260
Grapes, to mellow, require the cool dark of their leaves;
Neal wants balance; he throws his mind always too far,
Whisking out flocks of comets, but never a star;
He has so much muscle, and loves so to show it,
That he strips himself naked to prove he's a poet,
And, to show he could leap Art's wide ditch, if he tried,
Jumps clean o'er it, and into the hedge t' other side.
He has strength, but there's nothing about him in keeping;
One gets surelier onward by walking than leaping;
He has used his own sinews himself to distress,   270
And had done vastly more had he done vastly less;

---

240 **Neal,** John Neal (1793-1876), a hasty and highly productive author famous in his time as an outspoken critic of other American writers

In letters, too soon is as bad as too late;
Could he only have waited he might have been great;
But he plumped into Helicon up to the waist,
And muddied the stream ere he took his first taste.

Hawthorne

"There is Hawthorne, with genius so shrinking and rare
That you hardly at first see the strength that is there;
A frame so robust, with a nature so sweet,
So earnest, so graceful, so lithe and so fleet,
Is worth a descent from Olympus to meet;   280
'Tis as if a rough oak that for ages had stood,
With his gnarled bony branches like ribs of the wood,
Should bloom, after cycles of struggle and scathe,
With a single anemone trembly and rathe;
His strength is so tender, his wildness so meek,
That a suitable parallel sets one to seek, —
He's a John Bunyan Fouqué, a Puritan Tieck;
When Nature was shaping him, clay was not granted
For making so full-sized a man as she wanted,
So, to fill out her model, a little she spared   290
From some finer-grained stuff for a woman prepared,
And she could not have hit a more excellent plan
For making him fully and perfectly man.
The success of her scheme gave her so much delight,
That she tried it again, shortly after, in Dwight;
Only, while she was kneading and shaping the clay,
She sang to her work in her sweet childish way,
And found, when she'd put the last touch to his soul,
That the music had somehow got mixed with the whole.

Cooper

"Here's Cooper, who's written six volumes, to show   300
He's as good as a lord: well, let's grant that he's so;
If a person prefer that description of praise,
Why, a coronet's certainly cheaper than bays;
But he need take no pains to convince us he's not
(As his enemies say) the American Scott.

---

287 **John Bunyan Fouqué,** a combination of John Bunyan (1628-1688), author of the allegorical *Pilgrim's Progress,* and Baron de la Motte Fouqué (1777-1843), who wrote imaginative romances   287 **Tieck,** Ludwig Tieck. See note, p. 777   295 **Dwight,** John Sullivan Dwight (1813-1893), a Boston composer and music critic   305 **Scott,** Sir Walter Scott (1771-1832), popular Scottish novelist and poet

Choose any twelve men, and let C. read aloud
That one of his novels of which he's most proud,
And I'd lay any bet that, without ever quitting
Their box, they'd be all, to a man, for acquitting.
He has drawn you one character, though, that is new,   310
One wildflower he's plucked that is wet with the dew
Of this fresh Western world, and, the thing not to mince,
He has done naught but copy it ill ever since;
His Indians, with proper respect be it said,
Are just Natty Bumppo, daubed over with red,
And his very Long Toms are the same useful Nat,
Rigged up in duck pants and a sou'wester hat
(Though once in a Coffin, a good chance was found
To have slipped the old fellow away underground).
All his other men-figures are clothes upon sticks,   320
The *dernière chemise* of a man in a fix
(As a captain besieged, when his garrison's small
Sets up caps upon poles to be seen o'er the wall);
And the women he draws from one model don't vary,
All sappy as maples and flat as a prairie.
When a character's wanted, he goes to the task
As a cooper would do in composing a cask;
He picks out the staves, of their qualities heedful,
Just hoops them together as tight as is needful,
And, if the best fortune should crown the attempt, he   330
Has made at the most something wooden and empty,

    "Don't suppose I would underrate Cooper's abilities;
If I thought you'd do that, I should feel very ill at ease;
The men who have given to *one* character life
And objective existence are not very rife;
You may number them all, both prose-writers and singers,
Without overrunning the bounds of your fingers,
And Natty won't go to oblivion quicker
Than Adams the parson or Primrose the vicar.

    "There is one thing in Cooper I like, too, and that is   340
That on manners he lectures his countrymen gratis;
Not precisely so either, because, for a rarity,
He is paid for his tickets in unpopularity.

---

315 **Natty Bumppo,** Cooper's hero whose leggings gave the series title Leather-Stocking Tales to five
novels   316 **Long Toms.** Long Tom Coffin was the American sailor in *The Pilot* (1823)   321 **dernière
chemise,** last shirt   339 **Adams,** Parson Adams, a character in Fielding's *Joseph Andrews* (1742)   339
Primrose, the amiable, garrulous Dr. Primrose in Goldsmith's *The Vicar of Wakefield*

Now he may overcharge his American pictures,
But you'll grant there's a good deal of truth in his strictures;
And I honor the man who is willing to sink
Half his present repute for the freedom to think,
And, when he has thought, be his cause strong or weak,
Will risk t' other half for the freedom to speak,
Caring naught for what vengeance the mob has in store,   350
Let that mob be the upper ten thousand or lower.

Poe

"There comes Poe, with his raven, like Barnaby Rudge,
Three fifths of him genius and two fifths sheer fudge,
Who talks like a book of iambs and pentameters,
In a way to make people of common sense damn metres,
Who has written some things quite the best of their kind,
But the heart somehow seems all squeezed out by the mind,
Who — But hey-day! What's this? Messieurs Mathews and Poe,
You mustn't fling mud-balls at Longfellow so,
Does it make a man worse that his character's such   360
As to make his friends love him (as you think) too much?
Why, there is not a bard at this moment alive
More willing than he that his fellows should thrive;
While you are abusing him thus, even now
He would help either one of you out of a slough;
You may say that he's smooth and all that till you're hoarse,
But remember that elegance also is force;
After polishing granite as much as you will,
The heart keeps its tough old persistency still;
Deduct all you can, *that* still keeps you at bay;   370
Why, he'll live till men weary of Collins and Gray.
I'm not over-fond of Greek metres in English,
To me rhyme's a gain, so it be not too jinglish,
And your modern hexameter verses are no more
Like Greek ones than sleek Mr. Pope is like Homer;
As the roar of the sea to the coo of a pigeon is,
So, compared to your moderns, sounds old Melesigenes;
I may be too partial, the reason, perhaps, o't is

---

352 **Barnaby Rudge** (1841), a novel by Dickens in which a raven was important. See note, p. 760   358
Mathews, Cornelius Mathews (1817-1889), a New York author who, like Poe, created quite a stir by attack-
ing Longfellow   371 **Collins,** William Collins (1721-1759), English lyrical poet   371 **Gray,** Thomas
Gray (1716-1771), English poet, author of the famous elegy   375 **Pope,** Alexander Pope (1688-1744),
English poet whose translation of Homer was the standard one of his day   377 **Melesigenes,** Homer

That I've heard the old blind man recite his own rhapsodies,
And my ear with that music impregnate may be,   380
Like the poor exiled shell with the soul of the sea,
Or as one can't bear Strauss when his nature is cloven
To its deeps within deeps by the stroke of Beethoven;
But, set that aside, and 'tis truth that I speak,
Had Theocritus written in English, not Greek,
I believe that his exquisite sense would scarce change a line
In that rare, tender, virgin-like pastoral Evangeline.
That's not ancient nor modern, its place is apart
Where time has no sway, in the realm of pure Art,
'Tis a shrine of retreat from Earth's hubbub and strife   390
As quiet and chaste as the author's own life.

Irving

   "What! Irving? thrice welcome, warm heart and fine brain,
You bring back the happiest spirit from Spain,
And the gravest sweet humor, that ever was there
Since Cervantes met death in his gentle despair;
Nay, don't be embarrassed, nor look so beseeching,
I sha'n't run directly against my own preaching,
And having just laughed at their Raphaels and Dantes,
Go to setting you up beside matchless Cervantes;
But allow me to speak what I honestly feel, —   400
To a true poet-heart add the fun of Dick Steele,
Throw in all of Addison *minus* the chill,
With the whole of that partnership's honest good-will,
Mix well, and while stirring, hum o'er, as a spell,
The fine *old* English Gentleman, simmer it well,
Sweeten just to your own private liking, then strain,
That only the finest and clearest remain,
Let it stand out of doors till a soul it receives
From the warm lazy sun loitering down through green leaves,
And you'll find a choice nature, not wholly deserving   410
A name either English or Yankee, — just Irving.

---

382 **Strauss,** Johann Strauss (1804-1849), Viennese "Waltz King"   383 **Beethoven,** Ludwig von Beethoven
(1770-1827), German composer   385 **Theocritus,** a third-century B.C. Greek pastoral poet   393 **from
Spain** refers to Irving's return from that country in 1846   395 **Cervantes,** author of *Don Quixote.* See
note, p. 71. Cervantes, at the time of his death, was a monk   398 **Raphael** (1483-1520), Italian
painter   398 **Dante** (1265-1321), Italian poet   401 **Dick Steele . . . Addison.** Richard Steele (1672-
1729) and Joseph Addison (1672-1719) established *The Spectator,* a series of periodical essays   405 **English
Gentleman,** an essay by Irving

Holmes

"There's Holmes, who is matchless among you for wit;
A Leyden-jar always full-charged, from which flit
The electrical tingles of hit after hit;
In long poems 'tis painful sometimes, and invites
A thought of the way the new Telegraph writes,
Which pricks down its little sharp sentences spitefully
As if you got more than you'd title to rightfully,
And you find yourself hoping its wild father Lightning
Would flame in for a second and give you a fright'ning.   420
He has perfect sway of what *I* call a sham metre,
But many admire it, the English pentameter,
And Campbell, I think, wrote most commonly worse,
With less nerve, swing, and fire in the same kind of verse,
Nor e'er achieved aught in't so worthy of praise
As the tribute of Holmes to the grand *Marseillaise.*
You went crazy last year over Bulwer's New Timon; —
Why, if B., to the day of his dying, should rhyme on,
Heaping verses on verses and tomes upon tomes,
He could ne'er reach the best point and vigor of Holmes.   430
His are just the fine hands, too, to weave you a lyric
Full of fancy, fun, feeling, or spiced with satiric
In a measure so kindly, you doubt if the toes
That are trodden upon are your own or your foes'.

Lowell

"There is Lowell, who's striving Parnassus to climb
With a whole bale of *isms* tied together with rhyme,
He might get on alone, spite of brambles and boulders,
But he can't with that bundle he has on his shoulders,
The top of the hill he will ne'er come nigh reaching
Till he learns the distinction 'twixt singing and preaching;   440
His lyre has some chords that would ring pretty well,
But he'd rather by half make a drum of the shell,
And rattle away till he's old as Methusalem,
At the head of a march to the last new Jerusalem."

                                                 1847 – 1848, 1848

413 **Leyden-jar,** a glass jar which condenses electricity   416 **new Telegraph,** the Morse code   423
Campbell, Thomas Campbell (1777-1844), a British poet. Holmes' early poems are frequently reminiscent
of his poems   426 **tribute,** in Section II of Holmes' *Poetry: A Metrical Essay* (1836)   427 **Bulwer's
New Timon,** a satirical poem which had appeared in 1846   443 **Methusalem,** or Methuselah, according
to Genesis, died at "nine hundred sixty and nine years"

from The Biglow Papers, First Series

Written as a protest against the Mexican War and various political events connected with it, this series of poems had a success in the years of their appearance (1847-1848) which surprised and delighted their author. Lowell's earlier poems had been relatively unpopular. These he saw pinned up in workshops; he heard them quoted everywhere and their author-ship debated. They were effective propaganda.

They were effective partly because, like the writings of numerous humorists of New Eng-land at the time (notably Seba Smith, creator of Jack Downing), they appealed to the Yankee liking for Down East horse-sense philosophers who could voice their ideas — ideas of any sort arrived at by down-to-earth thinking — in amusing phrases. Chief among the characters exhibited by the papers was Hosea Biglow, intended by Lowell to represent New England's "homely common-sense vivified and heated by conscience." Biglow's rural way of feeling, thinking, and expressing himself was surefire appeal to an audience of Americans who had supreme respect for the intelligence of common men.

Other characters developed in the papers — a pedantic parson, for instance — were in-vented to serve in various ways as foils for the chief character and to attack Lowell's foes in ways impossible for the puritanical and unlearned Hosea. Birdofredum Sawin, to cite one more instance, was another Yankee farmer whom Lowell invented as "a mouthpiece of the mere drollery . . . meant to embody . . . that half-conscious unmorality which I have noticed as the recoil in gross natures from . . . puritanism." Sawin, unlike Biglow, was persuaded to join the army, and both during the War and after it his horrible experiences dragged him deeper and deeper into degradation. And the Rev. Homer Wilbur, Hosea's pastor, who edited his parishioner's poems, wrote in a learned, pedantic style which was amusingly in-congruous with the earthy patois of the poems.

Because of their style and their fictional excellence the verses have had an appeal more lasting than much political satire. An accomplished linguist, Lowell appreciated and repro-duced accurately the native idiom, which he praised as "racy with life and vigor and orig-inality, bucksome . . . to our new occasions." A keen observer of life in Yankeedom, he created characters, according to critic J. R. Dennet, writing in the Nation *(November 15, 1866, III, 397), "so life-like and, in the main, so true to nature — so good as individuals and as types that we know not where in literature to look for . . . others that excel them."*

No. 1, A Letter

From Mr. Ezekiel Biglow of Jaalam to the Hon. Joseph T. Buckingham, Editor of the Boston Courier, Enclosing A Poem of His Son, Mr. Hosea Biglow

Jaylem, june 1846

Mister Eddyter: — Our Hosea wuz down to Boston last week, and he see a cruetin Sarjunt a struttin round as popler as a hen with 1 chicking, with 2 fellers a drum-min and fifin arter him like all nater. the sarjunt he thout Hosea hedn't gut his i teeth cut cos he looked a kindo 's though he'd jest com down, so he cal'lated to hook him in, but Hosy woodn't take none o' his sarse for all he hed much as 20

---

1 **cruetin Sarjunt**, recruiting sergeant. Lowell was angered into writing this paper when, like Hosea, he saw a sergeant of the sort described trying to enlist men in Boston   3 **nater**, nature

Rooster's tales stuck onto his hat and eenamost enuf brass a bobbin up and down on his shoulders and figureed onto his coat and trousis, let alone wut nater hed sot in his featers, to make a 6 pounder out on.

wal, Hosea he com home considerabal riled, and arter I'd gone to bed I heern Him a thrashin round like a short-tailed Bull in flitime. The old Woman ses she to me ses she, Zekle, ses she, our Hosee's gut the chollery or suthin anuther ses she, don't you Bee skeered, ses I, he's oney amaking pottery [*Aut insanit, aut versos facit.* — H.W.] ses i, he's ollers on hand at that ere busynes like Da & martin, and shure enuf, cum mornin, Hosy he cum down stares full chizzle, hare on eend and cote tales flyin, and sot rite of to go reed his varses to Parson Wilbur bein he haint aney 10 grate shows o' book larnin himself, bimeby he cum back and sed the parson wuz dreffle tickled with 'em as i hoop you will Be, and said they wuz True grit.

Hosea ses taint hardly fair to call 'em hisn now, cos the parson kind o' slicked off sum O' the last varses, but he told Hosee he didn't want to put his ore in to tetch to the Rest on 'em, bein they wuz verry well As thay wuz, and then Hosy ses he sed suthin a nuther about Simplex Mundishes or sum such feller, but I guess Hosea kind o' didn't hear him, for I never hearn o' nobody o' that name in this village, and I've lived here man and boy 76 year cum next tater diggin, and thair aint no wheres a kitting spryer'n I be.

If you print 'em I wish you'd jest let folks know who hosy's father is, cuz my 20 ant Keziah used to say it's nater to be curus ses she, she aint livin though and he's a likely kind o' lad.
                                                                    EZEKIEL BIGLOW

Thrash away, you'll *hev* to rattle
  On them kittle-drums o' yourn, —
'Taint a knowin' kind o' cattle
  Thet is ketched with moldy corn;
Put in stiff, you fifer feller,
  Let folks see how spry you be, —
Guess you'll toot till you are yeller
  'Fore you git ahold o' me!

Thet air flag's a leetle rotten,
  Hope it aint your Sunday's best; — 10
Fact! it takes a sight o' cotton

---

1 **brass.** Ezekiel is pointing out that, both literally and figuratively, the sergeant had "a lot of brass"   7
pottery, poetry. Here, as elsewhere, the bad spelling makes possible a pun   7 **Aut . . . facit.** This note inserted by H. W., Parson Homer Wilbur, the pedantic editor of the text for book publication, is a slight misquotation from Horace's *Satires,* in which the poet's slave says of his master: "He is either mad or is making verses."   8 **Da & martin,** Day & Martin, who published rhymed advertisements of their shoe-blacking   9 **full chizzle,** full chisel, i.e., at headlong speed   12 **True grit,** an expression of highest praise extended figuratively from the meaning: grain of a certain quality   16 **Simplex Mundishes,** Hosea's Anglicized pronunciation of *simplex munditiis* — neat but not gaudy, unsophisticated
11 **takes . . . cotton.** The abolitionists charged that the real purpose of the Mexican War was to increase cotton-growing territory

To stuff out a soger's chest:
Sence we farmers hev to pay fer't,
  Ef you must wear humps like these,
Sposin' you should try salt hay fer't,
  It would du ez slick ez grease.

'Twouldn't suit them Southun fellers,
  They're a dreffle graspin' set,
We must ollers blow the bellers
  Wen they want their irons het;   20
May be it's all right ez preachin',
  But *my* narves it kind o' grates,
Wen I see the overreachin'
  O' them nigger-drivin' States.

Them thet rule us, them slave-traders,
  Haint they cut a thunderin' swarth,
(Helped by Yankee renegaders,)
  Thru the vartu o' the North!
We begin to think it's nater
  To take sarse an' not be riled; —   30
Who'd expect to see a tater
  All on eend at bein' biled?

Ez fer war, I call it murder, —
  There you hev it plain an' flat;
I don't want to go no furder
  Than my Testyment fer that;
God hez sed so plump an' fairly,
  It's ez long ez it is broad,
An' you've gut to git up airly
  If you want to take in God.   40

'Taint your eppyletts an' feathers
  Make the thing a grain more right;
'Taint afollerin' your bell-wethers
  Will excuse ye in His sight;
Ef you take a sword an' dror it,
  An' go stick a feller thru,
Guv'ment aint to answer for it,
  God'll send the bill to you.

Wut's the use o' meetin'-goin'
  Every Sabbath, wet or dry,   50

Ef it's right to go amowin'
　　Feller-men like oats an' rye?
I dunno but wut it's pooty
　　Trainin' round in bobtail coats, —
But it's curus Christian dooty
　　This 'ere cuttin' folks's throats.

They may talk o' Freedom's airy
　　Tell they'er pupple in the face, —
It's a grand gret cemetary
　　Fer the barthrights of our race;　　　60
They jest want this Californy
　　So's to lug new slave-states in
To abuse ye, an' to scorn ye,
　　An' to plunder ye like sin.

Aint it cute to see a Yankee
　　Take sech everlastin' pains,
All to git the Devil's thankee,
　　Helpin' on 'em weld their chains?
Wy, it's jest ez clear ez figgers,
　　Clear ez one an' one make two,　　　70
Chaps thet make black slaves o' niggers
　　Want to make wite slaves o' you.

Tell ye jest the eend I've come to
　　Arter cipherin' plaguy smart,
An' it makes a handy sum, tu,
　　Any gump could larn by heart;
Laborin' man an' laborin' woman
　　Hev one glory an' one shame,
Ev'y thin' thet's done inhuman
　　Injers all on 'em the same.　　　80

'Taint by turnin' out to hack folks
　　You're agoin' to git your right,
Nor by lookin' down on black folks
　　Coz you're put upon by wite;
Slavery aint o' nary color,
　　'Taint the hide thet makes it wus,

---

61 **want this Californy** refers to the claim that California was to be admitted to statehood only in order that more slave states might be formed　　65 **Yankee . . . thankee.** The Yankees had a widespread reputation for striking good bargains

All it keers fer in a feller
   'S jest to make him fill its pus.

Want to tackle *me* in, du ye?
   I expect you'll hev to wait;   90
Wen cold lead puts daylight thru ye
   You'll begin to kal'late;
'Spose the crows wun't fall to pickin'
   All the carkiss from your bones,
Coz you helped to give a lickin'
   To them poor half-Spanish drones?

Jest go home an' ask our Nancy
   Whether I'd be sech a goose
Ez to jine ye, — guess you'd fancy
   The etarnal bung was loose!   100
She wants me fer home consumption,
   Let alone the hay's to mow, —
Ef you're arter folks o' gumption,
   You've a darned long row to hoe.

Take them editors thet's crowin'
   Like a cockerel three months old, —
Don't ketch any on 'em goin',
   Though they *be* so blasted bold;
Aint they a prime lot o' fellers?
   'Fore they think on't guess they'll sprout, 110
(Like a peach thet's got the yellers)
   With the meanness bustin' out.

Wal, go 'long to help 'em stealin'
   Bigger pens to cram with slaves,
Help the men thet's ollers dealin'
   Insults on your fathers' graves;
Help the strong to grind the feeble,
   Help the many agin the few,
Help the men thet call your people
   Witewashed slaves an' peddlin' crew!   120

Massachusetts, God forgive her,
   She's akneeling with the rest,

---

88 **pus,** purse   92 **kal'late,** calculate   96 **half-Spanish drones,** the Mexicans   111 **yellers,** yellows,
a disease of peach trees accompanied by the sprouting of sterile shoots

She thet ough' to ha' clung ferever
   In her grand old eagle-nest;
She thet ough' to stand so fearless
   Wile the wracks are round her hurled,
Holdin' up a beacon peerless
   To the oppressed of all the world!

Ha'n't they sold your colored seamen?
   Ha'n't they made your env'ys wi'z?   130
Wut'll make ye act like free men?
   Wut'll git your dander riz?
Come, I'll tell ye wut I'm thinkin'
   Is our dooty in this fix,
They'd ha' done 't ez quick ez winkin'
   In the days o' seventy-six.

Clang the bells in every steeple,
   Call all true men to disown
The tradoocers of our people,
   The enslavers o' their own;   140
Let our dear old Bay State proudly
   Put the trumpet to her mouth,
Let her ring this messidge loudly
   In the ears of all the South: —

"I'll return ye good for evil
   Much ez we frail mortils can,
But I won't go help the Devil
   Makin' man the cus o' man;
Call me coward, call me traiter,
   Jest ez suits you mean idees, —   150
Here I stand a tyrant-hater,
   An' the friend o' God an' Peace!"
Ef I'd *my* way I hed ruther
   We should go to work an' part, —
They take one way, we take t'other, —
   Guess it wouldn't break my heart;
Man hed ough' to put asunder
   Them thet God has noways jined;
An' I shouldn't gretly wonder
   Ef there's thousands o' my mind.   160

---

130 **env'ys wi'z**, envoys whiz, a reference to the impolite treatment in the period of American envoys   154
We . . . part, an interesting advocacy, by Lowell, of disunion

[The first recruiting sergeant on record I conceive to have been that individual who is mentioned in the Book of Job as *going to and fro in the earth, and walking up and down in it.* Bishop Latimer will have him to have been a bishop, but to me that other calling would appear more congenial. The sect of Cainites is not yet extinct, who esteemed the first-born of Adam to be the most worthy, not only because of that privilege of primogeniture, but inasmuch as he was able to overcome and slay his younger brother. That was a wise saying of the famous Marquis Pescara to the Papal Legate, that *it was impossible for men to serve Mars and Christ at the same time.* Yet in time past the profession of arms was judged to be κατ᾽ ἐξοχὴν that of a
10 gentleman, nor does this opinion want for strenuous upholders even in our day. Must we suppose, then, that the profession of Christianity was only intended for losels, or, at best, to afford an opening for plebeian ambition? Or shall we hold with that nicely metaphysical Pomeranian, Captain Vratz, who was Count Konigsmark's chief instrument in the murder of Mr. Thynne, that the Scheme of Salvation had been arranged with an especial eye to the necessities of the upper classes, and that "God would consider *a gentleman* and deal with him suitably to the condition and profession, he had placed him in"? It may be said of us all, *Exemplo plus quam ratione vivimus.* — H. W.]

1846

---

1 **that individual . . . down in it.** The individual is Satan. See Job 1:17. The long footnote is Parson Wilbur's learned commentary on the poem   3 **Bishop Latimer,** Hugh Latimer. See note, p. 116   4 **Cainites,** a second-century religious sect which held that Cain represented the higher power   7 **Pescara,** Marquis Pescara (1489-1525), an Italian soldier   9 κατ᾽ ἐξοχὴν, especially   13 **Captain Vratz** a murderer who was executed in 1682   17 **Exemplo . . . vivimus.** We live more by example than by reason

from Keats

This essay on Keats was written in 1854, not long after study in Europe (1851-1852) had led Lowell to new perceptions of critical standards and procedures. He begins (in the portion of the essay not here printed) with a presentation of "those essential facts which underlie the life and make the individual man," noting particularly that Keats is a poet "in whom the moral seems to have so perfectly interfused the physical man, that you might almost say he could feel sorrow with his hands."

He then launches upon the evaluation here reprinted. In considering Keats' diction, he praises the poet for his eventual achievement of "the perfect mean of diction" — the "costly plainness" which combines richness with economy of language. Then he turns to a consideration of the poet himself, and describes his nature and his influence by contrasting him with Wordsworth and Byron. The paragraph of comparison which discriminates among the three poets offers an example of Lowell's precise though sometimes complex way of drawing distinctions. Keats, he notes, was remarkable for his "penetrative and sympathetic imagination," one which caused him, like Shakespeare, "to assimilate at a touch whatever could serve his purpose" — the things of the world as well as wisdom. Thus Keats had a sort of insight which serves a poet well. In addition, he had "the shaping faculty" which made his expression accord perfectly with his thought.

The faults of Keats' poetry are obvious enough, but it should be remembered that he died at twenty-five, and that he offends by superabundance and not poverty. That he was overlanguaged at first there can be no doubt, and in this was implied the possibility of falling back to the perfect mean of diction. It is only by the rich that the costly plainness, which at once satisfies the taste and the imagination, is attainable.

Whether Keats was original or not, I do not think it useful to discuss until it has been settled what originality is. Lord Houghton tells us that this merit [whatever it be] has been denied to Keats, because his poems take the color of the authors he happened to be reading at the time he wrote them. But men have their intellectual 10 ancestry, and the likeness of some one of them is forever unexpectedly flashing out in the features of a descendant; it may be after a gap of several generations. In the parliament of the present every man represents a constituency of the past. It is true that Keats has the accent of the men from whom he learned to speak, but this is to make originality a mere question of externals, and in this sense the author of a dictionary might bring an action of trover against every author who used his words. It is the man behind the words that gives them value, and if Shakespeare help himself to a verse or a phrase, it is with ears that have learned of him to listen that we feel the harmony of the one, and it is the mass of his intellect that makes the other weighty with meaning. Enough that we recognize in Keats that indefinable newness 20 and unexpectedness which we call genius. The sunset is original every evening, though for thousands of years it has built out of the same light and vapor its visionary cities with domes and pinnacles, and its delectable mountains which night shall utterly abase and destroy.

Three men, almost contemporaneous with each other. — Wordsworth, Keats, and Byron, — were the great means of bringing back English poetry from the sandy deserts of rhetoric, and recovering for her her triple inheritance of simplicity, sensuousness, and passion. Of these, Wordsworth was the only conscious reformer, and his hostility to the existing formalism injured his earlier poems by tingeing them with something of iconoclastic extravagance. He was the deepest thinker, Keats the 30 most essentially a poet, and Byron the most keenly intellectual of the three. Keats had the broadest mind, or at least his mind was open on more sides, and he was able to understand Wordsworth and judge Byron, equally conscious, through his artistic sense, of the greatnesses of the one and the many littlenesses of the other; while Wordsworth was isolated in a feeling of his prophetic character, and Byron had only an uneasy and jealous instinct of contemporary merit. The poems of Words-

---

8 **Lord Houghton.** Richard Monckton Milnes, Lord Houghton (1809-1885), English poet and prose writer, published his *Life of Keats* in 1848   17 **Shakespeare** was regarded by Lowell as one of the peerless poets of all time. Here Lowell notes that Shakespeare could borrow a line or a phrase from a predecessor and still give the expression new values indicative of his own personality   25 **Wordsworth.** William Wordsworth (1770-1850) rebelled against eighteenth-century poetry in his Preface to the 1800 edition of *Lyrical Ballads.* In 1875, Lowell was to note that throughout his two long, philosophical poems, "The Prelude" and "The Excursion," Wordsworth "seems striving to bind the wizard Imagination with the sand-ropes of dry disquisition." Nevertheless, Lowell ranked him fifth among the great English poets   26 **Byron.** George Gordon Byron, Lord Byron (1788-1824), English poet, was famous for brilliant satires upon the life of his period

worth, as he was the most individual, accordingly reflect the moods of his own nature; those of Keats, from sensitiveness of organization, the moods of his own taste and feeling; and those of Byron, who was impressible chiefly through the understanding, the intellectual and moral wants of the time in which he lived. Wordsworth has influenced most the ideas of succeeding poets; Keats, their forms; and Byron, interesting to men of imagination less for his writings than for what his writings indicate, reappears no more in poetry, but presents an ideal to youth made restless with vague desires not yet regulated by experience nor supplied with motives by the duties of life.

10   Keats certainly had more of the penetrative and sympathetic imagination which belongs to the poet, of that imagination which identifies itself with the momentary object of its contemplation, than any man of these later days. It is not merely that he has studied the Elizabethans and caught their turn of thought, but that he really sees things with their sovereign eye, and feels them with their electrified senses. His imagination was his bliss and bane. Was he cheerful, he "hops about the gravel with the sparrows"; was he morbid, he "would reject a Petrarcal coronation, — on account of my dying-day, and because women have cancers." So impressible was he as to say that he "had no nature" meaning character. But he knew what the faculty was worth, and says finely, "The imagination may be compared to Adam's dream: he awoke
20   and found it truth." He had an unerring instinct for the poetic uses of things, and for him they had no other use. We are apt to talk of the classic *renaissance* as of a phenomenon long past, nor ever to be renewed, and to think the Greeks and Romans alone had the mighty magic to work such a miracle. To me one of the most interesting aspects of Keats is that in him we have an example of the *renaissance* going on almost under our own eyes, and that the intellectual ferment was in him kindled by a purely English leaven. He had properly no scholarship, any more than Shakespeare had, but like him he assimilated at a touch whatever could serve his purpose. His delicate senses absorbed culture at every pore. Of the self-denial to which he trained himself [unexampled in one so young] the second draft of *Hyperion*
30   as compared with the first is a conclusive proof. And far indeed is his "Lamia" from the lavish indiscrimination of "Endymion." In his Odes he showed a sense of form and proportion which we seek vainly in almost any other English poet, and some of his sonnets (taking all qualities into consideration) are the most perfect in our language. No doubt there is something tropical and of strange overgrowth in his sudden maturity, but it *was* maturity nevertheless. Happy the young poet who has the saving fault of exuberance, if he have also the shaping faculty that sooner or later will amend it!

As every young person goes through all the world-old experiences, fancying them something peculiar and personal to himself, so it is with every new generation, whose
40   youth always finds its representatives in its poets. Keats rediscovered the delight

---

13 **the Elizabethans,** authors of the period of Queen Elizabeth of England, 1558-1603 — notably Shakespeare and Spenser, both of whom Keats admired greatly   16 **Petrarcal coronation** refers to Francesco Petrarca, or Petrarch (1304-1374), Italian poet   29 **Hyperion,** a poem left uncompleted, though partly revised, at Keat's death in 1821   30 **Lamia,** a narrative poem by Keats, published in 1820   31 **Endymion,** an early, rather formless poem by Keats, published in 1818

and wonder that lay enchanted in the dictionary. Wordsworth revolted at the poetic diction which he found in vogue, but his own language rarely rises above it, except when it is upborne by the thought. Keats had an instinct for fine words, which are in themselves pictures and ideas, and had more of the power of poetic expression than any modern English poet. And by poetic expression I do not mean merely a vividness in particulars, but the right feeling which heightens or subdues a passage or a whole poem to the proper tone, and gives entireness to the effect. There is a great deal more than is commonly supposed in this choice of words. Men's thoughts and opinions are in a great degree vassals of him who invents a new phrase or reapplies an old epithet. The thought or feeling a thousand times repeated be- 10 comes his at last who utters it best. This power of language is veiled in the old legends which make the invisible powers the servants of some word. As soon as we have discovered the word for our joy or sorrow we are no longer its serfs, but its lords. We reward the discoverer of an anaesthetic for the body and make him member of all the societies, but him who finds a nepenthe for the soul we elect into the small academy of the immortals.

The poems of Keats mark an epoch in English poetry; for, however often we may find traces of it in others, in them found its most unconscious expression that reaction against the barrel-organ style which had been reigning by a kind of sleepy divine right for half a century. The lowest point was indicated when there was such an 20 utter confounding of the common and the uncommon sense that Dr. Johnson wrote verse and Burke prose. The most profound gospel of criticism was, that nothing was good poetry that could not be translated into good prose, as if one should say that the test of sufficient moonlight was that tallow-candles could be made of it. We find Keats at first going to the other extreme, and endeavoring to extract green cucumbers from the rays of tallow; but we see also incontestable proof of the greatness and purity of his poetic gift in the constant return toward equilibrium and repose in his later poems. And it is a repose always lofty and clear-aired, like that of the eagle balanced in incommunicable sunshine. In him a vigorous understanding developed itself in equal measure with the divine faculty; thought emancipated 30 itself from expression without becoming in turn its tyrant; and music and meaning floated together, accordant as swan and shadow, on the smooth element of his verse. Without losing its sensuousness, his poetry refined itself and grew more inward, and the sensational was elevated into the typical by the control of that finer sense which underlies the senses and is the spirit of them.   1854

---

15 **nepenthe.** See note, p. 849   21 **Dr. Johnson,** Samuel Johnson (1709-1785), English author, whose verse was notable for its common sense rather than any noteworthy passion   22 **Burke,** Edmund Burke (1729-1797), political writer, many of whose speeches were eloquent and poetic

Review of "The Marble Faun"

This review, in the Atlantic Monthly, *April 1860, is one of many reviews embodying Lowell's evaluations of contemporary authors. Despite its brevity, it is a meaty commentary upon Hawthorne's work in general and upon* The Marble Faun *in particular. The second paragraph, which will recall part of the essay on Keats, defines Hawthorne's achievement in a Lowellian series of contrasts involving Poe, then Shakespeare, then Donne. Similarly, it comments upon Hawthorne's characterization by setting off his characters against those of authors ranging from ancient to modern times. The third paragraph offers a keen analysis of the way Hawthorne's works center around and develop "a ruling Idea." Thereafter Lowell turns to an illiminating discussion of* The Marble Faun.

Lowell's interest in Hawthorne was indicated by the fact that not long after Hawthorne's death, and again in 1887, he contemplated writing a biography of the novelist.

It is, we believe, more than thirty years since Mr. Hawthorne's first appearance as an author; it is twenty-three since he gave his first collection of "Twice-Told Tales" to the world. His works have received that surest warranty of genius and originality in the widening of their appreciation downward from a small circle of refined admirers and critics, till it embraced the whole community of readers. With just enough encouragement to confirm his faith in his own powers, those powers had time to ripen and to toughen themselves before the gales of popularity could twist them from the balance of a healthy and normal development. Happy the author whose earliest works are read and understood by the lustre thrown back upon them
10 from his latest! for then we receive the impression of continuity and cumulation of power, of peculiarity deepening to individuality, of promise more than justified in the keeping: unhappy, whose autumn shows only the aftermath and rowen of an earlier harvest, whose would-be replenishments are but thin dilutions of his fame!

The nineteenth century has produced no more purely original writer than Mr. Hawthorne. A shallow criticism has sometimes fancied a resemblance between him and Poe. But it seems to us that the difference between them is the immeasurable one between talent carried to its ultimate, and genius, — between a masterly adaptation of the world of sense and appearance to the purposes of Art, and a so thorough conception of the world of moral realities that Art becomes the interpreter of some-
20 thing profounder than herself. In this respect it is not extravagant to say that Hawthorne has something of kindred with Shakespeare. But that breadth of nature which made Shakespeare incapable of alienation from common human nature and actual life is wanting to Hawthorne. His is rather a denizen than a citizen of what men call the world. We are conscious of a certain remoteness in his writings, as in those of Donne, but with such a difference that we should call the one super- and the other subter-sensual. Hawthorne is psychological and metaphysical. Had he been born without the poetic imagination, he would have written treatises on the Origin of Evil. He does not draw characters, but rather conceives them and then shows them acted upon by crime, passion, or circumstances, as if the element of Fate were
30 as present to his imagination as to that of a Greek dramatist. Helen we know, and Antigone, and Benedick, and Falstaff, and Miranda, and Parson Adams, and Major Pendennis, — these people have walked on pavements or looked out of club-room windows; but what are these idiosyncrasies into which Mr. Hawthorne has breathed a necromantic life, and which he has endowed with the forms and attributes of men? And yet, grant him his premises, that is, let him once get his morbid tendency,

---

30 **Helen . . . Pendennis,** characters in the *Iliad,* in Sophocles' tragedies, Shakespeare's *Much Ado About Nothing, Henry IV,* and *The Tempest,* Fielding's *Joseph Andrews,* and Thackeray's *Pendennis*

whether inherited or the result of special experience, either incarnated as a new man or usurping all the faculties of one already in the flesh, and it is marvelous how subtilely and with what truth to as much of human nature as is included in a diseased consciousness he traces all the finest nerves of impulse and motive, how he compels every trivial circumstance into an accomplice of his art, and makes the sky flame with foreboding or the landscape chill and darken with remorse. It is impossible to think of Hawthorne without at the same time thinking of the few great masters of imaginative composition; his works, only not abstract because he has the genius to make them ideal, belong not specially to our clime or generation; it is their moral purpose alone, and perhaps their sadness, that mark him as the son 10 of New England and the Puritans.

It is commonly true of Hawthorne's romances that the interest centres in one strongly defined protagonist, to whom the other characters are accessory and subordinate, — perhaps we should rather say a ruling Idea, of which all the characters are fragmentary embodiments. They remind us of a symphony of Beethoven's, in which, though there be variety of parts, yet all are infused with the dominant motive, and heighten its impression by hints and far-away suggestions at the most unexpected moment. As in Rome the obelisks are placed at points toward which several streets converge, so in Mr. Hawthorne's stories the actors and incidents seem but vistas through which we see the moral from different points of view, — a moral 20 pointing skyward always, but inscribed with hieroglyphs mysteriously suggestive, whose incitement to conjecture, while they baffle it, we prefer to any prosaic solution.

Nothing could be more original or imaginative than the conception of the character of Donatello in Mr. Hawthorne's new romance. His likeness to the lovely statue of Praxiteles, his happy animal temperament, and the dim legend of his pedigree are combined with wonderful art to reconcile us to the notion of a Greek myth embodied in an Italian of the nineteenth century; and when at length a soul is created in this primeval pagan, this child of earth, this creature of mere instinct, awakened through sin to a conception of the necessity of atonement, we feel, that, while we looked to be entertained with the airiest of fictions, we were dealing with 30 the most august truths of psychology, with the most pregnant facts of modern history, and studying a profound parable of the development of the Christian Idea.

Everything suffers a sea-change in the depths of Mr. Hawthorne's mind, gets rimmed with an impalpable fringe of melancholy moss, and there is a tone of sadness in this book as in the rest, but it does not leave us sad. In a series of remarkable and characteristic works, it is perhaps the most remarkable and characteristic. If you had picked up and read a stray leaf of it anywhere, you would have exclaimed, "Hawthorne!"

The book is steeped in Italian atmosphere. There are many landscapes in it full of breadth and power, and criticisms of pictures and statues always delicate, often 40 profound. In the Preface, Mr. Hawthorne pays a well-deserved tribute of admiration to several of our sculptors, especially to Story and Akers. The hearty enthusiasm

---

25 **Praxiteles,** Greek sculptor of the third century B.C.   42 **Story and Akers,** William Wetmore Story (1819-1895) and Benjamin Paul Akers (1825-1861)

with which he elsewhere speaks of the former artist's "Cleopatra" is no surprise to Mr. Story's friends at home, though hardly less gratifying to them than it must be to the sculptor himself.

1860

from The Biglow Papers, Second Series **The Courtin'**

This most famous of the Biglow Papers *appeared in at least three versions. In the first, written to fill in a page of the book version of the first series, it contained what are now stanzas 2, 5, 4, 6, 14, and 15, in that order. In the second, these verses were supplemented with stanzas 16, 17, 19, 20, 21, and 24. Later, said Lowell, "I added other verses, into some of which I infused a little more sentiment in a homely way, and after a fashion completed the poem by sketching in the characters and making a connected story. Most likely I have spoiled it. . . ." The version below is the third.*

God makes sech nights, all white an' still
    Fur 'z you can look or listen,
Moonshine an' snow on field an' hill,
    All silence an' all glisten.

Zekle crep' up quite unbeknown
    An' peeked in thru' the winder,
An' there sot Huldy all alone,
    'ith no one nigh to hender.

A fireplace filled the room's one side
    With half a cord o' wood in —   10
There warn't no stoves (tell comfort died)
    To bake ye to a puddin'.

The wa'nut logs shot sparkles out
    Towards the pootiest, bless her,
An' leetle flames danced all about
    The chiny on the dresser.

Agin the chimbley crook-necks hung,
    An' in amongst 'em rusted
The ole queen's-arm thet gran'ther Young
    Fetched back from Concord busted.   20

The very room, coz she was in,
    Seemed warm from floor to ceilin',

---

17 **crook-necks,** gourds   19 **queen's-arm,** musket

An' she looked full ez rosy agin
  Ez the apples she was peelin'.

'Twas kin' o' kingdom-come to look
  On sech a blessed cretur,
A dogrose blushin' to a brook
  Ain't modester nor sweeter.

He was six foot o' man, A-1,
  Clear grit an' human natur';   30
None couldn't quicker pitch a ton
  Nor dror a furrer straighter.

He'd sparked it with full twenty gals,
  Hed squired 'em, danced 'em, druv 'em,
Fust this one, an' then thet, by spells —
  All is, he couldn't love 'em.

But long o' her his veins 'ould run
  All crinkly like curled maple,
The side she breshed felt full o' sun
  Ez a south slope in Ap'il.   40

She thought no v'ice hed sech a swing
  Ez hisn in the choir;
My! when he made Ole Hunderd ring,
  She *knowed* the Lord was nigher.

An' she'd blush scarlit, right in prayer,
  When her new meetin'-bunnet
Felt somehow thru' its crown a pair
  O' blue eyes sot upun it.

Thet night, I tell ye, she looked *some!*
  She seemed to've gut a new soul,   50
For she felt sartin-sure he'd come,
  Down to her very shoe-sole.

She heered a foot, an' knowed it tu,
  A-raspin' on the scraper, —
All ways to once her feelin's flew
  Like sparks in burnt-up paper.

---

30 **Clear grit,** the same meaning as "true grit." See note, p. 946   43 **Ole Hunderd,** "Old Hundred," the most famous New England Psalm, based on Psalm 100. The tune is also used for the doxology: "Praise God from whom all blessings flow"

He kin' o' l'itered on the mat
　Some doubtfle o' the sekle,
His heart kep' goin' pity-pat
　But hern went pity Zekle.　　　　60

An' yet she gin her cheer a jerk
　Ez though she wished him furder,
An' on her apples kep' to work,
　Parin' away like murder.

"You want to see my Pa, I s'pose?"
　"Wal. . . . no. . . . I come dasignin' "—
"To see my Ma? She's sprinklin' clo'es
　Agin to-morrer's i'nin'."

To say why gals acts so or so,
　Or don't, 'ould be presumin';　　　　70
Mebby to mean *yes* an' say *no*
　Comes nateral to women.

He stood a spell on one foot fust,
　Then stood a spell on t'other,
An' on which one he felt the wust
　He couldn't ha' told ye nuther.

Says he, "I'd better call agin";
　Says she, "Think likely, Mister":
Thet last word pricked him like a pin,
　An'. . . . Wal, he up an' kist her.　　　　80

When Ma bimeby upon 'em slips,
　Huldy sot pale ez ashes,
All kin' o' smily roun' the lips
　An' teary roun' the lashes.

For she was jes' the quiet kind
　Whose naturs never vary,
Like streams that keep a summer mind
　Snowhid in Jenooary.

The blood clost roun' her heart felt glued
　Too tight for all expressin',　　　　90
Tell mother see how metters stood,
　An' gin 'em both her blessin'.

Then her red come back like the tide
  Down to the Bay o' Fundy,
An' all I know is they was cried
  In meetin' come nex' Sunday.

———————————   1861

93 **like the tide** alludes to the huge tide in the Bay of Fundy

Sunthin' in the Pastoral Line

Parson Wilbur, in his introductory letter, asserts that the Puritans "showed remarkable practical sagacity as statesmen and founders." Hosea's poem, after a brilliant series of descriptive passages about the New England scene, tells of a dream. In this dream he is visited by "a Pilgrim Father," his ancestor, who advises him to battle against the injustice of slavery as the Puritans of old had battled against King Charles I.

To the Editors of the Atlantic Monthly

JAALAM, 17 May, 1862

Gentlemen, — At the special request of Mr. Biglow, I intended to inclose, together with his own contribution, (into which, at my suggestion, he has thrown a little more of pastoral sentiment than usual,) some passages from my sermon on the day of the National Fast, from the text, "Remember them that are in bonds, as bound with them," *Heb.* xiii. 3. But I have not leisure sufficient at present for the copying of them, even were I altogether satisfied with the production as it stands. I should prefer, I confess, to contribute the entire discourse to the pages of your respectable miscellany, if it should be found acceptable upon perusal, especially as I find the difficulty in selection of greater magnitude than I had anticipated. What passes without challenge in the fervour of oral delivery, cannot always stand the 10 colder criticism of the closet. I am not so great an enemy of Eloquence as my friend Mr. Biglow would appear to be from some passages in his contribution for the current month. I would not, indeed, hastily suspect him of covertly glancing at myself in his somewhat caustick animadversions, albeit some of the phrases he girds at are not entire strangers to my lips. I am a more hearty admirer of the Puritans than seems now to be the fashion, and believe that, if they Hebraized a little too much in their speech, they showed remarkable practical sagacity as statesmen and founders. But such phenomena as Puritanism are the results rather of great religious than of merely social convulsions, and do not long survive them. So soon as an earnest conviction has cooled into a phrase, its work is over, and the best that can be done 20 with it is to bury it. *Ite, missa est.* I am inclined to agree with Mr. Biglow that we cannot settle the great political questions which are now presenting themselves to the nation by the opinions of Jeremiah or Ezekiel as to the wants and duties of the

———————————

21 **Ite, missa est,** The final words of the mass: "Go, it is done."

Jews in their time, nor do I believe that an entire community with their feelings and views would be practicable or even agreeable at the present day. At the same time I could wish that their habit of subordinating the actual to the moral, the flesh to the spirit, and this world to the other, were more common. They had found out, at least, the great military secret that soul weighs more than body. — But I am suddenly called to a sick-bed in the household of a valued parishioner.

 With esteem and respect,

Your obedient servant,

HOMER WILBUR

Once git a smell o' musk into a draw,
An' it clings hold like precerdents in law:
Your gra'ma'am put it there, — when, goodness knows, —
To jes' this-worldify her Sunday-clo'es;
But the old chist wun't sarve her gran'son's wife,
(For, 'thout new funnitoor, wut good in life?)
An' so ole clawfoot, from the precinks dread
O' the spare chamber, slinks into the shed,
Where, dim with dust, it fust or last subsides
To holdin' seeds an' fifty things besides;   10
But better days stick fast in heart an' husk,
An' all you keep in 't gits a scent o' musk.

Jes' so with poets: wut they've airly read
Gits kind o' worked into their heart an' head,
So 's 't they can't seem to write but jest on sheers
With furrin countries or played-out ideers,
Nor hev a feelin', ef it doos n't smack
O' wut some critter chose to feel 'way back:
This makes 'em talk o' daisies, larks, an' things,
Ez though we 'd nothin' here that blows an' sings, — 20
(Why, I 'd give more for one live bobolink
Than a square mile o' larks in printer's ink,) —
This makes 'em think our fust o' May is May,
Which 't ain't, for all the almanicks can say.

O little city-gals, don't never go it
Blind on the word o' noospaper or poet!
They 're apt to puff, an' May-day seldom looks
Up in the country ez it doos in books;
They're no more like than hornets'-nests an' hives,
Or printed sarmons be to holy lives.   30
I, with my trousers perched on cowhide boots,
Tuggin' my foundered feet out by the roots,

Hev seen ye come to fling on April's hearse
Your muslin nosegays from the milliner's,
Puzzlin' to find dry ground your queen to choose,
An' dance your throats sore in morocker shoes:
I've seen ye an' felt proud, thet, come wut would,
Our Pilgrim stock wus pethed with hardihood.
Pleasure doos make us Yankees kind o' winch,
Ez though 't wuz sunthin' paid for by the inch;   40
But yit we du contrive to worry thru,
Ef Dooty tells us thet the thing's to du,
An' kerry a hollerday, ef we set out,
Ez stiddily ez though 't wuz a redoubt.

I, country-born an' bred, know where to find
Some blooms thet make the season suit the mind,
An' seem to metch the doubtin' blue-bird's notes, —
Half-vent'rin' liverworts in furry coats,
Bloodroots, whose rolled-up leaves ef you oncurl,
Each on 'em 's cradle to a baby-pearl, —   50
But these are jes' Spring's pickets; sure ez sin,
The rebble frosts 'll try to drive 'em in;
For half our May 's so awfully like May n't,
't would rile a Shaker or an evrige saint;
Though I own up I like our back'ard springs
Thet kind o' haggle with their greens an' things,
An' when you 'most give up, 'uthout more words
Toss the fields full o' blossoms, leaves, an' birds:
Thet's Northun natur', slow an' apt to doubt,
But when it *doos* git stirred, ther' 's no gin-out!   60

Fust come the blackbirds clatt'rin' in tall trees,
An' settlin' things in windy Congresses, —
Queer politicians, though, for I 'll be skinned
Ef all on 'em don't head aginst the wind.
'fore long the trees begin to show belief, —
The maple crimsons to a coral-reef.
Then saffern swarms swing off from all the willers
So plump they look like yaller caterpillars,
Then gray hossches'nuts leetle hands unfold
Softer 'n a baby's be at three days old: 70
Thet's robin-redbreast's almanick; he knows
Thet arter this ther' 's only blossom-snows;
So, choosin' out a handy crotch an' spouse,
He goes to plast'rin' his adobë house.

Then seems to come a hitch, — things lag behind,
Till some fine mornin' Spring makes up her mind,
An' ez, when snow-swelled rivers cresh their dams
Heaped-up with ice thet dovetails in an' jams,
A leak comes spirtin' thru some pin-hole cleft,
Grows stronger, fercer, tears out right an' left,   80
Then all the waters bow themselves an' come,
Suddin, in one gret slope o' shedderin' foam,
Jes' so our Spring gits everythin' in tune
An' gives one leap from Aperl into June:
Then all comes crowdin'; afore you think,
Young oak-leaves mist the side-hill woods with pink;
The catbird in the laylock-bush is loud;
The orchards turn to heaps o' rosy cloud;
Red-cedars blosom tu, though few folks know it,
An' look all dipt in sunshine like a poet;   90
The lime-trees pile their solid stacks o' shade
An' drows'ly simmer with the bees' sweet trade;
In ellum-shrouds the flashin' hangbird clings
An' for the summer vy'ge his hammock slings;
All down the loose-walled lanes in archin' bowers
The barb'ry droops its strings o' golden flowers,
Whose shrinkin' hearts the school-gals love to try
With pins, — they 'll worry yourn so, boys, bimeby!
But I don't love your cat'logue style, — do you? —
Ez ef to sell off Natur' by vendoo;   100
One word with blood in 't 's twice ez good ez two:
'nuff sed, June's bridesman, poet o' the year,
Gladness on wings, the bobolink, is here;
Half-hid in tip-top apple-blooms he swings,
Or climbs aginst the breeze with quiverin' wings,
Or, givin' way to 't in a mock despair,
Runs down, a brook o' laughter, thru the air.

I ollus feel the sap start in my veins
In Spring, with curus heats an' prickly pains,
Thet drive me, when I git a chance, to walk   110
Off by myself to hev a privit talk
With a queer critter thet can't seem to 'gree
Along o' me like most folks, — Mister Me.
Ther' 's times when I'm unsoshle ez a stone,
An' sort o' suffercate to be alone, —
I'm crowded jes' to think thet folks are nigh,

100 **vendoo,** vendue, public auction

An' can't bear nothin' closer than the sky;
Now the wind 's full ez shifty in the mind
Ez wut it is ou'-doors, ef I ain't blind,
An' sometimes, in the fairest sou'west weather,   120
My innard vane pints east for weeks together,
My natur' gits all goose-flesh, an' my sins
Come drizzlin' on my conscience sharp ez pins:
Wal, et sech times I jes' slip out o' sight
An' take it out in a fair stan'-up fight
With the one cuss I can't lay on the shelf,
The crook'dest stick in all the heap, — Myself.

'T wuz so las' Sabbath arter meetin'-time:
Findin' my feelin's would n't noways rhyme
With nobody's, but off the hendle flew   130
An' took things from an east-wind pint o' view,
I started off to lose me in the hills
Where the pines be, up back o' 'Siah's Mills:
Pines, ef you 're blue, are the best friends I know,
They mope an' sigh an' sheer your feelin's so, —
They hesh the ground beneath so, tu, I swan,
You half-forgit you 've gut a body on.
Ther' 's a small school'us' there where four roads meet,
The door-steps hollered out by little feet,
An' side-posts carved with names whose owners grew   140
To gret men, some on 'em, an' deacons, tu;
't ain't used no longer, coz the town hez gut
A high-school, where they teach the Lord knows wut:
Three-story larnin' 's pop'lar now; I guess
We thriv' ez wal on jes' two stories less,
For it strikes me ther' 's sech a thing ez sinnin'
By overloadin' children's underpinnin':
Wal, here it wuz I larned my A B C,
An' it 's a kind o' favorite spot with me.

We 're curus critters: Now ain't jes' the minute   150
Thet ever fits us easy while we 're in it;
Long ez 't wuz futur', 't would be perfect bliss, —
Soon ez it 's past, *thet* time 's wuth ten o' this;
An' yit there ain't a man thet need be told
Thet Now's the only bird lays eggs o' gold.
A knee-high lad, I used to plot an' plan
An' think 't wuz life's cap-sheaf to be a man;
Now, gittin' gray, there's nothin' I enjoy

Like dreamin' back along into a boy:
So the ole school'us' is a place I choose   160
Afore all others, ef I want to muse;
I set down where I used to set, an' git
My boyhood back, an' better things with it, —
Faith, Hope, an' sunthin', ef it is n't Cherrity,
It's want o' guile, an' thet 's ez gret a rerrity, —
While Fancy's cushin', free to Prince and Clown,
Makes the hard bench ez soft ez milkweed-down.
Now, 'fore I knowed, thet Sabbath arternoon
When I sot out to tramp myself in tune,
I found me in the school'us' on my seat,   170
Drummin' the march to No-wheres with my feet.
Thinkin' o' nothin', I've heerd ole folks say
Is a hard kind o' dooty in its way:
It 's thinkin' everythin' you ever knew,
Or ever hearn, to make your feelin's blue.
I sot there tryin' thet on for a spell:
I thought o' the Rebellion, then o' Hell,
Which some folks tell ye now is jest a metterfor
(A the'ry, p'raps, it wun't *feel* none the better for);
I thought o' Reconstruction, wut we 'd win   180
Patchin' our patent self-blow-up agin:
I thought ef this 'ere milkin' o' the wits,
So much a month, warn't givin' Natur' fits, —
Ef folks warn't druv, findin' their own milk fail,
To work the cow thet hez an iron tail,
An' ef idees 'thout ripenin' in the pan
Would send up cream to humor ary man:
From this to thet I let my worryin' creep,
Till finally I must ha' fell asleep.

Our lives in sleep are some like streams thet glide   190
'twixt flesh an' sperrit boundin' on each side,
Where both shores' shadders kind o' mix an' mingle
In sunthin' thet ain't jes' like either single;
An' when you cast off moorin's from To-day,
An' down towards To-morrer drift away,
The imiges thet tengle on the stream
Make a new upside-down'ard world o' dream:
Sometimes they seem like sunrise-streaks an' warnin's
O' wut 'll be in Heaven on Sabbath-mornin's,
An', mixed right in ez ef jest out o' spite,   200
Sunthin' thet says your supper ain't gone right.

I 'm gret on dreams, an' often when I wake,
I 've lived so much it makes my mem'ry ache,
An' can't skurce take a cat-nap in my cheer
'thout hevin' 'em, some good, some bad, all queer.

Now I wuz settin' where I 'd ben, it seemed,
An' ain't sure yit whether I r'ally dreamed,
Nor, ef I did, how long I might ha' slep',
When I hearn some un stompin' up the step,
An' lookin' 'round, ef two an' two make four,   210
I see a Pilgrim Father in the door.
He wore a steeple-hat, tall boots, an' spurs
With rowels to 'em big ez ches'nut-burrs,
An' his gret sword behind him sloped away
Long 'z a man's speech thet dunno wut to say. —
"Ef your name 's Biglow, an' your given-name
Hosee," sez he, "it 's arter you I came;
I 'm your gret-gran'ther multiplied by three." —
"My *wut?*" sez I. — "Your gret-gret-gret," sez he:
"You would n't ha' never ben here but for me.   220
Two hundred an' three year ago this May
The ship I come in sailed up Boston Bay;
I 'd been a cunnle in our Civil War, —
But wut an airth hev *you* gut up one for?
Coz we du things in England, 't ain't for you
To git a notion you can du 'em tu:
I 'm told you write in public prints: ef true,
It 's nateral you should know a thing or two." —
"Thet air 's an argymunt I can't endorse, —
't would prove, coz you wear spurs, you kep' a horse: 230
For brains," sez I, "wutever you may think,
Ain't boun' to cash the drafs o' pen-an'-ink, —
Though mos' folks write ez ef they hoped jes' quickenin'
The churn would argoo skim-milk into thickenin';
But skim-milk ain't a thing to change its view
O' wut it's meant for more'n a smoky flue.
But du pray tell me, 'fore we furder go,
How in all Natur' did you come to know
'bout our affairs," sez I, "in Kingdom-Come?" —
"Wal, I worked round at sperrit-rappin' some,   240
An' danced the tables till their legs wuz gone,
In hopes o' larnin' wut wuz goin' on,"
Sez he, "but mejums lie so like all-split

Thet I concluded it wuz best to quit.
But, come now, ef you wun't confess to knowin',
You 've some conjectures how the thing 's a-goin'." —
"Gran'ther," sez I, "a vane warnt never known
Nor asked to hev a jedgment of its own;
An' yit, ef 't ain't gut rusty in the jints,
It 's safe to trust its say on certin pints: 250
It knows the wind's opinions to a T,
An' the wind settles wut the weather 'll be."
"I never thought a scion of our stock
Could grow the wood to make a weather-cock;
When I wuz younger 'n you, skurce more 'n a shaver,
No airthly wind," sez he, "could make me waver!"
(Ez he said this, he clinched his jaw an' forehead,
Hitchin' his belt to bring his sword-hilt forrard.) —
"Jes so it wuz with me," sez I, "I swow,
When *I* wuz younger 'n wut you see me now, —   260
Nothin' from Adam's fall to Huldy's bonnet,
Thet I warn't full-cocked with my jedgment on it;
But now I 'm gittin' on in life, I find
It 's a sight harder to make up my mind, —
Nor I don't often try tu, when events
Will du it for me free of all expense.
The moral question 's ollus plain enough, —
It 's jes' the human-natur' side thet 's tough;
Wut 's best to think may n't puzzle me nor you, —
The pinch comes in decidin' wut to *du;*   270
Ef you *read* History, all runs smooth ez grease,
Coz there the men ain't nothin' more 'n idees, —
But come to *make* it, ez we must to-day,
Th' idees hev arms an' legs an' stop the way:
It 's easy fixin' things in facts an' figgers, —
They can't resist, nor warn't brought up with niggers;
But come to try your the'ry on, — why, then
Your facts an' figgers change to ign'ant men
Actin' ez ugly — " — "Smite 'em hip an' thigh!"
Sez gran'ther, "and let every man-child die!   280
Oh for three weeks o' Crommle an' the Lord!
Up, Isr'el, to your tents an' grind the sword!" —
"Thet kind o' thing worked wal in ole Judee,
But you forgit how long it 's ben A.D.;

---

281 **Crommle,** Oliver Cromwell (1599-1658), Puritan General, Lord Protector of the Commonwealth (1653-1658) during the Puritan rule

You think thet 's ellerkence, — I call it shoddy,
A thing," sez I, "wun't cover soul nor body;
I like the plain all-wool o' common-sense,
Thet warms ye now, an' will a twelve-month hence.
"You took to follerin' where the Prophets beckoned,
An', fust you knowed on, back come Charles the Second;   290
Now wut I want 's to hev all *we* gain stick,
An' not to start Millennium too quick;
We hain't to punish only, but to keep,
An' the cure 's gut to go a cent'ry deep."
"Wal, milk-an'-water ain't the best o' glue,"
Sez he, "an' so you 'll find before you 're thru;
Ef reshness venters sunthin', shilly-shally
Loses ez often wut 's ten times the vally.
Thet exe of ourn, when Charles's neck gut split,
Opened a gap thet ain't bridged over yit: 300
Slav'ry 's your Charles, the Lord hez gin the exe — "
"Our Charles," sez I, "hez gut eight million necks.
The hardest question ain't the black man's right,
The trouble is to 'mancipate the white;
One's chained in body an' can be sot free,
But t' other 's chained in soul to an idee:
It 's a long job, but we shall worry thru it;
Ef bagnets fail, the spellin'-book must du it."
"Hosee," sez he, "I think you're goin' to fail:
The rettlesnake ain't dangerous in the tail;   310
This 'ere rebellion 's nothin but the rettle, —
You 'll stomp on thet an' think you 've won the bettle;
It 's Slavery thet 's the fangs an' thinkin' head,
An' ef you want selvation, cresh it dead, —
An' cresh it suddin, or you 'll larn by waitin'
Thet Chance wun't stop to listen to debatin'!" —
"God's truth!" sez I, — "an' ef *I* held the club,
An' knowed jes' where to strike, — but there's the rub!" —
"Strike soon," sez he, "or you 'll be deadly ailin', —
Folks thet 's afeard to fail are sure o' failin';   320
God hates your sneakin' creturs thet believe
He 'll settle things they run away an' leave!"
He brought his foot down fercely, ez he spoke,
An' give me sech a startle thet I woke.

                                        1862

---

290 **Charles the Second** (1630-1685), king of Great Britain and Ireland (1660-1685) after the period
of Puritan rule

Ode Recited at the Harvard Commemoration

*This poem was read on July 21, 1865, to a group of friends and alumni who, in a broad
tent raised near the grounds of Harvard College, had gathered to pay tribute to the Harvard men who had served during the recently concluded Civil War. There can be no doubt
that Lowell was speaking sincerely in the ode. Former students of his were among those honored, and he himself had lost three nephews in the war.*

*In what is considered his greatest serious poem Lowell grapples with a question which
arises in all times of war — "What possible justification is there for the sacrifices of the men
who served?" He praises the faith of men which is made whole by brave actions, and sees
such faith made immortal not only in the lives of contemporaries but also in the race and
the nation which such men have served. In the sixth stanza, he pays reverent tribute to Lincoln, whom he cites as a great example of American insight and bravery.*

*Lowell tells of experiments with verse forms and justifies the form which he employed in
this account of the composition of the poem written to James B. Thayer in 1877: "A long
series of uniform stanzas (I am always speaking of public recitation) with regularly recurring rhymes produces somnolence among the men and a desperate resort to their fans on the
part of the women. . . . Now, my problem was to contrive a measure which should not be
tedious by uniformity, but which should vary with varying moods, in which the transitions
. . . should be managed without a jar. I at first thought of mixed rhymed and blank verses
of unequal measures, like those in the chorus of 'Samson Agonistes'. . . . I wrote some stanzas
. . . on this theory at first, leaving some verses without a rhyme to match. But my ear was
better pleased when the rhyme, coming at a longer interval, as a far-off echo rather than
instant reverberation, produced the same effect almost, and yet was grateful by unexpectedly
recalling an association and faint reminiscence of consonance."*

I

    Weak-winged is song,
Nor aims at that clear-ethered height
Whither the brave deed climbs for light:
    We seem to do them wrong,
Bringing our robin's-leaf to deck their hearse
Who in warm life-blood wrote their nobler verse,
Our trivial song to honor those who come
With ears attuned to strenuous trump and drum,
And shaped in squadron-strophes their desire,
Live battle-odes whose lines were steel and fire: 10
    Yet sometimes feathered words are strong,
A gracious memory to buoy up and save
From Lethe's dreamless ooze, the common grave
    Of the unventurous throng.

---

13 **Lethe's,** see note, p. 885

II

Today our Reverend Mother welcomes back
　　Her wisest Scholars, those who understood
The deeper teaching of her mystic tome,
　　　And offered their fresh lives to make it good:
　　　　No lore of Greece or Rome,
No science peddling with the names of things,   20
Or reading stars to find inglorious fates,
　　　　Can lift our life with wings
Far from Death's idle gulf that for the many waits,
　　　　And lengthen out our dates
With that clear fame whose memory sings
In manly hearts to come, and nerves them and dilates:
Nor such thy teaching, Mother of us all!
　　　　Not such the trumpet-call
　　　　Of thy diviner mood,
　　　　That could thy sons entice   30
From happy homes and toils, the fruitful nest
Of those half-virtues which the world calls best,
　　　　Into War's tumult rude;
　　　　But rather far that stern device
The sponsors chose that round thy cradle stood
　　　　In the dim, unventured wood,
　　　　The VERITAS that lurks beneath
　　　　The letter's unprolific sheath,
　　Life of whate'er makes life worth living,
Seed-grain of high emprise, immortal food,   40
　　One heavenly thing whereof earth hath the giving.

III

Many loved Truth, and lavished life's best oil
　　Amid the dust of books to find her,
Content at last, for guerdon of their toil,
　　With the cast mantle she hath left behind her.
　　　Many in sad faith sought for her,
　　　Many with crossed hands sighed for her;
　　　But these, our brothers, fought for her,
　　　At life's dear peril wrought for her,
　　　So loved her that they died for her,   50
　　　　Tasting the raptured fleetness
　　　　Of her divine completeness:
　　　　　Their higher instinct knew

---

15 **Reverend Mother,** Harvard, personified as the alma mater   37 **Veritas,** Truth — the motto of Harvard

Those love her best who to themselves are true,
And what they dare to dream of dare to do;
    They followed her and found her
    Where all may hope to find,
Not in the ashes of the burnt-out mind,
But beautiful, with danger's sweetness round her.
    Where faith made whole with deed   60
    Breathes its awakening breath
    Into the lifeless creed,
    They saw her plumed and mailed,
    With sweet, stern face unveiled,
And all-repaying eyes, look proud on them in death.

    IV
Our slender life runs rippling by, and glides
    Into the silent hollow of the past;
      What is there that abides
    To make the next age better for the last?
      Is earth too poor to give us   70
    Something to live for here that shall outlive us?
      Some more substantial boon
Than such as flows and ebbs with Fortune's fickle moon?
      The little that we see
      From doubt is never free;
      The little that we do
      Is but half-nobly true;
      With our laborious hiving
What men call treasure, and the gods call dross,
    Life seems a jest of Fate's contriving,   80
    Only secure in every one's conniving,
A long account of nothings paid with loss,
Where we poor puppets, jerked by unseen wires,
    After our little hour of strut and rave,
With all our pasteboard passions and desires,
Loves, hates, ambitions, and immortal fires,
    Are tossed pell-mell together in the grave.
    But stay! no age was e'er degenerate,
    Unless men held it at too cheap a rate,
    For in our likeness still we shape our fate.   90
      Ah, there is something here
    Unfathomed by the cynic's sneer,
    Something that gives our feeble light
    A high immunity from Night,

Something that leaps life's narrow bars
To claim its birthright with the hosts of heaven;
   A seed of sunshine that can leaven
   Our earthly dulness with the beams of stars,
     And glorify our clay
With light from fountains elder than the Day;   100
   A conscience more divine than we,
   A gladness fed with secret tears,
   A vexing, forward-reaching sense
   Of some more noble permanence;
     A light across the sea,
Which haunts the soul and will not let it be,
Still beaconing from the heights of undegenerate years.

   V

   Whither leads the path
   To ampler fates that leads?
   Not down through flowery meads,   110
     To reap an aftermath
   Of youth's vainglorious weeds,
   But up the steep, amid the wrath
And shock of deadly-hostile creeds,
Where the world's best hope and stay
By battle's flashes gropes a desperate way,
And every turf the fierce foot clings to bleeds.
   Peace hath her not ignoble wreath,
   Ere yet the sharp, decisive word
Light the black lips of cannon, and the sword   120
   Dreams in its easeful sheath;
But some day the live coal behind the thought,
   Whether from Baäl's stone obscene,
   Or from the shrine serene
   Of God's pure altar brought,
Bursts up in flame; the war of tongue and pen
Learns with what deadly purpose it was fraught,
And, helpless in the fiery passion caught,
Shakes all the pillared state with shock of men:
Some day the soft Ideal that we wooed   130
Confronts us fiercely, foe-beset, pursued,
And cries reproachful: "Was it, then, my praise,
And not myself was loved? Prove now thy truth;
I claim of thee the promise of thy youth;
Give me thy life, or cower in empty phrase,

123 **Baäl's stone obscene,** idol worshiped by the idolatrous Baalites. See Kings 18

The victim of thy genius, not its mate!"
   Life may be given in many ways,
   And loyalty to Truth be sealed '
As bravely in the closet as the field,
   So bountiful is Fate;   140
   But then to stand beside her,
   When craven churls deride her,
To front a lie in arms and not to yield,
     This shows, methinks, God's plan
     And measure of a stalwart man,
     Limbed like the old heroic breeds,
Who stands self-poised on manhood's solid earth,
Not forced to frame excuses for his birth,
     Fed from within with all the strength he needs.

   VI
Such was he, our Martyr-Chief,   150
   Whom late the Nation he had led,
   With ashes on her head,
Wept with the passion of an angry grief:
Forgive me, if from present things I turn
To speak what in my heart will beat and burn,
And hang my wreath on his world-honored urn.
     Nature, they say, doth dote,
     And cannot make a man
     Save on some worn-out plan,
     Repeating us by rote: 160
For him her Old-World moulds aside she threw,
   And, choosing sweet clay from the breast
     Of the unexhausted West,
With stuff untainted shaped a hero new,
Wise, steadfast in the strength of God, and true.
     How beautiful to see
Once more a shepherd of mankind indeed,
Who loved his charge but never loved to lead;
One whose meek flock the people joyed to be,
     Not lured by any cheat of birth,   170
     But by his clear-grained human worth,
And brave old wisdom of sincerity!
   They knew that outward grace is dust;
   They could not choose but trust
In that sure-footed mind's unfaltering skill,

---

150 **Martyr-Chief,** Lincoln, who had been assassinated April 14. This sixth section, perhaps the most famous
in the poem, was added after the public recital

     And supple-tempered will
That bent like perfect steel to spring again and thrust.
     His was no lonely mountain-peak of mind,
     Thrusting to thin air o'er our cloudly bars,
     A sea-mark now, now lost in vapors blind;   180
     Broad prairie rather, genial, level-lined,
     Fruitful and friendly for all human kind,
Yet also nigh to heaven and loved of loftiest stars.
     Nothing of Europe here,
Or, then, of Europe fronting mornward still,
     Ere any names of Serf and Peer
  Could Nature's equal scheme deface
  And thwart her genial will;
     Here was a type of the true elder race,
And one of Plutarch's men talked with us face to face. 190
     I praise him not; it were too late;
And some innative weakness there must be
In him who condescends to victory
Such as the Present gives, and cannot wait,
     Safe in himself as in a fate.
     So always firmly he:
     He knew to bide his time,
        And can his fame abide,
Still patient in his simple faith sublime,
        Till the wise years decide.   200
     Great captains, with their guns and drums,
     Disturb our judgment for the hour,
        But at last silence comes;
     These all are gone, and, standing like a tower,
     Our children shall behold his fame,
        The kindly-earnest, brave, foreseeing man,
Sagacious, patient, dreading praise, not blame,
     New birth of our new soil, the first American.

     VII
Long as man's hope insatiate can discern
     Or only guess some more inspiring goal   210
     Outside of Self, enduring as the pole,
Along whose course the flying axles burn
Of spirits bravely-pitched, earth's manlier brood;
     Long as below we cannot find
     The meed that stills the inexorable mind;

190 **one of . . . men,** a man worthy of comparison with the heroic Greeks and Romans celebrated in Plutarch's *Lives* (first century, A.D.)

So long this faith to some ideal Good,
Under whatever mortal names its masks,
Freedom, Law, Country, this ethereal mood
That thanks the Fates for their severer tasks,
 Feeling its challenged pulses leap   220
 While others skulk in subterfuges cheap,
And, set in Danger's van, has all the boon it asks,
 Shall win a man's praise and woman's love,
 Shall be a wisdom that we set above
All other skills and gifts to culture dear,
 A virtue round whose forehead we enwreathe
 Laurels that with a living passion breathe
When other crowns grow, while we twine them, sear.
 What brings us thronging these high rites to pay,
And seal these hours the noblest of our year,   230
 Save that our brothers found this better way?

 VIII
 We sit here in the Promised Land
That flows with Freedom's honey and milk;
 But 'twas they won it, sword in hand,
Making the nettle danger soft for us as silk.
 We welcome back our bravest and our best —
 Ah me! not all! some come not with the rest,
Who went forth brave and bright as any here!
I strive to mix some gladness with my strain,
 But the sad strings complain,   240
 And will not please the ear:
I sweep them for a pæan, but they wane
 Again and yet again
Into a dirge and die away in pain.
In these brave ranks I only see the gaps,
Thinking of dear ones whom the dumb turf wraps,
Dark to the triumph which they died to gain:
 Fitlier may others greet the living,
 For me the past is unforgiving;
  I with uncovered head   250
 Salute the sacred dead,
Who went, and who return not. — Say not so!
'Tis not the grapes of Canaan that repay,
But the high faith that failed not by the way;
Virtue treads paths that end not in the grave;
No ban of endless night exiles the brave;

---

232 **Promised Land,** the land sought by the children of Israel, the chosen people. See Exodus 13:5

And to the saner mind
We rather seem the dead that stayed behind.
Blow, trumpets, all your exultations blow!
For never shall their aureoled presence lack: 260
I see them muster in a gleaming row,
With ever-youthful brows that nobler show;
We find in our dull road their shining track;
      In every nobler mood
We feel the orient of their spirit glow,
Part of our life's unalterable good,
Of all our saintlier aspiration;
      They come transfigured back,
Secure from change in their high-hearted ways,
Beautiful evermore, and with the rays   270
Of morn on their white Shields of Expectation!

      IX
      But is there hope to save
Even this ethereal essence from the grave?
      Whatever 'scaped Oblivion's subtle wrong
Save a few clarion names, or golden threads of song?
         Before my musing eye
      The mighty ones of old sweep by,
Disvoiced now and insubstantial things,
As noisy once as we; poor ghosts of kings,
Shadows of empire wholly gone to dust,   280
And many races, nameless long ago,
To darkness driven by that imperious gust
Of ever-rushing Time that here doth blow:
O visionary world, condition strange,
Where naught abiding is but only Change,
Where the deep-bolted stars themselves still shift and range!
Shall we to more continuance make pretence?
Renown builds tombs; a life-estate is Wit;
      And, bit by bit,
The cunning years steal all from us but woe;   290
   Leaves are we, whose decays no harvest sow.
      But, when we vanish hence,
Shall they lie forceless in the dark below,
Save to make green their little length of sods,
Or deepen pansies for a year or two,
Who now to us are shining-sweet as gods?
Was dying all they had the skill to do?
That were not fruitless: but the Soul resents

Such short-lived service, as if blind events
Ruled without her, or earth could so endure;   300
She claims a more divine investiture
Of longer tenure than Fame's airy rents;
Whate'er she touches doth her nature share;
Her inspiration haunts the ennobled air,
    Gives eyes to mountains blind,
Ears to the deaf earth, voices to the wind,
And her clear trump sings succor everywhere
By lonely bivouacs to the wakeful mind;
For soul inherits all that soul could dare:
    Yea, Manhood hath a wider span   310
And larger privilege of life than man.
The single deed, the private sacrifice,
So radiant now through proudly-hidden tears,
Is covered up erelong from mortal eyes
With thoughtless drift of the deciduous years;
But that high privilege that makes all men peers,
That leap of heart whereby a people rise
    Up to a noble anger's height,
And, flamed on by the Fates, not shrink, but grow more bright,
    That swift validity in noble veins,   320
Of choosing danger and disdaining shame,
    Of being set on flame
By the pure fire that flies all contact base
But wraps its chosen with angelic might,
    These are imperishable gains,
Sure as the sun, medicinal as light,
These hold great futures in their lusty reins
And certify to earth a new imperial race.

    X
    Who now shall sneer?
    Who dare again to say we trace   330
    Our lines to a plebeian race?
    Roundhead and Cavalier!
Dumb are those names erewhile in battle loud;
Dream-footed as the shadow of a cloud,
    They flit across the ear:
That is best blood that hath most iron in't
To edge resolve with, pouring without stint
    For what makes manhood dear.

---

332 **Roundhead and Cavalier,** the Puritans and the followers of Charles I, here representing the New Englanders and the Southerners

Tell us not of Plantagenets,
Hapsburgs, and Guelfs, whose thin bloods crawl   340
Down from some victor in a border-brawl!
How poor their outworn coronets,
Matched with one leaf of that plain civic wreath
Our brave for honor's blazon shall bequeath,
Through whose desert a rescued Nation sets
Her heel on treason, and the trumpet hears
Shout victory, tingling Europe's sullen ears
With vain resentments and more vain regrets!

XI
Not in anger, not in pride,
Pure from passion's mixture rude   350
Ever to base earth allied,
But with far-heard gratitude,
Still with heart and voice renewed,
To heroes living and dear martyrs dead,
The strain should close that consecrates our brave.
Lift the heart and lift the head!
Lofty be its mood and grave,
Not without a martial ring,
Not without a prouder tread
And a peal of exultation: 360
Little right has he to sing
Through whose heart in such an hour
Beats no march of conscious power,
Sweeps no tumult of elation!
'Tis no Man we celebrate,
By his country's victories great,
A hero half, and half the whim of Fate,
But the pith and marrow of a Nation
Drawing force from all her men,
Highest, humblest, weakest, all,   370
For her time of need, and then
Pulsing it again through them,
Till the basest can no longer cower,
Feeling his soul spring up divinely tall,
Touched but in passing by her mantle-hem.
Come back, then, noble pride, for 'tis her dower!
How could poet ever tower,
If his passions, hopes, and fears,

---

339 **Plantagenets,** a line of English kings   340 **Hapsburgs, and Guelfs,** respectively, the royal family
which ruled the Holy Roman Empire and the papal party in medieval Italy

In his triumphs and his tears,
    Kept not measure with his people?   380
Boom, cannon, boom to all the winds and waves!
Clash out, glad bells, from every rocking steeple!
Banners, advance with triumph, bend your staves!
    And from every mountain-peak
    Let beacon-fire to answering beacon speak,
Katahdin tell Monadnock, Whiteface he,
And so leap on in light from sea to sea,
    Till the glad news be sent
      Across a kindling continent,
Making earth feel more firm and air breathe braver: 390
"Be proud! for she is saved, and all have helped to save her!
    She that lifts up the manhood of the poor,
    She of the open soul and open door,
    With room about her hearth for all mankind!
    The fire is dreadful in her eyes no more;
    From her bold front the helm she doth unbind,
    Sends all her handmaid armies back to spin,
    And bids her navies, that so lately hurled
    Their crashing battle, hold their thunders in,
    Swimming like birds of calm along the unharmful shore.   400
    No challenge sends she to the elder world,
    That looked askance and hated; a light scorn
    Plays on her mouth, as round her mighty knees
    She calls her children back, and waits the morn
Of nobler day, enthroned between her subject seas.'

    XII
Bow down, dear Land, for thou hast found release!
    Thy God, in these distempered days,
    Hath taught thee the sure wisdom of His ways,
And through thine enemies hath wrought thy peace!
    Bow down in prayer and praise!   410
No poorest in thy borders but may now
Lift to the juster skies a man's enfranchised brow.
O Beautiful! my Country! ours once more!
Smoothing thy gold of war-dishevelled hair
O'er such sweet brows as never other wore,
      And letting thy set lips,
      Freed from wrath's pale eclipse,
The rosy edges of their smile lay bare,
What words divine of lover or of poet

---

386 **Katahdin . . . Monadnock, Whiteface,** mountains in Maine, New Hampshire, and New York, respectively

Could tell our love and make thee know it,   420
Among the Nations bright beyond compare?
    What were our lives without thee?
    What all our lives to save thee?
    We reck not what we gave thee;
    We will not dare to doubt thee,
But ask whatever else, and we will dare!

                       1865

Auspex

My heart, I cannot still it,
Nest that had song-birds in it;
And when the last shall go,
The dreary days, to fill it,
Instead of lark or linnet,
Shall whirl dead leaves and snow.

Had they been swallows only,
Without the passion stronger
That skyward longs and sings, —
Woe's me, I shall be lonely   10
When I can feel no longer
The impatience of their wings!

A moment, sweet delusion,
Like birds the brown leaves hover,
But it will not be long
Before their wild confusion
Fall wavering down to cover
The poet and his song.

                1879, 1888

Democracy

In 1883, when he was serving as minister to Great Britain, Lowell was elected president of the Birmingham and Midland Institute. The following year, on October 6, 1884, he delivered an inaugural address which, like other addresses delivered by him in England, was admired for its felicity, wit, and learning. His discussion of democracy has been praised as an argument for "the most radical democratic principles as the ultimate logical result of the

British Constitution" presented "with a temper, an urbanity, a moderation, a precision of statement, and a courteous grace of humor." But though it was admirably ordered and phrased, the address will not seem very radical to modern readers. Most will notice that the ardor which had made young Jamie Lowell so ardent a democrat had cooled appreciably during the post-Civil War period.

He must be a born leader or misleader of men, or must have been sent into the world unfurnished with that modulating and restraining balance-wheel which we call a sense of humor, who, in old age, has as strong a confidence in his opinions and in the necessity of bringing the universe into conformity with them as he had in youth. In a world the very condition of whose being is that it should be in a perpetual flux, where all seems mirage, and the one abiding thing is the effort to distinguish realities from appearances, the elderly man must be indeed of a singularly tough and valid fibre who is certain that he has any clarified residuum of experience, any assured verdict of reflection, that deserves to be called an opinion, or who, even

10 if he had, feels that he is justified in holding mankind by the button while he is expounding it. And in a world of daily — nay, almost hourly — journalism, where every clever man, every man who thinks himself clever, or whom anybody else thinks clever, is called upon to deliver his judgment point-blank and at the word of command on every conceivable subject of human thought, or, on what sometimes seems to him very much the same thing, on every inconceivable display of human want of thought, there is such a spendthrift waste of all those commonplaces which furnish the permitted staple of public discourse that there is little chance of beguiling a new tune out of the one-stringed instrument on which we have been thrumming so long. In this desperate necessity one is often tempted to

20 think that, if all the words of the dictionary were tumbled down in a heap and then all those fortuitous juxtapositions and combinations that made tolerable sense were picked out and pieced together, we might find among them some poignant suggestions towards novelty of thought or expression. But, alas! it is only the great poets who seem to have this unsolicited profusion of unexpected and incalculable phrase, this infinite variety of topic. For everybody else everything has been said before, and said over again after. He who has read his Aristotle will be apt to think that observation has on most points of general applicability said its last word, and he who has mounted the tower of Plato to look abroad from it will never hope to climb another with so lofty a vantage of speculation. Where it is so simple if not so easy a thing

30 to hold one's peace, why add to the general confusion of tongues? There is something disheartening, too, in being expected to fill up not less than a certain measure of time, as if the mind were an hourglass, that need only be shaken and set on one end or the other, as the case may be, to run its allotted sixty minutes with decorous exactitude. I recollect being once told by the late eminent naturalist, Agassiz, that when he was to deliver his first lecture as professor (at Zürich, I believe) he had

---

18 **one-stringed instrument**, the tongue   26 **Aristotle . . . Plato,** Aristotle (384-322 B.C.) and Plato (429-347 B.C.), Greek philosophers, are contrasted as champions of observation and speculation, respectively   34 **Agassiz** actually gave his first lecture in Neufchatel. See note, p. 915

grave doubts of his ability to occupy the prescribed three quarters of an hour. He was speaking without notes, and glancing anxiously from time to time at the watch that lay before him on the desk. "When I had spoken a half hour," he said, "I had told them everything I knew in the world, everything! Then I began to repeat myself," he added, roguishly, "and I have done nothing else ever since." Beneath the humorous exaggeration of the story I seemed to see the face of a very serious and improving moral. And yet if one were to say only what he had to say and then stopped, his audience would feel defrauded of their honest measure. Let us take courage by the example of the French, whose exportation of Bordeaux wines increases as the area of their land in vineyards is diminished.   10

To me, somewhat hopelessly revolving these things, the undelayable year has rolled round, and I find myself called upon to say something in this place, where so many wiser men have spoken before me. Precluded, in my quality of national guest, by motives of taste and discretion, from dealing with any question of immediate and domestic concern, it seemed to me wisest, or at any rate most prudent, to choose a topic of comparatively abstract interest, and to ask your indulgence for a few somewhat generalized remarks on a matter concerning which I had some experimental knowledge, derived from the use of such eyes and ears as Nature had been pleased to endow me withal, and such report as I had been able to win from them. The subject which most readily suggested itself was the spirit and the work-   20 ing of those conceptions of life and polity which are lumped together, whether for reproach or commendation, under the name of Democracy. By temperament and education of a conservative turn, I saw the last years of that quaint Arcadia which French travellers saw with delighted amazement a century ago, and have watched the change (to me a sad one) from an agricultural to a proletary population. The testimony of Balaam should carry some conviction. I have grown to manhood and am now growing old with the growth of this system of government in my native land; have watched its advances, or what some would call its encroachments, gradual and irresistible as those of a glacier; have been an ear-witness to the forebodings of wise and good and timid men, and have lived to see those forebodings belied by   30 the course of events, which is apt to show itself humorously careless of the reputation of prophets. I recollect hearing a sagacious old gentleman say in 1840 that the doing away with the property qualification for suffrage twenty years before had been the ruin of the State of Massachusetts; that it had put public credit and private estate alike at the mercy of demagogues. I lived to see that Commonwealth twenty odd years later paying the interest on her bonds in gold, though it cost her sometimes nearly three for one to keep her faith, and that while suffering an unparalleled drain of men and treasure in helping to sustain the unity and self-respect of the nation.

If universal suffrage has worked ill in our larger cities, as it certainly has, this has   40

---

19 **to endow . . . withal,** an example of the kind of Shakespearian archaism Lowell often used   23 **Arcadia,** a Greek mountain region legend had endowed with great charm. French authors such as Chateaubriand (1768-1843) wrote lyrically about life in the United States   25 **proletary,** wage-earning   26 **Balaam.** See Numbers 23:8   33 **property . . . suffrage,** abolished in Massachusetts in 1820

been mainly because the hands that wielded it were untrained to its use. There the election of a majority of the trustees of the public money is controlled by the most ignorant and vicious of a population which has come to us from abroad, wholly unpracticed in self-government and incapable of assimilation by American habits and methods. But the finances of our towns, where the native tradition is still dominant and whose affairs are discussed and settled in a public assembly of the people, have been in general honestly and prudently administered. Even in manufacturing towns, where a majority of the voters live by their daily wages, it is not so often the recklessness as the moderation of public expenditure that surprises an old-
10 fashioned observer. "The beggar is in the saddle at last," cries Proverbial Wisdom. "Why, in the name of all former experience, doesn't he ride to the Devil?" Because in the very act of mounting he ceased to be a beggar and became part owner of the piece of property he bestrides. The last thing we need be anxious about is property. It always has friends or the means of making them. If riches have wings to fly away from their owner, they have wings also to escape danger.

I hear America sometimes playfully accused of sending you all your storms, and am in the habit of parrying the charge by alleging that we are enabled to do this because, in virtue of our protective system, we can afford to make better bad weather than anybody else. And what wiser use could we make of it than to export it in
20 return for the paupers which some European countries are good enough to send over to us who have not attained to the same skill in the manufacture of them? But bad weather is not the worst thing that is laid at our door. A French gentleman, not long ago, forgetting Burke's monition of how unwise it is to draw an indictment against a whole people, has charged us with the responsibility of whatever he finds disagreeable in the morals or manners of his countrymen. If M. Zola or some other competent witness would only go into the box and tell us what those morals and manners were before our example corrupted them! But I confess that I find little to interest and less to edify me in these international bandyings of "You're another."

I shall address myself to a single point only in the long list of offences of which
30 we are more or less gravely accused, because that really includes all the rest. It is that we are infecting the Old World with what seems to be thought the entirely new disease of Democracy. It is generally people who are in what are called easy circumstances who can afford the leisure to treat themselves to a handsome complaint, and these experience an immediate alleviation when once they have found a sonorous Greek name to abuse it by. There is something consolatory also, something flattering to their sense of personal dignity, and to that conceit of singularity which is the natural recoil from our uneasy consciousness of being commonplace, in thinking ourselves victims of a malady by which no one had ever suffered before. Accordingly they find it simpler to class under one comprehensive heading
40 whatever they find offensive to their nerves, their tastes, their interests, or what they

---

23 **Burke's monition.** In his "Speech on Conciliation" in 1775 Burke said: "I do not know the method of drawing up an indictment against a whole people."   25 **M. Zola,** Émile Zola (1840-1902), French naturalistic novelist. He attributed some of the excesses of the French Revolution to the bad example of the Americans. Lowell did not think Zola much of an authority on morals

suppose to be their opinions, and christen it Democracy, much as physicians label every obscure disease gout, or as cross-grained fellows lay their ill-temper to the weather. But is it really a new ailment, and, if it be, is America answerable for it? Even if she were, would it account for the phylloxera, and hoof-and-mouth disease, and bad harvests, and bad English, and the German bands, and the Boers, and all the other discomforts with which these later days have vexed the souls of them that go in chariots? Yet I have seen the evil example of Democracy in America cited as the source and origin of things quite as heterogeneous and quite as little connected with it by any sequence of cause and effect. Surely this ferment is nothing new. It has been at work for centuries, and we are more conscious of it only because in this 10 age of publicity, where the newspapers offer a rostrum to whoever has a grievance, or fancies that he has, the bubbles and scum thrown up by it are more noticeable on the surface than in those dumb ages when there was a cover of silence and suppression on the cauldron. Bernardo Navagero, speaking of the Provinces of Lower Austria in 1546, tells us that "in them there are five sorts of persons, Clergy, Barons, Nobles, Burghers, and Peasants. Of these last no account is made, *because they have no voice in the Diet.*"

Nor was it among the people that subversive or mistaken doctrines had their rise. A Father of the Church said that property was theft many centuries before Proudhon was born. Bourdaloue reaffirmed it. Montesquieu was the inventor of national 20 workshops, and of the theory that the State owed every man a living. Nay, was not the Church herself the first organized Democracy? A few centuries ago the chief end of man was to keep his soul alive, and then the little kernel of leaven that sets the gases at work was religious, and produced the Reformation. Even in that, farsighted persons like the Emperor Charles V. saw the germ of political and social revolution. Now that the chief end of man seems to have become the keeping of the body alive, and as comfortably alive as possible, the leaven also has become wholly political and social. But there had also been social upheavals before the Reformation and contemporaneously with it, especially among men of Teutonic race. The Reformation gave outlet and direction to an unrest already existing. For- 30 merly the immense majority of men — our brothers — knew only their sufferings, their wants, and their desires. They are beginning now to know their opportunity and their power. All persons who see deeper than their plates are rather inclined to thank God for it than to bewail it, for the sores of Lazarus have a poison in them against which Dives has no antidote.

There can be no doubt that the spectacle of a great and prosperous Democracy on the other side of the Atlantic must react powerfully on the aspirations and

---

4 **phylloxera,** plant lice that destroy grape vines   5 **Boers.** In 1877 England had annexed the Boer Transvaal in South Africa; the Boers rebelled and in 1881 England recognized their independence   6 **them . . . chariots,** national leaders   14 **Bernardo Navagero** (1507-1565), Italian diplomat and cardinal. Lowell cites the passage in a footnote   19 **Father . . . Church,** St. Ambrose (340-397), bishop of Milan   19 **Proudhon,** Pierre Joseph Proudhon (1809-1865), a French revolutionary socialist   20 **Bourdaloue,** Louis Bourdaloue (1632-1704), a French Jesuit preacher   20 **Montesquieu.** See note, p. 332   25 **Emperor Charles V** (1500-1558) of Spain in 1521 held the Diet of Worms at which Luther stated his position on religion   34 **Lazarus . . . Dives.** See Luke 16: 19-25

political theories of men in the Old World who do not find things to their mind;
but, whether for good or evil, it should not be overlooked that the acorn from which
it sprang was ripened on the British oak. Every successive swarm that has gone out
from this *officina gentium* has, when left to its own instincts — may I not call them
hereditary instincts? — assumed a more or less thoroughly democratic form. This
would seem to show, what I believe to be the fact, that the British Constitution,
under whatever disguises of prudence or decorum, is essentially democratic. England,
indeed, may be called a monarchy with democratic tendencies, the United States a
democracy with conservative instincts. People are continually saying that America is
10 in the air, and I am glad to think it is, since this means only that a clearer conception of human claims and human duties is beginning to be prevalent. The discontent
with the existing order of things, however, pervaded the atmosphere wherever the
conditions were favorable, long before Columbus, seeking the back door of Asia,
found himself knocking at the front door of America. I say wherever the conditions
were favorable, for it is certain that the germs of disease do not stick or find a prosperous field for their development and noxious activity unless where the simplest
sanitary precautions have been neglected. "For this effect defective comes by cause,"
as Polonius said long ago. It is only by instigation of the wrongs of men that what
are called the Rights of Man become turbulent and dangerous. It is then only that
20 they syllogize unwelcome truths. It is not the insurrections of ignorance that are
dangerous, but the revolts of intelligence: —

> The wicked and the weak rebel in vain,
> Slaves by their own compulsion.

Had the governing classes in France during the last century paid as much heed to
their proper business as to their pleasures or manners, the guillotine need never
have severed that spinal-marrow of orderly and secular tradition through which in
a normally constituted state the brain sympathizes with the extremities and sends
will and impulsion thither. It is only when the reasonable and practicable are denied that men demand the unreasonable and impracticable; only when the possible
30 is made difficult that they fancy the impossible to be easy. Fairy tales are made out
of the dreams of the poor. No; the sentiment which lies at the root of democracy
is nothing new. I am speaking always of a sentiment, a spirit, and not of a form
of government; for this was but the outgrowth of the other and not its cause. This
sentiment is merely an expression of the natural wish of people to have a hand, if
need be a controlling hand, in the management of their own affairs. What is new
is that they are more and more gaining that control, and learning more and more
how to be worthy of it. What we used to call the tendency or drift — what we are
being taught to call more wisely the evolution of things — has for some time been

---

4 **officina gentium,** manufactor of nations   18 **Polonius.** Hamlet, Act II, Scene 2, 1. 103   19 **The
Rights of Man,** an important discussion of the French Revolution by Thomas Paine, written in 1791   22
The wicked . . . compulsion. Lowell misquotes from Coleridge's *France: An Ode* (1798); the first line
reads "The Sensual and the Dark rebel in vain"

setting steadily in this direction. There is no good in arguing with the inevitable. The only argument available with an east wind is to put on your overcoat. And in this case, also, the prudent will prepare themselves to encounter what they cannot prevent. Some people advise us to put on the brakes, as if the movement of which we are conscious were that of a railway train running down an incline. But a metaphor is no argument, though it be sometimes the gunpowder to drive one home and imbed it in the memory. Our disquiet comes of what nurses and other experienced persons call growing-pains, and need not seriously alarm us. They are what every generation before us — certainly every generation since the invention of printing — has gone through with more or less good fortune. To the door of every gen-   10
eration there comes a knocking, and unless the household, like the Thane of Cawdor and his wife, have been doing some deed without a name, they need not shudder. It turns out at worst to be a poor relation who wishes to come in out of the cold. The porter always grumbles and is slow to open. "Who's there, in the name of Beelzebub?" he mutters. Not a change for the better in our human housekeeping has ever taken place that wise and good men have not opposed it, — have not prophesied with the alderman that the world would wake up to find its throat cut in consequence of it. The world, on the contrary, wakes up, rubs its eyes, yawns, stretches itself, and goes about its business as if nothing had happened. Suppression of the slave trade, abolition of slavery, trade unions, — at all of these excellent peo-   20
ple shook their heads despondingly, and murmured "Ichabod." But the trade unions are now debating instead of conspiring, and we all read their discussions with comfort and hope, sure that they are learning the business of citizenship and the difficulties of practical legislation.

One of the most curious of these frenzies of exclusion was that against the emancipation of the Jews. All share in the government of the world was denied for centuries to perhaps the ablest, certainly the most tenacious, race that had ever lived in it — the race to whom we owed our religion and the purest spiritual stimulus and consolation to be found in all literature — a race in which ability seems as natural and hereditary as the curve of their noses, and whose blood, furtively mingling   30
with the bluest bloods in Europe, has quickened them with its own indomitable impulsion. We drove them into a corner, but they had their revenge, as the wronged are always sure to have it sooner or later. They made their corner the counter and bankinghouse of the world, and thence they rule it and us with the ignobler sceptre of finance. Your grandfathers mobbed Priestley only that you might set up his statue and make Birmingham the headquarters of English Unitarianism. We hear it said sometimes that this is an age of transition, as if that made matters clearer; but can any one point us to an age that was not? If he could, he would show us an age of stagnation. The question for us, as it has been for all before us, is to make

---

11 **Thane . . . wife,** Macbeth and Lady Macbeth, *Macbeth,* Act IV, Scene 1, l. 48   13 **a poor relation.** See *Macbeth,* Act II, Scene 3   17 **the world . . . cut,** a reference to a remark of a London citizen commenting on the peril of living in France during the Revolution   21 **Ichabod,** a Hebrew word meaning "the glory has departed"   35 **Priestley,** Joseph Priestley (1738-1804), English scientist who in 1791 was attacked by a Birmingham mob because of his sympathy with the French revolutionists

the transition gradual and easy, to see that our points are right so that the train may not come to grief. For we should remember that nothing is more natural for people whose education has been neglected than to spell evolution with an initial "*r*." A great man struggling with the storms of fate has been called a sublime spectacle; but surely a great man wrestling with these new forces that have come into the world, mastering them and controlling them to beneficent ends, would be a yet sublimer. Here is not a danger, and if there were it would be only a better school of manhood, a nobler scope for ambition. I have hinted that what people are afraid of in democracy is less the thing itself than what they conceive to be its necessary
10 adjuncts and consequences. It is supposed to reduce all mankind to a dead level of mediocrity in character and culture, to vulgarize men's conceptions of life, and therefore their code of morals, manners, and conduct — to endanger the rights of property and possession. But I believe that the real gravamen of the charges lies in the habit it has of making itself generally disagreeable by asking the Powers that Be at the most inconvenient moment whether they are the powers that ought to be. If the powers that be are in a condition to give a satisfactory answer to this inevitable question, they need feel in no way discomfited by it.

Few people take the trouble of trying to find out what democracy really is. Yet this would be a great help, for it is our lawless and uncertain thoughts, it is the
20 indefiniteness of our impressions, that fill darkness, whether mental or physical, with spectres and hobgoblins. Democracy is nothing more than an experiment in government, more likely to succeed in a new soil, but likely to be tried in all soils, which must stand or fall on its own merits as others have done before it. For there is no trick of perpetual motion in politics any more than in mechanics. President Lincoln defined democracy to be "the government of the people by the people for the people." This is a sufficiently compact statement of it as a political arrangement. Theodore Parker said that "Democracy meant not 'I'm as good as you are,' but 'You're as good as I am.'" And this is the ethical conception of it, necessary as a complement of the other; a conception which, could it be made actual and practical, would
30 easily solve all the riddles that the old sphinx of political and social economy who sits by the roadside has been proposing to mankind from the beginning, and which mankind have shown such a singular talent for answering wrongly. In this sense Christ was the first true democrat that ever breathed, as the old dramatist Dekker said he was the first true gentleman. The characters may be easily doubled, so strong is the likeness between them. A beautiful and profound parable of the Persian poet Jellaladeen tells us that "One knocked at the Beloved's door, and a voice asked from within 'Who is there?' and he answered 'It is I.' Then the voice said, 'This house will not hold me and thee;' and the door was not opened. Then went the lover into the desert and fasted and prayed in solitude, and after a year he returned
40 and knocked again at the door; and again the voice asked 'Who is there?' and he said 'It is thyself;' and the door was opened to him." But that is idealism, you will

---

1 **points,** English term for railway switches   26 **Theodore Parker** (1810-1860), liberal Boston Unitarian minister   33 **Dekker,** Thomas Dekker (1572?-1632?), English dramatist, had a character speak thus of Christ in *The Honest Whore* (1604)   36 **Jellaladeen,** Jalal ed-Din Rumic (1207-1273), Persian poet

say, and this is an only too practical world. I grant it; but I am one of those who believe that the real will never find an irremovable basis till it rests on the ideal. It used to be thought that a democracy was possible only in a small territory, and this is doubtless true of a democracy strictly defined, for in such all the citizens decide directly upon every question of public concern in a general assembly. An example still survives in the tiny Swiss canton of Appenzell. But this immediate intervention of the people in their own affairs is not of the essence of democracy; it is not necessary, nor indeed, in most cases, practicable. Democracies to which Mr. Lincoln's definition would fairly enough apply have existed, and now exist, in which, though the supreme authority reside in the people, yet they can act only indirectly 10 on the national policy. This generation has seen a democracy with an imperial figurehead, and in all that have ever existed the body politic has never embraced all the inhabitants included within its territory: the right to share in the direction of affairs has been confined to citizens, and citizenship has been further restricted by various limitations, sometimes of property, sometimes of nativity, and always of age and sex.

The framers of the American Constitution were far from wishing or intending to found a democracy in the strict sense of the word, though, as was inevitable, every expansion of the scheme of government they elaborated has been in a democratical direction. But this has been generally the slow result of growth, and not the sudden 20 innovation of theory; in fact, they had a profound disbelief in theory, and knew better than to commit the folly of breaking with the past. They were not seduced by the French fallacy that a new system of government could be ordered like a new suit of clothes. They would as soon have thought of ordering a new suit of flesh and skin. It is only on the roaring loom of time that the stuff is woven for such a vesture of their thought and experience as they were meditating. They recognized fully the value of tradition and habit as the great allies of permanence and stability. They all had that distaste for innovation which belonged to their race, and many of them a distrust of human nature derived from their creed. The day of sentiment was over, and no dithyrambic affirmations or fine-drawn analyses of the Rights of Man 30 would serve their present turn. This was a practical question, and they addressed themselves to it as men of knowledge and judgment should. Their problem was how to adapt English principles and precedents to the new conditions of American life, and they solved it with singular discretion. They put as many obstacles as they could contrive, not in the way of the people's will, but of their whim. With few exceptions they probably admitted the logic of the then accepted syllogism, — democracy, anarchy, despotism. But this formula was framed upon the experience of small cities shut up to stew within their narrow walls, where the number of citizens made but an inconsiderable fraction of the inhabitants, where every passion was reverberated from house to house and from man to man with gathering rumor 40 till every impulse became gregarious and therefore inconsiderate, and every popular

---

6 **Appenzell** with a total area of 162 square miles was divided into two half-cantons, one Protestant and one Catholic   11 **imperial figurehead,** Louis Napoleon (1808-1873), elected emperor of France in 1852   25 **roaring . . . time,** from Carlyle's version of *Faust* in *Sartor Resartus,* Bk. I, Ch. 8

assembly needed but an infusion of eloquent sophistry to turn it into a mob, all the more dangerous because sanctified with the formality of law.

Fortunately their case was wholly different. They were to legislate for a widely scattered population and for States already practised in the discipline of a partial independence. They had an unequalled opportunity and enormous advantages. The material they had to work upon was already democratical by instinct and habitude. It was tempered to their hands by more than a century's schooling in self-government. They had but to give permanent and conservative form to a ductile mass. In giving impulse and direction to their new institutions, especially in supplying them
10 with checks and balances, they had a great help and safeguard in their federal organization. The different, sometimes conflicting, interests and social systems of the several States made existence as a Union and coalescence into a nation conditional on a constant practice of moderation and compromise. The very elements of disintegration were the best guides in political training. Their children learned the lesson of compromise only too well, and it was the application of it to a question of fundamental morals that cost us our civil war. We learned once for all that compromise makes a good umbrella but a poor roof; that it is a temporary expedient, often wise in party politics, almost sure to be unwise in statesmanship.

Has not the trial of democracy in America proved, on the whole, successful? If it
20 had not, would the Old World be vexed with any fears of its proving contagious? This trial would have been less severe could it have been made with a people homogeneous in race, language, and traditions, whereas the United States have been called on to absorb and assimilate enormous masses of foreign population, heterogeneous in all these respects, and drawn mainly from that class which might fairly say that the world was not their friend, nor the world's law. The previous condition too often justified the traditional Irishman, who, landing in New York and asked what his politics were, inquired if there was a Government there, and on being told that there was, retorted, "Thin I'm agin it!" We have taken from Europe the poorest, the most ignorant, the most turbulent of her people, and have made them over
30 into good citizens, who have added to our wealth, and who are ready to die in defence of a country and of institutions which they know to be worth dying for. The exceptions have been (and they are lamentable exceptions) where these hordes of ignorance and poverty have coagulated in great cities. But the social system is yet to seek which has not to look the same terrible wolf in the eyes. On the other hand, at this very moment Irish peasants are buying up the worn-out farms of Massachusetts, and making them productive again by the same virtues of industry and thrift that once made them profitable to the English ancestors of the men who are deserting them. To have achieved even these prosaic results (if you choose to call them so), and that out of materials the most discordant, — I might say the most recalci-
40 trant, — argues a certain beneficent virtue in the system that could do it, and is not

---

2 **law.** "The effect of the electric telegraph in reproducing this trooping of emotion and perhaps of opinion is yet to be measured. The effect of Darwinism as a disintegrator of humanitarianism is also to be reckoned with." — Lowell   25 **world . . . law.** *Romeo and Juliet*, Act IV, Sc. 1, 1. 72

to be accounted for by mere luck. Carlyle said scornfully that America meant only roast turkey every day for everybody. He forgot that States, as Bacon said of wars, go on their bellies. As for the security of property, it should be tolerably well secured in a country where every other man hopes to be rich, even though the only property qualification be the ownership of two hands that add to the general wealth. Is it not the best security for anything to interest the largest possible number of persons in its preservation and the smallest in its division? In point of fact, far-seeing men count the increasing power of wealth and its combinations as one of the chief dangers with which the institutions of the United States are threatened in the not distant future. The right of individual property is no doubt the very corner-stone of 10 civilization as hitherto understood, but I am a little impatient of being told that property is entitled to exceptional consideration because it bears all burdens of the State. It bears those, indeed, which can most easily be borne, but poverty pays with its person the chief expenses of war, pestilence, and famine. Wealth should not forget this, for poverty is beginning to think of it now and then. Let me not be misunderstood. I see as clearly as any man possibly can, and rate as highly, the value of wealth, and of hereditary wealth, as the security of refinement, the feeder of all those arts that ennoble and beautify life, and as making a country worth living in. Many an ancestral hall here in England has been a nursery of that culture which has been of example and benefit to all. Old gold has a civilizing virtue which new 20 gold must grow old to be capable of secreting.

I should not think of coming before you to defend or to criticise any form of government. All have their virtues, all their defects, and all have illustrated one period or another in the history of the race, with signal services to humanity and culture. There is not one that could stand a cynical cross-examination by an experienced criminal lawyer, except that of a perfectly wise and perfectly good despot, such as the world has never seen, except in that white-haired king of Browning's, who

> Lived long ago
> In the morning of the world,
> When Earth was nearer Heaven than now.   30

The English race, if they did not invent government by discussion, have at least carried it nearest to perfection in practice. It seems a very safe and reasonable contrivance for occupying the attention of the country, and is certainly a better way of settling questions than by push of pike. Yet, if one should ask it why it should not rather be called government by gabble, it would have to fumble in its pocket a good while before it found the change for a convincing reply. As matters stand, too, it is beginning to be doubtful whether Parliament and Congress sit at Westminster and Washington or in the editors' rooms of the leading journals, so thoroughly is everything debated before the authorized and responsible debaters get on their legs. And what shall we say of government by a majority of voices? To a person who in the 40

---

1 **Carlyle,** *Latter Day Pamphlets,* No. 1 (1850): ". . . in spite of 'roast-goose with apple-sauce' [America] is not much. . . ."   28 **Lived . . . now,** from Browning's *Pippa Passes* (1841), third song

last century would have called himself an Impartial Observer, a numerical preponderance seems, on the whole, as clumsy a way of arriving at truth as could well be devised, but experience has apparently shown it to be a convenient arrangement for determining what may be expedient or advisable or practicable at any given moment. Truth, after all, wears a different face to everybody, and it would be too tedious to wait till all were agreed. She is said to lie at the bottom of a well, for the very reason, perhaps, that whoever looks down in search of her sees his own image at the bottom, and is persuaded not only that he has seen the goddess, but that she is far better-looking than he had imagined.

10　　The arguments against universal suffrage are equally unanswerable. "What," we exclaim, "shall Tom, Dick, and Harry have as much weight in the scale as I?" Of course, nothing could be more absurd. And yet universal suffrage has not been the instrument of greater unwisdom than contrivances of a more select description. Assemblies could be mentioned composed entirely of Masters of Arts and Doctors in Divinity which have sometimes shown traces of human passion or prejudice in their votes. Have the Serene Highnesses and Enlightened Classes carried on the business of Mankind so well, then, that there is no use in trying a less costly method? The democratic theory is that those Constitutions are likely to prove steadiest which have the broadest base, that the right to vote makes a safety-valve of every voter, and 20 that the best way of teaching a man how to vote is to give him the chance of practice. For the question is no longer the academic one, "Is it wise to give every man the ballot?" but rather the practical one, "Is it prudent to deprive whole classes of it any longer?" It may be conjectured that it is cheaper in the long run to lift men up than to hold them down, and that the ballot in their hands is less dangerous to society than a sense of wrong in their heads. At any rate this is the dilemma to which the drift of opinion has been for some time sweeping us, and in politics a dilemma is a more unmanageable thing to hold by the horns than a wolf by the ears. It is said that the right of suffrage is not valued when it is indiscriminately bestowed, and there may be some truth in this, for I have observed that what men 30 prize most is a privilege, even if it be that of chief mourner at a funeral. But is there not danger that it will be valued at more than its worth if denied, and that some illegitimate way will be sought to make up for the want of it? Men who have a voice in public affairs are at once affiliated with one or other of the great parties between which society is divided, merge their individual hopes and opinions in its safer, because more generalized, hopes and opinions, are disciplined by its tactics, and acquire, to a certain degree, the orderly qualities of an army. They no longer belong to a class, but to a body corporate. Of one thing, at least, we may be certain, that, under whatever method of helping things to go wrong man's wit can contrive, those who have the divine right to govern will be found to govern in the end, and that 40 the highest privilege to which the majority of mankind can aspire is that of being governed by those wiser than they. Universal suffrage has in the United States sometimes been made the instrument of inconsiderate changes, under the notion of reform, and this from a misconception of the true meaning of popular government. One of these has been the substitution in many of the States of popular election for official selection in the choice of judges. The same system applied to military officers was the source of much evil during our civil war, and, I believe, had to be abandoned. But it has been also true that on all great questions of national policy a reserve of prudence and discretion has been brought out at the critical moment to turn the scale in favor of a wiser decision. An appeal to the reason of the people has never been known to fail in the long run. It is, perhaps, true that, by effacing the principle of passive obedience, democracy, ill understood, has slackened the spring of that ductility to discipline which is essential to "the unity and married calm of States." But I feel assured that experience and necessity will cure this evil, as they have shown their power to cure others. And under what frame of policy 10 have evils ever been remedied till they became intolerable, and shook men out of their indolent indifference through their fears?

We are told that the inevitable result of democracy is to sap the foundations of personal independence, to weaken the principle of authority, to lessen the respect due to eminence, whether in station, virtue, or genius. If these things were so, society could not hold together. Perhaps the best forcing-house of robust individuality would be where public opinion is inclined to be most overbearing, as he must be of heroic temper who should walk along Piccadilly at the height of the season in a soft hat. As for authority, it is one of the symptoms of the time that the religious reverence for it is declining everywhere, but this is due partly to the fact that state- 20 craft is no longer looked upon as a mystery, but as a business, and partly to the decay of superstition, by which I mean the habit of respecting what we are told to respect rather than what is respectable in itself. There is more rough and tumble in the American democracy than is altogether agreeable to people of sensitive nerves and refined habits, and the people take their political duties lightly and laughingly, as is, perhaps, neither unnatural nor unbecoming in a young giant. Democracies can no more jump away from their own shadows than the rest of us can. They no doubt sometimes make mistakes and pay honor to men who do not deserve it. But they do this because they believe them worthy of it, and though it be true that the idol is the measure of the worshipper, yet the worship has in it the germ of a nobler 30 religion. But is it democracies alone that fall into these errors? I, who have seen it proposed to erect a statue to Hudson, the railway king, and have heard Louis Napoleon hailed as the saviour of society by men who certainly had no democratic associations or leanings, am not ready to think so. But democracies have likewise their finer instincts. I have also seen the wisest statesman and most pregnant speaker of our generation, a man of humble birth and ungainly manners, of little culture beyond what his own genius supplied, become more absolute in power than any monarch of modern times through the reverence of his countrymen for his honesty, his wisdom, his sincerity, his faith in God and man, and the nobly humane simplicity of his character. And I remember another whom popular respect enveloped 40

---

8 **the unity . . . States,** Shakespeare's *Troilus and Cressida,* Act 1, Sc. 3, l. 100   18 **walk . . . hat.** The proper garb was a hard, high silk hat   32 **Hudson,** George Hudson (1800-1871), an English speculator in railroads. The proposal to erect a statue to him during his lifetime was met with fierce opposition and dropped

as with a halo, the least vulgar of men, the most austerely genial, and the most independent of opinion. Wherever he went he never met a stranger, but everywhere neighbors and friends proud of him as their ornament and decoration. Institutions which could bear and breed such men as Lincoln and Emerson had surely some energy for good. No, amid all the fruitless turmoil and miscarriage of the world, if there be one thing steadfast and of favorable omen, one thing to make optimism distrust its own obscure distrust, it is the rooted instinct in men to admire what is better and more beautiful than themselves. The touchstone of political and social institutions is their ability to supply them with worthy objects of this sentiment,
10 which is the very tap-root of civilization and progress. There would seem to be no readier way of feeding it with the elements of growth and vigor than such an organization of society as will enable men to respect themselves, and so to justify them in respecting others.

Such a result is quite possible under other conditions than those of an avowedly democratical Constitution. For I take it that the real essence of democracy was fairly enough defined by the First Napoleon when he said that the French Revolution meant "la carrière ouverte aux talents" — a clear pathway for merit of whatever kind. I should be inclined to paraphrase this by calling democracy that form of society, no matter what its political classification, in which every man had a chance and knew
20 that he had it. If a man can climb, and feels himself encouraged to climb, from a coal-pit to the highest position for which he is fitted, he can well afford to be indifferent what name is given to the government under which he lives. The Bailli of Mirabeau, uncle of the more famous tribune of that name, wrote in 1771: "The English are, in my opinion, a hundred times more agitated and more unfortunate than the very Algerines themselves, because they do not know and will not know till the destruction of their over-swollen power, which I believe very near, whether they are monarchy, aristocracy, or democracy, and wish to play the part of all three." England has not been obliging enough to fulfil the Bailli's prophecy, and perhaps it was this very carelessness about the name, and concern about the substance of popular government,
30 this skill in getting the best out of things as they are, in utilizing all the motives which influence men, and in giving one direction to many impulses, that has been a principal factor of her greatness and power. Perhaps it is fortunate to have an unwritten Constitution, for men are prone to be tinkering the work of their own hands, whereas they are more willing to let time and circumstance mend or modify what time and circumstance have made. All free governments, whatever their name, are in reality governments by public opinion, and it is on the quality of this public opinion that their prosperity depends. It is, therefore, their first duty to purify the element from which they draw the breath of life. With the growth of democracy grows also the fear, if not the danger, that this atmosphere may be corrupted with
40 poisonous exhalations from lower and more malarious levels, and the question of sanitation becomes more instant and pressing. Democracy in its best sense is merely

---

22 **Bailli of Mirabeau,** Jean-Antoine-Joseph-Charles-Elzear de Riquetti (1717-1794), who with his father, uncle, and adopted son was listed as an author of memoirs published in 1834-1835. The uncle was Jean Antoine Riquetti (1666-1737), Bailli de Mirabeau. The nephew figured prominently in the French Revolution

the letting in of light and air. Lord Sherbrooke, with his usual epigrammatic terse-
ness, bids you educate your future rulers. But would this alone be a sufficient safeguard? To educate the intelligence is to enlarge the horizon of its desires and wants.
And it is well that this should be so. But the enterprise must go deeper and prepare the way for satisfying those desires and wants in so far as they are legitimate.
What is really ominous of danger to the existing order of things is not democracy
(which, properly understood, is a conservative force), but the Socialism which may
find a fulcrum in it. If we cannot equalize conditions and fortunes any more than
we can equalize the brains of men — and a very sagacious person has said that
"where two men ride on a horse one must ride behind" — we can yet, perhaps, do   10
something to correct those methods and influences that lead to enormous inequalities, and to prevent their growing more enormous. It is all very well to pooh-pooh
Mr. George and to prove him mistaken in his political economy. I do not believe
that land should be divided because the quantity of it is limited by nature. Of what
may this not be said? *A fortiori,* we might on the same principle insist on a division
of human wit, for I have observed that the quantity of this has been even more
inconveniently limited. Mr. George himself has an inequitably large share of it. But
he is right in his impelling motive; right, also, I am convinced, in insisting that
humanity makes a part, by far the most important part, of political economy; and
in thinking man to be of more concern and more convincing than the longest column   20
of figures in the world. For unless you include human nature in your addition, your
total is sure to be wrong and your deductions from it fallacious. Communism means
barbarism, but Socialism means, or wishes to mean, co-operation and community
of interests, sympathy, the giving to the hands not so large a share as to the brains,
but a larger share than hitherto in the wealth they must combine to produce —
means, in short, the practical application of Christianity to life, and has in it the
secret of an orderly and benign reconstruction. State Socialism would cut off the
very roots in personal character — self-help, forethought, and frugality — which
nourish and sustain the trunk and branches of every vigorous Commonwealth.

I do not believe in violent changes, nor do I expect them. Things in possession   30
have a very firm grip. One of the strongest cements of society is the conviction of
mankind that the state of things into which they are born is a part of the order of
the universe, as natural, let us say, as that the sun should go round the earth. It is
a conviction that they will not surrender except on compulsion, and a wise society
should look to it that this compulsion be not put upon them. For the individual
man there is no radical cure, outside of human nature itself, for the evils to which
human nature is heir. The rule will always hold good that you must

Be your own palace or the world's your gaol.

1 **Lord Sherbrooke,** Robert Lowe, Viscount Sherbrooke (1811-1892), an English statesman   13 **Mr.**
George, Henry George (1839-1897), American advocate of tax reform who urged a single tax on real estate
in *The Land Question* (1883)   15 **A fortiori,** with stronger reasoning   38 **Be . . . gaol.** John Donne
(1517?-1631), English poet has in "Verse Letter to Sir Henry Wotton," "Be thine own palace, or the world's
thy jail"

But for artificial evils, for evils that spring from want of thought, thought must find a remedy somewhere. There has been no period of time in which wealth has been more sensible of its duties than now. It builds hospitals, it establishes missions among the poor, it endows schools. It is one of the advantages of accumulated wealth, and of the leisure it renders possible, that people have time to think of the wants and sorrows of their fellows. But all these remedies are partial and palliative merely. It is as if we should apply plasters to a single pustule of the small-pox with a view of driving out the disease. The true way is to discover and to extirpate the germs. As society is now constituted these are in the air it breathes, in the water it drinks, in things that seem, and which it has always believed, to be the most inno-cent and healthful. The evil elements it neglects corrupt these in their springs and pollute them in their courses. Let us be of good cheer, however, remembering that the misfortunes hardest to bear are those which never come. The world has out-lived much, and will outlive a great deal more, and men have contrived to be happy in it. It has shown the strength of its constitution in nothing more than in surviv-ing the quack medicines it has tried. In the scales of the destinies brawn will never weigh so much as brain. Our healing is not in the storm or in the whirlwind, it is not in monarchies, or aristocracies, or democracies, but will be revealed by the still small voice that speaks to the conscience and the heart, prompting us to a wider and wiser humanity.

1884, 1887

1807—1892 John Greenleaf Whittier

The Massachusetts farm house in which John Greenleaf Whittier was born on December 17, 1807, had been built of hand-hewn logs by his great-great grandfather more than a hundred years earlier. Whittier's birthplace was a fitting one, for this descendant of farm folk, himself a farmer and briefly a cobbler, remained a country man throughout his life, and his writings never lost a rough-hewn rural quality.

Pious but poor Quakers, the family and their son lived frugal lives and did more

than their fair share of harsh toil. Between farming chores the boy went to country schools and read and reread the few books in his home. As literary influences,
Quaker books urged devout thought combined with simplicity and directness of
style, and a well-thumbed Bible which met these demands became a model. In his
fifteenth year young Whittier encountered the poetry of Robert Burns. The Scottish poet was a kindred spirit who had lived as Whittier was living: he had worked
so hard on a farm as to ruin his health; he had been forced to content himself with
a sketchy education; he had found congenial poetic matter in the picturing of nature
and farm life, the recounting of country lore and the denunciation of hypocrisy and
intolerance. Burns', said Whittier, was "about the first poetry I had ever [heard], —
with the exception of the Bible . . . and it had a lasting influence on me." In addition, the words he used and his way of pronouncing them derived from Yankee
speech.

   The Whittiers subscribed to the Newburyport (Mass.) *Free Press,* edited by William Lloyd Garrison, who was destined to become a famous abolitionist leader. In
1826 Garrison accepted and printed Whittier's first published poems and urged the
youth to continue his education at nearby Haverhill Academy. After two years in
Haverhill, Whittier became a journalist, editing several newspapers and contributing
to others. In 1833, following additional urgings by Garrison, he became active in
the abolitionist movement, participating in politics, serving for a time in the state
legislature, appearing as a speaker, writing pamphlets and poems against slavery. In
1836 he moved to Amesbury, where he lived until his death.

   During the prewar years he not only published antislavery poems but also worked
for several abolitionist periodicals. Even his schoolboy poems had been widely
copied in newspapers: his poems against slavery were even more generally read, and
in 1837 he announced their inclusion in a book titled *Poems Written during the Progress of the Abolition Question.* Although abolition was the chief reform in which he
was interested, he advocated other reforms too in collections such as *Lays of My
Home* (1843), *Voices of Freedom* (1846), *Songs of Labor and Other Poems* (1850), and
In War Time and Other Poems (1863).

   Whittier's first book had been *Legends of New England* (1831), containing seven
prose sketches which dealt with romantic lore of his region. In 1848, he had reconstructed the lives of Quakers in colonial times in *Leaves from Margaret Smith's Journal.* During the 1850's and 1860's, he turned with increasing frequency to history,
country lore, and reminiscences. For *The Atlantic Monthly,* founded in 1857, he wrote
highly admired local color pieces such as "Skipper Ireson's Ride" (1857) and "Telling the Bees" (1858). His best poem, *Snow-Bound* (1867) was also his most widely
admired and remunerative one, bringing him $10,000 in royalties. Other postwar
books included *The Tent on the Beach and Other Poems* (1867), *Among the Hills and
Other Poems* (1869), *Ballads of New England* (1870) and *At Sundown* (1892 — the
year of his death).

The Writings of John Greenleaf Whittier, 7 vols., Boston, 1888-89   John B. Pickard, John Greenleaf
Whittier: An Introduction and Interpretation. New York, 1961   Lewis Leary, John Greenleaf Whittier. New York, 1961

Massachusetts to Virginia

Whittier printed the following explanatory note with a later edition of the poem: "Written on reading an account of the proceedings of the citizens of Norfolk, Virginia, in reference to George Latimer, the alleged fugitive slave, who was seized in Boston without warrant at the request of James B. Grey, of Norfolk, claiming to be his master. The case caused great excitement North and South, and led to the presentation of a petition to Congress, signed by more than fifty thousand citizens of Massachusetts, calling for such laws and proposed amendments to the Constitution as should relieve the Commonwealth from all further participation in the crime of oppression. George Latimer himself was finally given free papers for the sum of four hundred dollars."

"Massachusetts to Virginia" is one of the most stirring of Whittier's poems against slavery. The use of place names, rich in association, is particularly effective.

The blast from Freedom's Northern hills, upon its Southern way,
Bears greeting to Virginia from Massachusetts Bay;
No word of haughty challenging, nor battle bugle's peal,
Nor steady tread of marching files, nor clang of horsemen's steel.

No trains of deep-mouthed cannon along our highways go;
Around our silent arsenals untrodden lies the snow;
And to the land-breeze of our ports, upon their errands far,
A thousand sails of commerce swell, but none are spread for war.

We hear thy threats, Virginia! thy stormy words and high
Swell harshly on the Southern winds which melt along our sky;   10
Yet, not one brown, hard hand foregoes its honest labor here,
No hewer of our mountain oaks suspends his axe in fear.

Wild are the waves which lash the reefs along St. George's bank;
Cold on the shores of Labrador the fog lies white and dank;
Through storm, and wave, and blinding mist, stout are the hearts which man
The fishing-smacks of Marblehead, the sea-boats of Cape Ann.

The cold north light and wintry sun glare on their icy forms,
Bent grimly o'er their straining lines or wrestling with the storms;
Free as the winds they drive before, rough as the waves they roam,
They laugh to scorn the slaver's threat against their rocky home.   20

What means the Old Dominion? Hath she forgot the day
When o'er her conquered valleys swept the Briton's steel array?

---

13 **St. George's bank,** off Newfoundland   16 **Marblehead . . . Cape Ann,** on the Massachusetts coast

How side by side, with sons of hers, the Massachusetts men
Encountered Tarleton's charge of fire, and stout Cornwallis, then?

Forgets she how the Bay State, in answer to the call
Of her old House of Burgesses, spoke out from Faneuil Hall?
When, echoing back her Henry's cry, came pulsing in each breath
Of Northern winds the thrilling sounds of "Liberty or Death!"

What asks the Old Dominion? If now her sons have proved
False to their fathers' memory, false to the faith they loved;   30
If she can scoff at Freedom, and its great charter spurn,
Must we of Massachusetts from truth and duty turn?

We hunt your bondmen, flying from Slavery's hateful hell;
Our voices, at your bidding, take up the bloodhound's yell;
We gather, at your summons, above our fathers' graves,
From Freedom's holy altar-horns to tear your wretched slaves!

Thank God! not yet so vilely can Massachusetts bow;
The spirit of her early time is with her even now;
Dream not because her Pilgrim blood moves slow and calm and cool,
She thus can stoop her chainless neck, a sister's slave and tool!   40

All that a sister State should do, all that a free State may,
Heart, hand, and purse we proffer, as in our early day;
But that one dark loathsome burden ye must stagger with alone,
And reap the bitter harvest which ye yourselves have sown!

Hold, while ye may, your struggling slaves, and burden God's free air
With woman's shriek beneath the lash, and manhood's wild despair;
Cling closer to the "cleaving curse" that writes upon your plains
The blasting of Almighty wrath against a land of chains.

Still shame your gallant ancestry, the cavaliers of old,
By watching round the shambles where human flesh is sold;   50
Gloat o'er the newborn child, and count his market value, when
The maddened mother's cry of woe shall pierce the slaver's den!

---

24 **Tarleton . . . Cornwallis,** commanders of the British army in Virginia in the American Revolution
26 **Faneuil Hall,** in Boston, is famous as the scene of patriotic meetings   27 **Henry's cry,** an allusion to
Patrick Henry's "Speech in the Virginia Convention of Delegates," March 23, 1775   31 **great charter,**
translating England's Magna Charta, refers here to the Declaration of Independence   36 **altar-horns,** an
allusion to I Kings 1: 50-53, where Adonijah, fearing King Solomon, "caught hold on the horns of the altar," and was spared   44 **which . . . sown** seems less than fair in view of Massachusetts' and New
England's participation in the slave trade in colonial times   47 **cleaving curse,** a reference to Deuteronomy 13:17: "And there shall cleave nought of the cursed thing to thine hand"   50 **shambles,** strictly, a
place where butcher's meat is sold or animals are slaughtered for meat

Lower than plummet soundeth, sink the Virginia name;
Plant, if ye will, your fathers' graves with rankest weeds of shame;
Be, if ye will, the scandal of God's fair universe;
We wash our hands forever of your sin and shame and curse.

A voice from lips whereon the coal from Freedom's shrine hath been,
Thrilled, as but yesterday, the hearts of Berkshire's mountain men:
The echoes of that solemn voice are sadly lingering still
In all our sunny valleys, on every wind-swept hill.   60

And when the prowling man-thief came hunting for his prey
Beneath the very shadow of Bunker's shaft of gray,
How, through the free lips of the son, the father's warning spoke;
How, from its bonds of trade and sect, the Pilgrim city broke!

A hundred thousand right arms were lifted up on high,
A hundred thousand voices sent back their loud reply;
Through the thronged towns of Essex the startling summons rang,
And up from bench and loom and wheel her young mechanics sprang!

The voice of free, broad Middlesex, of thousands as of one,
The shaft of Bunker calling to that of Lexington;   70
From Norfolk's ancient villages, from Plymouth's rocky bound
To where Nantucket feels the arms of ocean close her round;

From rich and rural Worcester, where through the calm repose
Of cultured vales and fringing woods the gentle Nashua flows,
To where Wachuset's wintry blasts the mountain larches stir,
Swelled up to Heaven the thrilling cry of "God save Latimer!"

And sandy Barnstable rose up, wet with the salt sea spray;
And Bristol sent her answering shout down Narragansett Bay!
Along the broad Connecticut old Hampden felt the thrill,
And the cheer of Hampshire's woodmen swept down from Holyoke Hill. 80

The voice of Massachusetts! Of her free sons and daughters,
Deep calling unto deep aloud, the sound of many waters!

---

53 **Lower . . . soundeth** echoes The Tempest, Act III, Sc. iii, ll. 101-102: "I'll seek him deeper than e'er plummet sounded/And with him there lie mudded"   57 **lips . . . coal.** Compare Isaiah 6:6-7: "Then flew one of the seraphims unto me, having a live coal in his hand . . . And he laid it upon my mouth, and said, Lo, this hath touched thy lips; and thine iniquity is taken away, and thy sin purged"   58 **Berkshire . . . Essex . . . Middlesex . . . Norfolk . . . Plymouth . . . Worcester . . . Barnstable . . . Bristol . . . Hampden . . . Hampshire,** counties in Massachusetts   62 **Bunker's shaft,** the monument on Bunker Hill, near Boston   72 **Nantucket,** an island south of Cape Cod   75 **Wachuset,** a mountain near Fitchburg, Massachusetts   79 **Connecticut,** river which flows through Massachusetts   82 **Deep . . . waters.** Compare Psalms 42:7: "Deep calleth unto deep at the noise of thy waterspouts"

Against the burden of that voice what tyrant power shall stand?
No fetters in the Bay State! No slave upon her land!

Look to it well, Virginians! In calmness we have borne,
In answer to our faith and trust, your insult and your scorn;
You've spurned our kindest counsels; you've hunted for our lives;
And shaken round our hearths and homes your manacles and gyves!

We wage no war, we lift no arm, we fling no torch within
The fire-damps of the quaking mine beneath your soil of sin;   90
We leave ye with your bondmen, to wrestle, while ye can,
With the strong upward tendencies and god-like soul of man!

But for us and for our children, the vow which we have given
For freedom and humanity is registered in heaven;
No slave-hunt in our borders, — no pirate on our strand!
No fetters in the Bay State, — no slave upon our land!

                                                                      1843

_____

90 **fire-damps,** properly fire damp, a combustible gas formed by the decomposition of coal, or the explosive
mixture of this gas with air

Ichabod

"Ichabod" first appeared, May 2, 1850, in the National Era, *the organ of the "American
and Foreign Anti-Slavery Society," which was published in Washington and of which
Whittier was an editor. In his collected poems Whittier supplied the following note: "This
poem was the outcome of the surprise and grief and forecast of evil consequences which I felt
on reading the seventh of March speech of Daniel Webster in support of the 'compromise'
and the Fugitive Slave Bill. No partisan or personal enmity dictated it. On the contrary my
admiration of the splendid personality and intellectual power of the great senator was never
stronger than when I laid down his speech, and, in one of the saddest moments of my life,
penned my protest . . . in tones of stern and sorrowful rebuke."*
    *The title is taken from I Samuel 4:21: "And she named the child Ichabod, saying, the
glory is departed from Israel."*

So fallen! so lost! the light withdrawn
        Which once he wore!
The glory from his gray hairs gone
        Forevermore!

Revile him not, — the Tempter hath
        A snare for all;
And pitying tears, not scorn and wrath,
        Befit his fall!

Oh, dumb be passion's stormy rage,
    When he who might   10
Have lighted up and led his age,
    Falls back in night.

Scorn! would the angels laugh, to mark
    A bright soul driven,
Fiend-goaded, down the endless dark,
    From hope and heaven!

Let not the land once proud of him
    Insult him now,
Nor brand with deeper shame his dim,
    Dishonored brow.   20

But let its humbled sons, instead,
    From sea to lake,
A long lament, as for the dead,
    In sadness make.

Of all we loved and honored, naught
    Save power remains, —
A fallen angel's pride of thought,
    Still strong in chains.

All else is gone; from those great eyes
    The soul has fled: 30
When faith is lost, when honor dies,
    The man is dead!

Then, pay the reverence of old days
    To his dead fame;
Walk backward, with averted gaze,
    And hide the shame!

              1850

Skipper Ireson's Ride

This poem, Whittier said in a letter of 1880, twenty-three years after its publication, "was founded solely on a fragment of rhyme which I heard from one of my early schoolmasters, a native of Marblehead. I supposed the story to which it referred dated back at least a century. I knew nothing of the participators, and the narrative of the ballad was pure fancy."

The letter was addressed to Samuel Roads, Jr., who, in his History of Marblehead, *had stated that Ireson's crew, rather than the Captain, actually had been responsible for the abandonment of the vessel. Whittier was indebted to James Russell Lowell, then editor of the* Atlantic, *for the suggestion that the quoted refrain be phrased in Cape Ann dialect.*

Of all the rides since the birth of time,
Told in story or sung in rhyme, —
On Apuleius's Golden Ass,
Or one-eyed Calendar's horse of brass,
Witch astride of a human back,
Islam's prophet on Al-Borák, —
The strangest ride that ever was sped
Was Ireson's, out from Marblehead!
 Old Floyd Ireson, for his hard heart,
 Tarred and feathered and carried in a cart 10
  By the women of Marblehead!

Body of turkey, head of owl,
Wings a-droop like a rained-on fowl,
Feathered and ruffled in every part,
Skipper Ireson stood in the cart.
Scores of women, old and young,
Strong of muscle, and glib of tongue,
Pushed and pulled up the rocky lane.
Shouting and singing the shrill refrain:
 "Here's Flud Oirson, fur his horrd horrt, 20
 Torr'd an' futherr'd an' corr'd in a corrt
  By the women o' Morble'ead!"

Wrinkled scolds with hands on hips,
Girls in bloom of cheek and lips,
Wild-eyed, free-limbed, such as chase
Bacchus round some antique vase,
Brief of skirt, with ankles bare,
Loose of kerchief and loose of hair,
With conch-shells blowing and fish-horns' twang,
Over and over the Maenads sang: 30
 "Here's Flud Oirson, fur his horrd horrt,
 Torr'd an' futherr'd an' corr'd in a corrt
  By the women o' Morble'ead!"

---

3 **Apuleius's Golden Ass,** the ass into which a young man was transformed in Lucius Apuleius' Roman satire, *Metamorphoses* (155? A.D.) 4 **Calendar,** the story of "The Third Calendar" in *The Arabian Nights* 6 **Islam's . . . Al-Borák.** Mohammed, the prophet of Islam, was carried to the seventh heaven on a winged white animal called Al-Borák 26 **Bacchus,** god of wine, frequently depicted on ancient vases 30 **Maenads,** also called Bacchantes, the feminine followers of the god

Small pity for him! — He sailed away
From a leaking ship, in Chaleur Bay, —
Sailed away from a sinking wreck,
With his own town's-people on her deck!
"Lay by! lay by!" they called to him.
Back he answered, "Sink or swim!
Brag of your catch of fish again!"   40
And off he sailed through the fog and rain!
   Old Floyd Ireson, for his hard heart,
   Tarred and feathered and carried in a cart
     By the women of Marblehead!

Fathoms deep in dark Chaleur
That wreck shall lie forevermore.
Mother and sister, wife and maid,
Looked from the rocks of Marblehead
Over the moaning and rainy sea, —
Looked for the coming that might not be! 50
What did the winds and the sea-birds say
Of the cruel captain who sailed away? —
   Old Floyd Ireson, for his hard heart,
   Tarred and feathered and carried in a cart
     By the women of Marblehead!

Through the street, on either side,
Up flew windows, doors swung wide;
Sharp-tongued spinsters, old wives gray,
Treble lent the fish-horn's bray.
Sea-worn grandsires, cripple-bound,   60
Hulks of old sailors run aground,
Shook head, and fist, and hat, and cane,
And cracked with curses the hoarse refrain:
   "Here's Flud Oirson, fur his horrd horrt,
   Torr'd an' futherr'd an' corr'd in a corrt
     By the women o' Morble'ead!"

Sweetly along the Salem road
Bloom of orchard and lilac showed.
Little the wicked skipper knew
Of the fields so green and the sky so blue. 70
Riding there in his sorry trim,
Like an Indian idol glum and grim,
Scarcely he seemed the sound to hear

---

35 **Chaleur Bay,** inlet of the Gulf of St. Lawrence

Of voices shouting, far and near:
  "Here's Flud Oirson, fur his horrd horrt,
  Torr'd an' futherr'd an' corr'd in a corrt
    By the women o' Morble'ead!"

"Hear me, neighbors!" at last he cried, —
"What to me is this noisy ride?
What is the shame that clothes the skin   80
To the nameless horror that lives within?
Waking or sleeping, I see a wreck,
And hear a cry from a reeling deck!
Hate me and curse me, — I only dread
The hand of God and the face of the dead!"
  Said old Floyd Ireson, for his hard heart,
  Tarred and feathered and carried in a cart
    By the women of Marblehead!

Then the wife of the skipper lost at sea
Said, "God has touched him! —why should we?" 90
Said an old wife mourning her only son,
"Cut the rogue's tether and let him run!"
So with soft relentings and rude excuse,
Half scorn, half pity, they cut him loose,
And gave him a cloak to hide him in,
And left him alone with his shame and sin.
  Poor Floyd Ireson, for his hard heart,
  Tarred and feathered and carried in a cart
    By the women of Marblehead!

                                          1857

Telling the Bees

Samuel T. Pickard, Whittier's biographer, notes that the description at the beginning of this poem contains many details concerning the poet's own birthplace. The approach, the "gap in the old wall," "the stepping-stones," the garden and its daffodils, the red-barred gate, the poplars, the cattle-yard were all parts of the scene. But the story is wholly imaginative: Whittier's sister Mary was still living when the poem was written. The tale unfolded is of the returning lover who hears the chore-girl performing the Yankee ceremony of chanting to the bees the news of a death in the house. Only in the final lines does the lover discover that the one who has died is his beloved.

Here is the place; right over the hill
  Runs the path I took:

You can see the gap in the old wall still,
  And the stepping-stones in the shallow brook.

There is the house, with the gate red-barred,
  And the poplars tall;
And the barn's brown length, and the cattle-yard,
  And the white horns tossing above the wall.

There are the beehives ranged in the sun;
  And down by the brink   10
Of the brook are her poor flowers, weed o'errun,
  Pansy and daffodil, rose and pink.

A year has gone, as the tortoise goes,
  Heavy and slow;
And the same rose blows, and the same sun glows,
  And the same brook sings of a year ago.

There's the same sweet clover-smell in the breeze;
  And the June sun warm
Tangles his wings of fire in the trees,
  Setting, as then, over Fernside farm.   20

I mind me how with a lover's care
  From my Sunday coat
I brushed off the burrs, and smoothed my hair,
  And cooled at the brookside my brow and throat.

Since we parted, a month had passed, —
  To love, a year;
Down through the beeches I looked at last
  On the little red gate and the well-sweep near.

I can see it all now, — the slantwise rain
  Of light through the leaves,   30
The sundown's blaze on her window-pane,
  The bloom of her roses under the eaves.

Just the same as a month before, —
  The house and the trees,
The barn's brown gable, the vine by the door, —
  Nothing changed but the hives of bees.

Before them, under the garden wall,
  Forward and back,

Went drearily singing the chore-girl small,
  Draping each hive with a shred of black.   40

Trembling, I listened: the summer sun
  Had the chill of snow;
For I knew she was telling the bees of one
  Gone on the journey we all must go!

Then I said to myself, "My Mary weeps
  For the dead to-day:
Haply her blind old grandsire sleeps
  The fret and the pain of his age away."

But her dog whined low; on the doorway sill,
  With his cane to his chin,   50
The old man sat; and the chore-girl still
  Sung to the bees stealing out and in.

And the song she was singing ever since
  In my ear sounds on: —
"Stay at home, pretty bees, fly not hence!
  Mistress Mary is dead and gone!"

                                1857

Snow-Bound *A Winter Idyl*

Of this poem, Whittier wrote a friend, "It is a winter idyl — a picture of an old-fashioned farmer's fireside in winter — and if it were not mine I should call it pretty good." This memorial poem, written shortly after the death of two persons — his sister and his mother — whom the poet had loved very much, was a loving re-creation of the scenes and personalities of the poet's boyhood.

The manuscript was completed and sent to the publisher October 3, 1865, but before it reached print in 1866, the poet had made a number of careful revisions. Despite this care and his faith in the excellence of the poem, Whittier was astonished at the public reception. Because it was a poem which all could understand and because it expressed sentiments shared by many Americans, it sold widely. Whittier's first royalty check was for $10,000, and the poem continued to be popular for a number of years. It is still generally considered the best poem of its kind ever written in America.

Whittier wrote this note on the poem: "The inmates of the family at the Whittier homestead who are referred to . . . were my father, mother, my brother and two sisters, and my uncle and aunt, both unmarried. In addition, there was the district school-master, who boarded with us. The 'not unfeared, half-welcome guest' was Harriet Livermore . . . a young woman of fine natural ability, enthusiastic, eccentric, with slight control over her violent temper, which sometimes made her religious profession doubtful. . . . She early embraced the doctrine of the Second Advent, and felt it her duty to proclaim the Lord's speedy coming."

To the Memory of the Household It Describes, This Poem Is Dedicated by the Author

"As the Spirits of Darkness be stronger in the dark, so Good Spirits which be Angels of Light are augmented not only by the Divine light of the Sun, but also by our common VVood Fire: and as the Celestial Fire drives away dark spirits, so also this our Fire of VVood doth the same." —

COR. AGRIPPA, Occult Philosophy, Book I. ch. v.

"Announced by all the trumpets of the sky,
Arrives the snow; and, driving o'er the fields,
Seems nowhere to alight; the whited air
Hides hills and woods, the river and the heaven,
And veils the farm-house at the garden's end.
The sled and traveller stopped, the courier's feet
Delayed, all friends shut out, the housemates sit
Around the radiant fireplace, enclosed
In a tumultuous privacy of storm." —

EMERSON, The Snow-Storm

The sun that brief December day
Rose cheerless over hills of gray,
And, darkly circled, gave at noon
A sadder light than waning moon.
Slow tracing down the thickening sky
Its mute and ominous prophecy,
A portent seeming less than threat,
It sank from sight before it set.
A chill no coat, however stout,
Of homespun stuff could quite shut out,   10
A hard, dull bitterness of cold,
That checked, mid-vein, the circling race
Of life-blood in the sharpened face,
The coming of the snow-storm told.
The wind blew east; we heard the roar
Of Ocean on his wintry shore,
And felt the strong pulse throbbing there
Beat with low rhythm our inland air.

Meanwhile we did our nightly chores, —
Brought in the wood from out of doors,   20
Littered the stalls, and from the mows
Raked down the herd's-grass for the cows:

---

15 **wind blew east,** from the east. The home was about fifteen miles west of the ocean   22 **herd's-grass,** timothy

Heard the horse whinnying for his corn;
And, sharply clashing horn on horn,
Impatient down the stanchion rows
The cattle shake their walnut bows;
While, peering from his early perch
Upon the scaffold's pole of birch,
The cock his crested helmet bent
And down his querulous challenge sent.   30

Unwarmed by any sunset light
The gray day darkened into night,
A night made hoary with the swarm
And whirl-dance of the blinding storm,
As zigzag wavering to and fro
Crossed and recrossed the wingéd snow:
And ere the early bedtime came
The white drift piled the window-frame,
And through the glass the clothes-line posts
Looked in like tall and sheeted ghosts.   40

So all night long the storm roared on:
The morning broke without a sun;
In tiny spherule traced with lines
Of Nature's geometric signs,
In starry flake, and pellicle,
All day the hoary meteor fell;
And, when the second morning shone,
We looked upon a world unknown,
On nothing we could call our own.
Around the glistening wonder bent   50
The blue walls of the firmament,
No cloud above, no earth below, —
A universe of sky and snow!
The old familiar sights of ours
Took marvellous shapes; strange domes and towers
Rose up where sty or corn-crib stood,
Or garden-wall, or belt of wood;
A smooth white mound the brush-pile showed,
A fenceless drift what once was road;
The bridle-post an old man sat   60
With loose-flung coat and high cocked hat;
The well-curb had a Chinese roof;

---

26 **walnut bows** were fastened around the necks of the cows and affixed to the stanchions   28 **scaffold,**
barn loft

And even the long sweep, high aloof,
In its slant splendor, seemed to tell
Of Pisa's leaning miracle.

A prompt, decisive man, no breath
Our father wasted: "Boys, a path!"
Well pleased, (for when did farmer boy
Count such a summons less than joy?)
Our buskins on our feet we drew;   70
With mittened hands, and caps drawn low,
To guard our necks and ears from snow,
We cut the solid whiteness through.
And, where the drift was deepest, made
A tunnel walled and overlaid
With dazzling crystal: we had read
Of rare Aladdin's wondrous cave,
And to our own his name we gave,
With many a wish the luck were ours
To test his lamp's supernal powers.   80
We reached the barn with merry din,
And roused the prisoned brutes within.
The old horse thrust his long head out,
And grave with wonder gazed about;
The cock his lusty greeting said,
And forth his speckled harem led;
The oxen lashed their tails, and hooked,
And mild reproach of hunger looked;
The hornéd patiarch of the sheep,
Like Egypt's Amun roused from sleep,   90
Shook his sage head with gesture mute,
And emphasized with stamp of foot.

All day the gusty north-wind bore
The loosening drift its breath before;
Low circling round its southern zone,
The sun through dazzling snow-mist shone.
No church-bell lent its Christian tone
To the savage air, no social smoke
Curled over woods of snow-hung oak.
A solitude made more intense   100
By dreary-voicéd elements,
The shrieking of the mindless wind,

---

65 **Pisa's . . . miracle,** the leaning tower   77 **Aladdin's . . . cave** refers to the story in *The Arabian Nights* of Aladdin and his magic lamp   90 **Amun,** or Ammon, an Egyptian god with the head of a ram

The moaning tree-boughs swaying blind,
And on the glass the unmeaning beat
Of ghostly finger-tips of sleet.
Beyond the circle of our hearth
No welcome sound of toil or mirth
Unbound the spell, and testified
Of human life and thought outside.
We minded that the sharpest ear   110
The buried brooklet could not hear,
The music of whose liquid lip
Had been to us companionship,
And, in our lonely life, had grown
To have an almost human tone.

As night drew on, and, from the crest
Of wooded knolls that ridged the west,
The sun, a snow-blown traveller, sank
From sight beneath the smothering bank,
We piled, with care, our nightly stack   120
Of wood against the chimney-back, —
The oaken log, green, huge, and thick,
And on its top the stout back-stick;
The knotty forestick laid apart,
And filled between with curious art
The ragged brush; then, hovering near,
We watched the first red blaze appear,
Heard the sharp crackle, caught the gleam
On whitewashed wall and sagging beam,
Until the old, rude-furnished room   130
Burst, flower-like, into rosy bloom;
While radiant with a mimic flame
Outside the sparkling drift became,
And through the bare-boughed lilac-tree
Our own warm hearth seemed blazing free.
The crane and pendent trammels showed,
The Turks' heads on the andirons glowed;
While childish fancy, prompt to tell
The meaning of the miracle,
Whispered the old rhyme: *"Under the tree,*   140
When fire outdoors burns merrily,
There the witches are making tea."

The moon above the eastern wood
Shone at its full; the hill-range stood

---

137 **The Turks' heads.** The ornamented tops of the uprights resembled Turkish fezzes

Transfigured in the silver flood,
Its blown snows flashing cold and keen,
Dead white, save where some sharp ravine
Took shadow, or the sombre green
Of hemlocks turned to pitchy black
Against the whiteness at their back.   150
For such a world and such a night
Most fitting that unwarming light,
Which only seemed where'er it fell
To make the coldness visible.
Shut in from all the world without,
We sat the clean-winged hearth about,
Content to let the north-wind roar
In baffled rage at pane and door,
While the red logs before us beat
The frost-line back with tropic heat;   160
And ever, when a louder blast
Shook beam and rafter as it passed,
The merrier up its roaring draught
The great throat of the chimney laughed,
The house-dog on his paws outspread
Laid to the fire his drowsy head,
The cat's dark silhouette on the wall
A couchant tiger's seemed to fall;
And, for the winter fireside meet,
Between the andirons' straddling feet,   170
The mug of cider simmered slow,
The apples sputtered in a row,
And, close at hand, the basket stood
With nuts from brown October's wood.

What matter how the night behaved?
What matter how the north-wind raved?
Blow high, blow low, not all its snow
Could quench our hearth-fire's ruddy glow.
O Time and Change! — with hair as gray
As was my sire's that winter day,   180
How strange it seems, with so much gone
Of life and love, to still live on!
Ah, brother! only I and thou
Are left of all that circle now, —
The dear home faces whereupon

---

160 **frost-line,** the cold point at which the radiation from the fire ended   183 **brother,** Matthew Franklin
Whittier (1812-1883)

That fitful firelight paled and shone.
Henceforward, listen as we will,
The voices of that hearth are still;
Look where we may, the wide earth o'er
Those lighted faces smile no more.   190
We tread the paths their feet have worn,
   We sit beneath their orchard trees,
   We hear, like them, the hum of bees
And rustle of the bladed corn;
We turn the pages that they read,
   Their written words we linger o'er,
But in the sun they cast no shade,
No voice is heard, no sign is made,
   No step is on the conscious floor!
Yet Love will dream, and Faith will trust,   200
(Since He who knows our need is just,)
That somehow, somewhere, meet we must.
Alas for him who never sees
The stars shine through his cypress-trees!
Who, hopeless, lays his dead away,
Nor looks to see the breaking day
Across the mournful marbles play!
Who hath not learned in hours of faith
   The truth to flesh and sense unknown,
That Life is ever lord of Death,   210
   And Love can never lose its own!

We sped the time with stories old,
Wrought puzzles out, and riddles told,
Or stammered from our school-book lore
"The Chief of Gambia's golden shore."
How often since, when all the land
Was clay in Slavery's shaping hand,
As if a trumpet called, I've heard
Dame Mercy Warren's rousing word:
"Does not the voice of reason cry,   220
   Claim the first right which Nature gave
From the red scourge of bondage fly,
   Nor deign to live a burdened slave!"
Our father rode again his ride
On Memphremagog's wooded side;

---

215 **The Chief . . . shore.** This line and ll. 220-223 are from "The African Chief" by Sarah Wentworth Morton. Whittier incorrectly attributed them   224 **father,** John Whittier (1760-1830). As a young man he had made the trip which he recalls here.   225 **Memphremagog,** a lake in Canada and Vermont

Sat down again to moose and samp
In trapper's hut and Indian camp;
Lived o'er the old idyllic ease
Beneath St. François' hemlock-trees;
Again for him the moonlight shone   230
On Norman cap and bodiced zone;
Again he heard the violin play
Which led the village dance away,
And mingled in its merry whirl
The grandam and the laughing girl.
Or, nearer home, our steps he led
Where Salisbury's level marshes spread
  Mile-wide as flies the laden bee;
Where merry mowers, hale and strong,
Swept, scythe on scythe, their swaths along 240
  The low green prairies of the sea.
We shared the fishing off Boar's Head,
  And round the rocky Isles of Shoals
  The hake-broil on the drift-wood coals;
The chowder on the sand-beach made,
Dipped by the hungry, steaming hot,
With spoons of clam-shell from the pot.
We heard the tales of witchcraft old,
And dream and sign and marvel told.
To sleepy listeners as they lay   250
Stretched idly on the salted hay,
Adrift along the winding shores,
When favoring breezes deigned to blow
The square sail of the gundalow
And idle lay the useless oars.

Our mother, while she turned her wheel
Or run the new-knit stocking-heel,
Told how the Indian hordes came down
At midnight on Cocheco town,
And how her own great-uncle bore   260
His cruel scalp-mark to fourscore.
Recalling, in her fitting phrase,

226 **samp,** corn-meal mush   229 **St. Francois,** a river north of Lake Memphremagog   237 **Salisbury,** a town in northern Massachusetts near the Whittier farm   242 **Boar's Head,** a promontory on the New England coast between Salisbury and Portsmouth   243 **Isles of Shoals,** a group of islands near the Boar's Head   244 **hake,** a fish   254 **gundalow,** a large, flat-bottomed scow   256 **mother,** Abigail Hussey Whittier (1781-1857)   259 **Cocheco,** or Cochecho, a town near Dover, New Hampshire

So rich and picturesque and free,
    (The common unrhymed poetry
Of simple life and country ways,)
The story of her early days, —
She made us welcome to her home;
Old hearths grew wide to give us room;
We stole with her a frightened look
At the gray wizard's conjuring-book,   270
The fame whereof went far and wide
Through all the simple country side;
We heard the hawks at twilight play,
The boat-horn on Piscataqua,
The loon's weird laughter far away;
We fished her little trout-brook, knew
What flowers in wood and meadow grew,
What sunny hillsides autumn-brown
She climbed to shake the ripe nuts down,
Saw where in sheltered cove and bay   280
The ducks' black squadron anchored lay,
And heard the wild geese calling loud
Beneath the gray November cloud.
Then, haply, with a look more grave,
And soberer tone, some tale she gave
From painful Sewel's ancient tome,
Beloved in every Quaker home,
Of faith fire-winged by martyrdom,
Or Chalkley's Journal, old and quaint, —
Gentlest of skippers, rare sea-saint! —   290
Who, when the dreary calms prevailed,
And water-butt and bread-cask failed,
And cruel, hungry eyes pursued
His portly presence mad for food,
With dark hints muttered under breath
Of casting lots for life or death,
Offered, if Heaven withheld supplies,
To be himself the sacrifice.
Then, suddenly, as if to save

270 **conjuring-book.** Whittier's mother, the poet said, "described strange people who lived on the Piscataqua and Cocheco, among whom was Bantam the sorcerer. I have in my possession the wizard's 'conjuring book,' which he solemnly opened when consulted. It is a copy of Cornelius Agrippa's *Magic* printed in 1651." A quotation from this tome precedes this poem   274 **Piscataqua,** a new England river which runs its course chiefly in Maine and New Hampshire   286 **Sewel's . . . tome.** Willem Sewel (1650-1725) wrote the *History of the Christian People Called Quakers.* Whittier read an American edition published in Philadelphia in 1823   289 **Chalkley's Journal,** published in 1747, was by the Quaker preacher Thomas Chalkley (1675-1741)

The good man from his living grave,   300
A ripple on the water grew,
A school of porpoise flashed in view.
"Take, eat," he said, "and be content;
These fishes in my stead are sent
By Him who gave the tangled ram
To spare the child of Abraham."

Our uncle, innocent of books,
Was rich in lore of fields and brooks,
The ancient teachers never dumb
Of Nature's unhoused lyceum.   310
In moons and tides and weather wise,
He read the clouds as prophecies,
And foul or fair could well divine,
By many an occult hint and sign,
Holding the cunning-warded keys
To all the woodcraft mysteries;
Himself to Nature's heart so near
That all her voices in his ear
Of beast or bird had meanings clear,
Like Apollonius of old,   320
Who knew the tales the sparrows told,
Or Hermes who interpreted
What the sage cranes of Nilus said;
A simple, guileless, childlike man,
Content to live where life began;
Strong only on his native grounds,
The little world of sights and sounds
Whose girdle was the parish bounds,
Whereof his fondly partial pride
The common features magnified,   330
As Surrey hills to mountains grew
In White of Selborne's loving view, —
He told how teal and loon he shot,
And how the eagle's eggs he got,
The feats on pond and river done,
The prodigies of rod and gun;

---

305 **the tangled ram.** See Genesis 22:13: "And Abraham lifted up his eyes, and looked, and behold behind him a ram caught in a thicket by his horns; and Abraham went and took the ram, and offered him up for a burnt offering in the stead of his son"   307 **uncle,** Moses Whittier   320 **Apollonius,** Greek mystic of Tyana, first century A.D.   322 **Hermes,** Hermes Trismegistus, an Egyptian god to whom were attributed third-century books on medicine, ritual, and mystic subjects   332 **White,** Gilbert White (1720-1793), an English naturalist, author of the *Natural History and Antiquities of Selborne*

Till, warming with the tales he told,
Forgotten was the outside cold,
The bitter wind unheeded blew,
From ripening corn the pigeons flew,   340
The partridge drummed i' the wood, the mink
Went fishing down the river-brink.
In fields with bean or clover gay,
The woodchuck, like a hermit gray,
   Peered from the doorway of his cell;
The muskrat plied the mason's trade,
And tier by tier his mud-walls laid;
And from the shagbark overhead
   The grizzled squirrel dropped his shell.

Next, the dear aunt, whose smile of cheer   350
And voice in dreams I see and hear, —
The sweetest woman ever Fate
Perverse denied a household mate,
Who, lonely, homeless, not the less
Found peace in love's unselfishness,
And welcome wheresoe'er she went,
A calm and gracious element,
Whose presence seemed the sweet income
And womanly atmosphere of home, —
Called up her girlhood memories,   360
The huskings and the apple-bees,
The sleigh-rides and the summer sails,
Weaving through all the poor details
And homespun warp of circumstance
A golden woof-thread of romance.
For well she kept her genial mood
And simple faith of maidenhood;
Before her still a cloud-land lay,
The mirage loomed across her way;
The morning dew, that dried so soon   370
With others, glistened at her noon;
Through years of toil and soil and care,
From glossy tress to thin gray hair,
All unprofaned she held apart
The virgin fancies of the heart.
Be shame to him of woman born
Who hath for such but thought of scorn.

---

350 **aunt,** Mercy Evans Hussey, who died in 1846

There, too, our elder sister plied
Her evening task the stand beside;
A full, rich nature, free to trust,   380
Truthful and almost sternly just,
Impulsive, earnest, prompt to act,
And make her generous thought a fact,
Keeping with many a light disguise
The secret of self-sacrifice.
O heart sore-tried! thou hast the best
That Heaven itself could give thee, — rest,
Rest from all bitter thoughts and things!
   How many a poor one's blessing went
     With thee beneath the low green tent   390
Whose curtain never outward swings!
As one who held herself a part
Of all she saw, and let her heart
   Against the household bosom lean,
Upon the motley-braided mat
Our youngest and our dearest sat,
Lifting her large, sweet, asking eyes,
   Now bathed within the fadeless green
And holy peace of Paradise.
Oh, looking from some heavenly hill,   400
   Or from the shade of saintly palms,
   Or silver reach of river calms,
Do those large eyes behold me still?
With me one little year ago: —
The chill weight of the winter snow
   For months upon her grave has lain;
And now, when summer south-winds blow
   And brier and harebell bloom again,
I tread the pleasant paths we trod,
I see the violet-sprinkled sod   410
Whereon she leaned, too frail and weak
The hillside flowers she loved to seek,
Yet following me where'er I went
With dark eyes full of love's content.
The birds are glad; the brier-rose fills
The air with sweetness; all the hills
Stretch green to June's unclouded sky;
But still I wait with ear and eye
For something gone which should be nigh,

378 **elder sister,** Mary Whittier Caldwell (1806-1860)
the poet's closest companion until her death in 1864

396 **Our youngest,** Elizabeth Whittier, who was

A loss in all familiar things,   420
In flower that blooms, and bird that sings.
And yet, dear heart! remembering thee,
   Am I not richer than of old?
Safe in thy immortality,
    What change can reach the wealth I hold?
    What chance can mar the pearl and gold
Thy love hath left in trust with me?
And while in life's late afternoon,
   Where cool and long the shadows grow,
I walk to meet the night that soon   430
   Shall shape and shadow overflow,
I cannot feel that thou art far,
Since near at need the angels are;
And when the sunset gates unbar,
   Shall I not see thee waiting stand,
And, white against the evening star,
    The welcome of thy beckoning hand?

Brisk wielder of the birch and rule,
The master of the district school
Held at the fire his favored place,   440
Its warm glow lit a laughing face
Fresh-hued and fair, where scarce appeared
The uncertain prophecy of beard.
He teased the mitten-blinded cat,
Played cross-pins on my uncle's hat,
Sang songs, and told us what befalls
In classic Dartmouth's college halls.
Born the wild Northern hills among,
From whence his yeoman father wrung
By patient toil subsistence scant,   450
Not competence and yet not want,
He early gained the power to pay
His cheerful, self-reliant way;
Could doff at ease his scholar's gown
To peddle wares from town to town;
Or through the long vacation's reach
In lonely lowland districts teach,
Where all the droll experience found
At stranger hearths in boarding round,
The moonlit skater's keen delight,   460

439 **master,** George Haskell (1799-1876)   445 **cross-pins,** a game in which the object was to cause pins
lying in a hat to cross by tapping the hat

The sleigh-drive through the frosty night,
The rustic party, with its rough
Accompaniment of blind-man's-buff,
And whirling plate, and forfeits paid,
His winter task a pastime made.
Happy the snow-locked homes wherein
He tuned his merry violin,
Or played the athlete in the barn,
Or held the good dame's winding yarn,
Or mirth-provoking versions told   470
Of classic legends rare and old,
Wherein the scenes of Greece and Rome
Had all the commonplace of home,
And little seemed at best the odds
'Twixt Yankee pedlers and old gods;
Where Pindus-born Araxes took
The guise of any grist-mill brook,
And dread Olympus at his will
Became a huckleberry hill.

A careless boy that night he seemed;   480
   But at his desk he had the look
And air of one who wisely schemed,
   And hostage from the future took
   In trainèd thought and lore of book.
Large-brained, clear-eyed, —of such as he
Shall Freedom's young apostles be,
Who, following in War's bloody trail,
Shall every lingering wrong assail;
All chains from limb and spirit strike,
Uplift the black and white alike;   490
Scatter before their swift advance
The darkness and the Ignorance,
The pride, the lust, the squalid sloth,
Which nurtured Treason's monstrous growth,
Made murder pastime, and the hell
Of prison-torture possible;
The cruel lie of caste refute,
Old forms remould, and substitute
For Slavery's lash the freeman's will,
For blind routine, wise-handed skill;   500
A school-house plant on every hill,
Stretching in radiate nerve-lines thence

---

476 **Araxes,** or Arakthos, a river in Greece which originates in the Pindus mountain range

The quick wires of intelligence;
Till North and South together brought
Shall own the same electric thought,
In peace a common flag salute,
And, side by side in labor's free
And unresentful rivalry,
Harvest the fields wherein they fought.

Another guest that winter night   510
Flashed back from lustrous eyes the light.
Unmarked by time, and yet not young,
The honeyed music of her tongue
And words of meekness scarcely told
A nature passionate and bold,
Strong, self-concentred, spurning guide,
Its milder features dwarfed beside
Her unbent will's majestic pride.
She sat among us, at the best,
A not unfeared, half-welcome guest,   520
Rebuking with her cultured phrase
Our homeliness of words and ways.
A certain pard-like, treacherous grace
    Swayed the lithe limbs and dropped the lash,
    Lent the white teeth their dazzling flash;
    And under low brows, black with night,
    Rayed out at times a dangerous light;
The sharp heat-lightnings of her face
Presaging ill to him whom Fate
Condemned to share her love or hate.   530
A woman tropical, intense
In thought and act, in soul and sense,
She blended in a like degree
The vixen and the devotee,
Revealing with each freak or feint
    The temper of Petruchio's Kate,
The raptures of Siena's saint.
Her tapering hand and rounded wrist
Had facile power to form a fist;
The warm, dark languish of her eyes   540
Was never safe from wrath's surprise.
Brows saintly calm and lips devout

---

510 **Another guest,** Harriet Livermore   536 **Petruchio's Kate,** in Shakespeare's *The Taming of the Shrew,*
the violent tempered heroine, Kate, who was subdued by Petruchio   537 **Siena's saint,** St. Catherine
(1347-1380)

Knew every change of scowl and pout;
And the sweet voice had notes more high
And shrill for social battle-cry.

Since then what old cathedral town
Has missed her pilgrim staff and gown,
What convent-gate has held its lock
Against the challenge of her knock!
Through Smyrna's plague-hushed thoroughfares, 550
Up sea-set Malta's rocky stairs,
Gray olive slopes of hills that hem
Thy tombs and shrines, Jerusalem,
Or startling on her desert throne
The crazy Queen of Lebanon
With claims fantastic as her own,
Her tireless feet have held their way;
And still, unrestful, bowed, and gray,
She watches under Eastern skies,
   With hope each day renewed and fresh, 560
   The Lord's quick coming in the flesh,
Whereof she dreams and prophesies!
Where'er her troubled path may be,
   The Lord's sweet pity with her go!
The outward wayward life we see,
   The hidden springs we may not know.
Nor is it given us to discern
   What threads the fatal sisters spun,
   Through what ancestral years has run
The sorrow with the woman born, 570
What forged her cruel chain of moods,
What set her feet in solitudes,
   And held the love within her mute,
What mingled madness in the blood,
   A life-long discord and annoy,
   Water of tears with oil of joy,
And hid within the folded bud
   Perversities of flower and fruit.
It is not ours to separate
The tangled skein of will and fate, 580
To show what metes and bounds should stand
Upon the soul's debatable land,
And between choice and Providence

---

568 **fatal sisters**, the three Fates of Greek mythology who spun the thread of life, measured it, and snapped
it off

Divide the circle of events;
   But He who knows our frame is just,
Merciful and compassionate,
And full of sweet assurances
And hope for all the language is,
   That He remembereth we are dust!

At last the great logs, crumbling low,   590
Sent out a dull and duller glow,
The bull's-eye watch that hung in view
Ticking its weary circuit through,
Pointed with mutely warning sign
Its black hand to the hour of nine.
That sign the pleasant circle broke:
My uncle ceased his pipe to smoke,
Knocked from its bowl the refuse gray,
And laid it tenderly away,
Then roused himself to safely cover   600
The dull red brands with ashes over.
And while, with care, our mother laid
The work aside, her steps she stayed
One moment, seeking to express
Her grateful sense of happiness
For food and shelter, warmth and health,
And love's contentment more than wealth,
With simple wishes (not the weak,
Vain prayers which no fulfilment seek,
But such as warm the generous heart,   610
O'er-prompt to do with Heaven its part)
That none might lack, that bitter night,
For bread and clothing, warmth and light.
Within our beds awhile we heard
The wind that round the gables roared,
With now and then a ruder shock,
Which made our very bedsteads rock.
We heard the loosened clapboards tost,
The board-nails snapping in the frost;
And on us, through the unplastered wall,   620
Felt the light sifted snow-flakes fall.
But sleep stole on, as sleep will do
When hearts are light and life is new;
Faint and more faint the murmurs grew,
Till in the summer-land of dreams
They softened to the sound of streams,

Low stir of leaves, and dip of oars,
And lapsing waves on quiet shores.

Next morn we wakened with the shout
Of merry voices high and clear;   630
And saw the teamsters drawing near
To break the drifted highways out.
Down the long hillside treading slow
We saw the half-buried oxen go,
Shaking the snow from heads uptost,
Their straining nostrils white with frost.
Before our door the straggling train
Drew up, an added team to gain.
The elders threshed their hands a-cold,
    Passed, with the cider-mug, their jokes   640
    From lip to lip; the younger folks
Down the loose snow-banks, wrestling, rolled,
Then toiled again the cavalcade
    O'er windy hill, through clogged ravine,
    And woodland paths that wound between
Low drooping pine-boughs winter-weighed.
From every barn a team afoot,
At every house a new recruit,
Where, drawn by Nature's subtlest law
Haply the watchful young men saw   650
Sweet doorway pictures of the curls
And curious eyes of merry girls,
Lifting their hands in mock defence
Against the snow-ball's compliments,
And reading in each missive tost
The charm with Eden never lost.

We heard once more the sleigh-bells' sound;
    And, following where the teamsters led,
The wise old Doctor went his round,
Just pausing at our door to say,   660
In the brief autocratic way
Of one who, prompt at Duty's call,
Was free to urge her claim on all,
    That some poor neighbor sick abed
At night our mother's aid would need.
For, one in generous thought and deed,
    What mattered in the sufferer's sight
    The Quaker matron's inward light,

The Doctor's mail of Calvin's creed?
All hearts confess the saints elect   670
    Who, twain in faith, in love agree,
And melt not in an acid sect
    The Christian pearl of charity!

So days went on: a week had passed
Since the great world was heard from last.
The Almanac we studied o'er,
Read and reread our little store
Of books and pamphlets, scarce a score;
One harmless novel, mostly hid
From younger eyes, a book forbid,   680
And poetry, (or good or bad,
A single book was all we had,)
Where Ellwood's meek, drab-skirted Muse,
    A stranger to the heathen Nine,
    Sang, with a somewhat nasal whine,
The wars of David and the Jews.
At last the floundering carrier bore
The village paper to our door.
Lo! broadening outward as we read,
To warmer zones the horizon spread;   690
In panoramic length unrolled
We saw the marvels that it told.
Before us passed the painted Creeks,
    And daft McGregor on his raids
    In Costa Rica's everglades.
And up Taygetos winding slow
Rode Ypsilanti's Mainote Greeks,
A Turk's head at each saddle-bow!
Welcome to us its week-old news,
Its corner for the rustic Muse,   700
    Its monthly gauge of snow and rain,
Its record, mingling in a breath
The wedding knell and dirge of death;
Jest, anecdote, and love-lorn tale,
The latest culprit sent to jail;

---

683 **Ellwood,** Thomas Ellwood (1639-1714), English poet, who wrote *Davideis,* a pedestrian poem of King David's life   693 **Creeks,** an Indian tribe. The story probably told of their removal to an Indian reservation in 1821   694 **daft McGregor,** Sir Gregor McGregor, who in the 1820's tried to establish a colony in Costa Rica   696 **Taygetos . . . Greeks.** Taygetos is a Greek mountain near Maina, a district noted for its robbers and pirates. During the Greek struggle for independence from Turkey (1821-1833), the Greek General Ypsilanti sent a force of these mountaineers up Mount Taygetos against the Turks

Its hue and cry of stolen and lost,
Its vendue sales and goods at cost,
　　And traffic calling loud for gain.
We felt the stir of hall and street,
The pulse of life that round us beat;　　　710
The chill embargo of the snow
Was melted in the genial glow;
Wide swung again our ice-locked door,
And all the world was ours once more!

Clasp, Angel of the backward look
　　And folded wings of ashen gray
　　And voice of echoes far away,
The brazen covers of thy book;
The weird palimpsest old and vast,
Wherein thou hid'st the spectral past;　　　720
Where, closely mingling, pale and glow
The characters of joy and woe;
The monographs of outlived years,
Or smile-illumed or dim with tears,
　　Green hills of life that slope to death,
And haunts of home, whose vistaed trees
Shade off to mournful cypresses
　　With the white amaranths underneath.
Even while I look, I can but heed
　　The restless sands' incessant fall,　　　730
Importunate hours that hours succeed,
Each clamorous with its own sharp need,
　　And duty keeping pace with all.
Shut down and clasp the heavy lids;
I hear again the voice that bids
The dreamer leave his dream midway
For larger hopes and graver fears:
Life greatens in these later years,
The century's aloe flowers to-day!

Yet, haply, in some lull of life,　　　740
Some Truce of God which breaks its strife,
The worldling's eyes shall gather dew,
　　Dreaming in throngful city ways
Of winter joys his boyhood knew;

---

707 **vendue.** See note, p. 963　　727 **cypresses.** See note, p. 850　　728 **amaranths,** a flower associated
with immortality　　739 **century's aloe.** The century plant is reputed to bloom only once every hundred
years

And dear and early friends — the few
Who yet remain — shall pause to view
   These Flemish pictures of old days;
Sit with me by the homestead hearth,
And stretch the hands of memory forth
   To warm them at the wood-fire's blaze! 750
And thanks untraced to lips unknown
Shall greet me like the odors blown
From unseen meadows newly mown,
Or lilies floating in some pond,
Wood-fringed, the wayside gaze beyond;
The traveller owns the grateful sense
Of sweetness near, he knows not whence,
And, pausing, takes with forehead bare
The benediction of the air.

                                        1866

---

747 **Flemish pictures.** The Flemish School (the Van Eycks, Rubens, Van Dyck, and others) was noted for its detailed depiction of domestic scenes

Prelude to Among the Hills

*In its first form, entitled "The Wife: an Idyl of Bearcamp Water," the poem "*Among the Hills*" appeared in the* Atlantic, *January 1868. Before the volume* Among the Hills and Other Poems *appeared in December of the same year, Whittier made numerous changes. Says Pickard: "The inspiration . . . came to him in the summer of 1867. It is a tender and romantic love-story in verse, idealizing New England farm life; with a prelude which furnishes the darker shades needed to make the picture a faithful reproduction of the rural scenes he intended to portray. . . . In its original form there were sixty-four lines in the Prelude, and it did not deal with the prosaic and disagreeable side of farm life, as does the Prelude in its present form, which consists of one hundred and fifty-six lines. . . . The whole tenor of the Prelude is changed, so as to make it a new poem. . . . The ballad proper enlarges upon the sweet story originally told, making three hundred and forty-four lines instead of one hundred and sixty-eight, as at first."*

Although modern readers may find the poem itself rather too sweet for their taste, the Prelude, which is here printed separately, is clearly a forerunner of modern poems and stories which emphasize the drabness and the flinty quality of life on New England farms.

Along the roadside, like the flowers of gold
That tawny Incas for their gardens wrought,
Heavy with sunshine droops the golden-rod,
And the red pennons of the cardinal-flowers
Hang motionless upon their upright staves.
The sky is hot and hazy, and the wind,

---

2 **tawny Incas,** a Peruvian tribe of Indians noted for their handiwork in gold

Wing-weary with its long flight from the south,
Unfelt; yet, closely scanned, yon maple leaf
With faintest motion, as one stirs in dreams,
Confesses it. The locust by the wall   10
Stabs the noon-silence with his sharp alarm.
A single hay-cart down the dusty road
Creaks slowly, with its driver fast asleep
On the load's top. Against the neighboring hill,
Huddled along the stone wall's shady side,
The sheep show white, as if a snowdrift still
Defied the dog-star. Through the open door
A drowsy smell of flowers — gray heliotrope,
And white sweet clover, and shy mignonette —
Comes faintly in, and silent chorus lends   20
To the pervading symphony of peace.

No time is this for hands long overworn
To task their strength: and (unto Him be praise
Who giveth quietness!) the stress and strain
Of years that did the work of centuries
Have ceased, and we can draw our breath once more
Freely and full. So, as yon harvesters
Make glad their nooning underneath the elms
With tale and riddle and old snatch of song,
I lay aside grave themes, and idly turn   30
The leaves of memory's sketch-book, dreaming o'er
Old summer pictures of the quiet hills,
And human life, as quiet, at their feet.

And yet not idly all. A farmer's son,
Proud of field-lore and harvest craft, and feeling
All their fine possibilities, how rich
And restful even poverty and toil
Become when beauty, harmony, and love
Sit at their humble hearth as angels sat
At evening in the patriarch's tent, when man   40
Makes labor noble, and his farmer's frock
The symbol of a Christian chivalry
Tender and just and generous to her
Who clothes with grace all duty; still, I know
Too well the picture has another side, —
How wearily the grind of toil goes on
Where love is wanting, how the eye and ear

39 **angels . . . tent,** probably a reference to Genesis 18

And heart are starved amidst the plenitude
Of nature, and how hard and colorless
Is life without an atmosphere. I look   50
Across the lapse of half a century,
And call to mind old homesteads, where no flower
Told that the spring had come, but evil weeds,
Nightshade and rough-leaved burdock in the place
Of the sweet doorway greeting of the rose
And honeysuckle, where the house walls seemed
Blistering in sun, without a tree or vine
To cast the tremulous shadow of its leaves
Across the curtainless windows from whose panes
Fluttered the signal rags of shiftlessness;   60
Within, the cluttered kitchen-floor, unwashed
(Broom-clean I think they called it); the best room
Stifling with cellar damp, shut from the air
In hot midsummer, bookless, pictureless
Save the inevitable sampler hung
Over the fireplace, or a mourning piece,
A green-haired woman, peony-cheeked, beneath
Impossible willows; the wide-throated hearth
Bristling with faded pine-boughs half concealing
The piled-up rubbish at the chimney's back;   70
And, in sad keeping with all things about them,
Shrill, querulous women, sour and sullen men,
Untidy, loveless, old before their time,
With scarce a human interest save their own
Monotonous round of small economies,
Or the poor scandal of the neighborhood;
Blind to the beauty everywhere revealed,
Treading the May-flowers with regardless feet;
For them the song-sparrow and the bobolink
Sang not, nor winds made music in the leaves;   80
For them in vain October's holocaust
Burned, gold and crimson, over all the hills,
The sacramental mystery of the woods.
Church-goers, fearful of the unseen Powers,
But grumbling over pulpit-tax and pew-rent,
Saving, as shrewd economists, their souls
And winter pork with the least possible outlay
Of salt and sanctity; in daily life
Showing as little actual comprehension
Of Christian charity and love and duty,   90

_____

66 **mourning piece,** a drawing, frequently with verse, commemorating a death

As if the Sermon on the Mount had been
Out dated like a last year's almanac:
Rich in broad woodlands and in half-tilled fields,
And yet so pinched and bare and comfortless,
The veriest straggler limping on his rounds,
The sun and air his sole inheritance,
Laughed at a poverty that paid its taxes,
And hugged his rags in self-complacency!

Not such should be the homesteads of a land
Where whoso wisely wills and acts may dwell   100
As king and lawgiver, in broad-acred state,
With beauty, art, taste, culture, books, to make
His hours of leisure richer than a life
Of fourscore to the barons of old time,
Our yeoman should be equal to his home
Set in the fair, green valleys, purple walled,
A man to match his mountains, not to creep
Dwarfed and abased below them. I would fain
In this light way (of which I needs must own
With the knife-grinder of whom Canning sings,   110
"Story, God bless you! I have none to tell you!")
Invite the eye to see and the heart to feel
The beauty and the joy within their reach, —
Home, and home loves, and the beatitudes
Of nature free to all. Haply in years
That wait to take the places of our own,
Heard where some breezy balcony looks down
On happy homes, or where the lake in the moon
Sleeps dreaming of the mountains, fair as Ruth,
In the old Hebrew pastoral, at the feet   120
Of Boaz, even this simple lay of mine
May seem the burden of a prophecy,
Finding its late fulfillment in a change
Slow as the oak's growth lifting manhood up
Through broader culture, finer manners, love,
And reverence, to the level of the hills.
O Golden Age, whose light is of the dawn,
And not of sunset, forward, not behind,
Flood the new heavens and earth, and with thee bring
All the old virtues, whatsoever things   130

---

110 **knife-grinder . . . sings**, in "The Friend of Humanity and the Knife-Grinder," a parody written by
George Canning (1770-1827), a British statesman   118 **lake . . . moon.** In Whittier's day, the dark patches
on the moon were thought to be bodies of water   119 **Ruth . . . Boaz.** Ruth 3

Are pure and honest and of good repute,
But add thereto whatever bard has sung
Or seer has told of when in trance and dream
They saw the Happy Isles of prophecy!
Let Justice hold her scale, and Truth divide
Between the right and wrong; but give the heart
The freedom of its fair inheritance;
Let the poor prisoner, cramped and starved so long,
At Nature's table feast his ear and eye
With joy and wonder; let all harmonies   140
Of sound, form, color, motion, wait upon
The princely guest, whether in soft attire
Of leisure clad, or the coarse frock of toil,
And, lending life to the dead form of faith,
Give human nature reverence for the sake
Of One who bore it, making it divine
With the ineffable tenderness of God;
Let common need, the brotherhood of prayer,
The heirship of an unknown destiny,
The unsolved mystery round about us, make   150
A man more precious than the gold of Ophir.
Sacred, inviolate, unto whom all things
Should minister, as outward types and signs
Of the eternal beauty which fulfils
The one great purpose of creation, Love,
The sole necessity of Earth and Heaven!
                                                                    1868

---

151 **Ophir,** a region mentioned in the Old Testament as a source of gold and jewels, I Kings 9:28

The Meeting

The first printed version of this poem appeared in the Atlantic Monthly, *February 1868.
When the poem, as it is here printed, was prepared for publication in the book* Among the
Hills *(1868), Whittier inserted a number of lines. Says Whitman Bennett: "The man who
seriously wishes to understand Whittier's philosophic attachment to Quakerism should read,
line by line, 'The Meeting' . . . and get the information at the source."*

The elder folks shook hands at last,
Down seat by seat the signal passed.
To simple ways like ours unused,
Half solemnized and half amused,
With long-drawn breath and shrug, my guest

His sense of glad relief expressed.
Outside the hills lay warm in sun;
The cattle in the meadow-run
Stood half-leg deep; a single bird
The green repose above us stirred.   10
"What part or lot have you," he said,
"In these dull rites of drowsy-head?
Is silence worship? Seek it where
It soothes with dreams the summer air,
Not in this close and rude-benched hall,
But where soft lights and shadows fall,
And all the slow, sleep-walking hours
Glide soundless over grass and flowers!
From time and place and form apart,
Its holy ground the human heart,   20
Nor ritual-bound nor templeward
Walks the free spirit of the Lord!
Our common Master did not pen
His followers up from other men;
His service liberty indeed,
He built no church, he framed no creed;
But while the saintly Pharisee
Made broader his phylactery,
As from the synagogue was seen
The dusty-sandalled Nazarene   30
Through ripening cornfields lead the way
Upon the awful Sabbath day.
His sermons were the healthful talk
That shorter made the mountain-walk,
His wayside texts were flowers and birds,
Where mingled with His gracious words
The rustle of the tamarisk-tree
And ripple-wash of Galilee."

"Thy words are well, O friend," I said;
"Unmeasured and unlimited,   40
With noiseless slide of stone to stone,
The mystic Church of God has grown.
Invisible and silent stands
The temple never made with hands,
Unheard the voices still and small
Of its unseen confessional.
He needs no special place of prayer
Whose hearing ear is everywhere;

He brings not back the childish days
That ringed the earth with stones of praise, 50
Roofed Karnak's hall of gods, and laid
The plinths of Philae's colonnade.
Still less He owns the selfish good
And sickly growth of solitude, —
The worthless grace that, out of sight,
Flowers in the desert anchorite;
Dissevered from the suffering whole,
Love hath no power to save a soul.
Not out of Self, the origin
And native air and soil of sin,   60
The living waters spring and flow,
The trees with leaves of healing grow.

"Dream not, O friend, because I seek
This quiet shelter twice a week,
I better deem its pine-laid floor
Than breezy hill or sea-sung shore;
But nature is not solitude:
She crowds us with her thronging wood;
Her many hands reach out to us,
Her many tongues are garrulous;   70
Perpetual riddles of surprise
She offers to our ears and eyes;
She will not leave our senses still,
But drags them captive at her will:
And, making earth too great for heaven,
She hides the Giver in the given.

"And so, I find it well to come
For deeper rest to this still room,
For here the habit of the soul
Feels less the outer world's control;   80
The strength of mutual purpose pleads
More earnestly our common needs;
And from the silence multiplied
By these still forms on either side,
The world that time and sense have known
Falls off and leaves us God alone.

---

51 **Karnak's hall**, the great temple of Ammon on the east bank of the Nile, some three hundred and fifty
miles from Cairo   52 **Philae's colonnade.** Philae is a small island in the upper Egyptian Nile. The island,
now submerged most of the year because of the Aswan Dam, was sacred to the deity Isis and holds the remains of temples   67 **But nature. . . .** The lines from this point to l. 106 were added after the first version appeared

"Yet rarely through the charmed repose
Unmixed the stream of motive flows,
A flavor of its many springs,
The tints of earth and sky it brings;   90
In the still waters needs must be
Some shade of human sympathy;
And here, in its accustomed place,
I look on memory's dearest face;
The blind by-sitter guesseth not
What shadow haunts that vacant spot;
No eyes save mine alone can see
The love wherewith it welcomes me!
And still, with those alone my kin,
In doubt and weakness, want and sin,   100
I bow my head, my heart I bare
As when that face was living there,
And strive (too oft, alas! in vain)
The peace of simple trust to gain,
Fold fancy's restless wings, and lay
The idols of my heart away.

"Welcome the silence all unbroken,
Nor less the words of fitness spoken, —
Such golden words as hers for whom
Our autumn flowers have just made room;   110
Whose hopeful utterance through and through
The freshness of the morning blew;
Who loved not less the earth that light
Fell on it from the heavens in sight,
But saw in all fair forms more fair
The Eternal beauty mirrored there.
Whose eighty years but added grace
And saintlier meaning to her face, —
The look of one who bore away
Glad tidings from the hills of day,   120
While all our hearts went forth to meet
The coming of her beautiful feet!
Or haply hers, whose pilgrim tread
Is in the paths where Jesus led;
Who dreams her childhood's Sabbath dream
By Jordan's willow-shaded stream,
And, of the hymns of hope and faith,
Sung by the monks of Nazareth,

123 **Or haply hers.** . . . This line and the eleven following were added to the first version

Hears pious echoes, in the call
To prayer, from Moslem minarets fall,   130
Repeating where His works were wrought
The lesson that her Master taught,
Of whom an elder Sibyl gave,
The prophecies of Cumae's cave!

"I ask no organ's soulless breath
To drone the themes of life and death,
No altar candle-lit by day,
No ornate wordsman's rhetoric-play,
No cool philosophy to teach
Its bland audacities of speech   140
To double-tasked idolators
Themselves their gods and worshippers,
No pulpit hammered by the fist
Of loud-asserting dogmatist,
Who borrows from the hand of love
The smoking thunderbolts of Jove.
I know how well the fathers taught,
What work the later schoolmen wrought;
I reverence old-time faith and men,
But God is near us now as then;   150
His force of love is still unspent,
His hate of sin as imminent;
And still the measure of our needs
Outgrows the cramping bounds of creeds;
The manna gathered yesterday
Already savors of decay;
Doubts to the world's child-heart unknown
Question us now from star and stone;
Too little or too much we know,
And sight is swift and faith is slow;   160
The power is lost to self-deceive
With shallow forms of make-believe.
We walk at high noon, and the bells
Call to a thousand oracles,
But the sound deafens, and the light
Is stronger than our dazzled sight;
The letters of the sacred Book
Glimmer and swim beneath our look;
Still struggles in the Age's breast

---

134 **Cumae's cave.** Near Cumae, in Italy, was a cave where Aeneas consulted a Sibyl who uttered
dark prophecies

With deepening agony of quest   170
The old entreaty: 'Art thou He,
Or look we for the Christ to be?'

"God should be most where man is least:
So, where is neither church nor priest,
And never rag of form or creed
To clothe the nakedness of need, —
Where farmer-folk in silence meet, —
I turn my bell-unsummoned feet;
I lay the critic's glass aside,
I tread upon my lettered pride,   180
And, lowest-seated, testify
To the oneness of humanity;
Confess the universal want,
And share whatever Heaven may grant.
He findeth not who seeks his own,
The soul is lost that's saved alone.
Not on one favored forehead fell
Of old the fire-tongued miracle,
But flamed o'er all the thronging host
The baptism of the Holy Ghost;   190
Heart answers heart: in one desire
The blending lines of prayer aspire;
'Where, in my name, meet two or three,'
Our Lord hath said, 'I there will be!'

"So sometimes comes to soul and sense
The feeling which is evidence
That very near about us lies
The realm of spiritual mysteries.
The sphere of the supernal powers
Impinges on this world of ours.   200
The low and dark horizon lifts,
To light the scenic terror shifts;
The breath of a diviner air
Blows down the answer of a prayer:
That all our sorrow, pain, and doubt
A great compassion clasps about,
And law and goodness, love and force,
Are wedded fast beyond divorce.
When duty leaves to love its task,
The beggar Self forgets to ask;   210
With smile of trust and folded hands,

The passive soul in waiting stands
To feel, as flowers the sun and dew,
The One true Life its own renew.

"So, to the calmly gathered thought
The innermost of truth is taught,
The mystery dimly understood,
That love of God is love of good,
And, chiefly, its divinest trace
In Him of Nazareth's holy face;   220
That to be saved is only this, —
Salvation from our selfishness,
From more than elemental fire,
The soul's unsanctified desire,
From sin itself, and not the pain
That warns us of its chafing chain;
That worship's deeper meaning lies
In mercy, and not sacrifice,
Not proud humilities of sense
And posturing of penitence,   230
But love's unforced obedience;
That Book and Church and Day are given
For man, not God, — for earth, not heaven, —
The blessed means to holiest ends,
Not masters, but benignant friends;
That the dear Christ dwells not afar,
The king of some remoter star,
Listening, at times, with flattered ear
To homage wrung from selfish fear,
But here, amidst the poor and blind,   240
The bound and suffering of our kind,
In works we do, in prayers we pray,
Life of our life, he lives to-day."

                              1868

219 **And, chiefly.** . . . This line and the next were inserted after the first printing   223 **From more.** . . .
The passage through l. 231 was also inserted later

1803—1882 Ralph Waldo Emerson

R alph Waldo Emerson was descended from nine successive generations of ministers. His grandfather was a minister at Concord at the beginning of the American Revolution and gave encouragement to the embattled farmers who fired the shot heard around the world. His father, who was minister of the First Church, Unitarian, in Boston, Ralph Waldo's birthplace, died when Emerson was eight years old, leaving a widow and four sons in difficult financial circumstances. Nevertheless, all four sons went through Harvard, Ralph Waldo graduating in 1821. He taught school for a while, attended the Harvard Divinity School, spent a winter in Florida for his health, and, in 1829, became pastor of the Second Church of Boston and married Miss Ellen Tucker. His felicity at this time seemed perfect; in his journal he uneasily asked himself, "Can this hold?" It didn't hold, for in 1831 Ellen died, and in 1832 he resigned his pastorate because of his unwillingness to administer the Lord's Supper. In a remarkably candid sermon on the subject he said to his congregation: "It is my desire, in the office of a Christian minister, to do nothing which I cannot do with my whole heart. Having said this, I have said all. I have no hostility to this institution [the Lord's Supper]; I am only stating my want of sympathy with it."

Emerson at twenty-nine possibly looked like a failure; but, as Bliss Perry has happily observed, "he pulled himself together, being of the old, unbeatable Puritan stuff." In 1833 he went abroad and visited Landor in Italy, Coleridge and Wordsworth in England, and (most important of all, because the meeting was the beginning of a lifelong friendship) Carlyle in Scotland, at Craigenputtock, "amid desolate heathery hills, where the lonely scholar nourished his mighty heart" (see *English Traits*). Upon his return to America, he bought a house and two acres of land in Concord, married Miss Lydia Jackson, and in 1836 published his first volume, *Nature,* which Henry Seidel Canby has called "the most seminal of all American books." Except among Transcendentalists, *Nature* met with a mild reception; but the two challenging addresses which followed soon after, *The American Scholar* in 1837 and *The Divinity School Address* in 1838, made Emerson famous. *Essays, First Series* appeared in 1841, and *Essays, Second Series,* in 1844. From 1840 to 1842, he assisted Margaret Fuller in editing *The Dial,* the chief magazine of New England Transcendentalism, and was himself editor from 1842 to 1844. He lectured extensively and successfully in England in 1847-1848. In 1847 *Poems* appeared; in 1850, *Representative Men;* in 1856, *English Traits;* in 1860, *The Conduct of Life.*

In the 1840's and 1850's Emerson was in ever increasing demand as a lecturer on Lyceum platforms in New England, the middle Atlantic states, and the "Northwest." He met this demand heroically. An entry in his journal dated Beloit, Wisconsin, January 9, 1856, reads as follows: "Mercury varying from 20° to 30° below zero for the last week. . . . This climate and people are a new test for the wares of a man of letters. All his thin, watery matter freezes; 'tis only the smallest portion of alcohol that remains good. At the Lyceum, the stout Illinoisan, after a short trial, walks out of the hall." And another entry dated Kalamazoo, Michigan, February 1860: "My chief adventure was the necessity of riding in a buggy forty-eight miles to Grand Rapids; then, after the lecture, twenty more on the return; and the next morning getting back to Kalamazoo in time for the train at twelve. So I saw Michigan and its forests and Wolverines pretty thoroughly." One marvels at Emerson's hardihood and adaptability. He was enthusiastic about the development of civilization in the West. When Bret Harte accused him of naïveté, Emerson replied that he "spoke from Pilgrim experience, and knew on good grounds the resistless culture that religion effects."

Emerson kept aloof from the slavery controversy in the 1830's and 1840's. Why "this incredible tenderness for black folk a thousand miles off?" he asked in 1841; and in 1846 he had "quite other slaves to free than those Negroes, to wit, imprisoned spirits, imprisoned thoughts." But later events drove him inexorably into the ranks of the radical abolitionists. When Webster, who had previously been something of a hero in Emerson's eyes, supported the Fugitive Slave Law as a part of the Compromise of 1850, Emerson wrote of him scathingly in his journal: "The word *liberty* in the mouth of Mr. Webster sounds like the word *love* in the mouth of a courtezan." The law itself Emerson called a "filthy enactment," and he added, "I will not obey it, by God" (the only instance of profanity in his writings). In 1859 he took his stand publicly as a champion of John Brown. From 1861 to 1865 he was caught up in the general hysteria of war; "Emerson," Hawthorne said in 1861, "is breathing slaughter like the rest of us." On January 1, 1863, he read the "Boston Hymn" in the Boston Music Hall. Henry James remembered "the momentousness of the occasion, the vast excited multitude, the crowded platform, the tall spare figure of Emerson" and "the immense effect with which his beautiful voice pronounced the lines" — lines expressing the most intransigent of positions —

> Pay ransom to the owner
> And fill the bag to the brim.
> Who is the owner? The slave is owner,
> And ever was. Pay *him!*

In April 1865 he objected in his journal that Grant's terms of surrender were "a little too easy." Perhaps the world is yet to see the philosopher whose philosophy is proof against the excitements of war.

In his personal relations, Emerson has seemed to many readers to have been a little remote. "True love," he wrote in the essay on "Friendship," "dwells and broods on the eternal"; friends "descend to meet." Because his thoughts were so habitually fixed on the ideal, "actual society" was to him "a perpetual disappointment" — an attitude sufficiently illustrated in the references in his journal to his Concord friendships. His conversations with Margaret Fuller were "strange, cold-warm, attractive-repelling." Of his long and fruitful friendship with Thoreau he wrote in 1856, "All his resources of wit and invention are lost to me, in every experiment, year after year, that I make to hold intercourse with his mind." After the death of Hawthorne, with whom he had much less in common, he regretted that he had been unable to "conquer a friendship"; to him, the fault seemed to lie in Hawthorne's "unwillingness and caprice." To the more worldly Hawthorne, on the other hand, Emerson was "the mystic, stretching his hand out of cloud-land, in vain search for something real."

But whatever his human limitations and whatever the limitations of his thinking — "I could never give much reality to evil," he frankly admitted — as an idealist who insisted always upon the "beneficent tendency" in human life and as an inspirer of youth, Emerson was unquestionably great. James Russell Lowell, who was inclined to be skeptical of Emerson's philosophy as such, testified to the inspiring quality of his discourses. "He brought us *life,*" Lowell said in "Emerson the Lecturer," "gave us ravishing glimpses of an ideal under the dry husk of our New England; made us conscious of the supreme and everlasting originality of whatever bit of soul might be in any of us." After a lecture by Emerson, his hearers "walked homeward with prouder stride over the creaking snow." To Matthew Arnold as an undergraduate at Oxford, Emerson was one of the four most stimulating contemporary "voices."

"In all my lectures," Emerson wrote, "I have taught one doctrine, namely, the infinitude of the private man." And again, he said, "I gain my point, gain all points, whenever I can reach the young man with any statement which teaches him his own worth." Emerson had a genius, in the words of Henry James ("Emerson" in *Partial Portraits*), for "seeing character as a real and supreme thing." "He serves," James continued, "and will not wear out . . . indeed, we cannot afford to drop him. . . . He did something better than anyone else, he had a particular faculty, which has not been surpassed, for speaking to the soul in a voice of direction and authority." Emerson should be judged and appreciated, then, not primarily as a metaphysical philosopher, but as a moral teacher. If his moral teachings seem to have lost some of their early force, if Emerson for almost a generation has been "unfashionable" (T. S. Eliot could speak of the essays in 1919 as "already an encumbrance"), it is by no means certain that with a change of intellectual and moral "climate" Emerson may not regain much of his old authority and influence.

Other neglected achievements of his, however, have attracted new interest: his aesthetic and his poetry. He has given us in "The Poet" our best statement of the poem as organic form (". . . a thought so passionate and alive that . . . it has an architecture of its own, and adorns nature with a new thing"), and as his own poems are more clearly seen to embody such a concept, Emerson appears certain to gain greatly in stature as a poet.

The Complete Works of Ralph Waldo Emerson, Centenary Edition, 12 vols., Boston, 1904   The Journals of Ralph Waldo Emerson, 10 vols., Boston, 1909-1914   The Letters of Ralph Waldo Emerson, ed. R. L. Rusk, 7 vols., New York, 1939   The Journals and Miscellaneous Notebooks of Ralph Waldo Emerson, 1819-1834, ed. William H. Gilman and others, I-IV, Cambridge, 1960-1964 (the edition will comprise at least 15 volumes)   R. L. Rusk, Life of Ralph Waldo Emerson, New York, 1949   Vivian C. Hopkins, Spires of Form: A Study of Emerson's Aesthetic Theory, Cambridge, 1951   Sherman Paul, Emerson's Angle of Vision: Man and Nature in American Experience, Cambridge, 1952   S. E. Whicher, Freedom and Fate: An Inner Life of Ralph Waldo Emerson, Philadelphia, 1953   Floyd Stovall, "Emerson," in Eight American Authors, New York, 1956

Nature

Nature *was Emerson's first book. It was published in 1836 and soon became the bible of New England Transcendentalism. Emerson called it, in a letter to Carlyle, "an entering wedge, I hope, for something more worthy and significant." It contains, at least by implication, most of the ideas which Emerson was to develop later.*

Nature *has been called the most seminal book in American literature. Many writers — Thoreau and Whitman among them — have been influenced by its teachings, for it is probably the most important single statement in our literature of the idealistic viewpoint. Everywhere Emerson drives home the primacy of spirit, everywhere he insists eloquently upon the infinitude of the private man, drawing his texts impartially from Plato, the Christian Bible, Shakespeare, and other high sources. "Once inhale the upper air," he tells his readers, "being admitted to behold the absolute natures of justice and truth, and we learn that man has access to the entire mind of the Creator, is himself the creator in the finite." Idealism like this is inspiring, because it opens the door to many practical uses. The practicality of Emerson's idealism is perhaps its distinctive American trait.*

> A subtle chain of countless rings
> The next unto the farthest brings;
> The eye reads omens where it goes,
> And speaks all languages the rose;
> And, striving to be man, the worm
> Mounts through all the spires of form.

Introduction

Our age is retrospective. It builds the sepulchres of the fathers. It writes biographies, histories, and criticism. The foregoing generations beheld God and nature face to face; we, through their eyes. Why should not we also enjoy an original rela-

---

Motto: The first edition of 1836 used as motto the following quotation from Plotinus: "Nature is but an image or imitation of wisdom, the last thing of the soul; nature being a thing which doth only do, but not know." The present verse motto (suggested somewhat by his reading of the eighteenth-century evolutionist Lamarck) was substituted in the second edition of 1849

tion to the universe? Why should not we have a poetry and philosophy of insight and not of tradition, and a religion by revelation to us, and not the history of theirs? Embosomed for a season in nature, whose floods of life stream around and through us, and invite us, by the powers they supply, to action proportioned to nature, why should we grope among the dry bones of the past, or put the living generation into masquerade out of its faded wardrobe? The sun shines to-day also. There is more wool and flax in the fields. There are new lands, new men, new thoughts. Let us demand our own works and laws and worship.

10 Undoubtedly we have no questions to ask which are unanswerable. We must trust the perfection of the creation so far as to believe that whatever curiosity the order of things has awakened in our minds, the order of things can satisfy. Every man's condition is a solution in hieroglyphic to those inquiries he would put. He acts it as life, before he apprehends it as truth. In like manner, nature is already, in its forms and tendencies, describing its own design. Let us interrogate the great apparition that shines so peacefully around us. Let us inquire, to what end is nature?

All science has one aim, namely, to find a theory of nature. We have theories of races and of functions, but scarcely yet a remote approach to an idea of creation. We are now so far from the road to truth, that religious teachers dispute and hate each other, and speculative men are esteemed unsound and frivolous. But to a sound 20 judgment, the most abstract truth is the most practical. Whenever a true theory appears, it will be its own evidence. Its test is, that it will explain all phenomena. Now many are thought not only unexplained but inexplicable; as language, sleep, madness, dreams, beasts, sex.

Philosophically considered, the universe is composed of Nature and the Soul. Strictly speaking, therefore, all that is separate from us, all which Philosophy distinguishes as the NOT ME, that is, both nature and art, all other men and my own body, must be ranked under this name, NATURE. In enumerating the values of nature and casting up their sum, I shall use the word in both senses; — in its common and in its philosophical import. In inquiries so general as our present one, the 30 inaccuracy is not material; no confusion of thought will occur. *Nature,* in the common sense, refers to essences unchanged by man; space, the air, the river, the leaf. *Art* is applied to the mixture of his will with the same things, as in a house, a canal, a statue, a picture. But his operations taken together are so insignificant, a little chipping, baking, patching, and washing, that in an impression so grand as that of the world on the human mind, they do not vary the result.

I. Nature

To go into solitude, a man needs to retire as much from his chamber as from society. I am not solitary whilst I read and write, though nobody is with me. But if a man would be alone, let him look at the stars. The rays that come from those heavenly worlds will separate between him and what he touches. One might think 40 the atmosphere was made transparent with this design, to give man, in the heavenly bodies, the perpetual presence of the sublime. Seen in the streets of cities, how great they are! If the stars should appear one night in a thousand years, how would men believe and adore; and preserve for many generations, the remembrance of the city of God which had been shown! But every night come out these envoys of beauty, and light the universe with their admonishing smile.

The stars awaken a certain reverence, because though always present, they are inaccessible; but all natural objects make a kindred impression, when the mind is open to their influence. Nature never wears a mean appearance. Neither does the wisest man extort her secret, and lose his curiosity by finding out all her perfection. Nature never became a toy to a wise spirit. The flowers, the animals, the mountains, reflected the wisdom of his best hour, as much as they had delighted the simplicity 10 of his childhood.

When we speak of nature in this manner, we have a distinct but most poetical sense in the mind. We mean the integrity of impression made by manifold natural objects. It is this which distinguishes the stick of timber of the wood-cutter from the tree of the poet. The charming landscape which I saw this morning is indubitably made up of some twenty or thirty farms. Miller owns this field, Locke that, and Manning the woodland beyond. But none of them owns the landscape. There is a property in the horizon which no man has but he whose eye can integrate all the parts, that is, the poet. This is the best part of these men's farms, yet to this their warranty-deeds give no title.   20

To speak truly, few adult persons can see nature. Most persons do not see the sun. At least they have a very superficial seeing. The sun illuminates only the eye of the man, but shines into the eye and the heart of the child. The lover of nature is he whose inward and outward senses are still truly adjusted to each other; who has retained the spirit of infancy even into the era of manhood. His intercourse with heaven and earth becomes part of his daily food. In the presence of nature a wild delight runs through the man, in spite of real sorrows. Nature says, — he is my creature, and maugre all his impertinent griefs, he shall be glad with me. Not the sun or the summer alone, but every hour and season yields its tribute of delight; for every hour and change corresponds to and authorizes a different state of the 30 mind, from breathless noon to grimmest midnight. Nature is a setting that fits equally well a comic or a mourning piece. In good health, the air is a cordial of incredible virtue. Crossing a bare common, in snow puddles, at twilight, under a clouded sky, without having in my thoughts any occurrence of special good fortune, I have enjoyed a perfect exhilaration. I am glad to the brink of fear. In the woods, too, a man casts off his years, as the snake his slough, and at what period soever of life, is always a child. In the woods is perpetual youth. Within these plantations of God, a decorum and sanctity reign, a perennial festival is dressed, and the guest sees not how he should tire of them in a thousand years. In the woods, we return to reason and faith. There I feel that nothing can befall me in life, — no disgrace, no calamity 40 (leaving me my eyes), which nature cannot repair. Standing on the bare ground, — my head bathed by the blithe air, and uplifted into infinite space, — all mean egotism vanishes. I become a transparent eyeball; I am nothing; I see all; the currents of the Universal Being circulate through me; I am part or parcel of God. The name of the nearest friend sounds then foreign and accidental: to be brothers, to be acquaintances, — master or servant, is then a trifle and a disturbance. I am the lover of uncontained and immortal beauty. In the wilderness, I find something more dear and connate than in streets or villages. In the tranquil landscape, and especially in the distant line of the horizon, man beholds somewhat as beautiful as his own nature.

The greatest delight which the fields and woods minister is the suggestion of an occult relation between man and the vegetable. I am not alone and unacknowledged. They nod to me, and I to them. The waving of the boughs in the storm is new to me and old. It takes me by surprise, and yet is not unknown. Its effect is like that of
10 a higher thought or a better emotion coming over me, when I deemed I was thinking justly or doing right.

Yet it is certain that the power to produce this delight does not reside in nature, but in man, or in a harmony of both. It is necessary to use these pleasures with great temperance. For nature is not always tricked in holiday attire, but the same scene which yesterday breathed perfume and glittered as for the frolic of the nymphs, is overspread with melancholy to-day. Nature always wears the colors of the spirit. To a man laboring under calamity, the heat of his own fire hath sadness in it. Then there is a kind of contempt of the landscape felt by him who has just lost by death a dear friend. The sky is less grand as it shuts down over less worth in the population.

II. Commodity

20   Whoever considers the final cause of the world will discern a multitude of uses that enter as parts into that result. They all admit of being thrown into one of the following classes: Commodity; Beauty; Language; and Discipline.

Under the general name of commodity, I rank all those advantages which our senses owe to nature. This, of course, is a benefit which is temporary and mediate, not ultimate, like its service to the soul. Yet although low, it is perfect in its kind, and is the only use of nature which all men apprehend. The misery of man appears like childish petulance, when we explore the steady and prodigal provision that has been made for his support and delight on this green ball which floats him through the heavens. What angels invented these splendid ornaments, these rich conven-
30 iences, this ocean of air above, this ocean of water beneath, this firmament of earth between? this zodiac of lights, this tent of dropping clouds, this striped coat of climates, this fourfold year? Beasts, fire, water, stones, and corn serve him. The field is at once his floor, his work-yard, his play-ground, his garden, and his bed.

> "More servants wait on man
> Than he'll take notice of."

Nature, in its ministry to man, is not only the material, but is also the process and the result. All the parts incessantly work into each other's hands for the profit

---

4 **connate**, congenial   34 **More . . . of,** from the poem "Man" by George Herbert which Emerson quotes at greater length in the essay

of man. The wind sows the seed; the sun evaporates the sea; the wind blows the vapor to the field; the ice, on the other side of the planet, condenses rain on this; the rain feeds the plant; the plant feeds the animal; and thus the endless circulations of the divine charity nourish man.

The useful arts are reproductions or new combinations by the wit of man, of the same natural benefactors. He no longer waits for favoring gales, but by means of steam, he realizes the fable of Æolus's bag, and carries the two and thirty winds in the boiler of his boat. To diminish friction, he paves the road with iron bars, and mounting a coach with a ship-load of men, animals, and merchandise behind him, he darts through the country, from town to town, like an eagle or a swallow through 10 the air. By the aggregate of these aids, how is the face of the world changed, from the era of Noah to that of Napoleon! The private poor man hath cities, ships, canals, bridges, built for him. He goes to the post-office, and the human race run on his errands; to the book-shop, and the human race read and write of all that happens, for him; to the court-house, and nations repair his wrongs. He sets his house upon the road, and the human race go forth every morning, and shovel out the snow, and cut a path for him.

But there is no need of specifying particulars in this class of uses. The catalogue is endless, and the examples so obvious, that I shall leave them to the reader's reflection, with the general remark, that this mercenary benefit is one which has 20 respect to a farther good. A man is fed, not that he may be fed, but that he may work.

III. Beauty

A nobler want of man is served by nature, namely, the love of Beauty.

The ancient Greeks called the world κόσμος, beauty. Such is the constitution of all things, or such the plastic power of the human eye, that the primary forms, as the sky, the mountain, the tree, the animal, give us a delight *in and for themselves;* a pleasure arising from outline, color, motion, and grouping. This seems partly owing to the eye itself. The eye is the best of artists. By the mutual action of its structure and of the laws of light, perspective is produced, which integrates every mass of objects, of what character soever, into a well colored and shaded globe, so that where the particular objects are mean and unaffecting, the landscape which they compose 30 is round and symmetrical. And as the eye is the best composer, so light is the first of painters. There is no object so foul that intense light will not make beautiful. And the stimulus it affords to the sense, and a sort of infinitude which it hath, like space and time, make all matter gay. Even the corpse has its own beauty. But besides this general grace diffused over nature, almost all the individual forms are agreeable to the eye, as is proved by our endless imitations of some of them, as the acorn, the grape, the pine-cone, the wheat-ear, the egg, the wings and forms of most birds, the lion's claw, the serpent, the butterfly, sea-shells, flames, clouds, buds, leaves, and the forms of many trees, as the palm.

---

23 κόσμος, cosmos

For better consideration, we may distribute the aspects of Beauty in a threefold manner.

1. First, the simple perception of natural forms is a delight. The influence of the forms and actions in nature is so needful to man, that, in its lowest functions, it seems to lie on the confines of commodity and beauty. To the body and mind which have been cramped by noxious work or company, nature is medicinal and restores their tone. The tradesman, the attorney comes out of the din and craft of the street and sees the sky and the woods, and is a man again. In their eternal calm, he finds himself. The health of the eye seems to demand a horizon. We are never tired, so long
10 as we can see far enough.

But in other hours, Nature satisfies by its loveliness, and without any mixture of corporeal benefit. I see the spectacle of morning from the hilltop over against my house, from daybreak to sunrise, with emotions which an angel might share. The long slender bars of cloud float like fishes in the sea of crimson light. From the earth, as a shore, I look out into that silent sea. I seem to partake its rapid transformations; the active enchantment reaches my dust, and I dilate and conspire with the morning wind. How does Nature deify us with a few and cheap elements! Give me health and a day, and I will make the pomp of emperors ridiculous. The dawn is my Assyria; the sunset and moonrise my Paphos, and unimaginable realms of
20 faerie; broad noon shall be my England of the senses and the understanding; the night shall be my Germany of mystic philosophy and dreams.

Not less excellent, except for our less susceptibility in the afternoon, was the charm, last evening, of a January sunset. The western clouds divided and subdivided themselves into pink flakes modulated with tints of unspeakable softness, and the air had so much life and sweetness that it was a pain to come within doors. What was it that nature would say? Was there no meaning in the live repose of the valley behind the mill, and which Homer or Shakespeare could not re-form for me in words? The leafless trees become spires of flame in the sunset, with the blue east for their background, and the stars of the dead calices of flowers, and every withered stem
30 and stubble rimed with frost, contribute something to the mute music.

The inhabitants of cities suppose that the country landscape is pleasant only half the year. I please myself with the graces of the winter scenery, and believe that we are as much touched by it as by the genial influences of summer. To the attentive eye, each moment of the year has its own beauty, and in the same field, it beholds, every hour, a picture which was never seen before, and which shall never be seen again. The heavens change every moment, and reflect their glory or gloom on the plains beneath. The state of the crop in the surrounding farms alters the expression of the earth from week to week. The succession of native plants in the pastures and roadsides, which makes the silent clock by which time tells the summer hours, will
40 make even the divisions of the day sensible to a keen observer. The tribes of birds

---

20 **England . . . dreams.** To Emerson, England stood for a philosophy of rationalism, represented by such philosophers as Hobbes, Locke, and Hume; while Germany meant the idealism of Kant, Fichte, and Schelling. The English attitude he expresses by "understanding" or rational faculty; the German by his favorite "reason," the intuitive or transcendental apprehension of spiritual truth

and insects, like the plants punctual to their time, follow each other, and the year has room for all. By water-courses, the variety is greater. In July, the blue pontederia or pickerel-weed blooms in large beds in the shallow parts of our pleasant river, and swarms with yellow butterflies in continual motion. Art cannot rival this pomp of purple and gold. Indeed the river is a perpetual gala, and boasts each month a new ornament.

But this beauty of Nature which is seen and felt as beauty, is the least part. The shows of day, the dewy morning, the rainbow, mountains, orchards in blossom, stars, moonlight, shadows in still water, and the like, if too eagerly hunted, become shows merely, and mock us with their unreality. Go out of the house to see the 10 moon, and 'tis mere tinsel; it will not please as when its light shines upon your necessary journey. The beauty that shimmers in the yellow afternoons of October, who ever could clutch it? Go forth to find it, and it is gone; 'tis only a mirage as you look from the windows of diligence.

2. The presence of a higher, namely, of the spiritual element is essential to its perfection. The high and divine beauty which can be loved without effeminacy, is that which is found in combination with the human will. Beauty is the mark God sets upon virtue. Every natural action is graceful. Every heroic act is also decent, and causes the place and the bystanders to shine. We are taught by great actions that the universe is the property of every individual in it. Every rational creature has all 20 nature for his dowry and estate. It is his, if he will. He may divest himself of it; he may creep into a corner, and abdicate his kingdom, as most men do, but he is entitled to the world by his constitution. In proportion to the energy of his thought and will, he takes up the world into himself. "All those things for which men plough, build, or sail, obey virtue;" said Sallust. "The winds and waves," said Gibbon, "are always on the side of the ablest navigators." So are the sun and moon and all the stars of heaven. When a noble act is done, — perchance in a scene of great natural beauty; when Leonidas and his three hundred martyrs consume one day in dying, and the sun and moon come each and look at them once in the steep defile of Thermopylæ; when Arnold Winkelried, in the high Alps, under the shadow of 30 the avalanche, gathers in his side a sheaf of Austrian spears to break the line for his comrades; are not these heroes entitled to add the beauty of the scene to the beauty of the deed? When the bark of Columbus nears the shore of America; — before it, the beach lined with savages, fleeing out of all their huts of cane; the sea behind; and the purple mountains of the Indian Archipelago around, can we separate the man from the living picture? Does not the New World clothe his form with her palm-groves and savannahs as fit drapery? Ever does natural beauty steal in like air, and envelope great actions. When Sir Harry Vane was dragged up the Tower-hill,

---

24 **All . . . Sallust,** from *The Conspiracy of Catiline* (Chap. II), by Caius Sallustius Crispus, Roman historian of the first century B.C.   25 **The winds . . . navigators,** from *The Decline and Fall of the Roman Empire* (Chap. LXVIII), by Edward Gibbon, English historian of the eighteenth century   28 **Leonidas,** King of Sparta in the fifth century B.C. He died heroically while defending the pass of Thermopylae in 480 against the overwhelming Persian army of Xerxes   30 **Arnold Winkelried,** Swiss hero in the battle of Sempach in 1386 against the Austrians   38 **Sir Harry Vane . . . Lord Russell,** English statesmen and heroes; both were executed for treason in the reign of Charles II, the former in 1662, the latter in 1683

sitting on a sled, to suffer death as the champion of the English laws, one of the multitude cried out to him, "You never sate on so glorious a seat!" Charles II., to intimidate the citizens of London, caused the patriot Lord Russell to be drawn in an open coach through the principal streets of the city on his way to the scaffold. "But," his biographer says, "the multitude imagined they saw liberty and virtue sitting by his side." In private places, among sordid objects, an act of truth or heroism seems at once to draw to itself the sky as its temple, the sun as its candle. Nature stretches out her arms to embrace man, only let his thoughts be of equal greatness. Willingly does she follow his steps with the rose and the violet, and bend her lines
10 of grandeur and grace to the decoration of her darling child. Only let his thoughts be of equal scope, and the frame will suit the picture. A virtuous man is in unison with her works, and makes the central figure of the visible sphere. Homer, Pindar, Socrates, Phocion, associate themselves fitly in our memory with the geography and climate of Greece. The visible heavens and earth sympathize with Jesus. And in common life whosoever has seen a person of powerful character and happy genius, will have remarked how easily he took all things along with him, — the persons, the opinions, and the day, and nature became ancillary to a man.

3. There is still another aspect under which the beauty of the world may be viewed, namely, as it becomes an object of the intellect. Beside the relation of things to
20 virtue, they have a relation to thought. The intellect searches out the absolute order of things as they stand in the mind of God, and without the colors of affection. The intellectual and the active powers seem to succeed each other, and the exclusive activity of the one generates the exclusive activity of the other. There is something unfriendly in each to the other, but they are like the alternate periods of feeding and working in animals; each prepares and will be followed by the other. Therefore does beauty, which, in relation to actions, as we have seen, comes unsought, and comes because it is unsought, remain for the apprehension and pursuit of the intellect; and then again, in its turn, of the active power. Nothing divine dies. All good is eternally reproductive. The beauty of nature re-forms itself in the mind, and
30 not for barren contemplation, but for new creation.

All men are in some degree impressed by the face of the world; some men even to delight. This love of beauty is Taste. Others have the same love in such excess, that, not content with admiring, they seek to embody it in new forms. The creation of beauty is Art.

The production of a work of art throws a light upon the mystery of humanity. A work of art is an abstract or epitome of the world. It is the result or expression of nature, in miniature. For although the works of nature are innumerable and all different, the result or the expression of them all is similar and single. Nature is a sea of forms radically alike and even unique. A leaf, a sunbeam, a landscape, the ocean,
40 make an analogous impression on the mind. What is common to them all, — that perfectness and harmony, is beauty. The standard of beauty is the entire circuit of natural forms, — the totality of nature; which the Italians expressed by defining

12 **Pindar,** Greek lyric poet of the fifth and sixth centuries B.C.   13 **Phocion,** Athenian statesman and general of the fourth century B.C.

beauty "il più nell' uno."[1] Nothing is quite beautiful alone; nothing but is beautiful in the whole. A single object is only so far beautiful as it suggests this universal grace. The poet, the painter, the sculptor, the musician, the architect, seek each to concentrate this radiance of the world on one point, and each in his several work to satisfy the love of beauty which stimulates him to produce. Thus is Art a nature passed through the alembic of man. Thus in art does Nature work through the will of a man filled with the beauty of her first works.

The world thus exists to the soul to satisfy the desire of beauty. This element I call an ultimate end. No reason can be asked or given why the soul seeks beauty. Beauty, in its largest and profoundest sense, is one expression for the universe. God 10 is the all-fair. Truth, and goodness, and beauty, are but different faces of the same All. But beauty in nature is not ultimate. It is the herald of inward and eternal beauty, and is not alone a solid and satisfactory good. It must stand as a part, and not as yet the last or highest expression of the final cause of Nature.

IV. Language

Language is a third use which Nature subserves to man. Nature is the vehicle of thought, and in a simple, double, and threefold degree.

1. Words are signs of natural facts.
2. Particular natural facts are symbols of particular spiritual facts.
3. Nature is the symbol of spirit.

1. Words are signs of natural facts. The use of natural history is to give us aid in 20 supernatural history; the use of the outer creation, to give us language for the beings and changes of the inward creation. Every word which is used to express a moral or intellectual fact, if traced to its root, is found to be borrowed from some material appearance. *Right* means *straight; wrong* means *twisted. Spirit* primarily means *wind; transgression,* the crossing of a *line; supercilious,* the *raising of the eyebrow.* We say the *heart* to express emotion, the *head* to denote thought; and *thought* and *emotion* are words borrowed from sensible things, and now appropriated to spiritual nature. Most of the process by which this transformation is made, is hidden from us in the remote time when language was framed; but the same tendency may be daily observed in children. Children and savages use only nouns or names of things, 30 which they convert into verbs, and apply to analogous mental acts.

2. But this origin of all words that convey a spiritual import, — so conspicuous a fact in the history of language, — is our least debt to nature. It is not words only that are emblematic; it is things which are emblematic. Every natural fact is a symbol of some spiritual fact. Every appearance in nature corresponds to some state of the mind, and that state of the mind can only be described by presenting that natural appearance as its picture. An enraged man is a lion, a cunning man is a fox, a firm man is a rock, a learned man is a torch. A lamb is innocence; a snake is subtle spite; flowers express to us the delicate affections. Light and darkness are our familiar ex-

---

1 **il . . . uno,** the most in one

pression for knowledge and ignorance; and heat for love. Visible distance behind and before us, is respectively our image of memory and hope.

Who looks upon a river in a meditative hour and is not reminded of the flux of all things? Throw a stone into the stream, and the circles that propagate themselves are the beautiful type of all influence. Man is conscious of a universal soul within or behind his individual life, wherein, as in a firmament, the natures of Justice, Truth, Love, Freedom, arise and shine. This universal soul he calls Reason: it is not mine, or thine, or his, but we are its; we are its property and men. And the blue sky in which the private earth is buried, the sky with its eternal calm, and full of everlast-
10 ing orbs, is the type of Reason. That which intellectually considered we call Reason, considered in relation to nature, we call Spirit. Spirit is the Creator. Spirit hath life in itself. And man in all ages and countries embodies it in his language as the FATHER.

It is easily seen that there is nothing lucky or capricious in these analogies, but that they are constant, and pervade nature. These are not the dreams of a few poets, here and there, but man is an analogist, and studies relations in all objects. He is placed in the centre of beings, and a ray of relation passes from every other being to him. And neither can man be understood without these objects, nor these objects without man. All the facts in natural history taken by themselves, have no
20 value, but are barren, like a single sex. But marry it to human history, and it is full of life. Whole floras, all Linnæus' and Buffon's volumes, are dry catalogues of facts; but the most trivial of these facts, the habit of a plant, the organs, or work, or noise of an insect, applied to the illustration of a fact in intellectual philosophy, or in any way associated to human nature, affects us in the most lively and agreeable manner. The seed of a plant, — to what affecting analogies in the nature of man is that little fruit made use of, in all discourse, up to the voice of Paul, who calls the human corpse a seed, — "It is sown a natural body; it is raised a spiritual body." The motion of the earth round its axis and round the sun, makes the day and the year. These are certain amounts of brute light and heat. But is there no intent of an anal-
30 ogy between man's life and the seasons? And do the seasons gain no grandeur or pathos from that analogy? The instincts of the ant are very unimportant considered as the ant's; but the moment a ray of relation is seen to extend from it to man, and the little drudge is seen to be a monitor, a little body with a mighty heart, then all its habits, even that said to be recently observed, that it never sleeps, become sublime.

Because of this radical correspondence between visible things and human thoughts, savages, who have only what is necessary, converse in figures. As we go back in history, language becomes more picturesque, until its infancy, when it is all poetry; or all spiritual facts are represented by natural symbols. The same symbols are found to make the original elements of all languages. It has moreover been observed, that
40 the idioms of all languages approach each other in passages of the greatest eloquence and power. And as this is the first language, so is it the last. This immediate de-

---

7 **Reason.** Note Emerson's special distinction between "reason" and "understanding"   21 **Linnæus** . . . **Buffon,** Swedish and French naturalists, respectively, of the eighteenth century   26 **Paul** . . . **spiritual body.** I Corinthians 15:44

pendence of language upon nature, this conversion of an outward phenomenon into a type of somewhat in human life, never loses its power to affect us. It is this which gives that piquancy to the conversation of a strong-natured farmer or backwoodsman, which all men relish.

A man's power to connect his thought with its proper symbol, and so to utter it, depends on the simplicity of his character, that is, upon his love of truth and his desire to communicate it without loss. The corruption of man is followed by the corruption of language. When simplicity of character and the sovereignty of ideas is broken up by the prevalence of secondary desires, — the desire of riches, of pleasure, of power, and of praise, — and duplicity and falsehood take place of simplicity and 10 truth, the power over nature as an interpreter of the will is in a degree lost; new imagery ceases to be created, and old words are perverted to stand for things which are not; a paper currency is employed, when there is no bullion in the vaults. In due time the fraud is manifest, and words lose all power to stimulate the understanding or the affections. Hundreds of writers may be found in every long-civilized nation who for a short time believe and make others believe that they see and utter truths, who do not of themselves clothe one thought in its natural garment, but who feed unconsciously on the language created by the primary writers of the country, those, namely, who hold primarily on nature.

But wise men pierce this rotten diction and fasten words again to visible things; 20 so that picturesque language is at once a commanding certificate that he who employs it is a man in alliance with truth and God. The moment our discourse rises above the ground line of familiar facts and is inflamed with passion or exalted by thought, it clothes itself in images. A man conversing in earnest, if he watch his intellectual processes, will find that a material image more or less luminous arises in his mind, contemporaneous with every thought, which furnishes the vestment of the thought. Hence, good writing and brilliant discourse are perpetual allegories. This imagery is spontaneous. It is the blending of experience with the present action of the mind. It is proper creation. It is the working of the Original Cause through the instruments he has already made.   30

These facts may suggest the advantage which the country-life possesses, for a powerful mind, over the artificial and curtailed life of cities. We know more from nature than we can at will communicate. Its light flows into the mind evermore, and we forget its presence. The poet, the orator, bred in the woods, whose senses have been nourished by their fair and appeasing changes, year after year, without design and without heed, — shall not lose their lesson altogether, in the roar of cities or the broil of politics. Long hereafter, amidst agitation and terror in national councils, — in the hour of revolution, — these solemn images shall reappear in their morning lustre, as fit symbols and words of the thoughts which the passing events shall awaken. At the call of a noble sentiment, again the woods wave, the pines mur- 40 mur, the river rolls and shines, and the cattle low upon the mountains, as he saw and heard them in his infancy. And with these forms, the spells of persuasion, the keys of power are put into his hands.

3. We are thus assisted by natural objects in the expression of particular mean-

ings. But how great a language to convey such pepper-corn informations! Did it need such noble races of creatures, this profusion of forms, this host of orbs in heaven, to furnish man with the dictionary and grammar of his municipal speech? Whilst we use this grand cipher to expedite the affairs of our pot and kettle, we feel that we have not yet put it to its use, neither are able. We are like travellers using the cinders of a volcano to roast their eggs. Whilst we see that it always stands ready to clothe what we would say, we cannot avoid the question whether the characters are not significant of themselves. Have mountains, and waves, and skies, no significance but what we consciously give them when we employ them as emblems
10 of our thoughts? The world is emblematic. Parts of speech are metaphors, because the whole of nature is a metaphor of the human mind. The laws of moral nature answer to those of matter as face to face in a glass. "The visible world and the relation of its parts, is the dial plate of the invisible." The axioms of physics translate the laws of ethics. Thus, "the whole is greater than its part;" "reaction is equal to action;" "the smallest weight may be made to lift the greatest, the difference of weight being compensated by time;" and many the like propositions, which have an ethical as well as physical sense. These propositions have a much more extensive and universal sense when applied to human life, than when confined to technical use.

In like manner, the memorable words of history and the proverbs of nations con-
20 sist usually of a natural fact, selected as a picture or parable of a moral truth. Thus; A rolling stone gathers no moss; A bird in the hand is worth two in the bush; A cripple in the right way will beat a racer in the wrong; Make hay while the sun shines; 'Tis hard to carry a full cup even; Vinegar is the son of wine; The last ounce broke the camel's back; Long-lived trees make roots first; — and the like. In their primary sense these are trivial facts, but we repeat them for the value of their analogical import. What is true of proverbs, is true of all fables, parables, and allegories.

This relation between the mind and matter is not fancied by some poet, but stands in the will of God, and so is free to be known by all men. It appears to men, or it does not appear. When in fortunate hours we ponder this miracle, the wise
30 man doubts if at all other times he is not blind and deaf;

> "Can such things be,
> And overcome us like a summer's cloud,
> Without our special wonder?"

for the universe becomes transparent, and the light of higher laws than its own shines through it. It is the standing problem which has exercised the wonder and the study of every fine genius since the world began; from the era of the Egyptians and the Brahmins to that of Pythagoras, of Plato, of Bacon, of Leibnitz, of Swedenborg. There sits the Sphinx at the roadside, and from age to age, as each prophet comes by, he tries his fortune at reading her riddle. There seems to be a necessity in
40 spirit to manifest itself in material forms; and day and night, river and storm, beast and bird, acid and alkali, preëxist in necessary Ideas in the mind of God, and are

---

31 **Can . . . wonder?** *Macbeth,* Act III, sc. iv, ll. 110-112

what they are by virtue of preceding affections in the world of spirit. A Fact is the end or last issue of spirit. The visible creation is the terminus or the circumference of the invisible world. "Material objects," said a French philosopher, "are necessarily kinds of *scoriæ* of the substantial thoughts of the Creator, which must always preserve an exact relation to their first origin; in other words, visible nature must have a spiritual and moral side."

This doctrine is abstruse, and though the images of "garments," "scoriæ," "mirror," etc., may stimulate the fancy, we must summon the aid of subtler and more vital expositors to make it plain. "Every scripture is to be interpreted by the same spirit which gave it forth," — is the fundamental law of criticism. A life in harmony with 10 Nature, the love of truth and of virtue, will purge the eyes to understand her text. By degrees we may come to know the primitive sense of the permanent objects of nature, so that the world shall be to us an open book, and every form significant of its hidden life and final cause.

A new interest surprises us, whilst, under the view now suggested, we contemplate the fearful extent and multitude of objects; since "every object rightly seen, unlocks a new faculty of the soul." That which was unconscious truth, becomes, when interpreted and defined in an object, a part of the domain of knowledge, — a new weapon in the magazine of power.

V. Discipline

In view of the significance of nature, we arrive at once at a new fact, that nature 20 is a discipline. This use of the world includes the preceding uses, as parts of itself.

Space, time, society, labor, climate, food, locomotion, the animals, the mechanical forces, give us sincerest lessons, day by day, whose meaning is unlimited. They educate both the Understanding and the Reason. Every property of matter is a school for the understanding, — its solidity or resistance, its inertia, its extension, its figure, its divisibility. The understanding adds, divides, combines, measures, and finds nutriment and room for its activity in this worthy scene. Meantime, Reason transfers all these lessons into its own world of thought, by perceiving the analogy that marries Matter and Mind.

1. Nature is a discipline of the understanding in intellectual truths. Our dealing 30 with sensible objects is a constant exercise in the necessary lessons of difference, of likeness, of order, of being and seeming, of progressive arrangement; of ascent from particular to general; of combination to one end of manifold forces. Proportioned to the importance of the organ to be formed, is the extreme care with which its tuition is provided, — a care pretermitted in no single case. What tedious training, day after day, year after year, never ending, to form the common sense; what continual reproduction of annoyances, inconveniences, dilemmas; what rejoicing over us of little men; what disputing of prices, what reckonings of interest, — and all to

---

3 **French philosopher,** Guillaume Casper Lencry Oegger, in *The True Messiah* (see Emerson's *Journals*, III, 512)

form the Hand of the mind; — to instruct us that "good thoughts are no better than good dreams, unless they be executed!"

The same good office is performed by Property and its filial systems of debt and credit. Debt, grinding debt, whose iron face the widow, the orphan, and the sons of genius fear and hate; — debt, which consumes so much time, which so cripples and disheartens a great spirit with cares that seem so base, is a preceptor whose lessons cannot be foregone, and is needed most by those who suffer from it most. Moreover, property, which has been well compared to snow, — "if it fall level to-day, it will be blown into drifts to-morrow," — is the surface action of internal 10 machinery, like the index on the face of a clock. Whilst now it is the gymnastics of the understanding, it is hiving, in the foresight of the spirit, experience in profounder laws.

The whole character and fortune of the individual are affected by the least inequalities in the culture of the understanding; for example, in the perception of differences. Therefore is Space, and therefore Time, that man may know that things are not huddled and lumped, but sundered and individual. A bell and a plough have each their use, and neither can do the office of the other. Water is good to drink, coal to burn, wool to wear; but wool cannot be drunk, nor water spun, nor coal eaten. The wise man shows his wisdom in separation, in gradation, and his scale of 20 creatures and of merits is as wide as nature. The foolish have no range in their scale, but suppose every man is as every other man. What is not good they call the worst, and what is not hateful, they call the best.

In like manner, what good heed Nature forms in us! She pardons no mistakes. Her yea is yea, and her nay, nay.

The first steps in Agriculture, Astronomy, Zoölogy (those first steps which the farmer, the hunter, and the sailor take), teach that Nature's dice are always loaded; that in her heaps and rubbish are concealed sure and useful results.

How calmly and genially the mind apprehends one after another the laws of physics! What noble emotions dilate the mortal as he enters into the councils of 30 the creation, and feels by knowledge the privilege to BE! His insight refines him. The beauty of nature shines in his own breast. Man is greater that he can see this, and the universe less, because Time and Space relations vanish as laws are known.

Here again we are impressed and even daunted by the immense Universe to be explored. "What we know is a point to what we do not know." Open any recent journal of science, and weigh the problems suggested concerning Light, Heat, Electricity, Magnetism, Physiology, Geology, and judge whether the interest of natural science is likely to be soon exhausted.

Passing by many particulars of the discipline of nature, we must not omit to specify two.

40 The exercise of the Will, or the lesson of power, is taught in every event. From the child's successive possession of his several senses up to the hour when he saith, "Thy will be done!" he is learning the secret that he can reduce under his will not only particular events but great classes, nay, the whole series of events, and so conform all facts to his character. Nature is thoroughly mediate. It is made to serve. It

receives the dominion of man as meekly as the ass on which the Saviour rode. It offers all its kingdoms to man as the raw material which he may mould into what is useful. Man is never weary of working it up. He forges the subtile and delicate air into wise and melodious words, and gives them wing as angels of persuasion and command. One after another his victorious thought comes up with and reduces all things, until the world becomes at last only a realized will, — the double of the man.

2. Sensible objects conform to the premonitions of Reason and reflect the conscience. All things are moral; and in their boundless changes have an unceasing reference to spiritual nature. Therefore is nature glorious with form, color, and mo- 10 tion; that every globe in the remotest heaven, every chemical change from the rudest crystal up to the laws of life, every change of vegetation from the first principle of growth in the eye of a leaf, to the tropical forest and antediluvian coal-mine, every animal function from the sponge up to Hercules, shall hint or thunder to man the laws of right and wrong, and echo the Ten Commandments. Therefore is Nature ever the ally of Religion: lends all her pomp and riches to the religious sentiment. Prophet and priest, David, Isaiah, Jesus, have drawn deeply from this source. This ethical character so penetrates the bone and marrow of nature, as to seem the end for which it was made. Whatever private purpose is answered by any member or part, this is its public and universal function, and is never omitted. Nothing in na- 20 ture is exhausted in its first use. When a thing has served an end to the uttermost, it is wholly new for an ulterior service. In God, every end is converted into a new means. Thus the use of commodity, regarded by itself, is mean and squalid. But it is to the mind an education in the doctrine of Use, namely, that a thing is good only so far as it serves; that a conspiring of parts and efforts to the production of an end is essential to any being. The first and gross manifestation of this truth is our inevitable and hated training in values and wants, in corn and meat.

It has already been illustrated, that every natural process is a version of a moral sentence. The moral law lies at the centre of nature and radiates to the circumference. It is the pith and marrow of every substance, every relation, and every process. 30 All things with which we deal, preach to us. What is a farm but a mute gospel? The chaff and the wheat, weeds and plants, blight, rain, insects, sun, — it is a sacred emblem from the first furrow of spring to the last stack which the snow of winter overtakes in the fields. But the sailor, the shepherd, the miner, the merchant, in their several resorts, have each an experience precisely parallel, and leading to the same conclusion: because all organizations are radically alike. Nor can it be doubted that this moral sentiment which thus scents the air, grows in the grain, and impregnates the waters of the world, is caught by man and sinks into his soul. The moral influence of nature upon every individual is that amount of truth which it illustrates to him. Who can estimate this? Who can guess how much firmness the 40 sea-beaten rock has taught the fisherman? how much tranquillity has been reflected to man from the azure sky, over whose unspotted deeps the winds forevermore drive flocks of stormy clouds, and leave no wrinkle or stain? how much industry and

---

1 the ass. See Matthew 21:5

providence and affection we have caught from the pantomime of brutes? What a searching preacher of self-command is the varying phenomenon of Health!

Herein is especially apprehended the unity of Nature, — the unity in variety, — which meets us everywhere. All the endless variety of things make an identical impression. Xenophanes complained in his old age, that, look where he would, all things hastened back to Unity. He was weary of seeing the same entity in the tedious variety of forms. The fable of Proteus has a cordial truth. A leaf, a drop, a crystal, a moment of time, is related to the whole, and partakes of the perfection of the whole. Each particle is a microcosm, and faithfully renders the likeness of
10 the world.

Not only resemblances exist in things whose analogy is obvious, as when we detect the type of the human hand in the flipper of the fossil saurus, but also in objects wherein there is great superficial unlikeness. Thus architecture is called "frozen music," by De Staël and Goethe. Vitruvius thought an architect should be a musician. "A Gothic church," said Coleridge, "is a petrified religion." Michael Angelo maintained, that, to an architect, a knowledge of anatomy is essential. In Haydn's oratorios, the notes present to the imagination not only motions, as of the snake, the stag, and the elephant, but colors also; as the green grass. The law of harmonic sound reappears in the harmonic colors. The granite is differenced in its laws only
20 by the more or less of heat from the river that wears it away. The river, as it flows, resembles the air that flows over it; the air resembles the light which traverses it with more subtile currents; the light resembles the heat which rides with it through Space. Each creature is only a modification of the other; the likeness in them is more than the difference, and their radical law is one and the same. A rule of one art, or a law of one organization, holds true throughout nature. So intimate is this Unity, that, it is easily seen, it lies under the undermost garment of Nature, and betrays its source in Universal Spirit. For it pervades Thought also. Every universal truth which we express in words, implies or supposes every other truth. *Omne verum vero consonat.* It is like a great circle on a sphere, comprising all possible circles; which, however, may be drawn and comprise it in like manner. Every such truth is the
30 absolute Ens seen from one side. But it has innumerable sides.

The central Unity is still more conspicuous in actions. Words are finite organs of the infinite mind. They cannot cover the dimensions of what is in truth. They break, chop, and impoverish it. An action is the perfection and publication of thought. A right action seems to fill the eye, and to be related to all nature. "The wise man, in doing one thing, does all; or, in the one thing he does rightly, he sees the likeness of all which is done rightly."

Words and actions are not the attributes of brute nature. They introduce us to the human form, of which all other organizations appear to be degradations. When

---

5 **Xenophanes**, Greek philosopher of the fifth century B.C.   7 **Proteus**, sea god of classical mythology who when seized would assume different shapes   14 **De Staël . . . Goethe.** The quotation is from Madame de Staël's *Corinne,* Bk. IV, Chap. III and Goethe's *Conversations with Eckermann* (March 23, 1829)   14 **Vitruvius.** De architectura, Bk. I, Chap. I   15 **Coleridge,** in *Lecture on the General Character of the Gothic Mind in the Middle Ages*   28 **Omne . . . consonat,** every truth agrees with every other truth   31 **Ens,** a philosophical term for "being," in the most abstract sense

this appears among so many that surround it, the spirit prefers it to all others. It says, "From such as this have I drawn joy and knowledge; in such as this have I found and beheld myself; I will speak to it; it can speak again; it can yield me thought already formed and alive." In fact, the eye, — the mind, — is always accompanied by these forms, male and female; and these are incomparably the richest informations of the power and order that lie at the heart of things. Unfortunately every one of them bears the marks as of some injury; is marred and superficially defective. Nevertheless, far different from the deaf and dumb nature around them, these all rest like fountain-pipes on the unfathomed sea of thought and virtue whereto they alone, of all organizations, are the entrances.   10

It were a pleasant inquiry to follow into detail their ministry to our education, but where would it stop? We are associated in adolescent and adult life with some friends, who, like skies and waters are coextensive with our idea; who, answering each to a certain affection of the soul, satisfy our desire on that side; whom we lack power to put at such focal distance from us, that we can mend or even analyze them. We cannot choose but love them. When much intercourse with a friend has supplied us with a standard of excellence, and has increased our respect for the resources of God who thus sends a real person to outgo our ideal; when he has, moreover, become an object of thought, and, whilst his character retains all its unconscious effect, is converted in the mind into solid and sweet wisdom, — it is a sign to us that his   20 office is closing, and he is commonly withdrawn from our sight in a short time.

VI. Idealism

Thus is the unspeakable but intelligible and practicable meaning of the world conveyed to man, the immortal pupil, in every object of sense. To this one end of Discipline, all parts of nature conspire.

A noble doubt perpetually suggests itself, — whether this end be not the Final Cause of the Universe; and whether nature outwardly exists. It is a sufficient account of that Appearance we call the World, that God will teach a human mind, and so makes it the receiver of a certain number of congruent sensations, which we call sun and moon, man and woman, house and trade. In my utter impotence to test the authenticity of the report of my senses, to know whether the impressions they   30 make on me correspond with outlying objects, what difference does it make, whether Orion is up there in heaven, or some god paints the image in the firmament of the soul? The relations of parts and the end of the whole remaining the same, what is the difference, whether land and sea interact, and worlds revolve and intermingle without number or end, — deep yawning under deep, and galaxy balancing galaxy, throughout absolute space, — or whether, without relations of time and space, the same appearances are inscribed in the constant faith of man? Whether nature enjoy a substantial existence without, or is only in the apocalypse of the mind, it is alike useful and alike venerable to me. Be it what it may, it is ideal to me so long as I cannot try the accuracy of my senses.   40

The frivolous make themselves merry with the Ideal theory, as if its consequences were burlesque; as if it affected the stability of nature. It surely does not. God never jests with us, and will not compromise the end of nature by permitting any inconsequence in its procession. Any distrust of the permanence of laws would paralyze the faculties of man. Their permanence is sacredly respected, and his faith therein is perfect. The wheels and springs of man are all set to the hypothesis of the permanence of nature. We are not built like a ship to be tossed, but like a house to stand. It is a natural consequence of this structure, that so long as the active powers predominate over the reflective, we resist with indignation any hint that nature is more short-lived or mutable than spirit. The broker, the wheelwright, the carpenter, the tollman, are much displeased at the intimation.

But whilst we acquiesce entirely in the permanence of natural laws, the question of the absolute existence of nature still remains open. It is the uniform effect of culture on the human mind, not to shake our faith in the stability of particular phenomena, as of heat, water, azote; but to lead us to regard nature as a phenomenon, not a substance; to attribute necessary existence to spirit; to esteem nature as an accident and an effect.

To the senses and the unrenewed understanding, belongs a sort of instinctive belief in the absolute existence of nature. In their view man and nature are indissolubly joined. Things are ultimates, and they never look beyond their sphere. The presence of Reason mars this faith. The first effort of thought tends to relax this despotism of the senses which binds us to nature as if we were a part of it, and shows us nature aloof, and, as it were, afloat. Until this higher agency intervened, the animal eye sees, with wonderful accuracy, sharp outlines and colored surfaces. When the eye of Reason opens, to outline and surface are at once added grace and expression. These proceed from imagination and affection, and abate somewhat of the angular distinctness of objects. If the Reason be stimulated to more earnest vision, outlines and surfaces become transparent, and are no longer seen; causes and spirits are seen through them. The best moments of life are these delicious awakenings of the higher powers, and the reverential withdrawing of nature before its God.

Let us proceed to indicate the effects of culture.

1. Our first institution in the Ideal philosophy is a hint from Nature herself.

Nature is made to conspire with spirit to emancipate us. Certain mechanical changes, a small alteration in our local position, apprises us of a dualism. We are strangely affected by seeing the shore from a moving ship, from a balloon, or through the tints of an unusual sky. The least change in our point of view gives the whole world a pictorial air. A man who seldom rides, needs only to get into a coach and traverse his own town, to turn the street into a puppet-show. The men, the women, — talking, running, bartering, fighting, — the earnest mechanic, the lounger, the beggar, the boys, the dogs, are unrealized at once, or, at least, wholly detached from all relation to the observer, and seen as apparent, not substantial beings. What new thoughts are suggested by seeing a face of country quite familiar, in the rapid movement of the railroad car! Nay, the most wonted objects, (make a very slight change in the point of vision,) please us most. In a camera obscura, the butcher's cart, and the figure of one of our own family amuse us. So a portrait of a well-known face gratifies us. Turn the eyes upside down, by looking at the landscape through your legs, and how agreeable is the picture, though you have seen it any time these twenty years!

In these cases, by mechanical means, is suggested the difference between the observer and the spectacle — between man and nature. Hence arises a pleasure mixed with awe; I may say, a low degree of the sublime is felt, from the fact, probably, that man is hereby apprised that whilst the world is a spectacle, something in himself is stable.

2. In a higher manner the poet communicates the same pleasure. By a few strokes he delineates, as on air, the sun, the mountain, the camp, the city, the hero, the   10 maiden, not different from what we know them, but only lifted from the ground and afloat before the eye. He unfixes the land and the sea, makes them revolve around the axis of his primary thought, and disposes them anew. Possessed himself by a heroic passion, he uses matter as symbols of it. The sensual man conforms thoughts to things; the poet conforms things to his thoughts. The one esteems nature as rooted and fast; the other, as fluid, and impresses his being thereon. To him, the refractory world is ductile and flexible; he invests dust and stones with humanity, and makes them the words of the Reason. The Imagination may be defined to be the use which the Reason makes of the material world. Shakspeare possesses the power of subordinating nature for the purposes of expression, beyond all poets. His   20 imperial muse tosses the creation like a bauble from hand to hand, and uses it to embody any caprice of thought that is uppermost in his mind. The remotest spaces of nature are visited, and the farthest sundered things are brought together, by a subtile spiritual connection. We are made aware that magnitude of material things is relative, and all objects shrink and expand to serve the passion of the poet. Thus in his sonnets, the lays of birds, the scents and dyes of flowers he finds to be the *shadow* of his beloved; time, which keeps her from him, is his *chest;* the suspicion she has awakened, is her *ornament;*

> The ornament of beauty is Suspect,
> A crow which flies in heaven's sweetest air.   30

His passion is not the fruit of chance; it swells, as he speaks, to a city, or a state.

> No, it was builded far from accident;
> It suffers not in smiling pomp, nor falls
> Under the brow of thralling discontent;
> It fears not policy, that heretic,
> That works on leases of short numbered hours,
> But all alone stands hugely politic.

In the strength of his constancy, the Pyramids seem to him recent and transitory. The freshness of youth and love dazzles him with its resemblance to morning;

---

29 **The ornament . . . air,** from Shakespeare's *Sonnets,* number 70   32 **No . . . politic,** from Shakespeare's *Sonnets,* number 124

> Take those lips away
> Which so sweetly were forsworn;
> And those eyes, — the break of day,
> Lights that do mislead the morn.

The wild beauty of this hyperbole, I may say in passing, it would not be easy to match in literature.

This transfiguration which all material objects undergo through the passion of the poet, — this power which he exerts to dwarf the great, to magnify the small, — might be illustrated by a thousand examples from his Plays. I have before me the
10 Tempest, and will cite only these few lines.

> ARIEL. The strong based promontory
> Have I made shake, and by the spurs plucked up
> The pine and cedar.

Prospero calls for music to soothe the frantic Alonzo, and his companions;

> A solemn air, and the best comforter
> To an unsettled fancy, cure thy brains
> Now useless, boiled within thy skull.

Again;

> The charm dissolves apace,
20 And, as the morning steals upon the night,
> Melting the darkness, so their rising senses
> Begin to chase the ignorant fumes that mantle
> Their clearer reason.
>   Their understanding
> Begins to swell: and the approaching tide
> Will shortly fill the reasonable shores
> That now lie foul and muddy.

The perception of real affinities between events (that is to say, of *ideal* affinities, for those only are real), enables the poet thus to make free with the most imposing
30 forms and phenomena of the world, and to assert the predominance of the soul.

3. Whilst thus the poet animates nature with his own thoughts, he differs from the philosopher only herein, that the one proposes Beauty as his main end; the other Truth. But the philosopher, not less than the poet, postpones the apparent order and

---

1 **Take . . . morn.** Shakespeare's *Measure for Measure,* Act IV, sc. i, ll. 1-4   11 **Ariel.** The passage is spoken by Prospero, not Ariel; see Shakespeare's *The Tempest,* Act V, sc. i, ll. 46-48   11 **The strong . . . muddy.** These lines are spoken by Prospero in Shakespeare's *The Tempest,* Act V, sc. i, ll. 46-48, 58-60, 64-68, 79-82

relations of things to the empire of thought. "The problem of philosophy," according to Plato, "is, for all that exists conditionally, to find a ground unconditioned
and absolute." It proceeds on the faith that a law determines all phenomena, which
being known, the phenomena can be predicted. That law, when in the mind, is an
idea. Its beauty is infinite. The true philosopher and the true poet are one, and a
beauty, which is truth, and a truth, which is beauty, is the aim of both. Is not the
charm of one of Plato's or Aristotle's definitions strictly like that of the Antigone
of Sophocles? It is, in both cases, that a spiritual life has been imparted to nature;
that the solid seeming block of matter has been pervaded and dissolved by a thought;
that this feeble human being has penetrated the vast masses of nature with an in-   10
forming soul, and recognized itself in their harmony, that is, seized their law. In
physics, when this is attained, the memory disburthens itself of its cumbrous catalogues of particulars, and carries centuries of observation in a single formula.

    Thus even in physics, the material is degraded before the spiritual. The astronomer,
the geometer, rely on their irrefragable analysis, and disdain the results of observation. The sublime remark of Euler on his law of arches, "This will be found contrary to all experience, yet is true;" had already transferred nature into the mind,
and left matter like an outcast corpse.

    4. Intellectual science has been observed to beget invariably a doubt of the exist-
ence of matter. Turgot said, "He that has never doubted the existence of matter,   20
may be assured he has no aptitude for metaphysical inquiries." It fastens the attention upon immortal necessary uncreated natures, that is, upon Ideas; and in their
presence we feel that the outward circumstance is a dream and a shade. Whilst we
wait in this Olympus of gods, we think of nature as an appendix to the soul. We
ascend into their region, and know that these are the thoughts of the Supreme Being.
"These are they who were set up from everlasting, from the beginning, or ever the
earth was. When he prepared the heavens, they were there; when he established the
clouds above, when he strengthened the fountains of the deep. Then they were by
him, as one brought up with him. Of them took he counsel."

    Their influence is proportionate. As objects of science they are accessible to few   30
men. Yet all men are capable of being raised by piety or by passion, into their region.
And no man touches these divine natures, without becoming, in some degree, himself divine. Like a new soul, they renew the body. We become physically nimble
and lightsome; we tread on air; life is no longer irksome, and we think it will never
be so. No man fears age or misfortune or death in their serene company, for he is
transported out of the district of change. Whilst we behold unveiled the nature of
Justice and Truth, we learn the difference between the absolute and the conditional
or relative. We apprehend the absolute. As it were, for the first time, *we exist*. We
become immortal, for we learn that time and space are relations of matter; that with
a perception of truth or a virtuous will they have no affinity.   40

    5. Finally, religion and ethics, which may be fitly called the practice of ideas, or

---

2 **Plato.** See the Republic, Bk. V   16 **Euler,** Leonhard Euler, Swiss mathematician of the eighteenth century   20 **Turgot,** Robert Jacques Turgot, French economist of the eighteenth century   26 **These . . .**
counsel, quoted and adapted from Proverbs 8:23, 27, 28, 30

the introduction of ideas into life, have an analogous effect with all lower culture, in degrading nature and suggesting its dependence on spirit. Ethics and religion differ herein; that the one is the system of human duties commencing from man; the other, from God. Religion includes the personality of God; Ethics does not. They are one to our present design. They both put nature under foot. The first and last lesson of religion is, "The things that are seen, are temporal; the things that are unseen, are eternal." It puts an affront upon nature. It does that for the unschooled, which philosophy does for Berkeley and Viasa. The uniform language that may be heard in the churches of the most ignorant sects is, — "Contemn the unsubstantial
10 shows of the world; they are vanities, dreams, shadows, unrealities; seek the realities of religion." The devotee flouts nature. Some theosophists have arrived at a certain hostility and indignation towards matter, as the Manichean and Plotinus. They distrusted in themselves any looking back to these flesh-pots of Egypt. Plotinus was ashamed of his body. In short, they might all say of matter, what Michael Angelo said of external beauty, "It is the frail and weary weed, in which God dresses the soul which he has called into time."

It appears that motion, poetry, physical and intellectual science, and religion, all tend to affect our convictions of the reality of the external world. But I own there is something ungrateful in expanding too curiously the particulars of the general
20 proposition, that all culture tends to imbue us with idealism. I have no hostility to nature, but a child's love to it. I expand and live in the warm day like corn and melons. Let us speak her fair. I do not wish to fling stones at my beautiful mother, nor soil my gentle nest. I only wish to indicate the true position of nature in regard to man, wherein to establish man all right education tends; as the ground which to attain is the object of human life, that is, of man's connection with nature. Culture inverts the vulgar views of nature, and brings the mind to call that apparent which it uses to call real, and that real which it uses to call visionary. Children, it is true, believe in the external world. The belief that it appears only, is an afterthought, but with culture this faith will as surely arise on the mind as did the first.
30 The advantage of the ideal theory over the popular faith is this, that it presents the world in precisely that view which is most desirable to the mind. It is, in fact, the view which Reason, both speculative and practical, that is, philosophy and virtue, take. For seen in the light of thought, the world always is phenomenal; and virtue subordinates it to the mind. Idealism sees the world in God. It beholds the whole circle of persons and things, of actions and events, of country and religion, not as painfully accumulated, atom after atom, act after act, in an aged creeping Past, but as one vast picture which God paints on the instant eternity for the contemplation of the soul. Therefore the soul holds itself off from a too trivial and microscopic study of the universal tablet. It respects the end too much to immerse
40 itself in the means. It sees something more important in Christianity than the

6 **The things . . . eternal.** II Corinthians 4:18   8 **Berkeley . . . Viasa,** George Berkeley, British idealistic philosopher of the eighteenth century; Viasa, legendary Hindu seer   12 **Manichean,** a follower of Manichaeus, a Persian of the third century, who taught an extreme dualism of good and evil   12 **Plotinus,** a native of Egypt, was a Neoplatonic philosopher of the third century. He was a special favorite of Emerson's as the use of an epigraph from Plotinus for the first edition of *Nature* shows

scandals of ecclesiastical history or the niceties of criticism; and, very incurious concerning persons or miracles, and not at all disturbed by chasms of historical evidence, it accepts from God the phenomenon, as it finds it, as the pure and awful form of religion in the world. It is not hot and passionate at the appearance of what it calls its own good or bad fortune, at the union or opposition of other persons. No man is its enemy. It accepts whatsoever befalls, as part of its lesson. It is a watcher more than a doer, and it is a doer, only that it may the better watch.

VII. Spirit

It is essential to a true theory of nature and of man, that it should contain somewhat progressive. Uses that are exhausted or that may be, and facts that end in the statement, cannot be all that is true of this brave lodging wherein man is harbored, 10 and wherein all his faculties find appropriate and endless exercise. And all the uses of nature admit of being summed in one, which yields the activity of man an infinite scope. Through all its kingdoms, to the suburbs and outskirts of things, it is faithful to the cause whence it had its origin. It always speaks of Spirit. It suggests the absolute. It is a perpetual effect. It is a great shadow pointing always to the sun behind us.

The aspect of Nature is devout. Like the figure of Jesus, she stands with bended head, and hands folded upon the breast. The happiest man is he who learns from nature the lesson of worship.

Of that ineffable essence which we call Spirit, he that thinks most, will say least. 20 We can foresee God in the coarse, and, as it were, distant phenomena of matter; but when we try to define and describe himself, both language and thought desert us, and we are as helpless as fools and savages. That essence refuses to be recorded in propositions, but when man has worshipped him intellectually, the noblest ministry of nature is to stand as the apparition of God. It is the organ through which the universal spirit speaks to the individual, and strives to lead back the individual to it.

When we consider Spirit, we see that the views already presented do not include the whole circumference of man. We must add some related thoughts.

Three problems are put by nature to the mind: What is matter? Whence is it? 30 and Whereto? The first of these questions only, the ideal theory answers. Idealism saith: matter is a phenomenon, not a substance. Idealism acquaints us with the total disparity between the evidence of our own being and the evidence of the world's being. The one is perfect; the other, incapable of any assurance; the mind is a part of the nature of things; the world is a divine dream, from which we may presently awake to the glories and certainties of day. Idealism is a hypothesis to account for nature by other principles than those of carpentry and chemistry. Yet, if it only deny the existence of matter, it does not satisfy the demands of the spirit. It leaves God out of me. It leaves me in the splendid labyrinth of my perceptions, to wander without end. Then the heart resists it, because it balks the affections in denying sub- 40 stantive being to men and women. Nature is so pervaded with human life that there is something of humanity in all and in every particular. But this theory makes nature foreign to me, and does not account for that consanguinity which we acknowledge to it.

Let it stand then, in the present state of our knowledge, merely as a useful introductory hypothesis, serving to apprise us of the eternal distinction between the soul and the world.

But when, following the invisible steps of thought, we come to inquire, Whence is matter? and Whereto? many truths arise to us out of the recesses of consciousness. We learn that the highest is present to the soul of man; that the dread univer-
10 sal essence, which is not wisdom, or love, or beauty, or power, but all in one, and each entirely, is that for which all things exist, and that by which they are; that spirit creates; that behind nature, throughout nature, spirit is present; one and not compound it does not act upon us from without, that is, in space and time, but spiritually, or through ourselves: therefore, that spirit, that is, the Supreme Being, does not build up nature around us, but puts it forth through us, as the life of the tree puts forth new branches and leaves through the pores of the old. As a plant upon the earth, so a man rests upon the bosom of God; he is nourished by unfailing fountains, and draws at his need inexhaustible power. Who can set bounds to the possibilities of man? Once inhale the upper air, being admitted to behold the
20 absolute natures of justice and truth, and we learn that man has access to the entire mind of the Creator, is himself the creator in the finite. This view, which admonishes me where the sources of wisdom and power lie, and points to virtue as to

> "The golden key
> Which opes the palace of eternity,"

carries upon its face the highest certificate of truth, because it animates me to create my own world through the purification of my soul.

The world proceeds from the same spirit as the body of man. It is a remoter and inferior incarnation of God, a projection of God in the unconscious. But it differs from the body in one important respect. It is not, like that, now subjected to the
30 human will. Its serene order is inviolable by us. It is, therefore, to us, the present expositor of the divine mind. It is a fixed point whereby we may measure our departure. As we degenerate, the contrast between us and our house is more evident. We are as much strangers in nature as we are aliens from God. We do not understand the notes of birds. The fox and the deer run away from us; the bear and tiger rend us. We do not know the uses of more than a few plants, as corn and the apple, the potato and the vine. Is not the landscape, every glimpse of which hath a grandeur, a face of him? Yet this may show us what discord is between man and nature, for you cannot freely admire a noble landscape if laborers are digging in the field hard by. The poet finds something ridiculous in his delight until he is out of the
40 sight of men.

---

23 **The golden . . . eternity.** Milton's *Comus*, ll. 13-14

VIII. Prospects

In inquiries respecting the laws of the world and the frame of things, the highest reason is always the truest. That which seems faintly possible, it is so refined, is often faint and dim because it is deepest seated in the mind among the eternal verities. Empirical science is apt to cloud the sight, and by the very knowledge of functions and processes to bereave the student of the manly contemplation of the whole. The savant becomes unpoetic. But the best read naturalist who lends an entire and devout attention to truth, will see that there remains much to learn of his relation to the world, and that it is not to be learned by any addition or subtraction or other comparison of known quantities, but is arrived at by untaught sallies of the spirit, by a continual self-recovery, and by entire humility. He will perceive that there   10 are far more excellent qualities in the student than preciseness and infallibility; that a guess is often more fruitful than an indisputable affirmation, and that a dream may let us deeper into the secret of nature than a hundred concerted experiments.

For the problems to be solved are precisely those which the physiologist and the naturalist omit to state. It is not so pertinent to man to know all the individuals of the animal kingdom, as it is to know whence and whereto is this tyrannizing unity in his constitution, which evermore separates and classifies things, endeavoring to reduce the most diverse to one form. When I behold a rich landscape, it is less to my purpose to recite correctly the order and superposition of the strata, than to know why all thought of multitude is lost in a tranquil sense of unity. I cannot greatly   20 honor minuteness in details, so long as there is no hint to explain the relation between things and thoughts; no ray upon the *metaphysics* of conchology, of botany, of the arts, to show the relation of the forms of flowers, shells, animals, architecture, to the mind, and build science upon ideas. In a cabinet of natural history, we become sensible of a certain occult recognition and sympathy in regard to the most unwieldy and eccentric forms of beast, fish, and insect. The American who has been confined, in his own country, to the sight of buildings designed after foreign models, is surprised on entering York Minster or St. Peter's at Rome, by the feeling that these structures are imitations also, — faint copies of an invisible archetype. Nor has science sufficient humanity, so long as the naturalist overlooks that wonderful con-   30 gruity which subsists between man and the world; of which he is lord, not because he is the most subtile inhabitant, but because he is its head and heart, and finds something of himself in every great and small thing, in every mountain stratum, in every new law of color, fact of astronomy, or atmospheric influence which observation or analysis lays open. A perception of this mystery inspires the muse of George Herbert, the beautiful psalmist of the seventeenth century. The following lines are part of his little poem on Man.

> Man is all symmetry,
> Full of proportions, one limb to another,
> And all to all the world besides.   40

Each part may call the farthest, brother;
For head with foot hath private amity,
And both with moons and tides.

Nothing hath got so far
But man hath caught and kept it as his prey;
His eyes dismount the highest star:
He is in little all the sphere.
Herbs gladly cure our flesh, because that they
Find their acquaintance there.

10   For us, the winds do blow,
The earth doth rest, heaven move, and fountains flow;
Nothing we see, but means our good,
As our delight, or as our treasure;
The whole is either our cupboard of food,
Or cabinet of pleasure.

The stars have us to bed:
Night draws the curtain; which the sun withdraws.
Music and light attend our head.
All things unto our flesh are kind,
20   In their descent and being; to our mind,
In their ascent and cause.

More servants wait on man
Than he'll take notice of. In every path,
He treads down that which doth befriend him
When sickness makes him pale and wan.
Oh mighty love! Man is one world, and hath
Another to attend him.

The perception of this class of truths makes the attraction which draws men to science, but the end is lost sight of in attention to the means. In view of this half-
30 sight of science, we accept the sentence of Plato, that "poetry comes nearer to vital truth than history." Every surmise and vaticination of the mind is entitled to a certain respect, and we learn to prefer imperfect theories, and sentences which contain glimpses of truth, to digested systems which have no one valuable suggestion. A wise writer will feel that the ends of study and composition are best answered by announcing undiscovered regions of thought, and so communicating, through hope, new activity to the torpid spirit.

I shall therefore conclude this essay with some traditions of man and nature, which a certain poet sang to me; and which, as they have always been in the world, and perhaps reappear to every bard, may be both history and prophecy.

---

38 **a certain poet,** probably Emerson himself, although the following passages may owe something to Bronson Alcott's "Orphic Sayings." Compare Emerson's use of the same device in the essay "The Poet," p. 1112

"The foundations of man are not in matter, but in spirit. But the element of spirit is eternity. To it, therefore, the longest series of events, the oldest chronologies are young and recent. In the cycle of the universal man, from whom the known individuals proceed, centuries are points, and all history is but the epoch of one degradation.

"We distrust and deny inwardly our sympathy with nature. We own and disown our relation to it, by turns. We are like Nebuchadnezzar, dethroned, bereft of reason, and eating grass like an ox. But who can set limits to the remedial force of spirit?

"A man is a god in ruins. When men are innocent, life shall be longer, and shall   10
pass into the immortal as gently as we awake from dreams. Now, the world would be insane and rabid, if these disorganizations should last for hundreds of years. It is kept in check by death and infancy. Infancy is the perpetual Messiah, which comes into the arms of fallen men, and pleads with them to return to paradise.

"Man is the dwarf of himself. Once he was permeated and dissolved by spirit. He filled nature with his overflowing currents. Out of him sprang the sun and moon; from the man the sun, from the woman the moon. The laws of his mind, the periods of his actions externized themselves into day and night, into the year and the seasons. But, having made for himself this huge shell, his waters retired; he no longer fills the veins and veinlets; he is shrunk to a drop. He sees that the structure still   20
fits him, but fits him colossally. Say, rather, once it fitted him, now it corresponds to him from far and on high. He adores timidly his own work. Now is man the follower of the sun, and woman the follower of the moon. Yet sometimes he starts in his slumber, and wonders at himself and his house, and muses strangely at the resemblance betwixt him and it. He perceives that if his law is still paramount, if still he have elemental power, if his word is sterling yet in nature, it is not conscious power, it is not inferior but superior to his will. It is instinct." Thus my Orphic poet sang.

At present, man applies to nature but half his force. He works on the world with his understanding alone. He lives in it and masters it by a penny-wisdom; and the   30
that works most in it is but a half-man, and whilst his arms are strong and his digestion good, his mind is imbruted, and he is a selfish savage. His relation to nature, his power over it, is through the understanding, as by manure; the economic use of fire, wind, water, and the mariner's needle; steam, coal, chemical agriculture; the repairs of the human body by the dentist and the surgeon. This is such a resumption of power as if a banished king should buy his territories inch by inch, instead of vaulting at once into his throne. Meantime, in the thick darkness, there are not wanting gleams of a better light, — occasional examples of the action of man upon nature with his entire force, — with reason as well as understanding. Such examples are, the traditions of miracles in the earliest antiquity of all nations; the history of   40
Jesus Christ; the achievements of a principle, as in religious and political revolutions, and in the abolition of the slave-trade; the miracles of enthusiasm, as those

---

7 **Nebuchadnezzar.** See Daniel 4:33

reported of Swedenborg, Hohenlohe, and the Shakers; many obscure and yet contested facts, now arranged under the name of Animal Magnetism; prayer; eloquence; self-healing; and the wisdom of children. These are examples of Reason's momentary grasp of the sceptre; the exertions of a power which exists not in time or space, but an instantaneous in-streaming causing power. The difference between the actual and the ideal force of man is happily figured by the schoolmen, in saying, that the knowledge of man is an evening knowledge, *vespertina cognitio,* but that of God is a morning knowledge, *matutina cognitio.*

The problem of restoring to the world original and eternal beauty is solved by
10 the redemption of the soul. The ruin or the blank that we see when we look at nature, is in our own eye. The axis of vision is not coincident with the axis of things, and so they appear not transparent but opaque. The reason why the world lacks unity, and lies broken and in heaps, is because man is disunited with himself. He cannot be a naturalist until he satisfies all the demands of the spirit. Love is as much its demand as perception. Indeed, neither can be perfect without the other. In the uttermost meaning of the words, thought is devout, and devotion is thought. Deep calls unto deep. But in actual life, the marriage is not celebrated. There are innocent men who worship God after the tradition of their fathers, but their sense of duty has not yet extended to the use of all their faculties. And there are patient
20 naturalists, but they freeze their subject under the wintry light of the understanding. Is not prayer also a study of truth, — a sally of the soul into the unfound infinite? No man ever prayed heartily without learning something. But when a faithful thinker, resolute to detach every object from personal relations and see it in the light of thought, shall, at the same time, kindle science with the fire of the holiest affections, then will God go forth anew into the creation.

It will not need, when the mind is prepared for study, to search for objects. The invariable mark of wisdom is to see the miraculous in the common. What is a day? What is a year? What is summer? What is woman? What is a child? What is sleep? To our blindness, these things seem unaffecting. We make fables to hide the bald-
30 ness of the fact and conform it, as we say, to the higher law of the mind. But when the fact is seen under the light of an idea, the gaudy fable fades and shrivels. We behold the real higher law. To the wise, therefore, a fact is true poetry, and the most beautiful of fables. These wonders are brought to our own door. You also are a man. Man and woman and their social life, poverty, labor, sleep, fear, fortune, are known to you. Learn that none of these things is superficial, but that each phenomenon has its roots in the faculties and affections of the mind. Whilst the abstract question occupies your intellect, nature brings it in the concrete to be solved by your hands. It were a wise inquiry for the closet, to compare, point by point, especially at remarkable crises in life, our daily history with the rise and progress
40 of ideas in the mind.

---

1 **Hohenlohe,** Leopold Franz Emmerich, Prince of Hohenlohe-Waldenburg-Schillgsfurst (1794-1849), a reputed worker of miracles   1 **Shakers,** a religious society so called because of their violent singing, dancing, and marching during worship. They put a great emphasis on visions   16 **Deep . . . deep.** See Psalms 42:7

So shall we come to look at the world with new eyes. It shall answer the endless inquiry of the intellect, — What is truth? and of the affections, — What is good? by yielding itself passive to the educated Will. Then shall come to pass what my poet said: "Nature is not fixed but fluid. Spirit alters, moulds, makes it. The immobility or bruteness of nature is the absence of spirit; to pure spirit it is fluid, it is volatile, it is obedient. Every spirit builds itself a house, and beyond its house a world, and beyond its world a heaven. Know then that the world exists for you. For you is the phenomenon perfect. What we are, that only can we see. All that Adam had, all that Cæsar could, you have and can do. Adam called his house, heaven and earth; Cæsar called his house, Rome; you perhaps call yours, a cobbler's trade; a hundred acres of ploughed land; or a scholar's garret. Yet line for line and point for point your dominion is as great as theirs, though without fine names. Build therefore your own world. As fast as you conform your life to the pure idea in your mind, that will unfold its great proportions. A correspondent revolution in things will attend the influx of the spirit. So fast will disagreeable appearances, swine, spiders, snakes, pests, mad-houses, prisons, enemies, vanish; they are temporary and shall be no more seen. The sordor and filths of nature, the sun shall dry up and the wind exhale. As when the summer comes from the south the snowbanks melt and the face of the earth becomes green before it, so shall the advancing spirit create its ornaments along its path, and carry with it the beauty it visits and the song which enchants it; it shall draw beautiful faces, warm hearts, wise discourse, and heroic acts, around its way, until evil is no more seen. The kingdom of man over nature, which cometh not with observation, — a dominion such as now is beyond his dream of God, — he shall enter without more wonder than the blind man feels who is gradually restored to perfect sight."   1836

The American Scholar

An Oration Delivered Before the Phi Beta Kappa Society, at Cambridge, August 31, 1837

The American Scholar *was the most famous literary address of the century. "This grand oration," wrote Oliver Wendell Holmes, "was our intellectual Declaration of Independence. Nothing like it had been heard in the halls of Harvard since Samuel Adams supported the affirmative of the question, 'Whether it be lawful to resist the chief magistrate, if the commonwealth cannot otherwise be preserved.'" James Russell Lowell called it "our Yankee version of a lecture by Abelard." Thomas Carlyle wrote to Emerson, after having read* The American Scholar: *"I could have* wept *to read that speech; the clear high melody of it went tingling through my heart; I said to my wife, 'There, woman!' She read; and charges me to return for answer 'that there has been nothing met with like it since Schiller. . . .'"*

The circumstances of the delivery of The American Scholar *have been vividly reconstructed by Bliss Perry in "Emerson's Most Famous Speech,"* The Praise of Folly and Other Papers, *1923, 81-113.*

Mr. President and Gentlemen, I greet you on the recommencement of our literary
year. Our anniversary is one of hope, and, perhaps, not enough of labor. We do
not meet for games of strength or skill, for the recitation of histories, tragedies, and
odes, like the ancient Greeks; for parliaments of love and poesy, like the Troubadours; nor for the advancement of science, like our contemporaries in the British
and European capitals. Thus far, our holiday has been simply a friendly sign of the
survival of the love of letters amongst a people too busy to give to letters any more.
As such it is precious as the sign of an indestructible instinct. Perhaps the time is
already come when it ought to be, and will be, something else; when the sluggard
10 intellect of this continent will look from under its iron lids and fill the postponed
expectation of the world with something better than the exertions of mechanical
skill. Our day of dependence, our long apprenticeship to the learning of other lands,
draws to a close. The millions that around us are rushing into life, cannot always
be fed on the sere remains of foreign harvests. Events, actions arise, that must be
sung, that will sing themselves. Who can doubt that poetry will revive and lead in
a new age, as the star in the constellation Harp, which now flames in our zenith,
astronomers announce, shall one day be the pole-star for a thousand years?

In this hope I accept the topic which not only usage but the nature of our association seem to prescribe to this day, — the AMERICAN SCHOLAR. Year by year we
20 come up hither to read one more chapter of his biography. Let us inquire what light
new days and events have thrown on his character and his hopes.

It is one of those fables which out of an unknown antiquity convey an unlooked-
for wisdom, that the gods, in the beginning, divided Man into men, that he might
be more helpful to himself; just as the hand was divided into fingers, the better to
answer its end.

The old fable covers a doctrine ever new and sublime; that there is One Man, —
present to all particular men only partially, or through one faculty; and that you
must take the whole society to find the whole man. Man is not a farmer, or a professor, or an engineer, but he is all. Man is priest, and scholar, and statesman, and
30 producer, and soldier. In the *divided* or social state these functions are parcelled out
to individuals, each of whom aims to do his stint of the joint work, whilst each
other performs his. The fable implies that the individual, to possess himself, must
sometimes return from his own labor to embrace all the other laborers. But, unfortunately, this original unit, this fountain of power, has been so distributed to multitudes, has been so minutely subdivided and peddled out, that it is spilled into
drops, and cannot be gathered. The state of society is one in which the members
have suffered amputation from the trunk, and strut about so many walking monsters, — a good finger, a neck, a stomach, an elbow, but never a man.

Man is thus metamorphosed into a thing, into many things. The planter, who is

---

12 **Our . . . close.** Emerson's view that American literature should no longer follow European models but
should be indigenous to America was by no means original with him. Other writers had been saying the
same thing for a good many years. (See, for example, John C. McCloskey, "The Campaign of Periodicals
after the War of 1812 for National American Literature," *Publications of the Modern Language Association,*
March 1935.) Emerson has been remembered in this connection, while earlier writers have been forgotten,
because Emerson expressed the view more effectively

Man sent out into the field to gather food, is seldom cheered by any idea of the true dignity of his ministry. He sees his bushel and his cart, and nothing beyond, and sinks into the farmer, instead of Man on the farm. The tradesman scarcely ever gives an ideal worth to his work, but is ridden by the routine of his craft, and the soul is subject to dollars. The priest becomes a form; the attorney a statute-book; the mechanic a machine; the sailor a rope of the ship.

In this distribution of functions the scholar is the delegated intellect. In the right state he is *Man Thinking*. In the degenerate state, when the victim of society, he tends to become a mere thinker, or still worse, the parrot of other men's thinking.

In this view of him, as Man Thinking, the theory of his office is contained. Him 10 Nature solicits with all her placid, all her monitory pictures; him the past instructs; him the future invites. Is not indeed every man a student, and do not all things exist for the student's behoof? And, finally, is not the true scholar the only true master? But the old oracle said, "All things have two handles: beware of the wrong one." In life, too often, the scholar errs with mankind and forfeits his privilege. Let us see him in his school, and consider him in reference to the main influences he receives.

I. The first in time and the first in importance of the influences upon the mind is that of nature. Every day, the sun; and, after the sunset, Night and her stars. Ever the winds blow; ever the grass grows. Every day, men and women, conversing, behold- 20 ing and beholden. The scholar is he of all men whom this spectacle most engages. He must settle its value in his mind. What is nature to him? There is never a beginning, there is never an end, to the inexplicable continuity of this web of God, but always circular power returning into itself. Therein it resembles his own spirit, whose beginning, whose ending, he never can find, — so entire, so boundless. Far too as her splendors shine, system on system shooting like rays, upward, downward without centre, without circumference, — in the mass and in the particle, Nature hastens to render account of herself to the mind. Classification begins. To the young mind every thing is individual, stands by itself. By and by, it finds how to join two things and see in them one nature; then three, then three thousand; and so, tyran- 30 nized over by its own unifying instinct, it goes on tying things together, diminishing anomalies, discovering roots running under ground whereby contrary and remote things cohere and flower out from one stem. It presently learns that since the dawn of history there has been a constant accumulation and classifying of facts. But what is classification but the perceiving that these objects are not chaotic, and are not foreign, but have a law which is also a law of the human mind? The astronomer discovers that geometry, a pure abstraction of the human mind, is the measure of planetary motion. The chemist finds proportions and intelligible method throughout matter; and science is nothing but the finding of analogy, identity, in the most remote parts. The ambitious soul sits down before each refractory fact; one after 40 another reduces all strange constitutions, all new powers, to their class and their law, and goes on forever to animate the last fibre of organization, the outskirts of nature, by insight.

Thus to him, to this schoolboy under the bending dome of day, is suggested that

he and it proceed from one root; one is leaf and one is flower; relation, sympathy, stirring in every vein. And what is that root? Is not that the soul of his soul? A thought too bold; a dream too wild. Yet when this spiritual light shall have revealed the law of more earthly natures, —when he has learned to worship the soul, and to see that the natural philosophy that now is, is only the first gropings of its gigantic hand, he shall look forward to an ever expanding knowledge as to a becoming creator. He shall see that nature is the opposite of the soul, answering to it part for part. One is seal and one is print. Its beauty is the beauty of his own mind. Its laws are the laws of his own mind. Nature then becomes to him the measure of his attain-
10 ments. So much of nature as he is ignorant of, so much of his own mind does he not yet possess. And, in fine, the ancient precept, "Know thyself," and the modern precept, "Study nature," become at last one maxim.

II. The next great influence into the spirit of the scholar is the mind of the Past, — in whatever form, whether of literature, of art, of institutions, that mind is inscribed. Books are the best type of the influence of the past, and perhaps we shall get at the truth, — learn the amount of this influence more conveniently, — by considering their value alone.

The theory of books is noble. The scholar of the first age received into him the world around; brooded thereon; gave it the new arrangement of his own mind, and
20 uttered it again. It came into him life; it went out from him truth. It came to him short-lived actions; it went out from him immortal thoughts. It came to him business; it went from him poetry. It was dead fact; now, it is quick thought. It can stand, and it can go. It now endures, it now flies, it now inspires. Precisely in proportion to the depth of mind from which it issued, so high does it soar, so long does it sing.

Or, I might say, it depends on how far the process had gone, of transmuting life into truth. In proportion to the completeness of the distillation, so will the purity and imperishableness of the product be. But none is quite perfect. As no air-pump can by any means make a perfect vacuum, so neither can any artist entirely exclude the conventional, the local, the perishable from his book, or write a book of pure
30 thought, that shall be as efficient, in all respects, to a remote posterity, as to contemporaries, or rather to the second age. Each age, it is found, must write its own books; or rather, each generation for the next succeeding. The books of an older period will not fit this.

Yet hence arises a grave mischief. The sacredness which attaches to the act of creation, the act of thought, is transferred to the record. The poet chanting was felt to be a divine man: henceforth the chant is divine also. The writer was a just and wise spirit: henceforward it is settled the book is perfect; as love of the hero corrupts into worship of his statue. Instantly the book becomes noxious: the guide is a tyrant. The sluggish and perverted mind of the multitude, slow to open to the in-
40 cursions of Reason, having once so opened, having once received this book, stands upon it, and makes an outcry if it is disparaged. Colleges are built on it. Books are written on it by thinkers, not by Man Thinking; by men of talent, that is, who start

---

22 **quick,** living   40 **Reason.** In Emersonian usage, "Reason" is supra-rational, intuitive; "Understanding" is logical, scientific. See pp. 698-699

wrong, who set out from accepted dogmas, not from their own sight of principles.
Meek young men grow up in libraries, believing it their duty to accept the views
which Cicero, which Locke, which Bacon, have given; forgetful that Cicero, Locke,
and Bacon were only young men in libraries when they wrote these books.

Hence, instead of.Man Thinking, we have the bookworm. Hence the book-learned
class, who value books, as such; not as related to nature and the human constitution, but as making a sort of Third Estate with the world and the soul. Hence the
restorers of readings, the emendators, the bibliomaniacs of all degrees.

Books are the best of things, well used; abused, among the worst. What is the
right use? What is the one end which all means go to effect? They are for nothing   10
but to inspire. I had better never see a book than to be warped by its attraction
clean out of my own orbit, and made a satellite instead of a system. The one thing
in the world, of value, is the active soul. This every man is entitled to; this every
man contains within him, although in almost all men obstructed, and as yet unborn. The soul active sees absolute truth and utters truth, or creates. In this action
it is genius; not the privilege of here and there a favorite, but the sound estate of
every man. In its essence it is progressive. The book, the college, the school of art,
the institution of any kind, stop with some past utterance of genius. This is good,
say they, — let us hold by this. They pin me down. They look backward and not
forward. But genius looks forward: the eyes of man are set in his forehead, not in   20
his hindhead: man hopes: genius creates. Whatever talents may be, if the man create
not, the pure efflux of the Deity is not his; — cinders and smoke there may be, but
not yet flame. There are creative manners, there are creative actions, and creative
words; manners, actions, words, that is, indicative of no custom or authority, but
springing spontaneous from the mind's own sense of good and fair.

On the other part, instead of being its own seer, let it receive from another mind
its truth, though it were in torrents of light, without periods of solitude, inquest,
and self-recovery, and a fatal disservice is done. Genius is always sufficiently the
enemy of genius by over-influence. The literature of every nation bears me witness.
The English dramatic poets have Shakspearized now for two hundred years.   30

Undoubtedly there is a right way of reading, so it be sternly subordinated. Man
Thinking must not be subdued by his instruments. Books are for the scholar's idle
times. When he can read God directly, the hour is too precious to be wasted in
other men's transcripts of their readings. But when the intervals of darkness come,
as come they must, — when the sun is hid and the stars withdraw their shining, —
we repair to the lamps which were kindled by their ray, to guide our steps to the
East again, where the dawn is. We hear, that we may speak. The Arabian proverb
says, "A fig tree, looking on a fig tree, becometh fruitful."

It is remarkable, the character of the pleasure we derive from the best books. They
impress us with the conviction that one nature wrote and the same reads. We read   40
the verses of one of the great English poets, of Chaucer, of Marvell, of Dryden,

---

41 **Marvell.** Emerson's naming Andrew Marvell (1621-1678) as "one of the great English poets" is significant. For an informative study of Marvell's influence on Emerson, see Norman A. Brittin, "Emerson and
the Metaphysical Poets," *American Literature,* March, 1936

with the most modern joy, — with a pleasure, I mean, which is in great part caused by the abstraction of all *time* from their verses. There is some awe mixed with the joy of our surprise, when this poet, who lived in some past world, two or three hundred years ago, says that which lies close to my own soul, that which I also had well-nigh thought and said. But for the evidence thence afforded to the philosophical doctrine of the identity of all minds, we should suppose some pre-established harmony, some foresight of souls that were to be, and some preparation of stores for their future wants, like the fact observed in insects, who lay up food before death for the young grub they shall never see.

10   I would not be hurried by any love of system, by any exaggeration of instincts, to underrate the Book. We all know, that as the human body can be nourished on any food, though it were boiled grass and the broth of shoes, so the human mind can be fed by any knowledge. And great and heroic men have existed who had almost no other information than by the printed page. I only would say that it needs a strong head to bear that diet. One must be an inventor to read well. As the proverb says, "He that would bring home the wealth of the Indies, must carry out the wealth of the Indies." There is then creative reading as well as creative writing. When the mind is braced by labor and invention, the page of whatever book we read becomes luminous with manifold allusion. Every sentence is doubly significant,
20 and the sense of our author is as broad as the world. We then see, what is always true, that as the seer's hour of vision is short and rare among heavy days and months, so is its record, perchance, the least part of his volume. The discerning will read, in his Plato or Shakspeare, only that least part, — only the authentic utterances of the oracle; — all the rest he rejects, were it never so many times Plato's and Shakspeare's.

     Of course there is a portion of reading quite indispensable to a wise man. History and exact science he must learn by laborious reading. Colleges, in like manner, have their indispensable office, — to teach elements. But they can only highly serve us when they aim not to drill, but to create; when they gather from far every ray
30 of various genius to their hospitable halls, and by the concentrated fires, set the hearts of their youth on flame. Thought and knowledge are natures in which apparatus and pretension avail nothing. Gowns and pecuniary foundations, though of towns of gold, can never countervail the least sentence or syllable of wit. Forget this, and our American colleges will recede in their public importance, whilst they grow richer every year.

     III. There goes in the world a notion that the scholar should be a recluse, a valetudinarian, — as unfit for any handiwork, or public labor as a penknife for an axe. The so-called "practical men" sneer at speculative men, as if, because they speculate or *see,* they could do nothing. I have heard it said that the clergy, — who
40 are always, more universally than any other class, the scholars of their day, — are addressed as women; that the rough, spontaneous conversation of men they do not hear, but only a mincing and diluted speech. They are often virtually disfranchised;

---

32 **Gowns,** academic costume   33 **wit,** wisdom   39 **speculate or see.** "Speculate" is from the Latin, meaning to spy out, to observe

and indeed there are advocates for their celibacy. As far as this is true of the studious classes, it is not just and wise. Action is with the scholar subordinate, but it is essential. Without it he is not yet man. Without it thought can never ripen into truth. Whilst the world hangs before the eye as a cloud of beauty, we cannot even see its beauty. Inaction is cowardice, but there can be no scholar without the heroic mind. The preamble of thought, the transition through which it passes from the unconscious to the conscious, is action. Only so much do I know, as I have lived. Instantly we know whose words are loaded with life, and whose not.

The world, — this shadow of the soul, or *other me,* — lies wide around. Its attractions are the keys which unlock my thoughts and make me acquainted with myself. 10 I run eagerly into this resounding tumult. I grasp the hands of those next me, and take my place in the ring to suffer and to work, taught by an instinct that so shall the dumb abyss be vocal with speech. I pierce its order; I dissipate its fear; I dispose of it within the circuit of my expanding life. So much only of life as I know by experience, so much of the wilderness have I vanquished and planted, or so far have I extended my being, my dominion. I do not see how any man can afford, for the sake of his nerves and his nap, to spare any action in which he can partake. It is pearls and rubies to his discourse. Drudgery, calamity, exasperation, want, are instructors in eloquence and wisdom. The true scholar grudges every opportunity of action past by, as a loss of power. It is the raw material out of which the intellect 20 moulds her splendid products. A strange process too, this by which experience is converted into thought, as a mulberry leaf is converted into satin. The manufacture goes forward at all hours.

The actions and events of our childhood and youth are now matters of calmest observation. They lie like fair pictures in the air. Not so with our recent actions, — with the business which we now have in hand. On this we are quite unable to speculate. Our affections as yet circulate through it. We no more feel or know it than we feel the feet, or the hand, or the brain of our body. The new deed is yet a part of life, — remains for a time immersed in our unconscious life. In some contemplative hour it detaches itself from the life like a ripe fruit, to become a thought 30 of the mind. Instantly it is raised, transfigured; the corruptible has put on incorruption. Henceforth it is an object of beauty, however base its origin and neighborhood. Observe too the impossibility of antedating this act. In its grub state, it cannot fly, it cannot shine, it is a dull grub. But suddenly, without observation, the self-same thing unfurls beautiful wings, and is an angel of wisdom. So is there no fact, no event, in our private history, which shall not, sooner or later, lose its adhesive, inert form, and astonish us by soaring from our body into the empyrean. Cradle and infancy, school and playground, the fear of boys, and dogs, and ferules, the love of little maids and berries, and many another fact that once filled the whole sky, are gone already; friend and relative, profession and party, town and country, 40 nation and world, must also soar and sing.

---

31 **the corruptible . . . incorruption,** I Corinthians 15:53: "For this corruptible must put on incorruption . . ."

Of course, he who has put forth his total strength in fit actions has the richest return of wisdom. I will not shut myself out of this globe of action, and transplant an oak into a flower-pot, there to hunger and pine; nor trust the revenue of some single faculty, and exhaust one vein of thought, much like those Savoyards, who, getting their livelihood by carving shepherds, shepherdesses, and smoking Dutchmen, for all Europe, went out one day to the mountain to find stock, and discovered that they had whittled up the last of their pine trees. Authors we have, in numbers, who have written out their vein, and who, moved by a commendable prudence, sail for Greece or Palestine, follow the trapper into the prairie, or ramble round Algiers, to replenish their merchantable stock.

If it were only for a vocabulary, the scholar would be covetous of action. Life is our dictionary. Years are well spent in country labors; in town; in the insight into trades and manufactures; in frank intercourse with many men and women; in science; in art; to the one end of mastering in all their facts a language by which to illustrate and embody our perceptions. I learn immediately from any speaker how much he has already lived, through the poverty or the splendor of his speech. Life lies behind us as the quarry from whence we get tiles and copestones for the masonry of to-day. This is the way to learn grammar. Colleges and books only copy the language which the field and the work-yard made.

But the final value of action, like that of books, and better than books, is that it is a resource. The great principle of Undulation in nature, that shows itself in the inspiring and expiring of the breath; in desire and satiety; in the ebb and flow of the sea; in day and night; in heat and cold; and, as yet more deeply ingrained in every atom and every fluid, is known to us under the name of Polarity, — these "fits of easy transmission and reflection," as Newton called them, are the law of nature because they are the law of spirit.

The mind now thinks, now acts, and each fit reproduces the other. When the artist has exhausted his materials, when the fancy no longer paints, when thoughts are no longer apprehended and books are a weariness, — he has always the resource *to live*. Character is higher than intellect. Thinking is the function. Living is the functionary. The stream retreats to its source. A great soul will be strong to live, as well as strong to think. Does he lack organ or medium to impart his truths? He can still fall back on this elemental force of living them. This is a total act. Thinking is a partial act. Let the grandeur of justice shine in his affairs. Let the beauty of affection cheer his lowly roof. Those "far from fame," who dwell and act with him, will feel the force of his constitution in the doings and passages of the day better than it can be measured by any public and designed display. Time shall teach him that the scholar loses no hour which the man lives. Herein he unfolds the sacred germ of his instinct, screened from influence. What is lost in seemliness is gained in strength. Not out of those on whom systems of education have exhausted their culture, comes the helpful giant to destroy the old or to build the new, but out of

---

4 **Savoyards,** inhabitants of Savoy in northwestern Italy   25 **Newton,** Sir Isaac Newton (1642-1727), English philosopher and mathematician who discovered the laws of universal gravitation

unhandselled savage nature; out of terrible Druids and Berserkers come at last
Alfred and Shakspeare.

I hear therefore with joy whatever is beginning to be said of the dignity and necessity of labor to every citizen. There is virtue yet in the hoe and the spade, for
learned as well as for unlearned hands. And labor is everywhere welcome; always
we are invited to work; only be this limitation observed, that a man shall not for
the sake of wider activity sacrifice any opinion to the popular judgments and modes
of action.

I have now spoken of the education of the scholar by nature, by books, and by
action. It remains to say somewhat of his duties.   10

They are such as become Man Thinking. They may all be comprised in self-trust.
The office of the scholar is to cheer, to raise, and to guide men by showing them
facts amidst appearances. He plies the slow, unhonored, and unpaid task of observation. Flamsteed and Herschel, in their glazed observatories, may catalogue the stars
with the praise of all men, and the results being splendid and useful, honor is sure.
But he, in his private observatory, cataloguing obscure and nebulous stars of the
human mind, which as yet no man has thought of as such, — watching days and
months sometimes for a few facts; correcting still his old records; — must relinquish
display and immediate fame. In the long period of his preparation he must betray
often an ignorance of shiftlessness in popular arts, incurring the disdain of the able   20
who shoulder him aside. Long he must stammer in his speech; often forego the
living for the dead. Worst yet, he must accept — how often! — poverty and solitude.
For the ease and pleasure of treading the old road, accepting the fashions, the education, the religion of society, he takes the cross of making his own, and, of course,
the self-accusation, the faint heart, the frequent uncertainty and loss of time, which
are the nettles and tangling vines in the way of the self-relying and self-directed; and
the state of virtual hostility in which he seems to stand to society, and especially to
educated society. For all this loss and scorn, what offset? He is to find consolation
in exercising the highest functions of human nature. He is one who raises himself
from private considerations and breathes and lives on public and illustrious thoughts. 30
He is the world's eye. He is the world's heart. He is to resist the vulgar prosperity
that retrogrades ever to barbarism, by preserving and communicating heroic sentiments, noble biographies, melodious verse, and the conclusions of history. Whatsoever oracles the human heart, in all emergencies, in all solemn hours, has uttered
as its commentary on the world of actions, — these he shall receive and impart.
And whatsoever new verdict Reason from her inviolable seat pronounces on the
passing men and events of to-day, — this he shall hear and promulgate.

These being his functions, it becomes him to feel all confidence in himself, and
to defer never to the popular cry. He and he only knows the world. The world of
any moment is the merest appearance. Some great decorum, some fetish of a gov-   40

---

1 **unhandselled,** without "handsell" or gift made as a token of good luck; without, that is, artificial advantages or initial good auspices   14 **Flamsteed,** John Flamsteed (1646-1719), English astronomer   14
Herschel, Sir William Herschel (1738-1822), German astronomer in England, or his son, also a famous astronomer

ernment, some ephemeral trade, or war, or man, is cried up by half mankind and cried down by the other half, as if all depended on this particular up or down. The odds are that the whole question is not worth the poorest thought which the scholar has lost in listening to the controversy. Let him not quit his belief that a popgun is a popgun, though the ancient and honorable of the earth affirm it to be the crack of doom. In silence, in steadiness, in severe abstraction, let him hold by himself; add observation to observation, patient of neglect, patient of reproach, and bide his own time, — happy enough if he can satisfy himself alone that this day he has seen something truly. Success treads on every right step. For the instinct is sure, that

10 prompts him to tell his brother what he thinks. He then learns that in going down into the secrets of his own mind he has descended into the secrets of all minds. He learns that he who has mastered any law in his private thoughts, is master to that extent of all men whose language he speaks, and of all into whose language his own can be translated. The poet, in utter solitude remembering his spontaneous thoughts and recording them, is found to have recorded that which men in crowded cities find true for them also. The orator distrusts at first the fitness of his frank confessions, his want of knowledge of the persons he addresses, until he finds that he is the complement of his hearers; — that they drink his words because he fulfills for them their own nature; the deeper he dives into his privatest, secretest presenti-

20 ment, to his wonder he finds this is the most acceptable, most public, and universally true. The people delight in it; the better part of every man feels, This is my music; this is myself.

In self-trust all the virtues are comprehended. Free should the scholar be, — free and brave. Free even to the definition of freedom, "without any hindrance that does not arise out of his own constitution." Brave; for fear is a thing which a scholar by his very function puts behind him. Fear always springs from ignorance. It is a shame to him if his tranquillity, amid dangerous times, arise from the presumption that like children and women his is a protected class; or if he seek a temporary peace by the diversion of his thoughts from politics or vexed questions, hiding his

30 head like an ostrich in the flowering bushes, peeping into microscopes, and turning rhymes, as a boy whistles to keep his courage up. So is the danger a danger still; so is the fear worse. Manlike let him turn and face it. Let him look into its eye and search its nature, inspect its origin, — see the whelping of this lion, — which lies no great way back; he will then find in himself a perfect comprehension of its nature and extent; he will have made his hands meet on the other side, and can henceforth defy it and pass on superior. The world is his who can see through its pretension. What deafness, what stone-blind custom, what overgrown error you behold is there only by sufferance, — by your sufferance. See it to be a lie, and you have already dealt it its mortal blow.

40 Yes, we are the cowed, —we the trustless. It is a mischievous notion that we are come late into nature; that the world was finished a long time ago. As the world was plastic and fluid in the hands of God, so it is ever to so much of his attributes as we bring to it. To ignorance and sin, it is flint. They adapt themselves to it as they may; but in proportion as a man has any thing in him divine, the firmament

flows before him and takes his signet and form. Not he is great who can alter matter, but he who can alter my state of mind. They are the kings of the world who give the color of their present thought to all nature and all art, and persuade men by the cheerful serenity of their carrying the matter, that this thing which they do is the apple which the ages have desired to pluck, now at last ripe, and inviting nations to the harvest. The great man makes the great thing. Wherever Macdonald sits, there is the head of the table. Linnæus makes botany the most alluring of studies, and wins it from the farmer and the herbwoman; Davy, chemistry; and Cuvier, fossils. The day is always his who works in it with serenity and great aims. The unstable estimates of men crowd to him whose mind is filled with a truth, as 10 the heaped waves of the Atlantic follow the moon.

For this self-trust, the reason is deeper than can be fathomed, — darker than can be enlightened. I might not carry with me the feeling of my audience in stating my own belief. But I have already shown the ground of my hope, in adverting to the doctrine that man is one. I believe man has been wronged; he has wronged himself. He has almost lost the light that can lead him back to his prerogatives. Men are become of no account. Men in history, men in the world of to-day, are bugs, are spawn, and are called "the mass" and "the herd." In a century, in a millennium, one or two men; that is to say, one or two approximations to the right state of every man. All the rest behold in the hero or the poet their own green and crude being, 20 — ripened; yes, and are content to be less, so *that* may attain to its full stature. What a testimony, full of grandeur, full of pity, is borne to the demands of his own nature, by the poor clansman, the poor partisan, who rejoices in the glory of his chief. The poor and the low find some amends to their immense moral capacity, for their acquiescence in a political and social inferiority. They are content to be brushed like flies from the path of a great person, so that justice shall be done by him to that common nature which it is the dearest desire of all to see enlarged and glorified. They sun themselves in the great man's light, and feel it to be their own element. They cast the dignity of man from their downtrod selves upon the shoulders of a hero, and will perish to add one drop of blood to make that great heart beat, those 30 giant sinews combat and conquer. He lives for us, and we live in him.

Men such as they are, very naturally seek money or power; and power because it is as good as money, — the "spoils," so called, "of office." And why not? for they aspire to the highest, and this, in their sleep-walking, they dream is highest. Wake them and they shall quit the false good and leap to the true, and leave governments to clerks and desks. This revolution is to be wrought by the gradual domestication of the idea of Culture. The main enterprise of the world for splendor, for extent, is the upbuilding of a man. Here are the materials strewn along the ground. The private life of one man shall be a more illustrious monarchy, more formidable to its enemy, more sweet and serene in its influence to its friend, than any kingdom in 40 history. For a man, rightly viewed, comprehendeth the particular natures of all men.

---

6 **Wherever . . . table,** taken from a proverb   7 **Linnæus,** Carolus Linnæus (1707-1778), Swedish botanist   8 **Davy,** Sir Humphry Davy (1778-1829), English chemist   9 **Cuvier,** Georges Leopold Cuvier. See note, p. 821

Each philosopher, each bard, each actor has only done for me, as by a delegate, what one day I can do for myself. The books which once we valued more than the apple of the eye, we have quite exhausted. What is that but saying that we have come up with the point of view which the universal mind took through the eyes of one scribe; we have been that man, and have passed on. First, one, then another, we drain all cisterns, and waxing greater by all these supplies, we crave a better and more abundant food. The man has never lived that can feed us ever. The human mind cannot be enshrined in a person who shall set a barrier on any one side to this unbounded, unboundable empire. It is one central fire, which, flaming now out of the lips of Etna, lightens the capes of Sicily, and now out of the throat of Vesuvius, illuminates the towers and vineyards of Naples. It is one light which beams out of a thousand stars. It is one soul which animates all men.

But I have dwelt perhaps tediously upon this abstraction of the Scholar. I ought not to delay longer to add what I have to say of nearer reference to the time and to this country.

Historically, there is thought to be a difference in the ideas which predominate over successive epochs, and there are data for marking the genius of the Classic, of the Romantic, and now of the Reflective or Philosophical age. With the views I have intimated of the oneness or the identity of the mind through all individuals, I do not much dwell on these differences. In fact, I believe each individual passes through all three. The boy is a Greek; the youth, romantic; the adult, reflective. I deny not, however, that a revolution in the leading idea may be distinctly enough traced.

Our age is bewailed as the age of Introversion. Must that needs be evil? We, it seems, are critical; we are embarrassed with second thoughts; we cannot enjoy any thing for hankering to know whereof the pleasure consists; we are lined with eyes; we see with our feet; the time is infected with Hamlet's unhappiness, —

"Sicklied o'er with the pale cast of thought."

It is so bad then? Sight is the last thing to be pitied. Would we be blind? Do we fear lest we should outsee nature and God, and drink truth dry? I look upon the discontent of the literary class as a mere announcement of the fact that they find themselves not in the state of mind of their fathers, and regret the coming state as untried; as a boy dreads the water before he has learned that he can swim. If there is any period one would desire to be born in, is it not the age of Revolution; when the old and the new stand side by side and admit of being compared; when the energies of all men are searched by fear and by hope; when the historic glories of the old can be compensated by the rich possibilities of the new era? This time, like all times, is a very good one, if we but know what to do with it.

I read with some joy of the auspicious signs of the coming days, as they glimmer already through poetry and art, through philosophy and science, through church and state.

One of these signs is the fact that the same movement which effected the eleva-

27 Sicklied . . . thought. *Hamlet,* Act III, sc. i, l. 85

tion of what was called the lowest class in the state, assumed in literature a very marked and as benign an aspect. Instead of the sublime and beautiful, the near, the low, the common, was explored and poetized. That which had been negligently trodden under foot by those who were harnessing and provisioning themselves for long journeys into far countries, is suddenly found to be richer than all foreign parts. The literature of the poor, the feelings of the child, the philosophy of the street, the meaning of household life, are the topics of the time. It is a great stride. It is a sign — is it not? — of new vigor when the extremities are made active, when currents of warm life run into the hands and the feet. I ask not for the great, the remote, the romantic; what is doing in Italy or Arabia; what is Greek art, or Provençal 10 minstrelsy; I embrace the common, I explore and sit at the feet of the familiar, the low. Give me insight into to-day, and you may have the antique and future worlds. What would we really know the meaning of? The meal in the firkin; the milk in the pan; the ballad in the street; the news of the boat; the glance of the eye; the form and the gait of the body; — show me the ultimate reason of these matters; show me the sublime presence of the highest spiritual cause lurking, as always it does lurk, in these suburbs and extremities of nature; let me see every trifle bristling with the polarity that ranges it instantly on an eternal law; and the shop, the plough, and the ledger referred to the like cause by which light undulates and poets sing; — and the world lies no longer a dull miscellany and lumber room, but has form and 20 order; there is no trifle, there is no puzzle, but one design unites and animates the farthest pinnacle and the lowest trench.

This idea has inspired the genius of Goldsmith, Burns, Cowper, and in a newer time, of Goethe, Wordsworth, and Carlyle. This idea they have differently followed and with various success. In contrast with their writing, the style of Pope, of Johnson, of Gibbon, looks cold and pedantic. This writing is blood-warm. Man is surprised to find that things near are not less beautiful and wondrous than things remote. The near explains the far. The drop is a small ocean. A man is related to all nature. This perception of the worth of the vulgar is fruitful in discoveries. Goethe, in this very thing the most modern of the moderns, has shown us, as none ever did, the 30 genius of the ancients.

There is one man of genius who has done much for this philosophy of life, whose literary value has never yet been rightly estimated; —I mean Emanuel Swedenborg. The most imaginative of men, yet writing with the precision of a mathematician, he endeavored to engraft a purely philosophical Ethics on the popular Christianity of his time. Such an attempt of course must have difficulty which no genius could surmount. But he saw and showed the connection between nature and the affections of the soul. He pierced the emblematic or spiritual character of the visible, audible, tangible world. Especially did his shade-loving muse hover over and interpret the lower parts of nature; he showed the mysterious bond that allies moral evil to the 40 foul material forms, and has given in epical parables a theory of insanity, of beasts, of unclean and fearful things.

Another sign of our times, also marked by an analogous political movement, is

33 **Swedenborg** is the subject of an essay in Emerson's *Representative Men* (1850). See note p. 777

the new importance given to the single person. Every thing that tends to insulate the individual, — to surround him with barriers of natural respect, so that each man shall feel the world is his, and man shall treat with man as a sovereign state with a sovereign state, — tends to true union as well as greatness. "I learned," said the melancholy Pestalozzi, "that no man in God's wide earth is either willing or able to help any other man." Help must come from the bosom alone. The scholar is that man who must take up into himself all the ability of the time, all the contributions of the past, all the hopes of the future. He must be an university of knowledges. If there be one lesson more than another which should pierce his ear, it is,
10 The world is nothing, the man is all; in yourself is the law of all nature, and you know not yet how a globule of sap ascends; in yourself slumbers the whole of Reason; it is for you to know all; it is for you to dare all. Mr. President and Gentlemen, this confidence in the unsearched might of man belongs, by all motives, by all prophecy, by all preparation, to the American Scholar. We have listened too long to the courtly muses of Europe. The spirit of the American freeman is already suspected to be timid, imitative, tame. Public and private avarice make the air we breathe thick and fat. The scholar is decent, indolent, complaisant. See already the tragic consequence. The mind of this country, taught to aim at low objects, eats upon itself. There is no work for any but the decorous and the complaisant. Young
20 men of the fairest promise, who begin life upon our shores, inflated by the mountain winds, shined upon by all the stars of God, find the earth below not in unison with these, but are hindered from action by the disgust which the principles on which business is managed inspire, and turn drudges, or die of disgust, some of them suicides. What is the remedy? They did not yet see, and thousands of young men as hopeful now crowding to the barriers for the career do not yet see, that if the single man plant himself indomitably on his instincts, and there abide, the huge world will come round to him. Patience, — patience; with the shades of all the good and great for company; and for solace the perspective of your own infinite life; and for work the study and the communication of principles, the making those instincts
30 prevalent, the conversion of the world. Is it not the chief disgrace in the world, not to be an unit; — not to be reckoned one character; — not to yield that peculiar fruit which each man was created to bear, but to be reckoned in the gross, in the hundred, or the thousand, of the party, the section, to which we belong; and our opinion predicted geographically, as the north, or the south? Not so, brothers and friends, — please God, ours shall not be so. We will walk on our own feet; we will work with our own hands; we will speak our own minds. The study of letters shall be no longer a name for pity, for doubt, and for sensual indulgence. The dread of man and the love of man shall be a wall of defence and a wreath of joy around all. A nation of men will for the first time exist, because each believes himself inspired
40 by the Divine Soul which also inspires all men.

1837

---

5 **Pestalozzi,** Johann Heinrich Pestalozzi (1746-1827), Swiss educational reformer. His *Hints to Parents* influenced Bronson Alcott   17 **complaisant,** here in the unfavorable sense of too eager to please, too compliant with the wishes of others (not to be confused with "complacent")

The Divinity School Address

Delivered Before the Senior Class in Divinity College, Cambridge, Sunday Evening, July 15, 1838

Emerson wrote to Carlyle, October 17, 1838, concerning the reception of this address: "The publication of my Address to the Divinity College . . . has been the occasion of an out-cry in all our leading newspapers against my 'infidelity,' 'pantheism,' and 'atheism.' The writers warn all and sundry against me, and against whatever is supposed to be related to my connection of opinion, &c; against Transcendentalism, Goethe, and Carlyle. I am heartily sorry to see this last aspect of the storm in our washbowl." The opposition which Emerson refers to, it is important to notice, came from Unitarians as well as from the ortho-dox or "Calvinist" party; Emerson was not invited again to lecture at Unitarian Harvard until 1867. The core of his heresy was his denial of the special authority of the Christian revelation and his assertion of the supreme authority of the spiritual intuition belonging to each individual.

For an illuminating treatment of historical background, see C. H. Faust, "The Back-ground of the Unitarian Opposition to Transcendentalism," Modern Philology, *February 1938, XXXV, 297.*

In this refulgent summer, it has been a luxury to draw the breath of life. The grass grows, the buds burst, the meadow is spotted with fire and gold in the tint of flowers. The air is full of birds, and sweet with the breath of the pine, the balm-of-Gilead, and the new hay. Night brings no gloom to the heart with its welcome shade. Through the transparent darkness the stars pour their almost spiritual rays. Man under them seems a young child, and his huge globe a toy. The cool night bathes the world as with a river, and prepares his eyes again for the crimson dawn. The mystery of nature was never displayed more happily. The corn and the wine have been freely dealt to all creatures, and the never-broken silence with which the old bounty goes forward has not yielded yet one word of explanation. One is con- 10 strained to respect the perfection of this world in which our senses converse. How wide; how rich; what invitation from every property it gives to every faculty of man! In its fruitful soils; in its navigable sea; in its mountains of metal and stone; in its forests of all woods; in its animals; in its chemical ingredients; in the powers and path of light, heat, attraction and life, it is well worth the pith and heart of great men to subdue and enjoy it. The planters, the mechanics, the inventors, the astronomers, the builders of cities, and the captains, history delights to honor.

But when the mind opens and reveals the laws which traverse the universe and make things what they are, then shrinks the great world at once into a mere illustra-tion and fable of this mind. What am I? and What is? asks the human spirit with 20 a curiosity new-kindled, but never to be quenched. Behold these outrunning laws, which our imperfect apprehension can see tend this way and that, but not come full circle. Behold these infinite relations, so like, so unlike; many, yet one. I would study, I would know, I would admire forever. These works of thought have been the entertainments of the human spirit in all ages.

A more secret, sweet, and overpowering beauty appears to man when his heart and mind open to the sentiment of virtue. Then he is instructed in what is above him. He learns that his being is without bound; that to the good, to the perfect, he is born, low as he now lies in evil and weakness. That which he venerates is still his own, though he has not realized it yet. *He ought.* He knows the sense of that grand word, though his analysis fails to render account of it. When in inno-
10   cency or when by intellectual perception he attains to say, — "I love the Right; Truth is beautiful within and without for evermore. Virtue, I am thine; save me; use me; thee will I serve, day and night, in great, in small, that I may be not virtuous, but virtue"; — then is the end of the creation answered, and God is well pleased.

The sentiment of virtue is a reverence and delight in the presence of certain divine laws. It perceives that this homely game of life we play, covers, under what seem foolish details, principles that astonish. The child amidst his baubles is learning the action of light, motion, gravity, muscular force; and in the game of human life, love, fear, justice, appetite, man, and God, interact. These laws refuse to be adequately stated. They will not be written out on paper, or spoken by the tongue.
20   They elude our persevering thought; yet we read them hourly in each other's faces, in each other's actions, in our own remorse. The moral traits which are all globed into every virtuous act and thought, — in speech we must sever, and describe or suggest by painful enumeration of many particulars. Yet, as this sentiment is the essence of all religion, let me guide your eye to the precise objects of the sentiment, by an enumeration of some of those classes of facts in which this element is conspicuous.

The intuition of the moral sentiment is an insight of the perfection of the laws of the soul. These laws execute themselves. They are out of time, out of space, and not subject to circumstance. Thus in the soul of man there is a justice whose retributions are instant and entire. He who does a noble deed is instantly ennobled. He
30   who does a mean deed is by the action itself contracted. He who puts off impurity, thereby puts on purity. If a man is at heart just, then in so far is he God; the safety of God, the immortality of God, the majesty of God do enter into that man with justice. If a man dissemble, deceive, he deceives himself, and goes out of acquaintance with his own being. A man in the view of absolute goodness, adores, with total humility. Every step so downward, is a step upward. The man who renounces himself, comes to himself.

See how this rapid intrinsic energy worketh everywhere, righting wrongs, correcting appearances, and bringing up facts to a harmony with thoughts. Its operation in life, though slow to the senses, is at last as sure as in the soul. By it a man is made
40   the Providence to himself, dispensing good to his goodness, and evil to his sin. Character is always known. Thefts never enrich; alms never impoverish; murder will speak out of stone walls. The least admixture of a lie, — for example, the taint of vanity, any attempt to make a good impression, a favorable appearance, — will

---

35 **The . . . himself.** Compare Matthew 10:39: ". . . he that loseth his life for my sake shall find it"

instantly vitiate the effect. But speak the truth, and all nature and all spirits help you with unexpected furtherance. Speak the truth, and all things alive or brute are vouchers, and the very roots of the grass underground there do seem to stir and move to bear you witness. See again the perfection of the Law as it applies itself to the affections, and becomes the law of society. As we are, so we associate. The good, by affinity, seek the good; the vile, by affinity, the vile. Thus of their own volition, souls proceed into heaven, into hell.

These facts have always suggested to man the sublime creed that the world is not the product of manifold power, but of one will, of one mind; and that one mind is everywhere active, in each ray of the star, in each wavelet of the pool; and whatever 10 opposes that will is everywhere balked and baffled, because things are made so, and not otherwise. Good is positive. Evil is merely privative, not absolute: it is like cold, which is the privation of heat. All evil is so much death or nonentity. Benevolence is absolute and real. So much benevolence as a man hath, so much life hath he. For all things proceed out of this same spirit, which is differently named love, justice, temperance, in its different applications, just as the ocean receives different names on the several shores which it washes. All things proceed out of the same spirit, and all things conspire with it. Whilst a man seeks good ends, he is strong by the whole strength of nature. In so far as he roves from these ends, he bereaves himself of power, or auxiliaries; his being shrinks out of all remote channels, he 20 becomes less and less, a mote, a point, until absolute badness is absolute death.

The perception of this law of laws awakens in the mind a sentiment which we call the religious sentiment, and which makes our highest happiness. Wonderful is its power to charm and to command. It is a mountain air. It is the embalmer of the world. It is myrrh and storax, and chlorine and rosemary. It makes the sky and the hills sublime, and the silent song of the stars is it. But it is the universe made safe and habitable, not by science or power. Thought may work cold and intransitive in things, and find no end or unity; but the dawn of the sentiment of virtue on the heart, gives and is the assurance that Law is sovereign over all natures; and the worlds, time, space, eternity, do seem to break out into joy.   30

This sentiment is divine and deifying. It is the beatitude of man. It makes him illimitable. Through it, the soul first knows itself. It corrects the capital mistake of the infant man, who seeks to be great by following the great, and hopes to derive advantages *from another,* — by showing the fountain of all good to be in himself, and that he, equally with every man, is an inlet into the deeps of Reason. When he says, "I ought"; when love warms him; when he chooses, warned from on high, the good and great deed; then, deep melodies wander through his soul from Supreme Wisdom. — Then he can worship, and be enlarged by his worship; for he can never go behind this sentiment. In the sublimest flights of the soul, rectitude is never surmounted, love is never outgrown.   40

This sentiment lies at the foundation of society, and successively creates all forms of worship. The principle of veneration never dies out. Man fallen into superstition, into sensuality, is never quite without the visions of the moral sentiment. In like manner, all the expressions of this sentiment are sacred and permanent in proportion to their purity. The expressions of this sentiment affect us more than all other compositions. The sentences of the oldest time, which ejaculate this piety, are still fresh and fragrant. This thought dwelled always deepest in the minds of men in the devout and contemplative East; not alone in Palestine, where it reached its purest expression, but in Egypt, in Persia, in India, in China. Europe has always owed to oriental genius its divine impulses. What these holy bards said, all sane men found agreeable and true. And the unique impression of Jesus upon mankind, whose name is not so much written as ploughed into the history of this world, is proof of the subtle virtue of this infusion.

10 Meantime, whilst the doors of the temple stand open, day and night, before every man, and the oracles of this truth cease never, it is guarded by one stern condition; this, namely: it is an intuition. It cannot be received at second hand. Truly speaking, it is not instruction, but provocation, that I can receive from another soul. What he announces, I must find true in me, or reject; and on his word, or as his second, be he who he may, I can accept nothing. On the contrary, the absence of this primary faith is the presence of degradation. As is the flood, so is the ebb. Let this faith depart, and the very words it spake and the things it made become false and hurtful. Then falls the church, the state, art, letters, life. The doctrine of the divine nature being forgotten, a sickness infects and dwarfs the constitution. Once man 20 was all; now he is an appendage, a nuisance. And because the indwelling Supreme Spirit cannot wholly be got rid of, the doctrine of it suffers this perversion, that the divine nature is attributed to one or two persons, and denied to all the rest, and denied with fury. The doctrine of inspiration is lost; the base doctrine of the majority of voices usurps the place of the doctrine of the soul. Miracles, prophecy, poetry, the ideal life, the holy life, exist as ancient history merely; they are not in the belief, nor in the aspiration of society; but, when suggested, seem ridiculous. Life is comic or pitiful as soon as the high ends of being fade out of sight, and man becomes near-sighted, and can only attend to what addresses the senses.

These general views, which, whilst they are general, none will contest, find 30 abundant illustration in the history of religion, and especially in the history of the Christian church. In that, all of us have had our birth and nurture. The truth contained in that, you, my young friends, are now setting forth to teach. As the Cultus, or established worship of the civilized world, it has great historical interest for us. Of its blessed words, which have been the consolation of humanity, you need not that I should speak. I shall endeavor to discharge my duty to you on this occasion, by pointing out two errors in its administration, which daily appear more gross from the point of view we have just now taken.

Jesus Christ belonged to the true race of prophets. He saw with open eye the mystery of the soul. Drawn by its severe harmony, ravished with its beauty, 40 he lived in it, and had his being there. Alone in all history he estimated the greatness of man. One man was true to what is in you and me. He saw that God incarnates himself in man, and evermore goes forth anew to take possession of his World. He said, in this jubilee of sublime emotion, "I am divine. Through me,

43 **I . . . think.** The words are not Jesus' exact words, but Emerson's interpretation of Jesus' meaning

God acts; through me, speaks. Would you see God, see me; or see thee, when thou also thinkest as I now think." But what a distortion did his doctrine and memory suffer in the same, in the next, and the following ages! There is no doctrine of the Reason which will bear to be taught by the Understanding. The understanding caught this high chant from the poet's lips, and said, in the next age, "This was Jehovah come down out of heaven. I will kill you, if you say he was a man." The idioms of his language and the figures of his rhetoric have usurped the place of his truth; and churches are not built on his principles, but on his tropes. Christianity became a Mythus, as the poetic teaching of Greece and of Egypt, before. He spoke of miracles; for he felt that man's life was a miracle, and all that man doth, and he 10 knew that this daily miracle shines as the character ascends. But the word Miracle, as pronounced by Christian churches, gives a false impression; it is Monster. It is not one with the blowing clover and the falling rain.

He felt respect for Moses and the prophets, but no unfit tenderness at postponing their initial revelations to the hour and the man that now is; to the eternal revelation in the heart. Thus was he a true man. Having seen that the law in us is commanding, he would not suffer it to be commanded. Boldly, with hand, and heart, and life, he declared it was God. Thus is he, as I think, the only soul in history who has appreciated the worth of man.

1. In this point of view we become sensible of the first defect of historical Chris- 20 tianity. Historical Christianity has fallen into the error that corrupts all attempts to communicate religion. As it appears to us, and as it has appeared for ages, it is not the doctrine of the soul, but an exaggeration of the personal, the positive, the ritual. It has dwelt, it dwells, with noxious exaggeration about the *person* of Jesus. The soul knows no persons. It invites every man to expand to the full circle of the universe, and will have no preferences but those of spontaneous love. But by this eastern monarchy of a Christianity, which indolence and fear have built, the friend of man is made the injurer of man. The manner in which his name is surrounded with expressions which were once sallies of admiration and love, but are now petrified into official titles, kills all generous sympathy and liking. All who hear 30 me, feel that the language that describes Christ to Europe and America is not the style of friendship and enthusiasm to a good and noble heart, but is appropriated and formal, — paints a demigod, as the Orientals or the Greeks would describe Osiris or Apollo. Accept the injurious impositions of our early catechetical instruction, and even honesty and self-denial were but splendid sins, if they did not wear the Christian name. One would rather be

"A pagan, suckled in a creed outworn,"

than to be defrauded of his manly right in coming into nature and finding not names and places, not land and professions, but even virtue and truth foreclosed and

---

4 **Reason . . . Understanding.** See note, p. 1071   27 **friend of man.** When Elizabeth Peabody urged Emerson to write "friend" with a capital F, he replied, "If I did so, they would all go to sleep"   34 **catechetical instruction,** the questions and answers of the catechism, much in vogue in early New England   37 **A pagan . . . outworn,** Wordsworth's "The World Is Too Much with Us," l. 10

monopolized. You shall not be a man even. You shall not own the world; you shall not dare and live after the infinite Law that is in you, and in company with the infinite Beauty which heaven and earth reflect to you in all lovely forms; but you must subordinate your nature to Christ's nature; you must accept our interpretations, and take his portrait as the vulgar draw it.

That is always best which gives me to myself. The sublime is excited in me by the great stoical doctrine, Obey thyself. That which shows God in me, fortifies me. That which shows God out of me, makes me a wart and a wen. There is no longer a necessary reason for my being. Already the long shadows of untimely oblivion
10 creep over me, and I shall decease forever.

The divine bards are the friends of my virtue, of my intellect, of my strength. They admonish me that the gleams which flash across my mind are not mine, but God's; that they had the like, and were not disobedient to the heavenly vision. So I love them. Noble provocations go out from them, inviting me to resist evil; to subdue the world; and to Be. And thus, by his holy thoughts, Jesus serves us, and thus only. To aim to convert a man by miracles is a profanation of the soul. A true conversion, a true Christ, is now, as always, to be made by the reception of beautiful sentiments. It is true that a great and rich soul, like his, falling among the simple, does so preponderate, that, as his did, it names the world. The world seems to
20 exist for him, and they have not yet drunk so deeply of his sense as to see that only by coming again to themselves, or to God in themselves, can they grow forevermore. It is a low benefit to give me something; it is a high benefit to enable me to do somewhat of myself. The time is coming when all men will see that the gift of God to the soul is not a vaunting, overpowering, excluding sanctity, but a sweet, natural goodness, a goodness like thine and mine, and that so invites thine and mine to be and to grow.

The injustice of the vulgar tone of preaching is not less flagrant to Jesus than to the souls which it profanes. The preachers do not see that they make his gospel not glad, and shear him of the locks of beauty and the attributes of heaven. When I see
30 a majestic Epaminondas, or Washington; when I see among my contemporaries a true orator, an upright judge, a dear friend; when I vibrate to the melody and fancy of a poem; I see beauty that is to be desired. And so lovely, and yet with more entire consent of my human being, sounds in my ear the severe music of the bards that have sung of the true God in all ages. Now do not degrade the life and dialogues of Christ out of the circle of this charm, by insulation and peculiarity. Let them lie as they befell, alive and warm, part of human life and of the landscape and of the cheerful day.

2. The second defect of the traditional and limited way of using the mind of Christ is a consequence of the first; this namely: that the Moral Nature, that Law
40 of laws whose revelations introduce greatness — yea, God himself — into the open soul, is not explored as the fountain of the established teaching in society. Men have come to speak of the revelation as somewhat long ago given and done, as if

---

13 **not . . . vision.** Acts 26:19: "I was not disobedient unto the heavenly vision"   30 **Epaminondas,** Theban statesman and general (d. 362 B.C.)

God were dead. The injury to faith throttles the preacher; and the goodliest of institutions becomes an uncertain and inarticulate voice.

It is very certain that it is the effect of conversation with the beauty of the soul, to beget a desire and need to impart to others the same knowledge and love. If utterance is denied, the thought lies like a burden on the man. Always the seer is a sayer. Somehow his dream is told; somehow he publishes it with solemn joy: sometimes with pencil on canvas; sometimes with chisel on stone; sometimes in towers and aisles of granite, his soul's worship is builded; sometimes in anthems of indefinite music; but clearest and most permanent, in words.

The man enamored of this excellency becomes its priest or poet. The office is 10 coeval with the world. But observe the condition, the spiritual limitation of the office. The spirit only can teach. Not any profane man, not any sensual, not any liar, not any slave can teach, but only he can give, who has; he only can create, who is. The man on whom the soul descends, through whom the soul speaks, alone can teach. Courage, piety, love, wisdom, can teach; and every man can open his door to these angels, and they shall bring him the gift of tongues. But the man who aims to speak as books enable, as synods use, as the fashion guides, and as interest commands, babbles. Let him hush.

To this holy office you propose to devote yourselves. I wish you may feel your call in throbs of desire and hope. The office is the first in the world. It is of that 20 reality that it cannot suffer the deduction of any falsehood. And it is my duty to say to you that the need was never greater of new revelation than now. From the views I have already expressed, you will infer the sad conviction, which I share, I believe, with numbers, of the universal decay and now almost death of faith in society. The soul is not preached. The Church seems to totter to its fall, almost all life extinct. On this occasion, any complaisance would be criminal which told you, whose hope and commission it is to preach the faith of Christ, that the faith of Christ is preached.

It is time that this ill-suppressed murmur of all thoughtful men against the famine of our churches; — this moaning of the heart because it is bereaved of the consola- 30 tion, the hope, the grandeur that come alone out of the culture of the moral nature, — should be heard through the sleep of indolence, and over the din of routine. This great and perpetual office of the preacher is not discharged. Preaching is the expression of the moral sentiment in application to the duties of life. In how many churches, by how many prophets, tell me, is man made sensible that he is an infinite Soul; that the earth and heavens are passing into his mind; that he is drinking forever the soul of God? Where now sounds the persuasion, that by its very melody imparadises my heart, and so affirms its own origin in heaven? Where shall I hear words such as in elder ages drew men to leave all and follow, — father and mother, house and land, wife and child? Where shall I hear these august laws of moral being 40 so pronounced as to fill my ear, and I feel ennobled by the offer of my uttermost action and passion? The test of the true faith, certainly, should be its power to charm

---

25 **The Church . . . extinct.** Emerson wrote in his *Journals* of "the corpse-cold Unitarianism of Brattle Street"

and command the soul, as the laws of nature control the activity of the hands, —
so commanding that we find pleasure and honor in obeying. The faith should blend
with the light of rising and of setting suns, with the flying cloud, the singing bird,
and the breath of flowers. But now the priest's Sabbath has lost the splendor of
nature; it is unlovely; we are glad when it is done; we can make, we do make, even
sitting in our pews, a far better, holier, sweeter, for ourselves.

Whenever the pulpit is usurped by a formalist, then is the worshipper defrauded
and disconsolate. We shrink as soon as the prayers begin, which do not uplift, but
smite and offend us. We are fain to wrap our cloaks about us, and secure, as best
10 we can, a solitude that hears not. I once heard a preacher who sorely tempted me
to say I would go to church no more. Men go, thought I, where they are wont to
go, else had no soul entered the temple in the afternoon. A snow-storm was falling
around us. The snow-storm was real, the preacher merely spectral, and the eye felt
the sad contrast in looking at him, and then out of the window behind him into
the beautiful meteor of the snow. He had lived in vain. He had no one word intimating that he had laughed or wept, was married or in love, had been commended, or cheated, or chagrined. If he had ever lived and acted, we were none the
wiser for it. The capital secret of his profession, namely, to convert life into truth,
he had not learned. Not one fact in all his experience had he yet imported into his
20 doctrine. This man had ploughed and planted and talked and bought and sold; he
had read books; he had eaten and drunken; his head aches, his heart throbs; he
smiles and suffers; yet was there not a surmise, a hint, in all the discourse, that he
had ever lived at all. Not a line did he draw out of real history. The true preacher
can be known by this, that he deals out to his people his life, — life passed through
the fire of thought. But of the bad preacher, it could not be told from his sermon
what age of the world he fell in; whether he had a father or a child; whether he
was a freeholder or a pauper; whether he was a citizen or a countryman; or any
other fact of his biography. It seemed strange that the people should come to church.
It seemed as if their houses were very unentertaining, that they should prefer this
30 thoughtless clamor. It shows that there is a commanding attraction in the moral
sentiment, that can lend a faint tint of light to dullness and ignorance coming in its
name and place. The good hearer is sure he has been touched sometimes; is sure there
is somewhat to be reached, and some word that can reach it. When he listens to
these vain words, he comforts himself by their relation to his remembrance of better hours, and so they clatter and echo unchallenged.

I am not ignorant that when we preach unworthily, it is not always quite in vain.
There is a good ear, in some men, that draws supplies to virtue out of very indifferent nutriment. There is poetic truth concealed in all the commonplaces of prayer
and of sermons, and though foolishly spoken, they may be wisely heard; for each
40 is some select expression that broke out in a moment of piety from some stricken
or jubilant soul, and its excellency made it remembered. The prayers and even the
dogmas of our church are like the zodiac of Denderah and the astronomical monu-

42 **zodiac of Denderah,** Dendera, a village on the Nile, was the site of a temple to Hathor which held a
zodiacal table, now in the Louvre

ments of the Hindoos, wholly insulated from anything now extant in the life and business of the people. They mark the height to which the waters once rose. But this docility is a check upon the mischief from the good and devout. In a large portion of the community, the religious service gives rise to quite other thoughts and emotions. We need not chide the negligent servant. We are struck with pity, rather, at the swift retribution of his sloth. Alas for the unhappy man that is called to stand in the pulpit, and *not* give bread of life. Everything that befalls, accuses him. Would he ask contributions for the missions, foreign or domestic? Instantly his face is suffused with shame, to propose to his parish that they should send money a hundred or a thousand miles, to furnish such poor fare as they have at home and would do 10 well to go the hundred or the thousand miles to escape. Would he urge people to a godly way of living; — and can he ask a fellow-creature to come to Sabbath meetings, when he and they all know what is the poor uttermost they can hope for therein? Will he invite them privately to the Lord's Supper? He dares not. If no heart warm this rite, the hollow, dry, creaking formality is too plain, than that he can face a man of wit and energy and put the invitation without terror. In the street, what has he to say to the bold village blasphemer? The village blasphemer sees fear in the face, form, and gait of the minister.

Let me not taint the sincerity of this plea by any oversight of the claims of good men. I know and honor the purity and strict conscience of numbers of the clergy. 20 What life the public worship retains, it owes to the scattered company of pious men, who minister here and there in the churches, and who, sometimes accepting with too great tenderness the tenet of the elders, have not accepted from others, but from their own heart, the genuine impulses of virtue, and so still command our love and awe, to the sanctity of character. Moreover, the exceptions are not so much to be found in a few eminent preachers, as in the better hours, the truer inspirations of all, — nay, in the sincere moments of every man. But, with whatever exception, it is still true that tradition characterizes the preaching of this country; that it comes out of the memory, and not out of the soul; that it aims at what is usual, and not at what is necessary and eternal; that thus historical Christianity destroys 30 the power of preaching, by withdrawing it from the exploration of the moral nature of man; where the sublime is, where are the resources of astonishment and power. What a cruel injustice it is to that Law, the joy of the whole earth, which alone can make the thought dear and rich: that Law whose fatal sureness the astronomical orbits poorly emulate; — that it is travestied and depreciated, that it is behooted and behowled, and not a trait, not a word of it articulated. The pulpit in losing sight of this Law, loses its reason, and gropes after it knows not what. And for want of this culture the soul of the community is sick and faithless. It wants nothing so much as a stern, high, stoical, Christian discipline, to make it know itself and the divinity that speaks through it. Now man is ashamed of himself; he skulks and 40

---

14 **Lord's Supper.** Emerson had resigned the pastorate of the Second Church in Boston in 1832 because of a disagreement with his parishioners on the nature and importance of the Lord's Supper. In a sermon, "The Lord's Supper" (printed in *Miscellanies,* Centenary Edition his works), delivered to the Church, September 9, 1832, he gave the reasons for his "want of sympathy" with the sacrament

sneaks through the world, to be tolerated, to be pitied, and scarcely in a thousand years does any man dare to be wise and good, and so draw after him the tears and blessings of his kind.

Certainly there have been periods when, from the inactivity of the intellect on certain truths, a greater faith was possible in names and persons. The Puritans in England and America found in the Christ of the Catholic Church and in the dogmas inherited from Rome, scope for their austere piety and their longings for civil freedom. But their creed is passing away, and none arises in its room. I think no man can go with his thoughts about him into one of our churches, without feeling 10 that what hold the public worship had on men is gone, or going. It has lost its grasp on the affection of the good and the fear of the bad. In the country, neighborhoods, half parishes are *signing off,* to use the local term. It is already beginning to indicate character and religion to withdraw from the religious meetings. I have heard a devout person, who prized the Sabbath, say in bitterness of heart, "On Sundays, it seems wicked to go to church." And the motive that holds the best there is now only a hope and a waiting. What was once a mere circumstance, that the best and the worst men in the parish, the poor and the rich, the learned and the ignorant, young and old, should meet one day as fellows in one house, in sign of an equal right in the soul, has come to be a paramount motive for going thither.

20 My friends, in these two errors, I think, I find the causes of a decaying church and a wasting unbelief. And what greater calamity can fall upon a nation than the loss of worship? Then all things go to decay. Genius leaves the temple to haunt the senate or the market. Literature becomes frivolous. Science is cold. The eye of youth is not lighted by the hope of other worlds, and age is without honor. Society lives to trifles, and when men die we do not mention them.

And now, my brothers, you will ask, What in these desponding days can be done by us? The remedy is already declared in the ground of our complaint of the Church. We have contrasted the Church with the Soul. In the soul then let the redemption be sought. Wherever a man comes, there comes revolution. The old is for slaves. 30 When a man comes, all books are legible, all things transparent, all religions are forms. He is religious. Man is the wonderworker. He is seen amid miracles. All men bless and curse. He saith yea and nay, only. The stationariness of religion; the assumption that the age of inspiration is past, that the Bible is closed; the fear of degrading the character of Jesus by representing him as a man; — indicate with sufficient clearness the falsehood of our theology. It is the office of a true preacher to show us that God is, not was; that He speaketh, not spake. The true Christianity, — a faith like Christ's in the infinitude of man, — is lost. None believeth in the soul of man, but only in some man or person old and departed. Ah me! no man goeth alone. All men go in flocks to this saint or that poet, avoiding the God who 40 seeth in secret. They cannot see in secret; they love to be blind in public. They think society wiser than their soul, and know not that one soul, and their soul, is wiser than the whole word. See how nations and races flit by on the sea of time

---

14 **a devout person,** Mrs. Emerson, who is quoted in the *Journals* (December 3, 1837), as follows: "Lidian says, it is wicked to go to church Sundays"

and leave no ripple to tell where they floated or sunk, and one good soul shall make the name of Moses, or of Zeno, or of Zoroaster, reverend forever. None assayeth the stern ambition to be the Self of the nation and of nature, but each would be an easy secondary to some Christian scheme, or sectarian connection, or some eminent man. Once leave your own knowledge of God, your own sentiment, and take secondary knowledge, as St. Paul's or George Fox's or Swedenborg's, and you get wide from God with every year this secondary form lasts, and if, as now, for centuries, — the chasm yawns to that breadth, that men can scarcely be convinced there is in them anything divine.

Let me admonish you, first of all, to go alone; to refuse the good models, even 10 those which are sacred to the imagination of men, and dare to love God without mediator or veil. Friends enough you shall find who will hold up to your emulation Wesleys and Oberlins, Saints and Prophets. Thank God for these good men, but say, "I also am a man." Imitation cannot go above its model. The imitator dooms himself to hopeless mediocrity. The inventor did it because it was natural to him, and so in him it has a charm. In the imitator something else is natural, and he bereaves himself of his own beauty, to come short of another man's.

Yourself a newborn bard of the Holy Ghost, cast behind you all conformity, and acquaint men at first hand with Deity. Look to it first and only, that fashion, custom, authority, pleasure, and money, are nothing to you, — are not bandages over 20 your eyes, that you cannot see, — but live with the privilege of the immeasurable mind. Not too anxious to visit periodically all families and each family in your parish connection, — when you meet one of these men or women, be to them a divine man; be to them thought and virtue; let their timid aspirations find in you a friend; let their trampled instincts be genially tempted out in your atmosphere; let their doubts know that you have doubted, and their wonder feel that you have wondered. By trusting your own heart, you shall gain more confidence in other men. For all our penny-wisdom, for all our soul-destroying slavery to habit, it is not to be doubted that all men have sublime thoughts; that all men value the few real hours of life; they love to be heard; they love to be caught up into the vision of principles. We 30 mark with light in the memory the few interviews we have had, in the dreary years of routine and of sin, with souls that made our souls wiser; that spoke what we thought; that told us what we knew; that gave us leave to be what we inly were. Discharge to men the priestly office, and, present or absent, you shall be followed with their love as by an angel.

And, to this end, let us not aim at common degrees of merit. Can we not leave, to such as love it, the virtue that glitters for the commendation of society, and ourselves pierce the deep solitudes of absolute ability and worth? We easily come up to the standard of goodness in society. Society's praise can be cheaply secured, and almost all men are content with those easy merits; but the instant effect of con- 40

---

2 **Zeno,** Greek philosopher, founder of the Stoic School. See note, p. 342   2 **Zoroaster,** founder of the ancient Persian religion about 1000 B.C.   6 **George Fox.** See note, p. 937   13 **Wesley,** John Wesley. See note, p. 924   13 **Oberlin,** Jean Frédéric Oberlin (1740-1826), Franco-German clergyman and philanthropist, for whom Oberlin College was named

versing with God will be to put them away. There are persons who are not actors, not speakers, but influences; persons too great for fame, for display; who disdain eloquence; to whom all we call art and artist, seems too nearly allied to show and by-ends, to the exaggeration of the finite and selfish, and loss of the universal. The orators, the poets, the commanders encroach on us only as fair women do, by our allowance and homage. Slight them by preoccupation of mind, slight them, as you can well afford to do, by high and universal aims, and they instantly feel that you have right, and that it is in lower places that they must shine. They also feel your right; for they with you are open to the influx of the all-knowing Spirit, which an-
10 nihilates before its broad noon the little shades and gradations of intelligence in the compositions we call wiser and wisest.

   In such high communion let us study the grand strokes of rectitude: a bold benevolence, an independence of friends, so that not the unjust wishes of those who love us shall impair our freedom, but we shall resist for truth's sake the freest flow of kindness, and appeal to sympathies far in advance; and — what is the highest form in which we know this beautiful element, — a certain solidity of merit, that has nothing to do with opinion, and which is so essentially and manifestly virtue, that it is taken for granted that the right, the brave, the generous step will be taken by it, and nobody thinks of commending it. You would compliment a coxcomb doing
20 a good act, but you would not praise an angel. The silence that accepts merit as the most natural thing in the world, is the highest applause. Such souls, when they appear, are the Imperial Guard of Virtue, the perpetual reserve, the dictators of fortune. One needs not praise their courage, — they are the heart and soul of nature. O my friends, there are resources in us on which we have not drawn. There are men who rise refreshed on hearing a threat; men to whom a crisis which intimidates and paralyzes the majority, — demanding not the faculties of prudence and thrift, but comprehension, immovableness, the readiness of sacrifice, — comes graceful and beloved as a bride. Napoleon said of Massena, that he was not himself until the battle began to go against him; then, when the dead began to fall in ranks around
30 him, awoke his powers of combination, and he put on terror and victory as a robe. So it is in rugged crises, in unweariable endurance, and in aims which put sympathy out of the question, that the angel is shown. But these are heights that we can scarce remember and look up to without contrition and shame. Let us thank God that such things exist.

   And now let us do what we can to rekindle the smouldering, nigh quenched fire on the altar. The evils of the church that now is are manifest. The question returns, What shall we do? I confess, all attempts to project and establish a Cultus with new rites and forms, seem to me vain. Faith makes us, and not we it, and faith makes its own forms. All attempts to contrive a system are as cold as the new wor-
40 ship introduced by the French to the goddess of Reason, — today, pasteboard and filigree, and ending tomorrow in madness and murder. Rather let the breath of new

---

28 **Massena,** André Massena (1758-1817), Marshal of Napoleon I   39 **new . . . Reason.** The "worship of Reason" was instituted in France in 1793 in the midst of the Reign of Terror. The use of "Reason" in this connection is Deistic and is not to be confused with Emerson's use of the word

life be breathed by you through the forms already existing. For if once you are alive, you shall find they shall become plastic and new. The remedy to their deformity is first, soul, and second, soul, and evermore, soul. A whole popedom of forms one pulsation of virtue can uplift and vivify. Two inestimable advantages Christianity has given us; first the Sabbath, the jubilee of the whole world, whose light dawns welcome alike into the closet of the philosopher, into the garret of toil, and into prison-cells, and everywhere suggests, even to the vile, the dignity of spiritual being. Let it stand forevermore, a temple, which new love, new faith, new sight shall restore to more than its first splendor to mankind. And secondly, the institution of preaching, — the speech of man to men, — essentially the most flexible 10 of all organs, of all forms. What hinders that now, everywhere, in pulpits, in lecture-rooms, in houses, in fields, wherever the invitation of men or your own occasions lead you, you speak the very truth, as your life and conscience teach it, and cheer the waiting, fainting hearts of men with new hope and new revelation?

I look for the hour when that supreme Beauty which ravished the souls of those Eastern men, and chiefly of those Hebrews, and through their lips spoke oracles to all time, shall speak in the West also. The Hebrew and Greek Scriptures contain immortal sentences, that have been bread of life to millions. But they have no epical integrity; are fragmentary; are not shown in their order to the intellect. I look for the new Teacher that shall follow so far those shining laws that he shall see them 20 come full circle; shall see their rounding complete grace; shall see the world to be the mirror of the soul; shall see the identity of the law of gravitation with purity of heart; and shall show that the Ought, that Duty, is one thing with Science, with Beauty, and with Joy.

                                                                                                        1838

_____
17 Hebrew . . . Scriptures, the Old and New Testaments

Self-Reliance

Self-Reliance *has been in the past, and perhaps is still, the best-known and most often quoted essay in American literature. "Trust thyself; every heart vibrates to that iron string," and "Nothing can bring you peace but the triumph of principles" are only two among many examples of Emerson's gift for expressing spiritual truth in quotable form. "These lofty sentences of Emerson," Matthew Arnold wrote in 1884, "and a hundred others of like strain, I never have lost out of my memory; I never can lose them."*

Emerson's belief in self-reliance follows as the logical result of his doctrine of the "oversoul." According to this doctrine, every man has something of the divine in his nature and is capable of establishing a direct relationship with the universal spirit. By means of what Emerson liked to call "the intuition of the moral sentiment," every man is capable of perceiving the highest truth. To quote from the essay: "We lie in the lap of immense intelligence, which makes us receivers of its truth and organs of its activity." Every man, therefore, ought to rely upon his own spiritual perceptions, ought to be self-reliant.

Emerson was an individualist, and his Self-Reliance *is an extreme statement of the individualistic point of view. To the modern reader, the author may appear unmindful of*

social obligations when he says: "What I must do is all that concerns me, not what the peo-
ple think"; and again, "Are they my poor?" But Emerson was not indifferent to society. He
thought of society as composed of individuals. A good society would be a society composed of
good individuals. The primary *obligation of the individual, therefore, is to perfect his own*
life. Like his Puritan forbears, Emerson believed that social salvation could be achieved only
through the salvation of the individuals who compose society.

A superficial reading may leave one with the impression that Emerson's doctrine is fatally
easy. He appears to say, simply, "Do as you like." It should be remembered, however, that
Emerson, again like his Puritan forbears, is holding himself to an almost intolerably high
standard of thinking and living. The individual must obey his own highest *instinct, must*
"absolve" himself to himself. Self-imposed requirements, in the case of a conscientious person,
may be rigorous to the last degree. "If anyone imagines that this law is lax," says Emerson,
a little defiantly, "let him keep its commandment one day."

I read the other day some verses written by an eminent painter which were original
and not conventional. The soul always hears an admonition in such lines, let the subject be what it may. The sentiment they instil is of more value than any thought
they may contain. To believe your own thought, to believe that what is true for
you in your private heart is true for all men, — that is genius. Speak your latent
conviction, and it shall be the universal sense; for the inmost in due time becomes
the outmost, and our first thought is rendered back to us by the trumpets of the
Last Judgment. Familiar as the voice of the mind is to each, the highest merit we
ascribe to Moses, Plato and Milton is that they set at naught books and traditions,
10 and spoke not what men, but what *they* thought. A man should learn to detect and
watch that gleam of light which flashes across his mind from within, more than
the lustre of the firmament of bards and sages. Yet he dismisses without notice his
thought, because it is his. In every work of genius we recognize our own rejected
thoughts; they come back to us with a certain alienated majesty. Great works of art
have no more affecting lesson for us than this. They teach us to abide by our spontaneous impression with good-humored inflexibility then most when the whole cry
of voices is on the other side. Else to-morrow a stranger will say with masterly good
sense precisely what we have thought and felt all the time, and we shall be forced
to take with shame our own opinion from another.
20   There is a time in every man's education when he arrives at the conviction that
envy is ignorance; that imitation is suicide; that he must take himself for better for
worse as his portion; that though the wide universe is full of good, no kernel of
nourishing corn can come to him but through his toil bestowed on that plot of
ground which is given to him to till. The power which resides in him is new in
nature, and none but he knows what that is which he can do, nor does he know
until he has tried. Not for nothing one face, one character, one fact, makes much
impression on him, and another none. This sculpture in the memory is not without
preëstablished harmony. The eye was placed where one ray should fall, that it might
testify of that particular ray. We but half express ourselves, and are ashamed of that
30 divine idea which each of us represents. It may be safely trusted as proportionate

---

1 **eminent painter,** probably Washington Allston (1779-1843)

and of good issues, so it be faithfully imparted, but God will not have his work made manifest by cowards. A man is relieved and gay when he has put his heart into his work and done his best; but what he has said or done otherwise shall give him no peace. It is a deliverance which does not deliver. In the attempt his genius deserts him; no muse befriends; no invention, no hope.

Trust thyself: every heart vibrates to that iron string. Accept the place the divine providence has found for you, the society of your contemporaries, the connection of events. Great men have always done so, and confided themselves childlike to the genius of their age, betraying their perception that the absolutely trustworthy was seated at their heart, working through their hands, predominating in all their being. 10 And we are now men, and must accept in the highest mind the same transcendent destiny; and not minors and invalids in a protected corner nor cowards fleeing before a revolution, but guides, redeemers and benefactors, obeying the Almighty effort and advancing on Chaos and the Dark.

What pretty oracles nature yields us on this text in the face and behavior of children, babes, and even brutes! That divided and rebel mind, that distrust of a sentiment because our arithmetic has computed the strength and means opposed to our purpose, these have not. Their mind being whole, their eye is as yet unconquered, and when we look in their faces we are disconcerted. Infancy conforms to nobody; all conform to it; so that one babe commonly makes four or five out of the adults 20 who prattle and play to it. So God has armed youth and puberty and manhood no less with its own piquancy and charm, and made it enviable and gracious and its claims not to be put by, if it will stand by itself. Do not think the youth has no force, because he cannot speak to you and me. Hark! in the next room his voice is sufficiently clear and emphatic. It seems he knows how to speak to his contemporaries. Bashful or bold then, he will know how to make us seniors very unnecessary.

The nonchalance of boys who are sure of a dinner, and would disdain as much as a lord to do or say aught to conciliate one, is the healthy attitude of human nature. A boy is in the parlor what the pit is in the playhouse; independent, irresponsible, 30 looking out from his corner on such people and facts as pass by, he tries and sentences them on their merits, in the swift, summary way of boys, as good, bad, interesting, silly, eloquent, troublesome. He cumbers himself never about consequences, about interests; he gives an independent, genuine verdict. You must court him; he does not court you. But the man is as it were clapped into jail by his consciousness. As soon as he has once acted or spoken with *éclat* he is a committed person, watched by the sympathy or the hatreds of hundreds, whose affections must now enter into his account. There is no Lethe for this. Ah, that he could pass again into his neutrality! Who can thus avoid all pledges and, having observed, observe again from the same unaffected, unbiased, unbribable, unaffrighted innocence, — must always 40

---

14 **Chaos . . . Dark,** reminiscent of Milton's "Chaos and Old Night" in *Paradise Lost,* Bk. I, l. 543   30
pit, that part of the theater now usually known in the United States as the "orchestra." In Elizabethan times, the pit was the cheapest location in the house and was occupied by the "groundlings" (see *Hamlet,* Act III, sc. ii, l. 11), who were very outspoken in their judgments on the performance   38 **Lethe.** See note, p. 885

be formidable. He would utter opinions on all passing affairs, which being seen to be not private but necessary, would sink like darts into the ear of men and put them in fear.

These are the voices which we hear in solitude, but they grow faint and inaudible as we enter into the world. Society everywhere is in conspiracy against the manhood of every one of its members. Society is a joint-stock company, in which the members agree, for the better securing of his bread to each shareholder, to surrender the liberty and culture of the eater. The virtue in most request is conformity. Self-reliance is its aversion. It loves not realities and creators, but names and customs.

10 Whoso would be a man, must be a nonconformist. He who would gather immortal palms must not be hindered by the name of goodness, but must explore if it be goodness. Nothing is at last sacred but the integrity of your own mind. Absolve you to yourself, and you shall have the suffrage of the world. I remember an answer which when quite young I was prompted to make to a valued adviser who was wont to importune me with the dear old doctrines of the church. On my saying, "What have I to do with the sacredness of traditions, if I live wholly from within?" my friend suggested, — "But these impulses may be from below, not from above." I replied, "They do not seem to me to be such; but if I am the Devil's child, I will live then from the Devil." No law can be sacred to me but that of my nature. Good 20 and bad are but names very readily transferable to that or this; the only right is what is after my constitution; the only wrong what is against it. A man is to carry himself in the presence of all opposition as if every thing were titular and ephemeral but he. I am ashamed to think how easily we capitulate to badges and names, to large societies and dead institutions. Every decent and well-spoken individual affects and sways me more than is right. I ought to go upright and vital, and speak the rude truth in all ways. If malice and vanity wear the coat of philanthropy, shall that pass? If an angry bigot assumes this bountiful cause of Abolition, and comes to me with his last news from Barbadoes, why should I not say to him, "Go love thy infant; love thy woodchopper; be good-natured and modest; have that grace; 30 and never varnish your hard, uncharitable ambition with this incredible tenderness for black folk a thousand miles off. Thy love afar is spite at home." Rough and graceless would be such greeting, but truth is handsomer than the affectation of love. Your goodness must have some edge to it, — else it is none. The doctrine of hatred must be preached, as the counteraction of the doctrine of love, when that pules and whines. I shun father and mother and wife and brother when my genius calls me. I would write on the lintels of the door-post, *Whim.* I hope it is somewhat better than whim at last, but we cannot spend the day in explanation. Expect me not to show cause why I seek or why I exclude company. Then again, do not tell me, as a good man did to-day, of my obligation to put all poor men in good 40 situations. Are they *my* poor? I tell thee, thou foolish philanthropist, that I grudge the dollar, the dime, the cent I give to such men as do not belong to me and to whom I do not belong. There is a class of persons to whom by all spiritual affinity

11 **palms,** symbols of success   28 **Barbadoes,** an island in the British West Indies in which Negro slavery was abolished in 1834   36 **lintels.** A lintel is the crosspiece above a door

I am bought and sold; for them I will go to prison if need be; but your miscellaneous popular charities; the education at college of fools; the building of meeting-
houses to the vain end to which many now stand; alms to sots, and the thousand-
fold Relief Societies; — though I confess with shame I sometimes succumb and
give the dollar, it is a wicked dollar, which by and by I shall have the manhood
to withhold.

Virtues are, in the popular estimate, rather the exception than the rule. There is
the man *and* his virtues. Men do what is called a good action, as some piece of courage or charity, much as they would pay a fine in expiation of daily non-appearance
on parade. Their works are done as an apology or extenuation of their living in the 10
world, — as invalids and the insane pay a high board. Their virtues are penances. I
do not wish to expiate, but to live. My life is for itself and not for a spectacle. I
much prefer that it should be of a lower strain, so it be genuine and equal, than
that it should be glittering and unsteady. I wish it to be sound and sweet, and not
to need diet and bleeding. I ask primary evidence that you are a man, and refuse
this appeal from the man to his actions. I know that for myself it makes no difference whether I do or forbear those actions which are reckoned excellent. I cannot
consent to pay for a privilege where I have intrinsic right. Few and mean as my
gifts may be, I actually am, and do not need for my own assurance or the assur-
ance of my fellows any secondary testimony.   20

What I must do is all that concerns me, not what the people think. This rule,
equally arduous in actual and in intellectual life, may serve for the whole distinction between greatness and meanness. It is the harder because you will always find
those who think they know what is your duty better than you know it. It is easy
in the world to live after the world's opinion; it is easy in solitude to live after our
own; but the great man is he who in the midst of the crowd keeps with perfect
sweetness the independence of solitude.

The objection to conforming to usages that have become dead to you is that it
scatters your force. It loses your time and blurs the impression of your character. If
you maintain a dead church, contribute to a dead Bible-society, vote with a great 30
party either for the government or against it, spread your table like base house-
keepers, — under all these screens I have difficulty to detect the precise man you
are: and of course so much force is withdrawn from your proper life. But do your
work, and I shall know you. Do your work, and you shall reinforce yourself. A man
must consider what a blind-man's-buff is this game of conformity. If I know your
sect I anticipate your argument. I hear a preacher announce for his text and topic
the expediency of one of the institutions of his church. Do I not know beforehand
that not possibly can he say a new and spontaneous word? Do I not know that
with all this ostentation of examining the grounds of the institution he will do no
such thing? Do I not know that he is pledged to himself not to look but at one 40
side, the permitted side, not as a man, but as a parish minister? He is a retained
attorney, and these airs of the bench are the emptiest affectation. Well, most men
have bound their eyes with one or another handkerchief, and attached themselves

---

42 **bench,** the judge, who sits on the "bench"

to some one of these communities of opinion. This conformity makes them not false in a few particulars, authors of a few lies, but false in all particulars. Their every truth is not quite true. Their two is not the real two, their four is not the real four; so that every word they say chagrins us and we know not where to begin to set them right. Meantime nature is not slow to equip us in the prison-uniform of the party to which we adhere. We come to wear one cut of face and figure, and acquire by degrees the gentlest asinine expression. There is a mortifying experience in particular, which does not fail to wreak itself also in the general history; I mean "the foolish face of praise," the forced smile which we put on in company where
10 we do not feel at ease, in answer to conversation which does not interest us. The muscles, not spontaneously moved but moved by a low usurping wilfulness, grow tight about the outline of the face, with the most disagreeable sensation.

For nonconformity the world whips you with its displeasure. And therefore a man must know how to estimate a sour face. The by-standers look askance on him in the public street or in the friend's parlor. If this aversion had its origin in contempt and resistance like his own he might well go home with a sad countenance; but the sour faces of the multitude, like their sweet faces, have no deep cause, but are put on and off as the wind blows and a newspaper directs. Yet is the discontent of the multitude more formidable than that of the senate and the college. It is easy
20 enough for a firm man who knows the world to brook the rage of the cultivated classes. Their rage is decorous and prudent, for they are timid, as being very vulnerable themselves. But when to their feminine rage the indignation of the people is added, when the ignorant and the poor are aroused, when the unintelligent brute force that lies at the bottom of society is made to growl and mow, it needs the habit of magnanimity and religion to treat it godlike as a trifle of no concernment.

The other terror that scares us from self-trust is our consistency; a reverence for our past act or word because the eyes of others have no other data for computing our orbit than our past acts, and we are loth to disappoint them.

But why should you keep your head over your shoulder? Why drag about this
30 corpse of your memory, lest you contradict somewhat you have stated in this or that public place? Suppose you should contradict yourself, what then? It seems to be a rule of wisdom never to rely on your memory alone, scarcely even in acts of pure memory, but to bring the past for judgment into the thousand-eyed present, and live ever in a new day. In your metaphysics you have denied personality to the Deity, yet when the devout motions of the soul come, yield to them heart and life, though they should clothe God with shape and color. Leave your theory, as Joseph his coat in the hand of the harlot, and flee.

A foolish consistency is the hobgoblin of little minds, adored by little statesmen and philosophers and divines. With consistency a great soul has simply nothing to
40 do. He may as well concern himself with his shadow on the wall. Speak what you think now in hard words and to-morrow speak what to-morrow thinks in hard words again, though it contradict every thing you said to-day. — "Ah, so you shall

9 **the foolish . . . praise,** from Pope's famous satire on Addison in his "Epistle to Dr. Arbuthnot" 24 **mow,** make grimaces 36 **Joseph . . . flee.** The allusion is to Genesis 39:12

be sure to be misunderstood." — Is it so bad then to be misunderstood? Pythagoras
was misunderstood, and Socrates, and Jesus, and Luther, and Copernicus, and
Galileo, and Newton, and every pure and wise spirit that ever took flesh. To be
great is to be misunderstood.

I suppose no man can violate his nature. All the sallies of his will are rounded
in by the law of his being, as the inequalities of Andes and Himmaleh are insignificant in the curve of the sphere. Nor does it matter how you gauge and try him. A
character is like an acrostic or Alexandrian stanza; — read it forward, backward, or
across, it still spells the same thing. In this pleasing contrite wood-life which God
allows me, let me record day by day my honest thought without prospect or retro-   10
spect, and, I cannot doubt, it will be found symmetrical, though I mean it not and
see it not. My book should smell of pines and resound with the hum of insects.
The swallow over my window should interweave that thread or straw he carries in
his bill into my web also. We pass for what we are. Character teaches above our wills.
Men imagine that they communicate their virtue or vice only by overt actions, and
do not see that virtue or vice emit a breath every moment.

There will be an agreement in whatever variety of actions, so they be each honest
and natural in their hour. For of one will, the actions will be harmonious, however
unlike they seem. These varieties are lost sight of at a little distance, at a little height
of thought. One tendency unites them all. The voyage of the best ship is a zigzag   20
line of a hundred tacks. See the line from a sufficient distance, and it straightens
itself to the average tendency. Your genuine action will explain itself and will explain your other genuine actions. Your conformity explains nothing. Act singly,
and what you have already done singly will justify you now. Greatness appeals to
the future. If I can be firm enough to-day to do right and scorn eyes, I must have
done so much right before as to defend me now. Be it how it will, do right now.
Always scorn appearances and you always may. The force of character is cumulative. All the foregone days of virtue work their health into this. What makes the
majesty of the heroes of the senate and the field, which so fills the imagination?
The consciousness of a train of great days and victories behind. They shed a united   30
light on the advancing actor. He is attended as by a visible escort of angels. That is
it which throws thunder into Chatham's voice, and dignity into Washington's port,
and America into Adams's eye. Honor is venerable to us because it is no ephemera.
It is always ancient virtue. We worship it to-day because it is not of to-day. We love
it and pay it homage because it is not a trap for our love and homage, but is self-
dependent, self-derived, and therefore of an old immaculate pedigree, even if shown
in a young person.

I hope in these days we have heard the last of conformity and consistency. Let

1 **Pythagoras**. See note, p. 293   2 **Socrates**, Greek philosopher of the fifth century B.C.   2 **Luther**,
Martin Luther. See note, p. 116   2 **Copernicus**, Nikolaus Copernicus (1473-1543), Polish astronomer
whose system superseded the Ptolemaic   3 **Galileo** (1564-1642), Italian astronomer   3 **Newton**, Sir
Isaac Newton. See note, p. 1075   6 **Andes**, a mountain range in South America.   6 **Himmaleh**, or
Himalaya, a mountain range between India and China in which are found the world's highest moun-
tains   32 **Chatham**, William Pitt, first Earl of Chatham (1708-1788), English statesman   33 **Adams**,
Samuel Adams (1722-1803), Revolutionary patriot

the words be gazetted and ridiculous henceforward. Instead of the gong for dinner, let us hear a whistle from the Spartan fife. Let us never bow and apologize more. A great man is coming to eat at my house. I do not wish to please him; I wish that he should wish to please me. I will stand here for humanity, and though I would make it kind, I would make it true. Let us affront and reprimand the smooth mediocrity and squalid contentment of the times, and hurl in the face of custom and trade and office, the fact which is the upshot of all history, that there is a great responsibile Thinker and Actor working wherever a man works; that a true man belongs to no other time or place, but is the centre of things. Where he is, there is
10 nature. He measures you and all men and all events. Ordinarily, every body in society reminds us of somewhat else, or of some other person. Character, reality, reminds you of nothing else; it takes place of the whole creation. The man must be so much that he must make all circumstances indifferent. Every true man is a cause, a country, and an age; requires infinite spaces and numbers and time fully to accomplish his design; — and posterity seem to follow his steps as a train of clients. A man Cæsar is born, and for ages after we have a Roman Empire. Christ is born, and millions of minds so grow and cleave to his genius that he is confounded with virtue and the possible of man. An institution is the lengthened shadow of one man; as, Monachism, of the Hermit Antony; the Reformation, of Luther; Quakerism, of
20 Fox; Methodism, of Wesley; Abolition, of Clarkson. Scipio, Milton called "the height of Rome;" and all history resolves itself very easily into the biography of a few stout and earnest persons.

Let a man then know his worth, and keep things under his feet. Let him not peep or steal, or skulk up and down with the air of a charity-boy, a bastard, or an interloper in the world which exists for him. But the man in the street, finding no worth in himself which corresponds to the force which built a tower or sculptured a marble god, feels poor when he looks on these. To him a palace, a statue, or a costly book have an alien and forbidding air, much like a gay equipage, and seem to say like that, "Who are you, Sir?" Yet they all are his, suitors for his notice,
30 petitioners to his faculties that they will come out and take possession. The picture waits for my verdict; it is not to command me, but I am to settle its claims to praise. That popular fable of the sot who was picked up dead-drunk in the street, carried to the duke's house, washed and dressed and laid in the duke's bed, and, on his waking, treated with all obsequious ceremony like the duke, and assured that he had been insane, owes its popularity to the fact that it symbolizes so well the state of man, who is in the world a sort of sot, but now and then wakes up, exercises his reason and finds himself a true prince.

---

1 **gazetted,** announced in a gazette   19 **Monachism, . . . Antony,** St. Anthony (251-356?), Egyptian founder of monachism, or monasticism   20 **Fox,** George Fox. See note, p. 937   20 **Wesley,** John Wesley. See note, p. 924   20 **Clarkson,** Thomas Clarkson (1760-1846), English abolitionist   20 **Scipio** (185?-129? B.C.), Roman general who captured and destroyed Carthage   20 **the height of Rome,** from *Paradise Lost,* Bk. IX, l. 510   21 **all . . . persons.** Compare Carlyle's famous dictum at the beginning of *Heroes and Hero-Worship* (1841): "For, as I take it, Universal History, the history of what man has accomplished in this world, is at bottom the History of the Great Men who have worked here"   32 **fable.** Such a story is used by Shakespeare in the "Induction" of *Taming of the Shrew*

Our reading is mendicant and sycophantic. In history our imagination plays us false. Kingdom and lordship, power and estate, are a gaudier vocabulary than private John and Edward in a small house and common day's work; but the things of life are the same to both; the sum total of both is the same. Why all this deference to Alfred and Scanderbeg and Gustavus? Suppose they were virtuous; did they wear out virtue? As great a stake depends on your private act to-day as followed their public and renowned steps. When private men shall act with original views, the lustre will be transferred from the actions of kings to those of gentlemen.

The world has been instructed by its kings, who have so magnetized the eyes of nations. It has been taught by this colossal symbol the mutual reverence that is due 10
from man to man. The joyful loyalty with which men have everywhere suffered the king, the noble, or the great proprietor to walk among them by a law of his own, make his own scale of men and things and reverse theirs, pay for benefits not with money but with honor, and represent the law in his person, was the hieroglyphic by which they obscurely signified their consciousness of their own right and comeliness, the right of every man.

The magnetism which all original action exerts is explained when we inquire the reason of self-trust. Who is the Trustee? What is the aboriginal Self, on which a universal reliance may be grounded? What is the nature and power of that science-baffling star, without parallax, without calculable elements, which shoots a ray of 20
beauty even into trivial and impure actions, if the least mark of independence appear? The inquiry leads us to that source, at once the essence of genius, of virtue, and of life, which we call Spontaneity or Instinct. We denote this primary wisdom as Intuition, whilst all later teachings are tuitions. In that deep force, the last fact behind which analysis cannot go, all things find their common origin. For the sense of being which in calm hours rises, we know not how, in the soul, is not diverse from things, from space, from light, from time, from man, but one with them and proceeds obviously from the same source whence their life and being also proceed. We first share the life by which things exist and afterwards see them as appearances in nature and forget that we have shared their cause. Here is the fountain of action 30
and of thought. Here are the lungs of that inspiration which giveth man wisdom and which cannot be denied without impiety and atheism. We lie in the lap of immense intelligence, which makes us receivers of its truth and organs of its activity. When we discern justice, when we discern truth, we do nothing of ourselves, but allow a passage to its beams. If we ask whence this comes, if we seek to pry into the soul that causes, all philosophy is at fault. Its presence or its absence is all we can affirm. Every man discriminates between the voluntary acts of his mind and his involuntary perceptions, and knows that to his involuntary perceptions a perfect faith is due. He may err in the expression of them, but he knows that these things

---

5 **Alfred,** Alfred the Great (849-901), king of the West Saxons   5 **Scanderbeg** (1403-1468), Albanian patriot who opposed the Turks   5 **Gustavus,** Gustavus Adolphus (1594-1632), king of Sweden   20 **parallax,** the apparent displacement (or the difference in apparent direction) of an object as seen from two different points

are so, like day and night, not to be disputed. My wilful actions and acquisitions are but roving; — the idlest reverie, the faintest native emotion, command my curiosity and respect. Thoughtless people contradict as readily the statement of perceptions as of opinions, or rather much more readily; for they do not distinguish between perception and notion. They fancy that I choose to see this or that thing. But perception is not whimsical, but fatal. If I see a trait, my children will see it after me, and in course of time all mankind, — although it may chance that no one has seen it before me. For my perception of it is as much a fact as the sun.

The relations of the soul to the divine spirit are so pure that it is profane to seek
10 to interpose helps. It must be that when God speaketh he should communicate, not one thing, but all things; should fill the world with his voice; should scatter forth light, nature, time, souls, from the centre of the present thought; and new date and new create the whole. Whenever a mind is simple and receives a divine wisdom, old things pass away, — means, teachers, texts, temples fall; it lives now, and absorbs past and future into the present hour. All things are made sacred by relation to it, — one as much as another. All things are dissolved to their centre by their cause, and in the universal miracle petty and particular miracles disappear. If therefore a man claims to know and speak of God and carries you backward to the phraseology of some old mouldered nation in another country, in another world, believe him not.
20 Is the acorn better than the oak which is its fulness and completion? Is the parent better than the child into whom he has cast his ripened being? Whence then this worship of the past? The centuries are conspirators against the sanity and authority of the soul. Time and space are but physiological colors which the eye makes, but the soul is light: where it is, is day; where it was, is night; and history is an impertinence and an injury if it be any thing more than a cheerful apologue or parable of my being and becoming.

Man is timid and apologetic; he is no longer upright; he dares not say 'I think,' 'I am,' but quotes some saint or sage. He is ashamed before the blade of grass or the blowing rose. These roses under my window make no reference to former roses
30 or to better ones; they are for what they are; they exist with God to-day. There is no time to them. There is simply the rose; it is perfect in every moment of its existence. Before a leaf-bud has burst, its whole life acts; in the full-blown flower there is no more; in the leafless root there is no less. Its nature is satisfied and it satisfies nature in all moments alike. But man postpones or remembers; he does not live in the present, but with reverted eye laments the past, or, heedless of the riches that surround him, stands on tiptoe to foresee the future. He cannot be happy and strong until he too lives with nature in the present, above time.

This should be plain enough. Yet see what strong intellects dare not yet hear God himself unless he speak the phraseology of I know not what David, or Jeremiah,
40 or Paul. We shall not always set so great a price on a few texts, on a few lives. We are like children who repeat by rote the sentences of grandames and tutors, and, as they grow older, of the men of talents and character they chance to see, — painfully recollecting the exact words they spoke; afterwards, when they come into the point of view which those had who uttered these sayings, they understand them and are willing to let the words go; for at any time they can use words as good when occa-

sion comes. If we live truly, we shall see truly. It is as easy for the strong man to be strong, as it is for the weak to be weak. When we have no perception, we shall gladly disburden the memory of its hoarded treasures as old rubbish. When a man lives with God, his voice shall be as sweet as the murmur of the brook and the rustle of the corn.

And now at last the highest truth on this subject remains unsaid; probably cannot be said; for all that we say is the far-off remembering of the intuition. That thought by what I can now nearest approach to say it, is this. When good is near you, when you have life in yourself, it is not by any known or accustomed way; you shall not discern the footprints of any other; you shall not see the face of man; 10 you shall not hear any name;— the way, the thought, the good, shall be wholly strange and new. It shall exclude example and experience. You take the way from man, not to man. All persons that ever existed are its forgotten ministers. Fear and hope are alike beneath it. There is somewhat low even in hope. In the hour of vision there is nothing that can be called gratitude, nor properly joy. The soul raised over the passion beholds identity and eternal causation, perceives the self-existence of Truth and Right, and calms itself with knowing that all things go well. Vast spaces of nature, the Atlantic Ocean, the South Sea; long intervals of time, years, centuries, are of no account. This which I think and feel underlay every former state of life and circumstances, as it does underlie my present, and what is called 20 life and what is called death.

Life only avails, not the having lived. Power ceases in the instant of repose; it resides in the moment of transition from a past to a new state, in the shooting of the gulf, in the darting to an aim. This one fact the world hates; that the soul *becomes;* for that forever degrades the past, turns all riches to poverty, all reputation to a shame, confounds the saint with the rogue, shoves Jesus and Judas equally aside. Why then do we prate of self-reliance? Inasmuch as the soul is present there will be power not confident but agent. To talk of reliance is a poor external way of speaking. Speak rather of that which relies because it works and is. Who has more obedience than I masters me, though he should not raise his finger. Round him I 30 must revolve by the gravitation of spirits. We fancy it rhetoric when we speak of eminent virtue. We do not yet see that virtue is Height, and that a man or a company of men, plastic and permeable to principles, by the law of nature must overpower and ride all cities, nations, kings, rich men, poets, who are not.

This is the ultimate fact which we so quickly reach on this, as on every topic, the resolution of all into the ever-blessed ONE. Self-existence is the attribute of the Supreme Cause, and it constitutes the measure of good by the degree in which it enters into all lower forms. All things real are so by so much virtue as they contain. Commerce, husbandry, hunting, whaling, war, eloquence, personal weight, are somewhat, and engage my respect as examples of its presence and impure action. I 40 see the same law working in nature for conservation and growth. Power is, in nature, the essential measure of right. Nature suffers nothing to remain in her kingdoms which cannot help itself. The genesis and maturation of a planet, its poise and orbit, the bended tree recovering itself from the strong wind, the vital resources of every animal and vegetable, are demonstrations of the self-sufficing and therefore self-relying soul.

Thus all concentrates: let us not rove; let us sit at home with the cause. Let us stun and astonish the intruding rabble of men and books and institutions by a simple declaration of the divine fact. Bid the invaders take the shoes from off their feet, for God is here within. Let our simplicity judge them, and our docility to our own law demonstrate the poverty of nature and fortune beside our native riches.

But now we are a mob. Man does not stand in awe of man, nor is his genius admonished to stay at home, to put itself in communication with the internal ocean, but it goes abroad to beg a cup of water of the urns of other men. We must go alone. I like the silent church before the service begins, better than any preaching. How far off, how cool, how chaste the persons look, begirt each one with a precinct or sanctuary! So let us always sit. Why should we assume the faults of our friend, or wife, or father, or child, because they sit around our hearth, or are said to have the same blood? All men have my blood and I all men's. Not for that will I adopt their petulance or folly, even to the extent of being ashamed of it. But your isolation must not be mechanical, but spiritual, that is, must be elevation. At times the whole world seems to be in conspiracy to importune you with emphatic trifles. Friend, client, child, sickness, fear, want, charity, all knock at once at thy closet door and say, — 'Come out unto us.' But keep thy state; come not into their confusion. The power men possess to annoy me I give them by a weak curiosity. No man can come near me but through my act. "What we love that we have, but by desire we bereave ourselves of the love."

If we cannot at once rise to the sanctities of obedience and faith, let us at least resist our temptations; let us enter into the state of war and wake Thor and Woden, courage and constancy, in our Saxon breasts. This is to be done in our smooth times by speaking the truth. Check this lying hospitality and lying affection. Live no longer to the expectation of these deceived and deceiving people with whom we converse. Say to them, 'O father, O mother, O wife, O brother, O friend, I have lived with you after appearances hitherto. Henceforward I am the truth's. Be it known unto you that henceforward I obey no law less than the eternal law. I will have no covenants but proximities. I shall endeavor to nourish my parents, to support my family, to be the chaste husband of one wife, — but these relations I must fill after a new and unprecedented way. I appeal from your customs. I must be myself. I cannot break myself any longer for you, or you. If you can love me for what I am, we shall be the happier. If you cannot, I will still seek to deserve that you should. I will not hide my tastes or aversions. I will so trust that what is deep is holy, that I will do strongly before the sun and moon whatever inly rejoices me and the heart appoints. If you are noble, I will love you; if you are not, I will not hurt you and myself by hypocritical attentions. If you are true, but not in the same truth with

---

me, cleave to your companions; I will seek my own. I do this not selfishly but humbly and truly. It is alike your interest, and mine, and all men's, however long we have dwelt in lies, to live in truth. Does this sound harsh to-day? You will soon love what is dictated by your nature as well as mine, and if we follow the truth it will bring us out safe at last.' — But so may you give these friends pain. Yes, but I cannot sell my liberty and my power, to save their sensibility. Besides, all persons have their moments of reason, when they look out into the region of absolute truth; then will they justify me and do the same thing.

The populace think that your rejection of popular standards is a rejection of all standard, and mere antinomianism; and the bold sensualist will use the name of 10 philosophy to gild his crimes. But the law of consciousness abides. There are two confessionals, in one or the other of which we must be shriven. You may fulfill your round of duties by clearing yourself in the *direct,* or in the *reflex* way. Consider whether you have satisfied your relations to father, mother, cousin, neighbor, town, cat, and dog — whether any of these can upbraid you. But I may also neglect this reflex standard and absolve me to myself. I have my own stern claims and perfect circle. It denies the name of duty to many offices that are called duties. But if I can discharge its debts it enables me to dispense with the popular code. If any one imagines that this law is lax, let him keep its commandment one day.

And truly it demands something godlike in him who has cast off the common 20 motives of humanity and has ventured to trust himself for a taskmaster. High be his heart, faithful his will, clear his sight, that he may in good earnest be doctrine, society, law, to himself, that a simple purpose may be to him as strong as iron necessity is to others!

If any man consider the present aspects of what is called by distinction *society,* he will see the need of these ethics. The sinew and heart of man seem to be drawn out, and we are become timorous, desponding whimperers. We are afraid of truth, afraid of fortune, afraid of death, and afraid of each other. Our age yields no great and perfect persons. We want men and women who shall renovate life and our social state, but we see that most natures are insolvent, cannot satisfy their own wants, 30 have an ambition out of all proportion to their practical force and do lean and beg day and night continually. Our housekeeping is mendicant, our arts, our occupations, our marriages, our religion we have not chosen, but society has chosen for us. We are parlor soldiers. We shun the rugged battle of fate, where strength is born.

If our young men miscarry in their first enterprises they lose all heart. If the young merchant fails, men say he is *ruined.* If the finest genius studies at one of our colleges and is not installed in an office within one year afterwards in the cities or suburbs of Boston or New York, it seems to his friends and to himself that he is right in being disheartened and in complaining the rest of his life. A sturdy lad from New Hampshire or Vermont, who in turn tries all the professions, who *teams it,* 40 *farms it, peddles,* keeps a school, preaches, edits a newspaper, goes to Congress, buys a township, and so forth, in successive years, and always like a cat falls on his feet,

10 **antinomianism,** the doctrine that the moral law may be set aside on the ground that faith alone is necessary to salvation

is worth a hundred of these city dolls. He walks abreast with his days and feels no shame in not 'studying a profession,' for he does not postpone his life, but lives already. He has not one chance, but a hundred chances. Let a Stoic open the resources of man and tell men they are not leaning willows, but can and must detach themselves; that with the exercise of self-trust, new powers shall appear; that a man is the word made flesh, born to shed healing to the nations; that he should be ashamed of our compassion, and that the moment he acts from himself, tossing the laws, the books, idolatries and customs out of the window, we pity him no more but thank and revere him; — and that teacher shall restore the life of man to splendor
10 and make his name dear to all history.

It is easy to see that a greater self-reliance must work a revolution in all the offices and relations of men; in their religion; in their education; in their pursuits; their modes of living; their association; in their property; in their speculative views.

1. In what prayers do men allow themselves! That which they call a holy office is not so much as brave and manly. Prayer looks abroad and asks for some foreign addition to come through some foreign virtue, and loses itself in endless mazes of natural and supernatural, and mediatorial and miraculous. Prayer that craves a particular commodity, anything less than all good, is vicious. Prayer is the contemplation of the facts of life from the highest point of view. It is the soliloquy of a beholding
20 and jubilant soul. It is the spirit of God pronouncing his works good. But prayer as a means to effect a private end is meanness and theft. It supposes dualism and not unity in nature and consciousness. As soon as the man is at one with God, he will not beg. He will then see prayer in all action. The prayer of the farmer kneeling in his field to weed it, the prayer of the rower kneeling with the stroke of his oar, are true prayers heard throughout nature, though for cheap ends. Caratach, in Fletcher's "Bonduca," when admonished to inquire the mind of the god Audate, replies, —

> His hidden meaning lies in our endeavors;
> Our valors are our best gods.

Another sort of false prayers are our regrets. Discontent is the want of self-reliance:
30 it is infirmity of will. Regret calamities if you can thereby help the sufferer; if not, attend your own work and already the evil begins to be repaired. Our sympathy is just as base. We come to them who weep foolishly and sit down and cry for company, instead of imparting to them truth and health in rough electric shocks, putting them once more in communication with their own reason. The secret of fortune is joy in our hands. Welcome evermore to gods and men is the self-helping man. For him all doors are flung wide; him all tongues greet, all honors crown, all eyes follow with desire. Our love goes out to him and embraces him because he did not need it. We solicitously and apologetically caress and celebrate him because he held on

---

6 **word made flesh.** Compare John 1:14: "And the Word was made flesh, and dwelt among us . . ."   6 **healing . . . nations.** Compare Revelation 22:2: ". . . and the leaves of the tree [of life] were for the healing of the nations"   20 **God . . . good.** Compare Genesis 1:31: "And God saw everything that he had made, and behold, it was very good"   27 **His . . . gods,** from John Fletcher's *Bonduca* (1647), Act III, Sc. i, ll. 88-89

his way and scorned our disapprobation. The gods love him because men hated him. "To the persevering mortal," said Zoroaster, "the blessed Immortals are swift."

As men's prayers are a disease of the will, so are their creeds a disease of the intellect. They say with those foolish Israelites, 'Let not God speak to us, lest we die. Speak thou, speak any man with us, and we will obey.' Everywhere I am hindered of meeting God in my brother, because he has shut his own temple doors and recites fables merely to his brother's, or his brother's brother's God. Every new mind is a new classification. If it prove a mind of uncommon activity and power, a Locke, a Lavoisier, a Hutton, a Bentham, a Fourier, it imposes its classification on other men, and lo! a new system. In proportion to the depth of the thought, and so to   10 the number of the objects it touches and brings within reach of the pupil, is his complacency. But chiefly is this apparent in creeds and churches, which are also classifications of some powerful mind acting on the elemental thought of duty and man's relation to the Highest. Such is Calvinism, Quakerism, Swedenborgism. The pupil takes the same delight in subordinating every thing to the new terminology as a girl who has just learned botany in seeing a new earth and new seasons thereby. It will happen for a time that the pupil will find his intellectual power has grown by the study of his master's mind. But in all unbalanced minds the classification is idolized, passes for the end and not for a speedily exhaustible means, so that the walls of the system blend to their eye in the remote horizon with the walls of the   20 universe; the luminaries of heaven seem to them hung on the arch their master built. They cannot imagine how you aliens have any right to see, — how you can see; 'It must be somehow that you stole the light from us.' They do not yet perceive that light, unsystematic, indomitable, will break into any cabin, even into theirs. Let them chirp awhile and call it their own. If they are honest and do well, presently their neat new pinfold will be too strait and low, will crack, will lean, will rot and vanish, and the immortal light, all young and joyful, million-orbed, million-colored, will beam over the universe as on the first morning.

2. It is for want of self-culture that the superstition of Travelling, whose idols are Italy, England, Egypt, retains its fascination for all educated Americans. They who   30 made England, Italy, or Greece venerable in the imagination, did so by sticking fast where they were, like an axis of the earth. In manly hours we feel that duty is our place. The soul is no traveller; the wise man stays at home, and when his necessities, his duties, on any occasion call him from his house, or into foreign lands, he is at home still and shall make men sensible by the expression of his countenance that he goes, the missionary of wisdom and virtue, and visits cities and men like a sovereign and not like an interloper or a valet.

I have no churlish objection to the circumnavigation of the globe for the purposes of art, of study, and benevolence, so that the man is first domesticated, or does not go abroad with the hope of finding somewhat greater than he knows. He who travels   40

---

2 **Zoroaster.** See note, p. 1092   4 **Let . . . obey,** inaccurately quoted from Exodus 21:19   8 **Locke,** John Locke. See note, p. 284   9 **Lavoisier,** Antoine Lavoisier (1743-1794), French chemist   9 **Hutton,** James Hutton (1726-1797), English geologist   9 **Bentham,** Jeremy Bentham (1748-1832), English philosopher and jurist   9 **Fourier,** François Fourier (1772-1837), French socialist

to be amused, or to get somewhat which he does not carry, travels away from himself, and grows old even in youth among old things. In Thebes, in Palmyra, his
will and mind have become old and dilapidated as they. He carries ruins to ruins.

Travelling is a fool's paradise. Our first journeys discover to us the indifference of
places. At home I dream that at Naples, at Rome, I can be intoxicated with beauty
and lose my sadness. I pack my trunk, embrace my friends, embark on the sea and
at last wake up in Naples, and there beside me is the stern fact, the sad self, unre-
lenting, identical, that I fled from. I seek the Vatican and the palaces. I affect to be
intoxicated with sights and suggestions, but I am not intoxicated. My giant goes
10 with me wherever I go.

3. But the rage of travelling is a symptom of a deeper unsoundness affecting the
whole intellectual action. The intellect is vagabond, and our system of education
fosters restlessness. Our minds travel when our bodies are forced to stay at home.
We imitate; and what is imitation but the travelling of the mind? Our houses are
built with foreign taste; our shelves are garnished with foreign ornaments; our opinions, our tastes, our faculties, lean, and follow the Past and the Distant. The soul
created the arts wherever they have flourished. It was in his own mind that the artist
sought his model. It was an application of his own thought to the thing to be done
and the conditions to be observed. And why need we copy the Doric or the Gothic
20 model? Beauty, convenience, grandeur of thought and quaint expression are as near
to us as to any, and if the American artist will study with hope and love the precise
thing to be done by him, considering the climate, the soil, the length of the day,
the wants of the people, the habit and form of the government, he will create a
house in which all these will find themselves fitted, and taste and sentiment will
be satisfied also.

Insist on yourself; never imitate. Your own gift you can present every moment
with the cumulative force of a whole life's cultivation; but of the adopted talent of
another you have only an extemporaneous half possession. That which each can do
best, none but his Maker can teach him. No man yet knows what it is, nor can, till
30 that person has exhibited it. Where is the master who could have taught Shakspeare? Where is the master who could have instructed Franklin, or Washington,
or Bacon, or Newton? Every great man is a unique. The Scipionism of Scipio is
precisely that part he could not borrow. Shakspeare will never be made by the study
of Shakspeare. Do that which is assigned you, and you cannot hope too much or
dare too much. There is at this moment for you an utterance brave and grand as that
of the colossal chisel of Phidias, or trowel of the Egyptians, or the pen of Moses or
Dante, but different from all these. Not possibly will the soul, all rich, all eloquent,
with thousand-cloven tongue, deign to repeat itself; but if you can hear what these
patriarchs say, surely you can reply to them in the same pitch of voice; for the ear
40 and the tongue are two organs of one nature. Abide in the simple and noble regions
of thy life, obey thy heart, and thou shalt reproduce the Foreworld again.

---

2 **Thebes,** ancient ruined city in Egypt   2 **Palmyra,** ancient ruined city in Syria   19 **Doric,** Greek or
classic   19 **Gothic,** medieval   36 **Phidias,** Greek sculptor of the fifth century B.C.   36 **trowel . . .**
Egyptians, meaning the pyramids

4. As our Religion, our Education, our Art look abroad, so does our spirit of society. All men plume themselves on the improvement of society, and no man improves.

Society never advances. It recedes as fast on one side as it gains on the other. It undergoes continual changes; it is barbarous, it is civilized, it is christianized, it is rich, it is scientific, but this change is not amelioration. For every thing that is given something is taken. Society acquires new arts and loses old instincts. What a contrast between the well-clad, reading, writing, thinking American, with a watch, a pencil and a bill of exchange in his pocket, and the naked New Zealander, whose property is a club, a spear, a mat and an undivided twentieth of a shed to sleep un- 10 der! But compare the health of the two men and you shall see that the white man has lost his aboriginal strength. If the traveller tell us truly, strike the savage with a broad-axe and in a day or two the flesh shall unite and heal as if you struck the blow into soft pitch, and the same blow shall send the white to his grave.

The civilized man has built a coach, but has lost the use of his feet. He is supported on crutches, but lacks so much support of muscle. He has a fine Geneva watch, but he fails of the skill to tell the hour by the sun. A Greenwich nautical almanac he has, and so being sure of the information when he wants it, the man in the street does not know a star in the sky. The solstice he does not observe; the equinox he knows as little; and the whole bright calendar of the year is without a 20 dial in his mind. His note-books impair his memory; his libraries overload his wit; the insurance-office increases the number of accidents; and it may be a question whether machinery does not encumber; whether we have not lost by refinement some energy, by a Christianity, entrenched in establishments and forms, some vigor of wild virtue. For every Stoic was a Stoic; but in Christendom where is the Christian?

There is no more deviation in the moral standard than in the standard of height or bulk. No greater men are now than ever were. A singular equality may be observed between the great men of the first and of the last ages; nor can all the science, art, religion, and philosophy of the nineteenth century avail to educate greater men than Plutarch's heroes, three or four and twenty centuries ago. Not in time is the race 30 progressive. Phocion, Socrates, Anaxagoras, Diogenes, are great men, but they leave no class. He who is really of their class will not be called by their name, but will be his own man, and in his turn the founder of a sect. The arts and inventions of each period are only its costume and do not invigorate men. The harm of the improved machinery may compensate its good. Hudson and Behring accomplished so much in their fishing-boats as to astonish Parry and Franklin, whose equipment exhausted the resources of science and art. Galileo, with an opera-glass, discovered a more splendid series of celestial phenomena than any one since. Columbus found

---

30 **Plutarch's heroes,** the noble Greeks and Romans of Plutarch's *Lives*   31 **Phocion** (402?-317 B.C.), Greek philosopher   31 **Anaxagoras** (500?-428 B.C.), Greek philosopher   31 **Diogenes** (412?-323 B.C.), Greek Cynic philosopher   35 **Hudson,** Henry Hudson (d. 1611), English navigator. See note, p. 605   35 **Behring,** Vitus Jonassen Bering (1680-1741), Danish navigator who explored the Bering Sea   36 **Parry,** Sir William Edward Parry (1790-1855), English explorer of the Arctic   36 **Franklin,** Sir John Franklin (1786-1847), English explorer, was lost in the Arctic   37 **Galileo.** See note, p. 1100

the New World in an undecked boat. It is curious to see the periodical disuse and perishing of means and machinery which were introduced with loud laudation a few years or centuries before. The great genius returns to essential man. We reckoned the improvements of the art of war among the triumphs of science, and yet Napoleon conquered Europe by the bivouac, which consisted of falling back on naked valor and disencumbering it of all aids. The Emperor held it impossible to make a perfect army, says Las Cases, "without abolishing our arms, magazines, commissaries and carriages, until, in imitation of the Roman custom, the soldier should receive his supply of corn, grind it in his hand-mill and bake his bread himself."

10   Society is a wave. The wave moves onward, but the water of which it is composed does not. The same particle does not rise from the valley to the ridge. Its unity is only phenomenal. The persons who make up a nation to-day, next year die, and their experience dies with them.

And so the reliance on Property, including the reliance on governments which protect it, is the want of self-reliance. Men have looked away from themselves and at things so long that they have come to esteem the religious, learned and civil institutions as guards of property, and they deprecate assaults on these, because they feel them to be assaults on property. They measure their esteem of each other by what each has, and not by what each is. But a cultivated man becomes ashamed of
20   his property, out of new respect for his nature. Especially he hates what he has if he see that it is accidental, — came to him by inheritance, or gift, or crime; then he feels that it is not having; it does not belong to him, has no root in him and merely lies there because no revolution or no robber takes it away. But that which a man is, does always by necessity acquire; and what the man acquires, is living property, which does not wait the beck of rulers, or mobs, or revolutions, or fire, or storm, or bankruptcies, but perpetually renews itself wherever the man breathes. "Thy lot or portion of life," said the Caliph Ali, "is seeking after thee; therefore be at rest from seeking after it." Our dependence on these foreign goods leads us to our slavish respect for numbers. The political parties meet in numerous conven-
30   tions; the greater the concourse and with each new uproar of announcement, The delegation from Essex! The Democrats from New Hampshire! The Whigs of Maine! the young patriot feels himself stronger than before by a new thousand of eyes and arms. In like manner the reformers summon conventions and vote and resolve in multitude. Not so, O friends! will the God deign to enter and inhabit you, but by a method precisely the reverse. It is only as a man puts off all foreign support and stands alone that I see him to be strong and to prevail. He is weaker by every recruit to his banner. Is not a man better than a town? Ask nothing of men, and, in the endless mutation, thou only firm column must presently appear the upholder of all that surrounds thee. He who knows that power is inborn, that
40   he is weak because he has looked for good out of him and elsewhere, and, so per-

---

7 **Las Cases.** Marquis de Las Cases (1766-1842) recorded in *Mémorial de Ste. Hélène,* his conversations with the exiled Napoleon   27 **Caliph Ali,** Ali ben Abu Talic (602?-661),.fourth caliph of Mecca   31 **Essex,** a county in eastern Massachusetts   33 **reformers . . . conventions.** In 1840 some political abolitionists formed the Liberty Party and nominated a presidential candidate

ceiving, throws himself unhesitatingly on his thought, instantly rights himself, stands in the erect position, commands his limbs, works miracles; just as a man who stands on his feet is stronger than a man who stands on his head.

So use all that is called Fortune. Most men gamble with her, and gain all, and lose all, as her wheel rolls. But do thou leave as unlawful these winnings, and deal with Cause and Effect, the chancellors of God. In the Will work and acquire, and thou hast chained the wheel of Chance, and shall sit hereafter out of fear from her rotations. A political victory, a rise of rents, the recovery of your sick or the return of your absent friend, or some other favorable event raises your spirits, and you think good days are preparing for you. Do not believe it. Nothing can bring you peace 10 but yourself. Nothing can bring you peace but the triumph of principles.

1841

The Poet

Those who are esteemed umpires of taste are often persons who have acquired some knowledge of admired pictures or sculptures, and have an inclination for whatever is elegant; but if you inquire whether they are beautiful souls, and whether their own acts are like fair pictures, you learn that they are selfish and sensual. Their cultivation is local, as if you should rub a log of dry wood in one spot to produce fire, all the rest remaining cold. Their knowledge of the fine arts is some study of rules and particulars, or some limited judgment of color or form, which is exercised for amusement or for show. It is a proof of the shallowness of the doctrine of beauty, as it lies in the minds of our amateurs, that men seem to have lost the perception of the instant dependence of form upon soul. There is no doctrine of forms 10 in our philosophy. We were put into our bodies, as fire is put into a pan, to be carried about; but there is no accurate adjustment between the spirit and the organ, much less is the latter the germination of the former. So in regard to other forms, the intellectual men do not believe in any essential dependence of the material world on thought and volition. Theologians think it a pretty air-castle to talk of the spiritual meaning of a ship or a cloud, of a city or a contract, but they prefer to come again to the solid ground of historical evidence; and even the poets are contented with a civil and conformed manner of living, and to write poems from the fancy, at a safe distance from their own experience. But the highest minds of the world have never ceased to explore the double meaning, or, shall I say, the quad- 20 ruple, or the centuple, or much more manifold meaning, of every sensuous fact: Orpheus, Empedocles, Heraclitus, Plato, Plutarch, Dante, Swedenborg, and the masters of sculpture, picture, and poetry. For we are not pans and barrows, nor even

---

22 **Orpheus,** a Thracian poet and musician of Greek mythology, whose lyre could charm beasts and cause trees and rocks to move   22 **Empedocles, Heraclitus** Greek philosophers of the fifth century B.C.   22 **Plutarch.** See note, p. 159. Emerson was fond of lists of impressive names, some of which he seems to have used not very significantly. In the present list, only Swedenborg and Plato have a special importance for Emerson; each is the subject of an essay in *Representative Men.* In the essay on Plato, he said, "Plato is philosophy, and philosophy, Plato"

porters of the fire and torch-bearers, but children of the fire, made of it, and only the same divinity transmuted, and at two or three removes, when we know least about it. And this hidden truth, that the fountains whence all this river of Time, and its creatures, floweth, are intrinsically ideal and beautiful, draws us to the consideration of the nature and functions of the Poet, or the man of Beauty, to the means and materials he uses, and to the general aspect of the art in the present time.

The breadth of the problem is great, for the poet is representative. He stands among partial men for the complete man, and apprises us not of his wealth, but of the commonwealth. The young man reveres men of genius, because, to speak truly,
10 they are more himself than he is. They receive of the soul as he also receives, but they more. Nature enhances her beauty, to the eye of loving men, from their belief that the poet is beholding her shows at the same time. He is isolated among his contemporaries, by truth and by his art, but with this consolation in his pursuits, that they will draw all men sooner or later. For all men live by truth, and stand in need of expression. In love, in art, in avarice, in politics, in labor, in games, we study to utter our painful secret. The man is only half himself, the other half is his expression.

Notwithstanding this necessity to be published, adequate expression is rare. I know not how it is that we need an interpreter; but the great majority of men seem
20 to be minors, who have not yet come into possession of their own, or mutes, who cannot report the conversation they have had with nature. There is no man who does not anticipate a super-sensual utility in the sun, and stars, earth, and water. These stand and wait to render him a peculiar service. But there is some obstruction, or some excess of phlegm in our constitution, which does not suffer them to yield the due effect. Too feeble fall the impressions of nature on us to make us artists. Every touch should thrill. Every man should be so much an artist, that he could report in conversation what had befallen him. Yet, in our experience, the rays or appulses have sufficient force to arrive at the senses, but not enough to reach the quick, and compel the reproduction of themselves in speech. The poet is the
30 person in whom these powers are in balance, the man without impediment, who sees and handles that which others dream of, traverses the whole scale of experience, and is representative of man, in virtue of being the largest power to receive and to impart.

For the Universe has three children, born at one time, which reappear, under different names, in every system of thought, whether they be called cause, operation, and effect; or, more poetically, Jove, Pluto, Neptune; or theologically, the Father, the Spirit, and the Son; but which we will call here the Knower, the Doer, and the Sayer. These stand respectively for the love of truth, for the love of good, and for the love of beauty. These three are equal. Each is that which he is essentially, so
40 that he cannot be surmounted or analyzed, and each of these three has the power of the others latent in him, and his own patent.

The poet is the sayer, the namer, and represents beauty. He is a sovereign, and stands on the centre. For the world is not painted or adorned, but is from the beginning beautiful; and God has not made some beautiful things, but Beauty is the creator of the universe. Therefore the poet is not any permissive potentate, but is emperor in his own right. Criticism is infested with a cant of materialism, which assumes that manual skill and activity is the first merit of all men, and disparages such as say and do not, overlooking the fact, that some men, namely, poets, are natural sayers, sent into the world to the end of expression, and confounds them with those whose province is action, but who quit it to imitate the sayers. But Homer's words are as costly and admirable to Homer, as Agamemnon's victories are to Agamemnon. The poet does not wait for the hero or the sage, but, as they act and think primarily, so he writes primarily what will and must be spoken, reckoning the others, though primaries also, yet, in respect to him, secondaries and 10 servants; as sitters or models in the studio of a painter, or as assistants who bring building materials to an architect.

For poetry was all written before time was, and whenever we are so finely organized that we can penetrate into that region where the air is music, we hear those primal warblings, and attempt to write them down, but we lose ever and anon a word, or a verse, and substitute something of our own, and thus miswrite the poem. The men of more delicate ear write down these cadences more faithfully, and these transcripts, though imperfect, become the songs of the nations. For nature is as truly beautiful as it is good, or as it is reasonable, and must as much appear, as it must be done, or be known. Words and deeds are quite indifferent modes of the divine 20 energy. Words are also actions, and actions are a kind of words.

The sign and credentials of the poet are, that he announces that which no man foretold. He is the true and only doctor; he knows and tells; he is the only teller of news, for he was present and privy to the appearance which he describes. He is a beholder of ideas, and an utterer of the necessary and causal. For we do not speak now of men of poetical talents, or of industry and skill in metre, but of the true poet. I took part in a conversation, the other day, concerning a recent writer of lyrics, a man of subtle mind, whose head appeared to be a music-box of delicate tunes and rhythms, and whose skill, and command of language, we could not sufficiently praise. But when the question arose, whether he was not only a lyrist, but a 30 poet, we were obliged to confess that he is plainly a contemporary, not an eternal man. He does not stand out of our low limitations, like a Chimborazo under the line, running up from a torrid base though all the climates of the globe, with belts of the herbage of every latitude on its high and mottled sides; but this genius is the landscape-garden of a modern house, adorned with fountains and statues, with well-bred men and women standing and sitting in the walks and terraces. We hear, through all the varied music, the ground-tone of conventional life. Our poets are men of talents who sing, and not the children of music. The argument is secondary, the finish of the verses is primary.

For it is not metres, but a metre-making argument, that makes a poem, — a 40

---

27 **writer of lyrics,** probably Tennyson, of whose 1842 volume Emerson wrote in his *Journals* (June 1842): "It has many merits, but the question might remain whether it has *the* merit. One would say it was the poetry of an exquisite; that it was prettiness carried out to the infinite, but with no one great heroic stroke; a too vigorous exclusion of all mere natural influences"   32 **Chimborazo . . . line,** a mountain in Ecuador near the equator

thought so passionate and alive, that, like the spirit of a plant or an animal, it has an architecture of its own, and adorns nature with a new thing. The thought and the form are equal in the order of time, but in the order of genesis the thought is prior to the form. The poet has a new thought: he has a whole new experience to unfold; he will tell us how it was with him, and all men will be the richer in his fortune. For the experience of each new age requires a new confession, and the world seems always waiting for its poet. I remember, when I was young, how much I was moved one morning by tidings that genius had appeared in a youth who sat near me at table. He had left his work, and gone rambling none knew
10 whither, and had written hundreds of lines, but could not tell whether that which was in him was therein told: he could tell nothing but that all was changed, — man, beast, heaven, earth, and sea. How gladly we listened! how credulous! Society seemed to be compromised. We sat in the aurora of a sunrise which was to put out all the stars. Boston seemed to be at twice the distance it had the night before, or was much farther than that. Rome, — what was Rome? Plutarch and Shakspeare were in the yellow leaf, and Homer no more should be heard of. It is much to know that poetry has been written this very day, under this very roof, by your side. What! that wonderful spirit has not expired! these stony moments are still sparkling and animated! I had fancied that the oracles were all silent, and
20 nature had spent her fires; and behold! all night, from every pore, these fine auroras have been streaming. Every one has some interest in the advent of the poet, and no one knows how much it may concern him. We know that the secret of the world is profound, but who or what shall be our interpreter, we know not. A mountain ramble, a new style of the face, a new person, may put the key into our hands. Of course, the value of genius to us is in the veracity of its report. Talent may frolic and juggle; genius realizes and adds. Mankind, in good earnest, have availed so far in understanding themselves and their work, that the foremost watchman on the peak announces his news. It is the truest word ever spoken, and the phrase will be the fittest, most musical, and the unerring voice of the world for that time.
30 All that we call sacred history attests that the birth of a poet is the principal event in chronology. Man, never so often deceived, still watches for the arrival of a brother who can hold him steady to a truth, until he has made it his own. With what joy I begin to read a poem, which I confide in as an inspiration! And now my chains are to be broken; I shall mount above these clouds and opaque airs in which I live, — opaque, though they seem transparent, — and from the heaven of truth I shall see and comprehend my relations. That will reconcile me to life, and renovate nature, to see trifles animated by a tendency, and to know what I am doing. Life will no more be a noise; now I shall see men and women, and know the signs by which they may be discerned from fools and satans. This day shall be better than my birth-
40 day: then I became an animal: now I am invited into the science of the real. Such is the hope, but the fruition is postponed. Oftener it falls, that this winged man, who will carry me into the heaven, whirls me into mists, then leaps and frisks about

---

16 **yellow leaf.** Compare Macbeth, Act V, Sc. iii, ll. 22-23: "My way of life is fall'n into the sere, the yellow leaf"

with me as it were from cloud to cloud, still affirming that he is bound heavenward; and I, being myself a novice, am slow in perceiving that he does not know
the way into the heavens, and is merely bent that I should admire his skill to rise,
like a fowl or a flying fish, a little way from the ground or the water; but the all-
piercing, all-feeding, and ocular air of heaven, that man shall never inhabit. I tumble down again soon into my old nooks, and lead the life of exaggerations as before,
and have lost my faith in the possibility of any guide who can lead me thither where
I would be.

But, leaving these victims of vanity, let us, with new hope, observe how nature,
by worthier impulses, has insured the poet's fidelity to his office of announcement   10
and affirming, namely, by the beauty of things, which becomes a new and higher
beauty, when expressed. Nature offers all her creatures to him as a picture-language.
Being used as a type, a second wonderful value appears in the object, far better than
its old value, as the carpenter's stretched cord, if you hold your ear close enough, is
musical in the breeze. "Things more excellent than every image," says Jamblichus,
"are expressed through images." Things admit of being used as symbols, because
nature is a symbol, in the whole, and in every part. Every line we can draw in the
sand, has expression; and there is no body without its spirit or genius. All form is
an effect of character; all condition, of the quality of the life; all harmony, of health;
(and, for this reason, a perception of beauty should be sympathetic, or proper only   20
to the good.) The beautiful rests on the foundations of the necessary. The soul makes
the body, as the wise Spenser teaches:

> "So every spirit, as it is most pure,
> And hath in it the more of heavenly light,
> So it the fairer body doth procure
> To habit in, and it more fairly dight,
> With cheerful grace and amiable sight.
> For, of the soul, the body form doth take,
> For soul is form, and doth the body make."

Here we find ourselves, suddenly, not in a critical speculation, but in a holy place,   30
and should go very warily and reverently. We stand before the secret of the world,
there where Being passes into Appearance, and Unity into Variety.

The Universe is the externization of the soul. Wherever the life is, that bursts
into appearance around it. Our science is sensual, and therefore superficial. The earth
and the heavenly bodies, physics, and chemistry, we sensually treat, as if they were
self-existent; but these are the retinue of that Being we have. "The mighty heaven,"
said Proclus, "exhibits, in its transfigurations clear images of the splendor of intellectual perceptions, being moved in conjunction with the unapparent periods of

---

15 **Jamblichus,** one of the Neoplatonists who flourished in Alexandria in the fourth century   23 **So . . .**
make. Edmund Spenser's "An Hymn in Honour of Beautie," ll. 127-133   37 **Proclus** (411-485), another
Neoplatonist. The Neoplatonists (Plotinus, Proclus, Jamblichus, and Porphyry), whose works Emerson read
in the translations of Thomas Taylor, were one of the major influences on his thought

intellectual natures." Therefore, science always goes abreast with the just elevation of the man, keeping step with religion and metaphysics; or, the state of science is an index of our self-knowledge. Since everything in nature answers to a moral power, if any phenomenon remains brute and dark, it is because the corresponding faculty in the observer is not yet active.

No wonder, then, if these waters be so deep, that we hover over them with a religious regard. The beauty of the fable proves the importance of the sense; to the poet, and to all others; or, if you please, every man is so far a poet as to be susceptible of these enchantments of nature; for all men have the thoughts whereof
10 the universe is the celebration. I find that the fascination resides in the symbol. Who loves nature? Who does not? Is it only poets, and men of leisure and cultivation, who live with her? No; but also hunters, farmers, grooms, and butchers, though they express their affection in their choice of life, and not in their choice of words. The writer wonders what the coachman or the hunter values in riding, in horses, and dogs. It is not superficial qualities. When you talk with him, he holds these at as slight a rate as you. His worship is sympathetic; he has no definitions, but he is commanded in nature, by the living power which he feels to be there present. No imitation, or playing of these things, would content him; he loves the earnest of the north wind, of rain, of stone, and wood, and iron. A beauty not explicable is
20 dearer than a beauty which we can see to the end of. It is nature the symbol, nature certifying the supernatural, body overflowed by life, which he worships, with coarse, but sincere rites.

The inwardness and mystery of this attachment drives men of every class to the use of emblems. The schools of poets, and philosophers, are not more intoxicated with their symbols, than the populace with theirs. In our political parties, compute the power of badges and emblems. See the great ball which they roll from Baltimore to Bunker Hill! In the political processions, Lowell goes in a loom, and Lynn in a shoe, and Salem in a ship. Witness the cider-barrel, the log-chain, the hickory-stick, the palmetto, and all the cognizances of party. See the power of national emblems.
30 Some stars, lilies, leopards, a crescent, a lion, an eagle, or other figure, which came into credit God knows how, on an old rag of bunting, blowing in the wind, on a fort, at the ends of the earth, shall make the blood tingle under the rudest, or the most conventional exterior. The people fancy they hate poetry, and they are all poets and mystics!

Beyond this universality of the symbolic language, we are apprised of the divineness of this superior use of things, whereby the world is a temple whose walls are

---

26 **great . . . Hill,** the reference is to the Presidential election of 1840, in which the Whig candidate, Harrison, defeated the Democratic candidate, Van Buren. Emerson wrote in his *Journals:* "The most imposing part of this Harrison celebration of the Fourth of July in Concord, as in Baltimore, was this ball, twelve or thirteen feet in diameter, which, as it mounts the little heights and slopes of the road, draws all eyes with a certain sublime movement, especially as the imagination is incessantly addressed with its political significance"   27 **Lowell . . . ship,** signifying the textile industry of Lowell, the shoe factories of Lynn, and the maritime interests of Salem — all cities in Massachusetts   29 **the cognizances of party.** The cider barrel and the log cabin were used by the Whigs as emblems of Harrison; the hickory stick and the palmetto were Democratic symbols, associated, respectively, with Andrew Jackson and South Carolina   29 **national emblems,** lilies, of France; leopards, of Scotland; crescent, of Turkey; lion, of England

covered with emblems, pictures, and commandments of the Deity, in this, that there is no fact in nature which does not carry the whole sense of nature; and the distinctions which we make in events, and in affairs, of low and high, honest and base, disappear when nature is used as a symbol. Thought makes everything fit for use. The vocabulary of an omniscient man would embrace words and images excluded from polite conversation. What would be base, or even obscene, to the obscene, becomes illustrious, spoken in a new connection of thought. The piety of the Hebrew prophets purges their grossness. The circumcision is an example of the power of poetry to raise the low and offensive. Small and mean things serve as well as great symbols. The meaner the type by which a law is expressed, the more pun- 10 gent it is, and the more lasting in the memories of men: just as we choose the smallest box, or case, in which any needful utensil can be carried. Bare lists of words are found suggestive, to an imaginative and excited mind; as it is related of Lord Chatham, that he was accustomed to read in Bailey's Dictionary, when he was preparing to speak in Parliament. The poorest experience is rich enough for all the purposes of expressing thought. Why covet a knowledge of new facts? Day and night, house and garden, a few books, a few actions, serve us as well as would all trades and all spectacles. We are far from having exhausted the significance of the few symbols we use. We can come to use them yet with a terrible simplicity. It does not need that a poem should be long. Every word was once a poem. Every new relation is a 20 new word. Also, we use defects and deformities to a sacred purpose, so expressing our sense that the evils of the world are such only to the evil eye. In the old mythology, mythologists observe, defects are ascribed to divine natures, as lameness to Vulcan, blindness to Cupid, and the like, to signify exuberances.

For, as it is dislocation and detachment from the life of God, that makes things ugly, the poet, who re-attaches things to nature and the Whole, — re-attaching even artificial things, and violations of nature, to nature, by a deeper insight, — disposes very easily of the most disagreeable facts. Readers of poetry see the factory-village and the railway, and fancy that the poetry of the landscape is broken up by these; for these works of art are not yet consecrated in their reading; but the poet sees 30 them fall within the great Order not less than the beehive or the spider's geometrical web. Nature adopts them very fast into her vital circles, and the gliding train of cars she loves like her own. Besides, in a centred mind, it signifies nothing how many mechanical inventions you exhibit. Though you add millions, and never so surprising, the fact of mechanics has not gained a grain's weight. The spiritual fact remains unalterable, by many or by few particulars; as no mountain is of any appreciable height to break the curve of the sphere. A shrewd country-boy goes to the city for the first time, and the complacent citizen is not satisfied with his little wonder. It is not that he does not see all the fine houses, and know that he never saw such before, but he disposes of them as easily as the poet finds place for the rail- 40 way. The chief value of the new fact, is to enhance the great and constant fact of Life, which can dwarf any and every circumstance, and to which the belt of wampum, and the commerce of America, are alike.

---

13 **Lord Chatham,** William Pitt. See note p. 1100

The world being thus put under the mind for verb and noun, the poet is he who can articulate it. For, though life is great, and fascinates, and absorbs, — and though all men are intelligent of the symbols through which it is named, — yet they cannot originally use them. We are symbols, and inhabit symbols; workmen, work, and tools, words and things, birth and death, all are emblems; but we sympathize with the symbols, and, being infatuated with the economical uses of things, we do not know that they are thoughts. The poet, by an ulterior intellectual perception, gives them a power which makes their old use forgotten, and puts eyes, and a tongue, into every dumb and inanimate object. He perceives the independence of the thought on the symbol, the stability of the thought, the accidency and fugacity of the symbol. As the eyes of Lyncaeus were said to see through the earth, so the poet turns the world to glass, and shows us all things in their right series and procession. For, through that better perception, he stands one step nearer to things, and sees the flowing or metamorphosis; perceives that thought is multiform; that within the form of every creature is a force impelling it to ascend into a higher form: and, following with his eyes the life, uses the forms which express that life, and so his speech flows with the flowing of nature. All the facts of the animal economy, sex, nutriment, gestation, birth, growth, are symbols of the passage of the world into the soul of man, to suffer there a change, and reappear a new and higher fact. He uses forms according to the life, and not according to the form. This is true science. The poet alone knows astronomy, chemistry, vegetation, and animation, for he does not stop at these facts, but employs them as signs. He knows why the plain or meadow of space was strown with these flowers we call suns, and moons, and stars; why the great deep is adorned with animals, with men, and gods; for, in every word he speaks he rides on them as the horses of thought.

By virtue of this science the poet is the Namer or Language-maker, naming things sometimes after their appearance, sometimes after their essence, and giving to every one its own name and not another's, thereby rejoicing the intellect, which delights in detachment or boundary. The poets made all the words, and therefore language is the archives of history, and, if we must say it, a sort of tomb of the muses. For, though the origin of most of our words is forgotten, each word was at first a stroke of genius, and obtained currency, because for the moment it symbolized the world to the first speaker and to the hearer. The etymologist finds the deadest word to have been once a brilliant picture. Language is fossil poetry. As the limestone of the continent consists of infinite masses of the shells of animalcules, so language is made up of images, or tropes, which now, in their secondary use, have long ceased to remind us of their poetic origin. But the poet names the thing because he sees it, or comes one step nearer to it than any other. This expression, or naming, is not art, but a second nature, grown out of the first, as a leaf out of a tree. What we call nature, is a certain self-regulated motion, or change; and nature does all things by her own hands, and does not leave another to baptize her, but baptizes herself; and this through the metamorphosis again. I remember that a certain poet described it to me thus:

---

11 **Lyncaeus** was one of the mythological band who sailed in search of the Golden Fleece   42 **a certain poet,** Emerson himself

Genius is the activity which repairs the decays of things, whether wholly or partly of a material and finite kind. Nature, through all her kingdoms, insures herself. Nobody cares for planting the poor fungus: so she shakes down from the gills of one agaric countless spores, any one of which, being preserved, transmits new billions of spores to-morrow or next day. The new agaric of this hour has a chance which the old one had not. This atom of seed is thrown into a new place, not subject to the accidents which destroyed its parent two rods off. She makes a man; and having brought him to ripe age, she will no longer run the risk of losing this wonder at a blow, but she detaches from him a new self, that the kind may be safe from accidents to which the individual is exposed. So when the soul of the poet has come to   10
ripeness of thought, she detaches and sends away from it its poems or songs, — a fearless, sleepless, deathless progeny, which is not exposed to the accidents of the weary kingdom of time: a fearless, vivacious offspring, clad with wings (such was the virtue of the soul out of which they came), which carry them fast and far, and infix them irrecoverably into the hearts of men. These wings are the beauty of the poet's soul. The songs, thus flying immortal from their mortal parent, are pursued by clamorous flights of censures, which swarm in far greater numbers, and threaten to devour them; but these last are not winged. At the end of a very short leap they fall plump down, and rot, having received from the souls out of which they came no beautiful wings. But the melodies of the poet ascend, and leap, and pierce into   20
the deeps of infinite time.

So far the bard taught me, using his freer speech. But nature has a higher end, in the production of new individuals, than security, namely, *ascension,* or, the passage of the soul into higher forms. I knew, in my younger days, the sculptor who made the statue of the youth which stands in the public garden. He was, as I remember, unable to tell directly, what made him happy, or unhappy, but by wonderful indirections he could tell. He rose one day, according to his habit, before the dawn, and saw the morning break, grand as the eternity out of which it came, and, for many days after, he strove to express this tranquillity, and, lo! his chisel had fashioned out of marble the form of a beautiful youth, Phosphorus, whose aspect is such, that,   30
it is said, all persons who look on it become silent. The poet also resigns himself to his mood, and that thought which agitated him is expressed, but *alter idem,* in a manner totally new. The expression is organic, or, the new type which things themselves take when liberated. As, in the sun, objects paint their images on the retina of the eye, so they, sharing the aspiration of the whole universe, tend to paint a far more delicate copy of their essence in his mind. Like the metamorphosis of things into higher organic forms, is their change into melodies. Over everything stands its daemon, or soul, and, as the form of the thing is reflected by the eye, so the soul of the thing is reflected by a melody. The sea, the mountain-ridge, Niagara, and every flower-bed, pre-exist, or super-exist, in precantations, which sail like odors in   40
the air, and when any man goes by with an ear sufficiently fine, he overhears them, and endeavors to write down the notes, without diluting or depraving them. And herein is the legitimation of criticism, in the mind's faith, that the poems are a corrupt version of some text in nature, with which they ought to be made to tally. A

rhyme in one of our sonnets should not be less pleasing than the iterated nodes of a seashell, or the resembling difference of a group of flowers. The pairing of the birds is an idyl, not tedious as our idyls are; a tempest is a rough ode, without falsehood or rant: a summer, with its harvest sown, reaped, and stored, is an epic song, subordinating how many admirably executed parts. Why should not the symmetry and truth that modulate these, glide into our spirits, and we participate the invention of nature?

This insight, which expresses itself by what is called Imagination, is a very high sort of seeing, which does not come by study, but by the intellect being where and
10 what it sees, by sharing the path or circuit of things through forms, and so making them translucid to others. The path of things is silent. Will they suffer a speaker to go with them? A spy they will not suffer; a lover, a poet, is the transcendency of their own nature, — him they will suffer. The condition of true naming, on the poet's part, is his resigning himself to the divine *aura* which breathes through forms, and accompanying that.

It is a secret which every intellectual man quickly learns, that, beyond the energy of his possessed and conscious intellect, he is capable of a new energy (as of an intellect doubled on itself), by abandonment to the nature of things; that, beside his privacy of power as an individual man, there is a great public power, on which he
20 can draw, by unlocking, at all risks, his human doors, and suffering the ethereal tides to roll and circulate through him: then he is caught up into the life of the Universe, his speech is thunder, his thought is law, and his words are universally intelligible as the plants and animals. The poet knows that he speaks adequately, then, only when he speaks somewhat wildly, or, "with the flower of the mind;" not with the intellect, used as an organ, but with the intellect released from all service, and suffered to take its direction from its celestial life; or, as the ancients were wont to express themselves, not with intellect alone, but with the intellect inebriated by nectar. As the traveller who has lost his way throws his reins on his horse's neck, and trusts to the instinct of the animal to find his road, so much we do with the
30 divine animal who carries us through this world. For if in any manner we can stimulate this instinct, new passages are opened for us into nature, the mind flows into and through things hardest and highest, and the metamorphosis is possible.

This is the reason why bards love wine, mead, narcotics, coffee, tea, opium, the fumes of sandal-wood and tobacco, or whatever other procurers of animal exhilaration. All men avail themselves of such means as they can, to add this extraordinary power to their normal powers; and to this end they prize conversation, music, pictures, sculpture, dancing, theatres, travelling, war, mobs, fires, gaming, politics, or love, or science or animal intoxication which are several coarser or finer *quasi*-mechanical substitutes for the true nectar which is the ravishment of the intellect
40 by coming nearer to the fact. These are auxiliaries to the centrifugal tendency of a man, to his passage out into free space, and they help him to escape the custody of that body in which he is pent up, and of that jail-yard of individual relations in which he is enclosed. Hence a great number of such as were professionally expressers of Beauty, as painters, poets, musicians, and actors, have been more than others

wont to lead a life of pleasure and indulgence; all but the few who received the true nectar; and, as it was a spurious mode of attaining freedom, as it was an emancipation not into the heavens, but into the freedom of baser places, they were punished for that advantage they won, by a dissipation and deterioration. But never can any advantage be taken of nature by a trick. The spirit of the world, the great calm presence of the Creator, comes not forth to the sorceries of opium or of wine. The sublime vision comes to the pure and simple soul in a clean and chaste body. That is not an inspiration which we owe to narcotics, but some counterfeit excitement and fury. Milton says, that the lyric poet may drink wine and live generously, but the epic poet, he who shall sing of the gods, and their descent unto men, must drink 10 water out of a wooden bowl. For poetry is not 'Devil's wine,' but God's wine. It is with this as it is with toys. We fill the hands and nurseries of our children with all manner of dolls, drums, and horses, withdrawing their eyes from the plain face and sufficing objects of nature, the sun, and the moon, the animals, the water, and stones, which should be their toys. So the poet's habit of living should be set on a key so low, that the common influences should delight him. His cheerfulness should be the gift of the sunlight; the air should suffice for his inspiration, and he should be tipsy with water. That spirit which suffices quiet hearts, which seems to come forth to such from every dry knoll of sere grass, from every pine-stump, and half-imbedded stone, on which the dull March sun shines, comes forth to the poor and hungry, 20 and such as are of simple taste. If thou fill thy brain with Boston and New York, with fashion and covetousness, and wilt stimulate thy jaded senses with wine and French coffee, thou shalt find no radiance of wisdom in the lonely waste of the pinewoods.

If the imagination intoxicates the poet, it is not inactive in other men. The metamorphosis excites in the beholder an emotion of joy. The use of symbols has a certain power of emancipation and exhilaration for all men. We seem to be touched by a wand, which makes us dance and run about happily, like children. We are like persons who come out of a cave or cellar into the open air. This is the effect on us of tropes, fables, oracles, and all poetic forms. Poets are thus liberating gods. Men 30 have really got a new sense, and found within their world, another world, or nest of worlds; for, the metamorphosis once seen, we divine that it does not stop. I will not now consider how much this makes the charm of algebra and the mathematics, which also have their tropes, but it is felt in every definition; as, when Aristotle defines *space* to be an immovable vessel, in which things are contained; — or, when Plato defines a *line* to be a flowing point; or *figure* to be a bound of solid; and many the like. What a joyful sense of freedom we have, when Vitruvius announces the old opinion of artists that no architect can build any house well, who does not know something of anatomy. When Socrates, in Charmides, tells us that the soul is cured of its maladies by certain incantations, and that these incantations are beautiful rea- 40 sons, from which temperance is generated in souls; when Plato calls the world an animal; and Timaeus affirms that plants also are animals; or affirms a man to be a

9 **Milton says,** in the Sixth Latin Elegy, ll. 53-78   37 **Vitruvius** (fl. 46 B.C.), Roman author of a work on architecture   39 **Charmides,** a dialogue of Plato   42 **Timæus,** a dialogue of Plato

heavenly tree, growing with his root, which is his head, upward; and, as George Chapman, following him, writes, —

> "So in our tree of man, whose nervie root
> Springs in his top;"

when Orpheus speaks of hoariness as "that white flower which marks extreme old age;" when Proclus calls the universe the statue of the intellect; when Chaucer, in his praise of 'Gentilesse,' compares good blood in mean condition to fire, which, though carried to the darkest house betwixt this and the mount of Caucasus, will yet hold its natural office, and burn as bright as if twenty thousand men did it be-
10 hold; when John saw, in the Apocalypse, the ruin of the world through evil, and the stars fall from heaven, as the figtree casteth her untimely fruit; when Aesop reports the whole catalogue of common daily relations through the masquerade of birds and beasts; — we take the cheerful hint of the immortality of our essence, and its versatile habits and escapes, as when the gypsies say of themselves, "it is in vain to hang them, they cannot die."

The poets are thus liberating gods. The ancient British bards had for the title of their order, "Those who are free throughout the world." They are free, and they make free. An imaginative book renders us much more service at first, by stimulating us through its tropes, than afterward, when we arrive at the precise sense of the author.
20 I think nothing is of any value in books, excepting the transcendental and extraordinary. If a man is inflamed and cárried away by his thought, to that degree that he forgets the authors and the public, and heeds only this one dream, which holds him like an insanity, let me read his paper, and you may have all the arguments and histories and criticism. All the value which attaches to Pythagoras, Paracelsus, Cornelius Agrippa, Cardan, Kepler, Swedenborg, Schelling, Oken, or any other who introduces questionable facts into his cosmogony, as angels, devils, magic, astrology, palmistry, mesmerism, and so on, is the certificate we have of departure from routine, and that here is a new witness. That also is the best success in conversation, the magic of liberty, which puts the world, like a ball, in our hands. How cheap
30 even the liberty then seems; how mean to study, when an emotion communicates to the intellect the power to sap and upheave nature: how great the perspective! nations, times, systems, enter and disappear, like threads in tapestry of large figure

3 **So . . . top,** from the dedication of Chapman's *Homer*   5 **Orpheus.** See note, p. 1112   6 **Chaucer.** The reference is to the "Wife of Bath's Tale," ll. 283-289   10 **John . . . Apocalypse.** See Revelation 6:13   24 **Pythagoras.** See note, p. 293   24 **Paracelsus,** Philippus Paracelsus (1493?-1541), Swiss alchemist   25 **Cornelius Agrippa** (1486-1535), German physician   25 **Cardan,** Jerome Cardan (1501-1576), Italian mathematician   25 **Kepler,** Johannes Kepler (1571-1630), German astronomer   25 **Schelling,** Friedrich von Schelling (1775-1854), German philosopher   25 **Oken,** Lorenz Oken (1779-1851), German naturalist. Emerson, with characteristic whimsicality, lumps together philosophers, scientists, and charlatans

and many colors; dream delivers us to dream, and while the drunkenness lasts, we will sell our bed, our philosophy, our religion, in our opulence.

There is good reason why we should prize this liberation. The fate of the poor shepherd, who, blinded and lost in the snowstorm, perishes in a drift within a few feet of his cottage door, is an emblem of the state of man. On the brink of the waters of life and truth, we are miserably dying. The inaccessibleness of every thought but that we are in, is wonderful. What if you come near to it, — you are as remote when you are nearest as when you are farthest. Every thought is also a prison; every heaven is also a prison. Therefore we love the poet, the inventor, who in any form, whether in an ode, or in an action, or in looks and behavior, has yielded 10 us a new thought. He unlocks our chains, and admits us to a new scene.

This emancipation is dear to all men, and the power to impart it, as it must come from greater depth and scope of thought, is a measure of intellect. Therefore all books of the imagination endure, all which ascend to that truth that the writer sees nature beneath him, and uses it as his exponent. Every verse or sentence, possessing this virtue, will take care of its own immortality. The religions of the world are the ejaculations of a few imaginative men.

But the quality of the imagination is to flow, and not to freeze. The poet did not stop at the color, or the form, but read their meaning; neither may he rest in this meaning, but he makes the same objects exponents of his new thought. Here is the 20 difference betwixt the poet and the mystic, that the last nails a symbol to one sense, which was a true sense for a moment, but soon becomes old and false. For all symbols are fluxional; all language is vehicular and transitive, and is good, as ferries and horses are, for conveyance, not as farms and houses are, for homestead. Mysticism consists in the mistake of an accidental and individual symbol for a universal one. The morning-redness happens to be the favorite meteor to the eyes of Jacob Behmen, and comes to stand to him for truth and faith; and he believes should stand for the same realities to every reader. But the first reader prefers as naturally the symbol of a mother and child, or a gardener and his bulb, or a jeweller polishing a gem. Either of these, or of a myriad more, are equally good to the person to 30 whom they are significant. Only they must be held lightly, and be very willingly translated into the equivalent terms which others use. And the mystic must be steadily told, — All that you say is just as true without the tedious use of that symbol as with it. Let us have a little algebra, instead of this trite rhetoric, — universal signs, instead of these village symbols, — and we shall both be gainers. The history of hierarchies seems to show, that all religious error consisted in making the symbol too stark and solid, and, at last, nothing but an excess of the organ of language.

Swedenborg, of all men in the recent ages, stands eminently for the translator of nature into thought. I do not know the man in history to whom things stood so uniformly for words. Before him the metamorphosis continually plays. Every thing 40 on which his eye rests, obeys the impulses of moral nature. The figs become grapes whilst he eats them. When some of his angels affirmed a truth, the laurel twig which they held blossomed in their hands. The noise which, at a distance, appeared like

---

26 **Jacob Behmen** (1575-1624), German mystic

gnashing and thumping, on coming nearer was found to be the voice of disputants. The men, in one of his visions, seen in heavenly light, appeared like dragons, and seemed in darkness: but to each other they appeared as men, and, when the light from heaven shone into their cabin, they complained of the darkness, and were compelled to shut the window that they might see.

There was this perception in him, which makes the poet or seer, an object of awe and terror, namely, that the same men, or society of men, may wear one aspect to themselves and their companions, and a different aspect to higher intelligences. Certain priests, whom he describes as conversing very·learnedly together, appeared to
10 the children, who were at some distance, like dead horses; and many the like misappearances. And instantly the mind inquires, whether these fishes under the bridge, yonder oxen in the pasture, those dogs in the yard, are immutably fishes, oxen, and dogs, or only so appear to me, and perchance to themselves appear upright men; and whether I appear as a man to all eyes. The Brahmins and Pythagoras propounded the same question, and if any poet has witnessed the transformation, he doubtless found it in harmony with various experiences. We have all seen changes as considerable in wheat and caterpillars. He is the poet, and shall draw us with love and terror, who sees, through the flowing vest, the firm nature, and can declare it.

I look in vain for the poet whom I describe. We do not, with sufficient plainness,
20 or sufficient profoundness, address ourselves to life, nor dare we chaunt our own times and social circumstance. If we filled the day with bravery, we should not shrink from celebrating it. Time and nature yield us many gifts, but not yet the timely man, the new religion, the reconciler, whom all things await. Dante's praise is, that he dared to write his autobiography in colossal cipher, or into universality. We have yet had no genius in America, with tyrannous eye, which knew the value of our incomparable materials, and saw, in the barbarism and materialism of the times, another carnival of the same gods whose picture he so much admires in Homer; then in the middle age; then in Calvinism. Banks and tariffs, the newspaper and caucus, Methodism and Unitarianism, are flat and dull to dull people, but rest on
30 the same foundations of wonder as the town of Troy, and the temple of Delphi, and are as swiftly passing away. Our logrolling, our stumps and their politics, our fisheries, our Negroes, and Indians, our boats, and our repudiations, the wrath of rogues, and the pusillanimity of honest men, the northern trade, the southern planting, the western clearing, Oregon, and Texas, are yet unsung. Yet America is a poem in our eyes; its ample geography dazzles the imagination, and it will not wait long for metres. If I have not found that excellent combination of gifts in my countrymen which I seek, neither could I aid myself to fix the idea of the poet by reading now and then in Chalmers's collection of five centuries of English poets. These are wits, more than poets, though there have been poets among them. But when we adhere

25 **no . . . America.** The remainder of the paragraph seems remarkably prophetic of Whitman, whose *Leaves of Grass* appeared eleven years later   30 **temple of Delphi,** the seat of the oracles of Apollo   34 **Oregon and Texas.** In 1844, the date of this essay, Oregon and Texas were subjects of special interest. The Oregon boundary dispute with England was settled in 1846; Texas was admitted into the Union in 1845   38 **Chalmers's collection,** Alexander Chalmers' collection of English poets in twenty-one volumes, published in 1810

to the ideal of the poet, we have our difficulties even with Milton and Homer. Milton is too literary, and Homer too literal and historical.

But I am not wise enough for a national criticism, and must use the old largeness a little longer, to discharge my errand from the muse to the poet concerning his art.

Art is the path of the creator to his work. The paths, or methods, are ideal and eternal, though few men ever see them, not the artist himself, for years, or for a lifetime, unless he come into the conditions. The painter, the sculptor, the composer, the epic rhapsodist, the orator, all partake one desire, namely, to express themselves symmetrically and abundantly, not dwarfishly and fragmentarily. They found or put themselves in certain conditions, as, the painter and sculptor before some impressive 10 human figures; the orator, into the assembly of the people; and the others, in such scenes as each has found exciting to his intellect; and each presently feels the new desire. He hears a voice, he sees a beckoning. Then he is apprised, with wonder, what herds of daemons hem him in. He can no more rest; he says, with the old painter, "By God, it is in me, and must go forth of me." He pursues a beauty, half seen, which flies before him. The poet pours out verses in every solitude. Most of the things he says are conventional, no doubt; but by and by he says something which is original and beautiful. That charms him. He would say nothing else but such things. In our way of talking, we say, 'That is yours, this is mine;' but the poet knows well that it is not his; that it is as strange and beautiful to him as to 20 you; he would fain hear the like eloquence at length. Once having tasted this immortal ichor, he cannot have enough of it, and as an admirable creative power exists in these intellections, it is of the last importance that these things get spoken. What a little of all we know is said! What drops of all the sea of our science are baled up! and by what accident it is that these are exposed, when so many secrets sleep in nature! Hence the necessity of speech and song; hence these throbs and heartbeatings in the orator, at the door of the assembly, to the end, namely, that thought may be ejaculated as Logos, or Word.

Doubt not, O poet, but persist. Say 'It is in me, and shall out.' Stand there, balked and dumb, stuttering and stammering, hissed and hooted, stand and strive, until, 30 at last, rage draw out of thee that *dream*-power which every night shows thee is thine own; a power transcending all limit and privacy, and by virtue of which a man is the conductor of the whole river of electricity. Nothing walks, or creeps, or grows, or exists, which must not in turn arise and walk before him as exponent of his meaning. Comes he to that power, his genius is no longer exhaustible. All the creatures, by pairs and by tribes, pour into his mind as into a Noah's ark, to come forth again to people a new world. This is like the stock of air for our respiration, or for the combustion of our fireplace, not a measure of gallons, but the entire atmosphere if wanted. And therefore the rich poets, as Homer, Chaucer, Shakspeare, and Raphael, have obviously no limits to their works, except the limits of their life- 40 time, and resemble a mirror carried through the street, ready to render an image of every created thing.

---

28 **Logos,** Greek for "word." Emerson alludes to John 1:1: "In the beginning was the Word . . ."   40
Raphael. See note, p. 943. The inclusion of the painter Raphael in the present list seems whimsical

O poet! a new nobility is conferred in groves and pastures, and not in castles, or by the sword-blade, any longer. The conditions are hard, but equal. Thou shalt leave the world, and know the muse only. Thou shalt not know any longer the times, customs, graces, politics, or opinions of men, but shalt take all from the muse. For the time of towns is tolled from the world by funereal chimes, but in nature the universal hours are counted by succeeding tribes of animals and plants, and by growth of joy on joy. God wills also that thou abdicate a manifold and duplex life, and that thou be content that others speak for thee. Others shall be thy gentlemen, and shall represent all courtesy and worldly life for thee; others shall do the great
10 and resounding actions also. Thou shalt lie close hid with nature, and canst not be afforded to the Capitol or the Exchange. The world is full of renunciations and apprenticeships, and this is thine; thou must pass for a fool and a churl for a long season. This is the screen and sheath in which Pan has protected his well-beloved flower, and thou shalt be known only to thine own, and they shall console thee with tenderest love. And thou shalt not be able to rehearse the names of thy friends in thy verse, for an old shame before the holy ideal. And this is the reward: that the ideal shall be real to thee, and the impressions of the actual world shall fall like summer rain, copious, but not troublesome, to thy invulnerable essence. Thou shalt have the whole land for thy park and manor, the sea for thy bath and navigation,
20 without tax and without envy; the woods and the rivers thou shalt own; and thou shalt possess that wherein others are only tenants and boarders. Thou true land-lord! sea-lord! air-lord! Wherever snow falls, or water flows, or birds fly, wherever day and night meet in twilight, wherever the blue heaven is hung by clouds, or sown with stars, wherever are forms with transparent boundaries, wherever are out-lets into celestial space, wherever is danger, and awe, and love, there is Beauty, plente-ous as rain, shed for thee, and though thou shouldst walk the world over, thou shalt not be able to find a condition inopportune or ignoble. 1844

Plato; or, The Philosopher

Emerson's Representative Men, *published in 1850, consists of the chapters "Plato; or, The Philosopher," "Swedenborg; or, the Mystic," "Montaigne; or, the Sceptic," "Shakspeare; or, the Poet," "Napoleon; or, the Man of the World," and "Goethe; or, the Writer." Although modeled after the* Heroes and Hero-Worship *of his friend Thomas Carlyle, Emerson's book, as the word "representative" suggests, is more democratic: Carlyle's great men are demi-gods who, the author believed, ought to be worshiped and obeyed; Emerson's are embodiments of virtues which are attainable by all men.*

Of the six "representative men," Plato exerted by far the largest influence upon Emerson. Primarily a philosopher, Emerson derived his philosophy chiefly from Plato and his succes-sors — the Neo-Platonists and the Cambridge Platonists. The essay was written in an ex-pansive mood. No praise was too high for the great primary source of philosophical wisdom: "Plato is philosophy, and philosophy, Plato."

*So close was the relation between the subject and the author that Emerson seems in many
passages to have been writing about himself; many passages, at any rate, are as applicable
to him as to Plato and throw valuable light upon Emerson's philosophical ideas and methods.*

Among books, Plato only is entitled to Omar's fanatical compliment to the Koran,
when he said, "Burn the libraries, for their value is in this book." These sentences
contain the culture of nations; these are the corner-stone of schools; these are the
fountain-head of literatures. A discipline it is in logic, arithmetic, taste, symmetry,
poetry, language, rhetoric, ontology, morals, or practical wisdom. There was never
such range of speculation. Out of Plato come all things that are still written and
debated among men of thought. Great havoc makes he among our originalities. We
have reached the mountain from which all these drift boulders were detached. The
Bible of the learned for twenty-two hundred years, every brisk young man who says
in succession fine things to each reluctant generation, — Boethius, Rabelais, Erasmus, 10
Bruno, Locke, Rousseau, Alfieri, Coleridge, — is some reader of Plato, translating
into the vernacular, wittily, his good things. Even the men of grander proportion
suffer some deduction from the misfortune (shall I say?) of coming after this ex-
hausting generalizer. St. Augustine, Copernicus, Newton, Behmen, Swedenborg,
Goethe, are likewise his debtors, and must say after him. For it is fair to credit the
broadest generalizer with all the particulars deducible from his thesis.

Plato is philosophy and philosophy, Plato, — at once the glory and the shame of
mankind, since neither Saxon nor Roman have availed to add any idea to his categories. No wife, no children had he, and the thinkers of all civilized nations are his
posterity, and are tinged with his mind. How many great men Nature is incessantly 20
sending up out of night to be *his men,* — Platonists! the Alexandrians, a constellation of genius; the Elizabethans, not less; Sir Thomas More, Henry More, John Hales,
John Smith, Lord Bacon, Jeremy Taylor, Ralph Cudworth, Sydenham, Thomas
Taylor; Marcilius Ficinus, and Picus Mirandola. Calvinism is in his "Phædo:"
Christianity is in it. Mohametanism draws all its philosophy in its handbook of

---

1 **Omar,** caliph of Islam in the seventh century   1 **Koran,** the holy scriptures of Islam   10 **Boethius,**
Roman philosopher of the fifth century   10 **Rabelais,** François Rabelais (1490?-1553), French humorist
and satirist   10 **Erasmus,** Desiderius Erasmus. See note, p. 156   11 **Bruno,** Giordano Bruno (1548?-
1600), Italian philosopher   11 **Locke,** John Locke. See note, p. 285. Emerson had a low opinion of Locke
because of his denial of innate ideas   11 **Rousseau,** Jean Jacques Rousseau (1712-1778), French philoso-
pher and father of romanticism   11 **Alfieri,** Count Vittorio Alfieri (1749-1803), Italian dramatist   14
St. Augustine (354-430), bishop of Hippo and author of *The City of God*   14 **Copernicus,** Nikolaus
Copernicus. See note, p. 1100   14 **Newton,** Sir Isaac Newton. See note, p. 1075   14 **Behmen,** Jacob
Behmen. See note, p. 1124   14 **Swedenborg,** Emanuel Swedenborg. See note, p. 777   15 **Goethe,**
Johann Wolfgang von Goethe. (1749-1832), German author and philosopher   21 **Alexandrians,** the
Neoplatonists who flourished in Alexandria in the early centuries of the Christian era   22 **Sir Thomas
More** (1478-1535), English statesman and philosopher, author of *Utopia*   22 **Henry More** (1614-1687),
English philosopher and one of the Cambridge Platonists   22 **John Hales** (1584-1656), English divine
23 **John Smith,** Captain John Smith. See p. 43   23 **Jeremy Taylor** (1613-1667), English bishop. In his
poem "The Problem" Emerson called him "the Shakespeare of divines"   23 **Ralph Cudworth** (1617-
1688), another Cambridge Platonist   23 **Sydenham,** Thomas Sydenham (1624-1689), English physician
23 **Thomas Taylor** (1758-1835), English translator of Plato and the Neoplatonists whose translations
Emerson used and admired   24 **Marcilius Ficinus,** Marsilio Ficino (1433-1499), Italian Platonist   24
Picus Mirandola, Giovanni Pico della Mirandola (1463-1494), Italian humanist

morals, the Akhlak-y-Jalaly, from him. Mysticism finds in Plato all its texts. This citizen of a town in Greece is no villager nor patriot. An Englishman reads and says, "How English!" a German, "How Teutonic!" an Italian, "How Roman and how Greek!" As they say that Helen of Argos had that universal beauty that everybody felt related to her, so Plato seems, to a reader in New England, an American genius. His broad humanity transcends all sectional lines.

This range of Plato instructs us what to think of the vexed question concerning his reputed works, — what are genuine, what spurious. It is singular that wherever we find a man higher, by a whole head, than any of his contemporaries, it is sure
10 to come into doubt what are his real works. Thus Homer, Plato, Raffaelle, Shakspeare. For these men magnetize their contemporaries, so that their companions can do for them what they can never do for themselves; and the great man does thus live in several bodies, and write, or paint, or act by many hands: and after some time it is not easy to say what is the authentic work of the master, and what is only of his school.

Plato, too, like every great man, consumed his own times. What is a great man but one of great affinities, who takes up into himself all arts, sciences, all knowables, as his food? He can spare nothing; he can dispose of everything. What is not good for virtue is good for knowledge. Hence his contemporaries tax him with
20 plagiarism. But the inventor only knows how to borrow; and society is glad to forget the innumerable laborers who ministered to this architect, and reserves all its gratitude for him. When we are praising Plato it seems we are praising quotations from Solon, and Sophron, and Philolaus. Be it so. Every book is a quotation; and every house is a quotation out of all forests, and mines, and stone-quarries; and every man is a quotation from all his ancestors. And this grasping inventor puts all nations under contribution.

Plato absorbed the learning of his times — Philolaus, Timæus, Heraclitus, Parmenides, and what else; then his master, Socrates; and, finding himself still capable of a larger synthesis, — beyond all example then or since, — he travelled into Italy,
30 to gain what Pythagoras had for him; then into Egypt, and perhaps still farther east, to import the other element, which Europe wanted, into the European mind. This breadth entitles him to stand as the representative of philosophy. He says in the "Republic," "Such a genius as philosophers must of necessity have is wont but seldom, in all its parts, to meet in one man; but its different parts generally spring up in different persons." Every man who would do anything well must come to it from a higher ground. A philosopher must be more than a philosopher. Plato is clothed with the powers of a poet, stands upon the highest place of the poet, and (though I doubt he wanted the decisive gift of lyric expression) mainly is not a poet, because he chose to use the poetic gift to an ulterior purpose.

40 Great geniuses have the shortest biographies. Their cousins can tell you nothing about them. They lived in their writings, and so their house and street life was trivial and commonplace. If you would know their tastes and complexions, the most ad-

---

23 **Solon, Sophron, Philolaus,** Greek writers before Plato   27 **Timæus, Heraclitus, Parmenides,** Greek philosophers who flourished around 500 B.C.

miring of their readers most resembles them. Plato, especially, has no external biography. If he had lover, wife, or children, we hear nothing of them. He ground them all into paint. As a good chimney burns its smoke, so a philosopher converts the value of all his fortunes into his intellectual performances.

He was born 427, B.C., about the time of the death of Pericles; was of patrician connection in his times and city; and is said to have had an early inclination for war; but, in his twentieth year, meeting with Socrates, was easily dissuaded from this pursuit, and remained for ten years his scholar, until the death of Socrates. He then went to Megara, accepted the invitations of Dion and of Dionysius to the court of Sicily, and went thither three times, though very capriciously treated. He travelled into Italy, then into Egypt, where he stayed a long time; some say three, some say thirteen years. It is said he went farther, into Babylonia: this is uncertain. Returning to Athens, he gave lessons in the Academy to those whom his fame drew thither and died, as we have received it, in the act of writing, at eighty-one years.

But the biography of Plato is interior. We are to account for the supreme elevation of this man in the intellectual history of our race, — how it happens that, in proportion to the culture of men, they become his scholars; that, as our Jewish Bible has implanted itself in the table-talk and household life of every man and woman in the European and American nations, so the writings of Plato have pre-occupied every school of learning, every lover of thought, every church, every poet, — making it impossible to think, on certain levels, except through him. He stands between the truth and every man's mind, and has almost impressed language, and the primary forms of thought, with his name and seal. I am struck, in reading him, with the extreme modernness of his style and spirit. Here is the germ of that Europe we know so well, in its long history of arts and arms; here are all its traits, already discernible in the mind of Plato, — and in none before him. It has spread itself since into a hundred histories, but has added no new element. This perpetual modernness is the measure of merit in every work of art, since the author of it was not misled by anything short-lived or local, but abode by real and abiding traits. How Plato came thus to be Europe, and philosophy, and almost literature, is the problem for us to solve.

This could not have happened without a sound, sincere and catholic man, able to honour at the same time the ideal, or laws of the mind, and fate, or the order of nature. The first period of a nation, as of an individual, is the period of unconscious strength. Children cry, scream, and stamp with fury, unable to express their desires. As soon as they can speak and tell their want, and the reason of it, they become gentle. In adult life, whilst the perceptions are obtuse, men and women talk vehemently and superlatively, blunder and quarrel; their manners are full of desperation, their speech is full of oaths. As soon as, with culture, things have cleared up a little, and they see them no longer in lumps and masses, but accurately distributed, they desist from that weak vehemence, and explain their meaning in detail. If the tongue had not been framed for articulation man would still be a beast in the forest. The same weakness and want, on a higher plane, occurs daily in the education of ardent

9 **Megara**, a town in Greece   9 **Dion . . . Dionysius**, tyrants of Syracuse

young men and women. "Ah! you don't understand me; I have never met with any one who comprehends me;" and they sigh and weep, write verses, and walk alone, — fault of power to express their precise meaning. In a month or two, through the favor of their good genius, they meet some one so related as to assist their volcanic estate, and good communication being once established, they are thenceforward good citizens. It is ever thus. The progress is to accuracy, to skill, to truth, from blind force.

There is a moment, in the history of every nation, when proceeding out of this brute youth, the perceptive powers reach their ripeness, and have not yet become microscopic: so that man, at that instant, extends across the entire scale, and with his feet still planted on the immense forces of night, converses, by his eyes and brain, with solar and stellar creation. That is the moment of adult health, the culmination of power.

Such is the history of Europe in all points, and such in philosophy. Its early records, almost perished, are of the immigrations from Asia, bringing with them the dreams of barbarians; a confusion of crude notions of morals, and of natural philosophy, gradually subsiding through the partial insight of single teachers.

Before Pericles came the Seven Wise Masters, and we have the beginnings of geometry, metaphysics, and ethics: then the partialists, deducing the origin of things from flux or water, or from air, or from fire, or from mind. All mix with these causes mythologic pictures. At last comes Plato, the distributor, who needs no barbaric paint, or tattoo, or whooping; for he can define. He leaves with Asia the vast and superlative; he is the arrival of accuracy and intelligence. "He shall be as a god to me, who can rightly divide and define."

This defining is philosophy. Philosophy is the account which the human mind gives to itself of the constitution of the world. Two cardinal facts lie for ever at the base; the one, and the two. — 1. Unity, or Identity; and 2. Variety. We unite all things by perceiving the law which pervades them; by perceiving the superficial differences and the profound resemblances. But every mental act, — this very perception of identity or oneness, recognizes the difference of things. Oneness and otherness. It is impossible to speak or to think without embracing both.

The mind is urged to ask for one cause of many effects; then for the cause of that; and again the cause, diving still into the profound, self-assured that it shall arrive at an absolute and sufficient one, — a one that shall be all. "In the midst of the sun is the light, in the midst of the light is truth, and in the midst of truth is the imperishable being," say the Vedas. All philosophy, of east and west, has the same centripetence. Urged by an opposite necessity, the mind returns from the one to that which is not one, but other or many; from cause to effect; and affirms the necessary existence of variety, the self-existence of both, as each is involved in the other. These strictly-blended elements it is the problem of thought to separate and to reconcile. Their existence is mutually contradictory and exclusive; and each so fast slides into the other that we can never say what is one and what it is not. The Proteus is

17 **Seven Wise Masters,** characters in a collection of Eastern tales   36 **centripetence,** force directed toward the center   41 **Proteus.** See note, p. 1055

as nimble in the highest as in the lowest grounds, when we contemplate the one, the true, the good, — as in the surfaces and extremities of matter.

In all nations there are minds which incline to dwell in the conception of fundamental Unity. The raptures of prayer and ecstasy of devotion lose all being in one Being. This tendency finds its highest expression in the religious writings of the East, and chiefly in the Indian Scriptures, in the Vedas, the Bhagavat Geeta, and the Vishnu Purana. Those writings contain little else than this idea, and they rise to pure and sublime strains in celebrating it.

The Same, the Same: friend and foe are of one stuff; the ploughman, the plough, and the furrow are of one stuff; and the stuff is such, and so much, that the varia- 10 tions of form are unimportant. "You are fit" (says the supreme Krishna to a sage), "to apprehend that you are not distinct from me. That which I am thou art, and that also is this world, with its gods, and heroes, and mankind. Men contemplate distinctions, because they are stupefied with ignorance." "The words *I* and *mine* constitute ignorance. What is the great end of all you shall now learn from me. It is soul, — one in all bodies, pervading, uniform, perfect, pre-eminent over nature, exempt from birth, growth, and decay, omnipresent, made up of true knowledge, independent, unconnected with unrealities, with name, species, and the rest, in time past, present, and to come. The knowledge that this spirit, which is essentially one, is in one's own, and in all other bodies, is the wisdom of one who knows the unity of 20 things. As one diffusive air, passing through the perforations of a flute, is distinguished as the notes of a scale, so the nature of the Great Spirit is single, though its forms be manifold, arising from the consequences of acts. When the difference of the investing form, as that of god, or the rest, is destroyed, there is no distinction." "The whole world is but a manifestation of Vishnu, who is identical with all things, and is to be regarded by the wise as not differing from, but as the same as themselves. I neither am going nor coming; nor is my dwelling in any one place; nor art thou, thou: nor are others, others; nor am I, I." As if he had said, "All is for the soul, and the soul is Vishnu; and animals and stars are transient paintings; and light is whitewash; and durations are deceptive; and form is imprisonment; and 30 heaven itself a decoy." That which the soul seeks is resolution into being, above form, out of Tartarus, and out of heaven, — liberation from nature.

If speculation tends thus to a terrific unity, in which all things are absorbed, action tends directly backwards to diversity. The first is the course of gravitation of mind; the second is the power of nature. Nature is the manifold. The unity absorbs and melts or reduces. Nature opens and creates. These two principles reappear, and interpenetrate all things, all thought; the one, the many. One is being; the other, intellect: one is necessity; the other, freedom: one, rest; the other, motion: one, power; the other, distribution: one, strength; the other, pleasure: one, consciousness; the other, definition: one, genius; the other, talent: one, earnestness; the other, 40

---

9 **The Same . . . unimportant.** The same thought appears in Emerson's poem "Brahma" and is a close rendering of a passage from the *Bhagavad-Gita,* one of the Hindu scriptures   11 **Krishna,** a Hindu deity, the oracular source of the *Bhagavad-Gita*   25 **Vishnu,** a Hindu deity, of whom Krishna is an incarnation   32 **Tartarus,** the infernal regions

knowledge: one, possession; the other, trade: one, caste; the other, culture: one, king; the other, democracy: and if we dare carry these generalizations a step higher, and name the last tendency of both, we might say that the end of the one is escape from organization, — pure science; and the end of the other is the highest instrumentality, or use of means, or executive deity.

Each student adheres, by temperament and by habit, to the first or second of these gods of the mind. By religion, he tends to unity; by intellect, or by the senses, to the many. A too rapid unification, and an excessive appliance to parts and particulars, are the twin dangers of speculation.

10   To this partiality the history of nations corresponded. The country of unity, of immovable institutions, the seat of a philosophy delighting in abstractions, of men faithful in doctrine and in practice to the idea of a deaf, unimplorable, immense fate, is Asia; and it realizes this faith in the social institution of caste. On the other side, the genius of Europe is active and creative: it resists caste by culture; its philosophy was a discipline; it is a land of arts, inventions, trade, freedom. If the East loved infinity, the West delighted in boundaries.

European civility is the triumph of talent, the extension of system, the sharpened understanding, adaptive skill, delight in forms, delight in manifestation, in comprehensible results. Pericles, Athens, Greece, had been working in this element with
20   the joy of genius not yet chilled by any foresight of the detriment of an excess. They saw before them no sinister political economy; no ominous Malthus; no Paris or London; no pitiless subdivision of classes — the doom of the pinmakers, the doom of the weavers, of dressers, of stockingers, of carders, of spinners, of colliers; no Ireland; no Indian caste, superinduced by the efforts of Europe to throw it off. The understanding was in its health and prime. Art was in its splendid novelty. They cut the Pentelican marble as if it were snow, and their perfect works in architecture and sculpture seemed things of course, not more difficult than the completion of a new ship at the Medford yards, or new mills at Lowell. These things are in course, and may be taken for granted. The Roman legion, Byzantine legislation, English
30   trade, the saloons of Versailles, the cafés of Paris, the steam-mill, steam-boat, steam-coach, may all be seen in perspective; the town-meeting, the ballot-box, the newspaper and cheap press.

Meantime, Plato, in Egypt and in eastern pilgrimages, imbibed the idea of one Deity, in which all things are absorbed. The unity of Asia, and the detail of Europe; the infinitude of the Asiatic soul, and the defining, result-loving, machine-making, surface-seeking, opera-going Europe — Plato came to join, and by contact, to enhance the energy of each. The excellence of Europe and Asia are in his brain. Metaphysics and natural philosophy expressed the genius of Europe; he substructs the religion of Asia, as the base.

40   In short, a balanced soul was born, perceptive of the two elements. It is as easy to be great as to be small. The reason why we do not at once believe in admirable

---

21 **Malthus,** Thomas Robert Malthus (1766-1834), English political economist who predicted a disastrous population explosion   26 **Pentelican marble,** obtained from Mount Pentelicus, near Athens, and used in building the Parthenon   28 **Medford . . . Lowell,** shipbuilding and manufacturing cities in Massachusetts

souls, is because they are not in our experience. In actual life, they are so rare as to be incredible; but, primarily, there is not only no presumption against them, but the strongest presumption in favour of their appearance. But whether voices were heard in the sky, or not; whether his mother or his father dreamed that the infant man-child was the son of Apollo; whether a swarm of bees settled on his lips, or not; a man who could see two sides of a thing was born. The wonderful synthesis so familiar in nature; the upper and the under side of the medal of Jove; the union of impossibilities, which reappears in every object; its real and its ideal power — was now, also, transferred entire to the consciousness of a man.

The balanced soul came. If he loved abstract truth, he saved himself by propound- 10 ing the most popular of all principles, the absolute good, which rules rulers, and judges the judge. If he made transcendental distinctions, he fortified himself by drawing all his illustrations from sources disdained by orators and polite conversers; from mares and puppies; from pitchers and soup-ladles; from cooks and criers; the shops of potters, horse-doctors, butchers, and fishmongers. He cannot forgive in himself a partiality, but is resolved that the two poles of thought shall appear in his statement. His argument and his sentence are self-poised and spherical. The two poles appear; yes, and become two hands, to grasp and appropriate their own.

Every great artist has been such by synthesis. Our strength is transitional, alter- nating; or, shall I say, a thread of two strands. The sea-shore, sea seen from shore, 20 shore seen from sea; the taste of two metals in contact; and our enlarged powers at the approach and at the departure of a friend; the experience of poetic creativeness, which is not found in staying at home, nor yet in travelling, but in transitions from one to the other, which must therefore be adroitly managed to present as much transitional surface as possible; this command of two elements must explain the power and the charm of Plato. Art expresses the one, or the same by the different. Thought seeks to know unity in unity; poetry to show it by variety; that is, always by an object or symbol. Plato keeps the two vases, one of æther and one of pig- ment, at his side, and invariably uses both. Things added to things, as statistics, civil history, are inventories. Things used as language are inexhaustibly attractive. 30 Plato turns incessantly the obverse and the reverse of the medal of Jove.

To take an example: — The physical philosophers had sketched each his theory of the world; the theory of atoms, of fire, of flux, of spirit; theories mechanical and chemical in their genius. Plato, a master of mathematics, studious of all natural laws and causes, feels these, as second causes, to be no theories of the world, but bare inventories and lists. To the study of nature he therefore prefixes the dogma — "Let us declare the cause which led the Supreme Ordainer to produce and compose the universe. He was good; and he who is good has no kind of envy. Exempt from envy, he wished that all things should be as much as possible like himself. Who- soever, taught by wise men, shall admit this as the prime cause of the origin and 40 foundation of the world, will be in the truth." "All things are for the sake of the good, and it is the cause of everything beautiful." This dogma animates and imper- sonates his philosophy.

---

36 **Let us** . . . truth, from Plato's *Timaeus*

The synthesis which makes the character of his mind appears in all his talents. Where there is great compass of wit, we usually find excellencies that combine easily in the living man, but in description appear incompatible. The mind of Plato is not to be exhibited by a Chinese catalogue, but is to be apprehended by an original mind in the exercise of its original power. In him the freest abandonment is united with the precision of a geometer. His daring imagination gives him the more solid grasp of facts; as the birds of highest flight have the strongest alar bones. His patrician polish, his intrinsic elegance, edged by an irony so subtle that it stings and paralyzes, adorn the soundest health and strength of frame. According to the old
10 sentence, "If Jove should descend to the earth, he would speak in the style of Plato."

With this palatial air there is, for the direct aim of several of his works, and running through the tenor of them all, a certain earnestness, which mounts, in the "Republic," and in the "Phædo," to piety. He has been charged with feigning sickness at the time of the death of Socrates. But the anecdotes that have come down from the times attest his manly interference before the people in his master's behalf, since even the savage cry of the assembly to Plato is preserved; and the indignation towards popular government, in many of his pieces, expresses a personal exasperation. He has a probity, a native reverence for justice and honor, and a humanity which makes him tender for the superstitions of the people. Add to this, he believes that
20 poetry, prophecy, and the high insight, are from a wisdom of which man is not master; that the gods never philosophize; but, by a celestial mania, these miracles are accomplished. Horsed on these winged steeds, he sweeps the dim regions, visits worlds which flesh cannot enter; he saw the souls in pain; he hears the doom of the judge; he beholds the penal metempsychosis; the Fates, with the rock and shears; and hears the intoxicating hum of their spindle.

But his circumspection never forsook him. One would say, he had read the inscription on the gates of Busyrane — "Be bold;" and on the second gate — "Be bold, be bold, and evermore be bold:" and then again had paused well at the third gate — "Be not too bold." His strength is like the momentum of a falling planet;
30 and his discretion, the return of its due and perfect curve — so excellent is his Greek love of boundary, and his skill in definition. In reading logarithms, one is not more secure, than in following Plato in his flights. Nothing can be colder than his head, when the lightnings of his imagination are playing in the sky. He has finished his thinking, before he brings it to the reader; and he abounds in the surprises of a literary master. He has that opulence which furnishes, at every turn, the precise weapon he needs. As the rich man wears no more garments, drives no more horses, sits in no more chambers, than the poor— but has that one dress, or equipage, or instrument, which is fit for the hour and the need; so Plato, in his plenty, is never restricted, but has the fit word. There is, indeed, no weapon in all the armory of
40 wit which he did not possess and use — epic, analysis, mania, intuition, music, satire, and irony, down to the customary and polite. His illustrations are poetry, and his jests illustrations. Socrates' profession of obstetric art is good philosophy; and his

---

26 **inscription . . . too bold.** The inscriptions are in Spenser's *Faerie Queene*, Bk. III, Canto XI

finding that word "cookery," and "adulatory art," for rhetoric, in the "Gorgias," does us a substantial service still. No orator can measure in effect with him who can give good nicknames.

What moderation, and understatement, and checking his thunder in mid volley! He has good-naturedly furnished the courtier and citizen with all that can be said against the schools. "For philosophy is an elegant thing if any one modestly meddles with it; but, if he is conversant with it more than is becoming, it corrupts the man." He could well afford to be generous — he who, from the sunlike centrality and reach of vision, had a faith without cloud. Such as his perception, was his speech: he plays with the doubt, and makes the most of it: he paints and quibbles; and by- 10 and-by comes a sentence that moves the sea and land. The admirable earnest comes not only at intervals, in the perfect yes and no of the dialogue, but in bursts of light. "I, therefore, Callicles, am persuaded by these accounts, and consider how I may exhibit my soul before the judge in a healthy condition. Wherefore, disregarding the honors that most men value, and looking to the truth, I shall endeavor in reality to live as virtuously as I can; and, when I die, to die so. And I invite all other men to the utmost of my power; and you, too, I in turn invite to this contest, which, I affirm, surpasses all contests here."

He is a great average man; one who, to the best thinking, adds a proportion and equality in his faculties, so that men see in him their own dreams and glimpses 20 made available, and made to pass for what they are. A great common sense is his warrant and qualification to be the world's interpreter. He has reason, as all the philosophic and poetic class have: but he has, also, what they have not, — this strong solving sense to reconcile his poetry with the appearances of the world, and build a bridge from the streets of cities to the Atlantis. He omits never this graduation, but slopes his thought, however picturesque the precipice on one side, to an access from the plain. He never writes in ecstasy, or catches us up into poetic raptures.

Plato apprehended the cardinal facts. He could prostrate himself on the earth, and cover his eyes whilst he adored that which cannot be numbered, or gauged, or known, or named: that of which everything can be affirmed and denied: that "which is entity 30 and nonentity." He called it super-essential. He even stood ready, as in the "Parmenides," to demonstrate that it was so — that this Being exceeded the limits of intellect. No man ever more fully acknowledged the Ineffable. Having paid his homage, as for the human race, to the Illimitable, he then stood erect, and for the human race affirmed, "And yet things are knowable!" — that is, the Asia in his mind was first heartily honored — the ocean of love and power, before form, before will, before knowledge, the Same, the Good, the One; and now, refreshed and empowered by this worship, the instinct of Europe, namely, culture, returns; and he cries, Yet things are knowable! They are knowable, because, being from one, things correspond. There is a scale: and the correspondence of heaven to earth, of matter to 40 mind, of the part to the whole, is our guide. As there is a science of stars, called astronomy; a science of quantities, called mathematics; a science of qualities, called

---

1 **Gorgias,** one of Plato's works   18 **contests here.** The quotations in this paragraph are from the *Gorgias*   25 **Atlantis,** a mythical western continent mentioned by Plato and other ancient writers

chemistry; so there is a science of sciences, — I call it Dialectic, — which is the Intellect discriminating the false and the true. It rests on the observation of identity and diversity; for, to judge, is to unite to an object the notion which belongs to it. The sciences, even the best — mathematics and astronomy — are like sportsmen, who seize whatever prey offers, even without being able to make any use of it. Dialectic must teach the use of them. "This is of that rank that no intellectual man will enter on any study for its own sake, but only with a view to advance himself in that one sole science which embraces all."

"The essence or peculiarity of man is to comprehend a whole; or that which, in
10 the diversity of sensations, can be comprised under a rational unity." "The soul which has never perceived the truth cannot pass into the human form." I announce to men the Intellect. I announce the good of being interpenetrated by the mind that made nature: this benefit, namely, that it can understand nature, which it made and maketh. Nature is good, but intellect is better: as the law-giver is before the law-receiver. I give you joy, O sons of men! that truth is altogether wholesome; that we have hope to search out what might be the very self of everything. The misery of man is to be baulked of the sight of essence, and to be stuffed with conjectures: but the supreme good is reality; the supreme beauty is reality; and all virtue and all felicity depend on this science of the real: for courage is nothing else than knowl-
20 edge: the fairest fortune that can befall man, is to be guided by his dæmon to that which is truly his own. This also is the essence of justice — to attend every one his own; nay, the notion of virtue is not to be arrived at, except through direct contemplation of the divine essence. Courage, then! for, "the persuasion that we must search that which we do not know, will render us, beyond comparison, better, braver, and more industrious than if we thought it impossible to discover what we do not know, and useless to search for it." He secures a position not to be commanded, by his passion for reality; valuing philosophy only as it is the pleasure of conversing with real being.

Thus, full of the genius of Europe, he said, *Culture*. He saw the institutions of
30 Sparta, and recognized more genially, one would say, than any since, the hope of education. He delighted in every accomplishment, in every graceful and useful and truthful performance; above all, in the splendors of genius and intellectual achievement. "The whole of life, O Socrates, said Glauco, is, with the wise, the measure of hearing such discourses as these." What a price he sets on the feats of talent, on the powers of Pericles, of Isocrates, of Parmenides! What price, above price, on the talents themselves! He called the several faculties, gods, in his beautiful personation. What value he gives to the art of gymnastic in education; what to geometry; what to music; what to astronomy, whose appeasing and medicinal power he celebrates! In the "Timæus," he indicates the highest employment of the eyes. "By us it is as-
40 serted, that God invented and bestowed sight on us for this purpose — that, on surveying the circles of intelligence in the heavens, we might properly employ those

---

6 **This . . . all.** Compare Plato's *Republic,* Bk. VII   9 **The essence . . . form,** from Plato's *Phaedrus*   35
Pericles (c. 490-429 B.C.), Athenian statesman   35 **Isocrates** (436-338 B.C.), Athenian orator and teacher
of rhetoric   35 **Parmenides.** See note, p. 1129

of our own minds, which, though disturbed when compared with the others that
are uniform, are still allied to their circulations; and that, having thus learned, and
being naturally possessed of a correct reasoning faculty, we might, by imitating the
uniform revolutions of divinity, set right our own wanderings and blunders." And
in the "Republic" — "By each of these disciplines, a certain organ of the soul is
both purified and re-animated, which is blinded and buried by studies of another
kind; an organ better worth saving than ten thousand eyes, since truth is perceived
by this alone."

He said, Culture; but he first admitted its basis, and gave immeasurably the first
place to advantages of nature. His patrician tastes laid stress on the distinctions of 10
birth. In the doctrine of the organic character and disposition is the origin of caste.
"Such as were fit to govern, into their composition the informing Deity mingled
gold; into the military, silver; iron and brass for husbandmen and artificers." The
East confirms itself, in all ages, in this faith. The Koran is explicit on this point of
caste. "Men have their metal, as of gold and silver. Those of you who were the
worthy ones in the state of ignorance, will be the worthy ones in the state of faith, as
soon as you embrace it." Plato was not less firm. "Of the five orders of things, only
four can be taught to the generality of men." In the "Republic," he insists on the
temperaments of the youth, as first of the first.

A happier example of the stress laid on nature, is in the dialogue with the young 20
Theages, who wishes to receive lessons from Socrates. Socrates declares that, if some
have grown wise by associating with him, no thanks are due to him; but, simply,
whilst they were with him, they grew wise, not because of him; he pretends not to
know the way of it. "It is adverse to many, nor can those be benefited by associating
with me, whom the Dæmon opposes; so that it is not possible for me to live with
these. With many, however, he does not prevent me from conversing, who yet are
not at all benefited by associating with me. Such, O Theages, is the association
with me; for, if it pleases the God, you will make great and rapid proficiency; you
will not, if he does not please. Judge whether it is not safer to be instructed by
some one of those who have power over the benefit which they impart to men, than 30
by me, who benefit or not, just as it may happen." As if he had said, "I have no
system. I cannot be answerable for you. You will be what you must. If there is love
between us, inconceivably delicious and profitable will our intercourse be; if not,
your time is lost, and you will only annoy me. I shall seem to you stupid, and the
reputation I have, false. Quite above us, beyond the will of you or me, is this secret
affinity or repulsion laid. All my good is magnetic, and I educate, not by lessons,
but by going about my business."

He said, Culture; he said, Nature: and he failed not to add, "There is also the
divine." There is no thought in any mind, but it quickly tends to convert itself into
a power, and organizes a huge instrumentality of means. Plato, lover of limits, loved 40
the illimitable, saw the enlargement and nobility which come from truth itself, and
good itself, and attempted, as if on the part of the human intellect, once for all, to
do it adequate homage — homage fit for the immense soul to receive, and yet homage becoming the intellect to render. He said, then, "Our faculties run out into

infinity, and return to us thence. We can define but a little way; but here is a fact which will not be skipped, and which to shut our eyes upon is suicide. All things are in a scale; and, begin where we will, ascend and ascend. All things are symbolical; and what we call results are beginnings."

A key to the method and completeness of Plato is his twice-bisected line. After he has illustrated the relation between the absolute good and true, and the forms of the intelligible world, he says: — "Let there be a line cut in two unequal parts. Cut again each of these two parts — one representing the visible, the other the intelligible world — and these two new sections, representing the bright part and the dark
10 part of these worlds, you will have, for one of the sections of the visible world — images, that is, both shadows and reflections; for the other section, the objects of these images — that is, plants, animals, and the works of art and nature. Then divide the intelligible world in like manner; the one section will be of opinions and hypotheses, and the other section, of truths." To these four sections, the four operations of the soul correspond — conjecture, faith, understanding, reason. As every pool reflects the image of the sun, so every thought and thing restores us an image and creature of the supreme Good. The universe is perforated by a million channels for his activity. All things mount and mount.

All his thought has this ascension; in "Phædrus," teaching that "beauty is the
20 most lovely of all things, exciting hilarity, and shedding desire and confidence through the universe, wherever it enters; and it enters, in some degree, into all things: but that there is another, which is as much more beautiful than beauty, as beauty is than chaos; namely, wisdom, which our wonderful organ of sight cannot reach unto, but which, could it be seen, would ravish us with its perfect reality." He has the same regard to it as the source of excellence in works of art. "When an artificer, in the fabrication of any work, looks to that which always subsists according *to the same;* and, employing a model of this kind, expresses its idea and power in his work; it must follow, that his production should be beautiful. But when he beholds that which is born and dies, it will be far from beautiful."

30 Thus ever: the "Banquet" is a teaching in the same spirit, familiar now to all the poetry, and to all the sermons of the world, that the love of the sexes is initial; and symbolizes, at a distance, the passion of the soul for that immense lake of beauty it exists to seek. This faith in the Divinity is never out of mind, and constitutes the limitation of all his dogmas. Body cannot teach wisdom — God only. In the same mind, he constantly affirms that virtue cannot be taught; that it is not a science, but an inspiration; that the greatest goods are produced to us through mania, and are assigned to us by a divine gift.

This leads me to that central figure, which he has established in his Academy, as the organ through which every considered opinion shall be announced, and whose
40 biography he has likewise so labored, that the historic facts are lost in the light of Plato's mind. Socrates and Plato are the double star, which the most powerful instruments will not entirely separate. Socrates, again, in his traits and genius, is the

---

7 **Let . . . truths.** See Plato's *Republic,* Bk. VI   30 **Banquet,** another of Plato's works, more commonly known as the *Symposium*

best example of that synthesis which constitutes Plato's extraordinary power. Socrates, a man of humble stem, but honest enough; of the commonest history; of a personal homeliness so remarkable, as to be a cause of wit in others — the rather that his broad good nature and exquisite taste for a joke invited the sally, which was sure to be paid. The players personated him on the stage; the potters copied his ugly face on their stone jugs. He was a cool fellow, adding to his humor a perfect temper, and a knowledge of his man, be he who he might whom he talked with, which laid the companion open to certain defeat in any debate — and in debate he immoderately delighted. The young men are prodigiously fond of him, and invite him to their feasts, whither he goes for conversation. He can drink, too; has the 10 strongest head in Athens; and, after leaving the whole party under the table, goes away, as if nothing had happened, to begin new dialogues with somebody that is sober. In short, he was what our country-people call *an old one.*

He affected a good many citizen-like tastes, was monstrously fond of Athens, hated trees, never willingly went beyond the walls, knew the old characters, valued the bores and Philistines, thought everything in Athens a little better than anything in any other place. He was plain as a Quaker in habit and speech, affected low phrases, and illustrations from cocks and quails, soup-pans and sycamore-spoons, grooms and farriers, and unnameable offices — especially if he talked with any superfine person. He had a Franklin-like wisdom. Thus, he showed one who was afraid to go on foot 20 to Olympia, that it was no more than his daily walk within doors, if continuously extended, would easily reach.

Plain old uncle as he was, with his great ears — an immense talker — the rumor ran, that, on one or two occasions, in the war with Bœotia, he had shown a determination which had covered the retreat of a troop; and there was some story that, under cover of folly, he had, in the city government, when one day he chanced to hold a seat there, evinced a courage in opposing singly the popular voice, which had well-nigh ruined him. He is very poor; but then he is hardy as a soldier, and can,live on a few olives; usually, in the strictest sense, on bread and water, except when entertained by his friends. His necessary expenses were exceedingly small, and 30 no one could live as he did. He wore no under garment; his upper garment was the same for summer and winter; he went barefooted; and it is said that, to procure the pleasure, which he loves, of talking at his ease all day with the most elegant and cultivated young men, he will now and then return to his shop, and carve statues, good or bad, for sale. However that be, it is certain that he had grown to delight in nothing else than this conversation; and that, under his hypocritical pretence of knowing nothing, he attacks and brings down all the fine speakers, all of the fine philosophers of Athens, whether natives, or strangers from Asia Minor and the islands. Nobody can refuse to talk to him, he is so honest, and really curious to know; a man who was willingly confuted, if he did not speak the truth, and who 40 willingly confuted others, asserting what was false; and not less pleased when confuted than when confuting; for he thought not any evil happened to men, of such a magnitude as false opinion respecting the just and unjust. A pitiless disputant, who knows nothing, but the bounds of whose conquering intelligence no man had ever reached; whose temper was imperturbable; whose dreadful logic was always leisurely and sportive; so careless and ignorant, as to disarm the wariest, and draw them, in the pleasantest manner, into horrible doubts and confusion. But he always knew the way out; knew it, yet would not tell it. No escape; he drives them to terrible choices by his dilemmas, and tosses the Hippiases and Gorgiases, with their grand reputations, as a boy tosses his balls. The tyrannous realist! — Meno has discoursed a thousand times, at length, on virtue, before many companies, and very well, as it appeared to him; but, at this moment, he cannot even tell what it is — this crampfish of a Socrates has so bewitched him.

10   This hard-headed humorist, whose strange conceits, drollery, and *bonhommie* diverted the young patricians, whilst the rumor of his sayings and quibbles gets abroad every day, turns out, in the sequel, to have a probity as invincible as his logic, and to be either insane, or, at least, under cover of this play, enthusiastic in his religion. When accused before the judges of subverting the popular creed, he affirms the immortality of the soul, the future reward and punishment, and, refusing to recant, in a caprice of the popular government, was condemned to die, and sent to the prison. Socrates entered the prison, and took away all ignominy from the place, which could not be a prison whilst he was there. Crito bribed the jailer; but Socrates would not go out by treachery. "Whatever inconvenience ensue, nothing is to be preferred before jus-
20 tice. These things I hear like pipes and drums, whose sound makes me deaf to everything you say." The fame of this prison, the fame of the discourses there, and the drinking of the hemlock, are one of the most precious passages in the history of the world.

The rare coincidence, in one ugly body, of the droll and the martyr, the keen street and market debater with the sweetest saint known to any history at that time, had forcibly struck the mind of Plato, so capacious of these contrasts; and the figure of Socrates, by a necessity, placed itself in the foreground of the scene, as the fittest dispenser of the intellectual treasures he had to communicate. It was a rare fortune, that this Æsop of the mob, and this robed scholar, should meet, to make each other
30 immortal in their mutual faculty. The strange synthesis, in the character of Socrates, capped the synthesis in the mind of Plato. Moreover, by this means, he was able, in the direct way, and without envy, to avail himself of the wit and weight of Socrates, to which unquestionably his own debt was great; and these derived again their principal advantage from the perfect art of Plato.

It remains to say, that the defect of Plato in power is only that which results inevitably from his quality. He is intellectual in his aim; and, therefore, in expression, literary. Mounting into heaven, diving into the pit, expounding the laws of the state, the passion of love, the remorse of crime, the hope of the parting soul — he is literary, and never otherwise. It is almost the sole deduction from the merit of
40 Plato, that his writings have not — what is, no doubt, incident to this regnancy of intellect in his work — the vital authority which the screams of prophets and the sermons of unlettered Arabs and Jews possess. There is an interval; and to cohesion, contact is necessary.

---

5 **Hippiases, Gorgiases.** Hippias and Gorgias were early Greek philosophers

I know not what can be said in reply to this criticism, but that we have come to a fact in the nature of things; an oak is not an orange. The qualities of sugar remain with sugar, and those of salt, with salt.

In the second place, he has not a system. The dearest defenders and disciples are at fault. He attempted a theory of the universe, and his theory is not complete or self-evident. One man thinks he means this; and another, that: he has said one thing in one place, and the reverse of it in another place. He is charged with having failed to make the transition from ideas to matter. Here is the world, sound as a nut, perfect, not the smallest piece of chaos left, never a stitch nor an end, nor a mark of haste, or botching, or second thought; but the theory of the world is a thing of 10 shreds and patches.

The longest wave is quickly lost in the sea. Plato would willingly have a Platonism, a known and accurate expression for the world, and it should be accurate. It shall be the world passed through the mind of Plato — nothing less. Every atom shall have the Platonic tinge; every atom, every relation or quality you knew before, you shall know again, and find here, but now ordered; not nature, but art. And you shall feel that Alexander indeed overran, with men and horses, some countries of the planet; but countries, and things of which countries are made, elements, planet itself, laws of planet and of men, have passed through this man as bread into his body, and become no longer bread, but body: so all this mammoth morsel has be- 20 come Plato. He has clapped copyright on the world. This is the ambition of individualism. But the mouthful proves too large. *Boa constrictor* has good will to eat it, but he is foiled. He falls abroad in the attempt; and biting, gets strangled: the bitten world holds the biter fast by his own teeth. There he perishes: unconquered nature lives on, and forgets him. So it fares with all: so must it fare with Plato. In view of eternal nature, Plato turns out to be philosophical exercitations. He argues on this side, and on that. The acutest German, the lovingest disciple, could never tell what Platonism was; indeed, admirable texts can be quoted on both sides of every great question from him.

These things we are forced to say, if we must consider the effort of Plato, or of 30 any philosopher, to dispose of Nature — which will not be disposed of. No power of genius has ever yet had the smallest success in explaining existence. The perfect enigma remains. But there is an injustice in assuming this ambition for Plato. Let us not seem to treat with flippancy his venerable name. Men, in proportion to their intellect, have admitted his transcendent claims. The way to know him, is to compare him, not with nature, but with other men. How many ages have gone by, and he remains unapproached! A chief structure of human wit, like Karnac, or the mediæval cathedrals, or the Etrurian remains, it requires all the breadth of human faculty to know it. I think it is truliest seen, when seen with the most respect. His sense deepens, his merits multiply, with study. When we say, here is a fine collection of 40 fables; or, when we praise the style; or the common sense; or arithmetic; we speak as boys, and much of our impatient criticism of the dialectic, I suspect, is no better.

---

37 **Karnac**, Karnak, a village in Egypt which has given its name to the ruin of Thebes · 38 **Etrurian**, pertaining to the civilization of Italy before the rise of Rome

The criticism is like our impatience of miles, when we are in a hurry; but it is still best that a mile should have seventeen hundred and sixty yards. The great-eyed Plato proportioned the lights and shades after the genius of our life.

1845, 1850

The Rhodora: *On Being Asked, Whence Is the Flower?*

In May, when sea-winds pierced our solitudes,
I found the fresh Rhodora in the woods,
Spreading its leafless blooms in a damp nook,
To please the desert and the sluggish brook.
The purple petals, fallen in the pool,
Made the black water with their beauty gay;
Here might the red-bird come his plumes to cool,
And court the flower that cheapens his array.
Rhodora! if the sages ask thee why
This charm is wasted on the earth and sky,   10
Tell them, dear, that if eyes were made for seeing,
Then Beauty is its own excuse for being:
Why thou wert there, O rival of the rose!
I never thought to ask, I never knew:
But, in my simple ignorance, suppose
The self-same Power that brought me there brought you.

1834, 1839

---

12 **Beauty . . . being.** This often-quoted line hardly represents Emerson's usual attitude. More characteristic is the following from *Nature* (1836): "Beauty in nature is not ultimate. It is the herald of inward and eternal beauty, and is not alone a solid and satisfactory good"

Each and All

Little thinks, in the field, yon red-cloaked clown
Of thee from the hill-top looking down;
The heifer that lows in the upland farm,
Far-heard, lows not thine ear to charm;
The sexton, tolling his bell at noon,
Deems not that great Napoleon
Stops his horse, and lists with delight,
Whilst his files sweep round yon Alpine height;

Nor knowest thou what argument
Thy life to thy neighbor's creed has lent: 10
All are needed by each one;
Nothing is fair or good alone.
I thought the sparrow's note from heaven,
Singing at dawn on the alder bough;
I brought him home, in his nest, at even;
He sings the song, but it cheers not now,
For I did not bring home the river and sky; —
He sang to my ear, — they sang to my eye.
The delicate shells lay on the shore;
The bubbles of the latest wave   20
Fresh pearls to their enamel gave,
And the bellowing of the savage sea
Greeted their safe escape to me.
I wiped away the weeds and foam,
I fetched my sea-born treasures home;
But the poor, unsightly, noisome things
Had left their beauty on the shore
With the sun and the sand and the wild uproar.
The lover watched his graceful maid,
As 'mid the virgin train she strayed,   30
Nor knew her beauty's best attire
Was woven still by the snow-white choir.
At last she came to his hermitage,
Like the bird from the woodlands to the cage; —
The gay enchantment was undone,
A gentle wife, but fairy none.
Then I said, "I covet truth;
Beauty is unripe childhood's cheat;
I leave it behind with the games of youth": —
As I spoke, beneath my feet   40
The ground-pine curled its pretty wreath,
Running over the club-moss burrs;
I inhaled the violet's breath;
Around me stood the oaks and firs;
Pine-cones and acorns lay on the ground;
Over me soared the eternal sky,
Full of light and of deity;
Again I saw, again I heard,
The rolling river, the morning bird; —
Beauty through my senses stole;   50
I yielded myself to the perfect whole.

                        1834?, 1839

Concord Hymn *Sung at the Completion of the Battle Monument, July 4, 1837*

By the rude bridge that arched the flood,
    Their flag to April's breeze unfurled,
Here once the embattled farmers stood
    And fired the shot heard round the world.

The foe long since in silence slept;
    Alike the conqueror silent sleeps;
And Time the ruined bridge has swept
    Down the dark stream which seaward creeps.

On this green bank, by this soft stream,
    We set to-day a votive stone;   10
That memory may their deed redeem,
    When, like our sires, our sons are gone.

Spirit, that made those heroes dare
    To die, and leave their children free,
Bid Time and Nature gently spare
    The shaft we raise to them and thee.

                        1837

4 **fired . . . world.** The first armed clash of the American Revolution occurred at Lexington and Concord, April 19, 1775. After having retreated from Lexington, the minutemen rallied at Concord and drove the British back to Boston

The Problem

I like a church; I like a cowl;
I love a prophet of the soul;
And on my heart monastic aisles
Fall like sweet strains, or pensive smiles;
Yet not for all his faith can see
Would I that cowlèd churchman be.

Why should the vest on him allure,
Which I could not on me endure?

Not from a vain or shallow thought
His awful Jove young Phidias brought;   10

10 **Jove . . . Phidias,** statue of Zeus by Phidias. See note, p. 1109

Never from lips of cunning fell
The thrilling Delphic oracle;
Out from the heart of nature rolled
The burdens of the Bible old;
The litanies of nations came,
Like the volcano's tongue of flame,
Up from the burning core below, —
The canticles of love and woe:
The hand that rounded Peter's dome
And groined the aisles of Christian Rome   20
Wrought in a sad sincerity;
Himself from God he could not free;
He builded better than he knew; —
The conscious stone to beauty grew.
Know'st thou what wove yon woodbird's nest
Of leaves, and feathers from her breast?
Or how the fish outbuilt her shell,
Painting with morn each annual cell?
Or how the sacred pine-tree adds
To her old leaves new myriads?   30
Such and so grew these holy piles,
Whilst love and terror laid the tiles.
Earth proudly wears the Parthenon,
As the best gem upon her zone,
And Morning opes with haste her lids
To gaze upon the Pyramids;
O'er England's abbeys bends the sky,
As on its friends, with kindred eye;
For out of Thought's interior sphere
These wonders rose to upper air;   40
And Nature gladly gave them place,
Adopted them into her race,
And granted them an equal date
With Andes and with Ararat.

These temples grew as grows the grass;
Art might obey, but not surpass.
The passive Master lent his hand
To the vast soul that o'er him planned;
And the same power that reared the shrine
Bestrode the tribes that knelt within.   50
Ever the fiery Pentecost

---

12 **Delphic oracle.** See note, p. 1125   19 **hand . . . dome,** the famous dome of St. Peter's at Rome, designed by Michelangelo (1475-1564)   47 **Master,** the creative artist   51 **Pentecost.** See Acts 2 for the account of "the outpouring of the Spirit on the day of Pentecost"

Girds with one flame the countless host,
Trances the heart through chanting choirs,
And through the priest the mind inspires.
The word unto the prophet spoken
Was writ on tables yet unbroken;
The word by seers or sibyls told,
In groves of oak, or fanes of gold,
Still floats upon the morning wind,
Still whispers to the willing mind.   60
One accent of the Holy Ghost
The heedless world hath never lost.
I know what say the fathers wise, —
The Book itself before me lies,
Old *Chrysostom,* best Augustine,
And he who blent both in his line,
The younger *Golden Lips* or mines,
Taylor, the Shakspeare of divines.
His words are music in my ear,
I see his cowlèd portrait dear;   70
And yet, for all his faith could see,
I would not the good bishop be.

                              1839, 1840

<hr/>

55 **prophet,** Moses and the Commandments. See Exodus 32, 34   65 **Chrysostom.** The eloquent John of
Antioch (347-407), church father, was called "Chrysostom," meaning "Golden Lips"   65 **Augustine,** St.
Augustine. See note, p. 1128   68 **Taylor,** Jeremy Taylor. See note, p. 1128

The Snow-Storm

Announced by all the trumpets of the sky,
Arrives the snow, and, driving o'er the fields,
Seems nowhere to alight: the whited air
Hides hills and woods, the river, and the heaven,
And veils the farm-house at the garden's end.
The sled and traveller stopped, the courier's feet
Delayed, all friends shut out, the housemates sit
Around the radiant fireplace, enclosed
In a tumultuous privacy of storm.

    Come see the north wind's masonry.   10
Out of an unseen quarry evermore

Furnished with tile, the fierce artificer
Curves his white bastions with projected roof
Round every windward stake, or tree, or door.
Speeding, the myriad-handed, his wild work
So fanciful, so savage, nought cares he
For number or proportion. Mockingly,
On coop or kennel he hangs Parian wreaths;
A swan-like form invests the hidden thorn;
Fills up the farmer's lane from wall to wall,   20
Maugre the farmer's sighs; and at the gate
A tapering turret overtops the work.
And when his hours are numbered, and the world
Is all his own, retiring, as he were not,
Leaves, when the sun appears, astonished Art
To mimic in slow structures, stone by stone,
Built in an age, the mad wind's nightwork,
The frolic architecture of the snow.

                                                          1841

---

18 **Parian**, Parian marble was used for sculptures in ancient times

Grace

"Grace" was published in The Dial *for January 1842, but Emerson did not include it in his collected* Poems *(1847) or in later collections. His reason for "rejecting" it probably was that it expresses ideas contrary to those expressed elsewhere in his writings, especially in* Self-Reliance. *In the essay he says: "Society everywhere is in conspiracy against the manhood of every one of its members. . . . Whoso would be a man, must be a nonconformist. . . . What I must do is all that concerns me, not what the people think." Although one of his best poems, "Grace" expresses a view which must have been unusual with Emerson and which we may regard as uncharacteristic. The poem shows the influence of the English religious poets of the seventeenth century.*

How much, preventing God, how much I owe
To the defenses thou hast round me set;
Example, custom, fear, occasion slow, —
These scorned bondmen were my parapet.
I dare not peep over this parapet
To gauge with glance the roaring gulf below,
The depths of sin to which I had descended,
Had not these me against myself defended.

                                                          1842

Merlin

Emerson uses Merlin, famous prophet and magician of Arthurian romance, to typify the ideal poet. The ideas of the poem are similar to those of the essay on "The Poet."

I

Thy trivial harp will never please
Or fill my craving ear;
Its chords should ring as blows the breeze,
Free, peremptory, clear.
No jingling serenader's art,
Nor tinkle of piano strings,
Can make the wild blood start
In its mystic springs.
The kingly bard
Must smite the chords rudely and hard,   10
As with hammer or with mace;
That they may render back
Artful thunder, which conveys
Secrets of the solar track,
Sparks of the supersolar blaze.
Merlin's blows are strokes of fate,
Chiming with the forest tone,
When boughs buffet boughs in the wood;
Chiming with the gasp and moan
Of the ice-imprisoned flood;   20
With the pulse of manly hearts;
With the voice of orators;
With the din of city arts;
With the cannonade of wars;
With the marches of the brave;
And prayers of might from martyrs' cave.

Great is the art,
Great be the manners, of the bard.
He shall not his brain encumber
With the coil of rhythm and number;   30
But, leaving rule and pale forethought,
He shall aye climb

---

5 **No jingling . . . strings.** Possibly Emerson was thinking of Poe, whom he once called "the jingle man"   29 **He . . . number.** Compare "The Poet," p. 1114: ". . . it is not metres, but a metre-making argument that makes a poem"

For his rhyme.
"Pass in, pass in," the angels say,
"In to the upper doors,
Nor count compartments of the floors,
But mount to paradise
By the stairway of surprise."

Blameless master of the games,
King of sport that never shames,   40
He shall daily joy dispense
Hid in song's sweet influence.
Forms more cheerly live and go,
What time the subtle mind
Sings aloud the tune whereto
Their pulses beat,
And march their feet,
And their members are combined.

By Sybarites beguiled,
He shall no task decline;   50
Merlin's mighty line
Extremes of nature reconciled, —
Bereaved a tyrant of his will,
And made the lion mild.
Songs can the tempest still,
Scattered on the stormy air,
Mold the year to fair increase
And bring in poetic peace.

He shall not seek to weave,
In weak, unhappy times,   60
Efficacious rhymes;
Wait his returning strength.
Bird, that from the nadir's floor
To the zenith's top can soar,
The soaring orbit of the muse exceeds that journey's length.
Nor profane affect to hit
Or compass that, by meddling wit,
Which only the propitious mind
Publishes when 'tis inclined.

---

49 **Sybarites,** voluptuaries   51 **Merlin's mighty line** recalls "Marlowe's mighty line" (in Ben Jonson's
"To the Memory of My Beloved Master William Shakespeare," l. 30)   67 **meddling wit.** Emerson's doctrine of inspiration disparages the role of the intellect in artistic creation, the intellect being denoted by
"meddling wit" in the present passage and by "cunning" in "The Problem," l. 11

There are open hours   70
When the God's will sallies free,
And the dull idiot might see
The flowing fortunes of a thousand years; —
Sudden, at unawares,
Self-moved, fly-to the doors,
Nor sword of angels could reveal
What they conceal.

    II
The rhyme of the poet
Modulates the king's affairs;
Balance-loving Nature   80
Made all things in pairs.
To every foot its antipode;
Each color with its counter glowed;
To every tone beat answering tones,
Higher or graver;
Flavor gladly blends with flavor;
Leaf answers leaf upon the bough;
And match the paired cotyledons.
Hands to hands, and feet to feet,
In one body grooms and brides;   90
Eldest rite, two married sides
In every mortal meet.
Light's far furnace shines,
Smelting balls and bars,
Forging double stars,
Glittering twins and trines.
The animals are sick with love,
Lovesick with rhyme;
Each with all propitious Time
Into chorus wove.   100

Like the dancers' ordered band,
Thoughts come also hand in hand;
In equal couples mated,
Or else alternated;
Adding by their mutual gage,
One to other, health and age.
Solitary fancies go
Short-lived wandering to and fro,

---

78 **The rhyme . . . affairs,** a romantic conception of the power of the poet found elsewhere in the nineteenth century, as in Shelley's *Defense of Poetry:* "Poets are the unacknowledged legislators of the world"

Most like to bachelors,
Or an ungiven maid,   110
Not ancestors,
With no posterity to make the lie afraid,
Or keep truth undecayed.
Perfect-paired as eagle's wings,
Justice is the rhyme of things;
Trade and counting use
The selfsame tuneful muse;
And Nemesis,
Who with even matches odd,
Who athwart space redresses   120
The partial wrong,
Fills the just period,
And finishes the song.

Subtle rhymes, with ruin rife,
Murmur in the house of life,
Sung by the Sisters as they spin;
In perfect time and measure they
Build and unbuild our echoing clay,
As the two twilights of the day
Fold us music-drunken in.   130

                        1846, 1847
_____

118 **Nemesis**, Greek goddess of retribution   126 **Sisters**, the Fates, three sister goddesses of Greek mythology who determined the course of human life: Clotho spun the thread; Lachesis measured its length; and Atropos cut it off

Bacchus

Bring me wine, but wine which never grew
In the belly of the grape,
Or grew on vine whose tap-roots, reaching through
Under the Andes to the Cape,
Suffered no savor of the earth to scape.

Let its grapes the morn salute
From a nocturnal root,
Which feels the acrid juice
Of Styx and Erebus;
_____

9 **Styx**, in Greek mythology, the river which had to be crossed in passing to the regions of the dead   9 **Erebus,** in Greek mythology, the gloomy space through which souls passed to Hades

And turns the woe of Night,   10
By its own craft, to a more rich delight.

We buy ashes for bread;
We buy diluted wine;
Give me of the true, —
Whose ample leaves and tendrils curled
Among the silver hills of heaven
Draw everlasting dew;
Wine of wine,
Blood of the world,
Form of forms, and mould of statures,   20
That I intoxicated,
And by the draught assimilated,
May float at pleasure through all natures;
The bird-language rightly spell,
And that which roses say so well.

Wine that is shed
Like the torrents of the sun
Up the horizon walls,
Or like the Atlantic streams, which run
When the South Sea calls.   30

Water and bread,
Food which needs no transmuting,
Rainbow-flowering, wisdom-fruiting,
Wine which is already man,
Food which teach and reason can.

Wine which music is, —
Music and wine are one, —
That I, drinking this,
Shall hear far Chaos talk with me;
Kings unborn shall walk with me;   40
And the poor grass shall plot and plan
What it will do when it is man.
Quickened so, will I unlock
Every crypt of every rock.

I thank the joyful juice
For all I know; —
Winds of remembering
Of the ancient being blow,
And seeming-solid walls of use
Open and flow.   50

Pour, Bacchus! the remembering wine;
Retrieve the loss of me and mine!
Vine for vine be antidote,
And the grape requite the lote!
Haste to cure the old despair, —
Reason in Nature's lotus drenched,
The memory of ages quenched;
Give them again to shine;
Let wine repair what this undid; .
And where the infection slid,   60
A dazzling memory revive;
Refresh the faded tints,
Recut the aged prints,
And write my old adventures with the pen
Which on the first day drew,
Upon the tablets blue,
The dancing Pleiads and eternal men.
                                               1846, 1847

---

51 **remembering wine,** wine which causes the soul to remember. Emerson has in mind the Platonic doctrines of pre-existence and reminiscence   54 **lote.** The eating of the fruit of the lotus caused forgetfulness (compare Tennyson's poem, "The Lotos-Eaters")

Ode *Inscribed to W. H. Channing*

This poem was Emerson's answer to the Rev. William Henry Channing, and other reformers, who insisted that Emerson take an active part in the movement for the abolition of slavery.

Though loath to grieve
The evil time's sole patriot,
I cannot leave
My honeyed thought
For the priest's cant
Or statesman's rant.

If I refuse
My study for their politique,
Which at the best is trick,
The angry Muse   10
Puts confusion in my brain.

But who is he that prates
Of the culture of mankind,
Of better arts and life?

Go, blindworm, go,
Behold the famous States
Harrying Mexico
With rifle and with knife!

Or who, with accent bolder,
Dare praise the freedom-loving mountaineer? 20
I found by thee, O rushing Contoocook!
And in thy valleys, Agiochook!
The jackals of the Negro-holder.

The God who made New Hampshire
Taunted the lofty land
With little men; —
Small bat and wren
House in the oak: —
If earth-fire cleave
The upheaved land, and bury the folk, 30
The southern crocodile would grieve.
Virtue palters; Right is hence;
Freedom praised, but hid;
Funeral eloquence
Rattles the coffin-lid.

What boots thy zeal,
O glowing friend,
That would indignant rend
The northland from the south?
Wherefore? to what good end? 40
Boston Bay and Bunker Hill
Would serve things still; —
Things are of the snake.

The horseman serves the horse,
The neatherd serves the neat,
The merchant serves the purse,
The eater serves his meat;
'Tis the day of the chattel,
Web to weave, and corn to grind;

---

17 **Mexico.** War with Mexico began in April 1846 and was formally concluded in February 1848. In New England the war was strongly opposed (compare Lowell's *Biglow Papers,* First Series, 1846   21 **Contoo-cook,** a river rising in New Hampshire that flows into the Merrimack   22 **Agiochook,** Indian name for the White Mountains   23 **jackals.** The jackal, or wild dog, was once supposed to hunt game for the lion; the reference may be to the pursuit of fugitive slaves in New Hampshire, and in New England generally   45 **neat,** cattle

Things are in the saddle,   50
And ride mankind.

There are two laws discrete,
Not reconciled, —
Law for man, and law for thing;
The last builds town and fleet,
But it runs wild,
And doth the man unking.

'Tis fit the forest fall,
The steep be graded,
The mountain tunnelled,   60
The sand shaded,
The orchard planted,
The glebe tilled,
The prairie granted,
The steamer built.

Let man serve law for man;
Live for friendship, live for love,
For truth's and harmony's behoof;
The state may follow how it can,
As Olympus follows Jove.   70

   Yet do not I implore
The wrinkled shopman to my sounding woods,
Nor bid the unwilling senator
Ask votes of thrushes in the solitudes.
Every one to his chosen work; —
Foolish hands may mix and mar;
Wise and sure the issues are.
Round they roll till dark is light,
Sex to sex, and even to odd; —
The over-god   80
Who marries Right to Might,
Who peoples, unpeoples, —
He who exterminates
Races by stronger races,
Black by white faces, —
Knows to bring honey
Out of the lion;

---

75 **Every one . . . work.** William James justly noted Emerson's "fidelity to the limits of his genius"   86
honey . . . lion. Samson found "honey in the carcass of a lion" which he had slain. See Judges 14:5-9

Grafts gentlest scion
On pirate and Turk.

The Cossack eats Poland,   90
Like stolen fruit;
Her last noble is ruined,
Her last poet mute:
Straight, into double band
The victors divide;
Half for freedom strike and.stand; —
The astonished Muse finds thousands at her side.

                                                    1847

---

90 **Cossack eats Poland,** a frequent occurrence. Russia had appropriated Polish territory in 1772 ("the first partition of Poland"), in 1793 ("the second partition"), and 1795 ("the third partition"). A Polish revolution in 1830 had been suppressed by the czar

Hamatreya

"Hamatreya" is based upon a passage in the Vishnu Purana *(one of the sacred books of the Hindus), which Emerson transcribed in his* Journals *in 1845 as follows: "These and other kings who . . . have indulged the feeling that suggests 'This earth is mine — it is my son's — it belongs to my dynasty' — have all passed away. So, many who reigned before them, many who succeeded them, and many who are yet to come, have ceased or will cease to be. Earth laughs, as if smiling with autumnal flowers, to behold her Kings unable to effect the subjugation of themselves. I will repeat to you, Maitreya, the stanzas that were chanted by Earth. . . .*

" 'How great is the folly of princes who are endowed with the faculty of reason, to cherish the confidence of ambition when they themselves are but foam upon the wave. . . . Foolishness has been the character of every King who has boasted, "All this earth is mine — everything is mine — it will be in my house forever," — for he is dead. . . .'

"These were the verses, Maitreya, which Earth recited, and by listening to which ambitions fade away like snow before the sun."

Emerson's title is apparently a variant of "Maitreya" in the quoted passage.

Bulkeley, Hunt, Willard, Hosmer, Meriam, Flint
Possessed the land which rendered to their toil
Hay, corn, roots, hemp, flax, apples, wool and wood.
Each of these landlords walked amidst his farm,
Saying, " 'Tis mine, my children's and my name's.

---

1 **Bulkeley . . . Flint,** first settlers of Concord

How sweet the west wind sounds in my own trees!
How graceful climb those shadows on my hill!
I fancy these pure waters and the flags
Know me, as does my dog: we sympathize;
And, I affirm, my actions smack of the soil."   10

Where are these men? Asleep beneath their grounds:
And strangers, fond as they, their furrows plough.
Earth laughs in flowers, to see her boastful boys
Earth-proud, proud of the earth which is not theirs;
Who steer the plough, but cannot steer their feet
Clear of the grave.
They added ridge to valley, brook to pond,
And sighed for all that bounded their domain;
"This suits me for a pasture; that's my park;
We must have clay, lime, gravel, granite-ledge,   20
And misty lowland, where to go for peat.
The land is well, — lies fairly to the south.
'Tis good, when you have crossed the sea and back,
To find the sitfast acres where you left them."
Ah! the hot owner sees not Death, who adds
Him to his land, a lump of mould the more.
Hear what the Earth says: —

       EARTH-SONG
"Mine and yours;
Mine, not yours.
Earth endures;   30
Stars abide —
Shine down in the old sea;
Old are the shores;
But where are old men?
I who have seen much,
Such have I never seen.

"The lawyer's deed
Ran sure,
In tail,
To them, and to their heirs   40
Who shall succeed,
Without fail,
Forevermore.

---

12 **fond**, foolish   39 **In tail**, entail, limiting the inheritance of property strictly by blood line

"Here is the land,
Shaggy with wood,
With its old valley,
Mound and flood.
But the heritors? —
Fled like the flood's foam.
The lawyer, and the laws,   50
And the kingdom,
Clean swept herefrom.

"They called me theirs,
Who so controlled me;
Yet every one
Wished to stay, and is gone.
How am I theirs,
If they cannot hold me,
But I hold them?"

When I heard the Earth-song   60
I was no longer brave;
My avarice cooled
Like lust in the chill of the grave.

                    1847

---

63 **Like lust . . . grave.** Emerson seems to have taken this striking simile from Marvell's "To His Coy Mistress," ll. 29-32

Give All to Love

Give all to love;
Obey thy heart;
Friends, kindred, days,
Estate, good-fame,
Plans, credit and the Muse, —
Nothing refuse.

'Tis a brave master;
Let it have scope:
Follow it utterly,
Hope beyond hope: 10
High and more high
It dives into noon,

With wing unspent,
Untold intent;
But it is a god,
Knows its own path
And the outlets of the sky.

It was never for the mean;
It requireth courage stout.
Souls above doubt   20
Valor unbending,
It will reward, —
They shall return
More than they were,
And ever ascending.

Leave all for love;
Yet, hear me, yet, ·
One word more thy heart behoved,
One pulse more of firm endeavor, —
Keep thee to-day,   30
To-morrow, forever,
Free as an Arab
Of thy beloved.

Cling with life to the maid;
But when the surprise,
First vague shadow of surmise
Flits across her bosom young,
Of a joy apart from thee,
Free be she, fancy-free;
Nor thou detain her vesture's hem,   40
Nor the palest rose she flung
From her summer diadem.

Though thou loved her as thyself,
As a self of purer clay,
Though her parting dims the day,
Stealing grace from all alive;
Heartily know,
When half-gods go,
The gods arrive.

                          1847

---

48 **When . . . arrive.** Compare in the concluding paragraph of the essay "Friendship": "True love transcends the unworthy object and dwells and broods on the eternal . . ."

Days

"Days" is Emerson's version of a favorite theme of the early Puritans, who often preached on "redeeming the time."

Daughters of Time, the hypocritic Days,
Muffled and dumb like barefoot dervishes,
And marching single in an endless file,
Bring diadems and fagots in their hands.
To each they offer gifts after his will,
Bread, kingdoms, stars, and sky that holds them all.
I, in my pleached garden, watched the pomp,
Forgot my morning wishes, hastily
Took a few herbs and apples, and the Day
Turned and departed silent. I, too late,   10
Under her solemn fillet saw the scorn.

                                        1852?, 1857

Brahma

"Brahma" is the most notable expression of Hindu religious thought in Emerson's writings. Brahma is the underlying, unchanging reality; it can best be understood in contrast with Maya, the changing, illusory world of appearance, as shown in the following passage from the Hindu scriptures (quoted in Arthur Christy, The Orient in American Transcendentalism, *p. 91): "Brahma is without attribute and form, Maya is endowed with both; Brahma is infinite, Maya finite; Brahma is immaculate and serene, Maya fleeting and restless; Brahma is without adjuncts, Maya is full of them; Maya is visible, Brahma invisible; Maya perceptible, Brahma imperceptible; Maya perishable, Brahma imperishable; Maya groweth, Brahma waxeth not; Maya diminisheth, Brahma waneth not; Maya appealeth to the ignorant, Brahma attracts him not; Maya is born, Brahma is birthless; Maya dieth, Brahma is deathless; Maya descendeth into cognition, Brahma is beyond cognition; Maya fructifieth, Brahma doth not; Maya dissolveth, Brahma is indissoluble; Maya palleth, Brahma is a joy forever; Maya changeth, Brahma is immutable; Maya acteth, Brahma is beyond all activity; Maya assumeth various forms, Brahma is formless; Maya is . . . manifold, Brahma is one and eternal. . . . Maya is spread everywhere enveloping the Brahma, the sage alone can pierce through the mist."*

If the red slayer think he slays,
   Of if the slain think he is slain,
They know not well the subtle ways
   I keep, and pass, and turn again.

Far or forgot to me is near;
   Shadow and sunlight are the same;
The vanished gods to me appear;
   And one to me are shame and fame.

They reckon ill who leave me out;
   When me they fly, I am the wings;   10
I am the doubter and the doubt,
   And I the hymn the Brahmin sings.

The strong gods pine for my abode,
   And pine in vain the sacred Seven;
But thou, meek lover of the good!
   Find me, and turn thy back on heaven.

                         1856, 1857

---

8 **shame and fame.** Emerson intended an opposition: bad report and good report. The line must mean:
"Evil and Good are to me one and the same." Emerson is said to have suggested to a puzzled reader the
substitution of "Jehovah" for "Brahma," and E.W. Emerson (*Poems*, Centenary Edition, p. 467) tells with
approval the story of the child who said that the poem means simply "God everywhere." These suggestions
are seriously misleading. To Jehovah, or to the God of the Christian Bible, Good and Evil are not
the same   14 **sacred Seven**, the highest saints of the Hindu hierarchy

Terminus

The poem expresses an extraordinarily clear recognition of failing powers. Emerson was cor-
rect in thinking that at sixty-three he had reached and passed the peak of his achievement.
He lived on for sixteen years after "Terminus" without adding anything significant to his
literary output. A few months before his death, he lost his memory completely.
   The poem shows a strong vein of realism and Yankee common sense.

It is time to be old,
To take in sail: —
The god of bounds,
Who sets to seas a shore,
Came to me in his fatal rounds,
And said: "No more!
No farther shoot
Thy broad ambitious branches, and thy root.
Fancy departs: no more invent;
Contract thy firmament   10
To compass of a tent.
There's not enough for this and that,

---

3 **The god of bounds.** Terminus was the Roman god of boundaries   5 **fatal,** appointed by fate

Make thy option which of two;
Economize the failing river,
Not the less revere the Giver,
Leave the many and hold the few.
Timely wise accept the terms,
Soften the fall with wary foot;
A little while
Still plan and smile,   20
And, — fault of novel germs, —
Mature the unfallen fruit.
Curse, if thou wilt, thy sires,
Bad husbands of their fires,
Who when they gave thee breath,
Failed to bequeath
The needful sinew stark as once,
The Baresark marrow to thy bones,
But left a legacy of ebbing veins,
Inconstant heat and nerveless reins, —   30
Amid the Muses, left thee deaf and dumb,
Amid the gladiators, halt and numb."

As the bird trims her to the gale,
I trim myself to the storm of time,
I man the rudder, reef the sail,
Obey the voice at eve obeyed at prime:
"Lowly faithful, banish fear,
Right onward drive unharmed;
The port, well worth the cruise, is near,
And every wave is charmed."   40

1866, 1867

---

21 **fault of novel**, in the lack of new   30 **nerveless reins**, weak back

1817–1862 Henry David Thoreau

Henry David Thoreau was born in Concord, Massachusetts, July 12, 1817. The time and place of his birth pleased him enormously: "I have never got over my surprise that I should have been born into the most estimable place in all the world, and in the very nick of time, too." He was graduated without distinction from Harvard College in 1837, the year of *The American Scholar*. After graduation, he assisted his brother John for a while in teaching a private school. He also helped his father manufacture lead pencils in the 1840's; but when their product equaled, or perhaps surpassed, the best pencils on the market, he gave up pencil making because of a desire for fresh experiences. In 1839 he and John went on a famous journey, the literary record of which, *A Week on the Concord and Merrimack Rivers*, appeared ten years later. About the time of their journey together, both Henry and John fell in love with Ellen Sewall, who, perhaps wisely, refused them both.

Thoreau was a frequent contributor to *The Dial* from 1840 to 1844. In 1841, and again in 1847-1848, he was a member of Emerson's household, doing odd jobs. In 1842 John died. In 1838 Henry had delivered before the Concord Lyceum his first lecture, in which he described his neighbors as "newly shingled and clapboarded, but if you knock, no one is at home." He continued lecturing for many years; indeed, much of his writing, like Emerson's, was done with the intention of using it as lecture material. Henry Seidel Canby records lectures not only in Concord but in Boston, Salem, Portland, Bangor, Providence, Philadelphia, New Bedford, and Amherst (New Hampshire); at the last-named place, Thoreau lectured in December 1856 in the basement of the orthodox church, and, as he commented later, "helped to undermine it." But he was not very successful as a lecturer; much less successful and less popular than Emerson, to whom he remarked, with a little bitterness, that "whatever succeeded with the audience was bad." He concluded in 1858 that "audiences go to the Lyceum to suck a sugar-plum."

On July 4, 1845, Thoreau began his famous residence at Walden Pond. "I went to the woods," he explains in a great passage in *Walden,* "because I wished to live deliberately, to front only the essential facts of life. . . ." On September 6, 1847, he left Walden, not from a sense of failure or disappointment but, once more, because of a desire to explore new modes of living. "I left the woods," he wrote in the concluding chapter of his book, "for as good a reason as I went there. Perhaps it seemed to me that I had several more lives to live and could not spare any more time for that one. It is remarkable how easily and insensibly we fall into a particular route and make a beaten track for ourselves. I had not lived there a week before my feet wore a path from my door to the pond-side. . . . How worn and dusty, then, must be the highways of the world, how deep the ruts of tradition and conformity!" *Walden,* published in 1854, is the immortal record of Thoreau's rich, elemental experience. It is a mistake to think of Thoreau as a hermit during the Walden period, though he has frequently been called that. While he lived in the woods, he was often in the village, he received visitors at the Pond, and he continued to do, in and around Concord, the various odd jobs at which he was so adept: fence building, house painting, carpentering, gardening, berry picking, surveying. His aim was always, in his best phrase, to "adventure on life."

In 1846, during his residence at Walden, Thoreau was arrested because of his refusal to pay the poll tax and spent perforce a night in the Concord jail. The experience itself, as he tells us in "Civil Disobedience" (1849), was "novel and interesting enough." Through the grating of his prison cell, he saw his native village from a fresh point of view. The reason for his rebellion was his opposition to Negro slavery and the movement to increase slave territory in the Southwest. He helped at least one fugitive slave to evade the Boston police and escape into Canada (see Thoreau's *Journal,* October 1, 1851). Along with Emerson, he gave active support to John Brown. In his *Plea for Captain John Brown,* delivered in the Concord Town Hall, October 30, 1859, when Brown was under sentence of death, Thoreau likened him to Cromwell and the early New England Puritans. When the selectmen of the village refused to sanction a memorial service to Brown, Thoreau rang the bell of the Town Hall himself.

"I have traveled a good deal in Concord," Thoreau wrote in *Walden;* he traveled a good deal in other places, too. There were three excursions to the Maine Woods (in 1846, 1853, and 1857), and four excursions to Cape Cod (in 1849, 1850, 1855, and 1857). He frequently journeyed to Monadnock and the White Mountains. These excursions furnished material for much writing, which appeared in part in magazines during Thoreau's lifetime and was collected after his death (*Excursions,* 1863; *The Maine Woods,* 1864; *Cape Cod,* 1865). In 1856 he went to New York, where he saw Whitman; shortly after the visit, he wrote to a friend, "That Walt Whitman is the most interesting fact to me at present." In 1861 he traveled as far west as Minnesota; but his health was already failing. He died of tuberculosis in Concord, May 6, 1862, before he had reached his forty-fifth birthday. When asked in his last hours by his Aunt Louisa if he had "made his peace with God," he replied, "I have never quarrelled with Him."

It is only in comparatively recent years that Thoreau has attained his present high reputation in American literature. For more than a half century after his death, he was very generally regarded as an interesting eccentric and one of the minor Emersonians. This low estimate may be attributed in part to the influence of the derogatory essays of James Russell Lowell and Robert Louis Stevenson. Lowell, the cosmopolite, cleverly ridiculed Thoreau's provincialism and "morbid self-consciousness" ("Thoreau," *My Study Windows,* 1871). Stevenson, *bon vivant* and man of the world, objected that "Thoreau is dry, priggish, and selfish," — "in one word, a skulker" ("Henry David Thoreau," *Familiar Studies of Men and Books,* 1882). The growth of Thoreau's fame in the last several decades of the present century has no doubt been owing not only to a recognition of his fine literary qualities but also to various special appeals which his works make to modern readers. His lessons in simplicity and economy have appealed to those who are harassed by the complexity and expense of modern life. His almost primitive intimacy with nature has come home to a generation whose mode of life is largely artificial and divorced from natural influences. His sturdy, rebellious individualism has had a special attraction for members of an increasingly regimented society. His indigenousness, deeply rooted in a particular place, has been a warning and a rebuke to a generation so mobile and migratory that many people can scarcely be said to have roots anywhere. In short, we read Thoreau for those values which we have lost and which more and more seem necessary to our health and vigor and peace of mind.

The Writings of Henry David Thoreau, Walden Edition, 20 vols., Boston, 1906 (includes the complete Journals)   The Journal of Henry D. Thoreau, with a Foreword by Walter Harding, 14 vols. bound as 2, New York, 1962   H. S. Canby, Thoreau, Boston, 1939   Sherman Paul, The Shores of America: Thoreau's Inward Exploration, Urbana, 1958   Thoreau: A Century of Criticism, ed. Walter Harding   Walter Harding, A Thoreau Handbook, New York, 1959

from A Week on the Concord and Merrimack Rivers

In the following selections from A Week *Thoreau has some interesting things to say about good writing in both prose and verse. He evidently thinks that good prose should be efficient and functional. "A sentence should read," he says, "as if its author, had he held a plow instead of a pen, could have drawn a furrow deep and straight to the end." Thoreau himself did just this, in his best writing. His best sentences are lean and pithy, and free of extraneous ornament. They illustrate Thoreau's principle that the good prose writer, like the good wood chopper, husbands every stroke.*

Thoreau exalts the poetry of "inspiration" above that of mere "intellect and taste." Inspired poetry, he says, is "above criticism . . . is sacred, and to be read with reverence. . . ." Shakespeare and Burns are cited as examples of poets who were inspired. Thoreau here takes the position held by many "romantic" poets and critics: by Burns, for example, who exclaimed, "Gie me ae spark o' Nature's fire! / That's a' the learning I desire . . ."; and by Emerson, who in the essay "The Poet" and elsewhere expounded the doctrine of inspiration, as in the passage in the essay (see p. 1120) where he speaks of "a great public power" on which the poet "can draw, by unlocking, at all risks, his human doors, and suffering the ethereal tides to roll and circulate through him." It would be instructive to compare Emerson's development of the idea with Thoreau's, and to test out Emerson's self-deprecatory remark: "Thoreau illustrates with excellent images that which I convey in a sleepy generality."

From Sunday

Enough has been said in these days of the charm of fluent writing. We hear it complained of some works of genius that they have fine thoughts, but are irregular and have no flow. But even the mountain peaks in the horizon are, to the eye of science, parts of one range. We should consider that the flow of thought is more like a tidal wave than a prone river, and is the result of a celestial influence, not of any declivity in its channel. The river flows because it runs down hill, and flows the faster, the faster it descends. The reader who expects to float down-stream for the whole voyage may well complain of nauseating swells and choppings of the sea when his frail shore craft gets amidst the billows of the ocean stream, which flows
10 as much to sun and moon as lesser streams to it. But if we would appreciate the flow that is in these books, we must expect to feel it rise from the page like an exhalation, and wash away our critical brains like burr millstones, flowing to higher levels above and behind ourselves. There is many a book which ripples on like a freshet, and flows as glibly as a millstream sucking under a causeway; and when their authors are in the full tide of their discourse, Pythagoras and Plato and Jamblichus halt beside them. Their long, stringy, slimy sentences are of that consistency that they naturally flow and run together. They read as if written for military men, for men of business, there is such a dispatch in them. Compared with these, the grave thinkers and philosophers seem not to have got their swaddling-
20 clothes off; they are slower than a Roman army in its march, the rear camping tonight where the van camped last night. The wise Jamblichus eddies and gleams like a watery slough.

> 'How many thousands never heard the name
> Of Sidney, or of Spenser, or their books!
> And yet brave fellows, and presume of fame,
> And seem to bear down all the world with looks!'

The ready writer seizes the pen and shouts, 'Forward! Alamo and Fanning!' and after rolls the tide of war. The very walls and fences seem to travel. But the most rapid trot is no flow after all; and thither, reader, you and I, at least, will not follow.
30 A perfectly healthy sentence, it is true, is extremely rare. For the most part we miss the hue and fragrance of the thought; as if we could be satisfied with the dews of the morning or evening without their colors, or the heavens without their azure. The most attractive sentences are, perhaps, not the wisest, but the surest and roundest. They are spoken firmly and conclusively, as if the speaker had a right to know what he says, and if not wise, they have at least been well learned. Sir Walter

---

16 **Jamblichus.** See note, p. 1116   27 **Alamo and Fanning,** references to the Texas war of independence in 1836. The Mexicans massacred the garrison at the Alamo March 6, and on March 27 treacherously killed Col. James Walker Fannin and three hundred of his men at Goliad. These losses were avenged on April 21, when Gen. Sam Houston defeated Santa Anna at the battle of San Jacinto. Thoreau misspelled Fannin's name

Raleigh might well be studied, if only for the excellence of his style, for he is remarkable in the midst of so many masters. There is a natural emphasis in his style, like a man's tread, and a breathing space between the sentences, which the best of modern writing does not furnish. His chapters are like English parks, or say rather like a Western forest, where the larger growth keeps down the underwood, and one may ride on horseback through the openings. All the distinguished writers of that period possess a greater vigor and naturalness than the more modern — for it is allowed to slander our own time — and when we read a quotation from one of them in the midst of a modern author, we seem to have come suddenly upon a greener ground, a greater depth and strength of soil. It is as if a green bough were 10 laid across the page, and we are refreshed as by the sight of fresh grass in midwinter or early spring. You have constantly the warrant of life and experience in what you read. The little that is said is eked out by implication of the much that was done. The sentences are verdurous and blooming as evergreen and flowers, because they are rooted in fact and experience, but our false and florid sentences have only the tints of flowers without their sap or roots. All men are really most attracted by the beauty of plain speech, and they even write in a florid style in imitation of this. They prefer to be misunderstood rather than to come short of its exuberance. Hussein Effendi praised the epistolary style of Ibrahim Pasha to the French traveler Botta, because of 'the difficulty of understanding it; there was,' he said, 'but one person at 20 Jidda who was capable of understanding and explaining the Pasha's correspondence.' A man's whole life is taxed for the least thing well done. It is its net result. Every sentence is the result of a long probation. Where shall we look for standard English but to the words of a standard man? The word which is best said came nearest to not being spoken at all, for it is cousin to a deed which the speaker could have better done. Nay, almost it must have taken the place of a deed by some urgent necessity, even by some misfortune, so that the truest writer will be some captive knight, after all. And perhaps the fates had such a design, when, having stored Raleigh so richly with the substance of life and experience, they made him a fast prisoner, and compelled him to make his words his deeds, and transfer to his ex- 30 pression the emphasis and sincerity of his action.

Men have a respect for scholarship and learning greatly out of proportion to the use they commonly serve. We are amused to read how Ben Jonson engaged that the dull masks with which the royal family and nobility were to be entertained should be 'grounded upon antiquity and solid learning.' Can there be any greater reproach than an idle learning? Learn to split wood, at least. The necessity of labor and conversation with many men and things to the scholar is rarely well remembered; steady labor with the hands, which engrosses the attention also, is unquestionably the best method of removing palaver and sentimentality out of one's style, both of speaking and writing. If he has worked hard from morning till night, though he may have 40 grieved that he could not be watching the train of his thoughts during that time,

---

19 **Botta**, probably Paul Emile Botta (1802-1870), French archaeologist   29 **Raleigh**, Sir Walter Raleigh (1552?-1618), English soldier and courtier, who wrote his unfinished *History of the World* while in prison

yet the few hasty lines which at evening record his day's experience will be more musical and true than his freest but idle fancy could have furnished. Surely the writer is to address a world of laborers, and such therefore must be his own discipline. He will not idly dance at his work who has wood to cut and cord before nightfall in the short days of winter; but every stroke will be husbanded, and ring soberly through the wood; and so will the strokes of that scholar's pen, which at evening record the story of the day, ring soberly, yet cheerily, on the ear of the reader, long after the echoes of his axe have died away. The scholar may be sure that he writes the tougher truth for the calluses on his palms. They give firmness to the sentence.
10 Indeed, the mind never makes a great and successful effort, without a corresponding energy of the body. We are often struck by the force and precision of style to which hard-working men, unpracticed in writing, easily attain when required to make the effort. As if plainness and vigor and sincerity, the ornaments of style, were better learned on the farm and in the workshop than in the schools. The sentences written by such rude hands are nervous and tough, like hardened thongs, the sinews of the deer, or the roots of the pine. As for the graces of expression, a great thought is never found in a mean dress; but though it proceed from the lips of the Wolofs, the nine Muses and the three Graces will have conspired to clothe it in fit phrase. Its education has always been liberal, and its implied wit can endow a college. The
20 world, which the Greeks called Beauty, has been made such by being gradually divested of every ornament which was not fitted to endure. The Sibyl, 'speaking with inspired mouth, smileless, inornate, and unperfumed, pierces through centuries by the power of the god.' The scholar might frequently emulate the propriety and emphasis of the farmer's call to his team, and confess that if that were written it would surpass his labored sentences. Whose are the truly *labored* sentences? From the weak and flimsy periods of the politician and literary man, we are glad to turn even to the description of work, the simple record of the month's labor in the farmer's almanac, to restore our tone and spirits. A sentence should read as if its author, had he held a plow instead of a pen, could have drawn a furrow deep and
30 straight to the end. The scholar requires hard and serious labor to give an impetus to his thought. He will learn to grasp the pen firmly so, and wield it gracefully and effectively, as an axe or a sword. When we consider the weak and nerveless periods of some literary men, who perchance in feet and inches come up to the standard of their race, and are not deficient in girth also, we are amazed at the immense sacrifice of thews and sinews. What! these proportions, these bones — and this their work! Hands which could have felled an ox have hewed this fragile matter which would not have tasked a lady's fingers! Can this be a stalwart man's work, who has a marrow in his back and a tendon Achilles in his heel? They who set up the blocks of

---

17 **Wolofs,** a Negro tribe in the western Sudan   18 **nine Muses,** sister goddesses in Greek mythology who ruled over epic poetry and eloquence (Calliope), history (Clio), music and lyric poetry (Euterpe), love poetry (Erato), oratory and sacred music (Polyhymnia), tragedy (Melpomene), choral song and dance (Terpsichore), comedy (Thalia), and astronomy (Urania)   18 **three Graces,** Greek goddesses, associated with the Muses, representing bloom (Thalia), brilliance (Aglaia), and joy (Euphrosyne)   21 **Sibyl,** Greek mythology had many sibyls, prophetesses, the best known being the one at Cumae

Stonehenge did somewhat, if they only laid out their strength for once, and stretched themselves.

Yet, after all, the truly efficient laborer will not crowd his day with work, but will saunter to his task, surrounded by a wide halo of ease and leisure, and then do but what he loves best. He is anxious only about the fruitful kernels of time. Though the hen should sit all day, she could lay only one egg, and, besides, would not have picked up materials for another. Let a man take time enough for the most trivial deed, though it be but the paring of his nails. The buds swell imperceptibly, without hurry or confusion, as if the short spring days were an eternity.

> Then spend an age in whetting thy desire,   10
> Thou need'st not *hasten* if thou dost *stand* fast.

Some hours seem not to be occasion for any deed, but for resolves to draw breath in. We do not directly go about the execution of the purpose that thrills us, but shut our doors behind us and ramble with prepared mind, as if the half were already done. Our resolution is taking root or hold on the earth then, as seeds first send a shoot downward which is fed by their own albumen, ere they send one upward to the light.

There is a sort of homely truth and naturalness in some books which is very rare to find, and yet looks cheap enough. There may be nothing lofty in the sentiment, or fine in the expression, but it is careless country talk. Homeliness is almost as 20 great a merit in a book as in a house, if the reader would abide there. It is next to beauty, and a very high art. Some have this merit only. The scholar is not apt to make his most familiar experience come gracefully to the aid of his expression. Very few men can speak of Nature, for instance, with any truth. They overstep her modesty, somehow or other, and confer no favor. They do not speak a good word for her. Most cry better than they speak, and you can get more nature out of them by pinching than by addressing them. The surliness with which the woodchopper speaks of his woods, handling them as indifferently as his axe, is better than the mealy-mouthed enthusiasm of the lover of nature. Better that the primrose by the river's brim be a yellow primrose, and nothing more, than that it be something 30 less. Aubrey relates of Thomas Fuller that his was 'a very working head, insomuch that, walking and meditating before dinner, he would eat up a penny loaf, not knowing that he did it. His natural memory was very great, to which he added the art of memory. He would repeat to you forwards and backwards all the signs from Ludgate to Charing Cross.' He says of Mr. John Hales, that 'he loved Canarie,' and was buried 'under an altar monument of black marble . . . with a too long epitaph;'

---

4 **saunter.** See Thoreau's interesting discussion of this word and its etymology at the beginning of his essay "Walking"   10 **Then . . . fast.** These lines, and other lines of verse printed without quotation marks in *A Week* are by Thoreau himself. See *Collected Poems of Henry Thoreau,* ed. Carl Bode, Chicago, 1943; enlarged edition, 1964   24 **overstep her modesty,** an allusion to *Hamlet,* Act III, Sc. ii, l. 21   30 **yellow primrose,** an allusion to Wordsworth's poem "Peter Bell"   31 **Aubrey.** The quotations which follow are from *Brief Lives* by John Aubrey (1626-1697), an English antiquary. The passages can be found in Andrew Clark's edition, Oxford, 1898, vol. I, pp. 257, 280, 282, 404

of Edmund Halley, that he 'at sixteen could make a dial, and then, he said, he thought himself a brave fellow;' of William Holder, who wrote a book upon his curing one Popham who was deaf and dumb, 'he was beholding to no author; did only consult with nature.' For the most part, an author consults only with all who have written before him upon a subject, and his book is but the advice of so many. But a good book will never have been forestalled, but the topic itself will in one sense be new, and its author, by consulting with nature, will consult not only with those who have gone before, but with those who may come later. There is always room and occasion enough for a true book on any subject; as there is room for more light the brightest day, and more rays will not interfere with the first. . . .

From Friday

A true poem is distinguished not so much by a felicitous expression, or any thought it suggests, as by the atmosphere which surrounds it. Most have beauty of outline merely, and are striking as the form and bearing of a stranger; but true verses come toward us indistinctly, as the very breath of all friendliness, and envelop us in their spirit and fragrance. Much of our poetry has the very best manners, but no character. It is only an unusual precision and elasticity of speech, as if its author had taken, not an intoxicating draught, but an electuary. It has the distinct outline of sculpture, and chronicles an early hour. Under the influence of passion all men speak thus distinctly, but wrath is not always divine.

There are two classes of men called poets. The one cultivates life, the other art — one seeks food for nutriment, the other for flavor; one satisfies hunger, the other gratifies the palate. There are two kinds of writing, both great and rare — one that of genius, or the inspired, the other of intellect and taste, in the intervals of inspiration. The former is above criticism, always correct, giving the law to criticism. It vibrates and pulsates with life forever. It is sacred, and to be read with reverence, as the works of nature are studied. There are few instances of a sustained style of this kind; perhaps every man has spoken words, but the speaker is then careless of the record. Such a style removes us out of personal relations with its author; we do not take his words on our lips, but his sense into our hearts. It is the stream of inspiration, which bubbles out, now here, now there, now in this man, now in that. It matters not through what ice-crystals it is seen, now a fountain, now the ocean stream running underground. It is in Shakespeare, Alpheus, in Burns, Arethuse; but ever the same. The other is self-possessed and wise. It is reverent of genius, and greedy of inspiration. It is conscious in the highest and the least degree. It consists with the most perfect command of the faculties. It dwells in a repose as of the desert, and objects are as distinct in it as oases or palms in the horizon of sand. The train of thought moves with subdued and measured step, like a caravan. But the pen is

---

32 **Shakespeare . . Arethuse.** In Greek mythology, the god Alpheus, associated with the largest river of the Peloponnesus, fell in love with the nymph Arethusa. He pursued her as the river under the sea to Sicily where she was transformed to a fountain fed by the Alpheus. Thoreau's ideas on poetic inspiration were undoubtedly influenced somewhat by those of Carlyle in "The Hero as Poet" (in *Heroes and Hero-Worship*)

only an instrument in its hand, and not instinct with life, like a longer arm. It leaves a thin varnish or glaze over all its work. The works of Goethe furnish remarkable instances of the latter.

There is no just and serene criticism as yet. Nothing is considered simply as it lies in the lap of eternal beauty, but our thoughts, as well as our bodies, must be dressed after the latest fashions. Our taste is too delicate and particular. It says nay to the poet's work, but never yea to his hope. It invites him to adorn his deformities, and not to cast them off by expansion, as the tree its bark. We are a people who live in a bright light, in houses of pearl and porcelain, and drink only light wines, whose teeth are easily set on edge by the least natural sour. If we had been consulted, the backbone of the earth would have been made, not of granite, but of Bristol spar. A modern author would have died in infancy in a ruder age. But the poet is something more than a scald, 'a smoother and polisher of language'; he is a Cincinnatus in literature, and occupies no west end of the world. Like the sun, he will indifferently select his rhymes, and with a liberal taste weave into his verse the planet and the stubble.

In these old books the stucco has long since crumbled away, and we read what was sculptured in the granite. They are rude and massive in their proportions, rather than smooth and delicate in their finish. The workers in stone polish only their chimney ornaments, but their pyramids are roughly done. There is a soberness in a rough aspect, as of unhewn granite, which addresses a depth in us, but a polished surface hits only the ball of the eye. The true finish is the work of time, and the use to which a thing is put. The elements are still polishing the pyramids. Art may varnish and gild, but it can do no more. A work of genius is rough-hewn from the first, because it anticipates the lapse of time, and has an ingrained polish, which still appears when fragments are broken off, an essential quality of its substance. Its beauty is at the same time its strength, and it breaks with a lustre.

The great poem must have the stamp of greatness as well as its essence. The reader easily goes within the shallowest contemporary poetry, and informs it with all the life and promise of the day, as the pilgrim goes within the temple, and hears the faintest strains of the worshipers; but it will have to speak to posterity, traversing these deserts, through the ruins of its outmost walls, by the grandeur and beauty of its proportions.

But here on the stream of the Concord, where we have all the while been bodily, Nature, who is superior to all styles and ages, is now, with pensive face, composing her poem Autumn, with which no work of man will bear to be compared.

In summer we live out of doors, and have only impulses and feelings, which are all for action, and must wait commonly for the stillness and longer nights of autumn and winter before any thought will subside; we are sensible that behind the rustling leaves, and the stacks of grain, and the bare clusters of the grape, there is the field of a wholly new life, which no man has lived; that even this earth was

10

20

30

40

---

12 **Bristol spar.** Spar is translucent; granite, opaque   13 **scald,** skald, an ancient Scandinavian poet   14 **Cincinnatus,** Roman legendary patriot of the 5th century B.C. who once left his plowing to defend Rome

made for more mysterious and nobler inhabitants than men and women. In the hues
of October sunsets, we see the portals to other mansions than those which we occupy,
not far off geographically,

> 'There is a place beyond that flaming hill,
> From whence the stars their thin appearance shed,
> A place beyond all place, where never ill,
> Nor impure thought was ever harbored.'

Sometimes a mortal feels in himself Nature — not his Father but his Mother stirs
within him, and he becomes immortal with her immortality. From time to time she
10 claims kindredship with us, and some globule from her veins steals up into our own.

> I am the autumnal sun,
> With autumn gales my race is run;
> When will the hazel put forth its flowers,
> Or the grape ripen under my bowers?
> When will the harvest or the hunter's moon
> Turn my midnight into mid-noon?
> I am all sere and yellow,
> And to my core mellow.
> The mast is dropping within my woods,
20 The winter is lurking within my moods,
> And the rustling of the withered leaf
> Is the constant music of my grief.

To an unskillful rhymer the Muse thus spoke in prose:
The moon no longer reflects the day, but rises to her absolute rule, and the husbandman and hunter acknowledge her for their mistress. Asters and goldenrods reign
along the way, and the life-everlasting withers not. The fields are reaped and shorn
of their pride, but an inward verdure still crowns them. The thistle scatters its down
on the pool, and yellow leaves clothe the vine, and naught disturbs the serious life
of men. But behind the sheaves, and under the sod, there lurks a ripe fruit, which
30 the reapers have not gathered, the true harvest of the year, which it bears forever,
annually watering and maturing it, and man never severs the stalk which bears this
palatable fruit.
Men nowhere, east or west, live yet a *natural* life, round which the vine clings,
and which the elm willingly shadows. Man would desecrate it by his touch, and so
the beauty of the world remains veiled to him. He needs not only to be spiritualized but *naturalized,* on the soil of earth. Who shall conceive what kind of roof the
heavens might extend over him, what seasons minister to him, and what employment dignify his life! Only the convalescent raise the veil of nature. An immortality
in his life would confer immortality on his abode. The winds should be his breath,

---

26 **life-everlasting,** the purple-bloomed orpine

the seasons his moods, and he should impart of his serenity to Nature herself. But such as we know him he is ephemeral like the scenery which surrounds him, and does not aspire to an enduring existence. When we come down into the distant village, visible from the mountain-top, the nobler inhabitants with whom we peopled it have departed, and left only vermin in its desolate streets. It is the imagination of poets which puts those brave speeches into the mouths of their heroes. They may feign that Cato's last words were

> 'The earth, the air and seas, I know, and all
> The joys and horrors of their peace and wars;
> And now will view the Gods' state and the stars,'   10

but such are not the thoughts nor the destiny of common men. What is this heaven which they expect, if it is no better than they expect? Are they prepared for a better than they can now imagine? Where is the heaven of him who dies on a stage, in a theatre? Here or nowhere is our heaven.

> 'Although we see celestial bodies move
> Above the earth, the earth we till and love.'

We can conceive of nothing more fair than something which we have experienced. 'The remembrance of youth is a sigh.' We linger in manhood to tell the dreams of our childhood, and they are half forgotten ere we have learned the language. We have need to be earth-born as well as heaven-born, γηγενεῖς, as was said of 20 the Titans of old, or in a better sense than they. There have been heroes for whom this world seemed expressly prepared, as if creation had at last succeeded; whose daily life was the stuff of which our dreams are made, and whose presence enhanced the beauty and ampleness of Nature herself. Where they walked,

> 'Largior hic campos aether et lumine vestit
> Purpureo: Solemque suum, sua sidera norunt.'

'Here a more copious air invests the fields, and clothes with purple light; and they know their own sun and their own stars.' We love to hear some men speak, though we hear not what they say; the very air they breathe is rich and perfumed, and the sound of their voices falls on the ear like the rustling of leaves or 30 the crackling of the fire. They stand many deep. They have the heavens for their abettors, as those who have never stood from under them, and they look at the stars with an answering ray. Their eyes are like glowworms, and their motions graceful and flowing, as if a place were already found for them, like rivers flowing through valleys. The distinctions of morality, of right and wrong, sense and nonsense, are petty, and have lost their significance, beside these pure primeval natures. When I

---

20 γηγενεῖς, "earth-born," or "earth-sprung," said of the Titans and Giants in the Prometheus of Æschylus   27 Here . . . stars, a translation of the lines preceding from Virgil's *Æneid*, Bk. VI, ll. 640-641

consider the clouds stretched in stupendous masses across the sky, frowning with darkness or glowing with downy light, or gilded with the rays of the setting sun, like the battlements of a city in the heavens, their grandeur appears thrown away on the meanness of my employment; the drapery is altogether too rich for such poor acting. I am hardly worthy to be a suburban dweller outside those walls.

> 'Unless above himself he can
> Erect himself, how poor a thing is man!'

With our music we would fain challenge transiently another and finer sort of intercourse than our daily toil permits. The strains come back to us amended in the echo, as when a friend reads our verse. Why have they so painted the fruits, and freighted them with such fragrance as to satisfy a more than animal appetite?

> 'I asked the schoolman, his advice was free,
> But scored me out too intricate a way.'

These things imply, perchance, that we live on the verge of another and purer realm, from which these odors and sounds are wafted over to us. The borders of our plot are set with flowers, whose seeds were blown from more Elysian fields adjacent. They are the pot-herbs of the gods. Some fairer fruits and sweeter fragrances wafted over to us betray another realm's vicinity. There, too, does Echo dwell, and there is the abutment of the rainbow's arch.

> A finer race and finer fed
> Feast and revel o'er our head,
> And we titmen are only able
> To catch the fragments from their table.
> Theirs is the fragrance of the fruits,
> While we consume the pulp and roots.
> What are the moments that we stand
> Astonished on the Olympian land!

We need pray for no higher heaven than the pure senses can furnish, a *purely* sensuous life. Our present senses are but the rudiments of what they are destined to become. We are comparatively deaf and dumb and blind, and without smell or taste or feeling. Every generation makes the discovery that its divine vigor has been dissipated, and each sense and faculty misapplied and debauched. The ears were made, not for such trivial uses as men are wont to suppose, but to hear celestial sounds. The eyes were not made for such groveling uses as they are now put to and worn out by, but to behold beauty now invisible. May we not *see* God? Are we to be put off and amused in this life, as it were with a mere allegory? Is not Nature, rightly read, that of which she is commonly taken to be the symbol merely? When the

---

6 **Unless . . . man!** from Samuel Daniel's "To the Countess of Cumberland," st. 12

common man looks into the sky, which he has not so much profaned, he thinks it less gross than the earth, and with reverence speaks of 'the Heavens,' but the seer will in the same sense speak of 'the Earths,' and his Father who is in them. 'Did not he that made that which is *within* make that which is *without* also?' What is it, then, to educate but to develop these divine germs called the senses? for individuals and states to deal magnanimously with the rising generation, leading it not into temptation — not teach the eye to squint, nor attune the ear to profanity. But where is the instructed teacher? Where are the *normal* schools?

A Hindoo sage said, 'As a dancer, having exhibited herself to the spectator, desists from the dance, so does Nature desist, having manifested herself to soul. Noth- 1(ing, in my opinion, is more gentle than Nature; once aware of having been seen, she does not again expose herself to the gaze of soul.' . . .   1849

---

3 **Did . . . also.** See Luke 11:40   8 **normal.** Teachers' colleges were commonly known as "normal schools"

Civil Disobedience

"Civil Disobedience" was first published in Aesthetic Papers *(1849), a collection of essays edited by Elizabeth Peabody. " 'Civil Disobedience' attracted no attention at the time, but has since gone round the world. It was Gandhi's source-book in his Indian campaign for Civil Resistance, and has been read and pondered by thousands who hope to find some way to resist seemingly irresistible force" (Canby,* Thoreau, *p. 235).*

I heartily accept the motto, — "That government is best which governs least;" and I should like to see it acted up to more rapidly and systematically. Carried out, it finally amounts to this, which also I believe, — "That government is best which governs not at all;" and when men are prepared for it, that will be the kind of government which they will have. Government is at best but an expedient; but most governments are usually, and all governments are sometimes, inexpedient. The objections which have been brought against a standing army, and they are many and weighty, and deserve to prevail, may also at last be brought against a standing government. The standing army is only an arm of the standing government. The government itself, which is only the mode which the people have chosen to execute 10 their will, is equally liable to be abused and perverted before the people can act through it. Witness the present Mexican war, the work of comparatively a few individuals using the standing government as their tool; for, in the outset, the people would not have consented to this measure.

---

1 **That . . . least.** The idea is Jeffersonian. In his *First Inaugural* (1801) Jefferson advocated "a wise and frugal government, which shall restrain men from injuring one another, shall leave them otherwise free to regulate their own pursuits of industry and improvement, and shall not take from the mouth of labor the bread it has earned"   12 **Mexican war.** The Mexican War was unpopular in New England, where it was regarded as a device of the Southern Democrats to increase slave territory. Compare Lowell's protest in *The Biglow Papers, First Series*

This American government, — what is it but a tradition, though a recent one, endeavoring to transmit itself unimpaired to posterity, but each instant losing some of its integrity? It has not the vitality and force of a single living man; for a single man can bend it to his will. It is a sort of wooden gun to the people themselves. But it is not the less necessary for this; for the people must have some complicated machinery or other, and hear its din, to satisfy that idea of government which they have. Governments show thus how successfully men can be imposed on, even impose on themselves, for their own advantage. It is excellent, we must all allow. Yet this government never of itself furthered any enterprise, but by the alacrity with which it got out of its way. *It* does not keep the country free. *It* does not settle the West. *It* does not educate. The character inherent in the American people has done all that has been accomplished; and it would have done somewhat more, if the government had not sometimes got in its way. For government is an expedient by which men would fain succeed in letting one another alone; and, as has been said, when it is most expedient, the governed are most let alone by it. Trade and commerce, if they were not made of India-rubber, would never manage to bounce over the obstacles which legislators are continually putting in their way; and, if one were to judge these men wholly by the effects of their actions and not partly by their intentions, they would deserve to be classed and punished with those mischievous persons who put obstructions on the railroads.

But, to speak practically and as a citizen, unlike those who call themselves no-government men, I ask for, not at once no government, but *at once* a better government. Let every man make known what kind of government would command his respect, and that will be one step toward obtaining it.

After all, the practical reason why, when the power is once in the hands of the people, a majority are permitted, and for a long period continue, to rule is not because they are most likely to be in the right, nor because this seems fairest to the minority, but because they are physically the strongest. But a government in which the majority rule in all cases cannot be based on justice, even as far as men understand it. Can there not be a government in which majorities do not virtually decide right and wrong, but conscience? — in which majorities decide only those questions to which the rule of expediency is applicable? Must the citizen ever for a moment, or in the least degree, resign his conscience to the legislator? Why has every man a conscience, then? I think that we should be men first, and subjects afterward. It is not desirable to cultivate a respect for the law, so much as for the right. The only obligation which I have a right to assume is to do at any time what I think right. It is truly enough said, that a corporation has no conscience; but a corporation of conscientious men is a corporation *with* a conscience. Law never made men a whit more just; and, by means of their respect for it, even the well-disposed are daily made the agents of injustice. A common and natural result of an undue respect for law is, that you may see a file of soldiers, colonel, captain, corporal, privates, powder-monkeys, and all, marching in admirable order over hill and dale to the wars, against their wills, ay, against their common sense and consciences, which makes it very steep marching indeed, and produces a palpitation of the heart. They have no doubt that it is a damnable business in which they are concerned; they are all peaceably inclined. Now, what are they? Men at all? or small movable forts and magazines, at the service of some unscrupulous man in power? Visit the Navy-Yard, and behold a marine, such a man as an American government can make, or such as it can make a man with its black arts, — a mere shadow and reminiscence of humanity, a man laid out alive and standing, and already, as one may say, buried under arms with funeral accompaniments, though it may be, —

> "Not a drum was heard, not a funeral notè,
>   As his corse to the rampart we hurried;
> Not a soldier discharged his farewell shot   10
>   O'er the grave where our hero we buried."

The mass of men serve the state thus, not as men mainly, but as machines, with their bodies. They are the standing army, and the militia, jailors, constables, posse comitatus, etc. In most cases there is no free exercise whatever of the judgment or of the moral sense; but they put themselves on a level with wood and earth and stones; and wooden men can perhaps be manufactured that will serve the purpose as well. Such command no more respect than men of straw or a lump of dirt. They have the same sort of worth only as horses and dogs. Yet such as these even are commonly esteemed good citizens. Others — as most legislators, politicians, lawyers, ministers, and office-holders — serve the state chiefly with their heads; and, as they   20 rarely make any moral distinctions, they are as likely to serve the Devil, without *intending* it, as God. A very few, as heroes, patriots, martyrs, reformers in the great sense, and *men,* serve the state with their consciences also, and so necessarily resist it for the most part; and they are commonly treated as enemies by it. A wise man will only be useful as a man, and will not submit to be "clay," and "stop a hole to keep the wind away," but leave that office to his dust at least: —

> "I am too high-born to be propertied,
> To be a secondary at control,
> Or useful serving-man and instrument
> To any sovereign state throughout the world."   30

He who gives himself entirely to his fellow-men appears to them useless and self-ish; but he who gives himself partially to them is pronounced a benefactor and philanthropist.

How does it become a man to behave toward this American government to-day? I answer, that he cannot without disgrace be associated with it. I cannot for an instant recognize that political organization as *my* government ·which is the *slave's* government also.

---

8 **Not** . . . **buried,** from Charles Wolfe's "The Burial of Sir John Moore" (1817)   13 **posse comitatus,** inhabitants summoned by the sheriff to assist in preserving the peace   25 **clay** . . . **away.** Compare *Hamlet,* Act V, Sc. i, ll. 236-237: "Imperious Caesar, dead and turn'd to clay/ Might stop a hole to keep the wind away"   27 **I** . . . **world,** from Shakespeare's *King John,* Act V, Sc. ii, ll. 79-82

All men recognize the right of revolution; that is, the right to refuse allegiance to, and to resist, the government, when its tyranny or its inefficiency are great and unendurable. But almost all say that such is not the case now. But such was the case, they think, in the Revolution of '75. If one were to tell me that this was a bad government because it taxed certain foreign commodities brought to its ports, it is most probable that I should not make an ado about it, for I can do without them. All machines have their friction; and possibly this does enough good to counterbalance the evil. At any rate, it is a great evil to make a stir about it. But when the friction comes to have its machine, and oppression and robbery are organized, I say, let us not have such a machine any longer. In other words, when a sixth of the population of a nation which has undertaken to be the refuge of liberty are slaves, and a whole country is unjustly overrun and conquered by a foreign army, and subjected to military law, I think that it is not too soon for honest men to rebel and revolutionize. What makes this duty the more urgent is the fact that the country so overrun is not our own, but ours is the invading army.

Paley, a common authority with many on moral questions, in his chapter on the "Duty of Submission to Civil Government," resolves all civil obligation into expediency; and he proceeds to say, "that so long as the interest of the whole society requires it, that is, so long as the established government cannot be resisted or changed without public inconveniency, it is the will of God that the established government be obeyed, and no longer. . . . This principle being admitted, the justice of every particular case of resistance is reduced to a computation of the quantity of the danger and grievance on the one side, and of the probability and expense of redressing it on the other." Of this, he says, every man shall judge for himself. But Paley appears never to have contemplated those cases to which the rule of expediency does not apply, in which a people, as well as an individual, must do justice, cost what it may. If I have unjustly wrested a plank from a drowning man, I must restore it to him though I drown myself. This, according to Paley, would be inconvenient. But he that would save his life, in such a case, shall lose it. This people must cease to hold slaves, and to make war on Mexico, though it cost them their existence as a people.

In their practice, nations agree with Paley; but does any one think that Massachusetts does exactly what is right at the present crisis?

> "A drab of state, a cloth-o'-silver slut,
> To have her train borne up, and her soul trail in the dirt."

Practically speaking, the opponents to a reform in Massachusetts are not a hundred thousand politicians at the South, but a hundred thousand merchants and farmers here, who are more interested in commerce and agriculture than they are in human-

---

18 **that . . . other,** from *Principles of Moral and Political Philosophy* (1785) by William Paley (1743-1805), English theologian and moralist   29 **save . . . it.** Compare Matthew 10:39   37 **merchants.** Emerson wrote in his *Journal* (May 23, 1846): "Cotton thread holds the Union together; unites John C. Calhoun and Abbott Lawrence. Patriotism for Holidays and summer evenings, with music and rockets, but cotton thread is the Union"

ity, and are not prepared to do justice to the slave and to Mexico, *cost what it may*.
I quarrel not with far-off foes, but with those who, near at home, coöperate with,
and do the bidding of, those far away, and without whom the latter would be harmless. We are accustomed to say, that the mass of men are unprepared; but improvement is slow, because the few are not materially wiser or better than the many. It
is not so important that many should be as good as you, as that there be some absolute goodness somewhere; for that will leaven the whole lump. There are thousands who are *in opinion* opposed to slavery and to the war, who yet in effect do
nothing to put an end to them; who, esteeming themselves children of Washington
and Franklin, sit down with their hands in their pockets, and say that they know 10
not what to do, and do nothing; who even postpone the question of freedom to
the question of free-trade, and quietly read the prices-current along with the latest
advices from Mexico, after dinner, and, it may be, fall asleep over them both. What
is the price-current of an honest man and patriot to-day? They hesitate, and they
regret, and sometimes they petition; but they do nothing in earnest and with effect.
They will wait, well disposed, for others to remedy the evil, that they may no longer
have it to regret. At most, they give only a cheap vote, and a feeble countenance
and God-speed, to the right, as it goes by them. There are nine hundred and ninety-
nine patrons of virtue to one virtuous man. But it is easier to deal with the real
possessor of a thing than with the temporary guardian of it. 20

All voting is a sort of gaming, like checkers or backgammon, with a slight moral
tinge to it, a playing with right and wrong, with moral questions; and betting naturally accompanies it. The character of the voters is not staked. I cast my vote, perchance, as I think right; but I am not vitally concerned that that right should prevail.
I am willing to leave it to the majority. Its obligation, therefore, never exceeds that
of expediency. Even voting *for the right* is *doing* nothing for it. It is only expressing
to men feebly your desire that it should prevail. A wise man will not leave the right
to the mercy of chance, nor wish it to prevail through the power of the majority.
There is but little virtue in the action of masses of men. When the majority shall
at length vote for the abolition of slavery, it will be because they are indifferent to 30
slavery, or because there is but little slavery left to be abolished by their vote. *They*
will then be the only slaves. Only *his* vote can hasten the abolition of slavery who
asserts his own freedom by his vote.

I hear of a convention to be held at Baltimore, or elsewhere, for the selection of
a candidate for the Presidency, made up chiefly of editors, and men who are politicians by profession; but I think, what is it to any independent, intelligent, and
respectable man what decision they may come to? Shall we not have the advantage
of his wisdom and honesty, nevertheless? Can we not count upon some independent
votes? Are there not many individuals in the country who do not attend conventions? But no: I find that the respectable man, so called, has immediately drifted 40
from his position, and despairs of his country, when his country has more reason to
despair of him. He forthwith adopts one of the candidates thus selected as the only
available one, thus proving that he is himself *available* for any purposes of the

---

7 **leaven . . . lump.** Compare I Corinthians 5:6: "Know ye not that a little leaven leaveneth the whole lump?"

demagogue. His vote is of no more worth than that of any unprincipled foreigner or hireling native, who may have been bought. O for a man who is a *man,* and, as my neighbor says, has a bone in his back which you cannot pass your hand through! Our statistics are at fault: the population has been returned too large. How many *men* are there to a square thousand miles in this country? Hardly one. Does not America offer any inducement for men to settle here? The American has dwindled into an Odd Fellow, — one who may be known by the development of his organ of gregariousness, and a manifest lack of intellect and cheerful self-reliance; whose first and chief concern, on coming into the world, is to see that the Almshouses are in 10 good repair; and, before yet he has lawfully donned the virile garb, to collect a fund for the support of the widows and orphans that may be; who, in short, ventures to live only by the aid of the Mutual Insurance company, which has promised to bury him decently.

It is not a man's duty, as a matter of course, to devote himself to the eradication of any, even the most enormous wrong; he may still properly have other concerns to engage him; but it is his duty, at least, to wash his hands of it, and, if he gives it no thought longer, not to give it practically his support. If I devote myself to other pursuits and contemplations, I must first see, at least, that I do not pursue them sitting upon another man's shoulders. I must get off him first, that he may 20 pursue his contemplations too. See what gross inconsistency is tolerated. I have heard some of my townsmen say, "I should like to have them order me out to help put down an insurrection of the slaves, or to march to Mexico; — see if I would go;" and yet these very men have each, directly by their allegiance, and so indirectly, at least, by their money, furnished a substitute. The soldier is applauded who refuses to serve in an unjust war by those who do not refuse to sustain the unjust government which makes the war; is applauded by those whose own act and authority he disregards and sets at naught; as if the state were penitent to that degree that it hired one to scourge it while it sinned, but not to that degree that it left off sinning for a moment. Thus, under the name of Order and Civil Government, we are all made 30 at last to pay homage to and support our own meanness. After the first blush of sin comes its indifference; and from immoral it becomes, as it were, *un*moral, and not quite unnecessary to that life which we have made.

The broadest and most prevalent error requires the most disinterested virtue to sustain it. The slight reproach to which the virtue of patriotism is commonly liable, the noble are most likely to incur. Those who, while they disapprove of the character and measures of a government, yield to it their allegiance and support are undoubtedly its most conscientious supporters, and so frequently the most serious obstacles to reform. Some are petitioning the state to dissolve the Union, to disregard the requisitions of the President. Why do they not dissolve it themselves, — 40 the union between themselves and the state, — and refuse to pay their quota into

7 **Odd Fellow,** a member of a secret fraternity, the Independent Order of Odd Fellows, organized for mutual aid and social enjoyment, and comprising many lodges in England and America   10 **virile garb.** The *toga virilis,* or manly toga, was put on by Roman boys at the end of their fourteenth year   39 **requisitions . . . President,** President James K. Polk's call for volunteers for the war against Mexico

its treasury? Do not they stand in the same relation to the state that the state does to the Union? And have not the same reasons prevented the state from resisting the Union which have prevented them from resisting the state?

How can a man be satisfied to entertain an opinion merely, and enjoy *it?* Is there any enjoyment in it, if his opinion is that he is aggrieved? If you are cheated out of a single dollar by your neighbor, you do not rest satisfied with knowing that you are cheated, or with saying that you are cheated, or even with petitioning him to pay you your due; but you take effectual steps at once to obtain the full amount, and see that you are never cheated again. Action from principle, the perception and the performance of right, changes things and relations; it is essentially revolutionary, 10 and does not consist wholly with anything which was. It not only divides states and churches, it divides families; ay, it divides the *individual,* separating the diabolical in him from the divine.

Unjust laws exist: shall we be content to obey them, or shall we endeavor to amend them, and obey them until we have succeeded, or shall we transgress them at once? Men generally, under such a government as this, think that they ought to wait until they have persuaded the majority to alter them. They think that, if they should resist, the remedy would be worse than the evil. But it is the fault of the government itself that the remedy *is* worse than the evil. *It* makes it worse. Why is it not more apt to anticipate and provide for reform? Why does it not cherish its 20 wise minority? Why does it cry and resist before it is hurt? Why does it not encourage its citizens to be on the alert to point out its faults, and *do* better than *it* would have them? Why does it always crucify Christ, and excommunicate Copernicus and Luther, and pronounce Washington and Franklin rebels?

One would think, that a deliberate and practical denial of its authority was the only offense never contemplated by government; else, why has it not assigned its definite, its suitable and proportionate penalty? If a man who has no property refuses but once to earn nine shillings for the state, he is put in prison for a period unlimited by any law that I know, and determined only by the discretion of those who placed him there; but if he should steal ninety times nine shillings from the 30 state, he is soon permitted to go at large again.

If the injustice is part of the necessary friction of the machine of government, let it go, let it go: perchance it will wear smooth, — certainly the machine will wear out. If the injustice has a spring, or a pulley, or a rope, or a crank, exclusively for itself, then perhaps you may consider whether the remedy will not be worse than the evil; but if it is of such a nature that it requires you to be the agent of injustice to another, then, I say, break the law. Let your life be a counter friction to stop the machine. What I have to do is to see, at any rate, that I do not lend myself to the wrong which I condemn.

As for adopting the ways which the state has provided for remedying the evil, I 40 know not of such ways. They take too much time, and a man's life will be gone. I have other affairs to attend to. I came into this world, not chiefly to make this a good place to live in, but to live in it, be it good or bad. A man has not everything to do, but something; and because he cannot do *everything,* it is not necessary that he should do *something* wrong. It is not my business to be petitioning the Governor or the Legislature any more than it is theirs to petition me; and if they should not hear my petition, what should I do then? But in this case the state has provided no way: its very Constitution is the evil. This may seem to be harsh and stubborn and unconciliatory; but it is to treat with the utmost kindness and consideration the only spirit that can appreciate or deserves it. So is all change for the better, like birth and death, which convulse the body.

I do not hesitate to say, that those who call themselves Abolitionists should at once effectually withdraw their support, both in person and property, from the gov-
10 ernment of Massachusetts and not wait till they constitute a majority of one, before they suffer the right to prevail through them. I think that it is enough if they have God on their side, without waiting for that other one. Moreover, any man more right than his neighbors constitutes a majority of one already.

I meet this American government, or its representative, the state government, directly, and face to face, once a year — no more — in the person of its tax-gatherer; this is the only mode in which a man situated as I am necessarily meets it; and it then says distinctly, Recognize me; and the simplest, most effectual, and, in the present posture of affairs, the indispensablest mode of treating with it on this head, of expressing your little satisfaction with and love for it, is to deny it then. My
20 civil neighbor, the tax-gatherer, is the very man I have to deal with, — for it is, after all, with men and not with parchment that I quarrel, — and he has voluntarily chosen to be an agent of the government. How shall he ever know well what he is and does as an officer of the government, or as a man, until he is obliged to con-sider whether he shall treat me, his neighbor, for whom he has respect, as a neighbor and well-disposed man, or as a maniac and disturber of the peace, and see if he can get over this obstruction to his neighborliness without a ruder and more impetuous thought or speech corresponding with his action. I know this well, that if one thousand, if one hundred, if ten men whom I could name, — if ten *honest* men only, — if *one* HONEST man, in this State of Massachusetts, *ceasing to hold slaves,* were ac-
30 tually to withdraw from this copartnership, and be locked up in the county jail therefor, it would be the abolition of slavery in America. For it matters not how small the beginning may seem to be: what is once well done is done forever. But we love better to talk about it: that we say is our mission. Reform keeps many scores of newspapers in its service, but not one man. If my esteemed neighbor, the State's ambassador, who will devote his days to the settlement of the question of human rights in the Council Chamber, instead of being threatened with the prisons of Carolina, were to sit down the prisoner of Massachusetts, that State which is so anxious to foist the sin of slavery upon her sister, — though at present she can dis-cover only an act of inhospitality to be the ground of a quarrel with her, — the
40 Legislature would not wholly waive the subject the following winter.

---

35 **State's ambassador,** Samuel Hoar of Concord, sent to Charleston, South Carolina, in 1844 to protest against the seizure of Negro seamen from Massachusetts, and inhospitably expelled from Charleston by "a committee of leading citizens"

Under a government which imprisons any unjustly, the true place for a just man is also a prison. The proper place to-day, the only place which Massachusetts has provided for her freer and less desponding spirits, is in her prisons, to be put out and locked out of the State by her own act, as they have already put themselves out by their principles. It is there that the fugitive slave, and the Mexican prisoner on parole, and the Indian come to plead the wrongs of his race should find them; on that separate, but more free and honorable ground, where the State places those who are not *with* her, but *against* her, — the only house in a slave State in which a free man can abide with honor. If any think that their influence would be lost there, and their voices no longer afflict the ear of the State, that they would not be as an 10 enemy within its walls, they do not know by how much truth is stronger than error, nor how much more eloquently and effectively he can combat injustice who has experienced a little in his own person. Cast your whole vote, not a strip of paper merely, but your whole influence. A minority is powerless while it conforms to the majority; it is not even a minority then; but it is irresistible when it clogs by its whole weight. If the alternative is to keep all just men in prison, or give up war and slavery, the State will not hesitate which to choose. If a thousand men were not to pay their tax-bills this year, that would not be a violent and bloody measure, as it would be to pay them, and enable the State to commit violence and shed innocent blood. This is, in fact, the definition of a peaceable revolution, if any such 20 is possible. If the tax-gatherer, or any other public officer, asks me, as one has done, "But what shall I do?" my answer is, "If you really wish to do anything, resign your office." When the subject has refused allegiance, and the officer has resigned his office, then the revolution is accomplished. But even suppose blood should flow. Is there not a sort of blood shed when the conscience is wounded? Through this wound a man's real manhood and immortality flow out, and he bleeds to an everlasting death. I see this blood flowing now.

I have contemplated the imprisonment of the offender, rather than the seizure of his goods, — though both will serve the same purpose, — because they who assert the purest right, and consequently are most dangerous to a corrupt State, commonly 30 have not spent much time in accumulating property. To such the State renders comparatively small service, and a slight tax is wont to appear exorbitant, particularly if they are obliged to earn it by special labor with their hands. If there were one who lived wholly without the use of money, the State itself would hesitate to demand it of him. But the rich man — not to make any invidious comparison — is always sold to the institution which makes him rich. Absolutely speaking, the more money, the less virtue; for money comes between a man and his objects, and obtains them for him; and it was certainly no great virtue to obtain it. It puts to rest many questions which he would otherwise be taxed to answer; while the only new question which it puts is the hard but superfluous one, how to spend it. Thus his 40 moral ground is taken from under his feet. The opportunities of living are diminished in proportion as what are called the "means" are increased. The best thing a man can do for his culture when he is rich is to endeavor to carry out those schemes which he entertained when he was poor. Christ answered the Herodians according to their condition. "Show me the tribute-money," said he; — and one took a penny out of his pocket; — if you use the money which has the image of Cæsar on it and which he has made current and valuable, that is, *if you are men of the State,* and gladly enjoy the advantages of Cæsar's government, then pay him back some of his own when he demands it. "Render therefore to Cæsar that which is Cæsar's, and to God those things which are God's," — leaving them no wiser than before as to which was which; for they did not wish to know.

When I converse with the freest of my neighbors, I perceive that, whatever they may say about the magnitude and seriousness of the question, and their regard for
10 the public tranquillity, the long and the short of the matter is, that they cannot spare the protection of the existing government, and they dread the consequences to their property and families of disobedience to it. For my own part, I should not like to think that I ever rely on the protection of the State. But, if I deny the authority of the State when it presents its tax-bill, it will soon take and waste all my property, and so harass me and my children without end. This is hard. This makes it impossible for a man to live honestly, and at the same time comfortably, in outward respects. It will not be worth the while to accumulate property; that would be sure to go again. You must hire or squat somewhere, and raise but a small crop, and eat that soon. You must live within yourself, and depend upon
20 yourself always tucked up and ready for a start; and not have many affairs. A man may grow rich in Turkey even, if he will be in all respects a good subject of the Turkish government. Confucius said: "If a state is governed by the principles of reason, poverty and misery are subjects of shame; if a state is not governed by the principles of reason, riches and honors are the subjects of shame." No: until I want the protection of Massachusetts to be extended to me in some distant Southern port, where my liberty is endangered, or until I am bent solely on building up an estate at home by peaceful enterprise, I can afford to refuse allegiance to Massachusetts, and her right to my property and life. It costs me less in every sense to incur the penalty of disobedience to the State than it would to obey. I should feel as if I were
30 worth less in that case.

Some years ago, the State met me in behalf of the Church, and commanded me to pay a certain sum toward the support of a clergyman whose preaching my father attended, but never I myself. "Pay," it said, "or be locked up in the jail." I declined to pay. But, unfortunately, another man saw fit to pay it. I did not see why the schoolmaster should be taxed to support the priest, and not the priest the schoolmaster; for I was not the State's schoolmaster, but I supported myself by voluntary subscription. I did not see why the lyceum should not present its tax-bill, and have the State to back its demand, as well as the Church. However, at the request of the selectmen, I condescended to make some such statement as this in writing: — "Know
40 all men by these presents, that I, Henry Thoreau, do not wish to be regarded as a member of any incorporated society which I have not joined." This I gave to the town clerk; and he has it. The State, having thus learned that I did not wish to be regarded as a member of that church, has never made a like demand on me since;

1 **Show . . . God's.** See Matthew 22: 19-21

though it said that it must adhere to its original presumption that time. If I had known how to name them, I should then have signed off in detail from all the societies which I never signed on to; but I did not know where to find a complete list.

I have paid no poll-tax for six years. I was put into a jail once on this account, for one night; and, as I stood considering the walls of solid stone, two or three feet thick, the door of wood and iron, a foot thick, and the iron grating which strained the light, I could not help being struck with the foolishness of that institution which treated me as if I were mere flesh and blood and bones, to be locked up. I wondered that it should have concluded at length that this was the best use it could put me to, and had never thought to avail itself of my services in some way. I saw that, if there was a wall of stone between me and my townsmen, there was a still more difficult one to climb or break through before they could get to be as free as I was. I did not for a moment feel confined, and the walls seemed a great waste of stone and mortar. I felt as if I alone of all my townsmen had paid my tax. They plainly did not know how to treat me, but behaved like persons who are underbred. In every threat and in every compliment there was a blunder; for they thought that my chief desire was to stand the other side of that stone wall. I could not but smile to see how industriously they locked the door on my meditations, which followed them out again without let or hindrance, and *they* were really all that was dangerous. As they could not reach me, they had resolved to punish my body; just as boys, if they cannot come at some person against whom they have a spite, will abuse his dog. I saw that the State was half-witted, that it was timid as a lone woman with her silver spoons, and that it did not know its friends from its foes, and I lost all my remaining respect for it, and pitied it.

Thus the State never intentionally confronts a man's sense, intellectual or moral, but only his body, his senses. It is not armed with superior wit or honesty, but with superior physical strength. I was not born to be forced. I will breathe after my own fashion. Let us see who is the strongest. What force has a multitude? They only can force me who obey a higher law than I. They force me to become like themselves. I do not hear of *men* being *forced* to live this way or that by masses of men. What sort of life were that to live? When I meet a government which says to me, "Your money or your life," why should I be in haste to give it my money? It may be in a great strait, and not know what to do: I cannot help that. It must help itself; do as I do. It is not worth the while to snivel about it. I am not responsible for the successful working of the machinery of society. I am not the son of the engineer. I perceive that, when an acorn and a chestnut fall side by side, the one does not remain inert to make way for the other, but both obey their own laws, and spring and grow and flourish as best they can, till one, perchance, overshadows and destroys the other. If a plant cannot live according to its nature, it dies; and so a man.

The night in prison was novel and interesting enough. The prisoners in their shirt-sleeves were enjoying a chat and the evening air in the doorway, when I entered. But the jailer said, "Come, boys, it is time to lock up;" and so they dispersed,

---

4 I . . . **night.** H. S. Canby reckons that Thoreau's famous night in jail occurred on the 23rd or 24th of July, 1846 (*Thoreau*, p. 473)

and I heard the sound of their steps returning into the hollow apartments. My room-mate was introduced to me by the jailer as "a first-rate fellow and a clever man." When the door was locked, he showed me where to hang my hat, and how he managed matters there. The rooms were whitewashed once a month; and this one, at least, was the whitest, most simply furnished, and probably the neatest apartment in the town. He naturally wanted to know where I came from, and what brought me there; and, when I had told him, I asked him in my turn how he came there, presuming him to be an honest man, of course; and, as the world goes, I believe he was. "Why," said he, "they accuse me of burning a barn; but I never
10 did it." As near as I could discover, he had probably gone to bed in a barn when drunk, and smoked his pipe there; and so a barn was burnt. He had the reputation of being a clever man, had been there some three months waiting for his trial to come on, and would have to wait as much longer; but he was quite domesticated and contented, since he got his board for nothing, and thought that he was well treated.

He occupied one window, and I the other; and I saw that if one stayed there long, his principal business would be to look out the window. I had soon read all the tracts that were left there, and examined where former prisoners had broken out, and where a grate had been sawed off, and heard the history of the various occu-
20 pants of that room; for I found that even here there was a history and a gossip which never circulated beyond the walls of the jail. Probably this is the only house in the town where verses are composed, which are afterward printed in a circular form, but not published. I was shown quite a long list of verses which were composed by some young men who had been detected in an attempt to escape, who avenged themselves by singing them.

I pumped my fellow-prisoner as dry as I could, for fear I should never see him again; but at length he showed me which was my bed, and left me to blow out the lamp.

It was like traveling into a far country, such as I had never expected to behold, to
30 lie there for one night. It seemed to me that I never had heard the town-clock strike before, nor the evening sounds of the village; for we slept with the windows open, which were inside the grating. It was to see my native village in the light of the Middle Ages, and our Concord was turned into a Rhine stream, and visions of knights and castles passed before me. They were the voices of old burghers that I heard in the streets. I was an involuntary spectator and auditor of whatever was done and said in the kitchen of the adjacent village-inn, — a wholly new and rare experience to me. It was a closer view of my native town. I was fairly inside of it. I never had seen its institutions before. This is one of its peculiar institutions; for it is a shire town. I began to comprehend what its inhabitants were about.

40 In the morning, our breakfasts were put through the hole in the door, in small oblong-square tin pans, made to fit, and holding a pint of chocolate, with brown bread, and an iron spoon. When they called for the vessels again, I was green enough to return what bread I had left; but my comrade seized it, and said that I

2 **clever,** honest, kind, obliging; see *Dictionary of American English*

should lay that up for lunch or dinner. Soon after he was let out to work at haying in a neighboring field, whither he went every day, and would not be back till noon; so he bade me good-day, saying that he doubted if he should see me again.

When I came out of prison, — for some one interfered, and paid that tax, — I did not perceive that great changes had taken place on the common, such as he observed who went in a youth and emerged a tottering and grayheaded man; and yet a change had to my eyes come over the scene, — the town, and State, and country, — greater than any that mere time could effect. I saw yet more distinctly the State in which I lived. I saw to what extent the people among whom I lived could be trusted as good neighbors and friends; that their friendship was for summer 10 weather only; that they did not greatly propose to do right; that they were a distinct race from me by their prejudices and superstitions, as the Chinamen and Malays are; that in their sacrifices to humanity they ran no risks, not even to their property; that after all they were not so noble but they treated the thief as he had treated them, and hoped, by a certain outward observance and a few prayers, and by walking in a particular straight though useless path from time to time, to save their souls. This may be to judge my neighbors harshly; for I believe that many of them are not aware that they have such an institution as the jail in their village.

It was formerly the custom in our village, when a poor debtor came out of jail, for his acquaintances to salute him, looking through their fingers, which were 20 crossed to represent the grating of a jail window, "How do ye do?" My neighbors did not thus salute me, but first looked at me, and then at one another, as if I had returned from a long journey. I was put into jail as I was going to the shoemaker's to get a shoe which was mended. When I was let out the next morning, I proceeded to finish my errand, and, having put on my mended shoe, joined a huckleberry party, who were impatient to put themselves under my conduct; and in half an hour, — for the horse was soon tackled, — was in the midst of a huckleberry field, on one of our highest hills, two miles off, and then the State was nowhere to be seen.

This is the whole history of "My Prisons."   30

I have never declined paying the highway tax, because I am as desirous of being a good neighbor as I am of being a bad subject; and as for supporting schools, I am doing my part to educate my fellow-countrymen now. It is for no particular item in the tax-bill that I refuse to pay it. I simply wish to refuse allegiance to the State, to withdraw and stand aloof from it effectually. I do not care to trace the course of my dollar, if I could, till it buys a man or a musket to shoot with, — the dollar is innocent, — but I am concerned to trace the effects of my allegiance. In fact, I quietly declare war with the State, after my fashion, though I will still make what use and get what advantage of her I can, as is usual in such cases.

If others pay the tax which is demanded of me, from a sympathy with the State, 40

---

4 **some . . . tax.** According to one report his Aunt Maria, "putting a shawl over her head, went to the jailer's door, and paid the tax and fees to Ellen Staples, her father the jailer being absent" (Canby, *Thoreau*, p. 234)   30 **My Prisons.** Silvio Pellico (1789-1854), Italian patriot, told the story of his imprisonment by the Austrians in *Le Mie prigioni* (1832), to which Thoreau seems to allude

they do but what they have already done in their own case, or rather they abet injustice to a greater extent than the State requires. If they pay the tax from a mistaken interest in the individual taxed, to save his property, or prevent his going to jail, it is because they have not considered wisely how far they let their private feelings interfere with the public good.

This, then, is my position at present. But one cannot be too much on his guard in such a case, lest his action be biased by obstinacy or an undue regard for the opinions of men. Let him see that he does only what belongs to himself and to the hour.

10   I think sometimes, Why, this people mean well, they are only ignorant; they would do better if they knew how: why give your neighbors this pain to treat you as they are not inclined to? But I think again, This is no reason why I should do as they do, or permit others to suffer much greater pain of a different kind. Again, I sometimes say to myself, When many millions of men, without heat, without ill will, without personal feeling of any kind, demand of you a few shillings only, without the possibility, such is their constitution, of retracting or altering their present demand, and without the possibility, on your side, of appeal to any other millions, why expose yourself to this overwhelming brute force? You do not resist cold and hunger, the winds and the waves, thus obstinately; you quietly submit to a thou-
20   sand similar necessities. You do not put your head into the fire. But just in proportion as I regard this as not wholly a brute force, but partly a human force, and consider that I have relations to those millions as to so many millions of men, and not of mere brute or inanimate things, I see that appeal is possible, first and instantaneously, from them to the Maker of them, and, secondly, from them to themselves. But if I put my head deliberately into the fire, there is no appeal to fire or to the Maker of fire, and I have only myself to blame. If I could convince myself that I have any right to be satisfied with men as they are, and to treat them accordingly, and not according, in some respects, to my requisitions and expectations of what they and I ought to be, then, like a good Mussulman and fatalist, I should endeavor
30   to be satisfied with things as they are, and say it is the will of God. And, above all, there is this difference between resisting this and a purely brute or natural force, that I can resist this with some effect; but I cannot expect, like Orpheus, to change the nature of the rocks and trees and beasts.

I do not wish to quarrel with any man or nation. I do not wish to split hairs, to make fine distinctions, or set myself up as better than my neighbors. I seek rather, I may say, even an excuse for conforming to the laws of the land. I am but too ready to conform to them. Indeed, I have reason to suspect myself on this head; and each year, as the tax-gatherer comes round, I find myself disposed to review the acts and position of the general and State governments, and the spirit of the people, to
40   discover a pretext for conformity.

> "We must affect our country as our parents,
> And if at any time we alienate

---

32 **Orpheus.** See note, p. 1112

> Our love or industry from doing it honor,
> We must respect effects and teach the soul
> Matter of conscience and religion,
> And not desire of rule or benefit."

I believe that the State will soon be able to take all my work of this sort out of my hands, and then I shall be no better a patriot than my fellow-countrymen. Seen from a lower point of view, the Constitution, with all its faults, is very good; the law and the courts are very respectable; even this State and this American government are, in many respects, very admirable, and rare things, to be thankful for, such as a great many have described them; but seen from a point of view a little higher, they are what I have described them; seen from a higher still, and the highest, who shall say what they are, or that they are worth looking at or thinking of at all? 10

However, the government does not concern me much, and I shall bestow the fewest possible thoughts on it. It is not many moments that I live under a government, even in this world. If a man is thought-free, fancy-free, imagination-free, that which *is not* never for a long time appearing *to be* to him, unwise rulers or reformers cannot fatally interrupt him.

I know that most men think differently from myself; but those whose lives are by profession devoted to the study of these or kindred subjects content me as little as any. Statesmen and legislators, standing so completely within the institution, never distinctly and nakedly behold it. They speak of moving society, but have no resting-place without it. They may be men of a certain experience and discrimination, and have no doubt invented ingenious and even useful systems, for which we sincerely thank them; but all their wit and usefulness lie within certain not very wide limits. They are wont to forget that the world is not governed by policy and expediency. Webster never goes behind government, and so cannot speak with authority about it. His words are wisdom to those legislators who contemplate no essential reform in the existing government; but for thinkers, and those who legislate for all time, he never once glances at the subject. I know of those whose serene and wise speculations on this theme would soon reveal the limits of his mind's range and hospitality. 30 Yet, compared with the cheap professions of most reformers, and the still cheaper wisdom and eloquence of politicians in general, his are almost the only sensible and valuable words, and we thank Heaven for him. Comparatively, he is always strong, original, and, above all, practical. Still, his quality is not wisdom, but prudence. The lawyer's truth is not Truth, but consistency or a consistent expediency. Truth is always in harmony with herself, and is not concerned chiefly to reveal the justice that may consist with wrong-doing. He well deserves to be called, as he has been called, the Defender of the Constitution. There are really no blows to be given by him but defensive ones. He is not a leader, but a follower. His leaders are the men of '87. "I have never made an effort," he says, "and never propose to make an ef- 40 fort; I have never countenanced an effort, and never mean to countenance an effort, to disturb the arrangement as originally made, by which the various States came

26 **Webster.** See headnote to "Ichabod," p. 1000   39 **men of '87,** the framers of the Constitution in 1787

into the Union." Still thinking of the sanction which the Constitution gives to slavery, he says, "Because it was a part of the original compact, — let it stand." Notwithstanding his special acuteness and ability, he is unable to take a fact out of its merely political relations, and behold it as it lies absolutely to be disposed of by the intellect, — what, for instance, it behooves a man to do here in America to-day with regard to slavery, — but ventures, or is driven to make some such desperate answer as the following, while professing to speak absolutely, and as a private man, — from which what new and singular code of social duties might be inferred? "The manner," says he, "in which the governments of those States where slavery exists
10 are to regulate it is for their own consideration, under their responsibility to their constituents, to the general laws of propriety, humanity, and justice, and to God. Associations formed elsewhere, springing from a feeling of humanity, or other cause, have nothing whatever to do with it. They have never received any encouragement from me, and they never will."

They who know of no purer sources of truth, who have traced up its stream no higher, stand, and wisely stand, by the Bible and the Constitution, and drink at it there with reverence and humility; but they who behold where it comes trickling into this lake or that pool, gird up their loins once more, and continue their pilgrimage toward its fountain-head.

20 No man with a genius for legislation has appeared in America. They are rare in the history of the world. There are orators, politicians, and eloquent men, by the thousand; but the speaker has not yet opened his mouth to speak who is capable of settling the much-vexed questions of the day. We love eloquence for its own sake, and not for any truth which it may utter, or any heroism it may inspire. Our legislators have not yet learned the comparative value of free-trade and of freedom, of union, and of rectitude, to a nation. They have no genius or talent for comparatively humble questions of taxation and finance, commerce and manufactures and agriculture. If we were left solely to the wordy wit of legislators in Congress for our guidance, uncorrected by the seasonable experience and the effectual complaints of the
30 people, America would not long retain her rank among the nations. For eighteen hundred years, though perchance I have no right to say it, the New Testament has been written; yet where is the legislator who has wisdom and practical talent enough to avail himself of the light which it sheds on the science of legislation?

The authority of government, even such as I am willing to submit to, —for I will cheerfully obey those who know and can do better than I, and in many things even those who neither know nor can do so well, — is still an impure one: to be strictly just, it must have the sanction and consent of the governed. It can have no pure right over my person and property but what I concede to it. The progress from an absolute to a limited monarchy, from a limited monarchy to a democracy, is a
40 progress toward a true respect for the individual. Even the Chinese philosopher was wise enough to regard the individual as the basis of the empire. Is a democracy, such as we know it, the last improvement possible in government? Is it not possible to take a step further towards recognizing and organizing the rights of man? There will never be a really free and enlightened State until the State comes to recognize

the individual as a higher and independent power, from which all its own power and authority are derived, and treats him accordingly. I please myself with imagining a State at last which can afford to be just to all men, and to treat the individual with respect as a neighbor; which even would not think it inconsistent with its own repose if a few were to live aloof from it, not meddling with it, nor embraced by it, who fulfilled all the duties of neighbors and fellowmen. A State which bore this kind of fruit, and suffered it to drop off as fast as it ripened, would prepare the way for a still more perfect and glorious State, which also I have imagined, but not yet anywhere seen.   1849

from Walden *Where I Lived, and What I Lived For*

Walden, *the record of Thoreau's stay at Walden Pond from July 4, 1845, to September 6, 1847, was first published in 1854. It is Thoreau's best book and has come to be universally regarded as a great American classic. The book consists of eighteen chapters, as follows: "Economy," "Where I Lived and What I Lived For," "Reading," "Sounds," "Solitude," "Visitors," "The Bean Field," "The Village," "The Ponds," "Baker Farm," "Higher Laws," "Brute Neighbors," "House-Warming," "Former Inhabitants and Winter Visitors," "Winter Animals," "The Pond in Winter," "Spring," "Conclusion." Although "Thoreau's strength," as H. S. Canby has observed, "was in the sentence and paragraph, not in the ordered whole," F. O. Matthiessen (*American Renaissance, pp. 168-170) has ingeniously demonstrated "the firmness with which Thoreau binds his successive links" in* Walden.*
   "My purpose in going to Walden Pond," Thoreau wrote in the opening chapter, "was not to live cheaply nor to live dearly there, but to transact some private business with the fewest obstacles." The "private business" consisted chiefly of the study of nature and in reading and writing. "My residence," he added, "was more favourable, not only to thought, but to serious reading, than a university."*

   At a certain season of our life we are accustomed to consider every spot as the possible site of a house. I have thus surveyed the country on every side within a dozen miles of where I live. In imagination I have bought all the farms in succession, for all were to be bought, and I knew their price. I walked over each farmer's premises, tasted his wild apples, discoursed on husbandry with him, took his farm at his price, at any price, mortgaging it to him in my mind; even put a higher price on it, — took everything but a deed of it, — took his word for his deed, for I dearly love to talk, — cultivated it, and him too to some extent, I trust, and withdrew when I had enjoyed it long enough, leaving him to carry it on. This experience entitled me to be regarded as a sort of real-estate broker by my friends. Wherever I sat, there I   10
might live, and the landscape radiated from me accordingly. What is a house but a *sedes,* a seat? — better if a country seat. I discovered many a site for a house not likely to be soon improved, which some might have thought too far from the village, but to my eyes the village was too far from it. Well, there I might live, I said; and there I did live, for an hour, a summer and a winter life; saw how I could let

the years run off, buffet the winter through, and see the spring come in. The future inhabitants of this region, wherever they may place their houses, may be sure that they have been anticipated. An afternoon sufficed to lay out the land into orchard, wood-lot, and pasture, and to decide what fine oaks or pines should be left to stand before the door, and whence each blasted tree could be seen to the best advantage; and then I let it lie, fallow perchance, for a man is rich in proportion to the number of things which he can afford to let alone.

My imagination carried me so far that I even had the refusal of several farms, — the refusal was all I wanted, — but I never got my fingers burned by actual posses-
10 sion. The nearest that I came to actual possession was when I bought the Hollowell place, and had begun to sort my seeds, and collected materials with which to make a wheelbarrow to carry it on or off with; but before the owner gave me a deed of it, his wife — every man has such a wife — changed her mind and wished to keep it, and he offered me ten dollars to release him. Now, to speak the truth, I had but ten cents in the world, and it surpassed my arithmetic to tell, if I was that man who had ten cents, or who had a farm, or ten dollars, or all together. However, I let him keep the ten dollars and the farm too, for I had carried it far enough; or rather, to be generous, I sold him the farm for just what I gave for it, and, as he was not a rich man, made him a present of ten dollars, and still had my ten cents,
20 and seeds, and materials for a wheelbarrow left. I found thus that I had been a rich man without any damage to my poverty. But I retained the landscape, and I have since annually carried off what it yielded without a wheelbarrow. With respect to landscapes, —

"I am monarch of all I *survey,*
My right there is none to dispute."

I have frequently seen a poet withdraw, having enjoyed the most valuable part of a farm, while the crusty farmer supposed that he had got a few wild apples only. Why, the owner does not know it for many years when a poet has put his farm in rime, the most admirable kind of invisible fence, has fairly impounded it, milked it,
30 skimmed it, and got all the cream, and left the farmer only the skimmed milk.

The real attractions of the Hollowell farm, to me, were: its complete retirement, being about two miles from the village, half a mile from the nearest neighbor, and separated from the highway by a broad field; its bounding on the river, which the owner said protected it by its fogs from frosts in the spring, though that was nothing to me; the gray color and ruinous state of the house and barn, and the dilapidated fences, which put such an interval between me and the last occupant; the

---

24 **I . . . dispute,** from Cowper's "Verses supposed to be written by Alexander Selkirk (1782). By italicizing "survey," Thoreau makes a punning reference to his occupation as surveyor   28 **a poet . . . rime.** The thought is Emersonian. Compare, for example, in Emerson's "The Apology" (1846):
  One harvest from thy field
  Homeward brought the oxen strong;
  A second crop thine acres yield,
  While I gather in a song.

hollow and lichen-covered apple trees, gnawed by rabbits, showing what kind of neighbors I should have; but above all, the recollection I had of it from my earliest voyages up the river, when the house was concealed behind a dense grove of red maples, through which I heard the house-dog bark. I was in haste to buy it, before the proprietor finished getting out some rocks, cutting down the hollow apple trees, and grubbing up some young birches which had sprung up in the pasture, or, in short, had made any more of his improvements. To enjoy these advantages I was ready to carry it on; like Atlas, to take the world on my shoulders, — I never heard what compensation he received for that, — and do all those things which had no other motive or excuse but that I might pay for it and be unmolested in my pos-   10 session of it; for I knew all the while that it would yield the most abundant crop of the kind I wanted, if I could only afford to let it alone. But it turned out as I have said.

All that I could say, then, with respect to farming on a large scale — I have always cultivated a garden — was, that I had had my seeds ready. Many think that seeds improve with age. I have no doubt that time discriminates between the good and the bad; and when at last I shall plant, I shall be less likely to be disappointed. But I would say to my fellows, once for all, As long as possible live free and uncommitted. It makes but little difference whether you are committed to a farm or the county jail.   20

Old Cato, whose "De Re Rusticâ" is my "Cultivator," says, — and the only translation I have seen makes sheer nonsense of the passage, — "When you think of getting a farm turn it thus in your mind, not to buy greedily; nor spare your pains to look at it, and do not think it enough to go round it once. The oftener you go there the more it will please you, if it is good." I think I shall not buy greedily, but go round and round it as long as I live, and be buried in it first, that it may please me the more at last.

The present was my next experiment of this kind, which I purpose to describe more at length, for convenience putting the experience of two years into one. As I have said, I do not propose to write an ode to dejection, but to brag as lustily as   30 chanticleer in the morning, standing on his roost, if only to wake my neighbors up.

When first I took up my abode in the woods, that is, began to spend my nights as well as days there, which, by accident, was on Independence Day, or the Fourth of July, 1845, my house was not finished for winter, but was merely a defence against the rain, without plastering or chimney, the walls being of rough, weather-stained boards, with wide chinks, which made it cool at night. The upright white hewn studs and freshly planed door and window casings gave it a clean and airy look, especially in the morning, when its timbers were saturated with dew, so that I fancied that by noon some sweet gum would exude from them. To my imagination it retained throughout the day more or less of this auroral character, reminding me of   40

---

21 **Old Cato,** Marcus Porcius Cato (234-149 B.C.), Roman patriot   21 **De Re Rusticâ,** concerning country life   21 **Cultivator,** a farm implement   30 **ode to dejection.** Coleridge had written "Dejection: an Ode" (1802), and Shelley had composed "Stanzas Written in Dejection near Naples" (1824)

a certain house on a mountain which I had visited a year before. This was an airy and unplastered cabin, fit to entertain a travelling god, and where a goddess might trail her garments. The winds which passed over my dwelling were such as sweep over the ridges of mountains, bearing the broken strains, or celestial parts only, of terrestrial music. The morning wind forever blows, the poem of creation is uninterrupted; but few are the ears that hear it. Olympus is but the outside of the earth everywhere.

The only house I had been the owner of before, if I except a boat, was a tent, which I used occasionally when making excursions in the summer, and this is still
10 rolled up in my garret; but the boat, after passing from hand to hand, has gone down the stream of time. With this more substantial shelter about me, I had made some progress toward settling in the world. This frame, so slightly clad, was a sort of crystallization around me, and reacted on the builder. It was suggestive somewhat as a picture in outlines. I did not need to go outdoors to take the air, for the atmosphere within had lost none of its freshness. It was not so much within-doors as behind a door where I sat, even in the rainiest weather. The Harivansa says, "An abode without birds is like a meat without seasoning." Such was not my abode, for I found myself suddenly neighbor to the birds; not by having imprisoned one, but having caged myself near them. I was not only nearer to some of those which com-
20 monly frequent the garden and the orchard, but to those wilder and more thrilling songsters of the forest which never, or rarely, serenade a villager, — the wood thrush, the veery, the scarlet tanager, the field sparrow, the whip-poor-will, and many others.

I was seated by the shore of a small pond, about a mile and a half south of the village of Concord and somewhat higher than it, in the midst of an extensive wood between that town and Lincoln, and about two miles south of that our only field known to fame, Concord Battle Ground; but I was so low in the woods that the opposite shore, half a mile off, like the rest, covered with wood, was my most distant horizon. For the first week, whenever I looked out on the pond it impressed me
30 like a tarn high up on the side of a mountain, its bottom far above the surface of other lakes, and, as the sun arose, I saw it throwing off its nightly clothing of mist, and here and there, by degrees, its soft ripples or its smooth reflecting surface was revealed, while the mists, like ghosts, were stealthily withdrawing in every direction into the woods, as at the breaking up of some nocturnal conventicle. The very dew seemed to hang upon the trees later into the day than usual, as on the sides of mountains.

This small lake was of most value as a neighbor in the intervals of a gentle rainstorm in August, when, both air and water being perfectly still, but the sky overcast, mid-afternoon had all the serenity of evening, and the wood thrush sang
40 around, and was heard from shore to shore. A lake like this is never smoother than at such a time; and the clear portion of the air above it being shallow and darkened

---

10 **the boat.** The boat used in 1839 by Thoreau and his brother John on the famous voyage described in *A Week on the Concord and Merrimack Rivers* was purchased by Hawthorne in 1842 for seven dollars (see *The American Notebooks by Nathaniel Hawthorne*)   16 **Harivansa,** a Sanskrit epic poem of the fifth century

by clouds, the water, full of light and reflections, becomes a lower heaven itself so
much the more important. From a hilltop near by, where the wood had been recently
cut off, there was a pleasing vista southward across the pond, through a wide indentation in the hills which form the shore there, where their opposite sides sloping
toward each other suggested a stream flowing out in that direction through a
wooded valley, but stream there was none. That way I looked between and over
the near green hills to some distant and higher ones in the horizon, tinged with
blue. Indeed, by standing on tiptoe I could catch a glimpse of some of the peaks of
the still bluer and more distant mountain ranges in the northwest, those true-blue
coins from heaven's own mint, and also of some portion of the village. But in other   10
directions, even from this point, I could not see over or beyond the woods which
surrounded me. It is well to have some water in your neighborhood, to give buoyancy to and float the earth. One value even of the smallest well is, that when you
look into it you see that earth is not continent but insular. This is as important as
that it keeps butter cool. When I looked across the pond from this peak toward
the Sudbury meadows, which in time of flood I distinguished elevated perhaps by a
mirage in their seething valley, like a coin in a basin, all the earth beyond the pond
appeared like a thin crust insulated and floated even by this small sheet of intervening water, and I was reminded that this on which I dwelt was but *dry land.*

Though the view from my door was still more contracted, I did not feel crowded   20
or confined in the least. There was pasture enough for my imagination. The low
shrub oak plateau to which the opposite shore arose stretched away toward the
prairies of the West and the steppes of Tartary, affording ample room for all the
roving families of men. "There are none happy in the world but beings who enjoy
freely a vast horizon," — said Damodara, when his herds required new and larger
pastures.

Both place and time were changed, and I dwelt nearer to those parts of the universe and to those eras in history which had most attracted me. Where I lived was
as far off as many a region viewed nightly by astronomers. We are wont to imagine
rare and delectable places in some remote and more celestial corner of the system,   30
behind the constellation of Cassiopeia's Chair, far from noise and disturbance. I discovered that my house actually had its site in such a withdrawn, but forever new
and unprofaned, part of the universe. If it were worth the while to settle in those
parts near to the Pleiades or the Hyades, to Aldebaran or Altair, then I was really
there, or at an equal remoteness from the life which I had left behind, dwindled
and twinkling with as fine a ray to my nearest neighbor, and to be seen only in
moonless nights by him. Such was that part of creation where I had squatted; —

> "There was a shepherd that did live,
>   And held his thoughts as high
> As were the mounts whereon his flocks   40
>   Did hourly feed him by."

---

23 **Tartary,** an indefinitely defined region including Asia and Europe from the Sea of Japan to the Dnieper
River   25 **Damodara,** the Hindu divinity Krishna   34 **Pleiades . . . Hyades,** constellations   34
Aldebaran . . . Altair, bright stars

What should we think of the shepherd's life if his flocks always wandered to higher pastures than his thoughts?

Every morning was a cheerful invitation to make my life of equal simplicity, and I may say innocence, with Nature herself. I have been as sincere a worshipper of Aurora as the Greeks. I got up early and bathed in the pond; that was a religious exercise, and one of the best things which I did. They say that characters were engraven on the bathing tub of King Tching-thang to this effect: "Renew thyself completely each day; do it again, and again, and forever again." I can understand that. Morning brings back the heroic ages. I was as much affected by the faint hum of a mosquito making its invisible and unimaginable tour through my apartment at earliest dawn, when I was sitting with door and windows open, as I could be by any trumpet that ever sang of fame. It was Homer's requiem; itself an Iliad and Odyssey in the air, singing its own wrath and wanderings. There was something cosmical about it; a standing advertisement, till forbidden, of the everlasting vigor and fertility of the world. The morning, which is the most memorable season of the day, is the awakening hour. Then there is least somnolence in us; and for an hour, at least, some part of us awakes which slumbers all the rest of the day and night. Little is to be expected of that day, if it can be called a day, to which we are not awakened by our Genius, but by the mechanical nudgings of some servitor, are not awakened by our own newly acquired force and aspirations from within, accompanied by the undulations of celestial music, instead of factory bells, and a fragrance filling the air — to a higher life than we fell asleep from; and thus the darkness bear its fruit, and prove itself to be good, no less than the light. That man who does not believe that each day contains an earlier, more sacred, and auroral hour than he has yet profaned, has despaired of life, and is pursuing a descending and darkening way. After a partial cessation of his sensuous life, the soul of man, or its organs rather, are reinvigorated each day, and his Genius tries again what noble life it can make. All memorable events, I should say, transpire in morning time and in a morning atmosphere. The Vedas say, "All intelligences awake with the morning." Poetry and art, and the fairest and most memorable of the actions of men, date from such an hour. All poets and heroes, like Memnon, are the children of Aurora, and emit their music at sunrise. To him whose elastic and vigorous thought keeps pace with the sun, the day is a perpetual morning. It matters not what the clocks say or the attitudes and labors of men. Morning is when I am awake and there is a dawn in me. Moral reform is the effort to throw off sleep. Why is it that men give so poor an account of their day if they have not been slumbering? They are not such poor calculators. If they had not been overcome with drowsiness, they would have performed something. The millions are awake enough for physical labor; but only one in a million is awake enough for effective intellectual exertion, only one in a hundred millions to a poetic or divine life. To be awake is to be alive. I have never yet met a man who was quite awake. How could I have looked him in the face?

5 **Aurora,** Roman goddess of the dawn, corresponding to the Greek Eos   13 **singing . . . wanderings,** the wrath of Achilles in the *Iliad,* the wanderings of Odysseus in the *Odyssey*   29 **Vedas,** the sacred literature of the Hindus   31 **Memnon.** See note, p. 842. His statue made a harplike sound at sunrise

We must learn to reawaken and keep ourselves awake, not by mechanical aids, but by an infinite expectation of the dawn, which does not forsake us in our soundest sleep. I know of no more encouraging fact than the unquestionable ability of man to elevate his life by a conscious endeavor. It is something to be able to paint a particular picture, or to carve a statue, and so to make a few objects beautiful; but it is far more glorious to carve and paint the very atmosphere and medium through which we look, which morally we can do. To affect the quality of the day, that is the highest of arts. Every man is tasked to make his life, even in its details, worthy of the contemplation of his most elevated and critical hour. If we refused, or rather used up, such paltry information as we get, the oracles would distinctly inform us 10 how this might be done.

I went to the woods because I wished to live deliberately, to front only the essential facts of life, and see if I could not learn what it had to teach, and not, when I came to die, discover that I had not lived. I did not wish to live what was not life, living is so dear; nor did I wish to practise resignation, unless it was quite necessary. I wanted to live deep and suck out all the marrow of life, to live so sturdily and Spartan-like as to put to rout all that was not life, to cut a broad swath and shave close, to drive life into a corner, and reduce it to its lowest terms, and, if it proved to be mean, why then to get the whole and genuine meanness of it, and publish its meanness to the world; or if it were sublime, to know it by experience, 20 and be able to give a true account of it in my next excursion. For most men, it appears to me, are in a strange uncertainty about it, whether it is of the devil or of God, and have *somewhat hastily* concluded that it is the chief end of man here to "glorify God and enjoy him forever."

Still we live meanly, like ants; though the fable tells us that we were long ago changed into men; like pygmies we fight with cranes; it is error upon error, and clout upon clout, and our best virtue has for its occasion a superfluous and evitable wretchedness. Our life is frittered away by detail. An honest man has hardly need to count more than his ten fingers, or in extreme cases he may add his ten toes, and lump the rest. Simplicity, simplicity, simplicity! I say, let your affairs be as two or 30 three, and not a hundred or a thousand; instead of a million count half a dozen, and keep your accounts on your thumb-nail. In the midst of this chopping sea of civilized life, such are the clouds and storms and quicksands and thousand-and-one items to be allowed for, that a man has to live, if he would not founder and go to the bottom and not make his port at all, by dead reckoning, and he must be a great calculator indeed who succeeds. Simplify, simplify. Instead of three meals a day, if it be necessary eat but one; instead of a hundred dishes, five; and reduce other things in proportion. Our life is like a German Confederacy, made up of petty states, with

12 I . . . because. This paragraph should be compared with the following equally notable passage in the last chapter of Walden, beginning "I left the woods. . . ." See p. 1219   23 chief . . . forever, an allusion to the Westminster Catechism, formulated by the famous Westminster Assembly in 1643   26 like pygmies . . . cranes. In Greek fable, the pygmies were atacked every Spring by the cranes, who devoured them   35 dead reckoning, the method of finding the position of a ship without the aid of celestial observations, from a record of the courses sailed and the distance made on each course   38 German Confederacy. The German Confederation, set up by the Congress of Vienna in 1815, was loosely formed and inefficient. Modern, unified Germany dates from 1871

its boundary forever fluctuating, so that even a German cannot tell you how it is bounded at any moment. The nation itself, with all its so-called internal improvements, which, by the way, are all external and superficial, is just such an unwieldy and overgrown establishment, cluttered with furniture and tripped up by its own traps, ruined by luxury and heedless expense, by want of calculation and a worthy aim, as the million households in the land; and the only cure for it, as for them, is in a rigid economy, a stern and more than Spartan simplicity of life and elevation of purpose. It lives too fast. Men think that it is essential that the *Nation* have commerce, and export ice, and talk through a telegraph, and ride thirty miles an hour,
10 without a doubt, whether *they* do or not; but whether we should live like baboons or like men, is a little uncertain. If we do not get out sleepers, and forge rails, and devote days and nights to the work, but go to tinkering upon our *lives* to improve *them,* who will build railroads? And if railroads are not built, how shall we get to Heaven in season? But if we stay at home and mind our business, who will want railroads? We do not ride on the railroad; it rides upon us. Did you ever think what those sleepers are that underlie the railroad? Each one is a man, an Irishman, or a Yankee man. The rails are laid on them, and they are covered with sand, and the cars run smoothly over them. They are sound sleepers, I assure you. And every few years a new lot is laid down and run over; so that, if some have the pleasure of rid-
20 ing on a rail, others have the misfortune to be ridden upon. And when they run over a man that is walking in his sleep, a supernumerary sleeper in the wrong position, and wake him up, they suddenly stop the cars, and make a hue and cry about it, as if this were an exception. I am glad to know that it takes a gang of men for every five miles to keep the sleepers down and level in their beds as it is, for this is a sign that they may sometime get up again.

Why should we live with such hurry and waste of life? We are determined to be starved before we are hungry. Men say that a stitch in time saves nine, and so they take a thousand stitches to-day to save nine to-morrow. As for *work,* we haven't any of any consequence. We have the Saint Vitus' dance, and cannot possibly keep our
30 heads still. If I should only give a few pulls at the parish bell-rope, as for a fire, that is, without setting the bell, there is hardly a man on his farm in the outskirts of Concord, notwithstanding that press of engagements which was his excuse so many times this morning, nor a boy, nor a woman, I might almost say, but would forsake all and follow that sound, not mainly to save property from the flames, but, if we will confess the truth, much more to see it burn, since burn it must, and we, be it known, did not set it on fire, — or to see it put out, and have a hand in it, if

---

11 **sleepers,** the British term for railroad ties   13 **railroads . . . Heaven.** Thoreau perhaps remembered Hawthorne's satirical sketch, "The Celestial Railroad" (1843)   15 **We . . . us.** Emerson had expressed the same thought in the "Ode to Channing" (1846): "Things are in the saddle,/ And ride mankind." Despite Thoreau's disapproval of the railroad in theory, trains and trainmen had a romantic appeal for him. In the chapter "Sounds" in *Walden,* he wrote: "On this morning of the great Snow, . . . I hear the muffled tone of their engine bell from out the fog bank of their chilled breath, which announces that the cars *are coming,* without long delay, notwithstanding the veto of a New England northeast snow-storm, and I behold the plowmen covered with snow and rime, their heads peering above the mould-board . . . I am refreshed and expanded when the freight train rattles past me, and I smell the stores which go dispensing their odors all the way from Long Wharf to Lake Champlain . . ."

that is done as handsomely; yes, even if it were the parish church itself. Hardly a man takes a half-hour's nap after dinner, but when he wakes he holds up his head and asks, "What's the news?" as if the rest of mankind had stood his sentinels. Some give directions to be waked every half-hour, doubtless for no other purpose; and then, to pay for it, they tell what they have dreamed. After a night's sleep the news is as indispensable as the breakfast. "Pray tell me anything new that has happened to a man anywhere on this globe," — and he reads it over his coffee and rolls, that a man has had his eyes gouged out this morning on the Wachito River; never dreaming the while that he lives in the dark unfathomed mammoth cave of this world, and has but the rudiment of an eye himself.   10

For my part, I could easily do without the post-office. I think that there are very few important communications made through it. To speak critically, I never received more than one or two letters in my life — I wrote this some years ago — that were worth the postage. The penny-post is, commonly, an institution through which you seriously offer a man that penny for his thoughts which is so often safely offered in jest. And I am sure that I never read any memorable news in a newspaper. If we read of one man robbed, or murdered, or killed by accident, or one house burned, or one vessel wrecked, or one steamboat blown up, or one cow run over on the Western Railroad, or one mad dog killed, or one lot of grasshoppers in the winter, — we never need read of another. One is enough. If you are acquainted with 20 the principle, what do you care for a myriad instances and applications? To a philosopher all *news,* as it is called, is gossip, and they who edit and read it are old women over their tea. Yet not a few are greedy after this gossip. There was such a rush, as I hear, the other day at one of the offices to learn the foreign news by the last arrival, that several large squares of plate glass belonging to the establishment were broken by the pressure, — news which I seriously think a ready wit might write a twelve month, or twelve years, beforehand with sufficient accuracy. As for Spain, for instance, if you know how to throw in Don Carlos and the Infanta, and Don Pedro and Seville and Granada, from time to time in the right proportions, — they may have changed the names a little since I saw the papers, — and serve up a 30 bull-fight when other entertainments fail, it will be true to the letter, and give us as good an idea of the exact state or ruin of things in Spain as the most succinct and lucid reports under this head in the newspapers: and as for England, almost the last significant scrap of news from that quarter was the revolution of 1649; and if you have learned the history of her crops for an average year, you never need attend to that thing again, unless your speculations are of a merely pecuniary character. If one may judge who rarely looks into the newspapers, nothing new does ever happen in foreign parts, a French revolution not excepted.

---

8 **Wachito River,** Ouachita River in Arkansas, at that time a frontier region. A. B. Longstreet's "The Fight" in *Georgia Scenes* (1835) gives some notion of the brutality of the frontier in the old Southwest   9 **dark** . . . **cave,** a double allusion to the Mammoth Cave of Kentucky and "The dark unfathomed caves" of Gray's elegy   34 **revolution of 1649,** the English Civil War, which resulted in the victory of Cromwell and the execution of Charles I in 1649. The statement seems to show marked Puritan and democratic (or anti-royalist) sympathies   38 **French revolution.** Since the great revolution of 1789, there had been frequent changes in the French government, the latest having been the revolution of 1848 and the coup d'etat of 1851

What news! how much more important to know what that is which was never old! "Kieou-he-yu (great dignitary of the state of Wei) sent a man to Khoung-tseu to know his news. Khoung-tseu caused the messenger to be seated near him, and questioned him in these terms: What is your master doing? The messenger answered with respect: My master desires to diminish the number of his faults, but he cannot come to the end of them. The messenger being gone, the philosopher remarked: What a worthy messenger! What a worthy messenger!" The preacher, instead of vexing the ears of drowsy farmers on their day of rest at the end of the week, — for Sunday is the fit conclusion of an ill-spent week, and not the fresh and brave begin-
10 ning of a new one, — with this one other draggle-tail of a sermon, should shout with thundering voice, "Pause! Avast! Why so seeming fast, but deadly slow?"

Shams and delusions are esteemed for soundest truths, while reality is fabulous. If men would steadily observe realities only, and not allow themselves to be deluded, life, to compare it with such things as we know, would be like a fairy tale and the Arabian Nights' Entertainments. If we respected only what is inevitable and has a right to be, music and poetry would resound along the streets. When we are unhurried and wise, we perceive that only great and worthy things have any permanent and absolute existence, that petty fears and petty pleasures are but the shadow of the reality. This is always exhilarating and sublime. By closing the eyes and slum-
20 bering, and consenting to be deceived by shows, men establish and confirm their daily life of routine and habit everywhere, which still is built on purely illusory foundations. Children, who play life, discern its true law and relations more clearly than men, who fail to live it worthily, but who think that they are wiser by experience, that is, by failure. I have read in a Hindoo book, that "there was a king's son, who, being expelled in infancy from his native city, was brought up by a forester, and, growing up to maturity in that state, imagined himself to belong to the barbarous race with which he lived. One of his father's ministers having discovered him, revealed to him what he was, and the misconception of his character was removed, and he knew himself to be a prince. So soul," continues the Hindoo phi-
30 losopher, "from the circumstances in which it is placed, mistakes its own character, until the truth is revealed to it by some holy teacher, and then it knows itself to be *Brahme.*" I perceive that we inhabitants of New England live this mean life that we do because our vision does not penetrate the surface of things. We think that that *is* which *appears* to be. If a man should walk through this town and see only the reality, where, think you, would the "Mill-dam" go to? If he should give us an account of the realities he beheld there, we should not recognize the place in his description. Look at a meeting-house, or a court-house, or a jail, or a shop, or a dwelling-house, and say what that thing really is before a true gaze, and they would all go to pieces in your account of them. Men esteem truth remote, in the outskirts of the
40 system behind the farthest star, before Adam and after the last man. In eternity there is indeed something true and sublime. But all these times and places and occasions are now and here. God himself culminates in the present moment, and will never

---

2 **Kieou-he-yu** . . . **messenger,** from the Analects of Confucius   32 **Brahme,** compare Emerson's "Brahma" and the introductory note for that poem, p. 1161

be more divine in the lapse of all the ages. And we are enabled to apprehend at all
what is sublime and noble only by the perpetual instilling and drenching of the
reality that surrounds us. The universe constantly and obediently answers to our
conceptions; whether we travel fast or slow, the track is laid for us. Let us spend
our lives in conceiving then. The poet or the artist never yet had so fair and noble
a design but some of his posterity at least could accomplish it.

Let us spend one day as deliberately as Nature, and not be thrown off the track
by every nutshell and mosquito's wing that falls on the rails. Let us rise early and
fast, or break fast, gently and without perturbation; let company come and let company go, let the bells ring and the children cry, — determined to make a day of it.   10
Why should we knock under and go with the stream? Let us not be upset and overwhelmed in that terrible rapid and whirlpool called a dinner, situated in the meridian
shallows. Weather this danger and you are safe, for the rest of the way is down hill.
With unrelaxed nerves, with morning vigor, sail by it, looking another way, tied
to the mast like Ulysses. If the engine whistles, let it whistle till it is hoarse for its
pains. If the bell rings, why should we run? We will consider what kind of music
they are like. Let us settle ourselves, and work and wedge our feet downward
through the mud and slush of opinion, and prejudice, and tradition, and delusion,
and appearance, that alluvion which covers the globe, through Paris and London,
through New York and Boston and Concord, through Church and State, through   20
poetry and philosophy and religion, till we come to a hard bottom and rocks in
place, which we can call *reality,* and say, This is, and no mistake; and then begin,
having a *point d'appui,* below freshet and frost and fire, a place where you might
found a wall or a state, or set a lamp-post safely, or perhaps a gauge, not a Nilometer,
but Realometer, that future ages might know how deep a freshet of shams and appearances had gathered from time to time. If you stand right fronting and face to
face to a fact, you will see the sun glimmer on both its surfaces, as if it were
a cimeter, and feel its sweet edge dividing you through the heart and marrow, and
so you will happily conclude your mortal career. Be it life or death, we crave only
reality. If we are really dying, let us hear the rattle in our throats and feel cold in   30
the extremities; if we are alive, let us go about our business.

Time is but the stream I go a-fishing in. I drink at it; but while I drink I see the
sandy bottom and detect how shallow it is. Its thin current slides away, but eternity
remains. I would drink deeper; fish in the sky, whose bottom is pebbly with stars.
I cannot count one. I know not the first letter of the alphabet. I have always been
regretting that I was not as wise as the day I was born. The intellect is a cleaver; it
discerns and rifts its way into the secret of things. I do not wish to be any more
busy with my hands than is necessary. My head is hands and feet. I feel all my best
faculties concentrated in it. My instinct tells me that my head is an organ for burrowing, as some creatures use their snout and fore paws, and with it I would mine   40
and burrow my way through these hills. I think that the richest vein is somewhere

---

15 **Ulysses,** so tied as a defense against the song of the Sirens, in Bk. XII of the *Odyssey*   23 **point d'appui,**
a basis of operations   24 **Nilometer,** an instrument for measuring the height of water in the Nile during
the flood   28 **cimeter,** scimitar

hereabouts; so by the divining-rod and thin rising vapors I judge; and here I will
begin to mine.   1854

Higher Laws

    As I came home through the woods with my string of fish, trailing my pole, it
being now quite dark, I caught a glimpse of a woodchuck stealing across my path,
and felt a strange thrill of savage delight, and was strongly tempted to seize and
devour him raw; not that I was hungry then, except for that wildness which he
represented. Once or twice, however, while I lived at the pond, I found myself ranging the woods, like a half-starved hound, with a strange abandonment, seeking
10 some kind of venison which I might devour, and no morsel could have been too
savage for me. The wildest scenes had become unaccountably familiar. I found in
myself, and still find, an instinct toward a higher, or, as it is named, spiritual life,
as do most men, and another toward a primitive rank and savage one, and I reverence them both. I love the wild not less than the good. The wildness and adventure
that are in fishing still recommended it to me. I like sometimes to take rank hold
on life and spend my day more as the animals do. Perhaps I have owed to this employment and to hunting, when quite young, my closest acquaintance with Nature.
They early introduce us to and detain us in scenery with which otherwise, at that
age, we should have little acquaintance. Fishermen, hunters, wood-choppers, and
20 others, spending their lives in the fields and woods, in a peculiar sense a part of
Nature themselves, are often in a more favorable mood for observing her, in the
intervals of their pursuits, than philosophers or poets even, who approach her with
expectation. She is not afraid to exhibit herself to them. The traveller on the prairie
is naturally a hunter, on the head waters of the Missouri and Columbia a trapper,
and at the Falls of St. Mary a fisherman. He who is only a traveller learns things at
second-hand and by the halves, and is poor authority. We are most interested when
science reports what those men already know practically or instinctively, for that
alone is a true *humanity,* or account of human experience.
    They mistake who assert that the Yankee has few amusements, because he has
30 not so many public holidays, and men and boys do not play so many games as they
do in England, for here the more primitive but solitary amusements of hunting,
fishing, and the like have not yet given place to the former. Almost every New
England boy among my contemporaries shouldered a fowling-piece between the
ages of ten and fourteen; and his hunting and fishing grounds were not limited, like
the preserves of an English nobleman, but were more boundless even than those of a
savage. No wonder, then, that he did not oftener stay to play on the common. But
already a change is taking place, owing, not to an increased humanity, but to an
increased scarcity of game, for perhaps the hunter is the greatest friend of the animals hunted, not excepting the Humane Society.
40   Moreover, when at the pond, I wished sometimes to add fish to my fare for
variety. I have actually fished from the same kind of necessity that the first fishers

did. Whatever humanity I might conjure up against it was all factitious, and concerned my philosophy more than my feelings. I speak of fishing only now, for I
had long felt differently about fowling, and sold my gun before I went to the woods.
Not that I am less humane than others, but I did not perceive that my feelings
were much affected. I did not pity the fishes nor the worms. This was habit. As for
fowling, during the last years that I carried a gun my excuse was that I was studying
ornithology, and sought only new or rare birds. But I confess that I am now inclined
to think that there is a finer way of studying ornithology than this. It requires so
much closer attention to the habits of the birds, that, if for that reason only, I have
been willing to omit the gun. Yet notwithstanding the objection on the score of 10
humanity, I am compelled to doubt if equally valuable sports are ever substituted
for these; and when some of my friends have asked me anxiously about their boys,
whether they should let them hunt, I have answered, yes, — remembering that it
was one of the best parts of my education, — *make* them hunters, though sportsmen
only at first, if possible, mighty hunters at last, so that they shall not find game
large enough for them in this or any vegetable wilderness, — hunters as well
as fishers of men. Thus far I am of the opinion of Chaucer's nun, who

> "yave not of the text a pulled hen
> That saith that hunters ben not holy men."

There is a period in the history of the individual, as of the race, when the hunters are 20
the "best men," as the Algonquins called them. We cannot but pity the boy who
has never fired a gun; he is no more humane, while his education has been sadly
neglected. This was my answer with respect to those youths who were bent on this
pursuit, trusting that they would soon outgrow it. No humane being, past the
thoughtless age of boyhood, will wantonly murder any creature which holds its life
by the same tenure that he does. The hare in its extremity cries like a child. I warn
you, mothers, that my sympathies do not always make the usual *philanthropic*
distinctions.
     Such is oftenest the young man's introduction to the forest, and the most original
part of himself. He goes thither at first as a hunter and fisher, until at last, if he has 30
the seeds of a better life in him, he distinguishes his proper objects, as a poet or
naturalist it may be, and leaves the gun and fish-pole behind. The mass of men are
still and always young in this respect. In some countries a hunting parson is no
uncommon sight. Such a one might make a good shepherd's dog, but is far from
being the Good Shepherd. I have been surprised to consider that the only obvious
employment, except wood-chopping, ice-cutting, or the like business, which ever to
my knowledge detained at Walden Pond for a whole half-day any of my fellow-
citizens, whether fathers or children of the town, with just one exception, was fishing. Commonly they did not think that they were lucky, or well paid for their time,
unless they got a long string of fish, though they had the opportunity of seeing the 40
pond all the while. They might go there a thousand times before the sediment of

---

17 **Chaucer's nun.** The lines from the Prologue to Chaucer's *Canterbury Tales* describe not the Nun but the
Monk

fishing would sink to the bottom and leave their purpose pure; but no doubt such a clarifying process would be going on all the while. The Governor and his Council faintly remember the pond, for they went a-fishing there when they were boys; but now they are too old and dignified to go a-fishing, and so they know it no more forever. Yet even they expect to go to heaven at last. If the legislature regards it, it is chiefly to regulate the number of hooks to be used there; but they know nothing about the hook of hooks with which to angle for the pond itself, impaling the legislature for a bait. Thus, even in civilized communities, the embryo man passes through the hunter stage of development.

10 I have found repeatedly, of late years, that I cannot fish without falling a little in self-respect. I have tried it again and again. I have skill at it, and, like many of my fellows, a certain instinct for it, which revives from time to time, but always when I have done I feel that it would have been better if I had not fished. I think that I do not mistake. It is a faint intimation, yet so are the first streaks of morning. There is unquestionably this instinct in me which belongs to the lower orders of creation; yet with every year I am less a fisherman, though without more humanity or even wisdom; at present I am no fisherman at all. But I see that if I were to live in a wilderness I should again be tempted to become a fisher and hunter in earnest. Beside, there is something essentially unclean about this diet and all flesh, and I began 20 to see where housework commences, and whence the endeavor, which costs so much, to wear a tidy and respectable appearance each day, to keep the house sweet and free from all ill odors and sights. Having been my own butcher and scullion and cook, as well as the gentleman for whom the dishes were served up, I can speak from an unusually complete experience. The practical objection to animal food in my case was its uncleanness; and besides, when I had caught and cleaned and cooked and eaten my fish, they seemed not to have fed me essentially. It was insignificant and unnecessary, and cost more than it came to. A little bread or a few potatoes would have done as well, with less trouble and filth. Like many of my contemporaries, I had rarely for many years used animal food, or tea, or coffee, etc.; not so much be-30 cause of any ill effects which I had traced to them, as because they were not agreeable to my imagination. The repugnance to animal food is not the effect of experience, but is an instinct. It appeared more beautiful to live low and fare hard in many respects; and though I never did so, I went far enough to please my imagination. I believe that every man who has ever been earnest to preserve his higher or poetic faculties in the best condition has been particularly inclined to abstain from animal food, and from much food of any kind. It is a significant fact, stated by entomologists, — I find it in Kirby and Spence, — that "some insects in their perfect state, though furnished with organs of feeding, make no use of them;" and they lay it down as "a general rule, that almost all insects in this state eat much 40 less than in that of larvæ. The voracious caterpillar when transformed into a butterfly . . . and the gluttonous maggot when become a fly" content themselves with

---

37 **Kirby and Spence.** William Kirby (1759-1850), English clergyman and entomologist, and William Spence (1787-1860) wrote the four-volume *An Introduction to Entomology* (1815-1826), the standard work of its time

a drop or two of honey or some other sweet liquid. The abdomen under the wings of the butterfly still represents the larva. This is the tidbit which tempts his insectivorous fate. The gross feeder is a man in the larva state; and there are whole nations in that condition, nations without fancy or imagination, whose vast abdomens betray them.

It is hard to provide and cook so simple and clean a diet as will not offend the imagination; but this, I think, is to be fed when we feed the body; they should both sit down at the same table. Yet perhaps this may be done. The fruits eaten temperately need not make us ashamed of our appetites, nor interrupt the worthiest pursuits. But put an extra condiment into your dish, and it will poison you. It is 10 not worth the while to live by rich cookery. Most men would feel shame if caught preparing with their own hands precisely such a dinner, whether of animal or vegetable food, as is every day prepared for them by others. Yet till this is otherwise we are not civilized, and, if gentlemen and ladies, are not true men and women. This certainly suggests what change is to be made. It may be vain to ask why the imagination will not be reconciled to flesh and fat. I am satisfied that it is not. Is it not a reproach that man is a carnivorous animal? True, he can and does live, in a great measure, by preying on other animals; but this is a miserable way, — as any one who will go to snaring rabbits, or slaughtering lambs, may learn, — and he will be regarded as a benefactor of his race who shall teach man to confine himself to a 20 more innocent and wholesome diet. Whatever my own practice may be, I have no doubt that it is a part of the destiny of the human race, in its gradual improvement, to leave off eating animals, as surely as the savage tribes have left off eating each other when they came in contact with the more civilized.

If one listens to the faintest but constant suggestions of his genius, which are certainly true, he sees not to what extremes, or even insanity, it may lead him; and yet that way, as he grows more resolute and faithful, his road lies. The faintest assured objection which one healthy man feels will at length prevail over the arguments and customs of mankind. No man ever followed his genius till it misled him. Though the result were bodily weakness, yet perhaps no one can say that the con- 30 sequences were to be regretted, for these were a life in conformity to higher principles. If the day and the night are such that you greet them with joy, and life emits a fragrance like flowers and sweet-scented herbs, is more elastic, more starry, more immortal, — that is your success. All nature is your congratulation, and you have cause momentarily to bless yourself. The greatest gains and values are farthest from being appreciated. We easily come to doubt if they exist. We soon forget them. They are the highest reality. Perhaps the facts most astounding and most real are never communicated by man to man. The true harvest of my daily life is somewhat as intangible and indescribable as the tints of morning or evening. It is a little stardust caught, a segment of the rainbow which I have clutched. 40

Yet, for my part, I was never unusually squeamish; I could sometimes eat a fried rat with a good relish, if it were necessary. I am glad to have drunk water so long, for the same reason that I prefer the natural sky to an opium-eater's heaven. I would fain keep sober always; and there are infinite degrees of drunkenness. I believe that water is the only drink for a wise man; wine is not so noble a liquor; and think of dashing the hopes of a morning with a cup of warm coffee, or of an evening with a dish of tea! Ah, how low I fall when I am tempted by them! Even music may be intoxicating. Such apparently slight causes destroyed Greece and Rome, and will destroy England and America. Of all ebriosity, who does not prefer to be intoxicated by the air he breathes? I have found it to be the most serious objection to coarse labors long continued, that they compelled me to eat and drink coarsely also. But to tell the truth, I find myself at present somewhat less particular in these respects. I carry less religion to the table, ask no blessing; not because I am wiser than I was,

10 but, I am obliged to confess, because, however much it is to be regretted, with years I have grown more coarse and indifferent. Perhaps these questions are entertained only in youth, as most believe of poetry. My practice is "nowhere," my opinion is here. Nevertheless I am far from regarding myself as one of those privileged ones to whom the Ved refers when it says, that "he who has true faith in the Omnipresent Supreme Being may eat all that exists," that is, is not bound to inquire what is his food, or who prepares it; and even in their case it is to be observed, as a Hindoo commentator has remarked, that the Vedant limits this privilege to "the time of distress."

Who has not sometimes derived an inexpressible satisfaction from his food in
20 which appetite had no share? I have been thrilled to think that I owed a mental perception to the commonly gross sense of taste, that I have been inspired through the palate, that some berries which I had eaten on a hillside had fed my genius. "The soul not being mistress of herself," says Thseng-tseu, "one looks, and one does not see; one listens, and one does not hear; one eats, and one does not know the savor of food." He who distinguishes the true savor of his food can never be a glutton; he who does not cannot be otherwise. A puritan may go to his brown-bread crust with as gross an appetite as ever an alderman to his turtle. Not that food which entereth into the mouth defileth a man, but the appetite with which it is eaten. It is neither the quality nor the quantity, but the devotion to sensual savors;
30 when that which is eaten is not a viand to sustain our animal, or inspire our spiritual life, but food for the worms that possess us. If the hunter has a taste for mud-turtles, muskrats, and other such savage tidbits, the fine lady indulges a taste for jelly made of a calf's foot, or for sardines from over the sea, and they are even. He goes to the mill-pond, she to her preserve-pot. The wonder is how they, how you and I, can live this slimy, beastly life, eating and drinking.

Our whole life is startlingly moral. There is never an instant's truce between virtue and vice. Goodness is the only investment that never fails. In the music of the harp which trembles round the world it is the insisting on this which thrills us. The harp is the travelling patterer for the Universe's Insurance Company, recom-
40 mending its laws, and our little goodness is all the assessment that we pay. Though

---

14 **Ved**, Veda. See note, p. 1197   23 **Thseng-tseu,** Chuang-tze, a Chinese philosopher of the fourth century B.C.   31 **worms.** The Linnaean classification Vermes, including worms and all other invertebrates except arthropods, was in use through most of the nineteenth century. Despite terminological change, it is still true that the body holds many protozoans as commensals

the youth at last grows indifferent, the laws of the universe are not indifferent, but are forever on the side of the most sensitive. Listen to every zephyr for some reproof, for it is surely there, and he is unfortunate who does not hear it. We cannot touch a string or move a stop but the charming moral transfixes us. Many an irksome noise, go a long way off, is heard as music, a proud, sweet satire on the meanness of our lives.

We are conscious of an animal in us, which awakens in proportion as our higher nature slumbers. It is reptile and sensual, and perhaps cannot be wholly expelled; like the worms which, even in life and health, occupy our bodies. Possibly we may withdraw from it, but never change its nature. I fear that it may enjoy a certain 10 health of its own; that we may be well, yet not pure. The other day I picked up the lower jaw of a hog, with white and sound teeth and tusks, which suggested that there was an animal health and vigor distinct from the spiritual. This creature succeeded by other means than temperance and purity. "That in which men differ from brute beasts," says Mencius, "is a thing very inconsiderable; the common herd lose it very soon; superior men preserve it carefully." Who knows what sort of life would result if we had attained to purity? If I knew so wise a man as could teach me purity I would go to seek him forthwith. "A command over our passions, and over the external senses of the body, and good acts, are declared by the Ved to be indispensable in the mind's approximation to God." Yet the spirit can for the time 20 pervade and control every member and function of the body, and transmute what in form is the grossest sensuality into purity and devotion. The generative energy, which, when we are loose, dissipates and makes us unclean, when we are continent invigorates and inspires us. Chastity is the flowering of man; and what are called Genius, Heroism, Holiness, and the like, are but various fruits which succeed it. Man flows at once to God when the channel of purity is open. By turns our purity inspires and our impurity casts us down. He is blessed who is assured that the animal is dying out in him day by day, and the divine being established. Perhaps there is none but has cause for shame on account of the inferior and brutish nature to which he is allied. I fear that we are such gods or demigods only as fauns and satyrs, 30 the divine allied to beasts, the creatures of appetite, and that, to some extent, our very life is our disgrace. —

> "How happy's he who hath due place assigned
> To his beasts and disafforested his mind!
> .   .   .   .
> Can use his horse, goat, wolf, and ev'ry beast,
> And is not ass himself to all the rest!
> Else man not only is the herd of swine,
> But he's those devils too which did incline
> Them to a headlong rage, and made them worse."

---

15 **Mencius** (371?-288? B.C.), Chinese sage   33 **How . . . worse,** John Donne's "Letter to Sir Edward Herbert at Iulyers," ll. 9-10, 13-17

All sensuality is one, though it takes many forms; all purity is one. It is the same whether a man eat, or drink, or cohabit, or sleep sensually. They are but one appetite, and we only need to see a person do any one of these things to know how great a sensualist he is. The impure can neither stand nor sit with purity. When the reptile is attacked at one mouth of his burrow, he shows himself at another. If you would be chaste, you must be temperate. What is chastity? How shall a man know if he is chaste? He shall not know it. We have heard of this virtue, but we know not what it is. We speak conformably to the rumor which we have heard. From exertion come wisdom and purity; from sloth ignorance and sensuality. In the stu-
10 dent sensuality is a sluggish habit of mind. An unclean person is universally a slothful one, one who sits by a stove, whom the sun shines on prostrate, who reposes without being fatigued. If you would avoid uncleanness, and all the sins, work earnestly, though it be at cleaning a stable. Nature is hard to be overcome, but she must be overcome. What avails it that you are Christian, if you are not purer than the heathen, if you deny yourself no more, if you are not more religious? I know of many systems of religion esteemed heathenish whose precepts fill the reader with shame, and provoke him to new endeavors, though it be to the performance of rites merely.

I hesitate to say these things, but it is not because of the subject, — I care not
20 how obscene my *words* are, — but because I cannot speak of them without betraying my impurity. We discourse freely without shame of one form of sensuality, and are silent about another. We are so degraded that we cannot speak simply of the necessary functions of human nature. In earlier ages, in some countries, every function was reverently spoken of and regulated by law. Nothing was too trivial for the Hindoo lawgiver, however offensive it may be to modern taste. He teaches how to eat, drink, cohabit, void excrement and urine and the like, elevating what is mean, and does not falsely excuse himself by calling these things trifles.

Every man is the builder of a temple, called his body, to the god he worships, after a style purely his own, nor can he get off by hammering marble instead. We
30 are all sculptors and painters, and our material is our own flesh and blood and bones. Any nobleness begins at once to refine a man's features, any meanness or sensuality to imbrute them.

John Farmer sat at his door one September evening, after a hard day's work, his mind still running on his labor more or less. Having bathed, he sat down to recreate his intellectual man. It was a rather cool evening, and some of his neighbors were apprehending a frost. He had not attended to the train of his thoughts long when he heard some one playing on a flute, and that sound harmonized with his mood. Still he thought of his work; but the burden of his thought was, that though this kept running in his head, and he found himself planning and contriving
40 it against his will, yet it concerned him very little. It was no more than the scurf of his skin, which was constantly shuffled off. But the notes of the flute came home to his ears out of a different sphere from that he worked in, and suggested work for certain faculties which slumbered in him. They gently did away with the street, and the village, and the state in which he lived. A voice said to him, Why do you stay

here and live this mean moiling life, when a glorious existence is possible for you? Those same stars twinkle over other fields than these. — But how to come out of this condition and actually migrate thither? All that he could think of was to practice some new austerity, to let his mind descend into his body and redeem it, and treat himself with ever increasing respect.

Brute Neighbors

Sometimes I had a companion in my fishing, who came through the village to my house from the other side of the town, and the catching of the dinner was as much a social exercise as the eating of it.

Hermit. I wonder what the world is doing now. I have not heard so much as a locust over the sweet-fern these three hours. The pigeons are all asleep upon their 10 roosts, — no flutter from them. Was that a farmer's noon horn which sounded from beyond the woods just now? The hands are coming in to boiled salt beef and cider and Indian bread. Why will men worry themselves so? He that does not eat need not work. I wonder how much they have reaped. Who would live there where a body can never think for the barking of Bose? And oh, the housekeeping! to keep bright the devil's door-knobs, and scour his tubs this bright day! Better not keep a house. Say, some hollow tree; and then for morning calls and dinner-parties! Only a woodpecker tapping. Oh, they swarm; the sun is too warm there; they are born too far into life for me. I have water from the spring, and a loaf of brown bread on the shelf. — Hark! I hear a rustling of the leaves. Is it some ill-fed village hound 20 yielding to the instinct of the chase? or the lost pig which is said to be in these woods, whose tracks I saw after the rain? It comes on apace; my sumachs and sweet-briers tremble. — Eh, Mr. Poet, is it you? How do you like the world to-day?

Poet. See those clouds; how they hang! That's the greatest thing I have seen to-day. There's nothing like it in old paintings, nothing like it in foreign lands, — unless when we were off the coast of Spain. That's a true Mediterranean sky. I thought, as I have my living to get, and have not eaten to-day, that I might go a-fishing. That's the true industry for poets. It is the only trade I have learned. Come, let's along.

Hermit. I cannot resist. My brown bread will soon be gone. I will go with you 30 gladly soon, but I am just concluding a serious meditation. I think that I am near the end of it. Leave me alone, then, for a while. But that we may not be delayed, you shall be digging the bait meanwhile. Angleworms are rarely to be met with in these parts, where the soil was never fattened with manure; the race is nearly extinct. The sport of digging the bait is nearly equal to that of catching the fish, when one's appetite is not too keen; and this you may have all to yourself to-day. I would advise you to set in the spade down yonder among the ground-nuts, where you see the johnswort waving. I think that I may warrant you one worm to every three sods you turn up, if you look well in among the roots of the grass, as if you were

weeding. Or, if you choose to go farther, it will not be unwise, for I have found
the increase of fair bait to be very nearly as the squares of the distances.

Hermit alone. Let me see; where was I? Methinks I was nearly in this frame of
mind; the world lay about at this angle. Shall I go to heaven or a-fishing? If I should
soon bring this meditation to an end, would another so sweet occasion be likely to
offer? I was as near being resolved into the essence of things as ever I was in my
life. I fear my thoughts will not come back to me. If it would do any good, I would
whistle for them. When they make us an offer, is it wise to say, We will think of
it? My thoughts have left no track, and I cannot find the path again. What was it
10 that I was thinking of? It was a very hazy day. I will just try these three sentences
of Confutsee; they may fetch that state about again. I know not whether it was the
dumps or a budding ecstasy. Mem. There never is but one opportunity of a kind.

Poet. How now, Hermit, is it too soon? I have got just thirteen whole ones, beside several which are imperfect or undersized; but they will do for the smaller fry;
they do not cover up the hook so much. Those village worms are quite too large;
a shiner may make a meal off one without finding the skewer.

Hermit. Well, then, let's be off. Shall we to the Concord? There's good sport there if
the water be not too high.

Why do precisely these objects which we behold make a world? Why has man
20 just these species of animals for his neighbors; as if nothing but a mouse could have
filled this crevice? I suspect that Pilpay & Co. have put animals to their best use, for
they are all beasts of burden, in a sense, made to carry some portion of our thoughts.

The mice which haunted my house were not the common ones, which are said
to have been introduced into the country, but a wild native kind not found in the
village. I sent one to a distinguished naturalist, and it interested him much. When
I was building, one of these had its nest underneath the house, and before I had
laid the second floor, and swept out the shavings, would come out regularly at lunch
time and pick up the crumbs at my feet. It probably had never seen a man before;
and it soon became quite familiar, and would run over my shoes and up my clothes.
30 It could readily ascend the sides of the room by short impulses, like a squirrel, which
it resembled in its motions. At length, as I leaned with my elbow on the bench one
day, it ran up my clothes, and along my sleeve, and round and round the paper
which held my dinner, while I kept the latter close, and dodged and played at bo-
peep with it; and when at last I held still a piece of cheese between my thumb and
finger, it came and nibbled it, sitting in my hand, and afterward cleaned its face and
paws, like a fly, and walked away.

A phœbe soon built in my shed, and a robin for protection in a pine which grew
against the house. In June the partridge (*Tetrao umbellus*), which is so shy a bird,
led her brood past my windows, from the woods in the rear to the front of my house,
40 clucking and calling to them like a hen, and in all her behavior proving herself the

---

11 **Confutsee,** Confucius   12 **Mem.,** abbreviation of Latin memorandum, something to be remembered   21 **Pilpay & Co.** Pilpay or Bidpay, who in the eighth century wrote *Kalilah and Dininah,*
an Arabic version of the Sanskrit animal fables *Panchatantra,* and other fabulists   38 (**Tetrao umbellus**),
the ruffed grouse

hen of the woods. The young suddenly disperse on your approach, at a signal from the mother, as if a whirlwind had swept them away, and they so exactly resemble the dried leaves and twigs that many a traveller has placed his foot in the midst of a brood, and heard the whir of the old bird as she flew off, and her anxious calls and mewing, or seen her trail her wings to attract his attention, without suspecting their neighborhood. The parent will sometimes roll and spin round before you in such a dishabille, that you cannot, for a few moments, detect what kind of creature it is. The young squat still and flat, often running their heads under a leaf, and mind only their mother's directions given from a distance, nor will your approach make them run again and betray themselves. You may even tread on them, or have your   10 eyes on them for a minute, without discovering them. I have held them in my open hand at such a time, and still their only care, obedient to their mother and their instinct, was to squat there without fear or trembling. So perfect is this instinct, that once, when I had laid them on the leaves again, and one accidentally fell on its side, it was found with the rest in exactly the same position ten minutes afterward. They are not callow like the young of most birds, but more perfectly developed and precocious even than chickens. The remarkably adult yet innocent expression of their open and serene eyes is very memorable. All intelligence seems reflected in them. They suggest not merely the purity of infancy, but a wisdom clarified by experience. Such an eye was not born when the bird was, but is coeval with the sky it   20 reflects. The woods do not yield another such a gem. The traveller does not often look into such a limpid well. The ignorant or reckless sportsman often shoots the parent at such a time, and leaves these innocents to fall a prey to some prowling beast or bird, or gradually mingle with the decaying leaves which they so much resemble. It is said that when hatched by a hen they will directly disperse on some alarm, and so are lost, for they never hear the mother's call which gathers them again. These were my hens and chickens.

It is remarkable how many creatures live wild and free though secret in the woods, and still sustain themselves in the neighborhood of towns, suspected by hunters only. How retired the otter manages to live here! He grows to be four feet long, as big   30 as a small boy, perhaps without any human being getting a glimpse of him. I formerly saw the raccoon in the woods behind where my house is built, and probably still heard their whinnering at night. Commonly I rested an hour or two in the shade at noon, after planting, and ate my lunch, and read a little by a spring which was the source of a swamp and of a brook, oozing from under Brister's Hill, half a mile from my field. The approach to this was through a succession of descending grassy hollows, full of young pitch pines, into a larger wood about the swamp. There, in a very secluded and shaded spot, under a spreading white pine, there was yet a clean, firm sward to sit on. I had dug out the spring and made a well of clear gray water, where I could dip up a pailful without roiling it, and thither I went for this   40 purpose almost every day in midsummer, when the pond was warmest. Thither, too, the woodcock led her brood, to probe the mud for worms, flying but a foot above them down the bank, while they ran in a troop beneath; but at last, spying me, she would leave her young and circle round and round me, nearer and nearer

till within four or five feet, pretending broken wings and legs, to attract my attention, and get off her young, who would already have taken up their march, with faint,
wiry peep, single file through the swamp, as she directed. Or I heard the peep of
the young when I could not see the parent bird. There too the turtle doves sat over
the spring, or fluttered from bough to bough of the soft white pines over my head;
or the red squirrel, coursing down the nearest bough, was particularly familiar and
inquisitive. You only need sit still long enough in some attractive spot in the woods
that all its inhabitants may exhibit themselves to you by turns.

    I was witness to events of a less peaceful character. One day when I went out to
10 my wood-pile, or rather my pile of stumps, I observed two large ants, the one red,
the other much larger, nearly half an inch long, and black, fiercely contending with
one another. Having once got hold they never let go, but struggled and wrestled
and rolled on the chips incessantly. Looking farther, I was surprised to find that the
chips were covered with such combatants, that it was not a *duellum,* but a *bellum,* a
war between two races of ants, the red always pitted against the black, and frequently
two red ones to one black. The legions of these Myrmidons covered all the hills and
vales in my wood-yard, and the ground was already strewn with the dead and dying,
both red and black. It was the only battle which I have ever witnessed, the only
battle-field I ever trod while the battle was raging; internecine war; the red repub-
20 licans on the one hand, and the black imperialists on the other. On every side they
were engaged in deadly combat, yet without any noise that I could hear, and human soldiers never fought so resolutely. I watched a couple that were fast locked in
each other's embraces, in a little sunny valley amid the chips, now at noonday prepared to fight till the sun went down, or life went out. The smaller red champion
had fastened himself like a vise to his adversary's front, and through all the tum-
blings on that field never for an instant ceased to gnaw at one of his feelers near
the root, having already caused the other to go by the board; while the stronger
black one dashed him from side to side, and, as I saw on looking nearer, had already divested him of several of his members. They fought with more pertinacity
30 than bulldogs. Neither manifested the least disposition to retreat. It was evident
that their battle-cry was "Conquer or die." In the meanwhile there came along a
single red ant on the hillside of this valley, evidently full of excitement, who either
had despatched his foe, or had not yet taken part in the battle; probably the latter,
for he had lost none of his limbs; whose mother had charged him to return with
his shield or upon it. Or perchance he was some Achilles, who had nourished his
wrath apart, and had now come to avenge or rescue his Patroclus. He saw this unequal combat from afar, — for the blacks were nearly twice the size of the red, — he
drew near with rapid pace till he stood on his guard within half an inch of the combatants; then, watching his opportunity, he sprang upon the black warrior, and
40 commenced his operations near the root of his right fore leg, leaving the foe
to select among his own members; and so there were three united for life, as if a

---

16 **Myrmidons,** legendary followers of Achilles, said to be descended from ants   34 **to return . . . upon
it,** the injunction of Spartan mothers sending their sons to battle   35 **Achilles,** the Homeric hero, sulking in his tent, came out to avenge the loss of his friend Patroclus

new kind of attraction had been invented which put all other locks and cements to shame. I should not have wondered by this time to find that they had their respective musical bands stationed on some eminent chip, and playing their national airs the while, to excite the slow and cheer the dying combatants. I was myself excited somewhat even as if they had been men. The more you think of it, the less the difference. And certainly there is not the fight recorded in Concord history, at least, if in the history of America, that will bear a moment's comparison with this, whether for the numbers engaged in it, or for the patriotism and heroism displayed. For numbers and for carnage it was an Austerlitz or Dresden. Concord fight! Two killed on the patriots' side, and Luther Blanchard wounded! Why here every ant was a 10 Buttrick, — "Fire, for God's sake fire!" — and thousands shared the fate of Davis and Hosmer. There was not one hireling there. I have no doubt that it was a principle they fought for, as much as our ancestors, and not to avoid a three-penny tax on their tea; and the results of this battle will be as important and memorable to those whom it concerns as those of the battle of Bunker Hill, at least.

I took up the chip on which the three I have particularly described were struggling, carried it into my house, and placed it under a tumbler on my window-sill, in order to see the issue. Holding a microscope to the first-mentioned red ant, I saw that, though he was assiduously gnawing at the near fore leg of his enemy, having severed his remaining feeler, his own breast was all torn away, exposing what vitals 20 he had there to the jaws of the black warrior, whose breastplate was apparently too thick for him to pierce; and the dark carbuncles of the sufferer's eyes shone with ferocity such as war only could excite. They struggled half an hour longer under the tumbler, and when I looked again the black soldier had severed the heads of his foes from their bodies, and the still living heads were hanging on either side of him like ghastly trophies at his saddle-bow, still apparently as firmly fastened as ever, and he was endeavoring with feeble struggles, being without feelers and with only the remnant of a leg, and I know not how many other wounds, to divest himself of them; which at length, after half an hour or more, he accomplished. I raised the glass, and he went off over the window-sill in that crippled state. Whether he finally 30 survived that combat, and spent the remainder of his days in some Hôtel des Invalides, I do not know; but I thought that his industry would not be worth much thereafter. I never learned which party was victorious, nor the cause of the war; but I felt for the rest of that day as if I had had my feelings excited and harrowed by witnessing the struggle, the ferocity and carnage, of a human battle before my door.

Kirby and Spence tell us that the battles of ants have long been celebrated and the date of them recorded, though they say that Huber is the only modern author who appears to have witnessed them. "Æneas Sylvius," say they, "after giving a

---

9 **Austerlitz or Dresden.** The Battle of Austerlitz (1805) was Napoleon's greatest triumph over the Austrians and Russians; the Battle of Dresden (1813) was another of his victories over the Coalition   11 **Major John Buttrick** was in command at the Concord Bridge action   11 **Davis and Hosmer,** Isaac Davis and Abner Hosmer were the two killed at Concord   31 **Hôtel des Invalides,** a noted Paris landmark, built in the 17th century to house disabled veterans   37 **Huber,** François Huber (1750-1813), Swiss naturalist best known for his study of honeybees   38 **Æneas Sylvius,** the classical pseudonym of Enea Silvio de' Piccolomini (1405-1464), Italian humanist who became Pope Pius II, 1458-1464

very circumstantial account of one contested with great obstinacy by a great and small species on the trunk of a pear tree," adds that " 'this action was fought in the pontificate of Eugenius the Fourth, in the presence of Nicholas Pistoriensis, an eminent lawyer, who related the whole history of the battle with the greatest fidelity.' A similar engagement between great and small ants is recorded by Olaus Magnus, in which the small ones, being victorious, are said to have buried the bodies of their own soldiers, but left those of their giant enemies a prey to the birds. This event happened previous to the expulsion of the tyrant Christiern the Second from Sweden." The battle which I witnessed took place in the Presidency of Polk, five years before the passage of Webster's Fugitive-Slave Bill.

Many a village Bose, fit only to course a mud-turtle in a victualling cellar, sported his heavy quarters in the woods, without the knowledge of his master, and ineffectually smelled at old fox burrows and woodchucks' holes; led perchance by some slight cur which nimbly threaded the wood, and might still inspire a natural terror in its denizens; — now far behind his guide, barking like a canine bull toward some small squirrel which had treed itself for scrutiny, then, cantering off, bending the bushes with his weight, imagining that he is on the track of some stray member of the jerbilla family. Once I was surprised to see a cat walking along the stony shore of the pond, for they rarely wander so far from home. The surprise was mutual. Nevertheless the most domestic cat, which has lain on a rug all her days, appears quite at home in the woods, and, by her sly and stealthy behavior, proves herself more native there than the regular inhabitants. Once, when berrying, I met with a cat with young kittens in the woods, quite wild, and they all, like their mother, had their backs up and were fiercely spitting at me. A few years before I lived in the woods there was what was called a "winged cat" in one of the farmhouses in Lincoln nearest the pond, Mr. Gilian Baker's. When I called to see her in June, 1842, she was gone a-hunting in the woods, as was her wont (I am not sure whether it was a male or female, and so use the more common pronoun), but her mistress told me that she came into the neighborhood a little more than a year before, in April, and was finally taken into their house; that she was of a dark brownish-gray color, with a white spot on her throat, and white feet, and had a large bushy tail like a fox; that in the winter the fur grew thick and flatted out along her sides, forming strips ten or twelve inches long by two and a half wide, and under her chin like a muff, the upper side loose, the under matted like felt, and in the spring these appendages dropped off. They gave me a pair of her "wings," which I keep still. There is no appearance of a membrane about them. Some thought it was part flying squirrel or some other wild animal, which is not impossible, for, according to naturalists, prolific hybrids have been produced by the union of the marten and domestic cat. This would have been the right kind of cat for me to keep, if I had kept any; for why should not a poet's cat be winged as well as his horse?

---

3 **Eugenius the Fourth.** His pontificate was from 1431 to 1437   3 **Nicholas Pistoriensis,** later Pope Nicholas IV, 1447-1455   5 **Olaus Magnus** (1490-1557), Swedish churchman and historian   8 **Christiern the Second,** Christian II of Norway was expelled in 1523   9 **Presidency . . . Bill.** Polk was President, 1845-1849; the Fugitive Slave Bill passed in 1850; hence Thoreau's battle was observed in 1845   18 **jerbilla family,** gerbil, a family of Old World leaping rodents

In the fall the loon (*Colymbus glacialis*) came, as usual, to moult and bathe in the pond, making the woods ring with his wild laughter before I had risen. At rumor of his arrival all the Mill-dam sportsmen are on the alert, in gigs and on foot, two by two and three by three, with patent rifles and conical balls and spy-glasses. They come rustling through the woods like autumn leaves, at least ten men to one loon. Some station themselves on this side of the pond, some on that, for the poor bird cannot be omnipresent; if he dive here he must come up there. But now the kind October wind rises, rustling the leaves and rippling the surface of the water, so that no loon can be heard or seen, though his foes sweep the pond with spy-glasses, and make the woods resound with their discharges. The waves generously rise and dash 10 angrily, taking sides with all water-fowl, and our sportsmen must beat a retreat to town and shop and unfinished jobs. But they were too often successful. When I went to get a pail of water early in the morning I frequently saw this stately bird sailing out of my cove within a few rods. If I endeavored to overtake him in a boat, in order to see how he would manœuvre, he would dive and be completely lost, so that I did not discover him again, sometimes, till the latter part of the day. But I was more than a match for him on the surface. He commonly went off in a rain.

As I was paddling along the north shore one very calm October afternoon, for such days especially they settle on to the lakes, like the milkweed down, having looked in vain over the pond for a loon, suddenly one, sailing out from the shore 20 toward the middle a few rods in front of me, set up his wild laugh and betrayed himself. I pursued with a paddle and he dived, but when he came up I was nearer than before. He dived again, but I miscalculated the direction he would take, and we were fifty rods apart when he came to the surface this time, for I had helped to widen the interval; and again he laughed long and loud, and with more reason than before. He manœuvred so cunningly that I could not get within half a dozen rods of him. Each time, when he came to the surface, turning his head this way and that, he coolly surveyed the water and the land, and apparently chose his course so that he might come up where there was the widest expanse of water and at the greatest distance from the boat. It was surprising how quickly he made up his mind and 30 put his resolve into execution. He led me at once to the widest part of the pond, and could not be driven from it. While he was thinking one thing in his brain, I was endeavoring to divine his thought in mine. It was a pretty game, played on the smooth surface of the pond, a man against a loon. Suddenly your adversary's checker disappears beneath the board, and the problem is to place yours nearest to where his will appear again. Sometimes he would come up unexpectedly on the opposite side of me, having apparently passed directly under the boat. So long-winded was he and so unweariable, that when he had swum farthest he would immediately plunge again, nevertheless; and then no wit could divine where in the deep pond, beneath the smooth surface, he might be speeding his way like a fish, 40 for he had time and ability to visit the bottom of the pond in its deepest part. It is said that loons have been caught in the New York lakes eighty feet beneath the surface, with hooks set for trout, — though Walden is deeper than that. How surprised must the fishes be to see this ungainly visitor from another sphere speeding

his way amid their schools! Yet he appeared to know his course as surely under
water as on the surface, and swam much faster there. Once or twice I saw a ripple
where he approached the surface, just put his head out to reconnoitre, and instantly
dived again. I found that it was as well for me to rest on my oars and wait his reappearing as to endeavor to calculate where he would rise; for again and again, when
I was straining my eyes over the surface one way, I would suddenly be startled by
his unearthly laugh behind me. But why, after displaying so much cunning, did he
invariably betray himself the moment he came up by that loud laugh? Did not his
white breast enough betray him? He was indeed a silly loon, I thought. I could
10 commonly hear the splash of the water when he came up, and so also detected him.
But after an hour he seemed as fresh as ever, dived as willingly, and swam yet farther than at first. It was surprising to see how serenely he sailed off with unruffled
breast when he came to the surface, doing all the work with his webbed feet beneath. His usual note was this demoniac laughter, yet somewhat like that of a
water-fowl; but occasionally, when he had balked me most successfully and come
up a long way off, he uttered a long-drawn unearthly howl, probably more like that
of a wolf than any bird; as when a beast puts his muzzle to the ground and deliberately howls. This was his looning, — perhaps the wildest sound that is ever heard
here, making the woods ring far and wide. I concluded that he laughed in derision
20 of my efforts, confident of his own resources. Though the sky was by this time overcast, the pond was so smooth that I could see where he broke the surface when I
did not hear him. His white breast, the stillness of the air, and the smoothness of
the water were all against him. At length, having come up fifty rods off, he uttered
one of those prolonged howls, as if calling on the god of loons to aid him, and
immediately there came a wind from the east and rippled the surface, and filled the
whole air with misty rain, and I was impressed as if it were the prayer of the loon
answered, and his god was angry with me; and so I left him disappearing far away
on the tumultuous surface.

For hours, in fall days, I watched the ducks cunningly tack and veer and hold the
30 middle of the pond, far from the sportsman; tricks which they will have less need
to practise in Louisiana bayous. When compelled to rise they would sometimes
circle round and round and over the pond at a considerable height, from which they
could easily see to other ponds and the river, like black motes in the sky; and, when I
thought they had gone off thither long since, they would settle down by a slanting
flight of a quarter of a mile on to a distant part which was left free; but what beside safety they got by sailing in the middle of Walden I do not know, unless they
love its water for the same reason that I do.

Conclusion

To the sick the doctors wisely recommend a change of air and scenery. Thank
Heaven, here is not all the world. The buckeye does not grow in New England,
40 and the mockingbird is rarely heard here. The wild goose is more of a cosmopolite
than we; he breaks his fast in Canada, takes a luncheon in the Ohio, and plumes

himself for the night in a southern bayou. Even the bison, to some extent, keeps pace with the seasons, cropping the pastures of the Colorado only till a greener and sweeter grass awaits him by the Yellowstone. Yet we think that if rail fences are pulled down, and stone walls piled up on our farms, bounds are henceforth set to our lives and our fates decided. If you are chosen town clerk, forsooth, you cannot go to Tierra del Fuego this summer: but you may go to the land of infernal fire nevertheless. The universe is wider than our views of it.

Yet we should oftener look over the tafferel of our craft, like curious passengers, and not make the voyage like stupid sailors picking oakum. The other side of the globe is but the home of our correspondent. Our voyaging is only great-circle sail- 10 ing, and the doctors prescribe for diseases of the skin merely. One hastens to southern Africa to chase the giraffe; but surely that is not the game he would be after. How long, pray, would a man hunt giraffes if he could? Snipes and woodcocks also may afford rare sport; but I trust it would be nobler game to shoot one's self. —

> "Direct your eye right inward, and you'll find
> A thousand regions in your mind
> Yet undiscovered. Travel them, and be
> Expert in home-cosmography."

What does Africa, — what does the West stand for? Is not our own interior white on the chart? black though it may prove, like the coast, when discovered. Is it the 20 source of the Nile, or the Niger, or the Mississippi, or a Northwest Passage around this continent, that we would find? Are these the problems which most concern mankind? Is Franklin the only man who is lost, that his wife should be so earnest to find him? Does Mr. Grinnell know where he himself is? Be rather the Mungo Park, the Lewis and Clark and Frobisher, of your own streams and oceans; explore your own higher latitudes, — with shiploads of preserved meats to support you, if they be necessary; and pile the empty cans sky-high for a sign. Were preserved meats invented to preserve meat merely? Nay, be a Columbus to whole new continents and worlds within you, opening new channels, not of trade, but of thought. Every man is the lord of a realm beside which the earthly empire of the 30 Czar is but a petty state, a hummock left by the ice. Yet some can be patriotic who have no *self*-respect, and sacrifice the greater to the less. They love the soil which makes their graves, but have no sympathy with the spirit which may still animate their clay. Patriotism is a maggot in their heads. What was the meaning of that South-Sea Exploring Expedition, with all its parade and expense, but an indirect

---

6 **Tierra del Fuego**, an archipelago at the southern tip of South America   9 **picking oakum**, a make-work job on sailing ships, going over rope ends to retrieve usable fiber for caulking   23 **Franklin.** Sir John Franklin (1786-1847), English explorer, was lost while seeking the Northwest Passage in 1845. His wife was active in organizing search expeditions, two of which were financed by the American merchant Henry Grinnell (1800-1874). Records indicating Franklin died in 1847 were finally found   25 **Mungo Park** (1771-1806), British explorer of the Niger River   25 **Lewis and Clark.** Merriwether Lewis (1774-1809) and William Clark (1770-1838) led an expedition seeking a land route to the Pacific, 1803-1806   25 **Frobisher.** Sir Martin Frobisher (1535?-1594), English mariner, explored the Arctic seeking the Northwest Passage   35 **South-Sea Exploring Expedition**, fitted out by the United States in 1838, explored for four years

recognition of the fact that there are continents and seas in the moral world to which every man is an isthmus or an inlet, yet unexplored by him, but that it is easier to sail many thousand miles through cold and storm and cannibals, in a government ship, with five hundred men and boys to assist one, than it is to explore the private sea, the Atlantic and Pacific Ocean of one's being alone. —

> "Erret, et extremos alter scrutetur Iberos.
> Plus habet hic vitae, plus habet ille viae."

> Let them wander and scrutinize the outlandish Australians.
> I have more of God, they more of the road.

10   It is not worth the while to go round the world to count the cats in Zanzibar. Yet do this even till you can do better, and you may perhaps find some "Symmes' Hole" by which to get at the inside at last. England and France, Spain and Portugal, Gold Coast and Slave Coast, all front on this private sea; but no bark from them has ventured out of sight of land, though it is without doubt the direct way to India. If you would learn to speak all tongues and conform to the customs of all nations, if you would travel farther than all travellers, be naturalized in all climes, and cause the Sphinx to dash her head against a stone, even obey the precept of the old philosopher, and Explore thyself. Herein are demanded the eye and the nerve. Only the defeated and deserters go to the wars, cowards that run away and enlist. Start
20 now on that farthest western way, which does not pause at the Mississippi or the Pacific, nor conduct toward a worn-out China or Japan, but leads on direct, a tangent to this sphere, summer and winter, day and night, sun down, moon down, and at last earth down too.

It is said that Mirabeau took to highway robbery "to ascertain what degree of resolution was necessary in order to place one's self in formal opposition to the most sacred laws of society." He declared that "a soldier who fights in the ranks does not require half so much courage as a foot-pad," — "that honor and religion have never stood in the way of a well-considered and a firm resolve." This was manly, as the world goes; and yet it was idle, if not desperate. A saner man would have found
30 himself often enough "in formal opposition" to what are deemed "the most sacred laws of society," through obedience to yet more sacred laws, and so have tested his resolution without going out of his way. It is not for a man to put himself in such an attitude to society, but to maintain himself in whatever attitude he find himself through obedience to the laws of his being, which will never be one of opposition to a just government, if he should chance to meet with such.

I left the woods for as good a reason as I went there. Perhaps it seemed to me that I had several more lives to live, and could not spare any more time for that

---

6 **Erret . . . viae,** from Claudian's *On an Old Man of Verona.* Thoreau's translation of *vitae* (life, spirit) and *Iberos* (the Spanish) is free   11 **Symmes' Hole,** an alleged hole that was supposed to open from the North Pole into the concentric spheres of which the earth was then supposed to be composed   24 **Mirabeau,** Honoré Gabriel Riquetti, Comte de Mirabeau (1749-1791), French revolutionist

one. It is remarkable how easily and insensibly we fall into a particular route, and make a beaten track for ourselves. I had not lived there a week before my feet wore a path from my door to the pondside; and though it is five or six years since I trod it, it is still quite distinct. It is true, I fear, that others may have fallen into it, and so helped to keep it open. The surface of the earth is soft and impressible by the feet of men; and so with the paths which the mind travels. How worn and dusty, then, must be the highways of the world, how deep the ruts of tradition and conformity! I did not wish to take a cabin passage, but rather to go before the mast and on the deck of the world, for there I could best see the moonlight amid the mountains. I do not wish to go below now.   10

I learned this, at least, by my experiment: that if one advances confidently in the direction of his dreams, and endeavors to live the life which he has imagined, he will meet with a success unexpected in common hours. He will put some things behind, will pass an invisible boundary; new, universal, and more liberal laws will begin to establish themselves around and within him; or the old laws be expanded, and interpreted in his favor in a more liberal sense, and he will live with the license of a higher order of beings. In proportion as he simplifies his life, the laws of the universe will appear less complex, and solitude will not be solitude, nor poverty poverty, nor weakness weakness. If you have built castles in the air, your work need not be lost; that is where they should be. Now put the foundations under them. 20

It is a ridiculous demand which England and America make, that you shall speak so that they can understand you. Neither men nor toadstools grow so. As if that were important, and there were not enough to understand you without them. As if Nature could support but one order of understandings, could not sustain birds as well as quadrupeds, flying as well as creeping things, and *hush* and *who,* which Bright can understand, were the best English. As if there were safety in stupidity alone. I fear chiefly lest my expression may not be *extra-vagant* enough, may not wander far enough beyond the narrow limits of my daily experience, so as to be adequate to the truth of which I have been convinced. *Extra vagance!* it depends on how you are yarded. The migrating buffalo, which seeks new pastures in another 30 latitude, is not extravagant like the cow which kicks over the pail, leaps the cowyard fence, and runs after her calf, in milking time. I desire to speak somewhere *without* bounds; like a man in a waking moment, to men in their waking moments; for I am convinced that I cannot exaggerate enough even to lay the foundation of a true expression. Who that has heard a strain of music feared then lest he should speak extravagantly any more forever? In view of the future or possible, we should live quite laxly and undefined in front, our outlines dim and misty on that side; as our shadows reveal an insensible perspiration toward the sun. The volatile truth of our words should continually betray the inadequacy of the residual statement. Their truth is instantly *translated;* its literal monument alone remains. The words 40 which express our faith and piety are not definite; yet they are significant and fragrant like frankincense to superior natures.

Why level downward to our dullest perception always, and praise that as common sense? The commonest sense is the sense of men asleep, which they express by snoring. Sometimes we are inclined to class those who are once-and-a-half-witted with the half-witted, because we appreciate only a third part of their wit. Some would find fault with the morning red, if they ever got up early enough. "They pretend," as I hear, "that the verses of Kabir have four different senses; illusion, spirit, intellect, and the exotic doctrine of the Vedas;" but in this part of the world it is considered a ground for complaint if a man's writings admit of more than one interpretation. While England endeavors to cure the potato-rot, will not any endeavor to cure the brain-rot, which prevails so much more widely and fatally?

10   I do not suppose that I have attained to obscurity, but I should be proud if no more fatal fault were found with my pages on this score than was found with the Walden ice. Southern customers objected to its blue color, which is the evidence of its purity, as if it were muddy, and preferred the Cambridge ice, which is white, but tastes of weeds. The purity men love is like the mists which envelop the earth, and not like the azure ether beyond.

Some are dinning in our ears that we Americans, and moderns generally, are intellectual dwarfs compared with the ancients, or even the Elizabethan men. But what is that to the purpose? A living dog is better than a dead lion. Shall a man go and hang himself because he belongs to the race of pygmies, and not be the biggest pygmy that he can? Let every one mind his own business, and endeavor to 20 be what he was made.

Why should we be in such desperate haste to succeed and in such desperate enterprises? If a man does not keep pace with his companions, perhaps it is because he hears a different drummer. Let him step to the music which he hears, however measured or far away. It is not important that he should mature as soon as an apple tree or an oak. Shall he turn his spring into summer? If the condition of things which we were made for is not yet, what were any reality which we can substitute? We will not be shipwrecked on a vain reality. Shall we with pains erect a heaven of blue glass over ourselves, though when it is done we shall be sure to gaze still at the true ethereal heaven far above, as if the former were not?

30   There was an artist in the city of Kouroo who was disposed to strive after perfection. One day it came into his mind to make a staff. Having considered that in an imperfect work time is an ingredient, but into a perfect work time does not enter, he said to himself, It shall be perfect in all respects, though I should do nothing else in my life. He proceeded instantly to the forest for wood, being resolved that it should not be made of unsuitable material; and as he searched for and rejected stick after stick, his friends gradually deserted him, for they grew old in their works and died, but he grew not older by a moment. His singleness of purpose and resolution, and his elevated piety, endowed him, without his knowledge, with perennial youth. As he made no compromise with Time, Time kept out of his way, and only sighed 40 at a distance because he could not overcome him. Before he had found a stick in all respects suitable the city of Kouroo was a hoary ruin, and he sat on one of

---

4 **Kabir** (1450?-1518). Hindu reformer who tried to unite the Hindus and Moslems   7 **potato-rot.** Extensive and frantic efforts were made to offset the potato blight that produced famine in Ireland in the late 1840's

its mounds to peel the stick. Before he had given it the proper shape the dynasty of the Candahars was at an end, and with the point of the stick he wrote the name of the last of that race in the sand, and then resumed his work. By the time he had smoothed and polished the staff Kalpa was no longer the pole-star; and ere he had put on the ferule and the head adorned with precious stones, Brahma had awoke and slumbered many times. But why do I stay to mention these things? When the finishing stroke was put to his work, it suddenly expanded before the eyes of the astonished artist into the fairest of all the creations of Brahma. He had made a new system in making a staff, a world with full and fair proportions; in which, though the old cities and dynasties had passed away, fairer and more glorious ones had taken   10 their places. And now he saw by the heap of shavings still fresh at his feet, that, for him and his work, the former lapse of time had been an illusion, and that no more time had elapsed than is required for a single scintillation from the brain of Brahma to fall on and inflame the tinder of a mortal brain. The material was pure, and his art was pure; how could the result be other than wonderful?

No face which we can give to a matter will stead us so well at last as the truth. This alone wears well. For the most part, we are not where we are, but in a false position. Through an infirmity of our natures, we suppose a case, and put ourselves into it, and hence are in two cases at the same time, and it is doubly difficult to get out. In sane moments we regard only the facts, the case that is. Say what you have   20 to say, not what you ought. Any truth is better than make-believe. Tom Hyde, the tinker, standing on the gallows, was asked if he had anything to say. "Tell the tailors," said he, "to remember to make a knot in their thread before they take the first stitch." His companion's prayer is forgotten.

However mean your life is, meet it and live it; do not shun it and call it hard names. It is not so bad as you are. It looks poorest when you are richest. The fault-finder will find faults even in paradise. Love your life, poor as it is. You may perhaps have some pleasant, thrilling, glorious hours, even in a poor-house. The setting sun is reflected from the windows of the alms-house as brightly as from the rich man's abode; the snow melts before its door as early in the spring. I do not see but   30 a quiet mind may live as contentedly there, and have as cheering thoughts, as in a palace. The town's poor seem to me often to live the most independent lives of any. Maybe they are simply great enough to receive without misgiving. Most think that they are above being supported by the town; but it oftener happens that they are not above supporting themselves by dishonest means, which should be more disreputable. Cultivate poverty like a garden herb, like sage. Do not trouble yourself much to get new things, whether clothes or friends. Turn the old; return to them. Things do not change; we change. Sell your clothes and keep your thoughts. God will see that you do not want society. If I were confined to a corner of a garret all my days, like a spider, the world would be just as large to me while I had my   40 thoughts about me. The philosopher said: "From an army of three divisions one

2 **Candahars,** Kandahar, an Afghanistan city long ruled by the Durranis   4 **Kalpa,** in the Hindu cosmogony a day and a night of Brahma, or 4,320,000,000 solar years   5 **Brahma,** one of the three supreme Hindu gods, who is periodically reborn, thus many kalpas

can take away its general, and put it in disorder; from the man the most abject and vulgar one cannot take away his thought." Do not seek so anxiously to be developed, to subject yourself to many influences to be played on; it is all dissipation. Humility like darkness reveals the heavenly lights. The shadows of poverty and meanness gather around us, "and lo! creation widens to our view." We are often reminded that if there were bestowed on us the wealth of Crœsus, our aims must still be the same, and our means essentially the same. Moreover, if you are restricted in your range by poverty, if you cannot buy books and newspapers, for instance, you are but confined to the most significant and vital experiences; you are compelled to deal with the material which yields the most sugar and the most starch. It is life near the bone where it is sweetest. You are defended from being a trifler. No man loses ever on a lower level by magnanimity on a higher. Superfluous wealth can buy superfluities only. Money is not required to buy one necessary of the soul.

I live in the angle of a leaden wall, into whose composition was poured a little alloy of bell-metal. Often, in the repose of my mid-day, there reaches my ears a confused *tintinnabulum* from without. It is the noise of my contemporaries. My neighbors tell me of their adventures with famous gentlemen and ladies, what notabilities they met at the dinner-table; but I am no more interested in such things than in the contents of the Daily Times. The interest and the conversation are about costume and manners chiefly; but a goose is a goose still, dress it as you will. They tell me of California and Texas, of England and the Indies, of the Hon. Mr. _____ of Georgia or Massachusetts, all transient and fleeting phenomena, till I am ready to leap from their court-yard like the Mameluke bey. I delight to come to my bearings, — not walk in procession with pomp and parade, in a conspicuous place, but to walk even with the Builder of the universe, if I may, — not to live in this restless, nervous, bustling, trivial Nineteenth Century, but stand or sit thoughtfully while it goes by. What are men celebrating? They are all on a committee of arrangements, and hourly expect a speech from somebody. God is only the president of the day, and Webster is his orator. I love to weigh, to settle, to gravitate toward that which most strongly and rightfully attracts me, — not hang by the beam of the scale and try to weigh less, — not suppose a case, but take the case that is; to travel the only path I can, and that on which no power can resist me. It affords me no satisfaction to commence to spring an arch before I have got a solid foundation. Let us not play at kittly-benders. There is a solid bottom everywhere. We read that the traveller asked the boy if the swamp before him had a hard bottom. The boy replied that it had. But presently the traveller's horse sank in up to the girths, and he observed to the boy, "I thought you said that this bog had a hard bottom." "So it has," answered the latter, "but you have not got half way to it yet." So it is with the bogs and quicksands of society; but he is an old boy that knows it. Only what is thought, said, or done at a certain rare coincidence is good. I would not be one of those who will foolishly drive a nail into mere lath and plastering; such a deed

5 **and . . . view,** a slight misquotation from the Joseph Blanco White (1775-1841) sonnet "Night"   23 **Mameluke bey.** When Mohammed Ali massacred his comrades at Cairo in 1821, one bey escaped by jumping his horse over the parapet of an enclosed courtyard   29 **Webster.** See pp. 734-735

would keep me awake nights. Give me a hammer, and let me feel for the furring. Do not depend on the putty. Drive a nail home and clinch it so faithfully that you can wake up in the night and think of your work with satisfaction, — a work at which you would not be ashamed to invoke the Muse. So will help you God, and so only. Every nail driven should be as another rivet in the machine of the universe, you carrying on the work.

Rather than love, than money, than fame, give me truth: I sat at a table where were rich food and wine in abundance, an obsequious attendance, but sincerity and truth were not; and I went away hungry from the inhospitable board. The hospitality was as cold as the ices. I thought that there was no need of ice to freeze them. 10 They talked to me of the age of the wine and the fame of the vintage; but I thought of an older, a newer, and purer wine, of a more glorious vintage, which they had not got, and could not buy. The style, the house and grounds and "entertainment" pass for nothing with me. I called on the king, but he made me wait in his hall, and conducted like a man incapacitated for hospitality. There was a man in my neighborhood who lived in a hollow tree. His manners were truly regal. I should have done better had I called on him.

How long shall we sit in our porticoes practising idle and musty virtues, which any work would make impertinent? As if one were to begin the day with long-suffering, and hire a man to hoe his potatoes; and in the afternoon go forth to prac- 20 tise Christian meekness and charity with goodness aforethought! Consider the China pride and stagnant self-complacency of mankind. This generation inclines a little to congratulate itself on being the last of an illustrious line; and in Boston and London and Paris and Rome, thinking of its long descent, it speaks of its progress in art and science and literature with satisfaction. There are the Records of the Philosophical Societies, and the public Eulogies of *Great Men!* It is the good Adam contemplating his own virtue. "Yes, we have done great deeds, and sung divine songs, which shall never die," — that is, as long as *we* can remember them. The learned societies and great men of Assyria, — where are they? What youthful philosophers and experimentalists we are! There is not one of my readers who has yet lived a 30 whole human life. These may be but the spring months in the life of the race. If we have had the seven-years' itch, we have not seen the seventeen-year locust yet in Concord. We are acquainted with a mere pellicle of the globe on which we live. Most have not delved six feet beneath the surface, nor leaped as many above it. We know not where we are. Beside, we are sound asleep nearly half our time. Yet we esteem ourselves wise, and have an established order on the surface. Truly, we are deep thinkers, we are ambitious spirits! As I stand over the insect crawling amid the pine needles on the forest floor, and endeavoring to conceal itself from my sight, and ask myself why it will cherish those humble thoughts, and hide its head from me who might, perhaps, be its benefactor, and impart to its race some cheering in- 40 formation, I am reminded of the greater Benefactor and Intelligence that stands over me the human insect.

There is an incessant influx of novelty into the world, and yet we tolerate incredible dulness. I need only suggest what kind of sermons are still listened to in the most enlightened countries. There are such words as joy and sorrow, but they are only the burden of a psalm, sung with a nasal twang, while we believe in the ordinary and mean. We think that we can change our clothes only. It is said that the British Empire is very large and respectable, and that the United States are a first-rate power. We do not believe that a tide rises and falls behind every man which can float the British Empire like a chip, if he should ever harbor it in his mind. Who knows what sort of seventeen-year locust will next come out of the ground? The government of the world I live in was not framed, like that of Britain, in after-dinner conversations over the wine.

10   The life in us is like the water in the river. It may rise this year higher than man has ever known it, and flood the parched uplands; even this may be the eventful year, which will drown out all our muskrats. It was not always dry land where we dwell. I see far inland the banks which the stream anciently washed, before science began to record its freshets. Everyone has heard the story which has gone the rounds of New England, of a strong and beautiful bug which came out of the dry leaf of an old table of apple-tree wood, which had stood in a farmer's kitchen for sixty years, first in Connecticut, and afterward in Massachusetts, — from an egg deposited in the living tree many years earlier still, as appeared by counting the annual layers beyond it; which was heard gnawing out for several weeks, hatched perchance by 20 the heat of an urn. Who does not feel his faith in a resurrection and immortality strengthened by hearing of this? Who knows what beautiful and winged life, whose egg has been buried for ages under many concentric layers of woodenness in the dead dry life of society, deposited at first in the alburnum of the green and living tree, which has been gradually converted into the semblance of its well-seasoned tomb, — heard perchance gnawing out now for years by the astonished family of man, as they sat round the festive board, — may unexpectedly come forth from amidst society's most trivial and handselled furniture, to enjoy its perfect summer life at last!

I do not say that John or Jonathan will realize all this; but such is the character 30 of that morrow which mere lapse of time can never make to dawn. The light which puts out our eyes is darkness to us. Only that day dawns to which we are awake. There is more day to dawn. The sun is but a morning star.   1854

———
27 **handselled,** sold at auction

from The Journals

April 16, 1852

As I turned round the corner of Hubbard's Grove, saw a woodchuck, the first of the season, in the middle of the field, six or seven rods from the fence which bounds the wood, and twenty rods distant. I ran along the fence and cut him off, or rather overtook him, though he started at the same time. When I was only a rod and a half off, he stopped, and I did the same; then he ran again, and I ran up within three feet of him, when he stopped again, the fence being between us. I squatted down and surveyed him at my leisure. His eyes were dull black and rather inobvious, with a faint chestnut iris, with but little expression and that more of resignation than of anger. The general aspect was a coarse grayish brown, a sort of grisel. A lighter brown next the skin, then black or very dark brown and tipped with whitish rather loosely. The head between a squirrel and a bear, flat on the top and dark brown, and darker still or black on the tip of the nose. The whiskers black, two inches long. The ears very small and roundish, set far back and nearly buried in the fur. Black feet, with long and slender claws for digging. It appeared to tremble, or perchance shivered with cold. When I moved, it gritted its teeth quite loud, some- 10 times striking the under jaw against the other chatteringly, sometimes grinding one jaw on the other, yet as if more from instinct than anger. Whichever way I turned, that way it headed. I took a twig a foot long and touched its snout, at which it started forward and bit the stick, lessening the distance between us to two feet, and still it held all the ground it gained. I played with it tenderly awhile with the stick, trying to open its gritting jaws. Ever its long incisors, two above and two below, were presented. But I thought it would go to sleep if I stayed long enough. It did not sit upright as sometimes, but *standing* on its fore feet with its head down, *i.e.* half sitting, half standing. We sat looking at one another about half an hour, till we began to feel mesmeric influences. When I was tired, I moved away, wishing 20 to see him run, but I could not start him. He would not stir as long as I was looking at him or could see him. I walked round him; he turned as fast and fronted me still. I sat down by his side within a foot. I talked to him *quasi* forest lingo, babytalk, at any rate in a conciliatory tone, and thought that I had some influence on him. He gritted his teeth less. I chewed checkerberry leaves and presented them to his nose at last without a grit; though I saw that by so much gritting of the teeth he had worn them rapidly and they were covered with a fine white powder, which, if you measured it thus, would have made his anger terrible. He did not mind any noise I might make. With a little stick I lifted one of his paws to examine it, and held it up at pleasure. I turned him over to see what color he was beneath (darker 30 or more purely brown), though he turned himself back again sooner than I could have wished. His tail was also all brown, though not very dark, rat-tail like, with loose hairs standing out on all sides like a caterpillar brush. He had a rather mild look. I spoke to him kindly. I reached checkerberry leaves to his mouth. I stretched my hands over him, though he turned up his head and still gritted a little. I laid my hand on him, but immediately took it off again, instinct not being wholly overcome. If I had had a few fresh bean leaves, thus in advance of the season, I am sure I should have tamed him completely. It was a frizzly tail. His is a humble, terrestrial color like the partridge's, well concealed where dead wiry grass rises above darker brown or chestnut dead leaves, — a modest color. If I had had some food, I should 40 have ended with stroking him at my leisure. Could easily have wrapped him in my handkerchief. He was not fat nor particularly lean. I finally had to leave him without seeing him move from the place. A large, clumsy, burrowing squirrel. *Arctomys,* bearmouse. I respect him as one of the natives. He lies there, by his color and habits

so naturalized amid the dry leaves, the withered grass, and the bushes. A sound
nap, too, he has enjoyed in his native fields, the past winter. I think I might learn
some wisdom of him. His ancestors have lived here longer than mine. He is more
thoroughly acclimated and naturalized than I. Bean leaves the red man raised for
him, but he can do without them.

June 18, 1855

At 3 P.M., as I walked up the bank by the Hemlocks, I saw a painted tortoise just
beginning its hole; then another a dozen rods from the river on the bare barren field
near some pitch pines, where the earth was covered with cladonias, cinquefoil, sor-
rel, etc. Its hole was about two thirds done. I stooped down over it, and, to my sur-
10 prise, after a slight pause it proceeded in its work, directly under and within
eighteen inches of my face. I retained a constrained position for three quarters of
an hour or more for fear of alarming it. It rested on its fore legs, the front part of
its shell about one inch higher than the rear, and this position was not changed
essentially to the last. The hole was oval, broadest behind, about one inch wide
and one and three quarters long, and the dirt already removed was quite wet or
moistened. It made the hole and removed the dirt with its hind legs only, not using
its tail or shell, which last of course could not enter the hole, though there was
some dirt on it. It first scratched two or three times with one hind foot; then took
up a pinch of the loose sand and deposited it directly behind that leg, pushing it
20 backward to its full length and then deliberately opening it and letting the dirt fall;
then the same with the other hind foot. This it did rapidly, using each leg alternately with perfect regularity, standing on the other one the while, and thus tilting
up its shell each time, now to this side, then to that. There was half a minute or
a minute between each change. The hole was made as deep as the feet could reach,
or about two inches. It was very neat about its work, not scattering the dirt about
any more than was necessary. The completing of the hole occupied perhaps
five minutes.

It then without any pause drew its head completely into its shell, raised the rear
a little, and protruded and dropped a wet flesh-colored egg into the hole, one end
30 foremost, the red skin of its body being considerably protruded with it. Then it put
out its head again a little, slowly, and placed the egg at one side with one hind foot.
After a delay of about two minutes it again drew in its head and dropped another, and
so on to the fifth — drawing in its head each time, and pausing somewhat longer
between the last. The eggs were placed in the hole without any *particular* care, —
only well down flat and [each] out of the way of the next, — and I could plainly see
them from above.

After these ten minutes or more, it without pause or turning began to scrape the
moist earth into the hole with its hind legs, and, when it had half filled it, it carefully pressed it down with the edges of its hind feet, dancing on them alternately,
40 for some time, as on its knees, tilting from side to side, pressing by the whole weight
of the rear of its shell. When it had drawn in thus all the earth that had been

moistened, it stretched its hind legs further back and to each side, and drew in the dry and lichen-clad crust, and then danced upon and pressed that down, still not moving the rear of its shell more than one inch to right or left all the while, or changing the position of the forward part at all. The thoroughness with which the covering was done was remarkable. It persevered in drawing in and dancing on the dry surface which had never been disturbed, long after you thought it had done its duty, but it never moved its fore feet, not once looked round, nor saw the eggs it had laid. There were frequent pauses throughout the whole, when it rested, or ran out its head and looked about circumspectly, at any noise or motion. These pauses were especially long during the covering of its eggs, which occupied more than half 10 an hour. Perhaps it was hard work.

When it had done, it immediately started for the river at a pretty rapid rate (the suddenness with which it made these transitions was amusing), pausing from time to time, and I judged that it would reach it in fifteen minutes. It was not easy to detect that the ground had been disturbed there. An Indian could not have made his cache more skillfully. In a few minutes all traces of it would be lost to the eye.

The object of moistening the earth was perhaps to enable it to take it up in its hands, and also to prevent its falling back into the hole. Perhaps it also helped to make the ground more compact and harder when it was pressed down.

                                                                         1852-1855, 1906

Prayer from The Dial *for July 1842.*

Great God, I ask thee for no meaner pelf
Than that I may not disappoint myself,
That in my action I may soar as high
As I can now discern with this clear eye.

And next in value, which thy kindness lends,
That I may greatly disappoint my friends,
Howe'er they think or hope that it may be,
They may not dream how thou'st distinguished me.

That my weak hand may equal my firm faith,
And my life practise more than my tongue saith;   10
        That my low conduct may not show,
            Nor my relenting lines,
        That I thy purpose did not know,
            Or overrated thy designs.

                            1842

Rumors from an Æolian Harp

First printed in The Dial *for October 1842, the poem was reprinted in the chapter entitled "Monday" in* A Week on the Concord and Merrimack Rivers.

There is a vale which none hath seen,
Where foot of man has never been,
Such as here lives with toil and strife,
An anxious and a sinful life.

There every virtue has its birth,
Ere it descends upon the earth,
And thither every deed returns,
Which in the generous bosom burns.

There love is warm, and youth is young,
And poetry is yet unsung,   10
For Virtue still adventures there,
And freely breathes her native air.

And ever, if you hearken well,
You still may hear its vesper bell,
And tread of high-souled men go by,
Their thoughts conversing with the sky.
                                            1842

The Summer Rain

First printed in The Dial *for October 1842, "The Summer Rain" was reprinted in the chapter entitled "Thursday" in* A Week on the Concord and Merrimack Rivers.

My books I'd fain cast off, I cannot read,
    'Twixt every page my thoughts go stray at large
Down in the meadow, where is richer feed,
    And will not mind to hit their proper targe.

Plutarch was good, and so was Homer too,
    Our Shakespeare's life were rich to live again,

---

4 **targe,** target

What Plutarch read, that was not good nor true,
  Nor Shakespeare's books, unless his books were men.

Here while I lie beneath this walnut bough,
  What care I for the Greeks or for Troy town,   10
If juster battles are enacted now
  Between the ants upon this hummock's crown?

Bid Homer wait till I the issue learn,
  If red or black the gods will favor most,
Or yonder Ajax will the phalanx turn,
  Struggling to heave some rock against the host.

Tell Shakespeare to attend some leisure hour,
  For now I've business with this drop of dew,
And see you not, the clouds prepare a shower, —
  I'll meet him shortly when the sky is blue.   20

This bed of herdsgrass and wild oats was spread
  Last year with nicer skill than monarchs use,
A clover tuft is pillow for my head,
  And violets quite overtop my shoes.

And now the cordial clouds have shut all in,
  And gently swells the wind to say all's well;
The scattered drops are falling fast and thin,
  Some in the pool, some in the flower-bell.

I am well drenched upon my bed of oats;
  But see that globe come rolling down its stem,   30
Now like a lonely planet there it floats,
  And now it sinks into my garment's hem.

Drip, drip the trees for all the country round,
  And richness rare distills from every bough;
The wind alone it is makes every sound,
  Shaking down crystals on the leaves below.

For shame the sun will never show himself,
  Who could not with his beams e'er melt me so;
My dripping locks, — they would become an elf,
  Who in a beaded coat does gayly go.   40

                                                   1842

---

11 **battles** . . . **ants.** See pp. 1213-1214

Smoke

First printed in The Dial *for April 1843, "Smoke" was reprinted in Chapter XIII of* Walden.

Light-wingèd smoke, Icarian bird,
Melting thy pinions in thy upward flight,
Lark without song, and messenger of dawn,
Circling above the hamlets as thy nest;
Or else, departing dream, and shadowy form
Of midnight vision, gathering up thy skirts;
By night star-veiling, and by day
Darkening the light and blotting out the sun;
Go thou my incense upward from this hearth,
And ask the Gods to pardon this clear flame.   10
                                                        1843

---

1 **Icarian.** When Icarus, in Greek mythology, flew too near the sun, the wax of his artificial wings melted, and he fell into the sea and was drowned

Inspiration

Portions of "Inspiration" are found scattered through A Week on the Concord and Merrimack Rivers. *The poem should be compared with Emerson's "Merlin," p. 1149, noting especially the views of poetic composition expressed.*

Whate'er we leave to God, God does,
    And blesses us;
The work we choose should be our own,
    God leaves alone.

If with light head erect I sing,
    Though all the Muses lend their force,
From my poor love of anything,
    The verse is weak and shallow as its source.

But if with bended neck I grope
    Listening behind me for my wit,   10
With faith superior to hope,
    More anxious to keep back than forward it;

Making my soul accomplice there
   Unto the flame my heart hath lit,
Then will the verse forever wear —
   Time cannot bend the line which God hath writ.

Always the general show of things
   Floats in review before my mind,
And such true love and reverence brings,
   That sometimes I forget that I am blind.   20

But now there comes unsought, unseen,
   Some clear divine electuary,
And I, who had but sensual been,
   Grow sensible, and as God is, am wary.

I hearing get, who had but ears,
   And sight, who had but eyes before,
I moments live, who lived but years,
   And truth discern, who knew but learning's lore.

I hear beyond the range of sound,
   I see beyond the range of sight,   30
New earths and skies and seas around,
   And in my day the sun doth pale his light.

A clear and ancient harmony
   Pierces my soul through all its din,
As through its utmost melody, —
   Farther behind than they, farther within.

More swift its bolt than lightning is,
   Its voice than thunder is more loud,
It doth expand my privacies
   To all, and leave me single in the crowd.   40

It speaks with such authority,
   With so serene and lofty tone,
That idle Time runs gadding by,
   And leaves me with Eternity alone.

Now chiefly is my natal hour,
   And only now my prime of life;
Of manhood's strength it is the flower,
   'Tis peace's end and war's beginning strife.

It comes in summer's broadest noon,
   By a grey wall or some chance place,   50
Unseasoning Time, insulting June,
   And vexing day with its presuming face.

Such fragrance round my couch it makes,
   More rich than are Arabian drugs,
That my soul scents its life and wakes
   The body up beneath its perfumed rugs.

Such is the Muse, the heavenly maid,
   The star that guides our mortal course,
Which shows where life's true kernel's laid,
   Its wheat's fine flour, and its undying force.   60

She with one breath attunes the spheres,
   And also my poor human heart,
With one impulse propels the years
   Around, and gives my throbbing pulse its start.

I will not doubt for evermore,
   Nor falter from a steadfast faith,
For though the system be turned o'er,
   God takes not back the word which once He saith.

I will not doubt the love untold
   Which not my worth nor want has bought,   70
Which wooed me young, and wooes me old,
   And to this evening hath me brought.

My memory I'll educate
   To know the one historic truth,
Remembering to the latest date
   The only true and sole immortal youth.

Be but thy inspiration given,
   No matter through what danger sought,
I'll fathom hell or climb to heaven,
   And yet esteem that cheap which love has bought. 80

Fame cannot tempt the bard
   Who's famous with his God,
Nor laurel him reward
   Who has his Maker's nod.   1849

Though All the Fates

In the paragraph which precedes the poem, Thoreau tells of talking with some boatmen on the Merrimack who intended, when they reached the coast, possibly to embark for "the China seas." "What grievance," he asks, "has its root among the New Hampshire hills? . . . What is wanting to human life here, that these men should make haste to the antipodes?" (See A Week on the Concord and Merrimack Rivers.)

Though all the fates should prove unkind,
Leave not your native land behind.
The ship, becalmed, at length stands still;
The steed must rest beneath the hill;
But swiftly still our fortunes pace,
To find us out in every place.
The vessel, though her masts be firm,
Beneath her copper bears a worm;
Around the cape, across the line,
Till fields of ice her course confine;   10
It matters not how smooth the breeze,
How shallow or how deep the seas,
Whether she bears Manilla twine,
Or in her hold Madeira wine,
Or China teas, or Spanish hides,
In port or quarantine she rides;
Far from New England's blustering shore,
New England's worm her hulk shall bore,
And sink her in the Indian seas,
Twine, wine, and hides, and China teas.   20

                              1849

1804–1864 Nathaniel Hawthorne

Nathaniel Hawthorne's first American ancestor, William Hathorne, came to Massachusetts in 1630 and, as a magistrate of the Bay Colony, was active in the 1650's in the persecution of the Quakers. William Hathorne's son, John, was one of the "witch-judges" at Salem in 1692. The seventeenth-century Hathornes were obviously men of importance, though of a sinister kind. The family declined in prominence during the century which followed. Nathaniel Hawthorne's father, a sea captain, died in Dutch Guiana when Nathaniel was only four years of age, leaving at Salem a widow and three children in reduced circumstances. Hawthorne often thought of William Hathorne, "grave, bearded, sable-cloaked and steeple-crowned progenitor," and of John Hathorne, "so conspicuous in the martyrdom of the witches that their blood may fairly be said to have left a stain upon him." He wondered if their sins might have been to blame for his family's decline and if he might have inherited some of their guilt. "I take shame upon myself for their sakes," he wrote in "The Custom House," the prefatory essay to *The Scarlet Letter,* "and pray that any curse incurred by them — as I have heard, and as the dreary and unprosperous condition of the race, for many a long year back, would argue to exist — may be now and henceforth removed." And yet, however much he might deprecate the cruelties of these early progenitors (and however alien and distasteful to them might be a descendant who was "a writer of storybooks"), he could not escape his inheritance: "strong traits of their nature," he said, "have intertwined themselves with mine." This hereditary sense, no doubt, explains, at least in part, his preoccupation with guilt and somber tone.

He was graduated from Bowdoin College in 1825. Franklin Pierce was in the class of 1824; Longfellow was a classmate. After graduation, Hawthorne returned to his mother's house in Salem and lived there in comparative seclusion for twelve years. He later thought of himself as having been under a spell of enchantment. In a famous letter to Longfellow, written in 1837, he said: "By some witchcraft or other — for I really cannot assign any reasonable why and wherefore — I have been carried apart from the main current of life, and find it impossible to get back again. Since we last met . . . I have secluded myself from society; and yet I never meant any such thing, nor dreamed what sort of life I was going to lead. I have made a captive of myself and put me into a dungeon; and now I cannot find the key to let myself out — and if the door were open, I should be almost afraid to come out. . . . There is no fate in this world so horrible as to have no share in either its joys or sorrows. For the last ten years, I have not lived, but only dreamed about living." Those years, however, were not wasted. In his solitary chamber, Hawthorne put himself through a rigorous literary discipline. He read and wrote and destroyed much of what he had written. Recovering from a false start in *Fanshawe* (1828), a short novel based upon life at Bowdoin, he discovered the kind of composition in which he was to excel: the moral and psychological tale. After anonymous publication in magazines, his tales were first collected in *Twice-Told Tales* (1837). If they, as their author thought, "have the pale tint of flowers that blossomed in too retired a shade," they illustrate, nevertheless, his virtues of sharpness of insight and delicacy of treatment.

We need not regret the twelve solitary years; perhaps they were necessary to Hawthorne's development as an artist. The prolongation of the period of solitude, however, might have endangered both his literary growth and his mental health. Hawthorne evidently feared as much, for soon he was attempting, in his own phrase, "to open an intercourse with the world." In 1839-1840 he was "weigher and gauger" in the Boston Custom House; for several months in 1841 he worked in the potato patch and manure pile at Brook Farm. In the meantime, he had fallen in love with Miss Sophia Peabody, whom he married in 1842. Love and marriage more than anything else, he felt, saved him from the fate of the solitary. The idyllic life of the newlyweds at the Old Manse is recorded in *The American Notebooks.*

Hawthorne returned to Salem in 1845; and in 1846 appeared a second collection of tales, entitled *Mosses from an Old Manse.* This volume, like *Twice-Told Tales,* attracted so few readers that it was with some justice that Hawthorne believed himself to be "the obscurest man of letters in America." Because of financial need, he gladly accepted appointment as surveyor in the Salem Custom House. Since he held this appointment as a loyal Democrat under the administration of James K. Polk, he was dismissed from office in 1849, after three years' service, to make room for a Whig. Loss of this place was a blow to Hawthorne. But adversity discovers virtue. The three years which followed were the most productive of his life. *The Scarlet Letter* (1850), an intense, tragic study of the psychological effects of adultery upon four people, made Hawthorne famous. His fame was enhanced by *The House of the Seven Gables* (1851), a study of the decay of an old Salem family, and *The Blithedale Romance* (1852), a satire, in part, on the socialist community at Brook Farm. *The House of the Seven Gables* was written at Lenox, in the Berkshires, where Hawthorne enjoyed the stimulating companionship of Herman Melville.

From 1853 to 1857 Hawthorne was consul at Liverpool; he had been appointed to that post by his old college friend, Franklin Pierce, then President of the United States. The office was not much to Hawthorne's liking; but he made the most of the opportunity of seeing England, his impressions of which he recorded in the posthumously printed *English Notebooks* and in *Our Old Home* (1863), a collection of essays. He spent 1858-1859 in Italy and employed Italian backgrounds in his last complete novel, *The Marble Faun* (1860). He returned in 1860 to "The Wayside" in Concord, which he had purchased a short time before going abroad. The Civil War darkened his last years. He did not share the abolitionist zeal. "I always thought that the war should have been avoided," he said in 1863, "although since it has broken out, I have longed for military success as much as any man or woman of the North." His personal loyalty to Pierce, whose public opposition to the War seemed treacherous to many, was little short of heroic. His last attempts at fiction resulted in *The Ancestral Footstep, Septimius Felton, Doctor Grimshawe's Secret,* and *The Dolliver Romance,* all unfinished at his death.

Critics of Hawthorne have found a good deal to object to, but more to praise. Henry James, while deprecating Hawthorne's "provincialism" and his "abuse of the fanciful element," declared: "No one has had just that vision of life, and no one has had a literary form that more successfully expressed his vision." W. C. Brownell, the severest of Hawthorne's critics, objected to his "placidity" and his obsession with allegory, but found in *The Scarlet Letter* "our chief prose masterpiece." More recently, T. S. Eliot has said (in *The Athenaeum,* April 25, 1919): "Hawthorne had . . . the firmness, the true coldness, the hard coldness of the genuine artist. In consequence, the observation of moral life in *The Scarlet Letter,* in *The House of the Seven Gables,* and even in some of the tales and sketches, has solidity, has permanence, the permanence of art. It will always be of use. . . . The work of Hawthorne is truly a criticism — true because a fidelity of the artist and not a mere conviction of the man — of the Puritan morality, of the Transcendentalist morality, and of the world which Hawthorne knew. It is a criticism as Henry James's work is a criticism of the America of his times, and as the work of Turgenev and Flaubert is a criticism of the Russia and the France of theirs." Of all the writers of New England's flowering, Hawthorne seems the most certain to endure.

The Complete Works of Nathaniel Hawthorne, Riverside Edition, 13 vols., Boston, 1883   The American Notebooks by Nathaniel Hawthorne, ed. Randall Stewart, New Haven, 1932   The English Notebooks by Nathaniel Hawthorne, ed. Randall Stewart, New York, 1941   Henry James, Hawthorne, New York, 1879   Randall Stewart, Nathaniel Hawthorne: A Biography, New Haven, 1948   E. H. Davidson, Hawthorne's Last Phase, New Haven, 1949   F. O. Matthiessen, American Renaissance, New York, 1941   Richard H. Fogle, Hawthorne's Fiction: The Light and the Dark, Norman, Okla., 1952   Hyatt H. Waggoner, Hawthorne, A Critical Study, Cambridge, Mass., 1955   Roy R. Male, Jr., Hawthorne's Tragic Vision, Austin, Texas, 1957   Hubert H. Hoeltje, Inward Sky: The Mind and Heart of Nathaniel Hawthorne, Durham, N. C., 1962

The Gentle Boy

The author of this story stands apart from the warring sects of early New England. He condemns unbridled fanaticism, whether Puritan or Quaker. He recommends the golden mean of "rational piety."

"The Gentle Boy" was first published in the Token *for 1832 and was reprinted in* Twice-Told Tales *in 1837. Hawthorne's chief source of historical information was Willem Sewel's*

History of the Quakers *(see G. Harrison Orians, "The Sources and Themes of Haw-thorne's 'The Gentle Boy,'"* New England Quarterly, *December 1941).*

In the course of the year 1656 several of the people called Quakers, led, as they professed, by the inward movement of the Spirit, made their appearance in New England. Their reputation, as holders of mystic and pernicious principles, having spread before them, the Puritans early endeavored to banish and to prevent the further intrusion of the rising sect. But the measures by which it was intended to purge the land of heresy, though more than sufficiently vigorous, were entirely unsuccessful. The Quakers, esteeming persecution as a divine call to the post of danger, laid claim to a holy courage, unknown to the Puritans themselves, who had shunned the Cross, by providing for the peaceable exercise of their religion in a distant wilderness. Though it was the singular fact that every nation of the earth rejected the 10 wandering enthusiasts who practised peace towards all men, the place of greatest uneasiness and peril, and therefore in their eyes the most eligible, was the province of Massachusetts Bay.

The fines, imprisonments, and stripes, liberally distributed by our pious forefathers; the popular antipathy, so strong that it endured nearly a hundred years after actual persecution had ceased, were attractions as powerful for the Quakers as peace, honor, and reward would have been for the worldly-minded. Every European vessel brought new cargoes of the sect, eager to testify against the oppression which they hoped to share; and when shipmasters were restrained by heavy fines from affording them passage, they made long and circuitous journeys through the Indian country, and 20 appeared in the province as if conveyed by a supernatural power. Their enthusiasm, heightened almost to madness by the treatment which they received, produced actions contrary to the rules of decency as well as of rational religion, and presented a singular contrast to the calm and staid deportment of their sectarian successors of the present day. The command of the Spirit, inaudible except to the soul, and not to be controverted on grounds of human wisdom, was made a plea for most indecorous exhibitions, which, abstractedly considered, well deserved the moderate chastisement of the rod. These extravagances, and the persecution which was at once their cause and consequence, continued to increase, till, in the year 1659, the Government of Massachusetts Bay indulged two members of the Quaker sect with the 30 crown of martyrdom.

An indelible stain of blood is upon the hands of all who consented to this act, but a large share of the awful responsibility must rest upon the person then at the head of the government. He was a man of narrow mind and imperfect education, and his uncompromising bigotry was made hot and mischievous by violent and hasty passions; he exerted his influence indecorously and unjustifiably to compass the death of the enthusiasts, and his whole conduct in respect to them was marked by brutal cruelty. The Quakers, whose revengeful feelings were not less deep be-

---

14 **our . . . forefathers,** prominent among whom was Hawthorne's first American ancestor, William Hathorne (see note, p. 85). Hawthorne alludes to his acts of persecution in two essays: "Main Street" in *The Snow Image and Other Twice-Told Tales* and "The Custom House" (the prefatory essay to *The Scarlet Letter*)

cause they were inactive, remembered this man and his associates in aftertimes. The historian of the sect affirms that, by the wrath of Heaven, a blight fell upon the land in the vicinity of the "bloody town" of Boston, so that no wheat would grow there; and he takes his stand, as it were, among the graves of the ancient persecutors, and triumphantly recounts the judgments that overtook them in old age or at the parting hour. He tells us that they died suddenly, and violently, and in madness; but nothing can exceed the bitter mockery with which he records the loathsome disease and "death by rottenness" of the fierce and cruel governor.

On the evening of the autumn day that had witnessed the martyrdom of two men
10 of the Quaker persuasion, a Puritan settler was returning from the metropolis to the neighboring country town in which he resided. The air was cool, the sky clear, and the lingering twilight was made brighter by the rays of a young moon, which had now nearly reached the verge of the horizon. The traveller, a man of middle age, wrapped in a grey frieze coat, quickened his pace when he had reached the outskirts of the town, for a gloomy extent of nearly four miles lay between him and his home. The low, straw-thatched houses were scattered at considerable intervals along the road, and the country having been settled but about thirty years, the tracts of original forest still bore no small proportion to the cultivated ground. The autumn wind wandered among the branches, whirling away the leaves from all except the
20 pine-trees, and moaning as if it lamented the desolation of which it was the instrument. The road had penetrated the mass of woods that lay nearest to the town, and was just emerging into an open space, when the traveller's ears were saluted by a sound more mournful than even that of the wind. It was like the wailing of some one in distress, and it seemed to proceed from beneath a tall and lonely fir tree, in the centre of a cleared, but uninclosed and uncultivated field. The Puritan could not but remember that this was the very spot which had been made accursed a few hours before by the execution of the Quakers, whose bodies had been thrown together into one hasty grave, beneath the tree on which they suffered. He struggled, however, against the superstitious fears which belonged to the age, and compelled him-
30 self to pause and listen.

"The voice was most likely mortal, nor have I cause to tremble if it be otherwise," thought he, straining his eyes through the dim moonlight. "Methinks it is like the wailing of a child; some infant, it may be, which has strayed from its mother, and chanced upon the place of death. For the ease of mine own conscience, I must search this matter out."

He therefore left the path, and walked somewhat fearfully across the field. Though now so desolate, its soil was pressed down and trampled by the thousand footsteps of those who had witnessed the spectacle of that day, all of whom had now retired, leaving the dead to their loneliness. The traveller at length reached the fir tree, which
40 from the middle upward was covered with living branches, although a scaffold had been erected beneath, and other preparations made for the work of death. Under this unhappy tree, which in after-times was believed to drop poison with its dew,

---

2 **historian . . . sect,** William Sewel, author of *The History of the Quakers* (London, 1725)   8 **governor,**
John Endicott. See note, p. 78

sat the one solitary mourner for innocent blood. It was a slender and light-clad little boy, who leaned his face upon a hillock of fresh-turned and half-frozen earth,
and wailed bitterly, yet in a suppressed tone, as if his grief might receive the punishment of crime. The Puritan, whose approach had been unperceived, laid his hand
upon the child's shoulder, and addressed him compassionately.

"You have chosen a dreary lodging, my poor boy, and no wonder that you weep,"
said he. "But dry your eyes, and tell me where your mother dwells. I promise you,
if the journey be not too far, I will leave you in her arms to-night."

The boy had hushed his wailing at once, and turned his face upward to the stranger. It was a pale, bright-eyed countenance, certainly not more than six years old,   10
but sorrow, fear, and want, had destroyed much of its infantile expression. The
Puritan, seeing the boy's frightened gaze, and feeling that he trembled under his
hand, endeavored to reassure him.

"Nay, if I intended to do you harm, little lad, the readiest way were to leave you
here. What! you do not fear to sit beneath the gallows on a new-made grave, and
yet you tremble at a friend's touch. Take heart, child, and tell me what is your name,
and where is your home?"

"Friend," replied the little boy, in a sweet, though faltering voice, "they call me
Ilbrahim, and my home is here."

The pale, spiritual face, the eyes that seemed to mingle with the moonlight, the   20
sweet, airy voice, and the outlandish name, almost made the Puritan believe that
the boy was in truth a being which had sprung up out of the grave on which he
sat. But perceiving that the apparition stood the test of a short mental prayer, and
remembering that the arm which he had touched was lifelike, he adopted a more
rational supposition. "The poor child is stricken in his intellect," thought he; "but
verily his words are fearful, in a place like this." He then spoke soothingly, intending to humor the boy's fantasy.

"Your home will scarce be comfortable, Ilbrahim, this cold autumn night, and I
fear you are ill provided with food. I am hastening to a warm supper and bed, and
if you go with me, you shall share them!"   30

"I thank thee, friend, but though I be hungry and shivering with cold, thou wilt
not give me food nor lodging," replied the boy, in the quiet tone which despair had
taught him even so young. "My father was of the people whom all men hate. They
have laid him under this heap of earth, and here is my home."

The Puritan, who had laid hold of little Ilbrahim's hand, relinquished it as if he
were touching a loathsome reptile. But he possessed a compassionate heart, which
not even religious prejudice could harden into stone.

"God forbid that I should leave this child to perish, though he comes of the accursed sect," said he to himself. "Do we not all spring from an evil root? Are we
not all in darkness till the light doth shine upon us? He shall not perish, neither in   40
body, nor, if prayer and instruction may avail for him, in soul." He then spoke aloud
and kindly to Ilbrahim, who had again hid his face in the cold earth of the grave.
"Was every door in the land shut against you, my child, that you have wandered to
this unhallowed spot?"

"They drove me forth from prison when they took my father thence," said the boy; "and I stood afar off, watching the crowd of people, and when they were gone I came thither and found only his grave. I knew that my father was sleeping here, and I said, this shall be my home."

"No, child, no; not while I have a roof over my head, or a morsel to share with you!" exclaimed the Puritan, whose sympathies were now fully excited. "Rise up and come with me, and fear not any harm."

The boy wept afresh, and clung to the heap of earth, as if the cold heart beneath it were warmer to him than any in a living breast. The traveller, however, contin-
10 ued to entreat him tenderly, and seeming to acquire some degree of confidence, he at length arose. But his slender limbs tottered with weakness, his little head grew dizzy, and he leaned against the tree of death for support.

"My poor boy, are you so feeble?" said the Puritan. "When did you taste food last?"

"I ate bread and water with my father in the prison," replied Ilbrahim, "but they brought him none neither yesterday nor to-day, saying that he had eaten enough to bear him to his journey's end. Trouble not thyself for my hunger, kind friend, for I have lacked food many times ere now."

The traveller took the child in his arms and wrapped his cloak about him, while
20 his heart stirred with shame and anger against the gratuitous cruelty of the instruments in this persecution. In the awakened warmth of his feelings, he resolved that, at whatever risk, he would not forsake the poor little defenseless being whom Heaven had confided to his care. With this determination he left the accursed field, and resumed the homeward path from which the wailing of the boy had called him. The light and motionless burthen scarcely impeded his progress, and he soon beheld the fire-rays from the windows of the cottage which he, a native of a distant clime, had built in the western wilderness. It was surrounded by a considerable extent of cultivated ground, and the dwelling was situated in the nook of a wood-covered hill, whither it seemed to have crept for protection.

30 "Look up child," said the Puritan to Ilbrahim, whose faint head had sunk upon his shoulder; "there is our home."

At the word, "home," a thrill passed through the child's frame, but he continued silent. A few moments brought them to the cottage door, at which the owner knocked; for at that early period, when savages were wandering everywhere among the settlers, bolt and bar were indispensable to the security of a dwelling. The summons was answered by a bond-servant, a coarse-clad and dull-featured piece of humanity, who, after ascertaining that his master was the applicant, undid the door, and held a flaring pine-knot torch to light him in. Farther back in the passage-way the red blaze discovered a matronly woman, but no little crowd of children came
40 bounding forth to greet their father's return. As the Puritan entered, he thrust aside his cloak, and displayed Ilbrahim's face to the female.

"Dorothy, here is a little outcast, whom Providence hath put into our hands," observed he. "Be kind to him, even as if he were of those dear ones who have departed from us."

"What pale and bright-eyed little boy is this, Tobias?" she inquired. "Is he one whom the wilderness folk have ravished from some Christian mother?"

"No, Dorothy, this poor child is no captive from the wilderness," he replied. "The heathen savage would have given him to eat of his scanty morsel, and to drink of his birchen cup; but Christian men, alas? had cast him out to die."

Then he told her how he had found him beneath the gallows, upon his father's grave; and how his heart had prompted him, like the speaking of an inward voice, to take the little outcast home, and be kind to him. He acknowledged his resolutions to feed and clothe him, as if he were his own child, and to afford him the instruction which should counteract the pernicious errors hitherto instilled into his 10 infant mind. Dorothy was gifted with even a quicker tenderness than her husband, and she approved of all of his doings and intentions.

"Have you a mother, dear child?" she inquired.

The tears burst forth from his full heart as he attempted to reply; but Dorothy at length understood that he had a mother, who, like the rest of her sect, was a persecuted wanderer. She had been taken from the prison a short time before, carried into the uninhabited wilderness, and left to perish there by hunger or wild beasts; this was no uncommon method of disposing of the Quakers, and they were accustomed to boast that the inhabitants of the desert were more hospitable to them than civilized man.   20

"Fear not, little boy, you shall not need a mother, and a kind one," said Dorothy, when she had gathered this information. "Dry your tears, Ilbrahim, and be my child, as I will be your mother."

The good woman prepared the little bed from which her own children had successively been borne to another resting-place. Before Ilbrahim would consent to occupy it, he knelt down, and as Dorothy listened to his simple and affecting prayer, she marvelled how the parents that had taught it to him could have been judged worthy of death. When the boy had fallen asleep, she bent over his pale and spiritual countenance, pressed a kiss upon his white brow, drew the bedclothes up about his neck, and went away with a pensive gladness in her heart.   30

Tobias Pearson was not among the earliest emigrants from the old country. He had remained in England during the first years of the civil war, in which he had borne some share as a cornet of dragoons under Cromwell. But when the ambitious designs of his leader began to develop themselves, he quitted the army of the parliament and sought a refuge from the strife, which was no longer holy, among the people of his persuasion in the colony of Massachusetts. A more worldly consideration had perhaps an influence in drawing him thither; for New England offered advantages to men of unprosperous fortunes as well as to dissatisfied religionists, and Pearson had hitherto found it difficult to provide for a wife and increasing family. To this supposed impurity of motive, the more bigoted Puritans were in- 40 clined to impute the removal by death of all the children for whose earthly good the father had been over-thoughtful. They had left their native country blooming like roses, and like roses they had perished in a foreign soil. Those expounders of the ways of Providence, who had thus judged their brother, and attributed his domestic sorrows to his sin, were not more charitable when they saw him and Dorothy endeavoring to fill up the void in their hearts, by the adoption of an infant of the accursed sect. Nor did they fail to communicate their disapprobation to Tobias; but the latter, in reply, merely pointed at the little, quiet, lovely boy, whose appearance and deportment were indeed as powerful arguments as could possibly have been adduced in his own favor. Even his beauty, however, and his winning manners, sometimes produced an effect ultimately unfavorable; for the bigots, when the outer surfaces of their iron hearts had been softened and again grew hard, affirmed that no merely natural cause could have so worked upon them.

10   Their antipathy to the poor infant was also increased by the ill success of divers theological discussions, in which it was attempted to convince him of the errors of his sect. Ilbrahim, it is true, was not a skilful controversialist; but the feeling of his religion was strong as instinct in him, and he could neither be enticed nor driven from the faith which his father had died for. The odium of this stubbornness was shared in a great measure by the child's protectors, insomuch that Tobias and Dorothy very shortly began to experience a most bitter species of persecution, in the cold regards of many a friend whom they had valued. The common people manifested their opinions more openly. Pearson was a man of some consideration, being a Representative to the General Court, and an approved Lieutenant in the 20 trainbands, yet within a week after his adoption of Ilbrahim, he had been both hissed and hooted. Once, also, when walking through a solitary piece of woods, he heard a loud voice from some invisible speaker; and it cried, "What shall be done to the backslider? Lo! the scourge is knotted for him, even the whip of nine cords, and every cord three knots!" These insults irritated Pearson's temper for the moment; they entered also into his heart, and became imperceptible but powerful workers towards an end which his most secret thought had not yet whispered.

On the second Sabbath after Ilbrahim became a member of their family, Pearson and his wife deemed it proper that he should appear with them at public worship. They had anticipated some opposition to this measure from the boy, but he pre-30 pared himself in silence, and at the appointed hour was clad in the new mourning suit which Dorothy had wrought for him. As the parish was then, and during many subsequent years, unprovided with a bell, the signal for the commencement of religious exercises was the beat of a drum. At the first sound of that martial call to the place of holy and quiet thoughts, Tobias and Dorothy set forth, each holding a hand of little Ilbrahim, like two parents linked together by the infant of their love. On their path through the leafless woods, they were overtaken by many persons of their acquaintance, all of whom avoided them, and passed by on the other side; but a severer trial awaited their constancy when they had descended the hill, and drew near the pine-built and undecorated house of prayer. Around the door, from which 40 the drummer still sent forth his thundering summons, was drawn up a formidable phalanx, including several of the oldest members of the congregation, many of the middle-aged, and nearly all the younger males. Pearson found it difficult to sustain their united and disapproving gaze, but Dorothy, whose mind was differently circumstanced, merely drew the boy closer to her, and faltered not in her approach. As they entered the door, they overheard the muttered sentiments of the assemblage, and when the reviling voices of the little children smote Ilbrahim's ear, he wept.

The interior aspect of the meeting-house was rude. The low ceiling, the unplastered walls, the naked wood-work, and the undraperied pulpit, offered nothing to excite the devotion, which, without such external aids, often remains latent in the heart. The floor of the building was occupied by rows of long, cushionless benches, supplying the place of pews, and the broad aisle formed a sexual division, impassable except by children beneath a certain age.

Pearson and Dorothy separated at the door of the meeting-house, and Ilbrahim, being within the years of infancy, was retained under the care of the latter. The 10 wrinkled beldams involved themselves in their rusty cloaks as he passed by; even the mild-featured maidens seemed to dread contamination; and many a stern old man arose, and turned his repulsive and unheavenly countenance upon the gentle boy, as if the sanctuary were polluted by his presence. He was a sweet infant of the skies that had strayed away from his home, and all the inhabitants of this miserable world closed up their impure hearts against him, drew back their earth-soiled garments from his touch, and said, "We are holier than thou."

Ilbrahim, seated by the side of his adopted mother, and retaining fast hold of her hand, assumed a grave and decorous demeanor, such as might befit a person of matured taste and understanding, who should find himself in a temple dedicated to 20 some worship which he did not recognize, but felt himself bound to respect. The exercises had not yet commenced, however, when the boy's attention was arrested by an event, apparently of trifling interest. A woman having her face muffled in a hood, and a cloak drawn completely about her form, advanced slowly up the broad aisle, and took a place upon the foremost bench. Ilbrahim's faint color varied, his nerves fluttered, he was unable to turn his eyes from the muffled female.

When the preliminary prayer and hymn were over, the minister arose, and having turned the hour-glass which stood by the great Bible, commenced his discourse. He was now well stricken in years, a man of pale, thin countenance, and his grey hairs were closely covered by a black velvet skull-cap. In his younger days he had prac- 30 tically learned the meaning of persecution from Archbishop Laud, and he was not now disposed to forget the lesson against which he had murmured then. Introducing the often-discussed subject of the Quakers, he gave a history of that sect, and a description of their tenets, in which error predominated, and prejudice distorted the aspect of what was true. He adverted to the recent measures in the province, and cautioned his hearers of weaker parts against calling in question the just severity which God-fearing magistrates had at length been compelled to exercise. He spoke of the danger of pity, in some cases a commendable and Christian virtue but inapplicable to this pernicious sect. He observed that such was their devilish obstinacy in error, that even the little children, the sucking babes, were hardened and desperate 40 heretics. He affirmed that no man, without Heaven's especial warrant, should at-

---

11 **involved,** wrapped, enveloped (a Latinism)   31 **Archbishop Laud,** William Laud (1573-1645), Archbishop of Canterbury, whose acts of persecution caused many of the early Puritans to leave England

tempt their conversion, lest while he lent his hand to draw them from the slough, he should himself be precipitated into its lowest depths.

The sands of the second hour were principally in the lower half of the glass, when the sermon concluded. An approving murmur followed, and the clergyman, having given out a hymn, took his seat with much self-congratulation, and endeavored to read the effect of his eloquence in the visages of the people. But while voices from all parts of the house were tuning themselves to sing, a scene occurred which, though not very unusual at that period in the province, happened to be without precedent in this parish.

10   The muffled female, who had hitherto sat motionless in the front rank of the audience, now arose, and with slow, stately, and unwavering step, ascended the pulpit stairs. The quiverings of incipient harmony were hushed, and the divine sat in speechless and almost terrified astonishment, while she undid the door, and stood up in the sacred desk from which his maledictions had just been thundered. She then divested herself of the cloak and hood, and appeared in a most singular array. A shapeless robe of sackcloth was girded about her waist with a knotted cord; her raven hair fell down upon her shoulders, and its blackness was defiled by pale streaks of ashes, which she had strewn upon her head. Her eyebrows, dark and strongly defined added to the deathly whiteness of a countenance, which, emaciated with want,
20   and wild with enthusiasm and strange sorrows, retained no trace of earlier beauty. This figure stood gazing earnestly on the audience, and there was no sound, nor any movement, except a faint shuddering which every man observed in his neighbor, but was scarcely conscious of in himself. At length, when her fit of inspiration came, she spoke, for the first few moments, in a low voice, and not invariably distinct utterance. Her discourse gave evidence of an imagination hopelessly entangled with her reason; it was a vague and incomprehensible rhapsody, which, however, seemed to spread its own atmosphere round the hearer's soul, and to move his feeling by some influence unconnected with the words. As she proceeded, beautiful but shadowy images would sometimes be seen, like bright things moving in a turbid
30   river; or a strong and singularly shaped idea leapt forth, and seized at once on the understanding or the heart. But the course of her unearthly eloquence soon led her to the persecution of her sect, and from thence the step was short to her own peculiar sorrows. She was naturally a woman of mighty passions, and hatred and revenge now wrapped themselves in the garb of piety; the character of her speech was changed, her images became distinct though wild, and her denunciations had an almost hellish bitterness.

"The governor and his mighty men," she said, "have gathered together, taking counsel among themselves and saying, 'What shall we do unto this people — even unto the people that have come into this land to put our iniquity to the blush?'
40   And lo! the devil entereth into the council-chamber, like a lame man of low stature and gravely apparelled, with a dark and twisted countenance, and a bright, downcast eye. And he standeth up among the rulers; yea, he goeth to and fro, whispering to each; and every man lends his ear, for his word is, 'Slay, slay!' But I say unto ye, Woe to them that slay! Woe to them that shed the blood of saints! Woe to them

that have slain the husband, and cast forth the child, the tender infant, to wander homeless, and hungry, and cold, till he die; and have saved the mother alive, in the cruelty of their tender mercies! Woe to them in their lifetime, cursed are they in the delight and pleasure of their hearts! Woe to them in their death-hour, whether it come swiftly with blood and violence, or after long and lingering pain! Woe, in the dark house, in the rottenness of the grave, when the children's children shall revile the ashes of the fathers! Woe, woe, woe, at the judgment, when all the persecuted and all the slain in this bloody land, and the father, the mother, and the child, shall await them in the day that they cannot escape! Seed of the faith, seed of the faith, ye whose hearts are moving with a power that ye know not, arise, wash your   10
hands of this innocent blood! Lift your voices, chosen ones, cry aloud, and call down a woe and a judgment with me!'

Having thus given vent to the flood of malignity which she mistook for inspiration, the speaker was silent. Her voice was succeeded by the hysteric shrieks of several women, but the feelings of the audience generally had not been drawn onward in the current with her own. They remained stupefied, stranded, as it were, in the midst of a torrent, which deafened them by its roaring, but might not move them by its violence. The clergyman, who could not hitherto have ejected the usurper of his pulpit otherwise than by bodily force, now addressed her in the tone of just indignation and legitimate authority.   20

"Get you down, woman, from the holy place which you profane," he said. "Is it to the Lord's house that you come to pour forth the foulness of your heart, and the inspiration of the devil? Get you down, and remember that the sentence of death is on you; yea, and shall be executed, were it but for this day's work!"

"I go, friend, I go, for the voice hath had its utterance," replied she, in a depressed and even mild tone. "I have done my mission unto thee and to thy people. Reward me with stripes, imprisonment, or death, as ye shall be permitted."

The weakness of exhausted passion caused her steps to totter as she descended the pulpit stairs. The people in the meanwhile were stirring to and fro on the floor of the house, whispering among themselves and glancing towards the intruder. Many   30
of them now recognized her as the woman who had assaulted the governor with frightful language as he passed by the window of her prison; they knew, also, that she was adjudged to suffer death, and had been preserved only by an involuntary banishment into the wilderness. The new outrage by which she had provoked her fate seemed to render further lenity impossible; and a gentleman in military dress, with a stout man of inferior rank, drew towards the door of the meeting-house and awaited her approach. Scarcely did her feet press the floor, however, when an unexpected scene occurred. In that moment of her peril when every eye frowned with death, a little timid boy pressed forth and threw his arms round his mother.

"I am here, mother — it is I; and I will go with thee to prison," he exclaimed.   40

She gazed at him with a doubtful and almost frightened expression, for she knew that the boy had been cast out to perish, and she had not hoped to see his face again. She feared, perhaps, that it was but one of the happy visions with which her excited fancy had often deceived her, in the solitude of the desert or in prison. But when she felt his hand warm within her own, and heard his little eloquence of childish love, she began to know that she was yet a mother.

"Blessed art thou, my son," she sobbed. "My heart was withered; yea, dead with thee and with thy father; and now it leaps as in the first moment when I pressed thee to my bosom."

She knelt down and embraced him again and again, while the joy that could find no words expressed itself in broken accents, like the bubbles gushing up to vanish at the surface of a deep fountain. The sorrows of past years, and the darker peril that was nigh, cast not a shadow on the brightness of that fleeting moment. Soon, however, the spectators saw a change upon her face, as the consciousness of her sad estate returned, and grief supplied the fount of tears which joy had opened. By the words she uttered, it would seem that the indulgence of natural love had given her mind a momentary sense of its errors, and made her know how far she had strayed from duty in following the dictates of a wild fanaticism.

"In a doleful hour art thou returned to me, poor boy," she said, "for thy mother's path has gone darkening onward till now the end is death. Son, son, I have borne thee in my arms when my limbs were tottering, and I have fed thee with the food that I was fainting for; yet I have ill performed a mother's part by thee in life, and now I leave thee no inheritance but woe and shame. Thou wilt go seeking through the world, and find all hearts closed against thee, and their sweet affections turned to bitterness for my sake. My child, my child, how many a pang awaits thy gentle spirit, and I the cause of all!"

She hid her face on Ilbrahim's head, and her long, raven hair, discolored with the ashes of her mourning, fell down about him like a veil. A low and interrupted moan was the voice of her heart's anguish, and it did not fail to move the sympathies of many who mistook their involuntary virtue for a sin. Sobs were audible in the female section of the house, and every man who was a father drew his hand across his eyes. Tobias Pearson was agitated and uneasy, but a certain feeling like the consciousness of guilt oppressed him, so that he could not go forth and offer himself as the protector of the child. Dorothy, however, had watched her husband's eye. Her mind was free from the influence that had begun to work on his, and she drew near the Quaker woman, and addressed her in the hearing of all the congregation.

"Stranger, trust this boy to me, and I will be his mother," she said, taking Ilbrahim's hand. "Providence has signally marked out my husband to protect him, and he has fed at our table and lodged under our roof now many days, till our hearts have grown very strongly unto him. Leave the tender child with us, and be at ease concerning his welfare."

The Quaker rose from the ground, but drew the boy closer to her while she gazed earnestly in Dorothy's face. Her mild, but saddened features, and neat, matronly attire, harmonized together, and were like a verse of fireside poetry. Her very aspect proved that she was blameless, so far as mortal could be so, in respect to God and man; while the enthusiast, in her robe of sackcloth and girdle of knotted cord, had

---

42 **enthusiast** implied irrational and fanatical emotion and was a term of reproach in seventeenth-century Puritan usage as well as in the usage of eighteenth-century Neoclassicism

as evidently violated the duties of the present life and the future, by fixing her attention wholly on the latter. The two females, as they held each a hand of Ilbrahim, formed a practical allegory; it was rational piety and unbridled fanaticism contending for the empire of a young heart.

"Thou art not of our people," said the Quaker, mournfully.

"No, we are not of your people," replied Dorothy with mildness; "but we are Christians, looking upward to the same Heaven with you. Doubt not that your boy shall meet you there, if there be a blessing on our tender and prayerful guidance of him. Thither, I trust, my own children have gone before me, for I also have been a mother. I am no longer so," she added, in a faltering tone; "and your son will 10 have all my care."

"But will ye lead him in the path which his parents have trodden?" demanded the Quaker. "Can ye teach him the enlightened faith which his father has died for, and for which I, even I, am soon to become an unworthy martyr? The boy has been baptised in blood; will ye keep the mark fresh and ruddy upon his forehead?"

"I will not deceive you," answered Dorothy. "If your child become our child, we must breed him up in the instruction which Heaven has imparted to us; we must pray for him the prayers of our own faith; we must do towards him according to the dictates of our own consciences, and not of yours. Were we to act otherwise, we should abuse your trust even in complying with your wishes."   20

The mother looked down upon her boy with a troubled countenance, and then turned her eyes upward to heaven. She seemed to pray internally, and the contention of her soul was evident.

"Friend," she said at length to Dorothy, "I doubt not that my son shall receive all earthly tenderness at thy hands. Nay, I will believe that even thy imperfect lights may guide him to a better world; for surely thou art on the path thither. But thou hast spoken of a husband. Doth he stand here among this multitude of people? Let him come forth, for I must know to whom I commit this most precious trust."

She turned her face upon the male auditors, and after a momentary delay, Tobias Pearson came forth from among them. The Quaker saw the dress which marked his 30 military rank, and shook her head; but then she noted the hesitating air, the eyes that struggled with her own, and were vanquished; the color that went and came, and could find no resting-place. As she gazed, an unmirthful smile spread over her features, like sunshine that grows melancholy in some desolate spot. Her lips moved inaudibly, but at length she spake.

"I hear it, I hear it. The voice speaketh within me and saith, 'Leave thy child, Catherine, for his place is here, and go hence, for I have other work for thee. Break the bonds of natural affection, martyr thy love, and know that in all these things eternal wisdom hath its ends.' I go, friends, I go. Take ye my boy, my precious jewel.

---

3 **allegory.** Hawthorne's allegorical characters recall similar figures in Spenser's *Faerie Queene,* Bk. II, Canto II, where Elissa and Perissa represent opposite extremes of temperament and "the faire Medina" represents the golden mean. For a discussion of Spenser's influence on Hawthorne, see Randall Stewart, "Hawthorne and *The Faerie Queene,*" *Philological Quarterly,* April 1933

I go hence, trusting that all shall be well, and that even for his infant hands there is a labor in the vineyard."

She knelt down and whispered to Ilbrahim, who at first struggled and clung to his mother, with sobs and tears, but remained passive when she had kissed his cheek and arisen from the ground. Having held her hands over his head in mental prayer, she was ready to depart.

"Farewell, friends in mine extremity," she said to Pearson and his wife; "the good deed ye have done me is a treasure laid up in heaven, to be returned a thousand-fold hereafter. And farewell ye, mine enemies, to whom it is not permitted to harm
10 so much as a hair of my head nor to stay my footsteps even for a moment. The day is coming when ye shall call upon me to witness for ye to this one sin uncommitted, and I will rise up and answer."

She turned her steps towards the door, and the men, who had stationed themselves to guard it, withdrew, and suffered her to pass. A general sentiment of pity overcame the virulence of religious hatred. Sanctified by her love and her affliction, she went forth, and all the people gazed after her till she had journeyed up the hill, and was lost behind its brow. She went, the apostle of her own unquiet heart, to renew the wanderings of past years. For her voice had been already heard in many lands of Christendom; and she had pined in the cells of Catholic Inquisition, before
20 she felt the lash and lay in the dungeons of the Puritans. Her mission had extended also to the followers of the Prophet, and from them she had received the courtesy and kindness which all the contending sects of our purer religion united to deny her. Her husband and herself had resided many months in Turkey, where even the Sultan's countenance was gracious to them; in that pagan land, too, was Ilbrahim's birthplace, and his oriental name was a mark of gratitude for the good deeds of an unbeliever.

When Pearson and his wife had thus acquired all the rights over Ilbrahim that could be delegated, their affection for him became, like the memory of their native land, or their mild sorrow for the dead, a piece of the immovable furniture of their
30 hearts. The boy, also, after a week or two of mental disquiet, began to gratify his protectors by many inadvertent proofs that he considered them as parents, and their house as home. Before the winter snows were melted, the persecuted infant, the little wanderer from a remote and heathen country, seemed native in the New England cottage, and inseparable from the warmth and security of its hearth. Under the influence of kind treatment, and in the consciousness that he was loved, Ilbrahim's demeanor lost a premature manliness, which had resulted from his earlier situation; he became more childlike, and his natural character displayed itself with freedom. It was in many respects a beautiful one, yet the disordered imaginations of both his father and mother had perhaps propagated a certain unhealthiness in the mind of
40 the boy. In his general state, Ilbrahim would derive enjoyment from the most trifling events, and from every object about him; he seemed to discover rich treasures of happiness, by a faculty analogous to that of the witch-hazel, which points to hidden

---

21 **Prophet,** Mohammed, the founder of Islam

gold where all is barren to the eye. His airy gaiety, coming to him from a thousand sources, communicated itself to the family, and Ilbrahim was like a domesticated sunbeam, brightening moody countenances, and chasing away the gloom from the dark corners of the cottage.

On the other hand, as the susceptibility of pleasure is also that of pain, the exuberant cheerfulness of the boy's prevailing temper sometimes yielded to moments of deep depression. His sorrows could not always be followed up to their original source, but most frequently they appeared to flow, though Ilbrahim was young to be sad for such a cause, from wounded love. The flightiness of his mirth rendered him often guilty of offences against the decorum of a Puritan household, and on 10 these occasions he did not invariably escape rebuke. But the slightest word of real bitterness, which he was infallible in distinguishing from pretended anger, seemed to sink into his heart and poison all his enjoyments, till he became sensible that he was entirely forgiven. Of the malice which generally accompanies a superfluity of sensitiveness Ilbrahim was altogether destitute; when trodden upon, he would not turn; when wounded, he could but die. His mind was wanting in the stamina for self-support; it was a plant that would twine beautifully round something stronger than itself, but if repulsed, or torn away, it had no choice but to wither on the ground. Dorothy's acuteness taught her that severity would crush the spirit of the child, and she nurtured him with the gentle care of one who handles a butter- 20 fly. Her husband manifested an equal affection, although it grew daily less productive of familiar caresses.

The feelings of the neighboring people, in regard to the Quaker infant and his protectors, had not undergone a favorable change, in spite of the momentary triumph which the desolate mother had obtained over their sympathies. The scorn and bitterness of which he was the object were very grievous to Ilbrahim, especially when any circumstance made him sensible that the children, his equals in age, partook of the enmity of their parents. His tender and social nature had already overflowed in attachments to everything about him, and still there was a residue of unappropriated love, which he yearned to bestow upon the little ones who were taught to hate 30 him. As the warm days of spring came on, Ilbrahim was accustomed to remain for hours, silent and inactive, within hearing of the children's voices at their play; yet, with his usual delicacy of feeling, he avoided their notice, and would flee and hide himself from the smallest individual among them. Chance, however, at length seemed to open a medium of communication between his heart and theirs; it was by means of a boy about two years older than Ilbrahim, who was injured by a fall from a tree in the vicinity of Pearson's habitation. As the sufferer's own home was at some distance, Dorothy willingly received him under her roof, and became his tender and careful nurse.

Ilbrahim was the unconscious possessor of much skill in physiognomy, and it 40 would have deterred him, in other circumstances, from attempting to make a friend of this boy. The countenance of the latter immediately impressed a beholder dis-

---

2 **like . . . sunbeam,** a favorite figure of Hawthorne's. See Walter Blair, "Color, Light, and Shadow in Hawthorne's Fiction," *New England Quarterly,* March 1942

agreeably, but it required some examination to discover that the cause was a very slight distortion of the mouth, and the irregular, broken line and near approach of the eyebrows. Analogous, perhaps, to those trifling deformities was an almost imperceptible twist of every joint, and the uneven prominence of the breast; forming a body regular in its general outline, but faulty in almost all its details. The disposition of the boy was sullen and reserved, and the village schoolmaster stigmatized him as obtuse in intellect; although, at a later period of life, he evinced ambition and very peculiar talents. But whatever might be his personal or moral irregularities, Ilbrahim's heart seized upon, and clung to him, from the moment that he was brought
10 wounded into the cottage; the child of persecution seemed to compare his own fate with that of the sufferer, and to feel that even different modes of misfortune had created a sort of relationship between them. Food, rest, and the fresh air, for which he languished, were neglected; he nestled continually by the bedside of the little stranger, and, with a fond jealousy, endeavored to be the medium of all the cares that were bestowed upon him. As the boy became convalescent, Ilbrahim contrived games suitable to his situation, or amused him by a faculty which he had perhaps breathed in with the air of his barbaric birthplace. It was that of reciting imaginary adventures on the spur of the moment, and apparently in exhaustless succession. His tales were of course monstrous, disjointed, and without aim; but they were curi-
20 ous, on account of a vein of human tenderness which ran through them all, and was like a sweet, familiar face encountered in the midst of wild and unearthly scenery. The auditor paid much attention to these romances, and sometimes interrupted them by brief remarks upon the incidents, displaying shrewdness above his years, mingled with a moral obliquity which grated very harshly against Ilbrahim's instinctive rectitude. Nothing, however, could arrest the progress of the latter's affection, and there were many proofs that it met with a response from the dark and stubborn nature on which it was lavished. The boy's parents at length removed him, to complete his cure under their own roof.

Ilbrahim did not visit his new friend after his departure; but he made anxious
30 and continual inquiries respecting him, and informed himself of the day when he was to reappear among his playmates. On a pleasant summer afternoon, the children of the neighborhood had assembled in the little forest-crowned amphitheatre behind the meeting-house, and the recovering invalid was there, leaning on a staff. The glee of a score of untainted bosoms was heard in light and airy voices, which danced among the trees like sunshine become audible; the grown men of this weary world, as they journeyed by the spot, marvelled why life, beginning in such brightness, should proceed in gloom; and their hearts, or their imaginations, answered them and said, that the bliss of childhood gushes from its innocence. But it happened that an unexpected addition was made to the heavenly little band. It was Ilbrahim,
40 who came towards the children with a look of sweet confidence on his fair and spiritual face, as if, having manifested his love to one of them, he had no longer to fear a repulse from their society. A hush came over their mirth the moment they beheld him, and they stood whispering to each other while he drew nigh; but all at once the devil of their fathers entered into these unbreeched fanatics, and sending up a

fierce shrill cry, they rushed upon the poor Quaker child. In an instant he was the centre of a brood of baby-fiends, who lifted sticks against him, pelted him with stones, and displayed an instinct of destruction far more loathsome than the blood-thirstiness of manhood.

The invalid in the meanwhile stood apart from the tumult, crying out with a loud voice, "Fear not, Ilbrahim, come hither and take my hand;" and his unhappy friend endeavored to obey him. After watching the victim's struggling approach with a calm smile and unabashed eye, the foul-hearted little villain lifted his staff and struck Ilbrahim on the mouth so forcibly that the blood issued in a stream. The poor child's arms had been raised to guard his head from the storm of blows; but now he 10 dropped them at once. His persecutors beat him down, trampled upon him, dragged him by his long, fair locks, and Ilbrahim was on the point of becoming as veritable a martyr as ever entered bleeding into heaven. The uproar, however, attracted the notice of a few neighbors, who put themselves to the trouble of rescuing the little heretic, and of conveying him to Pearson's door.

Ilbrahim's bodily harm was severe, but long and careful nursing accomplished his recovery; the injury done to his sensitive spirit was more serious, though not so visible. Its signs were principally of a negative character, and to be discovered only by those who had previously known him. His gait was thenceforth slow, even, and unvaried by the sudden bursts of sprightlier motion which had once corresponded 20 to his overflowing gladness; his countenance was heavier, and its former play of expression, the dance of sunshine reflected from moving water, was destroyed by the cloud over his existence; his notice was attracted in a far less degree by passing events, and he appeared to find greater difficulty in comprehending what was new to him than at a happier period. A stranger, founding his judgment upon these circumstances, would have said that the dulness of the child's intellect widely contradicted the promise of his features; but the secret was in the direction of Ilbrahim's thoughts, which were brooding within him when they should naturally have been wandering abroad. An attempt of Dorothy to revive his former sportiveness was the single occasion on which his quiet demeanor yielded to a violent display of grief; 30 he burst into passionate weeping, and ran and hid himself, for his heart had become so miserably sore that even the hand of kindness tortured it like fire. Sometimes, at night and probably in his dreams, he was heard to cry, "Mother! Mother!" as if her place, which a stranger had supplied while Ilbrahim was happy, admitted of no substitute in his extreme affliction. Perhaps, among the many life-weary wretches then upon the earth, there was not one who combined innocence and misery like this poor, broken-hearted infant, so soon the victim of his own heavenly nature.

While this melancholy change had taken place in Ilbrahim, one of an earlier origin and of different character had come to its perfection in his adopted father. The incident with which this tale commences found Pearson in a state of religious dulness, 40 yet mentally disquieted, and longing for a more fervid faith than he possessed. The first effect of his kindness to Ilbrahim was to produce a softened feeling, an incipient love for the child's whole sect; but joined to this, and resulting perhaps from self-suspicion, was a proud and ostentatious contempt of their tenets and practical

extravagances. In the course of much thought, however, for the subject struggled irresistibly into his mind, the foolishness of the doctrine began to be less evident, and the points which had particularly offended his reason assumed another aspect, or vanished entirely away. The work within him appeared to go on even while he slept, and that which had been a doubt when he laid down to rest would often hold the place of a truth, confirmed by some forgotten demonstration, when he recalled his thoughts in the morning. But while he was thus becoming assimilated to the enthusiasts, his contempt, in no wise decreasing towards them, grew very fierce against himself; he imagined, also, that every face of his acquaintance wore a sneer, and
10 that every word addressed to him was a gibe. Such was his state of mind at the period of Ilbrahim's misfortune; and the emotions consequent upon that event completed the change, of which the child had been the original instrument.

In the meantime, neither the fierceness of the persecutors, nor the infatuation of their victims, had decreased. The dungeons were never empty; the streets of almost every village echoed daily with the lash; the life of a woman, whose mild and Christian spirit no cruelty could embitter, had been sacrificed; and more innocent blood was yet to pollute the hands that were so often raised in prayer. Early after the Restoration, the English Quakers represented to Charles II, that a "vein of blood was open in his dominions;" but though the displeasure of the voluptuous king
20 was roused, his interference was not prompt. And now the tale must stride forward over many months, leaving Pearson to encounter ignominy and misfortune; his wife to a firm endurance of a thousand sorrows; poor Ilbrahim to pine and droop like a cankered rosebud; his mother to wander on a mistaken errand, neglectful of the holiest trust which can be committed to a woman.

A winter evening, a night of storm, had darkened over Pearson's habitation, and there were no cheerful faces to drive the gloom from his broad hearth. The fire, it is true, sent forth a glowing heat and a ruddy light, and large logs, dripping with half-melted snow, lay ready to be cast upon the embers. But the apartment was saddened in its aspect by the absence of much of the homely wealth which had once adorned
30 it; for the exaction of repeated fines, and his own neglect of temporal affairs, had greatly impoverished the owner. And with the furniture of peace, the implements of war had likewise disappeared; the sword was broken, the helm and cuirass were cast away forever; the soldier had done with battles, and might not lift so much as his naked hand to guard his head. But the Holy Book remained, and the table on which it rested was drawn before the fire, while two of the persecuted sect sought comfort from its pages.

He who listened, while the other read, was the master of the house, now emaciated in form, and altered as to the expression and healthiness of his countenance; for his mind had dwelt too long among visionary thoughts, and his body had been worn by
40 imprisonment and stripes. The hale and weather-beaten old man who sat beside him had sustained less injury from a far longer course of the same mode of life. In person he was tall and dignified, and, which alone would have made him hateful to the Puritans, his grey locks fell from beneath the broad-brimmed hat, and rested on

his shoulders. As the old man read the sacred page, the snow drifted against the windows, or eddied in at the crevices of the door, while a blast kept laughing in the chimney, and the blaze leaped fiercely up to seek it. And sometimes, when the wind struck the hill at a certain angle, and swept down by the cottage across the wintry plain, its voice was the most doleful that can be conceived; it came as if the Past were speaking, as if the Dead had contributed each a whisper, as if the Desolation of Ages were breathed in that one lamenting sound.

The Quaker at length closed the book, retaining, however, his hand between the pages which he had been reading, while he looked steadfastly at Pearson. The attitude and features of the latter might have indicated the endurance of bodily pain; 10 he leaned his forehead on his hands, his teeth were firmly closed, and his frame was tremulous at intervals with a nervous agitation.

"Friend Tobias," inquired the old man, compassionately, "hast thou found no comfort in these many blessed passages of Scripture?"

"Thy voice has fallen on my ear like a sound afar off and indistinct," replied Pearson without lifting his eyes. "Yea, and when I have hearkened carefully, the words seemed cold and lifeless, and intended for another and a lesser grief than mine. Remove the book," he added, in a tone of sullen bitterness. "I have no part in its consolations, and they do but fret my sorrow the more."

"Nay, feeble brother, be not as one who hath never known the light," said the 20 elder Quaker, earnestly, but with mildness. "Art thou he that wouldst be content to give all, and endure all, for conscience' sake; desiring even peculiar trials, that thy faith might be purified, and thy heart weaned from worldly desires? And wilt thou sink beneath an affliction which happens alike to them that have their portion here below, and to them that lay up treasure in heaven? Faint not, for thy burthen is yet light."

"It is heavy! It is heavier than I can bear!" exclaimed Pearson, with the impatience of a variable spirit. "From my youth upward I have been a man marked out for wrath; and year by year, yea, day after day, I have endured sorrows, such as others know not in their lifetime. And now I speak not of the love that has been turned 30 to hatred, the honor to ignominy, the ease and plentifulness of all things to danger, want, and nakedness. All this I could have borne, and counted myself blessed. But when my heart was desolate with many losses, I fixed it upon the child of a stranger, and he became dearer to me than all my buried ones; and now he too must die as if my love were poison. Verily, I am an accursed man, and I will lay me down in the dust, and lift up my head no more."

"Thou sinnest, brother, but it is not for me to rebuke thee; for I also have had my hours of darkness, wherein I have murmured against the cross," said the old Quaker. He continued, perhaps in the hope of distracting his companion's thoughts from his own sorrows. "Even of late was the light obscured within me, when the 40 men of blood had banished me on pain of death, and the constables led me onward from village to village, towards the wilderness. A strong and cruel hand was wielding the knotted cords; they sunk deep into the flesh, and thou mightst have tracked every reel and totter of my footsteps by the blood that followed. As we went on —"

"Have I not borne all this, and have I murmured?" interrupted Pearson, impatiently.

"Nay, friend, but hear me," continued the other. "As we journeyed on, night darkened on our path, so that no man could see the rage of the persecutors, or the constancy of my endurance, though Heaven forbid that I should glory therein. The lights began to glimmer in the cottage windows, and I could discern the inmates as they gathered, in comfort and security, every man with his wife and children by their own evening hearth. At length we came to a tract of fertile land; in the dim light the forest was not visible around it; and behold! there was a straw-thatched dwell-
10 ing, which bore the very aspect of my home, far over the wild ocean, far in our own England. Then came bitter thoughts upon me; yea, remembrances that were like death to my soul. The happiness of my early days was painted to me; the disquiet of my manhood, the altered faith of my declining years. I remembered how I had been moved to go forth a wanderer, when my daughter, the youngest, the dearest of my flock, lay on her dying bed, and —"

"Couldst thou obey the command at such a moment?" exclaimed Pearson, shuddering.

"Yea, yea," replied the old man, hurriedly. "I was kneeling by her bedside when the voice spoke loud within me: but immediately I rose, and took my staff, and gat
20 me gone. Oh! that it were permitted me to forget her woful look when I thus withdrew my arm, and left her journeying through the dark valley alone! for her soul was faint, and she had leaned upon my prayers. Now in that night of horror I was assailed by the thought that I had been an erring Christian, and a cruel parent; yea, even my daughter, with her pale, dying features, seemed to stand by me and whisper, 'Father, you are deceived; go home and shelter your grey head.' Oh! Thou to whom I have looked in my farthest wanderings," continued the Quaker, raising his agitated eyes to heaven, "inflict not upon the bloodiest of our persecutors the unmitigated agony of my soul, when I believed that all I had done and suffered for Thee was at the instigation of a mocking fiend! But I yielded not; I knelt down
30 and wrestled with the tempter, while the scourge bit more fiercely into the flesh. My prayer was heard, and I went on in peace and joy towards the wilderness."

The old man, though his fanaticism had generally all the calmness of reason, was deeply moved while reciting this tale; and his unwonted emotion seemed to rebuke and keep down that of his companion. They sat in silence, with their faces to the fire, imagining perhaps, in its red embers, new scenes of persecution yet to be encountered. The snow still drifted hard against the windows, and sometimes, as the blaze of the logs had gradually sunk, came down the spacious chimney and hissed upon the hearth. A cautious footstep might now and then be heard in a neighboring apartment, and the sound invariably drew the eyes of both Quakers to the door
40 which led thither. When a fierce and riotous gust of wind had led his thoughts, by a natural association, to homeless travellers on such a night, Pearson resumed the conversation.

"I have well nigh sunk under my own share of this trial," observed he, sighing heavily; "yet I would that it might be doubled to me, if so the child's mother could be spared. Her wounds have been deep and many, but this will be the sorest of all."

"Fear not for Catherine," replied the old Quaker; "for I know that valiant woman, and have seen how she can bear the cross. A mother's heart, indeed, is strong in her, and may seem to contend mightily with her faith; but soon she will stand up and give thanks that her son has been thus early an accepted sacrifice. The boy hath done his work, and she will feel that he is taken hence in kindness both to him and her. Blessed, blessed are they that with so little suffering can enter into peace!"

The fitful rush of the wind was now disturbed by a portentous sound: it was a quick and heavy knocking at the outer door. Pearson's wan countenance grew paler, for many a visit of persecution had taught him what to dread; the old man, on the 10 other hand, stood up erect, and his glance was firm as that of the tried soldier who awaits his enemy.

"The men of blood have come to seek me," he observed, with calmness. "They have heard how I was moved to return from banishment; and now am I to be led to prison, and thence to death. It is an end I have long looked for. I will open unto them, lest they say, 'Lo, he feareth!'"

"Nay, I will present myself before them," said Pearson, with recovered fortitude. "It may be that they seek me alone, and know not that thou abidest with me."

"Let us go boldly, both one and the other," rejoined his companion. "It is not fitting that thou or I should shrink."   20

They therefore proceeded through the entry to the door, which they opened, bidding the applicant "Come in, in God's name!" A furious blast of wind drove the storm into their faces, and extinguished the lamp; they had barely time to discern a figure, so white from head to foot with the drifted snow, that it seemed like Winter's self, come in human shape to seek refuge from its own desolation.

"Enter, friend, and do thy errand, be it what it may," said Pearson. "It must needs be pressing, since thou comest on such a bitter night."

"Peace be with this household," said the stranger, when they stood on the floor of the inner apartment.

Pearson started, the elder Quaker stirred the slumbering embers of the fire, till 30 they sent up a clear and lofty blaze; it was a female voice that had spoken; it was a female form that shone out, cold and wintry, in that comfortable light.

"Catherine, blessed woman," exclaimed the old man, "art thou come to this darkened land again? art thou come to bear a valiant testimony as in former years? The scourge hath not prevailed against thee, and from the dungeon hast thou come forth triumphant; but strengthen, strengthen now thy heart, Catherine, for Heaven will prove thee yet this once, ere thou go to thy reward."

"Rejoice friends!" she replied. "Thou who hast long been of our people, and thou whom a little child hath led to us, rejoice! Lo! I come, the messenger of glad tidings, for the day of persecution is overpast. The heart of the king, even Charles, 40 hath been moved in gentleness toward us, and he hath sent forth his letters to stay the hands of the men of blood. A ship's company of our friends hath arrived at yonder town, and I also sailed joyfully among them."

As Catherine spoke, her eyes were roaming about the room, in search of him for whose sake security was dear to her. Pearson made a silent appeal to the old man, nor did the latter shrink from the painful task assigned him.

"Sister," he began, in a softened yet perfectly calm tone, "thou tellest us of His love, manifested in temporal good; and now must we speak to thee of that self-same love, displayed in chastenings. Hitherto, Catherine, thou hast been as one journeying in a darksome and difficult path, and leading an infant by the hand; fain wouldst thou have looked heavenward continually, but still the cares of that little child have drawn thine eyes, and thy affections, to the earth. Sister! go on rejoicing, for his tottering footsteps shall impede thine own no more."

10 But the unhappy mother was not thus to be consoled; she shook like a leaf, she turned white as the very snow that hung drifted into her hair. The firm old man extended his hand and held her up, keeping his eye upon hers, as if to repress any outbreak of passion.

"I am a woman, I am but a woman; will He try me above my strength?" said Catherine, very quickly, and almost in a whisper. "I have been wounded sore; I have suffered much; many things in the body, many in the mind; crucified in myself and in them that were dearest to me. Surely," added she, with a long shudder, "He hath spared me in this one thing." She broke forth with sudden and irrepressible violence. "Tell me, man of cold heart, what has God done to me? Hath He cast me

20 down, never to rise again? Hath He crushed my very heart in his hand? And thou, to whom I committed my child, how hast thou fulfilled thy trust? Give me back my boy, well, sound, alive, alive; or earth and heaven shall avenge me!"

The agonized shriek of Catherine was answered by the faint, the very faint voice of a child.

On this day it had become evident to Pearson, to his aged guest, and to Dorothy, that Ilbrahim's brief and troubled pilgrimage drew near its close. The two former would willingly have remained by him, to make use of the prayers and pious discourses which they deemed appropriate to the time, and which, if they be impotent as to the departing traveller's reception in the world whither it goes, may at least

30 sustain him in bidding adieu to earth. But though Ilbrahim uttered no complaint, he was disturbed by the faces that looked upon him; so that Dorothy's entreaties, and their own conviction that the child's feet might tread heaven's pavement and not soil it, had induced the two Quakers to remove. Ilbrahim then closed his eyes and grew calm, and, except for now and then a kind and low word to his nurse, might have been thought to slumber. As nightfall came on, however, and the storm began to rise, something seemed to trouble the repose of the boy's mind, and to render his sense of hearing active and acute. If a passing wind lingered to shake the casement, he strove to turn his head towards it; if the door jarred to and fro upon its hinges, he looked long and anxiously thitherward; if the heavy voice of the old

40 man, as he read the Scriptures, rose but a little higher, the child almost held his dying breath to listen; if a snowdrift swept by the cottage, with a sound like the trailing of a garment, Ilbrahim seemed to watch that some visitant should enter.

But, after a little time, he relinquished whatever secret hope had agitated him,

5 love . . . chastenings. Compare Hebrews 12:6: ". . . whome the Lord loveth, he chasteneth. . . ."

and, with one low, complaining whisper, turned his cheek upon the pillow. He then addressed Dorothy with his usual sweetness, and besought her to draw near him; she did so, and Ilbrahim took her hand in both of his, grasping it with a gentle pressure, as if to assure himself that he retained it. At intervals, and without disturbing the repose of his countenance, a very faint trembling passed over him from head to foot, as if a mild but somewhat cool wind had breathed upon him, and made him shiver. As the boy thus led her by the hand, in his quiet progress over the borders of eternity, Dorothy almost imagined that she could discern the near, though dim delightfulness, of the home he was about to reach; she would not have enticed the little wanderer back, though she bemoaned herself that she must leave him and re- 10 turn. But just when Ilbrahim's feet were pressing on the soil of paradise, he heard a voice behind him, and it recalled him a few, few paces of the weary path which he had travelled. As Dorothy looked upon his features, she perceived that their placid expression was again disturbed; her own thoughts had been so wrapt in him, that all sounds of the storm, and of human speech, were lost to her; but when Catherine's shriek pierced through the room, the boy strove to raise himself.

"Friend, she is come! Open unto her!" cried he.

In a moment his mother was kneeling by the bedside; she drew Ilbrahim to her bosom, and he nestled there, with no violence of joy, but contentedly as if he were hushing himself to sleep. He looked into her face, and reading its agony, said, with 20 feeble earnestness, "Mourn not, dearest mother. I am happy now." And with these words, the gentle boy was dead.

The king's mandate to stay the New England persecutors was effectual in preventing further martyrdoms; but the colonial authorities, trusting in the remoteness of their situation, and perhaps in the supposed instability of the royal government, shortly renewed their severities in all other respects. Catherine's fanaticism had become wilder by the sundering of all human ties; and wherever a scourge was lifted, there was she to receive the blow; and whenever a dungeon was unbarred, thither she came, to cast herself upon the floor. But in process of time a more Christian spirit — a spirit of forbearance, though not of cordiality or approbation, began to 30 pervade the land in regard to the persecuted sect. And then, when the rigid old Pilgrims eyed her rather in pity than in wrath; when the matrons fed her with the fragments of their children's food, and offered her a lodging on a hard and lowly bed; when no little crowd of schoolboys left their sports to cast stones after the roving enthusiast; then did Catherine return to Pearson's dwelling, and made that her home.

As if Ilbrahim's sweetness yet lingered round his ashes; as if his gentle spirit came down from Heaven to teach his parent a true religion, her fierce and vindictive nature was softened by the same griefs which had once irritated it. When the course of

---

27 **wherever . . . floor.** Hawthorne is on sound ground both psychologically and historically when he asserts that the more fanatical of the Quakers deliberately sought persecution and enjoyed it. A famous letter of 1657 from Rhode Island (where religious liberty was enjoyed by all) to Massachusetts states that the Quakers "begin to loathe this place for that they are not opposed by the civil authority" (quoted in J. T. Adams, *The Founding of New England*, p. 267)

years had made the features of the unobtrusive mourner familiar in the settlement, she became a subject of not deep, but general interest; a being on whom the otherwise superfluous sympathies of all might be bestowed. Every one spoke of her with that degree of pity which it is pleasant to experience; every one was ready to do her the little kindnesses which are not costly yet manifest goodwill; and when at last she died, a long train of her once bitter persecutors followed her, with decent sadness and tears that were not painful, to her place by Ilbrahim's green and sunken grave.   1831

6 **decent**, becoming, fitting

Roger Malvin's Burial

Hawthorne in 1829 offered "Roger Malvin's Burial" to a publisher as a unit to appear in Provincial Tales, *a collection which never was published. It was included, however, in an annual, the* Token, *for 1832, and the author placed it in* Mosses from An Old Manse *(1846). Like many other tales by its author, it raises questions for the attentive reader: "Concealment," says Hawthorne, "had imparted to a justifiable act much of the secret effect of guilt." Was Reuben Bourne justified, then, in concealing from Dorcas the actual circumstances of her father's death? And if he was, why was the "expiation" at the end necessary? "The symbolism of the tale," says Mark Van Doren, "is so concrete as to offend some readers"; but he holds that to object to it "is to miss the intensity with which Hawthorne, feeling his subject matter as he did, endowed every surrounding object with sensation. Like any good allegorist, he attributed life to all of the world that he knew, and never hesitated to use any of it as testimony. His worst allegories do this artificially and unconvincingly; his best ones are overwhelming, and 'Roger Malvin's Burial' is one of the best."*

One of the few incidents of Indian warfare naturally susceptible of the moonlight of romance was that expedition undertaken for the defence of the frontiers in the year 1725, which resulted in the well-remembered "Lovell's Fight." Imagination, by casting certain circumstances judicially into the shade, may see much to admire in the heroism of a little band who gave battle to twice their number in the heart of the enemy's country. The open bravery displayed by both parties was in accordance with civilized ideas of valor; and chivalry itself might not blush to record the deeds of one or two individuals. The battle, though so fatal to those who fought, was not unfortunate in its consequences to the country; for it broke the strength of 10 a tribe and conduced to the peace which subsisted during several ensuing years. History and tradition are unusually minute in their memorials of this affair; and the captain of a scouting party of frontier men has acquired as actual a military renown as many a victorious leader of thousands. Some of the incidents contained in the following pages will be recognized, notwithstanding the substitution of fictitious

3 "**Lovell's Fight**" was a ballad about an incident in the Penobscot War of 1725 by Professor Thomas C. Upham of Bowdoin College, published in 1824. Hawthorne also apparently read Thomas Symmes' *Historical Memoirs of the Late Fight at Piggwacket*, written in 1725 and included in the pamphlet containing the ballad

names, by such as have heard, from old men's lips, the fate of the few combatants who were in a condition to retreat after "Lovell's Fight."

The early sunbeams hovered cheerfully upon the tree-tops, beneath which two weary and wounded men had stretched their limbs the night before. Their bed of withered oak leaves was strewn upon the small level space, at the foot of a rock, situated near the summit of one of the gentle swells by which the face of the country is there diversified. The mass of granite, rearing its smooth, flat surface fifteen or twenty feet above their heads, was not unlike a gigantic gravestone, upon which the veins seemed to form an inscription in forgotten characters. On a tract of several acres around this rock, oaks and other hard-wood trees had supplied the place of the 10 pines, which were the usual growth of the land; and a young and vigorous sapling stood close beside the travellers.

The severe wound of the elder man had probably deprived him of sleep; for, so soon as the first ray of sunshine rested on the top of the highest tree, he reared himself painfully from his recumbent posture and sat erect. The deep lines of his countenance and the scattered gray of his hair marked him as past the middle age; but his muscular frame would, but for the effect of his wound, have been as capable of sustaining fatigue as in the early vigor of life. Languor and exhaustion now sat upon his haggard features; and the despairing glance which he sent forward through the depths of the forest proved his own conviction that his pilgrimage was at an end. 20 He next turned his eyes to the companion who reclined by his side. The youth — for he had scarcely attained the years of manhood — lay, with his head upon his arm, in the embrace of an unquiet sleep, which a thrill of pain from his wounds seemed each moment on the point of breaking. His right hand grasped a musket; and, to judge from the violent action of his features, his slumbers were bringing back a vision of the conflict of which he was one of the few survivors. A shout — deep and loud in his dreaming fancy — found its way in an imperfect murmur to his lips; and, starting even at the slight sound of his own voice, he suddenly awoke. The first act of reviving recollection was to make anxious inquiries respecting the condition of his wounded fellow-traveller. The latter shook his head.   30

"Reuben, my boy," said he, "this rock beneath which we sit will serve for an old hunter's gravestone. There is many and many a long mile of howling wilderness before us yet; nor would it avail me anything if the smoke of my own chimney were but on the other side of that swell of land. The Indian bullet was deadlier than I thought."

"You are weary with our three days' travel," replied the youth, "and a little longer rest will recruit you. Sit you here while I search the woods for the herbs and roots that must be our sustenance; and, having eaten, you shall lean on me, and we will turn our faces homeward. I doubt not that, with my help, you can attain to some one of the frontier garrisons."   40

"There is not two days' life in me, Reuben," said the other, calmly, "and I will no longer burden you with my useless body, when you can scarcely support your own. Your wounds are deep and your strength is failing fast; yet, if you hasten onward alone, you may be preserved. For me there is no hope, and I will await death here."

"If it must be so, I will remain and watch by you," said Reuben, resolutely.

"No, my son, no," rejoined his companion. "Let the wish of a dying man have weight with you; give me one grasp of your hand and get you hence. Think you that my last moments will be eased by the thought that I leave you to die a more lingering death? I have loved you like a father, Reuben; and at a time like this I should have something of a father's authority. I charge you to be gone that I may die in peace."

10 "And because you have been a father to me, should I therefore leave you to perish and to lie unburied in the wilderness?" exclaimed the youth. "No; if your end be in truth approaching, I will watch by you and receive your parting words. I will dig a grave here by the rock, in which, if my weakness overcome me, we will rest together; or, if Heaven gives me strength, I will seek my way home."

"In the cities and wherever men dwell," replied the other, "they bury their dead in the earth; they hide them from the sight of the living; but here, where no step may pass perhaps for a hundred years, wherefore should I not rest beneath the open sky, covered only by the oak leaves when the autumn winds shall strew them? And for a monument, here is this gray rock, on which my dying hand shall carve the

20 name of Roger Malvin; and the traveller in days to come will know that here sleeps a hunter and a warrior. Tarry not, then, for a folly like this, but hasten away, if not for your own sake, for hers who will else be desolate."

Malvin spoke the last few words in a faltering voice, and their effect upon his companion was strongly visible. They reminded him that there were other and less questionable duties than that of sharing the fate of a man whom his death could not benefit. Nor can it be affirmed that no selfish feeling strove to enter Reuben's heart, though the consciousness made him more earnestly resist his companion's entreaties.

"How terrible to wait the slow approach of death in this solitude!" exclaimed he.

30 "A brave man does not shrink in the battle; and, when friends stand round the bed, even women may die composedly; but here" —

"I shall not shrink even here, Reuben Bourne," interrupted Malvin. "I am a man of no weak heart, and, if I were, there is a surer support than that of earthly friends. You are young, and life is dear to you. Your last moments will need comfort far more than mine; and when you have laid me in the earth, and are alone, and night is settling on the forest, you will feel all the bitterness of the death that may now be escaped. But I will urge no selfish motive to your generous nature. Leave me for my sake, that, having said a prayer for your safety, I may have space to settle my account undisturbed by worldly sorrows."

40 "And your daughter, — how shall I dare to meet her eye?" exclaimed Reuben. "She will ask the fate of her father, whose life I vowed to defend with my own. Must I tell her that he travelled three days' march with me from the field of battle and that then I left him to perish in the wilderness? Were it not better to lie down and die by your side than to return safe and say this to Dorcas?"

"Tell my daughter," said Roger Malvin, "that, though yourself sore wounded, and weak, and weary, you led my tottering footsteps many a mile, and left me only at my earnest entreaty, because I would not have your blood upon my soul. Tell her that through pain and danger you were faithful, and that, if your lifeblood could have saved me, it would have flowed to its last drop; and tell her that you will be something dearer than a father, and that my blessing is with you both, and that my dying eyes can see a long and pleasant path in which you will journey together."

As Malvin spoke he almost raised himself from the ground, and the energy of his concluding words seemed to fill the wild and lonely forest with a vision of happi- 10 ness; but, when he sank exhausted upon his bed of oak leaves, the light which had kindled in Reuben's eye was quenched. He felt as if it were both sin and folly to think of happiness at such a moment. His companion watched his changing countenance, and sought with generous art to wile him to his own good.

"Perhaps I deceive myself in regard to the time I have to live," he resumed. "It may be that, with speedy assistance, I might recover of my wound. The foremost fugitives must, ere this, have carried tidings of our fatal battle to the frontiers, and parties will be out to succor those in like condition with ourselves. Should you meet one of these and guide them hither, who can tell but that I may sit by my own fireside again?" 20

A mournful smile strayed across the features of the dying man as he insinuated that unfounded hope, — which, however, was not without its effect on Reuben. No merely selfish motive, nor even the desolate condition of Dorcas, could have induced him to desert his companion at such a moment — but his wishes seized on the thought that Malvin's life might be preserved, and his sanguine nature heightened almost to certainty the remote possibility of procuring human aid.

"Surely there is reason, weighty reason, to hope that friends are not far distant," he said, half aloud. "There fled one coward, unwounded, in the beginning of the fight, and most probably he made good speed. Every true man on the frontier would shoulder his musket at the news; and, though no party may range so far into the 30 woods as this, I shall perhaps encounter them in one day's march. Counsel me faithfully," he added, turning to Malvin, in distrust of his own motives. "Were your situation mine, would you desert me while life remained?"

"It is now twenty years," replied Roger Malvin, — sighing, however, as he secretly acknowledged the wide dissimilarity between the two cases, — "it is now twenty years since I escaped with one dear friend from Indian captivity near Montreal. We journeyed many days through the woods, till at length overcome with hunger and weariness, my friend lay down and besought me to leave him; for he knew that, if I remained, we both must perish; and, with but little hope of obtaining succor, I heaped a pillow of dry leaves beneath his head and hastened on." 40

"And did you return in time to save him?" asked Reuben, hanging on Malvin's words as if they were to be prophetic of his own success.

"I did," answered the other. "I came upon the camp of a hunting party before sunset of the same day. I guided them to the spot where my comrade was expecting death; and he is now a hale and hearty man upon his own farm, far within the frontiers, while I lie wounded here in the depths of the wilderness."

This example, powerful in affecting Reuben's decision, was aided, unconsciously to himself, by the hidden strength of many another motive. Roger Malvin perceived that the victory was nearly won.

"Now, go, my son, and Heaven prosper you!" he said. "Turn not back with your friends when you meet them, lest your wounds and weariness overcome you; but send hitherward two or three, that may be spared, to search for me; and believe me,˙ Reuben, my heart will be lighter with every step you take towards home." Yet there
10 was, perhaps, a change both in his countenance and voice as he spoke thus; for, after all, it was a ghastly fate to be left expiring in the wilderness.

Reuben Bourne, but half convinced that he was acting rightly, at length raised himself from the ground and prepared himself for his departure. And first, though contrary to Malvin's wishes, he collected a stock of roots and herbs, which had been their only food during the last two days. This useless supply he placed within reach of the dying man, for whom, also, he swept together a bed of dry oak leaves. Then climbing to the summit of the rock, which on one side was rough and broken, he bent the oak sapling downward, and bound his handkerchief to the topmost branch. This precaution was not unnecessary to direct any who might come in search of
20 Malvin; for every part of the rock, except its broad, smooth front, was concealed at a little distance by the dense undergrowth of the forest. The handkerchief had been the bandage of a wound upon Reuben's arm; and, as he bound it to the tree, he vowed by the blood that stained it that he would return, either to save his companion's life or to lay his body in the grave. He then descended, and stood, with downcast eyes, to receive Roger Malvin's parting words.

The experience of the latter suggested much and minute advice respecting the youth's journey through the trackless forest. Upon this subject he spoke with calm earnestness, as if he were sending Reuben to the battle or the chase while he himself remained secure at home, and not as if the human countenance that was about
30 to leave him were the last he would ever behold. But his firmness was shaken before he concluded.

"Carry my blessing to Dorcas, and say that my last prayer shall be for her and you. Bid her to have no hard thoughts because you left me here," — Reuben's heart smote him, — "for that your life would not have weighed with you if its sacrifice could have done me good. She will marry you after she has mourned a little while for her father; and Heaven grant you long and happy days, and may your children's children stand round your death bed! And, Reuben," added he, as the weakness of mortality made its way at last, "return, when your wounds are healed and your weariness refreshed, — return to this wild rock, and lay my bones in the grave, and
40 say a prayer over them."

An almost superstitious regard, arising perhaps from the customs of the Indians, whose war was with the dead as well as the living, was paid by the frontier inhabitants to the rites of sepulture; and there are many instances of the sacrifice of life in the attempt to bury those who had fallen by the "sword of the wilderness." Reuben, therefore, felt the full importance of the promise which he most solemnly made to return and perform Roger Malvin's obsequies. It was remarkable that the latter, speaking his whole heart in his parting words, no longer endeavored to persuade the youth that even the speediest succor might avail to the preservation of his life. Reuben was internally convinced that he should see Malvin's living face no more. His generous nature would fain have delayed him, at whatever risk, till the dying scene were past; but the desire of existence and the hope of happiness had strengthened in his heart, and he was unable to resist them.

"It is enough," said Roger Malvin, having listened to Reuben's promise. "Go, and God speed you!"   10

The youth pressed his hand in silence, turned, and was departing. His slow and faltering steps, however, had borne him but a little way before Malvin's voice recalled him.

"Reuben, Reuben," said he, faintly; and Reuben returned and knelt down by the dying man.

"Raise me, and let me lean against the rock," was his last request. "My face will be turned towards home, and I shall see you a moment longer as you pass among the trees."

Reuben, having made the desired alteration in his companion's posture, again began his solitary pilgrimage. He walked more hastily at first than was consistent with 20 his strength; for a sort of guilty feeling, which sometimes torments men in their most justifiable acts, caused him to seek concealment from Malvin's eyes; but after he had trodden far upon the rustling forest leaves he crept back, impelled by a wild and painful curiosity, and, sheltered by the earthy roots of an uptorn tree, gazed earnestly at the desolate man. The morning sun was unclouded, and the trees and shrubs imbibed the sweet air of the month of May; yet there seemed a gloom on Nature's face, as if she sympathized with mortal pain and sorrow. Roger Malvin's hands were uplifted in a fervent prayer, some of the words of which stole through the stillness of the woods and entered Reuben's heart, torturing it with an unutterable pang. They were the broken accents of a petition for his own happiness and 30 that of Dorcas; and, as the youth listened, conscience, or something in its similitude, pleaded strongly with him to return and lie down again by the rock. He felt how hard was the doom of the kind and generous being whom he had deserted in his extremity. Death would come like the slow approach of a corpse, stealing gradually towards him through the forest, and showing its ghastly and motionless features from behind a nearer and yet a nearer tree. But such must have been Reuben's own fate had he tarried another sunset; and who shall impute blame to him if he shrink from so useless a sacrifice? As he gave a parting look, a breeze waved the little banner upon the sapling oak and reminded Reuben of his vow.

Many circumstances combined to retard the wounded traveller in his way to the 40 frontiers. On the second day the clouds, gathering densely over the sky, precluded the possibility of regulating his course by the position of the sun; and he knew not but that every effort of his almost exhausted strength was removing him farther from

the home he sought. His scanty sustenance was supplied by the berries and other
spontaneous products of the forest. Herds of deer, it is true, sometimes bounded
past him, and partridges frequently whirred up before his footsteps; but his ammunition had been expended in the fight, and he had no means of slaying them. His
wounds, irritated by the constant exertion in which lay the only hope of life, wore
away his strength and at intervals confused his reason. But, even in the wanderings
of intellect, Reuben's young heart clung strongly to existence; and it was only
through absolute incapacity of motion that he at last sank down beneath a tree,
compelled there to await death.

10   In this situation he was discovered by a party who, upon the first intelligence of
the fight, had been despatched to the relief of the survivors. They conveyed him to
the nearest settlement, which chanced to be that of his own residence.

    Dorcas, in the simplicity of the olden time, watched by the bedside of her wounded
lover, and administered all those comforts that are in the sole gift of woman's heart
and hand. During several days Reuben's recollection strayed drowsily among the
perils and hardships through which he had passed, and he was incapable of returning definite answers to the inquiries with which many were eager to harass him. No
authentic particulars of the battle had yet been circulated; nor could mothers, wives,
and children tell whether their loved ones were detained by captivity or by the
20 stronger chain of death. Dorcas nourished her apprehensions in silence till one afternoon when Reuben awoke from an unquiet sleep, and seemed to recognize her more
perfectly than at any previous time. She saw that his intellect had become composed, and she could no longer restrain her filial anxiety.

    "My father, Reuben?" she began; but the change in her lover's countenance made
her pause.

    The youth shrank as if with a bitter pain, and the blood gushed vividly into his
wan and hollow cheeks. His first impulse was to cover his face; but, apparently with
a desperate effort, he half raised himself and spoke vehemently, defending himself
against an imaginary accusation.

30   "Your father was sore wounded in the battle, Dorcas; and he bade me not burden myself with him, but only to lead him to the lakeside, that he might quench
his thirst and die. But I would not desert the old man in his extremity, and, though
bleeding myself, I supported him; I gave him half my strength, and led him away
with me. For three days we journeyed on together, and your father was sustained
beyond my hopes, but, awaking at sunrise on the fourth day, I found him faint and
exhausted; he was unable to proceed; his life had ebbed away fast; and" —

    "He died!" exclaimed Dorcas, faintly.

    Reuben felt it impossible to acknowledge that his selfish love of life had hurried
him away before her father's fate was decided. He spoke not; he only bowed his
40 head; and between shame and exhaustion, sank back and hid his face in the pillow.
Dorcas wept when her fears were thus confirmed; but the shock, as it had been long
anticipated, was on that account the less violent.

    "You dug a grave for my poor father in the wilderness, Reuben?" was the ques-
tion by which her filial piety manifested itself.

"My hands were weak; but I did what I could," replied the youth in a smothered tone. "There stands a noble tombstone above his head; and I would to Heaven I slept as soundly as he!"

Dorcas, perceiving the wildness of his latter words, inquired no further at the time; but her heart found ease in the thought that Roger Malvin had not lacked such funeral rites as it was possible to bestow. The tale of Reuben's courage and fidelity lost nothing when she communicated it to her friends; and the poor youth, tottering from his sick chamber to breathe the sunny air, experienced from every tongue the miserable and humiliating torture of unmerited praise. All acknowledged that he might worthily demand the hand of the fair maiden to whose father he had 10 been "faithful unto death;" and, as my tale is not of love, it shall suffice to say that in the space of a few months Reuben became the husband of Dorcas Malvin. During the marriage ceremony the bride was covered with blushes, but the bridegroom's face was pale.

There was now in the breast of Reuben Bourne an incommunicable thought — something which he was to conceal most heedfully from her whom he most loved and trusted. He regretted, deeply and bitterly, the moral cowardice that had restrained his words when he was about to disclose the truth to Dorcas; but pride, the fear of losing her affection, the dread of universal scorn, forbade him to rectify this falsehood. He felt that for leaving Roger Malvin he deserved no censure. His presence, 20 the gratuitous sacrifice of his own life, would have added only another and a needless agony to the last moments of the dying man; but concealment had imparted to a justifiable act much of the secret effect of guilt; and Reuben, while reason told him that he had done right, experienced in no small degree the mental horrors which punish the perpetrator of undiscovered crime. By a certain association of ideas, he at times almost imagined himself a murderer. For years, also, a thought would occasionally recur, which, though he perceived all its folly and extravagance, he had not power to banish from his mind. It was a haunting and torturing fancy that his father-in-law was yet sitting at the foot of the rock, on the withered forest leaves, alive, and awaiting his pledged assistance. These mental deceptions, however, came 30 and went, nor did he ever mistake them for realities, but in the calmest and clearest moods of his mind he was conscious that he had a deep vow unredeemed, and that an unburied corpse was calling to him out of the wilderness. Yet such was the consequence of his prevarication that he could not obey the call. It was now too late to require the assistance of Roger Malvin's friends in performing his long-deferred sepulture; and superstitious fears, of which none were more susceptible than the people of the outward settlements, forbade Reuben to go alone. Neither did he know where in the pathless and illimitable forest to seek that smooth and lettered rock at the base of which the body lay: his remembrance of every portion of his travel thence was indistinct, and the latter part had left no impression upon his mind. There was, 40 however, a continual impulse, a voice audible only to himself, commanding him to go forth and redeem his vow; and he had a strange impression that, were he to make the trial, he would be led straight to Malvin's bones. But year after year that summons, unheard but felt, was disobeyed. His one secret thought became like a chain binding down his spirit and like a serpent gnawing into his heart; and he was transformed into a sad and downcast yet irritable man.

In the course of a few years after their marriage changes began to be visible in the external prosperity of Reuben and Dorcas. The only riches of the former had been his stout heart and strong arm; but the latter, her father's sole heiress, had made her husband master of a farm, under older cultivation, larger, and better stocked than most of the frontier establishments. Reuben Bourne, however, was a neglectful husbandman; and, while the lands of the other settlers became annually more fruitful, his deteriorated in the same proportion. The discouragements to agriculture were greatly lessened by the cessation of Indian war, during which men held the plough in one hand and the musket in the other, and were fortunate if the products of their dangerous labor were not destroyed, either in the field or in the barn, by the savage enemy. But Reuben did not profit by the altered condition of the country; nor can it be denied that his intervals of industrious attention to his affairs were but scantily rewarded with success. The irritability by which he had recently become distinguished was another cause of his declining prosperity, as it occasioned frequent quarrels in his unavoidable intercourse with the neighboring settlers. The results of these were innumerable lawsuits; for the people of New England, in the earliest stages and wildest circumstances of the country, adopted, whenever attainable, the legal mode of deciding their differences. To be brief, the world did not go well with Reuben Bourne; and, though not till many years after his marriage, he was finally a ruined man, with but one remaining expedient against the evil fate that had pursued him. He was to throw sunlight into some deep recess of the forest, and seek subsistence from the virgin bosom of the wilderness.

The only child of Reuben and Dorcas was a son, now arrived at the age of fifteen years, beautiful in youth, and giving promise of a glorious manhood. He was peculiarly qualified for, and already began to excel in, the wild accomplishments of frontier life. His foot was fleet, his aim true, his apprehension quick, his heart glad and high; and all who anticipated the return of Indian war spoke of Cyrus Bourne as a future leader in the land. The boy was loved by his father with a deep and silent strength, as if whatever was good and happy in his own nature had been transferred to his child, carrying his affections with it. Even Dorcas, though loving and beloved, was far less dear to him; for Reuben's secret thoughts and insulated emotions had gradually made him a selfish man, and he could no longer love deeply except where he saw or imagined some reflection or likeness of his own mind. In Cyrus he recognized what he had himself been in other days; and at intervals he seemed to partake of the boy's spirit, and to be revived with a fresh and happy life. Reuben was accompanied by his son in the expedition, for the purpose of selecting a tract of land and felling and burning the timber, which necessarily preceded the removal of the household goods. Two months of autumn were thus occupied, after which Reuben Bourne and his young hunter returned to spend their last winter in the settlements.

It was early in the month of May that the little family snapped asunder whatever tendrils of affections had clung to inanimate objects, and bade farewell to the few who, in the blight of fortune, called themselves their friends. The sadness of the parting moment had, to each of the pilgrims, its peculiar alleviations. Reuben, a moody man, and misanthropic because unhappy, strode onward with his usual stern brow and downcast eye, feeling few regrets and disdaining to acknowledge any. Dorcas, while she wept abundantly over the broken ties by which her simple and affectionate nature had bound itself to everything, felt that the inhabitants of her inmost heart moved on with her, and that all else would be supplied wherever she might go. And the boy dashed one teardrop from his eye, and thought of the adventurous pleasures of the untrodden forest.

Oh, who, in the enthusiasm of a daydream, has not wished that he were a wan- 10 derer in a world of summer wilderness, with one fair and gentle being hanging lightly on his arm? In youth his free and exulting step would know no barrier but the rolling ocean or the snow-topped mountains; calmer manhood would choose a home where Nature had strewn a double wealth in the vale of some transparent stream; and when hoary age, after long, long years of that pure life, stole on and found him there, it would find him the father of a race, the patriarch of a people, the founder of a mighty nation yet to be. When death, like the sweet sleep which we welcome after a day of happiness, came over him, his far descendants would mourn over the venerated dust. Enveloped by tradition in mysterious attributes, the men of future generations would call him godlike; and remote posterity would see him standing, 20 dimly glorious, far up the valley of a hundred centuries.

The tangled and gloomy forest through which the personages of my tale were wandering differed widely from the dreamer's land of fantasy; yet there was something in their way of life that Nature asserted as her own, and the gnawing cares which went with them from the world were all that now obstructed their happiness. One stout and shaggy steed, the bearer of all their wealth, did not shrink from the added weight of Dorcas; although her hardy breeding sustained her, during the latter part of each day's journey, by her husband's side. Reuben and his son, their muskets on their shoulders and their axes slung behind them, kept an unwearied pace, each watching with a hunter's eye for the game that supplied their food. 30 When hunger bade, they halted and prepared their meal on the bank of some unpolluted forest brook, which, as they knelt down with thirsty lips to drink, murmured a sweet unwillingness, like a maiden at love's first kiss. They slept beneath a hut of branches, and awoke at peep of light refreshed for the toils of another day. Dorcas and the boy went on joyously, and even Reuben's spirit shone at intervals with an outward gladness; but inwardly there was a cold, cold sorrow, which he compared to the snowdrifts lying deep in the glens and hollows of the rivulets while the leaves were brightly green above.

Cyrus Bourne was sufficiently skilled in the travel of the woods to observe that his father did not adhere to the course they had pursued in their expedition of the 40 preceding autumn. They were now keeping farther to the north, striking out more directly from the settlements, and into a region of which savage beasts and savage men were as yet the sole possessors. The boy sometimes hinted his opinions upon the subject, and Reuben listened attentively, and once or twice altered the direction of their march in accordance with his son's counsel; but, having so done, he seemed ill at ease. His quick and wandering glances were sent forward, apparently in search of enemies lurking behind the tree trunks; and, seeing nothing there, he would cast his eyes backwards as if in fear of some pursuer. Cyrus, perceiving that his father gradually resumed the old direction, forbore to interfere; nor, though something began to weigh upon his heart, did his adventurous nature permit him to regret the increased length and the mystery of their way.

On the afternoon of the fifth day they halted, and made their simple encampment nearly an hour before sunset. The face of the country, for the last few miles, had been diversified by swells of land resembling huge waves of a petrified sea; and in one of the corresponding hollows, a wild and romantic spot, had the family reared their hut and kindled their fire. There is something chilling, and yet heart-warming, in the thought of these three, united by strong bands of love and insulated from all that breathe beside. The dark and gloomy pines looked down upon them, and, as the wind swept through their tops, a pitying sound was heard in the forest; or did those old trees groan in fear that men were come to lay the axe to their roots at last? Reuben and his son, while Dorcas made ready their meal, proposed to wander out in search of game, of which that day's march had afforded no supply. The boy, promising not to quit the vicinity of the encampment, bounded off with a step as light and elastic as that of the deer he hoped to slay; while his father, feeling a transient happiness as he gazed after him, was about to pursue an opposite direction. Dorcas, in the meanwhile, had seated herself near their fire of fallen branches, upon the mossgrown and mouldering trunk of a tree uprooted years before. Her employment, diversified by an occasional glance at the pot, now beginning to simmer over the blaze, was the perusal of the current year's Massachusetts Almanac, which, with the exception of an old black-letter Bible, comprised all the literary wealth of the family. None pay a greater regard to arbitrary divisions of time than those who are excluded from society; and Dorcas mentioned, as if the information were of importance, that it was now the twelfth of May. Her husband started.

"The twelfth of May! I should remember it well," muttered he, while many thoughts occasioned a momentary confusion in his mind. "Where am I? Whither am I wandering? Where did I leave him?"

Dorcas, too well accustomed to her husband's wayward moods to note any peculiarity of demeanor, now laid aside the almanac and addressed him in that mournful tone which the tender hearted appropriate to griefs long cold and dead.

"It was near this time of the month, eighteen years ago, that my poor father left this world for a better. He had a kind arm to hold his head and a kind voice to cheer him, Reuben, in his last moments; and the thought of the faithful care you took of him has comforted me many a time since. Oh, death would have been awful to a solitary man in a wild place like this!"

"Pray Heaven, Dorcas," said Reuben, in a broken voice, — "pray Heaven that neither of us three dies solitary and lies unburied in this howling wilderness!" And he hastened away, leaving her to watch the fire beneath the gloomy pines.

Reuben Bourne's rapid pace gradually slackened as the pang, unintentionally in-

flicted by the words of Dorcas, became less acute. Many strange reflections, however, thronged upon him; and, straying onward rather like a sleep walker than a
hunter, it was attributable to no care of his own that his devious course kept him
in the vicinity of the encampment. His steps were imperceptibly led almost in a
circle; nor did he observe that he was on the verge of a tract of land heavily timbered, but not with pinetrees. The place of the latter was here supplied by oaks and
other of the harder woods; and around their roots clustered a dense and bushy
under-growth, leaving, however, barren spaces between the trees, thick strewn with
withered leaves. Whenever the rustling of the branches or the creaking of the trunks
made a sound, as if the forest were waking from slumber, Reuben instinctively raised   10
the musket that rested on his arm, and cast a quick, sharp glance on every side; but,
convinced by a partial observation that no animal was near, he would again give
himself up to his thoughts. He was musing on the strange influence that had led
him away from his premeditated course, and so far into the depths of the wilderness. Unable to penetrate to the secret place of his soul where his motives lay hidden, he believed that a supernatural voice had called him onward, and that a
supernatural power had obstructed his retreat. He trusted that it was Heaven's intent to afford him an opportunity of expiating his sin; he hoped that he might find
the bones so long unburied; and that, having laid the earth over them, peace would
throw its sunlight into the sepulchre of his heart. From these thoughts he was   20
aroused by a rustling in the forest at some distance from the spot to which he had
wandered. Perceiving the motion of some object behind a thick veil of undergrowth,
he fired, with the instinct of a hunter and the aim of a practised marksman. A low
moan, which told his success, and by which even animals can express their dying
agony, was unheeded by Reuben Bourne. What were the recollections now breaking upon him?

The thicket into which Reuben had fired was near the summit of a swell of land,
and was clustered around the base of a rock, which, in the shape and smoothness
of one of its surfaces, was not unlike a gigantic gravestone. As if reflected in a mirror, its likeness was in Reuben's memory. He even recognized the veins which seemed   30
to form an inscription in forgotten characters: everything remained the same, except
that a thick covert of bushes shrouded the lower part of the rock, and would have
hidden Roger Malvin had he still been sitting there. Yet in the next moment
Reuben's eye was caught by another change that time had effected since he last
stood where he was now standing again behind the earthy roots of the uptorn tree.
The sapling to which he had bound the bloodstained symbol of his vow had increased and strengthened into an oak, far indeed from its maturity, but with no
mean spread of shadowy branches. There was one singularity observable in this tree
which made Reuben tremble. The middle and lower branches were in luxuriant life,
and an excess of vegetation had fringed the trunk almost to the ground; but a blight   40
had apparently stricken the upper part of the oak, and the very topmost bough was
withered, sapless, and utterly dead. Reuben remembered how the little banner had
fluttered on that topmost bough, when it was green and lovely, eighteen years before. Whose guilt had blasted it?

Dorcas, after the departure of the two hunters, continued her preparations for their evening repast. Her sylvan table was the moss-covered trunk of a large fallen tree, on the broadest part of which she had spread a snow-white cloth and arranged what were left of the bright pewter vessels that had been her pride in the settlements. It had a strange aspect, that one little spot of homely comfort in the desolate heart of Nature. The sunshine yet lingered upon the higher branches of the trees that grew on rising ground; but the shadows of evening had deepened into the hollow where the encampment was made, and the firelight began to redden as it gleamed up the tall trunks of the pines or hovered on the dense and obscure mass of foliage
10 that circled round the spot. The heart of Dorcas was not sad; for she felt that it was better to journey in the wilderness with two whom she loved than to be a lonely woman in a crowd that cared not for her. As she busied herself in arranging seats of mouldering wood, covered with leaves, for Reuben and her son, her voice danced through the gloomy forest in the measure of a song that she had learned in youth. The rude melody, the production of a bard who won no name, was descriptive of a winter evening in a frontier cottage, when, secured from savage inroad by the high-piled snow-drifts, the family rejoiced by their own fireside. The whole song possessed the nameless charm peculiar to unborrowed thought, but four continually-recurring lines shone out from the rest like the blaze of the hearth whose joys they
20 celebrated. Into them, working magic with a few simple words, the poet had instilled the very essence of domestic love and household happiness, and they were poetry and picture joined in one. As Dorcas sang, the walls of her forsaken home seemed to encircle her; she no longer saw the gloomy pines, nor heard the wind which still, as she began each verse, sent a heavy breath through the branches, and died away in a hollow moan from the burden of the song. She was aroused by the report of a gun in the vicinity of the encampment; and either the sudden sound, or her loneliness by the glowing fire, caused her to tremble violently. The next moment she laughed in the pride of a mother's heart.

"My beautiful young hunter! My boy has slain a deer!" she exclaimed, recollect-
30 ing that in the direction whence the shot proceeded Cyrus had gone to the chase.

She waited a reasonable time to hear her son's light step bounding over the rustling leaves to tell of his success. But he did not immediately appear; and she sent her cheerful voice among the trees in search of him.

"Cyrus! Cyrus!"

His coming was still delayed; and she determined, as the report had apparently been very near, to seek for him in person. Her assistance, also, might be necessary in bringing home the venison which she flattered herself he had obtained. She therefore set forward, directing her steps by the long-past sound, and singing as she went, in order that the boy might be aware of her approach and run to meet her.
40 From behind the trunk of every tree, and from every hiding-place in the thick foliage of the undergrowth, she hoped to discover the countenance of her son, laughing with the sportive mischief that is born of affection. The sun was now beneath the horizon, and the light that came down among the leaves was sufficiently dim to create many illusions in her expecting fancy. Several times she seemed indistinctly

to see his face gazing out from among the leaves; and once she imagined that he stood beckoning to her at the base of a craggy rock. Keeping her eyes on this object, however, it proved to be no more than the trunk of an oak fringed to the very ground with little branches, one of which, thrust out farther than the rest, was shaken by the breeze. Making her way round the foot of the rock, she suddenly found herself close to her husband, who had approached in another·direction. Leaning upon the butt of his gun, the muzzle of which rested upon the withered leaves, he was apparently absorbed in the contemplation of some object at his feet.

"How is this, Reuben? Have you slain the deer and fallen asleep over him?" exclaimed Dorcas, laughing cheerfully, on her first slight observation of his posture and appearance.

He stirred not, neither did he turn his eyes towards her; and a cold, shuddering fear, indefinite in its source and object, began to creep into her blood. She now perceived that her husband's face was ghastly pale, and his features were rigid, as if incapable of assuming any other expression than the strong despair which had hardened upon them. He gave not the slightest evidence that he was aware of her approach.

"For the love of Heaven, Reuben, speak to me!" cried Dorcas; and the strange sound of her own voice affrighted her even more than the dead silence.

Her husband started, stared into her face, drew her to the front of the rock, and pointed with his finger.

Oh, there lay the boy, asleep, but dreamless, upon the fallen forest leaves! His cheek rested upon his arm — his curled locks were thrown back from his brow — his limbs were slightly relaxed. Had a sudden weariness overcome the youthful hunter? Would his mother's voice arouse him? She knew that it was death.

"This broad rock is the gravestone of your near kindred, Dorcas," said her husband. "Your tears will fall at once over your father and your son."

She heard him not. With one wild shriek, that seemed to force its way from the sufferer's inmost soul, she sank insensible by the side of her dead boy. At that moment the withered topmost bough of the oak loosened itself in the stilly air, and fell in soft, light fragments upon the rock, upon the leaves, upon Reuben, upon his wife and child, and upon Roger Malvin's bones. Then Reuben's heart was stricken, and the tears gushed out like water from a rock. The vow that the wounded youth had made the blighted man had come to redeem. His sin was expiated, — the curse was gone from him; and in the hour when he had shed blood dearer to him than his own, a prayer, the first for years, went up to Heaven from the lips of Reuben Bourne.   1831

My Kinsman, Major Molineux

Long overlooked in Hawthorne's fiction, "My Kinsman, Major Molineux" is regarded today as one of his finest tales. Initially titled "My Uncle Molineux," it was published in the Token *for 1832. Later, with the title used here, it was included in the collection of tales,* The Snow Image.

After the kings of Great Britain had assumed the right of appointing the colonial governors, the measures of the latter seldom met with the ready and general approbation which had been paid to those of their predecessors, under the original charters. The people looked with most jealous scrutiny to the exercise of power which did not emanate from themselves, and they usually rewarded their rulers with slender gratitude for the compliances by which, in softening their instructions from beyond the sea, they had incurred the reprehension of those who gave them. The annals of Massachusetts Bay will inform us, that of six governors in the space of about forty years from the surrender of the old charter, under James II., two were
10 imprisoned by a popular insurrection; a third, as Hutchinson inclines to believe, was driven from the province by the whizzing of a musket-ball; a fourth, in the opinion of the same historian, was hastened to his grave by continual bickerings with the House of Representatives; and the remaining two, as well as their successors, till the Revolution, were favored with few and brief intervals of peaceful sway. The inferior members of the court party, in times of high political excitement, led scarcely a more desirable life. These remarks may serve as a preface to the following adventures, which chanced upon a summer night, not far from a hundred years ago. The reader, in order to avoid a long and dry detail of colonial affairs, is requested to dispense with an account of the train of circumstances that had caused much tem-
20 porary inflammation of the popular mind.

It was near nine o'clock of a moonlight evening, when a boat crossed the ferry with a single passenger, who had obtained his conveyance at that unusual hour by the promise of an extra fare. While he stood on the landing-place, searching in either pocket for the means of fulfilling his agreement, the ferryman lifted a lantern, by the aid of which, and the newly risen moon, he took a very accurate survey of the stranger's figure. He was a youth of barely eighteen years, evidently country-bred, and now, as it should seem, upon his first visit to town. He was clad in a coarse gray coat, well worn, but in excellent repair; his under garments were durably constructed of leather, and fitted tight to a pair of serviceable and well-shaped limbs;
30 his stockings of blue yarn were the incontrovertible work of a mother or a sister; and on his head was a three-cornered hat, which in its better days had perhaps sheltered the graver brow of the lad's father. Under his left arm was a heavy cudgel formed of an oak sapling, and retaining a part of the hardened root; and his equipment was completed by a wallet, not so abundantly stocked as to incommode the vigorous shoulders on which it hung. Brown, curly hair, well-shaped features, and bright, cheerful eyes were nature's gifts, and worth all that art could have done for his adornment.

The youth, one of whose names was Robin, finally drew from his pocket the half of a little province bill of five shillings, which, in the depreciation in that sort of
40 currency, did but satisfy the ferryman's demand, with the surplus of a sexangular piece of parchment, valued at three pence. He then walked forward into the town, with as light a step as if his day's journey had not already exceeded thirty miles,

---

10 **Hutchinson.** Thomas Hutchinson (1711-1780) wrote *History of the Colony of Massachusetts Bay, from its First Settlement in 1628 to the year 1750* (2 vols., 1764, 1767)

and with as eager an eye as if he were entering London city, instead of the little metropolis of a New England colony. Before Robin had proceeded far, however, it occurred to him that he knew not whither to direct his steps; so he paused, and looked up and down the narrow street, scrutinizing the small and mean wooden buildings that were scattered on either side.

"This low hovel cannot be my kinsman's dwelling," thought he, "nor yonder old house, where the moonlight enters at the broken casement; and truly I see none hereabouts that might be worthy of him. It would have been wise to inquire my way of the ferryman, and doubtless he would have gone with me, and earned a shilling from the Major for his pains. But the next man I meet will do as well." 10

He resumed his walk, and was glad to perceive that the street now became wider, and the houses more respectable in their appearance. He soon discerned a figure moving on moderately in advance, and hastened his steps to overtake it. As Robin drew nigh, he saw that the passenger was a man in years, with a full periwig of gray hair, a wide-skirted coat of dark cloth, and silk stockings rolled above his knees. He carried a long and polished cane, which he struck down perpendicularly before him at every step; and at regular intervals he uttered two successive hems, of a peculiarly solemn and sepulchral intonation. Having made these observations, Robin laid hold of the skirt of the old man's coat, just when the light from the open door and windows of a barber's shop fell upon both their figures. 20

"Good evening to you, honored sir," said he, making a low bow, and still retaining his hold of the skirt. "I pray you tell me whereabouts is the dwelling of my kinsman, Major Molineux."

The youth's question was uttered very loudly; and one of the barbers, whose razor was descending on a well-soaped chin, and another who was dressing a Ramillies wig, left their occupations, and came to the door. The citizen, in the mean time, turned a long-favored countenance upon Robin, and answered him in a tone of excessive anger and annoyance. His two sepulchral hems, however, broke into the very centre of his rebuke, with most singular effect, like a thought of the cold grave obtruding among wrathful passions. 30

"Let go my garment, fellow! I tell you, I know not the man you speak of. What! I have authority, I have — hem, hem — authority; and if this be the respect you show for your betters, your feet shall be brought acquainted with the stocks by daylight, tomorrow morning!"

Robin released the old man's skirt, and hastened away, pursued by an ill-mannered roar of laughter from the barber's shop. He was at first considerably surprised by the result of his question, but, being a shrewd youth, soon thought himself able to account for the mystery.

"This is some country representative," was his conclusion, "who has never seen the inside of my kinsman's door, and lacks the breeding to answer a stranger civilly. 40 The man is old, or verily — I might be tempted to turn back and smite him on the nose. Ah, Robin, Robin! even the barber's boys laugh at you for choosing such a guide! You will be wiser in time, friend Robin."

He now became entangled in a succession of crooked and narrow streets, which crossed each other, and meandered at no great distance from the water-side. The smell of tar was obvious to his nostrils, the masts of vessels pierced the moonlight above the tops of the buildings, and the numerous signs, which Robin paused to read, informed him that he was near the centre of business. But the streets were empty, the shops were closed, and lights were visible only in the second stories of a few dwelling-houses. At length, on the corner of a narrow lane, through which he was passing, he beheld the broad countenance of a British hero swinging before the door of an inn, whence proceeded the voices of many guests. The casement of one of the lower windows was thrown back, and a very thin curtain permitted Robin to

10 distinguish a party at supper, round a well-furnished table. The fragrance of the good cheer steamed forth into the outer air, and the youth could not fail to recollect that the last remnant of his travelling stock of provision had yielded to his morning appetite, and that noon had found and left him dinnerless.

"Oh, that a parchment three-penny might give me a right to sit down at yonder table!" said Robin, with a sigh. "But the Major will make me welcome to the best of his victuals; so I will even step boldly in, and inquire my way to his dwelling."

He entered the tavern, and was guided by the murmur of voices and the fumes of tobacco to the public-room. It was a long and low apartment, with oaken walls, grown dark in the continual smoke, and a floor which was thickly sanded, but of

20 no immaculate purity. A number of persons — the larger part of whom appeared to be mariners, or in some way connected with the sea — occupied the wooden benches, or leather-bottomed chairs, conversing on various matters, and occasionally lending their attention to some topic of general interest. Three or four little groups were draining as many bowls of punch, which the West India trade had long since made a familiar drink in the colony. Others, who had the appearance of men who lived by regular and laborious handicraft, preferred the insulated bliss of an unshared potation, and became more taciturn under its influence. Nearly all, in short, evinced a predilection for the Good Creature in some of its various shapes, for this is a vice to which, as Fast Day sermons of a hundred years ago will testify, we have a long

30 hereditary claim. The only guests to whom Robin's sympathies inclined him were two or three sheepish countrymen, who were using the inn somewhat after the fashion of a Turkish caravansary; they had gotten themselves into the darkest corner of the room, and heedless of the Nicotian atmosphere, were supping on the bread of their own ovens, and the bacon cured in their own chimney-smoke. But though Robin felt a sort of brotherhood with these strangers, his eyes were attracted from them to a person who stood near the door, holding whispered conversation with a group of ill-dressed associates. His features were separately striking almost to grotesqueness, and the whole face left a deep impression on the memory. The forehead bulged out into a double prominence, with a vale between; the nose came boldly

40 forth in an irregular curve, and its bridge was of more than a finger's breadth; the eyebrows were deep and shaggy, and the eyes glowed beneath them like fire in a cave.

---

28 **Good Creature,** food, drink, and other things ministering to material comfort; see I Timothy 4:4: "For every creature of God is good, and nothing to be refused, if it be received with thanksgiving"

While Robin deliberated of whom to inquire respecting his kinsman's dwelling, he was accosted by the innkeeper, a little man in a stained white apron, who had come to pay his professional welcome to the stranger. Being in the second generation from a French Protestant, he seemed to have inherited the courtesy of his parent nation; but no variety of circumstances was ever known to change his voice from the one shrill note in which he now addressed Robin.

"From the country, I presume, sir?" said he, with a profound bow. "Beg leave to congratulate you on your arrival, and trust you intend a long stay with us. Fine town here, sir, beautiful buildings, and much that may interest a stranger. May I hope for the honor of your commands in respect to supper?"   10

"The man sees a family likeness! the rogue has guessed that I am related to the Major!" thought Robin, who had hitherto experienced little superfluous civility.

All eyes were now turned on the country lad, standing at the door, in his worn three-cornered hat, gray coat, leather breeches, and blue yarn stockings, leaning on an oaken cudgel, and bearing a wallet on his back.

Robin replied to the courteous innkeeper, with such an assumption of confidence as befitted the Major's relative. "My honest friend," he said, "I shall make it a point to patronize your house on some occasion, when" — here he could not help lowering his voice — "when I may have more than a parchment three-pence in my pocket. My present business," continued he, speaking with lofty confidence, "is merely to   20 inquire my way to the dwelling of my kinsman, Major Molineux."

There was a sudden and general movement in the room, which Robin interpreted as expressing the eagerness of each individual to become his guide. But the innkeeper turned his eyes to a written paper on the wall, which he read, or seemed to read, with occasional recurrences to the young man's figure.

"What have we here?" said he, breaking his speech into little dry fragments. "'Left the house of the subscriber, bounden servant, Hezekiah Mudge, — had on, when he went away, gray coat, leather breeches, master's third-best hat. One pound currency reward to whosoever shall lodge him in any jail of the province.' Better trudge, boy; better trudge!"   30

Robin had begun to draw his hand towards the lighter end of the oak cudgel, but a strange hostility in every countenance induced him to relinquish his purpose of breaking the courteous innkeeper's head. As he turned to leave the room, he encountered a sneering glance from the bold-featured personage whom he had before noticed; and no sooner was he beyond the door, than he heard a general laugh, in which the innkeeper's voice might be distinguished, like the dropping of small stones into a kettle.

"Now, is it not strange," thought Robin, with his usual shrewdness, — "is it not strange that the confession of an empty pocket should outweigh the name of my kinsman, Major Molineux? Oh, if I had one of those grinning rascals in the woods,   40 where I and my oak sapling grew up together, I would teach him that my arm is heavy though my purse be light!"

On turning the corner of the narrow lane, Robin found himself in a spacious street, with an unbroken line of lofty houses on each side, and a steepled building

at the upper end, whence the ringing of a bell announced the hour of nine. The light of the moon, and the lamps from the numerous shop-windows, discovered people promenading on the pavement, and amongst them Robin hoped to recognize his hitherto inscrutable relative. The result of his former inquiries made him unwilling to hazard another, in a scene of such publicity, and he determined to walk slowly and silently up the street, thrusting his face close to that of every elderly gentleman, in search of the Major's lineaments. In his progress, Robin encountered many gay and gallant figures. Embroidered garments of showy colors, enormous periwigs, gold-laced hats, and silver-hilted swords glided past him and dazzled his
10 optics. Travelled youths, imitators of the European fine gentlemen of the period, trod jauntily along, half dancing to the fashionable tunes which they hummed, and making poor Robin ashamed of his quiet and natural gait. At length, after many pauses to examine the gorgeous display of goods in the shop-windows, and after suffering some rebukes for the impertinence of his scrutiny into people's faces, the Major's kinsman found himself near the steepled building, still unsuccessful in his search. As yet, however, he had seen only one side of the thronged street; so Robin crossed, and continued the same sort of inquisition down the opposite pavement, with stronger hopes than the philosopher seeking an honest man, but with no better fortune. He had arrived about midway towards the lower end, from which his
20 course began, when he overheard the approach of some one who struck down a cane on the flag-stones at every step, uttering, at regular intervals, two sepulchral hems.

"Mercy on us!" quoth Robin, recognizing the sound.

Turning a corner, which chanced to be close at his right hand, he hastened to pursue his researches in some other part of the town. His patience now was wearing low, and he seemed to feel more fatigue from his rambles since he crossed the ferry, than from his journey of several days on the other side. Hunger also pleaded loudly within him, and Robin began to balance the propriety of demanding, violently, and with lifted cudgel, the necessary guidance from the first solitary passen-
30 ger whom he should meet. While a resolution of this effect was gaining strength, he entered a street of mean appearance, on either side of which a row of ill-built houses was straggling towards the harbor. The moonlight fell upon no passenger along the whole extent, but in the third domicile which Robin passed there was a half-opened door, and his keen glance detected a woman's garment within.

"My luck may be better here," said he to himself.

Accordingly, he approached the door, and beheld it shut closer as he did so; yet an open space remained, sufficing for the fair occupant to observe the stranger, without a corresponding display on her part. All that Robin could discern was a strip of scarlet petticoat, and the occasional sparkle of an eye, as if the moonbeams were
40 trembling on some bright thing.

"Pretty mistress," for I may call her so with a good conscience, thought the shrewd youth, since I know nothing to the contrary, — "my sweet pretty mistress, will you

---

18 **philosopher,** Diogenes (c. 412-323 B.C.), Greek Cynic philosopher, who carried a lantern in daylight seeking an honest man

be kind enough to tell me whereabouts I must seek the dwelling of my kinsman, Major Molineux?"

Robin's voice was plaintive and winning, and the female, seeing nothing to be shunned in the handsome country youth, thrust open the door, and came forth into the moonlight. She was a dainty little figure, with a white neck, round arms, and a slender waist, at the extremity of which her scarlet petticoat jutted out over a hoop, as if she were standing in a balloon. Moreover, her face was oval and pretty, her hair dark beneath the little cap, and her bright eyes possessed a sly freedom, which triumphed over those of Robin.

"Major Molineux dwells here," said this fair woman.   10

Now, her voice was the sweetest Robin had heard that night, the airy counterpart of a stream of melted silver; yet he could not help doubting whether that sweet voice spoke Gospel truth. He looked up and down the mean street, and then surveyed the house before which they stood. It was a small, dark edifice of two stories, the second of which projected over the lower floor, and the front apartment had the aspect of a shop for petty commodities.

"Now, truly, I am in luck," replied Robin, cunningly, "and so indeed is my kinsman, the Major, in having so pretty a housekeeper. But I prithee trouble him to step to the door; I will deliver him a message from his friends in the country, and then go back to my lodgings at the inn."   20

"Nay, the Major has been abed this hour or more," said the lady of the scarlet petticoat; "and it would be to little purpose to disturb him to-night, seeing his evening draught was of the strongest. But he is a kind-hearted man, and it would be as much as my life's worth to let a kinsman of his turn away from the door. You are the good old gentleman's very picture, and I could swear that was his rainy-weather hat. Also he has garments very much resembling those leather small-clothes. But come in, I pray, for I bid you hearty welcome in his name."

So saying, the fair and hospitable dame took our hero by the hand; and the touch was light, and the force was gentleness, and though Robin read in her eyes what he did not hear in her words, yet the slender-waisted woman in the scarlet petticoat 30 proved stronger than the athletic country youth. She had drawn his half-willing footsteps nearly to the threshold, when the opening of a door in the neighborhood startled the Major's housekeeper, and, leaving the Major's kinsman, she vanished speedily into her own domicile. A heavy yawn preceded the appearance of a man, who, like the Moonshine of Pyramus and Thisbe, carried a lantern, needlessly aiding his sister luminary in the heavens. As he walked sleepily up the street, he turned his broad, dull face on Robin, and displayed a long staff, spiked at the end.

"Home, vagabond, home!" said the watchman, in accents that seemed to fall asleep as soon as they were uttered. "Home, or we'll set you in the stocks by peep of day!"   40

"This is the second hint of the kind," thought Robin. "I wish they would end my difficulties, by setting me there tonight."

Nevertheless, the youth felt an instinctive antipathy towards the guardian of mid-

---

35 **Moonshine of Pyramus.** See Shakespeare's *A Midsummer Night's Dream,* Act V, Sc. ii, l. 128ff.

night order, which at first prevented him from asking his usual question. But just when the man was about to vanish behind the corner, Robin resolved not to lose the opportunity, and shouted lustily after him —

"I say, friend! will you guide me to the house of my kinsman, Major Molineux?"

The watchman made no reply, but turned the corner and was gone; yet Robin seemed to hear the sound of drowsy laughter stealing along the solitary street. At that moment, also, a pleasant titter saluted him from the open window above his head; he looked up, and caught the sparkle of a saucy eye; a round arm beckoned to him, and next he heard light footsteps descending the staircase within. But
10 Robin, being of the household of a New England clergyman, was a good youth, as well as a shrewd one; so he resisted temptation, and fled away.

He now roamed desperately, and at random, through the town, almost ready to believe that a spell was on him, like that by which a wizard of his country had once kept three pursuers wandering a whole winter night, within twenty paces of the cottage which they sought. The streets lay before him, strange and desolate, and the lights were extinguished in almost every house. Twice, however, little parties of men, among whom Robin distinguished individuals in outlandish attire, came hurrying along; but, though on both occasions they paused to address him, such intercourse did not at all enlighten his perplexity. They did but utter a few words in some
20 language of which Robin knew nothing, and perceiving his inability to answer, bestowed a curse upon him in plain English and hastened away. Finally, the lad determined to knock at the door of every mansion that might appear worthy to be occupied by his kinsman, trusting that perseverance would overcome the fatality that had hitherto thwarted him. Firm in this resolve, he was passing beneath the walls of a church, which formed the corner of two streets, when, as he turned into the shade of its steeple, he encountered a bulky stranger, muffled in a cloak. The man was proceeding with the speed of earnest business, but Robin planted himself full before him, holding the oak cudgel with both hands across his body as a bar to further passage.

30 "Halt, honest man, and answer me a question," said he, very resolutely. "Tell me, this instant, whereabouts is the dwelling of my kinsman, Major Molineux!"

"Keep your tongue between your teeth, fool, and let me pass!" said a deep, gruff voice, which Robin partly remembered. "Let me pass, I say, or I'll strike you to the earth!"

"No, no, neighbor!" cried Robin, flourishing his cudgel, and then thrusting its larger end close to the man's muffled face. "No, no, I'm not the fool you take me for, nor do you pass till I have an answer to my question. Whereabouts is the dwelling of my kinsman, Major Molineux?"

The stranger, instead of attempting to force his passage, stepped back into the
40 moonlight, unmuffled his face, and stared full into that of Robin.

"Watch here an hour, and Major Molineux will pass by," said he.

Robin gazed with dismay and astonishment on the unprecedented physiognomy of the speaker. The forehead with its double prominence, the broad hooked nose, the shaggy eyebrows, and fiery eyes were those which he had noticed at the inn, but the man's complexion had undergone a singular, or, more properly, a twofold change. One side of the face blazed an intense red, while the other was black as midnight, the division line being in the broad bridge of the nose; and a mouth which seemed to extend from ear to ear was black or red, in contrast to the color of the cheek. The effect was as if two individual devils, a fiend of fire and a fiend of darkness, had united themselves to form this infernal visage. The stranger grinned in Robin's face, muffled his party-colored features, and was out of sight in a moment.

"Strange things we travellers see!" ejaculated Robin.

He seated himself, however, upon the steps of the church-door, resolving to wait 10 the appointed time for his kinsman. A few moments were consumed in philosophical speculations upon the species of man who had just left him; but having settled this point shrewdly, rationally, and satisfactorily, he was compelled to look elsewhere for his amusement. And first he threw his eyes along the street. It was of more respectable appearance than most of those into which he had wandered; and the moon, creating, like the imaginative power, a beautiful strangeness in familiar objects, gave something of romance to a scene that might not have possessed it in the light of day. The irregular and often quaint architecture of the houses, some of whose roofs were broken into numerous little peaks, while others ascended, steep and narrow, into a single point, and others again were square; the pure snow-white 20 of some of their complexions, the aged darkness of others, and the thousand sparklings, reflected from bright substances in the walls of many; these matters engaged Robin's attention for a while, and then began to grow wearisome. Next he endeavored to define the forms of distant objects, starting away, with almost ghostly indistinctness, just as his eye appeared to grasp them; and finally he took a minute survey of an edifice which stood on the opposite side of the street, directly in front of the church-door, where he was stationed. It was a large, square mansion, distinguished from its neighbors by a balcony, which rested on tall pillars, and by an elaborate Gothic window, communicating therewith.

"Perhaps this is the very house I have been seeking," thought Robin.   30

Then he strove to speed away the time, by listening to a murmur which swept continually along the street, yet was scarcely audible, except to an unaccustomed ear like his; it was a low, dull, dreamy sound, compounded of many noises, each of which was at too great a distance to be separately heard. Robin marvelled at this snore of a sleeping town, and marvelled more whenever its continuity was broken by now and then a distant shout, apparently loud where it originated. But altogether it was a sleep-inspiring sound, and, to shake off its drowsy influence, Robin arose, and climbed a window-frame, that he might view the interior of the church. There the moonbeams came trembling in, and fell down upon the deserted pews, and extended along the quiet aisles. A fainter yet more awful radiance was hovering around 40 the pulpit, and one solitary ray had dared to rest upon the open page of the great Bible. Had nature, in that deep hour, become a worshipper in the house which man had builded? Or was that heavenly light the visible sanctity of the place, — visible because no earthly and impure feet were within the walls? The scene made Robin's heart shiver with a sensation of loneliness stronger than he had ever felt in the remotest depths of his native woods; so he turned away and sat down again before the door. There were graves around the church, and now an uneasy thought obtruded into Robin's breast. What if the object of his search, which had been so often and so strangely thwarted, were all the time mouldering in his shroud? What if his kinsman should glide through yonder gate, and nod and smile to him in dimly passing by?

"Oh that any breathing thing were here with me!" said Robin.

Recalling his thoughts from this uncomfortable track, he sent them over forest, hill, and stream, and attempted to imagine how that evening of ambiguity and weariness had been spent by his father's household. He pictured them assembled at the door, beneath the tree, the great old tree, which had been spared for its huge twisted trunk and venerable shade, when a thousand leafy brethren fell. There, at the going down of the summer sun, it was his father's custom to perform domestic worship, that the neighbors might come and join with him like brothers of the family, and that the wayfaring man might pause to drink at that fountain, and keep his heart pure by freshening the memory of home. Robin distinguished the seat of every individual of the little audience; he saw the good man in the midst, holding the Scriptures in the golden light that fell from the western clouds; he beheld him close the book and all rise up to pray. He heard the old thanksgivings for daily mercies, the old supplications for their continuance, to which he had so often listened in weariness, but which were now among his dear remembrances. He perceived the slight inequality of his father's voice when he came to speak of the absent one; he noted how his mother turned her face to the broad and knotted trunk; how his elder brother scorned, because the beard was rough upon his upper lip, to permit his features to be moved; how the younger sister drew down a low hanging branch before her eyes; and how the little one of all, whose sports had hitherto broken the decorum of the scene, understood the prayer for her playmate, and burst into clamorous grief. Then he saw them go in at the door; and when Robin would have entered also, the latch tinkled into its place, and he was excluded from his home.

"Am I here, or there?" cried Robin, starting; for all at once, when his thoughts had become visible and audible in a dream, the long, wide, solitary street shone out before him.

He aroused himself, and endeavored to fix his attention steadily upon the large edifice which he had surveyed before. But still his mind kept vibrating between fancy and reality; by turns, the pillars of the balcony lengthened into the tall, bare stems of pines, dwindled down to human figures, settled again into their true shape and size, and then commenced a new succession of changes. For a single moment, when he deemed himself awake, he could have sworn that a visage — one which he seemed to remember, yet could not absolutely name as his kinsman's — was looking towards him from the Gothic window. A deeper sleep wrestled with and nearly overcame him, but fled at the sound of footsteps along the opposite pavement. Robin rubbed his eyes, discerned a man passing at the foot of the balcony, and addressed him in a loud, peevish, and lamentable cry.

"Hallo, friend! must I wait here all night for my kinsman, Major Molineux?"

The sleeping echoes awoke, and answered the voice; and the passenger, barely able to discern a figure sitting in the oblique shade of the steeple, traversed the street to obtain a nearer view. He was himself a gentleman in his prime, of open, intelligent, cheerful, and altogether prepossessing countenance. Perceiving a country youth, apparently homeless and without friends, he accosted him in a tone of real kindness, which had become strange to Robin's ears.

"Well, my good lad, why are you sitting here?" inquired he. "Can I be of service to you in any way?"

"I am afraid not, sir," replied Robin, despondingly; "yet I shall take it kindly, if 10 you'll answer me a single question. I've been searching, half the night, for one Major Molineux; now, sir, is there really such a person in these parts, or am I dreaming?"

"Major Molineux! The name is not altogether strange to me," said the gentleman, smiling. "Have you any objection to telling me the nature of your business with him?"

Then Robin briefly related that his father was a clergyman, settled on a small salary, at a long distance back in the country, and that he and Major Molineux were brothers' children. The Major, having inherited riches, and acquired civil and military rank, had visited his cousin, in great pomp, a year or two before; had manifested much interest in Robin and an elder brother, and, being childless himself, 20 had thrown out hints respecting the future establishment of one of them in life. The elder brother was destined to succeed to the farm which his father cultivated in the interval of sacred duties; it was therefore determined that Robin should profit by his kinsman's generous intentions, especially as he seemed to be rather the favorite, and was thought to possess other necessary endowments.

"For I have the name of being a shrewd youth," observed Robin, in this part of his story.

"I doubt not you deserve it," replied his new friend, good-naturedly; "but pray proceed."

"Well, sir, being nearly eighteen years old, and well grown, as you see," con- 30 tinued Robin, drawing himself up to his full height, "I thought it high time to begin the world. So my mother and sister put me in handsome trim, and my father gave me half the remnant of his last year's salary, and five days ago I started for this place, to pay the Major a visit. But, would you believe it, sir! I crossed the ferry a little after dark, and have yet found nobody that would show me the way to his dwelling; only, an hour or two since, I was told to wait here, and Major Molineux would pass by."

"Can you describe the man who told you this?" inquired the gentleman.

"Oh, he was a very ill-favored fellow, sir," replied Robin, "with two great bumps on his forehead, a hook nose, fiery eyes; and, what struck me as the strangest, his 40 face was of two different colors. Do you happen to know such a man, sir?"

"Not intimately," answered the stranger, "but I chanced to meet him a little time previous to your stopping me. I believe you may trust his word, and that the Major will very shortly pass through this street. In the mean time, as I have a singular curiosity to witness your meeting, I will sit down here upon the steps and bear you company."

He seated himself accordingly, and soon engaged his companion in animated discourse. It was but of brief continuance, however, for a noise of shouting, which had long been remotely audible, drew so much nearer that Robin inquired its cause.

"What may be the meaning of this uproar?" asked he. "Truly, if your town be always as noisy, I shall find little sleep while I am an inhabitant."

"Why, indeed, friend Robin, there do appear to be three or four riotous fellows
10 abroad to-night," replied the gentleman. "You must not expect all the stillness of your native woods here in our streets. But the watch will shortly be at the heels of these lads and" —

"Ay, and set them in the stocks by peep of day," interrupted Robin, recollecting his own encounter with the drowsy lantern-bearer. "But, dear sir, if I may trust my ears, an army of watchmen would never make head against such a multitude of rioters. There were at least a thousand voices went up to make that one shout."

"May not a man have several voices, Robin, as well as two complexions?" said his friend.

"Perhaps a man may; but Heaven forbid that a woman should!" responded the
20 shrewd youth, thinking of the seductive tones of the Major's housekeeper.

The sounds of a trumpet in some neighboring street now became so evident and continual, that Robin's curiosity was strongly excited. In addition to the shouts, he heard frequent bursts from many instruments of discord, and a wild and confused laughter filled up the intervals. Robin rose from the steps, and looked wistfully towards a point whither people seemed to be hastening.

"Surely some prodigious merry-making is going on," exclaimed he. "I have laughed very little since I left home, sir, and should be sorry to lose an opportunity. Shall we step round the corner by that darkish house, and take our share of the fun?"

"Sit down again, sit down, good Robin," replied the gentleman, laying his hand
30 on the skirt of the gray coat. "You forget that we must wait here for your kinsman; and there is reason to believe that he will pass by, in the course of a very few moments."

The near approach of the uproar had now disturbed the neighborhood; windows flew open on all sides; and many heads, in the attire of the pillow, and confused by sleep suddenly broken, were protruded to the gaze of whoever had leisure to observe them. Eager voices hailed each other from house to house, all demanding the explanation, which not a soul could give. Half-dressed men hurried towards the unknown commotion, stumbling as they went over the stone steps that thrust themselves into the narrow foot-walk. The shouts, the laughter, and the tuneless
40 bray, the antipodes of music, came onwards with increasing din, till scattered individuals, and then denser bodies, began to appear round a corner at the distance of a hundred yards.

"Will you recognize your kinsman, if he passes in this crowd?" inquired the gentleman.

"Indeed, I can't warrant it, sir; but I'll take my stand here, and keep a bright lookout," answered Robin, descending to the outer edge of the pavement.

A mighty stream of people now emptied into the street, and came rolling slowly towards the church. A single horseman wheeled the corner in the midst of them, and close behind him came a band of fearful wind-instruments, sending forth a fresher discord now that no intervening buildings kept it from the ear. Then a redder light disturbed the moonbeams, and a dense multitude of torches shone along the street, concealing, by their glare, whatever object they illuminated. The single horseman, clad in a military dress, and bearing a drawn sword, rode onward as the leader, and, by his fierce and variegated countenance, appeared like war personified; the red of one cheek was an emblem of fire and sword; the blackness of the other betokened the mourning that attends them. In his train were wild figures in the Indian dress, and many fantastic shapes without a model, giving the whole march a visionary air, as if a dream had broken forth from some feverish brain, and were sweeping visibly through the midnight streets. A mass of people, inactive, except as applauding spectators, hemmed the procession in; and several women ran along the sidewalk, piercing the confusion of heavier sounds with their shrill voices of mirth or terror.

"The double-faced fellow has his eye upon me," muttered Robin, with an indefinite but an uncomfortable idea that he was himself to bear a part in the pageantry.

The leader turned himself in the saddle, and fixed his glance full upon the country youth, as the steed went slowly by. When Robin had freed his eyes from those fiery ones, the musicians were passing before him, and the torches were close at hand; but the unsteady brightness of the latter formed a veil which he could not penetrate. The rattling of wheels over the stones sometimes found its way to his ear, and confused traces of a human form appeared at intervals, and then melted into the vivid light. A moment more, and the leader thundered a command to halt: the trumpets vomited a horrid breath, and then held their peace; the shouts and laughter of the people died away, and there remained only a universal hum, allied to silence. Right before Robin's eyes was an uncovered cart. There the torches blazed the brightest, there the moon shone out like day, and there, in tar-and-feathery dignity, sat his kinsman, Major Molineux!

He was an elderly man, of large and majestic person, and strong, square features, betokening a steady soul; but steady as it was, his enemies had found means to shake it. His face was pale as death, and far more ghastly; the broad forehead was contracted in his agony, so that his eyebrows formed one grizzled line; his eyes were red and wild, and the foam hung white upon his quivering lip. His whole frame was agitated by a quick and continual tremor, which his pride strove to quell, even in those circumstances of overwhelming humiliation. But perhaps the bitterest pang of all was when his eyes met those of Robin; for he evidently knew him on the instant, as the youth stood witnessing the foul disgrace of a head grown gray in honor. They stared at each other in silence, and Robin's knees shook, and his hair bristled, with a mixture of pity and terror. Soon, however, a bewildering excitement began to seize upon his mind; the preceding adventures of the night, the unexpected

appearance of the crowd, the torches, the confused din and the hush that followed, the spectre of his kinsman reviled by that great multitude, — all this, and, more than all, a perception of tremendous ridicule in the whole scene, affected him with a sort of mental inebriety. At that moment a voice of sluggish merriment saluted Robin's ears; he turned instinctively, and just behind the corner of the church stood the lantern-bearer, rubbing his eyes, and drowsily enjoying the lad's amazement. Then he heard a peal of laughter like the ringing of silvery bells; a woman twitched his arm, a saucy eye met his, and he saw the lady of the scarlet petticoat. A sharp, dry cachinnation appealed to his memory, and, standing on tip-toe in the crowd,
10 with his white apron over his head, he beheld the courteous little innkeeper. And lastly, there sailed over the heads of the multitude a great, broad laugh, broken in the midst by two sepulchral hems; thus, "Haw, haw, haw, — hem, hem, — haw, haw, haw, haw!"

The sound proceeded from the balcony of the opposite edifice, and thither Robin turned his eyes. In front of the Gothic window stood the old citizen, wrapped in a wide gown, his gray periwig exchanged for a nightcap, which was thrust back from his forehead, and his silk stockings hanging about his legs. He supported himself on his polished cane in a fit of convulsive merriment, which manifested itself on his solemn old features like a funny inscription on a tombstone. Then Robin seemed
20 to hear the voices of the barbers, of the guests of the inn, and of all who had made sport of him that night. The contagion was spreading among the multitude, when all at once, it seized upon Robin, and he sent forth a shout of laughter that echoed through the street, — every man shook his sides, every man emptied his lungs, but Robin's shout was the loudest there. The cloud-spirits peeped from their silvery islands, as the congregated mirth went roaring up the sky! The Man in the Moon heard the far bellow. "Oho," quoth he, "the old earth is frolicsome to-night!"

When there was a momentary calm in that tempestuous sea of sound, the leader gave the sign, the procession resumed its march. On they went, like fiends that throng in mockery around some dead potentate, mighty no more, but majestic still
30 in his agony. On they went, in counterfeited pomp, in senseless uproar, in frenzied merriment, trampling all on an old man's heart. On swept the tumult, and left a silent street behind.

"Well, Robin, are you dreaming?" inquired the gentleman, laying his hand on the youth's shoulder.

Robin started, and withdrew his arm from the stone post to which he had instinctively clung, as the living stream rolled by him. His cheek was somewhat pale, and his eye not quite as lively as in the earlier part of the evening.

"Will you be kind enough to show me the way to the ferry?" said he, after a moment's pause.
40 "You have, then, adopted a new subject of inquiry?" observed his companion, with a smile.

"Why, yes, sir," replied Robin, rather dryly. "Thanks to you, and to my other friends, I have at last met my kinsman, and he will scarce desire to see my face again. I begin to grow weary of a town life, sir. Will you show me the way to the ferry?"

"No, my good friend Robin, —not to-night, at least," said the gentleman. "Some few days hence, if you wish it, I will speed you on your journey. Or, if you prefer to remain with us, perhaps, as you are a shrewd youth, you may rise in the world without the help of your kinsman, Major Molineux."

1831

Young Goodman Brown

This story first appeared in the New England Magazine *for April 1835. Inexplicably, since it is generally considered to be one of his greatest tales, Hawthorne did not include it in the 1837 edition of* Twice Told Tales *or in the second enlarged edition of that collection which appeared in 1842; he postponed its appearance in a book until 1846 when* Mosses from an Old Manse *was issued. Here, in a remarkably small space and with great intensity, the author makes use of the tantalizing ambiguity of which he was a master.*

"Had Goodman Brown fallen asleep in the forest and only dreamed a wild dream of a witch meeting?" Hawthorne leaves the question open. But one thing is certain: Young Brown is never the same after the experience of the meeting, whether it is a dream or an actuality. "A stern, a sad, a darkly meditative, a distrustful, if not a desperate man, did he become the night of that fearful dream."

Young Goodman Brown came forth at sunset into the street at Salem village; but put his head back, after crossing the threshold, to exchange a parting kiss with his young wife. And Faith, as the wife was aptly named, thrust her own pretty head into the street, letting the wind play with the pink ribbons of her cap while she called to Goodman Brown.

"Dearest heart," whispered she, softly and rather sadly, when her lips were close to his ear, "prithee put off your journey until sunrise and sleep in your own bed to-night. A lone woman is troubled with such dreams and such thoughts that she's afeard of herself sometimes. Pray tarry with me this night, dear husband, of all nights in the year."   10

"My love and my Faith," replied young Goodman Brown, "of all nights in the year, this one night must I tarry away from thee. My journey, as thou callest it, forth and back again, must needs be done 'twixt now and sunrise. What, my sweet, pretty wife, dost thou doubt me already, and we but three months married?"

"Then God bless you!" said Faith, with the pink ribbons; "and may you find all well when you come back."

"Amen!" cried Goodman Brown. "Say thy prayers, dear Faith, and go to bed at dusk, and no harm will come to thee."

So they parted; and the young man pursued his way until, being about to turn the corner by the meeting-house, he looked back and saw the head of Faith still 20 peeping after him with a melancholy air, in spite of her pink ribbons.

"Poor little Faith!" thought he, for his heart smote him. "What a wretch am I to leave her on such an errand! She talks of dreams, too. Methought as she spoke there was trouble in her face, as if a dream had warned her what work is to be done to-night. But no, no; 't would kill her to think it. Well, she's a blessed angel on earth; and after this one night I'll cling to her skirts and follow her to heaven."

With this excellent resolve for the future, Goodman Brown felt himself justified in making more haste on his present evil purpose. He had taken a dreary road, darkened by all the gloomiest trees of the forest, which barely stood aside to let the narrow path creep through, and closed immediately behind. It was all as lonely as
10 could be; and there is this peculiarity in such a solitude, that the traveller knows not who may be concealed by the innumerable trunks and the thick boughs overhead; so that with lonely footsteps he may yet be passing through an unseen multitude.

"There may be a devilish Indian behind every tree," said Goodman Brown to himself; and he glanced fearfully behind him as he added, "What if the devil himself should be at my very elbow!"

His head being turned back, he passed a crook of the road, and, looking forward again, beheld the figure of a man, in grave and decent attire, seated at the foot of an old tree. He arose at Goodman Brown's approach and walked onward side by
20 side with him.

"You are late, Goodman Brown," said he. "The clock of the Old South was striking as I came through Boston, and that is full fifteen minutes agone."

"Faith kept me back a while," replied the young man, with a tremor in his voice, caused by the sudden appearance of his companion, though not wholly unexpected.

It was now deep dusk in the forest, and deepest in that part of it where these two were journeying. As nearly as could be discerned, the second traveller was about fifty years old, apparently in the same rank of life as Goodman Brown, and bearing a considerable resemblance to him, though perhaps more in expression than features. Still they might have been taken for father and son. And yet, though the elder per-
30 son was as simply clad as the younger, and as simple in manner too, he had an indescribable air of one who knew the world, and who would not have felt abashed at the governor's dinner table or in King William's court, were it possible that his affairs should call him thither. But the only thing about him that could be fixed upon as remarkable was his staff, which bore the likeness of a great black snake, so curiously wrought that it might almost be seen to twist and wriggle itself like a living serpent. This, of course, must have been an ocular deception, assisted by the uncertain light.

"Come, Goodman Brown," cried his fellow-traveller, "this is a dull pace for the beginning of a journey. Take my staff, if you are so soon weary."
40 "Friend," said the other, exchanging his slow pace for a full stop, "having kept covenant by meeting thee here, it is my purpose now to return whence I came. I have scruples touching the matter thou wot'st of."

"Sayest thou so?" replied he of the serpent, smiling apart. "Let us walk on, never-

---

32 **King William's court.** William III (1650-1702) reigned 1694-1702

theless, reasoning as we go; and if I convince thee not thou shalt turn back. We are but a little way in the forest yet."

"Too far! too far!" exclaimed the goodman, unconsciously resuming his walk. "My father never went into the woods on such an errand, nor his father before him. We have been a race of honest men and good Christians since the days of the martyrs; and shall I be the first of the name of Brown that ever took this path and kept" —

"Such company, thou wouldst say," observed the elder person, interpreting his pause. "Well said, Goodman Brown! I have been as well acquainted with your family as with ever a one among the Puritans; and that's no trifle to say. I helped your grandfather, the constable, when he lashed the Quaker woman so smartly through 10 the streets of Salem; and it was I that brought your father a pitch-pine knot, kindled at my own hearth, to set fire to an Indian village, in King Philip's war. They were my good friends, both; and many a pleasant walk have we had along this path, and returned merrily after midnight. I would fain be friends with you for their sake."

"If it be as thou sayest," replied Goodman Brown, "I marvel they never spoke of these matters; or, verily, I marvel not, seeing that the least rumor of the sort would have driven them from New England. We are a people of prayer, and good works to boot, and abide no such wickedness."

"Wickedness or not," said the traveller with the twisted staff, "I have a very general acquaintance here in New England. The deacons of many a church have drunk 20 the communion wine with me; the selectmen of divers towns make me their chairman; and a majority of the Great and General Court are firm supporters of my interest. The governor and I, too — But these are state secrets."

"Can this be so?" cried Goodman Brown, with a stare of amazement at his undisturbed companion. "Howbeit, I have nothing to do with the governor and council; they have their own ways, and are no rule for a simple husbandman like me. But, were I to go on with thee, how should I meet the eye of that good old man, our minister, at Salem village? Oh, his voice would make me tremble both Sabbath day and lecture day."

Thus far the elder traveller had listened with due gravity; but now burst into a fit 30 of irrepressible mirth, shaking himself so violently that his snake-like staff actually seemed to wriggle in sympathy.

"Ha! ha! ha!" shouted he again and again; then composing himself, "Well, go on, Goodman Brown, go on; but, prithee, don't kill me with laughing."

"Well, then, to end the matter at once," said Goodman Brown, considerably nettled, "there is my wife, Faith. It would break her dear little heart; and I'd rather break my own."

"Nay, if that be the case," answered the other, "e'en go thy ways, Goodman Brown. I would not for twenty old women like the one hobbling before us that Faith should come to any harm."   40

As he spoke he pointed his staff at a female figure on the path, in whom Goodman Brown recognized a very pious and exemplary dame, who had taught him his

---

5 days . . . martyrs, during the reign of Mary Tudor, 1553-1558   **12 King Philip's war,** between the Wampanoag Indian leader and the New England colonists, 1675-1676

catechism in youth, and was still his moral and spiritual adviser, jointly with the minister and Deacon Gookin.

"A marvel, truly, that Goody Cloyse should be so far in the wilderness at night-fall," said he. "But with your leave, friend, I shall take a cut through the woods until we have left this Christian woman behind. Being a stranger to you, she might ask whom I was consorting with and whither I was going."

"Be it so," said his fellow-traveller. "Betake you to the woods, and let me keep the path."

Accordingly the young man turned aside, but took care to watch his companion, 10 who advanced softly along the road until he had come within a staff's length of the old dame. She, meanwhile, was making the best of her way, with singular speed for so aged a woman, and mumbling some indistinct words — a prayer, doubtless — as she went. The traveller put forth his staff and touched her withered neck with what seemed the serpent's tail.

"The devil!" screamed the pious old lady.

"Then Goody Cloyse knows her old friend?" observed the traveller, confronting her and leaning on his writhing stick.

"Ah, forsooth, and is it your worship indeed?" cried the good dame. "Yea, truly is it, and in the very image of my old gossip, Goodman Brown, the grandfather of 20 the silly fellow that now is. But — would your worship believe it? — my broom-stick hath strangely disappeared, stolen, as I suspect, by that unhanged witch, Goody Cory, and that, too, when I was all anointed with the juice of smallage, and cinquefoil, and wolf's bane" —

"Mingled with fine wheat and the fat of a new-born babe," said the shape of old Goodman Brown.

"Ah, your worship knows the recipe," cried the old lady, cackling aloud. "So, as I was saying, being all ready for the meeting, and no horse to ride on, I made up my mind to foot it; for they tell me there is a nice young man to be taken into communion to-night. But now your good worship will lend me your arm, and we 30 shall be there in a twinkling."

"That can hardly be," answered her friend. "I may not spare you my arm, Goody Cloyse; but here is my staff, if you will."

So saying, he threw it down at her feet, where, perhaps, it assumed life, being one of the rods which its owner had formerly lent to the Egyptian magi. Of this fact, however, Goodman Brown could not take cognizance. He had cast up his eyes in astonishment, and, looking down again, beheld neither Goody Cloyse nor the ser-pentine staff, but his fellow-traveller alone, who waited for him as calmly as if noth-ing had happened.

"That old woman taught me my catechism," said the young man; and there was 40 a world of meaning in this simple comment.

They continued to walk onward, while the elder traveller exhorted his companion

---

3 **Goody Cloyse** was tried in Salem in 1692 for witchcraft and sentenced   26 **recipe.** This recipe comes from one of Cervantes' "exemplary novels," *The Conversation of the Dogs* and was reprinted by Hawthorne in the *American Magazine of Useful and Entertaining Knowledge* in 1836

to make good speed and persevere in the path, discoursing so aptly that his arguments seemed rather to spring up in the bosom of his auditor than to be suggested by himself. As they went, he plucked a branch of maple to serve for a walking stick, and began to strip it of the twigs and little boughs, which were wet with evening dew. The moment his fingers touched them they became strangely withered and dried up as with a week's sunshine. Thus the pair proceeded, at a good free pace, until suddenly, in a gloomy hollow of the road, Goodman Brown sat himself down on the stump of a tree and refused to go any farther.

"Friend," said he, stubbornly, "my mind is made up. Not another step will I budge on this errand. What if a wretched old woman do choose to go to the devil when I thought she was going to heaven: is that any reason why I should quit my dear Faith and go after her?"

"You will think better of this by and by," said his acquaintance, composedly. "Sit here and rest yourself a while; and when you feel like moving again, there is my staff to help you along."

Without more words, he threw his companion the maple stick, and was as speedily out of sight as if he had vanished into the deepening gloom. The young man sat a few moments by the roadside, applauding himself greatly, and thinking with how clear a conscience he should meet the minister in his morning walk, nor shrink from the eye of good old Deacon Gookin. And what calm sleep would be his that very night, which was to have been spent so wickedly, but so purely and sweetly now, in the arms of Faith! Amidst these pleasant and praiseworthy meditations, Goodman Brown heard the tramp of horses along the road, and deemed it advisable to conceal himself within the verge of the forest, conscious of the guilty purpose that had brought him thither, though now so happily turned from it.

On came the hoof tramps and the voices of the riders, two grave old voices, conversing soberly as they drew near. These mingled sounds appeared to pass along the road, within a few yards of the young man's hiding-place; but, owing doubtless to the depth of the gloom at that particular spot, neither the travellers nor their steeds were visible. Though their figures brushed the small boughs by the wayside, it could not be seen that they intercepted, even for a moment, the faint gleam from the strip of bright sky athwart which they must have passed. Goodman Brown alternately crouched and stood on tiptoe, pulling aside the branches and thrusting forth his head as far as he durst without discerning so much as a shadow. It vexed him the more, because he could have sworn, were such a thing possible, that he recognized the voices of the minister and Deacon Gookin, jogging along quietly, as they were wont to do, when bound to some ordination or ecclesiastical council. While yet within hearing, one of the riders stopped to pluck a switch.

"Of the two, reverend sir," said the voice like the deacon's, "I had rather miss an ordination dinner than to-night's meeting. They tell me that some of our community are to be here from Falmouth and beyond, and others from Connecticut and Rhode Island, besides several of the Indian powwows, who, after their fashion, know almost as much deviltry as the best of us. Moreover, there is a goodly young woman to be taken into communion."

"Mighty well, Deacon Gookin!" replied the solemn old tones of the minister. "Spur up, or we shall be late. Nothing can be done, you know, until I get on the ground."

The hoofs clattered again; and the voices, talking so strangely in the empty air, passed on through the forest, where no church had ever been gathered or solitary Christian prayed. Whither, then, could these holy men be journeying so deep into the heathen wilderness? Young Goodman Brown caught hold of a tree for support, being ready to sink down on the ground, faint and overburdened with the heavy sickness of his heart. He looked up to the sky, doubting whether there really was a heaven above him. Yet there was the blue arch, and the stars brightening in it.

10 "With heaven above and Faith below, I will yet stand firm against the devil!" cried Goodman Brown.

While he still gazed upward into the deep arch of the firmament and had lifted his hands to pray, a cloud, though no wind was stirring, hurried across the zenith and hid the brightening stars. The blue sky was still visible, except directly overhead, where this black mass of cloud was sweeping swiftly northward. Aloft in the air, as if from the depths of the cloud, came a confused and doubtful sound of voices. Once the listener fancied that he could distinguish the accents of towns-people of his own, men and women, both pious and ungodly, many of whom he had met at the communion table, and had seen others rioting at the tavern. The next moment,

20 so indistinct were the sounds, he doubted whether he had heard aught but the murmur of the old forest, whispering without a wind. Then came a stronger swell of those familiar tones, heard daily in the sunshine at Salem village, but never until now from a cloud of night. There was one voice, of a young woman, uttering lamentations, yet with an uncertain sorrow, and entreating for some favor, which, perhaps, it would grieve her to obtain; and all the unseen multitude, both saints and sinners, seemed to encourage her onward.

"Faith!" shouted Goodman Brown, in a voice of agony and desperation; and the echoes of the forest mocked him, crying, "Faith! Faith!" as if bewildered wretches were seeking her all through the wilderness.

30 The cry of grief, rage, and terror was yet piercing the night, when the unhappy husband held his breath for a response. There was a scream, drowned immediately in a louder murmur of voices, fading into far-off laughter, as the dark cloud swept away, leaving the clear and silent sky above Goodman Brown. But something fluttered lightly down through the air and caught on the branch of a tree. The young man seized it, and beheld a pink ribbon.

"My Faith is gone!" cried he, after one stupefied moment. "There is no good on earth; and sin is but a name. Come, devil; for to thee is this world given."

And, maddened with despair, so that he laughed loud and long, did Goodman Brown grasp his staff and set forth again, at such a rate that he seemed to fly along

40 the forest path rather than to walk or run. The road grew wilder and drearier and more faintly traced, and vanished at length, leaving him in the heart of the dark wilderness, still rushing onward with the instinct that guides mortal men to evil. The whole forest was peopled with frightful sounds — the creaking of the trees, the howling of wild beasts, and the yell of Indians; while sometimes the wind tolled

like a distant church bell, and sometimes gave a broad roar around the traveller, as if all Nature were laughing him to scorn. But he was himself the chief horror of the scene, and shrank not from its other horrors.

"Ha! ha! ha!" roared Goodman Brown when the wind laughed at him. "Let us hear which will laugh loudest. Think not to frighten me with your deviltry. Come witch, come wizard, come Indian powwow, come devil himself, and here comes Goodman Brown. You may as well fear him as he fear you."

In truth, all through the haunted forest there could be nothing more frightful than the figure of Goodman Brown. On he flew among the black pines, brandish- 10 ing his staff with frenzied gestures, now giving vent to an inspiration of horrid blasphemy, and now shouting forth such laughter as set all the echoes of the forest laughing like demons around him. The fiend in his own shape is less hideous than when he rages in the breast of man. Thus sped the demoniac on his course, until, quivering among the trees, he saw a red light before him, as when the felled trunks and branches of a clearing have been set on fire, and throw up their lurid blaze against the sky, at the hour of midnight. He paused, in a lull of the tempest that had driven him onward, and heard the swell of what seemed a hymn, rolling solemnly from a distance with the weight of many voices. He knew the tune; it was a familiar one in the choir of the village meeting-house. The verse died heavily away, and was lengthened by a chorus, not of human voices, but of all the sounds of the benighted 20 wilderness pealing in awful harmony together. Goodman Brown cried out, and his cry was lost to his own ear by its unison with the cry of the desert.

In the interval of silence he stole forward until the light glared full upon his eyes. At one extremity of an open space, hemmed in by the dark wall of the forest, arose a rock, bearing some rude, natural resemblance either to an altar or a pulpit, and surrounded by four blazing pines, their tops aflame, their stems untouched, like candles at an evening meeting. The mass of foliage that had overgrown the summit of the rock was all on fire, blazing high into the night and fitfully illuminating the whole field. Each pendent twig and leafy festoon was in a blaze. As the red light arose and fell, a numerous congregation alternately shone forth, then disappeared 30 in shadow, and again grew, as it were, out of the darkness, peopling the heart of the solitary woods at once.

"A grave and dark-clad company," quoth Goodman Brown.

In truth they were such. Among them, quivering to and fro between gloom and splendor, appeared faces that would be seen next day at the council board of the province, and others which, Sabbath after Sabbath, looked devoutly heavenward, and benignantly over the crowded pews, from the holiest pulpits in the land. Some affirm that the lady of the governor was there. At least there were high dames well known to her, and wives of honored husbands, and widows, a great multitude, and

---

37 **Some affirm.** . . . . Robert Calef in *More Wonders of the Invisible World* (1700), an attack on the witchcraft trials and Cotton Mather's book, says: "If it be true, what was said at the council-board in answer to the commendations of Sir William [Phips] for his stopping the proceedings about witchcraft, viz. that it was high time for him to stop it, his own lady being accused; if that assertion were a truth, then New-England may seem to be more beholden to the accusers for accusing her, and thereby necessitating a stop, than to Sir William, or to the advice that was given him by his pastor [Cotton Mather]"

ancient maidens, all of excellent repute, and fair young girls, who trembled lest their mothers should espy them. Either the sudden gleams of light flashing over the obscure field bedazzled Goodman Brown, or he recognized a score of the church members of Salem village famous for their especial sanctity. Good old Deacon Gookin had arrived, and waited at the skirts of that venerable saint, his revered pastor. But, irreverently consorting with these grave, reputable, and pious people, these elders of the church, these chaste dames and dewy virgins, there were men of dissolute lives and women of spotted fame, wretches given over to all mean and filthy vice, and suspected even of horrid crimes. It was strange to see that the good shrank not
10 from the wicked, nor were the sinners abashed by the saints. Scattered also among their palefaced enemies were the Indian priests, or powwows, who had often scared their native forest with more hideous incantations than any known to English witchcraft.

"But where is Faith?" thought Goodman Brown; and, as hope came into his heart, he trembled.

Another verse of the hymn arose, a slow and mournful strain, such as the pious love, but joined to words which expressed all that our nature can conceive of sin, and darkly hinted at far more. Unfathomable to mere mortals is the lore of fiends. Verse after verse was sung; and still the chorus of the desert swelled between like
20 the deepest tone of a mighty organ; and with the final peal of that dreadful anthem there came a sound, as if the roaring wind, the rushing streams, the howling beasts, and every other voice of the unconcerted wilderness were mingling and according with the voice of guilty man in homage to the prince of all. The four blazing pines threw up a loftier flame, and obscurely discovered shapes and visages of horror on the smoke wreaths above the impious assembly. At the same moment the fire on the rock shot redly forth and formed a glowing arch above its base, where now appeared a figure. With reverence be it spoken, the figure bore no slight similitude, both in garb and manner, to some grave divine of the New England churches.

"Bring forth the converts!" cried a voice that echoed through the field and rolled
30 into the forest.

At the word, Goodman Brown stepped forth from the shadow of the trees and approached the congregation, with whom he felt a loathful brotherhood by the sympathy of all that was wicked in his heart. He could have well-nigh sworn that the shape of his own dead father beckoned him to advance, looking downward from a smoke wreath, while a woman, with dim features of despair, threw out her hand to warn him back. Was it his mother? But he had no power to retreat one step, nor to resist, even in thought, when the minister and good old Deacon Gookin seized his arms and led him to the blazing rock. Thither came also the slender form of a veiled female, led between Goody Cloyse, that pious teacher of the catechism, and
40 Martha Carrier, who had received the devil's promise to be queen of hell. A rampant hag was she. And there stood the proselytes beneath the canopy of fire.

---

40 **Martha Carrier** was tried and hanged for witchcraft in Salem in 1692. Mather wrote in his record of the trial: "*Memorandum.* This *rampant hag,* Martha Carrier, was the person of whom the confessions of the witches, and of her own children among the rest, agreed that the devil had promised her she should be queen of hell."

"Welcome, my children," said the dark figure, "to the communion of your race. Ye have found thus young your nature and your destiny. My children, look behind you!"

They turned; and flashing forth, as it were, in a sheet of flame, the fiend worshippers were seen; the smile of welcome gleamed darkly on every visage.

"There," resumed the sable form, "are all whom ye have reverenced from youth. Ye deemed them holier than yourselves, and shrank from your own sin, contrasting it with their lives of righteousness and prayerful aspirations heavenward. Yet here are they all in my worshipping assembly. This night it shall be granted you to know their secret deeds: how hoary-bearded elders of the church have whispered 10 wanton words to the young maids of their households; how many a woman, eager for widows' weeds, has given her husband a drink at bedtime and let him sleep his last sleep on her bosom; how beardless youths have made haste to inherit their father's wealth; and how fair damsels — blush not, sweet ones — have dug little graves in the garden, and bidden me, the sole guest, to an infant's funeral. By the sympathy of your human hearts for sin ye shall scent out all the places — whether in church, bed-chamber, street, field, or forest — where crime has been committed, and shall exult to behold the whole earth one stain of guilt, one mighty blood spot. Far more than this. It shall be yours to penetrate, in every bosom, the deep mystery of sin, the fountain of all wicked arts, and which inexhaustibly supplies more evil 20 impulses than human power — than my power at its utmost — can make manifest in deeds. And now, my children, look upon each other."

They did so; and, by the blaze of the hell-kindled torches, the wretched man beheld his Faith, and the wife her husband, trembling before that unhallowed altar.

"Lo, there we stand, my children," said the figure, in a deep and solemn tone, almost sad with its despairing awfulness, as if his once angelic nature could yet mourn for our miserable race. "Depending upon one another's hearts, ye had still hoped that virtue were not all a dream. Now are ye undeceived. Evil is the nature of mankind. Evil must be your only happiness. Welcome again, my children, to the communion of your race."   30

"Welcome," repeated the fiend worshippers, in one cry of despair and triumph.

And there they stood, the only pair, as it seemed, who were yet hesitating on the verge of wickedness in this dark world. A basin was hollowed, naturally, in the rock. Did it contain water, reddened by the lurid light? or was it blood? or, perchance, a liquid flame? Herein did the shape of evil dip his hand and prepare to lay the mark of baptism upon their foreheads, that they might be partakers of the mystery of sin, more conscious of the secret guilt of others, both in deed and thought, than they could now be of their own. The husband cast one look at his pale wife, and Faith at him. What polluted wretches would the next glance show them to each other, shuddering alike at what they disclosed and what they saw!   40

"Faith! Faith!" cried the husband, "look up to heaven, and resist the wicked one."

Whether Faith obeyed he knew not. Hardly had he spoken when he found himself amid calm night and solitude, listening to a roar of the wind which died heavily away through the forest. He staggered against the rock, and felt it chill and damp;

while a hanging twig, that had been all on fire, besprinkled his cheek with the coldest dew.

The next morning young Goodman Brown came slowly into the street of Salem village, staring around him like a bewildered man. The good old minister was taking a walk along the graveyard to get an appetite for breakfast and meditate his sermon, and bestowed a blessing, as he passed, on Goodman Brown. He shrank from the venerable saint as if to avoid an anathema. Old Deacon Gookin was at domestic worship, and the holy words of his prayer were heard through the open window. "What God doth the wizard pray to?" quoth Goodman Brown. Goody Cloyse, that
10 excellent old Christian, stood in the early sunshine at her own lattice, catechizing a little girl who had brought her a pint of morning's milk. Goodman Brown snatched away the child as from the grasp of the fiend himself. Turning the corner by the meeting-house, he spied the head of Faith, with the pink ribbons, gazing anxiously forth, and bursting into such joy at sight of him that she skipped along the street and almost kissed her husband before the whole village. But Goodman Brown looked sternly and sadly into her face, and passed on without a greeting.

Had Goodman Brown fallen asleep in the forest and only dreamed a wild dream of a witch-meeting?

Be it so if you will; but, alas! it was a dream of evil omen for young Goodman
20 Brown. A stern, a sad, a darkly meditative, a distrustful, if not a desperate man did he become from the night of that fearful dream. On the Sabbath day, when the congregation were singing a holy psalm, he could not listen because an anthem of sin rushed loudly upon his ear and drowned all the blessed strain. When the minister spoke from the pulpit with power and fervid eloquence, and, with his hand on the open Bible, of the sacred truths of our religion, and of saint-like lives and triumphant deaths, and of future bliss or misery unutterable, then did Goodman Brown turn pale, dreading lest the roof should thunder down upon the gray blasphemer and his hearers. Often, awaking suddenly at midnight, he shrank from the bosom of Faith; and at morning or eventide, when the family knelt down at prayer,
30 he scowled and muttered to himself, and gazed sternly at his wife, and turned away. And when he had lived long, and was borne to his grave a hoary corpse, followed by Faith, an aged woman, and children and grandchildren, a goodly procession, besides neighbors not a few, they carved no hopeful verse upon his tombstone, for his dying hour was gloom.   1835

The Minister's Black Veil A Parable

"The Minister's Black Veil" was first published in the Token *for 1836 and was reprinted in* Twice-Told Tales *in 1837. Father Hooper is a prototype of Arthur Dimmesdale in* The Scarlet Letter *(see* The American Notebooks by Nathaniel Hawthorne, *pp. xlvii-xlviii).*

A Parable. "Another clergyman in New England, Mr. Joseph Moody, of York, Maine, who died about eighty years since, made himself remarkable by the same eccentricity that is here related of the Reverend Mr. Hooper. In his case, however, the symbol had a different import. In early life he had accidentally killed a beloved friend; and from that day till the hour of his own death he hid his face from men." — Hawthorne

The sexton stood in the porch of Milford meeting-house pulling lustily at the bell-rope. The old people of the village came stooping along the street. Children with bright faces tript merrily beside their parents, or mimicked a graver gait in the conscious dignity of their Sunday clothes. Spruce bachelors looked sidelong at the pretty maidens, and fancied that the Sabbath sunshine made them prettier than on week-days. When the throng had mostly streamed into the porch, the sexton began to toll the bell, keeping his eye on the Reverend Mr. Hooper's door. The first glimpse of the clergyman's figure was the signal for the bell to cease its summons.

"But what has good Parson Hooper got upon his face?" cried the sexton in as- 10 tonishment.

All within hearing immediately turned about, and beheld the semblance of Mr. Hooper pacing slowly in his meditative way towards the meeting-house. With one accord they started, expressing more wonder than if some strange minister were coming to dust the cushions of Mr. Hooper's pulpit.

"Are you sure it is our parson?" inquired Goodman Gray of the sexton.

"Of a certainty it is good Mr. Hooper," replied the sexton. "He was to have exchanged pulpits with Parson Shute, of Westbury; but Parson Shute sent to excuse himself yesterday, being to preach a funeral sermon."

The cause of so much amazement may appear sufficiently slight. Mr. Hooper, a 20 gentlemanly person of about thirty, though still a bachelor, was dressed with due clerical neatness, as if a careful wife had starched his band, and brushed the weekly dust from his Sunday's garb. There was but one thing remarkable in his appearance. Swathed about his forehead, and hanging down over his face so low as to be shaken by his breath, Mr. Hooper had on a black veil. On a nearer view it seemed to consist of two folds of crape, which entirely concealed his features except the mouth and chin, but probably did not intercept his sight farther than to give a darkened aspect to all living and inanimate things. With this gloomy shade before him, good Mr. Hooper walked onward at a slow and quiet pace, stooping somewhat and looking on the ground, as is customary with abstracted men, yet nodding kindly to those 30 of his parishioners who still waited on the meeting-house steps. But so wonderstruck were they that his greeting hardly met with a return.

"I can't really feel as if good Mr. Hooper's face was behind that piece of crape," said the sexton.

"I don't like it," muttered an old woman, as she hobbled into the meeting-house. "He has changed himself into something awful only by hiding his face."

"Our parson has gone mad!" cried Goodman Gray, following him across the threshold.

A rumor of some unaccountable phenomenon had preceded Mr. Hooper into the meeting-house, and set all the congregation astir. Few could refrain from twisting 40 their heads towards the door; many stood upright and turned directly about; while several little boys clambered upon the seats, and came down again with a terrible racket. There was a general bustle, a rustling of the women's gowns and shuffling of the men's feet, greatly at variance with that hushed repose which should attend

the entrance of the minister. But Mr. Hooper appeared not to notice the perturbation of his people. He entered with an almost noiseless step, bent his head mildly to the pews on each side, and bowed as he passed his oldest parishioner, a white-haired great-grandsire, who occupied an armchair in the centre of the aisle. It was strange to observe how slowly this venerable man became conscious of something singular in the appearance of his pastor. He seemed not fully to partake of the prevailing wonder till Mr. Hooper had ascended the stairs, and showed himself in the pulpit face to face with his congregation except for the black veil. That mysterious emblem was never once withdrawn. It shook with his measured breath as he gave
10 out the psalm; it threw its obscurity between him and the holy page as he read the Scriptures; and while he prayed, the veil lay heavily on his uplifted countenance. Did he seek to hide it from the dread Being whom he was addressing?

Such was the effect of this simple piece of crape that more than one woman of delicate nerves was forced to leave the meeting-house. Yet perhaps the pale-faced congregation was almost as fearful a sight to the minister as his black veil to them.

Mr. Hooper had the reputation of a good preacher, but not an energetic one: he strove to win his people heavenward by mild, persuasive influences, rather than to drive them thither by the thunders of the Word. The sermon which he now delivered was marked by the same characteristics of style and manner as the general series
20 of his pulpit oratory. But there was something either in the sentiment of the discourse itself, or in the imagination of the auditors, which made it greatly the most powerful effort that they had ever heard from their pastor's lips. It was tinged rather more darkly than usual with the gentle gloom of Mr. Hooper's temperament. The subject had reference to secret sin, and those sad mysteries which we hide from our nearest and dearest, and would fain conceal from our own consciousness, even forgetting that the Omniscient can detect them. A subtle power was breathed into his words. Each member of the congregation, the most innocent girl, and the man of hardened breast, felt as if the preacher had crept upon them behind his awful veil, and discovered their hoarded iniquity of deed or thought. Many spread their clasped
30 hands on their bosoms. There was nothing terrible in what Mr. Hooper said, at least, no violence; and yet, with every tremor of his melancholy voice the hearers quaked. An unsought pathos came hand in hand with awe. So sensible were the audience of some unwonted attribute in their minister, that they longed for a breath of wind to blow aside the veil, almost believing that a stranger's visage would be discovered, though the form, gesture, and voice were those of Mr. Hooper.

At the close of the service the people hurried out with indecorous confusion, eager to communicate their pent-up amazement, and conscious of lighter spirits the moment they lost sight of the black veil. Some gathered in little circles, huddled closely together, with their mouths all whispering in the centre; some went home-
40 ward alone, wrapt in silent meditation; some talked loudly, and profaned the Sabbath-day with ostentatious laughter. A few shook their sagacious heads, intimating that they could penetrate the mystery; while one or two affirmed that there was no mystery at all, but only that Mr. Hooper's eyes were so weakened by the midnight lamp as to require a shade. After a brief interval, forth came good Mr. Hooper also,

in the rear of his flock. Turning his veiled face from one group to another, he paid due reverence to the hoary heads, saluted the middle-aged with kind dignity, as their friend and spiritual guide, greeted the young with mingled authority and love, and laid his hands on the little children's heads to bless them. Such was always his custom on the Sabbath-day. Strange and bewildered looks repaid him for his courtesy. None, as on former occasions, aspired to the honor of walking by their pastor's side. Old Squire Saunders, doubtless by an accidental lapse of memory, neglected to invite Mr. Hooper to his table, where the good clergyman had been wont to bless the food almost every Sunday since his settlement. He returned, therefore, to the parsonage, and, at the moment of closing the door, was observed to look 10 back upon the people, all of whom had their eyes fixed upon the minister. A sad smile gleamed faintly from beneath the black veil, and flickered about his mouth, glimmering as he disappeared.

"How strange," said a lady, "that a simple black veil, such as any woman might wear on her bonnet, should become such a terrible thing on Mr. Hooper's face!"

"Something must surely be amiss with Mr. Hooper's intellects," observed her husband, the physician of the village. "But the strangest part of the affair is the effect of this vagary, even on a sober-minded man like myself. The black veil, though it covers only our pastor's face, throws its influence over his whole person, and makes him ghostlike from head to foot. Do you not feel it so?"   20

"Truly do I," replied the lady; "and I would not be alone with him for the world. I wonder he is not afraid to be alone with himself!"

"Men sometimes are so," said her husband.

The afternoon service was attended with similar circumstances. At its conclusion, the bell tolled for the funeral of a young lady. The relatives and friends were assembled in the house, and the more distant acquaintances stood about the door, speaking of the good qualities of the deceased, when their talk was interrupted by the appearance of Mr. Hooper, still covered with his black veil. It was now an appropriate emblem. The clergyman stepped into the room where the corpse was laid, and bent over the coffin to take a last farewell of his deceased parishioner. As he 30 stooped, the veil hung straight down from his forehead, so that, if her eyelids had not been closed for ever, the dead maiden might have seen his face. Could Mr. Hooper be fearful of her glance, that he so hastily caught back the black veil? A person who watched the interview between the dead and living scrupled not to affirm that, at the instant when the clergyman's features were disclosed, the corpse had slightly shuddered, rustling the shroud and muslin cap, though the countenance retained the composure of death. A superstitious old woman was the only witness of this prodigy. From the coffin Mr. Hooper passed into the chamber of the mourners, and thence to the head of the staircase, to make the funeral prayer. It was a tender and heart-dissolving prayer, full of sorrow, yet so imbued with celestial 40 hopes that the music of a heavenly harp, swept by the fingers of the dead, seemed faintly to be heard among the saddest accents of the minister. The people trembled, though they but darkly understood him, when he prayed that they, and himself, and all of mortal race, might be ready, as he trusted this young maiden had been, for

the dreadful hour that should snatch the veil from their faces. The bearers went
heavily forth, and the mourners followed, saddening all the street, with the dead
before them, and Mr. Hooper in the black veil behind.

"Why do you look back?" said one in the procession to his partner.

"I had a fancy," replied she, "that the minister and the maiden's spirit were walking hand in hand."

"And so had I at the same moment," said the other.

That night the handsomest couple in Milford village were to be joined in wedlock. Though reckoned a melancholy man, Mr. Hooper had a placid cheerfulness
for such occasions which often excited a sympathetic smile where livelier merriment would have been thrown away. There was no quality of his disposition which
made him more beloved than this. The company at the wedding awaited his arrival
with impatience, trusting that the strange awe which had gathered over him throughout the day would now be dispelled. But such was not the result. When Mr.
Hooper came, the first thing that their eyes rested on was the same horrible black
veil, which had added deeper gloom to the funeral, and could portend nothing but
evil to the wedding. Such was its immediate effect on the guests, that a cloud seemed
to have rolled duskily from beneath the black crape and dimmed the light of the
candles. The bridal pair stood up before the minister. But the bride's cold fingers
quivered in the tremulous hand of the bridegroom, and her deathlike paleness caused
a whisper that the maiden who had been buried a few hours before was come from
her grave to be married. If ever another wedding were so dismal, it was that famous
one where they tolled the wedding knell. After performing the ceremony, Mr.
Hooper raised a glass of wine to his lips, wishing happiness to the new-married
couple, in a strain of mild pleasantry that ought to have brightened the features of
the guests, like a cheerful gleam from the hearth. At that instant, catching a glimpse
of his figure in the looking-glass, the black veil involved his own spirit in the horror with which it overwhelmed all others. His frame shuddered — his lips grew
white — he spilt the untasted wine upon the carpet — and rushed forth into the
darkness. For the earth, too, had on her black veil.

The next day the whole village of Milford talked of little else than Parson
Hooper's black veil. That, and the mystery concealed behind it, supplied a topic for
discussion between acquaintances meeting in the street, and good women gossiping
at their open windows. It was the first item of news that the tavern-keeper told to
his guests. The children babbled of it on their way to school. One imitative little
imp covered his face with an old black handkerchief, thereby so affrighting his playmates that the panic seized himself, and he well-nigh lost his wits by his
own waggery.

It was remarkable that, of all the busybodies and impertinent people in the parish, not one ventured to put the plain question to Mr. Hooper, wherefore he did
this thing. Hitherto, whenever there appeared the slightest call for such interference,
he had never lacked advisers, nor shown himself averse to be guided by their judg-

---

22 **famous . . . knell.** The reference is to another story of Hawthorne's, "The Wedding Knell," which appeared in the same issue of the *Token*

ment. If he erred at all, it was by so painful a degree of self-distrust that even the mildest censure would lead him to consider an indifferent action as a crime. Yet, though so well acquainted with this amiable weakness, no individual among his parishioners chose to make the black veil a subject of friendly remonstrance. There was a feeling of dread, neither plainly confessed nor carefully concealed, which caused each to shift the responsibility upon another, till at length it was found expedient to send a deputation of the church, in order to deal with Mr. Hooper about the mystery before it should grow into a scandal. Never did an embassy so ill discharge its duties. The minister received them with friendly courtesy, but became silent after they were seated, leaving to his visitors the whole burden of introducing 1(their important business. The topic, it might be supposed, was obvious enough. There was the black veil swathed round Mr. Hooper's forehead, and concealing every feature above his placid mouth, on which at times they could perceive the glimmering of a melancholy smile. But that piece of crape, to their imagination, seemed to hang down before his heart, the symbol of a fearful secret between him and them. Were the veil but cast aside they might speak freely of it, but not till then. Thus they sat a considerable time, speechless, confused, and shrinking uneasily from Mr. Hooper's eye, which they felt to be fixed upon them with an invisible glance. Finally, the deputies returned abashed to their constituents, pronouncing the matter too weighty to be handled, except by a council of the churches, if indeed it might not 2 require a general synod.

But there was one person in the village unappalled by the awe with which the black veil had impressed all beside herself. When the deputies returned without an explanation, or even venturing to demand one, she, with the calm energy of her character, determined to chase away the strange cloud that appeared to be settling round Mr. Hooper, every moment more darkly than before. As his plighted wife, it should be her privilege to know what the black veil concealed. At the minister's first visit, therefore, she entered upon the subject with a direct simplicity which made the task easier both for him and her. After he had seated himself she fixed her eyes steadfastly upon the veil, but could discern nothing of the dreadful gloom 3(that had so overawed the multitude: it was but a double fold of crape, hanging down from his forehead to his mouth, and slightly stirring with his breath.

"No," said she aloud, and smiling, "there is nothing terrible in this piece of crape, except that it hides a face which I am always glad to look upon. Come, good sir, let the sun shine from behind the cloud. First lay aside your black veil: then tell me why you put it on."

Mr. Hooper's smile glimmered faintly.

"There is an hour to come," said he, "when all of us shall cast aside our veils. Take it not amiss, beloved friend, if I wear this piece of crape till then."

"Your words are a mystery too," returned the young lady. "Take away the veil 4 from them at least."

"Elizabeth, I will," said he, "so far as my vow may suffer me. Know, then, this veil is a type and a symbol, and I am bound to wear it ever, both in light and darkness, in solitude and before the gaze of multitudes, and as with strangers, so with my familiar friends. No mortal eye will see it withdrawn. This dismal shade must separate me from the world: even you, Elizabeth, can never come behind it!"

"What grievous affliction hath befallen you," she earnestly inquired, "that you should thus darken your eyes for ever?"

"If it be a sign of mourning," replied Mr. Hooper, "I, perhaps, like most other mortals, have sorrows dark enough to be typified by a black veil."

"But what if the world will not believe that it is the type of an innocent sorrow?" urged Elizabeth. "Beloved and respected as you are, there may be whispers that you hide your face under the consciousness of secret sin. For the sake of your holy office, do away with this scandal!"

The color rose into her cheeks as she intimated the nature of the rumors that were already abroad in the village. But Mr. Hooper's mildness did not forsake him. He even smiled again — that same sad smile, which always appeared like a faint glimmering of light proceeding from the obscurity beneath the veil.

"If I hide my face for sorrow, there is cause enough," he merely replied; "and if I cover it for secret sin, what mortal might not do the same?"

And with this gentle but unconquerable obstinacy did he resist all her entreaties. At length Elizabeth sat silent. For a few moments she appeared lost in thought, considering, probably, what new methods might be tried to withdraw her lover from so dark a fantasy, which, if it had no other meaning, was perhaps a symptom of mental disease. Though of a firmer character than his own, the tears rolled down her cheeks. But in an instant, as it were, a new feeling took the place of sorrow: her eyes were fixed insensibly on the black veil, when, like a sudden twilight in the air, its terrors fell around her. She arose, and stood trembling before him.

"And do you feel it then at last?" said he mournfully.

She made no reply, but covered her eyes with her hand, and turned to leave the room. He rushed forward and caught her arm.

"Have patience with me, Elizabeth!" cried he passionately. "Do not desert me, though this veil must be between us here on earth. Be mine, and hereafter there shall be no veil over my face, no darkness between our souls! It is but a mortal veil — it is not for eternity! Oh! you know not how lonely I am, and how frightened, to be alone behind my black veil. Do not leave me in this miserable obscurity for ever!"

"Lift the veil but once and look me in the face," said she.

"Never! It cannot be!" replied Mr. Hooper.

"Then, farewell!" said Elizabeth.

She withdrew her arm from his grasp and slowly departed, pausing at the door to give one long, shuddering gaze, that seemed almost to penetrate the mystery of the black veil. But even amid his grief Mr. Hooper smiled to think that only a material emblem had separated him from happiness, though the horrors which it shadowed forth must be drawn darkly between the fondest of lovers.

From that time no attempts were made to remove Mr. Hooper's black veil, or, by a direct appeal, to discover the secret which it was supposed to hide. By persons who claimed a superiority to popular prejudice it was reckoned merely an eccentric whim, such as often mingles with the sober actions of men otherwise rational, and tinges them all with its own semblance of insanity. But with the multitude good Mr. Hooper was irreparably a bugbear. He could not walk the streets with any peace of mind, so conscious was he that the gentle and timid would turn aside to avoid him, and that others would make it a point of hardihood to throw themselves in his way. The impertinence of the latter class compelled him to give up his customary walk at sunset to the burial-ground; for when he leaned pensively over the gate, there would always be faces behind the grave-stones peeping at his black veil. A fable went the rounds that the stare of the dead people drove him thence. It grieved him to the very depth of his kind heart to observe how the children fled from his approach, breaking up their merriest sports while his melancholy figure was yet afar off. Their instinctive dread caused him to feel more strongly than aught else that a preternatural horror was interwoven with the threads of the black crape. In truth, his own antipathy to the veil was known to be so great that he never willingly passed before a mirror, nor stooped to drink at a still fountain, lest in its peaceful bosom he should be affrighted by himself. This was what gave plausibility to the whispers, that Mr. Hooper's conscience tortured him for some great crime too horrible to be entirely concealed, or otherwise than so obscurely intimated. Thus from beneath the black veil there rolled a cloud into the sunshine, an ambiguity of sin or sorrow, which enveloped the poor minister, so that love or sympathy could never reach him. It was said that ghost and fiend consorted with him there. With self-shudderings and outward terrors he walked continually in its shadow, groping darkly within his own soul, or gazing through a medium that saddened the whole world. Even the lawless wind, it was believed, respected his dreadful secret and never blew aside the veil. But still good Mr. Hooper sadly smiled at the pale visages of the worldly throng as he passed by.

Among all its bad influences, the black veil had the one desirable effect of making its wearer a very efficient clergyman. By the aid of his mysterious emblem — for there was no other apparent cause — he became a man of awful power over souls that were in agony for sin. His converts always regarded him with a dread peculiar to themselves, affirming, though but figuratively, that, before he brought them to celestial light, they had been with him behind the black veil. Its gloom, indeed, enabled him to sympathize with all dark affections. Dying sinners cried aloud for Mr. Hooper, and would not yield their breath till he appeared; though ever, as he stooped to whisper consolation, they shuddered at the veiled face so near their own. Such were the terrors of the black veil, even when Death had bared his visage! Strangers came long distances to attend service at his church, with the mere idle purpose of gazing at his figure, because it was forbidden them to behold his face. But many were made to quake ere they departed! Once, during Governor Belcher's administration, Mr. Hooper was appointed to preach the election sermon. Covered

38 **Belcher,** Jonathan Belcher (1681-1757), royal governor of Massachusetts, 1730-1741   39 **election sermon,** delivered before the newly elected officers of state. An appointment to preach an election sermon was the highest honor that could be conferred upon a minister in colonial New England. See pp. 23-24. Election sermons were often published (see R.W.G. Vail, "A Check List of New England Election Sermons," *Proceedings of the Antiquarian Society,* October 1935). Compare the dramatic importance of the election sermon in *The Scarlet Letter*

with his black veil, he stood before the chief magistrate, the council, and the representatives, and wrought so deep an impression that the legislative measures of that year were characterized by all the gloom and piety of our earliest ancestral sway.

In this manner Mr. Hooper spent a long life, irreproachable in outward act, yet shrouded in dismal suspicions; kind and loving, though unloved, and dimly feared; a man apart from men, shunned in their health and joy, but ever summoned to their aid in mortal anguish. As years wore on, shedding their snows above his sable veil, he acquired a name throughout the New England churches, and they called him Father Hooper. Nearly all his parishioners who were of mature age when he
10 was settled had been borne away by many a funeral: he had one congregation in the church, and a more crowded one in the church-yard; and having wrought so late into the evening, and done his work so well, it was now good Father Hooper's turn to rest.

Several persons were visible by the shaded candlelight in the death-chamber of the old clergyman. Natural connections he had none. But there was the decorously grave though unmoved physician, seeking only to mitigate the last pangs of the patient whom he could not save. There were the deacons, and other eminently pious members of his church. There, also, was the Reverend Mr. Clark, of Westbury, a young and zealous divine, who had ridden in haste to pray by the bedside of the
20 expiring minister. There was the nurse, no hired handmaiden of death, but one whose calm affection had endured thus long in secrecy, in solitude, amid the chill of age, and would not perish, even at the dying hour. Who, but Elizabeth! And there lay the hoary head of good Father Hooper upon the death-pillow, with the black veil still swathed about his brow and reaching down over his face, so that each more difficult gasp of his faint breath caused it to stir. All through life that piece of crape had hung between him and the world: it had separated him from cheerful brotherhood and woman's love, and kept him in that saddest of all prisons, his own heart; and still it lay upon his face, as if to deepen the gloom of his darksome chamber, and shade him from the sunshine of eternity.

30 For some time previous his mind had been confused, wavering doubtfully between the past and the present, and hovering forward, as it were, at intervals, into the indistinctness of the world to come. There had been feverish turns, which tossed him from side to side, and wore away what little strength he had. But in his most convulsive struggles, and in the wildest vagaries of his intellect, when no other thought retained its sober influence, he still showed an awful solicitude lest the black veil should slip aside. Even if his bewildered soul could have forgotten, there was a faithful woman at his pillow, who, with averted eyes, would have covered that aged face, which she had last beheld in the comeliness of manhood. At length the death-stricken old man lay quietly in the torpor of mental and bodily exhaustion,
40 with an imperceptible pulse, and breath that grew fainter and fainter, except when a long, deep, and irregular inspiration seemed to prelude the flight of his spirit.

The minister of Westbury approached the bedside.

"Venerable Father Hooper," said he, "the moment of your release is at hand. Are you ready for the lifting of the veil that shuts in time from eternity?"

Father Hooper at first replied merely by a feeble motion of his head; then, apprehensive, perhaps, that his meaning might be doubtful, he exerted himself to speak.

"Yea," said he, in faint accents, "my soul hath a patient weariness until that veil be lifted."

"And is it fitting," resumed the Reverend Mr. Clark, "that a man so given to prayer, of such a blameless example, holy in deed and thought, so far as mortal judgment may pronounce; is it fitting that a father in the church should leave a shadow on his memory, that may seem to blacken a life so pure? I pray you, my venerable brother, let not this thing be! Suffer us to be gladdened by your triumphant aspect, as you go to your reward. Before the veil of eternity be lifted, let me   10
cast aside this black veil from your face!"

And thus speaking, the Reverend Mr. Clark bent forward to reveal the mystery of so many years. But exerting a sudden energy that made all the beholders stand aghast, Father Hooper snatched both his hands from beneath the bed-clothes, and pressed them strongly on the black veil, resolute to struggle if the minister of Westbury would contend with a dying man.

"Never!" cried the veiled clergyman. "On earth, never!"

"Dark old man!" exclaimed the affrighted minister, "with what horrible crime upon your soul are you now passing to the judgment?"

Father Hooper's breath heaved; it rattled in his throat; but with a might effort,   20
grasping forward with his hands, he caught hold of life, and held it back till he should speak. He even raised himself in bed; and there he sat, shivering with the arms of death around him, while the black veil hung down, awful, at the last moment, in the gathered terrors of a lifetime. And yet the faint, sad smile, so often there, now seemed to glimmer from its obscurity, and linger on Father Hooper's lips.

"Why do you tremble at me alone?" cried he, turning his veiled face round the circle of pale spectators. "Tremble also at each other! Have men avoided me, and women shown no pity, and children screamed and fled, only for my black veil? What but the mystery which it obscurely typifies has made this piece of crape so awful? When the friend shows his inmost heart to his friend; the lover to his best beloved;   30
when man does not vainly shrink from the eye of his Creator, loathsomely treasuring up the secret of his sin; then deem me a monster, for the symbol beneath which I have lived, and die! I look around me, and, lo! on every visage a black veil!"

While his auditors shrank from one another in mutual affright, Father Hooper fell back upon his pillow, a veiled corpse, with a faint smile lingering on the lips. Still veiled, they laid him in his coffin, and a veiled corpse they bore him to the grave. The grass of many years has sprung up and withered on that grave, the burial-stone is moss-grown, and good Mr. Hooper's face is dust; but awful is still the thought that it mouldered beneath the black veil!

                                                                          1835

---

26 **Why** . . . **black veil.** In his review of *Twice-Told Tales,* Poe commented on this story as follows: "The *moral* put into the mouth of the dying minister will be supposed to convey the *true* import of the narrative; and that a crime of dark dye (having reference to the 'young lady') has been committed, is a point which only minds congenial with that of the author will perceive." Poe's interpretation, though allowable, and even plausible, is by no means strictly necessary. Hawthorne here, as in so many places in his fiction, leaves the question open

The Celestial Railroad

John Bunyan's Pilgrim's Progress *(1678), of which "The Celestial Railroad" is an adaptation, tells the story of the journey of Christian from the City of Destruction to the Celestial City. In the course of the journey Christian struggled for a time in the Slough of Despond; passed through the Wicket-Gate; received religious instruction at the Interpreter's House; came to a Cross, where the great burden of sin fell from his back and dropped into the mouth of a Sepulchre; ascended the Hill Difficulty; visited the Palace Beautiful; fought with and overcame the foul fiend Apollyon in the Valley of Humiliation; traversed the Valley of the Shadow of Death, avoiding both "the ditch that was on the one hand and the quag that was on the other"; saw the cave of the two giants, Pope and Pagan; suffered persecution in Vanity Fair; refused the invitation of Demas to dig in the silver-mine on the hill called Lucre; was prisoner in the Doubting Castle of Giant Despair; talked with the shepherds of the Delectable Mountains; passed over the Enchanted Ground and through the country of Beulah; crossed the River of Death; and at last entered the Celestial City, where he was welcomed by the shining ones. It will be noticed that Hawthorne's story follows closely the stages of Bunyan's narrative; Hawthorne also uses, to a considerable extent, the actual language of Bunyan.*

The author's purpose was to satirize what might be called the new Emersonian liberalism: particularly the Unitarian liberalism, and incidentally the Transcendentalism so popular at the time in the cultivated circles of Boston and Concord. His sympathies were clearly with the older, Puritan school of religious thought, of which Bunyan was his favorite, and perhaps the best, representative in English prose. It is interesting to note that "The Celestial Railroad" was written in 1843, when the new liberalism was at its height; and in Concord, where Hawthorne was a neighbor of Emerson's.

The sketch abounds in telling satirical points. Incidental satire is directed against Transcendentalism ("Giant Transcendentalist" with his "strange phraseology"); against the current vogue of German and Oriental philosophies and the Lyceum lecture; and against the social respectability of Unitarianism. The body of the satire, however, is concerned with the romantic, liberal theology which denies original sin, asserts the natural goodness of man, and regards the Christian life as pleasant and not too difficult to attain. A bridge is built over the Slough of Despond; the burden of sin is deposited in the baggage car; a tunnel is constructed through the Hill Difficulty; the Valley of the Shadow of Death is illuminated by gas lamps. Hawthorne regards these "improvements" with Puritan disapproval.

"The Celestial Railroad" has enjoyed a considerable popularity among the more "orthodox" sects and has often been reprinted as a tract. There is reason to believe, also, that the sketch displeased the liberals. Hawthorne tells of a Unitarian clergyman who, very much to his relief, passed him by with only a curt greeting, and adds: "This is so unlike his deportment in times past, that I suspect the Celestial Railroad must have given him a pique; and if so, I shall feel as if Providence had sufficiently rewarded me for that pious labor."

Not a great while ago, passing through the gate of dreams, I visited that region of the earth in which lies the famous City of Destruction. It interested me much to learn that by the public spirit of some of the inhabitants a railroad has recently been established between this populous and flourishing town and the Celestial City.

Having a little time upon my hands, I resolved to gratify a liberal curiosity by making a trip thither. Accordingly, one fine morning after paying my bill at the hotel, and directing the porter to stow my luggage behind a coach, I took my seat in the vehicle and set out for the station-house. It was my good fortune to enjoy the company of a gentleman — one Mr. Smooth-it-away — who, though he had never actually visited the Celestial City, yet seemed as well acquainted with its laws, customs, policy, and statistics, as with those of the City of Destruction, of which he was a native townsman. Being, moreover, a director of the railroad corporation and one of its largest stockholders, he had it in his power to give me all desirable information respecting that praiseworthy enterprise.

Our coach rattled out of the city, and at a short distance from its outskirts passed over a bridge of elegant construction, but somewhat too slight, as I imagined, to sustain any considerable weight. On both sides lay an extensive quagmire, which could not have been more disagreeable, either to sight or smell, had all the kennels of the earth emptied their pollution there.

"This," remarked Mr. Smooth-it-away, "is the famous Slough of Despond — a disgrace to all the neighborhood; and the greater that it might so easily be converted into firm ground."

"I have understood," said I, "that efforts have been made for that purpose from time immemorial. Bunyan mentions that above twenty thousand cartloads of wholesome instructions had been thrown in here without effect."

"Very probably! And what effect could be anticipated from such unsubstantial stuff?" cried Mr. Smooth-it-away. "You observe this convenient bridge. We obtained a sufficient foundation for it by throwing into the slough some editions of books of morality; volumes of French philosophy and German rationalism; tracts, sermons, and essays of modern clergymen; extracts from Plato, Confucius, and various Hindoo sages, together with a few ingenious commentaries upon texts of Scripture, — all of which by some scientific process, have been converted into a mass like granite. The whole bog might be filled up with similar matter."

It really seemed to me, however, that the bridge vibrated and heaved up and down in a very formidable manner; and, in spite of Mr. Smooth-it-away's testimony to the solidity of its foundation, I should be loath to cross it in a crowded omnibus, especially if each passenger were encumbered with as heavy luggage as that gentleman and myself. Nevertheless we got over without accident, and soon found ourselves at the station-house. This very neat and spacious edifice is erected on the site of the little wicket gate, which formerly, as all old pilgrims will recollect, stood directly across the highway, and, by its inconvenient narrowness, was a great obstruction to the traveller of liberal mind and expansive stomach. The reader of John Bunyan will be glad to know that Christian's old friend Evangelist, who was accustomed to supply each pilgrim with a mystic roll, now presides at the ticket office.

---

5 **Mr. Smooth-it-away** recalls "Mr. Smooth-man," who was a citizen of the Vanity Fair in Bunyan's *Pilgrim's Progress*   39 **Evangelist . . . roll.** "Then Evangelist gave him [Christian] a parchment roll, and there was written within, Fly from the wrath to come." — *Pilgrim's Progress*

Some malicious persons it is true deny the identity of this reputable character with the Evangelist of old times, and even pretend to bring competent evidence of an imposture. Without involving myself in a dispute I shall merely observe that, so far as my experience goes, the square pieces of pasteboard now delivered to passengers are much more convenient and useful along the road than the antique roll of parchment. Whether they will be as readily received at the gate of the Celestial City I decline giving an opinion.

A large number of passengers were already at the station-house awaiting the departure of the cars. By the aspect and demeanor of these persons it was easy to
10 judge that the feelings of the community had undergone a very favorable change in reference to the celestial pilgrimage. It would have done Bunyan's heart good to see it. Instead of a lonely and ragged man with a huge burden on his back, plodding along sorrowfully on foot while the whole city hooted after him, here were parties of the first gentry and most respectable people in the neighborhood setting forth towards the Celestial City as cheerfully as if the pilgrimage were merely a summer tour. Among the gentlemen were characters of deserved eminence — magistrates, politicians, and men of wealth, by whose example religion could not but be greatly recommended to their meaner brethren. In the ladies' apartment, too, I rejoiced to distinguish some of those flowers of fashionable society who are so well fitted to
20 adorn the most elevated circles of the Celestial City. There was much pleasant conversation about the news of the day, topics of business and politics, or the lighter matters of amusement; while religion, though indubitably the main thing at heart, was thrown tastefully into the background. Even an infidel would have heard little or nothing to shock his sensibility.

One great convenience of the new method of going on pilgrimage I must not forget to mention. Our enormous burdens, instead of being carried on our shoulders as had been the custom of old, were all snugly deposited in the baggage car, and, as I was assured, would be delivered to their respective owners at the journey's end. Another thing, likewise, the benevolent reader will be delighted to understand. It
30 may be remembered that there was an ancient feud between Prince Beelzebub and the keeper of the wicket gate, and that the adherents of the former distinguished personage were accustomed to shoot deadly arrows at honest pilgrims while knocking at the door. This dispute, much to the credit as well of the illustrious potentate above mentioned as of the worthy and enlightened directors of the railroad, has been pacifically arranged on the principle of mutual compromise. The prince's subjects are now pretty numerously employed about the station-house, some in taking care of the baggage, others in collecting fuel, feeding the engines, and such congenial occupations; and I can conscientiously affirm that persons more attentive to their business, more willing to accommodate, or more generally agreeable to the passen-
40 gers, are not to be found on any railroad. Every good heart must surely exult at so satisfactory an arrangement of an immemorial difficulty.

---

30 **Beelzebub.** In Matthew 12:24, Beelzebub is called "the prince of devils"; in the council of devils in *Paradise Lost,* he is second only to Satan; in *Pilgrim's Progress,* he is captain of the castle near the Wicket-Gate

"Where is Mr. Greatheart?" inquired I. "Beyond a doubt the directors have engaged that famous old champion to be chief conductor on the railroad?"

"Why, no," said Mr. Smooth-it-away, with a dry cough. "He was offered the situation of brakeman; but, to tell you the truth, our friend Greatheart has grown preposterously stiff and narrow in his old age. He has so often guided pilgrims over the road on foot that he considers it a sin to travel in any other fashion. Besides, the old fellow had entered so heartily into the ancient feud with Prince Beelzebub that he would have been perpetually at blows or ill language with some of the prince's subjects, and thus have embroiled us anew. So, on the whole, we were not sorry when honest Greatheart went off to the Celestial City in a huff and   10 left us at liberty to choose a more suitable and accommodating man. Yonder comes the engineer of the train. You will probably recognize him at once."

The engine at this moment took its station in advance of the cars, looking, I must confess, much more like a sort of mechanical demon that would hurry us to the infernal regions than a laudable contrivance for smoothing our way to the Celestial City. On its top sat a personage almost enveloped in smoke and flame, which, not to startle the reader, appeared to gush from his own mouth and stomach as well as from the engine's brazen abdomen.

"Do my eyes deceive me?" cried I. "What on earth is this! A living creature? If so, he is own brother to the engine he rides upon!"   20

"Poh, poh, you are obtuse!" said Mr. Smooth-it-away, with a hearty laugh. "Don't you know Apollyon, Christian's old enemy, with whom he fought so fierce a battle in the Valley of Humiliation? He was the very fellow to manage the engine; and so we have reconciled him to the custom of going on pilgrimage, and engaged him as chief engineer."

"Bravo, bravo!" exclaimed I, with irrepressible enthusiasm; "this shows the liberality of the age; this proves, if anything can, that all musty prejudices are in a fair way to be obliterated. And how will Christian rejoice to hear of this happy transformation of his old antagonist! I promise myself great pleasure in informing him of it when we reach the Celestial City."   30

The passengers being all comfortably seated, we now rattled away merrily, accomplishing a greater distance in ten minutes than Christian probably trudged over in a day. It was laughable, while we glanced along, as it were, at the tail of a thunderbolt, to observe two dusty foot travelers in the old pilgrim guise, with cockle shell and staff, their mystic rolls of parchment in their hands and their intolerable burdens on their backs. The preposterous obstinacy of these honest people in persisting to groan and stumble along the difficult pathway rather than take advantage of modern improvements, excited great mirth among our wiser brotherhood. We greeted the two pilgrims with many pleasant gibes and a roar of laughter;

---

1 **Mr. Greatheart,** in the second part of *Pilgrim's Progress,* valiantly assists Christian's wife and sons on their journey to the Celestial City   17 **appeared . . . stomach.** Bunyan describes Apollyon as follows: ". . . he was clothed with scales like a fish . . . he had wings like a dragon, feet like a bear, and out of his belly came fire and smoke, and his mouth was as the mouth of a lion"   35 **cockle shell,** an emblem worn in the pilgrim's hat, often with a religious drawing on it, and serving also the practical purpose of a drinking vessel

whereupon they gazed at us with such woful and absurdly compassionate visages that our merriment grew tenfold more obstreperous. Apollyon also entered heartily into the fun, and contrived to flirt the smoke and flame of the engine, or of his own breath, into their faces, and envelop them in an atmosphere of scalding steam. These little practical jokes amused us mightily, and doubtless afforded the pilgrims the gratification of considering themselves martyrs.

At some distance from the railroad Mr. Smooth-it-away pointed to a large, antique edifice, which, he observed, was a tavern of long standing, and had formerly been a noted stopping-place for pilgrims. In Bunyan's road-book it is mentioned as the
10 Interpreter's House.

"I have long had a curiosity to visit that old mansion," remarked I.

"It is not one of our stations, as you perceive," said my companion. "The keeper was violently opposed to the railroad; and well he might be, as the track left his house of entertainment on one side, and thus was pretty certain to deprive him of all his reputable customers. But the footpath still passes his door, and the old gentleman now and then receives a call from some simple traveller, and entertains him with fare as old-fashioned as himself."

Before our talk on this subject came to a conclusion we were rushing by the place where Christian's burden fell from his shoulders at the sight of the Cross. This
20 served as a theme for Mr. Smooth-it-away, Mr. Live-for-the-world, Mr. Hide-sin-in-the-heart, Mr. Scaly-conscience, and a knot of gentlemen from the town of Shun-repentance, to descant upon the inestimable advantages resulting from the safety of our baggage. Myself, and all the passengers indeed, joined with great unanimity in this view of the matter; for our burdens were rich in many things esteemed precious throughout the world; and, especially, we each of us possessed a great variety of favorite Habits, which we trusted would not be out of fashion even in the polite circles of the Celestial City. It would have been a sad spectacle to see such an assortment of valuable articles tumbling into the sepulchre. Thus pleasantly conversing on the favorable circumstances of our position as compared with those of past
30 pilgrims and of narrow-minded ones at the present day, we soon found ourselves at the foot of the Hill Difficulty. Through the very heart of this rocky mountain a tunnel has been constructed of most admirable architecture, with a lofty arch and a spacious double track; so that, unless the earth and rocks should chance to crumble down, it will remain an eternal monument of the builder's skill and enterprise. It is a great though incidental advantage that the materials from the heart of the Hill Difficulty have been employed in filling up the Valley of Humiliation, thus obviating the necessity of descending into that disagreeable and unwholesome hollow.

"This is a wonderful improvement, indeed," said I. "Yet I should have been glad of an opportunity to visit the Palace Beautiful and be introduced to the charming
40 young ladies — Miss Prudence, Miss Piety, Miss Charity, and the rest — who have the kindness to entertain pilgrims there."

---

20 **Mr. Live-for-the-world.** . . . Here, as elsewhere, Hawthorne's names are similar to, but not identical with, Bunyan's. "Mr. Love-lust," "Mr. Live-loose," "Lord Time-server," "Mr. Facing-both-ways" are examples from *Pilgrim's Progress*

"Young ladies!" cried Mr. Smooth-it-away, as soon as he could speak for laughing. "And charming young ladies! Why, my dear fellow, they are old maids, every soul of them — prim, starched, dry, and angular; and not one of them, I will venture to say, has altered so much as the fashion of her gown since the days of Christian's pilgrimage."

"Ah, well," said I, much comforted, "then I can very readily dispense with their acquaintance."

The respectable Apollyon was now putting on the steam at a prodigious rate, anxious, perhaps, to get rid of the unpleasant reminiscences connected with the spot where he had so disastrously encountered Christian. Consulting Mr. Bunyan's road-   10
book, I perceived that we must now be within a few miles of the Valley of the Shadow of Death, into which doleful region, at our present speed, we should plunge much sooner than seemed at all desirable. In truth, I expected nothing better than to find myself in the ditch on one side or the quag on the other; but on communicating my apprehensions to Mr. Smooth-it-away, he assured me that the difficulties of this passage, even in its worst condition, had been vastly exaggerated, and that, in its present state of improvement, I might consider myself as safe as on any railroad in Christendom.

Even while we were speaking the train shot into the entrance of this dreaded Valley. Though I plead guilty to some foolish palpitations of the heart during our head-   20
long rush over the causeway here constructed, yet it were unjust to withhold the highest encomiums on the boldness of its original conception and the ingenuity of those who executed it. It was gratifying, likewise, to observe how much care had been taken to dispel the everlasting gloom and supply the defect of cheerful sunshine, not a ray of which has ever penetrated among these awful shadows. For this purpose, the inflammable gas which exudes plentifully from the soil is collected by means of pipes, and thence communicated to a quadruple row of lamps along the whole extent of the passage. Thus a radiance has been created even out of the fiery and sulphurous curse that rests forever upon the valley — a radiance hurtful, however, to the eyes, and somewhat bewildering, as I discovered by the changes which   30
it wrought in the visages of my companions. In this respect, as compared with natural daylight, there is the same difference as between truth and falsehood; but if the reader have ever travelled through the dark Valley, he will have learned to be thankful for any light that he could get — if not from the sky above, then from the blasted soil beneath. Such was the red brilliancy of these lamps that they appeared to build walls of fire on both sides of the track, between which we held our course at lightning speed, while a reverberating thunder filled the Valley with its echoes. Had the engine run off the track, — a catastrophe, it is whispered, by no means unprecedented, — the bottomless pit, if there be any such place, would undoubtedly have received us. Just as some dismal fooleries of this nature had made   40
my heart quake there came a tremendous shriek, careering along the valley as if a thousand devils had burst their lungs to utter it, but which proved to be merely the whistle of the engine on arriving at a stopping-place.

The spot where we had now paused is the same that our friend Bunyan —

a truthful man, but infected with many fantastic notions — has designated, in terms plainer than I like to repeat, as the mouth of the infernal region. This, however, must be a mistake, inasmuch as Mr. Smooth-it-away, while we remained in the smoky and lurid cavern, took occasion to prove that Tophet has not even a metaphorical existence. The place, he assured us, is no other than the crater of a half-extinct volcano, in which the directors had caused forges to be set up for the manufacture of railroad iron. Hence, also, is obtained a plentiful supply of fuel for the use of the engines. Whoever had gazed into the dismal obscurity of the broad cavern mouth, whence ever and anon darted huge tongues of dusky flame, and had
10 seen the strange, half-shaped monsters, and visions of faces horribly grotesque, into which the smoke seemed to wreathe itself, and had heard the awful murmurs, and shrieks, and deep, shuddering whispers of the blast, sometimes forming themselves into words almost articulate, would have seized upon Mr. Smooth-it-away's comfortable explanation as greedily as we did. The inhabitants of the cavern, moreover, were unlovely personages, dark, smoke-begrimed, generally deformed, with misshapen feet, and a glow of dusky redness in their eyes as if their hearts had caught fire and were blazing out of the upper windows. It struck me as a peculiarity that the laborers at the forge and those who brought fuel to the engine, when they began to draw short breath, positively emitted smoke from their mouth and nostrils.
20 Among the idlers about the train, most of whom were puffing cigars which they had lighted at the flame of the crater, I was perplexed to notice several who, to my certain knowledge, had heretofore set forth by railroad for the Celestial City. They looked dark, wild, and smoky, with a singular resemblance, indeed, to the native inhabitants, like whom, also, they had a disagreeable propensity to ill-natured gibes and sneers, the habit of which had wrought a settled contortion of their visages. Having been on speaking terms with one of these persons, — an indolent, good-for-nothing fellow, who went by the name of Take-it-easy, — I called him, and inquired what was his business there.

"Did you not start," said I, "for the Celestial City?"
30 "That's a fact," said Mr. Take-it-easy, carelessly puffing some smoke into my eyes. "But I heard such bad accounts that I never took pains to climb the hill on which the city stands. No business doing, no fun going on, nothing to drink, and no smoking allowed, and a thrumming of church music from morning till night. I would not stay in such a place if they offered me house room and living free."

"But, my good Mr. Take-it-easy," cried I, "why take up your residence here, of all places in the world?"

"Oh," said the loafer, with a grin, "it is very warm hereabouts, and I meet with plenty of old acquaintances, and altogether the place suits me. I hope to see you back again some day soon. A pleasant journey to you."
40 While he was speaking the bell of the engine rang, and we dashed away after dropping a few passengers, but receiving no new ones. Rattling onward through the Valley, we were dazzled with the fiercely gleaming gas lamps, as before. But some-

---

1 **terms . . . repeat.** Bunyan's statement is, "About the mist of this valley I perceived the mouth of hell to be, and it stood also hard by the wayside"   4 **Tophet,** here used for "hell"

times, in the dark of intense brightness, grim faces, that bore the aspect and expression of individual sins, or evil passions, seemed to thrust themselves through the veil of light, glaring upon us, and strétching forth a great, dusky hand, as if to impede our progress. I almost thought that they were my own sins that appalled me there. These were freaks of imagination — nothing more, certainly — mere delusions, which I ought to be heartily ashamed of; but all through the Dark Valley I was tormented, and pestered, and dolefully bewildered with the same kind of waking dreams. The mephitic gases of that region intoxicate the brain. As the light of natural day, however, began to struggle with the glow of the lanterns, these vain imaginations lost their vividness, and finally vanished from the first ray of sunshine 10 that greeted our escape from the Valley of the Shadow of Death. Ere we had gone a mile beyond it I could well-nigh have taken my oath that this whole gloomy passage was a dream.

At the end of the valley, as John Bunyan mentions, is a cavern, where, in his days, dwelt two cruel giants, Pope and Pagan, who had strown the ground about their residence with the bones of slaughtered pilgrims. These vile old troglodytes are no longer there; but into their deserted cave another terrible giant has thrust himself, and makes it his business to seize upon honest travellers and fatten them for his table with plentiful meals of smoke, mist, moonshine, raw potatoes, and sawdust. He is a German by birth, and is called Giant Transcendentalist; but as to 20 his form, his features, his substance, and his nature generally, it is the chief peculiarity of this huge miscreant that neither he for himself, nor anybody for him, has ever been able to describe them. As we rushed by the cavern's mouth we caught a hasty glimpse of him, looking somewhat like an ill-proportioned figure, but considerably more like a heap of fog and duskiness. He shouted after us, but in so strange a phraseology that we knew not what he meant, nor whether to be encouraged or affrighted.

It was late in the day when the train thundered into the ancient city of Vanity, where Vanity Fair is still at the height of prosperity, and exhibits an epitome of whatever is brilliant, gay, and fascinating beneath the sun. As I purposed to make 30 a considerable stay here, it gratified me to learn that there is no longer the want of harmony between the town's-people and pilgrims, which impelled the former to such lamentably mistaken measures as the persecution of Christian and the fiery martyrdom of Faithful. On the contrary, as the new railroad brings with it great trade and a constant influx of strangers, the lord of Vanity Fair is its chief patron, and the capitalists of the city are among the largest stockholders. Many passengers stop to take their pleasure or make their profit in the Fair, instead of going onward to the Celestial City. Indeed, such are the charms of the place that people often affirm it to be the true and only heaven; stoutly contending that there is no other, that those who seek further are mere dreamers, and that, if the fabled brightness of 40 the Celestial City lay but a bare mile beyond the gates of Vanity, they would not be fools enough to go thither. Without subscribing to these perhaps exaggerated encomiums, I can truly say that my abode in the city was mainly agreeable, and my intercourse with the inhabitants productive of much amusement and instruction.

Being naturally of a serious turn, my attention was directed to the solid advantages derivable from a residence here, rather than to the effervescent pleasures which are the grand object with too many visitants. The Christian reader, if he have had no accounts of the city later than Bunyan's time, will be surprised to hear that almost every street has its church, and that the reverend clergy are nowhere held in higher respect than at Vanity Fair. And well do they deserve such honorable estimation; for the maxims of wisdom and virtue which fall from their lips come from as deep a spiritual source, and tend to as lofty a religious aim, as those of the sagest philosophers of old. In justification of this high praise I need only mention the
10 names of the Rev. Mr. Shallow-deep, the Rev. Mr. Stumble-at-truth, the fine old clerical character the Rev. Mr. This-to-day, who expects shortly to resign his pulpit to the Rev. Mr. That-tomorrow; together with the Rev. Mr. Bewilderment, the Rev. Mr. Clog-the-spirit, and, last and greatest, the Rev. Dr. Wind-of-doctrine. The labors of these eminent divines are aided by those of innumerable lecturers, who diffuse such a various profundity, in all subjects of human or celestial science, that any man may acquire an omnigenous erudition without the trouble of even learning to read. Thus literature is etherealized by assuming for its medium the human voice; and knowledge, depositing all its heavier particles, except, doubtless, its gold, becomes exhaled into a sound, which forthwith steals into the ever-open ear of the
20 community. These ingenious methods constitute a sort of machinery, by which thought and study are done to every person's hand without his putting himself to the slightest inconvenience in the matter. There is another species of machine for the wholesale manufacture of individual morality. This excellent result is effected by societies for all manner of virtuous purposes, with which a man has merely to connect himself, throwing, as it were, his quota of virtue into the common stock, and the president and directors will take care that the aggregate amount be well applied. All these, and other wonderful improvements in ethics, religion, and literature, being made plain to my comprehension by the ingenious Mr. Smooth-it-away, inspired me with a vast admiration of Vanity Fair.
30   It would fill a volume, in an age of pamphlets, were I to record all my observations in this great capital of human business and pleasure. There was an unlimited range of society — the powerful, the wise, the witty, and the famous in every walk of life; princes, presidents, poets, generals, artists, actors, and philanthropists, — all making their own market at the fair, and deeming no price too exorbitant for such commodities as hit their fancy. It was well worth one's while, even if he had no idea of buying or selling, to loiter through the bazaars and observe the various sorts of traffic that were going forward.

Some of the purchasers, I thought, made very foolish bargains. For instance, a young man having inherited a splendid fortune, laid out a considerable portion of it
40 in the purchase of diseases, and finally spent all the rest for a heavy lot of repentance and a suit of rags. A very pretty girl bartered a heart as clear as crystal, and which seemed her most valuable possession, for another jewel of the same kind, but so worn and defaced as to be utterly worthless. In one shop there were a great

---

16 **omnigenous,** of all kinds

many crowns of laurel and myrtle, which soldiers, authors, statesmen, and various other people pressed eagerly to buy; some purchased these paltry wreaths with their lives, others by a toilsome servitude of years, and many sacrificed whatever was most valuable, yet finally slunk away without the crown. There was a sort of stock or scrip, called Conscience, which seemed to be in great demand, and would purchase almost anything. Indeed, few rich commodities were to be obtained without paying a heavy sum in this particular stock, and a man's business was seldom very lucrative unless he knew precisely when and how to throw his hoard of conscience into the market. Yet as this stock was the only thing of permanent value, whoever parted with it was sure to find himself a loser in the long run. Several of the speculations were of a questionable character. Occasionally a member of Congress recruited his pocket by the sale of his constituents; and I was assured that public officers have often sold their country at very moderate prices. Thousands sold their happiness for a whim. Gilded chains were in great demand, and purchased with almost any sacrifice. In truth, those who desired, according to the old adage, to sell anything valuable for a song, might find customers all over the Fair; and there were innumerable messes of pottage, piping hot, for such as chose to buy them with their birthrights. A few articles, however, could not be found genuine at Vanity Fair. If a customer wished to renew his stock of youth the dealers offered him a set of false teeth and an auburn wig; if he demanded peace of mind, they recommended opium or a brandy bottle.

Tracts of land and golden mansions, situate in the Celestial City, were often exchanged, at very disadvantageous rates, for a few years' lease of small, dismal, inconvenient tenements in Vanity Fair. Prince Beelzebub himself took great interest in this sort of traffic, and sometimes condescended to meddle with smaller matters. I once had the pleasure to see him bargaining with a miser for his soul, which, after much ingenious skirmishing on both sides, his highness succeeded in obtaining at about the value of sixpence. The prince remarked with a smile, that he was a loser by the transaction.

Day after day, as I walked the streets of Vanity, my manners and deportment became more and more like those of the inhabitants. The place began to seem like home; the idea of pursuing my travels to the Celestial City was almost obliterated from my mind. I was reminded of it, however, by the sight of the same pair of simple pilgrims at whom we had laughed so heartily when Apollyon puffed smoke and steam into their faces at the commencement of our journey. There they stood amidst the densest bustle of Vanity; the dealers offering them their purple and fine linen and jewels, the men of wit and humor gibing at them, a pair of buxom ladies ogling them askance, while the benevolent Mr. Smooth-it-away whispered some of his wisdom at their elbows, and pointed to a newly-erected temple; but there were these worthy simpletons, making the scene look wild and monstrous, merely by their sturdy repudiation of all part in its business or pleasures.

One of them — his name, was Stick-to-the-right — perceived in my face, I sup-

---

17 **messes . . . birthrights.** The allusion is to Esau, who sold his birthright to Jacob for a mess of pottage. See Genesis 25: 29-34

pose, a species of sympathy and almost admiration, which, to my own great surprise, I could not help feeling for this pragmatic couple. It prompted him to address me.

"Sir," inquired he, with a sad, yet mild and kindly voice, "do you call yourself a pilgrim?"

"Yes," I replied, "my right to that appellation is indubitable. I am merely a sojourner here in Vanity Fair, being bound to the Celestial City by the new railroad."

"Alas, friend," rejoined Mr. Stick-to-the-right, "I do assure you, and beseech you to receive the truth of my words, that that whole concern is a bubble. You may travel on it all your lifetime, were you to live thousands of years, and yet never get
10 beyond the limits of Vanity Fair. Yea, though you should deem yourself entering the gates of the blessed city, it will be nothing but a miserable delusion."

"The Lord of the Celestial City," began the other pilgrim, whose name was Mr. Foot-it-to-heaven, "has refused, and will ever refuse, to grant an act of incorporation for this railroad; and unless that be obtained, no passenger can ever hope to enter his dominions. Wherefore every man who buys a ticket must lay his account with losing the purchase money, which is the value of his own soul."

"Poh, nonsense!" said Mr. Smooth-it-away, taking my arm and leading me off, "these fellows ought to be indicted for a libel. If the law stood as it once did in Vanity Fair we should see them grinning through the iron bars of the prison window."
20 This incident made a considerable impression on my mind, and contributed with other circumstances to indispose me to a permanent residence in the city of Vanity; although, of course, I was not simple enough to give up my original plan of gliding along easily and commodiously by railroad. Still, I grew anxious to be gone. There was one strange thing that troubled me. Amid the occupations or amusements of the Fair, nothing was more common than for a person — whether at feast, theatre, or church, or trafficking for wealth and honors, or whatever he might be doing, and however unseasonable the interruption — suddenly to vanish like a soap bubble, and be never more seen of his fellows; and so accustomed were the latter to such little accidents that they went on with their business as quietly as if nothing
30 had happened. But it was otherwise with me.

Finally, after a pretty long residence at the Fair, I resumed my journey towards the Celestial City, still with Mr. Smooth-it-away at my side. At a short distance beyond the suburbs of Vanity we passed the ancient silver mine, of which Demas was the first discoverer, and which is now wrought to great advantage, supplying nearly all the coined currency of the world. A little further onward was the spot where Lot's wife had stood forever under the semblance of a pillar of salt. Curious travellers have long since carried it away piecemeal. Had all regrets been punished as rigorously as this poor dame's were, my yearning for the relinquished delights of Vanity Fair might have produced a similar change in my own corporeal substance, and left
40 me a warning to future pilgrims.

The next remarkable object was a large edifice, constructed of moss-grown stone, but in a modern and airy style of architecture. The engine came to a pause in its vicinity, with the usual tremendous shriek.

36 **Lot's wife,** looking back at Sodom, was turned into a pillar of salt. See Genesis 19:26

"This was formerly the castle of the redoubted giant Despair," observed Mr. Smooth-it-away; "but since his death Mr. Flimsy-faith has repaired it, and keeps an excellent house of entertainment here. It is one of our stopping-places."

"It seems but slightly put together," remarked I, looking at the frail yet ponderous walls. "I do not envy Mr. Flimsy-faith his habitation. Some day it will thunder down upon the heads of the occupants."

"We shall escape at all events," said Mr. Smooth-it-away, "for Apollyon is putting on the steam again."

The road now plunged into a gorge of the Delectable Mountains, and traversed the field where in former ages the blind men wandered and stumbled among the 10 tombs. One of these ancient tombstones had been thrust across the track by some malicious person, and gave the train of cars a terrible jolt. Far up the rugged side of a mountain I perceived a rusty iron door, half overgrown with bushes and creeping plants, but with smoke issuing from its crevices.

"Is that," inquired I, "the very door in the hill-side which the shepherds assured Christian was a by-way to hell?"

"That was a joke on the part of the shepherds," said Mr. Smooth-it-away, with a smile. "It is neither more nor less than the door of a cavern which they use as a smoke-house for the preparation of mutton hams."

My recollections of the journey are now, for a little space, dim and confused, inas- 20 much as a singular drowsiness here overcame me, owing to the fact that we were passing over the enchanted ground, the air of which encourages a disposition to sleep. I awoke, however, as soon as we crossed the borders of the pleasant land of Beulah. All the passengers were rubbing their eyes, comparing watches, and congratulating one another on the prospect of arriving so seasonably at the journey's end. The sweet breezes of this happy clime came refreshingly to our nostrils; we beheld the glimmering gush of silver fountains, overhung by trees of beautiful foliage and delicious fruit, which were propagated by grafts from the celestial gardens. Once, as we dashed onward like a hurricane, there was a flutter of wings and the bright appearance of an angel in the air, speeding forth on some heavenly mis- 30 sion. The engine now announced the close vicinity of the final station-house by one last and horrible scream, in which there seemed to be distinguishable every kind of wailing and woe, and bitter fierceness of wrath, all mixed up with the wild laughter of a devil or a madman. Throughout our journey, at every stopping-place, Apollyon had exercised his ingenuity in screwing the most abominable sounds out of the whistle of the steam-engine; but in this closing effort he outdid himself and created an infernal uproar, which, besides disturbing the peaceful inhabitants of Beulah, must have sent its discord even through the celestial gates.

While the horrid clamor was still ringing in our ears we heard an exulting strain, as if a thousand instruments of music, with height and depth and sweetness in their 40 tones, at once tender and triumphant, were struck in unison, to greet the approach of some illustrious hero, who had fought the good fight and won a glorious victory, and was come to lay aside his battered arms forever. Looking to ascertain what

42 **fought . . . fight.** See II Timothy 4:7

might be the occasion of this glad harmony, I perceived, on alighting from the cars, that a multitude of shining ones had assembled on the other side of the river, to welcome two poor pilgrims, who were just emerging from its depths. They were the same whom Apollyon and ourselves had persecuted with taunts, and gibes, and scalding steam, at the commencement of our journey — the same whose unworldly aspect and impressive words had stirred my conscience amid the wild revellers of Vanity Fair.

"How amazingly well those men have got on," cried I to Mr. Smooth-it-away. "I wish we were secure of as good a reception."

10   "Never fear, never fear!" answered my friend. "Come, make haste; the ferry boat will be off directly, and in three minutes you will be on the other side of the river. No doubt you will find coaches to carry you up to the city gates."

A steam ferry boat, the last improvement on this important route, lay at the river side, puffing, snorting, and emitting all those other disagreeable utterances which betoken the departure to be immediate. I hurried on board with the rest of the passengers, most of whom were in great perturbation: some bawling out for their baggage; some tearing their hair and exclaiming that the boat would explode or sink; some already pale with the heaving of the stream; some gazing affrighted at the ugly aspect of the steersman; and some still dizzy with the slumberous influences
20   of the Enchanted Ground. Looking back to the shore, I was amazed to discern Mr. Smooth-it-away waving his hand in token of farewell.

"Don't you go over to the Celestial City?" exclaimed I.

"Oh, no!" answered he with a queer smile, and that same disagreeable contortion of visage which I had remarked in the inhabitants of the Dark Valley. "Oh, no! I have come thus far only for the sake of your pleasant company. Good-by! We shall meet again."

And then did my excellent friend Mr. Smooth-it-away laugh outright, in the midst of which cachinnation a smoke-wreath issued from his mouth and nostrils, while a twinkle of lurid flame darted out of either eye, proving indubitably that his heart
30   was all of a red blaze. The impudent fiend! To deny the existence of Tophet, when he felt its fiery tortures raging within his breast. I rushed to the side of the boat, intending to fling myself on shore; but the wheels, as they began their revolutions, threw a dash of spray over me so cold — so deadly cold, with the chill that will never leave those waters until Death be drowned in his own river — that with a shiver and a heartquake I awoke. Thank Heaven it was a Dream!

                                                                                       1843

The Artist of the Beautiful

"The Artist of the Beautiful" was first published in the Democratic Review *in 1844 and was reprinted in* Mosses from an Old Manse *in 1846. The story may be profitably studied as an allegory of all art, and particularly as an allegory of Hawthorne's art. The delicacy of the true artist's perceptions, his meticulous attention to detail, his devotion to an artistic*

ideal, his lack of appreciation by a materialistic world, his ultimate satisfaction and reward, not in popular acclaim but in artistic creation itself, are some of the points suggested by the allegory, and all of these points are applicable in Hawthorne's own case.

An elderly man, with his pretty daughter on his arm, was passing along the street, and emerged from the gloom of the cloudy evening into the light that fell across the pavement from the window of a small shop. It was a projecting window; and on the inside were suspended a variety of watches, pinchbeck, silver, and one or two of gold, all with their faces turned from the streets, as if churlishly disinclined to inform the wayfarers what o'clock it was. Seated within the shop, sidelong to the window, with his pale face bent earnestly over some delicate piece of mechanism on which was thrown the concentrated lustre of a shade lamp, appeared a young man.

"What can Owen Warland be about?" muttered old Peter Hovenden, himself a 10 retired watchmaker, and the former master of this same young man whose occupation he was now wondering at. "What can the fellow be about? These six months past I have never come by his shop without seeing him just as steadily at work as now. It would be a flight beyond his usual foolery to seek for the perpetual motion; and yet I know enough of my old business to be certain that what he is now so busy with is no part of the machinery of a watch."

"Perhaps, father," said Annie, without showing much interest in the question, "Owen is inventing a new kind of timekeeper. I am sure he has ingenuity enough."

"Poh, child! He has not the sort of ingenuity to invent anything better than a Dutch toy," answered her father, who had formerly been put to much vexation by 20 Owen Warland's irregular genius. "A plague on such ingenuity! All the effect that ever I knew of it was to spoil the accuracy of some of the best watches in my shop. He would turn the sun out of its orbit and derange the whole course of time, if, as I said before, his ingenuity could grasp anything bigger than a child's toy!"

"Hush, father! He hears you!" whispered Annie, pressing the old man's arm. "His ears are as delicate as his feelings; and you know how easily disturbed they are. Do let us move on."

So Peter Hovenden and his daughter Annie plodded on without further conversation, until in a by-street of the town they found themselves passing the open door of a blacksmith's shop. Within was seen the forge, now blazing up and illuminat- 30 ing the high and dusky roof, and now confining its lustre to a narrow precinct of the coal-strewn floor, according as the breath of the bellows was puffed forth or again inhaled into its vast leathern lungs. In the intervals of brightness it was easy to distinguish objects in remote corners of the shop and the horseshoes that hung upon the wall; in the momentary gloom the fire seemed to be glimmering amidst the vagueness of uninclosed space. Moving about in this red glare and alternate dusk was the figure of the blacksmith, well worthy to be viewed in so picturesque

---

4 **pinchbeck,** an alloy of copper and zinc, used to imitate gold in cheap jewelry   14 **seek . . . motion,** the attempt, often made in times past, to invent a machine perpetually supplying its own motive forces independently of any action from without

an aspect of light and shade, where the bright blaze struggled with the black night, as if each would have snatched his comely strength from the other. Anon he drew a white-hot bar of iron from the coals, laid it on the anvil, uplifted his arm of might, and was soon enveloped in the myriads of sparks which the strokes of his hammer scattered into the surrounding gloom.

"Now, that is a pleasant sight," said the old watchmaker. "I know what it is to work in gold; but give me the worker in iron after all is said and done. He spends his labor upon a reality. What say you, daughter Annie?"

"Pray don't speak so loud, father," whispered Annie, "Robert Danforth will
10 hear you."

"And what if he should hear me?" said Peter Hovenden. "I say again, it is a good and a wholesome thing to depend upon main strength and reality, and to earn one's bread with the bare and brawny arm of a blacksmith. A watchmaker gets his brain puzzled by his wheels within a wheel, or loses his health or the nicety of his eyesight, as was my case, and finds himself at middle age, or a little after, past labor at his own trade and fit for nothing else, yet too poor to live at his ease. So I say once again, give me main strength for my money. And then, how it takes the nonsense out of a man! Did you ever hear of a blacksmith being such a fool as Owen Warland yonder?"

20 "Well said, uncle Hovenden!" shouted Robert Danforth from the forge, in a full, deep, merry voice, that made the roof re-echo. "And what says Miss Annie to that doctrine? She, I suppose, will think it a genteeler business to tinker up a lady's watch than to forge a horseshoe or make a gridiron."

Annie drew her father onward without giving him time for reply.

But we must return to Owen Warland's shop, and spend more meditation upon his history and character than either Peter Hovenden, or probably his daughter Annie, or Owen's old school-fellow, Robert Danforth, would have thought due to so slight a subject. From the time that his little fingers could grasp a penknife, Owen had been remarkable for a delicate ingenuity, which sometimes produced pretty
30 shapes in wood, principally figures of flowers and birds, and sometimes seemed to aim at the hidden mysteries of mechanism. But it was always for purposes of grace, and never with any mockery of the useful. He did not, like the crowd of school-boy artisans, construct little windmills on the angle of a barn or watermills across the neighboring brook. Those who discovered such peculiarity in the boy as to think it worth their while to observe him closely, sometimes saw reason to suppose that he was attempting to imitate the beautiful movements of Nature as exemplified in the flight of birds or the activity of little animals. It seemed, in fact, a new development of the love of the beautiful, such as might have made him a poet, a painter, or a sculptor, and which was as completely refined from all utilitarian coarseness as
40 it could have been in either of the fine arts. He looked with singular distaste at the stiff and regular processes of ordinary machinery. Being once carried to see a steam-engine, in the expectation that his intuitive comprehension of mechanical principles would be gratified, he turned pale and grew sick, as if something monstrous and unnatural had been presented to him. This horror was partly owing to the size and

terrible energy of the iron laborer; for the character of Owen's mind was microscopic, and tended naturally to the minute, in accordance with his diminutive frame and the marvellous smallness and delicate power of his fingers. Not that his sense of beauty was thereby diminished into a sense of prettiness. The beautiful idea has no relation to size, and may be as perfectly developed in a space too minute for any but microscopic investigation as within the ample verge that is measured by the arc of the rainbow. But, at all events, this characteristic minuteness of his objects and accomplishments made the world even more incapable than it might otherwise have been of appreciating Owen Warland's genius. The boy's relatives saw nothing better to be done — as perhaps there was not — than to bind him apprentice to 10 a watchmaker, hoping that his strange ingenuity might thus be regulated and put to utilitarian purposes.

Peter Hovenden's opinion of his apprentice has already been expressed. He could make nothing of the lad. Owen's apprehension of the professional mysteries, it is true, were inconceivably quick; but he altogether forgot or despised the grand object of a watchmaker's business, and cared no more for the measurement of time than if it had been merged into eternity. So long, however, as he remained under his old master's care, Owen's lack of sturdiness made it possible, by strict injunctions and sharp oversight, to restrain his creative eccentricity within bounds; but when his apprenticeship was served out, and he had taken the little shop which Peter 20 Hovenden's failing eyesight compelled him to relinquish, then did people recognize how unfit a person was Owen Warland to lead old blind Father Time along his daily course. One of his most rational projects was to connect a musical operation with the machinery of his watches, so that all the harsh dissonances of life might be rendered tuneful, and each flitting moment fall into the abyss of the past in golden drops of harmony. If a family clock was intrusted to him for repair, — one of those tall, ancient clocks that have grown nearly allied to human nature by measuring out the lifetime of many generations, — he would take upon himself to arrange a dance or funeral procession of figures across its venerable face, representing twelve mirthful or melancholy hours. Several freaks of this kind quite destroyed the young 30 watchmaker's credit with that steady and matter-of-fact class of people who hold the opinion that time is not to be trifled with, whether considered as the medium of advancement and prosperity in this world or preparation for the next. His custom rapidly diminished — a misfortune, however, that was probably reckoned among his better accidents by Owen Warland, who was becoming more and more absorbed in a secret occupation which drew all his science and manual dexterity into itself, and likewise gave full employment to the characteristic tendencies of his genius. This pursuit had already consumed many months.

After the old watchmaker and his pretty daughter had gazed at him out of the obscurity of the street, Owen Warland was seized with a fluttering of the nerves, 40

---

4 **The beautiful . . . rainbow.** Hawthorne perhaps thought of his work in the short tale as exemplifying this principle. The sentence is reminiscent of Ben Jonson's "In small proportions we just beauties see" from "A Pindaric Ode"

which made his hand tremble too violently to proceed with such delicate labor as he was now engaged upon.

"It was Annie herself!" murmured he. "I should have known it, by this throbbing of my heart, before I heard her father's voice. Ah, how it throbs! I shall scarcely be able to work again on this exquisite mechanism to-night. Annie! dearest Annie! thou shouldst give firmness to my heart and hand, and not shake them thus; for if I strive to put the very spirit of beauty into form and give it motion, it is for thy sake alone. O throbbing heart, be quiet! If my labor be thus thwarted, there will come vague and unsatisfied dreams which will leave me spiritless to-morrow."

10   As he was endeavoring to settle himself again to his task, the shop door opened and gave admittance to no other than the stalwart figure which Peter Hovenden had paused to admire, as seen amid the light and shadow of the blacksmith's shop. Robert Danforth had brought a little anvil of his own manufacture, and peculiarly constructed, which the young artist had recently bespoken. Owen examined the article and pronounced it fashioned according to his wish.

"Why, yes," said Robert Danforth, his strong voice filling the shop as with the sound of a bass viol, "I consider myself equal to anything in the way of my own trade; though I should have made but a poor figure at yours with such a fist as this," added he, laughing, as he laid his vast hand beside the delicate one of Owen. "But

20   what then? I put more main strength into one blow of my sledge hammer than all that you have expended since you were a 'prentice. Is not that the truth?"

"Very probably," answered the low and slender voice of Owen. "Strength is an earthly monster. I make no pretensions to it. My force, whatever there may be of it, is altogether spiritual."

"Well, but, Owen, what are you about?" asked his old school-fellow, still in such a hearty volume of tone that it made the artist shrink, especially as the question related to a subject so sacred as the absorbing dream of his imagination. "Folks do say that you are trying to discover the perpetual motion."

"The perpetual motion? Nonsense!" replied Owen Warland, with a movement of

30   disgust; for he was full of little petulances. "It can never be discovered. It is a dream that may delude men whose brains are mystified with matter, but not me. Besides, if such a discovery were possible, it would not be worth my while to make it only to have the secret turned to such purposes as are now effected by steam and water power. I am not ambitious to be honored with the paternity of a new kind of cotton machine."

"That would be droll enough!" cried the blacksmith, breaking out into such an uproar of laughter that Owen himself and the bell glasses on his work-board quivered in unison. "No, no, Owen! No child of yours will have iron joints and sinews. Well, I won't hinder you any more. Good night, Owen, and success, and if you

40   need any assistance, so far as a downright blow of hammer upon anvil will answer the purpose, I'm your man."

And with another laugh the man of main strength left the shop.

"How strange it is," whispered Owen Warland to himself, leaning his head upon his hand, "that all my musings, my purposes, my passion for the beautiful, my con-

sciousness of power to create it, — a finer, more ethereal power, of which this
earthly giant can have no conception, — all, all, look so vain and idle whenever my
path is crossed by Robert Danforth! He would drive me mad were I to meet him
often. His hard, brute force darkens and confuses the spiritual element within me;
but I, too, will be strong in my own way. I will not yield to him."

He took from beneath a glass a piece of minute machinery, which he set in the
condensed light of his lamp, and looking intently at it through a magnifying glass,
proceeded to operate with a delicate instrument of steel. In an instant, however, he
fell back in his chair and clasped his hands, with a look of horror on his face that
made its small features as impressive as those of a giant would have been.   10

"Heaven! What have I done?" exclaimed he. "The vapor, the influence of that
brute force, — it has bewildered me and obscured my perception. I have made the
very stroke — the fatal stroke — that I have dreaded from the first. It is all over —
the toil of months, the object of my life. I am ruined!"

And there he sat, in strange despair, until his lamp flickered in the socket and left
the Artist of the Beautiful in darkness.

Thus it is that ideas, which grow up within the imagination and appear so lovely
to it and of a value beyond whatever men call valuable, are exposed to be shattered
and annihilated by contact with the practical. It is requisite for the ideal artist to
possess a force of character that seems hardly compatible with its delicacy; he must   20
keep his faith in himself while the incredulous world assails him with its utter disbelief; he must stand up against mankind and be his own sole disciple, both as respects his genius and the objects to which it is directed.

For a time Owen Warland succumbed to this severe but inevitable test. He spent
a few sluggish weeks with his head so continually resting in his hands that the
towns-people had scarcely an opportunity to see his countenance. When at last it
was again uplifted to the light of day, a cold, dull, nameless change was perceptible
upon it. In the opinion of Peter Hovenden, however, and that order of sagacious
understandings who think that life should be regulated, like clockwork, with leaden
weights, the alteration was entirely for the better. Owen now, indeed, applied him-   30
self to business with dogged industry. It was marvellous to witness the obtuse gravity with which he would inspect the wheels of a great old silver watch; thereby delighting the owner, in whose fob it had been worn till he deemed it a portion of
his own life, and was accordingly jealous of its treatment. In consequence of the
good report thus acquired, Owen Warland was invited by the proper authorities to
regulate the clock in the church steeple. He succeeded so admirably in this matter
of public interest that the merchants gruffly acknowledged his merits on 'Change;
the nurse whispered his praises as she gave the potion in the sick-chamber; the lover
blessed him at the hour of appointed interview; and the town in general thanked
Owen for the punctuality of dinner time. In a word, the heavy weight upon his   40
spirits kept everything in order, not merely within his own system, but wheresoever
the iron accents of the church clock were audible. It was a circumstance, though
minute, yet characteristic of his present state, that, when employed to engrave
names or initials on silver spoons, he now wrote the requisite letters in the plainest

possible style, omitting a variety of fanciful flourishes that had heretofore distinguished his work in this kind.

One day, during the era of this happy transformation, old Peter Hovenden came to visit his former apprentice.

"Well, Owen," said he, "I am glad to hear such good accounts of you from all quarters, and especially from the town clock yonder, which speaks in your commendation every hour of the twenty-four. Only get rid altogether of your nonsensical trash about the beautiful, which I nor nobody else, nor yourself to boot, could ever understand, — only free yourself of that, and your success in life is as sure as
10 daylight. Why, if you go on in this way, I should even venture to let you doctor this precious old watch of mine, though, except my daughter Annie, I have nothing else so valuable in the world."

"I should hardly dare touch it, sir," replied Owen, in a depressed tone; for he was weighed down by his old master's presence.

"In time," said the latter, — "in time, you will be capable of it."

The old watchmaker, with the freedom naturally consequent on his former authority, went on inspecting the work which Owen had in hand at the moment, together with other matters that were in progress. The artist, meanwhile, could scarcely lift his head. There was nothing so antipodal to his nature as this man's cold, unimagi-
20 native sagacity, by contact with which everything was converted into a dream except the densest matter of the physical world. Owen groaned in spirit and prayed fervently to be delivered from him.

"But what is this?" cried Peter Hovenden abruptly, taking up a dusty bell glass, beneath which appeared a mechanical something, as delicate and minute as the system of a butterfly's anatomy. "What have we here? Owen! Owen! there is witchcraft in these little chains, and wheels, and paddles. See! with one pinch of my finger and thumb I am going to deliver you from all future peril."

"For Heaven's sake," screamed Owen Warland, springing up with wonderful energy, "as you would not drive me mad, do not touch it! The slightest pressure of
30 your finger would ruin me forever."

"Aha, young man! And is it so?" said the old watchmaker, looking at him with just enough of penetration to torture Owen's soul with the bitterness of worldly criticism. "Well, take your own course; but I warn you again that in this small piece of mechanism lives your evil spirit. Shall I exorcise him?"

"You are my evil spirit," answered Owen, much excited, — "you and the hard, coarse world! The leaden thoughts and the despondency that you fling upon me are my clogs, else I should long ago have achieved the task that I was created for."

Peter Hovenden shook his head, with the mixture of contempt and indignation which mankind, of whom he was partly a representative, deem themselves entitled to
40 feel towards all simpletons who seek other prizes than the dusty one along the highway. He then took his leave, with an uplifted finger and a sneer upon his face that haunted the artist's dreams for many a night afterwards. At the time of his old master's visit, Owen was probably on the point of taking up the relinquished task; but, by this sinister event, he was thrown back into the state whence he had been slowly emerging.

But the innate tendency of his soul had only been accumulating fresh vigor during its apparent sluggishness. As the summer advanced he almost totally relinquished his business, and permitted Father Time, so far as the old gentleman was represented by the clocks and watches under his control, to stray at random through human life, making infinite confusion among the train of bewildered hours. He wasted the sunshine, as people said, in wandering through the woods and fields and along the banks of streams. There, like a child, he found amusement in chasing butterflies or watching the motions of water insects. There was something truly mysterious in the intentness with which he contemplated these living playthings as they sported on the breeze or examined the structure of an imperial insect whom he had impris- 10 oned. The chase of butterflies was an apt emblem of the ideal pursuit in which he had spent so many golden hours; but would the beautiful idea ever be yielded to his hand like the butterfly that symbolized it? Sweet, doubtless, were these days, and congenial to the artist's soul. They were full of bright conceptions, which gleamed through his intellectual world as the butterflies gleamed through the outward atmosphere, and were real to him, for the instant, without the toil, and perplexity, and many disappointments of attempting to make them visible to the sensual eye. Alas that the artist, whether in poetry, or whatever other material, may not content himself with the inward enjoyment of the beautiful, but must chase the flitting mystery beyond the verge of his ethereal domain, and crush its frail 20 being in seizing it with material grasp. Owen Warland felt the impulse to give external reality to his ideas as irresistibly as any of the poets or painters who have arrayed the world in a dimmer and fainter beauty, imperfectly copied from the richness of their visions.

The night was now his time for the slow progress of re-creating the one idea to which all his intellectual activity referred itself. Always at the approach of dusk he stole into the town, locked himself within his shop, and wrought with patient delicacy of touch for many hours. Sometimes he was startled by the rap of the watchman, who, when all the world should be asleep, had caught the gleam of lamplight through the crevices of Owen Warland's shutters. Daylight, to the morbid sensi- 30 bility of his mind, seemed to have an intrusiveness that interfered with his pursuits. On cloudy and inclement days, therefore, he sat with his head upon his hands, muffling, as it were, his sensitive brain in a mist of indefinite musings; for it was a relief to escape from the sharp distinctness with which he was compelled to shape out his thoughts during his nightly toil.

From one of these fits of torpor he was aroused by the entrance of Annie Hovenden, who came into the shop with the freedom of a customer, and also with something of the familiarity of a childish friend. She had worn a hole through her silver thimble, and wanted Owen to repair it.

"But I don't know whether you will condescend to such a task," said she, laugh- 40 ing, "now that you are so taken up with the notion of putting spirit into machinery."

"Where did you get that idea, Annie?" said Owen, starting in surprise.

"Oh, out of my own head," answered she, "and from something that I heard you say, long ago, when you were but a boy and I a little child. But come; will you mend this poor thimble of mine?"

"Anything for your sake, Annie," said Owen Warland, — "anything, even were it to work at Robert Danforth's forge."

"And that would be a pretty sight!" retorted Annie, glancing with imperceptible slightness at the artist's small and slender frame. "Well, here is the thimble."

"But that is a strange idea of yours," said Owen, "about the spiritualization of matter."

And then the thought stole into his mind that this young girl possessed the gift
10   to comprehend him better than all the world besides. And what a help and strength would it be to him in his lonely toil if he could gain the sympathy of the only being whom he loved! To persons whose pursuits are insulated from the common business of life — who are either in advance of mankind or apart from it — there often comes a sensation of moral cold that makes the spirit shiver as if it had reached the frozen solitudes around the pole. What the prophet, the poet, the reformer, the criminal, or any other man with human yearnings, but separated from the multitude by a peculiar lot, might feel, poor Owen felt.

"Annie," cried he, growing pale as death at the thought, "how gladly would I tell you the secret of my pursuit! You, methinks, would estimate it rightly. You, I
20   know, would hear it with a reverence that I must not expect from the harsh material world."

"Would I not? to be sure I would!" replied Annie Hovenden, lightly laughing. "Come; explain to me quickly what is the meaning of this little whirligig, so delicately wrought that it might be a plaything for Queen Mab. See! I will put it in motion."

"Hold!" exclaimed Owen, "hold!"

Annie had but given the slightest possible touch, with the point of a needle, to the same minute portion of complicated machinery which has been more than once mentioned, when the artist seized her by the wrist with a force that made her scream
30   aloud. She was affrighted at the convulsion of intense rage and anguish that writhed across his features. The next instant he let his head sink upon his hands.

"Go, Annie," murmured he; "I have deceived myself, and must suffer for it. I yearned for sympathy and thought, and fancied, and dreamed that you might give it me; but you lack the talisman, Annie, that should admit you into my secrets. That touch has undone the toil of months and the thought of a lifetime! It was not your fault, Annie; but you have ruined me!"

Poor Owen Warland! He had indeed erred, yet pardonably; for if any human spirit could have sufficiently reverenced the processes so sacred in his eyes, it must have been a woman's. Even Annie Hovenden, possibly, might not have disappointed him
40   had she been enlightened by the deep intelligence of love.

The artist spent the ensuing winter in a way that satisfied any persons who had

---

24 **Queen Mab,** "the fairies' midwife," who delivers men of their dreams. See the famous description in *Romeo and Juliet,* Act I, Scene iv, ll. 53-94. Hawthorne's idea of a "spiritualized mechanism" as presented in this story may have owed something to Shakespeare's description of Queen Mab's chariot

hitherto retained a hopeful opinion of him that he was, in truth, irrevocably doomed to inutility as regarded the world, and to an evil destiny on his own part. The decease of a relative had put him in possession of a small inheritance. Thus freed from the necessity of toil, and having lost the steadfast influence of a great purpose, — great, at least, to him, — he abandoned himself to habits from which it might have been supposed the mere delicacy of his organization would have availed to secure him. But when the ethereal portion of a man of genius is obscured, the earthly part assumes an influence the more uncontrollable, because the character is now thrown off the balance to which Providence had so nicely adjusted it, and which, in coarser natures, is adjusted by some other method. Owen Warland made proof of whatever   10 show of bliss may be found in riot. He looked at the world through the golden medium of wine, and contemplated the visions that bubble up so gayly around the brim of the glass, and that people the air with shapes of pleasant madness, which so soon grow ghostly and forlorn. Even when this dismal and inevitable change had taken place, the young man might still have continued to quaff the cup of enchantments, though its vapor did but shroud life in gloom and fill the gloom with spectres that mocked at him. There was a certain irksomeness of spirit, which, being real, and the deepest sensation of which the artist was now conscious, was more intolerable than any fantastic miseries and horrors that the abuse of wine could summon up. In the latter case he could remember, even out of the midst of his   20 trouble, that all was but a delusion; in the former, the heavy anguish was his actual life.

From this perilous state he was redeemed by an incident which more than one person witnessed, but of which the shrewdest could not explain or conjecture the operation on Owen Warland's mind. It was very simple. On a warm afternoon of spring, as the artist sat among his riotous companions with a glass of wine before him, a splendid butterfly flew in at the open window and fluttered about his head.

"Ah," exclaimed Owen, who had drank freely, "are you alive again, child of the sun and playmate of the summer breeze, after your dismal winter's nap? Then it is time for me to be at work!"   30

And, leaving his unemptied glass upon the table, he departed and was never known to sip another drop of wine.

And now, again, he resumed his wanderings in the woods and fields. It might be fancied that the bright butterfly, which had come so spirit-like into the window as Owen sat with the rude revellers, was indeed a spirit commissioned to recall him to the pure, ideal life that had so etherealized him among men. It might be fancied that he went forth to seek this spirit in its sunny haunts; for still, as in the summer time gone by, he was seen to steal gently up wherever a butterfly had alighted, and lose himself in contemplation of it. When it took flight his eyes followed the winged vision, as if its airy track would show the path to heaven. But what could   40 be the purpose of the unseasonable toil, which was again resumed, as the watchman knew by the lines of lamplight through the crevices of Owen Warland's shutters? The towns-people had one comprehensive explanation of all these singularities. Owen Warland had gone mad! How universally efficacious — how satisfactory, too,

and soothing to the injured sensibility of narrowness and dulness — is this easy method of accounting for whatever lies beyond the world's most ordinary scope! From St. Paul's days down to our poor little Artist of the Beautiful, the same talisman had been applied to the elucidation of all mysteries in the words or deeds of men who spoke or acted too wisely or too well. In Owen Warland's case the judgment of his towns-people may have been correct. Perhaps he was mad. The lack of sympathy — that contrast between himself and his neighbors which took away the restraint of example — was enough to make him so. Or possibly he had caught just so much of the ethereal radiance as served to bewilder him, in an earthly sense, by
10 its intermixture with the common daylight.

One evening, when the artist had returned from a customary ramble and had just thrown the lustre of his lamp on the delicate piece of work so often interrupted, but still taken up again, as if his fate were embodied in its mechanism, he was surprised by the entrance of old Peter Hovenden. Owen never met this man without a shrinking of the heart. Of all the world he was most terrible, by reason of a keen understanding which saw so distinctly what it did see, and disbelieved so uncompromisingly in what it could not see. On this occasion the old watchmaker had merely a gracious word or two to say.

"Owen, my lad," said he, "we must see you at my house to-morrow night."
20 The artist began to mutter some excuse.

"Oh, but it must be so," quoth Peter Hovenden, "for the sake of the days when you were one of the household. What, my boy! don't you know that my daughter Annie is engaged to Robert Danforth? We are making an entertainment, in our humble way, to celebrate the event."

"Ah!" said Owen.

That little monosyllable was all he uttered; its tone seemed cold and unconcerned to an ear like Peter Hovenden's; and yet there was in it the stifled outcry of the poor artist's heart, which he compressed within him like a man holding down an evil spirit. One slight outbreak, however, imperceptible to the old watchmaker, he
30 allowed himself. Raising the instrument with which he was about to begin his work, he let it fall upon the little system of machinery that had, anew, cost him months of thought and toil. It was shattered by the stroke!

Owen Warland's story would have been no tolerable representation of the troubled life of those who strive to create the beautiful, if, amid all other thwarting influences, love had not interposed to steal the cunning from his head. Outwardly he had been no ardent or enterprising lover; the career of his passion had confined its tumults and vicissitudes so entirely within the artist's imagination that Annie herself had scarcely more than a woman's intuitive perception of it; but, in Owen's view, it covered the whole field of his life. Forgetful of the time when she had shown
40 herself incapable of any deep response, he had persisted in connecting all his dreams of artistical success with Annie's image; she was the visible shape in which the spiritual power that he worshipped, and on whose altar he hoped to lay a not unwor-

---

3 **St. Paul's.** The reference is to Acts 26:24: ". . . Festus said with a loud voice, Paul, thou art beside thyself; much learning doth make thee mad"

thy offering, was made manifest to him. Of course he had deceived himself; there were no such attributes in Annie Hovenden as his imagination had endowed her with. She, in the aspect which she wore to his inward vision, was as much a creature of his own as the mysterious piece of mechanism would be were it ever realized. Had he become convinced of his mistake through the medium of successful love, — had he won Annie to his bosom, and there beheld her fade from angel into ordinary woman, — the disappointment might have driven him back, with concentrated energy, upon his sole remaining object. On the other hand, had he found Annie what he fancied, his lot would have been so rich in beauty that out of its mere redundancy he might have wrought the beautiful into many a worthier type than he 10 had toiled for; but the guise in which his sorrow came to him, the sense that the angel of his life had been snatched away and given to a rude man of earth and iron, who could neither need nor appreciate her ministrations, — this was the very perversity of fate that makes human existence appear too absurd and contradictory to be the scene of one other hope or one other fear. There was nothing left for Owen Warland but to sit down like a man that had been stunned.

He went through a fit of illness. After his recovery his small slender frame assumed an obtuser garniture of flesh than it had ever before worn. His thin cheeks became round; his delicate little hand, so spiritually fashioned to achieve fairy task-work, grew plumper than the hand of a thriving infant. His aspect had a childishness such 20 as might have induced a stranger to pat him on the head — pausing, however, in the act, to wonder what manner of child was here. It was as if the spirit had gone out of him, leaving the body to flourish in a sort of vegetable existence. Not that Owen Warland was idiotic. He could talk, and not irrationally. Somewhat of a babbler, indeed, did people begin to think him; for he was apt to discourse at wearisome length of marvels of mechanism that he had read about in books, but which he had learned to consider as absolutely fabulous. Among them he enumerated the Man of Brass, constructed by Albertus Magnus, and the Brazen Head of Friar Bacon; and, coming down to later times, the automata of a little coach and horses, which it was pretended had been manufactured for the Dauphin of France; together with 30 an insect that buzzed about the ear like a living fly, and yet was but a contrivance of minute steel springs. There was a story, too, of a duck that waddled, and quacked, and ate; though, had any honest citizen purchased it for dinner, he would have found himself cheated with the mere mechanical apparition of a duck.

"But all these accounts," said Owen Warland, "I am now satisfied are mere impositions."

Then, in a mysterious way, he would confess that he once thought differently. In his idle and dreamy days he had considered it possible, in a certain sense, to spiritualize machinery, and to combine with the new species of life and motion thus produced a beauty that should attain to the ideal which Nature has proposed to herself in all her creatures, but has never taken pains to realize. He seemed, however, 40

---

28 **Albertus Magnus** (1193-1280), Bavarian philosopher and schoolman   28 **Brazen . . . Bacon.** Friar Bacon (1214-1294) was an English philosopher who, according to legend, made a head of brass   30 **Dauphin,** from 1349 to 1830, the title of the eldest son of the king of France; here the reference is specifically to the son of Louis XVI

to retain no very distinct perception either of the process of achieving this object
or of the design itself.

"I have thrown it all aside now," he would say. "It was a dream such as young
men are always mystifying themselves with. Now that I have acquired a little common sense, it makes me laugh to think of it."

Poor, poor and fallen Owen Warland! These were the symptoms that he had ceased
to be an inhabitant of the better sphere that lies unseen around us. He had lost his
faith in the invisible, and now prided himself, as such unfortunates invariably do,
in the wisdom which rejected much that even his eye could see, and trusted con-
10 fidently in nothing but what his hand could touch. This is the calamity of men
whose spiritual part dies out of them and leaves the grosser understanding to assimilate them more and more to the things of which alone it can take cognizance; but
in Owen Warland the spirit was not dead nor passed away; it only slept.

How it awoke again is not recorded. Perhaps the torpid slumber was broken by a
convulsive pain. Perhaps, as in a former instance, the butterfly came and hovered
about his head and reinspired him, — as indeed this creature of the sunshine had
always a mysterious mission for the artist, — reinspired him with the former purpose of his life. Whether it were pain or happiness that thrilled through his veins,
his first impulse was to thank Heaven for rendering him again the being of thought,
20 imagination, and keenest sensibility that he had long ceased to be.

"Now for my task," said he. "Never did I feel such strength for it as now."

Yet, strong as he felt himself, he was incited to toil the more diligently by an
anxiety lest death should surprise him in the midst of his labors. This anxiety, perhaps, is common to all men who set their hearts upon anything so high, in their
own view of it, that life becomes of importance only as conditional to its accomplishment. So long as we love life for itself, we seldom dread the losing it. When
we desire life for the attainment of an object, we recognize the frailty of its texture.
But, side by side with this sense of insecurity, there is a vital faith in our invul-
nerability to the shaft of death while engaged in any task that seems assigned by
30 Providence as our proper thing to do, and which the world would have cause to
mourn for should we leave it unaccomplished. Can the philosopher, big with the
inspiration of an idea that is to reform mankind, believe that he is to be beckoned
from this sensible existence at the very instant when he is mustering his breath to
speak the word of light? Should he perish so, the weary ages may pass away — the
world's, whose life sand may fall, drop by drop — before another intellect is prepared to develop the truth that might have been uttered then. But history affords
many an example where the most precious spirit, at any particular epoch manifested
in human shape, has gone hence untimely, without space allowed him, so far as
mortal judgment could discern, to perform his mission on the earth. The prophet
40 dies, and the man of torpid heart and sluggish brain lives on. The poet leaves his
song half sung, or finishes it, beyond the scope of mortal ears, in a celestial choir.
The painter — as Allston did — leaves half his conception on the canvas to sadden

---

31 **big**, pregnant   35 **sand**, of the hourglass   42 **Allston**, Washington Allston (1779-1843) left his
picture "Belshazzar's Feast" unfinished at his death

us with its imperfect beauty, and goes to picture forth the whole, if it be no irreverence to say so, in the hues of heaven. But rather such incomplete designs of this life will be perfected nowhere. This so frequent abortion of man's dearest projects must be taken as a proof that the deeds of earth, however etherealized by piety or genius, are without value, except as exercises and manifestations of the spirit. In heaven, all ordinary thought is higher and more melodious than Milton's song. Then, would he add another verse to any strain that he had left unfinished here?

But to return to Owen Warland. It was his fortune, good or ill, to achieve the purpose of his life. Pass we over a long space of intense thought, yearning effort, minute toil, and wasting anxiety, succeeded by an instant of solitary triumph: let 10 all this be imagined; and then behold the artist, on a winter evening, seeking admittance to Robert Danforth's fireside circle. There he found the man of iron, with his massive substance thoroughly warmed and attempered by domestic influences. And there was Annie, too, now transformed into a matron, with much of her husband's plain and sturdy nature, but imbued, as Owen Warland still believed, with a finer grace, that might enable her to be the interpreter between strength and beauty. It happened, likewise, that Old Peter Hovenden was a guest this evening at his daughter's fireside, and it was his well-remembered expression of keen, cold criticism that first encountered the artist's glance.

"My old friend Owen!" cried Robert Danforth, starting up, and compressing the 20 artist's delicate fingers within a hand that was accustomed to gripe bars of iron. "This is kind and neighborly to come to us at last. I was afraid your perpetual motion had bewitched you out of the remembrance of old times."

"We are glad to see you," said Annie, while a blush reddened her matronly cheek. "It was not like a friend to stay from us so long."

"Well, Owen," inquired the old watchmaker, as his first greeting, "how comes on the beautiful? Have you created it at last?"

The artist did not immediately reply, being startled by the apparition of a young child of strength that was tumbling about on the carpet, — a little personage who had come mysteriously out of the infinite, but with something so sturdy and real in 30 his composition that he seemed moulded out of the densest substance which earth could supply. This hopeful infant crawled towards the new-comer, and setting himself on end, as Robert Danforth expressed the posture, stared at Owen with a look of such sagacious observation that the mother could not help exchanging a proud glance with her husband. But the artist was disturbed by the child's look, as imagining a resemblance between it and Peter Hovenden's habitual expression. He could have fancied that the old watchmaker was compressed into this baby shape, and looking out of those baby eyes, and repeating, as he now did, the malicious question: —

"The beautiful, Owen! How comes on the beautiful? Have you succeeded in creat- 40 ing the beautiful?"

"I have succeeded," replied the artist, with a momentary light of triumph in his eyes and a smile of sunshine, yet steeped in such depth of thought that it was almost sadness. "Yes, my friends, it is the truth. I have succeeded."

"Indeed!" cried Annie, a look of maiden mirthfulness peeping out of her face again. "And is it lawful now, to inquire what the secret is?"

"Surely; it is to disclose it that I have come," answered Owen Warland. "You shall know, and see, and touch, and possess the secret! For, Annie, — if by that name I may still address the friend of my boyish years, — Annie, it is for your bridal gift that I have wrought this spiritualized mechanism, this harmony of motion, this mystery of beauty. It comes late, indeed; but it is as we go onward in life, when objects begin to lose their freshness of hue and our souls their delicacy of perception, that the spirit of beauty is most needed. If, — forgive me, Annie, — if you
10 know how to value this gift, it can never come too late."

He produced, as he spoke, what seemed a jewel box. It was carved richly out of ebony by his own hand, and inlaid with a fanciful tracery of pearl, representing a boy in pursuit of a butterfly, which, elsewhere, had become a winged spirit, and was flying heavenward; while the boy, or youth, had found such efficacy in his strong desire that he ascended from earth to cloud, and from cloud to celestial atmosphere, to win the beautiful. This case of ebony the artist opened, and bade Annie place her finger on its edge. She did so, but almost screamed as a butterfly fluttered forth, and, alighting on her finger's tip, sat waving the ample magnificence of its purple and gold-speckled wings, as if in prelude to a flight. It is impossible to express by
20 words the glory, the splendor, the delicate gorgeousness which were softened into the beauty of this object. Nature's ideal butterfly was here realized in all its perfection; not in the pattern of such faded insects as flit among earthly flowers, but of those which hover across the meads of paradise for child-angels and the spirits of departed infants to disport themselves with. The rich down was visible upon its wings; the lustre of its eyes seemed instinct with spirit. The firelight glimmered around this wonder — the candles gleamed upon it; but it glistened apparently by its own radiance, and illuminated the finger and outstretched hand on which it rested with a white gleam like that of precious stones. In its perfect beauty, the consideration of size was entirely lost. Had its wings overreached the firmament, the mind
30 could not have been more filled or satisfied.

"Beautiful! beautiful!" exclaimed Annie. "Is it alive? Is it alive?"

"Alive? To be sure it is," answered her husband. "Do you suppose any mortal has skill enough to make a butterfly, or would put himself to the trouble of making one, when any child may catch a score of them in a summer's afternoon? Alive? Certainly! But this pretty box is undoubtedly of our friend Owen's manufacture; and really it does him credit."

At this moment the butterfly waved its wings anew, with a motion so absolutely lifelike that Annie was startled, and even awestricken; for, in spite of her husband's opinion, she could not satisfy herself whether it was indeed a living creature or a
40 piece of wondrous mechanism.

"Is it alive?" she repeated, more earnestly than before.

"Judge for yourself," said Owen Warland, who stood gazing in her face with fixed attention.

The butterfly now flung itself upon the air, fluttered round Annie's head, and soared into a distant region of the parlor, still making itself perceptible to sight by the starry gleam in which the motion of its wings enveloped it. The infant on the floor followed its course with his sagacious little eyes. After flying about the room, it returned in a spiral curve and settled again on Annie's finger.

"But is it alive?" exclaimed she again; and the finger on which the gorgeous mystery had alighted was so tremulous that the butterfly was forced to balance himself with his wings. "Tell me if it be alive, or whether you created it."

"Wherefore ask who created it, so it be beautiful?" replied Owen Warland. "Alive? Yes, Annie; it may well be said to possess life, for it has absorbed my own being into itself; and in the secret of that butterfly, and in its beauty, — which is 10 not merely outward, but deep as its whole system, — is represented the intellect, the imagination, the sensibility, the soul of an Artist of the Beautiful! Yes; I created it. But" — and here his countenance somewhat changed — "this butterfly is not now to me what it was when I beheld it afar off in the day-dreams of my youth."

"Be it what it may, it is a pretty plaything," said the blacksmith, grinning with childlike delight. "I wonder whether it would condescend to alight on such a great clumsy finger as mine? Hold it hither, Annie."

By the artist's direction, Annie touched her finger's tip to that of her husband; and, after a momentary delay, the butterfly fluttered from one to the other. It preluded a second flight by a similar, yet not precisely the same, waving of wings as 20 in the first experiment; then, ascending from the blacksmith's stalwart finger, it rose in a gradually enlarging curve to the ceiling, made one wide sweep around the room, and returned with an undulating movement to the point whence it had started.

"Well, that does beat all nature!" cried Robert Danforth, bestowing the heartiest praise that he could find expression for; and, indeed, had he paused there, a man of finer words and nicer perception could not easily have said more. "That goes beyond me, I confess. But what then? There is more real use in one downright blow of my sledge hammer than in the whole five years' labor that our friend Owen has wasted on this butterfly."   30

Here the child clapped his hands and made a great babble of indistinct utterance, apparently demanding that the butterfly should be given him for a plaything.

Owen Warland, meanwhile, glanced sidelong at Annie, to discover whether she sympathized in her husband's estimate of the comparative value of the beautiful and the practical. There was, amid all her kindness towards himself, amid all the wonder and admiration with which she contemplated the marvelous work of his hands and incarnation of his idea, a secret scorn — too secret, perhaps, for her own consciousness, and perceptible only to such intuitive discernment as that of the artist. But Owen, in the latter stages of his pursuit, had risen out of the region in which such a discovery might have been torture. He knew that the world, and Annie as 40 the representative of the world, whatever praise might be bestowed, could never say the fitting word nor feel the fitting sentiment which should be the perfect recompense of an artist who, symbolizing a lofty moral by a material trifle, — converting what was earthly to spiritual gold, — had won the beautiful into his handiwork. Not at this latest moment was he to learn that the reward of all high performance must be sought within itself, or sought in vain. There was, however, a view of the matter which Annie and her husband, and even Peter Hovenden, might fully have understood, and which would have satisfied them that the toil of years had here been worthily bestowed. Owen Warland might have told them that this butterfly, this plaything, this bridal gift of a poor watchmaker to a blacksmith's wife, was, in truth, a gem of art that a monarch would have purchased with honors and abundant wealth, and have treasured it among the jewels of his kingdom as the most unique and wondrous of them all. But the artist smiled and kept the secret to himself.

"Father," said Annie, thinking that a word of praise from the old watchmaker might gratify his former apprentice, "do come and admire this pretty butterfly."

"Let us see," said Peter Hovenden, rising from his chair, with a sneer upon his face that always made people doubt, as he himself did, in everything but a material existence. "Here is my finger for it to alight upon. I shall understand it better when once I have touched it."

But, to the increased astonishment of Annie, when the tip of her father's finger was pressed against that of her husband, on which the butterfly still rested, the insect drooped its wings and seemed on the point of falling to the floor. Even the bright spots of gold upon its wings and body, unless her eyes deceived her, grew dim, and the glowing purple took a dusky hue, and the starry lustre that gleamed around the blacksmith's hand became faint and vanished.

"It is dying! it is dying!" cried Annie, in alarm.

"It has been delicately wrought," said the artist, calmly. "As I told you, it has imbibed a spiritual essence — call it magnetism, or what you will. In an atmosphere of doubt and mockery its exquisite susceptibility suffers torture, as does the soul of him who instilled his own life into it. It has already lost its beauty; in a few moments more its mechanism would be irreparably injured."

"Take away your hand, father!" entreated Annie, turning pale. "Here is my child; let it rest on his innocent hand. There, perhaps, its life will revive and its colors grow brighter than ever."

Her father, with an acrid smile, withdrew his finger. The butterfly then appeared to recover the power of voluntary motion, while its hues assumed much of their original lustre, and the gleam of starlight, which was its most ethereal attribute, again formed a halo round about it. At first, when transferred from Robert Danforth's hand to the small finger of the child, this radiance grew so powerful that it positively threw the little fellow's shadow back against the wall. He, meanwhile, extended his plump hand as he had seen his father and mother do, and watched the waving of the insect's wings with infantine delight. Nevertheless, there was a certain odd expression of sagacity that made Owen Warland feel as if here were old Peter Hovenden, partially, and but partially, redeemed from his hard scepticism into childish faith.

---

1 **the reward . . . itself.** Hawthorne here speaks in the tone of Milton's *Lycidas:* " 'But not the praise,' Phoebus replied, and touched my trembling ears;/ 'Fame is no plant that grows on mortal soil. . . .' " (ll. 76-78)

"How wise the little monkey looks!" whispered Robert Danforth to his wife.

"I never saw such a look on a child's face," answered Annie, admiring her own infant, and with good reason, far more than the artistic butterfly. "The darling knows more of the mystery than we do."

As if the butterfly, like the artist, were conscious of something not entirely congenial in the child's nature, it alternately sparkled and grew dim. At length it arose from the small hand of the infant with an airy motion that seemed to bear it upward without an effort, as if the ethereal instincts with which its master's spirit had endowed it impelled this fair vision involuntarily to a higher sphere. Had there been no obstruction, it might have soared into the sky and grown immortal. But 10 its lustre gleamed upon the ceiling; the exquisite texture of its wings brushed against that earthly medium; and a sparkle or two, as of stardust, floated downward and lay glimmering on the carpet. Then the butterfly came fluttering down, and, instead of returning to the infant, was apparently attracted towards the artist's hand.

"Not so! not so!" murmured Owen Warland, as if his handiwork could have understood him. "Thou has gone forth out of thy master's heart. There is no return for thee."

With a wavering movement, and emitting a tremulous radiance, the butterfly struggled, as it were, towards the infant, and was about to alight upon his finger; but while it still hovered in the air, the little child of strength, with his grandsire's sharp 20 and shrewd expression in his face, made a snatch at the marvellous insect and compressed it in his hand. Annie screamed. Old Peter Hovenden burst into a cold and scornful laugh. The blacksmith, by main force, unclosed the infant's hand, and found within the palm a small heap of glittering fragments, whence the mystery of beauty had fled forever. And as for Owen Warland, he looked placidly at what seemed the ruin of his life's labor, and which was yet no ruin. He had caught a far other butterfly than this. When the artist rose high enough to achieve the beautiful, the symbol by which he made it perceptible to mortal senses became of little value in his eyes while his spirit possessed itself in the enjoyment of the reality.

                                                                                                    1844

10 **soared . . . immortal,** reminiscent of Belinda's lock in Pope's *Rape of the Lock,* Canto V, ll. 113-150

Rappaccini's Daughter

"Rappaccini's Daughter" is perhaps Hawthorne's most vivid and forceful study of the tragic isolation of an abnormal personality. The poison in Beatrice's physical nature symbolizes this abnormality, which has been produced by her solitary life. The flowers possibly symbolize her thoughts, solitary thoughts which other people cannot share. The story seems to mean that it is tragic to be so unlike other people that one is cut from normal relations with them. "There was an awful doom," Hawthorne has Beatrice say, "the effect of my father's fatal love of science, which estranged me from all society of my kind. . . . I would fain have been loved, not feared." The story's interest is enhanced by the latitude of interpretation allowed the reader.

A secondary theme is Hawthorne's distrust of science, which he shared with other writers of the romantic generation, notably with Wordsworth ("A Poet's Epitaph"), Keats ("Lamia"), and Poe ("Sonnet to Science").

"Rappaccini's Daughter" was first published in the Democratic Review *in 1844 and was reprinted in* Mosses from an Old Manse *in 1846.*

A young man, named Giovanni Guasconti, came, very long ago, from the more southern region of Italy, to pursue his studies at the University of Padua. Giovanni, who had but a scanty supply of gold ducats in his pocket, took lodgings in a high and gloomy chamber of an old edifice which looked not unworthy to have been the palace of a Paduan noble, and which, in fact, exhibited over its entrance the armorial bearings of a family long since extinct. The young stranger, who was not unstudied in the great poem of his country, recollected that one of the ancestors of this family, and perhaps an occupant of this very mansion, had been pictured by Dante as a partaker of the immortal agonies of his Inferno. These reminiscences
10 and associations, together with the tendency to heartbreak natural to a young man for the first time out of his native sphere, caused Giovanni to sigh heavily as he looked around the desolate and ill-furnished apartment.

"Holy Virgin, signor!" cried old Dame Lisabetta, who, won by the youth's remarkable beauty of person, was kindly endeavoring to give the chamber a habitable air, "what a sigh was that to come out of a young man's heart! Do you find this old mansion gloomy? For the love of Heaven, then, put your head out of the window, and you will see as bright sunshine as you have left in Naples."

Guasconti mechanically did as the old woman advised, but could not quite agree with her that the Paduan sunshine was as cheerful as that of southern Italy. Such
20 as it was, however, it fell upon a garden beneath the window and expended its fostering influences on a variety of plants, which seemed to have been cultivated with exceeding care.

"Does this garden belong to the house?" asked Giovanni.

"Heaven, forbid, signor, unless it were fruitful of better pot herbs than any that grow there now," answered old Lisabetta. "No; that garden is cultivated by the own hands of Signor Giacomo Rappaccini, the famous doctor, who, I warrant him, has been heard of as far as Naples. It is said that he distils these plants into medicines that are as potent as a charm. Oftentimes you may see the signor doctor at work, and perchance the signora, his daughter, too, gathering the strange flowers that
30 grow in the garden."

The old woman had now done what she could for the aspect of the chamber; and, commending the young man to the protection of the saints, took her departure.

Giovanni still found no better occupation than to look down into the garden beneath his window. From its appearance, he judged it to be one of those botanic gardens which were of earlier date in Padua than elsewhere in Italy or in the world. Or, not improbably, it might once have been the pleasure-place of an opulent family; for there was the ruin of a marble fountain in the centre, sculptured with rare art but so wofully shattered that it was impossible to trace the original design from the chaos of remaining fragments. The water, however, continued to gush and sparkle into the sunbeams as cheerfully as ever. A little gurgling sound ascended to the young man's window, and made him feel as if the fountain were an immortal spirit that sung its song unceasingly and without heeding the vicissitudes around it, while one century imbodied it in marble and another scattered the perishable garniture on the soil. All about the pool into which the water subsided grew various plants, that seemed to require a plentiful supply of moisture for the nourishment of gigantic leaves, and, in some instances, flowers gorgeously magnificent. There was one shrub in particular, set in a marble vase in the midst of the pool, that bore a profusion of purple blossoms, each of which had the lustre and richness of a gem; 10 and the whole together made a show so resplendent that it seemed enough to illuminate the garden, even had there been no sunshine. Every portion of the soil was peopled with plants and herbs, which, if less beautiful, still bore tokens of assiduous care, as if all had their individual virtues, known to the scientific mind that fostered them. Some were placed in urns, rich with old carving, and others in common garden pots; some crept serpent-like along the ground or climbed on high, using whatever means of ascent was offered them. One plant had wreathed itself round a statue of Vertumnus, which was thus quite veiled and shrouded in a drapery of hanging foliage, so happily arranged that it might have served a sculptor for a study.   20

While Giovanni stood at the window he heard a rustling behind a screen of leaves, and became aware that a person was at work in the garden. His figure soon emerged into view, and showed itself to be that of no common laborer, but a tall, emaciated, sallow, and sickly-looking man, dressed in a scholar's garb of black. He was beyond the middle term of life, with grey hair, a thin, grey beard, and a face singularly marked with intellect and cultivation, but which could never, even in his more youthful days, have expressed much warmth of heart.

Nothing could exceed the intentness with which this scientific gardener examined every shrub which grew in his path: it seemed as if he was looking into their inmost nature, making observations in regard to their creative essence, and discover- 30 ing why one leaf grew in this shape and another in that, and wherefore such and such flowers differed among themselves in hue and perfume. Nevertheless, in spite of this deep intelligence on his part, there was no approach to intimacy between himself and these vegetable existences. On the contrary, he avoided their actual touch or the direct inhaling of their odors with a caution that impressed Giovanni most disagreeably; for the man's demeanor was that of one walking among malignant influences, such as savage beasts, or deadly snakes, or evil spirits, which, should he allow them one moment of license, would wreak upon him some terrible fatality. It was strangely frightful to the young man's imagination to see this air of insecurity in a person cultivating a garden, that most simple and innocent of human toils, 40 and which had been alike the joy and labor of the unfallen parents of the race. Was this garden, then, the Eden of the present world? And this man, with such a perception of harm in what his own hands caused to grow, — was he the Adam?

18 **Vertumnus,** Roman god of the changing year, or the seasons and their products

The distrustful gardener, while plucking away the dead leaves or pruning the too luxuriant growth of the shrubs, defended his hands with a pair of thick gloves. Nor were these his only armor. When, in his walk through the garden, he came to the magnificent plant that hung its purple gems beside the marble fountain, he placed a kind of mask over his mouth and nostrils, as if all this beauty did but conceal a deadlier malice; but, finding his task still too dangerous, he drew back, removed the mask, and called loudly, but in the infirm voice of a person affected with inward disease, —

"Beatrice! Beatrice!"

10   "Here am I, my father. What would you?" cried a rich and youthful voice from the window of the opposite house — a voice as rich as a tropical sunset, and which made Giovanni, though he knew not why, think of deep hues of purple or crimson and of perfumes heavily delectable. "Are you in the garden?"

"Yes, Beatrice," answered the gardener, "and I need your help."

Soon there emerged from under a sculptured portal the figure of a young girl, arrayed with as much richness of taste as the most splendid of the flowers, beautiful as the day, and with a bloom so deep and vivid that one shade more would have been too much. She looked redundant with life, health, and energy; all of which attributes were bound down and compressed, as it were, and girdled tensely, in their

20   luxuriance, by her virgin zone. Yet Giovanni's fancy must have grown morbid while he looked down into the garden; for the impression which the fair stranger made upon him was as if here were another flower, the human sister of those vegetable ones, as beautiful as they, more beautiful than the richest of them, but still to be touched only with a glove, nor to be approached without a mask. As Beatrice came down the garden path, it was observable that she handled and inhaled the odor of several of the plants which her father had most sedulously avoided.

"Here, Beatrice," said the latter, "see how many needful offices require to be done to our chief treasure. Yet, shattered as I am, my life might pay the penalty of approaching it so closely as circumstances demand. Henceforth, I fear, this plant must

30   be consigned to your sole charge."

"And gladly will I undertake it," cried again the rich tones of the young lady, as she bent towards the magnificent plant and opened her arms as if to embrace it. "Yes, my sister, my splendor, it shall be Beatrice's task to nurse and serve thee; and thou shalt reward her with thy kisses and perfumed breath, which to her is as the breath of life."

Then, with all the tenderness in her manner that was so strikingly expressed in her words, she busied herself with such attentions as the plant seemed to require; and Giovanni, at his lofty window, rubbed his eyes and almost doubted whether it were a girl tending her favorite flower, or one sister performing the duties of affec-

40   tion to another. The scene soon terminated. Whether Dr. Rappaccini had finished his labors in the garden, or that his watchful eye had caught the stranger's face, he now took his daughter's arm and retired. Night was already closing in; oppressive exhalations seemed to proceed from the plants and steal upward past the open window; and Giovanni, closing the lattice, went to his couch and dreamed of a rich

flower and beautiful girl. Flower and maiden were different, and yet the same, and fraught with some strange peril in either shape.

But there is an influence in the light of morning that tends to rectify whatever errors of fancy, or even of judgment, we may have incurred during the sun's decline, or among the shadows of the night, or in the less wholesome glow of moonshine. Giovanni's first movement, on starting from sleep, was to throw open the window and gaze down into the garden which his dreams had made so fertile of mysteries. He was surprised and a little ashamed to find how real and matter-of-fact an affair it proved to be, in the first rays of the sun which gilded the dew-drops that hung upon leaf and blossom, and, while giving a brighter beauty to each rare 10 flower, brought everything within the limits of ordinary experience. The young man rejoiced that, in the heart of the barren city, he had the privilege of overlooking this spot of lovely and luxuriant vegetation. It would serve, he said to himself, as a symbolic language to keep him in communion with Nature. Neither the sickly and thought-worn Dr. Giacomo Rappaccini, it is true, nor his brilliant daughter, were now visible; so that Giovanni could not determine how much of the singularity which he attributed to both was due to their own qualities and how much to his wonder-working fancy; but he was inclined to take a most rational view of the whole matter.

In the course of the day he paid his respects to Signor Pietro Baglioni, professor 20 of medicine in the university, a physician of eminent repute, to whom Giovanni had brought a letter of introduction. The professor was an elderly personage, apparently of genial nature, and habits that might almost be called jovial. He kept the young man to dinner, and made himself very agreeable by the freedom and liveliness of his conversation, especially when warmed by a flask or two of Tuscan wine. Giovanni, conceiving that men of science, inhabitants of the same city, must needs be on familiar terms with one another, took an opportunity to mention the name of Dr. Rappaccini. But the professor did not respond with so much cordiality as he had anticipated.

"Ill would it become a teacher of the divine art of medicine," said Professor Pietro 30 Baglioni, in answer to a question of Giovanni, "to withhold due and well-considered praise of a physician so eminently skilled as Rappaccini; but, on the other hand, I should answer it but scantily to my conscience were I to permit a worthy youth like yourself, Signor Giovanni, the son of an ancient friend, to imbibe erroneous ideas respecting a man who might hereafter chance to hold your life and death in his hands. The truth is, our worshipful Dr. Rappaccini has as much science as any member of the faculty — with perhaps one single exception — in Padua, or all Italy; but there are certain grave objections to his professional character."

"And what are they?" asked the young man.

"Has my friend Giovanni any disease of body or heart, that he is so inquisitive 40 about physicians?" said the professor, with a smile. "But as for Rappaccini, it is said of him — and I, who know the man well, can answer for its truth — that he cares infinitely more for science than for mankind. His patients are interesting to him only as subjects for some new experiment. He would sacrifice human life, his own among the rest, or whatever else was dearest to him, for the sake of adding so much as a grain of mustard seed to the great heap of his accumulated knowledge."

"Methinks he is an awful man indeed," remarked Guasconti, mentally recalling the cold and purely intellectual aspect of Rappaccini. "And yet, worshipful professor, is it not a noble spirit? Are there many men capable of so spiritual a love of science?"

"God forbid," answered the professor, somewhat testily; "at least, unless they take sounder views of the healing art than those adopted by Rappaccini. It is his theory that all medicinal virtues are comprised within those substances which we term vegetable poisons. These he cultivates with his own hands, and is said even to
10 have produced new varieties of poison, more horribly deleterious than Nature, without the assistance of this learned person, would ever have plagued the world withal. That the signor doctor does less mischief than might be expected with such dangerous substances is undeniable. Now and then, it must be owned, he has effected, or seemed to effect, a marvellous cure; but, to tell you my private mind, Signor Giovanni, he should receive little credit for such instances of success, — they being probably the work of chance, — but should be held strictly accountable for his failures, which may justly be considered his own work."

The youth might have taken Baglioni's opinions with many grains of allowance had he known that there was a professional warfare of long continuance between
20 him and Dr. Rappaccini, in which the latter was generally thought to have gained the advantage. If the reader be inclined to judge for himself, we refer him to certain black-letter tracts on both sides, preserved in the medical department of the University of Padua.

"I know not, most learned professor," returned Giovanni, after musing on what had been said of Rappaccini's exclusive zeal for science, — "I know not how dearly this physician may love his art; but surely there is one object more dear to him. He has a daughter."

"Aha!" cried the professor, with a laugh. "So now our friend Giovanni's secret is out. You have heard of this daughter, whom all the young men in Padua are wild
30 about, though not half a dozen have ever had the good hap to see her face. I know little of the Signora Beatrice save that Rappaccini is said to have instructed her deeply in his science, and that, young and beautiful as fame reports her, she is already qualified to fill a professor's chair. Perchance her father destines her for mine! Other absurd rumors there be, not worth talking about or listening to. So now, Signor Giovanni, drink off your glass of lachryma."

Guasconti returned to his lodgings somewhat heated with the wine he had quaffed, and which caused his brain to swim with strange fantasies in reference to Dr. Rappaccini and the beautiful Beatrice. On his way, happening to pass by a florist's, he bought a fresh bouquet of flowers.

40 Ascending to his chamber, he seated himself near the window, but within the shadow thrown by the depth of the wall, so that he could look down into the garden with little risk of being discovered. All beneath his eye was a solitude. The strange plants were basking in the sunshine, and now and then nodding gently to

---

35 **lachryma,** a rich, sweet Neapolitan wine

one another, as if in ackowledgment of sympathy and kindred. In the midst, by the shattered fountain, grew the magnificent shrub, with its purple gems clustering all over it; they glowed in the air, and gleamed back again out of the depths of the pool, which thus seemed to overflow with colored radiance from the rich reflection that was steeped in it. At first, as we have said, the garden was a solitude. Soon, however, — as Giovanni had half hoped, half feared, would be the case, — a figure appeared beneath the antique sculptured portal, and came down between the rows of plants, inhaling their various perfumes as if she were one of those beings of old classic fable that lived upon sweet odors. On again beholding Beatrice, the young man was even startled to perceive how much her beauty exceeded his recollection 10 of it; so brilliant, so vivid, was its character, that she glowed amid the sunlight, and, as Giovanni whispered to himself, positively illuminated the more shadowy intervals of the garden path. Her face being now more revealed than on the former occasion, he was struck by its expression of simplicity and sweetness, — qualities that had not entered into his idea of her character, and which made him ask anew what manner of mortal she might be. Nor did he fail again to observe, or imagine, an analogy between the beautiful girl and the gorgeous shrub that hung its gem-like flowers over the fountain, — a resemblance which Beatrice seemed to have indulged a fantastic humor in heightening, both by the arrangement of her dress and the selection of its hues.   20

Approaching the shrub, she threw open her arms, as with a passionate ardor, and drew its branches into an intimate embrace — so intimate that her features were hidden in its leafy bosom and her glistening ringlets all intermingled with the flowers.

"Give me thy breath, my sister," exclaimed Beatrice, "for I am faint with common air. And give me this flower of thine, which I separate with gentlest fingers from the stem and place it close beside my heart."

With these words the beautiful daughter of Rappaccini plucked one of the richest blossoms of the shrub, and was about to fasten it in her bosom. But now, unless Giovanni's draughts of wine had bewildered his senses, a singular incident occurred. 30 A small orange-colored reptile, of the lizard or chameleon species, chanced to be creeping along the path, just at the feet of Beatrice. It appeared to Giovanni, — but, at the distance from which he gazed, he could scarcely have seen anything so minute, — it appeared to him, however, that a drop or two of moisture from the broken stem of the flower descended upon the lizard's head. For an instant the reptile contorted itself violently, and then lay motionless in the sunshine. Beatrice observed this remarkable phenomenon, and crossed herself, sadly, but without surprise; nor did she therefore hesitate to arrange the fatal flower in her bosom. There it blushed, and almost glimmered with the dazzling effect of a precious stone, adding to her dress and aspect the one appropriate charm which nothing else in the 40 world could have supplied. But Giovanni, out of the shadow of his window, bent forward and shrank back, and murmured and trembled.

"Am I awake? Have I my senses?" said he to himself. "What is this being? Beautiful shall I call her, or inexpressibly terrible?"

Beatrice now strayed carelessly through the garden, approaching closer beneath Giovanni's window, so that he was compelled to thrust his head quite out of its concealment in order to gratify the intense and painful curiosity which she excited, At this moment there came a beautiful insect over the garden wall; it had, perhaps, wandered through the city, and found no flowers or verdure among those antique haunts of men until the heavy perfumes of Dr. Rappaccini's shrubs had lured it from afar. Without alighting on the flowers, this winged brightness seemed to be attracted by Beatrice, and lingered in the air and fluttered about her head. Now, here it could not be but that Giovanni Guasconti's eyes deceived him. Be that as it
10 might, he fancied that, while Beatrice was gazing at the insect with childish delight, it grew faint and fell at her feet; its bright wings shivered; it was dead — from no cause that he could discern, unless it were the atmosphere of her breath. Again Beatrice crossed herself and sighed heavily as she bent over the dead insect.

An impulsive movement of Giovanni drew her eyes to the window. There she beheld the beautiful head of the young man — rather a Grecian than an Italian head, with fair, regular features, and a glistening of gold among his ringlets — gazing down upon her like a being that hovered in mid air. Scarcely knowing what he did, Giovanni threw down the bouquet which he had hitherto held in his hand.

"Signora," said he, "there are pure and healthful flowers. Wear them for the sake
20 of Giovanni Guasconti."

"Thanks, signor," replied Beatrice, with her rich voice, that came forth as it were like a gush of music, and with a mirthful expression half childish and half womanlike. "I accept your gift, and would fain recompense it with this precious purple flower; but if I toss it into the air it will not reach you. So Signor Guasconti must even content himself with my thanks."

She lifted the bouquet from the ground, and then, as if inwardly ashamed at having stepped aside from her maidenly reserve to respond to a stranger's greeting, passed swiftly homeward through the garden. But few as the moments were, it seemed to Giovanni, when she was on the point of vanishing beneath the sculp-
30 tured portal, that his beautiful bouquet was already beginning to wither in her grasp. It was an idle thought; there could be no possibility of distinguishing a faded flower from a fresh one at so great a distance.

For many days after this incident the young man avoided the window that looked into Dr. Rappaccini's garden, as if something ugly and monstrous would have blasted his eyesight had he been betrayed into a glance. He felt conscious of having put himself, to a certain extent, within the influence of an unintelligible power by the communication which he had opened with Beatrice. The wisest course would have been, if his heart were in any real danger, to quit his lodgings and Padua itself at once; the next wiser, to have accustomed himself, as far as possible, to the famil-
40 iar and daylight view of Beatrice — thus bringing her rigidly and systematically within the limits of ordinary experience. Least of all, while avoiding her sight, ought Giovanni to have remained so near this extraordinary being that the proximity and possibility even of intercourse should give a kind of substance and reality to the wild vagaries which his imagination ran riot continually in producing. Guasconti

had not a deep heart — or, at all events, its depths were not sounded now; but he had a quick fancy and an ardent southern temperament, which rose every instant to a higher fever pitch. Whether or no Beatrice possessed those terrible attributes, that fatal breath, the affinity with those so beautiful and deadly flowers which were indicated by what Giovanni had witnessed, she had at least instilled a fierce and subtle poison in his system. It was not love, although her rich beauty was a madness to him; nor horror, even while he fancied her spirit to be imbued with the same baneful essence that seemed to pervade her physical frame; but a wild offspring of both love and horror that had each parent in it, and burned like one and shivered like the other. Giovanni knew not what to dread; still less did he know what to hope; 10 yet hope and dread kept a continual warfare in his breast, alternately vanquishing one another and starting up afresh to renew the contest. Blessed are all simple emotions, be they dark or bright! It is the lurid intermixture of the two that produces the illuminating blaze of the infernal regions.

Sometimes he endeavored to assuage the fever of his spirit by a rapid walk through the streets of Padua or beyond its gates: his footsteps kept time with the throbbings of his brain, so that the walk was apt to accelerate itself to a race. One day he found himself arrested; his arm was seized by a portly personage, who had turned back on recognizing the young man and expended much breath in overtaking him.   20

"Signor Giovanni! Stay, my young friend!" cried he. "Have you forgotten me? That might well be the case if I were as much altered as yourself."

It was Baglioni, whom Giovanni had avoided ever since their first meeting, from a doubt that the professor's sagacity would look too deeply into his secrets. Endeavoring to recover himself, he stared forth wildly from his inner world into the outer one and spoke like a man in a dream.

"Yes; I am Giovanni Guasconti. You are Professor Pietro Baglioni. Now let me pass!"

"Not yet, not yet, Signor Giovanni Guasconti," said the professor, smiling, but at the same time scrutinizing the youth with an earnest glance. "What! did I grow 30 up side by side with your father? and shall his son pass me like a stranger in these old streets of Padua? Stand still, Signor Giovanni; for we must have a word or two before we part."

"Speedily, then, most worshipful professor, speedily," said Giovanni, with feverish impatience. "Does not your worship see that I am in haste?"

Now, while he was speaking there came a man in black along the street, stooping and moving feebly like a person in inferior health. His face was all overspread with a most sickly and sallow hue, but yet so pervaded with an expression of piercing and active intellect that an observer might easily have overlooked the merely physical attributes and have seen only this wonderful energy. As he passed, this per- 40 son exchanged a cold and distant salutation with Baglioni, but fixed his eyes upon Giovanni with an intentness that seemed to bring out whatever was within him worthy of notice. Nevertheless, there was a peculiar quietness in the look, as if taking merely a speculative, not a human, interest in the young man.

"It is Dr. Rappaccini!" whispered the professor when the stranger had passed. "Has he ever seen your face before?"

"Not that I know," answered Giovanni, starting at the name.

"He *has* seen you! he must have seen you!" said Baglioni, hastily. "For some purpose or other, this man of science is making a study of you. I know that look of his! It is the same that coldly illuminates his face as he bends over a bird, a mouse, or a butterfly, which, in pursuance of some experiment, he has killed by the perfume of a flower; a look as deep as Nature itself, but without Nature's warmth of love. Signor Giovanni, I will stake my life upon it, you are the subject of one of
10 Rappaccini's experiments!"

"Will you make a fool of me?" cried Giovanni, passionately. "*That,* signor professor, were an untoward experiment."

"Patience! patience!" replied the imperturbable professor. "I tell thee, my poor Giovanni, that Rappaccini has a scientific interest in thee. Thou hast fallen into fearful hands! And the Signora Beatrice, — what part does she act in this mystery?"

But Guasconti, finding Baglioni's pertinacity intolerable, here broke away, and was gone before the professor could again seize his arm. He looked after the young man intently and shook his head.

"This must not be," said Baglioni to himself. "The youth is the son of my old
20 friend, and shall not come to any harm from which the arcana of medical science can preserve him. Besides, it is too insufferable an impertinence in Rappaccini, thus to snatch the lad out of my own hands, as I may say, and make use of him for his infernal experiments. This daughter of his! It shall be looked to. Perchance, most learned Rappaccini, I may foil you where you little dream of it!"

Meanwhile Giovanni had pursued a circuitous route, and at length found himself at the door of his lodgings. As he crossed the threshold he was met by old Lisabetta, who smirked and smiled, and was evidently desirous to attract his attention; vainly, however, as the ebullition of his feelings had momentarily subsided into a cold and dull vacuity. He turned his eyes full upon the withered face that was puckering
30 itself into a smile, but seemed to behold it not. The old dame, therefore, laid her grasp upon his cloak.

"Signor! signor!" whispered she, still with a smile over the whole breadth of her visage, so that it looked not unlike a grotesque carving in wood, darkened by centuries. "Listen, signor! There is a private entrance into the garden!"

"What do you say?" exclaimed Giovanni, turning quickly about, as if an inanimate thing should start into feverish life. "A private entrance into Dr. Rappaccini's garden?"

"Hush! hush! not so loud!" whispered Lisabetta, putting her hand over his mouth. "Yes; into the worshipful doctor's garden, where you may see all his fine shrubbery.
40 Many a young man in Padua would give gold to be admitted among those flowers."

Giovanni put a piece of gold into her hand.

"Show me the way," said he.

A surmise, probably excited by his conversation with Baglioni, crossed his mind, that this interposition of old Lisabetta might perchance be connected with the intrigue, whatever were its nature, in which the professor seemed to suppose that Dr. Rappaccini was involving him. But such a suspicion, though it disturbed Giovanni, was inadequate to restrain him. The instant that he was aware of the possibility of approaching Beatrice, it seemed an absolute necessity of his existence to do so. It mattered not whether she were angel or demon; he was irrevocably within her sphere, and must obey the law that whirled him onward, in ever-lessening circles, towards a result which he did not attempt to foreshadow; and yet, strange to say, there came across him a sudden doubt whether this intense interest on his part were not delusory; whether it were really of so deep and positive a nature as to justify him in now thrusting himself into an incalculable position; whether it were not 10 merely the fantasy of a young man's brain, only slightly or not at all connected with his heart.

He paused, hesitated, turned half about, but again went on. His withered guide led him along several obscure passages, and finally undid a door, through which, as it was opened, there came the sight and sound of rustling leaves, with the broken sunshine glimmering among them. Giovanni stepped forth, and, forcing himself through the entanglement of a shrub that wreathed its tendrils over the hidden entrance, stood beneath his own window in the open area of Dr. Rappaccini's garden.

How often is it the case that, when impossibilities have come to pass and dreams have condensed their misty substance into tangible realities, we find ourselves calm, 20 and even coldly self-possessed, amid circumstances which it would have been a delirium of joy or agony to anticipate! Fate delights to thwart us thus. Passion will choose his own time to rush upon the scene, and lingers sluggishly behind when an appropriate adjustment of events would seem to summon his appearance. So was it now with Giovanni. Day after day his pulses had throbbed with feverish blood at the improbable idea of an interview with Beatrice, and of standing with her, face to face, in this very garden, basking in the Oriental sunshine of her beauty, and snatching from her full gaze the mystery which he deemed the riddle of his own existence. But now there was a singular and untimely equanimity within his breast. He threw a glance around the garden to discover if Beatrice or her father were present, and, 30 perceiving that he was alone, began a critical observation of the plants.

The aspect of one and all of them dissatisfied him; their gorgeousness seemed fierce, passionate, and even unnatural. There was hardly an individual shrub which a wanderer, straying by himself through a forest, would not have been startled to find growing wild, as if an unearthly face had glared at him out of the thicket. Several also would have shocked a delicate instinct by an appearance of artificialness indicating that there had been such commixture, and, as it were, adultery, of various vegetable species, that the production was no longer of God's making, but the monstrous offspring of man's depraved fancy, glowing with only an evil mockery of beauty. They were probably the result of experiment, which in one or two cases had 40 succeeded in mingling plants individually lovely into a compound possessing the questionable and ominous character that distinguished the whole growth of the garden. In fine, Giovanni recognized but two or three plants in the collection, and those of a kind that he well knew to be poisonous. While busy with these contemplations he heard the rustling of a silken garment, and, turning, beheld Beatrice emerging from beneath the sculptured portal.

Giovanni had not considered with himself what should be his deportment; whether he should apologize for his intrusion into the garden, or assume that he was there with the privity at least, if not by the desire, of Dr. Rappaccini or his daughter; but Beatrice's manner placed him at his ease, though leaving him still in doubt by what agency he had gained admittance. She came lightly along the path and met him near the broken fountain. There was surprise in her face, but brightened by a simple and kind expression of pleasure.

10 "You are a connoisseur in flowers, signor," said Beatrice, with a smile, alluding to the bouquet which he had flung her from the window. "It is no marvel, therefore, if the sight of my father's rare collection has tempted you to take a nearer view. If he were here, he could tell you many strange and interesting facts as to the nature and habits of these shrubs; for he has spent a lifetime in such studies, and this garden is his world."

"And yourself, lady," observed Giovanni, "if fame says true, — you likewise are deeply skilled in the virtues indicated by these rich blossoms and these spicy perfumes. Would you deign to be my instructress, I should prove an apter scholar than if taught by Signor Rappaccini himself."

20 "Are there such idle rumors?" asked Beatrice, with the music of a pleasant laugh. "Do people say that I am skilled in my father's science of plants? What a jest is there! No; though I have grown up among these flowers, I know no more of them than their hues and perfume; and sometimes methinks I would fain rid myself of even that small knowledge. There are many flowers here, and those not the least brilliant, that shock and offend me when they meet my eye. But pray, signor, do not believe these stories about my science. Believe nothing of me save what you see with your own eyes."

"And must I believe all that I have seen with my own eyes?" asked Giovanni, pointedly, while the recollection of former scenes made him shrink. "No, signora; 30 you demand too little of me. Bid me believe nothing save what comes from your own lips."

It would appear that Beatrice understood him. There came a deep flush to her cheek; but she looked full into Giovanni's eyes, and responded to his gaze of uneasy suspicion with a queenlike haughtiness.

"I do so bid you, signor," she replied. "Forget whatever you may have fancied in regard to me. If true to the outward senses, still it may be false in its essence; but the words of Beatrice Rappaccini's lips are true from the depths of the heart outward. Those you may believe."

A fervor glowed in her whole aspect and beamed upon Giovanni's consciousness 40 like the light of truth itself; but while she spoke there was a fragrance in the atmosphere around her, rich and delightful, though evanescent, yet which the young man, from an indefinable reluctance, scarcely dared to draw into his lungs. It might be the odor of the flowers. Could it be Beatrice's breath which thus embalmed her words with a strange richness, as if by steeping them in her heart? A faintness passed like a shadow over Giovanni and flitted away; he seemed to gaze through the beautiful girl's eyes into her transparent soul, and felt no more doubt or fear.

The tinge of passion that had colored Beatrice's manner vanished; she became gay, and appeared to derive a pure delight from her communion with the youth not unlike what the maiden of a lonely island might have felt conversing with a voyager from the civilized world. Evidently her experience of life had been confined within the limits of that garden. She talked now about matters as simple as the daylight or summer clouds, and now asked questions in reference to the city, or Giovanni's distant home, his friends, his mother, and his sisters — questions indicating such seclusion, and such lack of familiarity with modes and forms, that 10 Giovanni responded as if to an infant. Her spirit gushed out before him like a fresh rill that was just catching its first glimpse of the sunlight and wondering at the reflections of earth and sky which were flung into its bosom. There came thoughts, too, from a deep source, and fantasies of a gemlike brilliancy, as if diamonds and rubies sparkled upward among the bubbles of the fountain. Ever and anon there gleamed across the young man's mind a sense of wonder that he should be walking side by side with the being who had so wrought upon his imagination, whom he had idealized in such hues of terror, in whom he had positively witnessed such manifestations of dreadful attributes, — that he should be conversing with Beatrice like a brother, and should find her so human and so maidenlike. But such reflections were 20 only momentary; the effect of her character was too real not to make itself familiar at once.

In this free intercourse they had strayed through the garden, and now, after many turns among its avenues, were come to the shattered fountain, beside which grew the magnificent shrub, with its treasury of glowing blossoms. A fragrance was diffused from it which Giovanni recognized as identical with that which he had attributed to Beatrice's breath, but incomparably more powerful. As her eyes fell upon it, Giovanni beheld her press her hand to her bosom as if her heart were throbbing suddenly and painfully.

"For the first time in my life," murmured she, addressing the shrub, "I had for- 30 gotten thee."

"I remember, signora," said Giovanni, "that you once promised to reward me with one of these living gems for the bouquet which I had the happy boldness to fling to your feet. Permit me now to pluck it as a memorial of this interview."

He made a step towards the shrub with extended hand; but Beatrice darted forward, uttering a shriek that went through his heart like a dagger. She caught his hand and drew it back with the whole force of her slender figure. Giovanni felt her touch thrilling through his fibres.

"Touch it not!" exclaimed she, in a voice of agony. "Not for thy life! It is fatal!"

Then, hiding her face, she fled from him and vanished beneath the sculptured 40 portal. As Giovanni followed her with his eyes, he beheld the emaciated figure and pale intelligence of Dr. Rappaccini, who had been watching the scene, he knew not how long, within the shadow of the entrance.

No sooner was Guasconti alone in his chamber than the image of Beatrice came

back to his passionate musings, invested with all the witchery that had been gathering around it ever since his first glimpse of her, and now likewise imbued with a tender warmth of girlish womanhood. She was human; her nature was endowed with all gentle and feminine qualities; she was worthiest to be worshipped; she was capable, surely, on her part, of the height and heroism of love. Those tokens which he had hitherto considered as proofs of a frightful peculiarity in her physical and moral system were now either forgotten, or, by the subtle sophistry of passion transmitted into a golden crown of enchantment, rendering Beatrice the more admirable by so much as she was the more unique. Whatever had looked ugly was now beau-
10 tiful; or, if incapable of such a change, it stole away and hid itself among those shapeless half ideas which throng the dim region beyond the daylight of our perfect consciousness. Thus did he spend the night, nor fell asleep until the dawn had begun to awake the slumbering flowers in Dr. Rappaccini's garden, whither Giovanni's dreams doubtless led him. Up rose the sun in his due season, and, flinging his beams upon the young man's eyelids, awoke him to a sense of pain. When thoroughly aroused, he became sensible of a burning and tingling agony in his hand — in his right hand — the very hand which Beatrice had grasped in her own when he was on the point of plucking one of the gemlike flowers. On the back of that hand there was now a purple print like that of four small fingers, and the likeness of a slender
20 thumb upon his wrist.

Oh, how stubbornly does love, — or even that cunning semblance of love which flourishes in the imagination, but strikes no depth of root into the heart, — how stubbornly does it hold its faith until the moment comes when it is doomed to vanish into thin mist! Giovanni wrapped a handkerchief about his hand and wondered what evil thing had stung him, and soon forgot his pain in a reverie of Beatrice.

After the first interview, a second was in the inevitable course of what we call fate. A third; a fourth; and a meeting with Beatrice in the garden was no longer an incident in Giovanni's daily life, but the whole space in which he might be said to live; for the anticipation and memory of that ecstatic hour made up the remainder. Nor
30 was it otherwise with the daughter of Rappaccini. She watched for the youth's appearance, and flew to his side with confidence as unreserved as if they had been playmates from early infancy — as if they were such playmates still. If, by any unwonted chance, he failed to come at the appointed moment, she stood beneath the window and sent up the rich sweetness of her tones to float around him in his chamber and echo and reverberate throughout his heart: "Giovanni! Giovanni! Why tarriest thou? Come down!" And down he hastened into that Eden of poisonous flowers.

But, with all this intimate familiarity, there was still a reserve in Beatrice's demeanor, so rigidly and invariably sustained that the idea of infringing it scarcely
40 occurred to his imagination. By all appreciable signs, they loved; they had looked love with eyes that conveyed the holy secret from the depths of one soul into the depths of the other, as if it were too sacred to be whispered by the way; they had even spoken love in those gushes of passion when their spirits darted forth in articulated breath like tongues of long-hidden flame; and yet there had been no seal

of lips, no clasp of hands, nor any slightest caress such as love claims and hallows. He had never touched one of the gleaming ringlets of her hair; her garment — so marked was the physical barrier between them — had never been waved against him by a breeze. On the few occasions when Giovanni had seemed tempted to overstep the limit, Beatrice grew so sad, so stern, and withal wore such a look of desolate separation, shuddering at itself, that not a spoken word was requisite to repel him. At such times he was startled at the horrible suspicions that rose, monster-like, out of the caverns of his heart and stared him in the face; his love grew thin and faint as the morning mist, his doubts alone had substance. But, when Beatrice's face brightened again after the momentary shadow, she was transformed at once from the mys- 10 terious, questionable being whom he had watched with so much awe and horror; she was now the beautiful and unsophisticated girl whom he felt that his spirit knew with a certainty beyond all other knowledge.

A considerable time had now passed since Giovanni's last meeting with Baglioni. One morning, however, he was disagreeably surprised by a visit from the professor, whom he had scarcely thought of for whole weeks, and would willingly have forgotten still longer. Given up as he had long been to a pervading excitement, he could tolerate no companions except upon condition of their perfect sympathy with his present state of feeling. Such sympathy was not to be expected from Professor Baglioni.   20

The visitor chatted carelessly for a few minutes about the gossip of the city and the university, and then took up another topic.

"I have been reading an old classic author lately," said he, "and met with a story that strangely interested me. Possibly you may remember it. It is of an Indian prince, who sent a beautiful woman as a present to Alexander the Great. She was as lovely as the dawn and gorgeous as the sunset; but what especially distinguished her was a certain rich perfume in her breath — richer than a garden of Persian roses. Alexander, as was natural to a youthful conqueror, fell in love at first sight with this magnificent stranger; but a certain sage physician, happening to be present, discovered a terrible secret in regard to her."   30

"And what was that?" asked Giovanni, turning his eyes downward to avoid those of the professor.

"That this lovely woman," continued Baglioni, with emphasis, "had been nourished with poisons from her birth upward, until her whole nature was so imbued with them that she herself had become the deadliest poison in existence. Poison was her element of life. With that rich perfume of her breath she blasted the very air. Her love would have been poison — her embrace death. Is not this a marvellous tale?"

"A childish fable," answered Giovanni, nervously starting from his chair. "I marvel how your worship finds time to read such nonsense among your graver studies." 40

---

23 **author.** The reference is to Sir Thomas Browne's *Pseudodoxia Epidemica,* Bk. VII, Ch. 17. Hawthorne had copied in his notebooks: "A story there passeth of an Indian King, that sent unto Alexander a fair woman fed with Aconites and other poysons, with this intent, either by converse or copulation complexionally to destroy him"

"By the by," said the professor, looking uneasily about him, "what singular fragrance is this in your apartment? Is it the perfume of your gloves? It is faint, but delicious; and yet, after all, by no means agreeable. Were I to breathe it long, methinks it would make me ill. It is like the breath of a flower; but I see no flowers in the chamber."

"Nor are there any," replied Giovanni, who had turned pale as the professor spoke; "nor, I think, is there any fragrance except in your worship's imagination. Odors, being a sort of element combined of the sensual and the spiritual, are apt to deceive us in this manner. The recollection of a perfume, the bare idea of it, may easily be
10 mistaken for a present reality."

"Ay; but my sober imagination does not often play such tricks," said Baglioni; "and, were I to fancy any kind of odor, it would be that of some vile apothecary drug, wherewith my fingers are likely enough to be imbued. Our worshipful friend Rappaccini, as I have heard, tinctures his medicaments with odors richer than those of Araby. Doubtless, likewise, the fair and learned Signora Beatrice would minister to her patients with draughts as sweet as a maiden's breath; but woe to him that sips them!"

Giovanni's face evinced many contending emotions. The tone in which the professor alluded to the pure and lovely daughter of Rappaccini was a torture to his
20 soul; and yet the intimation of a view of her character, opposite to his own, gave instantaneous distinctness to a thousand dim suspicions, which now grinned at him like so many demons. But he strove hard to quell them and to respond to Baglioni with a true lover's perfect faith.

"Signor professor," said he, "you were my father's friend; perchance, too, it is your purpose to act a friendly part towards his son. I would fain feel nothing towards you save respect and deference; but I pray you to observe, signor, that there is one subject on which we must not speak. You know not the Signora Beatrice. You cannot, therefore, estimate the wrong — the blasphemy, I may even say — that is offered to her character by a light or injurious word."

30 "Giovanni! my poor Giovanni!" answered the professor, with a calm expression of pity, "I know this wretched girl far better than yourself. You shall hear the truth in respect to the poisoner Rappaccini and his poisonous daughter; yes, poisonous as she is beautiful. Listen; for, even should you do violence to my gray hairs, it shall not silence me. That old fable of the Indian woman has become a truth by the deep and deadly science of Rappaccini and in the person of the lovely Beatrice."

Giovanni groaned and hid his face.

"Her father," continued Baglioni, "was not restrained by natural affection from offering up his child in this horrible manner as the victim of his insane zeal for science; for, let us do him justice, he is as true a man of science as ever distilled his
40 own heart in an alembic. What, then, will be your fate? Beyond a doubt you are selected as the material of some new experiment. Perhaps the result is to be death; perhaps a fate more awful still. Rappaccini, with what he calls the interest of science before his eyes, will hesitate at nothing."

---

14 **odors . . . Araby,** reminiscent of Shakespeare's "perfumes of Araby," *Macbeth,* Act V., sc. i, l. 57

"It is a dream," muttered Giovanni to himself; "surely it is a dream."

"But," resumed the professor, "be of good cheer, son of my friend. It is not yet too late for the rescue. Possibly we may even succeed in bringing back this miserable child within the limits of ordinary nature, from which her father's madness has estranged her. Behold this little silver vase! It was wrought by the hands of the renowned Benvenuto Cellini, and is well worthy to be a love gift to the fairest dame in Italy. But its contents are invaluable. One little sip of this antidote would have rendered the most virulent poisons of the Borgias innocuous. Doubt not that it will be as efficacious against those of Rappaccini. Bestow the vase, and the precious liquid within it, on your Beatrice, and hopefully await the result."   10

Baglioni laid a small, exquisitely wrought silver vial on the table and withdrew, leaving what he had said to produce its effect upon the young man's mind.

"We will thwart Rappaccini yet," thought he, chuckling to himself, as he descended the stairs; "but, let us confess the truth of him, he is a wonderful man — a wonderful man indeed; a vile empiric, however, in his practice, and therefore not to be tolerated by those who respect the good old rules of the medical profession."

Throughout Giovanni's whole acquaintance with Beatrice, he had occasionally, as we have said, been haunted by dark surmises as to her character; yet so thoroughly had she made herself felt by him as a simple, natural, most affectionate, and guileless creature, that the image now held up by Professor Baglioni looked as strange   20 and incredible as if it were not in accordance with his own original conception. True, there were ugly recollections connected with his first glimpses of the beautiful girl; he could not quite forget the bouquet that withered in her grasp, and the insect that perished amid the sunny air, by no ostensible agency save the fragrance of her breath. These incidents, however, dissolving in the pure light of her character, had no longer the efficacy of facts, but were acknowledged as mistaken fantasies, by whatever testimony of the senses they might appear to be substantiated. There is something truer and more real than what we can see with the eyes and touch with the finger. On such better evidence had Giovanni founded his confidence in Beatrice, though rather by the necessary force of her high attributes than by any deep and   30 generous faith on his part. But now his spirit was incapable of sustaining itself at the height to which the early enthusiasm of passion had exalted it; he fell down, grovelling among earthly doubts, and defiled therewith the pure whiteness of Beatrice's image. Not that he gave her up; he did but distrust. He resolved to institute some decisive test that should satisfy him, once for all, whether there were those dreadful peculiarities in her physical nature which could not be supposed to exist without some corresponding monstrosity of soul. His eyes, gazing down afar, might have deceived him as to the lizard, the insect, and the flowers; but if he could witness, at the distance of a few paces, the sudden blight of one fresh and healthful flower in Beatrice's hand, there would be room for no further question. With this   40

---

6 **Benvenuto Cellini** (1500-1571), Italian artist in metal and author   8 **Borgias,** Cesare Borgia (1476-1507), Italian cardinal and military leader, and his sister, Lucrezia Borgia (1480-1519); both were wicked and unscrupulous

idea he hastened to the florist's and purchased a bouquet that was still gemmed with the morning dew-drops.

It was now the customary hour of his daily interview with Beatrice. Before descending into the garden, Giovanni failed not to look at his figure in the mirror, — a vanity to be expected in a beautiful young man, yet, as displaying itself at that troubled and feverish moment, the token of a certain shallowness of feeling and insincerity of character. He did gaze, however, and said to himself that his features had never before possessed so rich a grace, nor his eyes such vivacity, nor his cheeks so warm a hue of superabundant life.

10 "As least," thought he, "her poison has not yet insinuated itself into my system. I am no flower to perish in her grasp."

With that thought he turned his eyes on the bouquet, which he had never once laid aside from his hand. A thrill of indefinable horror shot through his frame on perceiving that those dewy flowers were already beginning to droop; they wore the aspect of things that had been fresh and lovely yesterday. Giovanni grew white as marble, and stood motionless before the mirror, staring at his own reflection there as at the likeness of something frightful. He remembered Baglioni's remark about the fragrance that seemed to pervade the chamber. It must have been the poison in his breath! Then he shuddered — shuddered at himself. Recovering from his stupor,
20 he began to watch with curious eye a spider that was busily at work hanging its web from the antique cornice of the apartment, crossing and recrossing the artful system of interwoven lines — as vigorous and active a spider as ever dangled from an old ceiling. Giovanni bent towards the insect, and emitted a deep, long breath. The spider suddenly ceased its toil; the web vibrated with a tremor originating in the body of the small artisan. Again Giovanni sent forth a breath, deeper, longer, and imbued with a venomous feeling out of his heart: he knew not whether he were wicked, or only desperate. The spider made a convulsive gripe with his limbs and hung dead across the window.

"Accursed! accursed!" muttered Giovanni, addressing himself. "Hast thou grown
30 so poisonous that this deadly insect perished by thy breath?"

At that moment a rich, sweet voice came floating up from the garden.

"Giovanni! Giovanni! It is past the hour! Why tarriest thou? Come down!"

"Yes," muttered Giovanni again. "She is the only being whom my breath may not slay! Would that it might!"

He rushed down, and in an instant was standing before the bright and loving eyes of Beatrice. A moment ago his wrath and despair had been so fierce that he could have desired nothing so much as to wither her by a glance; but with her actual presence there came influences which had too real an existence to be at once shaken off: recollections of the delicate and benign power of her feminine nature, which had
40 so often enveloped him in a religious calm; recollections of many a holy and passionate outgush of her heart, when the pure fountain had been unsealed from its depths and made visible in its transparency to his mental eye; recollections which, had Giovanni known how to estimate them, would have assured him that all this ugly mystery was but an earthly illusion, and that, whatever mist of evil might seem

to have gathered over her, the real Beatrice was a heavenly angel. Incapable as he was of such high faith, still her presence had not utterly lost its magic. Giovanni's rage was quelled into an aspect of sullen insensibility. Beatrice, with a quick spiritual sense, immediately felt that there was a gulf of blackness between them which neither he nor she could pass. They walked on together, sad and silent, and came thus to the marble fountain and to its pool of water on the ground, in the midst of which grew the shrub that bore gem-like blossoms. Giovanni was affrighted at the eager enjoyment — the appetite, as it were — with which he found himself inhaling the fragrance of the flowers.

"Beatrice," asked he, abruptly, "whence came this shrub?"   10

"My father created it," answered she, with simplicity.

"Created it! created it!" repeated Giovanni. "What mean you, Beatrice?"

"He is a man fearfully acquainted with the secrets of Nature," replied Beatrice; "and, at the hour when I first drew breath, this plant sprang from the soil, the offspring of his science, of his intellect, while I was but his earthly child. Approach it not!" continued she, observing with terror that Giovanni was drawing nearer to the shrub. "It has qualities that you little dream of. But I, dearest Giovanni, — I grew up and blossomed with the plant and was nourished with its breath. It was my sister, and I loved it with a human affection; for, alas! — hast thou not suspected it? — there was an awful doom."   20

Here Giovanni frowned so darkly upon her that Beatrice paused and trembled. But her faith in his tenderness reassured her, and made her blush that she had doubted for an instant.

"There was an awful doom," she continued, "the effect of my father's fatal love of science, which estranged me from all society of my kind. Until Heaven sent thee, dearest Giovanni, oh, how lonely was thy poor Beatrice!"

"Was it a hard doom?" asked Giovanni, fixing his eyes upon her.

"Only of late have I known how hard it was," answered she, tenderly. "Oh, yes; but my heart was torpid, and therefore quiet."

Giovanni's rage broke forth from his sullen gloom like a lightning flash out of a 30
dark cloud.

"Accursed one!" cried he, with venomous scorn and anger. "And, finding thy solitude wearisome, thou hast severed me likewise from all the warmth of life and enticed me into thy region of unspeakable horror!"

"Giovanni!" exclaimed Beatrice, turning her large bright eyes upon his face. The force of his words had not found its way into her mind; she was merely thunderstruck.

"Yes, poisonous thing!" repeated Giovanni, beside himself with passion. "Thou hast done it! Thou hast blasted me! Thou hast filled my veins with poison! Thou hast made me as hateful, as ugly, as loathsome and deadly a creature as thyself — a world's wonder of hideous monstrosity! Now, if our breath be happily as fatal to 40
ourselves as to all others, let us join our lips in one kiss of unutterable hatred, and so die!"

"What has befallen me?" murmured Beatrice, with a low moan out of her heart. "Holy Virgin, pity me, a poor heart-broken child!"

"Thou, — dost thou pray?" cried Giovanni, still with the same fiendish scorn. "Thy very prayers, as they come from thy lips, taint the atmosphere with death. Yes, yes; let us pray! Let us to church and dip our fingers in the holy water at the portal! They that come after us will perish as by a pestilence! Let us sign crosses in the air! It will be scattering curses abroad in the likeness of holy symbols!"

"Giovanni," said Beatrice, calmly, for her grief was beyond passion, "why dost thou join thyself with me thus in those terrible words? I, it is true, am the horrible thing thou namest me. But thou, — what hast thou to do, save with one other shudder at my hideous misery to go forth out of the garden and mingle with thy race, and forget that there ever crawled on earth such a monster as poor Beatrice?"

"Dost thou pretend ignorance?" asked Giovanni, scowling upon her. "Behold! this power have I gained from the pure daughter of Rappaccini."

There was a swarm of summer insects flitting through the air in search of the food promised by the flower odors of the fatal garden. They circled round Giovanni's head, and were evidently attracted towards him by the same influence which had drawn them for an instant within the sphere of several of the shrubs. He sent forth a breath among them, and smiled bitterly at Beatrice as at least a score of the insects fell dead upon the ground.

"I see it! I see it!" shrieked Beatrice. "It is my father's fatal science! No, no, Giovanni; it was not I! Never! never! I dreamed only to love thee and be with thee a little time, and so to let thee pass away, leaving but thine image in mine heart; for, Giovani, believe it, though my body be nourished with poison, my spirit is God's creature, and craves love as its daily food. But my father, — he has united us in this fearful sympathy. Yes; spurn me, tread upon me, kill me! Oh, what is death after such words as thine? But it was not I. Not for a world of bliss would I have done it."

Giovanni's passion had exhausted itself in its outburst from his lips. There now came across him a sense, mournful, and not without tenderness, of the intimate and peculiar relationship between Beatrice and himself. They stood, as it were, in an utter solitude, which would be made none the less solitary by the densest throng of human life. Ought not, then, the desert of humanity around them to press this insulated pair closer together? If they should be cruel to one another, who was there to be kind to them? Besides, thought Giovanni, might there not still be a hope of his returning within the limits of ordinary nature, and leading Beatrice, the redeemed Beatrice, by the hand? O, weak, and selfish, and unworthy spirit, that could dream of an earthly union and earthly happiness as possible, after such deep love had been so bitterly wronged as was Beatrice's love by Giovanni's blighting words! No, no; there could be no such hope. She must pass heavily, with that broken heart, across the borders of Time — she must bathe her hurts in some fount of paradise, and forget her grief in the light of immortality, and *there* be well.

But Giovanni did not know it.

"Dear Beatrice," said he, approaching her, while she shrank away as always at his approach, but now with a different impulse, "dearest Beatrice, our fate is not yet so desperate. Behold! there is a medicine, potent, as a wise physician has assured me, and almost divine in its efficacy. It is composed of ingredients the most opposite to those by which thy awful father has brought this calamity upon thee and me. It is distilled of blessed herbs. Shall we not quaff it together, and thus be purified from evil?"

"Give it me!" said Beatrice, extending her hand to receive the little silver vial which Giovanni took from his bosom. She added, with a peculiar emphasis, "I will drink; but do thou await the result."

She put Baglioni's antidote to her lips; and, at the same moment, the figure of Rappaccini emerged from the portal and came slowly towards the marble fountain. As he drew near, the pale man of science seemed to gaze with a triumphant expression at the beautiful youth and maiden, as might an artist who should spend his life in achieving a picture or a group of statuary and finally be satisfied with his   10 success. He paused; his bent form grew erect with conscious power; he spread out his hands over them in the attitude of a father imploring a blessing upon his children; but those were the same hands that had thrown poison into the stream of their lives. Giovanni trembled. Beatrice shuddered nervously, and pressed her hand upon her heart.

"My daughter," said Rappaccini, "thou art no longer lonely in the world. Pluck one of those precious gems from thy sister shrub and bid thy bridegroom wear it in his bosom. It will not harm him now. My science and the sympathy between thee and him have so wrought within his system, that he now stands apart from common men, as thou dost, daughter of my pride and triumph, from ordinary women.   20 Pass on, then, through the world, most dear to one another and dreadful to all besides!"

"My father," said Beatrice, feebly, — and still as she spoke she kept her hand upon her heart, — "wherefore didst thou inflict this miserable doom upon thy child?"

"Miserable!" exclaimed Rappaccini. "What mean you, foolish girl? Dost thou deem it misery to be endowed with marvellous gifts against which no power nor strength could avail an enemy — misery, to be able to quell the mightiest with a breath — misery, to be as terrible as thou art beautiful? Wouldst thou, then, have preferred the condition of a weak woman, exposed to all evil and capable of none?"

"I would fain have been loved, not feared," murmured Beatrice, sinking down upon   30 the ground. "But now it matters not. I am going, father, where the evil which thou hast striven to mingle with my being will pass away like a dream — like the fragrance of these poisonous flowers, which will no longer taint my breath among the flowers of Eden. Farewell, Giovanni! Thy words of hatred are like lead within my heart; but they, too, will fall away as I ascend. Oh, was there not, from the first, more poison in thy nature than in mine?"

To Beatrice, — so radically had her earthly part been wrought upon by Rappaccini's skill, — as poison had been life, so the powerful antidote was death; and thus the poor victim of man's ingenuity and of thwarted nature, and of the fatality that attends all such efforts of perverted wisdom, perished there, at the feet of her father   40 and Giovanni. Just at that moment Professor Pietro Baglioni looked forth from the window, and called loudly, in a tone of triumph mixed with horror, to the thunder-stricken man of science, —

"Rappaccini! Rappaccini! and is *this* the upshot of your experiment!"   1844

The Old Manse

The Author Makes the Reader Acquainted with His Abode

The following essay is a pleasant account of Hawthorne's life at the Old Manse in Concord, where he took his bride, Sophia Peabody, upon their marriage in July 1842, and where they lived until the autumn of 1845. Drawn largely from the fuller and more intimate record preserved in The American Notebooks, *it was written after the author had moved back to Salem, and serves as an introduction to the collection of tales and sketches entitled* Mosses from an Old Manse, *published in 1846. Like many other examples in his writings — notably "The Custom House," which is prefatory to* The Scarlet Letter, *and the sketches in* Our Old Home *— "The Old Manse" shows Hawthorne's mastery of the informal essay: the delicate humor, the ripe wisdom, and the ease and naturalness of style make for excellence in this kind of writing.*

Between two tall gateposts of rough-hewn stone (the gate itself having fallen from its hinges at some unknown epoch) we beheld the gray front of the old parsonage terminating the vista of an avenue of black ash-trees. It was now a twelvemonth since the funeral procession of the venerable clergyman, its last inhabitant, had turned from that gateway towards the village burying-ground. The wheel-track leading to the door, as well as the whole breadth of the avenue, was almost overgrown with grass, affording dainty mouthfuls to two or three vagrant cows and an old white horse who had his own living to pick up along the roadside. The glimmering sha-dows that lay half asleep between the door of the house and the public highway
10 were a kind of spiritual medium, seen through which the edifice had not quite the aspect of belonging to the material world. Certainly it had little in common with those ordinary abodes which stand so imminent upon the road that every passer-by can thrust his head, as it were, into the domestic circle. From these quiet windows the figures of passing travellers looked too remote and dim to disturb the sense of privacy. In its near retirement and accessible seclusion it was the very spot for the residence of a clergyman, — a man not estranged from human life, yet enveloped in the midst of it with a veil woven of intermingled gloom and brightness. It was worthy to have been one of the time-honored parsonages of England in which, through many generations, a succession of holy occupants pass from youth to age,
20 and bequeath each an inheritance of sanctity to pervade the house and hover over it as with an atmosphere.

Nor, in truth, had the Old Manse ever been profaned by a lay occupant until that memorable summer afternoon when I entered it as my home. A priest had built it; a priest had succeeded to it; other priestly men from time to time had dwelt in it; and children born in its chambers had grown up to assume the priestly character. It was awful to reflect how many sermons must have been written there. The latest

---

4 **venerable clergyman,** the Rev. Ezra Ripley, who died in 1841, at the age of ninety   23 **A priest.** The Rev. William Emerson, grandfather of Ralph Waldo Emerson, built the house in 1765

inhabitant alone — he by whose translation to paradise the dwelling was left vacant — had penned nearly three thousand discourses, besides the better, if not the greater, number that gushed living from his lips. How often, no doubt, had he paced to and fro along the avenue, attuning his meditations to the sighs and gentle murmurs, and deep and solemn peals of the wind among the lofty tops of the trees! In that variety of natural utterances he could find something accordant with every passage of his sermon, were it of tenderness or reverential fear. The boughs over my head seemed shadowy with solemn thoughts as well as with rustling leaves. I took shame to myself for having been so long a writer of idle stories, and ventured to hope that wisdom would descend upon me with the falling leaves of the avenue, and   10 that I should light upon an intellectual treasure in the Old Manse well worth those hoards of long-hidden gold which people seek for in moss-grown houses. Profound treatises of morality; a layman's unprofessional and therefore unprejudiced views of religion; histories (such as Bancroft might have written had he taken up his abode here as he once purposed) bright with picture, gleaming over a depth of philosophic thought, — these were the works that might fitly have flowed from such a retirement. In the humblest event I resolved at least to achieve a novel that should evolve some deep lesson and should possess physical substance enough to stand alone.

In furtherance of my design, and as if to leave me no pretext for not fulfilling it, there was in the rear of the house the most delightful little nook of a study that   20 ever afforded its snug seclusion to a scholar. It was here that Emerson wrote Nature; for he was then an inhabitant of the Manse, and used to watch the Assyrian dawn and Paphian sunset and moonrise from the summit of our eastern hill. When I first saw the room its walls were blackened with the smoke of unnumbered years, and made still blacker by the grim prints of Puritan ministers that hung around. These worthies looked strangely like bad angels, or at least like men who had wrestled so continually and so sternly with the devil that somewhat of his sooty fierceness had been imparted to their own visages. They had all vanished now; a cheerful coat of paint and golden-tinted paper-hangings lighted up the small apartment; while the shadow of a willow-tree that swept against the overhanging eaves attempered the   30 cheery western sunshine. In place of the grim prints there was the sweet and lovely head of one of Raphael's Madonnas and two pleasant little pictures of the Lake of Como. The only other decorations were a purple vase of flowers, always fresh, and a bronze one containing graceful ferns. My books (few, and by no means choice; for they were chiefly such waifs as chance had thrown in my way) stood in order about the room, seldom to be disturbed.

The study had three windows, set with little, old-fashioned panes of glass, each with a crack across it. The two on the western side looked, or rather peeped, between the willow branches down into the orchard, with glimpses of the river through

---

14 **Bancroft,** George Bancroft (1800-1891), author of the *History of the United States* (1834-1876)   21
Nature. Emerson's first book, *Nature,* appeared in 1836   22 **Assyrian . . . sunset,** a graceful allusion to the passage in *Nature* in which Emerson said, "The dawn is my Assyria; the sunset and moonrise my Paphos." Assyria was an ancient civilization in Asia Minor, flourishing at the "dawn" of history; Paphos, an ancient city in Cyprus, had a temple to Aphrodite, goddess of love   32 **Lake of Como,** in Italy

the trees. The third, facing northward, commanded a broader view of the river at a spot where its hitherto obscure waters gleam forth into the light of history. It was at this window that the clergyman who then dwelt in the Manse stood watching the outbreak of a long and deadly struggle between two nations; he saw the irregular array of his parishioners on the farther side of the river and the glittering line of the British on the hither bank. He awaited in an agony of suspense the rattle of the musketry. It came, and there needed but a gentle wind to sweep the battle smoke around this quiet house.

Perhaps the reader, whom I cannot help considering as my guest in the Old Manse
10 and entitled to all courtesy in the way of sight-showing, — perhaps he will choose to take a nearer view of the memorable spot. We stand now on the river's brink. It may well be called the Concord, the river of peace and quietness; for it is certainly the most unexcitable and sluggish stream that ever loitered imperceptibly towards its eternity — the sea. Positively, I had lived three weeks beside it before it grew quite clear to my perception which way the current flowed. It never has a vivacious aspect except when a northwestern breeze is vexing its surface on a sunshiny day. From the incurable indolence of its nature, the stream is happily incapable of becoming the slave of human ingenuity, as is the fate of so many a wild, free mountain torrent. While all things else are compelled to subserve some useful purpose, it idles
20 its sluggish life away in lazy liberty, without turning a solitary spindle or affording even water-power enough to grind the corn that grows upon its banks. The torpor of its movement allows it nowhere a bright, pebbly shore, nor so much as a narrow strip of glistening sand, in any part of its course. It slumbers between broad prairies, kissing the long meadow grass, and bathes the overhanging boughs of elder bushes and willows or the roots of elms and ash-trees and clumps of maples. Flags and rushes grow along its plashy shore; the yellow water-lily spreads its broad, flat leaves on the margin; and the fragrant white pond-lily abounds, generally selecting a position just so far from the river's brink that it cannot be grasped save at the hazard of plunging in.
30 It is a marvel whence this perfect flower derives its loveliness and perfume, springing as it does from the black mud over which the river sleeps, and where lurk the slimy eel and speckled frog and the mud turtle, whom continual washing cannot cleanse. It is the very same black mud out of which the yellow lily sucks its obscene life and noisome odor. Thus we see, too, in the world that some persons assimilate only what is ugly and evil from the same moral circumstances which supply good and beautiful results — the fragrance of celestial flowers — to the daily life of others.

The reader must not, from any testimony of mine, contract a dislike towards our slumberous stream. In the light of a calm and golden sunset it becomes lovely beyond expression; the more lovely for the quietude that so well accords with the
40 hour, when even the wind, after blustering all day long, usually hushes itself to rest. Each tree and rock, and every blade of grass, is distinctly imaged, and, however unsightly in reality, assumes ideal beauty in the reflection. The minutest things of earth and the broad aspect of the firmament are pictured equally without effort and

---

4 **outbreak . . . struggle,** the Revolutionary War

with the same felicity of success. All the sky glows downward at our feet; the rich clouds float through the unruffled bosom of the stream like heavenly thoughts through a peaceful heart. We will not, then, malign our river as gross and impure while it can glorify itself with so adequate a picture of the heaven that broods above it; or, if we remember its tawny hue and the muddiness of its bed, let it be a symbol that the earthliest human soul has an infinite spiritual capacity and may contain the better world within its depths. But, indeed, the same lesson might be drawn out of any mud puddle in the streets of a city; and, being taught us everywhere, it must be true.

Come, we have pursued a somewhat devious track in our walk to the battleground. Here we are, at the point where the river was crossed by the old bridge, the possession of which was the immediate object of the contest. On the hither side grow two or three elms, throwing a wide circumference of shade, but which must have been planted at some period within the threescore years and ten that have passed since the battle day. On the farther shore, overhung by a clump of elder bushes, we discern the stone abutment of the bridge. Looking down into the river, I once discovered some heavy fragments of the timbers, all green with half a century's growth of water moss; for during that length of time the tramp of horses and human footsteps has ceased along this ancient highway. The stream has here about the breadth of twenty strokes of a swimmer's arm, — a space not too wide when the bullets were whistling across. Old people who dwell hereabouts will point out the very spots on the western bank where our countrymen fell down and died; and on this side of the river an obelisk of granite has grown up from the soil that was fertilized with British blood. The monument, not more than twenty feet in height, is such as it befitted the inhabitants of a village to erect in illustration of a matter of local interest rather than what was suitable to commemorate an epoch of national history. Still, by the fathers of the village this famous deed was done; and their descendants might rightfully claim the privilege of building a memorial.

A humbler token of the fight, yet a more interesting one than the granite obelisk, may be seen close under the stone-wall which separates the battleground from the precincts of the parsonage. It is the grave — marked by a small, mossgrown fragment of stone at the head and another at the foot — the grave of two British soldiers who were slain in the skirmish, and have ever since slept peacefully where Zechariah Brown and Thomas Davis buried them. Soon was their warfare ended; a weary night march from Boston, a rattling volley of musketry across the river, and then these many years of rest. In the long procession of slain invaders who passed into eternity from the battlefields of the revolution, these two nameless soldiers led the way.

Lowell, the poet, as we were once standing over this grave, told me a tradition in reference to one of the inhabitants below. The story has something deeply impressive, though its circumstances cannot altogether be reconciled with probability. A youth in the service of the clergyman happened to be chopping wood, that April morning, at the back door of the Manse, and when the noise of battle rang from side to side of the bridge he hastened across the intervening field to see what might

be going forward. It is rather strange, by the way, that this lad should have been so diligently at work when the whole population of town and country were startled out of their customary business by the advance of the British troops. Be that as it might, the tradition says that the lad now left his task and hurried to the battlefield with the axe still in his hand. The British had by this time retreated, the Americans were in pursuit; and the late scene of strife was thus deserted by both parties. Two soldiers lay on the ground — one was a corpse; but, as the young New Englander drew nigh, the other Briton raised himself painfully upon his hands and knees and gave a ghastly stare into his face. The boy, — it must have been a nervous impulse,
10 without purpose, without thought, and betokening a sensitive and impressible nature rather than a hardened one, — the boy uplifted his axe and dealt the wounded soldier a fierce and fatal blow upon the head.

I could wish that the grave might be opened; for I would fain know whether either of the skeleton soldiers has the mark of an axe in his skull. The story comes home to me like truth. Oftentimes, as an intellectual and moral exercise, I have sought to follow that poor youth through his subsequent career, and observe how his soul was tortured by the blood stain, contracted as it had been before the long custom of war had robbed human life of its sanctity, and while it still seemed murderous to slay a brother man. This one circumstance has borne more fruit for me than all
20 that history tells us of the fight.

Many strangers come in the summer time to view the battle-ground. For my own part, I have never found my imagination much excited by this or any other scene of historic celebrity; nor would the placid margin of the river have lost any of its charm for me had men never fought and died there. There is a wilder interest in the tract of land — perhaps a hundred yards in breadth — which extends between the battle-field and the northern face of our Old Manse, with its contiguous avenue and orchard. Here, in some unknown age, before the white man came, stood an Indian village, convenient to the river, whence its inhabitants must have drawn so large a part of their subsistence. The site is identified by the spear and arrowheads,
30 the chisels, and other implements of war, labor, and the chase, which the plough turns up from the soil. You see a splinter of stone, half hidden beneath a sod; it looks like nothing worthy of note; but, if you have faith enough to pick it up, behold a relic! Thoreau, who has a strange faculty of finding what the Indians have left behind them, first set me on the search; and I afterwards enriched myself with some very perfect specimens, so rudely wrought that it seemed almost as if chance had fashioned them. Their great charm consists in this rudeness and in the individuality of each article, so different from the productions of civilized machinery, which shapes everything on one pattern. There is exquisite delight, too, in picking up for one's self an arrowhead that was dropped centuries ago and has never been handled
40 since, and which we thus receive directly from the hand of the red hunter, who purposed to shoot it at his game or at an enemy. Such an incident builds up again the Indian village and its encircling forest, and recalls to life the painted chiefs and warriors, the squaws at their household toil, and the children sporting among the wigwams, while the little wind-rocked pappoose swings from the branch of the tree. It

can hardly be told whether it is a joy or a pain, after such a momentary vision, to gaze around in the broad daylight of reality and see stone fences, white houses, potato fields, and men doggedly hoeing in their shirt-sleeves and homespun pantaloons. But this is nonsense. The Old Manse is better than a thousand wigwams.

The Old Manse! We had almost forgotten it, but will return thither through the orchard. This was set out by the last clergyman, in the decline of his life, when the neighbors laughed at the hoary-headed man for planting trees from which he could have no prospect of gathering fruit. Even had that been the case, there was only so much the better motive for planting them, in the pure and unselfish hope of bene-fiting his successors, — an end so seldom achieved by more ambitious efforts. But 10 the old minister, before reaching his patriarchal age of ninety, ate the apples from this orchard during many years, and added silver and gold to his annual stipend by disposing of the superfluity. It is pleasant to think of him walking among the trees in the quiet afternoons of early autumn and picking up here and there a windfall, while he observes how heavily the branches are weighed down, and computes the number of empty flour barrels that will be filled by their burden. He loved each tree, doubtless, as if it had been his own child. An orchard has a relation to man-kind, and readily connects itself with matters of the heart. The trees possess a do-mestic character; they have lost the wild nature of their forest kindred, and have grown humanized by receiving the care of man as well as by contributing to his 20 wants. There is so much individuality of character, too, among apple-trees that it gives them an additional claim to be the objects of human interest. One is harsh and crabbed in its manifestations; another gives us fruit as mild as charity. One is churl-ish and illiberal, evidently grudging the few apples that it bears; another exhausts itself in free-hearted benevolence. The variety of grotesque shapes into which apple-trees contort themselves has its effect on those who get acquainted with them: they stretch out their crooked branches, and take such hold of the imagination that we remember them as humorists and odd-fellows. And what is more melancholy than the old apple-trees that linger about the spot where once stood a homestead, but where there is now only a ruined chimney rising out of a grassy and weed-grown 30 cellar? They offer their fruit to every wayfarer, — apples that are bitter sweet with the moral of Time's vicissitude.

I have met with no other such pleasant trouble in the world as that of finding myself, with only the two or three mouths which it was my privilege to feed, the sole inheritor of the old clergyman's wealth of fruits. Throughout the summer there were cherries and currants; and then came autumn, with his immense burden of apples, dropping them continually from his overladen shoulders as he trudged along. In the stillest afternoon, if I listened, the thump of a great apple was audible, falling without a breath of wind, from the mere necessity of perfect ripeness. And, besides, there were pear-trees, that flung down bushels upon bushels of heavy pears; and 40 peach-trees, which, in a good year, tormented me with peaches, neither to be eaten nor kept, nor, without labor and perplexity, to be given away. The idea of an infinite generosity and exhaustless bounty on the part of our Mother Nature was well worth obtaining through such cares as these. That feeling can be enjoyed in perfection only by the natives of summer islands, where the bread-fruit, the cocoa, the palm, and the orange grow spontaneously and hold forth the ever-ready meal; but likewise almost as well by a man long habituated to city life, who plunges into such a solitude as that of the Old Manse, where he plucks the fruit of trees that he did not plant, and which therefore, to my heterodox taste, bear the closest resemblance to those that grew in Eden. It has been an apothegm these five thousand years, that toil sweetens the bread it earns. For my part (speaking from hard experience, acquired while belaboring the rugged furrows of Brook Farm), I relish best the free gifts of Providence.

10 Not that it can be disputed that the light toil requisite to cultivate a moderately-sized garden imparts such zest to kitchen vegetables as is never found in those of the market gardener. Childless men, if they would know something of the bliss of paternity, should plant a seed, — be it squash, bean, Indian corn, or perhaps a mere flower or worthless weed, — should plant it with their own hands, and nurse it from infancy to maturity altogether by their own care. If there be not too many of them, each individual plant becomes an object of separate interest. My garden, that skirted the avenue of the Manse, was of precisely the right extent. An hour or two of morning labor was all that it required. But I used to visit and revisit it a dozen times a day, and stand in deep contemplation over my vegetable progeny with a love that
20 nobody could share or conceive of who had never taken part in the process of creation. It was one of the most bewitching sights in the world to observe a hill of beans thrusting aside the soil, or a row of early peas just peeping forth sufficiently to trace a line of delicate green. Later in the season the humming-birds were attracted by the blossoms of a peculiar variety of bean; and they were a joy to me, those little spiritual visitants, for deigning to sip airy food out of my nectar cups. Multitudes of bees used to bury themselves in the yellow blossoms of the summer squashes. This, too, was a deep satisfaction; although when they had laden themselves with sweets they flew away to some unknown hive, which would give back nothing in requital of what my garden had contributed. But I was glad thus to fling a benefac-
30 tion upon the passing breeze with the certainty that somebody must profit by it, and that there would be a little more honey in the world to allay the sourness and bitterness which mankind is always complaining of. Yes, indeed; my life was the sweeter for that honey.

Speaking of summer squashes, I must say a word of their beautiful and varied forms. They presented an endless diversity of urns and vases, shallow or deep, scalloped or plain, moulded in patterns which a sculptor would do well to copy, since Art has never invented anything more graceful. A hundred squashes in the garden were worthy, in my eyes at least, of being rendered indestructible in marble. If ever Providence (but I know it never will) should assign me a superfluity of gold, part
40 of it shall be expended for a service of plate, or most delicate porcelain, to be wrought into the shapes of summer squashes gathered from vines which I will plant with my own hands. As dishes for containing vegetables they would be peculiarly appropriate.

---

8 **Brook Farm.** Hawthorne spent most of 1841 in this socialist and utopian community

But not merely the squeamish love of the beautiful was gratified by my toil in the kitchen garden. There was a hearty enjoyment, likewise, in observing the growth of the crook-necked winter squashes, from the first little bulb, with the withered blossom adhering to it, until they lay strewn upon the soil, big, round fellows, hiding their heads beneath the leaves, but turning up their great yellow rotundities to the noontide sun. Gazing at them, I felt that by my agency something worth living for had been done. A new substance was born into the world. They were real and tangible existences, which the mind could seize hold of and rejoice in. A cabbage, too, — especially the early Dutch cabbage, which swells to a monstrous circumference, until its ambitious heart often bursts asunder, — is a matter to be proud of 10 when we can claim a share with the earth and sky in producing it. But, after all, the hugest pleasure is reserved until these vegetable children of ours are smoking on the table, and we, like Saturn, make a meal of them.

What with the river, the battle-field, the orchard and the garden, the reader begins to despair of finding his way back into the Old Manse. But in agreeable weather it is the truest hospitality to keep him out-of-doors. I never grew quite acquainted with my habitation till a long spell of sulky rain had confined me beneath its roof. There could not be a more sombre aspect of external Nature than as then seen from the windows of my study. The great willow-tree had caught and retained among its leaves a whole cataract of water, to be shaken down at intervals by the frequent gusts 20 of wind. All day long, and for a week together, the rain was drip-drip-dripping and splash-splash-splashing from the eaves, and bubbling and foaming into the tubs beneath the spouts. The old, unpainted shingles of the house and out-buildings were black with moisture; and the mosses of ancient growth upon the walls looked green and fresh, as if they were the newest things and afterthought of Time. The usually mirrored surface of the river was blurred by an infinity of raindrops; the whole landscape had a completely water-soaked appearance, conveying the impression that the earth was wet through like a sponge; while the summit of a wooded hill, about a mile distant, was enveloped in a dense mist, where the demon of the tempest seemed to have his abiding-place and to be plotting still direr inclemencies.   30

Nature has no kindness, no hospitality, during a rain. In the fiercest heat of sunny days she retains a secret mercy, and welcomes the wayfarer to shady nooks of the woods whither the sun cannot penetrate; but she provides no shelter against her storms. It makes us shiver to think of those deep, umbrageous recesses, those overshadowing banks, where we found such enjoyment during the sultry afternoons. Not a twig of foliage there but would dash a little shower into our faces. Looking reproachfully towards the impenetrable sky, — if sky there be above that dismal uniformity of cloud, — we are apt to murmur against the whole system of the universe, since it involves the extinction of so many summer days in so short a life by the hissing and spluttering rain. In such spells of weather — and it is to be supposed 40 such weather came — Eve's bower in paradise must have been but a cheerless and aguish kind of shelter, nowise comparable to the old parsonage, which had resources of its own to beguile the week's imprisonment. The idea of sleeping on a couch of wet roses!

Happy the man who in a rainy day can betake himself to a huge garret, stored, like that of the Manse, with lumber that each generation has left behind it from a period before the revolution. Our garret was an arched hall, dimly illuminated through small and dusty windows, it was but a twilight at the best; and there were nooks, or rather caverns, of deep obscurity, the secrets of which I never learned, being too reverent of their dust and cobwebs. The beams and rafters, roughly hewn and with strips of bark still on them, and the rude masonry of the chimneys, made the garret look wild and uncivilized, — an aspect unlike what was seen elsewhere in the quiet and decorous old house. But on one side there was a little whitewashed
10 apartment which bore the traditionary title of the Saint's Chamber, because holy men in their youth had slept and studied and prayed there. With its elevated retirement, its one window, its small fireplace, and its closet, convenient for an oratory, it was the very spot where a young man might inspire himself with solemn enthusiasm and cherish saintly dreams. The occupants, at various epochs, had left brief records and ejaculations inscribed upon the walls. There, too, hung a tattered and shrivelled roll of canvas, which on inspection proved to be the forcibly wrought picture of a clergyman, in wig, band, and gown, holding a Bible in his hand. As I turned his face towards the light he eyed me with an air of authority such as men of his profession seldom assume in our days. The original had been pastor of the
20 parish more than a century ago, a friend of Whitefield, and almost his equal in fervid eloquence. I bowed before the effigy of the dignified divine, and felt as if I had now met face to face with the ghost by whom, as there was reason to apprehend, the Manse was haunted.

Houses of any antiquity in New England are so invariably possessed with spirits that the matter seems hardly worth alluding to. Our ghost used to heave deep sighs in a particular corner of the parlor, and sometimes rustled paper, as if he were turning over a sermon in the long upper entry, — where nevertheless he was invisible in spite of the bright moonshine that fell through the eastern window. Not improbably he wished me to edit and publish a selection from a chest full of manu-
30 script discourses that stood in the garret. Once, while Hillard and other friends sat talking with us in the twilight, there came a rustling noise as of a minister's silk gown, sweeping through the very midst of the company so closely as almost to brush against the chairs. Still there was nothing visible. A yet stranger business was that of a ghostly servant maid, who used to be heard in the kitchen at deepest midnight, grinding coffee, cooking, ironing, — performing, in short, all kinds of domestic labor, — although no traces of anything accomplished could be detected the next morning. Some neglected duty of her servitude — some ill-starched ministerial band — disturbed the poor damsel in her grave and kept her at work without any wages.

But to return from this digression. A part of my predecessor's library was stored
40 in the garret, — no unfit receptacle indeed for such dreary trash as comprised the greater number of volumes. The old books would have been worth nothing at an

---

19 **original . . . Whitefield.** George Whitefield, the English revivalist (see p. 13), had preached in Concord at the invitation of the Rev. Daniel Bliss, the "original" referred to   30 **Hillard,** George Stillman Hillard (1808-1879), a Boston lawyer and the author of travel sketches

auction. In this venerable garret, however, they possessed an interest, quite apart from their literary value, as heirlooms, many of which had been transmitted down through a series of consecrated hands from the days of the mighty Puritan divines. Autographs of famous names were to be seen in faded ink on some of their fly-leaves; and there were marginal observations or interpolated pages closely covered with manuscript in illegible shorthand, perhaps concealing matter of profound truth and wisdom. The world will never be the better for it. A few of the books were Latin folios, written by Catholic authors; others demolished Papistry, as with a sledge-hammer, in plain English. A dissertation on the book of Job — which only Job himself could have had patience to read — filled at least a score of small, thick- 10
set quartos, at the rate of two or three volumes to a chapter. Then there was a vast folio body of divinity — too corpulent a body, it might be feared, to comprehend the spiritual element of religion. Volumes of this form dated back two hundred years or more, and were generally bound in black leather, exhibiting precisely such an appearance as we should attribute to books of enchantment. Others equally antique were of a size proper to be carried in the large waistcoat pockets of old times, — diminutive, but as black as their bulkier brethren, and abundantly inter-fused with Greek and Latin quotations. These little old volumes impressed me as if they had been intended for very large ones, but had been unfortunately blighted at an early stage of their growth.   20

The rain pattered upon the roof and the sky gloomed through the dusty garret windows, while I burrowed among these venerable books in search of any living thought which should burn like a coal of fire, or glow like an inextinguishable gem, beneath the dead trumpery that had long hidden it. But I found no such treasure; all was dead alike; and I could not but muse deeply and wonderingly upon the hu-miliating fact that the works of man's intellect decay like those of his hands. Thought grows mouldy. What was good and nourishing food for the spirits of one generation affords no sustenance for the next. Books of religion, however, cannot be considered a fair test of the enduring and vivacious properties of human thought, because such books so seldom really touch upon their ostensible subject, and have, 30
therefore, so little business to be written at all. So long as an unlettered soul can attain to saving grace, there would seem to be no deadly error in holding theolog-ical libraries to be accumulations of, for the most part, stupendous impertinence.

Many of the books had accrued in the latter years of the last clergyman's lifetime. These threatened to be of even less interest than the elder works, a century hence, to any curious inquirer who should then rummage them as I was doing now. Volumes of the "Liberal Preacher" and "Christian Examiner," occasional sermons, contro-versial pamphlets, tracts, and other productions of a like fugitive nature took the place of the thick and heavy volumes of past time. In a physical point of view there was much the same difference as between a feather and a lump of lead; but, intel- 40
lectually regarded, the specific gravity of old and new was about upon a par. Both also were alike frigid. The elder books, nevertheless, seemed to have been earnestly written, and might be conceived to have possessed warmth at some former period;

37 **Liberal Preacher** . . . Christian Examiner, theological magazines

although, with the lapse of time, the heated masses had cooled down even to the freezing point. The frigidity of the modern productions, on the other hand, was characteristic and inherent, and evidently had little to do with the writer's qualities of mind and heart. In fine, of this whole dusty heap of literature I tossed aside all the sacred part, and felt myself none the less a Christian for eschewing it. There appeared no hope of either mounting to the better world on a Gothic staircase of ancient folios or of flying thither on the wings of a modern tract.

Nothing, strange to say, retained any sap except what had been written for the passing day and year without the remotest pretension or idea of permanence. There were a few old newspapers, and still older almanacs, which reproduced to my mental eye the epochs when they had issued from the press with a distinctness that was altogether unaccountable. It was as if I had found bits of magic looking-glass among the books, with the images of a vanished century in them. I turned my eyes towards the tattered picture above mentioned, and asked of the austere divine wherefore it was that he and his brethren, after the most painful rummaging and groping into their minds, had been able to produce nothing half so real as these newspaper scribblers and almanac makers had thrown off in the effervescence of a moment. The portrait responded not; so I sought an answer for myself. It is the age itself that writes newspapers and almanacs, which, therefore, have a distinct purpose and meaning at the time, and a kind of intelligible truth for all times; whereas most other works — being written by men who, in the very act, set themselves apart from their age — are likely to possess little significance when new, and none at all when old. Genius, indeed, melts many ages into one, and thus effects something permanent, yet still with a similarity of office to that of the more ephemeral writer. A work of genius is but the newspaper of a century, or perchance of a hundred centuries.

Lightly as I have spoken of these old books, there yet lingers with me a superstitious reverence for literature of all kinds. A bound volume has a charm in my eyes similar to what scraps of manuscript possess for the good Mussulman. He imagines that those wind-wafted records are perhaps hallowed by some sacred verse; and I, that every new book or antique one may contain the "open sesame," — the spell to disclose treasures hidden in some unsuspected cave of Truth. Thus it was not without sadness that I turned away from the library of the Old Manse.

Blessed was the sunshine when it came again at the close of another stormy day, beaming from the edge of the western horizon; while the massive firmament of clouds threw down all the gloom it could, but served only to kindle the golden light into a more brilliant glow by the strongly contrasted shadows. Heaven smiled at the earth, so long unseen, from beneath its heavy eyelid. Tomorrow for the hill-tops and the wood paths.

Or it might be that Ellery Channing came up the avenue to join me in a fishing excursion on the river. Strange and happy times were those when we cast aside all irksome forms and strait-laced habitudes, and delivered ourselves up to the free air, to live like the Indians or any less conventional race during one bright semi-circle

---

28 **Mussulman**, a Moslem   39 **Ellery Channing**. William Ellery Channing (1818-1901), nephew of the famous Unitarian clergyman of the same name, was a poet of the Transcendental school

of the sun. Rowing our boat against the current, between wide meadows, we turned aside into the Assabeth. A more lovely stream than this, for a mile above its junction with the Concord, has never flowed on earth, — nowhere, indeed, except to lave the interior regions of a poet's imagination. It is sheltered from the breeze by woods and a hill-side; so that elsewhere there might be a hurricane, and here scarcely a ripple across the shaded water. The current lingers along so gently that the mere force of the boatman's will seems sufficient to propel his craft against it. It comes flowing softly through the mid-most privacy and deepest heart of a wood which whispers it to be quiet; while the stream whispers back again from its sedgy borders, as if river and wood were hushing one another to sleep. Yes; the river sleeps along 10 its course and dreams of the sky and of the clustering foliage, amid which fall showers of broken sunlight, imparting specks of vivid cheerfulness, in contrast with the quiet depth of the prevailing tint. Of all this scene, the slumbering river has a dream picture in its bosom. Which, after all, was the most real — the picture, or the original? — the objects palpable to our grosser senses, or their apotheosis in the stream beneath? Surely the disembodied images stand in closer relation to the soul. But both the original and the reflection had here an ideal charm; and, had it been a thought more wild, I could have fancied that this river had strayed forth out of the rich scenery of my companion's inner world; only the vegetation along its banks should then have had an Oriental character.   20

Gentle and unobtrusive as the river is, yet the tranquil woods seem hardly satisfied to allow it passage. The trees are rooted on the very verge of the water, and dip their pendent branches into it. At one spot there is a lofty bank, on the slope of which grow some hemlocks, declining across the stream with outstretched arms, as if resolute to take the plunge. In other places the banks are almost on a level with the water; so that the quiet congregation of trees set their feet in the flood, and are fringed with foliage down to the surface. Cardinal flowers kindle their spiral flames and illuminate the dark nooks among the shrubbery. The pond-lily grows abundantly along the margin — that delicious flower, which, as Thoreau tells me, opens its virgin bosom to the first sunlight and perfects its being through the magic 30 of that genial kiss. He has beheld beds of them unfolding in due succession as the sunrise stole gradually from flower to flower — a sight not to be hoped for unless when a poet adjusts his inward eye to a proper focus with the outward organ. Grapevines here and there twine themselves around shrub and tree and hang their clusters over the water within reach of the boatman's hand. Oftentimes they unite two trees of alien race in an inextricable twine, marrying the hemlock and the maple against their will, and enriching them with a purple offspring of which neither is the parent. One of these ambitious parasites has climbed into the upper branches of a tall, white pine, and is still ascending from bough to bough, unsatisfied till it shall crown the tree's airy summit with a wreath of its broad foliage and a cluster of its grapes. 40

The winding course of the stream continually shut out the scene behind us, and revealed as calm and lovely a one before. We glided from depth to depth, and

20 **Oriental character.** The reference is to the interest of the New England Transcendentalists in Oriental philosophy

breathed new seclusion at every turn. The shy kingfisher flew from the withered branch close at hand to another at a distance, uttering a shrill cry of anger or alarm. Ducks that had been floating there since the preceding eve were startled at our approach, and skimmed along the glassy river, breaking its dark surface with a bright streak. The pickerel leaped from among the lilypads. The turtle, sunning itself upon a rock or at the root of a tree, slid suddenly into the water with a plunge. The painted Indian who paddled his canoe along the Assabeth three hundred years ago could hardly have seen a wilder gentleness displayed upon its banks and reflected in its bosom than we did. Nor could the same Indian have prepared his noontide
10 meal with more simplicity. We drew up our skiff at some point where the overarching shade formed a natural bower, and there kindled a fire with the pine cones and decayed branches that lay strewn plentifully around. Soon the smoke ascended among the trees, impregnated with a savory incense, not heavy, dull, and surfeiting, like the steam of cookery within doors, but sprightly and piquant. The smell of our feast was akin to the woodland odors with which it mingled: there was no sacrilege committed by our intrusion there: the sacred solitude was hospitable, and granted us free leave to cook and eat in the recess that was at once our kitchen and banqueting hall. It is strange what humble offices may be performed in a beautiful scene without destroying its poetry. Our fire, red gleaming among the trees, and
20 we beside it, busied with culinary rites and spreading out our meal on a moss-grown log, all seemed in unison with the river gliding by and the foliage rustling over us. And, what was strangest, neither did our mirth seem to disturb the propriety of the solemn woods; although the hobgoblins of the old wilderness and the will-of-the-wisps that glimmered in the marshy places might have come trooping to share our table talk, and have added their shrill laughter to our merriment. It was the very spot in which to utter the extremest nonsense or the profoundest wisdom, or that ethereal product of the mind which partakes of both, and may become one or the other, in correspondence with the faith and insight of the auditor.

So amid sunshine and shadow, rustling leaves and sighing waters, up gushed our
30 talk like the babble of a fountain. The evanescent spray was Ellery's; and his, too, the lumps of golden thought that lay glimmering in the fountain's bed and brightened both our faces by the reflection. Could he have drawn out that virgin gold and stamped it with the mint mark that alone gives currency, the world might have had the profit, and he the fame. My mind was the richer merely by the knowledge that it was there. But the chief profit of those wild days to him and me lay, not in any definite idea, not in any angular or rounded truth, which we dug out of the shapeless mass of problematical stuff, but in the freedom which we thereby won from all custom and conventionalism and fettering influences of man on man. We were so free to-day that it was impossible to be slaves again to-morrow. When we crossed
40 the threshold of the house or trod the thronged pavements of a city, still the leaves of the trees that overhang the Assabeth were whispering to us, "Be free! be free!" Therefore along that shady river-bank there are spots, marked with a heap of ashes

---

7 **Assabeth.** The Assabeth River flows into the Concord River at Concord

and half-consumed brands, only less sacred in my remembrance than the hearth of a household fire.

And yet how sweet, as we floated homeward adown the golden river at sunset, — how sweet was it to return within the system of human society, not as to a dungeon and a chain, but as to a stately edifice, whence we could go forth at will into statelier simplicity! How gently, too, did the sight of the Old Manse, best seen from the river, overshadowed with its willow and all environed about with the foliage of its orchard and avenue, — how gently did its gray, homely aspect rebuke the speculative extravagances of the day! It had grown sacred in connection with the artificial life against which we inveighed; it had been a home for many years in spite of all; it was my home too; and, with these thoughts, it seemed to me that all the artifice and conventionalism of life was but an impalpable thinness upon its surface, and that the depth below was none the worse for it. Once, as we turned our boat to the bank, there was a cloud, in the shape of an immensely gigantic figure of a hound, couched above the house, as if keeping guard over it. Gazing at this symbol, I prayed that the upper influences might long protect the institutions that had grown out of the heart of mankind.

If ever my readers should decide to give up civilized life, cities, houses, and whatever moral or material enormities in addition to these the perverted ingenuity of our race has contrived, let it be in the early autumn. Then Nature will love him better than at any other season, and will take him to her bosom with a more motherly tenderness. I could scarcely endure the roof of the old house above me in those first autumnal days. How early in the summer, too, the prophecy of autumn comes! Earlier in some years than in others; sometimes even in the first weeks of July. There is no other feeling like what is caused by this faint, doubtful, yet real perception — if it be not rather a foreboding — of the year's decay, so blessedly sweet and sad in the same breath.

Did I say that there was no feeling like it? Ah, but there is a half-acknowledged melancholy like to this when we stand in the perfected vigor of our life and feel that Time has now given us all his flowers, and that the next work of his never idle fingers must be to steal them one by one away.

I have forgotten whether the song of the cricket be not as early a token of autumn's approach as any other, — that song which may be called an audible stillness; for though very loud and heard afar, yet the mind does not take note of it as a sound, so completely is its individual existence merged among the accompanying characteristics of the season. Alas for the pleasant summer time! In August the grass is still verdant on the hills and in the valleys; the foliage of the trees is as dense as ever, and as green; the flowers gleam forth in richer abundance along the margin of the river, and by the stone walls, and deep among the woods; the days, too, are as fervid now as they were a month ago; and yet in every breath of wind and in every beam of sunshine we hear the whispered farewell and behold the parting smile of a dear friend. There is a coolness amid all the heat, a mildness in the blazing noon. Not a breeze can stir but it thrills us with the breath of autumn. A pensive glory is seen in the far golden gleams; among the shadows of the trees. The flowers — even the brightest of them, and they are the most gorgeous of the year — have this gentle sadness wedded to their pomp, and typify the character of the delicious time each within itself. The brilliant cardinal flower has never seemed gay to me.

Still later in the season Nature's tenderness waxes stronger. It is impossible not to be fond of our mother now; for she is so fond of us! At other periods she does not make this impression on me, or only at rare intervals; but in those genial days of autumn, when she has perfected her harvests and accomplished every needful thing that was given her to do, then she overflows with a blessed superfluity of love. She has leisure to caress her children now. It is good to be alive at such times.
10   Thank Heaven for breath — yes, for mere breath — when it is made up of a heavenly breeze like this! It comes with a real kiss upon our cheeks; it would linger fondly around us if it might; but, since it must be gone, it embraces us with its whole kindly heart and passes onward to embrace likewise the next thing that it meets. A blessing is flung abroad and scattered far and wide over the earth, to be gathered up by all who choose. I recline upon the still unwithered grass and whisper to myself, "O perfect day! O beautiful world! O beneficent God!" And it is the promise of a blessed eternity; for our Creator would never have made such lovely days and have given us the deep hearts to enjoy them, above and beyond all thought, unless we were meant to be immortal. This sunshine is the golden pledge thereof.
20   It beams through the gates of paradise and shows us glimpses far inward.

By and by, in a little time, the outward world puts on a drear austerity. On some October morning there is a heavy hoar-frost on the grass and along the tops of the fences; and at sunrise the leaves fall from the trees of our avenue without a breath of wind, quietly descending by their own weight. All summer long they have murmured like the noise of waters; they have roared loudly while the branches were wrestling with the thunder gust; they have made music both glad and solemn; they have attuned my thoughts by their quiet sound as I paced to and fro beneath the arch of intermingling boughs. Now they can only rustle under my feet. Henceforth the gray parsonage begins to assume a larger importance, and draws to its fireside, —
30   for the abomination of the air-tight stove is reserved till wintry weather, — draws closer and closer to its fireside the vagrant impulses that had gone wandering about through the summer.

When summer was dead and buried the Old Manse became as lonely as a hermitage. Not that ever — in my time at least — it had been thronged with company; but, at no rare intervals, we welcomed some friend out of the dusty glare and tumult of the world, and rejoiced to share with him the transparent obscurity that was floating over us. In one respect our precincts were like the Enchanted Ground through which the pilgrim travelled on his way to the Celestial City! The guests, each and all, felt a slumberous influence upon them; they fell asleep in chairs, or
40   took a more deliberate siesta on the sofa, or were seen stretched among the shadows of the orchard, looking up dreamily through the boughs. They could not have

---

37 **Enchanted** . . . **City.** See p. 1316 for another allusion to the passage in *Pilgrim's Progress* where the shepherds on the Delectable Mountains warn the pilgrims to "take heed that they sleep not on the enchanted ground," for "the air naturally tended to make one drowsy"

paid a more acceptable compliment to my abode, nor to my own qualities as a host. I held it as a proof that they left their cares behind them as they passed between the stone gate-posts at the entrance of our avenue, and that the so powerful opiate was the abundance of peace and quiet within and all around us. Others could give them pleasure and amusement or instruction — these could be picked up anywhere; but it was for me to give them rest — in a life of trouble. What better could be done for those weary and world-worn spirits? — for him whose career of perpetual action was impeded and harassed by the rarest of his powers and the richest of his acquirements? — for another who had thrown his ardent heart from earliest youth into the strife of politics, and now, perchance, began to suspect that one lifetime is 10 too brief for the accomplishment of any lofty aim? — for her on whose feminine nature had been imposed the heavy gift of intellectual power, such as a strong man might have staggered under, and with it the necessity to act upon the world? — in a word, not to multiply instances, what better could be done for anybody who came within our magic circle than to throw the spell of a tranquil spirit over him? And when it had wrought its full effect, then we dismissed him, with but misty reminiscences, as if he had been dreaming of us.

Were I to adopt a pet idea, as so many people do, and fondle it in my embraces to the exclusion of all others, it would be, that the great want which mankind labors under at this present period is sleep. The world should recline its vast head on the 20 first convenient pillow and take an age-long nap. It has gone distracted through a morbid activity, and, while preternaturally wide awake, is nevertheless tormented by visions that seem real to it now, but would assume their true aspect and character were all things once set right by an interval of sound repose. This is the only method of getting rid of old delusions and avoiding new ones; of regenerating our race, so that it might in due time awake as an infant out of dewy slumber; of restoring to us the simple perception of what is right, and the single-hearted desire to achieve it, both of which have long been lost in consequence of this weary activity of brain and torpor or passion of the heart that now afflict the universe. Stimulants, the only mode of treatment hitherto attemped, cannot quell the disease; they do 30 but heighten the delirium.

Let not the above paragraph ever be quoted against the author; for, though tinctured with its modicum of truth, it is the result and expression of what he knew, while he was writing, to be but a distorted survey of the state and prospects of mankind. There were circumstances around me which made it difficult to view the world precisely as it exists; for, severe and sober as was the Old Manse, it was necessary to go but a little way beyond its threshold before meeting with stranger moral shapes of men than might have been encountered elsewhere in a circuit of a thousand miles.

---

7 **him**, Horatio Bridge, Bowdoin classmate and lifelong friend, whose *Journal of an African Cruiser*, edited by Hawthorne, had just been published. Bridge was an officer in the United States Navy, and Hawthorne perhaps intended to suggest that Bridge's literary talent was at odds with his professional career   9 **another**, Franklin Pierce (1804-1869), another associate at Bowdoin and friend of a lifetime, who rose through the state legislature of New Hampshire and the Congress to the Presidency of the United States, 1853-1857   11 **her**, Margaret Fuller (1810-1850), a Transcendentalist, editor of *The Dial*

These hobgoblins of flesh and blood were attracted thither by the widespreading influence of a great original thinker, who had his earthly abode at the opposite extremity of our village. His mind acted upon other minds of a certain constitution with wonderful magnetism, and drew many men upon long pilgrimages to speak with him face to face. Young visionaries — to whom just so much of insight had been imparted as to make life all a labyrinth around them — came to seek the clew that should guide them out of their self-involved bewilderment. Grayheaded theorists — whose systems, at first air, had finally imprisoned them in an iron frame-work — travelled painfully to his door, not to ask deliverance, but to invite the free spirit into their own thraldom. People that had lighted on a new thought, or a thought that they fancied new, came to Emerson, as the finder of a glittering gem hastens to a lapidary, to ascertain its quality and value. Uncertain, troubled, earnest wanderers through the midnight of the moral world beheld his intellectual fire as a beacon burning on a hill-top, and, climbing the difficult ascent, looked forth into the surrounding obscurity more hopefully than hitherto. The light revealed objects unseen before, — mountains, gleaming lakes, glimpses of a creation among the chaos; but, also, as was unavoidable, it attracted bats and owls and the whole host of night birds, which flapped their dusky wings against the gazer's eyes, and sometimes were mistaken for fowls of angelic feather. Such delusions always hover nigh whenever a beacon fire of truth is kindled.

For myself there had been epochs of my life when I, too, might have asked of this prophet the master word that should solve me the riddle of the universe; but now, being happy, I felt as if there were no question to be put, and therefore admired Emerson as a poet of deep beauty and austere tenderness, but sought nothing from him as a philosopher. It was good, nevertheless, to meet him in the woodpaths, or sometimes in our avenue, with that pure intellectual gleam diffused about his presence like the garment of a shining one; and he so quiet, so simple, so without pretension, encountering each man alive as if expecting to receive more than he could impart. And, in truth, the heart of many an ordinary man had, perchance, inscriptions which he could not read. But it was impossible to dwell in his vicinity without inhaling more or less the mountain atmosphere of his lofty thought, which, in the brains of some people, wrought a singular giddiness, — new truth being as heady as new wine. Never was a poor little country village infested with such a variety of queer, strangely-dressed, oddly-behaved mortals, most of whom took upon themselves to be important agents of the world's destiny, yet were simply bores of a very intense water. Such, I imagine, is the invariable character of persons who crowd so closely about an original thinker as to draw in his unuttered breath and thus become imbued with a false originality. This triteness of novelty is enough to make any man of common sense blaspheme at all ideas of less than a century's standing, and pray that the world may be petrified and rendered immovable in precisely the worst moral and physical state that it ever yet arrived at, rather than be benefited by such schemes of such philosophers.

And now I begin to feel -- and perhaps should have sooner felt — that we have talked enough of the Old Manse. Mine honored reader, it may be, will vilify the poor author as an egotist for babbling through so many pages about a moss-grown country parsonage, and his life within its walls and on the river and in the woods, and the influences that wrought upon him from all these sources. My conscience, however, does not reproach me with betraying anything too sacredly individual to be revealed by a human spirit to its brother or sister spirit. How narrow — how shallow and scanty too — is the stream of thought that has been flowing from my pen, compared with the broad tide of dim emotions, ideas, and associations which swell around me from that portion of my existence! How little have I told! and of that little, how almost nothing is even tinctured with any quality that makes it ex-clusively my own! Has the reader gone wandering, hand in hand with me, through 10 the inner passages of my being? and have we groped together into all its cham-bers and examined their treasures or their rubbish? Not so. We have been standing on the greensward, but just within the cavern's mouth, where the common sun-shine is free to penetrate, and where every footstep is therefore free to come. I have appealed to no sentiment or sensibilities save such as are diffused among us all. So far as I am a man of really individual attributes I veil my face; nor am I, nor have I ever been, one of those supremely hospitable people who serve up their own hearts, delicately fried, with brain sauce, as a tidbit for their beloved public.

Glancing back over what I have written, it seems but the scattered reminiscences of a single summer. In fairyland there is no measurement of time; and, in a spot so 20 sheltered from the turmoil of life's ocean, three years hastened away with a noise-less flight, as the breezy sunshine chases the cloud shadows across the depths of a still valley. Now came hints, growing more and more distinct, that the owner of the old house was pining for his native air. Carpenters next appeared, making a tremendous racket among the out-buildings, strewing the green grass with pine shavings and chips of chestnut joists, and vexing the whole antiquity of the place with their discordant renovations. Soon, moreover, they divested our abode of the veil of woodbine which had crept over a large portion of its southern face. All the aged mosses were cleared unsparingly away; and there were horrible whispers about brushing up the external walls with a coat of paint — a purpose as little to my 30 taste as might be that of rouging the venerable cheeks of one's grandmother. But the hand that renovates is always more sacrilegious than that which destroys. In fine, we gathered up our household goods, drank a farewell cup of tea in our pleas-ant little breakfast room, — delicately fragrant tea, an unpurchasable luxury, one of the many angel gifts that had fallen like dew upon us, — and passed forth between the tall stone gateposts as uncertain as the wandering Arabs where our tent might next be pitched. Providence took me by the hand, and — an oddity of dispensation which, I trust, there is no irreverence in smiling at — has led me, as the newspapers announce while I am writing, from the Old Manse into a custom house. As a story teller, I have often contrived strange vicissitudes for my imaginary personages, but 40 none like this.

The treasure of intellectual good which I hoped to find in our secluded dwelling had never come to light. No profound treatise of ethics, no philosophic history, no novel even, that could stand unsupported on its edges. All that I had to show, as a

man of letters, were these few tales and essays, which had blossomed out like flowers in the calm summer of my heart and mind. Save editing (an easy task) the journal of my friend of many years, the African Cruiser, I had done nothing else. With these idle weeds and withering blossoms I have intermixed some that were produced long ago, — old, faded things, reminding me of flowers pressed between the leaves of a book, — and now offer the bouquet, such as it is, to any whom it may please. These fitful sketches, with so little of external life about them, yet claiming no profundity of purpose, — so reserved, even while they sometimes seem so frank, — often but half in earnest, and never, even when most so, expressing satisfactorily the
10 thoughts which they profess to image, — such trifles, I truly feel, afford no solid basis for a literary reputation. Nevertheless, the public — if my limited number of readers, whom I venture to regard rather as a circle of friends, may be termed a public — will receive them the more kindly, as the last offering, the last collection, of this nature which it is my purpose ever to put forth. Unless I could do better, I have done enough in this kind. For myself the book will always retain one charm — as reminding me of the river, with its delightful solitudes, and of the avenue, the garden, and the orchard, and especially the dear Old Manse, with the little study on its western side, and the sunshine glimmering through the willow branches while I wrote.
20   Let the reader, if he will do me so much honor, imagine himself my guest, and that, having seen whatever may be worthy of notice within and about the Old Manse, he has finally been ushered into my study. There, after seating him in an antique elbow chair, an heirloom of the house, I take forth a roll of manuscript and entreat his attention to the following tales — an act of personal inhospitality, however, which I never was guilty of, nor ever will be, even to my worst enemy.

1846

Preface to "The House of the Seven Gables"

The following Preface is the best example of Hawthorne's criticism of his own writings. The critical points are generally applicable not only to The House of the Seven Gables *but to his works as a whole. Of particular interest is his distinction between the "Novel" and the "Romance." As examples of the Novel, Hawthorne had in mind no doubt the works of such writers as Thackeray and Trollope. His own works he preferred to call "Romances."*

When a writer calls his work a Romance, it need hardly be observed that he wishes to claim a certain latitude, both as to its fashion and material, which he would not have felt himself entitled to assume, had he professed to be writing a Novel. The latter form of composition is presumed to aim at a very minute fidelity, not merely to the possible, but to the probable and ordinary course of man's experience. The former — while, as a work of art, it must rigidly subject itself to laws, and while it sins unpardonably so far as it may swerve aside from the truth of the human heart — has fairly a right to present that truth under circumstances, to a great extent, of the writer's own choosing or creation. If he thinks fit, also, he may so manage his atmospherical medium as to bring out or mellow the lights, and deepen and enrich the shadows, of the picture. He will be wise, no doubt, to make a very moderate use of the privileges here stated, and, especially, to mingle the Marvelous rather as a slight, delicate, and evanescent flavor, than as any portion of the actual substance of the dish offered to the public. He can hardly be said, however, to commit a literary crime, even if he disregard this caution.

In the present work the author has proposed to himself — but with what success, fortunately, it is not for him to judge — to keep undeviatingly within his immunities. The point of view in which this tale comes under the Romantic definition 10 lies in the attempt to connect a bygone time with the very present that is flitting away from us. It is a legend, prolonging itself, from an epoch now gray in the distance down into our own broad daylight, and bringing along with it some of its legendary mist, which the reader, according to his pleasure, may either disregard or allow it to float almost imperceptibly about the characters and events for the sake of a picturesque effect. The narrative, it may be, is woven of so humble a texture as to require this advantage, and, at the same time, to render it the more difficult of attainment.

Many writers lay very great stress upon some definite moral purpose, at which they profess to aim their works. Not to be deficient in this particular, the author has 20 provided himself with a moral; — the truth, namely, that the wrongdoing of one generation lives into the successive ones, and, divesting itself of every temporary advantage, become a pure and uncontrollable mischief; — and he would feel it a singular gratification, if this romance might effectually convince mankind — or, indeed, any one man — of the folly of tumbling down an avalanche of ill-gotten gold, or real estate, on the heads of an unfortunate posterity, thereby to maim and crush them, until the accumulated mass shall be scattered abroad in its original atoms. In good faith, however, he is not sufficiently imaginative to flatter himself with the slightest hope of this kind. When romances do really teach anything, or produce any effective operation, it is usually through a far more subtle process than 30 the ostensible one. The author has considered it hardly worth his while, therefore, relentlessly to impale the story with its moral, as with an iron rod, — or, rather, as by sticking a pin through a butterfly, — thus at once depriving it of life, and causing it to stiffen in an ungainly and unnatural attitude. A high truth, indeed, fairly, finely, and skilfully wrought out, brightening at every step, and crowning the final development of a work of fiction, may add an artistic glory, but is never any truer, and seldom any more evident, at the last page than at the first.

The reader may perhaps choose to assign an actual locality to the imaginary events of this narrative. If permitted by the historical connection, — which, though slight, was essential to his plan, — the author would very willingly have avoided anything 40 of this nature. Not to speak of other objections, it exposes the romance to an inflexible and exceedingly dangerous species of criticism, by bringing his fancy-pictures almost into positive contact with the realities of the moment. It has been no part of his object, however, to describe local manners, nor in any way to meddle with the characteristics of a community for whom he cherishes a proper respect and a natural regard. He trusts not to be considered as unpardonably offending, by laying out a street that infringes upon nobody's private rights, and appropriating a lot of land which had no visible owner, and building a house, of materials long in use for constructing castles in the air. The personages of the tale — though they give themselves out to be of ancient stability and considerable prominence — are really of the author's own making, or, at all events, of his own mixing; their virtues can shed no luster, nor their defects redound, in the remotest degree, to the discredit of the venerable town of which they profess to be inhabitants. He would be glad, therefore, if — especially in the quarter to which he alludes — the book may be read strictly as a romance, having a great deal more to do with the clouds overhead than with any portion of the actual soil of the County of Essex.

1851

8 **venerable town**, Salem, Massachusetts

1819–1891 Herman Melville

H erman Melville, whom John Freeman has called "the most powerful of all the great American writers," was born in New York City in 1819. When he was eleven years of age, his family moved to Albany, where his father died in debt two years later. During the seven ensuing years the boy was occupied, clerking and working on his uncle's farm at Pittsfield, Massachusetts. At the age of twenty, he shipped as a sailor on a merchantman bound for Liverpool. The reasons for his doing so we can take from *Redburn,* which (though an imaginative work) contains a fair amount of autobiography: "Sad disappointments in several plans which I had sketched for my future life; the necessity of doing something for myself, united to a naturally roving disposition, had now conspired within me, to send me to sea as a sailor." After a short stay in Liverpool, where he was shocked by the brutality and misery of the great city, he returned with his ship, sobered and matured, one must believe, by this early introduction to a world of violence and crime. Following his return he taught school in Albany and Pittsfield, tried his hand at writing, and paid a visit to his uncle in Galena, Illinois.

The most decisive event of Melville's life came on January 3, 1841, when at the age of twenty-one he shipped at New Bedford on the *Acushnet,* a whaler, for the South Seas. This whale-ship was for him, in the words of Ishmael in *Moby Dick,* "my Yale College and my Harvard." Melville was gone three years and nine months, returning to Boston in October 1844. For his life during this period one is forced to draw largely upon *Typee, Omoo, White Jacket,* and *Moby Dick,* though C. R. Anderson has exposed some of the errors (in Lewis Mumford's biography, for example) which result from the unwary use of these fictional works for biographical purposes. The exact details of Melville's wanderings in the Pacific are in large measure still uncertain. But it is known that, after some eighteen months on the *Acushnet,* Melville deserted, July 9, 1842, at the Marquesas Islands. After a month or two among the cannibals he escaped to Tahiti; further travels may have taken him to

Japan. Finally, on August 17, 1843, he joined the crew of the frigate *United States* at Honolulu and remained with this ship until his arrival at Boston more than a year later.

The eight or nine years following his return from his voyage were Melville's great productive period. He poured forth a veritable torrent of books: *Typee* (1846), *Omoo* (1847), *Mardi* (1849), *Redburn* (1849), *White Jacket* (1850), *Moby Dick* (1851), and *Pierre* (1852). It was inevitable, perhaps, that there should be a falling off after such extraordinary productivity. Melville seemed to have a premonitory sense of this in 1851, when, at the age of thirty-two, he wrote to Hawthorne: "From my twenty-fifth year I date my life. Three weeks have scarcely passed, at any time between then and now, that I have not unfolded within myself. But I feel that I am now come to the inmost leaf of the bulb, and that shortly the flower must fall to the mold." He lived on for forty years; but he failed to write another book as great as *Moby Dick,* and his productivity steadily diminished: *Israel Potter* (1855); *The Piazza Tales* (1856), which includes "Benito Cereno"; *The Confidence-Man* (1857); two volumes of poetry, *Battle Pieces and Aspects of the War* (1866) and *Clarel* (1876); and *Billy Budd,* written near the end of his life and not published until 1924. From 1866 to 1885, he was Inspector of Customs in New York City.

Willard Thorp notes "five determining influences" in Melville's literary career: "the religious orthodoxy of his home, which left its imprint, though he revolted from it; his contact with the brutalities of a sailor's life and with savage societies which impelled him to question the premises of western civilization; his reading in philosophy and belles-lettres, which, though unmethodical, was prodigious between 1846 and 1851 [notably, Rabelais, Sir Thomas Browne, Shakespeare and other Elizabethan dramatists, the Bible, and Carlyle]; his friendships with artists and men of letters in New York who advanced his interests and educated him in his craft; and the sympathy of Hawthorne, which more than any other factor contributed to the fruition of his genius." This last influence is of special interest. From the summer of 1850 till the autumn of 1851, Melville and Hawthorne were near neighbors and frequent companions, the former residing at Pittsfield, the latter at Lenox. On more than one occasion the two men talked together "about time and eternity, things of this world and of the next, and books and publishers, and all possible and impossible matters" (Hawthorne's *American Notebooks*). Melville was somewhat extravagant in his admiration of his new friend (see his extraordinary letters to Hawthorne, in *The Letters*); Hawthorne, though reserved and older, gave to Melville a sympathetic understanding such as he had not known before and would never know again. *Moby Dick* was dedicated to Hawthorne, and Hawthorne's letter of acknowledgment and appreciation — unfortunately lost, as are all of his letters to Melville — was to Melville a "joy-giving and exultation-breeding letter." After Hawthorne left the Berkshires, their friendly intimacy was interrupted; but in 1856, when Melville was on a recuperative journey to Italy and the Holy Land, the two men met again in England. After this meeting, Hawthorne wrote in his journal the best contemporary characterization of Melville that we have: "We took a pretty long walk together, and sat down in a hollow among the sand hills (sheltering ourselves from the high, cool wind) and smoked a cigar. Melville, as he always does, began to reason of Providence and futurity, and of everything that lies beyond human ken, and informed me that he had 'pretty much made up his mind to be annihilated'; but still he does not seem to rest in that anticipation; and, I think, will never rest until he gets hold of a definite belief. It is strange how he persists — and has persisted ever since I knew him, and probably long before — in wandering to-and-fro over these deserts, as dismal and monotonous as the sand hills amid which we were sitting. He can neither believe, nor be comfortable in his unbelief; and he is too honest and courageous not to try to do one or the other . . . he has a very high and noble nature . . ." *(The English Notebooks).*

Melville began, in *Typee* and *Omoo,* with delightful narratives of travels in the South Seas, written in a straightforward style. There is no conscious allegory here, and no bitterness, except for occasional satirical sallies at the missionaries and the "civilized" nations. *Redburn* and *White Jacket,* also, are simple narratives, though imbued with darker elements: the former delves into the slums of Liverpool; the latter is an angry exposure of the cruelties practiced on board a frigate of the American Navy. The transition to deliberate allegory came in *Mardi* — an unsatisfying book, effective in parts, but lacking integration. Melville reached his full stature in *Moby Dick,* a powerful allegory of good and evil. By this time, too, his prose style had changed from one of Defoe-like simplicity to one of magnificent rhythms, which, while recalling Sir Thomas Browne's, were Melville's own. *Pierre,* in which Melville attempted for the first time the structure of the novel, has something of the power of *Moby Dick,* though it is much less successful as literary art. Among the productions after 1852, one may mention "Benito Cereno" (1856) and *Billy Budd* (1890?) as deserving to rank with his best work, always excepting the matchless *Moby Dick.* *Billy Budd* is of special interest because the book shows that Melville retained his creative power and also because it throws some light on Melville's state of mind in his old age. Some critics have argued that it represents Melville's "testament of acceptance"; others have maintained that it represents, like the earlier work, a reconciliation through compromise — a recognition that absolute innocence (or idealism) cannot survive the conditions of this world.

Melville's reputation as one of the very greatest of American writers dates from about 1920. His early works were enjoyed by many readers, most of whom, however, were estranged by the obscurity and pessimism of *Mardi, Moby Dick,* and *Pierre.* After about 1860, Melville was a forgotten author. There were always, to be sure, a few readers, particularly in England, who knew his books; but "oblivion" is hardly too strong a term to describe Melville's fate for a half century and more. The almost total eclipse of his fame is sufficiently attested by the fact that he was given just one sentence in Barrett Wendell's *Literary History of America,* published in 1900: "Herman Melville, with his books about the South Seas, which Robert Louis Stevenson is said to have declared the best ever written, and with his novels of maritime adventure, began a career of literary promise, which never came to fruition." The exciting rediscovery occurred in both England and America about the time of the centenary of Melville's birth. The enthusiasm of the 1920's may have been owing in part to the fact that the postwar mood of despair vibrated sympathetically with the mood of *Moby Dick* and *Pierre.*

Recent studies have found in Melville's writings a rich and inexhaustible mine of symbolical meanings.

The Works of Herman Melville, 16 vols., London, 1922-1924   R. M. Weaver, **Herman Melville, Mariner and Mystic,** New York, 1921   John Freeman, **Herman Melville,** London, 1926   Lewis Mumford, **Herman Melville,** New York, 1929   Willard Thorp, **Herman Melville, Representative Selections,** Cincinnati, 1938   C. R. Anderson, **Melville in the South Seas,** New York, 1939   Richard Chase, **Herman Melville: A Critical Study,** New York, 1949   Howard Vincent, **The Trying Out of Moby Dick,** New York, 1950   Newton Arvin, **Herman Melville,** New York, 1951   Leon Howard, **Herman Melville: A Biography,** Berkeley, 1951   Merrell R. Davis and William H. Gilman, eds., **The Letters of Herman Melville,** New Haven, 1960   Merlin Bowen, **The Long Encounter,** Chicago, 1960   James E. Miller, Jr., **A Reader's Guide to Herman Melville,** New York, 1962   The Hendricks House edition of Melville is in progress: **Collected Poems,** 1947, **The Piazza Tales,** 1948, **Pierre,** 1949, **Moby Dick,** 1952, **The Confidence-Man,** 1954, **Clarel,** 1961

Hawthorne and His Mosses By a Virginian Spending July in Vermont

The author of Hawthorne and His Mosses *was neither a Virginian nor a vacationer in Vermont, as the title would indicate, but Herman Melville, who had recently taken up his residence in Pittsfield and had about the same time "discovered" Hawthorne. His reaction to the first of Hawthorne's books which he read —* Mosses from an Old Manse — *was most enthusiastic, as will be seen in the following essay, which appeared in Duyckinck's* Literary World *in two installments, August 17 and 24, 1850. The essay is memorable, among other things, for its boldness in comparing Hawthorne with Shakespeare (like Shakespeare, Hawthorne "probes at the very axis of reality") and for its emphasis, as marked as Whitman's was a little later, upon the importance of Americanism in our literature ("Call* [Hawthorne] *an American and have done, for you cannot say a nobler thing of him.")*

Hawthorne and Melville met in early August 1850, the Hawthornes having recently moved into the little red farmhouse at Lenox, nearby, and the two writers soon became good friends. Hawthorne wrote to Duyckinck concerning the essay, before he was aware that his neighbor and newly made acquaintance was the author: "The writer is no common man, and, next to deserving his praise, it is good to have beguiled or bewitched such a man into praising me more than I deserve."

During their association in the Berkshires (in 1850-1851), Hawthorne wrote The House of the Seven Gables *and Melville finished* Moby Dick, *which he dedicated to Hawthorne. The friendly interest of each in the other's work undoubtedly helped to produce these masterpieces; the influence of Hawthorne on Melville, especially, has been generally recognized, though never demonstrated in detail.*

A papered chamber in a fine old farm-house, a mile from any other dwelling, and dipped to the eaves in foliage — surrounded by mountains, old woods, and Indian ponds, — this, surely, is the place to write of Hawthorne. Some charm is in this northern air, for love and duty seem both impelling to the task. A man of deep and noble nature has seized me in this seclusion. His wild, witch-voice rings through me; or, in softer cadences, I seem to hear it in the songs of the hill-side birds that sing in the larch trees at my window.

Would that all excellent books were foundlings, without father or mother, that so it might be we could glorify them, without including their ostensible authors! Nor would any true man take exception to this; least of all, he who writes, "When the Artist rises high enough to achieve the Beautiful, the symbol by which he makes it perceptible to mortal senses becomes of little value in his eyes, while his spirit possesses itself in the enjoyment of the reality."   10

But more than this. I know not what would be the right name to put on the title-page of an excellent book; but this I feel, that the names of all fine authors are fictitious ones, far more so than that of Junius; simply standing, as they do, for the mystical, ever-eluding spirit of all beauty, which ubiquitously possesses men of genius. Purely imaginative as this fancy may appear, it nevertheless seems to receive some warranty from the fact, that on a personal interview no great author has ever come up to the idea of his reader. But that dust of which our bodies are composed, how can it fitly express the nobler intelligences among us? With reverence be it spoken, that not even in the case of one deemed more than man, not even in our Saviour, did his visible frame betoken anything of the augustness of the nature within. Else,   20
how could those Jewish eye-witnesses fail to see heaven in his glance!

It is curious how a man may travel along a country road, and yet miss the grandest or sweetest of prospects by reason of an intervening hedge, so like all other hedges, as in no way to hint of the wide landscape beyond. So has it been with me concerning the enchanting landscape in the soul of this Hawthorne, this most excellent Man of Mosses. His "Old Manse" has been written now four years, but I never read it till a day or two since. I had seen it in the book-stores — heard of it often — even had it recommended to me by a tasteful friend, as a rare, quiet book, perhaps too deserving of popularity to be popular. But there are so many books called "excellent," and so much unpopular merit, that amid the thick stir of other things, the   30
hint of my tasteful friend was disregarded; and for four years the Mosses on the Old Manse never refreshed me with their perennial green. It may be, however, that all this while the book, like wine, was only improving in flavor and body. At any rate, it so chanced that this long procrastination eventuated in a happy result. At breakfast the other day, a mountain girl, a cousin of mine, who for the last two weeks has every morning helped me to strawberries and raspberries, which, like the roses and pearls in the fairy tale, seemed to fall into the saucer from those strawberry-beds, her cheeks — this delightful creature, this charming Cherry says to me —
"I see you spend your mornings in the hay-mow; and yesterday I found there

---

7 **When the Artist . . . reality.** This is the last sentence in Hawthorne's story "The Artist of the Beautiful" (see p. 1334), which is included in *Mosses from an Old Manse*   13 **Junius,** the pseudonym used by the author of *The Letters of Junius* (1769-1772), which attacked figures prominent in contemporary British politics. The author is now believed to have been Sir Philip Francis   28 **tasteful friend,** probably Evert A. Duyckinck, editor of *The Literary World,* who was instrumental in making Hawthorne and Melville acquainted with each other's works

'Dwight's Travels in New England.' Now I have something far better than that, something more congenial to our summer on these hills. Take these raspberries, and then I will give you some moss." "Moss!" said I. "Yes, and you must take it to the barn with you, and good-bye to 'Dwight.'"

With that she left me, and soon returned with a volume, verdantly bound, and garnished with a curious frontispiece in green; nothing less than a fragment of real moss, cunningly pressed to a fly-leaf. "Why, this," said I, spilling my raspberries, "this is the 'Mosses from an Old Manse.'" "Yes," said cousin Cherry, "yes, it is that flowery Hawthorne." "Hawthorne and Mosses," said I, "no more: it is morn-
10 ing: it is July in the country: and I am off for the barn."

Stretched on that new mown clover, the hill-side breeze blowing over me through the wide barn-door, and soothed by the hum of the bees in the meadows around, how magically stole over me this Mossy Man! and how amply, how bountifully, did he redeem that delicious promise to his guests in the Old Manse, of whom it is written — "Others could give them pleasure, or amusement, or instruction — these could be picked up anywhere — but it was for me to give them rest. Rest, in a life of trouble! What better could be done for weary and world-worn spirits? What better could be done for anybody, who came within our magic circle, than to throw the spell of a magic spirit over him?" So all that day, half-buried in the new clover,
20 I watched this Hawthorne's "Assyrian dawn, and Paphian sunset and moonrise, from the summit of our Eastern Hill."

The soft ravishments of the man spun me round about in a web of dreams, and when the book was closed, when the spell was over, this wizard "dismissed me with but misty reminiscences, as if I had been dreaming of him."

What a wild moonlight of contemplative humor bathes that Old Manse! the rich and rare distilment of a spicy and slowly-oozing heart. No rollicking rudeness, no gross fun fed on fat dinners, and bred in the lees of wine, — but a humor so spiritually gentle, so high, so deep, and yet so richly relishable, that it were hardly inappropriate in an angel. It is the very religion of mirth; for nothing so human but it
30 may be advanced to that. The orchard of the Old Manse seems the visible type of the fine mind that has described it — those twisted and contorted old trees, "that stretch out their crooked branches, and take such hold of the imagination, that we remember them as humorists and odd-fellows." And then, as surrounded by these grotesque forms, and hushed in the noon-day repose of this Hawthorne's spell, how aptly might the still fall of his ruddy thoughts into your soul be symbolized by "the thump of a great apple, in the stillest afternoon, falling without a breath of wind, from the mere necessity of perfect ripeness!" For no less ripe than ruddy are the apples of the thoughts and fancies in this sweet Man of Mosses —

---

1 **Dwight's Travels,** one of the more interesting and important works (4 vols., 1822) written by Timothy Dwight, president of Yale College and author of *Greenfield Hill* (see p. 536)   15 **Others . . . over him?** This quotation and several others in the essay were taken from "The old Manse" (see p. 1355), the first sketch in *Mosses.* Melville sometimes quotes inexactly   20 **Assyrian . . . Hill,** from "The Old Manse," where the passage refers to Emerson's having written *Nature* while residing at the Old Manse. Hawthorne's language, here quoted by Melville, is an adaptation of Emerson's "The dawn is my Assyria; the sunset and moonrise my Paphos. . . ." (see *Nature,* p. 1370)   23 **dismissed . . . him,** adapted from a passage in "The Old Manse" (see p. 1040)

"Buds and Bird-voices" —

What a delicious thing is that! "Will the world ever be so decayed, that Spring may not renew its greenness?" And the "Fire-Worship." Was ever the hearth so glorified into an altar before? The mere title of that piece is better than any common work in fifty folio volumes. How exquisite is this: — "Nor did it lessen the charm of his soft, familiar courtesy and helpfulness, that the mighty spirit, were opportunity offered him, would run riot through the peaceful house, wrap its inmates in his terrible embrace, and leave nothing of them save their whitened bones. This possibility of mad destruction only made his domestic kindness the more beautiful and touching. It was so sweet of him, being endowed with such power, to dwell, day after 10 day, and one long, lonesome night after another, on the dusky hearth, only now and then betraying his wild nature, by thrusting his red tongue out of the chimney-top! True, he had done much mischief in the world, and was pretty certain to do more, but his warm heart atoned for all; he was kindly to the race of man."

But he has still other apples, not quite so ruddy, though full as ripe; — apples, that have been left to wither on the tree, after the pleasant autumn gathering is past. The sketch of "The Old Apple-Dealer" is conceived in the subtlest spirit of sadness; he whose "subdued and nerveless boyhood prefigured his abortive prime, which, likewise, contained within itself the prophecy and image of his lean and torpid age." Such touches as are in this piece cannot proceed from any common heart. They 20 argue such a depth of tenderness, such a boundless sympathy with all forms of being, such an omnipresent love, that we must needs say that this Hawthorne is here almost alone in his generation, — at least, in the artistic manifestation of these things. Still more. Such touches as these, — and many, very many similar ones, all through his chapters — furnish clues whereby we enter a little way into the intricate, profound heart where they originated. And we see that suffering, some time or other and in some shape or other, — this only can enable any man to depict it in others. All over him, Hawthorne's melancholy rests like an Indian-summer, which, though bathing a whole country in one softness, still reveals the distinctive hue of every towering hill and each far-winding vale.   30

But it is the least part of genius that attracts admiration. Where Hawthorne is known, he seems to be deemed a pleasant writer, with a pleasant style, — a sequestered, harmless man, from whom any deep and weighty thing would hardly be anticipated — a man who means no meanings. But there is no man, in whom humor and love, like mountain peaks, soar to such a rapt height as to receive the irradiations of the upper skies; — there is no man in whom humor and love are developed in that high form called genius; no such man can exist without also possessing, as the indispensable complement of these, a great, deep intellect, which drops down into the universe like a plummet. Or, love and humor are only the eyes through which such an intellect views this world. The great beauty in such a mind is but 40 the product of its strength. What, to all readers, can be more charming than the

---

1 **Buds and Bird-voices,** one of the pieces in the collection *Mosses from an Old Manse;* the same is true of subsequent titles mentioned in this essay

piece entitled "Monsieur du Miroir"; and to a reader at all capable of fully fathoming it, what, at the same time, can possess more mystical depth of meaning? — yes, there he sits and looks at me, — this "shape of mystery," this "identical Monsieur du Miroir." "Methinks I should tremble now, were his wizard power of gliding through all impediments in search of me, to place him suddenly before my eyes."

How profound, nay appalling, is the moral evolved by the "Earth's Holocaust"; where — beginning with the hollow follies and affectations of the world, — all vanities and empty theories and forms are, one after another, and by an admirably graduated, growing comprehensiveness, thrown into the allegorical fire, till, at length,
10 nothing is left but the all-engendering heart of man; which remaining still unconsumed, the great conflagration is naught.

Of a piece with this, is the "Intelligence Office," a wondrous symbolizing of the secret workings in men's souls. There are other sketches still more charged with ponderous import.

"The Christmas Banquet," and "The Bosom Serpent," would be fine subjects for a curious and elaborate analysis, touching the conjectural parts of the mind that produced them. For spite of all the Indian-summer sunlight on the hither side of Hawthorne's soul, the other side — like the dark half of the physical sphere — is shrouded in a blackness, ten times black. But this darkness but gives more effect to
20 the ever-moving dawn, that for ever advances through it, and circumnavigates his world. Whether Hawthorne has simply availed himself of this mystical blackness as a means to the wondrous effects he makes it to produce in his lights and shades; or whether there really lurks in him, perhaps unknown to himself, a touch of Puritanic gloom, — this, I cannot altogether tell. Certain it is, however, that this great power of blackness in him derives its force from its appeal to that Calvinistic sense of Innate Depravity and Original Sin, from whose visitations, in some shape or other, no deeply thinking mind is always and wholly free. For, in certain moods, no man can weigh this world without throwing in something, somehow like Original Sin, to strike the uneven balance. At all events, perhaps no writer has ever wielded this
30 terrific thought with greater terror than this same harmless Hawthorne. Still more: this black conceit pervades him through and through. You may be witched by his sunlight, — transported by the bright gildings in the skies he builds over you; but there is the blackness of darkness beyond; and even his bright gildings but fringe and play upon the edges of thunderclouds. In one word, the world is mistaken in this Nathaniel Hawthorne. He himself must often have smiled at its absurd misconception of him. He is immeasurably deeper than the plummet of the mere critic. For it is not the brain that can test such a man; it is only the heart. You cannot come to know greatness by inspecting it; there is no glimpse to be caught of it, except by intuition; you need not ring it, you but touch it, and you find it is gold.
40 Now, it is that blackness in Hawthorne, of which I have spoken, that so fixes and fascinates me. It may be, nevertheless, that it is too largely developed in him. Perhaps he does not give us a ray of his light for every shade of his dark. But however this may be, this blackness it is that furnishes the infinite obscure of his background, — that back-ground, against which Shakspeare plays his grandest conceits,

the things that have made for Shakspeare his loftiest but most circumscribed renown, as the profoundest of thinkers. For by philosophers Shakspeare is not adored
as the great man of tragedy and comedy. — "Off with his head; so much for Buckingham!" This sort of rant, interlined by another hand, brings down the house, —
those mistaken souls, who dream of Shakspeare as a mere man of Richard-the-Third
humps and Macbeth daggers. But it is those deep far-away things in him; those
occasional flashings-forth of the intuitive Truth in him; those short, quick probings
at the very axis of reality; — these are the things that make Shakspeare, Shakspeare.
Through the mouths of the dark characters of Hamlet, Timon, Lear, and Iago, he
craftily says, or sometimes insinuates the things which we feel to be so terrifically 10
true, that it were all but madness for any good man, in his own proper character,
to utter, or even hint of them. Tormented into desperation, Lear, the frantic king,
tears off the mask, and speaks the same madness of vital truth. But, as I before said,
it is the least part of genius that attracts admiration. And so, much of the blind,
unbridled admiration that has been heaped upon Shakspeare, has been lavished upon
the least part of him. And few of his endless commentators and critics seem to have
remembered, or even perceived, that the immediate products of a great mind are
not so great as that undeveloped and sometimes undevelopable yet dimly-discernible
greatness, to which those immediate products are but the infallible indices. In
Shakspeare's tomb lies infinitely more than Shakspeare ever wrote. And if I mag- 20
nify Shakspeare, it is not so much for what he did do as for what he did not do,
or refrained from doing. For in this world of lies, Truth is forced to fly like a scared
white doe in the woodlands; and only by cunning glimpses will she reveal herself,
as in Shakspeare and other masters of the great Art of Telling the Truth, — even
though it be covertly and by snatches.

   But if this view of the all-popular Shakspeare be seldom taken by his readers, and
if very few who extol him have ever read him deeply, or perhaps, only have seen
him on the tricky stage (which alone made, and is still making him his mere mob
renown) — if few men have time, or patience, or palate, for the spiritual truth as it
is in that great genius; — it is then no matter of surprise, that in a contemporane- 30
ous age, Nathaniel Hawthorne is a man as yet almost utterly mistaken among men.
Here and there, in some quiet arm-chair in the noisy town, or some deep nook among
the noiseless mountains, he may be appreciated for something of what he is. But
unlike Shakspeare, who was forced to the contrary course by circumstances, Hawthorne (either from simple disinclination, or else from inaptitude) refrains from all
the popularizing noise and show of broad farce and blood-besmeared tragedy; content with the still, rich utterance of a great intellect in repose, and which sends few
thoughts into circulation, except they be arterialized at his large warm lungs, and
expanded in his honest heart.

   Nor need you fix upon that blackness in him, if it suit you not. Nor, indeed, will 40
all readers discern it; for it is, mostly, insinuated to those who may best understand
it, and account for it; it is not obtruded upon every one alike.

   Some may start to read of Shakspeare and Hawthorne on the same page. They
may say, that if an illustration were needed, a lesser light might have sufficed to

elucidate this Hawthorne, this small man of yesterday. But I am not willingly one
of those who, as touching Shakspeare at least, exemplify the maxim of Rochefou-
cauld, that "we exalt the reputation of some, in order to depress that of others"; —
who, to teach all noble-souled aspirants that there is no hope for them, pronounce
Shakspeare absolutely unapproachable. But Shakspeare has been approached. There
are minds that have gone as far as Shakspeare into the universe. And hardly a mortal man, who, at some time or other, has not felt as great thoughts in him as any
you will find in Hamlet. We must not inferentially malign mankind for the sake of
any one man, whoever he may be. This is too cheap a purchase of contentment for
10 conscious mediocrity to make. Besides, this absolute and unconditional adoration of
Shakspeare has grown to be a part of our Anglo-Saxon superstitions. The Thirty-
Nine Articles are now Forty. Intolerance has come to exist in this matter. You must
believe in Shakspeare's unapproachability, or quit the country. But what sort of a
belief is this for an American, a man who is bound to carry republican progressive-
ness into Literature as well as into Life? Believe me, my friends, that men, not very
much inferior to Shakspeare, are this day being born on the banks of the Ohio.
And the day will come when you shall say, Who reads a book by an Englishman
that is a modern? The great mistake seems to be, that even with those Americans
who look forward to the coming of a great literary genius among us, they somehow
20 fancy he will come in the costume of Queen Elizabeth's day; be a writer of dramas
founded upon old English history or the tales of Boccaccio. Whereas, great geniuses
are parts of the times, they themselves are the times, and possess a correspondent
coloring. It is of a piece with the Jews, who, while their Shiloh was meekly walking
in their streets, were still praying for his magnificent coming; looking for him in
a chariot, who was already among them on an ass. Nor must we forget that, in his
own lifetime, Shakspeare was not Shakspeare, but only Master William Shakspeare
of the shrewd, thriving business firm of Condell, Shakspeare & Co., proprietors of
the Globe Theatre in London; and by a courtly author, of the name of Chettle, was
looked at as an "upstart crow," beautified "with other birds' feathers." For, mark it
30 well, imitation is often the first charge brought against real originality. Why this is
so, there is not space to set forth here. You must have plenty of sea-room to tell
the Truth in; especially when it seems to have an aspect of newness, as America
did in 1492, though it was then just as old, and perhaps older than Asia, only those
sagacious philosophers, the common sailors, had never seen it before, swearing it
was all water and moonshine there.

Now I do not say that Nathaniel of Salem is a greater than William of Avon, or
as great. But the difference between the two men is by no means immeasurable.
Not a very great deal more, and Nathaniel were verily William.

This, too, I mean, that if Shakspeare has not been equalled, give the world time,
40 and he is sure to be surpassed, in one hemisphere or the other. Nor will it at all

---

11 **Thirty-Nine Articles,** the authoritative statement of the doctrines of the Church of England, dating
from the sixteenth century.   17 **Who reads . . . modern?** An adaptation of Sydney Smith's often-quoted
query, "Who reads an American book?"   23 **Shiloh,** one of the names for the Messiah; see Genesis
49:10   25 **ass.** Jesus entered Jerusalem sitting upon an ass; see Matthew 21   28 **Chettle . . . feathers,**
a famous aspersion made by Robert Greene, not Chettle, in *A Groatsworth of Wit*

do to say, that the world is getting grey and grizzled now, and has lost that fresh charm which she wore of old, and by virtue of which the great poets of past times made themselves what we esteem them to be. Not so. The world is as young to-day as when it was created; and this Vermont morning dew is as wet to my feet, as Eden's dew to Adam's. Nor has nature been all over ransacked by our progenitors, so that no new charms and mysteries remain for this latter generation to find. Far from it. The trillionth part has not yet been said; and all that has been said, but multiplies the avenues to what remains to be said. It is not so much paucity as super-abundance of material that seems to incapacitate modern authors.

Let America, then, prize and cherish her writers; yea, let her glorify them. They 10 are not so many in number as to exhaust her good-will. And while she has good kith and kin of her own, to take to her bosom, let her not lavish her embraces upon the household of an alien. For believe it or not, England, after all, is in many things an alien to us. China has more bonds of real love for us than she. But even were there no strong literary individualities among us, as there are some dozens at least, nevertheless, let America first praise mediocrity even, in her own children, before she praises (for everywhere, merit demands acknowledgment from every one) the best excellence in the children of any other land. Let her own authors, I say, have the priority of appreciation. I was much pleased with a hot-headed Carolina cousin of mine, who once said, — "If there were no other American to stand by, in literature, 20 why, then, I would stand by Pop Emmons and his 'Fredoniad,' and till a better epic came along, swear it was not very far behind the Iliad." Take away the words, and in spirit he was sound.

Not that American genius needs patronage in order to expand. For that explosive sort of stuff will expand though screwed up in a vice, and burst it, though it were triple steel. It is for the nation's sake, and not for her authors' sake, that I would have America be heedful of the increasing greatness among her writers. For how great the shame, if other nations should be before her, in crowning her heroes of the pen! But this is almost the case now. American authors have received more just and discriminating praise (however loftily and ridiculously given, in certain cases) 30 even from some Englishmen, than from their own countrymen. There are hardly five critics in America; and several of them are asleep. As for patronage, it is the American author who now patronizes his country, and not his country him. And if at times some among them appeal to the people for more recognition, it is not al-ways with selfish motives, but patriotic ones.

It is true, that but few of them as yet have evinced that decided originality which merits great praise. But that graceful writer, who perhaps of all Americans has re-ceived the most plaudits from his own country for his productions, — that very popular and amiable writer, however good and self-reliant in many things, perhaps owes his chief reputation to the self-acknowledged imitation of a foreign model, and 40

---

21 **Pop Emmons . . . Fredoniad.** It would probably be difficult to exceed the patriotism which praises *Fre-doniad, or Independence Preserved — An Epic Poem of the War of 1812,* by Richard Emmons   37 **graceful writer.** Melville was probably thinking of Washington Irving; in a letter to Duyckinck a little later, he said, "Irving is a grasshopper to him [Hawthorne]"

to the studied avoidance of all topics but smooth ones. But it is better to fail in originality than to succeed in imitation. He who has never failed somewhere, that man cannot be great. Failure is the true test of greatness. And if it be said, that continual success is a proof that a man wisely knows his powers, — it is only to be added, that, in that case, he knows them to be small. Let us believe it, then, once for all, that there is no hope for us in these smooth, pleasing writers that know their powers. Without malice, but to speak the plain fact, they but furnish an appendix to Goldsmith, and other English authors. And we want no American Goldsmiths: nay, we want no American Miltons. It were the vilest thing you could say
10 of a true American author, that he were an American Tompkins. Call him an American and have done, for you cannot say a nobler thing of him. But it is not meant that all American writers should studiously cleave to nationality in their writings; only this, no American writer should write like an Englishman or a Frenchman; let him write like a man, for then he will be sure to write like an American. Let us away with this leaven of literary flunkeyism towards England. If either must play the flunkey in this thing, let England do it, not us. While we are rapidly preparing for that political supremacy among the nations which prophetically awaits us at the close of the present century, in a literary point of view, we are deplorably unprepared for it; and we seem studious to remain so. Hitherto, reasons might have ex-
20 isted why this should be; but no good reason exists now. And all that is requisite to amendment in this matter, is simply this: that while freely acknowledging all excellence everywhere, we should refrain from unduly lauding foreign writers, and, at the same time, duly recognize meritorious writers that are our own; — those writers who breathe that unshackled, democratic spirit of Christianity in all things, which now takes the practical lead in this world, though at the same time led by ourselves — us Americans. Let us boldly contemn all imitation, though it comes to us graceful and fragrant as the morning; and foster all originality, though at first it be crabbed and ugly as our own pine knots. And if any of our authors fail, or seem to fail, then, in the words of my enthusiastic Carolina cousin, let us clap him on
30 the shoulder, and back him against all Europe for his second round. The truth is, that in one point of view, this matter of a national literature has come to such a pass with us, that in some sense we must turn bullies, else the day is lost, or superiority so far beyond us, that we can hardly say it will ever be ours.

And now, my countrymen, as an excellent author of your own flesh and blood, — an unimitating, and, perhaps, in his way, an inimitable man — whom better can I commend to you, in the first place, than Nathaniel Hawthorne. He is one of the new, and far better generation of your writers. The smell of your beeches and hemlocks is upon him; your own broad prairies are in his soul; and if you travel away inland into his deep and noble nature, you will hear the far roar of his Niagara.
40 Give not over to future generations the glad duty of acknowledging him for what he is. Take that joy to yourself, in your own generation; and so shall he feel those grateful impulses on him, that may possibly prompt him to the full flower of some still greater achievement in your eyes. And by confessing him you thereby confess

---

10 **Tompkins,** a name connoting an English butler; cf. **flunkeyism,** below

others; you brace the whole brotherhood. For genius, all over the world, stands hand in hand, and one shock of recognition runs the whole circle round.

In treating of Hawthorne, or rather of Hawthorne in his writings (for I never saw the man; and in the chances of a quiet plantation life, remote from his haunts, perhaps never shall); in treating of his works, I say, I have thus far omitted all mention of his "Twice Told Tales," and "Scarlet Letter." Both are excellent, but full of such manifold, strange, and diffusive beauties, that time would all but fail me to point the half of them out. But there are things in those two books, which, had they been written in England a century ago, Nathaniel Hawthorne had utterly displaced many of the bright names we now revere on authority. But I am content to 10 leave Hawthorne to himself, and to the infallible finding of posterity; and however great may be the praise I have bestowed upon him, I feel that in so doing I have more served and honored myself, than him. For, at bottom, great excellence is praise enough to itself; but the feeling of a sincere and appreciative love and admiration towards it, this is relieved by utterance; and warm, honest praise, ever leaves a pleasant flavor in the mouth; and it is an honorable thing to confess to what is honorable in others.

But I cannot leave my subject yet. No man can ever read a fine author, and relish him to his very bones while he reads, without subsequently fancying to himself some ideal image of the man and his mind. And if you rightly look for it, you will almost 20 always find that the author himself has somewhere furnished you with his own picture. For poets (whether in prose or verse), being painters of nature, are like their brethren of the pencil, the true portrait-painters, who, in the multitude of likenesses to be sketched, do not invariably omit their own; and in all high instances, they paint them without any vanity, though at times with a lurking something, that would take several pages to properly define.

I submit it, then, to those best acquainted with the man personally, whether the following is not Nathaniel Hawthorne; — and to himself, whether something involved in it does not express the temper of his mind, — that lasting temper of all true, candid men — a seeker, not a finder yet: —   30

"A man now entered, in neglected attire, with the aspect of a thinker, but somewhat too rough-hewn and brawny for a scholar. His face was full of sturdy vigor, with some finer and keener attribute beneath; though harsh at first, it was tempered with the glow of a large, warm heart, which had force enough to heat his powerful intellect through and through. He advanced to the Intelligencer, and looked at him with a glance of such stern sincerity, that perhaps few secrets were beyond its scope.

" 'I seek for Truth,' said he."

Twenty-four hours have elapsed since writing the foregoing. I have just returned from the hay-mow, charged more and more with love and admiration of Hawthorne. For I have just been gleaning through the Mosses, picking up many things here 40

---

31 **A man . . . said he.** The quotation is from "The Intelligence Office," a sketch in *Mosses from an Old Manse*

and there that had previously escaped me. And I found that but to glean after this man, is better than to be in at the harvest of others. To be frank (though, perhaps, rather foolish) notwithstanding what I wrote yesterday of these Mosses, I had not then culled them all; but had, nevertheless, been sufficiently sensible of the subtle essence in them, as to write as I did. To what infinite height of loving wonder and admiration I may yet be borne, when by repeatedly banqueting on these Mosses I shall have thoroughly incorporated their whole stuff into my being, — that, I cannot tell. But already I feel that this Hawthorne has dropped germinous seeds into my soul. He expands and deepens down, the more I contemplate him; and further and
10 further, shoots his strong New England roots in the hot soil of my Southern soul.

By careful reference to the "Table of Contents," I now find that I have gone through all the sketches; but that when I yesterday wrote, I had not at all read two particular pieces, to which I now desire to call special attention, — "A Select Party," and "Young Goodman Brown." Here, be it said to all those whom this poor fugitive scrawl of mine may tempt to the perusal of the "Mosses," that they must on no account suffer themselves to be trifled with, disappointed, or deceived by the triviality of many of the titles to these sketches. For in more than one instance, the title utterly belies the piece. It is as if rustic demijohns containing the very best and costliest of Falernian and Tokay, were labelled "Cider," "Perry," and "Elder-berry
20 wine." The truth seems to be, that like many other geniuses, this Man of Mosses takes great delight in hoodwinking the world, — at least, with respect to himself. Personally, I doubt not that he rather prefers to be generally esteemed but a so-so sort of author; being willing to reserve the thorough and acute appreciation of what he is, to that party most qualified to judge — that is, to himself. Besides, at the bottom of their natures, men like Hawthorne, in many things, deem the plaudits of the public such strong presumptive evidence of mediocrity in the object of them, that it would in some degree render them doubtful of their own powers, did they hear much and vociferous braying concerning them in the public pastures. True, I have been braying myself (if you please to be witty enough to have it so), but then
30 I claim to be the first that has so brayed in this particular matter; and therefore, while pleading guilty to the charge, still claim all the merit due to originality.

But with whatever motive, playful or profound, Nathaniel Hawthorne has chosen to entitle his pieces in the manner he has, it is certain that some of them are directly calculated to deceive — egregiously deceive, the superficial skimmer of pages. To be downright and candid once more, let me cheerfully say, that two of these titles did dolefully dupe no less an eagle-eyed reader than myself; and that, too, after I had been impressed with a sense of the great depth and breadth of this American man. "Who in the name of thunder" (as the country-people say in this neighborhood), "who in the name of thunder, would anticipate any marvel in a piece entitled
40 'Young Goodman Brown'?" You would of course suppose that it was a simple little tale, intended as a supplement to "Goody Two Shoes." Whereas, it is deep as Dante; nor can you finish it, without addressing the author in his own words — "It is yours to penetrate, in every bosom, the deep mystery of sin." And with Young Goodman, too, in allegorical pursuit of his Puritan wife, you cry out in your anguish:

"'Faith!' shouted Goodman Brown, in a voice of agony and desperation; and the echoes of the forest mocked him, crying, — 'Faith! Faith!' as if bewildered wretches were seeking her all through the wilderness."

Now this same piece, entitled "Young Goodman Brown," is one of the two that I had not all read yesterday; and I allude to it now, because it is, in itself, such a strong positive illustration of that blackness in Hawthorne, which I had assumed from the mere occasional shadows of it, as revealed in several of the other sketches. But had I previously perused "Young Goodman Brown," I should have been at no pains to draw the conclusion, which I came to at a time when I was ignorant that the book contained one such direct and unqualified manifestation of it.   10

The other piece of the two referred to, is entitled "A Select Party," which, in my first simplicity upon originally taking hold of the book, I fancied must treat of some pumpkin-pie party in old Salem, or some chowder-party on Cape Cod. Whereas, by all the gods of Peedee, it is the sweetest and sublimest thing that has been written since Spenser wrote. Nay, there is nothing in Spenser that surpasses it, perhaps nothing that equals it. And the test is this: read any canto in "The Faery Queen," and then read "A Select Party" and decide which pleases you the most, — that is, if you are qualified to judge. Do not be frightened at this; for when Spenser was alive, he was thought of very much as Hawthorne is now, — was generally accounted just such a "gentle" harmless man. It may be, that to common eyes, the sublimity of 20 Hawthorne seems lost in his sweetness, — as perhaps in that same "Select Party" of his; for whom he has builded so august a dome of sunset clouds, and served them on richer plate than Belshazzar's when he banqueted his lords in Babylon.

But my chief business now, is to point out a particular page in this piece, having reference to an honored guest, who under the name of "The Master Genius," but in the guise "of a young man of poor attire, with no insignia of rank or acknowledged eminence," is introduced to the man of Fancy, who is the giver of the feast. Now, the page having reference to this "Master Genius," so happily expresses much of what I yesterday wrote, touching the coming of the Literary Shiloh of America, that I cannot but be charmed by the coincidence; especially, when it shows such a 30 parity of ideas, at least in this one point, between a man like Hawthorne and a man like me.

And here, let me throw out another conceit of mine touching this American Shiloh, or "Master Genius," as Hawthorne calls him. May it not be, that this commanding mind has not been, is not, and never will be, individually developed in any one man? And would it, indeed, appear so unreasonable to suppose, that this great fulness and overflowing may be, or may be destined to be, shared by a plurality of men of genius? Surely, to take the very greatest example on record, Shakspeare cannot be regarded as in himself the concretion of all the genius of his time; nor as so immeasurably beyond Marlow, Webster, Ford, Beaumont, Jonson, that those great 40 men can be said to share none of his power? For one, I conceive that there were dramatists in Elizabeth's day, between whom and Shakspeare the distance was by

---

14 **Peedee,** the name of a river in North Carolina, but the word here probably has no significance other than that of a mild expletive   23 **Belshazzar's.** The reference is to Belshazzar's feast, described in Daniel 5

no means great. Let any one, hitherto little acquainted with those neglected old authors, for the first time read them thoroughly, or even read Charles Lamb's Specimens of them, and he will be amazed at the wondrous ability of those Anaks of men, and shocked at this renewed example of the fact, that Fortune has more to do with fame than merit, — though, without merit, lasting fame there can be none.

Nevertheless, it would argue too ill of my country were this maxim to hold good concerning Nathaniel Hawthorne, a man, who already, in some few minds, has shed "such a light, as never illuminates the earth save when a great heart burns as the household fire of a grand intellect."

10 The words are his, — in the "Select Party"; and they are a magnificent setting to a coincident sentiment of my own, but ramblingly expressed yesterday, in reference to himself. Gainsay it who will, as I now write, I am Posterity speaking by proxy — and after times will make it more than good, when I declare, that the American, who up to the present day has evinced, in literature, the largest brain with the largest heart, that man is Nathaniel Hawthorne. Moreover, that whatever Nathaniel Hawthorne may hereafter write, "The Mosses from an Old Manse" will be ultimately accounted his masterpiece. For there is a sure, though a secret sign in some works which proves the culmination of the powers (only the developable ones, however) that produced them. But I am by no means desirous of the glory of a prophet. I
20 pray Heaven that Hawthorne may *yet* prove me an impostor in this prediction. Especially, as I somehow cling to the strange fancy, that, in all men, hiddenly reside certain wondrous, occult properties — as in some plants and minerals — which by some happy but very rare accident (as bronze was discovered by the melting of the iron and brass at the burning of Corinth) may chance to be called forth here on earth; not entirely waiting for their better discovery in the more congenial, blessed atmosphere of heaven.

Once more — for it is hard to be finite upon an infinite subject, and all subjects are infinite. By some people this entire scrawl of mine may be esteemed altogether unnecessary, inasmuch "as years ago" (they may say) "we found out the rich and
30 rare stuff in this Hawthorne, whom you now parade forth, as if only *yourself* were the discoverer of this Portuguese diamond in our literature." But even granting all this — and adding to it, the assumption that the books of Hawthorne have sold by the five thousand, — what does that signify? They should be sold by the hundred thousand; and read by the million; and admired by every one who is capable of admiration. 1850

3 **Anaks**, a people of Palestine conquered by the Jews (see Joshua 11:21); Melville originally wrote "now half-forgotten men" (see Thorp's "Notes" in his Melville *Selections*), which was probably the meaning intended

The Agatha Letter

In "The Agatha Letter" Melville passed on to his friend Hawthorne the story of Agatha Hatch, the daughter of a lighthouse keeper on the Nantucket coast, who married a shipwrecked sailor and was deserted by him. Melville had heard the story from a New Bedford

lawyer while visiting in Nantucket in July 1852. Thinking the incidents more in Haw-thorne's "vein" than his own, a few weeks later he embodied them (with some suggestions for their handling) in the following letter to Hawthorne, then living at the Wayside, in Con-cord. In November 1852, Melville was a guest at the Wayside, where the two men talked over the possibilities of the story. Though interested, Hawthorne appeared reluctant to work it up (possibly because he felt that it was Melville's property), and their conversations ended with Hawthorne's urging Melville himself to do the story of Agatha. Shortly after his departure, Melville wrote saying that he would, and asking Hawthorne to return to him the memo-randa on the subject. But so far as is known, Melville did not carry out his intention, and the story of Agatha remains untold except in the following fragments.

Melville's suggestions give interesting insight into his literary methods. It is fascinating to see his imagination at work, tentatively yet masterfully sketching the opening action and in-sinuating a wealth of symbolic detail. Melville apparently intended to present with sympathy and admiration the patient resignation of Agatha; if so, the attitude contrasts sharply with the defiance of Moby Dick *and the despair of* Pierre. *It is easy to see why he thought the story would be a "natural" for Hawthorne (the author of many tales of the afflicted con-science) if told from the point of view of the wayward husband: Hawthorne would be the man who could most shrewdly "mark his trepidation and suspicion."*

The letter and the lawyer's accompanying memorandum are reprinted from the New England Quarterly *(II, April 1929, pp. 296-307), where they were edited by S. E. Mori-son from original manuscripts now preserved in the Houghton Library at Harvard. Two additional short letters by Melville to Hawthorne on the subject, together with some illumi-nating commentary, are given by Harrison Hayford in "The Significance of Melville's 'Agatha' Letters,"* Journal of English Literary History *(XIII, December 1946, pp. 299-310).*

Pittsfield Aug: 13th
1852

[Salutation torn off]

— While visiting Nantucket some four weeks ago, I made the acquaintance of a gentleman from New Bedford, a lawyer, who gave me considerable information upon several matters concerning which I was curious. One night we were talking, I think, of the great patience, & endurance, & resignedness of the women of the island in submitting so uncomplainingly to the long, long absences of their sailor husbands, when, by way of anecdote, this lawyer gave me a leaf from his professional experi-ence. Altho' his memory was a little confused with regard to some of the items of the story, yet he told me enough to awaken the most lively interest in me; and I begged him to be sure and send me a more full account so soon as he arrived home — 10 he having previously told me that at the time of the affair he had made a record in his books. —— I heard nothing more, till a few days after arriving here at Pittsfield I received thro' the Post Office the enclosed documents. — You will perceive by the gentleman's note to me that he assumed that I had purposed making literary use of the story; but I had not hinted anything of the kind to him, & my first spontane-ous interest in it arose from very different considerations. I confess, however, that since then I have a little turned the subject over in my mind with a view to a reg-ular story to be founded on these striking incidents. But, thinking again, it has occurred to me that this thing lies very much in a vein, with which you are peculiarly familiar. To be plump, I think that in this matter you would make a better hand at it than I would. —— Besides the thing seems naturally to gravitate towards you (to speak [*half a line torn*] should of right belong to you. I could [*half a line torn*] the Steward (?) to deliver it to you. ——

The very great interest I felt in this story while narrating to me, was heightened by the emotion of the gentleman who told it, who evinced the most unaffected sympathy in it, tho' now a matter of his past.— But perhaps this great interest of mine may have been largely helped by some accidental circumstance or other: so that,
10 possibly, to you the story may not seem to possess so much of pathos, & so much of depth. But you will see how it is. ——

In estimating the character of Robinson Charity should be allowed a liberal play. I take exception to that passage from the Diary which says that *"he must have received a portion of his punishment in this life"* — thus hinting of a future supplemental castigation. ——I do not at all suppose that his desertion of his wife was a premeditated thing. If it had been so, he would have changed his name, probably, after quitting her. — No: he was a weak man, & his temptations (tho' we know little of them) were strong. The whole sin stole upon him insensibly — so that it would perhaps have been hard for him to settle upon the exact day when he could say to
20 himself, *"Now* I have deserted my wife"; unless, indeed upon the day he wedded the Alexandria lady. — And here I am reminded of your *London husband:* tho' the cases so widely contrast. — Many more things might be mentioned; but I forbear; you will find out the suggestiveness for yourself; & all the better perhaps, for my not intermeddling. ——

If you should be suffic[ien]tly interested, to engage upon a regular story founded on this narration; then I consider you but fairly entitled to the following tributary items, collected by me, by chance, during my strolls thro the island; & which — as you will perceive — seem legitimately to belong to the story, in its rounded & beautified & thoroughly developed state; — but of all this you must of course be your
30 own judge — I but submit matter to you — I don't decide.

Supposing the story to open with the wreck — then there must be a storm; & it were well if some faint shadow of the preceding *calm* were thrown forth to lead the whole. — Now imagine a high cliff overhanging the sea & crowned with a pasture for sheep; a little way off — higher up, — a light-house, where resides the father of the future Mrs. Robinson the First. The afternoon is mild & warm. The sea with an air of solemn deliberation, with an elaborate deliberation, ceremoniously rolls upon the beach. The air is suppressedly charged with the sound of long lines of surf. There is no land over against the cliff short of Europe & the West Indies. Young Agatha (but you must give her some other name) comes wandering along
40 the cliff. She marks how the continual assaults of the sea have undermined it; so that the fences fall over, & have need of many shiftings inland. The sea has encroached also upon that part where their dwelling-house stands near the light-house. — Filled with meditations, she reclines along the edge of the cliff & gazes

---

21 **your London Husband.** See "Wakefield" in *Twice-Told Tales*

out seaward. She marks a handful of cloud on the horizon, presaging a storm thro'
all this quietude. (Of a maritime family & always dwelling on the coast, she is learned
in these matters). This again gives food for thought. Suddenly she catches the long
shadow of the cliff cast upon the beach 100 feet beneath her; and now she notes a
shadow moving along the shadow. It is cast by a sheep from the pasture. It has
advanced to the very edge of the cliff, & is sending a mild innocent glance far out
upon the water. There, in strange & beautiful contrast, we have the innocence of
the lamb placidly eyeing the malignity of the sea, (All this having poetic reference
to Agatha & her sea-lover, who is coming in the storm: the storm carries her lover
to her; she catches a dim distant glimpse of his ship ere quitting the cliff)   10

——

P. S. It were well, if from her knowledge of the deep miseries produced to wives
by marrying seafaring men, Agatha should have formed a young determination never
to marry a sailor; which resolve in her, however, is afterwards overborne by the
omnipotence of love. — P. S. no 2. Agatha should be active during the wreck, and
should, in some way, be made the saviour of young Robinson. He should be the
only survivor. He should be ministered to by Agatha at the house during the illness ensuing upon his injuries from the wreck. Now this wrecked ship has driven
over the shoals, & driven upon the beach where she goes to pieces, all but her stem-
part. This in course of time becomes embedded in the sand — after the lapse of
some years showing nothing but the sturdy stem (or, prow-bone) projecting some   20
two feet at low water. All the rest is filled and packed down with the sand. — So
that after her husband has disappeared the sad Agatha every day sees this melancholy
monument, with all its remindings. ——

Some few other items occur to me — but nothing material — and I fear to weary
you, if not, make you smile at my strange impertinent officiousness. — And it would
be so, were it not that these things do, in my mind, seem legitimately to belong
to the story; for they were visibly suggested to me by scenes I actually beheld while
on the very coast where the story of Agatha occurred. —— I do not, therefore, My
Dear Hawthorne, at all imagine that you will think that I am so silly as to flatter
myself I am giving you anything of my own. I am but restoring to you your own   30
property — which you would quickly enough have identified for yourself — had you
but been on the spot as I happened to be.

Let me conclude by saying that it seems to me that with your great power in these
things, you can construct a story of remarkable interest out of this material furnished
by the New Bedford lawyer. —— You have a skeleton of actual reality to build about
with fulness & veins & beauty. And if I thought I could do it as well as you, why,
I should not let you have it. — The narrative from the Diary is instinct with significance. — Consider the mention of the *shawls* —— & the inference drawn from it.
Ponder the conduct of this Robinson throughout. Mark his trepidation & suspicion
when anyone called upon him. — But why prate so — you will mark it all and mark   40
it deeper than I would, perhaps.

I have written all this in a great hurry; so you must spell it out the best way you may. ——

After a sufficient lapse of time — when Agatha has became alarmed about the protracted absence of her young husband & is fervently expecting a letter from — then we must introduce the mail-post — no, that phrase won't do, but here is the thing. —— Owing the remoteness of the lighthouse from any settled place no regular mail reaches it. But some mile or so distant there is a road leading between two post-towns. And at the junction of what we shall call the Light-House road with this Post Road, there stands a post surmounted with a little rude wood box
10 with a lid to it and a leather hinge. Into this box the Post boy drops all letters for the people of the light house & that vicinity of fishermen. To this post they must come for their letters. And, of course, daily young Agatha goes for seventeen years. She goes thither daily. As her hopes gradually decay in her, so does the post itself, & the little box decays. The post rots in the ground at last. Owing to its very little use — hardly used at all — grass grows rankly about it. At last a little bird nests in it. At last the post falls.
The father of Agatha must be an old widower — a man of the sea, but early driven away from it by repeated disasters. Hence, is he subdued & quiet & wise in his life. And now he tends a light house, to warn people from those very perils, from which
20 he himself has suffered.

The Lawyer's Story

May 28th 1842 Saturday. I have just returned from a visit to Falmouth with a Mr. Janney of M°. on one of the most interesting and romantic cases I ever expect to be engaged in. The gentleman from Missouri Mr. Janney came to my house last Sunday evening and related to myself and partner that he had married the daughter of a Mrs. Irvin formerly of Pittsburgh Pa. and that Mrs. Irvin had married a second husband by the name of Robertson. The latter deceased about two years since. He was appointed Adm^r. to his Estate which amounted to $20,000 — about 15 months afterwards Mrs. Robertson also died and in the meantime the Adm^r. had been en-
30 gaged in looking up heirs to the Estate. He learned that Robertson was an Englishman whose original name was Shinn — that he had resided at Alexandria D. C. where he had two nephews. He also wrote to England and had ascertained the history of genealogy of the family with much accuracy, when on going to the Post Office one day he found a letter directed to James Robertson the deceased, post marked Falmouth Mass^{tts}. On opening it he found it from a person signing herself Rebecca A. Gifford and addressing him as "Father." The existence of this girl had been known before by Mrs. Robertson and her husband had pronounced her to be illegitimate. The Adm^r. then addressed a letter to Mrs. Gifford informing her of the decease of her father. He was surprized soon after by the appearance in St. Louis of a shrewd Quaker from Falmouth named Dillingham with full powers and fortified

---

21 **The Lawyer's Story.** The following portion of the document was supplied by the New Bedford lawyer, in his handwriting

by letters and affidavits shewing the existence of a wife in Falmouth whom Robertson married in 1807 at Pembroke Mass & the legitimacy of the daughter who had married a Mr. Gifford and laying strong claims to the entire property.

The Adm^r. and his heirs having strong doubts arising from the declarations of Robertson during his lifetime & the peculiar expressions contained in the letters exhibited, as to the validity of the marriage & the claim based upon it, determined to resist and legal proceedings were at once commenced. The object of the visit of Mr. Janney was to attend the taking of depositions, upon a notice from the claimants. The Minister, Town Clerk and Witnesses present at the ceremony established the fact of a legal marriage and the birth of a child in wedlock, beyond all cavil or con- 10 troversy. All of the witnesses were of the highest respectability and the widow and daughter interested me very much.

It appeared that Robertson was wrecked on the coast of Pembroke where this girl, then Miss Agatha Hatch was living — that he was hospitably entertained and cared for, and that within a year after, he married her, in due form of law — that he went two short voyages to sea. About two years after the marriage, leaving his wife enceinte he started off in search of employment and from that time until seventeen years afterwards she never heard from him in any way whatsoever, directly or indirectly, not even a word. Being poor she went out nursing for her daily bread and yet contrived out of her small earnings to give her daughter a first rate education. 20 Having become connected with the Society of Friends she sent her to their most celebrated boarding school and when I saw her I found she had profited by all her advantages beyond most females. In the meantime Robertson had gone to Alexandria D. C. where he had entered into a successful and profitable business and married a second wife. At the expiration of this long period of 17 years which for the poor forsaken wife had glided wearily away, while she was engaged away from home, her Father rode up in a gig and informed her that her husband had returned and wished to see her and her child — but if she would not see him, to see her child at all events. They all returned together and encountered him on the way coming to meet them about half a mile from her father's house. This meeting was described 30 to me by the mother and daughter. — Every incident seemed branded upon the memories of both. He excused himself as well as he could for his long absence and silence, appeared very affectionate refused to tell where he was living and persuaded them not to make any inquiries. Gave them a handsome sum of money, promised to return for good and left the next day. — He appeared again in about a year, just on the eve of his daughter's marriage & gave her a bridal present. It was not long after this that his wife in Alexandria died. — He then wrote to his son-in-law to come there. — He did so — remained 2 days and brought back a gold watch and three handsome shawls which had been previously worn by some person. They all admitted that they had suspicions then & from this circumstance that he had been a 40 second time married.

Soon after this he visited Falmouth again & as it proved for the last time. He announced his intention of removing to Missouri & urged the whole family to go with him, promising money land and other assistance to his son-in-law. The offer was not accepted. He shed tears when he bade them farewell. From the time of his return to Missouri till the time of his death a constant correspondence was kept up money was remitted by him annually and he announced to them his marriage with Mrs. Irvin. He had no children by either of his last two wives.

Mr. Janney was entirely disappointed in the character of the evidence and the character of the claimants. He considered them, when he first came, as parties to the imposition practised upon Mrs. Irvin & her children. But I was satisfied and I think he was, that their motives in keeping silence were high and pure, creditable in every way to the true Mrs. Robertson. She stated the causes with a simplicity &
10 pathos which carried that conviction irresistibly to my mind. The only good(?) it could have done to expose him would have been to drive Robertson away and forever disgrace him & it would certainly have made Mrs. Irvin & her children wretched for rest of their days. "I had no wish," said the wife, "to make either of them unhappy, notwithstanding all I had suffered on his account." — It was to me a most striking instance of long continued & uncomplaining submission to wrong and anguish on the part of a wife, wch. made her in my eyes a heroine.

Janney informed me that R. and his last wife did not live very happily together and particularly that he seemed to be a very jealous suspicious man. That when a person called at his house he would never enter the room till he knew who it was
20 & "all about him." He must have received a portion of his punishment in this life. The fact came out in the course of examination that they had agreed to give Dillingham one half of what he might obtain deducting the expenses of his half. After the strength of the evidence became known Mr. Janney commenced the making of serious efforts to effect a compromise of the claims. What the result will be time will shew. This is, I suspect, the end of my connexion with the case.

New Bedford July 14th 1852
HERMAN MELVILLE

Dr. Sir

Above I send you the little story I promised you.
30   Respectfully yours
P. S.

The business was settled in a few weeks afterwards, in a most amicable and honorable manner, by a division of the property. I think Mrs. Robinson and her family refused to claim or receive anything that really belonged to Mrs. Irvin, or which Robinson had derived through her.

28 **Dr. Sir.** "This in the lawyer's hand is scratched out" — New England Quarterly   31 **P.S.** The postscript is Melville's

Benito Cereno

"Benito Cereno" was first printed serially in Putnam's Monthly Magazine *in October, November, and December 1855, and was reprinted, with minor revisions, in* Piazza Tales *in 1856. Melville derived the principal facts of his narrative from Chapter XVIII of* Amasa Delano's Narrative of Voyages and Travels in the Northern and Southern

Hemispheres . . ., *Boston, 1817; but the artistry which made of the facts a literary masterpiece was Melville's own. Delano's chapter is reprinted in Harold H. Scudder's "Melville's 'Benito Cereno' and Captain Delano's Voyages,"* Publications of the Modern Language Association, *June 1928, XLIII.*

The late Edward J. O'Brien regarded "Benito Cereno" as "the noblest short story in American literature" (Twenty-Five Finest Short Stories, *New York, 1931). The story is indeed remarkable for its atmosphere and suggestion, its cumulative suspense, its horror, its pictorial qualities, its portrayal of contrasting types of character. Only in* Moby Dick *perhaps is Melville's power more fully revealed.*

In the year 1799, Captain Amasa Delano, of Duxbury, in Massachusetts, commanding a large sealer and general trader, lay at anchor with a valuable cargo, in the harbor of St. Maria — a small, desert, uninhabited island towards the southern extremity of the long coast of Chili. There he had touched for water.

On the second day, not long after dawn, while lying in his berth, his mate came below, informing him that a strange sail was coming into the bay. Ships were then not so plenty in those waters as now. He rose, dressed, and went on deck.

The morning was one peculiar to that coast. Everything was mute and calm; everything gray. The sea, though undulated into long roods of swells, seemed fixed, and was sleeked at the surface like waved lead that has cooled and set in the smelt- 10 er's mould. The sky seemed a gray surtout. Flights of troubled gray fowl, kith and kin with flights of troubled gray vapors among which they were mixed, skimmed low and fitfully over the waters, as swallows over meadows before storms. Shadows present, foreshadowing deeper shadows to come.

To Captain Delano's surprise, the stranger, viewed through the glass, showed no colors; though to do so upon entering a haven, however unhabited in its shores, where but a single other ship might be lying, was the custom among peaceful seamen of all nations. Considering the lawlessness and loneliness of the spot, and the sort of stories, at that day, associated with those seas, Captain Delano's surprise might have deepened into some uneasiness had he not been a person of a singularly 20 undistrustful good nature, not liable, except on extraordinary and repeated incentives, and hardly then, to indulge in personal alarms, any way involving the imputation of malign evil in man. Whether, in view of what humanity is capable, such a trait implies, along with a benevolent heart, more than ordinary quickness and accuracy of intellectual perception, may be left to the wise to determine.

But whatever misgivings might have obtruded on first seeing the stranger, would almost, in any seaman's mind, have been dissipated by observing that the ship, in navigating into the harbor, was drawing too near the land; a sunken reef making out off her bow. This seemed to prove her a stranger, indeed, not only to the sealer, but the island; consequently, she could be no wonted freebooter on that ocean. 30 With no small interest, Captain Delano continued to watch her — a proceeding not much facilitated by the vapors partly mantling the hull, through which the far matin light from her cabin streamed equivocally enough; much like the sun — by this time hemisphered on the rim of the horizon, and, apparently, in company with the strange ship, entering the harbor — which, wimpled by the same low, creeping clouds, showed not unlike a Lima intriguante's one sinister eye peering across the Plaza from the Indian loop-hole of her dusk *saya-y-manta.*

It might have been but a deception of the vapors, but, the longer the stranger was watched the more singular appeared her manoeuvers. Ere long it seemed hard to decide whether she meant to come in or no — what she wanted, or what she was about. The wind, which had breezed up a little during the night, was now extremely light and baffling, which the more increased the apparent uncertainty of her movements.

10   Surmising, at last, that it might be a ship in distress, Captain Delano ordered his whale-boat to be dropped, and, much to the wary opposition of his mate, prepared to board her, and, at the least, pilot her in. On the night previous, a fishing-party of the seamen had gone a long distance to some detached rocks out of sight from the sealer, and, an hour or two before daybreak, had returned, having met with no small success. Presuming that the stranger might have been long off soundings, the good captain put several baskets of the fish, for presents, into his boat, and so pulled away. From her continuing too near the sunken reef, deeming her in danger, calling to his men, he made all haste to apprise those on board of their situation. But, some time ere the boat came up, the wind, light though it was, having
20 shifted, had headed the vessel off, as well as partly broken the vapors from about her.

Upon gaining a less remote view, the ship, when made signally visible on the verge of the leaden-hued swells, with the shreds of fog here and there raggedly furring her, appeared like a white-washed monastery after a thunderstorm, seen perched upon some dun cliff among the Pyrenees. But it was no purely fanciful resemblance which now, for a moment, almost led Captain Delano to think that nothing less than a ship-load of monks was before him. Peering over the bulwarks were what really seemed, in the hazy distance, throngs of dark cowls; while, fitfully revealed through the open port-holes, other dark moving figures were dimly descried, as of Black Friars pacing the cloisters.

30   Upon a still nigher approach, this appearance was modified, and the true character of the vessel was plain — a Spanish merchantman of the first class, carrying Negro slaves, amongst other valuable freight, from one colonial port to another. A very large, and, in its time, a very fine vessel, such as in those days were at intervals encountered along that main; sometimes superseded Acapulco treasure-ships, or retired frigates of the Spanish king's navy, which, like superannuated Italian palaces, still, under a decline of masters, preserved signs of former state.

As the whale-boat drew more and more nigh, the cause of the peculiar pipe-clayed aspect of the stranger was seen in the slovenly neglect pervading her. The spars, ropes, and great part of the bulwarks, looked woolly, from long unacquaintance
40 with the scraper, tar, and the brush. Her keel seemed laid, her ribs put together, and she launched, from Ezekiel's Valley of Dry Bones.

---

2 **Lima,** the capital of Peru   2 **intriguante,** a woman who carries on an illicit love affair   3 **saya-y-manta,** skirt and shawl   34 **Acapulco,** a Mexican port on the Pacific Ocean   41 **Ezekiel's . . . Bones.** See Ezekiel 37:1-10

In the present business in which she was engaged, the ship's general model and rig appeared to have undergone no material change from their original warlike and Froissart pattern. However, no guns were seen.

The tops were large, and were railed about with what had once been octagonal net-work, all now in sad disrepair. These tops hung overhead like three ruinous aviaries, in one of which was seen perched on a ratlin, a white noddy, a strange fowl, so called from its lethargic somnambulistic character, being frequently caught by hand at sea. Battered and mouldy, the castellated forecastle seemed some ancient turret, long ago taken by assault, and then left to decay. Toward the stern, two high-raised quarter galleries — the balustrades here and there covered with dry, 10 tindery sea-moss — opening out from the unoccupied state-cabin, whose dead-lights, for all the mild weather, were hermetically closed and calked — these tenantless balconies hung over the sea as if it were the grand Venetian canal. But the principal relic of faded grandeur was the ample oval of the shield-like stern-piece, intricately carved with the arms of Castile and Leon, medallioned about by groups of myth-ological or symbolical devices; uppermost and central of which was a dark satyr in a mask, holding his foot on the prostrate neck of a writhing figure, likewise masked.

Whether the ship had a figure-head, or only a plain beak, was not quite certain, owing to canvas wrapped about that part, either to protect it while undergoing a re-furbishing, or else decently to hide its decay. Rudely painted or chalked, as in a 20 sailor freak, along the forward side of a sort of pedestal below the canvas, was the sentence, *"Seguid vuestro jefe"* (follow your leader); while upon the tarnished head-boards, near by, appeared, in stately capitals, once gilt, the ship's name "SAN DOMI-NICK," each letter streakingly corroded with tricklings of copper-spike rust; while, like mourning weeds, dark festoons of sea-grass slimily swept to and fro over the name, with every hearse-like roll of the hull.

As, at last, the boat was hooked from the bow along toward the gangway amid-ship, its keel, while yet some inches separated from the hull, harshly grated as on a sunken coral reef. It proved a huge bunch of conglobated barnacles adhering below the water to the side like a wen — a token of baffling airs and long calms passed 30 somewhere in those seas.

Climbing the side, the visitor was at once surrounded by a clamorous throng of whites and blacks, but the latter outnumbering the former more than could have been expected, Negro transportation-ship as the stranger in port was. But, in one language, and as with one voice, all poured out a common tale of suffering; in which the Negresses, of whom there were not a few, exceeded the others in their dolorous vehemence. The scurvy, together with a fever, had swept off a great part of their number, more especially the Spaniards. Off Cape Horn, they had narrowly escaped shipwreck; then, for days together, they had lain tranced without wind; their pro-visions were low; their water next to none; their lips that moment were baked.   40

---

3 **Froissart,** Jean Froissart (1337-1410), author of the famous *Chronicles.* "Froissart pattern" apparently means that the ship was of medieval design   4 **tops,** platforms in the mast   11 **dead-lights,** shutters on the cabin windows to keep out water   15 **Castile and Leon,** formerly kingdoms in Spain

While Captain Delano was thus made the mark of all eager tongues, his one eager glance took in all the faces, with every other object about him.

Always upon first boarding a large and populous ship at sea, especially a foreign one, with a nondescript crew such as Lascars or Manilla men, the impression varies in a peculiar way from that produced by first entering a strange house with strange inmates in a strange land. Both house and ship — the one by its walls and blinds, the other by its high bulwarks like ramparts — hoard from view their interiors till the last moment; but in the case of the ship there is this addition: that the living spectacle it contains, upon its sudden and complete disclosure, has, in contrast with
10 the blank ocean which zones it, something of the effect of enchantment. The ship seems unreal; these strange costumes, gestures, and faces, but a shadowy tableau just emerged from the deep, which directly must receive back what it gave.

Perhaps it was some such influence, as above is attempted to be described, which, in Captain Delano's mind, heightened whatever, upon a staid scrutiny, might have seemed unusual; especially the conspicuous figures of four elderly grizzled Negroes, their heads like black, doddered willow tops, who, in venerable contrast to the tumult below them, were couched sphynx-like, one on the starboard cat-head, another on the larboard, and the remaining pair face to face on the opposite bulwarks above the main-chains. They each had bits of unstranded old junk in their hands,
20 and, with a sort of stoical self-content, were picking the junk into oakum, a small heap of which lay by their sides. They accompanied the task with a continuous, low, monotonous chant; droning and druling away like so many gray-headed bagpipers playing a funeral march.

The quarter-deck rose into an ample elevated poop, upon the forward verge of which, lifted, like the oakum-pickers, some eight feet above the general throng, sat along in a row, separated by regular spaces, the cross-legged figures of six other blacks; each with a rusty hatchet in his hand, which, with a bit of brick and a rag, he was engaged like a scullion in scouring; while between each two was a small stack of hatchets, their rusted edges turned forward awaiting a like operation.
30 Though occasionally the four oakum-pickers would briefly address some person or persons in the crowd below, yet the six hatchet-polishers neither spoke to others, nor breathed a whisper among themselves, but sat intent upon their task, except at intervals, when, with the peculiar love in Negroes of uniting industry with pastime, two-and-two they sideways clashed their hatchets together, like cymbals, with a barbarous din. All six, unlike the generality, had the raw aspect of unsophisticated Africans.

But that first comprehensive glance which took in those ten figures, with scores less conspicuous, rested but an instant upon them, as, impatient of the hubbub of voices, the visitor turned in quest of whomsoever it might be that commanded the
40 ship.

But as if not unwilling to let nature make known her own case among his suffering charge, or else in despair of restraining it for the time, the Spanish captain, a

---

4 **Lascars,** East Indian sailors   16 **doddered,** having lost their branches because of age or decay   19 **main-chains,** attached to the mainmast

gentlemanly, reserved-looking, and rather young man to a stranger's eye, dressed with singular richness, but bearing plain traces of recent sleepless cares and disquietudes, stood passively by, leaning against the mainmast, at one moment casting a dreary, spiritless look upon his excited people, at the next an unhappy glance toward his visitor. By his side stood a black of small stature, in whose rude face, as occasionally, like a shepherd's dog, he mutely turned it up into the Spaniard's, sorrow and affection were equally blended.

Struggling through the throng, the American advanced to the Spaniard, assuring him of his sympathies, and offering to render whatever assistance might be in his power. To which the Spaniard returned for the present but grave and ceremonious 10 acknowledgments, his national formality dusked by the saturnine mood of ill-health.

But losing no time in mere compliments, Captain Delano, returning to the gangway, had his basket of fish brought up; and as the wind still continued light, so that some hours at least must elapse ere the ship could be brought to the anchorage, he bade his men return to the sealer, and fetch back as much water as the whale-boat could carry, with whatever soft bread the steward might have, all the remaining pumpkins on board, with a box of sugar, and a dozen of his private bottles of cider.

Not many minutes after the boat's pushing off, to the vexation of all, the wind entirely died away, and the tide turning, began drifting back the ship helplessly seaward. But trusting this would not long last, Captain Delano sought, with good 20 hopes, to cheer up the strangers, feeling no small satisfaction that, with persons in their condition he could — thanks to his frequent voyages along the Spanish main — converse with some freedom in their native tongue.

While left alone with them, he was not long in observing some things tending to heighten his first impressions; but surprise was lost in pity, both for the Spaniards and blacks, alike evidently reduced from scarcity of water and provisions; while long-continued suffering seemed to have brought out the less good-natured qualities of the Negroes, besides, at the same time, impairing the Spaniard's authority over them. But, under the circumstances, precisely this condition of things was to have been anticipated. In armies, navies, cities, or families, in nature herself, nothing 30 more relaxes good order than misery. Still, Captain Delano was not without the idea, that had Benito Cereno been a man of greater energy, misrule would hardly have come to the present pass. But the debility, constitutional or induced by the hardships, bodily and mental, of the Spanish captain, was too obvious to be overlooked. A prey to settled dejection, as if long mocked with hope he would not now indulge it, even when it had ceased to be a mock, the prospect of that day or evening at furthest, lying at anchor, with plenty of water for his people, and a brother captain to counsel and befriend, seemed in no perceptible degree to encourage him. His mind appeared unstrung, if not still more seriously affected. Shut up in these oaken walls, chained to one dull round of command, whose unconditionality cloyed 40 him, like some hypochondriac abbot he moved slowly about, at times suddenly pausing, starting, or staring, biting his lip, biting his finger-nail, flushing, paling, twitching his beard, with other symptoms of an absent or moody mind. This distempered spirit was lodged, as before hinted, in as distempered a frame. He was

rather tall, but seemed never to have been robust, and now with nervous suffering was almost worn to a skeleton. A tendency to some pulmonary complaint appeared to have been lately confirmed. His voice was like that of one with lungs half gone — hoarsely suppressed, a husky whisper. No wonder that, as in this state he tottered about, his private servant apprehensively followed him. Sometimes the Negro gave his master his arm, or took his handkerchief out of his pocket for him; performing these and similar offices with that affectionate zeal which transmutes into something filial or fraternal acts in themselves but menial; and which has gained for the Negro the repute of making the most pleasing body-servant in the world, one, too, whom
10 a master need be on no stiffly superior terms with, but may treat with familiar trust; less a servant than a devoted companion.

Marking the noisy indocility of the blacks in general, as well as what seemed the sullen inefficiency of the whites, it was not without humane satisfaction that Captain Delano witnessed the steady good conduct of Babo.

But the good conduct of Babo, hardly more than the ill-behavior of others, seemed to withdraw the half-lunatic Don Benito from his cloudy languor. Not that such precisely was the impression made by the Spaniard on the mind of his visitor. The Spaniard's individual unrest was, for the present, but noted as a conspicuous feature in the ship's general affliction. Still, Captain Delano was not a little concerned at
20 what he could not help taking for the time to be Don Benito's unfriendly indifference toward himself. The Spaniard's manner, too, conveyed a sort of sour and gloomy disdain, which he seemed at no pains to disguise. But this the American in charity ascribed to the harassing effects of sickness, since, in former instances, he had noted that there are peculiar natures on whom prolonged physical suffering seems to cancel every social instinct of kindness; as if forced to black bread themselves, they deemed it but equity that each person coming nigh them should, indirectly, by some slight or affront, be made to partake of their fare.

But ere long Captain Delano bethought him that, indulgent as he was at the first, in judging the Spaniard, he might not, after all, have exercised charity enough. At
30 bottom it was Don Benito's reserve which displeased him; but the same reserve was shown toward all but his personal attendant. Even the formal reports which, according to sea-usage, were at stated times made to him by some petty underling, either a white, mulatto or black, he hardly had patience enough to listen to, without betraying contemptuous aversion. His manner upon such occasions was, in its degree, not unlike that which might be supposed to have been his imperial countryman's, Charles V, just previous to the anchoritish retirement of that monarch from the throne.

This splenetic disrelish of his place was evinced in almost every function pertaining to it. Proud as he was moody, he condescended to no personal mandate. What-
40 ever special orders were necessary, their delivery was delegated to his body-servant, who in turn transferred them to their ultimate destination, through runners, alert Spanish boys or slave boys, like pages or pilot-fish within easy call continually hov-

ering around Don Benito. So that to have beheld this undemonstrative invalid
gliding about, apathetic and mute, no landsman could have dreamed that in him
was lodged a dictatorship beyond which, while at sea, there was no earthly appeal.

Thus, the Spaniard, regarded in his reserve, seemed as the involuntary victim of
mental disorder. But, in fact, his reserve might, in some degree, have proceeded
from design. If so, then here was evinced the unhealthy climax of that icy though
conscientious policy, more or less adopted by all commanders of large ships, which,
except in signal emergencies, obliterates alike the manifestation of sway with every
trace of sociality; transforming the man into a block, or rather into a loaded cannon,
which, until there is call for thunder, has nothing to say.   10

Viewing him in this light, it seemed but a natural token of the perverse habit
induced by a long course of such hard self-restraint, that, notwithstanding the
present condition of his ship, the Spaniard should still persist in a demeanor, which,
however harmless, or it may be, appropriate, in a well-appointed vessel, such as the
San Dominick might have been at the outset of the voyage, was anything but
judicious now. But the Spaniard, perhaps, thought that it was with captains as with
gods: reserve, under all events, must still be their cue. But probably this appearance
of slumbering dominion might have been but an attempted disguise to conscious
imbecility — not deep policy, but shallow device. But be all this as it might, whether
Don Benito's manner was designed or not, the more Captain Delano noted its per-   20
vading reserve, the less he felt uneasiness at any particular manifestation of that
reserve toward himself.

Neither were his thoughts taken up by the captain alone. Wonted to the quiet
orderliness of the sealer's comfortable family of a crew, the noisy confusion of the
San Dominick's suffering host repeatedly challenged his eye. Some prominent
breaches, not only of discipline but of decency, were observed. These Captain
Delano could not but ascribe, in the main, to the absence of those subordinate deck-
officers to whom, along with higher duties, is entrusted what may be styled the
police department of a populous ship. True, the old oakum-pickers appeared at times
to act the part of monitorial constables to their countrymen, the blacks; but though   30
occasionally succeeding in allaying trifling outbreaks now and then between man
and man, they could do little or nothing toward establishing general quiet. The
San Dominick was in the condition of a transatlantic emigrant ship, among whose
multitude of living freight are some individuals, doubtless, as little troublesome as
crates and bales; but the friendly remonstrances of such with their ruder companions
are of not so much avail as the unfriendly arm of the mate. What the San Dominick wanted was, what the emigrant ship has, stern superior officers. But on these
decks not so much as a fourth-mate was to be seen.

The visitor's curiosity was roused to learn the particulars of those mishaps which
had brought about such absenteeism, with its consequences; because, though deriv-   40
ing some inkling of the voyage from the wails which at the first moment had
greeted him, yet of the details no clear understanding had been had. The best account would, doubtless, be given by the captain. Yet at first the visitor was loth to
ask it, unwilling to provoke some distant rebuff. But plucking up courage, he at

last accosted Don Benito, renewing the expression of his benevolent interest, adding, that did he (Captain Delano) but know the particulars of the ship's misfortunes, he would, perhaps, be better able in the end to relieve them. Would Don Benito favor him with the whole story.

Don Benito faltered; then, like some somnambulist suddenly interfered with, vacantly stared at his visitor, and ended by looking down on the deck. He maintained this posture so long, that Captain Delano, almost equally disconcerted, and involuntarily almost as rude, turned suddenly from him, walking forward to accost one of the Spanish seamen for the desired information. But he had hardly gone five
10 paces, when, with a sort of eagerness, Don Benito invited him back, regretting his momentary absence of mind, and professing readiness to gratify him.

While most part of the story was being given, the two captains stood on the after part of the main-deck, a privileged spot, no one being near but the servant.

"It is now a hundred and ninety days," began the Spaniard, in his husky whisper, "that this ship, well officered and well manned, with several cabin passengers — some fifty Spaniards in all — sailed from Buenos Ayres bound to Lima, with a general cargo, hardware, Paraguay tea and the like — and," pointing forward, "that parcel of Negroes, now not more than a hundred and fifty, as you see, but then numbering over three hundred souls. Off Cape Horn we had heavy gales. In one
20 moment, by night, three of my best officers, with fifteen sailors, were lost, with the main-yard; the spar snapping under them in the slings, as they sought, with heavers, to beat down the icy sail. To lighten the hull, the heavier sacks of mata were thrown into the sea, with most of the water-pipes lashed on deck at the time. And this last necessity it was, combined with the prolonged detentions afterwards experienced, which eventually brought about our chief causes of suffering. When —"

Here there was a sudden fainting attack of his cough, brought on, no doubt, by his mental distress. His servant sustained him, and drawing a cordial from his pocket placed it to his lips. He a little revived. But unwilling to leave him unsupported while yet imperfectly restored, the black with one arm still encircled his master, at
30 the same time keeping his eye fixed on his face, as if to watch for the first sign of complete restoration, or relapse, as the event might prove.

The Spaniard proceeded, but brokenly and obscurely, as one in a dream.

— "Oh, my God! rather than pass through what I have, with joy I would have hailed the most terrible gales; but —"

His cough returned and with increased violence; this subsiding, with reddened lips and closed eyes he fell heavily against his supporter.

"His mind wanders. He was thinking of the plague that followed the gales," plaintively sighed the servant; "my poor, poor master!" wringing one hand, and with the other wiping the mouth. "But be patient, Señor," again turning to Captain
40 Delano, "these fits do not last long; master will soon be himself."

Don Benito reviving, went on; but as this portion of the story was very brokenly delivered, the substance only will here be set down.

It appeared that after the ship had been many days tossed in storms off the Cape,

---

23 **water-pipes,** large casks of water

the scurvy broke out, carrying off numbers of the whites and blacks. When at last they had worked round into the Pacific, their spars and sails were so damaged, and so inadequately handled by the surviving mariners, most of whom were become invalids, that, unable to lay her northerly course by the wind, which was powerful, the unmanageable ship, for successive days and nights, was blown northwestward, where the breeze suddenly deserted her, in unknown waters, to sultry calms. The absence of the water-pipes now proved as fatal to life as before their presence had menaced it. Induced, or at least aggravated, by the more than scanty allowance of water, a malignant fever followed the scurvy; with the excessive heat of the length-ened calm, making such short work of it as to sweep away, as by billows, whole 10 families of the Africans, and a yet larger number, proportionably, of the Spaniards, in-cluding, by a luckless fatality, every remaining officer on board. Consequently, in the smart west winds eventually following the calm, the already rent sails, having to be simply dropped, not furled, at need, had been gradually reduced to the beggar's rags they were now. To procure substitutes for his lost sailors, as well as supplies of water and sails, the captain, at the earliest opportunity, had made for Baldivia, the southernmost civilized port of Chili and South America; but upon nearing the coast the thick weather had prevented him from so much as sighting that harbor. Since which period, almost without a crew, and almost without canvas and almost without water, and, at intervals, giving its added dead to the sea, the San Dominick 20 had been battle-dored about by contrary winds, inveigled by currents, or grown weedy in calms. Like a man lost in woods, more than once she had doubled upon her own track.

"But throughout these calamities," huskily continued Don Benito, painfully turn-ing in the half embrace of his servant, "I have to thank those Negroes you see, who, though to your inexperienced eyes appearing unruly, have, indeed, conducted themselves with less of restlessness than even their owner could have thought possi-ble under such circumstances."

Here he again fell faintly back. Again his mind wandered; but he rallied, and less obscurely proceeded.   30

"Yes, their owner was quite right in assuring me that no fetters would be needed with his blacks; so that while, as is wont in this transportation, these Negroes have always remained upon deck — not thrust below, as in the Guinea-men — they have, also, from the beginning, been freely permitted to range within given bounds at their pleasure."

Once more the faintness returned — his mind roved — but, recovering, he resumed:

"But it is Babo here to whom, under God, I owe not only my own preservation, but likewise to him, chiefly, the merit is due, of pacifying his more ignorant brethren, when at intervals tempted to murmurings."

"Ah, master," sighed the black, bowing his face, "don't speak of me; Babo is 40 nothing; what Babo has done was but duty."

"Faithful fellow!" cried Captain Delano. "Don Benito, I envy you such a friend; slave I cannot call him."

---

33 **Guinea-men,** ships trading with Guinea in West Africa

As master and man stood before him, the black upholding the white, Captain Delano could not but bethink him of the beauty of that relationship which could present such a spectacle of fidelity on the one hand and confidence on the other. The scene was heightened by the contrast in dress, denoting their relative positions. The Spaniard wore a loose Chili jacket of dark velvet; white small-clothes and stockings, with silver buckles at the knee and instep; a high-crowned sombrero, of fine grass; a slender sword, silver mounted, hung from a knot in his sash — the last being an almost invariable adjunct, more for utility than ornament, of a South American gentleman's dress to this hour. Excepting when his occasional nervous contortions
10 brought about disarray, there was a certain precision in his attire, curiously at variance with the unsightly disorder around: especially in the belittered Ghetto, forward of the mainmast, wholly occupied by the blacks.

The servant wore nothing but wide trowsers, apparently, from their coarseness and patches, made out of some old topsail; they were clean, and confined at the waist by a bit of unstranded rope, which, with his composed, deprecatory air at times, made him look something like a begging friar of St. Francis.

However unsuitable for the time and place, at least in the blunt-thinking American's eyes, and however strangely surviving in the midst of all his afflictions, the toilette of Don Benito might not, in fashion at least, have gone beyond the style of
20 the day among South Americans of his class. Though on the present voyage sailing from Buenos Ayres, he had avowed himself a native and resident of Chili, whose inhabitants had not so generally adopted the plain coat and once plebeian pantaloons; but, with a becoming modification, adhered to their provincial costume, picturesque as any in the world. Still, relatively to the pale history of the voyage, and his own pale face, there seemed something so incongruous in the Spaniard's apparel, as almost to suggest the image of an invalid courtier tottering about London streets in the time of the plague.

The portion of the narrative which, perhaps, most excited interest, as well as some surprise, considering the latitudes in question, was the long calms spoken of, and
30 more particularly the ship's so long drifting about. Without communicating the opinion, of course, the American could not but impute at least part of the detentions both to clumsy seamanship and faulty navigation. Eyeing Don Benito's small, yellow hands, he easily inferred that the young captain had not got into command at the hawse-hole but the cabin-window; and if so, why wonder at incompetence, in youth, sickness, and gentility united?

But drowning criticism in compassion, after a fresh repetition of his sympathies, Captain Delano, having heard out his story, not only engaged, as in the first place, to see Don Benito and his people supplied in their immediate bodily needs, but, also, now further promised to assist him in procuring a large permanent supply of
40 water, as well as some sails and rigging; and, though it would involve no small embarrassment to himself, yet he would spare three of his best seamen for tempo-

---

34 **hawse-hole,** one of the holes in the bow of a ship through which a cable passes. The statement means that the captain had had no experience as a common sailor

rary deck officers; so that without delay the ship might proceed to Conception, there fully to refit for Lima, her destined port.

Such generosity was not without its effect, even upon the invalid. His face lighted up; eager and hectic, he met the honest glance of his visitor. With gratitude he seemed overcome.

"This excitement is bad for master," whispered the servant, taking his arm, and with soothing words gently drawing him aside.

When Don Benito returned, the American was pained to observe that his hopefulness, like the sudden kindling in his cheek, was but febrile and transient.

Ere long, with a joyless mien, looking up towards the poop, the host invited his 10 guest to accompany him there, for the benefit of what little breath of wind might be stirring.

As, during the telling of the story, Captain Delano had once or twice started at the occasional cymballing of the hatchet-polishers, wondering why such an interruption should be allowed, especially in that part of the ship, and in the ears of an invalid; and moreover, as the hatchets had anything but an attractive look, and the handlers of them still less so, it was, therefore, to tell the truth, not without some lurking reluctance, or even shrinking, it may be, that Captain Delano, with apparent complaisance, acquiesced in his host's invitation. The more so, since, with an untimely caprice of punctilio, rendered distressing by his cadaverous aspect, Don 20 Benito, with Castilian bows, solemnly insisted upon his guest's preceding him up the ladder leading to the elevation; where, one on each side of the last step, sat for armorial supporters and sentries two of the ominous file. Gingerly enough stepped good Captain Delano between them, and in the instant of leaving them behind, like one running the gauntlet, he felt an apprehensive twitch in the calves of his legs.

But when, facing about, he saw the whole file, like so many organ-grinders, still stupidly intent on their work, unmindful of everything beside, he could not but smile at his late fidgety panic.

Presently, while standing with his host, looking forward upon the decks below, he was struck by one of those instances of insubordination previously alluded to. 30 Three black boys, with two Spanish boys, were sitting together on the hatches, scraping a rude wooden platter, in which some scanty mess had recently been cooked. Suddenly, one of the black boys, enraged at a word dropped by one of his white companions, seized a knife, and, though called to forbear by one of the oakumpickers, struck the lad over the head, inflicting a gash from which blood flowed.

In amazement, Captain Delano inquired what this meant. To which the pale Don Benito dully muttered, that it was merely the sport of the lad.

"Pretty serious sport, truly," rejoined Captain Delano. "Had such a thing happened on board the Bachelor's Delight, instant punishment would have followed."

At these words, the Spaniard turned upon the American one of his sudden, star- 40 ing, half-lunatic looks; then, relapsing into his torpor, answered, "Doubtless, doubtless, Señor."

Is it, thought Captain Delano, that this hapless man is one of those paper cap-

---

1 **Conception,** Concepción, a port in Chile

tains I've known, who by policy wink at what by power they cannot put down? I
know no sadder sight than a commander who has little of command but the name.

"I should think, Don Benito," he now said, glancing towards the oakum-picker
who had sought to interfere with the boys, "that you would find it advantageous to
keep all your blacks employed, especially the younger ones, no matter at what useless task, and no matter what happens to the ship. Why, even with my little band,
I find such a course indispensable. I once kept a crew on my quarter-deck thrumming mats for my cabin, when, for three days, I had given up my ship — mats,
men, and all — for a speedy loss, owing to the violence of a gale, in which we could
10 do nothing but helplessly drive before it."

"Doubtless, doubtless," muttered Don Benito.

"But," continued Captain Delano, again glancing upon the oakum-pickers and
then at the hatchet-polishers, near by, "I see you keep some, at least, of your host
employed."

"Yes," was again the vacant response.

"Those old men there, shaking their pows from their pulpits," continued Captain
Delano, pointing to the oakum-pickers, "seem to act the part of old dominies to the
rest, little heeded as their admonitions are at times. Is this voluntary on their part,
Don Benito, or have you appointed them shepherds to your flock of black sheep?"
20 "What posts they fill, I appointed them," rejoined the Spaniard in an acrid tone,
as if resenting some supposed satiric reflection.

"And these others, these Ashantee conjurors here," continued Captain Delano,
rather uneasily eyeing the brandished steel of the hatchet-polishers, where, in spots,
it had been brought to a shine, "this seems a curious business they are at,
Don Benito?"   ·

"In the gales we met," answered the Spaniard, "what of our general cargo was
not thrown overboard was much damaged by the brine. Since coming into calm
weather, I have had several cases of knives and hatchets daily brought up for overhauling and cleaning."
30 "A prudent idea, Don Benito. You are part owner of ship and cargo, I presume;
but not of the slaves, perhaps?"

"I am owner of all you see," impatiently returned Don Benito, "except the main
company of blacks, who belonged to my late friend Alexandro Aranda."

As he mentioned this name, his air was heart-broken; his knees shook; his servant supported him.

Thinking he divined the cause of such unusual emotion, to confirm his surmise,
Captain Delano, after a pause, said: "And may I ask, Don Benito, whether — since
awhile ago you spoke of some cabin passengers — the friend, whose loss so afflicts
you, at the outset of the voyage accompanied his blacks?"
40 "Yes."

"But died of the fever?"

"Died of the fever. — Oh, could I but —"

Again quivering, the Spaniard paused.

---

22 **Ashantee,** a native kingdom in West Africa

"Pardon me," said Captain Delano, lowly, "but I think that, by a sympathetic experience, I conjecture, Don Benito, what it is that gives the keener edge to your grief. It was once my hard fortune to lose, at sea, a dear friend, my own brother, then supercargo. Assured of the welfare of his spirit, its departure I could have borne like a man; but that honest eye, that honest hand — both of which had so often met mine — and that warm heart; all, all — like scraps to the dogs — to throw all to the sharks! It was then I vowed never to have for fellow-voyager a man I loved, unless, unbeknown to him, I had provided every requisite, in case of a fatality, for embalming his mortal part for interment on shore. Were your friend's remains now on board this ship, Don Benito, not thus strangely would the mention of his name 10 affect you."

"On board this ship?" echoed the Spaniard. Then, with horrified gestures, as directed against some spectre, he unconsciously fell into the ready arms of his attendant, who, with a silent appeal toward Captain Delano, seemed beseeching him not again to broach a theme so unspeakably distressing to his master.

This poor fellow now, thought the pained American, is the victim of that sad superstition which associates goblins with the deserted body of man, as ghosts with an abandoned house. How unlike are we made! What to me, in like case, would have been a solemn satisfaction, the bare suggestion, even, terrifies the Spaniard into this trance. Poor Alexandro Aranda! what would you say could you here see 20 your friend — who, on former voyages, when you, for months, were left behind, has, I dare say, often longed, and longed, for one peep at you — now transported with terror at the least thought of having you anyway nigh him.

At this moment, with a dreary grave-yard toll, betokening a flaw, the ship's forecastle bell, smote by one of the grizzled oakum-pickers, proclaimed ten o'clock, through the leaden calm; when Captain Delano's attention was caught by the moving figure of a gigantic black, emerging from the general crowd below, and slowly advancing toward the elevated poop. An iron collar was about his neck, from which depended a chain, thrice wound round his body; the terminating links padlocked together at a broad band of iron, his girdle.   30

"How like a mute Atufal moves," murmured the servant.

The black mounted the steps of the poop, and, like a brave prisoner, brought up to receive sentence, stood in unquailing muteness before Don Benito, now recovered from his attack.

At the first glimpse of his approach, Don Benito had started, a resentful shadow swept over his face; and, as with the sudden memory of bootless rage, his white lips glued together.

This is some mulish mutineer, thought Captain Delano, surveying, not without a mixture of admiration, the colossal form of the Negro.

"See, he waits your question, master," said the servant.   40

Thus reminded, Don Benito, nervously averting his glance, as if shunning, by anticipation, some rebellious response, in a disconcerted voice, thus spoke: —

---

4 **supercargo,** an officer in a merchant ship whose duty is to manage the business affairs of the voyage

"Atufal, will you ask my pardon now?"

The black was silent.

"Again, master," murmured the servant, with bitter upbraiding eyeing his countryman, "again, master; he will bend to master yet."

"Answer," said Don Benito, still averting his glance, "say but the one word, *pardon*, and your chains shall be off."

Upon this, the black, slowly raising both arms, let them lifelessly fall, his links clanking, his head bowed; as much as to say, "No, I am content."

"Go," said Don Benito, with inkept and unknown emotion.

10 Deliberately as he had come, the black obeyed.

"Excuse me, Don Benito," said Captain Delano, "but this scene surprises me; what means it, pray?"

"It means that that Negro alone, of all the band, has given me peculiar cause of offence. I have put him in chains; I — "

Here he paused; his hand to his head, as if there were a swimming there, or a sudden bewilderment of memory had come over him; but meeting his servant's kindly glance seemed reassured, and proceeded: —

"I could not scourge such a form. But I told him he must ask my pardon. As yet he has not. At my command, every two hours he stands before me."

20 "And how long has this been?"

"Some sixty days."

"And obedient in all else? And respectful?"

"Yes."

"Upon my conscience, then," exclaimed Captain Delano, impulsively, "he has a royal spirit in him, this fellow."

"He may have some right to it," bitterly returned Don Benito; "he says he was king in his own land."

"Yes," said the servant, entering a word, "those slits in Atufal's ears once held wedges of gold; but poor Babo here, in his own land, was only a poor slave; a black

30 man's slave was Babo, who now is the white's."

Somewhat annoyed by these conversational familiarities, Captain Delano turned curiously upon the attendant, then glanced inquiringly at his master; but, as if long wonted to these little informalities, neither master nor man seemed to understand him.

"What, pray, was Atufal's offence, Don Benito?" asked Captain Delano; "if it was not something very serious, take a fool's advice, and, in view of his general docility, as well as in some natural respect for his spirit, remit him his penalty."

"No, no, master never will do that," here murmured the servant to himself, "proud Atufal must first ask master's pardon. The slave there carries the padlock, but mas-

40 ter here carries the key."

His attention thus directed, Captain Delano now noticed for the first time, that, suspended by a slender silken cord, from Don Benito's neck, hung a key. At once, from the servant's muttered syllables, divining the key's purpose, he smiled and said: — "So, Don Benito — padlock and key — significant symbols, truly."

Biting his lip, Don Benito faltered.

Though the remark of Captain Delano, a man of such native simplicity as to be incapable of satire or irony, had been dropped in playful allusion to the Spaniard's singularly evidenced lordship over the black; yet the hypochondriac seemed in some way to have taken it as a malicious reflection upon his confessed inability thus far to break down, at least, on a verbal summons, the entrenched will of the slave. Deploring this supposed misconception, yet despairing of correcting it, Captain Delano shifted the subject; but finding his companion more than ever withdrawn, as if still sourly digesting the lees of the presumed affront above-mentioned, by-and-by Captain Delano likewise became less talkative, oppressed, against his own will, by what seemed the secret vindictiveness of the morbidly sensitive Spaniard. But the good sailor, himself of a quite contrary disposition, refrained, on his part, alike from the appearance as from the feeling of resentment, and if silent, was only so from contagion.

Presently the Spaniard, assisted by his servant, somewhat discourteously crossed over from his guest; a procedure which, sensibly enough, might have been allowed to pass for idle caprice of ill-humor, had not master and man, lingering round the corner of the elevated skylight, began whispering together in low voices. This was unpleasing. And more: the moody air of the Spaniard, which at times had not been without a sort of valetudinarian stateliness, now seemed anything but dignified; while the menial familiarity of the servant lost its original charm of simple-hearted attachment.

In his embarrassment, the visitor turned his face to the other side of the ship. By so doing, his glance accidentally fell on a young Spanish sailor, a coil of rope in his hand, just stepped from the deck to the first round of the mizzen-rigging. Perhaps the man would not have been particularly noticed, were it not that, during his ascent to one of the yards, he, with a sort of covert intentness, kept his eye fixed on Captain Delano, from whom, presently, it passed, as if by a natural sequence, to the two whisperers.

His own attention thus redirected to that quarter, Captain Delano gave a slight start. From something in Don Benito's manner just then, it seemed as if the visitor had, at least partly, been the subject of the withdrawn consultation going on — a conjecture as little agreeable to the guest as it was little flattering to the host.

The singular alternations of courtesy and ill-breeding in the Spanish captain were unaccountable, except on one of two suppositions — innocent lunacy, or wicked imposture.

But the first idea, though it might naturally have occurred to an indifferent observer, and, in some respects, had not hitherto been wholly a stranger to Captain Delano's mind, yet, now that, in an incipient way, he began to regard the stranger's conduct something in the light of an intentional affront, of course the idea of lunacy was virtually vacated. But if not a lunatic, what then? Under the circumstances, would a gentleman, nay, any honest boor, act the part now acted by his host? The man was an impostor. Some low-born adventurer, masquerading as an oceanic grandee; yet so ignorant of the first requisites of mere gentlemanhood as to be betrayed

into the present remarkable indecorum. That strange ceremoniousness, too, at other times evinced, seemed not uncharacteristic of one playing a part above his real level. Benito Cereno — Don Benito Cereno — a sounding name. One, too, at that period, not unknown, in the surname, to supercargoes and sea captains trading along the Spanish Main, as belonging to one of the most enterprising and extensive mercantile families in all those provinces; several members of it having titles; a sort of Castilian Rothschild, with a noble brother, or cousin, in every great trading town of South America. The alleged Don Benito was in early manhood, about twenty-nine or thirty. To assume a sort of roving cadetship in the maritime affairs of such
10 a house, what more likely scheme for a young knave of talent and spirit? But the Spaniard was a pale invalid. Never mind. For even to the degree of simulating mortal disease, the craft of some tricksters had been known to attain. To think that, under the aspect of infantile weakness, the most savage energies might be couched — those velvets of the Spaniard but the silky paw to his fangs.

From no train of thought did these fancies come; not from within, but from without; suddenly, too, and in one throng, like hoar frost; yet as soon to vanish as the mild sun of Captain Delano's good-nature regained its meridian.

Glancing over once more towards his host — whose side-face, revealed above the skylight, was now turned toward him — he was struck by the profile, whose clear-
20 ness of cut was refined by the thinness incident to ill-health, as well as ennobled about the chin by the beard. Away with suspicion. He was a true off-shoot of a true hidalgo Cereno.

Relieved by these and other better thoughts, the visitor, lightly humming a tune, now began indifferently pacing the poop, so as not to betray to Don Benito that he had at all mistrusted incivility, much less duplicity; for such mistrust would yet be proved illusory, and by the event; though, for the present, the circumstance which had provoked that distrust remained unexplained. But when that little mystery should have been cleared up, Captain Delano thought he might extremely regret it, did he allow Don Benito to become aware that he had indulged in ungenerous
30 surmises. In short, to the Spaniard's black-letter text, it was best, for a while, to leave open margin.

Presently, his pale face twitching and overcast, the Spaniard, still supported by his attendant, moved over towards his guest, when, with even more than his usual embarrassment, and a strange sort of intriguing intonation in his husky whisper, the following conversation began: —

"Señor, may I ask how long you have lain at this isle?"

"Oh, but a day or two, Don Benito."

"And from what port are you last?"

"Canton."

7 **Rothschild**, the Rothschilds, a family of wealthy bankers who flourished first in Germany and later in England from the eighteenth century to the present   22 **hidalgo**, a Spanish title of nobility   30 **black-letter**, a style of type, also known as Gothic or Old English, which was copied by the early printers from a form of manuscript hand current at the time. The phrase here connotes strangeness and unfamiliarity   31 **open margin**, without marginal gloss or commentary   39 **Canton**, in China

"And there, Señor, you exchanged your seal-skins for teas and silks, I think you said?"

"Yes. Silks, mostly."

"And the balance you took in specie, perhaps?"

Captain Delano, fidgeting a little, answered —

"Yes; some silver; not a very great deal, though."

"Ah — well. May I ask how many men have you, Señor?"

Captain Delano slightly started, but answered —

"About five-and-twenty, all told."

"And at present, Señor, all on board, I suppose?"   10

"All on board, Don Benito," replied the Captain, now with satisfaction.

"And will be to-night, Señor?"

At this last question, following so many pertinacious ones, for the soul of him Captain Delano could not but look very earnestly at the questioner, who, instead of meeting the glance, with every token of craven discomposure dropped his eyes to the deck; presenting an unworthy contrast to his servant, who, just then, was kneeling at his feet, adjusting a loose shoe-buckle; his disengaged face meantime, with humble curiosity, turned openly up into his master's downcast one.

The Spaniard, still with a guilty shuffle, repeated his question:

"And — and will be to-night, Señor?"   20

"Yes, for ought I know," returned Captain Delano — "but nay," rallying himself into fearless truth, "some of them talked of going off on another fishing party about midnight."

"Your ships generally go — go more or less armed, I believe, Señor?"

"Oh, a six-pounder or two, in case of emergency," was the intrepidly indifferent reply, "with a small stock of muskets, sealing-spears, and cutlasses, you know."

As he thus responded, Captain Delano again glanced at Don Benito, but the latter's eyes were averted; while abruptly and awkwardly shifting the subject, he made some peevish allusion to the calm, and then, without apology, once more, with his attendant, withdrew to the opposite bulwarks, where the whispering was resumed. 30

At this moment, and ere Captain Delano could cast a cool thought upon what had just passed, the young Spanish sailor, before mentioned, was seen descending from the rigging. In act of stooping over to spring inboard to the deck, his voluminous, unconfined frock, or shirt, of coarse woolen, much spotted with tar, opened out far down the chest, revealing a soiled under garment of what seemed the finest linen, edged, about the neck, with a narrow blue ribbon, sadly faded and worn. At this moment the young sailor's eye was again fixed on the whisperers, and Captain Delano thought he observed a lurking significance in it, as if silent signs, of some Freemason sort, had that instant been interchanged.

This once more impelled his own glance in the direction of Don Benito, and, as 40 before, he could not but infer that himself formed the subject of the conference. He paused. The sound of the hatchet-polishing fell on his ears. He cast another swift side-look at the two. They had the air of conspirators. In connection with the late questionings, and the incident of the young sailor, these things now begat such re-

turn of involuntary suspicion, that the singular guilelessness of the American could
not endure it. Plucking up a gay and humorous expression, he crossed over to the
two rapidly, saying: — "Ha, Don Benito, your black here seems high in your trust;
a sort of privy-counsellor, in fact."

Upon this, the servant looked up with a good-natured grin, but the master started
as from a venomous bite. It was a moment or two before the Spaniard sufficiently
recovered himself to reply; which he did, at last, with cold constraint: — "Yes,
Señor, I have trust in Babo."

Here Babo, changing his previous grin of mere animal humor into an intelligent
10 smile, not ungratefully eyed his master.

Finding that the Spaniard now stood silent and reserved, as if involuntarily, or
purposely giving hint that his guest's proximity was inconvenient just then, Captain
Delano, unwilling to appear uncivil even to incivility itself, made some trivial
remark and moved off; again and again turning over in his mind the mysterious demeanor of Don Benito Cereno.

He had descended from the poop, and, wrapped in thought, was passing near a
dark hatchway, leading down into the steerage, when, perceiving motion there, he
looked to see what moved. The same instant there was a sparkle in the shadowy
hatchway, and he saw one of the Spanish sailors, prowling there, hurriedly placing
20 his hand in the bosom of his frock, as if hiding something. Before the man could
have been certain who it was that was passing, he slunk below out of sight. But
enough was seen of him to make it sure that he was the same young sailor before
noticed in the rigging.

What was that which so sparkled? thought Captain Delano. It was no lamp —
no match — no live coal. Could it have been a jewel? But how come sailors with
jewels? — or with silk-trimmed under-shirts either? Has he been robbing the trunks
of the dead cabin-passengers? But if so, he would hardly wear one of the stolen articles on board ship here. Ah, ah — if, now, that was, indeed, a secret sign I saw
passing between this suspicious fellow and his captain awhile since; if I could only
30 be certain that, in my uneasiness, my senses did not deceive me, then —

Here, passing from one suspicious thing to another, his mind revolved the strange
questions put to him concerning his ship.

By a curious coincidence, as each point was recalled, the black wizards of Ashantee would strike up with their hatchets, as in ominous comment on the white stranger's thoughts. Pressed by such enigmas and portents, it would have been almost
against nature, had not, even into the least distrustful heart, some ugly misgivings
obtruded.

Observing the ship now helplessly fallen into a current, with enchanted sails, drifting with increased rapidity seaward; and noting that, from a lately intercepted projec-
40 tion of the land, the sealer was hidden, the stout mariner began to quake at thoughts
which he barely durst confess to himself. Above all, he began to feel a ghostly dread
of Don Benito. And yet when he roused himself, dilated his chest, felt himself strong on his legs, and coolly considered it — what did all these phantoms
amount to?

Had the Spaniard any sinister scheme, it must have reference not so much to him (Captain Delano) as to his ship (the Bachelor's Delight). Hence the present drifting away of the one ship from the other, instead of favoring any such possible scheme, was, for the time at least, opposed to it. Clearly any suspicion, combining such contradictions, must needs be delusive. Besides, was it not absurd to think of a vessel in distress — a vessel by sickness almost dismanned of her crew — a vessel whose inmates were parched for water — was it not a thousand times absurd that such a craft should, at present, be of a piratical character; or her commander, either for himself or those under him, cherish any desire but for speedy relief and refreshment? But then, might not general distress, and thirst in particular, be af- 10 fected? And might not that same undiminished Spanish crew, alleged to have perished off to a remnant, be at that very moment lurking in the hold? On heart-broken pretence of entreating a cup of cold water, fiends in human form had got into lonely dwellings, nor retired until a dark deed had been done. And among the Malay pirates, it was no unusual thing to lure ships after them into their treacherous harbors, or entice boarders from a declared enemy at sea, by the spectacle of thinly manned or vacant decks, beneath which prowled a hundred spears with yellow arms ready to upthrust them through the mats. Not that Captain Delano had entirely credited such things. He had heard of them — and now, as stories, they recurred. The present destination of the ship was the anchorage. There she would be near his own 20 vessel. Upon gaining that vicinity, might not the San Dominick, like a slumbering volcano, suddenly let loose energies now hid?

He recalled the Spaniard's manner while telling his story. There was a gloomy hesitancy and subterfuge about it. It was just the manner of one making up his tale for evil purposes, as he goes. But if that story was not true, what was the truth? That the ship had unlawfully come into the Spaniard's possession? But in many of its details, especially in reference to the more calamitous parts, such as the fatalities among the seamen, the consequent prolonged beating about, the past sufferings from obstinate calms, and still continued suffering from thirst; in all these points, as well as others, Don Benito's story had corroborated not only the wailing ejaculations of 30 the indiscriminate multitude, white and black, but likewise — what seemed impossible to be counterfeit — by the very expression and play of every human feature, which Captain Delano saw. If Don Benito's story was, throughout, an invention, then every soul on board, down to the youngest Negress, was his carefully drilled recruit in the plot: an incredible inference. And yet, if there was ground for mistrusting his veracity, that inference was a legitimate one.

But those questions of the Spaniard. There, indeed, one might pause. Did they not seem put with much the same object with which the burglar or assassin, by daytime, reconnoitres the walls of a house? But, with ill purposes, to solicit such information openly of the chief person endangered, and so, in effect, setting him on 40 his guard; how unlikely to procedure was that. Absurd, then, to suppose that those questions had been prompted by evil designs. Thus, the same conduct, which, in

---

10 **affected,** pretended

this instance, had raised the alarm, served to dispel it. In short, scarce any suspicion or uneasiness, however apparently reasonable at the time, which was not now, with equal apparent reason, dismissed.

At last, he began to laugh at his former forebodings; and laugh at the strange ship for, in its aspect someway siding with them, as it were; and laugh, too, at the odd-looking blacks, particularly those old scissors-grinders, the Ashantees; and those bed-ridden old knitting women, the oakum-pickers; and almost at the dark Spaniard himself, the central hobgoblin of all.

For the rest, whatever in a serious way seemed enigmatical, was now good-
10 naturedly explained away by the thought that, for the most part the poor invalid scarcely knew what he was about; either sulking in black vapors, or putting idle questions without sense or object. Evidently, for the present, the man was not fit to be entrusted with the ship. On some benevolent plea withdrawing the command from him, Captain Delano would yet have to send her to Conception in charge of his second mate, a worthy person and good navigator — a plan not more convenient for the San Dominick than for Don Benito; for, relieved from all anxiety, keeping wholly to his cabin, the sick man, under the good nursing of his servant, would probably, by the end of the passage, be in a measure restored to health, and with that he should also be restored to authority.

20 Such were the American's thoughts. They were tranquilizing. There was a difference between the idea of Don Benito's darkly pre-ordaining Captain Delano's fate, and Captain Delano's lightly arranging Don Benito's. Nevertheless, it was not without something of relief that the good seaman presently perceived his whale-boat in the distance. Its absence had been prolonged by unexpected detention at the sealer's side, as well as its returning trip lengthened by the continual recession of the goal.

The advancing speck was observed by the blacks. Their shouts attracted the attention of Don Benito, who, with a return of courtesy, approaching Captain Delano, expressed satisfaction at the coming of some supplies, slight and temporary as they must necessarily prove.

30 Captain Delano responded; but while doing so, his attention was drawn to something passing on the deck below: among the crowd climbing the landward bulwarks, anxiously watching the coming boat, two blacks, to all appearances accidentally incommoded by one of the sailors, violently pushed him aside, which the sailor someway resenting, they dashed him to the deck, despite the earnest cries of the oakum-pickers.

"Don Benito," said Captain Delano quickly, "do you see what is going on there? Look!"

But, seized by his cough, the Spaniard staggered, with both hands to his face, on the point of falling. Captain Delano would have supported him, but the servant
40 was more alert, who, with one hand sustaining his master, with the other applied the cordial. Don Benito restored, the black withdrew his support, slipping aside a little, but dutifully remaining within call of a whisper. Such discretion was here evinced as quite wiped away, in the visitor's eyes, any blemish of impropriety which might have attached to the attendant, from the indecorous conferences before men-

tioned; showing, too, that if the servant were to blame, it might be more the master's fault than his own, since, when left to himself, he could conduct thus well.

His glance called away from the spectacle of disorder to the more pleasing one before him, Captain Delano could not avoid again congratulating his host upon possessing such a servant, who, though perhaps a little too forward now and then, must upon the whole be invaluable to one in the invalid's situation.

"Tell me, Don Benito," he added, with a smile — "I should like to have your man here, myself — what will you take for him? Would fifty doubloons be any object?"

"Master wouldn't part with Babo for a thousand doubloons," murmured the black, overhearing the offer, and taking it in earnest, and, with the strange vanity of a 10 faithful slave, appreciated by his master, scorning to hear so paltry a valuation put upon him by a stranger. But Don Benito, apparently hardly yet completely restored, and again interrupted by his cough, made but some broken reply.

Soon his physical distress became so great, affecting his mind, too, apparently, that, as if to screen the sad spectacle, the servant gently conducted his master below.

Left to himself, the American, to while away the time till his boat should arrive, would have pleasantly accosted some one of the few Spanish seamen he saw; but recalling something that Don Benito had said touching their ill conduct, he refrained; as a ship-master indisposed to countenance cowardice or unfaithfulness in seamen.   20

While, with these thoughts, standing with eye directed forward toward that handful of sailors, suddenly he thought that one or two of them returned the glance and with a sort of meaning. He rubbed his eyes, and looked again; but again seemed to see the same thing. Under a new form, but more obscure than any previous one, the old suspicions recurred, but, in the absence of Don Benito, with less of panic than before. Despite the bad account given of the sailors, Captain Delano resolved forthwith to accost one of them. Descending the poop, he made his way through the blacks, his movement drawing a queer cry from the oakum-pickers, prompted by whom, the Negroes, twitching each other aside, divided before him; but, as if curious to see what was the object of this deliberate visit to their Ghetto, closing 30 in behind, in tolerable order, followed the white stranger up. His progress thus proclaimed as by mounted kings-at-arms, and escorted as by a Caffre guard of honor, Captain Delano, assuming a good-humored, off-handed air, continued to advance; now and then saying a blithe word to the Negroes, and his eye curiously surveying the white faces, here and there sparsely mixed in with the blacks, like stray white pawns venturously involved in the ranks of the chess-men opposed.

While thinking which of them to select for his purpose, he chanced to observe a sailor seated on the deck engaged in tarring the strap of a large block, a circle of blacks squatted round him inquisitively eyeing the process.

The mean employment of the man was in contrast with something superior in 40

---

2 **conduct.** According to Bartlett's *Dictionary of Americanisms* (1848) quoted in the *Dictionary of American English,* the intransitive use of the verb "conduct" without the reflexive pronoun was common in New England, both in speech and writing. Bartlett deplored the usage as an "offensive barbarism"   32 **kings-at-arms,** the chief heraldic officers of England   32 **Caffre,** Kafir, a tribe of South Africa

his figure. His hand, black with continually thrusting it into the tar-pot held for him by a Negro, seemed not naturally allied to his face, a face which would have been a very fine one but for its haggardness. Whether this haggardness had aught to do with criminality, could not be determined; since, as intense heat and cold, though unlike, produce like sensations, so innocence and guilt, when, through casual association with mental pain, stamping any visible impress, use one seal — a hacked one.

Not again that this reflection occurred to Captain Delano at the time, charitable man as he was. Rather another idea. Because observing so singular a haggardness
10 combined with a dark eye, averted as in trouble and shame, and then, again recalling Don Benito's confessed ill opinion of his crew, insensibly he was operated upon by certain general notions which, while disconnecting pain and abashment from virtue, invariably link them with vice.

If, indeed, there be any wickedness on board this ship, thought Captain Delano, be sure that man there has fouled his hand in it, even as now he fouls it in the pitch. I don't like to accost him. I will speak to this other, this old Jack here on the windlass.

He advanced to an old Barcelona tar, in ragged red breeches and dirty nightcap, cheeks trenched and bronzed, whiskers dense as thorn hedges. Seated between two sleepy-looking Africans, this mariner, like his younger shipmate, was employed upon
20 some rigging — splicing a cable — the sleepy-looking blacks performing the inferior function of holding the outer parts of the ropes for him.

Upon Captain Delano's approach, the man at once hung his head below its previous level; the one necessary for business. It appeared as if he desired to be thought absorbed, with more than common fidelity, in his task. Being addressed, he glanced up, but with what seemed a furtive, diffident air, which sat strangely enough on his weather-beaten visage, much as if a grizzly bear, instead of growling and biting, should simper and cast sheep's eyes. He was asked several questions concerning the voyage — questions purposely referring to several particulars in Don Benito's narrative, not previously corroborated by those impulsive cries greeting the visitor on
30 first coming on board. The questions were briefly answered, confirming all that remained to be confirmed of the story. The Negroes about the windlass joined in with the old sailor; but, as they became talkative, he by degrees became mute, and at length quite glum, seemed morosely unwilling to answer more questions, and yet, all the while, this ursine air was somehow mixed with his sheepish one.

Despairing of getting into unembarrassed talk with such a centaur, Captain Delano, after glancing round for a more promising countenance, but seeing none, spoke pleasantly to the blacks to make way for him; and so, amid various grins and grimaces, returned to the poop, feeling a little strange at first, he could hardly tell why, but upon the whole with regained confidence in Benito Cereno.
40 How plainly, thought he, did that old whiskerando yonder betray a consciousness of ill desert. No doubt, when he saw me coming, he dreaded lest I, apprised by his Captain of the crew's general misbehavior, came with sharp words for him, and so down with his head. And yet — and yet, now that I think of it, that very old fel-

---

17 **Barcelona,** a seaport in Spain

low, if I err not, was one of those who seemed so earnestly eyeing me here awhile since. Ah, these currents spin one's head around almost as much as they do the ship. Ha, there now's a pleasant sort of sunny sight; quite sociable, too.

His attention had been drawn to a slumbering Negress, partly disclosed through the lace-work of some rigging, lying, with youthful limbs carelessly disposed, under the lee of the bulwarks, like a doe in the shade of a woodland rock. Sprawling at her lapped breasts, was her wide-awake fawn, stark naked, its black little body half lifted from the deck, crosswise with its dam's; its hands, like two paws, clambering upon her; its mouth and nose ineffectually rooting to get at the mark; and meantime giving a vexatious half-grunt, blending with the composed snore of the Negress. 10

The uncommon vigor of the child at length roused the mother. She started up, at a distance facing Captain Delano. But as if not at all concerned at the attitude in which she had been caught, delightedly she caught the child up, with maternal transports, covering it with kisses.

There's naked nature, now; pure tenderness and love, thought Captain Delano, well pleased.

This incident prompted him to remark the other Negresses more particularly than before. He was gratified with their manners; like most uncivilized women, they seemed at once tender of heart and tough of constitution; equally ready to die for their infants or fight for them. Unsophisticated as leopardesses; loving as doves. Ah! 20 thought Captain Delano, these, perhaps, are some of the very women whom Ledyard saw in Africa, and gave such a noble account of.

These natural sights somehow insensibly deepened his confidence and ease. At last he looked to see how his boat was getting on; but it was still pretty remote. He turned to see if Don Benito had returned, but he had not.

To change the scene, as well as to please himself with a leisurely observation of the coming boat, stepping over into the mizzen-chains, he clambered his way into the starboard quarter-gallery — one of those abandoned Venetian-looking water-balconies previously mentioned — retreats cut off from the deck. As his foot pressed the half-damp, half-dry sea-mosses matting the place, and a chance phantom cats- 30 paw — an islet of breeze, unheralded, unfollowed — as this ghostly cats-paw came fanning his cheek; as his glance fell upon the row of small, round dead-lights — all closed like coppered eyes of the coffined — and the state-cabin door, once connecting with the gallery, even as the dead-lights had once looked out upon it, but now calked fast like a sarcophagus lid; and to a purple-black, tarred-over panel, threshold, and post; and he bethought him of the time, when that state-cabin and this state-balcony had heard the voices of the Spanish king's officers, and the forms of the Lima viceroy's daughters had perhaps leaned where he stood — as these and other images flitted through his mind, as the cats-paw through the calm, gradually he felt rising a dreamy inquietude, like that of one who alone on the prairie feels un- 40 rest from the repose of the noon.

He leaned against the carved balustrade, again looking off toward his boat; but found his eye falling upon the ribbon grass, trailing along the ship's waterline, straight

---

21 **Ledyard,** John Ledyard (1751-1789), American traveler

as a border of green box; and parterres of sea-weed, broad ovals and crescents, floating nigh and far, with what seemed long formal alleys between, crossing the terraces of swells, and sweeping round as if leading to the grottoes below. And overhanging all was the balustrade by his arm, which, partly stained with pitch and partly
embossed with moss, seemed the charred ruin of some summer-house in a grand garden long running to waste.

Trying to break one charm, he was but becharmed anew. Though upon the wide
sea, he seemed in some far inland country; prisoner in some deserted chateau, left
to stare at empty grounds, and peer out at vague roads, where never wagon or way-
10 farer passed.

But these enchantments were a little disenchanted as his eye fell on the corroded
main-chains. Of an ancient style, massy and rusty in link, shackle and bolt, they
seemed even more fit for the ship's present business than the one for which she had
been built.

Presently he thought something moved nigh the chains. He rubbed his eyes, and
looked hard. Groves of rigging were about the chains; and there, peering from behind a great stay, like an Indian from behind a hemlock, a Spanish sailor, a mar-
lingspike in his hand, was seen, who made what seemed an imperfect gesture toward the balcony, but immediately, as if alarmed by some advancing step along the
20 deck within, vanished into the recesses of the hempen forest, like a poacher.

What meant this? Something the man had sought to communicate, unbeknown
to any one, even to his captain. Did the secret involve aught unfavorable to his captain? Were those previous misgivings of Captain Delano's about to be verified? Or,
in his haunted mood at the moment, had some random, unintentional motion of
the man, while busy with the stay, as if repairing it, been mistaken for a significant beckoning?

Not unbewildered, again he gazed off for his boat. But it was temporarily hidden
by a rocky spur of the isle. As with some eagerness he bent forward, watching for
the first shooting view of its beak, the balustrade gave way before him like char-
30 coal. Had he not clutched an outreaching rope he would have fallen into the sea.
The crash, though feeble, and the fall, though hollow, of the rotten fragments, must
have been overheard. He glanced up. With sober curiosity peering down upon him
was one of the old oakum-pickers, slipped from his perch to an outside boom; while
below the old Negro, and, invisible to him, reconnoitering from a port-hole like a
fox from the mouth of its den, crouched the Spanish sailor again. From something
suddenly suggested by the man's air, the mad idea now darted into Captain Delano's
mind, that Don Benito's plea of indisposition, in withdrawing below, was but a
pretense: that he was engaged there maturing his plot, of which the sailor, by some
means gaining an inkling, had a mind to warn the stranger against; incited, it may
40 be, by gratitude for a kind word on first boarding the ship. Was it from foreseeing
some possible interference like this, that Don Benito had, beforehand, given such a
bad character of his sailors, while praising the Negroes; though, indeed, the former
seemed as docile as the latter the contrary? The whites, too, by nature, were the
shrewder race. A man with some evil design, would he not be likely to speak well

of that stupidity which was blind to his depravity, and malign that intelligence from which it might not be hidden? Not unlikely, perhaps. But if the whites had dark secrets concerning Don Benito, could then Don Benito be any way in complicity with the blacks? But they were too stupid. Besides, who ever heard of a white so far a renegade as to apostatize from his very species almost, by leaguing in against it with Negroes? These difficulties recalled former ones. Lost in their mazes, Captain Delano, who had now regained the deck, was uneasily advancing along it, when he observed a new face; an aged sailor seated cross-legged near the main hatchway. His skin was shrunk up with wrinkles like a pelican's empty pouch; his hair frosted; his countenance grave and composed. His hands were full of ropes, which he was working into a large knot. Some blacks were about him obligingly dipping the strands for him, here and there, as the exigencies of the operation demanded.   10

Captain Delano crossed over to him, and stood in silence surveying the knot; his mind, by a not uncongenial transition, passing from its own entanglements to those of the hemp. For intricacy such a knot he had never seen in an American ship, or indeed any other. The old man looked like an Egyptian priest, making Gordian knots for the temple of Ammon. The knot seemed a combination of double-bowline-knot, treble-crown-knot, back-handed-well-knot, knot-in-and-out-knot, and jamming-knot.

At last, puzzled to comprehend the meaning of such a knot, Captain Delano addressed the knotter: —   20

"What are you knotting there, my man?"

"The knot," was the brief reply, without looking up.

"So it seems; but what is it for?"

"For some one else to undo," muttered back the old man, plying his fingers harder than ever, the knot being now nearly completed.

While Captain Delano stood watching him, suddenly the old man threw the knot toward him, saying in broken English, — the first heard in the ship, — something to this effect: "Undo it, cut it, quick." It was said lowly, but with such condensation of rapidity, that the long, slow words in Spanish, which had preceded and followed, almost operated as covers to the brief English between.   30

For a moment, knot in hand, and knot in head, Captain Delano stood mute; while, without further heeding him the old man was now intent upon other ropes. Presently there was a slight stir behind Captain Delano. Turning, he saw the chained Negro, Atufal, standing quietly there. The next moment the old sailor rose, muttering, and, followed by his subordinate Negroes, removed to the forward part of the ship, where in the crowd he disappeared.

An elderly Negro, in a clout like an infant's, and with a pepper and salt head, and a kind of attorney air, now approached Captain Delano. In tolerable Spanish, and with a good-natured, knowing wink, he informed him that the old knotter was simple-witted, but harmless; often playing his odd tricks. The Negro concluded by   40
begging the knot, for of course the stranger would not care to be troubled with it.

---

16 **Gordian knot,** in classical mythology an intricately tied knot. An oracle predicted that the man who could untie it would rule Asia. Alexander the Great "untied" it with one blow of his sword   17 **Ammon,** Amen, an Egyptian deity

Unconsciously, it was handed to him. With a sort of congé, the Negro received it, and, turning his back, ferreted into it like a detective custom-house officer after smuggled laces. Soon, with some African word, equivalent to pshaw, he tossed the knot overboard.

All this is very queer now, thought Captain Delano, with a qualmish sort of emotion; but, as one feeling incipient sea-sickness, he strove, by ignoring the symptoms, to get rid of the malady. Once more he looked off for his boat. To his delight, it was now again in view, leaving the rocky spur astern.

The sensation here experienced, after at first relieving his uneasiness, with unfore-
10 seen efficacy soon began to remove it. The less distant sight of that well-known boat — showing it, not as before, half blended with the haze, but with outline defined, so that its individuality, like a man's, was manifest; that boat, *Rover* by name, which, though now in strange seas, had often pressed the beach of Captain Delano's home, and, brought to its threshold for repairs, had familiarly lain there, as a Newfoundland dog; the sight of that household boat evoked a thousand trustful associations, which, contrasted with previous suspicions, filled him not only with lightsome confidence, but somehow with half humorous self-reproaches, at his former lack of it.

"What, I, Amasa Delano — Jack of the Beach, as they called me when a lad — I,
20 Amasa; the same that, duck-satchel in hand, used to paddle along the waterside to the school-house made from the old hulk — I, little Jack of the Beach, that used to go berrying with cousin Nat and the rest; I to be murdered here at the ends of the earth, on board a haunted pirate-ship by a horrible Spaniard? Too nonsensical to think of! Who would murder Amasa Delano? His conscience is clean. There is some one above. Fie, fie, Jack of the Beach! you are a child indeed; a child of the second childhood, old boy; you are beginning to dote and drule, I'm afraid."

Light of heart and foot, he stepped aft, and there was met by Don Benito's servant, who, with a pleasing expression, responsive to his own present feelings, informed him that his master had recovered from the effects of his coughing fit, and
30 had just ordered him to go present his compliments to his good guest, Don Amasa, and say that he (Don Benito) would soon have the happiness to rejoin him.

There now, do you mark that? again thought Captain Delano, walking the poop. What a donkey I was. This kind gentleman who here sends me his kind compliments, he, but ten minutes ago, dark-lantern in hand, was dodging round some old grind-stone in the hold, sharpening a hatchet for me, I thought. Well, well; these long calms have a morbid effect on the mind, I've often heard, though I never believed it before. Ha! glancing towards the boat; there's *Rover;* good dog; a white bone in her mouth. A pretty big bone though, seems to me. — What? Yes, she has fallen afoul of the bubbling tide-rip there. It sets her the other way, too, for the
40 time. Patience.

It was now about noon, though, from the grayness of everything, it seemed to be getting toward dusk.

The calm was confirmed. In the far distance, away from the influence of land, the leaden ocean seemed laid out and leaded up, its course finished, soul gone, defunct.

But the current from landward, where the ship was, increased; silently sweeping her further and further toward the tranced waters beyond.

Still, from his knowledge of those latitudes, cherishing hopes of a breeze, and a fair and fresh one, at any moment, Captain Delano, despite present prospects, buoyantly counted upon bringing the San Dominick safely to anchor ere night. The distance swept over was nothing; since, with a good wind, ten minutes' sailing would retrace more than sixty minutes' drifting. Meantime, one moment turning to mark *Rover* fighting the tide-rip, and the next to see Don Benito approaching, he continued walking the poop.

Gradually he felt a vexation arising from the delay of his boat; this soon merged 10 into uneasiness; and at last — his eye falling continually, as from a stage-box into the pit, upon the strange crowd before and below him, and, by-and-by, recognizing there the face — now composed to indifference — of the Spanish sailor who had seemed to beckon from the main-chains — something of his old trepidations returned.

Ah, thought he — gravely enough — this is like the ague: because it went off, it follows not that it won't come back.

Though ashamed of the relapse, he could not altogether subdue it; and so, exerting his good-nature to the utmost, insensibly he came to a compromise.

Yes, this is a strange craft; a strange history, too, and strange folks on board. But — nothing more.   20

By way of keeping his mind out of mischief till the boat should arrive, he tried to occupy it with turning over and over, in a purely speculative sort of way, some lesser peculiarities of the captain and crew. Among others, four curious points recurred:

First, the affair of the Spanish lad assailed with a knife by the slave boy; an act winked at by Don Benito. Second, the tyranny in Don Benito's treatment of Atufal, the black; as if a child should lead a bull of the Nile by the ring in his nose. Third, the trampling of the sailor by the two Negroes; a piece of insolence passed over without so much as a reprimand. Fourth, the cringing submission to their master of all the ships' underlings, mostly blacks; as if by the least inadvertence they feared 30 to draw down his despotic displeasure.

Coupling these points, they seemed somewhat contradictory. But what then, thought Captain Delano, glancing toward his now nearing boat — what then? Why, Don Benito is a very capricious commander. But he is not the first of the sort I have seen; though it's true he rather exceeds any other. But as a nation — continued he in his reveries — these Spaniards are all an odd set; the very word Spaniard has a curious, conspirator, Guy-Fawkish twang to it. And yet, I dare say, Spaniards in the main are as good folks as any in Duxbury, Massachusetts. Ah, good! At last *Rover* has come.

As, with its welcome freight, the boat touched the side, the oakum-pickers, with 40 venerable gestures, sought to restrain the blacks, who, at the sight of three gurried

---

37 **Guy-Fawkish.** On November 5, 1605, Guy Fawkes attempted to set off barrels of gunpowder which had been placed under the English Houses of Parliament   41 **gurried,** fouled with gurry, the offal of fish

water-casks in its bottom, and a pile of wilted pumpkins in its bow, hung over the bulwarks in disorderly raptures.

Don Benito, with his servant, now appeared; his coming, perhaps, hastened by hearing the noise. Of him Captain Delano sought permission to serve out the water, so that all might share alike, and none injure themselves by unfair excess. But sensible, and, on Don Benito's account, kind as this offer was, it was received with what seemed impatience; as if aware that he lacked energy as a commander, Don Benito, with the true jealousy of weakness, resented as an affront any interference. So, at least, Captain Delano inferred.

10   In another moment the casks were being hoisted in, when some of the eager Negroes accidentally jostled Captain Delano, where he stood by the gangway; so that, unmindful of Don Benito, yielding to the impulse of the moment, with good-natured authority he bade the blacks stand back; to enforce his words making use of a half-mirthful, half-menacing gesture. Instantly the blacks paused, just where they were, each Negro and Negress suspended in his or her posture, exactly as the word had found them — for a few seconds continuing so — while, as between the responsive posts of a telegraph, an unknown syllable ran from man to man among the perched oakum-pickers. While the visitor's attention was fixed by this scene, suddenly the hatchet-polishers half rose, and a rapid cry came from Don Benito.

20   Thinking that at the signal of the Spaniard he was about to be massacred, Captain Delano would have sprung for his boat, but paused, as the oakum-pickers dropping down into the crowd with earnest exclamations, forced every white and every Negro back, at the same moment, with gestures friendly and familiar, almost jocose, bidding him, in substance, not be a fool. Simultaneously the hatchet-polishers resumed their seats, quietly as so many tailors, and at once, as if nothing had happened, the work of hoisting in the casks was resumed, whites and blacks singing at the tackle.

Captain Delano glanced toward Don Benito. As he saw his meagre form in the act of recovering itself from reclining in the servant's arms, into which the agitated

30 invalid had fallen, he could not but marvel at the panic by which himself had been surprised on the darting supposition that such a commander, who, upon a legitimate occasion, so trivial, too, as it now appeared, could lose all self-command, was, with energetic iniquity, going to bring about his murder.

The casks being on deck, Captain Delano was handed a number of jars and cups by one of the steward's aids, who, in the name of his captain, entreated him to do as he had proposed — dole out the water. He complied, with republican impartiality as to this republican element, which always seeks one level, serving the oldest white no better than the youngest black; excepting, indeed, poor Don Benito, whose condition, if not rank, demanded an extra allowance. To him, in the first place, Cap-

40 tain Delano presented a fair pitcher of the fluid; but, thirsting as he was for it, the Spaniard quaffed not a drop until after several grave bows and salutes. A reciprocation of courtesies which the sight-loving Africans hailed with clapping hands.

Two of the less wilted pumpkins being reserved for the cabin table, the residue were minced up on the spot for the general regalement. But the soft bread, sugar, and bottled cider, Captain Delano would have given the whites alone, and in chief Don Benito; but the latter objected; which disinterestedness not a little pleased the American; and so mouthfuls all around were given alike to whites and blacks; excepting one bottle of cider, which Babo insisted upon setting aside for his master.

Here it may be observed that as, on the first visit of the boat, the American had not permitted his men to board the ship, neither did he now; being unwilling to add to the confusion of the decks.

Not uninfluenced by the peculiar good-humor at present prevailing, and for the time oblivious of any but benevolent thoughts, Captain Delano, who, from recent indications, counted upon a breeze within an hour or two at furthest, dispatched 10 the boat back to the sealer, with orders for all the hands that could be spared immediately to set about rafting casks to the watering-place and filling them. Likewise he bade word be carried to his chief officer, that if, against present expectation, the ship was not brought to anchor by sunset, he need be under no concern; for as there was to be a full moon that night, he (Captain Delano) would remain on board ready to play the pilot, come the wind soon or late.

As the two captains stood together, observing the departing boat — the servant, as it happened, having just spied a spot on his master's velvet sleeve, and silently engaged rubbing it out — the American expressed his regrets that the San Dominick had no boats; none, at least, but the unseaworthy old hulk of the long-boat, which, 20 warped as a camel's skeleton in the desert, and almost as bleached, lay pot-wise inverted amidships, one side a little tipped, furnishing a subterraneous sort of den for family groups of the blacks, mostly women and small children; who, squatting on old mats below, or perched above in the dark dome, on the elevated seats, were descried, some distance within, like a social circle of bats, sheltering in some friendly cave; at intervals, ebon flights of naked boys and girls, three or four years old, darting in and out of the den's mouth.

"Had you three or four boats now, Don Benito," said Captain Delano, "I think that, by tugging at the oars, your Negroes here might help along matters some. Did you sail from port without boats, Don Benito?"   30

"They were stove in the gales, Señor."

"That was bad. Many men, too, you lost then. Boats and men. Those must have been hard gales, Don Benito."

"Past all speech," cringed the Spaniard.

"Tell me, Don Benito," continued his companion with increased interest, "tell me, were these gales immediately off the pitch of Cape Horn?"

"Cape Horn? — who spoke of Cape Horn?"

"Yourself did, when giving me an account of your voyage," answered Captain Delano, with almost equal astonishment at this eating of his own words, even as he ever seemed eating his own heart, on the part of the Spaniard. "You yourself, Don 40 Benito, spoke of Cape Horn," he emphatically repeated.

The Spaniard turned, in a sort of stooping posture, pausing an instant, as one about to make a plunging exchange of elements, as from air to water.

At this moment a messenger-boy, a white, hurried by, in the regular performance of his function carrying the last expired half-hour forward to the forecastle, from the cabin time-piece, to have it struck at the ship's large bell.

"Master," said the servant, discontinuing his work on the coat sleeve, and addressing the rapt Spaniard with a sort of timid apprehensiveness, as one charged with a duty, the discharge of which, it was foreseen, would prove irksome to the very person who had imposed it, and for whose benefit it was intended, "master told me never mind where he was, or how engaged, always to remind him, to a minute, when shaving-time comes. Miguel has gone to strike the half-hour afternoon. It is *now,* master. Will master go into the cuddy?"

10   "Ah — yes," answered the Spaniard, starting, as from dreams into realities; then turning upon Captain Delano, he said that ere long he would resume the conversation.

"Then if master means to talk more to Don Amasa," said the servant, "why not let Don Amasa sit by master in the cuddy, and master can talk, and Don Amasa can listen, while Babo here lathers and strops."

"Yes," said Captain Delano, not unpleased with this sociable plan, "yes, Don Benito, unless you had rather not, I will go with you."

"Be it so, Señor."

As the three passed aft, the American could not but think it another strange instance of his host's capriciousness, this being shaved with such uncommon punc-
20 tuality in the middle of the day. But he deemed it more than likely that the servant's anxious fidelity had something to do with the matter; inasmuch as the timely interruption served to rally his master from the mood which had evidently been coming upon him.

The place called the cuddy was a light deck-cabin formed by the poop, a sort of attic to the large cabin below. Part of it had formerly been the quarters of the officers; but since their death all the partitionings had been thrown down, and the whole interior converted into one spacious and airy marine hall; for absence of fine furniture and picturesque disarray of odd appurtenances, somewhat answering to the wide, cluttered hall of some eccentric bachelor-squire in the country, who
30 hangs his shooting-jacket and tobacco-pouch on deer antlers, and keeps his fishing-rod, tongs, and walking-stick in the same corner.

The similitude was heightened, if not originally suggested, by glimpses of the surrounding sea; since, in one aspect, the country and the ocean seem cousins-german.

The floor of the cuddy was matted. Overhead, four or five old muskets were stuck into horizontal holes along the beams. On one side was a claw-footed old table lashed to the deck; a thumbed missal on it, and over it a small, meagre crucifix attached to the bulk-head. Under the table lay a dented cutlass or two, with a hacked harpoon, among some melancholy old rigging, like a heap of poor friars' girdles.
40 There were also two long, sharp-ribbed settees of Malacca cane, black with age, and uncomfortable to look at as inquisitors' racks, with a large, misshapen arm-chair, which, furnished with a rude barber's crotch at the back, working with a screw, seemed some grotesque engine of torment. A flag locker was in one corner, open, exposing various colored bunting, some rolled up, others half unrolled, still others

tumbled. Opposite was a cumbrous washstand, of black mahogany, all of one block, with a pedestal, like a font, and over it a railed shelf, containing combs, brushes, and other implements of the toilet. A torn hammock of stained grass swung near; the sheets tossed, and the pillow wrinkled up like a brow, as if whoever slept here slept but illy, with alternate visitations of sad thoughts and bad dreams.

The further extremity of the cuddy, overhanging the ship's stern, was pierced with three openings, windows or port-holes, according as men or cannon might peer, socially or unsocially, out of them. At present neither men nor cannon were seen, though huge ring-bolts and other rusty iron fixtures of the woodwork hinted of twenty-four-pounders.   10

Glancing toward the hammock as he entered, Captain Delano said, "You sleep here, Don Benito?"

"Yes, Señor, since we got into mild weather."

"This seems a sort of dormitory, sitting-room, sail-loft, chapel, armory, and private closet all together, Don Benito," added Captain Delano, looking round.

"Yes, Señor; events have not been favorable to much order in my arrangements."

Here the servant, napkin on arm, made a motion as if waiting his master's good pleasure. Don Benito signified his readiness, when, seating him in the Malacca arm-chair, and for the guest's convenience drawing opposite one of the settees, the serv-ant commenced operations by throwing back his master's collar and loosening his   20 cravat.

There is something in the Negro which, in a peculiar way, fits him for avocations about one's person. Most Negroes are natural valets and hair-dressers; taking to the comb and brush congenially as to the castinets, and flourishing them apparently with almost equal satisfaction. There is, too, a smooth tact about them in this em-ployment, with a marvelous, noiseless, gliding briskness, not ungraceful in its way, singularly pleasing to behold, and still more so to be the manipulated subject of. And above all is the great gift of good-humor. Not the mere grin or laugh is here meant. Those were unsuitable. But a certain easy cheerfulness, harmonious in every glance and gesture; as though God had set the whole Negro to some pleasant tune.   30

When to this is added the docility arising from the unaspiring contentment of a limited mind, and that susceptibility of blind attachment sometimes inhering in in-disputable inferiors, one readily perceives why those hypochondriacs, Johnson and Byron — it may be something like the hypochondriac, Benito Cereno — took to their hearts, almost to the exclusion of the entire white race, their serving men, the Negroes, Barber and Fletcher. But if there be that in the Negro which exempts him from the inflicted sourness of the morbid or cynical mind, how, in his most pre-possessing aspects, must he appear to a benevolent one? When at ease with respect to exterior things, Captain Delano's nature was not only benign, but familiarly and humorously so. At home, he had often taken rare satisfaction in sitting in his door,   40 watching some free man of color at his work or play. If on a voyage he chanced to have a black sailor, invariably he was on chatty, and half-gamesome terms with him. In fact, like most men of a good, blithe heart, Captain Delano took to Negroes, not philanthropically, but genially, just as other men to Newfoundland dogs.

Hitherto the circumstances in which he found the San Dominick had repressed the tendency. But in the cuddy, relieved from his former uneasiness, and, for various reasons, more sociably inclined than at any previous period of the day, and seeing the colored servant, napkin on arm, so debonair about his master, in a business so familiar as that of shaving, too, all his old weakness for Negroes returned.

Among other things, he was amused with an odd instance of the African love of bright colors and fine shows, in the black's informally taking from the flag-locker a great piece of bunting of all hues, and lavishly tucking it under his master's chin for an apron.

10 The mode of shaving among the Spaniards is a little different from what it is with other nations. They have a basin, specifically called a barber's basin, which on one side is scooped out, so as accurately to receive the chin, against which it is closely held in lathering; which is done, not with a brush, but with soap dipped in the water of the basin and rubbed on the face.

In the present instance salt-water was used for lack of better; and the parts lathered were only the upper lip, and low down under the throat, all the rest being cultivated beard.

The preliminaries being somewhat novel to Captain Delano he sat curiously eying them, so that no conversation took place, nor, for the present, did Don Benito appear 20 disposed to renew any.

Setting down his basin, the Negro searched among the razors, as for the sharpest, and having found it, gave it an additional edge by expertly stropping it on the firm, smooth, oily skin of his open palm; he then made a gesture as if to begin, but midway stood suspended for an instant, one hand elevating the razor, the other professionally dabbling among the bubbling suds on the Spaniard's lank neck. Not unaffected by the close sight of the gleaming steel, Don Benito nervously shuddered; his usual ghastliness was heightened by the lather, which lather, again, was intensified in its hue by the contrasting sootiness of the Negro's body. Altogether the scene was somewhat peculiar, at least to Captain Delano, nor, as he saw the two thus 30 postured, could he resist the vagary, that in the black he saw a headsman, and in the white a man at the block. But this was one of those antic conceits, appearing and vanishing in a breath, from which, perhaps, the best regulated mind is not always free.

Meantime the agitation of the Spaniard had a little loosened the bunting from around him, so that one broad fold swept curtain-like over the chair-arm to the floor, revealing, amid a profusion of armorial bars and ground-colors — black, blue and yellow — a closed castle in a blood-red field diagonal with a lion rampant in a white.

"The castle and the lion," exclaimed Captain Delano — "why, Don Benito, this 40 is the flag of Spain you use here. It's well it's only I, and not the King, that sees this," he added with a smile, "but" — turning toward the black, — "it's all one, I suppose, so the colors be gay;" which playful remark did not fail somewhat to tickle the Negro.

"Now, master," he said, readjusting the flag, and pressing the head gently further back into the crotch of the chair; "now, master," and the steel glanced nigh the throat.

Again Don Benito faintly shuddered.

"You must not shake so, master. See, Don Amasa, master always shakes when I shave him. And yet master knows I never yet have drawn blood, though it's true, if master will shake so, I may some of these times. Now, master," he continued. "And now, Don Amasa, please go on with your talk about the gale, and all that; master can hear, and between times, master can answer."

"Ah yes, these gales," said Captain Delano; "but the more I think of your voyage, Don Benito, the more I wonder, not at the gales, terrible as they must have 10 been, but at the disastrous interval following them. For here, by your account, have you been these two months and more getting from Cape Horn to St. Maria, a distance which I myself, with a good wind, have sailed in a few days. True, you had calms, and long ones, but to be becalmed for two months, that is, at least, unusual. Why, Don Benito, had almost any other gentleman told me such a story, I should have been half disposed to a little incredulity."

Here an involuntary expression came over the Spaniard, similar to that just before on the deck, and whether it was the start he gave, or a sudden gawky roll of the hull in the calm, or a momentary unsteadiness of the servant's hand, however it was, just then the razor drew blood, spots of which stained the creamy lather under 20 the throat; immediately the black barber drew back his steel, and remaining in his professional attitude, back to Captain Delano, and face to Don Benito, held up the trickling razor, saying, with a sort of half humorous sorrow, "See, master — you shook so — here's Babo's first blood."

No sword drawn before James the First of England, no assassination in that timid King's presence, could have produced a more terrified aspect than was now presented by Don Benito.

Poor fellow, thought Captain Delano, so nervous he can't even bear the sight of barber's blood; and this unstrung, sick man, is it credible that I should have imagined he meant to spill all my blood, who can't endure the sight of one little drop 30 of his own? Surely, Amasa Delano, you have been beside yourself this day. Tell it not when you get home, sappy Amasa. Well, well, he looks like a murderer, doesn't he? More like as if himself were to be done for. Well, well, this day's experience shall be a good lesson.

Meantime, while these things were running through the honest seaman's mind, the servant had taken the napkin from his arm, and to Don Benito had said — "But answer Don Amasa, please, master, while I wipe this ugly stuff off the razor, and strop it again."

As he said the words, his face was turned half round, so as to be alike visible to the Spaniard and the American, and seemed, by its expression, to hint, that he was 40 desirous, by getting his master to go on with the conversation, considerately to withdraw his attention from the recent annoying accident. As if glad to snatch the offered relief, Don Benito resumed, rehearsing to Captain Delano, that not only were the calms of unusual duration, but the ship had fallen in with obstinate currents; and other things he added, some of which were but repetitions of former statements, to explain how it came to pass that the passage from Cape Horn to St. Maria had been so exceedingly long; now and then mingling with his words, incidental praises, less qualified than before, to the blacks, for their general good conduct. These particulars were not given consecutively, the servant, at convenient times, using his razor, and so, between the intervals of shaving, the story and panegyric went on with more than usual huskiness.

To Captain Delano's imagination, now again not wholly at rest, there was something so hollow in the Spaniard's manner, with apparently some reciprocal hollow-
10 ness in the servant's dusky comment of silence, that the idea flashed across him, that possibly master and man, for some unknown purpose, were acting out, both in word and deed, nay, to the very tremor of Don Benito's limbs, some juggling play before him. Neither did the suspicion of collusion lack apparent support, from the fact of those whispered conferences before mentioned. But then, what could be the object of enacting this play of the barber before him? At last, regarding the notion as a whimsy, insensibly suggested, perhaps, by the theatrical aspect of Don Benito in his harlequin ensign, Captain Delano speedily banished it.

The shaving over, the servant bestirred himself with a small bottle of scented waters, pouring a few drops on the head, and then diligently rubbing; the vehe-
20 mence of the exercise causing the muscles of his face to twitch rather strangely.

His next operation was with comb, scissors and brush; going round and round, smoothing a curl here, clipping an unruly whisker-hair there, giving a graceful sweep to the temple-lock, with other impromptu touches evincing the hand of a master; while, like any resigned gentleman in barber's hands, Don Benito bore all, much less uneasily, at least, than he had done the razoring; indeed, he sat so pale and rigid now, that the Negro seemed a Nubian sculptor finishing off a white statue-head.

All being over at last, the standard of Spain removed, tumbled up, and tossed back into the flag-locker, the Negro's warm breath blowing away any stray hair
30 which might have lodged down his master's neck; collar and cravat readjusted; a speck of lint whisked off the velvet lapel; all this being done; backing off a little space, and pausing with an expression of subdued self-complacency, the servant for a moment surveyed his master, as, in toilet at least, the creature of his own tasteful hands.

Captain Delano playfully complimented him upon his achievement; at the same time congratulating Don Benito.

But neither sweet waters, nor shampooing, nor fidelity, nor sociality, delighted the Spaniard. Seeing him relapsing into forbidding gloom, and still remaining seated, Captain Delano, thinking that his presence was undesired just then, withdrew, on
40 pretense of seeing whether, as he had prophesied, any signs of a breeze were visible.

Walking forward to the mainmast, he stood awhile thinking over the scene and not without some undefined misgivings, when he heard a noise near the cuddy, and turning, saw the Negro, his hand to his cheek. Advancing, Captain Delano perceived

26 **Nubian,** one of the Negro tribe of Nubia, in eastern Africa

that the cheek was bleeding. He wan about to ask the cause, when the Negro's wailing soliloquy enlightened him.

"Ah, when will master get better from his sickness; only the sour heart that sour sickness breeds made him serve Babo so; cutting Babo with the razor, because, only by accident, Babo had given master one little scratch; and for the first time in so many a day, too. Ah, ah, ah," holding his hand to his face.

Is it possible, thought Captain Delano; was it to wreak in private his Spanish spite against this poor friend of his, that Don Benito, by his sullen manner, impelled me to withdraw? Ah, this slavery breeds ugly passions in man. — Poor fellow!

He was about to speak in sympathy to the Negro, but with a timid reluctance he 10 now re-entered the cuddy.

Presently master and man came forth; Don Benito leaning on his servant as if nothing had happened.

But a sort of love-quarrel, after all, thought Captain Delano.

He accosted Don Benito, and they slowly walked together. They had gone but a few paces, when the steward — a tall, rajah-looking mulatto, orientally set off with a pagoda turban formed by three or four Madras handkerchiefs wound about his head, tier on tier — approaching with a salaam, announced lunch in the cabin.

On their way thither, the two captains were preceded by the mulatto, who, turning round as he advanced, with continual smiles and bows, ushered them on, a dis- 20 play of elegance which quite completed the insignificance of the small bare-headed Babo, who, as if not unconscious of inferiority, eyed askance the graceful steward. But in part, Captain Delano imputed his jealous watchfulness to that peculiar feeling which the full-blooded African entertains for the adulterated one. As for the steward, his manner, if not bespeaking much dignity of self-respect, yet evidenced his extreme desire to please; which is doubly meritorious, as at once Christian and Chesterfieldian.

Captain Delano observed with interest that while the complexion of the mulatto was hybrid, his physiognomy was European — classically so.

"Don Benito," whispered he, "I am glad to see this usher-of-the-golden-rod of 30 yours; the sight refutes an ugly remark once made to me by a Barbados planter; that when a mulatto has a regular European face, look out for him; he is a devil. But see, your steward here has features more regular than King George's of England; and yet there he nods, and bows, and smiles; a king, indeed — the king of kind hearts and polite fellows. What a pleasant voice he has, too!"

"He has, Señor."

"But, tell me, has he not, so far as you have known him, always proved a good, worthy fellow?" said Captain Delano, pausing, while with a final genuflexion the steward disappeared into the cabin; "come, for the reason just mentioned, I am curious to know."   40

"Francesco is a good man," rather sluggishly responded Don Benito, like a sort of phlegmatic appreciator, who would neither find fault nor flatter.

---

27 **Chesterfieldian.** Philip Dormer Stanhope, fourth Earl of Chesterfield (1694-1773) in *Letters to His Son* (1774) gave advice on how to get on in the world

"Ah, I thought so. For it were strange, indeed, and not very creditable to us white-skins, if a little of our blood mixed with the African's, should, far from improving the latter's quality, have the sad effect of pouring vitriolic acid into black broth; improving the hue, perhaps, but not the wholesomeness."

"Doubtless, doubtless, Señor, but" — glancing at Babo — "not to speak of Negroes, your planter's remark I have heard applied to the Spanish and Indian intermixtures in our provinces. But I know nothing about the matter," he listlessly added.

And here they entered the cabin.

The lunch was a frugal one. Some of Captain Delano's fresh fish and pumpkins, 10 biscuit and salt beef, the reserved bottle of cider, and the San Dominick's last bottle of Canary.

As they entered, Francesco, with two or three colored aids, was hovering over the table giving the last adjustments. Upon perceiving their master they withdrew, Francesco making a smiling congé, and the Spaniard, without condescending to notice it, fastidiously remarking to his companion that he relished not superfluous attendance.

Without companions, host and guest sat down, like a childless married couple, at opposite ends of the table, Don Benito waving Captain Delano to his place, and, weak as he was, insisting upon that gentleman being seated before himself.

The Negro placed a rug under Don Benito's feet, and a cushion behind his back, 20 and then stood behind, not his master's chair, but Captain Delano's. At first, this a little surprised the latter. But it was soon evident that, in taking his position, the black was still true to his master; since by facing him he could the more readily anticipate his slightest want.

"This is an uncommonly intelligent fellow of yours, Don Benito," whispered Captain Delano across the table.

"You say true, Señor."

During the repast, the guest again reverted to parts of Don Benito's story, begging further particulars here and there. He inquired how it was that the scurvy and fever should have committed such wholesale havoc upon the whites, while destroying less 30 than half of the blacks. As if this question reproduced the whole scene of plague before the Spaniard's eyes, miserably reminding him of his solitude in a cabin where before he had had so many friends and officers round him, his hand shook, his face became hueless, broken words escaped; but directly the sane memory of the past seemed replaced by insane terrors of the present. With starting eyes he stared before him at vacancy. For nothing was to be seen but the hand of his servant pushing the Canary over toward him. At length a few sips served partially to restore him. He made random reference to the different constitutions of races, enabling one to offer more resistance to certain maladies than another. The thought was new to his companion.

40 Presently Captain Delano, intending to say something to his host concerning the pecuniary part of the business he had undertaken for him, especially — since he was strictly accountable to his owners — with reference to the new suit of sails, and other things of that sort; and naturally preferring to conduct such affairs in private, was desirous that the servant should withdraw; imagining that Don Benito for a few

minutes could dispense with his attendance. He, however, waited awhile; thinking that, as the conversation proceeded, Don Benito, without being prompted, would perceive the propriety of the step.

But it was otherwise. At last catching his host's eye, Captain Delano, with a slight backward gesture of his thumb, whispered, "Don Benito, pardon me, but there is an interference with the full expression of what I have to say to you."

Upon this the Spaniard changed countenance; which was imputed to his resenting the hint, as in some way a reflection upon his servant. After a moment's pause, he assured his guest that the black's remaining with them could be of no disservice; because since losing his officers he had made Babo (whose original office, it now 10 appeared, had been captain of the slaves) not only his constant attendant and companion, but in all things his confidant.

After this, nothing more could be said; though, indeed, Captain Delano could hardly avoid some little tinge of irritation upon being left ungratified in so inconsiderable a wish, by one, too, for whom he intended such solid services. But it is only his querulousness, thought he; and so filling his glass he proceeded to business.

The price of the sails and other matters was fixed upon. But while this was being done, the American observed that, though his original offer of assistance had been hailed with hectic animation, yet now when it was reduced to a business transaction, indifference and apathy were betrayed. Don Benito, in fact, appeared to submit to 20 hearing the details more out of regard to common propriety, than from any impression that weighty benefit to himself and his voyage was involved.

Soon, his manner became still more reserved. The effort was vain to seek to draw him into social talk. Gnawed by his splenetic mood, he sat twitching his beard, while to little purpose the hand of his servant, mute as that on the wall, slowly pushed over the Canary.

Lunch being over, they sat down on the cushioned transom; the servant placing a pillow behind his master. The long continuance of the calm had now affected the atmosphere. Don Benito sighed heavily, as if for breath.

"Why not adjourn to the cuddy," said Captain Delano; "there is more air there." 30 But the host sat silent and motionless.

Meantime his servant knelt before him with a large fan of feathers. And Francesco coming in on tiptoes, handed the Negro a little cup of aromatic waters, with which at intervals he chafed his master's brow; smoothing the hair along the temples as a nurse does a child's. He spoke no word. He only rested his eye on his master's as if, amid all Don Benito's distress, a little to refresh his spirit by the silent sight of fidelity.

Presently the ship's bell sounded two o'clock; and through the cabin-windows a slight rippling of the sea was discerned; and from the desired direction.

"There," exclaimed Captain Delano, "I told you so, Don Benito, look!"

He had risen to his feet, speaking in a very animated tone, with a view the more 40 to rouse his companion. But though the crimson curtain of the stern-window near him that moment fluttered against his pale cheek, Don Benito seemed to have even less welcome for the breeze than the calm.

Poor fellow, thought Captain Delano, bitter experience has taught him that one ripple does not make a wind, any more than one swallow a summer. But he is mistaken for once. I will get his ship in for him, and prove it.

Briefly alluding to his weak condition, he urged his host to remain quietly where he was, since he (Captain Delano) would with pleasure take upon himself the responsibility of making the best use of the wind.

Upon gaining the deck, Captain Delano started at the unexpected figure of Atufal, monumentally fixed at the threshold, like one of those sculptured porters of black marble guarding the porches of Egyptian tombs.

But this time the start was, perhaps, purely physical. Atufal's presence, singularly
10 attesting docility even in sullenness, was contrasted with that of the hatchet-polishers, who in patience evinced their industry; while both spectacles showed, that lax as Don Benito's general authority might be, still, whenever he chose to exert it, no man so savage or colossal but must, more or less, bow.

Snatching a trumpet which hung from the bulwarks, with a free step Captain Delano advanced to the forward edge of the poop, issuing his orders in his best Spanish. The few sailors and many Negroes, all equally pleased, obediently set about heading the ship toward the harbour.

While giving some directions about setting a lower stu'n'-sail, suddenly Captain Delano heard a voice faithfully repeating his orders. Turning, he saw Babo, now for
20 the time acting, under the pilot, his original part of captain of the slaves. This assistance proved valuable. Tattered sails and warped yards were soon brought into some trim. And no brace or halyard was pulled but to the blithe songs of the inspirited Negroes.

Good fellows, thought Captain Delano, a little training would make fine sailors of them. Why see, the very women pull and sing, too. These must be some of those Ashantee Negresses that make such capital soldiers, I've heard. But who's at the helm? I must have a good hand there.

He went to see.

The San Dominick steered with a cumbrous tiller, with large horizontal pullies
30 attached. At each pulley-end stood a subordinate black, and between them, at the tiller-head, the responsible post, a Spanish seaman, whose countenance evinced his due share in the general hopefulness and confidence at the coming of the breeze.

He proved the same man who had behaved with so shame-faced an air on the windlass.

"Ah, — it is you, my man," exclaimed Captain Delano — "well, no more sheep's-eyes now; — look straight forward and keep the ship so. Good hand, I trust? And want to get into the harbor, don't you?"

The man assented with an inward chuckle, grasping the tiller-head firmly. Upon this, unperceived by the American, the two blacks eyed the sailor intently.
40 Finding all right at the helm, the pilot went forward to the forecastle, to see how matters stood there.

The ship now had way enough to breast the current. With the approach of evening the breeze would be sure to freshen.

18 **stu'n'-sail,** studding-sail

Having done all that was needed for the present, Captain Delano, giving his last orders to the sailors, turned aft to report affairs to Don Benito in the cabin; perhaps additionally incited to rejoin him by the hope of snatching a moment's private chat while his servant was engaged upon deck.

From opposite sides, there were, beneath the poop, two approaches to the cabin; one further forward than the other, and consequently communicating with a longer passage. Marking the servant still above, Captain Delano, taking the nighest entrance — the one last named, and at whose porch Atufal still stood — hurried on his way, till, arrived at the cabin threshold, he paused an instant, a little to recover from his eagerness. Then, with the words of his intended business upon his lips, he entered. 10 As he advanced toward the seated Spaniard, he heard another footstep, keeping time with his. From the opposite door, a salver in hand, the servant was likewise advancing.

"Confound the faithful fellow," thought Captain Delano; "what a vexatious coincidence."

Possibly, the vexation might have been something different, were it not for the brisk confidence inspired by the breeze. But even as it was, he felt a slight twinge, from a sudden indefinite association in his mind of Babo with Atufal.

"Don Benito," said he, "I give you joy; the breeze will hold, and will increase. By the way, your tall man and time-piece, Atufal, stands without. By your order, of 20 course?"

Don Benito recoiled, as if at some bland satirical touch, delivered with such adroit garnish of apparent good breeding as to present no handle for retort.

He is like one flayed alive, thought Captain Delano; where may one touch him without causing a shrink?

The servant moved before his master, adjusting a cushion; recalled to civility, the Spaniard stiffly replied: "You are right. The slave appears where you saw him, according to my command; which is, that if at the given hour I am below, he must take his stand and abide my coming."

"Ah now, pardon me, but that is treating the poor fellow like an ex-king indeed. 30 Ah, Don Benito," smiling, "for all the license you permit in some things, I fear lest, at bottom, you are a bitter hard master."

Again Don Benito shrank; and this time, as the good sailor thought, from a genuine twinge of his conscience.

Again conversation became constrained. In vain Captain Delano called attention to the now perceptible motion of the keel gently cleaving the sea; with lack-lustre eye, Don Benito returned words few and reserved.

By-and-by, the wind having steadily risen, and still blowing right into the harbour, bore the San Dominick swiftly on. Rounding a point of land, the sealer at distance came into open view.   40

Meantime Captain Delano had again repaired to the deck, remaining there some time. Having at last altered the ship's course, so as to give the reef a wide berth, he returned for a few moments below.

I will cheer up my poor friend, this time, thought he.

"Better and better, Don Benito," he cried as he blithely re-entered: "there will soon be an end to your cares, at least for awhile. For when, after a long, sad voyage, you know, the anchor drops into the haven, all its vast weight seems lifted from the captain's heart. We are getting on famously, Don Benito. My ship is in sight. Look through this side-light here; there she is; all a-taunt-o! The Bachelor's Delight, my good friend. Ah, how this wind braces one up. Come, you must take a cup of coffee with me this evening. My old steward will give you as fine a cup as ever any sultan tasted. What say you, Don Benito, will you?"

At first, the Spaniard glanced feverishly up, casting a longing look toward the sealer, while with mute concern his servant gazed into his face. Suddenly the old ague of coldness returned, and dropping back to his cushions he was silent.

"You do not answer. Come, all day you have been my host; would you have hospitality all on one side?"

"I cannot go," was the response.

"What? It will not fatigue you. The ships will lie together as near as they can, without swinging foul. It will be little more than stepping from deck to deck; which is but as from room to room. Come, come, you must not refuse me."

"I cannot go," decisively and repulsively repeated Don Benito.

Renouncing all but the last appearance of courtesy, with a sort of cadaverous sullenness, and biting his thin nails to the quick, he glanced, almost glared, at his guest, as if impatient that a stranger's presence should interfere with the full indulgence of his morbid hour. Meantime the sound of the parted waters came more and more gurglingly and merrily in at the windows; as reproaching him for his dark spleen; as telling him that, sulk as he might, and go mad with it, nature cared not a jot; since, whose fault was it, pray?

But the foul mood was now at its depth, as the fair wind at its height.

There was something in the man so far beyond any mere unsociality or sourness previously evinced, that even the forbearing good-nature of his guest could no longer endure it. Wholly at a loss to account for such demeanor, and deeming sickness with eccentricity, however extreme, no adequate excuse, well satisfied, too, that nothing in his own conduct could justify it, Captain Delano's pride began to be roused. Himself became reserved. But all seemed one to the Spaniard. Quitting him, therefore, Captain Delano once more went to the deck.

The ship was now within less than two miles of the sealer. The whale-boat was seen darting over the interval.

To be brief, the two vessels, thanks to the pilot's skill, ere long in neighborly style lay anchored together.

Before returning to his own vessel, Captain Delano had intended communicating to Don Benito the smaller details of the proposed services to be rendered. But, as it was, unwilling anew to subject himself to rebuffs, he resolved, now that he had seen the San Dominick safely moored, immediately to quit her, without further allusion to hospitality or business. Indefinitely postponing his ulterior plans, he would regulate his future actions according to future circumstances. His boat was ready to receive him; but his host still tarried below. Well, thought Captain Delano, if he has little breeding, the more need to show mine. He descended to the cabin to bid a ceremonious, and, it may be, tacitly rebukeful adieu. But to his great satisfaction, Don Benito, as if he began to feel the weight of that treatment with which his slighted guest had, not indecorously, retaliated upon him, now supported by his servant, rose to his feet, and grasping Captain Delano's hand, stood tremulous; too much agitated to speak. But the good augury hence drawn was suddenly dashed, by his resuming all his previous reserve, with augmented gloom, as, with half-averted eyes, he silently reseated himself on his cushions. With a corresponding return of his own chilled feelings, Captain Delano bowed and withdrew.

He was hardly midway in the narrow corridor, dim as a tunnel, leading from the 10 cabin to the stairs, when a sound, as of the tolling for execution in some jail-yard, fell on his ears. It was the echo of the ship's flawed bell, striking the hour, drearily reverberated in this subterranean vault. Instantly, by a fatality not to be withstood, his mind, responsive to the portent, swarmed with superstitious suspicions. He paused. In images far swifter than these sentences, the minutest details of all his former distrusts swept through him.

Hitherto, credulous good-nature had been too ready to furnish excuses for reasonable fears. Why was the Spaniard, so superfluously punctilious at times, now heedless of common propriety in not accompanying to the side his departing guest? Did indisposition forbid? Indisposition had not forbidden more irksome exertion that 20 day. His last equivocal demeanor recurred. He had risen to his feet, grasped his guest's hand, motioned toward his hat; then, in an instant, all was eclipsed in sinister muteness and gloom. Did this imply one brief, repentant relenting at the final moment, from some iniquitous plot, followed by remorseless return to it? His last glance seemed to express a calamitous, yet acquiescent farewell to Captain Delano forever. Why decline the invitation to visit the sealer that evening? Or was the Spaniard less hardened than the Jew, who refrained not from supping at the board of him whom the same night he meant to betray? What imported all those day-long enigmas and contradictions, except they were intended to mystify, preliminary to some stealthy blow? Atufal, the pretended rebel, but punctual shadow, that moment lurked 30 by the threshold without. He seemed a sentry, and more. Who, by his own confession, had stationed him there? Was the Negro now lying in wait?

The Spaniard behind — his creature before; to rush from darkness to light was the involuntary choice.

The next moment, with clenched jaw and hand, he passed Atufal, and stood unharmed in the light. As he saw his trim ship lying peacefully at her anchor, and almost within ordinary call; as he saw his household boat, with familiar faces in it, patiently rising and falling on the short waves by the San Dominick's side; and then, glancing about the decks where he stood, saw the oakum-pickers still gravely plying their fingers; and heard the low, buzzing whistle and industrious hum of the 40 hatchet-polishers, still bestirring themselves over their endless occupation; and more than all, as he saw the benign aspect of nature, taking her innocent repose in the evening; the screened sun in the quiet camp of the west shining out like the mild light

---

27 **the Jew . . . betray,** an allusion to Judas' betrayal of Jesus. See Matthew 26

from Abraham's tent; as his charmed eye and ear took in all these, with the chained figure of the black, the clenched jaw and hand relaxed. Once again he smiled at the phantoms which had mocked him, and felt something like a tinge of remorse, that, by harbouring them even for a moment, he should, by implication, have betrayed an atheist doubt of the everwatchful Providence above.

There was a few minutes' delay, while, in obedience to his orders, the boat was being hooked along to the gangway. During this interval, a sort of saddened satisfaction stole over Captain Delano, at thinking of the kindly offices he had that day discharged for a stranger. Ah, thought he, after good actions one's conscience is
10 never ungrateful, however much so the benefited party may be.

Presently, his foot, in the first act of descent into the boat, pressed the first round of the side-ladder, his face presented inward upon the deck. In the same moment, he heard his name courteously sounded; and, to his pleased surprise, saw Don Benito advancing — an unwonted energy in his air, as if, at the last moment, intent upon making amends for his recent discourtesy. With instinctive good feeling, Captain Delano, withdrawing his foot, turned and reciprocally advanced. As he did so, the Spaniard's nervous eagerness increased, but his vital energy failed; so that, the better to support him, the servant, placing his master's hand on his naked shoulder, and gently holding it there, formed himself into a sort of crutch.
20 When the two captains met, the Spaniard again fervently took the hand of the American, at the same time casting an earnest glance into his eyes, but, as before, too much overcome to speak.

I have done him wrong, self-reproachfully thought Captain Delano; his apparent coldness has deceived me; in no instance has he meant to offend.

Meantime, as if fearful the continuance of the scene might too much unstring his master, the servant seemed anxious to terminate it. And so, still presenting himself as a crutch, and walking between the two captains, he advanced with them toward the gangway; while still, as if full of kindly contrition, Don Benito would not let go the hand of Captain Delano, but retained it in his, across the black's body.
30 Soon they were standing by the side, looking over into the boat, whose crew turned up their curious eyes. Waiting a moment for the Spaniard to relinquish his hold, the now embarrassed Captain Delano lifted his foot, to overstep the threshold of the open gangway; but still Don Benito would not let go his hand. And yet, with an agitated tone, he said, "I can go no further; here I must bid you adieu. Adieu, my dear, dear Don Amasa. Go — go!" suddenly tearing his hand loose, "go, and God guard you better than me, my best friend."

Not unaffected, Captain Delano would now have lingered; but catching the meekly admonitory eye of the servant, with a hasty farewell he descended into his boat, followed by the continual adieus of Don Benito, standing rooted in the gangway.
40 Seating himself in the stern, Captain Delano, making a last salute, ordered the boat shoved off. The crew had their oars on end. The bowsmen pushed the boat a sufficient distance for the oars to be lengthwise dropped. The instant that was done, Don Benito sprang over the bulwarks, falling at the feet of Captain Delano; at the same time, calling toward his ship, but in tones so frenzied, that none in the

boat could understand him. But, as if not equally obtuse, three sailors, from three different and distant parts of the ship, splashed into the sea, swimming after their captain, as if intent upon his rescue.

The dismayed officer of the boat eagerly asked what this meant. To which Captain Delano, turning a disdainful smile upon the unaccountable Spaniard, answered that, for his part, he neither knew nor cared; but it seemed as if Don Benito had taken it into his head to produce the impression among his people that the boat wanted to kidnap him. "Or else — give way for your lives," he wildly added, starting at a clattering hubbub in the ship, above which rang the tocsin of the hatchet-polishers; and seizing Don Benito by the throat he added, "this plotting pirate means   10
murder!" Here, in apparent verification of the words, the servant, a dagger in his hand, was seen on the rail overhead, poised, in the act of leaping, as if with desperate fidelity to befriend his master to the last; while, seemingly to aid the black, the three white sailors were trying to clamber into the hampered bow. Meantime, the whole host of Negroes, as if inflamed at the sight of their jeopardized captain, impended in one sooty avalanche over the bulwarks.

All this, with what preceded, and what followed, occurred with such involutions of rapidity, that past, present, and future seemed one.

Seeing the Negro coming, Captain Delano had flung the Spaniard aside, almost in the very act of clutching him and, by the unconscious recoil, shifting his place,   20
with arms thrown up, so promptly grappled the servant in his descent, that with dagger presented at Captain Delano's heart, the black seemed of purpose to have leaped there as to his mark. But the weapon was wrenched away, and the assailant dashed down into the bottom of the boat, which now, with disentangled oars, began to speed through the sea.

At this juncture, the left hand of Captain Delano, on one side, again clutched the half-reclined Don Benito, heedless that he was in a speechless faint, while his right foot, on the other side, ground the prostrate Negro; and his right arm pressed for added speed on the after oar, his eye bent forward, encouraging his men to their utmost.   30

But here, the officer of the boat, who had at last succeeded in beating off the towing sailors, and was now, with face turned aft, assisting the bowsman at his oar, suddenly called to Captain Delano, to see what the black was about; while a Portuguese oarsman shouted to him to give heed to what the Spaniard was saying.

Glancing down at his feet, Captain Delano saw the freed hand of the servant aiming with a second dagger — a small one, before concealed in his wool — with this he was snakishly writhing up from the boat's bottom, at the heart of his master, his countenance lividly vindictive, expressing the centred purpose of his soul; while the Spaniard, half-choked, was vainly shrinking away, with husky words, incoherent to all but the Portuguese.   40

That moment, across the long-benighted mind of Captain Delano, a flash of revelation swept, illuminating in unanticipated clearness his host's whole mysterious demeanor, with every enigmatic event of the day, as well as the entire past voyage of the San Dominick. He smote Babo's hand down, but his own heart smote him harder. With infinite pity he withdrew his hold from Don Benito. Not Captain Delano, but Don Benito, the black, in leaping into the boat, had intended to stab.

Both the black's hands were held, as, glancing up towards the San Dominick, Captain Delano, now with the scales dropped from his eyes, saw the Negroes, not in misrule, not in tumult, not as if frantically concerned for Don Benito, but with mask torn away, flourishing hatchets and knives, in ferocious piratical revolt. Like delirious black dervishes, the six Ashantees danced on the poop. Prevented by their foes from springing into the water, the Spanish boys were hurrying up to the top-most spars, while such of the few Spanish sailors, not already in the sea, less alert,
10 were descried, helplessly mixed in, on deck, with the blacks.

Meantime Captain Delano hailed his own vessel, ordering the ports up, and the guns run out. But by this time the cable of the San Dominick had been cut; and the fag-end, in lashing out, whipped away the canvas shroud about the beak, sud-denly revealing, as the bleached hull swung round toward the open ocean, death for the figurehead, in a human skeleton; chalky comment on the chalked words be-low, *"Follow your leader."*

At the sight, Don Benito, covering his face, wailed out: " 'Tis he, Aranda! my murdered, unburied friend!"

Upon reaching the sealer, calling for ropes, Captain Delano bound the Negro,
20 who made no resistance, and had him hoisted to the deck. He would then have assisted the now almost helpless Don Benito up the side; but Don Benito, wan as he was, refused to move, or be moved, until the Negro should have been first put below out of view. When, presently assured that it was done, he no more shrank from the ascent.

The boat was immediately dispatched back to pick up the three swimming sailors. Meantime, the guns were in readiness, though, owing to the San Dominick having glided somewhat astern of the sealer, only the aftermost one could be brought to bear. With this, they fired six times; thinking to cripple the fugitive ship by bring-ing down her spars. But only a few inconsiderable ropes were shot away. Soon the
30 ship was beyond the gun's range, steering broad out of the bay; the blacks thickly clustering round the bowsprit, one moment with taunting cries toward the whites, the next with upthrown gestures hailing the now dusky moors of ocean — cawing crows escaped from the hand of the fowler.

The first impulse was to slip the cables and give chase. But, upon second thoughts, to pursue with whale-boat and yawl seemed more promising.

Upon inquiring of Don Benito what firearms they had on board the San Dominick, Captain Delano was answered that they had none that could be used; because, in the earlier stages of the mutiny, a cabin-passenger, since dead, had secretly put out of order the locks of what few muskets there were. But with all his remaining
40 strength, Don Benito entreated the American not to give chase, either with ship or boat; for the Negroes had already proved themselves such desperadoes, that, in case of a present assault, nothing but a total massacre of the whites could be looked for. But, regarding this warning as coming from one whose spirit had been crushed by misery, the American did not give up his design.

The boats were got ready and armed. Captain Delano ordered his men into them. He was going himself when Don Benito grasped his arm.

"What! have you saved my life, Señor, and are you now going to throw away your own?"

The officers also, for reasons connected with their interests and those of the voyage, and a duty owing to the owners, strongly objected against their commander's going. Weighing their remonstrances a moment, Captain Delano felt bound to remain; appointing his chief mate — an athletic and resolute man, who had been a privateer's-man — to head the party. The more to encourage the sailors, they were told, that the Spanish captain considered his ship as good as lost; that she and her   10
cargo, including some gold and silver, were worth more than a thousand doubloons. Take her, and no small part should be theirs. The sailors replied with a shout.

The fugitives had now almost gained an offing. It was nearly night; but the moon was rising. After hard, prolonged pulling, the boats came up on the ship's quarters, at a suitable distance laying upon their oars to discharge their muskets. Having no bullets to return, the Negroes sent their yells. But upon the second volley, Indian-like, they hurtled their hatchets. One took off a sailor's fingers. Another struck the whale-boat's bow, cutting off the rope there, and remaining stuck in the gunwale like a woodman's axe. Snatching it, quivering from its lodgment, the mate hurled it back. The returned gauntlet now stuck in the ship's broken quarter-gallery, and   20
so remained.

The Negroes giving too hot a reception, the whites kept a more respectful distance. Hovering now just out of reach of the hurtling hatchets, they, with a view to the close encounter which must soon come, sought to decoy the blacks into entirely disarming themselves of their most murderous weapons in a hand-to-hand fight, by foolishly flinging them, as missiles, short of the mark, into the sea. But ere long, perceiving the stratagem, the Negroes desisted, though not before many of them had to replace their lost hatchets with handspikes; an exchange which, as counted upon, proved, in the end, favorable to the assailants.

Meantime, with a strong wind, the ship still clove the water; the boats alternately   30
falling behind, and pulling up, to discharge fresh volleys.

The fire was mostly directed toward the stern, since there, chiefly, the Negroes, at present, were clustering. But to kill or maim the Negroes was not the object. To take them, with the ship, was the object. To do it, the ship must be boarded; which could not be done by boats while she was sailing so fast.

A thought now struck the mate. Observing the Spanish boys still aloft, high as they could get, he called to them to descend to the yards, and cut adrift the sails. It was done. About this time, owing to causes hereafter to be shown, two Spaniards, in the dress of sailors, and conspicuously showing themselves, were killed; not by volleys, but by deliberate marksman's shots; while, as it afterward appeared, by one   40
of the general discharges, Atufal, the black, and the Spaniard at the helm likewise were killed. What now, with the loss of the sails, and loss of leaders, the ship became unmanageable to the Negroes.

---

13 **offing,** a good distance from the shore where the water is deep and no pilot is needed

With creaking masts, she came heavily round to the wind; the prow slowly swinging into view of the boats, its skeleton gleaming in the horizontal moonlight, and casting a gigantic ribbed shadow upon the water. One extended arm of the ghost seemed beckoning the whites to avenge it.

"Follow your leader!" cried the mate; and, one on each bow, the boats boarded. Sealing-spears and cutlasses crossed hatchets and handspikes. Huddled upon the longboat amidships, the Negresses raised a wailing chant, whose chorus was the clash of the steel.

For a time, the attack wavered; the Negroes wedging themselves to beat it back; the half-repelled sailors, as yet unable to gain a footing, fighting as troopers in the saddle, one leg sideways flung over the bulwarks, and one without, plying their cutlasses like carters' whips. But in vain. They were almost overborne, when rallying themselves into a squad as one man, with a huzza, they sprang inboard, where, entangled, they involuntarily separated again. For a few breaths' space there was a vague, muffled, inner sound, as of submerged sword-fish rushing hither and thither through shoals of black-fish. Soon, in a reunited band, and joined by the Spanish seamen, the whites came to the surface, irresistibly driving the Negroes toward the stern. But a barricade of casks and sacks from side to side, had been thrown up by the mainmast. Here the Negroes faced about, and though scorning peace or truce, yet fain would have had respite. But, without pause, overleaping the barrier, the unflagging sailors again closed. Exhausted, the blacks now fought in despair. Their red tongues lolled, wolf-like, from their black mouths. But the pale sailors' teeth were set; not a word was spoken; and, in five minutes more, the ship was won.

Nearly a score of the Negroes were killed. Exclusive of those by the balls, many were mangled; their wounds — mostly inflicted by the long-edged sealing-spears — resembling those shaven ones of the English at Preston Pans, made by the poled scythes of the Highlanders. On the other side, none were killed, though several were wounded; some severely, including the mate. The surviving Negroes were temporarily secured, and the ship towed back into the harbor at midnight, once more lay anchored.

Omitting the incidents and arrangements ensuing, suffice it that, after two days spent in refitting, the ships sailed in company for Conception in Chili, and thence for Lima in Peru; where, before the vice-regal courts, the whole affair, from the beginning, underwent investigation.

Though, midway on the passage, the ill-fated Spaniard, relaxed from constraint, showed some signs of regaining health with free-will; yet, agreeably to his own foreboding, shortly before arriving at Lima, he relapsed, finally becoming so reduced as to be carried ashore in arms. Hearing of his story and plight, some of the many religious institutions of the City of Kings opened an hospitable refuge to him, where both physician and priest were his nurses, and a member of the order volunteered to be his one special guardian and consoler, by night and by day.

The following extracts, translated from one of the official Spanish documents, will,

---

26 **Preston Pans.** At the battle of Preston Pans in 1745, the Scottish Highlanders supported Charles Edward Stuart, grandson of James II, against the English

it is hoped, shed light on the preceding narrative, as well as, in the first place, reveal the true port of departure and true history of the San Dominick's voyage, down
to the time of her touching at the island of St. Maria.

But, ere the extracts come, it may be well to preface them with a remark.

The document selected, from among many others, for partial translation, contains
the deposition of Benito Cereno; the first taken in the case. Some disclosures therein
were, at the time, held dubious for both learned and natural reasons. The tribunal
inclined to the opinion that the deponent, not undisturbed in his mind by recent
events, raved of some things which could never have happened. But subsequent
depositions of the surviving sailors, bearing out the revelations of their captain in   10
several of the strangest particulars, gave credence to the rest. So that the tribunal,
in its final decision, rested its capital sentences upon statements which, had they lacked
confirmation, it would have deemed it but duty to reject.

I, DON JOSE DE ABOS AND PADILLA, His Majesty's Notary for the Royal Revenue, and Register of this Province, and Notary Public of the Holy Crusade of this
Bishopric, etc.

Do certify and declare, as much as is requisite in law, that, in the criminal cause
commenced the twenty-fourth of the month of September, in the year seventeen
hundred and ninety-nine, against the Negroes of the ship San Dominick, the following declaration before me was made: 20
Declaration of the first witness, DON BENITO CERENO.

The same day, and month, and year, His Honor, Doctor Juan Martinez de Rozas,
Councilor of the Royal Audience of this Kingdom, and learned in the law of this
Intendency, ordered the captain of the ship San Dominick, Don Benito Cereno, to
appear; which he did in his litter, attended by the monk Infelez; of whom he received the oath, which he took by God, our Lord, and a sign of the Cross; under
which he promised to tell the truth of whatever he should know and should be
asked; — and being interrogated agreeably to the tenor of the act commencing the
process, he said, that on the twentieth of May last, he set sail with his ship from
the port of Valparaiso, bound to that of Callao; loaded with the produce of the coun- 30
try besides thirty cases of hardware and one hundred and sixty blacks, of both sexes,
mostly belonging to Don Alexandro Aranda, gentleman, of the city of Mendoza;
that the crew of the ship consisted of thirty-six men, besides the persons who went
as passengers; that the Negroes were in part as follows: . . .

[*Here, in the original, follows a list of some fifty names, descriptions, and ages, compiled
from certain recovered documents of Aranda's, and also from recollections of the deponent,
from which portions only are extracted.*]

— One, from about eighteen to nineteen years, named José, and this was the man
that waited upon his master, Don Alexandro, and who speaks well the Spanish,
having served him four or five years; . . . A mulatto, named Francesco, the cabin   40
steward, of a good person and voice, having sung in the Valparaiso churches, native
of the province of Buenos Ayres, aged about thirty-five years. A smart Negro, named

---

36 [**Here . . . extracted.**] The brackets and bracketed material are Melville's throughout

Dago, who had been for many years a grave-digger among the Spaniards, aged forty-six years. . . . Four old Negroes, born in Africa, from sixty to seventy, but sound, caulkers by trade, whose names are as follows: — the first was named Muri, and he was killed (as was also his son named Diamelo); the second, Nacta; the third, Yola, likewise killed; the fourth, Ghofan; and six full-grown Negroes, aged from thirty to forty-five, all raw, and born among the Ashantees — Matiluqui, Yan, Lecbe, Mapenda, Yambaio, Akim; four of whom were killed; . . . a powerful Negro named Atufal, who being supposed to have been a chief in Africa, his owner set great store by him. . . . And a small Negro of Senegal, but some years among the Spaniards,
10 aged about thirty, which Negro's name was Babo; . . . that he does not remember the names of the others, but that still expecting the residue of Don Alexandro's papers will be found, will then take due account of them all, and remit to the court; . . . and thirty-nine women and children of all ages.

[*The catalogue over, the deposition goes on:*]

. . . That all the Negroes slept upon deck, as is customary in this navigation, and none wore fetters, because the owner, his friend Aranda, told him that they were all tractable; . . . that on the seventh day after leaving port, at three o'clock in the morning, all the Spaniards being asleep except the two officers on the watch, who were the boatswain, Juan Robles, and the carpenter, Juan Bautista Gayete, and the helms-
20 man and his boy, the Negroes revolted suddenly, wounded dangerously the boatswain and the carpenter, and successively killed eighteen men of those who were sleeping upon deck, some with hand-spikes and hatchets, and others by throwing them alive overboard, after tying them; that of the Spaniards upon deck, they left about seven, as he thinks, alive and tied, to manoeuvre the ship, and three or four more who hid themselves, remained also alive. Although in the act of revolt the Negroes made themselves masters of the hatchway, six or seven wounded went through it to the cockpit, without any hindrance on their part; that in the act of revolt, the mate and another person, whose name he does not recollect, attempted to come up through the hatchway, but being quickly wounded, were obliged to re-
30 turn to the cabin; that the deponent resolved at break of day to come up the companion-way, where the Negro Babo was, being the ringleader, and Atufal, who assisted him, and having spoken to them, exhorted them to cease committing such atrocities, asking them, at the same time, what they wanted and intended to do, offering, himself, to obey their commands; that, notwithstanding this, they threw, in his presence, three men, alive and tied, overboard; that they told the deponent to come up, and that they would not kill him; which having done, the Negro Babo asked him whether there were in those seas any Negro countries where they might be carried, and he answered them, No; that the Negro Babo afterward told him to carry them to Senegal, or to the neighbouring islands of St. Nicholas; and he an-
40 swered, that this was impossible, on account of the great distance, the necessity involved of rounding Cape Horn, the bad condition of the vessel, the want of provisions, sails, and water; but that the Negro Babo replied to him he must carry them in any way; that they would do and conform themselves to everything the deponent

---

9 **Senegal,** a province in West Africa

should require as to eating and drinking; that after a long conference, being absolutely compelled to please them, for they threatened to kill all the whites if they
were not, at all events, carried to Senegal, he told them that what was most wanting for the voyage was water; that they would go near the coast to take it and thence
they would proceed on their course; that the Negro Babo agreed to it; and the deponent steered toward the intermediate ports, hoping to meet some Spanish or foreign vessel that would save them; that within ten or eleven days they saw the land,
and continued their course by it in the vicinity of Nasca; that the deponent observed
that the Negroes were now restless and mutinous, because he did not effect the taking in of water, the Negro Babo having required, with threats, that it should be   10
done, without fail, the following day; he told him he saw plainly that the coast was
steep, and the rivers designated in the maps were not to be found, with other reasons suitable to the circumstances; that the best way would be to go to the island
of Santa Maria, where they might water easily, it being a solitary island, as the foreigners did; that the deponent did not go to Pisco, that was near, nor make any
other port of the coast, because the Negro Babo had intimated to him several times,
that he would kill all the whites the very moment he should perceive any city, town,
or settlement of any kind on the shores to which they should be carried: that having determined to go to the island of Santa Maria, as the deponent had planned, for
the purpose of trying whether, on the passage or near the island itself, they could 20
find any vessel that should favor them, or whether he could escape from it in a boat
to the neighbouring coast of Arruco, to adopt the necessary means he immediately
changed his course, steering for the island; that the Negroes Babo and Atufal held
daily conferences, in which they discussed what was necessary for their design of
returning to Senegal, whether they were to kill all the Spaniards, and particularly
the deponent; that eight days after parting with the coast of Nasca, the deponent
being on the watch a little after day-break, and soon after the Negroes had their
meeting, the Negro Babo came to the place where the deponent was, and told him
that he had determined to kill his master, Don Alexandro Aranda, both because he
and his companions could not otherwise be sure of their liberty, and that to keep   30
the seamen in subjection, he wanted to prepare a warning of what road they should
be made to take did they or any of them oppose him; and that, by means of the
death of Don Alexandro, that warning would best be given; but, that what this
last meant, the deponent did not at the time comprehend, nor could not, further
than that the death of Don Alexandro was intended; and moreover the Negro Babo
proposed to the deponent to call the mate Raneds, who was sleeping in the cabin,
before the thing was done, for fear, as the deponent understood it, that the mate,
who was a good navigator, should be killed with Don Alexandro and the rest; that
the deponent, who was the friend, from youth of Don Alexandro, prayed and conjured, but all was useless; for the Negro Babo answered him that the thing could   40
not be prevented, and that all the Spaniards risked their death if they should attempt to frustrate his will in this matter, or any other; that, in this conflict, the deponent called the mate, Raneds, who was forced to go apart, and immediately the
Negro Babo commanded the Ashantee Matiluqui and the Ashantee Lecbe to go and

commit the murder; that those two went down with hatchets to the berth of Don Alexandro; that, yet half alive and mangled, they dragged him on deck; that they were going to throw him overboard in that state, but the Negro Babo stopped them, bidding the murder be completed on the deck before him, which was done, when, by his orders, the body was carried below, forward; that nothing more was seen of it by the deponent for three days; . . . that Don Alonzo Sidonia, an old man, long resident at Valparaiso, and lately appointed to a civil office in Peru, whither he had taken passage, was at the time sleeping in the berth opposite Don Alexandro's; that awakening at his cries, surprised by them, and at the sight of the Negroes with
10 their bloody hatchets in their hands, he threw himself into the sea through a window which was near him and was drowned, without it being in the power of the deponent to assist or take him up; . . . that, a short time after killing Aranda, they brought upon deck his german-cousin, of middle-age, Don Francisco Masa, of Mendoza, and the young Don Joaquin, Marques de Aramboalaza, then lately from Spain, with his Spanish servant Ponce, and the three young clerks of Aranda, José Mozairi, Lorenzo Bargas, and Hermenegildo Gandix, all of Cadiz; that Don Joaquin and Hermenegildo Gandix, the Negro Babo, for purposes hereafter to appear, preserved alive; but Don Francisco Masa, José Mozairi, and Lorenzo Bargas, with Ponce the servant, besides the boatswain, Juan Robles, the boatswain's mates, Manuel Vis-
20 caya and Roderigo Hurta, and four of the sailors, the Negro Babo ordered to be thrown alive into the sea, although they made no resistance, nor begged for anything else but mercy; that the boatswain, Juan Robles, who knew how to swim, kept the longest above water, making acts of contrition, and, in the last words he uttered, charged this deponent to cause mass to be said for his soul to our Lady of Succour: . . . that, during the three days which followed, the deponent, uncertain what fate had befallen the remains of Don Alexandro, frequently asked the Negro Babo where they were, and, if still on board, whether they were to be preserved for interment ashore, entreating him so to order it; that the Negro Babo answered nothing till the fourth day, when at sunrise, the deponent coming on deck, the Negro
30 Babo showed him a skeleton, which had been substituted for the ship's proper figurehead — the image of Christopher Colon, the discoverer of the New World; that the Negro Babo asked him whose skeleton that was, and whether, from its whiteness, he should not think it a white's; that, upon discovering his face, the Negro Babo, coming close, said words to this effect: "Keep faith with the blacks from here to Senegal, or you shall in spirit, as now in body, follow your leader," pointing to the prow; . . . that the same morning the Negro Babo took by succession each Spaniard forward, and asked him whose skeleton that was, and whether, from its whiteness, he should not think it a white's; that each Spaniard covered his face; that then to each the Negro Babo repeated the words in the first place said to the deponent;
40 . . . that they (the Spaniards), being then assembled aft, the Negro Babo harangued them, saying that he had now done all; that the deponent (as navigator for the Negroes) might pursue his course, warning him and all of them that they should, soul and body, go the way of Don Alexandro, if he saw them (the Spaniards) speak or

6 **days;** . . . The dots indicating omissions are Melville's throughout

plot anything against them (the Negroes) — a threat which was repeated every day; that, before the events last mentioned, they had tied the cook to throw him overboard, for it is not known what thing they heard him speak, but finally the Negro Babo spared his life, at the request of the deponent; that a few days after, the deponent, endeavoring not to omit any means to preserve the lives of the remaining whites, spoke to the Negroes peace and tranquillity, and agreed to draw up a paper, signed by the deponent and the sailors who could write, as also by the Negro Babo, for himself and all the blacks, in which the deponent obliged himself to carry them to Senegal, and they not to kill any more, and he formally to make over to them the ship, with the cargo, with which they were for that time satisfied and quieted. 10 ... But the next day, the more surely to guard against the sailors' escape, the Negro Babo commanded all the boats to be destroyed but the long-boat, which was unseaworthy, and another, a cutter in good condition, which knowing it would yet be wanted for towing the water casks, he had it lowered down into the hold.

[*Various particulars of the prolonged and perplexed navigation ensuing here follow, with incidents of a calamitous calm, from which portion one passage is extracted, to wit:*]

— That on the fifth day of the calm, all on board suffering much from the heat, and want of water, and five having died in fits, and mad, the Negroes became irritable, and for a chance gesture, which they deemed suspicious — though it was harmless — made by the mate, Raneds, to the deponent in the act of handing 20 a quadrant, they killed him; but that for this they were afterwards sorry, the mate being the only remaining navigator on board, except the deponent.

— That omitting other events, which daily happened, and which can only serve uselessly to recall past misfortunes and conflicts, after seventy-three days' navigation, reckoned from the time they sailed from Nasca, during which they navigated under a scanty allowance of water, and were afflicted with the calms before mentioned, they at last arrived at the island of Santa Maria, on the seventeenth of the month of August, at about six o'clock in the afternoon, at which hour they cast anchor very near the American ship, Bachelor's Delight, which lay in the same bay, commanded by the generous Captain Amasa Delano; but at six o'clock in the morning, 30 they had already decried the port, and the Negroes became uneasy, as soon as at distance they saw the ship, not having expected to see one there; that the Negro Babo pacified them, assuring them that no fear need be had; that straightway he ordered the figure on the bow to be covered with canvas, as for repairs, and had the decks a little set in order; that for a time the Negro Babo and the Negro Atuful conferred; that the Negro Atuful was for sailing away, but the Negro Babo would not, and, by himself, cast about what to do; that at last he came to the deponent, proposing to him to say and do all that the deponent declares to have said and done to the American captain; ... that the Negro Babo warned him that if he varied in the least, or uttered any word, or gave any look that should give the least intima- 40 tion of the past events or present state, he would instantly kill him, with all his companions, showing a dagger, which he carried hid, saying something which, as he understood it, meant that that dagger would be alert as his eye; that the Negro Babo then announced the plan to all his companions, which pleased them; that he

then, the better to disguise the truth, devised many expedients, in some of them uniting deceit and defense; that of this sort was the device of the six Ashantees before named, who were his bravoes; that them he stationed on the break of the poop, as if to clean certain hatchets (in cases, which were part of the cargo), but in reality to use them, and distribute them at need, and at a given word he told them; that, among other devices, was the device of presenting Atufal, his right hand man, as chained, though in a moment the chains could be dropped; that in every particular he informed the deponent what part he was expected to enact in every device, and what story he was to tell on every occasion, always threatening him with instant
10 death if he varied in the least: that, conscious that many of the Negroes would be turbulent, the Negro Babo appointed the four aged Negroes, who were calkers, to keep what domestic order they could on the decks; that again and again he harangued the Spaniards and his companions, informing them of his intent, and of his devices, and of the invented story that this deponent was to tell; charging them lest any of them varied from that story; that these arrangements were made and matured during the interval of two or three hours, between their first sighting the ship and the arrival on board of Captain Amasa Delano; that this happened at about half-past seven o'clock in the morning, Captain Amasa Delano coming in his boat, and all gladly receiving him; that the deponent, as well as he could force himself, acting
20 then the part of principal owner, and a free captain of the ship, told Captain Amasa Delano, when called upon, that he came from Buenos Ayres, bound to Lima, with three hundred Negroes; that off Cape Horn, and in a subsequent fever, many Negroes had died; that also, by similar casualties, all the sea officers and the greatest part of the crew had died.

[*And so the deposition goes on, circumstantially recounting the fictitious story dictated to the deponent by Babo, and through the deponent imposed upon Captain Delano; and also recounting the friendly offers of Captain Delano, with other things, but all of which is here omitted. After the fictitious story, etc., the deposition proceeds:*]

— that the generous Captain Amasa Delano remained on board all the day, till
30 he left the ship anchored at six o'clock in the evening, deponent speaking to him always of his pretended misfortunes, under the forementioned principles, without having had it in his power to tell a single word, or give him the least hint, that he might know the truth and state of things; because the Negro Babo, performing the office of an officious servant with all the appearance of submission of the humble slave, did not leave the deponent one moment; that this was in order to observe the deponent's actions and words, for the Negro Babo understands well the Spanish; and besides, there were thereabouts some others who were constantly on the watch, and likewise understood the Spanish; . . . that upon one occasion, while deponent was standing on the deck conversing with Amasa Delano, by a secret sign
40 the Negro Babo drew him (the deponent) aside, the act appearing as if originating with the deponent; that then, he being drawn aside, the Negro Babo proposed to him to gain from Amasa Delano full particulars about his ship, and crew, and arms; that the deponent asked "For what?" that the Negro Babo answered he might conceive; that, grieved at the prospect of what might overtake the generous Captain

Amasa Delano, the deponent at first refused to ask the desired questions, and used every argument to induce the Negro Babo to give up this new design; that the Negro Babo showed the point of his dagger; that, after the information had been obtained the Negro Babo again drew him aside, telling him that that very night he (the deponent) would be captain of two ships instead of one, for that, great part of the American's ship's crew being to be absent fishing, the six Ashantees, without any one else, would easily take it; that at this time he said other things to the same purpose; that no entreaties availed; that before Amasa Delano's coming on board, no hint had been given touching the capture of the American ship: that to prevent this project the deponent was powerless; . . . — that in some things his memory is   10 confused, he cannot distinctly recall every event; . . . — that as soon as they had cast anchor at six of the clock in the evening, as has before been stated, the American Captain took leave, to return to his vessel; that upon a sudden impulse, which the deponent believes to have come from God and his angels, he, after the farewell had been said, followed the generous Captain Amasa Delano as far as the gunwale, where he stayed, under the pretense of taking leave, until Amasa Delano should have been seated in his boat; that on shoving off, the deponent sprang from the gunwale into the boat, and fell into it, he knows not how, God guarding him; that —

[*Here, in the original, follows the account of what further happened at the escape, and how the San Dominick was retaken, and of the passage to the coast; including in the recital*   20 *many expressions of "eternal gratitude" to the "generous Captain Amasa Delano." The deposition then proceeds with recapitulatory remarks, and a partial renumeration of the Negroes, making record of their individual part in the past events, with a view to furnishing, according to command of the court, the data whereon to found the criminal sentences to be pronounced. From this portion is the following:*]

— That he believes that all the Negroes, though not in the first place knowing to the design of revolt, when it was accomplished, approved it. . . . That the Negro, José, eighteen years old, and in the personal service of Don Alexandro, was the one who communicated the information to the Negro Babo, about the state of things in the cabin, before the revolt; that this is known, because, in the preceding midnight,   30 he used to come from his berth, which was under his master's, in the cabin, to the deck where the ringleader and his associates were, and had secret conversations with the Negro Babo, in which he was several times seen by the mate; that, one night, the mate drove him away twice; . . . that this same Negro José was the one who, without being commanded to do so by the Negro Babo, as Lecbe and Matiluqui were, stabbed his master, Don Alexandro, after he had been dragged half-lifeless to the deck; . . . that the mulatto steward, Francesco, was of the first band of revolters, that he was, in all things, the creature and tool of the Negro Babo; that, to make his court, he, just before a repast in the cabin, proposed, to the Negro Babo, poisoning a dish for the generous Captain Amasa Delano; this is known and believed, because   40 the Negroes have said it; but that the Negro Babo, having another design, forbade Francesco; . . . that the Ashantee Lecbe was one of the worst of them; for that, on the day the ship was retaken, he assisted in the defense of her, with a hatchet in each hand, with one of which he wounded, in the breast, the chief mate of Amasa

Delano, in the first act of boarding; this all knew; that, in sight of the deponent, Lecbe struck, with a hatchet, Don Francisco Masa when, by the Negro Babo's orders, he was carrying him to throw him overboard, alive; besides participating in the murder, before mentioned, of Don Alexandro Aranda, and others of the cabin-passengers; that, owing to the fury with which the Ashantees fought in the engagement with the boats, but this Lecbe and Yan survived; that Yan was bad as Lecbe; that Yan was the man who, by Babo's command, willingly prepared the skeleton of Don Alexandro, in a way the Negroes afterward told the deponent, but which he, so long as reason is left him, can never divulge; that Yan and Lecbe were the
10 two who, in a calm by night, riveted the skeleton to the bow; this also the Negroes told him; that the Negro Babo was he who traced the inscription below it; that the Negro Babo was the plotter from first to last; he ordered every murder, and was the helm and keel of the revolt; that Atufal was his lieutenant in all; but Atufal, with his own hand, committed no murder; nor did the Negro Babo; . . . that Atufal was shot, being killed in the fight with the boats, ere boarding; . . . that the Negresses, of age, were knowing to the revolt, and testified themselves satisfied at the death of their master, Don Alexandro; that, had the Negroes not restrained them, they would have tortured to death, instead of simply killing, the Spaniards slain by command of the Negro Babo; that the Negresses used their ut-
20 most influence to have the deponent made away with; that, in various acts of murder, they sang songs and danced — not gaily, but solemnly; and before the engagement with the boats, as well as during the action, they sang melancholy songs to the Negroes, and that this melancholy tone was more inflaming than a different one would have been, and was so intended; that all this is believed because the Negroes have said it.

— that of the thirty-six men of the crew, exclusive of the passengers (all of whom are now dead), which the deponent had knowledge of, six only remained alive, with four cabin-boys and ship-boys, not included with the crew; . . . — that the negroes broke an arm of one of the cabin-boys and gave him strokes with hatchets.
30 [*Then follow various random disclosures referring to various periods of time. The following are extracted:*]

— That during the presence of Captain Amasa Delano on board, some attempts were made by the sailors, and one by Hermenegildo Gandix, to convey hints to him of the true state of affairs; but that these attempts were ineffectual, owing to fear of incurring death, and, furthermore, owing to the devices which offered contradictions to the true state of affairs, as well as owing to the generosity and piety of Amasa Delano, incapable of sounding such wickedness; . . . that Luys Galgo, a sailor about sixty years of age, and formerly of the king's navy, was one of those who sought to convey tokens to Captain Amasa Delano; but his intent, though undiscovered, be-
40 ing suspected, he was, on a pretense, made to retire out of sight, and at last into the hold, and there was made away with. This the negroes have since said; . . . that one of the ship-boys feeling, from Captain Amasa Delano's presence, some hopes of release, and not having enough prudence, dropped some chanceword respecting his expectations, which being overheard and understood by a slave-boy with whom

he was eating at the time, the latter struck him on the head with a knife, inflicting
a bad wound, but of which the boy is now healing; that likewise, not long before
the ship was brought to anchor, one of the seamen, steering at the time, endangered
himself by letting the blacks remark some expression in his countenance, arising
from a cause similar to the above; but this sailor, by his heedful after conduct, escaped;
. . . that these statements are made to show the court that from the beginning to
the end of the revolt, it was impossible for the deponent and his men to act otherwise than they did; . . . — that the third clerk, Hermenegildo Gandix, who before
had been forced to live among the seamen, wearing a seaman's habit, and in all respects appearing to be one for the time; he, Gandix, was killed by a musket ball   10
fired through mistake from the boats before boarding, having in his fright run up
the mizzen-rigging, calling to the boats — "don't board," lest upon their boarding
the Negroes should kill him; that this inducing the Americans to believe he some
way favored the cause of the Negroes, they fired two balls at him, so that he fell
wounded from the rigging, and was drowned in the sea; . . . — that the young Don
Joaquin, Marques de Aramboalaza, like Hermenegildo Gandix, the third clerk, was
degraded to the office and appearance of a common seaman; that upon one occasion, when Don Joaquin shrank, the Negro Babo commanded the Ashantee Lecbe
to take tar and heat it, and pour it upon Don Joaquin's hands; . . . — that Don
Joaquin was killed owing to another mistake of the Americans, but one impossible   20
to be avoided, as upon the approach of the boats, Don Joaquin, with a hatchet tied
edge out and upright to his hand, was made by the Negroes to appear on the bulwarks; whereupon, seen with arms in his hands and in a questionable attitude, he
was shot for a renegade seaman; . . . — that on the person of Don Joaquin was
found secreted a jewel, which, by papers that were discovered, proved to have been
meant for the shrine of our Lady of Mercy in Lima; a votive offering, beforehand
prepared and guarded, to attest his gratitude, when he should have landed in Peru,
his last destination, for the safe conclusion of his entire voyage from Spain; . . . —
that the jewel, with the other effects of the late Don Joaquin, is in the custody of
the brethren of the Hospital de Sacerdotes, awaiting the disposition of the honor-   30
able court; . . . — that, owing to the condition of the deponent, as well as the haste
in which the boats departed for the attack, the Americans were not forewarned that
there were, among the apparent crew, a passenger and one of the clerks, disguised
by the Negro Babo; . . . — that, besides the Negroes killed in the action, some were
killed after the capture and re-anchoring at night, when shackled to the ring-bolts
on deck; that these deaths were committed by the sailors, ere they could be prevented. That so soon as informed of it, Captain Amasa Delano used all his authority, and, in particular with his own hand, struck down Martinez Gola, who, having
found a razor in the pocket of an old jacket of his, which one of the shackled Negroes
had on, was aiming it at the Negro's throat; that the noble Captain Amasa Delano   40
also wrenched from the hand of Bartholomew Barlo, a dagger secreted at the time
of the massacre of the whites, with which he was in the act of stabbing a shackled
Negro, who, the same day, with another Negro, had thrown him down and jumped
upon him; . . . — that, for all the events, befalling through so long a time, during

which the ship was in the hands of the Negro Babo, he cannot here give account; but that, what he has said is the most substantial of what occurs to him at present, and is the truth under the oath which he has taken; which declaration he affirmed and ratified, after hearing it read to him.

He said that he is twenty-nine years of age, and broken in body and mind; that when finally dismissed by the court, he shall not return home to Chili, but betake himself to the monastery on Mount Agonia without; and signed with his honor, and crossed himself, and for the time, departed as he came, in his litter, with the monk Infelez, to the Hospital de Sacerdotes.

BENITO CERENO

Doctor Rozas.

If the deposition have served as the key to fit into the lock of the complications which precede it, then, as a vault whose door has been flung back, the San Dominick's hull lies open to-day.

Hitherto the nature of this narrative besides rendering the intricacies in the beginning unavoidable, has more or less required that many things, instead of being set down in the order of occurrence, should be retrospectively, or irregularly given; this last is the case with the following passages, which will conclude the account:

During the long, mild voyage to Lima, there was, as before hinted, a period during which the sufferer a little recovered his health, or, at least in some degree, his tranquillity. Ere the decided relapse which came, the two captains had many cordial conversations — their fraternal unreserve in singular contrast with former withdrawments.

Again and again, it was repeated, how hard it had been to enact the part forced on the Spaniard by Babo.

"Ah, my dear friend," Don Benito once said, "at those very times when you thought me so morose and ungrateful, nay when, as you now admit, you half thought me plotting your murder, at those very times my heart was frozen; I could not look at you, thinking of what, both on board this ship and your own, hung, from other hands, over my kind benefactor. And as God lives, Don Amasa, I know not whether desire for my own safety alone could have nerved me to that leap into your boat, had it not been for the thought that, did you, unenlightened, return to your ship, you, my best friend, with all who might be with you, stolen upon, that night, in your hammocks, would never in this world have wakened again. Do but think how you walked this deck, how you sat in this cabin, every inch of ground mined into honeycombs under you. Had I dropped the least hint, made the least advance toward an understanding between us, death, explosive death — yours as mine — would have ended the scene."

"True, true," cried Captain Delano, starting, "you saved my life, Don Benito, more than I yours; saved it, too, against my knowledge and will."

"Nay, my friend," rejoined the Spaniard, courteous even to the point of religion, "God charmed your life, but you saved mine. To think of some things you did — those smilings and chattings, rash pointings and gesturings. For less than these, they slew my mate, Raneds; but you had the Prince of Heaven's safe conduct through all ambuscades."

"Yes, all is owing to Providence, I know; but the temper of my mind that morning was more than commonly pleasant, while the sight of so much suffering, more apparent than real, added to my good-nature, compassion, and charity, happily interweaving the three. Had it been otherwise, doubtless, as you hint, some of my interferences might have ended unhappily enough. Besides, those feelings I spoke of enabled me to get the better of momentary distrust, at times when acuteness might have cost me my life, without saving another's. Only at the end did my suspicions get the better of me, and you know how wide of the mark they then proved." 10

"Wide indeed," said Don Benito, sadly; "you were with me, all day; stood with me, sat with me, talked with me, looked at me, ate with me, drank with me; and yet your last act was to clutch for a monster, not only an innocent man, but the most pitiable of all men. To such degree many malign machinations and deceptions impose. So far may even the best men err, in judging the conduct of one with the recesses of whose condition he is not acquainted. But you were forced to it; and you were in time undeceived. Would that, in both respects, it was so ever, and with all men."

"You generalize, Don Benito; and mournfully enough. But the past is passed; why moralize upon it? Forget it. See, yon bright sun has forgotten it all, and the 20 blue sea, and the blue sky; these have turned over new leaves."

"Because they have no memory," he dejectedly replied; "because they are not human."

"But these mild trades that now fan your cheek, Don Benito, do they not come with a human-like healing to you? Warm friends, steadfast friends are the trades."

"With their steadfastness they but waft me to my tomb, Señor," was the foreboding response.

"You are saved," cried Captain Delano, more and more astonished and pained; "you are saved: what has cast such a shadow upon you?"

"The Negro." 30

There was silence, while the moody man sat, slowly and unconsciously gathering his mantle about him, as if it were a pall.

There was no more conversation that day.

But if the Spaniard's melancholy sometimes ended in muteness upon topics like the above, there were others upon which he never spoke at all; on which, indeed, all his old reserves were piled. Pass over the worst and, only to elucidate, let an item or two of these be cited. The dress so precise and costly, worn by him on the day whose events have been narrated, had not willingly been put on. And that silver-mounted sword, apparent symbol of despotic command, was not, indeed, a sword, but the ghost of one. The scabbard, artificially stiffened, was empty. 40

As for the black — whose brain, not body, had schemed and led the revolt, with the plot — his slight frame, inadequate to that which it held, had at once yielded to the superior muscular strength of his captor, in the boat. Seeing all was over, he uttered no sound, and could not be forced to. His aspect seemed to say, since I cannot do deeds, I will not speak words. Put in irons in the hold, with the rest, he was carried to Lima. During the passage, Don Benito did not visit him. Nor then, nor at any time after, would he look at him. Before the tribunal he refused. When pressed by the judges he fainted. On the testimony of the sailors alone rested the legal identity of Babo.

Some months after, dragged to the gibbet at the tail of a mule, the black met his voiceless end. The body was burned to ashes; but for many days, the head, that hive of subtlety, fixed on a pole in the Plaza, met, unabashed, the gaze of the whites; and across the Plaza looked towards St. Bartholomew's church, in whose vaults
10 slept then, as now, the recovered bones of Aranda: and across the Rimac bridge looked toward the monastery, on Mount Agonia without; where, three months after being dismissed by the court, Benito Cereno, borne on the bier, did, indeed, follow his leader.   1856

from Collected Poems

Melville published several volumes of poetry during his lifetime: Battle-Pieces and Aspects of the War *(1866), topical poems dealing with specific events of the Civil War;* Clarel *(1876), a two-volume narrative account of a trip through the Holy Land;* John Marr and Other Sailors *(1888), poems based on his youthful sea journeys; and* Timoleon *(1891), miscellaneous poems, many inspired by his earlier Mediterranean travels. During his life-time, Melville was not popular as a poet, and his last two volumes were privately printed in editions of twenty-five copies each. After his death, a large number of unpublished poems were found among his papers and these, together with the published volumes, have been edited by Howard P. Vincent and published in* Collected Poems of Herman Melville *(Hendricks House, 1947). In recent years, a critical revaluation of Melville as a poet has been in progress. Although there is not as yet a critical consensus as to his poetic achievement, there is general agreement that his poetry deserves far more than the oblivion to which his con-temporaries consigned it.*

The first four poems printed here are from Battle-Pieces *and were occasioned by the hanging of John Brown in 1859 ("The Portent"), the draft riots in New York in 1863 ("The House-Top"), Sherman's march through the South in 1864 ("The March to the Sea"), and the assassination of Abraham Lincoln in 1865 ("The Martyr"). "The Tuft of Kelp" is taken from* John Marr, *and the remaining poems from* Timoleon. *Worth special atten-tion are "After the Pleasure Party," about the unavoidable intrusiveness of an individual's sexuality; "Monody," a touching personal lament for a dead friend — probably Hawthorne; and "Art," on the strange paradoxes embodied in the creative act.*

The Portent (1859)

Hanging from the beam,
    Slowly swaying (such the law),
Gaunt the shadow on your green,

1859. After seizing Harper's Ferry, Va., and inciting slaves to rebel, abolitionist John Brown was captured, convicted of treason, and hanged December 2, 1859, at Charles Town, Va., now West Virginia

Shenandoah!
The cut is on the crown
      (Lo, John Brown),
And the stabs shall heal no more.

Hidden in the cap
      Is the anguish none can draw;
So your future veils its face,   10
      Shenandoah!
But the streaming beard is shown
      (Weird John Brown),
The meteor of the war.

_____   1866

4 **Shenandoah.** Brown's raid, trial, and execution all took place in the Shenandoah Valley   8 **cap,** executioner's hood

The House - Top

A Night Piece (July, 1863)

No sleep. The sultriness pervades the air
And binds the brain — a dense oppression, such
As tawny tigers feel in matted shades,
Vexing their blood and making apt for ravage.
Beneath the stars the roofy desert spreads
Vacant as Libya. All is hushed near by.
Yet fitfully from far breaks a mixed surf
Of muffled sound, the Atheist roar of riot.
Yonder, where parching Sirius set in drought,
Balefully glares red Arson — there — and there.   10
The Town is taken by its rats — ship-rats
And rats of the wharves. All civil charms
And priestly spells which late held hearts in awe —
Fear-bound, subjected to a better sway
Than sway of self; these like a dream dissolve,
And man rebounds whole æons back in nature.
Hail to the low dull rumble, dull and dead,
And ponderous drag that jars the wall.
Wise Draco comes, deep in the midnight roll
Of black artillery; he comes, though late;   20

July, 1863. The New York draft riots occurred July 11-13, when mobs rebelled against the Conscription
Act, which released from service anyone able to pay $300 for a substitute. Militia quelled the riots   19
Wise Draco, Athenian lawgiver (fl. 7th century B.C.), whose severe legal code was notable for excessive
reliance on the death penalty

In code corroborating Calvin's creed
And cynic tyrannies of honest kings;
He comes, nor parlies; and the Town, redeemed,
Gives thanks devout; nor, being thankful, heeds
The grimy slur on the Republic's faith implied,
Which holds that Man is naturally good,
And — more — is Nature's Roman, never to be scourged.

                                                    1866

The March to the Sea *(December, 1864)*

Not Kenesaw high-arching,
  Nor Allatoona's glen —
Though there the graves lie parching —
  Stayed Sherman's miles of men;
From charred Atlanta marching
  They launched the sword again.
        The columns streamed like rivers
          Which in their course agree,
        And they streamed until their flashing
          Met the flashing of the sea: 10
            It was glorious glad marching,
            That marching to the sea.

They brushed the foe before them
  (Shall gnats impede the bull?);
Their own good bridges bore them
  Over swamps or torrents full,
And the grand pines waving o'er them
  Bowed to axes keen and cool.
        The columns grooved their channels,
          Enforced their own decree,   20
        And their power met nothing larger
          Until it met the sea:
            It was glorious glad marching,
            A marching glad and free.

Kilpatrick's snare of riders
  In zigzags mazed the land,

December, 1864. Sherman's march to the sea, Nov. 16-Dec. 21, stretched from Atlanta to Savannah, cut communications of the South, and shortened the war   1 **Kenesaw,** Kennesaw Mountain, twenty-five miles northwest of Atlanta, where Sherman's attack was repulsed, June 27   2 **Allatoona's glen.** Sherman lost a third of a force of 2,000 men at Altoona on October 5   25 **Kilpatrick's snare.** Hugh Judson Kilpatrick (1836-1881) led one of Sherman's cavalry divisions

Perplexed the pale Southsiders
  With feints on every hand;
Vague menace awed the hiders
  In fort beyond command.   30
          To Sherman's shifting problem
            No foeman knew the key;
          But onward went the marching
            Unpausing to the sea:
              It was glorious glad marching,
              The swinging step was free.

The flankers ranged like pigeons
  In clouds through field or wood;
The flocks of all those regions,
  The herds and horses good,   40
Poured in and swelled the legions,
  For they caught the marching mood.
          A volley ahead! They hear it;
            And they hear the repartee:
          Fighting was but frolic
            In that marching to the sea:
              It was glorious glad marching,
              A marching bold and free.

All nature felt their coming,
  The birds like couriers flew,   50
And the banners brightly blooming
  The slaves by thousands drew,
And they marched beside the drumming,
  And they joined the armies blue.
          The cocks crowed from the cannon
            (Pets named from Grant and Lee),
          Plumed fighters and campaigners
            In that marching to the sea:
              It was glorious glad marching,
              For every man was free.   60

The foragers through calm lands
  Swept in tempest gay,
And they breathed the air of balm-lands
  Where rolled savannas lay,
And they helped themselves from farm-lands —
  As who should say them nay?
          The regiments uproarious

       Laughed in Plenty's glee;
   And they marched till their broad laughter
      Met the laughter of the sea: 70
         It was glorious glad marching,
         That marching to the sea.

The grain of endless acres
  Was threshed (as in the East)
By the trampling of the Takers,
  Strong march of man and beast;
The flails of those earth-shakers
  Left a famine where they ceased.
       The arsenals were yielded;
         The sword (that was to be),   80
       Arrested in the forging,
         Rued that marching to the sea:
         It was glorious glad marching,
         But ah, the stern decree!

For behind they left a wailing,
  A terror and a ban,
And blazing cinders sailing,
  And houseless households wan,
Wide zones of counties paling,
  And towns where maniacs ran,   90
       Was the havoc, retribution?
        But howsoe'er it be,
     They will long remember Sherman
      And his streaming columns free —
       They will long remember Sherman
       Marching to the sea.
               1866

The Martyr

Indicative of the Passion of the People on the 15th Day of April, 1865

Good Friday was the day
  Of the prodigy and crime,
When they killed him in his pity,
  When they killed him in his prime
Of clemency and calm —

15th Day of April, 1865. Abraham Lincoln, shot by John Wilkes Booth on April 14, died the next day

When with yearning he was filled
  To redeem the evil-willed,
And, though conqueror, be kind;
  But they killed him in his kindness,
  In their madness and their blindness, 10
And they killed him from behind.

  There is sobbing of the strong,
    And a pall upon the land;
  But the people in their weeping
    Bare the iron hand;
  Beware the People weeping
    When they bare the iron hand.

He lieth in his blood —
  The father in his face;
They have killed him, the Forgiver — 20
  The Avenger takes his place,
The Avenger wisely stern,
    Who in righteousness shall do
    What the heavens call him to,
And the parricides remand;
  For they killed him in his kindness,
  In their madness and their blindness,
And his blood is on their hand.

  There is sobbing of the strong,
    And a pall upon the land; 30
  But the People in their weeping
    Bare the iron hand:
  Beware the People weeping
    When they bare the iron hand.
               1866

The Tuft of Kelp

All dripping in tangles green,
  Cast up by a lonely sea
If purer for that, O Weed,
  Bitterer, too, are ye?
        1888

After the Pleasure Party

Lines Traced Under an Image of Amor Threatening

Fear me, virgin whosoever
Taking pride from love exempt,
  Fear me, slighted. Never, never
Brave me, nor my fury tempt:
Downy wings, but wroth they beat
Tempest even in reason's seat.

Behind the house the upland falls
With many an odorous tree —
White marbles gleaming through green halls,
Terrace by terrace, down and down,   10
And meets the starlit Mediterranean Sea.

  'Tis Paradise. In such an hour
Some pangs that rend might take release.
Nor less perturbed who keeps this bower
Of balm, nor finds balsamic peace?
From whom the passionate words in vent
After long revery's discontent?

  Tired of the homeless deep,
Look how their flight yon hurrying billows urge,
Hitherward but to reap   20
Passive repulse from the iron-bound verge!
Insensate, can they never know
'Tis mad to wreck the impulsion so?

  An art of memory is, they tell:
But to forget! forget the glade
Wherein Fate sprung Love's ambuscade,
The flout pale years of cloistral life
And flush me in this sensuous strife.
'Tis Vesta struck with Sappho's smart.

After the Pleasure Party. The poem seems to be a dramatic monologue, the speaker a woman who, in spite of long dedication to intellectual pursuits, especially astronomy, finds to her sorrow that "sex asserts itself"   **Amor,** another name for the Roman god of love, Cupid, whose weapon is the bow and arrow   29 **Vesta . . . smart.** Vesta is the Roman goddess of the hearth   29 **Sappho,** a Greek lyric poet (fl. 6th century B.C.) famous for her love poetry, according to legend leaped to her death from a cliff because of unfulfilled love

No fable her delirious leap: 30
With more of cause in desperate heart,
Myself could take it — but to sleep!

  Now first I feel, what all may ween,
That soon or late, if faded e'en,
One's sex asserts itself. Desire,
The dear desire through love to sway,
Is like the Geysers that aspire —
Through cold obstruction win their fervid way.
But baffled here — to take disdain,
To feel rule's instinct, yet not reign;   40
To dote, to come to this drear shame —
Hence the winged blaze that sweeps my soul
Like prairie fires that spurn control,
Where withering weeds incense the flame.

  And kept I long heaven's watch for this,
Contemning love, for this, even this?
O terrace chill in Northern air,
O reaching ranging tube I placed
Against yon skies, and fable chased
Till, fool, I hailed for sister there   50
Starred Cassiopea in Golden Chair.
In dream I throned me, nor I saw
In cell the idiot crowned with straw.

  And yet, ah yet scarce ill I reigned,
Through self-illusion self-sustained,
When now — enlightened, undeceived —
What gain I barrenly bereaved!
Than this can be yet lower decline —
Envy and spleen, can these be mine?

  The pleasant girl demure that trod   60
Beside our wheels that climbed the way,
And bore along a blossoming rod
That looked the sceptre of May-day —
On her — to fire this petty hell,
His softened glance how moistly fell!
The cheat! on briars her buds were strung;
And wiles peeped forth from mien how meek.

---

51 **Cassiopea. . . . Chair.** Cassiopea, an Ethiopian queen proud of her beauty, was placed after her death
in the constellation bearing her name; in the constellation is a group of stars resembling a chair

The innocent bare-foot! young, so young!
To girls, strong man's a novice weak.
To tell such beads! And more remain, 70
Sad rosary of belittling pain.

When after lunch and sallies gay,
Like the Decameron folk we lay
In sylvan groups; and I — let be!
O, dreams he, can he dream that one
Because not roseate feels no sun?
The plain lone bramble thrills with Spring
As much as vines that grapes shall bring.

Me now fair studies charm no more.
Shall great thoughts writ, or high themes sung 80
Damask wan cheeks — unlock his arm
About some radiant ninny flung?
How glad with all my starry lore,
I'd buy the veriest wanton's rose
Would but my bee therein repose.

Could I remake me! or set free
This sexless bound in sex, then plunge
Deeper than Sappho, in a lunge
Piercing Pan's paramount mystery!
For, Nature, in no shallow surge 90
Against thee either sex may urge,
Why hast thou made us but in halves —
Co-relatives? This makes us slaves.
If these co-relatives never meet
Self-hood itself seems incomplete.
And such the dicing of blind fate
Few matching halves here meet and mate.
What Cosmic jest or Anarch blunder
The human integral clove asunder
And shied the fractions through life's gate? 100

Ye stars that long your votary knew
Rapt in her vigil, see me here!
Whither is gone the spell ye threw
When rose before me Cassiopea?

---

73 **Like the Decameron folk.** In Boccaccio's *Decameron* (1353) a gathering of people who have fled Florence during the plague pass the time telling tales to each other   92 **Why hast . . . halves.** The allusion is to the legend told in Plato's *Symposium* that describes man as a four-legged round animal including both sexes, later split in two

Usurped on by love's stronger reign —
But lo, your very selves do wane:
Light breaks — truth breaks! Silvered no more,
But chilled by dawn that brings the gale
Shivers yon bramble above the vale,
And disillusion opens all the shore.   110

   One knows not if Urania yet
The pleasure-party may forget;
Or whether she lived down the strain
Of turbulent heart and rebel brain;
For Amor so resents a slight,
And her's had been such haught disdain,
He long may wreak his boyish spite,
And boy-like, little reck the pain.

   One knows not, no. But late in Rome
(For queens discrowned a congruous home)   120
Entering Albani's porch she stood
Fixed by an antique pagan stone
Colossal carved. No anchorite seer,
Not Thomas a Kempis, monk austere,
Religious more are in their tone;
Yet far, how far from Christian heart
That form august of heathen Art.
Swayed by its influence, long she stood,
Till surged emotion seething down,
She rallied and this mood she won: 130

   Languid in frame for me,
To-day by Mary's convent shrine,
Touched by her picture's moving plea
In that poor nerveless hour of mine,
I mused — A wanderer still must grieve.
Half I resolved to kneel and believe,
Believe and submit, the veil take on.
But thee, armed Virgin! less benign,
Thee now I invoke, thou mightier one.
Helmeted woman — if such term   140
Befit thee, far from strife
Of that which makes the sexual feud

---

111 **Urania,** the Greek muse of astronomy. Note that the speaker (as revealed in previous lines) has devoted her life to astronomy, thus identifying with Cassiopeia   121 **Albani's porch.** The Villa Albani,
near Rome, contains a notable collection of classical sculpture   124 **Thomas a Kempis,** German monk
(1380?-1471), the reputed author of *Imitation of Christ*

And clogs the aspirant life —
O self-reliant, strong and free,
Thou in whom power and peace unite,
Transcender! raise me up to thee,
Raise me and arm me!

                Fond appeal.
For never passion peace shall bring,
Nor Art inanimate for long   150
Inspire. Nothing may help or heal
While Amor incensed remembers wrong.
Vindictive, not himself he'll spare;
For scope to give his vengeance play
Himself he'll blaspheme and betray.

   Then for Urania, virgins everywhere,
O pray! Example take too,' and have care.   1891

In a Garret

Gems and jewels let them heap —
   Wax sumptuous as the Sophi:
For me, to grapple from Art's deep
   One dripping trophy: 1891

---

2 **Sophi,** Sophy, western name for the title of a Persian dynasty

Monody

To have known him, to have loved him
   After loneness long;
And then to be estranged in life,
   And neither in the wrong;
And now for death to set his seal —
   Ease me, a little ease, my song!

By wintry hills his hermit-mound
   The sheeted snow-drifts drape,
And houseless there the snow-bird flits
   Beneath the fir-trees' crape: 10
Glazed now with ice the cloistral vine
   That hid the shyest grape.   1891

---

11 **vine.** Persuasive evidence that the poem is about Hawthorne is the presence in Melville's *Clarel* of a Hawthorne-like character called Vine

Lone Founts

Though fast youth's glorious fable flies,
View not the world with worldling's eyes;
Nor turn with weather of the time.
Foreclose the coming of surprise:
Stand where Posterity shall stand;
Stand where the Ancients stood before,
And, dipping in lone founts thy hand,
Drink of the never-varying lore:
Wise once, and wise thence evermore.

1891

Art

In placid hours well-pleased we dream
Of many a brave unbodied scheme.
But form to lend, pulsed life create,
What unlike things must meet and mate:
A flame to melt — a wind to freeze;
Sad patience — joyous energies;
Humility — yet pride and scorn;
Instinct and study; love and hate;
Audacity — reverence. These must mate,
And fuse with Jacob's mystic heart,   10
To wrestle with the angel — Art.

1891

---

10 **Jacob's . . . angel.** See Genesis 32: 24-30

Buddha

> "FOR WHAT IS YOUR LIFE? IT IS EVEN A VAPOR THAT APPEARETH
> FOR A LITTLE TIME AND THEN VANISHETH AWAY."

Swooning swim to less and less,
  Aspirant to nothingness!
Sobs of the worlds, and dole of kinds
  That dumb endurers be —
Nirvana! absorb us in your skies,
  Annul us into thee.

1891

FOR WHAT. . . . VANISHETH AWAY. James 4:14

Billy Budd, Sailor

(An Inside Narrative)

From the time that he published his last novel, The Confidence Man, *in 1857, until his death, in 1891, Melville appeared to have given up writing fiction and to have devoted himself entirely to poetry. But in the 1920's, with the revival of interest in Melville, came the discovery among his papers of the manuscript for* Billy Budd. *It was first published in 1924. Apparently Melville wrote the work in the late 1880's, completing it (or at least abandoning it) only shortly before his death.*

Ever since the publication of Billy Budd, *its "meaning" has been in dispute. It appears to be one of those richly ambiguous and complex works whose meanings are inexhaustible — and about which the critics wage a constant battle. But however elusive its symbolic signifi-cance may be,* Billy Budd *remains a good story full of conflict and suspense. A sailor is falsely accused of mutiny at sea in wartime, strikes his accuser dead, and is sentenced by a drumhead court to be hanged. Stripped to its essence, the plot line seems simple enough. The complexity begins with the Christ-like character of the accused, Billy Budd; the Satanic nature of his accuser, Claggart; and the serenely balanced nature of the man who presides over the fateful events on his ship, Captain Vere. These brief descriptions, of course, are a radical over-simplification. Can Billy Budd be a Christ figure when he is afflicted with a stutter that is the "little card" of the "arch interferer"? But this is the kind of question which the reader himself must decide whether to pose and how to answer.*

However the story is read, it is certain that interpretation must depend on Melville's pre-cise wording. Fortunately, a reliable text (the most reliable possible) was finally published in 1962, superseding texts published in 1924 and 1948, which contained several major errors and many minor ones. The reader interested in the strange history of the Billy Budd *manuscript and its publication will find a fascinating account introducing the text (used in this volume) edited by Harrison Hayford and Merton M. Sealts, Jr. (University of Chicago Press, 1962).*

DEDICATED
TO

JACK CHASE
ENGLISHMAN

Wherever that great heart may now be
Here on Earth or harbored in Paradise

Captain of the Maintop
in the year 1843
in the U.S. Frigate
United States

1

In the time before steamships, or then more frequently than now, a stroller along the docks of any considerable seaport would occasionally have his attention arrested by a group of bronzed mariners, man-of-war's men or merchant sailors in holiday attire, ashore on liberty. In certain instances they would flank, or like a bodyguard quite surround, some superior figure of their own class, moving along with them like Aldebaran among the lesser lights of his constellation. That signal object was the "Handsome Sailor" of the less prosaic time alike of the military and merchant navies. With no perceptible trace of the vain-glorious about him, rather with the offhand unaffectedness of natural regality, he seemed to accept the spontaneous homage of his shipmates.   10

A somewhat remarkable instance recurs to me. In Liverpool, now half a century ago, I saw under the shadow of the great dingy street-wall of Prince's Dock (an obstruction long since removed) a common sailor so intensely black that he must needs have been a native African of the unadulterate blood of Ham — a symmetric figure much above the average height. The two ends of a gay silk handkerchief thrown loose about the neck danced upon the displayed ebony of his chest, in his ears were big hoops of gold, and a Highland bonnet with a tartan band set off his shapely head. It was a hot noon in July; and his face, lustrous with perspiration, beamed with barbaric good humor. In jovial sallies right and left, his white teeth flashing into view, he rollicked along, the center of a company of his shipmates. These were 20 made up of such an assortment of tribes and complexions as would have well fitted them to be marched up by Anacharsis Cloots before the bar of the first French Assembly as Representatives of the Human Race. At each spontaneous tribute rendered by the wayfarers to this black pagod of a fellow — the tribute of a pause and stare, and less frequently an exclamation — the motley retinue showed that they took that sort of pride in the evoker of it which the Assyrian priests doubtless showed for their grand sculptured Bull when the faithful prostrated themselves.

To return. If in some cases a bit of a nautical Murat in setting forth his person ashore, the Handsome Sailor of the period in question evinced nothing of the dandified Billy-be-Dam, an amusing character all but extinct now, but occasionally 30 to be encountered, and in a form yet more amusing than the original, at the tiller of the boats on the tempestuous Erie Canal or, more likely, vaporing in the groggeries along the towpath. Invariably a proficient in his perilous calling, he was also more or less of a mighty boxer or wrestler. It was strength and beauty. Tales of his prowess were recited. Ashore he was the champion; afloat the spokesman; on every

---

6 **Aldebaran**, the "eye" star in the constellation Taurus, the Bull   14 **blood of Ham.** Noah cursed his son Ham (see note, p. 116), and popular belief long attributed to this curse the black skin of Ham and his descendants   22 **Anacharsis Cloots**, or Clootz (1755-1794), a Prussian radical who presented to the Assembly during the French Revolution a group of assorted peoples he claimed to be representatives of the human race   24 **pagod**, archaic for pagoda, meaning either the temple or the idol contained therein   28 **Murat**, Joachim Murat (1767-1815), known as the "Dandy King," was appointed by Napoleon King of Naples

suitable occasion always foremost. Close-reefing topsails in a gale, there he was, astride the weather yardarm-end, foot in the Flemish horse as stirrup, both hands tugging at the earing as at a bridle, in very much the attitude of young Alexander curbing the fiery Bucephalus. A superb figure, tossed up as by the horns of Taurus against the thunderous sky, cheerily hallooing to the strenuous file along the spar.

The moral nature was seldom out of keeping with the physical make. Indeed, except as toned by the former, the comeliness and power, always attractive in masculine conjunction, hardly could have drawn the sort of honest homage the Handsome Sailor in some examples received from his less gifted associates.

10   Such a cynosure, at least in aspect, and something such too in nature, though with important variations made apparent as the story proceeds, was welkin-eyed Billy Budd — or Baby Budd, as more familiarly, under circumstances hereafter to be given, he at last came to be called — aged twenty-one, a foretopman of the British fleet toward the close of the last decade of the eighteenth century. It was not very long prior to the time of the narration that follows that he had entered the King's service, having been impressed on the Narrow Seas from a homeward-bound English merchantman into a seventy-four outward bound, H.M.S. *Bellipotent;* which ship, as was not unusual in those hurried days, having been obliged to put to sea short of her proper complement of men. Plump upon Billy at first sight in the
20   gangway the boarding officer, Lieutenant Ratcliffe, pounced, even before the merchantman's crew was formally mustered on the quarter-deck for his deliberate inspection. And him only he elected. For whether it was because the other men when ranged before him showed to ill advantage after Billy, or whether he had some scruples in view of the merchantman's being rather short-handed, however it might be, the officer contented himself with his first spontaneous choice. To the surprise of the ship's company, though much to the lieutenant's satisfaction, Billy made no demur. But, indeed, any demur would have been as idle as the protest of a goldfinch popped into a cage.

Noting this uncomplaining acquiescence, all but cheerful, one might say, the ship-
30   master turned a surprised glance of silent reproach at the sailor. The shipmaster was one of those worthy mortals found in every vocation, even the humbler ones — the sort of person whom everybody agrees in calling "a respectable man." And — nor so strange to report as it may appear to be — though a ploughman of the troubled waters, lifelong contending with the intractable elements, there was nothing this honest soul at heart loved better than simple peace and quiet. For the rest, he was fifty or thereabouts, a little inclined to corpulence, a prepossessing face, unwhiskered, and of an agreeable color — a rather full face, humanely intelligent in expression. On a fair day with a fair wind and all going well, a certain musical chime in his voice seemed to be the veritable unobstructed outcome of the innermost man. He
40   had much prudence, much conscientiousness, and there were occasions when these virtues were the cause of overmuch disquietude in him. On a passage, so long as

---

4 **Bucephalus,** Alexander the Great's favorite horse   4 **Taurus.** See first note, p. 1468   16 **the Narrow Seas,** channels separating Great Britain from Ireland and from continental Europe   17 **seventy-four,** a man-of-war bearing seventy-four guns

his craft was in any proximity to land, no sleep for Captain Graveling. He took to heart those serious responsibilities not so heavily borne by some shipmasters.

Now while Billy Budd was down in the forecastle getting his kit together, the *Bellipotent's* lieutenant, burly and bluff, nowise disconcerted by Captain Graveling's omitting to proffer the customary hospitalities on an occasion so unwelcome to him, an omission simply caused by preoccupation of thought, unceremoniously invited himself into the cabin, and also to a flask from the spirit locker, a receptacle which his experienced eye instantly discovered. In fact he was one of those sea dogs in whom all the hardship and peril of naval life in the great prolonged wars of his time never impaired the natural instinct for sensuous enjoyment. His duty he always faith- 10 fully did; but duty is sometimes a dry obligation, and he was for irrigating its aridity, whensoever possible, with a fertilizing decoction of strong waters. For the cabin's proprietor there was nothing left but to play the part of the enforced host with whatever grace and alacrity were practicable. As necessary adjuncts to the flask, he silently placed tumbler and water jug before the irrespressible guest. But excusing himself from partaking just then, he dismally watched the unembarrassed officer deliberately diluting his grog a little, then tossing it off in three swallows, pushing the empty tumbler away, yet not so far as to be beyond easy reach, at the same time settling himself in his seat and smacking his lips with high satisfaction, looking straight at the host.   20

These proceedings over, the master broke the silence; and there lurked a rueful reproach in the tone of his voice: "Lieutenant, you are going to take my best man from me, the jewel of 'em."

"Yes, I know," rejoined the other, immediately drawing back the tumbler preliminary to a replenishing. "Yes, I know. Sorry."

"Beg pardon, but you don't understand, Lieutenant. See here, now. Before I shipped that young fellow, my forecastle was a rat-pit of quarrels. It was black times, I tell you, aboard the *Rights* here. I was worried to that degree my pipe had no comfort for me. But Billy came; and it was like a Catholic priest striking peace in an Irish shindy. Not that he preached to them or said or did anything in particular; but a 30 virtue went out of him, sugaring the sour ones. They took to him like hornets to treacle; all but the buffer of the gang, the big shaggy chap with the fire-red whiskers. He indeed, out of envy, perhaps, of the newcomer, and thinking such a "sweet and pleasant fellow," as he mockingly designated him to the others, could hardly have the spirit of a gamecock, must needs bestir himself in trying to get up an ugly row with him. Billy forebore with him and reasoned with him in a pleasant way — he is something like myself, Lieutenant, to whom aught like a quarrel is hateful —but nothing served. So, in the second dogwatch one day, the Red Whiskers in presence of the others, under pretense of showing Billy just whence a sirloin steak was cut — for the fellow had once been a butcher — insultingly gave him a dig under the ribs. 40 Quick as lightning Billy let fly his arm. I dare say he never meant to do quite as much as he did, but anyhow he gave the burly fool a terrible drubbing. It took about half a minute, I should think. And, lord bless you, the lubber was astonished at the celerity. And will you believe it, Lieutenant, the Red Whiskers now really loves

Billy — loves him, or is the biggest hypocrite that ever I heard of. But they all love him. Some of 'em do his washing, darn his old trousers for him; the carpenter is at odd times making a pretty little chest of drawers for him. Anybody will do anything for Billy Budd; and it's the happy family here. But now, Lieutenant, if that young fellow goes — I know how it will be aboard the *Rights*. Not again very soon shall I, coming up from dinner, lean over the capstan smoking a quiet pipe — no, not very soon again, I think. Ay, Lieutenant, you are going to take away the jewel of 'em; you are going to take away my peacemaker!" And with that the good soul had really some ado in checking a rising sob.

10   "Well," said the lieutenant, who had listened with amused interest to all this and now was waxing merry with his tipple; "well, blessed are the peacemakers, especially the fighting peacemakers. And such are the seventy-four beauties some of which you see poking their noses out of the portholes of yonder warship lying to for me," pointing through the cabin window at the *Bellipotent*. "But courage! Don't look so downhearted, man. Why, I pledge you in advance the royal approbation. Rest assured that His Majesty will be delighted to know that in a time when his hardtack is not sought for by sailors with such avidity as should be, a time also when some shipmasters privily resent the borrowing from them a tar or two for the service; His Majesty, I say, will be delighted to learn that *one* shipmaster at least cheerfully
20   surrenders to the King the flower of his flock, a sailor who with equal loyalty makes no dissent. — But where's my beauty? Ah," looking through the cabin's open door, "here he comes; and, by Jove, lugging along his chest — Apollo with his portmanteau! — My man," stepping out to him, "you can't take that big box aboard a warship. The boxes there are mostly shot boxes. Put your duds in a bag, lad. Boot and saddle for the cavalryman, bag and hammock for the man-of-war's man."

The transfer from chest to bag was made. And, after seeing his man into the cutter and then following him down, the lieutenant pushed off from the *Rights-of-Man*. That was the merchant ship's name, though by her master and crew abbreviated in sailor fashion into the *Rights*. The hardheaded Dundee owner was a staunch admirer
30   of Thomas Paine, whose book in rejoinder to Burke's arraignment of the French Revolution had then been published for some time and had gone everywhere. In christening his vessel after the title of Paine's volume the man of Dundee was something like his contemporary shipowner, Stephen Girard of Philadelphia, whose sympathies, alike with his native land and its liberal philosophers, he evinced by naming his ships after Voltaire, Diderot, and so forth.

But now, when the boat swept under the merchantman's stern, and officer and oarsmen were noting — some bitterly and others with a grin — the name emblazoned there; just then it was that the new recruit jumped up from the bow where the coxswain had directed him to sit, and waving hat to his silent shipmates sor-
40   rowfully looking over at him from the taffrail, bade the lads a genial good-bye. Then,

---

30 **Paine . . . Revolution.** *The Rights of Man* (1791-1792)   33 **Stephen Girard,** French-born American patriot (1750-1830), who became a wealthy Philadelphia merchant, shipowner, and philanthropist   35 **Voltaire, Diderot.** François Marie Arouet de Voltaire (1694-1778), freethinking philosopher and writer, and Denis Diderot (1713-1784), encyclopedist, furnished much of the intellectual fuel for the French Revolution

making a salutation as to the ship herself, "And good-bye to you too, old *Rights-of-Man.*"

"Down, sir!" roared the lieutenant, instantly assuming all the rigor of his rank, though with difficulty repressing a smile.

To be sure, Billy's action was a terrible breach of naval decorum. But in that decorum he had never been instructed; in consideration of which the lieutenant would hardly have been so energetic in reproof but for the concluding farewell to the ship. This he rather took as meant to convey a covert sally on the new recruit's part, a sly slur at impressment in general, and that of himself in especial. And yet, more likely, if satire it was in effect, it was hardly so by intention, for Billy, though hap- 10 pily endowed with the gaiety of high health, youth, and a free heart, was yet by no means of a satirical turn. The will to it and the sinister dexterity were alike wanting. To deal in double meanings and insinuations of any sort was quite foreign to his nature.

As to his enforced enlistment, that he seemed to take pretty much as he was wont to take any vicissitude of weather. Like the animals, though no philosopher, he was, without knowing it, practically a fatalist. And it may be that he rather liked this adventurous turn in his affairs, which promised an opening into novel scenes and martial excitements.

Aboard the *Bellipotent* our merchant sailor was forthwith rated as an able seaman 20 and assigned to the starboard watch of the foretop. He was soon at home in the service, not at all disliked for his unpretentious good looks and a sort of genial happy-go-lucky air. No merrier man in his mess: in marked contrast to certain other individuals included like himself among the impressed portion of the ship's company; for these when not actively employed were sometimes, and more particularly in the last dogwatch when the drawing near of twilight induced revery, apt to fall into a saddish mood which in some partook of sullenness. But they were not so young as our foretopman, and no few of them must have known a hearth of some sort, others may have had wives and children left, too probably, in uncertain circumstances, and hardly any but must have had acknowledged kith and kin, while for Billy, as will 30 shortly be seen, his entire family was practically invested in himself.

2

Though our new-made foretopman was well received in the top and on the gun decks, hardly here was he that cynosure he had previously been among those minor ship's companies of the merchant marine, with which companies only had he hitherto consorted.

He was young; and despite his all but fully developed frame, in aspect looked even younger than he really was, owing to a lingering adolescent expression in the as yet smooth face all but feminine in purity of natural complexion but where, thanks to his seagoing, the lily was quite suppressed and the rose had some ado visibly to flush through the tan.   40

To one essentially such a novice in the complexities of factitious life, the abrupt transition from his former and simpler sphere to the ampler and more knowing world of a great warship; this might well have abashed him had there been any conceit or vanity in his composition. Among her miscellaneous multitude, the *Bellipotent* mustered several individuals who however inferior in grade were of no common natural stamp, sailors more signally susceptive of that air which continuous martial discipline and repeated presence in battle can in some degree impart even to the average man. As the Handsome Sailor, Billy Budd's position aboard the seventy-four was something analogous to that of a rustic beauty transplanted from the
10   provinces and brought into competition with the highborn dames of the court. But this change of circumstances he scarce noted. As little did he observe that something about him provoked an ambiguous smile in one or two harder faces among the bluejackets. Nor less unaware was he of the peculiar favorable effect his person and demeanor had upon the more intelligent gentlemen of the quarter-deck. Nor could this well have been otherwise. Cast in a mold peculiar to the finest physical examples of those Englishmen in whom the Saxon strain would seem not at all to partake of any Norman or other admixture, he showed in face that humane look of reposeful good nature which the Greek sculptor in some instances gave to his heroic strong man, Hercules. But this again was subtly modified by another and pervasive
20   quality. The ear, small and shapely, the arch of the foot, the curve in mouth and nostril, even the indurated hand dyed to the orange-tawny of the toucan's bill, a hand telling alike of the halyards and tar bucket; but, above all, something in the mobile expression, and every chance attitude and movement, something suggestive of a mother eminently favored by Love and the Graces; all this strangely indicated a lineage in direct contradiction to his lot. The mysteriousness here became less mysterious through a matter of fact elicited when Billy at the capstan was being formally mustered into the service. Asked by the officer, a small, brisk little gentleman as it chanced, among other questions, his place of birth, he replied, "Please, sir, I don't know."
30   "Don't know where you were born? Who was your father?"

"God knows, sir."

Struck by the straightforward simplicity of these replies, the officer next asked, "Do you know anything about your beginning?"

"No, sir. But I have heard that I was found in a pretty silk-lined basket hanging one morning from the knocker of a good man's door in Bristol."

"*Found,* say you? Well," throwing back his head and looking up and down the new recruit; "well, it turns out to have been a pretty good find. Hope they'll find some more like you, my man; the fleet sadly needs them."

Yes, Billy Budd was a foundling, a presumable by-blow, and, evidently, no igno-
40   ble one. Noble descent was as evident in him as in a blood horse.

For the rest, with little or no sharpness of faculty or any trace of the wisdom of the serpent, nor yet quite a dove, he possessed that kind and degree of intelligence going along with the unconventional rectitude of a sound human creature, one to whom not yet has been proffered the questionable apple of knowledge. He was illiterate; he could not read, but he could sing, and like the illiterate nightingale was sometimes the composer of his own song.

Of self-consciousness he seemed to have little or none, or about as much as we may reasonably impute to a dog of Saint Bernard's breed.

Habitually living with the elements and knowing little more of the land than as a beach, or, rather, that portion of the terraqueous globe providentially set apart for dance-houses, doxies, and tapsters, in short what sailors call a "fiddler's green," his simple nature remained unsophisticated by those moral obliquities which are not in every case incompatible with that manufacturable thing known as respectability. But are sailors, frequenters of fiddlers' greens, without vices? No; but less often than 10 with landsmen do their vices, so called, partake of crookedness of heart, seeming less to proceed from viciousness than exuberance of vitality after long constraint: frank manifestations in accordance with natural law. By his original constitution aided by the co-operating influences of his lot, Billy in many respects was little more than a sort of upright barbarian, much such perhaps as Adam presumably might have been ere the urbane Serpent wriggled himself into his company.

And here be it submitted that apparently going to corroborate the doctrine of man's Fall, a doctrine now popularly ignored, it is observable that where certain virtues pristine and unadulterate peculiarly characterize anybody in the external uniform of civilization, they will upon scrutiny seem not to be derived from custom or 20 convention, but rather to be out of keeping with these, as if indeed exceptionally transmitted from a period prior to Cain's city and citified man. The character marked by such qualities has to an unvitiated taste an untampered-with flavor like that of berries, while the man thoroughly civilized, even in a fair specimen of the breed, has to the same moral palate a questionable smack as of a compounded wine. To any stray inheritor of these primitive qualities found, like Caspar Hauser, wandering dazed in any Christian capital of our time, the good-natured poet's famous invocation, near two thousand years ago, of the good rustic out of his latitude in the Rome of the Caesars, still appropriately holds:

> Honest and poor, faithful in word and thought, 30
> What hath thee, Fabian, to the city brought?

Though our Handsome Sailor had as much of masculine beauty as one can expect anywhere to see; nevertheless, like the beautiful woman in one of Hawthorne's minor tales, there was just one thing amiss in him. No visible blemish indeed, as with the lady; no, but an occasional liability to a vocal defect. Though in the hour of elemental uproar or peril he was everything that a sailor should be, yet under sudden provocation of strong heart-feeling his voice, otherwise singularly musical, as if expressive of the harmony within, was apt to develop an organic hesitancy, in fact more or less of a stutter or even worse. In this particular Billy was a striking

22 **Cain's city.** Genesis 4:16-17 tells of Cain building a city after murdering his brother Abel   26 **Caspar Hauser,** German foundling discovered in Nuremberg in 1828, popularly believed to be of noble birth   30 **Honest . . . brought?** Martial, *Epigrams,* I, iv, ll. 1-2   33 **one . . . minor tales,** "The Birthmark"

instance that the arch interferer, the envious marplot of Eden, still has more or less to do with every human consignment to this planet of Earth. In every case, one way or another he is sure to slip in his little card, as much as to remind us — I too have a hand here.

The avowal of such an imperfection in the Handsome Sailor should be evidence not alone that he is not presented as a conventional hero, but also that the story in which he is the main figure is no romance.

3

At the time of Billy Budd's arbitrary enlistment into the *Bellipotent* that ship was on her way to join the Mediterranean fleet. No long time elapsed before the junc-
10 tion was effected. As one of that fleet the seventy-four participated in its movemens, though at times on account of her superior sailing qualities, in the absence of frigates, dispatched on separate duty as a scout and at times on less temporary service. But with all this the story has little concernment, restricted as it is to the inner life of one particular ship and the career of an individual sailor.

It was the summer of 1797. In the April of that year had occurred the commotion at Spithead followed in May by a second and yet more serious outbreak in the fleet at the Nore. The latter is known, and without exaggeration in the epithet, as "the Great Mutiny." It was indeed a demonstration more menacing to England than the contemporary manifestoes and conquering and proselyting armies of the French Direc-
20 tory. To the British Empire the Nore Mutiny was what a strike in the fire brigade would be to London threatened by general arson. In a crisis when the kingdom might well have anticipated the famous signal that some years later published along the naval line of battle what it was that upon occasion England expected of Englishmen; *that* was the time when at the mastheads of the three-deckers and seventy-fours moored in her own roadstead — a fleet the right arm of a Power then all but the sole free conservative one of the Old World — the bluejackets, to be numbered by thousands, ran up with huzzas the British colors with the union and cross wiped out; by that cancellation transmuting the flag of founded law and freedom defined, into the enemy's red meteor of unbridled and unbounded revolt. Reasonable discon-
30 tent growing out of practical grievances in the fleet had been ignited into irrational combustion as by live cinders blown across the Channel from France in flames.

The event converted into irony for a time those spirited strains of Dibdin — as a song-writer no mean auxiliary to the English government at that European conjuncture — strains celebrating, among other things, the patriotic devotion of the British tar: "And as for my life, 'tis the King's!"

Such an episode in the Island's grand naval story her naval historians naturally abridge, one of them (William James) candidly acknowledging that fain would he pass it over did not "impartiality forbid fastidiousness." And yet his mention is less

---

22 **famous signal.** Before the battle of Trafalgar (1805) Nelson's signal was "England expects that every man will do his duty"   32 **Dibdin,** Charles Dibdin (1745-1814), English song writer and playwright   37 **William James** (d. 1827), author of *The Naval History of Great Britain* (1822-1824)

a narration than a reference, having to do hardly at all with details. Nor are these readily to be found in the libraries. Like some other events in every age befalling states everywhere, including America, the Great Mutiny was of such character that national pride along with views of policy would fain shade it off into the historical background. Such events cannot be ignored, but there is a considerate way of historically treating them. If a well-constituted individual refrains from blazoning aught amiss or calamitous in his family, a nation in the like circumstance may without reproach be equally discreet.

Though after parleyings between government and the ring-leaders, and concessions by the former as to some glaring abuses, the first uprising — that at Spithead — 10 with difficulty was put down, or matters for the time pacified; yet at the Nore the unforeseen renewal of insurrection on a yet larger scale, and emphasized in the conferences that ensued by demands deemed by the authorities not only inadmissible but aggressively insolent, indicated — if the Red Flag did not sufficiently do so — what was the spirit animating the men. Final suppression, however, there was, but only made possible perhaps by the unswerving loyalty of the marine corps and a voluntary resumption of loyalty among influential sections of the crews.

To some extent the Nore Mutiny may be regarded as analogous to the distempering irruption of contagious fever in a frame constitutionally sound, and which anon throws it off.   20

At all events, of these thousands of mutineers were some of the tars who not so very long afterwards — whether wholly prompted thereto by patriotism, or pugnacious instinct, or by both — helped to win a coronet for Nelson at the Nile, and the naval crown of crowns for him at Trafalgar. To the mutineers, those battles and especially Trafalgar were a plenary absolution and a grand one. For all that goes to make up scenic naval display and heroic magnificence in arms, those battles, especially Trafalgar, stand unmatched in human annals.

4

In this matter of writing, resolve as one may to keep to the main road, some bypaths have an enticement not readily to be withstood. I am going to err into such a bypath. If the reader will keep me company I shall be glad. At the least, we can 30 promise ourselves that pleasure which is wickedly said to be in sinning, for a literary sin the divergence will be.

Very likely it is no new remark that the inventions of our time have at last brought about a change in sea warfare in degree corresponding to the revolution in all warfare effected by the original introduction from China into Europe of gunpowder. The first European firearm, a clumsy contrivance, was, as is well known, scouted by no few of the knights as a base implement, good enough peradventure for weavers too craven to stand up crossing steel with steel in frank fight. But as ashore knightly valor, though shorn of its blazonry, did not cease with the knights, neither on the seas — though nowadays in encounters there a certain kind of displayed gallantry 40

23 **coronet . . . crown of crowns.** Nelson's two great victories, the Nile and Trafalgar, won him a title and death

be fallen out of date as hardly applicable under changed circumstances — did the nobler qualities of such naval magnates as Don John of Austria, Doria, Van Tromp, Jean Bart, the long line of British admirals, and the American Decaturs of 1812 become obsolete with their wooden walls.

Nevertheless, to anybody who can hold the Present at its worth without being inappreciative of the Past, it may be forgiven, if to such an one the solitary old hulk at Portsmouth, Nelson's *Victory,* seems to float there, not alone as the decaying monument of a fame incorruptible, but also as a poetic reproach, softened by its picturesqueness, to the *Monitors* and yet mightier hulls of the European iron-
10 clads. And this not altogether because such craft are unsightly, unavoidably lacking the symmetry and grand lines of the old battleships, but equally for other reasons.

There are some, perhaps, who while not altogether inaccessible to that poetic reproach just alluded to, may yet on behalf of the new order be disposed to parry it; and this to the extent of iconoclasm, if need be. For example, prompted by the sight of the star inserted in the *Victory*'s quarter-deck designating the spot where the Great Sailor fell, these martial utilitarians may suggest considerations implying that Nelson's ornate publication of his person in battle was not only unnecessary, but not military, nay, savored of foolhardiness and vanity. They may add, too, that at Trafalgar it was in effect nothing less than a challenge to death; and death came; and that
20 but for his bravado the victorious admiral might possibly have survived the battle, and so, instead of having his sagacious dying injunctions overruled by his immediate successor in command, he himself when the contest was decided might have brought his shattered fleet to anchor, a proceeding which might have averted the deplorable loss of life by shipwreck in the elemental tempest that followed the martial one.

Well, should we set aside the more than disputable point whether for various reasons it was possible to anchor the fleet, then plausibly enough the Benthamites of war may urge the above. But the *might-have-been* is but boggy ground to build on. And, certainly, in foresight as to the larger issue of an encounter, and anxious prep-
30 arations for it — buoying the deadly way and mapping it out, as at Copenhagen — few commanders have been so painstakingly circumspect as this same reckless declarer of his person in fight.

Personal prudence, even when dictated by quite other than selfish considerations, surely is no special virtue in a military man; while an excessive love of glory, impassioning a less burning impulse, the honest sense of duty, is the first. If the name *Wellington* is not so much of a trumpet to the blood as the simpler name *Nelson*, the reason for this may perhaps be inferred from the above. Alfred in his funeral ode

---

2 **Don John . . . Decaturs.** Don John of Austria (1547?-1578), Spanish admiral, led the fleet of the Holy League that defeated the Turks at Lepanto in 1571; Andrea Doria (1468?-1560), Genoese admiral, assisted Spain against the Turks and the pirate Barbarossa; Maarten Tromp (1597-1653), Dutch admiral, fought against the English; Stephen Decatur (1779-1820), U. S. naval officer, fought the Tripoli pirates in 1803-1804 and in the War of 1812   27 **Benthamites.** Jeremy Bentham (1748-1832), was one of the chief exponents of utilitarianism   30 **Copenhagen.** Nelson made meticulous and elaborate preparation for the battle of Copenhagen in 1801   37 **Alfred,** Alfred Tennyson, first Baron Tennyson (1809-1892) in his laureate poem, "Ode on the Death of the Duke of Wellington" (1852)

on the victor of Waterloo ventures not to call him the greatest soldier of all time, though in the same ode he invokes Nelson as "the greatest sailor since our world began."

At Trafalgar Nelson on the brink of opening the fight sat down and wrote his last brief will and testament. If under the presentiment of the most magnificent of all victories to be crowned by his own glorious death, a sort of priestly motive led him to dress his person in the jewelled vouchers of his own shining deeds; if thus to have adorned himself for the altar and the sacrifice were indeed vainglory, then affectation and fustian is each more heroic line in the great epics and dramas, since in such lines the poet but embodies in verse those exaltations of sentiment that a 10 nature like Nelson, the opportunity being given, vitalizes into acts.

5

Yes, the outbreak at the Nore was put down. But not every grievance was re-dressed. If the contractors, for example, were no longer permitted to ply some prac-tices peculiar to their tribe everywhere, such as providing shoddy cloth, rations not sound, or false in the measure; not the less impressment, for one thing, went on. By custom sanctioned for centuries, and judicially maintained by a Lord Chancellor as late as Mansfield, that mode of manning the fleet, a mode now fallen into a sort of abeyance but never formally renounced, it was not practicable to give up in those years. Its abrogation would have crippled the indispensable fleet, one wholly under canvas, no steam power, its innumerable sails and thousands of cannon, everything 20 in short, worked by muscle alone; a fleet the more insatiate in demand for men, be-cause then multiplying its ships of all grades against contingencies present and to come of the convulsed Continent.

Discontent foreran the Two Mutinies, and more or less it lurkingly survived them. Hence it was not unreasonable to apprehend some return of trouble sporadic or general. One instance of such apprehensions: In the same year with this story, Nel-son, then Rear Admiral Sir Horatio, being with the fleet off the Spanish coast, was directed by the admiral in command to shift his pennant from the *Captain* to the *Theseus;* and for this reason: that the latter ship having newly arrived on the station from home, where it had taken part in the Great Mutiny, danger was apprehended 30 from the temper of the men; and it was thought that an officer like Nelson was the one, not indeed to terrorize the crew into base subjection, but to win them, by force of his mere presence and heroic personality, back to an allegiance if not as enthu-siastic as his own yet as true.

So it was that for a time, on more than one quarter-deck, anxiety did exist. At sea, precautionary vigilance was strained against relapse. At short notice an engage-ment might come on. When it did, the lieutenants assigned to batteries felt it in-cumbent on them, in some instances, to stand with drawn swords behind the men working the guns.

17 **Mansfield,** William Murray, Earl of Mansfield (1705-1793), Lord Chief Justice of Britain, 1756-1788

6

But on board the seventy-four in which Billy now swung his hammock, very little in the manner of the men and nothing obvious in the demeanor of the officers would have suggested to an ordinary observer that the Great Mutiny was a recent event. In their general bearing and conduct the commissioned officers of a warship naturally take their tone from the commander, that is if he have that ascendancy of character that ought to be his.

Captain the Honorable Edward Fairfax Vere, to give his full title, was a bachelor of forty or thereabouts, a sailor of distinction even in a time prolific of renowned seamen. Though allied to the higher nobility, his advancement had not been alto-
10 gether owing to influences connected with that circumstance. He had seen much service, been in various engagements, always acquitting himself as an officer mindful of the welfare of his men, but never tolerating an infraction of discipline; thoroughly versed in the science of his profession, and intrepid to the verge of temerity, though never injudiciously so. For his gallantry in the West Indian waters as flag lieutenant under Rodney in that admiral's crowning victory over De Grasse, he was made a post captain.

Ashore, in the garb of a civilian, scarce anyone would have taken him for a sailor, more especially that he never garnished unprofessional talk with nautical terms, and grave in his bearing, evinced little appreciation of mere humor. It was not out of
20 keeping with these traits that on a passage when nothing demanded his paramount action, he was the most undemonstrative of men. Any landsman observing this gentleman not conspicuous by his stature and wearing no pronounced insignia, emerging from his cabin to the open deck, and noting the silent deference of the officers retiring to leeward, might have taken him for the King's guest, a civilian aboard the King's ship, some highly honorable discreet envoy on his way to an important post. But in fact this unobtrusiveness of demeanor may have proceeded from a certain unaffected modesty of manhood sometimes accompanying a resolute nature, a modesty evinced at all times not calling for pronounced action, which shown in any rank of life suggests a virtue aristocratic in kind. As with some others engaged in various
30 departments of the world's more heroic activities, Captain Vere though practical enough upon occasion would at times betray a certain dreaminess of mood. Standing alone on the weather side of the quarter-deck, one hand holding by the rigging, he would absently gaze off at the blank sea. At the presentation to him then of some minor matter interrupting the current of his thoughts, he would show more or less irascibility; but instantly he would control it.

In the navy he was popularly known by the appellation "Starry Vere." How such a designation happened to fall upon one who whatever his sterling qualities was without any brilliant ones, was in this wise: A favorite kinsman, Lord Denton, a freehearted fellow, had been the first to meet and congratulate him upon his return

---

15 **Rodney . . . De Grasse.** British admiral George Brydges Rodney, 1st Baron Rodney (1719-1792), won a victory over French admiral François Joseph Paul de Grasse, comte de Grasse (1723-1788), in 1782 off Dominica

to England from his West Indian cruise; and but the day previous turning over a copy of Andrew Marvell's poems had lighted, not for the first time, however, upon the lines entitled "Appleton House," the name of one of the seats of their common ancestor, a hero in the German wars of the seventeenth century, in which poem occur the lines:

> This 'tis to have been from the first
> In a domestic heaven nursed,
> Under the discipline severe
> Of Fairfax and the starry Vere.

And so, upon embracing his cousin fresh from Rodney's great victory wherein he 10 had played so gallant a part, brimming over with just family pride in the sailor of their house, he exuberantly exclaimed, "Give ye joy, Ed; give ye joy, my starry Vere!" This got currency, and the novel prefix serving in familiar parlance readily to distinguish the *Bellipotent*'s captain from another Vere his senior, a distant relative, an officer of like rank in the navy, it remained permanently attached to the surname.

7

In view of the part that the commander of the *Bellipotent* plays in scenes shortly to follow, it may be well to fill out that sketch of him outlined in the previous chapter.

Aside from his qualities as a sea officer Captain Vere was an exceptional character. Unlike no few of England's renowned sailors, long and arduous service with signal 20 devotion to it had not resulted in absorbing and *salting* the entire man. He had a marked leaning toward everything intellectual. He loved books, never going to sea without a newly replenished library, compact but of the best. The isolated leisure, in some cases so wearisome, falling at intervals to commanders even during a war cruise, never was tedious to Captain Vere. With nothing of that literary taste which less heeds the thing conveyed than the vehicle, his bias was toward those books to which every serious mind of superior order occupying any active post of authority in the world naturally inclines: books treating of actual men and events no matter of what era — history, biography, and unconventional writers like Montaigne, who, free from cant and convention, honestly and in the spirit of common sense philoso- 30 phize upon realities. In this line of reading he found confirmation of his own more reserved thoughts — confirmation which he had vainly sought in social converse, so that as touching most fundamental topics, there had got to be established in him some positive convictions which he forefelt would abide in him essentially unmodified so long as his intelligent part remained unimpaired. In view of the troubled period in which his lot was cast, this was well for him. His settled convictions were as a dike against those invading waters of novel opinion social, political, and otherwise, which carried away as in a torrent no few minds in those days, minds by nature not inferior to his own. While other members of that aristocracy to which by birth he belonged were incensed at the innovators mainly because their theories were inimical to the privileged classes, Captain Vere disinterestedly opposed them not alone because they seemed to him insusceptible of embodiment in lasting institutions, but at war with the peace of the world and the true welfare of mankind.

With minds less stored than his and less earnest, some officers of his rank, with whom at times he would necessarily consort, found him lacking in the companionable quality, a dry and bookish gentleman, as they deemed. Upon any chance withdrawal from their company one would be apt to say to another something like this: "Vere is a noble fellow, Starry Vere. 'Spite the gazettes, Sir Horatio" (meaning him
10 who became Lord Nelson) "is at bottom scarce a better seaman or fighter. But between you and me now, don't you think there is a queer streak of the pedantic running through him? Yes, like the King's yarn in a coil of navy rope?"

Some apparent ground there was for this sort of confidential criticism; since not only did the captain's discourse never fall into the jocosely familiar, but in illustrating of any point touching the stirring personages and events of the time he would be as apt to cite some historic character or incident of antiquity as he would be to cite from the moderns. He seemed unmindful of the circumstance that to his bluff company such remote allusions, however pertinent they might really be, were altogether alien to men whose reading was mainly confined to the journals. But con-
20 siderateness in such matters is not easy to natures constituted like Captain Vere's. Their honesty prescribes to them directness, sometimes far-reaching like that of a migratory fowl that in its flight never heeds when it crosses a frontier.

8

The lieutenants and other commissioned gentlemen forming Captain Vere's staff it is not necessary here to particularize, nor needs it to make any mention of any of the warrant officers. But among the petty officers was one who, having much to do with the story, may as well be forthwith introduced. His portrait I essay, but shall never hit it. This was John Claggart, the master-at-arms. But that sea title may to landsmen seem somewhat equivocal. Originally, doubtless, that petty officer's function was the instruction of the men in the use of arms, sword or cutlass. But very
30 long ago, owing to the advance in gunnery making hand-to-hand encounters less frequent and giving to niter and sulphur the pre-eminence over steel, that function ceased; the master-at-arms of a great warship becoming a sort of chief of police charged among other matters with the duty of preserving order on the populous lower gun decks.

Claggart was a man about five-and-thirty, somewhat spare and tall, yet of no ill figure upon the whole. His hand was too small and shapely to have been accustomed to hard toil. The face was a notable one, the features all except the chin cleanly cut as those on a Greek medallion; yet the chin, beardless as Tecumseh's, had something of strange protuberant broadness in its make that recalled the prints of the
40 Reverend Dr. Titus Oates, the historic deponent with the clerical drawl in the time

---

38 **Tecumseh's.** Tecumseh, a Shawnee Indian chief (1768?-1813)

of Charles II and the fraud of the alleged Popish Plot. It served Claggart in his office that his eye could cast a tutoring glance. His brow was of the sort phrenologically associated with more than average intellect; silken jet curls partly clustering over it, making a foil to the pallor below, a pallor tinged with faint shade of amber akin to the hue of time-tinted marbles of old. This complexion, singularly contrasting with the red or deeply bronzed visages of the sailors, and in part the result of his official seclusion from the sunlight, though it was not exactly displeasing, nevertheless seemed to hint of something defective or abnormal in the constitution and blood. But his general aspect and manner were so suggestive of an education and career incongruous with his naval function that when not actively 10 engaged in it he looked like a man of high quality, social and moral, who for reasons of his own was keeping incog. Nothing was known of his former life. It might be that he was an Englishman; and yet there lurked a bit of accent in his speech suggesting that possibly he was not such by birth, but through naturalization in early childhood. Among certain grizzled sea gossips of the gun decks and forecastle went a rumor perdue that the master-at-arms was a *chevalier* who had volunteered into the King's navy by way of compounding for some mysterious swindle whereof he had been arraigned at the King's Bench. The fact that nobody could substantiate this report was, of course, nothing against its secret currency. Such a rumor once started on the gun decks in reference to almost anyone below the rank 20 of a commissioned officer would, during the period assigned to this narrative, have seemed not altogether wanting in credibility to the tarry old wiseacres of a man-of-war crew. And indeed a man of Claggart's accomplishments, without prior nautical experience entering the navy at mature life, as he did, and necessarily allotted at the start to the lowest grade in it; a man too who never made allusion to his previous life ashore; these were circumstances which in the dearth of exact knowledge as to his true antecedents opened to the invidious a vague field for unfavorable surmise.

But the sailors' dogwatch gossip concerning him derived a vague plausibility from the fact that now for some period the British navy could so little afford to be squeamish in the matter of keeping up the muster rolls, that not only were press 30 gangs notoriously abroad both afloat and ashore, but there was little or no secret about another matter, namely, that the London police were at liberty to capture any able-bodied suspect, any questionable fellow at large, and summarily ship him to the dockyard or fleet. Furthermore, even among voluntary enlistments there were instances where the motive thereto partook neither of patriotic impulse nor yet of a random desire to experience a bit of sea life and martial adventure. Insolvent debtors of minor grade, together with the promiscuous lame ducks of morality, found in the navy a convenient and secure refuge, secure because, once enlisted aboard a King's ship, they were as much in sanctuary as the transgressor of the Middle Ages harboring himself under the shadow of the altar. Such sanctioned 40 irregularities, which for obvious reasons the government would hardly think to parade at the time and which consequently, and as affecting the least influential class of mankind, have all but dropped into oblivion, lend color to something for the truth whereof I do not vouch, and hence have some scruple in stating; something I remember having seen in print though the book I cannot recall; but the same thing was personally communicated to me now more than forty years ago by an old pensioner in a cocked hat with whom I had a most interesting talk on the terrace at Greenwich, a Baltimore Negro, a Trafalgar man. It was to this effect: In the case of a warship short of hands whose speedy sailing was imperative, the deficient quota, in lack of any other way of making it good, would be eked out by drafts culled direct from the jails. For reasons previously suggested it would not perhaps be easy at the present day directly to prove or disprove the allegation. But allowed as a verity, how significant would it be of England's straits at the time confronted by those wars

10 which like a flight of harpies rose shrieking from the din and dust of the fallen Bastille. That era appears measurably clear to us who look back at it, and but read of it. But to the grandfathers of us graybeards, the more thoughtful of them, the genius of it presented an aspect like that of Camoëns' Spirit of the Cape, an eclipsing menace mysterious and prodigious. Not America was exempt from apprehension. At the height of Napoleon's unexampled conquests, there were Americans who had fought at Bunker Hill who looked forward to the possibility that the Atlantic might prove no barrier against the ultimate schemes of this French portentous upstart from the revolutionary chaos who seemed in act of fulfilling judgment prefigured in the Apocalypse.

20 But the less credence was to be given to the gun-deck talk touching Claggart, seeing that no man holding his office in a man-of-war can ever hope to be popular with the crew. Besides, in derogatory comments upon anyone against whom they have a grudge, or for any reason or no reason mislike, sailors are much like landsmen: they are apt to exaggerate or romance it.

About as much was really known to the *Bellipotent*'s tars of the master-at-arms' career before entering the service as an astronomer knows about a comet's travels prior to its first observable appearance in the sky. The verdict of the sea quidnuncs has been cited only by way of showing what sort of moral impression the man made upon rude uncultivated natures whose conceptions of human wickedness were nec-

30 essarily of the narrowest, limited to ideas of vulgar rascality — a thief among the swinging hammocks during a night watch, or the man-brokers and land-sharks of the seaports.

It was no gossip, however, but fact that though, as before hinted, Claggart upon his entrance into the navy was, as a novice, assigned to the least honorable section of a man-of-war's crew, embracing the drudgery, he did not long remain there. The superior capacity he immediately evinced, his constitutional sobriety, an ingratiating deference to superiors, together with a peculiar ferreting genius manifested on a singular occasion; all this, capped by a certain austere patriotism, abruptly advanced him to the position of master-at-arms.

40 Of this maritime chief of police the ship's corporals, so called, were the immediate subordinates, and compliant ones; and this, as is to be noted in some business de-

---

13 **Spirit of the Cape.** Adamastor, in the *Lusiads* (1572) of Luiz Vaz de Camoëns, Portuguese epic writer, embodied the violence of natural forces hostile to ships   31 **man-brokers and land-sharks,** those who arranged for and did the shanghaiing of seamen

partments ashore, almost to a degree inconsistent with entire moral volition. His place put various converging wires of underground influence under the chief's control, capable when astutely worked through his understrappers of operating to the mysterious discomfort, if nothing worse, of any of the sea commonalty.

9

Life in the foretop well agreed with Billy Budd. There, when not actually engaged on the yards yet higher aloft, the topmen, who as such had been picked out for youth and activity, constituted an aerial club lounging at ease against the smaller stun'sails rolled up into cushions, spinning yarns like the lazy gods, and frequently amused with what was going on in the busy world of the decks below. No wonder then that a young fellow of Billy's disposition was well content in such society. 10 Giving no cause of offense to anybody, he was always alert at a call. So in the merchant service it had been with him. But now such a punctiliousness in duty was shown that his topmates would sometimes good-naturedly laugh at him for it. This heightened alacrity had its cause, namely, the impression made upon him by the first formal gangway-punishment he had ever witnessed, which befell the day following his impressment. It had been incurred by a little fellow, young, a novice after-guardsman absent from his assigned post when the ship was being put about; a dereliction resulting in a rather serious hitch to that maneuver, one demanding instantaneous promptitude in letting go and making fast. When Billy saw the culprit's naked back under the scourge, gridironed with red welts and worse, when he 20 marked the dire expression in the liberated man's face as with his woolen shirt flung over him by the executioner he rushed forward from the spot to bury himself in the crowd, Billy was horrified. He resolved that never through remissness would he make himself liable to such a visitation or do or omit aught that might merit even verbal reproof. What then was his surprise and concern when ultimately he found himself getting into petty trouble occasionally about such matters as the stowage of his bag or something amiss in his hammock, matters under the police oversight of the ship's corporals of the lower decks, and which brought down on him a vague threat from one of them.

So heedful in all things as he was, how could this be? He could not understand 30 it, and it more than vexed him. When he spoke to his young topmates about it they were either lightly incredulous or found something comical in his unconcealed anxiety. "Is it your bag, Billy?" said one. "Well, sew yourself up in it, bully boy, and then you'll be sure to know if anybody meddles with it."

Now there was a veteran aboard who because his years began to disqualify him for more active work had been recently assigned duty as mainmastman in his watch, looking to the gear belayed at the rail roundabout that great spar near the deck. At off-times the foretopman had picked up some acquaintance with him, and now in his trouble it occurred to him that he might be the sort of person to go to for wise counsel. He was an old Dansker long anglicized in the service, of few words, many 40

---

40 **Dansker,** Dane

wrinkles, and some honorable scars. His wizened face, time-tinted and weather-stained to the complexion of an antique parchment, was here and there peppered blue by the chance explosion of a gun cartridge in action.

He was an *Agamemnon* man, some two years prior to the time of this story having served under Nelson when still captain in that ship immortal in naval memory, which dismantled and in part broken up to her bare ribs is seen a grand skeleton in Haden's etching. As one of a boarding party from the *Agamemnon* he had received a cut slantwise along one temple and cheek leaving a long pale scar like a streak of dawn's light falling athwart the dark visage. It was on account of that scar and the affair in which it was known that he had received it, as well as from his blue-peppered complexion, that the Dansker went among the *Bellipotent's* crew by the name of "Board-Her-in-the-Smoke."

Now the first time that his small weasel eyes happened to light on Billy Budd, a certain grim internal merriment set all his ancient wrinkles into antic play. Was it that his eccentric unsentimental old sapience, primitive in its kind, saw or thought it saw something which in contrast with the warship's environment looked oddly incongruous in the Handsome Sailor? But after slyly studying him at intervals, the old Merlin's equivocal merriment was modified; for now when the twain would meet, it would start in his face a quizzing sort of look, but it would be but momentary and sometimes replaced by an expression of speculative query as to what might eventually befall a nature like that, dropped into a world not without some mantraps and against whose subtleties simple courage lacking experience and address, and without any touch of defensive ugliness, is of little avail; and where such innocence as man is capable of does yet in a moral emergency not always sharpen the faculties or enlighten the will.

However it was, the Dansker in his ascetic way rather took to Billy. Nor was this only because of a certain philosophic interest in such a character. There was another cause. While the old man's eccentricities, sometimes bordering on the ursine, repelled the juniors, Billy, undeterred thereby, revering him as a salt hero, would make advances, never passing the old *Agamemnon* man without a salutation marked by that respect which is seldom lost on the aged, however crabbed at times or whatever their station in life.

There was a vein of dry humor, or what not, in the mastman; and, whether in freak of patriarchal irony touching Billy's youth and athletic frame, or for some other and more recondite reason, from the first in addressing him he always substituted *Baby* for Billy, the Dansker in fact being the originator of the name by which the foretopman eventually became known aboard ship.

Well then, in his mysterious little difficulty going in quest of the wrinkled one, Billy found him off duty in a dogwatch ruminating by himself, seated on a shot box of the upper gun deck, now and then surveying with a somewhat cynical regard certain of the more swaggering promenaders there. Billy recounted his trouble, again wondering how it all happened. The salt seer attentively listened, accompany-

---

7 **Haden's etching,** the masterpiece of Sir Francis Seymour Haden (1818-1910) was "Breaking Up of the *Agamemnon*," which had wide circulation

ing the foretopman's recital with queer twitchings of his wrinkles and problematical little sparkles of his small ferret eyes. Making an end of his story, the foretopman asked, "And now, Dansker, do tell me what you think of it."

The old man, shoving up the front of his tarpaulin and deliberately rubbing the long slant scar at the point where it entered the thin hair, laconically said, "Baby Budd, *Jemmy Legs*" (meaning the master-at-arms) "is down on you."

"*Jemmy Legs!*" ejaculated Billy, his welkin eyes expanding. "What for? Why, he calls me 'the sweet and pleasant young fellow,' they tell me."

"Does he so?" grinned the grizzled one; then said, "Ay, Baby lad, a sweet voice has Jemmy Legs."   10

"No, not always. But to me he has. I seldom pass him but there comes a pleasant word."

"And that's because he's down upon you, Baby Budd."

Such reiteration, along with the manner of it, incomprehensible to a novice, disturbed Billy almost as much as the mystery for which he had sought explanation. Something less unpleasingly oracular he tried to extract; but the old sea Chiron, thinking perhaps that for the nonce he had sufficiently instructed his young Achilles, pursed his lips, gathered all his wrinkles together, and would commit himself to nothing further.

Years, and those experiences which befall certain shrewder men subordinated life-   20 long to the will of superiors, all this had developed in the Dansker the pithy guarded cynicism that was his leading characteristic.

10

The next day an incident served to confirm Billy Budd in his incredulity as to the Dansker's strange summing up of the case submitted. The ship at noon, going large before the wind, was rolling on her course, and he below at dinner and engaged in some sportful talk with the members of his mess, chanced in a sudden lurch to spill the entire contents of his soup pan upon the new-scrubbed deck. Claggart, the master-at-arms, official rattan in hand, happened to be passing along the battery in a bay of which the mess was lodged, and the greasy liquid streamed just across his path. Stepping over it, he was proceeding on his way without comment, since the   30 matter was nothing to take notice of under the circumstances, when he happened to observe who it was that had done the spilling. His countenance changed. Pausing, he was about to ejaculate something hasty at the sailor, but checked himself, and pointing down to the streaming soup, playfully tapped him from behind with his rattan, saying in a low musical voice peculiar to him at times, "Handsomely done, my lad! And handsome is as handsome did it, too!" And with that passed on. Not noted by Billy as not coming within his view was the involuntary smile, or rather grimace, that accompanied Claggart's equivocal words. Aridly it drew down the thin corners of his shapely mouth. But everybody taking his remark as meant

---

6 **Jemmy Legs,** sailor's term for master-at-arms   16 **Chiron . . . Achilles,** a wise centaur, teacher of Achilles

for humorous, and at which therefore as coming from a superior they were bound to laugh "with counterfeited glee," acted accordingly; and Billy, tickled, it may be, by the allusion to his being the Handsome Sailor, merrily joined in; then addressing his messmates exclaimed, "There now, who says that Jemmy Legs is down on me!"

"And who said he was, Beauty?" demanded one Donald with some surprise. Whereat the foretopman looked a little foolish, recalling that it was only one person, Board-Her-in-the-Smoke, who had suggested what to him was the smoky idea that this master-at-arms was in any peculiar way hostile to him. Meantime that func-
10 tionary, resuming his path, must have momentarily worn some expression less guarded than that of the bitter smile, usurping the face from the heart — some distorting expression perhaps, for a drummer-boy heedlessly frolicking along from the opposite direction and chancing to come into light collision with his person was strangely disconcerted by his aspect. Nor was the impression lessened when the official, impetuously giving him a sharp cut with the rattan, vehemently exclaimed, "Look where you go!"

11

What was the matter with the master-at-arms? And, be the matter what it might, how could it have direct relation to Billy Budd, with whom prior to the affair of the spilled soup he had never come into any special contact official or otherwise?
20 What indeed could the trouble have to do with one so little inclined to give offense as the merchant-ship's "peacemaker," even him who in Claggart's own phrase was "the sweet and pleasant young fellow"? Yes, why should Jemmy Legs, to borrow the Dansker's expression, be "down" on the Handsome Sailor? But, at heart and not for nothing, as the late chance encounter may indicate to the discerning, down on him, secretly down on him, he assuredly was.

Now to invent something touching the more private career of Claggart, something involving Billy Budd, of which something the latter should be wholly ignorant, some romantic incident implying that Claggart's knowledge of the young bluejacket began at some period anterior to catching sight of him on board the seventy-
30 four — all this, not so difficult to do, might avail in a way more or less interesting to account for whatever of enigma may appear to lurk in the case. But in fact there was nothing of the sort. And yet the cause necessarily to be assumed as the sole one assignable is in its very realism as much charged with that prime element of Radcliffian romance, the mysterious, as any that the ingenuity of the author of *The Mysteries of Udolpho* could devise. For what can more partake of the mysterious than an antipathy spontaneous and profound such as is evoked in certain exceptional mortals by the mere aspect of some other mortal, however harmless he may be, if not called forth by this very harmlessness itself?

Now there can exist no irritating juxtaposition of dissimilar personalities com-

34 **Radcliffian romance.** Ann Radcliffe (1764-1823), wrote many popular Gothic romances, notably *The Mysteries of Udolpho*

parable to that which is possible aboard a great warship fully manned and at sea. There, every day among all ranks, almost every man comes into more or less of contact with almost every other man. Wholly there to avoid even the sight of an aggravating object one must needs give it Jonah's toss or jump overboard himself. Imagine how all this might eventually operate on some peculiar human creature the direct reverse of a saint!

But for the adequate comprehending of Claggart by a normal nature these hints are insufficient. To pass from a normal nature to him one must cross "the deadly space between." And this is best done by indirection.

Long ago an honest scholar, my senior, said to me in reference to one who like 10 himself is now no more, a man so unimpeachably respectable that against him nothing was ever openly said though among the few something was whispered, "Yes, X—— is a nut not to be cracked by the tap of a lady's fan. You are aware that I am the adherent of no organized religion, much less of any philosophy built into a system. Well, for all that, I think that to try and get into X——, enter his labyrinth and get out again, without a clue derived from some source other than what is known as 'knowledge of the world' — that were hardly possible, at least for me."

"Why," said I, "X——, however singular a study to some, is yet human, and knowledge of the world assuredly implies the knowledge of human nature, and in most of its varieties."   20

"Yes, but a superficial knowledge of it, serving ordinary purposes. But for anything deeper, I am not certain whether to know the world and to know human nature be not two distinct branches of knowledge, which while they may coexist in the same heart, yet either may exist with little or nothing of the other. Nay, in an average man of the world, his constant rubbing with it blunts that finer spiritual insight indispensable to the understanding of the essential in certain exceptional characters, whether evil ones or good. In a matter of some importance I have seen a girl wind an old lawyer about her little finger. Nor was it the dotage of senile love. Nothing of the sort. But he knew law better than he knew the girl's heart. Coke and Blackstone hardly shed so much light into obscure spiritual places as the Hebrew 30 prophets. And who were they? Mostly recluses."

At the time, my inexperience was such that I did not quite see the drift of all this. It may be that I see it now. And, indeed, if that lexicon which is based on Holy Writ were any longer popular, one might with less difficulty define and denominate certain phenomenal men. As it is, one must turn to some authority not liable to the charge of being tinctured with the biblical element.

In a list of definitions included in the authentic translation of Plato, a list attributed to him, occurs this: "Natural Depravity: a depravity according to nature," a definition which, though savoring of Calvinism, by no means involves Calvin's dogma as to total mankind. Evidently its intent makes it applicable but to individuals. Not 40 many are the examples of this depravity which the gallows and jail supply. At any rate, for notable instances, since these have no vulgar alloy of the brute in them,

---

4 **Jonah's toss.** See Jonah 1:12   29 **Coke and Blackstone,** noted British legal writers, Sir Edward Coke (1552-1634) and Sir William Blackstone (1723-1780)

but invariably are dominated by intellectuality, one must go elsewhere. Civilization, especially if of the austerer sort, is auspicious to it. It folds itself in the mantle of respectability. It has its certain negative virtues serving as silent auxiliaries. It never allows wine to get within its guard. It is not going too far to say that it is without vices or small sins. There is a phenomenal pride in it that excludes them. It is never mercenary or avaricious. In short, the depravity here meant partakes nothing of the sordid or sensual. It is serious, but free from acerbity. Though no flatterer of mankind it never speaks ill of it.

But the thing which in eminent instances signalizes so exceptional a nature is
10 this: Though the man's even temper and discreet bearing would seem to intimate a mind peculiarly subject to the law of reason, not the less in heart he would seem to riot in complete exemption from that law, having apparently little to do with reason further than to employ it as an ambidexter implement for effecting the irrational. That is to say: Toward the accomplishment of an aim which in wantonness of atrocity would seem to partake of the insane, he will direct a cool judgment sagacious and sound. These men are madmen, and of the most dangerous sort, for their lunacy is not continuous, but occasional, evoked by some special object; it is protectively secretive, which is as much as to say it is self-contained, so that when, moreover, most active it is to the average mind not distinguishable from sanity, and for the reason
20 above suggested: that whatever its aims may be — and the aim is never declared — the method and the outward proceeding are always perfectly rational.

Now something such an one was Claggart, in whom was the mania of an evil nature, not engendered by vicious training or corrupting books or licentious living, but born with him and innate, in short "a depravity according to nature."

Dark sayings are these, some will say. But why? Is it because they somewhat savor of Holy Writ in its phrase "mystery of iniquity"? If they do, such savor was far enough from being intended, for little will it commend these pages to many a reader of today.

The point of the present story turning on the hidden nature of the master-at-arms
30 has necessitated this chapter. With an added hint or two in connection with the incident at the mess, the resumed narrative must be left to vindicate, as it may, its own credibility.

12

That Claggart's figure was not amiss, and his face, save the chin, well molded, has already been said. Of these favorable points he seemed not insensible, for he was not only neat but careful in his dress. But the form of Billy Budd was heroic; and if his face was without the intellectual look of the pallid Claggart's, not the less was it lit, like his, from within, though from a different source. The bonfire in his heart made luminous the rose-tan in his cheek.

In view of the marked contrast between the persons of the twain, it is more than
40 probable that when the master-at-arms in the scene last given applied to the sailor

---

26 **mystery of iniquity.** See II Thessalonians 2:7

the proverb "Handsome is as handsome does," he there let escape an ironic inkling, not caught by the young sailors who heard it, as to what it was that had first moved him against Billy, namely, his significant personal beauty.

Now envy and antipathy, passions irreconcilable in reason, nevertheless in fact may spring conjoined like Chang and Eng in one birth. Is Envy then such a monster? Well, though many an arraigned mortal has in hopes of mitigated penalty pleaded guilty to horrible actions, did ever anybody seriously confess to envy? Something there is in it universally felt to be more shameful than even felonious crime. And not only does everybody disown it, but the better sort are inclined to incredulity when it is in earnest imputed to an intelligent man. But since its lodgment is in 10 the heart not the brain, no degree of intellect supplies a guarantee against it. But Claggart's was no vulgar form of the passion. Nor, as directed toward Billy Budd, did it partake of that streak of apprehensive jealousy that marred Saul's visage perturbedly brooding on the comely young David. Claggart's envy struck deeper. If askance he eyed the good looks, cheery health, and frank enjoyment of young life in Billy Budd, it was because these went along with a nature that, as Claggart magnetically felt, had in its simplicity never willed malice or experienced the reactionary bite of that serpent. To him, the spirit lodged within Billy, and looking out from his welkin eyes as from windows, that ineffability it was which made the dimple in his dyed cheek, suppled his joints, and dancing in his yellow curls made him pre- 20 eminently the Handsome Sailor. One person excepted, the master-at-arms was perhaps the only man in the ship intellectually capable of adequately appreciating the moral phenomenon presented in Billy Budd. And the insight but intensified his passion, which assuming various secret forms within him, at times assumed that of cynic disdain, disdain of innocence — to be nothing more than innocent! Yet in an aesthetic way he saw the charm of it, the courageous free-and-easy temper of it, and fain would have shared it, but he despaired of it.

With no power to annul the elemental evil in him, though readily enough he could hide it; apprehending the good, but powerless to be it; a nature like Claggart's, surcharged with energy as such natures almost invariably are, what recourse 30 is left to it but to recoil upon itself and, like the scorpion for which the Creator alone is responsible, act out to the end the part allotted it.

13

Passion, and passion in its profoundest, is not a thing demanding a palatial stage whereon to play its part. Down among the groundlings, among the beggars and rakers of the garbage, profound passion is enacted. And the circumstances that provoke it, however trivial or mean, are no measure of its power. In the present instance the stage is a scrubbed gun deck, and one of the external provocations a man-of-war's man's spilled soup.

5 **Chang and Eng,** Siamese twins (1811-1874) made famous by their exhibition in P. T. Barnum's circus   13 **Saul's visage.** See I Samuel 16:18, 18:8; Saul is described as envious of David's popularity and military accomplishment

Now when the master-at-arms noticed whence came that greasy fluid streaming before his feet, he must have taken it — to some extent wilfully, perhaps — not for the mere accident it assuredly was, but for the sly escape of a spontaneous feeling on Billy's part more or less answering to the antipathy on his own. In effect a foolish demonstration, he must have thought, and very harmless, like the futile kick of a heifer, which yet were the heifer a shod stallion would not be so harmless. Even so was it that into the gall of Claggart's envy he infused the vitriol of his contempt. But the incident confirmed to him certain telltale reports purveyed to his ear by "Squeak," one of his more cunning corporals, a grizzled little man, so nicknamed
10 by the sailors on account of his squeaky voice and sharp visage ferreting about the dark corners of the lower decks after interlopers, satirically suggesting to them the idea of a rat in a cellar.

From his chief's employing him as an implicit tool in laying little traps for the worriment of the foretopman — for it was from the master-at-arms that the petty persecutions heretofore adverted to had proceeded — the corporal, having naturally enough concluded that his master could have no love for the sailor, made it his business, faithful understrapper that he was, to foment the ill blood by perverting to his chief certain innocent frolics of the good-natured foretopman, besides inventing for his mouth sundry contumelious epithets he claimed to have overheard him
20 let fall. The master-at-arms never suspected the veracity of these reports, more especially as to the epithets, for he well knew how secretly unpopular may become a master-at-arms, at least a master-at-arms of those days, zealous in his function, and how the bluejackets shoot at him in private their raillery and wit; the nickname by which he goes among them (Jemmy Legs) implying under the form of merriment their cherished disrespect and dislike. But in view of the greediness of hate for pabulum it hardly needed a purveyor to feed Claggart's passion.

An uncommon prudence is habitual with the subtler depravity, for it has everything to hide. And in case of an injury but suspected, its secretiveness voluntarily cuts it off from enlightenment or disillusion; and, not unreluctantly, action is taken
30 upon surmise as upon certainty. And the retaliation is apt to be in monstrous disproportion to the supposed offense; for when in anybody was revenge in its exactions aught else but an inordinate usurer? But how with Claggart's conscience? For though consciences are unlike as foreheads, every intelligence, not excluding the scriptural devils who "believe and tremble," has one. But Claggart's conscience being but the lawyer to his will, made ogres of trifles, probably arguing that the motive imputed to Billy in spilling the soup just when he did, together with the epithets alleged, these, if nothing more, made a strong case against him; nay, justified animosity into a sort of retributive righteousness. The Pharisee is the Guy Fawkes prowling in the hid chambers underlying some natures like Claggart's. And they can really form
40 no conception of an unreciprocated malice. Probably the master-at-arms' clandestine persecution of Billy was started to try the temper of the man; but it had not developed any quality in him that enmity could make official use of or even pervert

---

38 **Pharisee . . . Fawkes.** A Pharisee is a self-righteous or hypocritical person, originally a member of an ancient Jewish sect that set itself apart. For Guy Fawkes, see note, p. 1424

into plausible self-justification; so that the occurrence at the mess, petty if it were, was a welcome one to that peculiar conscience assigned to be the private mentor of Claggart; and, for the rest, not improbably it put him upon new experiments.

14

Not many days after the last incident narrated, something befell Billy Budd that more graveled him than aught that had previously occurred.

It was a warm night for the latitude; and the foretopman, whose watch at the time was properly below, was dozing on the uppermost deck whither he had ascended from his hot hammock, one of hundreds suspended so closely wedged together over a lower gun deck that there was little or no swing to them. He lay as in the shadow of a hillside, stretched under the lee of the booms, a piled ridge of 10 spare spars amidships between foremast and mainmast among which the ship's largest boat, the launch, was stowed. Alongside of three other slumberers from below, he lay near that end of the booms which approaches the foremast; his station aloft on duty as a foretopman being just over the deck-station of the forecastlemen, entitling him according to usage to make himself more or less at home in that neighborhood.

Presently he was stirred into semiconsciousness by somebody, who must have previously sounded the sleep of the others, touching his shoulder, and then, as the foretopman raised his head, breathing into his ear in a quick whisper, "Slip into the lee forechains, Billy; there is something in the wind. Don't speak. Quick, I will meet 20 you there," and disappearing.

Now Billy, like sundry other essentially good-natured ones, had some of the weaknesses inseparable from essential good nature; and among these was a reluctance, almost an incapacity of plumply saying *no* to an abrupt proposition not obviously absurd on the face of it, nor obviously unfriendly, nor iniquitous. And being of warm blood, he had not the phlegm tacitly to negative any proposition by unresponsive inaction. Like his sense of fear, his apprehension as to aught outside of the honest and natural was seldom very quick. Besides, upon the present occasion, the drowse from his sleep still hung upon him.

However it was, he mechanically rose and, sleepily wondering what could be in 30 the wind, betook himself to the designated place, a narrow platform, one of six, outside of the high bulwarks and screened by the great deadeyes and multiple columned lanyards of the shrouds and backstays; and, in a great warship of that time, of dimensions commensurate to the hull's magnitude; a tarry balcony in short, overhanging the sea, and so secluded that one mariner of the *Bellipotent,* a Nonconformist old tar of a serious turn, made it even in daytime his private oratory.

In this retired nook the stranger soon joined Billy Budd. There was no moon as yet; a haze obscured the starlight. He could not distinctly see the stranger's face. Yet from something in the outline and carriage, Billy took him, and correctly, for one of the afterguard.   40

"Hist! Billy," said the man, in the same quick cautionary whisper as before. "You were impressed, weren't you? Well, so was I"; and he paused, as to mark the effect. But Billy, not knowing exactly what to make of this, said nothing. Then the other: "We are not the only impressed ones, Billy. There's a gang of us. — Couldn't you — help — at a pinch?"

"What do you mean?" demanded Billy, here thoroughly shaking off his drowse.

"Hist, hist!" the hurried whisper now growing husky. "See here," and the man held up two small objects faintly twinkling in the night-light; "see, they are yours, Billy, if you'll only ——"

But Billy broke in, and in his resentful eagerness to deliver himself his vocal in-
10 firmity somewhat intruded. "D—d—damme, I don't know what you are d—d—driving at, or what you mean, but you had better g—g—go where you belong!" For the moment the fellow, as confounded, did not stir; and Billy, springing to his feet, said, "If you d—don't start, I'll t—t—toss you back over the r—rail!" There was no mistaking this, and the mysterious emissary decamped, disappearing in the direction of the mainmast in the shadow of the booms.

"Hallo, what's the matter?" here came growling from a forecastleman awakened from his deck-doze by Billy's raised voice. And as the foretopman reappeared and was recognized by him: "Ah, Beauty, is it you? Well, something must have been the matter, for you st—st—stuttered."

20 "Oh," rejoined Billy, now mastering the impediment, "I found an afterguardsman in our part of the ship here, and I bid him be off where he belongs."

"And is that all you did about it, Foretopman?" gruffly demanded another, an irascible old fellow of brick-colored visage and hair who was known to his associate forecastlemen as "Red Pepper." "Such sneaks I should like to marry to the gunner's daughter!" — by that expression meaning that he would like to subject them to disciplinary castigation over a gun.

However, Billy's rendering of the matter satisfactorily accounted to these inquirers for the brief commotion, since of all the sections of a ship's company the forecastlemen, veterans for the most part and bigoted in their sea prejudices, are the most
30 jealous in resenting territorial encroachments, especially on the part of any of the afterguard, of whom they have but a sorry opinion — chiefly landsmen, never going aloft except to reef or furl the mainsail, and in no wise competent to handle a marlinspike or turn in a deadeye, say.

15

This incident sorely puzzled Billy Budd. It was an entirely new experience, the first time in his life that he had ever been personally approached in underhand intriguing fashion. Prior to this encounter he had known nothing of the afterguardsman, the two men being stationed wide apart, one forward and aloft during his watch, the other on deck and aft.

What could it mean? And could they really be guineas, those two glittering ob-
40 jects the interloper had held up to his (Billy's) eyes? Where could the fellow get guineas? Why, even spare buttons are not so plentiful at sea. The more he turned

the matter over, the more he was nonplussed, and made uneasy and discomfited. In his disgustful recoil from an overture which, though he but ill comprehended, he instinctively knew must involve evil of some sort, Billy Budd was like a young horse fresh from the pasture suddenly inhaling a vile whiff from some chemical factory, and by repeated snortings trying to get it out of his nostrils and lungs. This frame of mind barred all desire of holding further parley with the fellow, even were it but for the purpose of gaining some enlightenment as to his design in approaching him. And yet he was not without natural curiosity to see how such a visitor in the dark would look in broad day.

He espied him the following afternoon in his first dogwatch below, one of the 10 smokers on that forward part of the upper gun deck allotted to the pipe. He recognized him by his general cut and build more than by his round freckled face and glassy eyes of pale blue, veiled with lashes all but white. And yet Billy was a bit uncertain whether indeed it were he — yonder chap about his own age chatting and laughing in freehearted way, leaning against a gun; a genial young fellow enough to look at, and something of a rattlebrain, to all appearance. Rather chubby too for a sailor, even an afterguardsman. In short, the last man in the world, one would think, to be overburdened with thoughts, especially those perilous thoughts that must needs belong to a conspirator in any serious project, or even to the underling of such a conspirator.   20

Although Billy was not aware of it, the fellow, with a side long watchful glance, had perceived Billy first, and then noting that Billy was looking at him, thereupon nodded a familiar sort of friendly recognition as to an old acquaintance, without interrupting the talk he was engaged in with the group of smokers. A day or two afterwards, chancing in the evening promenade on a gun deck to pass Billy, he offered a flying word of good-fellowship, as it were, which by its unexpectedness, and equivocalness under the circumstances, so embarrassed Billy that he knew not how to respond to it, and let it go unnoticed.

Billy was now left more at a loss than before. The ineffectual speculations into which he was led were so disturbingly alien to him that he did his best to smother 30 them. It never entered his mind that here was a matter which, from its extreme questionableness, it was his duty as a loyal bluejacket to report in the proper quarter. And, probably, had such a step been suggested to him, he would have been deterred from taking it by the thought, one of novice magnanimity, that it would savor overmuch of the dirty work of a telltale. He kept the thing to himself. Yet upon one occasion he could not forbear a little disburdening himself to the old Dansker, tempted thereto perhaps by the influence of a balmy night when the ship lay becalmed; the twain, silent for the most part, sitting together on deck, their heads propped against the bulwarks. But it was only a partial and anonymous account that Billy gave, the unfounded scruples above referred to preventing full disclosure 40 to anybody. Upon hearing Billy's version, the sage Dansker seemed to divine more than he was told; and after a little meditation, during which his wrinkles were pursed as into a point, quite effacing for the time that quizzing expression his face sometimes wore: "Didn't I say so, Baby Budd?"

"Say what?" demanded Billy.

"Why, *Jemmy Legs* is *down* on you."

"And what," rejoined Billy in amazement, "has *Jemmy Legs* to do with that cracked afterguardsman?"

"Ho, it was an afterguardsman, then. A cat's-paw, a cat's-paw!" And with that exclamation, whether it had reference to a light puff of air just then coming over the calm sea, or a subtler relation to the afterguardsman, there is no telling, the old Merlin gave a twisting wrench with his black teeth at his plug of tobacco, vouch-safing no reply to Billy's impetuous question, though now repeated, for it was his
10 wont to relapse into grim silence when interrogated in skeptical sort as to any of his sententious oracles, not always very clear ones, rather partaking of that obscurity which invests most Delphic deliverances from any quarter.

Long experience had very likely brought this old man to that bitter prudence which never interferes in aught and never gives advice.

16

Yes, despite the Dansker's pithy insistence as to the master-at-arms being at the bottom of these strange experiences of Billy on board the *Bellipotent,* the young sailor was ready to ascribe them to almost anybody but the man who, to use Billy's own expression, "always had a pleasant word for him." This is to be wondered at. Yet not so much to be wondered at. In certain matters, some sailors even in mature life
20 remain unsophisticated enough. But a young seafarer of the disposition of our ath-letic foretopman is much of a child-man. And yet a child's utter innocence is but its blank ignorance, and the innocence more or less wanes as intelligence waxes. But in Billy Budd intelligence, such as it was, had advanced while yet his simple-mindedness remained for the most part unaffected. Experience is a teacher indeed; yet did Billy's years make his experience small. Besides, he had none of that intuitive knowledge of the bad which in natures not good or incompletely so foreruns experience, and therefore may pertain, as in some instances it too clearly does pertain, even to youth.

And what could Billy know of man except of man as a mere sailor? And the old-fashioned sailor, the veritable man before the mast, the sailor from boyhood up, he,
30 though indeed of the same species as a landsman, is in some respects singularly dis-tinct from him. The sailor is frankness, the landsman is finesse. Life is not a game with the sailor, demanding the long head — no intricate game of chess where few moves are made in straightforwardness and ends are attained by indirection, an oblique, tedious, barren game hardly worth that poor candle burnt out in playing it.

Yes, as a class, sailors are in character a juvenile race. Even their deviations are marked by juvenility, this more especially holding true with the sailors of Billy's time. Then too, certain things which apply to all sailors do more pointedly operate here and there upon the junior one. Every sailor, too, is accustomed to obey orders without debating them; his life afloat is externally ruled for him; he is not brought
40 into that promiscuous commerce with mankind where unobstructed free agency on

---

8 **Merlin,** a magician and seer in the Arthurian romances   12 **Delphic deliverances,** of the oracle at Delphi. See note, p. 921

equal terms — equal superficially, at least — soon teaches one that unless upon occasion he exercise a distrust keen in proportion to the fairness of the appearance, some foul turn may be served him. A ruled undemonstrative distrustfulness is so habitual, not with businessmen so much as with men who know their kind in less shallow relations than business, namely, certain men of the world, that they come at last to employ it all but unconsciously; and some of them would very likely feel real surprise at being charged with it as one of their general characteristics.

17

But after the little matter at the mess Billy Budd no more found himself in strange trouble at times about his hammock or his clothes bag or what not. As to that smile that occasionally sunned him, and the pleasant passing word, these were, if not 10 more frequent, yet if anything more pronounced than before.

But for all that, there were certain other demonstrations now. When Claggart's unobserved glance happened to light on belted Billy rolling along the upper gun deck in the leisure of the second dogwatch, exchanging passing broadsides of fun with other young promenaders in the crowd, that glance would follow the cheerful sea Hyperion with a settled meditative and melancholy expression, his eyes strangely suffused with incipient feverish tears. Then would Claggart look like the man of sorrows. Yes, and sometimes the melancholy expression would have in it a touch of soft yearning, as if Claggart could even have loved Billy but for fate and ban. But this was an evanescence, and quickly repented of, as it were, by an immitigable 20 look, pinching and shriveling the visage into the momentary semblance of a wrinkled walnut. But sometimes catching sight in advance of the foretopman coming in his direction, he would, upon their nearing, step aside a little to let him pass, dwelling upon Billy for the moment with the glittering dental satire of a Guise. But upon any abrupt unforeseen encounter a red light would flash forth from his eye like a spark from an anvil in a dusk smithy. That quick, fierce light was a strange one, darted from orbs which in repose were of a color nearest approaching a deeper violet, the softest of shades.

Though some of these caprices of the pit could not but be observed by their object, yet were they beyond the construing of such a nature. And the thews of Billy 30 were hardly compatible with that sort of sensitive spiritual organization which in some cases instinctively conveys to ignorant innocence an admonition of the proximity of the malign. He thought the master-at-arms acted in a manner rather queer at times. That was all. But the occasional frank air and pleasant word went for what they purported to be, the young sailor never having heard as yet of the "too fair-spoken man."

Had the foretopman been conscious of having done or said anything to provoke the ill will of the official, it would have been different with him, and his sight might have been purged if not sharpened. As it was, innocence was his blinder.

---

16 **Hyperion,** one of the Titans in Greek mythology   24 **dental . . . Guise.** The Guise were a French ducal family of the sixteenth and seventeenth centuries noted for conspiratorial schemes; hence the meaning here: smiles that conceal plots

So was it with him in yet another matter. Two minor officers, the armorer and captain of the hold, with whom he had never exchanged a word, his position in the ship not bringing him into contact with them, these men now for the first began to cast upon Billy, when they chanced to encounter him, that peculiar glance which evidences that the man from whom it comes has been some way tampered with, and to the prejudice of him upon whom the glance lights. Never did it occur to Billy as a thing to be noted or a thing suspicious, though he well knew the fact, that the armorer and captain of the hold, with the ship's yeoman, apothecary, and others of that grade, were by naval usage messmates of the master-at-arms, men
10 with ears convenient to his confidential tongue.

But the general popularity that came from our Handsome Sailor's manly forwardness upon occasion and irresistible good nature, indicating no mental superiority tending to excite an invidious feeling, this good will on the part of most of his shipmates made him the less to concern himself about such mute aspects toward him as those whereto allusion has just been made, aspects he could not so fathom as to infer their whole import.

As to the afterguardsman, though Billy for reasons already given necessarily saw little of him, yet when the two did happen to meet, invariably came the fellow's offhand cheerful recognition, sometimes accompanied by a passing pleasant word or
20 two. Whatever that equivocal young person's original design may really have been, or the design of which he might have been the deputy, certain it was from his manner upon these occasions that he had wholly dropped it.

It was as if his precocity of crookedness (and every vulgar villain is precocious) had for once deceived him, and the man he had sought to entrap as a simpleton had through his very simplicity ignominiously baffled him.

But shrewd ones may opine that it was hardly possible for Billy to refrain from going up to the afterguardsman and bluntly demanding to know his purpose in the initial interview so abruptly closed in the forechains. Shrewd ones may also think it but natural in Billy to set about sounding some of the other impressed men of the
30 ship in order to discover what basis, if any, there was for the emissary's obscure suggestions as to plotting disaffection aboard. Yes, shrewd ones may so think. But something more, or rather something else than mere shrewdness is perhaps needful for the due understanding of such a character as Billy Budd's.

As to Claggart, the monomania in the man — if that indeed it were — as involuntarily disclosed by starts in the manifestations detailed, yet in general covered over by his self-contained and rational demeanor; this, like a subterranean fire, was eating its way deeper and deeper in him. Something decisive must come of it.

18

After the mysterious interview in the forechains, the one so abruptly ended there by Billy, nothing especially germane to the story occurred until the events now about
40 to be narrated.

Elsewhere it has been said that in the lack of frigates (of course better sailers than line-of-battle ships) in the English squadron up the Straits at that period, the *Bel-lipotent* 74 was occasionally employed not only as an available substitute for a scout, but at times on detached service of more important kind. This was not alone because of her sailing qualities, not common in a ship of her rate, but quite as much, probably, that the character of her commander, it was thought, specially adapted him for any duty where under unforeseen difficulties a prompt initiative might have to be taken in some matter demanding knowledge and ability in addition to those qualities implied in good seamanship. It was on an expedition of the latter sort, a somewhat distant one, and when the *Bellipotent* was almost at her furthest remove from the fleet, that in the latter part of an afternoon watch she unexpectedly came in   10 sight of a ship of the enemy. It proved to be a frigate. The latter, perceiving through the glass that the weight of men and metal would be heavily against her, invoking her light heels crowded sail to get away. After a chase urged almost against hope and lasting until about the middle of the first dogwatch, she signally succeeded in effecting her escape.

Not long after the pursuit had been given up, and ere the excitement incident thereto had altogether waned away, the master-at-arms, ascending from his cavernous sphere, made his appearance cap in hand by the mainmast respectfully waiting the notice of Captain Vere, then solitary walking the weather side of the quarterdeck, doubtless somewhat chafed at the failure of the pursuit. The spot where Clag-   20 gart stood was the place allotted to men of lesser grades seeking some more particular interview either with the officer of the deck or the captain himself. But from the latter it was not often that a sailor or petty officer of those days would seek a hearing; only some exceptional cause would, according to established custom, have warranted that.

Presently, just as the commander, absorbed in his reflections, was on the point of turning aft in his promenade, he became sensible of Claggart's presence, and saw the doffed cap held in deferential expectancy. Here be it said that Captain Vere's personal knowledge of this petty officer had only begun at the time of the ship's last sailing from home, Claggart then for the first, in transfer from a ship detained for   30 repairs, supplying on board the *Bellipotent* the place of a previous master-at-arms disabled and ashore.

No sooner did the commander observe who it was that now deferentially stood awaiting his notice than a peculiar expression came over him. It was not unlike that which uncontrollably will flit across the countenance of one at unawares encountering a person who, though known to him indeed, has hardly been long enough known for thorough knowledge, but something in whose aspect nevertheless now for the first provokes a vaguely repellent distaste. But coming to a stand and resuming much of his wonted official manner, save that a sort of impatience lurked in the intonation of the opening word, he said "Well? What is it, Master-at-arms?"   40

With the air of a subordinate grieved at the necessity of being a messenger of ill tidings, and while conscientiously determined to be frank yet equally resolved upon shunning overstatement, Claggart at this invitation, or rather summons to disburden, spoke up. What he said, conveyed in the language of no uneducated man, was to the effect following, if not altogether in these words, namely, that during the chase and preparations for the possible encounter he had seen enough to convince him that at least one sailor aboard was a dangerous character in a ship mustering some who not only had taken a guilty part in the late serious troubles, but others also who, like the man in question, had entered His Majesty's service under another form than enlistment.

At this point Captain Vere with some impatience interrupted him: "Be direct, man; say *impressed men*."

Claggart made a gesture of subservience, and proceeded. Quite lately he (Clag-
10 gart) had begun to suspect that on the gun decks some sort of movement prompted by the sailor in question was covertly going on, but he had not thought himself warranted in reporting the suspicion so long as it remained indistinct. But from what he had that afternoon observed in the man referred to, the suspicion of some-thing clandestine going on had advanced to a point less removed from certainty. He deeply felt, he added, the serious responsibility assumed in making a report involv-ing such possible consequences to the individual mainly concerned, besides tending to augment those natural anxieties which every naval commander must feel in view of extraordinary outbreaks so recent as those which, he sorrowfully said it, it needed not to name.

20 Now at the first broaching of the matter Captain Vere, taken by surprise, could not wholly dissemble his disquietude. But as Claggart went on, the former's aspect changed into restiveness under something in the testifier's manner in giving his testimony. However, he refrained from interrupting him. And Claggart, continuing, concluded with this: "God forbid, your honor, that the *Bellipotent*'s should be the experience of the ——"

"Never mind that!" here peremptorily broke in the superior, his face altering with anger, instinctively divining the ship that the other was about to name, one in which the Nore Mutiny had assumed a singularly tragical character that for a time jeop-ardized the life of its commander. Under the circumstances he was indignant at the
30 purposed allusion. When the commissioned officers themselves were on all occa-sions very heedful how they referred to the recent events in the fleet, for a petty officer unnecessarily to allude to them in the presence of his captain, this struck him as a most immodest presumption. Besides, to his quick sense of self-respect it even looked under the circumstances something like an attempt to alarm him. Nor at first was he without some surprise that one who so far as he had hitherto come un-der his notice had shown considerable tact in his function should in this particular evince such lack of it.

But these thoughts and kindred dubious ones flitting across his mind were sud-denly replaced by an intuitional surmise which, though as yet obscure in form,
40 served practically to affect his reception of the ill tidings. Certain it is that, long versed in everything pertaining to the complicated gun-deck life, which like every other form of life has its secret mines and dubious side, the side popularly disclaimed, Captain Vere did not permit himself to be unduly disturbed by the general tenor of his subordinate's report.

Furthermore, if in view of recent events prompt action should be taken at the first palpable sign of recurring insubordination, for all that, not judicious would it be, he thought, to keep the idea of lingering disaffection alive by undue forwardness in crediting an informer, even if his own subordinate and charged among other things with police surveillance of the crew. This feeling would not perhaps have so prevailed with him were it not that upon a prior occasion the patriotic zeal officially evinced by Claggart had somewhat irritated him as appearing rather supersensible and strained. Furthermore, something even in the official's self-possessed and somewhat ostentatious manner in making his specifications strangely reminded him of a bandsman, a perjurous witness in a capital case before a court-martial ashore of which   10 when a lieutenant he (Captain Vere) had been a member.

Now the peremptory check given to Claggart in the matter of the arrested allusion was quickly followed up by this: "You say that there is at least one dangerous man aboard. Name him."

"William Budd, a foretopman, your honor."

"William Budd!" repeated Captain Vere with unfeigned astonishment. "And mean you the man that Lieutenant Ratcliffe took from the merchantman not very long ago, the young fellow who seems to be so popular with the men — Billy, the Handsome Sailor, as they call him?"

"The same, your honor; but for all his youth and good looks, a deep one. Not   20 for nothing does he insinuate himself into the good will of his shipmates, since at the least they will at a pinch say — all hands will — a good word for him, and at all hazards. Did Lieutenant Ratcliffe happen to tell your honor of that adroit fling of Budd's, jumping up in the cutter's bow under the merchantman's stern when he was being taken off? It is even masked by that sort of good-humored air that at heart he resents his impressment. You have but noted his fair cheek. A mantrap may be under the ruddy-tipped daisies."

Now the Handsome Sailor as a signal figure among the crew had naturally enough attracted the captain's attention from the first. Though in general not very demonstrative to his officers, he had congratulated Lieutenant Ratcliffe upon his good for-   30 tune in lighting on such a fine specimen of the *genus homo*, who in the nude might have posed for a statue of young Adam before the Fall. As to Billy's adieu to the ship *Rights-of-Man*, which the boarding lieutenant had indeed reported to him, but, in a deferential way, more as a good story than aught else, Captain Vere, though mistakenly understanding it as a satiric sally, had but thought so much the better of the impressed man for it; as a military sailor, admiring the spirit that could take an arbitrary enlistment so merrily and sensibly. The foretopman's conduct, too, so far as it had fallen under the captain's notice, had confirmed the first happy augury, while the new recruit's qualities as a "sailor-man" seemed to be such that he had thought of recommending him to the executive officer for promotion to a place   40 that would more frequently bring him under his own observation, namely, the captaincy of the mizzentop, replacing there in the starboard watch a man not so young whom partly for that reason he deemed less fitted for the post. Be it parenthesized here that since the mizzentopmen have not to handle such breadths of heavy canvas as the lower sails on the mainmast and foremast, a young man if of the right stuff not only seems best adapted to duty there, but in fact is generally selected for the captaincy of that top, and the company under him are light hands and often but striplings. In sum, Captain Vere had from the beginning deemed Billy Budd to be what in the naval parlance of the time was called a "King's bargain": that is to say, for His Britannic Majesty's navy a capital investment at small outlay or none at all.

After a brief pause, during which the reminiscences above mentioned passed vividly through his mind and he weighed the import of Claggart's last suggestion conveyed in the phrase "mantrap under the daisies," and the more he weighed it the
10 less reliance he felt in the informer's good faith, suddenly he turned upon him and in a low voice demanded: "Do you come to me, Master-at-arms, with so foggy a tale? As to Budd, cite me an act or spoken word of his confirmatory of what you in general charge against him. Stay," drawing nearer to him; "heed what you speak. Just now, and in a case like this, there is a yardarm-end for the false witness."

"Ah, your honor!" sighed Claggart, mildly shaking his shapely head as in sad deprecation of such unmerited severity of tone. Then, bridling — erecting himself as in virtuous self-assertion — he circumstantially alleged certain words and acts which collectively, if credited, led to presumptions mortally inculpating Budd. And for some of these averments, he added, substantiating proof was not far.

20 With gray eyes impatient and distrustful essaying to fathom to the bottom Claggart's calm violet ones, Captain Vere again heard him out; then for the moment stood ruminating. The mood he evinced, Claggart — himself for the time liberated from the other's scrutiny — steadily regarded with a look difficult to render: a look curious of the operation of his tactics, a look such as might have been that of the spokesman of the envious children of Jacob deceptively imposing upon the troubled patriarch the blood-dyed coat of young Joseph.

Though something exceptional in the moral quality of Captain Vere made him, in earnest encounter with a fellow man, a veritable touchstone of that man's essential nature, yet now as to Claggart and what was really going on in him his feeling
30 partook less of intuitional conviction than of strong suspicion clogged by strange dubieties. The perplexity he evinced proceeded less from aught touching the man informed against — as Claggart doubtless opined — than from considerations how best to act in regard to the informer. At first, indeed, he was naturally for summoning that substantiation of his allegations which Claggart said was at hand. But such a proceeding would result in the matter at once getting abroad, which in the present stage of it, he thought, might undesirably affect the ship's company. If Claggart was a false witness — that closed the affair. And therefore, before trying the accusation, he would first practically test the accuser; and he thought this could be done in a quiet, undemonstrative way.

40 The measure he determined upon involved a shifting of the scene, a transfer to a place less exposed to observation than the broad quarter-deck. For although the few gun-room officers there at the time had, in due observance of naval etiquette, with-

25 **Jacob . . . Joseph.** Genesis 37:31-32 describes Joseph's brothers, who after selling Joseph to the Ishmalites, deceived their father Jacob to make him believe that Joseph had been killed

drawn to leeward the moment Captain Vere had begun his promenade on the deck's weather side; and though during the colloquy with Claggart they of course ventured not to diminish the distance; and though throughout the interview Captain Vere's voice was far from high, and Claggart's silvery and low; and the wind in the cordage and the wash of the sea helped the more to put them beyond earshot; nevertheless, the interview's continuance already had attracted observation from some topmen aloft and other sailors in the waist or further forward.

Having determined upon his measures, Captain Vere forthwith took action. Abruptly turning to Claggart, he asked, "Master-at-arms, is it now Budd's watch aloft?"

"No, your honor."   10

Whereupon, "Mr. Wilkes!" summoning the nearest midshipman. "Tell Albert to come to me." Albert was the captain's hammock-boy, a sort of sea valet in whose discretion and fidelity his master had much confidence. The lad appeared.

"You know Budd, the foretopman?"

"I do, sir."

"Go find him. It is his watch off. Manage to tell him out of earshot that he is wanted aft. Contrive it that he speaks to nobody. Keep him in talk yourself. And not till you get well aft here, not till then let him know that the place where he is wanted is my cabin. You understand. Go. — Master-at-arms, show yourself on the decks below, and when you think it time for Albert to be coming with his man, 20 stand by quietly to follow the sailor in."

19

Now when the foretopman found himself in the cabin, closeted there, as it were, with the captain and Claggart, he was surprised enough. But it was a surprise unaccompanied by apprehension or distrust. To an immature nature essentially honest and humane, forewarning intimations of subtler danger from one's kind come tardily if at all. The only thing that took shape in the young sailor's mind was this: Yes, the captain, I have always thought, looks kindly upon me. Wonder if he's going to make me his coxswain. I should like that. And may be now he is going to ask the master-at-arms about me.

"Shut the door there, sentry," said the commander; "stand without, and let no- 30 body come in. — Now, Master-at-arms, tell this man to his face what you told of him to me," and stood prepared to scrutinize the mutually confronting visages.

With the measured step and calm collected air of an asylum physician approaching in the public hall some patient beginning to show indications of a coming paroxysm, Claggart deliberately advanced within short range of Billy and, mesmerically looking him in the eye, briefly recapitulated the accusation.

Not at first did Billy take it in. When he did, the rose-tan of his cheek looked struck as by white leprosy. He stood like one impaled and gagged. Meanwhile the accuser's eyes, removing not as yet from the blue dilated ones, underwent a phenomenal change, their wonted rich violet color blurring into a muddy purple. Those 40 lights of human intelligence, losing human expression, were gelidly protruding like the alien eyes of certain uncatalogued creatures of the deep. The first mesmeristic glance was one of serpent fascination; the last was as the paralyzing lurch of the torpedo fish.

"Speak, man!" said Captain Vere to the transfixed one, struck by his aspect even more than by Claggart's. "Speak! Defend yourself!" Which appeal caused but a strange dumb gesturing and gurgling in Billy; amazement at such an accusation so suddenly sprung on inexperienced nonage; this, and, it may be, horror of the accuser's eyes, serving to bring out his lurking defect and in this instance for the time intensifying it into a convulsed tongue-tie; while the intent head and entire form straining forward in an agony of ineffectual eagerness to obey the injunction to speak
10 and defend himself, gave an expression to the face like that of a condemned vestal priestess in the moment of being buried alive, and in the first struggle against suffocation.

Though at the time Captain Vere was quite ignorant of Billy's liability to vocal impediment, he now immediately divined it, since vividly Billy's aspect recalled to him that of a bright young schoolmate of his whom he had once seen struck by much the same startling impotence in the act of eagerly rising in the class to be foremost in response to a testing question put to it by the master. Going close up to the young sailor, and laying a soothing hand on his shoulder, he said, "There is no hurry, my boy. Take your time, take your time." Contrary to the effect intended,
20 these words so fatherly in tone, doubtless touching Billy's heart to the quick, prompted yet more violent efforts at utterance — efforts soon ending for the time in confirming the paralysis, and bringing to his face an expression which was as a crucifixion to behold. The next instant, quick as the flame from a discharged cannon at night, his right arm shot out, and Claggart dropped to the deck. Whether intentionally or but owing to the young athlete's superior height, the blow had taken effect full upon the forehead, so shapely and intellectual-looking a feature in the master-at-arms; so that the body fell over lengthwise, like a heavy plank tilted from erectness. A gasp or two, and he lay motionless.

"Fated boy," breathed Captain Vere in tone so low as to be almost a whisper,
30 "what have you done! But here, help me."

The twain raised the felled one from the loins up into a sitting position. The spare form flexibly acquiesced, but inertly. It was like handling a dead snake. They lowered it back. Regaining erectness, Captain Vere with one hand covering his face stood to all appearance as impassive as the object at his feet. Was he absorbed in taking in all the bearings of the event and what was best not only now at once to be done, but also in the sequel? Slowly he uncovered his face; and the effect was as if the moon emerging from eclipse should reappear with quite another aspect than that which had gone into hiding. The father in him, manifested towards Billy thus far in the scene, was replaced by the military disciplinarian. In his official tone he
40 bade the foretopman retire to a stateroom aft (pointing it out), and there remain till thence summoned. This order Billy in silence mechanically obeyed. Then going to the cabin door where it opened on the quarter-deck, Captain Vere said to the sentry without, "Tell somebody to send Albert here." When the lad appeared, his

---

2 **torpedo fish,** an electric fish that shocks its prey

master so contrived it that he should not catch sight of the prone one. "Albert," he said to him, "tell the surgeon I wish to see him. You need not come back till called."

When the surgeon entered — a self-poised character of that grave sense and experience that hardly anything could take him aback — Captain Vere advanced to meet him, thus unconsciously intercepting his view of Claggart, and, interrupting the other's wonted ceremonious salutation, said, "Nay. Tell me how it is with yonder man," directing his attention to the prostrate one.

The surgeon looked, and for all his self-command somewhat started at the abrupt revelation. On Claggart's always pallid complexion, thick black blood was now oozing from nostril and ear. To the gazer's professional eye it was unmistakably no 10 living man that he saw.

"Is it so, then?" said Captain Vere, intently watching him. "I thought it. But verify it." Whereupon the customary tests confirmed the surgeon's first glance, who now, looking up in unfeigned concern, cast a look of intense inquisitiveness upon his superior. But Captain Vere, with one hand to his brow, was standing motionless. Suddenly, catching the surgeon's arm convulsively, he exclaimed, pointing down to the body, "It is the divine judgment on Ananias! Look!"

Disturbed by the excited manner he had never before observed in the *Bellipotent's* captain, and as yet wholly ignorant of the affair, the prudent surgeon nevertheless held his peace, only again looking an earnest interrogatory as to what it was that 20 had resulted in such a tragedy.

But Captain Vere was now again motionless, standing absorbed in thought. Again starting, he vehemently exclaimed, "Struck dead by an angel of God! Yet the angel must hang!"

At these passionate interjections, mere incoherences to the listener as yet unapprised of the antecedents, the surgeon was profoundly discomposed. But now, as recollecting himself, Captain Vere in less passionate tone briefly related the circumstances leading up to the event. "But come; we must dispatch," he added. "Help me to remove him" (meaning the body) "to yonder compartment," designating one opposite that where the foretopman remained immured. Anew disturbed by a 30 request that, as implying a desire for secrecy, seemed unaccountably strange to him, there was nothing for the subordinate to do but comply.

"Go now," said Captain Vere with something of his wonted manner. "Go now. I presently shall call a drumhead court. Tell the lieutenants what has happened, and tell Mr. Mordant" (meaning the captain of marines), "and charge them to keep the matter to themselves."

20

Full of disquietude and misgiving, the surgeon left the cabin. Was Captain Vere suddenly affected in his mind, or was it but a transient excitement, brought about by so strange and extraordinary a tragedy? As to the drumhead court, it struck the

---

17 **the divine judgment on Ananias.** See Acts 5:3-5; when Peter told Ananias that he had lied to God, Ananias fell down and died   34 **drumhead court,** an immediate court-martial held in the field during war

surgeon as impolitic, if nothing more. The thing to do, he thought, was to place Billy Budd in confinement, and in a way dictated by usage, and postpone further action in so extraordinary a case to such time as they should rejoin the squadron, and then refer it to the admiral. He recalled the unwonted agitation of Captain Vere and his excited exclamations, so at variance with his normal manner. Was he unhinged?

But assuming that he is, it is not so susceptible of proof. What then can the surgeon do? No more trying situation is conceivable than that of an officer subordinate under a captain whom he suspects to be not mad, indeed, but yet not quite unaf-
10 fected in his intellects. To argue his order to him would be insolence. To resist him would be mutiny.

In obedience to Captain Vere, he communicated what had happened to the lieutenants and captain of marines, saying nothing as to the captain's state. They fully shared his own surprise and concern. Like him too, they seemed to think that such a matter should be referred to the admiral.

21

Who in the rainbow can draw the line where the violet tint ends and the orange tint begins? Distinctly we see the difference of the colors, but where exactly does the one first blendingly enter into the other? So with sanity and insanity. In pronounced cases there is no question about them. But in some supposed cases, in vari-
20 ous degrees supposedly less pronounced, to draw the exact line of demarcation few will undertake, though for a fee becoming considerate some professional experts will. There is nothing namable but that some men will, or undertake to, do it for pay.

Whether Captain Vere, as the surgeon professionally and privately surmised, was really the sudden victim of any degree of aberration, every one must determine for himself by such light as this narrative may afford.

That the unhappy event which has been narrated could not have happened at a worse juncture was but too true. For it was close on the heel of the suppressed insurrections, an aftertime very critical to naval authority, demanding from every
30 English sea commander two qualities not readily interfusable — prudence and rigor. Moreover, there was something crucial in the case.

In the jugglery of circumstances preceding and attending the event on board the *Bellipotent,* and in the light of that martial code whereby it was formally to be judged, innocence and guilt personified in Claggart and Budd in effect changed places. In a legal view the apparent victim of the tragedy was he who had sought to victimize a man blameless; and the indisputable deed of the latter, navally regarded, constituted the most heinous of military crimes. Yet more. The essential right and wrong involved in the matter, the clearer that might be, so much the worse for the responsibility of a loyal sea commander, inasmuch as he was not
40 authorized to determine the matter on that primitive basis.

Small wonder then that the *Bellipotent's* captain, though in general a man of rapid decision, felt that circumspectness not less than promptitude was necessary. Until he could decide upon his course, and in each detail; and not only so, but until the concluding measure was upon the point of being enacted, he deemed it advisable, in view of all the circumstances, to guard as much as possible against publicity. Here he may or may not have erred. Certain it is, however, that subsequently in the confidential talk of more than one or two gun rooms and cabins he was not a little criticized by some officers, a fact imputed by his friends and vehemently by his cousin Jack Denton to professional jealousy of Starry Vere. Some imaginative ground for invidious comment there was. The maintenance of secrecy in the matter, the confining all knowledge of it for a time to the place where the homicide occurred,   10 the quarter-deck cabin; in these particulars lurked some resemblance to the policy adopted in those tragedies of the palace which have occurred more than once in the capital founded by Peter the Barbarian.

The case indeed was such that fain would the *Bellipotent*'s captain have deferred taking any action whatever respecting it further than to keep the foretopman a close prisoner till the ship rejoined the squadron and then submitting the matter to the judgment of his admiral.

But a true military officer is in one particular like a true monk. Not with more of self-abnegation will the latter keep his vows of monastic obedience than the former his vows of allegiance to martial duty.   20

Feeling that unless quick action was taken on it, the deed of the foretopman, so soon as it should be known on the gun decks, would tend to awaken any slumbering embers of the Nore among the crew, a sense of the urgency of the case overruled in Captain Vere every other consideration. But though a conscientious disciplinarian, he was no lover of authority for mere authority's sake. Very far was he from embracing opportunities for monopolizing to himself the perils of moral responsibility, none at least that could properly be referred to an official superior or shared with him by his official equals or even subordinates. So thinking, he was glad it would not be at variance with usage to turn the matter over to a summary court of his own officers, reserving to himself, as the one on whom the ultimate   30 accountability would rest, the right of maintaining a supervision of it, or formally or informally interposing at need. Accordingly a drumhead court was summarily convened, he electing the individuals composing it: the first lieutenant, the captain of marines, and the sailing master.

In associating an officer of marines with the sea lieutenant and the sailing master in a case having to do with a sailor, the commander perhaps deviated from general custom. He was prompted thereto by the circumstance that he took that soldier to be a judicious person, thoughtful, and not altogether incapable of grappling with a difficult case unprecedented in his prior experience. Yet even as to him he was not without some latent misgiving, for withal he was an extremely good-natured man,   40 an enjoyer of his dinner, a sound sleeper, and inclined to obesity — a man who though he would always maintain his manhood in battle might not prove altogether reliable in a moral dilemma involving aught of the tragic. As to the first lieutenant

---

13 **Peter the Barbarian,** Peter the Great of Russia (1672-1725)

and the sailing master, Captain Vere could not but be aware that though honest natures, of approved gallantry upon occasion, their intelligence was mostly confined to the matter of active seamanship and the fighting demands of their profession.

The court was held in the same cabin where the unfortunate affair had taken place. This cabin, the commander's, embraced the entire area under the poop deck. Aft, and on either side, was a small stateroom, the one now temporarily a jail and the other a dead-house, and a yet smaller compartment, leaving a space between expanding forward into a goodly oblong of length coinciding with the ship's beam. A skylight of moderate dimension was overhead, and at each end of the oblong space were two sashed porthole windows easily convertible back into embrasures for short carronades.

All being quickly in readiness, Billy Budd was arraigned, Captain Vere necessarily appearing as the sole witness in the case, and as such temporarily sinking his rank, though singularly maintaining it in a matter apparently trivial, namely, that he testified from the ship's weather side, with that object having caused the court to sit on the lee side. Concisely he narrated all that had led up to the catastrophe, omitting nothing in Claggart's accusation and deposing as to the manner in which the prisoner had received it. At this testimony the three officers glanced with no little surprise at Billy Budd, the last man they would have suspected either of the mutinous design alleged by Claggart or the undeniable deed he himself had done. The first lieutenant, taking judicial primacy and turning toward the prisoner, said, "Captain Vere has spoken. Is it or is it not as Captain Vere says?"

In response came syllables not so much impeded in the utterance as might have been anticipated. They were these: "Captain Vere tells the truth. It is just as Captain Vere says, but it is not as the master-at-arms said. I have eaten the King's bread and I am true to the King."

"I believe you, my man," said the witness, his voice indicating a suppressed emotion not otherwise betrayed.

"God will bless you for that, your honor!" not without stammering said Billy, and all but broke down. But immediately he was recalled to self-control by another question, to which with the same emotional difficulty of utterance he said, "No, there was no malice between us. I never bore malice against the master-at-arms. I am sorry that he is dead. I did not mean to kill him. Could I have used my tongue I would not have struck him. But he foully lied to my face and in presence of my captain, and I had to say something, and I could only say it with a blow, God help me!"

In the impulsive aboveboard manner of the frank one the court saw confirmed all that was implied in words that just previously had perplexed them, coming as they did from the testifier to the tragedy and promptly following Billy's impassioned disclaimer of mutinous intent — Captain Vere's words, "I believe you, my man."

Next it was asked of him whether he knew of or suspected aught savoring of incipient trouble (meaning mutiny, though the explicit term was avoided) going on in any section of the ship's company.

The reply lingered. This was naturally imputed by the court to the same vocal embarrassment which had retarded or obstructed previous answers. But in main it was otherwise here, the question immediately recalling to Billy's mind the interview with the afterguardsman in the forechains. But an innate repugnance to playing a part at all approaching that of an informer against one's own shipmates — the same erring sense of uninstructed honor which had stood in the way of his reporting the matter at the time, though as a loyal man-of-war's man it was incumbent on him, and failure so to do, if charged against him and proven, would have subjected him to the heaviest of penalties; this, with the blind feeling now his that nothing really was being hatched, prevailed with him. When the answer came it was a negative.

"One question more," said the officer of marines, now first speaking and with a   10
troubled earnestness. "You tell us that what the master-at-arms said against you was a lie. Now why should he have so lied, so maliciously lied, since you declare there was no malice between you?"

At that question, unintentionally touching on a spiritual sphere wholly obscure to Billy's thoughts, he was nonplussed, evincing a confusion indeed that some observers, such as can readily be imagined, would have construed into involuntary evidence of hidden guilt. Nevertheless, he strove some way to answer, but all at once relinquished the vain endeavor, at the same time turning an appealing glance towards Captain Vere as deeming him his best helper and friend. Captain Vere, who had been seated for a time, rose to his feet, addressing the interrogator. "The question   20
you put to him comes naturally enough. But how can he rightly answer it? — or anybody else, unless indeed it be he who lies within there," designating the compartment where lay the corpse. "But the prone one there will not rise to our summons. In effect, though, as it seems to me, the point you make is hardly material. Quite aside from any conceivable motive actuating the master-at-arms, and irrespective of the provocation to the blow, a martial court must needs in the present case confine its attention to the blow's consequence, which consequence justly is to be deemed not otherwise than as the striker's deed."

This utterance, the full significance of which it was not at all likely that Billy took in, nevertheless caused him to turn a wistful interrogative look toward the   30
speaker, a look in its dumb expressiveness not unlike that which a dog of generous breed might turn upon his master, seeking in his face some elucidation of a previous gesture ambiguous to the canine intelligence. Nor was the same utterance without marked effect upon the three officers, more especially the soldier. Couched in it seemed to them a meaning unanticipated, involving a prejudgment on the speaker's part. It served to augment a mental disturbance previously evident enough.

The soldier once more spoke, in a tone of suggestive dubiety addressing at once his associates and Captain Vere: "Nobody is present — none of the ship's company, I mean — who might shed lateral light, if any is to be had, upon what remains mysterious in this matter."   40

"That is thoughtfully put," said Captain Vere; "I see your drift. Ay, there is a mystery; but, to use a scriptural phrase, it is a 'mystery of iniquity,' a matter for psychologic theologians to discuss. But what has a military court to do with it? Not to add that for us any possible investigation of it is cut off by the lasting tongue-tie of — him — in yonder," again designating the mortuary stateroom. "The prisoner's deed — with that alone we have to do."

To this, and particularly the closing reiteration, the marine soldier, knowing not how aptly to reply, sadly abstained from saying aught. The first lieutenant, who at the outset had not unnaturally assumed primacy in the court, now overrulingly instructed by a glance from Captain Vere, a glance more effective than words, resumed that primacy. Turning to the prisoner, "Budd," he said, and scarce in equable tones, "Budd, if you have aught further to say for yourself, say it now."

Upon this the young sailor turned another quick glance toward Captain Vere;
10 then, as taking a hint from that aspect, a hint confirming his own instinct that silence was now best, replied to the lieutenant, "I have said all, sir."

The marine — the same who had been the sentinel without the cabin door at the time that the foretopman, followed by the master-at-arms, entered it — he, standing by the sailor throughout these judicial proceedings, was now directed to take him back to the after compartment originally assigned to the prisoner and his custodian. As the twain disappeared from view, the three officers, as partially liberated from some inward constraint associated with Billy's mere presence, simultaneously stirred in their seats. They exchanged looks of troubled indecision, yet feeling that decide they must and without long delay. For Captain Vere, he for the time stood — un-
20 consciously with his back toward them, apparently in one of his absent fits — gazing out from a sashed porthole to windward upon the monotonous blank of the twilight sea. But the court's silence continuing, broken only at moments by brief consultations, in low earnest tones, this served to arouse him and energize him. Turning, he to-and-fro paced the cabin athwart; in the returning ascent to windward climbing the slant deck in the ship's lee roll, without knowing it symbolizing thus in his action a mind resolute to surmount difficulties even if against primitive instincts strong as the wind and the sea. Presently he came to a stand before the three. After scanning their faces he stood less as mustering his thoughts for expression than as one inly deliberating how best to put them to well-meaning men not intellectually
30 mature, men with whom it was necessary to demonstrate certain principles that were axioms to himself. Similar impatience as to talking is perhaps one reason that deters some minds from addressing any popular assemblies.

When speak he did, something, both in the substance of what he said and his manner of saying it, showed the influence of unshared studies modifying and tempering the practical training of an active career. This, along with his phraseology, now and then was suggestive of the grounds whereon rested that imputation of a certain pedantry socially alleged against him by certain naval men of wholly practical cast, captains who nevertheless would frankly concede that His Majesty's navy mustered no more efficient officer of their grade than Starry Vere.

40 What he said was to this effect: "Hitherto I have been but the witness, little more; and I should hardly think now to take another tone, that of your coadjutor for the time, did I not perceive in you — at the crisis too — a troubled hesitancy, proceeding, I doubt not, from the clash of military duty with moral scruple — scruple vitalized by compassion. For the compassion, how can I otherwise than share

it? But, mindful of paramount obligations, I strive against scruples that may tend to enervate decision. Not, gentlemen, that I hide from myself that the case is an exceptional one. Speculatively regarded, it well might be referred to a jury of casuists. But for us here, acting not as casuists or moralists, it is a case practical, and under martial law practically to be dealt with.

"But your scruples: do they move as in a dusk? Challenge them. Make them advance and declare themselves. Come now; do they import something like this: If, mindless of palliating circumstances, we are bound to regard the death of the master-at-arms as the prisoner's deed, then does that deed constitute a capital crime whereof the penalty is a mortal one. But in natural justice is nothing but the 10 prisoner's overt act to be considered? How can we adjudge to summary and shameful death a fellow creature innocent before God, and whom we feel to be so? — Does that state it aright? You sign sad assent. Well, I too feel that, the full force of that. It is Nature. But do these buttons that we wear attest that our allegiance is to Nature? No, to the King. Though the ocean, which is inviolate Nature primeval, though this be the element where we move and have our being as sailors, yet as the King's officers lies our duty in a sphere correspondingly natural? So little is that true, that in receiving our commissions we in the most important regards ceased to be natural free agents. When war is declared are we the commissioned fighters previously consulted? We fight at command. If our judgments approve the 20 war, that is but coincidence. So in other particulars. So now. For suppose condemnation to follow these present proceedings. Would it be so much we ourselves that would condemn as it would be martial law operating through us? For that law and the rigor of it, we are not responsible. Our vowed responsibility is in this: That however pitilessly that law may operate in any instances, we nevertheless adhere to it and administer it.

"But the exceptional in the matter moves the hearts within you. Even so too is mine moved. But let not warm hearts betray heads that should be cool. Ashore in a criminal case, will an upright judge allow himself off the bench to be waylaid by some tender kinswoman of the accused seeking to touch him with her tearful plea? 30 Well, the heart here, sometimes the feminine in man, is as that piteous woman, and hard though it be, she must here be ruled out."

He paused, earnestly studying them for a moment; then resumed.

"But something in your aspect seems to urge that it is not solely the heart that moves in you, but also the conscience, the private conscience. But tell me whether or not, occupying the position we do, private conscience should not yield to that imperial one formulated in the code under which alone we officially proceed?"

Here the three men moved in their seats, less convinced than agitated by the course of an argument troubling but the more the spontaneous conflict within.

Perceiving which, the speaker paused for a moment; then abruptly changing his 40 tone, went on.

"To steady us a bit, let us recur to the facts. — In wartime at sea a man-of-war's man strikes his superior in grade, and the blow kills. Apart from its effect the blow itself is, according to the Articles of War, a capital crime. Furthermore——"

"Ay, sir," emotionally broke in the officer of marines, "in one sense it was. But surely Budd purposed neither mutiny nor homicide."

"Surely not, my good man. And before a court less arbitrary and more merciful than a martial one, that plea would largely extenuate. At the Last Assizes it shall acquit. But how here? We proceed under the law of the Mutiny Act. In feature no child can resemble his father more than that Act resembles in spirit the thing from which it derives — War. In His Majesty's service — in this ship, indeed — there are Englishmen forced to fight for the King against their will. Against their conscience, for aught we know. Though as their fellow creatures some of us may appreciate
10   their position, yet as navy officers what reck we of it? Still less recks the enemy. Our impressed men he would fain cut down in the same swath with our volunteers. As regards the enemy's naval conscripts, some of whom may even share our own abhorrence of the regicidal French Directory, it is the same on our side. War looks but to the frontage, the appearance. And the Mutiny Act, War's child, takes after the father. Budd's intent or non-intent is nothing to the purpose.

"But while, put to it by those anxieties in you which I cannot but respect, I only repeat myself — while thus strangely we prolong proceedings that should be summary — the enemy may be sighted and an engagement result. We must do; and one of two things must we do — condemn or let go."
20   "Can we not convict and yet mitigate the penalty?" asked the sailing master, here speaking, and falteringly, for the first.

"Gentlemen, were that clearly lawful for us under the circumstances, consider the consequences of such clemency. The people" (meaning the ship's company) "have native sense; most of them are familiar with our naval usage and tradition; and how would they take it? Even could you explain to them — which our official position forbids — they, long molded by arbitrary discipline, have not that kind of intelligent responsiveness that might qualify them to comprehend and discriminate. No, to the people the foretopman's deed, however it be worded in the announcement, will be plain homicide committed in a flagrant act of mutiny. What penalty
30   for that should follow, they know. But it does not follow. *Why?* they will ruminate. You know what sailors are. Will they not revert to the recent outbreak at the Nore? Ay. They know the well-founded alarm — the panic it struck throughout England. Your clement sentence they would account pusillanimous. They would think that we flinch, that we are afraid of them — afraid of practicing a lawful rigor singularly demanded at this juncture, lest it should provoke new troubles. What shame to us such a conjecture on their part, and how deadly to discipline. You see then, whither, prompted by duty and the law, I steadfastly drive. But I beseech you, my friends, do not take me amiss. I feel as you do for this unfortunate boy. But did he know our hearts, I take him to be of that generous nature that he would feel even for us
40   on whom in this military necessity so heavy a compulsion is laid."

With that, crossing the deck he resumed his place by the sashed porthole, tacitly leaving the three to come to a decision. On the cabin's opposite side the troubled court sat silent. Loyal lieges, plain and practical, though at bottom they dissented from some points Captain Vere had put to them, they were without the faculty, hardly had the inclination, to gainsay one whom they felt to be an earnest man, one too not less their superior in mind than in naval rank. But it is not improbable that even such of his words as were not without influence over them, less came home to them than his closing appeal to their instinct as sea officers: in the fore-thought he threw out as to the practical consequences to discipline, considering the unconfirmed tone of the fleet at the time, should a man-of-war's man's violent kill-ing at sea of a superior in grade be allowed to pass for aught else than a capital crime demanding prompt infliction of the penalty.

Not unlikely they were brought to something more or less akin to that harassed frame of mind which in the year 1842 actuated the commander of the U.S. brig-of- 10 war *Somers* to resolve, under the so-called Articles of War, Articles modeled upon the English Mutiny Act, to resolve upon the execution at sea of a midshipman and two sailors as mutineers designing the seizure of the brig. Which resolution was carried out though in a time of peace and within not many days' sail of home. An act vindicated by a naval court of inquiry subsequently convened ashore. History, and here cited without comment. True, the circumstances on board the *Somers* were different from those on board the *Bellipotent*. But the urgency felt, well-warranted or otherwise, was much the same.

Says a writer whom few know, "Forty years after a battle it is easy for a noncom-batant to reason about how it ought to have been fought. It is another thing per- 20 sonally and under fire to have to direct the fighting while involved in the obscuring smoke of it. Much so with respect to other emergencies involving considerations both practical and moral, and when it is imperative promptly to act. The greater the fog the more it imperils the steamer, and speed is put on though at the hazard of running somebody down. Little ween the snug card players in the cabin of the responsibilities of the sleepless man on the bridge."

In brief, Billy Budd was formally convicted and sentenced to be hung at the yard-arm in the early morning watch, it being now night. Otherwise, as is customary in such cases, the sentence would forthwith have been carried out. In wartime on the field or in the fleet, a mortal punishment decreed by a drumhead court — on the 30 field sometimes decreed by but a nod from the general — follows without delay on the heel of conviction, without appeal.

22

It was Captain Vere himself who of his own motion communicated the finding of the court to the prisoner, for that purpose going to the compartment where he was in custody and bidding the marine there to withdraw for the time.

Beyond the communication of the sentence, what took place at this interview was never known. But in view of the character of the twain briefly closeted in that state-room, each radically sharing in the rarer qualities of our nature — so rare indeed as

---

11 **Somers.** In 1842, a young midshipman, a boatswain's mate, and a common seaman were hanged for mutiny on board the *Somers*. Melville's cousin, Guert Gansevoort, presided over the drumhead court that convicted the men. The harsh sentences became a subject of great controversy   19 **a writer whom few know,** apparently Melville himself

to be all but incredible to average minds however much cultivated — some conjectures may be ventured.

It would have been in consonance with the spirit of Captain Vere should he on this occasion have concealed nothing from the condemned one — should he indeed have frankly disclosed to him the part he himself had played in bringing about the decision, at the same time revealing his actuating motives. On Billy's side it is not improbable that such a confession would have been received in much the same spirit that prompted it. Not without a sort of joy, indeed, he might have appreciated the brave opinion of him implied in his captain's making such a confidant of him. Nor, as to the sentence itself, could he have been insensible that it was imparted to him as to one not afraid to die. Even more may have been. Captain Vere in end may have developed the passion sometimes latent under an exterior stoical or indifferent. He was old enough to have been Billy's father. The austere devotee of military duty, letting himself melt back into what remains primeval in our formalized humanity, may in end have caught Billy to his heart, even as Abraham may have caught young Isaac on the brink of resolutely offering him up in obedience to the exacting behest. But there is no telling the sacrament, seldom if in any case revealed to the gadding world, wherever under circumstances at all akin to those here attempted to be set forth two of great Nature's nobler order embrace. There is privacy at the time, inviolable to the survivor; and holy oblivion, the sequel to each diviner magnanimity, providentially covers all at last.

The first to encounter Captain Vere in act of leaving the compartment was the senior lieutenant. The face he beheld, for the moment one expressive of the agony of the strong, was to that officer, though a man of fifty, a startling revelation. That the condemned one suffered less than he who mainly had effected the condemnation was apparently indicated by the former's exclamation in the scene soon perforce to be touched upon.

23

Of a series of incidents within a brief term rapidly following each other, the adequate narration may take up a term less brief, especially if explanation or comment here and there seem requisite to the better understanding of such incidents. Between the entrance into the cabin of him who never left it alive, and him who when he did leave it left it as one condemned to die; between this and the closeted interview just given, less than an hour and a half had elapsed. It was an interval long enough, however, to awaken speculations among no few of the ship's company as to what it was that could be detaining in the cabin the master-at-arms and the sailor; for a rumor that both of them had been seen to enter it and neither of them had been seen to emerge, this rumor had got abroad upon the gun decks and in the tops, the people of a great warship being in one respect like villagers, taking microscopic note of every outward movement or non-movement going on. When therefore, in

15 **Abraham . . . behest.** See Genesis 22:1-18. God as a test commanded Abraham to offer his son Isaac up in sacrifice, and then as Abraham prepared to obey, withdrew the command

weather not at all tempestuous, all hands were called in the second dogwatch, a summons under such circumstances not usual in those hours, the crew were not wholly unprepared for some announcement extraordinary, one having connection too with the continued absence of the two men from their wonted haunts.

There was a moderate sea at the time; and the moon, newly risen and near to being at its full, silvered the white spar deck wherever not blotted by the clear-cut shadows horizontally thrown of fixtures and moving men. On either side the quarter-deck the marine guard under arms was drawn up; and Captain Vere, standing in his place surrounded by all the wardroom officers, addressed his men. In so doing, his manner showed neither more nor less than that properly pertaining to his su- 10 preme position aboard his own ship. In clear terms and concise he told them what had taken place in the cabin: that the master-at-arms was dead, that he who had killed him had been already tried by a summary court and condemned to death, and that the execution would take place in the early morning watch. The word *mutiny* was not named in what he said. He refrained too from making the occasion an opportunity for any preachment as to the maintenance of discipline, thinking perhaps that under existing circumstances in the navy the consequence of violating discipline should be made to speak for itself.

Their captain's announcement was listened to by the throng of standing sailors in a dumbness like that of a seated congregation of believers in hell listening to the 20 clergyman's announcement of his Calvinistic text.

At the close, however, a confused murmur went up. It began to wax. All but instantly, then, at a sign, it was pierced and suppressed by shrill whistles of the boatswain and his mates. The word was given to about ship.

To be prepared for burial Claggart's body was delivered to certain petty officers of his mess. And here, not to clog the sequel with lateral matters, it may be added that at a suitable hour, the master-at-arms was committed to the sea with every funeral honor properly belonging to his naval grade.

In this proceeding as in every public one growing out of the tragedy strict adherence to usage was observed. Nor in any point could it have been at all deviated 30 from, either with respect to Claggart or Billy Budd, without begetting undesirable speculations in the ship's company, sailors, and more particularly men-of-war's men, being of all men the greatest sticklers for usage. For similar cause, all communication between Captain Vere and the condemned one ended with the closeted interview already given, the latter being now surrendered to the ordinary routine preliminary to the end. His transfer under guard from the captain's quarters was effected without unusual precautions — at least no visible ones. If possible, not to let the men so much as surmise that their officers anticipate aught amiss from them is the tacit rule in a military ship. And the more that some sort of trouble should really be apprehended, the more do the officers keep that apprehension to themselves, though 40 not the less unostentatious vigilance may be augmented. In the present instance, the sentry placed over the prisoner had strict orders to let no one have communication with him but the chaplain. And certain unobtrusive measures were taken absolutely to insure this point.

24

In a seventy-four of the old order the deck known as the upper gun deck was the one covered over by the spar deck, which last, though not without its armament, was for the most part exposed to the weather. In general it was at all hours free from hammocks; those of the crew swinging on the lower gun deck and berth deck, the latter being not only a dormitory but also the place for the stowing of the sailors' bags, and on both sides lined with the large chests or movable pantries of the many messes of the men.

On the starboard side of the *Bellipotent's* upper gun deck, behold Billy Budd under sentry lying prone in irons in one of the bays formed by the regular spacing of
10 the guns comprising the batteries on either side. All these pieces were of the heavier caliber of that period. Mounted on lumbering wooden carriages, they were hampered with cumbersome harness of breeching and strong side-tackles for running them out. Guns and carriages, together with the long rammers and shorter linstocks lodged in loops overhead — all these, as customary, were painted black; and the heavy hempen breechings, tarred to the same tint, wore the like livery of the undertakers. In contrast with the funereal hue of these surroundings, the prone sailor's exterior apparel, white jumper and white duck trousers, each more or less soiled, dimly glimmered in the obscure light of the bay like a patch of discolored snow in early April lingering at some upland cave's black mouth. In effect he is already in
20 his shroud, or the garments that shall serve him in lieu of one. Over him but scarce illuminating him, two battle lanterns swing from two massive beams of the deck above. Fed with the oil supplied by the war contractors (whose gains, honest or otherwise, are in every land an anticipated portion of the harvest of death), with flickering splashes of dirty yellow light they pollute the pale moonshine all but ineffectually struggling in obstructed flecks through the open ports from which the tampioned cannon protrude. Other lanterns at intervals serve but to bring out somewhat the obscurer bays which, like small confessionals or side-chapels in a cathedral, branch from the long dim-vistaed broad aisle between the two batteries of that covered tier.
30 Such was the deck where now lay the Handsome Sailor. Through the rose-tan of his complexion no pallor could have shown. It would have taken days of sequestration from the winds and the sun to have brought about the effacement of that. But the skeleton in the cheekbone at the point of its angle was just beginning delicately to be defined under the warm-tinted skin. In fervid hearts self-contained, some brief experiences devour our human tissue as secret fire in a ship's hold consumes cotton in the bale.

But now lying between the two guns, as nipped in the vice of fate, Billy's agony, mainly proceeding from a generous young heart's virgin experience of the diabolical incarnate and effective in some men — the tension of that agony was over now. It
40 survived not the something healing in the closeted interview with Captain Vere. Without movement, he lay as in a trance, that adolescent expression previously

noted as his taking on something akin to the look of a slumbering child in the
cradle when the warm hearth-glow of the still chamber at night plays on the dimples that at whiles mysteriously form in the cheek, silently coming and going there.
For now and then in the gyved one's trance a serene happy light born of some wandering reminiscence or dream would diffuse itself over his face, and then wane away
only anew to return.

The chaplain, coming to see him and finding him thus, and perceiving no sign
that he was conscious of his presence, attentively regarded him for a space, then
slipping aside, withdrew for the time, peradventure feeling that even he, the minister of Christ though receiving his stipend from Mars, had no consolation to   10
proffer which could result in a peace transcending that which he beheld. But in the
small hours he came again. And the prisoner, now awake to his surroundings,
noticed his approach, and civilly, all but cheerfully, welcomed him. But it was to
little purpose that in the interview following, the good man sought to bring Billy
Budd to some godly understanding that he must die, and at dawn. True, Billy himself freely referred to his death as a thing close at hand; but it was something in
the way that children will refer to death in general, who yet among their other
sports will play a funeral with hearse and mourners.

Not that like children Billy was incapable of conceiving what death really is. No,
but he was wholly without irrational fear of it, a fear more prevalent in highly   20
civilized communities than those so-called barbarous ones which in all respects
stand nearer to unadulterate Nature. And, as elsewhere said, a barbarian Billy radically
was — as much so, for all the costume, as his countrymen the British captives, living trophies, made to march in the Roman triumph of Germanicus. Quite as much
so as those later barbarians, young men probably, and picked specimens among the
earlier British converts to Christianity, at least nominally such, taken to Rome (as
today converts from lesser isles of the sea may be taken to London), of whom the
Pope of that time, admiring the strangeness of their personal beauty so unlike the
Italian stamp, their clear ruddy complexion and curled flaxen locks, exclaimed,
"Angles," (meaning *English,* the modern derivative), "Angles, do you call them?   30
And is it because they look so like angels?" Had it been later in time, one would
think that the Pope had in mind Fra Angelico's seraphs, some of whom, plucking
apples in gardens of the Hesperides, have the faint rosebud complexion of the more
beautiful English girls.

If in vain the good chaplain sought to impress the young barbarian with ideas of
death akin to those conveyed in the skull, dial, and crossbones on old tombstones,
equally futile to all appearance were his efforts to bring home to him the thought
of salvation and a Savior. Billy listened, but less out of awe or reverence, perhaps,
than from a certain natural politeness, doubtless at bottom regarding all that in
much the same way that most mariners of his class take any discourse abstract or   40

---

24 **Germanicus,** Roman general (15 B.C.-19 A.D.), nephew of the Emperor Tiberius, famous for his campaign against the Germans; received a triumph in Rome, 17 A.D.   28 **Pope of that time,** Gregory I
whose pontificate was 590 to 604   32 **Fra Angelico's seraphs.** Giovanni da Fiesole, Fra Angelico (1387-
1455), Italian Renaissance painter   33 **Hesperides,** fabled gardens at the western extremity of the world,
where golden apples grew

out of the common tone of the workaday world. And this sailor way of taking clerical discourse is not wholly unlike the way in which the primer of Christianity, full
of transcendent miracles, was received long ago on tropic isles by any superior
savage, so called — a Tahitian, say, of Captain Cook's time or shortly after that time.
Out of natural courtesy he received, but did not appropriate. It was like a gift
placed in the palm of an outreached hand upon which the fingers do not close.

But the *Bellipotent's* chaplain was a discreet man possessing the good sense of a
good heart. So he insisted not in his vocation here. At the instance of Captain Vere,
a lieutenant had apprised him of pretty much everything as to Billy; and since he
10 felt that innocence was even a better thing than religion wherewith to go to Judgment, he reluctantly withdrew; but in his emotion not without first performing an
act strange enough in an Englishman, and under the circumstances yet more so in
any regular priest. Stooping over, he kissed on the fair cheek his fellow man, a felon
in martial law, one whom though on the confines of death he felt he could never
convert to a dogma; nor for all that did he fear for his future.

Marvel not that having been made acquainted with the young sailor's essential
innocence the worthy man lifted not a finger to avert the doom of such a martyr to
martial discipline. So to do would not only have been as idle as invoking the desert,
but would also have been an audacious transgression of the bounds of his function,
20 one as exactly prescribed to him by military law as that of the boatswain or any
other naval officer. Bluntly put, a chaplain is the minister of the Prince of Peace
serving in the host of the God of War — Mars. As such, he is as incongruous as a
musket would be on the altar at Christmas. Why, then, is he there? Because he indirectly subserves the purpose attested by the cannon; because too he lends the sanction of the religion of the meek to that which practically is the abrogation of everything but brute Force.

25

The night so luminous on the spar deck, but otherwise on the cavernous ones
below, levels so like the tiered galleries in a coal mine — the luminous night passed
away. But like the prophet in the chariot disappearing in heaven and dropping his
30 mantle to Elisha, the withdrawing night transferred its pale robe to the breaking
day. A meek, shy light appeared in the East, where stretched a diaphanous fleece of
white furrowed vapor. That light slowly waxed. Suddenly *eight bells* was struck aft,
responded to by one louder metallic stroke from forward. It was four o'clock in the
morning. Instantly the silver whistles were heard summoning all hands to witness
punishment. Up through the great hatchways rimmed with racks of heavy shot the
watch below came pouring, overspreading with the watch already on deck the space
between the mainmast and foremast including that occupied by the capacious launch
and the black booms tiered on either side of it, boat and booms making a summit
of observation for the powder-boys and younger tars. A different group comprising

4 **Captain Cook's time,** Captain James Cook (1728-1779), English explorer, first visited Tahiti in 1769   29
the prophet . . . Elisha. See II Kings 2:11-13. When the prophet Elijah "went up by a whirlwind into
Heaven," Elisha took up the mantle he dropped

one watch of topmen leaned over the rail of that sea balcony, no small one in a seventy-four, looking down on the crowd below. Man or boy, none spake but in whisper, and few spake at all. Captain Vere — as before, the central figure among the assembled commissioned officers — stood nigh the break of the poop deck facing forward. Just below him on the quarter-deck the marines in full equipment were drawn up much as at the scene of the promulgated sentence.

At sea in the old time, the execution by halter of a military sailor was generally from the foreyard. In the present instance, for special reasons the mainyard was assigned. Under an arm of that yard the prisoner was presently brought up, the chaplain attending him. It was noted at the time, and remarked upon afterwards, that 10 in this final scene the good man evinced little or nothing of the perfunctory. Brief speech indeed he had with the condemned one, but the genuine Gospel was less on his tongue than in his aspect and manner towards him. The final preparations personal to the latter being speedily brought to an end by two boatswain's mates, the consummation impended. Billy stood facing aft. At the penultimate moment, his words, his only ones, words wholly unobstructed in the utterance, were these: "God bless Captain Vere!" Syllables so unanticipated coming from one with the ignominious hemp about his neck — a conventional felon's benediction directed aft towards the quarters of honor; syllables too delivered in the clear melody of a singing bird on the point of launching from the twig — had a phenomenal effect, not un- 20 enhanced by the rare personal beauty of the young sailor, spiritualized now through late experiences so poignantly profound.

Without volition, as it were, as if indeed the ship's populace were but the vehicles of some vocal current electric, with one voice from alow and aloft came a resonant sympathetic echo: "God bless Captain Vere!" And yet at that instant Billy alone must have been in their hearts, even as in their eyes.

At the pronounced words and the spontaneous echo that voluminously rebounded them, Captain Vere, either through stoic self-control or a sort of momentary paralysis induced by emotional shock, stood erectly rigid as a musket in the shiparmorer's rack.

The hull, deliberately recovering from the periodic roll to leeward, was just re- 30 gaining an even keel when the last signal, a preconcerted dumb one, was given. At the same moment it chanced that the vapory fleece hanging low in the East was shot through with a soft glory as of the fleece of the Lamb of God seen in mystical vision, and simultaneously therewith, watched by the wedged mass of upturned faces, Billy ascended; and, ascending, took the full rose of the dawn.

In the pinioned figure arrived at the yard-end, to the wonder of all no motion was apparent, none save that created by the slow roll of the hull in moderate weather, so majestic in a great ship ponderously cannoned.

26

When some days afterwards, in reference to the singularity just mentioned, the purser, a rather ruddy, rotund person more accurate as an accountant than profound 40 as a philosopher, said at mess to the surgeon, "What testimony to the force lodged in will power," the latter, saturnine, spare, and tall, one in whom a discreet causticity went along with a manner less genial than polite, replied, "Your pardon, Mr. Purser. In a hanging scientifically conducted — and under special orders I myself directed how Budd's was to be effected — any movement following the completed suspension and originating in the body suspended, such movement indicates mechanical spasm in the muscular system. Hence the absence of that is no more attributable to will power, as you call it, than to horsepower — begging your pardon."

"But this muscular spasm you speak of, is not that in a degree more or less invariable in these cases?"

10   "Assuredly so, Mr. Purser."

"How then, my good sir, do you account for its absence in this instance?"

"Mr. Purser, it is clear that your sense of the singularity in this matter equals not mine. You account for it by what you call will power — a term not yet included in the lexicon of science. For me, I do not, with my present knowledge, pretend to account for it at all. Even should we assume the hypothesis that at the first touch of the halyards the action of Budd's heart, intensified by extraordinary emotion at its climax, abruptly stopped — much like a watch when in carelessly winding it up you strain at the finish, thus snapping the chain — even under that hypothesis how account for the phenomenon that followed?"

20   "You admit, then, that the absence of spasmodic movement was phenomenal."

"It was phenomenal, Mr. Purser, in the sense that it was an appearance the cause of which is not immediately to be assigned."

"But tell me, my dear sir," pertinaciously continued the other, "was the man's death effected by the halter, or was it a species of euthanasia?"

"*Euthanasia*, Mr. Purser, is something like your *will power:* I doubt its authenticity as a scientific term — begging your pardon again. It is at once imaginative and metaphysical — in short, Greek. — But," abruptly changing his tone, "there is a case in the sick bay that I do not care to leave to my assistants. Beg your pardon, but excuse me." And rising from the mess he formally withdrew.

27

30   The silence at the moment of execution and for a moment or two continuing thereafter, a silence but emphasized by the regular wash of the sea against the hull or the flutter of a sail caused by the helmsman's eyes being tempted astray, this emphasized silence was gradually disturbed by a sound not easily to be verbally rendered. Whoever has heard the freshet-wave of a torrent suddenly swelled by pouring showers in tropical mountains, showers not shared by the plain; whosoever has heard the first muffled murmur of its sloping advance through precipitous woods may form some conception of the sound now heard. The seeming remoteness of its source was because of its murmurous indistinctness, since it came from close by, even from the men massed on the ship's open deck. Being inarticulate, it was dubious in significance further than it seemed to indicate some capricious revulsion of thought or feeling such as mobs ashore are liable to, in the present instance pos

sibly implying a sullen revocation on the men's part of their involuntary echoing of Billy's benediction. But ere the murmur had time to wax into clamor it was met by a strategic command, the more telling that it came with abrupt unexpectedness: "Pipe down the starboard watch, Boatswain, and see that they go."

Shrill as the shriek of the sea hawk, the silver whistles of the boatswain and his mates pierced that ominous low sound, dissipating it; and yielding to the mechanism of discipline the throng was thinned by one-half. For the remainder, most of them were set to temporary employments connected with trimming the yards and so forth, business readily to be got up to serve occasion by any officer of the deck.

Now each proceeding that follows a mortal sentence pronounced at sea by a drum- 10 head court is characterized by promptitude not perceptibly merging into hurry, though bordering that. The hammock, the one which had been Billy's bed when alive, having already been ballasted with shot and otherwise prepared to serve for his canvas coffin, the last offices of the sea undertakers, the sailmaker's mates, were now speedily completed. When everything was in readiness a second call for all hands, made necessary by the strategic movement before mentioned, was sounded, now to witness burial.

The details of this closing formality it needs not to give. But when the tilted plank let slide its freight into the sea, a second strange human murmur was heard, blended now with another inarticulate sound proceeding from certain larger seafowl 20 who, their attention having been attracted by the peculiar commotion in the water resulting from the heavy sloped dive of the shotted hammock into the sea, flew screaming to the spot. So near the hull did they come, that the stridor or bony creak of their gaunt double-jointed pinions was audible. As the ship under light airs passed on, leaving the burial spot astern, they still kept circling it low down with the moving shadow of their outstretched wings and the croaked requiem of their cries.

Upon sailors as superstitious as those of the age preceding ours, men-of-war's men too who had just beheld the prodigy of repose in the form suspended in air, and now foundering in the deeps; to such mariners the action of the seafowl, though dictated by mere animal greed for prey, was big with no prosaic significance. An 30 uncertain movement began among them, in which some encroachment was made. It was tolerated but for a moment. For suddenly the drum beat to quarters, which familiar sound happening at least twice every day, had upon the present occasion a signal peremptoriness in it. True martial discipline long continued superinduces in average man a sort of impulse whose operation at the official word of command much resembles in its promptitude the effect of an instinct.

The drumbeat dissolved the multitude, distributing most of them along the batteries of the two covered gun decks. There, as wonted, the guns' crews stood by their respective cannon erect and silent. In due course the first officer, sword under arm and standing in his place on the quarter-deck, formally received the successive re- 40 ports of the sworded lieutenants commanding the sections of batteries below; the last of which reports being made, the summed report he delivered with the customary salute to the commander. All this occupied time, which in the present case was the object in beating to quarters at an hour prior to the customary one. That such variance from usage was authorized by an officer like Captain Vere, a martinet as some deemed him, was evidence of the necessity for unusual action implied in what he deemed to be temporarily the mood of his men. "With mankind," he would say, "forms, measured forms, are everything; and that is the import couched in the story of Orpheus with his lyre spellbinding the wild denizens of the wood." And this he once applied to the disruption of forms going on across the Channel and the consequences thereof.

At this unwonted muster at quarters, all proceeded as at the regular hour. The band on the quarter-deck played a sacred air, after which the chaplain went through
10 the customary morning service. That done, the drum beat the retreat; and toned by music and religious rites subserving the discipline and purposes of war, the men in their wonted orderly manner dispersed to the places allotted them when not at the guns.

And now it was full day. The fleece of low-hanging vapor had vanished, licked up by the sun that late had so glorified it. And the circumambient air in the clearness of its serenity was like smooth white marble in the polished block not yet removed from the marble-dealer's yard.

28

The symmetry of form attainable in pure fiction cannot so readily be achieved in a narration essentially having less to do with fable than with fact. Truth uncom-
20 promisingly told will always have its ragged edges; hence the conclusion of such a narration is apt to be less finished than an architectural finial.

How it fared with the Handsome Sailor during the year of the Great Mutiny has been faithfully given. But though properly the story ends with his life, something in way of sequel will not be amiss. Three brief chapters will suffice.

In the general rechristening under the Directory of the craft originally forming the navy of the French monarchy, the *St. Louis* line-of-battle ship was named the *Athée* (the *Atheist*). Such a name, like some other substituted ones in the Revolutionary fleet, while proclaiming the infidel audacity of the ruling power, was yet, though not so intended to be, the aptest name, if one consider it, ever given to a
30 warship; far more so indeed than the *Devastation,* the *Erebus* (the *Hell*), and similar names bestowed upon fighting ships.

On the return passage to the English fleet from the detached cruise during which occurred the events already recorded, the *Bellipotent* fell in with the *Athée*. An engagement ensued, during which Captain Vere, in the act of putting his ship alongside the enemy with a view of throwing his boarders across her bulwarks, was hit by a musket ball from a porthole of the enemy's main cabin. More than disabled, he dropped to the deck and was carried below to the same cockpit where some of his men already lay. The senior lieutenant took command. Under him the enemy was finally captured, and though much crippled was by rare good fortune success-
40 fully taken into Gibraltar, an English port not very distant from the scene of the

5 **story of Orpheus.** See note, p. 1112

fight. There, Captain Vere with the rest of the wounded was put ashore. He lingered for some days, but the end came. Unhappily he was cut off too early for the Nile and Trafalgar. The spirit that 'spite its philosophic austerity may yet have indulged in the most secret of all passions, ambition, never attained to the fulness of fame.

Not long before death, while lying under the influence of that magical drug which, soothing the physical frame, mysteriously operates on the subtler element in man, he was heard to murmur words inexplicable to his attendant: "Billy Budd, Billy Budd." That these were not the accents of remorse would seem clear from what the attendant said to the *Bellipotent*'s senior officer of marines, who, as the most reluc-   10
tant to condemn of the members of the drumhead court, too well knew, though here he kept the knowledge to himself, who Billy Budd was.

29

Some few weeks after the execution, among other matters under the head of "News from the Mediterranean," there appeared in a naval chronicle of the time, an authorized weekly publication, an account of the affair. It was doubtless for the most part written in good faith, though the medium, partly rumor, through which the facts must have reached the writer served to deflect and in part falsify them. The account was as follows:

"On the tenth of the last month a deplorable occurrence took place on board H.M.S. *Bellipotent*. John Claggart, the ship's master-at-arms, discovering that some   20
sort of plot was incipient among an inferior section of the ship's company, and that the ringleader was one William Budd; he, Claggart, in the act of arraigning the man before the captain, was vindictively stabbed to the heart by the suddenly drawn sheath knife of Budd.

"The deed and the implement employed sufficiently suggest that though mustered into the service under an English name the assassin was no Englishman, but one of those aliens adopting English cognomens whom the present extraordinary necessities of the service have caused to be admitted into it in considerable numbers.

"The enormity of the crime and the extreme depravity of the criminal appear the greater in view of the character of the victim, a middle-aged man respectable and   30
discreet, belonging to that minor official grade, the petty officers, upon whom, as none know better than the commissioned gentlemen, the efficiency of His Majesty's navy so largely depends. His function was a responsible one, at once onerous and thankless; and his fidelity in it the greater because of his strong patriotic impulse. In this instance as in so many other instances in these days, the character of this unfortunate man signally refutes, if refutation were needed, that peevish saying attributed to the late Dr. Johnson, that patriotism is the last refuge of a scoundrel.

"The criminal paid the penalty of his crime. The promptitude of the punishment has proved salutary. Nothing amiss is now apprehended aboard H.M.S. *Bellipotent*."

The above, appearing in a publication now long ago superannuated and forgot-   40
ten, is all that hitherto has stood in human record to attest what manner of men respectively were John Claggart and Billy Budd.

30

Everything is for a term venerated in navies. Any tangible object associated with some striking incident of the service is converted into a monument. The spar from which the foretopman was suspended was for some few years kept trace of by the bluejackets. Their knowledges followed it from ship to dockyard and again from dockyard to ship, still pursuing it even when at last reduced to a mere dockyard boom. To them a chip of it was as a piece of the Cross. Ignorant though they were of the secret facts of the tragedy, and not thinking but that the penalty was some-how unavoidably inflicted from the naval point of view, for all that, they instinc-tively felt that Billy was a sort of man as incapable of mutiny as of wilful murder.
10 They recalled the fresh young image of the Handsome Sailor, that face never de-formed by a sneer or subtler vile freak of the heart within. This impression of him was doubtless deepened by the fact that he was gone, and in a measure mysteriously gone. On the gun decks of the *Bellipotent* the general estimate of his nature and its unconscious simplicity eventually found rude utterance from another foretopman, one of his own watch, gifted, as some sailors are, with an artless *poetic* temperament. The tarry hand made some lines which, after circulating among the shipboard crews for a while, finally got rudely printed at Portsmouth as a ballad. The title given to it was the sailor's.

BILLY IN THE DARBIES

20   Good of the chaplain to enter Lone Bay
  And down on his marrowbones here and pray
  For the likes just o' me, Billy Budd. — But, look:
  Through the port comes the moonshine astray!
  It tips the guard's cutlass and silvers this nook;
  But 'twill die in the dawning of Billy's last day.
  A jewel-block they'll make of me tomorrow,
  Pendant pearl from the yardarm-end
  Like the eardrop I gave to Bristol Molly —
  O, 'tis me, not the sentence they'll suspend.
30   Ay, ay, all is up; and I must up too,
  Early in the morning, aloft from alow.
  On an empty stomach now never it would do.
  They'll give me a nibble — bit o' biscuit ere I go.
  Sure, a messmate will reach me the last parting cup;
  But, turning heads away from the hoist and the belay,
  Heaven knows who will have the running of me up!
  No pipe to those halyards. — But aren't it all sham?
  A blur's in my eyes; it is dreaming that I am.
  A hatchet to my hawser? All adrift to go?

---

19 **Darbies,** handcuffs

The drum roll to grog, and Billy never know?   40
But Donald he has promised to stand by the plank;
So I'll shake a friendly hand ere I sink.
But — no! It is dead then I'll be, come to think.
I remember Taff the Welshman when he sank.
And his cheek it was like the budding pink.
But me they'll lash in hammock, drop me deep.
Fathoms down, fathoms down, how I'll dream fast asleep.
I feel it stealing now. Sentry, are you there?
Just ease these darbies at the wrist,
And roll me over fair!   50
I am sleepy, and the oozy weeds about me twist.

1886-1891, 1924, 1962

HUMOR AND FOLKLORE
Smith
Crockett
Thompson
Harris
Thorpe
Singers of the West

1792—1868 Seba Smith

When, in January 1830, Editor Seba Smith of the *Portland* (Maine) *Courier* decided he should do something to stimulate interest in his languishing newspaper, he invented the humorous character Jack Downing to say his say about contemporary politics. The homespun commentator was such a success that from 1830 down to the eve of the Civil War Smith turned out the "Downing Letters," important in the development of American humor and of a type of political argument destined to prove very significant in our national history.

Jack and the members of the Downing family who exchanged letters with him were both believable and amusing. Smith's background had equipped him well for writing about Yankees, both authentically and humorously. Born in a Buckfield, Maine, log cabin, reared in Buckfield or other Down East towns until he was twenty-three, he was well acquainted with Yankee ways of thinking, talking, and living. The vividness with which he portrayed Downingville, the lifelikeness of the speech of the Downings, and the verisimilitude of their actions all made his rustics believable. (Emerson notes that his old Concord neighbor, Ezra Ripley, never could be persuaded that Jack was not a living man.) Smith's study at Bowdoin (1815-1818) and his travel in the South probably helped him acquire his objectivity.

In addition to the appeals of the characterization and the humor, there was the appeal of the political satire. At first Smith had his hero wander into the Maine legislature and write naïvely about state politics. Later he had Jack go to Washington, D. C., and comment on national issues and personalities. Writing of his adventures in the Kitchen Cabinet (unofficial advisers) of Jackson and of his friendships with public men, Downing wittingly or unwittingly said laughable things about the partisan struggles of the day — the fight against the national bank, the nullification struggle, and others. This illiterate but shrewd common man discoursing on national affairs appealed to readers not only in the Jacksonian period which produced him but also in later periods, as he continued his letters during succeeding administrations. Frequently, newspaper wits nominated him for the governorship or the Presidency, and early cartoonists of the day who wanted a symbol for the United States often pictured Jack. Even today, Uncle Sam is simply Jack Downing with whiskers. Jack was the ancestor of a whole series of horse sense humorists, such as Hosea Biglow, Bill Arp, Kin Hubbard, and Will Rogers, who have delighted great masses of Americans and influenced their political thinking.

My Thirty Years Out of the Senate, New York, 1859   Mary Alice Wyman, Two American Pioneers: Seba Smith and Elizabeth Oakes Smith, New York, 1927   Walter Blair, Horse Sense in American Humor, Chicago, 1942

from My Thirty Years Out of the Senate

Accompanied by a number of his official and unofficial advisers, President Jackson spent part of the summer of 1833 taking a trip which carried him to several of the chief cities of the North. At each stop there were large demonstrations, partly because of the President's personal popularity, partly because of general approval in the North of his recent stand on nullification. Jack Downing, in his letter dated June 10, tells of the reception at Philadelphia. Subsequent letters, here reprinted, offer additional details about the journey.

Major Downing Shakes Hands for the President at Philadelphia, While on the Grand Tour Down East

Philadelphia, June 10, 1833

To Uncle Joshua Downing, Postmaster, up in Downingville, in the State of Maine, with care and speed

Dear Uncle Joshua: — We are coming on, full chisel. I've been trying, ever since we started, to get a chance to write a little to you; but when we've been on the road I couldn't catch my breath hardly long enough to write my name, we kept flying so fast; and when we made any stop, there was such a jam around us there wasn't elbow room enough for a miskeeter to turn round without knocking his wings off.

I'm most afraid now we shall get to Downingville before this letter does, so that we shall be likely to catch you all in the suds before you think of it. But I under-   10 stand there is a *fast mail* goes on that way, and I mean to send it by that, so I'm in hopes you'll get it time enough to have the children's faces washed and their heads combed, and the gals get on their clean gowns. And if Sargent Joel *could* have time enough to call out my old Downingville company and get their uniforms brushed up a little, and come down the road as fur as your new barn to meet us, there's nothing that would please the President better. As for victuals, most anything won't come amiss; we are as hungry as bears after traveling a hundred miles a day. A little fried pork and eggs, or a pot of baked beans and an Indian pudding would suit us much better than the soft stuff they give here in these great cities.

The President wouldn't miss of seeing you for anything in the world, and he will   20 go to Downingville if he has legs and arms enough left when he goes to Portland

---

4 **full chisel.** See note, p. 946   10 **in the suds,** perplexed, in difficulty

to carry him there. But, for fear that anything should happen that he shouldn't be able to come, you had better meet us in Portland, say about the 22d; and then you can go up to Downingville with us.

This traveling with the President is capital fun, after all, if it wasn't so plaguy tiresome. We come into Baltimore on a railroad, and we flew over the ground like a harrycane. There isn't a horse in this country that could keep up with us, if he should go upon the clean clip. When we got to Baltimore, the streets were filled with folks as thick as the spruce trees down in your swamp. There we found Black Hawk, a little, old, dried up Indian king. And I thought the folks looked at him and the prophet about as much as they did at me and the President. I gave the President a wink that this Indian fellow was taking the shine off us a little; so we concluded we wouldn't have him with us any more, but go on without him.

I can't stop to tell you, in this letter, how we got along to Philadelphy, though we had a pretty easy time some of the way in the steamboats. And I can't stop to tell you of half of the fine things I have seen here. They took us up into a great hall this morning, as big as a meeting-house, and then the folks begun to pour in by thousands to shake hands with the President — Federalists and all, it made no difference. There was such a stream of 'em coming in that the hall was full in a few minutes, and it was so jammed up around the door that they couldn't get out again if they were to die. So they had to knock out some of the windows, and go out t'other way.

The President shook hands with all his might an hour or two, 'till he got so tired he couldn't hardly stand it. I took hold and shook for him once in a while to help him along, but at last he got so tired he had to lay down on a soft bench, covered with cloth, and shake as well as he could; and when he couldn't shake, he'd nod to 'em as they come along. And at last he got so beat out, he couldn't only wrinkle his forehead and wink. Then I kind of stood behind him, and reached my arm round under his, and shook for him for about half an hour as tight as I could spring. Then we concluded it was best to adjourn for to-day.

And I've made out to get away up into the garret in the tavern long enough to write this letter. We shall be off tomorrow or next day for York; and if I can possibly get breathing time enough there, I shall write to you again.

Give my love to all the folks in Downingville, and believe me your loving neffu,

MAJOR JACK DOWNING

1833

Major Downing Describes the Visit of the President at Boston

Boston, Tuesday, June 25, 1833

To the Editor of the Portland Courier

My Dear Old Friend: — I'm keeping house with the President to-day, and bein' he's getting considerable better, I thought I'd catch a chance when he was taking a knap, and write a little to let you know how we get along. This ere sickness of the President has been a bad pull-back to us. He hasn't been able to go out since

Sunday afternoon, and I've been watchin' with him this two nights, and if I wasn't as tough as a halter, I should be half dead by this time.

And if the President wasn't tougher than a catamount, he'd kick the bucket before he'd been round to see one half the notions there is in Boston. Poor man, he has a hard time of it; you've no idea how much he has to go through. It's worse than being dragged through forty knot-holes.

To be bamboozled about from four o'clock in the morning till midnight, rain or shine — jammed into one great house to eat a breakfast, and into another great house to eat a dinner, and into another to eat supper, and into two or three others between meals, to eat cooliations, and to have to go out and review three or four regiments 10 of troops, and then to be jammed into Funnel Hall two hours, and shake hands with three or four thousand folks, and then to go into the State House and stand there two or three hours, and see all Boston streaming through it like a river through a saw-mill, and then to ride about the city awhile in a fine painted covered wagon, with four or five horses to draw it, and then ride awhile in one without any cover to it, finney-fined off to the top notch, and then get on to the horses and ride awhile a horseback, and then run into a great picture-room and see more fine pictures than you could shake a stick at in a week, and then go into some grand gentleman's house, and shake hands a half an hour with a flock of ladies, and then after supper go and have a little still kind of a hubbub all alone with three or four hundred par- 20 ticular friends, and talk an hour or two, and take another cooliation, and then go home, and about midnight get ready to go to bed, and up again at four o'clock the next morning and at it. And if this aint enough to tucker a feller out, I don't know what is. The President wouldn't have stood it till this time, if he hadn't sent me and Mr. Van Buren to some of the parties, while he staid at home to rest.

The President's got so much better, I think we shall be able to start for Salem tomorrow, for we must go through with it now we've begun, as hard work as 'tis. I think we shall get to Portland about the 4th of July; so, if you get your guns and things all ready, you can kill two birds with one stone. I hope you'll be pretty careful there how you point your guns. They pointed 'em so careless at New York that 30 a wad come within six inches of making daylight shine through the President.

Now I think on't, there is the most rascally set of fellers skulking about somewhere in this part of the country that ever I heard of, and I wish you would blow 'em up. They are worse than the pickpockets. I mean them are fellers that's got to writing letters and putting my name to 'em, and sending of 'em to the printers. And I heard there was one sassy feller last Saturday, down to Newburyport, that got on to a horse, and rid about town calling himself Major Jack Downing, and all the soldiers and the folks marched up and shook hands with him, and thought it was me. Isn't it Mr. Shakespeare that says something about "he that steals my munnypus steals trash, but he that steals my name ought to have his head broke?" I wish you 40 would find that story and print it.

Your old friend,   MAJOR JACK DOWNING
                                                                           1833

---

10 **cooliations**, collations

The President and the Rest of 'Em Turn a Short Corner at Concord, and Set Their Faces Toward Washington

Concord, Nu Hamsheer, June 30, 1833

To the Editor of the Portland Courier

My Dear Old Friend: — The jig is all up about our going to Portland and Down-ingville, I've battled the watch with the President this two days about it, and told him he must go there if he had the breath of life in him; and he kept telling me he certainly would, if horses could carry him there.

But the President isn't very well, and that ain't the worst of it; there's been a lit-tle difficulty bruin' among us, and the President's got so riled about it, that he's finally concluded to start on his way back to-morrow. I can't help it; but I feel bad enough about it to cry a barrel of tears.

I don't know how they will stan' it in Downingville, when they come to get the
10 news. I'm afraid there will be a master uproar there, for you know they are all great Demokrats. But the stage is jest agoing to start.

In haste, from your friend,

MAJOR JACK DOWNING

1833

Cousin Nabby Describes the Unutterable Disappointment at Downingville Because the President Didn't Come

Downingville, July 8, 1833

To the Editor of the Portland Courier

Respectable Sir: — As Cousin Jack is always so mity budge in writing letters to you, and as he and the President showed us a most provoking trick, and run off like a stream of chalk, back to Washington, without coming here, after they had promised over and over again that they would come, and we had got all slicked up
20 and our clean gownds on, and more good victuals cooked than there ever was in all Downingville before — I say, Mr. Editor, I declare it's too bad; we are all as mad as blazes about it, and I mean to write and tell you all about it, if I live; and if Cousin Jack don't like it, he may lump it; so there now.

Ye see Cousin Jack writ to us that he and the President and some more gentle-men should be here the 4th of July, and we must spring to it and brush up and see how smart we could look, and how many fine things we could show to the Presi-dent. This was a Saturday before the 4th of July come a Thursday. The letter was to Uncle Joshua, the Postmaster. Most all the folks in Downingville were at the Post-Office waiting when the mail come in, for we expected to hear from Jack.
30 Uncle Joshua put on his spettacles and opened the mail, and hauled out the pa-pers and letters in a bunch. In a minute I see one to Uncle Joshua with the Presi-dent's name on the outside; so I knew it was from Jack, for the President always puts his name on Jack's letters. We all cried out to Uncle Joshua to open it, and

let us know what was in it. But he's such a provoking odd old man, he wouldn't touch it 'till he got every one of the papers and letters sorted and put up in their places. And then he took it and set down in his armchair, and took out his tobacker box and took a chaw of tobacker, and then he broke open the seal and sot and chawed and read to himself. We all stood tiptoe, with our hearts in our mouths, and he must needs read it over to himself three times, chawing his old quid, and once in a while giving us a knowing wink, before he would tell us what was in it. And he wouldn't tell us arter all, but, says he, "You must all be ready to put the best side out Thursday morning; there'll be business to attend to, such as Downingville never see before."   10

At that we all turned and run, and such a hubbub as we were in from that time 'till Thursday morning, I guess you never see. Such a washing and scrubbing, and making new clothes and mending old ones, and baking and cooking. Every thing seemed to be in a clutter all over the neighborhood. Sargent Joel flew round like a ravin' distracted rooster. He called out his company every morning before sunrise, and marched 'em up and down the road three hours every day. He sent to the store and got a whole new set of buttons, and had 'em sowed on to his regimental coat, and had a new piece of red put round the collar. And had his trowses washed and his boots greased, and looked as though he might take the shine off of most any-thing. But the greatest rumpus was at Uncle Joshua's; for they said the President 20 must stay there all night. And Ant Keziah was in such a pucker to have everything nice, I didn't know but she would fly off the handle.

She had every part of the house washed from garret to cellar, and the floors all sanded, and a bunch of green bushes put into all the fire places. And she baked three overn-full of dried punkin pies, besides a few dried huckleberry pies, and cake, and a great pot of pork and beans. But the worst trouble was to fix up the bed so as to look nice; for Ant Keziah declared the President should have as good a night's lodg-ing in her house as he had in New York or Boston. So she put on two feather beds on top the straw bed, and a bran-new calico quilt that she made the first summer after she was married, and never put it on a bed before. And to make it look as nice 30 as the New York beds, she took her red silk gown and ripped it up and made a blanket to spread over the top. And then she hung up some sheets all round the bedroom, and the gals brought in a whole handful of roses and pinks, and pinned 'em up round as thick as flies in August.

After we got things pretty much fixed, Uncle Joshua started off to meet Cousin Jack and the President, and left Sargent Joel to put matters to rights, and told us we must all be ready and be paraded in the road by nine o'clock Thursday morning. Well, Thursday morning come, and we all mustered as soon as it was daylight and dressed up. The children were all washed, and had their clean aprons on and their heads combed, and were put under the care of the schoolmarm, to be paraded along 40 with her scholars.

About eight o'clock, all the village got together down the road as fur as Uncle Joshua's new barn; and Sargent Joel told us how to stand, as he said, in military order. He placed Bill Johnson and Cousin Ephraim out a little ways in front, with each of 'em a great long fowling piece with a smart charge in to fire a salute, and told 'em as soon as the President hove in sight to let drive, only to be careful and pint their guns up, so as not to hurt anybody. Then come Sargent Joel and his company; and then come the schoolmarm and the children; and then come all the women and gals over sixteen with Ant Keziah at their head; and then come all the men in town that owned horses riding on horseback; and all the boys that Sargent Joel didn't think was large enough to walk in the procession got up and sot on the fences along by the side of the road.

There we stood 'till about nine o'clock, when, sure enough, we saw somebody
10 coming riding out of the woods down the hill. The boys all screamed, ready to split their throats, "Hoorah for Jackson," and Bill Johnson fired off his gun. Cousin Ephraim, who ain't so easily fluttered, held on to his and didn't fire, for he couldn't see anybody but Uncle Joshua on his old gray horse. Along come Uncle Joshua, on a slow trot, and we looked and looked, and couldn't see anybody coming behind him.

Then they all begun to look at one another as wild as hawks, and turn all manner of colors. When Uncle Joshua got up so we could see him pretty plain, he looked as cross as a thunder-cloud. He rid up to Sargent Joel, and says he, "You may all go home about your business, for Jack and the President are half way to Washington by this time."

20 My stars! what a time there was then. I never see so many folks boiling over mad before. Bill Johnson threw his gun over into the field as much as ten rods, and hopped up and down, and struck his fists together like all possessed. Sargent Joel marched back and forth across the road two or three times, growing redder and redder, till at last he drew out his sword and fetched a blow across a hemlock stump, and snapped it off like a pipe-stem. Ant Keziah fell down in a conniption fit; and it was an hour before we could bring her tu and get her into the house. And when she come to go round the house and see the victuals she had cooked up, and go into the bedroom and see her gown all cut up, she went into conniption fits again. But she's better to-day, and has gone to work to try to patch up her gown
30 again.

I thought I would jest let you know about these things, and if you are a mind to send word on to Cousin Jack and the President, I'm willing. You may tell 'em there aint five folks in Downingville that would hoorah for Jackson now, and hardly one that would vote for him, unless 'tis Uncle Joshua, and he wouldn't if he wasn't afraid of losing the Post-Office.

Your respected friend,

NABBY DOWNING

1833

1786—1836 David Crockett

In the days when Tennessee was still part of the Far West, David Crockett was born and reared in a Tennessee frontier log cabin. His schooling was meager, totaling altogether about one hundred days; but his lack of book learning did not keep him from becoming, in time, a United States congressman and a hero of the folk. Davy won followers in the period of coonskin democracy because, as a hunter, an Indian fighter, and a commoner who relied on good horse sense, he had abilities and ways particularly admired by his neighbors. His motto — "Be sure you're right, and then go ahead" — caught in a few words the spirit of the times.

Davy learned to farm and to hunt in boyhood. After fighting in the Creek War under Jackson (1813-1814), he was twice elected to the state legislature (1821-1823) and twice to Congress (1827-1831, 1833-1835). Newspapers of the day made much of his rough, homespun humor, and books about him — some by others, some by Davy himself — swelled his fame. When a Western critic read Crockett's autobiography, *Narrative of the Life of David Crockett of West Tennessee* (1834), he noticed that "the events are such . . . as we have seen acted over and over, and heard repeatedly recited by the firesides of our hardy backwoodsmen." The comment suggests Crockett's importance in literary history. His accounts did much to bring in the fireside yarn, with its authentic rendering of Western ways of living, thinking, talking, and narrating, as an eventual literary influence upon authors such as Harte and Clemens.

Furthermore, during Crockett's lifetime, and particularly after his heroic death in the Alamo in 1836, tall tales about him circulated in yarnspinning sessions and in print. He was pictured in such tales as a comic demigod, doing superhuman deeds imagined by exuberant storytellers. These tales combined imagination of the sort one finds in poetry with enough robust humor to make them palatable to ordinary men. They are related to the earlier whoppers of Samuel Peters, the later yarns of Mark Twain, and the present-day fantastic moving pictures of Walt Disney.

An Autobiography of Davy Crockett (containing Crockett's Narrative, A Tour of the North and Down East, 1834, and most of Colonel Crockett's Exploits and Adventures in Texas, 1836), ed. Hamlin Garland, New York, 1923   Davy Crockett: American Comic Legend, ed. R. M. Dorson, New York, 1939   Constance Rourke, Davy Crockett, New York, 1934   James A. Shackford, David Crockett: The Man and the Legend, Chapel Hill, 1956

Bear Hunting *from Narrative of the Life of David Crockett of West Tennessee*

In the morning I left my son at the camp, and we started on towards the harricane; and when we had went about a mile, we started a very large bear, but we got along mighty slow on account of the cracks in the earth occasioned by the earthquakes. We, however, made out to keep in hearing of the dogs for about three miles, and then we come to the harricane. Here we had to quit our horses, as old Nick himself couldn't have got through it without sneaking it along in the form that he put on, to make a fool of our old grandmother Eve. By this time several of my dogs had got tired and come back; but we went ahead on foot for some little time in the harricane, when we met a bear coming straight to us, and not more than twenty or
10 thirty yards off. I started my tired dogs after him, and McDaniel pursued them, and I went on to where my other dogs were. I had seen the track of the bear they were after, and I knowed he was a screamer. I followed on to about the middle of the harricane, but my dogs pursued him so close, that they made him climb an old stump about twenty feet high. I got in shooting distance of him and fired, but I was all over in such a flutter from fatigue and running, that I couldn't hold steady; but, however, I broke his shoulder, and he fell. I run up and loaded my gun as quick as possible, and shot him again and killed him. When I went to take out my knife to butcher him, I found I had lost it in coming through the harricane. The vines and briers was so thick that I would sometimes have to get down and crawl
20 like a varment to get through at all; and a vine had, as I supposed, caught in the handle and pulled it out. While I was standing and studying what to do, my friend came to me. He had followed my trail through the harricane, and had found my knife, which was mighty good news to me; as a hunter hates the worst in the world to lose a good dog, or any part of his hunting-tools. I now left McDaniel to butcher the bear, and I went after our horses, and brought them as near as the nature of case would allow. I then took our bags, and went back to where he was; and when we had skin'd the bear, we fleeced off the fat and carried it to our horses at several loads. We then packed it up on our horses, and had a heavy pack of it on each one. We now started and went on till about sunset, when I concluded we must be near
30 our camp; so I hollered and my son answered me, and we moved on in the direction to the camp. We had gone but a little way when I heard my dogs make a warm start again; and I jumped down from my horse and gave him up to my friend, and told him I would follow them. He went on to the camp, and I went ahead after my dogs with all my might for a considerable distance, till at last night came on. The woods were very rough and hilly, and all covered over with cane.

I now was compel'd to move on more slowly; and was frequently falling over logs, and into the cracks made by the earthquakes, so that I was very much afraid I would break my gun. However I went on about three miles, when I came to a good

---

1 **harricane,** hurricane

big creek, which I waded. It was very cold, and the creek was about knee-deep; but
I felt no great inconvenience from it just then, as I was all over wet with sweat from
running, and I felt hot enough. After I got over the creek and out of the cane, which
was very thick on all our creeks, I listened for my dogs. I found they had either
treed or brought the bear to a stop, as they continued barking in the same place. I
pushed on as near in the direction to the noise as I could, till I found the hill was
too steep for me to climb, and so I backed and went down the creek some distance
till I came to a hollow, and then took up that, till I come to a place where I could
climb up the hill. It was mighty dark, and was difficult to see my way or any thing
else. When I got up the hill, I found I had passed the dogs; and so I turned and   10
went to them. I found, when I got there, they had treed the bear in a large forked
poplar, and it was setting in the fork.

   I could see the lump, but not plain enough to shoot with any certainty, as there
was no moonlight; and so I set in to hunting for some dry brush to make me a
light; but I could find none, though I could find that the ground was torn mightily
to pieces by the cracks.

   At last I thought I could shoot by guess, and kill him; so I pointed as near the
lump as I could, and fired away. But the bear didn't come; he only clomb up higher
and got out on a limb, which helped me to see him better. I now loaded up again
and fired, but this time he didn't move at all. I commenced loading for a third fire,   20
but the first thing I knowed, the bear was down among the dogs, and they were
fighting all around me. I had my big butcher in my belt, and I had a pair of dressed
buckskin breeches on. So I took out my knife, and stood, determined, if he should
get hold of me, to defend myself in the best way I could. I stood there for some
time, and could now and then see a white dog I had, but the rest of them, and the
bear, which were dark coloured, I couldn't see at all, it was so miserable dark. They
still fought around me, and sometimes within three feet of me; but, at last, the bear
got down into one of the cracks, that the earthquakes had made in the ground,
about four feet deep, and I could tell the biting end of him by the hollering of my
dogs. So I took my gun and pushed the muzzle of it about, till I thought I had it   30
against the main part of his body, and fired; but it happened to be only the fleshy
part of his foreleg. With this, he jumped out of the crack, and he and the dogs had
another hard fight around me, as before. At last, however, they forced him back
into the crack again, as he was when I had shot.

   I had laid down my gun in the dark, and I now began to hunt for it; and while
hunting, I got hold of a pole, and I concluded I would punch him awhile with that.
I did so, and when I would punch him, the dogs would jump in on him, when he
would bite them badly, and they would jump out again. I concluded, as he would
take punching so patiently, it might be that he would lie still enough for me to get
down in the crack, and feel slowly along till I could find the right place to give him   40
a dig with my butcher. So I got down, and my dogs got in before him and kept his
head towards them, till I got along easily up to him; and placing my hand on his
rump, felt for his shoulder, just behind which I intended to stick him. I made a
lounge with my long knife, and fortunately stuck him right through the heart; at

which he just sank down, and I crawled out in a hurry. In a little time my dogs all come out too, and seemed satisfied, which was the way they always had of telling me that they had finished him.

I suffered very much that night with cold, as my leather breeches, and every thing else I had on, was wet and frozen. But I managed to get my bear out of this crack after several hard trials, and so I butchered him, and laid down to try to sleep. But my fire was very bad, and I couldn't find any thing that would burn well to make it any better; and I concluded I should freeze, if I didn't warm myself in some way by exercise. So I got up, and hollered a while, and then I would just jump up and
10 down with all my might, and throw myself into all sorts of motions. But all this wouldn't do; for my blood was now getting cold, and the chills coming all over me. I was so tired, too, that I could hardly walk; but I thought I would do the best I could to save my life, and then, if I died, nobody would be to blame. So I went to a tree about two feet through, and not a limb on it for thirty feet, and I would climb up it to the limbs, and then lock my arms together around it, and slide down to the bottom again. This would make the insides of my legs and arms feel mighty warm and good. I continued this till daylight in the morning, and how often I clomb up my tree and slid down I don't know, but I reckon at least a hundred times.

In the morning I got my bear hung up so as to be safe, and then set out to hunt
20 for my camp. I found it after a while, and McDaniel and my son were very much rejoiced to see me get back, for they were about to give me up for lost. We got our breakfasts, and then secured our meat by building a high scaffold, and covering it over. We had no fear of its spoiling, for the weather was so cold that it couldn't.

We now started after my other bear, which had caused me so much trouble and suffering; and before we got him, we got a start after another, and took him also. We went on to the creek I had crossed the night before and camped, and then went to where my bear was, that I had killed in the crack. When we examined the place, McDaniel said he wouldn't have gone into it, as I did, for all the bears in the woods.

We took the meat down to our camp and salted it and also the last one we had
30 killed; intending, in the morning, to make a hunt in the harricane again.

We prepared for resting that night, and I can assure the reader I was in need of it. We had laid down by our fire, and about ten o'clock there came a most terrible earthquake, which shook the earth so, that we were rocked about like we had been in a cradle. We were very much alarmed; for though we were accustomed to feel earthquakes, we were now right in the region which had been torn to pieces by them in 1812, and we thought it might take a notion and swallow us up, like the big fish did Jonah.

In the morning we packed up and moved to the harricane, where we made another camp, and turned out that evening and killed a very large bear, which made
40 *eight* we had now killed in this hunt.

The next morning we entered the harricane again, and in little or no time my dogs were in full cry. We pursued them, and soon came to a thick cane-brake, in which they had stop'd their bear. We got up close to him, as the cane was so thick that we couldn't see more than a few feet. Here I made my friend hold the cane a little open with his gun till I shot the bear, which was a mighty large one. I killed him dead in his tracks. We got him out and butchered him, and in a little time started another and killed him, which now made *ten* we had killed; and we know'd we couldn't pack any more home, as we had only five horses along; therefore we returned to the camp and salted up all our meat, to be ready for a start homeward next morning.

The morning came, and we packed our horses with the meat, and had as much as they could possibly carry, and sure enough cut out for home. It was about thirty miles, and we reached home the second day. I had now accommodated my neighbour with meat enough to do him, and had killed in all, up to that time, fifty-eight   10 bears, during the fall and winter.

As soon as the time come for them to quit their houses and come out again in the spring, I took a notion to hunt a little more, and in about one month I killed forty-seven more, which made one hundred and five bears I had killed in less than one year from that time.

                                                                                                        1834

from The Crockett Almanacs

Between 1835 and 1856 there appeared in various cities — Nashville, New York, Boston, Philadelphia, and others — almanacs put out by various publishers and called the Crockett Almanacs. *Like others, these almanacs contained data about the calendar year; unlike most others, they contained many tall tales, usually written as if in the language of Crockett or his unlearned frontier neighbors.*

Whether Crockett had anything to do with the earliest almanacs is not known, and certainly before long the tales were concocted by journalists, some of whom knew a good deal about frontier life and some of whom knew very little. The stories in the periodicals, however, all were purportedly told by the famous frontiersman. At their best these almanac humorists, whoever they were, caught the qualities of good yarnspinning sessions. The style was that of lively fireside talk, homely, relatively simple, but concrete, vigorous, full of conceits. The materials were typical combinations of earthy, even vulgar, reality with the unearthly inventions of soaring imaginations. The sort of literature in the almanacs, in other words, foreshadowed the widespread use of the American language of informal talk in print and the fantastic inventions of T. B. Thorpe, Joel Chandler Harris, Mark Twain, and Walt Disney. "A Sensible Varmint" and "Death of Crockett" are from Turner and Fisher almanacs, "Crockett's Morning Hunt" from a Cozans almanac; all appeared in New York.

A Sensible Varmint

Almost every body that knows the forest, understands parfectly well that Davy Crockett never loses powder and ball, havin' ben brought up to believe it a sin to throw away amminition, and that is the benefit of a vartuous eddikation. I war out in the forest one arternoon, and had jist got to a place called the Great Gap, when

I seed a rackkoon setting all alone upon a tree. I clapped the breech of Brown Betty to my shoulder, and war jist going to put a piece of lead between his shoulders, when he lifted one paw, and sez he, "Is your name Crockett?"

Sez I, "You are rite for wonst, my name is Davy Crockett."

"Then," sez he, "you needn't take no further trouble, for I may as well come down without another word." And the cretur walked rite down from the tree, for he considered himself shot.

I stoops down and pats him on the head, and sez I, "I hope I may be shot myself before I hurt a hair of your head, for I never had sich a compliment in my life."

10   "Seeing as how you say that," sez he, "I'll jist walk off for the present, not doubting your word a bit, d'ye see, but lest you should kinder happen to change your mind."

1841

Death of Crockett

Thar's a great rejoicin' among the bears of Kaintuck, and the alligators of the Mississippi rolls up thar shining ribs to the sun, and has grown so fat and lazy that they will hardly move out of the way for a steamboat. The rattlesnakes come up out of thar holes and frolic within ten foot of the clearings, and the foxes goes to sleep in the goose-pens. It is bekase the rifle of Crockett is silent forever, and the print of his moccasins is found no more in our woods. His old fox-skin cap hangs up in the cabin, and every hunter, whether he are a Puke, a Wolverine, or a Sucker, never looks at it without turnin' away his head and droppin' a salt tear.

20   Luke Wing entered the cabin the other day and took down old Killdevil to look at it. The muzzle was half stopped up with rust, and a great green spider run out of it and made his escape in the cracks of the wall. The varmints of the forest will fear it no more. His last act to defend it, war when the poor gallant Kurnill drew a bead on a pesky Mexican and brought him down. Crockett went to put "Big Butcher" into another, and the feller on the ground turned half over, and stuck a knife into him. Another come up behind and run his bayonet into Crockett's back, for the cretur would as soon have faced a hindred live mammoths as to have faced Crockett at any time.

Down fell the Kurnill like a lion struck by thunder and lightning. He never 30 spoke again. It war a great loss to the country, and the world, and to ole Kaintuck in particklar. Thar were never known such a member of Congress as Crockett, and never will be agin. The painters and bears will miss him, for he never missed them.

He died like a member o' Congress ought to die. While he war about to do his country some sarvice, and raise her name as high as her mountains, he war cut down in the prime o' life, and at a time when he war most wanted. His screams and yells are heard no more, and the whole country are clouded with a darkness for the gallant Kurnill. He war an ornament to the forest, and war never known to refuse his whiskey to a stranger. When he war alive, it war most beautiful to hear his scream coming through the forest; it would turn and twist itself into some of the most 40 splendifferous knots, and then untie itself and keep on till it got clar into nowhere.

But he are a dead man now, and if you want to see old Kaintuck's tears, go thar, and speak o' her gallant Kurnill, and thar's not a human but what will turn away and go behind some tree and dry up thar tears. He are dead now, and may he rest forever and a day arter.

1847

Crockett's Morning Hunt

One January morning it was so all-screwen-up cold that the forest trees war so stiff that they couldn't shake, and the very day-break froze fast as it war tryin' to dawn. The tinder-box in my cabin would no more ketch fire than a sunk raft at the bottom o' the sea. Seein' that daylight war so far behind time, I thought creation war in a fair way for freezin' fast.

"So," thinks I, "I must strike a leetle fire from my fingers, light my pipe, travel 10 out a few leagues, and see about it."

Then I brought my knuckles together like two thunder clouds, but the sparks froze up afore I could begin to collect 'em — so out I walked, and endeavored to keep myself unfriz by goin' at a hop, step and jump gait, and whistlin' the tune of "fire in the mountains!" as I went along in three double quick time. Well, arter I had walked about twenty-five miles up the peak o' Daybreak Hill, I soon discovered what war the matter. The airth had actually friz fast in her axis, and couldn't turn round; the sun had got jammed between two cakes o' ice under the wheels, an' thar he had bin shinin' and workin' to get loose, till he friz fast in his cold sweat.

"C-r-e-a-t-i-o-n!" thought I, "this are the toughest sort o' suspension, and it mustn't 20 be endured — somethin' must be done, or hum'an creation is done for."

It war then so antedeluvian and premature cold that my upper and lower teeth an' tongue war all collapsed together as tight as a friz oyster. I took a fresh twenty pound bear off o' my back that I'd picked up on the road, an' beat the animal agin the ice till the hot ile began to walk out on him at all sides. I then took an' held him over the airth's axes, an' squeezed him till I thaw'd 'em loose, poured about a ton on it over the sun's face, give the airth's cog-wheel one kick backward, till I got the sun loose — whistled "Push along, keep movin'!" an' in about fifteen seconds the airth gin a grunt, and begun movin' — the sun walked up beautiful, salutin' me with sich a wind o' gratitude that it made me sneeze. I lit my pipe by 30 the blaze o' his top-knot, shouldered my bear, an' walked home, introducin' the people to fresh daylight with a piece of sunrise in my pocket, with which I cooked my bear steaks, an' enjoyed one o' the best breakfasts I had tasted for some time. If I didn't, jist wake some mornin' and go with me to the office o' sunrise!

1853

1812–1882 William Tappan Thompson

I n 1842 William Tappan Thompson was an editor of a weekly newspaper, *The Southern Miscellany,* published in Madison, Georgia. Born in Ohio in 1812, orphaned at fourteen, Thompson had been prepared for editorship by work as a printer's devil, by political executive work in Tallahassee, Florida, and by newspaper, magazine, and printing work in Augusta. The readers to whom the *Miscellany* was intended to appeal, the citizens of surrounding Morgan County, were Scotch-Irish farmers who owned few or no slaves. Moderately educated, rustic, thrifty, rather stern in their Protestant morality, they were aptly nicknamed at the time "the Yankees of the South."

It was for such readers that Thompson prepared his most famous humorous pieces — the Major Jones letters — collected in *Major Jones's Courtship* (1843). *Major Jones's Sketches of Travel* (1848), first published in a Baltimore newspaper, used the same character to preach pro-Southern sentiments to a somewhat different audience. *The Chronicles of Pineville* (1845) was a collection of comic sketches and stories.

The letters, with their accurate use of the vernacular speech of Georgia, were clearly related to the humor, based on the oral tale, so popular in the Southwest at the time. Even closer to this prevalent sort of humor were a number of mock oral tales represented by "A Coon Hunt in a Fency Country," which had periodical publication in 1833 and, in the version used here, was included with a number of humorous narratives in an 1872 edition of Thompson's first book. These short, direct narratives, told in dialect, usually followed a formula thus described by Professor Henry Prentice Miller: "A single paragraph of general moralizing or crackerbox philosophizing; a quick, phrased sketching of the characters; a few statements about background; a single incident, and finally the point or nub, which ties up with the initial paragraph." Some of these economically told yarns deserve high rank among short humorous masterpieces. Thompson was much admired by Mark Twain. Chapter XIII of Twain's *A Tramp Abroad* evidently was influenced by "A Coon Hunt in a Fency Country," and other passages by America's greatest humorist echo other writings by Thompson.

H. P. Miller, **The Life and Works of William Tappan Thompson** (an unpublished doctoral dissertation done at the University of Chicago), 1941   J. H. Nelson, "William Tappan Thompson," **Dictionary of American Biography,** New York, 1935

A Coon Hunt in a Fency Country

It is really astonishin what a monstrous sight of mischief ther is in a bottle of rum. If one of 'em was to be submitted to a analization as the doctors calls it, it would be found to contain all manner of devilment that ever entered the head of man, from cussin and stealin up to murder and whippin his own mother, and nonsense enough to turn all the men in the world out of ther senses. If a man's got any badness in him, let him drink whiskey, and it will bring it out jest as sassafras tea does the measles; and if he's a good-for-nothin sort of a feller, without no bad traits in partickeler, it'll bring out all his foolishness. It affects different people in different ways — it makes some men monstrous brave and full of fight, and some it makes cowards — some it makes rich and happy and some pore and miserable. And   10 it has different effects on different people's eyes — some it makes see double, and some it makes so blind that they can't tell themselves from a side of bacon. One of the worst cases of rum-foolery that I've heard of for a long time tuck place in Pineville last fall.

Bill Sweeney and Tom Culpepper is the two greatest old conveys in our settlement for coon-huntin. The fact is, they don't do much of any thing else, and when *they* can't catch coons, it's a shore sign that coons is scarce. Well, one night they had every thing ready for a reglar hunt, but owin to some extra good fortin, Tom had got a pocket-pistol, as he called it, of genewine old Jimmaky rum. After takin a good startin horn, they went out on ther hunt, with ther lightwood torch a blazin,   20 and the dogs a barkin and yelpin like they was crazy. They struck out into the woods, gwine in the direction of old Starlin Jones's new ground, a great place for coons. Every now and then they would stop to wait for the dogs, and then they would drink one another's health, until they begun to feel first-rate. On they went, chattin away about one thing and another, takin a nip now and then from Tom's bottle, not mindin much whar they was gwine. Bimeby they come to a fence. Well, over they got without much difficulty.

"Who's fence is this?" ses Bill.

"Taint no matter," ses Tom, "let's take a drink."

After takin a pull at the bottle, they went on agin, wonderin what upon yeath   30 had come of the dogs. The next thing they come to was a terrible muddy branch. After gropin ther way through the bushes and briers and gittin on t'other side, they tuck another drink. Fixin up ther torch and startin on agin, they didn't go but a little ways before they come to another branch, as bad as the first one, and a little further they come to another fence — a monstrous high one this time.

"Whar upon yeath is we got to, Culpepper?" ses Bill; "I never seed sich a heap of fences and branches in these parts."

"Why," ses Tom, "it's old Starlin's doins; you know he's alway bildin fences and makin infernal improvements, as he calls 'em. But never mind; we's through 'em now."   40

"The devil we is," ses Bill; "why, here's the alfiredest high fence yit."

Shore enough, thar they was right agin another fence. By this time they begun to be considerable tired and limber in ther jints; and it was sich a terrible high fence. Tom drapped the last piece of the torch, and thar they was in the dark.

"Now you *is* done it!" ses Bill.

Tom knowd he had, but he thought it was no use to grieve over what couldn't be helped, so, ses he,

"Never mind, old hoss — come ahead, and I'll take you out," and the next minit, kerslash! he went into the water up to his neck.

Bill heard the splash, and he clung to the fence with both hands like he thought
10 it was slewin round to throw him off.

"Hellow, Tom!" ses he, "whar in creation has you got to?"

"Here I is!" ses Tom, spittin the water out of his mouth, and coughin like he'd swallered something. "Look out, ther's another dratted branch here."

"Name o' sense, whar is we?" ses Bill. "If this isn't a fency country, dad fetch my buttons!"

"Yes, and a branchy one, too!" ses Tom, "and they is the thickest and the highest and the deepest that I ever seed in all my born days."

After a good deal of cussin and gruntin Bill got himself loose from the fence.

"Which way is you?" ses he.

20 "Here, right over the branch," ses Tom.

The next minit in Bill went, up to his middle in the branch.

"Come ahead," ses Tom, "and let's go home."

"Come thunder!" ses Bill, "in sich a place as this, whar a feller hain't more'n got his coat-tail unhitched from a fence before he's over head and ears in a cussed branch."

Bill made a terrible job of gittin across the branch, which he swore was the deepest one yit. They managed to git together agin after feelin about in the dark a while, and, and, takin another drink, they sot out for home, cussin the fences and the branches, and helpin one another up now and then when they got ther legs tangled in the brush; but they hadn't gone more'n twenty yards before they found them-
30 selves in the middle of another branch. After gittin through the branch and gwine about twenty yards they was brung up all standin agin by another everlastin fence.

"Dad blame my picter," ses Bill, "if I don't think we's bewitched. Who upon yeath would go and build fences all over outdoors this way?"

It tuck 'em a long time to climb this fence, but when they got on top of it they found the ground on tother side without much trouble. This time the bottle was broke, and they come monstrous nigh havin a fight about the catastrofy. But it was a very good thing the licker was spilt, for after crossin three or four more branches and climbin as many more fences, it got to be daylight, when to ther great astonishment they found out that they had been climbin the same fence and wadin the same
40 branch all night, not more'n a hundred yards from the place whar they first come to 'em.

Bill Sweeney ses he can't account for it no other way but that the licker sort o' turned their heads; and he ses he really does believe if it hadn't gin out, they'd been climbin that same fence and wadin that same branch till now.   1847, 1872

1814—1869 George Washington Harris

At the age of five, George Washington Harris was taken from his birthplace in Allegheny City, Pennsylvania, to Knoxville, Tennessee. For forty years he lived in this sleepy village, coming to know intimately the life of its peaceful valley. He left its "Knobs" and mountains only when the economic stirrings preceding the Civil War forced him away.

Harris' wide and varied experience included an apprenticeship in a jewelry shop, the captaincy of a steamboat, farming, the operation of a metalworking shop, glass factory, and sawmill, service as postmaster, and, finally, work on a railroad. During his whole career, Harris had a deep interest in politics, and from 1839 until his death, whenever the political situation became crucial, he boisterously attacked forces which threatened the "good old days."

For a number of years Harris wrote humorous sketches for the New York *Spirit of the Times*. After 1854 his stories couched in the quaint language of his comic character, Sut Lovingood, obtained, according to one discerning critic of that period, "a circulation and popularity, throughout the country, which no similar productions, in modern times, have enjoyed." Sut, as a self-confessed "nat'ral born durn'd fool," delivered blows at the foibles of mankind from the vantage point of this "unassailable position." For his victims he reached as high as Abraham Lincoln and as low as a "durn'd, infurnel, hiperkritical, pot-bellied, scaley-hided, whisky-wastin'" circuit rider. In fact, most of humanity in some form or other can find itself "sloshin' about" in his caldron of comic situation. In a typical Lovingood story, the characters whom Sut disliked were comically portrayed and then, in all probability, physically maltreated. Sut's notion of the height of humor was a man whom he disliked surrounded by a knot of angry hornets and trying vainly to get away in a hurry. What Harris is admired for by modern enthusiasts about his yarns is his ability to put oral tales with all the art of their comic movement and all the poetry of their style onto the printed page.

Sut Lovingood Yarns, New York, 1867   Walter Blair, **Native American Humor (1800-1900),** Cincinnati, 1937   F. J. Meine, **Tall Tales of the Southwest,** New York, 1938   Numerous tales published only in newspapers are being issued annually as *Lovingood Papers* for the Sut Society by the University of Tennessee Press

Bart Davis's Dance

"Du yu know that bow-laiged boy on the fence thar?" said Sut.

"No; who is he?"

"That's Bart Davis's yungest son, name Obed. Jis' obsarve how his snout's skin'd an' his year slit an' so forth."

"Yes, I see; how did it happen?"

"Happen? hit didn't happen et all, hit wer dun a-pupos, permeditated a-pupos. Ther wer a dance et his dad's, las' Sat'day nite wer two weeks ago, what hed like tu bred a berryin ur two; the corpses wer mos' redy, an' nuffin but acksidint kep em frum bein finished. I wer thar mysef, an' kin say an' swar that the chances run mity
10 even, a-tween mirth an' mournin. Fur a spell hit wer the exhitenest time I ever seed on sich a ocashun, not tu hev no more whisky nur we hed. Thar warn't but 'bout half a barril when we begun, an' when we quit, we burnt the hoops an' staves tu dance the las' reel by.

"Everybody knows Bart is a durn'd no-count, jug-kerryin, slow-thinkin, flea-hurtin, herrin-eatin, Noth Calinian, plays a three-string fiddil wif a grasshopper jirk, while his wife totes the wood. He hes but two gifs wuf a durn: wun is, he'll vide his whisky wif yu down tu the las' half pint; thar he stops, fur that's jis a horn yu know; an' tuther is, he ain't feard ove enything a-livin, sept ole Peg. I don't wun-der et that, fur hit mus' take a man wif a onnatrally big melt, not tu be fear'd ove
20 his wife, onless she's blind ur hes a sweethart. Peg (she's his ole quilt, yu know) is a regular steeltrap ove an 'oman; she goes wif wun side ove her frock tucked up at the hips, her har down her back, an' a roasted hickory onder her arm tu scold the brats wif, an' tu skeer Bart. They's bof great on dancin ove Sat'day nites et home, an' sumwhar else on tuther nites. Ef thar's a frolic enywhar in five mile, Bart is sure tu be thar, an' Peg, too, ef she's in travilin fix, which ain't more nur five months in the year. She goes fur two reasons: wun is, tu eat an' dance, an' tuther tu watch Bart. He hes two reasons also: wun is tu suck in all the whisky floatin roun, an' tu du a heap ove things what needs watchin. They giner'lly hes a dermestic dis-cussun arter they gets home, in which, teeth, claws, an' beggin am the argymints,
30 an' 'I won't du so no more,' the aind ove hit. They am a lively an' even yok'd par. Nobody else on the green yeath orter be tied tu either ove em.

"Well they mounted that par ove hames yu see on the fence thar, the boy name Obed ontu a muel, an' sent him tu the still-hous, tu narrate hit that thar wud be a dance et home the nex nite, an' fur every feller what warn't married tu fetch a gal, an' them what wer married tu fetch two. Now this rangement show'd Bart's good sence, fur he know'd that hit takes more gals tu du married fellers then single wuns. Caze people what hes but one kind ove vittils et home, hit allers takes more tu du em abroad.

"When the nite cum they wer all thar, a hous' plum full, an' amung em a lot ove counter-hoppers wif strip'd sugar candy in their pockets, an' young lawyers wif cinamint ile ontu ther har; all on em frum town, an' jis' ole enuf tu begin tu strut an' gobble. Thunder and litnin, an' sun-flower pattrin calliker, mixed wif check an' stripe, homspun swept all about thar, wif one, jis' one black silk. They laid off two reels, wun call'd the leather shoe reel, an' tuther, the barfoot reel. I danced in the wun I nam'd las'."

"Why did they divide that way, Sut?"

"Why, durn hit, don't yu know that the dancin wud turn intu fitin afore the fust set got ofen the flure, ef they mix'd em? The shoes wud scronch the bar toes in dancin, an' rite then an' thar they'd mix fur a fite. A hard-shell preacher wif his   10
mouf mortised intu his face in shape like a muel's shoe, heels down, fotch hissef thar soon arter dark, an' made moshuns like he ment tu stay all nite. He got intu a corner, an' commenced a'tchunin up his sighin an' groanin aperatus, a-shakin ove his head, an' lookin like he hed the belly-ake. He cudn't hev look'd more solem-coly, ef his mam hed died that mornin a-owin him two dullars an' a 'alf. All these wimin an' luvely souns an' moshuns wer made on count ove the dancin, an' p'raps the cussin an' kissin. The whisky part ove that inturtainment he'd nuffin against. I *know'd* that, fur every time he roll'd his eyes to'ards the barril, he'd lick his lips sorter sloppy like, jis' es ef he'd been dippin his bill intu a crock ove chicken gravy, an' wer tryin tu save the stray draps, what hung outside his face. Oh! he wer jis'   20
a-honin arter that ball-face whisky; he'd a jis' kiss'd hit es sweet, an' es long, es ef hit hed been a willin gal. I sorter aidged up a-side him, an' sez I —

" 'Mister, will yu hev a few draps ove camfire, ur laudamy? Yu seems to be pow'-ful ailin in yer innards. Yu hesent swallered a live rat, ur a mole, hes yu?'

"He shook his head, an' fotch a sigh, what ainded in a groan. Sez I —

" 'Rats ur moles am onhelthy things tu swaller afore they'se departed this life.'

"He blow'd out a orful sigh, part outen his nose, but mos' ove hit out whar the toe ove the muel-shoe wer, an' sez he —

" 'This am a wicked an' a parvarse generashun ove vipurs, yung man.'

" 'An' gin up tu hardness ove hart, an' deviltry, an' belevin thunderin lies,' said   30
I; an' I puff'd out a big sigh, wif a little groan fur a tail. Sez he —

" 'Thar am no-o-o-o dancin in hell,' an sot intu shakin ove his head, till I thot he'd keep on fur everlastin, an' ever more. Sez I —

" 'Haint yu *slitely* mistaken'd in that las' re-mark ove yourn? Ef thar's es much hot truck, an' brimstone, an' cinders, an' hickory smoke, an' big hurtin, in hell es yu folks sez thar am, thar mus' be *sum* dancin, purtickelerly jigs an' quick-steps; they don't lack fur music, I reckon, fur I'se allers hearn hell wer full ove fiddlers, an' thar's Yankees enuf thar tu invent fire-proof fiddils fur em, so they don't want fur tchunes. All on yeath that bothers me is the rosim.'

" 'Ah, yung onregenerit man,' sez he, 'thar's more rosim in hell than thar's in all   40
Noth Caliny.'

" 'But hit ain't quite hard enuf tu rub ontu fiddil bows, is hit?' sez I.

---

1 **counter-hoppers,** store clerks   21 **ball-face,** bald-face, a poor grade

"He groan'd an' shook his head, an' sent one ove his eyes to'ards the whisky corner. I went an' fotch 'im a big slug intu a gourd. That shovel-shaped onder lip ove his'n jis' fell out'ards like ontu the fallin door ove a stone coal stove, an' he upsot the gourd inside ove his teef. I seed the mark ove the truck gwine down his froat jis' like a snake travelin thru a wet sassidge gut. He smelt intu the gourd a good long smell, turned up his eyes, an' sed 'Barlm ove life.'

"Thinks I, ole Sock, I know what fotch yu tu this frolic besides yu're hoss an' our whisky. Bart now cum up, an' Hardshell tole him he'd cum tu stay all nite, ef he suited all roun.

10 " 'Sartinly, oh yas, an' welcum,' sed Bart.

"The ole Sock, never alterin the shape ove the hole tore in his face, sed, mity sneerin like, 'Yu is hosspitabil.' I seed Bart sorter start, an' look at him, an' go off a-winkin at me tu foller him. We went outside the hous', intu a chimbly corner, an' thar wer two fellers, wun ove em a she, a-whisperin. We went tu tuther corner, an' thar were two more; then we went tu the stabil, an' hearn whisperin thar; hit mout been rats a-runnin in straw. So Bart cud hold in no longer. Sez he —

" 'Never mine, I don't keer a durn who hears me. I b'leve I'se been 'sulted in my own hous'; didn't that durn'd preachin mersheen call me a hoss?'

" 'That's jis' what he sed. He call'd yu a hoss-pitabil,' sez I.

20 " 'Pitabil, pitabil,' sez Bart, 'dam ef I don't b'leve that's wus nur the hoss.'

" 'Sartinly,' sez I, 'pitabil is a sorter Latin tail stuck tu hit so yu moutn't onderstand; hit means pitiful hoss in Inglish, an' ef I wer yu, I'd see that his stumack wer spiled fur Peg's fried chicken an' biskit. I'd go rite in an' show him how a hoss ken kick an' sich like.' He jis' gritted his teef, like he wer a'chompin aigshells, ur paragorick phials, an' put fur the hous', a-rollin up his shut-sleeves es he went, plum up to his arm-pit.

"The durn'd, hiperkritikil, groanin ole Hardshell raskil hed dun got the dancin stop't; he'd tuck the fiddil away frum the nigger, an' wer a-holdin hit by the naik in wun han, an' a-makin gesters wif the bow in tuther. He wer mounted ontu a
30 cheer, clost by the meal barril, an' wer exortin em orfully 'bout thar sins ove omishun an' cummishun, purtickerly the cummishun wuns, wif the dancin sins at the head, warin sunflower caliker wuns nex'; an' then cum thar smaller sins, sich es ridin a-hine fellers on the same hoss, whisperin outen doors, an' a-winkin a-hine fans, tuckey-tails an' hankerchers, an' sed that black silk wer plenty in hell, that hit wer used fur mournin thar, an' not tu dance in. The *he* sins, ove the small sort, wer cumin frum town ove nites, a-warin store clothes, smellin ove cinamint ile, an' a-totin striped sugar candy in thar pockets, tu turn the minds ove the weak gals, instead ove a flask ove that good holesum ole truck, what they'se got in towns, name 'coniack.'

40 "The wimmen folks wer backed up in bunches, in the corners, an' agin the beds, wif thar fingers in thar moufs, an' wun ur two ove the saftest ove em wer getting up a quiet sort ove dry cryin.

---

34 **tuckey-tails,** turkey-tails

"The he fellers all looked like they'd mos' es leave fite es not, ef they knew how tu start the thing, when in bounced Bart; he looked like a catamount; wun jump an' he stood a-top ove the meal barril, squar in frunt ove Hardshell, his har a-swayin about wif pure mad, like a patch ove ripe rye in a wind, an' his eyes wer es roun an' es red as a bull's when he's a-jinin in battil wif anuther bull frum Bashan. He struck wun fistes away out a-hine, an' wif tuther reachin at arm's laingth, he cummenc'd borin, like he hed a gimblit in his shot fis', rite onder the snout ove the thunderin Hardshell, like he wer tryin tu bore his mouf inter a better shape, an' a-narratin thru his teef these facs, in words what sounded like grittin hard co'n.

" 'Yu durn'd infunel, incumpassabil warter-dorg! yu cuss'd hiperkritikal, ongrate- 10
ful ole mus-rat! yu h-ll fir'd, divin, splatterin, pond-makin, iron-jacket'd ole son ove a mud-turtil, yu hes 'sulted me in my own hous', *an' in Latin et that,* an' then yu've tuck the imperdent liberty tu skare these yere children outen thar innersent mucement, (still borin away frum left tu right, wif that horny fis' ove his'n, an' the Hardshell's head gwine furder back every twist.) Call'd me a hoss — — Git ofen that cheer!'

"Es he sed 'git,' he loaned the passun a mos' tremenjus contushun, rite in the bull curl. I seed his shoe-soles a-gwine up each side ove Bart's fis' afore he hed time tu muve hit, arter he struck. Hit wer a lick, George, that hed hit been a kick, a four year ole muel wud hev been pow'ful proud ove. I seed ni ontu a gallon ove 20
sparks ove fire fly outen the passun's eyes mysef (he mus hev seed a bushel) when hit reached his curl. He let the fiddil go when he wer in the highes part ove his backward summerset, an' the nigger what hed been watchin up at hit all this time, wis'ful like, es a dorg watches a meat-skin when yu holds hit too high fur him tu grab, cotch his fiddil in bof hans afore hit toch the yeath.

" 'Dar by golly, you no git tu smash dis fiddil, wid yu durn fool fitin an' preachin.'

"An' holdin it wavinly abuv his head, he dodged outen the surkil ove imejut danger. The old Shell lit ontu his all fours, hit bein that much more nur a full summerset, an' *the* black silk lit a-stradil ove him. I know'd hit wer the black silk, bekase I seed the white stockins an' grey garters. Hev I mention'd that thar wer one 30
hundred an' twenty-five pouns ove live, black-eyed gal in under the black silk?"

"No, Sut."

"Well, thar wer, an' that she wer bof live an' willin, ole Dipper wer soon redy tu swar. 'Black silk in hell is thar,' scream'd she, a-hissin like ontu a cat, an' cummenced a-pullin up by the roots his long har, like hit wer flax, wif bof hans, an' a-shakin the bunches ofen her fingers, an' then gwine fur more, the hissin gittin a littil louder every pull. George, that were the fust spessamin ove a smokin mad gal I've seed in a hen's age; she kerried out my idear ove a fust-rate flax-puller, pullin agin two, fur a bet. I think she gin the ole Shell the idear that sum strong man body wer a-holden his head ni ontu the saws ove a activ cotton gin.   40

"Now the boy name Obed, with the hame laigs, hevin a sorter jestis' ove the peace turn ove mine, run in tu pull her off, an' cudn't du hit afore she made a rake

---

5 **Bashan,** a Biblical country famous for its cattle

fur his har, an' got hit. She jis' mixed the hanful wif the pile on the flure, an' gin
hersef back tu the job ove preparin the passun fur a wig. A hawk-billed, weazel-
eyed, rat-mouthed feller, what hed been a-struttin roun Black Silk all nite, a-trailin
wun wing, an' a-lickin his lips, seed the fool boy name Obed, a-trying tu git her tu
lite ofen the old Sock, so he jis' growl'd low, an' barked once, an' kiver'd him, an'
afore his mam Peg, an' me, an' five uther gals, cud git him loose, he hed made her
cub the speckterkil yu sees roostin on that ar fence, an' he's hed ni ontu three weeks
tu mend his looks in, by Jew David's plarster, sweet ile, an' the keer ove his mam.

"The fitin now got tu be gineral on mos' parts ove the field, an' es the cuppils
10 cum in frum outen doors, lookin sorter sneakin, an' pale, (frum the nise ove the
rumpus, I speck,) wun at leas', outen every par, got jump't on by sumbody. P'raps
a gal wud kiver a cumin in gal, anuther gal wud go fur the har an' skin ove a cumin
in he feller; then, agin, the fis' ove a he wud meet anuther cumin in he, right atween
the eyes, an' so on till the thing got tu be durn'dably mix'd up an' lively. Peg boun
up the boy name Obed's wouns, bruises, an' petrifyin sores, an' then went on wif
supper cookin, like all wer quiet on the Pertomack.

"Es soon es ole Shell begun to cum to, frum Bart's dubbil distill'd thunder-bolt,
the hurtin all over his head begun tu attrack his 'tenshun, an' soaked thru his skull,
an' in thar tuck the shape ove an idear; the idear shaped hitsef intu spoken wurds,
20 an' they wer, 'Gird up yer loins an' *git.*' I seek the wurkin ove his mind, so I jis'
shouted es loud es I could beller, 'The Pherlistshuns be upon yu Sampsin.' He hearn
hit, an' wer struck wif the force ove the remark, an' started fur the back door, still
on his all fours, in a single foot rack. Es soon es Black Silk felt him movin, she
cummenced spurrin him wif her heels; while she hilt tu his har wif wun han, she
tuck a pin outen her collar wif tuther, an' made a cushion fur hit in the hill, ontu
the north side ove the pint ove his back-bone; he kicked up an' snorted, an' changed
the single foot rack intu a tarin pace, loped outen the door intu outer darkness, an'
his heel-tops were the last I seed ove him. He stumbled an' fell down the log-steps,
an' flung Black Silk like onto a full balloon over his head, (I seed a heap ove white
30 shinin es she went.) He felt his way in the dark, thru the woods, fur more pleasant
places, an' she cum in larfin, 'Black silk in hell, hey?' wer every word she sed."

"Go on, Sut."

"That's all. I ain't like ole Glabbergab; when I'se spoke off what I knows, I stops
talkin."

"Well, what became of Hardshell?"

"Oh! es tu that, he made his 'pearance las' Sunday, in the pulpit, es bald es a jug,
wif a black spot aidged wif green an' yaller, 'bout the size ove a prickly par, on his
forehead, an' preach't bout the orful konsekenses ove Absalom's hevin long har,
human depravity, an' the Salt Lake; sed he wer gwine thar right off, an' *he'll du hit.*"

1845, 1867

---

38 **Absalom . . . har.** Absalom, David's son, was caught by the hair in overhanging oak boughs as he rode
and subsequently slain while thus helpless. See II Samuel 18:9ff.   39 **Salt Lake,** a play no doubt on the
Biblical Dead Sea and the lake of this name in Utah by which the Mormons settled

Mrs. Yardley's Quilting

"Thar's one durn'd nasty muddy job, an' I is jis' glad enuf tu take a ho'n ur two, on the straingth ove hit."

"What have you been doing, Sut?"

"Helpin tu salt ole Missis Yardley down."

"What do you mean by that?"

"Fixin her fur rotten cumfurtably, kiverin her up wif sile, tu keep the buzzards frum cheatin the wurms."

"Oh, you have been helping to bury a woman."

"That's hit, by golly! Now why the devil can't I 'splain mysef like yu? I ladles out my words at random, like a calf kickin at yaller-jackids; yu jis' rolls em out tu 10 the pint, like a feller a-layin bricks — every one fits. How is it that bricks fits so clost enyhow? Rocks won't ni du hit."

"Becaze they'se all ove a size," ventured a man with a wen over his eye.

"The devil yu say, hon'ey-head! haint reapin-mersheens ove a size? I'd like to see two ove em fit clost. Yu wait ontil yu sprouts tuther ho'n, afore yu venters tu 'splain mix'd questions. George, did yu know ole Missis Yardley?"

"No."

"Well, she wer a curious 'oman in her way, an' she wore shiney specks. Now jis' listen: Whenever yu see a ole 'oman ahine a par ove *shiney* specks, yu keep yer eye skinn'd: they am dang'rus in the extreme. Thar is jis' no knowin what they ken du. 20 I hed one a-stradil ove me onst, fur kissin her gal. She went fur my har, an' she went fur my skin, ontil I tho't she ment tu kill me, an' wud a-dun hit, ef my hollerin hadent fotch ole Dave Jordan, a *bacheler,* tu my aid. He, like a durn'd fool, cotch her by the laig, an' drug her back'ards ofen me. She jis' kivered him, an' I run, by golly! The nex time I seed him he wer bald headed, an' his face looked like he'd been a-fitin wildcats.

"Ole Missis Yardley wer a great noticer ove littil things, that nobody else ever seed. She'd say right in the middil ove sumbody's serious talk: 'Law sakes! thar goes that yaller slut ove a hen, a-flingin straws over her shoulder; she's arter settin now, an' haint laid but seven aigs. I'll disapint *her,* see ef I don't; I'll put a punkin in 30 her ne's, an' a feather in her nose. An' bless my soul! jis' look at that cow wif the wilted ho'n, a-flingin up dirt an' a-smellin the place whar hit cum frum, wif the rale ginuine still-wurim twis' in her tail, too; what upon the face ove the yeath kin she be arter now, the ole fool? watch her, Sally. An' sakes alive! jis' look at that ole sow; she's a-gwine in a fas' trot, wif her empty bag a-floppin agin her sides. Thar, she hes stop't, an's a-listenin! massy on us! what a long yearnis grunt she gin; hit cum frum way back ove her kidneys. Thar she goes agin; she's arter no good, sich kerryin on means no good.'

"An' so she wud gabble, no odds who wer a-listenin. She looked like she mout

been made at fust 'bout four foot long, an' the common thickness ove wimen when they's at tharsefs, an' then had her har tied 'tu a stump, a par ove steers hitched to her heels, an' then straiched out a-mos' two foot more — mos' ove the straichin cumin outen her laigs an' naik. Her stockins, a-hangin on the clothes-line tu dry, looked like a par ove sabre scabbards, an' her naik looked like a dry beef shank smoked, an' mout been ni ontu es tough. I never felt hit mysef, I didn't, I jis' jedges by looks. Her darter Sal wer bilt at fust 'bout the laingth ove her mam, but wer never straiched eny by a par ove steers an' she wer fat enuf tu kill; she wer taller lyin down than she wer a-standin up. Hit wer her who gin me the 'hump
10 shoulder.' Jis' look at me; haint I'se got a tech ove the dromedary back thar bad? haint I humpy? Well, a-stoopin tu kiss that squatty lardstan ove a gal is what dun hit tu me. She wer the fairest-lookin gal I ever seed. She allers wore thick woolin stockins 'bout six inches too long fur her laig; they rolled down over her garters, lookin like a par ove life-presarvers up thar. I tell yu she wer a tarin gal enyhow. Luved kissin, wrastlin, an' biled cabbige, an' hated tite clothes, hot weather, an' suckit-riders. B'leved strong in married folk's ways, cradles, an' the remishun ove sins, an' didn't b'leve in corsets, fleas, peaners, nur the fashun plates."

"What caused the death of Mrs. Yardley, Sut?"

"Nuffin, only her heart stop't beatin 'bout losin a nine dimunt quilt. True, she
20 got a skeer'd hoss tu run over her, but she'd a-got over that ef a quilt hadn't been mix'd up in the catastrophy. Yu see quilts wer wun ove her speshul gifts; she run strong on the bed-kiver question. Irish chain, star ove Texas, sun-flower, nine dimunt, saw teeth, checker board, an' shell quilts; blue, an' white, an' yaller an' black cover-lids, an' callickercumfurts reigned triumphan' 'bout her hous'. They wer packed in drawers, layin in shelfs full, wer hung four dubbil on lines in the lof, packed in chists, piled on cheers, an' wer everywhar, even ontu the beds, an' wer changed every bed-makin. She told everybody she cud git tu listen tu hit that she ment tu give every durn'd one ove them tu Sal when she got married. Oh, lordy! what es fat a gal es Sal Yardley cud ever du wif half ove em, an' sleepin wif a husbun at
30 that, is more nor I ever cud see through. Jis' think ove her onder twenty layer ove quilts in July, an' yu in thar too. Gewhillikins! George, look how I is sweatin' now, an' this is December. I'd 'bout es lief be shet up in a steam biler wif a three hundred pound bag ove lard, es tu make a bisiness ove sleepin wif that gal — 'twould kill a glass-blower.

"Well, tu cum tu the serious part ove this conversashun, that is how the old quilt-mersheen an' coverlid-loom cum tu stop operashuns on this yeath. She hed narrated hit thru the neighborhood that nex Saterday she'd gin a quiltin — three quilts an' one cumfurt tu tie. 'Goblers, fiddils, gals, an' whisky,' wer the words she sent tu the men-folk, an' more tetchin ur wakenin words never drap't ofen an 'oman's
40 tongue. She sed tu the gals, 'Sweet toddy, huggin, dancin, an' huggers in 'bundunce.' Them words struck the gals rite in the pit ove the stumick, an' spread a ticklin sen-sashun bof ways, ontil they scratched thar heads wif one han, an' thar heels wif tuther.

"Everybody, he an' she, what wer baptized b'levers in the righteousnes ove

---

22 **Irish chain . . . shell quilts,** the names of quilt patterns

quiltins wer thar, an' hit jis' so happen'd that everybody in them parts, frum fifteen
summers tu fifty winters, wer unannamus b'levers. Strange, warn't hit? Hit wer the
bigges' quiltin ever Missis Yardley hilt, an' she hed hilt hundreds; everybody wer
thar, 'scept the constibil an' suckit-rider, two dam easily-spared pussons; the numbers ni ontu even too; jis' a few more boys nur gals; that made hit more exhitin,
fur hit gin the gals a chance tu kick an' squeal a littil, wifout runnin eny risk ove
not gittin kissed at all, an' hit gin reasonabil grouns fur a few scrimmages amung
the he's. Now es kissin an' fitin am the pepper an' salt ove all soshul getherins, so
hit wer more espishully wif this ove ours. Es I swung my eyes over the crowd, George,
I thought quiltins, managed in a morril an' sensibil way, truly am good things —   10
good fur free drinkin, good fur free eatin, good fur free huggin, good fur free
dancin, good fur free fitin, an' goodest ove all fur poperlatin a country fas'.

   "Thar am a fur-seein wisdum in quiltins, ef they hes proper trimmins: 'vittils,
fiddils, an' sperrits in 'bundunce.' One holesum quiltin am wuf three old pray'r-
meetins on the poperlashun pint, purtickerly ef hits hilt in the dark ove the moon,
an' runs intu the night a few hours, an' April ur May am the time chosen.
The moon don't suit quiltins whar everybody is well acquainted an' already fur along
in courtin. She dus help pow'ful tu begin a courtin match onder, but when hit draws
ni ontu a head, nobody wants a moon but the ole mammys.

   "The mornin cum, still, saft, sunshiney; cocks crowin, hens singin, birds chirpin,   20
tuckeys gobblin — jis' the day tu sun quilts, kick, kiss, squeal, an' make love.

   "All the plow-lines an' clothes-lines wer straiched tu every post an' tree. Quilts
purvailed. Durn my gizzard ef two acres roun that ar house warn't jis' one solid
quilt, all out a-sunnin, an' tu be seed. They dazzled the eyes, skeered the hosses,
gin wimen the heart-burn, an' perdominated.

   "To'ards sundown the he's begun tu drap in. Yearnis' needil-drivin cummenced
tu lose groun; threads broke ofen, thimbils got los', an' quilts needed anuther roll.
Gigglin, winkin, whisperin, smoofin ove har, an' gals a-ticklin one anuther, wer
a-gainin every inch ove groun what the needils los'. Did yu ever notis, George, at
all sushul getherins, when the he's begin tu gather, that the young she's begin tu   30
tickil one anuther an' the ole maids swell thar tails, roach up thar backs, an' sharpen
thar nails ontu the bed-posts an' door jams, an' spit an' groan sorter like cats
a-courtin? Dus hit mean *rale* rath, ur is hit a dare tu the he's, sorter kivered up wif
the outside signs ove danger? I honestly b'leve that the young shes' ticklin means,
'Cum an' take this job ofen our hans.' But that swellin I jis' don't onderstan; dus
yu? Hit looks skeery, an' I never tetch one ove em when they am in the swellin
way. I may be mistaken'd 'bout the ticklin bisiness too; hit may be dun like a feller
chaws poplar bark when he haint got eny terbacker, a-sorter better nur nun make-
shif. I dus know one thing tu a certainty: that is, when the he's take hold the ticklin
quits, an' ef yu gits one ove the ole maids out tu hersef, then she subsides an' is   40
the smoofes, sleekes, saft thing yu ever seed, an' dam ef yu can't hear her purr, jis'
es plain!

   "But then, George, gals an' ole maids haint the things tu fool time away on. Hits
widders, by golly, what am the rale sensibil, steady-goin, never-skeerin, never-

kickin, willin, sperrited, smoof pacers. They cum clost up tu the hoss-block, standin still wif thar purty silky years playin, an' the naik-veins a-throbbin, an' waits fur the word, which ove course yu gives, arter yu finds yer feet well in the stirrup, an' away they moves like a cradil on cushioned rockers, ur a spring buggy runnin in damp san'. A tetch ove the bridil, an' they knows yu wants em tu turn, an' they dus hit es willin es ef the idear wer thar own. I be dod rabbited ef a man can't 'propriate happiness by the skinful ef he is in contack wif sumbody's widder, an' is smart. Gin me a willin widder, the yeath over: what they don't know, haint worth larnin. They hes all been tu Jamakey an' larnt how sugar's made, an' knows how tu sweeten
10 wif hit; an' by golly, they is always ready tu use hit. All yu hes tu du is tu find the spoon, an' then drink cumfort till yer blind. Nex tu good sperrits an' my laigs, I likes a twenty-five year ole widder, wif roun ankils, an' bright eyes, honestly an' squarly lookin intu yurn, an' sayin es plainly es a partrige sez 'Bob White,' 'Don't be afraid ove me; I hes been thar; yu know hit ef yu hes eny sense, an' thar's no use in eny humbug, ole feller — cum ahead!'

"Ef yu onderstans widder nater, they ken save yu a power ove troubil, onsartinty, an' time, en' ef yu is interprisin yu gits mons'rous well paid fur hit. The very soun ove thar littil shoe-heels speak full trainin, an' hes a knowin click as they tap the floor; an' the rustil ove thar dress sez, 'I dar yu tu ax me.'
20 "When yu hes made up yer mind tu court one, jis' go at hit like hit wer a job ove rail-maulin. Ware yer workin close, use yer common, every-day moshuns an' words, an' abuv all, fling away yer cinamint ile vial an' burn all yer love songs. No use in tryin tu fool em, fur they sees plum thru yu, a durn'd sight plainer than they dus thru thar veils. No use in a pasted shut; she's been thar. No use in borrowin a cavortin fat hoss; she's been thar. No use in har-dye; she's been thar. No use in cloves, tu kill whisky breff; she's been thar. No use in buyin clost curtains fur yer bed, fur she has been thar. Widders am a speshul means, George, fur ripenin green men, killin off weak ones, an makin 'ternally happy the soun ones.

"Well, es I sed afore I flew the track an' got ontu the widders. The fellers begun
30 tu ride up an' walk up, sorter slow, like they warn't in a hurry, the durn'd 'saitful raskils, hitchin thar critters tu enything they cud find. One red-comb'd, long-spurr'd, dominecker feller, frum town, in a red an' white gridiron jackid an' patent leather gaiters, hitched his hoss, a wild, skeery, wall-eyed devil, inside the yard palins, tu a cherry tree lim'. Thinks I, that hoss hes a skeer intu him big enuf tu run intu town, an' perhaps beyant hit, ef I kin only tetch hit off; so I sot intu thinkin.

"One aind ove a long clothes-line, wif nine dimunt quilts ontu hit, wer tied tu the same cherry tree that the hoss wer. I tuck my knife and socked hit thru every quilt, 'bout the middil, an' jis' below the rope, an' tied them thar wif bark, so they cudent slip. Then I went tu the back aind, an' ontied hit from the pos', knottin in
40 a hoe-handil, by the middil, tu keep the quilts frum slippin off ef my bark strings failed, an' laid hit on the groun. Then I went tu the tuther aind: thar were 'bout ten foot tu spar, a-lyin on the ground arter tyin tu the tree. I tuck hit atwix Wall-

---

9 **Jamakey,** Jamaica, the commonest source of sugar in the early days of the republic   24 **pasted shut,** stiff shirt   32 **dominecker,** Dominique, a breed of chicken with spectacular coloration

eye's hine laigs, an' tied hit fas' tu bof stirrups, an' then cut the cherry tree lim' be-
twix his bridil an' the tree, almos' off. Now, mine yu thar wer two ur three uther
ropes full ove quilts atween me an' the hous', so I wer purty well hid frum thar. I
jis' tore off a palin frum the fence, an' tuck hit in bof hans, an' arter raisin hit 'way
up yander, I fotch hit down, es hard es I cud, flatsided to'ards the groun, an' hit
acksidentally happen'd tu hit Wall-eye, 'bout nine inches ahead ove the root ove his
tail. Hit landed so hard that hit made my hans tingle, an' then busted intu splinters. The first thing I did, wer tu feel ove mysef, on the same spot whar hit hed
hit the hoss. I cudent help duin hit tu save my life, an' I swar I felt sum ove Wall-
eye's sensashun, jis' es plain. The fust thing he did, wer tu tare down the lim' wif   10
a twenty foot jump, his head to'ards the hous'. Thinks I, now yu hev dun hit, yu
durn'd wall-eyed fool! tarin down that lim' wer the beginin ove all the troubil, an'
the hoss did hit hissef; my conshuns felt clar es a mountin spring, an' I wer in a
frame ove mine tu obsarve things es they happen'd, an' they soon begun tu happen
purty clost arter one anuther rite then, an' thar, an' tharabouts, clean ontu town,
thru hit, an' still wer a-happenin, in the woods beyant thar ni ontu eleven mile frum
ole man Yardley's gate, an' four beyant town.

"The fust line ove quilts he tried tu jump, but broke hit down; the nex one he
ran onder; the rope cotch ontu the ho'n ove the saddil, broke at bof ainds, an' went
along wif the hoss, the cherry tree lim' an' the fust line ove quilts, what I   20
hed proverdensally tied fas' tu the rope. That's what I calls foresight, George. Right
furnint the frunt door he cum in contack wif ole Missis Yardley hersef, an' anuther
ole 'oman; they wer a-holdin a nine dimunt quilt spread out, a-'zaminin hit, an'
a-praisin hits purfeckshuns. The durn'd onmanerly, wall-eyed fool run plum over
Missis Yardley, frum ahine, stompt one hine foot through the quilt, takin hit along,
a-kickin ontil he made hits corners snap like a whip. The gals screamed, the men
hollered wo! an' the ole 'oman wer toted intu the hous' limber es a wet string, an'
every word she sed wer, 'Oh, my preshus nine dimunt quilt!'

"Wall-eye busted thru the palins, an' Dominicker sed 'im, made a mortal rush fur
his bitts, wer too late fur them, but in good time fur the strings ove flyin quilts,   30
got tangled amung em, an' the gridiron jackid patren wer los' tu my sight amung
star an' Irish chain quilts; he went frum that quiltin at the rate ove thuty miles tu
the hour. Nuffin lef on the lot ove the hole consarn, but a nine biler hat, a par ove
gloves, an' the jack ove hearts.

"What a onmanerly, suddin way ove leavin places sum folks hev got, enyhow.

"Thinks I, well, that fool hoss, tarin down that cherry tree lim', hes dun sum good,
enyhow; hit hes put the ole 'oman outen the way fur the balance ove the quiltin, an'
tuck Dominicker outen the way an' outen danger, fur that gridiron jackid wud a-bred
a scab on his nose afore midnite; hit wer morrily boun tu du hit.

"Two months arterwards, I tracked the route that hoss tuck in his kalamatus skeer,   40
by quilt rags, tufts ove cotton, bunches ove har, (human an' hoss,) an' scraps ove a
gridiron jackid stickin ontu the bushes, an' plum at the aind ove hit, whar all sign
gin out, I foun a piece ove watch chain an' a hosses head. The places what know'd
Dominicker, know'd 'im no more.

"Well, arter they'd tuck the ole 'oman up stairs an' camfired her tu sleep, things begun tu work agin. The widders broke the ice, an' arter a little gigilin, goblin, an' gabblin, the kissin begun. *Smack!* — 'Thar, now,' a widder sed that. *Pop!* — 'Oh, don't!' *Pfip!* — 'Oh, yu quit!' *Plosh!* — 'Go *way* yu awkerd critter, yu kissed me in the eye!' anuther widder sed that. *Bop!* 'Now yu ar satisfied, I recon, big mouf!' *Vip!* — 'That haint fair!' *Spat!* — 'Oh, lordy! May, cum pull Bill away; he's a-tanglin my har.' *Thut!* — 'I jis' d-a-r-e yu tu du that agin!' a widder sed that, too. Hit sounded all 'roun that room like poppin co'n in a hot skillet, an' wer pow'ful sujestif.

"Hit kep on ontil I be durn'd ef *my* bristils didn't begin tu rise, an' sumthin like
10 a cold buckshot wud run down the marrow in my back-bone 'bout every ten secons, an' then run up again, tolerabil hot. I kep a swallerin wif nuthin tu swaller, an' my face felt swell'd; an' yet I wer fear'd tu make a bulge. Thinks I, I'll ketch one out tu hersef torreckly, an' then I guess we'll rastil. Purty soon Sal Yardley started fur the smoke-'ous, so I jis' gin my head a few short shakes, let down one ove my wings a-trailin, an' sirkiled roun her wif a side twis' in my naik, steppin sidewise, an' a-fetchin up my hinmos' foot wif a sorter jerkin slide at every step. Sez I, 'Too coo-took a-too.' She onderstood hit, an stopt, sorter spreadin her shoulders. An' jis' es I hed pouch'd out my mouf, an wer a-reachin forrid wif hit, for the article hitsef, sunthin interfared wif me, hit did. George, wer yu ever ontu yer hans an' knees, an'
20 let a hell-tarin big, mad ram, wif a ten-yard run, but yu yearnis'ly, jis' onst, right squar ontu the pint ove yer back-bone?"

"No, you fool; why do you ask?"

"Kaze I wanted tu know ef yu cud hev a realizin' noshun ove my shock. Hits scarcely worth while tu try tu make yu onderstan the case by words only, onless yu hev been tetched in that way. Gr-eat golly! the fust thing I felt, I tuck hit tu be a back-ackshun yeathquake; an' the fust thing I seed wer my chaw'r terbacker a-flyin over Sal's head like a skeer'd bat. My mouf were pouch'd out, ready fur the article hitsef, yu know, an' hit went outen the roun hole like the wad outen a popgun — thug! an' the fust thing I know'd, I wer a flyin over Sal's head too, an' a-gainin on
30 the chaw'r terbacker fast. I wer straitened out strait, toes hinemos', middil finger-nails foremos', an' the fust thing I hearn wer, 'Yu dam Shanghi!' Great Jerus-a-lam! I lit ontu my all fours jis' in time tu but the yard gate ofen hits hinges, an' skeer loose sum more hosses — kep on in a four-footed gallop, clean acrost the lane afore I cud straiten up, an' yere I cotch up wif my chaw'r terbacker, stickin flat agin a fence-rail. I hed got so good a start that I thot hit a pity tu spile hit, so I jis' jump'd the fence an' tuck thru the orchurd. I tell yu I dusted these yere close, fur I tho't hit wer arter me.

"Arter runnin a spell, I ventered tu feel roun back thar, fur sum signs ove what hed happened tu me. George, arter two pow'ful hard tugs, I pull'd out the vamp an'
40 sole ove one ove old man Yardley's big brogans, what he hed los' amung my coat-tails. Dre'ful, dre'ful! Arter I got hit away frum thar, my flesh went fas' asleep, frum abuv my kidneys tu my knees; about now, fur the fust time, the idear struck me, what hit wer that hed interfar'd wif me, an' los' me the kiss. Hit wer ole Yardley hed kicked me. I walked fur a month like I wer straddlin a thorn hedge. Sich a shock,

at sich a time, an' on sich a place — jis' think ove hit! hit am tremenjus, haint hit? The place feels num, right now."

"Well, Sut, how did the quilting come out?"

"How the hell du yu 'speck me tu know? I warn't thar eny more."

1867

1815—1878 *Thomas Bangs Thorpe*

Although he was the author of the most famous tall tale of the pre-Civil War Southwest, "The Big Bear of Arkansas," Thomas Bangs Thorpe was born in the East — in Westfield, Massachusetts, in 1815. He left Wesleyan University, in Middletown, Connecticut, in 1836, when ill health made it necessary for him to move to a milder climate, and settled down in Baton Rouge, Louisiana. In Louisiana and other parts of what was then the Far West, Thorpe gathered material for both paintings and writings which won a fine reputation for him.

Thorpe had a varied career. He painted various frontier scenes and numerous portraits, among the most admired of which were one of Jenny Lind and one of his friend, Zachary Taylor. He edited several newspapers and wrote a number of sketches which were widely reprinted. He was in the army during the Mexican War. After the war, he returned to the East — to New York, where he was an editor until his death in 1878.

The Mysteries of the Backwoods; or Sketches of the Southwest including Character, Scenery and Rural Sports (1846) and *The Hive of the Bee Hunter* (1854) were Thorpe's best books — both of them collections of sketches detailing life in the backwoods. "The Big Bear of Arkansas," this author's masterpiece, first appeared in a great publication of masculine humor of the day, *The Spirit of the Times,* in 1841. Like many other pieces published in that journal, this narrative shows how the art of the oral tale gave shape and substance to narrative in print.

F. J. Meine, "Thomas Bangs Thorpe," **Dictionary of American Biography**, New York, 1935   Walter Blair, **Native American Humor** (1800-1900), Cincinnati, 1937   Milton Rickels, **Thomas Bangs Thorpe**, Baton Rouge, 1962

The Big Bear of Arkansas

In 1839 John Neal, an Eastern critic and fiction writer quite prominent at the time, published the article "Story-Telling" in the New York Mirror. *"Of all the stories I meet with," he testified, "none are so delightful to me as those I over-hear on board a steam-boat or a stage-coach . . . live stories, brimful of energy and vivacity." Thorpe's "Big Bear," published a couple of years later, conveyed much of the life and the gusto of a good yarn spun in the social hall of a steamboat.*

If, as many good critics agree, the essence of humor is incongruity, Thorpe's narrative contains that essence. One notes the disparity, for instance, between the various worlds in the story — worlds which are identified with various groups and various scenes. Contrasted are the heterogeneous world of the steamboat, realistically portrayed in the "literary" words of the author; the fashionable world of New Orleans, satirically described in the homely words of Jim Doggett; and the comic, wildly fantastic world of Shirt-tail Bend in Arkansas, imaginatively revealed by Jim's poetical invention. Each of these worlds has its own elements of amusement, and the juxtaposition underlines and contrasts these elements.

As Jim — a fascinating character in his own right — tells his tall tale, he becomes more and more imaginative. The "creation state" of Arkansas, as he pictures it, is astonishing compared with any other part of America, and Shirt-tail Bend is astonishing even for Arkansas. Ordinary bear hunts in Jim's section are truly extraordinary, but the great hunt here described is even more wonderful. And as the account of the Big Bear proceeds, even that monster takes on more and more of a supernatural aspect.

Just at the moment Jim's fancy soars into the empyrean, a homely detail — the loss of the valiant hunter's "inexpressibles" — contrasts his imaginative flight with mundane reality. But Jim, having started to soar, is carried along by his imaginings. At the end his yarn, which has started as a jest, has become so real to its creator that he is tremendously impressed by it.

A steamboat on the Mississippi frequently, in making her regular trips, carries between places varying from one to two thousand miles apart; and as these boats advertise to land passengers and freight at "all intermediate landings," the heterogeneous character of the passengers of one of these up-country boats can scarcely be imagined by one who has never seen it with his own eyes. Starting from New Orleans in one of these boats, you will find yourself associated with men from every state in the Union, and from every portion of the globe; and a man of observation need not lack for amusement or instruction in such a crowd, if he will take the trouble to read the great book of character so favourably opened before him. Here may be
10 seen jostling together the wealthy Southern planter, and the pedlar of tin-ware from New England — the Northern merchant, and the Southern jockey — a venerable bishop, and a desperate gambler, — the land speculator, and the honest farmer — professional men of all creeds and characters — Wolvereens, Suckers, Hoosiers, Buckeyes, and Corn-crackers, beside a "plentiful sprinkling" of the half-horse and half-alligator species of men, who are peculiar to "old Mississippi," and who appear

13 **Wolvereens** . . . **Corn-crackers,** natives, respectively, of Michigan, Illinois, Indiana, Ohio, and Kentucky

to gain a livelihood simply by going up and down the river. In the pursuit of pleasure or business, I have frequently found myself in such a crowd.

On one occasion, when in New Orleans, I had occasion to take a trip of a few miles up the Mississippi, and I hurried on board the well-known "high-pressure-and-beat-everything" steamboat *Invincible,* just as the last note of the last bell was sounding; and when the confusion and bustle that is natural to a boat's getting under way had subsided, I discovered that I was associated in as heterogeneous a crowd as was ever got together. As my trip was to be of a few hours' duration only, I made no endeavours to become acquainted with my fellow passengers, most of whom would be together many days. Instead of this, I took out of my pocket the "latest   10 paper," and more critically than usual examined its contents; my fellow passengers at the same time disposed themselves in little groups. While I was thus busily employed in reading, and my companions were more busily employed in discussing such subjects as suited their humours best, we were startled most unexpectedly by a loud Indian whoop, uttered in the "social hall," that part of the cabin fitted off for a bar; then was to be heard a loud crowing, which would not have continued to have interested us — such sounds being quite common in that place of spirits — had not the hero of these windy accomplishments stuck his head into the cabin and hallooed out, "Hurra for the Big Bar of Arkansaw!" and then might be heard a confused hum of voices, unintelligible, save in such broken sentences as "horse,"   20 "screamer," "lightning is slow" etc. As might have been expected, this continued interruption attracted the attention of every one in the cabin; all conversation dropped, and in the midst of this surprise the "Big Bar" walked into the cabin, took a chair, put his feet on the stove, and looking back over his shoulder, passed the general and familiar salute of "Strangers, how are you?" He then expressed himself as much at home as if he had been at "the Forks of Cypress," and "perhaps a little more so." Some of the company at this familiarity looked a little angry, and some astonished; but in a moment every face was wreathed in a smile. There was something about the intruder that won the heart on sight. He appeared to be a man enjoying perfect health and contentment: his eyes were as sparkling as diamonds, and   30 good-natured to simplicity. Then his perfect confidence in himself was irresistibly droll. "Perhaps," said he, "gentlemen," running on without a person speaking, "perhaps you have been to New Orleans often; I never made *the first visit before,* and I don't intend to make another in a crow's life. I am thrown away in that ar place, and useless, that ar a fact. Some of the gentlemen thar called me *green* — well, perhaps I am, said I, *but I arn't so at home;* and if I ain't off my trail much, the heads of them perlite chaps themselves wern't much the hardest; for according to my notion, they were real *know-nothings,* green as a pumpkin-vine — couldn't, in farming, I'll bet, raise a crop of turnips; and as for shooting, they'd miss a barn if the door was swinging, and that, too, with the best rifle in the country. And then they talked   40 to me 'bout hunting, and laughed at my calling the principal game in Arkansaw poker, and high-low-jack. 'Perhaps,' said I, 'you prefer chickens and rolette'; at this they laughed harder than ever, and asked me if I lived in the woods, and didn't

42 **chickens and rolette,** chicken hazard, a low stake game, and roulette

know what *game* was? At this I rather think I laughed. 'Yes,' I roared, and says, 'Strangers, if you'd asked me *how we got our meat* in Arkansaw, I'd a told you at once, and given you a list of varmints that would make a caravan, beginning with the bar, and ending off with the cat; that's *meat* though, not game.' Game, indeed, that's what city folks call it; and with them it means chippen-birds and shite-pokes; maybe such trash live in my diggens, but I arn't noticed them yet; a bird any way is too trifling. I never did shoot at but one, and I'd never forgiven myself for that, had it weighed less than forty pounds. I wouldn't draw a rifle on any thing less than that; and when I meet with another wild turkey of the same weight I will
10 drap him."

"A wild turkey weighing forty pounds!" exclaimed twenty voices in the cabin at once.

"Yes, strangers, and wasn't it a whopper? You see, the thing was so fat that it couldn't fly far; and when he fell out of the tree, after I shot him, on striking the ground he bust open behind, and the way the pound gobs of tallow rolled out of the opening was perfectly beautiful."

"Where did all that happen?" asked a cynical-looking Hoosier.

"Happen! happened in Arkansaw: where else could it have happened, but in the creation state, the finishing-up country — a state where the *sile* runs down to the
20 centre of the 'arth, and government gives you a title to every inch of it? Then its airs — just breathe them, and they will make you snort like a horse. It's a state without a fault, it is."

"Excepting mosquitoes," cried the Hoosier.

"Well, stranger, except them; for it ar a fact that they are rather *enormous*, and do push themselves in somewhat troublesome. But, stranger, they never stick twice in the same place; and give them a fair chance for a few months, and you will get as much above noticing them as an alligator. They can't hurt my feelings, for they lay under the skin; and I never knew but one case of injury resulting from them, and that was to a Yankee; and they take worse to foreigners, anyhow, than they do to
30 natives. But the way they used that fellow up! first they punched him until he swelled up and busted; then he su-per-a-ted, as the doctor called it, until he was as raw as beef; then he took the ager, owing to the warm weather, and finally he took a steamboat and left the country. He was the only man that ever took mosquitoes to heart that I know of. But mosquitoes is natur, and I never find fault with her. If they ar large, Arkansaw is large, her varmints ar large, her trees ar large, her rivers ar large, and a small mosquito would be of no more use in Arkansaw than preaching in a canebrake."

This knock-down argument in favour of big mosquitoes used the Hoosier up, and the logician started on a new track, to explain how numerous bear were in his "dig-
40 gins," where he represented them to be "about as plenty as blackberries, and a little plentifuler."

Upon the utterance of this assertion, a timid little man near me inquired if the bear in Arkansaw ever attacked the settlers in numbers.

---

5 **chippen-birds and shite-pokes,** chipping sparrows and green herons

"No," said our hero, warming with the subject, "no, stranger, for you see it ain't the natur of bar to go in droves; but the way they squander about in pairs and single ones is edifying. And then the way I hunt them the old black rascals know the crack of my gun as well as they know a pig's squealing. They grow thin in our parts, it frightens them so, and they do take the noise dreadfully, poor things. That gun of mine is perfect *epidemic among bar;* if not watched closely, it will go off as quick on a warm scent as my dog Bowie-knife will: and then that dog — whew! why the fellow thinks that the world is full of bar, he find them so easy. It's lucky he don't talk as well as think; for with his natural modesty, if he should suddenly learn how much he is acknowledged to be ahead of all other dogs in the universe, 10 he would be astonished to death in two minutes. Strangers, the dog knows a bar's way as well as a horse-jockey knows a woman's; he always barks at the right time, bites at the exact place, and whips without getting a scratch. I never could tell whether he was made expressly to hunt bar, or whether bar was made expressly for him to hunt; any way, I believe they were ordained to go together as naturally as Squire Jones says a man and woman is, when he moralizes in marrying a couple. In fact, Jones once said, said he, 'Marriage according to law is a civil contract of divine origin; it's common to all countries as well as Arkansaw, and people take to it as naturally as Jim Doggett's Bowie-knife takes to bar.' "

"What season of the year do your hunts take place?" inquired a gentlemanly for- 20 eigner, who, from some peculiarities of his baggage, I suspected to be an Englishman, on some hunting expedition, probably at the foot of the Rocky Mountains.

"The season for bar hunting, stranger," said the man of Arkansaw, "is generally all the year round, and the hunts take place about as regular. I read in history that varmints have their fat season, and their lean season. That is not the case in Arkansaw, feeding as they do upon the *spontenacious* productions of the sile, they have one continued fat season the year round; though in winter things in this way is rather more greasy than in summer, I must admit. For that reason bar with us run in warm weather, but in winter, they only waddle. Fat, fat! it's an enemy to speed; it tames everything that has plenty of it. I have seen wild turkeys, from its influence, as gen- 30 tle as chickens. Run a bar in this fat condition, and the way it improves the critter for eating is amazing; it sort of mixes the ile up with the meat, until you can't tell t'other from which. I've done this often. I recollect one perty morning in particular, of putting an old fellow on the stretch, and considering the weight he carried, he run well. But the dogs soon tired him down, and when I came up with him wasn't he in a beautiful sweat — I might say fever; and then to see his tongue sticking out of his mouth a feet, and his sides sinking and opening like bellows, and his cheeks so fat he couldn't look cross. In this fix I blazed at him, and pitch me naked into a briar path if the steam didn't come out of the bullet-hole ten foot in a straight line. The fellow, I reckon, was made on the high-pressure system, and the lead sort 40 of bust his biler."

"That column of steam was rather curious, or else the bear must have been *warm,*" observed the foreigner, with a laugh.

"Stranger, as you observe, that bar was WARM, and the blowing off of the steam show'd it, and also how hard the varmint had been run. I have no doubt if he had kept on two miles farther his insides would have been stewed; and I expect to meet with a varmint yet of extra bottom, who will run himself into a skinful of bar's grease: it is possible, much onlikelier things have happened."

"Whereabouts are these bears so abundant?" inquired the foreigner, with increasing interest.

"Why, stranger, they inhabit the neighbourhood of my settlement, one of the prettiest places on old Mississippi — a perfect location, and no mistake; a place that had some defects until the river made the 'cut-off' at 'Shirt-tail bend,' and that rem-
10 edied the evil, as it brought my cabin on the edge of the river — a great advantage in wet weather, I assure you, as you can now roll a barrel of whiskey into my yard in high water from a boat, as easy as falling off a log. It's a great improvement, as toting it by land in a jug, as I used to do, *evaporated* it too fast, and it became expensive. Just stop with me, stranger, a month or two, or a year if you like, and you will appreciate my place. I can give you plenty to eat; for beside hog and hominy, you can have bar-ham, and bar-sausages, and a mattrass of bar-skins to sleep on, and a wildcatskin, pulled off hull, stuffed with corn-shucks for a pillow. That bed would put you to sleep if you had the rheumatics in every joint in your body. I call that ar bed a *quietus*. Then look at my land — the government ain't got another such a
20 piece to dispose of. Such timber, and such bottom land, why you can't preserve any thing natural you plant in it unless you pick it young, things thar will grow out of shape so quick. I once planted in those diggins a few potatoes and beets; they took a fine start, and after that an ox team couldn't have kept them from growing. About that time I went off to old Kentuck on bisiness, and did not hear from them things in three months, when I accidentally stumbled on a fellow who had stopped at my place, with an idea of buying me out. 'How did you like things?' said I. 'Pretty well,' said he; 'the cabin is convenient, and the timber land is good; but that bottom land ain't worth the first red cent.' 'Why?' said I. ' 'Cause,' said he.

' 'Cause what?' said I. ' 'Cause it's full of cedar stumps and Indian mounds,' said
30 he, *'and it can't be cleared.'* 'Lord,' said I, 'Them ar "cedar stumps" is beets, and them ar "Indian mounds" ar tater hills.' As I expected, the crop was overgrown and useless; the sile is too rich, *and planting in Arkansaw is dangerous.* I had a good-sized sow killed in that same bottom land. The old thief stole an ear of corn, and took it down where she slept at night to eat. Well, she left a grain or two on the ground, and lay down on them; before morning the corn shot up, and the percussion killed her dead. I don't plant any more; natur intended Arkansaw for a hunting ground, and I go according to natur."

The questioner who thus elicited the description of our hero's settlement, seemed to be perfectly satisfied and said no more; but the "Big Bar of Arkansaw" rambled
40 on from one thing to another with a volubility perfectly astonishing, occasionally disputing with those around him, particularly with a "live Sucker" from Illinois, who had the daring to say that our Arkansaw friend's stories "smelt rather tall."

In this manner the evening was spent; but conscious that my own association with so singular a personage would probably end before morning, I asked him if he would not give me a description of some particular bear hunt; adding that I took great interest in such things, though I was no sportsman. The desire seemed to please him, and he squared himself round towards me, saying, that he could give me an idea of a bar hunt that was never beat in this world, or in any other. His manner was so singular, that half of his story consisted in his excellent way of telling it, the great peculiarity of which was the happy manner he had of emphasizing the prominent parts of his conversation. As near as I can recollect, I have italicized them, and given the story in his own words.

"Stranger," said he, "in bar hunts *I am numerous,* and which particular one, as you say, I shall tell, puzzles me. There was the old she devil I shot at the Hurricane   10 last fall — then there was the old hog thief I popped over at the Bloody Crossing, and then — Yes, I have it! I will give you an idea of a hunt, in which the greatest bar was killed that ever lived, *none excepted;* about an old fellow that I hunted more or less for two or three years; and if that ain't a particular bar hunt, I ain't got one to tell. But in the first place, stranger, let me say, I am pleased with you, because you ain't ashamed to gain information by asking, and listening, and that's what I say to Countess's pups every day when I'm home; and I have got great hopes of them ar pups, because they are continually *nosing* about; and though they stick it sometimes in the wrong place, they gain experience any how, and may learn something useful to boot. Well, as I was saying about this big bar, you see when I and   20 some more first settled in our region, we were drivin to hunting naturally; we soon liked it, and after that we found it an easy matter to make the thing our business. One old chap who had pioneered 'afore us, gave us to understand that we had settled in the right place. He dwelt upon its merits until it was affecting, and showed us, to prove his assertions, more marks on the sassafras trees than I ever saw on a tavern door 'lection time, 'Who keeps that ar reckoning?' said I. 'The bar,' said he. 'What for?' said I. 'Can't tell,' said he; 'but so it is; the bar bite the bark and wood too, at the highest point from the ground they can reach, and you can tell, by the marks,' said he, 'the length of the bar to an inch.' 'Enough,' said I; 'I've learned something here a'ready, and I'll put it in practice.'   30

"Well, stranger, just one month from that time I killed a bar, and told its exact length before I measured it, by those very marks; and when I did that, I swelled up considerable — I've been a prouder man ever since. So I went on, larning something every day, until I was reckoned a buster, and allowed to be decidedly the best bar hunter in my district; and that is a reputation as much harder to earn than to be reckoned first man in Congress, as an iron ramrod is harder than a toadstool. Did the varmints grow over-cunning by being fooled with by green-horn hunters, and by this means get troublesome, they send for me as a matter of course; and thus I do my own hunting, and most of my neighbours'. I walk into the varmints though, and it has become about as much the same to me as drinking. It is told in two   40 sentences — a bar is started, and he is killed. The thing is somewhat monotonous now — I know just how much they will run, where they will tire, how much they will growl, and what a thundering time I will have in getting them home. I could give you this history of the chase with all particulars at the commencement, I know the signs so well — *Stranger, I'm certain.* Once I met with a match though, and I will tell you about it; for a common hunt would not be worth relating.

"On a fine fall day, long time ago, I was trailing about for bar, and what should I see but fresh marks on the sassafras trees, about eight inches above any in the forests that I knew of. Says I, 'them marks is a hoax, or it indicates the d_____t bar that was ever grown.' In fact, stranger, I couldn't believe it was real, and I went on. Again I saw the same marks, at the same height, and *I knew the thing lived.* That conviction came home to my soul like an earthquake. Says I, 'here is something a-purpose for me: that bar is mine, or I give up the hunting business.' The very
10 next morning what should I see but a number of buzzards hovering over my corn-field. 'The rascal has been there,' said I, 'for that sign is certain:' and, sure enough, on examining, I found the bones of what had been as beautiful a hog the day be-fore, as was ever raised by a Buckeye. Then I tracked the critter out of the field to the woods, and all the marks he left behind, showed me that he was *the bar.*

"Well, stranger, the first fair chase I ever had with that big critter, I saw him no less than three distinct times at a distance: the dogs run him over eighteen miles and broke down, my horse gave out, and I was as nearly used up as a man can be, made on *my* principle, *which is patent.* Before this adventure, such things were un-known to me as possible; but, strange as it was, that bar got me used to it before
20 I was done with him; for he got so at last, that he would leave me on a long chase *quite easy.* How he did it, I never could understand. That a bar runs at all, is puz-zling; but how this one could tire down and bust up a pack of hounds and a horse, that were used to overhauling everything they started after in no time, was past my understanding. Well, stranger, that bar finally got so sassy, that he used to help himself to a hog off my premises whenever he wanted one; the buzzards followed after what he left, and so between *bar and buzzard,* I rather think I was *out of pork.*

"Well, missing that bar so often took hold of my vitals, and I wasted away. The thing had been carried too far, and it reduced me in flesh faster than an ager. I would see that bar in every thing I did; *he hunted me,* and that, too, like a devil,
30 which I began to think he was. While in this fix, I made preparations to give him a last brush, and be done with it. Having completed every thing to my satisfaction, I started at sunrise, and to my great joy, I discovered from the way the dogs run, that they were near him; finding his trail was nothing, for that had become as plain to the pack as a turnpike road. On we went, and coming to an open country, what should I see but the bar very leisurely ascending a hill, and the dogs close at his heels, either a match for him in speed, or else he did not care to get out of their way — I don't know which. But wasn't he a beauty, though? I loved him like a brother.

"On he went, until he came to a tree, the limbs of which formed a crotch about
40 six feet from the ground. Into this crotch he got and seated himself, the dogs yell-ing all around it; and there he sat eyeing them as quiet as a pond in low water. A green-horn friend of mine, in company, reached shooting distance before me, and blazed away, hitting the critter in the centre of his forehead. The bar shook his head as the ball struck it, and then walked down from that tree as gently as a lady

would from a carriage. 'Twas a beautiful sight to see him do that — he was in such
a rage that he seemed to be as little afraid of the dogs as if they had been sucking
pigs; and the dogs warn't slow in making a ring around him at a respectful distance, I
tell you; even Bowie-knife, himself, stood off. Then the way his eyes flashed — why
the fire of them would have singed a cat's hair; in fact that bar was in a *wrath all
over.* Only one pup came near him, and he was brushed out so totally with the bar's
left paw, that he entirely disappeared; and that made the old dogs more cautious
still. In the meantime, I came up, and taking deliberate aim as a man should do, at
his side, just back of his foreleg, *if my gun did not snap,* call me a coward, and I
won't take it personal. Yes, stranger, *it snapped,* and I could not find a cap about my 10
person. While in this predicament, I turned round to my fool friend — says I, 'Bill,'
says I, 'you're an ass — you're a fool — you might as well have tried to kill that bar
by barking the tree under his belly, as to have done it by hitting him in the head.
Your shot has made a tiger of him, and blast me, if a dog gets killed or wounded
when they come to blows, I will stick my knife into your liver, I will —' my wrath
was up. I had lost my caps, my gun had snapped, the fellow with me had fired at
the bar's head, and I expected every moment to see him close in with the dogs, and
kill a dozen of them at least. In this thing I was mistaken, for the bar leaped over
the ring formed by the dogs, and giving a fierce growl, was off — the pack, of
course, in full cry after him. The run this time was short, for coming to the edge 20
of a lake the varmint jumped in, and swam to a little island in the lake, which it
reached just a moment before the dogs. 'I'll have him now,' said I, for I had found
my caps in the *lining of my coat* — so, rolling a log into the lake, I paddled myself
across to the island, just as the dogs had cornered the bar in a thicket. I rushed up
and fired — at the same time the critter leaped over the dogs and came within three
feet of me, running like mad; he jumped into the lake, and tried to mount the log
I had just deserted, but every time he got half his body on it, it would roll over and
send him under; the dogs, too, got around him, and pulled him about, and finally
Bowie-knife clenched with him, and they sunk into the lake together. Stranger,
about this time, I was excited, and I stripped off my coat, drew my knife, and in- 30
tended to have taken a part with Bowie-knife myself, when the bar rose to the surface. But the varmint staid under — Bowie-knife came up alone, more dead than
alive, and with the pack came ashore. 'Thank God,' said I, 'the old villain has got
his deserts at last.' Determined to have the body, I cut a grape-vine for a rope, and
dove down where I could see the bar in the water, fastened my queer rope to his
leg, and fished him, with great difficulty, ashore. Stranger, may I be chawed to
death by young alligators, if the thing I looked at wasn't a *she bar, and not the old
critter after all.* The way matters got mixed on that island was onaccountably curious,
and thinking of it made me more than ever convinced that I was hunting the devil
himself. I went home that night and took to my bed — the thing was killing me. 40
The entire team of Arkansaw in barhunting, acknowledged himself used up, and the
fact sunk into my feelings like a snagged boat will in the Mississippi. I grew as
cross as a bar with two cubs and a sore tail. The thing got out 'mong my neighbours, and I was asked how come on that individu-al that never lost a bar when

once started? and if that same individ-u-al didn't wear telescopes when he turned a she bar, of ordinary size, into an old he one, a little larger than a horse? 'Perhaps,' said I, 'friends' — getting wrathy — 'perhaps you want to call somebody a liar.' 'Oh, no,' said they, 'we only heard such things as being *rather common* of late, but we don't believe one word of it; oh, no,' — and then they would ride off and laugh like so many hyenas over a dead nigger. It was too much, and I determined to catch that bar, go to Texas, or die, — and I made my preparations accordin'. I had the pack shut up and rested. I took my rifle to pieces and iled it. I put caps in every pocket about my person, *for fear of the lining.* I then told my neighbours, that on
10 Monday morning — naming the day — I would start THAT BAR, and bring him home with me, or they might divide my settlement among them, the owner having disappeared. Well, stranger, on the morning previous to the great day of my hunting expedition, I went into the woods near my house, taking my gun and Bowie-knife along, just *from habit,* and there sitting down also from habit, what should I see, getting over my fence, but *the bar!* Yes, the old varmint was within a hundred yards of me, and the way he walked *over the fence* — stranger, he loomed up like a *black mist,* he seemed so large, and he walked right towards me. I raised myself, took deliberate aim, and fired. Instantly the varmint wheeled, gave a yell, and *walked through the fence* like a falling tree would through a cobweb. I started after,
20 but was tripped up by my inexpressibles, which either from habit, or the excitement of the moment, were about my heels, and before I had really gathered myself up, I heard the old varmint groaning in a thicket near by, like a thousand sinners, and by the time I reached him he was a corpse. Stranger, it took five niggers and myself to put that carcase on a mule's back, and old long-ears waddled under the load, as if he was foundered in every leg of his body, and with a common whopper of a bar, he would have trotted off, and enjoyed himself. 'Twould astonish you to know how big he was: I made a *bedspread of his skin* and the way it used to cover my bar mattress, and leave several feet on each side to tuck up, would have delighted you. It was in fact a creation bar, and if it had lived in Samson's time, and had met
30 him, in a fair fight, it would have licked him in the twinkling of a dice-box. But, strangers, I never like the way I hunted, and *missed him.* There is something curious about, I could never understand, — and I never was satisfied at his giving in so easy at last. Perhaps, he had heard of my preparations to hunt him the next day, so he jist come in, like Capt. Scott's coon, to save his wind to grunt with in dying; but that ain't likely. My private opinion is, that that bar was an *unhuntable bar, and died when his time come.*"

When the story was ended, our hero sat some minutes with his auditors in a grave silence; I saw there was a mystery to him connected with the bear whose death he had just related, that had evidently made a strong impression on his mind. It
40 was also evident that there was some superstitious awe connected with the affair, — a feeling common with all "children of the wood," when they meet with any

---

34 **Capt. Scott's coon.** Oral lore pictured Captain Scott as such a great hunter that when he approached a raccoon, the animal shouted down to him, "Don't shoot! I'm a-comin' down." The same tall story was told about Davy Crockett (see p. 1532)

thing out of their everyday experience. He was the first one, however, to break the silence, and jumping up, he asked all present to "liquor" before going to bed, — a thing which he did, with a number of companions, evidently to his heart's content.

Long before day, I was put ashore at my place of destination, and I can only follow with the reader, in imagination, our Arkansas friend, in his adventures at the "Forks of Cypress" on the Mississippi.

1841

Singers of the West

In the new country being opened up by the emigrants, new songs were made which caught the spirit of the times in various ways. The four which follow show something of their variety: one was made for a political campaign, one was written by a composer of popular songs who was just starting his career in Cincinnati, two were the works of forgotten movers or settlers. All were ballads or ballad-like songs, and all, with the possible exception of "The Wolverine's Song," had widespread oral currency.

The Wolverine's Song

Most memorable, perhaps, of all Presidential campaigns before 1860 was the one of 1840, in which Harrison and Tyler, "Tippecanoe and Tyler, too," were elected. To the utmost, this campaign exploited the American enthusiasm about the frontier and the democratic spirit which flourished there.

A chance remark gave the campaign its cue. The Whig party, after having done badly in the local elections of 1839, met in December of that year and managed to nominate William Henry Harrison, hero of the battle of Tippecanoe, for the Presidency and John Tyler as his running mate. For several months Harrison's chances seemed hopeless even to the most enthusiastic Whigs. Then an opposition newspaper in Baltimore printed an attack on Harrison which hooted at his boorishness: "Give him a barrel of hard cider and a pension of two thousand a year, and, our word for it, he will sit the remainder of his days in a log cabin by the side of a sea coal fire and study moral philosophy."

Harrison was well-to-do and well-educated, but instead of pointing this out, his supporters made the remarks about his ignorance the basis of a campaign playing up Harrison as a

Western Indian fighter and log-cabin settler. The General discarded his high silk hat for a broad-brimmed one, and all the publicity about him made him the symbol of the log-cabin, hard-cider West. In every corner of the land there were log-cabin meetings, log-cabin floats in political processions, Log Cabin *newspapers,* Log Cabin Almanacs, *and log-cabin songs. Whig leaders also hit on the device of making Harrison's opponent, Martin Van Buren, a symbol of the moneyed aristocracy — one who dressed like a dandy, "strutted and swaggered like a crow in a gutter," "laced up in corsets, such as women in town wear," perfumed his whiskers, and dined with gold spoons. The electoral vote: Harrison, 234; Van Buren, 60.*

"The chief means of popular excitement," said a Harrison campaigner, "were the glee clubs, which never before or since have been so effectively used." Said a Van Buren supporter: "Songs rang in my ears wherever I went, morning, noon, and night. . . . Men, women, and children did nothing but sing. It worried, annoyed, dumfounded, crushed the Democrats, but there was no use trying to escape." One of the hundreds of such pieces, the song which follows, taken from The Log Cabin Minstrel, *appeals to the "Wolverines" — the Michigan men.*

Ye hard fisted, log cabin, Wolverine boys,
Whom slander and ridicule never annoys,
Now come up to the scratch, for your country demands
The prayers of your hearts and the work of your hands;
For a race of vile "soap-locks" and ruffle-gay knaves
Have seized on our birthrights, and made us all slaves!
Come, then, to the rescue — be fearless and true,
And we'll put them to flight with Old Tippecanoe!
     Make way for Tippecanoe!
He's death on a Tory, that Tippecanoe!   10

They call him a Granny — they say he is poor,
And lives in a Cabin befitting a boor!
And they say that he never drinks Port or Champagne,
But Cider as hard as his dwelling is plain! —
Well, what if he does? Still, his table is spread
With such as his purse will afford; and a bed —
Though coarser than Martin Van Buren's, 'tis true,
Is kept for the stranger by Tippecanoe!
     Huzza for Tippecanoe!
He's death on a Tory, that Tippecanoe!   20

We know that Van Buren can ride in his coach,
With servants, forbidding the vulgar's approach,
We know that his fortune such things will allow,
And we know that our candidate follows the plough;
But what if he does? Who was bolder to fight

---

5 **soap-locks**, hair made shiny and curly with the aid of soap   8 **Tippecanoe**, a two-hour battle in November 1811, during which the eleven hundred men under Harrison defeated the Indians led by Tecumseh. Harrison thus won his nickname

In his country's defence on that perilous night
When nought save his valor sufficed to subdue
Our foes at the battle of Tippecanoe?
      Huzza for Tippecanoe!
He dropped the red Locos at Tippecanoe!   30

They call him a coward, the dastardly slaves!
Whose courage preserved them from infantile graves,
   And gave them that life which they ignobly spend
Traducing their own and their Country's best friend.
But slander and ridicule ne'er can efface
That long-settled, well-settled, deep-settled trace
Of gratitude, marked on the heart that is true!
He's after you, Matty, that Tippecanoe!
      Make way for Tippecanoe!
He's death on a Tory, that Tippecanoe!   40
                           1840

---

30 **Locos,** abbreviation for Locofocos, a nickname of the anti-Whig Democratic party, 1835-1837   32
Whose . . . graves. The inspired poet exaggerated somewhat the results of Harrison's victory over the Indians

Oh! Susanna

Stephen Collins Foster   1826, 1864

"My Old Kentucky Home," "Swanee River," "Jeanie with the Light Brown Hair," "Beautiful Dreamer," "Old Black Joe" — these were only a few of the songs by Stephen Collins Foster, the most popular song writer in American history. Foster was born of Scotch-Irish parents in Pittsburgh, July 4, 1826. Though he was scantily educated, he discovered in the late 1840's his extraordinary gifts as a composer. Introduced, as a rule, by singers in minstrel shows, Foster's ballad-like compositions often became nationally famous, and many are still remembered and sung. Despite his popularity, Foster was abjectly poor when he died in 1864.

Foster was living in Cincinnati when his song "Oh! Susanna" was introduced in 1847 by singers in Andrew's Eagle Ice Cream Saloon in Pittsburgh. Within less than two years at least twenty editions had been published by various publishers, and several minstrel troupes were singing it wherever they stopped. It traveled across the ocean, and was translated into French, German, Italian, and modern Greek. Bayard Taylor, an American tourist, heard it sung in Delhi.

The song was becoming tremendously popular in January 1848, when gold was discovered in California. For the great throng of Forty-Niners who crossed the continent westward, this was the favorite song. The nonsense rhymes had no relevance whatever to the gold rush, but the amusing words and the jaunty tune made the song unforgettable.

I come from Alabama
Wid my banjo on my knee.
I'm gwan to Louisiana,
My true love for to see.
It rain'd all night the day I left,
The weather it was dry,
The sun so hot I froze to death,
Susanna, don't you cry

Chorus

     Oh! Susanna Oh! don't you cry for me,
     I've come from Alabama wid my banjo on my knee. 10

I jumped aboard de telegraph,
And trabbelled down de ribber,
De 'lectric fluid magnified,
And killed five hundred nigger.
De bullgine bust, de horse run off,
I really thought I'd die,
I shut my eyes to hold my breath,
Susanna, don't you cry.

I had a dream de odder night,
When eb'ry ting was still;   20
I thought I saw Susanna,
A-coming down de hill.
The buckwheat cake war in her mouth,
The tear was in her eye,
Says I, I'm coming from de South,
Susanna, don't you cry.

I soon will be in New Orleans,
And den I'll look all round,
And when I find Susanna,
I'll fall upon the ground.   30
But if I do not find her,
Dis darkie'll surely die,
And when I'm dead and buried,
Susanna, don't you cry.

              1847, 1848

---

15 **bullgine,** locomotive

Sweet Betsy from Pike

Pike County, Missouri, was the birthplace of many of the earliest emigrants to cross the plains, and the type of emigrants from this county was peculiar enough so that Westerners soon were talking of "Pikes." In 1855 the California humorist Phoenix, describing a migrating train from Pike County, said: "Each family consists of a man in butternut-colored clothing driving the oxen; a wife in butternut-colored clothing riding in the wagon, holding a butternut baby, and seventeen butternut children running promiscuously about the establishment; all are barefoot, dusty, and smell unpleasantly." In time "Pike" became the term for similar specimens not only from Missouri but also from other Middle Western or Southern states. "The Pike," said Bayard Taylor, "is the Anglo-Saxon relapsed into semi-barbarism . . . long, lathy, sallow . . . he takes naturally to whisky . . . has the 'shakes' his life long at home . . . distrusts men in 'store clothes.' . . ." An anonymous singer, in the 1850's, invented the following account of the travels Westward of two such poor whites. The chorus is the same as in the first stanza except in the instances where changed choruses appear.

Did you ever hear tell of Sweet Betsy from Pike,
Who crossed the wide prairies with her lover Ike,
And two yoke of cattle, a large yaller dog,
A tall, shanghai rooster, and one spotted hog.

Chorus

Saying, "Good-bye, Pike County, farewell for a while;
We'll come back again when we've panned out our pile."

One evening quite early they camped on the Platte,
'Twas near by the road on a green shady flat;
Where Betsy, quite tired, lay down for repose,
While with wonder Ike gazed on his Pike County rose.

They soon reached the desert, where Betsy gave out,
And down on the sand she lay rolling about;
While Ike in great terror looked on in surprise,
Saying, "Betsy, get up, you'll get sand in your eyes."

Chorus

Saying, "Good-bye, Pike County, farewell for a while;
I'd go back tonight, if it was but a mile."

Sweet Betsy got up in a great deal of pain,
And declared she'd go back to Pike County again;
Then Ike heaved a sigh and they fondly embraced,
And she traveled around with his arm round her waist.

The Injuns came down in a wild yelling horde,
And Betsy was skeered they would scalp her adored;

Behind the front wagon wheel Betsy did crawl,
And there she fought Injuns with musket and ball.

The alkali desert was burning and bare,
And Isaac's soul shrank from the death that lurked there:
"Dear old Pike County, I'll go back to you."
Says Betsy, "You'll go by yourself if you do."

The wagon tipped over with a terrible crash,
And out on the prairie rolled all sorts of trash;
A few baby clothes done up with great care
Looked rather suspicious; but 'twas all on the square.

The shanghai ran off and the cattle all died,
The last piece of bacon that morning was fried;
Poor Ike got discouraged, and Betsy got mad,
The dog wagged his tail and looked wonderfully sad.

They swam the wide rivers and crossed the tall peaks,
And camped on the prairie for weeks upon weeks.
Starvation and cholera and hard work and slaughter.
They reached California spite of hell and high water.

Long Ike and sweet Betsy got married of course,
But Ike getting jealous obtained a divorce;
And Betsy well satisfied, said with a shout:
"Good-bye, you big lummox, I'm glad you backed out!"

Chorus

>   Saying, "Good-bye, dear Isaac, farewell for a while,
>   But come back in time to replenish my pile."   1855?

Hell in Texas

*The year gold was discovered in California, Texas was ceded by Mexico to the United States.
The great stretch of territory thus secured had several climates, some of which were fairly
distressing. In "Hell in Texas," a ballad composer told in rollicking words a fanciful story
of the way Texas got some of its least attractive features.*

Oh, the Devil in hell they say he was chained,
And there for a thousand years he remained;
He neither complained nor did he groan,
But decided he'd start up a hell of his own,
Where he could torment the souls of men
Without being shut in a prison pen;
So he asked the Lord if He had any sand
Left over from making this great land.

The Lord He said, "Yes, I have plenty on hand,
But it's away down south on the Rio Grande,
And, to tell you the truth, the stuff is so poor
I doubt if 'twill do for hell any more."
The Devil went down and looked over the truck,
And he said if it came as a gift he was stuck,
For when he'd examined it carefully and well
He decided the place was too dry for a Hell.

But the Lord just to get the stuff off His hands
He promised the Devil He'd water the land,
For he had some old water that was of no use,
A regular bog hole that stunk like the deuce.
So the grant it was made and the deed it was given;
The Lord He returned to His place up in heaven.
The Devil soon saw he had everything needed
To make up a hell and so he proceeded.

He scattered tarantulas over the roads,
Put thorns on the cactus and horns on the toads,
He sprinkled the sands with millions of ants
So the man that sits down must wear soles on his pants.
He lengthened the horns of the Texas steer,
And added an inch to the jack rabbit's ear;
He put water puppies in all of the lakes,
And under the rocks he put rattlesnakes.

He hung thorns and brambles on all of the trees,
He mixed up the dust with jiggers and fleas;
The rattlesnake bites you, the scorpion stings,
The mosquito delights you by buzzing his wings.
The heat in the summer's a hundred and ten,
Too hot for the Devil and too hot for men;
And all who remained in that climate soon bore
Cuts, bites, stings, and scratches, and blisters galore.

He quickened the buck of the bronco steed,
And poisoned the feet of the centipede;
The wild boar roams in the black chaparral;
It's a hell of a place that we've got for a hell.
He planted red pepper beside of the brooks;
The Mexicans use them in all that they cook.
Just dine with a Greaser and then you will shout,
"I've hell on the inside as well as the out!"

1828—1867 Henry Timrod

No writer of equal stature in this country," Professor E. W. Parks observes, "has received so little attention" as Henry Timrod, the "Laureate of the Confederacy."

Timrod attended the Coates School in Charleston, South Carolina — his birthplace — and studied for a year and a half at the University of Georgia. After trying the law, he turned to tutoring in planters' families. Later he was a contributor to *Russell's Magazine* (1857-1860), a journal of literary promise published in Charleston and edited by his friend Paul Hamilton Hayne. In 1861 Timrod enlisted in the Confederate army, but because of ill health was able to serve less than a year. Undertaking the work of a war correspondent, he observed at close range the battle of Shiloh. In 1864 he edited a newspaper in Columbia, South Carolina; this position ended abruptly when Columbia was taken by Sherman's army. The three last years of his life were a losing struggle against poverty and disease. His poems were collected, with a memoir, by Paul Hamilton Hayne in 1873.

Timrod's early verses were imitative of Wordsworth. The war called forth his latent originality and inspired his best poems. These poems, though romantic in their ardor, are remarkable for certain classical qualities; indeed, it is the fusion of romantic and classical elements that gives to Timrod's poetry a special distinction. To quote Professor Parks again: "Although sincerity and throbbing emotion beat through his words in passionate undertones, the passion never carries the verse into formlessness of thought or reference. Instead an almost classic coolness and restraint appears, from first to last, in his war poems. . . . He saw a poem as a whole, yet as composed of lines, and his best poems combine a clear distinction of line with a sense of rounded completeness." Other noteworthy merits of Timrod's verse are the mastery of the sustained, or epic, simile and the classic purity of his diction.

Poems of Henry Timrod, ed. P. H. Hayne, New York, 1873   J. B. Hubbell, **The Last Years of Henry Timrod**, Durham, North Carolina, 1941   E. W. Parks, **Southern Poets**, Cincinnati, 1936   E. W. Parks, "Southern Poetry," **Segments of Southern Thought**, Athens, Georgia, 1938   E. W. Parks, **Henry Timrod**, New York, 1964

Ethnogenesis

Written During the Meeting of the First Southern Congress, at Montgomery, February, 1861

The following poem was first printed, with the title "Ode, on the Meeting of the Southern Congress," in the Charleston Mercury, *September 26, 1861. The title "Ethnogenesis," which was substituted when the poem was reprinted in the Charleston* Courier, *January 31, 1862, is a Greek coinage meaning "the birth of a nation." At once ardent and restrained, the poem expresses the patriotic spirit of the newly formed Confederate States of America.*

I

Hath not the morning dawned with added light?
And shall not evening call another star
Out of the infinite regions of the night,
To mark this day in Heaven? At last, we are
A nation among nations; and the world
Shall soon behold in many a distant port
   Another flag unfurled!
Now, come what may, whose favor need we court?
And, under God, whose thunder need we fear?
   Thank him who placed us here   10
Beneath so kind a sky — the very sun
Takes part with us; and on our errands run
All breezes of the ocean; dew and rain
Do noiseless battle for us; and the Year,
And all the gentle daughters in her train,
March in our ranks, and in our service wield
Long spears of golden grain!
A yellow blossom as her fairy shield,
June flings her azure banner to the wind,
   While in the order of their birth   20
Her sisters pass, and many an ample field
Grows white beneath their steps, till now, behold,
   Its endless sheets unfold
THE SNOW OF SOUTHERN SUMMERS! Let the earth
Rejoice! beneath those fleeces soft and warm
   Our happy land shall sleep
   In a repose as deep

---

24 **Snow** refers to cotton, of the importance of which to the South Timrod had an exaggerated conception. Contrast Lanier's later protest in "Corn" against the tyranny of "coquette cotton"

As if we lay intrenched behind
Whole leagues of Russian ice and Arctic storm!

II

And what if, mad with wrongs themselves have wrought, 30
    In their own treachery caught,
    By their own fears made bold,
    And leagued with him of old,
Who long since in the limits of the North
Set up his evil throne, and warred with God —
What if, both mad and blinded in their rage,
Our foes should fling us down their mortal gage,
And with a hostile step profane our sod!
We shall not shrink, my brothers, but go forth
To meet them, marshaled by the Lord of Hosts,   40
And overshadowed by the mighty ghosts
Of Moultrie and Eutaw — who shall foil
Auxiliars such as these? Nor these alone,
    But every stock and stone
    Shall help us; but the very soil,
And all the generous wealth it gives to toil,
And all for which we love our noble land,
Shall fight beside, and through us; sea and strand,
    The heart of woman, and her hand,
Tree, fruit, and flower, and every influence,   50
    Gentle, or grave, or grand;
    The winds in our defence
Shall seem to blow; to us the hills shall lend
    Their firmness and their calm;
And in our stiffened sinews we shall blend
    The strength of pine and palm!

III

Nor would we shun the battle-ground,
    Though weak as we are strong;
Call up the clashing elements around,

---

34 **limits . . . North.** When Satan (according to Milton) revolted in Heaven against God, he withdrew
with his followers to the North. See particularly *Paradise Lost,* Bk. V. l. 755: "At length into the limits of
the North/They came. . . ."   42 **Moultrie and Eutaw.** The repulse of the British at Sullivan's Island,
June 28, 1776, was led by General William Moultrie, for whom the fort on the island was later named.
Eutaw Springs was the scene of an American attack on a British outpost, September 8, 1781. Hence, the
"mighty ghosts" are those of Revolutionary patriots who fought at these places   44 **stock and stone,**
every senseless thing

And test the right and wrong!   60
On one side, creeds that dare to teach
What Christ and Paul refrained to preach;
Codes built upon a broken pledge,
And Charity that whets a poniard's edge;
Fair schemes that leave the neighboring poor
To starve and shiver at the schemer's door,
While in the world's most liberal ranks enrolled,
He turns some vast philanthropy to gold;
Religion, taking every mortal form
But that a pure and Christian faith makes warm,   70
Where not to vile fanatic passion urged,
Or not in vague philosophies submerged,
Repulsive with all Pharisaic leaven,
And making laws to stay the laws of Heaven!
And on the other, scorn of sordid gain,
Unblemished honor, truth without a stain,
Faith, justice, reverence, charitable wealth,
And, for the poor and humble, laws which give,
Not the mean right to buy the right to live,
    But life, and home, and health!   80
To doubt the end were want of trust in God,
        Who, if he has decreed
     That we must pass a redder sea
Than that which rang to Miriam's holy glee,
     Will surely raise at need
     A Moses with his rod!

IV

But let our fears — if fears we have — be still,
And turn us to the future! Could we climb
Some mighty Alp, and view the coming time,
The rapturous sight would fill   90
     Our eyes with happy tears!
Not only for the glories which the years
Shall bring us; not for lands from sea to sea,
And wealth, and power, and peace, though these shall be;
But for the distant peoples we shall bless,

---

61 **creeds . . . preach.** Timrod asserts that the creed of the abolitionists has no Biblical authority   63
pledge refers to the protection of slavery under the Constitution   65 **neighboring poor,** the underpaid
workers in Northern factories   75 **the other,** the other side, meaning the South   83 **redder sea.** The
reference is to the crossing of the Red Sea by the Israelites and their subsequent rejoicing, recorded
in Exodus 14:15. It is interesting to note that Whittier, speaking for the North, used the same Biblical
story in "Laus Deo"   95 **distant . . . bless,** presumably through the exportation of cotton

And the hushed murmurs of a world's distress:
For, to give labor to the poor,
   The whole sad planet o'er,
And save from want and crime the humblest door,
Is one among the many ends for which   100
   God makes us great and rich!
The hour perchance is not yet wholly ripe
When all shall own it, but the type
Whereby we shall be known in every land
Is that vast gulf which lips our Southern strand,
And through the cold, untempered ocean pours
Its genial streams, that far off Arctic shores
May sometimes catch upon the softened breeze
Strange tropic warmth and hints of summer seas.

                          1861

---

105 **gulf,** the Gulf Stream

The Cotton Boll

First printed in the Charleston Mercury, *September 3, 1861, "The Cotton Boll" is Timrod's most successful poem. It is remarkable, among other things, for its fluency and precision, its eloquence and restraint, and its mastery of the expanded or epic simile and a varied, flexible meter.*

While I recline
At ease beneath
This immemorial pine,
Small sphere!
(By dusky fingers brought this morning here
And shown with boastful smiles),
I turn thy cloven sheath,
Through which the soft white fibres peer,
That, with their gossamer bands,
Unite, like love, the sea-divided lands,   10
And slowly, thread by thread,
Draw forth the folded strands,
Than which the trembling line,
By whose frail help yon startled spider fled
Down the tall spear-grass from his swinging bed,
Is scarce more fine;
And as the tangled skein
Unravels in my hands,

---

5 **dusky fingers,** of a Negro slave

Betwixt me and the noonday light,
A veil seems lifted, and for miles and miles   20
The landscape broadens on my sight,
As, in the little boll, there lurked a spell
Like that which, in the ocean shell,
With mystic sound,
Breaks down the narrow walls that hem us round,
And turns some city lane
Into the restless main,
With all his capes and isles!

Yonder bird,
Which floats, as if at rest,   30
In those blue tracts above the thunder, where
No vapors cloud the stainless air,
And never sound is heard,
Unless at such rare time
When, from the City of the Blest,
Rings down some golden chime,
Sees not from his high place
So vast a cirque of summer space
As widens round me in one mighty field,
Which, rimmed by seas and sands,   40
Doth hail its earliest daylight in the beams
Of gray Atlantic dawns;
And, broad as realms made up of many lands,
Is lost afar
Behind the crimson hills and purple lawns
Of sunset, among plains which roll their streams
Against the Evening Star!
And lo!
To the remotest point of sight,
Although I gaze upon no waste of snow,   50
The endless field is white;
And the whole landscape glows,
For many a shining league away,
With such accumulated light
As Polar lands would flash beneath a tropic day!
Nor lack there (for the vision grows,
And the small charm within my hands —
More potent even than the fabled one,
Which oped whatever golden mystery
Lay hid in fairy wood or magic vale,   60

---

22 **As,** as if

The curious ointment of the Arabian tale —
Beyond all mortal sense
Doth stretch my sight's horizon, and I see,
Beneath its simple influence,
As if with Uriel's crown,
I stood in some great temple of the Sun,
And looked, as Uriel, down!)
Nor lack there pastures rich and fields all green
With all the common gifts of God,
For temperate airs and torrid sheen   70
Weave Edens of the sod;
Through lands which look one sea of billowy gold
Broad rivers wind their devious ways;
A hundred isles in their embraces fold
A hundred luminous bays;
And through yon purple haze
Vast mountains lift their plumèd peaks cloud-crowned;
And, save where up their sides the ploughman creeps,
An unhewn forest girds them grandly round,
In whose dark shades a future navy sleeps!   80
Ye Stars, which, though unseen, yet with me gaze
Upon this loveliest fragment of the earth!
Thou Sun, that kindlest all thy gentlest rays
Above it, as to light a favorite hearth!
Ye Clouds, that in your temples in the West
See nothing brighter than its humblest flowers!
And you, ye Winds, that on the ocean's breast
Are kissed to coolness ere ye reach its bowers!
Bear witness with me in my song of praise,
And tell the world that, since the world began   90
No fairer land hath fired a poet's lays,
Or given a home to man!

But these are charms already widely blown!
His be the meed whose pencil's trace
Hath touched our very swamps with grace,
And round whose tuneful way
All Southern laurels bloom;
The Poet of "The Woodlands," unto whom
Alike are known

---

61 **ointment . . . tale,** in the story describing the adventures of Haroun Al Rashid in the *Arabian Nights*   65 **Uriel,** regent of the Sun, described in Milton's *Paradise Lost,* Bk. III, ll. 622-629   98 **Poet . . . Woodlands,** a reference to William Gilmore Simms (1806-1870) and his country estate near Charleston. Simms wrote a good many poems (including a poem entitled "The Edge of the Swamp"), though he is best known for his prose romances

The flute's low breathing and the trumpet's tone,   100
And the soft west wind's sighs;
But who shall utter all the debt,
O Land wherein all powers are met
That bind a people's heart,
The world doth owe thee at this day,
And which it never can repay,
Yet scarcely deigns to own!
Where sleeps the poet who shall fitly sing
The source wherefrom doth spring
That mighty commerce which, confined   110
To the mean channels of no selfish mart,
Goes out to every shore
Of this broad earth, and throngs the sea with ships
That bear no thunders; hushes hungry lips
In alien lands;
Joins with a delicate web remotest strands;
And gladdening rich and poor,
Doth gild Parisian domes,
Or feed the cottage-smoke of English homes,
And only bounds its blessings by mankind!   120
In offices like these, thy mission lies,
My Country! and it shall not end
As long as rain shall fall and Heaven bend
In blue above thee; though thy foes be hard
And cruel as their weapons, it shall guard
Thy hearth-stones as a bulwark; make thee great
In white and bloodless state;
And haply, as the years increase —
Still working through its humbler reach
With that large wisdom which the ages teach —   130
Revive the half-dead dream of universal peace!
As men who labor in that mine
Of Cornwall, hollowed out beneath the bed
Of ocean, when a storm rolls overhead,
Hear the dull booming of the world of brine
Above them, and a mighty muffled roar
Of winds and waters, yet toil calmly on,
And split the rock, and pile the massive ore,
Or carve a niche, or shape the archèd roof;
So I, as calmly, weave my woof   140
Of song, chanting the days to come,
Unsilenced, though the quiet summer air

---

133 **Cornwall**, on the southwest coast of England

Stirs with the bruit of battles, and each dawn
Wakes from its starry silence to the hum
Of many gathering armies. Still,
In that we sometimes hear,
Upon the Northern winds, the voice of woe
Not wholly drowned in triumph, though I know
The end must crown us, and a few brief years
Dry all our tears,   150
I may not sing too gladly. To Thy will
Resigned, O Lord! we cannot all forget
That there is much even Victory must regret.
And, therefore, not too long
From the great burthen of our country's wrong
Delay our just release!
And, if it may be, save
These sacred fields of peace
From strain of patriot or of hostile blood!
Oh, help us, Lord! to roll the crimson flood   160
Back on its course, and while our banners wing
Northward, strike with us! till the Goth shall cling
To his own blasted altar-stones, and crave
Mercy; and we shall grant it, and dictate
The lenient future of his fate
There, where some rotting ships and crumbling quays
Shall one day mark the Port which ruled the Western seas.
                                                  1861

162 **Goth.** Timrod uses this uncomplimentary name to refer to the people of the North   167 **Port,** New York

Carolina

First printed in the Charleston Courier, *March 8, 1862, and reprinted there, November 12 of the same year, "Carolina" is perhaps the most fervid of all the patriotic lyrics written during the Civil War.*

I

The despot treads thy sacred sands,
Thy pines give shelter to his bands,
Thy sons stand by with idle hands,
                    Carolina!
He breathes at ease thy airs of balm,
He scorns the lances of thy palm;

Oh! who shall break thy craven calm,
    Carolina!
Thy ancient fame is growing dim,
A spot is on thy garment's rim;   10
Give to the winds thy battle hymn,
    Carolina!

  II

Call on thy children of the hill,
Wake swamp and river, coast and rill,
Rouse all thy strength and all thy skill,
    Carolina!
Cite wealth and science, trade and art,
Touch with thy fire the cautious mart,
And pour thee through the people's heart,
    Carolina!   20
Till even the coward spurns his fears,
And all thy fields and fens and meres
Shall bristle like thy palm with spears,
    Carolina!

  III

Hold up the glories of thy dead;
Say how thy elder children bled,
And point to Eutaw's battle-bed,
    Carolina!
Tell how the patriot's soul was tried,
And what his dauntless breast defied;   30
How Rutledge ruled and Laurens died,
    Carolina!
Cry! till thy summons, heard at last,
Shall fall like Marion's bugle-blast
Re-echoed from the haunted Past,
    Carolina!

  IV

I hear a murmur as of waves
That grope their way through sunless caves,

---

17 **Cite,** summon or call 27 **Eutaw's battle-bed.** See note, p. 1573 31 **Rutledge,** John Rutledge (1739-1800), governor of South Carolina 31 **Laurens,** John Laurens (1754-1782), Revolutionary soldier and South Carolinian, killed in battle 34 **Marion,** Francis Marion (1732-1795), Revolutionary general and South Carolinian

Like bodies struggling in their graves,
 Carolina!   40
And now it deepens; slow and grand
It swells, as, rolling to the land,
An ocean broke upon thy strand,
 Carolina!
Shout! let it reach the startled Huns!
And roar with all thy festal guns!
It is the answer of thy sons,
 Carolina!

V

They will not wait to hear thee call;
From Sachem's Head to Sumter's wall   50
Resounds the voice of hut and hall,
 Carolina!
No! thou hast not a stain, they say,
Or none save what the battle-day
Shall wash in seas of blood away,
 Carolina!
Thy skirts indeed the foe may part,
Thy robe be pierced with sword and dart,
They shall not touch thy noble heart,
 Carolina!   60

VI

Ere thou shalt own the tyrant's thrall
Ten times ten thousand men must fall;
Thy corpse may hearken to his call,
 Carolina!
When, by thy bier, in mournful throngs
The women chant thy mortal wrongs,
'Twill be their own funereal songs,
 Carolina!
From thy dead breast by ruffians trod
No helpless child shall look to God;   70
And shall be safe beneath thy sod,
 Carolina!

---

45 **Huns,** here applied to the soldiers of the North   50 **Sachem's . . . wall,** that is from the mountains
to the sea

VII

Girt with such wills to do and bear,
Assured in right, and mailed in prayer,
Thou wilt not bow thee to despair,
                    Carolina!
Throw thy bold banner to the breeze!
Front with thy ranks the threatening seas
Like thine own proud armorial trees,
                    Carolina!   80
Fling down thy gauntlet to the Huns,
And roar the challenge from thy guns;
Then leave the future to thy sons,
                    Carolina!
                              1862

---

74 **mailed . . . prayer,** reminiscent of St. Paul's Christian armor, described in Ephesians 6:11-17

Charleston

"Charleston" was first printed in the Charleston Mercury, *December 13, 1862.*

Calm as that second summer which precedes
    The first fall of the snow,
In the broad sunlight of heroic deeds
    The City bides the foe.

As yet, behind their ramparts stern and proud,
    Her bolted thunders sleep —
Dark Sumter, like a battlemented cloud,
    Looms o'er the solemn deep.

No Calpe frowns from lofty cliff or scar
    To guard the holy strand;   10
But Moultrie holds in leash her dogs of war
    Above the level sand.

And down the dunes a thousand guns lie couched
    Unseen beside the flood —
Like tigers in some Orient jungle crouched
    That wait and watch for blood.

---

7 **Sumter,** a fort on an island at the entrance of Charleston harbor, the firing upon which by the Confederates in April 1861 precipitated the Civil War   9 **Calpe,** Gibraltar   11 **Moultrie.** See note, p. 1573

Meanwhile, through streets still echoing with trade,
  Walk grave and thoughtful men
Whose hands may one day wield the patriot's blade
  As lightly as the pen.   20

And maidens with such eyes as would grow dim
  Over a bleeding hound
Seem each one to have caught the strength of him
  Whose sword she sadly bound.

Thus girt without and garrisoned at home,
  Day patient following day,
Old Charleston looks from roof and spire and dome
  Across her tranquil bay.

Ships, through a hundred foes, from Saxon lands
  And spicy Indian ports   30
Bring Saxon steel and iron to her hands
  And Summer to her courts.

But still, along yon dim Atlantic line,
  The only hostile smoke
Creeps like a harmless mist above the brine
  From some frail, floating oak.

Shall the Spring dawn, and she, still clad in smiles
  And with an unscathed brow,
Rest in the strong arms of her palm-crowned isles
  As fair and free as now?   40

We know not; in the temple of the Fates
  God has inscribed her doom;
And, all untroubled in her faith, she waits
  The triumph or the tomb.   1862

---

29 **foes,** the Federal blockade

Spring

"Spring" was first printed in the Charleston Southern Illustrated News, *April 4, 1863.*

Spring, with that nameless pathos in the air
Which dwells with all things fair,
Spring, with her golden suns and silver rain,
Is with us once again.

Out in the lonely woods the jasmine burns
Its fragrant lamps, and turns
Into a royal court with green festoons
The banks of dark lagoons.

In the deep heart of every forest tree
The blood is all aglee,   10
And there's a look about the leafless bowers
As if they dreamed of flowers.

Yet still on every side we trace the hand
Of Winter in the land,
Save where the maple reddens on the lawn,
Flushed by the season's dawn;

Or where, like those strange semblances we find
That age to childhood bind,
The elm puts on, as if in Nature's scorn,
The brown of Autumn corn.   20

As yet the turf is dark, although you know
That, not a span below,
A thousand germs are groping through the gloom,
And soon will burst their tomb.

Already, here and there, on frailest stems
Appear some azure gems,
Small as might deck, upon a gala day,
The forehead of a fay.

In gardens you may note amid the dearth
The crocus breaking earth;   30
And near the snowdrop's tender white and green,
The violet in its screen.

But many gleams and shadows need must pass
Along the budding grass,
And weeks go by, before the enamored South
Shall kiss the rose's mouth.

Still there's a sense of blossoms yet unborn
In the sweet airs of morn;
One almost looks to see the very street
Grow purple at his feet.   40

At times a fragrant breeze comes floating by,
And brings, you know not why,
A feeling as when eager crowds await
Before a palace gate

Some wondrous pageant; and you scarce would start,
If from a beech's heart,
A blue-eyed Dryad, stepping forth, should say,
"Behold me! I am May!"

Ah! who would couple thoughts of war and crime
With such a blessèd time!   50
Who in the west wind's aromatic breath
Could hear the call of Death!

Yet not more surely shall the Spring awake
The voice of wood and brake,
Then she shall rouse, for all her tranquil charms,
A million men to arms.

There shall be deeper hues upon her plains
Than all her sunlit rains,
And every gladdening influence around,
Can summon from the ground.   60

Oh! standing on this desecrated mould,
Methinks that I behold,
Lifting her bloody daisies up to God,
Spring kneeling on the sod,

And calling, with the voice of all her rills,
Upon the ancient hills
To fall and crush the tyrants and the slaves
Who turn her meads to graves.

                              1863

Ode

Mr. Parks says of the poem: "Timrod's 'Ode' has the supreme artistic merit of throbbing with vibrant emotion in its effect upon the reader, yet of possessing a classic coolness of phrase which might have been carved from stone. The poet indulges in no histrionic exhibitionism, but this controlled and inevitable verse leaves nothing to be said." The poem has been often compared with William Collins' "How Sleep the Brave."

The "Ode" was first printed in the Charleston Courier *as "Ode Sung on the Occasion of
Decorating the Graves of the Confederate Dead, at Magnolia Cemetery, Charleston, S. C."*

Sleep sweetly in your humble graves,
   Sleep, martyrs of a fallen cause;
Though yet no marble column craves
   The pilgrim here to pause.

In seeds of laurel in the earth,
   The blossom of your fame is blown,
And somewhere, waiting for its birth,
   The shaft is in the stone!

Meanwhile, behalf the tardy years
   Which keep in trust your storied tombs, 10
Behold! your sisters bring their tears,
   And these memorial blooms.

Small tributes! but your shades will smile
   More proudly on these wreaths today,
Than when some cannon-moulded pile
   Shall overlook this Bay.

Stoop, angels, hither from the skies!
   There is no holier spot of ground
Than where defeated valor lies,
   By mourning beauty crowned!   20

                              1866

Civil War Singers

Compared with Revolutionary War songs, those chanted by soldiers and
civilians during the Civil War had somewhat less courtliness, less of the
British manner about them. The colloquial language, however, which
had begun to influence much popular literature, was an element in remarkably few: words and phrases were still likely to be oratorical. The meters of
many were determined by the older tunes for which they were written — "The Star-
Spangled Banner," "The Campbells Are Coming," "Hearts of Oak," and so on. Al-

though there were exceptions — "The Battle Hymn of the Republic" and "Maryland," for instance — those best remembered were distinguished less for their sentiment and phrasing than for their rhythms and their tunes. Quite a large number continued to be popular down into modern times.

F. F. Browne, **Bugle Echoes, a Collection of Poems of the Civil War, Northern and Southern,** New York, 1886   G. E. Eggleston, **American War Ballads and Lyrics,** 2 vols., New York, 1889   E. A. Dolph, **Sound Off! 'Soldier Songs,** New York, 1929

Dixie *Daniel Decatur Emmett, 1815–1904*

On Broadway, in 1859, "Dixie," the most stirring tune associated with the war, had its first public performance. The author and composer of the first of many versions was Daniel Decatur Emmett, who was born, the son of an Irish blacksmith of Southern origin, in Mt. Vernon, Ohio, in 1815. Emmett had the most elementary sort of education before, at seventeen, he entered the United States army. He served for three years as a fifer. Discharged, he traveled with circus bands and in time became a composer and singer in minstrel troupes. It was for Bryant's Minstrels that he composed his famous song, a "walk-around," rendered by the whole company. The composition was introduced to the South by a chorus in John Brougham's New Orleans production of Pocahontas *shortly before the war began. The Confederate regiments of Louisiana marched to a military version of the song, and soon its use in Southern armies was widespread. The nonsense words as well as the lively tune evidently had great appeal.*

I wish I was in de land ob cotton,
Old times dar am not forgotten;
   Look away! Look away! Look away! Dixie Land!
In Dixie Land whar I was born in,
Early on one frosty mornin',
   Look away! Look away! Look away! Dixie Land!

Chorus

   Den I wish I was in Dixie! Hooray! Hooray!
   In Dixie's Land we'll take our stand, to lib an' die in Dixie.
   Away! away! away down South in Dixie.
   Away! away! away down South in Dixie.   10

Ole missus marry "Will-de-weaber";
Willum was a gay deceaber;
   Look away, look away, look away, Dixie Land!
But when he put his arm around her,
He smiled as fierce as a forty-pounder;
   Look away, look away, look away, Dixie Land!

His face was sharp as a butcher's cleaber;
But dat did not seem to greab her;
   Look away, look away, look away, Dixie Land!
Ole missus acted de foolish part,   20
And died for a man dat broke her heart;
   Look away, look away, look away, Dixie Land!

Now here's a health to de next ole missus,
An' all the gals dat want to kiss us;
   Look away, look away, look away, Dixie Land!
But if you want to drive 'way sorrow,
Come hear dis song tomorrow;
   Look away, look away, look away, Dixie Land!

Dar's buckwheat cakes and Injin batter,
Makes you fat or a little fatter;   .   30
   Look away, look away, look away, Dixie Land!
Den hoe it down an' scratch your grabble,
To Dixie's land I'm bound to trabble;
   Look away, look away, look away, Dixie Land!
                        1859

Dixie *Albert Pike, 1809–1891*

*The best-known "literary" version of "Dixie" was written by Albert Pike, born and edu-
cated in Massachusetts but transplanted to the South as a young man. Pike was a newspaper editor and a lawyer who had a commission in the Confederate army. His words for
the song were popular during the war, but in time they dropped from general memory in
favor of Emmett's humbler version written to the same tune.*

Southrons, hear your country call you!
Up! lest worse than death befall you!
   To arms! to arms! to arms! in Dixie!
Lo! all beacon fires are lighted,
Let our hearts be now united!
   To arms! to arms! to arms! in Dixie!

Chorus
      Advance the flag of Dixie!
        Hurrah! Hurrah!
      For Dixie's land we'll take our stand,
        To live or die for Dixie!   10
      To arms! To arms!
        And conquer peace for Dixie!

To arms! To arms!
　　And conquer peace for Dixie!

Hear the Northern thunders mutter!
Northern flags in South winds flutter!
　To arms! to arms! to arms! in Dixie!
Send them back your fierce defiance!
Stamp upon the cursed alliance!
　To arms! to arms! to arms! in Dixie!　20

Fear no danger! shun no labor!
Lift up rifle, pike and sabre!
　To arms! to arms! to arms! in Dixie!
Shoulder pressing close to shoulder,
Let the odds make each heart bolder!
　To arms! to arms! to arms! in Dixie!

How the South's great heart rejoices,
At your cannon's ringing voices;
　To arms! to arms! to arms! in Dixie!
For faith betrayed and pledges broken,　30
Wrongs inflicted, insults spoken!
　To arms! to arms! to arms! in Dixie!

Strong as lions, swift as eagles,
Back to their kennels hunt these beagles!
　To arms! to arms! to arms! in Dixie!
Cut the unequal bonds asunder!
Let them hence each other plunder!
　To arms! to arms! to arms! in Dixie!

Swear upon your country's altar,
Never to give up or falter;　40
　To arms! to arms! to arms! in Dixie!
Till the spoilers are defeated,
Till the Lord's work is completed.
　To arms! to arms! to arms! in Dixie!

Halt not till our Federation,
Secures among earth's Powers its station!
　To arms! to arms! to arms! in Dixie!
Then at peace and crowned with glory,
Hear your children tell the story!
　To arms! to arms! to arms! in Dixie!　50

If the loved ones weep in sadness,
Victory soon shall bring them gladness.
   To arms! to arms! to arms! in Dixie!
Exultant pride soon banish sorrow;
Smiles chase tears away tomorrow.
   To arms! to arms! to arms! in Dixie!

1861

My Maryland James Ryder Randall, 1839–1908

Upon hearing of the attack by the Massachusetts troops on his native city, Baltimore, James Ryder Randall wrote "My Maryland." At the time he composed the poem, Randall was a teacher in Louisiana, unacceptable for military duty because of poor health. He turned from teaching to journalism, and was in newspaper work until his death in 1908.

"My Maryland" appeared first in the New Orleans Delta, *but shortly it was reprinted in newspapers throughout the South. The tune for which the verses were designed was the German song "Tannenbaum, O Tannenbaum."*

The despot's heel is on thy shore,
   Maryland!
His torch is at thy temple door,
   Maryland!
Avenge the patriotic gore
That flecked the streets of Baltimore,
And be the battle-queen of yore,
   Maryland! My Maryland!

Hark, to an exiled son's appeal,
   Maryland!   10
My Mother-State, to thee I kneel,
   Maryland!
For life and death, for woe and weal,
Thy peerless chivalry reveal,
And gird thy beautious limbs with steel!
   Maryland! My Maryland!

Thou wilt not cower in the dust,
   Maryland!
Thy beaming sword shall never rust,
   Maryland!   20
Remember Carroll's sacred trust,

---

21 **Carroll,** Charles Carroll (1737-1832), a citizen of Maryland, the last surviving signer of the Declaration of Independence

Remember Howard's warlike thrust,
And all thy slumberers with the just,
   Maryland! My Maryland!

Come! 'tis the red dawn of the day,
   Maryland!
Come! with thy panoplied array,
   Maryland!
With Ringgold's spirit for the fray,
With Watson's blood at Monterey,   30
With fearless Lowe and dashing May,
   Maryland! My Maryland!

Dear Mother! burst the tyrant's chain,
   Maryland!
Virginia should not call in vain,
   Maryland!
She meets her sisters on the plain —
"Sic semper," 'tis the proud refrain
That baffles minions back amain,
   Maryland!   40
Arise, in majesty again,
   Maryland! My Maryland!

Come! for thy shield is bright and strong,
   Maryland!
Come! for thy dalliance does thee wrong,
   Maryland!
Come! to thine own heroic throng,
That stalks with Liberty along,
And ring thy dauntless Slogan-song, .
   Maryland! My Maryland!   50

I see the blush upon thy cheek,
   Maryland!
For thou wast ever bravely meek,
   Maryland!
But lo! there surges forth a shriek
From hill to hill, from creek to creek —
Potomac calls to Chesapeake,
   Maryland! My Maryland!

22 **Howard,** John Eager Howard, a military leader in the Revolution   29 **Ringgold . . . Watson . . .**
Lowe . . . May, Marylanders who fought with distinction in the Mexican War   38 **Sic semper,** the
opening words of the motto of Virginia, *Sic semper tyrannis* — Thus always to tyrants   57 **Potomac . . .**
Chesapeake, extreme boundaries of Maryland

Thou wilt not yield the Vandal toll,
    Maryland!   60
Thou wilt not crook to his control,
    Maryland!
Better the fire upon thee roll,
Better the shot, the blade, the bowl,
Than crucifixion of the soul,
    Maryland! My Maryland!

I hear the distant thunder-hum,
    Maryland!
The Old Line's bugle, fife, and drum,
    Maryland!   70
She is not dead, nor deaf, nor dumb —
    Huzza! she spurns the Northern scum!
She breathes — she burns! she'll come! she'll come!
    Maryland! My Maryland!

                          1861

Battle Hymn of the Republic *Julia Ward Howe, 1819—1910*

This poem was written by Mrs. Howe to accompany a well-established tune, that of the dog-gerel song, "John Brown's Body." Interestingly, this latter song had fitted its words to a Southern revival hymn, "Say, Brothers, Will You Meet Us?" popular throughout the United States in the 1850's. Soldiers of a Massachusetts regiment stationed in Boston worked out the words for "John Brown's Body" in 1861; when they sang them while marching through New York in July of the same year, the song began to have wide currency. The opening lines of the song were:

> *John Brown's body lies a-mold'ring in the grave,*
> *John Brown's body lies a-mold'ring in the grave,*
> *John Brown's body lies a-mold'ring in the grave,*
>   *His soul is marching on!*

Chorus
>   *Glory! Glory Hallelujah!*
>   *Glory! Glory Hallelujah!*
>   *Glory! Glory Hallelujah!*
>   *His soul is marching on.*

    Mrs. Howe, a Bostonian and descendant of a distinguished colonial family, had won dis-tinction before the war as a supporter of woman suffrage and other reforms, including aboli-tion. She wrote her poem one night after she had been stirred by a visit to an army camp

near Washington, D. C. Unlike Pike's "improvement" on the words of "Dixie," her words
replaced the initial ones in popular memory. "The Battle Hymn of the Republic" first was
published in the Atlantic Monthly, *February 1862.*

Mine eyes have seen the glory of the coming of the Lord:
He is trampling out the vintage where the grapes of wrath are stored;
He hath loosed the fateful lightning of his terrible swift sword;
    His truth is marching on.

Chorus

        Glory! glory! Hallelujah!
        Glory! glory! Hallelujah!
        Glory! glory! Hallelujah
            His truth is marching on!

I have seen him in the watch-fires of a hundred circling camps;
They have builded him an altar in the evening dews and damps;   10
I can read his righteous sentence by the dim and flaring lamps:
    His day is marching on.

I have read a fiery gospel, writ in burnished rows of steel:
"As ye deal with my contemners, so with you my grace shall deal;
Let the Hero, born of woman, crush the serpent with his heel,
    Since God is marching on."

He has sounded forth the trumpet that shall never call retreat;
He is sifting out the hearts of men before his judgment-seat;
Oh, be swift, my soul, to answer him! be jubilant, my feet!
    Our God is marching on.   20

In the beauty of the lilies Christ was born across the sea,
With a glory in his bosom that transfigures you and me:
As he died to make men holy, let us die to make men free,
    While God is marching on.

                                        1861, 1862

Three Hundred Thousand More James Sloan Gibbons, 1810—1892

On July 16, 1862, shortly after Lincoln had issued a call for three hundred thousand addi-
tional volunteers, this poem was published anonymously in the New York Evening Post.
William Cullen Bryant was credited with its authorship, but eventually it was attributed
to Gibbons, a Quaker editor and abolitionist. Stephen Collins Foster wrote a musical setting,
the most successful of his war songs.

We are coming, Father Abraham, three hundred thousand more,
From Mississippi's winding stream and from New England's shore;
We leave our plows and workshops, our wives and children dear,
With hearts too full for utterance, with but a silent tear;
We dare not look behind us, but steadfastly before:
We are coming, Father Abraham, three hundred thousand more!

If you look across the hill-tops that meet the northern sky,
Long moving lines of rising dust your vision may descry;
And now the wind, an instant, tears the cloudy veil aside,
And floats aloft our spangled flag in glory and in pride,   10
And bayonets in the sunlight gleam, and bands brave music pour:
We are coming, Father Abraham, three hundred thousand more!

If you look all up our valleys where the growing harvests shine,
You may see our sturdy farmer boys fast forming into line;
And children from their mother's knees are pulling at the weeds,
And learning how to reap and sow against their country's needs;
And a farewell group stands weeping at every cottage door:
We are coming, Father Abraham, three hundred thousand more!

You have called us, and we're coming, by Richmond's bloody tide
To lay us down, for Freedom's sake, our brothers' bones beside,   20
Or from foul treason's savage grasp to wrench the murderous blade,
And in the face of foreign foes its fragments to parade.
Six hundred thousand loyal men and true have gone before:
We are coming, Father Abraham, three hundred thousand more!

                                                                                                    1862

1809–1865 *Abraham Lincoln*

An autobiography which Lincoln wrote in 1859 tells the main details of his
early life in his characteristic style. It reads, in part:
        "I was born February 12, 1809, in Hardin County, Kentucky. My
parents were both born in Virginia, of undistinguished families. . . .
My mother, who died in my tenth year, was of a family of the name of Hanks. . . .
My father, at the death of his father, was but six years of age, and he grew up lit-

erally without education. He removed from Kentucky to what is now Spencer County, Indiana, in my eighth year. . . . It was a wild region, with many bears and other wild animals still in the woods. There I grew up. There were some schools, so called, but no qualification was ever required of a teacher beyond 'readin', writin', and cipherin',' to the rule of three. . . . There was absolutely nothing to excite ambition for education. Of course, when I came of age, I did not know much. Still, somehow, I could read, write, and cipher to the rule of three, but that was all. I have not been to school since. The little advance I now have upon this store of education, I have picked up from time to time under the pressure of necessity.

"I was raised to farm work, which I continued till I was twenty-two. At twenty-one I came to Illinois, Macon County. Then I got to New Salem . . . where I remained a year as a sort of clerk in a store. Then came The Black Hawk War; and I was elected a captain of volunteers, a success which gave me more pleasure than any I have had since. I went the campaign, was elected, ran for the legislature the same year (1832), and was beaten — the only time I ever have been beaten by the people. The next and three succeeding biennial elections I was elected to the legislature. I was not a candidate afterward. During this legislative period I had studied law, and removed to Springfield to practice it. In 1846 I was once elected to the lower House of Congress. Was not a candidate for reelection. From 1849 to 1854, both inclusive, practised law more assiduously than ever before. . . . I was losing interest in politics when the repeal of the Missouri Compromise aroused me again. What I have done since then is pretty well known.

"If my personal description of me is thought desirable, it may be said I am, in height, six feet four inches, nearly; lean in flesh, weighing on an average one hundred and eighty pounds; dark complexion, with coarse black hair and gray eyes. No other marks or brands recollected."

Lincoln's account breaks off at the time of the repeal of the Missouri Compromise (1854), a political move which caused him to return to public life when the Republican party was founded. In 1858 the Lincoln-Douglas debates, on the subject of popular sovereignty, attracted nation-wide attention and led to Lincoln's becoming a dark-horse candidate for the Presidential nomination. He was nominated in 1860, subsequently elected, and began to serve in 1861, as the Civil War was starting. His wartime leadership was rewarded by his reëlection in 1864. He was shot to death by John Wilkes Booth, in a Washington theater, about a month after his second inaugural.

One reason for his countrymen's idolizing Lincoln as they have is suggested in his claim, in his autobiography, that he had little book learning. Americans loved to think of him as a typical practical citizen. Joe Gillespie, an old friend, praised him in these words: "He had passed through all the grades of society when he reached the Presidency, and he had found common sense a sure reliance and he put it into practice. He acted all through his career upon just such principles as every man of good sense would approve. . . . Lincoln was a great common man." His ways of thinking were, indeed, much like those of ordinary Americans who distrust abstractions and rely upon experience and sound logic to help solve problems.

Yet Lincoln and many of his friends and worshipers probably underestimated the extent of his education. From boyhood, he was passionately fond of reading. He read the Bible, *Pilgrim's Progress,* and such fine writers as Milton, Gibbon, Voltaire, Paine, Hawthorne, and others with great appreciation. He knew much of Shakespeare and could recite long passages from the great plays. Finally, he had the urge to write well. As a young man, he wrote quite a number of poems. Of one poem which he read in 1846, he said, "I would give all I am worth and go in debt to be able to write so fine a piece. . . ." He took great pains with his writing. Mentor Graham, his teacher said, "I have known him . . . to study for hours the best way of three to express an idea." Such care is evident in his most famous utterances — most of them masterpieces of American oratory.

The Collected Works of Abraham Lincoln, ed. R. P. Basler, 9 vols., New Brunswick, 1953   Carl Sandburg, Abraham Lincoln: the Prairie Years, New York, 1926   Carl Sandburg, Abraham Lincoln: the War Years, New York, 1939   Nathaniel Stephenson, "Lincoln," Cambridge History of American Literature, New York, 1931

Farewell Address at Springfield, Illinois

Lincoln had been elected President in November 1860. The following month, South Carolina had seceded. By February 8, 1861, five additional states had seceded, and the Confederate government had been formed. Because it had been rumored that Lincoln would never be allowed to reach Washington alive, precautions had been taken to ensure his safety on the journey.

Such was the situation when, on February 11, the Presidential party went to the railroad station in Springfield to depart for Washington. There were dense clouds overhead, and a chilly drizzle of rain fell through the gray mist. From the platform of a car on the train, Lincoln spoke to the thousand townspeople who stood in the rain.

My Friends: No one, not in my situation, can appreciate my feeling of sadness at this parting. To this place, and the kindness of these people, I owe everything. Here I have lived a quarter of a century, and have passed from a young to an old man. Here my children have been born, and one is buried. I now leave, not knowing when or whether ever I may return, with a task before me greater than that which rested upon Washington. Without the assistance of that Divine Being who ever attended him, I cannot succeed. With that assistance, I cannot fail. Trusting in Him who can go with me, and remain with you, and be everywhere for good, let us confidently hope that all will yet be well. To His care commending you, as I hope in your prayers you will commend me, I bid you an affectionate farewell.

1861

First Inaugural Address

"The 4th of March has come and gone," wrote a Washington clerk, "and we have a live, Republican President. And, what is perhaps more singular, during the whole day we saw no one who appeared to manifest the least dislike to his living." The account reflects the gen-

eral fear in Washington on the day of the inauguration in 1861. During the parade and during the address, riflemen on rooftops along the Avenue and in windows of the Capitol Building watched the crowd for signs of violence. In addition to the fear for Lincoln's life, there was the tense feeling of a nation on the verge of war.

The speech, like most inaugurals, was addressed not only to the audience at Washington but also to a wider one. For the North, which half feared that he might be a waverer like his predecessor, Lincoln clearly stated his belief that the Union could not be dissolved and firmly defined the duty of the government in the face of a threat of dissolution. For the South, he made his account of the controversy dispassionate and offered in the closing lines the appeal for a continuance of peace. The address was revised in accordance with suggestions made by his advisers Browning and Seward, who chiefly urged more temperance of tone. The most notable indication of Lincoln's artistry is his rephrasing of the final paragraph from the form originally written out by Secretary of State Seward. (See footnote, p. 1603.)

Fellow Citizens of the United States: In compliance with a custom as old as the government itself, I appear before you to address you briefly, and to take in your presence the oath prescribed by the Constitution of the United States to be taken by the President "before he enters on the execution of his office."

I do not consider it necessary at present for me to discuss those matters of administration about which there is no special anxiety or excitement.

Apprehension seems to exist among the people of the Southern states that by the accession of a Republican administration their property and their peace and personal security are to be endangered. There has never been any reasonable cause for such
10 apprehension. Indeed, the most ample evidence to the contrary has all the while existed and been open to their inspection. It is found in nearly all the published speeches of him who now addresses you. I do but quote from one of those speeches when I declare that "I have no purpose, directly or indirectly, to interfere with the institution of slavery in the states where it exists. I believe I have no lawful right to do so, and I have no inclination to do so." Those who nominated and elected me did so with full knowledge that I had made this and many similar declarations, and had never recanted them. And, more than this, they placed in the platform for my acceptance, and as a law to themselves and to me, the clear and emphatic resolution which I now read:

20   *"Resolved,* That the maintenance inviolate of the rights of the states, and especially the right of each state to order and control its own domestic institutions according to its own judgment exclusively, is essential to that balance of power on which the perfection and endurance of our political fabric depend, and we denounce the lawless invasion by armed force of the soil of any state or territory, no matter under what pretext, as among the gravest of crimes."

I now reiterate these sentiments; and, in doing so, I only press upon the public attention the most conclusive evidence of which the case is susceptible, that the property, peace, and security of no section are to be in any wise endangered by the

_____

5 **I do not consider.** . . . . This paragraph was written and inserted after the main part of the address had been composed   7 **Apprehension seems.** . . . Marginal marks indicated that this paragraph was to receive special emphasis in reading

now incoming administration. I add, too, that all the protection which, consistently with the Constitution and the laws, can be given, will be cheerfully given to all the states when lawfully demanded, for whatever cause — as cheerfully to one section as to another.

There is much controversy about the delivering up of fugitives from service or labor. The clause I now read is as plainly written in the Constitution as any other of its provisions:

"No person held to service or labor in one state, under the laws thereof, escaping into another, shall in consequence of any law or regulation therein be discharged from such service or labor, but shall be delivered up on claim of the party to whom 10 such service or labor may be due."

It is scarcely questioned that this provision was intended by those who made it for the reclaiming of what we call fugitive slaves; and the intention of the lawgiver is the law. All members of Congress swear their support to the whole Constitution — to this provision as much as to any other. To the proposition, then, that slaves whose cases come within the terms of this clause "shall be delivered up," their oaths are unanimous. Now, if they would make the effort in good temper, could they not with nearly equal unanimity frame and pass a law by means of which to keep good that unanimous oath?

There is some difference of opinion whether this clause should be enforced by na- 20 tional or by state authority; but surely that difference is not a very material one. If the slave is to be surrendered, it can be of but little consequence to him or to others by which authority it is done. And should anyone in any case be content that his oath shall go unkept on a merely unsubstantial controversy as to how it shall be kept?

Again, in any law upon this subject, ought not all the safeguards of liberty known in civilized and humane jurisprudence to be introduced, so that a free man be not, in any case, surrendered as a slave? And might it not be well at the same time to provide by law for the enforcement of that clause in the Constitution which guarantees that "the citizen of each state shall be entitled to all privileges and immunities 30 of citizens in the several states"?

I take the official oath today with no mental reservations, and with no purpose to construe the Constitution or laws by any hypercritical rules. And while I do not choose now to specify particular acts of Congress as proper to be enforced, I do suggest that it will be much safer for all, both in official and private stations, to conform to and abide by all those acts which stand unrepealed, than to violate any of them, trusting to find impunity in having them held to be unconstitutional.

It is seventy-two years since the first inauguration of a president under our na-

---

5 **There is much controversy. . . .** Marginal marks show that this was another paragraph to be given emphasis   28 **And might . . . states.** This sentence was added after the first draft   32 **I take the official oath. . . .** This paragraph was originally marked for emphatic delivery, but the mark was crossed out   34 **choose,** originally, "think proper"   38 **It . . . years. . . .** This was marked for oral emphasis, but the mark was deleted

tional Constitution. During that period fifteen different and greatly distinguished citizens have, in succession, administered the executive branch of the government. They have conducted it through many perils, and generally with great success. Yet, with all this scope of precedent, I now enter upon the same task for the brief constitutional term of four years under great and peculiar difficulty. A disruption of the federal Union, heretofore only menaced, is now formidably attempted.

I hold that, in contemplation of universal law and of the Constitution, the union of these states is perpetual. Perpetuity is implied, if not expressed, in the fundamental law of all national governments. It is safe to assert that no government proper
10 ever had a provision in its organic law for its own termination. Continue to execute all the express provisions of our national Constitution, and the Union will endure forever — it being impossible to destroy it except by some action not provided for in the instrument itself.

Again, if the United States be not a government proper, but an association of states in the nature of contract merely, can it, as a contract, be peaceably unmade by less than all the parties who made it? One party to a contract may violate it — break it, so to speak; but does it not require all to lawfully rescind it?

Descending from these general principles, we find the proposition that, in legal contemplation the Union is perpetual confirmed by the history of the Union itself.
20 The Union is much older than the Constitution. It was formed, in fact, by the Articles of Association in 1774. It was matured and continued by the Declaration of Independence in 1776. It was further matured, and the faith of all the then thirteen states expressly plighted and engaged that it should be perpetual, by the Articles of Confederation in 1778. And, finally, in 1787 one of the declared objects for ordaining and establishing the Constitution was "to form a more perfect Union."

But if the destruction of the Union by one or by a part only of the states be lawfully possible, the Union is less perfect than before the Constitution, having lost the vital element of perpetuity.

It follows from these views that no state upon its own mere motion can lawfully
30 get out of the Union; that resolves and ordinances to that effect are legally void; and that acts of violence, within any state or states, against the authority of the United States, are insurrectionary or revolutionary, according to circumstances.

I therefore consider that, in view of the Constitution and the laws, the Union is unbroken and to the extent of my ability I shall take care, as the Constitution itself expressly enjoins upon me, that the laws of the Union be faithfully executed in all the states. Doing this I deem to be only a simple duty on my part; and I shall perform it so far as practicable, unless my rightful masters, the American people, shall withhold the requisite means, or in some authoritative manner direct the contrary. I trust this will not be regarded as a menace, but only as the declared purpose of
40 the Union that it will constitutionally defend and maintain itself.

In doing this there needs to be no bloodshed or violence; and there shall be none,

---

6 **heretofore only menaced** . . . and the rest of the sentence replaced an earlier, longer phrasing 33 **I therefore consider.** . . . This paragraph was added to the original draft

unless it be forced upon the national authority. The power confided to me will be used to hold, occupy, and possess the property and places belonging to the government, and to collect the duties and imposts; but beyond what may be necessary for these objects, there will be no invasion, no using of force against or among the people anywhere. Where hostility to the United States, in any interior locality, shall be so great and universal as to prevent competent resident citizens from holding the federal offices, there will be no attempt to force obnoxious strangers among the people for that object. While the strict legal right may exist in the government to enforce the exercise of these offices, the attempt to do so would be so irritating, and so nearly impracticable withal, that I deem it better to forego for the time the uses 10 of such offices.

The mails, unless repelled, will continue to be furnished in all parts of the Union. So far as possible, the people everywhere shall have that sense of perfect security which is most favorable to calm thought and reflection. The course here indicated will be followed unless current events and experience shall show a modification or change to be proper, and in every case and exigency my best discretion will be exercised according to circumstances actually existing, and with a view and a hope of a peaceful solution of the national troubles and the restoration of fraternal sympathies and affections.

That there are persons in one section or another who seek to destroy the Union 20 at all events, and are glad of any pretext to do it, I will neither affirm nor deny; but if there be such, I need address no word to them. To those, however, who really love the Union may I not speak?

Before entering upon so grave a matter as the destruction of our national fabric, with all its benefits, its memories, and its hopes, would it not be wise to ascertain precisely why we do it? Will you hazard so desperate a step while there is any possibility that any portion of the ills you fly from have no real existence? Will you, while the certain ills you fly to are greater than all the real ones you fly from — will you risk the commission of so fearful a mistake?

All profess to be content in the Union if all constitutional rights can be main- 30 tained. Is it true, then, that any right, plainly written in the Constitution, has been denied? I think not. Happily the human mind is so constituted that no party can reach to the audacity of doing this. Think, if you can, of a single instance in which a plainly written provision of the Constitution has ever been denied. If by the mere force of numbers a majority should deprive a minority of any clearly written constitutional right, it might, in a moral point of view, justify revolution — certainly would if such a right were a vital one. But such is not our case. All the vital rights of minorities and of individuals are so plainly assured to them by affirmations and negations, guarantees and prohibitions, in the Constitution, that controversies never

1 **The power confided.** . . . An earlier version read: "All the power at my disposal will be used to reclaim the public property and places which have fallen; to hold, occupy and possess these and all other properties and places belonging to the government." Senator Orville Browning of Illinois suggested the use of the less threatening version. The sentence nevertheless was considered by contemporaries the most warlike utterance in the speech   20 **That there are persons.** . . . Marginal marks indicated that Lincoln was to emphasize this paragraph

arise concerning them. But no organic law can ever be framed with a provision specifically applicable to every question which may occur in practical administration. No foresight can anticipate, nor any document of reasonable length contain, express provisions for all possible questions. Shall fugitives from labor be surrendered by national or by state authority? The Constitution does not expressly say. *May* Congress prohibit slavery in the territories? The Constitution does not expressly say. *Must* Congress protect slavery in the territories? The Constitution does not expressly say.

From questions of this class spring all our constitutional controversies, and we divide upon them into majorities and minorities. If the minority will not acquiesce,
10 the majority must, or the government must cease. There is no other alternative; for continuing the government is acquiescence on one side or the other.

If a minority in such case will secede rather than acquiesce, they make a precedent which in turn will divide and ruin them; for a minority of their own will secede from them whenever a majority refuses to be controlled by such minority. For instance, why may not any portion of a new confederacy a year or two hence arbitrarily secede again, precisely as portions of the present Union now claim to secede from it? All who cherish disunion sentiments are now being educated to the exact temper of doing this.

Is there such perfect identity of interests among the states to compose a
20 new Union, as to produce harmony only, and prevent renewed secession?

Plainly, the central idea of secession is the essence of anarchy. A majority held in restraint by constitutional checks and limitations, and always changing easily with deliberate changes of popular opinions and sentiments, is the only true sovereign of a free people. Whoever rejects it does, of necessity, fly to anarchy or to despotism. Unanimity is impossible; the rule of a minority, as a permanent arrangement, is wholly inadmissible; so that, rejecting the majority principle, anarchy or despotism in some form is all that is left.

I do not forget the position, assumed by some, that constitutional questions are to be decided by the Supreme Court; nor do I deny that such decisions must be
30 binding, in any case, upon the parties to a suit, as to the object of that suit, while they are also entitled to very high respect and consideration in all parallel cases by all other departments of the government. And while it is obviously possible that such decisions may be erroneous in any given case, still the evil effect following it, being limited to that particular case, with the chance that it may be overruled and never become a precedent for other cases, can better be borne than could the evils of a different practice. At the same time, the candid citizen must confess that if the policy of the government, upon vital questions affecting the whole people, is to be irrevocably fixed by decisions of the Supreme Court, the instant they are made, in ordinary litigation between parties in personal actions, the people will have ceased
40 to be their own rulers, having to that extent practically resigned their government into the hands of that eminent tribunal. Nor is there in this view any assault upon the court or the judges. It is a duty from which they may not shrink to decide cases properly brought before them, and it is no fault of theirs if others seek to turn their decisions to political purposes.

One section of our country believes slavery is right, and ought to be extended, while the other believes it is wrong, and ought not be extended. This is the only substantial dispute. The fugitive-slave clause of the Constitution, and the law for the suppression of the foreign slave-trade, are each as well enforced, perhaps, as any law can ever be in a community where the moral sense of the people imperfectly supports the law itself. The great body of the people abide by the dry legal obligation in both cases, and a few break over in each. This, I think, cannot be perfectly cured; and it would be worse in both cases after the separation of the sections than before. The foreign slave-trade, now imperfectly suppressed, would be ultimately revived, without restriction, in one section, while fugitive slaves, now only partially 10 surrendered, would not be surrendered at all by the other.

Physically speaking, we cannot separate. We cannot remove our respective sections from each other, nor build an impassable wall between them. A husband and wife may be divorced, and go out of the presence and beyond the reach of each other; but the different parts of our country cannot do this. They cannot but remain face to face, and intercourse, either amicable or hostile, must continue between them. Is it possible, then, to make that intercourse more advantageous or more satisfactory after separation than before? Can aliens make treaties easier than friends can make laws? Can treaties be more faithfully enforced between aliens than laws can among friends? Suppose you go to war, you cannot fight always; and when, after much loss 20 on both sides, and no gain on either, you cease fighting, the identical old questions as to terms of intercourse are again upon you.

This country, with its institutions, belongs to the people who inhabit it. Whenever they shall grow weary of the existing government, they can exercise their constitutional right of amending it, or their revolutionary right to dismember or overthrow it. I cannot be ignorant of the fact that many worthy and patriotic citizens are desirous of having the national Constitution amended. While I make no recommendation of amendments, I fully recognize the rightful authority of the people over the whole subject, to be exercised in either of the modes prescribed in the instrument itself; and I should, under existing circumstances, favor rather than oppose 30 a fair opportunity being afforded the people to act upon it. I will venture to add that to me the convention mode seems preferable, in that it allows amendments to originate with the people themselves, instead of only permitting them to take or reject propositions originated by others not especially chosen for the purpose, and which might not be precisely such as they would wish to either accept or refuse. I understand a proposed amendment to the Constitution — which amendment, however, I have not seen — has passed Congress, to the effect that the federal government shall never interfere with the domestic institutions of the states, including that of persons held to service. To avoid misconstruction of what I have said, I depart from my purpose not to speak of particular amendments so far as to say that, hold- 40 ing such a provision to now be implied constitutional law, I have no objections to its being made express and irrevocable.

The chief magistrate derives all his authority from the people, and they have conferred none upon him to fix terms for the separation of the states. The people themselves can do this also if they choose; but the executive, as such, has nothing to do with it. His duty is to administer the present government, as it came to his hands, and to transmit it, unimpaired by him, to his successor.

Why should there not be a patient confidence in the ultimate justice of the people? Is there any better or equal hope in the world? In our present differences is either party without faith of being in the right? If the Almighty Ruler of Nations, with His eternal truth and justice, be on your side of the North, or on yours of the South, that truth and that justice will surely prevail by the judgment of this great tribunal of the American people.

10   By the frame of the government under which we live, this same people have wisely given their public servants but little power for mischief; and have, with equal wisdom, provided for the return of that little to their own hands at very short intervals. While the people retain their virtue and vigilance, no administration, by any extreme of wickedness or folly, can very seriously injure the government in the short space of four years.

My countrymen, one and all, think calmly and well upon this whole subject. Nothing valuable can be lost by taking time. If there be an object to hurry any of you in hot haste to a step which you would never take deliberately, that object will be frustrated by taking time; but no good object can be frustrated by it. Such of you
20 as are now dissatisfied, still have the old Constitution unimpaired, and, on the sensitive point, the laws of your own framing under it; while the new administration will have no immediate power, if it would, to change either. If it were admitted that you who are dissatisfied hold the right side in the dispute, there still is no single good reason for precipitate action. Intelligence, patriotism, Christianity, and a firm reliance on Him who has never yet forsaken this favored land, are still competent to adjust in the best way all our present difficulty.

In your hands, my dissatisfied fellow-countrymen, and not in mine, is the momentous issue of civil war. The government will not assail you. You can have no conflict without being yourselves the aggressors. You have no oath registered in
30 heaven to destroy the government, while I shall have the most solemn one to "preserve, protect, and defend it."

I am loath to close. We are not enemies, but friends. We must not be enemies. Though passion may have strained, it must not break our bonds of affection. The mystic chords of memory, stretching from every battlefield and patriot grave to every living heart and hearthstone all over this broad land, will yet swell the chorus of the Union when again touched, as surely they will be, by the better angels of our nature.   1861

---

16 **My countrymen.** . . . The paragraph was marked for oral emphasis   32 **I am loath.** . . . This, at Seward's suggestion, replaced a more aggressive conclusion: "'You can forbear the assault up on it [the Government]; I cannot shrink from the defense of it.·With you, and not with me, is the solemn question of 'shall it be peace, or a sword?'" Seward, wanting "some words of affection, some of calm and cheerful confidence," suggested: "I close. We are not, we must not be aliens or enemies but fellow countrymen and brethren. Although passion has strained our bonds of affection too hardly they must not, I am sure they will not be broken. The mystic chords which proceeding from so many battle fields and so many patriot graves pass through all the hearts and all the hearths in this broad continent of ours will yet again harmonize in their ancient music when breathed upon by the guardian angel of the nation."

Open Letter to Horace Greeley

Horace Greeley, famous and influential editor of the New York Tribune, *in the issue of August 19, 1862, published an editorial — "The Prayer of 20,000,000 People." It urged complete emancipation of the slaves and indicated doubt concerning Lincoln's policies. Actually, the "Emancipation Proclamation" had already been written, and Lincoln was only waiting for a Union victory which would make politic its publication. The letter which Lincoln wrote in answer to Greeley's attack contains a clear and eloquent statement of the President's policy.*

Executive Mansion, Washington,
August 22, 1862

Hon. Horace Greeley.

Dear Sir: I have just read yours of the 19th, addressed to myself through the New York *Tribune.* If there be in it any statements or assumptions of fact which I may know to be erroneous, I do not, now and here, controvert them. If there be in it any inferences which I may believe to be falsely drawn, I do not, now and here, argue against them. If there be perceptible in it an impatient and dictatorial tone, I waive it in deference to an old friend whose heart I have always supposed to be right.

As to the policy I "seem to be pursuing," as you say, I have not meant to leave any one in doubt.

I would save the Union. I would save it the shortest way under the Constitution. The sooner the national authority can be restored, the nearer the Union will be "the 10 Union as it was." If there be those who would not save the Union unless they could at the same time save slavery, I do not agree with them. If there be those who would not save the Union unless they could at the same time destroy slavery, I do not agree with them. My paramount object in this struggle is to save the Union, and is not either to save or to destroy slavery. If I could save the Union without freeing any slave, I would do it; and if I could save it by freeing all the slaves, I would do it; and if I could save it by freeing some and leaving others alone, I would also do that. What I do about slavery and the coloured race, I do because I believe it helps to save the Union; and what I forbear, I forbear because I do not believe it would help to save the Union. I shall do less whenever I shall believe what I am doing 20 hurts the cause, and I shall do more whenever I shall believe doing more will help the cause. I shall try to correct errors when shown to be errors, and I shall adopt new views so fast as they shall appear to be true views.

I have here stated my purpose according to my view of official duty; and I intend no modification of my oft-expressed personal wish that all men everywhere could be free.

Yours,

A. LINCOLN
1862

The Gettysburg Address

In September 1863, the dedication of the Gettysburg National Cemetery was planned for the following October 23, but when Edward Everett, a renowned orator of the day, wrote that he could not prepare his oration in so short a time, the date was moved along to November 19. The request that Lincoln speak was an afterthought: the committee asked him, "as Chief Executive," to set apart the grounds "by a few appropriate remarks."

Busy with military and civil duties, the President found little time for composing his brief speech and actually did some work on it the night before its delivery. Lincoln, many of his friends, and most newsmen at the ceremonies thought it was not much of an address; but Everett wrote on November 20: "I should be glad if I could flatter myself that I came as near to the central idea of the occasion in two hours as you did in two minutes." Later, Americans were to come to regard the address as one of the noblest utterances in American history.

The simplicity of the diction, the impressive rhythm, and the majesty of the thought of the address account for much of its appeal. Important, too, is an ordering of the material more complex than at first evident. The treatment of the past, then the present, and, finally, the future is strengthened throughout by a subtle analogy of birth, death, and rebirth. In mentioning the continent, then the nation, then the battlefield, then a portion of the battlefield, Lincoln parallels in a sense the movement which begins with the great accomplishment of the founding fathers, then narrows down to the futile ceremonies at Gettysburg. He thus prepares for a triumphant conclusion which from another view enlarges the true significance of the occasion by noting the vast accomplishment of the heroic dead for the nation and for all the earth.

Four score and seven years ago our fathers brought forth on this continent a new nation, conceived in liberty, and dedicated to the proposition that all men are created equal.

Now we are engaged in a great civil war, testing whether that nation, or any nation so conceived and so dedicated, can long endure. We are met on a great battlefield of that war. We have come to dedicate a portion of that field as a final resting-place for those who here gave their lives that that nation might live. It is altogether fitting and proper that we should do this.

But in a larger sense we cannot dedicate, we cannot consecrate, we cannot hallow
10 this ground. The brave men, living and dead, who struggled here have consecrated it, far above our poor power to add or detract. The world will little note, nor long remember what we say here, but it can never forget what they did here. It is for us,

---

1 **Four score and seven years ago.** . . . Scholars have noted that Robert Toombs of Georgia in 1850 began a speech: "Sixty years ago our fathers joined together to form a more perfect Union and establish justice. . . . We have now met to put that government on trial. . . . In my judgment the verdict is such as to give hope to the friends of liberty throughout the world." Lincoln, speaking to a crowd of serenaders, four and a half months before the dedication, had mentioned the founding of the republic "eighty odd years since"   6 **We have come** . . . originally read, "We are met . . ."   7 **It is altogether fitting.** . . . The sentence replaced an earlier phrasing, "This we may, in all propriety do"

the living, rather, to be dedicated here to the unfinished work which they who fought here have thus far so nobly advanced. It is rather for us to be here dedicated to the great task remaining before us, — that from these honored dead we take increased devotion to that cause for which they gave the last full measure of devotion; that we here highly resolve that these dead shall not have died in vain; that this nation, under God, shall have a new birth of freedom; and that government of the people, by the people, and for the people, shall not perish from the earth.

1863

---

6 **under God.** The phrase was not in the copy from which Lincoln read; he apparently inserted it orally while reading   6 **a new birth of freedom.** The *Chicago Times* criticized this phrase as a misrepresentation of "the motives of men who were slain at Gettysburg." "They gave their lives," said the paper, "to maintain the old government, and the only Constitution and Union." Thus some, at least, saw Lincoln voicing in this phrase his "odious abolition doctrines"

Letter to Mrs. Bixby

This letter was written to a woman who purportedly had heard news of the death of five of her sons on the battlefield. James Bryce, a great English scholar and an admirer of Lincoln, called it "perhaps the most impressive" of Lincoln's letters, and added, "It is short, and it deals with a theme on which hundreds of letters were written daily. But I do not know where the nobility of self-sacrifice for a great cause, and of the consolation which the thought of a sacrifice so made may bring, is set forth with such simple and pathetic beauty."

Executive Mansion
Washington, Nov. 21, 1864

To Mrs. Bixby, Boston, Mass.

Dear Madam. I have been shown in the files of the War Department a statement of the Adjutant-General of Massachusetts that you are the mother of five sons who have died gloriously on the field of battle. I feel how weak and fruitless must be any word of mine which should attempt to beguile you from the grief of a loss so overwhelming. But I cannot refrain from tendering you the consolation that may be found in the thanks of the republic they died to save. I pray that our Heavenly Father may assuage the anguish of your bereavement, and leave you only the cherished memory of the loved and lost, and the solemn pride that must be yours to have laid so costly a sacrifice upon the altar of freedom.

Yours very sincerely and respectfully,
A. LINCOLN
1864

Second Inaugural Address

"What think you of the inaugural?" wrote Charles Francis Adams, Jr., to his father, shortly after its delivery, March 4, 1865. "That rail-splitting lawyer is one of the wonders of the day. Once at Gettyburg and now again on a greater occasion he has shown a capacity

for rising to the demands of the hour. . . . This inaugural strikes me in its grand simplicity and directness as being for all time the historical keynote of this war. . . ."

Mr. Carl Sandburg indicated the situation at the time the address was delivered when he said in his biography of Lincoln: "On Grant now menacing Lee before Richmond, on Sherman thrusting agony into the vitals of South Carolina — on these final struggles depended the length of the storm not yet spent. And on what the Chief Magistrate might have to say, on his words now, such had become his stature and place, depended much of the face of events and the character of what was to happen when the war was over. This no one understood more deeply and sensitively than Lincoln as he wrote his second inaugural address."

Fellow-Countrymen: At this second appearing to take the oath of the presidential office, there is less occasion for an extended address than there was at the first. Then a statement, somewhat in detail, of a course to be pursued, seemed fitting and proper. Now, at the expiration of four years, during which public declarations have been constantly called forth on every point and phase of the great contest which still absorbs the attention and engrosses the energies of the nation, little that is new could be presented. The progress of our arms, upon which all else chiefly depends, is as well known to the public as to myself; and it is, I trust, reasonably satisfactory and encouraging to all. With high hope for the future, no prediction in regard to it is
10   ventured.

On the occasion corresponding to this four years ago, all thoughts were anxiously directed to an impending civil war. All dreaded it — all sought to avert it. While the inaugural address was being delivered from this place, devoted altogether to saving the Union without war, insurgent agents were in the city seeking to destroy it without war — seeking to dissolve the Union, and divide effects, by negotiation. Both parties deprecated war; but one of them would make war rather than let the nation survive; and the other would accept war rather than let it perish. And the war came.

One eighth of the whole population were colored slaves, not distributed generally
20   over the Union, but localized in the southern part of it. These slaves constituted a peculiar and powerful interest. All knew that this interest was, somehow, the cause of the war. To strengthen, perpetuate, and extend this interest was the object for which the insurgents would rend the Union, even by war; while the government claimed no right to do more than to restrict the territorial enlargement of it.

Neither party expected for the war the magnitude or the duration which it has already attained. Neither anticipated that the cause of the conflict might cease with, or even before, the conflict itself should cease. Each looked for an easier triumph and a result less fundamental and astounding. Both read the same Bible, and pray to the same God; and each invokes his aid against the other. It may seem strange that
30   any man should dare to ask a just God's assistance in wringing their bread from the sweat of other men's faces; but let us judge not, that we be not judged. The prayers of both could not be answered — that of neither has been answered fully.

The Almighty has his own purposes. "Woe unto the world because of offenses! for it must needs be that offenses come; but woe to that man by whom the offense

---

33 **"Woe . . . cometh."** Matthew 18:7

cometh." If we shall suppose that American slavery is one of those offenses which in the providence of God, must needs come, but which, having continued through his appointed time, he now wills to remove, and that he gives to both North and South this terrible war, as the woe due to those by whom the offense came, shall we discern therein any departure from those divine attributes which the believers in a living God always ascribe to him? Fondly do we hope — fervently do we pray — that this mighty scourge of war may speedily pass away. Yet, if God wills that it continue until all the wealth piled by the bondman's two hundred and fifty years of unrequited toil shall be sunk, and until every drop of blood drawn with the lash shall be paid by another drawn with the sword, as was said three thousand years 10 ago, so still it must be said, "The judgments of the Lord are true and righteous altogether."

With malice toward none; with charity for all; with firmness in the right, as God gives us to see the right, let us strive on to finish the work we are in; to bind up the nation's wounds; to care for him who shall have borne the battle, and for his widow and his orphan — to do all which may achieve and cherish a just and lasting peace among ourselves, and with all nations.

1865

---

11 **"The judgments . . . altogether."** Cf. Revelation 16:7

Names of authors and titles of selections included in this volume are set in **boldface**. The **boldface** numbers refer to the pages on which the biographical sketch or selection appears.

Titles of works referred to but not included in this volume are set in *italic bold.*